Revenue Law—

Principles and Practice

Revenue Law—Principles and Practice

Thirty-fifth edition

General Editors

Anne Fairpo MA (Oxon), CTA (Fellow)
Barrister, Temple Tax Chambers

David Salter LLB (Hons)
Solicitor (non-practising), Emeritus Reader, University of Warwick

Contributors

Jackie Anderson LLB, ACA, CTA
LHA Consulting Limited

David Brookes FCA
Tax Partner, BDO LLP

Rosalind Connor
Partner, ARC Pensions Law LLP

George Duncan MA (Oxon), PhD, CTA
Partner, Charles Russell Speechlys LLP

Sandra Eden BA, LLB, CTA
Senior Lecturer, Edinburgh University

Graham Elliott CTA, MBA
Transaction Tax Consultant, Withers LLP

Michael Firth
Gray's Inn Tax Chambers

Hartley Foster MA (Hons)
Partner, Fieldfisher LLP

Mark Ife LLB MJur
Partner, Herbert Smith Freehills LLP

Colin Ives CTA ATT
Senior Professional Services Tax Partner, BDO LLP

Anna Jarrold CTA, FCCA
Head of Professional Services Tax, BDO LLP

Sarah Laing CTA

Jonathan Legg BA (Oxon), AIIT
Partner, Mishcon de Reya

Helen McGhee LLB, CTA
Senior Associate, Joseph Hage Aaronson LLP

Alison Paines MA (Cantab)
Principal, Withers LLP

Bradley Richardson MA (Cantab)
Senior Associate, Herbert Smith Freehills LLP

Anna Sumner BA
Solicitor, Withers LLP

Robin Vos
Solicitor, Macfarlanes LLP

Stephen Whitehead
Senior Manager, Tax, KPMG LLP (UK)

Robin Williamson MBE, CTA (Fellow)
Technical Director, Low Incomes Tax Reform Group

Martin Wilson MA, FCA
Chairman, The Capital Allowances Partnership Ltd

Iris Wünschmann-Lyall MA (Cantab)
Consultant, TaxAction

Bloomsbury Professional

Bloomsbury Professional
An imprint of Bloomsbury Publishing Plc

Bloomsbury Professional Ltd	Bloomsbury Publishing Plc
41–43 Boltro Road	50 Bedford Square
Haywards Heath	London
RH16 1BJ	WC1B 3DP
UK	UK

www.bloomsbury.com

BLOOMSBURY and the Diana logo are trademarks of
Bloomsbury Publishing Plc

© Bloomsbury Professional Ltd 2017

All rights reserved. No part of this publication may be reproduced or transmitted in any form or by any means, electronic or mechanical, including photocopying, recording, or any information storage or retrieval system, without prior permission in writing from the publishers.

While every care has been taken to ensure the accuracy of this work, no responsibility for loss or damage occasioned to any person acting or refraining from action as a result of any statement in it can be accepted by the authors, editors or publishers.

All UK Government legislation and other public sector information used in the work is Crown Copyright ©. All House of Lords and House of Commons information used in the work is Parliamentary Copyright ©. This information is reused under the terms of the Open Government Licence v3.0 (http://www.nationalarchives.gov.uk/doc/open-government-licence/version/3) except where otherwise stated.

All Eur-lex material used in the work is © European Union, http://eur-lex.europa.eu/, 1998–2017.

British Library Cataloguing-in-Publication Data

A catalogue record for this book is available from the British Library.

ISBN: PB: 978 1 52650 132 5
       ePDF: 978 1 52650 134 9
       ePub: 978 1 52650 133 2

Typeset by Compuscript Ltd, Shannon
Printed and bound in the United Kingdom by CPI Group (UK) Ltd, Croydon, CR0 4YY

To find out more about our authors and books visit www.bloomsburyprofessional.com. Here you will find extracts, author information, details of forthcoming events and the option to sign up for our newsletters

Authors

Jackie Anderson is a Chartered Accountant and Chartered Tax Adviser and her practice, LHA Consulting Limited, provides tax compliance and advisory services to a range of clients. Jackie is also the co-author of *Incorporating and Disincorporating a Business* from Bloomsbury Professional.

David Brookes is a fellow of the Institute of Chartered Accountants in England and Wales and is a tax partner at BDO LLP. David heads up the firm's specialist team advising on tax-efficient investments and particularly the EIS and VCT schemes. David worked with Treasury and HMRC representing the CBI on the tax law rewrite of the EIS and VCT legislation in ITA 2007. David is co-author of *Venture Capital Tax Reliefs* from Bloomsbury Professional.

Rosalind Connor is a partner at ARC Pensions Law, a boutique pensions law specialist firm established in 2015. Rosalind is the present chair of the Association of Pensions Law, and is also a Fellow of the Pensions Management Institute, where she has acted as secretary and then chair of its London Group. She is the co-author of *Global Issues in Employee Benefits Law* from West Academic Publishing, and of *Pensions and Corporate Insolvency: A Practitioner's Guide* from Jordan Publishing.

George Duncan is a Solicitor and Chartered Tax Adviser. He is a partner in the Private Client Service of Charles Russell Speechlys LLP. He graduated from Oxford University with a first class degree in Literae Humaniores (Greats) and was awarded a PhD by the Institute of Archaeology in London University. He has practised as a solicitor for more than 30 years covering a wide area of practice, especially the taxation of individuals and trustees, succession law, charity law and the law of trusts. He has considerable experience of advising on tax issues thrown up by divorce and relationship breakdown. He also contributes to Bloomsbury *Tax Planning*.

Sandra Eden is a senior lecturer at the University of Edinburgh where she teaches revenue law. She is a Chartered Tax Adviser and qualified as a solicitor in Scotland. She is also a member of the European Association of Tax Law Professors and is case note editor of the *British Tax Review*. She writes and lectures on a wide range of tax issues. She is co-author of *The Taxation of Pension Schemes*, and *Tax for Litigation Lawyers*.

Graham Elliott is a Chartered Tax Adviser and an MBA with 25 years' experience in advising clients on indirect taxes, and nearly 30 years' experience in the world of VAT. He has specialised in the affairs of charities for most of his career. He is widely recognised as a writer and lecturer on his subject areas, and was awarded 'Tax Writer of the Year' by LexisNexis in 2011. He joined Withers LLP in 2012 having held senior positions in accountancy firms previously.

Anne Fairpo, CTA (Fellow) is a barrister at Temple Tax Chambers. She advises a range of clients from listed multinationals to small start-ups on all areas of corporate tax, including cross-border taxation, and employment-related tax. She is a member and Past President of the CIOT Council and has authored many books, including *Taxation of Intellectual Property* (Bloomsbury Professional). Throughout her career, she has advised on tax issues relating to business structures, expansion, relocation and individual transactions, and in areas as diverse as the arts, biotechnology, online learning, telecoms, surgical equipment and reloadable payment systems.

Michael Firth is a barrister practising at Gray's Inn Tax Chambers, London and regularly appearing in the Tax Tribunals. He graduated from Oxford University with a first class degree in jurisprudence before studying for the BCL with a focus on tax. After qualifying as a barrister, he undertook pupillage at Gray's Inn Tax Chambers, passing the Chartered Tax Adviser exams at the same time.

Hartley Foster qualified as a barrister and then as a solicitor, after studying philosophy at the Universities of Edinburgh and East Anglia. He is Head of the Tax Disputes practice at Fieldfisher, and is responsible for the conduct of high profile complex tax litigation at all levels from the tax tribunals to the Supreme Court (and including the European Court of Justice). Hartley practises in all areas of revenue and VAT law. He writes and lectures widely on tax matters, particularly on the tax appeals system and international tax law, and is the author of a division of *Simon's Direct Tax Services*, and several chapters of *HMRC Investigations 2015–16*. Hartley is a member of the International Tax Sub-Committee of the Law Society, the VAT Practitioners Group and the Solicitors' Association of Higher Court Advocates.

Mark Ife is a partner in the Remuneration and Incentives group at Herbert Smith Freehills LLP. He is involved in advising on the establishment and continuing operation of a variety of employee incentive arrangements for both quoted and unquoted companies. In addition, he advises on the employee incentive aspects of corporate actions, corporate governance and financial services regulation. Mark is a member of the Share Plan Lawyers Group, is the author of *Employee Share Schemes* and is a regular speaker on share scheme issues. Mark is recognised as a leading individual by the *Chambers Guide to the UK Legal Profession* and by *Legal 500 UK*.

Anna Jarrold is a Chartered Tax Adviser and Chartered Certified Accountant having had 25 years of experience working in industry and practice. Anna is head of BDO LLP's Professional Services tax group and has a broad knowledge of corporate and personal taxation including that relating to shareholders or members of Limited Liability Partnerships. She acts for a variety of clients advising on numerous areas of taxation but often with regard to the use of LLPs in commercial structures. Anna is a main committee member and chairs the tax committee of the Association of Partnership Practitioners.

Sarah Laing is a Chartered Tax Adviser. She has been writing professionally since joining CCH Editions in 1998 as a Senior Technical Editor, contributing to a range of highly regarded publications including the *British Tax Reporter, Taxes – The Weekly Tax News*, the *Red & Green* legislation volumes, *Hardman's, International Tax Agreements* and many others. She became Publishing Manager for the tax and accounting portfolio in 2001 and later went on to help run CCH Seminars (including ABG Courses and Conferences). Sarah originally worked for the Inland Revenue in Newbury and Swindon Tax Offices, before moving out into practice in 1991. She has worked for both small and Big 5 firms, and now works as a freelance author providing technical writing services for the tax and accountancy profession.

Jonathan Legg is a Tax Partner at Mishcon de Reya. Jonathan read jurisprudence at Merton College, Oxford and has experience of all areas of corporate tax, with an emphasis on property investment, development, finance and funds work. He acts for a variety of institutional clients, investors, developers, local authorities and charities, and advises on both direct and indirect taxes (including Stamp Duty Land Tax and VAT). Jonathan contributes regular articles to various publications including *Estates Gazette, Tax Journal* and *De Voil Indirect Tax Intelligence*. Jonathan also speaks at various conferences. He is a Chartered Tax Adviser and is a member of both the VAT Practitioners Group and the Stamp Taxes Practitioners Group.

Helen McGhee is a solicitor and chartered tax advisor. She is a senior associate at the law firm Joseph Hage Aaronson LLP, where she specialises in UK and international tax disputes. Helen advises both individuals and corporates either engaged directly or as a consultant to other professional firms and financial institutions. Her specialism is the taxation of non doms but she advises on a wide range of tax issues, more recently focusing on film schemes, EBTs and HMRC's disclosure facilities. Helen was awarded the 2015 Taxation Rising Star accolade and was named one of Eprivate Client's top 35 under 35. Helen is also a member of the Society of Tax and Estate Practitioners.

Alison Paines is a partner at Withers LLP heading the Charities & Philanthropy team. She advises charities and other not-for-profit entities, their donors and those who have dealings with them on the legal aspects of their operations, including fiscal issues. She is particularly well known for her work with charities related to the NHS and central government and with international charity matters. She was Chairman of the Charity Law Association 2008–2011 and edits and contributes to *The Law and Practice of International Charitable Giving* (Oxford University Press, 2012).

Bradley Richardson is a senior associate in the Remuneration and Incentives team at Herbert Smith Freehills LLP. He advises on a broad range of share and cash based employee incentives arrangements, in respect of the taxation of incentive plans as well as the legal, regulatory and corporate governance aspects. Bradley is recognised as an 'associate to watch' by the *Chambers Guide to the UK Legal Profession* and is a member of the Share Plan Lawyers Group.

David Salter has enjoyed a long and stimulating career in higher education, specialising, for some time in the law of taxation. He retired as a Reader in Law at the University of Warwick in 2012, but continues to teach and research in tax law (UK and International) and has written widely on the subject. He is a member of the European Association of Tax Law Professors. David is also a part-time judge in the First-tier Tribunal of the Property Chamber (Residential Property).

Anna Sumner is an associate in the Charities & Philanthropy team at Withers LLP, working for domestic and international charities, high net worth individuals and businesses. Her practice involves establishing new charities, including those forming part of dual-qualified US/UK structures, and advising existing organisations on their governance, funding, and collaborative projects; and philanthropists on their grant making and cross-border issues. She has contributed to *Practical Will Precedents and Practical Trust Precedents* (Sweet & Maxwell) and *The Law and Practice of International Charitable Giving* (Oxford University Press, 2012) and is a member of the Charity Law Association.

Robin Vos is a solicitor in the Private Client team at Macfarlanes LLP. He qualified as a solicitor after studying law at the University of Southampton. He advises on all aspects of tax and estate planning. Much of his work has an international element. He has lectured in the UK, Continental Europe, Asia and North America. He has served on the Wills & Equity Committee of the Law Society of England and Wales and is the chair of the Technical Committee of the Society of Tax and Estate Practitioners.

Stephen Whitehead was formerly an Inspector of Taxes with the Inland Revenue. He subsequently joined KPMG, dealing with a variety of business and employment tax issues. He currently advises on a range of issues including corporate taxation and tax administration. KPMG LLP, a UK limited liability partnership, operates from 22 offices across the UK with approximately 13,500 partners and staff. KPMG is a global network of professional firms providing Audit, Tax, and Advisory services. It operates in 152 countries and has 189,000 professionals working in member firms around the world.

Robin Williamson is a Solicitor and a Fellow of the Chartered Institute of Taxation. He is Technical Director of the Low Incomes Tax Reform Group, an initiative of the Institute to give a voice to unrepresented taxpayers and tax credit claimants. In this capacity Robin directs the Group's work on all aspects of personal tax that affect individuals on low or modest incomes, including tax credits and how tax and welfare systems interact. He engages in consultations with HMRC and other Government agencies, lectures to tax and welfare rights audiences, appears in the press and broadcast media, gives evidence to Parliamentary committees, writes extensively in tax and other periodicals and has contributed to various professional publications. Robin previously worked as a technical author and editor with CCH where, from 1989 to 2002, he worked closely with the late Philip Hardman and others in developing CCH's annual Red and Green tax legislation books, *Hardman's Tax Rates and Tables* and other publications. Robin was awarded an MBE in the Queen's Birthday Honours in June 2015 for services to taxpayers.

Martin Wilson is a chartered accountant. After some 15 years with major accounting firms, he founded the Capital Allowances Partnership Limited, a specialist practice dealing with all aspects of capital allowances and tax depreciation. He is the author of many published works on the subject, including *Capital Allowances: Transactions & Planning* from Bloomsbury Professional (produced annually since 1998) and a contributor to *LexisPSL, Simon's Tax Planning* and the *Institute of Taxation Finance Act Commentaries.*

Iris Wünschmann-Lyall qualified as a solicitor after studying law at Cambridge University. She is a consultant with TaxAction (formerly IRIS Professional Tax Practice) specialising in the area of trust and estate taxation. She lectures on the STEP Taxation of Trusts and Estates Diploma course and the STEP Advanced Certificate of Will Drafting and is a member of STEP Practice Committee. Iris is a co-author of *Bloomsbury Professional Core Tax Annuals – Capital Gains Tax, Bloomsbury Professional Core Tax Annuals – Inheritance Tax*, and *Bloomsbury Professional Core Tax Annuals – Trusts and Estates.*

Contents

Authors v

Table of statutes xv

Table of statutory instruments liii

Table of cases lvii

References and abbreviations cv

Section 1 Introduction

1 UK taxation – structure and philosophy 3
2 Tax avoidance and the courts 15
3 Tax avoidance and legislation 63
4 Administrative machinery 91
5 Tax avoidance, the future and the disclosure rules 127

Section 2 Income tax

6 General principles 153
7 Computation charges, allowances and rates 159
8 Taxation of employment income 181
9 Employee participation: options, incentives and trusts 281
10 Trading income 335
11 Losses 391
12 Land 405
13 Miscellaneous income 429
14 Annual payments, patent royalties and savings income 441
15 Tax shelters and insurance products 465
16 Trusts and settlements 491
17 Estates in the course of administration 529
18 The overseas dimension 547

Section 3 Capital gains tax

19 CGT – basic principles 589
20 CGT – entrepreneurs' relief 635
21 CGT – death 659
22 CGT – exemptions and reliefs 683

xii   *Contents*

    23   CGT – the main residence   705
    24   CGT – gifts and sales at an undervalue   725
    25   CGT – settlements   745
    26   CGT – companies and shareholders   765
    27   CGT – Offshore matters for individuals   773
    27A   Offshore trusts and CGT   821

Section 4   Inheritance tax

       Introduction – from estate duty to inheritance tax   875
    28   IHT – lifetime transfers   877
    29   IHT – reservation of benefit   915
    30   IHT – death   935
    31   IHT – exemptions and reliefs   989
    32   IHT – settlements: definition and classification   1027
    33   IHT – settlements not subject to the relevant property regime   1041
    34   IHT – the relevant property regime   1063
    35   IHT – excluded property and the foreign element   1077
    36   Relief against double charges to IHT   1089

Section 5   VAT

    37   VAT – the foundations   1097
    38   VAT – UK provisions   1117
    39   VAT on property   1155
    40   Practical application of VAT   1181

Section 6   Business enterprise

    41   Corporation tax   1217
    42   Company distributions and shareholders   1267
    43   Corporate groups   1289
    44   The taxation of partnerships   1311
    45   Limited liability partnerships   1335
    46   Choice of business medium   1351
    47   Incorporations, acquisitions and demergers   1367
    48   Capital allowances   1381

Section 7   Stamp taxes

    49   Stamp taxes   1429

Section 8   Pensions

    50   Pensions   1479

Section 9   The family

    51   Taxation of the family unit   1505
    52   Matrimonial breakdown   1543

Section 10 Charities

53　Tax treatment of charities　1557

Section 11　Europe and human rights

54　The impact of EU law　1591
55　Human rights and taxation　1649

Index　1689

Table of statutes

	PARA
Charitable Uses Act 1601 (Statute of Elizabeth) preamble	53.1
Apportionment Act 1870	
s 2	17.3, 17.4
Married Women's Property Act 1882	52.79
Partnership Act 1890	8.23; 44.1; 45.2; 49.75
Stamp Act 1891	49.107, 49.108
s 12	49.112
14(4)	49.110
15, 15A	49.109
15B	49.109
(4), (5)	49.109
17	49.110
55	49.114
(1A)	49.114
57	49.114
75	2.43
Stamp Duties Management Act 1891	49.107
Limited Partnerships Act 1907	44.1; 45.2; 46.4; 49.75
Administration of Estates Act 1925	30.122
s 35	28.67
36(10)	21.105
Administration of Trusts Act 1925	16.76
Law of Property Act 1925	
s 34, 36	32.4
53(1)(b)	28.231
149	32.4
184	30.141, 30.143
Trustee Act 1925	
s 31	16.70, 16.73; 24.25; 21.2; 25.81, 33.67
(2)	16.97

	PARA
Trustee Act 1925 – *contd*	
s 33	33.118
36(1)	27A.34
37(1)(c)	27A.34, 27A.36
68	27A.37
Finance Act 1930	
s 42	49.78, 49.125
(2C)	49.125
Law Reform (Miscellaneous Provisions) Act 1934	14.6
Finance Act 1936	3.5
Finance Act 1937	3.29
Finance Act 1951	3.29
s 32	3.29
Income Tax Act 1952	
s 412, 413	28.102
Landlord and Tenant Act 1954	19.67
Finance (No 2) Act 1955	
s 4	3.29
Finance Act 1959	
s 23–26	3.29
Finance Act 1960	3.3; 8.149
s 21–24, 28, 29, 43	3.29
Continental Shelf Act 1964	18.48
Succession (Scotland) Act 1964	
s 14(3)	28.67
31	30.141
Finance Act 1965	19.2
s 42	27A.3
Sch 7	
para 6(2)	2.22
Finance Act 1967	
s 27(3)	49.125
Leasehold Reform Act 1967	19.41; 31.83
Theft Act 1968	
s 17	4.160
Finance Act 1969	3.7
Provisional Collection of Taxes Act 1968	6.22

Table of statutes

	PARA
Taxes Management Act 1970	4.1; 6.21; 51.39
s 1	55.44
7	4.26; 19.60
(1)	4.22
(9)	16.6
8(1), (1F), (1G)	4.22
9(2)	4.22
9A	4.22, 4.33, 4.163
9ZA, 9ZB	4.22
12AA	44.2
12AC	4.33, 4.163
12B	4.22
20(1)	55.62, 55.92
(3)	55.61
(8A)	4.54
20BA	4.157, 4.159
20C	4.58, 4.152; 55.61
(4)	4.155
20D(1)	4.159
28A	4.33, 4.178
(4)	4.33; 55.91
(6)	4.180
28B	4.33, 4.178, 4.180
(5)	4.33
28C	4.422
Pt IIIA (ss 28ZA–28ZE)	4.181
s 28ZA–28ZE	4.181
29	4.42
30B(1)	4.178
31(1)	4.33, 4.178
33	4.33; 55.23
33A	55.23
34	4.42
(1)	55.23
36	4.42; 20.7
(1A)	55.82
(a)	55.82
40	17.2
43	24.12
(1)	11.21
54	4.43, 4.184
55	4.182
59A	4.23
59A(2)	4.23
59B	8.201; 19.60; 24.29
59C	55.82, 55.83
61, 62, 65–68	4.24
74(1)	17.2
98C	5.4
106	14.27
(2)	14.27

	PARA
Taxes Management Act 1970 – contd	
Sch 1AA	
para 3–5	4.159
Sch 1AB	4.33; 55.23
para 2(4)	4.33
3A	4.24
European Communities	
Act 1972	54.2, 54.21, 54.24
s 2	54.21
(1)	2.44; 54.21
(4)	54.21
Finance Act 1972	38.1
s 9(1)	38.5
Domicile and Matrimonial Proceedings Act 1973	
s 1	18.29
(2)	18.29
4	35.3
Local Government (Scotland) Act 1973	40.99
s 226	40.99
235(1)	40.99
Matrimonial Causes Act 1973	52.15
s 25B–25D	52.12
31	52.23
(7B)	52.23
Finance Act 1975	
s 49(4)	31.24, 31.25
Sch 5	
para 4(2)	28.103
Inheritance (Provision for Family and other Dependants) Act 1975	17.59; 21.127; 30.67, 30.153; 51.131
s 2	30.67
19	21.127
Safety of Sports Grounds Act 1975	48.20
Industrial Common Ownership Act 1976	
s 2	7.47
Rent Act 1977	55.3
Capital Gains Tax Act 1979	19.2
Finance (No 2) Act 1979	
s 1(1)(b)	38.5
Housing Act 1980	28.72
Finance Act 1981	28.103; 31.62
s 80	27A.4
Senior Courts Act 1981	
s 35A	14.5
Supreme Court Act 1981 see Senior Courts Act 1981	

Table of statutes xvii

	PARA
Civil Jurisdiction and Judgments Act 1982	
s 41	27.2, 27.12, 27.14
Finance Act 1982	19.4, 19.24; 26.41, 26.42
Mental Health Act 1983	16.75
Value Added Tax Act 1983	38.1
Capital Transfer Tax Act 1984 *see* Inheritance Tax Act 1984	
County Courts Act 1984	
s 69	14.6
Inheritance Tax Act 1984	24.22; 28.1; 30.49; 55.43
s 1	28.2
2(1)	28.2, 28.151
3	47.8
(1)	28.3
(2)	35.2
(3)	28.4, 28.64; 31.6
(4)	28.3
3A	31.3; 32.91
(1)	28.42
(2)	28.43
(3A)	28.44
(5)	28.41
(6)	28.48
4	21.21; 28.231; 51.71
(1)	30.1
(2)	30.142, 30.143
5	31.44
(1)	28.61; 30.2; 33.24; 35.2
(2)	28.62; 29.101
(3)	35.41
(4)	28.63; 31.44
(5)	30.2, 30.13, 30.14; 31.67
6	28.25; 31.1
(1)	35.2, 35.4, 35.20, 35.85
(1A)	35.22
(2)	35.21
(3)	35.23
7(4)	30.21, 30.23
(5)	30.23
8	34.28
8B	30.28
8D–8I	30.28
8J	30.28
(1)	30.29
(4)	30.30
(6)	30.31
8K	30.28
(4)	30.29
8L–8M	30.28

	PARA
Inheritance Tax Act 1984 – *contd*	
s 10	28.4, 28.21; 33.16; 51.131
(1)	28.21, 28.22, 28.23, 28.24, 28.102, 28.105, 28.152; 31.72; 44.51
(2)	28.23
11	29.145; 31.7, 31.8; 33.25; 52.41
(1)(a)'	31.8
(b)	31.9
(2), (4)	31.9
(6)	31.10
12(2ZA)	28.4
13	9.116, 9.122
14	28.27
15	28.27; 46.54
16	31.72; 31.75
18	30.143; 31.41; 33.6, 33.9; 55.43
19	29.145; 31.3
(3A)(a), (b)	31.3
20	29.145; 31.5, 31.61
(4)	28.102
21	31.4
(2)	31.4
22	31.6
(4)	31.6
23	31.88; 33.12; 53.90
24	24.28; 31.87; 34.51
(3), (4)	31.87
25	31.79
(1)	31.86
26A	31.79
27	24.28; 31.85
28	9.116; 33.115
29	28.131
29A	30.67, 30.91; 51.77
30	22.5; 24.28
(3BA)	31.79
31	22.5
(1)	31.80
(a)–(e)	31.80
(4FA)	31.80, 31.81
(4FB)	31.80
32	31.79
(4)	31.86
35A	31.81
36	30.91, 30.96, 30.98, 30.99, 30.101, 30.102, 30.121, 30.156
37	30.91, 30.96, 30.98, 30.99, 30.101, 30.102, 30.121, 30.122, 30.156

Table of statutes

Inheritance Tax Act 1984 – *contd*

	PARA
s 37(2)	30.122
38	30.55, 30.91, 30.96, 30.98, 30.99, 30.101, 30.102, 30.121, 30.156
(2)	30.121
(3)	30.95
39	30.91, 30.96, 30.98, 30.101, 30.102, 30.121, 30.156
39A	30.97
(6)	30.98
40	30.91, 30.96, 30.98, 30.99, 30.101, 30.102, 30.121, 30.156
41	30.57, 30.58, 30.59, 30.91, 30.96, 30.98, 30.99, 30.101, 30.102, 30.103, 30.121, 30.156
42	30.91, 30.96, 30.98, 30.99, 30.101, 30.102, 30.121, 30.156
(1)	30.98
Pt III (ss 43–93)	28.26
s 43	32.2, 32.4
(2)	28.103; 32.4
(3)	35.84
44	28.102
(1)	28.103; 32.7
(2)	28.103; 32.7
45	32.4, 32.9
46	32.25
47	33.5; 35.82, 35.84
47A	28.62
48	28.103
(1)	35.84, 35.85; 52.75
(a)	33.62
(b)	15.24; 33.62
(c)	33.62; 35.84
(3)	32.8; 33.62; 35.20, 35.81, 35.85
(a), (b)	35.85
(3A), (4), (5)	35.22
49	33.5, 33.6
(1)	24.25; 29.42; 31.59; 33.4
49A	32.51
49C–49E	32.52
50	33.5
(1)	33.6
(3)	33.7
(6)	33.8
51(1)	33.13
52(1)	28.105; 33.12, 33.13

Inheritance Tax Act 1984 – *contd*

	PARA
s 52(2)	28.103, 33.14; 51.75
(3)	33.17, 33.18
53(1)	33.24
(2)	24.9; 33.14, 33.15
(3), (4)	33.21
(5)	33.21
(b)	28.103
54A	32.91; 33.18
(1A)	33.18
55	28.63
(1)	33.16
(2)	28.22
57	33.22
(3), (4)	33.22
(5)	31.85
57A	31.85
58	33.112, 33.116; 34.30
(1)	34.1
59	34.1, 34.30
60	34.30
61	34.30
(1), (2)	34.21
62	32.7; 34.30
62A–62C	34.24
63	33.116; 34.30
64	9.112; 34.26, 34.30
(4)	30.147
65	9.112; 34.23, 34.30, 34.72
(4)	34.25
(5)	34.23
66	34.27, 34.30, 34.35, 34.71
(2)	34.31
(6)	34.27
67	34.30, 34.33, 34.71
(1)	34.33
(4)	34.73
68	34.24, 34.30, 34.71
(4)(b)	34.24
(5)	34.24
(a)	34.35
(6)	34.72
69	34.28, 34.30
70	33.112
71	33.63
(1B)	33.67
71A	24.23, 24.27; 32.58; 33.71, 33.72
71B	32.58; 33.71, 33.72
(2)(b)	21.2
71C	32.58; 33.71, 33.72
71D	21.2; 24.23, 24.25, 24.27; 32.59; 33.71, 33.111

Inheritance Tax Act 1984 – contd	PARA	Inheritance Tax Act 1984 – contd	PARA
s 71E	24.25; 33.71, 33.111	s 105(3)	31.47, 31.58
(1)	33.111	(4)(b)	43.21
(2)	33.111	106–108	31.42, 31.46; 33.30
(b)	21.2	109	31.42, 31.47; 33.30
(3), (4)	33.111	110	31.42; 33.30
71F	24.25; 33.71, 33.111	(b)	31.44
(2)	21.2	111	31.42; 33.30; 43.21
(3)	33.111	112	31.42, 31.52; 33.30
(5A)	33.67	(2)(b)	31.52
71G	33.71, 33.111	113	31.42; 33.30; 44.51
72	9.112	114	31.42; 33.30
73	33.118	(1)	31.77
75	33.115; 34.51	115	31.62
76	33.112	(2)	31.62
(1)	34.51	(3)	31.67
(b)	34.51	116	31.62, 31.68, 31.69
77	33.117	(2)–(5)	31.75
78	24.28; 31.84	117	24.10; 31.62, 31.69
79	31.84	(1)	31.66
80	34.21	(a)	31.70
81	24.25; 33.114; 34.32	118	31.62
81A	32.94	119	31.62, 31.69
82	35.20	120	31.62, 31.71
83	34.21	121, 122	31.62
86	9.117; 33.115	123	31.62
87	34.114	(1)(b)	31.71
88	33.118	124	31.62
89	32.60; 33.113	125	31.21, 31.25
89A	33.113	(3)	31.21
89B	33.113	126	31.21
(1)(c), (d)	21.2	127	31.21, 31.22
90	32.94	128–130	31.21
92	30.143	131	30.24
93	30.155; 33.28, 33.29	141	30.144; 33.29
Pt IV (ss 94–102)	28.151	(3)	30.144
s 94	28.152	(4)	33.29
(1)	28.152	142	17.58; 30.153, 30.155, 30.157; 31.46; 33.28; 34.21; 53.85
(2)(a), (b)	28.152		
95, 96	28.152		
98	28.153, 28.171	(4)	30.157
(1)	28.171	143	30.151; 53.85, 53.92
(3)	28.153, 28.171	144	17.1, 17.58, 17.58, 17.59; 21.2, 21.104; 30.66, 30.145, 30.147, 30.149, 30.150, 30.151; 31.61
99(2)(a)	28.152		
102	28.151		
Pt V Ch 1 (ss 103–114)	31.58		
s 103	31.42; 33.30	(1)	34.51
104	31.42; 33.30	(2)	30.145
105	31.42; 33.30	146	21.127; 30.67
(1)(a)	31.43, 31.54, 31.58	150	28.28
(b)	31.43; 31.57, 31.58, 31.61	151	33.114
		153	31.25; 35.25
(bb)	31.43, 31.58	154	31.25
(cc), (d)	31.43	155	35.24

Table of statutes

Inheritance Tax Act 1984 – *contd*

	PARA
s 157	35.26
158, 159	35.41
Pt VI (ss 160–278)	38.65; 30.5
Pt VI Ch I (ss 160–170)	28.69
s 160	28.65; 30.3, 30.4
161	28.70
162(4)	28.66; 31.44, 31.67
(5)	35.61
162A, 162AA	30.15; 35.62
162B	30.15; 31.44
163	28.71
165	24.3
(1)	24.12
167	28.74
(2)	30.7
170	33.8; 35.84
171	30.6
(2)	30.7
173	35.62
174	21.1
175A	30.13
176	30.8
178	30.9
190	28.72; 30.10
(1)	21.23
197A	30.10
Pt VII (ss 199–214)	30.46
s 199	28.171; 29.146
(2)	30.28, 30.49
200	29.146
(1)	29.146
201(1)	32.71
203	28.171
204	30.46
211	30.56
(1)	29.146
(3)	29.146; 30.49, 30.56
212	28.171, 28.174
Pt VIII (ss 215–261)	31.58
s 216	28.172
(1)(bb)	30.28
(3)(b)	30.28
(3A)	30.12, 30.43
221	28.201
222	28.221
226	28.173
227	28.126; 28.174; 30.51; 31.58
(1A)	30.28, 30.54
(2)	31.58
(4)	28.174
228	30.51
(1)(a)–(d)	31.58

Inheritance Tax Act 1984 – *contd*

	PARA
s 228(3)	31.58
229	31.23, 31.58
230	28.176; 31.90
(1)	31.90
233	28.175
235	28.177
237	28.171
(1)(a)	30.50
(4)	28.171
238	28.171
239	28.171
(2)	30.53
(4)	30.155
240(2)	28.171
(4), (5)	28.171
242	28.221
251	52.78
247	30.43
262	28.127
263	31.4
264	28.129
266	28.128
(2)	28.128
267	35.4
(1)(a), (b)	35.4
(4)	35.23
267A	46.7
267ZA	18.28; 35.5
268	2.42; 3.1; 28.101, 28.102, 28.105; 29.44; 32.7
(1)(a)	28.104, 28.105
(b)	28.104, 28.105
(3)	28.105
269	31.55; 47.8
(1)	31.55, 31.58
270	28.21
272	28.62, 28.104; 32.7, 32.94
Sch 1	30.98
Sch 1A	30.30
Sch 2	
para 1A, 2	30.21
3	34.28
Sch 3	31.79, 31.86
Sch 4	33.117
para 1	31.85; 33.117
2–7	31.85
16	34.51
Sch 6	
para 2	30.158, 30.159; 33.23
Sch 19	
para 46	31.24, 31.25

Table of statutes xxi

	PARA
Police and Criminal Evidence Act 1984	4.52, 4.56, 4.152; 55.91
s 8	4.58, 4.140, 4.152, 4.154
(1) (d)	4.155
14(2)	4.157
14A	4.157
67	4.158
(11)	4.158
Sch 1	4.58, 4.140, 4.157, 4.159
para 7–14	4.157
Companies Act 1985	45.4
s 159	42.21
160	42.21
(4)	42.24
161–181	42.21
311	
Finance Act 1985	2.48; 48.67
s 83	51.91; 52.60
88	49.113
Finance Act 1986	28.1; 29.121; 49.92
s 66	42.31
67–72A	49.123
75	47.51; 49.79, 49.126
75A	49.85
76	49.79, 49.126
77	49.126
79	49.102
80	49.104
Pt IV (ss 86–99)	49.92
s 86(4)	49.101
87	49.92, 49.102
88A, 89A, 89AA	49.104
92	49.92
93, 96	49.103
97A	49.103, 49.123
97AA, 97B	49.103
99(3), (5)	49.102
(5A)	49.106
(b)	49.106
100	28.1
102	29.1, 29.128; 31.61
(1)	29.71
(b)	29.21
(3)	29.21; 35.21
(4)	35.21
(5)	29.138; 31.7
(a)	15.22
(b)	31.61
102A	29.130
(2)	29.131
(3)	29.72

	PARA
Finance Act 1986 – *contd*	
s 102A(5)	29.131
102B	29.130, 29.137
(3) (b)	29.72
(4)	29.138
102C	29.130
(3)	29.73
103	30.14; 36.4
(1), (5)	30.14
104	28.132; 36.1
(1) (d)	36.5
Sch 20	29.1, 29.121
para 1–4	29.101
5	29.101
(1)	29.42
(a)	29.72, 29.73, 29.145
(b)	29.73, 29.145
(c)	29.44
8	31.60, 31.61
Insolvency Act 1986	45.4, 45.5
s 110	47.52; 49.126
111	49.126
214	46.21
Finance (No 2) Act 1987	
s 62	54.21
97	31.90
Finance Act 1988	9.162; 14.7; 16.102; 19.4, 19.34
s 36	14.13
Income and Corporation Taxes Act 1988	6.2, 6.21, 6.43; 41.1, 41.24, 41.42; 50.6; 54.21
s 3	14.21
8(3)	41.21
16 Sch A	41.42, 41.62
18(1)	
Sch D	8.1, 8.22, 8.24; 9.123; 41.62
Case I	8.1; 10.2, 10.30; 13.15; 19.71; 47.3
Case II	8.1, 8.21; 10.2, 10.119
Case III	13.12; 14.6, 14.13
Case IV	18.31
Case V	8.66; 10.2; 18.31
Case VI	3.29; 13.1, 13.12, 13.15, 13.18, 13.22
19	8.41, 8.91, 8.102, 8.149
(1)	8.11, 8.13, 8.91, 8.149
Sch E	8.11, 8.22, 8.65, 8.149
20(2)	2.38
20 Sch F	2.38; 3.72; 9.81
74	48.80

Income and Corporation Taxes Act 1988 – contd

Section	PARA
s 74(1)(d)	10.142
(1)(j)	41.51
91A	10.67
131	8.91, 8.92
135	9.41, 9.51, 9.53
144A	9.43
145	8.112
148	8.149
(4)	8.149
154	8.102, 8.123, 8.124, 8.125; 9.12
155–158	8.123
160	8.123, 8.124
161–166	8.123
188	8.149
203(1)	2.37
208	42.28
209(2)(da)	41.98
219	42.28, 42.29
231(1)	18.78
248	48.10
249	48.10
266	14.41; 15.1
267	15.1
273	14.41
274	15.1
282A	51.54
313	8.134, 8.149
334	18.6; 27.14
336	27.13
338	2.37
342(2)	41.21
343	10.30; 41.66
347A	16.91
347B	55.43
348	14.13, 14.21; 16.8
349	14.13, 14.21, 14.23; 16.8
353	9.27; 10.28
(1A)	7.51
365	7.51
383(1)	8.124
388	2.37
393	41.62
410(2)	43.45
413(3)(b)	43.42
416(6)	24.19
501A	48.34
527	10.175
577(10)	1.41
578A	48.80
580A, 580B	8.133
595, 596A	8.149

Income and Corporation Taxes Act 1988 – contd

Section	PARA
s 615	5.7
619	14.41; 44.17
628	44.16
630–632, 634–655	44.17
656	14.41
659E	45.14
660A	16.93; 51.55
(1)	51.55
(2)	16.93
(3)(c)	51.55
(6)	51.55
660B(1)	16.93
660G(1), (2)	16.93
674	41.65
683	16.65
686	16.22, 16.33; 42.30, 42.147
(2)(a)	16.22
(d)	16.23
687	42.147, 42.152
690	31.85
703	2.47; 3.3, 3.29
704	3.3, 3.29
704D	3.34, 3.61
705	3.3, 3.29
706	3.3, 3.29; 4.173
707, 708	3.3, 3.29
709	3.3, 3.29
(2)	3.72
713	3.33
739	1.23; 2.32; 6.43; 18.113; 28.102
740	18.113
761(1)	51.44
765, 765A	3.29
767A, 767B	41.187
768, 768A	41.65
774	3.29
776	3.29
788(3)	54.21
821	14.26
824, 826	4.32
832(1)	10.21; 13.15; 20.13
839(7)	43.45
Sch 6	
para 7	8.120
Sch 15	15.1
para 8, 18	41.74
Sch 18	43.47
para 1	41.94
Sch 28AA	9.124

Table of statutes xxiii

	PARA
Finance Act 1989	9.113; 19.4; 39.1; 41.93
s 36(5)	8.13
43	9.123; 10.133
69	9.113
178	27A.112
Finance Act 1990	49.92
Finance Act 1991	9.112; 27A.8
s 13	38.5
Finance (No 2) Act 1992	
s 42	10.28
Social Security Contributions and Benefits Act 1992	
Sch 1	
para 3, 3A, 3B	9.44
Taxation of Chargeable Gains Act 1992	2.45; 9.45, 9.49; 19.2; 53.120
s 2	2.38; 19.6; 27.9, 27.43, 27.56; 27A.11
(1B)	19.6
(2)	19.13; 27A.11, 27A.55, 27A.118, 27A.128, 27A.127
2A	19.28
3	19.50; 25.152
(1), (2)	19.51
(7)	19.52
3A	19.62
4	19.49; 21.61
(1AA)	25.41
(3)	25.41
(6)	20.4
4B	20.4, 20.6; 21.81; 27A.95
4BB	25.41
8(6)	45.19
9	27.2, 27.10
(3), (5)	27.10
10	19.6; 27.44
10A	18.13; 19.6; 27.46, 27.56, 27.57, 27.59, 27.60, 27.61, 27.62
(9)	27.49
(9C)	27.49, 27.59
(10)	27.49, 27.57, 27.59
10AA	27.46
(1), (4)	27.49
10B	41.151, 41.162
12	27.81, 27.100
(1)	21.3
13	9.112; 21.3; 27.46, 27.62, 27.113; 41.161
(5)	27.112
(10)	27A.117, 27A.154
14A	27.112

	PARA
Taxation of Chargeable Gains Act 1992 – *contd*	
s 16(3)	27A.55, 27A.129
16A	19.48; 21.81
16ZA	27.86
16ZB	27.87
17	47.9; 8.129; 9.46, 9.47, 9.49, 9.51, 9.53, 9.76; 19.14, 19.70; 22.102; 51.61
(1)	9.46, 9.112, 9.116; 19.67; 42.145
(a)	19.14; 24.2
(b)	19.14
(2)	9.46; 19.14; 42.145
(b)	19.67
18	9.47; 19.14; 47.7; 51.61; 52.21
(2)	24.2
(3)	19.45; 25.22
19	19.16; 22.23; 43.132
(2)	19.16
(6)	43.133
20	43.132
21	19.7, 19.35; 22.2, 22.41; 27.101
(1)	19.8
22	8.148; 19.64, 19.65, 19.78; 27A.164
(1)	52.23
(c)	19.8
(3)	19.70
23	19.64; 27A.164
(4)–(6)	19.65
24	27A.164; 46.49
(1)	11.121; 19.65, 19.78
(1A)	19.69
(2)	11.121; 19.69; 26.21; 44.33
26	19.73
27	19.72
28	9.112; 19.17, 19.78
(1)	19.78
(2)	19.79
29	19.75; 26.61, 26.64
(2)	26.62, 26.63
(4)	26.63
30	19.75; 26.61, 26.64
(4)	26.64
31	19.75; 26.61, 26.64; 43.151
35	19.5, 19.31
(2)	19.20
(5)	19.33

Taxation of Chargeable Gains
Act 1992 – *contd*

	PARA
s 35A	19.25, 19.34
37	9.29, 9.48; 19.3; 42.28
(1)	9.57; 19.39; 42.29
(3)	44.34
38	9.47; 19.19, 19.22
(1)	19.70
(a)	19.20
(b)	19.21, 19.43
(c)	19.22
(2)	19.22
(3)	19.23
(4)	19.22; 25.53
39	19.23
42	19.35
44	19.37; 22.21
(1)(c)	22.21
45(1)	19.47; 22.21
(2), (3)	19.47; 22.21
46	19.48
47	19.37
48	19.17
(1)	19.17
49D	21.2
50	22.78
51	22.3
52(4)	22.73
52A	19.25
53	19.25
(1)	19.27
54	19.25, 19.26
55–57	19.25
58	19.14, 19.16; 24.2; 26.64; 51.58, 51.67, 51.131; 52.21, 52.63; 53.89
59	19.6; 44.31
59A	45.10, 45.15
60	19.12; 21.104; 25.2, 25.6; 52.71
(1)	25.47
(2)	21.105; 25.6, 25.7
62	19.63; 21.1, 21.22, 21.121, 21.125; 23.66
(1)	21.1
(a)	21.21
(2)	19.45, 19.58; 21.41
(3)	21.3
(4)	21.101, 21.105
(b)	21.64
(6)	21.121, 21.124, 21.127; 30.153
(a), (b)	21.121
(7)	21.122; 30.153

Taxation of Chargeable Gains
Act 1992 – *contd*

	PARA
s 62(8)	30.153
(9)	30.153
(10)	21.1
64(2)	21.102
(3)	21.105
65(2)	21.3
68A	25.2
68B	25.81; 27A.28
68C	21.126
69	27A.26
(1)	25.42; 27A.25, 27A.28, 27A.39
(2C)	27A.28
(2D)	18.19; 27A.30
(4)	25.141
70	25.21
71	19.22; 21.22, 21.103, 21.104; 24.9, 24.12; 25.44, 25.48, 25.55; 42.145, 42.147
(1)	2.38; 24.19, 24.25; 25.47, 25.49, 25.51, 25.54, 25.81, 25.113; 33.13; 52.74
(2)	25.44, 25.48
(2A)	25.44, 25.48
(2B)–(2D)	25.44
71B(2)(b)	21.2
71E(2)(b)	21.2
71F(2)	21.2
72	21.2; 25.54, 25.55
(1A)(b)	21.2
(1B)	21.2
73	21.2; 25.49
(1)(b)	25.50, 25.54
(2)	25.49
74	21.2; 24.19; 25.51
76	27A.10
(1)	25.111, 25.114, 25.118, 25.141; 27A.164; 33.13
(1A), (1B)	25.115
(2)	25.113, 25.114
(3)	25.115
76A	25.116, 25.141
76B	25.52; 27A.87
77	25.152; 27A.71, 27A.87, 27A.88, 27A.173
79A	25.45
79B	27.112
80	26.47; 27A.9, 27A.40, 27A.44, 27A.53
(2)	27A.38

	PARA		PARA
Taxation of Chargeable Gains Act 1992 – *contd*		Taxation of Chargeable Gains Act 1992 – *contd*	
s 81	27A.9, 27A.43	s 97(2)	27A.109, 27A.111, 27A.115
82	27A.9, 27A.41	(5)	27A.116
(3)	27A.41	(b)	27A.115
83	27A.9	(c)	27A.117
83A	27A.52	(6)	27A.55, 27A.129
84	27A.9	98A	27A.177
85	25.114; 27A.10, 27A.167, 28.168	100	19.12; 22.3
(1)	25.114, 25.115	(1)	15.124
(3)	25.114	104	9.46, 9.58; 26.43, 26.44, 26.45, 26.47
86	9.112; 21.126; 27.46, 27.49, 27.61, 27.100, 27.112; 27A.8, 27A.10, 27A.11, 27A.22, 27A.23, 27A.55, 27A.71, 27A.72, 27A.74, 27A.75, 27A.76, 27A.78, 27A.82, 27A.86, 27A.87, 27A.88, 27A.89, 27A.90, 27A.92, 27A.95, 27A.97, 27A.114, 27A.115, 27A.126, 27A.127, 27A.129, 27A.167, 27A.174; 35.21	(3)	9.55
		105	9.55; 26.46
		105A	9.55
		105B	9.55
		106A(5)	26.46, 26.47
		(5A)	26.47
		113	22.5
		115	22.3
		116	2.41; 41.96
		(10)	20.37, 20.38
		117	2.41; 22.45; 41.93
86A	27A.82	(1)(a), (b)	41.94
87	9.112; 18.125; 21.124, 21.125; 27.49, 27.62, 27.88, 27.100, 27.112; 27A.2, 27A.4, 27A.6, 27A.10, 27A.11, 27A.24, 27A.55, 27A.75, 27A.78, 27A.82, 27A.87, 27A.88, 27A.111, 27A.112, 27A.113, 27A.114, 27A.115, 27A.116, 27A.108, 27A.126, 27A.128, 27A.121, 27A.127, 27A.128, 27A.129, 27A.137, 27A.145, 27A.149, 27A.160, 27A.168, 27A.174, 27A.176	119A	9.29, 9.48
		(3)(d)	9.56
		120	9.51
		(4)	19.70
		121	22.2
		122	20.28; 47.71
		(1), (2), (4)	26.21
		(5)(b)	26.21
		123	26.21
		125	9.112
		126	26.2
		127	2.41; 20.39; 22.104; 26.2, 26.44; 42.141
		128–130	22.104; 26.2
		131	2.41; 26.2
		132	2.41; 14.6; 47.38
(2)	27A.128	(3)	22.44
(4)	27A.55, 27A.116, 27A.118, 27A.150	135	15.97; 19.34; 22.104; 26.3; 27.55; 41.96; 47.38, 47.39
(5)	27A.118		
(6)	27A.114		
(7)	27A.121	(1)	2.22
87A	27A.11, 27A.82, 27A.118, 27A.128	136	15.97; 19.34; 22.104; 26.3; 41.96; 47.38
87B	27A.114, 27A.150	137	19.34; 22.104; 26.3; 27.55; 41.96; 47.38
87C	27A.11		
89B(1)(c), (d)	21.2	(1)	27.56
90	27A.115, 27A.156, 27A.175, 27A.176	138	12.113; 26.3; 27.55; 47.38
(5)(a)	27A.174	138A	47.38
91	27A.152, 27A.160	139	49.126
97(1)	27A.109, 27A.111		

Taxation of Chargeable Gains Act 1992 – *contd*		Taxation of Chargeable Gains Act 1992 – *contd*	
s 140	41.155; 47.38, 47.51	s 165(4)	24.12
142	42.152	(8)(a)	24.10
144	9.49, 9.43; 19.70; 21.2	(10)	24.3, 24.17
144ZA	9.54; 19.70	165A	20.11; 24.10, 24.14
145	19.70	(2)	20.16
146	19.37, 19.70	(11)	20.17
147	19.70	166	24.18
149A	9.46, 9.49	167	24.19
149AA	9.46, 9.47	167A	24.18, 24.19; 47.8A
(1)	9.34	167LA	47.9
150A	15.52, 15.131, 15.132; 22.3	168	21.2; 24.18; 27.42
		(1)(b)	24.18
150B	15.52; 22.3	(2), (3), (5)	24.18
150C	15.52	(7)	21.2; 24.18
150E, 150F	15.128	(9)	24.18
150G	15.128; 51.50	168A	24.18
151A(1)	15.126	169A	45.17
152	12.64; 22.72, 22.74; 26.3; 27.46; 44.37; 46.62; 47.6, 47.32	169B–169G	24.21
		Pt V Ch III (ss 169H–169S)	9.87
		s 169H	44.39
(6)	22.75	169I	44.39
153	22.72; 26.3	(2)(b)	20.26
153A	22.80	(4)	20.24
154	22.72, 22.78; 26.3	(6)	20.9
155	22.72, 22.74; 26.3	(b)	20.10
156	22.72; 26.3	(7B)	20.28
156A	45.17	(8)	20.22
157, 158	22.72; 26.3	(a)–(c)	20.23
159	22.72, 22.76; 26.3	169J	44.39
(11)	22.75	169K	44.8, 44.39
161	10.118; 12.102; 19.71	(1A)	20.33
(3A)	19.71	(1B), (1D)	20.30
162	22.100, 22.102, 22.103; 26.4; 44.38; 47.4, 47.5, 47.8, 47.9, 47.10, 47.14	(3), (4)	20.30, 20.33
		(4A)	20.30, 20.33
		(5)	20.30, 20.33
		(6A)	20.30
162A	22.100, 22.103	169L	44.39
162B	19.10	(4)	20.25
162M(3)	22.103	169LA	20.20
165	9.53; 12.64; 21.2; 22.71, 22.99; 24.4, 24.5, 24.7, 24.12, 24.13, 24.15, 24.16, 24.17, 24.18, 24.19, 24.21, 24.23, 24.24, 24.30; 28.49; 29.44; 44.32, 44.33, 44.36; 47.7, 47.8, 47.9	(3)	20.23
		169M	20.7; 24.14; 44.39
		169N	44.39
		(1)	20.5
		(3)	19.49; 20.1
		(4A)	44.39
		(7), (8)	20.2
		(9)	15.94
(1)	24.12	169O	44.39
(2)	24.6	169P	20.32; 44.39
(b)(i)	24.6	(4)	20.34
(3)(ba)	24.5	169Q	20.39; 22.104; 26.2; 44.39
(d)	24.24	169R	20.36, 20.38; 44.39

Table of statutes xxvii

	PARA
Taxation of Chargeable Gains Act 1992 – *contd*	
s 169S	44.39
(2)	20.28
(3)	20.9
(4A)	20.17
(5)	20.2
169SA	20.1, 20.11, 20.17
169T–169V	20.40
170	43.121, 43.122
171	26.1, 26.64; 41.162; 43.122, 43.125, 43.126, 43.132; 47.35
171A	43.126
173	43.125
175	43.128
(1)	43.128
(2A)	43.128, 43.133
(2B)	43.130
(2C)	43.129
176	43.151
177A	43.127
179	26.1; 43.122; 47.35
(2A), (2B), (2ZA), (2ZB)	43.123
179ZA	43.122
184A–184F	43.125, 43.127
185	27A.38; 41.154
190	41.154
192	26.3
(2)	42.141; 47.51
192A	41.75
203(1)	23.83
205	19.23
210	15.8, 15.9; 22.3
222	12.113; 23.1, 23.44; 24.26; 52.63
(1)	23.22
(b)	23.61, 23.62
(4)	23.62
(5)	23.43
(6)	23.42; 51.62
(7)	21.104, 21.105
(a)	23.66, 23.82
223	23.1; 52.63
(1)	21.105; 23.44; 52.63
(3)	12.113; 23.84, 23.85
(3A)	23.85
(4)	23.64
(7)	23.81
224	23.1; 52.63
(3)	23.101
225	21.66, 21.81; 23.1, 23.62, 23.63; 52.71, 52.74

	PARA
Taxation of Chargeable Gains Act 1992 – *contd*	
s 225A	21.66; 23.65
225B	52.63. 52.64, 52.68
226	23.1
226A	23.121; 24.26
236A	9.82
236B1)	9.34
236H(4)	9.116
236P	9.116
237	22.3
237A	9.49
239	9.112
239ZA	9.112
240	19.39
241(3A)	20.14
242, 243	19.36
247	19.77; 22.82, 22.83; 43.131
248	19.77
248A	19.77; 22.83
248B, 248C	19.77
248D	19.77; 22.83
251	14.6; 22.42, 22.43, 22.44; 41.92, 41.93; 52.83
(3), (4)	22.42
252	22.3; 27.101
253	19.44; 22.43; 41.92; 46.49
(4)	22.43
254	41.96
256	19.12; 21.105; 22.3, 22.5; 53.41, 53.89
257	21.105; 22.4; 41.96; 53.89
257A	53.116
258(1A)	22.6
(2)	22.5
(b)	22.5
(3)	22.5; 31.79
(4)	22.5
260	21.2, 21.104; 24.13, 24.21, 24.22, 24.23, 24.24, 24.26, 24.30; 28.49; 31.85, 31.87; 32.93
(1) (c)	24.28
(2)	24.23, 24.28
(a)	24.23, 24.25, 24.27; 25.51
(d)	16.73; 24.27
(da)	24.27
(db)	24.27
261B	11.61, 11.81, 11.82; 19.45, 19.59
261C	11.61

	PARA		PARA
Taxation of Chargeable Gains Act 1992 – *contd*		Taxation of Chargeable Gains Act 1992 – *contd*	
s 261ZA	24.23	Sch 5A	27A.153, 27A.177
262(1)	22.22	Sch 5B	15.52
(3)	19.65	Sch 5BB	15.128; 51.50
(4)	22.23	Sch 7	
263	22.2	para 1	24.9
268, 269	22.3	5, 6	24.8
271(1A)	19.12	7	24.7
272	9.22; 19.16; 21.22	Sch 7A	43.127
273	19.16	Sch 7AC	41.47, 41.75
(3)	21.22	Sch 7C	9.82
274	21.22; 30.3	Sch 7D	9.75, 9.76
275A	27.83	para 5	9.81
279	27.42	Sch 7ZA	20.11, 20.17
279A	19.18, 19.45; 22.42	Pt 1 (paras 1, 2)	20.2
279B–279D	22.42	Pt 2 (paras 3–12)	20.17
280	19.17, 19.61; 47.34	Pt 3 (paras 13–23)	20.17
281	24.30	Sch 8	19.39
(2)	28.30	para 1	19.41
(3)	19.61; 28.30	(6)	19.41
(5), (7)	28.30	10(2)	19.40
282(2)	24.31	Sch 8A	27.101
283	4.32	Sch 9	22.3
286	19.15; 24.2; 28.21	Trade Union and Labour Relations Consolidation Act 1992	
(2)	19.15		
(4)	19.15; 44.32		
(5), (6)	19.15	s 189	8.42
Sch A1	19.28	Charities Act 1993	21.105
para 4(5)	21.63	Finance Act 1993	43.127
5(5)	21.63	Leasehold Reform, Housing and Urban Development Act 1993	31.83
Sch B1	25.41		
Sch BA1	25.41		
Sch 1	16.74; 19.53	Pension Schemes Act 1993	
para 1	33.113	s 71	50.19
Sch 2		Finance Act 1994	27A.177; 48.17
para 1–6	26.48	s 147(1)	2.48
16(3), (6)	19.29	147A(1)	2.48
18, 19	26.48	150A(1)	2.48
Sch 4	19.34	155	2.48
Sch 4A	25.116, 25.117, 25.141	(2)	2.48
Sch 4B	25.52; 27A.54, 27A.87, 27A.171, 27A.174, 27A.176	Local Government etc (Scotland) Act 1994	
		s 2	40.99
Sch 4C	27A.11, 27A.71, 27A.77, 27A.87, 27A.89, 27A.111, 27A.108, 27A.171, 27A.176	Value Added Tax Act 1994	5.24; 38.1, 38.2
		s 1	38.31
		(3)	38.101
Sch 5		2	38.29
para 1(6)	27A.55	(1), (2)	38.5
6	27A.73	3	38.27
9	27A.76	4(1)	38.21, 38.28
(2), (7)	27A.76	5	38.4
(10A)	27A.80	(2)	38.22

Table of statutes xxix

	PARA
Value Added Tax Act 1994 – *contd*	
s 5(2)(b)	38.24
(5)	38.30
6(2)–(4)	38.33
7	38.8
(2)	38.31
(5)	38.8
7A	38.8
(4)	38.8, 38.105
8	38.30, 38.101, 38.106
9	38.32
19(2)	38.29
(3)	38.29
21	38.103
(4)	38.4
25	38.84
(3)	38.3, 38.52
(6)	38.53
26	38.3, 38.84
(2)(c)	39.29
29A, 30	38.4
(6)	38.102
(8)	38.104
31	38.4
33	40.98, 40.101
(2)	39.29
(3)	40.98
33A	39.29
35	39.25, 39.42
36	38.59
41(2)	40.102
(3)	39.29
(6), (7)	40.102
41A	40.102
42	40.99
43	38.50; 43.191
45	38.27; 44.1
49	38.26; 47.13
50A	40.108
53(3)	40.110
60	55.82
80	38.52, 38.53; 55.23
(3)	38.52
(4)	38.53
83	4.178; 38.2
84(3)(c)	55.83
89	38.9
(3)	39.31
94	38.28
96(1)	40.65
(4)	40.99
97	38.2

	PARA
Value Added Tax Act 1994 – *contd*	
Sch 1	38.27, 38.49
para 9(a), (b)	38.49
11	38.51
13(2), (3)	38.51
14	38.49
Sch 3	
para 1	38.49
Sch 3B	38.34
Sch 4	38.23
para 1	38.25
(2)	38.25
3	38.25
4	38.23, 38.25
5(1)	38.25
(2)(a)	38.25
(4)	38.25
8(1)(a)	38.23
Sch 4A	38.106
para 1, 4	38.8
14A	40.43
Sch 6	
para 7	38.25
Sch 7A	37.5; 38.7
Group 2	38.6
Sch 8	38.6; 53.123
Group 1–3	38.7
Group 4	38.7; 53.123
Group 5	38.7
item 1	39.23
2	39.25, 39.25A
4	39.25
note (3), (4), (6)	39.23
(7), (7A)	39.23
(8), (9), (16), (18)	39.23
Group 6	38.7
item 1	39.24
2	39.25A
3	39.25
Group 7	38.7; 38.105
Group 8	38.7
item 3	53.123
Group 9–11	38.7
Group 12	38.7; 40.39
item 2, 2A, 4–7, 9, 11–13, 17–19	53.123
note 2A	40.39
Group 13, 14	38.7
Group 15	38.7
item 1, 1A	53.126
2, 4, 5, 8–8C, 9	53.123
Group 16	38.7
Group 17, 18	38.7

Table of statutes

	PARA
Value Added Tax Act 1994 – *contd*	
Sch 9	38.8
Group 1	38.8; 39.19, 39.21, 39.22, 39.27
item 1	39.21
Group 2	38.8; 40.56
item 1	40.78
3	40.78
4	40.81
note (2)	40.81
(9)	40.82
Group 3, 4	38.8
Group 5	38.8; 39.29
item 6	40.72
Group 6	38.8
note (1)	40.34
Group 7	38.8; 40.36
item 10	53.126
note (5)	40.34
Group 8–11	38.8
Group 9	38.8
para 1(e)	40.49; 53.126
Group 10	40.54
note (4)	40.54
Group 12	38.8; 53.42, 53.126
Group 13–15	38.8
Group 16	53.128
Sch 9A	43.191
Sch 10	39.1, 39.27
para 2	39.37; 49.42
5–11	39.29
27	39.28
Sch 11	
para 1	38.2
10(2)	4.168
(3)	4.58
11	4.157
Sch 11A	
para 3(1)	5.22
Finance Act 1995	43.129, 43.130, 43.131
s 91	50.2, 50.20
160	1.22
Pensions Act 1995	50.21; 52.10, 52.12
s 91	50.2, 50.20
166, 167	52.12
Employment Rights Act 1996	45.13; 47.14
Finance Act 1996	9.113; 31.59
154	18.20
Sch 13	2.38

	PARA
Trusts of Land and Appointment of Trustees Act 1996	27A.111
s 9	12.41
Sch 3	
para 3(12)	27A.37
Finance Act 1997	38.53; 42.30; 48.67
s 68	43.45
73	3.55
Finance (No 2) Act 1997	38.94
Finance Act 1998	8.149; 15.4; 19.25; 25.115; 26.44, 26.46; 27.45; 27A.10, 27A.74, 27A.82, 27A.85, 31.79, 31.80, 31.81; 43.123
117	41.181
132	27A.77
Sch 3	
para 12(4)	42.46
Sch 5	27A.77
Sch 14	
para 7	15.7
Sch 18	41.181
para 17	41.184
(2), (3)	4.202
18	41.184
19, 20	41.184
24	4.33, 4.163
30(3)	4.178
31A–31D	4.181
32	4.33, 4.178
33	4.33, 4.180
34(3)	4.33, 4.178
41	4.41
48	4.178
Sch 19	41.181
Human Rights Act 1998	17.2; 51.130; 55.1, 55.2, 55.3, 55.5, 55.44, 55.62, 55.93
s 2(1)	55.4
4	55.3
4	55.3
6	55.3
(1)	55.44
(2)(a), (b)	55.44
Late Payment of Commercial Debts (Interest) Act 1998	
s 1(1)	14.32
Social Security Act 1998	51.39
Access to Justice Act 1999	
s 54(4)	4.213
55	4.213

Table of statutes xxxi

	PARA
Finance Act 1999	12.87; 14.13, 14.31; 15.93; 29.44, 29.122, 29.137; 49.109
Sch 12	49.109
Sch 13	49.108
para 1	49.113
(1)	2.43
Sch 15	49.108
para 1	49.110
Sch 19	49.92, 49.102, 49.106
Welfare Reform and Pensions Act 1999	50.3, 50.23; 52.10, 52.12
Sch 3	
para 3	52.10
Finance Act 2000	9.1, 9.45; 14.13; 19.45; 25.52; 27.112; 27A.10, 27A.87, 27A.88, 27A.89, 27A.173, 27A.174; 41.157, 41.159; 43.42, 43.122, 43.126; 47.11; 48.63, 48.123; 49.125; 53.1, 53.79, 53.80, 53.87
s 63	41.72
122	49.117
144	55.82
Sch 15	41.72
para 8, 18	41.74
Financial Services and Markets Act 2000	50.3, 50.10
s 22	50.10
Limited Liability Partnerships Act 2000	44.1; 45.4, 45.12; 46.5; 49.75
s 1(5)	45.4
4(4)	45.11
5	45.6
12	45.23
Capital Allowances Act 2001	1.22; 2.38; 6.2, 6.21; 7.1; 48.1, 48.2, 48.3
Pt 2 (ss 1–10)	48.2
s 3(1)	48.6
5(1), (2), (5), (6)	48.7
6	48.7
9(1)	48.121
Pt 2 (ss 11–270)	48.2; 48.11
s 11(4)	2.38
13	48.21
14	48.14
15	48.12
(1)	48.12
21	48.17

	PARA
Capital Allowances Act 2001 – *contd*	
s 21(3)	48.18
22	48.17
(1)	48.15
23	48.15, 48.17
(1)	48.15
25	48.18
26(2), (3)	48.19
28	48.20, 48.60
30, 33	48.20
33A	48.60, 48.61
(3)	10.142
33B	48.3, 48.61
35	48.12
(2)	12.47
36	7.49
38A(3)(b)	45.16
44	48.30
45	2.38
45A	48.31
45B, 45C	48.31
45AA	48.31
45D	48.75, 48.79
45DA, 45DB	48.38, 48.74
45F, 45G	48.34
45H–45J	48.35
45K–45N	48.37
46	48.30, 48.31, 48.34, 48.35, 48.76
47–51	48.30
51A	48.28
52	48.30
53	48.54
(2)	48.54
54(3), (5), (6)	48.54
55(4)	48.53
56	48.38, 48.58
(1), (3), (4)	48.55
(5)	48.6
(6), (7)	48.56
57(1)	48.54
61(1)	48.53, 48.80
(2)	48.53, 48.54, 48.63
62	48.54
(1)	48.65, 48.68
63	48.53, 48.54
65	48.53
67	48.81
(1)	48.81
68, 69	48.81
Pt 2 Ch 8 (ss 74–82)	48.80
s 74, 75	48.80
76	48.80

	PARA		PARA
Capital Allowances Act 2001 – *contd*		Capital Allowances Act 2001 – *contd*	
s 76(4)	48.80	s 266	47.3; 48.58
77	48.80	267	48.58
(1), (2)	48.80	Pt 3 (ss 271–360)	48.2; 48.91
78–80	48.80	Pt 3 Ch 2 (ss 274–285)	48.92
81	48.76, 48.80	s 274	48.93
82	48.80	277	48.95
83	48.59	279–281	48.94
84	48.59, 48.74, 48.76	286–289	48.93
85–88	48.59	Pt 3A (ss 360A–360Z4)	48.2, 48.124
89	48.59	Pt 4 (ss 361–393)	48.2, 48.121
(2), (4)–(6)	48.59	s 362	48.121
90–95	48.62	Pt 4A (ss 393A–393W)	48.2
96	48.62, 48.74	Pt 5 (ss 394–436)	48.2
97	48.62	Pt 6 (ss 437–451)	48.2; 48.123
98	48.62	s 441–444	48.123
99–104	48.62	Pt 7 (ss 452–463)	48.2
104A	48.60, 48.61	Pt 8 (ss 464–483)	48.2
104F	48.77	Pt 9 (ss 484–489)	48.2
174	48.27	Pt 10 (ss 490–531)	48.2
(4)	48.23	Pt 11 (ss 532–543)	48.2, 48.4
175(1)	48.23	s 532, 534	48.4
176	48.26	536(5)	48.4
(1)	48.23, 48.24, 48.25, 48.27	537	48.4
(2), (3)	48.25	538(3)	48.4
177	48.27	Pt 12 (ss 544–581)	48.2
(1)	48.27	s 562	48.68, 48.65, 48.68, 48.70, 48.71
178(a), (b)	48.27		
179, 180	48.27	(2)	48.71
181	48.26	563	48.68
183	48.24, 48.26	Sch A1	48.36
184	48.24, 48.26	para 2	48.36
185	48.67, 48.68, 48.69, 48.70, 48.72	Sch 3	
		para 38	48.68
186	48.91	Criminal Justice and Police	
187A	48.54, 48.68, 48.72	Act 2001	4.152
189	48.26	s 50	4.152, 4.153
196(1)	48.53	52	4.153
197	48.70	Sch 1	4.152
198	48.70, 48.72	Pt I	4.152
199	48.72	Finance Act 2001	9.45, 9.85, 9.86; 27.112; 41.157; 48.31; 53.1
Pt 2 Ch 15 (ss 205–208)	48.63, 48.79		
s 205–207	48.63	s 78	9.45
208	48.63	Sch 25	45.22
212C	41.65	Sch 26	9.45
213(3)	48.14	Employee Share Schemes	
214–217	48.66	Act 2002	9.82
218	48.14, 48.66	Finance Act 2002	27A.92; 32.94; 39.1; 41.50; 48.32; 48.33, 48.34, 48.78; 49.126; 53.1
227, 228	48.66		
229(3)	48.81		
Pt 2 Ch 18 (ss 234–246)	48.5		
s 247–252	48.8	s 46	9.45
262	8.101	Sch 29	41.22

	PARA		PARA
Tax Credits Act 2002	51.39	Finance Act 2003 – *contd*	
s 3(5)	51.27	s 185	15.22
6(3)	52.16	Sch 2	38.34
7(3)(a)	51.38, 51.39	Sch 3	49.82, 49.90
(b)	51.39	para 3	52.65
39, 63	51.39	4	30.156
Finance Act 2003	2.38; 9.12, 9.45,	Sch 4	49.26, 49.41
	9.113, 9.121; 15.22;	para 5	49.45, 49.73
	19.70; 27A.10, 27A.87,	8	29.44; 49.48
	27A.89, 27A.118, 27A.175,	10	49.50
	27A.174; 32.94; 35.22;	(2A)	49.50
	49.22, 49.91	12	49.52
Pt IV (ss 42–124)	49.22	17	49.83
s 42(2)	49.25	Sch 5	49.65
43	49.25, 49.26, 49.33	para 2	49.66
(1)	49.31	3	49.68
(5)	49.34	Sch 6A	49.83
44	49.35, 49.37,	Sch 6B	49.83
	49.38, 49.39	Sch 7	43.211; 49.126
(3)	49.38	Pt 1 (paras 1–6)	49.79, 49.83
(4)	49.37	para 7, 9–13	49.83
(5)–(7), (9)	49.37	Sch 8	49.83
44A	49.39	para 1	21.105; 53.130
45	55.21	(1)	21.105
45A	49.39	2	53.130
46	49.40	Sch 9	49.83
(4)	49.40	Sch 10	49.90
48	49.31, 49.32	Pt 2 (paras 9–11)	49.90
(1)(a)	49.25	Pt 7 (paras 35–46)	4.178
51	49.56	para 35(1)	4.178
53	49.63, 49.82	Sch 11	
55	49.27	Pt 2 (paras 4–6)	49.90
57, 58A, 58D, 60, 61	49.83	Sch 15	49.83
62	49.79, 49.83	para 1–4	49.75
63, 64	49.83	Pt 3 (paras 9–14)	49.75
65	45.23; 49.83	para 9	49.75
75A	3.74; 49.75, 49.85	10	49.75
76	49.26, 49.90	(1)(a)–(c)	49.75
(1)	49.38	12A, 14, 17, 17A,	
77	49.26, 49.90	18, 25	49.75
(3)	30.156	27, 27A, 31, 32	49.75
77A	49.26, 49.90	33	49.75, 49.116
78	49.90	34(2)	49.75
80	49.60	Sch 17A	49.37, 49.65
86(1)	49.38	para 1	49.32
90	49.61	7	49.68, 49.69
108	49.64	10	49.53
119	49.26, 49.35	11	49.72
121	49.32	13	49.70
125	49.107	16	49.73
140	9.43	18	49.66
142(2)	9.113	Sch 19	49.91
157	9.54	Sch 22	9.11, 9.12
163	27A.176	para 12	9.43

xxxiv *Table of statutes*

	PARA
Finance Act 2003 – *contd*	
Sch 23..................	9.121, 9.123, 9.124
para 25, 33	9.124
Sch 24.............	9.121, 9.123
Income Tax (Earnings and Pensions) Act 2003..........	1.22; 6.2, 6.21, 6.41, 6.43; 7.1, 7.4, 7.21, 7.23; 8.1, 8.12, 8.21, 8.22, 8.32, 8.41, 8.61, 8.102, 8.104; 9.1, 9.49, 9.123; 10.41, 10.130; 28.152; 41.128; 55.45
Pt 2 (ss 3–61J)	8.12
s 4	8.22; 20.10
5	8.20, 8.32
(3)	20.10
7	8.101
(3)	8.132
(a)	8.41
(5)	8.132
9	8.11, 8.41, 8.42, 8.62, 8.93, 8.95, 8.149; 9.2, 9.27, 9.31, 9.41
(2)	8.41
11	8.11
(1)	8.11
12	8.11
Pt 2 Ch 4 (14–19)	8.11
s 14	8.11
15	18.43
(1)	8.11
16	8.13
17	6.41, 6.42; 8.13
(4)	8.13
18	8.12
(1)	8.12
19	8.12
Pt 2 Ch 5 (ss 20–41, 41ZA)	8.11
s 24	18.43
24A	18.43
25	18.43, 18.73
26	18.43, 18.47
27	18.46, 18.71
39	18.48
40	18.48
Pt 2 Ch 5A (ss 41A–41E)	9.13, 9.21, 9.27, 9.28, 9.41
Pt 2 Ch 5B (ss 41F–41L)	9.13, 9.43
Pt 2 Ch 7 (ss 44–47)	8.31
s 44	8.31
47(2)	8.31
Pt 2 Ch 8 (ss 48–61)	8.31; 44.13
s 50(3)	8.32

	PARA
Income Tax (Earnings and Pensions) Act 2003 – *contd*	
s 56	8.32
Pt 2 Ch 9 (ss 61A–61J)	8.34
S 61N, 61T	8.33
Pt 3 (ss 62–226)	41.127; 48.80
Pt 3 Ch 1 (s 62)	8.101; 9.46
s 62	8.120, 8.66, 8.91, 8.93, 8.120, 8.143
Pt 3 Ch 2 (ss 63–69)	8.141, 8.150
s 63(4)	8.124
64	8.62, 8.103
67	8.104
Pt 3 Ch 3 (ss 70–72)	8.141, 8.150
s 70, 71	8.105
72	8.13, 8.105, 8.141
Pt 3 Ch 4 (ss 73–96A)	8.108, 8.141, 8.150
s 73	8.102
78	9.115
81(1A)	8.106
85, 87	9.115
87A	8.106
93, 94	8.108
94A	8.106, 8.108
95, 96	8.108
Pt 3 Ch 5 (ss 97–113)	8.113, 8.141, 8.150; 49.52
s 97A	8.110
99(3)	8.114
102	8.109; 35.21
(1B)	8.106
103A(9)	8.106
105	8.112, 8.114
(2)	8.112
(4A), (4B)	8.112
105A, 105B	8.112
106	8.112
(2)	8.112
108	8.113
109	8.103, 8.113
Pt 3 Ch 6 (ss 114–172)....	8.108, 8.117, 8.141, 8.150
s 114	8.117, 8.119
(1A)	8.117
(3)	8.120
115(1)	8.119
117(3)	8.117
118	8.117
120	8.117, 8.119
120A	8.106
132	8.119, 8.120
132A	8.106

	PARA		PARA
Income Tax (Earnings and Pensions) Act 2003 – *contd*		Income Tax (Earnings and Pensions) Act 2003 – *contd*	
s 139	8.119	s 225(1)	8.134
143–145	8.120	226	8.134; 10.102, 10.134
147A	8.106	Pt 4 (ss 227–326B)	7.129; 8.41
149–153	8.122	s 228A	8.106
154	8.127, 8.128	(4), (5)	8.106
154A	8.106	229–236	8.121
155	8.123	237	8.122
156(2)	8.126	238	8.117
(5)(b)	8.129	239(4), (5)	8.122
(8)	8.126	240	8.95
158A	8.106	(4)	8.95
167, 168	8.118	241	8.95
Pt 3 Ch 7 (ss 173–191)	8.124, 8.141, 8.150; 9.27; 27A.112	248A	8.119
		250–260	8.95
		288	8.124
s 174	8.124	306	1.25
(1), (5)	8.124	307	8.146
175(1A)	8.106	309(3)	8.144
(2)	8.124	312B	9.117
176–179	8.124	315	8.114
178, 180	9.27	318	51.41
182, 183, 186, 188–190	8.124	326	8.126
Pt 3 Ch 8 (ss 192–197)	8.141, 8.150	Pt 5 (ss 327–385)	8.108
Pt 3 Ch 9 (ss 198–200)	8.141, 8.150	s 336	8.94, 8.95; 18.49
Pt 3 Ch 10 (ss 201–215)	8.61, 8.65, 8.119, 8.122, 8.124, 8.125, 8.141, 8.146, 8.150	337	18.49
		365	8.126
		367	8.94
		370, 371	18.49
s 201	8.125; 9.12; 50.11	386	8.145
(4)	8.128, 8.146	Pt 6 Ch 2 (ss 393–400)	50.51
202	8.125	Pt 6 Ch 3 (ss 401–416)	8.65, 8.148, 8.149, 8.151
203	8.114, 8.125, 8.126		
(2)	8.129	s 401	8.64, 8.144, 8.145, 8.148, 8.151, 8.153
203A	8.106		
(5)	8.106	(3)	8.148
204	8.126, 8.127	402(1)(b)	8.148
205(1B), (1C)	8.129	(2)	8.148
(3), (4)	8.129	402A–402E	8.141
205A, 205B	8.129	403	8.156
206(3)(a), (b)	8.129	404	8.155
207	8.129	(1), (4), (5)	8.154
211–215	8.130	405	8.151
Pt 3 Ch 11 (ss 216–220)	8.141, 8.150	406	8.151, 8.152
		407	8.151, 8.153
s 216	8.104	408–413	8.151
(3)	8.104	413A	8.148
217	8.104	414	8.151
Pt 3 Ch 12 (ss 221–226D)	8.132	Pt 7 (ss 417–554)	8.66, 8.101; 9.12, 9.13, 9.31, 9.41
s 221	8.133		
222	9.43	s 418(1)	9.41
225	8.65, 8.134, 8.14, 8.149; 10.102, 10.134	421	9.22
		421B(1)	9.12

	PARA		PARA
Income Tax (Earnings and Pensions) Act 2003 – *contd*		Income Tax (Earnings and Pensions) Act 2003 – *contd*	
s 412B(1)(b)	9.12	s 472	9.12
(3)	9.12	476	9.41, 9.87, 9.75
421C	9.12	477(2)	9.41
421E	9.21, 9.25	(3)(a)	9.41
421F	9.12	(b)	9.41, 9.43, 9.89
421G	9.41, 9.72	(c)	9.41
Pt 7 Ch 2 (ss 422–434)	2.38, 2.40; 9.12, 9.13, 9.21, 9.22, 9.23, 9.43, 9.56, 9.72; 47.71	479(3A)	9.32
		480	9.41
		481	9.41, 9.44
		483	9.24
s 423(2)	9.22, 9.46	Pt 7 Ch 6 (ss 488–515)	9.77
424	9.12	s 505, 506	9.81
(b)	9.22	515(a)(ii)	9.81
425	9.46	Pt 7 Ch 7 (ss 516–520)	9.75
(2)	9.23, 9.26	s 518, 519	9.75
(3)	9.23, 9.26	Pt 7 Ch 8 (ss 521–526)	9.76
427	9.24, 9.26	s 524	9.76
428	9.24	(2B), (2E)	9.76
428A	9.44	Pt 7 Ch 9 (ss 527–541)	9.83
429	9.12	s 530	9.87
431	9.24, 9.72	533	9.87
431A	9.72	Pt 7 Ch 10 (ss 542–548)	9.30
Pt 7 Ch 3 (ss 435–446)	9.12, 9.13, 9.23, 9.43, 9.56, 9.72	s 542	9.30
		Pt 7A (ss 554A–554Z1)	5.7; 8.1; 9.111; 50.51
s 438–440	9.25	s 555	7.42; 11.5
441	9.25	Pt 9 (ss 565–654)	8.11
(7)	9.26	s 575	18.50
442	9.25	Pt X (ss 655–681)	8.11
442A	9.44	s 656	8.133
Pt 7 Ch 3A (ss 446A–446J)	9.26, 9.44, 9.126	681B	7.125
		688A	8.34
Pt 7 Ch 3B (ss 446K–446P)	9.26, 9.44, 9.126	696	9.43
		698	9.43, 9.44
s 446A–446D	9.26	(1)(e), (ea)	9.43
446E	9.26	(2)	9.43
(1)	9.26	(3)(a)	9.43
446F–446K, 446N	9.26	700	9.44, 9.89
Pt 7 Ch 3C (ss 446Q–446W)	9.23, 9.27, 9.31, 9.43, 9.44, 9.126	(2)	9.43
		700A	9.43
		701	9.89
Pt 7 Ch 3D (ss 446X–446Z)	9.28, 9.29, 9.81, 9.126	(2)(c)	9.75
		(5A)–(5D)	9.43
s 446S, 446U	9.27	703	9.75
446UA	9.27, 9.43	710	9.43
Pt 7 Ch 4 (ss 447–470)	9.12, 9.13, 9.31, 9.43, 9.56, 9.72, 9.126	713–715	53.88
		721	18.43
		Sch 2	5.7
s 448	9.29	para 32(2)	9.80
Pt 7 Ch 4A (ss 451–460)	9.31	Pt 5–8 (paras 34–69)	9.78
Pt 7 Ch 5 (ss 471–487)	9.13, 9.23, 9.41, 9.51, 9.53, 9.56	para 99	9.80
		Sch 3	5.6; 9.75

Table of statutes xxxvii

	PARA
Income Tax (Earnings and Pensions) Act 2003 – contd	
Sch 4	5.6; 9.76
para 13	9.74
Sch 5	5.6; 9.83
para 4	9.72
11(2)	9.84
31	9.74
Pt 7 (paras 44–50)	9.87
Sch 7	
para 8	8.13
Child Trust Funds Act 2004	51.42
Civil Partnership Act 2004	31.41; 51.130; 55.43
Finance Act 2004	2.38; 5.1, 5.3, 5.5; 8.1, 8.149; 9.12, 9.41; 15.92; 16.1; 21.66; 23.121; 24.26; 41.182; 44.16; 49.39; 50.1, 50.3, 50.8, 50.12, 50.16, 50.22, 50.31, 50.32, 50.51
s 30	9.124
55	41.182
80	8.123
84	29.142
86	9.12
87	9.26
88	9.72, 9.89
(2)	9.72
(3), (12)	9.72
(13)	9.41
89	9.12
90	9.12
96	9.84
97–105	54.94
116	9.112
Pt 4 (ss 149–284)	50.5, 50.10
s 150	50.1
(5)	50.10
154	50.3
Pt 4 Ch 3 (ss 160–185J)	50.21
s 164(1)	50.10
(a), (b)	50.21
189(2)	7.23
196	50.11
209	55.25
214	50.16
215	50.16
222–224	8.101
229–237	50.12
237B	50.33
239	55.25
245	9.123

	PARA
Income Tax (Earnings and Pensions) Act 2003 – contd	
s 270	50.10
276	50.16
279	50.18
Pt 7 (ss 306–319)	5.4; 9.3; 10.28
s 306	55.62
306A	5.17
307	5.10; 55.62
308	55.62
308A	5.17
309, 310	55.62
311	5.4, 5.5; 55.62
312	5.4; 55.62
312A	5.5
(2A)	5.5
313	5.4; 55.62
313A	5.5, 5.17
313B	5.17
313C	5.17
313Z	5.4
313ZC	5.5
314	5.5; 55.62
314A	5.17
315	55.62
316–319	55.62
Sch 2	5.21, 5.24
Sch 5	41.44
Sch 14	8.123
Sch 15	29.142, 29.145
para 16	29.145
Sch 18	
para 12	15.92
Sch 21	9.112
Sch 28	
para 1	50.18
3(1)(d)	50.17
Sch 29A	50.15
para 1	50.4
Sch 36	
para 31	50.19
National Insurance Contributions and Statutory Payments Act 2004	9.44
Charities and Trustee Investment (Scotland) Act 2005	53.24
Commissioners for Revenue and Customs Act 2005	4.2
Finance Act 2005	11.122; 16.1, 16.96; 31.41; 41.50; 49.78
s 17	8.129
20	9.31
Pt 2 Ch 4 (ss 23–45)	16.74

	PARA
Finance Act 2005 – *contd*	
s 23, 24	25.149
25	16.96; 25.149
(1)	25.149
26–29	25.149
30	25.149, 25.150
(3)	25.150
31	25.149, 25.151
32	25.149, 25.152
33–37	25.149
38	16.75; 25.149
39–45	25.149
46–55	14.6
56, 57	14.6
Sch 1A	25.149
Finance (No 2) Act 2005	9.22; 27.46, 27.56; 27A.10; 41.57
s 11	53.84
26	9.129
32	27.60
(6)	27.59
51–65	54.99
Sch 2	9.12
Gambling Act 2005	53.42
Income Tax (Trading and Other Income) Act 2005	1.22; 2.38; 3.12; 6.2, 6.21, 6.41, 6.43; 7.1, 7.4, 7.21; 8.1, 8.21, 8.22, 8.23, 8.94; 10.2; 11.3; 12.87, 12.106; 13.1; 14.1; 15.1; 16.5, 16.26; 18.31; 19.71; 28.132; 41.1
Pt 2 (ss 3–359)	6.41; 7.23; 8.1; 10.2, 10.3, 10.130, 10.138; 12.22, 12.106, 12.106; 13.14, 13.15; 14.40
Pt 2 Ch 2 (ss 5–23)	12.24; 14.31; 18.72
s 5	10.3
6	10.3; 18.35
(2A)	10.3
7	10.61, 10.76, 10.101
9–12	10.42; 12.24
24	44.5
25	10.62; 44.5
25A	10.62, 10.73
27	10.78, 10.101
28	10.101
28A	10.101
29	44.11
31	10.132

	PARA
Income Tax (Trading and Other Income) Act 2005 – *contd*	
s 31A–31C	10.73
31D	10.73
(6)	10.74
31E	10.74, 10.78
32A	10.144
33	10.77, 10.130, 10.135, 10.142; 12.42, 12.43
33A	10.74
34	10.76, 10.117, 10.130, 10.130, 10.138, 10.148; 12.85; 14.46
(2)	10.137, 10.140; 44.13
35	10.144; 14.46
36, 37	10.132
38	10.133
(2A)	10.132
39–44	10.133
45–47	10.138
48	48.80
51A	10.74
53	10.152
54	10.156; 14.46
55	10.144, 10.149
55A	10.142
57	10.143
57B	10.74
60	10.140; 12.85; 48.3
61–65	10.140; 48.3
66, 67	10.140
69	10.134
70–72	10.152
73, 74	10.148
74E	10.74
76–80	10.152
81	10.149
82–86B	10.153
87, 88	10.154
89, 90	10.155
91	10.153
92	10.151, 10.153
93, 94	10.151
94B, 94C	10.62, 10.161
94D–94G	10.62 10.161, 10.162
94H	10.62, 10.161, 10.163
(5), (5A)	10.163
94I	10.62, 10.161, 10.164
(6A)	10.164
96	10.18
96A	10.74
97	10.109
97A, 97B	10.74
105(2A)	10.74

	PARA
Income Tax (Trading and Other Income) Act 2005 – *contd*	
s 108	53.96
160	10.73; 44.4
164A	8.34
172A	10.117, 10.119
172B	10.117, 10.119; 48.21
172C–172F	10.117, 10.119
173	10.30, 10.80, 10.114
(2A)–(2C)	10.114
174–181	10.30, 10.80, 10.114
182, 183	10.80
184	10.80, 10.114
185, 186	10.80, 10.114
191A, 192–194	10.108
197–203	10.192
204	10.192, 10.194
205	10.192, 10.195
206–213	10.192
214–217	10.192, 10.196
218	10.192, 10.196
(6)	10.196
219, 220	10.192, 10.196
221, 221A, 222A, 223, 224	10.172
225	10.102, 10.134, 10.172
Pt 2 Ch 17 (ss 226–240)	44.4
s 226	10.72, 10.102, 10.134
226–240	10.72
240A–240E	10.74
242–245	10.30, 10.80
246	10.30, 10.80
(2A)	10.74, 10.80
247	10.30, 10.80
248	10.30, 10.80, 10.81
249	10.30, 10.80
250	10.30, 10.80, 10.81
250A	48.12
251–253	10.30, 10.80
254	10.81
(2A)	10.74, 10.81
(2B)	10.81
257	10.80
Pt 3 (ss 260–364)	6.41; 10.140; 12.1, 12.22, 12.61; 19.3, 19.23, 19.42
s 264	12.1
265	12.24
266(2)	12.22
267	12.24
270(1)	12.41
271	12.41
272(1)	12.42
272A	7.48

	PARA
Income Tax (Trading and Other Income) Act 2005 – *contd*	
s 272A(1)–(4)	12.45
Pt 3 Ch 4 (ss 276–307)	12.1, 12.82; 19.42
s 277	12.82, 12.83, 12.86; 16.26, 16.29
278	12.83; 19.40
279–281	12.83
282	12.83, 12.85
(3)	12.83
284, 285	12.83
299	12.84
(3)	12.84
300, 303	12.83
308A–308C	12.47, 12.48
311A	12.47; 48.12
312	12.47; 48.126
Pt 3 Ch 6 (ss 322–328)	12.61
s 323	12.61; 48.12
324	48.12
325	12.62; 48.12
326	12.62
326A	12.62; 48.12
335	12.24
344	12.24
Pt 3 Ch 11 (ss 357–360)	18.37
Pt 4 (ss 365–573)	6.41; 14.2, 14.3, 14.4; 16.23; 42.1, 42.8, 42.152
s 369	14.6, 14.32; 17.42
(2), (3)	14.6
370A	14.35
371	14.3
380(3)	14.35
381A–381E	13.10
384B(2)(a)	7.49
(b)	7.48
385	42.76
392–396	9.81
396B	20.28
397	7.27
(1)	42.76
398	7.48
(1)	42.76
399	42.146
400	7.48; 42.121
401	42.121
Pt 4 Ch 4 (ss 402–408)	16.23
s 404A	20.28
405–408	9.81
409	42.151, 42.152
410	42.151, 42.152
(2)	42.9

Income Tax (Trading and Other Income) Act 2005 – *contd*	PARA
s 411–414	42.151, 42.152
422	14.41
423(1)	14.8
426	17.44
427	14.42
437(1), (3)	14.42
439(1), (4)	14.42
446	11.5
454(4)	11.5
Pt 4 Ch 9 (ss 461–546)	14.41
s 461	15.2
465	17.5
(1)	15.5
(3)	15.7
466	17.5
467	15.7
480	50.31
481, 482	15.9
498(2), (3)	9.81
508(2B)	9.81
539	55.25
541	15.9
Pt 5 (ss 574–689)	6.41; 10.41; 13.1, 13.4, 13.12, 13.14
s 574(1)	13.4
(4)	13.13
575	13.14
576	13.4
577	13.13
(2)–(4)	13.13
Pt 5 Ch 2 (ss 578–608)	13.13
s 578–586	13.4
587	10.175; 13.4; 14.40
588, 589	10.175; 13.4
590	10.175; 13.4; 14.40
591, 592	10.175; 13.4
593–608	13.4
Pt 5 Ch 3 (ss 609–613)	13.13
s 609	10.28; 13.4
610–612	13.4
612	13.4
Pt 5 Ch 4 (ss 614–618)	13.13
s 613–618	13.4
Pt 5 Ch 5 (ss 619–648)	3.1; 6.41; 13.13; 14.12, 14.13; 16.91, 16.93, 16.107; 18.115; 46.54; 51.54
s 619	13.4; 16.94, 16.106; 30.156; 32.91
620	13.4; 16.31, 16.93; 46.54
(1)	16.93, 16.96; 27A.114

Income Tax (Trading and Other Income) Act 2005 – *contd*	PARA
s 621–623	13.4
624	13.4; 16.98; 17.58 27A.73, 46.54, 46.61; 51.55
(1)	51.55
625	13.4; 16.93, 16.93, 16.98, 16.101, 16.102; 21.126; 51.55
(1)	16.93
(2)	16.104
(e)	16.105
(3)	16.104, 16.105
(4)	16.102
(a), (b)	16.102
(c)	51.55
(d)	16.102
626	13.4; 16.93, 16.98, 16.102; 46.61; 51.55
(2), (3)	16.102
627	13.4; 16.98
(1)	16.102, 16.104
(2)	16.103, 16.104; 44.15
628	13.4; 16.96
629	13.4; 16.24, 16.94, 16.95, 16.96, 16.98; 17.58; 51.44
(1)	16.93, 16.97
(7)	16.96
630	13.4
631	13.4; 16.95
632	13.4
(1)	16.97
633	13.4; 16.106
(3), (4)	16.106
634	13.4; 16.106
(1), (4)–(6), (7)	16.106
635, 636	13.4; 16.106
637	13.4; 16.106
(8)	16.106
638	13.4; 16.106
(1)–(3)	16.106
639–643	13.4; 16.106
644–647	13.4
648	13.4
(2)–(4)	16.105
(5)	6.41; 16.105
Pt 5 Ch 6 (ss 649–682A)	13.13
s 649–651	13.4; 17.41
652	13.4; 17.41, 17.52
653	13.4; 17.41
(2)	17.20
654, 655	13.4; 17.41, 17.49
656	13.4; 17.41, 17.53

Table of statutes xli

Income Tax (Trading and Other
  Income) Act 2005 – *contd*
s 657–662 .... 13.4; 17.41
  663 .... 13.4; 17.41, 17.54
  664, 665 .... 13.4; 17.41
  666 .... 13.4; 17.41, 17.42
  667 .... 13.4; 17.41, 17.53
  668 .... 13.4; 17.41
  669 .... 13.4; 17.3, 17.4, 17.41,
                                  17.54, 17.55
  670 .... 13.4; 17.41, 17.54
  671–675 .... 13.4; 17.41, 17.57
  676–678 .... 13.4; 17.41
  679 .... 13.4; 17.41, 17.53
  680 .... 13.4; 17.41
  681 .... 13.4; 17.41, 17.53
  682 .... 13.4; 17.41
Pt 5 Ch 7 (ss 683–686) 13.1;
                                  16.33, 16.64
s 683 .... 13.1, 13.2, 13.10, 13.13,
                     13.18, 13.24; 14.14,
                     14.16, 14.25; 16.65,
                              16.66; 52.3
  (1) 13.7; 14.14
  (2), (3) 13.7
  (4) 13.7; 14.14
  684(2), (3) 13.7
  685 .... 13.7
  685A 13.7; 16.65, 16.98
  686 .... 13.7
Pt 5 Ch 8 (ss 687–689) 13.1, 13.15
s 687 .... 13.1, 13.2, 13.10, 13.13,
                  13.15, 13.18, 13.22; 14.40
  (5) 13.10
  688 .... 13.10
  (2) 13.18
  689, 689A 13.10
Pt 6 (ss 690–783) 6.41, 6.43; 7.131
s 692–702 .... 7.131
  703 .... 7.131; 9.75
  704–712 .... 7.131
  713 .... 7.131; 18.77
  714–716 .... 7.131
  717 .... 7.131; 14.8,
                              14.41; 17.46
  718, 719 .... 7.131; 14.41
  720–726 .... 7.131
  727 .... 7.131; 14.14
  (1) 14.13, 14.15, 14.28
  728, 729 .... 7.131; 13.7
  730 .... 7.131; 13.7; 52.3
  731 .... 7.131; 13.7
  732 .... 7.131; 13.7; 14.6
  733 .... 7.131; 14.6

Income Tax (Trading and Other
  Income) Act 2005 – *contd*
s 734 .... 7.131; 13.7; 14.6
  735–748 .... 7.131; 13.7
  749, 479A, 751 .... 7.131
  752, 753, 753A 7.131
  756A 7.131
  757 .... 13.7; 54.94
  758 .... 13.7; 14.32,
                              14.40; 54.94
  759–762 .... 13.7; 14.32; 54.94
  763–767 .... 13.7; 54.94
  768 .... 13.10
  771, 772 .... 7.131
  776 .... 8.130; 13.7
  779 .... 13.10, 13.15
  782A, 782B 7.131
Pt 7 Ch 1 (ss 784–802) 12.47
Pt 8 (ss 829–845) 13.7
s 831, 832 .... 18.34
  841 .... 18.33
Pt 9 (ss 846–863) 18.18; 44.2
s 847 .... 44.13
  849 .... 18.17, 18.35
  850, 850A 44.9
  850C–850E 46.6
  858 .... 18.39
  860 .... 44.4
  863 .... 45.10, 45.11
  871 .... 13.17
  872 .... 13.20, 13.24
Sch 2
  para 28, 71 .... 12.87
Serious Organised Crime and
  Police Act 2005
Pt 2 Ch 1 (ss 60–70) 4.160
s 60 .... 4.160
  62(3) 4.160
  64 .... 4.160
  66(2) 4.160
  67 .... 4.160
Charities Act 2006 .... 53.1, 53.22,
                              53.26, 53.101
Companies Act 2006 .... 45.4, 45.7;
                        46.24, 46.56; 47.71
s 25 .... 46.21
  190 .... 47.13
  197 .... 41.128
  549, 617 .... 47.13
Pt 18 (ss 658–737) 42.21
s 688, 706 .... 42.24
  755(1) 46.2
Pt 26 (ss 895–901) 47.52
s 1159 .... 43.191

	PARA
Family Law (Scotland) Act 2006	
s 22	35.3
Finance Act 2006	15.21; 16.1, 16.2, 16.7, 16.73; 18.127; 19.48; 21.2; 24.20, 24.21, 24.23, 24.25; 26.46; 27A.22, 27A.25; 28.46; 30.153; 31.54; 32.1, 32.21, 32.51, 32.53; 33.2, 33.11, 33.30, 33.63, 33.71; 34.1, 34.35; 36.5; 38.30; 41.75; 43.44, 43.125; 45.23; 49.126; 53.1, 53.41, 53.42, 53.84, 53.116
s 57	53.42
93	9.128
Sch 9	48.22
para 11	48.33
Sch 12	21.126; 27A.26
Sch 20	28.42; 30.145
para 16	33.18
Finance Act 2007	4.55, 4.58, 4.159; 5.3, 5.4, 5.17; 8.31, 8.34; 19.48; 21.81; 41.184; 43.127; 45.22; 49.75
s 82(2)	4.58
83(2)	4.58
89	44.9
97	38.68
Sch 24	4.26; 38.68
para 3	4.26
Income Tax Act 2007	1.22; 6.2, 6.21, 6.41, 6.43; 7.1, 7.4; 8.1; 11.1, 11.61; 14.1, 14.40; 18.74; 45.22; 53.83, 53.116, 53.120
s 4	48.3
6	7.2
7	7.2, 7.26
8	7.2; 42.76
9	7.2; 9.112; 16.21
10	7.3
11	16.5
12	7.3, 7.26
12A, 12B	7.2, 7.25
13	7.27
13A	7.2, 7.27
14	7.27; 16.5
16	7.3, 7.25, 7.27
17	7.27
18, 19	18.36
Pt 2 Ch 3 (ss 22–32)	3.10; 52.3
s 23	7.4; 11.122; 14.23, 14.27
24	7.41; 11.5; 44.9; 51.22

	PARA
Income Tax Act 2007 – *contd*	
s 24A	7.42, 7.44, 7.83
25(2)–(4)	7.40
26	7.4; 51.22
27	51.22
30	7.4
32	7.126
38	7.105
45, 46	7.111
54	51.24
55A–55E	51.12
56	18.71, 18.78
57	7.101
58	7.111
Pt 4 (ss 59–155)	14.2,
s 64	7.42; 11.5, 11.21, 11.41, 11.61, 11.81, 11.82, 11.101, 11.102, 11.121, 11.122; 46.46, 46.47; 48.9
(2)	11.41
(a)–(c)	11.41
(3)	11.41
66, 67	7.83; 11.41
68, 69	7.83
71	11.61; 19.3; 48.9
72	7.42; 11.5, 11.81, 11.82, 11.121, 11.122; 46.46, 46.47; 48.9
73	11.81
74	11.81
(4)	11.81
74A	7.83; 48.9
74A(4)	11.122
74C	11.122
74ZA	7.83; 11.122; 48.9
83	11.21, 11.81, 11.82, 11.101; 48.9
85	11.102
86	11.101; 47.3
89	11.101, 11.102; 47.3
(3)	11.102
96	7.42; 10.81; 11.5
97, 98	10.81
98A	10.81
103B	44.9
103C	11.122; 45.13
105	44.9
107	45.13
118	12.46
120	7.42; 11.5; 12.46, 12.63; 48.10
123	11.3
125	7.42; 11.5; 12.63
127	12.61

	PARA
Income Tax Act 2007 – *contd*	
s 127A	12.46; 48.8, 48.10
127B	12.46
128	7.42; 8.175; 11.5
Pt 4 Ch 6 (ss 131–151)	7.42; 11.5, 11.121
s 131	11.121; 15.52, 15.131; 19.45; 46.49
(2)	11.121
132	11.121
150A	15.132
152	11.122; 13.20
(4)	13.20
(5)	11.122
153	13.20
154A	13.20
155	13.20
Pt 5 (ss 156–257)	14.2; 15.52; 46.50
s 165	15.57
170	15.53
173(2)	15.55
173A, 173AA	15.124
174	15.55
175A	15.54
177	15.57
(1)(a)	15.57
178, 178A	15.57
179	15.55
180A, 180B, 191A	15.56
197, 198, 198A	15.56
212A–212S	48.8
247–249	15.97
257BF	15.133
257C	15.57
257DK	20.41
257FP	15.134
Pt 6 (ss 258–332)	15.122
s 284	3.56; 16.23
285	3.56
286–292	3.56
Pt 8 Ch 1 (ss 383–412)	11.5
s 383	7.42; 10.28; 11.122; 14.31; 44.11; 47.71
384	7.42; 14.31
(1)	7.44
384A	14.31; 44.11
385–391	7.42
392	7.42, 7.45
(3), (3A)	7.45
393	7.42
393A	7.45
394	7.42
395	7.42
(2)	7.45

	PARA
Income Tax Act 2007 – *contd*	
s 396	7.42, 7.46; 14.31
397	7.42
398	7.42, 7.44, 7.48; 14.31; 44.11; 45.12
399	7.42; 45.12, 45.14
(2)	45.14, 45.22
(a)	45.14
(b)	45.12
(6)	45.14
400	7.42
401	7.42, 7.47; 47.71
402	7.42
403–405	7.42; 17.23; 30.52
406–408	7.42
409	7.42; 45.20
410–412	7.42
412A–412J	7.92
413	53.80
414	53.80
(2)	14.27
415–419	53.80
420, 421	53.80, 53.84
422–425	53.80
426	53.80, 53.102
427–429	53.80
430	7.128; 53.80
431	53.99
433, 434	53.100
438–440	53.99
Pt 8 Ch 4 (ss 447–452)	14.40, 14.45, 14.46; 16.8
s 448	14.14, 14.21, 14.22, 14.23, 14.25
Pt 8 Ch 5 (ss 453–456)	52.3
s 461	10.175
466	16.2
467	16.3
474	16.4; 27A.30
475	16.4; 18.19; 27A.30
(6)	18.19
476	18.19; 27A.30
Pt 9 Ch 3 (ss 479–483)	16.21; 42.147
s 479	16.21, 16.22, 16.25, 16.26, 16.29, 16.31, 16.32, 16.61, 16.73, 16.77, 16.96; 18.79; 42.30
(1)	16.21
480(3)	16.22, 16.24
481	6.43; 16.21, 16.26
482	6.43; 16.21, 16.26
486	16.23, 16.31
491	16.21, 16.32, 16.66, 16.96; 42.96

xliv *Table of statutes*

Income Tax Act 2007 – *contd*	PARA
s 492	16.21
Pt 9 Ch 7 (ss 493–498)	42.147, 42.152
s 493	18.79; 42.96
494	13.7; 16.96
496	16.61, 16.65, 16.66, 16.96
496A, 496B	9.112
504	14.44
417	12.109
Pt 9A (ss 517A–517U)	12.105
	12.108, 12.110, 12.111
s 517B	12.102, 12.103, 12.106
517C–517G	12.105
517L	12.108
517S	12.105
Pt 10 (ss 518–564)	7.128
s 520–522	53.41
523	55.41
524	55.41, 53.42
525, 526	53.41, 53.42
527, 528	53.41
529	53.41, 53.42
530	53.41, 53.42
531–533	53.41
535	51.44
540–564	53.61
Pt 11 Ch 4 (ss 596–606)	3.29
Pt 12 Ch 2 (ss 616–677)	3.4, 3.12, 3.29; 51.44
s 618, 639–641	3.12
681DL	3.36
Pt 13 Ch 1 (ss 682–686)	3.3, 3.29, 3.52, 3.71; 19.80
s 682	2.47; 3.3, 3.29, 3.30, 3.51
(1)	3.53
683	2.47; 3.3, 3.29, 3.30, 3.51, 3.55; 14.25
(3)	3.55
684	2.47; 3.3, 3.29, 3.30, 3.31, 3.33, 3.35, 3.51, 3.54, 3.60, 3.62, 3.63
(1)	3.54
(a)–(d)	3.32
(2)	3.33
(3)	3.55
685	2.47; 3.3, 3.29, 3.30, 3.31, 3.32, 3.33, 3.34, 3.51, 3.63
(2)	3.34
(3)	3.34
(4)	3.31, 3.34
(a)	3.31

Income Tax Act 2007 – *contd*	PARA
s 685(8)	3.34
686	2.47; 3.3, 3.29, 3.30, 3.31, 3.32, 3.36, 3.38, 3.51, 3.54, 3.61, 3.61, 3.72
687	3.3, 3.29, 3.30, 3.31, 3.35, 3.38, 3.51, 3.54; 5.7
688	3.3, 3.29, 3.30, 3.36, 3.38, 3.51, 3.54, 3.60, 3.61
689	3.3, 3.29, 3.30, 3.38, 3.51, 3.54, 3.61, 3.62
(6)	3.61
690	3.3, 3.31. 3.38, 3.51, 3.54, 3.60, 3.62
(2)	3.62
691	3.3, 3.30, 3.51, 3.61
692, 693	3.3, 3.30, 3.51, 3.58
694	3.3, 3.30, 3.38, 3.51
698	3.60
701	42.31
703(3)	3.72
704A	3.72
705(2)	3.71, 3.72
706	3.71, 3.72
709(2)	3.72
713	3.58, 3.72
Pt 13 Ch 2 (ss 714–751)	3.5, 3.38; 16.107; 18.110
s 714	18.116
715(1)(b)	18.111
718(2)	18.114
719	18.114
720	18.38, 18.111, 18.113, 18.114, 18.115, 18.119, 18.120, 18.127; 27A.24, 27A.113
(1)	18.111
721	18.111; 27A.113
(5)(c)	18.113
722	18.111; 27A.113
(3)	18.116
723	18.115, 18.116; 27A.113
724, 725	27A.113
726	18.119; 27A.113
727	18.120; 27A.113
728	18.111, 18.115, 18.117, 18.118; 27A.113
(3)	18.112
(c)	18.113
729, 730	27A.113
731	18.111, 18.115, 18.120, 18.125, 18.127; 27A.22, 27A.24, 27A.113, 27A.109, 27A.129, 27A.147

Table of statutes xlv

Income Tax Act 2007 – contd	PARA
s 732	18.120; 27A.24, 27A.113, 27A.109
(1)(e)	27A.176
733	27A.24, 27A.113, 27A.109
(1)	18.123
734	18.125; 27A.24, 27A.113, 27A.109
735	18.122; 27A.24, 27A.113, 27A.109
736	27A.113
737	18.113; 27A.113
(2), (3)	18.113
738	18.113; 27A.113
739	27A.113
(3)	18.118
740	18.113; 27A.113
741	18.113; 27A.113
742	27A.113
743	18.118, 18.124
(2)	18.118
744	18.118
748	18.126
(5)	18.126
Pt 13 Ch 3 (ss 752–772)	3.6; 12.103
s 755	53.43
756	53.43; 12.104
(2)	12.103
759(8)	12.113
760(2)	12.103
770	12.113
Pt 13 Ch 4 (ss 773–789)	3.7
s 776	12.107, 12.111
791–795, 797	11.122
802(2)	11.122
809B, 809C	27.81; 27A.145
809D	19.56; 27.81
809E	27.81
809G	19.56
809J	27.98
809L	27.82, 27.89; 27A.11, 27A.111, 27A.150
809M	27.93
(2)(e)	27.93
809Q	27.89
809T	27.100
809VA, 809VE, 809VH	27.96
809YA	27.97
809ZH–809ZR	53.116
811, 812	18.71; 41.163
813, 814	41.163
817	18.72
829	18.6; 27.2, 27.9, 27.14, 27.16

Income Tax Act 2007 – contd	PARA
s 830	27.2, 27.11
831	18.3; 27.2, 27.10, 27.15
(1)	18.5
(4)	27.10
832	18.3; 27.2, 27.10, 27.15
(1)	18.5
834	18.21; 21.3
836	7.22; 12.63; 51.54
(3)	51.54
837	7.22; 51.54
Pt 15 (ss 847–987)	11.21; 14.1
s 849(2)	14.26
858	18.39, 18.76
Pt 15 Ch 3 (873–888)	14.32
s 874(1)	17.42
(2)	14.32; 18.76
(5A), (5B)	14.32
(6)	14.32, 14.33
(6A)	14.32
875	14.32
876	14.32
(1)	14.32
877, 878	14.32
879	14.32
880–888	14.32
888A	14.32
889(4)	14.32
Pt 15 Ch 6 (ss 898–905)	11.21; 14.13, 14.21, 14.22, 14.23, 14.40; 16.8, 16.64; 48.3
s 899	18.80
900	14.23; 16.91; 18.80
(2)	14.26; 16.68
901	18.80; 42.152
(4)	14.32, 14.41
902–905	18.80
Pt 15 Ch 7 (ss 906–910)	14.40
s 906	18.80
(5)	14.32
907–909	18.80
910(2)	14.32
Pt 15 Ch 8 (ss 911–917)	14.40
s 914	14.40
928(2)	14.32
930(1)	14.32
933	14.32
939(6)	14.35
941	14.44
944(2)	12.113
Pt 15 Ch 15 (ss 945–962)	14.1, 14.45
s 951(3)	14.32

Table of statutes

Income Tax Act 2007 – *contd*
- Pt 15 Ch 16 (s 963) 14.1, 14.45
- s 963 .... 14.45
- (3) 14.32
- 963A 14.46
- Pt 15 Ch 17 (s 964) 14.1, 14.14
- s 964 .... 14.23
- (2), (3) 14.26
- 971 .... 18.75
- 975A 14.35
- 989 .... 10.21; 13.15; 20.14
- 993 .... 3.36; 10.114; 12.107, 12.09; 50.15
- 997 .... 10.62, 10.64
- 1004 .... 45.14
- 1011 .... 51.21
- 1016 .... 11.122; 13.20
- 1025, 1026 .... 14.24
- Sch 1
  - para 321 .... 12.106

Tribunals, Courts and Enforcement Act 2007 .... 4.173
- s 706 .... 4.173

Charities Act 2008 (Northern Ireland) 53.24

Energy Act 2008 .... 48.31

Finance Act 2008 .... 3.3; 4.55, 4.168; 5.4; 8.11; 9.83; 11.122; 19.4, 19.25; 24.12; 27.81, 27.82; 27A.2, 27A.2, 27A.11, 27A.11, 27A.113, 27A.114, 27A.118, 27A.152; 38.53; 41.42, 41.184; 44.9; 48.32, 48.60, 48.61; 49.75, 49.78, 49.90; 51.60; 52.60
- s 24 .... 18.11; 27.10
- 60, 61 .... 11.122
- 72 .... 48.29, 48.30
- 75 .... 48.33
- 87 .... 27A.116, 27A.119
- 98 .... 51.91
- 114 .... 4.163
- Sch 2 .... 9.45
- Sch 3
  - para 7 .... 20.36
- Sch 7 .... 27.86, 27.89
  - para 31 .... 9.21, 9.25
  - 62 .... 27.86
  - 86(4) 27.100
  - 112 .... 27A.138
  - 124 .... 27A.148, 27A.150
  - 125 .... 27A.149
  - 126 .... 27A.151, 27A.154
  - (9) 27A.159

Finance Act 2008 – *contd*
- Sch 21 .... 11.122
- Sch 25 .... 48.36
- Sch 36 .... 4.160, 4.163, 4.165; 28.202; 55.5
  - para 1 .... 4.162
  - 2 .... 4.164
  - 5 .... 4.54, 4.165
  - 6(2) 4.163
  - 7 .... 4.163
  - 10, 10A 4.167
  - 11 .... 4.168
  - 28 .... 4.167
  - 39, 40, 59 .... 4.163
  - 61A, 62 .... 4.167
  - 64 .... 4.162
- Sch 40 .... 4.26
- Sch 41 .... 4.26; 38.68

Pensions Act 2008 .... 50.3, 50.22

Planning Act 2008
- Pt 11 (ss 205–225) 53.131
- s 210 .... 53.131

Corporation Tax Act 2009 .... 1.22; 3.3; 6.2, 6.21, 6.41; 10.41; 13.1; 14.1; 41.1, 41.42; 43.99
- s 2 .... 10.76, 10.101
- (2) 41.41; 48.9
- 3 .... 18.72; 41.162
- 5 .... 10.4
- (1) 10.4
- (2), (3) 41.151
- 8(5) 41.21
- 14, 18 .... 18.16
- 18A–18S 41.155
- 19(3) 41.162
- Pt 2 Ch 3A (ss 18A–18S) 41.155
- Pt 3 (ss 34–201) 10.2, 10.4, 10.130, 10.138; 13.14, 13.15; 41.42, 41.46
- s 33 .... 10.21
- 34(1)(b) 10.30
- 35 .... 10.4, 10.61, 10.76, 10.101
- 36, 37 .... 10.42, 10.132
- 38, 39 .... 10.42, 100.133
- 40 .... 10.29, 10.133
- 41 .... 10.114, 10.133
- (2) 41.66
- 42–44 .... 10.133
- 46 .... 10.62; 48.80
- 48 .... 10.78, 10.101
- 49 .... 10.101
- 49A 10.101

	PARA		PARA
Corporation Tax Act 2009 – *contd*		Corporation Tax Act 2009 – *contd*	
Pt 3 Ch 4 (ss 53–60)	41.42	s 307	41.50
s 53	10.130, 10.135, 10.142	321A	41.128
54	10.76, 10.130, 10.138, 10.148	328	41.43
(2)	10.137, 10.140	374(1A)	41.56
56	48.80	443	41.44
56A	10.142	Pt 6 (ss 477–569)	14.5; 41.50
60	10.142	Pt 7 (ss 570–710)	41.43, 41.50
61	10.143	s 695A	41.53
62–65	10.140	Pt 8 (ss 711–906)	41.22, 41.42
69	10.134	s 747, 749	10.101
70–72	10.152	849B–849D	47.8A
74	10.148	907	10.108
76–81	10.152	908	10.108
82–86B	10.153	(1), (2)	10.108
87, 88	10.154	912–923	10.175
89, 90	10.155	Pt 9A (ss 931A–931W)	41.46; 42.91, 42.94
91, 92	10.153	Pt 10 (ss 932–982)	13.1, 13.5, 13.12, 13.13, 13.14
94	10.109		
101	10.29	932(1)	13.5
105, 106	53.96	934–975	13.5
107	53.97	Pt 10 Ch 7 (ss 976–978)	13.1
145	10.67	s 976	13.1, 13.2, 13.8, 13.13
155, 156	10.117	(2)	13.8
157	10.117; 48.21	977	13.8
158–160	10.117	(3)	13.8
161	10.117, 10.118	Pt 10 Ch 8 (ss 979–981)	13.1, 13.15
162	10.30, 10.80, 10.114	s 979	13.1, 13.2, 13.11, 13.13, 13.15
(2A)–(2C)	10.114		
163	10.30, 10.80, 10.114	980	13.11
(3)	10.114	981	13.11, 13.15
164–171	10.30, 10.80, 10.114	982	13.14
176	10.108	Pt 11 (ss 983–1000)	9.124
(3), (4)	10.108	s 989	9.82
177–179	10.108	Pt 12 (ss 1001–1038)	9.82, 9.117, 9.121, 9.127, 9.128, 9.129
180–187	10.72		
188	10.30, 10.80		
189–191	10.80	Pt 12 Ch 2	9.126
192	10.81	s 1008	9.127
193, 195	10.80	1009(3)	9.126
196	10.81	1016	9.127
Pt 4 (ss 202–291)	41.42, 41.46	1017(1), (2)	9.126
s 250A	12.47	1038	9.124
251	48.126	Pt 13 (ss 1039–1142)	10.154
265(3)	48.12	Pt 14 (ss 1143–1179)	41.42
267(1)–(6)	48.12	s 1217F–1217OB	13.24
268(1)–(5)	48.12	1223(1), (2)	41.69
268A	48.12	1248	41.69
Pt 5 (ss 292–476)	14.5; 41.43, 41.50	1259	45.10
		1285	41.46; 42.28, 42.91
s 297	10.101; 41.54	(3)	42.28
298(3)	10.42	1288	9.123; 41.45
301	41.55	1289	9.123
302	41.51		

Corporation Tax Act 2009 – *contd*	PARA
s 1290	9.121, 9.123, 9.127; 41.45
1290(2)	9.123
1291	9.121, 9.123, 9.127; 41.45
1292	9.121, 9.123, 9.124; 41.45
(4)	9.123
(6B)	9.117
1293–1297	9.121, 9.123, 9.124, 9.127; 41.45
1298–1300	10.138
1302	10.152
1303	10.156
1304	10.149
1305	10.138
1305A	41.42
Sch 2	
para 133, 140	9.123
Finance Act 2009	3.1, 3.73; 8.203; 14.31, 14.37, 14.41; 27.93; 38.32; 41.46, 41.62; 43.126; 44.9, 44.17; 49.83; 51.55; 55.23
s 100	55.23
106, 107	4.27
Sch 6	
para 3	41.62
Sch 11	
para 7, 8, 26	48.75
29, 31	48.74, 48.80
Sch 15	41.98
Sch 16	41.161
Sch 46	41.186
Sch 52	55.23
Sch 55	4.26; 17.7; 41.184
para 3–6	4.202
Sch 56	4.27; 8.199; 41.184
Constitutional Reform and Governance Act 2010	
Pt 4 (ss 41, 42)	27.11
Corporation Tax Act 2010	1.22; 3.30, 3.51; 6.2, 6.21, 6.41; 11.1; 41.1, 41.42; 43.44
Pt 2 Ch 4 (ss 5–17)	41.152
s 17(4)	41.152
18, 19	41.24
24(3)	41.24
25(5)	41.24
32	41.46
27	41.24
37	41.62, 41.63. 41.64; 43.43, 43.44; 48.9
37(7)	41.62
39(2)	41.62

Corporation Tax Act 2010 – *contd*	PARA
s 41	41.62
45	41.61, 41.63, 41.64; 48.9
46	41.61; 53.41
62	41.67; 48.10
Pt 4 Ch 5 (ss 68–90)	11.121
s 91	13.20; 41.67
Pt 5 (ss 97–188)	43.41
s 99	43.43; 47.35
105	43.43
107	43.42
(6A), (6B)	43.42
109	43.43
133	43.21
(5)–(8)	43.42
143, 144	43.41
148, 149	43.21
151(4)	43.41
153	43.21
(3)	43.21
154	43.47
155(3)	43.45
155A, 155B	43.47
Pt 5 Ch 6 (ss 157–182)	43.47
s 169	43.47
Pt 6 (ss 189–217)	41.57; 53.42
s 189(1), (2), (4)	41.59
190(2)	41.59
Pt 6 Ch 2 (ss 191–202)	41.60
Pt 7A (ss 269A–269CN)	41.60
s 199	53.42
203	53.99
205, 206	53.100
209–212	53.99
Pt 8ZB (ss 356OA–356OT)	12.105, 12.111
s 356OB	12.102, 12.104
356OJ	12.103
356OL	12.108
356OO	12.109
439	3.30, 3.37
(2), (3)	41.122
440–443	3.30, 3.37
444	3.30, 3.37
(4)	41.125
445–447	3.30, 3.37
448	41.124
449	26.62
450	24.19; 41.74
451	41.74
452	41.124, 41.127
453(4)	41.124
454	27.112; 41.124

	PARA
Corporation Tax Act 2010 – *contd*	
s 455	9.122; 41.128, 41.182; 45.16; 46.56
(1)(c)	46.57
456	51.51
464A–464D	41.128
468	7.128; 53.41
469–474	53.41
475, 476	7.128; 53.41
477	53.41
478	53.41, 53.42
479	53.41
480	53.41, 53.42
481, 482	53.41
483	53.41, 53.42
484	53.41, 53.42
485–489	53.41
490	7.128; 53.41
491, 492	53.41
493	53.41, 53.61
494–499	53.61
500, 501	53.61
502–516	53.61
517	12.103; 53.61
Pt 13 Ch 9 (ss 658–671)	53.101
Pt 14 Ch 2 (ss 673–676)	11.2
Pt 14 Ch 3 (ss 677–691)	41.42
s 628	41.21
648–671	7.128
665	19.12
673	3.8; 47.35
674	3.8; 41.65, 41.187
675, 676	3.8
682	41.70
683, 705C–705E	41.67
Pt 14 Ch 6 (ss 706–718)	41.187
Pt 14B (ss 730E–730H)	41.60
s 719, 724, 724A	41.65
729	42.4
730A–730D	41.65
Pt 15 (ss 731–751)	3.3, 3.29
s 731	3.29, 3.38, 3.51, 3.56; 5.7
732–742	3.29, 3.51
743–747	3.29, 3.51
748	3.29, 3.51; 12.113; 42.31
749–751	3.29, 3.51
Pt 16 (ss 752–779)	12.88
Pt 17 Ch 2 (ss 782–789)	3.11
Pt 18 (ss 815–833)	12.101; 53.43
s 816	12.106
819	12.103, 12.113
(2)(a)	12.106

	PARA
Corporation Tax Act 2010 – *contd*	
s 827	12.106
831	12.113
834–886	3.6, 10.141
939A–939I	53.116
940A	10.30
944, 948	41.66
Pt 23 Ch 2 (ss 998–1028)	42.1
s 999	47.51
1000(1)	42.3, 42.5, 42.7
(c), (d)	42.121
(1C), (1D)	42.5
1016	42.8
1017(1)	42.8
1020	42.6
1022	42.4
1026	42.3
Pt 23 Ch 3 (ss 1029–1063)	42.1
s 1030A, 1030B	20.28
1032	42.8
1033	3.35; 42.21, 42.27, 42.28, 42.29, 42.30, 42.31; 46.58
1042(1)	42.25
1063(1)	42.25
1064	41.127; 42.10
1072(4)	51.54
1074	47.51
1075	3.35; 42.141
1076–1085	42.141
1113(6)	51.54
1114(3), (6)	51.54
1115(1)	51.54
1117(1)	51.54
1119	20.13; 41.66
1122	10.114; 12.107
(3)	12.108
(4)	43.45
1127	10.62, 10.64
1136	42.121
1141–1153	27A.32
1154	20.13, 20.16; 43.21
Sch 1	
para 238	12.106
Equality Act 2010	9.32
Finance Act 2010	5.12, 5.17; 19.4; 27.93; 48.8; 53.1, 53.21, 53.23, 53.79, 53.99
s 8	28.121
34	27.101
39	9.74
42	9.82
56	5.4, 5.10

Table of statutes

	PARA
Finance Act 2010 – *contd*	
s 65	49.104
Sch 6	53.23, 53.91
para 1	53.23
Sch 17	5.4, 5.10
Finance (No 2) Act 2010	19.4, 19.55
s 3(1)	38.5
Sch 1	21.61, 21.102
para 22	27A.24, 27A.116
Sch 3	42.28
Finance (No 3) Act 2010	4.27
s 8	14.46
16	23.63
Sch 3	41.46; 42.28
Sch 7	48.38
Taxation (International and Other Provisions) Act 2010	1.22; 6.2, 6.21, 6.41; 41.1, 41.42
s 6	41.156; 54.21
9	41.156
12	18.37
18, 112	18.91
131	41.98
Pt 4 (ss 146–217)	3.8; 3.29; 9.122; 10.116, 10.118; 35.21; 41.44; 42.7
s 148	43.1
Pt 5 (ss 218–230)	41.44
s 249	9.129
Pt 7 (ss 260–353)	41.98
Pt 9A (ss 371AA–371VJ)	41.161
s 373SB(3)(a)	27.113
Sch 4	
para 2–5	3.6
Charities Act 2011	53.1, 53.22, 53.23, 53.24, 53.26
s 1	53.22, 53.24
2	53.23
5, 17	53.22
30(2)	53.21
177	53.23
Sch 3	53.21
Energy Act 2011	48.31
Finance Act 2011	3.1, 3.73; 8.1, 8.199; 12.61, 12.63; 19.4; 41.161; 43.122, 43.123, 43.127, 43.151; 47.35; 49.106; 53.84, 53.116
s 9	25.148
10	48.38
52	12.61, 12.63
55	41.24
Sch 2	9.111

	PARA
Finance Act 2011 – *contd*	
Sch 9	26.64
Sch 10	43.123
Sch 14	12.61, 12.63
Sch 18	50.22
Sch 23	4.165
National Insurance Contributions Act 2011	8.1
Finance Act 2012	12.63; 15.4, 15.54, 15.124; 16.103; 19.17; 22.3, 22.74; 30.30; 31.89; 41.161; 48.68; 51.45, 51.50; 55.21
s 10	12.63
Sch 12	27.81, 27.96, 27.97
Sch 14	22.6; 53.111
Sch 26	39.21
Sch 38	55.61
Welfare Reform Act 2012	1.4; 16.74; 51.2, 51.27
Finance Act 2013	1.23, 1.26; 3.74; 5.3, 5.17; 8.1, 8.11, 8.32, 8.199, 8.202; 9.32, 9.71, 9.74, 9.78, 9.80, 9.87; 16.74, 16.108; 18.13; 22.3; 25.149; 27.1, 27.46; 27A.121; 28.101; 41.21, 41.42, 41.128, 41.152; 44.1; 46.56; 48.32, 48.33; 49.38, 49.89; 51.50, 51.71
s 4	43.21
6	43.1
16	11.5; 12.46
110	18.13
194	55.21
203(3)(e)	28.101
Pt 5 (ss 206–215)	19.48; 27.46
s 206	3.77
207	3.77
(1), (2), (4), (5)	3.78
208–210	3.77
211	3.77
(1)(a)	3.78
(2)	3.77
212–215	3.77
223	
Sch 3	11.5; 12.46
para 1	8.175
Sch 11	14.35
Sch 42	16.75
Sch 43	3.77, 3.79
Sch 45	18.13
Growth and Infrastructure Act 2013	9.32; 51.130
Marriage (Same Sex Couples) Act 2013	51.2; 52.1

Table of statutes li

	PARA
Marriage (Same Sex Couples) Act 2013 – *contd*	
Sch 3 para 1(1)(b)	51.27
Trusts (Capital and Income) Act 2013	17.3, 17.4, 17.26; 42.149
s 2	42.149
Finance Act 2014	1.6, 1.23; 4.176, 4.182; 5.3, 5.4, 5.6, 5.28, 5.30; 8.1, 8.22, 8.23, 8.32, 8.119; 9.13 9.23, 9.71, 9.80, 9.81, 9.115, 9.116, 9.117, 9.126; 16.74. 16.75, 16.108; 22.3; 25.151; 34.1, 34.26; 44.1, 44.6, 44.9, 44.10, 44.17; 45.11, 45.12, 45.16; 46.5, 46.51; 47.5; 49.89, 49.106, 49.127; 51.2; 53.120
s 64(5)(a)	48.372
204(1)	5.29
National Insurance Contributions Act 2014	8.1
Taxation of Pensions Act 2014	50.17, 50.19, 50.32; 52.14
Finance Act 2015	1.26; 3.1, 3.77; 5.4, 5.5, 5.17, 5.28; 8.101, 8.104, 8.131, 8.169; 20.1, 20.17; 22.21; 23.44; 44.1, 44.8, 44.39; 53.83
s 7	23.44
22	11.122
37	23.2
24	18.34
40	19.37
41	44.39
42	44.39
43	44.39; 45.16
45	19.37
Pt 3 (ss 77–116)	4.178; 53.42
Sch 7	23.2
Sch 9	23.43, 23.44
Finance (No 2) Act 2015	4.24; 12.45; 28.104; 31.84; 32.92; 34.24; 43.42; 44.1; 45.2

	PARA
Charities (Protection and Social Investment) Bill (*draft*)	53.61
Charities (Protection and Social Investment) Act 2016	53.22
Finance Bill 2016 (*draft*)	12.45
Finance Act 2016	1.26; 2.1; 3.1, 3.33, 3.34, 3.35, 3.36, 3.38, 3.80; 8.110, 8.125, 8.131; 9.34; 12.4, 12.101; 14.32, 14.37, 14.40; 17.21, 17.53; 20.1, 20.17, 20.23, 20.33; 23.122; 25.41; 31.86; 38.6; 41.21; 44.1; 45.1, 45.2, 45.16; 49.28
s 35	20.28
65	48.37
66	48.53
69	48.12
70	48.12, 48.53
73	48.12
74	12.48
76–82	12.101
85	20.20
126	38.6
Finance Bill 2017 (*draft*)	12.43, 12.44; 15.57; 18.30, 18.34; 31.87; 35.4, 35.21; 41.98, 41.151; 50.12
Finance Act 2017	5.21, 5.26; 7.27, 7.120; 9.32; 27.81, 27.82; 27A.12, 27A.112; 31.87; 41.60, 41.75, 41.98, 41.151; 42.76; 53.120; 55.25, 55.49
Sch 2 para 62	8.106
(3)–(5)	8.106
Finance (No 2) Bill 2017	5.21, 5.26; 15.1, 15.57; 18.34; 44.1
Pension Schemes Act 2017	50.2
Small Charitable Donations and Childcare Payments Act 2017	53.81
European Union (Withdrawal) Bill 2017–2019	37.4; 50.14; 54.24
Finance Bill 2018	18.34

Table of statutory instruments

	PARA
Temporary Importation (Commercial Vehicles and Aircraft) Regulations 1961, SI 1961/1523	38.103
Value Added Tax (Change of Rate) Order 1974, SI 1974/1224	38.5
Value Added Tax (Imported Goods) Relief Order 1984, SI 1984/746	38.103
Stamp Duty Reserve Tax Regulations 1986, SI 1986/1711	49.92
Income Tax (Entertainers and Sportsmen) Regulations 1987, SI 1987/530	18.74
Inheritance Tax (Double Charges Relief) Regulations 1987, SI 1987/1130	36.1
reg 4	36.2
(3)(a)	36.2
5	36.3
6	36.4
7, 8	36.5
Value Added Tax (Cars) Order 1992, SI 1991/3122	38.30
Customs and Excise Duties (Personal Reliefs for Goods Permanently Imported) Order 1992, SI 1992/3193	38.103
Value Added Tax (Input Tax) Order 1992, SI 1992/3222	
art 6	39.25
Income Tax (Employments) Regulations 1993, SI 1993/744	
reg 6	8.194
Value Added Tax (Special Provisions) Order 1995, SI 1995/1268	38.26; 39.37; 40.126
reg 92	40.86

	PARA
Value Added Tax Regulations 1995, SI 1995/2518	38.84, 38.102, 38.103
reg 25	38.55
25A(6)	55.49
29	38.53
(1A)	38.53
55B(4)	38.30
55L(c)	38.30
55M	38.30
55N(3), (4)	38.30
55P–55S	38.30
Pt XI (regs 81–95)	38.33
reg 101	38.86
(3)	38.86
102	38.87
(3)	38.87
Pt XV (regs 112–116)	39.30
106	38.88
reg 113	39.30
Taxation of Income from Land (Non-residents) Regulations 1995, SI 1995/2902	18.75
reg 8(2)	18.75
9(4)	18.75
Stamp Duty and Stamp Duty Reserve Tax (Open-ended Investment Companies) Regulations 1997, SI 1997/1156	49.106
reg 4A	49.106
Corporation Tax (Instalment Payments) Regulations 1998, SI 1998/3175	41.183
Corporation Tax (Treatment of Unrelieved Surplus Advance Corporation Tax) Regulations 1999, SI 1999/358	42.46
reg 4(4)	42.46

liv Table of statutory instruments

	PARA
Social Security and Child Support (Decisions and Appeals) Regulations 1999, SI 1999/991	51.39
Inheritance Tax (Settled Property Income Yield) Order 2000, SI 2000/174	33.7
Donations to Charity by Individuals (Appropriate Declarations) Regulations 2000, SI 2000/2074	53.82
Orders for the Delivery of Documents (Procedure) Regulations 2000, SI 2000/2875 reg 7	4.159
Social Security (Contributions) Regulations 2001, SI 2001/1004	9.44
Limited Liability Partnership Regulations 2001, SI 2001/1090	45.5, 45.6
Value Added Tax (Refund of Tax to Museums and Galleries) Order 2001, SI 2001/2879	40.63
Value Added Tax (Amendment) (No. 2) Regulations 2002, SI 2002/1142	38.30; 53.129
Working Tax Credit (Entitlement and Maximum Rate) Regulations 2002, SI 2002/2005	8.169
Child Tax Credit Regulations 2002, SI 2002/2007 reg 3(1)	55.44
Tax Credits (Income Thresholds and Determination of Rates) Regulations 2002, SI 2002/2008	51.38
Tax Credit (Claims and Notifications) Regulations 2002, SI 2002/2014 reg 21	52.16
Individual Learning Accounts Wales Regulations 2003, SI 2003/918 (W119)	8.96
Value Added Tax (Amendment) (No 2) Regulations 2003, SI 2003/1069 reg 7	38.30
Social Security (Contributions) (Amendment No 4) Regulations 2003, SI 2003/1337	9.44

	PARA
Income Tax (Exemption of Minor Benefits) (Increase in Sums of Money) Order 2003, SI 2003/1361	8.168
Income Tax (Pay As You Earn) Regulations 2003, SI 2003/2682	8.191, 8.192
reg 21	8.201
23	8.196
37	8.156
41	8.199
61C	8.192
72	8.201
(3), (4)	8.201
72E–72G	8.24
81	8.201
82	8.199
85(4)	8.192
91	8.156
92(4)	8.156
Pt 6 (regs 105–117)	8.198
reg 185	8.201
Stamp Duty Land Tax (Administration) Regulations 2003, SI 2003/2837 Pt IV (regs 10–28)	49.61
Tax Avoidance Schemes (Promoters and Prescribed Circumstances) Regulations 2004, SI 2004/1865	5.5
Value Added Tax (Disclosure of Avoidance Schemes) Regulations 2004, SI 2004/1929	5.25
Value Added Tax (Groups: Eligibility) Order 2004, SI 2004/1931	38.50
Value Added Tax (Disclosure of Avoidance Schemes) (Designations) Order 2004, SI 2004/1933	5.23
Social Security (Contributions) (Amendment No 5) Regulations 2004, SI 2004/2246	9.44
Inheritance Tax (Delivery of Accounts) (Excepted Estates) Regulations 2004, SI 2004/2543	30.44
Tax Avoidance Schemes (Promoters and Prescribed Circumstances and Information) (Amendment) Regulations 2004, SI 2004/2613	5.5

Table of statutory instruments lv

	PARA
Tax and Civil Partnership Regulations 2005, SI 2005/3229	51.130
Registered Pension Schemes (Enhanced Lifetime Allowance) Regulations 2006, SI 2006/131	
reg 12	50.22
Transfer of Undertakings (Protection of Employment) Regulations 2006, SI 2006/246	47.14
Registered Pension Schemes (Modification of the Rules of Existing Schemes) Regulations 2006, SI 2006/364	50.8
Registered Pension Schemes (Authorised Surplus Payments) Regulations 2006, SI 2006/574	50.20
Authorised Investment Funds (Tax) Regulations 2006, SI 2006/964	14.32
Tax Avoidance Schemes (Prescribed Descriptions of Arrangements) Regulations 2006, SI 2006/1543	8.4
Tax Credit (Claims and Notifications) (Amendment) Regulations 2006, SI 2006/2689	52.16
National Insurance Contributions (Application of Part 7 of the Finance Act 2004) Regulations 2007, SI 2007/785	8.4
Business Premises Renovation Allowances Regulations 2007, SI 2007/945	48.124
Value Added Tax (Section 55A) (Specified Goods and Excepted Supplies) Order 2007, SI 2007/1417	38.30
Police and Criminal Evidence Act 1984 (Application to Revenue and Customs) Order 2007, SI 2007/3175	4.58
art 4	4.59
7	4.157
Inheritance Tax (Delivery of Accounts) (Excepted Transfers and Excepted Terminations) Regulations 2008, SI 2008/605	28.172; 33.22

	PARA
Inheritance Tax (Delivery of Accounts) (Excepted Settlements) Regulations 2008, SI 2008/606	28.172
Charities (Accounts and Reports) Regulations 2008, SI 2008/629	53.22
Energy-Saving Items (Corporation Tax) Regulations 2008, SI 2008/1520	48.126
National Insurance Contributions (Application of Part 7 of the Finance Act 2004) (Amendment) Regulations 2008, SI 2008/2678	8.4
Value Added Tax (Change of Rate) Order 2008, SI 2008/3020	38.5
Transfer of Tribunal Functions and Revenue and Customs Appeal Order 2009, SI 2009/56	51.39
Tribunal Procedure (First-tier Tribunal) (Tax Chamber) Rules 2009, SI 2009/273	4.201
r 10	4.208
Finance Act 2008, Schedule 36 (Appointed Day and Savings) Order 2009, SI 2009/404	4.161
Tax Avoidance Schemes (Information) (Amendment) Regulations 2009, SI 2009/611	5.10
Enactment of Extra-Statutory Concessions Order 2009, SI 2009/730	23.85
Offshore Funds (Tax) Regulations 2009, SI 2009/3001	
reg 34	21.1
Stamp Duty Land Tax Avoidance Schemes (Prescribed Descriptions of Arrangements) (Amendment) Regulations 2010, SI 2010/407	5.11
Tax Avoidance Schemes (Information) (Amendment) Regulations 2010, SI 2010/410	5.11
Value Added Tax (Buildings and Land) Order 2010, SI 2010/485	39.30

	PARA
Community Infrastructure Levy Regulations 2010, SI 2010/948 reg 44	53.131
Child Trust Funds (Amendment No 3) Regulations 2010, SI 2010/1894	51.42
Child Trust Funds (Amendment No 4) Regulations 2010, SI 2010/2599	51.43
National Insurance Contributions (Application of Part 7 of the Finance Act 2004) (Amendment) Regulations 2010, SI 2010/2927	8.4
Value Added Tax (Amendment) (No 4) Regulations 2010, SI 2010/3022	38.82
Income Tax (Pay as You Earn) (Amendment) (No 2) Regulations 2011, SI 2011/1054	8.156
Income Tax (Pay as You Earn) (Amendment) Regulations 2012, SI 2012/822	8.203
reg 65	8.156
Business Premises Renovation Allowances (Amendment) Regulations 2012, SI 2012/868	48.124
Income Tax (Limits for Enterprise Management Incentives) Order 2012, SI 2012/1360	9.83
Tax Avoidance Schemes (Information) Regulations 2012, SI 2012/1836	5.8
Taxation of Chargeable Gains (Gilt-edged Securities) Order 2012, SI 2012/1843	22.3
Annual Tax on Enveloped Dwellings Avoidance Schemes (Prescribed of Amendments) Regulations 2013, SI 2013/2571	5.16
Tax Avoidance Schemes (Information) (Amendment etc) Regulations 2012, SI 2013/2592	5.8, 5.15

	PARA
Small Companies (Micro-Entities' Accounts) Regulations 2013, SI 2013/3008	10.64
Income Tax (Pay As You Earn) and the Income Tax (Construction Industry Scheme) (Amendment) Regulations 2014, SI 2014/472	8.24
Public Bodies (Merger of the Director of Public Prosecutors and the Director of Revenue and Customs Prosecutions) Order 2014, SI 2014/834	4.160
Value Added Tax (Sport) Order 2014, SI 2014/3185	40.54
Capital Allowances Act 2001 (Extension of first-year allowances) (Amendment) Order 2015, SI 2015/60	48.32, 48.33
Community Amateur Sports Club Regulations 2015, SI 2015/725	53.101
Tax Avoidance Schemes (Information) (Amendment) Regulations 2015, SI 2015/948	5.7, 5.13
Police and Criminal Evidence Act 1984 (Application to Revenue and Customs) Order 2015, SI 2015/1783	4.59
art 4	4.59
6	4.157
Inheritance Tax Avoidance Schemes (Prescribed Descriptions of Arrangements) Regulations 2015 (*not yet in force*)	5.3, 5.12, 5.13
Tax Avoidance Schemes (Prescribed Descriptions of Arrangements) (Amendment) Regulations 2016, SI 2016/99	5.3, 5.7, 5.12, 5.13

Table of cases

Decisions of the European Court of Justice are listed numerically after the main table.

A

	PARA
A v R & C Comrs (2009)	8.148
A v R & C Comrs (2015)	8.42, 8.141, 8.157
AA Insurance Services Ltd v C & E Comrs [1999] BVC 2330, [1999] V & CR 361	39.20
AB v R & C Comrs [2011] UKFTT 685 (TC)	8.148
A-G v Black (1871) LR 6 Exch 308, 1 TC 54	13.13
A-G v Boden [1912] 1 KB 539, 105 LT 247	44.51
A-G v Johnson [1903] 1 KB 617	29.41
A-G v Seccombe [1911] 2 KB 688	29.44
A-G v Worrall [1895] 1 QB 99, CA	29.44
AK v Liechtenstein (9 July 2015)	55.83
AP, MP & TP v Switzerland (1998) 26 EHRR 541, [1998] EHRLR 88	55.82
ATP Pension Service A/S v Skatterministeriet (2014)	50.14
Abbey National plc v C & E Comrs (Case C-408/98) [2001] All ER (EC) 385, [2001] 1 WLR 769, [2001] STC 297, ECJ	38.26; 39.37
Abbott v IRC [1996] STC (SCD) 41n	10.137
Abbott v Philbin [1961] AC 352, 39 TC 82, HL	8.92; 9.41
Aberdeen Asset Management plc v R & C Comrs [2012] UKUT 43 (TCC), [2012] STC 650, [2012] BTC 1514	2.37; 8.129, 8.192
Aberdeen Construction Group Ltd v IRC [1977] STC 302, 52 TC 281, Ct of Sess; on appeal [1978] 1 All ER 962, [1978] STC 127, HL	22.44
Aberdeen Property Fininvest Alpha Oy, Proceedings brought by (Case C-303/07) [2009] STC 1945, [2009] ECR I-5145, [2009] 3 CMLR 34	54.62
Able (UK) Ltd v R & C Comrs [2007] EWCA Civ 1207, [2008] STC 136	10.103
Acornwood LLP v R & C Comrs [2014] UKFTT 416 (TC), [2014] SFTD 694	2.40, 2.46; 10.28
Adam & Co International Trustees Ltd v Theodore Goddard [2000] WTLR 349, [2000] 13 LS Gaz R 44, 144 Sol Jo LB 150	27A.34
Addy v IRC [1975] STC 601, 51 TC 71, 54 ATC 194	3.34, 3.61
Aeroassistance Logistics Ltd v R & C Comrs [2013] UKFTT 214 (TC)	10.157
Agassi v Robinson (2006)	18.1, 18.51, 18.74
Ahad v R & C Comrs [2009] UKFTT 353 (TC), [2010] STI 627	22.82
Ainslie v Buckley [2002] STC (SCD) 132	8.95
Air Jamaica v Charlton [1999] 1 WLR 1399, [1999] OPLR 11, [1999] Pens LR 247, (1999-2000) 2 ITELR 244	50.2
Akhtar Ali v R & C Comrs [2016] UKFTT 8 (TC), [2016] SFTD 335, [2016] STI 528	10.20
Alchemist (Devil's Gate) Film Partnership v R & C Comrs [2013] UKFTT 157 (TC)	10.67

	PARA
Al Fayed v Advocate General for Scotland (representing the IRC) [2002] STC 910, 2003 SC 1, 2003 SLT 745, Ct of Sess.	4.184
Alexander v IRC [1991] STC 112, [1991] 2 EGLR 179, [1991] 26 EG 141, CA	28.72
Ali & Begum v C & E Comrs [2002] V & DR 71	55.82, 55.101
Allgemeine Gold-und Silberscheidanstalt AG (AGOSI) v United Kingdom (1987) 9 EHRR	155.24
Alloway v Phillips [1980] 3 All ER 138, [1980] STC 490, CA	13.25
Allum v Marsh (Inspector of Taxes) [2005] STC (SCD) 191, [2005] STI 97	8.62, 8.145
Alpine Investments BV v Minister van Financien (Case C-384/93) [1995] All ER (EC) 543, [1995] ECR I-1141, ECJ	54.52
Altman Blane & Co v C & E Comrs (1994)	39.21
Amah (HL) v R & C Comrs (2014)	10.30
Amministrazione delle Finanze dello Stato v Simmenthal SpA (Case 106/77) [1978] ECR 629, [1978] 3 CMLR 263, ECJ	54.25
Anand v IRC [1997] STC (SCD) 58	30.2
Anderson v R & C Comrs [2016] UKFTT 335 (TC)	4.42
Anderton v Lamb [1981] STC 43, [1981] TR 393	22.75
Anise Ltd v Hammond (Inspector of Taxes) [2003] STC (SCD) 258	10.107; 13.13
Anson v R & C Comrs [2013] EWCA Civ 63, [2013] STC 557, [2013] BTC 81	45.8
Appellant v Inspector of Taxes [2001] STC (SCD) 21	8.147
Ardmore Construction Ltd v R & C Comrs [2015] UKUT 633 (TCC), [2016] STC 1044, [2015] BTC 536	14.33
Arnander v R & C Comrs [2007] RVR 208, [2006] STC (SCD) 800, [2007] WTLR 51	31.65, 31.66
Ashton Gas Co v A-G [1906] AC 10, 75 LJ Ch 1, HL	10.130
Aspden v Hildesley [1982] 2 All ER 53, [1982] STC 206	19.15; 52.21
Aspect Capital Ltd v R & C Comrs [2014] UKUT 81 (TCC), [2014] STC 1360, [2014] BTC 508	41.51
Asscher v Staatssecretaris van Financien (Case C-107/94) [1996] All ER (EC) 757, [1996] ECR I-3089, [1996] STC 1025, ECJ	54.56
Associated Portland Cement Manufacturers Ltd v Kerr [1946] 1 All ER 68, 27 TC 103, CA	10.134
Associated Provincial Picture Houses Ltd v Wednesbury Corpn [1948] 1 KB 223, [1947] 2 All ER 680, (1947) 63 TLR 623	55.46
Astall v R & C Comrs [2009] EWCA Civ 1010, [2010] STC 137	2.40, 2.46
Atherton v British Insulated & Helsby Cables Ltd *see* British Insulated & Helsby Cables Ltd v Atherton	
Atkinson v R & C Comrs [2011] UKUT 506 (TCC), [2012] STC 289, [2011] BTC 1917	31.69
Attwood v Anduff Car Wash Ltd [1997] STC 1167, 69 TC 575, CA	48.17
Audley v R & C Comrs [2011] UKFTT 219 (TC), [2011] SFTD 597	2.3, 2.40
Autoclenz v Belcher [2011] UKSC 41, [2011] 4 All ER 745, [2011] ICR 1157	8.22
Avoir Fiscal (1986)	54.57
Azam v R & C Comrs [2011] UKFTT 50 (TC)	10.137

B

BAT Industries plc v R & C Comrs [2017] UKFTT 558 (TC)	38.2; 54.8
BLP Group Ltd v C & E Comrs [1994] STC 41, CA (Case C–4/94): [1995] All ER (EC) 401, [1995] STC 424, ECJ	37.5

Table of cases lix

	PARA
BSC Footwear Ltd v Ridgway [1972] AC 544, [1971] 2 All ER 534, 47 TC 495, HL	10.112
BSM (1257) Ltd v Secretary of State for Social Services [1978] ICR 894	8.23
BT Pension Scheme (Trustes of) v R & C Comrs (2013)	54.11
BUPA Hospitals Ltd & Goldsborough Developments Ltd (Case C-419/02) [2002] ECJ 446	54.74
BUPA Purchasing Ltd v C & E Comrs [2003] EWHC 1957 (Ch), [2003] STC 120	2.44
Baars v Inspecteur der Belastingen Particulieren/Ondernemingen Gorinchem (Case C-251/98) [2000] ECR I-2787, [2002] 1 CMLR 1437, ECJ	54.31, 54.45, 54.49
Bachmann v Belgium (Case C-204/90) [1992] ECR I-249, [1994] STC 855, ECJ; apld *sub nom* Bachmann v Belgium [1994] 3 CMLR 263	54.61, 54.62
Baird's Executors v IRC 1991 SLT (Lands Tr) 9, [1991] 1 EGLR 201, [1991] 09 EG 129, 10 EG 153	28.73; 31.72
Baker v Archer-Shee [1927] AC 844, 96 LJKB 803, 11 TC 749, 6 ATC 621, HL	16.61, 16.62; 42.144, 42.149
Baker v Mabie Todd & Co Ltd (1927)	10.137
Balloon Promotions Ltd v Wilson (2006) SpC 524	22.74
Bamberg v R & C Comrs [2010] UKFTT 333 (TC), [2010] SFTD 1231, [2010] STI 2644	3.55, 3.61
Bambridge v IRC [1955] 3 All ER 812, 36 TC 313, HL	28.105
Bamford v ATA Advertising Ltd [1972] 3 All ER 535, 48 TC 359	10.145
Bancroft v Crutchfield [2002] STC (SCD) 347	55.82, 55.83
Barclays Bank plc v R & C Comrs (2007)	8.148
Barclays Bank Trust Co Ltd v IRC [1998] STC (SCD) 125	31.52
Barclays Mercantile Business Finance Ltd v Mawson [2002] EWHC 1527 (Ch), [2002] STC 1068; *revs'd* [2002] EWCA Civ 1853, [2003] STC 66; *aff'd* [2004] UKHL 51, [2005] STC 1	1.24; 2.2, 2.4, 2.37, 2.38, 2.39, 2.40, 2.41, 2.42, 2.43, 2.45, 2.46, 2.48; 6.21
Barnett v Brabyn [1996] STC 716, 69 TC 133	8.22, 8.23
Barrett v IRC (2005)	28.67
Barty-King v Ministry of Defence [1979] 2 All ER 80, [1979] STC 218	31.25
Bates van Winkelhof v Clyde & Co LLP [2012] IRLR 548	8.23
Batey v Wakefield [1982] 1 All ER 61, [1981] STC 521, CA	23.23, 23.24
Baxter (1999)	54.63
Baylis v Gregory [1989] AC 398, [1987] 3 All ER 27, [1987] STC 297, CA; *aff'd* [1989] AC 398, [1988] 3 All ER 495, [1988] STC 476, HL	2.25, 2.44
Beak v Robson [1943] AC 352, [1943] 1 All ER 46, 25 TC 33, HL	8.134
Beare (Inspector of Taxes) v Carter [1940] 2 KB 187	13.12
Beckman v IRC [2000] STC (SCD) 59	31.43
Belgium v Temco Europe SA (Case C-284/03) [2005] STC 1451, [2004] ECR I-11237, [2005] 1 CMLR 23	39.21
Belmonte v Italy (2010)	55.26
Beneficiary, A v IRC [1999] STC (SCD) 134	18.113
Benford v R & C Comrs [2011] UKFTT 457 (TC)	23.22, 23.42
Benham's Will Trusts, Re, Lockhart v Harker, Read & the Royal National Lifeboat Institution [1995] STC 210	30.58, 30.59, 30.60, 30.61, 30.62; 53.93
Bennett v IRC [1995] STC 54	31.4
Bennett v Ogston (1930) 15 TC 374, 9 ATC 182	14.6
Ben Nevis Forestry Ventures Ltd v CIR; Glenharrow Ltd v CIR (2007)	3.82

PARA

Benson v Counsell (Inspector of Taxes) [1942] 1 KB 364,
[1942] 1 All ER 435, 24 TC 178.. 13.12, 13.15
Bentleys, Stokes & Lowless v Beeson [1952] 2 All ER 82, 33 TC 491, CA.......... 10.137
Berlioz Investment Fund SA v Director of the Direct Tax Administration,
Luxembourg (Case C-682/15) [2017] BTC 15................................. 54.95; 55.84
Bernard & Shaw Ltd v Shaw [1951] 2 All ER 267, [1951] TR 205,
30 ATC 187... 8.202
Berry (Andrew) v R & C Comrs [2009] UKFTT 386 (TC),
[2010] STI 1449... 2.40, 2.46, 2.48
Best (Buller's Executor) v R & C Comrs [2014] UKFTT 77 (TC),
[2014] WTLR 409... 31.50
Beswick v Beswick [1968] AC 58, [1967] 2 All ER 1197, HL............................. 44.16
Beteiligungsgesellschaft Larentia + Minerva mbH KG v Finanzamt
Nordenham (Case C-108/14) [215] STC 2101, [2015] BVC 33.... 38.50; 43.191
Bhadra v Ellam [1988] STC 239, 60 TC 466 .... 8.31
Bhadra (t/a Admirals Locums) v R & C Comrs [2011] UKFTT 573 (TC) 10.30
Billingham (Inspector of Taxes) v Cooper [2001] EWCA Civ 1041,
[2001] STC 1177, 74 TC 139... 1.41; 27A.111
Billingham v John [1998] STC 120, 70 TC 380, [1998] 1 FCR 339,
[1998] 1 FLR 677.. 52.3
Bird v IRC [1985] STC 584; on appeal [1987] STC 168, CA; on appeal
[1989] AC 300, [1988] 2 All ER 670, [1988] STC 312, HL................... 2.47; 3.55
Bird v R & C Comrs [2009] STC (SCD) 81, [2008] STI 2792................ 16.93, 16.94,
16.95; 51.55
Bird v Martland [1982] STC 603, 56 TC 89 .... 8.65, 8.93
Black v Inspector of Taxes [2000] STC (SCD) 540... 8.194
Blackqueen Ltd v C & E Comrs [2002] BVC 2221, [2002] STI 1409 .... 54.74
Blackpool Marton Rotary Club v Martin [1990] STC 1, CA 41.1
Blackwell v R & C Comrs [2014] UKFTT 103 (TC), [2014] STI 1581 .... 19.21
Blakiston v Cooper [1909] AC 104, 5 TC 347, HL............................... 8.62, 8.105
Bloom v Kinder (Inspector of Taxes) (1958) 38 TC 77....................................... 13.13
Bluesparkle Ltd v R & C Comrs [2012] UKFTT 45 (TC)..................................... 10.77
Blum (MB) v R & C Comrs [2013] UKUT 304 (LC), [2014] RVR 137............... 19.31
Bluu Solutions Ltd v R & C Comrs [2015] UKFTT 95 (TC), [2015] STI 1582....... 55.82
Boake Allen Ltd v R & C Comrs [2007] UKHL 25, [2007] 1 WLR 1386,
[2007] 3 All ER 605... 54.49
Bond v Pickford [1982] STC 403, 57 TC 301; aff'd [1983] STC 517,
57 TC 301, CA.. 1.25; 25.82
Bond House Systems v Customs & Excise Comrs [2004] V&DR 125 .... 54.74
Booth v Ellard [1980] 3 All ER 569, [1980] STC 555, CA.......................... 25.5, 25.6
Bootle v Bye [1996] STC (SCD) 58... 8.92
Bosal Holdings BV v Staatssecretaris van Financien (Case C-168/01)
[2003] All ER (EC) 959, [2003] STC 1483, ECJ............................... 54.48, 54.49
Bouch, Re; Bouch v Sproule (1887) LR 12 App Cas 385 .... 42.152
Bowden v Russell & Russell [1965] 1 WLR 711, [1965] 2 All ER 258,
42 TC 301 .... 10.151
Bowerswood House Retirement Home Ltd v R & C Comrs
[2015] UKFTT 94 (TC) 48.65
Bowman v Fels [2005] EWCA Civ 226, [2005] 1 WLR 3083,
[2005] 4 All ER 609 .... 55.62
Bowman (t/a The Janitor Cleaning Co) v R & C Comrs
[2012] UKFTT 607 (TC) 10.131
Bowring v R & C Comrs [2013] UKFTT 366 (TC), [2014] SFTD 347,
[2013] STI 2889.. 27A.116, 27A.117, 27A.176

	PARA
Bradbury v Arnold (1957) 37 TC 665	13.25, 13.28
Bradley v London Electricity plc [1996] STC 1054, 70 TC 155	48.17
Bradley v R & C Comrs [2011] UKFTT 49 (TC)	23.22
Bradley (Susan) v R & C Comrs [2013] UKFTT 131 (TC)	23.22
Brady v Hart [1985] STC 498, 58 TC 518	8.31
Braithwaite (PW) v R & C Comrs [2008] STC (SCD) 707, [2008] STI 1233	13.19
Brander (Executor of Balfour), Re [2010] UKFTT 300 (TC), [2010] STC 666, 80 TC 163, [2010] BTC 1656	31.49, 31.50
Bray v Best [1986] STC 96; on appeal [1988] 2 All ER 105, [1988] STC 103, CA; aff'd [1989] 1 All ER 969, [1989] STC 159, HL	8.12, 8.41, 8.44
Bricom Holdings v IRC [1997] STC 1179, 70 TC 272, CA	18.91; 27.112
Briggenshaw v Crabb (1948) 30 TC 331	1.1
Brisal-Auto Estradas do Litoral SA v Fazanda Pública (Case C-18/15) [2016] STC 2078, [2017] 1 CMLR 20, [2016] BTC 39	54.48
British Dyestuffs Corpn (Blackley) v CIR (1924)	10.104, 10.108
British Insulated & Helsby Cables Ltd v Atherton [1926] AC 205, 4 ATC 47, sub nom Atherton v British Insulated & Helsby Cables Ltd (1925) 10 TC 155, HL	10.77, 10.131; 48.3
British Transport Commission v Gourley [1956] AC 185, [1955] 3 All ER 796, HL	8.157
Brockbank, Re [1948] 1 All ER 287	25.7
Brocklesby v Merricks (1934) 18 TC 576, CA	13.25, 13.28
Brodie's Will Trustees v IRC (1933) 17 TC 432, 12 ATC 140	16.67, 16.69; 17.47
Brooks v Brooks [1993] Fam 322, [1993] 4 All ER 917; on appeal [1995] Fam 70, [1994] 4 All ER 1065, CA; aff'd [1996] 1 AC 375, [1995] 3 All ER 257, HL	52.4
Brown v Bullock [1961] 1 All ER 206, 40 TC 1, [1960] TR 303; aff'd [1961] 3 All ER 129, 40 TC 1, CA	8.173
Brown v R & C Comrs [2013] UKFTT 208 (TC)	19.69
Brown v Ware [1995] STC (SCD) 155	8.120
Brown (1926) 11 TC 405	27.13, 27.14
Browne v Pritchard [1975] 3 All ER 721, [1975] 1 WLR 1366, CA	52.76
Brumby v Milner [1976] 3 All ER 636, [1976] 1 WLR 1096, [1976] STC 534, HL	8.44
Buccleuch (Duke) v IRC [1967] 1 AC 506, [1967] 1 All ER 129, [1966] TR 393, 45 ATC 472, HL	30.4
Buck v R & C Comrs [2009] STC (SCD) 6, [2009] WTLR 215	16.93; 46.54, 46.55; 51.55
Bucks v Bowers [1970] 2 All ER 202, 46 TC 267	7.23
Bulves AD v Bulgaria (3991/03) [2009] STC 1193, [2009] STI 1666	55.21
Burden & Burden v United Kingdom [2007] STC 252, [2005] 1 FCR 69, (2007) 44 EHRR 51	1.42; 31.41; 51.131; 55.21, 55.41, 55.43
Burdge v Pyne [1969] 1 WLR 364, [1969] 1 All ER 467, 45 TC 320	10.21
Burkinyoung (Executor of Burkinyoung) v IRC [1995] STC (SCD) 29	31.48
Burmah Steamship Co Ltd v IRC (1931) 16 TC 67	10.105
Burman v Westminster Press Ltd [1987] STC 669, 60 TC 418	19.47
Burrow v Burrow [1999] 2 FCR 549, [1999] 1 FLR 508	52.13
Burton v R & C Comrs [2009] UKFTT 203 (TC), [2009] SFTD 682, [2009] WTLR 1499	27A.87, 27A.116
Butler v Wildin [1989] STC 22, 61 TC 666	16.94
Butt v Haxby [1983] STC 239, 56 TC 547	11.82; 46.47

	PARA
Buzzoni v R & C Comrs [2011] UKFTT 267 (TC), [2011] SFTD 771, [2011] WTLR 1163	29.44, 29.71, 29.125, 29.131
Bye v Coren [1985] STC 113, 60 TC 116; *aff'd* [1986] STC 393, 60 TC 116, CA	19.3

C

C & E Comrs v Deutsche Ruck UK Reinsurance Co Ltd [1995] STC 495	40.82
C & E Comrs v Faith Construction Ltd [1989] 2 All ER 938, [1989] STC 539, CA	2.44
C & E Comrs v First National Bank of Chicago *see* First National Bank of Chicago v C & E Comrs	
C & E Comrs v Glassborow [1974] 1 All ER 1041, [1974] STC 142	44.71
C & E Comrs v Kingfisher plc [1994] STC 63	43.191
C & E Comrs v Leightons Ltd [1995] STC 458	40.37
C & E Comrs v Liverpool Institute for Performing Arts [1999] STC 424, CA; *aff'd* [2001] UKHL 28, [2001] 1 WLR 1187, [2001] 3 CMLR 75, [2001] STC 891	38.83
C & E Comrs v Lord Fisher [1981] 2 All ER 147, [1981] STC 238	38.28
C & E Comrs v Marchday Holdings Ltd [1997] STC 272, [1997] BTC 5054	39.24
C & E Comrs v Morrison's Academy Boarding Houses Association 1977 SC 279, 1977 SLT 197, [1978] STC 1	38.28
C & E Comrs v Professional Footballers' Association (Enterprises) Ltd [1993] 1 WLR 153, [1993] STC 86, HL	40.56
C & E Comrs v Samex ApS & Hanil Synthetic Fiber Industrial Co Ltd [1983] 3 CMLR 194	54.8
C & E Comrs v Schindler (Case C-275/92) [1994] QB 610, [1994] 2 All ER 193, [1994] ECR I-1039, ECJ	54.31
C & E Comrs v Sinclair Collis Ltd [1999] STC 701, CA; *revs'd* [2001] UKHL 30, [2001] STC 989, [2001] 3 CMLR 86	38.2; 39.21
C & E Comrs v Thorn Materials Supply Ltd & Thorn Resources Ltd [1996] STC 1490, CA; *aff'd* [1998] 3 All ER 342, [1998] 1 WLR 1106, [1998] STC 725, HL	2.44
CIR v Cleary [1968] AC 766, [1967] 2 WLR 1271, [1967] 2 All ER 48	3.34, 3.58
CIR v HIT Finance Ltd; CIR v Tai Hing Cotton Mill (Developments) Ltd (2007)	3.82
Cadbury-Schweppes v IRC (Case C-196/04) [2004] STC (SDC) 342	41.161; 54.8, 54.45, 54.64, 54.75, 54.76
Cadbury-Schweppes v IRC (2006)	27A.53
Caillebotte v Quinn [1975] 2 All ER 412, [1975] STC 265	10.137
Cairnsmill Caravan Park v R & C Comrs [2013] UKFTT 164 (TC)	10.142
Calvert v Wainwright [1947] KB 526, [1947] 1 All ER 282, 27 TC 475, 26 ATC 13	8.62
Camas plc v Atkinson (Inspector of Taxes) [2004] EWCA Civ 541, [2004] STC 860	41.69
Cameron v Prendergast *see* Prendergast v Cameron	
Campbell Connelly & Co Ltd v Barnett [1992] STC 316, 66 TC 380; *aff'd* [1994] STC 50, 66 TC 380, CA	1.25; 22.72; 43.128
Canada Safeway Ltd v IRC [1973] Ch 374, [1972] 1 All ER 666, [1971] TR 411	49.125
Canary Wharf Ltd v C & E Comrs [1996] V & DR 323	38.50
Cantor Fitzgerald International v C & E Comrs (Case C-108/99) [2002] QB 546, *sub nom* C & E Comrs v Cantor Fitzgerald International [2001] ECR I-7257, [2001] 3 CMLR 1441, [2001] STC 1453, ECJ	39.20

Table of cases lxiii

PARA

Capcount Trading v Evans [1993] 2 All ER 125, [1993] STC 11,
 65 TC 545, CA 19.17
Cape Brandy Syndicate v IRC [1921] 1 KB 64, 12 TC 358;
 aff'd [1921] 2 KB 403, 12 TC 358, CA 1.21; 10.26
Capital Air Services Ltd v R & C Comrs [2010] UKUT 373 (TCC),
 [2010] STC 2726, [2011] 1 Costs LO 21 .... 4.205
Card Protection Plan Ltd v C & E Comrs (Case C-349/96)
 [1999] 2 AC 601, [1999] All ER (EC) 339, [1999] STC 270, ECJ;
 apld *sub nom* Card Protection Plan Ltd v C & E Comrs
 [2001] UKHL 4, [2002] 1 AC 202, [2001] 2 All ER 143,
 [2001] 2 CMLR 19, [2001] STC 174 .... 13.12; 38.25; 40.37,
  40.78; 54.31
Carlisle & Silloth Golf Club v Smith [1913] 3 KB 75, 6 TC 198, CA 10.29
Carney v Nathan (Inspector of Taxes) [2003] STC (SCD) 28 .... 55.45
Carr (DH) v R & C Comrs (2005) (VAT decision 19267) 39.25A
Carter (Joseph) & Sons v Baird [1999] STC 120n 22.72
Carver v Duncan [1983] STC 310; on appeal [1984] STC 556, CA; *aff'd* [1985]
 AC 1082, [1985] STC 356, HL 16.23
Cartesio Okató és Szolgáltató bt v Hungary (Case C-210/06) [2009] Ch 354,
 [2009] 3 WLR 777, [2009] Bus LR 1233 .... 54.46
Carvill v IRC [2000] STC (SCD) 143 .... 18.113, 18.114, 18.115
Cassell v Crutchfield (No 2) [1997] STC 423n, 69 TC 259 .... 22.77
Castledine (Alan) v R & C Comrs [2016] UKFTT 145 (TC), [2016] SFTD 484,
 [2016] STI 1660 .... 20.9
Caton's Administrators v Couch [1997] STC 970,
 70 TC 10, CA 19.22; 21.22, 21.62
Cedar plc v Inspector of Taxes [1998] STC (SCD) 78 .... 2.42
Cenlon Finance Co Ltd v Ellwood [1962] AC 782, [1962] 1 All ER 854, HL 4.43
Central Sussex College v R & C Comrs [2014] UKFTT 1058 (TC),
 [2014] STI 3558 .... 39.23
Centro di Musicologia Walter Stauffer v Finanzamt München fur
 Korperschaften (Case C-386/04) [2008] STC 1439, [2006] ECR I-8203,
 [2009] 2 CMLR 31 .... 53.23
Centros Ltd v Erhvervs-Og Selskabsstyrelsen (Case C-212/97) [2000] Ch 446,
 [2000] All ER (EC) 481, [1999] ECR I-1459, ECJ 54.73
Chaloner v Pellipar Investments Ltd [1996] STC 234, 68 TC 238 .... 19.64, 19.78
Chandubhai Kumar Patel (Ajay) v C & E Comrs (2001) 55.91
Chaney v Watkis [1986] STC 89, 58 TC 707 .... 19.21
Chappell v R & C Comrs [2014] UKFTT 344 (TCC), [2015] STC 271,
 [2014] BTC 523, [2014] STI 2581 .... 2.2
Charkham v IRC [2000] RVR 7 .... 28.67
Charman v Charman (2007) 52.1, 52.13
Chepstow Plant International Ltd v R & C Comrs [2011] UKFTT 166 (TC),
 [2011] STI 1703 .... 8.125
Cherney v Deripaska [2007] EWHC 965 (Comm), [2007] 2 All ER
 (Comm) 785, [2007] ILPr 49 .... 27.2, 27.15
Cheshire Employer & Skills Development Ltd (formerly Total People Ltd)
 v R & C Comrs [2012] EWCA Civ 1429, [2013] BTC 1, [2012] STI 3229 ...... 8.122
Chesterfield Brewery Co v IRC [1899] 2 QB 7, 15 TLR 123 .... 49.117
Chesterfield's (Earl of) Trusts, Re (1883) 24 Ch D 643, 49 LT 261 .... 17.26
Chetwode (Lord) v IRC [1977] 1 All ER 638, [1977] STC 64, HL 18.118
Chevron Petroleum UK Ltd v BP Petroleum Ltd [1981] STC 689, 57 TC 137 ...... 14.6
Chick v Stamp Duties Comrs [1958] AC 435, [1958] 2 All ER 623, PC 29.122
Cholmondeley v IRC [1986] STC 384 .... 33.118

lxiv Table of cases

PARA

Cie de Saint-Gobain, Zweigniederlassung Deutschland v Finanzamt
  Aachen-Innenstadt (Case C-307/97) [1999] ECR I-6161,
  [2000] STC 854, ECJ 54.45, 54.61
Civil Engineer v IRC [2002] STC (SCD) 72, [2002] WTLR 491 .... 18.25
Clark (Executor of Clark dec'd) v Green [1995] STC (SCD) 99 .... 21.22
Clark v IRC [1979] 1 All ER 585, [1978] STC 614 .... 3.35, 3.64, 3.65
Clark v Oceanic Contractors Inc [1980] STC 656; revs'd [1982] STC 66,
  CA; on appeal [1983] 1 All ER 133, [1983] STC 35, HL 8.191;
                                                                                                         18.1, 18.51
Clarke (Inspector of Taxes) v British Telecom Pension Scheme
  [2000] STC 222, CA 13.15
Clarke v R & C Comrs [2014] UKFTT 949 (TC) 23.22
Clarke v United Real (Moorgate) Ltd [1988] STC 273, 61 TC 353 .... 19.40
Clavis Liberty 1LP (Acting through Cohen) v R & C Comrs [2016] UKFTT
  253 (TC), [2016] SFTD 558, [2016] STI 2068 .... 2.40
Clay (Peter) Discetionary Trust, Trustees of (2007) 16.23
Cleary v IRC [1968] AC 766, 44 TC 399, HL 3.55, 3.61
Cleveleys Investment Trust Co v IRC 1971 SC 233, 47 TC 300 .... 22.44
Clinch v IRC [1974] QB 76, [1973] 1 All ER 977, [1973] STC 155, 49 TC 52 .... 18.126
Clore (No 2), Re, Official Solicitor v Clore [1984] STC 609 .... 35.4
Coates v Arndale Properties Ltd [1982] STC 573; on appeal
  [1984] 1 WLR 537, [1984] STC 124, CA; aff'd [1985] 1 All ER 15,
  [1984] STC 637, HL 3.10; 43.125
Cochrane, Re [1906] 2 IR 200 .... 29.132; 32.94
Cochrane's Executors v IRC [1974] STC 335, 49 TC 299 .... 21.103
Coffey (t/a Coffey Builders) v R & C Comrs [2012] UKFTT 193 (TC),
  [2012] STI 1845 .... 10.102
Cohan's Executors v IRC (1924) 12 TC 602, 131 LT 377, CA 10.27
Coin-a-Drink v R & C Comrs [2015] UKFTT 495 (TC), [2016] SFTD 96 .... 10.102
Colaingrove Ltd v R & C Comrs [2013] UKFTT 343 (TC),
  [2013] SFTD 1182, [2013] STI 2349 .... 39.22
Cole Bros Ltd v Phillips [1980] STC 518, [1980] TR 171; varied
  [1981] STC 671, CA; aff'd [1982] 2 All ER 247, [1982] STC 307, HL 48.17
Coll v R & C Comrs [2010] UKUT 114 (TCC), [2010] STC 1849,
  [2010] BTC 1513 .... 27.55
Collector of Stamp Revenue v Arrowtown Assests Ltd [2003] FACV
  No 4 of 2003, HKCA 2.4, 2.37, 2.38, 2.41,
                                                                                                    2.43, 2.45; 6.21
Collins v Addies [1991] STC 445, 65 TC 190; aff'd [1992] STC 746,
  65 TC 190, CA 41.128
Colours Ltd (formerly Spectrum Ltd) v IRC [1998] STC (SCD) 93 .... 2.42
Colquhoun v Brooks (1889) 14 App Cas 493, [1886–90] All ER Rep 1063,
  2 TC 490, HL 18.18
Colquhon (Kenneth) v R & C Comrs (2010) 8.148
Commercial Union Assurance Co plc v Shaw [1998] STC 386,
  72 TC 101; aff'd [1999] STC 109, 72 TC 101, CA 41.42
Congreve v IRC [1946] 2 All ER 170, 30 TC 163; revs'd [1947] 1 All ER 168,
  30 TC 163, CA; on appeal [1948] 1 All ER 948, 30 TC 163, HL 18.115
Cook (Watkins' Executors) v IRC (SpC 319) [2002] SWTI 936 .... 30.154
Cook v Medway Housing Society Ltd [1997] STC 90, 69 TC 319 .... 41.69
Cooke v Secretary of State for Social Security (2001) EWCA Civ 734,
  [2002] 3 All ER 279 .... 4.213
Cooker v Foss [1998] STC (SCD) 189 .... 14.3
Cooling (Steven) v HMRC [2015] UKFTT 223 (TC) 19.14

                                                                                           PARA
Cooper v Cadwalader (1904) 5 TC 101, (1904) 7 F 146.............. 27.10, 27.13, 27.14
Cooper v Stubbs [1925] 2 KB 753, 10 TC 29, CA 13.15
Copeman v William J Flood & Sons Ltd [1941] 1 KB 202, 24 TC 53................. 10.137;
                                                                                     44.13; 46.44
Corbett's Executors v IRC [1943] 2 All ER 218, 25 TC 305, CA 18.115
Corbett (Susan) v R & C Comrs [2014] UKFTT 1056 (TC) 20.10
Costa v Ente Nazionale per l'Energia Elettrica (ENEL)
    (Case 6/64) [1964] ECR 585, [1964] CMLR 425 .... 54.21, 54.24, 54.25
Cottle v Coldicott [1995] STC (SCD) 239.. 31.76
Countrywide Estate Agents FS Ltd v R & C Comrs [2011] UKUT 470 (TCC),
    [2012] STC 511, [2012] BTC 1501 .... 10.104
Courtaulds Investments Ltd v Fleming [1969] 3 All ER 1281, [1969] 1 WLR
    1683, 46 TC 111.. 18.36
Courten v UK (2008) 51.131; 55.3, 55.43
Coventry City Council v IRC [1978] 1 All ER 1107, [1978] STC 151 .... 49.115
Cowan v Seymour (Inspector of Taxes) [1920] 1 KB 500 .... 8.145
Coxon v R & C Comrs [2013] UKFTT 112 (TC) 14.3
Craig (W) v R & C Comrs [2012] UKFTT 90 (TC) 10.63
Craven v White [1985] 3 All ER 125, [1985] STC 531; on appeffal
    [1989] AC 398, [1987] 3 All ER 27, [1987] STC 297, CA;
    aff'd [1989] AC 398, [1988] 3 All ER 495, [1988] 3 WLR 423,
    [1988] STC 476, 62 TC 1, HL.. 2.4, 2.25, 2.33,
                                                                                2.34, 2.35, 2.37, 2.39
Crompton v Revenue & Customs [2009] UKFTT 71 (TC), [2009]
    STC (SCD) 504.. 8.148
Crossland v IRC (1999) unreported, ECtHR 55.44
Crowe v Appleby [1975] 3 All ER 529, [1975] STC 502;
    aff'd [1976] 2 All ER 914, [1976] STC 301, CA.............................. 21.105; 25.7
Curnock (PR of Curnock dec'd) v IRC (2003) SWTI 1052................................. 28.231
Cunard's Trustees v IRC [1946] 1 All ER 159, 27 TC 122, CA 16.67, 16.69
Curtis v Oldfield (1933) 9 TC 319 .... 10.145
Curtis Brown Ltd v Jarvis (& cross appeals) (1929) 13.18

                                                    D
D v Inspecteur van be Belastingdienst (2005) 54.56
DB Group Services (UK) Ltd v R & C Comrs; R & C Comrs v UBS AG [2014]
    EWCA Civ 452, [2014] BTC 20, [2014] STI 1833 .... 2.40, 2.46; 8.66
DTE Financial Services Ltd v Wilson [2001] EWCA Civ 455,
    [2001] STC 777 .... 2.4, 2.37, 2.42;
                                                                                         8.192, 8.194
Daffodil (Daffodil's Administrator) v IRC [2002] STC (SCD) 224 .... 30.2
Dale v IRC [1954] AC 11, [1953] 2 All ER 671, 34 TC 468, HL.......................... 16.8
Dale v de Soissons [1950] 2 All ER 460, 32 TC 118, CA...................................... 8.142
Danner v Finland [2002] STC 1283... 54.60, 54.62
D'Arcy v R & C Comrs (2007) 3.12
Davenport v Chilver [1983] STC 426, 57 TC 661 .... 19.67
Davies v Braithwaite [1931] 2 KB 628, 18 TC 198...................................... 8.22; 18.35
Davies v Hicks [2005] EWHC 847 (Ch), [2005] STC 850, 78 TC 95.................. 26.47
Davies v Premier Investment Co Ltd [1945] 2 All ER 681, 27 TC 27 .... 14.6
Davies & James v R & C Comrs (2010) 18.7
Day (John Arthur) & Dalgety (Amanda Jane) v R & C Comrs [2015]
    UKFTT 142 (TC)... 19.22
De Baeck v Belgium (Case C-268/03) [2004] ECR I-5961,
    [2004] 2 CMLR 57... 54.45

lxvi Table of cases

	PARA
De Beers Consolidated Mines v Howe [1906] AC 455, 5 TC 198, HL	18.16
De Gezamenlijke Steenkolenmijnen in Limburg v High Authority (Case 30/59) [1961] ECR 1, ECJ	54.81
Degorce v R & C Comrs [2013] UKFTT 178 (TC), [2013] SFTD 806, [2013] STI 2050	10.28
De Lasteyrie du Saillant v Ministere de l'Economie, des Finances et de l'Industrie (Case C-9/02) [2005] STC 1722, [2004] ECR I-2409, [2004] 3 CMLR 39	27A.53; 54.45, 54.53, 54.63, 54.64, 54.67, 54.68
Demetriou v R & C Comrs [2011] UKFTT 394 (TC)	10.101
Demibourne Ltd v R & C Comrs [2005] STC (SCD) 667	8.24
Denkavit International BV v Ministre de l'Economie des Finances et de l'Industrie (Case C-170/05) [2007] STI 109	54.64
Dental IT v R & C Comrs [2011] UKFTT 128 (TC)	4.27
Devaraj (S) v R & C Comrs [2014] UKFTT 713 (TC)	10.77
De Vigier v IRC (1963) 42 TC 24, [1963] TR 415, CA; aff'd [1964] 2 All ER 907, 42 TC 24, HL	16.106
de Walden (Lord Howard) v IRC [1942] 1 All ER 287, 25 TC 121, CA	18.116
Dewar v IRC [1935] 2 KB 351, [1935] All ER Rep 568, 19 TC 561, 14 ATC 329, CA	14.3; 17.42
Dextra Accessories Ltd v Macdonald (Inspector of Taxes) [2002] STC (SCD) 413	9.123; 10.133
Dhendsa v Richardson [1997] STC (SCD) 265	10.131
Dickinson v Abel [1969] 1 All ER 484, 45 TC 353	13.13
Dickinson (Anne) v R & C Comrs [2013] UKFTT 653 (TC)	23.22, 23.61
Dingle v Turner [1972] AC 601, [1972] 1 All ER 878, HL	53.26
Direct Cosmetics Ltd & Laughtons Photographs Ltd v C & E Comrs (Cases 138/86 & 139/86) [1988] ECR 3937, [1988] STC 540, ECJ	37.5; 54.6
Dispit Ltd v R & C Comrs [2007] STC (SCD) 194, [2007] STI 349	10.67
Dixon v IRC [2002] STC (SCD) 53	31.63, 31.66
Donaghy (PG) v R & C Comrs [2011] UKFTT 283 (TC)	10.173
Donnelly v Williamson [1982] STC 88, 80 LGR 289	8.95, 8.141
Donovan & McLaren v R & C Comrs [2014] UKFTT 48 (TC)	16.93, 16.102; 46.54, 46.61; 51.55
Dougal, Re (Cowie's Trustees) [1981] STC 514	30.56
Dove (JT) Ltd v R & C Comrs [2011] UKFTT 16 (TC), [2011] SFTD 348, [2011] STI 1448	10.133
Down v Compston (1937)	10.21
Dubai Bank Ltd v Abbas [1996] EWCA Civ 1342	27.12, 27.13
Duckmanton v R & C Comrs [2011] UKFTT 664 (TC), [2012] SFTD 293, [2011] STI 3273	10.146
Dunlop International AG v Pardoe [1998] STC 459; aff'd [1999] STC 909, CA	43.123
Dunmore v McGowan [1976] STC 433; aff'd [1978] 2 All ER 85, [1978] STC 217, CA	14.3
Dunstall (Paul) Organisation Ltd v Hedges [1999] STC (SCD) 26	8.192, 8.194
Duple Motor Bodies Ltd v Ostime [1961] 1 All ER 167, 39 TC 537, HL	10.72, 10.112
Dutton-Forshaw v R & C Comrs [2015] UKFTT 478 (TC), [2016] STI 146	23.22
Drilling Global Consultant LLP v R & C Comrs [2014] UKFTT 888 (TC), [2014] STI 3363	48.28
Drown v R & C Comrs [2014] UKFTT 892 (TC), [2015] WTLR 775, [2014] STI 3707	21.41

Table of cases lxvii

PARA

Drummond (Inspector of Taxes) v Austin Brown [1985] Ch 52,
[1984] 3 WLR 381, [1984] 2 All ER 699 .... 19.64, 19.67
Drummond v IRC [2007] STC (SCD) 682, [2007] STI 1818............................... 15.8
Dunne (E) & Gray (V) v R & C Comrs [2015] EWHC 1204 (Admin) 5.28
Dyer (Roger & Jean) v R & C Comrs [2013] UKFTT 691 (TC).......................... 19.69
Dyson (Jack) v R & C Comrs [2015] UKFTT 131 (TC), [2015] SFTD 529,
[2015] STI 1738... 55.82

E

EC Commission v Belgium (Case 52/84) [1986] ECR 89,
[1987] 1 CMLR 710, ECJ 54.81
EC Commission v Belgium (2011).. 54.62
EC Commission v France (Case 270/83) [1986] ECR 273,
[1987] 1 CMLR 401, ECJ 54.45, 54.61, 54.64
EC Commission v Spain (2004) 54.48
EC Commission v United Kingdom (Case 333/85) [1988] 2 All ER 557,
[1988] ECR 817, [1988] STC 251, ECJ 38.25
EC Commission v United Kingdom (Case 416/85) [1990] 2 QB 130,
[1988] 3 WLR 1261, [1989] 1 All ER 364 .... 39.1
EC Commission v United Kingdom (Case C-86/11) 38.50; 43.191
EC Commission v UK (2014) 54.64
ECR Consulting Ltd v R & C Comrs [2011] UKFTT 313 (TC),
[2011] STI 2174... 8.32
EMI Group Electronics Ltd v Coldicott (Inspector of Taxes)
[1997] STC 1372, [1997] BTC 532 .... 8.41, 8.143, 8.144
Earlspring Properties Ltd v Guest [1993] STC 473, 67 TC 259;
aff'd [1995] STC 479, 67 TC 259, CA.. 10.137; 44.13; 46.44
Easinghall Ltd v R & C Comrs [2016] UKUT 105 (TCC),
[2016] STC 1476, [2016] BTC 504 .... 4.43
Eastham v Leigh London & Provincial Properties Ltd [1971] Ch 871,
[1971] 2 All ER 887, CA... 19.79
Ebrahimi v Westbourne Galleries Ltd [1973] AC 360, [1972] 2 All ER 492, HL...... 46.59
Ebsworth v R & C Comrs [2009] UKFTT 199, [2009] SFTD 602 .... 3.35
Eclipse Film Partners No 35 LLP v R & C Comrs [2012] UKFTT 270 (TC),
[2012] SFTD 823, [2012] STI 1607; *revs;d in part*
[2013] UKUT 639 (TCC), [2014] STC 1114, [2014] BTC 503;
aff'd [2015] UKFTT 401 (TC) 2.2; 6.21; 10.28
Ecotrade Srl v Altiforni Ferriere di Servola SpA (Case C-200/97)
[1998] ECR I-7907, [1999] 2 CMLR 804, ECJ... 54.81
Edinburgh Leisure South Lanarkshire Leisure & Renfrewshire Leisure,
Re (Joined Cases 03/22, 03/29 & 03/30) 40.50
Edwards v Bairstow & Harrison [1956] AC 14, 36 TC 207, HL........................ 10.18
Edwards v Clinch [1980] 3 All ER 278, [1980] STC 438, CA; *aff'd* [1981] 3 All
ER 543, [1981] STC 617, HL... 8.21
Edwards v Fisher *see* Billingham (Inspector of Taxes) v Cooper
Edwards v Warmsley, Henshall & Co [1967] 44 TC 431 .... 10.151
Eilbeck v Rawling [1980] 2 All ER 12, [1980] STC 192, CA; *aff'd* [1981] 1 All
ER 865, [1981] STC 174, HL... 2.4
Elf Enterprise Caledonia Ltd v IRC [1994] STC 785, 68 TC 328...................... 1.23
Elizabeth Moyne Ramsay v R & C Comrs [2013] UKUT 226 (TCC),
[2013] STI 1902... 47.5, 47.14
Ellis v R & C Comrs [2013] UKFTT 775 (TC), [2013] SFTD 144, [2013] STI
1251 .... 23.43

	PARA
Eloranta v Finland (2008)	55.91
Elson v Price's Tailors Ltd [1963] 1 All ER 231, 40 TC 671	10.107
Emery v IRC [1981] STC 150, 54 TC 607, [1980] TR 447	3.34, 3.55, 3.61
Emsland-Stärke GmbH v Hauptzollamt Hamburg-Jonas (Case C-110/99) [2000] ECR I-11569, ECJ	2.44; 54.72, 54.73, 54.74
Engel v Netherlands (1976) 1 EHRR 647, ECtHR	55.82
English Bridge Union Ltd v R & C Comrs (Case C-90/16)	40.54
Ensign Tankers (Leasing) Ltd v Stokes [1989] 1 WLR 1222, [1989] STC 705; revs'd [1991] 1 WLR 341, [1991] STC 136, CA; on appeal [1992] 1 AC 655, [1992] 2 All ER 275, [1992] STC 226, HL	2.1, 2.21, 2.40, 2.45; 3.10; 10.28
Essex (Somerset's Executors) v IRC [2002] STC (SCD) 39; aff'd sub nom IRC v Eversden (Greenstock's Executors) [2002] EWHC 1360 (Ch), [2002] STC 1109 aff'd [2003] EWCA Civ 668, [2003] STC 822	15.22; 29.121, 29.133; 32.28, 32.94
Euro Hotel (Belgravia) Ltd, Re [1975] 3 All ER 1075, [1975] STC 682, 51 TC 293	14.6
Eurofood IFSC (Case C-341/04) [2006] ECR I-3813	54.75
Eurowings Luftverkehrs AG v Finanzamt Dortmund-Unna (Case C-294/97) [1999] ECR I-7447, [2001] 3 CMLR 1669, ECJ	54.48, 54.61, 54.64
Evans v FCT (1989)	10.21
Executive Network (Consultants) Ltd v O'Connor (1996) SpC 56	10.157
Ezeh & Connors v UK (2004) 39 EHRR 1, 15 BHRC 145	55.82

F

FA & AB Ltd v Lupton [1971] 3 All ER 948, 47 TC 580, HL	3.10
FS Consulting Ltd v McCaul [2002] STC (SCD) 138	8.22
FWL de Groot v Staatssecretaris van Financiën (Case C-385/00) [2002] ECR I-11819, ECJ	54.56
Factortame Ltd v Secretary of State for Transport see R v Secretary of State for Transport, ex p Factortame Ltd	
Fall v Hitchen [1973] 1 All ER 368, [1973] STC 66	8.22
Fallon (Morgan's Executors) v Fellows [2001] STC (SCD) 45; revs'd [2001] STC 1409	49.126
Falmer Jeans Ltd v Rodin [1990] STC 270, 63 TC 55	41.66
Farmer (Farmer's Executors) v IRC [1999] STC (SCD) 321	20.15
Farmer (2009)	31.50
Faulkner (Adams's Trustee) v IRC [2001] STC (SCD) 112	32.28
Faulks v Faulks [1992] 1 EGLR 9, [1992] 15 EG 82	44.31
Favell v R & C Comrs [2010] UKFTT 360 (TC)	23.22
Felixstowe Dock & Rly Co Ltd v R & C Comrs [2014] UKFTT 452 (TC), [2014] STI 2524	43.42; 54.45
Fenech (Geoffrey Michael) v R & C Comrs (2013)	13.22
Ferguson v IRC [1970] AC 442, [1969] 1 All ER 1025, 46 TC 1, [1969] TR 63, HL	14.27
Ferguson v IRC (Bonus Payments) [2001] STC (SCD) 1, [2000] STI 1679	8.200
Ferrazzini v Italy [2001] STC 1314, E Ct HR	55.5, 55.83
Fetherstonehaugh v IRC [1984] STC 261, CA	31.43, 31.54; 33.30
Fidium Finanz AG (Case 452/04) [2007] All ER (EC) 239, [2006] ECR I-9521, [2007] 1 CMLR 15	54.31, 54.49
Figg v Clarke [1997] 1 WLR 603, [1997] STC 247, 68 TC 645	25.8

PARA

Finanzamt fur Korperschaften Ill in Berlin v Krankenheim Ruhesitz
am Wannsee-Seniorenheimstatt GmbH (Case C-157/07)
[2009] All ER (EC) 513, [2009] STC 138, [2008] ECR I-8061,
[2009] CEC 639, [2008] BTC 793, [2008] STI 2324.. 54.62
Finanzamt Köln-Altstadt v Schumacker (Case C-279/93) [1996] QB 28,
[1995] All ER (EC) 319, [1995] STC 306, ECJ.............................. 54.44, 54.56,
54.57, 54.58,
Finnish Tax Authorities v A (2012)... 54.63, 54.68
Firestone Tyre & Rubber Co Ltd v Lewellin [1957] 1 All ER 561,
37 TC 111, HL.. 18.72
First National Bank of Chicago v C & E Comrs (Case C-172/96) [1999] QB
570, [1998] All ER (EC) 744, [1998] STC 850, ECJ... 40.65
Fiscale Fenheid PPG Holdings BV CS Te Hoogezand v Inspecteur Va de
Belastingdienst / Noord / Kant Oor Groningen (2013) 50.14
Fisher v R & C Comrs [2014] UKFTT 813 (TC) 18.113
Fisher (Donald) (Ealing) Ltd v Spencer [1987] STC 423; aff'd [1989] STC
256, CA... 10.102
Fitton v Gilders & Heaton (1955) 34 ATC 215 .... 48.71
Fitzpatrick v IRC (No 2) [1994] 1 All ER 673, [1994] 1 WLR 306, [1994] STC
237, HL... 8.173
Fitzwilliam (Countess) v IRC [1990] STC 65; aff'd [1992] STC 185, CA;
on appeal [1993] 3 All ER 184, [1993] WLR 1189,
[1993] STC 502, HL... 2.4, 2.25, 2.29,
2.35, 2.42; 30.147
Flanagan (E) v R & C Comrs [2014] UKFTT 175 (TC), 82 TC 392,
[2014] SFTD 881, [2014] STI 1772... 10.28
Fleming v Associated Newspapers Ltd [1972] 2 All ER 574,
48 TC 382, HL... 1.41; 10.138
Fleming & Conde Nast Publications Ltd v Comrs of Customs & Excise [2008]
UKHL 2, [2008] 1 WLR 195 .... 38.53
Flix Innovations Ltd v R & C Comrs [2016] UKUT 301 (TCC), [2016] STC
2206, [2016] STC 612 .... 15.55
Floor v Davis [1979] 2 All ER 677, [1979] STC 379, HL... 26.62
Fokus Bank ASA v The Norweigan State, represented by Skattedirektoratet
(The Directorate of Taxes) (Case E-1/04) [2005] 1 CMLR 10........ 54.49, 54.64
Fountain v R & C Comrs [2015] UKFTT 419 (TC) 23.61
Fox's (Lady) Executors v IRC [1992] 1 EGLR 211, [1992] 19 EG 173,
20 EG 121, Lands Tribunal; on appeal sub nom IRC v Gray
[1994] STC 360, CA.. 30.4; 31.68, 31.74
Foxley v United Kingdom (2000) 31 EHRR 637, [2000] BPIR 1009,
8 BHRC 571, E CtHR.. 55.62
Frankland v IRC [1996] STC 735; aff'd [1997] STC 1450, CA........ 1.21; 2.36; 30.145
Fry v Salisbury House Estate Ltd [1930] AC 432, 15 TC 266, HL....................... 6.42
Fry v Shiels' Trustees 1915 SC 159, 6 TC 583 .... 16.6, 16.62
Fryer (Arnold's PR) v R & C Comrs [2010] UKFTT 87 (TC),
[2010] SFTD 632, [2010] WTLR 815... 28.4
Funke v France [1993] 1 CMLR 897, 16 EHRR 297, E Ct HR............................. 55.61
Furness v IRC [1999] STC (SCD) 232 .... 31.48
Furniss v Dawson [1982] STC 267; on appeal [1984] AC 474,
[1983] STC 549, CA; revs'd [1984] AC 474, [1984] 1 All ER 530,
[1984] STC 153, HL.. 1.24; 2.4, 2.22, 2.23,
2.29, 2.33, 2.34, 2.35, 2.37,
2.43, 2.45, 2.48; 43.125

PARA

Futter v Futter [2010] EWHC 449 (Ch). [2010] STC 982,
[2010] Pens LR 145.. 27A.126
Futura Participations SA, Singer v Administrations des Contributions
(Case C-250/95) [1997] ECR I-2471, [1997] STC 1301, ECJ.......... 54.56, 54.63,
54.66, 54.67
Fynn v IRC [1958] 1 All ER 270, 37 TC 629.. 18.114

G

G v G (2002).. 52.15, 52.21
GGN Builders Ltd R & C Comrs [2010] UKFTT 184 (TC)................................. 39.25A
GR Solutions Ltd v R & C Comrs [2013] UKUT 278 (TCC),
[2013] STC 2289, [2013] BTC 1926 .... 8.119
Gaines-Cooper v R & C Comrs (2006) SpC 568................................. 18.25; 27.5, 27.6
Gamble v Rowe [1998] STC (SCD) 116; *aff'd* [1998] STC 1247, 71 TC 190 ...... 11.81
Garforth (Inspector of Taxes) v Newsmith Stainless Ltd [1979] 1 WLR 409,
[1979] 2 All ER 73, [1979] STC 129 .... 8.194
Garner v Pounds Shipowners & Shipbreakers Ltd [1997] STC 551;
on appeal [1999] STC 19, CA; *aff'd* [2000] 3 All ER 218,
[2000] 1 WLR 1107, [2000] STC 420, 72 TC 561, HL......................... 19.21, 19.70
Garnett v IRC (1899) 81 LT 633, 48 WR 303... 49.116
Gartside v IRC [1968] AC 553, [1968] 2 WLR 277 .... 16.65; 29.133; 32.94
Gayen v R & C Comrs [2013] UKFTT 127 (TC)... 8.201
Gebhard v Consiglio dell 'Ordine degli Avvocati e Procuration di Milano
(Case C-55/94) [1996] All ER (EC) 189, [1995] ECR I-4165, ECJ............. 54.53,
54.61, 54.63, 54.64
Genovese v R & C Comrs [2009] STC (SCD) 373,
[2009] STI 1100.. 18.6, 18.14; 27.16
Georgiou (t/a Marios Chippery) v United Kingdom [2001] STC 80,
E Ct HR.. 55.21, 55.82
Ghaidan v Godin-Mendoza [2004] UKHL 30, [2004] 2 AC 557......................... 55.3
Gibson v R & C Comrs [2013] UKFTT 636 (TC), [2014] STI 440 .... 23.22
Gilbert v Hemsley [1981] STC 703, 55 TC 419 .... 8.117
Gilbert (t/a United Foods) v R & C Comrs [2011] UKFTT 705 (TC) 20.21
Gilchrist v R & C Comrs [2014] UKUT 169 (TCC), [2015] CH 183,
[2015] 2 WLR 1, [2014] 4 All ER 943, [2014] STC 1713,
[2014] BTC 513, 2014] WTLR 1209, [2014] STI 1875................................ 42.152
Gilly v Directeur des services fiscaux du Bas-Rhin (Case C-336/96)
(1998) ECR-I 2823... 54.53
Girvan v Orange Personal Communications Services Ltd [1998] STC 567,
70 TC... 14.3
Gissing v Gissing [1971] AC 886, [1970] 2 All ER 780, HL................................ 52.61
Gittos v Barclay [1982] STC 390, 55 TC 633 .... 12.23, 12.62
Gladstone v Bower [1960] 2 QB 384, [1960] 3 All ER 353, 58 LGR 313, CA 31.68
Glantre Engineering Ltd v Goodhand [1983] 1 All ER 542, [1983] STC 1........ 8.63
Glenboig Union Fireclay Co Ltd v IRC 1922 SC 112, 12 TC 427, HL.............. 10.105
Glyn v R & C Comrs [2013] UKFTT 645 (TC), [2014] STI 630 .... 18.7; 27.14
Gold v Inspector of Taxes [1998] STC (SCD) 222.. 41.128
Gold Coast Selection Trust Ltd v Humphrey (Inspector of Taxes)
[1948] AC 459 [1948] 2 All ER 379, 64 TLR 457.. 10.101
Golding v Kaufman [1985] STC 152, 58 TC 296 .... 19.70
Goldman (on the application of UK Uncut Legal Action Ltd) v R & C Comrs
[2012] EWHC 2017 (Admin), [2012] BTC 222.. 8.143
Goodwin v Curtis [1996] STC 1146, 70 TC 478; *aff'd* [1998] STC 475,
70 TC 478, CA... 23.22

Table of cases lxxi

	PARA
Gordon v IRC [1991] STC 174, 64 TC 173, Ct of Sess	22.102
Gordon & Blair Ltd v IRC (1962) 40 TC 358, [1962] TR 161	11.21
Gould (t/a Garry's Private Hire) v R & C Comrs (2007)	55.61
Grace v R & C Comrs [2008] EWHC 2708 (Ch), [2009] STC 213, [2008] BTC 843	18.6, 18.7; 27.9, 27.10, 27.13, 27.14, 27.15
Graf v Filzmoser Maschinenbau GmbH: C-190/98 [2000] All ER (EC) 170, [2000] ECR I-493, ECJ	54.52
Graham v Green (Inspector of Taxes) [1925] 2 KB 37, 9 TC 309	10.21; 13.13
Grant v Watton [1999] STC 330, 71 TC 333	8.124
Gray v Seymours Garden Centre (Horticulture) (a firm) [1995] STC 706, CA	48.17
Gray (surviving Executor of Lady Fox deceased) v IRC (1994) STC 360	21.22; 44.51
Gray's Timber Products Ltd v Revenue & Customs [2009] CSIH 11, [2009] STC 889	9.22, 9.26
Grey v Tiley (1932) 16 TC 412, CA	13.16
Green (W) v R & C Comrs [2011] UKFTT 660 (TC)	7.44
Greenberg v IRC [1972] AC 109, [1971] 3 All ER 136, 47 TC 240, 50 ATC 259, HL	3.33, 3.60, 3.63
Greenfield v Bains [1991] STC 445, 65 TC 190; aff'd [1992] STC 746, 65 TC 190, CA	41.128
Griffin v Citibank Investments Ltd [2000] STC 1010, 73 TC	2.23, 2.34, 2.37, 2.48
Griffin v Craig-Harvey [1994] STC 54, 66 TC 396	23.43
Griffiths v Dawson & Co [1993] 2 FCR 515, [1993] 2 FLR 315, [1993] Fam Law 476	52.4
Griffiths v JP Harrison (Watford) Ltd [1963] AC 1	3.10; 10.1
Griffiths v Jackson [1983] STC 184, 56 TC 583	6.43; 12.23
Grimwood-Taylor (Mallender's Executors) v IRC [2000] STC (SCD) 39	31.47
Grogan v R & C Comrs [2009] UKFTT 238 (TC), [2010] SFTD 115	3.35
Group Steria SCA (2015)	54.45
Grundig Italia (2002)	54.68
Gschwind v Finanzamt Aachen-Außenstadt (Case C-391/97) [1999] ECR I-5451, [2001] STC 331, ECJ	54.1, 54.56
Gubay v Kington [1981] STC 721, [1981] TR 291; on appeal [1983] 2 All ER 976, [1983] STC 443, CA; revs'd [1984] 1 All ER 513, [1984] STC 99, HL	52.21
Gurney (Inspector of Taxes) v Richards [1989] 1 WLR 1180, [1989] STC 682, 62 TC 287	8.119

H

HCB Ltd v Inspector of Taxes [1998] STC (SCD) 222	41.128
HSBC Trust Co v Twiddy [2006] RVR 308, [2006] WTLR 1533	28.67
HSBC Holdings plc & Mellon v R & C Comrs [2012] UKFTT 163 (TC)	49.103
HSBC Holdings plc, Vidacos Nominees Ltd v Comrs of R & C Comrs (Case C-569/07) [2008] STC (SCD) 502, [2008] STI 190	49.103, 49.123
Haahr Petroleum Ltd v Abenra Havn (Case C-90/94) [1997] ECR I-4085, [1998] 1 CMLR 771, ECJ	54.60
Hague v CIR [1969] 1 Ch 393, [1968] 3 WLR 576, [1968] 2 All ER 1252	3.58
Haig's (Earl) Trustees v IRC 1939 SC 676, 22 TC 725	13.12
Hakki v Secretary of State for Work & Pensions [2014] EWCA Civ 530, [2014] BTC 22	10.21
Hale v Shea [1965] 1 All ER 155, 42 TC 260	13.12
Halifax plc v C & E Comrs (Case C-255/02) [2006] Ch 387, [2006] 2 WLR 905, [2006] STC 919	2.44; 54.74

lxxii *Table of cases*

	PARA
Halifax plc v Davidson (2000) SpC 239	10.77
Hall v Lorimer [1992] 1 WLR 939, [1992] ICR 739, [1992] STC 599; *aff'd ov*[1994] 1 All ER 250, [1994] 1 WLR 209, [1994] STC 23, CA	8.22
Hall (Hall's Executors) v IRC [1997] STC (SCD) 126	31.48
Halpin v R & C Comrs [2011] UKFTT 512 (TC)	14.3
Hamblett v Godfrey [1987] 1 All ER 916, [1987] STC 60, CA	8.41, 8.65, 8.105
Hamlin (TD) v R & C Comrs (2011)	10.150
Han (t/a Murdishaw Supper Bar) v C & E Comrs [2001] EWCA Civ 1040, [2001] 4 All ER 687, [2001] 1 WLR 2253, *sub nom* C & E Comrs v Han [2001] STC 1188	55.4, 55.5, 55.82, 55.91, 55.92
Hanlon v Hanlon [1978] 2 All ER 889, [1978] 1 WLR 592, CA	52.67
Hanson v R & C Comrs [2012] UKFTT 314 (TC)	31.66
Hanson (Lord) v Mansworth (Inspector of Taxes) [2004] SWTI 1365	8.175
Hardcastle (Vernede's Executors) v IRC [2000] STC (SCD) 532	31.44
Harding v R & C Comrs [2008] EWCA Civ 1164, [2008] STC 3499, 79 TC 885	2.41
Harding (Loveday's Executors) v IRC [1997] STC (SCD) 321	30.151
Hardy (Anthony) v R & C Comrs [2015] UKFTT 250 (TC), [2015] STI 2576	19.78
Harris v R & C Comrs [2010] UKFTT 385 (TC), [2010] SFTD 1159, [2011] WTLR 55	53.85
Harrison v R & C Comrs [2015] UKFTT 539 (TC)	23.43
Harrold v IRC [1996] STC (SCD) 195	31.69
Harte v R & C Comrs [2012] UKFTT 258 (TC), [2012] STI 2219	23.22, 23.43
Hartland v R & C Comrs [2014] UKFTT 1099 (TC), [2015] STI 577	10.23, 10.26; 23.22
Hasloch v IRC (1971) 47 TC 50, 50 ATC 65, [1971] TR 45	3.63
Hastings-Bass (2011)	27A.126
Hatch, Re, Hatch v Hatch [1919] 1 Ch 351, 88 LJ Ch 147	14.26
Hatt v Newman [2000] STC 113, 72 TC 462	19.79
Hatton v IRC [1992] STC 140, 67 TC 759	2.37; 28.103, 28.105; 32.7
Hawkins, Re, Hawkins v Hawkins [1972] Ch 714, [1972] 3 All ER 386	14.6
Headley v R & C Comrs [2013] UKFTT 382 (TC)	10.23
Healey (Darrell) v R & C Comrs [2014] UKFTT 889 (TC)	18.7
Healy v R & C Comrs [2015] UKFTT 233 (TC); [2015] STI 2455	8.173; 10.137; 13.12
Heather v P E Consulting Group [1978] 1 All ER 8, 48 TC 320, CA	10.63, 10.133; 41.45
Heaton v Bell [1970] AC 728, [1969] 2 All ER 70, 46 TC 211, HL	8.93, 8.113, 8.119
Hector v Hector [1973] 3 All ER 1070, [1973] 1 WLR 1122, CA	52.76
Hencke v Revenue & Customs (2006)	23.61
Henley v Murray [1950] 1 All ER 908, 31 TC 351, CA	8.143
Herdman v IRC (1967) 45 TC 394, NI CA	28.102
Herman v R & C Comrs [2007] STC (SCD) 571, [2007] WTLR 1201, [2007] STI 1441	27A.116, 27A.176
Higgs v Olivier [1952] Ch 311, 33 TC 136, 31 ATC 8	10.102
Higginson's Exors v IRC [2002] STC (SCD) 483	31.66, 31.67
Higher Education Statistics Agency Ltd v C & E Comrs [2000] STC 332, QB	38.26
High Tech International AG v Deripaska [2006] EWHC 3276, [2007] EMLR 15	27.2, 27.15
Hill v Permanent Trustee of New South Wales Ltd [1930] AC 720, 99 LJPC 191, 144 LT 65, PC	42.142, 42.148, 42.152
Hirst v R & C Comrs [2014] UKFTT 924 (TC), [2015] STI 135	20.10
Hitch's Executors v Stone [1999] STC 431, 73 TC 600; *revs'd sub nom* Hitch v Stone [2001] EWCA Civ 63, [2001] STC 214, 73 TC 600	2.3; 19.80

Table of cases lxxv

	PARA
IRC v John Lewis Properties plc [2002] 1 WLR 35, [2001] STC 1118, *aff'd* [2003] STC 117	2.37; 12.88
IRC v Joiner [1975] 3 All ER 1050, [1975] 1 WLR 1701, [1975] STC 657, 50 TC 449, HL	3.33, 3.53
IRC v Lady Castlemaine [1943] 2 All ER 471, 25 TC 408	17.46
IRC v Laird Group plc [2000] STC (SCD) 75, [2000] STI 104, (2001) 98 (16) LSG 35; *aff'd* [1999] STC (SCD) 86; *aff'd* [2001] STC 689, [2001] BTC 137, [2001] STI 280; *revs'd* [2002] EWCA Civ 576, [2002] STC 722, [2002] BTC 208, 2002] STI 765, (2002) 99 (22) LSG 34, (2002) 146 SJLB 116; *revs'd* [2003] UKHL 54, [2003] 1 WLR 2476, [2003] 4 All ER 669, [2003] STC 1349, 75 TC 399, [2003] BTC 385, [2003] STI 1821, (2003) 100 (43) LSG 32	3.33, 3.71
IRC v Land Securities Investment Trust Ltd [1969] 2 All ER 430, 45 TC 495, HL	14.8
IRC v Lloyds Private Banking Ltd *see* Lloyds Private Banking Ltd v IRC	31.41; 32.28; 33.22
IRC v McGuickian [1994] STC 888, (N.I. CA); *revs'd* [1997] 3 All ER 817, [1997] 1 WLR 991, [1997] STC 908, HL	2.4, 2.32, 2.36, 2.37, 2.38; 3.38
IRC v Macpherson *see* Macpherson v IRC	
IRC v Matthew's Executors [1984] STC 386, 1984 SLT 414	21.103; 25.5
IRC v Maxse [1919] 1 KB 647, 12 TC 41, CA	10.41
IRC v Nelson 1939 SC 689, 22 TC 716	10.30
IRC v Oce Van Der Grinten NV [2000] STC 951	54.93
IRC v Parker [1966] AC 141, [1966] 1 All ER 399, 43 TC 396, HL	3.33, 3.34, 3.55, 3.58, 3.61
IRC v Pilkington (1941) 24 TC 160, CA	17.20
IRC v Plummer [1980] AC 896, [1979] 3 All ER 775, [1979] STC 793, 54 TC 1, HL	16.93; 51.55
IRC v Pratt [1982] STC 756, 57 TC 1	18.115
IRC v Quigley (1995) STC 931	8.120
IRC v Ramsay (1935) 20 TC 79, [1935] All ER Rep 847, 154 LT 141, CA	2.4, 2.21, 2.22, 2.23, 2.24, 2.25, 2.29, 2.32, 2.33, 2.34, 2.35, 2.36, 2.37, 2.38, 2.39, 2.40, 2.41, 2.42, 2.43, 2.44, 2.45, 2.46, 2.47, 2.48; 3.38; 8.66, 8.194; 14.8; 22.44
IRC v Regent Trust Co Ltd [1980] 1 WLR 688, [1980] STC 140, 53 TC 54	18.79
IRC v Reid's Trustees [1949] 1 All ER 354, 30 TC 431, HL	18.36
IRC v Reinhold 1953 SC 49, 34 TC 389	10.23
IRC v Richards' Executors [1971] 1 All ER 785, 46 TC 626, HL	19.22; 21.62
IRC v Rossminster Ltd [1980] 1 All ER 80, [1980] STC 42, HL	2.4
IRC v Schroder [1983] STC 480, 57 TC 94	18.20, 18.116
IRC v Scottish Provident Institution (2005)	2.25, 2.37, 2.39, 2.40, 2.46, 2.48; 6.21
IRC v Smith (Aubrey) (1930)	17.20; 21.1
IRC v Spencer-Nairn [1991] STC 60, Ct of Sess	28.21
IRC v Stannard [1984] 2 All ER 105, [1984] STC 245	30.46
IRC v Stype Investments (Jersey) Ltd [1981] 2 All ER 394, [1982] STC 310; *aff'd* [1982] 3 All ER 419, [1982] STC 625, CA	30.47
IRC v The 'Old Bushmills' Distillery Co Ltd (1927) 12 TC 1148	10.27
IRC v Titaghur Jute Factory Co Ltd 1978 SC 96, 1978 SLT 133, [1978] STC 166, 53 TC 675	10.67

lxxvi *Table of cases*

PARA

IRC v Trustees of Sema Group Pension Scheme [2002] EWHC 94 (Ch),
   [2002] STC 276 .... 3.35, 3.53,
   3.55, 3.58, 3.72
IRC v Universities Superannuation Scheme Ltd [1997] STC 1,
   70 TC 193 .... 3.55, 3.58, 3.72
IRC v Wattie [1999] 1 WLR 873, [1998] STC 1160, 72 TC 639, PC 12.87
IRC v Whitworth Park Coal Ltd [1959] 3 All ER 703 .... 14.8
IRC v Wiggins [1979] 2 All ER 245, [1979] 1 WLR 325, [1979] STC 244,
   53 TC 639 .... 3.34, 3.58, 3.61
IRC v Wilkinson [1992] STC 454, 65 TC 28, CA 19.3
IRC v Willoughby [1995] STC 143, 70 TC 57, CA; *aff'd* [1997] 4 All ER 65,
   [1997] 1 WLR 1071, [1997] STC 995, 70 TC 57, HL 1.23; 2.45; 3.4;
   18.112, 18.113
I/S Fini H v Skatterministeriet (Case C-32/03) [2005] STC 903,
   [2005] ECR I-1599, [2005] 2 CMLR 20 .... 38.81
Icebreaker 1 LLP v R & C Comrs [2010] UKFTT 6 (TC), [2010] STI 1520 .... 10.28
Imperial Chemical Industries plc v Colmer [1996] 2 All ER 23,
   [1996] 1 WLR 469, [1996] STC 352, HL; refd (Case C-264/96)
   [1998] All ER (EC) 585, [1998] STC 874, ECJ; apld [2000] 1 All ER 129,
   [1999] 1 WLR 2035, [1999] STC 1089, 72 TC 1, HL 1.42; 43.42; 54.25,
   54.45, 54.64; 55.5
Impossible TV v R & C Comrs [2011] UKFTT 413 (TC) 4.27
Income Tax Special Purposes Comrs v Pemsel [1891] AC 531, HL 53.1, 53.22
Independent Schools Council v Charity Commission (unreported, 2
   December 2011) 53.22
Ingram v IRC [1995] 4 All ER 334, [1995] STC 564; on appeal
   [1997] 4 All ER 395, [1997] STC 1234, CA; *revs'd*
   [1999] 1 All ER 297, [1999] STC 37, HL 2.36, 2.37, 2.43; 29.1,
   29.122, 29.123, 29.130, 29.131
Interfish Ltd v R & C Comrs [2010] UKFTT 219 (TC), [2010] STI 2397 .... 10.157
Internationale Handelsgesellschaft mbH v Einfuhr und Vorratsstelle für
   Getreide und Futtermittel (Case 11/70) [1970] ECR 1125,
   [1972] CMLR 255, ECJ 54.25, 54.68

J

JLJ Services Ltd v R & C Comrs [2011] UKFTT 766 (TC) 8.32
Jackman v Powell [2004] EWHC 550 (Ch), [2004] STC 645, 76 TC 87 .... 10.150
Jackson's Trustees v IRC (1942) 25 TC 13 .... 16.69
Jacobs v Templeton [1995] STC (SCD) 150; *revs'd sub nom* Templeton
   v Jacobs [1996] 1 WLR 1433, [1996] STC 991, 68 TC 735 .... 8.111, 8.125, 8.128
Jacques v R & C Comrs [2007] STC (SCD) 166, [2007] STI 263 .... 55.82
Jade Palace v R & C Comrs [2006] STC (SCD) 419, [2006] STI 1623 .... 4.180
Jaggers (t/a Shide Trees) v Ellis [1997] STC 1417, 71 TC 164 .... 12.24
Jain v R & C Comrs [2015] UKFTT 670 (TC) 10.150, 10.151
James Anderson v R & C Comrs [2013] UKFTT 126 (TC), [2013] STI 1812 .... 55.83
James H Donald (Darvel) Ltd v R & C Comrs [2015] UKUT 514 (TCC),
   [2016] STC 616, [2015] BTC 529 .... 2.40; 8.66
Janosevic v Sweden (2004) 38 EHRR 22 .... 55.82, 55.83
Jarrold v Boustead [1964] 3 All ER 76, 41 TC 701, CA 8.63
Jarvis (Linda) v R & C Comrs (2015) 55.82
Jasmine Trustees v Wells & Hind [2007] EWHC 38, [2008] Ch 194,
   [2007] 3 WLR 810 .... 27A.37
Jays the Jewellers Ltd v IRC [1947] 2 All ER 762, 29 TC 274 .... 10.107
Jeffs v Ringtons Ltd [1986] 1 All ER 144, [1985] STC 809 .... 10.133

	PARA
Jenkins v Brown [1989] 1 WLR 1163, [1989] STC 577	25.6
Jenkins v Horn [1979] 2 All ER 1141, [1979] STC 446	8.93
Jenners Princes Street Edinburgh Ltd v IRC [1998] STC (SCD) 196	10.67, 10.142
Jerome v Kelly [2002] EWHC 604 (Ch), [2002] STC 609	19.78
Jerome v Kelly (Inspector of Taxes) [2004] UKHL 25, [2004] 1 WLR 1409, [2004] 2 All ER 835	8.148
Johnson v Johnson [1946] P 205, [1946] 1 All ER 573, CA	14.26
Johnston v Britannia Airways Ltd [1994] STC 763, 67 TC 99	10.67
Johnston Publishing (North) Ltd v Revenue & Customs (2007)	43.123
John Wilkins (Motor Engineers) Ltd v R & C Comrs [2009] UKUT 175 (TCC), [2009] STC 2485, [2009] STI 2714	4.210
Jolaoso (Dr AS) v R & C Comrs [2011] UKFTT 44 (TC)	10.151
Jones (Balls' Administrators) v IRC [1997] STC 358	30.10
Jones v Garnett [2007] UKHL 35	16.93, 16.94, 16.102; 46.54, 46.60, 46.55, 46.61; 51.54, 51.55
Jones v Kernott [2011] UKSC 53, [2012] 1 AC 776, [2011] 3 WLR 1121	16.93; 52.1, 52.61
Jones v Leeming *see* Leeming v Jones	
Jones v R & C Comrs [2015] UKFTT 477 (TC)	10.150, 10.151
Jones v Wilcock [1996] STC (SCD) 389	23.101
Lobler v R & C Comrs [2015] UKUT 152 (TCC), [2015] STC 1893, [2015] BTC 515	55.25
Jowett v O'Neill & Brennan Construction Ltd [1998] STC 482, 70 TC 566	41.23
Joyce v R & C Comrs [2005] STC (SCD) 696	13.6
Jussila v Finland [2009] STC 29, (2007) 45 EHRR 39	55.82

K

Kamer van Koophandel en Fabrieken voor Amsterdam v Inspire Art Ltd (Case C-167/01) [2003] All ER (D) 64 (Oct), ECJ	54.73, 54.75
KapHag Renditefonds v Finanzamt Charlottenburg CJEC (Case C-442/01) [2003] All ER(D) 362 (Jun) (TVC 21.62)	37.6; 38.24
Kasperbauer v Griffith (Zorab) [2000] WTLR 333	27.13, 27.14
Keck & Mithouard (Cases C-267, 268/91) [1993] ECR I-6097, [1995] 1 CMLR 101, ECJ	54.52
Kelsall Parsons & Co v IRC 1938 SC 238, 1938 SLT 239, 21 TC 608, 17 ATC 87	10.106
Kenyon (A) v R & C Comrs [2011] UKFTT 91 (TC)	10.150
Kerr v Brown (Inspector of Taxes) [2002] STC (SCD) 434	8.119, 8.126, 8.129
Kerr v R & C Comrs [2011] UKFTT 40 (TC)	11.41
Ketko v Ukraine (2008)	55.5, 55.21
Key IP Ltd v R & C Comrs [2011] UKFTT 715 (TC), [2012] SFTD 305, [211] STI 3434	10.146
Khawaja v Secretary of State for the Home Department [1984] AC 74, [1983] 1 All ER 765, [1982] Imm AR 139, HL	55.91
Kidson v Macdonald [1974] 1 All ER 849, [1974] STC 54	25.5, 25.6; 52.71
Kildrummy (Jersey) Ltd v IRC [1990] STC 657, 1992 SLT 787	29.122, 29.126
King v Walden (Inspector of Taxes) [2001] STC 822	55.82
King v United Kingdom [2005] STC 438, (2005) 41 EHRR 2, 76 TC 699	55.82
Kirby v Thorn EMI plc [1986] STC 200; *revs'd* [1988] 2 All ER 947, [1987] STC 621, CA	19.8, 19.64
Kirkwood v Evans [2002] EWHC 30 (Ch), [2002] 1 WLR 1794, [2002] STC 231	8.173, 8.174
Kishore (D) v R & C Comrs [2013] UKFTT 465 (TC), [2013] STI 3520	10.30

lxxviii *Table of cases*

	PARA
Kleinwort Benson v Lincoln City Council [1998] 4 All ER 513, [1999] 2 AC 349, [1998] RVR 315, HL	8.202
Knight v R & C Comrs (2016)	19.21
Koenigsberger v Mellor [1993] STC 408; *aff'd* [1995] STC 547, CA	7.23
Konle v Austria (Case C-302/97) [1999] ECR I-3099	54.49
Koshal v R & C Comrs [2013] UKFTT 410 (TC)	51.54
Kothari v R & C Comrs [2016] UKFTT 127 (TC)	23.22
Kretztechnik AG v Finanzamt Linz (Case C-465/03) [2005] 1 WLR 3755, [2005] STC 1118, [2005] ECR I-4357	38.24; 40.72
Kuehne + Nagel Drinks Logistics Ltd v R & C Comrs [2012] EWCA Civ 34, [2012] STC 840, [2012] BTC 58	8.41, 8.42

L

LH Bishop Electrical Co Ltd AF Sheldon t/a Aztec Distributors v R & C Comrs (2013)	55.46, 44.49, 55.83
L/M Ferro Ltd v R & C Comrs [2013] UKFTT 463 (TC), [2013] STI 3468	8.66
LM Tenancies 1 plc v IRC [1996] STC 880, [1996] 2 EGLR 119, [1996] 46 EG 155; *aff'd* [1998] 1 WLR 1269, [1998] STC 326, CA	49.115
Laboratoires Fournier v Direction des Verifications Nationales et Internationales (Case C-39/04) [2006] STC 538, [2005] ECR I-2057, [2005] 2 CMLR 5	54.48, 54.56, 54.60, 54.61, 54.63, 54.68
Laerstate BV v R & C Comrs [2009] UKFTT 209 (TC), [2009] SFTD 551, [2009] STI 2669	18.16; 41.153
Laidler v Perry [1964] 3 All ER 329, 42 TC 351, CA; *aff'd* [1966] AC 16, [1965] 2 All ER 121, 42 TC 351, HL	8.62
Lake v Lake [1989] STC 865	30.157
Lancaster v IRC [2000] STC (SCD) 138	44.11
Land Management Ltd v Fox [2002] STC (SCD) 152	41.23
Lang v Rice [1984] STC 172, 57 TC 80, CA	10.103; 19.64
Langham v Veltema [2004] STC 544	4.42
Languard New Homes Ltd v R & C Comrs & DD & DM MacPherson v R& C Comrs [2017] UKUT 307 (TCC), [2017] STC 1769	39.23
Lankhorst-Hohorst GmbH v Finanzmt Steinfurt (Case C-324/00) [2002] ECR I-11779, [2003] STC 607, ECJ	54.45, 54.62, 54.67, 54.71
Larner v Warrington [1985] STC 442, 58 TC 557	19.69
Larsy v Institut National d'Assusurances Sociales pour Travailleurs Indépendants (INASTI) (Case C-118/00) [2001] ECR I-5063, ECJ	54.25
Larter v Skone James [1976] STC 220	21.21
Latilla v IRC [1943] 1 All ER 265, 25 TC 107, HL	18.116
Lau v R & C Comrs [2009] STC (SCD) 352, [2009] WTLR 627	30.155
Law Shipping Co Ltd v IRC 1924 SC 74, 12 TC 621	10.142; 12.43
Lawson (Inspector of Taxes) v Brooks [1992] STC 76, 64 TC 462, [1991] STI 1149	7.44
Lawson v Johnson Matthey plc [1992] 2 AC 324, [1992] 2 All ER 647, [1992] STC 466, HL	10.77, 10.132
Leach v Pogson (1962) 40 TC 585, [1962] TR 289	10.25
Lee v IRC (1941) 24 TC 207	18.116
Lee v Jewitt [2000] STC (SCD) 517	19.21
Lee v Lee's Air Farming Ltd [1961] AC 12, [1960] 3 All ER 420, PC	46.22
Leekes Ltd v R & C Comrs [2015] UKFTT 93 (TC), [2015] SFTD 433, [2015] STI 1564	10.30; 41.66
Leeming v Jones [1930] 1 KB 279, 15 TC 333, CA; *aff'd sub nom* Jones v Leeming [1930] AC 415, 15 TC 333, HL	13.15

	PARA
Lehigh Cement Ltd v R 2010 FCA 124	3.82
Leightons Ltd & Eye-Tech Opticians v C & E Comrs (2001) (VAT Decision 17498)	40.37
Leisureking Ltd v Cushing [1993] STC 46, 65 TC 400	22.43
Lennartz v Finanzamt Munchen III: C-97/90 [1991] ECR I-3795, [1995] STC 514, ECJ	37.5; 38.82
Lenz v Finanzlandesdirektion fur Tirol (Case C-315/02) [2004] All ER (D) 277 (Jul), ECJ	54.49, 54.57, 54.64, 54.68
Leur-Bloem v Inspecteur der Belastingdienst/Ondernemingen Amsterdam 2 (Case C-28/95) [1998] QB 182, [1997] All ER (EC) 738, [1997] STC 1205, ECJ	54.92
Levene v IRC [1928] AC 217, [1928] All ER Rep 746, 13 TC 486	27.2, 27.9, 27.12, 27.13, 27.14, 27.15
Levin v Secretary of State for Justice (Case 53/81) [1982] ECR 1035, [1982] 2 CMLR 454, ECJ	54.44
Lewis (Trustee of Redrow Staff Pension Scheme) v IRC [1999] STC (SCD) 349	3.65, 3.72
Lewis (Hazel Patricia) v R & C Comrs [2008] STC (SCD) 895, [2008] STI 1716	8.174
Lewis v Lady Rook [1992] 1 WLR 662, [1992] STC 171, CA	23.24
Lewis v Walters [1992] STC 97, 24 HLR 427	19.41
Lindsay v C & E Comrs [2002] EWCA Civ 267, [2002] 3 All ER 118, [2002] 1 WLR 1766, [2002] STC 588	55.24
Lindsay v United Kingdom (1986)	55.24, 55.43
Linslade Post Office & General Store (a firm) v R & C Comrs [2012] UKFTT 457 (TC)	10.146
Lints (J) v R & C Comrs [2012] UKFTT 491 (TC)	10.103
Lion Co v R & C Comrs [2009] UKFTT 357 (TC), [2010] SFTD 454, [2010] STI 683	10.142
Lipson v Canada (2009)	3.82
Lloyds Bank plc v Duker [1987] 1 WLR 1324	21.1; 25.7
Lloyds Bank plc v Rosset [1991] 1 AC 107, [1990] 1 All ER 1111, 60 P & CR 311, HL	52.61
Lloyds TSB (Antrobus) v IRC [2002] STC (SCD) 468	31.66
Lloyds UDT Finance Ltd v Chartered Finance Trust Holdings & others (Britax Int GmbH & another) [2002] EWCA Civ 806, [2002] STC 956, [2002] UKHRR 929, 74 TC 662, [2002] BTC 247, [2002] STI 853	10.63
Loffland Bros North Sea v Goodbrand [1997] STC 102; aff'd sub nom Goodbrand v Loffland Bros North Sea Inc [1998] STC 930, CA	19.17
Lomax v Peter Dixon & Son Ltd [1943] 2 All ER 255, 25 TC 353, CA	14.6
London & Thames Haven Oil Wharves Ltd v Attwooll [1967] 2 All ER 124, 43 TC 491	8.157; 10.103; 19.64, 19.68
Longson v Baker [2001] STC 6, 73 TC 415	23.61
Lord v Tustain [1993] STC 755, 65 TC 761	7.45; 47.71
Loring v Woodland Trust [2014] EWCA Civ 1314, [2015] 1 WLR 3238, [2015] 2 All ER 32, 2015] STC 598, [2015] WTLR 159, [2014] STI 3239	30.27
Lothian Chemical Co Ltd v Rogers (Inspector of Taxes) (1926) 11 TC 508, Ct of Sess	10.63
Lowe v J W Ashmore Ltd [1971] 1 All ER 1057, 46 TC 597	12.22
Lowenstein (1926) 10 TC 424	27.15

lxxx *Table of cases*

PARA

Lowry (Inspector of Taxes) v Consolidated African Selection Trust Ltd [1940] AC 648, [1940] 2 All ER 545, 23 TC 259, HL 9.121
Lubbock Fine v C & E Comrs (Case C-60/96) [1994] QB 571 .... 39.20
Lurcott v Wakely & Wheeler [1911] 1 KB 905, 104 LT 290, CA 10.142
Lütticke GmbH v Commission (Case 48/65) [1966] ECR 19, [1966] CMLR 378 .... 54.7
Lynall v IRC [1972] AC 680, [1971] 3 All ER 914, 47 TC 375, HL 28.72
Lyndale Fashion Manufacturers v Rich [1973] 1 All ER 33 .... 8.157
Lyon v Pettigrew [1985] STC 369, 58 TC 452 .... 19.72
Lysaght v IRC (1928) 13 TC 511 .... 27.2, 27.12, 27.13, 27.14

M

MA & 34 Others v Finland (2003) 55.26
MBF Design Services Ltd v R & C Comrs [2011] UKFTT 35 (TC), [2011] SFTD 383, [2011] STI 1552 .... 8.32
MC & LJ Ive Ltd v R & C Comrs [2014] UKFTT 400 (TC) 8.119
MJP Media Services v R & C Comrs [2012] EWCA Civ 1558, [2013] STC 2218, [2012] BTC 477 .... 41.51
McBride v Blackburn (Inspector of Taxes) [2003] STC (SCD) 139 .... 8.145
McCaig v University of Glasgow 1907 SC 231, 14 SLT 600, Ct of Sess 53.25
McCall (personal representatives of McLean) v R & C Comrs [2009] NICA 12 .... 31.43, 31.48
McCarthy v McCarthy & Stone plc [2007] EWCA Civ 664, [2008] 1 All ER 221 .... 8.202
McClure v Petre [1988] 1 WLR 1386, [1988] STC 749, 61 TC 226 .... 12.22
McDonald (Inspector of Taxes) v Dextra Accessories Ltd [2003] EWHC 872 (Ch), [2003] STC 749; revs'd [2004] EWCA Civ 22, [2004] STC 339 .... 41.45
McDowall v IRC [2004] STC (SCD) 22 .... 31.4
Macfarlane v IRC 1929 SC 453, 14 TC 532 .... 16.61
McFarlane v McFarlane [2003] EWHC 2410 (Fam) 52.1
McFarlane v McFarlane [2006] UKHL 24; [2006] 2 AC 618 .... 52.1, 52.13
McGarry v EF (1953) 13.28
McGowan v Brown & Cousins [1977] 3 All ER 844, [1977] STC 342 .... 10.102
McGregor v Randall [1984] 1 All ER 1092, [1984] STC 223 .... 8.65
MacGregor v United Kingdom (Application 30548/96) (3 December 1997, unreported), E Ct HR 55.44
McGregor (Her Majesty's Inspector of Taxes) v Adcock (1977) 51 TC 692 .... 20.21
McKelvey v R & C Comrs [2008] STC (SCD) 944, [2008] WTLR 1407, [2008] STI 1752 .... 31.8, 31.10
MacKinlay v Arthur Young McClelland Moores & Co [1986] STC 491; on appeal [1988] STC 116; revs'd [1990] 1 All ER 45, [1989] STC 898, HL 10.137; 44.3
McKnight v Sheppard [1997] STC 846, 71 TC 419, CA; aff'd [1999] 3 All ER 491, [1999] STC 669, 71 TC 419, HL 10.137, 10.146
McLaren Racing Ltd v R & C Comrs [2012] UKFTT 601 (TC), [2013] SFTD 18 .... 10.145
McLaughlin v R & C Comrs [2012] UKFTT 174 (TC), [2012] WTLR 855, [2012] STI 1711 .... 2.40, 2.46
MacLeod v IRC 1885 12 R (Ct of Sess) 105 .... 49.116
McMahon (P) v R & C Comrs [2013] UKFTT 403 (TC) 10.146
McManus v Griffiths [1997] STC 1089, 70 TC 218 .... 8.24
McMorris v R & C Comrs [2014] UKFTT 1116 (TC) 10.28

Table of cases lxxxi

PARA

McNiven (Inspector of Taxes) v Westmoreland Investments Ltd
[1997] STC 1103, 73 TC 1; *revs'd sub nom* Westmoreland Investments Ltd
v MacNiven (Inspector of Taxes) [1998] STC 1131, *sub nom*
McNiven (Inspector of Taxes) v Westmoreland Investments Ltd
73 TC 1, [1998] LS Gaz R 35, 142 Sol Jo LB 262, CA; *aff'd sub nom*
MacNiven (Inspector of Taxes) v Westmoreland Investments Ltd
[2001] UKHL 6 [2001] 1 All ER 865, [2001] 2 WLR 377,
[2001] STC 237, 73 TC 1, 145 Sol Jo LB 55, *sub nom* Westmoreland
Investments Ltd v MacNiven (Inspector of Taxes) [2001] NLJR 223........ 2.4, 2.34,
2.36, 2.37, 2.42,
2.43, 2.44, 2.45, 2.48;
4.184; 6.21; 8.194
MacPherson v Bond [1985] 1 WLR 1157, [1985] STC 678.................................... 14.3
Macpherson v IRC [1985] STC 471; on appeal [1987] STC 73, CA;
aff'd [1988] 2 All ER 753, [1988] STC 362, *sub nom* IRC v
Macpherson [1989] AC 159, HL.. 28.102; 33.17
Machon v McLoughlin (1926) 8.93
Mairs v Haughey [1992] STC 495, (N.I. CA); *aff'd* [1994] 1 AC 303,
[1993] 3 All ER 801, [1993] 3 WLR 393, [1993] STC 569,
66 TC 273, [1993] IRLR 551, HL............................... 8.41, 8.42, 8.65, 8.105,
8.125, 8.127, 8.140
8.143, 8.144, 8.162; 9.12
Makins v Elson [1977] 1 All ER 572, [1977] STC 46............................... 23.21, 23.22
Malam, Re, Malam v Hitchens [1894] 3 Ch 578, 63 LJCh 797, 71 LT 655.......... 42.152
Mallalieu v Drummond [1981] 1 WLR 908, [1981] STC 391;
on appeal [1983] 1 All ER 801, [1983] STC 124, CA; *revs'd*
[1983] 2 AC 861, [1983] STC 665, HL 10.137; 44.3
Manders (M) v R & C Comrs [2010] UKFTT 313 (TC) 10.150
Manduca (P) v R & C Comrs [2015] UKUT 262 (TCC);
[2015] BTC 519.. 8.63; 13.12
Manninen, proceedings brought by (Case C-319/02) [2005] Ch 236,
[2005] 2 WLR 670, [2004] ECR I-7477.................................. 54.49, 54.57, 54.62,
54.63, 54.64, 54.68
Mansworth v Jelley [2002] EWHC 442 (Ch), [2002] STC 1013;
aff'd [2002] EWCA Civ 1829, [2003] STC 53, 75 .... 9.46, 9.50,
9.53; 19.70
Manthorpe Building Products v R & C Comrs [2012] UKFTT 82 (TC) 2.40
Manzur (Dr KMA) v R & C Comrs [2010] UKFTT 580 (TC),
[2011] STI 1219.. 10.19
Market Investigations Ltd v Minister of Social Security [1969] 2 QB 173,
[1968] 3 All ER 732... 8.22
Markets South West (Holidngs) Ltd v R & C Comrs [2011] UKUT 257 (TCC),
[2011] STC 1469, [2011] BTC 1766 .... 10.77
Markey v Sanders [1987] 1 WLR 864, [1987] STC 256....................................... 23.24
Marks & Spencer plc v C & E Comrs [1999] 1 CMLR 1152, [1999] STC 205;
on appeal [2000] 1 CMLR 256, [2000] STC 16, CA........................... 55.101
Marks & Spencer plc v Halsey (Inspector of Taxes) (Case C-446/03) [2006]
Ch 184, [2006] 2 WLR 250, [2006] All ER (EC) 255 .... 1.42; 41.155;
43.42, 43.44; 54.8,
54.45, 54.57, 54.64,
54.65, 54.68; 55.5
Marquess of Linlithgow v R & C Comrs [2010] CSIH 19,
[2010] STC 1563, 2010 SC 391.. 28.231

PARA

Marren v Ingles [1979] STC 58, [1978] TR 233; on appeal
  [1979] 1 WLR 1131, [1979] STC 637, CA; aff'd
  [1980] 3 All ER 95, [1980] STC 500, HL........... 19.8, 19.18, 19.45, 19.61,
  19.64, 19.67; 22.41; 47.34, 47.38; 52.78
Marsden v IRC [1965] 2 All ER 364, 42 TC 326.. 8.174
Marshall v Kerr [1994] 3 All ER 106, [1994] STC 638, HL................. 17.58; 21.103,
                                                                    21.124, 21.126; 35.21
Marson v Morton [1986] 1 WLR 1343, [1986] STC 463 .... 10.23; 12.102
Martin (Moore's Executors) v IRC [1995] STC (SCD) 5 .... 31.48
Martin v Lowry [1926] 1 KB 550, 11 TC 297, CA; aff'd [1927] AC 312,
  11 TC 297, HL 10.19, 10.23, 10.26
Martin v Martin (1977)... 52.73
Martin v R & C Comrs [2014] UKFTT 1021 (TC) 8.143
Martin (Julian) v R & C Comrs [2013] UKFTT 40 (TC), [2013] SFTD 417,
  [2013] STI 1505 .... 8.175
Martin-Dye v Martin-Dye [2006] EWCA Civ 681, [2006] 1 WLR 3448,
  [2006] 4 All ER 779 .... 52.13
Marwood Homes Ltd v IRC [1997] STC (SCD) 37 .... 3.35, 3.64, 3.72
Marwood Homes Ltd v IRC (No 2) [1998] STC (SCD) 53 .... 3.72
Mason v Innes [1967] 2 All ER 926, 44 TC 326, CA 10.119
Matrix-Securities Ltd v IRC [1994] 1 All ER 769, [1994] 1 WLR 334,
  [1994] STC 272, HL.. 2.34
Matthews v R & C Comrs [2012] UKFTT 658 (TC), [2013] WTLR 93,
  [2013] STI 299 .... 10.102; 29.101
Matthews v Martin (1991) 30.157
Matthews v R & C Comrs [2011] UKFTT 24 (TC)...................... 10.102; 30.2
Mawsley Machinery Ltd v Robinson [1998] STC (SCD) 236 ...... 9.122; 10.133; 41.45
Mazurkiewicz v R & C Comrs [2011] UKFTT 807 (TC) 14.6
Meat Traders v Cushing (1997).. 10.67
Meilicke v Finanzamt Bonn-Innenstadt (Case C-292/04) [2008] STC 2267,
  [2007] ECR I-1835, [2007] 2 CMLR 19 .... 54.64
Mellor v R & C Comrs [2011] UKFTT 29 (TC) 10.150
Melville v IRC [2000] STC 628; aff'd, [2001] EWCA Civ 1247,
  [2002] 1 WLR 407, [2001] STC 1271 .... 28.62; 32.94; 33.62
Merseyside Cablevision Ltd v C & E Comrs [1987] 3 CMLR 290,
  [1987] VATTR 134 .... 38.49
Mesher v Mesher (1973) [1980] 1 All ER 126, CA 52.70
Metallgesellschaft Ltd v IRC (Case C-397/98) [2001] Ch 620,
  [2001] 2 WLR 1497, [2001] ECR I-1727, [2001] All ER (EC) 496,
  [2001] 2 CMLR 700, [2001] STC 452, [2001] All ER (D)
  96 (Mar), ECJ 54.45, 54.64, 54.65, 54.68
Methuen-Campbell v Walters [1979] QB 525, [1979] 2 WLR 113,
  [1979] 1 All ER 606 .... 23.24
Meynell-Smith v R & C Comrs [2013] UKFTT 113 (TC) 10.102
Miller v IRC [1987] STC 108.. 32.25, 32.27
Miller v Miller [2006] UKHL 24; [2006] 2 AC 618.......................... 52.1, 52.13
Milroy v Lord (1862) 7 LT 178.. 29.41
Milton v Chivers [1996] STC (SCD) 36... 22.72
Mimtec Ltd v IRC [2001] STC (SCD) 101.. 8.41
Minden Trust (Cayman) Ltd v IRC [1984] STC 434; aff'd
  [1985] STC 758, CA 32.6; 35.21
Miners v Atkinson [1995] STC (SCD) 64; aff'd [1997] STC 58, 68 TC 629 .... 8.174
Ministerio Fiscal v Bordessa (Case C-358/93) [1995] All ER (EC) 385,
  [1995] ECR I-361, [1996] 2 CMLR 13 .... 54.31

	PARA
Minister of National Revenue v Anaconda American Brass Ltd [1956] AC 85, [1956] 1 All ER 20, [1955] TR 339, 34 ATC 330, PC	10.66
Mirror Group plc v C & E Comrs (Case C-409/98) [2002] QB 546, *sub nom* C & E Comrs v Mirror Group plc [2001] ECR I-7175, [2001] 3 CMLR 1417, [2001] STC 1453, ECJ	39.20
Mitchell v B W Noble Ltd [1927] 1 KB 719, 11 TC 372, CA	10.132
Mitchell v Egyptian Hotels Ltd [1915] AC 1022, 6 TC 542, HL	18.35
Mitchell v Rosay (1954) 47 R & IT 508, 35 TC 496, (1954) 33 ATC 299	13.6
Mitchell & Edon v Ross [1959] 3 All ER 341, 40 TC 11; *aff'd* [1960] 2 All ER 218, 40 TC 11, CA; on appeal [1962] AC 814, [1961] 3 All ER 49, 40 TC 11, HL	6.42; 8.21
Mol v Inspecteur der Invoerrechten en Accijnzen, ECJ (Case C-269/86) [1988] ECR 3627, [1989] 3 CMLR 729	37.6
Mondero & others v France [2010] UKFTT 500 (TC)	55.27
Moonlight Textiles Ltd v R & C Comrs (2010)	10.142
Moore v Griffiths (Inspector of Taxes) [1972] 1 WLR 1024, [1972] 3 All ER 399, 48 TC 338	8.41, 8.62
Moore v R J Mackenzie & Sons Ltd [1972] 2 All ER 549, 48 TC 196	10.114
Moore v R & C Comrs [2010] UKFTT 271 (TC)	23.22
Moore (J) v R & C Comrs (2014)	20.10
Moore (TJ) v R & C Comrs (2011)	10.30
Moore v Thompson (Inspector of Taxes) [1986] STC 170, 60 TC 15, (1986) 83 LSG 1559	23.21
Moorhouse v Dooland [1955] 1 All ER 93, 36 TC 1, CA	8.62
Moorthy v R & C Comrs [2014] UKFTT 834 (TC), [2015] IRLR 4, [2014] Eq LR 640	8.148, 8.152
Morgan (David) v R & C Comrs [2013] UKFTT 181 (TC), [2013] STI 1851	23.22
Morgan Lloyd Trustees Ltd (as administrator of Wren Press Pension Scheme) v R & C Comrs [2017] UKFTT 131 (TC)	55.25
Morley v Tattersall [1938] 3 All ER 296, 22 TC 51, CA	10.107
Morrison v R & C Comrs [2014] CSIH 113, [2015] STC 659, 2015 SLT 169, [2015] BTC 1, 2015 GWD 2-56	19.23
Mortimore v IRC (1864) 33 LJ Ex 263	22.41
Moyles v R & C Comrs [2014] UKFTT 175 (TC), [2014] STI 1772	2.1, 2.41, 2.46
Mulloy v R & C Comrs [2016] UKFTT 243 (TC)	19.21
Munford (Paul) v R & C Comrs [2017] UKFTT 19 (TC)	23.22
Munro v Stamp Duties Comr [1934] AC 61, 103 LJPC 18, PC	29.122, 29.125
Murray v Goodhews [1976] STC 128; *aff'd* [1978] 2 All ER 40, [1978] STC 207, CA	10.102
Murray (Richard) v R & C Comrs [2014] UKFTT 338 (TC), [2014] STI 2118	10.28
Murtagh v R & C Comrs [2013] UKFTT 352 (TC)	10.20

N

N v Inspecteur van de Belastingdienst Oost (Case C-470/04) [2008] STC 436, [2006] ECR I-7409, [2006] 3 CMLR 49	54.45
N Brown Group plc v R & C Comrs [2016] UKFTT 445 (TC), [2016] STI 2174	4.208
NEC Semi-Conductors Ltd v IRC *sub nom* Boake Allen Ltd v IRC [2003] EWHC 2813 (Ch), [2004] STC 489, [2004] Eu LR 351	54.49
NKM v Hungary (application 66529/11) [2013] STC 1104	55.21, 55.25, 55.26
NMB Holdings Ltd v Secretary of State for Social Security (2000) 73 TC 85	8.192
Nabi v Heaton [1983] 1 WLR 626	7.111
Nadin v IRC [1997] STC (SCD) 107	31.4

	PARA
National & Provincial Building Society v United Kingdom (1997) 25 EHRR 127, [1997] STC 1466, ECtHR	1.42; 55.21
National Bank of Greece SA v Westminster Bank Executor & Trustee Co (Channel Islands) Ltd *see* Westminster Bank Executor & Trustee Co (Channel Islands) Ltd v National Bank of Greece SA	
National Grid Indus BV v Inspecteur van de Balstingdienst Rijnmond / Kantoor Rotterdam (Case C-371/10) [2012] STC 114, [2012] 1 CMLR 49, [2012] STI 107	54.46
Naturally Yours Cosmetics Ltd v C & E Comrs (Case C-230/87) [1988] ECR 6365, [1989] 1 CMLR 797, [1988] STC 879, ECJ	37.5; 38.2
Neely v Rourke [1987] STC 30; *aff'd* [1988] STC 216, CA	19.13
Nell Gwynn House Maintenance Fund (Trustees) v C & E Comrs [1999] 1 All ER 385, [1999] 1 WLR 174, [1999] STC 79, 32 HLR 13, HL	39.45
Nelson Dance Family Settlement Trustees v R & C Comrs [2009] EWHC 71 (Ch), [2009] STC 802, 79 TC 605	24.7; 31.43
Nessa v Chief Adjudication Officer [1999] 4 All ER 677, [1999] 1 WLR 1937, [1999] 3 FCR 538, [1999] 2 FLR 1116, HL	18.14
New York Life Insurance Co v Public Trustee [1924] 2 Ch 101, 40 TLR 430	35.83
New York Life Insurance Co v Styles (1889) LR 14 App Cas 381	10.29
Newman Manufacturing Company v Marrable [1931] 2 KB 297	1.21
News Datacom Ltd v R & C Comrs [2006] STC (SCD) 732, [2006] STI 2346	41.153
News International plc v Shepherd [1989] STC 617, 62 TC 495	43.127
Newsom v Robertson [1953] Ch 7, [1952] 2 All ER 728, 33 TC 452, CA	10.151
Nichols (deceased) v IRC [1975] 1 WLR 534, [1975] 2 All ER 120, [1975] STC 278	29.125
Nicoll v Austin (1935) 19 TC 531, 14 ATC 172	8.92, 8.94, 8.141
Nolder v Walters (1980) 15 TC 380	8.172
Norbury, Re [1939] Ch 528	30.56
Norris v Edgson [2000] STC 494, 72 TC 553, [2000] 2 FCR 445	52.3
Northend v White, Leonard & Corbin Greener [1975] 2 All ER 481, [1975] STC 317	7.23
Noved Investment Co v R & C Comrs [2006] STC (SCD) 120, [2006] STI 538	53.42
Nuclear Electric plc v Bradley [1996] 1 WLR 529, [1996] STC 405, 68 TC 670, HL	41.61

O

OJSC Oil Co Yugraneft v Abramovich [2008] EWHC 2613 (Comm)	27.2, 27.10, 27.14, 27.15
Oakes v Stamp Duties Comr of New South Wales [1954] AC 57, [1953] 2 All ER 1563, PC	29.134; 32.94
Oakley (as Personal Representative of Jossaume) v IRC [2005] STC (SCD) 343	32.24, 32.28
Oates v R & C Comrs [2014] UKUT 409 (LC), [2014] RVR 337, [2014] BTC 528, [2015] WTLR 89	23.62
O'Brien v Benson's Hosiery (Holdings) Ltd [1979] 3 All ER 652, [1979] STC 735, HL	19.8, 19.64, 19.67
Odeon Associated Theatres Ltd v Jones [1972] 1 All ER 681, 48 TC 257, CA	10.63, 10.142; 12.43
O'Driscoll v Manchester Insurance Committee [1915] 3 KB 499	22.41
Office of Fair Trading v Abbey National plc [2009] UKSC 6, [2010] 1 AC 696, [2009] 3 WLR 1215	8.143
Ogden v R & C Comrs [2011] UKFTT 212 (TC)	18.3

	PARA
Ogilvie v Kitton 1908 SC 1003, 5 TC 338	18.35
O'Grady v Bullcroft Main Collieries Ltd (1932) 17 TC 93	48.3
O'Grady v Markham Main Colliery Ltd (1932) 17 TC 93	10.142
O'Kane (J & R) & Co Ltd v IRC (1922) 12 TC 303, 126 LT 707, HL	10.30
O'Keeffe v Southport Printers Ltd [1984] STC 443, 58 TC 88	10.132
O'Leary v McKinlay [1991] STC 42, 63 TC 729	8.66, 8.124
Oliver v R & C Comrs [2016] UKFTT 796 (TC)	23.22
Olsson v Sweden (1988)	55.61
Omega Spielhallen und Automatenaufstellungs GmbH v Bundesstaft Bon (Case C-36/02) [2004] ECR I-9609	54.49
Oppenheim v Tobacco Securities Trust Co Ltd [1951] AC 297, [1951] 2 All ER 31, HL	33.115; 41.60
Optigen Ltd, Fulcrum Electronics Ltd, Bond House Systems Ltd v C & E Comrs (Cases C-354/03, 355/03, 484/03) [2006] Ch 218, [2006] 2 WLR 456, [2006] STC 419	37.6
Oram v Johnson [1980] 2 All ER 1, [1980] STC 222	19.22
Orthet Ltd v Vince-Cain [2005] ICR 374, [2004] IRLR 857	8.152
Ospelt v Unabhangiger Verwaltungssenat des Landes Vorarlberg (Case C-452/01) [2003] ECR I-9743	54.49
O'Rourke v Binks [1992] STC 703, 65 TC 165, CA	26.21
Otter v Andrews [1998] STC (SCD) 67	52.3
Owen v Elliott [1989] 1 WLR 162, [1989] STC 44; *revs'd* [1990] Ch 786, [1990] STC 469, CA	23.64
Owen v Pook [1970] AC 244, [1969] 2 All ER 1, 45 TC 571, HL	8.95, 8.173, 8.174
Owen (Inspector of Taxes) v Southern Rly of Peru Ltd [1957] AC 334, [1956] 3 WLR 389, [1956] 2 All ER 728, 49 R & IT 468, 36 TC 634, (1953) 32 ATC 147, [1956] TR 197, (1956) 100 SJ 527	10.67
Oxford Motors Ltd v Minister of National Revenue (1959) 18 DLR (2d) 712	6.1

P

PA Holdings v R & C Comrs [2011] EWCA Civ 1414, [2012] STC 582, [2011] BTC 705	2.40, 2.46; 8.66; 46.61
PM v UK [2005] STC 1566, [2005] 3 FCR 101, (2006) 42 EHRR 45	52.3; 55.42, 55.43
Padmore v IRC [1987] STC 36, 62 TC 352; *aff'd* [1989] STC 493, 62 TC 352, CA	18.39
Padmore v IRC (No 2) [2001] STC 280, 73 TC 470, [2001] BTC 36, 3 ITL Rep 315, [2001] STI 99, (2001) 98 (6) LSG 46, (2001) 145 SJLB 27	54.21
Page v Lowther [1983] STC 61; *aff'd* [1983] STC 799, CA	12.107, 12.110, 12.111, 12.112
Pardoe v Energy Power Development Corpn [2000] STC 286, 72 TC 617	12.112
Parkside Leasing Ltd v Smith [1985] 1 WLR 310, [1985] STC 63, 58 TC 282	14.3
Parnalls Solicitors Ltd v R & C Comrs [2009] UKFTT 318 (TC), [2010] SFTD 284, [2010] STI 378	10.67
Parsons v BMN Laboratories Ltd [1963] 2 All ER 658, [1963] TR 183, CA	8.157
Parsons (David S) v R & C Comrs [2010] UKFTT 110 (TC)	10.137
Partridge v Mallandaine (1886) 18 QBD 276, 2 TC 179	10.21, 10.41
Passant v Jackson [1985] STC 133, 59 TC 230; *aff'd* [1986] STC 164, 59 TC 230, CA	21.102
Patel v R & C Comrs [2016] UKFTT 78 (TC)	19.21
Patmore v R & C Comrs [2010] UKFTT 334 (TC), [2010] SFTD 1124, [2011] WTLR 125	16.93, 16.102; 51.55

Table of cases

	PARA
Pawlowski v Dunnington [1999] STC 550, CA	8.201
Pawson (deceased) v R & C Comrs [2012] UKFTT 51 (TC), [2012] WTLR 665	31.43, 31.48
Pearce v Woodall-Duckham Ltd [1978] 2 All ER 793, [1978] STC 372, 51 TC 271, CA	10.72
Pems Butler Ltd v R & C Comrs (unreported, 23 January 2012)	22.75
Pendragon plc v R & C Comrs [2009] UKFTT 192 (TC), [2010] SFTD 1, [2010] STI 1404	2.44
Pepper v Hart [1993] AC 593, [1993] 1 All ER 42, [1992] STC 898, HL	1.23; 8.126
Peracha v Miley [1989] STC 76, 63 TC 444; aff'd [1990] STC 512, 63 TC 444, CA	14.3
Perrin v R & C Comrs [2014] UKFTT 488 (TC)	14.33; 18.34
Perrons v Spackman [1981] 1 WLR 1411, [1981] STC 739	8.95
Perry v IRC [2005] SCD 474	29.101
Persche v Finanzamt Lüdenscheid (Case C-318/07) [2009] All ER (EC) 673	53.23; 54.63
Pertemps Recruitment Partnership Ltd v R & C Comrs [2011] STC 1346, [2011] BTC 1675, [2011] STI 739	10.107
Petrotim Securities Ltd v Ayres [1964] 1 All ER 269, 41 TC 389, CA	10.118
Pettit, Re, Le Fevre v Pettit [1922] 2 Ch 765, 127 LT 491	14.27; 17.45
Philips v Hamilton (Inspector of Taxes) [2003] SWTI 1052	8.174
Phillips Electronics UK Ltd v R & C Comrs (2006)	31.48
Phillips Electronics UK Ltd (2012) (Case C-18/11) [2013] STC 41, [2013] 1 CMLR 6, [2012] BTC 438, [2012] STI 2837, (2012) 109 (36) LSG17	43.42; 54.45, 54.64
Phizackerley v R & C Comrs [2007] STC (SCD) 328, [2007] WTLR 745, [2007] STI 559	30.14
Pickford v Quirke (1927) 138 LT 500, 13 TC 251, CA	10.25
Pi Consulting (Trustee Services) Ltd v Pensions Regulator [2013] EWHC 3181 (Ch), [2013] Pens LR 433	50.10
Pierce v Wood [2009] EWHC 3225 (Ch), [2010] WTLR 253	42.152
Piggott v Staines Investments Co Ltd [1995] STC 114, 68 TC 342	2.33
Pike (Nicholas) v R & C Comrs [2013] UKUT 225 (TCC), [2013] STI 1840	14.6
Pilkington v Randall (1966) 42 TC 662, CA	12.102
Pilkington Bros Ltd v IRC [1982] 1 All ER 715, [1982] STC 103, 55 TC 705, HL	43.47; 49.125
Pilkington, Re; Pearson v IRC [1981] 1 WLR 781, [1981] STC 219, [1980] TR 483	16.24; 32.22, 32.24, 32.25, 32.26, 32.27; 34.1
Pirelli v Oscar Faber [1983] 2 AC 1, [1983] 1 All ER 416, HL	19.67
Pitt v Holt [2011] EWCA Civ 197, [2011] 3 WLR 19, [2011] 2 All ER 450	27A.126; 55.25
Portuguese Republic v EC Commission (Case C-88/03) [2007] STC 1032, [2006] ECR I-7115, [2006] 3 CMLR 45	54.81
Postlethwaite's Executors v IRC [2007] STC (SCD) 83, [2007] WTLR 353, [2007] STI 346	28.21
Potel v IRC [1971] 2 All ER 504, 46 TC 658	17.3
Poulter v Gayjon Processes Ltd [1985] STC 174, 58 TC 350	10.102
Powell (1997)	31.48
Powlson v Welbeck Securities Ltd [1986] STC 423, 60 TC 269; aff'd [1987] STC 468, 60 TC 269, CA	19.65
Pratt (G) & Sons v R & C Comrs [2011] UKFTT 416 (TC)	10.142
Prendergast v Cameron [1939] 1 All ER 223, 23 TC 122, CA; on appeal sub nom Cameron v Prendergast [1940] 2 All ER 35, 23 TC 122, HL	8.65

Table of cases lxxxvii

	PARA
Prest v Bettinson [1980] STC 607, 53 TC 437	17.20; 21.105
Prest v Petrodel Resources Ltd [2013] UKSC 34, [2013] 3 WLR 1, (2013) 163 (7565) NLJ 27	46.21
Preston v IRC *see* R v IRC, ex p Preston	
Prestwich v Royal Bank of Canada Trust Co (17 December 1998)	27A.73
Price v R & C Comrs [2015] UKUT 164 (TCC), [2015] BTC 516	2.2
Price's Executor v R & C Comrs [2010] UKFTT 474 (TC), [2011] SFTD 52, [2011] WTLR 161	28.70
Prince v Mapp [1970] 1 All ER 519, 46 TC 169	10.137
Pritchard v Arundale [1971] 3 All ER 1011, 47 TC 680	8.63
Protec International Ltd v R & C Comrs [2010] UKFTT 628 (TC)	10.157
Prudential Assurance Co Ltd v R & C Comrs	41.46
Purchase v Tesco Stores Ltd [1984] STC 304, 58 TC 46	41.65
Purolite International Ltd v R & C Comrs [2012] UKFTT 475 (TC), 81 TC 562, [2012] STI 306	10.146

R

R v Allen [2000] QB 744, [1999] STC 846, CA; *aff'd* [2001] UKHL 45, [2002] 1 AC 509, [2001] 4 All ER 768, [2001] STC 1537	4.50; 8.104, 8.116; 35.21; 55.92
R v Barnet London Borough Council, ex p Nilish Shah [1983] 1 All ER 226	18.14; 27.2, 27.13, 27.14
R v C & E Comrs, ex p Greenwich Property Ltd (2001)	2.44
R v Canada Trustco Mortgage Co (205)	3.82
R v Dimsey [2000] QB 744, [2000] 3 WLR 273, [2000] 1 Cr App Rep 203, [1999] STC 846, CA	18.114; 35.21
R v HM Treasury, ex p Daily Mail & General Trust plc (Case C-81/87) [1989] QB 446, [1989] 1 All ER 328, [1988] STC 787, ECJ	54.44, 54.46
R v Henn & Darby (Case 34/79) [1981] AC 850, (1980) 71 Cr App Rep 44, [1980] 2 CMLR 229	38.2; 54.8
R v IRC, ex p Fulford-Dobson [1987] STC 344	1.25; 27.50
R v IRC, ex p Keys & Cook [1987] STC 434, 60 TC 405, [1987] BTC 339	8.201
R v IRC, ex p McVeigh [1996] STC 91, 68 TC 121	8.191, 8.201
R v IRC, ex p Mead & Cook [1992] STC 482, 65 TC 1	55.47
R v IRC, ex p Newfields Developments Ltd [2000] STC 52, 73 TC 532, CA; *revs'd* [2001] UKHL 27, [2001] 4 All ER 400, [2001] 1 WLR 1111, [2001] STC 901, 73 TC 532	41.23, 41.124
R v IRC, ex p Tamosius & Partners (a firm) *see* R v Crown Court at Middlesex Guildhall, ex p Tamosius & Partners (a firm) [2000] 1 WLR 453, [1999] STC 1077, [1ce999] BTC 404	4.155; 55.61
R v IRC, ex p Wilkinson [2005] UKHL 30	55.3, 55.44, 55.46
R v International Stock Exchange, ex p Else [1994] OB 534	54.8
R v Secretary of State for Transport, ex p Factortame Ltd [1990] 2 AC 85, [1989] 3 CMLR 1, *sub nom* Factortame Ltd v Secretary of State for Transport [1989] 2 All ER 692, HL; refd *sub nom* R v Secretary of State for Transport, ex p Factortame Ltd (No 2): C-213/89 [1991] 1 AC 603, *sub nom* Factortame Ltd v Secretary of State for Transport (No 2) [1991] 1 All ER 70, ECJ; apld *sub nom* R v Secretary of State for Transport, ex p Factortame Ltd (No 2) [1991] 1 AC 603, , *sub nom* Factortame Ltd v Secretary of State for Transport (No 2) [1991] 1 All ER 70, HL	54.24
R & C Comrs v Apollo Fuels Ltd [2016] EWCA Civ 157, [2016] 4 WLR 96, [2016] BTC 12	8.110, 8.117, 8.124, 8.125

lxxxviii *Table of cases*

	PARA
R & C Comrs v Banerjee [2010] EWCA Civ 843, [2011] 1 WLR 702, [2011] 1 All ER 985	8.173
R & C Comrs v Bridport & West Dorset Golf Club Ltd (Case C-495/12) [2014] STC 663, [2014] BVC 1, [2014] STI 257	40.54
R & C Comrs v Brockenhurst College (Case C-699/15) [2017] 4 WLR 96, [2017] STC 1112, [2017] BVC 20	40.23
R & C Comrs v Decadt [2007] EWHC 1659 (Ch), [2008] STC 1103	8.173
R & C Comrs v Drown & Leadley (2017)	19.69
R & C Comrs v FCE Bank plc (2012)	54.21
R & C Comrs v First Nationwide [2012] EWCA Civ 278, [2012] STC 1261, [2012] BTC 99	18.36
R & C Comrs v Hancock & Hancock [2016] UKUT 81 (TCC), [2016] STC 1433, [2016] BTC 503	2.41, 2.46
R & C Comrs v J Blackwell [2015] UKUT 418 (TCC), [2016] STC 598, [2015] BTC 526	19.21
R & C Comrs v Mayes [2011] EWCA Civ 407, [2011] STC 1269, [2011] BTC 261	f1.24; 2.40, 2.41, 2.46; 3.77; 6.21
R & C Comrs v Mertrux [2012] UKUT 274 (TCC), [2012] STC 2327, [2012] BTC 1701, [2012] STI 2590	22.74
R & C Comrs v Micro-Fusion 2004-1 Llp [2009] EWHC 1082 (Ch), [2009] STC 1741, [2009] BTC 237	10.28
R & C Comrs v Neton Dance (2009)	46.7
R & C Comrs v Rank Group plc (Case C-259/10) [2012] STC 23, [2011] ECR I-10947, [2012] CEC 884	40.27
R & C Comrs v Romie Tager [2015] UKUT 40 (TCC), [2015] BTC 509, [2015] STI 1258	4.163
R & C Comrs v Royal College of Paediatrics & Child Health, & Coleridge (Theobalds Road) Ltd [2015] UKUT 38 (TCC), [2015] STC 1243, [2015] BVC 507	39.37
R & C Comrs v Salaried Persons Postal Loans Ltd (2006)	41.23
R & C Comrs v Tower MCashback LLP1 [2011] UKSC 19, [2011] 2 WLR 1131, [2011] 3 All ER 171	1.24; 2.1, 2.4, 2.40, 2.41, 2.46; 6.21
R & C Comrs v Trigg [2016] UKUT 165 (TCC), [2016] STC 1310, [2016] BTC 505	41.94
R & C Comrs v Weald Leasing Ltd [2008] EWHC 30 (Ch)	2.44; 54.74
R & C Comrs v William Grant & Sons Distillers Ltd; Small (Inspector of Taxes) v Mars Ltd [2007] UKHL 15	10.136
R & C Comrs v Zurich Insurance (2007)	37.5
R (on the application of APVCO 19 Ltd) v R & C Comrs [2015] EWCA Civ 648, [2015] STC 2272, [2015] BTC 26	55.5, 55.21, 55.26, 55.83
R (on the application of Alconbury Developments Ltd) v R & C Comrs [2001] UKHL 23, [2003] 2 AC 295, [2001] 2 WLR 929	55.83
R (on the application of Barnett) v IRC [2003] EWHC 2581 (Admin), [2004] STC 763, 75 TC 796	22.72
R (on the application of Cooke) v R & C Comrs	55.61
R (on the application of Davies) v R & C Comrs *sub nom* R (on the application of Gaines-Cooper) v R & C Comrs [2010] EWCA Civ 83, [2010] STC 860, [2010] BTC 198	18.7, 18.25; 27.4, 27.5, 27.6, 27.9, 27.13, 27.14, 27.15, 27.16, 27.23

Table of cases lxxxix

PARA

R (on the application of Gaines-Cooper) v R & C Comrs *see* R (on the application of Davies) v R & C Comrs
R (on the application of H) v IRC (2002) 4.152
R (on the application of Higgs) v R & C Comrs [2015] UKUT 92 (TCC), [2015] STC 1600, [2015] BTC 510 .... 55.22
R (on the application of Hooper) v Secretary of State for Work & Pensions [2003] EWCA Civ 813, [2003] 3 All ER 673, [2003] 1 WLR 2623 .... 55.44
R (on the application of Hoverspeed Ltd) v C & E Comrs [2002] EWHC 1630 (Admin), [2002] 4 All ER 912, *sub nom* Hoverspeed Ltd v C & E Comrs [2002] 3 CMLR 395; *aff'd sub nom* R (on the application of Hoverspeed Ltd) v C & E Comrs [2002] EWCA Civ 1804, [2003] 2 All ER 553, [2003] 2 WLR 950, *sub nom* C & E Comrs v Hoverspeed Ltd [2003] 1 CMLR 742.. 55.24
R (on the application of Huitson) v R & C Comrs [2010] EWHC 97 (Admin), [2011] QB 174, [2010] 3 WLR 1015 .... 55.21, 55.26
R (on the application of McLaughlin (Siobhan)) v Department for Social Development [2016] NIQB 11 .... 55.43
R (on the application of Morgan Grenfell & Co Ltd) v Special Comr [2001] EWCA Civ 329, [2003] 1 AC 563, [2002] 1 All ER 776, [2001] STC 497; *revs'd sub nom* R (on the application of Morgan Grenfell & Co Ltd) v Special Comr of Income Tax [2002] UKHL 21, [2002] 3 All ER 1, [2002] 2 WLR 1299, [2002] STC 786.. 55.62
R (on the application of Professional Contractors Group Ltd) v IRC [2001] EWHC Admin 236, [2001] STC 629; *aff'd* [2001] EWCA Civ 1945, [2002] STC 165 .... 8.3, 8.31; 54.81; 55.22
R (on the application of Prudential plc & another) v Special Commissioner of Income Tax (2013) 55.48, 55.62
R (on the application of SG (previously JS)) v Secretary of State for Work & Pensions [2015] UKSC 16, [2015] 1 WLR 1449, [2015] PTSR 471, [2015] HRLR 5, [2015] HLR 21 .... 55.44
R (on the application of Shiner) v R & C Comrs [2011] EWCA Civ 892, [2011] STC 1878, [2012] 1 CMLR 9... 55.26
R (on the application of ToTel Ltd) v The First Tier Tribunal (Tax Chamber & HM Treasury) [2011] EWHC 652 (Admin) [2011] BVC 211, [2011] STI 1210... 55.5, 55.83
R (on the application of Wilkinson) v IRC [2002] EWHC 182 (Admin), [2002] STC 347; *aff'd* [2003] EWCA Civ 814, [2003] 3 All ER 719, [2003] 1 WLR 2683, [2003] STC 1113... 1.25; 55.41, 55.42, 55.44
RAL (Channel Islands) Ltgd v C & E Comrs (Case C-452/03) [2005] STC 1025, [2005] ECR I-3947, [2005] 2 CMLR 50................... 37.5; 54.74
RFC 2012 plc (in liquidation) v A-G for Scotland [2017] UKSC 45, [2017] 1 WLR 2767, [2017] STC 1566.. 8.94, 8.194
Rae v Lazard Investment Co Ltd [1963] 1 WLR 555, 41 TC 1, [1963] TR 149 .... 18.36
Ramsay (WT) Ltd v IRC [1982] AC 300, [1981] 1 All ER 865, [1981] STC 174, HL... 1.24; 2.4, 2.21, 2.22, 2.23, 2.24, 2.25, 2.29, 2.32, 2.33, 2.34, 2.35, 2.36, 2.37, 2.38, 2.39, 2.40, 2.41, 2.48; 22.44, 22.101; 27.56; 29.127; 43.127
Ramsay v R & C Comrs [2012] UKFTT 176 (TC), [2013] WTLR 307 .... 22.101
Ransom v Higgs [1974] 3 All ER 949, [1974] STC 539, HL................................. 10.18

	PARA
Ratcliffe v R & C Comrs [2013] UKFTT 420 (TC)	8.174
Ratcliffe, Re, Holmes v McMullan [1999] STC 262	30.61, 30.62; 53.93
Rawley v Rawley (1876) 1 QBD 460	22.41
Raynor (deceased) v R & C Comrs [2011] UKFTT 813 (TC), [2012] STI 166	10.146
Reed v Nova Securities Ltd (1985)	43.125
Reed Employment plc v R & C Comrs (2014)	8.95
Reed (HMIT) v Clark [1985] STC 323, 58 TC 528	18.6; 27.9, 27.13
Reed (S) v R & C Comrs [2011] UKFTT 92 (TC)	10.150
Reeves (William) v R & C Comrs [2017] UKFTT 192 (TC), [2017] STI 1123	24.19
Regan v R & C Comrs [2012] UKFTT 21 (TC)	23.22
Reid v R & C Comrs [2016] UKFTT 79 (TC), [2016] SFTD 312, [2016] STI 1268	8.42
Reisch (2004)	54.31
Rendell v Went (Inspector of Taxes) [1964] 1 WLR 650, [1964] 2 All ER 464, (1964) 43 ATC 123	8.125, 8.126
Republic National Bank of New York v C & E Comrs (unreported, 1998)	40.65
Rewe-Zentral AG v Bundesmonopolverwaltung für Branntwein (Cassis de Dijon) (Case 120/78) [1979] ECR 649, [1979] 3 CMLR 494, ECJ	54.59, 54.61, 54.63, 54.68
Reynaud v IRC [1999] STC (SCD) 185	2.37; 28.102
Rheinmuhlen-Dusseldorf v Einfuhr-und Vorratsstelle fur Getreide und Futtermittel (Case 166/73) [1974] ECR 33	54.8
Rice (Jeremy) v R & C Comrs [2014] UKFTT 133 (TC)	20.24
Richard v Mackay (Hon AB) [2008] WTLR 1667	27A.34
Richardson v Delaney [2001] STC 1328, [2001] IRLR 663	8.143
Richardson v Worrall [1985] STC 693, 58 TC 642	8.92
Riches v Westminster Bank Ltd [1947] 1 All ER 469, 28 TC 159, HL	14.6
Ricketts v Colquhoun [1925] 1 KB 725, 10 TC 118, CA; aff'd [1926] AC 1, 10 TC 118, HL	8.173, 8.174
Ridge Securities Ltd v IRC [1964] 1 All ER 275, 44 TC 373	10.118
Rignell v Andrews [1990] STC 410	7.111
Riskstop Consulting Ltd v R & C Comrs [2015] UKFTT 469 (TC), [2015] STI 2902	40.81
Robertson v IRC [2002] STC (SCD) 182	30.12, 30.43
Robertson v IRC (No 2) [2002] STC (SCD) 242	30.43
Robinson Family Ltd v R & C Comrs [2012] UKFTT 360 (TC), [2012] STI 2519	39.37
Robson v Dixon [1972] 3 All ER 671, 48 TC 527	18.7, 18.48
Rochdale Hornets Football Club Co Ltd v C & E Comrs [1975] VATTR 71	39.20
Roelich (Paul) v R & C Comrs (2014)	47.5
Rogge, Kent & JM Kent Settlement v R & C Comrs [2012] UKFTT 49 (TC), [2012] WTLR 537, [2012] STI 1206	16.98
Rolfe v Nagel [1982] STC 53, 55 TC 585, CA	10.106
Rompelman v Minister van Financiën (Case C-268/83) [1985] ECR 655, [1985] 3 CMLR 202, ECJ	37.5
Roome v Edwards [1979] 1 WLR 860, [1979] STC 546; on appeal [1980] 1 All ER 850, [1980] STC 99, CA; revs'd [1981] 1 All ER 736, [1981] STC 96, HL	1.25; 25.42, 25.82
Rosser v IRC (2003)	31.66
Rousseau-Wilmot SA v Caisse de Compensation de l'Organisation Autonome Nationale de l'Industrie et du Commerce (Organic) (Case C-295/84) [1988] 2 All ER 557, [1988] ECR 817, [1988] STC 251, ECJ	37.2

	PARA
Rowe & Maw v C & E Comrs [1975] 2 All ER 444, [1975] 1 WLR 129	40.97
Rowe, Worrall v R & C Comrs [2015] EWHC 1511 (Admin)	5.28; 55.21, 55.26, 55.83
Royal Bank of Canada v IRC [1972] 1 All ER 225, 47 TC 565	18.126
Royal Bank of Scotland v Greece (Case C-311/97) [1999] ECR I-2651, sub nom Royal Bank of Scotland v Greek State [2000] STC 733, ECJ	54.45
Rumbelow v R & C Comrs [2014] UKFTT 637 (TC)	18.7; 27.14
Rusling (Robert) v R & C Comrs [2014] UKFTT 692 (TC)	13.22
Russell v IRC (1988)	30.157
Russell (WSG) v R & C Comrs [2012] UKFTT 623 (TC)	20.21
Rutledge v IRC 1929 SC 379, 14 TC 490	10.23
Ryall v Hoare [1923] 2 KB 447, 8 TC 521	13.15
Ryan v Crabtree Denims Ltd [1987] STC 402, 60 TC 183	10.102
Rye v Rye [1962] AC 496, [1962] 1 All ER 146, HL	29.126; 44.8
Rysaffe Trustee Co (CI) Ltd v IRC [2002] EWHC 1114 (Ch), [2002] STC 872 *aff'd* [2003] STC 536, CA	28.104; 32.4, 32.7

S

SCA Packaging Ltd v R & C Comrs [2006] STC (SCD) 426, [2006] STI 1625	8.143
Safir v Skattemyndigheten i Dalarnas Lan (Case C-118/96) [1999] QB 451, [1998] ECR I-1897, [1998] STC 1043, ECJ	54.31, 54.49
Säger v Dennemeyer & Co Ltd (Case C-76/90) [1991] ECR I-4221, [1993] 3 CMLR 639, ECJ	54.61
Sainsbury (J) plc v O'Connor [1990] STC 516; *aff'd* [1991] 1 WLR 963, [1991] STC 318, CA	2.48; 43.47
St Aubyn v A-G [1952] AC 15, [1951] 2 All ER 473, HL	29.122
St Clair-ford (Youlden's Executor) v Ryder [2007] RVR 12, [2006] WTLR 1647	28.67
St Dunstan's v Major [1997] STC (SCD) 212	53.85
Salt v Chamberlain [1979] STC 750, 53 TC 143, [1979] TR 203	10.19
Salt v Fernandez [1997] STC (SCD) 271	10.41
Samadian (Dr S) v R & C Comrs [2013] UKFTT 115 (TC)	10.150, 10.151
Samarkand Film Partnership No 3 v R & C Comrs [2011] UKFTT 610 (TC), [2012] SFTD 1	10.28
Sansom v Peay [1976] 3 All ER 375, [1976] STC 494	23.62; 25.142
Sanz de Lera, criminal proceedings (Case C-163/94) [1995] ECR I-4821, [1996] 1 CMLR 631	54.49
Sargent v Barnes [1978] 2 All ER 737, [1978] STC 322	10.151
Saunders v C & E Comrs [1980] VATTR 53	44.71
Saunders v United Kingdom (19187/91) [1997] BCC 872, [1998] 1 BCLC 362, (1977) 23 EHRR 313	55.92
Saunders v Vautier (1841) Cr & Ph 240, 10 LJ Ch 354	25.4
Savarou v R & C Comrs (2011)	10.137
Schemepanel Trading Ltd v C & E Comrs [1996] STC 871	38.84
Schneider v Mills [1993] 3 All ER 377, [1993] STC 430	30.157
Schofield v R & C Comrs [2010] UKFTT 196 (TC), [2010] SFTD 772	2.40, 2.48
Schofield v R & C Comrs (2012)	27.56
Schouten & Meldrum v Netherlands (1994) 19 EHRR 432, E Ct HR	55.83
Scorer v Olin Energy Systems Ltd [1985] AC 645, [1985] 2 All ER 375, [1985] STC 218, HL	4.43
Scottish Provident Institution v IRC (2004)	1.24; 2.25, 2.48
Scotts Atlantic Management Ltd v R & C Comrs (and related appeals) [2013] UKFTT 299 (TC), [2014] SFTD 210, [2013] STi 2574	2.2; 10.133

	PARA
Sebright, Re, Public Trustee v Sebright [1944] Ch 287, [1944] 2 All ER 547	17.3
Sechiari, Re, Argenti v Sechiari [1950] 1 All ER 417, 94 Sol Jo 194, 66 (pt 1) TLR 531	42.142
Secretary of State in Council of India v Scoble [1903] AC 299, 4 TC 618, HL	14.8
Secret Hotels2 Ltd (formerly Med Hotels Ltd) v R & C Comrs [2014] UKSC 16, [2014] 2 All ER 685, [2014] STC 937	40.110
Seddon v R & C Comrs [2015] UKFTT 140 (TC), [2015] SFTD 539, [2015] WTLR 1103	42.152
Selectmove Ltd, Re [1995] 2 All ER 531, [1995] 1 WLR 474, [1995] STC 406, 66 TC 552, CA	4.24
Senex Investments Ltd v R & C Comrs (2011)	48.125
Sere Properties Ltd v R & C Comrs [2013] UKFTT 778 (TC), [2013] STI 1252	10.137
Seymour v Reed [1927] AC 554, 11 TC 625, HL	8.62, 8.105
Sharkey v R & C Comrs [2006] EWHC 300 (Ch), [2006] STC 2026, 77 TC 484	55.82
Sharkey v Wernher [1956] AC 58, [1955] 3 All ER 493, 36 TC 275, HL	3.8; 10.117, 10.119; 19.71
Shchokin v Ukraine (Application 23759/03) [2011] STC 401	55.21
Shepherd v R & C Comrs [2005] STC (SCD) 644	18.6; 27.5, 27.13, 27.16
Shepherd v Law Land plc [1990] STC 795, 63 TC 692	43.47
Sheppard v IRC (No 2) (1993)	3.55, 3.72
Sherwin v Barnes (1931)	13.28
Shilton v Wilmshurst [1989] 1 WLR 179, [1988] STC 868; on appeal [1990] 1 WLR 373, [1990] STC 55, CA; revs'd [1991] 1 AC 684, [1991] 3 All ER 148, [1991] STC 88, HL	8.41, 8.43, 8.44, 8.63
Shop Direct Group v R & C Comrs (and related appeals) [2013] EWHC 942 (Ch), [2013] STC 1709, [2013] BTC 1824	10.102
Shop Direct Group v R & C Comrs [2016] UKSC 7, [2016] 1 WLR 733, [2016] 2 All ER 725	8.41
Shortt v McIlgorm [1945] 1 All ER 391, 26 TC 262	8.173
Shove v Downs Surgical plc [1984] 1 All ER 7, [1984] ICR 532	8.157
Siebe Gorman & Co Ltd v Barclays Bank Ltd [1979] 2 Lloyd's Rep 142	46.23
Significant Ltd v Farrel (Inspector of Taxes) [2005] EWHC 3434 (Ch), [2006] STC 1626, [2006] BTC 755	55.5, 55.83
Sillars v IRC [2004] STC (SCD) 180	29.101
Silva v Charnock (Inspector of Taxes) [2002] STC (SCD) 426	8.96
Simpson v Tate [1925] 2 KB 214, 9 TC 314	8.173
Sinclair v Lee [1993] Ch 497, [1993] 3 All ER 926	42.148, 42.149; 47.51
Skandia America Corpn (USA) v Skatteverket (Case C-7/13) EU:C:2014:2225, [2015] STC 1163, [2014] BVC 43	38.50; 43.191
Skatterministeriet v Vestergaard (Case C-55/98) [1999] ECR I-7641, [2001] 3 CMLR 65	54.53
Skatteverket v A (Case C-101/05) [2008] All ER (EC) 638, [2009] STC 405, [2007] ECR I-11531, [2009] 1 CMLR 35, [2010] BTC 906, [2008] STI 99	54.49
Sloane Robinson Investment Services Ltd (formerly Sloane Robinson Investment Management Ltd) v R & C Comrs [2012] UKFTT 451 (TC), [2012] SFTD 1181, [2012] STI 2929	8.66
Smith v Abbott [1991] STC 661; on appeal [1993] 2 All ER 417, [1993] STC 316, CA; revs'd [1994] 1 All ER 673, [1994] STC 237, HL	8.173
Smith v Schofield [1992] 1 WLR 639, [1992] STC 249, CA; revs'd [1993] 1 WLR 399, [1993] STC 268, HL	
Smith (Herbert) (a firm) v Honour [1999] STC 173, 72 TC 130	10.67

Table of cases xciii

PARA

Smith (Leslie) v R & C Comrs [2010] UKFTT 92 (TC),
  [2010] STI 1672.. 10.63, 10.110
Smith & Williamson Corporate Services v R & C Comrs [2014] UKUT
  666 (TCC), [2016] STC 1393, [2015] BTC 539 .... 8.63; 13.22
Smith's Potato Estates Ltd v Bolland [1948] 2 All ER 367, 30 TC 267, HL......... 10.147
Smyth, Re, Leach v Leach [1898] 1 Ch 89, 77 LT 514....................................... 35.83
Snell v R & C Comrs [2006] EWHC 3350 (Ch), [2006] STC 1279,
  78 TC 294... 27.55, 27.56; 47.38
Snook (James) & Co Ltd v Blasdale [1952] TR 233, 33 TC 244, CA................... 8.158
Societe d'Importation Edouard Leclerc-Siplec v TF1 Publicite SA
  (Case C-412/93) [1995] All ER (EC) 343, [1995] ECR I-179,
  [1995] 3 CMLR 422... 54.52
Soering v United Kingdom (Application 14038/88) (1989) 11 EHRR 439,
  ECtHR... 54.68
Southern Aerial (Communications) Ltd v R & C Comrs [2015] UKFTT 538
  (TC), [2016] SFTD 114 .... 8.105
Southern Railway of Peru Ltd v Owen [1957] AC 334, [1956] 2 All ER 728,
  37 TC 602, HL.. 10.67
Soutter's Executry v IRC [2002] STC (SCD) 385, [2002] WTLR 1207, [2002]
  STI 1259.. 30.157
Sparekassernes Datacenter (SDC) v Skatteministeriet (Case C-2/95)
  [1997] All ER (EC) 610, [1997] STC 932, [1997] ECR I-3017,
  [1997] 3 CMLR 999, [1997] BTC 5395, [1997] BVC 509........................... 40.65
Sparrow Ltd v Inspector of Taxes [2001] STC (SCD) 206 .... 4.182
Spens v IRC [1970] 3 All ER 295, 46 TC 276 .... 17.42
Spritebeam Ltd v R & C Comrs *see* Versteegh Ltd v R & C Comrs
  [2015] UKUT 75 (TCC), [2015] STC 1222, [2015] BTC 507.................... 13.22
Staatssecretaris van Financiën v BGM Verkooijen (Case C-35/98)
  [2000] ECR I-4071, [2002] STC 654, ECJ................................ 54.49, 54.61, 54.62
Staatssecretaris van Financiën v Coöperatieve Aardappelenbewaarplaats
  GA (Case 154/80) [1981] ECR 445, [1981] 3 CMLR 337, ECJ................. 37.7
Staatssecretaris van Financiën v Hong Kong Trade Development Council
  (Case 89/81) [1982] ECR 1277, [1983] 1 CMLR 73, ECJ........................... 37.5
Staatsssecretaris van Financiën v X BV (Case C-651/11) [2013] STC 1893,
  [2013] BVC 209, [2013] STI 2072.. 38.26
Stack v Dowden [2007] UKHL 17, [2007] 2 AC 432,
  [2007] 2 WLR 831... 16.93; 51.55; 52.1, 52.61
Stamp Duties Comr (Queensland) v Livingston [1965] AC 694,
  [1964] 3 All ER 692, PC.. 21.103
Stamp Duties Comr of New South Wales v Owens (1953) 88 CLR 67............ 29.44
Stamp Duties Comr of New South Wales v Perpetual Trustee Co Ltd
  [1943] AC 425, [1943] 1 All ER 525, PC... 32.94
Stamp Duties Comr of New South Wales v Permanent Trustee Co [1956] AC
  512, [1956] 3 WLR 152, [1956] 2 All ER 512... 29.44
Stanley v IRC [1944] 1 All ER 230, 26 TC 12, CA.. 16.71
Starke (Brown's Executors) v IRC [1994] 1 WLR 888, [1994] STC 295;
  aff'd [1996] 1 All ER 622, [1995] STC 689, CA................. 31.63, 31.64, 31.66
Stec v UK (application 65731/01) (2006) 43 EHRR 47, 20 BHRC 348 .... 55.44
Steele v European Vinyls Corpn (Holdings) BV [1995] STC 31; on appeal
  sub nom Steele v EVC International [1996] STC 785, CA................. 41.23; 43.45
Steibelt v Paling [1999] STC 594, 71 TC 376... 22.72
Stekel v Ellice [1973] 1 All ER 465, [1973] 1 WLR 191..................................... 8.23
Stenhouse Holdings v IRC 1971 SLT 74.. 1.21

	PARA
Stephens v T Pittas Ltd [1983] STC 576, 56 TC 722	41.128
Stephenson v Barclays Bank Trust Co Ltd [1975] 1 All ER 625, [1975] STC 151	25.6, 25.7
Stevenson v Wishart [1986] 1 All ER 404, [1986] STC 74; aff'd [1987] 2 All ER 428, [1987] STC 266, CA	16.68
Stolkin v R & C Comrs [2011] UKFTT 831 (TC), [2012] SFTD 541, [2012] STI 223	22.71
Stones v Hall [1989] STC 138	8.111
Stonor (executors of Dickinson) v IRC [2001] STC (SCD) 199	21.23; 30.10
Strand Options & Futures Ltd v Vojak (Inspector of Taxes) [2003] EWHC 67 (Ch), [2003] STC 331	42.28
Strange v Openshaw [1983] STC 416, 57 TC 544	19.70
Street v Mountford [1985] [2 All ER 289, HL	49.32
Strong & Co of Romsey Ltd v Woodifield [1906] AC 448, 5 TC 215, HL	10.145
Sub One (t/a Subway) v R & C Comrs [2014] EWCA Civ 773, [2014] BVC 29, [2014] STI 2111	40.27
Sugden v Kent [2001] STC (SCD) 158	14.41
Sutherland & Partners' Appeal, Re [1993] STC 399, sub nom Sutherland & Partners v Barnes 66 TC 663; revs'd sub nom Sutherland v Gustar (Inspector of Taxes) [1994] Ch 304, [1994] 4 All ER 1, [1994] STC 387, 66 TC 663, CA	1.21
Sutton v R & C Comrs [2011] UKFTT 769 (TC)	14.6
Svensson & Gustavsson v Ministre du Logement et de l'Urbanisme (Case C-484/93) [1995] ECR I-3955, ECJ	54.31
Swires v Renton [1991] STC 490, 64 TC 315	25.82

T

T v T (financial relief: pensions) [1998] 2 FCR 364, [1998] 1 FLR 1072	52.13
T Settlement, Re (2002) 4 ITLR 820	27A.73, 27A.80
Talentcore Ltd (t/a Team Spirits) v R & C Comrs [2010] UKFTT 148 (TC), [2010] SFTD 744	8.31
Tamosius v United Kingdom [2002] STC 1307, ECtHR	55.61
Tapemaze Ltd v Melluish (Inspector of Taxes) [2000] STC 189, 73 TC 167	10.103
Tapsell (Mr & Mrs) & Lester (Mr) (t/a Partnership 'The Granleys') v R & C Comrs [2011] UKFTT 376 (TC)	48.71
Taylor v Good [1973] 2 All ER 785, [1973] STC 383; on appeal [1974] 1 All ER 1137, [1974] STC 148, CA	10.23, 10.26; 12.102, 12.110
Taylor v IRC [2004] EWCA Civ 174, [2004] STC 683	55.83
Taylor v Provan [1973] 2 All ER 65, [1973] STC 170, CA; revs'd [1974] 1 All ER 1201, [1974] STC 168, HL	8.21, 8.95, 8.174
Taylor v Taylor [1938] 1 KB 320, [1937] 3 All ER 571, CA	14.26
Taylor Clark International Ltd v Lewis [1997] STC 499, 71 TC 226; on appeal [1998] STC 1259, 71 TC 226, CA	22.44
Templeton v Jacobs see Jacobs v Templeton	
Tenbry Investments Ltd v Peugeot Talbot Motor Co Ltd [1992] STC 791, [1993] 1 EGLR 71, [1993] 06 EG 104	14.26; 18.75
Tennant v Smith [1892] AC 150, 3 TC 158, HL	8.92, 8.110, 8.114
Test Claimants in the CFC & Dividend Group Litigation Order v R & C Comrs (Case C-201/05) [2008] STC 1513, [2008] ECR I-2875, [2008] 2 CMLR 53	54.75
Test Claimants in the FII Group Litigation v IRC (Case C-446/04) [2007] STC 326, [2006] ECR I-11753, [2007] 1 CMLR 35	41.46; 54.49, 54.75, 54.76

Table of cases xcv

	PARA
Test Claimants in the Franked Investment Income Litigation v IRC [2013] EWHC 3757 (Ch), [2013] BTC 826, [2013] STI 3669	1.42
Test Claimants in Class IV of the ACT Group Litigation v IRC (Case C-374/04) [2007] All ER (EC) 351, [2007] STC 404, [2006] ECR I-11673	54.56, 54.64, 54.75
Test Claimants in the Thin Capitalisation Group Litigation (Case C-524/04) [2007] STC 906, [2007] ECR I-2107, [2007] 2 CMLR 31	41.98; 54.31, 54.45, 54.49, 54.75, 54.76
Teward v IRC [2001] STC (SCD) 36	9.41
Thomas v IRC [1981] STC 382, [1981] TR 83	32.7; 33.118
Thomas v Marshall [1953] 1 All ER 1102, 34 TC 178, HL	16.96
Thomas v R & C Comrs [2014] UKFTT 66 (TC)	14.3
Thompson v Magnesium Elektron Ltd [1944] 1 All ER 126, 26 TC 1, CA	10.104
Thorne v R & C Comrs [2014] UKFTT 730 (TC), [2014] STI 3025	10.28
Three H Aircraft Hire (a firm) v C & E Comrs [1982] STC 653	38.28
Three Rivers District Council v Governor & Company of the Bank of England (No 6) (2005)	55.62
Threlfall v Jones [1993] STC 199; revs'd [1994] Ch 107, [1993] STC 537, CA	10.63
Tiffin v Lester Aldridge LLP [2012] EWCA Civ 35, [2012] 1 WLR 1887, [2012] 2 All ER 1113	8.23
Tilley v Wales [1943] AC 386, 25 TC 136, HL	8.65
Timothy James Consulting Ltd v Wilton [2015] ICR 764, [2015] IRLR 368	8.152
Tod v Mudd [1987] STC 141, 60 TC 237	22.78
Tod (Inspector of Taxes) v South Essex Motors (Basildon) Ltd [1988] STC 392, 60 TC 598	4.184
Tomlinson v Glyns Executor & Trustee Co [1970] 1 All ER 381, 45 TC 600, CA	25.5
Tomlinson v R & C Comrs [2017] UKFTT 489 (TC)	8.22
Torkington (JS) v R & C Comrs [2010] UKFTT 441 (TC), [2010] STI 2925	7.45
Toronto-Dominion Bank v Oberoi (2004)	8.111
Total Mauritius Ltd v Mauritius Revenue Authority [2011] UKPC 40, [2012] STC 100, [2011] STI 2999	10.107
Totel Ltd v R & C Comrs [2014] UKUT 485 (TCC), [2015] STC 610, [2014] BVC 542	55.21
Tottenham Hotspur Ltd v R & C Comrs [2016] UKFTT 389 (TC), [2016] SFTD 803, [2016] STI 2499	8.143
Tower Radio Ltd; Total Property Support Services Ltd v R & C Comrs [2013] UKFT 387 (TC), [2014] SFTD 377, [2013] STI 3243	8.66
Tower Radio v R & C Comrs [2015] UKUT 60 (TCC), [2015] STC 1257, [2015] BTC 505	2.40
Townsend (Inspector of Taxes) v Grundy (1933) 18 TC 140	13.15
Travers Will Trust (trustees of) v R & C Comrs (2013)	16.22
Tuczka v R & C Comrs [2010] UKFTT 53 (TC), [2010] WTLR 715, [2010] STI 1594	18.6, 18.14; 27.16
Turner v Follett [1973] STC 148, 48 TC 614, CA	24.1, 24.2
Turvey v Dentons (1923) Ltd [1953] 1 QB 218, [1952] 2 All ER 1025	14.26

U

UBS AG v R & Comrs; DB Services (UK) Ltd v R & C Comrs [2016] UKSC 13, [2016] 1 WLR 1005, [2016] 3 All ER 1	2.46; 6.21
UK Storage Co (SW) Ltd v R & C Comrs [2012] UKUT 359 (TCC), [2013] STC 361, [2012] BVC 1955	39.21

PARA

Underwood v R & C Comrs [2008] EWCA Civ 1423, [2009] STC 239,
    79 TC 631.. 19.78
Unigate (Guernsey) Ltd v McGregor [1996] STC (SCD) 1..................... 41.153
Union Royale Belge des Societes de Football Association ASBL v Bosman
    (Case C-415/93) [1996] All ER (EC) 97, [1995] ECR I-4921, ECJ............ 54.52
Unit Construction Co Ltd v Bullock [1959] Ch 147, [1958] 3 All ER 186; on
    appeal [1959] Ch 315, [1959] 1 All ER 591, CA; revs'd [1960] AC 351,
    [1959] 3 All ER 831, HL.. 18.16
University of Huddersfield High Education Corporation v C & E Comr
    (Case C-223/03) [2006] Ch 387, [2006] 2 WLR 905, [2006] STC 980....... 2.44
Untelrab Ltd v McGregor [1996] STC (SCD) 1.......................... 18.16, 18.35; 41.153
Upjohn Co v United States 449 US 383 (1981).. 55.62

V

Vaines v R & C Comrs [2013] UKFTT 576 (TC)............................ 10.146; 44.3; 45.10
Van den Berghs Ltd v Clark [1935] AC 431, 19 TC 390, HL................ 10.106; 31.44
Van den Hout van Ejinsbergen v Staatsecretaris van Financien (Case
    C-444/04) [2007] STC 71, [2006] ECR I-3617, [2006] CEC 829................ 40.37
Van Dijk's Boekhuis BV v Staatssecretaris van Financiën (Case 139/84)
    [1987] ECR 1405, [1985] ECR 1405, [1986] 2 CMLR 575............................ 37.5
Van Hilten-Van der Heijden (Case C-513/03) [2008] STC 1245,
    [2006] ECR I-1957, [2006] WTLR 919.. 27A.53; 54.76
Varty v Lynes [1976] 3 All ER 447, [1976] STC 508.. 23.61
Vasili v Christensen (2003) SpC 377.. 8.119
Vastberga Taxi Association & Vlic v Sweden (2002) unreported............. 55.82, 55.83
Vaughan-Jones v Vaughan-Jones [2015] EWHC 1086 (Ch),
    [2015] STI 1883... 30.157
Vaughan-Neil v IRC [1979] 3 All ER 481, [1979] STC 644....................... 8.63, 8.134
Verder Lab Tec GmbH & Co KG v Finanzamt Hilden (Case C-657/13)
    EU:C:2015:331, [2015] BTC 18.. 54.46
Vereniging Happy Family v Inspecteur der Omzetbelasting (Case C- 289/86)
    [1988] ECR 3655, [1989] 3 CMLR 743, ECJ... 37.6
Vertigan v Brady [1988] STC 91.. 8.114
Vestey v IRC [1980] AC 1148, [1979] 3 All ER 976, [1980] STC 10, HL...... 1.25; 3.5;
                                                                                           18.111, 18.116, 18.120
Vestey's (Lord) Executors v IRC [1949] 1 All ER 1108, 31 TC 1, HL.............. 16.102
Vodafone 2 v R & C Comrs [2009] EWCA Civ 446, [2010] Ch 77,
    [2010] 2 WLR 288, [2010] Bus LR 96, [2009] STC 1480,
    [2010] Eu LR 110, [2009] BTC 273, [2009] STI 1795.................................. 1.42
Vodafone Cellular Ltd v Shaw [1995] STC 353, 69 TC 376;
    revs'd [1997] STC 734, 69 TC 376, CA... 41.42; 54.75

W

WHA Ltd v R & C Comrs (2007).. 2.44
Wagstaff v R & C Comrs [2014] UKFTT 43 (TC), [2014] WTLR 547,
    [2014] STI 883... 23.62; 25.2
Wakeling v Pearce [1995] STC (SCD) 96... 23.61
Walapu v R & C Comrs [2016] EWHC 658 (Admin), [2016] BTC 14,
    [2016] STI 1336.. 5.28; 55.5, 55.83,
                                                                                                55.91, 55.93
Walding's Executors v IRC [1996] STC 13... 31.55
Walker v Joint Credit Card Co Ltd [1982] STC 427, 55 TC 617....................... 10.131
Walker's Executors v IRC [2001] STC (SCD) 86... 31.55

Table of cases xcvii

PARA

Wallentin v Riksskatterverket (Case C-169/03) [2004] ECR I-6443, [2004] 3 CMLR 24.. 54.44
Walton v IRC [1996] STC 68, [1996] RVR 55, CA.................................. 28.73; 31.72
Wannell v Rothwell [1996] STC 450, 68 TC 719...................................... 11.41
Wardhaugh v Penrith Rugby Union Football Club [2002] EWHC 918 (Ch), [2002] STC 776 .... 22.78
Warrington v Sterland [1989] 1 WLR 1163, [1989] STC 577 .... 25.6
Wasa Liv Omsesidigt v Sweden (Application 13013/87) (1988) 58 DR 163, E Ct HR 55.25
Waterloo plc v IRC [2002] STC (SCD) 95 .... 9.122, 9.124
Watney Combe Reid & Co Ltd v Pike [1982] STC 733, 57 TC 372 .... 10.131
Watton v Tippett [1996] STC 101, 69 TC 491; *aff'd* [1997] STC 893, 69 TC 491, CA 22.73, 22.74
Weald Leasing & RBS Deutschland Holdings GmbH [2011] STC 596, [2011] BVC 118, [2011] STI 264... 54.74
Webb v Conelee Properties Ltd [1982] STC 913, 56 TC 149.................. 12.23
Weidert & Paulus (2004) 54.49, 54.61, 54.62, 54.81
Weight v Salmon (1935) 19 TC 174, 153 LT 55, HL................................. 9.2
Weightwatchers (UK) Ltd v R & C Comrs [2010] UKFTT 384 (TC), [2010] STI 2952... 8.22
Westcott (Inspector of Taxes) v Bryan [1969] 2 Ch 324, [1969] 3 WLR 255, [1969] 3 All ER 564.. 8.126
West (Inspector of Taxes) v Trennery [2005] UKHL 5, [2005] 1 All ER 827, [2005] STC 214 .... 27A.87
Westminster Bank Executor & Trustee Co (Channel Islands) Ltd v National Bank of Greece SA (1968) 46 TC 472; on appeal [1970] 1 QB 256, [1969] 3 All ER 504, 46 TC 472, CA; *aff'd sub nom* National Bank of Greece SA v Westminster Bank Executor & Trustee Co (Channel Islands) Ltd [1971] AC 945, [1971] 1 All ER 233, 46 TC 472, HL............... 14.33
Westmoreland Investments Ltd v Macniven *see* Macniven v Westmoreland Investments Ltd
Weston (Gordon L) v R & C Comrs [2014] UKFTT 11 (TC) 19.67, 19.69
Weston (Weston's Executors) v IRC [2000] STC 1064 .... 31.48
Wetherspoon (JD) plc v R & C Comrs [2008] STC (SCD) 460.............. 48.18
Wharf Properties Ltd v IRC [1997] AC 505, [1997] 2 WLR 334, [1997] STC 351, PC 12.45
Wheatley (Wheatley's Executors) v IRC [1998] STC (SCD) 60.............. 31.63
Wheels Common Investment Fund Trustees Ltd v R & C Comrs (Case C-424/11) [2014] STC 495, [2013] Pens LR 149, [2013] STI 589....... 50.14
White v White [2001] 1 AC 596, [2001] 1 All ER 1, [2000] 3 FCR 555, HL.. 52.1, 52.13
White (AJ) (VAT decision 15388/98).. 40.30
White (J) v R & C Comrs [2014] UKFTT 214 (TC), [2014] STI 1877 .... 10.137
White (Noel) v R & C Comrs [2014] UKFTT 214 (TC), [2014] STI 1877 .... 10.150, 10.151
Whitehead v Tubbs (Elastics) Ltd [1984] STC 1, 57 TC 472, CA 10.106
Whitehead's Will Trusts, Re [1971] 2 All ER 1334, [1971] 1 WLR 833............ 27A.34
Whitney v IRC [1926] AC 37, 10 TC 88, HL 18.1; 54.55
Whittles v Uniholdings Ltd (No 3) [1996] STC 914, 68 TC 528, CA...... 2.47
Wicks v Firth [1982] Ch 355, [1982] 2 All ER 9, [1982] STC 76, CA; on appeal [1983]2 AC 214, [1983] 1 All ER 151, [1983] STC 25, HL.. 8.105, 8.127

	PARA
Wielockx v Inspecteur der Directe Belastingen (Case C-80/94) [1995] All ER (EC) 769, [1995] STC 876, ECJ	54.45, 54.62
Wight v IRC [1984] RVR 163, 264 Estates Gazette 935, Lands Tribunal	28.67
Wilcock v Eve [1995] STC 18, 67 TC 223	8.41, 8.105; 9.41
Wilden Pump Engineering Co v Fusfield [1985] FSR 159	55.62
Wilkie v IRC [1952] Ch 153, [1952] 1 All ER 92, 32 TC 495	18.3
Wilkins v Rogerson [1961] 1 All ER 358, 39 TC 344, CA	8.93, 8.94, 8.104
Williams v Bullivant [1983] STC 107, 56 TC 159	19.69; 26.21
Williams v IRC [1980] 3 All ER 321, [1980] STC 535, 54 TC 257, [1980] TR 347, HL	3.33, 3.54, 3.55
Williams (personal representatives of Williams deceased) v IRC (2005)	31.64
Williams v Merrylees [1987] 1 WLR 1511, [1987] STC 445	23.23, 23.24
Williams v Simmonds [1981] STC 715, 55 TC 17, [1981] TR 33	8.142
Williams v Singer [1921] 1 AC 65, 7 TC 387, HL	18.38
Williams v Todd [1988] STC 676	8.124
Williams & Humbert Ltd v W & H Trade Marks (Jersey) Ltd [1986] AC 368, [1986] 1 All ER 129, HL	27A.73
Williamson & Soden Solicitors v Briars (unreported, 20 May 2011)	8.23
Willingdale v International Commercial Bank Ltd (1978)	14.6
Willis v Peeters Picture Frames Ltd [1983] STC 453, 56 TC 436, CA	41.65; 47.35
Willis v United Kingdom [2002] 2 FCR 743, E Ct HR	55.44
Willson v Hooker [1995] STC 1142	18.72
Wilson (Inspector of Taxes) v Clayton [2004] EWCA Civ 1657, [2005] STC 157, [2005] IRLR 108	8.41, 8.146
Wimpy International Ltd v Warland [1988] STC 149, 61 TC 51; aff'd [1989] STC 273, 61 TC 51, CA	48.17
Wing Hung Lai v Bale [1999] STC (SCD) 238	4.33
Winterton v Edwards [1980] 2 All ER 56, [1980] STC 206	12.107
Wisdom v Chamberlain [1969] 1 All ER 332, 45 TC 92, CA	10.24, 10.28
Withers (Inspector of Taxes) v Nethersole [1948] 1 All ER 400, 64 TLR 157, 41 R & IT 28	13.12
Withers v Wynard (1938) 21 TC 724	27.15
Wood v Holden (Inspector of Taxes) [2005] EWHC 547 (Ch), [2005] STC 443, [2006] 2 BCLC 210	18.16, 18.35; 41.153; 54.75
Wood v Owen [1941] 1 KB 42, 23 TC 541	17.4
Wood (Michael), decs'd, personal represetaties v R & C Comrs [2015] UKFTT 282 (TC)	55.82, 55.83
Woodhall (Woodhall's Personal Representative) v IRC [2000] STC (SCD) 558	32.28
Woodhouse v IRC (1936)	14.3

X

X v Belgium (1982) unreported, EC of HR	55.61
X v A (2000)	25.6
X v Y (2002)	54.45, 54.49, 54.64
XX v R & C Comrs (2010)	10.108
X-Wind Power Ltd v R & C Comrs [2016] UKFTT 317 (TC)	20.41

Y

Yarmouth v France (1887) 19 QBD 647, 4 TLR 1	22.21; 48.17
Yates v GCA International Ltd [1991] STC 157, 64 TC 37	18.91
Yates v R & C Comrs [2012] UKFTT 568 (TC), 15 ITL Rep 205, [2013] STI 196	27.14
Young v Pearce; Young v Scrutton [1996] STC 743, 70 TC 331	16.94, 16.102; 51.55

Table of cases xcix

PARA

Yuill v Fletcher [1983] STC 598, 58 TC 145; *aff'd* [1984] STC 401,
58 TC 145, CA 12.105
Yuill v Wilson [1980] 3 All ER 7, [1980] STC 460, HL 12.105, 12.109
Yukos v Russia (2011) 55.21

Z

ZM & AB v R & C Comrs (2013) 55.83
Zetland (Trustees of) v R & C Comrs [2013] UKFTT 284 (TC),
[2013] STI 2424 .... 31.48
Zim Properties Ltd v Proctor [1985] STC 90, 58 TC 371 .... 19.66, 19.67, 19.68,
19.69; 47.35
Zorab *see* Kasperbauer v Griffith

Decisions of the European Court of Justice are listed below numerically. These decisions are also included in the preceding alphabetical table.

30/59: De Gezamenlijke Steenkolenmijnen in Limburg v High Authority
[1961] ECR 1, ECJ 54.81
6/64: Costa v Ente Nazionale per l'Energia Elettrica (ENEL)
[1964] ECR 585, [1964] CMLR 425 .... 54.21, 54.24, 54.25
48/65: Lütticke GmbH v Commission [1966] ECR 19, [1966] CMLR 378 .... 54.7
11/70: Internationale Handelsgesellschaft mbH v Einfuhr und
Vorratsstelle für Getreide und Futtermittel [1970] ECR 1125,
[1972] CMLR 255, ECJ 54.25, 54.68
166/73: Rheinmuhlen-Dusseldorf v Einfuhr-und Vorratsstelle fur Getreide
und Futtermittel [1974] ECR 33 .... 54.8
106/77: Amministrazione delle Finanze dello Stato v Simmenthal SpA
[1978] ECR 629, [1978] 3 CMLR 263, ECJ 54.25
120/78: Rewe-Zentral AG v Bundesmonopolverwaltung für Branntwein
(Cassis de Dijon) [1979] ECR 649, [1979] 3 CMLR 494, ECJ 54.59, 54.61,
54.63, 54.68
34/79: R v Henn & Darby [1981] AC 850, (1980) 71 Cr App Rep 44,
[1980] 2 CMLR 229 .... 38.2; 54.8
154/80: Staatssecretaris van Financiën v Coöperatieve
Aardappelenbewaarplaats GA [1981] ECR 445, [1981] 3 CMLR
337, ECJ 37.7
53/81: Levin v Secretary of State for Justice [1982] ECR 1035,
[1982] 2 CMLR 454, ECJ 54.44
89/81: Staatssecretaris van Financiën v Hong Kong Trade Development
Council [1982] ECR 1277, [1983] 1 CMLR 73, ECJ 37.5
268/83: Rompelman v Minister van Financiën [1985] ECR 655,
[1985] 3 CMLR 202, ECJ 37.5
270/83: EC Commission v France [1986] ECR 273,
[1987] 1 CMLR 401, ECJ 54.45,
54.61, 54.64
52/84: EC Commission v Belgium [1986] ECR 89, [1987] 1 CMLR 710, ECJ 54.81
139/84: Van Dijk's Boekhuis BV v Staatssecretaris van Financiën
[1987] ECR 1405, [1985] ECR 1405, [1986] 2 CMLR 575 .... 37.5
295/84: Rousseau-Wilmot SA v Caisse de Compensation de l'Organisation
Autonome Nationale de l'Industrie et du Commerce (Organic)
[1986)353/85: EC Commission v United Kingdom [1988] 2 All ER 557,
[1988] ECR 817, [1988] STC 251, ECJ 37.2
416/85 EC Commission v United Kingdom [1990] 2 QB 130,
[1988] 3 WLR 1261, [1989] 1 All ER 364 .... 39.1

c   *Table of cases*

	PARA
C-138/86 & 139/86: Direct Cosmetics Ltd & Laughtons Photographs Ltd v C & E Comrs [1988] ECR 3937, [1988] STC 540, ECJ	37.5; 54.8
C-269/86: Mol v Inspecteur der Invoerrechten en Accijnzen, ECJ [1988] ECR 3627, [1989] 3 CMLR 729	37.6
C-289/86: Vereniging Happy Family v Inspecteur der Omzetbelasting [1988] ECR 3655, [1989] 3 CMLR 743, ECJ	37.6
C-81/87: R v HM Treasury, ex p Daily Mail & General Trust plc [1989] QB 446, [1989] 1 All ER 328, [1988] ECR 5483, [1988] STC 787, ECJ	54.44, 54.46
C-230/87: Naturally Yours Cosmetics Ltd v C & E Comrs [1988] ECR 6365, [1989] 1 CMLR 797, [1988] STC 879, ECJ	37.5; 38.2
C-76/90: Säger v Dennemeyer & Co Ltd [1991] ECR I-4221, [1993] 3 CMLR 639, ECJ	54.61
C-97/90: Lennartz v Finanzamt Munchen III [1991] ECR I-3795, [1993] 3 CMLR 689, [1995] STC 514, [1991] STI 700, ECJ	37.5; 38.82
C-204/90: Bachmann v Belgium [1992] ECR I-249, [[1994] STC 855, ECJ; apld *sub nom* Bachmann v Belgium [1994] 3 CMLR 263	54.61, 54.62
C-267/91 & 268/91: Keck v Mithouard [1993] ECR I-6097, [1995] 1 CMLR 101, ECJ	54.52
C-275/92: C & E Comrs v Schindler [1994] QB 610, [1994] 2 All ER 193, [1994] ECR I-1039, ECJ	54.31
C-279/93: Finanzamt Köln-Altstadt v Schumacker [1996] QB 28, [1995] All ER (EC) 319, [1995] STC 306, ECJ	54.44, 54.56, 54.57, 54.58
C-358/93: Ministerio Fiscal v Bordessa [1995] All ER (EC) 385, [1995] ECR I-361, [1996] 2 CMLR 13	54.31
C-384/93: Alpine Investments BV v Minister van Financien [1995] All ER (EC) 543, [1995] ECR I-1141, ECJ	54.52
C-412/93: Societe d'Importation Edouard Leclerc-Siplec v TF1 Publicite SA [1995] All ER (EC) 343, [1995] ECR I-179, [1995] 3 CMLR 422	54.52
C-415/93: Union Royale Belge des Societes de Football Association ASBL v Bosman [1996] All ER (EC) 97, [1995] ECR I-4921, ECJ	54.52
C-484/93: Svensson & Gustavsson v Ministre du Logement et de l'Urbanisme [1995] ECR I-3955, ECJ	54.31
C-4/94: BLP Group plc v C & E Comrs [1995] All ER (EC) 401, [1996] 1 WLR 174, [1995] STC 424, ECJ	37.5
C-55/94: Gebhard v Consiglio dell 'Ordine degli Avvocati e Procuration di Milano [1996] All ER (EC) 189, [1995] ECR I-4165, ECJ	54.53, 54.61, 54.63, 54.64
C-80/94: Wielockx v Inspecteur der Directe Belastingen [1995] All ER (EC) 769, [1996] 1 WLR 84, [1995] STC 876, ECJ	54.45, 54.62
C-90/94: Haahr Petroleum Ltd v Abenra Havn [1997] ECR I-4085, [1998] 1 CMLR 771, ECJ	54.60
C-107/94: Asscher v Staatssecretaris van Financien [1996] ECR I-3089, [1996] All ER (EC) 757, [1996] STC 1025, ECJ	54.56
C-163/94: Sanz de Lera, criminal proceedings [1995] ECR I-4821, [1996] 1 CMLR 631	54.49
C-2/95: Sparekassernes Datacenter (SDC) v Skatterministeriet [1997] All ER (EC) 610, [1997] STC 932, [1997] ECR I-3017, [1997] 3 CMLR 999, [1997] BTC 5395, [1997] BVC 509	40.65
C-28/95: Leur-Bloem v Inspecteur der Belastingdienst/Ondernemingen Amsterdam 2 [1998] QB 182, [1997] All ER (EC) 738, [1997] STC 1205, ECJ	54.92

Table of cases ci

PARA

C-250/95: Futura Participations SA, Singer v Administrations des
Contributions [1997] ECR I-2471, [1997] STC 1301, ECJ 54.56, 54.63,
54.66, 54.67
C-60/96: Lubbock Fine v C & E Comrs [1994] QB 571 .... 39.20
C-118/96: Safir v Skattemyndigheten i Dalarnas Lan [1999] QB 451,
[1998] ECR I-1897, [1998] STC 1043, ECJ... 54.31, 54.49
C-172/96: First National Bank of Chicago v C & E Comrs [1999] QB 570,
[1998] All ER (EC) 744, [1998] STC 850, ECJ... 40.65
C-264/96: Imperial Chemical Industries plc v Colmer
(Inspector of Taxes) [1998] All ER (EC) 585, [1998] STC 874,
ECJ; apld *sub nom* ICI plc v Colmer (Inspector of Taxes)
[2000] 1 All ER 129, [1999] STC 1089, HL.............................. 1.42; 43.42; 54.25,
54.45, 54.64; 55.5

C-336/96: Gilly v Directeur des services fiscaux du Bas-Rhin
(1998) ECR-I 2823... 54.53
C-349/96: Card Protection Plan Ltd v C & E Comrs: [1999] 2 AC 601,
[1999] All ER (EC) 339, [1999] STC 270, ECJ; apld *sub nom*
Card Protection Plan Ltd v C & E Comrs [2001] UKHL 4,
[2002] 1 AC 202, [2001] 2 All ER 143, [2001] 2 CMLR 19,
[2001] STC 174 .... 13.12; 38.25;
40.37, 40.78; 54.31
C-200/97: Ecotrade Srl v Altiforni Ferriere di Servola SpA
[1998] ECR I-7907, [1999] 2 CMLR 804, ECJ.. 54.81
C-212/97: Centros Ltd v Erhvervs-Og Selskabsstyrelsen [2000] Ch 446,
[2000] All ER (EC) 481, ECJ... 54.73
C-294/97: Eurowings Luftverkehrs AG v Finanzamt Dortmund-Unna
[1999] ECR I-7447, [2001] 3 CMLR 1669, ECJ.. 54.48,
54.61, 54.64
C-302/97: Konle v Austria [1999] ECR I-3099 .... 54.49
C-307/97: Cie de Saint-Gobain, Zweigniederlassung Deutschland v Finanzamt
Aachen-Innenstadt [1999] ECR I-6161, [2000] STC 854, ECJ 54.45, 54.61
C-311/97: Royal Bank of Scotland v Greece [1999] ECR I-2651 *sub nom*
Royal Bank of Scotland v Greek State [2000] STC 733, ECJ 54.45
C-391/97: Gschwind v Finanzamt Aachen-Außenstadt [1999] ECR I-5451,
[2001] STC 331, ECJ.. 54.1, 54.56
C-35/98: Staatssecretaris van Financiën v BGM Verkooijen
[2000] ECR I-4071, [2002] STC 654, ECJ......................... 54.49, 54.61, 54.62
C-55/98: Skatterministeriet v Vestergaard [1999] ECR I-7641,
[2001] 3 CMLR 65.. 54.53
C-190/98: Graf v Filzmoser Maschinenbau GmbH[2000] All ER (EC) 170,
[2000] ECR I-493, ECJ 54.52
C-251/98: Baars v Inspecteur der Belastingen Particulieren/
Ondernemingen Gorinchem [2000] ECR I-2787,
[2002] 1 CMLR 1437, ECJ 54.31, 54.45, 54.49
C-397/98: Metallgesellschaft Ltd v IRC [2001] Ch 620, [2001] 2 WLR 1497,
[2001] ECR I-1727, [2001] All ER (EC) 496, [2001] 2 CMLR 700,
[2001] STC 452, [2001] All ER (D) 96 (Mar), ECJ.................... 54.45, 54.64,
54.65, 54.68
C-408/98: Abbey National plc v C & E Comrs [2001] All ER (EC) 385,
[2001] 1 WLR 769, [2001] STC 297, ECJ 38.26; 39.37
C-409/98: Mirror Group plc v C & E Comrs [2002] QB 546, *sub nom*
C & E Comrs v Mirror Group plc [2001] ECR I-7175,
[2001] 3 CMLR 1417, [2001] STC 1453, ECJ... 39.20

cii *Table of cases*

PARA

C-108/99: Cantor Fitzgerald International v C & E Comrs [2002] QB 546,
sub nom C & E Comrs v Cantor Fitzgerald International
[2001] ECR I-7257, [2001] 3 CMLR 1441, [2001] STC 1453, ECJ 39.20
C-110/99: Emsland-Stärke GmbH v Hauptzollamt Hamburg-Jonas
[2000] ECR I-11569, ECJ 2.44; 54.72,
54.73, 54.74
C-118/00: Larsy v Institut National d'Assusurances Sociales pour Travailleurs
Indépendants (INASTI) [2001] ECR I-5063, ECJ 54.25
C-324/00: Lankhorst-Hohorst GmbH v Finanzmt Steinfurt
[2002] ECR I-11779, [2003] STC 607, ECJ 54.45, 54.62,
54.67, 54.71
C-385/00: FWL de Groot v Staatssecretaris van Financiën
[2002] ECR I-11819, ECJ 54.56
C-167/01: Kamer van Koophandel en Fabrieken voor Amsterdam v
Inspire Art Ltd [2003] All ER (D) 64 (Oct), ECJ 54.73, 54.75
C-168/01: Bosal Holdings BV v Staatssecretaris van Financien
[2003] All ER (EC) 959, [2003] STC 1483, ECJ 54.48, 54.49
C-442/01: KapHag Renditefonds v Finanzamt Charlottenburg CJEC
[2003] All ER(D) 362 (Jun) (TVC 21.62)C-167/01: Kamer van
Koophandel en Fabrieken voor Amsterdam v Inspire Art Ltd
[2003] All ER (D) 64 (Oct), ECJ 37.6; 38.24
C-452/01: Ospelt v Unabhangiger Verwaltungssenat des Landes
Vorarlberg [2003] ECR I-9743.. 54.49
C-9/02: De Lasteyrie du Saillant v Ministere de l'Economie, des Finances
et de l'Industrie [2005] STC 1722, [2004] ECR I-2409,
[2004] 3 CMLR 39.. 27A.53; 54.45, 54.53,
54.63, 54.64, 54.67, 54.68
C-36/02: Omega Spielhallen und Automatenaufstellungs GmbH v
Bundesstaft Bon [2004] ECR I-9609 .... 54.49
C-255/02: Halifax plc v C & E Comrs [2006] Ch 387, [2006] 2 WLR 905,
[2006] STC 919 .... 2.44; 54.74
C-315/02: Lenz v Finanzlandesdirektion fur Tirol [2004]
All ER (D) 277 (Jul), ECJ.. 54.49, 54.57,
54.64, 54.68
C-319/02: Manninen, proceedings brought by [2005] Ch 236,
[2005] 2 WLR 670, [2004] ECR I-7477................................. 54.49, 54.57, 54.62,
54.63, 54.64, 54.68
C-419/02: BUPA Hospitals Ltd & Goldsborough Developments Ltd
[2002] ECJ 446 .... 54.74
C-32/03: I/S Fini H v Skatterministeriet [2005] STC 903,
[2005] ECR I-1599, [2005] 2 CMLR 20 .... 38.81
C-88/03: Portuguese Republic v EC Commission [2007] STC 1032,
[2006] ECR I-7115, [2006] 3 CMLR 45 .... 54.81
C-169/03: Wallentin v Riksskatterverket [2004] ECR I-6443,
[2004] 3 CMLR 24... 54.44
C-223/03: University of Huddersfield High Education Corporation v
C & E Comr [2006] Ch 387, [2006] 2 WLR 905, [2006] STC 980.............. 2.44
C-268/03: De Baeck v Belgium [2004] ECR I-5961, [2004] 2 CMLR 57........... 54.45
C-284/03: Belgium v Temco Europe SA [2005] STC 1451, [2004] ECR
I-11237, [2005] 1 CMLR 23 .... 39.21
C-354/03, 355/03, 484/03: Optigen Ltd, Fulcrum Electronics Ltd, Bond
House Systems Ltd v C & E Comrs [2006] Ch 218, [2006] 2 WLR 456,
[2006] STC 419 .... 37.6

Table of cases ciii

PARA

C-446/03: Marks & Spencer plc v Halsey (Inspector of Taxes)
[2006] Ch 184, [2006] 2 WLR 250, [2006] All ER (EC) 255 .... 1.42; 41.155;
43.42, 43.44; 54.8
54.45, 54.57, 54.64,
54.65, 54.68; 55.5
C-452/03: RAL (Channel Islands) Ltd v C & E Comrs
[2005] STC 1025, [2005] ECR I-3947, [2005] 2 CMLR 50................. 37.5; 54.74
C-465/03: Kretztechnik AG v Finanzamt Linz [2005] 1 WLR 3755, [2005] STC
1118, [2005] ECR I-4357.. 38.24; 40.72
C-513/03: Van Hilten-Van der Heijden [2008] STC 1245,
[2006] ECR I-1957, [2006] WTLR 919 .... 27A.53; 54.76
C-39/04: Laboratoires Fournier v Direction des Verifications Nationales
et Internationales [2006] STC 538, [2005] ECR I-2057,
[2005] 2 CMLR 5 .... 54.48, 54.56,
54.60, 54.61,
54.63, 54.68
C-196/04: Cadbury-Schweppes v IRC [2004] STC (SDC) 342............... 41.161; 54.8,
54.45, 54.64,
54.75, 54.76

C-292/04: Meilicke v Finanzamt Bonn-Innenstadt [2008] STC 2267,
[2007] ECR I-1835, [2007] 2 CMLR 19 .... 54.64
C-341/04: Eurofood IFSC [2006] ECR I-3813 .... 54.75
C-374/04: Test Claimants in Class IV of the ACT Group Litigation v
Inland & Revenue Comrs [2007] All ER (EC) 351, [2007]
STC 404, [2006] ECR I-11673 .... 54.56, 54.64, 54.75
C-386/04: Centro di Musicologia Walter Stauffer v Finanzamt
München fur Korperschaften [2008] STC 1439,
[2006] ECR I-8203, [2009] 2 CMLR 31 .... 53.23
C-444/04: Van den Hout van Ejinsbergen v Staatsecretaris van Financien
[2007] STC 71, [2006] ECR I-3617, [2006] CEC 829..................... 40.37
C-446/04: Test Claimants in the FII Group Litigation v Inland Revenue
Comrs [2007] STC 326, [2006] ECR I-11753, [2006] 1
CMLR 35 .... 54.49, 54.75, 54.76
C-452/04: Fidium Finanz AG [2007] All ER (EC) 239,
[2006] ECR I-9521, [2007] 1 CMLR 15 .... 54.31, 54.49
C-470/04: N v Inspecteur van de Belastingdienst Oost [2008] STC 436,
[2006] ECR I-7409, [2006] 3 CMLR 49 .... 54.45
C-524/04: Test Claimants in the Thin Capitalisation Group Litigation
[2007] STC 906, [2007] ECR I-2107, [2007] 2 CMLR 31 .... 41.98; 54.31,
54.45, 54.49,
54.75, 54.76

C-101/05: Skatteverket v A [2008] All ER (EC) 638, [2009] STC 405,
[2007] ECR I-11531, [2009] 1 CMLR 35, [2010] BTC 906,
[2008] STI 99... 54.49
C-157/05: Holböck v Finanzamt Salzburg-Land [2008] STC 92, [2007] ECR
I-4051, [2008] 1 CMLR 24 .... 54.49
C-170/05: Denkavit International BV v Ministre de l'Economie des
Finances et de l'Industrie [2007] STI 109...................................... 54.64
C-201/05: CFC Test Claimants in the CFC & Dividend Group Litigation
Order v R & C Comrs [2008] STC 1513, [2008] ECR I-2875,
[2008] 2 CMLR 53... 54.75
C-210/06: Cartesio Okató és Szolgáltató bt v Hungary [2009] Ch 354,
[2009] 3 WLR 777, [2009] Bus LR 1233... 54.46

civ   *Table of cases*

	PARA
C-157/07: Finanzamt fur Korperschaften Ill in Berlin v Krankenheim Ruhesitz am Wannsee-Seniorenheimstatt GmbH [2009] All ER (EC) 513, [2009] STC 138, [2008] ECR I-8061, [2009] CEC 639, [2008] BTC 793, [2008] STI 2324	54.62
C-300/07: Proceedings brought by Aberdeen Property Fininvest Alpha Oy [2009] STC 1945, [2009] ECR I-5145, [2009] 3 CMLR 34	54.62
C-318/07: Persche v Finanzamt Lüdenscheid [2009] All ER (EC) 673	53.23; 54.63
C-569/07: HSBC Holdings plc, Vidacos Nominees Ltd v Comrs of R & C Comrs [2008] STC (SCD) 502, [2008] STI 190	49.103, 49.123
C-371/10: National Grid Indus BV v Inspecteur van de Balstingdienst Rijnmond/Kantoor Rotterdam [2012] STC 114, [2012] 1 CMLR 49, [2012] STI 107	54.46
C-18/11: Phillips Electronics UK Ltd (2012) [2013] STC 41, [2013] 1 CMLR 6, [2012] BTC 438, [2012] STI 2837, (2012) 109 (36) LSG17	43.42; 54.45, 54.64
C-65/11 European Commission v Netherlands	38.50
C-74/11: European Commission v Finland	38.50
C-85/11: European Commission v Ireland [2013] BVC 139, [2013] STI 1673	38.50
C-86/11 European Commission v UK	38.50; 43.191
C-95/11: European Commission v Denmark	38.50
C-109/11: European Commission v Czech Republic	38.50
C-657/13: Verder Lab Tec GmbH & Co KG v Finanzamt Hilden EU:C:2015:331, [2015] BTC 18	54.46
C-699/15: R & C Comrs v Brockenhurst College EU:C:2017:344, [2017] 4 WLR 96, [2017] STC 1112, [2017] BVC 20	40.23

References and abbreviations

All statutory references are given in the text.
The standard abbreviations are as follows:

ACT	=	Advance corporation tax
A&M trust	=	Accumulation and maintenance trust
ATED	=	Annual Tax on Enveloped Dwellings
BES	=	Business Expansion Scheme
BPR	=	Business property relief
CAA 2001	=	Capital Allowances Act 2001
CGT	=	Capital gains tax
CJEU	=	Court of Justice of the European Union
CTA (year)	=	Corporation Tax Act (year)
DPT	=	Diverted profits tax
DOTAS	=	Disclosure of Tax Avoidance Schemes
EBT	=	Employment benefit trusts
EFRBS	=	Employer-financed retirement benefits schemes
EIS	=	Enterprise Investment Scheme
ESC	=	Extra statutory concession
ER	=	Entrepreneurs' relief
FA (year)	=	Finance Act (year)
FCA	=	Financial Conduct Authority – the Financial Services Authority (FSA) was replaced by the Financial Conduct Authority in 2013
FID	=	Foreign income dividend
FII	=	Franked investment income
FURBS	=	Funded unapproved retirement benefits scheme
GAAR	=	General anti-abuse rule
HMRC	=	HM Revenue & Customs
IHT	=	Inheritance tax
IHTA 1984	=	Inheritance Tax Act 1984
IRC	=	Inland Revenue Commissioners
ITEPA 2003	=	Income Tax (Earnings and Pensions) Act 2003
ITA 2007	=	Income Tax Act 2007
ITTOIA 2005	=	Income Tax (Trading and Other Income) Act 2005
LPA 1925	=	Law of Property Act 1925
NIC	=	National Insurance contribution

OTS	=	Office for Tax Simplification
PAYE	=	Pay As You Earn
PET	=	Potentially exempt transfer
POTAS	=	Promoters of Tax Avoidance Schemes
PR	=	Personal representative
PSA	=	Personal savings allowance
RI	=	Revenue Interpretation
SA 1891	=	Stamp Act 1891
SDLT	=	Stamp Duty Land Tax
SDRT	=	Stamp Duty Reserve Tax
SEIS	=	Seed Enterprise Investment Scheme
SI	=	Statutory Instrument
SP	=	Statement of Practice
STI	=	Simon's Tax Intelligence
SWTI	=	Simon's Weekly Tax Intelligence
TA 1988	=	Income and Corporation Taxes Act 1988
TCGA 1992	=	Taxation of Chargeable Gains Act 1992
TFEU	=	Treaty on the Functioning of the European Union
TIOPA 2010	=	Taxation (International and Other Provisions) Act 2010
TLATA 1996	=	Trusts of Land and Appointment of Trustees Act 1996
TMA 1970	=	Taxes Management Act 1970
TPA 2014	=	Taxation of Pensions Act 2014
VADR	=	Value Added Tax Disclosure Rules
VAT	=	Value added tax
VATA 1994	=	Value Added Tax Act 1994
VCT	=	Venture Capital Trusts

References to the Manuals produced by HMRC are to the relevant manual (eg CG is Capital Gains Manual) followed by the relevant paragraph number.
Other abbreviations in the text are defined where they appear.

Section 1 Introduction

Chapters
1   UK taxation – structure and philosophy
2   Tax avoidance and the courts
3   Tax avoidance and legislation
4   Administrative machinery
5   Tax avoidance, the future and the disclosure rules

1 UK taxation – structure and philosophy

Updated by Anne Fairpo, Barrister

I   The UK tax picture [**1.2**]
II Features of the system [**1.21**]
III Conclusions [**1.41**]

'Singleton J – Your appeal must be dismissed. I will pass you back your documents. If I might add a word to you, it is that I hope you will not trouble your head further with tax matters, because you seem to have spent a lot of time in going through these various Acts, and if you go on spending your time on Finance Acts, and the like, it will drive you silly.

Mrs Briggenshaw – I will appeal to the higher court.

Singleton J – I cannot stop you, if I would. The advice which I gave you was for your own good, I thought. That is all.'

(*Briggenshaw v Crabb* (1948) 30 TC 331.)
[**1.1**]

I THE UK TAX PICTURE

1 Taxes in general

Taxes imposed in the UK may be classified in various ways. A tripartite division might be adopted into taxes on income, on capital and on expenditure. Alternatively, and arguably more satisfactorily, the classification might be into direct and indirect taxes. This book is concerned with the following direct taxes:

- income tax (**Chapters 6–18**)
- capital gains tax (CGT) (**Chapters 19–27A**)
- inheritance tax (IHT) (**Chapters 28–36**)
- corporation tax and the taxation of business enterprise (**Chapters 41–48**)
- stamp taxes (**Chapter 49**)

and there are also four chapters on VAT (an indirect tax: **Chapters 37–40**).

It omits indirect taxes such as car tax, landfill tax, climate change levy, insurance premium tax and customs and excise duties, as well as such direct taxes as petroleum revenue tax, the tonnage tax (the amount chargeable by shipping companies as if it was corporation tax) and the council tax. There is also a relatively new and further direct tax, the annual tax on enveloped dwellings which, since 1 April 2013, has been payable by companies that own high value residential property (see **[49.86]**). In principle, the distinction between direct and indirect taxes is that a direct tax is borne by the taxpayer and is not passed on to any other person, whereas an indirect tax is passed on by the payer so that the burden of the tax is ultimately borne by another, eg VAT which although paid by the business, is passed on to the customer. [1.2]

2 What is a tax?

The basic features of a tax may be simply stated. *First*, it is a compulsory levy. *Second*, it is imposed by government or, in the case of council tax, by a local authority. *Finally*, the money raised should be used either for public purposes or, if the purpose of the tax is not to raise money, it should aim to achieve social justice within the community (CGT, for instance, was specifically intended to have that effect). However, to describe the main features of a tax is not to define the concept. Thus, although not treated as taxes for parliamentary purposes, can it be said that social security contributions are, in reality, taxes? Tiley (*Revenue Law*, 2012) has suggested that, on the basis that they are now graduated in a way which does not relate directly to the graduation of the benefit, they *ought* to be treated as taxes; interesting, then, that in his 2011 Budget Speech, the then Chancellor of the Exchequer, the Rt Hon George Osborne MP, announced the implementation of a study into the integration of income tax and national insurance contributions. The initial period of consultation was completed, and an indicative timetable covering future periods was laid down. However, in the Autumn Statement on 5 December 2012, the Government announced that it would 'wait for further progress on planned operational changes to the tax system before formally consulting on the operational integration of income tax and NICs'. More recently, in March 2016 the Office of Tax Simplification published its recommendations on closer alignment of income tax and national insurance contributions following a simplification review (see **[1.26]**). Moreover, taxes shade off into fines and levies imposed for other purposes. So far as the distinction between fines and taxes is concerned, the line is often blurred. HLA Hart in *The Concept of Law* (Oxford, 1975) commented that:

> 'Taxes may be imposed not for revenue purposes but to discourage the activities taxed, though the law gives no express indications that these are to be abandoned as it does when it "makes them criminal". Conversely the fines payable for some criminal offence may, because of the depreciation of money, become so small that they are cheerfully paid. They are then perhaps felt to be "mere taxes", and "offences" are frequent, precisely because in these circumstances the sense is lost that the rule is, like the bulk of the criminal law, meant to be taken seriously as a standard of behaviour.'

It is not really surprising that this 'mere taxes' attitude has spawned the belief that all taxes can be avoided, or even evaded, with complete impunity (see **[1.24]** and **Chapters 2, 3** and **5**). [1.3]

3 The purpose of taxation

The primary object of taxation is to raise money for government expenditure, although it should be noted that capital gains tax was introduced in 1965 specifically on grounds of equity rather than for yield. The twentieth century witnessed increasing expenditure on social welfare whilst the use of taxation both as an economic regulator and for the promotion of the public good (or to discourage certain forms of conduct) may also be discerned in the legislation of the last century. Thus, alterations to the rate of VAT can affect the level of economic life in the community as much as adjustments to the money supply and credit regulation. Indeed, it was to stimulate the economy that, at the start of the most recent recession in 2008, the previous Labour Government introduced a temporary reduction in the rate of VAT and a temporary exemption from Stamp Duty Land Tax (SDLT) for acquisitions of residential property worth £175,000 or less.

Conversely, because the Coalition Government increased the rate of VAT to 20% in order to raise revenue, the measure was criticised on the basis that it would cause people to spend less at a time when, once again, the economy needs stimulating. The various tax incentives afforded for gifts to charities may be seen as the promotion of public good and altruism, whilst the duties levied on tobacco and alcohol may be seen as bordering on moral control. The trend of using tax as a regulator has continued into the 21st century, most notably with the announcement in the 2016 Budget of the proposed introduction of a sugar tax in 2018, as has the increase in social expenditure in the guise of tax credits, aimed at both reducing child poverty and encouraging work rather than welfare, although announcements made by the Chancellor of the Exchequer in his July 2015 Budget Speech revealed the intention for there to be to be a marked reduction in such expenditure over the next five years ([**51.27**] ff). It should be noted, however, that one of the effects of the Welfare Reform Act 2012, said to provide for the biggest change to the welfare system for over 60 years, is to replace the Child Tax Credit and Working Tax Credit with the new Universal Benefit, which will operate outside of the tax system.

[1.4]

4 Statistics

Who should pay the bill? Apportioning the burden of taxation fairly amongst the community can turn into the more radical contention that tax should operate as a method for effecting a redistribution of wealth or even the confiscation of wealth above a certain level. Historically, one striking feature of the statistics of direct taxation was that the vast proportion of the total yield was from income tax. More recently, whilst income tax continues to account for more than half of all tax receipts, it is only just more than one-half: receipts of income tax (including NICs) in 2016–17* amounted to 53% of the total sum raised by direct taxes; corporation tax 8.7% and CGT 1.5% (both rounded up).

Corporation tax receipts have fluctuated between a low of £28,077m in 2003–04 to a high of £47,036m in 2007–08; The £49,765m collected in 2016–17* was higher than that of any the previous seven years.

A greater fluctuation can be seen in capital gains tax receipts, ranging from £1,596m in 2002–03 to £7,852m in 2008–09, representing nearly a four-fold increase. The £8,703m collected in 2016–17* was substantially more than that collected in 2013–14.

IHT accounted for just 0.85% of the total direct tax raised in 2016–17,* compared to estate duty, which in its final year (1974–75) produced 2.38%. IHT receipts had been climbing steadily, reaching £3,833m in 2007–08. There followed a significant decline in 2008–09, partly as a consequence of falling house prices – it should be noted that one-third of the total value of taxpaying estates is made up of residential property – and, importantly, partly due to the introduction in 2007 of the transferrable nil-rate band, which provided that any unused part of the nil-rate band of the first spouse/civil partner to die could be transferred to the surviving spouse/civil partner. Nevertheless, receipts have continued to rise since 2009–10, in part due to a recovery in the housing market, particularly in London and the south-east where prices rose sharply, and also because of a relatively low nil rate band threshold that is frozen until 2020–21, as a result of which receipts of £4,835m for 2016–17* are now higher than the previous peak in 2007–08.

However, given the introduction in 2017–18 of an additional nil-rate band (also transferrable) when a residence is passed on death to a child or grandchild, another decline in IHT receipts can be expected for future years. Receipts from lifetime transfers (arising almost entirely on gifts to discretionary and other relevant property trusts, but occasionally including other immediately chargeable lifetime transfers and including the ten-yearly and proportionate charges on discretionary and other relevant property trusts) account for only 3.8% of inheritance tax receipts for 2014–15 (the latest figures available). This is unsurprising given the fact that outright lifetime transfers to another person made more than seven years before the transferor's death are exempt. SDLT, with strikingly low collection costs, raised £11,712m in 2016–17*.

The cost of collecting tax has dropped dramatically in recent years. In 1958, the administrative costs for tax collection (£ per £100 of revenue) was 1.16; in 2009, it was 1.14 (a fall of only 2% in just over 50 years). However, from a much lower cost of 0.87 in 2010–11, it has dropped to 0.6 for 2015–16, according to the National Audit Office report on HMRC's 2016-17 Accounts).

*The figures given for 2016–17 are provisional at the time of writing. [1.5]

5 The tax unit

Inherent in the question 'who should pay the bill' posed in [1.5] is the issue of the unit of taxation. At various times in the past, the basic taxpaying unit of the individual was expanded to comprise either the nuclear family or the married couple. Thus it was that, prior to the tax year 1972–73, the income of an unmarried infant who was not in regular employment was aggregated with that of its parents; after 1972–73, this ceased to be the case, and the infant became a taxpayer in its own right. However, until 1990–91, the incomes of husband and wife were aggregated, with the husband bearing the responsibility for the tax return and payment of the tax. The inequity of treating a married couple differently from an unmarried couple with equivalent income, together with the lack of privacy afforded to the married woman in her financial affairs, resulted in the current system of independent taxation, with every individual person a taxpayer in their own right. The idea of reintroducing tax breaks for married couples was contained in the

Conservative Party's Election 2010 manifesto, and FA 2014 provided that, from 2015–16, a spouse or civil partner has been able to elect to transfer part of their personal allowance to their spouse or civil partner (for 2016–17 and subsequent tax years the transferable amount is 10% of the basic personal allowance, ie £1,100 for 2016–17) provided that neither spouse pays higher or additional rate tax. The transferred allowance is given effect as a reduction to the recipient's income tax liability at the basic rate of tax.   [1.6]–[1.20]

II   FEATURES OF THE SYSTEM

1 Legislation

a) *Interpretation*

Fiscal legislation is both detailed and complex. The aim of the vast amount of detail is to ensure certainty: persons should know whether they are or are not subject to tax or duty on a particular transaction or sum of money; it is complex because the society within which it has to operate is complex. The result, however, has tended to be confusion for all! Historically, judges insisted upon a strict, literal, approach to the interpretation of taxing statutes. In a famous passage, Rowlatt J in *Cape Brandy Syndicate v IRC* (1921) expressed this rule as follows:

> '... It is urged ... that in a taxing Act clear words are necessary in order to tax the subject. Too wide and fanciful a construction is often sought to be given to that maxim, which does not mean that words are to be unduly restricted against the Crown, or that there is to be any discrimination against the Crown in those Acts. It simply means that in a taxing Act one has to look merely at what is clearly said. There is no room for any intendment. There is no equity about a tax. There is no presumption as to a tax. Nothing is to be read in, nothing is to be implied. One can only look fairly at the language used ...'

The reason commonly offered for this approach was that taxing statutes operate in a similar way to penal statutes, so if a taxpayer is to be charged to tax, this can only be achieved by the giving of very clear authority. Moreover, since taxing statutes were believed to be about revenue collection and nothing else, there could be no room for any further 'intendment'. Over the years, the practice became that where the meaning of the statute was clearly expressed, the court would not consider any contrary intention or belief of Parliament or, indeed, any contrary indication by the Revenue. Apart from this, the question of making allowance for the intendment of Parliament was not clear cut. There were two divergent views on this matter: on the one hand, there were those who viewed tax statutes to be about revenue collection and nothing else, and accordingly adhered to the literal approach to interpretation. This view can be summed up in the words of Lord Scarman who, in the course of a debate in 1981, said:

> 'If Parliament says one thing but means another, it is not, under the historic principles of the common law, for the courts to correct it. That general principle must surely be accepted in our society. We are to be governed not by Parliament's intentions but by Parliament's enactments.'

On the other hand, there were those who advocated the purposive approach. In *Stenhouse Holdings v IRC* (1972), Lord Reid considered the alternative to the literal approach to interpretation which, he said, was:

> 'to consider the ... general intendment of the provisions ... More recently courts have tended to give at least equal weight to more general considerations, because a strict literal interpretation has been found often to lead to a result which cannot really have been intended, and the object of statutory interpretation must be to find what was the intention of the legislature.'

A convergence of these views could be seen in cases revealing an actual *ambiguity* within a statutory provision (see, eg *Newman Manufacturing Company v Marrable* (1931)), but the two opposing approaches continued to be adopted in other cases. In *Frankland v IRC* (1997), while acknowledging that the inheritance tax legislation gave rise to an anomaly, Peter Gibson LJ refused to accept that it revealed any ambiguity. Accordingly, he dismissed the taxpayer's invitation to write words into the provision that would remove the anomaly and, pointing out that the 'court's function is to interpret the legislation and not to legislate under the guise of interpretation'. He concluded that it would be 'impermissible' for the court to write in words that some may conjecture parliament to have intended. In contrast, in *Sutherland v Gustar* (1994), where the statute was silent on the point at issue, the Court of Appeal decided that, in the interests of fairness and justice, it would not 'retreat into adopting a literal approach to the construction of the statutory provisions', but would interpret the legislation 'so as to give effect to Parliament's presumed intention'. In more recent years, the literal approach has all but given way to a more purposive approach. Importantly, it is the purposive approach that founded the so-called 'Ramsay' doctrine, which enshrined the judiciary's attempt to defeat artificial tax avoidance schemes (see **[1.24]** and **Chapters 2, 3** and **5**), and it is this approach that is being adopted generally in all other areas of the law. [1.21]

b) *Legislative simplification*

Following criticism from many sources, not least the Tax Law Review Committee of the Institute for Fiscal Studies in its Interim Report on Tax Legislation (1995), that tax law had become lengthy, complex and impenetrable, FA 1995 s 160 required the Inland Revenue to prepare a report on tax simplification. That report – *The Path to Tax Simplification* – was published in December 1995, and gave birth to the Tax Law Rewrite Project, which was charged with the task of rewriting most of the primary tax legislation falling within the remit of the then Inland Revenue (ie direct taxation). The Capital Allowances Act 2001 was the first piece of rewritten legislation to reach the statute book and this was followed by the Income Tax (Earnings and Pensions) Act 2003 (ITEPA 2003), the Income Tax (Trading and Other Income) Act 2005 (ITTOIA 2005), the Income Tax Act 2007 (ITA 2007), the Corporation Tax Act 2009 (CTA 2009), the Corporation Tax Act 2010 (CTA 2010) and the Taxation (International and Other Provisions) Act 2010 (TIOPA 2010). The final three Acts complete the work of the Tax Law Rewrite project, meaning that neither capital gains tax nor inheritance tax will undergo a complete rewrite. Unfortunately, whilst the rewritten legislation may be set out more clearly and logically, it has added to the length of tax legislation in the UK and rewriting words in plainer English has not solved the inherent complexity of the tax system (see **[1.26]–[1.40]**). **[1.22]**

c) *Use of Hansard*

As seen above (**[1.21]**), the courts now adopt a purposive approach in tax cases, which seeks to give effect to the purpose of the legislation. The difficulty with this approach is that the statutory purpose is not always discernible from the words used. Thus, the House of Lords in *Pepper v Hart* (1993) departed from the previous 'exclusionary' rule of disallowing references to parliamentary material as an aid to construction. Speaking for the majority (the then Lord Chancellor, Lord Mackay, dissenting), Lord Browne-Wilkinson accepted that the courts could look at Hansard for guidance on the interpretation of a statute in limited situations:

'I therefore reach the conclusion, subject to any question of parliamentary privilege, that the exclusionary rule should be relaxed so as to permit reference to parliamentary materials where:
(a) legislation is ambiguous or obscure, or leads to an absurdity;
(b) the material relied on consists of one or more statements by a minister or other promoter of the bill together, if necessary, with such other parliamentary material as is necessary to understand such statements and their effect;
(c) the statements relied on are clear.'

In *Elf Enterprise Caledonia Ltd v IRC* (1994), the court held that Inland Revenue Press Releases could *not* be used as an aid to statutory interpretation, whilst in *IRC v Willoughby* (1995) the Parliamentary Debates of 1936 (on the introduction of what is now TA 1988 s 739) were considered by the Court of Appeal to be of no value:

'Whatever might have been the intention of Ministers in 1936, the Court had decided in 1948 and again in 1969 that the words used by Parliament manifest a different intention. Yet in 1952 and again in 1970 the same formula is used and notwithstanding the changes made in 1969. In these circumstances it must be assumed that the original intention, whatever it was, was superseded by an acceptance of the decisions of the Courts' (*Morritt LJ*): note that the House of Lords did not need to consider this matter since they did not find any ambiguity in the statute.

Much of the complexity of recent tax legislation has been prompted by the growth of the tax avoidance industry. Whilst tax evasion is unlawful, the avoidance of tax is both lawful and widely practised. The growth of larger scale schemes, often devoid of all commercial reality, has promoted an increased amount of anti-avoidance legislation and, in 2004, the requirement for detailed advance disclosure of tax avoidance schemes. The FA 2013 contained the long-awaited General Anti Abuse Rule (GAAR), although critics argue that it is likely to be unworkable (see **Chapter 3**), and included in the FA 2014 are provisions that further strengthen HMRC's armoury of measures against avoiders. Statistics suggest that the strict approach towards tax avoidance has had the effect of reducing significantly the percentage tax gap between 2005–06 and 2013–14, representing an additional £57 billion in cumulative tax collected during this period; in 2013–14 alone, there was a saving of £2.7bn. The first Budget of the current Conservative Government (July 2015) made it clear that this approach would continue; indeed, the Chancellor of the Exchequer referred to tackling tax evasion, tax and avoidance *and* 'aggressive tax planning', thereby departing from the previous view that aggressive avoidance would not be tolerated but that tax planning was acceptable. [1.23]

2 Role of the courts – the 'new approach'

The role of the judiciary in the attack on artificial tax avoidance schemes has already been referred to above ([1.21]). The so-called 'Ramsay' doctrine (named after *Ramsay Ltd v IRC* (1981), the case in which it began to be developed) and otherwise known as 'the new approach', was a response to the burgeoning tax-avoidance industry in the 1970s, and to the marketing of a myriad of schemes wholly divorced from reality but obtaining a tax advantage because of the precise wording of the relevant legislation. It was felt by some that the methods used for attacking such schemes and neutralising this advantage, namely the canons of statutory construction and the use of limited anti-avoidance legislation, were wholly inadequate for the task. Hence the development of the new approach to tax-avoidance schemes in the House of Lords (now the Supreme Court) and, in particular, in the speeches of the Law Lords in *Furniss v Dawson* (1984) (see [2.22]). What the new approach was actually about and how it operated has been the subject of a number of high-profile House of Lords cases, culminating in *Barclays Mercantile Business Finance Ltd v Mawson* (2004) and *Scottish Provident Institution v IRC* (2004) and, more recently, *R & C Comrs v Tower MCashback LLP 1* (2011) and *R & C Comrs v Mayes* (2011) (see [2.38]). There were those critics who clearly believed that the early cases demonstrated a willingness on the part of their Lordships to engage in judge-made law and, it has to be said, with some justification as the following words of Lord Scarman demonstrate:

> 'I am aware, and the legal profession (and others) must understand, that the law in this area is in an early stage of development. Speeches in your Lordships' House and judgments in the appellate courts are concerned more to chart a way forward between principles accepted and not to be rejected, than to attempt anything so ambitious as to determine finally the limit beyond which the safe channel of acceptable tax avoidance shelves into the dangerous shallows of unacceptable tax evasion. The law will develop from case to case. Lord Wilberforce in *Ramsay's* case referred to "the emerging principle" of the law. What has been established is that the determination of what does, and what does not constitute unacceptable tax evasion is a subject suited to development by judicial process. Difficult though the task may be for judges, it is one which is beyond the power of the blunt instrument of legislation.'

Other and more recent members of the Judicial Committee of the House of Lords and subsequently the Supreme Court went out of their way to demonstrate that the *Ramsay* case did not give rise to a new principle, but was merely an example of purposive statutory interpretation. In response to those who were concerned about the appearance of judge-made anti-avoidance law, HMRC consulted on 'principle-based' anti-avoidance provisions with reference to financial products. All of this is discussed in far greater detail in **Chapter 2**. Suffice for now to say that the decision in *Ramsay* was critical in so far as, since that time, the courts have at least thought about the issue of artificial tax avoidance, expressed views on it and have brought a greater awareness about it both to advisors and taxpayers. Moreover, it would appear that fewer tax avoidance cases are now reaching the higher courts, with the First-tier and Upper Tax Tribunals determining the lion's share, and that the majority of all avoidance cases are being decided in favour of HMRC. [1.24]

3 **Practice**

Given the volume of legislation, it is not surprising that some provisions may impose hardship and cause unforeseen results in individual cases. As a result the Revenue operates a system of extra-statutory concessions (ESCs) and publishes Statements of Practice (SPs) and interpretations ('RI').

An ESC is a relaxation which gives taxpayers a reduction in tax liability to which they would not be entitled under the strict letter of the law: by contrast an SP explains the Revenue's interpretation of legislation and the way in which it is applied in practice (of course the taxpayer may disagree and is free to argue for a different interpretation before the courts!).

The current ESCs (as of 6 April 2017) are to be found at https://www.gov.uk/government/publications/extra-statutory-concessions-ex-inland-revenue. The effect of a concession is that tax is not charged despite the case falling within the provisions of a taxing statute. A number of concessions have been incorporated in the legislation, particularly in the rewritten legislation. An example would be ESC A6 that permitted miners to enjoy free coal or an allowance in lieu which would undoubtedly have been charged as emoluments. This is now the subject of a specific exemption in ITEPA 2003 s 306. It needs to be remembered that the published concessions are prefaced by a warning that 'a concession will not be given in any case where an attempt is made to use it for tax avoidance'. Thus in *R v IRC, ex p Fulford Dobson* (1987) an attempt to take advantage of a CGT concession, which, in certain cases, excluded from charge gains realised by a non-resident from the date of his departure from the UK, failed since the relevant asset had been transferred to the non resident by his spouse with the sole object of benefiting from that concession.

The fairness of concessions is open to question as is their constitutional legality. In a pungent judgment Walton J expressed the objection to ESCs as follows:

> 'I, in company with many other judges before me, am totally unable to understand upon what basis the Inland Revenue Commissioners are entitled to make extra-statutory concessions. To take a very simple example (since example is clearly called for), upon what basis have the commissioners taken it upon themselves to provide that income tax is not to be charged upon a miner's free coal and allowances in lieu thereof? That this should be the law is doubtless quite correct: I am not arguing the merits, or even suggesting that some other result, as a matter of equity, should be reached. But this, surely, ought to be a matter for Parliament, and not the commissioners. If this kind of concession can be made, where does it stop: and why are some groups favoured against others? ...

'... This is not a simple matter of tax law. What is happening is that, in effect, despite the words of Maitland, commenting on the Bill of Rights, "This is the last of the dispensing power", the Crown is now claiming just such a power ...' (*Vestey v IRC (No 2)* (1979)).

By contrast, in the *Fulford Dobson* case mentioned above, the judge (McNeill J) accepted the existence and indeed the necessity for extra-statutory concessions, concluding that they fell 'within the concept of good management or of administrative common sense' and that they could fairly be said to be made 'within the proper exercise of managerial discretion'. However, more recently the House of Lords in *R (on the application of Wilkinson) v IRC* (2005) (see [**55.44**]) made it clear that the scope of the administrative discretion of HMRC to make concessions that depart from the strict statutory position is not as wide as it had previously been thought. In light of that decision, HMRC has been reviewing its published concessions and, where an existing concession exceeds the scope of the discretion, the effect of the concession has been maintained by putting it on a legislative basis where it is appropriate to do so. In some cases, the ESC has been withdrawn altogether. Where this occurs, the change is not retrospective and an appropriate period of notice is given to allow taxpayers to review their affairs.

SPs set out the view that the Revenue takes of a particular provision and should be treated with caution since they may not accurately state the law (see, for instance, *Campbell Connelly & Co Ltd v Barnett* (1992)). The same can be said of the CGT consequences that ensue when trustees exercise a dispositive power, which were set out in a series of Revenue Statements. The first (SP 7/78) was withdrawn as a result of *Roome v Edwards* (1981); its successor (SP 9/81) suffered a similar fate after *Bond v Pickford* (1983); and current Revenue thinking is found in SP 7/84 (issued in October 1984).

There is an argument against inviting HMRC to express views upon the meaning to be given to particular provisions since in cases where HMRC indicates that tax is chargeable, it places professional advisers in a difficult position. Do they advise their clients that the HMRC is wrong and that the Supreme Court is bound to accept the taxpayer's arguments, or do they advise prudence in the face of the risk of protracted and expensive litigation? [**1.25**]

4 Tax simplification

Despite the fact that the work of the Tax Law Rewrite Project (see [**1.22**]) resulted in legislation that was easier to read and organised in a much more sensible fashion, the underlying tax structure remains complex. As the then Chancellor of the Exchequer, the Rt Hon George Osborne MP said:

'The previous Government took a complex tax system and made it even worse ... the tax affairs of millions of families and businesses across the UK [are] extremely complicated.' (July 2010)

Accordingly, in July 2010, the Office of Tax Simplification (OTS) was established, comprising a Board of tax experts whose responsibility it is to identify areas where complexities in the tax system for both business and individual taxpayers can be reduced. As one of the newly appointed Tax Directors commented at the time, a truly simple tax system for all is probably impossible given the complex world in which we live, but working towards a simpler system would help all who deal with it. Currently, the OTS can only make recommendations: it is Treasury ministers who actually make the decisions. However, finally the OTS has been put on a permanent and statutory footing by FA 2016.

Since its inception in 2010, the OTS has carried out extensive public consultations and engagement with a range of stakeholders. Its reports include reviews of employee expenses and benefits, tax reliefs, small business taxation, pensioner taxation and partnership taxation. It has also reviewed the competitiveness of UK tax administration and developed a complexity index for taxation as projects to inform the context of its work. In 2016, the OTS published its recommendations following a simplification review of small company taxation (focusing on the distortions between the personal and business tax systems) and on the closer alignment of income tax and national insurance contributions (this issue was the subject of an initial consultation in the Autumn of 2011, and the Next Steps Report (HM Treasury, HMRC, November 2011) set out an indicative timetable for reform, with final implementation occurring in 2017. If such reform were to be implemented, it would have an impact on every taxpayer in the UK and could render IR35 obsolete).

Of the 60 'big picture' recommendations already made by the OTS, 16 have been accepted, nine partially accepted, nine implemented and seven partially implemented. These include the repeal, in FA 2011, of a number of existing redundant reliefs and exemptions; allowing eligible small businesses to calculate their taxable income by taking business income received in a year and deducting business expenses paid in a year (the cash accounting basis. This means that they will not need to adjust for debtors, creditors and stock, and they will generally not have to distinguish between revenue and capital expenditure (see FA 2013 and [10.73])); the abolition of the £8,500 employee benefits threshold (see FA 2015 and [8.113] ff); the reduction in the 10% savings rate to 0% with an increase in the band to which it applies to £5,000; and, arising from its small business tax review, reform of the IR 35 administration (see [8.31]–[8.32]). [1.26]–[1.40]

III CONCLUSIONS

Tax is often seen as an ephemeral area: as a part of law devoid of principle and subject to the whims of politicians. In part this view is true; the annual (sometimes biannual, particularly in a General Election year like 2015) Finance Act often effects considerable changes. However, the underlying principles do remain and it is usually only the surface landscape that is altered. The bedrock of income tax, for instance, can be traced back to 1803 and although inheritance tax on gifts is of more recent origin, it is based upon a relatively simple conceptual structure. In understanding tax law the golden rule must be to ignore the form in favour of the substance (see, for instance, Robert Walker LJ giving the judgment of the Court of Appeal in

Billingham v Cooper (2001)). Given that the whole edifice is man-made and is designed to achieve practical ends, it should also follow that it is fully comprehensible. There is nothing here of the divine and, in the last resort, one should follow the approach of Lord Reid in the House of Lords in *Fleming v Associated Newspapers Ltd* (1972):

> 'On reading it [now TA 1988 s 577(10)] my first impression was that it is obscure to the point of unintelligibility and that impression has been confirmed by the able and prolonged arguments which were submitted to us ... I have suggested what may be a possible meaning, but if I am wrong about that I would not shrink from holding that the subsection is so obscure that no meaning can be given to it. I would rather do that than seek by twisting and contorting the words to give to the subsection an improbable meaning. Draftsmen as well as Homer can nod, and Parliament is so accustomed to obscure drafting in Finance Bills that no one may have noticed the defects in this subsection.' **[1.41]**

Finally, it may be noted that the long arm of Europe has increasingly been seen in direct tax matters. Fundamental principles of EU law impact into this area, as seen in the ECJ decision in *Marks & Spencer plc v Halsey* (2005) (and the subsequent application of it in the domestic courts). Following an unsuccessful appeal to the Special Commissioners by the UK-resident company, which had claimed group relief against its UK profits in respect of the losses of its non-resident subsidiaries, the High Court referred the case to the ECJ for a preliminary ruling on whether the UK group relief provisions were compatible with the provisions of the EU Treaty on freedom of establishment (Arts 43–49 since 2009). The ECJ held that the provisions in principle constituted a restriction on the right of establishment by deterring companies from setting up subsidiaries in other Member States, and went beyond what was necessary to attain the legitimate objectives that the relevant provision pursued (see also *ICI v Colmer* (1999) (see **[54.45]**), *Vodafone 2 v R & C Comrs* (2010) and *Test Claimants in the Franked Investment Income Litigation v IRC* (2013)). Moreover, when UK legislation creates manifest injustice (such as, for example, the settlor charge on offshore trusts: see **Chapter 27**), application to the European Court of Human Rights may be appropriate (compare *National and Provincial Building Society v UK* (1997) and see generally **Chapter 55**), but normally only when all other means of resolving the injustice have been tried and have failed (although see *Burden v UK* (2006, 2008), where the claimants took their case directly to the ECtHR, and **[55.43]**).

The Referendum of the 23 June 2016 resulted in a majority vote for the UK to leave the EU. As notification of leaving was given by the UK in March 2017, the two-year period for negotiations of possible trade and other deals is underway. Consequently, until at least March 2019, it is expected that the UK will remain subject to EU law in exactly the same way as before. **[1.42]**

2 Tax avoidance and the courts

Updated by Anne Fairpo, Barrister

I Introduction [**2.1**]
II Artificial schemes and the *Ramsay* principle [**2.21**]
III Limits to the *Ramsay* principle [**2.24**]
IV Reaffirmation of *Ramsay* [**2.32**]
V Meaning, scope and applicability of the *Ramsay* principle: the later cases [**2.34**]
VI Conclusions [**2.46**]

I INTRODUCTION

1 **The problem of tax avoidance**

'Aggressive tax avoidance is unacceptable, The majority of hardworking people in this country pay the right amount of tax and they quite rightly expect everyone else to do the same. But the behaviour of a small minority – both those who seek to avoid and those who devise and promote tax avoidance schemes – undermines the honesty of the majority.

As a key part of our long term economic plan, this government has taken significant strides to make the UK's tax system one of the most modern and competitive in the world. To maintain the integrity of this tax system, it must apply fairly and consistently to everyone.' ((The Exchequer Secretary to the Treasury, David Gauke MP, *Raising the stakes on tax avoidance: summary of responses and draft legislation*, January 2014)

The desire to escape the payment of tax need scarcely occasion surprise. In some cases, this may be achieved either by non-declaration or by the making of a fraudulent return (eg by deliberately under-declaring), both of which are examples of tax evasion, that is, illegal acts, subject to criminal sanctions. However, the greater number of situations concern attempts to avoid or minimise the payment of tax. Although there is currently an ongoing debate on questions of tax justice and tax morality, highlighted by the activities of pressure groups such as the Tax Justice Network and UK Uncut, tax avoidance remains something a taxpayer is legally entitled to do. As Lord Templeman said in *Ensign Tankers (Leasing) Ltd v Stokes* (1992), 'there is no morality in a tax and no illegality or immorality in a tax avoidance scheme'.

The policy of the former Labour Government had been to equate tax evasion *and* tax avoidance with non-compliance with a view to prosecuting both; although optimism was expressed by some that the Coalition Government (2010–2015) was likely to be more ready to maintain the historical clear focal divide between tax avoidance and tax evasion, this has not been the case. With the introduction of the general anti abuse rule (GAAR – see [**3.74**]), bringing with it a shift of emphasis from 'tax avoidance' *simpliciter* to 'abusive tax avoidance', the distinction between tax evasion and tax avoidance has become an even finer one. In light of cases such as *Moyles v R & C Comrs* (2014) (see [**2.38**]), this would seem justifiable despite the criticism by one commentator that this approach amounts to an 'abuse of rights' on the part of the authorities.

Accordingly, the distinction is now between on the one hand, 'tax planning', referring to the sensible use of the available exemptions and reliefs which Parliament intended and, on the other hand, aggressive tax avoidance where, often, the sums involved are greater, the methods adopted by the 'tax planning industry' to escape the fiscal net may take on a complexity that is beyond the comprehension of most individuals and may involve schemes which are divorced from reality (although this distinction too may now have become blurred following the Chancellor of the Exchequer's July 2015 Budget Speech when he referred to the need to combat tax evasion, avoidance *and* 'aggressive tax planning').

Indeed, in one Supreme Court case Lord Walker spoke of 'the unremitting ingenuity of tax consultants and investment bankers determined to test the limits of the capital allowances legislation' (*R & C Comrs v Tower MCashback LLP 1 and another* (2011), and the sentiment is not restricted to the capital allowances legislation but extends to most other tax legislation. Categorised now by HMRC as 'aggressive tax avoidance', this latter situation is clearly the one envisaged by the OECD, which suggests that such avoidance is 'the arrangement of a taxpayer's affairs that is intended to reduce his tax liability and ... although the arrangement could be strictly legal it is usually in contradiction with the intent of the law it purports to follow.'

Various Government publications for over a decade confirm that it is losing considerable amounts of revenue through tax avoidance practices such as these, as well as through tax evasion. In *Protecting Tax Revenues* (HMRC, March 2008) the Revenue explained why protecting tax revenues mattered:

> '... a strong and growing economy based on opportunity for all and a fair society in which everyone shares in rising national prosperity ... requires a modern tax system that encourages work and savings, keeps pace with business developments and globalisation and supports the provision of public services.
>
> For such a system to be effective, it needs to operate fairly and effectively. Those who attempt to pay less than their fair share through fraud or by undertaking artificial avoidance schemes undermine the ability of the tax system to deliver these objectives ...'

The effect of the behaviour of those who do not pay the tax they should (either through lack of care or understanding on the taxpayer's part or through the use of highly artificial avoidance schemes or through evasion or fraudulently obtaining tax repayments) results in a shortfall in tax revenues, requiring tax rates to be higher for other individuals and businesses in order to fund public services, thereby eroding the principle of fairness that underpins the tax system. The tax gap, the difference between the amount of tax that should in theory be collected by HMRC against that which is actually collected, and the tax gap as a percentage of tax liabilities is shown in the table below.

Tax gap and percentage of liabilities 2005–06 to 2013–14

Year	Tax Gap (bn)	Percentage of Liabilities
05–06	37	8.3
06–07	35	7.6
07–08	36	7.3
08–09	35	7.2
09–10	32	7.2
10–11	33	6.8
11–12	33	6.6
12–13	35	6.9
13–14	37	6.9
14–15	36	6.5

According to HMRC, the largest percentage gap reductions between 2013–14 and 2014–15 is to be found in PAYE (reduced by over a quarter). The largest part of the overall gap for 2013–14 (approximately half) is attributable to small and medium-sized enterprises, followed by large businesses (just over a quarter).

Of this tax gap, for 2014–15, tax avoidance is estimated to account for 6% of the overall tax gap (amounting to £2.2 billion); this is a reduction from the gap of £2.7bn or 8% in 2013–14. These figures are an estimate of what HMRC believes to be the tax gap; others have suggested that both the overall tax gap and the amount attributable to avoidance are much higher.

Over its five years in office, the Coalition Government described itself as being 'relentless in its crackdown on tax avoidance and evasion' and in its determination to reduce the incentives, and increase the penalties, for engaging in that kind of behaviour. It started by setting out its new anti-avoidance strategy (*Tackling Tax Avoidance*, HM Treasury and HM Revenue & Customs, March 2011), which comprised three elements: *first*, the prevention of avoidance at the outset where possible, including developing strategic defences against avoidance, such as principles-based legislation where appropriate (see [**3.73**]); *second*, detecting avoidance early where it persists, achievable through, amongst other things, maintaining the effectiveness of the rules on disclosure of tax avoidance schemes (DOTAS – see **Chapter 5**); and *third*, countering avoidance effectively through legislative change and challenge through litigation. Building upon that base, the Coalition Government made more than 40 changes, closing loopholes and introducing major reforms to the UK tax system. It was estimated that between 2010 and 2015 the measures taken to tackle avoidance should raise more than £12bn, although the figures for the tax gap have not yet shown such an increase.

Most notable of these measures is the general anti-abuse rule (GAAR – see [**3.74**] ff), which seeks to tackle the most egregious of tax avoidance arrangements and to deter those who may be tempted to use them. Other measures include the introduction of the accelerated payment regime (see [**5.26**]), under which certain taxpayers involved in marketed avoidance schemes are required to pay up front the tax they are disputing. As at 6 April 2017, more than 60,000 accelerated payment notices (APNs) to pay disputed tax had been issued since August 2014. The APN scheme was extended to NICs with effect from 12 April 2015 by the National Insurance Contributions Act 2015. In addition, HMRC:

- legislated for follower notices to encourage users of tax avoidance schemes to settle with HMRC after a relevant judicial ruling or risk facing a penalty if they lose (see [**5.27**]);
- set up a rigorous regime of penalties and monitoring requirements for high risk promoters of tax avoidance schemes, thereby tackling the supply as well as the use of marketed tax avoidance (see [**5.28**]) (HMRC has identified and issued with conduct notices the first risky promoters under the regime, requiring them to change their ways. If they fail to comply with these notices, they can be labelled as high-risk promoters, named and fined up to £1m);
- expanded and strengthened the DOTAS regime to ensure that it remains robust and to ensure that more promoters and users of avoidance schemes have to tell HMRC about their avoidance activities (the fact that the number of schemes being disclosed has declined significantly suggests that DOTAS is working successfully and that the market for tax avoidance schemes is in decline);
- increased HMRC's specialist transfer pricing team to better ensure that multinational enterprises (MNEs) pay the tax due and to prevent them from shifting profits outside of the UK; and
- introduced measures in FA 2016 to improve large business compliance, including a requirement that large businesses publish their tax strategies, a special measures regime for businesses that persistently engage in aggressive tax planning and a framework for cooperative compliance.

From an EU perspective, to ensure full tax transparency and cooperation, the Directive on Administrative Cooperation, effective from 1 January 2016, provides for the exchange of information between Member States tax administrations on all relevant financial income including interest, dividends and other similar types of income. Internationally, the UK has led efforts within the G20 group of countries to reform the international corporate tax rules through the OECD Base Erosion and Profit Shifting (BEPS) project, to make it harder for companies to avoid tax by hiding profits abroad. Whilst the European Commission's recent Anti-Tax Avoidance Directive, which provides for the automatic exchange of information on country-by-country reporting of multinational companies, is said to ensure a consistent and uniform implementation of the OECD recommendations across the EU, it may be seen by some as the Commission exploiting an opportunity to push its own agenda of a unified EU tax corporate tax policy.

As well as implementing and deploying the new powers granted to it, HMRC has been steadily defeating tax avoidance schemes in court. HMRC wins over 80% of cases that taxpayers choose to take to court, and it hopes that the publicity generated from these wins will act as a deterrent to those thinking of embarking on a tax avoidance scheme. Greater public awareness has undoubtedly contributed to changing attitudes towards avoidance over recent years.

Despite all of this, in its report on HMRC's progress in improving tax compliance and preventing tax avoidance (18 November 2014), the Public Accounts Committee (PAC) said that 'HMRC's action against tax avoiders continues to be unacceptably slow, putting tax revenues at risk'. Moreover, in its later report on the performance of HMRC for the year 2014–15 (3 November 2015), the PAC warned that HMRC's failure to gather intelligence on losses through aggressive tax avoidance is an obstacle to improving UK tax laws.

It can only be hoped that the creation in 2014 of a dedicated Counter-Avoidance Directorate within HMRC, which brings together policy, operational and technical expertise into a single directorate, will drive marketed avoidance further out of the system. This directorate, which also deals with specific issues around the GAAR and DOTAS is aimed, not at taxpayers who legitimately organise their tax affairs in the most efficient way, but rather at the people who use what HMRC calls 'specific avoidance schemes' and 'serial avoiders, and the highest risk promoters'.

This chapter analyses the way in which the courts have attempted to tackle tax avoidance; **Chapter 3** explores specific targeted legislative measures designed to neutralise avoidance; and **Chapter 5** provides an overview of the disclosure rules (DOTAS), effective from 1 August 2004, the regime against promoters of tax avoidance schemes (POTAS), accelerated payments and follower notices. [2.1]

2 Tackling tax avoidance

HMRC has three main weapons at its disposal when tackling tax avoidance. The first is legislative in the form of specific, targeted anti-avoidance measures and is considered in **Chapter 3**. The second is a group of measures that embrace the disclosure rules, rules that are aimed at promoters of tax avoidance schemes, accelerated payments and follower notices; **Chapter 5** provides an overview of all of these measures. The third weapon in HMRC's armoury, and the subject of this chapter, is to challenge in the courts the legal efficacy of avoidance schemes.

This chapter is largely historical: it charts the journey taken by the courts from a time when the Revenue was seldom successful in challenging tax avoidance ([**2.3**]) to the present day when it is winning far more cases than it loses. What happened on that journey is both interesting and instructive, and lays the foundation for the decisive HMRC victories that are being seen today.

See, for example, the recent decision of the Court of Appeal in *Eclipse Film Partners No 35 LLP v R & C Comrs* (2015) (note that the Supreme Court refused leave to appeal on the substantive issue (2016) – see [**10.28**]). This case concerned some high-profile tax planning schemes, The Eclipse schemes, which purported to be trading partnerships set up to sub-license films for a commercial profit. The 287 partners borrowed large sums from Barclays Bank to buy the licensing rights for a number of films. The interest on these loans created losses, for which they could then claim the special sideways tax relief introduced in 2005 to encourage investment in the British film industry. Each investor obtained £400,000 of tax relief for an investment of £173,000. However, HMRC challenged the £117m total of tax relief claims on the grounds that the partnership was not really a trading organisation; it claimed that the borrowed money simply earned interest which could then be returned to investors to pay the costs of their loans.

The First-tier Tax Tribunal agreed with HMRC and disallowed the relief; the Upper Tax Tribunal also held that the partnerships were not trading (although Eclipse's appeal was partially allowed on technical grounds – *Eclipse Film Partners No.35 LLP v R & C Comrs* (2013)).

On appeal to the Court of Appeal, Eclipse 35 advanced two arguments: *first*, the only reasonable conclusion from the facts was that it was trading; *second*, the activity of acquiring film rights and sub-licensing them for profit was inherently a trade as a matter of law. The Court rejected both arguments. On the first point, it decided that the activity of Eclipse 35 was of the character of a fixed-term investment, though some contingent receipts might be due later, depending on the success of the film. On the second point, the court found that there were no decided cases that justified the view that Eclipse 35's activity was inherently a trade. Following the approach taken by the House of Lords in *Barclays Mercantile Business Finance Ltd v Mawson* (2004) (*BMBF* – see **[2.38]**), a case that would appear to have offered definitive guidelines for future courts in deciding on issues of tax avoidance, the Chancellor of the High Court, Sir Terence Etherington, delivering the judgment of the whole Court, said that it was necessary to stand back and look at the whole picture and, having particular regard to what the taxpayer actually did, ask whether it constituted a trade. Having done that, the Court of Appeal concluded that there was no trade. Of the Court's decision to dismiss the appeal, Sir Terence Etherington warned that it had 'very serious fiscal consequences for the members of Eclipse 35. They will be taxed on the income from the arrangements without any relief for the interest they have already paid.'

In fact, the investors never actually received the partnership income and are therefore being taxed on large profits that they never received (and see *Scotts Atlantic Management Ltd (in members voluntary liquidation) & Ors* (2015), which concerned a tax avoidance scheme that routed profits of a tax advisory business through employee benefit trusts. Taking a purposive approach to the construction of the relevant provisions, the Upper Tribunal dismissed the taxpayers' appeal. See **[10.133]**; see also *Chappell v R & C Comrs* (2014), where a scheme involving a stock lending arrangement and manufactured dividend payment was held to be artificial with no commercial purpose and thus failed to achieve the income tax shelter it sought, and *Price v R & C Comrs* (2015), where, once again, following *BMBF*, the Upper Tribunal, taking a realistic view of the facts, dismissed the appellant taxpayers' claim that a payment of £6m for the acquisition of shares that were subsequently sold for £552 thereby created a £6m capital loss available for offset against taxable income. These are yet more examples of widely-marketed tax avoidance schemes to fail before the courts).

Finally in April 2016, the Supreme Court refused permission for an appeal against the Court of Appeal's judgement in *Eclipse 35* on the basis that

'We have heard nothing that persuades us that the Court of Appeal went wrong in this case' (per Lord Neuberger). [2.2]

3 Background

In the past the Revenue won few victories, in part because of the difficulty it had in putting forward the argument that transactions used to avoid tax should be viewed as shams. No matter how artificial a transaction may be, so long as it is genuine and properly implemented, it cannot be ignored as a sham (see, for example, *Hitch v Stone* (1999); *Audley v R & C Comrs* (2011)). The main reason for the Revenue's lack of success, however, was to be found in *IRC v Duke of Westminster* (1936). The object of the scheme in that case was to make servants' wages deductible in arriving at the Duke's total income by paying them by deed of covenant. Hence, although there was no binding agreement to that effect, it was accepted that so long as payments were made under the covenant they would not claim their wages. The House of Lords upheld the scheme saying that, in deciding the consequence of a transaction, the courts will look at the legal effect of the bargain that the parties have entered into and not take account of any supposed artificiality. [2.3]

4 The 'new approach' – an overview

Unsurprisingly, the *Westminster* case gave rise to what, in effect, could be called the very first 'taxpayer's charter', instilling a belief in those taxpayers that could afford to do so that the lengths to which they could go to avoid tax were limitless, provided they were not illegal. The growth in tax avoidance schemes became marked in the 1970s, and it seemed that legislative measures, which appeared to be insufficient to keep up with the problem, were met with even more ingenious schemes. In the early 1980s, however, the Revenue won some outstanding battles in the courts, most importantly before the House of Lords in the leading cases of *WT Ramsay Ltd v IRC, Eilbeck v Rawling* (1981), *IRC v Burmah Oil* (1982) and *Furniss v Dawson* (1984), from which cases there developed what became known as the *Ramsay* principle (named after the first case in the series, but which caused much confusion in later cases because many doubted the constitutional ability of the judiciary to develop such a principle). At that time, and most notably at the high point of *Furniss v Dawson*, in which case Lord Scarman commented that new law was gradually being developed and that the boundaries remained yet to be fully explored, it was felt that the new principle had sounded the death knell to artificial avoidance schemes. That feeling was given further credence by the high level of hostility shown by the Revenue to such schemes as evidenced by *IRC v Rossminster Ltd* (1980), and it was believed that potential customers would be deterred from purchasing avoidance packages. The status of the *Westminster* case was left unclear by these judgments, which showed that judicial attitudes to tax avoidance from the 1980s onwards were very different from those prevailing in the 1930s. Indeed, in *Furniss v Dawson*, Lord Roskill considered that 'the ghost of the Duke of Westminster has haunted the administration of this branch of the law for too long'.

Concern, however, was expressed that the development of the so-called *Ramsay* principle was nothing short of judicial legislation and, as such, an infringement of the Bill of Rights of 1689 (which established that there should be no taxation without representation). Not surprisingly therefore, subsequent decisions have been concerned with a close analysis of the true effect of *Ramsay* and the series of cases that followed. *Craven v White* (1989) and *Fitzwilliam v IRC* (1993), both of which were won by the taxpayer, left the precise ambit of the 'judicial associated operations rule' uncertain, with Lord Oliver in *Craven v White* seeking to explain that the *Ramsay* principle was simply an exercise in statutory construction. In *IRC v McGuckian* (1997), this view was used to the Revenue's advantage in the promotion of purposive statutory interpretation, which certain members of the House of Lords (notably, Lords Steyn and Cooke) believed to be the basis of the *Ramsay* decision. This approach would have given the Revenue almost guaranteed success in challenging tax avoidance schemes, as is evident from Lord Steyn's comment: 'Given the reasoning underlying the new approach it is wrong to regard the decisions of the House of Lords since the *Ramsay* case as necessarily marking the limit of the law on tax avoidance schemes.' Importantly, however, there could be seen an element of retreat in the decision of *MacNiven v Westmoreland* (2001), with Lord Nicholls commenting that 'the *Ramsay* approach is no more than a useful aid ... *Ramsay* did not introduce a new legal principle. It would be wrong, therefore, to set bounds to the circumstances in which the *Ramsay* approach may be appropriate and helpful'. Lord Hoffmann in the same case went further. In rejecting the view that *Ramsay* is a principle of construction, he commented: 'There is ultimately only one principle of construction, namely to ascertain what Parliament meant by using the language of the statute.' He explained further that the formulation of *Ramsay* given in *IRC v Burmah Oil* and *Furniss v Dawson* is simply 'a statement of the consequences of giving a commercial construction to a fiscal concept'. Whilst the approach taken by Lord Hoffmann was applied by the Court of Appeal in relation to a PAYE scheme in *DTE Financial Services Ltd v Wilson* (2001), the difficulties inherent in such an approach can be seen in the conflicting decisions of the High Court and the Court of Appeal in *Barclays Mercantile Business Finance Ltd v Mawson* (2002), and in the judgments of both Peter Gibson and Carnwath LLJ in the Court of Appeal in that case. And, whilst in *The Collector of Stamp Revenue v Arrowtown Assets Ltd* (2003) Lord Millett (sitting as a non-permanent judge in the Hong Kong Court of Final Appeal) delivered a challenge to Lord Hoffmann's approach, the House of Lords in *Barclays Mercantile Business Finance Ltd v Mawson* (2004) appeared finally to have laid to rest the notion that *Ramsay* had given birth to a special principle affecting tax statutes and tax law, affirming that the case had been decided on the normal basis of statutory construction, leading to the conclusion that the decisions of the House of Lords in *IRC v Burmah Oil* and *Furniss v Dawson*, which appeared to have created a principle lying outside the meaning of the statute whereby transactions or elements in transactions that had no commercial purpose were to be disregarded, were either incorrectly decided or had been misconstrued. Indeed, in *R & C Comrs v Tower MCashback LLP 1* (2011), Lord Walker commented that 'the clarity of Lord Wilberforce's insights [in *Ramsay*] was rather obscured by some subsequent decisions, especially (if I may respectfully say so) the opinion of Lord Brightman in *Furniss v Dawson* ...'. However, a recent spate of cases, including *Tower MCashback*, demonstrate that the application of *Barclays Mercantile Business Finance Ltd v Mawson* (2004) is by no means straightforward. **[2.4]–[2.20]**

II ARTIFICIAL SCHEMES AND THE *RAMSAY* 'PRINCIPLE'

1 The decisions in *Ramsay* and *Burmah Oil*

In both *Ramsay* and *Burmah Oil* the taxpayers sought to obtain the benefits of CGT loss relief, in the former case to wipe out large profits, in the latter to turn a large, non-allowable loss into an allowable one. To achieve this end both adopted schemes involving a series of steps to be carried out in rapid succession according to a pre-arranged timetable. Once started, it was intended that the schemes should be carried through to their conclusion that would be that a capital loss had been incurred. In reality, a comparison of the taxpayer's position at the start and finish showed that either no real loss was suffered, or, in *Ramsay's* case, that the only loss suffered was the professional fees paid for the implementation of the scheme! The House of Lords decided that such schemes should be viewed not as a series of separate transactions, none of which was a sham, but as a whole; the position of the taxpayer in real terms being compared at the start and at the finish. Thus, the scheme involved no real loss and was self-cancelling. In *Ramsay* Lord Wilberforce expounded this new approach to avoidance schemes and sought to explain the decision in *Westminster's* case:

> 'While obliging the court to accept documents or transactions, found to be genuine, as such, it does not compel the court to look at a document or a transaction in blinkers, isolated from any context to which it properly belongs. If it can be seen that a document or transaction was intended to have effect as part of a nexus or series of transactions, or as an ingredient of a wider transaction intended as a whole, there is nothing in the doctrine to prevent it being so regarded; to do so is not to prefer form to substance, or substance to form. It is the task of the court to ascertain the legal nature of any transaction to which it is sought to attach a tax, or a tax consequence, and if that emerges from a series, or combination of transactions, intended to operate as such, it is that series or combination which may be regarded.'
>
> ([1981] STC 174 at 180)

In *Ensign Tankers (Leasing) Ltd v Stokes* (1992) the House of Lords applied the *Ramsay* principle to the single composite transaction made up of 17 documents all dated the same day. **[2.21]**

2 Extending *Ramsay*: *Furniss v Dawson*

a) *The facts*

It was left to Lord Brightman in *Furniss v Dawson*, building upon the words of Lord Diplock in *Burmah Oil*, to set out the conditions necessary for the application of the *Ramsay* principle: *first*, there must be a pre-ordained series of transactions (or one single composite transaction); *second*, there must be steps inserted which have no commercial purpose other than the avoidance of tax.

24   *Tax avoidance and the courts*

Unlike the *Ramsay* and *Burmah Oil* cases, both of which involved circular self-cancelling schemes, the sole object of which was the avoidance of tax, *Furniss v Dawson* was concerned with the deferment of CGT by channelling the sale of chargeable assets through an intermediary company. The facts of the case are simple. The Dawsons decided to sell shares to Wood Bastow Holdings Ltd ('Wood Bastow') for £152,000. To defer the CGT that would otherwise have been payable, the shares were first sold to a newly incorporated Manx company ('Greenjacket') for the sum of £152,000 that was satisfied by an issue of shares in that company. The purchased shares were then immediately resold by Greenjacket to Wood Bastow for £152,000. The attraction of the scheme was that at no stage did any CGT liability arise: the sale to Greenjacket was specifically exempted from charge under FA 1965 Sch 7 para 6(2) (see now TCGA 1992 s 135(1)), whilst the resale by Greenjacket did not yield any profit to that company (the shares were purchased and sold for £152,000). As the price paid by Wood Bastow was received and retained by Greenjacket the scheme was not circular or self-cancelling: it involved a separate legal entity (Greenjacket) that ended up with the sale proceeds of the shares.   [2.22]

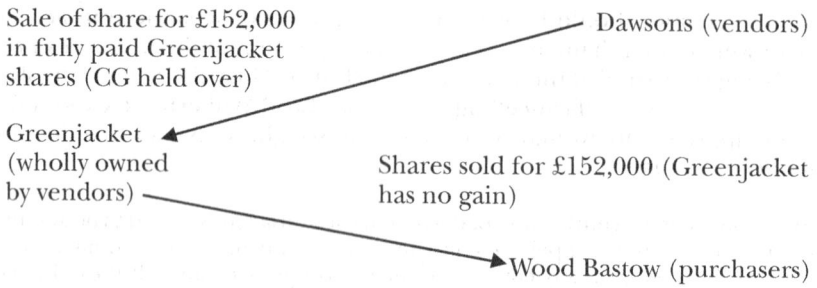

b) *The decision*

Before the Special Commissioners, Vinelott J, and a unanimous Court of Appeal, CGT was held not to be payable. The sale proceeds had been paid to Greenjacket and, in the phrase of Slade LJ in the Court of Appeal, the existence of Greenjacket had 'enduring legal consequences'. Before the House of Lords it was accepted that for a *scintilla temporis* legal and beneficial title to the shares passed to Greenjacket. Lord Brightman, however, in the only fully argued speech (which was concurred in by the other Lords) viewed the series of transactions as a pre-planned scheme:

'The whole process was planned and executed with faultless precision. The meetings began at 12.45pm on 20 December, at which time the shareholdings of the operating companies were still owned by the Dawsons unaffected by any contract of sale. They ended with the shareholdings in the ownership of Wood Bastow. The minutes do not disclose when the meeting ended but perhaps it was all over in time for lunch.'

As its purpose was to obtain a deferral of CGT, he concluded that the scheme should be viewed as a whole, that is as a composite transaction different from the actual transaction entered into by the parties, and that 'the court must then look at the end result. Precisely how the end result will be taxed will depend on the terms of the taxing statute sought to be applied'. Applying that test 'there was a disposal of the shares by the Dawsons in favour of Wood Bastow in consideration of a sum of money paid with the concurrence of the Dawsons to Greenjacket'. The gain on this disposal was subject to CGT. As already mentioned, Lord Brightman considered that there were two basic requirements for the application of the *Ramsay* principle. *First*, there must be a pre-ordained series of transactions ('a scheme'), although he stressed that, so long as a pre-planned tax saving scheme existed, no distinction should be drawn between the case where steps were carried out in pursuance of a contract and one where, although the steps were pre-ordained, separate binding contracts only arose at each stage. Although Greenjacket was not contractually bound to resell the shares to Wood Bastow, it was pre-ordained (ie there was an informal arrangement) that this would occur. Hence, 'the day is not saved for the taxpayer because the arrangement is unsigned or contains the magic words "this is not a binding contract"'. In a similar vein, Lord Fraser of Tulleybelton considered that 'the series of two transactions ... were planned as a single scheme and ... it should be viewed as a whole'. Furthermore, the scheme may include the attainment of a legitimate business end: the scheme in that case enabled shares to be sold from the Dawsons to Wood Bastow. *Second*, there must be steps in the scheme whose sole purpose is to avoid (or defer) a liability to tax. Such steps may have a 'business effect' but no 'business purpose'. The insertion of Greenjacket was such a step: in the words of Lord Brightman 'that inserted step had no business purpose apart from deferment of tax, although it had a business effect. If the sale had taken place in 1964 before CGT was introduced, there would have been no Greenjacket'.

An argument put forward by the Revenue in *Griffin v Citibank Investments Ltd* (2000), that *Ramsay* provided for a 'wider' analysis than *Furniss v Dawson*, and that the court should not be constrained by the preconditions set out therein, was rejected by Patten J in the High Court. He said that to accept that contention would be to convert genuine transactions into something quite different and would attribute to those transactions 'a substance and legal effect which they do not have and which ... the court would not give them upon the application of the ordinary principles of construction ...'.   **[2.23]**

III   LIMITS TO THE *RAMSAY* PRINCIPLE

1   **The difficulty in application**

Not only were the requirements just mentioned difficult to apply but, being almost in the nature of a statutory formulation, it was clearly open to later courts to interpret them in 'inventive' ways. Two of their Lordships considered that the *Westminster* case could be distinguished as involving a single and not a composite transaction. Certainly the covenant was a single transaction, but its sole purpose was the avoidance of income tax and it was only entered into on the 'understanding' that the gardeners would not seek to claim their wages. Hence the making of the covenant was a step that had no commercial purpose save for the avoidance of tax. It is arguable, however, that unlike

Greenjacket, which was an artificial person under the control of the Dawsons, the gardener's continuing right to sue for his wages serves to distinguish the case. Furthermore, as the covenant was to last for a period of seven years or the joint lives of the parties, it could have continued after the employment had terminated.

Any pre-arranged scheme which involves either tax avoidance, tax deferral or merely the preservation of an existing tax benefit was potentially within the *Ramsay* principle, but a single tax-efficient transaction presumably was not since the case does *not* state that persons must so organise their affairs that they pay the maximum amount of tax! [2.24]

2 A pre-ordained series of transactions

In the case of *Craven v White* (conjoined on appeal with *Baylis v Gregory* and *IRC v Bowater Property Developments Ltd*), the House of Lords was faced with the question of when a series of transactions forms part of a pre-planned scheme (or, alternatively, when it constitutes a single composite transaction). In all three of these cases, and for differing reasons, the ultimate purchaser remained unknown throughout the relevant transactions. For this reason, the House of Lords held that there could be no pre-ordained scheme. In reaching this conclusion, Lord Jauncey, expressing the view held by the majority, suggested the following definition of a 'composite transaction':

> 'A step in a linear transaction which has no business purpose apart from the avoidance or deferment of tax liability will be treated as forming part of a pre-ordained series of transactions or of a composite transaction if it was taken at a time when negotiations or arrangements for the carrying through as a continuous process of a subsequent transaction which actually takes place had reached a stage when there was no real likelihood that such subsequent transaction would not take place and if thereafter such negotiations or arrangements were carried through to completion without genuine interruption.'

This restrictive view of the meaning of a composite transaction would appear to give a taxpayer a way of surmounting the first part of Lord Brightman's test (see [2.23]), although *IRC v Scottish Provident* (2004) suggests that this may not always be successful (see [2.38]).

Fitzwilliam v IRC (1993) further demonstrates how easy it is to show that there is no composite scheme. Following the death of her husband a year earlier, Lady Fitzwilliam along with Lady Hastings (her daughter) and two beneficiaries, all of whom were the trustees of Lord Fitzwilliam's will, entered into a series of transactions involving five steps, devised by professional advisers, and intended to mitigate the ultimate capital transfer tax (CTT) bill. The transactions were to a large degree artificial (the appointment of interests for short periods) and in some cases circular and the end result was that some £7.8m had been distributed out of the residuary estate – £3.8m to Lady Hastings and £4m to Lady Fitzwilliam – without, it appeared, any CTT liability. The House of Lords held that this did not constitute a pre-ordained single composite transaction as formulated in *Ramsay*. Each step taken pursuant to the scheme had its own fiscal effect, imposing a charge to income tax on the relevant beneficiary for a limited period of time, and there was a potential charge to CTT on the estate of Lady Fitzwilliam in the event of her death while in possession of an interest appointed to her under the scheme. It was therefore not possible to treat the scheme as one composite whole.

For a fuller analysis of the cases discussed in this section, see earlier editions of this book. [2.25]–[2.28]

3 The insertion of steps with no business purpose

It may be remembered that, in considering whether steps inserted into a series of transactions had as their sole purpose tax avoidance, Lord Brightman made it clear that, for *Ramsay* to apply, such steps may have a 'business effect' but no 'business purpose' (see [2.23]–[2.24]). However, in *Fitzwilliam v IRC*, Lord Keith said:

> 'The fact of preordainment ... is not sufficient in itself, in my opinion, to negative the application of an exemption from liability to tax which the series of transactions is intended to create, unless the series is capable of being construed in a manner inconsistent with the application of the exemption ... in my opinion the series in the present case cannot be ... There is no question of running any two or more transactions together as in *Furniss v Dawson* or of disregarding any one or more of them.'

This crucial part of Lord Keith's judgment was strongly rejected by Lord Templeman. In his view, three of the inserted steps had no purpose other than the avoidance of CTT. In truth, none of the steps had any commercial purpose although they had 'enduring legal consequences' in that they gave rise, albeit for a very short period of time, to an income interest in favour of Lady Hastings or Lady Fitzwilliam. Clearly, the distinction drawn by Lord Brightman between *purpose* and *effect* appears to have been ignored by Lord Keith.

Although at the time it was possible to see the failure of the House of Lords to adapt *Ramsay* to the facts in *Fitzwilliam* as at root a failure of will, it can now possibly be better understood as part of a process of learning to understand what the exact effect of *Ramsay* was. [2.29]–[2.31]

IV REAFFIRMATION OF *RAMSAY*

1 *IRC v McGuckian*: the facts

The case involved numerous transactions, the strategy behind which was to reduce the assets held by a company (B), thus minimising the risk of exposure to a possible wealth tax on its shareholders, namely the taxpayer and his wife. At the same time to avoid an income tax liability on moneys paid out by B by ensuring that the proceeds were received in the form of capital rather than income. The main features of the scheme involved:

(1) the setting up of a trust under which B shares would be held for the benefit of the taxpayer and his wife by a trustee residing outside the jurisdiction; and

(2) a sale by the trustee of their rights to dividends expected to be declared and paid by B. This was in the form of a written assignment between the trustee and the purchaser, and for a consideration that only just fell short (by 1%) of the eventual dividend declared for that year by B.

The trustees were then – so it was argued – in receipt of a capital sum which could not be attributed to the settlor under eg TA 1988 s 739. As Lord Browne-Wilkinson observed, the crucial question was whether the money received by the trustee as consideration for the assignment of the right to the dividends from B was to be treated as the income of the trustee or as capital. As the proceeds of sale, the sum of money would appear to be capital; however, by applying the *Ramsay* principle, the inserted step (the assignment of the right to the dividends) would be excised, leaving the sum of money to be regarded as income. [2.32]

2 The House of Lords speeches

Unlike the majority of the Court of Appeal (Northern Ireland), Lord Browne-Wilkinson had no difficulty in applying the *Ramsay* principle; in his judgment, 'nothing in this case turns on the exact scope of the *Ramsay* principle. The case falls squarely within the classic requirements for the application of that principle as stated by Lord Brightman in *Furniss v Dawson* ...'. This was a view shared by Lord Steyn who, although feeling the necessity to analyse the basis of the *Ramsay* decision and to question the literal interpretation of taxation statutes, accepted that the present case was 'a classic case for the application of the *Ramsay* principle'. The inserted step had no commercial purpose apart from the avoidance of income tax, with the consequence that it had to be excised. The other members of the court reached the same conclusion, although the reasoning of each of the four Law Lords who delivered judgments was different in emphasis.

Worthy of particular note is the rejection by Lord Browne-Wilkinson of the taxpayer's argument that the *Ramsay* principle can only apply to a series of transactions in the absence of a statutory provision that would reverse the effect of such transactions. He said:

'The approach pioneered in *Ramsay* and subsequently developed in later decisions is an approach to construction, viz that in construing tax legislation, the statutory provisions are to be applied to the substance of the transaction, disregarding artificial steps in the composite transaction or series of transactions inserted only for the purpose of seeking to obtain a tax advantage. The question is not what was the effect of the insertion of the artificial steps but what was its purpose. Having identified the artificial steps inserted with that purpose and disregarded them, then what is left is to apply the statutory language of the taxing Act to the transaction carried through stripped of its artificial steps. It is irrelevant to consider whether or not the disregarded artificial steps would have been effective to achieve the tax saving purpose for which they were designed.' (See also Lord Cooke who considered that *Ramsay* was antecedent to or collateral with anti-avoidance provisions.)

The importance of *McGuckian* lies in the language used by the House of Lords in relation to tax avoidance schemes: in terms of clarifying when the principle operates, matters were left as unclear as they ever had been (see, for instance, *Piggott v Staines Investments* (1995) which at first glance would appear to fall within the principle but which was not appealed by the Revenue). Thus, in considering *Craven v White*, Lord Cooke noted that it involved facts 'distant from those of the present case' and categorised it as 'a difficult case, partly because of differences of opinion in Your Lordships' House'. **[2.33]**

V MEANING, SCOPE AND APPLICABILITY OF THE *RAMSAY* PRINCIPLE: THE LATER CASES

1 The earlier cases: a doctrine of fiscal nullity or statutory construction?

That there has been uncertainty as to the basis and extent of the *Ramsay* principle from the start, can be evidenced by the words of Lord Scarman in *Furniss v Dawson*:

> 'I am aware, and the legal profession (and others) must understand, that the law in this area is in an early stage of development. Speeches in your Lordships' House and judgments in the appellate courts are concerned more to chart a way forward between principles accepted and not to be rejected than to attempt anything so ambitious as to determine finally the limit beyond which the safe channel of acceptable tax avoidance shelves into the dangerous shallows of unacceptable tax evasion. The law will develop from case to case. Lord Wilberforce in *Ramsay's* case referred to "the emerging principle" of the law. What has been established with certainty by the House in *Ramsay's* case is that the determination of what does, and what does not, constitute unacceptable tax evasion is a subject suited to development by judicial process. Difficult though that task may be for judges, it is one which is beyond the power of the blunt instrument of legislation. Whatever a statute may provide, it has to be interpreted and applied by the courts and ultimately it will prove to be in this area of judge-made law that our elusive journey's end will be found.'

Not only does this passage reveal that Lord Scarman appeared to be giving a new meaning to the terms 'tax avoidance' and 'tax evasion', perhaps a forewarning of the current attitude of HMRC, but it also demonstrates a ready acceptance that new law was being created and that this was the proper function of the judiciary. Such sentiments did not, however, commend themselves to the majority of the House of Lords in the later case of *Craven v White* (and conjoined appeals). Indeed, the majority appeared anxious to distance themselves from any notion of judicial legislation, and sought to explain an alternative and more acceptable basis of the *Ramsay* decision. For instance, Lord Oliver commented that the basis was one of statutory construction:

> 'It has been said that *Furniss v Dawson* is "judge-made law". So it is, but judges are not legislators and if the result of a judicial decision is to contradict the express statutory consequences which have been declared by Parliament to attach to a particular transaction which has been found as a fact to have taken place, that can be justified only because, as a matter of construction of the statute, the court has ascertained that that which has taken place is not, within the meaning of the statute, the transaction to which those consequences attach.'

Having accepted that *Furniss v Dawson* had, in reality, extended the *Ramsay* principle in that it not only applied that principle to a 'linear' transaction, but it also reconstituted the actual constituent transactions into something that they were not in fact, Lord Oliver made this important observation:

> 'It seems ... that the first and critical point to be borne in mind in considering the true ratio of *Furniss v Dawson* is that it rests not upon some fancied principle that anything done with a mind to minimising tax is to be struck down but upon the premise that the intermediate transfer, whose statutory consequences would otherwise have resulted in payment of tax being postponed, did not, upon the true construction of the [statute], constitute a disposal attracting the consequences set out in [the relevant provision]. That is the first point. The second is that, in reaching the conclusion as a matter of construction, this House did not purport to be doing anything more than applying and explaining the principle that had been laid down ... in [*Ramsay*]. It was that decision that explains why and how the question of construction raised in *Furniss v Dawson* came to be answered in the way that it did and it is ... only if these two considerations are borne in mind that *Furniss v Dawson* itself can be properly understood or rationally justified as a proper exercise of the judicial function.'

It is difficult to fit the speeches in *Furniss v Dawson* into a purely constructional approach but, as later cases show, the fault rests with Lord Brightman (following Lord Diplock in *IRC v Burmah Oil Co Ltd* (1982)) in laying down a detailed, statute-like and fairly inflexible prescription of how the *Ramsay* principle works. As Lord Hoffmann said in *MacNiven v Westmoreland Investments Ltd* (2001) (see [**2.37**]):

> 'In the first flush of victory after the *Ramsay, Burmah* and *Furniss* cases, there was a tendency on the part of the Inland Revenue to treat Lord Brightman's words as if they were a broad spectrum antibiotic which killed off all tax avoidance schemes, whatever the tax and whatever the relevant provisions.'

Patten J, too, in *Griffin v Citibank Investments Ltd* (2000) made it clear that he did not believe that the decision in *Furniss* was in accord with either *IRC v Duke of Westminster* or the ordinary principles of construction and analysis that *Ramsay* applied.

The considerable level of disagreement on the ambit of the principle and the role of the courts in tax avoidance, was revealed by Lord Templeman in *Craven v White*:

> 'I have read the drafts of the speeches to be delivered in these present appeals. Three of those speeches accept the extreme argument of the taxpayer that *Furniss v Dawson* is limited to its own facts or is limited to a transaction which has reached an advanced stage of negotiation (whatever that expression means) before the preceding tax avoidance transaction is carried out. These limitations would distort the effect of *Furniss*, are not based on principle, are not to be derived from the speeches in *Furniss*, and if followed, would only revive a surprised tax avoidance industry and cost the general body of taxpayers hundreds of millions of pounds by enabling artificial tax avoidance schemes to alter the incidence of taxation. In *Furniss*, Lord Brightman was not alone in delivering a magisterial rebuke to those judges who sought to place limitations on *Ramsay* ... In my opinion, a knife-edged majority has no power to limit this principle which has been responsible for four decisions of this House approved by a large number of our predecessors.'

Lord Templeman always considered that the type of transactions envisaged by *Ramsay* and *Furniss v Dawson* were akin to sham transactions and should be treated accordingly. In *Matrix-Securities Ltd v IRC* (1994) he commented: 'Every tax avoidance scheme involves a trick and a pretence. It is the task of the Revenue to unravel the trick and the duty of the Court to ignore the pretence'. The dictionary definition of a 'sham' is a 'trick' or a 'pretence'. [2.34]

2 The later cases: statutory construction confirmed

Later cases, however, sought to lay this matter to rest. In *Fitzwilliam v IRC*, Nourse LJ summarised the position as follows:

'In *Craven v White* each of their Lordships said that the *Ramsay* principle is one of statutory construction. That is without doubt true in the sense that once the single composite transaction has been identified the question is whether it is caught by the taxing statute on which the Crown relies. However, it does not always or even usually involve a question of statutory construction in the sense that the meaning of the statute is in doubt. Usually the question is whether a statute whose meaning is clear applies to the single composite transaction. The principle might equally be described as one of statutory application.'

The approach taken by a majority of the House of Lords in *Fitzwilliam*, encapsulated in a statement by Lord Browne-Wilkinson, would appear to support this view:

'Whatever the exact scope of the principles laid down in *W T Ramsay Ltd v IRC* ... as developed and elucidated in *Furniss (HMIT) v Dawson* ... and *Craven (HMIT) v White*, the basic principle cannot be in doubt. The commissioners or the court must identify the real transaction carried out by the taxpayers and, if this real transaction is carried through by a series of artificial steps, apply the words of the taxing provisions to the real transaction, disregarding for fiscal purposes the steps artificially inserted. The provision of the taxing statute is to be construed as applying to the actual transaction the parties were effecting in the real world, not to the artificial forms in which the parties chose to clothe in the surrealist world of tax advisers.'

Of course, this view enabled the majority of the House of Lords to concentrate on matters of detail which, in turn, led to the decision that the transaction undertaken did not form one composite whole (see **[2.33]**) thus allowing £3.8m to pass tax free. As was previously observed (see **[2.34]**), the arrangements in *Fitzwilliam* fell clearly within the spirit and intendment of Lord Brightman's test laid down in *Dawson* and, had Lord Scarman's observations been followed (see **[2.36]**), would have been brought within the tax net. [2.35]

3 Purposive interpretation: *IRC v McGuckian*

That the approach pioneered in *Ramsay* and developed in later decisions is an approach to construction, was again reiterated by Lord Browne-Wilkinson in *IRC v McGuckian* (1997), expressing the view of the majority of the House of

Lords. However, in the same case, Lord Steyn (who would have decided the case without the benefit of the *Ramsay* principle) felt the necessity to analyse the basis of the *Ramsay* decision and to question the literal interpretation of taxation statutes. His view (of necessity an *obiter* view and one with which Lord Cooke concurred) was that *Ramsay* was important for two reasons. *First*, was the rejection by the House of pure literalism in the interpretation of tax statutes, and a move to a more purposive method of construction. This he identified in the following statement made by Lord Wilberforce: 'There may, indeed should, be considered the context and scheme of the relevant Act as a whole, and its purpose may, indeed should, be regarded.' *Second*, was the acceptance that a series of transactions, intended to be implemented as a whole, could be regarded for fiscal purposes as one composite transaction. Therefore, according to Lord Steyn, the *Ramsay* principle 'was not based on a linguistic analysis of the meaning of particular words in a statute. It was founded on a broad purposive interpretation, giving effect to the intention of Parliament. The principle enunciated in *Ramsay* was therefore based on an orthodox form of statutory interpretation'.

It would appear that the importance of *McGuckian* lies in the acceptance by at least two members of the House of Lords that, in applying *Ramsay*, the court should adopt a *purposive* approach to interpreting the relevant statutory provision. In the immediate aftermath of *McGuckian*, there were few signs of enthusiasm towards the purposive approach to statutory interpretation of fiscal statutes in general. For instance, neither the House of Lords in *Ingram v IRC* (1999) (see **[29.123]**) nor a unanimous Court of Appeal in *Frankland v IRC* (1997) (see **[30.147]**) were willing to apply 'a broad purposive approach' to the interpretation of the relevant statutory provisions before them. But, of course, neither of these cases was concerned with *Ramsay*. However, in the case of *MacNiven v Westmoreland Investments Ltd*, both Lord Hoffmann and Lord Nicholls endorsed the views of Lords Steyn and Cooke in *McGuckian*. Indeed, Lord Nicholls referred to 'the established purposive approach to the interpretation of statutes'. He continued:

> 'When searching for the meaning with which Parliament has used the statutory language in question, courts have regard to the underlying purpose that the statutory language is seeking to achieve. Likewise, Lord Cooke of Thorndon regarded *Ramsay* as an application to taxing Acts of the general approach to statutory interpretation whereby, in determining the natural meaning of particular expressions in their context, weight is given to the purpose and spirit of the legislation ...' **[2.36]**

4 *MacNiven v Westmoreland*: a commercial characterisation of fiscal concepts

The facts in *Westmoreland* (2001) revealed a pre-ordained series of transactions designed to secure a tax advantage to Westmoreland (WIL) in the guise of an allowable loss. WIL had incurred debts, including £40m arrears of interest on loans from a pension fund, the trustees of which were its only shareholders. Although WIL's losses were real, under TA 1988 s 338 they only became deductible for income tax purposes when actually paid. However, WIL had no assets upon which money could be raised to make the repayment, and thus a simple scheme was devised to make this possible: the pension fund lent money to WIL, which WIL then passed back as payment of interest. The intention was that such payment be a charge on income by virtue of TA 1988 s 338, thus creating a loss that WIL could set against any future profits of the company, even if there was a later change of ownership. (Note that, in making these payments of yearly interest, WIL was obliged to deduct tax at source. However, as the recipient pension fund was an exempt body, it could reclaim the tax. As Lord Hoffmann suggested, it was this to which the Revenue most objected.) Finding in favour of the taxpayer that there had been a payment within the section, the House of Lords rejected the argument advanced by the Revenue that the tax advantage gained by reason of the planned scheme should be vitiated by applying a wide formulation of the '*Ramsay* principle'.

Unlike *McGuckian*, the importance of *Westmoreland* lies in the fact that Lord Hoffmann, who gave the leading speech and with whom all of the members of the House concurred, took the opportunity to review the major cases decided since *Ramsay*, and sought to explain the true basis of that case. For him, as for all the other members of the House, that basis lies in statutory construction (nothing new at this point). However, he readily rejected the notion, advanced by the Revenue, that this principle of construction took the form of an overriding legal principle that sought to nullify any transaction, no matter how genuine, that is (or is part of) some pre-ordained, circular, self-cancelling transaction undertaken for no commercial purpose other than the obtaining of a tax advantage and irrespective of the language or purpose of any particular provision. As he said: 'There is ultimately only one principle of construction, namely to ascertain what Parliament meant by using the language of the statute'. Lord Nicholls was also insistent that '*Ramsay* did not introduce a new legal principle' of the kind advanced by the Revenue. Rather 'the *Ramsay* approach is no more than a useful aid [in ascertaining the legal nature of a transaction]'. Lord Hoffmann believed that some of the confusion that had abounded over the last two decades or so stemmed from the tendency to construe the conditions necessary for the application of *Ramsay* (see [**2.22**]) to particular statutory provisions 'as if it were itself a general principle, applicable to all tax legislation'. According to him, the essence of Lord Wilberforce's judgment in *Ramsay* was the distinction between commercial concepts and juristic analysis. Thus, in that case, it had to be determined whether there had been a 'disposal' giving rise to a 'loss'. By ascribing to those words a commercial meaning, it was permissible to view all the transactions together, rather than considering each step individually, and applying those words to the result of the overall transaction. As Lord Hoffmann explained:

> 'There had never been any commercial possibility that the transactions would not have cancelled each other out. Therefore, notwithstanding the juristic independence of each of the steps of the circular transaction, the commercial view would have been to lump them all together, as the parties themselves intended, and describe them as a composite transaction which had no financial consequences. The innovation in the *Ramsay* case was to give the statutory concepts of "disposal" and "loss" a commercial meaning. The new principle of construction was a recognition that the statutory language was intended to refer to commercial concepts, so that in the case of a concept such as "disposal", the court was required to take a view of the facts which transcended the juristic individuality of the various parts of a preplanned series of transactions.'

This approach taken by Lord Hoffmann was summarised by Lightman J at first instance in *IRC v John Lewis Properties plc* (2001) (whilst Lightman J's decision was upheld by the Court of Appeal in *John Lewis Properties plc v IRC* (2003), the reasoning was very different). The case concerned the question of whether a lump sum payment received by the company from a bank in return for the assignment of various leases to the bank was a capital or income payment (there now exist provisions directed at similar rent factoring schemes, which have the effect of taxing as income the price obtained on such assignments, but they did not have retrospective effect). In holding the payment to be capital, Lightman J explained that, following *Westmoreland*, the court was required as the first step in the purposive construction of the relevant statute:

> 'to identify the concept to which the statute refers and to determine whether the concept is a legally defined concept or a commercial concept, ie "a concept which Parliament intended to be given a commercial meaning". If the concept is a legally defined concept (eg "payment of interest"), the concept cannot (in the absence of expression of some statutory policy to the contrary) be given a wider or narrower meaning so as to disregard or cancel the effect of transactions answering that description because they have no commercial purpose other than to avoid tax. But if the concept is a commercial concept (eg "disposal" or "loss") and accordingly the statute applies the test of ordinary business, the court is required to look beyond the juristic individuality of component parts of a transaction: steps which have no commercial purpose but have been artificially inserted for tax purposes into a composite transaction will not affect the answer to the statutory question (eg whether there has been a profit or loss).'

In the Court of Appeal in *Barclays Mercantile Business Finance Ltd v Mawson* (2002) (see **[2.38]**, and note the difference in the approach taken by the Court of Appeal and the House of Lords), Peter Gibson LJ analysed the situation rather more succinctly. His view was that the *Ramsay* approach is applicable where:

> '... it is sought to attach a tax consequence to a transaction which typically consists of a series of pre-ordained transactions or a single composite transaction, in which steps have been inserted which have no business purpose apart from the avoidance of tax. The court gives effect to the statutory language, where the concept to which the statute refers is a commercial one, by disregarding the artificial steps.'

Having established that the attribution of commercial concepts to terms used in tax legislation (most notably the term 'profits or gains') had been occurring for some considerable time, Lord Hoffmann added: 'What was fresh and new about *Ramsay* was the realisation that such an approach need not be confined to well recognised accounting concepts such as profit and loss but could be the appropriate construction of other taxation concepts as well'. Whether such a construction can be applied to other provisions in the tax legislation must depend upon their language and purpose. Lord Hoffmann said that before applying Lord Brightman's conditions:

> '... it is first necessary to construe the statutory language and decide that it refers to a concept which Parliament intended to be given a commercial meaning capable

of transcending the juristic individuality of its component parts. But there are many terms in tax legislation which cannot be construed in this way. They refer to purely legal concepts which have no broader commercial meaning. In such cases, the *Ramsay* principle can have no application.'

In *Furniss v Dawson*, the relevant concept was whether the disposal that had undoubtedly been made was to one person (G) or to another (D) (see [**2.22**]). According to Lord Hoffmann's analysis, by giving a commercial characterisation to that concept, the House of Lords was able to answer the statutory question to whom was the disposal made by treating the intermediate step involving G as irrelevant. Of significance is the fact that Lord Hoffmann would not disregard or 'excise' the intermediate step; he was merely saying that for the purposes of determining the answer to a particular statutory question, that intermediate step is *irrelevant*. It is because of this rationalisation that Lord Hoffmann sympathised with the view of the Court of Appeal in *McGuckian* that the assignment by Shurltrust of its right to income to Mallard choice in return for a capital payment could not be disregarded (for the facts of *McGuckian*, see [**2.35**]). 'If the assignment had to be disregarded, one could not explain how Shurltrust had received any money at all.' Thus, whilst agreeing with the conclusion of the House of Lords in the same case that the application of the *Ramsay* principle vitiated any tax advantage to the taxpayers, Lord Hoffmann preferred to explain this on the basis that for the purpose of the fiscal concept in question, namely the character of the receipt as income, the assignment to Shurltrust was an irrelevance.

In *Westmoreland* itself, the question that had to be decided was quite simply whether there had been a payment. According to the above analysis, if a commercial attribution can be given to the term 'payment', then that term would be applied only to the end result, ignoring the all-important intermediate steps and, accordingly, no payment would be held to have been made. However, Lord Hoffmann said that a distinction had to be made between terms that could be construed commercially and those that should be interpreted juristically. In the present context, the term 'payment' was to be construed juristically and, according to its juristic meaning, there was a payment if the legal obligation to pay interest had been discharged.

Although the clear import of *Westmoreland* is that when applying a statutory provision, if a relevant concept is commercial, a transaction can be ignored if it has no commercial purpose apart from the avoidance of tax, Lord Hoffmann himself identified circumstances where that might not be the case. So, a transaction which comes within the statutory language, construed in the correct commercial sense, cannot be disregarded simply on the ground that it was entered into solely for tax reasons. Accordingly, in *Craven v White* (1989), although the initial disposal had no commercial purpose apart from laying the foundation for the avoidance of tax if and when there should be a further disposal to a third party, the transactions were so separate as to make it impossible to treat them in a commercial sense as a single disposal to the third party. Both the lapse of time between the two transactions and the lack of contemplation of any specific later disposal at the time of the first transaction were commercial realities. Similarly, in *Griffin v Citibank Investments Ltd* (2000) (see [**2.22**]), where it had to be decided, *inter alia*, whether two option contracts ('put' and 'call' options) undoubtedly entered into as part of a pre-planned scheme to produce a capital gain rather than an income profit, should be treated as a single composite transaction, Patten J held that 'it could not be said that there was no practical likelihood that the pre-planned events would not take place'.

It is also possible that the use of commercial concepts like 'income' and 'capital' may give the taxpayer a choice of structuring a transaction so as to come within one concept or the other. A transaction that, for the avoidance of tax, has been structured to produce capital, and does in fact produce capital in the ordinary commercial sense of that concept (which, of course, was *not* the position in *McGuckian*), cannot be recharacterised as producing income. Accordingly, in *Citibank Investments*, Patten J held that he was unable to conclude that the transaction (the combined effect of the put and call options) had no other purpose than tax mitigation. He said, 'There seems to me to be a real difference between the taxpayer who sets out to utilise a tax avoidance scheme in order to reduce or eliminate an already existing tax liability and one who makes a legitimate choice between investment options having regard to his own fiscal and financial position.'

The same conclusion was reached by Lightman J at first instance in *IRC v John Lewis Properties plc*, where he held that, for the avoidance of tax, the company was perfectly entitled to structure its commercial transaction with the bank so that in place of an income receipt of rent, it received a capital sum. The sum was not merely the bank's receipt of the rents from the lessees: it was a distinct sum paid out of the resources of the bank under a transaction that had commercial reality. As such, it was not open to the court to recharacterise the sum paid as income. Interestingly, although the majority of the Court of Appeal in *John Lewis Properties v IRC* (2003), agreed with Lightman J that the payment was one of capital, they reached their conclusion with no reference to *Ramsay*, *Westmoreland*, and commercial/legal concepts, basing their argument instead on the traditional and orthodox indicia of capital payments (see **[10.103]–[10.109]**). In contrast, Arden LJ, in her dissenting judgment in which she held the payment to be income, took the view that the conversion of rents into a lump sum had no 'commercial reality' as an exchange of income for capital despite the fact that she found a real commercial motive for the transaction. 'Commercial motive and commercial reality', she said, 'are different concepts'.

Despite the feeling that Lord Hoffmann's judgment in *Westmoreland* had provided a definitive view in respect of the application of *Ramsay*, subsequent cases, such as *DTE Financial Services v Wilson* (2001) and the Court of Session in *Scottish Provident v IRC* (2004), displayed a disparity of approach, and, moreover, it has to be accepted that there are real difficulties with this approach.

First, it has to be asked what the position is when the case is concerned with personal rather than commercial tax planning. The difficulty that has always existed is to apply in that context the second of Lord Brightman's conditions, namely that there must be a step inserted that has no business purpose. In *Hatton v IRC* (1992), Chadwick J excised a short-lived interest in possession commenting that neither of the two settlements involved 'had any practical (business) purpose other than the saving of tax'. In a similar fashion, Millett LJ in his dissenting Court of Appeal judgment in *Ingram v IRC*

(1997) sought to explain how the excising of inserted steps operated in a non-commercial context. He said:

> 'What is required to enable the court to disregard a transaction or step in a transaction is not the presence of a tax avoidance motive, but the absence of any other purpose. This is often described as the absence of any business purpose; but in this context "business purpose" does not mean "commercial purpose" but simply "non-fiscal purpose".' (See also *Reynaud v IRC* (1999).)

(The House of Lords in *Ingram v IRC* (1999) took the view that there was no need to discuss the scope of the *Ramsay* principle and the case was decided on the interpretation of the relevant statutory provision: see **Chapter 23**.) However, whilst those judgments are helpful in explaining the notion of business purpose in terms of 'non-fiscal purpose', we now know, of course, that it is wrong to talk of excising intermediate transactions. What has to be done instead is to apply, if permissible, a commercial interpretation to the relevant statutory provision. But, whilst the conditions necessary for the *Ramsay* approach to apply may be satisfied, there must be doubt about being able to characterise commercially a concept that is being applied in the context of a non-commercial transaction. This is not an issue that was addressed by Lord Hoffmann in *Westmoreland*.

Second, and substantively of the greatest importance, which particular words or concepts will lend themselves to a commercial rather than a juristic interpretation? It has already been seen that Lord Hoffmann spelt out the limitations of *Ramsay* by explaining that not all words or concepts will be capable of being interpreted commercially. However, there is nothing in his speech that lends any guidance to what will undoubtedly become a critical matter in future cases. In *DTE Financial Services Ltd v Wilson* (2001), one of the key issues was whether, in the context of the PAYE system, and for the purposes of TA 1988 s 203(1), the concept of 'payment' was a commercial or legalistic concept. The case concerned a scheme to avoid employer's PAYE on employee bonuses paid in the form of a contingent reversionary interest in an overseas trust. More specifically, the directors of DTE had 'contemplated' (but not, of course, decided) that DTE would pay each of them a bonus of £40,000. In accordance with the devised scheme, a contingent reversionary interest was created in an offshore discretionary settlement. On the following day, DTE took an assignment of the interest for a consideration of £40,600, £600 representing fees. The day after that, the interest was assigned to M, one of the directors. Two days later, the interest fell into possession, and £40,000 was remitted to M. DTE argued that the effect of the scheme was to provide M not with a cash payment of £40,000, but with a contingent reversionary interest and, accordingly, there was no 'payment' within TA 1988 s 203(1). A unanimous Court of Appeal accepted the Revenue's submission that the term 'payment' in the context of the PAYE system was a commercial concept. This conclusion was reached on the basis that the statutory provisions relating to PAYE focus on the actual transfer of money from employer to employee rather than on the discharge of an employer's obligation, and that the term 'payment' means cash or its equivalent (see also *Aberdeen Asset Management PLC v R & C Comrs* (2012)).

Given these difficulties, it came as no surprise that Lord Millett, at the time recently retired from the House of Lords and sitting as a non-permanent member of the Hong Kong Court of Final Appeal in *The Collector of Stamp Revenue v Arrowtown Assets Ltd* (2003), sought to destroy Lord Hoffmann's analysis. In this case, concerning the avoidance of Hong Kong stamp duty, the decision in which was that non-voting shares were not share capital and should accordingly be disregarded, Lord Millett said that Lord Hoffmann's approach had led to 'arid debates in an endeavour to fit the statutory language into one or other conceptual category'. In his view, whether a scheme is effective for tax purposes rather than falling foul of the *Ramsay* principle, had little to do with any distinction between juristic and commercial attribution to certain words in the statute, but depended upon whether 'it fell within the legislative intent of the relevant statutory provision purposively construed'. In a similar vein in the same case, and most frequently quoted, is the view of Ribeiro PJ, who said:

'... the driving principle in the *Ramsay* line of cases continues to involve a general rule of statutory construction and an unblinkered approach to the analysis of the facts. The ultimate question is whether the relevant statutory provisions, construed purposively, were intended to apply to the transaction viewed realistically.'

Applying that approach, in *Burmah Oil*, on a purposive construction of the statute, the relief for allowable losses was confined to transactions carried out for business purposes, and, therefore, did not apply to a transaction whose only purpose was to generate the tax relief. So also in *Furniss v Dawson*, the word 'disposal' was given its ordinary legal meaning, but was taken to refer to disposals occurring in the course of transactions undertaken for a business purpose other than the avoidance of tax. On this analysis, the share exchange with Greenjacket fell to be disregarded for tax purposes. In granting the tax relief for share exchanges, Parliament could not have intended to include a share exchange undertaken for the sole purpose of obtaining such relief. In distinction, Lord Millett explained why the *Ramsay* principle did not apply in *Westmoreland*. He said that there was nothing in the language or the context of the relevant statutory provision (TA 1988 s 338) to indicate that the purpose for which a payment of interest is made is material to the question of whether it should be allowed as a charge against profits. As a consequence, a genuine discharge of a debt (as opposed to a sham transaction) was not disqualified from being a 'payment' in this context merely because its only purpose was to secure a tax deduction under s 388; the granting of relief under this provision in the case of a payment made solely for the purpose of obtaining relief was within the intendment of the statute.

Lord Hoffmann's approach was finally laid to rest by the House of Lords in *Barclays Mercantile Business Finance Ltd v Mawson* (2004). Lord Nicholls, expressing the opinion of the judicial committee, said that Lord Hoffmann's approach was not 'intended to provide a substitute for a close analysis of what that statute means. It certainly does not justify the assumption that an answer can be obtained by classifying all concepts a priori as either "commercial" or "legal". That would be the very negation of purposive construction'. [2.37]

5 Barclays Mercantile Business Finance Ltd v Mawson: the final piece of the jigsaw?

a) *Analysis of* Barclays Mercantile Business Finance Ltd v Mawson

Writing extra-judicially, Lord Hoffmann has expressed the view that the decision of the House of Lords in *Barclays Mercantile Business Finance Ltd v Mawson* (*BMBF*) (2004) may well have 'killed off the *Ramsay* doctrine as a special theory of revenue law and subsumed it within the general theory of the interpretation of statutes …' (2005, BTR 197). The issue in *BMBF* was whether the lessor (BMBF) was entitled to capital allowances for expenditure on the purchase of a gas pipeline that was leased to the Irish Gas Board (BGE). BMBF was a company in the Barclays group whose principal activity was the provision of asset-based finance. Another member of the same group, BZW (the investment banking arm of the Barclays group), devised a series of transactions involving the various companies in the group under which BMBF agreed to acquire a gas pipeline that had already been constructed between Scotland and the Irish Republic from BGE. The total purchase price was some £91m. On the same date, BMBF borrowed £91m from Barclays. BMBF then leased the pipeline back to BGE on finance lease terms (the rate of which was made more attractive by the availability of capital allowances) and BGE subleased the pipeline to BGE(UK), a UK subsidiary.

This sublease was important because, had the end user of the pipeline been a company outside the UK (which BGE was), then BMBF would have been unable to claim capital allowances. It was then agreed that the rent due from BGE(UK) to BGE under the sublease would be paid directly to BMBF. BGE and BGE(UK) then entered into a transportation agreement, under which BGE(UK) would transport, handle and deliver gas to BGE's orders. This agreement provided BGE(UK) with a source of income from the use of the gas pipeline. The security for the lease and transportation agreements was provided by several other transactions, the overall effect of which was that an amount totalling some £91m was passed back to the Barclays group as a security deposit. From an overall perspective, an amount equal to the consideration received by BGE on the sale of the gas pipeline was recycled back to the Barclays group.

The Revenue refused BMBF's claim for writing-down allowances on the basis that, considering the whole finance lease transaction, there was in fact no finance. Both the Court of Appeal and the House of Lords reached the same decision in finding in favour of the taxpayer but, as Freedman has explained ((2007) LQR 53–90), did so by different routes. In the Court of Appeal, Carnwath LJ interpreted *Ramsay* as *a principle* in order to restrict its application. In dismissing the Revenue's appeal, the view of the House of Lords was that a taxing statute was to be applied by reference to the *ordinary principles of statutory construction*. The essence of the 'new approach' was to ascertain 'whether the relevant statutory provisions, construed purposively, were intended to apply to the transaction, viewed realistically' (Ribeiro PJ in *Collector of Stamp Revenue v Arrowtown Assets Ltd* (2003), quoted by Lord Nicholls in *BMBF*; and see [2.37]) and, in deciding whether the actual transaction answers the statutory description, this might involve a consideration of the overall effect of a number of elements intended to operate together. Whether it does involve such a consideration is the key issue. In summary, the question that must always be asked is whether, on its true construction, the relevant statutory provision applies to the facts found. As Lord Nicholls observed,

> 'The simplicity of this question, however difficult it might be to answer on the facts of a particular case, shows that the *Ramsay* case did not introduce a new doctrine operating within the special field of Revenue statutes. On the contrary, as Lord Steyn observed in *McGuckian* ... it rescued tax law from being "some island of literal interpretation" and brought it within generally applicable principles.'

Applying those principles to the case at hand, the House of Lords determined that the object of granting a capital allowance is to provide a tax equivalent to the normal accounting deductions from profits for the depreciation of machinery and plant used for the purposes of the trade. Consistently with that purpose, the relevant statutory provision requires that a trader should have incurred capital expenditure on the provision of machinery or plant for the purposes of the trade. In the case of a trade concerned with finance leasing, where the capital expenditure should have been incurred to acquire the machinery or plant for the purpose of leasing it in the course of the trade, these statutory requirements are concerned entirely with the acts and purposes of the lessor, who suffers the depreciation in the value of the plant and who is, therefore, entitled to the allowance. The Act is silent about what the lessee should do with the purchase price, how he should find the money to pay the rent or how he should use the plant and, accordingly, is not relevant. What arrangements the lessee chooses to make, even if they are pre-ordained, is of no concern to the lessor. [2.38]

b) IRC v Scottish Provident

The same principles were applied by the House of Lords in *IRC v Scottish Provident* (2004) on the very same day as *BMBF* and comprising the same members, but with a different conclusion. In that case, it had to be decided whether or not a loss arising from a scheme designed to take advantage of a transition to a new legislative regime, involving the use of cross-options in relation to gilts and a collateral loan, was deductible in calculating the taxpayer company's tax liability. One key factor was a contingency: the possibility that the taxpayer company's option might not be exercised because of its strike price. Finding against the taxpayer, Lord Nicholls, giving the judgment of the whole Court, explained the effect of *Ramsay*. He said:

> 'Since the decision of this House in *WT Ramsay Ltd v IRC* [1982] AC 300 it has been accepted that the language of a taxing statute will often have to be given a wide practical meaning ... which allows (and indeed requires) the court to have regard to the whole of a series of transactions which were intended to have commercial unity.'

In rejecting the argument of counsel for the taxpayer company that the scheme could not be viewed as one composite transaction because of the possibility that it would not proceed to completion (as in *Craven v White* – see [2.25]–[2.28]), the House of Lords chose to view the contingency as part of the composite transaction itself. Lord Nichol said:

'We think that it would destroy the value of the *Ramsay* principle of construing provisions ... as referring to the effect of composite transactions if their composite effect had to be disregarded simply because the parties had deliberately included a commercially irrelevant contingency, creating an acceptable risk that the scheme might not work as planned. We would be back in the world of artificial tax schemes, now equipped with anti-*Ramsay* devices. The composite effect of such a scheme should be considered as it was intended to operate and without regard to the possibility that, contrary to the intention and expectations of the parties, it might not work as planned.' [2.39]

c) *Explaining the different conclusions:* Astall v R & C Comrs

An explanation for these differing conclusions emerges quite clearly from a number of subsequent cases. In *Astall v R & C Comrs* (2009), and in similar fashion to *Scottish Provident*, circumstances and events were included in a series of transactions to ensure that a tax avoidance scheme was not a composite transaction. The taxpayers set up trusts to which they lent money in return for a security. Under the terms of issue, there were two occasions when the securities could potentially be redeemed for a deep gain for the purposes of the legislation. Those occasions were (1) on notice given within two months of the date of issue for a premium of 100.1/118 of the principal amount of the notes; and (2) on the final redemption date. This was normally 15 years after the date of issue. However, the terms of issue also provided that the holder could transfer the security to a third party. The third party could either redeem the security at approximately 5% of the issue price (or its then market value) or redeem the securities after 65 years (which then became the final redemption date). However, in an attempt to prevent the scheme from being treated as a pre-ordained series of transactions, a market change condition, which stood a 15% chance of not being fulfilled, was added and, as a further step in this attempt, no steps were taken to identify a purchaser until after the securities were issued.

The taxpayers argued that the securities were 'relevant discounted securities' (RDS) as defined by FA 1996 Sch 13 (since repealed and replaced by ITTOIA 2005 Ch 8). Because a loss incurred on a RDS is deductible for income tax purposes, the taxpayers sought to set the loss against other income. Accordingly, the appeal concerned the meaning of RDS as defined in the FA 1996 Sch 13.

The Court of Appeal held that the Special Commissioner had been correct in his application of the law to his finding of the facts and in ignoring those inserted conditions that had no real likelihood of ever being exercised. In discussing the application of *BMBF* and *Scottish Provident*, the Court of Appeal expressed the view that both cases emphasised the need to interpret the statute in question purposively, unless it was clear that that was not intended by Parliament. Arden LJ said that the court has to apply that interpretation to the actual transaction in issue, evaluated as a commercial unity, and not be distracted by any peripheral steps inserted by the actors that are in fact irrelevant to the way the scheme was intended to operate. *Scottish Provident* also illustrated another important point, namely that the fact that a real commercial possibility has been injected into a transaction does not mean that it can never be ignored. It can be disregarded if the parties have proceeded on the basis that it should be disregarded. There was little evidence of commercial reality to the scheme in *Schofield v R & C Comrs* (2012), in which case the Court of Appeal upheld the decisions of both the First-tier and Upper Tribunals. Following receipt in December 2002 of £10.7m on the disposal of his shares in his consulting company, the taxpayer entered into a series of transactions with a private bank in an attempt to offset the chargeable gain on the disposal.

The scheme involved creating an allowable capital loss for the taxpayer by setting up a sequence of put and call options. Two balancing options were exercised on 4 April 2003, and two more on 7 April 2003, resulting in the taxpayer paying out £65,589 more than he had received. HMRC disallowed the claim by the taxpayer to deduct an £11.3m loss from his gain. The First-tier Tribunal (2010) found as a matter of fact that the four options were parts of an overall preordained scheme designed to produce neither a gain nor a loss. Accordingly, the Tribunal concluded that the composite transaction was to be seen as the relevant transaction and it was in relation to that transaction that it was appropriate to ask whether it satisfied the requirements of TCGA 1992 s 2 so as to generate an allowable loss. It concluded that it did not. Upholding this decision, the Upper Tribunal (2011) made the following comment:

> 'We make clear that it is no part of our reasoning that steps are to be ignored for no other reason than that they are steps in a tax avoidance scheme. They are to be ignored in the present case, as we think that they were ignored in *Ramsay*, because the composite transaction in the present case is not one to which sections 2 and 16 TCGA 1992 apply so as to give rise to the loss claimed by Mr Schofield; and Mr Schofield fails to establish that the options code must be applied independently of the composite transaction.'

For its part, and on the basis of the facts found by the First-tier Tribunal, the Court of Appeal concluded that it would be wrong to adopt the step-by-step approach for which the taxpayer contended. In *Astall*, Arden LJ said that, in her judgment, applying a purposive interpretation involves two distinct steps: *first*, identifying the purpose of the relevant provision. In doing this, the court should assume that the provision had some purpose and Parliament did not legislate without a purpose. But the purpose must be discernible from the statute: the court must not infer one without a proper foundation for doing so. This is the key to cases such as *R & C Comrs v Mayes* (2011), below; as Lewison J explained in *Andrew Berry v R & C Comrs* (2011), 'the more comprehensively Parliament sets out the scope of a statutory provision or description, the less room there will be for an appeal to a purpose which is not the literal meaning of the words'.

Writing extra-judicially, Lord Hoffmann expressed the same view when he said, 'It is one thing to give a statute a purposive construction. It is another to rectify the terms of highly prescriptive legislation in order to include provisions which might have been included but are not actually there'. The same would apply if the provision in question is purely mechanistic of formulaic (*Mayes*). The *second* stage is to consider whether the transaction against the actual facts which occurred fulfils the statutory conditions. This does not entitle the court to treat any transaction as having some nature which in law it did not have, but it does entitle the court to assess it by reference to reality and not simply to its form (thus taking on board Ribeiro PJ's approach of viewing the facts

Meaning, scope and applicability of the Ramsay *principle: the later cases* 43

realistically). Arden LJ was aware that in *BMBF*, Lord Nicholls held that the court did not need to force its thinking into two separate compartments but, in her view, the process was likely to be an iterative one.

The same reasoning that applied in *Scottish Provident* and in *Astall* has been adopted in a number of subsequent cases. In *Andrew Berry v R & C Comrs* (2009 and 2011), the taxpayer took part in a tax avoidance scheme designed to realise an income loss on the transfer of a gilt strip where, in reality, no loss had actually been sustained by the taxpayer, no money had been paid by him for the gilt strips and there had been no actual transfer of the strips. In all the circumstances, there was no real risk that the parties to the transaction would suffer a real economic loss. There were three ingredients to the scheme, one of these designed as a call option with an option price equal to the loss required by the customer and a strike price of a lesser amount. Underpinning the project was the legal proposition that the grant of an option was separate from and not part of the transaction that occurred on the exercise of the option; the option price would not, therefore, come into the reckoning as an amount payable on the transfer of the gilt strip.

The FTT (2009) said that the decision in *BMBF* established that it is irrelevant to the construction of the particular provision that the arrangement is designed to produce a tax advantage or, absent any specific anti-avoidance wording, that one or more component parts of the transaction have no commercial or investment purpose but have been inserted for tax reasons. Nonetheless, in determining the reality of the transaction, the fact that the arrangements were designed and implemented as a scheme or package, whether to achieve a tax or some other advantage, would be a relevant consideration in determining as a factual matter the reality of the transaction. Viewing the transactions as part of a package, if the taxpayer's entitlement was bound to be cancelled by the exercise of an option, then in a practical sense the taxpayer would have no entitlement to the gilts. The implementation of the scheme was exactly as the parties had intended. The self-cancelling result was entirely in line with their expectations. The scheme was designed to ensure that no real money ever reached the taxpayer. Accordingly, looking at the transactions in the realistic manner required by the House of Lords in *BMBF* and *Scottish Provident*, and construing the relevant legislation in the light of what it required, no loss was sustained by the taxpayer.

In the Upper Tribunal (2011), Lewison J confirmed that in construing the relevant provision as they had done, the FTT had been correct in their interpretation. He said:

> 'This was not a case in which Parliament had used algebra (amount A and B) to create a notional profit or loss. It has used words which have a recognised commercial meaning; and it is to be expected that Parliament intended to tax (or relieve) real commercial outcomes. The FTT were right not to adopt a slavishly literal "tick-box" interpretation of the legislation. This is precisely how the *Ramsay* principle is meant to operate.'

The specific approach taken by Lewison J was adopted by the First-tier Tribunal in finding in favour of the taxpayer in *McLaughlin v R & C Comrs* (2012), which concerned a capital gains tax marketed avoidance scheme. It was contended by the taxpayer that a person (AG), who had been added as a beneficiary of a settlement and to whom an appointment was made by the trustees relating to part of the trust fund containing certain loan notes, had become absolutely entitled to the loan notes under TCGA 1992 s 71(1) and that the ultimate disposal of the loan notes was a disposal by AG. As AG was non-UK domiciled and the loan notes were situated outside the UK, no CGT was payable on the disposal. For its part, HMRC contended that under the 'composite' transaction AG had no right to call for or deal with the loan notes, which remained vested in the trustees, and did not have the necessary absolute entitlement. By looking at the purpose of the relevant legislation and viewing the facts 'actually and realistically', the First-tier Tribunal concluded that AG became absolutely entitled to the loan notes as against the trustees. What had been done answered the statutory description notwithstanding that there was an admitted tax avoidance motive.

The FTT used the same process of reasoning in *Audley v R & C Comrs* (2011). The case concerned a tax avoidance scheme comprising the transfer of a house valued at £1.8m and cash of £250,000 to trustees of a family trust (connected persons) and the issue of a loan note to the settlor at a price of £2,050,000, which the parties agreed was a relevant discounted security (RDI) for the purpose of FA 1996 Sch 13 (see now ITTOIA 2005 Ch 8). The loan note was valued at £35,700 as at three days after its issue (significantly less than its stated issue price), with the Tribunal finding that its value on the day of issue would been hardly different. The taxpayer claimed a loss on the subsequent disposal of the RDI to the trustees of a second family trust. HMRC refused to accept that the amount paid on acquisition was the issue price stipulated in the terms of the loan note. Accordingly, the issue before the FTT was the amount paid by the taxpayer in respect of his acquisition of the security having regard to the purpose of FA 1996 Sch 13 in computing the loss, if any, realised or sustained from the discount of the security claimed to have been issued to him. Sch 13 made explicit provision for market value to be substituted on a *transfer* of an RDS between connected persons, but there was no similar provision in relation to the *issue* of an RDS.

Taking a purposive view of the legislation, and a realistic view of the facts through an examination of 'the actual transaction in issue, evaluated as a commercial unity' (per Arden LJ in *Astall*, the Tribunal concluded that there was a gift of the house and cash by the taxpayer to his family trust. The only purpose of the trustees issuing the loan note was to try to sustain a loss for the purpose of claiming income tax relief under Sch 13 and the terms of the loan note were artificial. The amount paid by the taxpayer for the acquisition of the loan note was its true value, namely, £37,500 and, applying Sch 13, the loss on the subsequent transfer to the trustees of the second family trust was nil.

Reliance upon the dicta of Arden LJ in *Astall* by the Court of Appeal can be found in *R & C Comrs v PA Holdings* (2011), in which case the taxpayer company paid discretionary bonuses to its employees in the form of dividends from a UK company, relying on the former ICTA 1988 s 20(2), which gave priority to dividend tax treatment where a payment could be regarded as both dividend income and earnings from an employment (and which would have been more favourable to the employees). Whilst it was held by both the First-tier Tribunal and the Upper Tribunal that this provision should be applied, the Court of Appeal concluded that the payments in question were not capable of being taxed as both and held instead that, based on the substance and reality of the arrangement, the payments were in the nature of earnings from employment and should be taxed accordingly, ignoring the fact that the payments were received as dividends (see [**8.66**]). Of interest for this chapter is that the Court of Appeal considered, necessarily *obiter*, that the same result could be reached through the application of the *Ramsay* principle. Moses LJ, with whom Arden and Mummery LLJ agreed, applying the principles summarised by Arden LJ in *Astall*, said that the purpose of the relevant statutory provisions was to classify the income according to an appropriate mutually exclusive Schedule; viewed realistically, the payments in the present case were emoluments and the insertion of steps which created the form of dividends did not deprive the payments of their character as emoluments. The insertion had no fiscal effect because s 20, construed in its statutory context, did not charge emoluments under Schedule F (taxation of dividends) (see also *Manthorpe Building Products v R & C Comrs* (2012) and *James H Donald (Darvel) Ltd & Ors v R & C Comrs* (2015), but compare *Tower Radio Ltd v R & C Comrs* (2015), in which latter case the Upper Tribunal, as did the Court of Appeal in *R & C Comrs v Mayes* (2011) (see [**2.41**]), seemed to emphasise the prescriptive nature of the legislation in question in finding for the taxpayer). There was no appeal to the Supreme Court.

The same approach was applied by the Supreme Court in the recent case of *DB Group Services (UK) Ltd v R & C Comrs; R & C Comrs v UBS AG* (2016), overruling the previous decision of the Court of Appeal. The conjoined cases both concerned pre-conceived schemes (similar but not identical) designed to enable employers to provide bonuses to employees in a way that would escape liability to both income tax and national insurance contributions. This was to be achieved by awarding to employees shares in a special purpose vehicle offshore company, the shares being intended to be 'restricted securities' within the meaning of the special taxation regime in Chapter 2 of Part 7 of Income Tax (Earnings and Pensions) Act 2003 (ITEPA 2003). If the scheme succeeded, UK domiciled employees would only be subject to capital gains tax at 10% on the disposal of the shares and non-domiciled employees would escape tax entirely unless they chose to remit redemption amounts to the UK. (It should be noted that this PAYE and NICs avoidance scheme was briefly enabled by the newly-enacted restricted securities legislation in FA 2003; this was closed down by amendments in FA 2004.)

The Court of Appeal found for the taxpayer companies on the technical ground and rejected HMRC's argument that *Ramsay* should apply and that the employees should be treated as having received cash bonuses, upon which they would be chargeable to income tax and NICs. It was of the view that, contrary to the conclusion of the First-tier Tribunal that these schemes were ultimately mechanisms for the payment of a cash bonus, the reality was that participants had received shares, which clearly existed, and the structure meant that (certainly in the case of UBS) the amounts received on redemption could differ significantly from the cash bonus that might otherwise be received.

The Supreme Court took a different view. Giving the judgment of the Court, Lord Reed said that the exemption from tax on the acquisition of 'restricted securities' was designed to address the practical problem of valuing a benefit which was, for business or commercial reasons, subject to a restrictive condition involving a contingency. Accordingly, the relevant provisions had to be construed as being limited to a condition having a business or commercial purpose and not to commercially irrelevant conditions whose only purpose was the obtaining of the exemption. This meant that the forced sale in the *UBS* case and the 'leaver' provision in the *DB* case, neither of which had any business or commercial purpose, should be disregarded.

However, the Supreme Court did not accept HMRC's argument that the scheme should be viewed simply as the provision of cash bonuses and thus disregard other steps, but held that the recipients fell to be taxed in respect of their receipt of the shares in accordance with ordinary taxation principles, the value of the shares needing to be assessed as at the date of their acquisition, taking into account the restrictive conditions irrespective of the fact that those conditions were not intended to be commercially relevant. Lord Reed said that to disregard the conditions for these purposes would be to treat the employees as having received a more valuable benefit than they actually received (see also *Clavis Liberty 1LP (Acting through Cowen)* (2016).

The whole issue had previously been aired fully before the Supreme Court in *R & C Comrs v Tower MCashback LLP 1 and another* (2011). In this case, the taxpayers were limited liability partnerships (LLP 1 and LLP 2), which claimed first year capital allowances in respect of ICT expenditure as small enterprises pursuant to Capital Allowances Act (CAA) 2001 s 45. They claimed first year allowances (FYA) in respect of the full amount of the first year qualifying expenditure on completion of software licence agreements (SLA) entered into with the vendor of the software, MCashback (M). The consideration payable under the LLP 2's agreement with M was £27.5m. Pursuant to that agreement, LLP 2 acquired a right to receive 2.5% of the gross revenues from the software. Only 25% of the purchase price was funded by the investor members of the partnership from their own resources; non-recourse loans made to those members by a finance company provided the balance, the source of which was a series of circular transactions whereby that balance paid to M was funded by M out of the consideration itself.

The substantive issue in the case concerned the correct approach to determining whether expenditure had been 'incurred' for the purposes of the CAA 2001. Lord Hope summarised this with clarity:

> 'The issue, reduced to its simplest terms, is whether the whole of the £27.5m paid by LLP2 to MCashback under the terms of the software licence agreement was expenditure incurred by LLP2 on the provision of software within the meaning of the Capital Allowances Act 2001. The general rule itself is not in doubt. Expenditure is qualifying expenditure if it is capital expenditure on the provision of plant or machinery wholly or partly for the purposes of the qualifying activity carried on by the person incurring the expenditure: CAA, section 11(4). The problem that the facts of this case gives rise to is the extent to which surrounding circumstances, such as the source and destination of the funds expended and the commercial soundness of the transaction when looked at as a whole, may be taken into account in an assessment of the question whether the taxpayer was involved in expenditure that entitled it to the allowance claimed.'

The case for the LLPs was that transfer of ownership was itself enough to show that real expenditure was incurred. They also maintained that the source of the funds was irrelevant, as was what the purchaser did with the funds received by it (seeking to utilise *BMBF*). HMRC contended that the LLPs had not incurred expenditure in buying the software licences because their members had borrowed 75% of the funds against security provided by the seller, M, on uncommercial terms. Accepting the substance of this contention, the Special Commissioner decided that LLP 2 was limited to a FYA in respect only of the 25% of the first year qualifying expenditure it had actually incurred. Both the judge at first instance and the majority of the Court of Appeal took a different view and concluded that LLP 2 had incurred expenditure in the full amount claimed. Having tested a realistic view of the complex pre-ordained transaction against the wording of the statute, the Supreme Court found in favour of HMRC.

In reaching their conclusion, the court considered two previous decisions of the House of Lords, namely, *BMBF* and *Ensign Tankers (Leasing) Ltd v Stokes* (1992) (see [**2.45**]), a case concerning capital allowances and loans but the facts of which were different from those under consideration since there was not in that case 'in any meaningful sense' a loan at all, and confirmed that both remained good law. Accordingly, it is not enough for HMRC, in attacking a scheme of this sort, simply to point to money going round in a circle (*BMBF*), but nor is it the case that unless the transaction is found to be a sham, the only possible conclusion is that the whole of the consideration in the SLA was expenditure incurred on the provision of software (*Ensign Tankers*). In the context of a complex pre-ordained transaction, the court's task is to test the facts, realistically viewed, against the statutory test, purposively construed. Entitlement to capital allowances requires there to have been real expenditure for the real purpose of acquiring plant or machinery for use in a trade. Concerns about the valuation of what is being acquired and the commercial soundness of the transactions are relevant. The fact that rights in the software had been transferred by M to LLP2 demonstrated the reality of some expenditure on acquiring those rights, but did not conclusively show that the whole of consideration in the SLA was expenditure for that purpose. The Special Commissioner had found that the market value of the software was 'very materially below' £27.5m. He had also held that there was little chance that the members' loan would be repaid in full within ten years; he thought that as much as 60% might be unpaid, and waived, at the end of that period. These findings justified the conclusion that the money which the investor members borrowed was not used, in any meaningful sense, as expenditure in the acquisition of software rights. Instead, it went in a loop back to the lender in order to enable the LLPs to indulge in a tax avoidance scheme.

In an interesting closing remark, Lord Walker said:

'If a majority of the Court agrees with my conclusion, it is to be expected that commentators will complain that this Court has abandoned the clarity of *BMBF* and returned to the uncertainty of *Ensign*. I would disagree. Both are decisions of the House of Lords and both are good law. The composite transactions in this case, like that in *Ensign* (and unlike that in *BMBF*) did not, on a realistic appraisal of the facts, meet the test laid down by the CAA, which requires real expenditure for the real purpose of acquiring plant for use in a trade. Any uncertainty that there may be will arise from the unremitting ingenuity of tax consultants and investment bankers determined to test the limits of the capital allowances legislation.'

In the event, the Supreme Court reached a unanimous decision (See also *Acornwood LLP v R & C Comrs* ('*Icebreaker*') (2014). The schemes in this case, which were developed by entertainment firm Icebreaker Management and adopted by a large number of partnerships, purported to find finance for creative projects within the music industry and offer a return for investors, but in fact generated losses. More specifically, the partnerships entered into agreements for the acquisition and exploitation of certain intellectual property rights. Each partnership acquired a set of rights for a modest amount of money and for much larger payments agreed with an exploitation company that it would exploit the rights. The revenue from the exploitation was to be shared between the partnership and the exploitation company, which was also required to pay guaranteed sums to the partnership. In addition, each partnership entered into agreements with the promoter of the arrangements by which, in return for substantial payments, the promoter rendered various services to the partnership. The First-tier Tribunal said that the aim of the schemes was to secure sideways relief for members of all the partnerships and to inflate the scale of relief by unnecessary borrowing but that, for many reasons, in particular that the expenses were of a capital nature and so no income loss had been created, the schemes failed. This being the case, there was no need to decide upon *Ramsay*, but the Tribunal decided to do so and, noting the 'close parallel' between the case before them and *Tower MCashback*, the judges concluded, necessarily *obiter*, that had the *Ramsay* issue been a live one, the outcome would have been the same). **[2.40]**

d) *A case out on a limb:* R & C Comrs v Mayes

It might be thought that, finally, some clarity had been achieved in the application of *Ramsay*, but the comment by Mummery LJ in *R & C Comrs v Mayes* (2011) that 'it is unlikely that this test case will finally be resolved at this level of appeal' would suggest otherwise. The issue in the case was whether payments into and out of second-hand insurance policies through a pre-ordained, composite, artificial and tax-motivated series of transactions called SHIPS 2 should be disregarded for fiscal purposes or whether the deductible loss (in the form of corresponding deficiency relief) claimed by the taxpayer should be allowed. The only object of SHIPS 2 was to minimise the income tax liabilities of the participants as higher rate taxpayers (and also their liabilities to CGT – a second issue concerning relief against CGT is not discussed here). As described by Mummery LJ, the transaction comprised seven steps, some of which were self-cancelling. The steps to the creation of deductible losses, all of which were accepted to be genuine, included the payment of initial premiums for life assurance policies, the payment of additional 'top-up' premiums by a non-resident company (Step 3) and a partial surrender of the polices by that same company within a month (Step 4), thereby creating a potential for relief without triggering a charge to tax. This was later followed by a full surrender of the policies by taxpayer, who then claimed entitlement to income tax relief.

The argument advanced by HMRC did not rest upon the fact that the steps were pre-ordained and were inserted in order to avoid tax but, rather, that steps 3 and 4, relied on by the taxpayer for creating the corresponding deficiency relief, do not fall within a purposive construction of the relevant statutory provisions under which that relief was claimed and thus should be ignored. As a result, the main point of difference between the parties was how the *Ramsay* principle affects the construction of the relevant income tax provisions and how the principle should be applied to the facts of this case to the top-up premiums paid for the policies and the pre-arranged partial surrender of policies.

In holding for the taxpayer on this issue, the Court of Appeal applied the approach required by *BMBF*, namely that *Ramsay* did not lay down a special doctrine of revenue law striking down tax avoidance schemes on the ground that they are artificial composite transactions and that parts of them can be disregarded for fiscal purposes because they are self-cancelling and were inserted solely for tax avoidance purposes and for no commercial purpose. The *Ramsay* principle is the general principle of purposive and contextual construction of all legislation. The legislation in question in this case was no exception and was not immune from it. In applying that principle to the facts of the present case, the statutory provisions on the taxation of life insurance policies were to be given a purposive construction in order to determine the nature of the transaction to which they were intended to apply. On such a construction, the statutory requirements as to the transactions to which the provisions were intended to apply were far removed from the kind of case in which the focus is simply on an end result, such as a loss.

In this case the all-important corresponding deficiency relief was the product of real premiums paid at an earlier stage for real life policies and real surrenders made at an earlier stage. Although the corresponding deficiency was created solely to save tax, that alone did not entitle the court to disregard the fiscal consequences of payment of premium and the partial surrender which led to its creation. The court could not, as a matter of construction, deprive those events of their fiscal effects under the income tax legislation just because they were self-cancelling events that were commercially unreal and were inserted for a tax avoidance purpose in the pre-ordained programme that constituted SHIPS 2 (see also *Moyles v R & C Comrs* (2014), in which case the former Radio 1 DJ, Chris Moyles (and others) had used a marketed tax avoidance scheme (disclosed under the DOTAS scheme – see **Chapter 5**), concerning a supposed trade in second-hand cars designed to produce losses, which he sought to set against tax he owed on his substantial entertainment income. The First-tier Tribunal judge found for HMRC on the basis that there was no trade carried on by the taxpayer and that the technical basis of the scheme did not work. In addition, he found for HMRC on the basis of *Ramsay* although, in light of his previous findings, he did not need to consider the point.

Of importance was the judge's warning to HMRC that the mere fact that a transaction is part of a tax avoidance scheme, even one that is circular or self-cancelling and without commercial purpose, is not a sufficient ground for denying a tax advantage. Citing *BMBF*, *Mayes*, *Tower Mcashback* and *Arrowtown*, he said that the fact that the taxpayers had taken part in an acknowledged tax avoidance scheme did not change the approach that the tribunal should adopt, namely, to construe the legislation purposively and to apply it to the facts as viewed realistically. In the present case, 'the relevant statutory provisions, construed purposively, were not intended to apply to the transaction, viewed realistically').

HMRC's purposive construction of the relevant legislation was also rejected in *R & C Comrs v Hancock & Hancock* (2016), where the Upper Tribunal, whilst overruling the First-tier Tribunal on the technical issue, finding that a chargeable gain arose on the redemption of secured discounted loan notes, agreed with its approach to the *Ramsay* principle. The taxpayers sold their company in 2000 for an initial consideration in the form of guaranteed loan notes (the original loan notes), giving the holder the right to have them redeemed in US dollars. It was not in dispute that the provision for payment in a currency other than sterling and at an exchange rate other than that prevailing at redemption, prevented the loan notes from being Qualifying Corporate Bonds (QCBs – see [41.92]–[41.97]) for the purposes of TCGA 1992 s 117 and the gain which had accrued on the company shares was effectively rolled over under the share exchange provisions. The sale also provided for additional consideration based on the subsequent performance of the business. Accordingly, in March 2001, the taxpayers received a further issue of loan notes (the additional loan notes). Since these were identical to the original loan notes, these were also not QCBs. However, a deed of variation removed the right to redemption of the additional loan notes in US dollars, meaning that the additional loan notes became QCBs within s 117. In May 2003, the original and additional loan notes were exchanged for secured discounted loan notes (the secured notes), which did not carry any interest but provided for a premium to be paid on redemption and which were QCBs within s 117. The secured notes were redeemed shortly after on 30 June 2003.

The issues arising were whether:

(i) the conversion of the original and additional loan notes into the secured notes was to be treated as a single conversion or two; and

(ii) on a purposive construction of the relevant provisions and taking a realistic view of the facts, the exchange and redemption should be taxed as a single composite transaction.

On the first (and technical point with which this chapter is not really concerned), the Upper Tribunal did not accept the taxpayers' argument that there had been a single conversion. Accordingly, since there were two conversions and the conditions in s 116(1)(b) applied to each in turn, s 116 applied to the conversion of the original loan notes, which were not QCBs, and a gain was deemed to arise on the redemption of the secured notes which replaced them. Although this was sufficient to dispose of the case in favour of HMRC, the Upper Tribunal went on to consider the second issue concerning the *Ramsay* principle. The Revenue had argued that the conversion of the original loan notes and the further loan notes into secured notes and the subsequent redemption of the secured notes should be treated as a single composite transaction, with the result that the original loan notes should be treated as simply having been redeemed for cash, ignoring the intervening conversion.

The Upper Tribunal agreed with the First-tier Tribunal, who decided that whilst Parliament could not have intended that part of a gain rolled over should escape taxation altogether, it did not feel that it could invoke *Ramsay* and apply a purposive construction of the legislation because, in its view, s 116 was not intended to cover cases where both 'the original shares' and 'the new holding' included QCBs. The fact that the conversion process was intended to give rise to a tax advantage did not result in the transaction, viewed realistically, being anything other than a redemption of the secured notes. Taken in their context, the reorganisation provisions, along with s 116, provided a comprehensive code for the taxation of chargeable gains on reorganisations of securities, conversions, exchanges and reconstructions. A purposive construction of the reorganisation provisions could not produce any different result merely on the basis that the transactions entered into were intended, for tax avoidance reasons, to exploit an anomaly in the application of those rules. Also considered was whether the reorganisation provisions of ss 127, 131 and 132 could be purposively construed so as to exclude the conversion of the original and additional loan notes into the secured notes. It was found that they could not.

Importantly, the Upper Tribunal also made it clear that if the literal construction of a provision results in an obvious anomaly, particularly one that that does not arise only on a relatively unusual set of facts, and there is an alternative construction that avoids that anomaly, implements the general purpose of the legislation and does not suggest a counter-mischief, the alternative construction is to be preferred (see *Harding v R & C Comrs* (2008)), where the Upper Tribunal in *Hancock* did not consider that the Court of Appeal judgment in *Harding* cast doubt on the principle set out by the High Court in that case. [2.41]

6 Applicability to all taxes

a) *General*

Given that the House of Lords in *BMBF* (2004) seemed to state so decisively that the *Ramsay* line of authorities is based on ordinary principles of statutory construction, it must be the case that they are of common application depending on the facts of each particular case and on the wording of the relevant statutory provision.

Prior to this landmark decision, the Special Commissioners had applied *Ramsay* to a scheme aimed at maximising profit-related pay (see *Colours Ltd (formerly Spectrum Ltd) v IRC* (1998)) and upheld an assessment in a group company scheme designed to avoid the payment of ACT (*Cedar plc v IRC; Larch Ltd v IRC* (1998)), whilst the Court of Appeal has applied *Ramsay* (in the light of *Westmoreland*) to a scheme that sought to avoid having to account for tax on a bonus under the PAYE system (*DTE Financial Services Ltd v Wilson* (2001)). In *Fitzwilliam v IRC*, Lord Browne-Wilkinson queried the application of *Ramsay* to CTT/IHT given the existence of the wide-ranging associated operations provision in IHTA 1984 s 268. He said:

> 'This amounts to a statutory statement, in much wider terms, of the *Ramsay* principle which deals with transactions carried through by two or more operations which are inter-related ... it can therefore be argued that there is no room for the Court to adopt the *Ramsay* approach in construing an Act which expressly provides for the circumstances and occasions on which transfers carried through by "associated operations" are to be taxed. It is not necessary in the present case to express any concluded view on this point.'

However, he would appear to be the only member of the House of Lords/Supreme Court to have expressed such concern. Moreover, there seems to be no logical reason to assume that *Ramsay* cannot complement IHTA 1984 s 268 and *vice versa*. However, even if *Ramsay* can apply, there is no suggestion that the Revenue would seek to challenge the normal IHT arrangements between spouses designed to ensure that both make full use of the available exemptions and reliefs and nil rate band of tax. Similar arrangements may be entered into in order to take advantage of the independent taxation of spouses. [2.42]

b) *Stamp duty and stamp duty land tax*

It was thought that there was no room for the application of the *Ramsay* principle to stamp duty because, *inter alia*, it is a duty on documents not transactions. Since stamp duty land tax came into effect on 1 December 2003 (see [49.22]), the new tax created thereunder is levied on *transactions* in land rather than on written instruments. Accordingly, there is no longer any rational basis for that original view in relation to land transactions. However, even before that, there were indications that this was simply not the case. In *Ingram v IRC* (1985), Vinelott J held that a stamp duty scheme designed to avoid duty on the purchase of land by splitting the transaction into stages fell within *Furniss v Dawson* and was therefore ineffective. The scheme involved, *first*, the purchaser agreeing to take a 999-year lease of the property at a premium of £145,000 and small annual rent; *second*, the sale of the property subject to that lease to a company for 500; and *finally* the resale of the property by the company to the purchaser for 600. As a result of these transactions the taxpayer acquired full title to the land (by merger of the leasehold and freehold interests) but it was intended that the consideration paid for the long lease would escape duty (since agreements for leases exceeding 35 years were excluded from charge under the Stamp Act 1891 s 75) so that only the small sum paid on the transfer of the freehold would be subject to duty.

The judge held that, were it not for the *Ramsay* principle, it was clear that the taxpayer's contentions were correct and that the transfer was what it purported to be – ie of a freehold interest subject to the agreement for the lease which had reduced its value. An application of the *Ramsay* principle, however, required the composite transaction to be 'recharacterised'. Accordingly, the leasehold agreement should be excised as an artificial transaction, leaving the instrument of transfer subject to duty as a transfer of the entire freehold interest at the agreed price (ie £145,600).

Two important matters emerge from this judgment.

First, Vinelott J stated that the principle that, if a document was genuine, the court could not go behind it to some supposed underlying substance (derived from *IRC v Duke of Westminster*) had no application to composite transactions entered into for the purpose of avoiding tax and the result of the new approach of the House of Lords was that many decisions (including some of the House of Lords) needed reappraisal. In the light of the House of Lords decision in *Westmoreland*, in particular the speeches of Lords Hoffmann and Nicholls, this view must now be doubted.

Second, the view that *Ramsay* had no application in the field of stamp duty was rejected '*after considerable hesitation*'. Although the duty was levied on instruments not transactions, in order to determine the nature of a particular instrument, the court had to ascertain the substance of the transaction effected by it – a task which should be carried out by applying the *Ramsay* principle. Since 1 December 2003, stamp duty land tax has been levied on transactions and so, to that extent, there is little difference between this and other direct taxes where land transactions are concerned.

The *Westmoreland* decision threw the whole question of the applicability of *Ramsay* to stamp duty back into the melting pot. Lord Hoffmann in illustrating one expression of a taxing statute that referred to a purely legal concept used stamp duty payable upon a conveyance or transfer on sale as an example (FA 1999 Sch 13 para 1(1)). He continued:

> 'If a transaction falls within the legal description, it makes no difference that it has no business purpose. Having a business purpose is not part of the relevant concept. If the disregarded steps in *Furniss v Dawson* had involved the use of documents of a legal description which attracted stamp duty, stamp duty would have been payable.'

Given that stamp duty in relation to land transactions is no longer the classic tax on form rather than substance, scope for applying *Ramsay* today seems less limited than it had been previously, particularly in the light of *Barclays Mercantile Business Finance Ltd v Mawson* (2004) (it should also be noted as instructive that *Ramsay* was applied in the Hong Kong stamp duty case of *The Collector of Stamp Revenue v Arrowtown Assets Limited* (2004)). [2.43]

c) *VAT*

It has already been mentioned that the *Ramsay* doctrine is capable of applying to VAT. This was established in *C & E Comrs v Faith Construction Ltd* (1989), although it was not invoked in that case since the court decided that the relevant scheme amounted to a single genuine transaction. The particular arrangement was designed to avoid the VAT charge on building alterations that came into effect on 1 June 1984. Accordingly, the taxpayers arranged to be paid in full for the alterations before that date and this was achieved as part of an agreement under which the payment in question was lent back to the customer (under a commercial loan) and was then repaid by instalments equal to the amounts periodically certified as payable by the architects. In effect, therefore, payment for the work did occur after the deadline for the introduction of VAT but, because of the legal arrangements entered into, the taxpayers argued that the late instalments represented the repayment of a commercial loan. This abbreviated summary of the facts reveals the high level of artificiality involved in the case and accordingly the decision of the High Court that *Ramsay* did not apply is somewhat surprising. To categorise the scheme as a single transaction is in itself open to doubt and it was even accepted by the taxpayer that the sole reason for the arrangements was to avoid a VAT liability! (*C & E Comrs v Faith Construction Ltd* (1989): the Court of Appeal did not need to consider the possible application of *Ramsay*.)

An explanation for this decision, given by Lord Hoffmann in *Westmoreland*, that 'payment' in the *Faith Construction* case was a legal and not a commercial concept, clearly suggests that Lord Hoffmann considers that *Ramsay* can apply to VAT. Indeed, in the earlier case of *C & E Comrs v Thorn Materials Supply Ltd* (1998), whilst Lord Nolan said that there was no need, and in fact that it was undesirable, to consider the question of whether the *Ramsay* principle had any application to VAT until a case arose when it was necessary to do so,

Lord Hoffmann, in contrast, argued in his dissenting judgment that the *Ramsay* principle was potentially relevant, although not applicable on the facts of that particular case. (Note also that in the judicial review case of *R v C & E Comrs, ex p Greenwich Property Ltd* (2001), Collins J suggested that *Ramsay* could apply to VAT cases – although on the facts of the case, no attempt had been made to argue that the scheme in question did in fact fall within *Ramsay*.)

A complication with VAT is that it derives directly from the EC Sixth Directive (Directive 77/388), to which principles of European Law apply. Despite the comments made by Lord Hoffmann in *Westmoreland*, it has to be questioned whether these European law principles can incorporate *Ramsay* at all, or whether they would have the effect of restricting the *Ramsay* principle. Moreover, while it is clear that there exists within European law a principle of abuse of rights (defined recently by Lord Sumption as a principle that 'confines the exercise of legal rights to the purpose for which they exist, and precludes their use for a collateral purpose' (*R & C Comrs v Pendragon plc* (2015), and first applied to fiscal rights and obligations in *Emsland-Starke GmbH v Hauptzollamt Hamburg-Jonas* (2000)), the questions arise as to (i) whether this principle applies in the context of VAT, and (ii) if it does, is it in addition, or an alternative, to the *Ramsay* principle. Despite the *obiter* comment by Vinelott J in *Baylis v Gregory* (1986) that 'the doctrine of abuse of right by a taxpayer ... has no place in our jurisprudence', the first question appears to have been answered in the affirmative by the ECJ in the case of *Halifax plc v C & E Comrs* (2006) (discussed below). In a fiscal context, Lord Sumption, in *Pendragon*, drew attention to the 'difficult balance' to be drawn in the application of the principle to tax avoidance schemes between the need to recognise that frustrating the objective of a taxing provision by artificial means without falling foul of its language has significant social costs, on the one hand, and, on the other, the need for legal certainty, particularly when it comes to justifying the financial demands of the state. He continued:

> 'Artificiality, if it is to be deployed as a workable legal concept, has to be tested against some standard of transactional normality, and the search for such a standard is far from straightforward. Taxpayers faced with a choice between alternative ways of achieving some commercial objective are in principle entitled to select the one with the more tax-efficient statutory outcome. In particular, they are entitled to choose between exempt and taxable transactions in their own financial interest. Like any other tax, VAT is due only in so far as its imposition is authorised by statute. It follows that although the courts may examine the commercial reality of transactions without being unduly hidebound by labels, they do not as a general rule enlarge the scope of a taxing provision by reference to considerations which affect neither the construction of its language nor the characterisation of transactions to which it is said to apply. These dilemmas are particularly acute in the United Kingdom, where the drafting of tax legislation has traditionally depended not on the formulation of general principles but on the definition of taxable occasions with a high degree of specificity.'

It is the task of any court seeking to apply a principle of abuse of law to reconcile these competing considerations. The issue was fully debated in the leading case of *Halifax plc v C & E Comrs* (2006) and in a number of other cases heard at the same time, including *University of Huddersfield Higher Education Corp v C & E Comrs* and *BUPA Hospitals Ltd v C & E Comrs*. In all of these cases, the court had to consider various input tax planning arrangements for financial, educational and medical institutions. The court was of the view that a transaction that was wholly motivated by tax considerations was still an economic activity and a supply for the purposes of Article 4(1) of the Sixth Directive. However, although the ECJ did not explicitly consider the basis upon which HMRC may rely upon the principle of abuse of rights, it identified two conditions that needed to be satisfied before the principle could be of any relevance. These conditions are that, *first*, the transactions involved result in a tax advantage which is contrary to the purpose of the EU Directives and the domestic legislation implementing them, and *second*, the sole aim of the transactions is to obtain a tax advantage. The court was of the further view that: (i) the measures adopted by member states to ensure the correct levying and collection of tax and for the prevention of fraud, must go no further than is necessary to attain such objectives; and (ii) a finding of abusive practice must not lead to a penalty, but to an obligation to repay. In an interim judgment in 2004, the Court of Appeal in *WHA Ltd v C & E Comrs* found that the avoidance scheme (which concerned an insurance group that entered into a complex series of transactions with Gibraltar-based reinsurers to enable VAT to be claimed on motor breakdown insurance supplied to UK motorists, contrary to the VAT treatment of insurance. Gibraltar is part of the EU for some purposes but for VAT purposes it is treated as a non-EU jurisdiction) succeeded at face value but adjourned a final decision until after judgment had been handed down by the ECJ in *Halifax*. The court re-opened the hearing after *Halifax* when Lord Neuberger (2007) agreed with the Revenue's argument that although the Gibraltar deals had commercial benefits, they were consequential and the real purpose of the transactions was to avoid tax. The scheme was thus contrary to the EU principle of abuse of rights. He considered that the two conditions expressed in the judgment of the ECJ in *Halifax* gave rise to four questions: *first*, whether the scheme resulted in a tax advantage that was contrary to the provisions of the Sixth Directive; *second*, whether it was the 'essential aim' of the scheme to obtain the advantage; *third*, whether there were any special features that prevented the scheme from being an abuse; and *finally*, can and must the scheme be redefined. Having rejected WHA's request for a reference to the ECJ, in the main hearing of the appeal (2013), the Supreme Court reversed the Court of Appeal's 2004 judgment and held that the WHA avoidance scheme did not succeed at face value. Accordingly, there was no need to consider the abuse of rights principle, on which the Court of Appeal's 2007 judgment remains the leading authority in UK law. At issue in *R & C Comrs v Weald Leasing Ltd* (2008) was the significance, if any, of the scheme being outside *normal commercial operations*. In that case, the taxpayer was involved in a scheme (again, in relation to input tax planning), the sole aim of which was admitted to be the obtaining of a VAT advantage. The transactions that made up the scheme were not shams but were artificial in the sense that, but for their having the aim of securing a tax advantage, they would not otherwise have been made in any commercial context. Accordingly, HMRC made assessments relying on a redefinition of the transactions in question. HMRC accepted that, as a result of *Halifax*, a transaction was not to be denied its ordinary fiscal consequence merely because its essential aim was to obtain a tax advantage, but argued that the advantage could only accrue if the surrounding dealings represented *normal commercial operations*. Lindsay J rejected that argument, concluding that:

> 'where one is looking at a series of transactions the essential aim of which is to confer a tax advantage by way of deductibility of input tax, it does not, in my judgment, suffice to brand the series as abusive simply to add and to prove that the series was not in the "context of their normal operations".'

In other words, even when the essential aim is admitted and where the arrangements made are artificial, not at arm's length commercially and devoid of commercial motive other than as to the attainment of the essential aim, there is no abuse of rights unless in the circumstances, viewed as a whole, the grant of the tax advantage concerned would be contrary to the purposes of the Sixth Directive and the national legislation transposing it. The Court of Appeal referred this case to the ECJ for a ruling on whether the scheme concerned gave rise to a tax advantage within the *Halifax* principle, whether this was an abusive practice within the *Halifax* principle, and if it was an abusive practice, what should be the appropriate redefinition of the transactions making up the scheme. Holding that the leasing transaction was not of itself abusive because it was not contrary to the purpose of the Directive, the ECJ rejected HMRC's contention that the scheme involved a leasing transaction that was designed artificially to avoid the burden of input tax which would have been payable had the goods been purchased outright and, accordingly, was abusive and should be redefined to prevent any input tax recovery. It said:

> 'The leasing transactions come within the scope of the Sixth Directive and ... the tax advantage that could arise through recourse to such transactions does not, in itself, constitute a tax advantage the grant of which would be contrary to the purpose of the relevant provisions of that directive ... a taxable person cannot be criticised for choosing a leasing transaction which procures him an advantage consisting ... in spreading the payment of his tax liability, rather than a purchase transaction which does not procure him any such advantage, provided that the VAT on that leasing transaction is duly and fully paid.'

However, the introduction of non-commercial terms into the arrangements had the potential artificially to reduce or stagger the input tax charge even further, which could not be said to be within the contemplation of the Directive and would run counter to its purpose, calling for a redefinition. The court said that, in line with *Halifax*, such redefinition 'should go no further than is necessary for the correct charging of the VAT and the prevention of tax evasion'. Accordingly, the reconstruction was limited to the artificial elements of the leasing arrangements. That the courts continue to find difficulty in applying the principle can be seen in the long-running dispute in *Pendragon plc v R & C Comrs*: the First-tier Tax Tribunal (2010) found that transactions had been entered into for sound commercial reasons, albeit that a significant VAT advantage had been obtained. The Upper Tribunal (2012) reversed this decision, holding that the First-tier Tax Tribunal had erred in law. The Court of Appeal (2013) allowed the taxpayer company's appeal, but did not comment on whether the scheme was abusive; rather, it focused on the role of the Upper Tribunal as an appellate court. Because the First-tier

Tax Tribunal had found as a matter of fact that the purpose of the scheme was to obtain finance and not to obtain a tax advantage, it was not open to the Upper Tribunal to interfere with that finding. Accordingly, the Court of Appeal was bound to restore the decision of the First-tier Tax Tribunal. The Supreme Court (having concluded that the appeal to the Court of Appeal was from the decision of the Upper Tribunal, not from the First-tier Tribunal, and that the function of the Court of Appeal was to determine whether the Upper Tribunal had erred in law by looking at the merits of the reasoning of the Upper Tribunal in its own terms, rather than by reference to their evaluation of the First-tier Tax Tribunal's decision. Although the Upper Tribunal's jurisdiction to intervene had to begin from a finding of an error of 'law', that was not the main issue in the appeal, which was one of more general principle) finally followed the decision of the Upper Tribunal and, basing its decision on the principles established in *Halifax*, held that there had been an abuse of rights.

The difficulty with the judgments in *Halifax*, *WHA Ltd* and *Weald Leasing* was that none considered the question of precisely how the principle of abuse of rights could be relevant when interpreting the Sixth Directive, bearing in mind that a directive does not have direct effect against taxpayers. Although this appeared to be explained by Advocate-General Poiares Maduro who, in the course of his Opinion in *Halifax*, considered that HMRC were entitled to rely upon the doctrine of abuse of rights because of the obligation on national courts to interpret national law consistently with the Directive, no mention of this was made by Lord Neuberger in the course of his judgment in *WHA Ltd v R & C Comrs*. However, the issue was directly addressed in *Pendragon* by Lord Sumption, who reiterating the stand taken by Advocate-General Poiares Maduro, said:

> 'Value Added Tax is an EU tax imposed pursuant to successive Directives of the European Union, at the relevant time the Sixth Directive. The Directives are subject to the principle of abuse of law. By virtue of section 2(1) of the European Communities Act 1972 the same principle must apply to domestic legislation implementing the Directives.'

Such a definitive statement by a member of the Supreme Court, with whom all his fellow Justices agreed, must put paid to the views that the principle of abuse of rights can only be relied upon against taxpayers as an interpretive aid (*Tax Journal*, 20 August 2007), and that the message that planning must be associated with a genuine commercial justification is 'undiluted' by the *Halifax* cases, but that 'taxpayer choice, the right to mitigate, proportionality, immunity from penalty, and legal certainty come out of the case intact' (*Tax Journal*, 27 February 2006).

As far as the second question concerning the relationship between the abuse of rights doctrine and *Ramsay* is concerned, one commentator has suggested that the 'abuse' principle may move in the direction of the *Ramsay* principle, because *Ramsay* is arguably a more advanced and flexible principle in the sense that it allows the judges greater freedom to arrive at what they believe to be the 'correct' result (see *Tax Journal*, 12 March 2007 at pp 11–12). [2.44]

7 'Tax avoidance' versus 'tax mitigation'

Following the Privy Council case of *IRC v Challenge Corpn Ltd* (1986), a distinction emerged between tax mitigation on the one hand and tax avoidance on the other. According to Lord Nolan:

> 'The hallmark of tax avoidance is that the taxpayer reduces his liability to tax without incurring the economic consequences that Parliament intended to be suffered by any taxpayer qualifying for such reduction in his tax liability. The hallmark of tax mitigation, on the other hand, is that the taxpayer takes advantage of a fiscally attractive option afforded to him by the tax legislation, and genuinely suffers the economic consequences that Parliament intended to be suffered by those taking advantage of the option.' (*IRC v Willoughby* (1997)).

Having made the distinction between mitigation and avoidance, the question that then arises is precisely how the distinction affects the *Ramsay* principle. In *Ensign Tankers (Leasing) Ltd v Stokes* (1992), Lord Templeman made it clear that if steps were inserted in order to mitigate tax (and thus resulted in an actual loss or the incurring of actual expenditure) then such mitigation would be outside the *Ramsay* principle. However, where steps were inserted to avoid tax, and thus where the taxpayer sought to reduce his liability to tax without incurring any actual loss or expenditure contrary to the intention of Parliament, such steps would come within the principle. The difficulty with this distinction is that it provides no clear guidance as to the circumstances in which a taxpayer can be said to have suffered genuine economic consequences. Might not the creation of the intermediary company in *Furniss* be considered a genuine economic consequence? The distinction certainly found no favour with Lord Hoffmann who, in *MacNiven v Westmoreland Investments Ltd*, said that, unless the statutory provisions themselves contained words like 'avoidance' or 'mitigation', the terms were not particularly helpful. Thus, in *IRC v Willoughby* (1997), it was necessary for the House of Lords to determine what was meant by the term tax avoidance since the statute expressly provided that certain provisions having the effect of negating any advantage to the taxpayer should not apply if the taxpayer could show that he had not acted with 'the purpose of avoiding liability to tax'. And yet, the distinction may once again become important since it would appear to be the case that, in combating VAT avoidance pursuant to *Protecting Indirect Tax Revenues*, Customs & Excise were most definitely drawing a distinction between tax avoidance and tax mitigation. Their position was put thus:

> 'Some argue that there is no real difference between tax mitigation and tax avoidance, that these are just different ways of describing the same thing. But, while there may be some grey areas, the argument is entirely specious. Horses and donkeys have similarities, but most people can tell one from the other. In the same way, an objective observer generally has no problem telling an avoidance scheme – a contrived or artificial arrangement that exploits the letter of the law in ways contrary to its spirit and purpose – from tax mitigation.'
> (Chris Tailby, former Director of HMRC's Anti-Avoidance Group),
> *Tax Journal*, 2 December 2002.)

With the approach taken by the House of Lords in *Barclays Mercantile Business v Mawson* (2005) (adopted from the judgment of Ribeiro PJ in *Collector of Stamp Revenue v Arrowtown Assets Ltd* (2003)) (see **[2.38]**), this distinction may now be immaterial. **[2.45]**

VI CONCLUSIONS

1 Life after *Barclays Mercantile Business Finance Ltd*

It would appear to be the case that the hopes of the Revenue that a broad interpretation of *Ramsay* would permit either the preferment of substance over form (as in the USA) or some form of fiscal nullity doctrine have been dashed in the light of *Barclays Mercantile Business Finance Ltd v Mawson (BMBF)*. In that case, the House of Lords firmly rejected the view that transactions, or elements in a series of transactions, which have no commercial purpose are to be disregarded whatever the taxing statute in question happens to be. Rather, the court must *first* decide, on a purposive construction, precisely what transaction falls within the statutory description, and then, *second*, establish whether the particular transaction in question actually does so. If, as in *BMBF*, plant is purchased for the purpose of the purchaser's finance leasing trade, that is the only fact that is relevant to the statutory provision and it is of no consequence if the lessee chooses to make arrangements for the sale and leaseback of the plant, which result in the bulk of the purchase price being irrecoverable. There is no scope for the transaction to be disregarded. In contrast, where a taxpayer embarked upon an artificial scheme devised in 1995 to take advantage of a prospective change in the system of taxing gains on options to buy or sell bonds and Government securities ('gilts'), the House of Lords took the view that the relevant statutory provisions required the court to have regard to the whole of the series of transactions, including one that was to all intents and purposes not part of the series, that were intended to have a commercial unity (*IRV v Scottish Provident Institution* (2005): see **[42.48]**). That approach has been followed in a succession of cases including *Astall v R & C Comrs* (2009), *R & C Comrs v Tower MCashback LLP 1* (2011), *R & C Comrs v Mayes* (2011), *Andrew Berry v R & C Comrs* (2011), *R & C Comrs v PA Holdings Ltd* (2011), *McLaughlin v R & C Comrs* (2012), *DB Group Services (UK) Ltd v R & C Comrs; R & C Comrs v UBS AG* (2016) and *R & C Comrs v Hancock & Hancock* (2016) and was applied *obiter* in *Acornwood & Ors v R & C Comrs* (2014) and *Moyles v R & C Comrs* (2014) (see **[2.39]**), some of which have been decided in favour of HMRC and others in favour of the taxpayer. **[2.46]**

2 Use by taxpayer?

Although the majority of the Court of Appeal in *Whittles v Uniholdings Ltd (No 3)* (1996) found that the *Ramsay* principle had no application to the facts of that particular case, two of their Lordships were of the view that it could be applied in favour of the taxpayer in appropriate circumstances (see the judgments of Aldous LJ and Sir John Balcombe). In *Bird v IRC* (1985) Vinelott J at first instance, without expressing a concluded view on the matter, had thought it unlikely that when a taxpayer embarked on a series of transactions designed to avoid tax he could later argue (when those transactions were challenged under anti-avoidance legislation such as the transactions in securities provisions TA 1988 ss 703 ff, now ITA 2007 ss 682–686; see [**3.30**] ff) that they should be treated as a fiscal nullity. Further he expressed the view that a party cannot blow 'hot and cold' so that the Revenue could not argue that a scheme fell within the then TA 1988 s 703 (thereby accepting that all the steps were effective but that the end result was nullified by statute) and, as an alternative, seek to excise certain of those steps under the *Ramsay* approach. [**2.47**]

3 Options

In the wake of the *Furniss* decision the use of options in tax planning needed careful thought. It has in recent years become common to spread the sale of land over a number of years by means of options and part of the attraction has been to mitigate the vendor's CGT and (until its abolition in FA 1985) development land tax (DLT) liability by taking advantage of more than one annual exemption. Assume, for instance, that A wishes to sell Blackacre to B and will realise a gain of £14,000 on that sale. Were he to divide Blackacre into two equal portions and agree to sell the first portion in the tax year 2007–08 and, at the same time, grant a call option to purchase the second portion in the following tax year, it would appear that for CGT purposes the land has been disposed of in two different tax years and A will therefore have two annual exemptions available (notice that A could ensure that B is obliged to purchase the land by taking a 'put' option enabling him to require B to purchase the second parcel if he fails to exercise his 'call' option).

There is no doubt that such schemes amount to a pre-ordained series of transactions and arguably the options represent steps which have been inserted purely for the avoidance of tax, since, in the absence of CGT considerations, A would have sold the whole of Blackacre to B in 2007–08. From a pre-*Westmoreland* view if, under the *Furniss* approach, the steps are excised, it may be argued that there was effectively a sale of the land to B at the time when the contract of sale for the first parcel was made and the put and call options taken. Doubts have always been expressed about the validity of this argument and if the 'option-step' is excised it is by no means clear that the *Ramsay* principle permits the sale of all the land to be treated as occurring in 2007–08. These doubts are endorsed by the decision in *Griffin v Citibank Investments Ltd* (2000) in which Patten J refused to re-characterise the separate put and call options as a single composite transaction. He said that if he were to 'ignore the terms of each option contract which provide for its independent assignment and exercise, and concentrate instead on the fact that if exercised together the options are guaranteed to produce a fixed return in favour of the taxpayer, then it seems to me that I would be doing the very thing which Lord Wilberforce emphasised in *Ramsay* that the courts cannot do, ie to go behind the transactions and search for some supposed underlying substance which as a matter of ordinary legal analysis they do not possess.' Following *Westmoreland*, further support for this approach was taken by the Court of Session in *Scottish Provident Institution v IRC* (2004) when considering whether a loss arising from the use of cross-options in relation to gilts should be allowed under FA 1994 s 155. The Court was of the view that the term 'loss' in s 155(2) should be attributed with a legal meaning, but nonetheless pronounced on whether the *Ramsay* principle would apply had they decided that the provision employed a commercial concept. It was of the view that there was a 'genuine commercial possibility or practical likelihood' that the two options would be dealt with separately and should not be viewed as a composite transaction. However, on appeal (*IRC v Scottish Provident Institution* (2004)), the House of Lords (with the same Law Lords as those sitting in *Barclays Mercantile Business Finance Ltd*) took the opposite view. Proceeding on the basis that the matter was one of construction, they said that there could only be an allowable loss if the option was a 'qualifying contract' within the meaning of FA 1994 s 147(1) and by virtue of FA 1994 ss 147A(1) and 150A(1), for there to be a qualifying contract, the taxpayer had to have an 'entitlement' to gilts. In determining what the statute meant by the term 'entitlement', the Judicial Committee had this to say:

'Since the decision of this House in *W T Ramsay Ltd v Inland Revenue Comrs* [1982] AC 300 it has been accepted that the language of a taxing statute will often have to be given a wide practical meaning of this sort which allows (and indeed requires) the court to have regard to the whole of a series of transactions which were intended to have a commercial unity. Indeed, it is conceded by *(the taxpayer)* that the court is not confined to looking at the ... option in isolation. If the scheme amounted in practice to a single transaction, the court should look at the scheme as a whole. Mr Aaronson, who appeared for *(the taxpayer)*, accepted before the special commissioners that if there was "no genuine commercial possibility" of the two options not being exercised together, then the scheme must fail.'

They went on to conclude that there was no realistic possibility of the options not being exercised simultaneously and that, accordingly, the scheme should be regarded as a single composite transaction. They added that:

'it would destroy the value of the *Ramsay* principle of construing provisions such as section 150A(1) of the 1994 Act as referring to the effect of composite transactions if their composite effect had to be disregarded simply because the parties had deliberately included a commercially irrelevant contingency, creating an acceptable risk that the scheme might not work as planned. We would be back in the world of artificial tax schemes, now equipped with anti-*Ramsay* devices. The composite effect of such a scheme should be considered as it was intended to operate and without regard to the possibility that, contrary to the intention and expectations of the parties, it might not work as planned.'

(See also *Schofield v R & C Comrs* (2012) (**[2.39]**). Returning, then, to the example of Blackacre, it appears that an answer would depend upon the construction of the term 'disposal' in the context of TCGA 1992. Following *Scottish Provident Institution*, it may be possible to say that the disposal of both pieces of land occurred in 2007–08 since, to use the words of Millett J, 'from a commercial point of view, of course, the simultaneous creation of both put and call options puts the parties in much the same position as an unconditional contract of sale would do' (*J Sainsbury Ltd v O'Connor* (1990)). Alternatively, following *Citibank* the commercial context of the transactions may militate against such a conclusion.

In conclusion, commercial reasons may, in particular cases, justify the use of options and the *Ramsay* argument is obviously more difficult to sustain when cross-options are not employed but a call option alone is taken by the purchaser (but see *Andrew Berry v R & C Comrs* (2011) (**[2.39]**).   **[2.48]**

3 Tax avoidance and legislation
Updated by Anne Fairpo, Barrister

I   Introduction [**3.1**]
II   Statutory provisions to counter tax avoidance [**3.2**]
III Transactions in securities (ITA 2007 ss 682–686) [**3.28**]
IV   Principles-based legislation [**3.73**]
V   A general anti-abuse rule [**3.74**]

I INTRODUCTION

This chapter considers the use of legislative measures as a means of tackling tax avoidance. Tax avoidance legislation takes the form of enactments of five types: the first is directed at certain transactions, irrespective of whether or not the purpose of the taxpayer is to avoid tax, and an example of such legislation is to be found in ITTOIA Part 5 Chapter 5 relating to settlements (see [**16.91**]).

The second type targets specific avoidance schemes or specific areas (targeted anti-avoidance rules: TAARs), such as the provisions designed to prevent artificial transactions in land which are considered at [**12.101**]. These provisions complement the amendments (also) made by FA 2016 to the transactions in securities rules. The general characteristic of such legislation is that it is designed to deal with a specific problem, normally after it has arisen, but does not purport to prevent new schemes in different areas. Given a sophisticated legal profession, loopholes in such provisions will be exploited and need constant plugging.

IHT is unique in having a legislative provision of the third type: a widely drafted associated operations provision (see IHTA 1984 s 268).

The fourth type of enactment takes the form of principles-based legislation, which consists of shorter and more simply worded provisions, preceded by a statement of the principle underlying those provisions. Theoretically, because of the flexibility of this type of legislation, this should make the job of the judges in interpreting tax law much easier, and would be less likely to leave them open to criticisms of 'judge-made tax law' (see [**3.73**]). Two provisions in FA 2009 follow HMRC consultations on the use of principles-based drafting; the first is intended to combat schemes that are intended to disguise what is truly interest and thereby escape liability to income tax (disguised interest); the second seeks to treat as income receipts derived from a right to receive income and where no loss of capital is involved (transfer of income stream). A further such provision concerning group mismatch schemes can be found in FA 2011.

The final type of enactment is a general anti-avoidance rule or, more specifically for the UK, a general anti-abuse rule (GAAR). This is discussed at [**3.74**] ff. [3.1]

II STATUTORY PROVISIONS TO COUNTER TAX AVOIDANCE

1 The legislation

Some major provisions that have been enacted in attempts to deal with specific instances of tax avoidance are set out below. In many cases they were designed to prevent the conversion of income profits into capital gains taxed at a lower rate. Whilst the rates of the two taxes were harmonised, these provisions lost some of their force. However, with a top rate of CGT for individuals of 20% (28% for gains on residential property not eligible for principal private residence relief (see **Chapter 23**), and on carried interest) for those paying higher rate of income tax and with an extended entrepreneurs' relief (see **Chapter 20**), they are once again of some importance. [3.2]

Transactions in securities ITA 2007 Part 13 Chapter 1 (ss 682–686) and, for companies, CTA 2010 Pt 15 (ss 731–751) (the former TA 1988 ss 703–709 as amended) (see [**3.30**] ff). [3.3]

Accrued income profits (dealing with bond washing and dividend stripping) ITA 2007 Part 12 Chapter 2. [3.4]

Transfer of assets overseas Originally enacted in FA 1936, these provisions were amended in 1981 as a result of *Vestey v IRC* (1980) and again in 1997, partly as a result of the *Willoughby* litigation. They have now been rewritten in ITA 2007 Part 13 Chapter 2 (see **Chapter 18**). [3.5]

Artificial transactions in land ITA 2007 Part 13 Chapter 3, see **Chapter 12**. Statutory provisions also regulate sale and leaseback transactions (TIOPA 2010, Sch 4, paras 2–5 for income tax purposes; CTA 2010 ss 834–886 for corporation tax purposes); see **Chapter 10**. [3.6]

Sale of income derived from personal activities ITA 2007 Part 13 Chapter 4 (originally enacted in FA 1969) prevents the conversion of future taxable income into capital gains subject to CGT. The avoidance typically involved entertainers who sold their services to a company formed for that purpose and then sold the shares in that company. [3.7]

The use of tax losses and transfer pricing CTA 2010 ss 673–676 impose restrictions upon the purchase of tax loss companies (see **Chapter 41**). Sales at under or overvalue may be subject to challenge under TIOPA 2010 Part 4, and under the *Sharkey v Wernher* principle (see **Chapter 10**). [3.8]

2 Typical avoidance schemes involving securities

A company is a legal entity distinct from its shareholders and, therefore, provides fertile ground for such tax avoidance schemes as dividend stripping and bond washing. **[3.9]**

Dividend stripping The simplest illustration of dividend stripping is where A owns A Ltd that has profits available for distribution. A sells the shares to B who is a dealer in securities. A receives a capital sum which reflects the undistributed profits in the company. B will take out the profits from A Ltd (as a dividend) that will be taxed as income but the shares will now be worth less (reflecting the fact that they have been stripped of their dividend). B will, therefore, make a trading loss when he sells the shares that can be set off against the dividend income that B has received (usually under the provisions of ITA 2007 Part 2 Chapter 3). The result is that corporate profits have been extracted free of tax.

The courts were often invited to hold that the purchase and sale of the shares was not a trading transaction. In some cases they decided that it was trading; in others, not (contrast, eg *Griffiths v J P Harrison (Watford) Ltd* (1962) with *FA and AB Ltd v Lupton* (1971) and see *Coates v Arndale Properties Ltd* (1984) and, for consideration of the effect of fiscal motives, *Ensign Tankers (Leasing) Ltd v Stokes* (1991)). The close company legislation sought to tackle one part of the problem by preventing the accumulation of profits in close companies. The problem has also been addressed by legislation aimed at transactions in securities generally. (See further **[3.30]**.) **[3.10]**

Bond washing Dividends only become a taxpayer's income when they are due and payable; when that happens, the shareholder can claim the sum from the company as a debt. Usually there is a time gap between declaration and payment that provides an opportunity to wash the shares (or bonds) of their dividend. The washing process usually involves a taxpayer who is subject to no income tax or to lower rates only. Assume, for instance, that shares are owned by A, who is subject to income tax at a high rate. When a dividend is declared on his shares he sells them to his cousin, a student with unused personal allowances. A is, therefore, receiving a capital sum for the shares on which CGT rather than income tax will be charged. The dividends are paid to the cousin who suffers little if any income tax thereon. Finally, the shares may be repurchased by A after payment of the dividend. Legislative provisions (notably CTA 2010 Part 17 Chapter 2 and the accrued income scheme discussed below) prevent the most blatant examples of bond washing. (See further **[3.12]**.) **[3.11]**

3 The accrued income scheme

ITA 2007 Part 12 Chapter 2 (ss 616–677) is designed to prevent the bond washing of fixed interest securities.

The practice of bond washing involved the conversion of income into capital and resulted in that sum being taxed, if at all, to CGT (with the result that as most fixed interest securities were exempt from CGT if held for 12 months or more, tax was often avoided). Accordingly, these provisions treat interest on securities as accruing on a day-to-day basis between the interest payment dates. On a disposal, therefore, the vendor is subject to income tax on the interest accruing from the immediately preceding interest payment date to the date of disposal and the purchaser is treated as owning the income from that date.

It follows that when the sale is with accrued interest (*cum div*) the vendor is treated as entitled to extra interest and the purchaser gets relief for a corresponding amount. Conversely, if the sale is without accrued interest (*ex div*), the vendor will obtain relief on an amount equal to the interest to which the purchaser is regarded as entitled.

The apportioned sums are treated as received on the day when the interest period ends and are subject to tax for the chargeable period in which they are received. As a result of these provisions appropriate amendments are made in the computation of any capital gains on the disposal of the securities (gilt-edged securities and qualifying corporate bonds are generally exempt from CGT) and securities covered by the scheme are excluded from the anti-bond washing provisions which preceded this legislation.

EXAMPLE 3.1

Elena owns £100,000 in nominal value of Government stock paying interest at 5% pa on 30 June and 31 December. She sells that stock *cum div* to Henrietta on 30 September 2017 for £99,780.

(1) *Elena's tax position*: She is subject to income tax in 2017–18 on three months' accrued interest (£1,250) for the period from 30 June 2017 (the last payment date) to 30 September 2017 (disposal or settlement date).

(2) *Henrietta's tax position*: Assuming that she retains the stock until 31 December 2017, she will then be subject to income tax on the interest paid as follows:

Interest payment to 31 December 2017	=	£2,500
Deduct accrued interest purchased (1 July to 30 September)	=	£1,250
Reduced amount taxable	=	£1,250

(3) Had the sale been *ex div* so that the interest payment of £5,000 to 31 December 2017 was retained by Elena, she would be taxed on £1,250 of that figure and the balance of £1,250 (ie interest from the date of disposal to the date of sale) would be taxed in Henrietta's hands.

In *D'Arcy v R & C Comrs* (2007), the court held that the taxpayer, who had entered into transactions involving two acquisitions and disposals of gilts with a nominal value of £31,000,000 over a period of seven days, had ceased to be entitled to the gilts on the same day that she had become entitled to them. In the circumstances, their value would not count for the purpose of the exclusion in what is now ITA 2007 s 639 because there was nothing left at the end of the day for the accrued interest scheme to bite on.

The securities caught by these provisions are defined in ITA 2007 s 619 and include bearer bonds, UK and foreign securities, and securities whether secured or unsecured issued by governments, companies, local authorities and other institutions. Excluded from the provisions are ordinary or preference shares, National Savings Certificates, certificates of deposit, bills of exchange, Treasury bills, local authority bills and similar instruments.

Individuals (including trustees and PRs) resident or ordinarily resident in the UK are within the provisions, but there are specific exclusions for financial traders (whose profits on sale are taxed as trading income under ITTOIA 2005: ITA 2007 s 642) and for individuals, personal representatives and trustees of a disabled person's trust holding securities with a nominal value not exceeding £5,000 'on any day' (ITA 2007 ss 639–641).

Companies are not subject to these provisions, as the issue is dealt with in the corporate loan relationships rules. [3.12]

4 Bed and breakfasting

Bed and breakfasting, which allowed the selling of shares on one day (in order to crystallise a capital gain or loss) and the repurchase of those same shares on the following day, was stopped for disposals on or after 17 March 1998. Any shares of the same class in the same company sold and repurchased within a 30-day period are now matched, so that the shares sold cannot be identified with those already held. Curiously the rules would appear to be capable of circumvention, as follows, although such arrangements are now potentially subject to the GAAR:

(1) A sells his shares in X plc: he settles the sale proceeds on a life interest trust for himself and the trustees promptly buy back the shares.

(2) As in (1) except that A gives the sale proceeds to his wife who buys back the X plc shares. (See further [26.46]). [3.13]–[3.27]

III TRANSACTIONS IN SECURITIES (ITA 2007 SS 682–686)

1 Introduction

a) *Overview of the need for the rules*

From a general view, the transactions in securities rules are aimed at preventing shareholders of a company extracting profits in capital form *(taxed at rates of up to 20% for 2017–18)* when they should be paid out as dividend income *(taxed at rates up to 38.1% for 2016–17)*. [3.28]

b) *Outline history*

In order to better understand why we have legislation aimed at transactions in securities, it is instructive to start with the past.

It is 1950, rates of income tax (including surtax) are high and destined to rise further, accumulated profits (ie after payment of profits tax) retained in certain companies are subject to apportionment (as they have been since the 1920s) and there is no capital gains tax. This is, therefore, an ideal breeding ground for attempts to extract profits from companies in a manner that does not attract income tax.

A number of related techniques became commonplace, notably 'dividend stripping' (see [3.10]), 'bond washing' (see [3.11]) and 'stock stripping' (whereby B, who owns the shares in a company, which in turn owns a plot of land acquired for £20 and now worth £100, sells the shares to A for £100 thereby generating a capital profit free of tax (pre-1965) or chargeable at lower rates (post-1965); A can then extract the land (or profits on a sale) by way of dividend, free of tax (A is an exempt body or has tax losses) and sell the shares at a loss).

As is often the case when new 'problems' are identified by the Revenue, attempts were first made to deal with specific concerns. In 1951 the Revenue persuaded Parliament to give it (by FA 1951 s 32) wide discretionary powers where transactions were effected for the avoidance or reduction of liability to profits tax. This – a 'general anti-avoidance rule' or GAAR – was itself modelled on wartime provisions designed to prevent the avoidance of excess profits tax; provision was also made in FA 1951 to deal with the migration of companies (see now TA 1988 ss 765 and 765A) and transfer pricing (see now TIOPA 2010 Part 4). In 1955 legislation was introduced to deal with dividend stripping (see F(No 2)A 1955 s 4) and this is currently found in ITA 2007 Part 11 Chapter 4. In 1959, legislation was introduced to deal with bond washing (see FA 1959 ss 23–26, drawing on provisions in FA 1937) and this is also currently found in ITA 2007 Part 11 Chapter 4 (and see the 'accrued income scheme' in ITA 2007 Part 12 Chapter 2). In 1960, legislation was introduced to deal with stock stripping (see FA 1960 ss 21–24) and this is currently found (in a much more limited form) in TA 1988 ss 774, 776 as amended.

These measures were fine as far as they went but did not deal with the more sophisticated transactions. Accordingly, the Revenue persuaded Parliament to tackle the problem on a wider footing. The changes made in FA 1951 for profits tax purposes were the basis for FA 1960 ss 28–29, 43 which became TA 1988 ss 703–709. These provisions sought to ensure that the Revenue could counteract (by an assessment to income tax under the former Schedule D Case VI) any 'tax advantage' obtained by a person in consequence of a 'transaction in securities' in any of *four* circumstances (later increased to five) where the person could not show that the transaction was carried out for (a) 'bona fide commercial reasons or in the ordinary course of making and managing investments' *and* (b) the transaction did not have as its main object, or one of its main objects, 'to enable tax advantages to be obtained'. More recently, these provisions were the subject of the tax law rewrite project. For income tax purposes, the rewritten legislation was to be found in ITA 2007 Part 13 Chapter 1, ss 682–694. Since the rewrite, the rules regarding income tax advantages have been repealed by FA 2010 and replaced with different and much simpler ones (see ITA 2007 ss 686–689). For corporation tax purposes, equivalent rules are to be found in CTA 2010 Part 15, ss 731–742.

Provision is made for advance clearance by the Revenue and for counteraction notices. [3.29]

c) *The 2010 legislative changes*

The problem with the former legislation was that it brought potentially all transactions in securities within its ambit, and then used filters such as tax advantage, the five circumstances referred to above and an escape clause to take some of these transactions outside of the legislation. This meant that each and every circumstance had to be considered, involving unnecessary compliance costs. Moreover, and in addition to other problems, the use of the term 'relevant company' raised issues of EU compliance.

The Pre-Budget Report 2007 saw the launch of the Anti-Avoidance Simplification Review, the purpose of which was to consider how anti-avoidance legislation could best meet the twin aims of simplicity and revenue protection. Having concluded that new anti-avoidance legislation needed to be clear, effective and well-targeted, a consultation document was issued in July 2009, the ultimate aim of which was to simplify the transfer in securities legislation, and to clarify it by narrowing its scope so as to catch only those transactions undertaken with a main purpose of securing a tax advantage.

Following this consultation, the former provisions in ITA 2007 ss 682–694 were replaced by ss 682–688. These provisions, which were noticeably shorter than the ones they replaced, were drafted in plainer English and by reference to concepts and definitions that are familiar from elsewhere in the legislation. The main features of the revised legislation were the abolition of the five prescribed circumstances found in the former rules, the adoption of the definition of 'close company' found in CTA 2010 ss 439–447 in place of the term 'relevant company' and the removal from the rules of transactions that result from a fundamental change of ownership. The revised rules apply to income tax only. The Government has indicated that the CTA 2010 will be amended in due course to contain comparable rules for corporation tax, although no specific details have been released. [3.30]

d) *The 2016 legislative changes*

Following the announcement on 15 July 2015 by the Chancellor of the Exchequer of changes to the tax treatment of company distributions for income taxpayers (effective from 6 April 2016), resulting in an increase in the tax charged on many higher and additional rate taxpayers who receive dividends from UK and non-UK companies (see [7.27]), and foreseeing an increased incentive for taxpayers to structure transactions to receive a capital rather than an income return, HMRC issued a consultative document (*Company Distributions*, 9 December 2015). For the purposes of this chapter, the document focused on three potential problem areas, namely: (i) sales of companies with retained profits; (ii) distributions in a winding up, where distributable profits in excess of a company's needs are retained in the company; and (iii) repayments of share capital and premium, where HMRC is concerned that the rules that determine the amount of capital that is treated as paid up on shares for tax purposes is being manipulated.

The result of the consultation can now be found in FA 2016, which amends the 'gateway' provisions of ITA 2007 ss 684–687. The amendments:

- introduce a connected parties rule. The previous legislation required that the person who entered into the transaction was the one who obtained a tax advantage (ITA 2007 s 684(1)(d)). This is now extended so that tax advantages that accrue to an associate of a person who is a party to a transaction in securities can be counteracted;
- extend the types of transactions that can fall within the rules (see [3.33]);
- widen the scope of the legislation so that the test looks at the main purpose of the transaction rather than, as previously, of the person who entered into it (see [3.35]);
- extend the concept of relevant consideration. Relevant consideration equates, broadly, to the value of assets available for distribution by way

of dividend (ITA 2007 s 685(4)(a)). The amended legislation extends this to include amounts representing the value of assets available for distribution to the relevant company by way of dividend from any company it controls (see [**3.34**]);
- make changes to the exception from the rules for transactions which involve a fundamental change of ownership (see [**3.36**]).

The amendments apply to any transaction or series of transactions that takes place on or after 6 April 2016. Whilst the existing clearance is preserved, if a clearance application is made before 6 April 2016, but any of the relevant transactions occur on or after that date, the clearance is valid only if the transactions would not have been subject to counteraction under either the old or the new rules. If the transactions are caught by the new, but not the old, rules, any clearance given before 6 April 2016 is void and HMRC can counteract any tax advantage arising as a result of the new rules (see [**3.38**]).

[**3.31**]

2 The amended legislation for income tax advantages

a) *Key aspects of the amended legislation*

Transactions in securities will be counteracted where:
(1) a person ('the party') is a party to one or more transactions in securities (ITA 2007 s 684(1)(a));
(2) one of two prescribed conditions is met, both of which require the receipt of consideration (as specified in ITA 2007 s 685) (ITA 2007 s 684(1)(b));
(3) the main purpose, or one of the main purposes, of the transaction in securities, or any of the transactions in securities, is to obtain an income tax advantage (ITA 2007 s 684(1)(c));
(4) the party or any other person obtains an income tax advantage (ITA 2007 s 684(1)(d)); and
(5) there is no fundamental change of ownership (ITA 2007 s 686). [**3.32**]

b) *Transaction in securities*

As with the previous legislation, 'transaction in securities' extends to all forms of transaction (sale, exchange, purchase, issue, subscription, alteration of rights) involving 'securities' (ITA 2007 s 684(2)), and 'securities' includes shares, stock and any other interest of a member in a company. Nearly anything can be such a transaction, eg the redemption of debentures (*IRC v Parker* (1966)) and loans to shareholders (*Williams v IRC* (1980)) – and two or more steps can be looked at together to see if they amount to a 'transaction' (*IRC v Horrocks* (1968)).

FA 2016 has extended the types of transactions that can fall within the rules by including a repayment of share capital or share premium and a distribution made in a winding-up. As far as the first of those two additions is concerned, it is arguable that repayments of capital (including premium) paid up on shares have always qualified as transactions in securities and the new legislation merely clarifies this. In the case of the second addition, under the pre-amended legislation, the position was that an 'ordinary' liquidation would not be a transaction for these purposes (see *IRC v Joiner* (1975)).

is party to a transaction or transactions in securities was the obtaining of an income tax advantage. FA 2016 has widened the scope of the rules, so that the test now looks at the main purpose of *the transaction* (transactions) itself rather than that of the person who entered into it.

Since the existing case law concerns the pre-2010 law, it is questionable of what value it now is. Under that legislation, there could be no counteraction where there was *'no main object of obtaining a tax advantage'*. In commercial situations, the test of 'no main object of obtaining a tax advantage' was likely to be satisfied where the transactions were treated as an approved demerger (now CTA 2010 s 1075) or an approved purchase of own shares (now CTA 2010 s 1033). Corporate reorganisations would also usually pass the test where what was received was shares, although it was necessary to examine the particular transaction and not simply the surrounding circumstances: see *IRC v Trustees of the Sema Group Pension Scheme* (2003). In *Grogan v R & C Comrs* (2010), the Upper-tier tribunal held that it was enough if the tax advantage was obtained as the result of an overall series of transactions which were linked together to form a scheme and where the relevant transaction in securities was part of that scheme.

Neither the 2010 rules nor the amended rules contain a commercial test, and it was suggested that, as a consequence, it was difficult to relate the 2010 rules to the existing case law. However, despite the omission of the commercial test, those who are undertaking transactions would be well advised to be able to provide evidence of the genuine commercial purposes served. Under the former provisions, the '*bona fide* commercial' test was satisfied where, looking at the subjective intention of the taxpayer, there were genuine commercial reasons for what had been done (*IRC v Brebner* (1966)). In *Grogan v R & C Comrs* (2009), the First-tier Tribunal held that in the absence of evidence of the taxpayer's commitment to employee incentives, the taxpayer had failed to satisfy the tribunal on the balance of probabilities that the setting-up of a qualifying employee share-ownership trust (QUEST), which involved a reduction of the taxpayer's shareholding by way of sale of a block of his shares to the trust, was not a main object of the transaction.

If there are two possible courses, one which involves paying more tax than the other, merely choosing to take the latter course does not necessarily mean that the test is not satisfied. Examples of 'commercial' motives included the retention of family control of a company (*IRC v Goodwin* (1975)), the sale of shares to fund the purchase of a farm (*Clark v IRC* (1978)) and a corporate reorganisation to preserve the viability of the group (*Marwood Homes v IRC* (1997)) (but see [**43.171**]) In similar fashion, where the purpose of carrying out the transactions in question was to separate the personal and commercial interests of the taxpayer and his wife in a simple and commercially logical way on the occasion of their separation and divorce, the First-tier Tribunal held that the test was satisfied (*Ebsworth v R & C Comrs* (2009)).

(2) *Quantifying the income tax advantage* The definition of 'income tax advantage', seemingly adopted from HMRC practice, is now based on a notional calculation of the difference between the income tax which would have been payable in the absence of the avoidance and the capital

gains tax that is payable instead (ITA 2007 s 687). This does not apply where the tax advantage is in respect of chargeable gains. [3.35]

e) *Fundamental change of ownership*

The fundamental change in ownership test in ITA 2007 s 686, introduced in 2010 with the aim of reducing the number of pre-transaction clearance applications under s 701, provided that the transaction in securities rules would not apply if more than 75% of the shares in a close company were transferred to an unconnected party. Because the test failed to have the desired effect of reducing the number of clearance applications, FA 2016 has rewritten the rule so that, post-6 April 2016, the focus will be on the interest retained by the original holder or holders as opposed to the interest acquired by others.

Under the new rule, the transactions in securities legislation cannot apply where, after a transaction, an original shareholder (i) does not directly or indirectly hold more than 25% of the ordinary share capital of a close company; (ii) does not have an entitlement to more than 25% of the distributions that might be made by that company; and (iii) does not have more than 25% of the total voting rights. The test is concerned with both the original shareholder as well as any associates of that individual. What is an associate is based on the definition in ITA 2007 s 681DL and is thus wide, extending to business partners although, surprisingly, there is no reference to a trustee being associated with the beneficiaries.

In order that there should be a reasonable length of time to ensure that the fundamental change in ownership is substantive, the ownership change must be satisfied for two years after the transaction. [3.36]

f) *Close company*

By adopting the terminology of a 'close company', the 2010 legislation is now in line with the better-known definition in CTA 2010 ss 439–447, overcomes the previous problem of EU compliance and closes the former loop-hole of including a listed company in the group structure. [3.37]

g) *Counteraction*

Prior to 6 April 2016, HMRC could seek to counteract a tax advantage under the transactions in securities rules by sending to the taxpayer a notice to supply information, followed by a notification that a counteraction notice could be issued. If the taxpayer disputed the applicability of the rules, HMRC had to argue the case before the First-tier Tribunal before issuing a formal counteraction notice. FA 2016 has changed the process to make it similar to a self-assessment enquiry (although it should be noted that the transactions in securities scheme has been, and continues under the amended rules to be, outside of self-assessment). Under the new rules:

- HMRC can enquire into a transaction by issuing a notice, within six years of the end of the tax year to which the income tax advantage relates, of its intention to enquire if it believes that the transactions in securities provisions apply.

- If HMRC determines that the provisions do apply, it can counteract the advantage by making adjustments and issuing a counteraction notice to the taxpayer.
- If HMRC determines that no counteraction is required, it must issue a no-counteraction notice.
- The taxpayer can apply to the First-tier Tribunal for a direction requiring HMRC to issue a counteraction or no-counteraction notice.

Individual (and indeed corporate) shareholders should be aware of the risk that ITA 2007 s 684 (and CTA 2010 s 731 for companies) will apply as a result of a re-characterisation of the relevant steps under the *Ramsay* principle. While this has not yet happened in the Part 13 Chapter 1 context, it has in Part 13 Chapter 2 (transfer of assets abroad) (*IRC v McGuckian* (1997)) and there is no reason – given that *Ramsay* is a principle of statutory construction – why it does not apply to Part 13 Chapter 1. **[3.38]–[3.50]**

3 The legislation for corporation tax advantages: CTA 2010 ss 731–751; the former legislation for income tax advantages: ITA 2007 ss 682–694

Until the provisions in CTA 2010 are simplified, the law regarding transactions in securities for companies remains as it has been. As far as individuals are concerned, generally the former legislation in ITA 2007 ss 682–694 applied in relation to income tax advantages obtained prior to 24 March 2010. The sections below refer only to the former legislation in ITA 2007 ss 682–694, but the same principles (excluding Conditions A and B) apply for companies.

[3.51]

a) *Important cases and key points of interpretation*

There were numerous cases on the provisions mainly in the 'heyday' of tax avoidance from the 1960s to the early 1980s. The highlights are set out below. It should be noted that these cases were all decided prior to the original rewritten legislation in ITA 2007 Part 13 Chapter 1 and, consequently, the language used in the previous legislation is different, although the substance remains the same. **[3.52]**

'*Cancellation of a tax advantage*' rewritten as '*countering income tax advantages*' (ITA 2007 s 682(1)) – the general approach. The Court of Appeal confirmed that, since it was Parliament's intention when introducing the legislation in 1960 to provide for a 'wide and general attack on tax avoidance', ITA 2007 Part 13 Chapter 1 is targeted at all forms of tax avoidance which fall within its scope, and is not limited to contrived transactions carried out otherwise than on the open market (*Sema Group Pension Scheme Trustees v IRC* (2003), following *IRC v Joiner* (1975)). **[3.53]**

'*In consequence of … or the combined effect of …*' (ITA 2007 s 684(1)) A tax advantage will be regarded as being 'in consequence of' a transaction in securities where it is a product of it, whether or not there is a direct causal link (*Williams v IRC* (1980)). The exact scope of the term 'the combined effect of' is unclear. On the language of the statute, if one step is taken (Step 1) quite independently of a later step (Step 2) and a tax advantage then arises, the true test is whether there are any ss 686–690 'circumstances' and whether the tax advantage is the product of Steps 1 and 2. If it is, then s 684 applies unless *both* Steps satisfy the 'escape clause' in s 685 (see the phrase: 'the transaction or transactions' ...). The Revenue does not seem to take this line where the Steps are genuinely independent; if Step 2 was inevitable after Step 1 then the two are regarded as a single transaction (*IRC v Brebner* (1967)). [**3.54**]

'Income tax advantage' A person will obtain an 'income tax advantage' where he gets relief or greater relief from tax *or* repayment or greater repayment of tax *or* avoids or gets a reduced charge to tax *or* avoids an assessment or a possible assessment to tax – in the case of the last two, it does not matter whether the avoidance or reduction is effected by a tax-free receipt or a deduction from taxable profits or gains (s 683). It was not clear whether (as the Revenue long contended) an exempt body (eg a charity) would fall within the scope of a person who gets 'relief from' or 'repayment of' tax for these purposes. The High Court (Aldous J) said 'no' in *Sheppard v IRC (No 2)* (1993) on the basis that a person who has no liability to tax cannot gain a tax advantage ('relief') by avoiding what he is not subject to; this was 'reversed' by the High Court (Vinelott J) in *IRC v Universities Superannuation Scheme Ltd* (1997) on the basis that the anti-avoidance context required a broad approach to the term 'relief' and put beyond doubt by FA 1997 s 73 (see s 683(3))). This is further considered in the *IRC v Trustees of the Sema Group Pension Scheme* (2003) (see [**3.72**]).

The advantage may arise as a result of one or more transactions or a transaction combined with the liquidation of the company (see s 684(3)). What matters is whether the person has received in non-taxable form cash or property he could have received in a taxable form; it does not matter that what he actually receives is different in nature to what he could have received provided that, in some way, the former represents the latter (*IRC v Parker* (1966), *Emery v IRC* (1981) and *Cleary v IRC* (1987)). In *Cleary* the taxpayers received as capital, in the form of consideration for the sale of shares to the company, sums which would have been received as income, in the form of dividends; notwithstanding that the net assets of the company were not reduced by the transaction, this amounted to a 'tax advantage' (according to the House of Lords) (see also *Bamberg v R & C Comrs* (2010)).

The amount of the income tax advantage is to be computed by looking at all the circumstances – this can be a receipt in cash or kind or even in the form of a loan by a company to a shareholder where the loan is unlikely to be repaid (see *IRC v Williams* (1980) and *Bird v IRC* (1988)). [**3.55**]

'Income tax' The original rewritten legislation in ITA 2007 ss 284–292 applies to individuals who gain income tax advantages; equivalent legislation for companies is found in CTA 2010 ss 731–742. Neither set of provisions include capital gains tax. [**3.56**]

'Transaction in securities' See [**3.33**] above. [**3.57**]

Circumstance s 686 (circumstance A) Circumstance A was aimed at dividend stripping where the taxpayer received an abnormal amount by the way of dividend. There must have been a purchase or sale of securities followed by the sale or purchase respectively of the same or other securities, the distribution, transfer or realisation of assets of a company or the application of such assets in the discharge of liabilities in connection with which a person received an abnormal dividend the amount of which was used in gaining exemption from, relief from or a reduction in tax (eg a charity buys shares, receives the dividend and claims the tax back on the dividend).

The legislation treated these requirements as being exhaustive, in line with the existing case law (see, for example, *IRC v Parker* (1966), *IRC v Cleary* (1967), *Hague v IRC* (1968), *IRC v Horrocks* (1968) and *IRC v Wiggins* (1978). A dividend was 'abnormal' if it was at an excessive fixed rate or greater than a normal return on the consideration given for the shares, measured by reference to the period of ownership of the shares (ss 692, 693) (and see *IRC v Trustees of the Sema Group Pension Scheme* (2003) at **[3.55]**). 'Dividend' encompassed other distributions and interest (s 713), eg a purchase of own shares (*IRC v Universities Superannuation Scheme Ltd* (1997)). **[3.58]**

Circumstance s 687 (circumstance B) Circumstance B was aimed at dividend stripping (or stock stripping) where the taxpayer became entitled to a deduction in calculating profits or gains as a result of the payment of a dividend or from dealing in the assets of a company. The entitlement must have arisen in connection with a sale or purchase of securities followed by the purchase and sale of the same or similar securities, the distribution, transfer or realisation of assets of a company or the application of such assets in the discharge of liabilities. **[3.59]**

Circumstance s 688 (circumstance C) Circumstance C was aimed at the 'other party' to the dividend stripping arrangement. Thus if the purchaser of shares fell within circumstances A or B, the vendor (it is intended) should have fallen within C. It operated where: (1) a person received consideration in a form not chargeable to income tax; (2) the consideration represented assets of a company available for distribution (dividend stripping), future receipts of a company (forward stripping – see *Greenberg v IRC* (1972)) or trading stock of a company (stock stripping); (3) in consequence of a transaction involving shares in a company whereby; (4) another person received an abnormal dividend (ie Circumstance A) or a deduction in profits attributable to a fall in value of shares (ie Circumstance B). There must have been a close enough causal link between the relevant transactions and the abnormal dividend or a deduction in profits (see *IRC v Garvin* (1981)).

The terms of s 688 (and s 690) ensured that a company could not reduce its distributable reserves in anticipation of a transaction which would otherwise be caught by s 684. If, however, the reserves were reduced, say, two years before the other transaction at a time when that later transaction was not contemplated, those reserves would not have been relevant for s 684 purposes. The legislation could not – did not – apply to all reserves which a company had ever had; what these provisions were aimed at were artificial steps to reduce reserves. Clearance should therefore have been given since this was not a transaction that would attract a counteraction notice (s 698). **[3.60]**

Circumstance s 689 (circumstance D) Circumstance D was not limited to dividend and stock-stripping activities. It applied to the receipt of consideration, in money or money's worth, 'in connection' with the distribution, transfer or realisation of assets of a relevant company (see s 691 for the meaning of 'relevant company' for the purposes of both s 689 and s 690; it was a company under the control of not more than five persons or any other company none of whose shares or stock were listed in the Official List of the Stock Exchange and dealt in on the Stock Exchange regularly or from time to time) or the application of such assets in the discharge of liabilities where the receipt was or represented assets available for distribution or future receipts of the company or trading stock of the company.

As with s 686, the requirements as to what the receipt must have been in connection with were exhaustive. The term 'consideration' included non-contractual receipts of money or money's worth (s 689(6)). The full extent of the provision was spelt out in the speech of Lord Upjohn in *Cleary v IRC* (1967):

> 'In connection with the distribution, transfer or realisation, including application in discharge of liabilities, of profits, income, reserves or other assets of a company to which this paragraph applies, the person in question so receives ... that he does not pay or bear tax on it as income ... a consideration in money or money's worth which either is, or represents the value of, assets which are (or apart from anything done by the company in question would have been) available for distribution by way of dividend or is received in respect of future receipts of the company or is or represents the value of trading stock of the company.'

In *Cleary v IRC* two sisters owned all the share capital of two companies G (which had substantial accumulated profits) and M. They sold the shares of M to G for cash that would otherwise have been available to pay dividends and counteraction was taken under circumstance s 704D of TA 1988 (now ITA 2007 s 689) in respect of the consideration for the sale of shares of M. The House of Lords (after commenting on the scope of the imprecise language used in s 704D) rejected the taxpayer's argument that circumstance D only applied if the transfer of assets diminished the company's assets.

In *Bamberg v R & C Comrs* (2010) the taxpayer, who owned a company (A) with distributable reserves, purchased loan stock from and (for a nominal amount) the shares of a company (B) with negative distributable reserves, no assets and a liability to repay loan stock, and then sold them to A. A then made loans to B, which were used to repay part of B's loan stock to the taxpayer. Later the trade of A was hived-down to B, which continued the trade, and further repayments of its loan stock were made to the taxpayer. Until the hive-down, immediately before each repayment of loan stock by B, A lent a corresponding amount to B. Following the hive-down, A ceased to trade. The First-tier tribunal held that the fact that assets had been lent by A to B or transferred on the hive-down in consideration of a debt did not prevent those assets from continuing to represent assets available for distribution by A by way of dividend.

Counteraction was taken in cases of capital distributions (*Addy v IRC* (1975)), a bonus issue of debentures (*Parker v IRC* (1966)) and indirect receipts of proceeds representing trading stock (*IRC v Wiggins* (1979) where the owner of a company procured the transfer of all its business and assets bar one to Newco and then sold the company; the sale proceeds were held to represent the trading stock of the company).

The receipt of consideration was 'in connection with' the distribution of profits if there was a causal connection which did not need to be as strong as that required by 'whereby' in s 688 (*Emery v IRC* (1981)). There had to be a *link* but it did not have to be *the cause*. [3.61]

Circumstance s 690 (circumstance E) Circumstance E was aimed at transactions that did not fall within s 689 (eg because the person concerned received shares or securities and not money or money's worth). It applied where a person received, in connection with the transfer of assets of a relevant company see [3.60] to another such company, consideration consisting of any share capital or security issued by a relevant company which was not chargeable to income tax but which represented the assets available for distribution of such a company. The classic case covered by s 690 was the sale of the shares of relevant company which had assets available for distribution to another company in return for shares or securities. In effect the assets available for distribution of company A were received in the form of shares in company B.

The provision operated at the time of the receipt of redeemable share capital or securities (they were regarded as 'near cash') or at the time of repayment (on a winding up or otherwise) of non-redeemable share capital (see s 690(2): 'The person *receives* consideration ...'). The deferral operated on the latter only. If the receipt of shares or securities gave rise to a charge under s 684 no charge would arise on the redemption of such shares or securities. [3.62]

The 'escape clause' (ITA 2007 s 685) This section provided an exception to s 684 provided that two cumulative conditions were satisfied: the first was that the transactions were effected for genuine commercial reasons or in the ordinary course of making or managing investments; the second was that gaining a tax benefit as not the main object of the transactions. Clearly, it was only necessary to meet the second condition if the first was satisfied. Thus, a taxpayer may have had a commercial purpose or the transactions must have been in the ordinary course of making or managing investments where a tax advantage was a feature of the transactions but not a main object (the latter was merely a step on the way to the former); in such a case the clause would be satisfied. However, if the taxpayer had both a commercial purpose and a main tax object – they were separate goals in themselves – the clause was not satisfied (see *Hasloch v IRC* (1971)). The heavy burden of proof lay on the taxpayer. Note that the term 'effected' had been used in place of 'carried out', following *Greenberg v IRC* (1971) and for the purposes of consistency with other provisions. [3.63]

Genuine commercial reasons: the 'bona fide commercial' test The *'bona fide* commercial' test was satisfied where, looking at the subjective intention of the taxpayer, there were genuine commercial reasons for what had been done (*IRC v Brebner* (1966)). If there were two possible courses, one which involved paying more tax than the other, merely choosing to take the latter course did not necessarily mean that the test was not satisfied. Examples of 'commercial' motives included the retention of family control of a company (*IRC v Goodwin* (1975)), the sale of shares to fund the purchase of a farm (*Clark v IRC* (1978)) and a corporate reorganisation to preserve the viability of the group (*Marwood Homes v IRC* (1997)) (but see [**43.171**]). [**3.64**]

The 'ordinary course of making and managing investments' test This test was satisfied where the taxpayer took an ordinary, sensible, investment decision (the 'prudent investor') divorced from tax considerations. In *Clark v IRC* two brothers owned the shares in a company; one, the farming brother, wanted to sell the shares to purchase a farm; the other, the non-farming brother, felt that he had to sell to avoid being left with a less valuable investment. This satisfied the 'making and managing investments' test (see also *Lewis (Trustee of Redrow Staff Pension Scheme) v IRC* (1999)). [**3.65**]

The 'no main object of obtaining a tax advantage' test See [**3.35**] above. [**3.66**]

Counteraction See [**3.38**] above. [**3.67**]–[**3.70**]

4 Application of ITA 2007 ss 682–687 and of CTA 2010 ss 731–742

a) *Notable cases*

Transactions in securities In *Laird Group plc v IRC* (1999) the Special Commissioners held that where L purchased all of the shares in S Co for *bona fide* commercial reasons, S Co paid an abnormal amount by way of dividend (plus tax credit) to L on 17 December 1990 (outside a group income election) and L gained a tax advantage by setting off the dividend received and tax credit against a dividend and ACT paid to its shareholders on 5 December 1990, there were transactions in securities which failed to satisfy either limb of the escape clause. L plc sought a rehearing in front of the s 703 Tribunal (ITA 2007 Part 13 Chapter 1 Tribunal for the purposes of income tax) (under s 705(2), now ITA 2007 s 706). The Tribunal held that the counteraction notice should be struck down since the payment of a dividend is not a transaction in securities, S Ltd's dividend was for *bona fide* commercial reasons since it allowed L plc to avoid surplus ACT and thus prevent the erosion of L plc's earnings per share but that the dividend had as one of its main objects the securing of the tax advantage. On appeal Lightman J upheld the Tribunal's decisions on the basis that a dividend is not a transaction in securities since it merely gives effect to existing rights attached to securities.

The House of Lords (*IRC v Laird Group plc* (2003)) set aside the decision of the Court of Appeal that the declaration or payment of a dividend was plainly a transaction related to securities in the form of the shares in respect of which it was paid, and that it did not just give effect to a shareholder's pre-existing rights, and decided to the contrary that the payment of a dividend was neither a transaction *in* securities, nor a transaction *relating to* securities, Lord Millett (who gave the only full judgment) reached this conclusion by comparing the distribution of profits on an ordinary liquidation (which is not a transaction in securities) with the declaration of a dividend. He said:

'Whether the company is in liquidation or continuing to carry on business as a going concern .... the distribution of the undistributed profits of a company to the shareholders entitled thereto merely gives effect to the rights attached to the shares. The funds are released, in the one case from the liquidator's discretion to retain them for the purpose of the winding up, and in the other from the directors' discretion to retain them for the purposes of the undertaking. Given that the former is not 'a transaction relating to securities', neither in my opinion is the latter. The relationship between the payment and the shares in respect of which it is paid is the same in both cases.'

The implications of this important decision are great for those engaged in merger and acquisition planning, although it should be noted that an abnormal dividend could still bring the issue within circumstances A–D where there is already a transaction in securities giving rise to a tax advantage.

[3.71]

The exception The saga of *Marwood Homes* is a stark reminder of the importance of identifying all relevant evidence *before* commencing litigation in this area. The basic facts were these: Marwood Homes Ltd (MHL) was making heavy losses; as a way of solving those financial difficulties it acquired four companies from its parent and then procured the payment of dividends by those companies (outside the group income election) and the sale by those companies of their trades and assets. The dividends were, as a result of the reorganisation, necessarily abnormal; the tax credit attaching to them was set against MHL's trading losses. The Revenue (who had refused clearance) issued a notice on the basis of s 704A (ITA 2007 s 686) and the company appealed on the basis that it fell within the escape clause (referred to in the rewritten legislation as an 'exception').

In *Marwood Homes Ltd v IRC* (1997) the Special Commissioners held that the transactions were carried out for *bona fide* commercial reasons (getting sufficient funds into MHL to allow it to survive) and did not have a main object of securing a tax advantage; the Revenue, being dissatisfied with this, sought a rehearing (by virtue of s 705(2) (ITA 2007 s 706)) before the Special Commissioners. The taxpayer challenged this as an abuse of process (on the basis that the reasons given by the Revenue for the rehearing were ones which could have advanced at the first hearing but were not) but this was rejected (see *Marwood Homes (No 2)* (1998)). At the rehearing the Revenue produced evidence – found in an internal note in the files of the taxpayer's accountants – that suggested that the commercial rationale for the transactions had been 'beefed up' so as to outweigh the tax motivation. On the basis of this (and other evidence) the Tribunal overturned the decision of the Special Commissioners and restored the counteraction notice (see *Marwood Homes Ltd v IRC* (1999)). In effect the Tribunal was not satisfied that the tax advantages were not one of the main purposes of the steps taken by MHL. For a discussion of the main purpose test, see (2007) *Tax Journal*, 12 March, pp 8–10

In *Lewis (Trustee of Redrow Staff Pension Scheme) v IRC* (1999), it was held that the tax advantage obtained by the trustees of a staff pension scheme on their sale of shares in the employer company to the employer company should not be counteracted, because the transaction was carried out for *bona fide* commercial reasons, the trustees were acting in the ordinary course of managing investments and the tax advantage was not the only or main reason for the transaction. The trustees of the scheme held shares in R plc which represented 8.9% of the value of the pension scheme funds. As R plc was about to float, the trustees were told by the Occupational Pensions Board to reduce the employer-related investment to 5% or below as soon as R plc was listed. This was done by a purchase of own shares (which allowed the trustees to reclaim the tax credit) rather than a sale on the flotation. This meant that the trustees did not have to become involved in the flotation and saved them the substantial associated disposal costs. The trustees' appeal against the Revenue's notice under s 703(3) (ITA 2007 ss 695, 698) and assessment under the former Schedule F was allowed as the purchase of own shares relieved the trustees of the burden of extra work and the costs involved in the flotation; and the obtaining of a tax advantage was not the main object or one of the main objects in making that choice. The trustees took the simplest and cheapest option available to them, and in doing so were acting in the ordinary course of managing investments. A wish to reduce the excessive holding of employer-related investments was a *bona fide* commercial reason.

In *IRC v Trustees of the Sema Group Pension Scheme* (2003) the trustees of an exempt pension scheme had acquired quoted shares in the market. The company concerned (Powergen) then announced a buy-back of its shares and the trustees sold their shares. The proceeds of sale in excess of the paid up capital of the shares were treated as a distribution in the hands of the trustees that gave them an entitlement to reclaim the tax credit. The Revenue contended that circumstance s 704A (ITA 2007 s 686) was relevant on the basis that the trustees had obtained an abnormal amount by way of dividend. The Special Commissioners decided that the dividend was not abnormal but that the trustees had obtained a 'tax advantage' (in the form of the tax credit repayable to them by virtue of their exempt status) and that had been one of their main objects in selling the shares in the buy-back. The Revenue appealed and the trustees cross-appealed. In the High Court, Lightman J concluded that the normalcy (or otherwise) of the dividend had to be determined by looking at the sum received excluding the tax credit but that, on the facts, the dividend was abnormal since it represented a one-off return, by way of distribution, of what was, in reality, capital.

Further the judge concluded: (1) although minded to decide otherwise, he was bound to follow the later decision in *IRC v Universities Superannuation Scheme Ltd* (1997) (rather than the earlier one in *Sheppard v IRC (No 2)* (1993)) to the effect that an exemption from tax can be regarded as a 'relief' and thus within the definition of 'tax advantage'; and (2) the Special Commissioners were entitled on the facts to decide that the obtaining of the tax advantage had been a main object of the trustees in deciding to sell in the buy-back. The Court of Appeal, in allowing the trustees' appeal, rejected the view of Lightman J that the amounts in question had to be treated *as if they were dividends*. Section 704(A) (ITA 2007 s 686) requires that the normality of the amount 'received by way of dividends' should be considered. Section 709(2) (ITA 2007 s 713) provides that 'references to dividends include references to other qualifying distributions'. Accordingly, what had to be considered on the facts of the present case was the normality of the amount received by the trustee by way of a qualifying distribution of the kind that in fact occurred. The Court of Appeal did, however, agree with Lightman J on the two further issues. *First*, in holding that the tax credit to which the trustees were entitled was a 'relief from tax', Jonathan Parker LJ opined that:

'what the draftsman was manifestly trying to do when defining "tax advantage" ... was to cover every situation in which the position of the taxpayer vis-à-vis the Revenue is improved in consequence of the particular transaction or transactions.'

Second, it was held that the Special Commissioners were entitled to hold that the tax credits were crucial to the decision to sell into the buy-backs, and so one of the main objects of the sales was to enable tax advantages to be obtained. These were findings that they were fully entitled to reach on the evidence before them, and there was no basis on which an appellate court could interfere. [3.72]

IV PRINCIPLES-BASED LEGISLATION

It has to be accepted that the current statutory method of dealing with tax avoidance results, in effect, in a game of cat and mouse between HMRC on the one hand, and the taxpayer on the other: the more detailed the statutory provision, the more refined the avoidance scheme becomes and so on. Prior to the election of the Coalition Government and the enactment in 2013 of a General Anti-Abuse Rule (GAAR), there had been a proposed move to a different type of legislation. In its consultative document *Principles-based approach to financial products avoidance* (December 2007), HMRC stated:

> 'Principles-based legislation would embody a principle of UK taxation, and would be accompanied by a statement of how the legislation intends to operate by reference to that principle. It would do this in such a way that it would be clear, on a first reading, what was being addressed and with what outcome in mind.
>
> The principles-based legislation ... should improve certainty – even if taxpayers were to find that some of the detail of their specific case was not mentioned in the legislation, they would know whether and, if so, how to apply the legislation, as they would understand the underlying principle ...
>
> Making the principle apparent on the face of the legislation would eliminate the need to have lots of detailed rules. This would promote fairness and consistency in tax treatment ... New principles-based legislation could be shorter and less complex. And it should be more difficult for avoiders to argue that a scheme does not contravene principles than to argue that a scheme meets the literal requirements of the statute.'

A principles-based approach to tax avoidance brings with it flexibility (for HMRC) and a defence for the judiciary against claims of 'judge-made law' in tax avoidance cases. On the other hand, from the taxpayer's point of view, it could be argued that such legislation is vague in its scope and would lead to uncertainty. As one commentator has pointed out, HMRC are bound to publish guidance in respect of principles-based provisions. Whilst these will be helpful, 'there is a fine line between helpful interpretation and legislation by guidance. We have a legislative process which, whatever its limitations, should be used to determine the amount of tax payable; Parliament's power should not be usurped by HMRC.' ((2008) *Tax Journal*, 7 January.) Moreover, the only way in which a taxpayer could seek redress in respect of HMRC's guidance is to seek judicial review. This is a costly and time-consuming process, which is effectively unavailable to most potential applicants because 'potential applicants do not know about it, cannot understand it, cannot afford it, or find the prospect of going to the High Court too daunting'. (Tracey Bowler *Countering Tax Avoidance in the UK: Which Way Forward?* (Tax Law Review Committee, 2009)).

Following further consultation, provisions seeking to combat financial products avoidance were included in FA 2009. The draft legislation, which contained short statements of principles, was described as being not 'very "principles-based" at all' (Sara Luder (2008) *Tax Journal*, 7 January). Worse was to follow: heralded as the first attempt at principles-based drafting, neither of the two provisions in FA 2009 contains any statement of principle at all, and the legislation appears to be no different than any other TAAR in that it is focused and complex. It can only be assumed that this has come about as a result of the consultation process (see, for example, the criticism of Roger Muray in (2008) *Tax Journal*, 4 February, when he wrote of an inconsistency between the clearly stated principle and the detailed legislation). Further principles-based legislation concerning group mismatch schemes was included in FA 2011.

Despite the introduction of the GAAR, it is envisaged that principles-based legislation will continue to be one of a number of proposed measures (see **[2.1]**) to tackle tax avoidance along with the widening of the disclosure rules regime (see **Chapter 5**), That it should continue as part of the Government's strategy was confirmed by the Economic Affairs Committee: when discussing the Finance Bill 2011, it agreed that 'principles-based drafting is an approach that should be developed for the future in appropriate situations. It seems likely that the more it is used, the easier the approach will be to develop in a wider range of situations'. **[3.73]**

V A GENERAL ANTI-ABUSE RULE

1 Introduction

The then Chancellor of the Exchequer, the Rt Hon Gordon Brown MP, announced in his Budget speech in July 1997 that it was his intention to curb generally 'the leakage' and avoidance of direct taxes. He said:

> 'I have also instructed the Inland Revenue to carry out a wide-ranging review of areas of tax avoidance, with a view to further legislation in future Finance Bills. I have specifically asked them to consider a general anti-avoidance rule.'

Further to this instruction, the then Inland Revenue published in 1998 a Consultation Paper on the proposed general anti-avoidance rule (GAAR). The GAAR, initially planned to apply to direct corporate taxes only, was intended to introduce provisions in the legislation that can be used to strike at tax schemes which the Revenue view as being unacceptable. (Customs and Excise produced their own Consultation Paper on a series of mini-GAARs.) Although this document was based on a 1997 report from the Tax Law Reform Committee (set up in 1994 by the Institute for Fiscal Studies to keep under review the state and operation of tax law), that very same committee subsequently announced that it would be unable to support a GAAR of the type proposed in the consultation. Other professional bodies also criticised the proposed changes, most notably the Tax Faculty of the Institute of Chartered Accountants, which described the proposals as 'worryingly wide-ranging' with the potential to catch legitimate tax planning. In particular, it was doubted whether the proposed system of pre-transaction rulings would be quick or cheap enough to allow for all taxpayers to make use of it.

Possibly because of the negative response to the Consultation Paper, the former Labour Government did not legislate for a GAAR to deal with the main direct taxes, namely, income tax, corporation tax and capital gains tax, although a GAAR was introduced by secondary legislation into stamp duty land tax (SDLT) in the form of FA 2003 s 75A (see **Chapter 49**). This provision was described at the time as 'fundamentally deficient' and it was believed at the time that the section was 'almost unworkable in practice'; it was amended in 2006.

However, as part of the Coalition Government's commitment to tackle tax avoidance, and following a consultation (the consultation document being the result of the work of a study group chaired by Graham Aaronson QC) on whether a GAAR could be framed so as to be effective in the UK tax system, FA 2013 introduced legislation providing for an anti-abuse rule (see **[3.75]**).
[**3.74**]

2 The Aaaronson Report

a) *Background*

Against a backdrop of acute suffering by many due to the terrible economic climate and an increasing awareness by the public at large (due partly to the likes of groups such as the Tax Justice Network and UK Uncut) of tax avoidance by both corporations and wealthy individuals, in December 2010 Graham Aaronson QC was asked to lead a study programme to establish whether a GAAR could be framed so as to be effective in the UK tax system and, if so, how the provisions of such a GAAR might be framed. In particular, the Group was asked to develop rules that would be effective, fair and certain, and that would not erode the attractiveness of the UK and its tax regime to the global business community. In addition, it was required to keep any increase in resources for HMRC to an acceptable level. [**3.75**]

b) *The Report's conclusions*

The Report, presented in November 2011, estimated that there were currently in the region of 300 targeted anti-avoidance rules and that these, together with purposive interpretation (see **Chapter 2**) and the Disclosure of Tax Avoidance Schemes (DOTAS: see **Chapter 5**) did reduce the scope for tax avoidance. However, these tools had proved ineffective in preventing 'intolerable' tax avoidance, and something more was required. With all of this in mind, the conclusion reached by the Aaronson study group was that a broad spectrum GAAR would undermine the ability of business and individuals to carry out sensible and responsible tax planning, thereby causing the UK to lose some of its attractiveness as a place to reside and to do business. Instead, it proposed a general anti-abuse rule aimed at attacking

the most heinous of tax arrangements. The benefits of a targeted anti-abuse rule were perceived as:
(i) deterring or counteracting contrived and artificial schemes;
(ii) providing a more level playing field for business;
(iii) reducing the risk of stretched judicial interpretation and the uncertainty that entails (see **Chapter 2**);
(iv) obviating the need for further complex legislation dealing with particular abusive schemes and thereby simplifying legislation. Although it was recognised that there would still be a need for specific legislation, it was thought that a GAAR would operate better where such rules are clear, and that this would encourage legislators and drafters to consider more carefully the principles behind the rules;
(v) eventually reducing and simplifying the existing body of anti-avoidance rules;
(vi) not requiring a comprehensive system of clearances;
(vii) helping to inform the public debate about tax avoidance and abusive practices and building trust between taxpayers and HMRC as the boundaries between acceptable and unacceptable behaviours are clarified.

It was proposed that a targeted general anti-abuse rule (GAAR) should apply initially to the main direct taxes (income tax, corporation tax, capital gains tax and petroleum revenue tax) together with national insurance contributions, which would need separate legislation, and could later apply to other taxes including stamp duty land tax (SDLT). It was believed that it should not apply to VAT, which is already subject to the EU abuse rules (see **[2.44]**). [3.76]

3 The general anti-abuse rule (GAAR) (FA 2013 ss 206–215 and Sch 43)

a) *General overview*

The GAAR, which has effect in respect of tax arrangements entered into on or after 17 July 2013, is designed to counteract tax advantages arising from tax arrangements that are abusive. It is a separate rule, which operates when the application of the normal rules would fail to prevent the achievement of the abusive tax result. Thus, counteraction under the GAAR would come into effect only if the application to the arrangement of the particular tax rules given their purposive interpretation would produce an abusive result (for example, had one been in effect, a GAAR could have counteracted the result in *Mayes v R & C Comrs* (2011) (see **[2.39]**).

Tax advantages include relief or increased relief from tax; repayment or increased repayment of tax; avoidance or reduction of a charge to tax or to an assessment to tax; deferral of a payment of tax or advancement of a repayment of tax; and avoidance of an obligation to deduct or account for tax (FA 2013 s 208).

An independent advisory board (the Advisory Panel) appointed by HMRC, but with no HMRC representation on the panel, helps taxpayers and HMRC to identify the limits of acceptable tax avoidance, thereby avoiding giving greater discretionary powers to HMRC. Specifically, the Advisory Panel has two formal functions. *First*, it gives opinions (see **[3.79]**); *second*, it approves HMRC guidance on the application of the GAAR. In addition, and importantly, the panel members bring with them a deep knowledge of the way in which the system works.

HMRC have provided guidance on the GAAR (amended with effect from 30 January 2015 and running to 191 pages, the majority of which must be, and have been, approved by the Advisory Panel), and which a court or tribunal *must* take account in determining any issue in connection with the GAAR (FA 2013 s 211(2)).

Where the GAAR applies, adjustments are made on a 'just and reasonable' basis in order to counteract any tax advantages that would otherwise arise from abusive tax arrangements (FA 2013 s 209). These are likely to reflect the tax result that would have prevailed had the abusive tax arrangements not been entered into.

The breadth of the GAAR is greater than originally envisaged by the Aaronson report, applying to income tax; capital gains tax; inheritance tax; corporation tax and any amount treated as if it were corporation tax, eg a CFC charge, the bank levy, the oil supplementary charge and tonnage tax; petroleum revenue tax; stamp duty land tax; the annual tax on enveloped dwellings; and the new diverted profits tax (introduced by FA 2015; see **[41.64]–[41.180]**). **[3.77]**

b) *Scope of the GAAR*

Much of the criticism levelled at the GAAR has stemmed from the difficulty of defining 'abusive tax avoidance', causing concern about the width of the rule. In proceedings before a court or tribunal, the burden of proof rests with HMRC to demonstrate that tax arrangements are abusive (FA 2013 s 211(1)(a)). The scope of the GAAR turns on the meaning of the terms 'tax arrangements', defined by the 'main purpose' rule and 'abusive', defined by the 'double reasonableness' test.

(i) *The 'main purpose' rule* This determines whether the obtaining of a tax advantage was the main purpose, or one of the main purposes, of the arrangements entered into, thereby turning it into a tax arrangement (FA 2013 s 207(1)).

(ii) *The 'double reasonableness' test* It has to be decided, ultimately by a court, whether there can be a reasonably held view that the tax arrangements are a reasonable course of action in relation to the relevant tax provisions, having regard to all the circumstances (a non-exhaustive list of examples of such circumstances are given in the legislation, including whether the means of achieving the tax advantage involves one or more contrived or abnormal steps) (FA 2013 s 207(2)). If there is no such reasonably held view, the arrangements are 'abusive'. Unlike a single reasonableness test, the personal view of the judge is irrelevant. Accordingly, if a court heard conflicting expert evidence and both views were reasonable, irrespective of which view the judge might prefer, the GAAR could not apply to the arrangements in question.

FA 2013 s 207(4) provides examples of indicators that tax arrangements are abusive; the fact that tax arrangements accord with established practice and HMRC had, at the time the arrangements were entered into, indicated its acceptance of that practice, is an example of something which might indicate that the arrangements are not abusive (FA 2013 s 207(5)). It is believed that the GAAR would catch a number of marketed tax avoidance schemes involving individuals and, on the corporate front, transactions that seek to create a tax deduction when there has been no economic loss (according to a representative of HMRC giving evidence to the House of Lords Finance Bill Sub-Committee). What it is unlikely to cover are the arrangements that enable multinational companies (such as Amazon, Google and Starbucks) to escape tax on the profits that have accrued to them in the UK, and the deferring of the payment of bonuses (ensuring that a bonus is received, and thus assessable to tax, in a year when the rate of tax is lower). The reason for this is that the taxation of multinationals and the deferral of bonuses concern the very structure of the tax system, which a GAAR cannot address, rather than avoidance involving manipulation of loopholes in the legislation. [3.78]

c) *GAAR operating procedures*

Schedule 43 to FA 2013 sets out the procedure for applying the GAAR, and can be summarised in stages as follows:
(i) Written notification to a taxpayer that a designated officer considers that the GAAR may apply, including reasons and proposed counteraction) and inviting a written response.
(ii) Written response from the taxpayer.
(iii) If the taxpayer has made:
 (a) no written response, a designated officer must refer the matter to the Advisory Panel;
 (b) a written response, if, after considering it, the designated officer remains of the view that the GAAR should apply, he must refer the matter to the Advisory Panel.
(iv) A sub-panel of three members of the Advisory Panel gives its opinion(s) to HMRC and the taxpayer on whether the entering into and carrying out of the tax arrangements is a reasonable course of action in relation to the relevant tax provisions.
(v) The opinion(s) of the sub-panel are considered by the designated officer, who then gives notice to the taxpayer of whether the relevant tax advantages are to be counteracted, including any adjustments required to give effect to the counteraction. [3.79]

d) *Other matters*

(i) No account is taken of transactions, or part of transactions, entered into before 17 July 2013 except where referring to those earlier arrangements would help to show that the later arrangements were not abusive.
(ii) Despite concerns expressed by a number of witnesses appearing before the House of Lords Finance Bill Sub-Committee about the uncertainty over whether or not particular arrangements would fall within the ambit of the GAAR, there is no clearance procedure. This is justified on the basis that the GAAR is narrowly focused and the existence of other safeguards, namely, the role of the independent Advisory Panel, requiring HMRC to establish that the arrangements are abusive and the application of the 'double reasonableness test'.
(iii) Arguments were raised over whether the GAAR could override the UK's international obligations already written into its double taxation agreements (DTAs), and thus liable to be held unlawful. HMRC guidance notes make it clear that the abusive use of DTAs is ineffective.

Since most double tax treaties are based on the OECD model, and under the accompanying guidelines, treaty benefits are denied where they have been obtained by abusive transactions, there should be no conflict. Moreover, for those DTAs that operate outside of the OECD, it is a general principle that OECD guidelines are referred to as a general international framework.

(iv) Only a designated HMRC official can authorise any prospective use of a GAAR to ensure consistency and responsibility in the use by HMRC of a GAAR.

(v) Until 6 April 2016, no special penalties applied to tax recovered through the application of a GAAR. It had been considered that, whilst this would increase its deterrent effect, it could be seen as a temptation for HMRC to use a GAAR as a weapon rather than a shield. Nevertheless, FA 2016 has introduced, with effect from the date of Royal Assent, a penalty of 60% of all the tax due (with special rules to calculate this figure where the arrangements result in an unused loss or deferral of tax due) in all cases which are successfully brought within the scope of the GAAR. The GAAR penalty will be charged in addition to any 'normal' penalties issued in accordance with existing penalty rules (see **[4.25]** ff), and also in addition to the new serial tax avoiders penalty introduced by FA 2016. Total penalties will be restricted to 100% of the tax, or the maximum allowed under existing legislation if this is higher.

HMRC will give notice that a taxpayer may be within the scope of the GAAR, and the taxpayer will be given the opportunity to correct their tax position up until the point that their arrangements are referred to the GAAR Advisory Panel. If they do correct their tax position they will not be liable to a GAAR penalty.

(vi) FA 2016 has made small changes to the existing legislation to increase the effectiveness of the GAAR in dealing with marketed avoidance schemes. **[3.80]**

e) *Thoughts on the GAAR legislation*

The likes of the Tax Justice Network and UK Uncut are not wholly supportive of the legislation since they see it as too restrictive, being insensitive to the stated need of preventing erosion of the UK's attractiveness to do business and not understanding that the GAAR is unable to cure all the ills of the tax system (that enable the likes of Amazon, Google and Starbucks to escape UK tax on profits generated in the UK). On the other hand, supporters of the GAAR would argue that the rapid growth in complex and often obscure legislation, frequently leading to avoidance possibilities, could be viewed as a greater evil than the possible uncertainty generated by the new legislation. Finally, it would seem that the role of the Advisory Panel appears to be more circumscribed than originally expected, being limited to expressing an opinion on whether the tax arrangements were a reasonable course of action in relation to the legislation. If their opinion was to be sought, instead, on whether the GAAR applied or not, this might allay concerns that there could be an eventual drift to cover sensible tax planning.

It is suggested that the success of the newly enacted GAAR turns on it remaining a narrowly-focused rule aimed at egregious tax avoidance. However, whether this is likely to be the case must be questionable in light of the announcement by the Chancellor of the Exchequer in his July 2015 Budget Speech that the Government was determined upon tackling aggressive *tax planning* in addition to tax evasion and tax avoidance, and that the GAAR is to be strengthened. Nevertheless, despite the prediction in 2013 of Colin Bishopp, President of the Tax Chamber of the First-tier Tribunal, that the Tribunal would by 2014 have begun to see appeals generated by the GAAR, there have been none, and the President believes that the signs now are that such cases will be rare. [3.81]

4 The experience of other jurisdictions

Other jurisdictions, notably Canada, Australia, Hong Kong, New Zealand, South Africa and, very recently, India have introduced general anti-avoidance provisions to combat the ever-increasing amount of tax avoidance, but with only varying degrees of success. The current Australian provision, which focuses on the concept of a tax avoidance 'scheme', replaced the previous legislation which was so widely worded that the courts tended to restrict its operation so that it became a weak weapon in the hands of the revenue authorities. However, its replacement relies heavily on judicial discretion with the result that there is a great deal of uncertainty surrounding the provision. In addition, in 2006 a promoter penalty regime was introduced adding to the tax already collected under the GAAR a penalty of 50% of the tax avoided or 25% if the case was 'reasonably arguable'. Of the cases heard by the High Court, three have been decided in favour of the Australian Tax Office and just one for the taxpayer, although more cases have been decided in favour of the taxpayer in the Federal Courts.

As far as Canada is concerned, despite the fact that, as with Australia, Hong Kong and New Zealand, more recently the highest courts have upheld the application of the relevant GAAR (see *Lipson v Canada* (2009), *CIR v HIT Finance Ltd; CIR v Tai Hing Cotton Mill (Developments) Ltd* (2007) and *Ben Nevis Forestry Ventures Ltd v CIR; Glenharrow Ltd v CIR* (2007) respectively), the case of *The Queen v Canada Trustco Mortgage Co* (2005) highlights just how difficult the application of their GAAR can be. In *Lipson*, although the Supreme Court of Canada found in favour of the Canada Revenue Agency, it was significantly divided on the question of whether a particular series of transactions resulted in a 'misuse or abuse' (a key term in the Canadian GAAR) of one or more of the relevant provisions. Cases since *Lipson*, including *Lehigh Cement Limited v R* (2010), a case heard by the Federal Court of Appeal, reflect a similar lack of consensus within the judiciary regarding the scope of the GAAR and the application of the misuse and abuse test, and would suggest that, in seeking to apply it, the higher Canadian courts are facing exactly the same difficulties with respect to the proper approach to the interpretation of tax statutes as the UK courts did when developing the so-called judicial anti-avoidance doctrine (see **Chapter 2**).

One further point of interest is that none of these other jurisdictions (with the exception of India where the GAAR has only fairly recently been introduced) has seen a decline in the complexity of legislation, reducing and simplifying existing complex anti-avoidance legislation, being one of the factors Aaronson had pointed to as being a distinct benefit of the proposed GAAR. [3.82]

4 Administrative machinery

Written by Hartley Foster, Partner, Fieldfisher LLP

I   Introduction [4.1]
II   General structure of Her Majesty's Revenue and Customs [4.2]
III Assessment and collection of tax [4.21]
IV The information powers of HMRC [4.55]
V   The tax appeals system [4.173]

I INTRODUCTION

This chapter on the administrative machinery of the UK tax system comprises four sections.

The first section contains an outline of the general structure of Her Majesty's Revenue and Customs (HMRC), and the second explains how direct tax is collected and administered. The third and fourth sections comprise respectively an outline of the system of information powers of HMRC and the system of tax litigation. Both of these systems have been fundamentally reformed in recent years, primarily with effect from 1 April 2009.

All statutory references in this chapter are to the Taxes Management Act 1970 (TMA 1970), unless otherwise indicated. References to HMRC include references to its statutory predecessors.

The Commissioners of HMRC are responsible for the 'collection and management' of the taxes considered in this book, namely VAT, income tax, corporation tax, capital gains tax, inheritance tax and stamp taxes. However, this chapter considers the collection and administration of income tax and capital gains tax only; the procedures for corporation tax, inheritance tax and stamp taxes are dealt with in the appropriate chapters on those taxes. VAT is considered in **Chapter 38**. The sections in relation to the information powers of HMRC and the tax appeals system relate to all taxes. [4.1]

II GENERAL STRUCTURE OF HER MAJESTY'S REVENUE AND CUSTOMS

1 The creation of HMRC

In the 2004 Budget, plans to integrate the two tax departments (HM Customs and Excise and the Inland Revenue) were introduced and subsequently, the

Commissioners for Revenue and Customs Act 2005 (CRCA 2005) received Royal Assent. This Act provided the legal basis for the integrated department – HMRC – and for the new independent prosecutions office, the Revenue and Customs Prosecutions Office (RCPO). In 2010, the RCPO merged with the Crown Prosecution Service (CPS). Since 2010, the CPS has been the entity that is responsible for the prosecution function.

HMRC is responsible for all the functions (bar prosecutions) that were previously the responsibility of the Commissioners of Inland Revenue and the Commissioners of Customs and Excise, each of which had different functions and responsibilities. On merging the two departments, the powers of the Inland Revenue and of HM Customs and Excise were transferred unchanged to HMRC; the actual integration of the two has been an ongoing process since 2005.

The Government recognised the importance of rationalising the heterogeneous powers of the predecessor departments, not least because it makes it easier for taxpayers to understand and comply with their tax obligations. In order to facilitate this, fundamental changes to HMRC's powers, deterrents and safeguards have been introduced since 2005. These include a new single penalty regime and a new single regime of information powers for the purposes of tax collection. As a further step towards rationalisation, the tax appeal system was reformed fundamentally: a single UK-wide tribunal system was introduced in 2009, with one set of procedural rules, and with the competence to hear every form of tax appeal by either the taxpayer or HMRC.

The Commissioners of HMRC, currently seven in number (often referred to, albeit inaccurately, as 'the Board'), are assisted by a departmental board that has twelve members (including six non-executives, and a further three non-executives who serve only on the boards' committees).

Revenue Scotland is a non-ministerial department of the Scottish Administration. It is responsible for the devolved taxes, currently Land and Buildings Transactions Tax (LBTT) which has replaced Stamp Duty Land Tax (SDLT) and Scottish Landfill Tax (SLfT) which has replaced UK Landfill Tax (LfT). [4.2]–[4.20]

III ASSESSMENT AND COLLECTION OF TAX

1 The self-assessment system

The accountability of HMRC to the taxpaying public rests upon the premises that the system of taxation that they administer can be understood clearly and that the way in which it is administered is fair.

As far as the second premise is concerned, the 1990s saw a significant reform of the machinery of administration, particularly in the system for assessing personal tax. The essence of the reform was that those taxpayers who used to be required to make an annual return of their income (on the basis of which an Inspector of Taxes calculated the tax that they were liable to pay) are now instead required to include a self-assessment of the amount of the tax. Self-assessment has reduced the costs of tax administration in the public sector and improved the government's cash-flow, as tax payments are made more promptly than they were under the old system. The costs to the private sector, reflected either in taxpayers' own time or in the amounts expended in employing professional advisers, have, however, increased substantially. On 18 March 2015, the Chancellor of the Exchequer announced that the self-assessment tax return would be abolished and replaced with an online tax account for each taxpayer. The accomplishment of this aim is anticipated to be some years in the future. The consequences as regards the compliance burden are currently unclear. [4.21]

2 Returns

a) *Introduction*

As indicated above, the key feature of the self-assessment system is that the primary responsibility for making an assessment of the tax payable each year falls on the individual taxpayer, not on HMRC. HMRC describe their approach as 'process now, check later'; it is only after receipt and processing of the return that HMRC may make enquiries into its accuracy.

b) *Time limits*

The self-assessment cycle for income and capital gains tax purposes is started in April of each year by HMRC sending notices to taxpayers to complete tax returns for the immediately preceding tax year (which runs from 6 April to the following 5 April). If a taxpayer does not receive such a notice, but does have taxable income or gains, then he must notify HMRC (under TMA 1970 s 7(1)) within six months from the end of the relevant tax year, so that a return can be issued and completed within the normal time limits.

There are different filing dates for electronic and non-electronic self-assessment tax returns. In general, paper (ie non-electronic) returns are due on or before 31 October following the end of the tax year concerned; electronic returns are due on or before the following 31 January (ie 31 January 2018 for the 2016–17 tax year) (TMA 1970 s 8(1D)). The taxpayer must pay any tax due (and any balancing payment for the previous year – see [4.23]) by 31 January following the end of the year of assessment; the deadline for payment is the same for both returns filed by paper and returns filed online. The tax return operates as a source of information and is the basis of a debt payable by the taxpayer; the liability to pay tax arises on submission of the return without HMRC having to take any further action.

If the returns are issued late, then the filing dates are as follows. Where notice to make a return is given after 31 July, but on or before 31 October, any paper return must be delivered during the period of three months beginning with the date of the notice (TMA 1970 s 8(1F)). An electronic return is due as normal (ie on or before 31 January). Where notice is given after 31 October then the return (whether in electronic format or not) must be delivered within three months of the date of the notice (TMA 1970 s 8(1G)).

A taxpayer may amend his self-assessment return within 12 months of the filing date for any reason (TMA 1970 s 9ZA). Also, HMRC may amend a self-assessment return, so as to correct any obvious errors or omissions in the return within nine months of receipt (s 9ZB).

c) *Calculation of the tax liability*

If a taxpayer wants HMRC to calculate his tax liability, on the basis of the information provided by his tax return, and to notify him of the tax payable before the due date for payment, then the taxpayer must submit a paper return by 31 October after the year of assessment (ie 31 October 2017 for the 2016–17 tax year) or two months from the date of issue of the return, if later (see TMA 1970 s 9(2)). In either case, the taxpayer must ask HMRC to calculate his tax liability, or they will not do so. HMRC will then calculate the tax due on the basis of the information provided in the return and will issue the taxpayer with a tax calculation set out on form SA302. The software used to file a return electronically (either via HMRC's website or acquired commercially) will calculate the self-assessment for those taxpayers who file online.

All relevant figures will be needed for the self-assessment form to be completed; accordingly business accounts made up to (say) 31 March 2017 must be ready before 31 January 2018.

d) *Use of provisional figures*

HMRC accept that a return is not invalid simply because it contains provisional or estimated figures. However, if provisional figures are used, then, in order for HMRC to accept the return (and for the taxpayer to avoid a possible penalty), the taxpayer must provide an acceptable explanation for supplying provisional figures and the taxpayer should send the final figures as soon as possible. The omission of information is a factor that is taken into account in deciding whether or not to open an enquiry into the return.

e) *Record keeping*

There is a duty to preserve the records that were needed to complete the return properly; generally, this duty can be fulfilled by retaining copy documents, but certain original documents must be retained (see TMA 1970 s 12B). If the taxpayer is carrying on a trade, profession or business, then all relevant documents must be kept until the fifth anniversary of the filing date or the sixth anniversary of the end of the period (ie records for 2016–17 must be kept until 31 January 2023). In the case of other records, these must be kept for 12 months from the filing date of 31 January.

Failure to keep records renders the taxpayer potentially liable to the imposition of a penalty of up to £3,000. HMRC have indicated that the imposition of a penalty, however, is not automatic; and that the maximum penalty will be imposed only 'in the more serious cases'. HMRC have issued guidance with regard to keeping records: 'A general guide to keeping records for your tax return' which can be regarded as promoting 'best practice'.

In April 2011, a pilot programme of business records checks on small and medium-sized enterprises was undertaken. The aim was to inspect the adequacy of businesses' record keeping by pre-return checks (which would be quicker than opening formal enquiries), and with penalties being imposed for only the most serious record-keeping failures. However, the pilot was unpopular. HMRC agreed to undertake a review with a view to formulating a new approach focussing primarily on high-risk businesses. A new approach was rolled out from November 2012. Customers who HMRC consider are more likely to be at risk of having inadequate records are now contacted by letter to arrange for HMRC to call them to go through a short questionnaire. The calls take about 15 minutes and the questions are not specific to the tax return of the taxpayer concerned; they are designed to enable HMRC to work out whether or not the taxpayer is keeping satisfactory records. Customers who are assessed as being at risk of keeping inadequate records will be told so immediately and a business record check scheduled. [4.22]

3 Payment of tax

Under self-assessment, all income is taxed for the year of assessment in which it arises. As the amount of income to be charged to tax for a year of assessment is not known until after the end of that year, and because the date for payment of tax is set at 31 January following the end of the year, to ensure that the Government's ongoing financing needs are met, payments on account of income tax are required to be made (under TMA 1970 s 59A).

Under TMA 1970 s 59A(2), taxpayers are not required to pay payments on account of more than 50% of the relevant amount for the preceding year, even if it may already be clear, at the time that the payments are made, that the actual liability for the year will exceed that for the preceding year.

The payments on account are made in two equal instalments:
(1) on or before 31 January in the year of assessment; and
(2) on or before 31 July next following.

The amount to be paid on account is the sum of:
(a) the amount of income tax in the self-assessment for the immediately preceding year minus the amount of income tax deducted at source; and
(b) the amount of any discovery assessment made for the immediately preceding year.

EXAMPLE 4.1

The self-assessment for Bill, a self-employed taxpayer, shows the following for 2016–17.
(1) Gross income tax assessed: £29,627
(2) Gross Class 4 NICs: £4,215
(3) Gross Class 2 NICs: £143
(4) Tax deducted at source £4,000

The relevant amount is income tax assessed for 2015–16 less income tax deducted at source for 2016–17.

The relevant amount of income tax for 2016–17 is £25,627 (£29,627 – £4,000); the relevant amount of Class 4 NICs for 2016–17 is: £4,215 and Class 2 NICs £143

Therefore the payments on account required for 2017–18 are:
31 January 2018: £12,813.50+ £2107+ £71.50
31 July 2018: £12,813.50+ £2108+ £71.50

Taxpayers who have filed returns are excused from making payments on account if the amount of income tax payable for the previous year which was not deducted at source (eg under the PAYE regime) does not exceed £1,000 or 20% of the total tax assessed.

A taxpayer can reduce the interim payments of tax based on the previous year's income, if he believes that his current year's income is lower than his previous year's, by making a claim specifying the reason for the reduction (TMA 1970 s 59A(3)). HMRC cannot refuse the reduction, but it can impose a penalty of up to 100% of the difference between the amount of income tax that is shown to be due and the amount paid as reduced payments on account if the claim to reduce the instalment was made carelessly or deliberately (TMA 1970 s 59A(6)). HMRC have made it clear that the intention of this penalty is to prevent gross or persistent abuse (see eg the HMRC Self Assessment: Legal Framework Manual at SALF 303). [4.23]

4 Collection of tax

Once the amount of tax due has been finalised, HMRC has a number of powers that it can use to collect the tax (but see *Re Selectmove Ltd* (1995) on the restrictions on HMRC's power to agree to a proposal to pay arrears of tax in instalments). If the taxpayer fails to pay the tax due then HMRC can levy distress (TMA 1970 s 61) or, if the taxpayer is an employee, arrange for the tax to be deducted from his earnings. Alternatively, the tax charged can be recovered in the magistrates' court (for amounts up to £2,000), the county court (without limit, but rarely used for amounts above £50,000) or the High Court for amounts over £50,000) (TMA 1970 ss 65–68).

The insolvency of the taxpayer is no bar to HMRC pursuing the debt. However, the former status given to HMRC as a preferential creditor on insolvency has been abolished.

Where HMRC have issued a determination of tax where no return has been delivered (see [4.41]), the amount determined is in excess of what would otherwise have been due had a return been filed and the taxpayer is unable to adjust the amount due (because, for example, the time limit for filing a return has past), the taxpayer may make a claim for 'special relief' under TMA 1970 Sch 1AB para 3A. Paragraph 3A replaces the previous non-statutory practice of granting 'equitable relief' in these circumstances. However, HMRC are not liable to give effect to a claim for special relief unless (i) in the opinion of HMRC it would be unconscionable for them to seek to recover the amount determined; (ii) the taxpayer's tax affairs are otherwise up to date, or arrangements have been put in place to bring them up to date; and (iii) the taxpayer has not claimed special relief previously (or, if they have, the circumstances exceptionally allow the taxpayer to claim special relief again).

These powers have been amended by F(No 2)A 2015 Sch 8, which allows the direct recovery of tax debt (DRD) without a court order from the bank accounts (and ISAs) of those who owe the tax debt. The power can be used only to recover debts of more than £1,000, and is subject to a number of statutory safeguards. Only debtors who: (a) have received a face-to-face visit; (b) have not been identified as vulnerable; (c) have sufficient money in their accounts; and (d) have still refused to settle their debts, will be considered for debt recovery through DRD. Debtors have 30 days to object before any money is transferred to HMRC, and HMRC must always leave a minimum of £5,000 across a debtor's accounts above the amount that has been held. If debtors

do not agree with HMRC's decision, then they can appeal to a county court on specified grounds, including hardship and third party rights. DRD enables recovery of up to 50% of assets held in joint accounts. The DRD powers are available to HMRC to use against individuals, businesses and partnerships.
[4.24]

5 **Penalties and interest**

In order to ensure that taxpayers comply with their obligations regarding the filing of returns and paying of taxes, a system of penalties and interest is in place. (To ensure that the correct amount of tax is collected, HMRC has wide powers to obtain information, not only from taxpayers, but also from third parties. These powers are examined in [4.161]–[4.172].) [4.25]

a) *Penalties*

The penalty regime is premised, predominantly, on the degree of culpability of the taxpayer (for more details, see HMRC's Compliance Manual (CH) at CH 81012, CH 81013, and CH 81014).

The penalty regime can be split into four broad areas:
- errors in returns or documents (introduced initially in relation to income and capital gains tax, corporation tax and VAT (FA 2007 Sch 24) but subsequently extended to cover all taxes (FA 2008 Sch 40));
- failure to notify (eg failure to give notice under TMA 1970 s 7 of liability to income tax or capital gains tax (see [4.22])) (relates to all taxes: FA 2008 Sch 41);
- failure to make returns (this was introduced by FA 2009 Sch 55; it covers income tax, capital gains tax returns, PAYE (in relation to Forms P14 and P35, corporation tax returns and inheritance tax accounts.)
- failure to make payments on time (this was introduced by FA 2009 Sch 56; it covers income tax, capital gains tax, PAYE, NICs, student loan deductions, Construction Industry Scheme (CIS) and a number of other taxes.

Potential lost revenue

Penalties for errors and failures to notify are calculated as a percentage of the 'potential lost revenue', ie the amount of additional tax due as a result of correcting the error or the tax unpaid as a consequence of failing to notify.

Degrees of culpability

The regime focuses on taxpayer behaviour, with the degree of culpability of the taxpayer in the potential loss of revenue forming the basis for calculating the penalty due. So if a taxpayer deliberately files a return containing an error, then he will suffer a higher penalty than if the error in the return was brought about by carelessness in preparing that return.

The actual percentage used to calculate the penalty can be reduced if the taxpayer makes a disclosure in relation to the inaccuracy. 'Disclosure' means telling HMRC about the error, helping them to quantify the amount involved and allowing them access to records to ensure the inaccuracy is fully corrected. Disclosures may be either 'prompted' or 'unprompted'. An unprompted disclosure is one made at a time when the person making it had no reason to believe that HMRC have discovered or are about to discover the inaccuracy.

If they 'think it right because of special circumstances', HMRC can also reduce a penalty still further but it is clear from their manuals that HMRC consider special circumstances to be 'uncommon or exceptional, or where the strict application of the penalty law produces a result that is contrary to the clear compliance intention of that penalty law' and that 'the circumstances in question must apply to the particular individual and not be general circumstances that apply to many taxpayers by virtue of the penalty legislation'. If an officer considers that a special reduction may be applicable, he must submit the case to Central Policy, Tax Administration Advice, before any reduction can be applied.

Examples of what constitutes special circumstances are provided in HMRC's manuals, but they add little in terms of general guidance:

> 'Brian included a careless inaccuracy in his return. He made a prompted disclosure and received full reduction for that disclosure. So he was liable to a 15% minimum penalty. Due to the precise facts relating to Brian's circumstances, after very careful consideration and with authorisation at the appropriate level under remission procedures... HMRC decided not to collect the understated tax.'

The legislation sets out the percentage of tax payable for different taxpayer behaviours, and the possible reductions for disclosure:

For error penalties:
- an inaccuracy in a return that appears despite reasonable care having been taken will attract no penalty;
- carelessness will merit a penalty of 30% of the potential lost revenue (mitigable to 15% for prompted disclosure or to nil for unprompted disclosure);
- deliberate action without concealment will attract a penalty of 70% of potential lost revenue (mitigable to 35% for prompted disclosure or 20% for unprompted disclosure); and
- 100% will be imposed for deliberate action with concealment (mitigable to 50% for prompted disclosure or 30% for unprompted disclosure).

For failure to notify penalties:
- non-deliberate failure with a reasonable excuse will attract no penalty;
- non-deliberate failure with no reasonable excuse will give rise to a penalty of 30% (which may be reduced to 10% for prompted disclosure within 12 months of the tax being due, (20% thereafter) or nil for unprompted disclosure within 12 months of the tax being due (10% thereafter);
- deliberate failure will give rise to a penalty of 70% (which may reduced to 35% for prompted disclosure or 20% for unprompted disclosure); and
- deliberate and concealed failure will result in a 100% penalty (which is mitigable to 50% if disclosure is prompted or 30% if unprompted).

A penalty for a careless inaccuracy can be suspended in whole or in part for up to two years, where compliance with a condition of the suspension would help the relevant person to 'avoid becoming liable to further penalties' for careless inaccuracy (for example by changing its accounting systems). If the

826 and TCGA 1992 s 283). However, the rate of interest on tax repaid is less than the rate of interest on overdue tax (and is currently zero).

Usually, repayments will be made automatically. A claim for repayment must be made within four years from the end of the tax year in question; repayments of tax will only be made in respect of claims made outside this time limit where the overpayment of tax has indisputably arisen as a result of error by HMRC or another government department (ESC B41). **[4.32]**

6 Enquiries

A 'compliance check' is the general term that HMRC uses for its investigations. 'Compliance checks' can take place at any time, but will be carried out only when HMRC has identified a risk or when a check is required as part of HMRC's random programme. HMRC will telephone or write to a taxpayer to tell them that they have started a check.

An 'enquiry' is a particular type of 'compliance check'. There is a statutory procedure that allows HMRC to enquire into the accuracy of a return. An 'enquiry' can be only into a tax return; accordingly, it can only take place after a tax return has been filed. An enquiry will always start with a written notification. There is no requirement that there be any reason to believe that a return is incorrect before an enquiry can be commenced. Some enquiries will be made on a random basis, whereas others will arise because of specific queries on a particular return. The relevant provisions are TMA 1970 s 9A in relation to a personal or trustee return, s 12AC for a partnership return and FA 1998 Sch 18 para 24 for a company tax return.

Notice of any such enquiry must be given to the taxpayer 'within the time allowed'. The time allowed is up to 12 months after the day on which the return was delivered or, if the return was delivered late, up to and including the quarter day next following the first anniversary of the day the return was delivered. However, for companies that are not a member of a small group, the 12-month period does not commence until the filing date for the return (as opposed to the day the return is actually delivered). If the notice is not delivered within the requisite time period it will be invalid (see *Wing Hung Lai v Bale* (1999) and *Holly v Inspector of Taxes* (2000)). If no enquiry notice is served within the statutory time period, then (unless the return is incorrect because of the taxpayer (or agent) having acted carelessly or deliberately) the tax return will become final, subject to the power of discovery (see **[4.42]**) and the taxpayer's ability to make a claim for overpaid tax within four years from the end of the relevant tax year (under TMA 1970 s 33 and Sch 1AB). It should be noted that, under TMA 1970 Sch 1AB para 2(4), HMRC can refuse a claim to relief for overpaid tax where the claimant could have sought relief in an earlier period and knew or ought reasonably to have known that such relief was available.

Under TMA 1970 s 28A, an enquiry into a personal or trustee return is completed when, by closure notice, the Officer informs the taxpayer that he has completed his enquiries and states his conclusions (see s 28B for a partnership return and FA 1998 Sch 18 para 32 for a company return). The closure notice either must state that no amendment of the return is required or make the requisite amendments of the return to give effect to his conclusions.

The taxpayer then may appeal (under TMA 1970 s 31(1) or FA 1998 Sch 18 para 34(3) as applicable) any amendments of the return (see V below).

Section 28A(4) (or TMA 1970 s 28B(5) or FA 1998 Sch 18 para 33 as applicable) enables the taxpayer to apply to the tribunal, during the enquiry, for a direction that the enquiry should be closed (see V below). The burden of proof lies on HMRC to persuade the tribunal that it should not direct that a closure notice be issued. **[4.33]–[4.40]**

7 Discovery assessments

Whilst generally HMRC will not issue assessments under the self-assessment regime, it has the power to make 'discovery assessments' under TMA 1970 s 29 (as amended) if it 'discovers' that income or capital gains that ought to have been assessed have not or that any relief has become excessive (HMRC has a similar discovery power in relation to corporation tax assessments at FA 1998 Sch 18 para 41). The principle is that HMRC should be able to make assessments to prevent there being any loss of tax. **[4.41]**

If a taxpayer has made a self-assessment, then a discovery assessment cannot be made unless either a loss of tax has been brought about carelessly or deliberately by the taxpayer (or a person acting on his behalf) or the 'officer could not have been reasonably expected, on the basis of the information made available to him' before the final date for opening an enquiry (see above) to be aware that additional tax was due. However, this latter precondition has been interpreted in a way that does not restrict significantly an Officer's ability to raise a discovery assessment. In *Langham v Veltema* (2004) the Court of Appeal held that an inspector reasonably can be expected to have been aware of tax issues only where there is an actual insufficiency that has been highlighted in the return. There is no obligation on an inspector to make an enquiry, however routine, unless the insufficiency of tax is apparent on the basis of the information before him. Accordingly, in order to prevent a discovery assessment being raised, a taxpayer needs to flag, for the Officer's benefit, the fact that a figure in his return may turn out to be incorrect. Following this decision, HMRC issued a guidance note (SP 1/06) on what taxpayers can do to reduce or remove the risk of discovery in some fairly common circumstances.

In *Anderson v R & C Comrs* (2016), the First-tier Tribunal held that HMRC was not entitled to issue a discovery assessment, as the taxpayer had not been careless. The tribunal considered that the taxpayer's actions were the same as those which would be expected of a person acting reasonably and diligently in the circumstances under consideration. He had relied on the advice of his professional advisers, which was entirely reasonable in the circumstances.

HMRC must make their discovery assessment no later than four years after the end of the year of assessment to which it relates (s 34), unless the loss of tax has been brought about carelessly or deliberately, in which case the four-year time period is extended to six years and 20 years respectively (s 36). If no self-assessment return has been returned by the taxpayer, an HMRC officer may make a determination of the amount chargeable to income tax and capital gains tax and the amount of tax payable to the best of his information and belief (s 28C). Such a determination will have effect as if it were a self-assessment, unless or until a taxpayer files a self-assessment return to supersede the determination. [4.42]

Where HMRC has reached a settlement with a taxpayer by agreement (s 54) in respect of a particular issue, HMRC is not able to reopen that settlement (provided that there has been full disclosure by the taxpayer). In *Easinghall Limited v R & C Comrs* (2016), the Upper Tribunal confirmed that where an agreement has been reached with HMRC under TMA 1970, s 54, HMRC cannot commence an enquiry or issue a discovery assessment unless either concerns an issue that was not the subject of the agreement.

The relationship between s 54 and s 29 (before its self-assessment amendment) was considered by the House of Lords in *Cenlon Finance Co Ltd v Ellwood* (1962). In *Cenlon*, the House of Lords held that an issue in dispute that had been agreed under s 54 could not be re-opened for that year of assessment by the Revenue raising a further assessment. However, the taxpayer is protected only for the particular issue (or issues) agreed and only in respect of the year (or years) that form the subject of the s 54 agreement.

Scorer v Olin Energy Systems Ltd (1985) involved the making of a further assessment by a later inspector, after a s 54 agreement had been entered into on what was discovered to have been an erroneous basis (namely allowing a claim for losses to be carried forward from one division of the business to another). The House of Lords held that the Revenue was precluded from making the further assessment. If the Revenue leads the taxpayer reasonably to believe that they are making an offer on particular terms, then they will be estopped from saying subsequently that they did not intend that consequence. Lord Keith (with whom all their Lordships agreed) said that the relevant question was whether the parties had come to an agreement in respect of the claim; and that the test was an objective one:

> 'The situation must be viewed objectively, from the point of view of whether the inspector's agreement to the relevant computation, having regard to the surrounding circumstances including all the material known to be in his possession, was such as to lead a reasonable man to the conclusion that he had decided to admit the claim which had been made.'

As the accounts submitted on behalf of the taxpayer set out all the facts relevant to the claim for carry forward of losses, a reasonable man would have concluded that the inspector had agreed to that claim. Thus, the Revenue was bound by the s 54 agreement. (See SP 8/91.) [4.43]–[4.49]

8 From Hansard to the Contractual Disclosure Facility

a) *The Hansard procedure*

What became known as the Hansard procedure was first introduced on 19 July 1923. It took its name from the official record of parliamentary debates and was set out in a statement made by the Chancellor of the Exchequer (recorded in Hansard). The statement set out the policy of the Board of Inland Revenue as regards serious tax fraud. In short, taxpayers who were suspected of serious tax fraud, were encouraged to make a full confession, and to make good any tax that they had failed to disclose in past years (and, in addition, to pay a

104   *Administrative machinery*

substantial penalty (potentially up to 100% of the historic tax lost through their suspected fraud)) in return for an effective immunity from prosecution. The Hansard process was not a 'criminal' process in the sense that that term is widely understood; it was offered in circumstances where the tax authority was not seeking to prosecute the taxpayer. As a result of comments made by Lord Hutton in *R v Allen* (2001), a revised Hansard statement was made on 7 November 2002. It provided an explicit guarantee that if the taxpayer made a full and complete disclosure of all tax irregularities, then he would not be prosecuted. [4.50]–[4.51]

b)   *Code of Practice 9*

With effect from 1 September 2005, following consultation with the relevant professional bodies, HMRC introduced a new combined code, Code of Practice 9 (COP 9), governing the civil investigation of fraud. It replaced both the Hansard procedure and HM Customs and Excise's civil evasion procedures.

Although many of the features of the old Hansard procedure appeared in COP 9, two important differences were as follows. *First*, once the decision had been made to follow the civil route for investigation and the procedure was offered to the taxpayer, no underlying threat of prosecution for the original tax loss remained (although there remained a prosecution sanction for making a materially false disclosure (including deliberate false statements) during the course of the investigation or furnishing false documents at the conclusion of that investigation). The *second* was the absence of the Police and Criminal Evidence At 1984 (PACE) procedures. Accordingly meetings were not tape recorded, nor was the taxpayer cautioned as to his rights.

Taxpayers were encouraged to co-operate fully with HMRC during a COP9 investigation. Full co-operation was likely to lead to lower penalties being charged and reduced the risk that the taxpayer would have his details published by HMRC as someone who deliberately evaded their tax obligations (this relates to inaccuracies that have taken place in periods starting after 1 April 2010). The COP9 procedure remains in force, subject to the amendments introduced in January 2012. [4.52]

c)   *The Contractual Disclosure Facility*

A revised COP9 procedure, the Contractual Disclosure Facility (CDF), was introduced with effect from 31 January 2012. Under CDF, HMRC no longer gives an absolute guarantee at the outset of an investigation under COP9 that a taxpayer will not be investigated criminally with a view to prosecution for the suspected tax fraud. Such a guarantee is only given to a taxpayer who enters into a contractual arrangement to disclose, and who has made an outline disclosure under that arrangement. If the taxpayer agrees to the terms of the CDF, HMRC will undertake not to pursue a criminal investigation in return.

At the start of any COP9 investigation that is commenced after 31 January 2012, a CDF outline disclosure form and guidance notes are issued with the COP9 opening letter. The taxpayer has 60 days within which to accept the standard terms of the CDF.

Between 31 January 2012 and 30 June 2014, there were three possible responses to a COP9 letter. The first was to admit the deliberate evasion of tax and agree to co-operate with HMRC (generally in return for immunity from prosecution). The second was to deny fraud, but agree to co-operate with HMRC (the 'denial with co-operation' option). The third was to deny fraud and refuse to co-operate with HMRC. The 'denial with co-operation' option was withdrawn on 30 June 2014. The withdrawal of this option gives rise to a particular issue for regulated professionals, who have been offered COP 9 in relation to a tax structure that they participated in, but which HMRC consider is fraudulent. Co-operating with HMRC requires an admission of fraud. But the incautious making of a decision to participate in a tax structure does not, by itself, constitute conspiracy to cheat the public revenue; and admitting to fraud (even in a civil context) can often be career-ending, since it requires the individual to self-report an admission of dishonesty to his professional bodies.

The CDF consists of two stages; the Outline Disclosure and the Certified Disclosure. The Outline Disclosure must be submitted to HMRC within the same 60-day time limit as is allowed for acceptance of HMRC's offer. It must set out as clearly as possible the specific tax frauds committed by the taxpayer and a formal admission of deliberately bringing about a loss of tax must be included. If HMRC consider that the Outline Disclosure does not include details of all tax frauds that have been disclosed, they may send it to the HMRC Criminal Investigation team to consider a criminal investigation of those frauds that have not been disclosed.

Where HMRC do not consider that the Outline Disclosure under CDF discloses all the tax frauds committed, the criminal investigators to whom the disclosure is to be sent are to investigate only the frauds that have not been disclosed. Given this, where a taxpayer is prosecuted after having provided an Outline Disclosure, it is considered that the circumstances when he will be able to argue successfully that the Crown should not be able to rely on evidence of his admission in the outline disclosure will be rare. [4.53]

d) *Disclosure opportunities*

In recent years, HMRC have undertaken a number of initiatives whereby certain groups of taxpayers are encouraged to disclose tax irregularities (and pay the tax due) in return for a reduced penalty and immunity from prosecution. The initiatives have typically been consequent on large information-gathering exercises having been undertaken by HMRC. The first such project was the Offshore Disclosure Facility (ODF) (in 2007). It was followed up by the New Disclosure Opportunity (NDO) (in 2009) and also by the Liechtenstein Disclosure Facility (LDF) (also in 2009). All three disclosure opportunities related to individuals who had a UK address and a non UK bank account (specifically in Liechtenstein as regards the LDF). ODF and NDO were consequent on HMRC having obtained significant amounts of data from financial institutions through the issue of notices under TMA 1970 s 20(8A) and subsequently under FA 2008 Sch 36, para 5. Other disclosure opportunities have been aimed at medical professionals and plumbers (although they were, in fact, available to virtually all taxpayers).

Those who have not taken advantage of an applicable disclosure opportunity, in circumstances where they were aware of that opportunity, face a considerably higher chance of prosecution should they have filed deliberately incorrect tax returns. [4.54]

IV THE INFORMATION POWERS OF HMRC

1 Introduction – the new system

Prior to 1 April 2009, HMRC had a wide range of powers that it could call on to ascertain the quantum of tax due from a particular taxpayer. There were distinct powers for direct and indirect taxes, with a number of significant differences between them (for example, HMRC had powers of inspection for VAT purposes but did not have a like power for corporation tax purposes). HMRC considered that the fact their existing powers were not aligned hindered their effectiveness (particularly when more than one tax was at issue). FA 2007 introduced enabling legislation under which HMRC's powers of investigation (relating to criminal matters) in England, Wales and Northern Ireland became based on the powers contained in PACE; and FA 2008 introduced a new regime of information powers for the purposes of tax collection (ie relating to civil matters). The fundamental underlying principle of the changes is that it is the nature of the activity, rather than the tax, that determines the ambit of the statutory power. [4.55]

2 Criminal investigatory powers

a) *Introduction*

HMRC criminal investigations are now subject to the statutory codes of practice and safeguards that attach to criminal investigations generally. A notable change is therefore that HMRC officers now have the PACE 1984 powers of search, seizure and arrest in connection with ex-Inland Revenue matters. [4.56]

In 'Criminal Investigation Powers: Publication of Draft Clauses and Explanatory Notes' (which was published on 17 January 2007), it was proposed that the use of the PACE powers would be restricted to suitably trained officers authorised by the Commissioners of HMRC. HMRC subsequently issued a release in which it was stated, inter alia:

> **'Authorisation to use powers**
>
> The criminal investigation powers can be used only by officers who are authorised to use them. An authorised officer is an officer of HM Revenue and Customs, appropriately trained and engaged on operational duties in Criminal Investigation, Detection, Risk and Intelligence and Internal Governance Directorates. PACE provides that some powers can be exercised only by police constables of a particular rank. When those powers are applied to HMRC the police ranks are converted to HMRC grades of an equivalent authority—
>
> - Sergeant   Officer
> - Inspector   Higher Officer
> - Chief Inspector   Higher Officer
> - Superintendent   Senior Officer
>
> HMRC has set internal authorisation levels requiring an authorised officer to get the approval of a higher graded officer before using certain powers. The authority levels for HMRC are set no lower than the authority levels in the police, the primary user of PACE powers. However in most cases HMRC has set the main authority

level required at a minimum of Senior Officer grade, for example applications to a magistrate or court for a production order or search warrant. The majority of authorities in the police service are held at Inspector level, equivalent to HMRC's Higher Officer grade.'

It was revealed that, at that time, approximately 1,500 HMRC officers had powers of arrest. [4.57]

The amendments in FA 2007 increased the powers available to ex-Inland Revenue investigators; and meant that HMRC no longer needed to follow different procedures in the same investigation where both direct and indirect tax fraud are suspected. FA 2007 enabled the Treasury to make orders applying the provisions of PACE to investigations conducted by officers of HMRC (under FA 2007 ss 82(2) and 83(2)). The Police and Criminal Evidence Act 1984 (Application to Revenue and Customs) Order 2007 (SI 2007/3175) applies the relevant provisions of PACE to all functions of HMRC (except where the department acts as an agent for other government departments), with effect from 1 December 2007.

Thus, since 1 December 2007, HMRC officers have had access to the appropriate powers in PACE to investigate all tax matters where criminal activity is suspected. In particular, from that date, search warrants are now obtained under PACE s 8 and Sch 1, rather than TMA 1970 s 20C (for offences concerning direct tax) or VATA 1994 Sch 11 para 10(3) (for offences concerning indirect tax).

The changes introduced by FA 2007 resolved a number of the problems that arose when HMRC officers sought to investigate combined instances of direct and indirect tax fraud. For example, prior to the introduction of these changes, if a taxpayer was suspected of both VAT and corporation tax fraud, separate warrants for each of these offences were required to search and seize evidence from the same premises and, arguably, the taxpayer had to be arrested twice (once by the police for the suspected direct tax offence and once by HMRC officers for the suspected indirect tax offence). [4.58]

b) *PACE powers*

Not all the powers that are available to the police under PACE are available to HMRC officers. In particular, the power to take fingerprints, and the power to charge and bail suspects have not been made available to HMRC officers. Article 4 of the Police and Criminal Evidence Act 1984 (Application to Revenue and Customs) Order 2007 ensured that HMRC officers do not have powers to charge a person, release a person on bail or to detain a person after charge. The Police and Criminal Evidence Act 1984 (Application to Revenue and Customs) Order 2015 repealed that Order with effect from 4 November 4 2015; art 4 replicates these exceptions. PACE has been amended so as to apply four categories of PACE powers to all taxes. These categories are:

(1) search warrants;
(2) production orders;
(3) arrest powers; and
(4) search and entry powers in order to arrest. [4.59]–[4.139]

i) The PACE power to search

Applications for search warrants by HMRC must be made under PACE s 8 or Sch 1. On an application by an HMRC officer, a magistrate may issue a warrant for the HMRC officer to enter and search premises if he has reasonable grounds for believing that an indictable tax offence has been committed and that there is material on the specified premises that is likely to be of substantial value (whether by itself or together with other material) to the investigation of the offence and is likely to be admissible at the trial for the offence. [4.140]–[4.151]

The powers of seizure under PACE were considerably extended by Sch 1 to the Criminal Justice and Police Act 2001 (CJPA 2001). Under CJPA 2001 Sch 1 Part 1, the s 50 powers of seizure under that Act are extended to PACE s 8. The consequence of that is that it is lawful to seize something where it is not reasonably practicable to determine on the premises whether the material is, or contains, something HMRC is entitled to seize. The aim is to overcome the problems that arose either where it could not be conveniently determined in situ whether a particular item (such as a computer) was subject to seizure or where there were issues relating to whether or not material was protected by reason of legal professional privilege. In *R (on the application of H) v IRC* (2002), which concerned a warrant under TMA 1970 s 20C, the High Court held that a hard disk could not be regarded as simply a container of the files visible to the computer's operating system. It was a single object: a single thing. The fact that there was also on the hard disk irrelevant material did not make the computer any less of a thing that might be required as evidence for the purposes of criminal proceedings. Accordingly, if a Revenue officer who entered into premises under the authority of a warrant under s 20C found a computer, and he had reasonable cause to believe that the data on the computer's hard disk might be required as evidence for the purpose of relevant proceedings, he might seize and remove that computer even though it contained irrelevant material also. It is considered that the ratio of this case applies to PACE warrants. [4.152]

Once the material is removed from the premises, HMRC is empowered to sift the material to determine whether it contains any relevant items that it wishes to seize. When powers of seizure under CJPA 2001 s 50 are exercised by an HMRC officer, the taxpayer or third party must be provided with a written notice of this in accordance with CJPA 2001 s 52. The warrant must be endorsed to provide a record of those documents or items that have been removed. [4.153]

Access to all the documents or items may be permitted, on request and under supervision. Copies may be taken at the time of access, or requested. If requested, the copies must be provided within a reasonable time. There is no right to allow a copy to be taken at the time of search.

An HMRC officer exercising powers under PACE s 8 is bound by the Codes of Practice of PACE. Code B provides, inter alia, that a person from whom any items are seized must, on request, be provided with a list or description of the property within a reasonable time. If an original document has been removed and is of such a nature that a copy would be sufficient (1) for use as evidence at a trial for an offence, or (2) for forensic examination or for investigation in connection with an offence, it shall not be retained longer than is necessary to establish that fact and to obtain the copy. [4.154]

Section 8(1)(d) of PACE protects privileged materials. In *R v IRC and Middlesex Guildhall Crown Court, ex parte Tamosius and Partners* (1999) (and see also [55.61]–[55.80]), the High Court held that s 20C(4) prevented only the removal of documents with respect to which a claim to professional privilege could be 'maintained' – the seizure did not become unlawful merely because the firm of American lawyers that had been raided claimed that the documents were privileged. HMRC will often adopt the practice of applying in advance to the Attorney-General to nominate an 'independent counsel' and then using that counsel to review material to determine whether or not legal privilege applies. However, this process is undertaken only to protect HMRC; it does not preclude a taxpayer or third party challenging a decision by counsel that material is not privileged. If there is a dispute during a search as to whether legal privilege applies, the taxpayer should ask HMRC to put the material in an opaque, sealed, envelope (a process colloquially known as 'blue-bagging') to allow the issue of privilege to be resolved subsequently (ultimately before a judge if necessary). [4.155]–[4.156]

ii) Production orders

'Special procedure material', items subject to legal professional privilege, and 'excluded material' are excluded from the scope of a s 8 warrant. Special procedure material consists broadly of business records that are held by a person under an obligation of confidence to a third party (see PACE s 14(2)). If it is suspected that special procedure material needs to be obtained, HMRC can apply to a circuit judge (without notice) for a warrant under PACE Sch 1 paras 12–14. If granted, this enables an officer to enter premises and search for excluded material or other special procedure material (there are a number of conditions as to access and other criteria that must be satisfied (see Code B of the PACE Codes of Practice)).

An alternative to an order authorising such material to be seized under a search and seizure exercise is a production order (under PACE Sch 1 paras 7–11). If a circuit judge is satisfied that there are reasonable grounds for believing that an indictable tax offence has been committed, he may consent to the issue of a PACE production order. The hearing before the judge is with notice (in contrast to applications under s 20BA (see below)).

Currently, the production order powers under TMA 1970 s 20BA, (direct tax) and VATA Sch 11 para 11 are preserved. However, if the documents sought are believed to include special procedure material, then those documents may not be obtained under the s 20BA or para 11 production orders; a production order under PACE Sch 1 paras 12–14 must be used instead. Prior to its repeal, Article 7 of the Police and Criminal Evidence Act 1984 (Application to Revenue and Customs) Order 2007 provided that PACE is to be interpreted as if a 's 14B' was inserted after s14A, with s 14B (which is specific to HMRC) providing that an HMRC officer may make an application under TMA 1970 s 20BA or VATA Sch 11 para 11 only if the officer considers that an application under PACE Sch 1 would not succeed because the material required does not consist of or include special procedure material. Article 6 of the Police and Criminal Evidence Act 1984 (Application to Revenue and Customs) Order 2015 provides the like provision. [4.157]

iii) Safeguards

The PACE Codes of Practice apply when PACE powers are exercised by HMRC officers and when HMRC officers are investigating tax offences (see PACE s 67). They contain detailed regulations on the exercise of PACE powers and notes for guidance. They are admissible in evidence and any relevant provision must be taken into account by a court (under PACE s 67(11)). PACE Code B deals with the powers to search premises and to seize and retain property found on premises and persons. [4.158]

c) *Section 20BA, TMA – the production power*

Section 20BA allows HMRC to apply to a judge for an order requiring a third party, who may have evidence relating to suspected fraud to deliver the documents to HMRC, without the need for a search and seizure warrant to obtain documents from the third party. The appropriate judicial authority (a circuit judge in England and Wales (see s 20D(1))) may, if satisfied on information on oath given by an authorised officer of the Board of the grounds set out below, make an order under s 20BA requiring a person who appears to have in his possession or power the documents specified in the order to deliver them to a specified HMRC officer within ten working days (working days exclude Saturdays, Sundays and public holidays), or such other period as may be specified. Section 20BA was intended to limit the occasions on which it is necessary for HMRC to enter the premises of persons not themselves suspected of fraud. Section 20BA is amended in one regard following the changes introduced by FA 2007: the procedure under s 20BA cannot be used to obtain 'special procedure material' (see art 6 of the Police and Criminal Evidence Act 1984 (Application to Revenue and Customs) Order 2015 and further above); instead an application under PACE Sch 1 must be made.

The grounds for issuing the order are that:
(1) there is reasonable ground for suspecting that an offence involving serious fraud in connection with, or in relation to, tax is being, has been or is about to be committed; and
(2) documents which may be required as evidence for the purposes of any proceedings in respect of such an offence are or may be in the power or possession of any person.

A person is entitled to notice of the intention to apply for an order against him under s 20BA and to appear and be heard at the hearing of the application, unless the appropriate judicial authority is satisfied that this would seriously prejudice the investigation of the offence (under TMA 1970 Sch 1AA, para 3).

A recipient of the notice of intention to apply for an order must not do any of the following:
(1) conceal, destroy, alter or dispose of any document to which the application relates; or

(2) disclose to any other person information or any other matter likely to prejudice the investigation of the offence to which the application relates (under Sch 1AA para 4) unless permission is obtained from the appropriate court, or in writing from an HMRC officer, or after the application has been dismissed or abandoned, or after any order has been complied with.

There is an exception to the anti-tipping off provision in the case of professional legal advisers. A professional legal adviser may disclose information to his client in connection with the giving by the adviser of legal advice, or to any other person in contemplation of, or in connection with, legal proceedings and for the purposes of those proceedings. However, this exception does not apply in circumstances where disclosures are made with a view to furthering a criminal purpose.

Schedule 1AA, para 5 provides protection to privileged materials with regard to the exercise of a power under s 20BA. In addition, reg 7 of the Orders for the Delivery of Documents (Procedure) Regulations 2000 (as amended) sets out a procedure for the resolution of disputes as to legal privilege. If there is a dispute as to whether any document or parts of documents are protected by legal privilege, the person concerned may apply to the appropriate judicial authority (in England and Wales, a circuit judge) to resolve the dispute. If the application is made within the time allowed for the delivery of the documents, then they are deemed to have been delivered in accordance with the notice until the dispute is resolved. In the meantime, all the documents concerned are to be lodged with and held by the court. The Board of HMRC is entitled to at least five working days' notice of the hearing of the application, and to attend and be heard at the hearing. If the authority upholds the claim for legal privilege in whole or in part, the costs of the application are to be met by the Board of HMRC. Before the hearing of the dispute, it may be resolved by agreement between the Board and the applicant. Failure to comply with an order made under s 20BA and with the obligations under Sch 1AA, para 4 is punishable as a contempt of court. [4.159]

d) *SOCPA powers*

Under the Serious Organised Crime and Police Act 2005 (SOCPA) Part 2, Chapter 1 ss 60–70, new investigatory powers in relation to tax crimes were introduced. As enacted, SOCPA s 60 enabled use of these powers to be delegated by the DPP to any Revenue and Customs Prosecution Office (RCPO) prosecutor. RCPO was subsumed subsequently into the CPS and s 60(3) ceased to have effect: see the Public Bodies (Merger of the Director of Public Prosecutors and the Director of Revenue and Customs (Prosecutions) Order 2014 (SI 2014/834). The offences to which the powers (now exercisable by the CPS) pertain include the common law offence of cheating the public revenue, and false accounting contrary to the Theft Act 1968 s 17, provided that, in the opinion of the investigating officer, the potential loss to the public revenue is of an amount not less than £5,000.

A Crown prosecutor can give, or authorise an officer of HMRC to give, a disclosure notice to any person who has information which relates to a matter relevant to the investigation of the offence, provided that there are reasonable grounds for belief that the information in question, whether or not by itself, is likely to be of 'substantial value' to the investigation. A recipient of the notice will not only have to produce documents relevant to the investigation, but also to 'answer questions with respect to any matter relevant to the investigation' and to 'provide information with respect to any such matter as is specified in the notice' (under SOCPA s 62(3)). Under SOCPA s 64, there is protection for privileged information or documents; a person may not be required to answer any privileged question, or provide any privileged information, or produce any privileged document (except that a lawyer may be required to provide the name and address of his client).

Two offences are created with regard to SOCPA disclosure notices (s 67). The *first* is failure to comply with the requirements set out in a disclosure notice (punishable by a maximum sentence of 51 weeks' imprisonment, with a 'reasonable excuse' for failure to comply being a defence); and the *second* is making a false or misleading statement in response to the requirements imposed by a disclosure notice (punishable by a maximum of two years' imprisonment).

If the recipient of a disclosure notice fails to comply with its terms, then the HMRC prosecutor will be able to obtain a search and seize warrant from a Justice of the Peace. Such a warrant will enable an HMRC prosecutor to enter and search premises, using force where necessary, and to take possession of any documents that appear to be of a description specified in the disclosure notice, or to take any other steps that appear to be necessary for preserving, or preventing interference with, any such documents. A warrant will also be able to be issued if it is not practicable to issue a disclosure notice, or where the service of a disclosure notice might seriously prejudice the investigation (under SOCPA s 66(2)).

The intention was that these powers would be used primarily against third parties, including professional advisers (see the comments of the Parliamentary Under-Secretary of State for the Home Department at the Committee stage of the Serious Organised Crime and Police Bill). [4.160]

3 Civil investigatory powers

Schedule 36 to FA 2008 introduced a new regime of information powers for the purposes of tax collection. Schedule 36 contains powers that enable officers of HMRC to obtain information and documents for the purpose of 'checking a taxpayer's tax position'. The new rules apply to enquiries into income tax, corporation tax, capital gains tax, VAT, insurance premium tax, inheritance tax, SDLT, SDRT, petroleum revenue tax, aggregates levy, climate change levy, landfill tax (and relevant foreign taxes). The Finance Act 2008, Schedule 36 (Appointed Day and Savings) Order 2009 brought FA 2008 Sch 36 into force with effect from 1 April 2009. It also repealed (with effect from the same date) the main previous information powers, with savings provisions (the effect of which is to keep in force the rules regarding appeals and penalties that previously applied in relation to all information notices that have been issued on or before 31 March 2009).

Schedule 36 introduces two classes of powers:
(1) the power to obtain information and documents; and
(2) the power to inspect businesses. [4.161]

a)   *The power to obtain information and documents*

Sch 36 para 1 – 'the Taxpayer Notice'

An HMRC officer may by written notice require a taxpayer to provide information or to produce a document reasonably required for checking the taxpayer's tax position.

'Tax position' is defined in FA 2008 Sch 36 para 64 as a past, present or future liability to pay any tax, penalties and other amounts, claims, elections, applications and notices and deductions or repayments required under PAYE, CIS or under any other provisions of the Taxes Act. **[4.162]**

It is important to note that:
(1) The issue of an information notice is not required to be related to the issue of a notice of enquiry (under TMA 1970 s 9A or 12AC or FA 1998 Sch 18 para 24) and para 1 notices can apply to 'future liabilities' to pay any tax.
(2) HMRC are not restricted to the seeking of existing identifiable documents. The information that can be requested by a para 1 notice may be specified or 'described' by HMRC (FA 2008 Sch 36 para 6(2)). As is indicated in the Explanatory Notes to the Finance Bill 2008, 'information' includes both explanations and the creation of schedules or documents that do not already exist. Paragraph 1 bestows on HMRC a free-standing power to obtain information and documents; it allows HMRC to obtain documents and information before a tax return is filed.
(3) There is no statutory precondition that the taxpayer must have been asked to provide the information and or documents voluntarily before service of a para 1 notice; however, it is usual for HMRC to issue an informal request for information or documents before serving a statutory information notice.
(4) There is no obligation on HMRC to obtain prior judicial approval of the notice. The HMRC officer can choose whether or not seek to approval from the tribunal in advance; whether or not the officer has sought approval will have consequences for the ability of the taxpayer to appeal the notice to the tribunal.
(5) Documents more than six years old are able to be required to be produced, provided only that the request is made by an 'authorised officer' of HMRC (defined in FA 2008 Sch 36 para 59 as an HMRC officer who has been authorised by HMRC for the purposes of FA 2008 Sch 36).
(6) A taxpayer who is required to provide information or documents must do so within the period, and at the time, by such means and in such form as is reasonably specified in the notice (under FA 2008 Sch 36 para 7). Section 114 of FA 2008 gives HMRC, at any reasonable time, access to computers used in connection with relevant documents and a power to insist (with threat of a penalty for obstruction) on 'reasonable assistance' in relation to the same.

Failure to comply with information notices can lead to the imposition of a penalty under FA 2008 Sch 36 para 39 (in the sum of £300) or, for continued non-compliance, under para 40 (up to £60 per day). For serious and persistent non-compliance a punitive tax-geared penalty may be imposed pursuant to an application to the Upper Tribunal. The first such occasion where HMRC made such an application is reported as *R & C Comrs v Romie Tager* (2015), where penalties of almost £1.25m were imposed on the taxpayer for non-compliance with information notices. **[4.163]**

Sch 36, para 2 – 'the third-party notice'

An HMRC officer may by written notice to any person require that person to provide information or to produce a document if that is reasonably required for checking the position of a known person.

The points that are set out above in relation to taxpayer notices apply, mutatis mutandis, to the third party notice regimes.

Ordinarily, HMRC are required to name in the third-party notice the taxpayer to whom it relates and give a copy of the notice to the taxpayer. HMRC are not required to name the taxpayer or provide a copy of the notice to the taxpayer if the requirements to do so have been disapplied by the tribunal. In order to disapply these requirements, the tribunal must be satisfied that the HMRC officer has reasonable grounds for believing that naming the taxpayer might seriously prejudice the assessment or collection of tax and, in disapplying the requirement to copy the notice to the taxpayer, that to do so might prejudice the assessment or collection of tax. **[4.164]**

Sch 36, para 5 – 'the identity unknown notice'

An HMRC officer may issue a notice to a third party requesting information or documents in relation to a taxpayer/taxpayers unknown. The information or documents requested must be reasonably required by the officer for the purpose of checking the UK tax position of a person or a class of persons whose identities are not known to the officer. HMRC have used 'identity unknown notices' to obtain information from financial institutions in relation to customers with overseas bank accounts.

HMRC require the approval of the tribunal to issue an identity unknown notice. In order to approve the giving of an 'identity unknown notice', the tribunal must be satisfied that:
(1) the information or documents requested in the notice are reasonably required for checking the tax position of the relevant taxpayer(s);
(2) there are reasonable grounds for believing that the person or any of the class of persons to whom the notice relates may fail or may have failed to comply with any enactment relating to UK tax;
(3) any such failure is likely to have led or lead to serious prejudice to the assessment or collection of UK tax; and
(4) the information or document required by the notice is not readily available from another source.

An application to the tribunal for approval of an identity unknown notice may be made without notice.

A recipient of an identity unknown notice may appeal against the notice or any requirement contained in the notice on the ground that it would be 'unduly onerous' to comply with the notice or requirement.

FA 2011 Sch 23 introduced additional data gathering powers, under which HMRC can obtain information from various 'data holders'. Data holders include employers and third parties who make payments to another's employees in relation to salary, fee and commission payments and lessees and land agents in relation to payments arising from land. These powers are in addition to HMRC's Sch 36 powers. This legislation came into force with effect from 1 April 2012. [4.165]

b) *The power to inspect businesses*

FA 2008 Sch 36 Part 2 introduced the new inspection power. VAT and PAYE inspections habitually involved visits to premises to check records; now inspections can take place in relation to all taxes covered by Sch 36. 'Inspect' means to examine; this power does not give HMRC the right to force entry, or to search. [4.166]

Sch 36 para 10 – the power to inspect

Paragraph 10 provides that an HMRC officer may enter a person's business premises and inspect the premises, business assets and business documents on the premises if the inspection is reasonably required for the purpose of checking that person's tax position.

The premises that HMRC can inspect are those used by the person whose liability is being checked and (under para 10A) the business premises of 'involved third parties' (para 61A provides a list of 'involved third parties' who will, broadly, be intermediaries of taxpayers) for checking the position of any person or class of persons. The inspection power does not extend to inspection of any part of the premises used solely as a dwelling.

Business premises, assets and documents are defined for these purposes. 'Premises' means any premises (or a part thereof) used in connection with the carrying on of a business. It includes land, buildings, and 'means of transport'. 'Business documents' means documents that relate to the carrying on of a business by any person and that form part of any person's 'statutory records' (statutory records are defined in para 62 as information or documents required to be kept and preserved under the Taxes Acts and any other enactment relating to tax). Thus, any person's business records can be reviewed if they are found on the inspected premises.

HMRC are precluded from reviewing such documents that could not have been required to be produced had the occupier been given an information notice at the time of inspection (under para 28).

Inspections should normally take place at a reasonable time agreed with the occupier of the premises or with at least seven days' notice. However, inspections can be made without advance warning. No external judicial authorisation is required for unannounced visits, and there is also no provision for a right of appeal to the tribunal. Such visits need only the agreement of an 'authorised' HMRC officer. In 2008, HMRC noted in a consultation document entitled 'A New Approach to Compliance Checks: Responses to Consultation and Proposals' that unannounced visits would be 'the exception'. [4.167]

Sch 36 para 11 – inspection of premises used in connection with taxable supplies

Paragraph 11 provides for the inspection of premises used in connection with taxable supplies where an HMRC officer has reason to believe that:

(1) the premises are used in connection with the taxable supply of goods and such goods are on those premises;
(2) the premises are used in connection with the taxable acquisition of goods from other Member States and such goods are on those premises; or
(3) the premises are used as a fiscal warehouse.

This reproduces the power in VATA 1994 Sch 11 para 10(2). In the Explanatory Notes to FA 2008, it was stated that it is important that HMRC retain the power to inspect third party premises, goods on the premises and documents relating to those goods, in order to combat certain VAT frauds (in particular missing trader intra-community fraud). **[4.168]–[4.172]**

V THE TAX APPEALS SYSTEM

1 Introduction

On 19 July 2007, the Tribunals, Courts and Enforcement Act 2007 (TCE 2007) received Royal Assent. TCE 2007 is an enabling Act, under which the General Commissioners and Special Commissioners (which heard disputes relating to direct tax), and the VAT and Duties Tribunal (which heard disputes relating to indirect tax) were abolished and replaced by a unified tribunal (comprising a First-tier and an Upper Tribunal) with a single consistent procedure across all tribunal jurisdictions. The 'tax chapter' of that tribunal system, the First-tier Tribunal (Tax) (the 'First-tier Tribunal') and the Upper Tribunal (Tax and Chancery Chamber), (the 'Upper Tribunal')) replaced the General and Special Commissioners, the s 706 Tribunal, the VAT and Duties Tribunal, and (to a large extent) the High Court for tax matters. **[4.173]–[4.175]**

2 Summary of the tribunal system

Following the changes, a single UK-wide first-instance tribunal with the competence to hear every form of tax appeal and every tax-related application by either the taxpayer or HMRC with one set of procedural rules was introduced.

The First-tier Tribunal is the first instance tribunal for most jurisdictions; the majority of appeals will commence in this tier. In essence, the First-tier Tribunal replaced the General and Special Commissioners, the VAT and Duties Tribunal, and the s 706 Tribunal. Appeals from the First-tier Tribunal to the Upper Tribunal are possible only on points of law and with permission from the First-tier Tribunal, or, if refused, from the Upper Tribunal itself. The First-tier Tribunal is not a court of record; and decisions of the First-tier Tribunal are not binding. However, FA 2014 enables HMRC to issue a 'follower notice' requiring a taxpayer to pay the disputed tax where HMRC determines that an unappealed decision in favour of HMRC of, for example, the First-tier Tribunal, is sufficiently similar to the taxpayer's appeal (see **[4.181]**).

The role of the Upper Tribunal is primarily to hear appeals from the decisions of the First-tier Tribunal. However, it also hears some first-instance appeals in more complex tax cases and may have transferred to it some judicial review proceedings started before the High Court. The chamber president can decide the criteria for those classes of case which will always be heard in the Upper Tribunal (although parties will be able to make special applications in respect of other types of cases). The Upper Tribunal is a superior court of record. Its decisions are binding on the First-tier Tribunal. **[4.176]–[4.177]**

3 The preliminary stages

a) *The right to appeal*

For enquiries into personal tax returns (and partnership returns) there is a right of appeal against:
(a) an amendment to a self-assessment by HMRC made during an enquiry to prevent loss of tax;
(b) any conclusion stated or amendment made by a closure notice under TMA 1970 s 28A or 28B (amendment by HMRC on completion of an enquiry);
(c) any amendment of a partnership return under s 30B(1) (amendment by HMRC where a loss of tax is discovered); or
(d) any assessment to tax which is not a self-assessment (see TMA 1970 s 31(1)). An appeal has to be made in writing to HMRC within 30 days of the date of issue of the relevant notice by HMRC.

For enquiries into corporate tax returns an appeal may be brought against:
(a) an amendment to a self-assessment by HMRC made during an enquiry to prevent loss of tax;
(b) any conclusion stated or amendment made by a closure notice (under FA 1998 Sch 18 para 32); or
(c) any assessment to tax on a company which is not a self-assessment (FA 1998 Sch 18 paras 30(3), 34(3) and 48).

A taxpayer may also bring an appeal against any decision of HMRC that a penalty is exigible.

There is only a severely curtailed right of appeal in respect of the imposition of a charge under the diverted profits tax rules that were introduced (on 1 April 2015) pursuant to Part 3 of FA 2015.

VATA 1994 s 83(1) contains a list of the VAT matters in respect of which an appeal lies to the Tax Tribunal. An appeal is made directly to the Tax Tribunal against an HMRC decision relating to an indirect tax.

FA 2003 Sch 10 Part 7 contains the appeal provisions relating to stamp duty land tax. See, in particular para 35(1). **[4.178]–[4.179]**

b) *Closure notice applications*

HMRC not only has very wide powers during the enquiry stage, but also considerable scope for prolonging that stage. This is significant for taxpayers, as, in general, they can appeal only after the enquiry has been completed (ie when a closure notice has been issued). However, valuable protection is provided to the taxpayer against HMRC by s 28A(6) (and s 28(B) for partnerships and FA 1998 Sch 18 para 33 for companies), which enables the taxpayer to apply to the Tax Tribunal, during an enquiry, for a direction that HMRC give a closure notice within a specified period. The burden of proof is then on HMRC to show that there are 'reasonable grounds' for not giving a closure notice within a specified period. As the Special Commissioner noted in *Jade Palace v R & C Comrs* (2006):

> '... the issue on [a closure notice] application is not simply whether a closure notice should be directed, but whether it should be directed within a specified period. The reasonable grounds must cover the setting of a period.'

This procedural rule is intended to protect taxpayers against protracted and unfocused enquiries and to enable taxpayers to take control of a dispute with HMRC. It is a powerful tool in the context of resolving a dispute with HMRC.

There is no similar provision for indirect taxes; a taxpayer's only route here is to apply for judicial review on the basis that HMRC have failed to reach a decision within a reasonable time period. **[4.180]**

c) *Referral of questions during enquiry*

TMA Part IIIA allows for a referral to the tribunal, by agreement between the parties, during an enquiry. Sections 28ZA to 28ZE set out a procedure for personal self-assessment that enables questions relating to the subject matter of an enquiry to be referred to the Tax Tribunal whilst the enquiry is still in progress. A similar procedure of referral was introduced with regard to corporation tax self-assessment (see FA 1998 Sch 18 paras 31A–31D).

Referral only can be made jointly by the taxpayer and HMRC. Whilst proceedings on a referral are in progress in relation to an enquiry and until the matter referred is finally determined, no closure notice will be issued, nor can an application for a direction to give such a notice be made. The determination is binding on both parties, subject to any further appeal rights. **[4.181]**

d) *Application for postponement of tax*

Where the taxpayer has lodged an appeal and he considers that the tax charged is excessive, he can apply, under TMA 1970 s 55, for postponement of the payment of part or all of the tax charged, pending the determination of the appeal. HMRC may agree with the taxpayer the amount of tax in respect of which payment may be postponed; and most cases are determined in this way. However, if agreement cannot be reached, then the taxpayer may apply to the Tax Tribunal for a determination of the amount of tax to be postponed pending the determination of the appeal. Before the Tax Tribunal, the taxpayer does not have to prove all the facts or succeed in the legal arguments that will have to be proved or established at the substantive appeal; instead, the taxpayer just must show 'reasonable grounds' for believing that he has been overcharged to tax. 'Reasonable' means that the grounds must be based on reason and must not be irrational, absurd or ridiculous (see *Sparrow Ltd v Inspector of Taxes* (2001)).

For indirect taxes, an appeal may not proceed before the Tax Tribunal if the liability to pay the amount in dispute is outstanding, unless HMRC or the Tax Tribunal consent to the appeal proceeding following a 'hardship application' by the taxpayer. A hardship application will be accepted where HMRC are satisfied (or the Tax Tribunal decides if HMRC are not satisfied) that the requirement to pay or deposit the amount determined would cause the taxpayer to suffer hardship. In order to satisfy HMRC as to hardship, a taxpayer will usually be required to present information to HMRC with regard to his financial situation, such as bank statements, details of assets and trading accounts.

FA 2014 introduced the concept of 'follower notices', which HMRC may give to a taxpayer where it considers that a judicial ruling is 'relevant to' a tax 'arrangement' entered into by the taxpayer. If such a notice is issued (which is at HMRC's discretion) the taxpayer must either withdraw their appeal against HMRC's decision that tax is payable or face additional penalties for not doing so if the appeal is eventually unsuccessful.

FA 2014 also introduced the power for HMRC to issue 'accelerated payment notices'. These require the disputed tax to be paid in advance of resolution of an appeal. HMRC may (and is likely to) issue an accelerated payment notice when a follower notice has been given.

HMRC may also issue an accelerated payment notice where the arrangements are such that a Disclosure of Tax Avoidance Scheme (DOTAS) notification has been given or a GAAR counteraction notice has been given (see **Chapters 3** and **5** respectively for an explanation of the GAAR and DOTAS). [4.182]

e) *HMRC'S litigation and settlement strategy*

HMRC's Litigation and Settlement Strategy (LSS) was published in June 2007 and 'refreshed' in July 2011. The LSS sets out the strategy that HMRC now adopts in contentious matters. In an article in the *Tax Journal* (11 June 2007), Dave Hartnett (who was, at the time, HMRC Director General) set out the aims of HMRC's LLS strategy:

> 'The LSS sets consistent standards for the way we settle disputes with our customers, whether by agreement or litigation. It ensures that where we are confident about the strength of our case and the disputed point is a significant one, we will insist on 100% of the tax or other liabilities that HMRC believes to be due. Where we accept that we do not have strong grounds for our position or the issue is less important to us, we will aim to avoid disputes altogether.'

In July 2011, HMRC 'refreshed' the LSS, following the criticism that there was not a clear understanding by HMRC officers as to the flexibility permitted in settling disputes. The relaunch of the LSS was intended to make the message clearer. It does not involve any significant revisions to the stated strategy.

The focus of the LSS is on promoting positive customer behaviours and deterring non-compliance with the tax laws. The LSS covers all types of dispute about liability to pay taxes or duties, or entitlement to tax credits, absent litigation to recover debts or concerning employment matters and the term 'dispute' means any situation where HMRC and a taxpayer are in disagreement over what is the 'right tax at the right time'.

The two fundamental aspects of the LSS are as follows:
(1) Each dispute will be settled on its own merits. There will be no 'package deals' that settle a range of issues for a single undifferentiated sum of money.
(2) If HMRC considers that it is likely to succeed in litigation and that litigation will be both effective and efficient, it will insist on 100% of the tax or other liabilities that it believes to be due; it will not compromise on this figure. Disputes that genuinely have an 'all-or-nothing' character that will be decided one way or the other by the courts must be settled on 'all-or-nothing' basis. Thus, for example, no discount will be provided for an agreement not to litigate.

If HMRC consider that they are unlikely to succeed in litigation, then they will not pursue the case unless it can be justified by the particular circumstances, such as a very large amount of tax in question (in the case itself or from immediate precedent value), or a fundamental point of principle at stake. However, the nature of taxation being what it is (a series of general rules with individual application), a surprisingly high proportion of cases fall into these two categories. [4.183]

f) *Agreements settling appeals*

Litigation which has been commenced by notice of appeal can be validly settled by agreement only if the agreement complies with the relevant statutory provision, namely s 54. In short, a s 54 agreement has the same consequences as a determination to the same effect by the Tax Tribunal; and the agreement binds the parties to it in the same way as a determination binds the parties to an appeal (see *Tod v South Essex Motors (Basildon) Ltd* (1988)). It cannot be determinative of tax liabilities for years after that to which the assessment in question relates (see *MacNiven v Westmoreland Investments Ltd* (2001) (see [2.37]) in which, although the inspector's reasoning in the agreement referred to the amount of excess management expenses that were intended to be carried forward, the court held that this did not bind HMRC to take those into account in future years).

An agreement between HMRC and a taxpayer made outside s 54 will be binding only in limited circumstances. Whilst HMRC, under its care and management powers, may enter into 'back duty' agreements (whereby it agrees to settle for less than the tax that may be due), HMRC does not have power to enter into 'forward tax agreements' (where it is agreed, in advance, that specified amounts will be paid annually in lieu of tax that otherwise would be due (see *Al Fayed v Advocate General for Scotland* (2004)), HMRC does not have power to agree not to perform its duty to collect tax in accordance with the statutory procedure. If a taxpayer enters into such an agreement, it will be enforceable only by way of judicial review proceedings, and HMRC will be bound only if their failure or refusal to abide by the agreement amounts to an abuse of power. [4.184]

g) *The review procedure*

The review procedure is a voluntary procedure that applies before any notification of an appeal to the First-tier Tribunal. This review procedure applies to nearly all direct and indirect taxes (previously the only review procedures were the mandatory review procedure for customs and excise cases and the extra-statutory procedure for the review of VAT cases). The review will be carried out by an HMRC case officer who has no connection to the decision under review.

In the case of an HMRC decision relating to an indirect tax, HMRC must offer the taxpayer a review of the decision. Following that review, or if the taxpayer chooses not to avail itself of the opportunity for the decision to be reviewed, the taxpayer may make an appeal against the decision (or review conclusion) to the Tax Tribunal. The time period for making the appeal is within 30 days of the date of the decision, or if a review is undertaken, within 30 days of the date of the conclusion of that review.

Accordingly, for direct taxes, after a taxpayer has notified HMRC of its decision to appeal, he has three options:
(1)   to request that HMRC reviews its decision;
(2)   to respond to any offer from HMRC to review its decision; or
(3)   to bypass the review procedure by notifying the First-tier Tribunal of the appeal.

If the taxpayer decides that a review would not be worthwhile, then he notifies the First-tier Tribunal of the appeal. This starts the appeal process. However, if the taxpayer proceeds to a review, then it will not be possible to notify the First-tier Tribunal of the appeal until after the review has been concluded.

If the taxpayer disagrees with HMRC's post-review decision, then it is the taxpayer's responsibility to notify the First-tier Tribunal of the appeal within 30 days. Failure to do so means that HMRC's original decision stands.
[4.185]–[4.200]

6   The First-tier Tribunal

The First-tier Tribunal is the court of first instance for nearly all tax appeals. The judges, for every appeal, are selected on a case-by-case basis from a pool that comprises both legally qualified and non-legally qualified members. All members of the Upper Tribunal are able to sit as members of the First-tier Tribunal. A substantial number of the previous Special Commissioners transferred to the First-tier Tribunal (but virtually no-one who sat as a General Commissioner did). The First-tier Tribunal sits in local centres, with larger centres in London, Manchester and Edinburgh that deal with matters of greater complexity. There is also a new central processing centre based in Birmingham, which handles the administration of most appeals.

To commence the appeal process the taxpayer submits a Notice of Appeal to the tribunal. Once the First-tier Tribunal has been notified of the appeal, it will allocate the appeal to one of four categories (see r 23 of the Tribunal Procedure (First-tier Tribunal) (Tax Chamber) Rules 2009 (SI 2009/273)) (the 'First-tier Tribunal Rules'). [4.201]

a)   *Default paper cases*

The simplest appeals (such as fixed penalties) are dealt with under this track. They are dealt with by means of written submissions only, unless either party requests a hearing. Appeals against, for example, penalties for late income tax and corporation tax self-assessment returns (including penalties under FA 2009, Sch 55 paras 3–6) and FA 1998 Sch 18 para 17(2) and (3)) must be allocated as paper cases, unless the tribunal considers that there is a reason why it is appropriate to allocate the case to a different category. [4.202]

b) *Basic cases*

All standard tax penalties that are not suitable for the paper category are allocated as basic cases. Applications for closure notices are typically allocated to the basic category. All cases will go to a hearing unless the taxpayer chooses otherwise, but the requirements for documentary exchange are minimal.
[4.203]

c) *Standard cases*

Any case that does not fall within the basic or paper categories will, as a rule, be allocated to the standard case category. [4.204]

d) *Complex cases*

The tribunal may allocate a case as a complex case only if it considers that: the case will require lengthy or complex evidence or a lengthy hearing; involves a complex or important principle or issue; or involves a large financial sum. If an appeal has been allocated to the complex track, the First-tier Tribunal may, with the agreement of the parties, refer the case to the chamber president with a request that the case be transferred directly to the Upper Tribunal.

The circumstances when it is appropriate to categorise a case as complex were considered by the First-tier Tribunal and the Upper Tribunal in *Capital Air Services Limited v R & C Comrs* (2010). The First-tier Tribunal declined to categorise the case as complex, holding that, in order to be complex, it must be the type of case that ought to be treated exceptionally and start in the Upper Tribunal. The Upper Tribunal disagreed. It allocated the case as a complex case. The Upper Tribunal also made a number of observations regarding the general approach that should be taken to allocation.

(1) A case has to satisfy one or more of the three criteria. Accordingly, a case which is, overall, complex within the ordinary meaning of the word but does not quite meet any of the criteria separately cannot be allocated as a complex case.

(2) Alternatively, a case that is not complex in the ordinary meaning, but which nonetheless satisfies one or more of the criteria could be allocated as complex. However, if for example, a case would involve no lengthy or complex evidence and no complex or important principle or issue, then it may be appropriate not to allocate the matter as complex simply because it involves a large amount of tax. This could be either because a case must be complex, as that term is ordinarily understood, in order to be allocated to the complex category or because the First-tier Tribunal has a discretion not to allocate such a case to the complex category (it is considered by the author that the latter is the better justification).

(3) There is an element of objectivity to be applied. Thus, for example, a hearing of half a day can never be 'lengthy', whereas a three-month hearing always would be. Likewise, a case involving tax of £1,000 could never be said to involve a large financial sum and a case involving tax of

£100 million always would. Absent broad indicative limits such as these, there is not a single 'right' answer that could be ascertained objectively as a matter of law.

Once a case has been allocated to a category either party may apply (or the tribunal may decide on its own initiative) for the case to be re-allocated to a different category. [4.205]

e) *Procedure*

For all categories but the basic category, HMRC must file a statement of case that sets out the grounds for its original decision.

Standard or complex cases may also require substantial case management, documentary evidence and a hearing. As regards case management, the First-tier Tribunal has wide-ranging powers, such as the ability to require expert evidence, to compel the production of documentary evidence or the attendance of witnesses, and to select preliminary issues, consolidate cases and appoint lead cases. [4.206]

f) *The decision*

The First-tier Tribunal must provide to each party a decision notice which states its decision and notifies the party of any right to appeal within 28 days after making the decision (or as soon as reasonably practicable). The decision must include a summary of the findings of fact and the reasons for the decision, unless each party agrees that it is unnecessary.

Tribunal decisions are reported on its website and most decisions are also reported (in *Simon's First-tier Tax Decisions*). [4.207]

g) *Costs of First-tier Tribunal proceedings*

There is a 'no costs' environment for paper, basic and standard cases. Costs will be awarded only if the First-tier Tribunal considers either that a party has acted unreasonably or that a wasted costs order is appropriate (First-tier Tribunal Rules r 10). This will happen only exceptionally.

In the complex track, the default costs approach is the normal High Court costs rules: the losing party pays the costs of the successful party. However, a taxpayer can elect to opt out of the default approach and submit to a 'no costs' environment, as for paper, basic and standard cases. If the taxpayer opts out, that is irrevocable (*N Brown Group plc v R & C Comrs* (2016)). [4.208]

h) *Appealing a First-tier Tribunal decision*

There is no automatic right of appeal to the Upper Tribunal. Accordingly, if the unsuccessful party wishes to appeal, then it must apply first to the First-tier Tribunal. On receipt of an application for permission to appeal, the First-tier Tribunal must first consider whether to review the decision; it will only do so if it is satisfied that there was an error of law in the decision. If the First-tier Tribunal decides not to review the decision, or does conduct a review and decides to take no action in relation to the decision, it will then consider whether to give permission to appeal; if it refuses permission, then the taxpayer may then apply to the Upper Tribunal for permission to appeal.
[4.209]

7 The Upper Tribunal

The Upper Tribunal's main role is to act as a court of appeal from the First-tier Tribunal. It replaces the High Court in this regard.

In addition, some cases go directly to the Upper Tribunal:

(1) Direct referrals: a small number of appeals have been referred directly to the Upper Tribunal by the First-tier Tribunal. For a case to qualify for such a referral, it has to (1) raise a point of law of wide importance or particular complexity; and (2) not involve a complex factual dispute. The first appeal to be heard in the Upper Tribunal, *John Wilkins (Motor Engineers) Ltd v R & C Comrs* (2009) was so transferred. The first President of the First-tier Tribunal, Sir Stephen Oliver QC, indicated that such a referral normally would be made where the parties were in agreement that it should.

(2) Conflicting decisions: appeals in which there are conflicting First-tier Tribunal decisions.

(3) Tax-related judicial review cases: An initial application must be made to the High Court to transfer the case for a decision by the Upper Tribunal, if it considers that it is appropriate to do so.

Generally, it is expected that most cases will be heard by one judge, but the chamber president may require a hearing before up to three judges. **[4.210]**

a) *Publication of decisions*

Following any appeal hearing, the Upper Tribunal issues its decision to the parties as soon as reasonably practicable, along with written reasons (unless the parties have consented otherwise) for that decision. Decisions of the Upper Tribunal will be published on its website and in *Simon's Tax Cases*.

[4.211]

b) *Costs in the Upper Tribunal*

The Upper Tribunal has full costs jurisdiction. It may not make an order for costs against a person without first (i) giving that person an opportunity to make representations and (ii) if the proceedings were a judicial review, or if a party has acted unreasonably, considering the person's financial means.

[4.212]

c) *Appeals from the Upper Tribunal*

Following the Upper Tribunal's decision, the unsuccessful party has one month in which to appeal. Permission to appeal must be sought from the Upper Tribunal, but, if that is refused, the party may then apply to the Court of Appeal. The available grounds for appeal are the same as those currently for an appeal from the High Court (as set out in s 55 of the Access to Justice Act 1999). It must be an appeal on a point of law, and the proposed appeal raises an important point of principle or practice, or is some other compelling reason for the Court of Appeal to hear the appeal.

The Court of Appeal appears to have adopted a more stringent approach to granting permission for appeals from the Upper Tribunal than it did for appeals from the High Court. The general rule is that appeals from specialist tribunals should be approached with 'an appropriate degree of caution' (per Hale LJ, *Cooke v Secretary of State for Social Security* (2001)) and it may be that the Court of Appeal takes note of this when considering applications for permission.

Section 54(4) of the Access to Justice Act 1999 provides that there is no appeal from a decision of the Court of Appeal refusing permission to appeal to that court. Consequently, if the Court of Appeal refuses to grant permission, the appeal process ends. **[4.213]**

5 Tax avoidance, the future and the disclosure rules

Updated by Anne Fairpo, Barrister

I   Introduction [5.1]
II   The direct tax rules [5.4]
III The indirect tax rules (VADR) [5.21]
IV   Strengthening the rules: accelerated payments and follower notices [5.27]
V   Promoters of tax avoidance schemes rules (POTAS) [5.30]
VI   Assessment of the rules [5.31]

'These new disclosure rules, which are part of an overall package of measures intended to reduce the tax lost from tax avoidance, form a central component in the Revenue's increasingly strategic approach to managing the risk to tax revenues from avoidance. They will help to maintain the integrity of the tax system and ensure that everyone pays their fair share of tax and so contributes to the UK's needs.'
(*Regulatory Impact Assessment: Tackling Tax Avoidance – Disclosure Requirements*, Inland Revenue, April 2004.)

'The Government's objective is to increase transparency in the tax system. The new rules will provide Customs & Excise with information about tax avoidance schemes, and those using them, much earlier than at present to enable swifter and more effective investigation and, where appropriate, counter action.'
(*Tax Avoidance Impact Assessment*, HM Customs & Excise, July 2004.)

'DOTAS has been in place for 10 years and has been revised at various times. We believe that now is the right time to look at its hallmarks to see whether they still work properly or whether they need updating. We also want to look at how compliance can be updated.'
(*Strengthening the Tax Avoidance Disclosure Regimes*, HM Revenue & Customs, July 2014.)

I INTRODUCTION

1 The background

With tax avoidance causing severe losses to the Exchequer, it had been the clear intention of the then Chancellor of the Exchequer, the Rt Hon Gordon

Brown MP, to introduce into the UK a general anti-avoidance rule, something the Inland Revenue consulted upon in 1998 (see **[3.74]** ff for a full discussion of the current general anti-abuse rule (GAAR)). Very probably because of the negative responses to the consultation paper, the former Labour Government chose a different method of tackling avoidance. With respect to both direct and indirect taxation, the approach appears to have been a 'strategic' one, namely, to identify areas of the tax system where the potential loss of revenue is high, and target resources and compliance activity accordingly.

In *Fairness in Taxation – Protecting Tax Revenues* (Treasury, 9 April 2003), it was announced that additional resources would be deployed in three particular areas, namely, (i) protecting the Exchequer from non-payment of tax and NICs debts and from failure to file tax returns; (ii) tackling fraud involving concealment of undeclared income or profits offshore; and (iii) countering avoidance of corporation tax and of NICs and tax on employment income. FA 2004 (as amended) sought to start to tackle the third of these by the introduction of new disclosure rules in addition to targeted anti-avoidance rules (TAARs: see **[3.2]–[3.8]**) to combat particular types of schemes (see, eg measures to prevent the use of losses in avoidance schemes: **[11.122]**, finance leasebacks, manufactured dividends and gilt strips).

Further measures that have been aimed at reducing tax avoidance generally include an increase in the rate applicable to trusts (see **[16.21]**), an income tax charge where the former owner continues to enjoy the benefits of ownership of an asset (see **[29.142]**), restricting the IHT benefits arising from accumulation and maintenance trusts (see **[32.53]**) and a tax on enveloped dwellings (ATED – see **[49.86]**).   **[5.1]–[5.2]**

2   The disclosure rules

Broadly, the DOTAS regime requires that a scheme must be disclosed if it falls within any of the descriptions (hallmarks) prescribed in regulations, might be expected to enable any person to obtain a tax advantage and obtaining that advantage is one of the main benefits that might be expected to arise. Those who use certain listed or hallmarked VAT schemes must disclose under the value added tax disclosure rules (VADR), which currently differ from DOTAS.

The disclosure rules were introduced (i) to enable HMRC to identify avoidance schemes sooner than had previously been the case to allow the Government to make a swifter and more targeted response to deliberate abuses of the tax system; and (ii) to identify the users of those schemes, enabling HMRC to prioritise and co-ordinate enquiries into such users. Essentially, the rules are aimed at detecting marketed (ie off-the-peg) avoidance schemes, such as those that have recently been tested before the tax tribunals (eg the 'Working Wheels', 'Icebreaker' and 'Eclipse' schemes: see **[2.2]**, **[2.39]**).

The main objective of the Government of the time was said to be obtaining transparency in the tax system, although some of its detractors would argue that it was 'about the Treasury trying to instil a behavioural change to discourage taxpayers from indulging in "abusive" tax planning as a follow through to the morality campaign'. (*Tax Journal*, 17 May 2004). This view becomes all the more pertinent in light of the additional disclosure rules introduced by FA 2007 (see **[5.4]**, **[5.11]**, **[5.12]**, **[5.15]**). Once identified, these schemes and arrangements may then be challenged through the courts or with new legislation where appropriate; unlike the GAAR (see [3.74] ff) the new rules do not give HMRC additional powers of challenge.

When first introduced, the rules applied to income tax, corporation tax and capital gains tax, but were limited to schemes that concerned employment and certain financial products. As from 1 August 2006, these limitations were removed, meaning that the disclosure regime now covers the whole of income tax, corporation tax and capital gains tax. Stamp duty land tax, in relation to commercial property, was added with effect from 1 August 2005 (see [5.11]), the scheme was extended still further with effect from 1 April 2010 to include arrangements where the subject matter is residential property (with a market value of at least £1m) or mixed use property where the subject matter of the arrangements contains non-residential property with a market value of at least £5m and/or residential property with a market value of at least £1m (see [49.87]–[49.89]), from 1 April 2013, it was extended yet again to cover ATED, introduced by FA 2013.

Further, since 6 April 2011, the regime has also covered inheritance tax on lifetime transfers by individuals to relevant property trusts (primary legislation is not necessary because FA 2004 includes IHT within the regime and allows HM Treasury to define notifiable arrangements for IHT by regulation) and the Inheritance Tax Avoidance Schemes (Prescribed Descriptions of Arrangements) Regulations 2015 as amended by the Tax Avoidance Schemes (Prescribed Descriptions of Arrangements) (Amendment) Regulations 2016 bring IHT fully within the DOTAS rules.

Separate disclosure regimes exist for VAT (see [5.21]–[5.25]), and for National Insurance Contributions (which are outside the scope of this book).

In its consultative document (*Disclosure of Tax Avoidance Schemes* (DOTAS), December 2009), HMRC suggested that DOTAS had changed the economics of avoidance. It highlighted how successful the scheme had been to date (recent figures provided in a further HMRC consultative document, *Strengthening the Tax Avoidance Disclosure Regimes,* July 2014, suggest that more than 2,500 direct and 900 indirect tax schemes had been identified under DOTAS, resulting in more than 60 legislative changes, closing over £12.5b in avoidance opportunities), and stated that it was the (then) Government's intention that DOTAS, in conjunction with VADR, should eventually provide a comprehensive regime applying to all parts of the tax system at risk from avoidance.

In line with this and as mentioned above, in respect of the direct tax rules, the Coalition Government (i) brought within the regime inheritance tax on the creation of certain trusts (see below [5.12]–[5.14]) and ATED (see [49.86]); (ii) made substantive changes to (and thus improved) the targeting of the existing descriptions of schemes required to be disclosed (hallmarks: see [5.7]); (iii) amended the information regulations by bringing forward the earliest date that information relating to a disclosable scheme must be provided and requiring promoters of schemes to provide HMRC periodically with client lists detailing information relating to promoters' clients who have implemented a disclosable scheme and which should have had a scheme reference number allocated to it; (iv) increased penalties for failing to comply with the disclosure regime; provided for an accelerated payment of tax in cases where HMRC challenge an avoidance scheme disclosed by a taxpayer (see [5.27]); and introduced the promoters of tax avoidance schemes rules

(POTAS), aimed at deterring the development and use of avoidance schemes by influencing the behaviour of promoters, their intermediaries and clients (see [5.28]). Taxpayers are free to continue to make their case to the tribunal or court and, if successful, their money will be returned with interest.

This work of ever-honing the DOTAS rules has been continued by successive Governments. Following HMRC's *Technical consultation on draft hallmarks for the Disclosure of Tax Avoidance Schemes regime*, July 2015, the Tax Avoidance Schemes (Prescribed Descriptions of Arrangements) (Amendment) Regulations 2016 (effective from 26 February 2016) strengthen the existing hallmarks, including the IHT hallmark, to ensure that schemes seeking to avoid IHT charges following death as well as during a person's lifetime have to be disclosed, and add to the list the financial products hallmark (see [5.7]). A further HMRC consultation, *Strengthening the Tax Avoidance Disclosure Regimes for Indirect Taxes and Inheritance Tax*, April 2016, proposed the revision of the Inheritance Tax Hallmark following responses to the previous 2015 consultation, a reform of VADR to ensure it remains effective and an extension of the scope of the scheme to include other indirect taxes. [5.3]

II THE DIRECT TAX RULES

The essence of the rules is that a promoter of a scheme is required to provide details of certain prescribed arrangements to HMRC within a specified time limit (see [5.10]). Where a non-UK based promoter does not disclose a scheme, or where the promoter is a lawyer and LLP prevents him from providing all or part of the prescribed information to HMRC, the client (the user) is required to disclose the scheme. In the case where there is no promoter, namely, where the scheme is devised 'in-house' for use within that entity or a corporate group to which it belongs, the scheme must be disclosed by the scheme user.

The details that are to be provided must include a description of the scheme, including information about each element involved, the expected tax consequences and the statutory provisions sought to be relied upon. HMRC will then register the scheme and allocate it a scheme reference number (SRN) (FA 2004 s 311); this helps HMRC to identify users of schemes. The promoter will then be required to provide the SRN to any taxpayer client who uses the scheme or arrangement. This requirement will apply even though the promoter has ceased to provide services to a client by the later of either the date the promoter became aware of a transaction involving the client forming part of the arrangement or the date the reference number was notified to the promoter (FA 2008). For his part, the taxpayer will only be required to include the SRN on his tax return if he has devised the scheme himself or the scheme was provided by a foreign promoter who has not registered with HMRC, when the taxpayer will himself be required to disclose the details of the scheme together with his tax return.

Where a person currently fails, without reasonable excuse, to disclose a scheme as required, an initial daily penalty not exceeding £600 for each day during the 'initial period' is charged. This period is the period of non-compliance beginning on the day after the deadline for complying, and ending when the penalty is determined or, if earlier, the date on which the person complies (TMA 1970 s 98C as amended by FA 2010 s 56 and Sch 17). If this is not considered to be a sufficient deterrent, there may be a higher penalty not exceeding £1 million. After the initial period, a secondary daily penalty not exceeding £600 may be charged. In cases where a Tribunal has issued a disclosure notice, and no disclosure has been made within ten days of the order, both the maximum initial daily penalty and the secondary daily penalty increase to £5,000 each day.

Users of tax avoidance schemes who fail to correctly provide information about the reference number to HMRC under FA 2004 s 313 are liable to a penalty: of £100 for each scheme to which the failure relates for a first occasion; £500 per scheme on the second occasion, within three years, whether or not it relates to the same scheme involved in the previous occasion; and £1,000 per scheme on the third and subsequent occasions whether or not the failure relates to schemes involved in a previous occasion

For other failures to comply with the regime in respect of the provision of information, there may be imposed an initial penalty not exceeding £5,000 and a daily penalty not exceeding £600 for each day after failure to provide information continues after an initial penalty has been determined. The maximum daily penalty is increased to £5,000 per day where a Tribunal has issued an order.

Following a consultation document published in December 2006, in which HMRC highlighted their concern that notifiable schemes they believed were being promoted were not being disclosed, and of their inability to take any action against those who denied being promoters of such schemes, FA 2007 included rules that give HMRC the power to take the necessary action (see [5.17]).

FA 2008 made amendments to FA 2004 Part 7 to ensure that *all* users receive SRNs and understand their obligations under the scheme. Importantly, promoters who rely upon the co-promoter rule, which relieves promoters of the duty to disclose schemes to HMRC in certain circumstances where there is more than one promoter in relation to a scheme, now receive SRNs either directly from HMRC or from the promoter who has disclosed the scheme. Those promoters in turn will then be required by FA 2004 s 312 to pass on the SRNs to clients to whom they provide services in connection with the scheme. Furthermore, FA 2004 s 312A imposes duties on clients of promoters of a notifiable scheme to pass SRNs to other parties to the scheme who receive a tax advantage from it. Finally, FA 2004 s 313Z addresses what were seen by HMRC as continued weaknesses in the SRN system by requiring, from 1 January 2011, promoters to provide periodic lists of clients to whom they have issued reference numbers.

As previously mentioned, the Coalition Government's aim was to strengthen the DOTAS regime. To this end, FA 2014 introduced a sister regime, POTAS (see [5.29]) and, following a consultation by HMRC (*Strengthening the Tax Avoidance Regimes*, July 2014), FA 2015 contains a number of further measures. Significantly, provision is made for persons to voluntarily provide information or documents to HMRC, which they suspect may assist HMRC in determining whether there has been a breach of any of the DOTAS requirements. FA 2015 also enables HMRC to publish information about promoters and schemes that are notified under DOTAS and which have been issued with a reference number. HMRC must inform a promoter before publishing any information which would identify that person as a promoter, and may not publish any information that will identify scheme users. Other provisions are included in the sections below. [5.4]

1 A promoter

In practice, promoters are likely to be accountants, tax advisers, solicitors and barristers if they provide services relating to taxation, including those who are non-UK resident. Regulations (SI 2004/1865 as amended by SI 2004/2613) seek to ensure that, for example, a member of a firm who provides advice, but not tax advice, in respect of an arrangement, is not treated as a promoter. They also provide that in-house planning need only be disclosed with corporation tax self-assessment filing, thereby relieving each company within a group from the burden of disclosure.

Since 1 January 2011, persons who introduce scheme promoters to clients (ie intermediaries) have been required to identify the scheme promoters (FA 2004 s 313A). FA 2004 s 314 (as amended) expressly preserves legal professional privilege (LPP), so that where the promoter believes the relevant information is covered by LPP, the rules require clients to make a disclosure in place of the promoter. These rules (as amended) are designed to ensure that all promoters of schemes, including the legal profession, can comply with their obligations to HMRC without revealing privileged information.

FA 2015 amended FA 2004 by introducing the following new requirements:
(i) promoters must notify HMRC within 30 days if the name of a scheme, or the name or address of a promoter, changes after a reference number has been issued under s 311 of FA 2004 (FA 2004 s 310C);
(ii) where an employer receives, or might reasonably be expected to receive, a tax advantage from notifiable arrangements relating to an employee's employment, the employer must provide prescribed information to the employee (FA 2004 s 312A(2A));
(iii) employers must provide HMRC with prescribed information at the prescribed time about each employee to whom they have provided information in accordance with FA 2004 s 312A (FA 2004 s 313ZC).
[5.5]

FA 2014 introduced a new regime, the promoters of tax avoidance schemes rules (POTAS), aimed at 'high risk' promoters with a view to deterring the development and use of avoidance schemes by influencing the behaviour of promoters, their intermediaries and their clients. These rules are discussed at [5.27]. [5.6]

2 Schemes and arrangements subject to the disclosure rules

A scheme or arrangement, or a proposal for such a scheme or arrangement relating to income tax, corporation tax, capital gains, stamp duty land tax (in respect of commercial property arrangements where the subject matter is residential property with a market value of at least £1m or mixed use property where the subject matter of the arrangements contains non-residential property with a market value of at least £5m and/or residential property with

a market value of at least £1m), the annual tax on enveloped dwellings and inheritance tax has to be disclosed if:
(1) it will, or might be expected to, enable a person to obtain a tax advantage. The definition of 'tax advantage' is based upon ITA 2007 s 687 and CTA 2010 s 732 (relief from income tax or increased relief from income tax, a repayment of income tax or increased repayment of income tax, the avoidance or reduction of a charge to income tax or an assessment to income tax, or the avoidance of a possible assessment to income tax) although there is also specific reference to the deferral of tax and the avoidance of an obligation to deduct tax. The term 'advantage', then, is wider than avoidance;
(2) the tax advantage is, or might be expected to be, the main benefit or one of the main benefits of the arrangement; and
(3) the tax arrangement falls within any description prescribed in the regulations (the 'hallmarks').

(For SDLT arrangements, see [5.11] and [49.87]–[49.89]; for IHT arrangements, see [5.12]–[5.14]; for ATED, see [5.15] and [49.89].)

Arrangements across the whole spectrum of income tax, corporation tax and capital gains tax are required to be disclosed if one of the following 'hallmarks' applies:
(1) it would be expected that a promoter would wish any element of the arrangements giving rise to the tax advantage to be kept confidential from any competitor or from HMRC. There does not need to be an explicit confidentiality agreement between the promoter and the user about the arrangement before the test is met. This hallmark does not apply where the arrangements are designed 'in-house' for use by the business that devised it. The Tax Avoidance Schemes (Prescribed Descriptions of Arrangements) (Amendment) Regulations 2016 expand this hallmark to include schemes involving IHT;
(2) there is no promoter and the intended user is a business, which is not small or medium-sized, who intends any element of the arrangements giving rise to the tax advantage to be kept confidential from HMRC. This hallmark only applies to schemes devised for use 'in-house';
(3) they are likely to command the payment of a fee, the amount of which is contingent on or attributable to a tax saving by a client with experience of purchasing sophisticated tax services. The question is whether it might reasonably be expected that a promoter could charge a premium fee if he wished to; the test does not depend on a premium fee actually being received. The Tax Avoidance Schemes (Prescribed Descriptions of Arrangements) (Amendment) Regulations 2016 expand this hallmark to include schemes involving IHT;
(4) the hallmark concerning off market terms has been abolished;
(5) they are mass-marketed tax products, their fundamental characteristic being their ease of replication rather than the number of times they have been adopted. Such schemes are historically associated with unacceptable tax avoidance and, accordingly, a number of exceptions are specified, encompassing arrangements under approved share incentive plans, approved SAYE option schemes or approved CSOP schemes under ITEPA 2003 Schs 2 (see [9.77]), 3 (see [9.75]) and 4 (see [9.76]) respectively, enterprise management incentives under ITEPA

2003 Sch 5, registered pension schemes, overseas pension schemes in respect of which tax relief is granted in the UK under ICTA 1988 s 615, pension schemes which are relevant non-UK pension schemes, periodical payments of personal injury damages, enterprise investment schemes, venture capital trusts and the corporate venturing scheme (see **Chapter 15**), arrangements consisting solely of one or more plant or machinery leases, arrangements qualifying for community investment tax relief, and accounts which satisfy the Individual Savings Account Regulations.

To ensure that promoters cannot argue that small changes to documentation, to a sequence of transactions or the way in which a product is described make the product non-standardised and remove the requirement to disclose, the Tax Avoidance Schemes (Prescribed Descriptions of Arrangements) (Amendment) Regulations 2016 change how the hallmark works by requiring the informed observer to consider all aspects of the test, rather than the previous position where the observer was required only to consider the purpose of the arrangements.

In addition, the changes remove an existing 'grandfathering' provision, which exempts schemes from disclosure under this hallmark if the same or a substantially similar scheme was made available by any person before the hallmark was introduced. Arrangements involving Social Investment Tax Relief (SITR), Seed Enterprise Investment Schemes (SEIS), Quoted Eurobonds, or Excluded Indexed Securities are unlikely to fall within the redrafted hallmark. As with the first and second hallmarks, this hallmark does not apply where the arrangements are designed 'in-house' for use by the business that devised it;

(6) there are involved loss-making schemes of the type commonly used by high-wealth individuals to reduce their income tax or capital gains tax liability. To ensure that promoters cannot argue that the projection of a theoretical profit under the arrangements at some point in the distant future exempts them from disclosing the scheme, amendments to the 2006 Regulations during 2015 (see the Tax Avoidance Schemes (Prescribed Descriptions of Arrangements) (Amendment) Regulations) 2016 substitute a new description of the Loss Scheme hallmark.

This refines the targeting of the hallmark by requiring the informed observer to consider whether the provision of losses is *a* main benefit, rather than *the* main benefit, and to consider whether the arrangements or their structure contain elements which are unlikely to have been entered into were it not for the provision of those losses. This hallmark does not apply where the arrangements are designed 'in-house' for use by the business that devised it;

(7) they concern leasing arrangements, which concern the lease of high-value plant and machinery and which contain features commonly associated with avoidance. This 'hallmark' will apply where an arrangement includes a plant or machinery lease and:
   (a) one of the parties to the arrangement has, or would have, a right or entitlement to claim capital allowances in respect of the expenditure incurred on the plant or machinery, and another party is not, or will not be, within the charge to corporation tax;

(b) either the lower of the cost to the lessor or the market value of any one asset forming part of the plant and machinery leased is at least £10m, or the aggregate of the lower of the costs to the lessor, or the market values, of all the assets forming part of the plant and machinery leased is at least £25m; and

(c) the lease is not a short-term lease. For the purpose of these rules, a lease for two years or less is a short-term lease unless it is structured in such a way that the term *may* exceed two years. A leasing arrangement will not be notifiable where there is no promoter in relation to it and the tax advantage which may be obtained therefrom is intended to be obtained by an individual or a business which is a small or medium-sized enterprise.

This hallmark applies both to promoted and 'in-house' arrangements but, in respect of the latter, it does not apply where the person intended to obtain the tax advantage is a small or medium-sized enterprise;

(8) this hallmark, concerning pensions and the special annual allowance charge, which has been abolished, has been revoked.

(9) where they are intended to circumvent the employment 'disguised remuneration' rules in ITEPA 2003 Part 7A (see **[9.111]**) and none of the Part 7A exclusions apply (this hallmark came into force on 4 November 2013 and applies where there is a duty to provide prescribed information on a notifiable proposal or becomes aware of a transaction forming part of notifiable arrangements on or after 4 November 2013).

(10) The Tax Avoidance Schemes (Prescribed Descriptions of Arrangements) (Amendment) Regulations 2016, which came into force on 23 February 2016, introduced a new hallmark aimed at schemes using financial products that include terms unlikely to have been entered into were it not for the tax advantage, and schemes using financial products which include contrived or abnormal steps without which the tax advantage could not be obtained. Under the regulations, in order for a financial product to be disclosable it must be reasonable to expect an informed observer (having regard to all relevant circumstances) to conclude that certain conditions are met. *The first step* is that the informed observer would have to be reasonably expected to conclude that both of the following conditions are met:

- **condition 1**: that arrangements include at least one of the specified financial products; and
- **condition 2**: that the main benefit, or one of the main benefits, of including a specified financial product in the arrangements is to give rise to a tax advantage.

The second step is that the informed observer would also have to be reasonably expected to conclude that either of the following conditions are met:

- **condition 3**: a specified financial product included in the arrangements contains at least one term unlikely to have been entered into but for the tax advantage;
- **condition 4**: arrangements involve one or more contrived or abnormal steps without which the tax advantage could not be obtained.

136   *Tax avoidance, the future and the disclosure rules*

There are some specific exclusions to ensure that the ordinary use of certain financial products or arrangements is not caught by this hallmark. These are:
- The sale of a business in exchange for financial products which allow deferral (roll-over) of a gain until later disposal.
- Setting the term over which a long-dated debt matures to below 50 years, so that it is not subject to the equity note legislation.
- Arrangements comprising the hiving down of a trading division to obtain the benefit of the substantial shareholding exemption which would otherwise meet condition 4, so long as condition 3 is not met.
- Arrangements consisting only of the issuing of shares to hedge the currency risk from a loan relationship or a derivative contract, where the shares are accounted for as a liability. This would not, however, apply where condition 3 is met (eg where the shares contain terms unlikely to have been entered into but for the tax advantage).
- Financial Products including a term providing for conversion into, or redemption in, a foreign currency which would otherwise meet conditions 3 and 4 (this would apply in particular to a term included to ensure that a security or loan agreement is not treated as a Qualifying Corporate Bond (QCB) for chargeable gains purposes).

The nature of these 'hallmarks' mean that there is no requirement to disclose routine tax planning. Routine planning refers to the situation where taxpayers pay for advice tailored to their particular circumstances and for the implementation of that advice, and must be contrasted with 'off the peg' advice where the taxpayer normally pays a 'premium fee' for making the elements of the scheme itself available and where the promoter wishes to keep the scheme hidden from other promoters. Further, HMRC is of the view that 'everyday tax advice' would also be excluded from the obligation to disclose, and the type of products that are deemed acceptable include salary sacrifice arrangements for cars, computers, childcare vouchers or pension funds and standard dual contract arrangements. [5.7]

3   The information that needs to be disclosed

The details (set out in SI 2012/8136 (as amended by SI 2013/2592) that must be given to HMRC in writing are: (i) the name and address of the promoter and, if different, the person giving the notification (in those cases where the *user* is required to make the disclosure); (ii) details of the provision of the disclosure rules under which the scheme is notifiable; (iii) a summary of the scheme and, if it has one, its name or title; (iv) information regarding each step of the arrangement. The regulations do not make it clear whether this is restricted to 'tax-steps' or would include other steps taken for other legal reasons; and (v) the relevant statutory provision relied upon. [5.8]

4   Form of disclosure

Disclosures, which will be handled by HMRC's Counter-Avoidance Directorate (Intelligence), must be made on the specified form (obtainable from HMRC's website or from the Directorate). [5.9]

5 When to disclose a notifiable scheme

A promoter must disclose a notifiable scheme or arrangement to HMRC generally within five days of the earlier of making the proposal available for implementation, or the date on which the promoter first became aware of any transaction forming part of the proposed arrangements (note the exceptions to the five-day rule in the Tax Avoidance Schemes (Information) (Amendment) Regulations 2009, SI 2009/611).

Difficulties may well arise with this provision. What if, say, a barrister is asked to advise on an arrangement structured by an accountant. To the extent that he merely agrees with the arrangement without having to make any changes, he has not initiated the proposal. Does this mean that he can never be said to have made it available for implementation, so that he will only be required to make a disclosure when he becomes aware that a transaction under the arrangement has been implemented, or is he making the proposal available for implementation by simply advising his client that he sees no reason for not going ahead with the arrangement? This lack of clarity raises an important issue, particularly bearing in mind the penalty provisions discussed above at [5.4].

Apart from certain SDLT schemes, a promoter need only disclose the same scheme once, meaning that minor changes made to fit the requirements of different clients need not be separately disclosed provided that the revised scheme remains substantially the same.

It is possible that there may be more than one promoter in respect of the same, or substantially the same, scheme whether or not it is made available to the same person. In this case, there is an option for a single disclosure only to be made.

In order to prevent scheme promoters from delaying in making a disclosure, from 1 January 2011, FA 2004 s 307 (as amended by FA 2010 s 56 and Sch 17) accelerates the time at which an actively marketed scheme has to be disclosed to HMRC to the point at which a promoter makes a firm approach to another person in relation to the implementation of the scheme irrespective of whether it is possible for that person to implement the scheme at that time. Schemes that are not actively marketed require to be disclosed only within five days of the date on which the scheme is made available for implementation (as under the original rules). [5.10]

6 Stamp duty land tax

Tax schemes seeking a stamp duty land tax advantage are required to be disclosed when they concern property (i) that is not residential property and which has a market value of at least £5m and (ii) (from 1 April 2010) that is residential property with a value of at least £1m (Stamp Duty Land Tax Avoidance Schemes (Prescribed Descriptions of Arrangements) (Amendment) Regulations 2010, SI 2010/407). The rules have also been amended so that certain schemes involving 'sub-sale' relief, which previously did not have to be disclosed under the so-called 'grandfathering' rules, now have to be disclosed.

Until 1 April 2010, in distinction to schemes concerning income tax, corporation tax and capital gains tax, HMRC did not issue SRNs, and promoters of SDLT arrangements had no obligation to convey a reference number to a client. As a consequence, users were not generally under an obligation to provide the Revenue with information unless either the promoter was offshore, or the user had devised the scheme in-house, or the promoter was a lawyer bound by legal privilege (although the client could waive the right to privilege and permit the lawyer to make the disclosure).

From 1 April 2010, the SRN system is extended to schemes that concern SDLT (Tax Avoidance Schemes (Information) (Amendment) Regulations 2010, SI 2010/410). These regulations prescribe the information a purchaser who has used a disclosed SDLT scheme must provide to HMRC, including the SRN itself, the address, title number and market value. They also prescribe that the purchaser must provide the required information within 30 days of the later of the effective date of the first land transaction forming part of the scheme or the date the purchaser receives the SRN. [5.11]

7 Inheritance tax

a) Introduction

DOTAS was extended in 2011 to cover IHT as it relates to trusts to ensure that legislation included in FA 2010 to make ineffective tax avoidance schemes used to avoid the IHT charge arising when property is transferred into trust was targeted at the main risks. Whilst arrangements involving IHT have been brought into the Confidentiality and Premium Fee hallmarks (see The Tax Avoidance Schemes (Prescribed Descriptions of Arrangements) (Amendment) Regulations 2016; see [5.7]), in 2016 HMRC also consulted again on expanding the IHT hallmark through a revised set of the Inheritance Tax Avoidance Schemes (Prescribed Descriptions of Arrangements) Regulations. Respondents to the previous consultation were of the view that the draft regulations were not sufficiently targeted and risked catching ordinary, non-abusive, IHT tax planning. [5.12]

b) Description of arrangements

Since 6 April 2011, the regime has applied where property becomes relevant property (as defined in the IHT legislation; see **Chapter 34**), and a main benefit of those arrangements is an advantage in relation to the IHT entry charge (but *not* to the ten-yearly and exit charges on the trustees). An advantage is the avoidance, reduction or deferral of a charge to tax. Arrangements consisting only of a transfer of property into trust where the charge is removed because of any one of business property relief, agricultural property relief, conditional exemption or exemption on a transfer into a heritage maintenance fund do not fall within the description of arrangements that have to be disclosed. Schemes that are the same or substantially the same as arrangements made available before 6 April 2011 are exempted from disclosure.

The draft regulations that had been proposed in 2015, were dropped owing to the overwhelmingly negative reaction to them. It was believed that the regulations cast the net far too wide, and were liable to catch conventional IHT planning methods that have always been regarded as normal, prudent planning within the spirit of the existing tax legislation. The draft regulations (the Inheritance Tax Avoidance Schemes (Prescribed Descriptions of Arrangements) Regulations 2016, which were the subject of a 2016 consultation), provide that, for the purposes of DOTAS, arrangements

are prescribed in relation to IHT if an informed observer, having studied the arrangements and having regard to all the relevant circumstances, could reasonably be expected to conclude that two conditions are met. These are:
- **Condition 1**: A main purpose of the arrangements is obtaining an IHT advantage; and
- **Condition 2**: The arrangements must be contrived or abnormal or involve one or more contrived or abnormal steps without which a tax advantage could not be obtained.

Certain arrangements are excepted from being prescribed under the regulations; these are loan trusts, discounted gift schemes, flexible reversionary trusts and split or retained interest trusts which, presumably, would otherwise be reportable since they would be viewed as abnormal means of circumventing the reservation of benefit rules. It was envisaged that these regulations were likely to come into force in the later part of 2016 but, at the time of writing, the regulations have still not come into force. [5.13]

c) *Required information*

The existing information rules (see [5.8]) broadly apply as they apply to other taxes, and the existing requirements for promoters to provide information to clients, or clients of promoters, to provide information to users, also apply to IHT. However, because there is no IHT annual reporting requirement, users of a notifiable IHT scheme must disclose its implementation by providing HMRC with the scheme reference number outside an IHT return in a stand-alone form. [5.14]

8 The annual tax on enveloped dwellings (ATED)

a) *Introduction*

ATED is a tax payable, from 1 April 2013, by companies that own high value residential property ('dwellings') that are physically located in the UK. The main purpose of the new tax was to 'encourage individuals who have put such high value property into envelopes for reasons including tax avoidance to take them out, thereby ensuring that the onward sale of the property is subject to SDLT' (*Ensuring the fair taxation of residential property transactions*, HM Treasury, May 2012). ATED only needs to be paid when the property is owned by:
(a) a company or other corporate body (however, a company that owns property in its capacity as a trustee of a settlement is not included in ATED. If a company holds property as a trustee of a bare trust, it is the person who beneficially owns the property who may be within ATED);
(b) a collective investment vehicle (such as a unit trust or an open ended investment company);
(c) a partnership which includes one, or more, of (a) and (b).

The amount of ATED is based on a banding system based on the value of property. FA added ATED to the list of taxes to be covered by DOTAS (with retrospective effect). In most circumstances a user must report the use of a notifiable ATED scheme on the ATED return. However, in some circumstances a user must report the use of the scheme separately from the return, for example where no ATED return is due or where the filing date has already passed. [5.15]

b) *Description of arrangements*

The types of ATED schemes requiring disclosure, and those that will not are set out in the Annual Tax on Enveloped Dwellings Avoidance Schemes (Prescribed Descriptions of Arrangements) Regulations 2013 (SI 2013/2571) and the Tax Avoidance Schemes (Information) (Amendment) Regulations 2013 (SI 2013/2592). These regulations are aimed at planning which attempts to avoid or minimise the ATED charge by:
- removing residential property worth more than £500,000 from the ownership by a chargeable person;
- reducing the taxable value to under £500,000;
- reducing the taxable value so that a lower charging band applies.

The regulations identify planning which would not require disclosure, for example:
- arm's length transactions between unconnected parties; or
- company distributions to individuals. [5.16]

9 Information powers

Powers introduced in FA 2007, FA 2010 and FA 2013 enable HMRC to:
(1) require a person who has introduced a client to a promoter to identify the person who provided them with information relating to the scheme. For the purposes of gaining information, a new category of person, an 'introducer', was included in FA 2010. An introducer is a person, possibly an independent financial adviser, who has not been involved in the design of the scheme and may not know how the scheme is intended to work. Their role does not extend to that of a promoter, but is simply to market the scheme to potential users and put them in touch with the promoter. The disclosure rules do not impose any automatic reporting obligations on an introducer, although an introducer can be required to provide HMRC with information in response to an information notice from HMRC. To strengthen HMRC's gathering of information powers, FA 2015 enables HMRC to require a person suspected of being an introducer in relation to a notifiable proposed scheme to provide prescribed information about those with whom they have made a marketing contact (FA 2004 s 313C);
(2) apply to the Tax Tribunal for an order requiring a promoter to provide further information or documents in circumstances where HMRC does not believe that a promoter of a notifiable scheme has provided all the required information (FA 2004 s 308A);
(3) require a person they suspect of being a promoter of a notifiable scheme to state whether or not in his opinion the scheme is notifiable. If his answer is in the negative, HMRC can require him to state his reasons and provide sufficient information (a legal opinion that a scheme is not notifiable will not be sufficient for these purposes) to enable them to confirm the assertion (FA 2004 s 313A). HMRC may also apply to the Tax Tribunal for an order requiring the person to produce information or documents supporting his reasons (FA 2004 s 313B);
(4) apply for an order that a scheme is notifiable. The Tribunal must be satisfied that, on the evidence, the scheme is indeed disclosable (FA 2004 s 314A);

(5) apply for an order that a tax avoidance proposal or arrangement is to be treated as if it were notifiable. HMRC must have reasonable grounds for their suspicion and have taken all reasonable steps to establish whether the arrangements are notifiable (FA 2004 s 306A);
(6) request further information from the promoter on the end user of a proposal or arrangement.

The penalty provisions ([**5.4**]) apply with equal force for failure to comply with these rules. [**5.17**]–[**5.20**]

III THE INDIRECT TAX RULES (VADR)

The VAT Disclosure Regime (VADR) was introduced at the same time as DOTAS but its structure and the way it works are different. The principal differences are that VADR requires disclosure by the scheme user after implementation rather than by a promoter prior to implementation, and includes a list of known schemes which require disclosure rather than relying solely on hallmarks. VADR also makes use of hallmarks to provide information about new schemes and their users and schemes which were too complex to include in the listed schemes.

The general thrust of this set of rules is to require all businesses with an annual turnover of more than £600,000 to notify Customs when they use one of eight designated schemes, and all businesses with an annual turnover of more than £10 million to notify HMRC when they carry out a scheme that includes, or is associated with, a provision that has been designated as being tainted with tax avoidance. Both sets of rules refer to schemes entered into to obtain a 'tax advantage', the term 'scheme' being defined so as to include a single supply, whilst 'obtaining a tax advantage' is defined in such a way that any transaction that does not maximise the tax payable is potentially caught (FA 2004 Sch 2).

These rules have been the subject of a recent consultation, *Strengthening the Tax Avoidance Disclosure Regimes for Indirect Taxes and Inheritance Tax*, HMRC 2016 (see [**5.26**]), and major changes to the rules had been planned to be introduced in Finance Act 2017. However, due to truncation of the Finance Bill as a result of the general election, the rules are now anticipated to be included in the Finance (No2) Bill 2017, and are expected to have effect from 1 September 2017. [**5.21**]

1 Designated transactions (listed schemes)

Businesses with an annual turnover of more than £600,000 are required to notify HMRC when they use one of the ten designated schemes, all of which are considered by HMRC to be 'abusive'. They are:
(1) first grant of a major interest in a building;
(2) credit card or cash handling services;
(3) value shifting (ie where a retailer supplies a package of goods or services for a single price where part is standard-rated and part zero-rated or exempt);
(4) leaseback agreements (ie, the sale and leaseback of goods by a business making both taxable and exempt supplies);

(5) extended approval period (ie, where a retailer supplies goods on approval or sale or return, receives payment, but defers the tax point until the end of the approval period);
(6) groups; third party suppliers (ie, the anti out-sourcing provision);
(7) exempt education or vocational training by a non-profit making body;
(8) taxable education or vocational training by a non-eligible body;
(9) property transactions between connected persons; and
(10) issue of face-value vouchers.

The last two were added to the original list of eight by virtue of VATA 1994 Sch 11A para 3(1), which gives the Treasury power to add to the list of designated schemes further schemes that they believe to be abusive, including those that which they believe as a matter of law could not be tax advantageous!

It is questionable whether some of these schemes can truly be described as being 'abusive'. For example, a value shifting scheme could quite easily cover a normal commercial promotion where a free book (zero-rated) is given away with the sale of a DVD (standard-rated). Because the retailer is charging less overall than had the goods been sold separately, he will account to HMRC for less VAT and will accordingly fall within the 'tax advantage' test, and will be required to notify HMRC. It is interesting to note that for income tax purposes, such a disposal of stock on justifiable commercial grounds will not attract the rigour of the market value rule (see [10.117]).

Businesses in this category will not have to worry too much about whether or not a tax advantage has been obtained for reporting purposes, since the designated schemes are deemed to produce such an advantage. However, on a failure to report, that advantage will become material, since the 15% penalty is calculated by reference to the VAT saved. For a discussion of the definition of 'tax advantage', see [5.21]. [5.22]

2 Generally notifiable transactions (hallmarked schemes)

In addition to reporting the ten listed schemes, businesses with an annual turnover exceeding £10m are also required to report *any* transaction in any VAT accounting period that has as it main purpose, or one of its main purposes, the gaining of a tax advantage and that is tainted with avoidance because either:
(1) there is a confidentiality condition in an agreement; or
(2) it entails the sharing of the tax advantage with another party to the scheme or with the promoter; or
(3) it concerns a contingent fee arrangement; or
(4) there is a prepayment between connected parties; or
(5) it concerns funding by loan or share subscriptions;
(6) it is an off-shore loop; or finally
(7) it concerns construction work connected with a property transaction between connected persons (SI 2004/1933).
(8) it concerns the issue of face-value vouchers.

The concern, once again, is that normal commercial transactions are likely to be caught within one of these categories, making notification appear to be a universal requirement. Further, the inclusion of the words 'main purpose, or one of its main purposes' (not defined by HMRC on the basis that they believe that it is a matter for the business using the tax scheme to decide whether gaining a tax advantage is a main purpose) is likely to result in large numbers of transactions undertaken by businesses requiring notification on the basis that, given different ways of structuring a particular business objective, the one involving the least amount of tax will clearly be chosen. Failure to make the required notification for a general transaction will result in a fixed penalty of £5,000. [5.23]

3 The tax advantage

A tax advantage is obtained by a person who is, or is liable to be, registered for VAT in any VAT accounting period where:
(1) the VAT payable (output tax less input tax) is less than it would otherwise have been;
(2) the VAT repayable (input tax less output tax) is more than it would otherwise have been;
(3) where the business is the customer, the period of time between which he accounts for the input tax and the supplier accounts for the output tax is greater than would otherwise have been the case (FA 2004 Sch 2). There would appear to be a significant lack of clarity in this 'definition', since there is no indication as to what is meant by 'otherwise' in this context; or
(4) the amount of non-deductible tax (that is, input tax for which the taxable person is not entitled to credit and the VAT incurred on goods and services which is not input tax and for which the taxable person is not entitled to a refund) is less than it would otherwise have been.

A person who is not liable to be registered for VAT will also obtain a tax advantage if his non-refundable tax is less than it would otherwise be. The term 'non-refundable tax' means the VAT on: (1) goods and services supplied to him; (2) goods acquired by him from other Member States; and (3) goods imported by him from outside the Member States. It excludes any VAT that he is entitled to be refunded under a provision in the VATA 1994. [5.24]

4 Notification

Businesses must report the details of the offending scheme or provision to HMRC within 30 days of the due date for filing the VAT return or, where there is a claim for repayment of output tax or an increased input tax claim, within 30 days of making the claim. For a generally notifiable transaction, the details must include:
(1) the particular provision that taints the scheme with tax avoidance;
(2) how the scheme gave rise to a tax advantage, which will require a description of each arrangement, transaction or series of transactions, their sequence, their timing or the intervals between them and the goods and services involved;
(3) the parties involved; and
(4) the statutory provision relied upon that gives rise to the tax advantage (SI 2004/1929).

Surprisingly, perhaps, although SI 2004/1929 makes provision for HMRC to publish details of the required form and manner in which notification of designated schemes has to be made, no such details are included in those regulations. [5.25]

5 Strengthening VADR

Unlike the DOTAS rules, the VADR regime has not been the subject of revision since its introduction in 2004 but, in light of the dramatic reduction in the number of new disclosures each year, HMRC consulted on how the scheme could be strengthened (*Strengthening the Tax Avoidance Regimes*, July 2014). Given that, in terms of providing HMRC with information, there is no intrinsic difference between VAT and the taxes included within DOTAS, it was proposed that the policy objectives of VADR and DOTAS should be more closely aligned, and that VADR should be amended accordingly.

The approach favoured by HMRC was to re-design the regime to operate on a promoter basis in order to place the disclosure responsibility with a small number of promoters who design and promote avoidance arrangements rather than, as is currently the position, requiring a much larger number of users, each disclosing potentially similar information, with the aim of relieving the administrative burden for business more widely. Users of disclosed schemes would report their actual use of a scheme by simply notifying HMRC of the scheme reference number (SRN) and the period in which they expect the tax advantage to arise. A promoter-based regime could be achieved by retaining VADR as a discrete regime, adopting many of the design features of DOTAS to make it work on a promoter basis, or by expanding DOTAS to cover VAT as well as income and corporation tax, CGT, NICs, SDLT, Inheritance Tax, ATED and diverted profits tax

More closely aligning VADR with DOTAS was also the theme in HMRC's most recent consultation document on the subject, *Strengthening the Tax Avoidance Disclosure Regimes for Indirect Taxes and Inheritance Tax*, April 2016, in which it was proposed that, to ensure the system remains effective, the obligation to disclose schemes should be moved from users to scheme promoters. Views were also sought on proposals to extend the scope of the regime to include other indirect taxes. These changes to the rules had been planned to be introduced in Finance Act 2017. However, due to truncation of the Finance Bill as a result of the general election, the rules are now anticipated to be included in the Finance (No2) Bill 2017, and are expected to have effect from 1 September 2017 [5.26]

IV STRENGTHENING THE RULES: ACCELERATED PAYMENTS AND FOLLOWER NOTICES

1 Introduction

In a further attempt to make the use of tax avoidance schemes less attractive, by virtue of FA 2014, HMRC now has the power to require payment of tax or NICs upfront, before a dispute about the efficacy of a tax scheme has been settled by the courts. It can also require payment of tax from a taxpayer where it has succeeded in the courts against other taxpayers using similar schemes.
[5.27]

2 Accelerated payments

Taxpayers subject to the PAYE system or who pay VAT and interest on bank accounts pay tax immediately even if they then wish to dispute the amount that is payable. However, under the self-assessment systems for income tax, Class 4 NICs, capital gains tax, corporation tax, stamp duty land tax and the annual tax on enveloped dwellings, the position has been that the taxpayer can usually retain the amount of tax payable whilst the dispute is resolved.

The Government's view was that taxpayers believed to have been involved in avoidance schemes that were notifiable under DOTAS or subject to the GAAR should not be able to enjoy the use of the money they are trying to avoid paying during the period in which HMRC is enquiring into, investigating or litigating such arrangements.

Accordingly, FA 2014 introduced provisions, known as the accelerated payment notice scheme (APN) and associated partner payment notice scheme (PPN), effective from 17 July 2014 for income tax, CGT, corporation tax, IHT, SDLT and ATED and from 12 April 2015 for NICs, that permit HMRC to demand upfront payment of disputed tax by the issue of a 'Notice to Pay' to any taxpayer for whom there is an open enquiry, or the matter is under appeal, and who has claimed a tax advantage by the use of arrangements that either fall to be disclosed under DOTAS, or HMRC counteracts under the GAAR following an opinion of the GAAR Advisory Panel that, in the Panel's opinion, the arrangements are not a reasonable course of action, or to whom a follower notice has been issued.

Such a notice to pay requires the taxpayer to pay the tax in dispute within 90 days, or a further 30 days where the taxpayer requests that HMRC should reconsider the amount of the payment notice. Where the matter is under appeal, the measure operates to remove any postponement of the disputed tax. Penalties of up to 15% of the tax payable apply for late payment. As Green J explained in *Walapu v R & C Comrs* (2016):

> 'The express objective of the Chancellor of the Exchequer, in promoting this legislation, was to alter the economics of tax avoidance by stripping from parties to such schemes all of the liquidity advantages that they, hitherto, enjoyed. An important consideration leading to the new provisions was the experience of HMRC of dealing with aggressive delaying tactics and strategies engaged in by tax avoidance scheme promoters. Documentary evidence placed before this Court by the Revenue showed that, not infrequently, the unravelling of tax avoidance schemes could take many years prior to HMRC being in a position to assess a taxpayer's liability and then obtain payment. In the interim participants held money that HMRC considered was due to the State and promoters of tax avoidance schemes continued to be in a position to promote their schemes as having longevity.'

To ensure that the accelerated payment legislation operates effectively where the benefit of a loss or other amount is surrendered as group relief, FA 2015 provides that by taking a group of companies as a whole, the disputed tax will sit with the Exchequer during a dispute.

In its impact statement, HMRC estimate that this measure, together with a further measure included in FA 2014 that enables HMRC to issue a 'follower notice' (see [**55.28**]), will require Payment Notices to be issued to around 43,000 taxpayers involved in avoidance schemes currently under dispute with HMRC. In fact, according to an HMRC press release of September 2015, it was announced that more than 25,000 APNs/PPNs had already been issued since August 2014, with HMRC collecting £1 billion in tax payments from users of tax avoidance schemes, and that by the end of 2016, HMRC expect to have completed issuing around 64,000 such notices, bringing forward £5.5 billion in payments for the Exchequer by March 2020.

Although at the time of writing these measures have been in force for only three years, they have already been the subject of various judicial review proceedings. In *Rowe Worrall & Others v R & C Comrs* (2015) (see **[55.21]** and **[55.83]**, a number of investors in various Ingenious Film Partnerships challenged through judicial review HMRC's issue of PPNs requiring up-front payments of tax pending the resolution of enquiries into the tax arrangements entered into by the investors. They argued that the APN/PPN system was unlawful because it defeated natural justice, was ultra vires, irrational, violated legitimate expectations, and was incompatible with human rights including retrospection and proportionality. In firmly rejecting all of these arguments, Simler J clearly made known her view of the merits of the case when, in relation to retrospection, she said:

> 'The claimants assert that "if they had known that participating in a business notified under DOTAS meant that monies contributed would be claimed by executive act some ten years later at short notice and prior even to any enquiry or assessment to tax it is highly unlikely that they would have made the investment". *That is untenable* [my emphasis]. The primary risk to the claimants was not precisely when they might have to pay the relevant tax, but whether they would have to pay it. That was a risk that must have been well understood and for which financial provision can be expected to have been made.'

Although the outcome was the same in *Walapu v R & C Comrs* (2016) (see **[55.83]**), the factual situation was different in that, unlike the previous case, where HMRC had formally *assessed* the taxpayers' tax liability and what was then in dispute, by way of appeal, was a crystallised tax liability owed by the taxpayers, in *Walapu* the taxpayer had claimed relief against past income tax assessments but he had not had the present claim formally assessed. Accordingly, he argued that the APN imposed upon him required payment on account of an unassessed tax liability that had not yet accrued and that this was a fundamentally different position to the case of an assessment which was under appeal and was a violation of his human rights. His application for judicial review claimed that the APN system gave HMRC powers that it was using unfairly and unjustly, and which gave him no right of appeal. Green J dismissed these arguments, noting that the established APN procedures allowed recipients either to complain to HMRC or to use TMA 1970 s 28A(4) to compel HMRC to issue a closure notice within a specified period, triggering the normal rights of appeal, although neither course of action would cause cancellation of the APN. However, he added that the taxpayer had produced nothing to suggest he would be denied the right to put his arguments to the appellate tribunal.

Green J also dismissed an alternative argument advanced by the taxpayer that the tax avoidance scheme he had used was substantially the same as an earlier one that had been notified under DOTAS, and that the later one was thus exempt from being notifiable and that therefore the APN regime could not apply. The judge said that to construe the DOTAS regulations in this way 'would create a gaping hole in their efficacy' and would prevent HMRC from issuing APNs to thousands of other taxpayers. The judicial review application was accordingly dismissed.

Whilst it is open to anybody else to challenge the issue of an APN/PPN, in light of the strength of these judgments, it is suggested that further challenges would be pointless. It should also be noted that the issue of judicial review proceedings does not halt the due date for the payment of an APN so that by the time any appeal could be heard, the tax demanded would already have become payable (see *E Dunne and V Gray v R & C Comrs* (2015)). [5.28]

3 Follower notices

A 'follower notice' informs the taxpayer that in HMRC's opinion another judicial decision is relevant to their case, that the decision determines their dispute and that the taxpayer should amend their return or agree to resolve their appeal in line with the court's decision. If the taxpayer chooses not to do so, HMRC can then issue an APN and the taxpayer will be required to pay the disputed amount under the accelerated payment rules. HMRC may serve a notice on a taxpayer under FA 2014 s 204(1) provided four conditions are met. These conditions are:

(i) there must either be an enquiry in progress into a tax return or claim made by the taxpayer or there must be an on-going appeal with HMRC or the tribunal;

(ii) the return, claim or appeal are in respect of tax arrangements that leads to a tax advantage;

(iii) HMRC are of the opinion that there is a judicial ruling that is relevant to the taxpayer's tax arrangements. A judicial ruling is 'relevant' to the chosen arrangements if: (a) it relates to tax arrangements; (b) the principles laid down, or reasoning given, in the ruling would, if applied to the chosen arrangements, deny the asserted advantage or a part of that advantage; and (c) it is a final ruling. A ruling is final if it a decision of the Supreme Court or, if it is the decision of another court or tribunal, either no appeal can be made or there can be no appeal because, for example, the time has expired or the appeal has been abandoned; and

(iv) No previous follower notice has been given to the same person in the same circumstances.

A follower notice, which must identify the ruling that, in HMRC's opinion, is relevant to the tax arrangements, must be given within 12 months of the later of the date the claim, return or notice of appeal was received. The taxpayer has 90 days from the date of the notice to make representations in writing to HMRC objecting on the grounds that: (a) conditions (i), (ii) or (iv) are not met; (b) the judicial ruling specified in the notice is not relevant to the arrangements entered into by the taxpayer; or (c) the notice was given outside the 12-month limit. Having considered the representations, HMRC must then confirm or withdraw the notice. There is no right to appeal against a follower notice, with the only right of challenge being by way of an application for judicial review.

If no corrective action is taken, the taxpayer will be liable to a penalty of between 10% and 50% of the value of the tax advantage that has been denied.

[5.29]

V PROMOTERS OF TAX AVOIDANCE SCHEMES RULES (POTAS)

FA 2014 contains rules that apply to promoters of tax avoidance schemes and aim to deter the development and use of high risk avoidance schemes by influencing the behaviour of promoters, their intermediaries and clients. The regime builds on the existing DOTAS regime, drawing on and reinforcing existing disclosure obligations and sharing many similar definitions.

The regime involves a graduated series of sanctions, with two key steps:

(i) *A conduct notice* This is issued where a promoter meets a threshold condition (eg the promoter breaches the Banking Code of Practice in respect of schemes that it promotes; the promoter fails to meet DOTAS obligations; a professional body of which the promoter is a member takes certain disciplinary action against it; the promoter fails to comply with an information notice). A conduct notice is issued by an authorised officer of HMRC and imposes conditions on a promoter that must be complied with. There is no right of appeal against the issue of a conduct notice, which can last for up to two years.

(ii) *A monitoring notice* This is issued by an authorised officer of HMRC where a promoter breaches one or more conditions in a conduct notice and approval is obtained from the First-tier Tribunal. There is a right of appeal against a decision of the First-tier Tribunal to do so. A promoter that is subject to a monitoring notice is referred to as a monitored promoter. If a monitoring notice is issued, the monitored promoter is subject to a more stringent regime that includes publication by HMRC of information about the promoter (but only after the promoter's appeal rights have been exhausted). There is a duty on the promoter to tell clients that it is a monitored promoter and to provide them with a promoter reference number (PRN). There is then a corresponding duty on clients to put the PRN on their returns or otherwise to report the PRN to HMRC.

HMRC expects that few promoters will be issued with conduct notices and the great majority of those who are will comply with the conditions in the notices. This would mean that the much more rigorous sanctions consequent on a monitoring notice will be imposed in only a very few cases and subject to prior approval by the First-tier Tribunal that the issue of the notice is justified.

[5.30]

VI ASSESSMENT OF THE RULES

From the view of HMRC, the disclosure rules have been a success, reportedly closing over £12.5 billion in avoidance opportunities and enabling swift and effective action once a scheme has been notified. However, as far as taxpayers and their advisers are concerned, it is a very different picture that is painted. The overwhelming view of practitioners is that the rules place too great a burden on tax advisers to provide vast amounts of information in respect of transactions which, it must be remembered, are in accordance with the law, and which could in any event be discerned by HMRC from tax returns. Moreover, there is real concern that the rules amount to broadly-based transaction reporting rules that go beyond their US counterparts, and could be counter-productive in so far as the more widely the disclosure legislation is drawn, the less easy it will become to identify the real abuses that most of the profession had been led to believe were the motivating force behind the introduction of the new rules.

More specifically, and of vital importance is the fact that both the primary legislation and the regulations leave much room for doubt about certain definitions (eg what is meant by an 'informed observer', language used in a number of hallmarks). On a final note, it has been submitted by one commentator that an argument could be maintained that the rules are inconsistent with Art 8 of the European Convention on Human Rights (this article secures the right to respect for private and family life; see **[55.61]**), particularly now that they have been extended (see *Tax Journal*, 13 March 2006). This view must have even greater force since the introduction of the additional disclosure rules for, although they are likely to affect relatively few people (in their December 2006 consultative document, HMRC reported that they had identified over 100 entities where there was evidence of involvement in promoting notifiable schemes but where there had been no disclosure; this has to be viewed in the context of a total of over 2,400 direct tax disclosures between 1 August 2004 and 30 September 2014), their effect is that disclosure is now required not only of schemes that fall within the statutory definition, but also any that HMRC *reasonably suspect* may do so. **[5.31]**

Section 2 Income tax

Chapters
6   General principles
7   Computation charges, allowances and rates
8   Taxation of employment income
9   Employee participation: options, incentives and trusts
10 Trading income
11 Losses
12 Land
13 Miscellaneous income
14 Annual payments, patent royalties and savings income
15 Tax shelters and insurance products
16 Trusts and settlements
17 Estates in the course of administration
18 The overseas dimension

Section 2 Income tax

6 General principles
Updated by Helen McGhee, Senior Associate, Joseph Hage Aaronson LLP

I History **[6.2]**
II Statutory basis of the tax **[6.21]**
III Categories of income **[6.41]**

'No one has ever been able to define income in terms sufficiently concrete to be of value for taxation purposes ... where it has to be ascertained whether a gain is to be classified as an income gain or a capital gain, the determination of that question must depend in large measure upon the particular facts of the particular case.'
(Abbott J in *Oxford Motors Ltd v Minister of National Revenue*
(1959) 18 DLR (2d) 712.)
[6.1]

I HISTORY

Income tax is sometimes referred to as the 'tax which beat Napoleon'. Such claims amount to a gross exaggeration although it is true that the tax was first introduced in 1799 by Pitt the Younger as a wartime measure. Pitt's tax was not wholly innovative; there had always been a tradition of direct taxation even if it had been applied spasmodically. The origins of income tax may be seen in land tax and in the Triple Assessment of 1798.

Early yields were disappointing; estimates predicted a yield of £10m in the first year, but under £6m was actually raised. Although the tax was repealed when peace with France was concluded in 1802, it was reintroduced by Addington when hostilities recommenced in the following year. Addington included two basic changes which have survived more or less intact: *first*, a requirement that returns should be of income from particular sources and not just a lump sum; and *second*, provisions for deduction of tax at source.

The final cessation of hostilities in 1816 led to the repeal of the tax with the resulting financial deficit being made good by increased yields from Customs and Excise. Income tax was brought back, this time for good, by Peel in 1842. It was not revived because of its own inherent merits, but as a first step towards the repeal of the Corn Laws in 1846.

By the end of the century, income tax, although an accepted part of the fiscal landscape, raised less than either customs or excise. The twentieth century with the extraordinary demands of war and welfare transformed the picture. By the end of the 1914–18 War, the income tax yield was some £585m as compared with the pre-war figure of £34m and the complexity of the modern tax had been established with earned income relief, supertax, a range of personal allowances, and a primitive system of capital allowances. The process of further developing the tax was accelerated by the 1939–45 War with the yield rising from £371m in 1938 to £1,426m in 1945. PAYE was introduced in 1944 and the tax avoidance industry maintained a steady growth.

Today, the flood of income tax legislation shows little sign of diminishing; the statutory material was consolidated in 1952, in 1970, and again in 1988 (TA 1988). Any further consolidation has been overtaken by the complete redraft of the legislation on a piecemeal basis – see the Capital Allowances Act (CAA) 2001, the Income Tax (Earnings and Pensions) Act (ITEPA) 2003, the Income Tax (Trading and Other Income) Act (ITTOIA) 2005, the Income Tax Act (ITA) 2007, the Corporation Tax Act (CTA) 2009, the Corporation Tax Act (CTA) 2010 and the Taxation (International and Other Provisions) Act (TIOPA) 2010. [6.2]–[6.20]

II STATUTORY BASIS OF THE TAX

1 The statutes and case law

The authority for imposing taxation is by Act of Parliament and, the statutory basis for levying tax is now to be found in CAA 2001 (see **Chapter 48**), ITEPA 2003 (see **Chapters 8** and **50**), ITTOIA 2005 (see **Chapter 10**), ITA 2007 (incorporating most of the remaining parts of income tax, including the calculation of income tax liability), CTA 2009 and 2010, TIOPA 2010 and TA 1988 (now containing only very minor income tax provisions). TMA 1970 deals with the administration of the tax.

The meaning of the statute is primarily a question for the judiciary that sit in the various courts from the Appeal Tribunals to the Supreme Court. Many concepts are not defined by statute (eg what is a trade? what is an income receipt/expense?), many provisions are obscure, and it is the role of the judiciary to resolve such difficulties. It is questionable whether it should be the job of the courts to create law to deal with sophisticated avoidance schemes but some would say it is a task, which over the last decade or so, they have undertaken with varying degrees of enthusiasm (see, *MacNiven v Westmoreland Investments Ltd* (2001), the Hong Kong case of *Collector of Stamp Revenue v Arrowtown Assets Ltd* (2004) and the more recent cases of *Barclays Mercantile Business Finance Ltd v Mawson* (2005), *IRC v Scottish Provident Institution* (2005), *R & C Comrs v Tower MCashback LLP 1* (2011), *R & C Comrs v Mayes* (2011), *Eclipse Film Partners No 35 v R & C Comrs* (2015) (in which case the taxpayers were refused leave to appeal by the Supreme Court (2016)) and *UBS AG v R & C Comrs; DB Services (UK) Ltd v R & C Comrs* (2016) (see **Chapter 2**)).
[6.21]

2 Years and rates

The income tax year runs from 6 April to the following 5 April and is termed the 'year of assessment' or simply the 'tax year'. It is referred to by reference to both the calendar years that it straddles – hence, the year of assessment beginning on 6 April 2017 is referred to as the tax year 2017–18. The curious starting date for the year (6 April) is explicable, as is so much of income tax, on historical grounds. The tax year originally ended on Lady Day 25th March but, on the change from the Julian to the Gregorian calendar in 1752, 11 days were lost and the tax year was extended by 11 days, taking it to 5 April.

Income tax needs annual renewal by Parliament. The annual Finance Act receives Royal Assent, normally in late July. By virtue of the Provisional Collection of Taxes Act 1968, the Budget resolutions (such as the rates of tax) are given limited statutory force from the beginning of a tax year until the Finance Act is enacted. It is intended from 2018 that the Finance Act will be enacted before the start of the tax year after the introduction of the Autumn Budget from 2017 as announced by the Chancellor at the Autumn Statement 2016. **[6.22]–[6.40]**

III CATEGORIES OF INCOME

1 The source doctrine

For both income tax and corporation tax purposes, income is categorised according to its source. For income tax purposes, the various types of income are charged as follows.

Income category	Income charged	Basis of assessment	Legislation
Employment	Employment, pension and social security income	Current year	ITEPA 2003
Trading	Profits of a trade, profession or vocation	Current year	ITTOIA 2005 Part 2
Property	Rents and income from land	Current year	ITTOIA 2005 Part 3
Savings and investment income	Interest, dividends, distributions, securities, deposits, purchased life annuities, life insurance gains, futures and options	Current year	ITTOIA 2005 Part 4
Miscellaneous	Intellectual property, non-trade film recordings, telecommunication rights, settlements, income from estates in administration, annual payments and income not otherwise charged	Current year	ITTOIA 2005 Part 5
Exempt income	National savings, individual investment plans, FOTRA securities, life annuities, annual payments and other income	N/A	ITTOIA 2005 Part 6

One of the reasons for such categorisation is that different rules apply to the computation of income in each category. ITEPA 2003, ITTOIA 2005 and

ITA 2007 all have their own rules for determining the amount of income and the allowable deductions (if any). Property income, for example, is charged to tax by reference to the rents and other receipts which arise as a result of the ownership of land (or of an interest therein) and the landlord may deduct expenses such as repairs to the property.

The doctrine of source encompasses the idea that, unless income has a source in a tax year, it is not liable to tax. With the enactment of ITEPA 2003, ITTOIA 2005, ITA 2007, CTA 2009, CTA 2010 and TIOPA 2010 (the rewritten legislation – see [1.22]) income is categorised by description. In arriving at the total income of a taxpayer, it is necessary to categorise his income as falling within one of the charging statutes and, by applying the rules of the relevant provisions, to calculate the income arising under each one. It is always said that tax is charged only so long as a taxpayer possesses a source of the income. However, this principle has been modified over the years by legislation seeking to curtail tax avoidance opportunities which arise from it. For instance, although the sale of trading stock after the permanent cessation of the relevant trade would not on general principles fall within trading income (because the source – the trade – had ceased when the sale occurred), there is express provision to bring into the tax net the value of stock unsold at the date of the discontinuance. Similar tax avoidance opportunities in connection with earnings (see *Example 6.1* below) and on income arising under ITTOIA 2005 Part 5 Chapter 5 are curtailed by specific rules. Until 6 April 2008 the source doctrine was able to provide an advantage for non-UK domiciliaries taxed on the remittance basis (see **Chapter 18**), but the comprehensive changes to the remittance basis for 2008–09 and subsequent years, eliminate those advantages. In any event those opportunities did not apply to earnings by reason of ITEPA 2003 s 17, which applies to charge emoluments received after an employment has ceased, nor to income within the settlements legislation by reason of ITTOIA 2005 s 648(5), which is treated as arising in the year it is remitted. [6.41]

EXAMPLE 6.1

B, having been employed by G Ltd for 20 years, is transferred together with all the other employees to the employment of G Ltd's parent company in the tax year 2016–17. The trustees of a fund for the benefit of employees of G Ltd, including B, brought that trust to an end and made distributions to B in the following tax year (ie in 2017–18). That distribution will be employment income (see **Chapter 8**), and although there was no source of income in the year of receipt, ITEPA 2003 s 17 applies the charge to income tax on earnings, even though the employee did not hold the employment in the year of assessment.

2 The mutually exclusive rule

The heads of charge of income are mutually exclusive with the result that HMRC cannot assess income to tax under any provision other than the one to which that income is properly attributable (*Fry v Salisbury House Estate Ltd* (1930)). The same principle applies to the taxpayer who may not deduct expenses attributable to a different source nor opt to have his income taxed under a different provision (*Mitchell and Edon v Ross* (1962)). **[6.42]**

EXAMPLE 6.2

(1) Roger lets several properties to university students and works full time in the management of the properties. Tax must be charged as property income (which applies to rent and other receipts from land), not as trading income, because there cannot be a trade of letting properties (see *Griffiths v Jackson* (1983), **[12.23]**).

(2) A firm of solicitors acted as secretary for a number of companies. The profits from the profession of solicitors are assessed as trading income; remuneration from the office of company secretary is, however, charged under ITEPA 2003 (*IRC v Brander and Cruickshank* (1971); see **[8.21]** and ESC A37 for the tax treatment of directors' fees received in such cases).

3 What is income?

The term 'income' is not defined in the legislation. Furthermore, any definition is a matter for acute debate by both economists and philosophers. How, therefore, can income tax operate if the subject matter of the tax is not defined? The answer is that income for this purpose means all the sums calculated under ITEPA 2003, ITTOIA 2005, ITA 2007 and the Taxes Act 1988. Hence, a sum of money falling under these provisions is subject to tax (and is, therefore, 'income'), whilst a sum which escapes them is untaxed (and may, therefore, be termed 'capital'). Critics of income tax (notably the Meade Committee in its report in 1979 on the Structure and Reform of Direct Taxation) argue that it is the distinction between capital and income that has been used to greater effect than many other devices to avoid tax.

Because of the tax avoidance possibilities, the concept of 'income' is extended in certain cases, so that capital sums such as premiums are treated as property income and golden handshakes and restrictive covenant payments under ITEPA 2003 are deemed to be income for the purposes of the tax. This extended definition of 'income' also sometimes results in a divergence between the income tax rules and ordinary principles of trust law that identify what sums are income. Take, for instance, ITA 2007 s 481 which imposes an additional charge on income received by discretionary or accumulation trusts. Because the section was limited to 'income arising to the trustees' it was limited to income 'in a trust sense' and hence did not catch profits of a capital nature (eg lease premiums) albeit that those profits are deemed to be income for basic rate purposes in the hands of the trustees (see **Chapter 16**). Under ITA 2007 s 482 such profits are brought into charge as income at the dividend trust rate of 38.1% (for 2017–18). Specific tax avoidance provisions aimed at transactions in securities, transfers of assets abroad and artificial transactions in land can all be found in ITA 2007.

Some income is deemed to be exempt such as National Savings ordinary account interest, individual investment plans and FOTRA securities under ITTOIA 2005 Part 6.

The lack of a definition of income results in various difficulties including, for example, when the legislation prescribes that only income receipts are subject to tax or only income expenses can be deducted (for example, with property income and trading and professional income the tax is levied on the profits that remain after income deductions have been taken from income receipts). The meaning of 'income' has accordingly been debated frequently before the courts and the various tests that have been suggested for resolving the problem are considered in **Chapter 10**. [6.43]

7 Computation charges, allowances and rates

Updated by Sarah Laing, CTA, Chartered Tax Advisor

I   Introduction [**7.1**]
II Total income [**7.21**]
III Net income [**7.40**]
IV Personal reliefs [**7.101**]
V   Method of charging taxable income [**7.120**]

I INTRODUCTION

1 General

The income tax legislation is mainly located in the Income Tax Act 2007 (ITA 2007). This legislation, together with the Capital Allowances Act 2001, Income Tax (Earnings and Pensions) Act 2003 (ITEPA 2003) and the Income Tax (Trading and Other Income) Act 2005 (ITTOIA 2005) contains most of the income tax provisions. A principal feature of ITA 2007 is the tax calculation, which sets out how amounts liable to income tax and eligible for relief are combined to compute a person's income tax liability. Unless otherwise indicated, all references are to ITA 2007. [**7.1**]

2 Tax rates

For 2017–18, income tax is levied at three main rates: a basic rate of 20%, a higher rate of 40% and a 45% additional rate charged on taxpayers with taxable income above £150,000 (s 6). In certain circumstances savings income is not taxed (s 7, s 12 and ss 12A–12B). Basic rate taxpayers are entitled to a personal savings allowance (PSA) of £1,000 in 2017–18 and higher rate taxpayers to a PSA of £500 (see [**7.25**]). Interest received up to these thresholds is taxed at 0%. Savings income above the thresholds is taxed at the taxpayers' marginal tax rate (20%, 40% or 45%). There is also a starting rate for savings of 0% with a £5,000 limit in 2017–18 (s 12) (see [**7.26**]). Dividend income is tax-free up to a limit of £5,000 in 2017–18. Where dividends exceed this threshold, the tax rates are 7.5% for basic rate taxpayers, 32.5% for higher rate taxpayers and 38.1% for individuals paying additional rate tax (s 8 and s 13A) (see [**7.27**]). There are also two trust tax rates (s 9). In 2017–18 the trust rate is 45% and trust dividends are taxed at the dividend trust rate of 38.1% (s 9) (see [**16.21**]). [**7.2**]

The basic and higher tax rates are applied to bands of income determined by reference to the basic rate limit, whilst the additional tax rate of tax is charged on income over a higher rate limit (s 10) (see [**7.120**]). The 0% starting rate for savings applies where the £5,000 limit is not exhausted by non-savings income (s 12) (see [**7.26**]). The legislation prescribes which source of income is liable at the highest rate. Investment income, and in particular dividend income, is taxable as the top slice (s 16). [**7.3**]

3 Stages of the income tax calculation

The following steps are involved in calculating the taxpayer's income and in working out their annual income tax liability (s 23):

Step 1 Identify the individual sources of income liable to income tax for the tax year under ITEPA 2003, ITTOIA 2005 and ITA 2007. The sum of these components constitutes the taxpayer's 'total income'.

Step 2 From the total in Step 1 deduct any relief due to the taxpayer for the allowable payments listed in s 24. These include loss relief, and certain interest and annual payments. The sum left at the end of this step is the taxpayer's 'net income'. The maximum relief that can be deducted at this step is limited to the greater of £50,000 or 25% of the individual's 'adjusted total income' for the tax year (s 24A) (see [**7.42**]).

Step 3 From the total in Step 2 deduct any personal reliefs which the taxpayer is entitled to under Part 3 Chapter 2 (personal allowances and blind person's allowance).

Step 4 For each of the components left after Step 3, calculate income tax at the applicable rates described in [**7.2**] and [**7.120**]. If the taxpayer is a trustee, special provisions apply.

Step 5 Add together the amounts of tax calculated at Step 4.

Step 6 From the tax calculated at Step 5 deduct any reductions due to the taxpayer under s 26 in so far as there is sufficient tax available to permit the deduction (see [**7.124**]). Possible reductions include that for older married couples and civil partners, the transferable tax allowance, qualifying maintenance payments, top slicing relief and relief attributable to investments in the enterprise investment scheme, seed enterprise investment scheme and venture capital trusts (as to which see **Chapter 15**).

Step 7 To the amount of any tax left after *Step 6* add on any additional tax liability which the taxpayer has under any provision listed in s 30 such as charges under certain gift aid and pension provisions (see [**7.125**]). The final result is the taxpayer's liability to income tax for the tax year.

The calculation does not deal with the tax actually paid by a taxpayer under PAYE or deducted at source on certain income such as trusts, investment trusts, some annuities, royalties and annual payments. The tax deducted is off-set against the total tax liability for the year to arrive at the amount of tax owed by the individual.

The above steps involve terms requiring explanation, and the various stages in the income tax calculation will now be considered in detail. The income tax liability due on the transactions listed in s 32 (withdrawal of certain reliefs etc) does not form part of the calculation (see [7.126]). [7.4]–[7.20]

II TOTAL INCOME (*STEP 1*)

1 Combining income from all sources

Total income consists of the taxpayer's income for a tax year (6 April to 5 April) from all sources, calculated according to the provisions under which it arises and after deducting expenses appropriate to the particular source of income. The provisions governing the taxation of employment income, pensions and social security payments are found in ITEPA 2003, whilst the tax treatment of self-employed and partnership profits, property, savings and investment, miscellaneous and exempt income are to be found in ITTOIA 2005. Special rules apply to interest (see [7.24]) and dividends (see [7.27]). [7.21]

2 Taxation of couples

Irrespective of a person's marital status (single, cohabiting, married or in a civil partnership) all taxpayers are taxed as separate individuals (see **Chapter 51**). Where property is jointly owned there is a presumption of equal entitlement in some circumstances with each individual taxed on 50% of the income. This presumption can be rebutted by a joint declaration of unequal beneficial ownership (ss 836–837; see [51.54]). In spite of there being a general principle of separate taxation, some overlap occurs in the affairs of married couples and civil partners in connection with the transferrable allowance (see [7.115]), the tax reduction for older married couples and civil partners (see [7.111]) and in connection with the higher income child benefit charge (see [7.125]). [7.22]

3 Earned and investment income

The distinction between earned and investment income is only relevant in a few situations, such as in calculating relevant UK earnings for pension purposes (FA 2004 s 189(2)). Earnings fall into two main categories:
(1) Any income charged to tax under ITEPA 2003 (employment, pension and social security income).
(2) Profits charged under ITTOIA 2005 Part 2 (income from a trade, profession or vocation) whether as an individual or as a partner.

The borderline between earned and unearned income is not always easy to draw. In *Koenigsberger v Mellor* (1993) the court held that earned income must be received because of 'personal exertions' (see also *Northend v White, Leonard and Corbin Greener* (1975) and *Bucks v Bowers* (1970)). Generally, income from a trade, profession or vocation is earned income, whereas income from property, interest, trusts and foreign securities such as dividends and dividends from UK companies constitutes investment income. Rent from 'furnished holiday lettings' in the UK and EEA is specifically treated as earned income (see **[12.61]**).

Consider the case of a company director who is also the controlling shareholder where there may be a choice between receiving a salary (earned income) and dividends (unearned income). There will be income tax implications according to whether the director receives employment income or dividends (see **[7.2]**) as well as consequences for pension contributions and National Insurance. The General Anti-Avoidance Rule (GAAR) should be borne in mind if there is a tax avoidance motive in selecting one type of income over another (see **[3.77]** ff). **[7.23]**

4 Savings income

a) *Interest*

Until 2015–16, interest paid to individuals by building societies, banks and other deposit-takers was paid net of basic rate income tax (20%). Non-taxpayers and those liable to tax at the starting rate for savings (see **[7.26]**) were entitled to recover this tax on submitting the appropriate claim, whilst higher and additional rate taxpayers had to pay extra tax of the difference between their marginal tax rate (40% or 45%) and the 20% income tax deducted at source. From 2016–17 alongside the introduction of the PSA (see **[7.25]**), banks, building societies and NS&I pay interest without the deduction of tax. For 2016–17, basic rate tax was still deducted at source from authorised investment funds, investment trusts and peer-to-peer loans but this also ceased from 6 April 2017 (FA 2017 s 11 and Sch 5). Where a taxpayer receives interest net of tax, the income has to be grossed up so that the full amount of income is included in the tax calculation. The tax deducted is then off-set against the taxpayer's total tax liability for the year. Grossing up involves multiplying the net interest by 100 and dividing the result by100-R where R is the rate of tax withheld from the interest (eg where tax of 20% is deducted at source and the net interest is £20 × 100/80 = £25)). **[7.24]**

b) *Personal savings allowance and the savings nil rate*

From 2016–2017 where an individual receives bank or building society interest in excess of their personal allowance (see **[7.101]**) or they do not qualify for the starting rate for savings (see **[7.26]**), a savings nil rate of 0% applies to savings income up to the amount of their PSA (ss 12A–12B). Basic rate taxpayers receive a PSA of £1,000 and higher rate taxpayers an allowance of £500. Additional tax taxpayers do not receive an allowance. This means that small amounts of interest paid to basic and higher rate taxpayers are tax-free whilst additional rate taxpayers are taxed on all their savings income. Where an individual's interest exceeds their PSA, the income is taxed at their marginal tax rate (ss 6 and 10). For the purpose of calculating the taxpayer's marginal tax rate, savings income is treated as the highest part of a taxpayer's income but ranking below dividend income where the taxpayer has both sources of income (s 16). **[7.25]**

EXAMPLE 7.1

Jasmine, a basic rate taxpayer, receives a salary of £21,000 in 2017–18. She has £19,000 in a savings account with a building society and receives interest (gross) of £700 in 2017–18. Jasmine is a basic rate taxpayer so she is entitled to a PSA of £1,000. As her interest is less than the PSA it is taxed at the savings nil rate (0%) and Jasmine owes no tax on the building society interest.

If Jasmine was a higher rate taxpayer the tax charged on her interest would be £80 in 2017–18 (40% of the £200 received in excess of the PSA of £500).

If Jasmine was an additional rate taxpayer all of the £700 of interest would be taxed at 45% giving her a tax liability of £315.

c) *Starting rate for savings*

Some lower income taxpayers can receive up to £5,000 of interest tax-free. Where an individual's non-savings income (such as employment income, self-employed or partnership profits) is less than the starting rate for savings limit (£5,000 in 2016–17 and 2017–18), up to £5,000 of their savings income is taxed at the 0% starting rate for savings (ss 7 and 12). Savings income in excess of £5,000 is taxed at the taxpayer's marginal tax rate taking interest as the highest part of their income apart from dividends (s 16). Where a taxpayer is eligible for the starting rate for savings, there is no need to apply the PSA or the savings nil rate described at **[7.25]**. If a taxpayer's non-savings income (employed, self-employed etc) exceeds the starting rate for savings limit, the PSA and the savings nil rate apply with any excess income being taxed at the taxpayer's marginal tax rate. **[7.26]**

EXAMPLE 7.2

In 2017–18 the following people are each entitled to the basic personal allowance of £11,500 (see **[7.120]**).
- Lulu has employment income of £21,000. The starting rate of income tax does not affect her because it only applies to savings income.
- Mario's only source of income is building society interest of £21,500. His taxable income after deducting his personal allowance is £10,000. The first £5,000 of his taxable income is taxed at the starting rate for savings (0%) and the rest is taxed at the basic rate (20%). His tax liability is £1,000 (£5,000 × 0% = £0 + £5,000 × 20% = £1,000).
- Nora has employment income of £21,500 and savings income of £3,000 giving her taxable income after deducting her personal allowance of £13,000. Since the personal allowance is first allocated against her employment income, Nora's taxable employment income is £10,000 (£21,500 – £11,500). This exceeds the starting rate for savings income threshold so none of her savings income is taxed at the nil rate. Nora is however entitled to a PSA of £1,000 (see **[7.25]**), which means that she is taxed on £2,000 of interest at 20% = £400.

- Oliver has employment income of £8,500 and bank interest of £13,000. His taxable income after deducting the personal allowance is £10,000. The personal allowance is first allocated against his employment income and then against his savings income. None of the employment income is taxable. £10,000 of the savings income is taxable. The first £5,000 of Oliver's savings income is taxed at the starting rate for savings (0%) and the rest is taxed at the basic rate (20%). His tax liability is £1,000 (£5,000 × 0% = £0 + £5,000 × 20% = £1,000).
- Pandora has employment income of £11,700 and bank interest of £4,900. Her taxable income after deducting the personal allowance is £5,100. The personal allowance is first allocated against Pandora's employment income and then against her savings income. £200 of her employment income is taxable at 20% = £40. Her non-savings income does not exceed the starting rate for savings income band so she is eligible for the 0% starting rate for savings. £200 from the employment income is taxable leaving £4,800 (£5,000 – £200) of her savings income taxable at the nil rate. The remaining £100 of the savings income is taxed at the 20% basic rate giving a tax liability on this portion of her income of £20. Pandora's total tax liability is therefore £60 (£40 + £20).

5 Dividend income

Until 5 April 2016 dividends and other company distributions were paid with a tax credit of 10%. The credit was treated as satisfying the taxpayer's basic rate liability so that no further tax was charged unless the taxpayer was a higher or additional rate taxpayer (ss 13, 14 and ITTOIA 2005 s 397). The tax credit was, however, irrecoverable and could not be refunded to non-taxpayers or taxpayers paying tax at the starting rate for savings.

The tax regime for dividend income changed significantly on 6 April 2016. From 2016–17 the first £5,000 of dividend income is taxed at the dividend nil rate, effectively giving all individuals up to £5,000 of dividend income tax free (s 13A). Where dividend income exceeds the £5,000 allowance the rates of tax in 2016–17 and 2017–18 are: 7.5% (the dividend basic rate); 32.5% (the dividend higher rate); and 38.1% (the dividend additional rate) (see **[7.120]**). When calculating a taxpayer's marginal tax rate, dividend income is treated as the highest part of their income (s 16). It was announced at the Spring 2017 Budget that the dividend nil rate band will be reduced to £2,000 from April 2018. This change was not, however included in the much-reduced Finance Act 2017, which received Royal Assent on 27 April 2017.

[7.27]–[7.39]

EXAMPLE 7.3

In 2017–18 Ali has self-employed profits of £80,000 and also receives dividend income of £4,200. The income comes within the limit for the dividend nil rate (£5,000 in 2017–18), and as a result he owes no tax on his dividend income.

If Ali's dividends were £7,200 in 2017–18, £5,000 of the dividend income would be taxed at 0%. The remaining £2,200 of the dividends would be taxed at 32.5% as Ali is a higher rate taxpayer. In this situation Ali would have a tax liability on this source of income of £715 (£2,200 × 32.5%).

III NET INCOME (*STEP 2*)

1 **General**

Allowable payments are amounts that fall to be deducted from an individual's total income before personal reliefs so as to arrive at a taxpayer's net income. After relief is given at *Step 2*, the individual deducts personal allowances from his net income at *Step 3* before calculating his income tax liability at *Steps 4 and 5*.

Allowable payments may be deducted in the way which results in the biggest reduction of the taxpayer's income tax liability (s 25(2)), subject to specific provisions in the legislation which restrict the way in which relief is to be given, for example with regard to loss relief (s 25(3)) (see **[7.81]**). A deduction can only be made to eliminate a taxpayer's total income, so the extent of the relief depends on there being sufficient income available (s 25(4)). Any amount that is unabsorbed receives no tax relief and cannot be carried forward to a future year. [7.40]

2 **Deductible reliefs**

The sums deductible at *Step 2* are set out in s 24 and include:
- loss reliefs (from trades, property, employments, shares and securities);
- relief for irrecoverable peer-to-peer loans (see **[7.92]**–**[7.100]**);
- gifts of shares, securities and real estate to charities;
- payments to trade unions or police organisations;
- pension payments;
- post-cessation reliefs;
- interest payments;
- annual payments;
- manufactured interest and dividends and special leasing of plant and machinery. [7.41]

a) *Restriction on deductible reliefs*

Some of the reliefs deductible at *Step 2* are restricted to 25% of an individual's 'adjusted total income' or £50,000 whichever is the greater figure (s 24A). 'Adjusted total income' is the taxpayer's total income adjusted for payroll giving and pensions.

The restricted reliefs are: trading losses (s 64) and (s 72), post-cessation reliefs (s 96) and (s 125), property loss relief (s 120), qualifying loan interest (ss 383–412), employment loss relief (s 128), deduction for liabilities by former employees (ITEPA 2003 s 555), share loss relief on non-EIS/SEIS shares (Part 4 Chapter 6) and losses on deeply discounted securities (ITTOIA 2005 s 446 and s 454(4)). When calculating the restricted reliefs, business premises renovation allowances and relief for overlap profits are excluded.
[7.42]

3 **Calculation**

The following example illustrates the computational aspects involved in *Step 2*. [7.43]

EXAMPLE 7.4

Viola a solicitor has total income of £232,000 in 2017–18. She pays interest of £60,000 a year on a loan to purchase her partnership share (s 398) (see [**7.48**]).

The £60,000 loan interest is restricted to the greater of £58,000 (£232,000 × 25%) and £50,000 (s 24A).

Viola's net income to be carried through to *Step 3* is:

	£
Step 1 – Total income	232,000
Step 2 – Deduct allowable payment – loan interest (s 398) restricted to 25% of total income (s 24A)	58,000
Net income	**£174,000**

From this sum, Viola may deduct her personal allowance at *Step 3* and she will be taxed on the balance at *Step 4*. £2,000 of the loan interest does not receive tax relief.

4 Certain interest payments

An individual obtains income tax relief for certain interest payments by deducting them from his total income at *Step 2*, except in the case of interest paid on a loan to purchase a life annuity prior to 9 March 1999 when relief is given as an income tax reduction at *Step 6* (see [**7.51**]). The maximum relief that can be deducted at *Step 2* is limited to the greater of £50,000 or 25% of the individual's 'adjusted total income' for the tax year (see [**7.42**]). Some interest payments are deductible in computing income from a particular source only (eg interest payments made for the purposes of a trade are deductible in computing the profits of that trade). Most interest payments, however, receive no tax relief including interest paid on loans to purchase a main residence. Ordinary bank overdraft, credit card interest, and hire-purchase interest payments, for example, also receive no relief (except, if appropriate, as a trading expense) (s 384(1)). This includes the transfer of an overdraft to a loan account: see *Lawson v Brooks* (1992) and *W Green v R & C Comrs* (2011).

The rules governing the deductibility of interest are complex (see Part 8). To be deductible the interest must be payable on a loan made for one of the specified purposes dealt with below. The character of the interest or the status of the lender is irrelevant. As a general rule, interest that is eligible for tax relief is paid gross. [**7.44**]

a) *Loans to buy an interest in a close company (s 392)*

An individual may obtain income tax relief for the interest paid on a loan to acquire ordinary share capital in a UK close trading company providing that it is not a close investment-holding company (s 393A), including from 6 April 2014, a company resident in an EEA state (s 392(4)). It has to be shown that the company exists wholly or mainly for the purpose of carrying on a trade: see *Lord v Tustain* (1993)). Tax relief is available for a loan raised to lend money to such a company so long as it is used wholly and exclusively for the business of the company (or of an associated company which is likewise a qualifying close company: see *JS Torkington v R & C Comrs* (2010)). Interest relief also applies to replacement loans.

To qualify for relief, the borrower has to show *either* that he is a shareholder and works for the greater part of his time in the management or conduct of the company (s 393) *or* that he controls more than 5% (a 'material interest') of the ordinary share capital (in the latter case the borrower need not work for the company) (s 394).To calculate whether the individual has the necessary material interest, shares of associates must generally be aggregated with his own shares. 'Associates' include an individual's relatives, partners, trustees of a settlement which he created, and trustees of a settlement holding shares for the benefit of that individual. However, shares in which the individual has an interest only under an employee benefit trust are not included in deciding whether he has a material interest in the company (s 395(2)).

To the extent that the borrower recovers any capital from the company during that time (eg by repayment of ordinary share capital), he is treated as having repaid the loan and the amount of interest available for relief is reduced accordingly (s 393(2)). Relief is not withdrawn if the company subsequently ceases to be close (see SP 3/78). It is not possible to obtain double tax relief, for example by using the loan to purchase shares qualifying for relief under EIS (Enterprise Investment Scheme) or by reinvesting gains in social enterprises (ss 392(3) and 392(3A)). [7.45]

EXAMPLE 7.5

Gatty Ltd is the family trading company of the Gatty family. Sam Freebie, a full-time working director owning no shares in the company, borrows £50,000 from his bank to subscribe for ordinary shares. He will own a 4% shareholding and tax relief is available on the interest he pays. If, however, Jack Floor, the caretaker of the company's factory, were to subscribe for a similar number of shares no relief will be available because he is not concerned in the management or conduct of the company.

b) *Loan to buy an interest in an employee-controlled company (s 396)*

Relief is available for interest payments on a loan taken out by an individual to acquire ordinary shares in an employee-controlled company (which must be a UK resident unquoted trading company, or from 6 April 2014 a company resident in an EEA state). An employee-controlled company is one where full-time employees own more than 50% of the ordinary share capital and voting power of the company. When an employee owns more than 10% of the issued share capital, the excess is treated as not being owned by a full-time employee. Other conditions for relief are that the shares must be acquired within 12 months of the company becoming employee-controlled and that the taxpayer or his or her spouse/civil partner must be full-time employees of the company from the time when the loan is applied to the date when interest is paid. Furthermore, in the year of assessment in which the interest is paid the company must either first become employee-controlled or be such a company for at least nine months. Accordingly, interest relief will be withdrawn when the company ceases to be employee-controlled. To the extent that the individual recovers any capital from the company, the same rule operates as for close companies and partnerships. [7.46]

c) *Loan to invest in a co-operative (s 401)*

Relief is available for interest payments made on a loan to acquire an interest in a co-operative, or to be used wholly and exclusively for the business of that body or a subsidiary. A co-operative is defined as a common ownership enterprise or a co-operative enterprise within the meaning of the Industrial Common Ownership Act 1976 s 2. Relief is available only if the individual shows that from the application of the loan to the payment of the interest he has worked for the greater part of his time as an employee in that co-operative or in a subsidiary thereof. [7.47]

d) *Loan to invest in a partnership (s 398)*

Interest relief is available to an individual on a loan used to purchase a share in a partnership or to contribute capital or make a loan to the partnership, if it is used wholly and exclusively for the business purposes of the partnership and provided that cash accounting (see **[10.73]**) is not used (s 384B(2)(b)). Relief is available only if, from the application of the loan to the payment of interest, the individual has been a member of the partnership (otherwise than as a limited partner or a partner in an investment LLP) and has not recovered any capital from the partnership. If the partnership is a film partnership as described in s 400, only 40% of the interest which would otherwise be eligible for relief is available as a deduction if a partner's income share is small in relation to their capital contribution.

The payment of interest on borrowings to finance the business can be relieved in one of two ways: either under s 398 as described or, alternatively, as a deduction in the partnership accounts. The s 398 deduction has the attraction of enabling the interest to be set against the total income of the individual rather than against the profits of the firm only. In some circumstances the interest relief may be restricted (see **[7.42]**). From 6 April 2017 interest paid on loans to fund residential property to let only receives relief at the basic rate of tax (20%) limiting the tax relief that landlords with higher incomes can receive (ITTOIA 2005 s 272A). The restriction is being phased in over a four-year period commencing in 2017–18 (s 399A) (see **[12.45]** for details). For the position of LLPs, see **[45.12]**.

Where a partnership is subsequently incorporated into a close company and the loan remains outstanding, relief continues to be available so long as relief would be available under the close company provisions considered at **[7.45]** if the loan were a new loan taken out on incorporation. [7.48]

e) *Loan to purchase plant or machinery (ss 388 and 390)*

Where a partner borrows money to purchase a car or other items of machinery or plant for which capital allowances are available, he can claim interest relief on that loan for up to three years after the end of the tax year when the debt was incurred providing that cash accounting (see **[10.73]**) is not used (s 384B(2)(a)). (Note that for a sole trader interest on loans to purchase plant and machinery is a deductible business expense.)

An employee can claim interest relief on a loan to purchase plant and machinery necessarily provided for use in the performance of the duties of their employment (CAA 2001 s 36). For example, a violinist employed by an orchestra could claim interest relief on a loan to purchase a violin. **[7.49]**

f) *Loan to pay inheritance tax (s 403)*

Personal representatives are eligible for interest relief on a loan used by them to pay IHT attributable to personal property situated in the UK to which the deceased was beneficially entitled and which has vested in them. The relief is limited to a 12-month period. **[7.50]**

g) *Loan to purchase a life annuity (TA 1988 s 353(1A) and s 365)*

Interest relief is available on loans taken out before 9 March 1999 not exceeding £30,000 by a person aged 65 or over in order to purchase an annuity on his life provided that at least nine-tenths of the loan proceeds are used to buy the annuity and that the annuity is secured on land in the UK (or Republic of Ireland) in which he has an interest and uses as his only or main residence at the time when the interest is paid. Relief is not lost if, after 27 July 1999, the taxpayer ceases to occupy the property as his only or main residence provided it was his only or main residence on 9 March 1999. Relief is given on a replacement loan where at least 90% of the new loan repays the old loan and the above conditions are satisfied. Tax relief is available at 23%, however the interest paid does not reduce the taxpayer's income. Instead relief is given by way of an income tax reduction (see *Step 6* below).
[7.51]–[7.80]

5 Losses

a) *Property losses*

As indicated at **[7.40]**, some losses are deductible only in computing profits from the same source. **[7.81]**

EXAMPLE 7.6

Anita receives a salary as a lecturer (employment income) of £50,000 pa. She also owns a house which she rents to tenants. In the current tax year her allowable expenses on the property exceeded her rental income by £1,000. Her total and net income for the current year are:

	£
Employment income	50,000
Property income (loss £1,000)	Nil
Total and Net income	£50,000

Anita cannot deduct her £1,000 loss on her property income (ITTOIA 2005 Part 3) from her income from any other source. All she can do is carry the loss forward to a subsequent year and deduct it from her property income of that year (s 118).

Thus, if in the following year her rental income exceeds her allowable expenses by £12,000, Anita's total and net income are as follows:

	£	£
Employment income		50,000
Property income: profit	12,000	
		12,000
Total income (*Step 1*)		62,000
Less: loss brought forward	1,000	
		–1,000
Net income (*Step 2*)		£61,000

b) *Trading losses deducted from general income*

Where the individual makes a loss in his trade, profession or vocation, however, he may choose to deduct that loss from his total income from all sources before deducting personal reliefs (see s 64). The danger with claiming this loss relief is that it may so reduce total income that personal allowances are unused. [7.82]

There are various restrictions on the use of trading losses under s 64 including where the cash basis of accounting (see [10.73]) is used (see ss 66–69, s 74ZA, s 74A, s 74E and s 115). As described at [7.42] the use of trading losses against other income is also restricted to 25% of an individual's 'adjusted total income' or £50,000 whichever is the greater (s 24A). [7.83]–[7.90]

EXAMPLE 7.7

Andrew is a barrister and a part-time lecturer (employment income) with a salary for 2017–18 of £30,000 pa. In 2017–18 he also makes a loss in his first year at the Bar of £20,000 which he chooses to deduct from his total income under s 64. His income tax calculation is as follows:

	£
Employment income	30,000
Trading income (loss £20,000)	Nil
Total income (*Step 1*)	30,000
Less: loss (s 64)	–20,000
Net income (*Step 2*)	£10,000

The loss is relieved in full and not restricted because it is less than £50,000 (see [7.42]). However, as Andrew has only £10,000 income from which he can deduct his personal reliefs, £1,500 of his personal allowance (£11,500 in 2017–18) will be wasted (see [7.101]). The detailed loss relief rules and the variety of potential claims are set out in **Chapter 11**. [7.91]

6 Relief for irrecoverable peer-to-peer loans

Peer-to-peer loans (P2P) are web-based intermediary services that connect investors with money to lend to individuals or small businesses who need to borrow money. The lender invests a lump sum which in turn is lent in smaller sub-loans to a number of borrowers. This diversification spreads the risk of default across a number of loans. P2P loans are regulated by the Financial Conduct Authority. From 6 April 2015 losses from P2P loans that become irrecoverable can be offset against interest received subject to making a claim. If no claim is made the deficit may be treated as a capital loss. From 6 April 2016 losses from irrecoverable loans will automatically be relieved against P2P interest received through the same platform and will not be eligible for relief as a capital loss (ss 412A–412J). Sideways and carry forward relief may be claimed against P2P loans held through other platforms in certain circumstances. **[7.92]–[7.100]**

IV PERSONAL RELIEFS (*STEP 3 OR STEP 6*)

1 General

Individuals resident in the UK (and currently some non-residents, see s 56(3) and **[18.71]**) can deduct personal reliefs from their net income at *Step 3* or *Step 6*. The availability of these reliefs depends on the taxpayer's personal circumstances and in some cases the amount of their income (see **[7.101]–[7.102]**). The personal allowance and blind person's allowance operate by way of deduction from net income at *Step 3*. The tax reduction for married couples and civil partners is given by subtracting 10% of the allowance from the individual's total tax liability at *Step 6* (see **[7.111]–[7.112]**). The deduction for the transferable tax allowance for married couples and civil partners, also given at *Step 6*, is 20% of the allowance (see **[7.115]–[7.119]**). Blind person's allowance and the tax reduction and transferable tax allowance for married couples and civil partners have to be claimed. Taxpayers using the remittance basis of tax do not have automatic entitlement to personal reliefs (see **[18.47]**). If personal allowances exceed the taxpayer's total income, the surplus is unused and cannot be carried forward for use in future years.

A summary of the personal reliefs available for 2017–18 is set out below. Reliefs (marked with a (●)) are linked to increases in the Consumer Prices Index (CPI) between September preceding the year of assessment and the previous September (s 57) but automatic indexation of the reliefs is frequently overridden in the Finance Act.

- ● Personal allowance[1]   £11,500
- ● Blind person's allowance   £2,320
- ● Transferable tax allowance for married couples and civil partners[2]   £1,150
- ● Tax reduction for married couples and civil partners (born before 6 April 1935)[3,4]   £8,445

- Tax reduction for married couples and civil   £3,260
  partners born before 6 April 1935 (minimum amount)[4]
- Income limit for the personal allowance   £100,000
- Income limit for the tax reduction for older   £28,000
  married couples and civil partners

[1]   Reduced if the taxpayer's income exceeds the income limit for the personal allowance.
[2]   Tax reduced by 20% of the allowance.
[3]   Reduced if the taxpayer's income exceeds the income limit for the tax reduction for older married couples and civil partners.
[4]   Tax reduction restricted to 10%.

[7.101]–[7.102]

2 The reliefs given at Step 3

a) *Personal allowance (s 35)*

The personal allowance for individuals in 2017–18 is £11,500. The personal allowance is available to all taxpayers resident in the UK irrespective of their age, including minor children. It can also be claimed by some non-residents. The allowance can be set against any form of income but any surplus is wasted since it cannot be used in any other tax year. The personal allowance is withdrawn from taxpayers with 'adjusted net income' (see [**7.104**]) above £100,000 at the rate of £1 for every £2 above the income limit until no allowance remains. A taxpayer with income of £123,000 in 2017–18 therefore receives no personal allowance. Basic rate taxpayers can elect to transfer 10% of their personal allowance to their spouse or civil partner (see [**7.115**]).

[7.103]–[7.104]

b) *Blind person's allowance (s 38)*

A taxpayer who is a registered with their local council as a blind or severely sight-impaired person for the whole or part of the year of assessment receives an additional relief of £2,320 for 2017–18. If a husband and wife or civil partners, are both registered they can each claim the allowance. A blind or severely sight-impaired person who is married or in a civil partnership may transfer any surplus allowance to their spouse or civil partner irrespective of whether the spouse or civil partner is themselves blind or severely sight impaired (s 39).   [7.105]–[7.110]

3 The personal reliefs given at Step 6

a) *Tax reduction for older married couples and civil partners (ss 45 and 46)*

A tax reduction can be claimed by married couples, and from 5 December 2005 registered civil partners, provided one party was born before 6 April 1935. Different rules apply to pre-5 December 2005 marriages (s 45) and to post-5 December 2005 marriages and civil partnerships (s 46). The way in which relief is given and how it is divided and can be transferred between the couple is considered at [**51.23**]. For these purposes a couple are treated as living together unless they are separated under a court order, written deed, or are in fact separated in such circumstances that the separation is likely to be permanent (s 1011). Accordingly, this allowance cannot be claimed by a spouse or civil partner who, though separated from his or her spouse or civil partner, continues to maintain them: see further [52.2]. The availability of relief for married couples was confirmed in a case where a man had two wives, see *Nabi v Heaton* (1983). In *Rignell v Andrews* (1990), however, a taxpayer who had lived with the same woman for 11 years and who treated her as his common law wife was not entitled to the allowance as he was not married.

The level of the tax reduction depends on the age of the older spouse/civil partner in the relevant tax year. In 2017–18 it is 10% of £8,445 where the older spouse/civil partner was born before 6 April 1935. Where the claimant's 'adjusted net income' exceeds £28,000 in 2017–18 the tax reduction is reduced by half of the difference between the taxpayer's 'adjusted net income' and the income limit (ie a reduction of £1 of allowance for every £2 of income above £28,000). 'Adjusted net income' is defined in s 58 as follows: net income at *Step 2* is adjusted by deducting gross gift aid payments and pension contributions and by adding back relief already given in the calculation for contributions to trade unions or police organisations. In such cases the tax reduction is restricted by reference to the husband's total income (for pre-5 December 2005 marriages) or the taxpayer with the highest total income (for post-5 December 2005 marriages and civil partnerships). At worst, the restriction will leave the couple with an allowance of £3,260. It should be noted that a couple married before 5 December 2005 can elect to be taxed as if they were married after 5 December 2005 (s 44). Finally, it should be borne in mind that married couples and civil partners cannot transfer any unused part of their income limits to each other. **[7.111]–[7.112]**

EXAMPLE 7.8

(1) Fred was born on 10 July 1940; his partner, Wilma, was born on 20 March 1935. In 2017–18 Fred has income of £18,000; Wilma has an income of £28,000.
  (a) Fred and Wilma are both entitled to a personal allowance of £11,500.
  (b) As the couple are not married they are not entitled to the married couples and civil partners' tax reduction, even though they meet the age criteria.
(2) In 2017–18 Robert who was born on 3 June 1934 has an income of £105,000; his wife, Alison, was born on 26 August 1939 and has an income of £5,500.
  (a) Alison will be entitled to a personal allowance of £11,500 of which £6,000 will be wasted.
  (b) Robert's personal allowance of £11,500 will be reduced by £2,500 to £9,000 because his income of £105,000 exceeds the £100,000 threshold for the personal allowance by £5,000. The married couple's allowance of £8,445 will be reduced to £3,260 because Robert's income also exceeds the £28,000 income threshold for older taxpayers.

[7.113]–[7.114]

b) *Transferable tax allowance for married couples and civil partners (ss 55A–55E)*

Taxpayers who are married or in a civil partnership can elect to transfer a fixed part of their personal allowance to their spouse or civil partner provided that certain conditions are met (s 55B). Both parties must be liable to pay tax below the higher rates (in other words they must have income of less than £45,000 in 2017–18), they must be UK resident (s 56) and neither party can claim the tax reduction for older married couples and civil partners; see [**7.111**]. The transferable sum for 2017–18 is £1,150 (10% of the personal allowance). [**7.115**]–[**7.116**]

EXAMPLE 7.9

In 2017–18 Jake who was born on 5 October 1965 has income of £8,500. His civil partner, Liam, who was born on 17 April 1957, has income of £28,000.
(a) Jake is entitled to a personal allowance of £11,500 but as his taxable income is only £8,500 he will waste £3,000 of the allowance unless he elects to reduce his allowance by £1,150 and transfers it to Liam. His personal allowance then becomes £10,350 resulting in only £1,850 of the allowance being wasted.
(b) Liam is also entitled to a personal allowance of £11,500. As he is a basic rate taxpayer he can claim a tax reduction of £1,150 for the transferable tax allowance at *Step 6* of the tax calculation saving him tax of £230 (£1,150 × 20%). [**7.117**]–[**7.119**]

V METHOD OF CHARGING TAXABLE INCOME (*STEPS 4 AND 5*)

1 Rates of tax

Income tax is charged on an individual's taxable income after deducting allowable payments at *Step 2* and personal reliefs at *Step 3*. For 2017–18 the following tax rates apply to earned income and pensions:

	Income band
On the first £33,500 at 20% (basic rate)	£1–£33,500
Between £33,501 and £150,000 at 40% (higher rate)	£33,501–£150,000
On the remainder at 45% (additional rate)	Excess over £150,000

For 2017–18 the following tax rates apply to non-dividend savings income in excess of the savings allowance (see [**7.25**]):

	Income band
On the first £5,000 at 0% (where the starting rate for savings applies, see [**7.26**])	£1–£5,000
On the next £28,500 at the basic rate of 20% (where the starting rate for savings applies, see [**7.26**])	£5,001–£28,500
On the first £33,500 at the basic rate of 20% (where no starting rate for savings applies)	£1–£33,500
Between £33,501 and £150,000 at the higher rate of 40%	£33,501–£150,000
On the remainder at the additional rate of 45%	Excess over £150,000

In accordance with Spring Budget 2017 announcements, it was expected that the dividend allowance would be reduced to £2,000 from April 2018. However, no provision was made in the much-reduced version of Finance Act 2017, which received Royal Assent on 27 April 2017. This measure may be included in a future Finance Bill, with the effective date to be confirmed.

From 2016–17 (remaining unchanged for 2017–18) a PSA of £1,000 applies to basic rate taxpayers and higher rate taxpayers receive an allowance of £500. Additional rate taxpayers do not receive an allowance. Savings income below the allowance suffers no tax as it is charged at the savings nil rate (0%). Savings income in excess of the allowance is taxed at the taxpayer's marginal tax rate (20%, 40% or 45%), see **[7.25]**.

From 2016–17 onwards a £5,000 dividend allowance applies to all taxpayers (see **[7.27]**). For 2017–18, where dividend income exceeds the allowance, the rates of tax are as shown in the following table:

	Income band
On the first £33,500 at 7.5% (dividend ordinary rate)	£1–£33,500
On the next £116,500 at 32.5% (dividend upper rate)	£33,500–£150,000
On the remainder at 38.1% (dividend additional rate)	Excess over £150,000

Increases in the rate bands are usually linked to the increase in the Consumer Prices Index (CPI) between the September before the year of assessment and the previous September. The indexed rises are, however, subject to a negative resolution of Parliament (ie they occur 'unless Parliament otherwise determines'; s 21). **[7.120]**

Where payments are made by the taxpayer under deduction of tax at source (eg gifts to charities under Gift Aid) those payments are added back to the taxpayer's taxable income for basic rate tax purposes, thereby effectively extending the basic rate band by increasing the figure chargeable to basic rate tax above £33,500 (2017–18). Where payments are received by the taxpayer after deduction at source (generally pre-6 April 2016), the tax due from the payee will be reduced by the tax already paid on his behalf by the payer.
[7.121]

EXAMPLE 7.10

Brian has a net income for 2017–18 of £51,500. He makes gross Gift Aid payments to charity of £3,000 (£2,400 net of 20% tax relief) and is entitled to a personal allowance of £11,500. His income tax calculation is as follows:

	£
Net income (*Step 2*)	51,500
Less: personal reliefs (*Step 3*)	11,500
Taxable income	£40,000
Tax payable:	£
First £33,500 + £3,000 = £36,500 at 20%	7,300
Balance of £3,500 at 40%	1,400
Tax liability (*Steps 4 and 5*)	£8,700

2 Dates for payment of tax

The due date for the payment of income tax is currently 31 January following the year of assessment. Self-employed individuals, partners and landlords usually pay tax in two interim payments falling due on 31 January in the year of assessment and 31 July immediately following that year (TMA 1970 ss 59A–59B). HMRC are introducing digital tax accounts and self-employed people, partners and landlords keeping digital records and providing HMRC with regular updates, will be able to pay their tax on a 'pay-as-you-go' basis so that they can arrange their tax payments to suit their businesses and cash flow.

Tax on employment earnings, pension and social security income is collected under the PAYE system on a current year basis (ITEPA 2003). If the taxpayer's only source of income is from employment, the correct amount of tax can usually be collected under this system necessitating no further adjustment. Where the taxpayer has other sources of income, either too much or too little tax may be deducted, giving rise to the need for a subsequent adjustment. [7.122]

3 Specimen income tax calculation

Applying the steps listed at [7.1] it is now possible to calculate an individual's income tax liability for a tax year. [7.123]

EXAMPLE 7.11

Rory has the following income for 2017–18:

		£
(i)	Pensions (employment, pensions and social security income)	32,500
(ii)	Author (trading income)	5,000
(iii)	Rents from houses (property income)	14,000
(iv)	Dividends from Smarttec Ltd	11,000

Rory was born on 1 October 1934. He is married to Lydia who was born on 10 April 1945. He makes a gift of shares valued at £1,000 to the RSPCA (a registered charity).

	£
Employment, pensions and social security income [1]	32,500
Trading income	5,000
Property income	14,000
Savings and investment income [2]	6,000
Step 1: Total income from all sources	57,500
Step 2: Deduct allowable payment – shares to RSPCA	1,000
Step 2: Net income	56,500
Step 3: Deduct personal reliefs:	
Personal allowance	11,500
Step 3: Taxable income	£45,000

		£
Tax chargeable at *Step 4*:		
	First £33,500 at 20%	6,700
	Balance of £5,500 at 40%	2,200
	£6,000 at 32.5% [2]	1,950
	Step 5: Tax on £45,000	10,850
Step 6: Deduct 10% of additional allowance (£3,260) [3]		(326)
Step 7: Income tax liability for the tax year [1]		£10,524

Notes:
(1)   Tax would have been deducted at source under the PAYE system in respect of the pensions. Credit will be given for this tax, thereby affecting the actual tax due from Rory by self-assessment. Nevertheless, Rory is actually liable (however it is collected) for tax of £10,828 in 2017–18.
(2)   The first £5,000 of Rory's dividend income is covered by the dividend allowance leaving £6,000 (£11,000 – £5,000) liable to tax at the dividend upper rate of 32.5%.
(3)   The tax reduction for married couples and civil partners is restricted as Rory's income exceeds £28,000. Relief is given at the 10% rate: hence it is deducted at *Step 6*.

4   Other tax reductions (Step 6)

The tax reduction given to older married couples and civil partners is not the only reduction in an individual's tax liability to be given at *Step 6*. The transferable tax allowance is deducted at this stage (see **[7.115]**). The reductions detailed in s 26 are also deducted at *Step 6*. These include Enterprise Investment Scheme (EIS) relief, Seed Enterprise Investment Scheme (SEIS) relief, relief for social investments, Venture Capital Trust (VCT) relief, Community Investment Scheme Relief (CISR), relief for non-deductible interest on a loan to invest in a partnership with residential property business, relief for qualifying maintenance payments, the spreading of patent royalty receipts, relief for interest on a loan to buy a life annuity (see **[7.51]**), relief for a property business for the non-deductible costs of a dwelling-related loan, and top slicing relief. Relief is given in the way which results in the greatest tax reduction for the individual (s 27). Tax relief on investments in the EIS, SEIS and in VCTs is considered in **Chapter 15**. **[7.124]**

5   Additional tax liabilities (Step 7)

The final stage in the calculation of an individual's income tax liability is to add to the result of *Step 6* any additional amount of tax to which the taxpayer is liable under s 30. These include the gift aid charge to tax, various liabilities arising under the pension's legislation such as the unauthorised payments charge, lifetime allowance charge and annual allowance charge plus the high income child benefit charge. The high income child benefit charge applies to taxpayers who receive child benefit for at least one week per tax year where their adjusted net income for the tax year exceeds £50,000, and to those with income above £50,000 whose partner receives child benefit (ITEPA 2003 s 681B). **[7.125]**

6 Liabilities not dealt with in the calculation

A number of tax liabilities fall to be taxed outside the individual's tax calculation. These are scheduled in s 32 and include withdrawal of relief for EIS, SEIS, VCT, social investments, CISR and capital allowances, and transactions in securities. [7.126]

7 Exemptions from income tax

There are a number of exemptions from income tax in the form of exempt organisations and exempt income. [7.127]

a) *Exempt organisations*

The Crown is not within the tax legislation and charities are generally exempt from income tax in respect of:
(1) income from land and investment income provided that it is applied for charitable purposes only; and
(2) trading profits applied purely for charitable purposes where either the trade is part of the main purpose of the charity, or the work is carried out mainly by the beneficiaries (Part 10 and CTA 2010 ss 478–489).

Other exempt organisations include the National Heritage Memorial Fund, Historic Buildings and Monuments Commission for England and Community Amateur Sports Clubs (s 430 and CTA 2010 s 468, ss 475–476, s 490 and ss 648–671). [7.128]

b) *Exempt income*

Exempt income includes certain employment-related payments to members of parliament, elected representatives, government minsters and members of local authorities; members of the armed forces; consular officials, foreign agents and visiting forces; crown employees; detached national experts and live-in carers (ITEPA 2003 Part 4). Payments to non-resident accredited competitors in various sporting events are also exempt. [7.129]

A wide-range of earnings-only exemptions apply to employees under ITEPA 2003 Part 4 (ss 227–326B) including certain payments for: mileage, parking, travel, personal incidental overnight expenses, education, training and advice, recreation and health, childcare, trivial benefits costing less than £50, phone and office costs, removal expenses and living accommodation in some circumstances. More significant employment-related exemptions are statutory redundancy (ITEPA 2003 s 309), compensation for loss of office to the extent that the payments do not exceed £30,000 (ITEPA 2003 s 403) and the first £100,000 of sporting testimonials for professional sports people subject to conditions (s 306B). Pensions and other payments under German, Austrian or Dutch law for the victims of persecution (ITEPA 2003 ss 642–642A) are exempt and so are some social security benefits (ITEPA 2003 s 677 and Table B). [7.130]

Other items that are exempt from income tax are set out in ITTOIA 2005 Part 6, including:
(a) National Savings and Ulster Savings Certificates (ITTOIA 2005 ss 692–693);
(b) income and individual investment funds, including Individual Savings Accounts (ISAs) (ITTOIA 2005 ss 694–701);
(c) SAYE interest (ITTOIA 2005 ss 702–708);
(d) venture capital trust dividends (ITTOIA 2005 ss 709–712);
(e) income from FOTRA securities (ITTOIA 2005 ss 713–716);
(f) purchased life annuity payments and immediate needs annuities (ITTOIA 2005 ss 717–726);
(g) certain annual payments including foreign maintenance (ITTOIA 2005 ss 727–730);
(h) periodical payments for personal injury and damages including compensation and payment from trusts (ITTOIA 2005 ss 731–734);
(i) benefits paid under sickness and unemployment insurance policies (ITTOIA 2005 ss 735–743);
(j) payments to adopters and other carers by local authorities and adoption agencies (ITTOIA 2005 ss 744–747);
(k) repayment supplement and interest on tax overpaid (ITTOIA 2005 ss 749-749A and 777);
(l) interest on damages for personal injury (ITTOIA 2005 s 751);
(m) interest under employees' share schemes (ITTOIA 2005 s 752);
(n) interest on repayment of student loans (ITTOIA 2005 s 753);
(o) interest on certain unpaid pension contributions (ITTOIA 2005 s 753A);
(p) interest on certain deposits of the victims of National-Socialist Persecution (ITTOIA 2005 s 756A);
(q) the relevant foreign income of consular officers and employees (ITTOIA 2005 ss 771–772); and
(r) the sale of electricity from domestic microgeneration (ITTOIA 2005 ss 782A–782B). [7.131]

c) *Exempt products*

The exemptions applicable to life assurance policies and ISAs are considered in **Chapter 15**. [7.132]

8 Taxation of employment income

Updated by Michael L Firth BA (Oxon) BCL (Oxon), Barrister, CTA

I   Introductory points [**8.1**]
II   The structure of the charges to tax on employment income [**8.8**]
III   Office or employment [**8.20**]
IV   Agency workers, personal service companies and managed service companies [**8.31**]
V   Are the earnings *from* employment? [**8.40**]
VI   Problem cases [**8.61**]
VII   What are earnings? [**8.91**]
VIII   Amounts treated as earnings or counted as employment income [**8.101**]
IX   Termination payments [**8.141**]
X   Exemptions [**8.161**]
XI   Deductions from earnings [**8.171**]
XII   Collection of tax [**8.191**]

I INTRODUCTORY POINTS

1 General introduction

Earnings from an office or employment are taxed under ITEPA 2003 (and, unless otherwise specified, all statutory references in this chapter are to ITEPA 2003). About 90% of total income tax per annum is raised from such earnings mainly through a deduction-at-source system (Pay As You Earn or PAYE) which ensures timely receipt of the tax by the Treasury. Earnings are currently taxed at 20% up to £33,500 per annum, and 40% above this amount, with a personal allowance of £11,500. An additional rate of 45% applies to taxable income over £150,000. There is also a gradual reduction of the personal allowance for those with taxable income over £100,000. For 2015–16 and subsequent tax years it is possible to transfer an amount, presently up to £1,150, of personal allowance between married couples or civil partners who are both basic rate taxpayers (see [**51.12**]).   [**8.1**]

2 National insurance contributions

Whenever an employee receives earnings, National Insurance contributions (NICs) also have to be considered. NICs are categorised into Classes:

Classes 2 and 4 relate to profits from self-employment; Class 3 is a voluntary contribution (for instance, to cover a period when a person has been out of the country). Classes 1, 1A and 1B relate to employment income: both employees and employers pay Class 1 NICs but Class 1A and 1B are employer-only liabilities. Whilst NICs are in theory separate from income tax, from an employee's perspective they seem very similar: primary Class 1 NICs (often known as employees' NICs) are deducted from his salary under the PAYE system and paid to the government. There are, however, differences.

First, not all employee receipts from employment are subject to Class 1 NICs. *Second*, for the 2017–18 tax year, employees pay primary Class 1 NICs at a nil rate on annual earnings of £8,164 and below, at the rate of 12% on earnings above £8,164 and up to £43,000 per annum and at 2% on annual earnings above £45,000. Until 5 April 2016, if the employee was contracted out of the State Second Pension then the rate fell to 10.6% on earnings of up to £770 per week. Contracting out is now no longer an option.

Employers pay secondary Class 1 NICs at 13.8% on their employees' earnings above £8,164 per year (prior to 5 April 2016 this could be reduced to 10.4% on earnings of up to £770 per week depending on the type of pension arrangements the employee had). Secondary Class 1 NICs represent a real cost to an employer and many of the tax avoidance schemes in the employment field have had the primary aim of reducing the employers' NIC obligations. A number of measures have been directed at reducing this burden in a targeted way.

First, in September 2010, a new national insurance 'holiday' was created for businesses established in certain parts of the UK. This was designed to promote new enterprise in areas that had been most reliant on public sector employment. Under the scheme, companies could claim a deduction of up to £5,000 from their employers' NICs bill for each of the first ten employees they engaged. The scheme ended on 5 September 2013 but it is still possible to make a retrospective claim for relief until 4 September 2017.

Second, since 6 April 2014, each employer has been entitled to an 'Employment Allowance' which enables them to claim a deduction from their NICs bill of up to, currently, £3,000 each tax year. One Employment Allowance is allowed for each PAYE scheme and it is only available in respect of one company within a group. From 6 April 2016 the allowance is no longer available to companies where the director is the only employee paid earnings above the threshold for secondary Class 1 NICs.

Third, from 6 April 2015, a new measure applies which means that employers with employees under 21 years old will no longer have to pay employers' NICs on earnings of, currently, up to £45,000.

The combination of high marginal tax rates and the PAYE system led to employers providing benefits in kind to minimise the employee's tax or, where tax was payable, escape the PAYE net (and thus give him a cash flow advantage) and avoid NICs. The natural consequence has been frequent legislation making such benefits taxable and widening the PAYE net; further, over the years some benefits in kind were specifically made subject to Class 1 NICs; and since 6 April 2000 the majority of the others have been made subject to Class 1A contributions.

Many have questioned the justification for having separate tax and social security regimes and in 2011, the Chancellor of the Exchequer initiated a consultation on merging income tax with NICs. As a result, the Next Steps Report (HM Treasury, HMRC, November 2011) set out an indicative timetable for reform, with final implementation occurring in 2017. Following the July 2015 budget, the Office for Tax Simplification (OTS) was asked to focus on the issues and impact of a closer alignment between income tax and NICs (note that it was not asked to make recommendations). Initial proposals for changes to NICs for the self-employed in early 2017 were quickly withdrawn by the Government. [8.2]

3 The effect of the employed/self-employed distinction

In the meantime, the more the government seeks to increase the tax and NICs raised from employees, the more some workers try to bring themselves within the self-employed regime. HMRC's attitude is predictable. The courts' approach has varied over the years.

The tensions created by taxpayers' desire to avoid being taxed as employees and the government's desire to raise as much tax as possible through this source created a regime in which the principles originally at play were swamped by the detailed legislation. The need for a fundamental review arises not only from increasingly sophisticated attempts to avoid classification as an employee (for instance, by taking advantage of the beneficial tax regime obtainable through providing a worker's services through his own one-man company) but also from more complex and flexible working patterns in general.

To create a level playing field for all workers, it will be necessary to introduce an approach where people performing the same economic function are treated in the same way. Robert Walker LJ's suggestion in *R (on the application of Professional Contractors Group Ltd) v IRC* (2002), might be the way forward:

> '[I] wonder whether it might not have been possible to bring forward measures which accorded some recognition to the existence of a sort of no man's land between Sch D [the Schedule under which the self-employed used to be taxed] and Sch E [the Schedule under which employees and office-holders used to be taxed] rather than insisting on the gulf which exists in theory (but not, always, in practice) between them.'

The major development in this area was the enactment (with effect from 6 April 2003) of the Income Tax (Earnings and Pensions) Act 2003 (ITEPA 2003). Although it made very few changes to the substantive law in this area (it is a consolidation Act, enacted as part of the Tax Law Rewrite Project (see [1.22])), it has restructured the whole regime and in the process abolished its bedrocks – emoluments, Cases and even Schedule E itself (along with all the other Schedules).

This issue has assumed greater relevance with the rise of the 'gig economy' whereby individuals perform freelance work on a regular basis for the same business (for example, driving cars for Uber). In this context, the business may seek to ensure that the worker is self-employed so as to avoid certain employment law obligations arising (for example, holiday pay, minimum wage) whereas the worker wishes to be employed precisely in order to obtain those rights. The recent Taylor *Review of Modern Working Practices* has looked at this area and has recommended, inter alia, the creation of a category of 'dependent contractor' for employment law purposes and closer alignment of the taxation of the employed and self-employed. It contains few details on how this might be achieved, but does suggest increasing the tax burden on those who engage self-employed workers. The recent furore over proposals to increase NICs on the self-employed confirms that any such proposals will be difficult to implement. As is often noted, the losers will always shout the loudest. [8.3]

4 Anti-avoidance measures

A subsidiary development is the introduction of tax avoidance scheme disclosure obligation (DOTAS; see **Chapter 5**). Since 1 August 2004 the DOTAS regime has applied to provide HMRC with information about potential tax avoidance products. The principle behind the regime is for disclosure to be made of 'notifiable arrangements' (and 'notifiable proposals') that have as their main expected benefit the obtaining of a UK tax advantage. Much of the detail of who has the obligation to provide information to HMRC and exactly what arrangements have to be disclosed is set out in statutory instruments. The Tax Avoidance Schemes (Prescribed Descriptions of Arrangements) Regulations 2006 (SI 2006/1543) is the principal regulatory instrument in relation to tax avoidance. It prescribes six types of arrangement: arrangements involving confidentiality in cases involving a promoter; arrangements involving confidentiality in cases not involving a promoter; arrangements involving a premium fee; arrangements involving standardised tax products; arrangements involving loss schemes; and leasing arrangements. Details on the regulations regarding these arrangements can be found in regs 6 to 13. These regulations were amended by SI 2013/2595 which came into force on 4 November 2013 and requires the disclosure of schemes with a new 'employment income' hallmark. These are, broadly, schemes designed to circumvent the disguised remuneration rules found in ITEPA 2003 Part 7A (see **[5.7]**). On 1 January 2011, four further statutory instruments came into force with the intention of strengthening the disclosure regime established by SI 2006/1543. Additional strengthening measures were included in the 2015 Finance Act and proposals to widen the standardised products hallmark and to introduce a new financial product hallmark were also announced.

Similar regulations apply to NIC avoidance schemes. These can be found in the National Insurance Contributions (Application of Part 7 of the Finance Act 2004) Regulations 2007 (SI 2007/785) (as amended by SI 2008/2678 and SI 2010/2927). In summary, the NIC disclosure obligations need to be considered in relation to the promotion or use of arrangements (including any scheme, transaction or series of transactions) that will, or are intended to, provide an advantage in relation to NICs when compared to carrying on a different course of action, and the main benefit or one of the main benefits that might be expected to arise from those arrangements is the obtaining of that advantage. An 'advantage' is broadly the avoidance, reduction or deferral of NICs.

Technically the legislation covers all classes of NICs but in practice it is likely that schemes which are required to be disclosed under the regulations will only arise in respect of class 1 and class 1A contributions. The guidance and rules for NICs largely parallel similar rules to those that apply to disclosure for the other main taxes.

Anyone advising in this area on arrangements involving shares, payments to trustees and intermediaries or loans to employees which may give rise to a tax or NICs advantage should consider whether a disclosure obligation arises. HMRC has published updated guidance on disclosure with effect from 14 May 2014. Since April 2009 HMRC has also published regular 'spotlights' on selected avoidance schemes that it believes to be ineffective. In June 2015, a 'spotlight' was published in relation to a scheme designed to exploit the Employment Allowance. Irrespective of whether disclosure obligations arise, any such arrangements may give rise to income tax charges under the disguised remuneration rules which are set out at Part 7A of ITEPA (as enacted by FA 2011). For a more detailed examination of the disguised remuneration rules please refer to **Chapter 9**.

Practitioners must also consider the general anti-abuse rule ('GAAR') introduced by FA 2013 (see **[3.74]** ff), which applies to a range of taxes including income tax and, following the entering into force of the National Insurance Contributions Act 2014, NICs (this operates such that the provisions in FA 2013 relating to the GAAR include a reference to NICs). In brief, the GAAR applies if there is an arrangement which has the main purpose of giving rise to a tax advantage and is abusive. It is for HMRC to show, on the balance of probabilities, that an arrangement is abusive. An arrangement will be abusive if it cannot reasonably be regarded as a reasonable course of action in relation to the relevant tax provisions, having regard to all the circumstances. This is known as the 'double reasonableness' test. HMRC have published guidance on the application of the GAAR, including worked examples which may be helpful in providing a framework for advisers to use when analysing arrangements.

From 27 March 2015 new provisions have applied in relation to promoters of high-risk tax avoidance schemes under which HMRC has been given additional information gathering powers following disclosures and the ability to issue conduct notices to high risk promoters who meet certain conditions and to monitor promoters who breach a conduct notice. If a conduct notice has been breached, sanctions aimed at affecting the reputation of the high-risk promoter and deterring its clients from entering into avoidance schemes may apply, for example the promoter will be publicly named by HMRC and required to inform its clients that it is being monitored. Legislation has also been introduced designed to promote the early settlement of tax avoidance cases by way of 'Accelerated Payment Notices' and, in certain situations, to require payment of the disputed tax immediately where a similar scheme has been defeated in the courts by the issue of a 'Follower Notice' (see *Tax Journal*, Issue 1215, 9, where it is suggested that these notices will provide a 'hefty deterrent against engaging in future schemes'. Whether this will be the case remains to be seen). **[8.4]**

5 Other introductory points

HMRC's view on the interpretation and application of ITEPA 2003 can be found in its Employment Income Manual, available on its website (www.hmrc.gov.uk and also, now, the www.gov.uk website). This replaces the old Schedule

E Manual which should only be used when dealing with the application of the old provisions. References in this chapter to the former manual have the prefix EIM and to the latter SE.

Readers of this chapter need also to be aware of the enactment of another consolidation Act, the Income Tax (Trading and Other Income) Act 2005 (ITTOIA 2005) (see further Chapter 10). This has restructured the regime for taxing trading income. Persons carrying out a trade, profession or vocation used to be taxed under Case I or II of Schedule D but are now taxed under ITTOIA 2005 Part 2: references to only the new regime will appear in this chapter.

In addition to these, there has been a further consolidation enactment in the form of the Income Tax Act 2007 (ITA 2007). This covers the remaining income tax provisions of TA 1988 which were not included in ITEPA 2003 or most of ITTOIA 2005. In the main, as with much of the Tax Law Rewrite Project, ITA 2007 does not change the effect of the law, but rather corrects anomalies and incorporates extra statutory concessions, as well as attempting to simplify the language of the law. [8.5]–[8.7]

II THE STRUCTURE OF THE CHARGES TO TAX ON EMPLOYMENT INCOME

1 A framework

When approaching the charge to tax on employment income, one needs to consider a number of questions in a logical order:

(1) Is there an employment or an office? Without an employment or an office (eg a company directorship), and subject to the rules dealing with specific situations, such as agency contracts, there can be no charge to tax on employment income (one should consider other charges to tax instead). Whether or not there is an employment depends upon a multi-factoral enquiry involving a balancing of a number of different indicators of employment.

(2) If there is no employment, is there nevertheless deemed to be one? Due to the tax advantages of being self-employed (for example, no employer's NICs and more generous rules for deducting expenses) persons may seek to structure their arrangements such that they are classified as a self-employment rather than an employment (for example, workers engaged through an agency). Alternatively, even if there is an employment, the worker may seek to receive earned income in a form that is not taxable as employment income (for example dividends from a company of which the worker is the sole shareholder, director and employee). To combat perceived avoidance in this area, there are special tax codes dealing with agency workers, personal service companies and managed service companies.

(3) What are 'earnings'? The primary charge to tax on employment income applies to 'earnings'. Not everything an employee receives is taxable as earnings. Salary/wages are obviously earnings, but there are broader categories of earnings including a benefit of any kind 'if it is money or money's worth' (ITEPA 2003 s 62). As will be seen, this treats a

benefit received by an employee as earnings if and to the extent that it is convertible to money, but not otherwise.

(4) Are the earnings 'from' employment? The required link between the employment and the benefit is that it must be 'from' employment. Generally this means that the benefit is a reward for service, but that phrase is not necessarily apt to cover all circumstances. On the one hand, a salary or bonus is obviously a reward for service, but more difficult questions arise in relation to, for example, benefits presented as gifts.

(5) Does the benefits code apply to tax a benefit? The benefits code is a section of the legislation (ITEPA 2003 ss 63–220) that specifically targets and taxes benefits in kind (ie non-monetary benefits) provided by reason of employment. Some sections identify and bring into charge specific types of benefit, using special rules for the calculation of the value of the benefit (such as the use of a car or living accommodation), but there is also a sweep-up charge for any other benefits provided by reason of employment. Generally, the code operates in a residual way such that where a benefit gives rise to general earnings (based on its convertible value) only the difference between the benefits code value and the general earnings value is taxed under the benefits code. Such a difference may arise because of the specific calculation rules for a particular benefit or because the sweep-up charge bases the taxable value on the cost to the employer of providing the benefit rather than the convertible value of the benefit.

(6) Does any other provision cause a payment or benefit to be treated or counted as employment income? In addition to general earnings and the benefits code, there are also statutory provisions that seek to bring into charge specific types of payment and benefit. For example, sick pay (s 221), payments of PAYE by an employer where the employer did not deduct the tax from earnings (s 222) and payments for restrictive undertakings (s 225). Of great practical importance are the specific provisions dealing with payments made to employees in connection with the termination of their employment or a change of duties/earnings (ss 401–416 – considered at [8.141] ff) and the provisions dealing with the taxation of shares or other securities given to employees (ss 417–553 considered at **Chapter 9**).

(7) Is the employee entitled to any exemptions? Certain amounts that would otherwise be treated as income may be exempted by specific provisions. Often this is for policy reasons rather than reflecting any general principle.

(8) Is the employee entitled to any deductions? An employee may incur expenditure related to the performance of the duties of his or her employment, for example, the cost of getting to his/her place of employment or the cost of clothing required to be worn during the hours of employment. There are strict rules that determine whether and to what extent such expenses are deductible in calculating the employee's taxable income. Generally it is necessary for the expense to have been incurred, wholly, exclusively and necessarily in the performance of the duties of the employment. This excludes, for example, the cost of travelling from home to work and the cost of ordinary clothes worn at work. [8.8]

188 *Taxation of employment income*

The structure of the charging provisions (in ITEPA 2003, Part 2) is relatively complex, requiring multiple cross-references, but in essence:
- Tax is charged on general earnings and specific employment income (s 6(1)).
- General earnings consist of earnings (s 62) and amounts treated as earnings (eg the benefits code) (s 7(3)). Specific employment income consists of amounts that 'count' as employment income (eg some payments on termination of employment and some employee-share awards) (s 7(4)). The difference between amounts treated as earnings and amounts that count as employment income is important for certain purposes, eg the taxation of non-residents.
- The amount that is charged in a particular tax year is the total of the net taxable earnings and net taxable specific income from an employment in the year (s 9).
- 'Net' taxable earnings and net taxable specific income mean taxable earnings/taxable specific income less permitted deductions (ss 11–12).
- Taxable earnings refers to general earnings adjusted to take account of the employee's residence status (s 10(2) and ss 14–41ZA), whereas taxable specific income refers to specific employment income (and note that the rules for calculating specific employment income incorporate their own rules about residence and domicile etc) (s 10(3) although see also s 41A).
- Residence status affects the taxability of general earnings based on the employee's residence status in the tax year for which the earnings are 'for' (s 15 – there is a need to distinguish the 'for' question and the 'from' question, discussed in the next bullet point). Generally, earnings are 'for' the period in which they were earned (s 16), but see **[8.12]–[8.20]** on the source doctrine.
- Taxable earnings are 'from an employment in a tax year' if they are received in that tax year (s 15(2) – the receipts basis has been in use since the tax year 1989–90). Further rules specify when earnings are treated as received, and the general rule for monetary earnings is that they are received at the earlier of when payment is made on account of the earnings or when a person becomes entitled to payment of or on account of the earnings (s 18). Additional rules apply to employees who are directors and non-monetary earnings.

In so far as employment income involves a foreign element, readers are also referred to **Chapter 18**; this chapter is limited to the tax position of employees and office-holders who are UK tax resident according to the 'statutory residence test' introduced by FA 2013 (for further details, see **Chapter 18**).

[8.9]

In light of the continuing importance of older cases, it is also worth having a basic understanding of the previous terminology of the employment tax legislation. One will see numerous references to 'Schedule E' which can be taken as synonymous with the charge to tax on employment income. The name arises from earlier income tax acts in which the charges to tax were set out in schedules to the Act. Even when the charging provisions were incorporated into the body of the Act itself (for example TA 1988 s 19(1)), the legislation retained the reference to 'Schedule E'. ITEPA 2003, however,

rewrote the structure of the charge to tax on employment income (generally without changing the substance) and forewent reference to Schedule E.
[8.10]

2 **Basis of assessment**

Since the 1989–90 tax year, employment income is charged to tax on a receipts basis.

Only general earnings which are 'for a tax year' in which the employee is UK tax resident under the statutory residence test fall within ITEPA 2003 Part 2. In case of a 'split year' under the statutory residence test, earnings attributable to the overseas part (and meeting certain conditions) do not fall to be taxed under ITEPA 2003. Earnings which do fall within ITEPA 2003 are subject to charge when they are received (rather than when they are earned), even if they are not 'for' that tax year (as to which see [8.13]–[8.20]) and even if the employment is not held at the time of receipt.

Not surprisingly, there is a detailed definition of when a payment is received for these purposes (s 18 for money earnings and s 19 for others). In the case of directors, for instance, payment is treated as made when the sum is credited in the company's accounts or records – hence crediting the director's account with that sum will constitute a payment for these purposes (s 18(1)). [8.11]

3 **The source doctrine**

One of the hallowed principles of income tax (see [6.41]) is that a charge can only be made if the source of the income is continuing. This principle has, of course, been much modified by statute. Thus, the possibility of a barrister (who would normally be self-employed) ceasing to practise and, at some time during his peaceful retirement, receiving arrears of fees which, because the source of the fees had ceased, escaped tax, has long since gone under the post-cessation receipts rules. The case of *Bray v Best* (1988) (see *Example 8.1*) revealed an unsuspected gap in the Schedule E legislation where employees were paid emoluments after the cessation of their employment. That gap was quickly closed by the introduction of para 4A into TA 1988 s 19(1). As a result of FA 1989 s 36(5) this only applied in relation to 1989–90 onwards. Unfortunately, when paragraph 4A was consolidated into ITEPA 2003 s 17, this time limit was not included (though it was included in s 30 (the equivalent provision for employees resident or domiciled outside the UK) as a result of ITEPA 2003 Sch 7 para 8), but it is understood that HMRC intends to correct this in due course. Apart from this small omission, ITEPA 2003 clarifies the position further.

Section 16 sets out the rules for determining whether general earnings are 'for' a particular tax year. Section 16 can be overridden by any provision in ITEPA 2003 Part 3 which specifies when an amount is to be treated as earnings for a particular tax year (s 16(5)). If general earnings are paid to an employee before his employment commences, they will be treated for the purposes of s 9 as earnings for the first year of that employment: if paid after the employment has ceased, they will be related back to the last year of employment (s 17). Accordingly, should the facts of *Bray v Best* recur in the future, the payment will be related back to the last year of the employment. Note, however, that this change merely extends the source doctrine to catch the payment; the tax itself will still remain charged in the year of receipt. The principle that tax is charged in the year of receipt but that the source of the income must be determined in the year when it is earned, applies to the facts of the following example.

EXAMPLE 8.1

(1) In 2016–17, Bert is UK tax resident according to the statutory residence test when his UK job ceases. In 2017–18 he becomes non-resident. A bonus paid in 2017–18 in relation to the UK job falls within Part 2 Chapter 4 and is taxed in year of receipt.

(2) Take the opposite case: ie in 2016–17, Henri is non-UK resident when his full-time job in Paris ceases. He comes to the UK in 2017–18 when he receives a bonus in respect of 2016–17. He is not subject to UK tax since he was outside the tax net when the money was earned.

It should be noted that the general rule in s 17 does not apply for the purposes of the benefits code (see Section VIII Part 3) (s 17(4)). Many of the provisions in that code only apply if the benefit is provided in a year when the employment is held: the Chapters of Part 3 identify the year the earnings are 'for' (see, eg s 72). [8.12]–[8.19]

III OFFICE OR EMPLOYMENT

The starting point is that the charges to tax on employment income require the existence of either an employment or an office. In the latter case, this is because 'the provisions of the employment income Parts that are expressed to apply to employments apply equally to offices, unless otherwise indicated' (ITEPA 2003, s 5). [8.20]

1 Meaning of 'office'

The basic meaning of an 'office' is that it is a position which has an existence independent of the person who holds it and may be filled by successive holders (ITEPA 2003 s 5(3)). This includes trustees, personal representatives, company directors, company secretaries, NHS consultants (*Mitchell & Edon v Ross* (1959)), MPs and independent officials such as judges. An office holder may also be an employee if there is a contract of service (for example, it is relatively common for company directors to both hold office as a director and have a contract of employment with the same company).

However, s 5(3) is only an 'inclusive' definition. It is possible, therefore, for an office to exist that lacks some element of independence and/or continuity. Whilst in *Edwards v Clinch* (1981), a civil engineer appointed to act as an inspector of an ad hoc public inquiry did not hold an office because the post had no existence independent of the holder, in *Taylor v Provan* (1974) a directorship was created specifically and solely for the person who occupied it, but was nevertheless an office. The difference is between being appointed to execute a specific task (*Edwards v Clinch*) and performing a certain type of work (*Taylor v Provan*).

This distinction was relied on by the Court of Session in *IRC v Brander & Cruickshank* (1971) (affirmed by the House of Lords) in a case dealing with the difficulties which arise when a taxpayer acquires an 'office' by reason of his particular profession: eg solicitor partners (then taxable under Schedule D Case II, now under ITTOIA 2005) who assume trusteeships. Each office will be separately assessed under ITEPA 2003 and not taxed under ITTOIA 2005, unless that office is assumed as an integral part of the trade or profession. In practice, HMRC allows partnerships which receive directors' fees to enter those fees in their self-employed assessment so long as the directorship is a normal incident of the profession and of the particular practice, the fees form only a small part of total profits, and under the partnership agreement the fees are pooled for division amongst the partners (see ESC A37). [8.21]

2 Employed or self-employed?

ITEPA 2003 makes no attempt to define 'employment' but s 4 does (in HMRC's view) provide 'a non-exhaustive explanation which [gives] an indication of the *core* meaning of "employment" by listing certain arrangements that on any view constitute an employment.' (Explanatory Notes to the Act.)

The arrangements listed in s 4 are any employment under a contract of service or contract of apprenticeship, or in the service of the Crown. This leaves open the most significant question: when is there a contract of service? (Note the common terminological distinction between a contract of service (employment) and a contract to provide services (self-employment), which is sometimes collapsed to simply the distinction between 'service' and 'services' – a subtle difference that is ripe to cause confusion).

Ultimately, whether there is a contract of service/employment is a multifactorial enquiry and the best approach is generally to look at each specific factor in turn before stepping back and viewing the picture as a whole. Factors to consider are as follows (see, inter alia, *Market Investigations Ltd v Minister of Social Security* (1969)):

(a) Mutuality of obligation (ie the obligations to provide and accept work) – this factor is of greater relevance in an employment law context where it is necessary to prove a particular length of employment for some purposes. Even a relatively short engagement may, in the right circumstances, give rise to an employment.

(b) Degree of control (or the right of control) as regards the manner in which work is done is an important factor in showing the existence of employment.

(c) Autonomous hours points towards self-employment (*Barnett v Brabyn* (1996)) whereas the lack of autonomous hours may be a neutral factor if the hours are dictated by the nature of the work.

(d) Degree of integration into the potential employer's business – the greater the degree of integration (for example, having an allocated desk), the more likely there is employment.

(e) Provision of own capital/equipment – employees do not usually invest their own capital or provide their own substantial pieces of equipment.

(f) Opportunity for profit/risk of loss – employees do not usually take the risk of making a loss and the opportunity to make a profit by, for example, efficient working is usually limited (bonuses aside). An interesting case is *Tomlinson v R & C Comrs* (2017) where HMRC successfully argued that a double-glazing salesman who worked on commission for a single provider, using their showrooms, was self-employed. They relied on the fact that hours worked were determined by customer need, not company instructions and that the company had no control over how he sold the windows. What appeared to weigh most heavily with the Tribunal was the fact that Mr Tomlinson was paid solely on the basis of commissions and thus took a significant financial risk (and the parties' longstanding view – see below).

(g) Personal service/right to provide a substitute – a genuine right to provide a substitute (ie one that the parties contemplated may operate in practice rather than inserted in attempt to create self-employment) points against employment as the work will not necessarily be done by that particular worker.

(h) Contractual terms such as sick pay, holiday etc point towards employment.

(i) Number of contracts with the same client – see below.

(j) Number of clients – discussed below.

(k) The parties' view of the arrangement – this is usually no more than a tie breaker. Indeed, it was explicitly relied upon as such in *Tomlinson v R & C Comrs* (2017).

Difficult issues arise when a taxpayer works for more than one person, either consecutively or concurrently. In *Davies v Braithwaite* (1931), for instance, an actress who entered into a series of separate engagements to appear on film, stage and radio was held to be taxable under Schedule D. Rowlatt J looked at her total commitments during the year and, as the number was considerable, decided that each was a mere engagement in the course of exercising her profession.

This may be contrasted with *Fall v Hitchen* (1973) where the taxpayer was employed as a professional ballet dancer by Sadler's Wells under a contract which only allowed him to take other work with their consent (which was not to be unreasonably withheld). Pennycuick V-C looked at the characteristics of the contract in isolation and held that the taxpayer was taxable under Schedule E; undoubtedly, one reason for the decision was that the taxpayer had only one contract which provided for a first call on his time.

The Revenue, adopting this approach of looking at each contract in isolation, tried to bring persons traditionally taxed under Schedule D (eg actors) within the old Schedule E. However, the courts reverted to taking an overview and, in *Hall v Lorimer* (1994), the Revenue's attempt to recategorise technical workers in the film industry as Schedule E taxpayers, whatever the number and nature of their engagements each year, was successfully resisted. The Court of Appeal held that the duration of each engagement and the number of people by whom Mr Lorimer was engaged were of critical importance. It said that, in these types of case, the question of whether the taxpayer was 'dependent on or independent of a particular paymaster for the financial exploitation of his talents may well be significant' and that this was a more useful test than the 'business on own account' one since persons who exercise a profession or vocation will often do so 'without any of the normal trappings of a business'. Thus, although the taxpayer only supplied his own expertise, he could still be treated as self-employed.

Self-employed status may be established even where the number of contracts are few, provided that there is other evidence of self-employment, including that the worker does not have the protections normally given to an employee (eg sick pay or holiday entitlement).

Lightman J's decision in *Barnett v Brabyn* (1996) underlines the need for careful analysis. In that case the taxpayer's situation lacked some of the factors identified in *Market Investigations*, but Mr Barnett worked only for one employer and their relationship involved many factors indicating employment, including receipt of holiday pay. Nevertheless, the court felt that the taxpayer's contractual right to work as much or as little as he liked (which right he exercised) and the parties' agreement that he should be self-employed (as to which, see **[8.23]**) were sufficient to ensure that status. On the other hand, the Special Commissioners' decision in *FS Consulting Ltd v McCaul* (2002) is a reminder that if a person enters into a full-time contract which requires him to obtain the other party's consent to any absence, he, like Mr Hitchen, will find it hard to prove his self-employed status.

The Supreme Court has more recently ruled on the issue of employment status in *Autoclenz v Belcher* (2011). It confirmed that employment tribunals may disregard the express terms of a contract that do not reflect the actual legal relationship (for example, a substitution clause that was never genuinely intended to be operated). Whilst this judgment was given in the context of a claim brought under employment law, it could have wider implications to employment status claims under tax law.

See also *Weight Watchers (UK) Ltd v R & C Comrs* (2011), which examined whether teachers taking Weight Watchers classes are self-employed or employees of Weight Watchers UK Ltd. The Upper Tribunal (upholding the decision of the First-tier Tribunal) held that, on balance, the teachers were in fact employees of Weight Watchers focusing on the fact that Weight Watchers dictated the way classes were run, imposed strict limits on the right of substitution and set the prices of its products (thereby limiting the potential for profit).

HMRC's manuals contain extensive guidance on the way they interpret and apply the employment/self-employment distinction and they have has also published an 'Employment Status Indicator' which can be accessed through its website to help taxpayers decide their employment status for tax purposes. While the conclusions of the Employment Status Indicator may be indicative of a person's employment status, they are by no means determinative. The Employment Status Indicator has been known to categorise someone as an 'employee' where the courts regard him as 'self-employed'!

In March 2015, the Office of Tax Simplification (OTS) carried out a review for HMRC into the divide between employment and self-employment. In its final report it noted that the area is difficult and requires further work although it did not make any specific recommendations on status. However, it did suggest that unifying National Insurance treatment with that of income tax or introducing a statutory test might solve the problem of incorrect employment status. The OTS has now been charged with looking at the effects of unification. **[8.22]**

3 Taxing a partner

Prior to the introduction in FA 2014 of the new rules relating to salaried members of LLPs (for which see below), a partner in a business was presumed to be self-employed and, therefore, assessable under ITTOIA 2005. LLP members are now treated differently and these new rules are outlined at the end of this section. All other partners are still presumed to be self-employed (see generally **Chapter 45**). Difficulties may arise, however, as to the status of a salaried partner. Whether he is an employee or is self-employed does not *necessarily* depend upon the labels used or whether his salary is taxed at source under PAYE. However, in a non-partnership case, *Barnett v Brabyn* (1996), Lightman J stated that whilst the parties' agreement on status:

> 'cannot contradict the effect of a contract as a whole and must be disregarded if inconsistent with the substantive terms or general effect of the contract as a whole, when the terms and general effect of the contract as a whole are consistent with either relationship, the parties' label may be decisive'.

In *Stekel v Ellice* (1973), although the agreement referred to 'salaried partner' and a 'fixed salary', the court found that it was, in substance, a partnership agreement rather than a contract of employment. In *Horner v Hasted* (1995) the rules of the ICAEW prevented a firm of accountants from appointing a non-qualified person as a partner (such an appointment would have led to the firm breaching various statutory rules), so the firm, therefore, went out of its way technically to preserve Mr Horner's employment status (eg by paying employers' NICs). These factors significantly influenced Lightman J's confirmation of his employment status when otherwise he had a 'status in the firm equivalent to that of a partner', including receiving a 'salary' that was a share of the profits, attending and voting at partners' meetings and being held out to clients as a partner! Accordingly, provided that the partnership determines the new partner's status in advance and drafts the agreement accordingly, its terms are likely to be conclusive unless there is strong factual evidence to the contrary (*BSM (1257) Ltd v Secretary of State for Social Services* (1978)). If the partners are in any doubt on the matter, they should seek confirmation of status from HMRC.

The Employment Appeal Tribunal in *Williamson & Soden Solicitors v Briars* (2011) deemed a solicitor who was a partner to be an employee. The Tribunal held that the label given by the parties was not determinative of the individual's employment status. Surprisingly, little weight was given to exploring whether Mr Briars was a fixed equity partner. This decision should be contrasted with that of *Tiffin v Lester Aldridge LLP* (2012) where the Court of Appeal agreed with the Employment Appeal Tribunal that a fixed share partner, in an arguably similar position to Mr Briars, was not an employee. This position was followed in *Bates van Winkelhof v Clyde & Co LLP* (2012), in which case the Court of Appeal found that a member of an LLP who would have been a partner under the Partnership Act 1890 could not be an employee. It held that as the partnership was not a separate legal entity, in order to be an employee, a partner would have to be both workman and employer which was a legal impossibility. Whilst the decisions in these cases were in the context of claims brought under employment law, they have wider potential implications to the corresponding tax analysis.

FA 2014 brought with it fundamental changes to the rules relating to the taxation of LLP members, removing the presumption of self-employment for LLP members from 6 April 2014 in order to combat the disguising of employment relationships through LLPs. Instead of the presumption of self-employment for LLP members, HMRC has introduced a new category of 'salaried member' which applies if three conditions are met; (1) it is reasonable to expect that at least 80% of the total amount payable by the LLP for the member's services will be 'disguised salary', ie a fixed salary rather than a profit share; (2) the member does not have significant influence over the affairs of the LLP; and (3) the member's contribution to the LLP is less than 25% of the anticipated disguised salary (examining the level of risk which the member has assumed). With effect from 6 April 2014, a 'salaried member' is liable to income tax and primary Class 1 NICs as an employee and the LLP is liable to pay secondary Class 1 NICs as employer. Accordingly, the LLP now has to operate PAYE in respect of the salaried member. FA 2014 also introduced a targeted anti-avoidance rule to deter LLPs from introducing arrangements with a main purpose of falling outside the 'salaried member' conditions (see [45.12]). [8.23]

4 **Reclassification**

If the classification assumed by the parties is later proved to have been wrong, the tax and NIC treatment throughout the relationship will have to be revised (see *Taxation*, 9 October 1997, pp 32–35). Where self-employed status is reclassified as employment, this can cause severe problems for the (newly designated) employer who will be primarily responsible (under the PAYE system) for accounting to HMRC for any unpaid income tax and employees' NICs but will have difficulties recovering that from the (possibly former) worker (see further [8.202]), as well as having the extra cost of employers' NICs (which it would be unlawful to recover from him) – see *Demibourne v R & C Comrs* (2005). *McManus v Griffiths* (1997) illustrates the opposite situation. A golf club stewardess provided catering services at the club under a 'contract of employment' drafted by the club secretary. When she was found to be self-employed, she had to pay interest on 12 years of Schedule D assessments. A simple error of judgment can in this context, because of the uncertainties inherent in any system of classification, have severe financial repercussions.

In response to the *Demibourne* decision, legislation was introduced, which permits income tax paid by a worker, believing that he/she was self-employed, to be set-off against an employer's obligation to account for PAYE income tax where the worker is found to be an employee of the employer. See regs 72E–72G of the Income Tax (Pay As You Earn) Regulations 2003 (SI 2003/2682). These regulations have since been amended by the Income Tax (Pay As You Earn) and the Income Tax (Construction Industry Scheme) (Amendment) Regulations 2014 (SI 2014/472) which came into force on 6 April 2014. These regulations provide that HMRC can now simply issue a *Demibourne* direction transferring the tax liability by stating the employment concerned rather than being required to state the specific year to which the direction relates and the amount of tax paid. [8.24]–[8.30]

IV AGENCY WORKERS, PERSONAL SERVICE COMPANIES AND MANAGED SERVICE COMPANIES

1 Introduction

As discussed in Section I, pressures to avoid taxation as an employee have long existed. Tax avoidance is not, of course, unknown in this area.

ITEPA 2003 Part 2 Chapter 7 provides that where a worker receives remuneration under a contract with an agency to render personal services to a client under supervision he is taxable under ITEPA 2003 (see s 44); the agency has to operate PAYE (*Brady v Hart* (1985) and, on the supervision requirement, see *Bhadra v Ellam* (1988) and *Talentcore Ltd (t/a Team Spirits) v R & C Comrs* (2011)). Certain workers (such as entertainers) are excluded from the operation of the section (s 47(2)); special rules also apply to self-employed persons working in the construction industry.

At the time of the 1999 Budget, the government announced that it would be introducing provisions to 'counter avoidance in the area of personal service provision', primarily through the use of one-man companies. The effect of using a company to provide a worker's services, rather than those services being provided directly to the client, was that the agency rules would not apply (because there was no contract for the worker to supply his personal services to the client) and the agency could, therefore, pay the company a fee without deducting PAYE or being liable to account for NICs. The worker could take his money out of the personal service company in the form of dividends, which are not subject to NICs, would benefit from the delay before having to pay the higher rate tax to HMRC, and would often pay an overall lower rate of income tax on his income. The government announcement was made in Budget Press Release IR35 and much of the subsequent discussion has used the term 'IR35' as a catch-all phrase to refer to this whole issue. The legislation itself is now in ITEPA 2003 Part 2 Chapter 8.

Such was the opposition to the introduction of this legislation that judicial review proceedings were brought (*R (on the application of Professional Contractors Group Ltd) v IRC* (2002)), alleging that it infringed EC law on state aid and freedom of establishment and was a breach of Art 1, Protocol No 1 of the European Convention on Human Rights. The Court of Appeal dismissed the application.

After the introduction of the IR35 rules, a number of specialist intermediaries started providing packaged service companies. In exchange for a fee, these intermediaries calculate salary, National Insurance, PAYE, profits, corporation tax and dividends, and liaise with agencies or clients. The worker is paid in the form of dividends, expenses and a salary by the intermediary on a periodic (usually weekly) basis. Some of these companies, known as managed service companies ('MSCs'), have only one worker. As there are a number of tax advantages for people working in quasi self-employed roles, MSCs became very popular.

FA 2007 included provisions which attempted to increase regulation of both single-person MSCs and other personal service companies with more than one worker. The main upshot of the new legislation is that, as of 6 April 2007, all earnings, including dividends, of an MSC should be subject to PAYE income tax and National Insurance contributions (see **[8.33]**).

The agency rules apply where a worker provides services to a client through a third party in such a way that the worker is not technically the employee of either. The purpose of the agency rules is to treat the worker, for tax purposes, as an employee of the third party. Certain conditions have to be met for the agency rules to apply. The government became concerned that the rules were being abused with the result that the agency legislation was being circumvented. As a result, in 2014, changes were introduced that strengthen the agency rules and to prevent abuse of them. The amended legislation also includes provisions to ensure the correct payment of tax where offshore employment intermediaries are utilised. Essentially the UK agency in the contractual chain is responsible for operating PAYE and NIC, except where there are multiple UK agencies, in which case the agency which contracts with the end client shoulders the responsibility. If there is no UK agency involved, the responsibility falls on the end client. [8.31]

2 The operation of the IR35 rules

The aim of the legislation is to bring into the ITEPA 2003, PAYE and Class 1 NIC nets workers who provide their services to clients through intermediaries when they would have been classified as employees if they had been providing those services directly to the clients. The essential issue of when a worker would have been classified as an employee is not addressed by the legislation, so that the common law position governs it (see Section III above and note that in some agency and IR35-type situations the courts have implied an employment contract between the worker and the client (*Taxation*, 26 May 2005 p 214)), subject to the fact that the decision has to be made within the legislative matrix. HMRC will advise on a person's status before arrangements are implemented.

There is no statutory definition of 'intermediary'. Individuals, companies and partnerships can be intermediaries. It should be noted that it is not only one-man companies that are caught. If the intermediary is a company, it can fall within the statutory provisions if the worker has a 'material interest' in it (basically, 5%); even if he has no interest in the intermediary, the legislation will apply if the intermediary pays him and that pay 'can reasonably be taken to represent remuneration for services provided by the worker to the intermediary's client'.

If the legislation applies and the intermediary receives payments for the worker's services which are not paid to the worker as employment income, the legislation classifies the difference between the receipts of the intermediary and those of the worker as a 'deemed employment payment'. There are detailed rules as to how to calculate the amount of that deemed payment: for instance, one has to take into account not only payments and benefits in kind received by the intermediary in respect of relevant engagements but also those received by the worker and his family from someone other than the intermediary (compare the wide net for 'higher-paid' employees: see [8.125]). Expenses incurred and paid for by the intermediary and those borne by the worker and reimbursed by the intermediary are deductible in calculating the deemed payment (provided they would have been deductible in a straightforward employment situation (see Section XI) and see *Tax Bulletin*, December 2004, pp 1165–1168 on claims for travel and subsistence costs).

The deemed employment payment is generally treated as received at the end of the tax year, though in certain cases it can be treated as received earlier (eg if the connection between the worker and intermediary comes to an end before then) (s 50(3)). ITEPA 2003 s 56 sets out how the PAYE provisions apply.

The legislation is particularly complex and this is only a brief summary of it. One difficulty with IR35 is that it is applied on a contract-by-contract basis. This makes it labour intensive for HMRC to monitor. In May 2012, following a recommendation of the OTS, HMRC published guidance on its risk based approach to checking compliance with IR35. Where a taxpayer could show that it was either outside IR35 or there was a low risk of it applying by reference to a series of business entity tests, HMRC would close any IR35 review and not undertake a further review in the next three years. However, following research by the IR35 Forum (set up to improve the administration of IR35) it became apparent that the tests were not fulfilling this purpose. As a result, they were withdrawn from 6 April 2015. In the summer Budget of 2015, the government announced that HMRC would start a dialogue with businesses on how to improve the effectiveness of the existing intermediaries legislation. On 17 July 2015 HMRC published a discussion document to explore the possible options to improve compliance. One such option is to make the end client responsible for collecting the tax and NICs due. It is, however, clear that the government has no current intention of abolishing IR35. Decisions of the First-tier Tribunal also demonstrate the unpredictable nature of this area of law and illustrate that each case depends on its own facts: *ECR Consulting Limited v R & C Comrs* (2011) and *MBF Design Services Ltd v R & C Comrs* (2011). *ECR Consulting* also highlighted the importance of the contract between the intermediary and the client. In this case, the First-tier Tribunal gave little weight to a four-week termination notice clause in the agreement, even though it was coupled with a right to terminate without notice on payment in lieu. In *JLJ Services Limited v R & C Comrs* (2011) the First-tier Tribunal determined that the status of a contractor providing services through his personal service company changed from self-employed, at the outset of his engagement, to employed, during his engagement. This decision highlights the importance of continually monitoring the status of contractors. Working for a single client for a substantial period of time brings with it the risk that a contractor's status could transform into that of an employee.

FA 2013 introduced changes to IR35 intended to bring office-holders within the rules so that where a worker who provides services to a client through an intermediary is an office-holder with that client, they will be subject to deduction of PAYE and NICs at source. Previously, deduction of PAYE income tax has only applied to situations where 'the worker would be regarded for income tax purposes as an employee of the client'. Office-holders such as non-executive directors (who are not normally regarded as employees) are not covered by the deeming provisions in ITEPA 2003, s 5 (which state that the Employment Income parts expressed to apply to employments apply equally to office holdings) as the intermediaries legislation is not expressed to apply to 'employments'. This contrasts with the NICs provisions, where a charge arises where the worker would be regarded as employed in employed earner's employment (the term 'employed earner' including office-holder). HMRC have therefore sought to realign the income tax and NICs treatment of office-holders whose personal services are provided through an intermediary. According to the HMRC FAQs on IR35, the changes apply from 6 April 2013 where (i) a worker is personally appointed to perform the duties of an office; (ii) an intermediary is appointed as a corporate office-holder, provides the worker to perform the duties of that office and the worker's personal services are required; (iii) a worker is engaged both as an office-holder and to perform other duties in circumstances when they would be regarded as an employee if they were engaged directly by the client; or (iv) a worker has earnings from an employment that have already been subject to PAYE/NICs by a client but they are also engaged by that client as an office-holder. The other rules relating to IR35 remain unchanged and only apply in circumstances where the worker would be regarded as an employee if they had been engaged directly by the client.

Although the agency rules can apply to those with personal service companies in practice they fall outside the strict terms of the legislation. For example, one feature of the agency rules is that they treat any remuneration received by a worker in respect of providing the services as employment income. In practice, it is more likely for a worker under a PSC arrangement to receive income in the form of dividends. HMRC have confirmed that in their view the amended agency rules will not generally apply to a worker engaged by a PSC and that genuine dividends from the PSC would not normally be considered to be remuneration for the purposes of the agency legislation.

There are also now increased reporting requirements for agencies, and the legislation amends the PAYE regulations to allow for any unpaid tax to be collected from the directors personally where they have provided false information. Separate rules also apply in relation to those employed in the UK gas and oil industry on the continental shelf. [8.32]

3 Services provided to public sector authorities through intermediaries

Under the IR35 rules it is the worker/intermediary rather than the client who has to consider whether or not the contract gives rise to a deemed employment. From 2017–18, however, where the client is a public authority, the obligations to deduct and account for PAYE on a deemed payment of earnings move up the chain from the intermediary to the first person in the 'chain' who is resident in or has a place in the UK (and thus within the territorial scope of PAYE) and who is not controlled by the worker (alone or with associates) or in which the worker has a material interest (s 61N).

In a typical case, the obligations could move to the public authority client itself and that is the intention of the rules, as it means that the public authority will have to consider whether the worker is caught by IR35. Furthermore, there is now an explicit obligation on the client to consider whether or not, if the services were provided directly to the client by the worker, the worker would be regarded as an employee (s 61T). The client must inform its contractual party of its conclusion. [8.33]

4 The managed service companies legislation

The use of managed service companies (MSCs) may become less popular as a consequence of the MSC legislation enacted as part of the Finance Act 2007 in an attempt to prevent MSCs becoming tax avoidance schemes.

As mentioned in [8.31], workers supplied through an MSC could previously reduce their income tax and NICs liability by taking their remuneration in the form of dividends and expenses instead of salaries. HMRC was concerned that this kind of arrangement was essentially disguised employment, and that income tax and NICs should be paid on this remuneration through the PAYE system.

Following HMRC's consultation paper on 'Tackling Managed Service Companies' (December 2006) a new tax regime was introduced in relation to the taxation of an MSC. The provisions (namely ITEPA 2003 Chapter 9 Part 2 (ss 61A–61J) and s 688A, Income Tax (Pay As You Earn) Regulations 2003 and ITTOIA 2005 s 164A) are wide, and encompass the taxation of MSCs and their workers and the treatment of travel and subsistence costs relating to these workers.

The purpose of the legislation is to ensure that those individuals who provide services through MSCs are taxed as employees and pay income tax and NICs accordingly. Whilst the IR35 legislation (see [8.32]) should have achieved this, as it applies equally to an MSC as it does to a personal service company, HMRC considered that IR35 was not being complied with by the majority of MSCs and, where non-compliance was identified, enforcement against the MSC was impractical or impossible and very 'resource intensive' for HMRC. In order to combat this non-compliance and lack of enforceability the MSC legislation casts the net wide.

An MSC provider includes businesses which are involved in promoting or facilitating the use of companies to provide the services of individuals. The MSC legislation also sets out how the deemed employment payment (which can include travelling expenses) should be calculated. In contrast with the IR35 rules, the deemed employment income calculation and the operation of the PAYE system must be undertaken when an individual receives a payment and not after the end of the relevant tax year. Excluded from being defined as an MSC provider are (i) entities which provide legal and accountancy services in a professional capacity, and (ii) employment agencies and employment businesses to the extent that they do no more than an employment business or employment agency would normally do in pursuit of its business of placing work-seekers who wish to obtain their services, and provided that they do not influence or control the finances of the MSC or the way in which payments to individuals are made.

Under the MSC legislation, HMRC has the power to recover unpaid PAYE income tax and NICs debts which an MSC should have paid from those who are involved with MSCs. ITEPA 2003 s 688A ('the transfer of debt provision') specifically provides for the recovery of unpaid income tax debts from third parties. Third parties can include a director or other office-holder, or an associate, of the MSC, an MSC provider, or even 'a person who (directly or indirectly) has encouraged or been actively involved in the provision by the MSC of the services of the individual' – this wording can clearly be interpreted very widely to include a range of third parties who could become potentially liable for any unpaid PAYE income tax and NICs. It is this provision which is most likely to discourage people from using or dealing with MSCs, as they will not want to risk opening themselves up to becoming potentially liable for unpaid PAYE income tax and NICs liabilities. Certain third parties are excluded from the remit of the transfer of debt provisions. The nature of these persons is similar to those who are excluded from the definition of an MSC provider (see above).

Following attempts to circumvent the MSC legislation, HMRC published guidance stating that they will investigate companies and partnerships that otherwise fall within the MSC legislation but claim not to be MSCs because the provider is an officer/partner of the intermediary (and therefore claim that there is no separate MSC provider). HMRC state that where necessary in these situations they will invoke the transfer of debt provisions in order to collect PAYE from associated persons.

After the 2014 Autumn Statement, the government published a discussion paper on the use of umbrella companies and other employment intermediaries to change a series of permanent workplaces into temporary workplaces with the result that relief is available for expenditure on travel and subsistence. Those proposals have since been implemented by FA 2016, with effect for the tax year 2016–17 and subsequent years (see [8.174]).

The government has also announced that it will consult on proposals to require employment intermediaries to provide workers with more information on how they are engaged and what they are paid. This is amid concerns that many individuals do not understand their working arrangements and how it impacts on the income they receive. [8.34]–[8.39]

V   ARE THE EARNINGS *FROM* EMPLOYMENT?

1 Introduction

Historically, tax was charged 'in respect of any office or employment on emoluments therefrom …' (see, for example, TA 1988 s 19(1)). This wording gave rise to a great body of case law on what it meant for an emolument to be 'from' employment. Following the re-write, and despite the widespread acceptance that the test is still whether earnings are 'from' employment in the sense considered by earlier authorities, it is difficult to find the legislative basis for the continued application of this test.

There is a reference to 'net taxable earnings from an employment in the year' in s 9(2) but this would not appear to incorporate the 'from' employment test because that phrase is defined, for UK residents, in s 15(2) exclusively in terms of what is received in the year (signposted in s 10(2)). Note also that if the continuing relevance of the 'from' employment test is derived from s 9(2), ITEPA 2003 would also incorporate the 'from' test in relation to 'specific employment income' by virtue of s 9(4). In turn that would override the intention behind, for example, s 403, which is aimed at charging payments on the termination of employment that are not 'from' employment in the case law sense (see below).

Similarly, there is no explicit qualification in the definition of earnings in s 62 limiting it to the categories there identified if they are 'from' employment.

Nevertheless, in light of the facts that:
(1) there does need to be some test to identify a relevant link between an amount falling within the definition of 'earnings' and an employment;
(2) there was no intention to abrogate such a fundamental part of the pre-existing law; and
(3) there is a widespread acceptance (perhaps assumption) that the 'from' employment test continues to apply, including from HMRC who would be the beneficiaries of any widening of the scope of the charge to tax (Employment Income Manual EIM 00600)

it is reasonably safe to proceed on the basis that the 'from' test is implicit in ITEPA 2003, most likely in the definition of earnings in s 62. [8.40]

2 General principles: 'reward for service' or a broader test?

In *Hochstrasser v Mayes* (1960), Upjohn J said that, in order for a payment received by an employee to be a profit arising from his employment, 'it must be something in the nature of a reward for services past, present or future'. When considering the appeal in the House of Lords, Viscount Simonds approved this analysis of the law (subject to a possible qualification relating to past service considered below) and Lord Radcliffe stated:

> 'While it is not sufficient to render a payment assessable that an employee would not have received it unless he had been an employee, it is assessable if it has been paid to him in return for acting as or being an employee.'

The essence of these two statements is that a payment is not taxable merely because it would not have been paid if the recipient had not been an employee – there must be some additional factor to bring the payment within the tax net. The *Hochstrasser* case itself related to a scheme whereby if an employee was transferred within the group, ICI would buy his house at a fair valuation and would also reimburse any capital loss on the sale. Mr Mayes was reimbursed following a move – he would not have received that money unless he was an employee of ICI but that was not sufficient to make it taxable.

The difficulty arises in categorising the additional element that is required to bring a payment within the tax net. The courts have been fairly consistent in their requirement that the payment must be a 'reward for services'. Lord Templeman in *Shilton v Wilmshurst* (1991) (for the facts see [8.43]) said:

> 'Section [19] is not limited to emoluments provided in the course of the employment; the section must therefore apply first to an emolument which is paid as a reward for past services and as an inducement to continue to perform services and, second, to an emolument which is paid as an inducement to enter a contract of employment and to perform services in the future. The result is that an emolument "from employment" means an emolument "from being or becoming an employee". The authorities are consistent with this analysis and are concerned to distinguish in each case between an emolument which is derived "from being or becoming an employee" on the one hand and an emolument which is attributable to something else on the other hand, for example, to a desire on the part of the provider of the emolument to relieve distress or to provide assistance to a home buyer.'

In *Mairs v Haughey* (1993), the House of Lords reaffirmed that payments to compensate for loss or to relieve distress were not taxable under general principles, certainly if they were only payable in certain circumstances after the employment came to an end (the relative significance of these factors was not explained in the judgment). The case involved payments made to employees to compensate them for giving up their contingent rights under a non-statutory redundancy scheme but, in reaching its decision, the House of Lords also considered whether the redundancy payments themselves would have been taxable (because of the 'replacement principle', considered below at **8.42**). Lord Woolf, delivering the judgment of the House, held that they would not have been as 'a characteristic of a redundancy payment is that it is to compensate or relieve an employee for what can be the unfortunate consequences of becoming unemployed'.

More recent authority can be found in the Court of Appeal decision in *Wilson v Clayton* (2005) (discussed below) and see also the following dicta in the Supreme Court decision in *Shop Direct Group v R & C Comrs* (2016):

'Rule 1 of the Schedule spoke of a charge on a "person having or exercising an office or employment" in respect of "salaries ... perquisites or profits whatsoever *therefrom*" (emphasis added). The question was whether the employee has received money or money's worth representing remuneration for his services.'

It would be neat to be able to conclude at this point that a payment is 'from' employment if it is a reward for providing, or an inducement to provide, services, and not otherwise. However, in *Hamblett v Godfrey* (1987), the Court of Appeal held that a payment of £1,000 made to each employee of GCHQ who relinquished the right to join a trade union was taxable. The Court explained this decision on the basis that the payment was for the loss of the right and that right went directly to the employment of the taxpayer with the employer, therefore the source of the payment was the employment:

'The right to join a union, in my judgment, also falls directly to be considered as in connection with that employment, because without the employment there is no purpose in joining the union except for esoteric or personal reasons which are not relevant in this case.'

There are three approaches one could take to *Hamblett v Godfrey*:
(1) Accept the result and the reasoning – this was the approach of the High Court in both *Wilcock v Eve* (1995) and *EMI Group Electronics v Coldicott* (1997). In the former case, Carnwath J asked himself whether the share option rights were 'intimately connected with the employment'. He decided that the value derived from exercising share options would not have been from employment, therefore, applying the replacement principle, nor was compensation for the loss of those rights. In the latter case, Neuberger J noted that the House of Lords appeared to approve *Hamblett* in *Bray v Best* (1989).
(2) Accept the result but not the reasoning – this was the approach taken by Lord Hutton CJ in the Court of Appeal of Northern Ireland in *Mairs v Haughey* where emphasis was placed on Neill LJ's reference, in his judgment in *Hamblett*, to the payment being received 'as a recognition of the fact that she had lost certain rights as an employee, *and* by reason of the further fact that she had elected to remain in her employment at GCHQ' (emphasis added). In doing this, Lord Hutton CJ was implicitly

rejecting the dominant reasoning in *Hamblett*, which revolved around the fact that the right given up related wholly and exclusively to the employment relationship, and instead seeking to characterise the payment as one made to induce the employee to continue providing services. Relying on *Mairs v Haughey*, the same approach was taken by the High Court in *Wilson v Clayton*.

(3) Reject the result and the reasoning – this view is advocated in [1998] BTR 364 in essence on the basis that *Hochstrasser* established a 'reward for services' test and the Court of Appeal in *Hamblett* did not explain why it was able to apply a broader test. Further, it is argued, the reference to *Hamblett* in *Bray v Best* was simply to illustrate that remuneration did not need to be periodic in order to be from employment.

Overall, it is suggested that the best view on the current authorities is that *Hamblett* did show that a payment can be 'from' employment even if it is not a reward for service or an inducement to provide service where no other source can be identified for a payment that is otherwise directly connected with the employment.

This is supported by the way *Hochstrasser* was dealt with in *Hamblett*. Knox J observed:

> '... all their Lordships, except Lord Keith, who merely agreed presumably with the conclusion rather than all the reasoning in all the speeches, and Lord Denning, who could see no profit from employment, found a separate source for the payment in question, namely the housing agreement, and that dealt with Mr. Mayes' individual position as householder. In this case there is no such independent source other than the Crown's [in the form of GCHQ] desire to recognise the loss of rights intimately linked with employment.'

Similarly, Purchas LJ interpreted *Hochstrasser* as follows:

> 'That authority directs one's attention to the expression "from no other source" which is to be found elsewhere in the authorities.'

The narrowness of this extension is, however, demonstrated by more recent decisions. The Revenue's attempt to apply *Hamblett* to payments made by an employer to replace the protective awards that could have been claimed under the Trade Union and Labour Relations (Consolidation) Act 1992 s 189 (for failure to go through the stipulated consultation process when redundancies are planned) was rejected by the Special Commissioner in *Mimtec v IRC* (2001)). Whilst he was, of course, unable to ignore *Hamblett*, the Special Commissioner sought to narrow its application by holding that it does not apply to payments received under statutory provisions in connection with the termination of employment.

In *Wilson v Clayton* (2005) the Court of Appeal had to decide whether a payment of compensation under a compromise agreement for unfair dismissal in 1997 was taxable under the general charging provision (then TA 1988 s 19). Peter Gibson LJ (with whom the other two members of the Court of Appeal agreed), reasserted the role of the 'reward for services' test:

> 'It is not enough that Mr Clayton would not have received [the payment] but for having been an employee. It is not a payment in return or as a reward for past services. It is not a payment in return for acting as or being an employee. It is not an

inducement to enter into employment – he was already employed* – or to provide future services. If one looks for what reason it was paid, the answer is obvious ... it was to compensate Mr Clayton for the unfair dismissal.' (*The employer and Mr Clayton had entered into a new contract of employment in 1997.)

These cases show that if the source is the termination of the employment, employment (in the sense of being or becoming an employee) is not the source. Other examples of non-employment sources (discussed below in more detail) include:
- Personal gifts (*Moore v Griffiths* (1972))
- Payments to alleviate distress (*Hochstrasser v Mayes*).
- Payments to compensate for discrimination (*A v R & C Comrs* (2015))
- Voluntary payments to alleviate the unfortunate consequences of becoming unemployed (*Mairs v Haughey* (1993)).

Where a payment is made for more than one reason, only one of which is 'from employment', the present position is as follows:
- If the reason that 'is not "from employment"' is dissociable from the reason that 'is "from employment"' in the sense that part of the payment was caused exclusively by that reason (whether or not the part can be quantified), the payment should be apportioned and that part is not earnings from employment.
- To the extent that the reasons are not dissociable (for example, where one reason entails the other reason), then as long the 'from employment' reason is a substantial cause of the payment, the payment is taxable. It need not be the main cause or the dominant cause.

Both points are illustrated by *Kuehne + Nagel Drinks Logistics Ltd v R & C Comrs* (2012) in which a payment of £5,000 was made by the former employer on the occasion of the transfer of employees to a new employer. £200 was compensation for the loss of a beer allowance. The remainder arose out of a dispute over the loss of pension rights. This part was secured by a threat of industrial action and the First-tier Tribunal found that the desire to secure the continued willing service of the employees was a 'substantial cause'. It was common ground that the compensation for the loss of the beer allowance was taxable, and this did not depend upon the taxability of the remainder. The reason for this part was dissociable. In respect of the £4,800, compensating the employees for their loss of pension rights (not a taxable reason, applying the replacement principle) was the means by which the employer secured the continued willing service (which was a taxable reason). These reasons were not dissociable and because the desire to secure service was a substantial reason, the £4,800 was taxable in full. [8.41]

3 The replacement principle

The key statement of the replacement principle is by Lord Woolf in *Mairs v Haughey* (1994):

> 'It is inevitable that if a payment is made in substitution for a payment which might, subject to a contingency, have been payable, that the nature of the payment which is made in lieu will be affected by the nature of the payment which might otherwise have been made. There will usually be no legitimate reason for treating the two payments in a different way.'

More recently, in *Kuehne* (2012) in the First-tier Tribunal (and also *Reid v R & C Comrs* (2016)), it was accepted that:

> '[I]f the payment in this appeal were one which could be said to have been made only to recognise the removal of the pension rights then it would have derived its character from the nature of the rights for which it compensated.'

There is thus a principle that a payment made only to recognise/compensate for the removal or surrender of another contingent payment derives its character for tax purposes from the payment it replaces because that other payment is its source.

Note, however, that if the payment is instead made in respect of an obligation to compensate the employee for a legal wrong, the legal wrong is the source. Thus, as will be seen, compensation for terminating an employment without giving the required notice derives from the unlawful termination of the employment and is thus not 'from employment'. Similarly, compensation for discrimination that occurs during the course of an employment derives from the discrimination rather than the employment, even when calculated to compensate for reduced earnings that would have been taxable (*A v R & C Comrs* (2015)). [8.42]

4 Third party payments

Tips normally form part of an employee's taxable earnings and in some businesses form a substantial part of take-home pay. In such cases, the payment is made by a third party rather than by the employer. In *Shilton v Wilmshurst* (1991) the House of Lords decided that such payments could amount to emoluments even if the third party did not have an interest in the performance of the employment contract. The case concerned Peter Shilton, the former England goalkeeper, who, on his transfer from Nottingham Forest to Southampton, received a payment of £75,000 from Nottingham Forest. Deciding that this sum was an emolument Lord Templeman stressed that:

> 'there is nothing in [the section] or the authorities to justify the inference that an "emolument from employment" only applies to an emolument provided by a person who has an interest in the performance by the employee of the services which he becomes bound to perform when he enters into the contract of employment ... so far as the taxpayer is concerned, both the emoluments of £80,000 from Southampton and £75,000 from Nottingham Forest were paid to him for the same purpose and had the same effect, namely, as an inducement to him to agree to become an employee of Southampton.' [8.43]

5 Past services

The debate about past services does not, of course, relate to the normal case where salary is paid in arrears. What is in issue is the taxability of a payment which relates to a period of employment for which payment has already been received.

In *Hochstrasser v Mayes* (1960) Viscount Simonds quoted Upjohn J as soundly reflecting the law when he said:

'Indeed, in my judgment, the authorities show that to be a profit arising from the employment the payment must be made in reference to the services the employee renders by virtue of his office, and it must be something in the nature of a reward for services past, present or future.'

Viscount Simonds' only reservation was that 'in this passage the single word "past" may be open to question'.

In *Shilton v Wilmshurst*, Lord Templeman stated that:

'Section 181 is not limited to emoluments provided in the course of employment; the section must therefore apply first to an emolument which is paid as a reward for past services and as an inducement to continue to perform services and, second, to an emolument which is paid as an inducement to enter into a contract of employment and to perform services in the future. The result is that an emolument "from employment" means an emolument "from being or becoming an employee".'

This can be interpreted as saying that in order for a reward for past services to be an emolument it must also be an inducement for future services. Slightly further on Lord Templeman is more ambiguous:

'if an emolument is not paid as a reward for past services or as an inducement to enter into employment and provide future services but is paid for some other reason, then the emolument is not received "from the employment".'

Taking Lord Templeman's speech as a whole it does not appear that he was deliberately intending to provide support for Viscount Simonds' comment in *Hochstrasser*. Further, it is not clear why a reward for past services should not be taxable.

In *Brumby v Milner* (1976), the House of Lords held that payments made from an employee trust when it was wound up, to employees who were still in employment, were taxable. In *Bray v Best* (1989), payments in similar circumstances were made to *former* employees. Lord Oliver said:

'Although before the Special Commissioners and High Court the taxpayer had contested that the sum paid constituted an emolument from his employment, the decision ... in Brumby v Milner ... effectively precludes further argument on this point and the question has not been pursued either before the Court of Appeal or before your Lordships.'

Overall, the most sensible position is that a reward for past service is a reward for service, but the fact that a payment is given after the service has been performed, with no prior obligation, may be a factor pointing to the payment being a personal gift. **[8.44]–[8.60]**

VI PROBLEM CASES

1 Introduction

This Section examines the case law on when particular types of payments can be said to be '*from employment*' and therefore taxable as earnings. When many of these cases were decided, if a payment or benefit did not satisfy that test, it fell outside the income tax net altogether. This is no longer the case: if a payment or benefit is not taxable as earnings, it may well be taxable under another, more specific, provision. If it is not caught by a specific provision in ITEPA 2003 relating to certain types of benefits commonly provided, it may fall within the residual provision bringing benefits within the tax net in Part 3 Chapter 10 or be a payment treated as earnings within Chapter 12. If none of those apply, it could be some form of unapproved retirement payment or benefit taxable under Part 6 Chapter 2. Finally, if the payment or benefit relates to termination of employment (or a change in its nature), it could fall within Part 6 Chapter 3. Since the taxation of termination payments is particularly complicated, the application of the different charging provisions to such payments is considered separately in Section IX. Accordingly, when reading the rest of this Section, it should not be assumed that just because a receipt is not 'from employment' it is not taxable. The complex issues arising from employment-related shares and securities are considered at [**8.66**].

[**8.61**]

2 Gifts

There is a basic distinction between a payment which is a *reward for services* and which is, therefore, taxable under ITEPA 2003 s 9 as earnings and one which is made *in appreciation of an individual's personal qualities*, which is not so taxable (the taxability of a payment made in appreciation of services rendered was considered in *Allum v Marsh* (see further [**8.145**])). Various factors are relevant in drawing this distinction (see also *Taxation*, 5 June 2008, p 606).

First, where the payment is made once only it is more likely to escape tax than where it is recurring:

> 'The payment had no foreseeable element of recurrence. Recurrence, or the possibility of recurrence, is not of course essential to tax liability in this type of case, but is a relevant factor and a not uncommon factor in the reported cases where the decision has favoured the crown.' (*Moore v Griffiths* (1972)).

Second, a payment is more likely to be taxed where it is made to a whole class of employees rather than to only one employee. For instance, in *Laidler v Perry* (1966), all the employees received a £10 voucher at Christmas instead of the turkey that they had received in previous years. The employees were taxed on the cash value of the voucher.

On the other hand, in *Moore v Griffiths*, which concerned bonuses paid by the FA to England's 1966 World Cup winning team, reliance was placed on the fact that the same amount was given to every player irrespective of whether he played or not, in order to justify finding that the payment was not a reward for service and thus not from employment.

Third, if the payment is by the employer there is a strong presumption that it constitutes earnings, whereas if it is from a third party, it is easier to show that it is a gift for personal qualities. However, tips are generally regarded as being in return for services and so taxable, even though made voluntarily by someone other than the employer. In *Calvert v Wainwright* (1947), a taxi driver was taxable on tips received from customers:

'A tip is in the ordinary way given as a remuneration for services rendered. Similarly, a waiter may expect to receive, and will usually receive, gratuities from those whom he serves; the waiter receives the gratuities in respect of his services; he receives them by way of remuneration for his services, even though the payments are voluntary and are not made by the employer of the waiter.'

The relevant point appears to be that even though such tips are voluntary they are, nevertheless, customary. This is supported by the fact that the court suggested that a particularly generous tip from a special customer (eg at Christmas) might escape tax (see also *Blakiston v Cooper* (1909)).

In a related vein, a payment by a person whose primary interest does not lie in deriving a benefit from the services of the payee is more likely to be a personal gift. This was noted by Brightman J in *Moore v Griffiths* (1972):

'the principal function of the FA is to promote the sport of football, and not to derive a benefit from the services of footballers.'

Fourth, a payment to which the employee is entitled under the terms of his contract of employment will usually be taxable as a part of his earnings (*Moorhouse v Dooland* (1955)), although this is subject to exceptions (see [8.42]–[8.43]).

Fifth, an unexpected benefit is less likely to be a reward for services. Thus in *Moore v Griffiths*, Brightman J gave the fact that the payments to the England team were not announced until after the World Cup as one reason why it was not remuneration. Nevertheless, even if an expectation can be shown throughout the relevant period, this is not necessarily a substantial argument in favour of taxing the payment. In *Seymour v Reed* (1927) the court recognised that there may have been an expectation of payment, but given that it was not a contractual entitlement, it did not carry great weight and the taxpayer won.

Sixth, the relative size of the benefit may be relevant if it is either very large compared to the employee's regular salary (as in *Seymour v Reed*) or very small, as was noted in *Laidler v Perry* (1966):

'But now suppose that, instead of £100, it was a box of chocolates or a bottle of whisky or £2, it might be merely a gesture of goodwill at Christmas without regard to services at all. So it is a question of degree. It seems to me that in this case when one finds that £10 a year was paid to each of the staff year after year, each of them must have come to expect the £10 as a regular payment, which went with their services.'

The explanation is that a payment that is either very small relative to the normal salary or very large is unlikely to be a reward for service.

Seventh, a voluntary payment may be a personal gift even if it is in recognition of an employee's long service. This is, after all, usually the point of a testimonial, as was noted in *Moorhouse*. Such payments recognise the personal qualities demonstrated through, for example, the long service and the personal qualities are the source.

EXAMPLE 8.2

(1) Ham has played cricket for Gloucestershire for many years. At the end of his distinguished career the county grants him a benefit match (ie he is entitled to all the receipts from a particular game). The benefit is a testimonial paid for Ham's personal qualities and not earnings from employment (see *Seymour v Reed* (1927) – although see now s 226E which would treat this amount as earnings subject to an exemption for £100,000). *Compare*:

(2) Mercenary plays as a professional in the Lancashire League and under the terms of his contract is entitled to have the 'hat passed round' (ie a collection taken) every time he scores 50 runs or takes five wickets in an innings. The sums that he receives will be taxed as earnings because he is entitled to them in his contract of employment (see *Moorhouse v Dooland* (1955)).

Finally, the gift rules overlap with the benefit in kind rules. In deciding whether tax is chargeable under ITEPA 2003, the gift rules should be applied first and then the benefit in kind rules (see Sections VII and VIII of this Chapter (particularly *Example 8.13*) and ITEPA 2003 s 64). A gift connected with the termination of an employment is considered at [8.145].   [8.62]

3 Inducement payments

Shilton v Wilmshurst (1991) (see [8.43] and [8.44]) illustrates that payments which are made (even by a third party) for 'being or becoming an employee' are taxable. However, payments made to compensate the taxpayer for some sacrifice that he has made by taking up an employment are generally not taxable because they are not in return for services. In *Jarrold v Boustead* (1964) an international rugby union player was not taxable on a £3,000 signing-on fee paid to him when he turned professional. The payment was not an emolument but was to compensate him for permanent loss of his amateur status.

The same principle was applied in *Pritchard v Arundale* (1971) where a chartered accountant was not taxed on a large shareholding transferred to him in return for signing a service contract as managing director of the company. The benefit was held to accrue to him, not for future services as managing director which were to be adequately rewarded, but as compensation for loss of his professional status as a chartered accountant. It may also be noted that the shares were to be transferred in return for the taxpayer's signing the service contract. Hence, even if he had died without performing any services for the company, the shares would have been transferable to his estate. Further, they were given by a third party not by the new employer (see also *Vaughan-Neil v IRC* (1979) at [8.134]).

In *Jarrold* Lord Denning MR said (*obiter*) that a church organist appointed for seven months at £10 per month would not be taxable on £500 paid to him in return for giving up golf *for the rest of his life*. On the face of it, *Pritchard* is

hard to reconcile with this example, but perhaps the following conclusions can be supported:
(1) Mr Arundale had been the senior partner in a firm of chartered accountants. Although he could have resumed his status as a chartered accountant on leaving the employment, his age (48) in practice made it 'most unlikely' that he would 'be able to pick up his former profession as soon as his other activities' ended; the organist in Lord Denning's example could never again play golf on a Sunday. In both cases, therefore, the compensation was, in effect, for a permanent loss to the taxpayer. If the loss is merely restricted to the period of the contract, the payment is likely to be viewed as advance remuneration.
(2) Mr Arundale was fully rewarded for his services under the contract. It seems likely that £10 per month was a reasonable payment, in 1964, for an organist. If the salary is not fair remuneration, again the payment is likely to be viewed as advance remuneration.

In *Glantre Engineering Ltd v Goodhand* (1983) an inducement payment made to a chartered accountant was held to be an emolument as the taxpayer failed to show that he had provided consideration in return for the payment since he was merely moving from one employment to another. It therefore seems that once the taxpayer fails to show that he has been permanently deprived of something akin to amateur status or the status of being a partner, it must follow that the payment is a reward for future services in the new employment.

A related issue arises where a new employee purports to sell something to his/her new employer. In *Hose v Warwick* (1946), an insurance broker who had built up considerable personal connections during his career took up employment and brought those connections with him. Subsequently, the company wished for him to become the managing director, which would involve him ceasing to make use of his client relationships (as he would manage the whole operation) and for the rest of the company to be allowed to use them. A £30,000 payment to recognise this was held not to be a reward for service 'but was a sum paid for abandoning to the company his personal connection'.

In *Manduca v R & C Comrs* (2013), HMRC accepted that a payment made to an employee for facilitating the transfer of a business, in circumstances where the taxpayer was an employee of the vendor and became an employee of the purchaser, was not taxable as employment income (but it was taxable as miscellaneous income).

On the other hand, in *Smith Williamson Corporate Services v R & C Comrs* (2015), which concerned an agreement with a new employee under which a payment was made purportedly for agreeing to deliver to the new employer the employee's existing client relationships, the Upper Tribunal rejected the submission that this should be regarded as a purchase of goodwill (and thus not from employment) and held, instead, that introducing the client connections was not a separate source of income but the provision of a service as part of the employment. The payment was thus earnings from employment.

[8.63]

4 Compensation for other losses

Compensation for loss caused to the employee may escape tax even when not paid as part of an inducement payment. The cases discussed at [**8.42**] illustrate that compensation paid for a personal loss suffered by an employee (eg compensation for loss on the sale of a house as in *Hochstrasser v Mayes* (1960)) will usually not be taxable as earnings. Further, compensation for various forms of discrimination prohibited by statute will be taxable, if at all, only under ITEPA 2003 s 401 (see further [**8.148**]). [**8.64**]

> **EXAMPLE 8.3**
>
> Num Ltd paid its employee, Sid, £1,000 to compensate him for the anguish he suffered as a result of his wife running off with the milkman. The payment may be non-taxable in Sid's hands as compensation for his suffering rather than a reward for services.

5 Payments on variation of terms of employment

Payments are sometimes made to employees when a benefit is withdrawn (and note *Hamblett v Godfrey* (1987), discussed at [**8.41**], which relates to compensation paid when a right was relinquished).

Where the employee agrees to receive a smaller salary in the future in return for a lump sum, as in *Cameron v Prendergast* (1940) and part of the payment in *Tilley v Wales* (1943), the lump sum is taxable. In *Bird v Martland* (1982) compensation was paid following withdrawal of company cars; in *McGregor v Randall* (1984) a contractual right to receive commission was withdrawn: in both cases the compensation was taxable. All these cases can be explained on the basis of the replacement principle whereby the payment made solely to recognise the surrender of a right to a benefit that would have been 'from employment' is itself 'from employment' (see [**8.43**]).

Lump sum compensation payments have, however, been held not to be taxable where the taxpayer gave up a contingent right which would have provided him with a benefit *after* his employment had ceased, even if the benefit would have been taxable. In *Hunter v Dewhurst* (1932), the director of a company wished to retire, upon which he would have been entitled to a lump sum equal to his total remuneration in the preceding five years. This amount would have been taxable as earnings from employment (as a majority of their Lordships acknowledged). To persuade him to remain as a director at a reduced salary, the company paid a lump sum of £10,000 in return for him giving up his right to this sum on retirement. The House of Lords held that the payment was not taxable.

This case is at odds with at least one generally accepted principle of employment taxation. Lord Atkin and Lord Thankerton reasoned that a sum paid to obtain release from a contingent liability under a contract of employment is not received under the contract of employment which is at odds with the replacement principle. Lord Warrington, however, appeared to reason that it was a capital sum and, therefore, not a profit from employment, which is at odds with acceptance that the capital/income distinction is not relevant to employment taxation of earnings.

In *Mairs v Haughey*, the Northern Ireland Court of Appeal held that 'even if a payment under the enhanced redundancy scheme was taxable, a payment to secure the termination of [the employee's] rights under the scheme would not be taxable as an emolument from the employment' on the basis of *Hunter v Dewhurst* (above). Although not necessary to the decision, Lord Woolf in *Mairs* indicated that he was not:

> 'persuaded that this aspect of the Court of Appeal of Northern Ireland's decision was incorrect or that Hunter v Dewhurst was wrongly decided. This is because for the Revenue to succeed, the Revenue would have to establish, contrary to my provisional view, that the lump sum payment was in the nature of an income payment before it could begin to qualify as being chargeable to tax under Schedule E.'

This is an unorthodox approach: the income/capital distinction has generally been considered irrelevant to the issue of the taxability of employment income. Given that this was only his provisional view, Lord Woolf's suggestion that the nature of the payment affected whether it was taxable under Schedule E should not be relied on too heavily, particularly as the end-result could be difficult to reconcile with the replacement principle he previously had enunciated.

Finally, as these sorts of compensation payments may be taxable under Part 3 Chapter 10, s 225 (restrictive undertakings) or Part 6 Chapter 3 if not taxable under the general charging provision, the reader is referred to Section IX Parts 3–5 ([**8.146**]–[**8.160**]) of this Chapter. [**8.65**]

6 Avoidance cases

A number of cases are of interest because they illustrate attempts to avoid charges to tax on employment income, and how the courts have addressed such attempts. The issues in these cases do not necessarily all relate to the 'from' employment test, but in the absence of a better place to put them, they are considered here.

David O'Leary, like Peter Shilton, was a professional footballer. He was domiciled in the Republic of Ireland and entered into an arrangement, designed to avoid income tax, with his employers, Arsenal FC. An offshore trust was established with O'Leary as life tenant and the sum of £266,000 was lent to the trust by Arsenal, interest-free and repayable on demand. The income produced by this sum (£28,985 pa) was payable to O'Leary but, so it was argued, because the sum fell to be taxed under Schedule D Case V and because O'Leary was non-UK domiciled, tax would not arise unless and until that sum was remitted to the UK (see [**18.34**]). Once O'Leary ceased to be employed by Arsenal the loan would be repaid. Vinelott J decided that the annual interest was correctly assessed as an emolument. He commented:

> 'The fallacy which I think underlies Counsel for the taxpayer's submission can be shortly stated. If an employer lends money to an employee free of interest or at a favourable rate of interest and if the employee is free to exploit the money in any manner he chooses his employment cannot be said to have been the source of the income derived from the exploitation; the employer is the source of the money

and the taxpayer is assessable to tax under Schedule E on the benefit to him of obtaining the loan on the terms on which the loan was made; but if the loan is repayable on demand that benefit cannot be quantified and form the basis of an assessment under Schedule E [but see **[8.124]** as employer loans are now subject to tax]. By contrast if an employer were to lend money to a bank on terms that interest was paid to the employee until further order the interest paid to him while he remains an employee would almost inevitably be taxable as an emolument of his employment ...' (*O'Leary v McKinlay* (1991))

A more recent case where a similar issue of attempting to have employment income classified as something else arose is that of *R & C Comrs v PA Holdings* (2011). This case involved the payment of discretionary bonuses in the form of dividends from a UK company during the 1999–00 tax year. The tax treatment of the dividend payments received by the employees relied on what was TA 1988 s 20(2), which gave priority to dividend tax treatment where a payment could be regarded as both dividend income and earnings from an employment. Whilst this was accepted by the First-tier Tribunal and the Upper Tribunal, the Court of Appeal concluded that in determining the nature of a payment, one was required to look at the substance and not be seduced by the form. Looking at the character of the payment in the employee's hands, it was earnings from employment and not a dividend, therefore the priority rule did not apply. This was followed by the Upper Tribunal in *Sloane Robinson Investment Services Ltd v R & C Comrs* (2012) and *James H Donald (Darvel) Ltd v R & C Comrs* (2015).

Interestingly, the Court of Appeal in PA Holdings stated (*obiter*) that even if their analysis was incorrect, the same end result could be arrived at by application of the principle in *Ramsay v IRC* (1981) (see **Chapter 2**), ie when the arrangement is considered as a whole (as opposed to each of its constituent steps) the payments represented by the dividends constituted earnings from employment and therefore should be taxed as such.

However, a different approach has been taken in *DB Group Services (UK) Ltd v R & C Comrs; R & C Comrs v UBS AG* (2016) where bonuses were delivered in the form of shares, the Supreme Court holding that the form of the transaction had to be respected – the shares were real and could not be treated as money. On the facts, however, the scheme failed because it depended upon the shares being subject to a restriction (ie a risk of forfeiture if certain events did not happen), so as to fall within Chapter 2 the employment-related securities legislation in ITEPA 2003 Part 7. The Supreme Court held that, on a realistic view of the facts, the restrictions were completely artificial, having no commercial purpose, and thus could be disregarded.

The same conclusion, that shares could not be treated as money, was reached by the Upper Tribunal in the earlier case of *Tower Radio Ltd, Total Property Support Services Ltd v R & C Comrs* (2015).

It is unclear, in light of *DB Group Services (UK) Ltd* and *Tower Radio Ltd* whether *LM Ferro Ltd v R & C Comrs* (2013), a First-tier Tribunal decision, can be regarded as correctly decided. There, too, a bonus was awarded in the form of shares but the FTT held that it was a 'money in, money out' scheme and thus could be treated as money. [8.66]–[8.90]

VII WHAT ARE EARNINGS?

1 Introduction

TA 1988 s 19(1) para 1 taxed 'emoluments' from an office or employment. That term was partially defined in s 131 as including 'all salaries, fees, wages, perquisites and profits whatsoever'. This was wide enough to cover benefits in kind as well as cash payments. Limits were, however, imposed on its meaning by the courts. The major restriction was that a benefit to an employee was only taxable under s 19 if it was convertible into money or was of direct monetary value to the employee (the prime example of the latter being the discharge of a personal debt of the employee).

ITEPA 2003 s 9 taxes 'general earnings' from an employment. General earnings are defined in s 7 and are made up of 'earnings' and amounts treated as earnings. The former replaces 'emoluments' and is defined in s 62 as follows:

'(2) "earnings" means (a) any salary, wages or fee, (b) any gratuity or other profit or incidental benefit of any kind obtained by the employee if it is money or money's worth, or (c) anything else that constitutes an emolument of the employment.

(3) "money's worth" means something that is (a) of direct monetary value to the employee, or (b) capable of being converted into money or something of direct monetary value to the employee.'

The change in wording at the beginning of (2)(b) reflects the Rewrite Project's aim of modernising the language of the legislation; the additional words at the end reflect the way the common law had interpreted 'emoluments'; (c) is to ensure that anything which would have been an emolument under the old law but does not fall within (a) or (b) will still be caught, though it is hard to imagine what that could be, given the width of (b). The old authorities on the meaning of emoluments and those on how an emolument is to be valued for tax purposes, which are all reflected in (3), are discussed in **[8.92]** and **[8.93]**.

Clearly, not all the types of benefits that an employee might receive will be 'earnings', so it is not surprising that over the years the legislature has brought other benefits within the tax net; in the main, those statutory provisions now apply to all employees, though 'lower-paid' employees escape some of them. That statutory regime and its relationship with the general charging provision is considered in Section VIII. The remainder of this Section considers further the general principles which apply to all employees. **[8.91]**

2 The general principles

a) *Money or money's worth*

Tennant v Smith (1892) is the leading case on the convertibility requirement. In that case, the House of Lords, in interpreting the equivalent of the old s 131, held that the benefit of a house, which the employee was required by his employment to occupy but which he could not assign or sub-let, did not constitute an emolument since it was not convertible into money. The test is whether the benefit *could* be lawfully converted; it is irrelevant whether the employee actually converts it into money. Consider, for instance, a rail season ticket which cannot be sold because it is non-assignable, but which can be converted into cash by surrender.

Although in *Abbott v Philbin* (1961) Lord Reid stated 'if a right can be turned to pecuniary account that in itself is enough to make it a perquisite', the Special Commissioner in *Bootle v Bye* (1996) thought that this was not intended to apply 'regardless of whether any payment obtainable would be heavily depreciated'. He accordingly held that a right to receive a cash sum if the employing company was sold (an event over which the taxpayer had no control) was not a perquisite as, realistically, any payment he could obtain from a third party in relation to that right would in no way reflect the right's intrinsic value. It will be interesting to see whether higher courts adopt this approach.

Abbott v Philbin demonstrates that a benefit may be convertible in ways other than simple sale as in that case the employee received an option to acquire shares which was non-assignable but its value could be realised in other ways, for example, by raising money on the right to call for the shares.

Nicoll v Austin (1935) shows how a payment of direct monetary benefit to an employee will be taxable. In that case a managing director told his employer company that he would have to sell his imposing house, where he entertained potential customers, because he could no longer afford to pay for its upkeep. To prevent the sale, the company paid the outgoings on the house and the employee was taxed on this sum as if he had been given the money to pay the bills himself. Similarly in *Richardson v Worrall* (1985) payment for petrol using an employer's credit card was held taxable since it discharged the taxpayer's liability to the garage. [8.92]

EXAMPLE 8.4

Simon is employed as a butler at a wage of £100 pw. He is required to 'live in' and £20 is deducted per week for board and lodging. Simon is assessed to tax on £100 pw (see *Machon v McLoughlin* (1926)). Compare the case of Rosie, who is employed as a housemaid and is paid a weekly wage of £95. She is required to live in but is not charged for board and lodging. She is taxed on £95; the board and lodging is a non-convertible benefit in kind which, therefore, escapes tax as earnings from employment (although see the benefits code, below).

b) *Valuing the benefit*

If the benefit is convertible, tax is levied on the value of the benefit to the employee: this is taken to be its second-hand value. In *Wilkins v Rogerson* (1961) the company arranged with a firm of tailors that each employee would be permitted to obtain clothes of up to £15 in value. The contract provided for payment directly by the company. When HMRC sought to tax an employee on a suit costing £14.50 the court held that the benefit was convertible into money, because the taxpayer could sell the suit, but that he could only be taxed on the secondhand value, estimated at £5 (see also *Jenkins v Horn* (1979), where this test operated to the taxpayer's disadvantage).

The practical application of these two principles can cause problems. For instance, the provision of a non-convertible benefit, such as the free use of a car, is not chargeable as earnings, whereas the provision of money to enable the employee to purchase such a benefit does constitute earnings (see *Bird v Martland* (1982)). A further problem (which mainly arises where an employee agrees to reduce his cash salary in return for a benefit – often known as 'salary sacrifice') is that it may be difficult to decide whether particular facts involve the rules on benefits in kind or not. This is illustrated by the case of *Heaton v Bell* (1970) where a company operated a scheme under which its employees were offered the use of fully insured company cars. If they accepted the offer they thereupon received reduced wages. An employee could withdraw from the scheme on giving 14 days' notice whereupon he would revert to his original wage. The House of Lords by a majority of four to one held that an employee who joined the scheme was entitled to his original unamended wage and that he had merely chosen to spend a portion of that wage on the hire of a car (but see Lord Reid's dissenting judgment). Thus tax was charged on the full wage since what the taxpayer chooses to spend his wages on is not tax-deductible! Three members of the House also considered that, if the full wage was not taxable, then the car was a taxable benefit in kind because, even though the right to use the car could not be assigned, it could be converted into money by withdrawing from the scheme and receiving the original wage again. The value of the benefit was the wage foregone. **[8.93]**

EXAMPLE 8.5
(1) Employees are given £40 to buy clothes to wear to work. The sum is earnings.
(2) Employees buy clothes on credit and they send the bills to the employer for payment. As the debt has been incurred by the employee, tax will be charged in accordance with *Nicoll v Austin* (1935).
(3) The employer enters into an arrangement with Sparks and Menacer Co Ltd that it will pay for work outfits chosen by its employees up to £100 each. The employees are taxable but on the second-hand value of the clothes, not their cost.
NB It is assumed that the exemption in ITEPA 2003 s 367 for special clothing does not apply.

c) *Redirection of earnings*

In *RFC 2012 Plc (in liquidation) v Advocate General for Scotland* (2017), the Supreme Court held that payments to a discretionary trust whose beneficiaries included players of the Rangers FC football team and their families constituted earnings of the players. The Court's starting point was that there was no requirement in the legislation for earnings to be paid to the employee or for the employee to be entitled to receive the earnings. Consequently, the charge applies to:

'money that the employee is entitled to have paid as his or her remuneration whether it is paid to the employee or a third party.'

Following this logic through, when a footballer negotiated payment terms that included their employer making a specified payment to the discretionary trust, that money was paid as part of the employee's remuneration package and was earnings from his employment.

Surprisingly, however, when the Court came to apply the law to the facts the focus was on the fact that 'the Scheme was designed to give each footballer access without delay to the money paid into the Principal Trust' (para 64) and did so (through sub-trusts and loans). On the above principle, however, it ought to have been irrelevant whether the footballers gained access to the redirected earnings.

Similarly, the risk that the trustees may not have exercised their discretion in favour of a footballer ought to have been irrelevant, yet the Supreme Court felt it necessary to apply the principle that 'composite schemes should be considered as they were intended to operate' in order to disregard this risk (para 65).

A judgment that appears to begin by setting out a point of high principle thus descends into the ad hoc world of taking a 'realistic view of the facts' when actually deciding the case. One may be left justifiably confused by the contradiction between the Court, on the one hand, saying that it does not matter if the employee receives the earnings and on the other deciding the case on the basis that the tax scheme was intended to and did deliver money to the employee.

A clue lies in the fact that alongside the footballers, who had contractual rights to trust contributions being made, there were executives being given voluntary bonuses in the form of trust contributions. On the 'entitlement' principle, the executive had no entitlement to the trust contribution being made – there was thus no redirection of earnings. That did not matter:

> 'For the same reasons as those which cause the footballers' remuneration paid to the Principal Trust to be subject to taxation, the bonuses which were paid to the employees through the trust mechanism fall within the tax charge as emoluments or earnings when paid to the Principal Trust.'

In other words, the realistic view of the facts analysis was necessary to catch the executives.

Although the Supreme Court said that they were 'essentially' upholding the reasons of the Inner House, there is in fact an important clarification. The Court of Session decided:

> 'For the respondents it was submitted that it was necessary for liability to income tax on a bonus that there should be a present entitlement to payment of money or money's worth. We disagree with that proposition. The fact that a payment is made is sufficient to produce a liability to income tax.'

This raised the problem of what the analysis should be where an employer makes a payment to a third party to procure a benefit for an employee. On the Court of Session's reasoning one could argue that when the employer in *Wilkins v Rogerson* (1961) paid the tailor £14.50 to purchase a suit for the employee that was a redirection of £14.50 of earnings.

The Supreme Court confirmed that payments to procure benefits in kind are not taxable as earnings – it is the benefit that is taxable as earnings (on its convertible value, if any). The situation would only be different if the employee had a contractual entitlement to the employer making a specified payment in order to procure the benefit. [8.94]

3 Amounts in respect of expenses

a) *What counts as earnings?*

Where an employee incurs expenses which the employer reimburses, those reimbursements will not be taxed as earnings, provided that the employee could have deducted the money he spent from his employment income as an expense of the employment. In such cases it can be said that the employee has derived no personal profit from the reimbursement (in the sense that he is no better off) and, in addition, no practical purpose would be served by deciding that the reimbursement is earnings but then permitting the employee to reduce those earnings to nil by setting off an equivalent expense (see ITEPA 2003 s 336 and Section XI for a discussion of what expenditure is deductible and [8.104] for the position of employees and directors who are not lower-paid). This principle does not apply to a flat rate allowance that is paid whether or not the expense is incurred.

It has been suggested that payments to an employee to reimburse him for the cost of using his home as an office are in fact taxable under ITTOIA 2005, thus avoiding these problems (see *Taxation*, 13 July 2000, p 386 and note that the absence of 'a separate agreement with a specific payment for an office involving use by persons in addition to the taxpayer' was fatal to the claim in *Ainslie v Buckley* (2002)).

In *Pook v Owen* (1970) a doctor holding a part-time hospital appointment and who had to attend the hospital several times a week was reimbursed two-thirds of his travelling expenses. It was held that the reimbursements were not emoluments because he was no 'better off' as a result of them. They were (partial) repayments of actual expenditure which would have been deductible in arriving at the emoluments of the taxpayer.

Other cases, however, have suggested that a reimbursement is not an emolument even though the relevant expenditure would not have been deductible by the employee. Thus, in *Donnelly v Williamson* (1982), a teacher was reimbursed for travelling expenses incurred in attending out-of-school functions was not taxable on the reimbursements. Walton J held that they were not emoluments because:

(a) they were not derived from her employment (she attended the functions voluntarily); and,

(b) they were a genuine attempt to compensate her for actual expenditure (irrespective of whether it was deductible).

This latter conclusion was doubted by the Upper Tribunal in *Reed Employment plc v R & C Comrs* (2014) on the basis that it was obiter and inconsistent with *Taylor v Provan* (1973), in which *Pook v Owen* was interpreted as a case in which it was crucial that the travel was between two places of work. The Upper Tribunal rejected a suggestion that reimbursement of expenditure did not constitute an emolument even if the expenditure was not deductible, as long as the expenditure was by reason of employment. The Court of Appeal did not need to consider this issue.

In *Perrons v Spackman* (1981) a mileage allowance paid by the council to one of its rent officers was held to be an emolument because it contained a profit element. **[8.95]**

EXAMPLE 8.6

Justinian, a part-time law lecturer, attends a legal conference and his university employers refund the cost of the conference which he had paid. The reimbursements are taxable as earnings from employment unless attending the conference is part of the duties of Justinian's employment and attends exclusively for that reason (see **[8.173]**).

If the university had instead paid for the conference so that he had received a benefit in kind, Justinian would be taxed on it only to the extent that it was convertible.

b) *Exemptions*

ITEPA 2003 s 240 provides a specific exemption where an employer reimburses (or pays directly for) incidental expenses (eg for newspapers and private telephone calls) incurred by an employee during overnight absences, up to an allowable maximum (currently, £5 for stays in the UK and £10 for those abroad): such expenditure would not normally be deductible under s 336 as it would not be necessarily incurred in the performance of the employee's duties. If the maxima are exceeded, the exemption does not apply to *any* part of the payment (s 241); nor does it apply if the costs of the employee's travel to his overnight rest place are not deductible (unless that is because of an exemption) (s 240(4)). HMRC seem to accept that the exemption applies to round sum allowances to be used to pay such expenses (EIM 02730).

ITEPA 2003 ss 250–254 provide an exemption from income tax where the employer (or a third party – for instance, when a manufacturer organises training for a retailer's staff) reimburses (or pays directly for) the cost of 'work-related training' or 'related costs' (see *Tax Bulletin*, April 2003, p 1022 on the application of these provisions where an employer reimburses the cost of training before the employment began, in response to the Special Commissioners' decision in *Silva v Charnock* (2002)). Sections 255–260 exist merely to deal with situations where the employer wishes to contribute to 'non-work-related training' undertaken by employees who are individual learning account holders (eg skills development courses) ('work-related training' is covered by ss 250–254). Individual learning accounts were discontinued throughout the UK in 2001, but were reintroduced in Wales by the Welsh Assembly in 2003 by way of Welsh SI 2003/918.

Reimbursement of expenditure calculated in an approved way can now result in exemption from liability to income tax (see **[8.107]**). **[8.96]–[8.100]**

VIII AMOUNTS TREATED AS EARNINGS OR COUNTED AS EMPLOYMENT INCOME

1 Introduction

Employees are taxed on 'employment income' and this is made up of:
(1) earnings (defined in s 62, which constitutes Part 3 Chapter 1 of the Act, and has already been considered in Section VII);

(2) amounts treated as earnings; and
(3) 'amounts which count as employment income' (ITEPA 2003 s 7 and see [**8.11**]).

This Section considers the majority of the taxing provisions covered by the last two categories; others are dealt with elsewhere because of the nature of the benefit to which they relate.

Category (2) incorporates the 'benefits code' (the provisions in Part 3 Chapters 2–11 of ITEPA 2003) which brings certain benefits in kind within the employment tax net. Unfortunately, the neat label 'benefits code' does not encompass all the provisions within (2) (see s 7(5)). As well as the benefits code, the following provisions also treat amounts received as earnings:

- those relating to agency workers and intermediaries (see Section IV);
- payments (NB not 'amounts') treated as earnings under Part 3 Chapter 12 (ss 221, 225 and 226 are discussed in this Section, ss 222 and 223 in Section XII and s 224 in **Chapter 50**); and
- capital allowances balancing charges covered by CAA 2001 s 262.

Category (3) covers share-related income (ITEPA 2003 Part 7, considered in **Chapter 9**) and 'income which is not earnings or share-related' as set out in Part 6 of the Act (Chapters 1 and 2 of which are considered in **Chapter 50** and Chapter 3 of which is considered in Section IX of this Chapter).

Not all payments and benefits which would be 'employment income' are actually taxed as there is a wide range of exemptions. Many can be found in ITEPA 2003 Part 4 (see Section X) but others are scattered throughout the Act. It is therefore important to check carefully whether any exemptions apply when calculating taxable earnings. [**8.101**]

2 The purpose of the special rules

The general purpose of the rules discussed in this Section is to extend the scope of the charge to tax on employment.

They do this in two main ways. *First*, whereas the causation test for the general charge to tax is 'from' employment (see Section V) the special rules cast their nets wider by using different concepts.

For example, the general causation test under the benefits code asks whether the benefit is provided 'by reason of employment' (instead of whether it is 'from' employment) and this is further supplemented by what is, in most cases, an irrebuttable presumption that benefits provided by the employer are provided 'by reason of employment'.

Similarly, the provisions relating to termination payments etc (s 401 onwards) apply to payments made 'in connection with' the termination of the employment which, again, is intended to catch payments that would not be caught by the 'from employment' test.

Second, even where a benefit was 'from' employment, the amount brought into tax depended upon the 'convertibility' principle (see Section VII). This resulted in no tax charge for benefits that were not convertible (such as a personal right to use living accommodation) or a charge to tax based on, for example, the second hand value of the benefit. The benefits code contains specific rules for calculating the taxable benefit for a number of common benefits in kind (such as living accommodation) and a residual charge based on the cost to the employer of providing the benefit (rather than its convertible value).

Furthermore, for arrangements entered into on or after 6 April 2017 (with transitional periods for arrangements entered into before that date and not renewed or varied afterwards), there are additional rules to deal with arrangements whereby the employee accepts a benefit instead of an amount of earnings. In essence, tax is charged on the higher of the amount of earnings 'surrendered' and the modified cash value under the benefits code (see [8.105]). Importantly, a number of exemptions do not apply to benefits charged under the optional remuneration arrangement rules, removing significant potential tax savings.

The effect of the benefits code is to bring many benefits in kind within the income tax net *even if not convertible into cash* or increase the taxable value of those already within that net. [8.102]

3 The benefits code

a) *Interaction with the charge on earnings from employment*

Except in the case of living accommodation, if the same benefit gives rise to an amount of earnings and an amount to be treated as earnings under the benefits code, it will first be taxed as earnings and only the excess will be taxed under the benefits code (ITEPA 2003, s 64 – resolving any previously existing ambiguity).

In respect of living accommodation, the priority is reversed such that the cash equivalent under the benefits code is treated as earnings, in full, and only the excess (if any) of the amount that would constitute earnings from employment under the general charge (ie the convertible value) is taxed under the general charge (s 109). [8.103]

EXAMPLE 8.7

The facts are as in *Wilkinson v Rogerson* (1961) (where the employer spent £14.50 providing an employee with a suit that had a second-hand value of £5 – see [8.93]):
(1) Prior to 6 April 2016, a lower-paid employee would still be taxed on £5 whereas any other employee would be taxed on £5 as earnings and £9.50 as an amount to be treated as earnings.
(2) Post 5 April 2016, any employee will be taxed on £5 as earnings and £9.50 as an amount to be treated as earnings.

b) *Who is excluded from the benefits code?*

From the 2016–17 tax year onwards, the benefits code applies in full to all employees and office holders (including shadow directors – *R v Allen* (2001)) except certain lower-paid ministers of religion (for the effect and meaning of which, see ITEPA 2003 s 290C–290G).

Previously, lower-paid employees (employees with earnings for the year of less than £8,500) and certain lower-paid directors were exempt from all but certain chapters of the benefits code including, significantly, the residual charge. When first introduced in 1948, the threshold was £2,000, many times greater than average earnings, however, due to fiscal drag the threshold became stuck at £8,500 and it was the case that very few employees or directors benefited from the exemptions. Implementing an OTS recommendation, FA 2015, s 13 repealed ITEPA 2003 ss 216–220, which previously dealt with this subject. For details of the pre-existing regime, readers are referred to previous editions of this book. [8.104]

c) *'By reason of employment'*

Every chapter of the benefits code, other than Chapter 7 (employment-related loans) requires the benefit in question to have been provided 'by reason of employment'. Where the benefit is provided by the employer, it is deemed to be 'by reason of employment' unless the employer is an individual and the benefit is provided in the normal course of the employer's domestic, family or personal relationships (see, for example, s 71).

In other cases, the question arises as to what is meant by 'by reason of employment'. At least three approaches can be detected in the case law:

(1) The test is one of 'but-for' causation. Support for this approach can be found in the judgment of Lord Denning MR in *Wicks v Firth* (1982):

> 'The words cover cases where the fact of employment is the causa sine qua non of the fringe benefits, that is, where the employee would not have received fringe benefits unless he had been an employee.'

(2) The test is wider than 'from employment' but not as wide as a 'but-for' test. In *Wicks v Firth*, Oliver LJ accepted that the test was wider than 'from' employment:

> '... the obvious intention of this legislation – presumably in an attempt to produce fairness between taxpayers – is to impose tax on the value of those otherwise untaxed advantages which the employee enjoys because he is employed, advantages which may not even accrue to him directly but which, because of their receipt by a member of his household, benefit him by relieving him of an expense which he might otherwise expect to bear out of his own resources ...'

Instead, he elaborated on the test as asking 'what is it that enables the person concerned to enjoy the benefit?'. This was also the formulation preferred by Hutton LCJ in the Court of Appeal in *Mairs v Haughey*:

> 'I prefer, with respect, the test suggested by Oliver LJ, which involves asking the question "What is it that enables the person concerned to enjoy the benefit?" than the causa sine qua non test suggested by Lord Denning ... I consider, with respect, that the causa sine qua non test suggested by Lord Denning is too wide and could let in a factor in the past which, in ordinary language, would not constitute a "reason" for the provision of the benefit.'

(3) The test is the same as the 'from employment' test. In *Wilcock v Eve* (1995), Carnwath J, although finding Oliver LJ's test 'more helpful', went on to say that:

> '... the difference between these formulations [of the "from" test] and the expression "by reason of" is hard to detect. It may be that we have moved beyond *Wicks v Firth*, to a point where there is very little difference, if any, between the two tests.'

It will be apparent that the difference between approaches (2) and (3) depends not upon the breadth of the 'by reason of' test but on one's approach to the 'from employment' test. Thus, if one limits the 'from' test to rewards for service, the 'by reason of' test will be broader whereas if one takes the broader *Hamblett v Godfrey* approach to 'from' employment (see **[8.41]**), as Carnwath J did in *Wilcock v Eve*, one can argue that the tests are largely indistinguishable.

As between the 'but-for' approach in (1) and the 'what is it that enables the person to enjoy the benefit?' test in (2) and (3), it is suggested that if Parliament had intended a 'but-for' test of causation it would have been a simple matter to say so. That it chose to express a different concept supports Oliver LJ's approach in *Wicks v Firth*. Notably, in a recent First-tier Tribunal case, HMRC are recorded as preferring, and indeed relying upon, the judgment of Oliver LJ on this point (*Southern Aerial (Communications) Ltd v R & C Comrs* (2016)).

What is interesting about the proposition that the 'by reason of' test is the same as the broader 'from' test is that, even on the broader 'from' test, there are well established categories of payment that are not 'from' employment, such as personal gifts (see **[8.62]**). Logically, if the two tests are indistinguishable, such payments will also not be 'by reason of' employment.

This conclusion is lent some support by the fact that prior to Schedule E referring to 'emoluments therefrom' it referred to 'profits by reason of ...'. The change to 'therefrom' was interpreted as only a slight variation:

> 'That word "therefrom" is a slight variation from the old Section which stood before the Consolidating Act of 1918 came into force, the words previously being "profits by reason of his office." We have now to consider as taxable "profit whatsoever" from the office which is an employment of profit.' (*Reed v Seymour*, per Lord Hanworth MR in the Court of Appeal)

By way of example, in *Cooper v Blakiston* (1907) the statutory question was whether Easter offerings to the incumbent Vicar were 'by reason of' his office. It was held that they were not because they were personal gifts.

Of course, the statutory context when introducing the benefits code provisions was different (being a deliberate attempt to cast a wider net), but these cases do provide some indications of the possible limits on the phrase 'by reason of'. In practice, this issue arises relatively infrequently because it is usually only relevant where the benefit is provided by a third party. **[8.105]**

d) *Optional remuneration arrangements*

An optional remuneration arrangement is an arrangement under which either:
(a) the employee gives up the right (or a future right) to receive an amount of earnings in return for a benefit; or
(b) other arrangements under which the employee agrees to be provided with the benefit rather than an amount of earnings.

The difference between the two is not always clear cut but, for example, if an employee gives up salary in return for a benefit, that is a type A arrangement; whereas if the employee has the option of receiving a cash allowance instead of a benefit, that is a type B arrangement.

If, in circumstances where there is such an optional remuneration arrangement, the employee selects the benefit, then he/she will generally be taxed on the higher of:

Benefit	Amount (a)	Amount (b)
Cash voucher (s 81(1A))	Sum of money for which the voucher is capable of being exchanged.	The amount foregone.
Non-cash voucher (s 87A)	Cost of provision less the amount made good.	The amount foregone less the amount made good.
Credit token (s 94A)	Relevant cost of provision.	The amount foregone less the amount made good.
Living accommodation (s 102(1B))	Cash equivalent (but this amount only applies if the modified cash equivalent (essentially the cash equivalent before deducting any amount made good) is equal to or higher than the amount foregone).	The amount foregone less the 'deductible amount'. The deductible amount means any amount made good; however, if the cost of providing the accommodation exceeds £75,000 and the amount made good exceeds the rental value, the deductible amount is limited to the rental value plus rent paid in excess of the rental value (s 103A(9)).
Cars other than low emission cars (s 120A) (Note the separate provisions relating to classic cars in s 147A)	Cash equivalent (but this amount only applies if the modified cash equivalent (essentially the cash equivalent before deducting capital contributions and payments in respect of private use) is equal to or higher than the amount foregone).	The amount foregone less deductible capital contributions made by the employee under s 132A and less payments for private use under s 144.
Fuel (ss 149A, 160A)	Cash equivalent.	Amount foregone.
Van (s 154A)	Cash equivalent (but this amount only applies if the modified cash equivalent (essentially the cash equivalent before deducting payments in respect of private use) is equal to or higher than the amount foregone.	Amount foregone less amounts paid in respect of private use under s 158A.

Benefit	Amount (a)	Amount (b)
Loans (s 175(1A))	Cash equivalent (but this amount only applies if the modified cash equivalent (essentially equal to interest at the official rate) is equal to or higher than the amount foregone).	Amount foregone less any interest actually paid on the loan for the tax year.
Other benefits (s 203A)	Cost of the employment-related benefit.	Amount foregone less any part of the cost made good by the employee.

These new rules can result in harsh outcomes. For example, assume an employee is offered a choice between £400 per month cash allowance for fuel based on expected mileage or car fuel as needed. The cash equivalent could be, say, 20% of £22,200 (£4,520) under s 150 but the employee will be taxed on the higher amount foregone of £4,800, irrespective of whether he/she did use that much fuel.

In addition, a number of exemptions do not apply to benefits provided pursuant to optional remuneration arrangements. Indeed, the way in which s 228A operates is by stating that no exemption in Part 4 applies unless it is listed in s 228A(4) or (5). Furthermore, where a benefit would be exempt from income tax but for s 228A, the amount taxed is always the amount in column (b) above (see, for example, s 203A(5)).

This means that, for example, an employee who is offered the choice between a car parking space at work or a cash alternative will be taxed on the cash alternative if he/she takes the car parking space, but an employee who is simply offered a car parking space will not be taxed on any benefit (s 237). Arrangements under which salary was surrendered in return for an exempt benefit were one of the main targets of these new rules.

Where a benefit is provided only partly under optional remuneration arrangements, the benefit is apportioned on a just and reasonable basis between the normal benefits code (to the extent it is not provided under optional remuneration arrangements) and the modified benefits code set out above.

Benefits provided pursuant to arrangements entered into, varied or renewed on or after 6 April 2017 are caught by the new rules in full from 2017–18 (FA 2017 Sch 2 para 62). For pre-6 April 2017 arrangements, the new rules apply with effect from 2018–19 or 2021–22 for cars, vans, living accommodation and school fees (see FA 2017 Sch 2, para 62(3)–(5)). **[8.106]**

e) *Making good*

With effect from 2017–18 there is a time limit on the period during which the employee can make good a benefit and obtain a deduction for that making good. The time limit will be 6 July following the relevant tax year. This rule already exists in respect of optional remuneration arrangements and is expected to be introduced for the ordinary benefits code in Autumn 2017, with effect from 6 April 2017. **[8.107]**

f) *Expense payments*

If an employee or director receives an expense allowance or a reimbursement of expenses that he has incurred, he is taxed on it in full as an amount treated as earnings under the benefits code (ITEPA 2003 ss 70–72), subject to the ability to claim a deduction in respect of such expenses. This reverses the position under the basic charge on earnings from employment where such reimbursement is unlikely to involve any element of profit and thus earnings (see [**8.95**]). However, from 2016–17 there are two specific exemptions for payments in respect of expenses, the effect of which is that no liability to income tax arises in respect of such amounts.

First, an amount paid or reimbursed in respect of an expense is exempt from charge under the benefits code if the expense reimbursed would give rise to an allowable deduction and the reimbursement is not part of a salary sacrifice arrangement (s 289A(1)). A similar rule applies to non-expense related benefits that give rise to a deduction (s 289D).

Second, an amount paid or reimbursed in respect of an expense is exempt from income tax (not just under the benefits code) if it is calculated in an approved way, is not part of a salary sacrifice arrangement and the payer or another person operates a system for checking that the employee is incurring and paying amounts that would be deductible expenses in respect of expenses of the same kind (s 289A(2)). This is intended to provide a simplified system for flat rate expenses. To prevent abuse, however, the exemption does not apply if the payer or person operating the system could reasonably be expected to know or suspect that the employee has not incurred or paid amounts in respect of the expenses or that a deduction would not be permitted.

In both cases, a targeted anti-avoidance rule applies to arrangements with a main purpose of avoiding tax or NICs (s 289E).

Previously, either the employer would have to claim a dispensation in relation to the reimbursement of expenditure under ITEPA 2003 s 65 or else the employee would have to claim a deduction under the rules discussed below.

There is also an exemption for reimbursements of actual expenditure on 'incidental overnight expenses', up to the permitted maximum (see [**8.95**]).

[**8.108**]

EXAMPLE 8.9

Andy has a salary of £9,000 pa and an expense allowance of £4,000 pa. For 2015–16, he would have been taxed on £13,000 pa as an amount treated as earnings unless he could deduct any expenses under ITEPA 2003 Part 5. For 2016–17 and subsequent years, £4,000 will be exempt from (a) the benefits code provided that the expense reimbursed would give rise to an allowable deduction and the reimbursement is not part of a salary sacrifice arrangement; and (b) from income tax generally provided they are qualifying business expense under s 289A(2).

g) *Vouchers and credit tokens*

An employee or office-holder who (or a member of whose family) receives a benefit in the form of a voucher or credit token may be charged to tax thereon. The tax charge crystallises when the voucher is received or the token used (unless there is a dispensation under s 96), and therefore the receipt of money, goods or services resulting from its use is not taxable (s 95): this avoids double taxation.

Where the employee receives a cash voucher (ie a voucher which can be exchanged for a sum of money not substantially less than the cost to the person providing it), he is taxed on its exchange value (s 81).

Where he receives a non-cash voucher (ie a voucher or similar document which can be exchanged for goods or services only and not for cash), he is taxed on the cost to the employer of providing the voucher rather than on its exchange value (s 87). Cheque vouchers (ie a cheque provided for an employee to be used by him to obtain goods or services) are treated as non-cash vouchers by s 84 and are therefore similarly charged as earnings.

Where the employee receives a credit token (including a credit card), he is taxed on the cost to the employer of providing the goods, money and services obtained by the use of that credit token less any part of the cost made good by the employee (s 94).

The employee will not be taxed if the voucher or token is made available to the public generally and he (or a member of his family) does not receive it on more favourable terms (ss 78, 85 and 93). Part 3 Chapter 4 contains other exemptions: for instance, a cash voucher is not taxable if it is intended to enable the employee to obtain a payment which would not have been taxable if paid to him directly (s 80). Other exemptions can be found in ITEPA 2003 Part 4, particularly Chapter 6.

In addition, HMRC has the power to exempt the provision of certain vouchers and credit tokens as representing a taxable benefit where the voucher or credit token enables an employee to obtain specified benefits which are exempt from taxation under the benefits code (s 96A). HMRC will specify on a case-by-case basis (by way of regulations) the vouchers and credit tokens which benefit from this exemption. **[8.109]**

h) *Living accommodation*

The leading case on a benefit escaping the general charging provision because it was not convertible into money or money's worth related to employer-provided accommodation (*Tennant v Smith* (1892) – see **[8.92]** and *Taxation*, 5 January 2012). It is not therefore surprising to find that there has long been a statutory provision bringing such a benefit within the tax net.

As a result of ITEPA 2003 s 102, the cash equivalent of the benefit of accommodation is to be treated as earnings for all employees. Following *R & C Comrs v Apollo Fuels Ltd* (2016) it might be thought that if the employee pays a market rent for use of the living accommodation that is a fair bargain and thus no benefits code charge arises. FA 2016 introduces ITEPA 2003 s 97A specifying that Chapter 5 (ie living accommodation) applies irrespective of whether the accommodation is provided pursuant to a fair bargain. As noted below, on a literal interpretation the legislation has misfired (see **[8.125]**).

The charge is divided into two parts: the first calculates the benefit derived from accommodation where the cost of providing it does not exceed £75,000; the second calculates the benefit received when the accommodation costs more than that (see below for how the 'cost' of a property is ascertained).

An employee is only taxed on accommodation provided whilst he is actually in employment (s 102(1)). [8.110]

i) The basic charge

If an employer *provides* his employee with living accommodation, the employee is taxed on the value to him of that accommodation less any sum that he 'makes good' (normally by paying for the use of the property) (ITEPA 2003 s 105).

In *Stones v Hall* (1989), the court concluded that the provision of services in return for accommodation was, for the purposes of TA 1988 s 145(1) (now ITEPA 2003 ss 105(2) and 106(2)), neither the payment of rent nor the making good of the cost to the company of providing that accommodation. Accordingly, the taxpayer was charged on the value of the accommodation.

If the employee owns a share of the property, so that he and the employer each have an undivided beneficial share in it, there is an argument that, since the employee already has a right to occupy the accommodation rent-free, it is not '*provided*' by the employer. It is clear from HMRC's Employment Income Manual that HMRC sometimes equates 'provided' with 'being available' and claims a tax charge based on the period of availability, not actual use: see *Taxation*, 18 October 2001, pp 51–53 and 15 November 2001, p 170 for two criticisms; and note the interpretation of 'provided' in TA 1988 s 154 in *Templeton v Jacobs* ((1996) – see [8.125]).

The value on which the employee is charged was the higher of the rental value of the premises (defined in s 105(3) as based on the annual value, which itself is defined in s 110) and the rent paid by the employer for that accommodation (s 105) (see *Toronto-Dominion Bank v Oberoi* (2004) where the employing bank successfully converted rental payments into a premium and thus reduced the charge under TA 1988 s 145). However, from 22 April 2009, structuring the payment as a lease premium will not avoid a benefit in kind charge (s 105(4A)–(4B), s 105A, s 105B). Where a lease is for 10 years or less, or contains a relevant break clause, the rental amount on which the employee is charged will be the amount of the lease premium spread over the duration of the lease plus the amount of any rent paid by the person at whose cost the accommodation is provided less any amount made good by the employee.
[8.111]

ii) The additional charge

Special rules apply in cases where the cost of providing the accommodation exceeds £75,000 (s 106). First, what would be the cash equivalent under s 105 is calculated. Then, broadly, additional earnings are calculated by applying the official rate of interest (as under beneficial loans – see [8.124]) to the amount by which the cost of providing the accommodation exceeds £75,000. Cost for these purposes will usually be the cost of acquiring the property (though there are special rules in s 107 for calculating the cost under s 106 if the person providing the accommodation has held an interest in it for at least six years when the employee first occupies it). The two amounts added together constitute the taxable benefit.

EXAMPLE 8.10

Giles, the managing director of Clam Ltd, sells to the company his house in Manchester for its market value of £160,000. He is granted an option to buy the property back in ten years' time for its present value. The rental value of the house is £750 and Giles continues to live in the property. Giles is assessed to tax under ITEPA 2003 on earnings of £750 pa plus (say) 5% of £85,000 (£160,000 − £75,000), ie £4,250 pa. **[8.112]**

iii) Increasing and decreasing the charge

At one time, employers were offering employees a low cash alternative to accommodation, in the hope of reducing the tax charge on accommodation actually occupied (relying on *Heaton v Bell* (1970) – see **[8.119]**). Now Part 3 Chapter 5 applies even in that situation. Of course, if the cash offered is *higher* than the amount taxable thereunder, that higher amount will be taxed (s 109)!

Where employer-provided accommodation is in multiple occupation, s 108 limits the total amount chargeable to what it would have been if it was occupied by one employee; and this is then apportioned amongst the employees in accordance with what is 'just and reasonable'. **[8.113]**

iv) Exemptions

The charge under s 105 does not catch the provision of ancillary services such as cleaning, repairs and furniture. However, if the employee or director is not lower-paid, the cost to the employer of providing those services (less any amount paid by the employee for them) will fall within ITEPA 2003 s 203 (but note that there is a cap on the taxable amount if the employee is in 'representative accommodation' – s 315).

No charge arises for 'representative occupation'. This means occupation falling within ss 99(1) and (2) and 100, ie accommodation which is:
(1) necessary for the proper performance of the employee's duties (eg a caretaker and see *Tennant v Smith* (1892) at **[8.92]**); or
(2) customary for the better performance of the employee's duties (eg a police officer who occupies a police house adjacent to the police station – see also *Taxation*, 4 August 2011); or
(3) where there is a special threat to his security and special security arrangements are in force as a result of which he resides in that accommodation.

A director can only be a representative occupier under (1) or (2) above if he has no material interest and he is either employed full-time or the company is either non-profit-making or charitable (s 99(3)).

In *Vertigan v Brady* (1988) the owner of a nursery site near Norwich provided his 'right-hand man' with a rent-free bungalow some three miles from the nursery. That employee was in direct charge of the plants and their propagation and was on standby at all hours during the week and on two out of three weekends to make adjustments to the heating and ventilation of the greenhouses. He was able to reach the nursery within five minutes of leaving the bungalow. There was evidence that he had been unable to obtain council accommodation in the area when he took the job and could not afford to buy a house in the vicinity. The court decided that the benefit of the rent-free accommodation was taxable since the exception for accommodation which was customarily provided ((2) above) did not apply. What was customary depended upon three main factors: statistical evidence (how common was the practice?); how long the practice had existed (a custom does not grow up overnight!); and whether the relevant employer accepted the customary practice. In this case, although statistical evidence showed that approximately two-thirds of all key nursery workers were provided with rent-free accommodation, there was insufficient evidence to show that the practice had become so normal as to be an established custom. **[8.114]–[8.115]**

v) Non-domiciliaries

Whether the charge on living accommodation is capable of applying to shadow directors has long been a matter of debate: the issue is especially important when a non-UK domiciliary purchases a UK house for personal occupation through a foreign company. If it can be shown that he is a shadow director of that company, can he then be assessed on benefits derived from occupying the property? In *R v Allen* (2001) the House of Lords answered this question in the affirmative. However, it should be noted that in that case the money to purchase the UK property derived from the trading profits of the offshore company whereas in most cases it derives from money given or lent to the company by the non-UK domiciliary. For an interesting argument as to whether, in such cases, it can be said that the property is provided at the 'cost' of the non-UK company, as the legislation requires, or whether, if it is, the shadow director 'makes good' that cost, see Brandon, *Offshore and International Taxation Review* (2000) 135 and see *Example 36.2*. **[8.116]**

i) *Vehicles and fuel*

ITEPA 2003 Part 3 Chapter 6 brings into the tax net, for employees and directors, the benefit that they derive from an employer-provided car or van which is available for their private use (s 114). Tax is not, therefore, charged if the employee can prove that he was forbidden to use the vehicle for private use and did not so use it (*Gilbert v Hemsley* (1981) and see s 118). Generally, any benefit received from the private use of a 'heavier commercial vehicle' is exempt from tax, provided the employee's use of the vehicle is not wholly or mainly private use (s 238).

Furthermore, it was previously the case that if the vehicle is provided on commercial terms that amount to a fair bargain, there is no 'benefit' and thus no charge under the benefits code (see *R & C Comrs v Apollo Fuels Ltd* (2016) and **[8.125]**).

With effect from the 2016–17 tax year, however, s 114(1A) will provide that Chapter 7 applies irrespective of whether or not the car is made available on terms that constitute a fair bargain. It appears, however, that the legislation has misfired because the reasoning in *Apollo Fuels Ltd* was not that Chapter 7 did not apply, but that when one came to calculate the tax charge in s 120 there was no 'benefit' for which a cash equivalent could be calculated. Arguably that reasoning still applies, although the Finance Bill 2016 notes indicate an intention to reverse *Apollo Fuels*; thus the courts may well hold that the statutory context of s 120 is now different.

In place of the fair bargain rule is a much more limited exclusion where the employer carries on a business of vehicle hire to the public and the car/van is hired to the employee in the normal course of that business in circumstances where the employee is acting as an ordinary member of the public (new ITEPA 2003 s 117(3) with effect from the 2016–17 tax year). [8.117]

i) Pooled cars and vans

The legislation distinguishes between two categories of car and van: the pooled car or van and all others. A pooled vehicle is one which is made available to different employees, is normally garaged overnight at the employer's premises, and any private use is merely incidental to its business use (see ss 167 and 168 for the exact conditions – and see SP 2/96 and s 295 in relation particularly to the position when a pooled car is used for chauffeur-driven home to work journeys for a senior employee; and IR 480 for a discussion of what is 'merely incidental' private use). When these conditions are satisfied, the benefits of using pooled cars or vans are not taxable. [8.118]

ii) Non-pooled cars

If a non-pooled car is available for the private use of an employee or his family or household, he is taxed on the cash equivalent of the car as fixed by statute (ITEPA 2003 ss 114 and 120). Section 114 (1)(a) limits the application of Part 3 Chapter 6 to a car which is made available to the employee 'without any transfer of the property in it'. In *Vasili v Christensen* the courts had to decide whether the purchase by the employee of a 5% interest in a car owned by his employer prevented the company car provisions applying (and, if so, whether the (smaller) residual benefit in kind charge applied instead). The Special Commissioner (2003) held that the company car provisions did not apply but the benefits in kind ones did; but the High Court (2004) overturned that decision and held that the former continued to apply on the basis that s 132 must be taken to deal with the situation where the employee acquires an interest in the car following a capital contribution to its purchase. This point was raised again in *GR Solutions Ltd v R & C Comrs* (2013) where it was held that if the employee owned a car outright, transferred 90% of the interest in the car to his employer but continued to use the car, tax and Class 1A NIC was due on the benefit.

In *MC & LJ Ive Ltd v R & C Comrs* (2014) it was held that where a car was leased in the name of the company but the employee paid all costs associated with the vehicle, a benefit had been provided by reason of employment and this therefore fell within ITEPA 2003 s 114.

In *Kerr v Brown* (2002), the Special Commissioners held that the use of vehicles provided to senior officers in the fire brigade which, it was agreed, were not 'cars' for the purposes of these provisions (because they were not commonly used as private vehicles and were unsuitable to be so used – see now s 115(1)) was caught by the general benefits in kind charge (now ITEPA 2003 Part 3 Chapter 10). ITEPA 2003 s 248A now contains an exemption where members of the emergency services take home emergency vehicles when on call.

Vehicles with emergency flashing lights permanently attached to their roofs are not cars for the purposes of Chapter 6 because they are not of a type commonly used as a private vehicle and are unsuitable to be so used – indeed, the use of such cars by members of the public on a road would be unlawful (*Gurney v Richards* (1989)).

There are two regimes in ITEPA 2003 for taxing company cars. Readers are referred to earlier editions of this book for that relating to cars registered before 1 January 1998. This edition considers the regime for cars registered after 31 December 1997. The policy behind this regime is to 'help tackle global warming and improve local air quality'. Therefore, the tax charge is linked to the car's CO_2 emissions. The starting-point is the car's list price but the percentage of that which is the 'cash equivalent' (the amount to be treated as earnings) depends on the level of CO_2 emissions (see s 139); it ranges from 10 to 35%. High business mileage or the fact that the car is older will not decrease the cash equivalent as it did under the old regime; use of a diesel car will in general increase it beyond what it would be based on the CO_2 emissions (as diesels emit greater quantities of air pollutants); cars which are capable of running on 'alternative' fuel (such as electric, hybrid and bi-fuel cars) attract a reduced percentage; for the five-year period which commenced on 6 April 2010, employees who have electric cars available to them for private use will not be subject to a benefit in kind charge on the basis that electric cars have zero CO_2 emissions. FA 2014 introduced a new reduced rate of 5% of the car's list price for ultra-low emission cars in addition to an increase of 2% to the remaining percentage bands, up to a new maximum of 37%. These rates apply for the 2015–16 and subsequent tax years.

In order to avoid the statutory charge (and Class 1A NICs), some employers offered a (low) cash alternative, so that under *Heaton v Bell* (1970) (see **[8.94]**) earnings would be based only on (and the employers' NICs based on) the salary foregone. Section 119 means that the mere fact that a cash alternative is offered will not make the use of a company car taxable as earnings under the general charging provision. The employee will pay tax on what he actually receives – the car or the cash. **[8.119]**

iii) Reducing the tax charge

The amount of tax payable can be reduced if the employee is required to make a payment for the private use of the vehicle or if it is unavailable for at least 30 days (ss 143 and 144 and see s 145 where the car is temporarily replaced); or if the employee makes capital contributions (s 132). These contributions must be made within the relevant tax year from 2014–15 onwards. Reliance on any of these provisions is not straightforward: for instance, any payments must clearly be for private use, so a payment for insurance premiums, required by the agreement with the employer, did not reduce the cash equivalent in *IRC v Quigley* (1995) because they were made 'in exchange for the insurance of the vehicle, not for the use of it'.

Problems also arise where contributions are made in order to receive a more expensive car. While HMRC may allow these to be deducted from the cash equivalent if the agreement is properly worded (see *Tax Bulletin*, November 1991, p 3), it is easy to fail to satisfy the (literally interpreted) words of s 144 (previously TA 1988 Sch 6 para 7 – see *Brown v Ware* (1995)). It is not even certain that *monthly* contributions will count as capital payments for the purpose of s 132.

HMRC interprets 'unavailability' in s 143 strictly, so the fact that, for instance, the employee is out of the country for three months and cannot in fact then use the car may not be sufficient.

Prior to 6 April 2014, an employee was prevented from falling within the car benefits charge if the benefit was taxable as earnings under ITEPA 2003 s 62. However, following FA 2014 this is no longer the case as s 114(3) has been repealed. An employee who has leased a car and paid full market value for the lease will now fall within the car benefits regime and will therefore be unable to claim tax-free mileage payments. [8.120]

iv) Use of own car

If employees use their own car for business travel, they may get tax relief for their journeys (see [8.174]). If the employer reimburses expenses, the employee will be taxable on any profit element. To support a claim for relief or to calculate if there is any profit, a statutory system of mileage rates now applies (and this extends to payments made to an employee because he carries another employee who is travelling on business) (see ss 229–236 and IR 124). [8.121]

v) Fuel and other benefits

There is a separate scale charge on the provision of petrol for private use in an employer's car (ss 149–153) which is linked to the CO_2 emissions of the company car. See HMRC's guide: *Company Cars – Advisory Fuel Rates* (1 June 2017) for current advisory fuel rates for company cars. These rates can be used by employers to either reimburse employees for business travel in their company cars and/or require employees to repay the cost of fuel used for private travel.

Reimbursement/repayment made within these rates should prevent an employment income and Class 1 NICs charge (see *Cheshire Employer and Skills Development Limited (formerly Total People Limited) v R & C Comrs* (2012), where the Court of Appeal re-affirmed the conclusion in the First-tier Tribunal which discussed how such arrangements should be structured in order to avoid an NIC charge; see also *Tax Journal*, 23 November 2012 for a discussion of this case).

The provision of a personal chauffeur for an employee is a taxable benefit under Part 3 Chapter 10 (but see the comment on pooled cars above). The employee is not taxed on other benefits provided in connection with the car such as insurance, road fund tax and a car parking space provided by the employer (ss 237, 239(4) and (5)). HMRC has confirmed that payment by the employer of the London Congestion Charge, in relation to a non-pooled car (or van) the provision of which gives rise to a benefit charge, is not a taxable benefit ([2003] STI 292 and 303). [8.122]

vi) Non-pooled vans

Vans available for private use were previously taxed under TA 1988 ss 154–166. Basically, the cash equivalent was £500 if the van was less than four years old at the end of the year; £350 if aged four or more years. There were special provisions to deal with shared vans. In May 2003, the government issued a consultation document on reforming the tax treatment of employer-provided vans to simplify the system and take into account the environmental impact of vans. As a consequence FA 2004 s 80 and Sch 14 substantially changed the tax treatment. From 6 April 2005 there is now no tax charge if any private use of the van other than for 'ordinary commuting' is 'insignificant' (see *Tax Bulletin*, October 2004, pp 1160 and 1161 for how to assess whether other private use is 'insignificant'); and the van is mainly used for the purposes of the employee's business travel (ITEPA 2003 s 155 as amended). If unrestricted private use is allowed, the old scale charges continue to apply and to include any private fuel provided by the employer. However, from 6 April 2007, the scale charge increased to £3,000 and a separate fuel charge of £550 applied where fuel was provided for unrestricted private use (see *Taxation*, 1 February 2007, p 133). From 6 April 2014, this charge increased to £3,090 with a fuel benefit of £581. For zero emission vans, from 2015–16, zero emission vans will be charged at a special rate of 20% of the van benefit charge, which rate will then increase each year until April 2020 when the zero emission rate matches the full van benefit charge.

The cash equivalent is reduced when the van is unavailable or is shared, and is adjusted if the employee makes payments for its private use. There are similar provisions in relation to the fuel charge. Many of the points made in iii), iv) and v) will also apply in relation to these provisions. [8.123]

j) Beneficial loan arrangements

Interest-free (or cheap) loans to employees were not caught under TA 1988 s 154 (the old general benefits in kind charge, now the residual liability in ITEPA 2003 Part 3 Chapter 10): if the loan is repayable on demand, the benefit cannot be quantified (see extract from *O'Leary v McKinlay* (1991) at [8.66]); in any event, if the money comes from the employer's own funds, then foregoing the opportunity to earn interest may not have been a 'cost' to the employer within s 154. Accordingly, a specific charging provision was introduced (originally TA 1988 s 160, now ITEPA 2003 Part 3 Chapter 7). This provides that where an employee or director obtains a loan by reason of his employment (as to which, see s 174), either interest-free or at a low rate of interest, he is taxed on the cash equivalent of the benefit of that loan. This is defined as the difference between interest for the year calculated at the 'official rate' and any interest actually paid by the employee. The 'official rate' is set by the Treasury under FA 1989 s 178 and is linked to commercial mortgage rates, so accordingly varies from time to time.

The main circumstances in which a loan will be employment-related is if it is made by the employer or a person within the same group as the employer (parent company, subsidiary or sibling company). Careful attention needs to be paid to the terms of s 174 outside these core cases, however, as other situations are caught (in particular, in relation to close companies).

For the purposes of these provisions 'loan' includes 'any form of credit' (s 173(2)). The width of this definition is illustrated by *Grant v Watton* (1999), in which a service company paid the expenses of a partnership and was reimbursed haphazardly during the year, with the total service fee not being fixed until after the end of the year. It was held that this amounted to the provision of credit to a director of the service company who was also one of the partners because, in the absence of an agreement, the partnership owed the company money as soon as it was expended by the service company.

As with other provisions of the benefits code, the charge applies to 'the cash equivalent of the benefit ...'. However, unlike other provisions of the benefits code, the reference to 'benefit' does not exclude a fair bargain (ie a loan at a commercial rate of interest). The Court of Appeal has said that it is 'a perfectly ordinary use of language to speak of a borrower receiving the benefit of a loan, even if it is at a full commercial rate' (*R & C Comrs v Apollo Fuels Ltd* (2016) considering the decision in *Williams v Todd* (1988) – and see with effect from 2016–17 tax year, s 173(1A)). Instead, credit is given for interest actually paid when calculating the cash equivalent (s 175(3) and note that if interest is paid at the official rate, it is not a 'taxable cheap loan' for which a cash equivalent needs to be calculated).

This can result in fixed rate loans that were made on commercial terms at the outset giving rise to a tax charge either because the official rate is higher than the commercial rate for a loan of that length or because the official rate rises after the loan was initially made.

There are two methods of calculating what would be the amount of interest due on the loan at the official rate – the normal and alternative methods (ss 182 and 183 and see s 186 in relation to replacement loans), the latter giving a more accurate figure where the amount outstanding fluctuates during the year. The following example deals with a straightforward situation, using the normal method of calculation. (See *Taxation*, 11 September 2008, p 276 for further examples.)

EXAMPLE 8.11

Day, an employee of Digday Ltd, borrows £25,000 from his employer to purchase a suite of Italian furniture. He pays interest at 2% pa and the capital is to be repaid on demand. For 2016–17, Day has received an amount to be treated as earnings equal to:

	£
Interest at official rate of 3% on £25,000	750.00
Less: interest paid at 2% pa	500.00
Taxable amount	£250.00

A loan to a relative of the employee is also taxed unless the employee can show that he derived no benefit from it (s 174(1) and (5)).

If a loan to a relevant employee or director is released or written off, he is treated as receiving earnings equivalent to that amount, even if the release is made after the employment has become an 'excluded employment' (ie lower-paid – see s 63(4)) or on (or after) the termination of his employment (unless the termination is due to his death) (ss 188, 189 and s 190). 'Golden handshakes' given in the form of the release of a loan will not have the benefit of the £30,000 exemption under Part 6 Chapter 3 (see [8.154]) and should, therefore, be avoided. It may, therefore, be more tax-efficient to make a tax-free payment to the employee which he then uses to repay the loan.

There is no charge to tax where the aggregate amount of all taxable cheap loans (ie loans to which the exceptions in ss 176–179 do not apply – see s 175(2)) outstanding at any time in the tax year does not exceed £10,000 (this threshold was raised from £5,000 with effect from 6 April 2014 and applies to both future and existing loans); or if the aggregate of 'non-qualifying' loans does not exceed such amount (s 180). This enables small loans (eg to buy a season ticket) to escape the tax net even if the employee has a larger 'qualifying' loan (eg a cheap mortgage). There are special rules on the aggregation of loans by a close company to a director (s 187). Loans provided on 'ordinary commercial terms' are exempted from the charge (s 176). This is to prevent an employee being subject to a tax charge if the rate of interest normally charged by his employer (being in the business of lending money or supplying goods or services on credit) is less than the official rate. There is also an exemption for certain types of fixed interest loan (s 177).

Sums advanced by the employer to cover expenses that will be necessarily incurred in the employment are not treated as earnings provided that the sum advanced is less than £1,000 and that the advance is spent within six months (these conditions may be relaxed on an application by the employer) (s 179).

There has always been a problem reconciling the beneficial loan charge with the provisions which give relief for 'qualifying loans' (basically, loans on which interest is eligible for relief under ITA 2007 s 383(1)) when the employee uses the loan for a qualifying purpose. The position now is that loans will not be taxed if interest on the loan would qualify for relief if it were in fact payable and paid (s 178 and see s 184).

The benefit of a cheap or interest-free bridging loan provided when an employee has to move house because of his job may be exempted from tax: see ITEPA 2003 s 288 (see [8.162]). [8.124]

k) Taxable benefits – residual liability

i) Introduction

The object of Part 3 Chapter 10 is to tax all benefits (except those which are taxed under Chapters 3 to 7, or would be but for an exception (s 202)) 'provided by reason of the employment' by any person (not just the employer) to an employee who is not lower-paid or his family *and whether or not convertible into cash.* These are called 'employment-related benefits' (s 201(2)).

Four questions arise out of this:
(1)   What is a 'benefit'?
(2)   When is a benefit 'provided'?
(3)   When is a benefit provided 'by reason of employment'?
(4)   On what amount is tax charged?

First, as regards (1), in many cases it will be obvious whether a benefit has been provided or not. It is, however, established and accepted that 'fair bargains' are excluded because they do not involve a benefit:

> 'HMRC does not dispute that fair bargains are excluded from the meaning of "employment-related benefit" in section 203 for the purposes of Chapter 10 of Part 3, dealing with benefits not covered by the specific earlier Chapters, but they say that that is not the case with all or most of the other Chapters.' (*HMRC v Apollo Fuels Ltd* (2016))

The Court of Appeal went on to hold, contrary to HMRC's submission, that references to 'benefit' in Chapter 6 of the benefits code (cars, vans etc) also excluded a fair bargain and, where an employee paid market value for a car lease, that was a fair bargain (although note the attempt to reverse *Apollo Fuels* in FA 2016 for living accommodation, cars and vans, discussed at [8.110]–[8.123]). Similarly, in *Mairs v Haughey* (1992), the Northern Ireland Court of Appeal held that reasonable compensation for employees surrendering rights under a non-statutory redundancy scheme was a fair bargain and thus not a benefit.

It should be noted that, whilst HMRC practice is not to apply s 201 to compensation payments on termination of employment (see [8.146]), it will seek to apply it to compensation for a change to the terms of an ongoing employment (see *Tax Bulletin*, June 2003, pp 1036 and 1037).

A further point in relation to the meaning of 'benefit' is that it is unnecessary for the employee to have requested the benefit and it is generally irrelevant that the employee could have obtained the benefit cheaper elsewhere (although if the employee could have obtained the benefit free elsewhere, there would appear to be no advantage). Thus, in *Rendell v Went* (1964) the managing director of a company had a car accident and was prosecuted at the Old Bailey for dangerous driving. The company paid for the legal services for him and he was acquitted. He was taxed on the cost to the company of providing the legal services (a non-convertible benefit in kind) although he did not request the benefit and could have found cheaper services elsewhere. All their Lordships did, however, emphasise that the sum in question was not extravagant or unreasonable for the purpose.

An unusual example is provided by *Chepstow Plant International Ltd v R & C Comrs* (2011), where the First-tier Tribunal held that being the registered owner of a race horse (but not the beneficial owner) was not a benefit because the taxpayer had no interest in horses. If he had had an interest, there would have been a benefit.

Second, a benefit is 'provided' to an employee when the benefit in question becomes available to be enjoyed by the taxpayer, not (if earlier) when the employer has done everything it had to do to secure the provision of the benefit (*Templeton v Jacobs* (1996) – an employer agreed to provide an employee with an office at home by means of a loft conversion, the Revenue successfully argued that the loft conversion was provided when completed, not when the employer engaged and paid the builder. The assessment had, therefore, been made for the right tax year.)

Third, the question of when a benefit is provided 'by reason of employment' has been considered above (see [8.41]).

Finally, the amount charged to tax is generally the cost incurred in providing the benefit, subject to a deduction for any payment made by the employee (s 203). This is considered in more detail in the following section. [8.125]

ii) *The cost of providing the benefit*

ITEPA 2003 s 203 provides as follows:

'(1) The cash equivalent of an employment-related benefit is to be treated as earnings from the employment ...

(2) The cash equivalent ... is the cost of the benefit less any part of that cost made good by the employee ...'

Section 204 provides:

'The cost of an employment-related benefit is the expense incurred in or in connection with provision of the benefit (including a proper proportion of any expense relating partly to provision of the benefit and partly to other matters).'

What the legislation does not explain is what is meant by 'expense incurred'. This presents a particular problem in cases where the employer provides an in-house benefit, for example, where the employee is a teacher at a school and the school allows the employee's child to attend the school for 20% of the normal school fees. In theory, one could argue that the cost means:

- The marginal cost – ie how much extra expense is incurred by the school to educate the extra child.
- The average cost – ie a rateable proportion of the expenses incurred in providing the school facilities that were enjoyed generally by *all* the pupils.
- The opportunity cost – ie if the child fills a school place that would otherwise have been taken by a fee-paying pupil, providing the benefit has cost those fees in full.

These were the facts of *Pepper v Hart* (1992). The House of Lords held that, in the case of in-house benefits, the cost of the benefit to the employer was the additional (or marginal) cost and not a *pro rata* share of all the costs of the employer. On the facts, the 20% fee more than covered the direct additional costs resulting from the boys' presence in the school.

It is notable that *Pepper v Hart* was heard in two stages before the House of Lords. During the first hearing, five law lords sat and a majority were in favour of the Revenue's view that the cost was a proportionate part of the cost of running the whole school.

After the hearing, however, their Lordships became aware that during the Parliamentary consideration of what became FA 1976, a clause providing for in-house benefits to be taxed at market value was deliberately dropped and the Financial Secretary explicitly told Parliament (as recorded in Hansard):

'The removal of clause 54(4) will affect the position of a child of one of the teachers at the child's school, because now the benefit will be assessed on the cost to the employer, which would be very small indeed in this case.' (Column 1098.)

Their Lordships reconvened the case before a panel of seven law lords who unanimously held that reference to Hansard should be permitted in certain circumstances as an aide to interpretation and, in the present case, since the words of the statute were capable of being interpreted as referring to the marginal cost, that is how they were interpreted. In reaching this conclusion, Lord Browne-Wilkinson (with whom a majority agreed) was explicit that this did not depend upon the children occupying surplus places (such that there was no opportunity cost).

The marginal cost approach can lead to difficult questions in some circumstances. For example, if an employer takes advantage of an offer whereby the purchase of one new suit provides a discount of 50% on the next purchase, is the first employee taxed on the full cost of the suit whereas the second employee taxed on 50% (unless the convertible value is higher)?

A further point that should be noted is that s 204 provides for 'a proper proportion of any expenses relating partly to provision of the benefit and partly to other matters' to be taken into account. This allows apportionment where the same expenditure is also used for matters other than providing the benefit to the employee in question, for example:

- A benefit shared with other employees or persons who are not employees.
- A benefit provided for only part of a tax year.
- The product of the expenditure is used partly for the purposes of the employer's business and partly to provide the benefit.

For example, in *Westcott v Bryan* (1969), the taxpayer was the managing director of a pottery company. A house was bought by the company both for the purpose of providing the taxpayer with somewhere to live and to use to entertain the company's overseas customers. The Revenue assessed the taxpayer on the basis that all the expenditure on the house was a benefit because no part of the expenditure was severable and thus could be related solely to the company's purposes. This was rejected by the Court of Appeal: the expenditure was incurred for two distinct objects only one of which was of benefit to the taxpayer. Accordingly, and even though no part of the expenditure could be severed and attributed solely to the company's purposes, an apportionment was required.

By way of contrast, in *Rendell v Went* (1964) where the employer paid for the legal defence of one of its employees against criminal charges, the benefit to the employer arose though the provision of the benefit to the employee or, as Lord Denning MR explained in *Westcott* '[i]n that case every part of the £641 was spent for the director's benefit'.

In *Kerr v Brown* (2002), which concerned the use of emergency vehicles by firemen, the availability of the car to be called to an emergency whilst being driven between the fire station and home did not justify any apportionment of the driving expenses because that 'availability' did not result in any expense (the car would have been available whether or not the journey was undertaken). However, apportionment of the standing costs of the vehicle to exclude days when the car was not at all available for private use was appropriate.

HMRC state (at EIM 21200):

> 'where a benefit is provided to a director or employee to perform the duties of his employment it remains a benefit and not an "other matter" to be apportioned. The director or employee is entitled to a deduction under Section 365 ITEPA if all or part of his use of the benefit relates to use for business purposes – see EIM21637 – but this does not affect the calculation of the cash equivalent of the benefit. All use by the director or employee remains a benefit, whether that use is for business or private reasons.'

It is difficult to understand what HMRC mean or what they have in mind. When an employee uses a 'benefit' to perform the duties of his employment, he is using it for his employer's purposes and not his own. If there is no private use, it is difficult to see why there is a benefit. If there is also private use, applying *Westcott v Bryan*, an apportionment is required.

As HMRC indicate, however, s 365 permits a deduction in respect of amounts treated as earnings under the residual benefits code charge where, had the employee incurred and paid the cost of the benefit, the whole or part of the amount paid would have been deductible. **[8.126]**

iii) Are cash payments caught?

The wording of s 204 would seem to indicate that s 203 does not apply to cash payments (it is odd to think of an expense being incurred in the provision of cash or how that would be calculated if the cash was obtained through trading activities). However, the Court of Appeal held in *Wicks v Firth* (1982) that the old s 154 did apply to cash benefits (the House of Lords did not have to decide the point) and this approach was also taken by the Northern Ireland Court of Appeal in *Mairs v Haughey* (1992).

Arguably, applying the marginal cost test, the expense incurred should take account of the employer's profit margin. Thus if the employer makes computers at a marginal cost of £400 per extra computer and sells them for £1,000, the expense incurred in providing £1,000 of cash is £400. Of course, this issue only becomes relevant if the payment escapes the 'from employment' general charge but is nevertheless 'by reason of employment' (or deemed to be so), for example, a personal gift provided by the employer. **[8.127]**

iv) Do the rules apply before commencement and after termination?

A Special Commissioner held, in *Jacobs v Templeton* (1995), that benefits 'provided' to *future* employees in the tax year *before* the employment commenced were not caught by s 154. This point was not considered by the High Court (because it interpreted 'provided' differently) but the Commissioner's view is now made explicit in ITEPA 2003 s 201(4). Benefits provided 'by reason of the employment' to a prospective employee in the tax year in which the employment commences will be caught, the inference being that they will not be caught if paid in a year prior to the commencement of the employment.

Employers sometimes provide benefits to former employees – for instance, a redundant employee may be allowed to continue his cheap mortgage; a retired employee may still have his private medical insurance premiums paid. For a discussion of whether such benefits could be taxed under the benefits in kind legislation, see **[8.146]**. **[8.128]**

v) Special rules for use or transfer of an asset

When the benefit consists of the private *use* of an asset without transfer of ownership, the cash equivalent treated as earnings from the employment is the higher of the actual cost to the employer in providing the asset (eg the cost of hiring it) and the 'annual value' of the use of the asset (s 205): see *Tax Bulletin*, October 2000 for HMRC's view that, under the old s 156(5)(b) (now ITEPA 2003 s 205(4)), only the marginal additional cost of running expenses have to be taken into account when calculating the cash equivalent; and *Kerr v Brown* (2002) for the Special Commissioners' interpretation of these difficult provisions.

From 2017–18, there is an exclusion for assets made available under terms that prohibit private use throughout the year (as long as no private use is in fact made of the asset) (s 205(1B)) and there is a proportionate reduction of the amount charged where the asset was not available for private use throughout the tax year (s 205(1C) and s 205A). Similarly, where an asset is available for the private use of more than one employee, the amount charged is apportioned on a just and reasonable basis (s 205B).

In the case of land, its annual value is defined in s 207. For any other asset, the annual value is 20% of its market (capital) value when it is first put at the employee's disposal (s 205(3)). This could apply, for example, to furniture provided in living accommodation.

If assets which have previously been used or have depreciated are *transferred* to an employee, the cash equivalent is the market value of the asset *at the date of transfer* less any sum paid by the employee (s 206 and 203(2) although do not forget to consider the general charge on the convertible value first). If, however, the employee (or some other person) has previously been subject to an income tax charge for the use of the asset, he is taxed on its market value *at the date when he first used it* less the sum of the annual value(s) on which he has already been taxed (s 206(3)) if this is higher than the market value when transferred.

This alternative method of calculating the taxable benefit does not, however, apply if the asset transferred is an 'excluded asset' (see s 206(6) – cars, certain computer equipment, and cycles/cycle safety equipment). In such a case, no tax charge will arise provided the employee buys the asset for market value.

Note that s 206 only applies to transfers of assets that have been 'used' or have 'depreciated'; where an asset that has not been used but has increased in value is transferred, the benefits code cost will be based on the expense incurred at the time of acquisition by the employer (ie before the increase) (*Aberdeen Asset Management plc v R & C Comrs* (2012)). It is likely, however, that the full current value will be taxable under s 62.

EXAMPLE 8.12

On 6 April 2015, Mr C Rash was given by his employer the use of a hi-fi system costing £2,000. In October 2017, the employer transferred the system to Mr Rash free of charge when its market value was £800.

Market value at the date when first used by Mr Rash, ie cost	£2,000
*Benefit in kind in 2015–16: 20% × £2,000	£400
*Benefit in kind in 2016–17: 20% × £2,000	£400
Benefit in kind in 2017–18: £2,000 – £400 – £400 (remember that the second hand value will be taxed as earnings under s 62)	£1,200

*If the employer had rented the system at £500 pa, this higher figure would be taxed as earnings.

Whenever an employer transfers an asset to an employee, the former's CGT position should be considered in the light of TCGA 1992 s 17, given that HMRC has withdrawn its former concessionary treatment whereby that section was not applied if the employee paid less than market value and was subject to income tax on the difference (*Tax Bulletin*, December 1994, p 181). [8.129]

vi) Scholarships

Scholarship income is exempt from tax (ITTOIA 2005 s 776 – see [8.164] in relation to HMRC practice where employers make payments to employees who are in full-time education). However, scholarships provided under arrangements entered into by the employer which are awarded to the children of employees and directors who are not lower-paid are taxed as earnings of the parents unless not more than 25% of the total payments from the fund are to children of any employees and the award is fortuitous, ie not resulting from the employment (ITEPA 2003 ss 211–215: see further [1984] STI 62). [8.130]

vii) Trivial benefits

With effect from the tax year 2016–17, ITEPA 2003 ss 323A–323C (inserted by FA 2016) exempt trivial benefits provided to employees or members of their family or household (s). This replaces a previous non-statutory and rather ambiguous policy of excluding 'trivial' benefits.

That ambiguity is replaced with three dense sections of legislation, the essence of which is that a benefit is exempt if:
(a) it is not cash or a cash voucher;
(b) the cost of the benefit does not exceed £50;
(c) it is not provided pursuant to a salary sacrifice arrangement;
(d) the benefit is not provided in recognition or anticipation of particular services; and
(e) where the employer is a close company and the employee is a director/ office holder or a member of the family/household of such a person, total trivial benefits provided in the tax year in respect of that employee do not cost in excess of £300.

This might cover, for example, sending a bunch of flowers when an employee is ill. [8.131]

4 Payments treated as earnings

a) Introduction

Part 3 Chapter 12 sets out those payments which are treated as earnings. These are a sub-set of the category 'amounts treated as earnings' (s 7(5)) and, therefore, form part of 'general earnings' under s 7(3). Not all the provisions of Chapter 12 are considered here: for the whereabouts of the remainder, see [8.101]. [8.132]

b) Sick pay and permanent health insurance

Sick pay is taxable, whether paid by the employer, a Friendly Society, an insurance company or a third person, if it is paid as a result of arrangements entered into by the employer (ITEPA 2003 s 221). Where an employer runs a sick pay scheme to which both employer and employee contribute, sums paid to him or his family are not treated as earnings to the extent that the sums reflect contributions made by the employee (s 221(4)).

Similarly, if the employee receives *income* benefits under a permanent health insurance policy which he has taken out then, provided the cost of the insurance premiums was not met by the employer, benefits will be exempt from tax as long as they are only paid while the individual is sick or disabled (ITTOIA 2005 s 735). See *Tax Bulletin*, December 1996, p 377, on the types of insurance benefits not covered by the exemption and when and how gross payments can be received.

Statutory sick, maternity, paternity and adoption pay are all taxable under ITEPA 2003 s 656, although as social security (rather than employment) income. **[8.133]**

c) *Restrictive undertakings*

Payments in respect of the giving or fulfilment of a restrictive undertaking in connection with an individual's current, future or past employment is treated as earnings from the employment for the tax year in which it is made (ITEPA 2003 s 225). Similar provision is made in s 226 where 'valuable consideration' (as defined) is given for a restrictive undertaking instead of a payment.

These provisions reverse the position under the general charge according to which payments under restrictive covenants are not usually a reward for service (see the House of Lords decision in *Beak v Robson* (1943)). Depending on whether the payment was classified as income or capital for the employer, it may or may not be deductible by the employer for its tax purposes (see **[10.135]**).

Nevertheless, gaps may still arise. For example, a payment of £40,000 in *Vaughan-Neil v IRC* (1979) to a barrister to induce him to leave the planning Bar and work for a company as an employee was not taxed because (a) it was not a reward for service, and (b) the barrister did not give an undertaking (his inability to practise at the Bar was the consequence of accepting the employment).

HMRC has in the past argued that the provision charging payments for restrictive covenants applies if the employee gives any sort of undertaking not to sue for breach of contract. This is most likely to occur in a termination agreement, though it could also be a provision in an agreement to change the terms of an ongoing employment: in relation to the former, see **[8.147]**.

[8.134]

d) *Sporting testimonial payments*

From 2016–17 a sporting testimonial payment that is not otherwise earnings from employment is treated as earnings under s 226E, subject to an exemption for £100,000 (s 306B). **[8.135]**

5 Conclusions on the treatment of benefits

The present system presents a bewildering range of possibilities and a number of grey areas in relation to important statutory terms, although the removal of the category of lower-paid employees does reduce some of the complexity.

Consider, for instance, the following examples (no account is taken of exemptions potentially applicable in the first example). **[8.136]–[8.140]**

EXAMPLE 8.13

Rod wants his part-time computer operator, Julie, to work late two evenings per week. Her salary is £4,500 pa. He plans to provide her with meals or a meal allowance on those two evenings. So far as Rod is concerned, the sum that he expends will be a deductible business expense, but Julie's tax position depends upon how the provision is made:
(1) If Rod, the employer, pays a cash allowance, that sum is earnings.
(2) If Rod pays the bill incurred by Julie, that sum is earnings (*Nicoll v Austin* (1935)).
(3) If Rod gives Julie a voucher exchangeable at a restaurant, the cost incurred by Rod in providing the voucher amounts to earnings.
(4) If Julie buys the food herself and is reimbursed, the reimbursement will be earnings (although see the discussion of *Donnelly v Williamson* (1982) – see [**8.95**]).
(5) If the employer has an arrangement with the restaurant, so that food is provided and the expense is directly met by the employer, there is a benefit in kind charge based on the cost. Prior to the tax year 2016–17, as a lower paid employee, there would have been no charge.

EXAMPLE 8.14

Free Range Ltd gives all its employees a 25lb turkey at Christmas. In deciding whether tax is charged: (1) apply the gift rules (ie is the turkey given in return for services or is it for personal qualities?); then (2) apply the benefit in kind rules (ie is the turkey convertible into money; if not, is it caught by ITEPA 2003 Part 3 Chapters 2–11?). If it is decided that the benefit is a gift, the benefits code is applicable and the cost of providing the turkey will be deemed to be a benefit provided by reason of employment.

IX TERMINATION PAYMENTS

1 Introduction

When an employment terminates a number of different payments may be made for a number of different reasons. Each payment or element of a payment needs to be identified and analysed separately. A summary of common types of payment and their *typical* tax treatment is as follows:

Unpaid salary	Taxable in full as s 62 earnings.
Contractual amount payable on termination for any reason	Taxable in full as s 62 earnings.
Salary during notice period	Taxable in full as s 62 earnings.
Contractual payment in lieu of notice	Taxable in full as s 62 earnings.

Damages for failure to give contractual notice of termination and failure to pay PILON (if any)	Not taxable as s 62 earnings. Taxable as an amount in connection with termination of employment under s 401 (subject to the £30,000 exemption) (EIM 12970). It is anticipated that this treatment will be reversed with effect from 2018–19 by new ss 402A–402E.
Statutory redundancy payment	Not taxable as s 62 earnings (s 309). Taxable under s 401 (subject to the £30,000 exemption).
Non-statutory redundancy payment	Not taxable as s 62 earnings (*Mairs v Haughey* and EIM 13750). Taxable under s 401 (subject to the £30,000 exemption).
Payment for a restrictive covenant	Treated as earnings under s 225 and taxed in full.
Benefit in kind provided or continued after termination	If pursuant to a right under the terms of employment, the convertible value (if any) is taxed as s 62 earnings and the cash equivalent under the benefits code is taxed under s 401 (see s 415, but note the slightly different treatment for living accommodation), subject to the £30,000 exemption. If part of a redundancy package, the higher of the convertible value and the benefits code cash equivalent is taxed under s 401 (see s 415) subject to the £30,000 exemption.
Damages relating to termination (eg unfair dismissal)	Taxable under s 401, subject to the £30,000 exemption.
Damages for events occurring prior to termination	Generally not taxable (*A v R & C Comrs* (2015) and EIM 12965).
Other amount that the employer is accustomed to make and/or the employee could reasonably have expected to receive	If the payment has the character of damages, it is taxed under s 401. If the payment does not have the character of damages, it is likely to be taxable as s 62 earnings (for example, a termination bonus).

It is not uncommon for the employer to pay a single lump sum in settlement of all and any claims the employee may have. In such cases, it is a question of judgment as to how the sum should be apportioned between the various different claims. Where feasible, the parties should seek to agree their own apportionment in the compromise agreement as this will at least provide a starting point in the event of an enquiry by HMRC. Labels that do not reflect reality will, however, be disregarded. [8.141]

2   The general charging provision

a)   *Deferred remuneration and contractual payments on termination*

A payment made after the termination of employment is earnings if it is in the nature of 'deferred remuneration'. Similarly, as a general proposition, a payment made under the contract of employment will be taxed in full, even though it is paid because of the termination of the employment. In *Dale v de Soissons* (1950), followed in *Williams v Simmonds* (1981), a director's service agreement provided for him to be paid £10,000 if it should be prematurely terminated. The taxpayer argued that the payment was not in return for services. It was held, however, that as the payment was one to which he was contractually entitled, it was taxable. The status of this general proposition is not entirely clear at the moment (see **[8.42]**) but, in view of the generous tax and NIC treatment of non-contractual payments on a termination of employment, it will generally still be advisable from a tax point of view to omit such compensation clauses from contracts of employment (see *4* below (**[8.147]**)). [8.142]

b)   *Payments in lieu of notice ('PILONs')*

If correct notice is given to the employee and he works out that period or remains employed but on 'garden leave', payments that he receives are earnings under general principles. If the employer terminates the contract without giving the required notice and in circumstances where there is no contractual provision permitting a payment to be made in lieu of notice, a payment to recognise that the required notice was not given is, prima facie, damages and thus not earnings from employment (see *Henley v Murray* (1950)).

However, HMRC's view is that if the employer has a practice of automatically making payments instead of giving contractually required notice, the payment may be categorised as earnings from employment. This is on the basis that if the payment is automatic and does not involve an assessment of the loss suffered by the particular employee, then it is not in the nature of damages. HMRC recognise, however, that sometimes it is impractical to consider each individual case and adjust the net earnings for the notice period to arrive at an amount of damages (EIM 12977).

Where the contract permits the employer to terminate the employment either by giving notice or by making a payment in lieu of notice, it has been held by the Court of Appeal that a payment in lieu of notice is taxable as earnings from employment on the basis that the right to notice or a PILON was the security required by the employee as an inducement to become an employee in the first place (*EMI Group Electronics Ltd v Coldicott* (1999)). This point is considered further in the following section in light of the decision in *Mairs v Haughey* that a contractual redundancy payment is not earnings from employment.

If the contract provides for a notice period or a PILON and the employer gives notice but then the parties enter into negotiations and agree a compromise to bring the employment to an immediate end with a payment not very different to the PILON, it has been held that the payment is earnings from employment (*Richardson v Delaney* (2001); a similar result was reached by the FTT in *Brian Goldman v R & C Comrs* (2012)). Lloyd J reasoned that there was no breach of contract nor any good reason why this 'intermediate' course should escape taxation when the salary during the notice period and the PILON would both be subject to tax. Arguably this was an application of the replacement principle.

On the other hand, in *Martin v R & C Comrs* (2014), Warren J rejected a submission by HMRC that there is 'a material distinction between cases where the payment arises as a result of something which one or other of the parties is permitted to do in accordance with the terms of the contract ... and a case which involves a breach of contract', noting that *Henley v Murray* had not involved a breach of contract. The First-tier tribunal in *Tottenham Hotspur Ltd v R & C Comrs* (2016) preferred the decision in *Martin* to the decision in *Richardson* in holding that a payment under a mutual agreement to terminate a football player's contract was not from employment because it was made to abrogate the employment.

In reality, a search for good reasons for the distinctions drawn in this area is likely to end in failure, for example, HMRC's position is that where the employer and employee negotiate a compromise to bring the employment to an end in circumstances where there was no contractual alternative for a PILON, the payment is treated as damages (EIM 12979).

It is possible that the contract does not give the employer the right to make a payment in lieu of notice but does purport to quantify the damages that will be payable in the event that the employer breaches the requirement to give notice. Such liquidated damages clauses are enforceable as long as they are a genuine estimate of the loss that will be suffered (and there is a real distinction between a payment which is part of the price of the contract and liquidated damages provisions – see *The Office of Fair Trading v Abbey National plc* (2009)).

In *Martin v R & C Comrs* (2014), the question was whether a payment by an employee upon termination of his employment to the employer was negative general earnings. The Upper Tribunal held that one determines whether something is negative earnings by applying the concept of earnings with the roles reversed. HMRC themselves argued that the payment the employee was required to make upon termination was liquidated damages and thus not negative earnings (by analogy with *Henley v Murray*) indicating that HMRC accept that liquidated damages are not earnings from employment. The Upper Tribunal appeared to accept the premise that liquidated damages would not be negative earnings but disagreed that the payment in question was liquidated damages.

It thus appears that a genuine liquidated damages clause will not give rise to 'earnings from employment'. This is another example of fine distinctions without obvious good reason. However, *SCA Packaging Ltd v R & C Comrs* (2006) demonstrates that care will be required in drafting a provision that is accepted as a liquidated damages clause (on the facts, the clause was not a liquidated damages clause because, inter alia, it used the language of a right to payment rather than any loss sustained).

HMRC, clearly unhappy at the distinction between PILONs and damages for failure to give notice, have proposed that the law will be changed with effect from 2018–19 such that an amount of a termination award (other than a redundancy award) will be taxed as earnings insofar as it is 'post-employment notice pay' (new ITEPA ss 402A–402E, expected in the next Finance Act). Post-employment notice pay will be calculated by reference to the pay that the employee would have received if they had worked the minimum notice period required to terminate the contract. A deduction will be given for any part of the termination award that is otherwise taxed as earnings (other than holiday pay and termination bonuses). [8.143]

c) *Redundancy payments*

Redundancy refers to a situation where the employer has reduced need for employees, for example, due to the cessation of part of a business or the introduction of new working methods (see Employment Rights Act 1996 s 139).

Statutory redundancy payments can only be taxed as termination payments within s 401 (ITEPA 2003 s 309(3)). Following the House of Lords' decision in *Mairs v Haughey* (1993), HMRC accept that lump sum payments under non-statutory schemes will also only fall within s 401, provided they are made on a genuine redundancy and are genuinely made to compensate for the employment lost through redundancy (SP 1/94). Advance clearance for schemes can be obtained. Presumably, genuine one-off redundancy payments will be taxed in the same way but the Statement of Practice does not mention them. In either situation, HMRC will have to be convinced that no part of the payment is what it refers to as a 'terminal bonus' (HMRC will seek to tax such amounts as earnings from employment) and that the employee is not really 'retiring' (see **[8.145]**).

One may legitimately question why a contractual redundancy payment and a contractual PILON are treated differently. In *EMI Group Electronics Ltd v Coldicutt* (1997), Chadwick LJ's justification for treating a contractual PILON as earnings from employment was that the contractual PILON was 'the security, or continuity, of salary which [the employee] required as an inducement to enter the employment'. This was a general proposition, not based on any investigation of the particular facts in that case, which begs the question as to why a contractual redundancy payment would not also be capable of being explained in the same way?

When it came to distinguishing *Mairs v Haughey*, Chadwick LJ reasoned that whereas a redundancy payment had the purpose (in part at least) of relieving an employee from the hardship consequent upon being unemployed, an obligation to give notice or pay a PILON did not. Instead it 'gives recognition to the obvious fact that it is likely to take time to find other employment'. *First*, that does not explain why a contractual or non-statutory redundancy scheme would not also act as an inducement to take up employment (Chadwick LJ's reason for treating a PILON as earnings from employment). *Second*, it seems obvious that a redundancy payment is also recognition that it is likely to take time to find other employment – that is why there is hardship.

Perhaps a better explanation is that by agreeing to a PILON clause, the employee is voluntarily agreeing to allow the employer to replace taxable salary with a lump sum and thus the taxability of a PILON is another application of the replacement principle. [8.144]

d) Ex gratia payments on termination

In contrast to payments for redundancy or breach of contract, *ex gratia* payments may be made as a testimonial or present to the employee – to the employee as an individual rather than in return for services rendered (see [**8.62**]). An *ex gratia* payment made to an employee on termination of employment will not be taxable under general principles (see *Cowan v Seymour* (1920)). *McBride v Blackburn* (2003) and *Allum v Marsh* (2005) show how important the payer's description of the reasons for the payment can be in deciding whether it was a gift in recognition of services performed rather than a reward for them.

If, at the time the employee's employment has come to an end, he is treated as 'retiring', then any ex-gratia payment made to him could be treated as being made under an unapproved retirement benefits scheme, and it will be taxable in full under the retirement benefits provisions (ITEPA 2003 s 386 ff) without the benefit of any £30,000 exemption, since s 401 (see 5(b)(iv) below ([**8.154**])) only applies if the payment is not otherwise taxable. [**8.145**]

3 The benefits code

Can benefits provided to former employees be taxed under ITEPA 2003 Part 3 Chapter 10? Pensions, lump sums and 'other like' benefits provided to the employee, or his family or dependants, on his death or 'retirement' cannot be so taxed, as a result of s 307.

Certain termination payments *may* escape Chapter 10 as being 'fair bargains' (see [**8.125**]). In *Wilson v Clayton* (2005), the Court of Appeal supported excluding from the scope of s 154 payments made pursuant to 'fair bargains' and concluded that payments made pursuant to a 'genuine' compromise agreement to settle a dispute could not be a 'benefit'. Peter Gibson LJ did not, however, 'rule out the possibility that it might be shown in some cases that the reason for the payment was to confer a gratuitous benefit within a compromise agreement so that to that extent [Part 3 Chapter 10] might apply'.

In relation to other benefits within Part 3 Chapter 10, s 201(4) makes it clear that the Chapter cannot apply in a year of assessment when the taxpayer has not been employed at all. However, what is the position if benefits which would fall within Chapter 10 are provided in the remainder of the tax year following termination? This will most commonly occur because a pre-termination benefit (for instance, a beneficial loan or use of a car) continues after termination; but could also arise when a new benefit is provided at that time. Whilst s 201(4) suggests that such benefits fall within Chapter 10 for the remainder of the tax year following termination, HMRC has made it clear that it will continue its previous practice of not applying s 201 to 'payments or benefits related to the termination of employment' (*Tax Bulletin*, June 2003, pp 1036–1037). That practice of excluding the benefit in kind charge covered not only benefits newly provided on termination but also the continued provision of a pre-termination benefit (see SE 12815, now EIM 12815) (unless, as when beneficial loans are written off, there is a specific provision making that taxable under the benefits code even though the employment has ceased (see, eg ITEPA 2003 s 188)). It is likely that, in most cases, this practice will reflect the strict legal position: the deeming provision in s 201(3) will not apply because an ex-employer is not an 'employer'; and such benefits will not be provided 'by reason of employment'. [8.146]

4 Other payments treated as earnings

If neither the general charging provision nor the residual benefits code charge applies, could the termination payment (or part of it) be regarded as a payment for a restrictive covenant within s 225? Some Revenue officers used to argue that s 225 had a wide ambit and applied, inter alia, where an employee agreed, on receiving a compensation payment, to give up his right to claim damages. It appeared from SP 3/96 that HMRC would no longer take this approach. The SP states that 'no chargeable value will be attributed under s [225]' to undertakings to give up legal claims or reaffirmations of restrictive covenants which were in the contract when employment commenced. However, the Special Commissioner in *Appellant v Inspector of Taxes* (2001) held that the SP does not apply if the parties attached a value to the undertakings, an unexpected interpretation of the wording in the SP. Further, whilst there was some evidence that HMRC was seeking to apply s 225 if the ex-employee had to repay the whole (or part of the) termination payment if he commenced legal proceedings, HMRC now 'accepts that such a charge will not arise other than in very exceptional cases' (*Tax Bulletin*, October 2003, p 1063). [8.147]

5 Amounts counted as employment income

a) *Introduction*

Part 6 Chapter 3 (ss 401–416) applies to payments and benefits received in connection with:
(a) the termination of a person's employment
(b) a change in the duties of a person's employment; or
(c) a change in the earnings from a person's employment.

These provisions are most often considered in relation to termination payments, but their relevance to payment on a change of duties or change of earnings should not be overlooked.

Part 6 Chapter 3 sets out a residual liability to tax: it does not apply if the payment or benefit is otherwise chargeable (s 401(3)). Therefore, it has first to be established that no other provision applies before considering the applicability of this charge.

The following questions arise:
(1) What counts as a 'benefit' for these purposes?
(2) When is a payment 'received directly or indirectly in consideration or in consequence of, or otherwise in connection with' the termination of employment.
(3) How much is charged?
(4) What exceptions are there?

Section 402 provides a non-exhaustive definition of benefit (a point HMRC emphasise in their manuals). According to s 402, benefit includes anything that would be taxable as earnings if it were received for the performance of duties or would be so taxable but for an 'earnings-only exemption'. An earnings only exemption is an exemption that prevents liability to tax arising in respect of earnings either by virtue a particular provision (such as a Chapter of the benefits code) or at all, but does not prevent liability to tax arising in respect of other income (such as under s 403, for example) (s 227). It follows that for a benefit to be exempt under s 401, it must be the subject of a Chapter 6 specific exception (see **[8.151]** ff) or an employment income exemption (as defined in s 227(3)).

Certain benefits are nevertheless specifically excluded from the definition of benefit, such as certain removal expenses (s 402(2)–(3)).

Turning to the meaning of 'in connection with', the Upper Tribunal held in *Moorthy v R & C Comrs* (2016) that any kind of connection between a payment/benefit and the termination (for example) is sufficient to bring the payment into charge. In doing so, it agreed with the Upper Tribunal in *Kenneth Colquhoun v R & C Comrs* (2010):

> 'The statutory language of section 148(2) [the predecessor to s 401] has been broadly drawn. That can be seen from the use of words and phrases such as *indirectly* and *otherwise in connection with. Otherwise* may simply mean *in any way* and is consistent with the Parliamentary intention to catch a wide range of payments.'

In fact, authority indicates that the link required by the words 'in connection with' depends upon the context and does not necessarily cover every link (*Barclays Bank Plc v R & C Comrs* (2007)). Even in the context of s 401, it seems obvious that not every link is sufficient. For example, in *Crompton v R & C Comrs* (2009) an army employee was wrongly overlooked by selection boards and pursued a claim for those failures when he was made redundant from an alternative role in the army that he had taken. HMRC's attempt to tax the payment under s 401 was rejected:

> 'Even if I assume he would not have pursued the claim if he had stayed in the army the fact that he left was only a circumstance that occasioned his decision to make the claim. It had nothing to do with the merits of the claim or whether it would succeed. That circumstance does not constitute a linkage between the payment and the termination of his employment of the sort envisaged by the legislation.'

On the facts of *Moorthy*, the taxpayer received a payment for alleged discrimination on grounds of age during a redundancy process. The Upper Tribunal confirmed the First-tier Tribunal's decision that this payment, including the payment for injury to feelings, was in connection with the termination of his employment. For an argument that the payment for injury to feelings ought not to have been considered connected with the termination of employment see [2016] BTR 152.

In *Colquhoun*, the Upper Tribunal applied the replacement principle to hold that a payment for the loss of redundancy payment rights took its character from the rights given up and thus was in connection with the termination of employment (even though at the time no actual termination was in prospect).

The *Crompton* case illustrates a vitally important point, namely, that a payment in respect of, for example, discrimination arising during the course of the employment is not taxable under s 401. Thus in *A v R & C Comrs* (2015), a banker's employment was terminated at which point he decided to pursue the bank for racial discrimination occurring during the course of his employment. That discrimination had manifested itself in the form of, inter alia, lower bonuses. Consistently with their guidance (EIM 12965), HMRC did not argue that the payment was connected with termination, accepting that it was related to discrimination occurring during the course of the employment. The First-tier Tribunal found that it was also not earnings from employment (see also *AB v R & C Comrs* (2011)).

In terms of how much is charged, subject to exceptions (the most important of which is usually the £30,000 exception), it is the amount of the payment or the benefit. The value of a non-cash benefit is the higher of the value that would be ascribed to it under the common law valuation principles for earnings (see Section VII) or under the benefits code (ie Part 3 Chapters 2 to 11), subject to a small alteration in respect of living accommodation (s 415(7)). Section 401 amounts are treated as the highest part of the person's total income (s 404A).

The payment or benefit is taxed in the year it is received (s 403(2)) irrespective of whether the employment has terminated or whether the employee is UK resident. There is, however, the possibility of an exception or reduction for an employee who provided foreign service (s 413 and s 414).

A payment is treated as received when it is paid or (presumably only if earlier) when the recipient becomes entitled to require payment of or on account of it. It is suggested that this is merely a timing rule and that if the payment is ultimately never received (for instance if the employer becomes insolvent), then it is not deemed to be received (see *Jerome v Kelly* (2004)).

[8.148]–[8.150]

b) *The exceptions*

i) *Introduction*

Whilst ITEPA 2003 Part 6 Chapter 3 contains detailed information on the exceptions from s 401 (ss 402 and 405–414), the list is not comprehensive. Payments and benefits subject to 'employment income exemptions' are also excluded (see **[8.148]** and Section X) and there are specific exemptions in Part 4 Chapter 10.

As there is now a wide range of exceptions from s 401, it is not proposed to list them all here but only to consider those that apply most often in practice; readers considering the taxability of any particular payment made in connection with either the termination of an employment or a change in its duties or earnings should check all the applicable exceptions. **[8.151]**

ii) *Death, injury and disability*

Section 406 exempts payments and benefits provided in connection with the death of an employee or 'on account of injury to, or disability of, an employee'. Lightman J's view, in *Horner v Hasted* (1995), on the last exemption was that it had to be established as an objective fact that there was a 'relevant disability' (which, reflecting SP 10/81, he considered to be one affecting an employee's ability to perform his duties) and as a subjective fact that the disability was the motive for the payment.

Similarly, the Upper Tribunal took the view in *Moorthy v R & C Comrs* (2016) that 'injury' was limited to cases where there was a recognised medical condition and thus a payment for injury to feelings caused by discrimination in connection with the termination of an employment was not exempt. In doing so, the Upper Tribunal was disagreeing with two decisions of the Employment Appeals Tribunal that the exception did apply to injury to feelings payments (*Orthet Ltd v Vince-Cain* (2005) and *Timothy James Consulting Ltd v Wilton* (2015)). It is difficult to find a convincing reason for this limited approach to the meaning of 'injury' or to think of a good reason why such a payment, if genuinely made to compensate for injury to feelings caused by discrimination, should be subject to employment income tax. Any such reservations will shortly become moot, however, as s 406 is to be amended to explicitly include psychiatric injury but exclude injured feelings. [8.152]

iii) Pension benefits from and contributions to approved schemes

Pensions received from approved retirement benefits schemes do not fall within s 401 because they are taxed under other provisions. Section 407 exempts from s 401 a lump sum benefit from an approved scheme provided that it can 'properly [be] regarded as earned by past service'; or if it is 'by way of compensation for loss of employment or loss or diminution of earnings and the loss or diminution is due to ill-health' (which may require an objective assessment of why the payment was made (as well as of whether the ill-health caused the loss, in contrast to the position where payments are made 'on account of injury or disability'). There is no blanket exemption for lump sum payments from approved schemes in order to prevent them, in effect, being manipulated to provide non-taxable compensation payments on termination.

Section 408 exempts contributions made to approved pension plans as part of arrangements relating to the termination of employment. These special contributions are often made to ensure that the plan is sufficiently funded if the pension is to be drawn earlier than was expected; and they now provide a tax-efficient method of making a termination payment. Since 6 April 2014, the maximum amount on which an individual can make tax relieved savings in a registered pension scheme has been £40,000. Excess contributions will be subject to an annual allowance charge by which tax relief is effectively recovered. From 6 April 2016, the annual allowance will be tapered for individuals with higher incomes by reducing it by £1 for every £2 of income above £150,000 with a maximum reduction of £30,000. Effectively this means that those with an income of £210,000 or more have an annual allowance of £10,000. [8.153]

iv) First £30,000

The exemption which is still likely to be invoked most often is that for the first £30,000 of payments or benefits received (the threshold is applied to the aggregate of payments made in respect of the same office or employment or made by the same or associated employers – s 404(1)). As termination and compensation payments can now be taxed in more than one year of assessment, the application of this exemption has become more complex but, in essence, the exemption, to the extent that it is not used up by cash and benefits received in the first year of assessment when a charge arises, is applied to successive payments and benefits and, whenever more than one payment or benefit is received in a tax year, it is used first against cash (ss 404(4) and (5)).

HMRC are expected to be given the power to vary the £30,000 threshold in the near future. This will include the power to reduce it by regulations laid before and approved by a resolution of the House of Commons. [8.154]

EXAMPLE 8.15

During the year 2016–17, Joanne has earnings of £25,000 and receives a lump sum payment of £20,000 on termination of her employment. No tax is payable on the £20,000 termination payment.

The next tax year (2017–18) Joanne receives a further £25,000 of her termination payment. Assuming she has found another job at a salary of £30,000, then to calculate the tax payable on the further instalment of the termination payment:
(1) Calculate amount of exemption: £30,000 − £20,000 (used in 2016–17) = £10,000 for 2017–18.
(2) Calculate taxable slice: £25,000 − £10,000 = £15,000.

		£
Earnings from employment		30,000.00
Other income		Nil
Taxable lump sum on termination of employment		15,000.00
Personal allowance		11,000.00
Tax payable:		
Taxable income		45,000.00
Less:		11,000.00
		34,000.00
Tax payable:	first £32,000 at 20%	6,400.00
	remaining £2,000 at 40%	800.00
		£7,200.00

v) Legal advice

Legal costs of the employee can be paid tax-free by the employer (see ITEPA 2003 s 413A) provided they are incurred exclusively in connection with the termination of employment and the payment is made either pursuant to (i) a court or tribunal order; or (ii) a compromise agreement which provides for the payment to be made by the employer directly to the former employee's solicitor. It would appear that HMRC does not interpret the exemption for legal costs generously, with HMRC stating that it does not cover legal advice in relation to taxation of the termination payment, for example. [8.155]

c) *PAYE and reporting requirements*

PAYE has to be operated on cash termination payments but does not have to be operated on such payments which benefit from the £30,000 exemption.

ITEPA 2003 s 404 provides for the £30,000 exemption to be allocated to cash payments in priority to benefits in kind, but employers might still face difficulties in deciding whether the exemption has been used up: for instance, if cash of £28,000 is provided at the time of termination plus continuing benefits and a cash payment is due at the beginning of the next tax year, the employer might find it difficult to calculate how much of that exceeds the tax-free band. The difficulty is exacerbated as the obligation to operate PAYE extends to the provision of 'readily convertible assets' to ex-employees, particularly as, if the employer pays the tax, he can only recover it from cash payments made in the same income tax month and there may well not be any when such assets are provided to ex-employees (see generally Section XII). In the absence of a satisfactory statutory right to recover PAYE from an employee, the need for tax indemnities in termination agreements has become more important (or even a right to retain and realise assets to pay tax, since the employee could remain taxable even if he were non-resident and therefore difficult to pursue – see [8.149]).

If the payment is made before the employment has ceased, the deduction should be in accordance with the employee's code for the relevant period; if after, it should be deducted at the non-cumulative '0T' tax code (Income Tax (Pay As You Earn) Regulations 2003, SI 2003/2682, reg 37, as amended by the Income Tax (Pay As You Earn) (Amendment) (No 2) Regulations 2011, SI 2011/1054 and reg 65 of the Income Tax (Pay as You Earn) (Amendment) Regulations 2012, SI 2012/822). Regulation 91 requires a one-off report if the termination settlement includes non-cash benefits and it is estimated that their value will in total exceed £30,000 (this has to be filed if those conditions were not originally fulfilled but are fulfilled later as a result of some change in the arrangements). Further reports are only required if there is a 'material change in the amount of the payments awarded or the nature and amounts of other benefits awarded' (reg 92(4)).

See the October 1998 issue of *Tax Bulletin* which gives HMRC's views on how to apply the £30,000 exemption when operating PAYE and the reporting requirements. [8.156]

d) *Interaction of £30,000 exemption and a damages claim*

The exemption for the first £30,000 of a termination payment which falls within s 401 can cause problems when assessing the damages payable for breach of the employment contract. *British Transport Commission v Gourley* (1956) and subsequent cases are concerned with the determination of the amount of damages awarded by the courts in tort and for breach of contract. The cases are not concerned with the tax treatment of the sum once it has been awarded.

As has been explained, damages are generally not subject to tax as earnings because there is usually a source other than employment (for example, a personal injury, an unfair dismissal or a discriminatory act). This is so even where the damages are calculated by reference to lost earnings (*A v R & C Comrs* (2015)). The principle applicable to trading income expressed in *London and Thames Haven Oil Wharves Ltd v Attwooll* (1967) at [10.103] is therefore not applicable in the employment income context. Section 401 is, however, applicable to damages payments.

Damages should compensate the innocent party for a breach of contract; they should not normally penalise the contract-breaker. Hence, if an employment contract has been broken, the damages should reflect the fact that, had the employee performed the contract, he would only have been left with the benefit of a net sum after payment of tax. Therefore, the damages awarded should be computed by reference to that net sum. Obviously, this will adequately compensate the claimant so long as the damages are not themselves taxed; if they are, the net sum will be insufficient.

It could be argued that, once a payment is subject to charge (as termination payments are by virtue of s 401), there is no room for the application of the *Gourley* rule and a gross sum should be paid. The courts, however, have generally distinguished between termination payments of less than £30,000 and those in excess of £30,000. A payment below £30,000 is free of tax and, therefore, the amount awarded should be calculated on *Gourley* principles (see *Parsons v BNM Laboratories* (1963)). EIM 13070 supports this approach, though HMRC recognise that in the real world negotiations take place that may result in the *Gourley* adjustments not being made. Whilst this does not necessarily prevent the payment being damages, and may simply mean that the employee is over compensated, if none of the adjustments normally accepted for a damages payment are made then HMRC may call the nature of the payment into question. *Lyndale Fashion Manufacturers v Rich* (1973) shows that the calculation should proceed as if the damages are compensation for income which formed the highest slice of the recipient's income for the year (see *Law Society's Gazette*, 1983, p 346). If the net damages exceed £30,000 (after making the appropriate Gourley adjustment for tax), those damages must be increased by a sum equal to the estimated income tax that will be charged on the award under s 403. This final net award will represent, as realistically as possible, the actual loss suffered (*Shove v Downs Surgical plc* (1984) and see (1984) *Modern Law Review* 471 where the conflicting decisions of the courts are discussed).

Raising the unfair dismissal compensatory award ceiling to (currently) £78,962 means that this issue has to be addressed in that context now as well.
[8.157]

e) *Contemporaneous share sale*

Problems may arise when the employee is also a substantial shareholder in the employer company and a termination payment is made on the change of ownership of that company. In such cases, a payment ostensibly for termination of his service contract may be challenged on the grounds that it represents partial consideration for the shares transferred. To the extent that the challenge is successful, the payment will not be deductible as a business expense of the company (see *James Snook & Co Ltd v Blasdale* (1952)) and will not qualify for the £30,000 exemption. To avoid this, it may be desirable to separate, so far as possible, arrangements for the share sale from the question of compensation for loss of office. [8.158]

f) *Internationally mobile employees*

Issues relating to the taxation of termination payments can be further complicated where there is an international element. The OECD has recently published a discussion draft highlighting the key issues relating to these payments in an international context and suggesting how the OECD model tax treaty might apply. The draft focuses on the OECD's concern that the lack of clarity over how these payments will be taxed creates a potential for double taxation, and attempts to resolve this problem by proposing changes to the commentary to the model tax treaty with the effect that remuneration for previous work will be taxable in the state where the employee carried out the work and PILON payments will be taxed in the state where it was reasonable to assume that the employee would have worked during the notice period (see *Tax Journal*, 15 November 2013, for a more detailed overview of the discussion draft). [8.159]

g) *Recommendations for Reform*

In 2014 the Office for Tax Simplification (OTS) published a report recommending reform in the context of termination payments. One of these recommendations was to replace the £30,000 exemption with an income tax relief that is available only in the event of a statutory redundancy. The exemption would apply to all payments received in a statutory redundancy situation and regardless of whether the payment was contractual or statutory. The OTS recommended that the limit for the new relief should be calculated as a multiple of the statutory redundancy payment that the individual would be entitled to. Another recommendation of the OTS was whether the other existing exemptions (eg payment on death) should be retained. It remains to be seen whether the government will adopt these recommendations. [8.160]

X EXEMPTIONS

1 Introduction

ITEPA 2003 Part 4 is headed 'Employment income: exemptions'. It is however important to note that not all exemptions are set out in this Part: some can be found in other Parts of the Act – for instance, those in Part 6 Chapter 3 (discussed in Section IX part 5 d) and those in Part 7 listed in s 227(4); others in Extra-Statutory Concessions (though many of these have been incorporated into ITEPA 2003 (see Annex 3 to the Explanatory Notes), some remain in force as they would have taken a disproportionate amount of legislation to enact them).

Part 4 contains two types of exemptions: 'earnings-only exemptions' and 'employment income exemptions' (s 227). The former prevent 'liability to tax arising in respect of earnings, either by virtue of one or more particular provisions (such as a Chapter of the benefits code) or at all', but do 'not prevent liability to tax arising in respect of other employment income' (s 227(2)); the latter prevent 'liability to tax arising in respect of employment income of any kind at all'. Although this distinction is not as clear as it might be. Employment income exemptions provide complete exemption from charge under ITEPA 2003. The title 'earnings-only exemption' might lead one to think that they only provide exemption from earnings within Part 3 Chapter 1: however, it is clear from the wording of s 227(2) itself that they also apply to provisions under which amounts are treated as earnings; in other words, they provide an exemption from 'general earnings' (not just 'earnings') but do not provide an exemption from the charges on 'specific employment'. The real distinction in practice (given the nature of the exemptions) is that the earnings-only exemptions do not provide exemption from the charge on termination payments under Part 6 Chapter 3 (though, in fact, even they will apply to that charge if they are listed in s 402) but the employment income exemptions do provide such an exemption.

How is the nature (earnings-only or employment income) of any particular exemption determined? By looking at the wording of the exemption provision. Section 247 provides an example of each: sub-s (2) states that '*no liability to income tax arises by virtue of Chapter 6 or 10 of Part 3 ...* in respect of the benefit [(provision of a car for disabled employees)] if conditions A to C are met' (an earnings-only exemption); sub-s (3) states that '*no liability to income tax arises* in respect of (a) the provision of fuel for the car, or (b) the payment or reimbursement of expenses incurred in connection with it, if conditions A to C are met' (an employment income exception).

Section 228 lists benefits which are exempt from income tax under all statutes, not just ITEPA 2003.

Not all the exemptions in Part 4 will be examined here in detail. To give a flavour of their extent, the headings of the various Chapters are listed below. A few of the exemptions will be considered further in the remainder of this Section. The Chapter headings are:

(1) mileage allowances and passenger payments (see [**8.117**]–[**8.123**]);
(2) other transport, travel and subsistence (see [**8.96**] and [**8.123**] in relation to some of these);
(3) education and training (see [**8.96**] in relation to some of these);
(4) recreational benefits;
(5) non-cash vouchers and credit tokens;
(6) removal benefits and expenses;
(7) special kinds of employees;
(8) pension provision;
(9) termination of employment; and
(10) miscellaneous exemptions. [**8.161**]

2 **Relocation costs**

The taxation of benefits provided to a relocating employee is complex.

If the employer offers a guaranteed selling price (GSP) scheme (which normally involves the employer or a relocation company buying the house and subsequently selling it – the employer taking the risk of price fluctuations) then, even if the price paid is no more than the market value of the property, other costs incurred by the employer could be taxable under Part 3 Chapter 10 (eg his legal costs) – see [**8.126**]. However, as a result of s 326, many of these costs will be ignored.

Benefits not covered by s 326, whether or not arising under a GSP scheme, may be relieved under ss 277–289. However, only 'eligible' expenses and benefits are relieved and the maximum relief is limited to £8,000.

Reimbursement of a capital loss is not covered. HMRC's view is that if the employer (or relocation company) pays more than the market value (usually because the house has fallen in value since it was bought), the difference is subject to income tax (*Tax Bulletin*, May 1994, pp 122–124) but this does not seem essentially different from the employee selling to a third party at a loss and being reimbursed by his employer, as in *Hochstrasser v Mayes* (1960) (see **[8.41]**). It is not clear whether HMRC considers that the House of Lords would reverse its previous decision or that the situation would be likely to arise only where Part 3 Chapter 10 applied so that compensation would be taxable thereunder. Even the latter view would not be uncontroversial, particularly if the payment were not made by the employer (see the Northern Ireland Court of Appeal's discussion of the scope of s 154 (the predecessor to Part 3 Chapter 10) in *Mairs v Haughey* (1992)).

Note that Stamp Duty Land Tax may also be in issue (see *Tolley's Practical Tax Newsletter*, 27 February 2004). **[8.162]**

3 Outplacement counselling

When employees are made redundant, employers sometimes arrange 'outplacement counselling' for them. This is a service provided by a third party to help the employee, for instance, by providing counselling to help him adjust to the redundancy or providing assistance in the preparation of his CV. Section 310 exempts the provision of these services from income tax, provided certain conditions are satisfied. It was extended to cover part-time employees by FA 2005 s 18(2). In addition, the employer can claim a statutory deduction for their cost (see ITTOIA 2005 ss 31 and 73). **[8.163]**

4 Training

If an employer pays up to £15,480 (for the 2007–08 and subsequent academic years) of certain costs for employees attending full-time educational courses at universities or technical colleges etc, any benefit which would otherwise be chargeable to tax under ITEPA 2003 is not treated as earnings (SP 4/86, revised 16 March 2005). Where an employer meets the cost of a qualifying training course undertaken by his employee or former employee to retrain in skills needed for a new job or self-employment following termination of employment, that payment or reimbursement will not give rise to an income tax charge if the conditions in s 311 are satisfied. This exemption was extended by FA 2005 s 18(3) to cover part-time employees and courses lasting up to two years (rather than one). Relief for other types of external training is given by ss 250–260 (see **[8.96]**). **[8.164]**

5 Homeworker's additional expenses

Section 316A exempts from income tax payments in respect of reasonable additional household expenses incurred in working from home under 'homeworking arrangements'. An employer can pay up to £216 pa (£18 per month) tax-free without having to prove the costs the employee has incurred: higher amounts will have to be justified by supporting evidence (see also *Tax Bulletin*, December 2003, pp 1068 and 1069). **[8.165]**

6 Use of assets

Special treatment applies to the use of certain assets. Section 319 exempts the provision of a mobile phone to an employee. Prior to 6 April 2006, this exemption extended to the provision of mobile phones to members of the employee's family and household. However, FA 2006 narrowed the exemption so as to only apply to employees except where the mobile phone was provided to the employee's family or household member before 6 April 2006. HMRC accept that smart phones (such as a 'BlackBerry') are mobile phones for these purposes (see *Taxation*, 13 January 2005, p 345 and Revenue & Customs Brief 02/12).

There is no exemption where computer equipment (or any other peripheral device) is made available to an employee unless it was first made available to the employee before 6 April 2006, when the first £500 of the annual value is exempt (subject to the proviso that, at the time, the arrangement was not confined to directors (or those connected with them) and they could not obtain use of the equipment on more favourable terms than other employees.

To benefit from the exemption for bicycles and cycling safety equipment (s 244), the equipment must be made available generally to all staff and must be mainly used for journeys from home to work or between workplaces (s 249). [8.166]

7 Childcare

Employees who are entitled to Working Tax Credit and who incur childcare costs are entitled to a credit in relation thereto (see **Chapter 51**). For all employees who have children, the deductibility of childcare costs, and the taxability of childcare provided by the employer, is of interest.

Certain employer-provided nursery facilities are excluded from tax by s 318; neither is there any charge when similar provisions are available for older children after school. Whilst the facilities can be provided away from the workplace and jointly with other persons, mere payment of nursery fees to a third party is not enough, nor is a more structured buying-in of places; in HMRC's view s 318(7)(c) requires 'some real and substantial commitment to funding the facility or providing it with capital' (see *Tax Bulletin*, April 1998, p 531). The exemption does not, of course, apply if the employer provides cash to enable his employee to pay for nursery facilities (and HMRC is looking closely at situations where the employee's salary is cut in return for the employer paying for nursery facilities: this may be taxed as if the employee had received the cost as salary). Similar costs incurred by a self-employed taxpayer do not qualify as deductible expenditure, nor can an individual employee deduct the costs of a nanny or child help in the home.

Two related exemptions were introduced by FA 2004, as amended by FA 2005 ss 15 and 16). Section 318A (as amended) exempts from Part 3 Chapter 10 (the residual benefits charge) the first £55 per week of approved childcare contracted for by the employer, provided that specified conditions are met. Section 270A (as amended) exempts the first £55 per week of qualifying childcare vouchers.

For any of these exemptions to apply, the facility will have to be available to the employer's employees generally or to all those working at a particular location (see s 318(8)).

As this area is now so complex, HMRC have issued a booklet for employees (IR 115) and guidance for employers (E18 (2012)).

The introduction of a new 'Tax-Free Childcare' regime was announced in the 2014 Budget, and will slowly be rolled out from early 2017. The Government will cover 20% of working families' childcare costs, up to an annual limit of £2,000 for each child. Tax-Free Childcare is intended to replace the current system described above of Employer-Supported Childcare. Parents will register with the Government and open an online account, which will then be 'topped up' by government payments into this account at a rate of 20p for every 80p that families pay in, up to the annual limit. Parents will not be able to benefit from the scheme where either parent is an additional rate taxpayer (taking into account income from all sources).

Once Tax-Free Childcare becomes available, employer related schemes will close, although employer-provided nursery facilities can continue alongside the new scheme. It is important to note that since the salary sacrifice element of the previous regime will no longer be present, the NIC advantages currently enjoyed by both employer and employee will be lost (see *Taxation*, 10 April 2014, 11). [8.167]

8 Annual parties and functions, long service awards, subsidised meals and small gifts from third parties

Sections 264, 323 and 324 provide limited exemptions for annual parties and functions, long service awards and small gifts from third parties, based on their cost.

As a result of ITEPA 2003 s 716, these limits can be increased by Treasury Order. SI 2003/1361 is such an Order and increased the limits to £150, £50 for each year of service, and £250, respectively. It should be noted that, if the limits in ss 264 and 324 are exceeded, the full cost becomes a taxable benefit (for more detail on the latest developments, see *Taxation*, 14 December 2006, p 284, and see *Taxation*, 18 December 2008, p 651 generally).

Section 317 exempts free or subsidised meals provided in a workplace canteen, subject to the proviso that they are available to employees generally.
[8.168]

9 Minor benefits

Section 316 exempts any benefit obtained from the use of assets and services which is 'not significant' (as to which see *Tax Bulletin*, October 2000), provided that the sole purpose of providing the benefit was to enable the employee to perform his duties and it is not an excluded benefit (for instance, the provision of an aircraft!). Section 210 allows for the exemption by regulation of 'minor benefits' provided they are made available to all employees on similar terms: welfare counselling; cyclists' breakfasts provided on days designated by the employer; lunchtime use of works buses; the private use of equipment or facilities provided to disabled employees to enable them to carry out their duties; the provision of no more than £150 worth of pensions advice per employee per year; and using recreational facilities or being provided with free or subsidised meals on the premises of another employer have all been exempted (see SI 2002/2005, as amended from time to time).

The new exemption for trivial benefits has already been noted (see [8.131]).

[8.169]–[8.170]

XI DEDUCTIONS FROM EARNINGS

1 Introduction

ITEPA 2003 Part 5 sets out the deductions allowed from earnings in computing taxable income. Section 9 charges 'net taxable earnings' and 'net taxable specific income' and so these deductions (as well as the others referred to in s 327) must be taken into account to ascertain the amount ultimately taxable under ITEPA 2003 (see further ss 10–12 and [8.11]). In general, the deductions listed in Part 5 can be made from any earnings from the employment in question (s 328), though there are limitations (ss 328–331). Section 329 provides that the amount of allowable deductions may not exceed the earnings from which they are deductible (so that it is not possible to create a loss to offset against other income).

The final provision of Part 5 Chapter 1 lists the 'deductibility provisions'. These are provisions in other Parts of ITEPA 2003 which relieve an employee from liability to income tax on a benefit received *provided* that, had the employee paid for the benefit, the cost would have been deductible under Part 5 (eg s 310(6)). [8.171]

2 Deductions for an employee's expenses

To be deductible, the amount must be (s 333):
(1) paid by the employee; or
(2) paid by someone else on the employee's behalf but constitutes earnings.

If the employee is reimbursed for the expense, he is only considered to have paid the expense (and thus to be entitled to a deduction) if the reimbursement is included in his earnings (s 334). The benefits code will normally ensure that this is the case, although note the possibility of applying an exemption to the reimbursement instead of claiming a deduction (see [8.96]).

General expenses are dealt with in s 336 whereas travelling expenses are dealt with in s 337. HMRC treats subsistence expenses attributable to business travel in the same way that it treats the travel expenses because it regards them as necessary travelling expenses (EIM 31815 referring to *Nolder v Walters* (1980)). [8.172]

a) *Expenses other than travelling expenses*

Subject to special provisions, a deduction is allowed only if (s 336):
(a) the employee is obliged to incur and pay the expense as holder of the employment; and
(b) the amount is incurred wholly, exclusively and necessarily in the performance of the duties of the employment.

It will be noted that this test is stricter than that applicable to trading income expenses insofar as (1) the employee must be obliged to incur the expense as holder of the employment, and (2) the amount must also be incurred necessarily in the performance of the duties.

The test can usefully be considered in three stages.

First, the 'wholly and exclusively' element is the same question as arises in relation to trading income. under ITTOIA 2005. The cases make it clear that in deciding what is 'wholly and exclusively' in the performance of duties, the court must look at whether there is any duality of purpose in the payment (see, for example, *R & C Comrs v Healy* (2015) – note that this case was initially heard by the First-tier Tribunal in 2012 and decided in favour of the taxpayer; HMRC appealed to the Upper Tribunal who, in 2013, remitted it to the First-tier Tribunal) and, more generally, **[10.137]**).

Second, the 'obliged to incur' and 'necessarily' elements can be taken together (indeed, the legislation previously referred to expenses that the employee was 'necessarily obliged to incur'). These are objective tests: the expenditure must arise from the nature of the employment and not from the personal choice of the taxpayer. In other words, the expense must be one which each and every occupant of the particular office is necessarily obliged to incur (see Lord Blanesburgh in *Ricketts v Colquhoun* (1926), as clarified by Lord Wilberforce in *Owen v Pook* (1970) – for more detailed consideration of these cases, see below under travelling expenses).

Nor is it sufficient that the employer requires the expenditure – the nature of the duties must require it. In *Brown v Bullock* (1961), a bank manager was required by his employer to join a London club. He could not deduct his subscription because it was not necessary for the performance of his duties. On the other hand, in *R & C Comrs v Banerjee* (2010) it was part of the duties of a specialist register to attend training courses thus the expenditure was incurred necessarily.

Third, as regards the 'in the performance of the duties' requirement, no deduction is allowed for expenses which enable the employee to prepare for his duties or to be better equipped to carry them out. In order to determine whether an activity is preparation or performance, however, one must first determine what the duties of the employment are.

As noted above, in *R & C Comrs v Banerjee* (2010), the Court of Appeal accepted that a specialist registrar was a training post and thus attendance at training courses was in the performance of the duties:

> 'I can also see no reason in principle why Dr Banerjee's successive contracts during the five-year training period cannot and should not be characterised as "training" contracts by which she was employed – and paid - to undergo both practical *and* theoretical exercises whose ultimate aim was the generation of a supply of qualified dermatology consultants for the benefit of the National Health Service. Once the contracts are so characterised, I can equally see no reason why the incurring by Dr Banerjee of the expenses in question was not necessarily incurred in the performance of her duties under those contracts.'

The Court of Appeal also accepted (by a majority) that any consideration of professional advancement was incidental to the intention to perform her duties and thus the expenditure was incurred 'exclusively' in the performance of duties:

> 'It is also clear law that it does not follow from the fact that a taxpayer receives an incidental personal benefit from the expenditure, that the obtaining of the benefit necessarily becomes a "purpose" which defeats the "exclusivity" requirement. If the law were otherwise it is unlikely that any (honest) taxpayer would be able to satisfy the "exclusivity" requirement.'

Rimer LJ acknowledged that it was likely an earlier case on similar facts, *R & C Comrs v Decadt* (2008), had reached an 'irreconcilable' decision.

By way of contrast, fees paid to an employment agency were not deductible in *Shortt v McIlgorm* (1945) (although note ITEPA 2003 s 352 allowing agents' fees paid by actors and other theatrical artists taxed under ITEPA 2003 to be deducted).

In *Simpson v Tate* (1952) a medical officer could not deduct the cost of joining learned societies which would enable him to perform his duties better (note the partial reversal of this decision by ITEPA 2003 s 344 and that s 343 permits a deduction for specified professional membership fees (though HMRC did issue a Technical Note in December 2003 to prompt a discussion on how the rules might be changed to provide 'an incentive for membership bodies to provide workforce development')).

The House of Lords adopted a similarly strict approach in *Fitzpatrick v IRC (No 2)* and *Smith v Abbott* (1994), which concerned expenses incurred by journalists in purchasing newspapers and journals. It held that when a journalist reads newspapers and periodicals he is *preparing* to perform his duties efficiently but not actually acting 'in the performance of' his duties. Parts of Lord Templeman's speech indicate that the House was to some extent influenced by the amount of tax that would be lost if the journalists' claims were allowed:

> 'If a journalist or other employee were allowed to deduct expenses incurred by him in his spare time in improving his usefulness to his employer, the imposition of income tax would be distorted and the amount of the expenses claimed by the individual would depend only on his own choice ... if each [journalist] spends £1,000 a year the total deduction for 30,000 journalists will be £30m a year ... the principle of the decision in the present cases does not apply only to journalists; the ramifications of [a] decision in their favour would be enormous.'

This contrasts with the approach of Nolan LJ in the Court of Appeal in *Smith v Abbott* (1993):

> 'The submission that the reading by the taxpayers of other newspapers and periodicals could only reasonably be regarded as a means of adding to their general qualifications seems to me to ignore the short-lived and almost ephemeral nature of the benefits which they thus acquired.
>
> The purpose which their reading was designed to serve, and did serve, was the production of the next edition of the *Daily Mail* or the *Mail on Sunday*. In these circumstances, the reading seems to me to constitute preparation for a particular assignment.'

Few expenses will satisfy all three conditions. In *Kirkwood v Evans* (2002), Patten J refused a claim for home office expenses by a civil servant who opted to join a homeworking scheme. The judge considered that the expenses were not necessarily incurred, even though the scheme required him to provide his own office accommodation at his home, because the scheme itself was voluntary. Further, even ignoring the optional nature of the scheme, it did not oblige Mr Evans to maintain a *separate* room in which to work and therefore he could not claim heating and lighting costs relating to the work space. The case illustrates not only the difficulty of claiming such expenses, but also how strictly the conditions are interpreted in general. See *Taxation*, 5 June 2008 for further examples. See also *Tax Bulletin*, October 2005, p 1231 which sets out the conditions which HMRC require to be satisfied in order to claim tax relief under s 336 for unreimbursed homeworking (including additional household) expenses. Even if tax relief is not available under s 336 then relief may be available under ITEPA 2003 s 316A – see **[8.165]**.

Also, other statutory deductions (eg the flat rate allowance for the costs of tools and special clothing in s 367) mitigate the effect of the way in which s 336 has been interpreted. The principal statutory deductions are:

i) Liability payments

A person can claim relief if he pays the premiums on liability insurance (including 'D&O' insurance) or pays uninsured work-related liabilities, even for payments made after employment has ceased (at least if made before the end of the sixth year of assessment following that in which the employment ceased) (ss 346–350 – and see *Tax Bulletin*, October 1995, p 257 for HMRC's interpretation of the original provisions). It is also possible to claim a deduction for the cost of indemnity insurance premiums in relation to liabilities arising from a previous employment (and for actual payment of liabilities) (ITEPA 2003 Part 8). Since there will rarely be earnings from which to deduct the cost, the deduction is allowed from 'total income' (s 555). From 2017–18, it is anticipated that these provisions will extend to costs relating to proceedings or investigations in which the employee will give evidence or where his/her acts are under consideration.

ii) Payroll deduction scheme

The so-called 'payroll deduction scheme' is designed to encourage charitable giving. So long as a recognised scheme is operated by their employer, employees can make donations to the charity of their choice of any amount. These sums are deductible expenses for the employee and are paid gross to an approved charitable agent which then distributes the sums to the charity of the employee's choice (ITEPA 2003 ss 713–715).

The main statutory *restriction* on claiming as a deduction an expense which would be allowable under s 336 is that relating to the expenses of business entertaining in ss 356–358. This also applies to expenses claimed by the self-employed and is discussed at **[10.138]**; for HMRC's view of its application to employees see *Tax Bulletin*, August 1999, pp 679–682. **[8.173]**

b) Travelling expenses

A deduction for travelling expenses is allowed if:
(a) the employee is obliged to incur and pay them as holder of the employment; and either
(b) they are expenses necessarily incurred on travelling in the performance of the duties of the employment (s 337); or
(c) they are attributable to the employee's necessary attendance at any place in the performance of the duties of the employment and are not expenses of ordinary commuting or private travel (s 338).

The s 337 test is almost as strict as the s 336 test, but the absence of the 'wholly and exclusively' requirement may, in some cases prove a little more lenient. The requirement that the expenses be incurred 'in the performance' of the duties excludes a deduction for the expense of travelling to work because it is incurred before, rather than in, the performance of the duties.

In contrast, travelling between places of work in the course of a single employment is deductible. Section 340 gives some relief for the expenses of an employee of two companies in a group who travels between those companies (and see also s 340A for directors travelling between certain companies). The main people, however, who can regularly claim relief under s 337 are those with 'travelling appointments' (eg sales representatives or service engineers).

EXAMPLE 8.16

(1) Sally is employed as a lecturer by the Midtech University and gives seminars at both branches of the University which are two miles apart. Her travelling costs between both branches are deductible under s 337.

(2) Jim works as a postman and as a barman in a local pub. The cost of travelling between the sorting office and the pub is not deductible under s 337 since Jim has two different jobs and is not therefore travelling between centres of work in the course of a single employment.

The requirement that travelling expenditure be 'necessarily incurred' has been considered in three House of Lords cases. In *Ricketts v Colquhoun* (1926), the travelling expenses of a barrister to and from Portsmouth where he had been appointed Recorder were not deductible. In *Owen v Pook* (1970), a general medical practitioner was allowed to deduct the expenses of travelling to a hospital where he held a part-time appointment, because some of the functions of that post were performed at his home so that he was travelling between two centres of work. Finally, in *Taylor v Provan* (1974) a Canadian director of a UK company was allowed to deduct his travelling expenses to the UK because he performed part of his duties in Canada.

What emerges from these cases is that travelling expenses for getting to work will not be deductible under s 337: where a person resides is his personal choice and therefore the expenses of travelling to work will not satisfy the objective test established by the courts (see [8.173]). Further, a job will not be treated as having two centres just because the taxpayer *chooses* to perform some of its functions at his home. In *Miners v Atkinson* (1997), the court agreed with the extreme interpretation given to this rule by the Special Commissioner: even if it is an objective requirement of the job that duties are performed at home, if the duties could be performed equally well wherever the taxpayer lived, then doing the work at that precise address should be treated as a matter of personal choice and, therefore, the costs of travelling thereto and therefrom are not deductible (for a criticism of the Special Commissioner's reasoning, see *Taxation*, 27 April 1995, p 79). This decision is, however, in line with HMRC's view that it is extremely difficult to establish home as a place of work except where the employee has a 'travelling appointment' (paras 2.13 and 2.14 of the Consultative Document on travel and subsistence issued in April 1996).

Whilst the costs of getting to the employee's permanent workplace from home (or of private travel) along with the cost of ordinary commuting are, and always have been, non-deductible, s 338, which replaced previous rules that were unduly restrictive, allows an employee to claim a deduction when he makes a journey from home to a place he has to attend to carry out the duties of his employment (or *vice versa*) – unless the journey is 'for practical purposes substantially ordinary commuting or private travel': in that case it is treated as such and is non-deductible (see [1998] BTR 425 at 427 for examples of how this operates).

So, if an employed solicitor has to attend a meeting at a client's head office and goes there directly from home, his expenses will be deductible, provided the journey was not substantially ordinary commuting (only if he went there from his own office would the costs be deductible under s 337). For the purposes of s 338, the client's office would be designated a 'temporary workplace', and a place can remain 'temporary' even if the employee attends it regularly, provided he only goes there to perform 'a task of limited duration or for some other temporary purpose' (s 339(3)).

There are, however, rules which further circumscribe when a workplace can remain 'temporary' (see *Tax Bulletin*, December 2004, pp 1165–1168 for a detailed discussion of these rules (in relation to composite and managed service companies but nevertheless of general interest)). If an employee spends (or is likely to spend) a significant amount of his time (40% or more, in HMRC's view – see Booklet 490) performing the duties of his employment at a place for more than 24 months, it will become a 'permanent workplace' and the costs of travelling from home will cease to be deductible (see *Tax Bulletin*, December 2000 on how HMRC applies these provisions to employees seconded to the UK for up to 24 months). Further, a place cannot be a temporary workplace if the employee's attendance there is 'in the course of a period of continuous work at that place comprising all or almost all of the period for which the employee is likely to hold the employment' (s 339(5)(a)(ii) – discussed in *Philips v Hamilton* (2003) and *Ratcliffe v R & C Comrs* (2013)).

The meaning of many of these phrases was considered by Patten J in *Kirkwood v Evans* (2002) (see **[8.173]**) in relation to Mr Evans' weekly trip to his employer's office in Leeds. The decision makes it clear that even under s 338 an employee will face substantial difficulties in claiming a deduction for travel from his home office to his employer's office (although HMRC has pointed out that for many homeworkers the employer's office may not be a permanent workplace, so that the costs of travel thereto could be deductible – *Tax Bulletin*, December 2003, pp 1068 and 1069). See also *Hazel Patricia Lewis* *v R & C Comrs* (2008) where a Revenue employee claimed a deduction for travel between her home (and office) and the Revenue's office. Despite the appellant only taking the job because an alternative working pattern was offered, it was held that this was simply an option available to the appellant and not an inherent part of the job. To have been deductible, the appellant would have to show that every holder of the job would be required to have two workplaces. The expenses were therefore expenses of 'ordinary commuting'.

EXAMPLE 8.17*

(1) Ernie, who works for Heartless & Co, solicitors, is asked to be at Downsizing Ltd's office at 7 am to deliver the finance director's P45 and ensure he departs without removing any confidential material. He leaves directly from home: his costs of travel are deductible.

(2) Downsizing Ltd decide to implement a voluntary redundancy programme and changes to the employees' conditions of employment. Over a six-month period, Ernie regularly attends Downsizing's office to meet management, staff and unions. Most meetings are early in the morning, as the company does not want to disrupt the working day, and Ernie travels directly from home. His travel costs are deductible.

(3) HMRC disputes the taxability of compensation paid for the changes to employment terms, the unions consider that correct procedures were not adopted in relation to the redundancies and the company is sued for failing to meet order deadlines (due to lack of staff). Ernie is sent to work at the company full-time to deal with the legal ramifications and is expected to be there for 30 months. Although he is, in fact, able to leave after eight months when all the cases settle, none of his travel costs for that period are deductible because his attendance was expected to exceed 24 months at the time they were initially incurred (s 339(5)(b)).

*It is assumed none of these journeys are 'substantially ordinary commuting'.

If there is a place regularly attended by employees as their base or to receive their allocation of duties (eg bus drivers attending the bus depot at the beginning and end of each shift), that place is deemed to be a permanent workplace and the costs of travel between home and there are not deductible (s 339(4)). Where a person's job is defined by reference to a particular geographical area (eg a relief manager for a brewery's pubs in Kent), the whole of that area is treated as the permanent workplace so that all travel within it is deductible, but the costs of getting to the edge of it (if, eg the employee lives outside it) are treated as ordinary commuting costs and not deductible.

Section 338 also provides relief for travel to a temporary workplace when the employee does not in fact have a permanent workplace to go back to. This is of benefit to site-based employees (eg bank relief staff who are called at home and told to attend a branch where there is a staff shortage).

With effect from the 2016–17 tax year, ITEPA 2003 s 339A (inserted by FA 2016 s 14), provides, subject to exceptions, that individuals who provide services through an employment intermediary will be treated as having separate employments in respect of each engagement for the purposes of ss 338–339. The effect will be to make it more likely that, vis à vis each deemed separate employment, the place of work will be a permanent workplace,

270 *Taxation of employment income*

thereby preventing a deduction arising under s 338. This provision is justified on the basis that:

> 'It is an established principle in the UK tax system that people should not be able to claim relief on their regular commute from home-to-work, therefore this relief is not generally available to other workers.' (Explanatory Notes to clause 14 of Finance Bill 2016).

Travelling expenses raise two further problems. *First*, allowable expenditure has to be reasonable. In *Marsden v IRC* (1965) an Inland Revenue investigator could not deduct the full cost of travelling by car to perform his duties because he could have used a cheaper form of transport. This is not to say that the cheapest form must always be used, since the matter is one of fact and degree and allowance must be made for the inconvenience of certain forms of transport. For expenditure to be reasonable, the shortest route does not necessarily have to be taken, if the longer route is taken for a good business reason (see Booklet 490, paras 5.11–5.15). *Second*, the relationship between the rules for deductibility of expenditure and the taxation of reimbursements should be carefully noted (see **[8.96]** and **[8.172]**). In the case of employees and directors who are not lower-paid, such reimbursements are automatically treated as earnings (ITEPA 2003 s 70).

It is worth noting that, as a result of s 231, mileage allowance relief can be claimed if an employee uses his own car for business travel and is not reimbursed the full tax-free mileage allowance payments permissible. If that relief is available or if an employee uses his own car and receives mileage allowance payments, no deduction can be claimed under the 'travel deduction provisions' (s 359). **[8.174]**

3 Other deductions

Further provisions relating to deductions are grouped in the remaining Chapters of Part 5 according to the type of deduction. Chapter 3 allows deductions where the employee is taxed under the benefits code but could have claimed a deduction under Part 5 Chapter 2 or 5 if he had paid for the goods or services provided as a benefit in kind. Chapter 4 covers deductions for which an allowance is fixed by Treasury Order (eg if there is a specified allowance for maintaining work equipment for a specified type of employment). Chapter 5 allows a deduction in certain limited circumstances where the employer (or a third party) has paid for something and that payment is treated as earnings. In the main it relates to travel and accommodation expenses where duties are performed abroad, though s 377 relates to the provision of personal security assets and services (for an in-depth discussion of the application of its predecessor, FA 1989 s 50, see the Special Commissioners' decision in *Lord Hanson v Mansworth* (2004)). Chapter 6 relates specifically to seafarers.

Within Chapter 3, s 11 provides that relief is available under ITA 2007 s 128 where taxable earnings are negative. In the case of *Martin v R & C Comrs* (2014), the Upper Tribunal found that an employee re-paying a signing bonus should receive tax relief because the repayment amounted to 'negative pay' for the employee. The Tribunal noted that 'negative taxable earnings' was 'extraordinarily undefined' by the legislation and there was no HMRC guidance published on its meaning. HMRC has stated that it will provide guidance to clarify the uncertain tax treatment of clawbacks.

In addition, FA 2013 Sch 3 para 1 has since amended Chapter 3 of Part 2 of ITA 2007 in order to limit the amount of income tax relief available under various sections, including s 128. The amount deducted for the reliefs to which the amendment applies (less certain allowances) must not exceed £50,000 or, if more, 25% of the taxpayer's 'adjusted total income' for the tax year. **[8.175]–[8.190]**

XII COLLECTION OF TAX

1 **The scope of the provisions**

Tax relating to employment income is collected by a sophisticated method of deduction at source operated by the employer and known as the PAYE system (ITEPA 2003 Part 11). The employer used to be required by statute to 'deduct' tax when he made a payment (TA 1988 s 203), with the detailed operation of the deduction system being set out in regulations. Most peculiarly, there is no longer primary legislation requiring PAYE to be operated: s 684(1) imposes an obligation on HMRC to make regulations with respect to the collection of all 'PAYE income' and s 684(2) includes in the list of what they may include in those regulations 'provision for requiring persons making payments of PAYE income to make, at the time of the payment, deductions of ... income tax', but this is not quite the same as what the legislation previously required. A payment is treated as made at the earlier of the time when it is made or the person becomes entitled to it (s 686, mirroring s 18 – see **[8.12]**).

There are difficulties in establishing that there has been a 'deduction' when no actual payment is made at the time of the deemed payment, particularly when money is never actually handed over but a credit is merely given against drawings already made on a director's loan account (see *R v IRC, ex p McVeigh* (1996)).

The system generally applies to all taxable earnings and taxable specific income (defined in s 10). There are far-reaching provisions which extend the PAYE net to cover situations where it would normally be difficult for HMRC to collect the tax due (for instance, if the employer is outside the UK).

Section 689 provides that if the employer (or, if applicable, the person paying the earnings on behalf of the employer) is not subject to the Income Tax (Employments) Regulations 2003, SI 2003/2682 (the PAYE Regulations) (as to which, see *Clark v Oceanic Contractors* (1983), discussed at **[18.51]**), and does not collect PAYE voluntarily, then the person for whom the employee 'works' (in the UK) is treated as making the payment and is, therefore, required to operate PAYE. Typically, this will catch the employee seconded to a UK subsidiary. Section 690 deals with the situation where a non-UK resident employee is liable to UK income tax on his UK earnings because he performs part of his duties in the UK. The employer is required to apply to HMRC for a direction agreeing 'what part of his remuneration is liable to UK income tax'; if no direction is applied for, the employer must operate PAYE in respect of the entire salary. Section 691 enables HMRC to subject a person for whom an employee works (but who is not his employer) to the PAYE Regulations even if the actual employer is taxed in the UK and therefore subject to the PAYE Regulations. HMRC can direct that person to operate PAYE 'if it is likely that income tax will not be deducted or accounted for in accordance with the Regulations'.

ITEPA 2003 s 692 allows regulations to make provision for PAYE to be operated where tips are collected and shared amongst employees. The obligation to operate PAYE can be imposed on the person running the arrangement, with a residual liability on the actual employer. This provision used to be in the PAYE Regulations dealing with these arrangements under which the organiser was called the 'troncmaster' (see HMRC Booklet E24).

[8.191]

2 Problem cases

a) *Benefits in kind*

Benefits in kind were generally seen as excluded from the PAYE regime on the basis that there was no payment (but see *Paul Dunstall Organisation Ltd v Hedges* (1999), considered below). However, PAYE has now been imposed where assessable income is provided in the form of 'readily convertible assets' (s 696): PAYE is also imposed where non-cash vouchers and credit tokens which may be exchanged for such assets (or money, in the case of credit tokens) are obtained and where cash vouchers to which Part 3 Chapter 4 applies are received (ss 693–695).

Part 11 Chapter 4 and the PAYE Regulations provide how and when the employer is to account for PAYE on these 'notional payments'. They also exclude certain benefits from the scope of these provisions (eg cash vouchers used to defray expenses if the amount for which the voucher can be exchanged would not, if it had been paid directly by the employer to the employee, have been taxable except under Chapter 3 Part 10; some shares received through approved employee share schemes or on exercise of some options granted before 27 November 1996).

Deciding whether or not an asset is readily convertible can be difficult. The definition is set out in s 702 and includes assets for which 'trading arrangements' exist (or are likely to come into existence). On the difficult question of what constitutes 'trading arrangements' see *DTE Financial Services Ltd v Wilson* (2001) (see [8.194]) and *NMB Holdings Ltd v Secretary of State for Social Security* (2000) (but note that these relate to the legislation before it was amended in 1998). HMRC's interpretation of 'readily convertible' can be seen in *Tax Bulletin*, August 1998, pp 563–567 and April 2000, pp 735 and 736: but it should be noted that in some situations it now views that test as more easily satisfied than there indicated; and that the definition was amended by FA 2003 Sch 22 para 15 so as to include any share the provision of which would not entitle the employing company to a corporation tax deduction under FA 2003 Sch 23 (the main target of this being shares in an unquoted subsidiary of an unquoted parent).

The Upper Tribunal held in *Aberdeen Asset Management Plc v R & C Comrs* (2012) that shares in a cash-box company awarded to employees as part of an avoidance scheme were readily convertible assets.

To prevent avoidance, s 697 imposes PAYE where an asset that the employee already owns is enhanced in value, if the asset falls within the definition of 'readily convertible assets'.

With effect from 6 April 2016, employers have had the option of applying to operate PAYE in respect of the cash equivalent of certain benefits in kind. An application to become authorised to make such deductions must be made to HMRC in advance, specifying the benefits and employees in respect of which deductions are proposed to be made (PAYE Regulations, r 61C). For 2015–16 the option applied Chapter 6 benefits (cars, vans and related benefits) and benefits treated as earnings under Chapter 10 (which includes the residual charge). From 2016–17 it will also cover non-cash vouchers and credit tokens. HMRC have the power to extend this legislation to cover any chapter of the benefits code.

Benefits in kind that are treated as giving rise to PAYE income in this way must be reported in real time to HMRC but are excluded from the P11D (r 85(4)). [**8.192**]

b) *Part only of a payment taxed*

Another exclusion derives from the House of Lords decision in *IRC v Herd* (1993). It was held that any payment 'only part of which is assessable to income tax under Schedule E' is excluded from the system because there is no machinery for distinguishing the part that is taxable from the part that is not. In such a situation there is no obligation on the payer to operate PAYE in relation to the taxable part. This type of situation used to arise (as it did in *Herd*) where an employee sells shares acquired by reason of his employment and part only of the purchase price is taxable (eg under ITEPA 2003 Part 7 Chapter 3D – see [**9.28**]) but note that the PAYE treatment changed in that situation as a result of the amendments effected to ITEPA 2003 ss 698 and 700 by FA 2003 (see [**9.43**])).

The decision in *IRC v Herd* (1993) cast doubt on the practice under which employers operated PAYE on part of an employee's remuneration where the other part was not subject to UK tax (because he performed some of his duties abroad and was not resident or not ordinarily resident). What is now s 690 was therefore introduced to deal with this situation (see [**8.191**]).

As a result of these legislative changes, there is now little scope for the principle established in *IRC v Herd* (1993) to operate. [**8.193**]

c) *What is a 'payment'?*

As a general rule, one may say that a payment has been made when money is placed unreservedly at the disposal of another. The Supreme Court clarified in *RFC 2012 Plc (in liquidation) v Advocate General for Scotland* (2017) that it need not be placed unreservedly at the disposal of the employee if the earnings in question have been redirected to another person (in that case to trustees of an employee benefit trust). Similarly, in *Garforth v Newsmith Stainless Ltd* (1979), there was a 'payment' when sums were credited to directors' loan accounts, even though the money had not been drawn down.

Even prior to the introduction of the anti-avoidance provisions, HMRC would try to collect PAYE despite the fact that the employee had not actually received cash from the employer (see Press Release IR 24 (30 November 1993) for some examples of the wide interpretation HMRC gave to the word 'payment'). One particularly popular attack was to ascertain whether there had been a declaration of a monetary amount due to the employee (say a bonus of £500,000) which had then been commuted into an asset (say gold bars): HMRC argued that the mere declaration of the amount counted as a 'payment'.

In *Paul Dunstall Organisation Ltd v Hedges* (1999), this was in essence what happened (except the payment was in land which the employee immediately sold), but the finding by the Special Commissioners in favour of HMRC was not based on such an approach. Instead, the Special Commissioners seemed to take the view that, since regulation 6 of the (then) PAYE Regulations (SI 1993/744) required the operation of PAYE on the payment of emoluments and that term included non-cash assets, the PAYE obligation extended to such assets (one of the two Special Commissioners in that case applied the same reasoning in *Black v Inspector of Taxes* (2000)). This ignored the fact that it was only emoluments which were 'paid' which triggered the obligation and the reasoning in this part of the decision has been much criticised (see *Taxation*, 4 February 1999, p 429 and 6 May 1999, p 148).

Of course, inserting land in place of cash remuneration could have been regarded as an inserted step under the *Ramsay* principle (as the Commissioners mentioned *obiter* in *Dunstall*). Adopting the approach in *MacNiven v Westmoreland Investments Ltd* (2001) (to ascertain first whether the concept used in the legislation (in this case 'payment') is a practical commercial one and, only if it is, to apply *Ramsay* to the composite transaction), the Court of Appeal in *DTE Financial Services Ltd v Wilson* (2001) found that, when the company satisfied bonuses by assigning its beneficial interest in an offshore trust to the employee, who then received £40,000 from the trustees when his interest fell in, a PAYE liability was triggered. The court's robust approach was to interpret the sequence of events as the company deciding to pay the employee a £40,000 bonus and the employee receiving that bonus – the cash payment received by him was a payment of employment income, so PAYE applied. [8.194]

3 Coding and accounting for tax due

a) *PAYE coding*

PAYE is an effective tax collection system which reduces the opportunity and incentive for tax evasion. The employer is given a code for each employee which represents the amount of his (tax-free) allowances less taxable benefits in kind (of which HMRC are aware) for the tax year. This code and the amount of tax paid to date in the tax year determine the amount of tax to be deducted at source. PAYE can be used to collect underpayments of tax by the employee in previous years or tax due on other income by reducing (or eliminating completely) the amount of the employee's (tax-free) allowances for the current year. [8.195]

b) *K codes*

A K code is applied if the employee receives benefits in kind (or has other income not subject to PAYE) the value of which exceeds his personal allowances. The K code is a negative code: normally a non-K code results in a deduction from earnings to arrive at the amount subject to PAYE; the K code results in an addition to earnings, thereby increasing the amount of tax collected. However, an employee's salary cannot entirely be applied in paying tax on his benefits in kind: tax deducted from any payment cannot exceed 50% of the payment (except where tax is being collected on 'notional payments' (PAYE Regulations reg 23). [8.196]

c) *Returns*

Each year the employer must complete form P11D giving details of benefits in kind in respect of which voluntary payrolling is not operated and details payments by way of expenses (except those for which a dispensation has been granted: see ITEPA 2003 s 65, P11DX and EIM 30050). Previously, form P9D was used for employees earning less than £8,500.

Other returns may also be required (for instance, in relation to company cars and termination payments). A Form P60 must be given to each employee working for the employer on 5 April, giving details of earnings subject to PAYE and the tax paid; a Form P45 (giving similar details for the tax year to date) is given on cessation of employment. [8.197]

d) *PAYE settlement agreements*

Certain employers regularly agree to pay their employees' tax liabilities on minor items (for instance, the cost of office parties which exceed the exempt amount (see [8.168]) – a lump sum is paid for all employees on a grossed-up basis – under what are known as 'PAYE settlement agreements' (or 'PSAs') (ITEPA 2003 ss 703–707). The detailed rules are set out in the PAYE Regulations Part 6 and SP5/96. [8.198]

e) *Accounting to HMRC*

Normally, an employer has to account to HMRC within 14 days of the end of the income tax month during which he should have deducted the tax (ie normally by the 19th of the following month); a 17-day delay applies if the employer pays electronically. However, where the amount due is relatively low, the employer can account on a quarterly basis (PAYE Regulations reg 41).

In the event of an overpayment of tax in a previous year, this will be corrected between HMRC and the employee himself either by direct repayment or by set-off against other tax liabilities of that year; alternatively, the employee's code for the current year can be adjusted to take the repayment due into account. If the PAYE due for the tax year is not paid by the following 19 April (22 April if payment is made electronically), interest is payable (PAYE Regulations reg 82).

Penalties can be levied for (i) late payment of PAYE; (ii) inaccurate returns; and (iii) late filing of in-year real time information (RTI) returns.

A uniform penalty regime for late paid in-year PAYE was introduced by FA 2009 Sch 56 with effect from 6 April 2010. This charges fixed penalties by reference to the number of defaults during the tax year. The initial default does not trigger a penalty but, if between one and three defaults is made there is a penalty of 1% of the total tax unpaid. This rises to 4% if ten or more defaults occur, with further penalties of 5% if tax remains unpaid six and twelve months from the penalty date. These penalties are imposed manually at the end of every tax year. FA 2013 amended the late payment penalties regime with effect from 6 April 2015 to 'ring-fence' each penalty. This means that if there is a further default in the tax year, the earlier penalties are not re-calculated.

Penalties of up to 100% of the tax liability can be levied for inaccurate returns. The amount of the penalty will vary accordingly to the culpability of the employer, ie penalties are higher if the failure to submit a correct return was deliberate and concealed as opposed to simply careless. There are also reductions in the level of penalty imposed depending upon the level of disclosure made by the company.

A separate penalty regime for failing to file in-year real time information (RTI) returns on time took effect from 6 October 2014 (for employers with at least 50 employees on that date) and 6 March 2015 (for employers with fewer than 50 employees on 6 October). In earlier tax years, there was only a penalty if the annual or final RTI submission was late; there was no penalty if an in-year RTI return was filed late. The penalties for late RTI returns are calculated by reference to the number of employees ranging from £100 for employers with under 10 employees to £400 for those with 250 or more employees. **[8.199]**

f)   *Non-deduction of PAYE*

Special provisions operate to ensure that PAYE is operated on remuneration paid to directors. Section 223 provides that, whenever tax on a director's earnings should have been deducted in accordance with the regulations and the whole, or part, of the amount due was not deducted but was accounted for to HMRC by a person other than the director, then, unless the director makes good the tax paid, he will be treated as receiving further earnings equal to the amount of tax that has been accounted for to HMRC. This provision only applies to directors not excluded from the benefits code by Part 3 Chapter 11 (see **[8.103]**).

There is a similar provision if an employer is treated as making a 'notional payment' to an employee or director (generally, a payment treated as made under ss 687, 689, 693–700: see s 710(2)(a)). The employer is required to account for the tax due; and if that tax is neither deducted from actual payments made nor made good by the employee within 90 days, the tax payable is treated as a taxable benefit (s 222) (see *Ferguson v IRC* (2001) for what may be regarded as a liberal interpretation of 'making good'; and EIM 11952 for HMRC's harsher view of whether a credit balance in a director's loan account is sufficient to satisfy the statutory requirement that the tax due is 'made good'). Unfortunately for the employer, he only has a statutory right to deduct the tax due from cash payments made in the same income tax month as the notional payment (s 710(7) and see *Tax Bulletin*, April 2000, pp 734 and 735 for a discussion of whether the uncollected tax could be treated as a loan). As the PAYE obligation extends to notional payments made to ex-employees (who may well not be in receipt of cash payments), it has become increasingly important for employers to ensure they have some enforceable means of collecting tax paid from the recipients of these notional payments (see **[8.202]**). **[8.200]**

g) *When the employee can be directly assessed*

Under the PAYE system, the liability of the employer to deduct and account for the correct amount of tax is usually exclusive, so that HMRC cannot assess an employee for unpaid tax. Exceptions are provided for in regulations 72(3), (4) and 81 of the PAYE Regulations. Regulation 72(3), which applies when an employee receives the earnings knowing that the employer has wilfully failed to deduct the proper amount of tax, is often relied on by HMRC. In *R v IRC, ex p McVeigh* (1996), May J commented that this provision 'would normally operate where the employer had wilfully paid an employee gross and the employee knew this'. Regulation 81's prime role is to allow an inspector to determine an amount of PAYE due from an employer if he believes tax is payable; but if the tax so determined is not paid by the employer, it can be collected from the employee if the same conditions as those in reg 72(4) are satisfied. An employee can appeal against a direction under reg 72 or 81.

A heavy burden is placed on HMRC if reg 72(4) (or reg 81) is to be satisfied, since not only is actual knowledge on the part of the employee required but also an element of blameworthiness on the part of the employer must be shown. This burden was satisfied in the cases of *R v IRC, ex p Keys and ex p Cook* (1987) where the employees in question were the controlling directors of the employer company which had failed over a number of years to operate PAYE in respect of their salaries (for the public law defence available to an employee in such cases, see *Pawlowski v Dunnington* (1999)).

Regulation 72(3), which can be applied by HMRC if satisfied that the employer took reasonable care to comply with the regulations and the error was made in good faith, is rarely applied. However, an employer can request HMRC to make a direction if the employer considers an error was made in good faith, so more use may now be made of this mode of recovery.

In the case of *Gayen v R & C Comrs* (2013), the First-tier Tribunal found that an employee, Dr Gayen, was not liable for income tax that should have been deducted by his employer under PAYE. Under TMA 1970, s 59B, a taxpayer is required to pay the difference between (i) the amount of income tax and capital gains tax contained in their self-assessment and (ii) the aggregate of any income tax deducted at source (which includes income tax treated as deducted from any income). Regulation 185 of the PAYE Regulations provides that 'income tax treated as deducted' includes income tax which the employer was liable to deduct from payments but failed to do so. No direction had been made under reg 72 or 81 and therefore the amount to be treated as deducted was the amount the employer was liable to deduct, rather than the amount actually deducted. The employer should have deducted tax by reference to the employee's tax code in accordance with reg 21. The tribunal therefore held that the amount of tax due from Dr Gayen should be varied, so that the amount of unpaid tax would be reduced by the amount the employer should have deducted and did not. This case acts as a reminder that the responsibility for collecting and accounting for PAYE rests with the employer and, as discussed below, the courts will only permit redress against an employee in very limited circumstances. **[8.201]**

h) *Recovery of tax from the employee*

A perennial problem faced by employers is how to recover from employees tax paid over to HMRC but not deducted from their salaries. The statutory rights are extremely limited. Whether recovery is possible at common law was until recently open to debate. In *Bernard & Shaw Ltd v Shaw* (1951) a company failed in a restitutionary claim, but this was not surprising since it had not actually paid over the tax to HMRC; the judge left open the possibility that, if it had done so, it might have been successful in an action for 'money paid to the use of the employee' on the basis that the employee was 'ultimately responsible' for the tax. In the more recent case of *McCarthy v McCarthy & Stone plc* (2007) the employer successfully recovered, from a former director, PAYE income tax and NICs payments it had made to HMRC based on a restitutionary claim. The High Court and Court of Appeal's decisions followed the possibility left open in *Bernard & Shaw Ltd v Shaw*. The courts accepted that the PAYE payments made by the employer were payments for which the director was 'ultimately responsible', and therefore the employer was entitled to recover the same from the employee.

A restitutionary action based on mistake of fact will often not be appropriate (as there has not normally been such a mistake), but the removal of the bar to restitutionary claims based on mistakes of law effected by the House of Lords in *Kleinwort Benson v Lincoln City Council* (1998) could also prove helpful to employers (see *Taxation*, 18 March 1999, p 595 and 22 March 2001, p 601 for details of two successful restitutionary claims).

In May 2014, HMRC published a consultation document relating to a new power called 'direct recovery of debts', which would enable them to recover overdue tax from a taxpayer's bank account where there is a tax or tax credit debt of £1,000 or more due to HMRC. Provision for this contentious power was included in the summer 2015 Finance Bill.

See also **[8.24]–[8.30]** in relation to the recovery of PAYE income tax from workers reclassified as employees. **[8.202]**

4 Real-time information and future reform

Operating PAYE is a burden for employers, not only because of the uncertainties touched on above and the fact that getting it wrong can be expensive (see *Taxation*, 22 February 2001, p 483 but note the possible right of recovery discussed at **[8.202]**) but also because the basic system is cumulative, aiming to ensure that at any given week in a tax year the tax paid by an employee matches his liabilities. The Treasury's Sixth Report on HMRC advised that, unless the PAYE system could adapt to deal more easily with people commencing and leaving employment during a tax year, 'it may in the longer term, be necessary to consider moving to non-cumulative collection of PAYE or to a form of collection direct from employees'. In an attempt to rectify the problem, developments have been underway to put PAYE online: from 6 April 2008, employers with 50 or more employees have had to send their employee starting and leaving details and some pension information to HMRC online. From 2010, every employer has had to do the same (see Revenue & Customs Brief 15/07).

Furthermore, under the Income Tax (Pay As You Earn) (Amendment) Regulations 2012, SI 2012/822, HMRC introduced a regime which allows the collection of real-time PAYE information (RTI), whereby employers send to HMRC information concerning the payments and deductions they make under PAYE at the same time as making a payment to an employee. From 6 October 2013 (for most employers), information on payments made to employees has to be provided to HMRC in real time. The employer will normally be required to send HMRC (electronically) details of payments made to employees 'on or before' the time each payment is made to the employee. Employers are no longer required to file form P35 – instead when they submit a final Full Payment Submission (FPS) at the end of the year, they must report that it is the final submission for the tax year and answer end of year declarations and questions. In addition, employers are no longer required to submit P45s to HMRC, although they will continue to provide these to employees when they cease employment. Starter and leaver information is provided to HMRC as part of the RTI submission. FA 2013 included provisions to introduce a new model for late filing penalties in relation to RTI. This amends FA 2009, Sch 55 so that penalties for late filing of RTI will (i) be based on the number of employees in the employer's PAYE scheme rather than the number of filing defaults; (ii) allow the first default in a tax year to be unpenalised; (iii) apply only one penalty each tax month (regardless of the number of defaults); (iv) charge penalties quarterly; and (v) provide for an extra penalty where a return is more than three months late. The new penalty regime took effect from October 2014. [8.203]

9 Employee participation: options, incentives and trusts

Updated by Mark Ife, LLB MJur, Partner and Bradley Richardson, MA, Senior Associate, Herbert Smith Freehills LLP

I Introduction [9.1]
II Non tax-advantaged share schemes [9.11]
III Tax-advantaged share schemes [9.71]
IV Employee trusts and treasury shares [9.111]
V Corporation tax [9.121]
VI Choice of scheme [9.151]

I INTRODUCTION

1 Encouraging employee share ownership

Over the last 30 years there has been a substantial growth in employee share option and share incentive schemes. The major attraction of such schemes was stated by the then Chancellor in his Foreword to a consultation document on employee share ownership (December 1998) as follows: 'Share ownership offers employees a real stake in their company with shareholders, managers and employees working towards common goals.' Despite this growth, 'only a fraction of British employees and an even smaller minority of those outside senior management own shares in the companies they work in'. Therefore, the Government's emphasis turned towards encouraging companies to introduce schemes which benefit all their employees and on restricting tax relief for schemes which enable large benefits to be provided to senior management, unless the Government perceives substantial macro-economic benefits may result (as with Enterprise Management Incentives (EMIs) introduced by FA 2000). The Government also encourages employees to invest in their employers by enabling such investment to be made out of pre-tax salary through Share Incentive Plans (SIPs), also introduced in 2000.

The Government continues to believe that productivity will be increased by encouraging employee participation. The research report 'Employee ownership, motivation and productivity' (November 2002) for Employees Direct by Birkbeck College, University of London and The Work Foundation concluded that there is 'undoubtedly' evidence to support this belief.

Employee ownership has formed a key aspect of the 'mutualisation' of certain Government functions, with Cabinet Office minister Francis Maude expressing the view that '[w]e know that employees who have a stake in their business, or take ownership of it completely, have more power and motivation to improve the service they run'.

Recent years have seen the Government renew its focus on employee ownership of both shares and of the business in which they are employed. In April 2014 the Government raised the permitted levels of participation in the most popular tax-advantaged 'all-employee' share plans. In response to a review of employee-ownership in 2012, the Government has taken steps designed to facilitate the transfer of businesses into employees' hands, most recently with the introduction of tax reliefs available in connection with businesses owned by employee-ownership trusts.

Although not supported by the tax regime in the same way as is wider employee share ownership, executive share ownership also continues to be seen, particularly by institutional investors, as creating a positive alignment between owners and managers, and so continues to be an important aspect within the wider topic of employee share participation.

Various HMRC Manuals deal with share schemes: the Employment Related Securities Manual (ERSM prefix) now deals with all arrangements other than tax-advantaged plans, which are covered by the Tax-Advantaged Share Scheme Manual (ETASSUM prefix), which is the updated version of the previous Employee Share Schemes Unit Manual (ESSUM prefix). These manuals are available at www.gov.uk/government/collections/hmrc-manuals. [9.1]

2 Taxation of share incentives and options

An individual who is given shares by his employer receives taxable earnings if the shares are 'from employment' and will suffer income tax on the market value of those shares on the date when he receives them: *Weight v Salmon* (1935) and ITEPA 2003 s 9. Similarly, an employee who is sold shares by his employer at an undervalue receives earnings equal to the difference between the price paid and the market value of the shares at the date of purchase. These types of arrangement, where the employee receives shares not share options, are referred to in this Chapter 9 as *share incentives*.

Various schemes, including the use of *share options*, were introduced by employers in an attempt to circumvent the income tax net. Inevitably, anti-avoidance legislation was then passed in an attempt to widen that net!

Certain employee share schemes are given favourable tax treatment. These tax-advantaged schemes are also referred to as 'approved schemes' as, until 6 April 2014, prior approval to operate such schemes was required from HMRC; this requirement has now been replaced with a self-certification regime. Profits made by employees under such schemes are, provided the relevant criteria are met, treated as capital gains: employees who acquire shares under such arrangements have the benefit of not realising any taxable amount until shares are sold and then being taxed at CGT rates of, since 6 April 2016, 10% and 20%, rather than income tax and National Insurance at combined rates of up to 47%. In addition, where such profits fall to be taxed within the CGT regime, the individual will also benefit from the CGT annual exemption. Except for the minority of employees who are eligible to receive

Enterprise Management Incentive options, however, the potential to make very large gains is only obtainable under non tax-advantaged schemes.

Where employees are offered the opportunity to buy shares they may borrow to finance their acquisition. Readers are referred to [7.44] for a discussion of the tax relief available for interest paid on such loans where the company is a close company and to [8.123] for a discussion of the tax treatment for employees where the loan is provided interest-free. [9.2]

3 Reporting obligations

At the same time that the taxation of non tax-advantaged schemes was fundamentally changed by FA 2003 (see Section II), new reporting requirements were also introduced. These requirements have since been amended to provide for online reporting for tax years from 6 April 2014. Online filing first requires all schemes (both tax-advantaged and non tax-advantaged) to be notified to HMRC, itself an online process. The notification for tax-advantaged schemes must also include a self-certification of compliance with the regulatory requirements (in place of the previous HMRC approval process), which is explained in more detail at [9.73].

Returns are required to be filed by 6 July following the end of the tax year in which the reportable event occurs (and, therefore, notification to HMRC of a new scheme is also required by this deadline). Penalties may be chargeable for failure to make a timely, complete and accurate filing. It is worth noting that the reporting obligations are not limited to shares acquired through specific schemes but will also apply, for instance, to shares acquired through an 'earn-out' (see [9.12] (7)). Indeed, the reporting requirements are not limited to cases where an income tax charge arises: they may apply whenever an employee or director acquires shares. Guidance in respect of the online notification and filing requirements are available at www.gov.uk/business-tax/employment-related-securities.

The anti-avoidance reporting obligations introduced by FA 2004 Part 7 (see [5.3] ff) may also apply to employee share scheme arrangements. [9.3]–[9.10]

II   NON TAX-ADVANTAGED SHARE SCHEMES

1   Introduction

a)   *Background*

The income tax treatment of non-tax-advantaged schemes was introduced on a piecemeal basis mainly in response to varied attempts over the years to devise arrangements that escaped the income tax net. Although still viewed as complex, this piecemeal approach was replaced with the provisions set out in FA 2003 Sch 22.

> 'By far the lengthiest and most complex part of this year's Finance Bill is Schedule 22 which completely rewrites the rules relating to the tax treatment of non-approved employee share schemes. This is an area of tax law which has always been an active battleground between the Revenue and taxpayers. The Revenue's abiding concern is that share schemes will be used to remunerate employees in a

way which avoids income tax. Taxpayer motivation to do just that has been raised by the generous terms on which CGT taper relief has been extended to employee shareholders and by the imposition of national insurance on share schemes.

The main purpose of Schedule 22 is, of course, to close loopholes. But the Revenue accepts that the income tax net should only catch gains which are artificially engineered as opposed to those arising from "real" increases in share values generated by corporate performance.'

(*Tax Journal*, 5 May 2003)
[9.11]

b) *General points on the legislation*

In the remainder of this Section, the operation of the amended Chapters of Part 7 of ITEPA 2003 is examined. It is assumed throughout these Chapters that they, and only they, apply to the shares in question. Therefore, the operative date for each amended provision to come into force is not set out, nor the shares to which each apply (some only apply to shares acquired after 16 April 2003, some to shares whenever acquired). Readers for whom the exact details of the application of a particular provision are important will need to consult FA 2003 Sch 22. Further, whilst in general the provisions of ITEPA 2003 before it was amended by FA 2003 reflected the old legislation, there were one or two changes; and those changes in some cases only applied from 6 April 2003 to 9 or 16 April 2003 and were subject to their own transitional provisions! In relation to the changes effected by ITEPA 2003, readers are referred to *Tax Journal*, 14 April 2003.

There are seven further points of general application:
(1) In the majority of cases employees are given *shares* but as advantage was being taken of the fact that the anti-avoidance legislation only applied to shares, ITEPA 2003 Part 7 now extends to 'securities', as defined in s 420 (and interests therein). However, to reflect the usual position, this Chapter 9 refers to shares.
(2) In appropriate circumstances it used to be possible to argue that employees/directors had not acquired shares in their company by reason of that status but rather as investors (for instance, on a management buy-out). In most cases such an argument will no longer be possible: now any right or opportunity to acquire shares which is made available by a person's employer (or someone connected with it) will be deemed to be available '**by reason of employment**' (the prerequisite to taxability – s 421B(1)), unless provided by an individual 'in the normal course of the domestic, family or personal relationships' of that individual (s 421B(3)). The proviso might apply, for instance, when a son received shares in his employing company from his father. If the deeming provision does not apply, the Northern Ireland Court of Appeal's consideration of the analogous wording in TA 1988 s 154 (now, ITEPA 2003 s 201) in *Mairs v Haughey* (1992) may provide helpful guidance as to the meaning of the phrase 'by reason of employment'. As a result of this change, ITEPA 2003 Part 7 is wider in scope than the previous provisions which has meant that the Government has had to introduce specific legislation (for example in relation to research institution spinout companies (FA 2005 s 20) – see **[9.31]**) to limit the extent of this legislation.

(3) Closely connected to (2), section 421B applies Chapters 2 to 4 of Part 7 if shares are acquired 'where the right or opportunity to acquire [them] is **available**' by reason of employment. An almost identical phrase in the old legislation was considered by the Court of Session in *IRC v Herd* (1992). The argument centred around whether an opportunity was 'available' by reason of employment when the employee had stipulated that he must receive the shares as a precondition to taking up the appointment: not surprisingly, the court declined to interpret the provision as requiring it to investigate who instigated the idea of providing share benefits to the employee. However, it should be noted that by virtue of s 421B(2)(b), 'employment' is also taken to cover former and prospective employment.

(4) There are exceptions from the income tax charges if the event (which would otherwise be a **chargeable** event) affects all shares of the same class as the employee's shares, provided certain conditions are satisfied. Those conditions were amended with effect from 7 May 2004 by FA 2004 s 86 as it was thought that the previous exceptions were being exploited to provide an exemption from income tax when employees received value from their shares. Now the exception only applies if: (a) 'the avoidance of tax or national insurance contributions was not the main purpose, or one of the main purposes, of the arrangements under which the right or opportunity to acquire' the employee shares was made available; and (b) either the company is employee-controlled by virtue of shares of that class or the majority of the shares of that class are not held by employees (see, for example, ITEPA 2003 s 429 as amended by FA 2004). Similar anti-avoidance provisions (where HMRC consider avoidance of tax and NIC to be a 'main purpose') were introduced by F(No 2)A 2005 Sch 2, for example in relation to restricted securities (ITEPA 2003 s 424), convertible securities (ITEPA 2003 s 437) and acquisitions at less than market value (ITEPA 2003 s 446R and s 446UA).

(5) Prior to FA 2004, ITEPA 2003 s 421F excluded shares acquired on a public offer from the application of Part 7 Chapters 2–4. As a result of FA 2004 s 89, with effect from 18 June 2004 (but in relation to shares whenever acquired), only Chapters 2, 3 and 3C are disapplied and then only if tax or NIC avoidance is not the main purpose of the arrangements under which the shares are acquired or held.

(6) In most cases, the charge imposed by Part 7 will arise whether it is the employee or an associate of his who acquires the shares. It is worth noting that, most peculiarly, the legislation does not draw a distinction between the employee and his associates: instead, the employee himself is included in the definition of 'associated person' in s 421C: as a result, on a casual reading of the sections which describe the circumstances when a charge arises and which refer only to an 'associated person' acquiring etc the shares, it looks as if there are no charges when the employee himself holds the shares! Since, in fact, it will usually be the employee himself who acquires the shares, this Chapter 9 refers only to him.

Sections 421C and 472 (which define 'associated persons' for the purposes of ITEPA 2003 Part 7 Chapter 3) were amended by FA 2004 s 90 to extend the definition of who are 'associated' persons. The current term covers the person who acquires the shares, the employee (if different) and any 'relevant linked person' (ie a current or former connected person or member of the same household). HMRC's reasons for making this change were set out in News Release 30/4:

> 'The changes will ensure that charges cannot be avoided by ensuring that persons, once associated, remain associated and also provide for a charge on a benefit received through the ownership of securities options.'

(7) There are several types of arrangement that could fall within more than one Chapter of Part 7. One example is 'equity ratchets'. These are commonly found in management buyouts and take various forms but all have the same aim – the managers' proportion of the ordinary share capital will increase (and that of the other investors will fall) if certain performance targets are met. Other examples are 'earn-outs' (where the number of shares a purchaser provides to the vendor as consideration for the purchase, or the amount it pays, varies depending on how the company acquired performs) and 'flowering shares' (where rights provisionally attach to shares when they are acquired but whether they become unconditionally attached depends on future events). How arrangements are structured will affect how, if at all, Part 7 applies. The Memorandum of Understanding between the British Venture Capital Association and the Inland Revenue dated 25 July 2003 and ERSM 30520 discuss how some of those arrangements may be taxed. [9.12]

c) *New approach to residency conditions*

Prior to 6 April 2015, the provisions of Part 7 were subject to a number of exclusions where the employee was not UK resident, so that (broadly) the chapters of Part 7 that deal with non tax-advantaged schemes (Chapters 2 to 5) applied only where the employee was UK resident at the time of acquisition of the shares or grant of the option. Where the employee was subject to tax on the remittance basis, Part 2 Chapter 5A may then also have applied, pursuant to which it may have been possible to treat a portion of the amount otherwise subject to tax under Part 7 as non-taxable.

However, the application of Part 7 to employees whose residence status changes between acquisition of the shares (or grant of the option) and the relevant chargeable event (commonly referred to as 'internationally mobile employees') was complex and lead to anomalous results (as well as being out of step with the OECD's recommendations on the application of double-tax treaties to employee share plans). An example of such an anomaly was that the option-taxing provisions (Part 7 Chapter 5) did not apply where an individual was not UK tax resident at the time of grant even though he may have become UK tax resident by the time of exercise, whilst, strictly, that same provision would tax in full any gain made on exercise of an option granted to a previously UK resident employee where the employee was no longer resident or holding UK duties by the time of exercise. HMRC addressed some of these issues through guidance and accepted practice, but this did not provide a complete solution.

To address these issues, the provisions governing how Part 7 Chapters 2 to 5 apply to internationally mobile employees were amended with effect from 6 April 2015 by FA 2014.

The first aspect of the new regime is the removal of the current residency requirements that previously applied to these Chapters (as noted, broadly being that, in order for Part 7 to apply, the employee had to be resident at the time of acquisition of the shares or grant of an option). The second aspect is the replacement of Part 2 Chapter 5A with a new Part 2 Chapter 5B which applies to a wider range of internationally mobile employees. The new regime applies to all taxable events that occur on or after 6 April 2015, including, for example, on the exercise after such date of an option that was granted prior to 6 April 2015.

The new Chapter 5B applies if any one of three specified 'international mobility conditions' are satisfied during the 'relevant period'.

The 'relevant period' is, generally, the period over which the relevant employment income is treated as arising, and is defined separately for the purposes of each Chapter of Part 7. For the purposes of Part 7 Chapter 2 (restricted securities) and Chapter 3 (convertible securities), the relevant period is the period from acquisition of the shares to the date of the chargeable event. For the purposes of Chapter 5 (securities options) the relevant period is the vesting period of the option – being the period from the grant of the option to the date on which the option is exercised or, if earlier, the date on which it becomes capable of exercise. Specific definitions of the 'relevant period' apply for the other Chapters of Part 7.

The three 'international mobility conditions' that trigger the application of Part 2 Chapter 5B are that any part of the relevant period: (i) falls within a tax year in which the employee is taxed on the remittance basis; (ii) falls within a tax year in which the employee is non-resident; or (iii) falls within the overseas part of a tax year that is a split year (see further **Chapter 18**). The conditions can, therefore, be satisfied without the employee's tax residence changing during the relevant period.

Where one or more of the international mobility conditions is satisfied, Part 2 Chapter 5B apportions the taxable value under Part 7 over the relevant period on a daily basis, with the employee's tax status during the relevant portions of the relevant period governing how the value attributable to such part of the relevant period is taxed. Therefore, depending on the individual's tax status during the relevant period, part of the amount may not be chargeable to UK income tax (for example, where the individual is non-resident and performing duties outside the UK for part of the relevant period) or may be subject to charge on the remittance basis (where the employee is able to rely on those rules during part of the relevant period). [9.13]–[9.20]

2 Share Incentives

a) *Restricted shares*

Some forms of long-term incentive plans (particularly in private companies) involve employees receiving shares subject to a restriction on the employees' ability to dispose of them for a certain period and to their being forfeited if the employee leaves service before the end of that period. Sometimes the shares will be held in trust until the end of the period but with the employee being entitled to receive dividends and instruct the trustees how to vote in the meantime. These restricted share schemes not only act as an incentive to the employee to remain in service but also ensure an immediate identity of interest between him and the company. Further, just as companies can make exercisability of non tax-advantaged options subject to satisfying performance criteria, so shares held under these schemes can also be made subject to forfeiture if such criteria are not met. ITEPA 2003 Part 7 Chapter 2 imposes income tax charges in relation to shares that are 'restricted' when the shares become unrestricted.

Long-term incentives plans may, rather than involving employees receiving restricted shares, involve employees being given a right to acquire shares in the future. In such cases, a tax charge on acquiring the shares will arise under the 'option' regime (see [**9.41**]) or as a general employment income charge. If the shares then acquired are restricted, post-acquisition charges can also arise under Part 7 Chapter 2.

Prior to 6 April 2008, Part 7 Chapter 2 provisions only applied if the employee was resident and ordinarily resident in the UK at the time of acquisition of the restricted shares. From 6 April 2008 until 5 April 2015, by virtue of FA 2008 Sch 7 para 31, these provisions were extended to acquisitions by all employees who were UK resident (s 421E). From 6 April 2015, the requirement for the employee to have been UK resident at the time of the acquisition of the restricted shares was removed, so that Part 7 Chapter 2 now applies irrespective of the residency status of the employee, and this is the case even in respect of restricted shares acquired prior to 6 April 2015. Where one or more of the international mobility conditions is satisfied, as described above at [**9.13**], Part 2 Chapter 5 apportions the taxable value over the relevant period, in the case of restricted shares being from the date of acquisition of the restricted shares to the date of the taxable event. The employee's tax status during the relevant period will then govern how the taxable value attributable to each portion of the relevant period is taxed. [**9.21**]

i) Meaning of restriction

Pursuant to s 423(2), shares are restricted if they are subject to a 'contract, agreement, arrangement or condition' which causes their value to be less than it would be but for the restriction, and whereby:

(a) the shares may be forfeit or the employee can be compelled to sell them for less than their market value at the time of sale (the forfeiture provision);

(b) their dividend, voting, transfer or any other rights are restricted, or the employee can be compelled to sell the shares (whatever the price); or

(c) the disposal or retention of the shares or the exercise of rights attached to them may result in some other type of disadvantage.

Shares will not be restricted merely because the employee can be forced to sell them on termination of employment for misconduct at less than their then market value (s 424(b)). This exemption is narrow and does not apply where employers want to 'punish' employees who resign/are dismissed for other reasons, such as poor performance. Section 424 also provides that forfeiture for non-payment of calls on nil or partly paid shares do not count as restrictions. Previously this also included an exemption for the possibility of redeemable shares being redeemed, but this was removed by F(No 2)A 2005.

In order for a 'contract, agreement, arrangement or condition' to constitute a 'restriction' it must cause the market value of the shares to be lower than it would otherwise have been. This leads to the question of how market value is to be determined for these purposes and what type of provision is capable of affecting such market value. Whilst s 421 imports the TCGA 1992 s 272 definition of market value, which would ignore any personal or employee-specific restriction (such as the terms in an incentive plan), it is clear that HMRC is of the view that a restriction contained in an incentive plan (such as a forfeiture condition or a no-sale period) will constitute a restriction for these purposes, so as to engage Part 7 Chapter 2. Therefore, and in light of the Supreme Court's comment in *Gray's Timber Products Ltd v R & C Comrs* (2010) that the concept market value should be interpreted independently (and, indeed, differently) within each Chapter of Part 7, the cautious approach would be to take a broad reading of the provisions requiring a reduction in market value, such that any personal, or employee-specific, restrictions should not be dismissed as irrelevant to the valuation. **[9.22]**

ii)   The tax charge – acquisition

Normally, there would be an income tax charge under s 9 on the acquisition of restricted shares if the employee did not pay their (restricted) market value. However, this general position is reversed for shares that are restricted by virtue of a restriction that falls within category (a) listed in **[9.22]** (generally referred to as 'forfeitable shares'). There will not be an income tax charge on the acquisition of forfeitable shares if the forfeiture restriction will fall away within five years (even if the shares would remain restricted for another reason) (s 425(2)), unless there is an election under s 425(3). Under this provision it is, therefore, possible for an employee to receive a gift of shares that are subject to forfeiture without paying any tax until the forfeiture provision is lifted or falls away. Even if there is no income tax charge on acquisition under Part 7 Chapter 2, there may still be such a charge if the shares fall within Chapters 3, 3C or 5 (see below). **[9.23]**

iii) The tax charge – chargeable events

Whatever the reason for the shares being restricted, whenever there is a 'chargeable event', the taxable amount calculated under s 428 will 'count as employment income' (see **[8.11]**). There is such an event on the shares ceasing to be restricted, a restriction being varied or lifted, or on an arm's length sale (s 427). Section 428 sets out a formula for calculating the taxable amount which, basically, results in the taxable amount being the same percentage of the unrestricted market value of the shares immediately after the chargeable event (or percentage of the sale proceeds, if lower) as the percentage difference between the unrestricted market value of the shares when they were acquired and their actual (restricted) value at that time (ie the untaxed proportion).

The policy behind this approach is that the employee should be able to benefit in the same way as an investor would from any increase in value in that part of the share for which he has paid (directly or by paying income tax on its value), so that only the increase in value attributable to that part for which he has not so paid should be within the income tax net.

FA 2014 introduced a new exemption from the charge to income tax where restricted shares are disposed of in consideration of the acquisition of further shares which are also restricted and which have the same market value (and, where the consideration is part-shares and part-cash, the exemption will apply accordingly on a proportionate basis). This exemption was introduced to enable restricted securities to be 'rolled-over' (most commonly, where the company that issued the restricted shares is acquired by another company which wants to continue the long-term incentive arrangement over shares in the acquiror), and will replicate the effect of s 483 which already applies the same principle to share options.

EXAMPLE 9.1

Albert is given shares in his employer, Consort Ltd, which would have an unrestricted market value of £2.50. As the shares have no dividend or voting rights for the first five years, they are actually only worth £1.50. Albert therefore has to pay income tax on £1.50, but does not pay income tax on the balance of the unrestricted market value of £1 (the proportion not subject to income tax is therefore two-fifths of the unrestricted value).

Three years later, the restrictions are removed and thereafter the shares are worth £5. Albert will be treated as having employment income of £2 (two-fifths of £5). If the shares were sold at £5, £1.50 (£5 less £1.50 and £2) would be chargeable to CGT (see **[9.48]**).

NB If the shares had been sold before the restrictions were lifted, the same calculation has to be done but, as would normally be the case with this type of restriction, the restrictions will have the same proportionate effect on the share value at the time of the sale as they did at the time of acquisition, and the calculation will need to take this into consideration in determining any charge to income tax: this is in line with the policy objective identified above.

Tax charges after acquisition can, however, be avoided by making an election under s 431 for full disapplication of Chapter 2 on acquisition, so that the full unrestricted market value of the shares (or the difference between that value and the price the employee paid) is then taxed on acquisition as a general charge to income tax under s 9. Alternatively, the tax charge after acquisition can be reduced by electing for a partial disapplication (ie that the market value on acquisition should be calculated as if some of the restrictions did not apply). The benefit of making such an election is that any future increase in value will generally be subject only to CGT. However, if the share price was to fall, the income tax already paid cannot be reclaimed.

EXAMPLE 9.2

Assume that Albert made an election under s 431 for full disapplication on acquisition.

He would have had to pay income tax on £2.50 on acquisition but there would be no further charges under Chapter 2. If the shares were sold at £5, £2.50 (£5 less £2.50) would be chargeable to CGT. **[9.24]**

b) *Convertible shares*

The issue of convertible shares to employees, while unusual, is normally associated with the imposition of performance conditions and is most commonly found when the directors have acquired the company with funding from a venture capitalist. It might be the case that the latter holds ordinary shares and the directors have preference shares which will convert to ordinary shares (thus reducing the percentage held by the venture capitalist) on the achievement of performance targets.

HMRC treats convertible shares as two separate assets: the share itself, ignoring the right to convert; and the right to convert. The former is taxed on receipt in the usual way, so the charge will depend upon what, if anything, the employee pays for the shares. Although the latter has a value on receipt, in general it is not taxed until conversion occurs: there is an income tax charge on the conversion or sale of the convertible shares or if the entitlement to convert is released for consideration or if the employee receives a benefit in connection with that entitlement (ss 438–439).

Prior to 6 April 2008, these provisions only applied if the employee was resident and ordinarily resident in the UK at the time of acquisition. From 6 April 2008 to 5 April 2015, by virtue of FA 2008 Sch 7 para 31, they were also extended to acquisitions by all employees who were UK resident (s 421E). From 6 April 2015, the requirement for the employee to have been UK resident at the time of the acquisition of the convertible shares was removed, so that Part 7 Chapter 2 now applies irrespective of the residency status of the employee, and this is the case even in respect of convertible shares acquired prior to 6 April 2015. Where one or more of the international mobility conditions is satisfied, as described above at **[9.13]**, Part 2 Chapter 5 apportions the taxable value over the relevant period, in the case of convertible shares being from the date of acquisition of the convertible shares to the date of the taxable event. The employee's tax status during the relevant period will then govern how the taxable value attributable to each portion of the relevant period is taxed.

Sections 440–442 set out how to calculate the taxable amount on the occurrence of the chargeable event. Where the shares have been converted, s 441 taxes only the difference in value between the shares converted and the shares acquired. **[9.25]**

EXAMPLE 9.3

Albert buys 100 preference shares (which are convertible into ordinary shares on achieving performance targets) for £100 (their market value). Ignoring the conversion right, they are worth £150 when he converts them to 100 ordinary shares worth £1,000. He will be charged to income tax on £850.

NB (1) The preference shares are valued as if they were not convertible (s 441(7)) as otherwise the added value that could be acquired by converting would increase their market value to that of the ordinary shares once the right to convert became unrestricted.

(2) It may be possible to avoid any income tax charge by structuring the arrangements differently: see the Memorandum of Understanding referred to at (7) in **[9.12]**.

c) *Artificial depression or enhancement of market value*

Part 7 Chapters 3A and 3B cover the situation when the value of employee shares is enhanced or depressed because of things done other than for genuine commercial reasons. Both Chapters (ss 446A and 446K) include a non-exhaustive definition of 'things that are ... done otherwise than for genuine commercial purposes': this includes where one of the main purposes is the avoidance of tax or NICs; and non-arm's length transactions between group companies.

Section 446B applies to impose a charge on acquisition if, within the seven years preceding the employee's acquisition, the market value of the shares has been artificially depressed by at least 10%. It does not apply if the shares are restricted and fall within s 425(2) where a forfeiture provision applies, provided no election has been made under s 425(3) (see **[9.23]**). The fact that s 446B applies does not prevent other charges applying (for instance, the ongoing notional loan charge under Chapter 3C (see **[9.27]**)).

Section 446C sets out how to calculate the taxable amount on acquisition (although the formula varies if the shares in question are restricted or convertible (s 446D)). That calculation results in the employee having taxable income equal to the difference between what would have been the market value but for its artificial depression and the actual market value of the shares (or the price paid, if higher). The rest of Chapter 3A sets out how other tax charges (including under ITEPA 2003 s 427 *as originally enacted*) have to be adjusted if the value of the share is artificially depressed *after* acquisition. Further, if the shares are restricted (as will often be the case), a depreciatory transaction will result in a tax charge every 5 April (s 446E).

FA 2004 s 87 introduced an anti-avoidance provision into Chapter 3A. ITEPA 2003 s 446E(1) is amended to introduce other occasions when the market value of the shares which are restricted has to be assessed: when the shares are disposed of in circumstances which are not a chargeable event under Chapter 2 and when they are cancelled. If either of those happens when the shares are restricted and the market value is artificially depressed, there will be a tax charge.

Chapter 3B treats the difference between the actual market value of employee shares on 5 April each year and what would have been their market value if there had not been any non-commercial increases in value during the tax year as employment income for that tax year, even though that increase in value has not been realised (s 446N). No charge arises unless the market value of the shares has been enhanced by at least 10% in the tax year. **[9.26]**

d) *Shares acquired for less than market value*

If fully paid shares are issued to a director or employee for less than their market value at that date, the difference between that value and any consideration paid is taxable under s 9. If shares are acquired by a director or 'higher paid' employee and the consideration to be paid is left outstanding as a debt, ITEPA 2003 Part 3 Chapter 7 may apply to that loan. However, if shares are issued at market value but only part of that price is payable on issue (so that the shares are issued partly paid), the resultant benefit to such a director or employee does not fall within either of the foregoing situations but is dealt with by the special provisions in ITEPA 2003 Part 7 Chapter 3C. If these apply, there is deemed to be an interest-free loan, taxable on the same basis as under Part 3 Chapter 7, equal to the undervalue.

Broadly, Chapter 3C applies when a person acquires shares at an undervalue as a result of a right or opportunity made available because of his employment: undervalue is defined as the difference between the market value of fully paid shares of the same class and the amount (if any) actually paid at the time of issue. It should be noted that Chapter 3C will not apply to the extent that the acquisition of the shares is already taxed as earnings under other provisions; and if the aggregate value of the notional loan and any actual loans is no more than (currently) £10,000, or if money borrowed to purchase the shares would have qualified for relief under TA 1988 s 353 or ITA 2007 s 383, no charge arises (s 446S applies ss 178 and 180).

Where a notional loan arises, income tax will be due on the deemed interest (the benefit to the employee) at the official rate of (at 30 June 2017) 2.5% pa.

Generally, the deemed loan remains outstanding until either:

(1) the employee dies or the 'loan' is repaid (when liability to income tax will cease); or
(2) the beneficial interest in the shares is transferred or, in respect of shares that were issued partly-paid, the obligation to pay is released (when the amount of the notional loan outstanding is taxed as employment income of the employee, subject to the provisions of ITEPA 2003 Part 2 Chapter 5B applicable where one or more of the international mobility conditions are satisfied – see [9.13]) (s 446U).

Prior to 17 July 2014, these provisions dealt imperfectly with a number of situations. *First*, where shares subject to the outstanding obligation were sold for a price reflecting that obligation, an income tax charge still arose on the full amount of the outstanding obligation. *Second*, where Chapter 3C applied in respect of shares which were not partly-paid (a common situation under joint ownership plans – see [9.45]) it was not possible to bring the application of Chapter 3C to an end by releasing the obligation (as any such release was ignored by s 446U, with the tax charges continuing to arise). Solutions to these problems were included in FA 2014, applying from the date of Royal Assent, by creating an exemption from the tax charge that applies on a transfer of the shares where the consideration reflects the on-going liability to pay, and by removing the distinction between partly-paid and other shares.

ITEPA 2003 s 446UA was introduced as an anti-avoidance provision by F(No2)A 2005 and provides that where HMRC considers that the avoidance of tax and NIC is a 'main purpose' of the arrangements, the full amount of what would have been the notional loan is treated as employment income and taxed upfront. [9.27]

e) *Shares disposed of for more than market value*

When shares are acquired by reason of employment, there will be a tax charge if they are subsequently disposed of for more than their market value (ITEPA 2003 Part 7 Chapter 3D), subject to the provisions of ITEPA 2003

Part 2 Chapter 5B applicable where one or more of the international mobility conditions are satisfied – see [9.13]. The charge is on the difference between the price received and their then market value. This prevents the use of 'stop-loss' protection under which shares acquired under an incentive scheme are bought back by the company if they fall in value. However, the charge applies irrespective of who the purchaser is. Unless there are additional rights attaching to the shares in question that are acquired by the purchaser, amounts received by the employee for his shares in excess of what would be paid for shares held by any other shareholder will be caught by Chapter 3D (*Gray's Timber Products Ltd v R & C Comrs* (2010)). [9.28]

EXAMPLE 9.4

Sandy, the buying manager of Cosifabrics Ltd, is allotted 10,000 £1 shares in the company in 2014. The purchase price of the shares is the market value of £2.25 each but the shares are issued partly paid and Sandy pays only 50p per share. In 2016 he pays a further 50p per share to the company. The tax position is as follows:
(1) *From 2014 to 2016:* the notional loan per share is £2.25 – 50p = £1.75. This amounts to £17,500 so the deemed interest on that sum at the official rate is treated as employment income each year.
(2) *After 2016:* the payment of a further 50p per share reduces the notional loan by £5,000 to £12,500. Thereafter, the official rate of interest on that figure is treated as employment income.
In 2017, when the market value of each share is £3, he sells the shares to an employee trust for £4 each. He will pay income tax:
(1) under Chapter 3C on £12,500; and
(2) under Chapter 3D on £10,000.
His gain for CGT purposes will be reduced by £22,500 as a result of TCGA 1992 ss 37 and 119A.

f) *Post-acquisition benefits*

Part 7 Chapter 4 applies whenever a benefit is received 'by virtue of the ownership' of employee shares (the causal connection that this requires has not been considered by the courts but for a discussion of how other provisions imposing a causal connection test have been interpreted, see [8.42] and [8.112]), if the benefit is not otherwise chargeable to income tax. In such a case, the market value of the benefit counts as employment income(s 448), although is subject to the provisions of ITEPA 2003 Part 2 Chapter 5B applicable where one or more of the international mobility conditions are satisfied – see [9.13]. The predecessor to this provision was rarely invoked by HMRC, but it has indicated that it may seek to apply this charge in a wide range of circumstances, for instance when an equity ratchet operates to increase the managers' share of the ordinary share capital (see [9.12] (7)). [9.29]

g) *Priority share allocations*

When shares in a company are first offered to the public, employees are sometimes given priority and/or discount offers. Under general principles, the employees would be taxable on the benefit of a priority allocation: if they receive more shares than they would have done as members of the public, then if the share value at the date of allocation is higher than the price paid, they will have received a benefit by reason of their employment. As a result of ITEPA 2003 Part 7 Chapter 10, however, no charge arises merely because of the priority allocation, provided certain conditions are complied with (the statutory provisions are set out in s 542 and are complicated because provisions were added to the previous legislation as privatisations were structured in different ways, so that the employees would continue to be protected). However, if the employees pay less for their shares than members of the public, there will be an income tax charge on that discount. **[9.30]**

h) *Research institution spinout companies (FA 2005 s 20)*

As noted above, the provisions of Part 7 are much wider than the previous legislation and this has led the Government into having to introduce specific legislation to deal with certain situations – for example, in relation to university spinout companies.

Universities and similar research institutions often develop their intellectual property (IP) through companies ('spinout' or 'spin-off' companies) created in association with a researcher. There is usually an agreement under which the researcher either shares in the royalties generated by the use of the IP or, where the IP is developed through a spinout into which IP has been transferred, receives shares in that company.

If a researcher is employed by a research institution, acquires shares in a spinout and the research institution transfers IP to that spinout, a charge to income tax could arise under Part 7 Chapter 4 (as a result of the increase in value of existing shares held by the researcher), under s 9 or Chapter 3C (because the shares acquired reflect the value of IP, but are acquired by a researcher at a discount) or under Chapter 5 (if the shares are acquired as a result of the exercise of an option (see below)). The charge would be based on current values when the shares are acquired or the IP transferred.

From 2 December 2004, however, an income tax charge is prevented from arising on an increase in the value of existing shares in a spinout that is due to the transfer of designated IP or where researchers acquire shares following any IP transfer. ITEPA 2003 Part 7 Chapter 4A sets out the detailed provisions and acts to prevent the value of the IP from being reflected in any consideration as to whether the shares have been acquired at an undervalue, deeming the market value to be the value that the shares would have had if the IP had not been transferred.

The provisions relate to the researcher's position and do not affect the position of the research institution itself for capital gains tax or corporation tax purposes (although it may make a NIC saving – see **[9.44]**). The spinout company and the researcher's shares, remain within the scope of Part 7 in all other respects. **[9.31]**

i) *Employee-shareholder status*

The Growth and Infrastructure Act 2013 (GIA 2013) 'created a new employment status of employee shareholder in order to increase the range of employment options companies may use as they grow and adapt their workforce' (GIA 2013 Explanatory Notes) and shares issued in consideration of the agreement to become an employee-shareholder benefited from tax reliefs introduced by FA 2013. These tax reliefs were, however, abolished by

FA 2017 in respect of shares acquired as consideration for entering into an employee-shareholder agreement made (generally) on or after 1 December 2016. This abolition of the tax reliefs was 'in response to evidence [that the reliefs were] primarily being used for tax-planning purposes by high-earning individuals' (Autumn Statement 2016).

Employee-shareholder status – which continues to be available notwithstanding the abolition of the tax reliefs – is achieved by the employee and employer agreeing that the employee will take on the new status, thereby waiving a number of the statutory employment protections normally available to employees, in consideration for which the employer must issue at least £2,000 worth of shares in the employer (or its parent company) to the employee. Other than the requirements as to which company must issue the shares there are no restrictions on the type of share that may be issued to the employee.

An employee-shareholder remains an employee (and so will continue to be subject to employment income tax provisions) and, in fact, retains the majority of the statutory employment rights afforded to employees. In summary, the main rights that an employee-shareholder foregoes are the right to statutory redundancy payments and, save in certain circumstances, the right not to be unfairly dismissed (in particular, an employee-shareholder would retain rights where the dismissal is in breach of the Equality Act 2010). The employee-shareholder also does not have the right to request time off to study or to request flexible working (with some exceptions in connection with parental leave). It is possible for an employer to agree to give back these foregone rights to an employee-shareholder, on a contractual (rather than statutory) basis, apparently without prejudicing the availability of the tax reliefs. **[9.32]**

(i) Tax reliefs and abolition

Prior to the tax reliefs being abolished, the first £2,000 of shares issued to the employee in consideration of the agreement to become an employee-shareholder could benefit from income tax and NIC relief on acquisition, and up to £50,000 of shares issued to the employee could benefit from CGT relief on disposal (but, for shares issued as consideration for employee-shareholder agreements entered into on or after 16 March 2016, with relief limited to a lifetime cap of £100,000 of gains).

These reliefs were abolished in respect of shares acquired in consideration for entering into an employee-shareholder agreement made on or after 1 December 2016 (or on or after 2 December 2017 where the independent legal advice required as part of the process of becoming an employee-shareholder was provided before 1.30pm on 2 December 2016). The income tax relief on acquisition is therefore now obsolete. (Readers desiring more information on that relief are referred to previous editions.) The exemption from CGT on disposal, however, continues to apply to shares acquired pursuant to employee-shareholder agreements made before such time.**[9.33]**

(ii) CGT relief on disposal

To the extent it remains applicable, an exemption from CGT is available in respect of the first disposal of employee-shareholder shares which, on acquisition, had an actual (ie restricted) market value of up to £50,000 (TCGA 1992 s 236B(1)). Where employee-shareholder shares were acquired with an actual market value of greater than £50,000, the exemption is available in respect of a corresponding proportion of the number of shares acquired. Employee-shareholder shares which qualify for the exemption are referred to as 'exempt employee-shareholder shares'.

The exemption is not available if the employee had a material interest in the company at the time of, or within one year prior to, the acquisition of the employee-shareholder shares.

The exemption is subject to a lifetime cap introduced by FA 2016, which limits the relief available on gains made on shares acquired as consideration for entering into an employee-shareholder agreement on or after 16 March 2016 to £100,000 of gains.

Where the employee-shareholder disposes of shares of the same class, where only some of which are exempt employee-shareholder shares, the usual share identification rules are disapplied and instead the employee-shareholder is entitled to elect whether or not he is to be treated as disposing of the exempt employee-shareholder shares.

Where employee-shareholder shares are not exempt from CGT, for example, on shares in excess of the £50,000 limit, the base cost of the shares will be the amount on which the income tax charge arose on acquisition (TCGA 1992 s 149AA(1A)), with the employee-shareholder not being treated as having given any further consideration. **[9.34]–[9.40]**

3 Share options and other rights to acquire shares

In *Abbott v Philbin* (1961), the House of Lords held that options are subject to income tax on their value (if any) at the time of grant and that any benefit resulting from the exercise of an option (ie because the shares had grown in value during the option period) was not so taxable. Naturally, legislation was introduced to reverse this decision.

ITEPA 2003 Part 7 Chapter 5 provides that if, by reason of employment, an individual is granted options to acquire shares, he is not taxed on the value of the options *at that time*. However, the notional gain made on the shares will be subject to income tax *when the option is exercised*. The amount taxed will be reduced by: the price (if any) paid for the option; the price paid for the shares; any relevant expenses (s 480); and any employers' NICs paid by the employee (s 481) – see **[9.44]**.

Prior to 6 April 2015, Part 7 Chapter 5 applied only where the individual to whom the option was granted was resident in the UK at the time of grant (and prior to 6 April 2008, this provision applied only to employees who were resident *and* ordinarily resident in the UK at the time of grant). From 6 April 2015, the requirement for the employee to have been UK resident at the time of grant of the option was removed, so that Part 7 Chapter 2 now applies irrespective of the residency status of the employee, and this applies even in respect of a share option granted prior to 6 April 2015. Where one or more of the international mobility conditions is satisfied, as described above at **[9.13]**, Part 2 Chapter 5 apportions the taxable value over the relevant period, in the case of a share option being from the date of grant of the share option to the date on which the option is exercised or, if earlier, to the date on which the option became capable of exercise. The employee's tax status during the relevant period will then govern how the taxable value attributable to each portion of the relevant period is taxed.

The previous legislation (TA 1988 s 135) imposed a tax charge on the 'exercise' of a right to acquire shares. Part 7 Chapter 5 applies whenever shares are acquired pursuant to a right to acquire them (s 477(3)(a)) and thus disposing of arguments that either an amount must be paid or something must actually be done by the employee in order to effect an 'exercise'. Thus, if there is a *right* to receive shares after the expiry of a period of time, on meeting performance conditions or under a long-term incentive plan (or otherwise), the receipt of the shares will be a chargeable event under Chapter 5. In that Chapter the term 'employment-related securities option' is used to describe any type of right to acquire shares to which the Chapter applies.

EXAMPLE 9.5

John is granted an option to acquire 10,000 shares in a company at 30p per share. The option can be exercised at any time in the next six years. The price of the shares is fixed at their current market value on grant. John pays £10 for the option, which he exercises five years later when the shares are worth 75p. He sells the shares six months later for 85p per share.

(1) There is no income tax charge on the grant of the option.
(2) When the option is exercised, the sum taxed as employment income is calculated as follows:

Market value of shares at exercise:		
10,000 × 75p		£7,500
Deduct:		
Option price	£10	
Price paid 10,000 × 30p	£3,000	£3,010
Sum assessed to income tax under		
ITEPA 2003		£4,490

Note: Tax is charged on the above sum *despite the fact that the shares have not been sold by the employee;* and it is assumed that the company bears its own NIC liability.

(3) On the subsequent sale of the shares any further gain is subject to CGT:

Sale proceeds: 10,000 × 85p		£8,500
Deduct:		
Option price	£10	
Price paid	£3,000	
Sum assessed to income tax	£4,490	
		£7,500
Gain subject to CGT		£1,000

Note: No account is taken of any reliefs or allowable CGT expenses in this example.

If a person holding an employment-related securities option realises a gain by assigning or releasing it (for instance, he might receive a cash payment in return for surrendering his option if his employing company is taken over), that gain also falls within Chapter 5 (s 477(3)(b)).

Wilcock v Eve (1995) illustrated the situation where the general charging provisions used to be relevant. The court held that the old charging provision (TA 1988 s 135) did not apply where an *ex gratia* compensation payment was made following lapse of options under the rules of a scheme (in this case because the employing company had left the group). However, this has been overtaken by s 477(3)(c) which states that there is a chargeable event (for the purposes of s 476) if the employee receives 'a benefit in money or money's worth in connection with' an employment-related securities option. It should be noted that, under the old legislation, when a new employer compensated a new recruit for the share scheme benefits he lost as a result of moving from his former employment, the Special Commissioner was able to find that the payment was an inducement payment and therefore taxable under (now) s 9 (*Teward v IRC* (2001)). It is not entirely clear which of s 9 or Part 7 would now apply if such a payment related to lost securities options, as a result of s 418(1).

There is no charge under Part 7 Chapter 5 where an option is exercised, assigned or released following the death of the employee (s 477(2)).

A subsequent increase in the value of shares acquired by an employee under an employment-related securities option may be subject to income tax, rather than capital gains tax, if other provisions of Part 7 apply (see 2 above). Prior to FA 2004, an exemption from Chapters 2–4 applied in relation to shares acquired under a tax-advantaged scheme (see **[9.72]**), but this exemption (s 421G) was removed by FA 2004 s 88(13). **[9.41]**

4 **PAYE and NICs**

Prior to December 1996, the provision of share benefits to employees triggered significant cost and cash flow advantages for both parties since 'own company shares' were outside both the PAYE and NIC nets. A plethora of primary and secondary legislation has since reversed that position to a significant extent.
[9.42]

a) *PAYE*

Since 27 November 1996, PAYE has had to be operated where an employee acquires shares that are readily convertible assets (RCAs) (ss 700(2) and 696). The term 'readily convertible asset' is defined in s 702. It is sometimes difficult to decide whether unquoted shares are readily convertible. HMRC's views on this issue are given in *Tax Bulletin*, August 1998, p 563 and April 2000, pp 735 and 736, but it should be noted that in some situations it now views the PAYE net as rather wider than there indicated (for instance, in relation to the effect of an employee trust). Certain shares that would not have previously been RCAs have, since the addition of s 702(5A) to (5D) by FA 2003 s 140, become RCAs. Essentially this covers shares in respect of which a statutory corporation tax deduction is not available (see **[9.124]** ff). If a tax charge arises under ss 477(3)(b) or (c) because an employee has received consideration in return for assigning or releasing an option, PAYE has to be operated even if the shares subject to the option were not RCAs (s 700(2)).

ITEPA 2003 s 698 sets out the PAYE obligations that apply whenever tax charges arise under Part 7 Chapters 2–4 in relation to shares acquired on or after 16 April 2003 (s 699 applies to the old convertible securities regime – see FA 2003 Sch 22 para 12). When the charges listed in s 698(1) arise, PAYE has to be operated if the shares are RCAs (s 698(2) and s 696). However, if an amount counts as employment income by virtue of the provisions listed in s 698(3)(a), an obligation to operate PAYE can arise even if the shares are not readily convertible.

Where there is a notional loan charge on the acquisition of shares at an undervalue (ITEPA 2003 Part 7 Chapter 3C), the status of the shares is irrelevant and this tax is collected under the self-assessment regime unless the notional loan on partly paid shares is written off (s 698(1)(e)) or the anti-avoidance provisions of ITEPA 2003 s 446UA apply (s 698(1)(ea)).

Where Part 2 Chapter 5B applies, ITEPA 2003 s 700A provides that the PAYE obligation arises in respect of an amount calculated as the best estimate of the total amount which counts as employment income, less the best estimate of the amount of such income which will count as foreign securities income (ie that is either not taxable in the UK or which would only be taxed under the remittance basis), and see HMRC's guidance at ERSM 162820 as to how this assessment can be undertaken.

Employers may face difficulties in recovering from employees (and former employees) the PAYE they have been obliged to pay to HMRC under the above provisions. The statutory right of recovery can only be exercised against cash payments made to the employees in the income tax month in which the notional payment is deemed to have been made (see ITEPA 2003 s 710) and such cash will often be insufficient to cover the PAYE in respect of a substantial share award. It is possible for the terms of the relevant scheme to provide that, by accepting the share award, an employee becomes obliged to reimburse the employer for the amount of tax due. In the absence of such a statutory or contractual right, in certain circumstances a restitutionary claim may be possible.

If the employee does not in fact 'make good' the tax due within 90 days of the end of the tax year in which the original tax charge is triggered, ITEPA 2003 s 222 results in the employee being taxable on the tax paid (for HMRC's responses to questions raised on the predecessor to this provision, TA 1988 s 144A, see *Tax Bulletin*, April 2000, p 734). Where the date on which the original tax charge was triggered was prior to 6 April 2014, the employee was required to make good the tax due within 90 days from such date. HMRC has issued guidance at EIM 11966 on the meaning of 'making good' in this context, which explains that this does not necessarily require the employee to pay the amount of tax due to the employer as a monetary amount and, in particular, that in some cases the employee giving an indemnity in respect of such amount will have been sufficient for the employee to have 'made good'.

[9.43]

b) *National Insurance contributions*

Since 1996 there have been periods of time when the PAYE and NIC obligations in relation to share scheme benefits have diverged but over time they have been brought more into line. The PAYE and NIC treatment of non tax-advantaged benefits is therefore almost completely aligned, so that whenever there is a PAYE liability under ss 698 or 700, Class 1 NICs are payable.

Although there is no PAYE liability when there is a notional loan charge under ITEPA 2003 Part 7 Chapter 3C, Class 1A employer NICs are payable.

The effect of extending NICs to employee share benefits is to impose a real cost on employers who cannot, or choose not to, use tax-advantaged share schemes. It used to be the case that that cost could not be passed on to employees as there was a statutory bar on their reimbursing employers' NICs. Perhaps worse than the fact of this extra cost is its unpredictability. This is a particular strain for small companies if they use share incentives to attract high quality managers and the shares grow significantly in value: the potential NIC charge 'could put at risk investment strategies, damage their future growth by deterring investors and even make them insolvent' (Budget 2000 Press Release 3).

The statutory bar on recovering employers' NICs from employees was removed in 2000 but initially only in relation to employment-related securities options (see Social Security Contributions and Benefits Act 1992 (SSCBA) Sch 1 paras 3A and 3B). The usual method will be by the employee agreeing to pay the company's liability, so that the company can recover the amount due from him. It is possible for the parties to sign a joint election that will actually transfer the liability to the employee so that the company will no longer have any responsibility for it. The election needs prior HMRC approval. It was introduced to deal with the problem faced by some non-UK companies whose accounting rules required that, unless the liability is transferred completely, it still has to be shown in the company's accounts.

Employees can deduct the amount paid to the company (provided that was done no later than 60 days after the year of assessment of the chargeable event) or for which the liability has been undertaken when calculating the amount of gain subject to income tax on option exercise (see **[9.41]**) (ITEPA 2003 s 481). Employee contributions are not deductible.

The National Insurance Contributions and Statutory Payments Act 2004 (NICSPA 2004) amended, from 1 September 2004, SSCBA 1992 Sch 1 paras 3A and 3B to allow agreements and elections to be made in respect of post-acquisition charges relating to restricted securities and convertible securities. Charges on the acquisition of restricted or convertible securities are excluded. As with options, employees will enjoy income tax relief in respect of any payment of employers' NICs (ss 428A and 442A and *Tax Bulletin*, June 2004, p 1118).

In relation to employees' NICs, these must be paid to HMRC in the same manner as PAYE. Although an employer is able to immediately recover such amounts from a *cash* payment, it is more difficult when the payment is made in *shares*. In such cases the employer is able to make a recovery from any cash payments made in the same tax year and the next tax year. The addition of this second year for recovery was introduced by SI 2003/1337. If recovery is not made by this time, the amounts become the employer's liability and there is no further right of recovery.

Following the introduction of the additional 2% employees' NICs charge that also applies, uncapped, to earnings over the UEL, the ability to recover NICs from employees became even more important for employers. The

National Insurance Contributions and Statutory Payments Act 2004 paved the way to extending the right of recovery when employees and ex-employees receive shares. It amended SSCBA 1992 Sch 1 para 3, which in turn enabled the necessary amendments to be made to the Social Security (Contributions) Regulations 2001, in order for NICs to be recovered, with the agreement of the employee, by the withholding of sufficient shares rather than from cash payments (SI 2004/2246). [9.44]

5 Capital gains tax

a) Introduction

The capital gains tax rules were significantly overhauled with effect from 6 April 2008, to introduce a much simplified system for taxing capital gains (see FA 2008 Sch 2). One effect of this, however, was that for the first time since 1982 there were no longer any reliefs which relate to the length of time an asset has been held. This generally remains the case, although since 6 April 2013 entrepreneurs' relief has been available in respect of the disposal of shares acquired pursuant to Enterprise Management Incentive arrangements (see [9.75]).

The (now abolished) taper relief provisions introduced in FA 2000 had a significant effect on the way the provision of employee share benefits were structured; and on the decision by employees as to whether to keep or sell their shares. With the abolition of taper relief, there are now only limited benefits (for example, the ability to use more than one annual exemption) associated with share ownership on a long-term basis, something which had previously been encouraged by the Government as being beneficial for UK businesses.

When taper relief was introduced, an employee shareholding only counted as a business asset if the employee owned at least 5% of the shares. FA 2000 extended business asset taper relief to all shareholdings in unquoted trading companies and to employees' holdings in trading companies by which they are employed whilst they are in employment, whilst at the same time reducing the time for which assets had to be held to qualify for the full relief (from ten to four years). FA 2001 retrospectively (to 6 April 2000) extended the relief further so that an employee's holding in his non-trading employing company became a business asset provided the employee did not have a material interest (basically a holding of more than 10%) (FA 2001 s 78 and Sch 26). FA 2002 s 46 then reduced the four-year period for full business asset taper to only two years in the case of disposals occurring after 5 April 2002.

These changes gave non tax-advantaged share incentive schemes a significant advantage over share option schemes as, in the latter case, the qualifying period for taper relief purposes would only start to run once the option has been exercised. For options granted under Enterprise Management Incentive arrangements (see [9.87]), an additional benefit was that taper relief ran from the date of option grant, thus making these schemes extremely attractive. With the abolition of taper relief and the share identification rules (see generally **Chapter 20**), these benefits have been revoked.

Since April 2013 the disposal of shares acquired pursuant to Enterprise Management Incentive options has qualified for entrepreneurs' relief (see generally **Chapter 20**) provided that certain conditions have been met (as further described at **[9.87]**).

From 6 April 2016 a flat rate of CGT applies to tax chargeable gains at 10%, or 20% for higher and additional rate tax payers. There is, therefore, a benefit in holding shares (where gains will generally be chargeable to CGT) as compared with non tax-advantaged share options (where gains will generally be chargeable to income tax and National Insurance). Tax-advantaged options have also become more attractive as a result of their income tax reliefs, as have 'growth shares' (a separate class of shares acquired by employees which have rights only to a proportion of the increase in the value of the company from acquisition) and joint ownership arrangements (under which shares are jointly owned between the employee and a third party, with the employee holding the portion of the share representing any increase in the share's value from acquisition and the third party retaining the portion representing the residual value). Each of these arrangements result in the employee acquiring a security, rather than a right to a share, and so are subject to income tax on acquisition under the restricted securities regime (see **[9.21]** to **[9.24]**) with future gains within the CGT regime.

In some cases, the amount of gain subject to CGT can be reduced by the employee transferring some of his/her shares to his/her spouse or civil partner (so that he/she can make use of his/her annual exemption if he/she would not do so otherwise and/or take advantage of lower tax rates).

As already discussed, FA 2003 introduced a new regime for the taxation of non tax-advantaged share benefits and TCGA 1992 was amended in consequence. FA 2003 also amended the CGT treatment when shares are acquired pursuant to a pre-existing right (most often an option). The CGT position set out below is that which applies to shares wholly within the new regime, so that the operative date for the new sections, any transitional provisions and details of shares to which they apply are not set out: for that information, readers will need to consult FA 2003. **[9.45]**

b) *Employee acquires shares otherwise than pursuant to pre-existing right*

The employee The employee is subject to income tax under ITEPA 2003 Part 3 Chapter 1 (ie the general charging provision) on the difference between the market value of the shares and the price, if any, he pays for them (unless the shares are restricted shares by reason of ITEPA 2003 s 423(2), the restrictions are not capable of lasting more than five years and the employee has not elected to be taxed on acquisition (under s 425) – see **[9.23]**). When he has acquired existing shares which are not restricted or convertible (as to which, see below), his base cost will be their market value as a result of the operation of TCGA 1992 s 17(1). Although the share identification rules have been abolished from 6 April 2008, it remains important to be able to calculate the individual base costs of shares for same-day disposals and also to enable a correct calculation of the average acquisition cost of all shares held within the 's 104 pool' (see TCGA 1992 s 104).

Establishing the CGT position where the employee acquires newly issued shares has always been difficult as TCGA 1992 s 17(2) seems to disapply the deemed market value in s 17(1). However, HMRC's position appears to be that s 17(2) does not apply (see CG 56321 but note the position on public offers at CG 56330 ff) on the rather unexpected basis (it would seem, in light of TCGA 1992 s 149A (see **[9.49]**)) that the employee provides market value for the shares in the form of his services; therefore, since one of the two limbs of s 17(2) is not satisfied, s 17(1) applies to uplift the employee's base cost. As a consequence, whether the shares acquired by the employee are newly issued or existing, his base cost is the value by reference to which he pays income tax under the general charging provision (but see below if they are restricted or convertible). HMRC's belief that s 17 applies when newly issued shares are acquired was confirmed in its News Releases on *Mansworth v Jelley* (2003) (see **[9.53]**); the fact that HMRC felt the need to enact TCGA 1992 s 149AA is further confirmation.

When restricted or convertible shares are acquired, TCGA 1992 s 149AA states that the consideration the employee provided for the shares shall be treated as the aggregate of the price the employee paid and any amount charged to income tax under the general charging provision: this total will be taken into account under TCGA 1992 s 38 and will constitute the employee's base cost (plus any other expenditure allowed under that section). It would seem that s 149AA was introduced to prevent TCGA 1992 s 17 applying when these types of shares are acquired, whether they are *newly issued or existing*. Although, on its face, s 149AA applies if the shares are restricted but employer and employee have elected to ignore all the restrictions (because it applies to 'restricted securities' as defined in Chapter 2 and that definition depends on the nature of the restrictions, not whether or not there is a tax charge under general principles on acquisition), the HMRC view seems to be that s 149AA does not apply (presumably because there will be a tax charge under general principles) and the position set out in the preceding two paragraphs will then apply.

There is one final point in relation to the acquisition of shares. If there is a charge on acquisition because the shares fall within Part 7 Chapter 3A, TCGA 1992 s 119A does not give a CGT uplift for the amount on which tax is charged; nor will there be an uplift under s 149AA even if the shares are restricted or convertible because the taxable amount under Chapter 3A is not 'earnings' under ITEPA 2003 Part 3 Chapter 1 but rather 'counts as employment income' (s 446B) and is, therefore, 'specific employment income'. **[9.46]**

The transferor or issuer The transferor of existing shares will be treated as receiving a market value consideration if the requirements of TCGA 1992 s 17 or s 18 are satisfied (as they normally will be). Section 149AA 'is to be disregarded in calculating the consideration received' by the transferor, so s 17 will continue to apply when he transfers restricted or convertible shares. There are no CGT consequences for the issuer when new shares are issued to the employee since there will not be a disposal. **[9.47]**

c) *Income tax charges following acquisition otherwise than pursuant to pre-existing right*

TCGA 1992 s 119A increases the expenditure to be taken into account under s 38 by reference to any amount taxable under Chapters 2 and 3 and when a notional loan is discharged under ITEPA 2003 Part 7 Chapter 3C.

Section 119A does not cover Chapters 3A, 3B, 3D and the ongoing loan charge under Chapter 3C nor Chapter 4. If shares are sold for more than their market value in circumstances giving rise to a charge under Chapter 3D, the excess over market value will be deducted from the sale price in calculating the employee's gain as a result of TCGA 1992 s 37; but in the other cases not covered by s 119A, the income tax charges will not be taken into account for capital gains tax purposes. [9.48]

d) *Grant of right to acquire shares to employee*

As a preliminary matter it must be noted that the income tax treatment whenever shares are acquired pursuant to a pre-existing right was aligned with that of options by FA 2003 (see [9.32]). As a consequence, TCGA 1992 was amended, so that every right which falls within ITEPA 2003 Part 7 Chapter 5 will be treated as an option for the purposes of TCGA 1992. In ITEPA 2003 such rights are called 'employment-related securities options' and that terminology is used here.

The CGT position of both the grantor and the employee is established according to normal principles, save that the grant *is* treated as a disposal as a result of TCGA 1992 s 144. The consideration received by the grantor and the employee's base cost are both calculated by reference to what the employee pays for the employment-related securities option, as a result of TCGA 1992 s 149A which disapplies the market value rule in TCGA 1992 s 17 *and* excludes the value of the employee's services in calculating the consideration. It appears that s 149A is sufficient to exclude a deemed market value consideration even if the employment-related securities option is granted to a connected person (within s 18).

If an employment-related securities option is granted in return for the release of an existing option, TCGA 1992 s 237A excludes that release when calculating the consideration received by the grantor. From the point of view of the employee, the section allows him to roll over his employment-related securities option: it states that his allowable expenditure for the new option will be any consideration he gave for the original option and 'any consideration paid for the acquisition' of the new option (this excludes the value of the option released). Finally, the new employment-related securities option is disregarded when calculating the consideration received by the employee for releasing the existing option. [9.49]

e) *Acquisition of shares pursuant to employment-related securities options*

i) *Introduction*

This subject is complex because the decision in *Mansworth v Jelley* (2003) upset the widely-held view as to the CGT consequences of an employee exercising an option. Amending legislation was introduced but the decision in that case continues to apply to certain options. Paragraphs 12396 et seq in HMRC's Capital Gains Manual set out in detail its view of the CGT position in relation to options. [9.50]

ii) *The old position*

The employee HMRC's view was that the deemed market value rule in TCGA 1992 s 17 did not apply to an employee's acquisition of existing shares on exercising an option as he acquired those shares as an optionholder, not an employee, and through an arm's length bargain. Accordingly, whether he acquired newly-issued or existing shares, the employee's base cost should be the price paid for the option plus the price paid for the shares plus any amount taxed under TA 1988 s 135 (now ITEPA 2003 Part 7 Chapter 5) (see TCGA 1992 s 120). [9.51]

The grantor From the point of view of the grantor, grant and exercise of the employment-related securities option are treated as one event as a result of s 144. If the grantor issues new shares to the employee, there is no disposal and, because of the 'one transaction' rule, any CGT assessment raised on the grant of the option will be discharged, so the grantor has no CGT liability, either on payments received on grant of the option or on payments received on its exercise. If existing shares are transferred by the grantor of the option, HMRC's view was that the consideration received by the grantor should be the price he received for the option plus the price he received for the shares.
[9.52]

iii) Mansworth v Jelley (2003)

When Mr Jelley exercised his unapproved option he was not subject to income tax under TA 1988 s 135 (now ITEPA 2003 Part 7 Chapter 5) as he was not a UK resident at grant and so, applying the principles above, his base cost for the shares acquired would have been the price he paid for them (plus anything he paid for the option). He argued (in a bid to reduce the CGT payable on subsequent sale, by which time he was UK resident and subject to CGT) that TCGA 1992 s 17 applied to the exercise, so that his base cost was the market value of the shares at that date. The Court of Appeal's acceptance of his argument, whilst good news for anyone like Mr Jelley who is outside the income tax net but inside the CGT one, gave rise to the following unsatisfactory results in other circumstances (though not on exercise of a tax-advantaged SAYE or Company Share Option Plan options as s 17 was specifically excluded in those cases):

(1) If existing shares were transferred on exercise, the transferor would be deemed to have received not the actual exercise price but market value, thus increasing his taxable gain (unless hold-over relief under TCGA 1992 s 165 was available).

(2) A bizarre outcome of HMRC's interpretation of the effect of the case (see News Releases: 8 January, 17 March and 8 August 2003) was that an employee within s 135 could get a double uplift to his base cost: s 17 would deem him to have paid market value; and s 120 would add to that the amount on which he paid income tax.

The effect of this reversal of HMRC's previous view was that gains previously made on exercise of non tax-advantaged (and Enterprise Management Incentive – see [9.87]) options should have been lower and in some cases there would have been a capital loss.

In what seems a final twist to the tale, HMRC issued Revenue & Customs Brief 30/09, which stated that, following legal advice, HMRC had reversed its interpretation and now considers that, where shares are treated as having been acquired at market value, that value is the full measure of their deemed cost of acquisition and there should be no augmentation by any amount chargeable to income tax on the exercise of the option. [9.53]

iv) FA 2003

Given the above, it is not surprising that FA 2003 s 157 inserted s 144ZA into TCGA 1992 to prevent s 17 applying whatever type of option is exercised on or after 10 April 2003. The old position as set out above therefore applies again. HMRC has now also issued guidance at CG 12397 that s 144ZA is capable of applying where the trustee of an employee benefit trust, or possibly a majority shareholder, transfers shares to an employee in satisfaction of an option granted by the employing company. **[9.54]**

v) Exercise of employment-related securities options on same day

When a person acquires assets of the same type on the same day, they are usually pooled and the total acquisition costs averaged to provide the base cost for each (TCGA 1992 s 105), but will not form part of an existing 's 104 pool' (TCGA 1992 s 104(3)). This is disadvantageous to an employee who exercises either a tax-advantaged option and non tax-advantaged employment-related securities option on the same day or two tax-advantaged options with different exercise prices (which will most often occur in the context of a takeover): the total CGT he has to pay on subsequent sale of the shares acquired could be reduced (and the payment thereof delayed) if the shares could be kept separate and he could sell those with the highest base cost first. This is particularly the case in the first scenario when there will be no chargeable gain if the shares acquired on exercise of the non tax-advantaged employment-related securities option are immediately sold (as they often are to pay the exercise price and income tax due) because their base cost will usually be their then market value (see above); and if the employee can hold on to the shares acquired on exercise of the tax-advantaged option, he may well be able to take advantage of CGT reliefs to reduce the tax payable on later sale (see Explanatory Notes issued by the Inland Revenue on clause 49 of the Finance Bill 2002 for an example).

In relation to shares acquired on or after 6 April 2002, TCGA 1992 ss 105A and 105B have remedied the position in relation to the first scenario by allowing the employee to opt to treat the shares with the higher base cost as disposed of first. The election must be made by the next but one 31 January following the end of the tax year in which the first disposal of (some of) the shares acquired takes place. Unfortunately, it does not extend to the second scenario. **[9.55]**

f) *Income tax charges following acquisition of shares pursuant to employment-related securities option*

ITEPA 2003 Part 7 Chapters 2–4 can apply to shares acquired pursuant to an employment-related securities option: the effect on the employee's base cost will be the same as where they apply following a share acquisition (see **[9.48]**). It would be possible to avoid later charges under Chapter 2 by making an election under s 431 (see **[9.24]**). Such an election when shares are acquired pursuant to an employment-related securities option may increase the income tax charge on acquisition under Chapter 5 by deeming the value of the shares acquired to be increased. This would feed through to the employee's base cost via TCGA 1992 s 119A(3)(d). **[9.56]**

308 *Employee participation: options, incentives and trusts*

g)   *Calculating the chargeable gain on eventual sale*

The gain is found by deducting the allowable expenditure from the disposal consideration. The effect of the provisions discussed above is to increase the employee's allowable expenditure and hence his base cost (except for s 37(1) which reduces the amount of the disposal consideration that is taken into account).

To calculate chargeable gains for a year, losses are first deducted from gains. A person's annual exemption is then set against his gains. For more detailed information on how the CGT liability is calculated, please see **Chapters 19** and **20**. For further detail on CGT arising on a disposal of shares, particularly in relation to the share identification and pooling rules, please see **Chapter 26**.

The following example assumes there are no losses to be used in the relevant years. **[9.57]**

EXAMPLE 9.6

In September 2016, Mog exercises non tax-advantaged options over 1,000 shares in his employing company, Haythrop Ltd, paying £1 per share when the market value is £2. The option was granted by deed.

	£
Cost	1,000
Income tax payable on	1,000
Mog's base cost	£2,000

In May 2018, Mog sells 50 of those shares at £5 per share, realising £250. The remaining 950 shares are worth £4,750. The proportion of qualifying expenditure attributable to the shares to be sold is:

$$\frac{£250}{£5000} \times £2{,}000 = £100$$

Mog therefore realises a gain of £150.

In July 2019, Mog is given 500 shares of the same class by Haythrop Ltd. The market value is still £5 per share. He pays income tax under ITEPA 2003 s 9 on £2,500.

As Mog now holds shares of the same class which were acquired at different times, for capital gains tax purposes the base costs are (as a result of the 2008 CGT reforms) pooled under TCGA 1992 s 104 as follows:

The September 2016 shares

Remaining number of shares	950
Base cost of remaining shares	£1,900

The July 2019 shares

Number of shares	500
Base cost of shares	£2,500

Aggregate number of shares 1,450
Aggregate base cost £4,400

In August 2020, Mog sells 750 shares at £10 each, realising £7,500. The remaining 700 shares are worth £7,000. The proportion of qualifying expenditure attributable to the shares to be sold is:

$$\frac{£7500}{£14500} \times £4,400 = £2,276$$

Mog therefore realises a gain of £5,224.

6 Reassessment of non tax-advantaged schemes

Although the imposition of NICs shifted the balance of advantage back towards tax-advantaged schemes, the change to the rules on reimbursement of employers' NICs went some way to redressing that. The 10% and 20% rates of CGT from 6 April 2016 compared to a top income tax rate of 45% (plus 2% NICs) means that there is currently a clear advantage in using tax-advantaged schemes. Between the non tax-advantaged schemes themselves, the (now abolished) CGT taper relief, under which all shares acquired by employees counted as business assets, tipped the balance in favour of share incentive, rather than share option, schemes with an increase in the number of restricted shares schemes including a forfeiture provision (as taper relief ran from the date of the acquisition). This balance was redressed in 2008, and has since favoured a move back towards share option arrangements (particularly where these supplement tax-advantaged option schemes). For those companies able to take advantage of Enterprise Management Incentives, there is now also the added benefit of optionholders being able to take advantage of entrepreneurs' relief – see [9.87].

Many companies have, alternatively, sought to take advantage of the capital gains tax regime whilst maintaining the flexibility of non tax-advantaged arrangements by using 'growth share' and 'joint ownership' plans (see [9.45]), although these arrangements are more complex to establish and require a valuation exercise to be undertaken to ensure the correct upfront income tax treatment under the restricted securities regime.

The great benefit non tax-advantaged schemes offer is flexibility: they can be selective in any way the employer wishes (subject to the requirements of EC and UK non-discrimination legislation); they can relate to any type of share; and they can be more flexible in relation to adjustable performance targets.

[9.58]–[9.70]

III TAX-ADVANTAGED SHARE SCHEMES

1 Tax treatment – general

a) *Recent deregulation*

Recent years have seen a significant deregulatory approach to tax-advantaged share schemes. These changes stem from a review of tax-advantaged share schemes carried out by the Office of Tax Simplification ('OTS') during 2012. The OTS terms of reference began:

> 'The OTS consultations with business have found that employee share schemes are perceived to be a highly complex area of the tax code. This complexity is seen as a frequent cause of error in tax returns and as a source of administrative burdens on employers, their advisers and employees.'

The OTS was tasked with identifying areas where the legislation creates complexities or a disproportionate administrative burden, and then making proposals for simplification.

The OTS's main proposal was replacing the requirement to obtain prior approval from HMRC to operate a tax-advantaged share scheme with a requirement on companies to retrospectively self-certify that such schemes comply with the legislative provisions to qualify for the tax advantages. This proposal was the primary change to the tax-advantaged share scheme legislation included in FA 2014 (which became effective from 6 April 2014).

FA 2013 addressed other OTS recommendations and removed a number of restrictions on how tax-advantaged schemes can be operated, and of particular note included changes intended to allow a wider range of private companies to be able to use the tax-advantaged schemes by removing conditions as to the types of shares that can awarded under tax-advantaged schemes (in some cases, deficiently, with provisions included in FA 2014 attempting to address some of the issues). [9.71]

b) *The tax regime*

The overriding benefit of tax-advantaged share schemes is that, provided the rules of the scheme and the requirements of the legislation are complied with, any profit made by the employees on disposal of shares acquired through such schemes will be *subject to CGT and not income tax*.

Whilst there are circumstances where an income tax charge can arise when shares are acquired under a tax-advantaged scheme (see further below), prior to 18 June 2004 the charges imposed by ITEPA 2003 Part 7 Chapters 2–4 (see Section II 2 above) did not apply to shares acquired under tax-advantaged schemes, as a result of s 421G. However, the Government removed that exclusion with effect from 18 June 2004 (in relation to shares whenever acquired) because shares acquired through tax-advantaged schemes were being used 'to give a cash bonus to employees free of tax and National Insurance contributions' (News Release 30/04) (FA 2004 s 88(2)). However, if restricted shares are acquired from a tax-advantaged scheme after 17 June 2003, in circumstances in which no liability to income tax arises, the election under ITEPA 2003 s 431 (see [9.24]) is deemed to be made (ITEPA 2004 s 431A, inserted by FA 2004 s 88(3)). Further, as the revocation of s 421G applies to all shares, whenever acquired, a s 431 election is deemed to have been made in relation to those on 18 June 2004 (FA 2004 s 88(12)). The deemed election in both cases exempts the shares to which it relates from the application of ITEPA 2003 Part 7 Chapter 2 when restrictions are lifted or varied thereafter. However, the other Chapters of Part 7 will apply.

It used to be the case that the charges under Chapters 2–4 could apply to shares acquired on exercise of an Enterprise Management Incentive (EMI) being able to grant awards or options over more shares and/or with lower option exercise prices.

(3) *The exclusion of persons holding a material interest* Prior to 23 July 2013, it was the case that an individual who at the date of grant holds (or has within the previous 12 months held) a material interest in a close company which is *either* the company which issues the shares *or* a company which controls the issuing company, is not eligible to participate in a tax-advantaged scheme. This condition has now been repealed in respect of SAYE schemes and SIPs, and so since 23 July 2013 only applies in respect of CSOPs and Enterprise Management Incentive (EMI) schemes. An individual holds a material interest for these purposes if he either alone, or together with associates, beneficially owns or controls 30% of the ordinary share capital of the company (prior to 23 July 2013, for SAYE schemes, SIPs and CSOPs, the test was 25%). 'Associate' means, broadly, a relative or partner or trustee of any settlement in which the employee has an interest. However, an individual who is a beneficiary under an employee trust which owns shares in the company will not have an interest in those shares for these purposes (ITEPA 2003 Sch 4 para 13 and Sch 5 para 31). **[9.74]**

3 Savings-Related Share Option Schemes (ITEPA 2003 Part 7 Chapter 7 and Sch 3)

SAYE schemes are funded by contributions from the employees themselves. These are accumulated in standard Save-As-You-Earn savings arrangements (ITTOIA 2005 s 703) that are entered into at the time the options are granted. These arrangements require a person to save a regular fixed monthly contribution and are designed to pay out a tax-free bonus: however, as a result of low market interest rates, for arrangements entered into on or after 1 August 2012, the bonus rates are nil on all contracts. The bonus rates are adjusted automatically on an annual basis (taking effect generally from 1 September) by linking them to 3- or 5-year market swap rates (the market reference swap rates). There are, however, mechanisms for allowing bonus rates to be adjusted if the market reference swap rates move dramatically. The proceeds of the savings arrangements are used to provide funds for the exercise of the options to acquire ordinary shares in the employer company. The maximum permitted monthly contribution into all savings arrangements is (as at 30 June 2017) £500 (increased, from 6 April 2014, from £250).

The *price* of the shares must be fixed at the time *when the employee is granted* the option and must not be less than 80% of the market value of the shares at that time (calculated ignoring the effect on value of any restrictions on the shares). Generally, the option must not be exercisable until the SAYE savings arrangements mature at the end of three or five years (the previous possibility of a seven-year contract was removed from 23 July 2013). The employee is *exempt from any charge to income tax* on the grant (s 518) and, in most cases, on the exercise of the option (s 519). A charge to income tax under s 476 will apply where the option is exercised before the third anniversary of grant, otherwise than in certain specified circumstances. However, by virtue of s 701(2)(c), shares acquired under an SAYE scheme are not classed as RCAs and so there are no NICs or PAYE, and so gains on exercise are accounted for under self-assessment. Where income tax relief applies the only charge is to CGT *if and when the shares are sold* (see TCGA 1992 Sch 7D for the disapplication of TCGA 1992 s 17 in such a case) and in many cases the employee will be able to take advantage of the annual exemption.

In order to qualify as a tax-advantaged SAYE scheme, the scheme must be open to *all* employees and full-time directors; participation of part-time directors remains at the discretion of the company. The scheme may restrict participation to employees who have been in employment for a period of up to five years and it must satisfy the detailed conditions set out in Sch 3.

These schemes are attractive because the employee is not required to find a large sum of money to exercise his option as sufficient funds will have accrued through the SAYE savings arrangements. This encourages the employee to *retain* his shares, since he is not forced to sell to repay a loan or deferred finance arrangements taken out to acquire them. [9.75]

4 Company Share Option Plans (ITEPA 2003 Part 7 Chapter 8 and Sch 4)

Options granted under these plans can only qualify as tax-advantaged if: (a) the value of shares subject to options held by any one employee (value to be measured at date of option grant) does not exceed £30,000 (see *Share Focus*, Issue 2 (December 2003) for HMRC's view of the effect of granting options with an aggregate market value which exceeds this limit); and (b) the option exercise price is not manifestly less than the market value of the shares at date of option grant. The market value is calculated ignoring the effect on value of any restrictions on the shares.

Participation in Company Share Option Plans remains subject to the company's discretion: it used to be that a plan could only allow 'qualifying' employees (required to work at least 20 hours per week) and 'full-time' working directors (normally required to devote at least 25 hours per week to their duties) to obtain rights under it; options may, however, be granted to part-time employees (but not directors).

As with SAYE schemes, there is *no income tax* charge on the *exercise* of the option. The only charge is to *CGT if and when the shares are sold* (see TCGA 1992 Sch 7D for the disapplication of TCGA 1992 s 17 in such a case). The detailed requirements with which a scheme must comply in order to qualify as tax-advantaged are set out in Sch 4; and for tax relief in s 524.

To avoid income tax charges on these options, they not only have to be granted under a tax-advantaged plan but the requirements of s 524 must also be satisfied. To avoid the charges which normally arise on exercise of a non tax-advantaged option when a Company Share Option Plan option is exercised:

(1) the option must be exercised between the third and tenth anniversaries of the date of grant; or
(2) if it is exercised within three years of grant, either:
    (i) the employee must be a 'good leaver' within the meaning of s 524(2B) (for instance, leaving as a result of disability, retirement or redundancy); or
    (ii) with effect from 23 July 2013, the exercise must occur pursuant to a takeover of the company, or a scheme of arrangement affecting the company, which satisfies the requirements of s 524(2E).

Where an income tax charge arises on exercise, the employee will be taxed in the same way as on exercise of a non tax-advantaged option (see Section II) and NICs and PAYE will apply if the shares are RCAs. **[9.76]**

5 Share Incentive Plans (ITEPA 2003 Part 7 Chapter 6 and Sch 2)

a) *Introduction*

To operate a Share Incentive Plan (SIP) the company must establish a trust that buys shares and holds them as trustee for the relevant employees to whom they have been awarded or by whom they have been purchased. **[9.77]**

b) *Benefits to be provided*

Employees may receive up to four types of share benefits under a SIP:
(1) Employers can give up to £3,600 (increased from £3,000, from 6 April 2014) worth of shares each year to each employee (Free Shares – Sch 2 Part 5). The award of some or all of these shares can be linked to performance.
(2) If the company allows, employees can use up to £1,800 per year (increased from £3,000, from 6 April 2014), or 10% of salary if that is lower, of pre-tax income to buy shares (Partnership Shares – Sch 2 Part 6).
(3) If the company chooses, it can give up to two shares for every one Partnership Share purchased (Matching Shares – Sch 2 Part 7).
(4) If the company allows, dividends received on plan shares each year can be reinvested in further shares without the employee paying income tax thereon (Dividend Shares – Sch 2 Part 8). Prior to 23 July 2013 a limit on the value of dividends that could be reinvested of £1,500 applied, but this was removed by FA 2013. The attractiveness of the reinvestment of dividends on a tax-free basis is likely to have been lessened for many SIP participants as a result of the introduction of a £5,000 dividend allowance as part of the changes to the taxation of dividends from 6 April 2016 – see **[7.27]**. **[9.78]**

c) *Restrictions and the holding period*

As noted at **[9.71]**–**[9.74]**, prior to 23 July 2013 a condition for obtaining tax-advantaged status was that shares subject to a SIP could not be subject to restrictions (subject to limited exemptions). At the same time, the SIP legislative requirements required the plan to impose a no-sale period (referred to as the 'holding period') of between three and five years to be imposed on Free and Matching Shares. The result, prior to 23 July 2013, was that Free and Matching Shares had to be subject to a holding period of between three and five years, but that it was not permissible to impose any such restriction on Partnership or Dividend Shares.

With the removal of the general prohibition on using restricted shares from 23 July 2013, there is now much greater flexibility, and Partnership and Dividend Shares can now be subject to restrictions (although they cannot be subject to provision pursuant to which they may be forfeited, other than in specific circumstances – see **[9.80]**). The requirement to impose a holding period of at least three years on Free and Matching Shares, however, continues to apply, so this provision now sets the minimum restriction to which these shares must be subject. **[9.79]**

d) *Forfeiture and compulsory transfer*

Prior to 23 July 2013, a SIP could (but did not have to) provide for Free and/or Matching Shares to be forfeited if the employment is terminated within three years (or a shorter period if the company wished), unless the employee was a 'good leaver' (for instance, leaving as a result of disability, retirement or redundancy – see Sch 2 para 32(2) (now repealed)). Further, whilst Partnership Shares could not be forfeited (as the employee had used his own money to buy them), the rules could impose forfeiture of Matching Shares if the Partnership Shares to which they were linked are withdrawn from the plan within three years.

As described at **[9.71]–[9.74]**, since 23 July 2013 the condition that shares subject to a SIP cannot be subject to restrictions was repealed, and consequently there are now no limitations on the circumstances in which a SIP can provide that Free and/or Matching Shares will be forfeit. To protect the position of Partnership and Dividend Shares (which are acquired by employees for value), provisions were introduced by FA 2013 to the effect that Partnership and Dividend Shares cannot be subject to forfeiture. This inadvertently reversed the ability to impose mandatory sale provisions, which private company articles will commonly apply in cases such as the employee leaving or as a sweep-up of minority shareholdings following a purchase of the company, as a result of the wide definition of 'forfeiture' (Sch 2 para 99)). This position was rectified by FA 2014 (with effect from 6 April 2014) permitting Partnership and Dividend Shares to be subject to a provision pursuant to which the shares can be required to be sold for an amount that is at least equal to the amount of partnership share money (or dividends) used in acquiring such shares or, if lower, the market value of the shares at the time they are offered for sale. **[9.80]**

e) *Taxation of the employees*

Withdrawal of shares from the plan has tax consequences. Employees are able to withdraw their Partnership Shares at any time (even if the shares are subject to sale restrictions) but have to agree to keep both Free Shares and Matching Shares during a holding period of between three and five years. Whenever employment ceases, however, all shares are then deemed to have been removed from the plan. The timing of the removal affects the tax liability.

(1) *Free and Matching Shares (s 505)* No income tax is payable on these shares if they remain in the plan for at least five years. If they are removed between three and five years, tax is payable based on their market value at the time they were originally awarded to the employee (or current market value if that is lower); before then, the tax charge is based on the market value at the date of removal.

(2) *Partnership Shares (s 506)* These are subject to a similar regime: if removal is within three years, tax is charged on market value at time of withdrawal; on removal between three and five years, tax is charged on the amount used to buy the shares (or current market value if lower); no income tax is charged on withdrawal after five years.

(3) *Dividend Shares (s 515(a)(ii))* If Dividend Shares leave the plan within three years of acquisition, the amount of dividend used to acquire the shares is treated as dividend income in the year in which the shares leave the plan. Removal thereafter is not treated as the receipt of dividend income.

In cases (1) and (2), PAYE and NICs apply if the shares are then 'readily convertible' (see **[9.43]**); in case (3) tax is charged in accordance with ITTOIA 2005 ss 392 to 396 or ss 405 to 408 (previously known as Schedule F) in the same way as dividends. Consequently, from 6 April 2016, dividend shares which cease to be subject to the SIP within three years will be subject to tax if the value of the dividend used to acquire the shares, when added to value of other dividends received in the tax year in which the shares cease to be subject to the plan, exceeds the personal allowance of £5,000 (see **[7.27]** on the taxation of dividends from 6 April 2016). The trustees must supply the employee with sufficient information in this respect. In addition, in all three cases no income tax charge arises if either: (i) the employee is a 'good leaver' (s 498(2)); or (ii) from 23 July 2013, the shares are withdrawn in connection with a takeover or scheme of arrangement of the company, where the conditions of s 498(3) are satisfied. On removal of shares from the plan an employee's base cost for CGT purposes is uplifted to their then market value (TCGA 1992 Sch 7D para 5).

Where partnership shares cease to be subject to the SIP by virtue of a forced sale provision (see **[9.80]**), ITEPA 2003 s 506(2B) has been introduced, with effect from 6 April 2014, in place of the normal provisions to tax the lesser of the amount of partnership share money applied in acquiring the shares and market value at the time the shares are offered for sale. Equivalent provisions have been introduced as ITTOIA 2005 s 394(3A) in respect of dividend shares.

[9.81]

f) *Funding the SIP trust*

Tax benefits are given to three types of funding:

(1) In computing their taxable profits, companies are able to claim a deduction for the costs of setting up and administering the plan, as with SAYE schemes and CSOPs.

(2) When SIPs were introduced, one novel feature was that the company could claim a statutory corporation tax deduction, at the time either Free Share or Matching Shares were awarded, for the market value of those shares at the time they were acquired by the SIP trustee. This deduction continues to be available (CTA 2009 Part 11 Chapter 1) and indeed takes precedence over the more generally available relief for share acquisitions set out in CTA 2009 Part 12 (see Section V of this Chapter 9). Further, in order to enable SIP trusts to acquire large blocks of shares for distribution over a long period (which private companies might want to do) without substantially delaying the corporation tax deduction, the Employee Share Schemes Act 2002 introduced an *immediate* corporation tax deduction for contributions to a SIP trust after 5 April 2003, provided: the SIP trust acquires at least 10% of the ordinary shares in the year following the first acquisition funded by the contribution; and 30% of the shares are distributed in five years and all within ten to avoid a clawback of the deduction (CTA 2009 s 989). As a result of perceived tax avoidance, limitations were introduced in

FA 2010 s 42 to deal with, for example, situations where SIPs were funded and a deduction claimed without the general intention of delivering shares to employees.
(3) A CGT roll-over relief is available for transfers to a SIP trust provided that the rather restrictive conditions are satisfied (see TCGA 1992 s 236A and Sch 7C). **[9.82]**

6 Enterprise Management Incentives (ITEPA 2003 Part 7 Chapter 9 and Sch 5)

a) *Introduction*

The Government not only wants to extend the use of all-employee share schemes but also wishes to encourage 'high-quality managers to share in the risks and rewards of running small- and medium-sized enterprises, particularly early stage high-technology companies, by supporting equity-based remuneration' (Pre-Budget Report 1998). This is the role for Enterprise Management Incentives (EMIs) under which options over up to £250,000 worth of shares can be granted to an individual employee, subject to a beneficial tax regime (the original limit of £100,000 was increased to £120,000 for grants from 6 April 2008 under FA 2008, and the current limit has applied from 16 June 2012 under the Income Tax (Limits for Enterprise Management Incentives) Order 2012 (SI 2012/1360)).

Companies that wish to award EMI options may enter into individual option agreements with selected employees, although many companies continue to prefer to establish a scheme under which options are granted. The main features are discussed below. **[9.83]**

b) *Qualifying companies*

Given the government's aim, the types of company that can grant EMIs are, of course, limited. Broadly, to qualify a company's gross assets must not exceed £30m; it must be independent; it cannot undertake certain activities (eg dealing in land); and it must have a 'permanent establishment' in the UK (prior to 16 December 2010 EMIs were limited to companies whose trading activities were conducted wholly or mainly in the UK). It used to be the case that shares in a parent company could only be used if it owned at least 75% of all its subsidiaries. FA 2004 s 96 amended ITEPA 2003 Sch 5 para 11(2), so that, for EMI options granted after 16 March 2004, most subsidiaries need only be 51% owned. The same section introduced requirements where there is a property managing subsidiary. It is possible to obtain advance assurance from HMRC that a company qualifies. A further restriction was introduced under FA 2008 in order to comply with EU legislation on state aids which restricts EMI options to companies with fewer than 250 'full-time equivalent' employees. **[9.84]**

c) *Eligible employees*

Prior to FA 2001, options could only be granted 'for commercial reasons in order to recruit or retain a *key* employee'. Now they can be granted to any employee who has committed to work at least 25 hours a week for the company (or 75% of his working time, if that is less) and who does not have a material interest (essentially, owning or controlling 30% or more of the ordinary share capital of the company). **[9.85]**

d) *Maximum value of options*

Prior to FA 2001, the maximum value of options that a company could grant was limited by the fact that only 15 'key' employees could have EMIs. Now any number of 'eligible employees' can benefit (up to an individual limit of £250,000) but the maximum value of shares over which there can be unexercised EMI options is limited to £3m (the value to be measured at the time of option grant). **[9.86]**

e) *Tax treatment of employees*

The basic position is that if an option granted at market value is exercised within ten years of grant and there are no intervening 'disqualifying events' (see s 533), no income tax charge arises on option grant or exercise (s 530). This applies no matter how short a time the option has been held but, of course, companies will normally impose a contractual retention period. It is important to note, however, that if HMRC is not notified of the grant of the option within 92 days in accordance with the statutory procedure (Sch 5 Part 7), the beneficial tax treatment is lost.

If the option is granted at a discount, the discount will be taxed under ITEPA 2003 s 476 at the time of option exercise. Additionally, if the option is exercised after ten years, s 476 will apply.

If there has been a 'disqualifying event' before the option is exercised and the option is not exercised within 90 days of that event (previously 40 days), there is an income tax charge on exercise but it is based only on the amount (if any) by which the market value of the shares when the option is exercised exceeds their market value immediately before the disqualifying event.

FA 2013 introduced into TCGA 1992 Part V Chapter 3 provisions enabling shares acquired pursuant to EMI qualifying options which are exercised on or after 6 April 2013 to qualify for entrepreneurs' relief (see **Chapter 20**). Transitional provisions extended, in certain circumstances, this relief to shares acquired on an exercise of EMI options during the 2012/2013 tax year: readers should refer to the FA 2013 provisions and, importantly, HMRC's guidance (which sets out HMRC's more restrictive interpretation of certain of the transitional provisions). The condition for entrepreneurs' relief that the individual must hold at least a 5% stake in the company (ie the 'personal company' condition) does not apply in respect of EMI option shares. The usual one-year qualifying period is also replaced with a requirement that the EMI option was granted at least one year prior to the disposal of the shares. The usual employment requirement and the trading company requirement need to be satisfied during that one-year period. Therefore, where these conditions are satisfied, and provided that the EMI option has been held for at least one year, entrepreneurs' relief will be available where shares acquired on exercise of such an EMI option are sold immediately following exercise. There are circumstances in which entrepreneurs' relief on an EMI option may be lost, including where a 'disqualifying event' occurs within one year of the grant of the option. Even where the disqualifying event occurs more

320 *Employee participation: options, incentives and trusts*

than one year after grant, the option must be exercised no later than 90 days following such event in order for the shares to benefit from entrepreneurs' relief. **[9.87]**

7 PAYE and NICs

Originally, benefits from tax-advantaged schemes fell wholly outside the PAYE and NICs nets but this position has changed significantly over the years. **[9.88]**

a) *PAYE*

PAYE has always applied whenever there is an income tax charge when benefits are acquired from Share Incentive Plans and on the exercise of Enterprise Management Incentive options, provided the shares acquired are readily convertible assets (RCAs – see further **[9.43]**). PAYE now has to be operated in most cases if there is an income tax charge on the exercise of a Company Share Option Plan (CSOP) option, if the shares are RCAs; and PAYE will also apply if there are income tax charges thereafter, in accordance with the usual principles (see **[9.43]**) (ITEPA 2003 s 701, as amended by FA 2004 s 88). However, it is still the case that, even if there is an income tax charge on the exercise of an SAYE option, PAYE is not operated; but it will apply in the usual way if there are charges thereafter (see again **[9.43]**).

Whenever a payment is made for the surrender of any EMI or tax-advantaged option, there is an income tax charge under ITEPA 2003 s 477(3)(b) and, in such a case, PAYE will apply, whatever the nature of the shares that would have been acquired on exercise of the option (see ITEPA 2003 s 700). **[9.89]**

b) *NICs*

The NIC treatment of tax-advantaged benefits follows the PAYE treatment discussed above. In relation to CSOP and EMI options, it is possible for the employee to agree to bear the cost of employer NICs whenever there is an income tax charge (see further **[9.44]**). **[9.90]–[9.110]**

IV EMPLOYEE TRUSTS AND TREASURY SHARES

1 Employee trusts

a) *Introduction*

The term 'employee trust' has no statutory definition but, in broad terms, an employee trust is a discretionary trust the actual and potential beneficiaries of which are defined by reference to employment. Such trusts may enjoy favoured treatment for IHT, CGT, income tax and corporation tax. The use of employee trusts has been significantly limited by the introduction of ITEPA 2003 Part 7A (pursuant to FA 2011 Sch 2), which imposes an income tax charge on certain payments, asset transfers and the 'earmarking' of assets for employees by any third party, which would include the trustees of an employee trust. This legislation, known as the 'disguised remuneration' legislation, is extremely widely drafted, but seeks to permit certain share-based incentives provided by third parties through a series of exemptions. HMRC have also confirmed that hedging arrangements, the primary use of most employee trusts, should not be caught by the provisions provided that the trustee does not have sufficient information to be deemed to have earmarked trust assets against awards made to individual employees. The provision of assets other than in connection with employees' share schemes is not considered further in this chapter.

There are several other important functions of employee trusts. *First*, they offer non-quoted companies the opportunity of creating a market for the sale and purchase of their shares: without such a market, non-quoted companies cannot effectively embark upon any share scheme unless current shareholders or the company itself would be prepared to buy shares from employees wishing to sell. *Second*, unlike treasury shares (see below) that are treated in the same way as new issue shares, the use of existing shares through a trust does not affect the 'headroom' limits usually contained in the rules of listed companies' schemes (see **[9.164]**). *Third*, they can be used to build up a large shareholding in friendly hands so that the company will be protected against any unwanted takeovers and outside interference. *Finally*, they promote good relations between employer and employee since they can be viewed as a demonstration of an employer's concern for the welfare of its staff. Employee trusts have previously been used to provide a cost-efficient means for the company to finance a scheme: the tax deductibility of company contributions is considered in Section V of this Chapter 9. **[9.111]**

b) *Taxation of the trust*

Trustees pay tax at 45% on any income received other than dividend income that is taxed at 38.1% (ITA 2007 s 9) (see *Tax Bulletin*, April 2004, p 1113 on what items of expenditure may properly be claimed as trust management expenses by the trustees of discretionary trusts). By ITA 2007 ss 496A and 496B (previously ESC A68), to avoid an effective double tax charge UK resident trustees may reclaim tax paid by them when payments made to employees are treated as earnings (which will normally be the case). Where discretionary payments are made by non-resident trustees, the recipient may be able to make a claim for a tax credit under a similar principle set out in ESC B18.

If trustees distribute shares to employees, the employee will normally be liable to income tax on the market value of the shares and that value will be treated as his base cost for CGT purposes (TCGA 1992 s 17(1)). UK resident trustees will be liable to CGT on the difference between the market value at the date of distribution and their base cost. TCGA 1992 s 239ZA (previously ESC D35) relieves the trustees from this CGT liability where the employee is liable to income tax on the full market value of the shares (thus removing the double tax charge). The relief will not be available where shares are used to satisfy options held by employees because payment of the option price will mean the employee will not be taxable on the *full* market value of the shares acquired (but see *Tax Bulletin*, April 2000, p 738 for this and other points relating to the provisions previously contained in ESC D35). Where an employee trust is to be used to supply shares for a share scheme, particularly an option scheme, consideration should be given as to whether establishing the trust offshore would avoid this double tax charge. The CGT treatment of offshore employee trusts has been problematical, particularly after the changes introduced by FA 1991, but HMRC's view that, if there is no element of bounty (as with genuine commercial arrangements), TCGA 1992 ss 86–87 do not apply, is helpful (*Tax Bulletin*, April 1995, p 204).

Transfers of shares or other assets to an employee trust can have CGT consequences for the transferor. TCGA 1992 s 239 will often prevent the market value rule in s 17 being applied, so that the transferor's gain will be based on the actual consideration received and, in the case of close companies, it will limit the effect of s 125. Hold-over relief under TCGA 1992 s 165 may be available when shares are transferred to an employee trust (even if it has a corporate trustee – see *Tax Bulletin*, December 2000, p 815). Following the restrictions on hold-over relief under TCGA 1992 s 165 (and s 260) introduced by FA 2004 s 116 and Sch 21, care will be needed when determining whether the relief is available if any individual who has (or may acquire) an interest in the employee trust has ever contributed property to it (see further **[25.21]** ff).

When dealing with trusts, IHT is an additional tax consideration. To qualify for favoured treatment, an employee trust must satisfy the conditions set out in IHTA 1984 s 86, especially the requirement that *all or most* of the employees of the establishing employer *must be* within the class of potential beneficiaries. If the trust falls outside s 86, or s 13 or s 28 are not satisfied, contributions to the trust may be transfers of value for IHT purposes (eg if the employer is a close company). Further, if s 86 does not apply the trust will be subject to an IHT charge on each ten-year anniversary (s 64) and to an exit charge when capital is distributed (s 65). Even if the trust falls within s 86, an exit charge may, in certain circumstances, arise under s 72 if a transfer of property is made to an excluded person where the transfer is not classed as income. **[9.112]**

2 Employee share ownership plans

FA 1989 introduced the concept of qualifying employee share ownership plans (QUESTs). The main advantage that a QUEST had over a non-statutory employee trust was a guaranteed corporation tax deduction for company contributions. However, to benefit from that statutory deduction, numerous conditions had to be satisfied. As a result, very few QUESTs were established until a change introduced by FA 1996 enabled them to be used in conjunction with SAYE schemes, so that the company could obtain a corporation tax deduction for providing the shares to satisfy the SAYE options. As FA 2003 introduced a more general corporation tax relief, the specific relief for QUESTs is no longer available (see further Section V below). Since this was the *raison d'être* of most QUESTs, very few remain in existence (most having been wound up – FA 2003 s 142(2) (by amending FA 1989 s 69) allowed the assets held by QUESTs on 26 November 2002 to be transferred to a Share Incentive Plan trust): they are not considered further. Readers desiring more information are referred to previous editions. **[9.113]**

3 Treasury shares

Since 1 December 2003, UK listed companies (and, since 30 April 2013, private companies) have been able to hold their shares 'in treasury'. This means that they do not have to cancel shares they purchase from shareholders but are able to retain them. The shares can then later be sold, cancelled or transferred pursuant to an employee share scheme. The guidelines on share incentive schemes issued by the Investment Association require the use of treasury shares to count towards the 'headroom' limits contained in scheme rules (see [9.164]). As a result, few listed companies are making use of treasury shares over shares acquired by a trust. [9.114]

4 Employee-ownership trusts

In June 2012 the Government commissioned a report on ways to encourage companies to adopt employee-owned status, and published its response to that report in October 2012. In the 2013 Autumn Statement it was announced that, in addition to the existing tax-advantaged share schemes, the Government would make available £70m annually to support employee ownership models and, this in turn, lead to two related measures being introduced by the FA 2014. [9.115]

a) *Transfer of ownership interest into employee-ownership trusts*

The first measure introduced by FA 2014 is an exemption from CGT where shares constituting a controlling interest in a business are transferred to a trust which operates for the benefit of employees of that company (referred to as an 'employee-ownership trust'). TCGA 1992 s 17(1) would normally apply in respect of a gift of shares to an employee trust, and would deem the transfer to have been made at market value. Under the new provisions, where five specified relief requirements are met (TCGA 1992 s 236H(4)), s 17(1) is disapplied in respect of transfers of shares into a qualifying employee-ownership trust made within a single tax year. The first three relief requirements determine whether the trust qualifies for the relief; these are: (1) that the company is a trading company or the principal company of a trading group; (2) that the trust holds a controlling interest in the company at the end of the tax year, whilst not having done so at the start of the tax year (the 'controlling interest requirement'); and (3) that the trust meets the 'all-employee benefit requirement'. The other relief requirements relate to the transfer and transferor; these govern the position where the transferor is a participator in the company and provide that the relief is available only once in respect of a company (or, where applicable, companies in the same group).

The 'all-employee benefit requirement' requires the terms of the employee trust not to permit the trust property to be applied other than to benefit, on the same terms, all of the employees (but excluding, broadly, any employee who is a participator in the company and who holds an interest of 5% or more in the company). The terms of the trust must also comply with certain other requirements, including having no power to make loans to beneficiaries. The 'all-employee benefit requirement' is, therefore, stricter than the requirements for a trust to fall within IHTA 1984 s 86, as it requires equality of treatment between beneficiaries. Many existing employee benefit trusts will not meet this requirement due to the wide discretionary powers normally granted to trustees. To ensure that existing employee benefit trusts which already hold a stake in a company are not prejudiced, but without requiring amendments to the terms of the existing trust, a deeming rule (TCGA 1992 s 236P) provides that a IHTA 1984 s 86 trust established prior to 10 December 2013 and which on that date held a significant (generally, 10% or greater) interest in a qualifying company will be treated as satisfying the 'all-employee benefit requirement' provided that, within 12 months prior to a qualifying transfer of shares into the trust, the trustees do not exercise the trust powers in a way that would have been prohibited by the 'all-employee benefit requirement'. Certain anti-avoidance rules also apply governing the position where, generally, the relief requirements cease to be met in the tax year following that in which the transfer of shares to the trust occurs.

Provisions are also included to ensure that qualifying employee-ownership trusts can benefit from the same favoured treatment under the IHT regime as is available to employee benefit trusts, in particular in respect of IHTA 1984 ss 13, 28 and 86 (see [9.112]). [9.116]

b) *Bonus payments by employee-ownership trust controlled employers*

The second employee ownership measure introduced by FA 2014 created an income tax exemption in respect of bonuses paid, on an all-employee basis, by an employer which is owned by an employee-ownership trust that qualifies for the CGT and IHT reliefs. The relief is available for bonus payments made on or after 1 October 2014. The exemption is limited to bonuses of £3,600 per tax year per employee, and is therefore consistent with the value that can be awarded as Free Shares under a Share Incentive Plan. In order to qualify for the relief a number of conditions must be met (ITEPA 2003 s 312B). In addition to the company having to meet the trading company requirement, and being controlled by an employee-ownership trust that meets the 'all-employee benefit requirement' and the controlling interest requirement (see [9.116]), these conditions include a requirement that the bonus must be awarded to all employees on the same terms, although, in line with the SIP legislation, the bonus scheme may impose a minimum qualifying service requirement of up to 12 months, and, subject to certain conditions, may determine bonus amounts by reference to each employee's remuneration, length of service and/or hours worked.

There is no corresponding relief from employee's or employer's National Insurance. A bonus which qualifies for the income tax relief will, however, constitute qualifying benefits for the purposes of CTA 2009 Part 12, such that a corporation tax deduction will still be available (CTA 2009 s 1292(6B)).
[9.117]–[9.120]

V CORPORATION TAX

1 **Introduction**

Lowry v Consolidated African Selection Trust Ltd (1940) established that a company cannot claim a corporation tax deduction for the notional loss it suffers when it issues shares to employees for less than their market value. In order to obtain such a deduction, some companies operating employee share schemes therefore established employee trusts: they contributed cash to the trust which then purchased shares and distributed them via the share scheme.

Prior to FA 2003, a statutory corporation tax deduction was available for contributions to tax-advantaged Share Incentive Plans (SIPs), but the deductibility of company contributions to a discretionary employee trust depended on the application of general principles. FA 2003 introduced a general statutory corporation tax deduction when certain types of employee share benefits are provided to employees (Sch 23); and prevents or delays any deduction for contributions to trusts to provide other sorts of benefits which would be available under general principles (Sch 24). These provisions have been rewritten into CTA 2009 Part 12 and ss 1290–1297 respectively. **[9.121]**

2 Deductibility under general principles

Subject to what is said in 3 below, payments by a company to an employee trust are deductible under normal principles if they are of a revenue (income) nature and are wholly and exclusively for the purposes of the trade. In *Mawsley Machinery Ltd v Robinson* (1998), the Special Commissioner disallowed a small company's contributions to a trust on both grounds: the purpose of the payments was to enable the trust to purchase the controlling shareholder's shares when he retired as managing director, which made them both capital in nature and partially for the purpose of enabling him to sell his shares without trouble when he retired (so not exclusively for the purposes of the trade).

Employer contributions to a trust should not be made under a binding legal obligation nor expressed as instalments of a lump sum. The best policy is to make regular payments geared to a variable factor – eg a percentage of profits. Funding by close companies requires special care in view of IHTA 1984 s 13 and CTA 2010 s 455. To avoid CGT, employee trusts are often established offshore (see **[9.112]**).

The Special Commissioner's decision in *Waterloo plc v IRC* (2002) acts as a reminder that the transfer-pricing provisions in TIOPA 2010 Part 4 apply if the trust provides benefits to employees of subsidiaries but is funded only by contributions from the parent company, although the practical implications of this may be limited by the guidance from HMRC discussed below (see **[9.124]**).

These general principles will continue to apply when specific statutory provisions do not. **[9.122]**

3 Restriction of tax relief

Prior to the introduction of the anti-avoidance legislation in CTA 2009 ss 1290–1297 (formerly FA 2003 Sch 24), a company could obtain a corporation tax deduction (and other, non-corporate, employers could claim a deduction in computing their Schedule D income tax profits) under general principles when it made a contribution to an employee benefit trust. However, two things could affect the timing of the deduction. The first was FA 1989 s 43 which delayed the deduction if the company paid 'potential emoluments' to an 'intermediary'; the second, the accounting treatment (see **[9.160]**).

In *Dextra Accessories v Macdonald* (2002) the Special Commissioners held that s 43 was not widely enough drawn to prevent a company claiming a corporation tax deduction even though the employees suffered no income tax on the benefits provided by the trustees of an employee benefit trust. Not prepared to wait for the decision of the High Court ((2003) – which did in fact uphold the Commissioners), nor the Court of Appeal ((2004) – which allowed HMRC's appeal), nor the House of Lords ((2005) – which upheld the Court of Appeal decision in favour of HMRC), draft legislation was issued at the time of the 2002 Pre-Budget Report and this became Sch 24 to FA 2003. This sequence of events explains why the new rules apply to contributions made on or after 27 November 2002. However, they do not apply where the rules in CTA 2009 Part 12 (previously FA 2003 Sch 23) apply (see 4 below).

CTA 2009 ss 1290–1297 contains anti-avoidance legislation, the main aim of which is to prevent an employer claiming a tax deduction for contributions to an employee benefit trust (and other arrangements – see definition of 'employee benefit scheme' in CTA 2009 s 1291), that would potentially be allowable under general principles, unless and until an employee receives 'qualifying benefits'. A deduction for a contribution is allowed only to the extent that it is used to provide 'qualifying benefits' or pay 'qualifying expenses' during the accounting period when the deduction would be allowed under general principles or within nine months from the end of it (CTA 2009 s 1290(2)); or if it is subsequently used to provide 'qualifying benefits'.

'Qualifying benefits' are defined in CTA 2009 s 1292 and are basically limited to money or assets which: give rise to both an income tax and NIC charge (or would do so if the employee were resident and ordinarily resident in the UK); are provided on a termination of employment or (from 6 April 2006) are provided under an employer-financed retirement benefit scheme (FA 2004 s 245). CTA 2009 s 1292(4) sets out payments to which the provisions of CTA 2009 ss 1290–1297 do not apply (for instance, contributions to an accident benefit scheme). What is surprisingly absent is a provision allowing the deduction to be claimed (assuming it is allowable under general principles) if the employee is exempt from income tax for some reason other than non-residence (for instance, because of the nature of the benefit or because of an exemption in ITEPA 2003); or if he would not be subject to NICs even if resident in the UK because of a tax treaty between his home country and the UK. Companies providing share benefits to employees in circumstances which do not qualify for relief under CTA 2009 Part 12, and all employers providing other types of benefits via a trust, will need to consider the tax and NIC position of their employees carefully before seeking to claim a deduction.

CTA 2009 ss 1288–1289 (as supplemented by CTA 2009 Sch 2 paras 133 and 140) applies to delay a deduction until the earnings are actually paid where an employer reserves an amount for earnings in its accounts. **[9.123]**

4 Statutory corporation tax relief

a) *Interaction with other provisions*

FA 2003 Sch 23 (now CTA 2009 Part 12) introduced a new regime for claiming corporation tax relief for all accounting periods beginning after 31 December 2002. The relief is available if the conditions set out in CTA 2009 Part 12 are satisfied. If they are not, then relief may still be available under general principles but subject to the restrictions set out in CTA 2009 ss 1290–1297.

If relief can be claimed under CTA 2009 Part 12 in respect of the cost of providing shares, no other relief can be claimed (CTA 2009 s 1038), save that the deductions available under CTA 2009 Part 11 in relation to SIPs (see **[9.82]**) take priority. This provision (originally FA 2003 Sch 23 para 25) resulted in a concern arising in relation to the extension of the transfer pricing regime to UK-UK transactions (FA 2004 s 30). A company that operates a share scheme in which employees of its subsidiary participate needs to recharge the subsidiary or be subject to a deemed receipt under TIOPA 2010 Part 4 (see *Waterloo plc v IRC* (2002)). In other types of intra-group transaction this receipt by the parent company would be included in its corporation tax calculation, but the subsidiary would receive a corresponding deduction for the payment. However, in the case of a share-based transaction, CTA 2009 s 1038 denies the subsidiary the corresponding deduction (although the CTA 2009 Part 12 deduction outlined below will be available). This issue does not arise for accounting periods after 1 January 2005 as a result of the accounting treatment of share-based payments under IFRS 2/FRS 20 (now FRS 102). HMRC has issued guidance which states that, as any recharge (or transfer pricing adjustment) relating to a grant or award is now accounted for within reserves by the parent company (see **[9.160]**), this element is treated as 'capital' and, therefore, not subject to corporation tax. This effectively avoids the double tax problem (as well as having led HMRC to accept that in this position there is no need to calculate the transfer pricing charge).

It remains possible to claim relief under general principles for other costs, such as fees and stamp duty. **[9.124]**

b) *Availability of relief*

The availability of the relief depends upon the tax position of the employee and the type of shares being acquired. **[9.125]**

i) *Tax position of employee*

The basic idea behind the legislation is that a company can claim a corporation tax deduction for the value of shares received by its employees but only if and when the employee is taxed thereon. This is subject to two caveats. *First*, the deduction is available even if the employee is not taxed because either the shares were acquired on exercise of a tax-advantaged option (CTA 2009 s 1017(1)) or he is not resident (CTA 2009 ss 1009(3) and 1017(2)). *Second*, not all income tax charges under ITEPA 2003 Part 7 count for these purposes. CTA 2009 Part 12 Chapter 2 gives relief where there is an income tax charge in respect of the *award* or *acquisition* of shares; Chapter 3 where there is a charge in relation to the exercise of an option; Chapter 4 where there is a charge on acquisition of restricted securities or where there is a chargeable event under Part 7 Chapter 2; and Chapter 5 in relation to convertible shares. Therefore, no corporation tax relief can be claimed when the employee is taxed under ITEPA 2003 Part 7 Chapters 3A, 3B, 3C, 3D and 4 (see **[9.26]–[9.29]**).

FA 2014 amended CTA 2009 Part 12 with effect from 6 April 2015 to address an asymmetry that previously existed where a UK income tax charge arises on the acquisition of shares by an employee of a company that is not within the scope of UK corporation tax (such that no deduction corresponding to the income tax charge was available). From 6 April 2015, where the income tax charge arises as a result of such an employee working for (but without being employed by) a company that is within the scope of UK corporation tax, that 'host company' will, subject to certain conditions, be able to claim a corporation tax deduction up to the extent of the overseas employee's UK income tax liability. A similar extension to the availability of the deductions under Part 12 was also introduced where an employee of a company within the scope of UK corporation tax incurs, because of that employment, a liability to UK income tax on the exercise of an option, or in respect of restricted or convertible shares, which was acquired by virtue of a previous overseas employment (which, as the option or shares are not acquired because of the employment with the UK company, would not otherwise qualify for a deduction). **[9.126]**

ii) Type of shares

CTA 2009 Part 12 only gives relief where *shares* are acquired – not when the range of securities covered by ITEPA 2003 Part 7 are acquired. Only certain types of shares qualify (CTA 2009 ss 1008 and 1016): in essence, these are the same type that can be used for SAYE Option Schemes and Share Incentive Plans (see **[9.74]** (1)), although the rules relating to consortium companies are slightly different. The most notable absence is shares in an unlisted subsidiary of an unlisted parent – if such a company wants to distribute its own shares to employees, it will still have to rely on general principles to claim a deduction and will be subject to CTA 2009 ss 1290–1297. **[9.127]**

c) *Amount and timing of relief*

The employing company (not, if different, the company whose shares are acquired) will obtain a corporation tax deduction equal to the amount on which the employee is (or would be) taxed if the conditions in **[9.126]** are satisfied. The relief will be claimable for the accounting period in which the employee is (or would be) taxed. Thus, except in the case of SIPs (as to which see **[9.82]**), tax-advantaged (including EMI) options and non-residents (as to whom see above), there will be symmetry between the employing company's corporation tax deduction and the employee's tax charge. FA 2006 s 93 amended Sch 23 to correct an oversight in drafting in relation to discounted EMI options over restricted or convertible shares. EMI gains are now in line with other options under CTA 2009 Part 12, allowing the employing company a deduction for the full gain realised by the employee and not solely for the amount of the upfront discount on which the employee is taxed (see **[9.87]**).
[9.128]

d) *Arbitrage receipts rules*

The arbitrage receipts rules were introduced by F(No 2)A 2005 s 26 (now TIOPA 2010 s 249) to counter tax arbitrage where a UK-resident company receives a benefit from a payment that is not fully taxable as income or gains, but where the payee has received a tax deduction. The legislation allows HMRC to issue the UK company with a 'notice' requiring the company to compute its income or gains for tax purposes as if it had received taxable income equal to any untaxed amount.

HMRC does not expect the arbitrage receipts rules to apply generally to recharge payments from the employing company to its UK parent where shares are provided by the parent company to its employees, provided that the amount of any tax deduction available to the employing company (the payer) is based on the economic value of what is provided (the shares or options).

Any recharge arrangements made on the basis of the transfer pricing provisions referred to above (see **[9.124]**) would not, therefore, be caught, nor would recharge arrangements between two UK companies, as a result of the operation of CTA 2009 Part 12. However, an example of where the arbitrage receipts rules may apply is where a non-UK employing company is required to make a payment (which is tax deductible) to a UK company in respect of the 'spread' at the time of exercise (the difference between the exercise price and the market value of the shares acquired), and this exceeds the fair value of the options at the time of grant. **[9.129]–[9.150]**

VI CHOICE OF SCHEME

1 Non-tax aspects

Whenever any commercial transaction is considered it is vital to look at the tax implications from all angles. However, no transaction can or should be entirely tax-driven. Thus, an employer should first decide what commercial objective he is seeking by his scheme of employee participation. Set out below is a list of the likely objectives, together with a note of the schemes (tax-advantaged and non tax-advantaged) that may go some way towards achieving them. **[9.151]**

a) *Tax-efficient bonus scheme*

Tax-advantaged schemes are the most efficient schemes to operate. In some cases, the selectivity offered by EMIs and Company Share Option Plans may be the deciding factor (see **[9.159]**)). **[9.152]**

b) *Performance-related incentives*

Non tax-advantaged schemes are better in this regard because targets can be changed and directly related to individual performance. With all tax-advantaged schemes, targets must be fixed at the outset (although the decision in *IRC v Burton Group plc* (1990) affords some flexibility). If looking to the profitability of the company, rather than individual employees, an employee trust may be preferred, since this enables the amount passing into the trust for the benefit of the employees to be directly related to the company's performance. **[9.153]**

c) *Reward for growth in share value*

Share incentive schemes or share options may be used and, again, the selectivity of EMIs and Company Share Option Plans may make them the more attractive of the tax-advantaged schemes. Market value share options focus on the growth in value of the underlying shares. Fulfilling a similar role are the more complex 'growth share' and joint ownership arrangements (see [9.45]). [9.154]

d) *Retention of employees*

Long-running schemes are required. Most schemes will be appropriate where they operate over a long period and are made subject to the employee remaining with the company. Non tax-advantaged share incentives with restrictions on sale could also be used. [9.155]

e) *Creation of 'friendly' shareholdings*

Shares may be sold immediately after exercise of options and it is therefore better to use an employee trust or a SIP to create a friendly block holding of shares. This has the added benefit of the shares of the employees being 'co-ordinated' through trustees. Alternatively, SAYE schemes tend not to result in an immediate sale because the employee does not need to raise funds to exercise the option. [9.156]

f) *Creation of market in non-quoted shares*

Any arrangement involving the use of a trust would be ideal as the trust can be funded to acquire shares from employees where no other market exists. Often a private company's articles of association will restrict the sale of shares other than to existing shareholders or to an employee trust. [9.157]

g) *Generation of sense of identity between employees and the company*

Any form of share ownership should promote this and the normal procedure would be to tie this into a long-term commitment as suggested above. The employee trust is particularly useful in this respect. On an all-employee basis, the SIP provides tax benefits whilst aligning the interests of employees with those of the company as they share the risks through their investments. Many employees, however, prefer to participate in option schemes, particularly an SAYE, on the basis that they are not at risk of making a loss – if the share price falls employees do not need to exercise their options and those employees participating in an SAYE are able to recover their contributions and tax-free bonus. [9.158]

h) *Selective employee participation*

One problem with tax-advantaged SIPs and SAYE schemes is that they must apply to *all* employees (subject to qualifying periods of employment). EMIs and Company Share Option Plans permit selectivity. Should that type of scheme not be suitable, companies may consider a non tax-advantaged scheme that provides *total* flexibility on this matter. [9.159]

i) *Accounting treatment*

'Share-based payments' must be provided for in UK companies' accounts in accordance with accounting standard FRS 102 (Section 26), which replaced

FRS 20 with effect from 1 January 2015, mirroring the international standard IFRS 2.

IFRS 2 and FRS 102 require that an expense be charged in the company's profit and loss account whenever it enters into any share-based obligation. The expense will have to be measured as the 'fair value' of the equity instrument (the share or option) at the grant date and will be derived from the market value of the instrument, where this can be determined (eg for a share) or, in the case of an option, as calculated by using a valuation technique or model. This value will be accrued in the accounts over the performance period: the charge to the profit and loss account will be finalised on vesting depending on the proportion of the shares or option which vest as a result of the application of (non-market based) vesting conditions.

The accounting treatment of employee trusts is addressed by IFRS 10 on a group consolidated basis and, from 1 January 2015, FRS 102 (and prior to 1 January 2015 was the subject of Abstract 38 ('Accounting for ESOP Trusts') and Abstract 32 ('Employee benefit trusts and other intermediate payment arrangements') issued by the Urgent Issues Task Force of the ASB).

Although no longer current from 1 January 2015, UITF Abstract 25 addressed the accounting treatment of employers' NICs. UITF 25 provided that companies have to make provision for the liability, unless there has been an election to transfer the employer's liability to the employee; if the employee agreed to reimburse the employer's liability, then that promise would appear as an asset if receipt is virtually certain. [9.160]

2 Tax aspects

Having determined what type of scheme can best meet its commercial objectives, the employer will need to look at the relative tax benefits of the various schemes available. Two main questions need to be asked: *first*, do tax-advantaged schemes offer real tax benefits in comparison with non tax-advantaged schemes; and, *second*, if they do, which of the tax-advantaged schemes is most beneficial? [9.161]

a) *Tax-advantaged or not?*

So far as share-based schemes are concerned, it has been explained that the benefits provided under *tax-advantaged* schemes will usually be subject only to *CGT* in the employee's hands, and that any charge will arise only if and when the relevant shares are *sold*. By contrast, benefits provided for an employee under a *non tax-advantaged* scheme will usually be taxed as *income* and charges can arise even *before sale*.

Prior to FA 1988, with a top rate of income tax of 60%, compared with a CGT rate of only 30%, the attractions of tax-advantaged schemes from an employee's point of view were obvious. From 1988–89 to 2008, capital gains were generally charged at the employee's marginal income tax rate and the distinction between tax-advantaged and non tax-advantaged became somewhat blurred. With CGT rates of 10% and 20%, compared to the highest rate of income tax at 45% and in the additional 2% in National Insurance, the benefits of approved schemes have been reintroduced.

A capital gain rather than an income profit will also be advantageous for the following reasons.

First, the due date for payment of the two taxes differs: earnings under ITEPA 2003 may attract an immediate tax charge under PAYE, whereas any capital gain realised will only fall into charge on 31 January following the tax year in which the disposal occurred, as CGT is collected under self-assessment. *Second*, in arriving at the chargeable gain, an individual will be entitled to an annual exemption of (currently) £11,300. *Third*, the taxation of benefits received under tax-advantaged schemes is only triggered on the disposal of the shares: accordingly, as long as the employee or director intends to retain the shares over a period of years, it may be possible to reduce, or even eliminate, the charge. In due course, that individual may be able to arrange for disposals to occur in different tax years (thereby taking advantage of more than one annual exemption) and for disposals to be channelled through a spouse or civil partner.

These advantages are further enhanced by the difference in the treatment of tax-advantaged and non tax-advantaged schemes for national insurance purposes (cf [9.44] and [9.90]), and particularly in the real extra cost to employers of operating non tax-advantaged schemes. [9.162]

b) *Which tax-advantaged scheme?*

If the employer decides that his overall objectives fit within the structure of a tax-advantaged scheme, which scheme should be chosen? This question should be answered by looking at the non-tax aspects of the matter noted above.

The main difference between the various tax-advantaged share schemes lies in the amount of relief available and whether or not benefits can be given on a selective basis.

If shares are retained in a SIP for the period necessary to avoid an income tax charge and sold immediately on removal, the effect of the 100% CGT base cost uplift will be to make the gain tax-free. Shares may be retained in the SIP trust generally for as long as the employee remains in employment. This is the only way of *ensuring* a tax-free benefit for an employee irrespective of his own tax position. However, in many cases benefits from tax-advantaged schemes *will be* tax-free as there will be no income tax liability and the gains will be within the recipient's (unused) annual CGT exemption. [9.163]

3 Other shareholders

The presence of institutional shareholders may be a further factor for a company considering setting up an employee participation scheme to consider. Any listed company will not only have to comply with the Listing Rules, the Disclosure and Transparency Rules and the Prospectus Rules but will also usually feel obliged to follow the guidelines issued by committees representing institutional investors. The Listing Rules require prior shareholder approval for any employee share scheme which involves or may involve the issue of new shares or transfer of treasury shares, and for any long-term incentive scheme in which at least one director is eligible to participate. This will cover an employee trust which has the power to subscribe for shares in the company as well as those schemes more obviously involving new issues.

Institutional investor guidelines impose limits ('headroom limits') as to the number of shares that can be issued under employee share schemes and, broadly, set the ceiling at 10% of issued share capital in any ten-year period (or 5% for discretionary schemes). Further, institutional investors generally do not accept the use of shares in subsidiaries for incentive schemes.

Guidelines issued by institutional investors cover matters other than the number of shares that can be used for incentive schemes, in particular the circumstance when discretionary share options may be exercised. Institutional investors are adamant that this should depend on performance targets being met. The key point is the requirement for performance conditions which require the 'achievement of appropriately challenging financial performance' with awards subject to lapse if the conditions are not met at the end of a fixed performance measurement period (see Principle of Executive Remuneration, October 2014, issued by the Investment Management Association (now the Investment Association), which follows the previous Association of British Insurers' guidelines). **[9.164]**

10 Trading income
Updated by Anne Fairpo, Barrister

I   Introduction [**10.2**]
II What is a trade? [**10.18**]
III Computation of profits [**10.61**]
IV Trading receipts [**10.101**]
V   Stock and work in progress [**10.110**]
VI Deductible expenses [**10.130**]
VII Relief for fluctuating profits [**10.171**]
VIII Basis of assessment (sole-traders and partnerships) [**10.192**]

'… take a gang of burglars. Are they engaged in trade or an adventure in the nature of trade? They have an organisation. They spend money on equipment. They acquire goods by their efforts. They sell the goods. They make a profit. What detail is lacking in their adventure? You may say it lacks legality, but it has been held that legality is not an essential characteristic of a trade. You cannot point to any detail that it lacks. But still it is not a trade, nor an adventure in the nature of trade. And how does it help to ask the question: If it is not a trade, what is it? It is burglary and that is all there is to say about it.'

(Lord Denning in *Griffiths v Harrison* (1963)).

[**10.1**]

I INTRODUCTION

The law relating to the taxation of trading income differs according to whether a business is unincorporated or a limited company. For income tax purposes, trading income is dealt with under Part 2 of the Income Tax (Trading and Other Income) Act 2005 (ITTOIA 2005) from 2005–06 onwards. For corporation tax, trading income is computed under Part 3 of the Corporation Tax Act 2009 (CTA 2009) for accounting periods ending on or after 1 April 2009. Previously trading income was taxed under Schedule D Cases I (trades) and II (professions and vocations). Trades, professions and vocations carried on wholly abroad by a UK resident taxpayer or company were taxed under Schedule D Case V. From the above dates no sources of trading, professional or vocational income are taxed under the scheduler system. Reference to Schedule D Cases I and II is, however, required in connection with the extensive, early case law; references to Schedule D Case I include Schedule D Case II unless otherwise stated.

In this chapter trade includes profession and vocation (for a definition see [10.41]). [10.2]

1 Income tax

Income tax is charged under the trading income provisions of ITTOIA 2005 Part 2 on the profits of a trade, profession or vocation (ITTOIA 2005 s 5). Accordingly all sole-traders and partnerships have 'trading' income regardless of their business activities. The profits of a trade arising to a UK resident person are chargeable to tax under these provisions irrespective of where in the world the trade is carried on. The trading profits of a non-UK resident person are chargeable to income tax only if they arise from a trade carried on wholly in the UK, or if it is carried on partly in the UK and partly abroad, from the part carried on in the UK (ITTOIA 2005 s 6). If a person is partly UK resident and partly non-resident during a split tax year, for the overseas part of the year, the individual is treated as non-UK resident (ITTOIA 2005 s 6(2A)). [10.3]

2 Corporation tax

Corporation tax is charged under the trading income provisions of CTA 2009 Part 3 on the profits of a trade, (CTA 2009 s 35). In contrast to the income tax provisions, there are no references to profession or vocation in the corporation tax legislation. The profits of UK resident companies are chargeable to corporation tax irrespective of where in the world the trade is carried on, subject to exemptions for foreign permanent establishments (CTA 2009 s 5(1)). The trading profits of non-UK resident companies are chargeable to corporation tax only if they arise from a trade carried on by a 'permanent establishment' in the UK (CTA 2009 s 5). [10.4]–[10.17]

II WHAT IS A TRADE?

1 The problems involved

a) *Definition*

'Trade' is not precisely defined in the legislation although there are a few signposts indicating what does and does not constitute a trade, see [10.42]. CTA 2009 s 33 indicates that a trade includes an office and the holding of an office. In ITA 2007 s 989 a somewhat circular and limited definition is given with 'trade' being defined as 'any venture in the nature of trade'.

In the absence of a clear statutory definition of 'trade' reference must be had to the significant case law. In *Ransom v Higgs* (1974) Lord Wilberforce considered that a trading transaction would usually exhibit the following features:

> 'Trade normally involves the exchange of goods or services for reward ... there must be something which the trade offers to provide by way of business. Trade moreover presupposes a customer ...'

The Final Report of the Royal Commission on the Taxation of Profits and Income (1955: Cmnd 9474) concluded that there could be no single test that points to a trade but suggested certain objective tests or hallmarks. These have become know as 'the badges of trade', see **[10.22]**. Before considering these tests, two general matters should be noted in connection with the case law. *First*, when the case is concerned with whether a taxpayer carried on a trade or not, caution needs to be exercised in citing it as precedent since the finding of the First-tier Tribunal is a decision of fact, which will rarely be overturned on appeal (see *Edwards v Bairstow and Harrison* (1956)). *Second*, before the introduction of CGT in 1965, the question whether or not a person engaged in a trade was of fundamental significance. If he was trading, any profit was charged under Case I; if not, income tax was inapplicable so that the (capital) profit escaped tax altogether. Since 1965 the choice is normally between paying income tax and CGT. The taxpayer's preference for one or the other will depend on the availability of various reliefs and losses. Capital receipts, although they may suffer CGT, are not charged to income tax as trading income (ITTOIA 2005 s 96), see also **[10.103]**.

HMRC's Business Income Manual BIM 20051 ff should be referred to for their interpretation of 'trading'. [10.18]

b) *Single activity*

In spite of implying that 'trade' cannot be precisely defined, the legislation is useful in that it indicates that a single activity may constitute a trade (see eg *Martin v Lowry* (1927) below) although the opposite conclusion was reached in *Salt v Chamberlain* (1979) and *Dr KMA Manzur v R & C Comrs* (2010).
[10.19]

c) *Commonsense and commercial approach*

Often a commonsense approach to the question 'what is a trade' is adopted. In *PI Murtagh v R & C Comrs* (2013) a pharmacist's claim to deduct trading losses incurred in managing his two sons who were professional golfers was rejected. The First-tier Tribunal found that he was not carrying on 'a trading venture' and his activities were undertaken simply to foster his sons' careers. In contrast in *Akhtar Ali v R & C Comrs* (2016), a pharmacist who used the profits from his business to buy and sell shares was held to be operating a commercial share dealing trade. The First-tier Tribunal held that the fact that the dealing was unsuccessful and unsophisticated did not mean that it was not a trading activity. Mr A may have been a risk-taker and over-confident in his abilities, but as these are often qualities of self-made individuals who become entrepreneurs, they are indicative of a trading venture. It was clear that the appellant aimed to make a profit and that he pursued the activity in a sufficiently organised way such that it did not amount to gambling (see **[10.21]**). [10.20]

d) *Gambling*

It has long been held that betting and gambling do not amount to a trade. In *Graham v Green* (1925), Rowlatt J said in the case of an appellant who gambled on horses, 'a bet is merely an irrational agreement that one person should pay another on the happening of an event'. This view was upheld in *Down v Compston* (1937) a case involving a professional golfer and in an Australian case, *Evans v FCT* (1989). In contrast, a bookmaker who runs an organised activity to profit from the gaming public is likely to be trading, see *Partridge v Mallandaine* (1886). A similar decision was reached in *Burdge v Pyne* (1969), in which the proprietor of a registered club provided a card room where he regularly won against members at three-card brag. The question of whether the income of a poker player was organised as a self-employment was considered by the Court of Appeal in *Hakki v Secretary of State for Work and Pensions* (2014). It was held that the appellant's winnings did not amount to a self-employment for the purposes of the Child Support Agency in spite of the fact that he played poker three or four days a week, made television appearances and had a website. [10.21]

2 The 'badges of trade'

The Royal Commission identified six 'badges' designed to determine whether or not the purchase and sale of property has the hallmarks of a trading transaction. [10.22]

a) *The subject matter of the transaction*

Property that neither yields an income nor gives personal enjoyment to its owner is more likely to form the subject matter of a trading transaction. Other property (typically land, works of art, and shares) may be acquired for the income and/or enjoyment that it provides.

In *Rutledge v IRC* (1929), the taxpayer was a businessman connected with the film industry. Whilst in Berlin he purchased 1 million toilet rolls for £1,000 that he resold in the UK at a profit of approximately £11,000. The Court of Session held that the taxpayer had engaged in an adventure in the nature of a trade so that the profits were assessable under Case I. They stressed that such a quantity of goods must have been intended for resale. Similarly, in *Martin v Lowry* (1927), the gigantic speculation involved in the purchase and sale of 44 million yards of Government surplus aeroplane linen, at a profit of £1,600,000, amounted to a trade largely because of the nature of the subject matter and the commercial methods employed to sell it.

The purchase and sale of land causes more difficulty since owning land in quantity does not raise a presumption that trading is intended. In *IRC v Reinhold* (1953), for instance, despite the taxpayer having bought four houses over two years, admittedly for sale, the Court of Session concluded that 'heritable property is not an uncommon subject of investment' and that the taxpayer was not trading. In *A Headley v R & C Comrs* (2013) the appellant purchased a house in 2001, let it to tenants and then sold it in 2005. He appealed against HMRC's capital gains tax assessment claiming that he had a property-dealing trade. The First-tier Tribunal found that the property was acquired because of the prospect of rental income (an investment motive) and that as the appellant had continued to hold the house as an investment until it was sold there was no trade. Renovating and developing property may, however, be indicative of a trade: see *TA Hartland v R & C Comrs* (2014) at [10.26].

In *Taylor v Good* (1974) the taxpayer was held not to be trading when he sold at a considerable profit, because he had obtained planning permission, a house which he had purchased with the original intention of using it as a residence. The Court of Appeal took the view that a person intending to sell property is entitled to take steps to ensure that he obtains the best possible price for it. In particular, the court decided that the house did not become his trading stock merely because he had applied for planning permission before the sale. As Lord Russell LJ said:

> 'If you find a trade in the purchase and sale of land, it may not be difficult to find that properties originally owned (for example) by inheritance, or bought for investment only, have been brought into the stock in trade of that trade. But where, as here, there is no question at all of absorption into a trade of dealing in land or lands previously acquired with no thought of dealing, there is no ground at all for holding that activities such as those in the present case, designed only to enhance the value of the land in the market, are to be taken as pointing to, still less as establishing, an adventure in the nature of trade.'

The definition of a trade was further limited in this area in *Marson v Morton* (1986). The taxpayer was a potato merchant and on advice from an estate agent friend, purchased land suitable for development. He paid £65,000: £35,000 out of his own resources and £30,000 on a mortgage arranged by the estate agent. At the time of the purchase the taxpayer said that he intended to make a medium to long-term investment in the land. However, two months later, on advice from the same estate agent, the land was sold for £100,000. Both the commissioners and Sir Nicolas Browne-Wilkinson V-C held that the taxpayer was not trading and that land could be held as an investment even though it produced no income. **[10.23]**

b) *Length of ownership*

A quick sale is more consistent with a trading activity rather than an investment that is more likely to be long term. The reason for sale may be special and could rebut such a presumption (see *Wisdom v Chamberlain* (1969), a case involving the purchase and sale of silver bullion, and see also **[10.28]**). **[10.24]**

c) *Frequency of similar transactions*

Repeated transactions in the same subject matter point to a trade. Since a single adventure may amount to a trade this 'badge' will be applicable only in circumstances where that would not otherwise be the case. In *Pickford v Quirke* (1927) the court held that although a single purchase and sale by a syndicate of four cotton mills did not amount to trading, the series viewed as a whole did. Note also that later transactions may colour earlier transactions and may trigger a trading income liability on those earlier transactions (see also *Leach v Pogson* (1962) in which the founding and subsequent sale of 30 driving schools consecutively, was held to be trading). **[10.25]**

d) *Work done on the property*

When work is done to the property in order to make it more marketable, or when an organisation is set up to sell the asset, there is some evidence of trading (see *Martin v Lowry* (1927): compare *Taylor v Good* (1974)). In *Cape Brandy Syndicate v IRC* (1921) three individuals engaged in the wine trade who formed a syndicate and purchased some £3,000 casks of Cape brandy which they blended (with French brandy), recasked, and sold in lots over an 18-month period were held to be trading. Work done to improve property before sale can also be evidence of trading. In *TA Hartland v R & C Comrs* (2014) H, a builder, bought a number of properties and either renovated or demolished and rebuilt them before selling them on or advertising them for sale. H claimed that he had occupied two of the properties as his private residence. The First-tier Tribunal found that one had been purchased, reconstructed and sold in the course of a trade. [10.26]

e) *Circumstances responsible for the realisation*

A forced sale to raise cash for an emergency raises a presumption that the transaction is not a trade. Sales by executors in the course of winding up the deceased's estate and by liquidators and receivers in the administration of an insolvent company will often fall into this category (see *Cohan's Executors v IRC* (1924) and *IRC v The 'Old Bushmills' Distillery Co Ltd* (1927)). [10.27]

f) *Motive*

If the transaction was undertaken in order to realise a profit that is some evidence of trading. The absence of a profit motive does not prevent a commercial operation from amounting to a trade (see, for instance, dividend stripping and for the effect of fiscal motives, *Ensign Tankers (Leasing) Ltd v Stokes* (1992)); conversely, the mere fact that an asset is purchased with the intention of ultimate resale at a profit will not of itself lead to a finding of trading (see, for example, *Richard Murray v R & C Comrs* (2014), in which case the First-tier Tribunal rejected the taxpayer's claim for relief in relation to losses incurred in racehorse training and breeding. Although the taxpayer claimed that he had intended to make a profit, the economic downturn and a lack of income led the Tribunal to be scornful of the argument that the activities would be sustainable if the losses were allowed and to conclude that the activities did not amount to trading on a commercial basis with a view to making a profit. See also *McMorris v R & C Comrs* (2014) and *Thorne v R & C Comrs* (2014), concerning horse ownership and breeding respectively). Often the subject matter involved will be decisive. In *Wisdom v Chamberlain* (1968) the taxpayer (a comedian) who bought £200,000 of silver bullion as a 'hedge' against an expected devaluation of sterling and three months later sold it realising a profit of £50,000 was held to be trading. His claim that he had made no profit, but rather that the pound had fallen in value, was rejected.

The creation of a substantial loss may lead to a claim that an entity is not trading, particularly if there is a tax avoidance motive. This is particularly the case with partnerships designed to create substantial losses or claims to tax relief by the exploitation of film and other intellectual property rights. A limited liability partnership (LLP) made a loss of more than £13 million on film production. The High Court held that there was no trade in films because the business had simply sold the master negative of a film to a distribution company. The Court of Appeal held that the LLP was not carrying on a trade or business which 'consisted of or included the exploitation of films within F(No2)A 1992 s 42'. The film did not constitute trading stock of the trade within s 42(8) because copyright remained vested in the business that exploited the film, *R & C Comrs v Micro-Fusion 2004-1 LLP* (2009). A similar issue also arose in *Icebreaker 1 LLP v R & C Comrs* (2010). The LLP was formed with the aim of trading in film distribution. It made a large loss. The Upper Tribunal held that a payment of more than £1 million made under a distribution agreement was not allowable as it was not expended for trading purposes. This decision was followed by the First-tier Tribunal in the related case of *Acornwood LLP v R & C Comrs (and related appeals)* (2014) where it was held that certain partnerships had participated in a tax avoidance scheme, the aim of which was to secure sideways loss relief for the members inflated by unnecessary borrowing. The scheme was structured to give the illusion that the borrowed money was available to exploit intellectual property rights by the device of a large production fee offset by an equally large share of revenue.

In *Samarkand Film Partnership No 3 v R & C Comrs (and related appeals)* (2015), the Upper Tribunal, confirming the decision of the First-tier Tribunal, decided that the sale and leaseback of films was not carried out on a commercial basis with a view to profit. Accordingly loss relief was denied and an application for a judicial review was dismissed. In *Eclipse Film Partners No 35 LLP v R & C Comrs* (2015), the Court of Appeal, upholding the decisions of the First-tier and Upper Tribunals, held that a complex series of transactions relating to the licensing and distribution of film rights did not have the speculative aspect required to make them trading transactions and the taxpayer had not been trading in a meaningful way. The Court of Appeal confirmed that in deciding whether an activity amounts to a trade, it is necessary to consider the totality of the business activities and in this case the activities were those of a 'non-trade business' within the provisions of ITTOIA 2005 s 609. As such the income was taxable as miscellaneous and not trading income. Furthermore, the tax relief claimed by the individual partners for qualifying interest payments under ITA 2007 s 383 (formerly TA 1988 s 353) was denied. The Supreme Court has refused leave to appeal, making this the most significant case on the question of whether film exploitation schemes are trading transactions.

In *Patrick Degorce v R & C Comrs* (2015), involving another marketed tax avoidance scheme, a company sold the rights in two films to the appellant hedge fund manager. Nearly 80% of the purchase price was funded by a loan from an associated company. Later in the same day the hedge fund manager assigned the film rights to an associated company generating a substantial loss. The appellant claimed he was carrying on a trade of acquiring and exploiting film distribution rights. This assertion was rejected by the First-tier Tribunal, which decision was upheld in the Upper Tribunal where it was found that obtaining advice and negotiating a transaction did not transform the purchase of an asset into a trading activity. The speculative element was insufficient to turn the transaction into trading income and the sole purpose of entering into the complex transactions was to shelter taxable income. In *E Flanagan v R & C Comrs (and related appeals)* (2014), the appellant had entered into a tax avoidance scheme notified to HMRC under FA 2004 Part 7 (see **Chapter 5**). He also commenced self-employment as a car dealer, making a loss of £5 million attributable mainly to finance costs with no turnover. The

First-tier Tribunal rejected the loss claim on the basis that the business was not a serious trade pursued with a view to profit but a means of securing tax relief. Furthermore no money had really been put at risk. **[10.28]**

3 Mutual trading

No man can trade with himself. Thus, when persons join together in an association and jointly contribute to a common fund for their mutual benefit, any surplus received by the members on a division of that fund is tax-free (*New York Life Insurance Co v Styles* (1889)) but equally there is no relief for losses, and capital allowances cannot be claimed. Legislation confirms that if a credit union holds deposits or invests surplus member funds this is not treated as a trade (CTA 2009 s 40). If however, an association trades with non-members, the profits attributable to that activity are taxable. In *Carlisle and Silloth Golf Club v Smith* (1913), fees paid by visitors for the use of the club facilities were held to be trading receipts. CTA 2009 s 101 prevents the mutual trading rules from being used to avoid tax, by imposing a charge on the return of surplus assets in circumstances when the original contributions were tax deductible. For HMRC's view of mutual trading see BIM 24000. **[10.29]**

4 Trading after a discontinuance

The realisation of assets after the permanent discontinuance of the business is not trading. Hence, in *IRC v Nelson* (1938) income tax under the then Case I was not charged when a whisky broker, who because of ill-health had closed his business, sold the entire business including the stock in trade. By contrast, a sale of stock *with a view to* the cessation of trading (a 'closing-down sale') is chargeable because the trade is still continuing (see *J & R O'Kane & Co Ltd v IRC* (1922)).

Whether or not a trade is continuing or has ceased is an issue that has required consideration by the courts particularly where losses are claimed. In *TJ Moore v R & C Comrs* (2011), a musician's income declined and he started working as a music teacher. HMRC attempted to disallow most of his expenses on the basis that the trade of musician had ended. The First-tier Tribunal upheld the musician's appeal and found that regardless of a significant decrease in income he had not ceased to be a musician. In contrast in *T Bhadra (t/a Admirals Locums) v R & C Comrs* (2011) the First-tier Tribunal found that a doctor who had been struck off the register of medical practitioners by the General Medical Council in 2006 was no longer trading in 2008–09. In *D Kishore v R and C Comrs* (2013) terminal losses of some £24 million were claimed by the appellant who traded in mobile phones on the basis that the trade had ceased in 2006. He resumed active trading in 2009 and remained VAT registered throughout. The First-tier Tribunal found that the business had not ceased trading in 2006 but rather had continued as a single trade. In *HL Amah v R & C Comrs* (2014), a franchisee dispensing optician made a loss in his final accounting period and subsequently commenced working as a freelance locum optician. The First-tier Tribunal held that there was 'very clearly' a cessation of one business activity and the commencement of another. As a result, the loss could not be carried forward to be deducted from the new self-employment.

The case of *Leekes Ltd v R & C Comrs* (2015) illustrates the difficulties in offsetting losses even where all the parties agree that that there has been a succession to the trade. L Ltd ran department stores, and in November 2009 purchased C Ltd, which operated furniture stores and warehousing. C Ltd hived its business up to L Ltd and became dormant. L Ltd refurbished the stores previously run by C Ltd and rebranded them in its name. C Ltd had current and brought forward losses, and L Ltd claimed to offset them against its trading profits. HMRC considered that losses could only be off-set against the post succession trading profits of C Ltd. The First-tier Tribunal held that as L Ltd had succeeded to C Ltd's business and there was a single new trade, all the losses should be available for off-set. They considered that creating two notional trades for the purpose of determining the use of the losses was not what the legislation intended. The Upper Tribunal (2016), however, overturned the decision and took the view that the legislation (CTA 2010 s 940A (formerly TA 1988 s 343)) only permitted loss relief to be set against the profits that would have been made by the transferor if it had continued to carry on the trade transferred. Although the legislation does not specifically refer to streaming of losses, the Upper Tribunal took the view that it was unnecessary for it do so, as the transferor's trade could still be identified in the enlarged business through appropriate bookkeeping.

For HMRC's view of whether a business continues or ceases see BIM 90005.

Tax is charged on income received after the cessation of a trade in certain circumstances under the post-cessation income provisions (ITTOIA 2005 ss 242–253; CTA 2009 s 34(1)(b) and s 188): see BIM 90010 and [**10.80**]). Special rules also operate for the valuation of trading stock held at the date of cessation of a business (ITTOIA 2005 ss 173–181; CTA 2009 ss 162–171: see [**10.114**]). [**10.30**]–[**10.40**]

5 Meaning of 'profession' and 'vocation'

Trading income encompasses profits from a profession or vocation and there will rarely be a need to distinguish one from the other (see [**10.3**]). In common with 'trade', neither 'profession' nor 'vocation' is statutorily defined. 'Profession' has been judicially described as involving 'the idea of an occupation requiring either purely intellectual skill or manual skill controlled by the intellectual skill of the operator' (see Scrutton LJ in *IRC v Maxse* (1919)). This definition can be misleading, because a person exercising an occupation in those terms (such as a solicitor) may be doing so as an employee assessable under ITEPA 2003 (see [**8.22**]). A profession has been said to differ from a trade as it involves an element of continuity but this is disputed by HMRC, see BIM 80585. Casual profits and fees arising from an isolated professional or vocational transaction may be taxed as miscellaneous income under ITTOIA 2005 Part 5 if they are insufficient to constitute a trade. For an examination of when an author becomes a publisher, see *Salt v Fernandez* (1997).

'Vocation' has been judicially defined by Denman J in *Partridge v Mallandaine* (1886) as '… the way in which a man passes his life'. This definition is somewhat unhelpful as it would embrace a very wide variety of activities not all of which would be vocations.

A review of the corporate tax case law relating to the meaning of 'profession' can be found in CTA 2009 Explanatory Notes Annex 1, Change 2. [**10.41**]

344 Trading income

6 Statute

In a few limited respects the legislation specifies activities that do and do not amount to a trade. A trade includes:
- farming and market gardening except that carried on by an insurance company on land held for the purposes of its long-term business (ITTOIA 2005 s 9; CTA 2009 s 36);
- the commercial occupation of land other than woodland (ITTOIA 2005 ss 10–11; CTA 2009 ss 37–38);
- profits of land used for mining, quarrying, waterworks, canals, docks, fishing rights, markets, bridges, tolls, railways and similar concerns except that carried on by an insurance company on land held for the purposes of its long-term business (ITTOIA 2005 s 12; CTA 2009 s 39).

For the purposes of the loan relationship regime any mutual trading or any mutual insurance or other mutual business which is not life assurance business does not constitute the whole or any part of a trade (CTA 2009 s 298(3)). [10.42]–[10.60]

III COMPUTATION OF PROFITS

1 The accounts

Income tax is charged on the 'full amount' of the trading profits (ITTOIA 2005 s 7). The charge to corporation tax simply applies to the 'profits of a trade' (CTA 2009 s 35). The amount of the trading profit is usually arrived at by preparing accounts that show trading income and expenses with adjustments for stock and work-in-progress, amounts due and sums owing. Smaller businesses run by individuals do not always prepare formal trading accounts. Often all that is required for tax purposes is that they make the relevant entries on the tax return. Some small businesses can elect to prepare their accounts on a cash basis, see [10.73].

Where accounts are prepared for commercial purposes and in accordance with generally accepted accountancy practice (see [10.62]) they will rarely show the taxable trading profits. Some items that have been deducted in the accounts may not be deductible for tax purposes (such as entertainment expenses: see [10.138]). Other items are treated differently for taxation purposes: expenditure on a capital asset, for instance, is written off annually over the life of the asset as depreciation under generally accepted accounting practice but is deductible for income tax and corporation tax only to the extent that it falls within the system of capital allowances (see **Chapter 48**). The taxpayer's trading accounts must therefore be adjusted for tax purposes by adding back deductions that are not allowable and, where appropriate, by making permitted deductions (such as capital allowances). [10.61]

2 Generally accepted accounting practice (GAAP)

Trading profits must be computed in accordance with generally accepted accounting practice (GAAP) subject to any necessary adjustment required or authorised by law for the calculation of trading profits (ITTOIA 2005 s 25;

CTA 2009 s 46). Certain small businesses can elect to use a simpler cash basis (ITTOIA 2005 s 25A). Deductions are allowed at a fixed rate in some cases (ITTOIA 2005 ss 94B–94I). For income tax purposes generally accepted accounting practice (GAAP) is defined in ITA 2007 s 997. For corporation tax purposes it is defined in CTA 2010 s 1127. Trading profits must be prepared in accordance with UK and international financial reporting standards and take into account the concept of materiality, see **[10.64]**–**[10.65]**. Compliance with GAAP does not for the purpose of computing income tax or corporation tax require the accounts to be audited or disclosure to be made under either the Companies Acts or the financial reporting standards (ITTOIA 2005 s 25; CTA 2009 s 46). GAAP does not lay down specific rules for the calculation of profits for any specific type of business (CTA 2009 s 46).

Trading profits must be computed on the earnings basis in order to comply with GAAP. This means that the accounts must reflect debtors, creditors, stock and work-in-progress. From 2013–14 eligible small businesses may prepare cash accounts instead of accounting under GAAP, see **[10.73]**. Cash accounts are comparatively simple to prepare and in most cases require few or no adjustments to arrive at the taxable trading profit. Payments are deducted from income receipts and no account is taken of debtors, creditors, stock or work-in-progress. **[10.62]**

3 Accounting practice

a) *Introduction*

As described at **[10.62]**, trading profits must be computed in accordance with generally acceptable accounting practice (GAAP) unless there are exceptional circumstances or the cash basis of accounting is used (see **[10.73]**). Historically, in computing trading profits, the starting point is the profit as shown by the accounts drawn up in accordance with the principles and practice of commercial accounting and taking into account the specific provisions of tax law (*Heather v P-E Consulting Group Ltd* (1972)). This concept was established by case law long before it was given statutory effect (*Lothian Chemical Co Ltd v Rogers* (1926), *Odeon Associated Theatres Ltd v Jones* (1972); *Threlfall v Jones* (1993), *Lloyds UDT Finance Ltd v Chartered Finance Trust Holdings and ors (Britax Int. GmbH and anor)* (2002)). GAAP accounting now requires compliance with UK and international financial reporting standards (see **[10.64]**).

During the course of an enquiry HMRC may check whether trading accounts comply with GAAP. In *Leslie Smith v R & C Comrs* (2011) the Upper Tribunal dismissed the taxpayer's appeal against the decision of the First-tier Tribunal and held that the accounts of a construction industry ground works contractor had not been prepared in accordance with GAAP because they did not include a value for work-in-progress as required by SSAP 9 and FRS 5 (see **[10.64]** and **[10.113]**). The result was that trading profits were increased by more than £200,000 for the years in question. The taxpayer's accountant was found guilty of 'negligent conduct'. In *W Craig v R & C Comrs* (2012), the First-tier Tribunal found that an invoice for services provided by an associated company to a landscape designer had not been correctly apportioned to the relevant accounting periods and as a result the accounts had not been prepared in accordance with GAAP. **[10.63]**

346 Trading income

b) *Financial reporting standards*

Generally accepted accounting practice has no legal definition in the UK beyond the somewhat limited provisions in ITA 2007 s 997 and CTA 2010 s 1127 (see **[10.62]**). GAAP means UK generally accepted accounting practice in relation to the accounts of UK companies that are intended to give a true and fair view. Accounts drawn up in accordance with the micro-entity provisions of company law are presumed to give a true and fair view. In the case of companies preparing accounts in accordance with International Accounting Standards (IAS) it means generally accepted accounting practice in relation to IAS accounts. The definitions extend to individuals, entities that are not companies and companies that are not UK companies. GAAP thus encompasses the principles and practice set out in the financial reporting standards and other statements issued by the Financial Reporting Council (FRC) and in addition includes the requirements of company law, industry-specific requirements, regulatory factors and pronouncements by HMRC. The Foreword to Accounting Standards states, 'The whole essence of accounting standards is to provide for recognition, measurement, presentation and disclosure for specific aspects of financial reporting in a way that reflects economic reality and hence provides a true and fair view.' When considering compliance with GAAP, the relevant question to ask is 'how would accountants present the trading profit in practice?'

All entities, regardless of whether they are incorporated or not, must take into account the financial reporting standards (FRSs) and related statements when computing their trading profits unless they use the cash basis of accounting (see **[10.73]**).

Financial reporting standards are continually evolving and as new ones are published they will need to be taken into account. A full list of current statements is available on the FRC website at www.frc.org.uk. Financial reporting in the UK and Republic of Ireland was substantially revised from 2012, with almost all the previous standards being replaced by the following Financial Reporting Standards, although some previous standards remain in place for accounting periods beginning before 1 January 2015 (1 January 2016 for the Financial Reporting Standard for Smaller Entities (FRSSE)). The current reporting standards are:

- FRS 100 – Application of Financial Reporting Requirements for UK and Republic of Ireland entities (last updated September 2015);
- FRS 101 – Reduced Disclosure Framework (for subsidiaries and ultimate parent companies) (last updated September 2015);
- FRS 102 – The Financial Reporting Standard Applicable in the UK and Republic of Ireland (applicable to the financial statements of entities that are not applying the FRSSE, EU-adopted IFRS or FRS 101) (last updated September 2015; (Fair Value hierarchy disclosure updated March 2016));
- FRS 103 – Insurance Contracts (consolidated accounting and reporting requirements for entities in the UK and Republic of Ireland issuing insurance contracts) (March 2014);
- FRS 104 – Interim Financial Reporting (March 2015); and
- FRS 105 – Financial Reporting Standard Applicable to the Micro-Entities Regime (July 2015).

FRS 105 replaces the FRSSE and is effective for accounting periods beginning on or after 1 January 2016 with permitted earlier use for accounting periods beginning after 1 January 2015. It enables certain micro-entities to apply exemptions in the preparation of their financial statements whilst still complying with GAAP. Micro-entities are companies which do not exceed two of the following criteria in a year: turnover £632,000, balance sheet total £316,000 and number of employees ten.

Listed companies must draw up their consolidated accounts in accordance with EU-adopted international financial reporting standards (IFRS), international accounting standards (IAS) and the related interpretations (IFRIC and SIC interpretations) (EU Regulation (EC) No 1606/2002). Non-listed companies can choose whether to adopt IFRS or prepare their accounts in accordance with UK GAAP. Non-consolidated accounts can also be prepared under UK GAAP. Companies using IAS are taxed in an equivalent way to companies using UK GAAP.

Entities not using FRS 105 or IFRS must prepare their financial statements in accordance with FRS 102 (or FRS 101 for subsidiaries and ultimate parent companies). **[10.64]**

c) *Materiality*

Materiality is an accounting concept and is relevant to the preparation of accounts which form the starting point for the computation of taxable trading profits. An item is material if its misstatement or omission would affect a reader's view of the accounts. The extent to which materiality impacts on the accounts is a matter of judgement but a certain level of materiality should not be assumed as there are no quantitative guidelines. Materiality does not sit comfortably with HMRC's view of the tax legislation which requires accuracy, ultimately to be determined by the First-tier Tribunal. HMRC permit some relaxation in the requirement for complete accuracy in large businesses where rounding to £1,000 is permitted in some circumstances, see Statement of Practice (SP 15/93). **[10.65]**

d) *Accounting policies*

Financial reporting standard FRS 102 Section 10 provides guidance to help businesses to select and apply suitable accounting policies. These are the specific principles, bases, conventions, rules and practices used by an entity to prepare and present their financial statements. FRS 102 states that an entity's management should use its judgement to develop and apply accounting policies so that they produce accounting information that is relevant to the economic decision-making needs of users and reliable. Reliability means that the financial statements should: faithfully represent the entity's financial position, financial performance and cash flow; include the genuine economic substance of transactions; and be neutral (free from bias), prudent and complete in all respects. When choosing an accounting policy, management should take into account guidance in FRS 102 Section 10, any relevant Statement of Recommended Practice (SORP), FRS 102 Section 2 (Concepts and Pervasive Principles) and in certain cases EU-adopted IFRS and IAS in that order. One aspect in choosing accounting policies is comparability with previous financial statements produced by the same entity and with other similar trades. The accounting policies should be reviewed regularly to ensure that they remain appropriate to the business transactions and a new policy should be implemented if changes in circumstances make it more appropriate (see [10.72]).

The accounting policies adopted must have sufficient regard to the facts. In *Minister of National Revenue v Anaconda American Brass Ltd* (1956), it was held that the stock valuation policy that the company adopted in its statutory accounts was based on a theoretical pattern of stock use, 'last in first out' (LIFO), which disregarded the facts. The Privy Council concluded that the basis to be used for tax purposes was 'first in first out' (FIFO): see also [10.112]. [10.66]

e) *Provisions*

The inclusion of provisions in accounts is governed by FRS 102 Section 21. Before the introduction of financial reporting standards the cases of *Owen v Southern Railway of Peru Ltd* (1957) and *IRC v The Titaghur Jute Factory Co Ltd* (1978) established that a deduction may be allowed for a contingent liability provided that:
(1) the profit would not be adequately stated if the obligation was not taken into account; and
(2) it has been possible to arrive at a sufficiently reliable figure.

The admissibility of provisions was also considered in *Johnston v Britannia Airways Ltd* (1994) (provision for future repairs), *Jenners Princes Street (Edinburgh) v IRC* (1998) (provision for refurbishment expenditure) and *Herbert Smith v Honour* (1999) (provision for onerous leases). As accounting profits must now accord with GAAP this negates the effect of much of the previous case law.

Under FRS 102 Section 21 provisions can only be made when:
(a) the entity has an obligation at the reporting date as a result of a past event;
(b) it is probable (ie more likely than not) that the entity will be required to transfer economic benefits in settlement; and
(c) the amount of the obligation can be estimated reliably.

Satisfying condition (a) requires the entity to have no realistic alternative other than to settle the obligation. The obligation must be a present obligation as the result of a past event and not one that arises from the future conduct of the business however likely it is to occur. For example, where a company because of commercial pressure or legal requirements needs to install new equipment such as smoke filters in a factory, no provision is required because the company can avoid the expense by its future actions such as selling the factory or operating in a different way. This means that *Johnston v Britannia Airways Ltd* (1994) no longer applies. Provisions for future restructuring costs can be made where the entity has a detailed development plan. Provisions for onerous contracts are permitted provided that a reliable estimate can be made of the costs: *Herbert Smith v Honour* (1999). No provision can be made for future operating losses: *Meat Traders v Cushing* (1997).

Expenditure can only be provided where there is an unconditional obligation to pay it. In *Alchemist (Devil's Gate) Film Partnership v R & C Comrs* (2013) a significant deduction was made in the accounts for deferred payments to the cast and crew. Sir Stephen Oliver observed that as expenditure is only deductible when there is an unconditional obligation to pay it the financial statements failed to comply with GAAP. The provision for the production expenses should have been removed before the accounts were used to calculate the partnership loss. Furthermore at the time when the accounts were approved the deferred amounts were unascertainable and the partnership had not incurred the expenditure.

The expenditure being provided must be revenue and not capital. In *Parnalls Solicitors Ltd v R & C Comrs* (2009) a company acquired a partnership of solicitors. One of the former partners was entitled to an annuity. The company decided to commute the annuity rights by paying a lump sum of over £1 million. A provision was duly made in the company's accounts. The First-tier Tribunal held that the obligation to pay the annuity was assumed as part of the consideration for the partnership's business. Accordingly it was capital expenditure.

Provisions for expenditure are not tax deductible in all situations even if they comply with financial reporting standards. In *Dispit Ltd v R & C Comrs* (2007), the Special Commissioners rejected an accounting provision of £600,000 for future expenditure to reinstate a landfill site because CTA 2009 s 145 (formerly TA 1988 s 91A) relating to relief for site restoration payments was confined to the actual payments made. **[10.67]–[10.71]**

f) *Change of accounting basis*

Changes in accounting policies are dealt with by FRS 102 Section 10 but the need for consistency in accounts was recognised by the courts in *Ostime v Duple Motor Bodies Ltd* (1961) and *Pearce v Woodall Duckham Ltd* (1978).These cases established the principle that where:
(1) there has been a change, from one valid accounting basis to another; and
(2) as a result a profit or loss is recognised in the period in which the change is made (usually by being shown as a prior year adjustment in the accounts),

then the profit or loss should be included in the computation of the assessable profit of the period in which the change was made. The legislation regarding a change of accounting basis is now found in ITTOIA 2005 ss 226–240 and CTA 2009 ss 180–187.

A change occurs where there is, from one period of account to the next, a change of basis in computing taxable trading profits, the old basis accorded with the law or practice applicable in relation to the period of account before the change, and the new basis accords with the law and practice applicable to the period of account following the change.

A change of basis for these purposes consists of either a change of accounting principle or practice in accordance with generally accepted accounting practice giving rise to a prior period adjustment, or a change resulting from a change of view as to application of the statute. In recent years this has included:
- the adoption of international accounting standards (see **[10.64]**); and
- the introduction of the cash basis for small businesses (see **[10.73]**).

350 Trading income

Where a change of accounting basis gives rise to a positive adjustment, tax is charged on the full amount of any adjustment as trading income. A negative adjustment is treated as a trading expense. There are modifications to this rule where expenses are spread over more than one period of account after the change, where an adjustment is not required until an asset is realised or written off and on a change from realisation basis to mark to market. Spreading relief is available in some cases. **[10.72]**

4 The cash basis for small businesses

a) *Making an election*

Although the general rule is that accounts must be prepared on an earnings basis to comply with generally accepted accounting practice, eligible unincorporated businesses can choose to prepare their accounts on a cash basis (ITTOIA 2005 s 25A). The cash basis replaces the alternative basis of accounting used by barristers in the early years of practice under ITTOIA 2005 s 160 subject to transitional protection.

A cash basis election can be made provided that the cash receipts of all the businesses carried on by the applicant do not exceed a 'relevant maximum' limit and so long as the person is not excluded from making a claim (ITTOIA 2005 s 31A). Where it applies, the 'relevant maximum' limit is the VAT threshold for the tax year (£85,000 in 2017–18), or double that threshold where the person claims Universal Credit (£170,000 in 2017–18) (ITTOIA 2005 s 31B).The thresholds are proportionally adjusted for short accounting periods. The 'relevant maximum' threshold applies where no cash basis election was made in the previous year and also where a cash basis election was made in the previous year but the cash receipts exceeded twice the VAT threshold for that year. Excluded persons include partnerships where one of the partners is a company, limited liability partnerships, Lloyd's underwriters and those who have made certain tax claims including profit averaging (see **[10.172]**) (ITTOIA 2005 s 31C). Once an election has been made, it continues until the claimant's circumstances change (ITTOIA 2005 s 31D). **[10.73]**

b) *Calculating profits on a cash basis*

The profit calculation for the cash basis involves two stages: *Step 1*, calculate the total trading receipts for the accounting period for the tax year; *Step 2*, deduct the trading expenses paid during the same period (ITTOIA 2005 s 31E). This calculation is subject to any adjustments required by law; for example. entertaining expenses must still be excluded (see **[10.138]**). There is no need to deduct bad or doubtful debts as the accounts do not include debtors (see **[10.144]**). The trader can treat income as received and expenses paid at the date of his choosing provided that it is consistent. For example a receipt or expense may be treated as paid when the entry shows on the bank statement or alternatively recognised when a card transaction is made (see BIM 70005).

When accounting on a cash basis, capital purchases are deducted as if they were any other payment provided that they are qualifying expenditure for the purposes of plant and machinery capital allowances (ITTOIA 2005 s 33A; see **[48.11]**–**[48.90]**). No deduction is given for the purchase of a car but capital allowances can be claimed (ITTOIA 2005 s 31D(6)). Specific rules apply to capital receipts and grants including income from asset disposals (ITTOIA 2005 s 96A and s 105(2A)). Capital allowances on plant and equipment are subject to special rules when a business joins and leaves the cash accounting scheme. Any unrelieved capital expenditure for capital purchases made prior to joining the cash accounting scheme can usually be treated as a deduction provided that the asset is paid for in full (ITTOIA 2005 ss 240A–240E).

No deduction is allowed for the payment of loan interest but, where it is disallowed, or it would be because it is not incurred wholly and exclusively for the trade, a deduction of up to £500 is permitted for the interest and the incidental costs of obtaining finance (ITTOIA 2005 s 51A and s 57B). Interest payments on trade purchases are not subject to the £500 limit provided that the purchase is an allowable expense. This includes hire purchase and leasing charges, credit card interest and trade credit charges. The interest must be apportioned where the item purchased is used privately (see BIM 70040).

A trader using the cash accounting scheme can deduct vehicle and use of home expenses at a fixed rate rather than accounting for the actual costs, see [10.161].

When a business moves from the cash basis to GAAP accounting adjustments have to be made to ensure that business income is taxed, and expenses relieved, only once (ITTOIA 2005 s 231). A negative adjustment is deducted from the taxable profits of the first accruals accounts. A positive amount is adjustment income which can be spread over six tax years (ITTOIA 2005 s 239A). When a business using cash accounting ceases to trade, the value of stock on hand or work-in-progress is treated as a business receipt (ITTOIA 2005 ss 97A–97B) (see [10.114]). Post-cessation receipts and expenses are treated as though the business was still in the cash accounting scheme (ITTOIA 2005 s 246(2A) and s 254(2A)) (see [10.80]–[10.81]).

The legislation details many tax provisions that do not apply to cash accounts, including profit averaging for farmers and creative artists; see [10.172]. There are also restrictions on the use of losses which can only be relieved against future profits from the same trade unless the business ceases (ITA 2007 s 74E), see [7.83].

The following example illustrates how the cash basis of accounting operates.

EXAMPLE 10.1

Martin, a solicitor who commenced in business as a mediator on 1 May 2014, makes up his accounts to 31 March each year. He elects to use the cash basis of accounting for 2014–15 and the election continues in force for subsequent tax years. His cash receipts for 2014–15, 2015–16 and 2016–17 are below the VAT threshold for the year in question. For 2017–18 he received fees of £72,000 and is owed a further £50,000 at 31 March 2018; he has paid bills of £12,000, but owes a further £5,000 at 31 March 2018. Under the cash basis Martin deducts his expenses from his income and the accounts show a profit as follows:

Cash receipts *(Step 1)*	72,000
Cash payments *(Step 2)*	<u>12,000</u>[1]
Profit	<u>£60,000</u>[2]

[1] Martin takes out a bank loan to purchase a new computer system which he uses for work 80% of the time and privately for 20% of the time. Martin pays interest on the loan in 2017–18 of £600. He

can deduct £500 of the interest as a cash payment. No apportionment for the business/private use is necessary (see BIM 70040).

2   The profit would be reduced to £55,000 (£60,000 – £5,000) were Martin to pay off all his outstanding liabilities on 31 March 2018.

If Martin's accounts were prepared on the earnings basis, his profits would be £45,000 (£105,000 – £60,000) higher than under the cash basis. The cash basis gives him a substantial cash-flow advantage whilst his profits are on a rising trend and is illustrated as follows:

Fees rendered:	Received		72,000
	Outstanding		50,000
			122,000
Expenses:	Paid	12,000	
	Outstanding	5,000	
			17,000
Profits			£105,000

In 2018–19 Martin receives income of £210,000 which significantly exceeds the VAT threshold for that year. He can continue to use cash accounting for 2018–19 but must change to GAAP accounting for 2019–20 unless his receipts for that year are less that the VAT threshold (see BIM 70055). **[10.74]**

c) *Moving to the cash basis*

Where the trader's previous accounts were prepared under GAAP or accruals accounting, adjustments will be required to the first cash accounts to ensure that business income is not taxed and expenses relieved twice.

EXAMPLE 10.2

Nona sells jewellery and prepares her trading accounts to 31 March. In the first year of using the cash basis she receives income from customers of £35,000 of which £1,000 was owed at the end of the previous year. Last year's accounts included closing stock of £5,000. She pays suppliers £15,000 during the year and at the end of the previous year had owed them £2,000. During the year Nona paid her accountant £800 and at the end of the previous year she owed him £400. The adjustments required to the figures for cash accounting are as follows:

	Accounting entry	Opening adjustment	Adjusted cash basis
	£	£	£
Cash receipts	35,000	-1,000	34,000
Cash payments[1]	15,000	5,000 – 2,000 = 3,000	18,000
Accountancy	800	-400	400

1   The payments are adjusted for the stock on hand and the amount owed to suppliers at the end of the previous year. Assuming no other accounting entries, Nona's trading profit is £15,600 (£34,000 – £18,000 – £400). Had she not made these adjustments her trading profit would have been £19,200 (£35,000 – £15,000 – £800).

If Nona had purchased a car in a previous accounting period and had unrelieved capital expenditure of £3,000, she cannot write off the £3,000 in her cash accounts. Instead she continues to claim capital allowances on the vehicle in the usual way.

[10.75]

5 Expenditure

a) *Deductibility*

Expenditure cannot be deducted in computing the trading profits of a business if it falls within the scope of any of the prohibitions specified in the tax legislation, or it violates a rule of tax law derived by the courts (ITTOIA 2005 s 7 and s 34; CTA 2009 s 2, s 35 and s 54). **[10.76]**

b) *Capital or revenue*

Capital expenditure is not allowable as a deduction in computing the profits of a trade (ITTOIA 2005 s 33; CTA 2009 s 53). The only exception is where a small business uses cash accounting; see **[10.74]**.

Whether expenditure is of a capital nature is ultimately a question of law to be determined in the light of the facts of an individual case. There is no single test to be applied in distinguishing capital from revenue expenditure. For determining profits for accountancy purposes, the important issue is whether expenditure is 'consumed', ie used up, and, therefore, when it must be charged to the profit and loss account or whether the expenditure brings into existence an asset or advantage for the enduring benefit of the trade: see *Atherton v British Insulation Helsby Cables Ltd* (1925). Other more recent cases which considered this issue include *Lawson v Johnson Matthey* (1992), *Halifax plc v Davidson* (2000) and *S Devaraj v R & C Comrs* (2014), where the First-tier Tribunal held that a payment for the goodwill of a shop and sub-post office was capital expenditure. In *Markets South West (Holdings) Ltd v R & C Comrs* (2011), the Upper Tribunal rejected HMRC's view that legal and professional costs incurred in applying for planning permission to run a weekly market were wholly capital costs. It was held that the expenditure could be apportioned between revenue and capital as some costs were incurred to maintain the company's asset. Judge Avery Jones said that there was an analogy with 'expenditure on a building that is partly an improvement and partly repairs'. In *Bluesparkle Ltd v R & C Comrs* (2012), the company sought to deduct a part payment for the purchase of the freehold of a hospital from a subsidiary company on the basis that it was a 'premium'. The First-tier Tribunal held that the sum was a capital payment for the purchase of a capital asset. Judge Cornwell-Kelly observed 'on the face of it, any payment under a sale agreement must in the hands of the payer be presumed to be in the nature of capital unless it is clearly otherwise'. **[10.77]**

c) *Date at which allowable*

Expenditure included in the accounts of a trader is generally deductible for tax purposes in the accounting period covered by the accounts if they have been prepared in accordance with generally acceptable accounting practice including the benefit of hindsight to the extent permissible by FRS 102 Section 32. For GAAP-compliant accounts expenditure does not need to be paid in order to be deducted; it only has to be incurred and accounted for as a 'debit' (ITTOIA 2005 s 27; CTA 2009 s 48).

In the case of accounts prepared on a cash basis by an eligible small business, the expenditure must have been paid in order to be deductible (ITTOIA 2005 s 31E), see **[10.74]**. **[10.78]–[10.79]**

6 Post-cessation receipts and expenses

a) *Receipts*

Sums received in respect of a trade after its discontinuance which would not otherwise be charged to tax because the source of the income no longer exists, are taxed as trading income (ITTOIA 2005 ss 242–253; CTA 2009 ss 188–191). For the purpose of the post-cessation rules, a debt released after a discontinuance is treated as a receipt (ITTOIA 2005 s 249; CTA 2009 s 193). Certain sums are excluded from the rules; in particular, receipts on the transfer of stock or work-in-progress in order to avoid an overlap with ITTOIA 2005 ss 173–186 and CTA 2009 ss 162–171 (see ITTOIA 2005 s 252; CTA 2009 s 195 and [10.114]). For the post-cessation receipt of VAT paid in error and statutory interest see [10.102].

Post-cessation receipts are generally taxed in the year of receipt or, if a taxpayer elects, in the year of discontinuance so long as that discontinuance has not occurred more than six years before the receipt (ITTOIA 2005 s 257; CTA 2009 s 198). For small businesses using the cash accounting scheme, post-cessation receipts are accounted for as though the business was still in the cash accounting scheme (ITTOIA 2005 s 246(2A)); see [10.74]. [10.80]

b) *Expenses*

Expenditure that would have been deductible if the trade had not discontinued may be offset against post-cessation receipts (ITTOIA 2005 s 254; CTA 2009 s 196). Relief against total income is available for certain payments made by an unincorporated business within seven years after cessation. Relief is given for the year in which the payment is made and unused relief cannot be carried forward (ITTOIA 2005 s 250; ITA 2007 ss 96–98). Payments qualifying for relief are those made wholly and exclusively to remedy defective work done, goods supplied or services rendered or by way of damages for defective work; to meet legal and professional fees in connection with a claim for defective work; to insure against claims and to collect debts of the former trade. Relief is not available for payments made in connection with tax avoidance arrangements (ITA 2007 s 98A).

The expenditure provisions also apply to debts of the business which are, after discontinuance, shown to be bad. The relief must be claimed and is given against income of the year of assessment in which the expenditure is incurred although the taxpayer may claim for the excess to be treated as an allowable capital loss of the same year if there is insufficient income in that year (ITTOIA 2005 s 248; CTA 2009 s 192).

Where small businesses use cash accounting, post-cessation expenses are treated as though the business was still in the cash accounting scheme (ITTOIA 2005 s 254(2A)); see [10.74]. Where the post-cessation expense relates to a vehicle and immediately before the trade ceased a deduction was claimed at a fixed rate, the fixed rate provisions continue to apply (ITTOIA 2005 s 254(2B); see [10.161]). [10.81]–[10.100]

IV TRADING RECEIPTS

To be a 'trading receipt' a sum must generally possess two characteristics:
- it must be derived from the trade (ITTOIA 2005 s 7; CTA 2009 s 2 and s 35); and
- it must not be capital (ITTOIA 2005 s 28; CTA 2009 s 49).

With regard to the calculation of company profits, credits in respect of loan relationships (CTA 2009 s 297), derivative contracts (CTA 2009 s 573) and intangible assets (CTA 2009 ss 747 and 749) are trading receipts and are brought into account in computing the trading profits.

Trading income received in a non-monetary form must be accounted for in full and treated as if it were a monetary payment: *Gold Coast Selection Trust Ltd v Humphrey* (1948). From 16 March 2016 this principle has statutory effect (ITTOIA 2005 s 28A; CTA 2009 s 49A).

Unless a small business uses the cash basis of accounting (see **[10.73]**), income does not need to be received in order to be treated as trading income; it only has to be accounted for as a 'credit' (ITTOIA 2005 s 27; CTA 2009 s 48). This point was considered in *D Demetriou v R & C Comrs* (2011). D, a partner in a firm of solicitors, withdrew £90,000 from the firm without authorisation. The firm took legal action and he was also struck off by the Law Society. D was entitled to receive a share of partnership profits. Instead of paying their former partner most of this sum the firm deducted the amount it was owed plus legal costs. D did not include any of the amounts retained on his tax return. Following an enquiry HMRC amended his self-assessment to tax the full amount of his trading profits. D's appeal was rejected by the First-tier Tribunal on the basis that he was entitled to the money regardless of whether he had actually received it. **[10.101]**

1 The sum must be derived from the trade

If the payment is in return for services or goods it is a trading receipt, whereas if it is made voluntarily in recognition of some personal quality of the taxpayer it is not (compare this with the rules for employment income at **[8.61]**). In *Murray v Goodhews* (1976), for instance, Watneys brewery took back tied tenancies (mainly pubs) from their tenant traders as they fell vacant and made *ex gratia* lump sum payments to the traders which were held not to be trading receipts; they were paid voluntarily by Watneys to acknowledge the good relationship with the traders and to maintain their good name. (As to whether the payments were deductible expenditure of the payer, see **[10.131]**.) By contrast, in *McGowan v Brown and Cousins* (1977) the taxpayer, an estate agent, found sites for a company for which he was paid a low fee because it was expected that he would handle the subsequent lettings for the company. The company, however, found another agent to do the letting and 'paid off' the taxpayer with £2,500. This was held to be a trading receipt: it was a reward for services even though paid in pursuance of a moral rather than a legal obligation.

In *Higgs v Olivier* (1952) Laurence Olivier was paid £15,000 by a film company not to appear in any other film for a period of 18 months.

The amount was held not to be a receipt of his profession but compensation for not exercising that profession and it therefore escaped tax. Such a receipt would now be taxed as income from an employment under the payment for restrictive undertakings provisions in ITEPA 2003 ss 225–226 (see [8.133]). In other cases, individuals have contended that they are employed rather than self-employed and in receipt of trading income. In *Matthews v R & C Comrs (and related appeals)* (2012), two entertainers working on cruise ships claimed that they should be treated as employees. The Upper Tribunal upheld the decision of the First-tier Tribunal that they were self-employed. Similar decisions were reached in *T Coffey (t/a Coffey Builders) v R & C Comrs* (2012), where a builder refurbishing a doctor's clinic claimed to be an employee of the doctor rather than self-employed, and *LC Meynell-Smith v R & C Comrs* (2013) where the First-tier Tribunal rejected the appellant's claim that he was employed as a toolmaker in a car plant.

A receipt which is not in return for services or goods may nevertheless be a trading receipt if it is intended to be used in the taxpayer's business. Thus, in *Poulter v Gayjon Processes Ltd* (1985), a Government subsidy paid to encourage a shoe manufacturer to retain persons in employment was held to be a taxable trading receipt (see also *Ryan v Crabtree Denims Ltd* (1987)). In *Donald Fisher (Ealing) Ltd v Spencer* (1989), compensation paid by an agent whose negligence had resulted in the taxpayer becoming liable to pay substantially increased rent on its business premises was held to be a trading receipt. In the course of his judgment, subsequently upheld in the Court of Appeal, Walton J stated that:

> 'If compensation is received which is in substance payable in respect of either the non-receipt of what ought to have been received or the extra expense which would not have been incurred if all had gone properly, it seems to me that the principle is exactly the same.'

Substantial repayments of incorrectly paid VAT and statutory interest received by four companies who acted as the representative members of large retail groups were held to be trading receipts by the Supreme Court, upholding the decision of the Court of Appeal. The courts took a broad interpretation of the legislation and held that the sums in question arose from the carrying on of the discontinued trades of the companies that had made the overpayments and as such were taxable trading receipts: *Shop Direct Group v R & C Comrs* (2016). EU law arguments, which had not been put forward in the *Shop Direct* case, were considered and dismissed by the First-tier Tribunal in *Coin-a-Drink v R & C Comrs* (2015), a decision which was upheld by the Upper Tribunal (2017). [10.102]

2 The sum must be income not capital

The difficulty of determining whether payments are income receipts or capital receipts was forcibly expressed by Greene MR in *IRC v British Salmson Aero Engines Ltd* (1938):

> '... in many cases it is almost true to say that the spin of a coin would decide the matter almost as satisfactorily as an attempt to find reasons'.

A number of tests have been suggested. The classic test is the distinction between a sale of the fixed capital of the business and of its circulating capital. Sale of the circulating capital produces income receipts. The defect with this test is that the classification of the asset (is it fixed or circulating?) depends upon the particular trade.

EXAMPLE 10.3

(1) Ziggy, a bookseller, owns a bookshop in Bristol. The books are his circulating capital (his stock in trade) so that the sale proceeds are trade receipts. The shop premises represent his fixed capital, the sale of which would give rise to a CGT liability.

(2) Yvonne buys vacant premises in Bristol which she renovates and sells as shops. She is trading in the sale of shops that are her circulating capital so that the receipts are income receipts.

Other tests are but variations on the original theme and contain the same defect. For example, whether or not the expenditure brings into existence an enduring asset for the benefit of the trade (see **[10.76]**), and the 'trees and fruit' test (the tree is the capital producing the fruit which is income).

The case law is considerable and characterised by subtle distinctions. Many involve compensation receipts where the question is whether the receipt is for the loss of a permanent asset (capital), or is in lieu of trading profits (income) (see also *Tapemaze Ltd v Melluish* (2000)). In *London and Thames Haven Oil Wharves Ltd v Attwooll* (1967), the taxpayer owned jetties used by oil tankers. A tanker crashed into and badly damaged a jetty. The taxpayer received compensation of £100,000, £80,000 to rebuild the jetty (capital) and £20,000 to compensate him for lost tanker fees (income).

In *Lang v Rice* (1984) the taxpayer ran two clubs in Belfast until they were destroyed by bombings. He did not resume trading thereafter and received compensation from the Northern Ireland Office for 'consequential loss'. The then Revenue argued that the payment was a once and for all capital payment to compensate the taxpayer for the permanent loss of his business. The Northern Ireland Court of Appeal held that the payment was designed to compensate the taxpayer for loss of profit during the period that would elapse before business could be resumed. Accordingly, the fact that business did not recommence had no effect on the nature of the payment. An air of some unreality pervades this decision since, as the premises had been totally destroyed and the taxpayer held only a short lease, there was never any question of the business being resumed.

A more representative case is *Able (UK) Ltd v R & C Comrs* (2008). A water company (N) made a compulsory purchase of land owned by an unrelated company (L). N subsequently vacated the site and the compulsory purchase order was rescinded. L was awarded £2,185,000 in compensation by the Lands Tribunal which it treated as a capital receipt. The tax authorities subsequently assessed the sum as income and this treatment was upheld on appeal by the General Commissioners, the High Court and Court of Appeal on the basis that the interruption to L's use of its land was only temporary. In *J Lints v R & C Comrs* (2012) a solicitor whose office premises were on the route of the Edinburgh Tramway received compensation of £4,000 for possible disruption during its construction. HMRC ruled that the sum was a trading receipt and this was upheld by the First-tier Tribunal on the basis that the payment was 'a surrogatum for business turnover'. **[10.103]**

The remainder of the decided cases can be considered under the following headings:

Restrictions on activity: If, as part of his trading arrangements, the taxpayer agrees to restrict his activities in return for payments made to him, the payments are trade receipts. In *Thompson v Magnesium Elektron Ltd* (1944), the taxpayers manufactured magnesium that required chlorine, a by-product of which is caustic soda. ICI agreed to supply the chlorine at below market value and paid the taxpayers a lump sum to prevent them from making their own chlorine and caustic soda, sales of which would compete with those of ICI. The sum was a taxable receipt paid as compensation for profits that the taxpayers would have made on the sale of caustic soda. In *IRC v Biggar* (1982), a payment to a farmer, under EC regulations, to compensate him for changing from milk to meat farming was a trade receipt, being compensation for lost profits. In *Countrywide Estate Agents Ltd v R & C Comrs*, the appellant received £25 million from a life insurance company in exchange for entering into an exclusivity agreement. The company treated the sum as a capital receipt. HMRC contended that the sum was a trading receipt. The First-tier Tribunal (2010) dismissed the estate agent's appeal finding that it had not disposed of a capital asset and applied the principles set out in *British Dyestuffs Corporation (Blackley) Ltd v CIR* (1924) (see **[10.108]**). Their decision was confirmed by the Upper Tribunal (2011), where Sales J held that the payment was 'income earned by the appellant from use of its goodwill, not a capital sum received by it in return for giving up any part of its goodwill'. **[10.104]**

Sterilisation of an asset: A payment for the permanent restriction on the use of an asset is capital even though the sum is computed by reference to loss of profits. In *Glenboig Union Fireclay Co Ltd v IRC* (1922), fireclay manufacturers who received compensation for the permanent loss of their right to work fireclay under neighbouring land were held to have received a capital sum. If the compensation is for the temporary loss of an asset, however, it is a trade receipt. Hence, in *Burmah Steamship Co Ltd v IRC* (1931), repairers of a vessel over-ran the contractual date for completion of the work and paid compensation for the lost profits of the owners. The payments were trade receipts. **[10.105]**

Cancellation of a business contract or connection: When a taxpayer receives compensation for the cancellation of a contract, the nature of the receipt depends upon the significance of the cancelled contract to the business. If it relates to the whole structure of the profit making apparatus, the compensation is capital. Thus in *Van den Berghs Ltd v Clark* (1935) a Dutch and an English company (both manufacturing margarine) had contracted to trade in different areas so as to avoid competition. The Dutch company cancelled the contract, which had 13 years to run, and paid £450,000 in compensation. It was held to be a capital receipt because the contract had provided the means whereby profits were produced; the English company had lost the equivalent of a fixed asset of the business (see also *Whitehead v Tubbs Elastics Ltd* (1984)).

However, if the contract is merely one of many and of short duration, the compensation received is income. In *Kelsall Parsons & Co v IRC* (1938) the taxpayer was a manufacturers' agent who had contracts with different manufacturers and received commission on a sale of their products. One such contract was terminated a year early and the manufacturer paid £15,000 compensation. It was held to be a trade receipt. The contract was the source of profits and the compensation equalled the estimated profit that the taxpayer would have made. Likewise in *Rolfe v Nagel* (1982) a payment to compensate a diamond broker for a client transferring his business elsewhere was taxable as a payment in lieu of profits. **[10.106]**

Deposits and advances: Sums are often received from customers as deposits to be used later in part payment towards the price of goods supplied. If they can be forfeited, because of the customer's failure to take delivery of the goods, they are trade receipts in the year of payment (*Elson v Price's Tailors Ltd* (1962)). If at the time of receipt, a deposit is not a trade receipt, it does not later become one by appropriation, unless its nature has been changed by statute. Thus in *Morley v Tattersall* (1938), deposits taken by auctioneers remained clients' money and were not trading receipts even though unclaimed and appropriated by the auctioneers. See also *Anise Ltd v Hammond* (2003) where unclaimed overpayments written off to the profit and loss account were not taxable receipts; they were not received as part of the trading activities before they were written off and writing them off did not make them taxable. In *Total Mauritius Ltd v Mauritius Revenue Authority* (2011) the Privy Council held that deposits paid by customers for lpg gas bottles were not trading receipts. The sums paid belonged to the customers and although the company had the use of the deposits they would ultimately be repaid without reduction. Contrast *Jays the Jewellers Ltd v IRC* (1947) where pawnbrokers' pledges, although originally customers' money, became trading receipts when rendered irrecoverable by statute. In *Pertemps Recruitment Partnership Ltd v R & C Comrs* (2011) some of the customers of a recruitment agency made overpayments which were not always refunded to them. Initially the agency included the overpayments as trading receipts but they later claimed error and mistake relief on the basis of the decision in *Morley v Tattersall*. The Upper Tribunal distinguishing *Morley v Tattersall* (on the basis that the deposits in that case were held in a fiduciary capacity) and disapproving of aspects of *Anise v Hammond*, held that the agency was legally entitled to receive and keep the mistaken overpayments until such time as the customers claimed repayment. As such the overpayments were trading receipts. **[10.107]**

Where a trader disposes of know-how but continues to trade, any receipt is a trading receipt (ITTOIA 2005 ss 193–194; CTA 2009 ss 176–179 and ss 907–910), but where he disposes of know-how as one of the assets of his business which he is selling as an entity, it is treated as a sale of goodwill. In the latter case liability will be to CGT, unless the trader elects to treat the sum as a trading receipt. Any sum received as consideration for a restriction on the vendor's freedom of activity (following a sale of know-how) is treated as a payment for know-how (ITTOIA 2005 s 192; CTA 2009 s 176(3)–(4) and ss 908(1)–(2)). These provisions only apply to GAAP accounts and not where cash accounts (see [**10.73**]) are prepared (ITTOIA 2005 s 191A).

In *British Dyestuffs Corporation (Blackley) Ltd v CIR* (1924), a UK company agreed to exchange information on patents and secret processes with an American company in return for a payment of £25,000 a year for 10 years. The Revenue assessed the sums as trading profits. The company contended that they were instalments of a capital sum for the disposal of an asset. Upholding the decision of the Special Commissioners, the Court of Appeal confirmed that the income was a series of trading receipts. A similar decision was reached in *XX v R & C Comrs (and related appeals)* (2010). In that case, X invented a specialist item which he licensed to a company of which he was the managing director and his wife was the controlling shareholder. The company then sold the product to the US Government Department of Defence. X was paid sums described as 'license fees'. The First-tier Tribunal held that since the beneficial ownership of all the intellectual property rights remained with X as the inventor, the fees were taxable on him as trading income. [**10.108**]

A debt owed by the trader which has been deducted as a trade expense and later released, becomes a trade receipt in the year of its release (ITTOIA 2005 s 97; CTA 2009 s 94). HMRC's view is that the writing back of a trade debt in the accounts will be treated as a trading receipt of the year in which it is recognised as such in the accounts whether it is formally released or not (BIM 40265). ITTOIA 2005 s 97 and CTA 2009 s 94 do not apply to debts released as part of a statutory insolvency arrangement (ie such debts are *not* treated as receipts of the debtor's trade; see BIM 42701).

EXAMPLE 10.4

Bob, a greengrocer, obtains lettuces from his brother Bart who runs a market garden. In 2013–14 he incurs debts of £50,000 to Bart which is a trading expense. In 2017–18 Bart agrees to forgo the debt because of the critical state of Bob's business; £50,000 will be a trading receipt in Bob's 2017–18 accounts. [**10.109**]

V STOCK AND WORK IN PROGRESS

The calculation of trading income in accordance with GAAP requires adjustments to be made for stock and work-in-progress except when the accounts are prepared on a cash basis (see [**10.73**]). See *Leslie Smith v R & C Comrs* (2011) at [**10.63**] for the consequences of not including work-in-progress in trading accounts. [**10.110**]

1 Trading stock

a) *Why value stock?*

Taxpayers must value their unsold stock at the end of the accounting period, otherwise the business could spend all its receipts on the purchase of new stock, thereby increasing its deductible expenses and reducing the taxable profits to nil. The same principle applies to work-in-progress.

EXAMPLE 10.5

In year 1 Zac, a trader, buys 100,000 units of stock at £1 each. During the year he sells 50,000 units at £2 each.

Stock not valued	£
Receipts (sales)	100,000
Less: Expenses (purchases)	100,000
Result	£Nil

The trader appears to have made no profit whereas, in fact, his profit is £50,000. At the end of the accounting year, the cost of his unsold (closing) stock must be deducted from the cost of his total purchases. Hence, the profit becomes:

Stock valued	£	£
Sales		100,000
Purchases	100,000	
Less: closing stock	50,000	
Cost of sales		50,000
Profit		£50,000

At the start of the next accounting period the stock-in-hand (opening stock) must be entered into the accounts for that year at the same figure (ie £50,000 from *Example 10.5*). **[10.111]**

EXAMPLE 10.6

Continuing *Example 10.5*, in year 2, Zac has opening stock of 50,000 units at a cost of £1 each. His purchases during the year are 150,000 units of stock at £1 each and he sells 100,000 units at £2 each.

	£	£
Sales		200,000
Opening stock	50,000	
Purchases	150,000	
Less: closing stock	(100,000)	
Cost of sales		100,000
Profit		£100,000

b) *Method of stock valuation*

The method of stock and inventory valuation is not provided for in statute except on a discontinuance of the trade (see **[10.114]**). FRS 102 Section 13 provides for each item of unsold stock to be valued at the lower of its cost price and market value (see **[10.64]**). This principle was originally established in *IRC v Cock Russell & Co Ltd* (1949) and, in effect, allows losses but not profits to be anticipated, ie the trader can apply 'cost' to items that have increased in value and 'market value' to items that have fallen in value. Cost is the original acquisition price. This should include not only the cost of materials and direct labour but the costs of conversion and the fixed production overheads incurred in bringing the stock to its present location and condition (FRS 102 Section 13.11) and *Duple Motor Bodies v Ostime* (1961). Costs excluded from inventories are: abnormal wastage, storage unless this is necessary during the production process, administrative overheads that do not contribute to bringing the items to their present location and condition and selling costs. Market value means the best price obtainable in the market in which the trader sells – for instance, a retailer in the retail and a wholesaler in the wholesale market (*BSC Footwear v Ridgway* (1972)).

Where the price of stock has altered during the accounting period it is necessary to identify which stock is left. There are a number of methods of valuing stock including: the trader treats the stock sold as the stock first bought (first in first out, ie FIFO); the opposite, last in first out (LIFO) which is not acceptable under FRS 102, and weighted average. Standard costing, the retail method and the most recent purchase price can be used in the calculation if they approximate to cost. Special rules apply to biological assets related to agricultural activities and to financial instruments. **[10.112]**

2 Work-in-progress

The basis of valuing work-in-progress is not provided for in statute except when a trade is discontinued (see **[10.114]**). Long-term contracts (for example construction contracts) are valued in accordance with FRS 102, Section 23. This provides for income to be recorded in the accounts as the contract progresses and means that where the outcome of a contract can be predicted with reasonable certainty, some of the profit on the contract will be included in the accounts before the contract is completed.

All businesses including service providers and professionals such as solicitors and accountants must include the value of their ongoing unbilled work in their accounts as income unless they are eligible for cash accounting; see **[10.73]**. Special rules apply to insurance contracts. The valuation must be based on the proportion of the work completed at the accounting date in a similar way to the valuation of work-in-progress for long-term construction contracts. This means that an appropriate part of the profit on the contract will be included as it progresses rather than at the end when the work is billed (FRS 102, Section 23.14). **[10.113]**

3 Valuation on a discontinuance

On discontinuance of a trade (which includes a deemed discontinuance under CTA 2009 s 41) the rule in *IRC v Cock Russell* does not apply and trading stock unsold must be entered into the final GAAP accounts at the amount realised on its sale or transfer or at market value (ITTOIA 2005 ss 173–181; CTA 2009 ss 162–171 and *Moore v R J Mackenzie & Sons Ltd* (1972)). A similar rule applies to work-in-progress (ITTOIA 2005 ss 182–186; CTA 2009 s 163(3)). Where the transfer pricing rules apply (see [10.116]), a business ceasing to trade after 8 July 2015 may have to make a further adjustment to its accounts to ensure that the full value of the stock is accounted for (ITTOIA 2005 s 173(2A)–(2C); CTA 2009 s 162(2A)–(2C)). Where a business uses cash accounting (see [10.73]), the value of any stock or work-in-progress on cessation must be accounted for as a trading receipt in the final accounts valued on a just and reasonable basis (ITTOIA 2005 ss 97A–97B). These provisions are designed to prevent tax avoidance by the taxpayer discontinuing his business, entering his unsold stock or work-in-progress at cost in the final accounts and then selling it privately at a tax-free profit.

Where the stock is sold to another UK trader for valuable consideration so that it will appear in his accounts for tax purposes anyway, tax could be avoided by a manipulation of the price. Typically where the parties are connected an undervalue might be agreed in order to ensure a loss for the vendor which could be relieved against past profits of his business. Alternatively the sale could be at overvalue in order to absorb losses of the vendor and, in effect, to pass losses to the purchaser. At the very least, it could be used as a way of deferring the tax liability into the next accounting period. ITTOIA 2005 s 177 and s 184; CTA 2009 ss 166–168 provide that disposals between connected persons (as defined in ITA 2007 s 993; CTA 2010 s 1122) will be taken to be for the amount which would have been realised if the sale had been at arm's length. This 'arm's length rule' can be excluded by joint election of the parties if the arm's length value exceeds both (a) the actual price paid, and (b) the acquisition value of the stock. If an election is made arm's length value will be replaced by the greater of (a) and (b). [10.114]

EXAMPLE 10.7

Aldred ceases trading and sells his stock of women's shoes to his great rival Bertrum and his stock of men's shoes to his son Caldo. Both Bertrum and Caldo carry on business in the UK and so far as the sale to Bertrum (an unconnected person) is concerned, the actual sale price will be taken. The arm's length rule will apply to the Caldo sale unless that produces a figure that is higher than both the actual sale price and Aldred's acquisition costs in which case the joint election referred to above may be made.

4 Gifts and dispositions for less than market value

A trader has no duty to make the maximum profit and normally tax is assessed according to the actual sum received on a disposal of his stock (including any non-monetary consideration (see [10.101])). There are, however, certain exceptions to this rule. [10.115]

a) *Transfer pricing*

The Taxation (International and Other Provisions) Act (TIOPA) 2010 ss 146–217 prevents certain related companies, including multi-nationals and partnerships, from obtaining a tax advantage by trading with each other. The transfer pricing rules apply to all transactions – cross-border and domestic.

There is, however, a let-out for many small and medium-sized enterprises and some dormant companies (based on the EU definition). **[10.116]**

b) *The market value rule*

If an item of trading stock is disposed of otherwise than in the ordinary course of the taxpayer's trade, it must be included in GAAP accounts as a trading receipt at its market value at the date of the disposal. The market value rule originated in the case of *Sharkey v Wernher* (1956) but in relation to changes in stock occurring on or after 12 March 2008, the principle is enshrined in ITTOIA 2005 ss 172A–172F; CTA 2009 ss 156–161. In *Sharkey v Wernher* (1956) the taxpayer carried on the trade of a stud farm. She also raced horses for pleasure and she transferred five horses from the stud farm to the racing stable. The House of Lords held that the market value as opposed to the cost price of the horses at the date when they left the stud farm must be entered in the accounts of the trade as a receipt.

The market value rule in ITTOIA 2005 ss 172A–172F; CTA 2009 ss 156–161 does not apply in every case or where accounts are prepared on the cash basis (ITTOIA 2005 s 172AA). The definition of 'trading stock' specifically excludes materials used in the manufacture, preparation or construction of anything, any services performed in the ordinary course of the trade or any article produced or material used in the performance of any such services. Instead of the accounts including a trading receipt at market value, certain expenditure may be disallowed under the 'wholly and exclusively' rule (ITTOIA 2005 s 34; CTA 2009 s 54). Where services are rendered to the trader personally or to his household or meals are provided for the proprietors of hotels, pubs, restaurants and members of their families only the costs in question are disallowed. Where expenditure is incurred by a trader on the construction of an asset which is to be used as a fixed asset in the trade the costs should be disallowed as a revenue expense but may be eligible for capital allowances (BIM 33630). **[10.117]**

EXAMPLE 10.8

(1) Rex is a diamond merchant and on the occasion of his daughter's wedding he gives her a diamond which cost him £80,000 and has a market value of £110,000. As the disposal is not a trading transaction, the market value (£110,000) is a trading receipt. The result is that Rex is treated as making a taxable profit of £30,000 on the stone. There is no distinction between the trader using the goods himself and giving them away to a friend or relative: see *Petrotim Securities Ltd v Ayres* (1964).

(2) Company A sells an asset forming part of its trading stock for which it had paid £400,000 to an associated UK trading company (company B) for £200,000. The asset then had a market value of £800,000. The following points should be noted:

   (i) The transfer pricing rules are inapplicable since the purchaser company is a UK-resident trading company and there is no tax advantage (TIOPA 2010 ss 146–217). If the transfer pricing rules did apply (see **[10.116]**) they would take precedence over the market value rule (CTA 2009 s 161).

(ii) The sale will be caught by the market value rule in CTA 2009 ss 156–161 (see comments above) which applies to both gifts of trading stock and to sales at undervalue (see *Petrotim v Ayres* (1964) and also TCGA 1992 s 161).
(iii) The recipient of trading stock caught by the market value rule is treated as receiving the goods for their market value. Hence, company B is treated as having paid £800,000 (see *Ridge Securities Ltd v IRC* (1964)).
(iv) In extreme cases both the purchase and the resale may be expunged from the accounts of the trader if neither constitutes a genuine trading transaction (see the Y transaction in *Petrotim v Ayres* (1964)).

The market value rule is subject to two major qualifications. *First*, it is only appropriate when the disposal of stock is not a genuine trading transaction. So long as the disposal can be justified on commercial grounds the general principle remains that a trader is free to charge what he likes for his goods.
[10.118]

EXAMPLE 10.9

Yang runs a business selling electronic goods. In an attempt to encourage custom he gives away a smart phone (market value £200) to any customer who purchases an item costing more than £2,000. The gift is a commercial disposition and outside the scope of the market value rule. Accordingly, Yang is not required to enter the market value of the smart phone as a trading receipt. There may, however, be a VAT liability on the 'gift' (see [**38.23**]).

Second, the rule does not apply to professional persons. In *Mason v Innes* (1967), Hammond Innes, a novelist, began writing *The Doomed Oasis* in 1958 and incurred deductible travelling expenses in obtaining background material. When the manuscript was completed in 1960 he assigned it to his father in consideration of natural love and affection when it had a market value of about £15,000. Innes was taxed under Case II and rendered accounts prepared on the cash basis applicable at the time. When the then Revenue sought to tax the market value of the copyright as a receipt of his profession the Court of Appeal held that the market value rule was limited to traders and to dispositions of trading stock. In rejecting the Revenue's argument, Lord Denning MR said:

'Suppose an artist paints a picture of his mother and gives it to her. He does not receive a penny for it. Is he to pay tax on the value of it? It is unthinkable. Suppose he paints a picture which he does not like when he has finished it and destroys it. Is he liable to pay tax on the value of it? Clearly not. These instances ... show that ... *Sharkey v Wernher* does not apply to professional men.' [**10.119**]–[**10.129**]

EXAMPLE 10.10

Keen, a partner in the solicitors' firm of Keen, Lax & Muddle, purchases a house. All the conveyancing work is done by his firm free of charge. The market value rule in ITTOIA 2005 ss 172A–172F does not apply but the costs of undertaking the work may, however, not be deductible as a business expense (ITTOIA 2005 s 34).

VI DEDUCTIBLE EXPENSES

1 Basic principles

An expense will be deductible in arriving at the taxpayer's trading profits only if:
(1) It is an income and not a capital expense (ITTOIA 2005 s 33; CTA 2009 s 53) (see **[10.77]** and **[10.131]**).
(2) It is incurred wholly and exclusively for the purpose of the trade (ITTOIA 2005 s 34; CTA 2009 s 54), (see **[10.137]**).
(3) Its deduction is not prohibited by statute (see generally ITTOIA 2005 s 34; CTA 2009 s 54).

Expenses are only deductible from trading income by implication from the charging sections which impose tax on 'profits' (see **[10.61]**) and from ITTOIA 2005 Part 2 and CTA 2009 Part 3 which contain a list of prohibited deductions. These rules are more generous than under the employment income provisions in ITEPA 2003 (see **[8.171]**).

A distinction is drawn between expenses incurred in earning the profits (which may be deductible) and expenses incurred after the profits have been earned, which are not deductible. For example, the payment of income tax is an application of profit which has been earned and is, therefore, not deductible (*Ashton Gas Co v A-G* (1906)). Other taxes, such as rates and stamp duties, may be paid in the course of earning the profits and so may be deductible. **[10.130]**

2 The expense must be income not capital

a) General

Similar tests are applied for classifying expenditure as income or capital as those for deciding whether a receipt is income or capital (see **[10.103]**). Hence, a distinction is drawn between the fixed and the circulating capital of the business. A payment is capital if it is made to bring into existence an asset for the enduring advantage of the trade (see *British Insulated and Helsby Cables v Atherton* (1926)). The asset may be intangible as in *Walker v Joint Credit Card Co Ltd* (1982) where a payment by a credit card company to preserve its goodwill was held to be a capital payment.

A once and for all payment, even though it brings no enduring asset into existence, is more likely to be of a capital nature than a recurring expense. In *Watney Combe Reid & Co Ltd v Pike* (1982), *ex gratia* payments made by Watneys brewery to tenants of tied houses to compensate them for the termination of their tenancies were held to be capital, because their purpose was to render capital assets (the premises) more valuable. In *Dhendsa v Richardson* (1997) an introductory payment paid to Post Office Counters Ltd by a new sub-postmaster was considered capital. In *G Bowman (t/a The Janitor Cleaning Co) v R & C Comrs* (2012) a payment of £11,000 described as a consultancy fee paid to an American for helping to secure a major contract was also held to be capital expenditure by the First-tier Tribunal, Judge Tildesley finding that the payment was intended to produce an enduring benefit for the business. **[10.131]**

b) *Employee payments*

These are generally deductible in computing the profits of the employer, so long as they are paid for the purposes of the business. In *Mitchell v B W Noble Ltd* (1927), a company deducted the sum of £19,500 paid to a director to induce him to resign. It was held to be in the interests of the company to get rid of him and to avoid undesirable publicity by encouraging him to 'go quietly'. For similar reasons, the House of Lords in *Lawson v Johnson Matthey plc* (1992) decided that the sum of £50m was a deductible revenue expense being paid to save its business (by removing an obstacle to successful trading). It was not, as the lower courts had concluded, a sum paid to get rid of a burdensome capital asset (which would itself have been capital).

Problems may arise when the payments in question are linked to the cessation of the business; in particular, such payments may not satisfy the 'wholly and exclusively' test (discussed below at **[10.137]**). In *O'Keeffe v Southport Printers Ltd* (1984) payments made to employees in lieu of notice were deductible by the employer since they were incurred as part of the orderly conduct of the business prior to its termination (see also on severance payments, *IRC v Cosmotron Manufacturing Co Ltd* (1997)).

No deduction is allowed for an amount charged in the accounts in respect of employees' remuneration unless it is paid no later than nine months after the end of the period of account. Remuneration paid at a later time is deductible when it is paid (ITTOIA 2005 ss 31 and 36–37; CTA 2009 ss 36–37). These provisions do not apply to cash accounts (see **[10.74]**). Where cash accounting is used, employee benefit contributions can only be deducted if paid in the accounting period (ITTOIA 2005 s 38(2A)). **[10.132]**

c) *Employee trusts*

In *Heather v PE Consulting Group* (1978) payments made by a company to a trust created in order to acquire shares in that company for the benefit of employees and to prevent outside interference in the affairs of the company were deductible expenses because, *inter alia*, they encouraged the recruitment of well-qualified staff (see also *Jeffs v Ringtons Ltd* (1985)). However, in *Mawsley Machinery Ltd v Robinson* (1998) it was held that the objective of the payment to the trust was to provide the shareholder/vendor with a means to dispose of his shareholding. It was thus a capital payment. In *MacDonald v Dextra Accessories Ltd* (2005), at the High Court, contributions made to an employee benefit trust were allowed on the grounds that they were made to motivate the company's employees. Various awards were made out of the trust to employees, some of which gave rise to tax, but others (such as loans) did not. The then Inland Revenue argued that the then applicable measures in FA 1989 s 43 prevented the deduction of the payments until such time as the employees were taxed on the amounts as emoluments. Their view was upheld in the Court of Appeal and House of Lords. In *JT Dove Ltd v R & C Comrs* (2011), the First-tier Tribunal followed the *Dextra* case in rejecting a claim for a deduction of £3 million paid to an employee benefit trust on the basis that the payment was only deductible if paid within nine months of the end of the accounting period concerned (see also **[10.132]**).

ITTOIA 2005 ss 38–44 and CTA 2009 ss 38–44 deny relief for payments to an employee benefit trust unless the employee is taxed on 'qualifying benefits' received within nine months of the accounting period: see generally [**9.123**].

Payments may be rejected where they are part of a 'highly contrived' tax avoidance scheme. Substantial payments to employee benefit trusts in favour of their controlling directors by two companies that promoted film finance schemes were rejected by the Upper Tribunal, substantially upholding the decision of the First-tier Tribunal: see *Scotts Atlantic Management Ltd v R & C Comrs (and related appeals)* (2015). [**10.133**]

d) *Restrictive covenants*

Associated Portland Cement Manufacturers Ltd v Kerr (1946) involved payments to two retiring directors in return for covenants that they would not compete with the company for the rest of their lives. The payments were held not to be deductible as they were a capital expenditure being payments to enhance the company's goodwill. Had the covenant been for a shorter period the expenditure might have been of an income nature and therefore deductible. To prevent the making of restrictive covenant payments instead of salary increases (which could result in the deduction of the payment by the employer even though it was not fully taxed in the hands of the employee), ITTOIA 2005 s 69 and CTA 2009 s 69 now provide that such payments are tax deductible by the employer and taxed in the hands of the employee where the payments are within ITEPA 2003 ss 225–226 (see [**8.133**]). [**10.134**]

e) *Capital allowances*

Capital expenditure is not generally deductible and provisions for depreciation are not allowable (ITTOIA 2005 s 33; CTA 2009 s 53). Tax relief may, however, be given in accordance with the rules governing capital allowances (see **Chapter 48**). If 100% annual investment allowances or 100% first year allowances on green technologies can be claimed, the taxable profits will be the same irrespective of whether a particular item of expenditure is of an income or of a capital nature. Where allowances on plant and machinery can only be claimed at a lower rate, the taxpayer will prefer to claim that the expense is of an income nature so that it can immediately be deducted in full.
[**10.135**]

f) *Depreciation in stock and work in progress*

Sometimes the depreciation charge in the trading and profit and loss account is reduced by capitalising part of it and including it in the balance sheet in the stock valuation. The tax treatment of the capitalised element was considered in *R & C Comrs v William Grant and Sons Distillers Ltd; Small (Inspector of Taxes) v Mars Ltd* (2007). HMRC contended that, where part of the depreciation charge is carried forward in stock, it must be added back in the tax computation as a disallowable expense, along with the depreciation charged to the profit and loss account as an expense (the gross adjustment). The cases went to the House of Lords, where they were decided in the taxpayers' favour. Their Lordships held that only the depreciation deducted in the profit and loss account (and not the part capitalised in the stock valuation) had to be added back in the tax computation (the net adjustment). The court held that there is nothing preventing depreciation being carried forward to and then deducted in a subsequent tax year provided that the profits are calculated on a true and fair basis. HMRC now require all businesses to apply these decisions. If an element of the depreciation charged in respect of fixed assets is capitalised in stock the tax computation must be adjusted for the net and not the gross depreciation, see BIM 33190. [10.136]

3 Expense must have been incurred 'wholly and exclusively' for business purposes

The courts have generally interpreted the 'wholly and exclusively' requirement strictly, so that the *sole* reason for the expenditure must be a business purpose. This test therefore denies a deduction for personal expenditure: see *PT Savarou v R & C Comrs* (2011), which concerned domestic mortgage interest, and *C Huhtala v R & C Comrs (No 2)* (2012), considering which expenses could be deducted in connection with an author's boat where he lived whilst writing about his experiences. In other circumstances costs are not deductible because the expenditure has both business and personal elements (dual purposes expenditure). This is particularly relevant where the necessities of life are involved such as food, rent, health and clothing. In *T Healy v R & C Comrs* (2015), an actor who lived in Cheshire initially succeeded at the First-tier Tribunal in his claim that a flat rented one mile from a London theatre where he was acting in a play was rented 'wholly and exclusively in connection with his profession as an actor'; however the decision was subsequently set aside by the Upper Tribunal and remitted to the First-tier Tribunal for a fresh hearing where the fact that he had rented a three bedroom flat in order to have guests to stay meant that the expenditure failed the 'wholly and exclusively' test. Had he rented a one bedroom flat, this issue would not have arisen. Where the personal element is less obvious such as event sponsorship, a tax deduction may also be denied (see [10.157]).

In *Bentleys, Stokes & Lowless v Beeson* (1952), Romer LJ explained the requirements that have to be satisfied for an expense to be deductible as follows:

> 'it is quite clear that the purpose must be the sole purpose. The paragraph says so in clear terms. If the activity be undertaken with the object both of promoting business and also with some other purpose, for example, with the object of indulging an independent wish of entertaining a friend or stranger or of supporting a charitable or benevolent object, then the paragraph is not satisfied though in the mind of the actor the business motive may predominate. For the statute so prescribes. Per contra, if, in truth, the sole object is business promotion, the expenditure is not disqualified because the nature of the activity necessarily involves some other result, or the attainment or furtherance of some other objective, since the latter result or objective is necessarily inherent in the act.'

Dual purpose expenditure is not deductible and there are numerous cases where this rule has been strictly applied. In *Caillebotte v Quinn* (1975) a self-employed carpenter worked on sites 40 miles from home. He ate lunch at a nearby café which cost him 40p per day instead of the usual 10p which it cost him at home. His claim to deduct the extra 30p per day as an expense was disallowed on the grounds that he ate to live as well as to work so that the expenditure was incurred for dual purposes. Similarly, in *Prince v Mapp* (1970) a guitarist in a pop group could not deduct the cost of an operation on his little finger because he played the guitar partly for business, but partly for pleasure. In *Mallalieu v Drummond* (1983) the House of Lords held that expenditure on clothing to be worn in court by a female barrister was not deductible. Although she only wore the clothes for business purposes and that was her sole conscious purpose when she purchased the garments, Lord Brightman concluded that 'she needed the clothes to travel to work and clothes to wear at work ... it is inescapable that one object though not a conscious motive, was the provision of the clothing that she needed as a human being'. In practice, the cost of protective clothing is deductible where the 'wholly and exclusively' test is met. In *Parsons v R & C Comrs* (2010) the First-tier Tribunal held that medical expenses for a knee injury, chiropractic and massage costs for a back injury and certain dental costs were 'wholly and exclusively' laid out for business purposes by a stunt performer working in television and film productions. In contrast his general health and fitness costs were held to be dual purpose expenditure and not tax deductible. In *Azam v R & C Comrs* (2011), a deduction for counselling expenses were claimed by the owner of a beauty salon on the basis that the costs were to help her to deal with staff issues. The First-tier Tribunal rejected the claim on the basis that the taxpayer had undertaken the counselling for a dual purpose, part of which was her own wellbeing.

The same test for deductible expenditure is applied whether the business is run as a sole trade or partnership. In *MacKinlay v Arthur Young McClelland Moores & Co* (1990) the Court of Appeal had allowed a partnership to deduct removal costs paid to encourage two partners to move house: in one case from London to Southampton, in the other from Newcastle to Bristol. In both cases the move was desirable from the point of view of the firm's business and neither partner would have agreed to move had his relocation expenses not been borne by the firm. This decision was not easy to reconcile with earlier authorities and its reversal by the House of Lords was scarcely surprising. Their Lordships restated the principles underlying the rules governing deductible expenditure and stressed that the same rules applied to individuals and to unincorporated partnerships.

The 'dual purpose' cases show that it is not possible to split a purpose: ie if the taxpayer incurs the expenditure for two purposes, one business and the other personal, none of the expenditure is deductible. It may, however, be possible to split a payment into a portion which is incurred for business purposes and a portion which is not. This approach was apparent in *Copeman v Flood* (1941) where the son and daughter of the managing director of a small private company were employed as directors at salaries of £2,600 each pa. The son was aged 24 and had some business experience; the daughter was only 17. Although both performed duties for the company, the then Revenue claimed that the entire salary was not an expense incurred by the company 'wholly and exclusively' for business purposes. Lawrence J remitted the case to the commissioners for them to decide, as a question of fact, to what extent the payments were deductible expenses of the trade. He accepted that the expenditure could be apportioned into allowable and non-allowable parts (see also *Earlspring Properties Ltd v Guest* (1994) and contrast *Abbott v IRC* (1996)). This approach is now enshrined in ITTOIA 2005 s 34(2) and CTA 2009 s 54(2) which provide that if an expense is incurred for more than one purpose a deduction can be made for any identifiable part or identifiable proportion of the expense which is incurred wholly and exclusively for the purposes of the trade. In practice, payments are regularly split in this fashion when a car is used both for business and private use and when a business is run from the taxpayer's home and he claims to deduct a proportion of the overheads of the house (alternatively a fixed rate deduction can be made for car and home costs, see [**10.161**]). If the 'wholly and exclusively' test is satisfied there is no further test – based on the expenditure being 'sufficiently connected' with the business – to be satisfied: *McKnight v Sheppard* (1997) (see [**10.146**]).

In corporate cases, the courts distinguish between costs incurred for activities that are part of the business and those that are not. In *Baker v Mabie Todd and Co Ltd* (1927), a company made loans to an associated company which proved irrecoverable. The company claimed that the irrecoverable amount was a deductible expense. The High Court rejected the claim holding that financing an associate was not part of the company's business. A similar decision was reached in *Sere Properties Ltd v R & C Comrs* (2013) where a company claimed a deduction for rent arrears owed by an associated company. In *J White v R & C Comrs* (2014) a sole trader who owned a skip-hire business claimed a deduction for bad debts allegedly owed by a company owned by his father. The First-tier Tribunal upheld HMRC's rejection of the claim on the basis that the loans had not been incurred wholly and exclusively for the purposes of the skip hire trade. Furthermore the appellant was managing the company on behalf of his father and no evidence of how the loans had been incurred was provided. [**10.137**]

4 Deduction of the expense must not be prohibited by statute

The deduction of expenses against trading income is permitted by implication. ITTOIA 2005 Part 2 and CTA 2009 Part 3 include details of non-deductible expenses and expenditure where a limited deduction is permitted. In particular, expenditure incurred for private as opposed to business purposes is non-deductible, ITTOIA 2005 s 34; CTA 2009 s 54. Dividends and distributions are expressly not tax deductible (CTA 2009 s 1305).

The deduction of business gifts and entertainment expenses is severely curtailed by ITTOIA 2005 s 45; CTA 2009 s 1298. The legislation is widely drafted although a number of exceptions are permitted (ITTOIA 2005 ss 46–47; CTA 2009 ss 1299–1300) and see *Fleming v Associated Newspapers Ltd* (1972). [**10.138**]

5 Illustrations of deductible expenditure

Expenditure on heating and lighting business premises, rates on those premises and the wages paid to employees are obvious examples of allowable expenditure. Other expenditure may be more problematic, as the examples considered below show. [**10.139**]

a) Business premises

Rent is deductible and it may be apportioned if part of the premises is used for non-business activities (ITTOIA 2005 s 34(2); CTA 2009 s 54(2)); alternatively a fixed-rate deduction can be made (see [10.164]). An individual's private house may, of course, be used in part for business purposes and a portion of the overheads may be claimed as allowable expenditure, with the option of a standard deduction applying instead (see [10.163]). So long as no part of the house is used exclusively for business purposes the full CGT main residence exemption will still be available.

When the taxpayer pays a premium in return for the grant of a lease, a portion of the premium (corresponding to the portion that is taxed under the property income provisions of ITTOIA 2005 Part 3 or CTA 2009 Part 4 in the case of companies; see [12.85]) may be deducted as an expense (ITTOIA 2005 ss 60–67; CTA 2009 ss 62–65).   [10.140]

b) Sale and leaseback arrangements

Specific provisions were enacted to deal with the problems caused by sale and leaseback, and surrender and leaseback arrangements. The attraction of such schemes stemmed from booming land values which encouraged the owner of the land (or of an interest therein) to sell (or surrender) it, thereby realising a capital sum, and immediately to take a leaseback of the same property. CTA 2010 ss 834–886 prohibit the deduction of rent in excess of a commercial level and in certain circumstances CTA 2010 s 850 imposes a tax charge on a capital sum received in return for surrendering a lease which has less than 50 years to run, when a leaseback for a term not exceeding 15 years is taken.   [10.141]

c) Repairs and improvements

Sums expended on the repair of business assets are deductible. Replacing part of a worn-out asset is a repair but replacing the whole asset is capital expenditure. In each case it is necessary to determine whether the work has affected the 'entirety' of the asset (BIM 46910). Repair work often involves new materials or technology. These do not necessarily render the repair costs disallowable provided that the asset as a whole has not been improved. The question to ask is does the asset do the same job as it did before the expenditure was incurred? In *G Pratt and Sons v R & C Comrs* (2011) the First-tier Tribunal held that the cost of resurfacing a farm driveway was a revenue expense and therefore deductible. In *Hopegar Properties Ltd v R & C Comrs* (2013), the First-tier Tribunal allowed expenditure on resurfacing a carriageway on an industrial estate, resiting a car park, diverting cabling and reinstating a footpath as revenue expenditure. The cost of replacing grass in a caravan park with a hard surface was treated as a revenue deduction by the First-tier Tribunal on the basis that the new surface had not enhanced the park, had less visual appeal and had generated customer complaints, see *Cairnsmill Caravan Park v R & C Comrs* (2013).

Provisions for future repairs are not deductible unless they comply with FRS 102, Section 21 (see [10.67]). The case of *Jenners Princes Street (Edinburgh) v IRC* (1998) which considered this point no longer applies.

The cost of improvement, alteration or reconstruction of an asset is not allowable as a revenue deduction being capital expenditure (ITTOIA 2005 s 33; CTA 2009 s 53). The borderline between repairs on the one hand and capital expenditure on the other is a difficult factual question which depends upon the nature of the asset and the importance of the work in relation to it (see *Lurcott v Wakely and Wheeler* (1911) on the duty to repair and *O'Grady v Markham Main Colliery Ltd* (1932)). A repair is generally considered to be restoration of an asset by renewal or the replacement of parts. Renewal or improvement on the other hand refers to reconstruction, not necessarily of the whole asset but substantially all of it. In *Moonlight Textiles Ltd v R & C Comrs* (2010), the First-tier Tribunal rejected the company's claim to deduct the cost of substantial alterations and improvements to its business premises as a repair. A claim to deduct expenditure on repairs and improvements to a property later transferred to its controlling director as a bonus were similarly rejected as capital costs, see *Lion Co v R & C Comrs* (2009).

The cost incurred on initial repairs carried out to a business asset may also cause difficulties. In *Law Shipping Co Ltd v IRC* (1924), a vessel purchased for £97,000 was in such a state of disrepair that a further £51,000 had to be spent before it could obtain its Lloyd's Certificate. The Court of Session disallowed most of the subsequent expenditure; as Lord Cullen stated:

'It is in substance the equivalent of an addition to the price. If the ship had not been in need of the repairs in question when bought, the appellants would have had to pay a correspondingly larger price.'

By way of contrast, in *Odeon Associated Theatres Ltd v Jones* (1972) subsequent repair work on a cinema, which had been purchased in a run-down condition after the war, was allowed. There are three points of distinction from the *Law Shipping* case: *first*, the cinema was a profit-earning asset when purchased despite its disrepair; *second*, the purchase price was not reduced because of that disrepair; and *third*, the Court of Appeal accepted that the expenses were deductible in accordance with the principles of proper commercial accounting.

No deduction is allowed for expenditure on integral features in a building or structure coming within CAA 2001 s 33A(3) (ITTOIA 2005 s 55A; CTA 2009 s 60).

EXAMPLE 10.11

XYZ Ltd trades as a tile warehouse from premises that consist of a showroom, warehouse and office. The company contracts to modernise the property. The leaky roof is replaced and the office painted and refurbished. The showroom is extended by demolishing an interior wall and a new false ceiling is installed. Which costs are revenue and which are capital?
(1) The new roof is a repair as it simply returns the roof to its original condition.
(2) The refurbishment and redecoration of the office is also a repair.
(3) The showroom is now extended and of a higher standard. This work improves and alters the building and is capital expenditure. **[10.142]**

d) Pre-trading expenditure

Under ITTOIA 2005 s 57 and CTA 2009 s 61 revenue expenditure incurred in the seven years before a trade, profession or vocation commences is treated as incurred on the day on which the business commences (see also BIM 46351).

[10.143]

e) Bad and doubtful debts and impairment losses

For income tax purposes debts are deducted from accounts prepared in accordance with GAAP when they are bad, estimated to be bad or the debt is released wholly and exclusively for the purposes of the trade as part of a statutory insolvency arrangement (ITTOIA 2005 s 35). If the debt is later paid it is treated as a trading receipt for that later year. Where the debtor is bankrupt or insolvent the release of a trade debt is fully deductible by the creditor (except for any amount reasonably expected to be received from the insolvency) and does not give rise to a taxable receipt in the hands of the debtor. In the case of cash accounts income is accounted for when it is received so there is no need to write off bad debts (ITTOIA 2005 s 32A), (see [10.73]). For corporation tax purposes no deduction is allowed in respect of a debt owed to the company that does not come within the loan relationship regime as a derivative contract or an intangible fixed asset except for impairment losses (CTA 2009 s 55). Tax relief is also due to the extent that a debt is released wholly and exclusively for the purposes of the trade as part of a statutory insolvency arrangement. [10.144]

f) Damages, fines and losses

The issue of whether damages, fines and losses incurred in the course of a trade are tax deductible is complex. The case law illustrates some of the difficulties.

In *Strong & Co of Romsey Ltd v Woodifield* (1906) damages paid to an hotel guest injured by the fall of a chimney from the building were not deductible. Lord Loreburn, somewhat unsympathetically, observed that 'the loss sustained by the appellants ... fell upon them in their character not of traders but of householders' whilst Lord Davey rejected the claim because 'the expense must be incurred for the purpose of earning the profits'. Had the guest suffered food poisoning from the hotel restaurant any compensation would have been deductible! In practice, the *Strong v Woodifield* case will be avoided by the trader carrying insurance to cover compensation claims; further, the premiums that he pays for such insurance will be deductible.

Most fines are not allowable as deductions against trading income. A fine of £32 million imposed by the FIA (the governing body of Formula 1 motor racing) for breaking the rules of its International Sporting Code was unusually held to be tax deductible by a single casting vote in the First-tier Tribunal but the decision was reversed in the Upper Tribunal (*McLaren Racing Ltd v R & C Comrs* (2014)).

Theft by employees causes particular difficulties. Petty theft by subordinates, so that money never finds its way into the till, will result in reduced profits for tax purposes, but defalcations by directors will not be similarly allowable (*Curtis v Oldfield* (1933); *Bamford v ATA Advertising* (1972)). [10.145]

g) *Legal costs*

Where individuals are concerned, the availability of a deduction for legal costs depends on whether they were incurred in a business or personal capacity. In *MA and Mrs BC Raynor v R & C Comrs* (2011), a husband and wife partnership traded as haulage contractors. The husband was convicted of polluting a river with insecticide causing the death of fish. The partnership claimed a deduction for the costs of defending the criminal proceedings. This was rejected by the First-tier Tribunal on the basis that the prosecution had been against the husband as an individual and his defence costs were incurred for personal as well as business reasons. A similar outcome was reached in *Duckmanton v R & C Comrs* (2013). D, a sole-trader, operated a vehicle transport business and one of his lorries killed a pedestrian. D was charged with, and acquitted of, manslaughter but convicted of attempting to pervert the course of justice. He claimed a deduction for his legal costs. This was rejected by the First-tier Tribunal and upheld by the Upper Tribunal on the basis that the costs were incurred primarily to protect D's liberty and personal reputation. In *P McMahon v R & C Comrs* (2013) an employee became self-employed and incurred expenditure to settle a claim by his former employer that he had breached an undertaking not to canvass any contacts made whilst he was an employee. The First-tier Tribunal denied the appellant's claim to deduct the legal costs on the basis that the expense arose partly out of his employment contract and not wholly as a result of the trade.

In a corporate context the question is whether the legal costs are incurred wholly and exclusively for the purposes of the trade. In *Purolite International Ltd v R & C Comrs* (2012), the company made a contribution of over £3.8 million towards legal costs incurred by its Delaware parent company in unsuccessfully defending proceedings that the group had traded illegally with Cuba. The First-tier Tribunal held that the legal costs were not tax deductible as they had not been incurred wholly and exclusively for the purposes of the company's trade.

If the legal costs are incurred to protect a business or its reputation, the costs are deductible because they are expended for the purposes of the trade. This was the case in *McKnight v Sheppard* (1997) where the House of Lords held that legal expenses incurred at disciplinary hearings involving the taxpayer, a stockbroker, were deductible. In contrast where costs are incurred personally they are not incurred wholly and exclusively for the trade and are therefore not tax deductible. In *Vaines v R & C Comrs* (2016) the First-tier Tribunal initially allowed a solicitor to deduct a payment to a German bank in full settlement of all claims against him as a revenue expense on the basis that the payment was made to protect his professional career by preventing him becoming bankrupt. The decision was reversed by the Upper Tribunal, which found that the payment had been made personally and not by the law firm in which V was a partner. The fact that the law firm had lent V the money indicated that they took no responsibility for the settlement and furthermore V had not discussed the payment with the other members of the firm.

In *Linslade Post Office and General Store v R & C Comrs* (2012), the First-tier Tribunal held that legal costs incurred in defending the assets of the business from a claim by an outsider (the partners' sister) were deductible. Money spent trying to preserve a trade from destruction would thus appear to satisfy the wholly and exclusively rule irrespective of whether the case was successful. Legal expenses were also held to be deductible in *Key IP Ltd v R & C Comrs* (2011). This case involved allegations of e-mail defamation between the Board members of two companies. The dispute was settled in court under an agreement in which each side paid their own costs. The legal costs were held to be allowable by the First-tier Tribunal on the basis that the case had been brought to protect K's business reputation and not because of personal hurt. **[10.146]**

h) *Tax and accounting costs*

The professional costs involved in drawing up a trader's commercial accounts and other accountancy services are tax deductible, but the costs of computing and agreeing the tax liability on those profits are not (BIM 46450). However, there is a longstanding practice of allowing such costs to be deducted in order to avoid the difficulty of apportioning the fees (see *Smith's Potato Estates Ltd v Bolland* (1948)). The cost of completing a personal tax return is not deductible. Fees incurred in connection with compliance checks and enquiries are not deductible where the enquiry reveals discrepancies and additional tax liabilities arising from negligence or fraud, or careless or deliberate behaviour. Where no addition to profits results from the enquiry and there is no negligence, fraud or careless or deliberate conduct, additional accountancy expenses are tax deductible (EM 3981). **[10.147]**

i) *Work training and outplacement counselling*

The costs of training an employee in skills relating to present or future duties of his job are deductible. In addition, the costs of retraining an employee or former employee for a new job with another employer (or for self-employment) are in certain circumstances deductible (see further **[8.164]**: ITTOIA 2005 s 74; CTA 2009 s 74). Training costs incurred in the course of a trade are deductible in computing profits, provided the costs are incurred wholly and exclusively for the purposes of the trade or profession (ITTOIA 2005 s 34; CTA 2009 s 54). The provision of outplacement counselling services to employees who are made redundant is not a taxable benefit for that employee and the costs are deductible by the employer (ITTOIA 2005 s 73; CTA 2009 s 73 and BIM 47217). **[10.148]**

j) *Expenditure involving crime and security*

A payment (such as a bribe), which involves the commission of a crime in the UK (or which if paid overseas would amount to a crime if it were paid in the UK), is not deductible. Nor is a payment made as a result of blackmail (such as a payment made under duress to terrorist groups): ITTOIA 2005 s 55; CTA 2009 s 1304.

If an individual or partner experiences a special threat to their physical security as a result of the particular trade in which they are engaged a deduction is given for certain services and assets designed to improve their safety (ITTOIA 2005 s 81). **[10.149]**

k) *Travelling expenses*

Case law establishes two general propositions. *First*, that the cost of travelling *to the place of business* is not deductible; *second*, that the cost of travelling *in the course of the business* is deductible. The leading authority on this important issue is *Horton v Young* (1971), in which case a labour-only sub-contractor who operated from his home was entitled to deduct expenses incurred in collecting his team of bricklayers and travelling to the building site. As Salmon LJ put it:

> 'Since *[his home]* was his business base and the place where his chief, and indeed only, customers knew that he was always to be found, it would be understandable that exclusively for the purposes of his business he would think it right to return to his base at night from any site on which he was working during the day.'

This approach was followed in *P Mellor v R & C Comrs* (2011), in which case a self-employed electrician who worked for various building contractors was also allowed to deduct the cost of driving from his home to the sites where he worked. The First-tier Tribunal found that the taxpayer could not have coordinated his business activities without having somewhere to receive the electrical drawings which allowed him to make quotes (see also *A Kenyon v R & C Comrs* (2011), where travelling but not subsistence expenses were allowed for a self-employed pipe fitter and *S Reed v R & C Comrs* (2011), where both travel and subsistence expenses were deductible by a scaffolder).

In contrast, a milkman was not allowed to deduct the cost of travelling between his home and the depot from which he collected his supplies (*Jackman v Powell* (2004)), and in *M Manders v R & C Comrs* (2010) a claim by a market trader to deduct the cost of travel between his home and market stall was rejected. It was held that the market stall was the main place of business in spite of the taxpayer's contention that his place of business was where he kept his stock and trailer (an industrial site four miles from his home). In *TD Hamlin v R & C Comrs* (2011) the First-tier Tribunal denied travel and subsistence claims for a self-employed subcontractor who lived in Coventry but worked for a single contractor in Kent, distinguishing *Horton v Young* on the basis that the appellant had been working in one place for several years rather than working for several different clients.

Horton v Young was also distinguished in *Dr S Samadian v R & C Comrs* (2014). Dr Samadian worked full-time as an employee for the NHS at two hospitals in London where he had a permanent NHS office. He also looked after private patients as a self-employed consultant at two private hospitals where he held weekly out-patient sessions, and had a dedicated office in his home for his professional activity. He claimed expenses for travelling between the NHS hospitals and the private hospitals, and between his home and the private hospitals. The Upper Tribunal upheld the decision of the First-tier Tribunal which regarded the journeys between the NHS hospitals and the private hospitals as non-deductible on the grounds that 'the object of the travel is to put the appellant into a position where he can carry on his business away from his place of employment; the travel is not an integral part of the business itself'.

Further, and most importantly, the First-tier Tribunal concluded that this case differed from *Horton v Young* in that Dr Samadian had places of business other than in his home, namely, at the two private hospitals. The Tribunal accepted that Dr Samadian's home office was necessary for his professional activity but took the view that *Horton v Young* is good authority only for the limited proposition that a taxpayer who can establish that he has no place of business other than his home can generally claim a deduction for business-related travel between his home and other places attended from time to time for the purposes of his business.

Accordingly, since there must have been a 'mixed object' in travelling between his home and the private hospitals, because part of the object of the journeys must 'inescapably' have been to maintain a home in a separate location, his claim failed. In the Upper Tribunal the mixed motive was emphasised; the journeys between the taxpayer's home and the private hospitals were partly to conduct his private practice and partly to enable him to maintain his home at a location of choice. This decision has had an impact on many self-employed professions where there is a home office and another business base from which they operate on a regular basis; see *David Jones v R & C Comrs* (2015) where a similar decision was reached in the case of an anaesthetist. In *Dr Sharat Jain v R & C Comrs* (2015) minor differences in the way that another hospital consultant conducted his work were held not to be significant and the First-tier Tribunal disallowed expenditure claimed for travel, accommodation and subsistence. The *Samadian* case does not only affect hospital consultants. In *Noel White v R & C Comrs* (2014) the First-tier Tribunal rejected a claim for a flying instructor's costs of travelling between his home (where he had his office) and two airports (where he gave lessons) on the basis that his attendance at the airports was regular and predictable. Unfortunately it is not stipulated how often attendance is required before it becomes 'regular and predictable'. [10.150]

EXAMPLE 10.12

Wig is a barrister who travels into chambers each day from his home in Isleworth. He also travels from chambers to courts in the London area.

(1) The cost of travelling from Isleworth to chambers is not deductible because chambers is his base. It does not matter that he does a substantial amount of work at home (including report writing and research) and that he claims a deduction for a portion of the expenses of the house (see *Newsom v Robertson* (1953), *Dr S Samadian v R & C Comrs* (2014), *David Jones v R & C Comrs* (2015), *Dr Sharat Jain v R & C Comrs* (2015) and *Noel White v R & C Comrs* (2014)).

(2) Expenses in travelling from chambers to court are deductible (contrast *Horton v Young* (1971): travelling between two centres of work).

(3) If he were regularly to go from Isleworth to a case at Westminster Magistrates' Court and then on to chambers could he deduct all the travelling expenses? The difficult case of *Sargent v Barnes* (1978) in which a dental surgeon was unable to deduct travelling expenses to collect false teeth from a laboratory on his way to work, suggests that the answer is no, although it should be noted that the laboratory was not a place of work whereas the court is. A claim for travelling from the court to chambers might succeed. In BIM 37630 HMRC emphasise that visiting a supplier during the course of a 'home to office' journey does not convert an otherwise disallowable cost into an allowable one.

The 'dual purpose' rule (see [10.137]) will cause the disallowance of the entire cost of a journey with a material private purpose. In practice most costs can be split into those that have a business purpose and those that relate to private use. It then remains to agree an appropriate division of the costs with HMRC: see *Dr AS Jolaoso v R & C Comrs* (2011) where 10% of motoring costs were held to be deductible rather than the 50% originally claimed.

A solicitor's expenses incurred in travelling abroad partly for a holiday and partly to attend professional conferences were disallowed: *Bowden v Russell & Russell* (1965). Contrast this with the expenses incurred by an accountant in attending a professional conference abroad which were allowed: *Edwards v Warmsley, Henshall & Co* (1967).

Certain travel, hotel and subsistence expenses are deductible by individuals and partners where they are absent from the UK because they are carrying out a foreign trade (ITTOIA 2005 ss 92–93). If the trader is absent from the UK for a continuous period of 60 days or more the travel expenses of a spouse, civil partner or child under the age of 18 are also tax deductible up to the limit of no more than two return journeys made by the same person in a tax year (ITTOIA 2005 s 94). [10.151]

l) *Employee costs*

National insurance contributions (secondary Class 1, Class 1A and Class 1B) paid by an employer in respect of his employees are a deductible business expense (ITTOIA 2005 s 53; CTA 2009 s 1302).

If employees are temporarily seconded to a charity or educational establishment, a deduction is given for the employee's employment expenses during the period of the secondment (ITTOIA 2005 ss 70–71; CTA 2009 ss 70–71).

The legislation specifically permits a deduction for redundancy and other approved contractual payments in connection with the termination of an employee's employment (ITTOIA 2005 ss 76–80; CTA 2009 ss 76–81).

Where an employer operates the payroll giving scheme for payments to charity, a deduction is allowed for expenses paid to an approved agent (ITTOIA 2005 s 72; CTA 2009 s 72). [10.152]

m) *Payments to organisations*

A deduction is allowed for payments to local enterprise organisations and urban regeneration companies. This is subject to adjustment where the contributor or a connected person receives or is entitled to receive a disqualifying benefit (ITTOIA 2005 ss 82–86; CTA 2009 ss 82–86). From 1 January 2015 contributions to flood and coastal erosion risk management projects are deductible expenses (ITTOIA 2005 ss 86A–86B; CTA 2009 ss 86A–86B).

Payments to the Export Credit Guarantee Department are deductible (ITTOIA 2005 s 91; CTA 2009 s 91) as are levies paid under the Financial Services and Markets Act 2000 (CTA 2009 s 92). [10.153]

n) Research and development

Revenue expenses incurred on research and development are tax deductible (ITTOIA 2005 s 87; CTA 2009 s 87). Certain companies incurring expenditure on research and development are also entitled to tax credits (CTA 2009 ss 1039–1142) and enhanced capital allowances (see [48.123]). Payments to approved research associations and universities are deductible from the trading profits (ITTOIA 2005 s 88; CTA 2009 s 88). [10.154]

o) Patents, designs and trade marks

A deduction is given for expenses incurred in obtaining a patent or extension to a patent's term provided it is obtained for the purposes of the trade (ITTOIA 2005 s 89; CTA 2009 s 89). A deduction can also be obtained for abandoned or rejected applications. A tax deduction is given for the registration of a design or trade mark, the extension of a period for which the right to a registered design subsists and the renewal of the registration of a trade mark (ITTOIA 2005 s 90; CTA 2009 s 90). [10.155]

p) Penalties, interest and surcharges

No deduction is given for certain tax penalties, interest or VAT surcharges set out in the tables in ITTOIA 2005 s 54 and CTA 2009 s 1303. [10.156]

q) Sponsorship

No deduction is given for the sponsorship of events where there is a dual purpose. In *Executive Network (Consultants) Ltd v O'Connor* (1996), the company sponsored an equestrian business whose riders included the wife and children of the majority shareholder. Tax relief for the payments was denied on the basis that the non-business advantage to the family was at least one of the objects of the expenditure. This was the case even though more than a third of the company's business came from clients involved in equestrian sponsorship. The decision was cited in *Protec International Ltd v R & C Comrs* (2010) where the First-tier Tribunal held that sponsorship of a motor rallying company by a business operating in the construction industry was not wholly and exclusively laid out for business purposes. In *Interfish Ltd v R & C Comrs* (2014) a deduction for payments by a business in the fishing industry to sponsor a rugby club were denied by the Court of Appeal because the company had a dual purpose in making the payments; the company's controlling director was keen on rugby and wanted to strengthen the club financially. Furthermore, the benefits to the business of the sponsorship deal were hard to quantify. In *Aeroassistance Logistics Ltd v R & C Comrs* (2013) the taxpayer company invited clients to attend a power boat grand prix in Tunisia and claimed tax relief for the costs. The deduction was denied by the First-tier Tribunal on the basis that the expenditure was akin to business entertainment. [10.157]–[10.160]

6 Expenditure deductible at a fixed rate

Individuals and partnerships of individuals can choose to deduct expenses at a fixed rate when calculating trading profits instead of apportioning their actual expenditure (ITTOIA 2005 ss 94B–94I). This is the case irrespective of whether the trader uses GAAP accounting (see **[10.62]**) or cash accounting (see **[10.73]**). The provisions apply to those in professions as well as traders. No upper limit of business income applies to simplified expenses. The categories covered by the rules are: vehicle expenditure (see **[10.162]**); use of home for business purposes (see **[10.163]**) and private use of business premises (see **[10.164]**). **[10.161]**

a) *Vehicle expenditure*

Instead of accounting for the actual costs of running a car, motor cycle or goods vehicle for business purposes, a deduction can be made based on the business mileage multiplied by an appropriate mileage rate. For a car or goods vehicle this is 45p for the first 10,000 miles and 25p for each business mile after that. For a motorcycle the rate is 24p per mile irrespective of the mileage (ITTOIA 2005 ss 94D–94G). The number of people travelling in the vehicle does not affect the rate. The fixed rate deduction covers the cost of buying, running and maintaining the vehicle including repairs, insurance, MOT and depreciation. It does not cover items such as tolls, parking and congestion charges which can be deducted separately where they are incurred solely for business purposes. The business proportion of finance charges paid under a hire purchase agreement or finance lease may also be claimed as a deduction (see BIM 75005). Simplified expenses cannot be used if capital allowances have been claimed on the vehicle, or if the cost of a motor cycle or goods vehicle has been deducted as an expense under cash accounting as the mileage rates include an allowance for depreciation. Once the simplified basis has been adopted it must be applied consistently year to year. If a trader has started to use the fixed rate scheme he can only deduct the actual expenditure when the vehicle is replaced.

The fixed rate applies to 'business mileage'. This means 'any journey or any identifiable part or proportion of a journey, that is made wholly and exclusively for the purposes of the trade'. No deduction can be claimed for home to work travel or for journeys with a dual purpose. The main advantage of making a fixed rate deduction is the simplicity of record-keeping. Records of business and private mileage should nevertheless still be retained to support the claim.

[10.162]

b) *Use of home for business purposes*

As an alternative to claiming the cost of working from home under the usual trading income rules, a deduction for the use of the home of a sole trader or partner can be based on the number of hours spent on qualifying work by the person, a partner or any employee wholly and exclusively for the purposes of the trade (ITTOIA 2005 s 94H). Qualifying work relates to core business activities including providing goods and services, maintaining business records and marketing. The deduction includes costs for heat, light, power, telephone and broadband/internet and does not prevent a separate deduction for a proportion of council tax, insurance and mortgage interest where this is considered appropriate (see BIM 75010). If a person or partner has more than one home the properties are treated as a single home (ITTOIA 2005 s 94H(5)). Where a fixed deduction is used for one partner's home, the simplified rules must also be used for the other partners' homes (ITTOIA

2005 s 94H(5A)). Where two partners share a home, only one deduction is permitted (see BIM 75010).

The deductible amount for a month (or part of a month) is given by the following table:

Number of hours worked in a month	Applicable amount per month
25 or more	£10
51 or more	£18
101 or more	£26

[10.163]

c) *Use of business premises as a home*

Where business premises are used by a sole trader or a partner partly as a home, a deduction can be made for the total running costs of the premises (such as mortgage interest, rent, business rates and council tax) less a standard deduction for the non-business use (ITTOIA 2005 s 94I). The simplified formula can be used instead of calculating the business proportion of the costs under the usual trading income rules and might be used where for example a landlord and her family live in a flat above a pub, as well as for bed and breakfast establishments, guest houses and small nursing/care homes.

The flat rate adjustments reflect the non-business proportion of household goods, services, rent, utilities, food and non-alcoholic drinks (see BIM 75015) and are set out in the following table. A 'relevant occupant' is a person (including children and guests) who lives in the premises as a home or stays in there other than in a trading capacity.

Number of relevant occupants	Applicable amount per month or part month
1	£350
2	£500
3 or more	£650

Where the simplified calculation is used for one partner's home, the same rules must be used for the homes of the other partners (ITTOIA 2005 s 94I(6A)). [10.164]

EXAMPLE 10.13

Jane is a self-employed tax writer who works from her home where she has an office. She works 130 hours each month. She uses her car for business purposes, calculating that she drives 1,200 business miles each year. To simplify her tax affairs, Jane decides to calculate her vehicle and use of home expenses based on the fixed rate regime.

She claims the following deductions:
(1) Car costs – 1,200 miles x 45p per mile = £540
(2) Use of home (130 hours worked per month) = 12 months x £26 = £312

EXAMPLE 10.14

Rachel runs a guest house and lives on the premises with her partner Gwen. Her son Ben who is a student stays with her for three months during the university vacation. Her total household expenditure on food, utilities etc is £20,000 for the year to 31 March 2018. The allowable proportion of the expenditure is calculated as follows:

Flat rate deduction:
(1) Sue and Gwen (2 people) for 9 months x £500 = £4,500.
(2) Sue, Gwen and Ben (3 people) for 3 months x £650 = £1,950
Total flat rate deduction (£4,500 + £1,950) = £6,450
Allowable expenses (£20,000 – £6,450) = £13,550. **[10.165]–[10.170]**

VII RELIEF FOR FLUCTUATING PROFITS

The profits earned from certain businesses are so irregular that it would be unfair to tax them all in the year of receipt. Instead, they are deemed to have been received over a longer period ('averaged'). **[10.171]**

1 Farmers, market gardeners and creative artists

ITTOIA 2005 ss 221–225 allows farmers, market gardeners and creative artists etc to compare the profits of consecutive years of assessment and, if conditions are met to average the profits. 'Profit' means profit before deducting loss relief and capital allowances. Farmers (including those rearing livestock and fish) and market gardeners can claim to average their profits over two years, or from 6 April 2016 over five, consecutive years (ITTOIA 2005 s 222A). Creative artists can average over a two year period. For two year averaging the relevant profits of one of the years must be less than 75% of the other, or one of the years must show no profit (or a loss). For five year averaging the profits must be 'volatile'. This means that the average of the first four years profits or the profit of the last of the tax years to which the claim relates is less than 75% of the other, or one or more of the five tax years shows no profit (or a loss). The trader must claim the relief before the first anniversary of the 31 January filing date for the last of the tax years to which the claim relates. No averaging claim can be made for opening or closing years of assessment (see **[10.194]**), or where trading profits are accounted for on the cash basis (ITTOIA 2005 s 221A), see **[10.73]**. **[10.172]**

EXAMPLE 10.15

An artist's profits in year 1 are £6,000 and in year 2 £36,000. £6,000 is less than 75% of £36,000. Therefore profits are averaged and in years 1 and 2 she is taxed on profits of £21,000 (£6,000 + £36,000 = £42,000 ÷ 2).

Where losses are involved in one of the averaged years, the outcome of the averaging exercise may not be as expected. In *PG Donaghy v R & C Comrs* (2012) a farmer made a trading profit of £20,244 in year 1 and a trading loss of £10,315 in year 2. He claimed averaging relief contending that since the total profit for the two years was £9,929 he should be treated as having a taxable profit of £4,964.50 per year. The Upper Tribunal rejected his claim, confirming HMRC's ruling that he had taxable profits of £10,122 in both years 1 and 2 less a deduction of £10,122 in the second year for the loss, leaving £193 of the loss to carry forward. **[10.173]**

EXAMPLE 10.16

A farmer's profits are as set out in the following table. For tax years up to 2016–17 the profits have not been averaged. From 2017–18 the farmer opts to average his profits over a five year period.

Year	2013–14 £	2014–15 £	2015–16 £	2016–17 £	2017–18 £	Total £
Original profit	20,000	50,000	20,000	50,000	60,000	200,000
Averaged profit	40,000	40,000	40,000	40,000	40,000	200,000

The farmer can average over five years because the average profit of the four years 2013–14 to 2016–17 is less than 75% of the profit in year five. **[10.174]**

2 Inventors

Similar provisions apply to lump sums received by inventors for the exploitation of their patents. A sum received in return for patent rights is spread over the year of receipt and the next five years (ITTOIA 2005 ss 587–592; CTA 2009 ss 912–923). Sums received for the use of a patent for a period of at least six years may be spread back over six years (ITA 2007 s 461; TA 1988 s 527).
[10.175]–[10.191]

VIII BASIS OF ASSESSMENT (SOLE-TRADERS AND PARTNERSHIPS)

1 Background

A taxpayer can commence or cease his business at any time and adopt an accounting date of his choosing. It is not necessary that this date coincide with the tax year. In the first and closing years and upon a change of accounting date the accounts may not necessarily be of 12 months duration. This flexibility about accounting gives rise to two difficulties in some cases:
(1) the actual profits made in a year of assessment may only be arrived at by splitting two accounting years and taking the proportions which fall into the assessment year;
(2) the calculation of the taxpayer's liability has to await the completion of the accounts. For this reason many traders choose to prepare their accounts to coincide with the tax year (or 31 March) which is treated as if it were the same date as 5 April.

Tax is assessed and calculated on a current year basis under ITTOIA 2005 ss 197–220. There are special rules for the opening and closing years of a business and upon a change of accounting date. **[10.192]**

2 How the current year basis operates

a) *The position of a continuing business*

EXAMPLE 10.17

Jon makes his accounts up to 30 April each year. For the accounting year ending 30 April 2017 his profits are £50,000. As that accounting period ends in the tax year 2017–18, those profits will be assessed to tax in that year. The tax is payable in three instalments: two being estimated on the basis of the previous year's tax on 31 January 2018 and 31 July 2018 with a balancing payment (or refund) on submission of the tax return on 31 January 2019. [10.193]

b) *Opening years of a new business*

EXAMPLE 10.18

Assume that Myrcella begins her millinery business on 1 July 2014 making up her accounts to the following 30 June. Her profits are as follows:

	£
y/e 30.6.15	16,000
y/e 30.6.16	19,500
y/e 30.6.17	22,500

For the *first tax year* of the business (2014–15) Myrcella is taxed on her profits from the date of commencement (1 July 2014) to the following 5 April, ie:
9/12 × £16,000 = £12,000

For the *second year* (2015–16) the current year basis applies so that the first year's profit of £16,000 is subject to tax.

When the accounting date chosen is not 5 April (as in *Example 10.16*) the first year's profits are used as the basis for part of the tax charge in both the first and second years (in this case £12,000 is taxed twice). This is contrary to the principle that profits taxed must equal profits earned and accordingly a limited relief is available for these doubly taxed profits (*'overlap relief'*: see [10.201]), ITTOIA 2005 s 204. If there is an accounting date in the second year which falls less than 12 months after the commencement, the basis period for this year is the profits of the first 12 months of trading. For the third (and subsequent) years of assessment tax is calculated on a current year basis, which means that the profits for the year ended 30 June 2016 of £19,500 are taxed in 2016–17 and profits for the year ended 30 June 2017 of £22,500 are taxed in 2017–18. [10.194]

c) *The closing years of a business*

In the final tax year, profits from the end of the basis period of the preceding year until the date of cessation are taxed.

EXAMPLE 10.19

Assume that Ellaria, who has previously made up her accounts to 30 April, ceases trading on 30 September 2017. Her final accounts are as follows:

	£
to 30.4.16	10,000
to 30.4.17	4,500
to 30.9.17	1,500

Her tax position is as follows:

Tax year	Taxed profits (£)
2016–17	10,000 (current year basis)
2017–18	6,000 (final period)

Note that Ellaria may be entitled to 'overlap relief' (see *Example 10.17*) which will reduce the taxable profit in her final tax year, ITTOIA 2005 s 205 (see also **[10.201]**).

If the business ceases in its second tax year, the assessment is on profit from the end of the commencement year until cessation. If the business starts and finishes in the same tax year, the basis period is the actual profits earned.

[10.195]

3 Accounting dates

A taxpayer is free to choose whatever accounting date he wishes. There are, however, statutory provisions concerning changes of accounting date, ITTOIA 2005 s 214–220.

First, a change of accounting date in the second or third year of a business is permitted without restriction thereby enabling a business to make suitable adjustments when the original date turns out to be impractical.

Second, in all other cases a change will only have a fiscal effect if certain prescribed conditions are satisfied. Otherwise the change is disregarded and tax computations continue on the basis of the old date (thereby necessitating apportionments). There are four conditions: both conditions I and II must be satisfied together with either condition III or condition IV.

Condition I: The first accounting period ending on the new (changed) date must not exceed 18 months.

Condition II: Notice of the change must be given to an officer of HMRC by 31 January following the year of change. The 'year of change' is the first year in which accounts are made up to the new date or, if there is a year without an accounting date, it is that year.

Condition III: Either no accounting date change occurred in any of the five preceding tax years *or* any such change was fiscally ineffective (ie because these conditions were not met).

Condition IV: The notice under condition II must set out the reasons for the change and HMRC then has 60 days to decide whether they are satisfied that the change is for '*bona fide* commercial reasons'. If they are not so satisfied they must give the taxpayer notice of the fact: if he or she does not respond at all within this period the change is effective. The taxpayer can appeal against HMRC's notice of dissatisfaction within 30 days and the tribunal then has to decide if there are *bona fide* commercial reasons for the change. 'Obtaining a tax advantage' is *not* regarded as a *bona fide* commercial reason for a change

Basis of assessment (sole-traders and partnerships) 387

(ITTOIA 2005 s 218(6)) and HMRC has indicated that this includes the obtaining of a cashflow benefit as well as a reduction in liability. Bearing in mind, however, that condition IV is irrelevant if condition III is satisfied, so it is possible to make one change for purely fiscal *reasons* every five years.

How are effective changes of date treated for income tax purposes? Consider the following situations. **[10.196]**

Situation 1 If the accounting period of change is under 12 months (or the change occurs in the second year of business) the basis period is 12 months to the new accounting date. **[10.197]**

EXAMPLE 10.20

Theon's business, having made up its accounts to 31 October, changes its accounting date to 30 April in 2017. Its profits are as follows:

	£
y/e 31.10.16	28,500
p/e 30.4.17	14,500
y/e 30.4.18	30,500

The tax assessments are:

Tax year	Accounting period	£
2016–17	y/e 31.10.16	28,500
2017–18	y/e 30.4.17 (ie six months' accounts to 30.4.17 + 6/12 of profit to 31.10.16)	28,750
2018–19	y/e 30.4.18	30,500

Situation 2 If, as a result of the change, no account ends in the next financial year, this is the year in which the change is deemed to take effect and the basis period is 12 months to the new accounting date. **[10.198]**

EXAMPLE 10.21

If Theon had prepared an 18-month account to 30 April 2018 the position would be:

	£
y/e 31.10.16	28,500
p/e 30.4.18	36,000

and the tax assessment would be:

Tax year	Accounting period	£
2016–17	y/e 31.10.16	28,500
2017–18	12-month period to	

	30.4.17 (ie 6/12 of £28,500 (as before) + 6/18 of £36,000)	26,250
2018–19	12-month period to 30.4.18 (ie 12/18 of £36,000)	24,000

Situation 3 If the accounting period exceeds 12 months but ends in the next tax year, profits of that accounting period are assessed. If, for instance, Theon had made up accounts to 31 December 2017, profits of the period from 1 November 2016 to that date would be taxed in the tax year 2017–18. **[10.199]**

Situation 4 If the new period is a short one so that there are two accounting periods ending in the same tax year, the two are treated as a single period ending on the new date. **[10.200]**

4 Overlap relief

This is given where the same profits are used twice as the basis of assessment (as for instance in *Example 10.18*). The relief for the overlap, which is calculated in money terms and is not index-linked, is given on the earlier of:
(1) a change of accounting date which results in an assessment for a period of *more than* 12 months; or
(2) a cessation of the trade or business.

If none or not all the overlap is used in (1) above, then it can be carried forward for use in (2). **[10.201]**

5 Taxing partners and the position of partners joining the firm

Taxable profits or losses are allocated amongst partners according to their interest in the partnership during the accounting period not according to the shares in the tax year for which that period is the basis period. Each partner is treated as carrying on a notional sole trade which begins when he becomes a partner and ends when he ceases to be a partner. As a result initial overlap relief can be given on leaving and terminal loss relief is likewise available on leaving the partnership even though the business itself may continue.

[10.202]

EXAMPLE 10.22

Firm ABC makes up accounts to 30 June each year. On 1 January 2017 D joined the firm. Assume profits always split equally.
(1) *Tax year 2016–17*
ABC taxed on profits of the accounts to 30 June 2016: profits divided equally.

D taxed on his share of the profits when he became a partner (1 January 2017) to following 5 April. Hence profits for the year ended 30 June 2017 must be divided as follows:
(a) 1 July 2016 to 31 December 2016 (6/12) divided equally between ABC and taxed in the year 2016–17.

(b) 1 January 2017 to 5 April 2017 (3/12) divided equally between ABCD and D's share taxed in the year 2016–17.

(2) *Tax year 2017–18*

ABC taxed on their profit share for year to 30 June 2017: being one-third each to 31 December 2016 and thereafter one-quarter each.

D will be taxed on his share of the profits to 30 June 2017 (being one half of one-quarter) and in addition on his share of the profit for the following six months to 31 December 2017 (this will be one half of one-quarter of the profits to 30 June 2018). These accounts will require speedy completion in order for D to meet the tax return filing date.

(3) *D's position*
(a) He will receive credit for profits doubly taxed on commencement, ie on his profit of the year to 30 June 2017 (taxed in 2016–17 plus a six-month share of profits for the year to 30 June 2018 (since those profits will be taxed in full in the year 2018–19).

He will receive overlap relief on the earlier of:
(i) when he leaves the firm;
(ii) when the firm's business ceases;
(iii) on a change to a later accounting date (relief may only be partial).

(b) For D no accounting period fell within the period of 12 months from the date when his notional trade began hence he only reaches the current year basis in the third tax year (being 2018–19).

6 Partners leaving the firm

Given that each partner is treated as carrying on a notional sole trade, the usual principles apply. **[10.203]**

EXAMPLE 10.23

XYZ make up their accounts to 30 June each year. Profits are divided equally. On 31 December 2017 Z retires and X and Y continue the business splitting the profits equally.

Position of Z

He is taxed on the basis of his share of the profits from the end of the basis period of the preceding year until 31 December 2017, ie profits from 1 July 2016 to 31 December 2017 (18 months).

Overlap relief will be due from when he joined the firm on 1 January 2002. This will amount to approximately nine months. In theory therefore he is taxed on retirement on the nine-month period from 5 April to 31 December 2017 (but note that there is no necessary link between profits at the start and at the end and there is no index-linking of overlap relief).

7 Partnership changes

When there is a change in the persons carrying on a trade and at least one person was a member of the firm before and after the change, there is a continuing partnership, ie there is no deemed discontinuance and recommencement. Accordingly, it is only *actual* discontinuances which have tax consequences. These occur when:
(1) all the partners sell out;
(2) on the death of a sole trader;

(3) on an actual discontinuance: for instance on a merger (or demerger) when there results a change in the nature of the business carried on by the two firms engaged in the merger (or demerger): see for instance *George Humphries Ltd v Cook* (1934); Statement of Practice SP 9/86 and BIM 82435. **[10.204]–[10.250]**

11 Losses

Updated by Sarah Laing, CTA, Chartered Tax Advisor

I   Introductory **[11.1]**
II Relief under ITA 2007 s 83: carry-forward **[11.21]**
III Relief under ITA 2007 s 64: carry-across **[11.41]**
IV Relief against capital gains (ITA 2007 s 71) **[11.61]**
V   Relief for losses in the early years (ITA 2007 s 72) **[11.81]**
VI Relief for losses in the final years (ITA 2007 s 89) **[11.101]**
VII Investment in unquoted corporate trades (ITA 2007 Part 4 Chapter 6; CTA 2010 Part 4 Chapter 5) **[11.121]**
VIII Anti-avoidance **[11.122]**

I INTRODUCTORY

1 General

Whenever an individual or partnership makes a loss (ie where allowable expenses in an accounting period exceed taxable receipts) there are two repercussions.

First, any year of assessment using that accounting period as its basis period will have a nil tax assessment.

Second, the loss may be used to reduce tax assessments of that or other years of assessment so that the taxpayer will either pay less tax or be able to reclaim tax that he has previously paid. Losses are, however, personal to the taxpayer. They are not in any sense an asset that can be bought and sold.

The income tax provisions dealing with relief for losses are contained in the Income Tax Act 2007 (ITA 2007). The corporation tax provisions dealing with relief for losses made by companies, limited partners and members of limited liability partnerships, are contained in the Corporation Tax Act 2010 (CTA 2010). **[11.1]**

2 Companies

Companies are subject to a separate regime governing the use of losses – see **[41.60]**.

As a matter of planning, it should be noted that when the loss is made by a trading company it is not available for use by individual shareholders (even in a 'one man' company). Hence, when it is proposed to start a business and early losses are anticipated the advantages of income tax relief for the losses must be weighed against the protection of limited liability. This is particularly the case where a limited liability partnership (LLP) is being considered so that the benefits of limited liability may be obtained, whilst retaining the transparency of a partnership (see [45.11]). To prevent companies with accumulated losses being sold to a purchaser who wishes to use the losses to shelter his own profits (by injecting income or profits into the company) CTA 2010, Part 14, Chapter 2 imposes a series of conditions for the utilisation of the losses. In broad terms, where during a period of three years there is a change in the ownership of the company and a major change in the nature or conduct of the company's trade, the brought-forward losses will not be available for relief (see [41.63]). [11.2]

3 Loss relief on income from property

The loss reliefs available for the landlord are discussed at [12.46]. It should be noted, however, that losses under the income from property provisions of ITTOIA 2005 are 'ring fenced', ie they can only be set against profits from the property business (unless attributable to certain capital allowances or in relation to an agricultural estate as defined in ITA 2007 s 123). [11.3]

4 Losses in a trade profession and vocation

This chapter concentrates on the loss reliefs available against profits from trades, professions or vocations. When seeking to apply relief under these provisions it is important to realise that the loss may be eligible for relief under more than one provision and that the choice will usually rest with the taxpayer. The reliefs apply, with some modification, to members of a partnership in respect of their share of any business losses. [11.4]

5 Restriction on income tax reliefs 2013–14 onwards

From 6 April 2013, a cap applies to certain previously unlimited income tax reliefs that may be deducted from income under ITA 2007 s 24 (FA 2013 s 16 and Sch 3). The cap is set at £50,000 or 25% of income, whichever is greater. The reliefs affected by the cap are as follows:
(a) ITA 2007 s 64 (trade loss relief against general income);
(b) ITA 2007 s 72 (early trade losses relief);
(c) ITA 2007 s 96 (post-cessation trade relief);
(d) ITA 2007 s 120 (property loss relief against general income);
(e) ITA 2007 s 125 (post-cessation property relief);
(f) ITA 2007 s 128 (employment loss relief against general income);
(g) relief under ITA 2007 Part 4 Chapter 6 (share loss relief);
(h) relief under ITA 2007 Part 8 Chapter 1 (interest payments);
(i) ITEPA 2003 s 555 (deduction for liabilities relating to former employment);
(j) ITTOIA 2005 s 446 (strips of government securities: relief for losses); and

(k) ITTOIA 2005 s 454(4) (listed securities held since 26 March 2003: relief for losses: persons other than trustees). **[11.5]–[11.20]**

II RELIEF UNDER ITA 2007 S 83: CARRY-FORWARD

A loss that is sustained in carrying on a trade, profession or vocation can be carried forward under s 83 and set off against the first available profits of the same trade, profession or vocation without time limit. The loss must be deducted as far as possible from the earliest subsequent profits with the result that the taxpayer may not be able to make use of his personal allowance.

EXAMPLE 11.1

Scrooge's accounts are as follows:

Accounting period	£
Year to 31 December 2013	2,000 profit
Year to 31 December 2014	(6,000) loss
Year to 31 December 2015	1,600 profit
Year to 31 December 2016	3,600 profit
Year to 31 December 2017	4,000 profit

The income tax assessments are:

Tax year	Taxable profit (loss)
	£
2013–14	2,000
2014–15	nil (6,000 loss c/f)
2015–16	nil (1,600–1,600 loss)
2016–17	nil (3,600–3,600 loss)
2017–18	3,200 (4,000–800 loss)

Scrooge would lose the benefit of his personal allowance in 2014–15, 2015–16 and 2016–17 if he had no other income against which to set it. In 2013–14 and 2017–18 his personal allowance would be used to reduce this taxable income to nil, the remainder would be lost.

In calculating the loss to be carried forward under s 83, certain items may be treated as losses. For instance, an annual payment which is made wholly and exclusively for the purpose of the business and assessed under ITA 2007, Part 15 (because the taxpayer has no income) and which cannot be relieved because there are no profits against which to set it, may be treated as a loss for s 83. The same principle applies to unrelieved interest payments (ITA 2007 s 88).

EXAMPLE 11.2

Oliver makes a loss of £10,000 in his accounting year ended 31 July 2017 and is expected to make a loss in the year to 31 July 2018. He makes an annual payment each year on 1 June of £1,000. In 2017–18 there will be a nil assessment on his business profits, but under ITA 2007 Part 15 Chapter 6, HMRC require Oliver to pay basic rate income tax on £1,000 at 20% (£200). As he made a loss of £10,000 and has paid out £1,000 in total, Oliver's loss to be carried forward under s 83 is £11,000.

Losses can only be carried forward under s 83 against future profits from the *same* business. Thus, if the nature of the business changes in a future year, there can be no carry-forward of losses. In *Gordon and Blair Ltd v IRC* (1962) brewing losses could not be carried forward against bottling profits. Similarly, if the business ceases, there can be no carry-forward.

There are two major drawbacks to loss relief under s 83. *First*, it is only available against profits from the same business and not against any other income of the taxpayer. *Second*, the relief is not immediate. Even assuming that the business makes profits in the future, full loss relief may not be obtained for some years (see *Example 11.1*). In inflationary times, this delay renders the loss relief less valuable in real terms (cp ITA 2007 s 64).

The time limit for making a claim under s 83 is four years after the end of the year of assessment to which the loss relates, as laid down in TMA 1970 s 43(1). Once an effective claim has been made the loss will then be carried forward and utilised each year until extinguished without the need for any further claim. [11.21]–[11.40]

III RELIEF UNDER ITA 2007 S 64: CARRY-ACROSS

Under s 64(2), trading losses may be set against the taxpayer's total income of the year in which the loss arises or (see s 64(2)(b)) of the *preceding year*, or both (s 64(2)(c)). From 2013–14, the amount of relief that may be claimed is restricted to the greater of £50,000 or 25% of income (see [11.5]). It is possible to choose the year in which the loss is to be set off – for instance, the claim may indicate that the loss is to be allowed in the preceding year. If the claim is for relief in both years, the claim for relief in the current year takes precedence over that for the preceding year (s 64(3)); claims for relief must generally be made within 12 months from 31 January following the end of the tax year in which the loss arose.

EXAMPLE 11.3

Confused makes his account up to 5 October each year. For the year to 5 October 2017 a loss of £24,000 is suffered; for the previous year a loss of £18,000.
(i)   *The loss of £18,000*
Given that these accounts are the basis period for tax year 2016–17, loss relief may be claimed as follows:
(a)   against Confused's other income for 2016–17 under s 64(2)(a); or
(b)   against his income for 2015–16 (under s 64(2)(b)).
He may choose the year in which relief is given in the claim: namely by stipulating that the loss is to be relieved in (or as far as possible in) 2016–17.
(ii) *The loss of £24,000*

The rules are the same with the qualification that if relief is claimed for both a loss in the current year and a loss in the preceding year, the current year is given priority. Accordingly if relief was claimed for the £18,000 loss in 2016–17 that would take priority over a claim to relief for the £24,000 loss in that year.

Certain restrictions are placed on the availability of s 64 relief in order to prevent a taxpayer indulging in a 'hobby' trade. ITA 2007 s 66 denies the relief unless the taxpayer can show that the loss-making business was run on a commercial basis with a view to profit (although a reasonable expectation of profit is conclusive evidence of this (see *Wannell v Rothwell* (1996); and more recently *Kerr v R & C Comrs* (2011)). By ITA 2007 s 67, a farmer or market gardener will automatically lose the relief if he incurs a loss in each of the preceding five years unless he can show that any competent farmer or market gardener would have made the same losses. The moral here is 'let your losses be those of the reasonable man or make a profit every sixth year!'

[11.41]–[11.60]

IV RELIEF AGAINST CAPITAL GAINS (ITA 2007 S 71)

ITA 2007 allows a person who cannot deduct all of a loss under a claim for trade loss relief against general income (under s 64) to treat the unused part as an allowable loss for capital gains tax purposes (under TCGA 1992 ss 261B and 261C).

The manner in which CGT is charged does not involve a joining together of the taxes themselves. The taxes remain distinct so that income losses cannot generally be offset against chargeable gains and nor can capital losses be offset against income. The position is slightly different for companies – see **[41.62]**.

Trading losses of an individual can be offset against his capital gains in the tax year when the loss arises and in one preceding year. The following matters are particularly worthy of note concerning this relief:

(1) The relief depends upon an election being made by the taxpayer and this claim for relief may only be made if a claim is also submitted under ITA 2007 s 64 (ie to set the loss against the taxpayer's other income). Capital gains may only be used to the extent that the trading loss cannot be used against the taxpayer's other income for the year (this is 'the relevant amount').

(2) Relief is obtained by setting the trading loss against the amount which would otherwise be subject to a CGT charge – ie after deducting current year and losses carried forward – but *disregarding for this purpose the taxpayer's annual exemption* (this is referred to as 'the maximum amount'). For these purposes the trading losses are treated as an allowable capital loss made in that year.

(3) To the extent that full relief is not available in the year when the trading loss is incurred, any unrelieved balance may then be carried back and set against gains in the immediately preceding tax year in accordance with the s 64 procedure.   **[11.61]–[11.80]**

EXAMPLE 11.4

Curious' tax position for 2016–17 is as follows:

		£
Taxable income		50,000
Trading losses		75,000
Chargeable gains		120,000
Allowable capital losses	(current year)	30,000
	(brought forward)	25,000

He makes claims under s 64 and s 261B in respect of the trading loss.
(1) *Assessable income:* reduced to nil (hence a loss of personal allowances) and the 'relevant amount' for s 261B is £25,000.
(2) *The 'maximum amount':* £120,000 − (£30,000 + £25,000) = £65,000. Accordingly relief is not restricted.

Hence £25,000 of trading losses are treated as allowable (capital) losses. Curious' gains for the year are therefore £40,000.

V RELIEF FOR LOSSES IN THE EARLY YEARS

1 ITA 2007 s 72: initial loss relief

A business will often make losses in its early years, and ITA 2007 s 72 provides relief where a loss is sustained in the year of assessment in which the business is first carried on, or in any of the next three years of assessment, as an alternative to relief under ITA 2007 s 64, 83 and TCGA 1992 s 261B. The relief is obtained by a set-off against the taxpayer's total income of the three years of assessment preceding the year of loss (ITA 2007 s 73). The set-off is against earlier years before later years (the loss can, of course, only be relieved once: see *Gamble v Rowe* (1998)). The effect of the relief is to revise earlier income tax computations and to obtain a tax refund. Relief under s 72 is available to individuals (including partners) for a maximum of four years only and is not available to a limited company. Therefore, where early losses are envisaged, it may be worth starting as a sole trader (or partnership) and at a later stage incorporating the business. From 2013–14 the amount of relief that may be claimed is restricted to the greater of £50,000 or 25% of income (see **[11.5]**).

Relief under s 72 requires a specific election by 31 January in the second tax year following the year of assessment in which the loss is sustained. Relief is denied unless it can be shown that the business was conducted on a commercial basis with a view to profit (ITA 2007 s 74). The relief cannot be extended by the taxpayer transferring the business to the spouse or civil partner after the first four years (ITA 2007 s 74(4)). **[11.81]**

EXAMPLE 11.5

Fergus began business as a sole practitioner on 1 July 2016. His results for the first 12 months showed a loss of £36,000. This is apportioned as follows:
  2016–17: loss £27,000 (ie 1 July 2016–5 April 2017)
  2017–18: loss £9,000.

Relief for losses in the early years 397

Before beginning his own business, Fergus was employed as an assistant solicitor. He worked increasingly part-time as he prepared to launch his business. Salary from his job was as follows:

	Salary
2013–14	£20,000
2014–15	£15,000
2015–16	£10,000

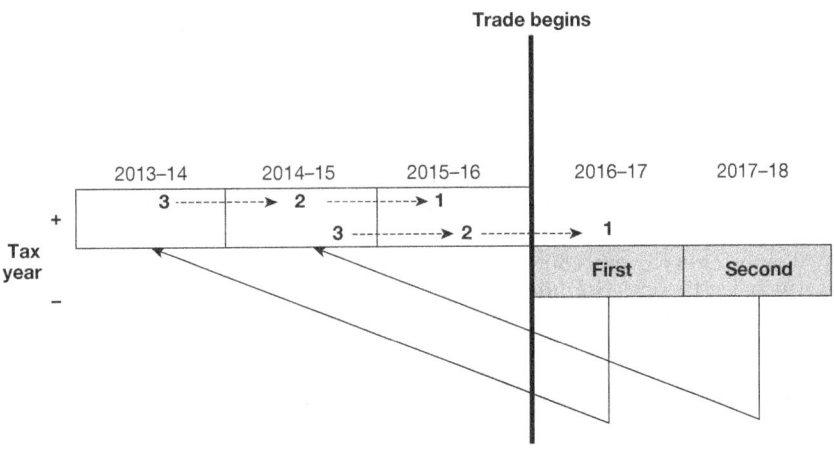

The position is as follows:

	£
2013–14	
Salary	20,000
Less: 2016–17 loss carried back (part)	(20,000)
Revised liability	NIL
2014–15	
Salary	15,000
Less: 2016–17 loss carried back (remaining)	(7,000)
	8,000
Less: 2017–18 loss carried back (part)	8,000
Revised liability	NIL
2015–16	
Salary	10,000
Less: 2017–18 loss (remaining)	1,000
Revised liability	£9,000

2 Relationship of s 72 with ss 64 and 83

As with s 64, relief under s 72 requires a specific election. The election need only be made for one year of loss, but, once made, that loss must be carried back against the taxpayer's income in the earlier years without limit, which may result in a loss of personal allowances.

Sections 72 and 64 are alternatives so that the same portion of any loss cannot be relieved under both sections (ie twice). Where, however, relief has been given as far as possible under one section, any surplus loss remaining can be relieved by a specific election under the other section (see *Butt v Haxby* (1983)). Any surplus loss still unrelieved will then be carried forward under s 83.

EXAMPLE 11.6

Angus begins trading on 1 August 2017 and in the period to 5 April 2018 makes a loss of £15,000. His income in the preceding three years (2014–15 onwards) amounted to £10,000. If Angus elects for s 72 relief he will have wasted his personal allowances in the preceding years. He will be left with an unrelieved loss of £5,000 which can be relieved under s 64 against any other income which he may have in 2017–18. To the extent that relief is not given under s 64, the surplus loss will be carried forward under s 83.

Which relief the taxpayer chooses will depend upon his circumstances. Section 72 relief is advantageous when the taxpayer has a large pre-trading income, since it will ensure a cash refund. Alternatively, if his other income/gains in the year(s) of loss is large, relief under ITA 2007 s 64/TCGA 1992 s 261B may be more attractive. Changes in income tax rates are also an important factor to bear in mind. [11.82]–[11.100]

VI RELIEF FOR LOSSES IN THE FINAL YEARS

1 ITA 2007 s 86: transfer of a business to a company

The general rule is that loss relief is personal to the taxpayer who sustains the loss; it cannot be 'sold' with the business or otherwise transferred. Thus, if a business is incorporated, any unabsorbed loss of the old business that ceases to trade cannot be carried forward under s 83 by the company. However, ITA 2007 s 86 provides that, where the business of a sole trader or a partnership is transferred to a company and the whole or main consideration for the transfer is the allotment of shares to the former proprietor, he can set his unrelieved losses against income which he receives from the company for any year throughout which he owns the shares allotted to him and during which the company continues to trade. The set-off must be used first against direct assessments (eg on director's fees, etc) with any balance set against dividends, etc from the company. HMRC have confirmed that even if the vending agreement refers to a cash consideration, provided that shares are taken relief is available and that this relief will be allowed provided that the taxpayer keeps shares which represent more than 80% of the consideration received for the business (BIM 85060).

EXAMPLE 11.7

Evans incorporates his business on 30 September 2016. He has brought-forward losses of £50,000, although the business is now trading profitably. The company issues 80,000 £1 shares to him and a director's loan account of £20,000 is created. The company trades profitably and Evans takes a salary of £25,000 in each of the next two years. The losses may be set against the salary under s 86, but Class 1 NIC is still payable.

Frank is also a sole trader with brought-forward losses of £50,000 and he, too, is now trading profitably. He also decides to incorporate but, for personal reasons, one of the business assets is kept out of the company. The remainder of the business is transferred for a consideration that is left outstanding on loan account. The company trades profitably and he takes a salary of £25,000 in each of the next two years. Because of the manner of incorporation, the losses cannot be set against the salary and the benefit of them is effectively lost.

Relief under s 86 is given automatically (as an extension of s 83) as if the original business had not ceased and as if the income derived from the company were profits of that business. However, for all other purposes the business has discontinued and, if the taxpayer wants relief for his business loss in the year of discontinuance under s 64, or terminal relief under s 89 (see [**11.102**]), he must make a specific election to that effect. Section 86 relief is, of course, given to the individual taxpayer who sustains the loss and affords no relief for losses made by the newly formed company. [**11.101**]

2 ITA 2007 s 89: terminal loss relief

If a loss is sustained in the last 12 months of a business, the unrelieved loss of that period, so far as not otherwise relieved (eg under ITA 2007 s 64/TCGA 1992 s 261B, in the year of discontinuance), may be relieved by set-off against the business profits in the year of cessation and the three preceding years of assessment. Relief is given as far as possible against later rather than earlier years. A terminal loss is defined as one sustained in the year of assessment in which the trade discontinued together with such proportion of any loss sustained in the previous year beginning 12 months before the discontinuance (if in either case there was a profit then nil is entered in calculating the terminal loss).

The claim is for the total amount of terminal losses made in the trade by the person to be deducted in calculating the person's net income for the final tax year and the three previous tax years. A deduction for that purpose is to be made only from profits of the trade (s 89(3)). If profits of a preceding year are insufficient to absorb the loss, trade-related interest and dividends are treated as profits for the purposes of obtaining a repayment of income tax (ITA 2007 s 85).

Relief may be claimed under ITA 2007 s 89 as an alternative to relief under ITA 2007 s 86 (transfer to a company) and any unused loss can be relieved under s 86.

EXAMPLE 11.8

Dolly closes down her hairdressing business on 5 June 2017. Her results for the four years ending 5 December 2016 and for her final six months of business were:

Accounting period	Profit/loss	Tax years	Original Assessments
Year to 5 December 2013	£11,000 profit	2013–14	£11,000
Year to 5 December 2014	£7,000 profit	2014–15	£7,000
Year to 5 December 2015	£3,000 profit	2015–16	£3,000
Year to 5 December 2016	£1,000 profit	2016–17	£1,000
Six months to 5 June 2017	£(12,000) loss	2017–18	nil

The terminal loss is calculated as:
(i) loss in year of discontinuance:
$2/6 \times £(12,000) = £(4,000)$

plus
(ii) loss in preceding year of assessment:
$4/6 \times £(12,000) = £(8,000)$

plus

$9/12 \times £1,000 = $ nil
ie £12,000 terminal loss
That loss is relieved as follows:

Tax year	Fiscal assessment
2017–18	Nil
2016–17	
2015–16	– profits for these years (starting with 2014–15) reduced by the terminal loss of £12,000.
2014–15	

[11.102]–[11.120]

VII INVESTMENT IN UNQUOTED CORPORATE TRADES (ITA 2007 PART 4 CHAPTER 6; CTA 2010 PART 4 CHAPTER 5)

As a general rule, a person who subscribes for shares in a company and later disposes of them at a loss can only claim CGT relief for his loss. In an attempt to stimulate investment in corporate trades, ITA 2007 s 131 enables an individual to obtain income tax relief for his loss in certain circumstances. Broadly, the section allows an individual who has made a loss on the disposal of shares in an 'eligible trading company' (or shares to which Enterprise Investment Scheme (EIS) relief is attributable (s 131(2)), to deduct the loss from his total income in the year of assessment in which the loss is incurred or against total income of the preceding year (s 132 and see *Hobart v Williams* (1997)). This relief contains a number of restrictions (s 131):

(1) It is available only to an individual who subscribes for shares in a company for money or money's worth, including one who acquires the shares from a subscribing spouse or civil partner; it is not available to a subsequent purchaser of the shares.

(2) The disposal giving rise to the loss must be by way of a bargain made at arm's length; or a distribution from the company on a dissolution or a winding up; or a deemed disposal under TCGA 1992 s 24(1) (entire loss, destruction, dissipation or extinction of asset); or a deemed disposal

under TCGA 1992 s 24(2) where the shares have become of negligible value.
(3) The company must satisfy the complex requirements set out in ITA 2007 Part 4 Chapter 6. Basically, it must be an eligible trading company, carrying on its business wholly or mainly in the UK, which does not trade in certain prohibited items such as land or shares and which is not a building society, or a registered industrial and provident society. An eligible company is, broadly, one that satisfies the requirements to be a qualifying company for the purposes of the EIS. The company must be unquoted at the time of issue and no arrangements must then exist for it to cease to be unquoted. However, there is no requirement that the company remain unquoted.

If these conditions are satisfied, the allowable loss is calculated on CGT principles and is deducted in priority to relief under ITA 2007 s 64 or 72.

The deduction is given in accordance with the s 64 rules, ie against income of the year of assessment in which the loss arises and income of the previous year. A claim must be made by notice given within 12 months from 31 January of the tax year following the disposal. Relief may be claimed against either or both of the income tax years: to the extent that part of the loss is unrelieved the capital gains tax rules apply (see [19.44]).

To prevent the taxpayer from obtaining double tax relief on his investment, any income tax relief he received on the acquisition of the shares under the EIS must be deducted from the base value of the shares when calculating an allowable loss for CGT. [11.121]

VIII ANTI-AVOIDANCE

Over recent years the Government has seen evidence of schemes and arrangements involving the use of losses to avoid tax. To counter such arrangements various anti-avoidance provisions relating to individuals and partnerships are now contained in the legislation. The provisions to date include the following:

(a) *Partnership losses: non-active partners.* Loss relief under ITA 2007 s 64 or 72 (and interest relief under ITA 2007 s 383) is restricted in the case of an individual partner who does not devote 'a significant amount of time' to the trade (professions are not affected). The relief available is restricted to the amount of the partner's 'contribution to the trade' as at the end of the tax year in which the loss is sustained. The restriction applies to losses sustained in the tax year in which the partner first carries on the trade and in any of the next three tax years. The restricted losses may be carried forward and used against profits of the same trade, or used against general income or chargeable gains to the extent that the partner makes a further contribution to the trade.

The rules give HMRC power to set out in regulations details of the kind of contributions that are excluded in computing the amount of the individual's contribution to the trade for this purpose. Partners whose loss relief may be restricted in this way are limited partners, members of a limited liability partnership and other partners who do not spend a significant amount of time personally engaged in carrying on the trade.

Excess relief will be recovered if, after loss relief has been claimed, the partner's capital contribution is reduced by the exclusion of amounts under the provisions outlined above. Excess relief is recovered by means of an income tax charge on the partner. The chargeable amount is computed under ITA 2007 s 793 and is taxable as income of the partner arising otherwise than from the trade for the tax year in which the relevant decrease in the partner's capital contribution occurred. Partners whose excess loss relief may be recovered in this way are those who have claimed relief for trading losses sustained in periods beginning on or after 2 December 2004 during which they were limited partners, members of a limited liability partnership, or did not spend a significant amount of time personally engaged in carrying on the trade.

For the treatment of partnership losses generally, see **[44.9]**.

(b) *Partnership losses from exploiting a licence: non-active partners.* These rules are designed to tackle schemes used by partners to reduce the tax charge on income from a licence or similar agreement. The schemes aim to generate trading losses followed by a disposal of the licence or related income rights for a sum not otherwise chargeable to income tax. The legislation ensures that the disposal of income rights is charged to income tax, but only in relation to a partner who does not devote 'a significant amount of time' to the trade (professions are not affected) at the time the losses are generated.

(c) *Partnership losses derived from exploiting films: non-active partners.* Relief under ITA 2007 s 64 or 72 for trading losses derived from exploiting films is restricted in certain circumstances in the case of an individual partner who does not devote 'a significant amount of time' to the trade. Such relief can be given only against income consisting of profits from the trade in question and not against other income or against chargeable gains. The restriction applies to losses sustained in the tax year in which the partner first carries on the trade and in any of the next three tax years. FA 2004 provisions were further extended by FA 2005. HMRC now have the power (ITA 2007 s 802(2)) to set out in regulations details of the kind of contributions that are excluded in computing the amount of the partner's contribution to the trade for this purpose.

(d) *Film-related losses: disposal of a right to profits.* There is a potential exit charge, under ITA 2007 s 797, where an individual has claimed loss relief under ITA 2007 s 64 or 72 for a trade that has benefited from the special reliefs available for certain films and subsequently disposes of a right to profits arising from the trade. A charge may also arise where the losses claimed exceed the individual's capital contribution to the trade.

(e) *Restrictions on interest relief.* ITA 2007 ss 791–795 remove restrictions on the amount of interest relief that an individual can claim in respect of a loan to buy into a partnership. The provisions also disregard such interest relief in computing any restrictions on the amount of loss relief that an individual partner can set off against their other income or capital gains. The measures apply to interest paid by a partner on or after 2 December 2004 and to restrictions on the amount of loss relief that a partner can set off in respect of trading losses sustained in periods beginning on or after 2 December 2004 (see ITA 2007 s 795).

(f) *Individuals: Non-active traders.* Finance Act 2008 made changes, to the rules for 'sideways loss relief' claimable by individuals who, otherwise than in a partnership, carry on trades in a non-active capacity (as defined in s 74C) (FA 2008 s 60, 61 and Sch 21). These rules are designed to prevent individuals using these activities to generate losses that can be offset against their other taxable income or capital gains. The restriction applies if an individual carries on a trade, otherwise than as a partner in a firm, in a non-active capacity, and the individual makes a loss in the trade in a tax year that arises directly or indirectly in consequence of, or otherwise in connection with, relevant tax avoidance arrangements (as defined in s 74ZA). Broadly, the measure means that no sideways relief or capital gains relief will be given to the individual for that loss. In addition, the total amount of sideways relief and capital gains relief for all affected losses of an individual for a tax year must not exceed the cap for that tax year. The cap is currently set at £25,000 (s 74A(4)). No relief is due where the cash basis (under ITTOIA 2005 s 25A) has been made (s 74E).

Where the individual is a non-active partner or limited partner in a firm and the loss is subject to restriction under ITA 2007 s 103C, the cap is reduced by the amount of that loss that is given as sideways relief or capital gains relief. This means that the amount of a loss for a tax year that may be allowed for 'sideways loss relief' from affected losses, incurred as a non-active partner, a limited partner, or a non-active sole trader, cannot exceed £25,000 for a tax year.

(g) A targeted anti-avoidance rule ('TAAR'), designed to prevent post-cessation trade relief from being available where a payment, or event, for which relief is sought arises from relevant tax avoidance arrangements, applies to payments made, and events occurring, on or after 12 January 2012.

(h) From 2013–14 onwards, income tax reliefs, which an individual may claim under step 2 of the income tax calculation in ITA 2007 s 23, are restricted to £50,000 or, if more, 25% of the taxpayer's adjusted total income for the tax year (see [11.5]).

(i) From 3 December 2014, loss relief is not allowed under ITA 2007 s 152 where a loss arises as a result of relevant tax avoidance arrangements.

In addition, the miscellaneous income against which loss relief under s 152 can be deducted will be limited to an individual's 'relevant miscellaneous income' rather than 'miscellaneous income', as previously defined in s 152(5). 'Relevant miscellaneous income' is so much of the individual's total income as is income or gains arising from transactions and income on which income tax is charged under, or by virtue of, the same provision in ITA 2007 s 1016 as a profit or other income arising from the relevant loss-making transaction would have been charged, if the loss on the transaction had been profits or income. This change took effect from 6 April 2015 (FA 2015 s 22). **[11.122]**

12 Land

Updated by Sarah Laing, CTA, Chartered Tax Advisor

I   Application of trading principles [**12.1**]
II Chargeable persons and computation [**12.41**]
III Furnished holiday lettings [**12.61**]
IV The taxation of premiums and rent factoring [**12.81**]
V   Transactions in UK land [**12.101**]

I APPLICATION OF TRADING PRINCIPLES

1 Ambit of income from property rules

ITTOIA 2005 Part 3 charges income tax on the *profits of a property business*, which includes isolated or casual lettings, income from furnished lettings and certain lease premiums. ITTOIA 2005 s 264 provides: 'A person's UK property business consists of every business which the person carries on for generating income from land in the United Kingdom, and every transaction which the person enters into for that purpose otherwise than in the course of such a business.' The following matters should be noted.

First, the tax is not levied by reference to income produced from individual properties but instead looks at *all* properties owned by the individual under the umbrella of a 'property income business'.

Second, that business includes isolated transactions provided that they are entered into 'for generating income from land'. (Insofar as the term 'a business' implies continuous activities, it is, therefore, something of a misnomer.)

Third, rents from furnished lettings come within the ITTOIA 2005 Part 3 provisions.

Finally, 'other receipts', not just rent, are caught by the ITTOIA 2005 provisions although given that the charge is on *annual* profits or gains, it is only receipts of an *income* nature that are caught (subject to the special rules in ITTOIA 2005 Part 3 Chapter 4 governing lease premiums: see [**12.81**] ff).

[**12.1**]–[**12.21**]

EXAMPLE 12.1

(1) Rustic sells turves from his land: he falls within ITTOIA 2005 Part 3 and the payments are of an income nature being received for the exploitation of rights in UK land (*Lowe v J W Ashmore Ltd* (1971)). Contrast the position of Campo who received a 'one-off' payment in return for a licence to tip. This payment is of a capital nature and, therefore, outside the income from property business rules – see *McClure v Petre* (1988) in which Sir Nicolas Browne-Wilkinson V-C concluded that:

> 'The substance of the present matter is that the payments were received by the taxpayer as consideration for a once and for all disposal of a right or advantage appurtenant to the land; namely the right or advantage of using it for dumping. Immediately before the licence was granted, the value of the land itself included the value of the right to turn it to advantage by using it for dumping. After the licence that right or advantage had gone forever in return for a lump sum. True the acreage of land and the taxpayer's interest remain the same; but it was shorn of this valuable advantage. It was in truth a realisation of part of the value of the freehold. That strikes me as a disposal of a capital nature ...'

(2) Junius lets flats and the tenants pay a service charge aimed at recouping Junius's costs of maintenance, insurance and repairs. These payments fall within ITTOIA 2005 Part 3 (see ITTOIA 2005 s 266(2)). Contrast the position if Junius provided other services, such as a caretaker, when he would be carrying on a trade and so payments made in return for such services would be assessed under ITTOIA 2005 Part 2 (Trading Income).

2 The income is unearned

The concept of the 'property income business' is limited in that, although the tax charge is computed on normal trading principles, the income is not itself treated as earned income. As a result income tax benefits associated with earned income (for example, pension entitlement) and the CGT business reliefs (such as roll-over relief and entrepreneurs' relief) do not apply. Special rules, however, apply to 'furnished holiday lettings' in the UK (see **[12.61]** and **[12.63]**). Whether property lettings qualify for IHT business property relief is considered elsewhere (see **[31.42]** ff). [12.22]

3 Lettings outside trading provisions

A line of cases decided in the early 1980s examined the nature, and consequential treatment for tax purposes, of letting income. These cases include *Webb v Conelee Properties Ltd* (1982), in which the court held that there was no such trade as 'the letting of properties producing a rent'. That is precisely what is charged to tax and the taxpayer had conducted no other activities which could have amounted to a trade. Similarly, in *Griffiths v Jackson* (1983), income from letting furnished flats or bedsitting rooms to students was held to be income from land and not trading income (see also *Gittos v Barclay* (1982)). Unless a landlord can establish that either he is running an hotel or guest house or can bring himself within the holiday letting provisions, then all his income from land (apart from charges for ancillary services constituting a trade, such as caretaking) will be taxed as the unearned income of a property income business. **[12.23]**

4 Exclusions from the property income charge

ITTOIA 2005 s 267 expressly excludes certain income from the property income charge: namely, profits from the occupation of land; profits and gains arising from mines, quarries and certain other concerns such as markets, tolls, bridges and ferries (which by ITTOIA 2005 s 12 are taxed under ITTOIA 2005 Part 2 Chapter 2 (Trades and Trade Profits)); mineral rent and royalties (taxed half as income from trade and half as capital) and miscellaneous receipts such as income from wayleaves or tolls, which is received after basic rate income tax has been deducted at source by the payer under ITTOIA 2005 s 335 (and see ITTOIA 2005 s 344 in relation to payment for wayleaves for electricity cables, telephone lines, etc).

Rental income from land outside the UK is charged to tax under ITTOIA 2005 s 265. Specifically, s 265 states that: 'a person's overseas property business consists of every business which the person carries on for generating income from land outside the United Kingdom, and every transaction which the person enters into for that purpose otherwise than in the course of such a business'.

Letting property abroad is treated as a separate trade with the same rules for computing receipts and expenses. The lease premium rules also apply to property outside the UK (see **[18.37]**).

Profits from the occupation of land such as farming are taxed as a trade under ITTOIA 2005 s 9. There is a specific exemption from this charge in the case of 'the occupation of land which comprises woodlands or is being prepared for use for forestry purposes' (ITTOIA 2005 s 10–11) but in *Jaggers (t/a Shide Trees) v Ellis* (1997) this was held not to cover the planting and cultivating of conifers for Christmas. This activity was taxable as a trade.
[12.24]–[12.40]

II CHARGEABLE PERSONS AND COMPUTATION

1 Chargeable persons

ITTOIA 2005 s 271 provides for the tax to be charged on and paid by 'the person receiving or entitled to the profits', whilst s 270(1) provides for the tax to be computed on 'the full amount of the profits arising in the tax year'.

In the application of these rules to settlements comprising land HMRC considers that it will normally be the trustees who are carrying on the business save where there is an old style strict settlement or where the trustees have delegated their management powers to the life tenant under TLATA 1996 s 9. In both these cases the business will be carried on by the beneficiary. This distinction will be significant in cases where a life tenant personally owns land on which he makes a loss. Only in these two exceptional cases does HMRC consider that he is entitled to set his loss against the property income in the settlement. **[12.41]**

2 Computation: accountancy practice

So far as computation is concerned, ITTOIA 2005 s 272(1) states that: 'profits of a property business are calculated in the same way as the profits of a trade'.

As a result, property business profits must be computed on the basis of generally accepted accountancy practice (GAAP) that will, in the absence of express statutory provision, decide what is a taxable receipt and what is an allowable expense. The trade and trade receipts principles are applicable (see **[10.61]** ff) so that deduction is available for items of expenditure incurred wholly and exclusively for the purpose of the property business provided that the particular type of expenditure is not prohibited by the statute (eg capital expenditure incurred in the making of improvements or acquiring the premises: ITTOIA 2005 s 33). **[12.42]**

EXAMPLE 12.2

Julia acquires a Fulham flat for letting. It is in a rundown condition and she expends substantial sums restoring it to its former glory. These sums will be deductible expenses provided that the property was capable of letting without repair works having to be carried out. Otherwise they would be capital and disallowable under ITTOIA 2005 s 33 (see generally the cases of *Law Shipping Co Ltd v IRC* (1924) and *Odeon Associated Theatres Ltd v Jones* (1972) discussed at **[10.142]**).

3 Proposed property income allowance

At March Budget 2016, the Government announced the introduction of a £1,000 allowance for property income, with an expected start date of 6 April 2017. Under the proposals, individuals with property income below £1,000 in a tax year will no longer be required to declare or pay tax on that income. Those with income above the allowance will calculate their taxable profit either by deducting their expenses in the normal way or by deducting the allowance from their gross income. Although this measure was contained in the original publication of the Finance Bill 2017, it had been dropped from the much reduced version, which received Royal Assent on 27 April 2017. It is anticipated that the measure will reappear in a Finance Bill later this year, pending the outcome of the General Election on 8 June 2017. **[12.43]**

4 Consultation on cash basis

In August 2016, the Government launched a consultation on proposals to introduce a more comprehensive cash basis of taxation of rental business profits, modelled on the cash basis for unincorporated trades. The proposals would see the taxpayer concentrate on receipts and payments only, in order to derive taxable profits, rather than working with invoices, provisions and accruals, etc. The consultation indicated that legislation would be contained in Finance Bill 2017, but this was not to be the case. The proposals appear to have been temporarily shelved, but may be introduced at some later stage.
[12.44]

5 Interest payments

A deduction is currently permitted for interest paid on loans where the money borrowed is 'wholly and exclusively' incurred for the purposes of the property business. Linking interest payments to rent from a particular property is unnecessary: indeed the particular property acquired by means of the relevant loan may be sold but it may be that relief will continue provided that the property business continues (in this connection consider, however, *Wharf Properties v IRC* (1997)).

From April 2017 the amount of relief on finance costs (such as mortgage interest, interest on loans to buy furnishings and fees incurred when taking out or repaying mortgages or loans) that individual landlords of residential property can claim is restricted to the basic rate of tax. The new restriction is being phased in over four years, starting from 6 April 2017 (ITTOIA 2005 s 272A(1)–(4)). The legislation was originally enacted in F(No 2)A 2015 ss 274A–274C, but was subsequently partly substituted by FA 2016 to clarify that the basic rate tax reduction will be available to beneficiaries of deceased persons' estates, and ensure the basic rate tax reduction will apply and be calculated 'as intended'.

Under the reform, landlords will be able to obtain relief as follows:

- in 2017–18, the deduction from property income will be restricted to 75% of finance costs, with the remaining 25% being available as a basic rate tax reduction;
- in 2018–19, 50% finance costs deduction and 50% given as a basic rate tax reduction;
- in 2019–20, 25% finance costs deduction and 75% given as a basic rate tax reduction;
- from 2020–21, all financing costs incurred by a landlord will be given as a basic rate tax reduction.

A separate restriction applies from April 2017, for investment loan interest in the case of property partnerships.

Furnished holiday lettings are excluded from this reform.   [12.45]

EXAMPLE 12.3

Jennie borrows substantial sums to acquire property A, to renovate property B and to re-roof property C. During the year, despite her best endeavours, property A remains unlet whilst property C is sold. Property B is let throughout the year. Jennie is carrying on a property business and all the interest payments are deductible in computing her profit.

6 Losses

The general principle is that losses incurred in a property business can only be offset against future profits of that business (ITA 2007 s 118). Relief against other income is only available in two cases (ITA 2007 s 120): *first*, losses resulting from claims to capital allowances; and, *second*, for 'agricultural expenses' incurred in connection with the management of an agricultural estate. From 6 April 2013, a cap applies to the amount of relief that may be claimed to certain previously unlimited income tax reliefs that may be deducted from income under ITA 2007 s 120 (property loss relief against general income) (FA 2013 s 16 and Sch 3). The cap is set at £50,000 or 25% of income, whichever is greater.

There is no right to carry back unrelieved property business losses. The trade rules for bad debts and pre-business expenditure apply.

Property loss relief against general income is denied where the loss is attributable to the annual investment allowance (ITA 2007 s 127A).

In relation to arrangements entered into on or after 13 March 2012 (or any transaction forming part of arrangements which is entered into on or after that date), property loss relief against general income is denied for agricultural expenses and post-cessation property relief where expenses, or a payment or event for which relief is sought, arise from relevant tax avoidance arrangements (see [12.63]) (ITA 2007 s 127B). [12.46]

7 Capital allowances

Capital allowances for machinery and plant used in the management of property will be given as a property business expense, as part of the profit calculation. Capital allowances are not available for plant or machinery let in a dwelling house (CAA 2001 s 35(2)) so, until 5 April 2016, the renewals basis or the wear and tear allowances for furnished lettings were given instead (ITTOIA 2005 ss 308A–308C). Under the renewals basis the entire cost of replacing furniture, furnishings and chattels (excluding any additions or improvements) could be deducted in arriving at the profits from the lettings in the year when that expense was incurred. The alternative method, the allowance for depreciation, permits the deduction of 10% of the gross rent less expenses in relation to utilities, council tax or anything else the cost of which is, in the case of a furnished letting, normally borne by the lessee (ITTOIA 2005 s 308C). In addition to this 10% allowance, the landlord may claim the cost of renewing fixtures such as baths, washbasins and toilets. Once a taxpayer has claimed allowances on one of these two bases, the practice is for that basis to continue.

From April 2016, the wear and tear allowance has been replaced with a new relief allowing all residential landlords to deduct the actual costs of replacing furnishings (ITTOIA 2005 s 311A; CTA 2009 s 250A) (see [12.48]). Capital allowances continue to apply for landlords of furnished holiday lets. Until April 2015, landlords could claim the Landlord's Energy Saving Allowance (LESA) of up to £1,500 per property per tax year for expenditure incurred in respect of energy-saving items (such as loft and cavity wall insulation, draught proofing and insulation for hot water systems and floor insulation), where the expenditure was incurred in the course of a property income business. Where more than one person had an interest in the building concerned, the allowance could be apportioned accordingly (ITTOIA 2005 s 312). [12.47]

8 Replacement domestic items relief

FA 2016, s 74 repealed the statutory wear and tear allowance in ITTOIA 2005 ss 308A-308C with effect from 2016/17 onwards (see [12.47]). The new rules make provision for a deduction for expenditure on the replacement of domestic items such as furniture, furnishings, appliances (including white goods) and kitchenware in a let dwelling-house. The deduction applies for expenditure incurred on or after 6 April 2016 for income tax payers and 1 April 2016 for corporation tax payers on an item that is substantially the same as the item being replaced, plus any costs incurred in disposing of, or less any proceeds received for, the item being replaced (see Example 12.4).

The availability of the relief is conditional on certain conditions being met:
- the expenditure must relate to the replacement of a domestic item for use solely by the lessee in the let property;
- the old item must no longer be available;
- the expenditure is capital in nature and incurred wholly and exclusively for the purposes of the property business;
- capital allowances are not available in respect of the expenditure; and
- rent-a-room relief has not been claimed.

Where the replacement is superior to the old item, the deduction is limited to the cost of an equivalent replacement.

EXAMPLE 12.4

Rakeman replaces a washing machine in one of his buy-to-let (BTL) properties with a washer-dryer, which cost £500. The washing machine-only version would cost just £400, so Bill can claim only £400 replacement domestic items relief.

However, when he comes in turn to replace that washer-dryer with a new model washer-dryer a few years later, this time for £650, then the full amount will be allowable, since it will then be a like-for-like replacement.

EXAMPLE 12.5

George is the landlord of a furnished property. In 2017–18, he replaces the sofa at a cost of £600 and the washing machine at a cost of £300. He pays £20 to dispose of the old washing machine and he sells the old sofa for £50.

For 2017–18, George can claim a deduction of £870 (the cost of the replacement items (£600 + £300), plus the cost of disposing of the washing machine (£20), less the proceeds from the sale of the old sofa (£50)).

The legislation accommodates part-exchanges and letting arrangements without a formal lease and clarifies that the item being replaced should no longer be available for use in the dwelling-house. [12.48]

9 Rent-a-room relief (ITTOIA 2005 Part 7 Chapter 1)

Designed as a tax incentive to encourage owner-occupiers and tenants who have a spare room in their home to let it out, gross annual rents not exceeding £7,500 are currently exempt from income tax (SI 2015/1539). Prior to 6 April 2016 the annual threshold was £4,250.

In the 2017 Spring Budget, the government announced that it will consult on proposals to redesign rent-a-room relief, to ensure it is better targeted to support longer-term lettings. This will align the relief more closely with its intended purpose, to increase supply of affordable long-term lodgings.

As the current rules stand, the following conditions must be satisfied:
(1) relief is available to *individuals* on a letting of *furnished* accommodation;
(2) the individual does not derive any taxable income other than rent-a-room receipts from a relevant trade, letting or agreement;
(3) the letting must be in the individual's *'only or main residence'* in the *'basis period'* (ie in the current year: letting for office accommodation does not qualify);
(4) the gross income limit will be halved if more than one person lets rooms in the same house. A husband and wife may so arrange matters that the income is either wholly the wife's or wholly the husband's;
(5) the individual can elect for this exemption not to apply (he may wish to do so, for instance, in order to claim loss relief for the relevant period);
(6) if gross annual receipts exceed the annual limit, the individual can choose either to pay tax in the normal way (on gross receipts less actual expenses) or, alternatively, on gross receipts less £7,500 (this is termed 'the alternative basis'). An election must be made on or before the first anniversary of the 31 January next following the year of assessment for which it is made (or such later date as the Board may allow) if the alternative basis is to apply. Such election remains in force until withdrawn. **[12.49]–[12.60]**

III FURNISHED HOLIDAY LETTINGS

1 Introduction

Historically, ITA 2007 s 127 provided that a UK furnished holiday lettings business could be treated as a trade and as a consequence, UK landlords benefited from the special rules governing trades for tax purposes. However, landlords with income from furnished holiday accommodation elsewhere in the European Economic Area (EEA) could not benefit from similar treatment – they were instead treated in the same way as landlords of other types of overseas property, under the property income rules. In consequence, a plan emerged to end the system altogether but, following representations from various interested groups, it was decided to retain the system, extending it to include both UK and EEA properties but tightening up the rules (FA 2011 s 52 and Sch 14).

A 'UK furnished holiday lettings business' is defined as one which consists of, or so far as it includes, the commercial letting of furnished holiday accommodation (within the meaning of ITTOIA 2005 Part 3 Chapter 6). ITTOIA 2005 s 323 defines the meaning of 'commercial letting of furnished holiday accommodation'. The provisions apply to lettings by individuals and by companies. The property business rules do not affect these provisions and owners of property suitable for letting as holiday accommodation are advised to satisfy the conditions of s 323 wherever possible so that full (rather than restricted) loss relief is available; the income qualifies as earned for pension purposes and the CGT reliefs are available. **[12.61]**

2 Qualifying holiday lettings

Accommodation will only qualify if all of the following conditions are satisfied (ITTOIA 2005 s 325):

(a) the accommodation must be available to let for commercial letting by the public for at least 210 days in a tax year;

(b) the accommodation must actually be let for at least 105 days in a tax year, ignoring lettings in the same occupation exceeding 31 days unless it is due to illness, accident or similarly unusual/unforeseen circumstance; and

(c) the accommodation must not be occupied for more than 155 days in the relevant period, for periods in excess of 31 days; however, the test is based on the lessor's intentions, rather than actual occupation accidentally or occasionally exceeding 31 days, and this would not necessarily preclude extensive personal occupation by the owner 'out of season'.

These periods need not be continuous and accordingly both winter and summer holiday accommodation may qualify. To ensure a 'genuine' holiday letting, it must not 'normally' (undefined) be let to the same person continuously in any seven months of the year (but including the 105-day period above) for more than 31 days. In the remaining five months of the tax year, therefore, landlords may do what they wish with the property, eg let it continuously, keep it empty or go into occupation themselves. The above requirements will normally exclude student accommodation. The letting of caravans is included, in so far as it is not taxed as a trade under the trading income provisions, but not the letting of sites nor residential caravans for long-term occupation (IR Press Release [1984] STI 386).

There is an 'averaging election' which can be made for any year where one or more properties fail the 'qualifying period' test (ITTOIA 2005 s 326). The 'election' treats each of the properties as satisfying the 'day count' test for that year. In the situation where furnished holiday lettings are owned both in the UK and EEA, the averaging election is made separately for each of the two categories of property.

There is a 'period of grace' which will help properties that may meet the 'qualifying period' rules for one year but fail the next. An election needs to be made on or before the 31 January self-assessment filing date for the tax year which will allow the property to be treated as satisfying the 'letting condition' for that coming year. The 'period of grace' can include the following year if required, but must not be made should the 'averaging election' above have already been made. If the election is made for the first year, it need not be made for the second; however, it cannot be made for the second year without also having been made for the first (ITTOIA 2005 s 326A).

The term 'holiday' accommodation is undefined; if the above conditions are satisfied, it will be deemed to be a holiday letting (see eg *Gittos v Barclay* (1982) where these requirements were satisfied). 'Letting' means occupation by a person other than the landlord and includes granting a licence to occupy.

Whether the accommodation qualifies as a holiday let in any tax year is judged on the facts of that year (for company landlords, the financial year). However, where the letting begins in a tax year (eg on 1 August 2016), it may qualify as a holiday let for that year if it satisfies the above requirements within the following 12 months (ie between 1 August 2016 and 31 July 2017).

Likewise, a letting that ends in a tax year must satisfy the necessary conditions during the previous 12 months. [12.62]

3 **Other measures**

Although the 2011 Budget confirmed that the existing system for taxing furnished holiday lettings would be retained, it has been extended to include both UK and EEA properties (see above). In addition FA 2011 contained various measures to tighten up the rules as follows (FA 2011 s 52 and Sch 14):

- From April 2011 the use of loss relief is restricted such that losses can only be carried forward against future profits of the same trade. Sideways relief against general income, terminal loss relief and corporation tax relief for the offset of losses against total profits is no longer allowed.
- Losses cannot be offset against profits from other non-furnished lettings property income. However, where a business ceases to qualify for one tax year any losses previously incurred will be available for offset against subsequent profits made from the same property (ie they will not be 'lost').
- Income from property held jointly by married couples or civil partners living together is treated as arising in equal shares under ITA 2007 s 836. The exception to this general rule is for income from furnished holiday lettings in the UK. The Finance Act 2011 confirmed this exception for income from EEA furnished holiday lettings.
- Where a person owns and uses plant or machinery at different types of property business (ie both furnished and non-furnished lettings in either the UK or EU), for capital allowance purposes the capital expenditure is to be treated as though the expenditure had been incurred on the date that it was used (or reused) in the second business when it ceased being used in the first business. The amount of qualifying expenditure is treated as the market value of the plant or machinery or the amount of the original expenditure if lower.
- The valuable capital gain tax reliefs such as roll-over relief and entrepreneurs' relief which are usually only allowed for trading companies are retained and expanded to include both UK and non-UK furnished holiday letting businesses.

FA 2012 included targeted anti-avoidance rules ('TAARs') that deny property loss relief against general income for agricultural expenses and post-cessation property relief where expenses, or a payment or event for which relief is sought, arise from relevant tax avoidance arrangements (FA 2012 s 10). These measures seek to deny relief for a post-cessation property business loss (under ITA 2007 s 125) and a loss in property business with an 'agricultural connection' (under ITA 2007 s 120) where there are 'relevant tax avoidance arrangements'. Such arrangements are widely defined and are those which have as one of their main purposes the obtaining of one of those reliefs. The restrictions on relief will have effect in respect of events occurring and payments made on or after 13 March 2012 (unless paid under an unconditional contract made prior to that date).

The restriction on relief for finance costs (and for investment loan interest in partnership cases), applicable from 2017–18 onwards (see [12.45]) does not apply to the furnished holiday lettings regime. [12.63]

4 Tax treatment

Tax is charged on the full amount of the profits arising in the tax year. Such profits are treated as trading profits and, therefore, receive most of the benefits of an assessment under the income from trade provisions. Thus, the income is earned income. The tax is usually payable in two equal instalments in January and July each year.

For CGT purposes the letting is treated as a trade in any year when it satisfies the above conditions or would do so but for the fact that the property is under construction or repair. Thus, roll-over (replacement of business assets) relief (TCGA 1992 ss 152 ff) and hold-over relief on a gift of business assets (TCGA 1992 s 165) may be available on a disposal. However, a landlord who claims roll-over relief and occupies the property himself may not claim the main residence exemption against the entire gain on a subsequent disposal. In such a case the rolled-over gain is chargeable and the exemption applies only to any remaining gain. No special relief is given from IHT and property lettings do not generally qualify for business property relief.

EXAMPLE 12.6

'Seaview' is purchased for £40,000 in 1997 and let as furnished holiday accommodation until 2004. It is then sold for £60,000 and the proceeds used in the purchase of 'Belvedere' for £85,000 that is similarly let. In 2006 the landlord takes possession and lives there until 2010 when he sells it for £145,000.

In 2004, the gain on 'Seaview' is rolled over into the purchase of 'Belvedere' giving it a base cost for CGT of £65,000. On the sale of 'Belvedere' in 2010 the gain is £80,000, of which £20,000 (rolled over from 'Seaview') is chargeable. The remaining gain is apportioned between the period of occupation that is exempt (ie 4/6 = £40,000) and the let period (ie 2/6 = £20,000) that is chargeable.

Where the same landlord lets several 'qualifying' properties, they are taxed as one trade. Should one or more properties qualify as furnished holiday lettings in the tax year and others not, because they fail to satisfy the former 70-day requirement, the landlord can claim, within two years of the end of the relevant tax year, for the days of letting to be averaged between all or any of the properties thereby enabling all the properties to qualify. Thus, if property A had been let in 2010–11 for 90 days and properties B and C for 50 days each respectively, A and B or A and C can be averaged so that two properties qualify; there are insufficient letting days for all three to qualify. **[12.64]–[12.80]**

IV THE TAXATION OF PREMIUMS AND RENT FACTORING

1 Introductory

A premium is a capital sum paid by a tenant to a landlord in connection with the grant of a lease. To understand the income tax treatment of premiums, it should be remembered that the original provision was introduced before CGT so that a landlord could have avoided paying any tax by extracting a capital sum from the tenant instead of rent. Accordingly, certain premiums are deemed to be income and so chargeable to income tax. In so far as a premium is not chargeable as income it may be subject to CGT. Income tax and capital gains tax rates, whilst currently at similar levels, do differ. So, whilst the importance of the distinction between the taxes is not large, it does exist and could be used to advantage. For instance, when a landlord is entitled to substantial interest relief or has incurred deductible expenditure, he may prefer any premium to be taxed as rent. The rules on taxing a premium are something of a minefield (see the remarks of Lightman J in *Hurlingham Estates Ltd v Wilde & Partners* (1997):

> '... I would expect any reasonably competent solicitor practising in the field of conveyancing or commercial law to be aware of this concealed trap for the unwary. It is a matter he should have in mind for any transaction involving the grant of a lease and a related payment by the lessee to the lessor.') [12.81]

2 The charge (ITTOIA 2005 s 277)

If a lease is granted for a period not exceeding 50 years and the consideration includes a premium, a proportion of that premium is treated as additional rent taxable under ITTOIA 2005 Part 3 Chapter 4. This proportion is the amount that is left after deducting 2% of the premium for each complete year of the lease other than the first. The effect of the 2% discount is that the amount of premium charged to income tax falls with the length of the lease. For a 1-year lease all the premium is taxed and for a 50-year lease 2%.

EXAMPLE 12.7

Lease 16 years; premium £3,000.
Discount 2% of £3,000 over 15 years = £3,000 × $\frac{2}{100}$ × 15 = £900
Chargeable slice: £3,000 − £900 = £2,100

The grant of a sub-lease of 50 years or less will, as a general rule, be taxed in the same way as the grant of a head lease. If, however, a premium on the grant of the head lease was taxed under the property business rules, this is taken into account when taxing any premium on the grant of the sub-lease. [12.82]

3 Anti-avoidance provisions

There are elaborate provisions designed to prevent the charge to income tax on premiums from being circumvented.

First, a landlord cannot avoid the ITTOIA 2005 s 277 charge by disguising the length of the lease. If its length can be shortened by an option to surrender or to terminate, the option will be taken into account only in so far as it is likely to be exercised (ITTOIA 2005 s 303).

EXAMPLE 12.8

L grants a lease to T for 60 years at a premium of £20,000 and a rent of £1,000 pa for the first ten years and thereafter at an annual rent of ten times the then market rent. T has an option to surrender the lease after ten years. For income tax purposes this is treated as a ten-year lease since the tenant is likely to exercise the option to surrender in view of the penal increase in the rent after ten years.

Second, where a landlord, instead of taking a premium on the grant of a lease for 50 years or less, requires the tenant to make improvements to the premises, the amount by which the value of the landlord's reversion is increased as a result of those improvements is treated as a premium (ITTOIA 2005 s 278). This provision does not, however, apply if the tenant is required to make improvements to another property of the landlord; if the obligation is not imposed by the lease or if the expenditure would have been a deductible expense of the landlord.

EXAMPLE 12.9

Property is let from 1 June 2016, for seven years. Under the terms of the lease the tenant is required to carry out certain structural alterations, as a result of which the value of the landlord's interest in the premises is increased by £2,000.

Increase:	£2,000
Less: discount: 2/100 × £2,000 × 6:	£240
Included in 2016–17 property business profits:	£1,760

Third, ITTOIA 2005 ss 279–281 charge 'delayed premiums' as income. If a premium becomes payable at some date during the currency of the lease or the tenant has to pay a sum for the waiver or variation of any terms of the lease, the sum is treated as a premium and in both cases the premium is taxed in the year of receipt as a premium for the then unexpired period of the lease. If a tenant has to pay a sum for the surrender of a lease it is taxed as a premium on a lease running from the date of commencement to the date of surrender.

Fourth, the assignment of a lease, which has been granted at an undervalue is charged under ITTOIA 2005 s 282. The charge under s 277 could be circumvented by a landlord granting a lease to, say, his spouse or to a company that he owns. No premium would be charged on the grant but the lease could then be assigned to the intended tenant and a premium taken. Section 277 only applies to a premium paid on the grant of a lease not on its assignment. However, s 282 provides that, when a lease is granted for less than its market premium, tax is charged under the property business provisions on assignors of the lease up to the amount of premium forgone by the landlord and to the extent that such assignors have made a profit on that assignment. Section 282(3) ensures that receipts are taxed in the tax year in which the consideration for the assignment becomes payable.

EXAMPLE 12.10

A grants B a 21-year lease at a premium of £2,000 although he could have charged £3,000. Therefore, the 'amount foregone' is £1,000. A is chargeable on the premium that he actually receives.

Two years later B assigns the lease to C charging a premium of £2,800. B receives £800 more than he paid; that is within the 'amount foregone'.

B is, therefore, chargeable on:
£800 − (2/100 × 20 × £800) = £480

Notice that the 'amount foregone' still outstanding is £200 and that the period of the lease remains at the original length (namely 21 years) for the purpose of discounting. Two years later C assigns the lease to D charging a premium of £3,200. He has received £400 more than he paid but only £200 of that is caught under ITTOIA 2005 s 282 since that exhausts the 'amount forgone' by A. C is chargeable, therefore, on:

£200 − (2/100 × 20 × £200) = £120

An assignee should, therefore, ensure (so far as possible) that the lease was not granted at an undervalue, and if necessary should take advantage of the clearance procedure under ITTOIA 2005 s 300.

The *final* anti-avoidance provision prevents the grant of a lease from being disguised as a sale (ITTOIA 2005 s 284). If D sells land (freehold or leasehold) to E with a right to have the property reconveyed to him in the future, any difference between the price paid by E and the reconveyance price payable by D is treated as a premium on a lease for the period between the sale and the reconveyance and is taxed accordingly.

ITTOIA 2005 s 285 extends ITTOIA 2005 s 284 so that if D sells land to E with a right for him (or a person connected with him) to take a leaseback of the property in the future, any difference between the price paid by E and the aggregate of the premium (if any) payable on the grant of a lease by E, together with the value of the reversion in E's hands, is treated as a premium on a lease for the period between the sale and leaseback and is taxed under the property business provisions. So as not to prejudice a commercial sale and leaseback, this provision does not apply where the leaseback is within one month of the sale. [12.83]

EXAMPLE 12.11

D sells land to E for £40,000 with a right to take a 20-year lease of the property after 11 years for a premium of £8,000. The value of E's reversionary interest subject to the lease is £2,000. There is a deemed premium under ITTOIA 2005 s 285 of £30,000 (£40,000 − (£8,000 + £2,000)) on a lease of 11 years. D is chargeable on:

£30,000 − (2/100 × £30,000 × 10) = £24,000

4 Premium payable in instalments

If a premium is payable in instalments, the taxpayer may opt to pay the tax in such instalments as HMRC may allow (ITTOIA 2005 s 299). The instalment period may not exceed eight years, and must end not later than the time the last instalment of the premium is payable (ITTOIA 2005 s 299(3)). [12.84]

5 Relief for traders paying a premium on trading premises (ITTOIA 2005 s 60)

Rent is an allowable deduction from the trading income of a trader (ITTOIA 2005 s 34). If a trader is granted a lease of business premises for 50 years or less at a premium, he can treat a portion of the premium as an annual rent and deduct it from his trading income (ITTOIA 2005 s 60). This portion is the amount of the premium that is charged to income tax in the landlord's hands under the property business provisions divided by the unexpired term of the lease. The rest of the premium is a capital expense.

A premium paid by a trader who takes an assignment of a lease is not allowable as a deduction from trading income unless the premium is caught by s 282. [12.85]

EXAMPLE 12.12

L grants T a lease of business premises for ten years at an annual rent of £100 and a premium of £10,000.

L is chargeable under ITTOIA 2005 on £8,200 of the premium (see ITTOIA 2005 s 277). The yearly equivalent of this sum, £820 (£8,200 ÷ 10), can be treated by T as additional rent so that each year he can deduct rent of £920 (£820 + £100) from his trading receipts.

6 Position of trusts

Lease premiums received by trustees are a capital receipt as a matter of general law. Hence whilst the trustees will run a property income business so that basic rate income tax will be charged on the income deemed to arise from the premium, that deemed income will not be subject to the 'surcharge' under ITTOIA 2005 s 568 and, in the case of interest in possession trusts, will not lead to a higher rate liability in the hands of the life tenant. And, of course, the sum received will form part of the trust capital. [12.86]

7 Reverse premiums (ITTOIA 2005 Sch 2 paras 28 and 71)

A reverse premium is a sum paid by a landlord to a prospective tenant as an inducement to enter into a lease. In *IRC v Wattie* (1998) the Judicial Committee of the Privy Council held that although the premium was linked to an increased rent payable by the tenant it was a capital sum. As a result the premium would be subject to neither income tax nor capital gains tax. FA 1999 reversed this decision by treating them as income receipts taxable under ITTOIA 2005. Note the following:
(1) the definition of a reverse premium for these purposes is 'an inducement in connection with a transaction being entered into' by the recipient or a connected person. It is not thought that the paying of a sum to cover fitting-out costs would fall within this definition;
(2) if the premium is taken into account to reduce the amount qualifying for capital allowances it is not taxed as an income receipt under these rules (thereby avoiding an effective double charge). [12.87]

8 Rent factoring (CTA 2010 Part 16)

EXAMPLE 12.13

(1) Dumb Ltd borrows £100,000 for the purposes of its property business. The interest is tax deductible in arriving at the profits of the company but repayments of capital are not.

(2) Smart Ltd disposes of its right to receive the rents of its portfolio properties for seven years in consideration for the payment of a lump sum (in effect a loan which will be repaid – as to both principal and interest – out of future rents) which the company then argues is chargeable to corporation tax as capital gains and which is therefore offset by available losses and reliefs (see *IRC v John Lewis Properties plc* (2003)).

Anti-avoidance legislation prevents Smart Ltd from obtaining these benefits by providing that the sum received (ie the capital sum) is to be taxed as income. There are detailed rules to ensure that there is no double taxation where the sum forms part of a company's trading profits or falls within other specific property business legislation. The legislation applies to a 'rent factoring transaction' that is identified by reference to its correct accounting treatment in the accounts of Smart. It does not apply to rent factoring arrangements entered into by partnerships or individuals nor to factoring agreements that exceed 15 years. **[12.88]–[12.100]**

V TRANSACTIONS IN UK LAND

1 Transactions in UK land

Finance Act 2016 introduced provisions, which radically change the way in which profits from trading and development in UK land are taxed (FA 2016 ss 76–82). The rules seek to level the playing field between resident and non-resident companies or individuals, by basing the charge on the location of the land rather than the residence of the taxpayer making the disposal. The territorial scope of corporation tax (in CTA 2009 s 5) has been amended to include non-UK resident companies which carry on a trade of dealing in or developing UK land. Subject to transitional provisions, the new rules took effect from 5 July 2016, replacing the previous provisions contained in ITA 2017 Part 13 Chapter 3 and CTA 2010 Part 18. **[12.101]**

2 Trading transactions

The anti-avoidance provisions do not apply to trading transactions which are of a capital nature. The definition of a trade has been restrictively interpreted in *Marson v Morton* (1986) in which the judge stated that:

> 'the mere fact that land is not income producing should not be decisive or even virtually decisive on the question whether it was bought as an investment.'

However, land originally acquired for a non-trading purpose (eg investment) may subsequently be appropriated to trading stock. At this point a CGT charge may arise under TCGA 1992 s 161 although this can be avoided by the election to transfer the land at no gain/no loss. In *Taylor v Good* (1974), discussed at **[10.23]**, the house in question did not become trading stock merely because the taxpayer had applied for planning permission before the sale:

> 'If you find a trade in the purchase and sale of land, it may not be difficult to find that properties originally owned (for example) by inheritance, or bought for

investment only, have been brought into the stock in trade of that trade. But where, as here, there is no question at all of absorption into a trade of dealing in land or lands previously acquired with no thought of dealing, there is no ground at all for holding that activities such as those in the present case, designed only to enhance the value of the land in the market, are to be taken as pointing to, still less as establishing, an adventure in the nature of trade.' (Russell LJ)

By contrast, in *Pilkington v Randall* (1966) land was held in a will trust for a brother and sister absolutely. It was sold at different times and roads and drains were constructed prior to the sales. Furthermore, the brother bought parcels of the land from his sister. He was held to be trading. At first instance, Cross J stated:

'I do not think that one can lay down hard and fast rules, such as that the construction of roads and sewers and the installation of services can never be enough to make the case one of embarking upon a trade. One has to look at the whole picture and say whether the amount of money spent on the development before sale and the objects for which and the circumstances in which the money was spent are such as to make it reasonable to say that what was inherited has changed its character and become part of the raw material or stock in trade of a business.'

In the Court of Appeal, Danckwerts LJ likewise stated that there was no general proposition of law to the effect that whenever a property owner develops his land by making roads and laying sewers and selling plots he can never be carrying on a trade:

'This would be opening the door very wide to modern property developers. I think the highest it can be put is that usually in such circumstances the property owner is not carrying on a trade, but whether in the particular case he is or is not doing so must depend on the facts of the particular case. It is essentially a question of fact and degree.'

It is apparent from the foregoing cases that how the land came to be owned by the taxpayer is an important factor in determining whether he is trading. If it is acquired by *inheritance* or *gift* HMRC will have to show that it has at some point been appropriated to trading stock (in such cases it may also be argued that the land has not been 'acquired' as required by ITA 2007 s 517B for income tax or CTA 2010 s 356OB for corporation tax purposes). On the other hand, if acquired *by purchase* the taxpayer's motive at that time will be relevant. If it is clear that it was acquired as an investment, again the burden will be on HMRC to show that at a subsequent stage it was appropriated to trading stock. Furthermore, if land was originally acquired as an investment, the mere act of obtaining planning permission prior to a sale will not by itself result in an appropriation of the land to trading stock. Generally the taxpayer is entitled to get the best possible price for the land (*Taylor v Good*, above).

Care needs to be exercised if, as a prelude to sale to a developer, the taxpayer decides to acquire adjacent parcels of land. Such extra parcels will have been acquired purely for resale and there is a risk therefore that the taxpayer will be treated as a trader (and not just in relation to those portions but also in relation to the previously owned land). The purchase of small areas of land need not necessarily create problems: the taxpayer may merely be taking steps to obtain the best possible price for his existing land as in *Taylor v Good*. However, it would naturally be advisable, whenever practicable, to arrange for the developer to acquire any extra land that will be needed for the development. [12.102]

3 The effect of falling within the transactions in UK land provisions

The legislation converts a gain that would otherwise be of a capital nature (and therefore in the case of an individual subject to CGT) into an income profit subject to income tax for the chargeable period in which that gain is realised (ITA 2007 Part 9A; CTA 2010 Part 8ZB for CT). The gain is to be computed by such method as is 'just and reasonable' in all the circumstances (ITA 2007 s 517J; CTA 2010 s 356OJ for CT) so that CGT computational rules will not necessarily apply.

The effect of taxing the gain as income is that for an *individual* the maximum rate of charge is 45% (2013–14 onwards). The lower rates applicable to corporation tax may make it advantageous to shelter the gain in a company. If the gain is realised by *trustees*, income tax will be charged at basic rate. If there is an interest in possession, as a matter of trust law the capital sum will not belong to the life tenant and it is not thought that the amount charged on the trustees by reason of ITA 2007 Part 13 Chapter 3 can be treated as the income of the beneficiary. In general, therefore, gains realised through the medium of a trust will escape income tax at the top rate (subject to an exception where the trust income is deemed under the tax legislation to be that of the settlor: see further **Chapter 16**).

The gain is taxed as unearned income so that, although it may be reduced by other unearned income losses, it cannot be reduced by pension contributions nor by trading losses. [12.103]

4 When do the anti-avoidance rules apply?

The following conditions must be satisfied (ITA 2007 s 517B; CTA 2010 s 356OB for CT):
(1) A person within (2) below realises a profit or gain from a disposal of any land in the United Kingdom, and any of conditions A to D is met in relation to the land.
(2) The persons referred to in (1) above are:
    (a) the person acquiring, holding or developing the land,
    (b) a person who is associated with the person in paragraph (a) at a relevant time, and
    (c) a person who is a party to, or concerned in, an arrangement within (3) below.
(3) A transaction is treated as an arrangement if:
    (a) it is effected with respect to all or part of the land, and
    (b) it enables a profit or gain to be realised:
        (i) by any indirect method, or
        (ii) by any series of transactions.

The conditions are as follows:

Condition A is that the main purpose, or one of the main purposes, of acquiring the land was to realise a profit or gain from disposing of the land.

Condition B is that the main purpose, or one of the main purposes, of acquiring any property deriving its value from the land was to realise a profit or gain from disposing of the land.

Condition C is that the land is held as trading stock.

Condition D is that (in a case where the land has been developed) the main purpose, or one of the main purposes, of developing the land was to realise a profit or gain from disposing of the land when developed. **[12.104]**

5 Disposal of land

For a charge under this anti-avoidance condition there must be a disposal of land. Land is disposed of if the property in the land or control over the land is effectively disposed of by one or more transactions, or by any arrangement or scheme (ITA 2007 ss 517C–517G). This may include the disposal of shares in a land company and an interest in a company, partnership or trust which is wound up (ITA 2007 s 517S).

Land is also deemed to be disposed of if, as a result of arrangements and schemes falling within ITA 2007 Part 9A (CTA 2010 Part 8ZB for CT), there is an effective disposal of the land itself or control over the land. It is a moot point whether the letting of land at a rack rent is a disposal. Given that the value of the property in the hands of the taxpayer is unchanged, it may be argued that such a lease does not involve any disposal of land despite the fact that such a letting does confer rights in land on the tenant.

For tax to be imposed it is also necessary for a gain to be *realised*. This will only occur when a person can effectively enjoy or dispose of money or money's worth. In the case of the right to future sums the question is, therefore, whether such sums can be valued and treated as part of the disposal proceeds (see *Yuill v Wilson* (1980)). A further disposal for the purposes of the anti-avoidance legislation will occur when sums become quantifiable (see *Yuill v Fletcher* (1984)). **[12.105]**

6 Trading stock

If land is held as trading stock or obtained with the main purpose of selling at a profit, that profit will be subject to tax under the trading income provisions of ITTOIA 2005 in the majority of cases (see **[12.102]**). However, a disposal of land is widened in s 517B (CTA 2010 s 356OB for CT) to include transactions, arrangements, and schemes concerning the land or property deriving its value from the land as a result of which there is a disposal of the land or control over the land. Hence, it is likely that the income provisions will apply in cases where the land (or more likely property deriving its value from the land) is acquired with the intent of transferring control over the land by some indirect means.

An owner-occupier who decides to develop his land will naturally fall within ITA 2007 Part 9A. It is specified that the relevant gain is that arising after the intention to develop is formed. Apart from the difficulties of determining when this occurs, the formation of this intention may result in the land becoming trading stock, with the result that any charge will arise under ITTOIA 2005 Part 2 (see also ITA 2007 Sch 1 para 321; CTA 2010 Sch 1 para 238 for CT). The owner-occupier who sells his land for development by a third party will not normally fall within this provision unless he stipulates for some future payment linked to the value of the land after it has been developed (see [12.107]). [12.106]

7 Connected persons

The person who holds or develops the land may be caught as may a person connected with him (for 'connected persons', see ITA 2007 s 993; CTA 2010 s 1122 for CT purposes). In addition, a gain realised through a scheme or arrangement by an indirect method, or as a result of a series of transactions, will lead to a tax charge on any person concerned in that scheme or arrangement. In such cases, tax is imposed to the extent of the gain realised by the particular individual as can be seen by the case of *Winterton v Edwards* (1980). In that case L was the prime mover in a complicated tax avoidance scheme and owned all the shares in the relevant property company except for two small holdings owned by W and B. He acquired two sites outside the company for development and when W and B protested at this he arranged to give them a share in any sale proceeds from the land. (Former) section 776 assessments on W and B were upheld because, although they were not parties to L's various transactions, they were *concerned in* the transactions as a result of their small interests in the proceeds of sale. Hence, if one person intends to realise a gain within (former) s 776 (in this case both acquiring and developing land with the intention of realising a gain on its disposal) other persons may then be caught, even though they lack that intention, if they participate in the arrangement.

The phrase 'scheme or arrangement' is wide enough to catch a vendor or landowner who retains a share of the ultimate development profits. In *Page v Lowther* (1983), trustees owned four houses forming a site suitable for redevelopment. They granted a 99-year lease to the developers who in turn granted underleases of new dwellings when constructed at premiums payable partly to the trustees and partly to the developers. In all, the trustees received premiums totalling £1.2m. On these facts, the Court of Appeal held that the expression 'an arrangement or scheme' had no sinister overtones so that the grant of the lease by the trustees to the developers was such an arrangement. Further, the grant of the underlease was a disposal (albeit not by the trustees) in return for a capital sum so that the trustees were held liable on their share under former s 776. The Court of Appeal did not accept that the duty of the trustees to obtain the best possible price afforded any defence to them. The case is authority for the proposition that the section is not limited to artificial transactions, nor need tax avoidance be a motive on the part of the taxpayer (see [12.101]). For the rate of tax charged on the trustees, see [12.103].
[12.107]

8 Shares in landholding companies

There is a disposal of land if control over it is disposed of. Hence the disposal of a controlling shareholding in a landowning company is treated as a disposal of the land.

The further requirement, that a gain of a capital nature must be obtained from the disposal by a person owning that land *or by any connected person*, may be satisfied when shares in a landowning company are sold if the vendor controls that company. In such a case he will then be a connected person (ITA 2007 s 993; CTA 2010 s 1122(3) for CT). If two or more shareholders act together their interests may be aggregated in order to determine whether they have control for these purposes: the agreement of a number of minority shareholders to sell their shares may amount to an 'arrangement' under ITA 2007 Part 9A (CTA 2010 Part 8ZB).

There is an exemption from charge under s 517L (CTA 2010 s 356OL for CT) when land is held as trading stock by a company and there is a disposal of the shares in that company *provided* that the land is subsequently disposed of by the company in the normal course of its trade in order to ensure that all opportunity of profit in respect of that land arises to the company. To take advantage of this exemption it is normal when selling a property dealing company to obtain from the purchaser a warranty that the trading stock (ie the land) will be sold in the normal course of the trade. However, it is obviously difficult to draft such warranties and the vendor remains very much in the hands of the purchaser. It should also be noted that this exemption does not furnish any defence when a scheme or arrangement has been entered into. [12.108]

9 Providing an opportunity

A gain may be obtained for another person (ITA 2007 s 517P; CTA 2010 s 356OO) (eg trusts are treated as distinct entities from the beneficiaries). In general, a gain is obtained in such circumstances if the opportunity of making that gain is transmitted by premature sale or otherwise. For example, if B allows value to pass out of his land into A's land whereupon A makes a gain falling within the section, all or part of that gain may be attributed to B. In such cases, B is given a right of recovery against A for the tax that he suffers, although this may prove to be worthless if A is a non-resident.

The opportunity of making a gain is not presumably transmitted merely because land is sold even when it is possible that a gain will be made in the future. As the following case illustrates, however, it is no defence to claim under this section that the land was transferred for full consideration.

In *Yuill v Wilson* (1980), Mr Yuill, who controlled various UK companies, arranged for land to be sold to Guernsey companies who thereupon obtained planning consent for redevelopment and sold the land back to a Yuill UK company at a substantial profit. This profit constituted a gain of a capital nature and Mr Yuill was treated as a person who indirectly furnished the opportunity for the making of that gain. It was Yuill personally who was subject to charge not the companies which he controlled and which actually transferred the land to the Guernsey company. Note also that all these transactions were at market value. It is somewhat surprising that sales at full value can be regarded as a transfer of an opportunity to make a gain simply because at some later date the market value of the land increases.

Does an outright sale of land with the benefit of planning permission constitute the transmission of an opportunity? It is generally thought that the answer to this question is no, so long as the sale is a genuine transaction to an unconnected person for which full consideration is paid. [12.109]

10 Typical situations

First, a landowner may sell his land for a capital sum at a time when there is obviously development potential. That sale will not usually be a trading transaction (assuming that there are no other trading factors present) and ITA 2007 Part 9A will also be inapplicable assuming that it is on arm's length terms to an unconnected person (see [12.109]).

Second, the landowner may obtain planning permission and then sell the land. This is not usually trading (see *Taylor v Good*, [12.102]) and the anti-avoidance provisions will not apply if the sale is at arm's length etc (see [12.109]).

Third, the landowner may develop his own land. On an eventual disposal of the land or an interest therein he will be subject to an income tax charge either as a trader or under ITA 2007 Part 9A. In both cases his gain will be computed from the time when the intention to develop was formed. If a landowner buys extra land with a view to developing the enlarged site he may then become a trader (see [12.102]). Similarly, there is a risk of trading if agreements are entered into with an adjacent landowner (such agreements may even result in the formation of a trading partnership) although a mere agreement to find a single purchaser for two parcels of land should not have this result.

Finally, a vendor or landowner who intends to sell but who wishes to obtain a slice of any future development profits runs the risk of falling within *Page v Lowther* (see [12.107]). In this case the courts proposed a fairly general test for the applicability of former s 776: for instance 'has a gain of a capital nature been derived from the relevant disposal?' (which will usually be the leasing of the developed site) and 'did the (original landowner) obtain any gain from the disposals effected by the under-leases?' [12.110]

11 Possible ways of avoiding ITA 2007 Part 9A and/or CTA 2010 Part 8ZB, but still obtaining 'a slice of the action'

A vendor could insert a covenant against development into the contract of sale and subsequently agree to release this in return for a capital sum. Although this arrangement may offer advantages when there is no immediate prospect of the purchaser wishing to develop the land it is impractical if that is his immediate intention. Furthermore, such restrictions may not be commercially acceptable to the purchaser.

Alternatively, provision could be made in the original sale agreement for a further sum to be payable based on a proportion of the market value of the land after it has been developed. Arguably this does not constitute a gain of a capital nature derived from a disposal of land falling within ITA 2007 Part 9A (or CTA 2010 Part 8ZB). Further, even if this sum is calculated by reference to rents achieved, it is thought that the capital sum is still not derived from a *particular disposal*.

There are two major objections to this arrangement. *First*, the developer may find it unacceptable since it imposes an obligation on him to pay a capital sum unrelated to moneys received for letting the developed site. (Thus it will be payable even if he fails to let or sell that site.) *Second*, this may be a scheme or arrangement sufficient to be caught on the reasoning in *Page v Lowther* (see **[12.107]**). *Third*, it has been suggested that the arrangement involves the landowner in trading. This view may be doubted: if it is correct it is difficult to see why *Page v Lowther* was argued under former s 776 since the arrangements in that case would be trading transactions.

A further possibility is to shelter the gain by transferring the land to a trading company. This operation should be carried out before any development is undertaken and the result will then be that the land is held as trading stock so that any profit from the development will be an income receipt of that company (but taxed, at most, at 19% (from 1 April 2017)) and therefore a gain of a capital nature will not have been obtained. This arrangement depends upon the existence of a suitable company and there is obviously a risk of a tax charge if the shares in that company are subsequently sold for a capital sum (see **[12.108]**).

As an alternative sheltering device, ensure that any gain is realised by trustees. Only the basic rate of tax will be payable unless the anti-avoidance provisions can be invoked by HMRC (see **[12.103]**).

Finally, ensure that a capital sum is not received from a disposal of the developed land. Assume, for instance, that the purchaser/developer agrees that he would only take a rack rent (not premiums) on lettings of the developed site. For ITA 2007 Part 9A to apply in this case, a capital sum received by the taxpayer would have to fall within s 517B(7). Under that provision it is necessary for land to be developed: 'the main purpose, or one of the main purposes, of developing the land was to realise a profit or gain from disposing of the land when developed'. It is arguable that the grant of leases at a rack rent is not a disposal and furthermore, that the receipt of rents will not amount to the realisation of a *gain* for the purpose of the subsection. The difficulties with this arrangement are, *first*, will the purchaser agree to accept only a rental return? And *second*, the original vendor remains entitled on the properties being let to a capital sum based upon a multiple of the rental value. Thus, it is arguable that *Page v Lowther* may apply since he will then have obtained a capital sum from a disposal of the developed land, albeit that that sum was paid by the original purchaser not the sub-lessee. **[12.111]**

12 Other matters

Although there is a clearance procedure under ITA 2007 s 770 (CTA 2010 s 831 for CT), opinions vary as to whether it should be used. In *Page v Lowther*, for instance, clearance was refused, the scheme went ahead and was then challenged. There are those who feel that applying for clearance merely puts HMRC on notice. Unlike the other clearance procedures (eg under CTA 2010 s 748 and TCGA 1992 s 138) the application must be made to the local tax office: ie the matter is considered at a much lower level where there is obviously a temptation simply to issue a blanket refusal giving no reasons.

The anti-avoidance rules apply to non-UK residents if all or any part of the land is situated in the UK (s 759(8); CTA 2010 s 819). When the person entitled to the consideration is not resident in the UK, HMRC can require the payer to deduct income tax at the basic rate from the consideration and pay it over to HMRC (s 944(2) and see *Pardoe v Entergy Power Development Corp* (2000)). This can apply even if the recipient is not the taxable person but HMRC obviously need to know about the transaction in advance and this will not normally be the case. ITA 2007 Part 13 Chapter 3 does not apply to a gain arising to an individual on the disposal of his principal private residence which is exempt from CGT (TCGA 1992 ss 222 ff), or (generously) which would be exempt from CGT were it not that the property was acquired with the intention of making a gain on its disposal (TCGA 1992 s 223(3)). [12.112]

13 Miscellaneous income
Updated by David Salter, Emeritus Reader, University of Warwick

I   Scope [13.1]
II The various charges [13.2]
III Procedural aspects [13.16]
IV Specific cases [13.23]

I SCOPE

The rules on miscellaneous income are expressed differently for income tax and corporation tax and are found in different Acts. The income tax rules on miscellaneous income are contained in ITTOIA 2005 Part 5 and took effect from 2005–06 onwards. The corporation tax rules on miscellaneous income are to be found in CTA 2009 Part 10 and are effective for accounting periods ending on or after 1 April 2009. Prior to these dates miscellaneous income was taxed under Schedule D Case VI. The provisions in both ITTOIA 2005 and CTA 2009 mirror each other with specific rules for some sources of miscellaneous income, and general measures to catch income not otherwise charged.

For income tax purposes, the residual rules are found in ITTOIA 2005 Part 5 Chapters 7–8, which subject to various exemptions charge tax on any annual payments that are not charged to income tax under any other provision (s 683) and any income from any source (ie excluding annual payments) that is not charged to income tax under any other provision (s 687). For corporation tax purposes, the 'sweeping-up' rules are found in CTA 2009 Part 10 Chapters 7–8, which subject to various exemptions charge tax on annual payments not otherwise liable to corporation tax (s 976) and on any income that is not charged to corporation tax under any other provision (s 979). Much of the discussion in this chapter deals with the principles surrounding this residual or 'sweeping-up' role.

The miscellaneous income provisions in ITTOIA 2005 and CTA 2009 do not provide just a default head of charge. ITTOIA 2005 Part 5 and CTA 2009 Part 10 contain specific charges to tax under the 'miscellaneous' heading, in addition to the catch-all provisions described in the previous paragraph. This chapter contains an outline discussion of these specific charges many of which are also discussed in more detail elsewhere in this book. The concluding sections of this chapter deal with certain procedural aspects of

430 *Miscellaneous income*

the miscellaneous income provisions: see **[13.16]** and specific sources of miscellaneous income: see **[13.23]**. **[13.1]**

II THE VARIOUS CHARGES

1 Charging options

A source of income may fall within one of the specific sources of miscellaneous income described at **[13.4]**–**[13.5]** or it could be taxable as:
- an annual payment not otherwise charged to income tax or corporation tax (ITTOIA 2005 s 683; CTA 2009 s 976): see **[13.6]**–**[13.8]**; or
- income not otherwise charged to income tax or corporation tax: see **[13.10]**–**[13.11]** (ITTOIA 2005 s 687; CTA 2009 s 979).

Some income that might otherwise appear to be miscellaneous income may be taxed as trading income, property income, investment income or employment income: see **[13.14]**. Various exemptions apply to exclude certain income from the miscellaneous income charge: see **[13.9]**–**[13.11]**.
[13.2]

2 Specific charging provisions

The legislation specifically taxes a number of sources of income under the miscellaneous income heading. **[13.3]**

a) *Income tax*

ITTOIA 2005 Part 5 charges income tax on the following sources of income (s 574(1)):
(1) receipts from intellectual property (Chapter 2, ss 578–608);
(2) films and sound recordings (otherwise than from a trade) (Chapter 3, ss 609–613);
(3) telecommunications rights (otherwise than from a trade) (Chapter 4, ss 614–618);
(4) settlement income where it is treated as income of the settlor (Chapter 5, ss 619–648);
(5) beneficiaries' income from estates in administration (Chapter 6, ss 649–682).

Where income could be taxed both as a receipt from intellectual property and as income from a film or sound recording, it is dealt with under Chapter 3 (ITTOIA 2005 s 576). **[13.4]**

b) *Corporation tax*

CTA 2009 Part 10 charges corporation tax on the following specific sources of income (s 932(1)):
(1) beneficiaries' income from estates in administration (Chapter 3, ss 934–968);
(2) income from the holding of an office (Chapter 4, ss 969–970);
(3) income treated as arising from the sale or other realisation of dividend coupons in respect of foreign holdings (Chapter 6, ss 974–975). **[13.5]**

3 Annual payments not otherwise charged

If the income is not specifically taxed under the provisions described at **[13.4]–[13.5]** it may still be taxed as miscellaneous income if it is an annual payment. See *Mitchell v Rosay* (1954) where the Court of Appeal held that receipts from the exploitation of a film were annual payments and not capital and *Joyce v HMRC* (2005) where compensation paid monthly by an employer to an employee for incorrectly calculating his pension on early retirement was considered an annual payment by the Special Commissioner, and not capital as alleged by the appellant. Certain renewal commissions rebated to investors in collective investment schemes, insurance policies and other investment products by fund managers, advisors and intermediaries, are considered to be annual payments liable to tax under the miscellaneous income rules, HMRC Brief 04/13. **[13.6]**

a) *Income tax*

Income tax under the miscellaneous income provisions is charged on annual payments that are not otherwise charged to tax, for example as trading income (ITTOIA 2005 s 683(1)–(2)). In determining whether the sums are annual payments the frequency with which payments are made is ignored (ITTOIA 2005 s 683(3)).

Tax is charged on the full amount of the annual payment unless it is foreign income within the remittance basis rules in ITTOIA 2005 Part 8 (ITTOIA 2005 s 684(2)). If the annual payment is a discretionary payment made by trustees the payment is grossed up in accordance with ITA 2007 s 494 (ITTOIA 2005 s 684(3)). Where the annual payment has income tax deducted at source this is available to be off-set against any tax liability (ITTOIA 2005 s 686). (See **Chapter 14** for the taxation of annual payments.)

The person liable to pay the tax is the person receiving or entitled to receive the payment (ITTOIA 2005 s 685) subject to special rules applicable to settlor-interested settlements (ITTOIA 2005 s 685A).

The following sources of income are specifically exempt from tax as miscellaneous income (ITTOIA 2005 s 683(4)):

- certain annual payments made by individuals including commercial payments (s 728), payments for non-taxable consideration (s 729) and foreign maintenance payments (s 730);
- periodical payments of personal injury damages (s 731);
- compensation awards (s 732);
- payments from trusts for injured persons (s 734);
- health and employment insurance payments (ss 735–743);
- payments to adopters, special guardians and those caring for children under a residence order (ss 744–747);
- certain interest and royalty payments (ss 757–767); and
- scholarship income (s 776). **[13.7]**

b) *Corporation tax*

Corporation tax under the miscellaneous income provisions is charged on annual payments not otherwise within the charge to corporation tax (CTA 2009 ss 976–977). In determining whether the sums are annual payments the frequency with which payments are made is ignored (CTA 2009 s 977(3)). Where tax is deducted at source from the annual payment this is taken into account in certain cases (CTA 2009 s 976(2)). [13.8]

4 Income not otherwise charged

Ultimately, if income is not taxed elsewhere it may still fall to be taxed as miscellaneous income. [13.9]

a) *Income tax*

There is a further residual charge on income not otherwise charged to tax. The income tax charge is on income from any source that is not charged to income tax excluding annual payments within ITTOIA 2005 s 683, disguised interest under ITTOIA 2005 ss 381A–381E, income taxed under another provision and amounts that are treated as income either expressly or by implication (ITTOIA 2005 s 687). Income tax is charged on the amount of miscellaneous income arising in the year with modifications for income within the rent-a-room, qualifying care relief or remittance basis provisions (ITTOIA 2005 s 688). The person liable for the tax is the person receiving or entitled to the income (ITTOIA 2005 s 689). Certain close company distributions paid whilst an individual (or their associate) is temporarily non-resident (and not otherwise liable to tax under the miscellaneous income provisions) are taxed under ITTOIA 2005 s 689A.

Specific exemptions from these provisions apply to the commercial occupation of woodlands under ITTOIA 2005 s 768 and gains on commodity and financial futures under ITTOIA 2005 s 779 (ITTOIA 2005 s 687(5)).
[13.10]

b) *Corporation tax*

The 'sweeping-up' corporation tax charge taxes income that is not otherwise liable to corporation tax excluding annual payments, exempt and deemed income (CTA 2009 s 979). The commercial occupation of woodland (CTA 2009 s 980) and gains arising in the course of dealing in financial futures, traded options or financial options (CTA 2009 s 981) are exempt from a corporation tax charge under these provisions. [13.11]

5 Income rather than capital

The legislation in ITTOIA 2005 Part 5 and CTA 2009 Part 10 expressly taxes income. Therefore, the principles discussed in **[10.103]** on the boundary between income and capital apply equally here. Where profits are derived from the provision of services or the exploitation of a capital asset, then those profits will be treated as having an income quality. Where profits are derived instead from the disposal of a capital asset, or a sufficiently substantial interest in a capital asset, they will be treated as of a capital nature and so are not taxable as income at all (but may be taxed as chargeable gains). A high proportion of the reported cases turn on the distinction between income and capital. The first question to ask is, 'does the transaction generate "income" taxable under the miscellaneous income provisions, or is it a capital transaction?'

This question was considered in *P Manduca v R & C Comrs* (2015), where the Upper Tribunal, upholding the decision of the First-tier Tribunal, held that compensation given to a hedge fund manager for an 'investment bonus' (owed for introducing certain business to his employer but not paid because he was made redundant) was taxable under then applicable Schedule D Case VI rules. The bonus, and thus the compensation, was found to be a reward and not a capital sum. In *Hobbs v Hussey* (1942) a solicitor's clerk (who was not an author by vocation) contracted with a newspaper to write his memoirs; the payment that he received was income taxable under Schedule D Case VI as a payment for services. In *Benson v Counsell* (1942), the sale of stud rights in a stallion in which the taxpayer had a part-share was also held to be an activity taxable under Case VI, being the exploitation of the taxpayer's rights arising under a capital asset: the interest in the stallion itself. In contrast, in *Trustees of Earl Haig v IRC* (1939), the trustees of Earl Haig's estate allowed an author to use Earl Haig's diaries for the purposes of writing a biography. It was held that the sums they received were capital in nature, being the sale price for the part-disposal of a pre-existing capital asset (the copyright in the diaries). It was clear that this was a disposal of a sufficiently important interest in that asset; three of the four members of the Court of Session expressly noted that this transaction largely exhausted the publication value of the diaries. The capital versus income argument also succeeded in *Beare v Carter* (1940) (writing fee) and *Nethersole v Withers* (1948) (sale of copyright). In *Healey v R & C Comrs* (2015), the taxpayers' profit of £2.21m on a floating-rate promissory note purchased for less than its face value was agreed by both parties to be a profit on a discount – the question was whether the discount was of a capital or income nature. The Upper Tribunal held that the discount was income and therefore taxable under the then applicable Schedule D Case III rules.

In certain circumstances, an activity may be partly an income transaction and partly a capital transaction because it has aspects of both the provision of services and the sale of a capital asset. In this case, it is important to determine whether the profits are to be treated as income, or capital, or to be split between the two. In *Hobbs v Hussey* (1942), the taxpayer not only provided services to the newspaper, but also assigned (or at least licensed) the copyright in his words to them. Based on the facts, the court found that the assignment of copyright was of little importance. It characterised the transaction as one that involved, in substance, the provision of services, and imposed a tax treatment accordingly. By contrast, in *Hale v Shea* (1964) the court sought to apportion the taxpayer's profits between two separate aspects (even though this was not possible on the facts). The cases do not provide a clear test for when one aspect of a mixed transaction is to be subsumed within the other. On the other hand the very helpful test set out by the ECJ in another context in the case of *Card Protection Plan Ltd v Customs and Excise Commissioners* (1999) (see [38.25] and [40.37]) could well be of assistance. [13.12]

6. **A taxable source**

The early case law considered that there would only be a liability to income tax if the income arose from a taxable source, see *Attorney-General v Black* (1871). This resulted in several cases where income was held not to be taxable because it did not come from a 'source', see *Graham v Green* (1925), *Bloom v Kinder* (1958), *Dickinson v Abel* (1969) and *Anise v Hammond* (2003) where gambling winnings and introductory fees were found to be unsolicited gifts, ex-gratia payments or received by chance. This rationale could still be the case for a purely voluntary payment such as a 'thank you' gift which HMRC considers not to be taxable as miscellaneous income; see BIM 100110 and **[13.25]**.

The need to consider whether there is a 'source' of income does not apply the specific charges in ITTOIA 2005 Part 5 Chapters 2–6 (see **[13.4]**–**[13.5]**). In relation to the residual charges, the legislation appears to catch only income from a 'source' (for ITTOIA 2005 s 683 annual payments and for ITTOIA 2005 s 687 'any other source') but in ascertaining the territorial scope of the charge ITTOIA 2005 s 577(1) specifically states that the miscellaneous income charge applies to UK residents 'whether or not it is from a source in the United Kingdom'. The charge also applies to non-UK residents but only if the income is from a UK source (ITTOIA 2005 s 574(4) and s 577(2)). Where income arises in the overseas part of a split year, it is treated as arising to a non-UK resident (s 577(2A)). If income does not have a source it refers to income which has a comparable connection to the UK (ITTOIA 2005 s 577(3)).

The requirement for a taxable source does not fall to be considered for the purposes of corporation tax (CTA 2009 Part 10). The legislation applies to annual payments (s 976) but the need for there to be a 'source' is not specifically mentioned in s 979. This section simply states that 'the charge to corporation tax on income applies to income that is not otherwise within the application of that charge under the Corporation Tax Acts'.

It therefore seems that in order to contend that that there is no 'source' of income under ITTOIA 2005 s 687 it is now necessary to show that ITTOIA 2005 s 577 is limited to ascertaining the territorial scope of the provisions and some cases might now be decided differently. **[13.13]**

7 Taxing priority

a) *Alternative charges*

Even if profits are of an income nature, whether or not from a taxable source, they will not be taxable as miscellaneous income (ie under ITTOIA 2005 Part 5 or CTA 2009 Part 10) if they are taxed under another head. Where there is a choice between taxing income as miscellaneous income or some other category, the trading income, property income, savings income and employment income provisions all take priority over the miscellaneous income charge (ITTOIA 2005 s 575 and CTA 2009 s 982).

For both income tax and corporation tax purposes, the principal challenge is (and always has been) to determine whether profits are really trading profits (including the profits of a profession or vocation). In other words the question is whether the income is caught by the trading income provisions of ITTOIA 2005 Part 2 or CTA 2009 Part 3. In practice the need to compare the miscellaneous category and the other heads of charge does not arise frequently. **[13.14]**

b) *Trading or miscellaneous income?*

Certain quasi-trading (including quasi-professional and quasi-vocational) profits will not be caught by ITTOIA 2005 Part 2 or CTA 2009 Part 3, and so will be taxable under ITTOIA 2005 s 687 or CTA 2009 s 979 instead.

Transactions carried out otherwise than with a profit motive may not be treated as trading transactions. In *Ryall v Hoare* (1923), Rowlatt J held that a fee paid to company directors for guaranteeing the company's overdraft was taxable under Schedule D Case VI, relying on the fact that the directors had given the guarantee only by way of a favour. Similarly, in *Clarke v British Telecom Pension Scheme Trustees* (2000), fees paid to the taxpayer for providing certain services were held to fall within Case VI on the basis that the taxpayer had provided the services not with a view to profit, but so as to protect the value of other investments. In *CIR v Forth Conservancy Board No 2* (1931) the House of Lords held that fees paid to a statutory body were taxable under Case VI rather than Case I, as it was not constituted as a profit-making body.

In addition, there are cases where profit-motivated quasi-trading activities have been taxed under Case VI on the basis that they do not amount to a trade. In *Benson v Counsell* (above) profits from the sale of stud rights were held to be taxable under Case VI. In *Cooper v Stubbs* (1925) and *Townsend v Grundy* (1933), profits from transactions in cotton futures were held to be capable of being taxed under Case VI (and the profits in question in those cases were taxed in that way). It is notable, in particular, that these were not considered to be gambling profits. These decisions have now been reversed on their facts by ITTOIA 2005 s 779 and CTA 2009 s 981, which provide that dealings in commodity and financial futures, traded options and financial options which are not part of a trade and so to be taxed as such are to be charged to CGT rather than under ITTOIA Part 5 Chapter 8 or CTA 2009 Part 10 Chapter 8. However, *Cooper v Stubbs*, like *Benson v Counsell*, still stands as authority for the proposition that certain items of quasi-trading income will be taxable under ITTOIA 2005 Part 5 Chapter 8 or CTA 2009 Part 10 Chapter 8. It is necessary in such instances simply to consider whether the taxpayer can truly be said to be trading, which will be a question of fact in each case (see [10.21]–[10.31]).

In *Leeming v Jones* (1930) the taxpayer acquired rubber estates for resale at a profit, and then resold them at the hoped-for profit. The General Commissioners found that the taxpayer had not been trading, and the Revenue then sought to argue that the profit was assessable under Schedule D Case VI. The House of Lords held for the taxpayer, relying in part on the definition of 'trade' in TA 1988 s 832(1) (see ITA 2007 s 989 for income tax purposes), which encompasses an adventure/venture in the nature of a trade. They said that either this transaction was 'an adventure in the nature of a trade' in which case the profit was a trading receipt taxable under Schedule D Case I (see [10.21]–[10.31]), or a capital transaction. Either way, Case VI was not applicable. However, it is quite clear from the speeches in the House of Lords that this is very much a decision on its own facts. Their Lordships had no doubt that the purchase of assets for resale is either a trading activity or a capital activity, and they held that, in this case, it was a capital activity. *Leeming v Jones* says nothing whatsoever about whether a particular activity producing profits of an income character might be something different from a trade, and so taxable as miscellaneous income (as it was in *Cooper v Stubbs*). **[13.15]**

III PROCEDURAL ASPECTS

1 Earnings basis

From an income tax perspective the charge is on miscellaneous income 'arising' in the period for the specific and residual charges. There is limited authority for the proposition that profits are taxable when received, rather than when they become due (*Grey v Tiley* (1932)), and as small businesses have the option of preparing their trading accounts on a cash basis (see **[10.73]**), accounting for miscellaneous profits when received could be appropriate for some individuals. For corporation tax purposes there is no reference to the charge being on income 'arising' in the period but the earnings rather than the cash basis will be the appropriate method of accounting for miscellaneous income arising in the corporate context. **[13.16]**

2 Apportionment

Income tax charged under the miscellaneous income provisions may in some cases be based on accounting profits. Where accounts are drawn up for an accounting period that does not coincide with the tax year, the profits or losses may be apportioned to a tax year by reference to the number of days in the relevant period (ITTOIA 2005 s 871). A different method of apportionment can also be used if it is reasonable to do so and it is used consistently. **[13.17]**

3 Expenses

HMRC's view is that in most cases the trading income rules (see **Chapter 10**) apply to determine whether expenses are deductible in relation to miscellaneous income. Interest payments would however be unlikely to satisfy the 'wholly and exclusively' test for casual or occasional profits and there is normally no entitlement to capital allowances (see BIM 100155).

Expenses incurred wholly and exclusively in relation to income from films and sound recordings (ITTOIA 2005 s 612) and telecommunication rights (ITTOIA 2005 s 617) are deductible providing that had they been incurred for a trade they would have been deductible (see **[13.4]**). No deductions can be made where the income from telecommunications rights consists of annual payments, and in determining this the frequency with which the payments are made is ignored.

The principle established in *Curtis Brown Ltd v Jarvis (and cross-appeals)* (1929) that expenses are deductible on the same basis as trading income also appears to apply to other miscellaneous income where expenses are incurred. Apart from some specific exclusions in s 688(2) relating to rent a room relief, qualifying care relief for foster and other carers and foreign income, there is no express rule on the deductibility of expenses for the residual charges. For s 687 there is obviously no question of deducting expenses in respect of s 683 income but not much seems to be made of this in practice and under the former Schedule D Case VI legislation the words 'profits or gains' implied a surplus of income after deducting expenses (see, for instance, *CIR v Forth Conservancy Board* (above)). For corporation tax purposes no reference is made with regard to the deductibility of expenses. [13.18]

4 Full amount of the income

Miscellaneous income is taxable on the recipient in full. An attempt to assign 50% of the royalty payments for development of an inhaler to the taxpayer's wife failed (*PW Braithwaite v R & C Comrs* (2008)). Non-cash receipts, for example a holiday provided as an alternative to a cash payment, are however likely to be taxable as miscellaneous income based on the amount of the cash alternative. Non transferable, non convertible items are not taxable (see BIM 100150). [13.19]

5 Losses

For income tax purposes miscellaneous losses are calculated in the same way as miscellaneous profits (ITTOIA 2005 s 872). From 2015–16 relief for losses from relevant miscellaneous transactions (as defined by ITA 2007 s 1016) is given against relevant miscellaneous income (ITA 2007 s 152(1)). This means that the losses can only be off-set against miscellaneous income of the same type as the loss (ITA 2007 s 152(4)). The losses can be deducted from relevant miscellaneous income for the loss-making year, the next tax year and subsequent tax years until they are fully utilised (ITA 2007 s 153). Relief must be claimed within four years (ITA 2007 s 155). From 3 December 2014, no tax relief is available if the loss arises as the result of relevant tax avoidance arrangements (ITA 2007 s 154A). If the miscellaneous loss is made by a partner in a partnership, it can only be deducted from other partnership transactions (ITA 2007 s 152(6)). A corporation tax loss arising from a miscellaneous transaction which had it resulted in a gain would have been treated as miscellaneous income (other than an offshore income gain), can similarly only be used against other miscellaneous income in the same tax year or in future years (CTA 2010 s 91). There is no general right to set losses against other income or gains (unlike the position for trading income losses, see **Chapter 11**. [13.20]

EXAMPLE 13.1

In 2017–18 James, who is employed as a film funding manager, received a payment of £5,000 for allowing shots of the exterior of his distinctive home to be used in a film. He and his neighbours also received from the film company a share of £1,000 plus a selection of vouchers for restaurants and movies for the inconvenience of having film crews and vehicles parked in their street for a weekend. Following the release of the film later the same year, James was interviewed by two lifestyle magazines and received further one-off payments of £4,000 and £5,000 for the interviews and photographs. During 2017–18 James thought that he might be able to license a sound recording to a company but he has so far been unable to do so. His marketing and finance costs have mounted and he has made a loss of £25,000, with no income.

How are the income and the losses to be treated assuming that none of the sources are trading income?

(1) The £5,000 for the filming of his house is miscellaneous income; see [13.12] and [13.26].

(2) The payment and vouchers to compensate James and his neighbours for inconvenience during filming are probably ex-gratia and not taxable; see [13.19] and [13.26].

(3) The two interviews totalling £9,000 are miscellaneous income; see [13.25].

(4) The loss of £25,000 for the sound recording cannot be off-set against the filming income or the income from the interviews. It can only be carried forward against any future sound recording income; see [13.20].

In 2017–18 James is taxable on £14,000 of miscellaneous income (£5,000 + £9,000). The £25,000 of losses can be carried forward but may never receive relief. [13.21]

6 Legal proceedings

When a question of whether a source of income is taxable comes before the courts it is common practice for HMRC to include the 'catch-all' claim discussed at [13.9] that the income is taxable as miscellaneous income (see for instance *Smith and Williamson Corporate Services v R & C Comrs* (2015), *Robert Rusling v R & C Comrs* (2014) and *Geoffrey Michael Fenech v R & C Comrs* (2013). Often the case is decided without the need to consider whether the income is in fact miscellaneous income but the miscellaneous income provisions provide a useful 'back-stop' to prevent income escaping an income tax or corporation tax charge should the primary argument fail. In *Spritebeam Ltd & Other v R & C Comrs* (2015) the Upper Tribunal reviewed a corporation tax avoidance scheme and confirmed the First-tier Tribunal decision that the scheme was ineffective. Under the scheme one company in a group lent money to another under a loan agreement. No interest was payable while the loan was outstanding but, instead, irredeemable preference shares equal in value to a commercial rate of interest on the loan were to be issued to a third group company. The lender and share recipient maintained that neither of them was liable for tax on the interest or an equivalent sum. Analysis of two anti-avoidance provisions and legislation, which has since been replaced, led to the conclusion that the tax outcome should be determined by the loan relationship rules. However, because the value of the preference shares were credited to capital there was no income to be taxed. The Schedule D Case VI 'catch-all' provisions then became relevant, with the Upper Tribunal holding that the company receiving the shares was taxable on their receipt being analogous to interest received under Schedule D Case VI. The shares did not have the characteristics of a voluntary payment as the borrower company was legally obliged to issue them under the loan agreement. [13.22]

IV SPECIFIC CASES

Whilst the statutory provisions and case law describe and illustrate aspects of the scope of the miscellaneous provisions, there are other non-statutory sources to consider in order to understand the extent of the charge and the interaction with other potential charges particularly trading income. For further details see HMRC's Business Income Manual BIM 100000. [13.23]

1 Theatrical 'angels'

A person who backs a theatrical production (called an 'angel') and who is not trading is strictly assessable under ITTOIA 2005 s 683 (see [**13.7**]) on any return received over and above the original investment. Losses are dealt with under the capital gains tax rules. Until 5 April 2017 Extra Statutory Concession (ESC) A94 permits the profits of angels to be taxed under ITTOIA 2005 s 687 (see [**13.10**]) and allows losses to be calculated under ITTOIA 2005 s 872 and relieved against miscellaneous income for the year or carried forward. Where the concession is used the losses are not relieved as capital losses. From 6 April 2017 ESC A94 is withdrawn as a result of statutory relief for corporate investment in theatre productions being available from 1 September 2014 (CTA 2009 ss 1217F–1217OB). For further details about the taxation of theatre backers see BIM 66601. [**13.24**]

2 Writing and publishing

Publishing, even if it is in small quantities or a one-off piece, may be trading income. If not the income is likely to be taxed under the miscellaneous income provisions unless it is a capital transaction, see [**13.12**]. Payments for newspaper stories are usually taxable as miscellaneous income, see *Hobbs v Hussey* (1942), *Housden v Marshall* (1958), *Alloway v Phillips* (1980) and BIM 100230, as are receipts from self-publishing, vanity publishing or print on demand books, see BIM 100205. The fact that a publishing agreement does not require much work to be done does not prevent the income being taxable miscellaneous income (see *Brocklesby v Merricks* (1934) and *Bradbury v Arnold* (1957)). [**13.25**]

3 Photography and filming

Sale of a photograph other than as part of a trade is assessable as miscellaneous income unless the copyright of the photograph is sold (also not as part of a trade) when the transaction is a capital disposal (BIM 100235). See also at [**13.12**].

Fees paid for allowing a property to be used for filming will either be property income or miscellaneous income. Payments, for example to a group of residents for disturbance during a film shoot, are likely to be gratuitous and not taxable as miscellaneous income (see BIM 100245). [**13.26**]

4 Hire of equipment and toll charges

The casual hire of equipment (not as part of a trade) is taxed under the miscellaneous income provisions (BIM 100220). Profits from the charging of tolls which do not arise from the ownership of land and are not taxable as trading income, are also likely to be taxed as miscellaneous income (BIM 100250). [**13.27**]

5 Cash-backs, commissions and fees

Cash-backs that are not trading income and which are not gratuitous may be assessable as miscellaneous income, see Statement of Practice 4/97. This includes introductory fees (see **[13.15]**) and rebated commission from 6 April 2013 (see **[13.6]**) but not inducements in the course of ordinary retail business (BIM 100210). Commission not taxed elsewhere is taxable as miscellaneous income, see *Brocklesby v Merricks* (1934) and *Hugh v Rogers* (1958) unless it can be argued that it is ex-gratia, see *McGarry v EF* (1953), or capital, see *Bradbury v Arnold* (1957). A reward paid to a person who acts as a guarantor is taxed as miscellaneous income if not otherwise assessable; see *Sherwin v Barnes* (1931), BIM 100215 and **[13.15]**. **[13.28]**

6 Volunteer drivers

Volunteer drivers (for hospital journeys or the elderly) are paid mileage allowances. The drivers are not considered to be employees and are unlikely to be trading; as such they are taxable on any profit made over and above the statutory tax-free mileage and passenger rates. **[13.29]**

The potential issues outlined in this chapter seem unlikely to cause many problems in practice, and if they do the dispute usually relates to the distinction between income and capital. Miscellaneous income is now closely focused on a few specific sources of income not taxed elsewhere in the legislation, and whilst the sweeping-up provisions remain, in the majority of cases it is likely that the income under discussion will usually be taxed as trading income.

[13.30]

14 Annual payments, patent royalties and savings income

Updated by Anne Fairpo, Barrister

I   General [**14.1**]
II Terminology [**14.6**]
III Taxation of annual payments [**14.11**]
IV Deduction of tax at source for annual payments (ITA 2007 Part 15 Chapter 6 and s 448; Chapter 17) [**14.21**]
V   Taxation of interest payments [**14.31**]
VI Intellectual property royalties [**14.40**]
VII Other savings income [**14.41**]
VIII Collection of tax deducted at source: ITA 2007 Part 15 Chapters 15, 16 and 17 [**14.45**]

I   GENERAL

1   **Introduction**

Interest, annuities and other annual payments are charged to tax under the Income Tax (Trading and Other Income) Act 2005 (ITTOIA 2005) (for corporation tax purposes, see the Corporation Tax Act 2009 (CTA 2009)). The Income Tax Act 2007 (ITA 2007) also has a considerable impact upon the way in which tax is paid in respect of annual and certain other payments. The rules in ITA 2007 relating to deduction of tax from a variety of different types of payment are to be found in Part 15; those relating specifically to deduction of tax from annual payments and patent royalties are dealt with in Chapter 6 of Part 15. The rules under which the tax deducted is to be collected can be found in Part 15 Chs 15–17 (see [**14.45**]). [**14.1**]

2   **Ambit of charge to tax on annual payments and savings income**

ITTOIA 2005 Part 5 imposes a charge to tax on miscellaneous income, which includes annual payments not otherwise charged to tax. Part 4 of the Act provides for 'savings and investment income'. This includes, amongst other things, charges to tax on interest, purchased life annuities, discounted securities and distributions from unauthorised unit trusts. All of these will be discussed in this chapter. Other heads of charge include dividends from resident and non-UK resident companies (see **Chapter 42**), loans to participators in a close company which are waived (see [**7.25**]), gains from contracts for life insurance, etc (see [**15.2**]), transactions in deposits, disposals of futures and options involving guaranteed returns (see [**14.6**]) and sales of foreign dividend coupons (see **Chapter 18**).

Income discussed in this chapter is often termed 'pure income' because it is not normally reduced by any deductible expenses; it is pure profit. Annual payments are sometimes referred to as settlements of income since they can operate to reduce the income of the payer and increase that of the payee. Hence, the payer may be seen as settling an income sum on the payee.

[**14.2**]

3 The tax is on income arising

Income tax is charged under ITTOIA 2005 Part 4 in respect of savings and investment income. In particular, it is charged on the full amount of interest arising in the tax year (s 370) on the person receiving or entitled to receive the income in question (s 371). Income 'arises' when it is received; in the case of payment by cheque the sum is received when it is credited to the account of the recipient (*Parkside Leasing v Smith* (1984). However, the term 'arising' has a wider meaning than this; for example, where interest accrues in respect of a bank or building society account, it is received at the date when it is credited, notwithstanding that it may not be paid to the account holders until a future date; it is just as much theirs whether it is paid to them at that time or not (*Dunmore v McGowan* (1978); *Halpin v R & C Comrs* (2011)). If the payment is not made at all, there is no liability to tax (*Woodhouse v IRC* (1936)).

The phrase 'receiving or entitled to' has been considered at length by the courts, although no clear definition of it appears to have emerged. In earlier cases, the courts placed greater emphasis on the concept of receipt than on entitlement (see, for example, *Dewar v Commissioners of Inland Revenue* (1935)), but more recent cases, such as *MacPherson v Bond* (1985) have hinged on whether or not any benefit has accrued to the taxpayer. In that case a bank held a charge on the taxpayer's deposit account as security for a loan to a company. The taxpayer had not personally guaranteed this loan and accordingly interest earned on the deposit account and which was credited to it could not be said to reduce his personal liability. In the event, the company debt finally absorbed the whole of the deposit account plus interest but as Vinelott J explained:

> 'Even before the liability of the company to the bank had been finally determined ... the taxpayer's only prospect was that he would in time become entitled to repayment of so much of the deposit as was not required to meet the company's liability to the bank and to interest on that part of the deposit. The crediting of interest on the whole of the deposit could therefore be aptly described as a mere book entry: a matter of convenience of accounting for the bank.'

On the facts of the case, because the taxpayer was not entitled to the interest, he was not subject to any tax charge thereon. See also *Girvan v Orange Personal Communications Services Ltd* (1998) where, due to a renegotiated agreement between the taxpayer and its bank, interest on deposit accounts was compounded quarterly and not paid until the accounts were closed. Since the compounded interest was retained by the bank, it was not income which arose until it was actually paid to the taxpayer on closure of the relevant accounts. Nor was the decision altered by the fact that the agreement had been renegotiated in order to gain a tax advantage. By contrast, if the security is backed up by a personal guarantee, interest credited to the account is not then a mere book entry but can be seen as reducing the sum payable by the taxpayer under the guarantee. It will, therefore, be subject to income tax in the hands of the taxpayer as it arises even though he does not actually receive it! So, in *Peracha v Miley* (1990), an amount was deposited by the taxpayer with a London bank as security for a loan to the taxpayer's company, which had been expropriated by the taxation years in question. Interest which had been credited by the bank to the taxpayer benefited him to the extent that his continuing liability to repay the loans was reduced. The taxpayer therefore was the person entitled to the interest although he did not receive it (and on the general position of receipts and payments under guarantees, see *Taxation*, 1992, p 157).

In *Coxon v R & C Comrs* (2013), the taxpayer had entered into a contract to purchase a new build residential property in Cyprus and paid a substantial deposit with the balance of the purchase price to be funded by a loan. The deposit was paid into an escrow bank account in the name of the taxpayer by a Cypriot lawyer acting under a power of attorney. Interest was credited to the account and under the terms of the arrangement was to have been used to offset the sums due under the loan agreement. Even though the property development had not progressed beyond a shell, most of the escrow account had been passed to the developer, who appeared to have become insolvent. In reply to HMRC's claim that he should pay income tax on the interest that was credited to the escrow account, the taxpayer argued that he had never had access to the escrow account or the funds in it and thus could not be viewed as having either received the interest or derived any benefit from it. The Tribunal dismissed the taxpayer's argument, applying *Dunmore v McGowan*; interest credited to the account was received by and belonged to the taxpayer even if it was not actually paid to him (see also the identical case of *Thomas v R & C Comrs* (2014)). The taxpayer in both of these cases had also argued that the loan was in the nature of an offset mortgage, where savings are offset against what is owed on a mortgage thereby reducing the overall amount of interest paid by paying interest only on the difference and eliminating a tax charge on the savings. The Tribunal in each case held that for the offset arrangements to be effective for tax purposes, the offset had to be of the balances owed to and from the bank with the interest being charged or paid by reference to the net amount; it is not enough for two separate amounts of interest to be calculated and then subsequently offset, which was the situation in both of these cases (see also *Cooker v Foss* (1998)). [14.3]

4 Basis of assessment

Income assessable under Part 4 and in respect of annual payments in Part 5 is charged to tax on the actual income of the fiscal year. [14.4]

5 Companies

Special rules apply for corporation tax purposes: see 'loan relationships' and CTA 2009, Parts 5 and 6 (see [41.50]–[41.56]). [14.5]

II TERMINOLOGY

1 Interest

Apart from payments treated as interest for certain purposes (ITTOIA 2005 s 369(2) and see FA 2005 ss 46–57 which provide that the same rules that apply for interest will apply to alternative finance arrangements) and specified exemptions (ITTOIA 2005 s 369(3)), the term 'interest' is not statutorily defined. It has been described as 'payment by time for the use of money' (*per* Rowlatt J in *Bennett v Ogston* (1930)). More precisely, interest:

> 'may be regarded either as representing the profit the lender might have made if he had had the use of the money, or conversely, the loss he suffered because he had not that use. The general idea is that he is entitled to compensation for the deprivation' (*per* Lord Wright in *Riches v Westminster Bank Ltd* (1947) 28 TC 159 at 189).

In *Nicholas Pike v R & C Comrs* (2013), where it was held that the payment of a premium on the redemption of loan stock was interest (and thus not a relevant discounted security), the Upper Tribunal found that the term 'interest' does not have a special meaning and, from observations in decided cases, identified the following characteristics of an amount payable by interest:
- interest is calculated by reference to an underlying debt (see, for instance, *Re Euro Hotel (Belgravia) Ltd* (1975));
- the payment that is made by reference to that debt is payment made according to time (*Bennett v Ogston* and *Re Euro Hotel (Belgravia) Ltd*);
- the sum payable accrues from day to day, or at other periodic intervals (*Willingdale v International Commercial Bank Ltd* (1978);
- whilst interest accrues from day to day, or at other fixed intervals, it does not have to be paid at particular intervals (*Davies v Premier Investment Co Ltd* (1945);
- what the return is called is not determinative of its nature (*Davies v Premier Investment Co Ltd, Re Euro Hotel (Belgravia) Ltd*; but see also *Sutton v R & C Comrs* (2011), concerning a sum of money received by the taxpayer from an insurance company representing a refund in full for premiums paid on a Lifetime Care policy, the documentation for which failed to warn of the true risk involved in purchasing such a policy, together with 'interest'. The First-tier Tribunal held that since the agreement under

which the sum was paid referred to the additional payment as interest and that it was precisely calculated as to rate and period, it was difficult to escape the conclusion that this additional payment was interest!).
- the mere fact that the payment by way of interest may be aggregated with a payment of a different nature does not alter the nature of that part of the payment that is interest (*Chevron Petroleum UK Ltd v BP Petroleum Development Ltd* (1981) and *Sutton v R & C Comrs*).

A common question is whether a lump sum awarded as compensation or damages (by a court or tribunal or under an out-of-court settlement) contains an element of interest. Although compensation itself will normally be a capital sum, interest on it will be taxable as 'interest of money'. This was established by the *Riches* case, where it was held that interest awarded by the court under the Law Reform (Miscellaneous Provisions) Act 1934 fell within the then Schedule D Case III charge, now ITTOIA 2005 s 369 (today the award is under either the Supreme Court Act 1981 s 35A or the County Courts Act 1984 s 69, but note that interest on damages paid for personal injuries or death is not taxed (ITTOIA 2005 ss 732–734)). Whether something is 'interest of money' depends on the facts of the arrangement, or sometimes on specific statutory provisions (so eg there may be a statutory requirement for a local authority to pay interest on compulsory purchase payments). (For changes made to the tax rules on the deduction of income tax from yearly interest in respect of compensation payments, see **[14.32]–[14.33]**.)

EXAMPLE 14.1

Bigco Ltd executes a debenture deed in favour of Mr Big who has made a secured loan to the company of £10,000. The deed provides for repayment of the loan together with a 'premium' of £2,000 by the end of 2015 and interest at 10% pa on the full redemption figure (£12,000) until 2015. The interest falls within ITTOIA 2005 s 369 and the repayment of £10,000 is a capital sum. The so-called 'premium' may be seen as deferred interest or, alternatively, as a capital sum paid as compensation for the capital risk taken by Mr Big.

The true nature of the payment is a matter of fact and the terms used by the parties are not conclusive (see *Lomax v Peter Dixon & Son Ltd* (1943) and *Davies v Premier Investment Co Ltd* (1945). See also *Mazurkiewicz v R & C Comrs* (2011), where the First-tier Tribunal concluded that income arising in respect of a disastrous venture of lending money to a gun company to finance the purchase of guns, which was then automatically reinvested under a number of transactions without ever being paid to the lender, was interest rather than the profits of a trade. Whilst this ruled out the carrying back of losses, with the result that the eventual losses would eliminate earlier profits and the ability to set any excess losses against other income in the year they were incurred, the Tribunal also held that since the taxpayer lost everything, realistically no interest was ever received).

So long as the rate of interest charged is commercial, it is likely that the sum on which the interest is calculated will be treated as capital and will escape both income tax and CGT unless the debt is a 'debt on a security' within the meaning of TCGA 1992 s 132 (see TCGA 1992 s 251 and **[22.44]**).

Finally, it should be noted that if the principal debtor defaults so that the moneys are paid under a contract of indemnity the sum will still be taxed as interest; if paid by a guarantor, the position is unclear (see *Re Hawkins, Hawkins v Hawkins* (1972) on indemnities and contrast *Holder v IRC* (1932) on guarantors). [14.6]

2 Purchased life annuities

Annuities fall into two broad categories. *First*, a purchased annuity usually arising from a contract with an insurance company under which a capital sum is paid in return for a right to income (an annuity) for a stated period of time (see [14.41]). *Second*, annuities payable under an instrument, such as an annuity provided for in a will. The changes made by FA 1988 in the treatment of annual payments (see [14.13]) did not affect annuities, and such annuities fall within the ambit of annual payments. [14.7]

3 Annual payments not otherwise charged to tax

Despite the fact that most annual payments have been taken outside the tax net altogether (see [14.13]), it is still important to be able to identify a certain sum of money as an annual payment. If such a sum is an annual payment, it cannot then fall within any other head of charge and be classified, for example, as trading or earned income; it will simply remain outside of the tax net. As the name suggests, annual payments not otherwise charged to tax comprise a residual category, although the term is wide enough to include an annuity. Hence, all annuities may be described as annual payments but not all annual payments as annuities. The main features of annual payments were laid down by Jenkins LJ in *IRC v Whitworth Park Coal Co Ltd* (1958):

'(1) To come within the rule as an "other annual payment" the payment in question must be *ejusdem generis* with the specific instances given in the shape of interest of money and annuities ...
(2) The payment in question must fall to be made under some binding legal obligation as distinct from being a mere voluntary payment ...
(3) The fact that the obligation to pay is imposed by an order of the court and does not arise by virtue of a contract does not exclude the payment ...
(4) The payment in question must possess the essential quality of recurrence implied by the description "annual" ... A payment is annual if it is recurrent or is capable of recurrence. Payments made at intervals of less than a year will still be "annual" provided that they may continue beyond a year. Only payments that are income in the hands of the recipient are included. Payments may, therefore, be annual income payments; or they may represent instalments of a capital sum; or they may represent part income and part capital (in the latter case the income element will usually be interest on a debt which is being repaid in instalments). ... In considering whether payments constitute capital and/or income, the form of the document drawn up by the parties is not conclusive and a payment may represent a capital expenditure of the payer, but an income receipt for the payee and, presumably, *vice versa*.
(5) The payment in question must be in the nature of a "pure income" profit in the hands of the recipient. Accordingly, the recipient must not have incurred

allowable expenditure in return for the payment. This proposition prevents any attempt to disguise trading receipts as annual payments (see Scrutton LJ in *Howe v IRC* (1919)).'

EXAMPLE 14.2

Denis wants to sell his dental practice (which is worth £30,000) to Flossie and retire. The contract could be drawn up in a variety of different forms, eg:
(1) Flossie is to pay the purchase price of £30,000 over five years, at £6,000 pa. Each payment is a capital sum (see generally *IRC v Ramsay* (1935)).
(2) Flossie is to pay by instalments as in (1) above, but is to pay five instalments of £6,250 (so that the total sum to be paid will be £31,250). Each payment probably represents a capital and an income element and must accordingly be dissected. £6,000 is an instalment of capital and £250 interest on the unpaid balance (see *Secretary of State in Council of India v Scoble* (1903)).
(3) Denis agrees to be paid by Flossie either 15% of the profits of the business each year for the rest of his life or £1,000 pa whichever is the higher. Denis is in effect purchasing a life annuity so that the payments each year will be income in his hands (see *IRC v Church Comrs for England* (1977): ITTOIA 2005 s 717 (see [**14.41**]) does not apply by reason of s 423(1)); Flossie's payments are instalments of capital (see *IRC v Land Securities Investment Trust Ltd* (1969)). [**14.8**]–[**14.10**]

III TAXATION OF ANNUAL PAYMENTS

1 Annual payments in a modern context

a) *The former attractions of annual payments*

One of the key features of annual payments has always been the way in which tax is collected. Historically, this has been effected by deduction of basic rate income tax at source (although from 6 April 2007, the source concept has been abolished; see [**14.21**]), the origins of which can be found in the concept of alienation of income, thus forging a distinction between the person on whom the burden of taxation falls on the one hand and, on the other, the person from whom it is actually collected. In the case of annuities and annual payments, the payer was looked upon as having alienated that part of his income representing the annuity or annual payment. This resulted in such payments being deductible in computing the total income of the payer with the burden of both basic and higher rate tax thereby falling on the payee (but with basic rate tax being collected from the payer).

As a consequence, annual payments were used over the years for the purposes of avoiding or minimising tax. A taxpayer, subject to the higher rates of tax, would assign a part of his income, eg by deed of covenant, to a taxpayer who paid no income tax, such as a charity, or to one who paid at the lower rates of tax. In *IRC v Duke of Westminster* (1936), for instance, gardeners were paid by the Duke, their employer, by means of a deed of covenant in lieu of wages, with the advantageous tax result that the Duke escaped paying higher rate taxes on the covenanted sums. [**14.11**]

b) The growth of anti-avoidance legislation

The ability to avoid tax in this way was reduced over the years by the enactment of provisions (now found in ITTOIA Part 5 Chapter 5 (see **[16.91]** ff) designed to prevent income tax benefits being obtained by:
(1) short-term covenants not capable of lasting for more than six – or in the case of charities, three – years;
(2) revocable settlements (including covenants);
(3) an assignment of income to the infant unmarried child of the settlor (see **Chapter 16**);
(4) covenants to trustees who do not distribute income.

Other annual payments not caught by these provisions were nevertheless limited in their effect by a provision that the taxpayer should be subject to excess liability (ie the difference between the higher rate and the basic rate of income tax) on the payment. So, if in 1987 a taxpayer had executed a seven-year covenant in favour of, say, his niece, while the recipient, the niece, would bear the burden of basic rate tax (collected at source from the payer), the taxpayer would be liable for any excess liability on the covenanted sum. Despite these endeavours of the legislature, annual payments continued to be used for tax avoidance purposes, notably covenants by grandparents in favour of their grandchildren for the payment of school fees, and by parents in favour of their adult children to support them during their time at college or university. **[14.12]**

c) The 1988 and subsequent changes

The process culminated in the enactment of FA 1988 s 36 (now ITTOIA 2005 s 727(1)) which had the dramatic effect of taking most annual payments by individuals outside the tax net altogether. Two further categories of annual payment have been removed from the tax net by more recent legislation. *First*, by virtue of FA 1999, relief for maintenance payments under a court order or agreement made prior to 15 March 1988 was withdrawn, generally from 6 April 2000. *Second*, FA 2000 took covenanted payments to charity outside of the charge under the former Schedule D Case III and incorporated them into the Gift Aid rules. As a result, the provisions now to be found in ITA 2007 Part 15 Chapter 6 (formerly TA 1988 ss 348 and 349) and ITA 2007 s 448, which provide respectively for deduction of tax from the annual payment and relief in respect the payment (see **[14.21]**), along with the anti-avoidance provisions in ITTOIA Part 5 Chapter 5, have lost much of their impact. **[14.13]**

2 The charge to tax

ITTOIA 2005 s 683(1) imposes a charge to tax on annual payments not otherwise charged to income tax. Section 683(4) provides for exemptions to the charge, including certain annual payments by individuals, but to this there are also exceptions (ss 727–730). In effect, what this means is that most individuals in receipt of annual payments will not suffer a charge under s 683. The payment will have been made out of the taxed income of the payer. There are exceptional cases, however, where the annual payment remains effective (see **[14.15]**–**[14.16]**) and in respect of which a sum representing income tax at the basic rate will be deducted by the payer from the payment, and income tax equivalent to that sum will be collected through the payer's self-assessment return under ITA 2007 Part 15 Chapter 17 (see [14.45]). Under ITA 2007 s 448, relief for the annual payment is given as a deduction in calculating the payer's net income (see [14.21]). In these cases, the anti-avoidance rules will remain of importance. It should also be borne in mind that the provisions in ITTOIA 2005 Part 5 Chapter 5 are concerned with capital as well as income settlements. This breadth of coverage is inevitable since, if it is desired to stop a particular income settlement from attracting fiscal benefit, it is necessary to cover a settlement of income-producing assets (ie capital) that might otherwise achieve the same result. The provisions in the context of capital settlements are considered in **Chapter 16**.

ITTOIA 2005 s 727 provides that:

'(1) No liability to income tax arises under Part 5 (s 683) in respect of an annual payment if it –
(a)   is made by an individual, and
(b)   arises in the United Kingdom.'

As already stated, the majority of annual payments now fall wholly outside the tax system. The section is, however, subject to the following exceptions.
[14.14]

a)   *The annual payment must be made by an individual*

ITTOIA 2005 s 727(1) is limited to annual payments made by individuals. Annuities, whether purchased or payable out of a deceased's estate, are therefore unaffected and, similarly, the beneficiary of a discretionary trust who receives income payments from the trustees will be charged to tax under s 683. [14.15]

b)   *Bona fide commercial payments*

Annual payments made for *bona fide* commercial reasons in connection with a trade, profession or vocation continue to fall within s 683. The main examples are annuities payable under partnership agreements to outgoing partners.
[14.16]

c)   *The payment of interest*

These changes made over the years only applied to annual payments: the tax treatment of interest has continued unchanged (see [14.31]). [14.17]–[14.20]

IV   DEDUCTION OF TAX AT SOURCE FOR ANNUAL PAYMENTS
(ITA 2007 PART 15 CHAPTER 6 AND S 448; CHAPTER 17)

1   **Introduction**

Historically, one of the characteristic features of annual payments, although not applicable to all such payments, was that basic rate income tax was not directly assessed on the recipient but, rather, was deducted and collected at source from the payer by virtue of the former provisions in TA 1988 ss 348 and 349 (and s 3). Under both of these sections, which were designed to achieve the same objective, the Revenue collected basic rate income tax from the payer on the annual payment and the payer was permitted to deduct that sum from the amount paid to the payee. Section 348 applied where the payment was made wholly out of taxable profits or gains.

The concept of alienation that underpinned s 348 was that an amount of income equal to the amount of the 'charge on income' (the payment) was regarded as no longer being the income of the payer but, rather, of the payee. The tax that the payer deducted (and although it was not mandatory under s 348 to make a deduction, it was in the payer's best interest to do so) enabled the payee to be regarded as receiving the payment under deduction of tax. All of the payer's income was subject to tax, without the annual payment being deducted, and the payment was always charged at the basic rate to ensure that the tax was collected from the payer.

Generally, therefore, the payee would receive a net sum together with a credit for the basic rate income tax that had been deducted at source and paid to the Revenue on his behalf. Loosely, s 349 applied where the payer had insufficient income to cover the charge on income; in this case, deduction of income tax was mandatory, and the tax was collected by direct assessment on the payer. For a full explanation of deduction of tax at source, see earlier editions of this book.

The Tax Law Rewrite team highlighted various difficulties with this system:

(a)   The concept of alienation of income and deduction *at source* do not rest easily with a system that no longer assesses different sources of income, but looks instead to total income.
(b)   Where a payment fell between the boundary of ss 348 and 349, the payer was not always sure which regime applied.
(c)   The multiplicity of provisions requiring an understanding of charges on income were not justified given that the range of payments treated in this way was now very narrow. [14.21]

2   Deduction at source: ITA 2007 Part 15 Chapter 6 and s 448

ITA 2007 replaced the former scheme relating to charges on income (see [7.40]) with a deduction in calculating net income. [14.22]

3   Operation of ITA 2007 Part 15 Chapter 6 and s 448 for the payer

There is a duty upon the payer of a qualifying annual payment (that is, an annual payment not otherwise charged to tax) made to an individual for genuine commercial reasons in connection with that individual's trade, profession or vocation, to deduct from it in all cases a sum representing income tax at the basic rate in force for the tax year in which it is made (ITA 2007 s 900).

The sum deducted is then collected as part of the payer's self-assessment return (see [14.45]). Mandatory deduction in all cases should dispense with the need for direct assessment that used to exist with TA 1988 s 349 (see [14.31]), although see proposals for the reform to the machinery for collection ([14.46]).

Provided that the payment is not deductible in calculating the payer's income from a trade etc, relief for the payment is then given by way of a deduction, equal to the gross amount of the payment, in computing the payer's net income (ITA 2007 s 448) at Step 2 of the tax calculation (ITA 2007 s 23) (see [7.40]). Relief is dependent upon whether the payer has taxable income that is sufficient overall to cover the payment.

EXAMPLE 14.3

In 2017–18, under a commercial partnership agreement, Wilbur pays to his former partner, Oscar, an annuity of £1,000 pa. Wilbur has income in that year of £50,000.

Step 1: By virtue of ITA 2007 s 900, Wilbur is under a duty to deduct from the £1,000 a sum equal to the basic rate tax thereon for the year in which the payment is made. Hence, for 2017–18, Wilbur can deduct £200 (20% × £1,000). He will, therefore, give Oscar £800.

Step 2: Income tax equivalent to the sum deducted (£200) will be collected through Wilbur's self-assessment return (ITA 2007 s 964).

Step 3: Since Wilbur's income is sufficient overall to cover the annuity, he can deduct the gross amount of the annuity (£1,000) in calculating his 'net income'. It follows that his 'net income' is £49,000 and that he can set his personal allowances against that sum (ITA 2007 s 23). Wilbur's own tax will, therefore, be calculated on the income that is left.

The result is that the total cost of the covenant to Wilbur is £1,000 since he handed £800 to Oscar at *Step 1* and £200 to the Revenue at *Step 2*. The relief given to him by the deduction of the gross amount of the payment in calculating his 'net income' means that he will not be liable to higher rate tax on that sum. [14.23]

Where only *some* income is subject to income tax, relief is limited to the payer's 'modified net income' (ITA 2007 s 1025); in determining the payer's modified net income, the relief being considered and any 'non-qualifying income' (ITA 2007 s 1026) is ignored. [14.24]

EXAMPLE 14.4

Wilbur (see *Example 14.3*) falls on hard times and receives only £500 for 2017–18. He remains bound to pay the annuity to Oscar. When he makes the next annual payment:

Step 1: Wilbur must deduct the basic rate tax (£200) on that annual sum and pay Oscar £800 only.

Step 2: Income tax equivalent to the sum deducted (£200) will be collected through Wilbur's self-assessment return (ITA 2007 s 964).

Step 3: Wilbur's 'modified net income' is £500; accordingly, the relief under ITA 2007 s 448 is limited to £500.

The total cost of the annuity is £1,000 made up of £800 paid to Oscar and £200 to the Revenue.

4 Position of the recipient

The recipient of an annual payment falling under s 683 will have income under s 683 equivalent to the gross value of the payment (not just of the sum that is actually received) and will be given a tax credit equal to the basic rate income tax deducted from the payment by the payer. Accordingly, the recipient may be entitled to reclaim that tax (eg if the recipient has unused personal allowances); or the tax may exactly discharge his tax liability; or he may be liable to extra income tax at the higher or additional rate. **[14.25]**

EXAMPLE 14.5

Watson received £800 from Holmes in respect of an annuity of £1,000 payable under a partnership agreement on his retirement. The £200 basic rate income tax has been collected by the Revenue through Holmes' self-assessment return.

Watson's income under s 683 is £1,000 and he has a credit for income tax paid of £200. Therefore, his tax position will be as follows:

(1) If he is subject to tax at the basic rate (ie if he has no unused allowances or charges), there is no further liability to tax and no question of a refund.
(2) If he has no other income and so has available personal allowances he can reclaim the £200 tax paid on his behalf by Holmes. If he had (say) £200 of unused allowances he would have taxable income of £800 (£1,000 − £200) on which tax at 20% would be £160. As the tax credit of £200 exceeds his tax liability by £160, he can obtain a refund of £160 of the tax deducted at source.
(3) If he has other income so that, say, he is paying income tax at the higher or additional rate (40% and 45% respectively for 2017–18), he will be liable to excess liability on the annuity, ie the difference between the higher or additional and basic rates of tax. On present rates, such excess liability would be 20% or 25% × £1,000.

5 Issues arising in connection with the deduction of tax from the payment

a) *Effect of failure to deduct tax from the payment*

It has been seen that the deduction of basic rate income tax from an annual payment is mandatory (ITA 2007 s 900(2)), and is collected through the payer's self-assessment return. To support this, ITA 2007 s 964(2), (3) provides that the income tax to be deducted is to be treated as if it were income tax charged on the payer, and that the tax must be taken into account for the purposes of the payer's return and assessment to income tax. Accordingly, failure to account for the tax will be subject to the normal penalties for non-declaration. In these circumstances, since basic rate income tax on the payment will be collected from the payer in any event, it is in his own interest to make this deduction.

Failure to deduct tax will, of course, affect the parties *inter se*. In general, if the payee has been overpaid, that overpayment cannot be reclaimed or corrected from later payments; it is a payment made under a mistake of law, and the excess is treated as a perfected gift which cannot be undone (*Re Hatch* (1919)). There are a few exceptions to this general principle: if the mistake is one of fact, recovery is possible (*Turvey v Dentons (1923) Ltd* (1953)); if the basic rate of tax increases after the payment, the excess can be recovered (TA 1988 s 821 as amended; this provision survives the newly rewritten provisions: see ITA 2007 s 849(2)), but it appears that under-deductions cannot be recouped from later payments made in that tax year (*Johnson v Johnson* (1946) explaining *Taylor v Taylor* (1938) and see *Tenbry Investments Ltd v Peugeot Talbot*

Motor Co Ltd (1992)). There is of course nothing to stop a recipient who has been overpaid from reimbursing the payer! **[14.26]**

EXAMPLE 14.6

Wilton has income of £5,000 for the tax year 2017–18. He pays to Twist an annuity of £1,000 under a partnership agreement on his retirement from which he fails to deduct basic rate income tax.

(1) Wilton must account for basic rate income tax on the payment in his self-assessment return. If he does not, he will face the usual penalties for an incorrect return (see **[4.26]**).

(2) In the event of Wilton paying the tax, Twist's income is £1,000 with a credit for £200 tax paid. The extra £200 that Twist has received is ignored; it is a tax-free gift.

b) *Use of formulae*

TMA 1970 s 106(2) provides that 'every agreement for payment of interest ... or other annual payment in full without allowing any such deduction shall be void'. The parties may not, therefore, agree that the payer will not deduct basic rate income tax from the payment. If s 106(2) is infringed, the instrument is void only as to the provision seeking to oust the deduction machinery. The section is also limited in that it only applies to 'agreements', so that payments under court orders and wills are outside its terms (see **Chapter 17**).

Despite s 106, the parties will often wish to ensure that a fixed sum is paid each year to the recipient regardless of fluctuations in the basic rate of income tax. Say, for instance, that Felix is paying an annuity to Hope, his former partner, under the terms of the partnership agreement, and wants to ensure that it receives £800 each year. Whilst the basic rate is 20%, a covenant to pay £1,000 pa would achieve this result. Were the basic rate to rise to 35%, however, Hope would only receive £650. As it is not possible to agree to pay £800 and not to deduct tax, the only way of achieving what Felix wants is to use a formula in the covenant. The standard formula would be that 'Felix agrees to pay Hope such sum as will after deduction of income tax at the basic rate for the time being in force leave £800'. This takes effect as an undertaking to pay the gross sum which after deducting the appropriate income tax leaves Hope with £800. What Hope receives is, therefore, constant; what will vary with the rate of tax is the sum paid to the Revenue and, therefore, the total cost of the annuity to Felix.

An alternative formula would be to agree to pay Hope £800 'free of tax', which takes effect as an undertaking to pay such sum as after deduction of income tax leaves £800 (*Ferguson v IRC* (1969)). One danger if such a formula is employed is that it is arguable that a promise to pay £800 free of tax means that the recipient should in any event end up with neither more nor less than £800. It follows that if the recipient is liable to higher rate income tax on the annual payment the payer must reimburse him for that tax, whilst conversely, any repayment of tax should be returned to the payer (the rule in *Re Pettit* (1922)).

If a covenant were made in favour of a charity after 5 April 2000 (the charge upon which has now been removed: see **[14.13]**), it should no longer use a formula of the type just described. Since such a covenant will be subject to the Gift Aid rules if tax relief is to be available and, if a formula were to be used, the payer would be liable to pay the whole of the grossed-up value, which would then be further grossed up under ITA 2007, ss 23 and 414(2).

[14.27]

6 Payments outside the tax net – ITTOIA 2005 s 727(1)

The result of the majority of annual payments being outside the tax system is illustrated in the following example: [14.28]–[14.30]

EXAMPLE 14.7

On 20 June 2017, Toby, with an annual income of £50,000, entered into a deed of covenant to pay £1,000 pa to his nephew, Jacques. Jacques has no income. The sum falls outside the charge under s 683 with the following result:

(1) Toby is taxed on £50,000 without any deduction for the annual payment. As the payment has to be discharged out of taxed income, the gross cost to Toby (in 2017–18) is, therefore, £1,667 (Toby is a higher rate taxpayer).
(2) The sum of £1,000 is paid over to Jacques and is not taxed in his hands.
(3) Jacques has no income so that his personal allowances remain unused.

V TAXATION OF INTEREST PAYMENTS

1 Tax relief for payment of interest

Tax relief for the payment of interest is only given in certain limited cases (ITA 2007 ss 383, 384) and, depending upon the purpose for which the loan was taken out, interest is accorded different tax treatment:

(1) payment of interest in respect of, eg a bank overdraft or credit card interest, receives no tax relief;
(2) payment of interest made, eg for the purposes of a trade, receives relief by allowing the payment as a deduction in computing the profits of that trade under ITOIA 2005 Part 2 (similar rules apply to a landlord: see **Chapter 12**). Interest relief on loans to buy land, etc was repealed by FA 1999 with effect from 6 April 2000.
(3) interest paid by individuals on loans used to invest in small businesses carried on by close companies or partnerships may qualify for relief against the individual's other income (ITA 2007 ss 396, 398) provided there exists significant uncertainty as to whether the level of return will secure a post-tax surplus for the investor. This proviso is the effect of ITA 2007 s 384A (inserted by FA 2009), and would, for example, deny relief for interest if the loan is made as part of arrangements that are certain (apart from any insignificant risk) to produce a post-tax surplus for the investor by virtue of the interest being eligible for relief, provided that the arrangement seems designed to reduce tax to which the borrower would have been liable apart from the arrangements. [14.31]

2 Deduction of tax at source

ITA 2007 Part 15 Chapter 3, s 874(1) provides for the circumstances where basic rate tax must be deducted from the payment of interest when it is made. Many yearly interest payments are not subject to deduction under Part 15 Chapter 3; ss 875–888 provide a list of circumstances where the duty to deduct is excluded. By virtue of ITA 2007 s 876(1) (as amended by FA 2016), savings income paid or credited on or after 6 April 2016 to their customers by banks, building societies and National Savings and Investments will no longer be paid net of basic rate tax (see **[7.24]**). ITA 2007 s 874(1), (6) requires basic rate to be deducted where there is a payment of yearly interest chargeable to tax under ITTOIA 2005 s 369 and it is paid either:

(1) by a company otherwise than in a fiduciary or representative capacity, eg debenture interest; or
(2) by a local authority otherwise than in a fiduciary or representative capacity, eg debenture interest; or
(3) by or on behalf of a partnership of which a company is a member; or
(4) by any person to another person whose usual place of abode is outside the UK.

A payment of interest which is payable to an individual in respect of compensation is to be treated as a payment of yearly interest regardless of whether the interest is actually paid yearly (ITA 2007 s 874(5A)) unless HMRC Commissioners make regulations to disapply the provision in circumstances prescribed in the regulations (ITA 2007 s 874(5B)), For ITA 2007 s 874(1) to operate, the income must arise in the UK, and must be 'yearly'. In determining whether a payment of interest arises in the UK, no account is taken of the location of the deed recording the obligation to pay the interest (ITA 2007 s 874(6A) inserted by FA 2013 Sch 11, with effect from the 17 July 2013). As far as yearly interest is concerned, the distinction between 'yearly' and 'short' interest depends upon the degree of permanence of the loan. The crucial question is whether it is stated or expected, that the loan will last, or is capable of lasting for 12 months or longer and in this connection the intention of the parties is crucial (see *Tax Journal*, 30 March 1995, p 14).

The rate of tax deducted is the basic rate of tax in force for the year in which the payment is made (20% for 2016–17) (ITA 2007 s 901(4)).

Payments made gross

Even if the payment falls within one of the four categories of interest payments listed in s 874(1), the duty to deduct a sum representing tax at the basic rate will be disapplied in the circumstances set out in ITA 2007 ss 875–888A. These are:

(1) interest paid by banks, building societies and National Savings and Investments (deposit takers) (ITA 2007 s 876 (as amended by FA 2016);
(2) other forms of interest paid on money debts by building societies, unless it is treated as a payment of yearly interest paid to an individual in respect of compensation (ITA 2007 s 875); and interest paid by banks if the payment is made in the ordinary course of its business (ITA 2007 s 878);

(3) interest payable on an advance from a building society (ITA 2007 s 880) and interest payable on an advance from a bank if the person beneficially entitled to the interest is within the charge to corporation tax on that interest (ITA 2007 s 879);
(4) UK public revenue dividends (ITA 2007 s 877);
(5) National Savings Bank interest (ITA 2007 s 881);
(6) quoted Eurobond interest (ITA 2007 s 882). Although HMRC consulted on the proposal to amend this exemption so that it would not apply to Eurobonds listed on stock exchanges where there is no substantial or regular trading (eg the Channel Islands and the Cayman Islands), in light of the responses it received, the Government decided not to proceed with the proposed restriction. However, it is to consider further the wider question of the extent to which tax is withheld from interest in a cross-border context;
(7) interest on a loan to purchase a life annuity (ITA 2007 s 883);
(8) relevant foreign income (ITA 2007 s 884);
(9) authorised persons dealing in financial instruments (ITA 2007 s 885);
(10) interest paid by recognised clearing houses (ITA 2007 s 886);
(11) industrial and provident society payments (ITA 2007 s 887); and
(12) statutory interest (ie payment of interest by virtue of the contractual term implied by the Late Payment of Commercial Debt (Interest) Act 1998 s 1(1)) (ITA 2007 s 888).
(13) interest on private qualifying payments (ITA 2007 s 888A, which provision will come into force on a day yet to be appointed by secondary legislation). Such payments are a form of selective, direct lending to non-individual borrowers. When the provision comes into force, payments may be paid without withholding tax provided: (i) the interest is paid on a security; (ii) that security must represent a loan relationship to which a company is party as debtor; and (iii) the security must not be listed on a recognised stock exchange. It is understood that the Revenue view is that although the term 'security' is used in the legislation, it will not prevent the exception applying also to loans.

Company payments made gross

The duty imposed on companies to deduct tax at the basic rate applies in respect of certain payments of yearly interest (ITA 2007 s 874(2)); payments in respect of building society securities (ITA 2007 s 889(4)); annual payments made by persons other than individuals (ITA 2007 s 901(4)); patent royalties (ITA 2007 s 903(7)); certain royalty payments where the owner lives abroad (ITA 2007 s 906(5)); proceeds of sale of patent rights paid to non-UK residents (ITA 2007 s 910(2)); payments by UK residents of manufactured interest in UK securities (ITA 2007 s 919(2); and chargeable payments connected with exempt distributions (ITA 2007 s 928(2)). The duty to deduct does not apply where the company making the payment believes, at the time of the payment, that it is an excepted payment (ITA 2007 s 930(1)). A payment is an excepted payment where:
(1) the person beneficially entitled to the income is a UK resident company (ITA 2007 s 933);

(2) the person beneficially entitled to the income is a non-UK resident company *and* it carries on trade in the UK through a permanent establishment *and* the payment is one that is required to be brought into account in calculating its chargeable profits (ITA 2007 s 934).

There is a further disapplication of the duty to deduct in respect of certain authorised investment funds (see the Authorised Investment Funds (Tax) Regulations 2006).

Assessment

Where payment by a company is concerned, income tax representing the sum deducted is payable by that company without direct assessment by HMRC (ITA 2007 s 951(3)); in other cases, a direct assessment will be made (ITA 2007 s 963(3): see **[14.45]** and **[14.46]**).

No liability to income tax arising

No liability to income tax arises (and thus no duty to deduct tax) in respect of a payment of interest or a payment of a royalty where the payment is made by a UK company (or a UK permanent establishment of an EU company) to an EU company (or a non-UK permanent establishment of such a company), provided that the Revenue has first issued an 'exemption notice' following a request by the recipient of a payment (see ITTOIA 2005 ss 758–762). These provisions enable UK companies to make payments to associated companies in EU Member States without deduction of tax, where previously existing double tax treaties did not eliminate UK withholding. **[14.32]**

3 **Source of the interest**

The obligation to deduct tax from the interest payment when made, and the availability of tax relief, depends on whether the interest arises in the UK. In deciding whether this is the case, it is provided that no account is to be taken of the location of any deed recording the obligation to pay the interest (ITA 2007 s 874(6)). Apart from that, other factors to be considered were discussed in *Westminster Bank Executor & Trustee Co (Channel Islands) Ltd v National Bank of Greece SA* (1968 (High Court) and 1971 (House of Lords)) (and SAIM 9090 ff) as follows:

> 'The factors considered relevant in that case (leading to the conclusion that the income involved did not have a UK source) were
> - there was an obligation undertaken by a principal debtor which was a foreign corporation
> - the obligation was guaranteed by another foreign corporation with no place of business in the UK
> - the obligation was secured on lands and public revenues outside the UK
> - funds for payments by the principal debtor of principal or interest to residents outside Greece would have been provided either by a remittance from Greece or funds remitted by debtors from abroad (even though a cheque might be drawn in London).

Although the Greek Bank case was concerned with income which turned out not to have a UK source, inferences can be drawn from that case about the factors which would support the existence of a UK source and we regard the most important as
- the residence of the debtor, ie the place in which the debt will be enforced
- the source from which interest is paid
- where the interest is paid, and
- the nature and location of the security for the debt.

If all of these are located in the UK then it is likely that the interest will have a UK source.'

The issue of whether interest paid by a UK taxpayer to a lender outside of the UK arose in the UK resulting in a requirement to withhold tax from the payments was fully discussed in two cases, the appeals in each being heard together before the Upper Tribunal in *Ardmore Construction Ltd and Perrin v R & C Comrs* (2015). In the case of *Perrin*, the taxpayer was resident and domiciled in the UK. He borrowed money from an employer-funded retirement benefit scheme, the trustee of which was an Isle of Man company. The loan was unsecured and not guaranteed by anyone, and the agreement was governed by Isle of Man law. The taxpayer had an Isle of Man bank account from which the first few interest payments were made. This account contained sufficient money to pay the majority of the interest on the loan but not the capital, and the taxpayer's other assets and sources of income were almost wholly to be found in the UK. The principal place of enforcement of the interest and/or capital would therefore have been the UK. *Ardmore* involved circular financing arrangements in which Ardmore, a UK resident company trading in the UK, subscribed over £8m for shares in two BVI incorporated companies owned by Gibraltar trusts in which the beneficiaries were Ardmore's two directors. The BVI companies lent the money to the trusts which, in turn, lent it to Ardmore at 2% above base rate. There was no security and no guarantor. The shares acquired by Ardmore were converted into valueless deferred shares and the purpose of the arrangement appears to have been for Ardmore to pay amounts for the benefit of the directors via their trusts.

The parties attempted to prevent the interest payable having a UK source by stipulating that the loans were governed by the law of Gibraltar, that the courts of Gibraltar had exclusive jurisdiction and that payments by Ardmore had to be made in Gibraltar and from a source outside the UK. Ardmore paid interest from its UK bank account funded from UK trading profits. The absence of security over those UK assets was not sufficient to prevent the conclusion that enforcement of payment of interest and repayment of principal would have to be against UK assets.

In dismissing the taxpayers' appeals, the Upper Tribunal found that the First-tier Tribunal, which had placed great weight on the speech of Lord Hailsham in *Westminster Bank Executor & Trustee Co (Channel Islands) Ltd v National Bank of Greece SA*, and thereby concluded that the interest arose from a source outside of the UK, was correct to take a multi-factorial approach and that, in applying that approach, was correct to give weight to the residence of the debtor and source of funds for payment and enforcement, over the place of residence or activity of the creditor, the place where the credit was advanced or the place of the payment of interest. [14.33]

4 Interest on legacies

For the tax treatment of interest paid by PRs on pecuniary legacies left in a will, see **Chapter 17**. [14.34]

5 Interest in kind and funding bonds

To overcome the difficulties in valuing interest paid in the form of goods and services, which is taxable in the same way as interest paid in cash, an interest payment made on or after 17 July 2013 is treated as the face value (retail or market price) of those goods or services and, where a voucher is issued, the interest is the face value of the voucher or, if higher, the cash equivalent of the goods and services that can be obtained in exchange (ITTOIA 2005 s 370A).

Both ITTOIA 205 s 380(3) and ITA 2007 s 939(6) have been amended so as to distinguish between interest in kind and funding bonds, that is, shares or loan notes issued by a debtor to pay interest, in order to retain the current treatment of funding bonds whereby the issue of a funding bond is treated as a payment of interest equal to the market value of the funding bond at issue (FA 2013 Sch 11). A person paying interest in kind or by funding bond is required to issue a certificate of value showing the gross amount of interest paid and amount of tax deducted, if any (ITA 2007 s 975A inserted by FA 2013 Sch 11). [14.35]

6 Disguised interest

ITTOIA 2005 Chapter 2A provides for income tax to be charged on returns produced from arrangements that provide amounts equivalent to interest, in order to deal with the many tax avoidance schemes that are developed to ensure that an interest-like return will be taxed, if at all, as something other than interest. The provisions are modelled broadly on the anti-avoidance rule addressing disguised interest for the purposes of the corporation tax rules on loan relationships introduced in FA 2009 (see **[41.50]** ff). [14.36]

7 The future

Following the announcement in the March 2015 Budget of the abolition (with effect from 6 April 2016 – see now FA 2016 and **[14.32]**) of the obligation to deduct tax under the Tax Deduction of Savings Interest scheme (TDSI) so that most interest will be paid gross (although the obligation to provide information to HMRC would remain), HMRC published a consultation document in July 2015 concerning options for dealing with other, non-TDSI, deduction at source arrangements in such a way as to balance the interests of savers, financial institutions and the Exchequer. This document put forward a number of options including retaining the current deduction arrangements for non-TDSI interest; removing them for all non-TDSI interest; removing them below a specified limit; and allowing individuals to choose whether to receive such interest gross or net of tax.

From the responses received, the Government concluded that the consultation did not point to a clear way forward and that, for most non-TDSI savings income, the issue was best left to be addressed once further progress had been made on the design and implementation of the new digital tax accounts (it is the government's intention to modernise the tax system by replacing tax returns with digital tax accounts (see HMRC, *Making tax digital,* July 2015), which will represent a major modernisation of the way in which taxpayers interact with HMRC). The Government added that it had:

> 'not yet reached a decision on this question in respect of authorised investment funds, investment trusts and P2P (peer to peer) lending. The government is continuing to analyse information provided to understand fully the impact of potential changes, and an announcement will be made as soon as possible.'
> (HMRC, *Deduction of income tax from savings income: implementation of the Personal Savings Allowance: A Summary of Responses,* December 2015, para 3.9)

In respect of peer to peer (P2P) lending in particular (P2P lending enables individuals and businesses to lend to each other through the intermediary of an internet platform, providing new opportunities for investors and new sources of finance to borrowers), it is the Government's intention to amend legislation to clarify how any obligations will apply in the future. However, in the period prior to such amendment, interest payments made on P2P loans may be made without deduction of tax. This will apply to interest payments made by a UK borrower to a UK P2P platform; a UK P2P platform to whoever; and any intermediary to or from a UK P2P platform.   [14.37]–[14.39]

VI INTELLECTUAL PROPERTY ROYALTIES

Patent royalties: Under ITA 2007, generally, patent royalties have been treated in the same way as annual payments: there is a requirement for a sum equal to the basic rate of income tax to be deducted on the payment of patent royalties (ITA 2007 Part 15 Chapter 6). Until December 2012, relief was afforded by the deduction of the amount of such royalties in calculating the payer's net income (ITA 2007 Part 8 Chapter 4), but this applied only to payments that were not deducted in calculating income tax liability from any source (for example, a trade). As an anti-avoidance measure, with effect from 5 December 2012, income tax relief is abolished for payments of patent royalties by individuals and other persons, such as trustees, personal representatives and non-resident companies who are within the charge to income tax that are not deductible in computing income from any source.

For collection of tax deducted at source, see [14.45]. Such payments may be annual payments, but will usually fall within ITTOIA 2005 Part 2 as receipts of a trade or profession. There are 'spreading provisions' in certain cases where lump sums are received (ITTOIA 2005 ss 587, 590, see [10.173]). Payments of royalties by a UK company (or a UK permanent establishment of an EU company) to an EU company (or a non-UK permanent establishment of such a company) may be made without deduction of income tax at source (see ITA 2007 s 914 and [14.32]). No advance approval needs to be obtained by HMRC; it is sufficient that the payer had a reasonable belief that ITTOIA 2005 s 758 applies to exempt the payments and that the recipient is entitled to receive the payment gross. However, if the payment is not in fact exempt from income tax, no matter how reasonable the belief of the payer company is, the right to pay without deduction is treated as never having existed.

Copyright royalties: Unless the owner of the right is outside the UK (see ITA 2007 Part 15 Chapters 7 and 8), copyright royalties are payable without deduction of tax. The recipient will be taxed under either ITTOIA 2005 Part 2 (if a professional author) or otherwise under ITTOIA 2005 s 687 (income not otherwise charged to tax). Again, spreading provisions are available for certain of these lump sum payments (ITTOIA 2005 s 590); see [**10.172**]).

Intellectual property royalties generally, from 28 June 2016: In order to align the UK deduction of tax at source regime in respect of royalties with the UK taxing rights over such income and to counteract contrived arrangements that are used by groups (typically by large multi-national enterprises) that result in the erosion of the UK tax base, a measure was included in FA 2016 to provide additional obligations to deduct income tax at source from any intellectual property royalties paid to non-resident persons where either:
- the category of royalty is not currently one of those in respect of which there is an obligation to deduct tax under UK law;
- arrangements have been entered into which exploit the UK's double taxation agreements (DTAs) in order to ensure that little or no tax is paid on royalties either in the UK or anywhere in the world;
- royalties which do not have otherwise have a source in the UK are connected with the business that a non-UK resident person carries on in the UK through a permanent establishment in the UK. [**14.40**]

VII OTHER SAVINGS INCOME

1 Purchased life annuities (ITTOIA 2005 s 717)

Purchased life annuities were formerly taxed as income with no allowance being given for their capital cost. ITTOIA 2005 ss 717, 719 (formerly TA 1988 s 656) permit the amount of any annuity payment which fall within their scope to be dissected into an income and a capital amount. The capital amount in each payment is found by dividing the cost of the annuity by the life expectancy of the annuitant at that time, calculated according to Government mortality tables. The balance is treated as income taxable under the rules of ITTOIA 2005 s 422, with income tax deductible from the payment under ITA Part 15 Chapter 6.

It is necessary to distinguish between a purchased life annuity on the one hand and, on the other, an investment of capital, with annual payments being in the nature of a return of that capital. In *Sugden v Kent* (2001), the taxpayer invested £200,000 with an insurance company and, at the commencement of the policy, he decided to effect annual partial surrenders of about £20,000. He argued that these annual amounts were of a capital nature, and so were partial surrenders within the provisions of ITTOIA 2005 Part 4 Chapter 9 (see **Chapter 7**). The Revenue took the view that each payment was an annuity, and probably a purchased life annuity under TA 1988 s 656 (now ITTOIA 2005 s 717), with it then being open to the taxpayer to make a claim under that section. In holding for the taxpayer, the Special Commissioner distinguished an annuity on the grounds that, *first*, in this case, the initial investment did not cease to exist; the amount that the taxpayer would receive over the term of the contract was £200,000, plus or minus the value of the units in the linked fund. If he died before receiving the full value, the value of the remaining units would be payable to his trustees. This is not the case where income is purchased with a sum of money that then ceases to exist; and, *second*, there was no possibility that the insurance company in the present case would have a liability greater than the amount of the initial investment, however long the taxpayer should live.

Generally, s 717 does not apply if the annuity has already been given tax relief (as is the case with purchased annuities for a fixed term of years which have always been dissected); or, if the annuity was not purchased by the annuitant but by a third party (eg if it was purchased as the result of a direction in a will); or, if the premiums qualified for tax relief under TA 1988 s 266, s 273 or s 619 when they were paid or if the annuity is payable under approved personal pension arrangements (ITTOIA 2005 s 718).

For 2008–09 and subsequent tax years, the rate at which tax must be deducted at source on the payment of a purchased life annuity and other annuities (apart from those to which PAYE applies), is the basic rate of tax in force at the time the payment is made (20% for 2017–18: ITA 2007 s 901(4) and FA 2009). **[14.41]**

2 Deeply discounted securities

Income tax is charged on the profits on the disposal of 'deeply discounted securities' (ITTOIA 2005 s 427). In simple terms, a deeply discounted security is one where the amount that would (or might) be payable on redemption exceeds the issue price by a particular percentage. A profit may be realised in the year of disposal (defined as: (i) the redemption of the deeply discounted security; (ii) its transfer by way of any sale, gift, exchange 'or otherwise'; and (iii) to its conversion into shares in a company or other securities (unless covered by (i) or (ii)) (ITTOIA 2005 s 437(1)). It is specifically provided that, on death, the individual is treated as transferring the security for market value immediately before death (ITTOIA 2005 s 437(3)).

The taxed profit is the proceeds of transfer or redemption less the amount paid on acquisition. Only incidental expenses on longstanding securities can be taken into account, as the expense must have been incurred before 27 March 2003 to be allowable (ITTOIA 2005 s 439(1), (4)) (see generally SIM 3020 (HMRC)). **[14.42]–[14.43]**

3 Unauthorised unit trusts

Unit trusts provide a form of pooled investment and, being trusts in the strict legal sense, operate according to the terms of the trust deed. Unit trusts that are now authorised by the Financial Services Authority (FSA) were first introduced as vehicles for investment by individuals, and the tax rules were designed to ensure that tax-paying individuals fared no worse by investing via an authorised unit trust than would have been the case had they invested in a company directly. Those rules involve treating authorised unit trusts like companies for taxation purposes. In contrast, by definition, unauthorised unit trusts are unit trusts not authorised by the FSA, and are taxed as trusts.

This means that when trustees receive income from a unit trust, they are liable to pay income tax on it at the basic rate of tax (ITA 2007 s 504). Distributions of income to unit holders are deemed to have been paid as annual payments under deduction of income tax at the basic rate (ITA 2007 s 941). **[14.44]**

VIII COLLECTION OF TAX DEDUCTED AT SOURCE: ITA 2007 PART 15 CHAPTERS 15, 16 AND 17

1 The current situation

a) *Chapter 17: Qualifying annual payments and patent royalties*

Where tax is deducted at source by an individual from a qualifying annual payment or a patent royalty (see **[14.40]**), the sum withheld is treated as if it were income tax charged on that person and is collected through the person's self-assessment tax return for the year in which the payment is made (ITA 2007 s 963). Where the qualifying annual payment is made for genuine commercial reasons in connection with a person's trade, profession or vocation or where tax is required to be deducted from patent royalties, tax relief can be claimed on the gross amount of the payment (ITA 2007 Pt 8 Ch 4). However, this is only permitted if the payment is not deductible in calculating income from any source, such as where the person making the payment may deduct it in computing trade profits.

b) *Chapter 16: payments of interest*

When a person makes a payment of interest, they are required to deliver an account of the payment to HMRC 'without delay'. No specific form is prescribed for the delivery of the account, and the tax is not payable with the delivery of the account. HMRC may make an assessment of the amount equal to the sum required to be deducted.

c) *Chapter 15: payments by companies and other financial institutions*

Chapter 15, which is in contrast to the mechanism provided for in Chapter 16 and 17, requires banks, building societies and companies to deliver a return (the CT61 Return) of the tax deducted at source within 14 days of the end of the return period, along with the tax payable. The return is issued each quarter automatically by HMRC to registered companies. **[14.45]**

2 Reform

For individuals and non-corporate taxpayers, the difficulty with the present mechanism for collecting tax deducted at source is the possibility of claiming tax relief twice, once under ITA 2007 Part 8 Ch 4 (relief for qualifying annual payments) and again as a trade expense under ITTOIA 2005 ss 34, 35 and 54. In its consultation document (*Changes to the tax rules on the deduction of Income Tax at source*, March 2010), HMRC advanced alternative proposals to avoid that problem. The main proposal was to align the system for collecting tax on interest paid by individuals with that for companies. This would mean that individuals would use a designated form on which to deliver to HMRC an account of tax deducted, and the tax would be payable without an assessment. This process could also extend to cover tax currently collected through the self-assessment form in respect of annual payments and patent royalties. Alternatively, both the requirement to deduct tax from qualifying annual payments and the associated tax relief for such payments could be abolished.

Following the consultation, HMRC is now provided with a power to make regulations to amend how and when a person should report income tax deducted from certain payments (ITA 2007 s 963A (inserted by FA (No 3) Act 2010 s 8). At the time of writing, no such regulations have been made, but the Government may issue further proposals on the matter in due course.

[14.46]

15 Tax shelters and insurance products
Updated by David Brookes FCA, Tax Partner, BDO LLP

I   Insurance products [15.1]
II   Investment and savings products [15.21]
III Enterprise investment scheme (EIS) [15.51]
IV   CGT reinvestment and deferral relief [15.82]
V   Venture capital trusts [15.121]
VI   Seed Enterprise Investment Scheme (SEIS) [15.128]

I INSURANCE PRODUCTS

1 Life assurance policies

a) *Treatment of qualifying policies*

Tax relief is available for premiums paid by a UK resident on a 'qualifying' life assurance policy made *before* 14 March 1984 (TA 1988 ss 266–267 and, for the definition of a 'qualifying policy', Sch 15 as amended by ITTOIA 2005). The relief is given by allowing the policyholder to deduct and retain 12 1/2% of the premium, provided that the total annual premiums payable do not exceed the greater of £1,500 and one-sixth of his total income (TA 1988 s 274). The insurer reclaims the deduction from HMRC. The relief is not available for policies made after 13 March 1984, nor for those made before that date where the holder subsequently alters the policy to increase the benefits secured or to extend the term. In such cases premiums will be paid without the 12 1/2% deduction.

The proceeds of a qualifying policy are not normally subject to income tax and so, even without tax relief on premiums payable, qualifying policies have remained popular.

For policies taken out after 15 March 1984 to be qualifying policies the term must be ten or more years and regular payments must be made for three-quarters of the term, or the first ten years, whichever is the shorter. For policies issued after 5 April 2013 there is also an annual premium limit of £3,600 and transitional rules will apply to policies issued between 21 March 2012 and 5 April 2013.   [15.1]

b) *Non-qualifying policies (ITTOIA 2005 s 461 et seq)*

The typical example of a non-qualifying policy is the single premium insurance bond or with-profits investment bond. Not only is no relief available on the sum invested, but any gain realised by the policyholder, net of premiums paid, on the occasion of a 'chargeable event' (eg on surrender, maturity, assignment or death) may be subject to income tax at higher rate (but tax at the basic rate, or, for 2005–06 to 2007–08 at the lower rate, is deemed to have been paid) subject to top slicing relief. Annual tax-free withdrawals are allowed up to the value of the original investment so long as they do not exceed 5% of the premium paid for each year of the policy (ie the tax-free withdrawals cease after 20 years). Single premium bonds therefore provide shelter for income in the case of higher rate taxpayers. However, for non-taxpayers they are not necessarily the most tax efficient investments since the underlying assets held by the life insurance company are subject to tax (see [15.3]).

Provisions were introduced in the Finance Bill 2017 to allow taxpayers to ask HMRC to recalculate the taxable amount on a chargeable event where the assessable figure is considered to be disproportionate on a partial surrender or partial assignment. The amendment was dropped when Finance Bill 2017 was truncated when the 2017 general election was called, and, at the time of writing is in Finance (No 2) Bill 2017. [15.2]

c) *Taxation of insurance companies*

The rate of corporation tax on the relevant profits (both income and capital) of a life assurance company is equal to the basic rate of income tax (20% in 2017–18). The policyholder is not charged on these accumulating profits.
[15.3]

d) *Anti-avoidance*

FA 1998 contained measures aimed at preventing 'avoidance loopholes', ie:
(1) in the case of policies held in trust it was possible to avoid any charge by the 'dead settlor trick' (see [15.7]). From 6 April 1998 this is prevented by gains being taxed on the trustees or beneficiaries who receive benefits;
(2) special rules for 'personal portfolio bonds' (ie a life policy where benefits are linked to a portfolio of assets that is personal to the policyholder). In such cases an annual tax charge on the basis of deemed gains is imposed;
(3) compliance rules aimed at non-UK insurance companies who sell insurance in the UK and special rules for overseas life assurance business if the policyholder becomes UK resident.

Further anti-avoidance measures were introduced by FA 2012. Rules regarding the calculation of chargeable events have been clarified so that previous chargeable events are only deductible to the extent that they are attributable to one of the persons chargeable to tax. Additionally, interdependent policies issued on or after 21 March 2012 are treated as a single policy. [15.4]

2 General treatment of non-qualifying insurance policies

Gains arising from dealings in non-qualifying policies are subject to higher rate tax if there is a chargeable event. Basic rate tax (lower rate for years 2005–06 to 2007–08) is deemed to have been paid but is not recoverable.

A chargeable event occurs when there is a surrender, a death giving rise to benefits under the policy, maturity or assignment for consideration.

EXAMPLE 15.1

Elizabeth, a higher rate taxpayer, takes out a non-qualifying single premium life contract in June 2004 for £20,000. She withdraws 5% each year for two years, ie a total of £2,000. She takes no further amounts.

In June 2015 she surrenders the policy for, say, £24,000.

The total withdrawals are £26,000, ie £2,000 plus surrender proceeds of £24,000.

Deduct premium paid of £20,000. No gains previously charged, so no further deduction. Chargeable gains are £6,000 top sliced over nine years.

IPost 5 April 2005, individuals who are non-UK resident throughout a year of assessment are not liable to UK tax on gains on chargeable events even on UK non-qualifying policies (ITTOIA 2005 s 465(1),; previously this was an extra statutory concession, ESC B53). If the policy has been assigned by that individual to a trust the position is usually more adverse. **[15.5]**

a) *Offshore policies*

A policy issued by an offshore life office that does not trade in the UK is not subject to tax on the income and gains from the investments underlying the policy. The chargeable events legislation still applies so that gains realised when the policy matures, is surrendered, or assigned for consideration will be taxable. **[15.6]**

b) *Trusts*

Any gain on the policy is taxed as the income of an individual if immediately before the chargeable event he or a trust created by him owns the policy (ITTOIA 2005 s 465(3)). Note that there is still a charge on the settlor even if he cannot benefit from the trust although he has a right of reimbursement. Therefore trustees should be careful before taking out policies where the settlor is still alive.

If the settlor has died or is non resident, then the gain on the policy is chargeable at the rate for trusts and assessed on the trustees (ITTOIA 2005 s 467).

However, if the trust had taken out a policy with funds left by a settlor who died prior to 17 March 1998 and the policy was issued before 17 March 1998 and has not subsequently been varied, then there is no tax payable (see FA 1998 Sch 14 para 7). This is the so-called dead settlor trick. **[15.7]**

c) *Capital losses*

With effect from 9 April 2003, TCGA 1992 s 210 prevents capital losses being generated in relation to life insurance policies and deferred annuity contracts which exceed the amount of any economic loss and also prevent gains escaping a charge to tax simply because the person making the disposal has received the policy or contract by way of gift. Capital losses generated prior to 9 April 2003 have also been successfully challenged by HMRC in the Court of Appeal (*Drummond v IRC* (2009)).

EXAMPLE 15.2

Miss X takes out a new life insurance policy paying a single premium of £500,000. The policy is one liable to income tax on a chargeable event gain. She sells it to Mr Y for £525,000, Mr Y surrenders the policy back to the insurance company and receives £502,000 in cash. Mr Y is treated as making a chargeable event gain of £2,000 on which he is liable to income tax (£502,000 less the amount of the premium paid of £500,000). Under the old rules for capital gains tax he was treated as receiving £502,000 but this was taken into account in calculating his chargeable gain so was disregarded for capital gains tax purposes. His cost of acquiring the policy of £525,000 was not taken into account in the income tax calculations so it is not disregarded for capital gains tax purposes. Therefore under the old legislation he made an allowable loss of £525,000. Following amended s 210 the income tax position is unchanged but his allowable loss is restricted to £23,000, ie £525,000 less the amount he received on surrender of the policy of £502,000.

EXAMPLE 15.3

Mrs Z buys a second-hand life insurance policy for £20,000. It is not a policy which attracts liability to income tax but she is liable to capital gains tax on any gain because she is not the original owner and she paid cash to acquire it. Just before maturity she gives the policy to her husband and he receives £36,000 from the insurance company. Mr Z does not have an income tax liability but makes a gain of £16,000. Under the old rules this gain was not liable to capital gains tax because Mr Z did not give any actual consideration to acquire the policy. Under new s 210 neither of them will have any income tax liability but Mr Z is now treated as having made a gain of £16,000 liable to capital gains tax because, although he gave nothing to acquire the property, his spouse (or civil partner from 5 December 2005) has given actual consideration to acquire the policy. [15.8]

d) *Deficiency relief*

There is a limit on the amount of relief that can be set off against the income of the individual in circumstances where there is a deficiency when the insurance policy, life annuity contract or capital redemption policy comes to an end (ITTOIA 2005, s 541). Broadly, the amount of the relief to which the individual is entitled cannot be greater than the total amounts of earlier gains made on the insurance policy, life annuity contract or capital redemption policy which formed part of the individual's income in an earlier year of assessment. Earlier gains may have arisen as a result of earlier part surrenders of the policy or contract.

This amendment has effect from 3 March 2004 in relation to all new life insurance policies, capital redemption policies and life annuity contracts. It also applies to life insurance policies, capital redemption policies and life annuity contracts that existed at 3 March 2004 if:

(a) the life insurance policies, capital redemption policies or life annuity contracts are varied on or after 3 March 2004 so as to increase the benefits secured;

(b) all or part of the rights conferred by the life insurance policies, capital redemption policies or life annuity contracts are assigned on or after 3 March 2004; or

(c) all or part of the right conferred by the life insurance policies, capital redemption policies or life annuity contracts come to be held as security in relation to a debt on or after 3 March 2004. [15.9]

3 Group life policies

Many partnerships have inadequate life cover in the event that one of their partners dies in service before retirement. The occupational death in service approved life insurance options are not open to them because they are self-employed and each partner has therefore traditionally had to take out life cover individually on his own life for the benefit of his dependants. Increasingly, partnerships instead want to take out some form of group life cover that insures the lives of all their partners and pays benefits on more than one death. This can be obtained more cheaply on a group rather than an individual basis.

Provided a group life policy qualifies as an excepted group life policy within ITTOIA 2005 ss 481–482, it is outside the scope of the income tax charge if there is a chargeable event such as a death. If structured properly the group life assurance scheme can also be held in trust to pay out benefits to the dependants of the deceased partner on a discretionary basis in order to obtain maximum inheritance tax advantages. In order to qualify as an excepted group life policy a number of conditions must be satisfied.

Condition 1 provides that under the policy, sums or other benefits of a capital nature must be payable on the death of each of the individuals insured under the policy but only if the individual dies before reaching his or her 75th birthday. The same method of calculation must be used for calculating each of the death benefits payable under the policy. Generally no sums or benefits may be paid or conferred under the policy other than on death. The recipients of the death benefits paid must be individuals or charities so, if the death benefits have been written in trust, care will be needed on payment out of those benefits to ensure that the payments are made outright rather than on trusts to the partners' dependants. This could cause problems if such dependants are minor children. It is not possible to allow another partner who has survived the deceased partner to receive any benefits on payment out unless such other partner receives the death benefits for another reason – for example, they are the spouse of an insured person who has died. [15.10]–[15.20]

II INVESTMENT AND SAVINGS PRODUCTS

1 Investment products and IHT planning

There are a number of insurance products or 'schemes' currently in the marketplace which centre round the idea of the investor giving a cash sum into trust but continuing to benefit from the funds, allegedly without inheritance or other tax problems.

These products generally involve some type of single premium non-qualifying endowment policy written in some form of trust.

The initial minimum premiums invested are often quite high – £50,000 is not atypical. The idea is that the investor is limited to his 5% 'tax-free' withdrawal. If withdrawals exceed 5% of the premium paid, there is the usual higher rate income tax charge on the excess subject to top-slicing relief. In addition, the life assurance company, unless based abroad, usually pays tax on the relevant underlying profits currently at the rate of 20%. However, provided the 5% limits are not exceeded, the investor is not charged to any income tax or gains even though the trust is settlor interested because the trust holds all its assets in the wrapper of the bond. Thus the underlying gains (if any) realised within the bond itself are not taxable on the settlor.

The types of scheme are described below. It should be noted, however, that FA 2006 had a profound effect on new trust arrangements for life assurance based products, which are subject to the inheritance tax regime for trusts. For pre-22 March 2006 interest-in-possession trusts holding pre-22 March 2006 contracts of life assurance, even where premiums are paid on or after that date, measures exist in FA 2006 which effectively exclude them from the new regime for the inheritance taxation of interest-in-possession trusts so long as there have been no changes to the terms of the policies (see **Chapter 33**). Nor will ongoing premium payments affect the transitional provisions applicable to pre-22 March accumulation and maintenance trusts (see **Chapter 34**).

[15.21]

a) *Spousal interest trust*

Such trusts are no longer possible to set up from 20 June 2003 due to FA 2003 s 185. Under the 'old scheme', the donor, eg the husband, effected a capital investment bond which was written on interest-in-possession trusts under which his wife was entitled to the interest in possession. The settlor was among the class of potential beneficiaries. Say six months later the trustees exercised their powers of appointment to terminate her interest in possession in favour of the settlor's children who would take interests in possession. The wife would no longer benefit and was treated as having made a PET when her interest in possession was ended by the trustees. If she survived seven years the initial value of the bond fell outside her estate for inheritance tax purposes. The idea was that any later growth in the bond should also fall outside the couple's estate for inheritance tax purposes whether or not she survived seven years.

The husband continued to benefit and from time to time the trustees could use their 5% withdrawal facility to make partial encashments from the bond and appoint such capital out to the settlor. Provided the encashments did not exceed 5%, there was no income tax charge on the settlor.

The idea behind this scheme was that the gifts with reservation (GWR) provisions were avoided due to the initial gift being to the settlor's spouse. Therefore FA 1986 s 102(5)(a) arguably applied which says that to the extent any gift is covered by the spouse exemption then no GWR will occur.

The Revenue did not accept this analysis and argued that there was a reservation of benefit. The point went to the High Court and then the Court of Appeal in the context of family homes – see *IRC v Eversden* (2003) considered at **[29.140]**).

The scheme was effectively stopped by FA 2003 s 185. For further details on this section see **[29.140]**. Insurance bonds taken out and settled prior to 20 June 2003 are not affected by the FA 2003 changes. **[15.22]**

b) *Gift and loan scheme*

The investor as settlor sets up a trust for the benefit of his children. He cannot benefit from the trust. The settlor then makes an interest-free loan repayable on demand to the trustees who use this money to invest in a bond normally written on the lives of the named beneficiaries under the trust. The idea is that the loan is not a diminution in the settlor's estate and therefore effectively no transfer of value has been made under this arrangement.

From time to time, the settlor demands repayment of part of the loan. To finance this, the trustees will make a part surrender of the bond within their 5% entitlement. Normally repayment of loans to a settlor can cause income tax problems for the settlor, but as before the idea is that the trust 'income' is restricted to the 5% withdrawal, at least while the settlor is alive.

As the settlor receives loan repayments and spends them, his taxable estate will reduce and the growth in value of the bond will be outside his estate. He can ask for the whole of the loan back at any time although this may trigger income tax charges if the bond has grown in value since the trustees will be forced to encash it.

The trust and loan documentation has to be drafted carefully to ensure that it does not breach any anti-avoidance legislation. And this is of course only an estate freezing exercise. There is no immediate inheritance tax benefit because the loan still forms part of the settlor's estate. It is the growth in value of the investment product which will be outside his estate.

The inheritance tax planning is rather inflexible. The settlor may not in fact need repayment of the entire loan but it will still form part of his estate. Alternatively, he may end up needing some of the capital growth in the bond as well but cannot get access to this. Or he may want to be repaid on the loan at a greater rate than 5% of the initial premium each year. Calling for repayment at a greater rate than 5% could, as noted above, generate income tax charges. Many clients might also feel unhappy about basing their inheritance tax planning on the idea that investment products they take out really will grow in value in the future!

If the settlor dies shortly after the product is taken out then some thought needs to be given as to what happens regarding this loan. It will be necessary to avoid a situation where the loan is automatically called in by his executors because this will result in the trustees being forced to encash the bond early. This could be expensive in terms of tax and commission charges. To avoid this, the settlor could leave his right to receive loan repayments to another beneficiary under his will, eg his spouse. If he leaves the benefit of the loan back to the trust then this will be a chargeable transfer under the terms of his will and (even if it does not jeopardise the inheritance tax planning) may result in unnecessary tax charges if his nil rate band has already been exhausted. **[15.23]**

c) *Trust carve out*

There are many varieties of the carve out idea. In some the settlor takes out a cluster of single premium non-qualifying endowment life assurance policies maturing at regular intervals. The policies are assigned by the settlor to a trust. The terms of the trust provide that the settlor can take if living at the maturity date, but otherwise he has no interest in the policy. He cannot benefit in any other circumstances. The trustees, but not the settlor, have the option of deferring the maturity date and can surrender the policies at any time. In either event the settlor receives nothing. He can only benefit if the policy actually matures.

The beneficiaries of the trust are usually his children who take immediate vested interests in possession. The idea is that if the settlor requires some income, then the trustees will let a policy mature and he will take the proceeds. If he does not require income, the policy is extended by the trustees and the settlor receives nothing. The argument is that the settlor has 'carved out' or retained a reversionary interest under the trust, but this interest is liable to be defeated in a number of ways by the exercise of powers vested in the trustees. Therefore although the retained reversionary interest is not excluded property (see IHTA 1984 s 48(1)(b)), it has little or no value. The beneficiaries take the benefit of an insurance policy which is shorn of a reversionary interest retained by the settlor.

HMRC appears to accept that the retention by the settlor of a reversionary interest under a trust is not a reservation of benefit (see letter to the Law Society dated 18 May 1987). The settlor has retained actual property rather than reserved a benefit in the policy gifted. There is some question as to whether HMRC may argue that the effecting of the bond, the assignment into trust and the extension of the maturity date are associated operations giving rise to a chargeable transfer at the date of the last operation, ie the extension date.

In addition, there is a potential double inheritance tax charge if the settlor dies within seven years of settling the property but in that time has received the policy proceeds back on maturity. The Double Charges Regulations (see **Chapter 34**) would not appear strictly to give relief in this situation.   [15.24]

d) *Discounted gift schemes*

There are also a number of schemes combining a carve out with a discounted gift. Under this route, the settlor takes out a life insurance linked bond and retains from the outset certain rights, typically the right to receive the 5% tax-free withdrawals, which add up to more than just a reversionary interest.

The bond is split into two defined parts, with certain rights (eg the right to withdraw a specified amount each year) belonging to the settlor outright, and all other rights under the bond are gifted to a trust for the residuary beneficiaries. These persons do not include the settlor. When the settlor makes the investment he is retaining certain rights under the trust (eg the right to withdraw a specified amount each year – once fixed the amount cannot be varied) and therefore the loss to his estate is not the full capital value of the bond. The gift of the residuary fund is treated as less than the face value. The discount depends on the donor's life expectancy. The longer he is likely to live and draw on the benefits, the greater the discount on the gift. The discount is immediately exempt from IHT.

HMRC contend that no discount applies to settlors of 90 years of age or more. All of these schemes involve complex provisions, have certain disadvantages and risks and may only be suitable in very limited circumstances. Specialist advice should always be sought. **[15.25]**

2 ISAs, PEPs, TESSAs and SAYE

a) *Individual Savings Accounts (ISAs)*

These were announced by the Government in the July 1997 Budget: the intention being to 'build on' the experience of TESSAs and PEPs (see below) and for the new account to provide a tax-favoured environment for savings. The scheme came into effect on 6 April 1999 when the rules permitting tax credits to be repaid to individuals in respect of company distributions ceased. Initially introduced for 10 years, the Government has announced that ISAs will remain indefinitely. Since being introduced, the range of ISAs has expanded and various rules have been changed, but the basic premise has remained throughout: they are tax-free accounts for individuals to hold savings or investments.

There are now five key types of ISA (discussed below):
- Cash
- Stocks and shares
- Help-to-buy
- Lifetime
- Innovative finance

These are available to individuals over 18 (16 for Cash ISAs) who are resident in the UK.

Each tax year there is an investment limit – for 2017–18 this is £20,000. If, for a given tax year, the full amount is not utilised it is lost, ie the unused proportion cannot be rolled forward to subsequent tax years. However, with effect from April 2016 providers are permitted to offer 'flexible' ISAs, which allow an individual who withdraws funds to subsequently put them back into the same account in the same tax year without penalty (aside from a potential loss of interest).

Savers are now able to apportion their investment of up to the annual limit (£20,000 for 2017–18) how they wish between the different types of ISA, subject to a limit of £4,000 for the Lifetime ISA.

There is also a Junior ISA for children, which works in a similar way. For 2017–18 the subscription limit is £4,128. **[15.26]**

Cash ISA

A Cash ISA is simply a savings account. Any interest credited to the account is exempt from income tax.

For many individuals the tax advantage has been eroded by the introduction of the Personal Savings Allowance (PSA) from 6 April 2016 which means that individuals can earn up to the following amounts of interest each year tax-free: basic rate taxpayers £1,000; higher rate taxpayers £500. (Additional rate taxpayers' PSA is restricted to nil.)

In addition, at present, many standard savings accounts offer higher rates of interest than cash ISA accounts. **[15.27]**

Stocks and shares ISA

With Stocks and shares ISAs, investments can be made in assets including shares, funds and corporate and government bonds.

Any income received in a stocks and shares ISA is exempt from income tax and any gains made (that are not covered by an individual's annual exemption) are exempt from CGT. [15.28]

Help-to-buy ISA

A Help-to-buy ISA was launched in 2015 to help first-time buyers save up for their first home (their only residence, not a buy-to-let).

Individuals aged 16 or over can save up to £200 per month, to which the Government adds a 25% tax-free bonus, from a minimum of £400 up to a maximum amount of £3,000 on £12,000 of savings.

£1,200 can be credited to the account in the first month and then up to £200 per month subsequently.

The bonus is paid directly to the mortgage lender when the home is purchased. The bonus is available on UK home purchases of up to £450,000 in London and up to £250,000 outside London.

The Lifetime ISA (see below) has subsequently been launched, but Help-to-buy ISAs remain available. [15.29]

Lifetime ISA

A Lifetime ISA was announced in the 2016 Budget with a view to encouraging people under the age of 40 to save. Such accounts are sheltered from tax and have been available from April 2017.

A lifetime ISA can be opened by anyone between the ages of 18 and 40, with any savings paid into the ISA before the age of 50 receiving a 25% bonus from the government. The maximum that can be paid into an account each year is £4,000 (meaning a £1,000 bonus would be received).

Individuals can use the money in a lifetime ISA to buy their first home, up to the value of £450,000, or to save until reaching the age of 60. If the money is withdrawn and not used for one of these purposes, any bonuses received (including any growth and interest thereon) will have to be repaid to the government, along with a 5% charge.

An individual can only have one account; however, two first-time buyers can both use their lifetime ISA when buying together. Individuals who have already taken out a help to buy ISA can continue saving into this account but only one ISA (either a lifetime ISA or a help to buy ISA) can be used to purchase their first property.

An existing help-to-buy ISA can be transferred into a lifetime ISA. [15.30]

Innovative finance ISA

Innovative ISAs (IFISAs) were launched in April 2016. These allow individuals to use a proportion of their annual ISA allowance, £20,000 in 2017–18, to lend funds through the peer-to-peer lending market. It does not include equity-based investing.

Any income or gains which result from the lending are exempt from income tax and CGT.

It is anticipated that the rates of return from investing in an IFISA will be higher than from a Cash ISA. However, it has a higher risk profile – a lender's capital is entirely at risk and they may receive back less than they originally lent. [15.31]

Junior ISA

Since Autumn 2011 a Junior ISA has been available for children aged under 18 who do not have a Child Trust Fund. The maximum per child is £4,128 per year for 2017–18. Children aged 16 to 18 can contribute to both a cash ISA and a junior cash ISA.

Withdrawals can be made without forfeiting tax relief. [15.32]

b) *Personal Equity Plans (PEPs), Tax Exempt Special Savings Accounts (TESSAs), Save as You Earn (SAYE)*

Personal Equity Plans were abolished on 5 April 1999, though existing plans remain effective and can be transferred between managers. PEPs allowed tax-free dividends and capital gains on annual investment in equities, stock and bonds of up to £9,000 per year. From 6 April 2008, all PEP accounts automatically became Stocks and shares ISAs, and are now subject to ISA rules.

TESSAs were also abolished on 5 April 1999. They allowed tax-free savings on up to £9,000 per year, subject to restrictions. Existing TESSAs were allowed to continue, and there was provision to allow transfer into a 'TESSA only ISA' when their term expired.

SAYE schemes were abolished in November 1994, although schemes linked to approved employee share option schemes ('SAYE Sharesave Schemes') remain available. [15.33]–[15.50]

III ENTERPRISE INVESTMENT SCHEME (EIS)

The Enterprise Investment Scheme (EIS) was introduced in 1994 to encourage individuals to invest in unquoted trading companies by offering tax reliefs. The EIS allows a company (a 'qualifying company') that meets certain conditions to raise funds by issuing full-risk ordinary shares to the individual investors previously unconnected with the company. It also allows individuals to be paid directors in the companies in which they invest and yet retain the tax reliefs, provided certain conditions are met. [15.51]

1 **The relief**

The EIS legislation is set out in ITA 2007 Part 5 and TCGA 1992 ss 150A–150C and Sch 5B.

EIS applies to new eligible shares issued in qualifying companies and from 6 April 2011 provides income tax relief at 30%. Prior to 6 April 2011 the relief was given at 20%. The maximum qualifying investment from 6 April 2012 is £1m per year (previously £500,000 per year).

To calculate the available relief, an individual's taxable income is arrived at by deducting charges on income and other allowances which afford relief at the highest rate (ie the personal allowance and the blind person's allowance). EIS relief is then given *after* venture capital trust relief (see [15.122]). The relief can only be utilised to the extent that the investor's income tax liability is reduced to nil.

Any gain made by an investor on the eventual disposal of his qualifying shares, provided that these are held for three years and income tax has been given and not withdrawn on those shares, is exempt from CGT. If the shares are sold at a loss (on cost) the cost of the shares is treated as reduced by the EIS relief given (TCGA 1992 s 150A). Subject to that, the loss can be offset against CGT gains or relief may be obtained under ITA 2007 s 131 (see [11.121]) against the taxpayer's income. A claim to offset the loss against income rather than gains is likely to be beneficial since the top rate of CGT is now 20% (28% for gains on residential investment properties and carried interest) with effect from 6 April 2016 (28% prior to that date).

Loss relief against income on shares qualifying for EIS income tax relief will not be subject to the cap introduced from 6 April 2013.

However, if an individual has only claimed EIS deferral relief, their income tax loss relief is restricted in any tax year to either £50,000 or 25% of earnings, whichever is greater. In practice, because the loss can also be set against income of the previous year, the individual has two tranches of £50,000 or 25% of earnings, whichever is greater.

EXAMPLE 15.4

Eddy Investor puts £150,000 into an EIS investment in June 2010. In the tax year 2017–18 he sells the shares for either (a) £200,000 or (b) £100,000. His tax position is as follows:

(1) *The original investment:* EIS relief at 20% was available so that Eddy's net investment cost was £120,000.
(2) *The sale for £200,000:* Given that the shares have been owned for more than three years the gain is tax free.
(3) *The sale for £100,000:* A capital loss of £50,000 minus £30,000 (being the EIS relief) is available for offset against Eddy's chargeable gains in 2017–18 or, most likely preferably, against his income under ITA 2007 s 131.

An investor may elect to carry-back his relief to the previous tax year, subject only to the maximum investment limit.. [15.52]

2 Qualifying individuals

EIS income tax relief is available to individual investors (and not therefore trustees or companies) who are liable for UK income tax, whether or not they are actually resident in the UK, who are not connected with the company (contrast CGT deferral: see [15.89]). Broadly an individual is so connected if he, or an associate of his, is an employee or paid director of the company; or if he and his associates possess more than 30% of the share capital or voting power of the company (see ITA 2007 s 170). For shares issued prior to 6 April 2012 the 30% test also applies to combined share and loan capital.

For these purposes, an associate excludes brothers and sisters but otherwise has a close company meaning [**41.121**] whilst a director is not debarred from the relief if the only payments that he receives from the company are for travelling and other tax deductible expenses. Certain individuals (commonly called 'business angels') will, however, qualify for the tax relief even though they are connected with the company by being paid directors. (They must not, however, be connected with a company or its trade at any time *before* the shares were issued.)

With effect from 18 November 2015, an investor cannot claim relief on a subscription unless all of the existing shares he holds at the time of the investment:
(1) were issued under EIS or SEIS; or
(2) are subscriber shares, ie the original shares that were issued on incorporation of the company. [**15.53**]

3 Qualifying company

The relevant company must be unquoted at the time of issue; it must not be controlled by another company and must not control any company that is not a qualifying subsidiary. It can be a qualifying holding company only if its subsidiaries qualify. It need not be UK registered but, from 6 April 2011, the issuing company must have a UK permanent establishment (see below). For shares issued prior to 6 April 2011, the requirement was that the trade had to be carried on mainly in the UK. The company must exist wholly for the purpose of carrying on one or more qualifying trades and generally must do so for three years from the date of issue of the shares or from the commencement of the qualifying activity (whichever is later).

For shares issued on or after 18 November 2015, a company must, unless it meets one of three exceptions, not exceed the maximum permitted age, defined by ITA 2007 s 175A as:
(1) seven years from the date of the issuing company's first commercial sale (including 51% subsidiaries and acquired trades); or
(2) 10 years from the date of the issuing company's first commercial sale (including 51% subsidiaries and acquired trades), in the case of a knowledge-intensive company.

In order for the maximum permitted age restriction not to apply, the company must meet one of Conditions A, B or C:
- Condition A is that the company must have received relevant State aid (including SEIS, SITR, EIS and VCT) investment in the seven years since its 'first relevant commercial sale'.
- Condition B is that the company must meet the turnover test; it is raising more than 50% of its average turnover over the last five years, and the funds are to be used for entering a new product market and/or geographic market (in the case of a group, the five year average turnover must include the turnover of a subsidiary company before it became a subsidiary if it became a subsidiary within the five year period).
- *Condition C* is that Condition B was met in connection with a previous share issue.

The 'relevant first commercial sale' means the first sale by any trade or subsidiary of the company or group.

The 'average turnover amount' means one-fifth of the total relevant turnover amount for the five-year period which ends:
(1) immediately before the beginning of the last accounts filing period, or
(2) if later, 12 months before the issue date.

A company is a 'knowledge-intensive' company at the date of the share issue if:
(1) it meets one or both of the following 'operating cost conditions':
   (a) in any one or more of the three previous years at least 15% of the relevant operating costs was spent on research and development or innovation;
   (b) in each of the previous three years at least 10% of the relevant operating costs was spent on research and development or innovation

   and
(2) it meets both of the following 'innovation conditions':
   (a) the company (or a subsidiary company within the group) is engaged in intellectual property creation at the date of issue, and
   (b) it is reasonable to assume that within 10 years the exploitation or utilisation of the intellectual property will form the greater part of the company's business (or the business of the group taken together)

   and/or
(3) the 'skilled employee condition' is met, ie at least 20% of the full-time equivalent employees are 'skilled employees'. Skilled employees are defined as individuals with a relevant higher education qualification (broadly, a Master's degree or higher) who are engaged directly in research, development or innovation activities.

The company's 'gross assets' must be less than £15m immediately before the share issue and £16m immediately after (prior to 6 April 2012 the limits were £7m and £8m respectively). If there are qualifying subsidiaries, the gross assets of the company and those subsidiaries must be aggregated for these purposes.

The company issuing the EIS shares ('the qualifying company') or a qualifying directly held 90% subsidiary of that qualifying company (or post 6 April 2007 a 100% subsidiary of a 90% subsidiary or vice versa) must, during the relevant period, carry on the qualifying activity which is funded by the money raised by the EIS share issue. Additionally, for shares issued on or after 6 April 2012, the use of money raised to acquire shares in another company is no longer a qualifying activity. This does not prevent money being used to subscribe for new shares in a company which as a result becomes a 90% qualifying subsidiary, as long as the funds are used for a qualifying purpose within that company. The requirement that shares must be issued in order to raise money for the purposes of a qualifying business activity was amended in relation to shares issued on or after 18 November 2015, with the effect that the issue of shares must also be used to promote the growth and development of the group if all of the group activities are looked at together. It is no longer possible to use money raised from the issue of EIS or VCT shares on or after 18 November 2015 to acquire a business by a trade and assets acquisition. This includes the acquisition of any goodwill, intellectual property or other intangible assets employed for the purposes of a trade.

Further, a company can be a qualifying subsidiary if it is a 51% subsidiary of an EIS company. This rule does not apply to a company that actually carries on the trade or research and development in question nor to a company which is a property management company. In order for such companies to be qualifying subsidiaries, they must be 90% subsidiaries.

A company must have fewer than 250 full-time equivalent employees at the time of the share issue (increased from 50 prior to from 6 April 2012) or, with effect from 18 November 2015, fewer than 500 employees if it is a knowledge-intensive company. A qualifying company can raise no more than £5m (increased from £2m from 6 April 2012) in total from the EIS, VCTs and other State Aid in a 12-month period ending on the date of the relevant investment. This rule applies to all VCTs, regardless of when their funds were raised and a VCT which invests in a company which breaks this rule will itself be disqualified as a VCT, with effect from Royal Assent to the 2012 Finance Act.

Additionally, with effect from 18 November 2015, a new lifetime cap applies to the total amount of investments a company or group can raise via any combination of EIS, SEIS, VCT or other State aid of £12 million, for most companies, or £20 million for knowledge-intensive companies (as defined above). Account must be taken of all State aid investment received by any company within a group or business that has been acquired. [15.54]

4 Eligible shares

From 6 April 2012, shares must be new shares and from the date of issue there can be no rights to redemption, no preferential rights to assets on a winding up and no preferential rights to dividends if the amount or timing of the dividend depends on a decision by the company or any other person, and the dividends are not cumulative. Effectively dividends of a fixed amount, with a fixed payment date are no longer deemed to be preferential. For further information on preferential rights, with particular regard to deferred shares, see *Flix Innovations Ltd v R & C Comrs* (2016), which illustrates how even an apparently trivial preferential right can result in the loss of EIS relief.

Prior to 6 April 2012, shares had to be new shares and during three years from the date of the issue there could be no preferential rights to dividends or to the company's assets on a winding up, and there must be no right to redeem the shares (ITA 2007 s 173(2)).

The shares must be subscribed for wholly in cash and be fully paid up at the time of subscription (other than, for shares issued after 16 March 2004, any of them which are bonus shares) and all shares comprised in that issue (once again, other than bonus shares) must be issued in order to raise money for a 'qualifying business activity' (see ITA 2007 ss 174, 179). For shares issued on or after 22 April 2009 only the EIS shares issued must raise money for a qualifying business activity and there is no requirement in relation to non-qualifying shares issued on the same day.

In November 2015, a 'sunset' clause was introduced so that income tax relief can only be obtained in respect of shares issued before 6 April 2025. [15.55]

5 Qualifying activities

Although the company need not be incorporated or resident in the UK, it must have a UK permanent establishment (ITA 2007 s 180A). Prior to 6 April 2011, the requirement was that the company using the funds raised had to carry on trading or research and development activities wholly or mainly in the UK. The definition of permanent establishment used is based on Article 5 of the OECD Model Tax Convention on Income and on Capital and is written into the EIS legislation at ITA 2007 s 191A. The relevant trading activities, which for shares issued after 6 April 2011 may be undertaken outside the UK, must either be carried on, or intended to be carried on and actually carried on, within two years of the date of issue of the shares.

Certain trading activities are prohibited including: (a) dealing in shares, securities or land; (b) dealing in goods otherwise than in the course of an ordinary trade or wholesale or retail distribution; (c) banking or other financial activities; (d) provision of legal or accountancy services and leasing; (e) property development; (f) farming and market gardening; (g) forestry and timber production; (h) hotel keeping, guest houses etc (but see ITA 2007 s 197); (i) the operation and management of nursing or residential care homes (but see ITA 2007 s 198); (j) coal production; (k) steel production; (l) generation or exporting electricity, or production of heat, fuel or gas; (m) shipbuilding; and (n) the provision of services to a connected party conducting any of the above trades.

A company must meet the financial health requirement of ITA 2007 s 180B. The issuing company is 'in difficulty' if it is reasonable to assume that it would be regarded as a firm in difficulty for the purposes of the Community Guidelines on State Aid for Rescuing and Restructuring Firms in Difficulty (2004/C 244/02). It should be noted that HMRC's view is that the financial health requirement will be met if the company is within the first three years of operations in the relevant field of activity and/or it has been able to raise funds from its existing shareholders or from the market sufficient to meet its anticipated funding requirements at that time. [15.56]

6 Anti-avoidance and pre-arranged exits

ITA 2007 ss 165 and 178 contain an anti-avoidance rule. It provides that relief is not given to an individual in respect of any shares unless those shares are subscribed for and issued for genuine commercial purposes and not as part of a scheme or arrangement the main purpose of which (or one of the main purposes of which) is the avoidance of tax. Provisions deny EIS relief on investments affording the investor undue protection in the form of:
(1) arrangements providing the investor with an exit route;
(2) predetermined plans for the disposal of the underlying trade;
(3) third party guarantees or assurances;
(4) sub-contracting the activities to a third party with which any of the preceding arrangements have been made. See generally ITA 2007 s 177.

HMRC took a view that articles allowing for a conversion of shares, on an IPO or otherwise, were an arrangement for the disposal of shares and therefore contravened ITA 2007 s 177(1)(a). An amendment to ITA 2007 s 177 was introduced in Finance Bill 2017, in order to allow such conversion clauses, with effect from 5 December 2016. However, the Finance Bill 2017 was truncated following the announcement of the 2017 general election. At the time of writing, the amendment forms part of Finance (No 2) Bill 2017. The SEIS legislation at ITA 2007 s 257CD will be amended in the same way.

The No Disqualifying Arrangements Requirement (ITA 2007 s 178A) provides that the shares must not be issued in consequence of or otherwise in connection with 'disqualifying arrangements'. Arrangements are 'disqualifying' if the main purpose or one of the main purposes of any person being party to them is to secure that the issuing company is a qualifying company and that EIS relief is obtainable by one or more persons, and one or both of conditions A or B are satisfied. Condition A is that as a direct or indirect result of the share issue an amount representing the whole or a majority of the amount raised is paid to or for the benefit of a party to the arrangements. Condition B is that in the absence of the arrangements it is reasonable to assume that the relevant qualifying business activity would have been carried on as part of another business, by a person who is a party to the arrangements or a person connected with such a party. [15.57]–[15.81]

IV CGT REINVESTMENT AND DEFERRAL RELIEF

1 Reinvestment relief

The position for acquisitions *prior to 6 April 1998* is that to obtain relief a *chargeable gain* must accrue to an individual (or to trustees) on a *disposal of (any) assets*, and that person must then reinvest in a *qualifying investment* in the *qualifying period* and make the appropriate claim for relief.

This relief is not considered further, except in the context of clawbacks of reinvestment relief claimed prior to 5 April 1998. [15.82]–[15.87]

a) *Clawback of gain*

Due to the passage of time, clawback of pre 6 April 1998 reinvestment relief can now only occur on the disposal of the asset. The effect is the same as arises on the disposal of EIS shares on which EIS deferral relief has been claimed (see 2(g) below). [15.88]

2 Deferral relief under the Enterprise Investment Scheme

a) *The two codes*

There are now two separate codes in operation:
(1) Income tax and CGT exemption: these rules are considered at [15.52];
(2) CGT deferral relief (see [15.90]). It is important to appreciate that for the purpose of deferral there is no prohibition on the investor being connected with the company and the £1m pa (£500,000 pre 2012–13) subscription limit does not apply. [15.89]

b) *The relief*

The deferral relief operates to defer a CGT charge on a gain arising on disposals by an individual (the investor) where that gain is rolled over into a qualifying investment within the qualifying time. There is no limit on the amount of gains that may be sheltered (but see the investment limit and gross assets test described in [15.54]). [15.90]

c) *A disposal*

The gain must accrue to the investor (which may include a trustee – see [15.99]) on the disposal of *any* asset, or upon the occurrence of a chargeable event in respect of gains previously deferred by an investment in EIS shares or VCT shares or where, in respect of shares acquired prior to 6 April 1998 as a qualifying investment for reinvestment relief, there has been a clawback of the reinvestment relief. [15.91]

d) *Qualifying investment*

Relief is available only if within *the qualifying time*, that is, a one-year period before or the three-year period following the disposal upon which the gain has arisen (*the accrual time*) a *qualifying investment* is made. A qualifying investment is made where:

(1) the investor subscribes wholly in cash (other than, for shares issued after 16 March 2004, any bonus shares) for eligible shares (ie ordinary, non-preferential shares; there is no requirement that they should be shares to which EIS income tax relief is attributable);

(2) the company issuing the shares is a company which is a qualifying company for the purposes of EIS income tax relief (see [15.54]) in relation to those shares. For instance, the company's gross assets before the issue of new shares after 5 April 2012 must be no more than £15m and after the issue no more than £16m;

(3) the shares on which relief is claimed are subscribed for wholly in cash and are fully paid up at issue (other than, for shares issued after 16 March 2004, any of them which are bonus shares). An undertaking to pay cash at a future date will not qualify the shares as fully paid up;

(4) where the investment is made before the accrual time, the shares are still held by the investor at accrual time;

(5) the company issuing the shares or its qualifying 90% subsidiary must carry on the qualifying trade or research and development (see [15.54] and [15.56]);

(6) all qualifying shares (other than bonus shares, as above) are issued in order to fund a 'qualifying business activity' carried on by the issuing company or its 90% subsidiary (see below and at [15.56]);

(7) the proceeds of the issue are applied wholly (or practically wholly) for that activity within the two-year period required for income tax purposes;

(8) the subscription and issue are made for genuine commercial purposes and not as part of a tax avoidance scheme.

It is not a requirement that the investor must not be connected with the company in which the investment is being made (contrast income tax relief: see [15.52]). The main limitation in respect of the relief is in the exclusion of certain trade activities. Some of these were already excluded under the previous legislation, but some were added. Crucially, these comprise property development, farming and market gardening and forestry and timber production. Also excluded are hotel-keeping and the management of nursing or residential care homes, but only where the person operating such an establishment has either a property interest in it or is in occupation of it. Certain financial activities such as insurance and money-lending are excluded, but not the giving of financial advice.

FA 2004 introduced some changes to the deferral relief rules in order to bring them into line with the changes made for income tax purposes. These amendments are found at FA 2004 Sch 18 para 12 et seq. Broadly, deferral relief can be obtained by trustees of some trusts and by individuals who have a pre-existing connection with the company. [15.92]

e) *Taper relief and EIS investments*

Prior to FA 1999, where an individual disposed of an investment in a company qualifying for EIS relief and reinvested the proceeds in another company qualifying for EIS relief, whilst the gain on the disposal could be deferred, the holding period for taper relief would be limited to the period for which the investor held the original shares.

However, where shares in the first EIS company were issued after 5 April 1998 and are disposed of after 5 April 1999, individuals will be able to benefit from taper relief on a cumulative basis. The amount of the deferred gain which becomes chargeable to tax when the shares in the second EIS company are sold will be calculated for taper relief purposes as though the holding period began when the shares in the first company were acquired and ended when the shares in the second company were sold.

Taper relief was abolished in respect of disposals occurring after 5 April 2008. [15.93]

f) *Entrepreneurs' relief and EIS Investments*

Entrepreneurs' relief is available in connection with disposals taking place on or after 6 April 2008 (see **Chapter 20**). Entrepreneurs' relief now operates by reducing the rate of tax rather than the amount of the taxable gain. Prior to 6 April 2008, where EIS deferral relief was given the amount of gain to be deferred was the amount before deducting taper relief.

For share disposals on or after 3 December 2014 an individual may defer a gain which would be eligible for entrepreneurs' relief and, when the gain comes back into charge, the deferred gain will be eligible for entrepreneurs' relief. Entrepreneurs' relief must be claimed the first time that any part of the deferred gain comes back into charge, even if there is no tax to pay (eg due to the annual exemption or available losses). If relief is not claimed the first time, it cannot be claimed subsequently in respect of any of the remaining gain.

Prior to 3 December 2014, any gain on which entrepreneurs' relief is claimed is ineligible for EIS deferral relief (TCGA 1992 s 169N(9)). A choice must be made between claiming entrepreneurs' relief or claiming EIS deferral. [15.94]

g) *Withdrawal of relief*

Shares cease to be eligible and deferral relief may be withdrawn in the following circumstances:
(1) where, during the qualifying period, the company is no longer a qualifying company;

(2) where, during the qualifying period, the qualifying trade or research and development is not being carried on by the qualifying company or a qualifying 90% subsidiary;
(3) where, for shares issued before 22 April 2009, less than 80% of the proceeds of the issue have been applied towards a qualifying business activity within one year and the balance within the following year or where, for shares issued on or after 22 April 2009, less than 100% of the proceeds of the issue have been applied towards a qualifying business activity within two years;
(4) where not all the shares (other than, for shares issued after 16 March 2004, any of them which are bonus shares) were issued in order to fund a qualifying business.

In cases (1)–(3), shares cease to be eligible at the time of the relevant event; in (4), deferral relief is deemed never to have been available.

Relief can only be withdrawn where the company concerned has given notice to the inspector where required to do so, or where the inspector has given notice to the company that, in his opinion, relief should be withdrawn.
[15.95]

h) *Appeals*

A notice from an inspector is treated as a decision to refuse a claim by the investee company and provides grounds for an appeal. If an appeal has been determined in respect of the parallel income tax provisions, that determination is decisive in relation to the same issue on a CGT appeal and vice versa. [15.96]

i) *Clawback of gain*

A chargeable event, giving rise to a chargeable gain, may be triggered *first*, when the investor disposes of the EIS shares otherwise than by way of an inter-spouse (including civil partner from 5 December 2005) transfer; *second*, when shares issued cease to be eligible shares (see [15.95]); *third*, when either the investor or the investor's spouse (or civil partner from 5 December 2005) who has acquired the shares from the investor becomes non-resident less than three years (five years for shares issued prior to 5 April 2000) from the date of issue of the shares; and *fourth* where the investor (or any associate of the investor) receives any value from the company (or any person connected with it) at any time during the 'period of restriction', namely, the period beginning one year prior to the share issue and ending on the termination date relating to the shares.

The rules that determine the amount of the value received correspond to the rules for EIS income tax relief. Receipts of 'insignificant value' will not trigger a chargeable event unless there have been a number of such receipts in the period of restriction in question and a receipt of their aggregate value would not be construed as insignificant. The rules for determining whether a receipt is of insignificant value are broadly the same as those for EIS income tax relief, with one exception. Where the amount received exceeds £1,000, for deferral relief purposes the amount received is compared with the total amount of any gains deferred in respect of the subscription for the shares.

The identification of share rules that apply on disposals that may give rise to a chargeable gain after a chargeable event are aligned with the identification rules for EIS income tax purposes.

Where EIS shares are disposed of by means of a 'share-for-share' exchange under TCGA 1992 s 135 or 136, the deferred gain will be brought back into charge. Additionally, for shares issued before 22 April 2009, a disposal of EIS shares in a share-for-share exchange also gave rise to a disposal of the EIS shares since s 135 or 136 were disapplied for EIS purposes. Shares issued on or after 22 April 2009 can, however, benefit from the relief offered by TCGA 1992 ss 135 and 136 and no gain or loss will be brought into charge in respect of the disposal of shares that form the subject of the exchange. EIS reliefs may only be retained on a share for share exchange in two specific circumstances (ITA 2007 ss 247–249). **[15.97]**

j) Anti-avoidance

A number of rules exist to prevent, *inter alia, first,* the obtaining of deferral relief in respect of a gain from shares or securities where the reinvestment is in the same company as that in which the shares or securities disposed of subsisted or in a company in the same group and, *second,* obtaining deferral relief where the investor takes little or no risk in making the investment due to a guaranteed exit route (see **[15.57]**). **[15.98]**

k) Trustees

Trustees may obtain deferral relief on the disposal of trust assets where either:
(1) the trust is a discretionary trust, provided that all those who may benefit are individuals or charities; or
(2) the trust is an interest-in-possession trust (which, for these purposes, excludes an interest for a fixed term) where any of the beneficiaries is an individual or a charity. Where not all of the beneficiaries are individuals or charities, then only the 'relevant proportion' of the gain may qualify for relief. The 'relevant proportion' is the proportion that the income accruing to beneficiaries who are individuals or charities bears to the total income of the trust. **[15.99]**

l) Claims

The procedure for claiming relief is the same as for EIS income tax relief.
[15.100]–[15.120]

V VENTURE CAPITAL TRUSTS

1 Background

The Venture Capital Trust (VCT) scheme was introduced on 6 April 1995 in order to assist small businesses by channelling investment into qualifying unlisted trading companies. Investors acquire shares in a VCT, whose professional managers use the funds to invest in a range of 'small' unquoted companies, enabling investors to spread their risk.

The qualifying conditions with which VCT investee companies have to comply mirror those of the EIS scheme. [15.121]

2 The provisions in outline

The legislation relating to VCTs is now contained in ITA 2007 Part 6.

a) *Income tax*

Individual investors are exempt from tax on dividends received from shares in a VCT (whether the shares have been acquired by subscription or purchase) and are also entitled to relief at 30% for investment in *new* ordinary shares in a VCT. This relief is limited to investments of up to £200,000 in any tax year and requires the shares to be retained for five years. The investment relief is given in priority to other deductions and reliefs available to the taxpayer which are given in terms of a tax offset (such as EIS relief). To the extent that full relief is not available it is not possible to carry forward any unused portion.

With effect from 6 April 2014, relief for investment is restricted where an individual has made a 'linked sale'. Broadly a linked sale is a sale of shares in the same VCT (or a successor VCT), where either the sale was conditional upon the purchase, or the sale and purchase took place within six months of each other.

Also, with effect from 17 July 2014 investors are able to subscribe for VCT shares via nominees. This enables individuals to subscribe for VCT shares through brokers. [15.122]

b) *Capital gains*

The individual investor is exempt from CGT on disposals of ordinary shares in a VCT (whether the shares were acquired by subscription or purchase and so that losses will equally not be allowable) so long as the VCT was and has remained approved by HMRC throughout. In addition reinvestment relief was available to an individual who after 5 April 1995 had crystallised a chargeable gain. That gain could be deferred either in whole or part by matching it against a subscription for eligible shares in a VCT subject to the permitted maximum limit: that investment must take place within a qualifying period of 12 months before and 12 months after the chargeable event. This two-year period may straddle three tax years so that it was possible to shelter a gain of up to £300,000. However, deferral relief was abolished in relation to VCT shares issued after 5 April 2004. [15.123]

3 The venture capital trust

A VCT must be listed on a regulated market (prior to 6 April 2011 the requirement was that they had to be listed on the official UK list) and, in general, will enjoy the same exemption from corporation tax on its capital gains as investment trusts (TCGA 1992 s 100(1)). At least 70% of the investments of VCTs must be in unquoted trading companies ('qualifying holdings' as defined in ITA 2007 Part 6 Chapter 4 which exclude securities relating to a guaranteed loan) with not more than 15% in any one company or group of companies. From 6 April 2007 there was a relaxation such that, if a VCT makes a cash realisation on the disposal of an investment that has been part of its qualifying holdings for at least six months, the disposal will be ignored for the next six months for the purposes of the 70% test. At least 10% of the total investment in any one company must be in ordinary non-preference shares. The investments may include both equity and loans with a minimum term of five years but at least 70% (30% for pre 6 April 2011 VCTs) of the investments must be in new qualifying shares. VCTs will initially have up to three years to meet the 70% unquoted trading company and 30% qualifying share requirements. Investments in unquoted trading companies held by VCTs at a time when such companies become quoted may be treated as investments in unquoted trading companies for up to a further five years.

With effect from 6 April 2014, there are anti-avoidance rules which operate to remove a VCT's status if it returns capital that does not relate to profits on investments (eg by a repayment of share capital or share premium) within three years of the end of the accounting period in which shares were issued to investors.

From 18 November 2015, the permitted age requirement (see above) must be met by investee companies. In broad terms, the investee companies must be less than seven years old unless:
(1) they have previously issued shares that are SEIS, EIS and/or VCT qualifying shares; or
(2) they are raising more than 50% of their five-year average turnover in EIS/VCT investment and will spend the money on a new product and/or geographic market.

Finally, there are requirements about the size of the companies in which VCTs may invest to qualify for tax relief:
- The investee company's gross assets must not exceed £15m immediately before the share issue and £16m immediately afterwards.
- The investee company must have fewer than 250 full time equivalent employees or, with effect from 18 November 2015, fewer than 500 employees if it is a knowledge-intensive company.
- The investee company may raise no more than £5m from all State aid investment (including EIS, VCT and SEIS) in any 12-month period. After Royal Assent to FA 2012 a VCT which invests in a company which exceeds this limit can lose its status as a VCT (ITA 2007 s 173A).
- The investee company may raise no more than £12m in total from all State aid sources (including EIS, VCT and SEIS) in any 12-month period. After 17 July 2012, a VCT which invests in a company which exceeds this limit can lose its status as a VCT (ITA 2007 s 173AA).

These limits apply to all VCTs regardless of when they raised their funds. The following example illustrates how the VCT rules operate.

EXAMPLE 15.5

Mr Smith acquires existing VCT shares for the value of £30,000 on 1 May 2016. He is entitled to relief on distributions and CGT relief on disposals of those shares. He also subscribes £200,000 for new VCT shares issued on 1 October 2016. He is entitled to relief on distributions and relief on disposals for £170,000 of that subscription. He can claim income tax investment relief on the full £200,000 subscription. **[15.124]**

4 CGT aspects

a) *The trust itself*

Chargeable gains realised by the trust are exempt provided that it has not lost its approval. **[15.125]**

b) *Relief on disposals by investors*

An individual (aged 18 or over) is exempt from CGT on gains arising from a disposal of ordinary shares in a VCT (whether or not acquired as a new issue) provided that it retains approval until the date of disposal and the shares disposed of were not acquired in excess of the permitted maximum (ie investments not exceeding £200,000 in any tax year from 2004–05 onwards – see **[15.122]**) (TCGA 1992 s 151A(1) as amended).

Capital losses are not allowable. **[15.126]**

c) *Deferred CGT relief on reinvestment in a VCT*

Deferral relief was abolished with effect in relation to shares issued after 5 April 2004. Earlier editions of this book contain details of how the relief worked. **[15.127]**

VI SEED ENTERPRISE INVESTMENT SCHEME (SEIS)

The Seed Enterprise Investment Scheme (SEIS) was introduced with effect from 6 April 2012 in response to a perceived need to give further incentives to encourage individuals to invest in seed stage companies. It has effect in relation to shares issued on or after 6 April 2012 and was initially introduced with a fixed five year term but this 'sunset' clause has now been removed and SEIS is a permanent relief.

The SEIS legislation is set out at ITA 2007 Part 5A and TCGA 1992 ss 150E–150G and Sch 5BB. **[15.128]**

1 Qualifying companies

The SEIS requirements for qualifying companies mirror those of the EIS, except in a few aspects. In addition to meeting the EIS qualifying criteria, an SEIS qualifying company must also, or where applicable instead, meet the following conditions.

An SEIS qualifying company must have fewer than 25 employees at the date of the share issue (rather than fewer than 250 under the EIS scheme) and its gross assets must not exceed £200,000 before the share issue (rather than £15m under the EIS). The maximum a company can raise under the SEIS is £150,000. This is effectively a lifetime limit because it applies to all State aid received in a three-year period.

In addition, an SEIS company must conduct a new qualifying trade, being a trade which commenced less than two years before the share issue, and which was not previously carried on by any other person. Additionally, a company cannot have carried on any other trade.

An SEIS qualifying company must also never have been under the control of another company. From 6 April 2013, this rule was relaxed so that a period when the company had only issued subscriber shares and had not traded nor begun preparations to carry on a trade is ignored. This relaxation was introduced to avoid 'off the shelf' companies being unintentionally disqualified.

The company must not have issued any shares under either the EIS or VCT schemes at any time. With effect from 6 April 2015, once SEIS shares have been issued, the company can issue shares under EIS and/or VCT as long as this is at least one day later than the SEIS share issue. Until 6 April 2015, the company could not issue shares under either the EIS or VCT schemes until it had spent at least 70% of the SEIS money raised. **[15.129]**

2 The tax reliefs

a) *Income tax relief*

SEIS applies to new eligible shares issued in qualifying companies from 6 April 2012 and provides income tax relief at 50% on qualifying investments of up to £100,000. To calculate the available relief, an individual's taxable income is arrived at by deducting charges on income and other allowances which afford relief at the highest rate (ie the personal allowance and the blind person's allowance). SEIS relief is then given *after* VCT relief (see **[15.122]**), and EIS relief. The relief can only be utilised to the extent that the investor's income tax liability is reduced to nil. Carry back provisions mirror those of the EIS. **[15.130]**

b) *Capital gains tax exemption*

As with the EIS, any gain made by an investor on the eventual disposal of his SEIS qualifying shares, provided that these are held for three years and income tax has been given and not withdrawn, is exempt from CGT. If the shares are sold at a loss (on cost) the cost of the shares is treated as reduced by the SEIS relief given (TCGA 1992 s 150A). Subject to that, the loss can be offset against CGT gains or relief may be obtained against the taxpayer's income by making an election under ITA 2007 s 131 (see **[11.121]**). A claim to offset the loss against income rather than gains is likely to be beneficial since the top rate of CGT is now 20%, or 28% for gains on residential investment properties and carried interest (28% prior to 6 April 2016). **[15.131]**

c) *Capital gains tax re-investment relief*

An individual may claim 50% exemption from capital gains tax on the disposal of any asset on a qualifying SEIS investment.

If SEIS shares are sold at a loss, the cost of shares is treated as reduced by the SEIS relief given (TCGA 1992 s 150A). The net loss can be off-set against capital gains or against the taxpayer's income under ITA 2007 s 131). Loss relief against income for SEIS shares will not be subject to the cap introduced from 6 April 2013. [15.132]

3 Qualifying investors – company directors

SEIS requirements for qualifying investors mirror those of the EIS except that, unlike the EIS, individuals who are directors of the issuing company may claim SEIS relief for qualifying investments, provided only that they meet the 30% test. As with the EIS, broadly, an individual will fail the 30% test if he and his associates possess more than 30% of the share capital or voting power of the company (see ITA 2007 s 257BF). For these purposes, an associate excludes brothers and sisters but otherwise has a close company meaning (see [41.121]). [15.133]

4 Anti Avoidance

Anti-avoidance legislation at ITA 2007 s 257FP et seq applies, broadly, so that SEIS relief is withdrawn from an investor if a qualifying company acquires the trade or assets of another business or the shares in another company, and that investor and his associates previously had an interest in that trade or company. [15.134]

16 Trusts and settlements

Updated by Sandra Eden, Senior Lecturer, University of Edinburgh

---

I   Introduction – trust modernisation [**16.1**]
II Definitions [**16.2**]
III General principles [**16.5**]
IV Income arising to trustees which is taxed at special rates (ITA 2007 Part 9 Chapter 3) [**16.21**]
V   The taxation of beneficiaries [**16.61**]
VI Trusts with vulnerable beneficiaries [**16.74**]
VII The anti-avoidance provisions (ITTOIA 2005 Part 5 Chapter 5) [**16.91**]
VIII Reform [**16.108**]

I   INTRODUCTION – TRUST MODERNISATION

Provisions were included in the Finance Acts of 2004, 2005 and 2006 aimed at 'trust modernisation' for income and capital gains tax purposes. In addition to the stated aim of simplifying the tax regime for UK trusts, the main thrust behind the these provisions was to move towards a more 'tax neutral' system, in which the amount of income or capital gains tax chargeable should not vary to any great extent depending on whether the property upon which it arises is held under a trust or directly by an individual. In achieving this goal, the Government sought to strike a balance between a system that does not provide artificial incentives to set up a trust, and one that avoids artificial obstacles to the use of trusts where significant non-tax benefits could be gained. Reform began with FA 2004, which increased the special rate applicable for certain trusts ([**16.21**] ff) to bring it in line with the higher rate of income tax. In order to mitigate the possible harsh effects of this measure on smaller trusts and trusts with vulnerable beneficiaries, FA 2005 introduced a lower rate band for all trusts that pay tax at the trust or dividend trust rate ([**16.21**]), and a new regime for trusts with vulnerable beneficiaries ([**16.74**] ff). The later stage in the process of reform, provided for in FA 2006 and aimed at reducing the burden of administering the taxation of trusts, was an attempt to bring the main trust-related definitions for tax on income and chargeable gains into line with each other, along with an increase in the standard rate band for trustees. [**16.1**]

II DEFINITIONS

1 What is a settlement?

Although the term settlement is not statutorily defined, the idea behind the provisions in FA 2006 is the alignment of what is treated as a settlement for the general purposes of income tax and tax on chargeable gains. This is achieved through a common definition of 'settled property', being any property held in trust other than property held by one person as nominee for another, or held by a person as trustee for another person who is absolutely entitled to the property as against the trustee, or as a trustee for another who, but for being an infant or under some disability, is absolutely entitled against the trustee (ITA 2007 s 466). This definition mirrors the equivalent capital gains tax provisions ([**25.2**]). [**16.2**]

2 The settlor

A person is a settlor in relation to a settlement if the settlement was made, or is treated as having been made, by that person. A person is treated as having made a settlement if he has made or directly or indirectly entered into it, if he has provided, or undertaken to provide, property directly or indirectly for the purposes of the settlement, or if the settlement arose on his death and any of the settled property is, or is derived from, property of which he was competent to dispose immediately before his death (ITA 2007 s 467). Once again, the provisions are almost identical to their capital gains tax counterparts ([**25.21**]–[**25.40**]). [**16.3**]

3 The trustees

ITA 2007 s 474 provides that the trustees of a settlement are to be treated as a single person, meaning that the trustees are distinct from the persons who may from time to time be trustees of the settlement. A common test to determine whether the trustees of a settlement are resident in the UK is provided by ITA 2007 s 475 ([**18.13**]–[**18.15**]). [**16.4**]

III GENERAL PRINCIPLES

1 Trustees' liability at basic rate

The starting position is that trustees are subject to the basic rate of income tax (ITA 2007 s 11, currently 20%) or the dividend ordinary rate (ITA 2007 s 14, currently 7.5%) on all the income produced by the fund regardless of their own personal tax position and that of the beneficiary. The basis for taxing trustees under ITTOIA 2005 is that although not *beneficially* entitled to the income, they are 'persons receiving or entitled to' the income. Trustees are 'persons' but not individuals – hence, subject to special rules, discussed later, their liability is limited to tax at the basic rate and they have no personal allowances (the trust income is, after all, not their property) (see *Trusts, Settlements and Estates Manual* (TSEM) 3610). However, there are significant exceptions to this treatment and it is largely limited to trusts where the trustees have no discretion over the distribution of income (ie trusts in which there is an interest in possession) and other trusts are subject to different regimes (see **[16.21]–[16.60]** for the discretionary trust and **[16.74]–[16.90]** for trusts with vulnerable beneficiaries).

A beneficiary, entitled to the income under the terms of the trust, enjoys a credit for the tax paid by the trustees – see **[16.62]**.

Expenses incurred in administering the fund may not be deducted in computing the tax liability of the trustees and are, therefore, paid out of taxed income (see TSEM 8010 ff). **[16.5]**

EXAMPLE 16.1

(1) The trustees of the Jenkinson family trust run a bakery. The profits of that business will be calculated in accordance with the normal rules applicable to trading income under ITTOIA 2005 and be subject to basic rate income tax in the trustees' hands (but note that the profits of a business carried on by trustees are not 'earned income': see *Fry v Shiels' Trustees* (1915)).

(2) A and B, trustees of the Joel family settlement, farm trust land in partnership with Sir Joel (head of the family) who owns adjacent land. Normal rules of partnership taxation apply and, as the trustees have entered the partnership agreement *qua* trustees, any change in their composition will not lead to a cessation of a trade carried on by that retiring trustee. In the event of losses arising, the relevant proportion may be set against other trust income.

2 Trust returns, direct assessment and deduction at source

Trustees have always been assessed directly on income from certain sources, for example trading income and property income. Prior to 2016–17, however, tax would have been deducted at source on savings income and, similarly the tax credit available on dividend income would have satisfied the trustees' liability to pay tax at the basic rate. From 6 April 2016, most forms of investment income will no longer carry a tax credit and some trustees who did not previously complete a tax return or make informal payments to HMRC face new reporting requirements. In order to ease the burden on such trustees, as an interim arrangement for the tax year 2016–2017 HMRC will not require notification from trustees where the only source of income is savings interest and the tax liability is below £100. The longer term position is currently being reviewed.

Unlike individuals, trustees do not qualify for either the personal savings allowance or the tax-free dividend allowance (see **[7.27]**). The normal self-assessment rules apply to trustees, but note that every person who was a trustee when the income arose or who subsequently becomes one is responsible for making trust returns etc (TMA 1970 s 7(9)). However, anything done by one trustee satisfies the liability of all and penalties can only be recovered once (from a person who was a trustee when the penalty was triggered). Trustees are generally required to complete the trust and estate tax return: there is, however, no requirement on bare trustees to complete a self-assessment tax return or to make any payment on account unless they choose to do so (see *Tax Bulletin*, February 1997, p 395 and *Tax Bulletin*, December 1997). [16.6]

3 Exceptional cases

In exceptional cases trustees do not have to complete a return. The main situation is where professional trustees are acting; there is no untaxed income or any such income is mandated directly to a beneficiary; it is clear because of the small value of the fund that CGT will not arise and the trustees undertake to notify the Revenue of any change in their circumstances. A similar rule is applied where the sole or main asset is a residential property, which is occupied rent free by a beneficiary under the terms of the trust. In cases not falling within the above but where the payment of untaxed income is made directly to an interest in possession beneficiary under the authority of the trustee, that income is excluded from the trust and estate tax return and the beneficiary will be directly assessed on that income. This practice has been extended to trustees of settlor interested trusts where the settlor (or the settlor's spouse or civil partner) is also an interest in possession beneficiary and the trust income is mandated to them (see TSEM 3040). Where trustees receive income which is covered by the standard rate band and which has suffered deduction of basic rate tax at source or comes with a non-repayable tax credit (ie dividends), trustees do not have to make a return every year, although this will have little relevance from 2016–17 with the removal of the interest and dividend tax credit (TSEM 3014). [16.7]

4 Trustees' remuneration

If a trust instrument authorises the remuneration of a trustee, the payment will be regarded as an annual payment subject to deduction of income tax at source (ITA 2007 Part 15 Chapter 6 and Part 8 Chapter 4, formerly TA 1988 ss 348–349; see [14.21]), but is nonetheless treated as earned income in the trustees' hands (*Dale v IRC* (1954) and see TSEM 6237). [16.8]

5 Other matters

The UK treatment of non-resident trustees is discussed at [18.79]; and the treatment of foreign source income received by trustees at [18.38].
[16.9]–[16.20]

IV INCOME ARISING TO TRUSTEES WHICH IS TAXED AT SPECIAL RATES (ITA 2007 PART 9 CHAPTER 3)

1 The charge imposed by ITA 2007 s 479

a) *Special rates: the 'trust rate' and the 'dividend trust rate'*

As noted above, trustees are not liable to income tax at the higher or additional rate because they are not individuals. Trustees receiving income falling within s 479(1) (see [16.22]) are, however, liable to pay income tax at the trust rates.

Income	First £1,000 of income (ITA 2007 s 491)	Income over £1,000 (ITA 2007 s 9)
Income other than dividends	20%	45% (the trust rate)
Dividend income (treated as highest slice of income)	7.5%	38.1% (the dividend trust rate)

Where the settlor has made more than one settlement which exist in the tax year, the £1,000 band is shared between them, subject to a minimum of £200 per settlement (ITA 2007 s 492).

Effectively, this means that trustees pay tax at the same rates as basic rate taxpayers on the first £1,000 of income and at the additional rates of tax on the rest of their income (see [42.76]).

The charge is on net income, ie income after the deduction of permitted expenses (see further [16.23]) and includes capital payments which are deemed to be income (ITA 2007 ss 481, 482, see further [16.26]). [16.21]

b) *Which trusts are caught?*

ITA 2007 s 479 provides that the special rates for trustees apply if the income arising under a trust, not being one that is established for charitable purposes only, is accumulated or discretionary income. By virtue of s 480(1), income is accumulated or discretionary income in so far as:

'(a) it must be accumulated, or
(b) it is payable at the discretion of the trustees or any other person, and it is not excluded by subsection (3).'

Section 480(2) provides guidance as to when income is payable at the discretion of the trustees or any other person. These will include:

'cases where the trustees have, or any other person has, any discretion over one or more of the following matters –
(a) whether, or the extent to which, the income is to be accumulated,
(b) the persons to whom the income is to be paid, and
(c) how much of the income is to be paid to any person.'

Income excluded by s 480(3) includes income that, before being distributed, is the income of any person other than the trustees.

Settlements containing a power for trustees to accumulate income, and those which give the trustees a discretion over the distribution of the income are caught. The result is not only to increase the cost of accumulating income in such settlements but, with the trust rate standing at 45%, the effect is to remove altogether any tax advantage that might otherwise have been enjoyed.

EXAMPLE 16.2

Magnus is a wealthy individual who pays income tax at the additional (highest) rate (currently 45%). He settles income-producing assets on discretionary trusts for his children, giving the trustees power to accumulate the income for 21 years. As a result of s 479, however, the trustees have to pay the same marginal rate of tax as Magnus, so that the attractions of the settlement are wholly removed.

The ambit of the predecessor provision to ITA 2007 ss 479, 480 (ICTA 1988 s 686(2)(a)) was considered in *IRC v Berrill* (1982) and more recently in *The Trustees of Mrs PL Travers Will Trust v R & C Comrs* (2013). In the former case, the settlor's son was entitled to the income from the fund unless the trustees exercised a power to accumulate it. Vinelott J held that the section applied since the income was 'income ... which is payable at the discretion of the trustees'. 'Discretion' is wide enough to cover a discretion or power to withhold income. The rewritten legislation makes it absolutely clear that accumulated income refers to income which the trustees are under a positive duty to accumulate. A mere power to accumulate is not sufficient, although it will usually mean that the income 'is payable at the discretion of the trustees' within para (b). *The Trustees of Mrs PL Travers Will Trust v R & C Comrs* (2013) concerned royalties received by the Will Trust in respect of a stage musical based on the Marry Poppins books. The main thrust of the case was to determine whether the royalties were of an income or capital nature; if they were income, it then had to be decided whether a direction not to distribute the royalties as income was a direction to 'accumulate' income. In 1994 the author of the Mary Poppins books agreed a licence to enable a company to produce a stage musical based on the books. The author died before the musical was staged, leaving her literary estate in trust with instructions to pay income to certain beneficiaries for 80 years and then to distribute the capital to selected beneficiaries. In 2004 the trustees amended the 1994 agreement and assigned the right to stage the musical in exchange for royalties. The trustees treated the royalties as capital for tax purposes. HMRC took the view that the royalties should be taxed as income. The First-tier Tribunal followed the decisions in a line of Scottish cases, concerned, in the main, with mining, which held that where an existing mine was put into trust, the receipts were income and payable to the life tenant. However, where the trustees opened new mines or granted new rights, the receipts were capital for the benefit of the remaindermen. Applying those principles, which had been approved by the House of Lords, to the facts of the case before it, the Tribunal held that the receipts prior to the 2004 agreement were income whereas the royalties paid under the terms of the 2004 agreement were not income. In relation to those royalties that were income, the Tribunal rejected the trustees' argument that the manner in which the Trustees were required to deal with the receipts could not amount to accumulation because copyright has a limited life and the building up of a fund to replace such a wasting asset does not amount to an accumulation, and held that the former TA 1988 s 686 (now ITA 2007 s 479) and the rate applicable to trusts applied. [16.22]

c) *Management expenses*

Expenses which are properly chargeable to income by statute or case law (which includes, for instance, the cost of preparing trust accounts) are not deductible against the trustees' liability to tax at the basic rate but may be deducted in arriving at the amount of income chargeable at the special rates for trustees (ITA 2007 s 484).

In *Carver v Duncan* (1985) trustees paid premiums on policies of life assurance out of the income of the fund as they were permitted to do under the trust deed. The House of Lords held that the payments did not fall to be deducted under s 686(2)(d) (forerunner of ITA 2007 s 484) which was limited to expenses which were properly chargeable to income under the general law. As the life assurance premiums were for 'the benefit of the whole estate' they should, as a matter of principle, be borne by capital and accordingly, the express authority in the instrument did not bring the sums within the section. The all-important question of what is for 'the benefit of the whole estate' was considered in *Trustees of the Peter Clay Discretionary Trust* (2008). The High Court in that case accepted that accountancy fees and bank charges were not *wholly* incurred for the benefit of the whole estate, and could thus be apportioned so as fairly to attribute part of the expense to capital and part to income. However, at issue before the Court of Appeal were the fees (fixed in amount) paid to non-executive trustees of a discretionary trust and investment management fees, which the trustees had argued related partly to income, and should thus be apportioned fairly between income and capital, with the part attributable to income being deductible. Chadwick LJ said that 'when the purpose or object for which the expense is incurred is to confer benefit both on the income beneficiaries and on those entitled to capital on determination of the income trusts', the expense is undoubtedly incurred 'for the benefit of the whole estate' and cannot therefore be deducted. By the time of the trustees' appeal to the Court of Appeal, the Revenue had conceded that the rule that an expense incurred for the benefit of both the income and capital beneficiaries must be regarded as incurred for the benefit of the whole estate did not preclude the apportionment of a single expense. This concession is not based on any notion of fairness between beneficiaries but, rather, upon the ability to demonstrate that part of the expenses relates to the trustee's duties to income beneficiaries alone. Thus it was that apportionment of the executive trustee's fee (which varied considerably depending on actual work undertaken) was permissible. Since the non-executive trustees also spent time addressing matters relating exclusively to the income beneficiaries, the Court of Appeal held that, despite the fact that the fees were fixed, part should similarly be attributed to income and be deductible. Investment management fees, however, were a different story. Since, in the present case, the advice was being given in relation to the investment of capital and of income already accumulated, no part of the expenses could be said to have been incurred exclusively for the benefit of the income beneficiaries. The advice inured for the benefit of the whole estate; for the capital beneficiaries because the capital of the trust would be augmented and for the benefit of the income beneficiaries because the income of the trust would be increased because of the augmentation of the capital. Had the expenses been incurred *before* the trustees had taken the decision to accumulate the income (which was not so in the present case), to the extent that the expenses could be said to be incurred for the purpose of temporarily investing income whilst the trustees were deciding whether or not to accumulate, in the event that the income was distributed and not accumulated, the expenses could be said to have been incurred exclusively for the benefit of the income beneficiaries.

A further example of an income expense is the cost of collecting and distributing the income. The costs of preparing the trust accounts (which had previously been accepted as a concession by HMRC) has now been endorsed by the court in *Peter Clay* and reflected in HMRC guidance (TSEM 8120 ff). Against which sources of income should allowable expenses be met? ITA 2007 s 486 provides that the order is:
(1) against dividend income (ITTOIA 2005 Part 4);
(2) against dividends from non-UK resident companies (as defined in ITTOIA 2005 Part 4 Chapter 4);
(3) against savings income; and finally
(4) against other income. [16.23]

d) *Income of a person other than the trustees*

The special rates for trustees will not apply to income that is treated as that of any person other than the trustees before being distributed (ITA 2007 s 480(3)). This will apply to income arising to a bare trust, to an interest in possession trust and to a settlor-interested trust (treated as the income of the settlor – see **[16.98]–[16.105]**). Excluded from this exception are trusts in favour of the settlor's unmarried minor child. Under the rules in ITTOIA 2005 s 629 (see **[16.95]–[16.97]**), income will only be treated as that of the settlor for income tax purposes if it is actually paid to or for the benefit of the children so such income is not the income of the settlor before being distributed. This means it is subject to the higher rates of tax (although such distributions will carry with them tax credits, discussed below in Part V).

These cases must be contrasted with the settlement in *Pearson v IRC* (1981), in which the income of a life tenant could be taken from him after it had arisen by the exercise of a power to accumulate it. Accordingly, it would be subject to the trust rate as the income still 'belongs' to the trustees. [16.24]

e) *Will trusts*

ITA 2007 s 479 does not apply to the income of an estate of a deceased person during administration: of course if distributed to the trustees by the personal representatives, it will then be subject to the 45% rate (with a credit for tax suffered by the personal representatives). [16.25]

f) *What is 'income' for s 479 purposes?*

Although the section only applies to income in a trust sense, and generally would not apply to capital sums treated as income under a provision in ITTOIA 2005, ITA 2007 s 481 provides specifically that certain payments will be treated as income for the purposes of s 479, and s 482 sets out the types of amounts to be charged at the special rates for trustees. Thus it is that the payment of a lease premium (treated as an income receipt under ITTOIA 2005 s 277) on or after 6 April 2006 will also be treated as income for the purposes of the special rates for trustees. This has not always been the case. Further examples include certain deemed income receipts of employee share ownership trusts, profits or gains from the disposal of interests in certain offshore funds and gains from contracts for life insurance. It should be noted that the lower rates applicable to the first £1,000 of income apply equally to such deemed income ([16.21]). [16.26]–[16.28]

EXAMPLE 16.3

Discretionary trustees granted a lease for 35 years over a commercial property taking a premium on the grant of £100,000. For income tax purposes a part of that premium is taxed as income (see ITTOIA 2005 s 277 [12.82]). The receipt is treated as income for s 479 purposes, with the result that the trustees will suffer a further charge. Thus, assuming the trustees receive no other income during 2017–18, their liability would be as follows:

		£
Deemed income		100,000
Tax at first slice rate	£1,000 at 20% =	200
Tax at the trust rate	£99,000 at 45% =	44,550
Tax liability		44,750

2 Dividends and the s 479 charge

a) *The 6 April 2016 changes*

Prior to 6 April 2016 distributions from UK companies were paid with an irrecoverable tax credit of 10%, and the dividend trust rate payable by trustees under s 479 was 37.5%. From 6 April 2016, dividends are paid gross with a dividend tax rate of 38.1%. The following tables compare these two positions. In each case, the trustees actually receive from the distributing company £9,000. It will be seen that the trustees are left with less after-tax income tax under the new regime:

Dividends paid pre-6 April 2016

Dividend		£9,000
Tax credit (10%)		£1,000
Income taxed		£10,000
£1,000 at 10%	£ 100	
£9,000 at 37.5%	£3,375	
	£3,475	
Less: tax credit		£1,000
Tax to pay		£2,475
Trust receipt		£9,000
Less: tax paid		£2,475
After-tax income		£6,525

Dividends paid post-6 April 2016

		£
Dividend		9,000
£1,000 at 7.5% =	£ 75	
£8,000 at 38.1% =	£3,048	3,123
After-tax income		£5,877

The withdrawal of the 10% dividend tax credit along with an increase in the dividend trust rate to 38.1% (albeit that the first £1,000 of income is taxed at the dividend ordinary rate of 7.5%) clearly means that trustees pay more income tax.

However, should the income be *distributed* to the beneficiaries, the pre- and post- 6 April 2016 position is the same: see *Example 16.5*. **[16.29]**

b) *The removal of the tax credit*

Prior to 6 April 2016, although dividends were received by the trustees with a tax credit of 10%, that tax credit did not enter the trust tax pool (the 'tax pool' is considered at **[16.32]**). Further, since management expenses (considered at **[16.23]**) are regarded as being paid out of income after it has suffered tax at the normal rate, the amount of income arising to trustees which is applied in defraying expenses is an amount of income sufficient to meet both the tax and the expenses. Accordingly, in order to arrive at that amount of income, the expenses have to be grossed up at the appropriate rate, namely 10% prior to 6 April 2016 and 7.5% on or after 6 April 2016 (ITA 2007 s 486).

Since dividends are paid gross on and after 6 April 2016: (i) necessarily there is no tax credit; and (ii) the amount of tax paid applying the dividend ordinary rate to the first £1,000 of dividends and the dividend trust rate of 38.1% will enter the trust tax pool. **[16.30]**

3 The charge imposed by ITA 2007 s 496

a) *The charge*

Section 496 imposes a charge to income tax on income payments made at the trustees' discretion to the extent that the amount of income tax treated as having been paid under s 494 exceeds the amount of the tax pool available for the year in question.

Section 494 provides that:

'(1) The discretionary payment is treated as if it were made after the deduction of a sum representing income tax at the trust rate on the grossed up amount of the discretionary payment.
(2) The grossed up amount of the discretionary payment is the actual amount of the discretionary payment grossed up by reference to the trust rate.
(3) The person mentioned in subsection (4) is treated as having paid income tax of an amount equal to the sum deducted as mentioned in subsection (1).'

The person mentioned in subsection (4) is the discretionary beneficiary and the settlor where the income has been paid to children of the settlor, and the income is thereby treated as that of the settlor under ITTOIA 2005 s 620 (see [16.95]). [16.31]

b) *'The tax pool'*

The 'tax pool' is the sum of the tax suffered by the trustees on income that has been taxed under ss 479 and 491 (less, of course, any amount already used to 'frank' the s 496 charge). The tax pool includes tax actually paid by the trustees together with recoverable tax credits and for many trusts (which have accumulated income) the tax pool will be substantial. Apart from dividend income, which is considered below, the fact that the first £1,000 of income liable to the special rates for trustees is subject to a lower rate band (see [16.21]), means that where income is received and distributed within the same tax year, the tax due under s 479 will no longer be equivalent to the s 496 set-off (compare scenario 1 and 3, below). The result is then the same as that where income is received in one tax year, but distributed in another when the tax rate has increased (see scenario 2, below). Scenario 4 is an example of the position for 2013–14 and subsequent years, when the trust rate is 45%.
[16.32]

EXAMPLE 16.4

Scenario 1

In 2004–05 trustees of the newly established Jenkins family discretionary trust received rental income of £2,000 that was (in the same tax year) distributed to Gilly Jenkins. The tax position of the trustees was as follows:
(1) Under the former ICTA 1988 s 686 (ITA 2007 s 479) they would have been liable to pay tax at 40% = £800.
(2) On distributing the net income remaining to Gilly Jenkins (£1,200) they would have been taxed under the former ICTA 1988 s 687 (ITA 2007 s 496) on the sum distributed grossed up at 40% (so that £1,200 would have been grossed up to £2,000 – ITA 2007 s 494) with tax at 40% being charged on the gross sum. The tax charge under what is now s 496 would therefore have been £800 which could have been reduced by sums standing in the 'tax pool'. Given that £800 was in the pool, tax under what is now s 496 would have been reduced to zero (and the pool – assuming no previous credits – reduced to zero).

Scenario 2

Assume now that the distribution of £1,200 was made in a later tax year when the rate of tax suffered by discretionary trustees had increased to 60%. The gross sum treated as distributed would accordingly have been £3,000 on which tax of £1,800 would have been payable under what is now s 496 but from which could have been deducted the tax pool of £800, leaving the trustees with a liability of £1,000.

Scenario 3

Assume the same facts as in scenario 1, but they occur in 2017–18. The tax position of the trustees is as follows:
(1) Under ss 479 and 491, they will be liable to pay tax at:
    (a) 20% (the basic rate) on the first £1,000 = £200; and
    (b) 45% on £1,000 (the excess over £1,000) = £450.

(2) On distributing the net income remaining to Gilly Jenkins (£1,350) they are taxed under s 496 on the sum distributed grossed up (ITA 2007 s 494) at 45% (so that £1,350 is grossed up to £2,454) with tax at 45% being charged on the gross sum. The tax charge under s 496 is, therefore, £1,104, that can be reduced by sums standing in the 'tax pool'. Given that £650 is in the pool, tax under s 496 is reduced to £454 (and the pool – assuming no previous credits – reduced to zero).

c) *Dividends and the s 496 charge*

As already discussed, dividends from UK companies are now (since 6 April 2016) received gross and taxed under s 479 at the rate of 38.1% (for 2017–18). It is important to realise that if distributed to beneficiaries, the net sum must still be grossed up at 45% because such a payment is treated as an annual payment under ITTOIA 2005 Part 5 Chapter 7, with the result that by passing through the trust the sum has lost its character as a dividend. However, in comparison with the position prior to 6 April 2016, when dividends carried a tax credit of 10%, which was irrecoverable and therefore did not enter the tax pool, for 2016–17 and subsequent tax years, the whole amount of the tax paid on the dividend at the dividend tax rate (38.1% for 2017–18) will enter the tax pool. **[16.33]–[16.60]**

EXAMPLE 16.5

The trustees of the Roberts Trusts receive a dividend payment of £9,000. They propose to distribute the entire available trust income.
(1) If the dividends were received before 6 April 2016, the position is as follows:
The dividends are treated as £10,000 of gross income which is taxed as follows:

10% (the dividend ordinary rate) on the first £1,000 =	£ 100
37.5% on the remaining £9,000	£3,375
	£3,475
Less: tax credit	£1,000
Tax payable	£2,475

This £2,475 enters the tax pool, in contrast to the former dividend tax credit.
Because the trustees have to give a tax credit on any distribution of 45%, the maximum they can distribute is 55% of the £9,000 received, or £4,950.
The tax credit of £4,050 is met partly by the £2,475 in the tax pool (the tax paid by the trustees on the dividends) and the balance of £1,575 is payable by the trustees.

	£
Distribution to beneficiary (£9,000 × 55%)	4,950
Addition for tax at 45% under s 496	4,050
Gross distribution	£9,000

	£
Tax due under s 496	4,050
Less: credit in tax pool	2,475
Balance payable	£ 1,575

The net income left in the trustees' hands after the s 479 charge has been used:
  (a) to distribute £4,950 to the beneficiary; and
  (b) to pay the s 496 tax of £1,575.

(2) If the dividends were received from 6 April 2016, the position is as follows:
The £9,000 of dividends received are taxed as follows:

7.5% (the dividend ordinary rate) on the first £1,000 =	£ 75
38.1% on the remaining £8,000 =	£3,048
Tax payable	£3,123

(No tax credit)

This £3,123 enters the tax pool
As above, only £4,950 of the £9,000 receipt can be distributed and the 45% tax credit of £4,050 on the distribution is met partly by the £3,123 in the tax pool with the balance of £927 being payable by the trustees.

It can be seen that the overall position of the beneficiary is the same before and after the 2016 changes.

V THE TAXATION OF BENEFICIARIES

1 Taxing a beneficiary who is entitled to trust income

a) *General rule*

A beneficiary who is entitled to the income of a trust as it arises (or is entitled to have it applied for his benefit) is subject to income tax for the year of assessment in which that income arises, even if none of the money is paid to him during that year (*Baker v Archer-Shee* (1927)). The sum to which the beneficiary is entitled is that which is left in the trustees' hands after they have paid administration expenses and discharged their income tax liability. The beneficiary is, as a result, entitled to a net sum which must be grossed up at the basic rate of income tax in order to find the sum which enters his total income computation and to a credit for some of the income tax paid by the trustees; not, it should be noted, for the full amount in cases where management expenses have been deducted (*Macfarlane v IRC* (1929)). Where the beneficiary is entitled to trust income, it retains its character so, for example, dividend income passing through a trust continues to be dividend income in the hands of the beneficiary. This is important for the new personal savings allowance (see [7.25]) and dividend allowance (see [7.27]–[7.39]).
[16.61]

b) *Calculating tax (reclaim) of the beneficiary*

Depending upon his other income and allowances, a beneficiary may be entitled to reclaim all or some of the tax paid by the trustees (although not, of course, the pre 2016 irrecoverable credit on dividends). Alternatively, he may be liable for tax at the higher rate. The income that he receives from the trust will be unearned even if it arises from a trade run by the trustees (see *Fry v Shiels' Trustees* (1915), but note also *Baker v Archer-Shee* (1927) which indicates that if a beneficiary is entitled to the income as it arises, he will be taxed according to the rules of the statutory provision appropriate to that source of income). [16.62]

EXAMPLE 16.6

(1) Zac is entitled to the income of a trust fund. In 2017–18, £6,000 of property business income is produced and the trustees incur administrative expenses (properly chargeable against income: see **[16.23]**) of £1,000. The trustees are taxed at 20% on the income of £6,000. The balance of the income available for Zac will be:

	£	£
Gross income		6,000
Less: tax	1,200	
expenses	1,000	2,200
		£3,800

Zac, is, therefore, taxed on £3,800 grossed up by tax at 20%, ie:

$$\frac{£3{,}800 \times 100}{80} = £4{,}750$$

He will be given a credit for that portion of the basic rate tax paid by the trustees which is attributable to £4,750, ie £950, but does not receive a credit for the rest of the tax paid by the trustees (£1,200 − £950 = £250) and the result is that management expenses have been paid out of taxed income so that the total cost of these expenses is £1,250.

(2) Trustees receive gross dividend income of £1,000 and pay tax at the dividend ordinary rate of 7.5% (£75 for 2017–18). Assuming Zac, the life tenant, has used up his dividend allowance, he is taxed on a gross income of £1,000 and, if a basic rate taxpayer, will suffer no further tax charge; if a non-taxpayer, he will be able to obtain a repayment of the £75 paid by the trustees; if a higher rate taxpayer, he will be taxed at 32.5% (the higher rate applicable to dividend income on an income of £1,000 and may deduct the £75 already paid. He suffers additional tax of £250. If Zac's taxable income exceeds £150,000 he will then be taxed at 38.1% (the additional rate for dividends: see **[42.76]**), which will result in additional tax of £306.

c) *What is income?*

'Income' for these purposes will not (in the absence of an express provision to the contrary) include items which are capital profits under trust law although income tax may have been charged on them in the hands of the trustees: see **[16.26]**. [16.63]

EXAMPLE 16.7

The Wonker Trust is a cash fund. The trustees are offered a run-down city centre property in Liverpool which they purchase for £1m (being the entire trust fund). At the time of purchase they were already in negotiations to sell the site to Norwest Developers and the sale is completed the next day for £10m. The trustees have realised a profit of £9m that will be taxed as follows:

(1) in the *trustees' hands* as a trading receipt on which they will suffer income tax at basic rate (see **Chapter 10** for a consideration of 'one-off' trading transactions);

(2) so far as the *beneficiaries* are concerned the £10m is trust capital and the profit of £9m will not be distributed to the Wonker life tenant.

2 Taxing an annuitant

An annuitant under a trust is not entitled to income of the trust as it arises; he is taxed under ITTOIA 2005 Part 5 Chapter 7 on the income that he receives. As basic rate income tax will be deducted from the annuity by the trustees under ITA 2007 Part 15 Chapter 6, an assessment for basic rate tax on the beneficiary will be precluded. He has a tax credit for the basic rate tax deducted at source in the usual way. **[16.64]**

3 Taxing a discretionary beneficiary

a) *General rules*

A discretionary beneficiary has no right to a specific amount of income but is merely entitled to be considered (*Gartside v IRC* (1968)). The Revenue therefore considers that any payments that he receives will be charged as his income under ITTOIA 2005 s 683 (presumably they are annual payments since they may recur) and he will receive a credit for the tax paid by the trustees under ITA 2007 s 496 which is attributable to that payment. The effect is to encourage trustees to distribute income to beneficiaries who are subject to income tax at less than 45% (for 2015–16 and subsequent years) so that all or a part of the surcharge can be repaid. If, however, the payment is received from a settlor-interested trust, it will not be charged to tax in the hands of the beneficiary (ITTOIA 2005 s 685A and see **[16.98]** ff)

Once an irrevocable decision has been taken by the trustees to retain income as a part of the capital of the fund, the sum accumulated loses its character as income and is treated in the same way as the original fund, ie as capital. It follows, therefore, that the income tax suffered by that income (at 45% from 2015–16) is irrecoverable and that no further income tax will be charged on the accumulations when they are eventually paid out to the beneficiaries as capital (although such distributions may have CGT and IHT consequences). In deciding whether it is more advantageous to accumulate income or to pay it out to beneficiaries under their discretionary powers, trustees need to consider, *inter alia*, the tax position of the individual beneficiaries. **[16.65]**

EXAMPLE 16.8

Trustees are proposing to distribute £6,300 (net) of trust income. There are four discretionary beneficiaries, Ding, Dang, Dong and Dung. Ding has no other income and has an unused personal allowance; Dang is a basic rate taxpayer; Dong is a higher rate taxpayer; and Dung is an additional rate taxpayer (45% for 2017–18). The trustees are deciding whether to pay income to any one or more of the beneficiaries or whether to accumulate it. The following tax consequences will ensue:
(1) The trustees have paid 20% on the first £1,000 of trust income and 45% tax on the remainder of the trust income (ie £4,700 tax) since none of the income is from dividends.

(2) If the trustees decide to pay all the income to Ding (who has no other income) he will be entitled to a repayment of tax as follows:

	£
Income (ITTOIA 2005 s 683)	11,000
Less: personal allowance	11,000
Total income	£0
Income tax	0
Less: tax credit	4,700
Tax refund	£(4,700)

(3) If the trustees pay the income to Dang (the basic rate taxpayer), he will not be entitled to a refund of any basic rate tax, but, depending upon the amount of his other income, he may obtain a refund of such part of the rate applicable to trusts as exceeds the basic rate of tax.

(4) If the trustees pay the income to Dong (the higher rate taxpayer), like Dang, he will not be entitled to a refund of any basic rate tax, but, depending upon the amount of his other income, he may obtain a refund of such part of the rate applicable to trusts as exceeds the higher rate of tax.

(5) If the trustees pay the income to Dung (the additional rate taxpayer), no extra tax will be levied since the rate of tax on the trust income (45%) is the same as his own marginal rate.

(6) If the trustees accumulate the income, the £4,700 tax paid will be irrecoverable and the net income of £6,300 will be converted into capital.

From a tax perspective, the trustees will consider appointing all or part of the income to Ding, Dang and Dong. They should avoid payments to Dung (since there will be no advantage whatever), and should also avoid accumulating the income.

b) *Dividends and other company distributions*

The tax treatment of dividends (and other company distributions) in the hands of the trustees has been considered at **[16.29]**. If the net sum is retained by the trustees as an accumulation, the position is, broadly speaking, no different from that which applies to other trust income. In many cases, however, the trusts will either be required or will wish to distribute that income to their beneficiaries (eg in the case of a discretionary trust, the power to accumulate may have ended, whilst in trusts for bereaved minors it may be required for the education of the beneficiaries). If this occurs because what is distributed is considered to be a new source of income (not therefore dividends, and therefore no dividend allowance is available), a 45% rate of charge is imposed under s 496, as a result of which the income suffers a further substantial tax charge. **[16.66]**

EXAMPLE 16.9

Continuing *Example 16.8* above, assume that the trustees distribute £2,200 of dividend income (with a credit for 45% tax paid under s 496 of £1,800) to each of the four beneficiaries as follows:

(1) *To Ding a non taxpayer* He will recover all the tax paid by the trustees on the sum that he receives and so ends up with £4,000, putting him in exactly the

same position as an individual non-taxpayer shareholder in a company who receives a cash dividend of £4,000. Trusts for bereaved minors which, eg, pay the beneficiaries school fees may, therefore, not be adversely affected by these rules provided that the sums involved will fall within the beneficiaries' personal allowances.

(2) *To Dang a basic rate taxpayer* He recovers £1,000 (the difference between 20% and 45%) of the tax deducted by the trustees. This, however, means that he receives in total £3,200, which compares less favourably with a basic rate taxpayer who directly owns shares in the company, who would be left with £3,700 (should the dividend income be taxed at 7.5%) or £4,000 (should the dividend be covered by the dividend allowance).

(3) *To Dong a higher rate taxpayer* He recovers £200 (the difference between 40% and 45%) of the tax deducted by the trustees. This means that, in total, he receives £2,400. When compared with a higher rate individual shareholder liable for tax at the dividend upper rate of 32.5% (whose liability to tax will amount to £1,300, leaving him with £2,700) or zero, if the dividend allowance is available, Dong is worse off.

(4) *To Dung an additional rate taxpayer* Since the rate applicable to trusts is the same as an individual's additional rate, he suffers no further tax charge. He will thus have just £2,200, leaving him worse off than an additional rate individual shareholder, who will only be liable for tax at the dividend additional rate of 38.1% (who would be left with £2,476) or, again, £4,000 with the dividend allowance (see [42.76]).

Notes:
(a) For some (old) trusts these problems will be alleviated by a substantial tax pool.
(b) Consider whether the problems can be overcome by accumulating income and making only capital payments to beneficiaries (see [16.67]).
(c) Does mandating the income avoid the problem? See *Taxation*, 15 April 1999, and subsequent correspondence.
(d) Given that these rules only apply to dividend income, trustees may consider switching their investments but need to beware of the CGT costs involved.

4 The dangers of supplementing income out of capital

a) *The problem*

Capital payments will not generally be subject to income tax. However, if a beneficiary is given a fixed amount of income each year and is entitled to have that sum made up out of capital should the trust fail to produce the requisite amount of income, such 'topping up' payments will be taxed as income in the hands of the beneficiary (see *Brodie's Will Trustees v IRC* (1933) and *Cunard's Trustees v IRC* (1946)). [16.67]

EXAMPLE 16.10

(1) The settlor's widow is given an annuity of £4,000 pa; the trustees have a discretion to pay it out of the capital of the fund if the income is insufficient. The widow will be assessed to income tax on the payments that she receives, whether paid out of income or capital, since they will be annual payments (to the extent that there is insufficient income in the trust, they are paid out of capital). However, deduction of income tax by the trustees is mandatory (ITA 2007 s 900(2); see [14.23] and [14.24]).

(2) The settlor's widow is given an annuity of £4,000 pa and, in addition, the trustees have the power 'to apply capital for the benefit of the widow in such manner as they shall in their absolute discretion think fit'. Any supplements out of capital will now escape income tax since the widow has an interest in both income and capital, and payments out of capital will, therefore, be treated as advances of capital rather than as income payments.

b) *Stevenson v Wishart*

At one time the Revenue sought to argue that payments made out of trust capital could be taxed as income in the hands of the recipient beneficiary even when the payments were not paid in augmentation of an income interest. This argument was based on its view that the income nature of the payment in the hands of the recipient could be discovered by looking at the size, recurrence, and purpose of the payments. *Stevenson v Wishart* (1987) provided a test case for this view since the discretionary trust income was there paid out in full each year to a charity and capital sums were then paid to one of the beneficiaries who had suffered a heart attack. The purpose of the payments was to cover medical expenses and the cost of living in a nursing home. The Revenue's view that these sums were paid out for an income purpose and were therefore subject to income tax was rejected both at first instance and by the Court of Appeal. Fox LJ stated that:

> 'There is nothing in the present case which indicates that the payments were of an income nature except their recurrence. I do not think that is sufficient. The trustees were disposing of capital in exercise of a power over capital. They did not create a recurring interest in property. If, in exercise of a power over capital, they chose to make at their discretion regular payments of capital to deal with the specific problems of the beneficiary's last years rather than release a single sum to her of a large amount, that does not seem to me to create an income interest. Their power was to appoint capital. What they appointed remained capital.'

The Court of Appeal did stress the exceptional nature of nursing home payments. Fox LJ, for instance, stated that such expenditure, although involving day-to-day maintenance, was emergency expenditure of very substantial amounts that would usually fall outside normal income resources. It may be, therefore, that if the expenditure was not of an emergency nature the court would consider the payments to be income. A typical example is the payment of school fees out of a trust fund where the Revenue argued for a number of years that lump sum payments could be taxed as the income of the recipient beneficiary in the year when that payment was made. **[16.68]**

c) *Current position*

The Revenue currently treats advances or appointments out of trust capital as capital in the hands of the recipient beneficiary unless the payments in question fall within one of the following two categories. *First*, when they are designed to augment income as in the *Brodie* case; *second*, if the trust instrument contains a provision authorising the use of capital to maintain a beneficiary in the same degree of comfort as had been the case in the past (the *Cunard* case) (see TSEM 3758).Further, if the capital payment in question really amounts to an annuity, the payment will be looked upon as income in the hands of the beneficiary (see *Jackson's Trustees v IRC* (1942)). [16.69]

5 The effects of Trustee Act 1925 s 31

This section is concerned with trustees' powers of maintenance. It can be excluded by the trust instrument: in practice it is commonly amended. The section can have both a vesting and a divesting effect on the income of beneficiaries. [16.70]

a) *Divesting effect*

A beneficiary with a vested interest in income (not, notice, in capital) is treated as enjoying a contingent interest only until attaining the age of 18. This is illustrated in *Example 16.11(1)*: see *Stanley v IRC* (1944). [16.71]

b) *Vesting effects*

By contrast, a beneficiary who is contingently entitled to the capital of the settlement at an age greater than 18 (in the situation where no prior interest exists) is treated as entitled to the income at age 18. This vesting effect of the section is illustrated in *Example 16.11(2)*. [16.72]

c) *Tax treatment*

When entitlement to income is postponed (the divesting effect) ITA 2007 s 479 will apply to the income. When income vests in a beneficiary at 18, that section ceases to apply.

EXAMPLE 16.11

(1) Property in a settlement is held on trust for Barbara (aged six) for life with remainder to her Uncle Silas. As Barbara, the life tenant, has only a vested interest in income and s 31 has not been modified in the trust deed, the trustees will be liable for tax at 45%. Barbara will not be subject to tax on the income and will not, therefore, be able to reclaim any of the tax paid by the trustees, except to the extent that income is applied for her maintenance (this illustrates the divesting effect of the section).

(2) Tilley is entitled to the Biggins Trust Fund when she becomes 30. On attaining 18 she will be entitled to income under TA 1925 s 31: as a result, ITA 2007 s 479 will cease to apply to that income (which will now be taxed at basic rate in the trustees' hands and at higher or additional rate (if appropriate) on Tilley). Note also the consequences for capital taxes, and compare the difference of treatment before and after FA 2006:

Before FA 2006:
 (a) *at 18* Tilley has an interest in possession for IHT purposes;
 (b) *at 30* When she becomes entitled to the capital – there will be a deemed disposal under TCGA 1992 s 71 for CGT purposes (see **[25.47]** and **[33.28]**).

After FA 2006, unless the terms on which this trust are held are modified to ensure that Tilley becomes absolutely entitled to the property at 18 (when the current IHT treatment will continue and hold-over relief under TCGA 1992 s 260(2)(d) will be available), the trust property will become subject to a 4.2% IHT charge in respect of the period between Tilley's 18th and 25th birthdays.

New post-22 March 2006 A&M trusts will only qualify for special IHT treatment if they arise on intestacy or are established under the will of a deceased parent for the benefit of a minor child who will become absolutely entitled to the assets at the age of 18. This means that special treatment will no longer be accorded to an A&M trust established by a grandparent, when its creation will incur an immediate IHT charge (at 20% unless the value transferred is within the settlor's nil rate band). **[16.73]**

VI TRUSTS WITH VULNERABLE BENEFICIARIES

1 Background

It is unusual (and undesirable) that the whole of the income arising in any one year under trusts established for the long-term benefit of the disabled and for the benefit of minors who have lost a parent (or both parents) should be paid out to those beneficiaries. The result is that for income tax purposes, the retained income suffers income tax at the trust rate and the dividend trust rate. In order to protect vulnerable beneficiaries from these high rates (45% and 38.1% respectively) (for 2016–17 and subsequent years), FA 2005 Part 2 Chapter 4 provides for special tax treatment for qualifying trusts with vulnerable beneficiaries, backdated to 6 April 2004, the effect of which is to ensure that the amount of tax charged on income (and capital gains) arising to the trustees is no more than it would have been had the income and gains arisen directly to the vulnerable person.

In light of the introduction of the personal independence payment (PIP) by the Welfare Reform Act 2012, which replaces disability living allowance for people of working age (16–64), and following HMRC's consultation on vulnerable beneficiary trusts (August 2012), FA 2013 and FA 2014 have extended the definition of 'disabled person' (see **[16.75]**). FA 2013 also harmonised rules that limit how the income and capital of a trust with a vulnerable beneficiary may be applied (see **[16.76]**). This is particularly pertinent for IHT purposes: see **[32.59]**–**[32.70]**). For income tax purposes discussed in this chapter (and also for CGT purposes and the application of the annual exempt amount under TCGA 1992 Sch 1), the changes in FA 2013 took effect from 6 April 2013 but only in respect of trusts created on or after 8 April 2013. For trusts created by a will executed prior to 8 April 2013, the rules applying before that date are preserved even where there is a codicil to a will or a new will provided that a qualifying vulnerable beneficiary trust is established. The changes in FA 2014 have effect for the tax year 2014–15 and subsequent years. **[16.74]**

2 Who are vulnerable beneficiaries?

Vulnerable beneficiaries fall into two categories:
(1) *Disabled persons.* For trusts established before 8 April 2013, disabled persons are defined as persons who are incapable of administering their

property or managing their affairs because they have a mental disorder within the meaning of the Mental Health Act 1983 and persons in receipt of an attendance allowance or of a disability living allowance by virtue of entitlement to the care component at the highest or middle rate. In addition, a person may be treated as being in receipt of an attendance allowance or disability living allowance provided that they would be entitled to receive the relevant allowances if they were to meet the necessary residence requirements (see TSEM 3422). For trusts established on or after 8 April 2013, persons in receipt of the personal independence payment by virtue of entitlement to the daily living component, constant attendance allowance or armed forces independence payment are added to the definition of disabled persons that applied previously (FA 2005 s 38 as amended by FA 2013 Sch 42). A person remains a 'disabled person' if he would be entitled to receive a qualifying welfare benefit but for him being resident outside of the UK or in a care home, hospital or prison. FA 2014 contains provisions that extend the range of trusts that qualify. As from 6 April 2014 the definition of 'disabled person' includes those in receipt of the mobility component of disability living allowance at the higher rate, or the mobility component of personal independence payment at either the standard or enhanced rate.

(2) *Relevant minors.* These are young persons who have not yet reached the age of 18 and who have lost at least one parent.

A beneficiary does not have to be resident in the UK to be a vulnerable person for the purposes of the special tax regime. [16.75]

3 What are qualifying trusts?

a) *Trusts created prior to 8 April 2013*

In the case of a disabled person, trusts will be qualifying trusts provided that, during the disabled person's lifetime or until the earlier termination of the trusts, any property applied for the benefit of a beneficiary must be applied for the benefit of the disabled person *and* either the disabled person is entitled to all of the income (if there is any) or the income may not be applied for the benefit of any other person.

Trusts for relevant minors qualify, subject to conditions, if either they were established under the will of a deceased parent of the minor or under the Criminal Injuries Compensation Scheme, or are statutory trusts arising under the Administration of Trusts Act 1925 in favour of a minor whose parent (or parents) has died intestate. The conditions are: (i) that the minor will, on reaching 18, become absolutely entitled to the property, any income arising from it and any income accumulated for his or her benefit before that time; (ii) until that time, any of the property that is applied during the minor's lifetime must be applied for his or her benefit; and (iii) until that time, and while the minor is alive, either the minor must be entitled to all of the income (if any) arising from any of the property, or no such income may be applied for the benefit of any other person.

b) Trusts created on or after 8 April 2013

For all vulnerable beneficiary trusts, the rules are aligned so that if any income arising from the settled property is applied for the benefit of a beneficiary, it must be applied for the benefit of the vulnerable beneficiary (for example, the bereaved minor or disabled person) with the proviso that in any tax year the trustees may apply the 'annual limit', which is the lesser of £3,000 and 3% of the settled property (whether income or capital) for the benefit of another person (perhaps a carer).

Where there is more than one beneficiary, the property held for the benefit of the disabled person or relevant minor, as the case may be, must be held in a separate fund or in some other defined part of the settled property. A ring-fenced fund for a disabled person within a trust is not a separate trust for tax purposes. [16.76]

4 Special treatment of income arising under trusts for vulnerable persons

The trustees and the vulnerable person may make a joint and irrevocable election (see TSEM 3450 ff) that the trustees' tax liability will be brought into line with what the beneficiary's tax liability would have been had he or she received the income directly and relief is given by way of a reduction in the trustees' liability. The amount of the relief is the difference between the total tax paid by the trustees and the vulnerable beneficiary without the special treatment, and the amount that would be paid if the trust income was deemed to be that of the vulnerable beneficiary. The amount of income tax paid should be reduced considerably since the trustees will be able to take into account the beneficiary's personal allowances and starting and basic rate income tax bands (similar provisions apply for chargeable gains: see **Chapter 27**). The following example shows how the relief is given.

EXAMPLE 16.12

Under the terms of her father's will, property is held on trust for Anastasia on attaining the age of 18. Anastasia, who is ten years of age, lost both of her parents in a car accident in 2010. During the tax year 2017–18, the trustees receive dividend income amounting to £15,000, which they decide to accumulate since Anastasia receives other income of £12,000 from a trust established for her benefit by her grandfather.

A joint election is made for special treatment and this will be given by way of a reduction in the income tax liability of the trustees. The amount of the reduction is calculated by deducting the vulnerable person's liability (b) from the liability that the trustees would suffer without the special treatment (a). The vulnerable person's liability is calculated by deducting the total tax liability of the vulnerable person (d) from the income tax to which the vulnerable person would be liable if the special treatment applied (c).

		£	£
Trustees liability (the s 479 charge):			
Income			15,000.00
Liability to the dividend trust rate:	£1,000@ 7.5%	75.00	
	£14,000@ 38.1%	5,334.00	
			5,409.00 (a)

Anastasia's liability if the special treatment applied:		
Income		27,000.00
Less: personal allowance		11,500
		15,500.00
Income tax liability:	£ 15,500 @ 20%	3,100.00 (c)
Anastasia's tax liability without special treatment:		
Income		12,000.00
Less: personal allowance		11,500.00
		500.00
Income tax liability:	£500 @ 20%	100.00 (d)
Vulnerable person's liability: (c–d)		3,000.00 (b)
Relief: (a–b)		2,409.00

The trustees liability to income tax will be reduced by £2,409.

Note:

In calculating the beneficiary's liability to tax in (c) and (d), no account is taken of:

(i) any distribution to the vulnerable beneficiary of income that has arisen to the trustees in that year; and

(ii) any income tax relief which is given by way of a reduction in the income tax payable by the vulnerable beneficiary (eg the married couple's allowance).

[16.77]–[16.90]

VII THE ANTI-AVOIDANCE PROVISIONS (ITTOIA 2005 PART 5 CHAPTER 5)

1 **Introductory**

a) *Background*

Prior to 15 March 1988, a wealthy individual paying income tax at a top rate of 60% who wished to transfer a part of his income, eg to a grandchild, could have done so in one of two ways. *First*, by entering into a deed of covenant (ie an income settlement); or, *second*, by transferring capital assets that produced the required amount of income to trustees to hold for the benefit of the chosen grandchild for a stated period. Inevitably, the legislation that sought to restrict the efficacy of covenants was also drafted so as to deal with capital settlements. Income settlements were generally rendered tax ineffective by the former TA 1988 s 347A (now ITA 2007 s 900) (see **[14.23]**) so that the only choice open to the wealthy taxpayer was whether or not to create a capital settlement. **[16.91]**

b) *Effect of the rules applying*

When the anti-avoidance rules apply, they generally deem the income of a capital settlement to be that of the settlor and enable him to recover from the trustees any tax that he suffers on that income in excess of the basic rate.

[16.92]

c) What is a 'settlement' for these purposes?

The term 'settlement' is widely defined for these purposes to include any 'disposition, trust, covenant, agreement, arrangement or transfer of assets', and 'settlor' has a similarly wide meaning as well as including reciprocal settlors (ITTOIA 2005 s 620(1)). Although as a matter of general law a settlement can be established even though created for consideration, according to cases such as *IRC v Plummer* (1979), liability under Part 5 Chapter 5 depends upon there being some element of bounty.

The Arctic Systems case: Jones v Garnett

In the case of *Jones v Garnett* (2007), the taxpayer, an information technology specialist, and his wife each owned one share in a company that earned profits by providing the taxpayer's personal services to clients. He drew a comparatively small salary so that the company earned profits, which were then distributed as dividends. His wife, the company secretary, received half. HMRC contended that the 'arrangement' amounted to a settlement within ITTOIA 2005 s 625 (formerly TA 1988 s 660A) and that, accordingly, dividends paid to his wife were to be treated as his income for tax purposes. The House of Lords, reversing the judgment of the Court of Appeal, upheld the Revenue's contention. Lord Hoffmann's view, contrary to that of the Court of Appeal but which was shared by his learned brethren (although with some doubt on the part of Baroness Hale), was that the transaction entered into by the taxpayers was no 'normal commercial transaction between two adults'. In his words, it was not

> 'an arrangement into which Mr Jones would ever have entered with someone with whom he was dealing at arms' length. It was only "natural love and affection" which provided the consideration for the benefit he intended to confer upon his wife. That is sufficient to provide the necessary "element of bounty".'

Accordingly, despite its commercial appearance, this case is not so very different from *Example 16.13* below.

Elaborating on the statutory definition of 'settlement' as including an 'arrangement', Lords Walker and Neuberger were of the opinion that an alleged arrangement should be identified at the time it was made, and that subsequent events may be evidence of the intention of the parties at the time of the arrangement, but not part of the arrangement itself. Applying that principle to the facts of the current case, Lord Walker was of the view that the establishment by the taxpayers of the corporate set-up, together with their admitted common intention that they would use it to minimise tax, was the essential arrangement; what happened subsequently was that the arrangement was put to that intended use (see [**51.55**]).(The taxpayer's successful contention that ITTOIA 2005 s 626, which excludes from the effect of s 625 outright gifts by one spouse to the other, should apply is discussed at [**16.102**].)

Similar issues arise with a transfer or issue of shares to the minor children of a settlor (or trusts for their benefit). In *Bird v R & C Comrs* Mr and Mrs Bird were the initial shareholders of a company, owning one share each.

The company issued a further 98 shares at par, 19 shares each to Mr and Mrs Bird, and 20 shares to each of their three minor daughters. The Revenue argued successfully that the dividends paid to the daughters (until they reached the age of 18) constituted income arising under a settlement which, under s 660B(1) (now ITTOIA 2005 s 629(1)), should be treated as Mr and Mrs Bird's income. In reaching his conclusion, the Special Commissioner said that arranging for their minor daughters to take 60% of the company enabled them to share in the profits of the business previously owned by Mr and Mrs Bird. By doing this, Mr and Mrs Bird made an arrangement within the scope of the settlement provisions. Since it was unlikely that Mr and Mrs Bird would have entered the same arrangement with another person at arm's length, the Special Commissioner was able to determine that the element of bounty was satisfied.

Dividend waivers: Buck v R & C Comrs; Donovan & McLaren v R & C Comrs

Although dividend waivers can provide a legitimate way for one or more shareholders to waive their dividend entitlement to retain additional profits within the company, tax problems occur when waivers are used to distribute funds to shareholders on a 'disproportionate' basis. Such was the case in both *Buck v R & C Comrs* (2008) and *Donovan & McLaren v R & C Comrs* (2014), where the Special Commissioner and the First-tier Tribunal (respectively) held that income had arisen under an arrangement coming within the definition of settlement in the former TA 1988 s 660G(1) (in *Buck*), now ITTOIA 2005 s 620(1) (in *Donovan & McLaren*). In the former case, the taxpayer owned 9,999 of the issued shares in a company of which he was sole director, whilst his former wife owned just one. In each of the two relevant tax years, the taxpayer waived his dividend entitlement by formal notice in writing, and thereafter resolved at a director's 'meeting' that a dividend of £35,000 per share be paid. The result of this was that the taxpayer's former wife received enhanced dividends for the years in question, whilst he received none because of his waivers. The two questions to be determined in this case were (1) whether the dividend income was income arising under an arrangement within s 660G(1), and (2) if the dividend income did so arise, whether it arose from property in which the taxpayer had an interest. Taking Lord Hoffmann's realistic view of the facts, the Special Commissioner concluded that the taxpayer's waiver of his right to dividends on two occasions was the first step in his plan for dividend income to become payable to his former wife, and thus amounted to an arrangement with respect to each dividend. Given that there was no commercial purpose for either of the waivers, and that it was unlikely that they would have taken place in a transaction at arm's length, the arrangement contained the necessary element of bounty. As far as the second question was concerned, the taxpayer had an interest by virtue of s 660A(2) (now ITTOIA 2005 s 625(1)), which treats the settlor as having retained an interest if the property from which the income arises may be payable to or applicable for his spouse. In *Donovan & McLaren v R & C Comrs*, the taxpayers each had a 50% shareholding in their company. In 2001, they agreed to issue a 10% shareholding in the company to each of their wives and in subsequent tax years, dividends were paid to the four shareholders.

However, the taxpayers made annual dividend waivers, enabling their wives to receive a larger share of the total dividend than would have been due by reference to their 10% holdings. HMRC was of the view that the waivers of dividend by the taxpayers and payment of dividends to their wives constituted an 'arrangement' under ITTOIA 2005 s 620 and that the dividend income paid to the taxpayers' wives from their shares together with the dividend rights attached to them constituted property in which the taxpayers had an interest under ITTOIA 2005 s 625, which treats the settlor as having retained an interest if the property from which the income arises may be payable to his spouse. For their part, the taxpayers argued that a commercial decision to waive the dividends had been taken to ensure that the company maintained workable reserves and cash balances in order to accumulate sufficient of each to fund the purchase of the company's own freehold property. The First-tier Tribunal agreed with HMRC that the taxpayers' contention that the waivers were motivated by commercial reasons was unconvincing and that they were clearly intended to take advantage of the wives' lower income tax rate band in order to save income tax, The arrangement would not have been entered into with someone at arm's length and it therefore plainly contained an element of bounty. Accordingly, the waivers of dividend by the directors and payment of dividends to their wives constituted an 'arrangement' under ITTOIA 2005 s 620.

HMRC's further contention in *Jones v Garnett*, that ITTOIA 2005 s 626, which excludes from the effect of s 625 outright gifts by one spouse to the other, did not apply in this case, was not accepted by the House of Lords and is discussed at [16.102].

Patmore v R & C Comrs (2010)

Possibly in light of the lack of any legislation designed to reverse the effect of *Jones v Garnett*, the Revenue again sought to argue the same point in *Patmore v R & C Comrs* (2010). In this case, on the retirement of its controlling shareholder, the taxpayer and his wife purchased a small company of which the taxpayer was a director. The purchase was funded partly by a mortgage on their home, which they owned jointly. Following the purchase, although the wife was equally liable for the loans raised to purchase the company, she received a much smaller percentage of the shares in the company than the taxpayer. The company's shares were reorganised into two classes, with the wife owning 2% of the A shares and 10% of the non-voting B shares, in respect of which dividends were paid in the tax years 1999–2003. The dividends were paid immediately into the taxpayer's loan account to set against the outstanding payments in relation to the purchase of the company.

HMRC argued that the taxpayer was liable to tax on the dividend paid in respect of the B shares as the settlor under a settlement within TA 1988 s 660A (now ITTOIA 2005 s 625) on the basis that the taxpayer owned the company and used his control of it to declare significant dividends in favour of his wife so that they would attract a lower rate of income tax. However, his wife never received the dividends because they were effectively retained by the taxpayer to repay the purchase debt. Accordingly, the issues to be decided by the Tribunal were whether there was a settlement of (i) the B shares and (ii) the dividends from those shares for the purpose of s 660A.

In respect of the first issue, the First-Tier Tribunal judge, having decided that there was an arrangement between the taxpayer and his wife that would never have been the subject of a commercial, arm's length deal, held that it amounted to a settlement. However, and crucially, in distinction to the cases of *Buck* and *Bird*, the judge could find no element of bounty. This was because she held that there was a constructive trust in the wife's favour: she contributed half of the capital to buy the shares by being jointly liable with her husband on the purchase loan and on the mortgage of the jointly owned house. The purchase of the company was a joint enterprise by the taxpayer and his wife to secure their financial future. The wife did not intend to give her half-share to her husband. The couple took the advice of their accountant, which was to allot to her B shares rather than transfer to her half of the 85 A shares they had jointly purchased. The B shares were not a fair recognition of her investment as they were almost valueless, carrying no voting rights and no rights to any dividend; any dividend paid was entirely at the taxpayer's discretion. As a result, there arose a constructive trust over half of the A shares in the wife's favour when they were purchased; she was entitled to half of the A shares but she received only two and a promise of almost valueless B shares. Accordingly, when the 10 B shares were allotted to the wife, although the arrangement was not commercial, it was not gratuitous either: it was a recognition of her rights to shares in the company. If the taxpayer had transferred to her 42.5 of his A shares it would not have been gratuitous as she was entitled to them (under the constructive trust); the judge said that it followed that the allotment instead of the almost valueless B shares (presumably in lieu) could not therefore be gratuitous.

As to the second issue of whether the *dividends* from the B shares were settled on the wife, following the approach of Lord Hoffmann in taking 'a broad and realistic view of the arrangements', the judge found that, consistently with the decision in *Buck*, choosing to pay a dividend on only one kind of share (the B shares) could amount to a settlement of that dividend. However, as with the allotment of the shares themselves, s 660A could only apply where there was present in the arrangement some element of bounty or gratuity. Because the taxpayer held the A shares in trust for his wife, the dividends he caused to have paid to her, albeit on the B shares, were dividends to which she was entitled, at least in part. Thus, to the extent that she was entitled to the dividends, there was no gratuity and therefore no settlement within s 660A.

It should be noted that the learned judge seemed to apply a 'fairness' approach in quantifying the wife's interest under the constructive trust she said existed, an approach expressly rejected by the House of Lords in *Stack v Dowden* (2007) and by the Supreme Court in *Jones v Kernott* (2011). Further, the judge might be seen to have confused constructive trusts with resulting trusts; where there is a contribution to property at the time of its purchase, a presumption of resulting trust arises (as opposed to the imposition of a constructive trust). Would this make a difference? In the event of a resulting trust, it is perhaps harder to understand how an interest in the A shares could so easily be inferred to exist in the B shares (although this writer thinks that a similar argument could be made with respect to the constructive trust). **[16.93]**

EXAMPLE 16.13

Sirius establishes a company (SE Ltd) of which he is the managing director. He takes 100 £1 shares and his four infant children subscribe for the remaining 400 issued shares. The subscription moneys are given to the children by their grandparents. Thanks to Sirius's enterprise and skill the company is profitable and dividends (equal to their personal allowances) are paid to the children. Sirius has created a settlement in favour of his infant children and the income will be taxed as his (see ITTOIA 2005 s 629 considered at [16.95]–[16.97] and *Butler v Wildin* (1989); see also *Young v Pearce, Young v Scrutton* (1996), *Jones v Garnett* (2005) and *Bird v R & C Comrs* (2008) considered at [16.102]).

d) *The charge to tax*

The charge to tax is imposed by ITTOIA 2005 s 619 and contains rules which apply:
(1) where the unmarried minor children of the settlor receive a benefit from the settlement ([16.95]–[16.97]);
(2) where the settlor or his spouse has retained an interest in the settlement or where the settlor transfers income not capital ([16.98]); and
(3) where the settlor or his spouse or minor child have received a capital payment or benefit from the settlement ([16.106]). [16.94]

2 Benefits received by unmarried infant children from parental settlements (ITTOIA 2005 s 629)

a) *Basic rule*

Payments of income made to or for the benefit of the settlor's own unmarried infant child will be treated as the income of the settlor (see *Bird v R & C Comrs* (2008)). The rule applies to settlements whenever made, but where the total income paid to the child under such a settlement does not exceed £100 in any year, it will not be treated as that of the settlor. If income is accumulated under a capital settlement in favour of unmarried infant children, the income is not treated as that of the settlor until paid out, eg to maintain the child, although note that payments of capital out of the fund will be treated as the income of the settlor to the extent that they can be matched against any available undistributed income.

There will be taken to be available retained or accumulated income so long as the total amount of settlement income arising since the settlement was made is more than the aggregate of:
(1) the amounts treated as income of the settlor;
(2) payments treated as the income of other beneficiaries;
(3) payments of expenses properly charged to income (ITTOIA 2005 s 631). [16.95]

EXAMPLE 16.14

Darien settles property for the benefit of his three children: Amien, Darien Jr and Arres in equal shares contingent upon them attaining the age of 21. They are all infants and unmarried. Assuming the income of the fund of £10,000 pa is not dividend income, the income tax position is as follows:
(1) The trustees will be liable for income tax at the basic rate on the first £1,000 and a rate of 45% on the remaining income (ITA 2007 ss 479, 491).

(2) If the balance of the income (after the payment of tax) is accumulated, it will not be treated as the income of the settlor. Hence, so long as the income is retained in the trust no further income tax is payable.

(3) If any of the income is paid to a child, it is treated as income of Darien. Say, for instance, that £1,500 is paid to, or for the benefit of, Amien. The result will be that Darien's income is increased by £2,727.27 (£1,500 grossed up at 45%). He has a tax credit for the £1,227.27 tax paid by the trustees (ITA 2007 ss 494, 496). Since the rate applicable to trusts is now equivalent to an individual's additional rate, he will not be charged to further income tax on that sum.

(4) ITA 2007 s 494 makes no distinction between the settlor of a resident trust and the settlor of a non-resident trust; accordingly, each can claim credit against his income tax liability arising under ITTOIA 2005 s 629 for income tax paid by the trustees.

(5) If all the net income (say, £5,600) is distributed amongst the three beneficiaries, it is treated as Darien's income. Once the income treated as that of the settlor (together with any payments becoming the income of other beneficiaries and payment of expenses properly charged to income) exceeds the aggregate amount of income which has arisen under the settlement since it was made, any further distributions to the beneficiaries will be capital advancements and thus *not* treated as the income of the settlor.

(6) This settlement is currently a former A&M trust for IHT purposes; but this does not bestow any income tax advantages. It will now enjoy IHT advantages only if it was modified by 6 April 2008 so that the beneficiaries will become entitled to the trust assets *at the age of 18*. If it is not, the trust property will become subject to a 4.2% IHT charge in respect of the period between each beneficiary's 18th and 21st birthdays.

(7) It should be noted that references to 'payments' include payments in money *or money's worth*. Thus a non-cash distribution *in specie* will be caught (ITTOIA 2005 s 629(7)).

b) *Vulnerable beneficiaries*

Discretionary income payments made on or after 6 April 2006 to unmarried minor children of a settlor, where that child is a vulnerable person for the purposes of FA 2005 and the trustees have made a successful claim under FA 2005 s 25 for special income tax treatment ([**16.74**] ff), do not give rise to a charge to tax on the settlor under ITTOIA 2005 s 629.

c) *Other points*

Four other general matters should be noted. *First*, that income covenants by the settlor/parent in favour of trustees will be ineffective annual payments in accordance with the rules discussed in **Chapter 14**. *Second*, 'child' is widely defined to include 'a stepchild, an adopted child, and an illegitimate child' (ITTOIA 2005 s 629(7)), but does not include a foster child. *Third*, the definition of settlement includes a transfer of assets (ITTOIA 2005 s 620(1)); and see *Thomas v Marshall* (1953)). *Finally*, if the settlor is not the parent of the infant beneficiary, ITTOIA 2005 s 629 is not applicable; grandparental settlements may, therefore, be advantageous from an income tax point of view (albeit no longer for the purposes of IHT). [**16.96**]

d) *Bare trusts for infants*

Prior to 9 March 1999 there were advantages for parents who established a bare trust for their infant child (a bare trust is one in which the child is absolutely entitled to the assets or income and only prevented from claiming them because of infancy). The position is illustrated in the following example:

EXAMPLE 16.15

Dad's marginal rate of income tax is 40%. In 1996 he settled property, which produced an income of £1,000 gross, upon trust for his infant daughter, Daisy, absolutely. The income is retained by the trustees (Daisy cannot, of course, give a good receipt for the income).
(1) If Dad had received the income, the income tax payable would have been £400, so that he would have been left with £600.
(2) As the income is settled upon trust for Daisy absolutely, the income was treated as belonging to her so long as it was not used for her benefit but retained by the trustees. As a result, she was able to set her allowances against the income that resulted in no income tax being charged. (The rate applicable to trusts did not apply because the income belonged to a beneficiary.) If the settlor did not want the assets to become the absolute property of the child (bearing in mind that once Daisy became 18 she could call for the assets), similar income tax advantages were obtained if the child was given a vested income entitlement only (which involved the exclusion of Trustee Act 1925 s 31(2)). At 18 she was merely entitled to sums representing accrued income but the capital remained in trust.

These arrangements are now prevented by ITTOIA 2005 ss 629(1) and 631(1)), as a result of which:
(1) bare trusts already in existence before 9 March 1999 are not affected although no further property should be added;
(2) income produced by such trusts established on or after 9 March 1999 is taxed on the settlor as it arises. [16.97]

3 Settlements in which the settlor retains an interest

a) *Basics*

The charging rules are to be found in ITTOIA 2005 ss 624–628. In outline, these sections provide that where during the life of a settlor any property subject to a settlement, or any 'derived property', can become payable to, or applicable for the benefit of, the settlor or spouse or civil partner of the settlor in any circumstances whatsoever, the income of the settlement is treated as the settlor's income for all income tax purposes. The First-tier Tribunal rejected an argument that because the settlor had provided the funds for the trust, he could not then be taxed on the income arising that he never actually received, and that this was akin to the case of profits of a 'mutual trade' which do not attract tax (*Rogge, Kent and JM Kent Settlement v R & C Comrs* (2012)). The tribunal judge, expressing some sympathy with this argument, nevertheless felt constrained by the words of the legislation (the predecessor provision to s 624), suggesting that the appeals in question 'fall within those cases to which

Lawrence Collins LJ referred in which the anomaly cannot be avoided by any legitimate process of interpretation'. ITTOIA 2005 s 685A seeks to ensure that discretionary income payments to beneficiaries from a settlement where the settlor is chargeable to tax under s 624 are not also chargeable in the hands of the beneficiaries. In effect, such payments are treated as gifts of income from the settlor to the beneficiary. [16.98]

b) *Other taxes*

The CGT rules for settlor-interested UK settlements were repealed in 2008 as trust gains are taxed at the highest rates of CGT, although there are wide-ranging CGT rules for offshore trusts (see **Chapter 27A**). In some circumstances the retention of a benefit may result in the settlor being caught, for IHT purposes, by the reservation of benefit rules (see **Chapter 29**). [16.99]

c) *Inter-relationship with the former rules*

For a discussion of a comparison between the rules that existed prior to the tax year 1995–96 and the existing rules, see earlier editions of this book. The important points to note are: (i) the current rules apply to settlements *whenever made*; (ii) under the existing provisions, the income is treated as that of the settlor's for *all* income tax purposes, although the settlor may claim reimbursement from the trustees of any tax paid in respect of that income. Settlors are under an obligation to notify their tax office of any liability under these provisions even if they do not normally receive a tax return. [16.100]

d) *Retention of benefit*

ITTOIA 2005 s 625 provides that if property or any related property is, or will or may become, payable to or applicable for the benefit of the settlor or his spouse or civil partner in any circumstances, then the income from that property is taxed as his for all income tax purposes. [16.101]

EXAMPLE 16.16

Jasper wishes to make provision for his son, Jonas, who is going up to Cambridge to read law. A covenant to pay Jonas £1,000 pa so long as he is studying law is, since FA 1988, ineffective for tax purposes. Accordingly, Jasper proposes to settle ICI shares on trust for Jonas for so long as he is reading law at Cambridge with a provision that thereafter the shares will revert to him. Because the property will revert to the settlor on the ending of Jonas' university career, Jasper will be taxed on the income. The section does not apply in cases where there has been an absolute divesting: hence, were the property to pass on Jonas finishing his law studies to, eg Jasper's adult daughter, the income would then fall outside the provision and be taxed as that of Jonas so long as he was studying law. Where Jasper has retained an interest but subsequently ceases to do so for whatever reason, ITTOIA 2005 s 625 will then cease to treat the income of the settled property as his for income tax purposes.

e) *Benefit to spouse or civil partner*

The settlor is treated as having an interest in settled property if his spouse or civil partner is capable of benefiting from it (ITTOIA 2005 s 625 as amended), unless that benefit derives from an outright gift made to the spouse or civil partner (ITTOIA 2005 s 626 as amended). Section 626 will only apply if the gift of property carries a right to the whole of the income (s 626(2)) and the property is not wholly or substantially a right to the income (s 626(3)).

EXAMPLE 16.17

In January 2002 Popeye settled property on trust for his wife, Olive, for life, with remainder to his children. Because a benefit from the settlement is being received by the spouse of the settlor (and there is no outright gift to that person) the income will be taxed as Popeye's under ITTOIA 2005 s 625.

In *Young v Pearce, Young v Scrutton* (1996) the spouses of two directors who ran a tooling company were allocated preference shares in the company by special resolution. This arrangement constituted a 'settlement' (for the wide meaning of 'settlement', see [16.93]). In the subsequent three years, they received dividends amounting to more than 30% of the net profits of the company. The spouses had no voting powers and, apart from the preferential rights to dividends, their only other entitlement was to repayment of the sums subscribed for the preference shares in a liquidation of the company. Accordingly, although the allotment of the preference shares did amount to an outright gift to the spouses, it was property which was 'wholly or substantially a right to income', and Vinelott J concluded that the dividends on the shares were caught by the anti-avoidance provisions. The key point in the decision was the absence of rights, apart from the right to income, attaching to the preference shares. He observed, '[A]s a matter of strict legal principle, the preference shares were assets distinct from the income derived from them ... '. However, he concluded that 'in reality they could never have been realised'. The decision has to be read in the context of this particular anti-avoidance legislation and, for a similar scheme to succeed, it will be necessary to ensure that greater rights attach to the shares, eg by making the preference shares convertible or by giving a right to participate in capital on a winding up of the company. The issue was considered further in *Jones v Garnett* (2007) (see [16.93]). Having concluded that this was an arrangement giving rise to a settlement within s 625, the House of Lords then had to consider whether the taxpayers fell within the exception created by ITTOIA 2005 s 626. Their unanimous verdict was that: (i) despite the fact that Mrs Jones paid £1 for her share, it was Mr Jones' consent to the transfer of a share with expectations of dividends to Mrs Jones which gave the transfer the 'element of bounty' that brought the arrangement within s 625 (see [16.93]) – by the same token, this also made the transfer a 'gift'; (ii) the transfer of the share was the essence of the arrangement, which did not include subsequent events – the expectation of other future events gave the transfer the necessary element of bounty, but the events themselves did not form part of the arrangement; and (iii) the share given to Mrs Jones was not simply 'wholly or substantially a right to income' – this was an ordinary share, which conferred (amongst other things) the right to vote, to participate in the distribution of assets on a winding up of the company and to block a special resolution. Lord Hoffmann said that these are rights 'over and above the right to income', and distinguished the ordinary share of Mrs Jones with the preference shares in *Young v Pearce*. This point was stressed by Lord Hope who said:

'... so long as the shares from which [*the*] income arises are ordinary shares, and not shares carrying contractual rights which are restricted wholly or substantially to a right to income, the settlement will fall within the exception created by section [*626*]. This is an important point of general public interest ...'

In *Patmore v R & C Comrs* (2010) (see **[16.93]**) the First-tier Tribunal judge concluded that dividends paid by the taxpayer to his wife were dividends to which she was entitled as beneficial owner (through a constructive trust of other shares), at least in part and, to the extent that she was so entitled, there was no gratuity and therefore no settlement within s 660A (now ITTOIA 2005 s 625). However, to the extent that the dividends exceeded the wife's entitlement, there was a settlement within s 625 and, because the property given, dividends, was 'wholly or substantially a right to income', the judge concluded that the exception in s 660A(b) (now ITTOIA 2005 s 626) for outright gifts could not apply. She said:

'It may at first glance seem illogical that statute allows an exemption for giving away capital from which income is derived (such as a gift of shares) but not the lesser gift of just the income ... I assume that this is because Parliament wished to allow a person to entirely divest themselves of property in favour of their spouse so that for all purposes separate taxation would then apply. What Parliament did not want is for a spouse to decide year on year that his or her income could be given to the spouse in order to get a lower rate of tax.'

The issue was again considered, albeit briefly, in *Donovan & McLaren* (2014 and see **[16.93]**), where the Tribunal drew a distinction between an allotment of shares (as in *Jones v Garnett*) and dividend waivers. The latter cannot fall within the 'outright gifts between spouses' exemption because they are merely a right to income.

Since the decision in *Jones v Garnett*, HMRC has consulted on draft anti-avoidance provisions designed to prevent income shifting between spouses and civil partners. No such provisions have been included in any subsequent Finance Acts, possibly due to the fact that there were grave concerns at the time that the premises upon which the draft provisions were founded were very unsound (see [2007] BTR 680).

ITTOIA 2005 s 625(4) restricts the definition of a spouse or civil partner of the settlor. It does not include a widow or widower or survivor of a civil partnership, so that a possibility of benefit for the widow or widower or surviving civil partner of the settlor will not cause the income of the settled property to be taxable as the settlor's (and see *Lord Vestey's Executors v IRC* (1949)). In a similar fashion, s 625(4)(d) excludes a prospective spouse or civil partner, and s 625(4)(a) and (b) a separated spouse or civil partner. An exception for settlements made by one party to a marriage or civil partnership to provide for the other after divorce, termination of a civil partnership or separation, where the income is being paid to that other, is to be found in ITTOIA 2005 s 627(1) (see below, **[16.103]** for further exceptions). So, on the break-up of a marriage, one party to the marriage can make a settlement to provide for the other under which the income is paid to that other, but under which the settled property may revert to the settlor, without the income being taxed as the settlor's. [16.102]

f) *Exceptions for certain types of income*

Further exceptions are made by ITTOIA 2005 s 627(2). Thus there is no charge on the settlor in relation to income:
(i) of the trust that is given to a charity in the year of assessment in which it arises or which is income to which the charity is entitled under the terms of the trust;
(ii) that consists of annual payments made by an individual for commercial reasons in connection with the individual's trade, profession or vocation;
(iii) that consists of a benefit under a relevant pension scheme; or
(iv) originating from any settlor who is not an individual. This provision was added by FA 2012 to prevent taxpayers from using the anti-avoidance rule to their own advantage in order to reduce the amount of tax paid overall by arranging for a company to be the settlor. The rate of tax payable on the income by the company settlor will frequently be less than the rate paid by the beneficiaries or the trustees. Thus, with effect from 21 March 2012, a corporate settlor will not be taxable on the income of the trust; instead the trustees or the beneficiaries will be chargeable. [16.103]

g) *When the settlor is not to be regarded as retaining an interest*

In addition to the exceptions provided by s 627(1) and (2) (see [16.102] and [16.103]), ITTOIA 2005 s 625(2) deals with the possibility of a settlor becoming entitled to settled property on a disposition, bankruptcy or death by or of beneficiaries, or on the death of his own child or children over the age of 25 where the child has, for example, a life interest, in which circumstances the settlor will not be regarded as retaining an interest. Moreover, the settlor will not be regarded as retaining an interest while there is a living beneficiary under the age of 25 during whose life the settled property cannot be paid to or applied for the benefit of the settlor except in the events mentioned above (ITTOIA 2005 s 625(3)). [16.104]

EXAMPLE 16.18

Tybalt settles property upon trust for such of his three children as attain the age of 25 and if more than one in equal shares absolutely and subject thereto for the benefit of the settlor.

As a result of s 625(3) Tybalt is not treated as having retained an interest in the fund. Even if the children took only life interests so that the property would revert to Tybalt on death, he is not taxed on the income (ITTOIA 2005 s 625(2)(e)).

h) *Non-domiciled settlors*

A non-domiciled settlor cannot be taxed on foreign income accumulated overseas even if he had an interest in the settlement. *However*, it is provided that if such income is subsequently remitted to the UK in a year of assessment in which the settlor is resident in the UK, it is to be treated as income arising *in that year* and chargeable to tax as the settlor's income. This means that although the income might have arisen in a year when the settlor had *no* connection with the UK, it will be taxed if there is a remittance after the settlor has acquired such a connection (ITTOIA 2005 s 648(2)–(5) and *Tax Journal*, 30 March 1995, p 9). [16.105]

4 Receipt of capital benefits (ITTOIA 2005 ss 633–643)

These provisions prevent the settlor obtaining any benefit of a capital nature from a settlement in which the income may be taxed at a lower rate than that which would have applied had the settlor retained the income. In effect, capital payments to the settlor (or his spouse) from the fund are matched with undistributed income of the fund and taxed as the settlor's income under ITTOIA 2005 s 619. The sum is grossed up at the rate applicable to trusts but the settlor is entitled to a credit for tax paid by the trustees – although not to any repayment! There are no provisions enabling the settlor to recover any tax that he may have to pay.

A 'capital sum' covers any sum paid by way of loan or repayment of a loan and any sum paid otherwise than as income and which is not paid for full consideration in money or money's worth (ITTOIA 2005 s 634(1)–(4)(7)). A capital sum is treated as paid to the settlor if it is paid at his direction, or as a result of his assignment, to a third party (ITTOIA 2005 s 634(4)–(6)).

The capital sum will only be caught by s 633 to the extent that it is less than, or equals, the income available in the settlement; this means the undistributed income of the fund from any relevant year. Any excess will not be charged in the year of receipt but it may be charged later if income becomes available in any of the next 11 years (ITTOIA 2005 s 633(3)–(4)).

EXAMPLE 16.19

The undistributed net income of a settlement is as follows:

Year 1	£10,000
Year 2	£2,500
Year 3	£15,000
Year 4	£6,000
Year 5	£7,000

In year 3, the trustees lend the settlor £45,000. That loan is a capital sum and, therefore, the settlor is charged to income tax in year 3 on that sum to the extent that it represents available income. As the available income is £27,500 (years 1–3) he will be taxed on £27,500 grossed up at 45% – ie on £50,000. Although he is not entitled to any repayment of tax, he will receive a tax credit for tax paid by the trustees.

The remaining £17,500 is carried forward to be taxed in succeeding years when income becomes available; in year 4, for instance, £6,000 is available. If the loan is repaid, there will be no further charge on available income in subsequent years, but any tax paid during the loan period cannot be recovered (s 638(1)–(3)).

Section 633 ff also applies to a capital sum received by the settlor from a body corporate connected with the settlement. Generally, a company will be connected with a settlement if it is a close company and the participators include the trustees of the settlement (ITTOIA 2005 s 637(8)). The width of s 633 ff and its somewhat capricious nature (see eg *De Vigier v IRC* (1964)) means that settlements will often contain a clause prohibiting the payment of capital sums to the settlor or his spouse. **[16.106]**

5 General conclusions

(1) With the demise of the income settlement, the transfer of income-producing capital assets has assumed greater importance. So long as the settlor is prepared to sever all interest in the property settled, the anti-avoidance provisions considered above need not cause problems in the majority of cases. In light of the fact that, for 2017–18, income over £150,000 is taxed at 45% (38.1% on dividends) and that the basic personal allowance is restricted for those with income over £100,000, tapering down to zero, it would seem sensible to give a beneficiary whose income is less than £100,000, or who has no income at all, an entitlement to income. Particularly attractive settlements include those made by grandparents on their infant grandchildren through which use is made of the grandchild's personal allowance to ensure that income in the settlement is either tax free or taxed only at the grandchild's lower marginal rate of tax. By contrast, parental discretionary settlements in favour of the settlor's own infant unmarried children are less attractive: the income is either retained in the trust where it will attract trust tax rates or, if distributed, it attracts tax at the settlor's rate. Given that such income is likely to suffer high rates of tax in either event, there is no longer anything to justify the expenses involved in creating and running the relevant trust. Note also the fact that, for the purposes of IHT, almost all inter-vivos trusts the settlor will incur an immediate IHT charge at 20%, unless he is still able to utilise his nil rate band.

(2) The increase in the special rates for trustees (45% on ordinary income and 38.1% on dividends and other company distributions for 2017–18) will largely affect those, typically, smaller trusts with beneficiaries who either pay no tax at all, or who are liable at lower rates on income and gains received by them in their non-beneficial capacity. However, it has been suggested that the effect of the first slice rate band on the first £1,000 of income taxable at the special rates for trustees has reduced the number of trusts currently liable to tax at the special rates by around one-third because their total income falls below this threshold. Moreover, that percentage might be higher given that the standard rate band applies after deduction for allowable trust management expenses. In other cases, there is likely to be an advantage in distributing available income.

(3) Consider investing in assets that are subject to CGT at 20% or 28% rather than income tax at 45%.

(4) The provisions of ITTOIA 2005 Part 5 Chapter 5 involve 'looking through' a settlement and treating the income as that of the settlor:

similar provisions are found in the CGT treatment of UK resident trusts and more draconian provisions in the case of non-resident trusts.

(5) ITTOIA 2005 Part 5 Chapter 5 is capable of applying to foreign as well as UK trusts. For instance, in a case where assets are transferred to non-resident trustees, these provisions need to be considered as, of course, does ITA 2007 Part 13 Chapter 2 (see [18.111] ff). Unlike the latter provision, ITTOIA 2005 Part 5 Chapter 5 is only concerned with the income of the settlement and does not catch income retained in a company that is owned by the settlement. [16.107]

VIII REFORM

Much of the reform proposed in the various discussion and consultation documents since December 2003 has now been implemented. This embraces increasing the trust and dividend trust rates (originally to 40% and 32.5% respectively, now 45% and 38.1%), the introduction of a first slice rate band for the first £1,000 of income taxable at the trust and dividend trust rates (for 2006–07 and subsequent years), legislation providing for special treatment of trusts for the most vulnerable beneficiaries (now amended by FA 2013 and FA 2014) and the harmonisation of the main definitions and tests for trusts and trustees used in the taxation of UK personal resident trusts. Other measures which were discussed, including income streaming, are not currently being taken forward. The rise in the special rate for trusts and the dividend trust rate to 50% and 42.5% respectively for 2010–11 until 5 April 2013 had less to do with the reform of the taxation of trusts, and was more an attempt to recoup revenue following the bailing out of the country's ailing banks during 2008 and 2009. [16.108]

＃ 17 Estates in the course of administration

Updated by Iris Wünschmann-Lyall, MA (Cantab), TEP

I   The deceased's income [17.2]
II The administration period [17.20]
III Taxation of distributions to beneficiaries [17.41]
IV Disclaimers, variations and appointments under IHTA 1984 s 144 [17.58]
V   Clearances [17.60]

Personal representatives (PRs, meaning both executors and administrators) are under a duty to administer a deceased's estate. From the point of view of taxation this involves:
(1) Settling the deceased's outstanding tax liabilities to the date of death. Although this chapter is concerned primarily with income tax, PRs may also have to settle any outstanding CGT liabilities (see **Chapter 21**). PRs cannot generally obtain a grant of probate until any IHT, payable on their application for a grant, has been accounted for (see **Chapter 30**).
(2) Liability to income tax on any income produced during the administration period. In addition, the PRs may incur CGT liabilities (see **Chapter 21**) and the original IHT bill may require adjustment as a result of events happening after the death (see [**30.63**]).

Apart from considering the PRs' liability to pay income tax, this chapter also considers the liability of beneficiaries to tax on any income distributed to them from the estate. [17.1]

I THE DECEASED'S INCOME

The PRs are accountable for any income tax owed by the deceased (TMA 1970 s 74(1)). They should report the death to the appropriate tax office and complete an ordinary income tax return on behalf of the deceased for the period from 6 April preceding his death to the date of death, and for earlier tax years (if necessary!). In computing the income tax of the deceased, normal principles operate and full personal allowances are available for the year of death.

530 *Estates in the course of administration*

Any outstanding income tax is a debt of the estate thereby reducing the value of that estate for IHT purposes. Conversely, any repayment of income tax will increase the assets of the estate and may increase the IHT liability on death. HMRC can assess the PRs, at any time within four years after 31 January following the year of assessment in which the death occurred, for any tax that is owing for a period ending within six years of the date of death (TMA 1970 s 40). Following a review, it is now agreed by HMRC that, as a result of the Human Rights Act 1998, penalties are no longer collectable.

From 13 October 2014, it will not be necessary for the PRs to complete Form R27. Instead, any outstanding income tax liabilities/repayments of the deceased will be dealt with automatically for PAYE cases with a more tailored service for self-assessment cases. [17.2]

EXAMPLE 17.1

A died on 28 September 2017 (tax year 2017–18). If HMRC assesses his PRs on 31 January 2019 they can recover back tax to the tax year 2011–12 but no further.

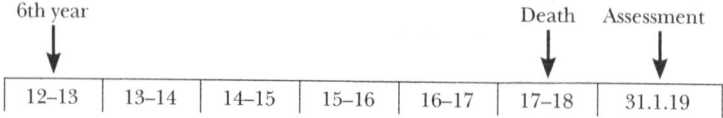

1 Dividends

Dividends received before the deceased's death form part of the deceased's income. For IHT purposes any quoted securities in the deceased's estate must be valued at death; if that valuation was *ex div* (ie it did not include the value of a declared dividend) the outstanding dividend must be added to the value of the security. This problem does not arise when the shares were valued at death *cum div* since the valuation includes any accruing dividend to date.

Prior to the enactment of the Trusts (Capital and Income) Act 2013, which came into effect on 1 October 2013, it may have been necessary to apportion dividends paid after death but which relate to a period partly before and partly after death (Apportionment Act 1870 s 2). The portion which relates to the period prior to death may be chargeable to inheritance tax. The apportionment rules are cumbersome and expensive to administer, and most wills and trust documents therefore exclude them. For wills and trusts executed after 1 October 2013 there is no need to disapply the apportionment rules.

However, whether or not the dividend is apportioned for succession purposes, any dividend paid after the deceased's death is treated as the *income of the estate and not of the deceased* and must not be included in the deceased's tax return (*IRC v Henderson's Executors* (1931)). This rule follows from the fact that, as the dividends were never owed to the deceased, they never became a part of his income.

Only in cases where a dividend is declared due before death, but paid after that death, will it be taxed as the deceased's income (see, for instance, *Re Sebright* (1944) and contrast *Potel v IRC* (1971)). Similarly, certain other investment income paid after death but relating to the period before death (eg bank deposit interest) should be apportioned for succession purposes, but included as estate income for tax purposes. This may lead to some double taxation in that the income which is deemed for succession purposes to accrue before death is charged both to IHT (as part of the deceased's estate on death) and also to income tax in the hands of the PRs and beneficiaries. ITTOIA 2005 s 669 affords some relief against such double taxation but only to an absolutely entitled residuary beneficiary who is a higher rate taxpayer (see [17.54]). [17.3]

EXAMPLE 17.2

T died on 30 May 2017 leaving his residuary estate (including 1,000 shares in Z Ltd) to his brother B absolutely. On 15 May 2017, Z Ltd declared a dividend on those shares of £450 in respect of the year ending on 30 June. The dividend was paid on 28 July 2017.

Of this dividend, 11/12ths (£412.50) is deemed to have accrued before T's death and will be reflected in the value of the shares in T's estate which will have been valued *cum div*. For inheritance tax it will thus be taxed as part of the capital in T's estate.

However, for income tax purposes the whole dividend is taxed as the income of the estate, albeit with some relief for double taxation against any higher rate liability of B under ITTOIA 2005 s 669.

2 Trust income

Where the deceased was a life tenant under a trust, any income that was received by the trustees before his death is treated as the deceased's income and must be included in the PRs' tax return to the date of death.

For trusts created prior to 1 October 2013, where the Apportionment Act s 2 was not excluded, any income paid to the trustees after death, but attributable in part to the period before death, the actual apportionment determines the tax payable. Any income that is apportioned to the deceased life tenant is taxed as the income of the estate – and not of the deceased (*Wood v Owen* (1941)).

Income that is apportioned to the deceased life tenant forms an asset of his estate, thereby increasing his IHT liability. This could result in an element of double IHT because the apportioned income also will affect the value of the trust assets on which the trustees pay IHT on the life tenant's death. This double taxation is avoided by deducting the apportioned income from the value of the settled assets.

For trusts created prior to 1 October 2013, where s 2 of the Apportionment Act 1870 is excluded, so that all the income is paid to either a subsequent life tenant or a remainderman, income tax follows the actual payment made. Therefore, any income paid after the date of death of the life tenant, is not taxed as part of the deceased life tenant's estate but, rather, as income of either the subsequent life tenant or remainderman.

Trusts created after 1 October 2013 can rely on the Trusts (Capital and Income) Act 2013 which excludes the apportionment rules and provides that income tax follows the actual payment made.

EXAMPLE 17.3

T, who died on 30 June 2016, was the life tenant of a trust which was established in 2004, where s 2 of the Apportionment Act 1870 was not excluded. Included in the settled assets was debenture stock in Z Ltd. On 31 December 2016, Z Ltd paid the trustees annual interest of £100 gross. This interest was apportioned by the trustees as to half (£50) to T and half (£50) to the remainderman R.

The £50 apportioned to T will have to be taxed by the trustees at the basic income tax rate of 20%, which leaves £40 net representing estate income. Notice, also, that the £40 (net after income tax) increases the value of the trust fund on which the trustees may have to pay IHT at T's rates, if it is a pre 22 March 2006 interest in possession settlement or an immediate post death interest (see [33.10]).

If the settlement was a lifetime settlement set up after 22 March 2006 and therefore is subject to the relevant property regime, the trustees will have to include the apportioned income when calculating the exit charge for IHT on the death of a life tenant. To avoid the £40 being charged twice to IHT, it is deducted from the value of the settled assets. (If T's free estate passes to a residuary beneficiary absolutely, the latter may be entitled to relief under ITTOIA 2005 s 669).

EXAMPLE 17.4

T died on 30 June 2017. He was the life tenant of a trust which was set up on his uncle's death on 1 November 2014, which was after the Trusts (Capital and Income) Act 2013 came into force. Again, the settled fund included debenture stock in Z Ltd and on 31 October 2016 Z Ltd paid the trustees annual interest of £100 gross. The income tax follows the actual payment made and it is therefore taxed on the remainderman. [17.4]

3 Sole traders and partners

A sole trader's business is discontinued as a result of death: tax for the year of death is based on profits for the previous basis period to the date of death less any overlap profits (see generally [10.201]). Unused losses or capital allowances are not available for use by the PRs but can be carried back as a terminal loss (see [11.102]). If the business is carried on by the surviving spouse capital allowances are given on the basis that the spouse acquired the assets at probate value. If the deceased had been a member of a partnership his death is treated as the discontinuance of the separate trade carried on by him alone. [17.5]

4 Life insurance policy or life annuity contracts

The chargeable event legislation is complex and any liability to income tax depends on a number of factors.

In most cases the insured person and the beneficial owner are the same individuals. In these circumstances, if any rights are extinguished by the death of the insured person and the policy is not held on trust, the chargeable event gain will be that of the deceased person in the period to date of death rather than that of the PRs (ITTOIA 2005 s 465).

PRs are only liable in cases where the insured person is different from the beneficial owner, or the policy is a capital redemption policy and the policy continues to run following the death of the beneficial owner and it passes into the estate of the deceased. Any chargeable event arising on the policy will be treated as estate income (ITTOIA 2005 s 466).

In the very common scenario where the policy is held on trust, and a chargeable event gain arises on the death of the settlor, the settlor will be chargeable to income tax on the chargeable event gain. It is not the tax liability of the estate or the trustees.

If a policy is subject to a UK resident trust and continues after the death of the settlor, but the chargeable event gain occurs before the end of the tax year in which the settlor died, the gain will be chargeable as part of the total income of the deceased settlor for that tax year.

If a policy is held on a UK resident trust, a chargeable event gain will only be chargeable on the trustees if the settlor is 'absent' (eg where he is non-UK resident or has died and the chargeable event gain occurred after the end of the tax year in which the settlor died).

There are transitional provisions that apply where both the trust and the policy were in existence before 17 March 1998 and
- at least one of its creators was an individual, and
- one of the creators died before 17 March 1998.

In such cases, provided the policy has not been varied on or after 17 March 1998 to increase benefits or extend its term, there is no chargeable event gain and proceeds therefore escape a charge to income tax in the hands of the trustees.

Special anti-avoidance provisions (see ITA 2007 Chapter 2, Part 13) are in force in relation to policies which are held on non-UK resident trusts, where:
- trustees would have been chargeable under the chargeable event regime had they been UK-resident when the event took place, or
- in relation to certain rights under a policy or contract, where:
  - a foreign institution beneficially owns a share in those rights;
  - the rights are held for the purposes of a foreign institution; or
  - a share in the rights is held as security for a foreign institution's debt.

These provisions are designed to prevent avoidance of tax where an individual who is ordinarily UK resident benefits from a transfer of assets and provide that:
- in the case of non-UK resident trustees, to treat the gain as becoming payable to the trustees, as if income arose to the trustees in the tax year in which the gain arises
- in the case of a foreign institution, to treat the gain as becoming payable to the institution, and as if income arose to the institution in the tax year in which the gain arises. [17.6]

5 **Administrative issues**

In cases where the PRs have to pay income tax for the period to the date of death, but they cannot pay until they have obtained grant of probate or letters of administration, by concession, HMRC will not charge interest until the normal due date or 30 days from the grant of probate or letters of administration, whichever is the later (ESC A17 – now obsolete and replaced by FA 2009 Sch 53 Part 2). [17.7]–[17.19]

II THE ADMINISTRATION PERIOD

1 Duration of administration

The administration period is the period from the date of death until the date when the residue is ascertained and ready for distribution. Until that time no beneficiary is entitled to the income or to any property comprised in the estate and, accordingly, is generally not liable to income tax unless income is actually distributed to him. Identifying precisely when completion of the administration of the estate occurs can present problems. In respect of Scottish estates the administration is considered complete, when debts, specific legacies and liabilities of the estate have been discharged or provided for and the residuary estate can be ascertained (see ITTOIA 2005 s 653(2)). This also seems to be the position in England and Wales, see, for instance, *The Commissioner of Inland Revenue v Sir Aubrey Smith* (1930), *IRC v Pilkington* (1941) and *Prest v Bettinson* (1980) and HMRC Manual CG 30700. [17.20]

2 Taxing PRs during administration

During the administration period, the PRs are liable, in a representative capacity, to income tax on all the income of the estate computed in the usual way.

Prior to 6 April 2008 the basic rate of tax of 22% was charged on rents, royalties and profits from trading, whilst savings income was taxed at the 20% lower rate. UK dividend income was paid with a 10% tax credit that covered the tax due.

From 6 April 2008 to 5 April 2016 the basic rate of 20% applied to all income except for dividends, which were taxed at 10%. UK dividend income was paid with a 10% tax credit that covered the tax due.

FA 2016 introduced changes to the way dividends and bank or building society interest is paid from 6 April 2016. It also introduced a new tax rate of 7.5% on all dividends (the basic rate for all other income remained at 20%) and any interest or dividends paid on or after 6 April 2016 is paid gross of tax. The PRs will have to account for any income tax due in the usual way. However the result of these changes is that some estates that did not have to file tax returns may now have to report untaxed interest and dividends. HMRC announced transitional measures for the tax years 2016–17 and 2017–18, meaning that PRs will not need to return estate income, if the only source of income of the estate is interest income and the tax liability is less than £100.

Tax liabilities arise even when the beneficiaries are not liable to income tax, for example charities or non-tax paying beneficiaries. In such cases the tax paid (apart from any non-repayable tax credit on dividends) can be reclaimed by the beneficiaries.

Some income received by the PRs will already have borne tax: in those cases the PRs have no further tax to pay. Generally such income falls into two categories:
(1) bank/building society interest received prior to 6 April 2016 which has borne tax at the basic rate; and
(2) dividends received prior to 6 April 2016 which carried non-repayable 10% tax credits.

The main examples of income on which PRs are directly assessed are:
(a) gross interest from banks or building societies;
(b) UK dividends received after 6 April 2016;
(c) rents from property;
(d) foreign source income;
(e) interest (eg from National Savings) which is paid gross; and
(f) royalties. [17.21]

3 Which tax office?

HMRC has introduced the Trusts Registration Service in July 2017 which will be an online service for PRs. However only complex estates will need to be registered including estates that have already registered with HMRC, but where the administration has not been finalised.

An estate is considered complex, if:
(a) the probate/confirmation value of the estate exceeds £2.5m; or
(b) the tax payable by the PRs in respect of the administration period exceeds £10,000; or
(c) the proceeds of assets sold in any one tax year for dates of death up to 6 April 2016 exceeds £250,000 or £500,000 for dates of death on or after 6 April 2016.

If the estate is considered complex, PRs have to complete full self-assessment returns and HMRC Administration of Estates Cardiff will be the appropriate office.

If the estate is not complex, it is not necessary for the PRs to complete a formal tax return. It is sufficient to report the relevant details in a simple letter to HMRC using the informal procedure and making a one-off payment. Informal payments are usually accepted by the tax office that dealt with the tax affairs of the deceased during his lifetime – see HMRC Manual TSEM 7411.

If a trust arises under the terms of the will (or intestacy) the PRs should account to the relevant trust office which normally is HMRC Trust and Estates Nottingham and which from 1 March 2017 deals with all trusts including non-resident trusts.

If the deceased was a Lloyd's underwriter, the PRs may need to account to the High Net Worth Unit Bradford West Yorkshire or Public Department 1.

Finally if the estate does not fall into any of the above categories but it cannot easily be dealt with under the informal payments procedures, advice should be obtained from HMRC Administration of Estates Cardiff. [17.22]

4 Interest relief

If PRs raised a loan for IHT payable on delivery of the PRs' account, tax relief is available for interest paid within one year from the making of the loan. Interest on loans to pay inheritance tax after the grant of representation does not qualify for relief. The tax relief for which the loan is required must be attributable to personal property owned beneficially by the deceased and which vests in his PRs (ITA 2007 s 403). Relief is given against the income of the estate for the year in which the interest is paid but where that income is insufficient relief may be given against income of the preceding year and then against the future income of the estate (ITA 2007 s 405). In practice this is normally the only deduction that can be made against the estate income: expenses incurred by the PRs in administering the estate are not deductible, except for the purpose of determining residuary beneficiaries' shares of the income for their own tax purposes. [17.23]

5 Trading

When the PRs carry on a business after the death of a sole trader in order to sell it as a going concern or to transfer it to a beneficiary, they must pay basic rate tax on any profits calculated in the usual way. Hence, they can deduct business expenses and claim loss relief in the usual way. [17.24]

6 Letting

Similarly, any expenses incurred directly in connection with the letting of freehold or leasehold property may be deducted in arriving at the net income liable to tax. [17.25]

7 Apportionments

Dividends and certain other income received by the PRs after the death in respect of a period wholly or partly before death is taxed as the income of the estate whether or not it is apportioned for succession purposes. Similarly, trust income received by the trustees after the deceased life tenant's death and apportioned to him is taxed as the income of the estate for trusts created prior to 1 October 2013 (see [16.4]).

When property which produces no income is left to persons in succession (eg to A for life, remainder to B), part of the capital sum realised on the sale of that property may be treated for trust purposes as income, eg the rules in *Howe v Dartmouth* (1802) and *Re Earl of Chesterfield's Trusts* (1883) since, otherwise, the life tenant would receive nothing. Income apportioned to the life tenant may be liable to basic rate tax if it is of a recurring nature as in the case of a *Howe v Dartmouth* apportionment, but if it is paid as a one-off lump sum from capital by way of compensation as in the case of a *Re Chesterfield* apportionment it is not liable to tax.

Following the enactment of the Trust (Capital and Income) Act 2013, these apportionment rules are automatically disapplied for trusts created after 1 October 2013. Prior to this date, most wills and trust deeds expressly excluded these rules. [17.26]–[17.40]

III TAXATION OF DISTRIBUTIONS TO BENEFICIARIES

1 The basic principles

Income received by the PRs suffers the equivalent of basic rate tax either by deduction at source (if received prior to 6 April 2016) or by direct assessment in their hands, with dividends being taxed at the rate of 7.5% from 6 April 2016 (10% prior to 6 April 2016). From this taxed income the PRs deduct administration expenses chargeable against income, leaving a net sum available for distribution to beneficiaries entitled to the income from the estate. These different types of income fall to be divided between beneficiaries as is just and reasonable having regard to their different interests (ITTOIA 2005 ss 664 to 670). The legislation does not specify against which types of income administration expenses are to be deducted. For income received prior to 6 April 2016 the best approach was to set expenses first against income carrying a non-reclaimable credit (ie dividend income received prior to 6 April 2016), then against income bearing tax at basic rate (this order was accepted by HMRC).

For income received on or after 6 April 2016 the position is more complex. If the beneficiary benefits from the savings allowance (£5,000, £1,000 or £500) or the dividend allowance of £5,000, it may be more beneficial to use estate income against non-savings income first, then savings income and dividend income. The income tax position of the beneficiary will determine the most tax efficient use of administration expenses.

If the PRs have a discretion whether to deduct administration expenses from income or capital they may consider the tax position of a beneficiary (if any) absolutely entitled to the residue of the estate. When that beneficiary has a large income, they may deduct their expenses from income so as to reduce his income and, therefore, his higher-rate tax bill. Conversely, if the beneficiary has only a small income or is a charity, they may deduct expenses from capital so as not to prejudice any claim that he may have for a repayment of income tax.

The relevant provisions can be found in ITTOIA 2005 ss 649–682. **[17.41]**

2 General legatees

A general legatee is a person who is entitled to a sum of money (a pecuniary legacy) not charged on any particular fund. This sum is capital and the legatee is generally not entitled to any interest unless:
(1) the will directs the PRs to pay him interest; or
(2) the legacy remains unpaid at the end of the executor's year, in which case he is entitled to interest at the rate payable on funds in court in the absence of a contrary direction; or
(3) the legacy is a 'statutory legacy' arising on intestacy (eg to a surviving spouse) in which case he is similarly entitled to interest at the rate indicated above from the date of death to the date of payment.

Interest is paid gross by the PRs and the legatee is assessed directly to tax under ITTOIA 2005 s 369 on the interest (unless the interest is paid to a person whose usual place of abode is outside the UK when basic rate tax must be deducted by the PRs: see ITA 2007 s 874(1)). If that interest is neither claimed nor paid, there is no income to be assessed in the beneficiary's hands (*Dewar v IRC* (1935)). Once a sum has been set aside to pay the legacy it may, however, be too late to disclaim any income (*Spens v IRC* (1970)). For the PRs, interest is ignored in computing their tax liability and so does not appear on their tax returns: this follows from the basic principle that the payment of interest does not attract tax relief (see further **[7.44]**). Such interest may, however, be treated as an administration expense and properly be deducted from the net income that is available for allocation and vouching to the residuary beneficiaries (ITTOIA 2005 s 666). [17.42]

3 Specific legatees

A specific legatee is entitled to a particular item of property and to any income produced by it as from the date of death. Therefore, once the PRs vest the asset in the beneficiary, any income from it that arose during the administration period is related back and taxed as the legatee's income for the tax year(s) when it arose (*IRC v Hawley* (1928)). It will have suffered tax either through deduction at source or as a result of direct assessment on the PRs. Accordingly, the net income will be passed to the beneficiary together with a tax deduction certificate Form R185 completed by the PRs. [17.43]

EXAMPLE 17.5

A died in September 2016 leaving his 1,000 shares in B Ltd to his nephew N. A dividend of £100 gross is paid in respect of the shares in January 2017. The administration is completed and the shares vest in N in May 2017 together with the net dividend of £92.50 and the tax credit for the £7.50 tax that has been deducted. N must include the £100 dividend with the 7.5% tax credit in his income tax return for the tax year 2016–17 (when the dividend was paid) and not 2017–18 (when N received it).

4 Annuitants

a) *Definition*

An annuity is a pecuniary legacy payable by instalments. The payments are income from which the PRs must deduct basic rate income tax (ITTOIA 2005 s 426). The net sum will be paid to the annuitant who will be given a certificate of tax deducted.

Modern wills rarely provide for the payment of an annuity. [17.44]

b) *Use of formula*

A testator may want the annuitant to receive a constant sum despite fluctuations in the tax rates. The two methods most commonly employed are:
(1) The testator provides for the payment of 'such sum as will after deduction of income tax at the basic rate for the time being in force leave (say) £1,000 pa'.

The PRs must pay £1,000 grossed up at the current basic rate to give a gross equivalent of £1,250. They must pay basic rate tax on that grossed-up figure but they are not liable to indemnify the annuitant against any higher rate income tax for which he may be liable. Conversely, if the annuitant can reclaim all or any of the basic rate tax paid, he need not account for it to the PRs.
(2) If the testator provides for the payment of '£1,000 pa free from income tax' this imposes an obligation on the PRs to pay such sum as after deducting basic rate income tax leaves £1,000. However, it also means that the annuitant can recover from the PRs any higher rate tax that he may have to pay on the annuity and any basic rate tax that he reclaims

must be repaid to the PRs. In effect, he will never be left with more nor with less than £1,000 (see *Re Pettit, Le Fevre v Pettit* (1922)). [17.45]

c) *Setting aside a capital sum and purchased life annuities*

An annuitant can insist on a capital sum being set aside to provide for his annuity (thereby creating an interest in possession trust for IHT purposes: see **Chapter 32**). If the capital in the estate is insufficient he can demand that the actuarial value of the annuity be paid to him, abated if necessary (*IRC v Lady Castlemaine* (1943)). This capitalised annuity is not subject to income tax either in the PRs' or in the annuitant's hands.

If the will directs the PRs to purchase an annuity for the beneficiary, he will be charged to income tax on the full amount of each annual payment and cannot claim relief under ITTOIA 2005 s 717 which taxes only the income element. The beneficiary should, therefore, request that the PRs give him the appropriate capital sum so that he can buy the annuity himself and claim s 717 relief. [17.46]

d) *Beware top-ups!*

Where there is insufficient income in the estate to pay the annuity in full, the will may direct the PRs to make up the income from capital. If they do so, that capital is treated as income from which basic rate tax must be deducted (*Brodie's Will Trusts v IRC* (1933)). The unfortunate result of such 'top-up' provisions is to convert capital into income and it is, therefore, better to give the PRs a discretion to make good any shortfall in the annuity by capital advances (see **[16.68]**). [17.47]

5 Residuary beneficiaries

A beneficiary may have a limited, an absolute, or a discretionary interest in residue. A limited interest exists where he is entitled to income only, eg if the will leaves residue to 'my wife for life, remainder to my children', the wife is entitled only to income from the estate. An absolute interest exists when the beneficiary is entitled to both the income and capital of the residue, as where the residue is left to 'my wife absolutely'. A discretionary interest exists where a discretion must be exercised in favour of a residuary beneficiary to pay any income to him. [17.48]

a) *Beneficiary with a limited interest in residue*

Any income paid to the beneficiary during the administration period will be paid net of tax deducted by the PRs. The beneficiary must gross up these sums, at the tax rate applicable in the year of *receipt by him* to that category of income, as part of his total income in the year of receipt for the purposes of his excess liability or to obtain a repayment of tax (as appropriate). Where any sum remains payable on completion of administration, it is treated as being the income of the beneficiary in the tax year in which the administration ends (ITTOIA 2005 ss 654–655). [17.49]–[17.51]

EXAMPLE 17.6

Mandy died on 6 March 2016 leaving her residuary estate to Shirley for life with remainder to Jemima. The interest income of the estate was:

Tax year	Amount before tax (£)	Amount after tax (£)
2015–16 (net of tax)	3,000	3,000
2016–17 (gross)*	12,500	10,000
2017–18 (gross)*	1,000	800
Total	£16,500	£13,800

* As the tax liability for 2016–17 and 2017–18 exceeds £100, the transitional measure announced by HMRC does not apply (see [17.21]). The PRs will have to pay income tax of £2,500 in 2016–17 and £200 in 2017–18 on the interest received, thereby leaving £10,000 in 2016–17 and £800 in 2017–18 to be distributed to Shirley.

However, payments made to Shirley were:

Tax year	Amount (£)
2015–16	nil
2016–17	9,000
2017–18	4,800
Total	£13,800

Shirley is taxed on the payments in the tax years of receipt, ie in 2016–17 and 2017–18.

Note: If at the end of administration there is an undistributed income balance it is deemed to have been paid to the beneficiary in the tax year when the administration ended (this being the one exception to the receipts basis). For instance, if the administration of Mandy's estate was completed on 4 April 2017, the undistributed income balance of £4,800 would be taxed on Shirley in 2016–17 even though she did not receive it until the following tax year.

b) *Beneficiary with an absolute interest in residue*

Such a beneficiary is entitled to receive both income and capital from the estate. He can, of course, only be charged to income tax in so far as any payments that he receives represent income. The position is that:

(1) payments during administration are taxed as income up to the amount of the aggregate income entitlement of the beneficiary for the year of assessment in which the sum is paid (see ITTOIA 2005 s 652): ('*aggregate income entitlement*' means the net income to which the beneficiary is entitled);

(2) if on completion of the administration the beneficiary has not received his full aggregate entitlement to income, the shortfall is treated as having been paid to him immediately before the end of the administration period; and

(3) the beneficiary must gross up the sums treated as income, at the tax rate applicable in the year of *receipt by him* to that category of income, as part

of his total income in the year of receipt for the purposes of his excess liability or to obtain a repayment of tax (as appropriate). **[17.52]**

EXAMPLE 17.7

Simon died on 6 March 2016 leaving his entire estate to Dorothy. The PRs transfer a painting worth £63,000 to Dorothy on 5 April 2017. Interest income arising to the estate was as follows:

Tax year	Amount before tax (£)	Amount after tax (£)
2015–16 (net of tax)	3,000	3,000
2016–17 (gross)*	12,500	10,000
2017–18 (gross)*	1,000	800
Total	£16,500	13,800

* The transitional measure does not apply to the income of Simon's estate, as the tax liability exceeds £100 (see **[17.21]**). The PRs will have to pay £2,500 income tax in 2016–17 and £200 income tax in 2017–18 on the gross interest received, thereby leaving £10,000 and £800 respectively to be distributed to Dorothy.

(1) *Tax year 2015–16* Assuming that no payment is made to Dorothy, £3,000 is carried forward to 2016–17. Therefore as at 5 April 2016 Dorothy's aggregated income entitlement is £3,000.

(2) *Tax year 2016–17* At 6 April 2017 Dorothy's aggregated income entitlement, assuming no payments were made in 2016–17, is £13,000. One would assume that the transfer of the painting represents capital rather than income. However, following ITTOIA 2005 s 681, the first £13,000 of the value of the painting is treated as income.

(3) *Tax year 2017–18* Assuming the administration period has ended and the estate is distributed, Dorothy will be taxed on the remaining income of £800 (£1,000 received gross less tax due of £200).

Notes:
(a) The timing of the payment in the tax year is irrelevant: it could for instance occur on 6 April 2016 but nonetheless it is Dorothy's aggregated income entitlement at 5 April 2016 that is crucial.
(b) The rules apply to the payment of 'any sum': it is not possible for the PRs to specify that the payment is 'of capital'. Furthermore, HMRC considers that for these purposes the payment of 'any sum' includes a transfer of assets or release of a debt. It will therefore treat the value of such assets as income up to the amount of the beneficiary's aggregated income entitlement (ITTOIA 2005 s 681).

Position when a multiplicity of beneficiaries: In this situation income arising during administration must be split between beneficiaries in the same proportion as their capital shares (see ITTOIA 2005 s 667 referring to a 'proportionate part' of the residuary income). Further complexity arises from the different types of estate income: this too needs to be split proportionately between the beneficiaries (see ITTOIA 2005 ss 656 and 679). Section 679 determines the order of distributions in that payments are first made from income bearing tax at the basic rate and then income bearing tax at the dividend ordinary rate. **[17.53]**

EXAMPLE 17.8

Adam's estate is to be divided between Betty (50%); Claude (25%) and David (25%). In 2015–16 the net income of the estate was £16,000 made up of:

Rental income	£4,000 after tax. The PRs paid tax at 20% on £5,000 gross rental income.
Savings income	£2,000 (credit for 20%)
Dividends	£10,000 (credit for 10% non-reclaimable divided tax)

(i) Aggregated income entitlement for 2015–16

Type of income (net)	Betty (50%)	Claude (25%)	David (25%)
Non-savings income	2,000.00	1,000.00	1,000.00
Savings income	1,000.00	500.00	500.00
Dividend income	5,000.00	2,500.00	2,500.00
£16,000	£8,000.00	£4,000.00	£4,000.00

(ii) Treatment of income distribution in the year

Assuming that during the same year, 2015–16, each beneficiary received one half of his aggregated income entitlement for the year, the position would be:

	Betty (£)	Claude (£)	David (£)
Receipt	4,000.00	2,000.00	2,000.00
made up of:			
Basic rate income	3,000.00	1,500.00	1,500.00
–grossed-up equivalent at 20%	3,750.00	1,875.00	1,875.00
–20% tax credit	750.00	375.00	375.00
Non-reclaimable dividend	1,000.00	500.00	500.00
–grossed-up equivalent at 10%	1,111.11	555.55	555.55
–10% tax credit	111.11	55.55	55.55

Notes:
(1) Each beneficiary would carry forward any aggregated income entitlement to the next tax year: in Betty's case this would be £4,000 of dividend income.
(2) Each beneficiary is considered separately and a distribution to one beneficiary may not be matched by an equivalent distribution to another in that tax year. For instance, in 2015–16 the PRs may distribute income to Claude but not to Betty or David. Of course, ultimately income of the estate must be split in the ratio 50:25:25 and so the other beneficiaries' shares must be made good in the future.
(3) What if tax rates change between receipt of income by PRs and its distribution? ITTOIA 2005 ss 663 and 670 provide for income to be paid with the appropriate credit for rates of tax current in the year of payment not in the year of receipt by PRs.

Here the beneficiaries receive the remaining income during the 2016–17 tax year, when the tax rate for dividends has changed from a notional tax credit of 10% to a tax rate of 7.5%.

The 7.5% tax due on the dividends from 6 April 2016 is refundable and will be credited to the beneficiary but the now reduced 7.5% tax credit on dividends received prior to 6 April will be non-refundable.

The administration of Adam's estate continues in 2016–17 and the income of the estate is as follows. The administration period comes to an end on 30 March 2017.

	Gross	Tax	Net
Rental income	£2,000	£400	£1,600
Savings income	£500	£100	£400
Dividends	£5,000	£375	£4,625
Total	£7,500	£875	£6,625

(iii) Aggregated income entitlement for 2016–17

Type of income (net)	Betty (50%)	Claude (25%)	David (25%)
Non-savings income	800.00	400.00	400.00
Savings income	200.00	100.00	100.00
Non-reclaimable dividend income for 2015–16	4,000.00	2,000.00	2,000.00
Reclaimable dividend income for 2016–17	2,312.50	1,156.25	1,156.25
£14,625	£7,312.50	£3,656.25	£3,656.25

	Betty (£)	Claude (£)	David (£)
Receipt	7,312.50	3,656.25	3,656.25
made up of:			
Rental income	800.00	400.00	400.00
– *grossed-up equivalent at 20%*	*1,000.00*	*500.00*	*500.00*
– *20% tax credit*	*200.00*	*100.00*	*100.00*
Savings income	200.00	100.00	100.00
– *grossed-up equivalent at 20%*	*250.00*	*125.00*	*125.00*
– *20% tax credit*	*50.00*	*25.00*	*25.00*
Non-reclaimable dividend rate	4,000.00	2,000.00	2,000.00
– *grossed-up equivalent at 7.5%*	*4,324.32*	*2,162.16*	*2,162.16*
– *7.5% non-reclaimable tax credit*	*324.32*	*162.16*	*162.16*
Reclaimable dividend rate	2,312.50	1,156.25	1,156.25
– *grossed-up equivalent at 7.5%*	*2,500.00*	*1,250.00*	*1,250.00*
– *7.5% reclaimable tax credit*	*187.50*	*93.75*	*93.75*

Note that the dividends carried forward from 2015–16 will be distributed with a non-reclaimable tax credit of 7.5% rather than 10%. The tax paid on the dividends received during 2016–17 will be recoverable by the beneficiaries if they have the relevant dividends allowance of £5,000 during 2016–17 available.

(c) *Relief against a double charge*

Income which accrued before death, but is received by the PRs after death, is included in the value of the deceased's estate for IHT purposes and is also taxed as the income of the estate (see **[17.3]**). Some relief against this double taxation is provided by ITTOIA 2005 s 669 that allows a reduction in the residuary income for the purposes of any liability to higher rate tax of a residuary beneficiary absolutely entitled to residue. The reduction is of an amount equal to the IHT chargeable on that income at the estate rate and the resultant sum is then grossed up at the basic rate of income tax or dividend ordinary rate) for the tax year in which the charge to higher rate arises. **[17.54]**

EXAMPLE 17.9

Xavier died on 30 April 2017. His will was dated 1 April 2006 and the apportionment rules were not excluded. He left his residuary estate including 1,000 debentures in B Ltd to his daughter Deborah. His PRs received interest of £200 gross from B Ltd in November 2017. (B Ltd's accounting year ended 31 October 2017). The whole interest is taxed as the income of the estate but, as half the interest accrued before death, that portion is included in Xavier's estate for IHT purposes. Under ITTOIA 2005 s 669, if Deborah is a higher rate taxpayer, one half of the interest is eligible for relief. Assume that the estate rate of IHT is 30%.

	£
Interest (gross)	£200
Sum accrued before death	100
Less: income tax for year of death	20
	£80
The relief is calculated as:	£
£80 × 30% (IHT estate rate)	24
Grossed-up (at 20%) amount that can be deducted from the residuary income to reduce D's liability to higher rate income tax only	£30

(d) *Beneficiary with a discretionary interest in residue*

A beneficiary with a discretionary interest in residue is taxed on the amount paid to him in the tax year the discretion was exercised. The beneficiary is assessed on the basic amount grossed up at the applicable tax rate.

6 Conclusions

a) *Position of PRs*

The payments basis of assessment for residuary beneficiaries means that the dates of payment or conclusion of administration are critical: if all payments are bunched in a single tax year this may push the beneficiary into the higher rate of income tax.

When deciding upon the timing of distributions, therefore, PRs need to consider the effect of 'bunching' and what effect distributions of income during the administration period have on the tax position of the beneficiaries. To do this the PRs will need to know the financial and fiscal circumstances of each beneficiary. **[17.55]–[17.56]**

b) *Successive interests in residue*

ITTOIA 2005 ss 671–675 provide for the situation where an interest in the whole or part of the residue is held successively by different persons during the course of administration. In the case of instruments of variation (as to which see [30.153]) the result is that, provided no distributions have been made to the original beneficiary before the variation, all income will be assessed on the new beneficiary. The same applies to a change of beneficiary as the result of an exercise by the PRs of a power of appointment. In the case of a beneficiary with a limited interest in residue, eg a life tenant, dying during the course of the administration, any income that would otherwise be due to the deceased life tenant, up to and including the day he died, is payable (in the absence of a contrary indication in the will) to his own PRs and assessable on them accordingly. [17.57]

IV DISCLAIMERS, VARIATIONS AND APPOINTMENTS UNDER IHTA 1984 S 144

1 Income tax consequences of disclaimers, variations and appointments under IHTA 1984 s 144

For inheritance tax (see [30.153]) and certain aspects of capital gains tax (see [21.121]) a variation rewrites the provisions of the will and therefore is deemed to be effected by the deceased, and a disclaimed benefit is treated as though it had never been conferred, if certain conditions are complied with. In a similar fashion for appointments under IHTA 1984 s 144, where an appointment is made out of a discretionary will trust within two years of date of death, the appointment is read back to the date of death for IHT purposes and there is no CGT disposal.

A variation, however, has no effect for income tax or capital gains tax purposes (*Marshall v Kerr* (1994) – see [21.124]). Therefore, if the original beneficiary effects a variation which creates a settlement where either he or his spouse can benefit, the settlement will be subject to the anti-avoidance provisions in ITTOIA 2005 s 624 (see [16.98] ff) and any income of the settlement will continue to be taxed on the original beneficiary.

EXAMPLE 17.10

Fred dies leaving his estate absolutely to his wife Daisy. For asset protection purposes the solicitor dealing with the estate advises Daisy to effect a deed of variation to pass £325,000 (the available nil rate band at the date of Fred's death) into a discretionary trust with Daisy and her adult children as beneficiaries.

Following ITTOIA 2005 s 624, this settlement will be treated as 'settlor-interested' for income tax purposes and all the income will have to be treated as Daisy's and will have to be included in her tax return.

The anti-avoidance provisions in ITTOIA 2005 s 629 provide that where a parent effects a deed of variation or disclaims his interest in an estate in favour of an unmarried minor child, the income will be assessed on the parent during an unmarried child's minority.

EXAMPLE 17.11

Jennifer is the sole beneficiary of her father's substantial estate. As Jennifer has no need for the money, she would like either to vary her father's will or to disclaim her interest and to pass the estate to her twin children Jack and Jill who are 7 years old.

This 'writing-back' works well for inheritance tax under IHTA 1984 s 142, but for income tax purposes it is deemed to be a parental settlement under ITTOIA 2005 s 629 and the income of the fund will be taxed on Jennifer during her unmarried twins' minority. These provisions apply even if the income is not distributed but accumulated. [17.58]

2 Treatment of income up to the date of variation, disclaimer or s 144 appointment

As it is not possible to disclaim an interest in an estate once benefit under it has been accepted, it is generally acknowledged that any income accruing up to the date of disclaimer is transferred to the person who will benefit from the disclaimed interest and liability will fall on him accordingly.

Where an instrument of variation has been effected, any income up to the date of variation will be deemed the income of the original beneficiary unless the variation provides otherwise. Any transferred income will be taxed on the new beneficiary. The same applies to appointments under s 144.

Where the gift is made out of a specific legacy or devise, the income/interest up to the date of variation remains that of the original beneficiary regardless of its treatment under the variation.

In cases where the gift is made out of residue, the interest/income will be that of the original beneficiary to the extent that it can be identified with any distribution to him on account of that entitlement, regardless of whether it subsequently passes elsewhere under the variation.

In contrast, court orders made under the Inheritance (Provisions for Family and Dependants) Act 1975 are retrospective to the date of death, even for income tax purposes. [17.59]

V CLEARANCES

Before completing the distribution of an estate the PRs should obtain clearance from HMRC. They should write to the relevant tax office requesting confirmation that the tax affairs of both the deceased for the period to the date of death, and of the PRs for the administration period, are clear. Notwithstanding the normal time limits within which HMRC are entitled to enquire into a return, in circumstances where it is desired to complete the distribution of an estate they will normally grant early confirmation that they do not intend to enquire into a return. However, this does not preclude HMRC from opening an enquiry at a later stage. [17.60]

18 The overseas dimension

Updated by Helen McGhee, Senior Associate, Joseph Hage Aaronson LLP

I   Residence and domicile [**18.2**]
II Taxation of foreign income [**18.31**]
III Taxation of the non-resident taxpayer [**18.71**]
IV Double taxation relief [**18.91**]
V   Anti-avoidance legislation: transfer of assets abroad (ITA 2007 Part 13 Chapter 2) [**18.110**]

'The [UK resident] is taxed because (whether he be a British subject or not) he enjoys the benefit of our laws for the protection of his person and his property. The [non-UK resident] is taxed because in respect of his property in the United Kingdom he enjoys the benefit of our laws for the protection of that property.'
(*Whitney v IRC* (1926) 10 TC 88 at 112.)

The territorial scope of any tax raises both theoretical and practical questions. A strong element of practical reality inevitably permeates this area: theoretically the UK could impose a tax on the Chinese income of a Chinaman resident in China but little revenue would be raised from that source! The practical constraints upon tax collection and enforcement are well illustrated in the House of Lords' speeches in *Clark v Oceanic Contractors Inc* (1983): see [**18.51**] – but see also *Agassi v Robinson* (2006).

The 'connecting factors' that determine the extent to which the individual should be subject to income tax are now residence and domicile and the meaning of these terms will be considered in this chapter. Ordinary residence used to be relevant but this concept has now been abolished. This discussion will also be relevant when the territorial scope of CGT, IHT and corporation tax are considered (in **Chapter 41**).

As a general rule, a UK resident is subject to UK income tax on all his income worldwide wherever its source, whereas a foreign resident is only liable to UK income tax on income arising to him in the UK. In some circumstances, a foreign domiciled but UK resident individual may be taxed on foreign income if it is remitted to the UK. [**18.1**]

I RESIDENCE AND DOMICILE

1 Residence: introduction

Until 6 April 2013, when the statutory residence test took effect, the meaning of 'residence', not being defined in any statute, had to be determined from decisions of the courts, with guidance as to the practice of HMRC set out in HMRC 6 and, for earlier periods, IR 20. The dictionary definition of the word 'resident' was usually adopted for taxation purposes. Questions of residence do not generally depend upon any mental element (unlike domicile), hence the American who finds himself stuck in the UK because of extra work commitments may become resident here although his intention is to return to America as soon as those commitments are over.

A person can be resident in more than one country at the same time so that the individual who spends the winter months in Manchester and the summer in the Costa del Sol could be resident both in the UK and in Spain. Alternatively, an individual may not be resident anywhere as in the case of the travel writer who spends two years exploring South America by bus and is, therefore, continually on the move. Residence is related to particular tax years. It is possible to split tax years into periods of residence and non-residence under the statutory residence test but under general principles the individual who is resident for any part of a tax year is treated as being resident for the whole of that year.

Before April 2013, the splitting of tax years with periods of residence and non-residence for income tax purposes was applied by concession under ESC A11. This applied when an individual left the UK for permanent residence abroad or when an individual came to the UK for permanent residence or to stay for at least two years. In the former case, UK residence was treated as ceasing on the day following the day of departure from the UK: in the latter, UK residence was treated as having been acquired from the day of arrival. A similar splitting of the tax year could occur when an individual left the UK to take up full-time employment abroad or to work full time in a trade or profession.

The position for CGT was slightly different. There was a corresponding concession (ESC D2) which provided for the tax year to be split in a similar fashion, but only where the individual leaving the UK had not been resident or ordinarily resident for at least four out of the seven years preceding the year of departure. For individuals coming to the UK, to benefit from split year treatment for CGT purposes they had to be non-resident for at least five years prior to the year of arrival.

This concessionary practice does not apply for the tax year 2013–14 and subsequent years (but remains applicable for earlier years). As mentioned, since 6 April 2013 there is a statutory split year provision which enables individuals in certain cases to claim split year treatment and this statutory provision replaces the concessionary practice.

The statutory residence test applies for income tax and capital gains tax but not for the purposes of national insurance contributions (NICs). The concept of ordinary residence has been abolished from 6 April 2013 for income tax and capital gains tax purposes but not for NICs. **[18.2]**

2 The position prior to 6 April 2013

a) *Who is a UK resident?*

An individual would be regarded as a resident in the UK in the following circumstances:

(i) The '183-day' rule

If he spent more than 182 days here (even in a leap year), an individual would be resident in the UK. This rule is derived from ITA 2007 ss 831 and 832. Until 6 April 2008 it was possible to count hours and minutes in determining whether the 183-day limit had been breached: see *Wilkie v IRC* (1952). From 6 April 2008 the days are counted on the basis of nights spent in the UK – although presence in the UK in transit would be disregarded providing while in transit the individual did not engage in activities that were to a substantial extent unrelated to their passage through the UK.

This 183-day rule was absolute and applied even if the days in the UK were for exceptional circumstances (for example by reason of the illness of the taxpayer or a member of his immediate family). See *Ogden v R & C Comrs* (2011). [18.3]

(ii) The '91-day' rule

A person who had left the UK for permanent residence abroad was regarded as resident here if his visits to the UK averaged 91 days or more per tax year over a four-year period. In cases where it was clear that the taxpayer intended to make such visits he was treated as resident either from the year of his arrival or from the year when he formed that intention (if later). For this purpose 'any days spent in the UK because of *exceptional circumstances beyond an individual's control* (such as illness) were excluded from the calculation'.
[18.4]

EXAMPLE 18.1

(1) Barry comes to England from America to study law at London University. The course is to last three years. As Barry will be present in the UK for more than six months in each of those tax years he is UK resident from the date of his arrival.

(2) Ellie regularly comes to the UK on holiday from America. Her visits do not exceed two months per annum. She would not be treated as UK resident.

(iii) Available accommodation

The individual who had UK accommodation available for his use and who merely set foot in this country (even if he did not visit that accommodation) used to be treated as UK resident.

In 1993 the 'available accommodation' test was abolished. In establishing an individual's residence in the UK, no regard shall be paid to living accommodation available for that person's use in the UK (see ITA 2007 ss 831(1) and 832(1)).

However, the existence of living accommodation continued to be relevant for all other purposes and was regarded as significant by HMRC in judging the intentions of the individual even though intention was not a determinant of residence. [18.5]

EXAMPLE 18.2

Toki, an international playboy, comes to London each year for 'the season'. If he rents a flat in London for the period, that will not by itself make him UK resident and, provided that he does not remain in the UK for 91 days in any tax year, he will not become resident.

(iv) Occasional Residence Abroad

The absence of a person from the UK *throughout* a tax year was evidence that he was not resident in that year.

Under ITA 2007 s 829 an individual who had been resident and ordinarily resident in the UK and who left for *occasional residence* abroad continued to be liable to income tax in the same way as a UK resident. In *Reed v Clark* (1985), it was held that TA 1988 s 334 (now ITA 2007 s 829) was a charging provision and was not limited to persons who were out of the UK for part only of a tax year but could equally apply to persons living abroad throughout a year of assessment. In that case, the taxpayer (the pop star Dave Clark) left the UK with the deliberate intention of living and working abroad for a limited period in excess of one tax year and then returning to the UK. The judge held that his absence could not be described as for the purpose of merely occasional residence abroad so he was not treated as UK resident under TA 1988 s 334 (now ITA 2007 s 829). Occasional residence under this section was to be contrasted with ordinary or settled residence.

> 'The presence of a tax avoidance intention may help to show, for instance, why a person went abroad at all or at the particular time he did, how long he intended to remain away, or where his home in fact was in the year of assessment. But residence abroad for a carefully chosen limited period of work there ... is no less residence abroad for that period because the major reason for it was the avoidance of tax.
>
> (Nicholls J, at 346.)

Where the individual had *not* become resident elsewhere it was difficult to show that he did not remain UK resident. For the tax treatment of mobile workers (those who come to the UK during the week to work and live elsewhere, or those who live in the UK but spend the working week abroad) see *Tax Bulletin*, April 2001, p 836 and *Taxation*, 26 April 2001, p 81. See also *Shepherd v R & C Comrs* (2005) and *Grace v R & C Comrs* (2008) where the Special Commissioner summarised the principles to be adopted in determining residence.

In *Tuczka v R & C Comrs* (2011) the Upper Tribunal confirmed that coming to the UK for the purpose of an employment is a settled purpose sufficient to make the person ordinarily resident shortly after his arrival. This decision contrasts with *Genovese v R & C Comrs* (2009) where it was held that ordinary residence did not arise until three years after the arrival in the UK. [18.6]

b) *Acquiring and losing resident status*

An individual who came to the UK with the intention of taking up permanent residence was by concession regarded as both resident and ordinarily resident only from the date of his arrival. By contrast, a short-term visitor would not become UK resident unless he fell within the 91-day rule. The casual UK resident (eg one who spends an isolated six months here) would lose his resident status simply by returning abroad.

Where a person left the UK seeking to establish residence in another country it was not enough merely to restrict the visits to the UK to fewer than 91 days. This would have appeared to be the rule from IR20 but following the publication of HMRC Brief 01/07, HMRC explained their view that the 91-day test was not applicable to a person leaving the UK; it only applies to somebody who has left the UK, became non-resident and subsequently made short visits to the UK. This view was upheld by the Supreme Court in *Gaines-Cooper v R & C Comrs* (2011). No guidance was provided by HMRC regarding the meaning of leaving the UK other than the need for there to be a distinct break in the pattern of the taxpayer's life. There was accordingly no safe number of days for which a departing resident could return to the UK while seeking to establish non-residence.

This point was reinforced by the decision in *Grace v R & C Comrs* (2011). Despite the fact that Mr Grace returned to the UK for only 41 days, 71 days and 70 days in the three years of assessment after his departure, he was nevertheless held to be resident because his visits to the UK were not for a temporary purpose but for the purposes of his employment.

In *Gaines-Cooper v R & C Comrs* (2010) the Court of Appeal said that to lose UK residence it was necessary to 'sever social and family ties' with the UK but this test was held by the Supreme Court to be too strong a test. A distinct break is necessary but this only involves a substantive loosening of ties with the UK (see *Rumbelow v R & C Comrs* (2013) for a further discussion on the meaning of these concepts). The First-tier Tribunal thought that the taxpayer in *Glyn v R & C Comrs* (2013) had changed his pattern of life to a satisfactory extent by careful planning and documentation and therefore was able to demonstrate his distinct break, but the Upper Tribunal have since allowed HMRC's appeal in this case and found that the First-tier Tribunal made errors in determining Mr Glynn to be non UK resident in the relevant years (2015).

Where an individual went abroad to work, the HMRC practice was clearer. An individual may go abroad for full-time service under a contract of employment that requires all the duties of his employment to be performed abroad (with any UK duties being merely incidental). Providing his absence from the UK lasted for a complete tax year with interim visits to the UK not exceeding six months in any tax year (or an average of 91 days per tax year for four years), he would normally be regarded as neither resident nor ordinarily resident in the UK from the day following the date of his departure. (For the meaning of 'incidental duties', see *Robson v Dixon* (1972)).

In April 2011 HMRC stated that their practice was that, in determining whether an employment is being carried out full time abroad, they disregarded ten days of work in the UK whether or not they represented incidental duties.

It was confirmed in *Davies and James v R & C Comrs* (2010) that if an individual took up full time employment abroad, that would be sufficient to effect a distinct break and no further loosening of ties would be necessary. Whether this view taken by HMRC was reasonable was brought into question in *Darrell Healey v R & C Comrs* (2014). [18.7]

3 The position from 6 April 2013: the statutory residence test

The statutory residence test comprises three tests. The first test can make an individual conclusively non-resident; the second can make him conclusively resident; if neither of these is determinative, resort must be had to the third test where the number of days an individual is allowed in the UK will depend on a number of connecting factors called 'UK ties'. The general idea is that someone who has been UK resident for three years will find it more difficult to shed UK residence status than someone who has not. [18.8]

a) *The first test: automatic non-residence*

An individual will be automatically non-resident for the tax year if:
(i) he was resident in none of the previous 3 years and spent fewer than 46 days in the tax year in the UK; or
(ii) he was resident in any of the last 3 years and spent fewer than 16 days in the UK; or
(iii) he left the UK to carry out full time work abroad and spent fewer than 91 days in the tax year and no more than 30 working days in the UK.

If the individual satisfies any of these conditions he will be conclusively non-resident whatever else may happen. If he should die during the tax year, special rules apply.

If the individual is in breach of any of these conditions, he cannot satisfy this test and would not be conclusively non-resident. However, that would not make him resident, it would mean moving to the second test. [18.9]

b) *The second test: automatic residence*

An individual will be automatically resident for the tax year if:
(i) he spends more than 182 days in the UK; or
(ii) he has only one home, which is in the UK and he is present there for 30 days in the tax year; or
(iii) he has a home in the UK in which he is present throughout any period of 91 consecutive days (of which at least 30 days are in the tax year) and either he has no home overseas, or if he does, he spends fewer than 30 days there in the tax year; or
(iv) he carries out full time work in the UK.

If an individual dies during the tax year, special rules apply. If the individual satisfies both these automatic tests, the first test takes priority and he will be conclusively non-resident. Where neither of the above tests conclusively determines a person's residence, the third test must be applied. [18.10]

c) *The third test: UK ties*

This test provides five UK ties:
(i) spouse or minor children being resident in the UK;
(ii) the existence and use of place to live in the UK;

(iii) work in the UK for at least 40 days;
(iv) presence in the UK for more than 90 days in either of the previous two years;
(v) more days in the UK than any other single country (this is applicable to 'leavers' only).

The importance of these UK ties depends upon whether an individual is an 'arriver' (someone who was not resident for the last three tax years) or a 'leaver' (someone who was resident in UK in any of the last three tax years). If the individual dies during the tax year, special rules apply.

An arriver will be resident by reference to a combination of day count and the UK ties according to the following table:

Days in the UK	Ties
0–45	Always non resident
46–90	4 factors = resident
91–120	3 factors = resident
121–182	2 factors = resident
over 182	Always resident

A leaver will be resident by reference to a combination of day count and the UK ties according to the following table:

Days in the UK	Ties
0–15	Always non resident
16–45	4 factors = resident
46–90	3 factors = resident
91–120	2 factors = resident
121–182	1 factor = resident
over 182	Always resident

The following points need to be taken into account when drawing conclusions from the above:
- Full time work in the UK for the automatic tests means 35 hours a week for more than 365 days (excluding holidays) with no significant breaks.
- Work in the UK means 40 working days in the tax year for the ties test.
- A working day is more than 3 hours – and counts whether or not an individual is in the UK at midnight. What constitutes work is unclear; it can include travelling if the person is working during the journey.
- The statutory day (or rather, night) count rules in FA 2008 s 24 will apply in the same way to determine the number of days in the UK. These have therefore become much more important because they are now relevant to every figure in the above tables and not only the 183-day test for which they were introduced. They will need to be subject to much closer examination, particularly in relation to transit visits where days in the UK can be disregarded if they consist of engaging in 'activities that are to a substantial extent unrelated to the individual's passage through the UK'.

- There is a further deeming rule which applies when determining the number of days in the UK under certain circumstances. If a person has more than three UK ties and has been resident in the UK in any one of the previous three years (ie a leaver), any days of presence spent in the UK in excess of 30 will be counted. In that case, any day of presence in the UK (not including midnight) in excess of 30 will be treated as a day in the UK for determining the day count in the above tables.
- There is no definition of 'home' for the automatic tests but it includes any building, vehicle, vessel or structure used as a home and with a sufficient degree of permanence or stability to count as a home. It does not include a holiday home or a temporary retreat. A home is certainly not the same as having a place to live for the UK ties test. A 'place to live' includes anywhere where the individual can live (including a holiday home and even a hotel room) and is available for a continuous period of more than 91 days (and he actually spends one night there) during the year. The continuous period is not really continuous – gaps of up to 15 days will be counted. It also includes staying with relatives for more than 15 nights during the year.
- There are some transitional provisions. These new rules will only determine the position for 2013–14 and subsequent years, but where residence for an earlier year is relevant, it is possible to elect for the new tests to be used for that purpose. However, this election is only for assisting with the determination of the individual's absence for 2013–14 and subsequent years; it has no effect on the actual residence for prior years.
- There is an exclusion for exceptional days, ie those days spent in the UK for reasons outside of an individual's control, but limited to 60 days. This is a much stricter test than the previous HMRC practice. **[18.11]**

d) *Split year treatment*

There are some special rules which enable the tax year to be split into resident and non-resident periods for people arriving or leaving the UK. There are eight different circumstances in which split year treatment can apply, three dealing with leaving the UK and five dealing with arriving in the UK. They include arriving and leaving the UK for work, and, include provisions for the accompanying spouse.

Where split year treatment applies the tax year will be divided into periods of residence and non-residence and the individual will only be taxable in the UK on income referable to the period of residence. **[18.12]**

e) *Temporary non residence*

Under FA 2013 s 110 and Sch 45, where an individual has been non-resident for five years or fewer and was previously resident for four out of the prior seven years, certain income arising during his period of non-residence can be taxed in the year of return. This resonates with the capital gains tax rule for temporary non residence in TCGA 1992 s 10A and with the similar rule that applies to income on the remittance basis – but this FA 2013 rule is for five years or fewer, which means that to escape these provisions the period of absence must be for at least six years. **[18.13]**

4 Ordinary residence

Ordinary residence has been abolished from 6 April 2013 for income tax and capital gains tax purposes (but not for NIC). Those provisions which previously referred to ordinary residence such as those relating to FOTRA Securities, the transfer of assets abroad legislation, earnings related provisions and numerous others will now apply to individuals resident in the UK.

Although largely now of historical significance only, it is worth briefly outlining some principles regarding ordinary residence.

Before 6 April 2013, ordinary residence meant a choice of abode adopted voluntarily and which had a settled purpose and formed part of the regular order of an individual's life (see, in particular, *R v Barnet London Borough Council, ex p Nilish Shah* (1983)). A person could be resident without being ordinarily resident in the UK and probably *vice versa*. HMRC 6 stated at para 3.2 that an individual would be ordinarily resident if:

(a) he comes to the UK voluntarily – which includes coming to the UK at the request of the employer;
(b) the presence in the UK has a settled purpose – even for a limited period;
(c) the presence in the UK forms part of the regular and habitual mode of the individual's life.

It was also suggested by HMRC that coming to the UK to live and work for three years or more would establish an habitual mode of life in the UK. This view was supported by the Special Commissioners in *Genovese v R & C Comrs* (2009) but with regards to the timing of the commencement of residence *Genovese* was held to be wrongly decided in *Tuczka v R & C Comrs* (2011) which held that ordinary residence commences almost immediately on arrival in the UK if the individual comes to this country to work.

In *Nessa v Chief Adjudication Officer* (2000) the House of Lords considered the meaning of 'habitual residence' in the context of the Income Support Regulations and concluded that a mere intention to live in a place was insufficient: there must be actual residence for a period which showed that it had become habitual. A similar construction is likely to apply to ordinary residence which casts doubt on HMRC's view that a person who comes to the UK permanently was both resident and ordinarily resident from his date of arrival (see HMRC 6 para 7.2).

EXAMPLE 18.4

(1) Bonzo has lived in Hackney for many years. He sold his terraced house in February 2010 and went on a world cruise for 18 months. He may have ceased to be UK resident (see **[18.7]**) but he would have remained ordinarily resident.
(2) Claude, a French student, visited the UK for six months in 2012–13 to study the eating habits of the natives. He became UK resident but not ordinarily resident. **[18.14]**

Although not in name, the concept of ordinary residence has been somewhat preserved by a statutory relief introduced to preserve the remittance basis for foreign domiciled individuals only who have not been UK resident for three years prior to their arrival. This 'overseas work day relief' allows overseas earnings to qualify for the remittance basis for two years following the individual's arrival in the UK. [18.15]

5 Corporations

Prior to 15 March 1988, any company was resident in the UK (and therefore subject to corporation tax on its worldwide profits) if its central management and control was located in the UK. Central management and control was considered to be located at the place where board meetings were held and not necessarily where the company was incorporated or registered (see *De Beers Consolidated Mines v Howe* (1906) and SP 1/90 and *Wood v Holden* (2006)).

EXAMPLE 18.5

The directors of a Kenyan subsidiary company always held meetings in Kenya but in fact the company was managed, in breach of its articles, by its UK parent company. The company was therefore resident in the UK since the question was where the actual control and management was located. *Unit Construction Co Ltd v Bullock* (1959) and *Untelrab Ltd v McGregor* (1996) give details on this scenario, although in the latter case HMRC failed to prove that a subsidiary was managed and controlled by its UK parent company. This was supported more recently in *Wood v Holden* (2006).

From 15 March 1988 this control and management test was supplemented by a further test based on the place of company incorporation (see CTA 2009 ss 14 and 18). Companies incorporated in the UK will always be UK resident and will remain UK resident even if control and management is exercised abroad unless under the terms of a 'tie-breaker' article in a double tax treaty they would be treated as resident in the other treaty country. Foreign incorporated companies may become resident, as before, if their central management and control is situated in the UK. (See also *Laerstate BV v R & C Comrs* (2009) and HMRC guidance note July 2010). [18.16]

6 Partnerships

a) *Non-resident partnerships*

A similar central management and control test applies to partnerships. If the management and control of the business is exercised abroad, the firm is deemed to be non-resident even though individual partners may be resident in the UK. Conversely, a firm established abroad will be treated as resident in the UK if managed and controlled here. However, as a partnership is not normally taxed as a separate entity, the residence of the individual partners is much more important: ITTOIA 2005 s 849.

It appears that the forerunner of s 849 was aimed at clarifying the source classification of income from foreign controlled partnerships rather than altering the liability to tax of the individual partners. In practice, a foreign source is attributed to profits from foreign trading operations even when the firm also trades in the UK (this being treated as a UK source). This departs from the normal analysis of a trade as a single indivisible source. [18.17]

b) *Fiscal transparency*

HMRC will look through a partnership to the residence of its individual members for the purpose of determining the tax liability of each partner. So far as *UK source* income is concerned, individual members of a partnership will be subject to income tax whether UK resident or not. So far as *non-UK source* income is concerned, UK residents will be subject to tax in the UK whereas partners who are non-UK resident will not, although they may be taxable in the country where the profits are earned or, alternatively, in the country of their residence. In the case of a trading partnership which is itself managed and controlled in the UK, it is highly unlikely that a trade carried on, for instance, in France would be treated as being carried on wholly outside the UK and therefore the profits will attract tax under ITTOIA 2005 Part 9 (*Colquhoun v Brooks* (1889)). [18.18]

7 Trustees and personal representatives

a) *Residence of trustees*

The residence of a trust for income tax and capital gains tax purposes was aligned with effect from 5 April 2007; for income tax purposes, see ITA 2007 ss 475, 476. Where the settlor is resident and domiciled in the UK all the trustees must be resident outside the UK for the trust to be regarded as non resident. If the settlor is not resident and not domiciled, the trust will be UK resident only if all the trustees are UK resident; only one non resident trustee is sufficient to make the trust non resident in these circumstances. Where the settlor is not UK domiciled but is UK resident when establishing the trust, it will be UK resident if any of the trustees are UK resident at a time when funds are added to the trust. Assessments may be made in the name of any one or more of the trustees. A trustee will be treated as UK resident if he acts as trustee in the course of a business which he carries on through a branch, agency or permanent establishment in the UK: TCGA 1992 s 69(2D) and ITA 2007 s 475(6). The terms 'branch' and 'agency' apply to individual trustees and the reference to 'permanent establishment' applies to corporate trustees. Both expressions refer to the business of providing professional trustee services generally for a fee and not the business of the particular trust. It is necessary to consider those activities which are the core activities of a trustee and not activities which are merely preparatory. The core activities of a trustee would include the general administration of the trust, the investment strategy, monitoring the performance of the investments and making decisions about how the trust income should be dealt with. The approach of HMRC is to look at where these core activities are physically carried out and if they are carried out through a branch, agency or permanent establishment in the UK, the trustee will be treated as UK resident. [18.19]

EXAMPLE 18.6

(1) The de Vere family trust was set up in 1990 when the settlor was, and remains, neither resident nor domiciled in the UK. All the trustees are UK resident except one. The trust will not be resident in the UK.

(2) The Walpole trust was set up by a UK-resident unmarried settlor who is excluded from any benefit under the trust. It has since been exported and currently all the trustees are non-UK resident and there is no UK source income. There is no liability to UK income tax.

(3) The Vigo Trust was set up in May 2007 by a foreign domiciled settlor who is resident in the UK. There are two non-resident trustees and one UK-resident trustee. The trust will be UK resident.

b) *Tax status of trusts*

For income tax purposes the position is complicated by the distinction between trusts where the beneficiary has an immediate entitlement to the income (where the trustees are only liable for UK income tax at the basic rate) and other trusts (discretionary and accumulation) where liability to UK tax may be imposed in full on the trustees. Where the settlor and his spouse are incapable of benefiting from the trust it is only in the case of such 'other trusts' that the residence of trustees is of critical importance and in this connection it should be borne in mind that income arising in the UK is always subject to UK tax subject only to specific exemptions (for instance, income arising on FOTRA ('Free of Tax to Residents Abroad') securities under FA 1996 s 154). Non-resident trustees do not qualify for 'excluded income' treatment (see [**18.71**]) if a relevant beneficiary is UK resident.

Some trusts have a protector who may be UK resident. Save in exceptional circumstances (when the protector is given – or exercises – wider powers than normal) this will not cause the trust to be UK resident. The powers of a protector are fiduciary in nature (see *IRC v Schroder* (1983)). [**18.20**]

c) *Personal representatives*

ITA 2007 s 834 extended the residence rules for trustees to personal representatives and in so doing created an apparent injustice. Assume, for instance, that Dan Dare is an American domiciliary who comes to the UK to work or to start up a business. As it is envisaged that he will stay in this country for a number of years he acquires a house and other assets here and, accordingly, is advised to make a UK will (with UK personal representatives) disposing of this property. The bulk of his assets remain in America and a separate American will disposing of this property is also made. Assume then that Dan dies without having altered these arrangements. Under s 834, UK tax will be imposed on *all the income produced by his estate* passing under *both* wills since under his English will UK resident personal representatives have been appointed. As Dan is resident in the UK the conditions laid down for the operation of the section are satisfied given that the definition of personal representatives includes not just the UK appointees but also (in relation to another country) 'the persons having under its law any functions corresponding to the functions for administration purposes of personal representatives'. The end result appears unjust: surely UK tax should only be charged on UK source income arising under his UK estate? In practice, although no formal statement has been made, it is understood that HMRC apply the legislation in this way. [**18.21**]

8 Double tax treaties

A person may be resident in more than one country at the same time so most double tax treaties contain a provision to determine in which of the contracting countries a person is to be treated as resident (sometimes referred to as 'tie-breaker' clauses). It is important to realise that although the treaty may therefore lead to the person being treated as resident in one of the two countries, this will only apply for the purposes of the taxes and types of income and gains covered by the relevant treaty. For other purposes, the individual may still be treated as resident in the other country. [18.22]

9 Domicile

a) *Introduction*

The concept of domicile is extremely important having regard to the tax advantages that are allowed to individuals with a foreign domicile. A foreign domiciled individual resident in the UK can elect to be chargeable to UK tax on his foreign income and capital gains on the remittance basis, ie only if the income or gains are actually brought to or enjoyed in the UK.

Domicile is not the same as residence or nationality and should not be confused with either of them. An individual's domicile is generally the country that he regards as his home. It is where he has his closest ties and when he is away, the place to which he intends to return – although maybe not for some time.

There is a great deal talked about giving up clubs, changing nationality, selling property or even arranging to be buried in a foreign country. Whilst these things are relevant, they are rarely crucial except in marginal cases. Where an individual leaves the UK to live in another country, the maintenance of these connections could indicate some continuity of association with the UK that can be taken into account in deciding whether an expressed intention to reside permanently abroad is real or imaginary. In most cases, however, it will not be necessary to suffer the personal inconvenience and possibly the financial disadvantage of giving up these things. The UK might be a good place to invest, so investing money here should not necessarily indicate an intention to return (or a lack of intention to stay away). Many foreign domiciled individuals are members of clubs in the UK because when they visit the UK they can be assured of the use of the club's facilities. The ability to just turn up at a familiar club without making prior arrangements is obviously very convenient – all the more so if he is settled in another country and does not visit the UK very often.

Domicile is not specifically defined for tax purposes but takes its meaning from the general law which has developed over a very long period. There are various types of domicile and they all have different characteristics. [18.23]

b) *Domicile of origin*

The most important type of domicile is the domicile of origin which is acquired by an individual usually by reference to the domicile of his father at the time of his birth – where he was actually born has little or nothing to do with his domicile of origin. Accordingly if an individual is claiming to have a foreign domicile of origin, the circumstances of his parents at the time of his birth must be investigated – and account must also be taken of what he has done and where he has lived since reaching the age of 16 which is the age when an individual is able to acquire an independent domicile.

A domicile of origin is retained unless and until it is abandoned by the acquisition of a domicile of choice. In that event the domicile of origin goes into a kind of limbo, able to be revived if the domicile of choice is later abandoned without the acquisition of a further domicile of choice. An individual can never be without a domicile so if he were unable to satisfy the conditions for a domicile of choice, his domicile of origin would revive, even if he has no continuing connection with that country. The strange effects of this rule are explained in more detail below. [18.24]

c) *Domicile of choice*

A domicile of choice is acquired by satisfying two tests:
(1) physical residence in the chosen territory; and
(2) an intention of permanent or indefinite residence in that territory.

It is virtually impossible to acquire a domicile of choice in a country without actually residing there – so an individual cannot claim a foreign domicile of choice unless he has at least established a residence in that country.

It is also necessary to show an intention of permanent or indefinite residence in that country. Intention is a subjective matter and is therefore difficult to prove. It is not enough just to claim the necessary intention; HMRC will require positive proof and actions speak louder than words. It is obviously fatal to a claim for a domicile of choice in some foreign territory if there is an intention to return to the country of origin or indeed if there is an intention to leave and live somewhere else. If such an intention does exist the domicile of origin will continue. The actual conduct must therefore support the expressed intention to reside there permanently. If a person has a home in one country and visits it occasionally but spends most of their time somewhere else, it may be difficult to argue that there is sufficient commitment to that country to demonstrate an intention of permanent residence.

The individual may want to avoid acquiring a domicile of choice. Many people coming to live in the UK would prefer not to acquire a UK domicile of choice because of the substantial tax privileges that would immediately be lost. For those individuals it will be necessary to demonstrate that their period in the UK is for a specific or limited purpose and that their long-term intention is to leave the UK and either return to their country of origin, or to live somewhere else. Note that to avoid the acquisition of a UK domicile it is not necessary to show an intention to return to your country of origin; an intention to live anywhere but the UK, or indeed no intention at all, will do. The test is a positive one, ie to intend to reside permanently or indefinitely in the UK. However, again actions speak louder than words and after a long period of UK residence HMRC may well take the view that the expressed intentions of leaving are a mere hope or aspiration and the reality is that the taxpayer is intending to stay. It is therefore necessary either to preserve ties in the country of origin or develop ties elsewhere, both of which would indicate a lack of commitment to the UK. (For an example of a claim to a domicile of choice and a summary of all the main issues see *Civil Engineer v IRC* (2002) and *Personal Tax Planning Review* Volume 8 Issue 3 and *Gaines-Cooper v R & C Comrs* (2007) and (2010).) [18.25]

d) *Losing a domicile of choice*

It can be just as important for someone who has acquired a domicile of choice, not to lose it before they want to. This would be particularly important to those individuals who for example have a UK domicile of origin but acquired a domicile of choice in (say) Hong Kong by reason of being permanently settled there for many years. If they were to leave, they might find that their Hong Kong domicile disappears. The test is very specific. A domicile of choice is lost by the combination of:
(1) ceasing to reside in the country in question; and
(2) ceasing to intend to reside there permanently or indefinitely, but not otherwise.

Note that there are two different conditions – and both need to be satisfied if the domicile of choice is to be lost. Ceasing to reside sounds like a plain question of fact, but it may not be quite as simple as that. The individual might leave Hong Kong to live in the UK but retain some residential accommodation for occasional visits for social or business purposes. Will this mean he continues to reside in Hong Kong? Possibly, but it may not matter because there is the other condition to consider as well. Has he ceased to intend to reside in Hong Kong? If he retains residential accommodation there and visits regularly, this would be very supportive of a claim that he had not ceased to intend to reside there permanently; he is just away for a while. Even if he does not retain any ties or accommodation there, this does not mean that he had necessarily ceased to intend to reside there permanently. He may intend to return, for example when his children are settled in school or have finished their education. It is only when he has decided not to return, or his actions indicate that resuming residence there is not a reality, that his domicile of choice will be lost. On that occasion, either the domicile of origin will revive or he will acquire a new domicile of choice. If therefore his domicile of origin is not the UK but (say) Australia, the loss of a Hong Kong domicile by taking up residence in the UK is more likely to mean the revival of the Australian domicile of origin than the acquisition of a UK domicile of choice. [18.26]

e) *Special situations*

If an individual with a foreign domicile of origin intends to come to the UK to take up permanent residence he may become UK domiciled as soon as he arrives. That is possible if when he arrives he comes with the settled intention of residing in the UK on a permanent basis. However, in many cases this will be an over-simplification. It is more likely that a domicile of choice in the UK will not be acquired until he has been in the UK for some time and is sure that he has made the right decision. Before he arrives the foreign domiciled individual cannot possibly become UK domiciled because he would not satisfy the requirement of physical residence in this country.

Some people have ties in a number of different countries and this can create confusion about their domicile.

EXAMPLE 18.7

A had a domicile of origin in the UK but subsequently acquired a domicile of choice in Singapore. He decides to leave Singapore and retire to France. He will spend five months every year in France, three months in Italy and the rest of the year in other parts of the world. Where does this leave his domicile?

When A leaves Singapore, he ceases to reside there and ceases to intend to reside there permanently, so his Singapore domicile of choice will be abandoned. He cannot be without a domicile so either his Singapore domicile of choice will be replaced by a new domicile of choice, or his domicile of origin will revive. If it is his intention to reside permanently (although not exclusively) in France, and he has sufficient knowledge and experience of France to be able to make an informed judgment on the matter, he may acquire a French domicile immediately he arrives in France. If however his intentions are less clear and he merely wants to divide his time between a number of different countries and enjoy his retirement, he may not have the necessary firmness of intention to acquire a French domicile of choice. In the absence of any other suitable territory his UK domicile of origin will revive – even though he has no intention of returning to the UK permanently; indeed even if he was determined never to set foot in the UK again.

He may think that if he is never going to live in the UK and will not be resident there, he need not worry about UK tax. That is true for income tax and CGT but it could still be a problem for IHT and it is clearly something to be avoided, or at the very least prepared for by action before it happens. It would be a mistake to think that HMRC would be unable to collect any IHT. If he had any property in the UK, HMRC would have no difficulty in getting its hands on it in satisfaction of the tax. Even if he had no UK property but those who will inherit his estate live in the UK, HMRC would be able to collect the tax from them.

It is important to appreciate the crucial distinction in *Example 18.7* above between a domicile of origin and a domicile of choice. A domicile of origin is extremely adhesive and will be retained unless and until positive steps are taken to acquire a domicile of choice. An individual can leave his country of origin vowing never to return but he will keep his domicile of origin until a domicile of choice is acquired elsewhere. There is a clear contrast here with a domicile of choice that can be much more easily abandoned. [18.27]

f) *Deemed domicile*

A special rule applies for IHT which is that an individual will be deemed to be domiciled in the UK if he has been resident for tax purposes for 17 out of the preceding 20 years (this is set to change shortly – see [18.30]). In calculating the years of residence there is no requirement to count any year in which residence occurred only by reason of the existence of available accommodation under the pre 2013 rules. In these circumstances the real domicile is disregarded and liability to IHT is determined as if he were UK domiciled. This means that he becomes chargeable to IHT on the whole of his worldwide assets.

There is a further deemed domicile rule for IHT, that a person with a UK domicile who leaves the UK and acquires a domicile in another country will continue to be regarded as UK domiciled (and therefore within the charge to IHT) for three years following the acquisition of his new domicile (see further [35.4]).

The 17-year rule is overridden on death under certain Estate Tax Double Taxation Treaties, namely those with India, Pakistan, Italy and France.

FA 2013 contained provisions which allow non-UK domiciled individuals to elect to be treated as UK domiciled for the purposes of IHT and transfers of assets between spouses in certain circumstances. The new section (IHTA 1984 s 267ZA) resolves the problems of the restriction on the value of assets passing between mixed domicile spouses (otherwise limited to the nil rate band), but there are other factors to be considered when a spouse makes such an election. [18.28]

g) *Married women*

Where a marriage took place before January 1974 the wife took her husband's domicile automatically at the time of her marriage. If the marriage took place on or after 1 January 1974 the domicile of a married woman is determined independently of her husband and is based on her own intentions and circumstances (see the Domicile and Matrimonial Proceedings Act 1973 s 1). However, this does not mean that marriage is wholly irrelevant to her domicile. Whilst the ceremony of marriage itself is no longer capable of causing a change in her domicile, the fact of getting married can do so. She may not acquire the domicile of her husband, but a decision to marry may represent a sufficient indication of her intentions to enable a domicile of choice to be acquired on general principles. If a woman marries a man who lives in the UK and continues to do so, her decision to reside in the UK with him may well be sufficient evidence for the acquisition of a UK domicile of choice under the normal rules (the same applies for married men in this latter instance).

For a woman who was married before 1 January 1974, her domicile did not necessarily change on that date – it just changed its nature from a domicile of dependence to a domicile of choice (see Domicile and Matrimonial Proceedings Act 1973 s 1(2)). This is a strange rule because the wife of a UK domiciled husband might never have set foot in the UK and could not therefore have acquired a UK domicile of choice under general principles (see [18.25]); she will nevertheless have acquired a UK domicile of choice on 1 January 1974. This gives rise to some complex implications but it is fair to say that a married woman who acquired a UK domicile of choice on 1 January 1974 and has continued to live abroad since that time, will almost certainly have abandoned this domicile of choice either immediately or shortly after it was imposed upon her (see *IRC v Duchess of Portland* (1982) and *Taxation*, 17 January 1988). [18.29]

h) *The proposed 2017–18 changes*

On 8 July 2015 the UK Chancellor announced that there would be a major overhaul to the taxation of non-UK domiciled individuals and non resident trusts which would apply from 6 April 2017. The changes essentially fall into four categories:
(1) Non-UK domiciled individuals who have been resident in the UK for 15 out of the past 20 tax years will after April 2017 be deemed to be domiciled in the UK for income tax, capital gains tax and inheritance tax purposes.

(2) Individuals with a UK domicile of origin who have left the UK and acquired a non-UK domicile of choice will be treated as UK deemed domiciled when they return to the UK, even if they returned to the UK before 6 April 2017, and trusts created whilst the individual was non-domiciled will lose excluded property status once the individual is treated as UK deemed domicile for IHT purposes.

(3) The way that UK residents are taxed on benefits they receive from non-UK trusts will be overhauled.

(4) UK residential property owned indirectly by non-UK domiciled individuals through an offshore company, partnership or offshore property trust will fall within the charge to UK IHT.

As a result of the June 2017 general election the anticipated changes were put on hold and it remains to be seen if, how and when they will be implemented – this could be in a second finance bill in 2017 or perhaps with some alteration, in 2018. [18.30]

II TAXATION OF FOREIGN INCOME

1 Relevant foreign income

Before 6 April 2005 Case IV charged income arising from foreign securities and Case V charged income arising from foreign possessions but the distinction has now been abolished by ITTOIA 2005 and both types of income are now described as 'relevant foreign income'. 'Foreign possessions' includes land, shares, interests in foreign partnerships and interests under non-resident discretionary trusts. [18.31]

2 Calculation of liability

A current year basis applies in respect of unearned income (ie on the whole amount arising or received in the tax year). In the case of a trade carried on abroad the assessment is by reference to the accounting period (see [10.192] ff). [18.32]

Deductible expenses (including travelling expenses if, broadly, the same conditions are met as in the case of an employee working abroad (see below)), capital allowances and losses are calculated in the normal way but loss relief is only given against other foreign income. Where, despite the endeavours of the taxpayer, income cannot be remitted to the UK because of foreign laws, executive action of an overseas government, or the non-availability of foreign currency, the payment of tax may be postponed until that problem passes (ITTOIA 2005 s 841). [18.33]

3 The remittance basis

If the taxpayer is UK resident, but not UK domiciled, he may claim to be taxed on the remittance basis: ie on income received or otherwise enjoyed in the UK (ITTOIA 2005 s 832). From 6 April 2008 where an individual has been resident in the UK for seven out of the previous nine tax years, he will only be able to claim the remittance basis if he pays a special £30,000 charge each year. The charge increased to £50,000 from 6 April 2012 for those who have been resident in the UK for 12 out of the previous 14 tax years. FA 2015 s 24 increased this £50,000 charge to £60,000 and introduced a new levy of £90,000 to be payable by taxpayers who have been UK resident for 17 out of the previous 20 tax years. The proposed 2017–18 changes will render this £90,000 charge superfluous. Unless income is actually brought to or enjoyed in the UK there is no tax charge. Such a taxpayer may therefore arrange for income to be reinvested or spent abroad.

On 6 April 2008 the taxation of UK resident individuals with a foreign domicile was profoundly changed. The remittance basis was entirely recast so as to bring foreign income and capital gains into charge to UK tax in a much wider set of circumstances. The definition of a remittance has been enlarged considerably to include circumstances where money or other property is brought to or received or used in the UK or any services provided in the UK where it derives from foreign income or gains (see RDRM 33050 for HMRC's interpretation of some practical examples of what constitutes a remittance).

Where a chattel is purchased with foreign income outside the UK and then brought to the UK, that now represents a remittance of the income even though it does not represent a sum of money. There is an exemption for personal effects, assets costing less than £1,000, assets brought into the UK for repair and assets which are in the UK for less than nine months; in addition any asset purchased out of untaxed relevant foreign income which was owned by the taxpayer on 11 March 2008 can be brought to the UK without charge – unless it is sold in the UK.

The source ceasing rules were also modified on 6 April 2008. Prior to this date no tax liability could arise if the source of the income which is remitted did not exist in the tax year. A common example would be a bank deposit or shareholding which gives rise to interest or dividends. If the account had been closed or the shares were sold and the accumulated interest and dividends were remitted to the UK in the following year, no tax would arise because in the year of remittance the source of the income would not exist. This rule has not applied for some years in respect of employment income nor in the case of some trust income, but from 6 April 2008 all such income will be taxed in the year it is remitted whether or not the source exists in that year. It is worth noting that the question of the source of income in the context of debts was recently debated in the case of *Perrin v R & C Comrs* (2014) (see **[14.33]**). Remittances from a fund which contains a mixture of income, capital and capital gains have always been problematic, with different rules and practices applying to the income and capital gains. A statutory rule has applied from 6 April 2008 to determine how much of a transfer from a mixed fund is treated as income or gain.

For income to be taxed in the UK it has to be remitted by or on behalf of a person entitled to the income. A gift of income to a third party (an outright and absolute gift completed outside the UK) could be remitted by the donee without any charge to tax. The amount remitted would not be the income of the donee and therefore not taxable, nor could it be taxed on the donor as it did not belong to them. From 6 April 2008, where foreign income and gains are alienated by a transfer to an offshore vehicle, which the individual's spouse or civil partner or children under 18 or grandchildren under 18 can benefit from, it will be treated as a remittance by the donor if the donee remits the money to the UK.

Where a resident but not domiciled individual has a foreign loan for his use in the UK, any repayments of principal out of foreign income or gains will be treated as a remittance. Before 6 April 2008 this was not the case in respect of payments of interest on such a foreign loan. From 6 April 2008 the payment of interest on a foreign loan which has been used in the UK will be a taxable remittance. These 2008 rules do not apply where interest is paid on pre 2008 mortgages which are secured on a residential property in the UK provided that the terms of the loan are not varied, no further advances are made and that the loan continues to be secured on the same property. From 4 August 2014, HMRC without warning withdrew the concessionary treatment of remittances on the taxation of non domiciled individuals using foreign income/gains as collateral for borrowings used in the UK. From this date, as well as any foreign income/gains used to pay interest on or repay the collateral being treated as a remittance, the actual funds used to secure the loan will also be treated as a remittance. In October 2015 HMRC responded to staunch industry opposition to this sudden and legally questionable change of approach by conceding that if the loans were in place before August 2014, so long as there were no significant variations to the terms HMRC would not seek to tax the collateral as a remittance. The £90,000 charge is set to be abolished under the proposed 2017–18 changes.

Despite the 2008 changes, the traditional technique of segregating capital from income and remitting only capital (which would not be chargeable to income tax) continues to apply and will be a principal source of planning for UK resident foreign domiciled individuals.

Profound changes were also made from 6 April 2008 to the taxation of offshore trusts by UK resident foreign domiciled individuals, and even more drastic changes are expected to be included in either F(No 2)A 2017 or FA 2018.

Remittance Basis Charge

Foreign domiciled individuals who have been resident in the UK for seven out of the last nine tax years will only be able to benefit from the remittance basis if they pay £30,000 pa for the privilege. From 6 April 2015 onwards, those who have been resident in the UK for 12 out of the previous 14 tax years are to pay £60,000 pa, and those individuals who have been resident for 17 out of the previous 20 tax years will pay £90,000 pa (this last charge will be abolished when the deemed domicile rules come into effect). Those who do not pay the £30,000, £60,000 or £90,000 'non-dom' charge will be chargeable to tax on their worldwide income and capital gains – subject to the normal double taxation relief for tax paid in other countries on that income.

Those who have not been resident in the UK for seven out of nine years will continue to benefit from the remittance basis without charge and so will those who have unremitted foreign income and gains of less than £2,000 per annum. Where an individual claims the remittance basis (whether they pay the non-dom charge or not) they will forfeit the right to their personal allowance and their capital gains tax annual exemption. This will not apply to anybody under the age of 18 who will continue to benefit from the remittance basis without any supplementary charge.

An individual will be able to claim the remittance basis each year (providing they pay the non-dom charge) but any income not taxed by reason of a claim in one year which is subsequently remitted in a year when the remittance basis is not claimed will continue to be taxable in the UK.

The remittance of funds to pay the non-dom charge will generally represent a remittance – unless the non-dom charge is paid direct to HMRC from an offshore bank account by cheque or electronic transfer.

The non-dom charge is not a tax but it will be collected in the same manner as a tax. However, the individual must nominate the particular unremitted income or gains to which the non-dom charge will relate. The purpose of this nomination is to facilitate double taxation relief for the charge although this will depend upon the relevant double taxation agreement and domestic rules in the other countries.

EXAMPLE 18.8

(1) Jacques, domiciled in France, but resident in England carries on his business in France. Out of the profits of his business he buys a Picasso painting in France that he brings to England. Before 6 April 2008 this would not have been a remittance (unless he were to sell the painting in the UK); from 6 April 2008 the use or enjoyment of the asset in the UK will be a remittance of the income used to purchase it.

(2) Diego, resident but not domiciled in the UK, retains his savings abroad. Should he need to remit foreign moneys he will still avoid UK income tax if the remitted sum is capital. He may be able to arrange this by operating a number of separate overseas bank accounts. If all the income is paid into one account and the receipts from disposal of capital assets are paid into a separate account, remittances from the latter are capital (and not subject to UK income tax – although a CGT charge may arise). **[18.34]**

4 Particular categories of income

a) *Profits of a trade, profession or vocation*

A UK resident is assessed on trading or professional income on all his profits arising from a trade, profession or vocation ('trade') carried on by him in the UK, despite some of the profits being attributable to overseas business: ITTOIA 2005 s 6.

For a trader to be assessed on the income as foreign income, he must be resident in the UK, but the trade must be carried on *wholly* abroad. This is a question of fact, and for the sole trader who is resident in the UK and who has the sole right to manage and control the business it will be difficult to argue that the trade is wholly carried on abroad (*Ogilvie v Kitton* (1908)).

A UK resident company may, however, be able to show that it is trading wholly abroad (*Mitchell v Egyptian Hotels Ltd* (1915)). Where the company establishes a foreign subsidiary (as opposed to a branch) it is a question of fact whether that subsidiary is carrying on its own trade or acting merely as agent for the parent company. To avoid the risk of the subsidiary being treated as UK resident it is prudent to ensure that UK resident directors are not in a majority on the subsidiary's board; that the non-resident directors of the subsidiary are men of substance who are capable of independent thought and judgment; and that board meetings (where 'real' decisions and not just 'rubber stampings' occur) should be held outside the UK (see **[41.153]** and *Untelrab v McGregor* (1996) and *Wood v Holden* (2006)).

Where a partner is a UK-resident individual the profits of the firm are calculated as if the firm were a UK resident individual; the opposite applies in the case of non-UK resident individuals: ITTOIA 2005 s 849.

EXAMPLE 18.9

Wino and Co, a French partnership, have one partner resident in London who arranges for sales of their wine in the UK. In deciding whether the firm is trading in the UK the precise mechanics of the wine sales are important. If contracts are made in the UK it is likely that a business in the UK is being carried on, whereas if the orders are merely solicited here and the actual contracts are made in France, the firm may be trading with the UK so that any assessment to UK tax will be as foreign income (see generally the problem of when non-UK residents trade within the UK discussed at **[18.72]**).

Although 'trade' is used here to include professions and vocations, in practice, profits arising from a profession will rarely be taxed as foreign income because the individual exercising his profession wholly abroad is unlikely to be a UK resident and hence will not be chargeable to UK income tax at all (see *Davies v Braithwaite* (1931)). **[18.35]**

b) *Distributions from companies*

A distribution will only be chargeable to income tax if it is income. This is decided by applying the local law to see whether or not the *corpus* of the asset is left intact after the distribution: if it is, the payment will be taxed as income; if not, it is capital (*IRC v Reid's Trustees* (1949); *IRC v Burrell; Rae v Lazard Investment Co Ltd* (1963) and *Courtaulds Investments Ltd v Fleming* (1969); see also *R & C Comrs v First Nationwide* (2012)).

Dividends received from a foreign company are subject to UK tax at 7.5% *only* (to the extent it exceeds £5,000 under the new dividend tax regime for 2016–17 onwards) until the dividend (treated as a top slice of income) brings the recipient into the 32.5% or the 38.1% band (ITA 2007 ss 18 and 19): for the treatment of dividends generally, see **Chapter 42**). **[18.36]**

EXAMPLE 18.10

Fergus has employment income of £12,000 and dividends from a UK company of £36,000 in 2017–18. His tax position is:

	£
Total income	48,000
Less: personal allowance	11,500
Taxable Income	£36,500

The tax charge is as follows:

	£
employment income	
£500 at 20% (basic rate)	100
dividend income	0
£5,000 at 0%	
£28,000 at 7.5%	2,100
£3,000 at 32.5%	975
	3,075
	£3,175

Notes:
(1) The taxation of foreign dividends at the ordinary and upper rates does not apply to income charged on the remittance basis.
(2) If a foreign dividend has suffered withholding tax, credit will be given for that foreign tax against any liability to UK tax.
(3) The dividend may have borne tax at two levels: *first*, the company's profits may have suffered tax and, *second*, the dividend itself may have been taxed. Relief from the former ('underlying tax') may be given to UK corporate shareholders (TIOPA 2010 s 12) but not to individual shareholders unless provided by a double tax treaty.

c) *Income from foreign land and unsecured loans*

This income is taxable overseas property income and is computed in accordance with the rules relating to property income (ITTOIA 2005 Part 3 Chapter 11)). The same deductions in arriving at profits will be made and lease premiums and analogous receipts will also be taxed (interest paid on a loan to acquire the property may for instance be deducted in arriving at the income). However a UK property income business is wholly separate thereby preventing foreign losses being offset against UK gains (see [**12.24**]).
[**18.37**]

d) *Income from a foreign trust*

If a UK resident beneficiary has an absolute right to all or part of the income of the foreign trust (one where the trustees are non-UK resident and the assets are abroad), he is taxed on the foreign income as it arises whether or not he receives it (*Williams v Singer* (1921)). Similar principles apply to a discretionary beneficiary in whose favour the trustees have exercised their discretion to appoint income (see further [**18.79**]).

In appropriate cases income tax may be charged on a UK settlor under the settlement provisions (see [**16.61**]); under ITA 2007 s 720 (see [**18.111**]) or on the beneficiary under ITA 2007 s 731 in respect of benefits received from the trust.
[**18.38**]

e) *Income from a foreign partnership*

In *Padmore v IRC* (1987) it was held that a UK resident partner was not subject to income tax on his share of the profits of an overseas partnership as foreign income because of the Jersey double tax treaty. The decision was reversed retrospectively and the present position is that such treaties do not affect the taxation of a UK partner's share of overseas profits or gains (see ITTOIA 2005 s 858). [18.39]

f) *Offshore 'roll-up' funds*

The tax treatment of a UK investor is considered in **Chapter 13**. [18.40]

g) *Miscellany*

Certain pensions (see [18.50]) and alimony ordered by a foreign court are taxed as foreign income. [18.41]

h) *Coming to the UK*

In cases where an individual becomes UK resident during the course of a tax year there are complex rules that identify the overseas investment income that thereupon becomes subject to UK tax. Arrangements should be made *before* becoming UK resident to maximise the amount of income arising in the non-resident period. [18.42]

5 Employment income

The earnings of an individual who is resident in the UK are chargeable to income tax wherever earned or received, whether in respect of that year or an earlier year and whether or not the employment is held at the time the earnings are received, (ITEPA 2003 s 15).

Where the employee is not domiciled in the UK and the employment is with a foreign employer, earnings and amounts treated as earnings may be taxable on a remittance basis (see ITEPA 2003 s 25 and [18.46] and [18.47]). A foreign employer is defined in ITEPA 2003 s 721 as meaning:

> 'an individual partnership or body of person resident outside the UK and not resident in the UK'.

For such earnings to be chargeable on the remittance basis, it is necessary to establish, *first*, that the duties of the office are performed wholly outside the UK; *second*, that the employment is with a foreign employer; and, *third*, that the individual is not domiciled in the UK. In the case of an individual who needs to work both abroad and in the UK, it is sensible to ensure that the overseas duties are carried out under a separate contract of employment. Care needs to be taken in drafting the terms of any such contract because HMRC has power to ensure that the earnings are not artificially weighted in favour of the overseas contract (see ITEPA 2003 s 24). See also *Tax Bulletin* 76 (April 2005) for the HMRC approach to dual contracts where they explain their intention to scrutinise such contracts to identify whether there is in fact only one contract. Since 5 April 2014, ITEPA 2003 s 24A has further tightened up the availability of the remittance basis with respect to overseas employment where an individual has both UK and overseas employments with the same or an associated employer and the foreign tax payable on the overseas income is less than 65% of the UK's top rate of 45% tax (ie taxed at less than 29.25%). This provision will not apply to overseas income which falls within ITEPA 2003 s 26 and qualifies for overseas workday relief, meaning that the remittance basis is available for an arriving foreign domicile for the year of arrival and the following two years. **[18.43]–[18.45]**

a) *Earnings for duties performed in the UK:*

Where a person is not resident in the UK, he is taxable only on the earnings in respect of duties performed in the UK (see ITEPA 2003 s 27). He is not, however, chargeable to UK tax on general earnings for overseas duties.

The rules relating to the taxation of employment related securities for internationally mobile employees were changed with effect from 6 April 2015. Regardless of when an award of shares or an option to acquire shares was made, if the employee has worked in the UK at any time prior to vesting, income tax arising on the vesting must be apportioned over the employment period and taxed in the UK with respect to any time spent working in the UK in this period. **[18.46]**

b) *The remittance basis*

For UK resident employees who are not UK domiciled in the UK, earnings from overseas on overseas employment are taxable under ITEPA 2003 s 26 to the extent that they are remitted to the UK. Remittances, for the purposes of the charge on earnings, include earnings paid, used or enjoyed in the UK in any manner or form. Remittances of earnings are assessed on a current year basis and will be subject to tax even if the earnings were for some previous year or the employment has ceased. **[18.47]**

c) *Place of work*

In deciding whether the duties of an employment are in substance performed wholly abroad, merely incidental duties performed in the UK are ignored (ITEPA 2003 s 39 and see *Robson v Dixon* (1972); see also the HMRC Statement of April 2011).

By ITEPA 2003 s 40 some duties are deemed to be performed in the UK. Generally, crews of ships and aircraft will be treated as performing their duties abroad in respect of any part of a voyage that does not begin *and* end in the UK. Areas designated under the Continental Shelf Act 1964 are regarded as part of the UK (eg workers on oil rigs in the UK sector of the North Sea are deemed to work in the UK). **[18.48]**

d) *Deductible expenses*

The general rule is that a deduction from earnings is allowed for expenditure which the employee is obliged to incur and pay as the holder of the employment and the amount is incurred wholly, exclusively and necessarily in the performance of the duties of the employment (ITEPA 2003 s 336). An identical rule applies for deductions in respect of travel expenses (ITEPA 2003 s 337).

Non-UK residents and seafarers entitled to the long absence deduction will not suffer UK tax on reimbursements by their employer for travelling expenses incurred during those periods. A UK resident individual who is wholly employed abroad, will still be liable to tax on such expenses (and reimbursements) (because they will not be 'necessarily' incurred in the performance of the duties). ITEPA 2003 s 370, therefore, provides that he can deduct his costs of travelling to and from the UK to take up or leave the employment. If the expenses of board and lodging incurred in carrying out the duties abroad are paid or reimbursed by the employer, the employee will be entitled to a deduction so that those payments will not be emoluments. In addition, s 371 provides that where he spends 60 or more continuous days outside the UK, the expenses of travel of his spouse and children under 18 are not taxable if met by his employer (limited to two trips in each year of assessment). Any number of other journeys made by the employee between the place of work and the UK can be paid for by the employer without such payments being taxed as emoluments (though notice that the employee cannot deduct the costs of such journeys where he pays for them).

The travelling expenses available to non-UK domiciled employees working in the UK broadly mirror the provisions discussed above for UK residents who work abroad. Accordingly, so long as the employer bears the cost of (any number of) journeys undertaken between the employee's usual place of abode and the UK such sums will not be taxed as earnings and there are similar provisions to those already discussed for visits by spouses and children. However, for foreign domiciled employees who perform duties in the UK, a relaxed interpretation exists in respect of the continuous period of 60 days; for such employees it is sufficient to spend two-thirds of their working days in the UK over a period of 60 days provided they are present in the UK at the beginning and end of the period (see *Tax Bulletin* 56, December 2001). It should be noted that the reliefs for expatriates are limited to a period of two years from the date of the expatriate's arrival in the UK. **[18.49]**

e) *Foreign pensions and annuities*

Foreign pensions and annuities are taxed on 90% of the income arising (ITEPA 2003 s 575). However, such income will be taxable elsewhere in ITEPA 2003 if it is payable in the UK through a department or agent of a Commonwealth government. **[18.50]**

f) *Collection of tax*

Tax on earnings is generally collected at source from the employer under the PAYE system (see **Chapter 8**). Accordingly where an employer is resident in the UK he must as a general rule operate PAYE in respect of all his employees' assessable earnings.

The application of PAYE to a non-resident employer, was considered in *Clark v Oceanic Contractors Inc* (1983). In that case a non-resident company made payments abroad to employees engaged in performing duties in the UK sector of the North Sea and so within the UK for the purpose of liability to tax on earnings. The House of Lords held that PAYE applied to the employer company so that it should have deducted tax from the payments. The only limit on the territorial scope of the legislation is whether it can effectively be enforced. It will, therefore, apply to the non-resident employer who maintains a 'trading presence' in the UK. This was so in the *Oceanic* case: the company carried on activities in the UK and in the UK sector of the North Sea; was liable to corporation tax on its profits; and had an address for service in the UK (see further **Chapter 8**). See also *Agassi v Robinson* (2006). [18.51]

New legislation was introduced by the Government with effect from 6 April 2014 to tackle a practice used by employment intermediaries knows as 'false self employment' where PAYE, NICs and income tax obligations are avoided using contracts classifying workers as 'self employed' when such status may not be genuine.

The effect of these rules is to widen the scope of the existing agency legislation and ensure that the 'end users' of the workers' skills have a PAYE obligation enforced upon them. [18.52]–[18.70]

III TAXATION OF THE NON-RESIDENT TAXPAYER

The following general rules apply to an individual who is not resident in the UK:
(1) He is not charged to UK income tax on foreign source income.
(2) So far as *earned income* is concerned, tax is charged on UK pensions and employments where the duties are carried on in the UK (see ITEPA 2003 s 27: **[18.73]**). Tax is also charged on the profits of a trade or profession which is not carried on wholly outside the UK (see **[18.72]**).
(3) For *investment income*, with the exception of UK rental income (as to which see **[18.75]**), the general rule is that the tax is limited to the amount (if any) deducted at source ('excluded income': see ITA 2007 s 811):
  (a) If the taxpayer has other fully taxed UK source income any personal allowances to which he is entitled (as to which, see below) will be first set against excluded income (although not so as to result in any tax refund).
  (b) If the taxpayer is resident in a country with which the UK has a double tax treaty, then he may be entitled to exemption or relief from tax on UK investment income (although not on income from land).
  (c) These rules do not apply to non-resident trustees when a 'relevant beneficiary' (broadly speaking, one who is or may be entitled to income) is resident in the UK (ITA 2007 s 812).

Non-residents are entitled to personal allowances in the circumstances set out in ITA 2007 s 56 generally to Commonwealth citizens: citizens of a state within the European Economic Area and residents of the Isle of Man or Channel Islands.

The Government is consulting on restricting a non-resident's entitlement to the UK personal allowance, but legislation is not expected imminently.
[18.71]

1 Profits of a trade, profession or vocation

As an application of the source doctrine, the foreign resident taxpayer will be taxable on trading or professional income on the profits of any trade carried on *within* as opposed to *with* the UK. For these purposes, however, maintaining an administrative or representative office as opposed to a branch in the UK will not *per se* constitute trading within the UK. The same principle applies to the exercise of a profession or vocation although the exercise of either in the UK would normally render the taxpayer UK resident.

The majority of cases in this area have been concerned with the sale of goods by a non-resident to a person in the UK. The courts have tended to say that the trade is carried on in the place where, under English law, the contract is made. This is the place where acceptance of the offer is communicated. In general terms, acceptance by post occurs at the place of posting, whereas acceptance by any other form occurs at the place where acceptance is received. Accordingly, the non-resident who faxes his acceptance of an order to a UK customer is in danger of trading within the UK, whereas the non-resident who posts his acceptance to such a customer from outside the UK would appear to be merely trading with the UK. However, the place where contracts are made is only one (albeit important) factor to be considered and is of greater significance where the trade consists simply of the purchase and resale of goods. The better test is whether the trading operations that give rise to the profits take place in the UK (*Firestone Tyre and Rubber Co Ltd v Lewellin* (1957)). It is likely, for instance, that if land in the UK is acquired, developed and then sold, the trade will take place in the UK irrespective of where the contract of sale was entered into.

When a trade is carried on within the UK, the profits are computed under the normal rules under ITTOIA 2005 Part 2 Chapter 2. The tax charge is limited to the profits from the part of the trade carried on in the UK measured on an arm's length basis.

When a foreign taxpayer is assessed to tax on trading income, the tax can be levied on the branch or agency within the UK through which the trade is being carried on although certain agents, eg independent brokers, are excepted from this provision (ITA 2007 s 817 and see *Willson v Hooker* (1995)).

So far as non-resident companies are concerned, even if they are trading within the UK, there will be no liability to UK corporation tax unless that trade is carried on through a permanent establishment in the UK. If that is not the case the liability will be to income tax at the basic rate not corporation tax (CTA 2009 s 3). In the latter case, as the company will not have any UK presence, HMRC may be presented with problems of tax collection. **[18.72]**

2 Employment income

The foreign resident taxpayer is chargeable under ITEPA 2003 s 25 on emoluments he receives for duties performed in the UK (see **[18.46]**). This provision has the effect of treating the UK duties as a source of income that would otherwise escape tax completely. **[18.73]**

3 Non-resident entertainers and sportsmen

The UK has encountered difficulties (also experienced by other countries) in securing tax payments from non-resident entertainers and sportsmen and women (eg tennis players, golfers, actors and pop stars) who only pay short visits to the country and who have often left before tax can be assessed and collected. Accordingly, a withholding tax applies in ITA 2007 chapter 18;

SI 1987/530. In general, the payer of the money is obliged to make returns to HMRC at quarterly intervals and to account for basic rate income tax that he should deduct from the payment made to the entertainer. There is a *de minimis* provision that ensures that these rules do not operate if the total payments made in the tax year to an entertainer do not exceed £1,000. (See also *Agassi v Robinson* (2006) in respect of payments to third parties.) **[18.74]**

4 Income from land in the UK (ITA 2007 s 971; SI 1995/2902)

Profits from letting property in the UK are subject to income tax at basic and higher rate as appropriate.

(1) *Position of the landlord*: A non-resident landlord (including a person whose usual place of abode is outside the UK) can apply to HMRC for confirmation that the rental income can be paid gross. HMRC must be satisfied that his tax affairs are up to date; or that he has never had UK tax obligations; or that he does not expect to be subject to UK tax.

(2) *Position of tenants and agents*: In the absence of any agreement with HMRC for the rent to be paid gross overseas, a tenant paying rent direct to his landlord should deduct tax at the basic rate and account for the tax to HMRC.

The burden is on the tenant to know the landlord's usual place of abode: if the tenant fails to deduct tax from an instalment of rent the right to deduct is lost and cannot be made good out of later rent payments (*Tenbry Investments Ltd v Peugeot Talbot Motor Co Ltd* (1992)). A repayment to the landlord may be made in the event of the tax deducted exceeding the landlord's liability (for example, because of deductible expenses).

In cases where an agent is employed to collect the rent, the agent is responsible for making a tax return and then liable to pay the relevant tax after taking into account all allowable deductions.

(3) *Deductible expenses*: Letting agents must pay tax at basic rate on rental income less deductible expenses: by contrast tenants must account for basic rate tax on all rent directly paid to the landlord together with basic rate tax on rental income paid to third parties which is not a deductible expense. In general an expense can only be deducted when the letting agent/tenant can reasonably be satisfied that it is allowable in computing the profits of the landlord's letting business (SI 1995/2902 regs 9(4), 8(2)). Note also that deduction is only permitted if the expense is borne by the tenant/letting agent and not if it is directly paid by the landlord.

(4) *Assessment on the landlord*: The tax deducted at source by the tenant or letting agent will usually not represent the correct liability of the landlord so an adjustment will be needed. For instance, letting agents cannot deduct expenses paid by the landlord and landlords who are individuals may be subject to the higher rate of income tax whilst discretionary trustees may suffer the additional rate of tax for trusts. A non-resident company is normally subject to income tax at basic rate on its profits from UK lettings because it will not be chargeable to corporation tax in the absence of any trade carried on in the UK through a permanent establishment. **[18.75]**

5 Interest from UK banks and building societies

Interest can be paid gross provided that an appropriate declaration is made that the taxpayer is not resident in the UK (ITA 2007 s 858). Absent such a declaration the paying institution may be required to deduct tax at the basic rate of 20% from the outbound interest payment under the withholding tax regime. ITA 2007 s 874(2) requires witholding where there is a payment of yearly interest that arises in the UK made by any person to another person whose usual place of abode is outside the UK. There has been notable recent case law (*Perrin v R & C Comrs, Ardmore Construction Ltd v R & C Comrs* (2015)) examining the question of whether the payment has properly arisen in the UK. There are circumstances when the withholding tax regime may be overridden (or the rate reduced), most commonly as a result of an applicable double taxation agreement. [18.76]

6 UK government securities

Tax is not chargeable on certain government securities owned by persons not resident in the UK (FOTRA securities: ITTOIA 2005 s 713). [18.77]

7 Dividends paid by UK companies

A non-UK resident is not entitled to the £5,000 tax free dividend allowance in respect of a qualifying distribution from a UK company unless he is entitled to personal allowances under ITA 2007 s 56 (see [18.71] and TA 1988 s 231(1)). This position may be altered by a double tax treaty. [18.78]

8 Non-resident discretionary trusts

Non-resident trusts that fall within ITA 2007 s 479 are liable to the rate applicable to trusts in respect of UK source income (*IRC v Regent Trust Co Ltd* (1979)). Of course, HMRC may face enforcement problems in such cases. A UK beneficiary receiving payments out of such a trust may claim credit under ESC B18 for tax actually paid by the trustees on the income out of which the payment is made (as if the payment came from a UK trust and fell within ITA 2007 s 493) but only if the trustees have made tax returns and paid all relevant tax. It may be inferred from this concession that HMRC accepts that s 493 (see [16.29]) does not apply to payments out of non-resident trusts.
[18.79]

9 Witholding tax on royalties

There is also an obligation to deduct income tax at source from payments to a non-UK resident person in respect of royalties and other income from intellectual property as set out at ITA 2007 ss 899–909. Where an applicable double tax treaty is in place such deduction need not be made. Due to perceived abuses FA 2016 restricted the use of double tax treaties in certain avoidance scenarios within groups of companies. [18.80]–[18.90]

IV DOUBLE TAXATION RELIEF

Overseas income may be taxed in its country of origin and if UK tax is also chargeable on the same income, the taxpayer is entitled to relief in one of three ways.

First, under the double tax treaty with the other country. The treaties differ in detail but generally provide that certain categories of income will be taxed in only one of the countries concerned (usually where the taxpayer is resident). Other income will be taxable in both countries, but with a credit for one amount of tax against the other (the application of a treaty to income (or gains) covered by a 'deeming' provision needs careful consideration: see *Bricom Holdings v IRC* (1997)).

Second, if there is no treaty in force, 'unilateral relief' is given under TIOPA 2010 s 18. This takes the form of a credit against the UK tax equal to the foreign tax paid (see SP 7/91). Whereas a double tax treaty specifies the taxes which are covered by the agreement, s 18 relief is limited to taxes which are similar to UK taxes against which the relief is claimed (see, for instance, *Yates v GCA International Ltd* (1991) and SP 7/91).

Third, if neither of the above applies, unilateral relief may be given under TIOPA 2010 s 112 by way of deduction (from the foreign income which is assessable to UK tax) of the amount of foreign tax paid. Relief by deduction is less advantageous to the taxpayer than relief by credit.   [18.91]–[18.109]

V ANTI-AVOIDANCE LEGISLATION: TRANSFER OF ASSETS ABROAD (ITA 2007 PART 13 CHAPTER 2)

1 Introduction

The legislation on this subject was redrawn by the Tax Law Rewrite Committee and is now contained in Chapter 2 of ITA 2007.   [18.110]

2 General

a) *The mischief*

A person who is not resident in the UK cannot be assessed to UK income tax on income that arises from a source outside the UK. Accordingly, an individual resident in the UK could seek to avoid UK income tax by transferring income-producing assets to a non-UK resident who is not subject to UK income tax. The relevant wording in ITA 2007 s 720(1) is as follows:

> 'The charge under this section applies for the purpose of preventing the avoiding of liability to income tax by individuals who are UK resident by means of relevant transfers.'

EXAMPLE 18.11

(1) Toby, who is resident in the UK, owns land in Barbados that produces a substantial income. He transfers it to a non-UK resident company in return for an allotment of shares.

(2) Toby also owns shares in a German company which he transfers to a non-UK resident trust in which he is one of the beneficiaries.

To prevent such arrangements being effective in avoiding tax, these sections operate to treat the income of the company in (1) or the trust in (2) above as Toby's income. ITA 2007 s 720 provides that if an individual transfers assets and as a result of that transfer, or of associated operations (ITA 2007 s 715(1)(b)), income becomes payable to any person resident or domiciled outside the UK and the transferor has either power to enjoy that income (ITA 2007 ss 721, 722) or receives a capital sum (ITA 2007 s 728), the income of the non resident person is taxed as that of the transferor. The scope of the original legislation was restricted as a result of the House of Lords decision in *Vestey v IRC* (1980) to the original transferor of the assets or his spouse. As a result, fresh legislation (ITA 2007 s 731) was introduced to bring into charge those individuals (other than the transferor) who receive benefits as a result of the arrangements. [18.111]

b) *'Individuals resident in the UK'*

The legislation applies even if the transfer occurred at a time when the individual was not resident in the UK. (ITA 2007 s 728(3) reversing the decision of the House of Lords in *IRC v Willoughby* (1997).) [18.112]

c) *Purpose*

An individual will avoid liability under these sections if *either* it would not be reasonable to conclude from all the circumstances that avoidance of tax was the purpose, or one of the purposes, for effecting the relevant transactions, *or* that the relevant transactions were genuine commercial transactions and that it would not be reasonable to conclude that any of the relevant transactions were more than incidentally designed for the purpose of avoidance of tax (ITA 2007 s 737(2), (3); see s 738 for the meaning of a 'commercial transaction'). The test is an objective one. There is no clearance procedure and the onus of proof is on the taxpayer. In *IRC v Willoughby* (1997) the court accepted that if the overall objective was not tax avoidance the motive defence could apply even if the objective was achieved in a tax-efficient manner. In the course of rejecting HMRC's submission that a tax avoidance motive must attach to an individual who invested in a personal portfolio bond with a non-resident life office, Lord Nolan commented:

'it would be absurd in the context of [s 741 (now ITA 2007 s 737)] to describe as tax avoidance the acceptance of an offer of freedom from tax which Parliament has deliberately made. Tax avoidance within the meaning of s 741 is a course of action designed to conflict with or defeat the evident intention of Parliament'.

If a purpose of the taxpayer is to avoid any UK tax, the defence will not apply: by contrast, avoiding foreign tax falls within the genuine commercial transaction defence! (*IRC v Herdman* (1969) and, putting the matter beyond doubt, ITA 2007 ss 721(5)(c), 728(3)(c).)

EXAMPLE 18.12

G was domiciled and resident in Japan and opened a substantial sterling bank account in London for the benefit of his granddaughter. He transferred the moneys to the Channel Islands and then established a Channel Islands trust (into which the money was paid) for the benefit of his granddaughter. The Special Commissioners concluded that avoiding a liability to tax was not the purpose, or one of the purposes, for which the transfer was effected. The test to be applied was subjective and the creation of the settlement was prompted by a wish to ensure the financial independence of his granddaughter. There was no evidence that on this matter he had sought UK tax advice (see *A Beneficiary v IRC* (1999) and *Carvill v IRC* (2000). However, this decision must now be considered in the light of ITA 2007 s 737 which provides an objective test in determining the purpose of the relevant transactions).

The defence under ITA 2007 s 737 only applies if the individual 'shows in writing or otherwise to the satisfaction of the Board' that its conditions are fulfilled. It cannot simply be assumed. See *Tax Bulletin* 40, April 1999, on the view of the Revenue on disclosure for this purpose:

'Taxpayers are required to disclose clearly in their self assessment return if there is any income or benefit assessable under Section 739 (now ITA s 720) or 740 (now ITA s 731), and whether reliance is being placed on Section [737] to exclude income or benefit from assessment. Where such a disclosure has been made and exemption under Section 741 claimed, the Revenue will make any necessary enquiries about that exemption in the statutory period allowed, and will not seek to reopen that year's return on discovery grounds if the Section [737]) exemption has to be reconsidered in later years.'

The defence can be very difficult to prove as was discovered by the taxpayers in the First-tier Tribunal in *Fisher v R & C Comrs* (2014) where a commercially sensible decision to move a family bookmaking business to Gibraltar did not prevent there being a tax avoidance motive. [18.113]

3 Liability of the transferor (ITA 2007 s 720)

a) *General*

There are two preconditions.

First, there must be a transfer of assets by an individual. This means a transfer of property or rights of any kind but also includes the creation of those rights so that the incorporation of a company or formation of a partnership will be caught. In *IRC v Brackett* (1986), the taxpayer, by entering into a contract of employment with a Jersey company, fell within the section since rights created under that contract were assets and, as 'transfer' included the creation of rights, those assets were transferred to a non-UK resident person. The assets need not be situated in the UK.

Second, as a result of the transfer, either alone or together with associated operations, income must become payable to a non-UK resident or non-UK domiciled person. 'Person' includes a company and, for these purposes, a company incorporated outside the UK is always considered non-resident even if it is in fact resident in the UK (ITA 2007 s 718(2)) and, for the implications of this deeming, see *R v Dimsey; R v Allen* (1999)).

'Associated operations' is widely defined in s 719. Basically, any operation (except death) which is carried out by any person (not necessarily the transferor) is capable of being an associated operation, provided only that, together with the transfer, it results in income becoming payable to a person resident or domiciled outside the UK; (for cases where this did not happen see *Fynn v IRC* (1958) and *Carvill v IRC* (2000)). Whether the operation has this result is judged objectively without regard to the intention of the person effecting the operation. **[18.114]**

EXAMPLE 18.13
(1) Sam settles overseas property on a UK trust under which he can benefit. Subsequently overseas trustees are appointed so that the trust becomes non-UK resident. Income produced in the trust may be taxed as Sam's under ITA 2007 s 720 (note that there may be an overlap in such cases with the settlement provisions in ITTOIA 2005 Part 5 Chapter 5: when this is the case HMRC practice is to apply the settlement provisions and not s 720).
(2) A transfers assets to a UK resident company, B Ltd, in consideration for an allotment of shares. Some years later B Ltd sells the assets to a non-resident company, C Ltd, in return for shares in C Ltd. The transfer by B Ltd to C Ltd is associated with the transfer of assets from A to B Ltd although the operations were not contemplated as part of a single scheme at the time of the transfer (*Corbett's Executors v IRC* (1943)).
(3) A sells foreign investments to an overseas company in return for shares in that company. He makes a will leaving the shares to a non-resident trust for the benefit of his daughter. The making of the will, although not the death, is an operation associated with the transfer of the assets abroad. Hence, on the death of A the daughter is within the scope of s 731 in respect of any benefits received from the trust.

b) *The liability is that of the transferor*

Once there has been a transfer of assets resulting in income becoming payable to a non-UK resident, s 720 will then apply if the transferor has the power to enjoy the income (s 723) *or* receives or is entitled to receive a capital sum (s 728).

Who is a transferor? The key cases are *Congreve v IRC* (1948), *Pratt v IRC* (1982) and *Carvill v IRC* (2000) which show that the term may include a person who acts through an agent as well as a person who owns all or practically all the share capital of the company which makes the transfer (see *Example 18.14(2)* above).

In *Pratt*, Walton J commented on *Congreve* as follows:

'The only authority dealing with quasi-transferors so far as a company is concerned – or indeed, at all – is *Congreve's case*, and what that case does is, whilst recognising that a transfer by an individual, even one holding 99.9 per cent of the shares of the company, is not the same as a transfer by the company, to hold that a transfer by the company "procured" by a quasi-transferor holding the vast majority of the shares in the company is to be regarded as having been made by the quasi-transferor himself.'

In *Carvill* the Special Commissioner stressed that cases where an individual had such influence over another that he should be regarded as the transferor of that other's shares were 'exceptional': the majority shareholder in that case was not to be treated as the transferor of the minority shareholders' shares.

As was pointed out in *Pratt* joint assessments are not possible under ITA 2007 s 728 and there can only be a single transferor to consider at a time. Given that no apportionments are provided for, it must follow that for the section to apply an identifiable part of the asset transferred must be attributed to a particular transferor. For this reason it is not considered that discretionary beneficiaries can be transferors. [18.115]

c)   *Power to enjoy: ITA 2007 s 723*

A tax charge will only apply if, given that the above conditions are satisfied, an individual resident in the UK has 'power to enjoy the income of a person resident or domiciled outside the UK' (for an illustration of when a settlor was considered to have such a power, see *IRC v Botnar* (1999)). The income caught by the section need not be derived directly from the assets transferred, but the power of enjoyment must be held by the transferor or his spouse (*Vestey v IRC* (1980); ITA 2007 s 714). An individual has the power to enjoy income if any of the five conditions in s 723 are satisfied. Generally, they apply to any situation whereby the transferor receives, or is entitled to receive, any benefit in any form from the income:

(1)   The income is dealt with by any person so that it will at some time benefit the individual in some manner, whether in the form of income or not.

EXAMPLE 18.14

A non-resident company accumulates its profits for the purpose of redeeming the debentures of the transferor. This is a benefit within (1) because it results from a use of the income (*Latilla v IRC* (1943)).

(2)   Where assets that he holds, or which are held for his benefit, increase in value as a result of the income becoming payable to the non-UK resident.

EXAMPLE 18.15

(a)   X Ltd, a non-resident company, is in debt to A, a UK resident. When income becomes payable to X Ltd, A's *chose in action* (the debt) increases in value (unless X Ltd had sufficient funds to repay the debt) because X Ltd is more likely to be able to honour its obligations (*Lord Howard de Walden v IRC* (1942)).

(b)   As in (a) save that A also owned shares in X Ltd which he transferred to a discretionary trust for the benefit of himself and his family. The section applies because the value of the shares is increased and they are assets held for his benefit.

(3)   Where he receives, or is entitled to receive at any time, any benefit from the income or the assets representing the income.

EXAMPLE 18.16

(a) C, who is resident in the UK, holds 90% of the issued shares of a non-UK resident company, B Ltd, which gives him the right to a dividend when declared. C is entitled to receive a benefit within (3) (*Lee v IRC* (1941)). Similarly, if, after he has transferred his shares, the directors make a gift to him, C has then received a benefit and it does not matter that the directors were acting *ultra vires*.

(b) Trustees of a non-UK resident trust exercise their discretion to pay income to a UK resident settlor B. B has received a benefit within (3) above.

(4) Where he is or may become entitled to some of the income as a result of the exercise of discretions by any persons. Even if the discretions are never exercised so that the transferor never benefits, he is still within (4). Thus, in *Example 18.16(b)*, B has power to enjoy the income whether or not he receives a benefit. This paragraph also catches revocable settlements and settlements where trustees have power to appoint absolute or income interests back to the settlor as well as settlements where the settlor is within the class of discretionary beneficiary – although in those cases ITTOIA 2005 Part 5 Chapter 5 is also likely to apply.

(5) Where he can control the application of the income in any way, not necessarily for his own benefit. This does not include a right to direct the investments nor a power of appointment that is concerned with capital rather than income payments (*Lord Vestey's Executors v IRC* (1949)). Thus, in *Example 18.16(a)*, C has power to enjoy B Ltd's income through his ability to replace the existing directors by virtue of his 90% shareholding (contrast the power to appoint trustees; *IRC v Schroder* (1983)).

When applying these tests regard must be had to the substantial result and effect of all the relevant transactions (ITA 2007 s 722(3)). In *Seesurrun v R & C Comrs* (2014), the transfer of funds into an offshore structure and the taking of loans resulted in the provisions of s 714 ff being triggered. **[18.116]**

d) *Capital sums: s 728*

Section 728 applies where, in connection with a transfer of assets abroad, the transferor or his spouse receives or is entitled to receive a capital sum, whether before or after the relevant transfer. 'Capital sum' is defined as a sum paid or payable by way of loan or repayment of a loan; or any sum (not being income) which is paid or payable otherwise than for full consideration in money or money's worth. **[18.117]**

EXAMPLE 18.17

B, who is resident in the UK, has transferred income-producing assets to a non-UK resident trust. A loan is made to his wife from the trust. B falls within s 739(3).

e) *Computation of the income chargeable under ITA 2007 s 728*

When a transferor is caught by s 728, he will be assessed to income tax on the non-resident's income to the extent that it arose by virtue or in consequence of the relevant transfer of assets and any associated operation(s) (see *Tax Bulletin*, April 1999, p 651). Hence, the purchase of an existing offshore company with an existing income stream is not within the section.

If s 728 applies, the assessment is not limited to the amount of the capital sum and includes income arising in the year when the capital sum was paid or payable and *all* such income arising thereafter (see *Private Client Business*, 1995, p 209).

Should HMRC assess both the transferor and his spouse under either subsection, it cannot tax the same income twice (ITA 2007 s 743), but must charge it in such proportions as it considers 'just and reasonable'.

In computing the income of the non-resident which is chargeable under s 728, the transferor is only entitled to such deductions and reliefs as he would have been allowed had he, and not the non-resident, actually received the income (see *Lord Chetwode v IRC* (1977); management charges of a non-resident company were not deductible by a UK resident individual, and see s 743(2). If, however, the income has already suffered basic rate tax, this will not be collected again from the UK resident (s 744). **[18.118]**

f) *Remittance basis for non-domiciliaries*

ITA 2007 s 726 provides that a non-UK domiciliary is not chargeable 'in respect of any income ... if he would not, by reason of his being so domiciled, have been chargeable to tax in respect of it if it had in fact been his income'. The wording may be tortuous, but the effect is to preserve the remittance basis to income caught by ITA 2007 s 720. However, from 6 April 2008 the individual may need to pay the £30,000 (or £60,000) charge to enjoy the benefit of the remittance basis, in the same way as would have applied to his income generally. **[18.119]**

4 Liability of non-transferors: s 731

a) *Ambit*

This provision was designed to fill the gaps in the legislation revealed in *Vestey v IRC* (1980). The section has effect where a relevant transfer occurs, and an individual resident in the UK, who is not liable to tax under section 720 or 727, receives a benefit provided out of assets available for the purpose as a result of the transfer or associated operations (ITA 2007 s 732). **[18.120]**

b) *A receipts basis*

The important limitation in s 731 is that such an individual is only assessed to income tax *to the extent of any benefit that he receives*. It should be realised therefore that the section leaves open planning opportunities (and it may be noted that the CGT rules are now far more restrictive given the definition of a 'defined person'). An overseas settlement (in which the settlor and his spouse do not have power to enjoy the income) in which the income is accumulated will be free from UK income tax unless and until benefits are conferred on a UK resident beneficiary (so at the very least there will be a deferment of UK tax). **[18.121]**

c) *What is a 'benefit'?*

The term 'benefit' is not defined. A cash advance or the transfer of an asset *in specie* will be caught and HMRC also considers that the free use of property constitutes a benefit. In general, tax is charged even if the benefit is received and kept abroad. This is subject to limited protection for non-domiciliaries under s 735 who will remain taxable in such cases unless the benefit is received outside the UK and all the relevant income is foreign source income which has not been remitted to the UK. If some of the relevant income is UK source income or is remitted, then the benefit is taxable to the extent of such income. Again the £30,000 (or £60,000) charge may need to be paid for the individual to benefit from the remittance basis on this income. **[18.122]**

d) *'Relevant income'*

The benefit is taxed as the income of the UK resident in the year of receipt to the extent that it does not exceed the 'relevant income' of the non-resident in the tax years up to and including the year when the benefit is paid. In so far as it exceeds the relevant income of those years, any excess is carried forward and set against the first available relevant income of future years until it is finally absorbed. HMRC consider that the tax charge cannot be relieved by double tax relief.

'Relevant income' means, in relation to an individual, income arising in any year of assessment to the non-resident and which, as a result of the transfer of assets, can be used to provide a benefit to that individual (s 733(1)). **[18.123]**

e) *Apportionment of liability*

The same income cannot be charged to tax twice (s 743). Therefore, where several beneficiaries receive benefits, the relevant income is allocated amongst them by HMRC in such proportions as may be just and reasonable (in the first instance they will seek to agree the division of liability with the taxpayer). The taxpayer may appeal against the apportionment. **[18.124]**

EXAMPLE 18.18

A non-resident discretionary trust has relevant income in three consecutive years of £6,000, £6,000 and £12,000 respectively. It makes payments to two UK resident beneficiaries in *Year 2*. It is assumed that the apportionment provisions would be applied *pro rata* and not according to the order in which the payments are made. The benefits are taxed as follows:

	A	B
	£	£
Year 1		
Benefits paid	Nil	Nil
Relevant income £6,000 (unapportioned)		

Year 2				
Benefits			6,000	12,000
Relevant income	£6,000			
Plus income brought forward	£6,000			
	£12,000	apportioned	4,000	8,000
Untaxed benefit carried forward			2,000	4,000
Year 3				
Benefits paid			Nil	Nil
Relevant income	£12,000			
	£6,000	apportioned	2,000	4,000
Relevant income carried forward	£6,000		Nil	Nil

In *Year 2* A and B are assessed to income tax on £4,000 and £8,000 of their respective benefits. The balance is assessed in *Year 3*.

f) *CGT tie-in*

If the benefit is of a capital nature and results from a capital gain made by the non-resident, the same sum is not charged to both income tax under s 731 and CGT under TCGA 1992 s 87. To the extent that the benefit exceeds relevant income it is charged to CGT, in which case, it cannot be treated as income in a subsequent year under s 731 (s 734). **[18.125]**

5 Powers of HMRC to obtain information (ITA 2007 s 748)

HMRC has wide investigatory powers for the purposes of this section which are exercisable against a taxpayer, and also against his advisers. It can demand, at 28 days' notice, such particulars as it deems necessary.

A solicitor is exempt from these powers and can only be compelled to state that he was acting on his client's behalf and to give the client's name and address. However, he is only exempt to the extent that he is acting *qua* solicitor. Thus, a solicitor would not be able to claim the exemption in respect of his own affairs.

A bank is also exempt from providing details of ordinary banking transactions (s 748(5)), except to the extent that it has acted for a customer in connection with either the formation and management of a non-resident company which would be close if resident in the UK and is not a trading company, or the creation or execution of a trust which may be used for schemes under these provisions. The banks' exemption was narrowly construed in *Royal Bank of Canada v IRC* (1972) and in *Clinch v IRC* (1973) where a 'fishing expedition' was upheld in the courts. Other advisers, eg accountants, have no exemption from s 748. **[18.126]**

6 The legislation – an overview

It is interesting to note that a UK domiciliary may still employ an offshore trust to obtain an income tax advantage for his family without falling within

s 720 although s 731 will still apply to benefits received by beneficiaries. The following factors should be borne in mind:
(1) the trust must be discretionary; all trustees must be non-resident and income must be foreign source;
(2) the settlor and his spouse must be excluded from all benefit; they must not receive any benefit; nor be entitled to control the application of the income;
(3) UK tax is avoided provided that the income is accumulated or distributions are made only to non-residents or to non UK domiciliaries who do not remit the income to the UK.
(4) The inheritance tax and capital gains tax implications of such a transfer need also to be considered particularly following the changes in FA 2006 to the application of inheritance tax to trusts. [18.127]

The proposed 2017–18 changes are expected to overhaul the way that the transfer of assets abroad legislation operates to tax benefits received from offshore trusts. [18.128]

Section 3 Capital gains tax

Chapters
19   CGT – basic principles
20   CGT – entrepreneurs' relief
21   CGT – death
22   CGT – exemptions and reliefs
23   CGT – the main residence
24   CGT – gifts and sales at an undervalue
25   CGT – settlements
26   CGT – companies and shareholders
27   CGT – offshore matters for individuals
27A Offshore trusts and CGT

Section 5 Capital gains tax

19 CGT – basic principles

Updated by Jackie Anderson, Chartered Accountant and Chartered Tax Advisor, LHA Consulting Ltd

I Introduction [19.2]
II Calculation of the gain [19.13]
III Losses for CGT [19.44]
IV Calculating the tax payable [19.49]
V Meaning of 'disposal' [19.63]
VI Capital gain or income profit? [19.80]

> 'The Income Tax Acts proceeded on the principle that to be chargeable as income, receipts must be derived from an identified "source". Receipts so derived, the "fruit" of the "tree", were income, but the source itself was a capital asset, and a profit from the sale of the source was a capital profit.'
> (Capital Gains Manual 10200 – Reason for legislation)

[19.1]

I INTRODUCTION

1 Background

Prior to 1962 all capital gains were free of tax. During the period 1962 to 1965 short-term capital gains were charged to income tax. A separate tax, capital gains tax (CGT), was introduced in FA 1965 to cover all capital gains, both short-term and long-term; the CGT legislation has since been consolidated, first in the Capital Gains Tax Act 1979 and then again in the Taxation of Chargeable Gains Act 1992 (TCGA 1992). It was largely introduced to tax profits left untaxed by income tax. Income tax, in the much quoted dictum of Lord Macnaghten, is 'a tax on income' and does not (save in exceptional cases where capital is deemed to be income) tax the profit made on a disposal of a capital asset.

The then Chancellor of the Exchequer, James Callaghan, in his 1965 Budget speech introducing CGT, explained:

> 'Yield is not my main purpose ... The failure to tax capital gains is ... the greatest blot on our existing system of direct taxation. There is little dispute nowadays that capital gains confer much the same kind of benefit on the recipient as taxed

earnings more hardly won. Yet earnings pay tax in full while capital gains go free ... This new tax will provide a background of equity and fair play ... ' [19.2]

a) *Overlap with income tax*

CGT aims to tax only what is untaxed by income tax and, normally, there will be no CGT on a transaction that is chargeable to income tax. Hence, in the case of certain transactions which might attract both taxes, CGT is chargeable on only so much of the transaction as is not charged to income tax, as is the case, for instance, on the sale of assets which qualify for capital allowances (see [19.47]), and on the grant of leases at a premium where part of the premium is chargeable to income tax under the property income provisions of Income Tax (Trading and Other Income) Act 2005 (ITTOIA 2005), Pt 3: see [12.81] and [19.42]).

There is no general rule against double taxation that prevents the same sum from being subject to two different taxes and in *Bye v Coren* (1986) Scott J (whose judgment was upheld in the Court of Appeal) held that 'whether it is so subject is a matter of construction of the statute or statutes which have imposed the taxes'. However, TCGA 1992 s 37 will provide relief in most cases since its effect is that once an income tax assessment has become final in respect of a sum of money the same person cannot be subject to a CGT assessment on that same sum. There is, of course, nothing to prevent HMRC from raising alternative assessments (eg to income tax and CGT) on the same sum of money (*Bye v Coren*, above, and *IRC v Wilkinson* (1992)).

For the use of trading losses to reduce chargeable gains, see Income Tax Act 2007 (ITA 2007) s 71 which is discussed at [11.61]. [19.3]

b) *The changing face of CGT*

The scope of the tax has fluctuated greatly since its introduction in 1965. The rate of CGT has likewise changed since its introduction. Initially tax on chargeable gains was levied at a flat rate of 30% and this prevailed up to 1987–88. FA 1988 then abolished this separate rate of tax for individuals and charged gains to income tax by treating an individual's gains as the top slice of his income.

The charge on death was removed in 1971. The taxation of inflationary gains was originally largely removed by the introduction of an indexation allowance (FA 1982), and the re-basing of the acquisition cost of an asset to its market value on 31 March 1982 (instead of 1965) (FA 1988).

This trend towards limiting the scope of the tax was, however, reversed by changes made in FA 1989. These concerned lifetime gifts where the position from 1980 had been that in most cases tax could be postponed by the exercise of a hold-over election. It is now only possible to make such an election in a limited number of cases (see **Chapter 24**). As a result, CGT may be charged on a gift of assets where hold-over relief is not available so that the curious position is reached that a tax aimed at catching profits will often apply to gifts (deemed profits) whereas the tax intended to catch all gifts (IHT, see **Chapter 28**) will only apply to certain lifetime gifts.

Further major reforms to both the scope and the effective rate of CGT took place in 1998 following a widespread consultation initiated by the then

Chancellor, Gordon Brown. Taper relief was introduced for individuals (and trustees and personal representatives) but not for companies, replacing the indexation allowance in respect of periods of ownership after April 1998, and linking the amount of gain chargeable to CGT to the type of asset and the number of years it was held. The amount of taper relief was significantly more generous for 'business assets' than for 'non-business assets', so that a gain on sale of a business asset that had been owned by a higher rate taxpayer for at least two years was charged to tax at an effective top rate of just 10%. The effective top rate of tax for a non-business asset varied from 40% to 24% depending on how long the asset had been owned.

The system introduced by Gordon Brown proved very complex and taper relief was subject to major revisions in each Finance Act from 2000 to 2003 (inclusive). The then Chancellor, Alistair Darling, announced a simplification of the CGT legislation in his Pre-Budget Report of October 2007. Taper relief and the indexation allowance (in respect of periods of ownership up to April 1998) were withdrawn for individuals, trustees and personal representatives with effect from 6 April 2008 and, instead, a simple CGT rate of 18% was introduced for all disposals from that date, irrespective of the period for which the asset has been held (except of course for disposals by companies which pay corporation tax on chargeable gains).

The major 'losers' from these changes were those who prior to 6 April 2008 were prospectively entitled, through the operation of taper relief, to an effective tax rate of 10% on their future disposal of business assets. Compensation was provided for such taxpayers in the form of the new 'entrepreneurs' relief', introduced by FA 2008, also introduced with effect from 6 April 2008, which had the effect of restoring the 10% rate on the first £1m of gains from the disposal of business assets that qualified for the relief (though it should be noted that several assets which qualified for business asset taper relief do not qualify for entrepreneurs' relief). The lifetime limit of £1m was increased to £2m by FA 2010 following Alistair Darling's final Budget but it was widely thought that, given the considerable disparity between the then top rate of income tax of 50% (from April 2010) and the current rate of CGT of 18%, the newly elected Coalition Government would announce an increase in the rate of CGT in the first post-election Budget to implement their commitment to 'tax non-business capital gains at rates similar or close to those applied to income'. In the result the Chancellor, George Osborne, did not really do that; the new rate of CGT for higher rate taxpayers was increased by F(No 2)A 2010 to just 28%. The same rate of 28% applied to trustees and personal representatives. Basic rate taxpayers still paid CGT at 18%. The 28% rate applied to gains from disposals made on and after 23 June 2010. The introduction of a new rate of CGT part way through a tax year gave rise to complexities and some transitional provisions which were generally, though not invariably, helpful to the taxpayer.

At the same time, F(No 2)A 2010 further increased the lifetime limit for entrepreneurs' relief from £2m to £5m, an extension widely seen as very generous. George Osborne confirmed that the 28% rate would stay for the remainder of that parliament, and an initial report by the Office for Tax Simplification stated that any further changes to the CGT regime would be undesirable. Other than the further increase in the lifetime allowance for entrepreneurs' relief to £10m by FA 2011, the then Coalition Government appeared to favour a period of relative stability until the General Election in May 2015.

The first majority Conservative government since 1997 was elected in May 2015, and has continued the CGT squeeze on buy-to-let investors and second-home owners (see [19.60]), non-resident residential property owners (see [19.6]) and non-individual vehicles used to hold UK residential property (see [19.6]). It has also signalled encouragement for non-residential property investors by reducing CGT rates (see [19.49]) and extending entrepreneurs' relief (see **Chapter 20**). [19.4]

2 Basic principles

CGT is charged on any gain resulting when a **chargeable person** makes a **chargeable disposal** of a **chargeable asset**. Tax is charged on so much of the gain as is left after taking into account any exemptions or reliefs and after deducting any allowable losses.

CGT is payable on 31 January following the year of assessment in which the gain becomes chargeable (see [19.60]).

When the tax was introduced in 1965 it was not retrospective. Accordingly, it only taxed gains arising on or after 6 April in that year. Thus, where an individual acquired an asset in 1960 for £10,000 and sold it in 1970 for £20,000, thereby realising a gain of £10,000, only such part of the gain as accrued after 6 April 1965 was charged (see [19.29]). For assets owned on 31 March 1982, the chargeable gain is computed on the basis that the asset in question had been acquired in March 1982 at its then market value (TCGA 1992, s 35). This re-basing of the tax (discussed in detail at [19.30]) means that gains accruing between 1965 and 1982 have been removed from the tax charge. [19.5]

a) *Who is a 'chargeable person'? (TCGA 1992 s 2)*

Chargeable persons include individuals, trustees and personal representatives who meet the 'residence condition' – which is broadly that they are resident in the UK during the tax year in question. UK residents who are also domiciled in the UK are liable to CGT on their worldwide chargeable gains.

Non-residents were generally not taxed on the disposal of UK-situs assets unless they were carrying on a business in the UK through a permanent establishment (TCGA 1992 s 10). However, non-UK residents – including non-resident individuals, partnerships, trustees and personal representatives, and some non-resident companies – became subject to CGT on gains arising on disposals of UK residential property from 6 April 2015 onwards.

Strictly, individuals are taxed as UK residents for the whole tax year even when they are present here for only part of it. However, there is a 'split year' treatment which relates to chargeable gains arising to individuals who arrive in, or leave, the UK during the year. If the year is a split year, the individual is not charged to CGT in respect of their chargeable gains which accrue during the overseas part of that year (TCGA 1992 s 2(1B)).

There is a further provision that charges CGT on the gains of 'temporary non-residents', namely those who become temporarily non-resident (for less than five tax years) on assets owned before they left the UK (TCGA 1992 s 10A).

Introduction 593

In the case of partners, each partner is charged separately in respect of his share of the partnership gains (TCGA 1992 s 59, see **Chapter 44**).

Charities, pension funds and certain investment vehicles are generally exempt from CGT on their gains (see **[19.12]**).

Although companies are not chargeable persons for CGT purposes, the corporation tax to which they are subject is levied on corporate profits that include chargeable gains. Companies calculate their chargeable gains using broadly the same principles as individuals.

The Government is consulting during 2017 as to whether the UK property income of non-UK resident companies should become chargeable to corporation tax (rather than to income tax as is currently the case). This could bring non-resident companies within the charge to CGT (to the extent that they are not already subject to CGT, such as in respect of UK residential property).

With effect from 1 April 2013, CGT is charged (at 28%) on the disposal of properties to which the annual tax on enveloped dwellings (ATED) rules apply which, broadly, are residential properties valued at more than £2 million which are held by 'non-natural persons' (including companies, partnerships with company members and Collective Investment Schemes). This £2 million threshold fell to £1 million from 6 April 2015, and then down to £500,000 from 6 April 2016. These provisions apply to both UK and offshore persons.

For further consideration of the taxation of non-residents see **Chapter 27** and **Chapter 27A**. [19.6]

b) *What is a 'chargeable disposal'?*

A chargeable gain can potentially arise whenever a person disposes of an asset or an interest in an asset, for example, by sale or gift, but 'disposal' for these purposes (while not defined in the legislation) extends to include any transaction as a result of which the person ceases to own the asset or an interest in the asset.

Hence, a 'disposal' can include a part disposal (TCGA 1992 s 21), a gift, a transfer to a third party, an exchange, the creation of rights over an asset (eg by way of trust) and the distribution of an asset by a company to a shareholder (see also **[19.63]**).

'Disposal' is extended to include cases where a capital sum is derived from an asset (for instance, insurance money paid for the damage to or destruction of an asset) (see **[19.64]**), the total loss or destruction of an asset (see **[19.65]**), and the receipt of compensation and damages (see **[19.66]**). [19.7]

c) *What is a 'chargeable asset'? (TCGA 1992 s 21(1))*

All forms of property are assets for CGT purposes including options, debts, intangible property, currency (other than sterling), and any form of property created by the person disposing of it (for example, goodwill), or otherwise being owned without having been acquired (TCGA 1992 s 21(1)).

Examples of assets chargeable to CGT include shares and securities, land and property (and interests therein), milk quotas, business and professional goodwill, and copyright.

The gain on the disposal of certain other assets is exempt from charge (see **[19.9]** and **Chapter 22**).

An asset which cannot be transferred by sale or gift may be within the tax charge. In *O'Brien v Benson's Hosiery (Holdings) Ltd* (1979), for instance, a director under a seven-year service contract paid his employer £50,000 to be released from his obligations. The employer was charged to CGT on the basis that the contract, despite being non-assignable, was an asset under TCGA 1992 s 21(1) so that the release of those rights resulted in 'a capital sum being received in return for the forfeiture or surrender of rights' (TCGA 1992 s 22(1)(c); see further **[19.64]**).

In *Marren v Ingles* (1980) shares in a private company were sold for £750 per share, payable at the time of the sale, plus a further sum if the company obtained a Stock Exchange quotation; the market value of the shares at that time was in excess of £750 per share. Two years later a quotation was obtained and a further £2,825 per share was paid. The House of Lords held that the taxpayers were initially liable to CGT calculated on the original sale price of £750 per share plus the value of the contingent right to receive a further sum – that right was a separate asset, a *chose in action*, which was disposed of for £2,825 per share two years later, leading to a further CGT liability (see **[19.18]**).

A 'right' may be used in both a colloquial and a legal sense. In its wider colloquial sense a right is not an asset for CGT purposes: it must be legally enforceable and capable of being turned into money. In *Kirby v Thorn EMI plc* (1988) HMRC initially argued that the right to engage in commercial activity was an asset for CGT purposes with the result that if the taxpayers agreed to restrict their commercial activities in return for a capital payment, that sum would be brought into charge to tax. This argument was rejected on the basis that freedom to indulge in commercial activity was not a legal right constituting an asset for CGT purposes. On appeal, HMRC produced an alternative argument that the taxpayers had derived a capital sum from the firm's goodwill so that the payment in question was chargeable to CGT. In this argument it was successful (see **[19.64]**). **[19.8]**

3 CGT exemptions and reliefs

a) *CGT exemptions*

CGT exemptions are discussed in full in **Chapters 22 AND 23.** Gains arising on the disposal of exempt assets are not liable to CGT but, by the same token, no capital loss relief will be available on the disposal of exempt assets. **[19.9]**

b) *CGT reliefs*

The main CGT reliefs are as follows:
(1) Entrepreneurs' relief (see **Chapter 20**).
(2) Disposals on death (see **Chapter 21**).
(3) Roll-over relief for replacement of business assets (see **Chapter 22**).
(4) Roll-over relief on the transfer of business assets ('incorporation relief') (see **Chapter 22**).
(5) Private residence relief (see **Chapter 23**).
(6) Hold-over relief for gifts of business assets (see **Chapter 24**).
(7) Hold-over relief for gifts attracting an immediate IHT charge (see **Chapter 24**).

(8) Company 'reorganisations' (see **Chapter 26**).
(9) Disincorporation relief (TCGA 1992 ss 162B) (see **Chapter 22**).
(10) Substantial Shareholding Exemption (see **Chapter 41**).
(11) Seed Enterprise Investment Scheme reinvestment of gains (see **Chapter 15**). [19.10]

c) *No gain/no loss transactions*

No gain/no loss transactions are deemed by law to take place on such a basis that neither a gain, nor a loss, arises to the transferor, and include the following:
(1) Transfers between married persons (or civil partners) living together (see **Chapter 51**).
(2) Disposals between companies within a 75% group (see **Chapter 43**). [19.11]

d) *Exempt persons*

Gains are not liable to CGT where they arise to the following exempt persons:
(1) Charities (TCGA 1992 s 256).
(2) Community Amateur Sports Clubs (CASCs) (CTA 2010 s 665).
(3) Pension funds (TCGA 1992 271(1A)).
(4) Nominees or bare trustees (TCGA 1992 s 60).
(5) Authorised unit trusts, investments trusts, etc (TCGA 1992 s 100). [19.12]

II CALCULATION OF THE GAIN

The chargeable gain is found by taking the disposal consideration of the asset and deducting from that figure the allowable expenditure (often called the '*base cost*').

A pro forma CGT computation could be set out as follows:

	£	£
Disposal/sale proceeds (or market value)		X
Less: Incidental costs of disposal/sale		(X)
Net disposal proceeds		X
Less: Allowable expenditure		
Acquisition cost (or 31 March 1982 value)	X	
Incidental cost of acquisition	X	
Improvement costs	X	
		(X)
Gain or loss		X
CGT elections/reliefs		(X)
Net gain		X
Less: Annual exemption		(X)
Taxable gain		X

The disponer's acquisition cost is usually the main item of expenditure. If the allowable expenditure exceeds the disposal consideration, the disponer has made a loss for CGT purposes which may be used to reduce the chargeable gains that he has made on disposals of other assets (see TCGA 1992 s 2(2) and [19.44]).

In addition, the allowable expenditure of companies may be increased by indexation relief (see [19.24]).

EXAMPLE 19.1

A sells a painting for £20,000 (the disposal consideration). He bought it six months ago for £14,000 (the acquisition cost) and has incurred no other deductible expenses. His chargeable gain is £6,000. If A sold the picture for £10,000 he would have an allowable loss of £4,000.

The onus is on the taxpayer to establish what (if any) part of the disposal consideration is not within the charge to CGT (see *Neely v Rourke* (1987)).

[19.13]

1 What is the consideration for the disposal?

a) *General*

When the disposal is by way of a sale at arm's length, the consideration for the disposal will be the proceeds of sale.

For disposals between married couples and civil partners the disposal consideration is deemed to be the sum which results in neither a gain nor a loss arising provided they have been living together at some time during the tax year of disposal (TCGA 1992 s 58). This rule applies irrespective of the actual consideration given (if any). This effectively means that the transferee inherits the transferor's base cost. This rule does not apply to co-habiting couples (see **Chapter 51**). Gains and losses on property owned jointly by spouses or civil partners are calculated according to the underlying beneficial ownership.

Any other disposal which is not 'at arm's length' is deemed to be for a consideration equal to the market value of the asset at that date (TCGA 1992 s 17). This applies to gifts, to disposals between 'connected persons' (TCGA 1992 s 18) (where the disposal is *always* deemed to be made otherwise than by way of a bargain at arm's length), to transfers of assets by a settlor into a settlement, and to certain distributions by a company in respect of shares (TCGA 1992 s 17(1)(a)).

In the case of disposals by persons who are exempt from CGT (see [19.12]), the recipient is taken to acquire the asset at market value.

EXAMPLE 19.2

(1) Sarah gives her husband a Richard Eurich painting for which she had paid £10,000. He is deemed to acquire the picture for such sum as ensures neither gain nor loss results to Sarah (ie £10,000).

(2) A gives a Ming vase worth £40,000 to his son. A has made a gift to a 'connected person' and so the deemed consideration for the disposal would be £40,000.

The market value of the asset is also taken to be the disposal consideration whenever the actual consideration cannot be valued, or where the consideration is the provision of services as an employee or director (TCGA 1992 s 17(1)(b), but note that this provision does not apply to the exercise of an option: see [19.70]).

EXAMPLE 19.3

A, an antiques dealer, gives B, a fellow dealer, his country cottage worth £40,000 in consideration of B entering into a restrictive covenant with A, whereby B agrees not to open an antique shop in competition with A. The consideration for the disposal is taken to be £40,000.

This market value rule can work to a taxpayer's advantage by giving the recipient a high acquisition cost for any future disposal in a transaction where the disponer is not charged to CGT on the gain (known as '*reverse Nairn Williamson*' arrangements). To some extent this is prevented by TCGA 1992 s 17(2) which provides that, where there is an acquisition without a disposal (eg the issue of shares by a company) and either no consideration is given for the asset, or the consideration is less than its market value, the actual consideration (if any) given prevails (see CG 14550).

EXAMPLE 19.4

A Ltd issues 1,000 £1 ordinary shares to B at par when their market value is £2 per share. The issue of shares by a company is not a disposal. This is, therefore, an acquisition of a chargeable asset by B without a disposal. Were it not for s 17(2), B's acquisition cost of the shares would be £2,000. As it is, B's acquisition cost is what he actually paid for the shares: ie £1,000.

In *Steven Cooling v R & C Comrs* (2015), the First-tier Tribunal confirmed that the waiver of a debt was part of the consideration for the sale of the taxpayer's shares in the target company for CGT purposes, where the share purchase agreement provided that debt owed by the taxpayer under a related asset purchase agreement would not be recovered by the target company. [19.14]

b) *Connected persons*

'Connected persons' for CGT purposes fall into four categories (TCGA 1992 s 286):
(1) An individual is connected with their spouse or civil partner, their own relatives, the relatives of their spouse or civil partner, and the spouses or civil partners of their relatives (s 286(2)). Relatives include siblings, ancestors (parents, grandparents) and lineal descendants (children, grandchildren) (s 286(8), but not lateral relatives (uncles, aunts, nephews and nieces). Married status continues for these purposes until the final divorce (see *Aspden v Hildesley* (1982)).

(2) A company is connected with another company if both are under common control (s 286(5)). A company is connected with another person if the person (either alone or with other persons connected with him) controls that company (s 286(6)).

(3) A business partner is connected with their fellow partner(s), and their partner's spouse or civil partner, and the partners' relatives, except in relation to acquisitions and disposals of partnership assets (for example, goodwill for a new partner) under bona fide commercial arrangements (s 286(4)).

(4) A trustee is connected with the settlor, with any person connected with the settlor, and with any close company in which the trustee is a participator (for the definition of close company and participator, see **Chapter 41**). A trustee is not automatically connected with a beneficiary and, once the settlor dies, ceases to be connected with persons connected with the settlor (CG 14590).

EXAMPLE 19.5

A would like to 'unlock' the unrealised losses on a number of his assets. He disposes of the assets into a trust in which he enjoys a life interest. The result is to crystallise the loss but, because of the connected persons rule, that loss will only be available to set against gains on disposals *between the same parties* (see **[19.45]**). Accordingly, A disposes of assets showing a gain to the same trustees. Now the loss can be offset against that gain and, if those assets are immediately sold by the trustees, no chargeable gain will result to them. **[19.15]**

c) *The market value of assets*

Market value is the price for which the asset could be sold on the open market (TCGA 1992 s 272).

The market value of shares and securities listed in The Stock Exchange Daily Official List is taken as the lesser of:

(1) the lower of the two prices quoted for that security in the Daily Official List plus one quarter of the difference between the two prices ('quarter-up'); and

(2) half way between the highest and lowest prices at which bargains were recorded in that security on the relevant date (excluding bargains at special prices) ('mid-price').

Unquoted shares and securities are valued on a number of criteria including the size of the holding and the degree of control of the company (TCGA 1992 s 273).

TCGA 1992, s 19 modifies the basic rule for 'linked transactions', applying when assets are fragmented (ie when one transferor makes two or more transfers to connected persons and the transfers occur within six years of each other).

EXAMPLE 19.6

Alf owned a pair of Ming vases which as a pair were worth £100,000 but separately each was worth only £40,000. In January 2017, he gave one to his daughter and in the following July the other to his son.

(1) The disposal to his daughter was for an original market value of £40,000. However, as it is linked to the later disposal to his son, the assets disposed of by the two disposals are valued as if they were disposed of by one disposal and the value attributed to each disposal is the appropriate proportion of that value. The market value of the two vases is £100,000 and the appropriate proportion is £50,000. (This revaluation of an earlier transaction will lead to an additional CGT liability.)

(2) The later disposal to Alf's son, occurring within six years, is a linked transaction. Again the original market value (£40,000) is replaced by the appropriate proportion (£50,000).

Disposals to a spouse or civil partner are treated as giving rise to neither gain nor loss (TCGA 1992, s 58: see [**19.14**]) but may form part of a series in order to determine the value of any of the other transactions in that series (TCGA 1992 s 19(2)). [**19.16**]

d) *Deferred consideration*

Where the consideration for the disposal is known at the date of the disposal (which will normally be the date of contract: TCGA 1992 s 28 and see [**19.78**]) but is payable in instalments (TCGA 1992 s 280: see [**19.61**]) or is subject to a contingency (TCGA 1992 s 48), the disponer is taxed on a gain calculated by reference to the full amount of the consideration receivable with no discount for the fact that payment is postponed. If, in fact, they never receive the full consideration then their original CGT liability is adjusted (TCGA 1992 s 48(1)).

EXAMPLE 19.7

(1) A bought land two years ago for £50,000. He sells it today for £100,000 payable in two years' time. A is taxed now on a gain of £50,000 despite the fact that he has received nothing and with no discount for the fact that the right to £100,000 in two years' time is not worth £100,000 today. If A had been 'connected' with his purchaser, market value would be substituted for the actual consideration under s 17 thereby enabling a 'discount' to be taken into account.

(2) Mucky sells four oil rigs for a consideration of $38.6m payable by instalments over nine years. At exchange rates prevailing at the date of disposal this produced a gain of £6.7m. Taking rates at the time when each instalment was paid, however, Mucky realised a loss of £2.7m. The basic CGT rule for foreign currency transactions is that the gain is to be computed by taking the exchange rate equivalent of the allowable expenditure at the time when it was incurred and the rate equivalent of the disposal consideration at the date of disposal (see *Capcount Trading v Evans* (1993)). Accepting this position, will Mucky succeed in arguing that because of the change in exchange rates part of his consideration was irrecoverable under TCGA 1992 s 48? Not according to the Court of Appeal who held that 'consideration' meant what was promised (ie dollars) rather than any sterling equivalent (see *Loffland Bros North Sea Inc v Goodbrand* (1998)). (It is thought that this decision would not be affected by the provisions of FA 2012, which exempt from charge gains made on withdrawals from foreign currency bank accounts (see [**19.9**]).

[**19.17**]

e) *Marren v Ingles*

It may be that the deferred consideration cannot be valued because it is dependent on some future contingency. In *Marren v Ingles* (1980) (see **[19.8]**) part of the payment for the disposal of shares was to be calculated by reference to the price of the shares if and when the company obtained a Stock Exchange listing. The taxpayer's gain at the time of the disposal of the shares could not be calculated by reference to such unquantifiable consideration. Accordingly he was treated as making two separate disposals. The first was the disposal of the shares. The consideration for this was the payment that the taxpayer actually received plus the value (if any) of the right to receive the future deferred sum (a *chose in action*). The value of the *chose in action* then formed the acquisition cost of that asset. Hence, once the deferred consideration became payable, the taxpayer was treated as making a second disposal, this time of the *chose in action*. He was, therefore, chargeable on the difference between the consideration received and whatever was the acquisition cost of that asset.

The House of Lords did not attempt to value the *chose in action*. The value has to be agreed with the Shares Valuation Division (SVD) of HMRC. In some cases the deferred consideration is so uncertain that the value of it at the time of the sale of the shares is nominal, with the result that on the first disposal (of the shares) the gain is calculated by reference only to the cash received, whilst on the second disposal (of the *chose in action*) any consideration received is entirely gain. There is no element of double taxation involved in the *Marren v Ingles* situation. Instead, the CGT is collected (in effect) in two instalments with the result that the taxpayer may be better off than A in *Example 19.7(1)*, above, who is taxed on money years before receiving it.

The *Marren v Ingles* principle applies most commonly to 'earn-out' deals, where the seller of shares receives a fixed sum on completion, with further sums being paid at a later date calculated by reference to a formula which takes into account the actual results of the business over the period from completion. In these cases the *chose in action* (the 'earn-out' right) usually has some value at the time of the sale of the shares and this means the seller can be taxed on the SVD-agreed value of the 'earn-out' right before he has received any consideration from the 'earn-out'.

In the event that the earn-out consideration received is *less* than the initial value of the earn-out right agreed with SVD, the seller will make a loss for CGT purposes, and relief may be available against the gain on the disposal of the original shares (see TCGA 1992 ss 279A). **[19.18]**

2 What expenditure is deductible?

Once the disposal consideration is known, the chargeable gain (or allowable loss) can be calculated by deducting allowable expenditure. This is defined in TCGA 1992 s 38 as 'expenditure incurred wholly and exclusively' in: **[19.19]**

a) *Acquiring the asset*

The purchase price (or market value), including certain incidental costs of acquisition (see **[19.22]**), or the cost of creating or providing it where the asset was created rather than acquired (for example, a painting), is deductible

(TCGA 1992 s 38(1)(a)). In certain circumstances a deemed acquisition cost will be deducted, for example, when an asset is acquired by inheritance (probate value being the acquisition cost) and when the 31 March 1982 re-basing rules apply (TCGA 1992 s 35(2)). **[19.20]**

b) *Enhancing the value of the asset*

Enhancement expenditure is an allowable deduction provided that the expenditure is reflected in the state or nature of the asset at the time of its disposal (TCGA 1992 s 38(1)(b)). (It is presupposed that the asset is in existence when the expenditure is incurred (*Garner v Pounds Shipowners and Shipbreakers Ltd* (2000)).) Thus, in the case of land, the costs of an application for planning permission which is never granted are not deductible, whereas the costs of building an extension are. Also deductible under this head are the costs of 'establishing, preserving or defending' title to the asset (for example, the costs of a boundary dispute and, in the case of personal representatives, a proportion of probate expenses or, following *Lee v Jewitt* (2000), where the costs of a partnership dispute were incurred in defending the taxpayer's title to goodwill).

In *Chaney v Watkis* (1986) the taxpayer agreed to pay his mother-in-law a cash sum (£9,400) if she surrendered up vacant possession of a house which he owned and wished to sell. Between exchange of contracts for the sale of the property and completion this agreement was varied by mutual consent. Instead of the cash sum, the taxpayer agreed to build an extension onto his own home and allow her to occupy it rent-free for life. It was held that the cash sum would have been deductible in arriving at his gain on sale of the house if it had been paid (since vacant possession enhanced the value of the house). The same principle applied to a consideration in money's worth (the rent-free accommodation) and the case was remitted to the Commissioners for them to determine the value of this consideration. Two matters are worthy of note: *first*, that expenditure incurred post-contract but pre-completion of the sale was taken into account and the phrase 'at the time of the disposal' in TCGA 1992 s 38(1)(b) must be construed accordingly; and, *second*, that the taxpayer's mother-in-law was a protected tenant of the property (and had been before he purchased the house) and hence the agreement with her was a commercial arrangement.

In the more recent case of *R & C Comrs v J Blackwell* (2015), the taxpayer sought to deduct a substantial sum of money spent to release himself from an agreement to sell certain shares so that he could accept a much higher bid from another purchaser. In finding for the taxpayer, the First-tier Tribunal agreed that the expenditure had enhanced the value of the shares because it had enabled a higher bid to be accepted, and found also that although the 'nature' of the shares remained the same, the expenditure had changed their 'state' in much the same way that allowable expenditure incurred making roadworthy a car unfit to be driven would change its state rather than its nature. However, the Upper Tribunal found that the First-tier Tribunal had made an error of law as the shares needed to be looked at from the perspective of the purchaser, and their 'state' had not changed in that respect, so the payment made should not form part of the computation of his gain. The taxpayer then appealed to the Court of Appeal which similarly dismissed his appeal.

HMRC won a further victory in *Patel & Others v R & C Comrs* (2016) when, the First-tier Tribunal held that compensation paid by the taxpayer for the loss of the taxpayer-controlled company's ability to trade from his property was not enhancement expenditure on the property, as the payment neither enhanced the value of the asset nor was reflected in the state or nature of the asset at the time of disposal.

In *Mulloy v R & C Comrs* (2016), a claim for allowable expenditure in relation to improvements to leasehold premises failed as the leasehold was about to expire, meaning its value was not enhanced.

The case of *Knight v R & C Comrs* (2016) showed that in computing capital gains on foreign assets, enhancement expenditure should be converted into sterling on the date that the expenditure was incurred, rather than being offset against sale proceeds with the net gain then being converted into sterling. **[19.21]**

c) *Disposing of the asset*

The incidental costs of making the disposal are deductible (TCGA 1992 s 38(1)(c)).

Allowable incidental costs of acquisition or disposal include professional fees paid to a surveyor, valuer, auctioneer, accountant, agent or legal adviser, together with the costs of the transfer or conveyance (including stamp duty or stamp duty land tax) (TCGA 1992 s 38(2)). In addition, the costs of advertising to find a buyer or seller, and any costs incurred in making valuations or apportionments necessary for calculating CGT, are allowable. Expenses incurred in making a valuation include the costs of an initial valuation to enable a tax return to be submitted, or for the purposes of a post transaction valuation check, but include neither the costs of agreeing or negotiating that value with HMRC, nor the costs of appealing an assessment (*Caton's Administrators v Couch* (1997)). In the recent case of *John Arthur Day and Amanda Jane Dalgety v R & C Comrs* (2015), the First-tier Tribunal found that mortgage fees were not deductible. Other taxes, such as IHT on a gift, are also not deductible.

The requirement in TCGA 1992 s 38 that expenditure must be 'wholly and exclusively' incurred has been interpreted relatively liberally. In *IRC v Richards' Executors* (1971), personal representatives who sold shares at a profit claimed to deduct from the sale proceeds the cost of valuing the relevant part of the deceased's estate for probate. The House of Lords held that they could do so even though the valuation was for the purposes of estate duty as well as for establishing title (ie even though the costs were 'dual purpose expenditure').

'Expenditure' within TCGA 1992 s 38 must be something that reduces the taxpayer's estate in some quantifiable way. Thus in *Oram v Johnson* (1980) the taxpayer who bought a second home for £2,500, renovated it himself and later sold it for £11,500 could not deduct the notional cost of his own labour.

On a deemed disposal and reacquisition (see **[25.41]**) notional expenses are not deductible (TCGA 1992 s 38(4)), but actual expenses are. Thus, in *IRC v Chubb's Settlement Trustees* (1971), where the life tenant and the remainderman ended a settlement by dividing the capital between them so that there was a deemed disposal under (now) TCGA 1992 s 71, the costs of preparing the deed of variation of the settlement were deductible. **[19.22]**

d) Disallowed expenditure

The deduction of certain items of expenditure is specifically prohibited including, for example, interest on a loan to acquire the asset (TCGA 1992 s 38(3)). In addition, any sums that a person can deduct in calculating his income for income tax are excluded (TCGA 1992 s 39). Additionally, no sum is deductible for CGT purposes which would be deductible for income tax if the disponer were in fact using the relevant asset in a trade.

EXAMPLE 19.8

A buys a country cottage in 2009 for £200,000 to rent to high net worth individuals. He spends £30,000 on installing a gold plated bathroom and £14,000 on mending the leaking roof. Over the following years he spends a further £500 on repairing leaking radiators and £400 on general maintenance. He pays a total of £3,000 on property insurance. He sells it in May 2017 for £650,000.
His chargeable gain is:

	£	£
Sale proceeds		650,000
Less:		
Acquisition cost	200,000	
Cost of improvements	30,000	230,000
		£420,000

The cost of repairs, maintenance and insurance are not deductible for CGT because they are deductible in computing his income under the property income rules of ITTOIA 2005 Part 3. The insurance premiums are specifically disallowed under TCGA 1992 s 205.

If A had bought the cottage as a second home, and not to rent out, his gain on sale would still be £420,000; the other items are disallowed as deductions for CGT because they are of an income nature.

In the recent case of *Morrison v R & C Comrs* (2014), the Scottish Court of Session considered s 49, under which a gain can be reduced where a contingent liability subsequently arises and is enforced. In that case, it was held that the gain could be reduced by a claim against the vendor, a major shareholder and chairman and chief executive of Morrison plc, in relation to some profit forecasts which 'falsely misrepresented' how much the company was worth. [19.23]

3 The indexation of allowable expenditure: abolished for disposals by individuals, trustees and PRs on and after 6 April 2008

a) *Rationale for an indexation allowance*

Before 1982 CGT made no allowance for the effects of inflation on the value of chargeable assets and, accordingly, it taxed both 'real' and 'paper' profits. FA 1982 afforded a measure of relief from April 1982 by introducing an indexation allowance for disposals of assets made by individuals, trustees, personal representatives and companies. Hence, allowable expenditure became index-linked (to rises in the Retail Prices Index) so that only 'real' profits were subject to CGT. [19.24]

b) *The changes of FA 1998 and FA 2008*

For individuals, trustees and personal representatives, FA 1998 froze the indexation allowance as at April 1998 so that it was available only in relation to increases in the RPI between the month of acquisition (or, if later, 31 March 1982) and April 1998, even if the disposal took place after April 1998. Assets acquired in April 1998 or later did not benefit from the allowance (they attracted taper relief instead: see **Chapter 20**). FA 2008 then abolished both the indexation allowance and taper relief altogether for disposals by individuals, trustees and personal representatives taking place on and after 6 April 2008. Only the frozen element of the indexation allowance on interspousal transfers made before 6 April 2008 survived (TCGA 1992 s 35A).

However, the indexation allowance continues to apply in calculating the chargeable gains of companies (TCGA 1992 ss 52A–57). [19.25]

c) *Basic rules of indexation*

For disposals made by companies (and by individuals, trustees and personal representatives before 6 April 2008), the indexation allowance is calculated as follows (TCGA 1992 s 54):

$$\frac{RD - RI}{RI}$$

where RD is the index for the month in which the disposal occurs and RI is the index for the month in which the item of expenditure was incurred, or March 1982 if later. (This fraction, calculated to three decimal places, produces the 'indexed rise' decimal which is published by HMRC each month).

Assuming that the RPI increases over this period, the allowable expenditure is multiplied by the fraction and the resultant figure (known as the 'indexation allowance') is a further allowable deduction in arriving at the chargeable gain on disposal of the asset.

EXAMPLE 19.9

A chargeable asset was bought by a company for £20,000 on 10 April 1992 and was sold for £100,000 on 31 March 2017. The RPI for April 1992 was 138.8, and for March 2017 was 269.3. The indexed rise was:

$$\frac{269.3 - 138.8}{138.8} = 0.940 \text{ (correct to three decimal places)}$$

Indexation allowance is: £20,000 × 0.940 = £18,800

Therefore, the chargeable gain was:

	£	£
Sale proceeds		100,000
Less:		
Acquisition cost	20,000	
Indexation allowance	18,800	38,800
Chargeable gain		£61,200

Assume that the asset was enhanced on 12 November 2004 for £2,000. RPI for November 2004 was 189.0. As well as the indexation allowance of £18,800 above, there would be a further indexation allowance on the enhancement costs, as follows:

$$£2,000 \times \frac{269.3 - 189.0}{189.0} = £850$$

Therefore, the chargeable gain would be £58,350 (£61,200 – £2,000 – £850).

As the indexation allowance is applied to allowable expenditure, it follows that where an asset had a nil base cost (for instance, goodwill created by the company) there could be no indexation allowance. **[19.26]**

d) *The indexation allowance and capital losses*

The indexation allowance cannot (and for individuals, trustees and personal representatives could not) create or increase a capital loss: it only operates to reduce or extinguish capital gains (TCGA 1992 s 53(1)). **[19.27]**

4 **Taper relief (TCGA 1992 s 2A; Sch A1): abolished for disposals by individuals, trustees and personal representatives on and after 6 April 2008**

These provisions and the effect of their abolition are considered in detail in **Chapter 20**. **[19.28]**

5 **Calculation of gains for assets acquired before 6 April 1965**

When CGT was introduced in 1965 it was not retrospective in its effect. Hence the general principle was that only gains after 6 April 1965 were chargeable. Accordingly, for assets acquired before 6 April 1965, the legislation contained rules determining how much gain was deemed to have accrued since that date.

However, these rules now only apply to companies. For disposals by individuals, trustees and personal representatives on and after 6 April 2008 the rules have been abolished in light of the provisions for universal re-basing to March 1982 market values (see **[19.30]**).

Generally, the gain is deemed to accrue evenly over the whole period of ownership (the so-called 'straight-line' method: TCGA 1992 Sch 2 para 16(3)).

The chargeable gain is, therefore, a proportion of the gross gain calculated by the formula:

$$\text{Gross gain} \times \frac{\text{period of ownership since 6 April 1965}}{\text{total period of ownership}} = \text{chargeable gain}$$

EXAMPLE 19.10

(Indexation allowance and 1982 re-basing has been ignored.)

	£
A company bought a picture on 5 April 1964 for	5,000
It sold it on 5 April 2017 for	19,000
Its gain was	£14,000

Its chargeable gain was: £14,000 × 52/53 = £13,735.85 (rounded up).

In applying this formula, the ownership of the asset could never be treated as beginning earlier than 6 April 1945 (TCGA 1992 Sch 2 para 16(6)) so that if it was acquired before that date it was deemed to have been acquired on that date. **[19.29]**

6 Calculation of gains on assets owned on 31 March 1982 ('re-basing')

The following rules apply to disposals of assets that were owned on 31 March 1982 by the person making the disposal. **[19.30]**

a) *Basic rule*

Assets that the taxpayer owned on 31 March 1982 are deemed to have been sold by him and immediately reacquired at market value on that date. Re-basing means that the taxpayer, on disposal, must agree with HMRC a valuation figure for the relevant asset as at March 1982 (TCGA 1992 s 35).

EXAMPLE 19.11

Jacques' valuable collection of porcelain cost £12,000 in 1963; it was worth £100,000 on 31 March 1982 and has just been sold for £175,000. In computing Jacques' capital gain arising from his disposal, re-basing to March 1982 will result in a reduction in the gain from £163,000 to £75,000.

In the case of *MB Blum v R & C Comrs* (2013), an individual purchased a property in Harrow in 1970, which he subsequently converted first into offices and then into flats. He sold the property in 2006 and self-assessed his capital gain on the basis that its market value at 31 March 1982 was £200,000. HMRC issued an amended assessment assuming the 31 March 1982 value to be £100,000. The Upper Tribunal determined that the 31 March 1982 value should be calculated as a multiple of the annual rental value of the property of £11,000 and 12.5 (being the expected 8% yield for that part of London), totalling £137,500. **[19.31]**

b) *Qualification: abolished for disposals by individuals, trustees and PRs on and after 6 April 2008*

Until 5 April 2008, in cases where a computation based on the actual costs and ignoring 1982 values would produce a smaller gain or loss, re-basing did not generally apply and it was that smaller gain or loss which was relevant. In cases where one computation would produce a gain and the other a loss, there was deemed to be neither.

For disposals on or after 6 April 2008 these qualifications apply only to companies. For individuals etc re-basing to March 1982 market values is now mandatory. [19.32]

c) *The election: abolished for disposals by individuals, trustees and PRs on and after 6 April 2008*

Because the qualifications discussed above required the taxpayer to keep pre-1982 records and usually involved alternative calculations, the taxpayer was able to make an election for re-basing to apply to all assets which he held on 31 March 1982. This election could be made at any time before 6 April 1990 or (if no relevant disposal was made by that time) by the 31 January two years after the end of the tax year of the first relevant disposal (or within such longer period as HMRC might allow). The 'first relevant disposal' meant the first disposal by the taxpayer of assets held by him on 31 March 1982, but HMRC issued a Statement of Practice 4/92 setting out certain types of disposal which they disregarded for the purpose of applying this time limit and also clarifying the circumstances in which they exercised their discretion to extend the time limit.

The election was irrevocable and applied to all assets owned on 31 March 1982 by the particular taxpayer (TCGA 1992 s 35(5)).

In light of universal re-basing to March 1982 market values for individuals, etc in relation to disposals on or after 6 April 2008, the election is now available only to companies. [19.33]

d) *Technical matters*

In exceptional cases, the re-basing to March 1982 market value is applied to a previous owner of the asset. These are situations where the disponer acquired the asset as a result of a no gain/no loss disposal that took place after 31 March 1982, and was made by a transferor who had owned the asset before that date (TCGA 1992 s 35A).

EXAMPLE 19.12

Doris inherited a gold snuff box on the death of her father in 1977. Its probate value was £10,000. In 1983 she gave it to her husband, Sid, on their wedding anniversary. In March 1982, the box was worth £25,000 and in 1983 £28,000. Sid sold the box for £35,000.

(1) In calculating Sid's gain on sale, it is assumed that the market value at 31 March 1982 (£25,000) applied to Doris for the purpose of the transfer to Sid in 1983.

(2) The 1983 transfer between spouses was made at no gain/no loss so that Sid is treated as having acquired the box for £25,000.

In certain other situations ownership of an asset may be related back to an earlier date: generally these are cases where the asset is treated as forming part of or replacing an earlier asset. This, for instance, is the case where securities are issued as the consideration for a company takeover under TCGA 1992 ss 135–137 (see **Chapter 26**).

Re-basing of the acquisition cost to market value on 31 March 1982 was introduced by FA 1988 in relation to disposals on and after 6 April 1988. Accordingly, where an asset held on 31 March 1982 had been disposed of before 6 April 1988 no re-basing would have applied; but FA 1988 (now TCGA 1992 Sch 4) provided that where the gain on such a disposal had been held-over or rolled-over, the gain ultimately realised was relieved by deducting half of that held-over or rolled-over gain. This was because part of the held-over etc gain would have related to an increase in value before 31 March 1982 and the 'halving relief' was a rough-and-ready substitute for re-computing the held-over or rolled-over gain so as to give effect to March 1982 re-basing.

For disposals on or after 6 April 2008 'halving relief' applies only to companies, not to individuals, trustees or personal representatives. [**19.34**]

7 Part disposals

a) *General rule*

The term 'disposal' includes a part disposal, so that whenever part of an asset or an interest in an asset is disposed of it is necessary to calculate the original cost of the part sold before any gain can be computed (TCGA 1992 ss 21, 42). This applies, for instance, to a sale of part of a landholding or to the grant of a lease (see [**19.39**]).

The formula used for calculating the deductible cost of the part sold is:

$$C \times \frac{A}{A + B}$$

Where
C = all the deductible expenditure on the whole asset
A = consideration of the part of the asset disposed of
B = market value of part retained (at the time when the part is sold).

EXAMPLE 19.13

Ten acres of land were bought for £10,000 on 1 January 1992. Four acres of land were sold for £12,000 on 1 January 2017 (the remaining six acres were then worth £24,000).

Acquisition cost of the four acres sold is:

$$£10,000 \times \frac{£12,000}{£36,000} = £3,333$$

Therefore the chargeable gain is:

	£	£
Sale proceeds		12,000
Less:		
Acquisition cost		3,333
		£8,667

The indexation provisions apply in the same way for part disposals as for disposals of the whole, except that only the apportioned expenditure is index-linked. [19.35]

b) *Cases when the formula is not used*

The part disposal formula need not be used (thereby removing the need to value the part of the asset not disposed of) when the cost of the part disposed of can easily be calculated. In particular, there are special rules relating to a part disposal of shares of the same class in the same company (see **Chapter 26**).

Further, the rules will not be applied to small part disposals of land (TCGA 1992 s 242) if the taxpayer so elects. Where the consideration received is 20% or less of the value of the entire holding and does not exceed £20,000 (or is 'small' in the case of a disposal to an authority with compulsory powers of acquisition: see s 243) the transaction need not be treated as a disposal at all. Instead, the taxpayer can elect to deduct the consideration received from the allowable expenditure applicable to the land on any later disposal.

Similar principles apply to small capital distributions made by companies (see **[26.21]** and for the meaning of 'small', see RI 164, February 1997).
[19.36]

8 Wasting assets (TCGA 1992 ss 44–47)

a) *Definition*

A wasting asset is one with a predictable useful life not exceeding 50 years (TCGA 1992 s 44 and see **[22.21]**).

Freehold land can never be a wasting asset, whereas plant and machinery is always treated as a wasting asset.

Tangible moveable property which is a wasting asset (such as a television or washing machine) is not subject to CGT. However, this exemption does not apply to such assets which have been used solely for the purposes of a trade, in which case there are special rules where the asset qualified for capital allowances (TCGA 1992 s 47, see **[19.47]**). Short leases of land are likewise subject to their own rules (see **[19.41]**).

The main types of asset subject to the ordinary wasting asset rules are intangible assets such as options (TCGA 1992 s 146), patent rights and copyrights.

In the case of *R & C Comrs v The Executors of Lord Howard of Henderskelfe* (2014), the Court of Appeal confirmed the Upper Tribunal decision that *Portrait of Omai*, a Joshua Reynolds painting, which had been lent by the executors of Lord Howard (the sellers) to an associated trading company for public display at Castle Howard, was an item of 'plant' which had to be treated as a wasting asset, and was thereby exempt from CGT on its subsequent sale by the executors. In response to this decision, FA 2015 s 40 has now amended s 45 such that, with effect from April 2015, the exemption for wasting assets will only now apply if the asset has been used in the seller's own business.

[19.37]

b)   *Calculation of gain on disposal*

On disposal of a chargeable wasting asset (other than those where special rules apply), any gain is calculated on the basis that the allowable expenditure on the asset is written down at a uniform daily rate over its expected useful life so that any claim for loss relief will be limited (TCGA 1992 s 46).

EXAMPLE 19.14

Copyright (19 years unexpired) of a novel was bought by Fred for £2,800 on 1 April 1999. The copyright was sold by Fred for £2,600 on 1 April 2017. Fred's gain on disposal is calculated as follows:

Calculate written down acquisition cost:

$$£2,800 - \left(£2,800 \times \frac{18 \text{ years}}{19 \text{ years}}\right) = £147$$

Therefore the chargeable gain is:

	£	£
Sale proceeds		2,600
Less:		
Acquisition cost		147
Chargeable gain		£2,453

Consistent with the general principles that apply to such assets, it was only the written down expenditure (£147 in the example) that, for a disposal by individuals, trustees and personal representatives before 6 April 2008, was entitled to the indexation allowance for pre-April 1998 periods of ownership.

[19.38]

9   Rules for leases of land (TCGA 1992 s 240, Sch 8)

a)   *Basic rules*

The grant of a lease out of a freehold or superior lease is a part disposal. The grant of a lease for a 'rack rent' and no premium will not attract any CGT charge: sums charged to income tax are excluded from the consideration in computing the gain for CGT (TCGA 1992 s 37(1)). [19.39]

b)   *CGT on premiums*

The gain is computed by deducting from the disposal consideration (ie the premium) the cost of the part disposed of, calculated as for any part disposal (see [**19.35**]). Included in the denominator of the formula as a part of the market value of the land undisposed of is the value of any right to receive rent under the lease.

In *Clarke v United Real (Moorgate) Ltd* (1988), the court held that a premium included any 'sum' paid by a tenant to his landlord in consideration for the grant of a lease and therefore caught payments to the landlord covering past and future development costs. The definition of 'premium' in TCGA 1992 Sch 8 para 10(2) does not address the giving of consideration other than by payment of a sum, eg where a lease is granted in consideration of the tenant undertaking works of improvement to the demised or other premises. This is in contrast to the position for income tax where the value (to the landlord) of an undertaking by the tenant to carry out development or improvement works to the demised premises (though not to other premises of the landlord) is treated as a premium (ITTOIA 2005 s 278 and see [**8.83**]). On general principles the value of a tenant's undertaking to carry out development or improvement works would constitute consideration for the lease; and in so far as this notional premium is not subject to income tax (for example, because the works relate to other premises of the landlord) it would be taken into account in computing the landlord's chargeable gain (or allowable loss) on the part-disposal arising from the grant of the lease. [**19.40**]

c) *The wasting asset rules for leases*

A lease which has 50 or less years to run is a wasting asset. It does not depreciate evenly over time, however, so that on any assignment of it, its cost is written down not as described in [**19.38**], but according to a special table in TCGA 1992 Sch 8 para 1(6). (On the duration of a lease, see *Lewis v Walters* (1992) which decided that the possibility of extending the term under the Leasehold Reform Act 1967 – now the Leasehold Reform, Housing and Urban Development Act 1993 – should be ignored).

Where a sub-lease is granted out of a lease that is a wasting asset, the ordinary part disposal formula is not applied. Instead, any gain is calculated by deducting, from the consideration received for the sub-lease, that part of the allowable expenditure on the head lease that will waste away, according to the special table, over the period of the sub-lease.

EXAMPLE 19.15

A acquires a lease of premises for 40 years for £5,000 (that lease is, therefore, a wasting asset). After ten years he grants a sub-lease to B for ten years at a premium of £1,000.

A's gain is calculated by deducting from the consideration on the part disposal (ie £1,000), such part of £5,000 as will waste away (in accordance with TCGA 1992 Sch 8 para 1) on a lease dropping from 30 years to 20 years. [**19.41**]

d) *Income tax overlap*

Any part of a premium that is chargeable to income tax under the property income provisions of ITTOIA 2005 Part 3 (see **Chapter 12**) is not charged to CGT. Thus, on the grant of a short lease out of an interest that is not a wasting asset (eg the freehold) there must be deducted from the premium received such part of it as is taxed under ITTOIA 2005 Part 3 Chapter 4. The part disposal formula is then applied (see [**19.35**]) but in the numerator (though not in the denominator) the sum representing the sale proceeds of the part disposal is the premium received *less* that part taxed under ITTOIA 2005.

EXAMPLE 19.16

A buys freehold premises for £200,000. He grants a lease of the premises for 21 years at a premium of £100,000 and a rent. The value of the freehold subject to the lease and including the right to receive rent is now £150,000.

Of the premium of £100,000, £60,000 is taxed under ITTOIA 2005 Part 3, Chapter 4 (ie the premium less 2% x 20 ie less 40%: see [**12.82**]).

A's chargeable gain is, therefore:

	£
Consideration received	100,000
Less: amount taxed under ITTOIA 2005	(60,000)
	40,000
Less: cost of the part disposed of	
$£200,000 \times \dfrac{£40,000}{£100,000 + £150,000}$:	(32,000)
Chargeable gain	£8,000

[**19.42**]

e) *Tenants and lease surrenders/regrants*

For the position of a tenant who extends his lease, often by surrendering the old lease in return for the grant of a new long lease and payment of a premium, see ESC D39 ([**19.76**]); for the calculation of his indexation allowance (for disposals before 6 April 2008) see ESC D42. A reverse premium received by a tenant as an inducement to enter into the lease will not normally attract a CGT charge: see CG 70835 and for the income tax rules, see [**12.87**]. The payment of the reverse premium by the landlord will normally be deductible under TCGA 1992 s 38(1)(b) as being expenditure incurred to enhance the value of his interest in the land. [**19.43**]

III LOSSES FOR CGT

1 When does a loss arise?

A loss arises whenever the consideration for the disposal of a chargeable asset is less than the allowable expenditure incurred by the taxpayer.

The same rules generally apply for calculating capital losses as for gains. However, for disposals before 6 April 2008 (and for disposals at any time by companies) the indexation of allowable expenditure could (and for companies still can) operate only to reduce a gain – at most, to nil – and not to create a loss.

EXAMPLE 19.17

If an antique desk was bought for £12,000, restored for £1,000 and then sold for £11,000, a loss of £2,000 would result.

The disposal of a debt (other than a debt on a security) is usually exempt from CGT – so that any gain is not chargeable and any loss is not allowable. However, a loss that is made on a qualifying loan to a trader may be treated as a capital loss (see TCGA 1992 s 253 and [**22.43**]).

If an asset is destroyed or extinguished, or abandoned in the case of options that are not wasting assets (see [**19.70**]), or if its value has become negligible (see [**19.69**]), the taxpayer may claim to have incurred an allowable loss.

[**19.44**]

2 Use of losses

Losses must be relieved primarily against gains of the taxpayer in the same year, but any surplus loss can be carried forward and set against the first available gains of future years without time limit.

Losses cannot be carried back and set against gains of previous years except for the net losses incurred by an individual in the year of his death (TCGA 1992 s 62(2) and [**21.41**]). Losses cannot be transferred between spouses.

Capital losses cannot generally be set against the taxpayer's income for tax purposes. The only exception is for losses arising as a result of investment in a corporate trade under ITA 2007 s 131 (see [**11.121**]). Similarly, income losses cannot generally be set against an individual's capital gains: although this rule is also subject to an important exception whereby trading losses which cannot be relieved against the taxpayer's income may be set against his chargeable gains for both the year when the loss was incurred and one preceding tax year (see TCGA 1992 s 261B and see [**11.61**]).

Also, as a result of changes in FA 2000, payments under the Gift Aid scheme may be covered by tax on chargeable gains (see [**53.89**]).

An important restriction on the availability of loss relief is that a loss incurred on a disposal to a connected person can only be set against any gains on subsequent disposals to the same person (TCGA 1992 s 18(3) and see [**19.15**]).

For the exceptional relief when a loss arises on the disposal of certain rights to unascertainable consideration (as in *Marren v Ingles* situations) see TCGA 1992 s 279A.

[**19.45**]

3 Losses and taper relief

Taper relief has been abolished for disposals on and after 6 April 2008 (see **Chapter 20**). Losses on disposals before that date, unlike gains, were not tapered.

[**19.46**]

4 Restriction of losses: capital allowances

Generally, chattels that are wasting assets are exempt from CGT (TCGA 1992 s 45(1), see [**22.21**]). That exemption does not, however, extend to an item of plant or machinery if throughout the taxpayer's period of ownership it has been used in a trade and the taxpayer has claimed (or could have claimed) capital allowances in respect of any expenditure on the asset (TCGA 1992 s 45(2)). It follows that if capital allowances are not available (for example, because the asset is never brought into use in the business) the CGT exemption will apply: see *Burman v Westminster Press Ltd* (1987). Other non-wasting assets that qualify for capital allowances are chargeable assets.

However, a gain that is charged to income tax will not be charged to CGT; and a loss will not be allowable for CGT if it is deductible for income tax. Thus, for CGT purposes the gain on a disposal of plant and machinery and other assets qualifying for capital allowances is calculated in the usual way with the gain charged to CGT only to the extent that it exceeds the original cost of the asset. The original cost is not written down as it is with most wasting assets ([**19.38**]).

EXAMPLE 19.18

	£
Year 1: Machine bought for	10,000
WDA at 18%	1,800
Year 2: Machine sold for	12,000

There is a balancing charge for income tax of £1,800 (ie to the extent of the capital allowance given – see further **Chapter 41**). The excess of the sale price over the acquisition cost (£2,000) is chargeable to CGT. The acquisition cost (£10,000) is not written down in order to calculate the gain.

However, it is rare for plant and machinery to be sold at a gain; it is more likely to be sold at a loss, in which case the loss is not allowable for CGT to the extent that it is covered by capital allowances. Capital allowances may reduce a loss to nil, but they cannot produce a gain.

EXAMPLE 19.19

	£
Machine cost	4,000
Sale proceeds	2,000
Capital allowance claimed	2,000
Loss for CGT is:	
Disposal proceeds	2,000
Less: acquisition cost	4,000
Capital loss	(2,000)
Credit for capital allowances	2,000
Allowable loss	£Nil

[19.47]

5 Restriction of losses: targeted anti-avoidance rule

FA 2006 had already introduced 'targeted anti-avoidance rules' (TAAR) restricting losses of corporate bodies. The extended TAAR introduced by FA 2007 aims to block all capital gains tax loss schemes, whether undertaken by companies, individuals, trustees or personal representatives. The 2007 rules apply to any transaction effected on or after 6 December 2006.

TCGA 1992 s 16A, which replaced the FA 2006 legislation affecting companies, provides that a loss on a disposal will not be allowable if:
(i) it accrues as a result of, or in connection with, any arrangements; and
(ii) the main purpose or one of the main purposes of the arrangements is the securing of a tax advantage.

'Arrangements' is defined very widely and 'includes any agreement, understanding, scheme, transaction or series of transactions (whether or not legally enforceable)'.

'Purpose' is not defined, but in HMRC's view is wider than 'motive' and imports an objective test which looks not only at the parties' subjective intentions but also at the overall context and surrounding circumstances.

For the purpose of the definition of 'tax advantage', 'tax' means capital gains tax, corporation tax, or income tax. The reference to income tax is included to ensure artificial capital losses cannot reduce an income tax liability.

Note that it does not matter for whom the tax advantage is secured, nor that the loss accrues at a time when there are no chargeable gains from which it could otherwise be deducted. The main difficulty, however, is the extraordinary breadth of the two conditions. Given that any loss will necessarily arise as a result of some 'arrangement' (as defined) – thus satisfying condition (i) above – and the effect of any loss will be to reduce an actual or prospective chargeable gain – thus constituting a 'tax advantage' (as defined) in condition (ii) – it would seem that on a proper construction of the legislation no loss is now allowable unless the taxpayer can show that the ability to deduct the loss was not one of the main purposes of the disposal or deemed disposal.

Contrary to what was suggested in HMRC's Guidance Notes to the FA 2007 legislation (see HMRC's Capital Gains Manual, Appendix 9), the legislation is not targeted at capital losses realised only 'where a person enters deliberately and knowingly into arrangements to gain a tax advantage' or where there is no 'genuine commercial loss'. The Guidance uses these words but the legislation does not. In any event, gains are not charged merely on 'genuine commercial' transactions but, for example, on deemed disposals by trustees, and so losses can also be easily realised on deemed disposals. Individuals and trustees holding normal portfolios can unwittingly be caught by the legislation, and uncertainty abounds.

EXAMPLE 19.20

An individual, R, who has realised a chargeable gain in a particular tax year, sells shares in a company, X plc, which are standing at a loss, to an unconnected third party. R wishes to offset the resulting capital loss against the other chargeable gain. Thirty-one days later, R buys back the same number of shares in X plc, again from an unconnected third party.

This is Example 9 in HMRC's Guidance Notes. There is an arrangement (the sale of the shares in X plc). There is a tax advantage (R obtains relief from CGT). Securing that relief is one of the main purposes of the transaction (R would not have sold the shares in X plc were it not for the ability to offset the loss, as demonstrated by the fact that he buys the shares back). However, HMRC say the legislation is not intended to apply because R has incurred a real economic loss on a genuine disposal. The Guidance goes on to suggest that the loss would not be allowable 'if R had entered into some form of arrangement ... to ensure that he is not exposed to a genuine commercial risk'. Given the wording of the legislation, however, it is difficult to see why the fact that he has been exposed to market fluctuations should make any difference. The legislation makes no reference either to 'real economic loss' or to 'genuine commercial risk'.

Again, HMRC's Example 4 visualises a husband selling shares to crystallise a loss in order to offset this against other gains he has made and 'unbeknown to him' his wife buys back shares of the same class a few days later at the same price. The Guidance states the arrangements do not fall foul of the TAAR but, on a strict reading of the legislation, the sale by the husband would be caught.

TAAR was a major milestone on the path away from taxation by legislation towards non-taxation by HMRC concession. Another such milestone has now been reached with the legislation for the 'general anti-abuse rule' (GAAR) contained in FA 2013 Part 5, which requires a court to take account of HMRC's published guidance on the GAAR in determining any issue relating to the GAAR that comes before it. **[19.48]**

IV CALCULATING THE TAX PAYABLE

1 Rates (TCGA 1992 s 4)

Recent years' CGT rates can be summarised as follows:

Tax Year	Tax rate paid by Individuals within: Basic rate band %	Higher tax bands %	Trustees and PR's %
2017–18	10	20	20
2016–17	10	20	20
2015–16	18	28	28
2014–15	18	28	28
2013–14	18	28	28
2012–13	18	28	28
2011–12	18	28	28
2010–11 (23 June 2010 to 5 April 2011)	18	28	28
2010–11 (6 April to 22 June 2010)	18	18	18
2009–10	18	18	18
2008–09	18	18	18

Notes:

Individuals

For disposals on or after 6 April 2016, the rate of CGT has been reduced, with individuals paying at a rate of 10% or 20% depending on whether they are basic or higher rate taxpayers. For disposals on or after 23 June 2010 but before 6 April 2016, the rates of CGT were 18% or 28%. In order to calculate whether or not an individual is a higher rate taxpayer for CGT purposes, gains have to be added to income in order to see whether the higher rate threshold (£43,000 for most individuals in 2016–17) has been reached. If and to the extent that gains fall below the individual's higher rate threshold the rate of CGT was 18%. For gains that are above the threshold the rate of CGT was 28%.

The reduction in the CGT rates to 10% and 20% does not apply to gains arising on (i) the disposal of residential properties which do not qualify for private residence relief (mainly buy-to-let properties and second homes), nor (ii) the receipt of 'carried interest' (ie performance-based rewards for investment fund managers), which both continue to be subject to the 18% and 28% rates.

All ATED-related gains are charged at 28% (see **[19.6]**).

Entrepreneurs' relief

A 10% rate of CGT applies from 23 June 2010 in respect of gains qualifying for entrepreneurs' relief (TCGA 1992 s 169N(3)), see **Chapter 20**.

Earlier years

For 2007–08 and earlier tax years, capital gains were taxed as the top slice of income at income tax rates.

Companies

Companies are subject to corporation tax, not CGT, but corporation tax is charged on corporate profits including chargeable gains. The rate of tax charged on such gains in the financial year to 31 March 2014 (financial year 2013) was either 20% (small profits rate) or 23% (full rate), or somewhere between the two if the company had profits (including its chargeable gains) falling between the upper limit for the small profits rate (£300,000) and the threshold for the full rate (£1.5m). The small company rate remained at 20% while the main rate was reduced to 21% with effect from 1 April 2014 (financial year 2014). The corporation tax rates were effectively combined when the main rate reduced further to 20% from 1 April 2015. The corporation tax rate fell to 19% from 1 April 2017. **[19.49]**

2 The annual exemption (TCGA 1992 s 3)

The amount of the annual exemption depends on the capacity of the person making the gain.

Recent years' CGT annual exemptions can be summarised as follows:

Tax Year	Annual exempt amount	
	Individuals, personal representatives and trusts for disabled	General trusts
	£	£
2017–18	11,300	5,650
2016–17	11,100	5,550
2015–16	11,100	5,550
2014–15	11,000	5,500
2013–14	10,900	5,450
2012–13	10,600	5,300
2011–12	10,600	5,300
2010–11	10,100	5,050
2009–10	10,100	5,050
2008–09	9,600	4,800

[19.50]

a) *Individuals*

The first £11,300 (for 2017–18) of the total gains in a tax year are exempt from CGT (TCGA 1992 s 3(1), (2)). (However, for 'remittance basis users' see [19.56])

EXAMPLE 19.21

	£	£
A sells a painting in July 2017 for		25,150
Original cost of painting in 1996		(9,700)
Chargeable gain		15,450
Less: annual exemption for 2017–18		(11,300)
Gain charged to CGT		£4,150

If the exemption is unused in a tax year it is lost since there is no provision to carry it forward. [19.51]

b) *Personal representatives*

In the tax year of the deceased's death, and the two following tax years, personal representatives have the same annual exemption as an individual. In the third and following tax years they have no annual exemption and so are charged to CGT on all chargeable gains they make (TCGA 1992 s 3(7), see [21.64]). [19.52]

c) *Trustees*

Trustees generally enjoy only half the annual exemption available to an individual (£5,650 for 2017–18) (TCGA 1992 Sch 1). Where the same settlor has created more than one settlement since 6 June 1978 the annual exemption is divided equally between them. Two post-June 1978 settlements, for instance, would each have an exemption of £2,825 in 2017–18. This is subject to a minimum exemption per trust of one-tenth of the individual's annual exemption, ie £1,130 (for 2017–18). Thus, if a settlor creates 12 settlements they will each have an exemption of £1,130.

Where the settlement is for the mentally or physically disabled, the trustees have the same exemption as an individual, ie £11,300 (for 2017–18) (subject to similar rules for groups of settlements). **[19.53]**

d) *Husband and wife and civil partners*

Husband and wife are both entitled to a full exemption (see further **Chapter 51**). Any unused annual exemption cannot be transferred to the other spouse. **[19.54]**

e) *Split tax years*

F(No 2)A 2010 provides that if gains accruing to a person (including trustees and PRs) in any tax year are chargeable to CGT at different rates the taxpayer may use the annual exemption in the way that is most beneficial to him/them. **[19.55]**

f) *Remittance basis users*

From 2008–09, an individual who claims to use the remittance basis for a tax year is not entitled to the annual capital gains exemption for that year (ITA 2007 s 809G). However the annual exempt amount remains available where the remittance basis applies without a claim (for example, where the individual's unremitted foreign income and gains are less than £2,000 for the year) (ITA 2007 s 809D) (see **Chapter 27**). **[19.56]**

g) *Companies*

No annual exemption is available to companies. **[19.57]**

3 Order of set-off of capital losses

Current year losses must be deducted from current year gains in full.

EXAMPLE 19.22

A makes chargeable gains of £4,000 and incurs allowable losses of £3,000 in the tax year. His gain is reduced to £1,000 and is further reduced to zero by £1,000 of his annual exemption. He is forced to set his loss against gains for the year even though the gains would in any event have escaped tax because of the annual exemption.

Unrelieved losses in any tax year can be carried forward to future tax years without time limit though they must be deducted from the first available gains. However, the loss need only be used to reduce later gains to the amount covered by the annual exemption and not to zero. Losses carried back from the year of death are treated in the same way (TCGA 1992 s 62(2)). Losses of one spouse can only be used to reduce the gains of that spouse – they cannot be set against gains of the other spouse.

EXAMPLE 19.23

A makes the following gains and losses:

Tax year	Gain £	Loss £
2012–13 (Year 1)	4,000	16,000
2013–14 (Year 2)	10,000	3,000
2014–15 (Year 3)	14,000	Nil
2015–16 (Year 4)	21,000	Nil
2016–17 (Year 5)	10,000	Nil
2017–18 (Year 6)	5,000	Nil

In *Year 1* A pays no CGT and carries forward an unused loss of £12,000. His annual exemption for that year is wasted. In *Year 2* A's gain is reduced to £7,000 by his loss in that year and he pays no CGT as this is covered by his annual exemption. The unused £12,000 loss from *Year 1* does not reduce his gain to zero; it still remains unused and so is carried forward to *Year 3*. In *Year 3* £3,000 of the £12,000 loss brought forward from *Year 1* is used to reduce his gain to £11,000, the amount of the annual exemption in 2014–15. He has £9,000 of loss remaining to carry forward to *Year 4*, reducing his gain in that year to £12,000, of which £11,100 is covered by the annual exemption for 2015–16, leaving £900 to be charged to CGT at 18% (or 28% if A is a higher rate taxpayer). No CGT is payable in *Years 5 and 6* as the gains are below the annual exemption for those years of £11,100 and £11,300 respectively. [19.58]

4 Use of trading losses

The relief enabling trading losses to be offset against capital gains under TCGA 1992 s 261B is considered at [11.61]. [19.59]

5 When is CGT payable?

a) *General rule*

CGT is assessed on a current year basis and is normally payable in full by 31 January following the year of assessment. However, there is an extended due date where a notice to make a return is issued after 31 October following the year of assessment and there has been no failure to notify chargeability (under TMA 1970 s 7). In that case, the payable date is extended to three months from the date of the issue of the notice to make a return (TMA 1970 s 59B).

Interest is charged on tax remaining unpaid after the due date, and any tax remaining unpaid 31 days later will attract a 5% late payment penalty.

CGT does not impact on an individual's payment on account for the following tax year as these are based on their income tax and NIC liabilities.

In its Autumn Statement 2015, the Government announced plans to bring forward the CGT payment date on the sale of residential properties from April 2019 to within 30 days of the date of completion. The proposals cover both buy-to-let properties and second homes (but not properties subject to private residence relief). The Government is still consulting on this proposal.

[19.60]

b) *Payment by instalments*

CGT may be paid in instalments in two cases.

First, when (part of) the consideration for the disposal is payable in instalments over a period exceeding 18 months, running from the date of the disposal or later, and the taxpayer elects to pay by instalments. The instalments of tax can be spread (at the discretion of the Board) over a maximum of eight years provided that the final instalment of tax is not payable after the final instalment of the disposal consideration is payable (TCGA 1992 s 280). Interest would be payable on any instalments paid late.

Second, CGT may be paid by 10 equal annual instalments when there is a gift of any of the following assets, and where either hold-over relief is not available on the disposal, or where it is available but where the held-over gain is less than the otherwise chargeable gain (TCGA 1992 s 281(3)):

(1) land;
(2) a controlling shareholding in any company; and
(3) a minority holding in an unquoted company.

In these cases, the outstanding instalments carry interest. In addition, all outstanding instalments plus interest become payable in full if the gifted asset is sold (even if sold by someone other than the donee) unless the gift was made to a donee who was not 'connected with' the donor.

Finally, in a *Marren v Ingles* type case (see [19.18]) an incidental result of there being two disposals is that tax on the overall gain of the disponor will be paid in two or more stages. [19.61]

c) *Reporting requirements (TCGA 1992 s 3A)*

Individuals do not need to report the sale or disposal of assets not liable to CGT. This includes their main home provided it is covered by principal private residence relief.

For individuals who do not normally complete a self assessment tax return, there are no reporting requirements to HMRC of gains or disposals if there is no CGT to pay. However, if there is a CGT liability, they will need to register for self assessment, if they have not done so already, and then report the gain on their return.

Individuals who do normally complete a self assessment tax return will not normally have to complete the CGT section of their tax return if:

(1) their chargeable gains (before deducting any losses) for the year do not exceed the annual exemption; and

(2) the total proceeds from their chargeable disposals in the year do not exceed four times the annual exemption.

There are corresponding provisions for PRs and trustees.

From 6 April 2015 onwards, non-residents subject to CGT on gains arising on the disposal of UK residential property are required to report to HMRC and pay any CGT due within 30 days of the conveyance of the property. If, however, they have been issued with a self-assessment tax return by HMRC, then they must report the CGT liability through their tax return instead, and pay the CGT on the normal due date.

In its Autumn Statement 2015, the Government announced that it will give powers to HMRC to set circumstances in which a CGT return is not required by non-residents. [19.62]

V MEANING OF 'DISPOSAL'

1 General

A 'disposal' is not defined for CGT. Giving the word its natural meaning, there will be a disposal of an asset whenever its ownership changes or whenever an owner divests himself of rights in, or interests over, an asset (usually by sale, gift or exchange). Additionally, the term is extended by the legislation to cover certain transactions which would not fall within its common sense meaning, eg trustees of a settlement are treated as having disposed of and immediately reacquired settlement assets at their market value in certain circumstances (deemed disposals: see [25.41]).

A part disposal of an asset is charged as a disposal according to the rules considered earlier ([19.35]).

Death does not give rise to a chargeable disposal (TCGA 1992 s 62, see **Chapter 21**). [19.63]

2 Capital sums derived from assets (TCGA 1992 s 22)

When a capital sum is derived from an asset there is a disposal for CGT. This is so whether or not the person who pays the capital sum receives anything in return for his payment (see *Marren v Ingles* (1980)).

All legal rights that can be turned to account by the extraction of a capital sum are assets for CGT purposes. The test is whether such rights can be converted into money or money's worth and the mere fact that they are non-assignable does not matter so long as consideration can be obtained in some other way (for instance, by surrendering the right). This is apparent from the case of *O'Brien v Benson's Hosiery (Holdings) Ltd* (1979) (see [19.8]). In *Marren v Ingles* (1980) (see [19.18]) the right to receive an unquantifiable sum in the future was considered to be an asset, a *chose in action*, from which a capital sum was derived when the right matured.

The rights must, however, be legally enforceable. Thus, the receipt of a sum by a person in return for his agreement to restrict his future activities, say, is not a disposal because the right to work is not a legal right and so there is no disposal of an asset. The position is different, however, if the restrictive agreement means that a capital sum has been derived from the goodwill (an asset) of the taxpayer's business. In this case there will be a disposal under TCGA 1992 s 22 (see *Kirby v Thorn EMI plc* (1988)).

Four specific instances of disposals are given in s 22:
(1) Where a capital sum is received by way of compensation for the loss of, or damage to, an asset (for example, on the receipt of damages as compensation for the destruction of an asset). It should be noted that there is only a disposal where a capital sum is received so that if the receipt is of an income nature, it is charged to income tax and not to CGT (eg compensation received by a trader for loss of trading profits in *London and Thames Haven Oil Wharves Ltd v Attwooll* (1967) and *Lang v Rice* (1984)) (see **[10.103]**).
(2) Where a capital sum is received under an insurance policy for loss of or damage to an asset.
(3) Where a capital sum is received in return for the forfeiture or surrender of rights. This category includes payments received in return for releasing another person from a contract (*O'Brien v Benson's Hosiery (Holdings) Ltd* (1979)); or from a restrictive covenant; but not a statutory payment on the termination of a business tenancy since that sum is not derived from the lease (*Drummond v Austin Brown* (1984)).
(4) Where a capital sum is received for the use or exploitation of assets (for example, for the right to exploit a copyright). In *Chaloner v Pellipar Investments Ltd* (1996) Rattee J commented of this provision 'those words are apt to include capital sums received as consideration for the use or exploitation of assets, title to which remains unaffected in their owner ... but are not apt to include capital sums received as consideration for a grant of the owner's title to the assets, whether in perpetuity, or for a term of years'. He therefore held that the subsection did not catch consideration for the grant of a lease which took the form of the agreement by a developer to develop other land owned by the lessor (see **[19.40]**).

In the case of disposals falling within (1)–(4) above, the time of disposal is when the capital sum is received, and not when the contract (if any) was made (see **[19.78]**).

The receipt of a capital sum from an asset under categories (1) and (2) above – compensation and insurance – need not be treated as a disposal or part disposal if the asset has not been totally lost or destroyed. Instead, the taxpayer can elect to deduct the capital sum from the acquisition cost of the asset thereby postponing a charge to CGT until the eventual disposal of the asset (TCGA 1992 s 23). However, this relief is only available if one of three conditions is satisfied:
- the capital sum (ie the compensation or insurance) is wholly used to restore the asset; or
- if the full amount of the capital sum is not used to restore the asset but the amount unused is not reasonably required to do so, and is 'small' (ie does not exceed 5%) compared to the sum received. Where the sum unused exceeds 5%, the asset is treated as being partly disposed of for a consideration equivalent to the unused sum; or
- the capital sum is 'small' (ie does not exceed 5%) compared with the value of the asset.

Note that RI 164 (February 1997) confirms HMRC's view that 'small' does not exceed 5% and also states that, from 24 February 1997, HMRC regard a receipt as 'small' where it is £3,000 or less, regardless of whether it would meet the 5% test.

EXAMPLE 19.24

A buys a picture for £20,000 that is now worth £30,000. It is damaged by rain from a leaking roof and A receives £8,000 compensation with which he restores the picture. The £8,000 received is deducted from the cost of the asset (reducing £20,000 to £12,000), but its expenditure on restoration qualifies as allowable expenditure on a future disposal so that for CGT the total allowable expenditure of the asset remains £20,000 and A is in the same position as if the damage had never occurred.

Assume, however, that A restores the picture for £7,600. The £400 unused does not exceed 5% of £8,000 (and is less than £3,000 anyway). The full £8,000 is, therefore, deducted from the cost of the asset (reducing £20,000 to £12,000). The restoration expenditure qualifying as allowable expenditure is of course just £7,600 so the total allowable expenditure on a future disposal of the asset is £19,600.

Assume, alternatively, that A restores the picture for £3,000 and it regains its £30,000 value. The £5,000 unused exceeds 5% of £8,000 (and £3,000) and there would therefore be a disposal of the picture under s 22. A could however elect under s 23(3) to have his disposal consideration limited to the £5,000 (hence a part-disposal only) with the £3,000 being deducted from the acquisition cost on a future disposal of the picture. A's total allowable expenditure at the time of the part-disposal would be £23,000 (£20,000 + £3,000) and the proportion of that which would be deductible from the £5,000 consideration in order to calculate the gain would be:

$$\frac{5,000}{5,000 + 30,000} \times 23,000 = £3,285.71 \text{ (see [19.35])}$$

Alternatively, if A received compensation of just £1,500 which he does not use to restore the picture, A need not treat this receipt as a part disposal (since the amount is 'small'). Instead, he can elect to deduct £1,500 from his acquisition cost, so that the picture has a base value of £18,500 on a subsequent disposal.

[19.64]

3 Total loss or destruction of an asset (TCGA 1992 s 24(1))

Total loss or destruction of an asset is a disposal for CGT purposes and, where the owner of the asset receives no compensation, it may give rise to an allowable loss equal to the base cost of the taxpayer. Where the asset is tangible movable property, however, the owner is deemed to dispose of it for £6,000 for loss relief purposes, thereby restricting his loss relief if his base cost was greater than £6,000 (TCGA 1992 s 262(3)). This limitation derives from the fact that gains on such assets are exempt from CGT in so far as the consideration does not exceed £6,000 (see [22.22]). As a corollary, therefore, loss relief on the disposal of these assets is not available to the extent that the consideration received is less than £6,000.

EXAMPLE 19.25

A buys a picture for £10,000 which is destroyed by fire; A is uninsured. Although the picture is now worthless, A's allowable loss is restricted to £4,000.

Land and the buildings on it are treated as separate assets for these purposes. Where the building is totally destroyed both assets are separately deemed to have been disposed of and reacquired, and it is the overall gain or loss which is taken into account.

Where the taxpayer later receives compensation or insurance moneys for an asset which is totally lost or destroyed, this would appear to be a further disposal for CGT purposes under TCGA 1992 s 22 since it is a capital sum derived from an asset (the right under the insurance contract). In practice, however, HMRC treats both disposals (ie the entire loss of the asset and the receipt of capital moneys) as one transaction (see also the discussion of this problem by Hoffmann J in *Powlson v Welbeck Securities Ltd* (1986)).

If the taxpayer uses the capital sum within one year of receipt to acquire a replacement asset, he may claim to roll over any gain made on the disposal of the destroyed asset against the cost of the replacement asset; this relief does not apply to wasting assets. If only part of the capital sum is used in replacement, only partial roll-over is available (TCGA 1992 s 23(4)). 'Replacement' is not defined in the legislation, but HMRC state in CG 15745 that it can be 'interpreted reasonably' and will cover a claim in respect of a replacement asset which is of similar function and type to the original asset.

EXAMPLE 19.26

A buys a picture for £6,000 that is destroyed when its value is £10,000. He receives insurance money of £10,000 and uses it towards the purchase of a similar picture for £12,000. A has made a gain of £4,000 on the original picture (£10,000 – £6,000) on which he need not pay CGT. Instead he may deduct the gain from the cost of the new picture so that his base cost becomes £8,000 (£12,000 – £4,000).

Assume that A buys the new picture for only £7,500 and claims roll-over relief.

Amount of insurance money not applied in replacement = £2,500 (£10,000 – £7,500).

£2,500 is therefore A's chargeable gain, instead of the £4,000 he made on the picture. The roll-over relief is limited to the amount by which the gain on the original picture is reduced (ie to £1,500) which is given by reducing A's base value for the new picture from £7,500 to £6,000.

The same relief applies where the asset destroyed is a building. The gain on the old building can be rolled over against the cost of the new building. Any gain deemed to have been made on the land cannot, however, be so treated and will, therefore, be chargeable (TCGA 1992 s 23(6)). **[19.65]**

4 Compensation, damages and Zim Properties

a) *The Zim case*

In *Zim Properties v Procter* (1985) a firm of solicitors acting for the taxpayer in a conveyancing transaction were allegedly negligent, with the result that a sale of three properties owned by the taxpayer fell through. An action in negligence against the solicitors was eventually compromised and compensation of £69,000 was paid to the taxpayer. Undoubtedly, this was a capital sum, but was it derived from the disposal of an asset? Warner J held that it arose from the right of action against the solicitors which, as it could be turned into a capital sum by negotiating a compromise, was an asset for CGT purposes. Although the ownership of the properties put the taxpayer in the position to enjoy that right of action, the sum was not derived from the properties themselves, because, after receipt of that sum, the taxpayer still owned the properties.

[19.66]

b) *The difficulties created by the Zim decision*

First, not all rights to payment or compensation are themselves 'assets' for CGT purposes. Warner J cited as an example the right of a seller of property to payment of the price. The relevant asset in such a case must be the property itself (contrast, however, *Marren v Ingles*, discussed at **[19.18]**). A further example is shown by *Drummond v Austin Brown* (1984) where a tenant's right to statutory compensation on the termination of his lease under the Landlord and Tenant Act 1954 was not subject to CGT; it was neither compensation for loss of the lease, nor was it derived from that lease (contrast *Davenport v Chilver* (1983) where the right to statutory compensation for confiscated property was held to be an asset). There are also a number of statutory exemptions: eg for damages following personal injury. See also the recent *Gordon L Weston* case (**[19.69]**) as to what constitutes a right of action following the *Zim Properties* case.

Second, the date of acquisition of the right of action will in many cases be unclear. In *Zim*, Warner J held that the asset was acquired at the time when the taxpayer acted upon the allegedly negligent advice – entered into the sale contracts – although this matter is not free from doubt (see the House of Lords judgments in *Pirelli v Oscar Faber* (1983)).

Third, the question of how to calculate the acquisition cost of this asset, namely the taxpayer's right to sue, was left unclear (see also *Marren v Ingles* and *O'Brien v Benson's Hosiery*). Arguably, it was acquired otherwise than by bargain at arm's length, so that the market value (if any) of the right should be taken at the moment of its acquisition (see TCGA 1992 s 17(1), discussed at **[19.14]**: it may be doubted, however, whether the taxpayer is able to satisfy the requirements in s 17(2)(b) and failure to do so would result in a nil acquisition cost).

Finally, as the purpose of damages is to compensate the claimant, the award in such cases would need to be grossed up if the damages themselves are to be reduced by taxation.

[19.67]

c) *ESC D33*

Some of the difficulties resulting from the *Zim* case have been solved by ESC D33 that affords relief from CGT in two ways.

First, 'where the right of action arises by reason of the total or partial loss or destruction of or damage to a form of property which is an asset for CGT purposes, or because the claimant suffered some loss or disadvantage in connection with such a form of property, any gain or loss on the disposal of the right of action may by concession be computed as if the compensation derived from that asset and not from the right of action'. As a consequence, part of the acquisition cost of the chargeable asset may be deducted from the gain in accordance with the usual part-disposal rules (see [**19.35**]); alternatively, the compensation may be exempt from CGT.

EXAMPLE 19.27

(1) Because of the negligence of his land agent, Lord Q's sale of a plot of land to Out of Town Supermarkets Ltd falls through. The agent is forced to pay £70,000 in compensation to Lord Q. Instead of treating this sum as consideration on the disposal of a separate *chose in action* it may be treated as arising on a part disposal of the land itself. Accordingly, part of the expenditure attributable to that land may be deducted in arriving at Lord Q's chargeable gain.

(2) Zara, because of the negligence of her solicitor, ends up with less money from the sale of her main residence than would otherwise have been the case. Because the underlying asset (her main residence) is exempt from CGT (see **Chapter 23**) any compensation paid by the solicitor will likewise escape tax.

Second, if there is no underlying asset, any gain accruing on the disposal of the right of action will be exempt from CGT. However, in this respect ESC D33 has changed with effect from 27 January 2014, and only the first £500,000 of this kind of capital compensation will be exempt. However, these changes do not apply to compensation for personal injury, which remains fully exempt from CGT. (Note that during 2014, HMRC consulted both on legislating the relief given by ESC D33, and on introducing a limit of £1m exemption with amounts in excess of this liable to CG; the feedback received was mostly negative, and the issue remains to be determined.)

EXAMPLE 19.28

Zappy, a wealthy taxpayer, suffers a massive income tax liability because his professional adviser negligently fails to shelter that income from tax by arranging for Zappy to invest in an EIS and in an industrial building in an enterprise zone. Substantial compensation is therefore paid to Zappy and because there is no underlying property that is an asset for CGT purposes, the sum is not subject to charge.

The logic behind this is that as the compensation merely puts the taxpayer into the position he would have been in but for the negligence, there should be no tax charge since the benefit which he was entitled to (a lesser income tax liability) is not itself subject to charge. It should be noted that the *Zim* case has no application to compensation payments that attract an income tax charge (see, for instance, *London and Thames Haven Oil Wharves Ltd v Attwooll* (1967) at [**10.103**]) whilst its application in the context of warranties and indemnities on a company takeover is discussed in **Chapter 47**. [**19.68**]

5 Assets becoming of negligible value (TCGA 1992 s 24(1A))

Where an asset becomes of negligible value (eg shares and securities in an insolvent company) the taxpayer is deemed to have disposed of and immediately reacquired the asset at its market value (nil) thus enabling him to claim loss relief.

This disposal is deemed to occur in the tax year in which HMRC accepts the claim or at any earlier time specified in the claim provided that: (a) the taxpayer owned the asset at that earlier time; (b) the asset had become of negligible value at that earlier time; and (c) that earlier time was not more than two years before the beginning of the year of assessment in which the claim is made (*Williams v Bullivant* (1983) and see *Larner v Warrington* (1985)).

HMRC considers that 'negligible' means considerably less than 5% of the original cost (or March 1982 value).

The First-tier Tribunal has had to consider negligible value claims in three recent cases. *First*, in *Roger and Jean Dyer v R & C Comrs* (2016), the Tribunal upheld HMRC's decision to deny a negligible value claim on the grounds that the shares in question had not become negligible in value, but had been of negligible value when they were first acquired by the taxpayers; the Upper Tribunal dismissed the taxpayer's subsequent appeal; *second*, in *Brown v R & C Comrs* (2013), the Tribunal decided that the shares could be of negligible value without the company having ceased trading, nor having been put into liquidation, provided that they had no market value; and *finally*, in *Gordon L Weston v R & C Comrs* (2014), the Tribunal held that no negligible value claim could be made in relation to the individual's irrecoverable investment in a certificate of deposit in the Stanford International Bank, which had gone into liquidation. The certificate of deposit was held not to be a chargeable asset for CGT purposes, and neither was the investor's right of action against the bank (applying *Zim Properties*) in relation to its fraudulent activities.

In the case of *R & C Comrs v Peter Drown and Mrs RE Leadley* (2017), the Upper Tribunal found that Mr Leadley's executors were not able to make a negligible value claim on his behalf as he no longer owned the assets following his death.

Should the value of the asset subsequently increase, the result of claiming relief under s 24(2) will be that on a later disposal the base value will be nil so that all the consideration received will be treated as a gain. [19.69]

6 Options (TCGA 1992 ss 144–147)

The grant of an option (whether to buy or to sell an asset) is a disposal, not of a part of the asset that is subject to the option, but of a separate asset, namely, the option itself at the date of the grant. The gain will be the consideration paid for the grant of the option less any incidental expenses (see *Strange v Openshaw* (1983)). In *Garner v Pounds Shipowners and Shipbreakers Ltd* (2000) P Ltd granted an option to M to purchase its land which included a term that P Ltd was to use its best endeavours to obtain the release of restrictive covenants and would only receive the option fee if it was successful. In the event the covenants were released in return for a payment of £90,000 by P Ltd, the option fee (£399,750) was paid by M, but the option was never exercised so that the option fee was retained by P Ltd. The House of Lords held that P Ltd's obligations regarding the release of the covenants, even though involving the probable payment of sums to third parties, did not affect the amount of consideration received for the grant of the option (ie the option fee), nor were the sums paid by P Ltd deductible under TCGA 1992 s 38(1): the expenditure was not incurred in *providing* the asset disposed of (the option), nor was the expenditure reflected in the state or nature of the option at the time it was granted (see **[19.20]** and **[19.21]**).

EXAMPLE 19.29

(1) A grants to B for £3,000 an option to buy A's country cottage in two years' time for £30,000 which is its current market value. A has made a gain of £3,000 from which he can deduct any incidental expenses involved in granting the option. (This is an option to buy.)

(2) B grants to A for £3,000 an option enabling A to require B to buy that country cottage in two years' time for £30,000. (This is an option to sell.) B has made a gain of £3,000 less any incidental expenses.

If the option is exercised, the grant and the exercise are treated as a single transaction for both grantor and grantee. In the case of an option to buy (ie binding the grantor to sell) the consideration received for the grant of the option is treated as part of the consideration for the sale. Any CGT that has been charged on the grant itself will be either set off or repaid.

In the case of an option to sell (ie binding the grantor to buy) the consideration received for the option is deducted from the acquisition cost of the asset to the grantor.

EXAMPLE 19.30

As in *Example 19.29*, assuming that A had allowable expenditure of £15,000:

(1) When B exercises the option and pays A £30,000 for the house, A's gain is:

	£
Proceeds from sale of house	30,000
Consideration for option	3,000
	33,000
Less: allowable expenditure	15,000
Chargeable gain	£18,000

B's acquisition cost is £30,000 plus the cost of the option, ie £33,000.

(2) When A exercises the option and sells the house to B for £30,000, A's gain is:

	£	£
Proceeds of sale		30,000
Less: cost of option	3,000	
allowable expenditure	15,000	18,000
Chargeable gain		£12,000

B's acquisition cost of the cottage is only £27,000 (ie £30,000 reduced by the amount that he received for the option).

HMRC took the view that the market value rule in TCGA 1992 s 17 (see **[19.14]**) did not normally apply to shares acquired as a result of the exercise of an option but this view was not upheld by the Court of Appeal in *Mansworth v Jelley* (2003). As a consequence the taxpayer's acquisition of the shares on exercising the option was deemed to be at market value so that on his immediate disposal of the shares no gain arose. Moreover, the acquisition cost, according to HMRC's published view at the time, was further enhanced by TCGA 1992 s 120(4) to include the amount on which the employee paid income tax. This was generally the same figure as the market value and so the bizarre consequence in many cases was that the taxpayer was able to establish a substantial, though unreal, loss for CGT. TCGA 1992 s 144ZA, inserted by FA 2003, reversed the effect of *Mansworth v Jelley* and, broadly speaking, disapplies the market value rule (in cases where it would otherwise apply) in relation to options exercised after 9 April 2003. In *Mansworth v Jelley*-type circumstances the taxpayer's gain is now calculated by deducting from the sale proceeds the sum actually paid on the exercise of the option plus any amount charged to income tax as a result of the exercise of the option (but not also the market value of the shares acquired).

An option is a chargeable asset so that, if disposed of other than by exercise or abandonment (see below), there may be a chargeable gain or allowable loss on ordinary principles. In particular, an option which has a predictable life of 50 years or less will be a wasting asset unless it is an option to subscribe for shares that is listed on a recognised stock exchange; a traded option; a financial option; or it is an option to acquire assets to be used in a trade. Consequently the cost of acquiring the option will be written down over its predictable life on a straight-line basis (see **[19.38]**).

The abandonment of an option that is a wasting asset is not a disposal (but notice that a capital sum received for relinquishing an option will be chargeable under TCGA 1992 s 22(3): see *Golding v Kaufman* (1985) and CG 12340). **[19.70]**

7 Appropriations to and from a trader's stock in trade (TCGA 1992 s 161)

There are two cases to consider. *First*, where a trader acquires an asset for private use and later appropriates it to his trade. As a general rule, this is a disposal and CGT is payable on the difference between the market value of the asset at the date of appropriation and its original cost.

EXAMPLE 19.31

A owns a picture gallery. He buys a picture for private use for £5,000 and transfers it to the gallery when it is worth £15,000. He has made a chargeable gain of £10,000. Later he sells the picture to a customer for £30,000. The profit on sale of £15,000 (£30,000 – £15,000) is chargeable to income tax under ITTOIA 2005 (former Schedule D Case I).

However, the trader can elect to avoid paying CGT at the date of appropriation by transferring the asset into his business at a no gain/no loss value (see s 161(3A) for time limits in making the election). When the asset is eventually sold, the total profit will be charged to income tax as a trading receipt. So, in the above example, were A to make the election he would pay no CGT, but instead he would be liable to income tax on a profit of £25,000 (£30,000 – £5,000). The effect of the election is that the total gain is deferred and charged to income tax; hence, for appropriations made in tax years up to and including 2007–08, the taper relief that had accrued was permanently lost by an election.

Whether the election should be exercised or not must depend upon the particular facts of each case. In many cases CGT would appear to be the lesser of two evils because of its annual exemption and the 10% or 20% tax rate, but income tax will be paid later (on eventual sale), and the profit so made may be offset against personal allowances or unused capital allowances.

Second, where an asset originally acquired as trading stock is taken out for the trader's private use. In this case, there is no election and the transfer is treated as a sale at market value for income tax purposes (see *Sharkey v Wernher* (1956) at [**10.117**]). The taxpayer will have market value as his CGT base cost.

EXAMPLE 19.32

One of the pictures in A's gallery cost him £6,000. He removes it to hang it in his dining room when its market value is £16,000. He later sells it privately for £30,000.

On the appropriation out of trading stock, A is treated as selling the picture for its market value (£16,000) and the profit (£10,000) is assessed to income tax. The gain on the subsequent sale (£30,000 – £16,000 = £14,000) is chargeable to CGT.
[**19.71**]

8 Miscellaneous cases

a) *Hire-purchase agreements (TCGA 1992 s 27)*

Although the hirer does not own the asset until he pays all the instalments, the owner is treated as having disposed of the asset at the date when the hirer is first able to use it (usually the date of the contract). The consideration for the disposal is the cash price payable under the contract. These transactions rarely give rise to a CGT charge, however, either because the asset is exempt (eg a private car or a chattel worth less than £6,000) or because it is a wasting asset. Further, the contract will normally be a trading transaction falling within the income tax charge (for an illustration where these provisions were held to apply to the sale of a taxi-driver's licences, see *Lyon v Pettigrew* (1985)).

In the rare case where there is a CGT charge and the hire term ends without title passing (eg because the hirer defaults) tax is adjusted, or discharged, according to the amount the owner actually received. [**19.72**]

b) *Mortgages and charges (TCGA 1992 s 26)*

Neither the grant nor the redemption of a mortgage is a disposal. Where the property is sold by a mortgagee or his receiver, the sale is treated as a disposal by the mortgagor. [**19.73**]

632   *CGT – basic principles*

c)   *Settled property*

On the happening of certain events the trustees are deemed to have disposed of the trust assets and immediately reacquired them (see **Chapter 25**).
[19.74]

d)   *Value shifting (TCGA 1992 ss 29–31)*

There are anti-avoidance provisions intended to charge a person who passes value to another without actually making a disposal (see **[26.61]**).   [19.75]

e)   *Lease extensions (ESC D39)*

The ESC provides that a tenant who surrenders his lease in return for the grant of a new lease over the same premises does not make a disposal or part disposal of the old lease provided that the terms of the new lease (other than its duration and the amount of rent) are the same as those of the old lease. It does not address the position of the landlord. The concession can apply to transactions between connected persons provided that the terms of the transaction are equivalent to those that would have been made between unconnected parties bargaining at arm's length.   [19.76]

f)   *Relief for exchanges of joint interests in land (TCGA 1992 ss 248A–248E)*

Roll-over relief along the lines of that in TCGA 1992 ss 247–248 in the case of compulsory acquisitions (see **[22.82]**) is available when a joint holding of land is partitioned (so that each joint owner becomes a sole owner of part of the land) or when a number of separate joint holdings are partitioned.   [19.77]

9   Time of disposal

a)   *Timing – the general rule*

A disposal under a contract of sale takes place for CGT purposes at the date of the contract, not completion, with an adjustment of tax if completion never occurs (TCGA 1992 s 28(1)). By contrast, a disposal arising from the receipt of a capital sum under TCGA 1992 s 22 is treated as taking place when the capital sum is received (see *Chaloner v Pellipar Investments Ltd* (1996)). A disposal occurs on the date of destruction where an asset is destroyed without compensation being payable (TCGA 1992 s 24(1)).

See *Jerome v Kelly* (2004) for authority for the proposition that TCGA 1992 s 28 not only serves to fix the time of a disposal but also the identity of the person making the disposal for CGT purposes. However *Jerome v Kelly* makes clear, as has been confirmed by the Court of Appeal in *Underwood v R & C Comrs* (2009), that s 28(1) is only a deeming provision stating, where there has been a disposal, when the disposal is deemed to have been made. It does not define the disposal to be the contract. For there to be a disposal there must be a transfer of the taxpayer's entire beneficial interest in the asset. Hence if, as happened in *Underwood*, a sale contract of land is never completed there will have been no disposal and so no possibility of an allowable loss. The Court of Appeal's decision is not easy to reconcile with the long-established treatment of bed-and-breakfast transactions and sub-sales in both of which assets are regarded as being disposed of under a sale contract.

In *Anthony Hardy v R & C Comrs* (2015), the First-tier Tribunal had found that there was no loss on a disposal for CGT purposes where the taxpayer lost his deposit as a result of failing to complete a contract. They referred to the decision in *Jerome v Kelly* to support the principle that TCGA 1992 s 28 only fixes the time of disposal at the time when a contract is made if the exchange of contracts is followed by completion. The Upper Tribunal (2016) subsequently dismissed the taxpayer's appeal, finding that there was no disposal of an asset, but just something more like an abandonment of an option to purchase. **[19.78]**

b) *Conditional contracts*

If the contract is conditional, the disposal takes place when the condition is fulfilled (s 28(2) and see *Hatt v Newman* (2000)). The subsection specifically provides that when a contract is conditional on the exercise of an option (eg a put or call option) the disposal occurs when that option is exercised. In order to decide whether a contract is conditional for these purposes the contract in question has to be construed in order to determine whether any conditions stipulated therein are truly conditions precedent to any legal liability or whether they are merely conditions precedent to completion. In the former case there is a conditional contract for CGT purposes: in the latter, the contract is unconditional (*Eastham v Leigh London and Provincial Properties Ltd* (1971)).

EXAMPLE 19.33

Lord W agrees to grant a lease to Concrete (Development Company) Ltd if they obtain satisfactory planning permission to develop the relevant land as a business park. The contract to grant the lease is conditional on satisfactory permission being obtained and so the relevant part disposal will occur only if and when that happens.

Where a local authority compulsorily acquires land (other than under a contract), the disposal occurs when the compensation is agreed or when the authority enters the land (if earlier). In the case of gifts, disposal occurs when the ownership of the asset passes to the donee (usually the date of the gift).
[19.79]

VI CAPITAL GAIN OR INCOME PROFIT?

One reason for the linking of CGT in 1988 to the income tax rates of the taxpayer was to render redundant much conventional tax planning designed to ensure that capital profits rather than income were received by a taxpayer. As a result, some of the anti-avoidance sections, including ITA 2007, Pt 13, Ch 1 (transactions in securities) and Ch 3 (transactions in land)) became of reduced importance. With the advent of the flat CGT rate of 18% from 6 April 2008, this anti-avoidance legislation became very relevant again. Even with the increase in the rate of CGT to 28% for higher rate taxpayers as from

23 June 2010, the attraction of schemes to convert income to capital is still considerable given the 45% additional rate of income tax that currently applies to taxable income in excess of £150,000 p.a. The recent reduction in individual CGT rates to 10% and 20% has further increased the potential attractiveness of capital disposals for tax purposes.

The distinction between capital and income receipts is also important for other reasons, and set out below are two of the factors to bear in mind. As will be apparent, the facts of each individual case will largely determine whether the taxpayer is better off receiving a sum as capital or income. (See *Hitch v Stone* (2001) for an example of agreements being entered into with the object of converting capital sums into income. The agreements were dismissed by the Court of Appeal as shams.)

All arrangements designed to convert income to capital which are made after 17 July 2013 are potentially subject to the new 'general anti-abuse rule' (GAAR). [19.80]

1 Consequences of realising a capital gain

Tax on the gain will not be due until 31 January of the following tax year and in computing the chargeable gain the annual exemption may be deducted. By contrast, tax on income profits is largely due on 31 January in the tax year of receipt and on the following 31 July, and without any equivalent annual exemption. It is also important to remember that CGT is only levied when a disposal has occurred and therefore it may be possible to arrange disposals in the most advantageous tax year. There is also the ability to defer the gain from CGT by rolling it over into a qualifying investment under the amended EIS provisions (see [15.89]). [19.81]

2 Taxation of income profits

Receiving a profit as income may be advantageous for the taxpayer in that the sum may be reduced by personal allowances, charges on income, unused losses, and there is the possibility of obtaining limited income tax relief by investing in an EIS (see [15.52]). [19.82]

20 CGT – entrepreneurs' relief
Updated by Sarah Laing CTA

I   Introduction [20.1]
II   General principles [20.2]

I INTRODUCTION

Entrepreneurs' relief is a relief from capital gains tax arising on the disposal of a business. The relief replaced taper relief with effect from 6 April 2008. Broadly, it was designed to run alongside the Government's capital gains tax (CGT) reform programme, which was announced in the 2007 Pre-Budget Report.

Entrepreneurs' relief is a kind of resurrection of the old retirement relief, which was phased out between 1998 and 2003, but the rules are designed to be simpler. There is no minimum age limit for entrepreneurs' relief (under retirement relief the claimant generally had to be 50 plus, or on his death-bed to get relief). Moreover, entrepreneurs' relief will generally be available where the relevant conditions are met for a period of one year, instead of the former retirement relief qualifying period of up to 10 years.

In summary, entrepreneurs' relief applies to:
- gains made on the disposal of all or part of a business; or
- gains made on disposals of assets following the cessation of a business;

by certain individuals who were involved in running the business.

The amount of relief available is limited to the lifetime threshold in force at the time of disposal, from which the amount of any net relevant gains on previous disposals is deducted. Recent lifetime limits on relief are as follows:
- £1m for disposals occurring in the period 6 April 2008 to 5 April 2010;
- £2m for disposals occurring in the period 6 April 2010 to 22 June 2010;
- £5m for disposals occurring on or after 23 June 2010; and
- £10m for disposals occurring on or after 6 April 2011.

Qualifying gains arising on disposals occurring on or after 23 June 2010 are charged to CGT at a rate of 10%. Where the net gains arose on disposals before that date, the resulting net gains were to be reduced by 4/9ths, which meant that only 5/9ths of the net relevant gains were chargeable gains (TCGA 1992 s 169N(3)) and were charged at the 18% CGT rate then in force. This gave an effective rate of 10% on the full amount of the gains.

The Finance Acts in 2015 and 2016 have altered the application of entrepreneurs' relief in the following situations:
- gains arising on the transfer of goodwill from individuals to a company, particularly as part of an incorporation;
- disposal of a business asset by shareholder or partner at the same time as disposing of shares or partnership interest;
- disposal of shares held through a joint venture company or corporate partnership; and
- gains deferred by investing under venture capital schemes which later fall back into charge.

Note that provisions in FA 2016 change some of the FA 2015 amendments made to entrepreneurs' relief, with retrospective effect from the date those amendments originally took effect, ie 3 December 2014 or 18 March 2015.

[20.1]

II GENERAL PRINCIPLES

1 Outline

The relief applies to gains arising on disposals of the whole or part of a trading business (including professions and vocations, but not including a property letting business) that is carried on by an individual, either alone or in partnership. Where a business is not disposed of as a going concern, but simply ceases, relief will be available on gains on assets formerly used in the business and disposed of within three years of the cessation of the business.

The relief will also apply to gains on disposals of shares (and securities) in a trading company (or the holding company of a trading group) provided that the individual making the disposal:
- has been an officer or employee of the company, or of a company in the same group of companies, and
- owns at least 5% of the ordinary share capital of the company and that holding enables the individual to exercise at least 5% of the voting rights in that company.

The terms 'trading company', 'holding company' and 'trading group' have the same meaning as they did for the purposes of the former taper relief on business assets (TCGA 1992 s 169S(5)). For the meaning of 'trading company' and 'trading group', see now s 169SA and Sch 7ZA, Part 1. Because of this, there is no requirement to restrict the gains on shares by reference to any non-trading assets held, as was the case for retirement relief.

Where an individual qualifies for entrepreneurs' relief on a disposal of shares or securities under the previous paragraph, relief will also be available in respect of any 'associated disposal' of an asset that was used in the company's (or group's) business. For example, if a company director who owns the premises from which the company carries on its business sells the premises at the same time as he sells his shares in the company, the sale of the premises may count as an 'associated disposal' and any gain attract entrepreneurs' relief. The relief due on an associated disposal will be restricted where the asset in question was not wholly in business use throughout the period it was owned.

General principles 637

A similar rule allows relief on an 'associated disposal' by a member of a partnership who is entitled to relief on disposal of his interest in the assets of the partnership. (Again, relief will be restricted where the asset in question was not wholly in business use throughout the period of ownership.)

Trustees may also benefit from entrepreneurs' relief on gains on assets used in a business. However, trustees are not entitled to the 'lifetime allowance' of relief in the same way as individuals. Any relief given to trustees is treated as having been given to a 'qualifying beneficiary' and serves to reduce the beneficiary's entitlement for future disposals (TCGA 1992 s 169N(7)).

Where two qualifying disposals are made on the same day, one by the trustees and the other by an individual who is also a qualifying beneficiary of that trust, the trustees' disposal will be treated as having occurred after the one made by the individual (TCGA 1992 s 169N(8)). These rules serve to restrict an individual's lifetime relief threshold by the relief granted to trustees of a settlement of which he is a qualifying beneficiary. **[20.2]**

2 Operation of the relief

Which disposals qualify

Entrepreneurs' relief is available on gains made by individuals arising from qualifying business disposals, which consist of:
(1) all or part of a sole trader business (see **[20.19]**);
(2) all or part of an interest in a partnership, including an interest in an LLP (see **[20.22]**);
(3) shares or securities held in the shareholder's personal company (see **[20.28]**);
(4) certain post-cessation disposals of former business assets (see **[20.24]**); and
(5) associated disposals (see **[20.29]**) which are disposals of assets owned by the individual but used in the business of either:
   - a partnership of which he was a member; or
   - his personal company.

In addition, disposals of certain business assets by trustees can qualify for entrepreneurs' relief, but only where there is a qualifying beneficiary who also holds enough shares in their own right for the company to qualify as his personal company, or operates or has operated the business that used the assets.

A disposal for entrepreneurs' relief can be:
- a sale;
- a gift or transfer at undervalue;
- where a capital distribution is received in respect of shares held in a company, for example on the liquidation of that company; or
- a capital sum derived from an asset. **[20.3]**

How the relief is calculated

Where gains were made between 6 April 2008 and 22 June 2010, entrepreneurs' relief is given by reducing the amount of the capital gain by 4/9ths, leaving the residue of 5/9ths to be charged to CGT at 18%, before deduction of unrelated losses and the annual exemption. As the rate of CGT increased to 28% for higher rate taxpayers on 23 June 2010, this fractional reduction would no longer produce a 10% rate for taxpayers subject to the higher rate. Gains that accrue on and after 23 June 2010 and are subject to entrepreneurs' relief are taxed at 10%, irrespective of the level of the taxpayers' other income for the year.

However, when calculating taxpayers' available basic rate band to determine the rate of CGT to apply to gains (18% or 28%), those gains subject to entrepreneurs' relief are deemed to take priority over the available basic rate band before other gains (TCGA 1992 s 4(6)).

Taxpayers can choose which gains should absorb their annual exemption or losses to achieve the lowest possible charge to CGT (TCGA 1992 s 4B).

EXAMPLE 20.1

Milo gave 25% of the shares in his company M Ltd to his son on 10 May 2010, and sold the remaining shares in M Ltd on 12 July 2016 for £3 million. Milo formed M Ltd in 1980 and was a director until the sale in July 2016. The 31 March 1982 value of M Ltd was £400,000. The market value of the gift in May 2010 is judged to be £1 million. Milo claims entrepreneurs' relief on both disposals, and chooses to set his annual exemption against other unrelated gains in both tax years. His CGT liability on the gains made on the disposal of M Ltd is calculated as follows:

		May 2010 £	July 2016 £
Lifetime limit		2,000,000	10,000,000
Market value/proceeds		1,000,000	3,000,000
31 March 1982 value		(100,000)	(300,000)
Gain		900,000	2,700,000
Entrepreneurs' relief reduction	4/9 × £900,000	(400,000)	–
Taxable gain:		500,000	2,700,000
Tax due at 18%/10%		90,000	270,000

The effective or actual rate of CGT on both gains is 10%. **[20.4]**

Aggregation of gains and losses

When a business is sold some assets may crystallise gains and other disposals may create losses. Before calculating entrepreneurs' relief the gains and losses arising on the same business disposal must be aggregated (TCGA 1992 s 169N(1)). There is no requirement for the disposal of the business to be made in a single contract to qualify for entrepreneurs' relief. In practice, the business assets may be sold to a number of different purchasers over a period of time. The disposal of a single business could conceivably be spread over two tax years. However, a distinction must be drawn between assets that are disposed of as part of the business, and assets that are disposed of after cessation of the business. The taxpayer may claim entrepreneurs' relief on several qualifying disposals, as long as the lifetime limit is not breached. The difficulty in practice will be distinguishing between the disposal of parts of the business which each separately qualify for entrepreneurs' relief, and the disposal of qualifying assets after the business has ceased trading. The gains and losses realised by disposing of separate parts of the business should not be aggregated before the relief is applied; but, where assets comprising of a single business disposal accrue both gains and losses, those should be aggregated before the relief is applied. [20.5]

Interaction with losses

Once the losses arising on the disposal of the assets of a single business have been aggregated with gains from that business (see [20.5]), any other allowable capital losses brought forward or arising in the same tax year may be offset against the gains in the year as the taxpayer chooses (TCGA 1992 s 4B). [20.6]

3 Claiming the relief

Entrepreneurs' relief must be claimed by the individual who makes the gain, although in the case of gains made by trustees the claim must be signed by both the trustee and the qualifying beneficiary (TCGA 1992 s 169M). The claim will normally be attached to the tax return for the tax year in which the gain arose. There is a template for the claim in HMRC helpsheet HS275 to assist with this. Where no tax return is issued, or the return has already been submitted, the claim may be made by letter to HMRC.

The claim must be made by the first anniversary of 31 January following the tax year in which the gain arose. The claim may be amended or withdrawn within the same period. If an assessment is made under TMA 1970 s 36 to make good a loss of tax, the time limit for the claim may be extended (HMRC Capital Gains Manual CG 63970). [20.7]

4 Shareholders

In order for a shareholder to claim entrepreneurs' relief on the disposal of shares or securities (referred to as shares from here on) the following conditions must all be met:
(a) the company in which those shares are held must be the individual's personal company (see [20.9]);
(b) the shareholder must be an employee or officer of the company, or of a company in the same group throughout the period of 1 year ending with the date of the disposal (see [20.10]); and
(c) the company must be a trading company or a holding company of a trading group (see [20.11]).

All three of these conditions must be met for the whole of a 12-month period that ends with one of the following events:
- the disposal of the shares;
- the cessation of the trade; or
- the company leaving the trading group and not becoming a member of another trading group.

There is a relaxation of condition (a) for shares acquired through the exercise of qualifying EMI options after 5 April 2013.

The relief may also be claimed if the business has ceased trading when the shares are disposed of, if the disposal date falls up to three years after the date the company ceased to be a trading company or to be a member of a trading group (see [**20.17**]). The relief can thus apply to distributions made where the company has been liquidated, or to distributions made in anticipation of an informal company dissolution, where the total distribution does not exceed £25,000. [**20.8**]

Personal company

A company is the personal company of the individual at any time when both (1), and (2) below apply (TCGA 1992 s 169S(3)) where:
(1) the individual holds at least 5% of the ordinary shares of the company;
(2) the individual controls at least 5% of the voting rights of the company that are associated with those ordinary shares.

The shareholding must meet the 5% threshold without including shares held by associates or shares held in another capacity, for instance as a trustee of a settlement. Where shares are held in the joint names of a married couple or civil partners, each spouse or partner is deemed to have a 50% beneficial interest in the whole shareholding.

The shares disposed of by the individual do not have to be ordinary shares for the gain to qualify for entrepreneurs' relief. As long as ordinary shares in the company are held at the minimum threshold level of 5%, any other disposals of shares or securities in the company can qualify for the relief. The shareholder may make several disposals of shares in the same company and claim entrepreneurs' relief on all gains made as long as the employment requirement is met for the required one-year period in respect of each disposal.

In the recent case of *Alan Castledine v R & C Comrs* (2016), the First-tier Tribunal found that a holding of ordinary shares that could only meet the 5% ownership test (necessary to satisfy the 'personal company' requirements of TCGA 1992 s 169I(6)) if the existence of deferred ordinary shares was ignored, did not qualify for entrepreneurs' relief. [**20.9**]

5 **Employment requirement**

The shareholder must be either an officer or employee of the company in which he disposed of shares (TCGA 1992 s169I(6)(b)). However, if the company was a member of a trading group (see [**20.17**]), the employment requirement is satisfied where the shareholder was employed by another member company of that trading group.

EXAMPLE 20.2

Pauline has worked for Laundrette Ltd for 20 years and owns 7% of the ordinary shares and voting rights. She also owns 5% of the ordinary shares in Handwash Ltd, but she does not work for Handwash Ltd. The remaining shares in Laundrette and Handwash are held by the holding company East Ltd. When Laundrette and Handwash are sold Pauline will qualify for entrepreneurs' relief in respect of her shareholdings in both companies, as she has satisfied the employment requirement by working for either the actual trading company or another trading company in the same trading group.

Whether an individual was an officer of the company (director or company secretary) should easily be confirmed by records held at Companies House. The position of company secretary became optional for private companies from 6 April 2008. Private family companies may consider retaining this post, so a member of the family can hold the office of company secretary and qualify for entrepreneurs' relief.

Non-executive directors count as officers of the company, but shadow directors do not (ITEPA 2003 s 5(3)). In *Hirst v R & C Comrs* (2014), it was argued that Richard Hirst was a 'de facto director' as he was viewed by third parties as a decision maker on behalf of the company. The Tribunal did not accept that he was a director, but did agree that there was an employment relationship between Hirst and the company and entrepreneurs' relief was due.

An employee is defined in ITEPA 2003 s 4 but, for the purposes of entrepreneurs' relief, the employment does not need to be full time or cover any minimum hours (CG 64110). There is also no requirement for the shareholder/employee to be paid although, without a contract of employment, it may be difficult to show that an individual who received no pay was actually employed. This was explored in *Susan Corbett v R & C Comrs* (2014), where the Tribunal decided that Susan continued to be an employee of the company even though her name had been removed from the payroll and her husband's pay was increased to compensate the family for the work that she did.

The requirements of the national minimum wage will normally mean that the company has to make some payment to all of its employees who are not directors of the company.

The shareholder who makes several disposals of shares in the same company may claim entrepreneurs' relief on all gains made, as long as the employment requirement is met for the required one-year period in respect of each disposal. It is essential that a director doesn't resign from his post before he disposes of his shares, as he must hold the directorship for a full year ending with the date of disposal for the relief to be due: see *J Moore v R & C Comrs* (2014). [20.10]

6 Trading company

The definitions of trading company, trading group and holding company are found in TCGA 1992 s 169SA and Sch 7ZA. Joint venture companies may not form part of a trading group from 18 March 2015. At present there are no decided tax cases that examine the question of whether a company is a trading company for entrepreneurs' relief purposes, but it may be possible to obtain a ruling from HMRC on this point (see [20.18]).

Trading company means a company carrying on 'trading activities' whose activities do not include to a substantial extent (see [20.15]) activities other than trading activities. [20.11]

Trading activities

HMRC interpret 'activities' as meaning 'what a company does'. Activities would include 'engaging in trading operations, making and holding investments, planning, holding meetings and so forth'.

Trading activities are those carried on by the company in the course of, or for the purposes of, a trade that it is carrying on or is preparing to carry on. HMRC regard such activities as including (1) certain activities that a company has to carry out before it can start trading, and (2) cases where an existing trade is to be acquired from another person, where trading activities may include developing a business plan, acquiring premises, hiring staff, ordering materials and incurring pre-trading expenditure. HMRC also provide guidance at CG 64060 on the question whether the generation of investment income constitutes a trading or investment activity.

Trading activities also include activities undertaken with a view to the company acquiring or starting to carry on a trade, or with a view to its acquiring a 'significant interest' (see [20.13]) in the share capital of another company that is a trading company or the holding company (see [20.17]) of a trading group (so long as, where the acquiring company is a member of a group of companies, it is not a member of the target company's group). These activities qualify as trading activities only if the acquisition is made, or (as the case may be) the company starts to carry on the trade, as soon as is reasonably practicable. HMRC accept that a company that has disposed of its trade and invested the proceeds and is 'actively seeking' to acquire a new trade or trading subsidiary might still be a trading company if it does not have substantial non-trading activities. What is 'reasonably practicable in the circumstances' will depend on the particular facts of the case. See [20.15] regarding the letting of surplus business property. [20.12]

Significant interest

An acquisition by a company (A) of a 'significant interest' in the share capital of another company (B) is an acquisition of ordinary share capital in company B that would make company B a 51% subsidiary of company A, or would give company A a 'qualifying shareholding in a joint venture company' (see below) without making the two companies members of the same group of companies. Ordinary share capital takes the meaning given by CTA 2010 s 1119). A 51% subsidiary takes its meaning from CTA 2010 s 1154, so that for former taper relief purposes, a company (B) is a 51% subsidiary of another company (A) if company A owns directly or indirectly more than 50% of company B's ordinary share capital. [20.13]

Trade

Trade means anything which:
- is a trade profession or vocation within the meaning of the Income Tax Acts; and
- is conducted on a commercial basis with a view to the realisation of profits (ITA 2007 s 169S(1)).

For entrepreneurs' relief, a trade also includes the commercial letting of furnished holiday accommodation (TCGA 1992 s 241(3A)). For the purposes of this relief, the persons who carry on the furnished holiday lettings are generally treated as sole traders (see [12.61]) even where the property is jointly owned. [20.14]

Substantial extent

Where a company carries on activities other than trading activities, the existence of those non-trading activities will not disturb the trade status of the company if they are not carried on to a substantial extent. HMRC regard 'substantial extent' as meaning more than 20% (CG 64090). There is no hard-and-fast rule about what must be considered in ascertaining a company's trading status, but HMRC indicate the following may be indicators:
- income from non-trading activities;
- the company's asset base;
- expenses incurred, or time spent, by officers and employees of the company in undertaking its activities; and
- the company's history.

These measures should not be regarded as individual tests that all need to be passed; they are just factors that may point one way or the other. The HMRC officer is instructed to weigh up the relevance of each measure in the context of the individual case and judge the matter 'in the round' as demonstrated by the approach of the Special Commissioner in *Farmer (Farmer's Executors) v IRC* (1999).

Where a company lets property surplus to its current requirements, HMRC do not consider that the following necessarily consist of non-trading activities (CG 64085):
- letting part of the trading premises;
- letting properties that are no longer required for the purpose of the trade, where the company's objective is to sell them;
- subletting property where it would be impractical or uneconomic in terms of the trade to assign or surrender the lease;
- the acquisition of property (whether vacant or already let) where it can be shown that the intention is that it will be brought into use for trading activities. **[20.15]**

Holding company and subsidiaries

A holding company is a company that has one or more 51% subsidiaries (TCGA 1992 s 165A(2)).

A 51% subsidiary is, as defined in CTA 2010 s 1154, a company where more than 50% of its ordinary share capital is owned directly or indirectly by another body corporate. Thus a company where 50.1% of its ordinary shares were held by another company would count as a 51% subsidiary. **[20.16]**

Trading group

A group of companies means a company that has one or more 51% subsidiaries. It is important to determine that the companies where the shareholder is employed are members of the same group based on the 51% subsidiary definition, and are not just associated companies.

When looking at whether the group is trading all the activities of the members of the group are taken together as one business (TCGA 1992 s 165A(11)). This allows the group to contain one or more companies that are not trading and still qualify as a trading group. The intra-group transactions are also ignored.

From 18 March 2015, the activities of joint venture companies and corporate partnerships are not necessarily attributed to the trade of the full group (TCGA 1992 Sch 7ZA Pt 2). This change was designed to block management feeder company structures, which allowed a group of shareholders who directly owned less than 5% of the trading company, to each hold at least 5% of the feeder company, and thus qualify for the relief.

FA 2016 has modified this position with retrospective effect from 18 March 2015. Now the activities of a joint venture company can be attributed to the activities of the whole group. As long as an individual shareholder directly or indirectly holds at least 5% of the ordinary share capital and votes of the joint venture, he will qualify for the relief.

For the activities of a partnership to be attributed to the corporate partner, that corporate partner must be a member of the partnership for at least 12 months prior to the disposal date (TCGA 1992 Sch 7ZA Pt 3). Also the individual partner in that partnership must pass two tests. The partner must:
- have an interest in at least 5% of the partnership assets and profits; and
- control 5% or more of the voting power in the corporate partners of the partnership.

The legislation is complex and includes a number of formulas to determine the direct and indirect holding percentages. [20.17]

HMRC ruling

Where a taxpayer has disposed of, or plans to dispose of shares, and is unsure whether the company would qualify as a trading company during the relevant period, he should in the first instance apply to the company for confirmation. HMRC suggest that where the company cannot confirm its trading status the taxpayer should record this fact on the additional information area of their tax return, and take a view themselves on the trading status in order to complete their claim for relief (CG 64100). This seems a particularly unsatisfactory solution for the taxpayer, as it provides him with no certainty that his claim for entrepreneurs' relief is valid, and hence whether he has self-assessed the right amount of CGT.

An alternative approach is for the individual to apply to HMRC for a ruling under its non-statutory clearance service. This procedure is limited to guidance on tax legislation passed in the last four years. However, HMRC will provide views on circumstances which are not covered in the published HMRC guidance, and there is uncertainty about the right tax treatment.

Where a company wishes to clarify its trading status, it may ask HMRC for an opinion in accordance with the non-statutory clearance service, as described in the HMRC Non-statutory Business Clearance Guidance Manual (NBCG). HMRC have confirmed that clearance will be given under the NBCG procedure, if a company wishes to confirm its trading status for entrepreneurs' relief to be claimed by its shareholders, or for SSE to be claimed by the company. [20.18]

7 Sole traders

A sole trader may qualify for entrepreneurs' relief on gains arising in three specific circumstances:
- on the disposal of his whole business;

- on the disposal of part of his business;
- on the disposal of qualifying business assets up to three years after the cessation of his business. **[20.19]**

Disposal of a business

The disposal of a business will qualify for entrepreneurs' relief if the following conditions are met at the date of disposal:
(1) the business has been owned by the individual who is making the claim for relief for at least 12 months; and
(2) the disposal includes at least one relevant business asset (see **[20.25]**).

The disposal of the business does not need to be made as a going concern, and all of the assets do not have to be sold to the same purchaser. Where several purchasers are involved, careful timing of the disposals of the main assets will be required.

Where some assets are sold well before the main part of the business and the trade continues after those disposals, the gains on those early disposals may not qualify for entrepreneurs' relief. This applies where those early disposals do not comprise 'part of a business' and the assets were not in use in the business at the time the business ceases to trade.

HMRC are prepared to accept that the disposal of a business may be spread over several weeks, in which case the delay between disposals should not prevent the relief from applying to all the assets.

Entrepreneurs' relief has always been available to apply to gains that arise on the incorporation of a business so long as that business was operating for at least 12 months before the date it ceased and the assets were transferred to the company within three years of that date. Those assets may well include goodwill created within the unincorporated business, which is notoriously difficult to value.

For incorporations undertaken on and after 3 December 2014 where the assets are transferred by an individual or partnership to a close company, any goodwill included in that transfer is not necessarily a relevant asset. If the goodwill is not a relevant asset, any gain arising on its disposal will not qualify for entrepreneurs' relief (TCGA 1992 s 169LA, amended by FA 2016 s 85).

The test of whether goodwill is a relevant asset depends on the relationship between the individual vendor (P) and the close company (C) that acquires the goodwill. There are three possible outcomes:

P holds 5% or more of C

Where immediately after the incorporation of the business P and any relevant connected persons hold 5% or more of C's ordinary share capital or voting rights, or 5% or more of the ordinary share capital or voting rights of any company which is a member of the same group as C, then the goodwill is not treated as a relevant asset, and the relief is not due. The connected persons include other companies or trustees connected to P, but not other individuals such as family members.

P holds less than 5% of C

Where immediately after the incorporation P and any relevant connected persons own less than 5% of the ordinary share capital or votes of C or of any company in the same group as C, then P can claim entrepreneurs' relief on the gains arising on the transfer of goodwill.

This allows a business to be incorporated as part of a family succession plan and entrepreneurs' relief to be claimed on the transfer of goodwill. Where the vendor (P) acquires less than 5% of the ordinary share capital, the relief can be claimed, even if the vendor is related to other individuals who hold larger shareholdings in the company.

Where C is sold on

If the incorporation is part of an arrangement to sell the business, entrepreneurs' relief can be claimed irrespective of the shareholdings in C that P acquires. However, C must be sold on to another company (A) within a 28-day period that starts with the incorporation, or another longer period that HMRC may allow.

After C is sold, neither P nor any person connected with P must hold any of C's ordinary shares. This does not bar C from holding shares in company A that acquires C. However, if A is a close company P and his connected parties must not hold more than 5% of A's ordinary share capital or votes or more than 5% of share capital or votes in another company in the same group as A.

Entrepreneurs' relief is still available for gains arising from the transfer of other assets on incorporation on and after 3 December 2014. Also entrepreneurs' relief is still available on the sale or transfer of a business including goodwill, where the successor to the business is not a close company or on the formation of a partnership, or on the introduction of new partners.

[20.20]

Disposal of part of a business

It is often difficult to distinguish between the disposal of a collection of business assets and the disposal of 'part of a business'. The disposal of one or more business assets will not attract the relief if those assets were either not in use when business ceased, or the business has not ceased, whilst the disposal of 'part of a business' will attract entrepreneurs' relief. There is no clear definition of 'part of a business' and, as this term has been imported from the retirement relief provisions, the tax cases on this issue concerning retirement relief are now considered to be relevant to entrepreneurs' relief (see CG 64010).

In particular the case of *McGregor (Her Majesty's Inspector of Taxes) v Adcock* (1977) established the 'interference test', where the HMRC officer would look at the impact of the sale on the business and establish what had changed. If the sale made a significant difference to the way the business operated then there had been a sale of part of the business; if not, then the sale was probably one of assets out of the business, which would not qualify for relief.

There were many cases of farmland disposals under retirement relief and an unofficial practice emerged of treating disposals of 50% or more of the farmland occupied by the farm as a disposal of part of the business, although the facts would have to be established in each case. In *WSG Russell v R & C Comrs* (2012), just 35% of the farmland was disposed of, but the owner claimed entrepreneurs' relief. The claim was rejected on the basis that the disposal was not part of a business, but merely an asset used in the business.

A key case concerning entrepreneurs' relief on the disposal of part of a business is *M Gilbert (T/A United Foods) v R & C Comrs* (2011). Mr Gilbert acted as an independent sales representative for nine different wholesale food suppliers, and had about 120 customers. He sold the business that related to one of these suppliers as a going concern. This included customer lists, goodwill and trademarks, and the benefit and burden of unperformed contracts. The tribunal judge rejected the interference test established by *McGregor v Adcock*, above as being only relevant to the disposal of farmland. Instead, the judge looked for a 'viable section' test to see whether the part of the business disposed of could operate as a separate business. The fact that the assets disposed of were treated as a going concern for VAT purposes appeared to influence his decision to agree the taxpayer's claim for entrepreneurs' relief. [20.21]

8 Partners

Disposals by the partnership of the whole or part of the business attracts entrepreneurs' relief as the whole partnership was one sole trader. However, there are special rules in TCGA 1992 s 169I(8) that are there to ensure certain disposals made by an individual partner attract relief as if he had been a sole trader (see [20.19]). The taxation of gains made by partners and members of LLPS is dealt with in **Chapter 44** and **Chapter 45** respectively. [20.22]

Special rules

The circumstances that attract entrepreneurs' relief for established or new partners are as follows:
(1) where an individual transfers assets to a partnership, on the occasion of him joining that partnership and the partnership takes over his business (TCGA 1992 s 169I(8)(a));
(2) where a partner disposes of the whole of his interest in the partnership, he is treated as if he had disposed of the whole of a business (TCGA 1992 s 169I(8)(b));
(3) where a partner disposes of part of his interest in the partnership, he is treated as if he had disposed of part of a business; and
(4) where the partnership disposes of the whole or part of the partnership business, the partners are each treated as if they owned the whole of the partnership business (TCGA 1992 s 169I(8)(c)).

Note that the special rules for retiring partners on incorporation of a business (TCGA 1992 s 169LA(3)) were removed by FA 2016.

The situation in (1) would provide relief for the capital gains that arise when a new partner introduces an asset to the partnership as the whole or part of his capital contribution. Prior to 21 January 2008 it was thought that a gain would not arise in this situation using the well-established practice in SP D12. However, Revenue and Customs Brief 03/08 sets out details of a revised practice in this area.

Where a sole trader merges his business with an established partnership, the provisions in (1) and (3) above will ensure that any gains arising on the transfer of assets between those partners, either the new partner transferring his assets into the partnership or the existing partners transferring an interest in the partnership assets (such as goodwill) to the new partner, will be covered by entrepreneurs' relief.

On the other hand, HMRC argue that the disposal (or part disposal) of an individual partner's interest in one or more particular assets owned collectively by the partnership, rather than a disposal of his entire interest in all the partnership assets, would not qualify for the relief (CG 64040).

A partner may qualify for relief on the disposal of an asset owned personally, but which was used by the partnership, when that disposal is associated with his exit from the partnership business or the reduction in his interest in the partnership.

The rule described in (3) above is required to ensure that every partner in the partnership qualifies for the relief where there is a disposal of all or part of the partnership business, but the following conditions must also apply:

(a) the partnership business has been carried on for at least a year at the date of disposal; and
(b) the disposal consists of one or more relevant assets.

Where a partnership business ceases and, within three years after that cessation, the partnership disposes of some assets which were in use at the time the business ceased, entrepreneurs' relief should be available to the gains realised by all the partners. The rules follow those that apply for sole traders (see below). [20.23]

9 Post-cessation disposals

Business assets

Where the owners of an unincorporated business cease trading, they may retain certain business assets to be disposed of at a later date. Entrepreneurs' relief can still apply to these later disposals if they occur within three years after the date the business ceased (TCGA 1992 s 169I(4)) and the other conditions listed below apply.

It is vital to accurately identify the business cessation date.

Any disposals outside the three-year period will not qualify for entrepreneurs' relief, even if the asset can be clearly linked to the disposal of the main business.

HMRC have no discretion to extend the three-year period for post-cessation disposals.

According to HMRC, the date the business ceased is a question of fact (CG 64045), but there will be cases where the cessation date is not clear cut. Further guidance on this issue is given in the HMRC Business Income Manual at BIM 80565–BIM 80585. The cessation of the business does not have to fall after the commencement of entrepreneurs' relief, so long as the disposal of the asset does.

This was illustrated in the case of *Rice v R & C Comrs* (2014). The taxpayer had run a second-hand car business for over 30 years from Fletton Avenue. In early 2005 he started to wind down the business, which took a number of months. The First-tier Tribunal had to decide whether the trade ceased before or after 29 April 2005 to allow the claim for entrepreneurs' relief on the sale of the Fletton Avenue site on 29 April 2008. No cessation accounts had been prepared and no cessation date was noted on his tax returns. In spite of the lack of evidence of a distinct cessation date, the Tribunal decided in favour of the taxpayer.

The other conditions that must apply for the gain on the disposal of the asset to qualify for entrepreneurs' relief are:
(a) the asset must have been a relevant business asset for the business;
(b) the asset must have been in use at the time the business ceased; and
(c) the owner of the asset must have owned the business for at least 12 months ending with the date the business ceased. **[20.24]**

Relevant business asset

Relevant business assets can include any assets including goodwill used for the purposes of the business carried on by the sole trader or partnership, but not including 'excluded assets' that are:
- shares and securities; and
- other assets held as investments (TCGA 1992 s 169L(4)).

Shares and securities held by a sole trader or partnership will never be relevant business assets even if there is some business-related reason for holding the shares. For example a farmer may hold shares in a milk marketing co-operative. **[20.25]**

Used in the business

For the asset to qualify under (b) in **[20.24]** it does not have to be used for any particular length of time before the business ceased, it just needs to be in use at the date the business ceased (TCGA 1992 s 169I(2)(b)).

Assets that have a mixed business and non-business use can qualify as relevant business assets. There is no restriction that requires the asset to be used wholly for the purposes of the business at the date of cessation. **[20.26]**

Use after the business ceased

There is no restriction on the use to which the asset is put between the date the business ceased and the disposal of that asset. This period can be up to three years, so the owner is free to let the asset at a commercial rent for that three-year period and still claim entrepreneurs' relief on the disposal of the asset. The asset could even be used in a different business operated and owned by the asset owner, and then when it is sold relief is claimed in respect of the use of the asset in the ceased business. **[20.27]**

Shares

Shares or securities in a company may be disposed of after the company has ceased trading on the occasion of the liquidation or winding up of the company. The shareholder is treated as if he had disposed of his interest in the shares when he receives the distribution from the liquidation (TCGA 1992 s 122). That receipt will generally be treated as capital, but be aware of the TAAR that can apply to distributions made on and after 6 April 2016, which may cause the receipt to be taxed as income (FA 2016 s 35; ITTOIA 2005 ss 396B, 404A).

On an informal winding up, the distributions made to shareholders can only be treated as capital for tax purposes where the total of all the distributions from the company in anticipation of the winding up do not exceed £25,000. Otherwise, all the distributions made in anticipation of the winding up are subject to income tax (CTA 2010 ss 1030A, 1030B).

Where the distribution is treated as a capital payment, it can qualify for entrepreneurs' relief under TCGA 1992 s 169S(2) if the conditions listed below apply:
(1) the company must have been the individual's personal company (see [20.9]);
(2) the shareholder must have been an employee or officer of the company, or of a company in the same group (see [20.10]); and
(3) the company must have been a trading company or a holding company of a trading group (see [20.17]).

All of these three conditions must apply for the whole of a 12-month period that ends with either the cessation of the trade of the company, or the date the company left the trading group and did not continue to trade outside of that group. This date must also fall not more than three years before the date the shares are treated as being disposed of, which will normally be the date the shareholder receives the capital distribution.

However, where the shares disposed of were acquired through EMI qualifying options on or after 6 April 2012, condition (1) above is not required. In such a case, the EMI shares will qualify for entrepreneurs' relief if the option grant date fell at least one year before the cessation date (ie on or after 6 April 2013), and the other conditions are met (TCGA 1992 s 169I(7B)). [20.28]

10 Associated disposals

This is a tricky concept and it is not well explained in the legislation. An associated disposal of business assets can only occur in connection with:
- the disposal of shares or securities in a company (see [20.8]); or
- the disposal of a partnership interest (see [20.22]).

The relief cannot apply on the disposal of assets following the disposal of a sole trader business, as such a disposal would fall into the more flexible post-cessation rules: see [20.24]–[20.28]. [20.29]

Disposal of shares

If a shareholder who is also an employee or officer of his personal company disposes of shares or securities in that company, the gain arising will be eligible for entrepreneurs' relief if the other conditions apply (see [20.8]). Where that individual disposes of an asset which was used by the company at around the same time as the share disposal (see [20.32]), the gain on that asset will qualify for the relief as an associated disposal, if all of the following conditions also apply:
(a) the asset is disposed of as part of the shareholder's withdrawal from participation in the business carried on by his personal company or the business carried on by the trading group (TCGA 1992 s 169K(3), (5));
(b) the asset was used for the purpose of the business for at least one year to the date of disposal of the shares, or to the date of cessation of the company's business if earlier (TCGA 1992 s 169K(4));

(c) for disposals made on and after 18 March 2015 the share disposal must consist of at least 5% of the company's ordinary share capital which carries at least 5% of the voting rights. For a disposal of securities the disposal must consist of at least 5% of the value of securities of the company but no disposal of voting rights is required. In both cases there must be no share purchase arrangements in existence (TCGA 1992 s 169K(1B), (1D)); and

(d) for assets acquired on or after 13 June 2015 which are used for the business, when that asset is disposed of, it must have been owned by the shareholder throughout a three-year period ending with the date of disposal (TCGA 1992, s 169K(4A), as amended by FA 2016).

To summarise:

- the first disposal of shares must qualify for entrepreneurs' relief (and for disposals made on or after 18 March 2015, meet condition (c) above), but this disposal does not have to generate a taxable gain; and
- the associated disposal of the privately held asset must meet conditions (a) and (b), and for assets acquired on and after 13 June 2016, and thus disposed of after that date, condition (d) must also be met.

'Share purchase arrangements' means an arrangement, agreement or understanding under which the individual (P) who disposes of the shares or securities in company A is entitled to acquire shares or securities in company A or in another company which is in the same trading group as company A. If the associated disposal takes place before the material disposal of shares, the disposal of shares is not treated as a 'share purchase arrangement' (TCGA 1992 s 169K(6A)).

This condition also applies if a person connected with P (as defined in TCGA 1992 s 286) is the person entitled to acquire the shares or securities in company A or a company in the same group as company A. **[20.30]**

Withdrawal from participation in the business

This condition is imposed to prevent a shareholder from disposing of a single asset and claiming it was an associated disposal because he also disposed of a small number of shares at the same time. The term 'withdrawal from participation in the business' is not defined and what HMRC take it to mean may become clearer in the future. The HMRC guidance (CG 63995) says it is not necessary for the individual to actually reduce the amount of work they may do for the business for this condition to be met.

EXAMPLE 20.3

Lewpyn has owned the intellectual property used by his internet games company Level 6 Ltd (his personal company) since it was created on 6 April 2012. He sold a 50% holding in Level 6 Ltd on 6 August 2016, and on the same date he sold the intellectual property used by the company. Lewpyn remains the technical director for the company.

Lewpyn has withdrawn from the business of the company because he has disposed of at least 5% of the ordinary share capital and, in connection with that disposal, he sold his interest in the IP used by the company. The disposal of the IP therefore qualifies as an associated disposal, and the gain realised on that disposal will qualify for entrepreneurs' relief. [20.31]

Time limit

The legislation does not give a time limit during which the associated disposal must be made, but the HMRC guidance (CG 63995) stipulates that both the disposal of the shares and the associated disposal of the asset must be caused by the same event and there should be no significant time interval between the disposals. It is also implied in the HMRC guidance that the event causing the disposal should be withdrawal from participation in the business, although the legislation only says the asset disposal must be connected with the withdrawal from the business.

However, HMRC realise that there will often be a delay between the disposal of the shares, perhaps on the cessation of the business, and the disposal of the asset which potentially qualifies as the associated disposal. They have therefore laid down some guidelines as to when a later disposal of an asset can be accepted as an associated disposal.

The disposal may be an associated disposal if the disposal occurs:
- within one year of the cessation of business, or
- within three years of the cessation of business and the asset has not been leased or used for any other purpose at any time after business ceased;
- where the business has not ceased within three years of the material disposal provided the asset has not been used for any purpose other than that of the business.

These extra-statutory conditions are not as flexible as the legally imposed conditions relating to the post-cessation disposals for a sole trader business (see [20.24]). HMRC guidance (CG 36995) indicates that any significant use of the asset, other than for the business of the company, between the first disposal of shares and the disposal of the asset, will disqualify that asset from being an associated disposal. This is in addition to the legislative restrictions imposed by TCGA 1992 s 169P (see [20.34]). [20.32]

Disposal of partnership interest

Where a partner disposes of his interest in the partnership or part of that interest so the disposal would qualify for entrepreneurs' relief where a gain arises (see [20.22]), a disposal of an asset held personally may qualify for as an associated disposal for the relief if the following conditions apply:

(a) the asset is disposed of as part of the partner's withdrawal from participation in the business carried on by the partnership (TCGA 1992 s 169K(3), (5));

(b) the asset was used for the purpose of the partnership business for at least one year to the date of disposal of the partnership interest, or to the date or cessation of the partnership business if earlier (TCGA 1992 s 169K(4));

(c) for disposals on and after 18 March 2015, the partner must have held at least a 5% interest in the partnership's assets for a period of three years in the eight years ending with the disposal, and there must be no partnership purchase arrangements in existence at the date of that disposal (TCGA 1992 s 169K(1A));

(d) for assets acquired on and after 13 June 2016 the partner must have held the asset for a continuous period of at least three years ending with the date of disposal (TCGA 1992 s 169K(4A) as amended by FA 2016).

The definition of withdrawal from the business of the partnership is similar to that discussed with reference to a company (see [20.31]). The HMRC guidance (CG 63995) indicates that the partner does not have to step down as a partner completely.

Note that for a partner to claim entrepreneurs' relief on the disposal of his partnership interest, or part of that partnership interest, he is not required to hold any particular percentage of the partnership assets. He could be a partner with an entitlement to just 1% of the partnership assets and still qualify for the relief. However, to qualify for the relief on an associated disposal made on or after 18 March 2015, the partner must have held at least 5% of the partnership assets for a three-year period in the last eight years preceding the disposal.

This condition is relaxed when the partner is retiring and has already disposed of all but a small percentage of his partnership interest. Where that last fraction of the partner's interest in the partnership amounts to less than 5%, he will be able to claim relief on an associated disposal, if he also disposes of all of his interest in the partnership at the same time as he makes the associated disposal.

EXAMPLE 20.4

Graham has been in partnership with his son Tristan for 10 years, sharing the profits: 80% Graham and 20% Tristan. Graham owns the office that the partnership trades from. On his 60th birthday, Graham gave the office to his son (treated as a disposal at market value as they are connected persons), and the profit-sharing ratios are changed to 25% Graham and 75% Tristan.

The reduction by Graham of his interest in the partnership is a material disposal, as he has reduced his interest in the partnership by at least 5%. The disposal of the office to Tristan thus qualifies as an associated disposal and any gains arising on that will qualify for entrepreneurs' relief. Both the disposals are caused by the same event: Graham partially withdrawing from participation in the partnership business.

The time period in which the associate disposal must take place is subject to the same restrictions as apply to disposals associated with the withdrawal from the business of a trading company (see [20.31]). [20.33]

Restrictions

Where there is a material disposal of shares or of a partnership interest, there are four additional restrictions on the use of any asset that is the subject of the associated disposal (TCGA 1992 s 169P(4)). If any of the following apply the amount of the gain arising on the associated disposal of the asset, which would be subject to entrepreneurs' relief, is reduced on a just and reasonable basis:
(1) the asset has only been used by the business for part of the period of ownership by the individual, in which case the gain taken into account will reflect the period of business use;
(2) only part of the asset has been used for the purposes of the business, so the gain taken into account will reflect the proportion of the asset used for business purposes;

(3) the individual concerned has only been involved in the business as a partner of the partnership or employee/officer of the company for part of the time during which the asset was used by the business. This is less likely than situations (1) or (2), but is possible where an individual was a salaried partner before becoming a full partner;
(4) any payment of rent was made for the use of the asset by the personal company or partnership for a period after 5 April 2008.

The payment of 'rent' in restriction (4) means any form of consideration paid for the use of the asset, including licence fees for the use of intellectual property. Where the rent paid is less than a full market rent for the use of the asset the gain is restricted proportionately.

The restriction in (4) is likely to cause the most aggravation as it was good tax planning practice under former taper relief to hold business property outside of the company, and to charge the company a commercial rent for its use. Full business asset taper relief would apply on any gain made on the disposal of the let property and the rent paid was a useful way to extract funds free of NIC from the company.

Now that situation is turned on its head, so property owners must calculate whether the reduction in the eventual rate of CGT down to 10% using entrepreneurs' relief is worth more than the short-term benefit of NIC-free rent. There may be strong commercial reasons for keeping the property in personal hands. Even if it was desirable to not hold the property within the company, the transfer may well involve high transactional costs such as Stamp Duty Land Tax, mortgage and valuation fees, and it will create a personal capital gain that will not qualify for entrepreneurs' relief. [20.34]

11 Deferred gains

Where a gain is rolled over or deferred on the acquisition of new shares or corporate bonds, the eventual crystallisation of that gain may not qualify for entrepreneurs' relief as the disposal of the new security will not meet the necessary qualifying conditions. In these cases special provisions may apply to give entrepreneurs' relief in respect of gains deferred by acquiring the following shares or securities:
- qualifying corporate bonds (QCBs) (see [20.36]);
- share exchanges (see [20.39]);
- Enterprise Investment Scheme (EIS) or Venture Capital Trust (VCT) shares (see [20.40]). [20.35]

Qualifying corporate bonds

When a shareholder sells his personal company, he may well receive qualifying corporate bonds (QCBs) in exchange for some or all of his shares. The gain that arises on the disposal of those shares is then rolled into the QCBs and only crystallises when the QCBs are exchanged for cash, normally on the maturity of the bonds. Under the taper relief rules the gain on the disposal of the shares was frozen and taper relief would apply when the gain crystallised, but only in relation to the period the shares were held, not the period the QCBs were held. QCBs exchanged for shares prior to 6 April 2008 thus present a problem, as the gain is frozen, but taper relief now no longer applies.

This problem is eased by a special relief for QCBs that were exchanged for shares before 6 April 2008 (FA 2008 Sch 3 para 7). There is also a separate relief for QCBs exchanged for shares on or after 6 April 2008 (TCGA 1992 s 169R).

HMRC have produced two tables that summarise the CGT position where a deferred gain comes into charge following a disposal of QCBs or EIS or VCT shares (see TAXGUIDE 1/12). [20.36]

Post-6 April 2008 QCBs

Where an individual acquires QCBs in exchange for shares in his personal company on or after 6 April 2008, the gain inherent in those personal company shares is rolled into the QCBs and falls into charge to CGT when the QCBs are disposed of (TCGA 1992 s 116(10)). On the disposal of those QCBs, the tests for entrepreneurs' relief to apply to the deferred gain would normally look at the individual's shareholding and employment conditions in the company that issued the QCBs, not the original personal company. The individual must meet both shareholding and employment tests (see [20.8] and [20.10]), for the company that issued the QCBs, to claim entrepreneurs' relief on the gain realised on disposal of the QCBs. [20.37]

Taxpayer election

If the taxpayer elects for the gain to crystallise under TCGA 1992 s 169R, the gain arising on the disposal of the personal company shares is not deferred at all. That gain is subject to entrepreneurs' relief at the time of the share for QCB exchange (if all the conditions apply), and bears CGT at the entrepreneurs' relief rate of 10%.

If the taxpayer makes the election under s 169R, CGT is paid on the gain realised on the disposal of the shares, potentially at the ER rate of 10%, if the entrepreneurs' relief conditions apply.

As the consideration for the shares is QCBs and not cash, the taxpayer may not have the cash to pay the tax due on that part of the deal, until some of the QCBs are disposed of.

The alternative is not to elect under s 169R, and to accept the automatic deferral of the gain under TCGA 1992 s 116(10). The deferred gain can then fall into charge as and when the QCBs are gradually cashed, but that gain will be subject to CGT at the normal rates:10% or 20% (for 2017–18), depending on the taxpayer's level of income and gains for the tax year of encashment. Entrepreneurs' relief is unlikely to apply when the QCBs are cashed, unless the taxpayer holds 5% of the company that issued the QCBs and the other conditions in [20.8] are met (see HMRC Capital Gains Manual at CG 64161). [20.38]

Share exchanges

Another situation where gains may be deferred is on a share-for-share exchange, which often occurs on the takeover of a company. A shareholder may exchange shares (or debentures) in his personal company (the old shares) for a small holding of shares (new shares) issued by the acquiring company.

No capital gain arises at the time of the share exchange as the new shares are considered to stand in the shoes of the old shares (TCGA 1992 s 127). However, on disposal of the new shares, entrepreneurs' relief may not apply if the minority shareholder does not hold 5% of the ordinary share capital of the acquiring company.

In this situation, the shareholder can choose whether to defer the gain using s 127 or to disapply s 127 (using the election under TCGA 1992 s 169Q) and claim entrepreneurs' relief on the gain as it arises on the disposal of the old shares. This will make the effective rate of CGT on that gain 10%, whether the share exchange occurs before or after 23 June 2010.

If the shareholder elects under s 169Q to disapply the deferral of the gain under s 127, he will have to pay CGT on the residue of the gain at 10%, if the entrepreneurs' relief conditions apply at that time.

The shareholder may have difficulty in funding the CGT due, as he has not received cash proceeds for those old shares. [20.39]

Venture capital schemes

There are now four venture capital schemes under which investors can achieve income tax relief, and certain capital gains tax reliefs. These are:
- Seed Enterprise investment scheme (SEIS);
- Enterprise investment scheme (EIS);
- Social investment tax relief (SITR); and
- Venture capital trust (VCT) – only for shares acquired before 6 April 2006.

Where gains that potentially qualify for entrepreneurs' relief are invested under those schemes, the relief is generally lost as the gain falls back into charge on exiting the venture capital scheme, and no longer has the attributes that make it qualify for the relief. However, gains arising in the following two periods can retain the ability to qualify for entrepreneurs' relief when the gain falls back into charge after a period of deferral using a venture capital relief.

Where a gain arises on or after 3 December 2014 (the underlying disposal), which would qualify for entrepreneurs' relief (based on the law existing at the date of that disposal), that relief may be preserved when the taxpayer defers the gain by investing in shares issued under EIS, or shares or debt issued under SITR (TCGA 1992 ss 169T–169V). The underlying disposal must not be a chargeable event under EIS or SITR.

The taxpayer must make a claim for entrepreneurs' relief to apply when the first part of that deferred gain falls back into charge to CGT. The claim must be made by the first anniversary of 31 January following the tax year in which the first part of the deferred gain falls back into charge to CGT. The taxpayer who makes the claim for entrepreneurs' relief must be the same person that made the original underlying disposal. [20.40]

12 Order of use of schemes

The rules for SEIS have been designed to mirror those for EIS, so that a company which has used SEIS can go on to use EIS to raise additional funding. However, it is essential to use those two venture capital schemes in the right order, ie utilise SEIS before EIS, or proceed directly to using the EIS.

The requirements for an SEIS qualifying company specify that it must have no previous other risk capital investments, using the EIS or VCT schemes (ITA 2007 s 257DK). If SEIS is to be used by a small company, the application for that SEIS relief must be submitted before any application for EIS. The SEIS shares must be issued before the EIS shares, and shares under those two schemes must not be issued on the same day. A mix-up between the forms required to apply for approval under SEIS and EIS will result in the SEIS tax relief being denied: see *X-Wind Power Ltd v R & C Comrs* (2015). **[20.41]**

21 CGT – death

Updated by Robin Vos, Macfarlanes LLP

I   General [**21.1**]
II   Valuation of chargeable assets at death [**21.21**]
III CGT losses of the deceased [**21.41**]
IV Sale of deceased's assets by PRs [**21.61**]
V   Losses of the PRs [**21.81**]
VI Transfers to legatees (TCGA 1992 s 62(4)) [**21.101**]
VII Disclaimers and variations (TCGA 1992 s 62(6)); Claims under the Inheritance (Provision for Family and Dependants) Act 1975 [**21.121**]

I GENERAL

1 Basic principles

On death, the assets of the deceased of which he was competent to dispose are deemed to be acquired by the personal representatives (PRs) at their market value at death. There is an acquisition without a corresponding disposal: an uplift in the value of the assets but no charge to CGT (TCGA 1992 s 62(1)).

Hence, death generally wipes out capital gains with no charge to tax.

The position is different for offshore income gains (gains on offshore funds that do not have 'reporting status'). If an individual dies owning an offshore fund personally, reg 34 of the Offshore Funds (Tax) Regulations 2009 (SI 2009/3001) deems there to be a disposal at market value but an income tax charge arises on the deemed disposal if a profit arises. This is deductible for inheritance tax purposes (see IHTA 1984 s 174).

The deceased is not treated as being competent to dispose of assets over which he had a power of appointment (s 62(10)) but is regarded as being competent to dispose of his share of jointly owned property (even if on his death the share passes automatically to the other joint owner).

As will be seen below, special tax rules apply to the PRs during the period of administration. One difficulty is in determining whether the administration of the estate is completed. If the administration of the estate is complete then the PRs do not dispose of assets as PRs, but as bare trustees for the legatee. This can make a significant difference to the rate of tax payable on a disposal (see CG 30700 and *IRC v Aubrey Smith* (1930)).

In order for the administration of the estate to be complete, the residue of the estate must be ascertained even if no formal assent has been made to the relevant legatee. Where the distribution of the estate is being challenged or the full extent of the assets or liabilities of the deceased is not yet clear, the administration is not complete.

There are exceptional cases where it is accepted that the period of administration is continuing despite the fact that all the figures are apparently available to enable residue to be ascertained. One example (given by CG 30710) is where:

> 'distributing shares in accordance with legatees' fractional entitlements to residue would result in one legatee receiving a majority shareholding whilst the other legatees would only receive minority holdings. Because of the disparity in values between majority and minority holdings it may be necessary for the personal representatives to apply the rule from *Lloyd's Bank Plc v Duker and others* [1987] 3 All ER 193 Ch D. This would require them to sell these shares rather than distributing them in specie.
>
> The period of administration would continue in such a case until the shares were sold and the Capital Gains Tax liability arising to the personal representatives was quantified.'

As CG 30710 states, the rule referred to above is of fairly limited application. The fact that a majority shareholding would be broken into minority holdings on distribution should not be accepted as preventing distribution of shares and thus the ending of the period of administration. Nor should minor valuation differences between minority shareholdings passing to the legatees be accepted as covered by the rule in the *Duker* case, above. **[21.1]**

EXAMPLE 21.1

Included in T's estate on his death in November 2016 is a rare first edition of *Ulysses* that T had acquired in 1997 for £10,000. It is worth £100,000 at death. The gain of £90,000 is not chargeable on T's death. Instead his PRs acquire the asset at a new base value of £100,000.

Although gains on assets accruing over a trust's period of ownership where the life tenant has a 'qualifying' interest in possession (see below) are also generally wiped out on the death of the life tenant, provided the property does not revert to the original 'disponer' or settlor (see TCGA 1992 ss 72–73) and the trust funds in question do not comprise offshore funds, held over gains on entry into a trust are not wiped out on the death of the life tenant.

EXAMPLE 21.2

Using the facts in the example above, T was the life tenant of a pre-22 March 2006 interest in possession trust and the book had been given to the trust by his mother in1982 with the benefit of a holdover claim. The gain held over was £20,000. On T's death, the held over gain of £20,000 becomes chargeable and only the balance of the gain (£70,000) is wiped out on death (see TCGA 1992 s 74).

It may be possible to make another holdover claim to avoid paying tax on the £20,000 if T's death is a chargeable transfer (TCGA 1992 s 260). In most cases the transfer on T's death will be chargeable to inheritance tax unless the asset passes on interest in possession trusts to the spouse (in which case it will be a transitional serial interest and spouse exempt) or outright to his spouse. Hence in most cases a further hold over claim can be made.

Contrast the position if mother had given T the book outright rather than into trust and claimed holdover relief (such a claim on gifts to an individual is now only possible on business or agricultural assets). In these circumstances there is no clawback of the held over gain on T's death.

If an individual donor gives business or agricultural assets to the donee and claims holdover relief under TCGA 1992 s 165 there is a clawback of relief if the donee becomes non-UK resident before he has disposed of the asset and within six years of the end of the tax year of the disposal (s 168). If the donee does not discharge the liability the donor will be liable (s 168(7)) with a right of reimbursement against the donee. However, it is thought that HMRC accept that no liability can attach to the donor's PRs in respect of that liability if no assessment has been raised during the lifetime of the deceased donor.

When is a capital gains tax uplift available on the death of a beneficiary?
When the inheritance tax rules relating to trusts were radically changed in 2006, FA 2006 amended TCGA 1992 ss 72 and 73 so that if the interest in possession arises on or after 22 March 2006 there is no deemed disposal or base cost uplift to market value on the death of the interest in possession beneficiary unless the interest is:
(a)   an immediate post-death interest (IPDI); or
(b)   a transitional serial interest (TSI); or
(c)   a disabled person's interest within IHTA 1984 s 89B(1)(c) or (d); or
(d)   an 18–25 trust where the beneficiary has an interest in possession and dies under 18; or
(e)   a bereaved minor trust and the minor has an interest in possession and then dies before reaching 18.

If the deceased had an interest within (a) to (e) above or a pre-22 March 2006 interest in possession then on his death by virtue of TCGA 1992 ss 72–73 there is a deemed disposal and reacquisition by the trustees at market value but no chargeable gain arises on the disposal.

If the trust assets comprise offshore funds which do not have reporting status and these show a profit then an offshore income gain is deemed to accrue. Any tax on this gain is not deductible for inheritance tax purposes unless the deceased was the settlor of the trust. Contrast the position if the individual owned the offshore funds.

The effects of all this can be summarised as follows:

EXAMPLE 21.3

(1)   Husband dies in 2016 leaving his assets on interest in possession trusts for his wife in his will. This is an IPDI. On the death of the wife, inheritance tax will be chargeable and capital gains tax base cost uplift is available.

(2)   Husband dies in 2016 leaving assets on trust for his child at 18. This is not an IPDI even if the child is entitled to income while a minor. It is a bereaved minor trust. On the death of the child no inheritance tax will be chargeable but capital gains tax base cost uplift is available if the child was entitled to the income (see *Example 21.5* below).

(3)   Husband dies in 2016 leaving assets on interest in possession trusts for his child at 30. Section 31 of the Trustee Act 1925 has been excluded so that

the child takes entitlement to income while a minor. This is an IPDI. On the death of the child, inheritance tax will be chargeable and capital gains tax base cost uplift is available.

If the wife's interest in example (1) above is terminated during lifetime and the remainder beneficiaries take absolutely this is a PET and a disposal for capital gains tax purposes at market value. No holdover relief is available unless the settled property is business or agricultural property qualifying for relief under TCGA 1992 s 165.

EXAMPLE 21.4

Husband has an interest in possession under a pre-March 2006 trust. He dies in 2016 and his wife takes a successive interest in possession. This is a transitional serial interest under IHTA 1984 s 49D and, on each of husband and wife's death, there is a base cost uplift for capital gains tax purposes.

EXAMPLE 21.5

Father dies leaving his estate on a bereaved minor trust for his two children, Amy and John. They are each given entitlement to income before they are 18 and Amy dies at 17. Note that this is not an immediate post-death interest because a bereaved minor interest takes priority over an immediate post-death interest. There is no inheritance tax charge (IHTA 1984 s 71B(2)(b)) but there is a base cost uplift for capital gains tax purposes (TCGA 1992 s 72(1B)).

EXAMPLE 21.6

Mother dies leaving her estate on trust for her only child Mary at 25 and, subject thereto, to her nephew. Under the terms of the trust Mary is to become entitled to the income from the age of 16 and receive capital at 25. If Mary dies under 18, having already become entitled to income but not on or within two years of mother's death, she takes a s 71D (18–25 trust) interest rather than an immediate post death interest. A base cost uplift for capital gains tax purposes is available under TCGA 1992 s 72(1A)(b) even if the property remains settled. There is no inheritance tax charge (IHTA 1984 s 71E(2)(b)).

Note that, if Mary is entitled to the income immediately on the death of mother or becomes so entitled within two years of mother's death, this will be an immediate post-death interest and there would be inheritance tax payable on Mary's subsequent death if the funds are of sufficient value to exceed the nil rate band threshold when cumulated with her free estate. This is because the immediate post-death interest rules take priority over the s 71D (18–25 trust) rules. Therefore if the mother dies when Mary is 14 the interest taken by Mary is an IPDI because she has become entitled within two years of death and the effect of reading back under IHTA 1984 s 144 is that she is deemed to have always been entitled to the income from death.

If Mary dies after reaching 18 having taken a s 71D (18–25 trust) interest rather than an immediate post death interest (because she did not become entitled to the income on or within two years of death) but before 25 there is no base cost uplift for capital gains tax purposes but there is an inheritance tax exit charge even though the trust continues in favour of the nephew (IHTA 1984 s 71F(2)).

If the 18–25 trust is extended so that Mary does not take outright at 25 but is living at that date, there is an inheritance tax charge then (maximum rate is 4.2%). If she later dies after 25, retaining her interest in possession, there is no inheritance tax charge on her death unless the trust ends (in which case there is an exit charge at maximum 6%) and no capital gains tax uplift since the property is within the relevant property regime and her interest in possession is not qualifying. Contrast the position if she takes an interest in possession immediately on the death of her mother or within two years of her mother's death, in which case the reading-back provisions under IHTA 1984 s 144 apply; she takes an IPDI and on her death at any subsequent age a capital gains tax uplift is available and inheritance tax is payable (if the trust assets are of sufficient value to exceed the nil rate band threshold when cumulated with her free estate).

EXAMPLE 21.7

Mother leaves her estate on trust for Mary at 30, with Mary taking entitlement to income at 18. Note that, unless Mary becomes 18 within two years of mother's death even though she eventually takes an interest in possession, it is not *qualifying* for inheritance tax purposes and this is not an 18–25 trust. The only exception would be if Mary took entitlement to income within two years of her mother's death (eg she was 17 when her mother died and became entitled to the income by virtue of Trustee Act 1925 s 31 or the trustees conferred entitlement on her by exercise of their dispositive powers). In these circumstances the effect of the reading back provision in IHTA 1984 s 144 is such that Mary is deemed to have taken an IPDI immediately on her mother's death. Assuming Mary did not take entitlement to income within two years of her mother's death, on Mary's death there is no inheritance tax payable unless the trust ends (in which case there is an exit charge at 6% maximum) and no base cost uplift for capital gains tax purposes. If the trust does end on Mary's death, holdover relief would be available under TCGA 1992 s 260.

EXAMPLE 21.8

In 2016 H set up a trust during his lifetime giving his adult child an immediate interest in possession. Unless the conditions for a disabled trust are satisfied, the gift into trust is a chargeable transfer for inheritance tax purposes. It may fall within H's nil rate band. On the death of the child there is no base cost uplift for capital gains tax purposes, but there is no inheritance tax charge either, unless the trust ends, in which case there is an exit charge but the property is *not* taxed at 40% as part of the child's estate. If the child's interest in possession is revoked during his lifetime and the trust becomes discretionary or someone else takes an interest in possession, this has no capital gains tax or inheritance tax effects provided there is no resettlement. If the assets are resettled this has no inheritance tax effect unless the new trust is a disabled trust but there would be a disposal of the settled property for capital gains tax purposes. [21.2]

2 Residence and domicile status of PRs

PRs are deemed to have the same residence and domicile status as the deceased had at the date of death for capital gains tax purposes irrespective of their actual residence (TCGA 1992 s 62(3)), but the remittance basis – which is available to a UK-resident but non-domiciled individual in respect of a disposal of non-UK *situs* assets – does not apply to personal representatives (PRs). This is because the exclusion for non-domiciliaries only applies to individuals (see TCGA 1992 s 12(1); s 65(2) and **[27.1]**).

This contrasts with the income tax position, where PRs are UK resident if all are UK resident, and non-UK resident if all are non-UK resident; if the estate has both resident and non-resident PRs the position is governed by ITA 2007 s 834 such that if the deceased was resident or domiciled in the UK then any UK resident PR means that all the PRs are treated as resident in the UK.

Note that PRs treated as UK resident are also charged on the gains of non-resident companies apportioned to them under TCGA 1992 s 13 (see Section IV of Chapter 27 for more information on the operation of TCGA 1992 s 13). Although the base cost of the shares in the company may be uplifted for capital gains tax purposes, the assets held by the company will not. Significant tax liabilities could therefore arise on a disposal of assets by the company shortly after death.

Like trustees, PRs are treated as a single and continuing body of persons, and liability can be imposed on any PR: HMRC will, therefore, assess UK PRs on the estate's worldwide gains even though those PRs may have no control over foreign assets which are vested in foreign PRs. Any one of them is assessable and chargeable on behalf of the body as a whole.

Because PRs are deemed to take the deceased's residence status, UK-resident personal representatives of a non-resident deceased are outside the charge to capital gains tax in respect of most assets, the notable exception (since 6 April 2015) being UK residential property on which all non-residents are taxable. However, this only applies while they are acting in their capacity as PRs; if they become trustees (eg assets are assented to them as trustees), they are taxed as UK residents unless the deceased was both resident and domiciled outside the UK and there is at least one non-resident trustee. The vesting of property by the PRs in non-resident trustees pursuant to the provisions of the will is not a capital gains tax disposal. **[21.3]–[21.20]**

II VALUATION OF CHARGEABLE ASSETS AT DEATH

1 Basic rule

The assets of the deceased are valued at their open market value at the date of death (TCGA 1992 s 62(1)(a)). Unlike inheritance tax where the deceased is deemed to make the transfer of value immediately before death (IHTA 1984 s 4), for capital gains tax purposes the notional acquisition occurs at the moment after death. See *Larter v Skone James* [1976] STC 220 where the taxpayer tried to argue the contrary in order to sustain an argument that a Revenue assessment for capital gains tax due on death was out of time. (At that time there was capital gains tax due on death.) **[21.21]**

2 Value ascertained for inheritance tax purposes

If the value of an asset which forms part of the deceased's estate has been 'ascertained' for the purposes of inheritance tax that value will constitute the CGT acquisition cost of the deceased's PRs (TCGA 1992 s 274). When the

IHT related property rules apply the resultant figure may be artificially high (see **[28.70]**). In cases where the deceased's estate does not attract IHT (eg because it is wholly left to a surviving spouse or a charity or where the property qualifies for 100% agricultural or business relief) the value will not have been ascertained and so the figure returned on the IHT account will not fix the CGT value (see *Tax Bulletin*, April 1995, p 209).

There is no reduction in the CGT cost just because business or agricultural property relief reduces the value transferred for IHT purposes.

If the value of the assets is not ascertained for inheritance tax purposes then the normal capital gains tax valuation rules apply (TCGA 1992 s 272). Market value is defined as the price which any asset might reasonably be expected to fetch on a sale in the open market. There is no reduction just because the whole of the assets are placed on the market at the same time. Assets are valued without foreknowledge of imminence of death. However, special purchasers need to be taken into account. If an asset is subject to a restriction (eg a lease owned by the deceased is non-assignable) it still has value. The lease must be valued as if a hypothetical purchaser could buy it but subject to that restriction.

In the case of unquoted securities the level of information available to a prospective purchaser in the hypothetical market is deemed to be 'all the information which a prudent prospective purchaser of an asset might reasonably require if he were proposing to purchase it from a willing vendor by private treaty and at arm's length' (TCGA 1992 s 273(3)). See *Clark (executor of Clark deceased) v Green* [1995] STC (SCD) 99 and *Administrators of the Estate of Caton deceased v Couch* [1995] STC (SCD) 34 regarding the level of information this involves.

HMRC considered the relationship between inheritance tax and capital gains tax valuations in *Tax Bulletin* August 1996 in the context of *Gray (surviving Executor of Lady Fox deceased) v IRC* (1994). They noted:

> 'The principle that emerged from Gray is that two or more different assets comprised in an estate can be treated as a single unit of property if disposal as one unit was the course that a prudent hypothetical vendor would have adopted in order to obtain the most favourable price without undue expenditure of time and effort. This principle will be applicable to capital gains tax valuations in which the statutory hypothesis on which the valuation is based deems two or more assets to be disposed of together.
>
> Examples will include an acquisition by personal representatives or legatees under s 62 TCGA 1992 of assets of which a deceased person was competent to dispose, an acquisition of settled property under s 71 TCGA 1992 on the occasion of a person becoming absolutely entitled to that settled property.' **[21.22]**

3 IHT revaluations

Where property valued on death as 'related property' is sold within three years after the death, or land is sold within four years of death, or listed securities within one year, for less than the death valuation, the PRs may substitute a lower figure for the death valuation and so obtain a reduction in the IHT paid on death (see **[30.7]**). Not surprisingly, this lower figure will also form the death value for CGT so that the PRs cannot claim CGT loss relief. As an alternative to reducing the estate valuation, the PRs may prefer to claim a CGT loss on the disposal. This would be advantageous where they have made chargeable gains on disposals of other assets in the estate and where no repayment of IHT would result from amending the value of the death estate.

Note, though, *Stonor (executors of Dickinson) v IRC* (2001) where it was held that the executors could not substitute a *higher* sale price for probate value where the estate was left to charity because no values had been 'ascertained' for inheritance tax purposes. A higher sale price can only be substituted where more inheritance tax is then paid. This decision is based on the principle that substitution of the sale proceeds can only be allowed for inheritance tax purposes on a claim made by an 'appropriate person' defined as a person who is liable for inheritance tax (IHTA 1984 s 190(1)). Presumably in that case the executors had wanted to increase the probate value in order to avoid a capital gains tax problem on a subsequent sale by them when the assets had increased in value from probate. Unless the executors could show that the value was actually wrong at the date of death and was in fact a higher value, the fact that the asset had increased in value since death did not mean they could substitute the higher value for probate purposes (see IHTM 33026). The problems raised by this are discussed further below – see *Example 21.15*.

[21.23]

4 General conclusion

Ideally, for CGT purposes, the PRs want a high value for the assets because of the tax-free uplift, whereas in the case of estates where IHT is payable they want as low a value as possible. Generally, since IHT will be levied on the entire value and not just on the gain and charged at 40% rather than 20% a low valuation is usually preferable for inheritance tax purposes unless the assets in question qualify for business property relief or agricultural property relief, fall within the nil rate band or are otherwise exempt, eg because of spouse exemption. [21.24]–[21.40]

III CGT LOSSES OF THE DECEASED

Losses of the deceased in the tax year of his death must be set against gains of that year. Any surplus loss at the end of the year of death can be carried back and set against chargeable gains of the deceased in the three tax years preceding the year of death, taking the most recent year first (TCGA 1992 s 62(2)). Any tax thus reclaimed will, of course, fall into the deceased's estate for IHT purposes! Losses carried back are not set against the gains of any year if and to the extent that they would cause the annual capital gains tax exemption to be wasted.

It was established in *Drown v R & C Comrs* (2017) that the personal representatives of the deceased cannot make a negligible value claim in respect of shares held by the deceased even where the shares became of negligible value before the death of the deceased. This means that no losses can be realised and so cannot be used to offset gains realised by the deceased.

[21.41]–[21.60]

IV SALE OF DECEASED'S ASSETS BY PRS

1 Rate of tax

A sale of the deceased's chargeable assets by his PRs is a disposal for CGT purposes and will be subject to CGT on the difference between the sale consideration and the market value at death. PRs paid tax at a rate of 34% until 6 April 2004. For disposals on or after that date until 6 April 2008 the rate of tax increased to 40% but taper relief was available, although rarely relevant for PRs. For disposals from 6 April 2008 until 22 June 2010 inclusive the rate of tax was 18%. For disposals on or after 23 June 2010 up to 5 April 2016, PRs pay tax at 28%. (See F(No 2)A 2010 Sch 1 amending TCGA 1992 s 4.) From 6 April 2016, PRs pay tax at 20% except on gains realised on residential property which are still taxed at 28%.

These rules apply to disposals by the PRs even if the beneficiaries under the will would not themselves be subject to CGT (for example where the legatee is an individual who has an unused capital gains tax exemption, is a basic rate taxpayer and would therefore pay capital gains tax at 10% (or 18% on residential property) rather than 20% (or 28% on residential property), has personal losses, is a remittance basis user and the asset is non-UK situated, or is a charity or non-resident).

In appropriate cases, therefore, assets should be vested in the beneficiary by assent before sale even if the administration is not yet complete provided the PRs retain sufficient assets to satisfy their liabilities (see **[21.105]**). (Note that if the administration of the estate is complete, then even without a formal assent the PRs are treated as disposing of the asset as bare trustee for the beneficiary.) **[21.61]**

2 Deductions and allowances

a) *Incidental expenses*

The normal deductions for the incidental expenses of sale are available and PRs can also deduct an appropriate proportion of the cost of the administration of the estate that is necessary to put themselves in the position of being able to sell, eg solicitor's costs of obtaining probate and of obtaining valuations (*IRC v Richards' Executors* (1971) and see *Administrators of the Estate of Caton v Couch* (1997)). Although HMRC publish a scale of allowable expenses for the cost of establishing title (see SP 02/04), PRs may claim to deduct more than the 'scale' figure when higher expenses have been incurred. A deduction for the costs of obtaining the grant is only available where the PRs themselves sell the assets in the course of administration not where the beneficiaries under the will dispose of the asset. Nor is the cost of obtaining probate allowable where the asset is transferred to a beneficiary under the will. See SP 2/04.

Where an asset is transferred to a legatee the PRs may either deduct the cost of the transfer from the gains accruing to them on the sale of other assets or the beneficiary can add the cost of the transfer to the market value at which he is deemed to acquire the asset and thereby reduce his future chargeable gain.

There is no deduction for the expenses of negotiating with HMRC or any related proceedings concerning valuation. See the Court of Appeal decision in *Caton v Crouch* [1997] STC 970. **[21.62]**

b) *Abolition of indexation and taper*

For deaths before 6 April 1998, the PRs enjoyed the benefit of the indexation allowance. As with individuals that relief was replaced with taper relief until 6 April 2008 (see **Chapter 19**). From 6 April 2008 taper relief was also abolished and on the *sale* of an asset by the PRs the full amount of all gains arising since death are taxed. **[21.63]**

c) *Entrepreneurs' relief*

PRs are not entitled to entrepreneurs' relief.

For the purposes of calculating a legatee's period of ownership, he is treated as acquiring the asset at the date of death (TCGA 1992 s 62(4)(b)). For entrepreneurs' relief purposes, the period of ownership by the PRs can therefore be incorporated within the legatee's period so as to allow the relief to be available on the shares which have been inherited but only if the legatee has separately since before the death owned at least 5% of the voting shares in the trading group in his own right and is an officer or employee of the company.

It is understood that HMRC take the view that if the PRs assented, say, a 5% shareholding to a beneficiary after death and that beneficiary satisfied all other conditions but did not own 5% of the shares until the assent, the legatee would need to hold the shares for a further 12 months from the date of assent before relief would be available. It is questionable whether this is correct. The question for entrepreneurs' relief purposes is whether the legatee is deemed to have all the voting rights of the PRs since the date of death by virtue of s 62(4)(b) which states 'the legatee shall be treated as if the PRs' acquisition of the asset had been his acquisition of it.' (Contrast the taper relief provisions and see in particular TCGA 1992 Sch A1 paras 4(5)) and 5(5).) **[21.64]**

EXAMPLE 21.9

In 2014 Marx left 10% of the shares in CP Ltd to the managing director, Engels. The shares are vested in Engels two years after Marx's death and he promptly sells them. Although Engels' ownership period is related back to Marx's death, for Engels to get entrepreneurs' relief HMRC argue that the company must already have been his personal company, ie Engels must own personally at least 5% voting rights in the company for one year prior to the sale of any shares. Either he has to hold these shares for a further 12 months before sale or have owned at least 5% other voting shares in his own right for at least 12 months.

d) *Annual exemption*

PRs enjoy an annual exemption from CGT of £11,300 in the tax year of death (for 2017–18) and in each of the two following tax years they receive the same annual CGT exemption applicable to individuals. Thereafter they have no exemption, so that if it is intended to sell property in the estate and that sale will result in a chargeable gain, it may be advantageous to vest the asset in the appropriate beneficiary for him to sell if he has an unused annual capital gains tax exemption. [21.65]

EXAMPLE 21.10
(1) Dougall died in May 2012. In July 2017 a valuable Ming vase then worth £90,000 (probate value in 2012 £45,000) is to be sold. Administration of the estate has not been completed. The proceeds of sale will be split equally between Dougall's three children. The following possibilities should be considered:
  (a) the PRs could themselves sell the vase and realise gains of £45,000. No annual exemption will be available (since more than three years have elapsed since death) and the rate of CGT will be 20%. *Accordingly, the maximum tax bill will be £9,000*; or
  (b) the PRs could first appropriate the vase to the three children who could then sell it taking advantage of three CGT annual exemptions (£33,900 in all being £11,300 each in 2017–18). The resultant taxable gain (£11,100) is attributed equally between the children and, even if they are all higher rate taxpayers and taxed at 20%, *the maximum total tax bill will be £2,220*. The gain may be reduced still further if the children transfer part of their share to a spouse or civil partner after assent to them but prior to sale, thus obtaining an additional annual capital gains tax exemption. Even if the children have already used their annual capital gains tax exemptions, it may well be that some of them are basic rate taxpayers and therefore some or all of the gain is only chargeable at 10%.
(2) Different issues arise when an asset is to be sold and the residuary beneficiary who will be entitled to all or the bulk of the proceeds of sale is not subject to CGT (eg because they are a UK charity or non-UK-resident): see [**21.105**] and [**53.41**]. Note that the tax on residential property gains of certain non-residents which was introduced in 2013 does not apply to non-resident individuals who can therefore sell UK real estate tax free until 2015. All non-residents however have to pay tax on gains arising from disposals of UK residential property after 5 April 2015 (but only on any increase in value since that date).

3 The principal private residence

Where PRs dispose of a private dwelling house which, both before and after the death, was occupied by a person who is entitled as a result of the death to the whole, or substantially the whole, of the proceeds of sale from the house, either absolutely or for life, PRs were by concession given the benefit of the private residence exemption from CGT (ESC D5 and for principal private residence exemption, see **Chapter 23**). The concession addressed the sort of situation where a house-owner died and his widow and perhaps some children occupied the house. 'Substantially the whole' meant 75% of the proceeds. The concession did not cover disposals of part of the house or an interest in the house or grounds. Nor did it help the child who moved into the house after the death of the mother.

FA 2004 gave statutory force to the ESC (with effect from 10 December 2003) and ensured that the position for PRs is more consistent with the capital gains tax exemption available to trustees under TCGA 1992 s 225.

Section 225A provides that relief is available if the person or persons who occupied the house as their main residence immediately before and after the death are together entitled to at least 75% of the net proceeds of disposal (or an interest in possession in the same). Disposals of part of an interest in a house are covered. A specific claim for relief is required by the PRs. Net proceeds of disposal are the disposal proceeds realised by the PRs less any allowable incidental costs, but on the assumption that none of the proceeds is needed to meet the liabilities of the estate, including any inheritance tax liability. Any election for main residence treatment is to be a joint notice by the PRs and the individuals entitled to occupy. If principal private residence relief is not available because a relevant beneficiary of the estate was not in occupation before the death but is now in occupation, an option is for the PRs to assent the house to the beneficiary and let him carry out the sale (but see [21.104] below if the beneficiary was the spouse of the deceased). [21.66]–[21.80]

EXAMPLE 21.11

(1) Bill and his brother Ben live in Bill's house. On his death, Bill leaves the house to Ben who goes on living in it. The property has to be sold by the PRs to pay for Bill's funeral. Any gain will be exempt. If Ben was not in occupation at the date of death but is now in occupation, the PRs could assent the house to Ben, and Ben sells the house. Even if he has not been in occupation for the entire period since death, the fact that the last 18 months of ownership will be exempt in any event should mean that Ben obtains principal private residence relief if he has occupied the property for at least some of that period. However, the PRs may have insufficient left in the estate to pay all the costs and tax. The difficulty is that the PRs cannot easily assent part of the house to Ben and retain part to pay costs: HMRC (wrongly, in the author's view) do not accept that this is a valid appropriation. Similar issues arise in relation to appropriations of part to charities (discussed below).

(2) F dies, leaving his Dorset estate including a farmhouse to his two children Eric and Ernie. Eric lives in the house and Ernie lives in London. The two sons want to retain the house for the foreseeable future. If the house is simply assented to both of them jointly, Eric obtains principal private residence relief on his share but there is no principal private residence relief on Ernie's share on a future sale. If, instead, Eric and Ernie enter into a deed of variation and vary the house into a trust where each takes an immediate post-death interest (eg entitlement to income with power to advance them capital), the inheritance tax position is no different, but TCGA 1992 s 225 means that principal private residence relief will be available in future on the entire gain when the trustees sell the house (as long as Eric occupies as his main residence), even though Ernie is not in occupation and indeed occupies his London house as his main residence.

Contrast the above with the position where a life tenant with a qualifying interest in possession dies and the trust fund includes a house occupied by the deceased life tenant. If the house is disposed of by the trustees at a gain there is no main residence relief even if the disposal takes place within 18 months of the life tenant ceasing to occupy. The trustees are deemed to have disposed of the property and reacquired it at market value at death but main residence relief is only available going forward if a beneficiary has occupied it as his main residence since the death.

On the other hand, if the trust is discretionary or if the life tenant does not have a 'qualifying' interest in possession (eg the trust was set up after 2006) the trustees will get full main residence relief as long as the disposal takes place within 18 months of the beneficiary ceasing to occupy the property.

V LOSSES OF THE PRS

Losses made by the PRs on disposals of chargeable assets during administration can be set off against chargeable gains on other sales made by them. Any surplus losses at the end of the administration period cannot be transferred to beneficiaries. Accordingly, when PRs anticipate that a loss will not be relieved, they may prefer to transfer the loss-making asset to the relevant beneficiary so that he can sell it and obtain the loss relief. If PRs do realise losses then they should ensure that they sell an asset that shows a gain before the administration of the estate is complete in order to utilise fully the loss relief. Even if the asset has not been formally assented to a beneficiary, if the administration of the estate is complete and residue ascertained, HMRC may argue that the loss is not allowable against the gain realised later on the basis that the later disposal is being done by the PRs as bare trustees for the beneficiaries and at their direction. See CG 30750.

Note that artificially created losses on disposals after 5 December 2006 may be restricted under FA 2007 which inserts TCGA 1992 s 16A, and see guidance notes issued by HMRC on 19 July 2007.

TCGA 1992 s 4B provides that PRs may deduct losses in the most beneficial way and therefore, from 6 April 2016, may choose to set losses against gains on residential property which will be charged at 28% rather than gains on other assets which will be taxable at 20% (see **[21.61]**). **[21.81]–[21.100]**

VI TRANSFERS TO LEGATEES (TCGA 1992 S 62(4))

1 Basic rule

On the transfer of an asset to a legatee, the PRs make neither a gain nor loss for CGT purposes and the legatee acquires the asset at the PRs' base value together with the expenses of transferring the asset to him. The base cost will in appropriate cases be a fraction of the probate value: for instance, if a 60% shareholding (valued at death as a majority holding) was split between the deceased's four sons each would receive a 15% holding with a base cost equal to one-quarter of the probate valuation of the 60% holding. **[21.101]**

EXAMPLE 21.12

The PRs transfer the book (see *Example 21.1*) to the legatee (L) under the will in March 2017 when it is worth £130,000. The cost of valuing the book as a part of the whole estate in November 2015 was £1,000 and the PRs incurred incidental expenses involved in the transfer of the book in March 2017 of £150. L sells the book in July 2018 for £140,000. On the transfer by the PRs to L, no chargeable gain accrues to the PRs and L's base cost is:

	£
Market value at death	100,000
Valuation cost	1,000
Expenses of transfer	150
Base cost of L	£101,150

When L sells the book in July 2018 for £140,000 he is charged to CGT on his gain that is £38,850 (£140,000 − £101,150) as reduced by any allowable expenditure that he has incurred or available annual CGT exemption. The rate of tax on the net gain will be 20% unless he is a basic rate taxpayer in which case gains up to the amount of the unused basic rate band will be charged at 10%.

2 Who is a legatee?

A legatee is defined in TCGA 1992 s 64(2) as any person taking under a testamentary disposition or on intestacy or partial intestacy, whether beneficially or as a trustee. This definition covers only property passing under the will or on an intestacy to a beneficiary so that to the extent a beneficiary contracts with the PRs to purchase a particular asset or to obtain a greater share in an asset he is not taking that asset *qua* legatee.

In CG 30770 HMRC cite *Passant v Jackson* (1986) as authority for the view that, where a residuary legatee pays some balancing sum to the executors in order to acquire a property in the deceased's estate, he does not acquire the asset *qua* legatee.

In that case, a residuary legatee wished to retain a property worth more than the net value of the estate. He paid the executors a balancing payment to cover the shortfall and they executed an assent in his favour. On a subsequent disposal, the legatee sought to include both the probate value of the property and the sum he paid to the executors in his acquisition cost but this claim was rejected. However, the court said nothing to suggest that on the original acquisition by him from the executors he did not acquire *qua* legatee. He was not allowed to include the cash sum he paid the executors to reduce the overall gain on the *later* sale, but that is a very different point. The HMRC Manual seems incorrect on this point: see CG 30770 and CG 31175.

A *donatio mortis causa* is also treated for these purposes as a testamentary disposition and not as a gift, so that the donee acquires the asset at its market value on the donor's death and the donor is not treated as having made a chargeable gain. **[21.102]**

3 Taking under a will trust

Difficult questions may arise when a person receives assets under a trust created either by will or under the intestacy rules. Does he receive them as a legatee (in which case there is no charge to capital gains tax since the legatee acquires the asset at the PRs base cost together with the expenses of transferring it to him) or as a beneficiary absolutely entitled as against the trustee, in which case there is a deemed disposal under TCGA 1992 s 71 which may be chargeable if the property has increased in value since death (see **Chapter 25**)? The answer depends upon the status of the PRs (have they turned into trustees at the relevant time?) and the terms of the will (see *Cochrane's Executors v IRC* (1974) and *IRC v Matthew's Executors* (1984)).

During the course of administration PRs are the sole owners of the deceased's assets, albeit in a fiduciary capacity (*Stamp Duties Comr (Queensland) v Livingston* (1965)) so that there is no trust of particular assets at that time (although the beneficiaries will own a *chose in action*). Accordingly, if, before the completion of administration or the vesting of assets in themselves as trustees (whichever first occurs), the property ceases to be settled for CGT purposes, when it is transferred to the relevant beneficiary he will take *qua* legatee (see *Example 21.13(2)* below and *Marshall v Kerr* (1994) at **[21.124]**).

[21.103]

EXAMPLE 21.13

(1) T dies leaving his house to executors on trust for his three children all of whom are over 18, in equal shares absolutely. Whether the children receive the assets before the administration is completed or after the executors have assented the assets to themselves as bare trustees for the children does not matter since they take as legatees. For CGT purposes joint ownership does not result in the property being settled (TCGA 1992 s 60: see further **Chapter 25**). Suppose that the house is assented to the three children a year after death and one of the children ('A') decides to occupy the property immediately as his main residence and the property is then sold three years later (ie four years after death) with the child still in occupation. Main residence relief for A is restricted to three-quarters of the gain on his share since no relief is available for the first year after death when he was not in occupation (see CG 64925). On the other hand, if the PRs assent the property to the children 6 months after death, the children occupy it as their main residence and sell within 18 months of T's death, then the entire gain is exempt because once the property has been their main residence, the last 18 months are exempt in any event (see **[23.83]**).

(2) T dies in 2007 leaving his property to executors on trust for his widow for life and then for his three children absolutely, all of whom are over 18. If the widow dies *before the executors become trustees*, any distributions to the children will be received by them as legatees since, for CGT purposes, the trust ended on the widow's death. If, however, the widow dies *after* the executors have become trustees, the property is settled, so that the children receive assets as persons absolutely entitled as against the trustees with a consequent deemed disposal under TCGA 1992 s 71 (there will be no charge in this case even if the assets have increased in value since T's death because the event leading to their entitlement was the death of the life tenant who took an IPDI so there is rebasing: contrast the position if the interest had terminated *inter vivos* – see **Chapter 25**).

(3) Z leaves his residuary estate on discretionary trusts. Within two years of his death the assets are distributed amongst his children so that:

(a) for IHT purposes, IHTA 1984 s 144 ensures that the distributions are 'read back' into Z's will (see **[30.145]**);

(b) although holdover relief under TCGA 1992 s 260 will not be available (see **[24.22]**), provided that the children become entitled during the administration period and the assets are not vested in the trustees first, HMRC accept that the children will take *qua* legatees. The normal way would be for the trustees to make an appointment directing the executors (usually themselves) to hold the asset absolutely for the children. When the administration is complete, the executors transfer the asset to the children pursuant to that appointment who then take *qua* legatees. Furthermore HMRC's view is that such appointment is not a disposal of a chose in action of the legatee (which would be disastrous since such chose would have a nil base cost as the right has been acquired in circumstances where there is no corresponding disposal). *See Taxation Practitioner,* September 1995, p 23.

4 The deceased's main residence

When the former matrimonial home of the deceased passes to his surviving spouse there is an uplift in the base value of the property on death in the usual way. On a subsequent disposal by that spouse, it might be expected that any gain since death will be wholly exempt from CGT if the house has been occupied as that spouse's main residence. However TCGA 1992 s 222(7) provides that the deceased's period of ownership is deemed to be that of the surviving spouse in deciding what proportion of the gain (if any) is chargeable (see **[23.82]**). Occupation by the deceased as his main residence can be treated as occupation by the surviving spouse. This can be both a relieving and a charging provision. **[21.104]**

EXAMPLE 21.14

T bought a house in 2004 for £50,000. It was his main residence until his death in 2007 when it was worth £150,000. His wife (W) whom he married just before his death never lived there with him, but became entitled to the house on his intestacy. T's administrators transferred the house to W in 2008. She occupied it as her main residence since T's death until 2009 and then went abroad until 2014 when she returned and sold the house for £250,000.

For the purpose of the main residence exemption, W can claim that she has occupied the house as her main residence for six and a half out of the ten years that it has been in the ownership of herself or T, ie:

2004–2007 (3 years)	Occupied by T as his main residence
2007–2009 (2 years)	Occupation by W.
2009–2014 (5 years)	Abroad from 2009 but last 18 months of ownership disregarded (TCGA 1992 s 223(1))

W is, therefore, charged on a proportion of the gain:
(1) Sale consideration (£250,000) – base cost (£150,000) = £100,000 (assuming no other allowable expenses).
(2) Fraction chargeable: £100,000 × $^{3.5}/_{10}$ = £35,000.
Were it not for s 222(7), she would be charged on a larger proportion of the gain, ie:

$$100{,}000 \times \frac{3.5}{7 \ (\textit{length of her ownership})} = 50{,}000$$

Of course, if the husband or wife had not occupied it as their main residence prior to T's death then, s 222(7) could prove disadvantageous to the wife. For example if W occupied the property continuously after T's death as her main residence but it had not been the couple's main residence while T was alive, then 3 out of 10 years ownership does not qualify for exemption. Hence 3/10ths of the gain (calculated on the basis of an acquisition cost as at T's death) is chargeable (see CG 64955).

5 Exempt legatees

Assume that the estate includes shares which are showing a substantial gain over probate value and which are to be sold. The relevant beneficiary is a UK charity. If the PRs sell the shares in the course of the administration, tax at a rate of 20% will be payable: by contrast if the shares are assented to the charity which sells them no CGT will be payable (see TCGA 1992 s 256). In cases where the estate is to be divided amongst several charities the PRs may appropriate the shares in partial or entire satisfaction of the charities' entitlement and hold them as bare trustees for those charities. The sale will then be taxed on the basis that it was made by the charities so that the s 256 exemption will apply (for the CGT treatment of bare trusts, see [25.3]). See *Prest v Bettinson* [1980] STC 607 where the deceased left the residuary estate to be divided between four charities and one non-charitable body. The PRs were held to be assessable on the entire gain. The PRs needed to appropriate the entirety of the assets showing gains to the charities and non-charity to obtain exemption.

Similar considerations apply if the legatee is non-UK-resident and so outside the CGT net unless the asset is UK residential property (on which, since 2015, non-residents pay CGT).

What if the PRs need part of the sale proceeds (eg to pay administration costs), and the estate comprises land which has increased in value since death? One suggestion is to appropriate part of the land *before* sale to the charity. Unfortunately, HMRC seem to dispute that an appropriation of a share in land in England and Wales works for capital gains tax purposes. They argue that *Crowe v Appleby* applies so that the charity does not become absolutely entitled to the land *qua* legatee. The decision in *Crowe v Appleby* (1976) CA (and see High Court decision of Goff J) is authority for the proposition that in order for someone to become absolutely entitled as against the trustees, in the case of land it is not enough for the beneficiary to become absolutely entitled to the settled property. HMRC argue that unless the charities can direct how their share in the property is to be dealt with, then they are not absolutely entitled as against the personal representatives and the gain does not then accrue to the charities but to the executors in their capacity as trustees of the estate. In other words the land is treated as being subject to continuing trusts of administration and the PRs would still be liable for capital gains tax on the entire gain.

In the author's view, while the charities do not have a beneficial interest in the assets in the executors' hands during the course of administration, once they have been appropriated assets it is not clear that their position is comparable to a beneficiary under a trust – TCGA 1992 s 60(2) is dealing with settled property not property where the beneficiaries of the residuary estate are absolutely entitled. It cannot simply be the case that any person holding an undivided share in land is subject to *Crowe v Appleby* principles.

For example *Crowe v Appleby* does not apply in relation to equitable interests in land held by trustees (eg two joint owners hold land equally; one settles his 50% share on continuing trusts; this does not mean the other 50% owner is suddenly no longer absolutely entitled). Even if the charities are not absolutely entitled it is arguable that they still acquire the assets as legatees within TCGA 1992 s 62(4) and hence the charity is treated as if the executors' acquisition of the asset had been its acquisition (see s 64(3)). This depends on the appropriation itself having been valid. There are a number of other arguments but the author suggests that HMRC's view should be challenged.

EXAMPLE 21.15
A dies leaving a house worth £1,300,000 at his death (the main asset) and his will leaves his residuary estate to charity after specific cash gifts totalling £800,000, all of which are chargeable. The executors need to sell the house to raise cash to pay the inheritance tax and the cash gifts in the will. Two years after A's death, the house has increased in value by £300,000. The executors do not want to incur capital gains tax on the sale but have calculated that it is not tax efficient to substitute the increased sale price even if they could do so. If the charity sells the house, there is no capital gains tax payable. As a matter of general law, there is, of course, no difficulty in any executor appropriating 'any part of the real or personal estate' of the testator in or towards satisfaction of any legacy or any other interest or share in his property. Accordingly, in the author's view the executors could appropriate a specified share in the house to charity and charitable exemption could subsequently be claimed on that share.

HMRC say that the appropriation is not effective for capital gains tax purposes (even if effective under general law) on the basis of *Crowe v Appleby* (1975) (see **[25.7]**). As noted earlier, the author doubts that this is correct, but practitioners should be aware of the potential problem. None of the alternatives are satisfactory. The PRs can under the Administration of Estates Act 1925 s 36(10) assent the whole of the interest in the house to the relevant charity, subject to a legal charge for the PRs' debts and liabilities, including payment of the legacies to the non-charitable beneficiaries. *Crowe v Appleby* does not apply because there are no continuing trusts. Ideally, the charge should be fixed in amount rather than floating. The charity will then direct the PRs as bare trustees to sell the house, and any gain on the sale will then clearly accrue to the charities and not to the PRs (TCGA 1992 s 256). The fixed amount is paid to the PRs on sale, who then use this to pay out the expenses and legacies.

The difficulty with this approach is that, arguably, although the gain accrues to the charity, the second condition in s 256 is not satisfied because the proceeds are not entirely applicable and applied for charitable purposes. Some of the proceeds are ultimately applied for non-charitable purposes such as payment of expenses and discharge of non-charitable legacies. It is not that the charity is in breach of any charity law by satisfying the charge (because it takes the land subject to such charge in the first place), but it is hard to say that the proceeds are all being applied for charitable purposes. (The position is different from the more common situation where a charge is granted by the charity to secure borrowings taken out by the charity and those borrowings are used by the charity for other charitable purposes.)

This would not be a problem for a non-resident legatee although it is likely that SDLT would be payable on the amount of the charge. In addition, since 6 April 2015, non-residents are taxable on a gain arising on a sale of UK residential property (but not any other sort of land or other property) although only on any increase in value since that date.

An alternative approach is to divide the land up into physically divisible parts if possible. The charity could be made absolutely entitled by declaration of trust to the *entirety* of one part of the land rather than the undivided share, and the PRs could retain the separate land and sell it (paying capital gains tax on that part alone).

Another option is for the PRs to sell the land at base cost to the charities. The sale would usually be more than sufficient to cover the pecuniary legacies and any tax and debts. Any surplus could eventually be distributed back to the charities. No chargeable gain will arise on the sale by the PRs (TCGA 1992 s 257). The personal representatives can then use the purchase price to pay out the legacies and the debts, and distribute any balance left to the charity. The charity will then clearly sell on the land in its capacity as a charity, without having to pay anything back to the personal representatives. Thus, the entire gain accrues to the charity and is applied for charitable purposes. This raises a number of practical issues, eg does the charity have to pay the cash upfront to the executors before it has received cash from the sale? In addition, it seems that there is an SDLT charge (see **Chapter 49**) on the sale to the charity because the charity does not hold the land for qualifying charitable purposes or as an investment from which the profits are applied to the charitable purposes of the purchaser (FA 2003 Sch 8 para 1(1)). So, where property is acquired by the charity and then sold off by the charity, HMRC may deny SDLT relief on the basis that the purchase is not an investment but speculation.

In any event, if the assets are vested in the charity, HMRC may require evidence that the charity has approved the sale and complied with the provisions of the Charities Act 1993.

Where there is more than one residuary legatee not all of whom are charities it may be desirable (if there are sufficient powers in the will) to appropriate the assets showing the highest capital gains to the charities in satisfaction of their share. The non-charitable beneficiaries of the estate can then receive cash or property that does not show a gain. The charity can sell the asset and realise the gains free of tax. [21.105]–[21.120]

VII DISCLAIMERS AND VARIATIONS (TCGA 1992 S 62(6)); CLAIMS UNDER THE INHERITANCE (PROVISION FOR FAMILY AND DEPENDANTS) ACT 1975

1 Basic rule

Subject to conditions, which are the same as for IHT (see [30.153]), any variation of the deceased's will or of the intestacy rules, or any disclaimer, made in both cases within two years of the deceased's death may be treated:
(1) as if it were not a disposal (s 62(6)(a)); and
(2) (for the purposes of TCGA s 62) as if it had been effected by the deceased or, in the case of a disclaimer, as if the disclaimed benefit had never been conferred (s 62(6)(b)).

This is sometimes referred to as 'reading back'. As with inheritance tax, the instrument must be made in writing within two years of the death and the variation (or disclaimer) must not be made for consideration in money or money's worth other than consideration consisting of the making of a variation or disclaimer in respect of another of the dispositions.

The variation can be made regardless of whether the administration of the estate is complete or whether the property has already been distributed in accordance with the original disposition. The same property cannot be subject to more than one variation. Although a variation can be made over jointly owned property, HMRC deny reading back for capital gains tax purposes in respect of settled property over which the deceased had a general power of appointment (although such property is capable of variation for inheritance tax purposes). HMRC also deny reading back for capital gains tax purposes in relation to an interest in partnership assets which passes automatically to the surviving partners although a variation of such property is capable of reading back for inheritance tax purposes. See CG 30362 and compare IHTM 35073.

[21.121]

EXAMPLE 21.16

A dies leaving a house (Blackacre) to B and a house (Whiteacre) to C. B would rather have Whiteacre and C would rather have Blackacre. They enter into a deed of variation such that A is deemed to have left Whiteacre to B and Blackacre to C. Although each one does the variation in consideration of the other beneficiary also varying his interest, this does not prevent reading back. Accordingly, each takes the other's house at probate value.

EXAMPLE 21.17

The deceased T leaves L a book worth £100,000. Within two years of T's death L varies the will so that the book (now worth £140,000) passes to his brother B. Provided that the appropriate statement for reading back (formerly election) is made (see [21.122]) this will be treated for capital gains tax purposes as if T's will had provided for the book to pass to B. Accordingly, B acquires the asset at its market value at death (£100,000) as legatee plus any additional expenses of the PRs. If the book has increased in value since the death by no more than L's annual exemption, he should not opt to read back for capital gains tax purposes since the gain is then exempt and B will acquire the asset at its market value at the date of the variation.

2 'Reading back' (TCGA 1992 s 62(7) as amended)

a) *The 'reading back' decision*

If 'reading back' is desired the instrument of variation itself must so provide.

[21.122]

b) *To read back or not*

In many cases, it will be desirable that the variation is read back for both CGT and IHT purposes. This is not necessary, however, since the decisions are independent of each other with the result that a taxpayer may decide to read back for IHT purposes (so that the gift is treated as a transfer by the deceased) without doing so for CGT and *vice versa*. Careful thought should be given to this problem. Consider the following: **[21.123]**

EXAMPLE 21.18

(1) A's will leaves quoted shares worth £100,000 to the testator's daughter. She transfers the shares within two years to her mother (the testator's surviving spouse). The shares are then worth £106,000.

For IHT reading back will be desirable as the result will be to reduce the testator's chargeable estate at death by £100,000 since the shares are now an exempt transfer to a surviving spouse.

For CGT the election to read the disposal back should *not* be made since, if the daughter makes a chargeable disposal, her gain will be £106,000 − £100,000 = £6,000 which will be more than covered by her annual CGT exemption. Her mother will then acquire the shares at the higher base cost of £106,000.

(2) B's will leaves quoted shares worth £100,000 to the testator's surviving spouse. After they have risen in value to £140,000 she decides (within the permitted time limit) to vary the will in favour of her daughter.

For IHT it is debatable whether the disposition should be read back. If it is, £100,000 will constitute a chargeable death transfer made by B so that, assuming that the nil rate band has already been exhausted, tax will be charged at 40%. If it is not, the widow will make a lifetime potentially exempt transfer of £140,000 that, if she survives by seven years, will be free of all tax. On the other hand, if it is likely that she will only survive her husband by a few weeks, then it will be necessary to consider whether it is better for £100,000 to be taxed as part of her dead husband's estate or for £140,000 to be taxed on her death. With the introduction of the transferable nil rate band (see **Chapter 31**) it is less likely to make a difference since any unused nil rate band of the husband can be transferred and used on the wife's death.

For CGT the disposal should be read back into the will since otherwise there will be a chargeable gain of £140,000 − £100,000 = £40,000. Generally reading back is desirable for capital gains tax purposes when the administration of the estate is not completed in order to avoid certain 'chose in action' problems. See CG 31900 onwards for a somewhat puzzling interpretation of the position.

3 Marshall v Kerr (1994) – who is the settlor of a trust created by a variation?

a) *The issue*

The case of *Marshall v Kerr* raised the question of who was the settlor of a trust for capital gains tax purposes when a deed of variation with election for reading back was made. The testator died in 1977 domiciled in Jersey, and Mrs Kerr (UK-resident and domiciled) became entitled to one half of the residuary estate. By a deed of family arrangement executed in January 1978 made before the administration of the estate had been completed, her half share was to be retained by the PRs (a Jersey resident company) as trustees for, *inter alia*, Mrs Kerr. In due course, gains were realised by those trustees and capital advanced to Mrs Kerr. If the settlement had been created by Mrs Kerr, the rules of TCGA 1992 s 87 applied and capital payments made to her attracted a CGT charge (see **Chapter 27**). Given that she had transferred property to trustees, on general principles she would be treated as the settlor of that trust: but was this conclusion displaced by the deeming provision in s 62(6)? This provides that if a variation is made within two years of death and there is reading back, it takes effect 'as if the variation had been effected by the deceased'. [21.124]

The Inland Revenue successfully argued in the House of Lords that Mrs Kerr rather than the deceased was the settlor for capital gains tax purposes. While accepting that s 87 took effect subject to the various deeming provisions contained in s 62, the Revenue argued that there was nothing in the latter section to prevent Mrs Kerr from being treated as the settlor. [21.125]

EXAMPLE 21.19

Boris, domiciled in France, leaves his villa in Tuscany and moneys in his Swiss bank account to his son Gaspard, UK-resident and domiciled. By a variation of the terms of his will made within two years of Boris' death, the property is settled on discretionary trusts where the trustees are resident in Jersey for the benefit of Gaspard and his family.

For IHT purposes, reading back ensures that the settlement is of excluded property made by Boris as the foreign domiciled settlor. Hence on Gaspard's death the trust is not subject to UK tax and there is no 10-year anniversary or exit charge provided that no UK situs assets are held on those dates (see **[35.5]**). Although the reading back provision applies only for the purposes of the IHTA 1984 rather than FA 1986, HMRC appear to accept that reservation of benefit (see **Chapter 29**) does not apply even though Gaspard is the actual settlor and continues to benefit.

For CGT purposes, the settlement has been created by Gaspard, a UK-resident domiciliary, so that the charging provisions in TCGA 1992 s 86 ff (see **Chapter 27**) will apply given that he and other defined persons can benefit from the trust.

For *income tax* purposes, the settlement has been created by Gaspard and as he and his wife can benefit all trust income will be taxed on him wherever the trustees are resident or the assets are situated.

Note that there is no need for the Trustees to be non-resident to obtain continuing favourable inheritance tax treatment – the requirements for excluded property for inheritance tax purposes are simply that Boris (the settlor) must not be UK domiciled or deemed domiciled at his death (when he is treated as establishing the trust) and that the assets are non-UK situs. Hence for capital gains tax reasons it may be easier to have UK-resident trustees in order to avoid any offshore tax implications. If the trustees are UK resident, Gaspard will not be subject to capital gains tax on any trust gains (the trustees will be taxable) He will however, be subject to income tax on trust income: see ITTOIA 2005 s 625.

The *Marshall v Kerr* case therefore does not affect the IHT treatment of instruments of variation and disclaimer: see RI 101 (February 1995).

The question of who is the settlor for income and capital gains tax purposes was put on a statutory footing in 2006. Schedule 12 to the Finance Act 2006 introduced provisions on identification of the settlor where there is a variation of a will or intestacy which sets up new trusts – see TCGA 1992 s 68C as amended. If property becomes settled property as a result of the variation, the person making the variation is treated as the settlor. If property was already settled under the will or intestacy and then becomes comprised in another trust as a result of the variation, the deceased person, not the person making the variation, is treated as the settlor for capital gains tax purposes. This is presumably on the basis that, if several persons act to vary their entitlements under a will trust and settle the assets in a new trust, it would be difficult to establish who is the settlor. The position is less clear where the person making the variation, eg the life tenant, simply varies their own interest under the settlement. Suppose the life tenant assigns her interest to a discretionary trust under which income is rolled up. If the trustees then make gains, it would appear that she is not taxed on those gains even though she may be a beneficiary under the trust. [21.126]

4 Claims under the Inheritance (Provision for Family and Dependants) Act 1975

For inheritance tax purposes the terms of any court order are read back to the date of death under IHTA 1984 s 146 and similarly for capital gains tax purposes (see IPFDA 1975 s 19). This means that the terms of the order are deemed to have applied since death for all purposes and there is no option to elect for different tax treatment. There is no capital gains tax disposal on making the order and it does not matter how long the interval between death and the making of the court order.

However, if there is not a full hearing and a compromise is reached that is embodied in a consent order, HMRC somewhat controversially treat such consent orders as outside s 19 unless involving minors, and a specific positive obligation is imposed on the parties to follow the terms of the compromise (see CG 31820). If the compromise is reached within two years of death, HMRC accept that it can qualify for reading back under s 62(6) as a variation; otherwise the terms of the order are not treated as retrospective to the date of death. The settlement of a claim without a court order may then raise some difficult capital gains tax issues around whether the claimant has disposed of his chose in action (the right to take the proceedings which has a nil base cost) in consideration of receiving cash, or disposed of an asset of the estate.

[21.127]

22 CGT – exemptions and reliefs

Updated by Jackie Anderson, Chartered Accountant and Chartered Tax Adviser, LHA Consulting Ltd

I   Miscellaneous exemptions [**22.2**]
II Chattels [**22.21**]
III Debts [**22.41**]
IV Business reliefs [**22.71**]

In many cases a gain on the disposal of an asset will not be chargeable either because the gain itself is exempt or because the asset is not chargeable. Even if a gain is chargeable, there are various reliefs whereby the tax can be minimised or deferred indefinitely.

As already noted at [**19.50**], there is an annual exemption for an individual whose gains do not exceed £11,300 (for 2017–18) in the tax year; trustees are generally entitled to half of the exemption available to individuals: ie £5,650 unless they are trustees of settlements for the disabled when they enjoy the same exempt amount as individuals (see [**19.53**]).

Private residence relief is considered in **Chapter 23**.   [**22.1**]

I MISCELLANEOUS EXEMPTIONS

1 Exempt assets

Exempt assets are not chargeable to CGT. The taxpayer, therefore, realises no chargeable gain or, often more significantly, no allowable loss on their disposal.

Non-chargeable assets include sterling (TCGA 1992 s 21), National Savings Certificates, Premium Bonds and Save As You Earn deposits (s 121), and private motor vehicles (s 263). Gains and losses arising on the disposal of investments in an Individual Savings Account and a Junior Individual Savings Account are disregarded.   [**22.2**]

2 Exempt gains

The following gains are exempt from CGT:
(1) capital sums paid as compensation or damages for any wrong or injury suffered by an individual in his personal or professional capacity. Until 27 January 2014, where compensation could not be linked to an asset

chargeable to CGT, ESC D33 treated the full amount of any compensation as exempt from CGT. Since 27 January 2014, only the first £500,000 of this kind of capital compensation is exempt, although a person who receives compensation of more than that amount and thinks he should not be chargeable to CGT may make a claim in writing to HMRC, who will then consider whether further relief can be given. Compensation for personal injury will continue to enjoy full CGT exemption (s 51 and see ESC D33 as amended). (Note that during 2014, HMRC consulted both on legislating the relief given by ESC D33, and on introducing a limit of £1m exemption with amounts in excess of this liable to CGT; the feedback received was mostly negative, and the issue remains to be determined.) (See **[19.66]–[19.68]**.);

(2) gains on the disposal of decorations for valour unless the decoration was acquired for money or money's worth (s 268);

(3) gains on the disposal of foreign currency by individuals, trustees or personal representatives (s 252 as amended by FA 2012). A foreign currency bank account is a chargeable asset (a debt) and, accordingly, every disposal therefrom is potentially chargeable to CGT. Although there has been a limited exemption for the personal expenditure of an individual or his family outside the UK, many individuals have bank accounts in a foreign currency for a variety of other reasons, for which the exemption has not applied. FA 2012 extended the exemption to all individuals, trustees or personal representatives who hold a bank account in a foreign currency irrespective of the reason for the account;

(4) gains on the disposal of gilt-edged securities (s 115 and Sch 9; Taxation of Chargeable Gains (Gilt-Edged Securities) Order 2012 (SI 2012/1843): the exemption also applies to futures and options in these instruments;

(5) gains on the disposal of ordinary shares in a venture capital trust are exempt from CGT (see **Chapter 15**). There is also a qualified exemption for shares acquired under the complementary Enterprise Investment Scheme (EIS) and the Seed Enterprise Investment Scheme (as extended by FA 2013 and FA 2014) (see **Chapter 15**) (see TCGA 1992 ss 150A, 150B);

(6) the disposal of pension rights, annuity rights and annual payments will not generally give rise to a chargeable gain (s 237);

(7) any gain on the disposal of a life policy, a deferred annuity policy, or any rights under such policies, unless the disposal is by someone other than the original beneficial owner and *that person* acquired the interest or right for money or money's worth (s 210 and CG 69040); and

(8) gains are exempt if made *by* such bodies as authorised unit trusts and investment trusts (s 100), and charities where the gain is applied for charitable purposes (s 256). **[22.3]**

3 Charities

Disposals *to* charities and to certain national institutions are treated as made on a no gain/no loss basis (s 257 and see **[53.89]**). **[22.4]**

4 Heritage property and woodlands

The exemptions for heritage property are basically the same as for IHT (see **Chapter 31**).

First, where property which has been designated by the Treasury to be of national interest is given (or sold by private treaty) to a non-profit making body (including a charity or other national institution mentioned in s 256) any gain will be exempt from CGT (s 258(2)). *Second,* any gain on a disposal of such property may be conditionally exempt from CGT in the same way as for IHT (s 258(3), (4): see IHTA 1984 ss 30, 31). *Third,* the gain on any property that is accepted by the Treasury in satisfaction of IHT is exempt from CGT (s 258(2)(b)).

Consideration received for a disposal of trees (or saleable underwood) is excluded from any CGT computation provided that the disponer is the occupier who manages the woodlands on a commercial basis with a view to profit (s 113). [22.5]

5 The Cultural Gifts Scheme

When a donor makes a lifetime gift on or after 1 April 2012 to the nation of pre-eminent objects in accordance with the Cultural Gifts Scheme (CGS), the donor receives a reduction in his liability to income tax and CGT, the maximum value of which is 30% of the agreed value of the object that is being donated. For individuals, the tax reduction can be spread across a maximum of five tax years, beginning with the tax year in which the offer is formally registered by the Arts Council, to whom applications to donate must be made. If the individual does not express any preference, the tax reduction will be applied first to the individual's income tax liability and thereafter to any capital gains tax (FA 2012 Sch 14). Further, on the making of the donation, TCGA 1992 s 258(1A) exempts from CGT the chargeable gain that would otherwise arise on the disposal of a chargeable asset. According to the Department of Culture, Media and Sport, the CGS is not appropriate for gifts of land and buildings which may, in suitable circumstances and subject to certain conditions, qualify for other forms of tax relief. [22.6]–[22.20]

II CHATTELS

1 Chattels that are wasting assets

A gain on the disposal of a chattel that is a wasting asset is generally exempt from CGT, the rationale being that since the taxpayer has enjoyed the use of the chattel, he should not be entitled to claim any loss in respect of it. A wasting asset is one with a predictable useful life of 50 years or less and includes yachts, caravans, washing machines, animals and all plant and machinery (provided that it is not plant and machinery used by a business that has, or could have, claimed capital allowances). This includes, in the Revenue's view, such assets as antique clocks and watches, certain vintage cars and (generally) shotguns (see TCGA 1992 ss 44, 45; CG 76720 ff; and **[19.37]**).

For gains accruing on or after 6 April 2015 (for CGT purposes; 1 April 2015 for corporation tax purposes), FA 2015 includes provisions which make clear that the exemption applies only where the asset being disposed of has been used in the business of the person disposing of it. These new provisions were rendered necessary because of the decisions of the Upper Tribunal (2013) and Court of Appeal (2014) in *The Executors of Lord Howard of Henderskelfe (Decd) v R & C Comrs*.

In that case, it was argued by the appellants that a work of art by Sir Joshua Reynolds, situated in a stately house owned by a company carrying on the trade of opening the greater part of the house and the exhibiting of works of art (owned by the appellant executors) within that part to the general public, was 'plant' and thus had a predictable life of less than 50 years (TCGA 1992 s 44(1)(c)). It was further contended that since capital allowances were never available to the appellants, the removal and restriction of the exemption under s 45(2) and s 45(3) respectively did not apply and, accordingly, the gain accruing on the sale of the painting was exempt as a wasting asset.

Having noted that 'plant' does not have the same innate quality as does machinery, and that it is 'merely an asset that is put to a particular use in a particular context and acquires its colour from the context in which it is used', the First-tier Tribunal (2011) dismissed the appellants' argument on the grounds that (i) since the painting was not owned by the company but was loaned to it on an informal basis by the appellant executors and could be removed by them at any time, there was absent the degree of permanence that was required for an asset to be termed 'plant' (*Yarmouth v France* (1887) *per* Lindley LJ); and (ii) to be 'plant', the asset had to be owned by a business or formally leased to it; the appellant executors did not carry on a business.

The Tribunal further concluded that just because an asset may be 'plant' in the hands of one person this did not mean that it was necessarily of the same character in someone else's hands. The Upper Tribunal (2013) and the Court of Appeal (2014), finding for the executors, took a different view. The Upper Tribunal held that the picture was used for the promotion of the company's trade and that in the company's hands it passed the permanence test; accordingly, it was 'plant' within s 44(1)(c) and thus deemed a wasting asset within the meaning of s 44. Morgan J then went on to hold that this entitled the executors to claim that the gain realised on their disposal of the picture was exempt from CGT by virtue of s 45(1), rejecting HMRC's argument that *if* the picture was plant in the hands of the company (which they disputed), it was not plant in the hands of the executors since they carried on no trade or business. He said:

> 'the meaning of plant in section 44(1)(c) of the 1992 Act does not permit a finding that an asset is plant in the hands of a person using the asset in business but, at the same time, not plant in the hands of the owner of the asset.'

On appeal, HMRC argued that the painting was not plant because (i) its enjoyment by the company was not sufficiently permanent in that the company had only a precarious right to enjoy it; (ii) there was no relevant identity between the interest in the plant held by the company and the interest in the asset sold by the executors (as the company was entitled to a limited interest only (terminable at will), whereas what the executors sold was the picture itself); and (iii) s 44 contemplates that what is plant is an asset with a limited life that wastes away with use; an old master, such as the picture, cannot fit such a description. The Court of Appeal rejected all three of these arguments. With respect to the first, it held that permanence related to the quality of the asset concerned, distinguishing it from the circulating nature of a trader's stock in trade. As for the second, the court was of the view that the plant kept by the company for use in its trade was not merely a limited interest but the painting itself and thus exactly of the same nature as the asset sold by the executors. Finally, the court rejected the notion that 'plant' is not identified by the predictable life of a chattel but, rather, whether or not it passes the *Yarmouth v France* test of permanence; an item is capable of doing so irrespective of its predictable life. Once an item qualifies as 'plant', it is then in every case deemed to be a wasting asset by s 44(1)(c). HMRC's further argument that even if the picture was plant in the hands of the company, it was not plant in the hands of the executors since they were not carrying on a trade that engaged its use was also rejected. The Court of Appeal could find nothing in the statutory provisions from which could be derived a legislative intent to limit the exemption to a disposal by the trader who had used the plant.

The result of this decision was that the capital gain arising on the sale of the painting was exempt. As Briggs LJ said in the case itself, '[I]t is ... surprising to those unfamiliar with the workings of Capital Gains Tax, that a famous Old Master like Omai should qualify for exemption from tax on the ground that it is is either "plant" or a wasting asset ...'. It has been suggested that it was also surprising to those who are familiar with the workings of CGT (see *Private Client Business* (2013) 163). It was clearly surprising to HMRC, and the amendment to the original legislation is to be welcomed for the purpose of clarity as well as common sense. **[22.21]**

2 Non-wasting chattels

In the case of non-wasting chattels (eg items of jewellery, fine wine, antiques etc), if the disposal consideration is £6,000 or less, any gain is exempt and so does not enter the computation of the taxpayer's total gains in a tax year (TCGA 1992 s 262(1)). CGT is as a result easier and less costly to administer as there is no need to calculate gains and losses on assets of relatively low value. In so far as the disposal consideration exceeds £6,000, the chargeable gain is limited to 5/3 of the excess of that consideration over £6,000.

Where a loss is made on the disposal of a chattel and the disposal consideration is *less than* £6,000, the sum of £6,000 is substituted for that consideration so as to limit a claim for loss relief. **[22.22]**

EXAMPLE 22.1

(1) A bought a necklace for £4,600 and later sold it for £7,200 so making a total gain of £2,600. The chargeable gain is reduced to 5/3 × £1,200 (£7,200 − £6,000) = £2,000.

(2) A bought a brooch for £8,000 and sold it for £4,600 so making an actual loss of £3,400. He is deemed to have sold it for £6,000 so that his allowable loss is restricted to £2,000 (£8,000 − £6,000).

3 Chattels comprising a set

The taxpayer cannot dispose of a set of articles to the same person by a series of separate transactions so as to take advantage of the £6,000 exemption on each disposal. Whether the disposals are to the same person or to connected persons (albeit on different occasions), they are regarded as a single transaction (see also TCGA 1992 s 19 and [19.16]). The meaning of 'a set' is not always obvious: a valuable collection of lead toy soldiers, for instance, is arguably not a set. Whether bottles of fine wine amount to a set would appear to be a question of fact depending on (a) whether the bottles are 'similar and complementary', requiring them to have been produced from the same vineyard in the same vintage year; and (b) whether the bottles are of greater worth when sold collectively than when sold individually (see CG 76632. See also *Tax Bulletin*, August 1999 and February 2000, which considers the treatment of a pair of shotguns). More generally, the wording of s 262(4) suggests that at least three articles are required for a set. [22.23]–[22.40]

EXAMPLE 22.2

A owns three Rousseau paintings which, as a set, have a market value of £30,000. He paid £4,000 for each of the paintings that individually are now worth £6,000. He sells all three paintings at different times to his sister B for £6,000 each. He thereby appears to fall within the chattel exemption on each disposal. The Revenue can, however, treat the three disposals as a single disposal of an asset worth £30,000 with a base value of £12,000 so that A has made a gain of £18,000.

III DEBTS

1 What is a debt?

A debt is a chargeable asset (TCGA 1992 s 21). It is not defined and bears the common law meaning of 'a sum payable in respect of a liquidated money demand recoverable by action' (*Rawley v Rawley* (1876)). It can include a right to receive a sum of money that is not yet ascertained (*O'Driscoll v Manchester Insurance Committee* (1915)) or a contingent right to receive a definite sum (*Mortimore v IRC* (1864)). However, for the purposes of CGT, it cannot include a right to receive an uncertain sum at an unascertained date; there must be a liability, either present or contingent, to pay a sum which is ascertained or capable of being ascertained at the time of disposal (*Marren v Ingles* (1980): see [19.18]). [22.41]

EXAMPLE 22.3

Barry agrees to sell his Ming vase to Bruce for £15,000 plus one half of any profits that Bruce realises if he resells the vase in the next ten years. The disposal consideration received for the vase is £15,000 plus the value of a *chose in action*. As that *chose* is both contingent (on resale occurring) and for an unascertained sum (half of any profits), it is not a debt. The *chose in action* is a separate asset and a CGT charge may arise on its disposal (see [19.18] and note that if that disposal results in a loss, relief may be available against gains of earlier years: see TCGA 1992 s 279A–279D).

2 The general principle

A disposal of a debt by the original creditor, his personal representatives or legatee is exempt from CGT unless it is a debt on a security (see [21.44]). 'Disposal' includes repayment of the debt (TCGA 1992 s 251). Since a contractual debt will normally give a creditor merely the right to repayment of the sum lent, together with interest, the disposal of a debt will rarely generate a gain and the aim of s 251 is to exclude the more likely claim for loss relief, particularly where the debt is never repaid. This provision only applies to the original creditor so that an assignee of a debt can claim an allowable loss if the debtor defaults, unless the assignee and the creditor are connected persons (s 251(4)).

If the debt is satisfied by a transfer of property, that property is acquired by the creditor at its market value. Since this could operate harshly for an original creditor who can claim no allowable loss, s 251(3) provides that on a subsequent disposal of the property, its base value is taken as the value of the debt. [22.42]

EXAMPLE 22.4

A owes B £30,000 and in full satisfaction of the debt he gives B a painting worth £22,000. B does not have an allowable loss of £8,000. However, if B later sells the painting for £40,000 he is taxed on a gain of £10,000 only (£40,000 – £30,000).

3 Loans to traders

The harshness of TCGA 1992 s 251 is mitigated by s 253, allowing original creditors to claim loss relief in respect of a qualifying loan. The loan must have become irrecoverable and the creditor must not have assigned his rights. Creditor and debtor must not be married to each other nor be companies in the same group. A 'qualifying loan' must be used by a UK-resident borrower *wholly for the purpose of a trade* (not being moneylending) carried on by him and the debt must not be 'on a security'. The relief is extended to include a loss arising from the guaranteeing of a 'qualifying loan' (see s 253(4) and *Leisureking Ltd v Cushing* (1993)). [22.43]

4 Debt on a security

The legislation distinguishes between debts that can normally only decrease in value and those which may be disposed of at a profit. It, therefore, provides that a 'debt on a security' is chargeable to CGT even in the hands of the original creditor (TCGA 1992 s 251).

The term 'debt on a security' lacks both statutory and satisfactory judicial interpretation despite a number of cases (for instance, *Cleveleys Investment Trust Co v IRC* (1971); *Aberdeen Construction Group Ltd v IRC* (1978); *W T Ramsay Ltd v IRC* (1981)). It has a limited and technical meaning and '[it] is not a synonym for a secured debt' *per* Lord Wilberforce in *Aberdeen Construction Group Ltd v IRC* above. The word 'security' is defined in TCGA 1992 s 132(3) as including 'any loan stock or similar security whether of the Government of the UK or elsewhere, or of any company, and whether secured or unsecured'. Despite the word '*including*' the Revenue has stated that it regards the definition as exhaustive (see CCAB June 1969 although this is not referred to in CG 53421 which refers to this definition as being 'of limited use').

In *Taylor Clark International Ltd v Lewis* (1998) Robert Walker J, whose views were upheld by the Court of Appeal, concluded that the basic requirements for a debt on security were:
(1) the debt had to be capable of being assigned;
(2) it had to carry interest;
(3) to have a structure of permanence; and
(4) to provide proprietary security.

Relief was denied in this case which involved an interest-bearing loan with security from a parent company to its subsidiary. The loan was essentially impermanent and not intended to be marketable or dealt in even though it was assignable. However, the fact that it was in a foreign currency was not significant.

For the Revenue's views on the meaning of a 'debt on security', see CG 53425 and see **[47.39]**–**[47.50]**.

Because of the regime for the taxation of company loan relationships, most debt held by companies has been removed from the capital gains charge: instead profits and losses on such debt together with interest are charged or allowed as income (see **[41.50]**–**[41.56]**). [22.44]

5 Qualifying corporate bonds

Gains on the disposal of a 'qualifying corporate bond' (which includes most company debentures) are exempt from CGT under TCGA 1992 s 117 (see **[41.92]**). [22.45]–[22.70]

IV BUSINESS RELIEFS

1 The problems and the taxes

A number of CGT reliefs relate to businesses both incorporated and unincorporated. Their aim is to enable businesses to be carried on and transferred without being threatened by taxation. This chapter is concerned only with CGT reliefs: bear in mind a disposal of a business will normally involve other taxes.

A disposal may be by way of gift or by sale. If by way of *gift*, the relevant taxes will be CGT, income tax and IHT. For CGT, hold-over relief under TCGA 1992 s 165 (as amended) may be available on a lifetime gift. Where the transfer is a *sale*, income tax and CGT may apply.

On death, there will be no CGT (see **Chapter 19**).

The CGT business reliefs may apply to a disposal of:
(1) a sole trade/profession;
(2) a part of a trade/profession (eg a partnership share);
(3) shares in a company; and
(4) assets used by a company or partnership in which the owner of the assets either owns shares or is a partner.

In a number of cases relief is given by a deferment of the CGT charge and this is usually done by deducting the otherwise chargeable gain from the acquisition cost of a new or replacement asset (roll-over or hold-over relief). For the Revenue's views on the order of reliefs, see CG 60210. For disposals of assets before 6 April 2008, careful note should be taken of the impact on taper relief when roll-over or hold-over relief applies (see *Stolkin v R & C Comrs* (2011) for the interaction of taper relief and the EIS); for disposals after that date, taper relief has been abolished and the problem does not arise, but consideration should be given to the interaction between roll-over and hold-over relief and entrepreneurs' relief (see [20.41]). [22.71]

2 Roll-over (replacement of business assets) (TCGA 1992 ss 152–159)

a) *Basic conditions for relief*

Where certain assets of a business are sold and the proceeds of sale wholly reinvested in acquiring a 'new' asset to be used in a business and, where relevant, occupied for the purposes of the business (see, below, [22.75]), the taxpayer can elect to roll over the gain and deduct it from the acquisition cost of the new asset. Tax is, therefore, postponed until that asset is sold and no replacement qualifying asset purchased. The new asset must be bought within one year *before* or three years *after* the disposal of the old one, and once it is acquired, it must 'on the acquisition' be taken into use for the purposes of the taxpayer's trade. The Revenue has the power to extend this time limit and, whilst the exercise of the power can be challenged by judicial review, the Commissioners cannot themselves exercise it (*Steibelt v Paling* (1999)). This point was reiterated in *R (on the application of Barnett) v IRC* (2004), in which case, it was made clear that, although the Board was under a duty to take into account relevant findings by the Commissioners, the issue of whether the taxpayer had been prevented from re-investing in further property by circumstances beyond his control was a question for the Revenue and it was entitled to conclude that such circumstances did not exist. A gap between the time of acquisition and the time when it is used in the trade will mean that the exemption will not be available (see *Campbell Connelly Co Ltd v Barnett* (1993) and *Milton v Chivers* (1996) holding that while 'on the acquisition' did not imply immediacy, it did exclude dilatoriness: see also *Joseph Carter & Sons v Baird* (1999)). [22.72]

EXAMPLE 22.5

A makes a gain of £50,000 on the sale of factory 1, but he immediately buys factory 2 for £120,000. He can roll the gain of £50,000 into the purchase price of factory 2 thereby reducing it to £70,000 (actual cost £120,000 minus rolled-over gain of £50,000). Note that the gain that is rolled over takes no account of any taper relief (abolished for disposals on or after 5 April 2008) that would have been available to A. This matter is considered further at [21.79].

b) *Prior acquisitions of replacement assets*

It will be appreciated that the 'new' asset can be acquired before the disposal of the old asset – the Revenue accepts that the requirements are met if 'the old assets, or the proceeds of the old assets, are part of the resources available to the taxpayer when the new assets are acquired'. An important limitation on the relief was, however, confirmed by the Court of Appeal in *Watton v Tippett* (1997) where the taxpayer, having purchased certain freehold land and buildings (unit 1) for a single unapportioned consideration, within 12 months of that purchase sold part of the same land and buildings (unit 1A) and claimed to roll over the gain made on that disposal into the land and buildings retained by him (unit 1B). Rejecting this claim the court held that it was critical to identify the asset acquired and disposed of and unit 1B had not been acquired as such. The position would have been different if two separate properties had been purchased albeit for a single unapportioned consideration given that this could be apportioned under TCGA 1992 s 52(4).

[22.73]

EXAMPLE 22.6

If A acquires factory 1 (as in the above example), but almost immediately sells part of it, he cannot roll any gain over into the acquisition cost of the remainder of the factory retained by him. It is a part disposal of a single asset; the consideration for that single asset cannot, according to *Watton v Tippett* (above), be apportioned.

If A acquires two adjacent factories (1 and 2) at the same time but under separate contracts, and immediately sells factory 2, A can roll over any gain into the acquisition cost of factory 1: this is *not* a part disposal of a single asset, but rather a disposal of a severable part of the taxpayer's assets, with separate consideration attributable to the 'old' asset (factory 2) and 'other' assets (factory 1). *Note* that s 152 does not as such require 'new' assets to be acquired; rather it refers to the consideration being applied in acquiring *other* assets (and see, for instance, ESC D22 permitting expenditure on improvement to existing assets).

c) *Qualifying assets*

The assets must be comprised in the list of business assets in TCGA 1992 s 155. These are land and buildings; fixed plant and machinery; ships; aircraft; hovercraft; goodwill; satellites, space stations and spacecraft; milk and potato quotas, fish quota and certain EU quotas. Lloyds syndicate capacity and Lloyds members' agent pooling arrangements may also qualify. This list can be added to by Treasury Order.

The old and new assets need not be of the same type, however, eg a gain on the sale of an aircraft can be rolled over into the purchase of a hovercraft. Further, although the old asset must have been used in the taxpayer's trade during the whole time that he owned it (otherwise only partial roll-over is allowed), it could have been used in successive trades provided that the gap between them did not exceed three years.

For a discussion of whether part of a taxpayer's chargeable gains related to the sale of goodwill, see the Special Commissioners decision in *Balloon Promotions Ltd v Wilson* (2006); see also *R & C Comrs v Mertrux Ltd* (2012), where the Upper Tribunal held that a payment received by the taxpayer for the sale of its motor dealership did not consist wholly of consideration for the goodwill in respect of which roll-over relief was available; half of the payment was compensation for termination of its dealer agreement in respect of which relief was not available. Note also that corporate goodwill will not qualify where intangible fixed assets are acquired or disposed of on or after 1 April 2002.

Qualifying EU quotas include the premium given to producers of ewes and suckler cows and payment entitlements under 'the single payment scheme' (a system of support for farmers under the EU Common Agricultural Policy. Amendments to the legislation have been made by FA 2012 to take account of EU replacement regulations made in 2009. Payment entitlements under the single payment scheme will cease in 2014, to be replaced with new payment entitlements under the Basic Payment Scheme: by virtue of FA 2014, these are included within the classes of qualifying assets in s 155). **[22.74]**

EXAMPLE 22.7

A inherited a freehold shop in 2000 when its value was £36,000. The shop was kept empty until 2004 when he started a fish and chip shop. He sold the shop in October 2016 for £60,000 and purchased new premises for £75,000.

His total gain in 2016 is £24,000 and the premises have been used for business purposes during twelve-sixteenths of the ownership period. Hence £18,000 of the gain is rolled over but the balance (£6,000) is taxed.

d) *Occupation for business purposes*

The assets that are sold must be occupied as well as used for the purposes of the taxpayer's business (for a discussion of these requirements, see *Pems Butler Ltd v R & C Comrs* (2012)). If the property is occupied by his partner or employee, he must be able to show that their occupation is *representative* (ie attributed to him) to obtain the relief. For occupation to be representative it must *either* (1) be essential for the partner or employee to occupy the property to perform his duties; *or* (2) be an express term of the employment contract (or partnership agreement) that he should do so, and the occupation must enable him to perform his duties better. If either of these conditions is proved, the Revenue accepts that the property is used for the purpose of the owner's trade (see *Anderton v Lamb* (1981)).

The new asset need not be used in the same trade as the old but can be used in another trade carried on by the taxpayer simultaneously or successively, provided in the latter case that there is not more than a three-year gap between the ceasing of one trade and the start of another (see SP 8/81). There is nothing to prevent the taxpayer from rolling his gain into the purchase of more than one asset or to require him to continue to use the new asset in a trade throughout his period of ownership. ESC D22–25 extend the relief, *inter alia*, to cover improvements to, or capital expenditure to enhance the value of, existing assets; the acquisition of a further interest in an asset already used for the purposes of the trade; and the partition of land on the dissolution of a partnership.

Where only part of the premises are actually used for business purposes, only those parts are to be treated as both used and occupied for business purposes and, in making an apportionment under s 152(6), which must, by virtue of s 159(11), be made in a just and reasonable manner, only those issues relating to the nature and value of the property and the bargain under which it was bought, are to be taken into account (*Pems Butler Ltd v R & C Comrs* (2012)). **[22.75]**

e) *Non residents and foreign assets*

Relief is not available to a non-UK resident who sells a chargeable asset (ie one used in a trade carried on through a UK branch or agency) and then purchases a new asset that is not chargeable because it is situated outside the UK (TCGA 1992 s 159). Relief is, however, available if he acquires further UK branch or agency assets and is also given to a UK resident who rolls over into the acquisition of a qualifying asset wherever situated (and even though he may be non resident at the time of acquisition: see CG 60270 and CG 61350 ff). **[22.76]**

f) *Partnerships, companies and employees*

This relief is available to partnerships and to companies and it can be claimed for an asset that is owned by an individual and used by his partnership or personal company. In such cases, however, the relief is only available to the individual and the replacement asset cannot be purchased by the partnership or company (*Cassell v Crutchfield (No 2)* (1997)). Employees may claim the relief for assets owned by them so long as the assets are used (or, in the case of land and buildings, occupied) only for the purposes of the employment. (Note, however, that it is not necessary for the asset to be used *exclusively* by the employee in the course of his employment so that relief may apply even if the asset is provided for the general use of the employer: see SP 5/86.) **[22.77]**

g) *Restrictions on the relief*

There are certain restrictions on the relief.

First, if the new asset is a depreciating asset (defined as a 'wasting asset' – see **[19.37]** – or one which will become a wasting asset within ten years, such as a lease with 60 years unexpired) the gain on the old asset cannot be deducted from the cost of the new. Instead, tax on the gain is postponed until the earliest of the three following events:

(1) ten years elapse from the date of the purchase of the new asset; or
(2) the taxpayer disposes of the new asset; or
(3) the taxpayer ceases to use the new asset for the purposes of a trade.

When the new asset ceases to be used in a trade because of the death of the taxpayer, no gain arises under s 154(2) because the gain is already exempted by s 62(1)(b).

If, before the deferred gain becomes chargeable, a new asset is acquired (whether the depreciating asset is sold or not), the deferred gain may be rolled into the new asset (see TCGA 1992 s 154).

EXAMPLE 22.8

Sam sells his freehold fish and chip shop for £25,000 thereby making a gain of £12,000. One year later he buys a 55-year lease on new premises for £27,000 and seven years after that acquires a further freehold shop for £35,000.
(1) The 55-year lease is a depreciating asset. The gain of £12,000 on the sale of the original shop is, therefore, held in suspense for ten years.

(2) As the purchase of the freehold shop occurs within ten years of the gain, roll-over relief is available so that the purchase price is reduced to £23,000.

Second, if the whole of the proceeds of sale are not reinvested in acquiring the new asset there is a chargeable gain equivalent to the amount not reinvested and it is only the balance that is rolled over. Accordingly, if the purchase price of the new asset does not exceed the acquisition cost of the old, all the gain is chargeable and there is nothing to roll over. TCGA 1992 s 50 excludes from the computation of the gain expenditure on the acquisition of an asset met by a public authority. It does not reduce the cost of acquisition of the asset with the effect of limiting any hold-over relief available (*Wardhaugh v Penrith Rugby Union Football Club* (2002)). The new asset must, of course, be purchased for use in a business so that if there is an element of non-business user relief will be restricted accordingly.

EXAMPLE 22.9

A buys factory 1 for £50,000 and sells it for £100,000 thereby making a gain of £50,000. A buys factory 2 for £80,000. The amount not reinvested (£20,000, ie £100,000 – £80,000) is chargeable. The balance of the gain (£30,000) is rolled over so that the acquisition cost of factory 2 is £50,000. If factory 2 had only cost £50,000 the amount not reinvested would equal the gain (ie £50,000) and may be chargeable.

In *Tod v Mudd* (1987) the taxpayer sold his accountancy practice and with his wife bought premises to carry on business as hoteliers in partnership. The premises were bought as tenants in common with a 75% interest being held by Mr Mudd and 25% by his wife and it was agreed that they would be used as to 75% for business purposes and 25% for private purposes. The partnership agreement stated that the business of the partnership should be conducted on that portion of the premises attributable to Mr Mudd's share. The court held that roll-over relief should be given to Mr Mudd but only on 75% of 75% of the purchase price because his interest as a tenant in common constituted a share in the whole property and not in a distinct 75% portion thereof. Accordingly, because of the way in which this arrangement had been structured, roll-over relief was restricted. There are a number of ways in which matters could have been organised so that full relief would have been given to Mr Mudd. *First*, he could have bought the whole of the new premises for business use and then given 25% to his wife. *Second*, he could have purchased an identified and separate portion of the premises (75% thereof) in his sole name and for business use leaving his wife to purchase the remaining portion for private purposes. Finally, the defective arrangement could have been cured had Mr Mudd bought out Mrs Mudd's 25% share within three years of the disposal of his accountancy practice.

If the taxpayer knows that the price of the new asset will be too low to enable him to claim roll-over (or full roll-over) relief and he is married, it may be advantageous to transfer a share in the old asset to his wife before it is sold (subject to challenge under the *Ramsay* principle, **Chapter 2**). [22.78]

EXAMPLE 22.10

H buys factory 1 for £50,000 and transfers 2/5 of it to his wife W. The factory is sold for £100,000. H's gain is £30,000 ([3/5 × £100,000]-[3/5 × £50,000]). W's gain is £20,000 ([2/5 × £100,000]-[2/5 × £50,000]).

H's share of the proceeds of sale is £60,000. H then buys factory 2 for £50,000. The proceeds of sale are not wholly reinvested in factory 2 and, therefore, H is charged to CGT on £10,000 (£60,000 – £50,000). The balance of his gain £20,000 (£30,000 – £10,000) can be rolled over, leaving him with a base value for factory 2 of £30,000. H and W between them are taxed on a gain of £30,000 instead of (as in *Example 22.9*) H being taxed on a gain of £50,000.

h) *Problems if the relief is claimed*

Roll-over relief should not be claimed where the taxpayer makes an allowable loss on the sale of the old asset since he cannot add this loss to the base value of the new asset, and nor should he claim the relief where the gain does not exceed his annual exemption. **[22.79]**

i) *Self-assessment and provisional relief where an intention to reinvest*

TCGA 1992 s 153A allows taxpayers to obtain provisional relief in advance of the reinvestment of the proceeds from the sale of the assets. At such time as the conditions for the granting of the relief have been satisfied, the provisional relief will be replaced by that actual relief. **[22.80]–[22.81]**

3 Roll-over relief on compulsory acquisition of land (TCGA 1992 s 247)

This form of roll-over relief is limited to the disposal of land (or an interest in land) to an authority exercising or able to exercise compulsory purchase powers. Any gain arising can be rolled over into the cost of acquiring replacement land (*Ahad v R & C Comrs* (2009)). Similar restrictions to those which apply to the replacement of business assets roll-over relief (see **[21.72]**) apply: for instance, the replacement asset must not have a limited life expectancy and, for full relief, all the disposal consideration must be reinvested. Further, reinvestment into property qualifying for the main residence relief is not allowed. **[22.82]**

4 Extensions of TCGA 1992 s 247

The Revenue allows s 247 relief to be claimed by landlords when leasehold tenants exercise their statutory rights to acquire the freehold reversion (see CG 61940), and when two or more persons sever their joint interests in land (s 248A) (or in milk quotas: s 248D). No charge arises irrespective of the s 247 concession when persons pool their resources and subsequently extract their shares from the pool. (See *Example 25.3(2)* and the cases there cited.) **[22.83]**

5 Retirement relief

Following a five-year period of phased withdrawal, retirement relief is no longer available for 2003–04 and subsequent years. For details of the relief, reference should be made to earlier editions of this book. **[22.84]**

6 Entrepreneurs' relief

Entrepreneurs' relief replaced taper and pre-1998 indexation relief and is available in three circumstances. *First*, in respect of gains made on the disposal of all or part of a business; *second*, in respect of gains made on the disposal of assets following the cessation of a business; and *finally* in respect of gains made by an individual on the disposal of shares in a trading company where that individual was an officer or employee of the company and held at least 5% of its shares and voting rights.

Qualifying gains made on or after 23 June 2010 are charged to CGT at a rate of 10% (for gains arising before that date, relief was given by reducing the gain by 4/9ths) on the first £10m of gains (for disposals on or after 6 April 2011; for disposals prior to that date but on or after 23 June 2010, the relief applied to the first £5m of gains; for gains arising on or before 6 April 2008, only the first £1m of gains were subject to the relief).

This relief appears at first to look rather more favourable than the former retirement relief in that it will not be based on any age or illness conditions and the qualifying holding period will only be one year. However, there are some serious drawbacks. First, entrepreneurs' relief is available on gains of £10m. Whilst this is very much more generous than the previous limits of £1m and £5m, taper relief was subject to no such limit, although the former retirement relief was. Moreover, the £10m limit is a lifetime limit, and may be of less benefit to the entrepreneur who sells more than one successful business in a lifetime. Secondly, to take advantage of the new relief, an individual needs to sell the whole or part of the business he carried on as a sole trader or in partnership, and not just the assets unless the business has come to an end. This, again, differs from the former taper relief.

Entrepreneurs' relief is considered in **Chapter 20**.   [22.85]–[22.98]

7 Postponement of CGT on gifts and sales at an undervalue (TCGA 1992 s 165)

This provision is considered in detail in **Chapter 24**.   [22.99]

8 Roll-over relief on the incorporation of a business (TCGA 1992 ss 162 and 162A)

a) *The relief*

The purpose of this relief is to postpone, rather than exempt, the actual charge to CGT where there is a disposal of an unincorporated business (whether by a sole trader, a partnership, or trustees but *not* by an unincorporated association) to a company and that disposal is wholly or partly in return for shares in that company. Any gains made on the disposal of chargeable business assets will be deducted from the value of the shares received (the gain is 'rolled into' the shares) and the relevant assets are acquired by the company at market value (ie there is a 'step-up' in their value).   [22.100]

b) Conditions to be satisfied

The business must be transferred as a going concern; a mere transfer of assets is insufficient. Further, all the assets of the business (excluding only cash) must be transferred to the company. As only a gain on business assets can be held over, it will be advisable to take investment assets out of the business before incorporation. The Revenue accepts that 'business' has a wider meaning than 'trade': managing a landed estate would, for instance, qualify as a business (see CG 65710), and in *Ramsay v R & C Comrs* (2013) the Upper Tribunal, overturning the First-tier Tribunal's decision (2012), held that 'the proper approach ... is to construe "business" broadly, according to its unvarnished ordinary meaning'. In that case the taxpayer who, together with her husband, owned a large house divided into flats and let out, spent about 20 hours per week attending to the building, cleaning the communal areas, forwarding post to tenants who no longer lived there, ensuring that the property was insured and complied with fire regulations and collected the rent. On a transfer of the property to a company in exchange for shares in the company, incorporation relief was claimed. The question that was required to be addressed was whether the activities of the taxpayer in relation to the property constituted a business. Agreeing with HMRC that the property was an investment not a business, the First-tier Tribunal concerned itself with the rather different question of whether the property activities were sufficient to be taxed as trading income (rather than property income) and whether the property would have attracted business property relief. The judge of the Upper Tribunal said that the findings of the First-tier Tribunal were based on an error or errors of law.

EXAMPLE 22.11

On the incorporation of a business in consideration for the issue of fully paid shares, there is a gain on business assets of £50,000. The market value of the shares is £150,000. The gain is rolled over by deducting it from the value of the shares so that the acquisition cost of the shares becomes £100,000 (£150,000 – £50,000). The assets are acquired by the company at market value of (say) £150,000.

Where only a part of the total consideration given by the company is in shares (the rest being in cash or debentures), only a corresponding part of the chargeable gain can be rolled forward and deducted from the value of the shares. That part is found by applying the formula:

$$\text{Gain rolled forward} = \text{total gain} \times \frac{\text{market value of shares}}{\text{total consideration for transfer}}$$

In practice, the assumption of liabilities by the company is not treated as consideration for this purpose (see CG 65745 and ESC D32).

EXAMPLE 22.12

A transfers his hotel business to Strong Ltd in return for £160,000, consisting of £10,000 shares (market value £120,000) and £40,000 cash. The chargeable business assets transferred are the premises (market value £130,000), the goodwill (market value £10,000) and furniture, fixtures etc (market value £20,000). On the premises and the goodwill A makes chargeable gains of £35,000 and £5,000 respectively.

$$£40,000 - \left(£40,000 \times \frac{£120,000}{£160,000}\right) = £40,000 - £30,000 = £10,000$$

and the acquisition cost of the shares is £120,000 − £30,000 = £90,000 (ie £9 per share).

Entrepreneurs' relief may be available on a subsequent disposal of the shares if the relevant conditions are satisfied (see **Chapter 20**). **[22.101]**

c) *Deferring tax on the sale of an unincorporated business*

If it is desired to sell an unincorporated business s 162 may be used to defer any CGT liability on the sale. The business is first incorporated and s 162 ensures that the vendors will not be subject to CGT until they dispose of their shares in that company. As the company acquires the business assets at market value, however (under TCGA 1992 s 17: see **[19.14]**), the trade can immediately be resold to the intended purchaser without any CGT charge (see *Gordon v IRC* (1991)). **[22.102]**

d) *Election to disapply the s 162 roll-over relief*

Arrangements may be structured so that roll-over relief is given on incorporation, but TCGA 1992 s 162A enables a taxpayer subsequently to opt out of this relief where a business is transferred after 5 April 2002. This provision was designed specifically to allow a taxpayer to preserve the benefits of taper relief. By comparing the same scenario, but with the transactions taking place at different times, the following example (which takes no account of the annual exempt amount) explains how valuable s 162A once was and why it may no longer be of any importance.

EXAMPLE 22.13

(1) Incorporation and subsequent sale of shares both occur before 6 April 2008
On 25 April 2007, B incorporates his trade as Y Ltd. He transfers all the assets of the business to the company in consideration for all the shares of Y Ltd. CGT incorporation relief applies.

Incorporation of business

Value of shares received in consideration		£1,500,000
Acquisition cost of assets used in the business (6 April 1998)	less	£200,000
Net chargeable gains on disposal of business assets (rolled-over into deemed acquisition cost of shares)		£1,300,000

On 20 May 2007, B receives an unexpected offer to sell his shares in Y Ltd.

Sale of shares

Consideration		£1,800,000
Acquisition cost of shares	£1,500,000	
less net chargeable gain rolled Over	£1,300,000	
	£200,000	
Deemed acquisition cost	less	£200,000
Gain chargeable to tax (after less than one year no taper relief: 100% of gain chargeable)		£1,600,000
CGT at 40%		**£640,000**

Instead, B elects on 31 October 2007 for incorporation relief not to apply. Therefore the two disposals above are recalculated as follows.

Transfer of unincorporated business

Value of shares received in Consideration		£1,500,000
Acquisition cost of assets of business (6 April 1998)	less	£200,000
Net chargeable gains on disposal of business assets		£1,300,000
Untapered gain chargeable to tax		£1,300,000
Gains chargeable (after two years business asset taper relief: 25% of gain chargeable)		£325,000

Sale of shares

Consideration		£1,800,000
Acquisition cost of shares	less	£1,500,000
Untapered gain chargeable to tax		£300,000
(after less than one year no taper relief: 100% of gain chargeable)		
Total gains chargeable to tax		£625,000
CGT at 40%		**£250,000**

(2) Incorporation occurs before 6 April 2008, and the sale of the shares after 6 April 2008
If, instead, B had incorporated his trade as Y Ltd in December 2007, and received an offer to sell his shares in Y Ltd in May, 2008, the result would be the same as in the first scenario, except that, provided all the conditions were satisfied, B could claim entrepreneurs' relief (see **Chapter 20**). Accordingly, B elects on 31 October 2008 for incorporation relief not to apply and, instead, for entrepreneurs' relief.

Transfer of unincorporated business

Value of shares received in Consideration		£1,500,000
Acquisition cost of assets of business (6 April 1998)	less	£200,000
Net chargeable gains on disposal		

of business assets		£1,300,000
Untapered gain chargeable to tax		£1,300,000
Gains chargeable (after two years, business asset taper relief: 25% of gain chargeable)		£325,000
CGT at 40%		£130,000
Sale of shares		
Consideration		£1,800,000
Acquisition cost of shares	less	£1,500,000
Gain chargeable to tax (taper relief abolished)		£300,000
Entrepreneurs' relief (reduces gain by 4/9)		£166,667
CGT at 10%		£16,667
Total CGT on incorporation and sale of shares		**£146,667**

(3) Both incorporation and the sale of the shares occur on or after 6 April 2008

Incorporation of business (May 2008)

Value of shares received in consideration		£1,500,000
Acquisition cost of assets used in the business (6 April 1998)	less	£200,000
Net chargeable gains on disposal of business assets (rolled-over into deemed acquisition cost of shares)		£1,300,000

Sale of shares (March 2015)

Consideration		£1,800,000
Acquisition cost of shares	£1,500,000	
less net chargeable gain rolled Over	£1,300,000	
Deemed acquisition cost	£200,000	
	less	£200,000
Gain chargeable to tax (taper relief abolished)		£1,600,000
Entrepreneurs' relief (limited to first £10,000,000 of gains)		£1,600,000
CGT: 10% x £1,600,000		£160,000
Total CGT		**£160,000**

Notes

(1) It can be seen that
   (a) In the transitional period, ie, where incorporation occurred prior to 6 April 2008, but the sale of the shares took place after that date, an election for incorporation roll-over relief not to apply, together with a further election for entrepreneurs' relief, minimises the CGT significantly. Tax planning on this basis will be restricted because of the time limits set for opting out of s 162 relief (see below).
   (b) If both incorporation and the sale of the shares occur after 6 April 2008, there will be no advantage in B electing for

incorporation roll-over relief not to apply. He should, however, elect for entrepreneurs' relief (if the conditions are satisfied – see **Chapter 20**).

(c) By comparing (1) and (3) above, it can be seen that the increase in entrepreneurs' relief to over its original £1m limit has made entrepreneurs' relief more beneficial than taper relief in these circumstances.

(2) The time limits for opting out of s 162 relief are as follows:
  (a) Generally, an election to disapply s 162 must be made by the second anniversary of the 31 January next following the year of assessment in which the transfer took place. For example, if the business was transferred in the year ending 5 April 2015, the election must therefore be made by 31 January 2018.
  (b) If all the shares acquired on incorporation have been disposed of before the end of the tax year following incorporation, the election must be made no later than 31 January following the end of the later tax year. (Hence, if incorporation was in 2014–15 and the sale occurred in 2015–16, the election has to be made at the latest on 31 January 2017).

(3) A claim for entrepreneurs' relief must be made on or before the first anniversary of the 31 January following the tax year in which the disposal for which relief is sought is made (TCGA 1992 s 169M(3)). Thus, in the third part of the example above, B would have to claim entrepreneurs' relief no later than 31 January 2017. [22.103]

9 Relief on company reconstructions, amalgamations and takeovers

The relief afforded by TCGA 1992 ss 135–137 in respect of 'paper for paper exchanges' is considered in **Chapter 47**. Worthy of note here, however, is the relevance of entrepreneurs' relief in the structuring of deferred consideration on company takeovers. For various reasons, the seller of shares on the takeover of a private company may take all or part of the price for the shares by way of deferred remuneration. The effect of taper relief was that the agreement would be structured to enable the seller to have the deferred remuneration satisfied by the issue of a loan note in order to defer the CGT charge. With the abolition of taper relief, the availability of entrepreneurs' relief may be equally important in the structuring of deferred consideration post 6 April 2008. Generally, whilst loan notes may still be the preferred option where the deferred consideration is ascertainable (subject to HMRC clearance under s 135), where the consideration is unascertainable (eg an earn-out), this may not be the case bearing in mind particularly that entrepreneurs' relief has now become a significant factor, with the maximum saving per individual being £1.8m. However, it is possible that the relief may have been used up in an earlier transaction or transactions, in which case loan notes may still have an important role in deferring the CGT charge. If there is a bonus or rights issue so that the existing shareholders are allotted shares or debentures in proportion to that existing holding, the new securities are treated as acquired when the original shares were acquired. The price for this combined holding will then be the sum originally paid for the original shares plus whatever is paid for the new securities (TCGA 1992 ss 127–130). However, if there is an election under TCGA 1992, s 169Q, a claim for entrepreneurs' relief can be made as if the re-organisation involved a disposal of the original shares, and s 127 will not apply (see **[26.2]**).

Altering the rights attached to a class of shares or the conversion of securities can similarly be achieved without an immediate charge to CGT (TCGA 1992 ss 133–135). **[22.104]**

23 CGT – the main residence

Updated by Jackie Anderson, Chartered Accountant and Chartered Tax Adviser, LHA Consulting Ltd

I   When is the exemption available? **[23.1]**
II Meaning of 'dwelling house' and 'residence' **[23.21]**
III How many residences can qualify for the exemption? **[23.42]**
IV Miscellaneous problems **[23.61]**
V   Effect of periods of absence **[23.81]**
VI Expenditure with a profit-making motive **[23.101]**
VII Second homes **[23.121]**
VIII Link up with IHT schemes **[23.141]**

I WHEN IS THE EXEMPTION AVAILABLE?

1 Introduction

'Private residence relief' is the most important exemption from CGT for the individual taxpayer, and one that probably affects more taxpayers than any other (TCGA 1992 ss 222–226). There is no similar relief for IHT purposes.

The CGT exemption is available for any gain arising on the gift or sale by a taxpayer of his only or main residence, including grounds of up to half a hectare (or such larger area as is required for the reasonable enjoyment of the dwelling house) (TCGA 1992 s 222). **[23.1]**

2 The new charge on non-residents and consequent changes to the conditions for relief

From 6 April 2015, all non-UK residents are taxable on gains realised on a disposal of UK residential property (the 'non-resident CGT' charge; FA 2015 s 37 and Sch 7). However, only the increase in value of the property since 6 April 2015 is subject to the charge. CGT did not apply to non-residents prior to the non-resident CGT charge, apart from (i) on those carrying on a trade in the UK and, (ii) on a company subject to the 'annual tax on enveloped dwellings' (ATED) charge. The extension of the CGT charge is intended to harmonise the UK system with other jurisdictions that charge tax on the basis of where the property is located rather than where the owner is resident (see generally **[27.43]**).

Necessary changes to private residence relief have been made to prevent non-residents with properties in and outside of the UK from avoiding a charge to CGT on the UK property (see **[23.43]–[23.60]** and **[23.81]–[23.100]**).

[23.2]–[23.20]

II MEANING OF 'DWELLING HOUSE' AND 'RESIDENCE'

1 Meaning of a 'dwelling house'

What qualifies as a dwelling house is a question of fact. In *Makins v Elson* (1977) the taxpayer bought land intending to build a house on it. In the meantime, he lived there in a caravan. He never built the house and later sold both land and caravan at a profit. On the facts, the caravan was held to be a dwelling house, the most significant of these facts being that it was connected to the mains services as well as to the telephone system and that it was resting on bricks so that it was not movable. In contrast, in *Moore v Thompson* (1986) the court held that since there was no supply of water or electricity, the caravan in question was not a dwelling house. [23.21]

2 'Residence': a degree of permanence

To qualify for the relief, the property must have been occupied by the taxpayer at some stage during his ownership as his only or main residence. Ownership *per se* is not sufficient; for example, a taxpayer may own property but may be trading in that property. In those circumstances, the property cannot be called a residence (see *Hartland v R & C Comrs* (2014)).

In this context, 'residence' is given its ordinary meaning although, as Millet LJ observed in *Goodwin v Curtis* (1998), 'the question whether occupation is sufficient to make *[the taxpayer]* resident is one of fact and degree of the commissioners to decide'. According to the First-tier Tribunal, for an individual 'this is the dwelling in which that person habitually lives; in other words, their home' (*Bradley v R & C Comrs* (2011); see also *Moore v R & C Comrs* (2010), *Benford v R & C Comrs* (2011), *Harte v R & C Comrs* (2011), *Kothari v R & C Comrs* (2016) and *Oliver v R & C Comrs* (2016)).

It follows, then, that although permanent residence is not a *condition* for the application of relief, a distinction has to be drawn between a permanent residence and temporary accommodation. In *Goodwin v Curtis* (1998), the taxpayer agreed to purchase (by way of sub-sale) a farmhouse from a company with which he was connected. The purchase by the company was completed on 7 March and the taxpayer put the property on the market at that time, only completing his purchase on 1 April. The taxpayer then occupied the property living there seven days a week and had a telephone connected. On 3 April, however, he completed the purchase of a small cottage to which he moved when he sold the farmhouse on 3 May 1985. The taxpayer paid £70,000 for the farmhouse and sold it for £177,000. The Court of Appeal confirmed the findings of the commissioners that relief was not available notwithstanding the taxpayer's occupation of the property. There was not the required 'degree of permanence, continuity and the expectation of continuity' (to use the language of Vinelott J in the High Court) for the occupation to amount to a residence. According to Millett LJ, the nature of the taxpayer's personal circumstances together with the size of the house indicated that his occupation was a 'stop gap measure' (in passing it may be suggested that size of the house should not be a factor of any significance: a single person should qualify for relief on an eight-bedroom mansion!). This case demonstrates that the intention of the taxpayer at the time of acquisition is central to the availability of the relief.

However, in *Regan v R & C Comrs* (2012), the First-tier Tribunal was of the view that the need for permanence or continuity should not be overstated and that the issue of whether a property is or has been a residence is a matter of fact that should be determined by reference to the quality (and not merely the length) of the occupation. In that case, a builder and his wife purchased house A in May 2000 and lived there until June 2003. In September 2002, they purchased house B, which was uninhabitable and upon which they worked for the next two years. A scheme of development by a family company required the demolition of house A and, needing somewhere to live, they purchased the house next door, house C. Whilst still living in house A, the taxpayers carried out work on house C to make it habitable – they replaced the kitchen and bathroom, installed gas central heating and double glazing, and decorated and laid carpets. They moved into house C in June 2003 and lived there until April 2004, at which time they moved into house B. After moving out of house C, they added an extension to it and eventually sold that house in August 2006. The issue in the case being whether house C was the *residence* of the taxpayers *at all*, somewhat surprisingly the First-tier Tribunal found that although the taxpayers always intended to move into house B when they could, that intention did not disqualify house C from being a residence. In view of the fact that the taxpayers were in occupation of house C for nine to ten months, it was more than a stop gap or temporary place of occupation. This case appears to depart from placing weight on the taxpayer's intention, moving to a notion of 'quality' of occupation.

It might have been expected that a similar decision would be reached in *Susan Bradley v R & C Comrs* (2013), but the First-tier Tribunal, in this case placing much reliance on *Goodwin v Curtis* and the taxpayer's intention, denied the PPR relief sought despite a clear difference in facts: the taxpayer had moved into a perfectly suitable home, took steps to make it more of a home and lived there from April 2008 to November 2008 without any intention of moving out unless the house should unexpectedly be sold. Nevertheless, the Tribunal decided that she did not occupy the property as her residence since she had already placed it on the market and, had somebody offered her the asking price, she would have sold it. The tribunal judge considered that she never intended to live permanently in the property; it was only ever going to be a temporary home and, therefore, it was never her residence. Similarly, in *Clarke v R & C Comrs* (2014) the extent and the substantial expense of the refurbishment of two houses purchased in succession, the short length of the period of ownership of those houses (11 and 17 months respectively), the fact that both houses were purchased with the aid of short-term loan finance, that no domestic rates had been paid, that gas bills indicated low consumption and no other utility bills were produced and that the taxpayer remained in occupation of her flat all amounted to the view that the houses had been purchased as investments to be sold on at a profit after each had been refurbished. Accordingly, the First-tier Tribunal held that PPR relief was not due.

Although once again based on intention, a different conclusion, and a somewhat surprising one, was reached in *David Morgan v R & C Comrs* (2013), in which case the taxpayer, in preparing to purchase a property where he intended to live when he and his fiancée were married, sold his own flat and moved in with his fiancée's family. Two weeks before the purchase, the relationship ended and the taxpayer went to live with his parents. He continued with the purchase of the property and moved in for two months, specifically to prepare the house for renting, after which he moved back to live with his parents. The property was let and eventually sold. HMRC argued that the quality of the taxpayer's occupation was insufficient because, at the time of moving in, he had already decided to let (and ultimately sell) it and, accordingly, his intention at the time of purchase could not have been to live there. Contrary to *Regan*, the Tribunal was of the view that it was not so much the quality of the occupation but, rather, intention that mattered. On the evidence, they believed that the taxpayer continued to hold out hope that the relationship with his ex-fiancée could be repaired and that the couple would live together in the property. Thus, despite the taxpayer's brief occupancy, the Tribunal allowed PPR relief in what they called this 'extremely finely balanced' case. It would appear that, with the exception of *Regan*, the intention of the taxpayer continues to be the paramount consideration. However, its application seems to have led to judgments that might be considered perverse.

Where, unlike in *Regan*, there is a clear intention to reside permanently in a dwelling house, relief will be available even if that intention is thwarted after only a brief period of occupation. In *Favell v R & C Comrs* (2010), the First-tier Tribunal suggested in an *obiter dictum* that proof of occupation for a mere seven months could amount to residence for the purpose of the relief. On the facts of that case, the taxpayer failed to discharge the burden of proof required to demonstrate occupation at any time during his ownership of the house in question and so the question did not arise. What is required is *an intention* for continuity of occupation.

In *Dutton-Forshaw v R & C Comrs* (2015), the First-tier Tribunal reiterated the need for 'some assumption of permanence, some degree of continuity and some expectation of continuity' to satisfy the requirement for 'residence' but, as in *Regan*, felt that the need for permanence or continuity should not be overstated. The Tribunal accepted that, although the property was occupied for only seven weeks, the taxpayer had moved into it in the hope of living there on a continuous basis and therefore there was some expectation of continuity albeit the possibility that the occupation might be cut short. In this case, great store was set by the taxpayer's application for a parking permit; since such applications were policed very carefully by the relevant local authority and action had been taken against people who had not been entirely truthful in their applications, the Tribunal concluded that the taxpayer would not have made an application for a parking permit in circumstances where he did not consider the property in question to be his residence. Clearly, then, even actual occupation for a reasonable period may be insufficient to attract the relief where no continuity of occupation is intended. Although in *Daniel Regan* (2013), the First-tier Tribunal held that temporary absences for the purpose of staying at another's house over Christmas or spending time in a property owned by the taxpayer's girlfriend did not disentitle the taxpayer to relief bearing in mind that he spent some nights each week in the property claimed as the main residence and it was the place to which his post was sent and where he kept his belongings.

That HMRC is targeting the availability of principal private residence relief (PPR) at all costs is demonstrated very clearly by the cases of *Anne Dickinson v R & C Comrs* (2013) (considered at [**23.61**]) and *Gibson v R & C Comrs* (2013). In the latter case, the taxpayer purchased a house in 2003 with the help of a mortgage and a significant loan from a friend and moved into the property about one month after purchase with the intention of renovating it and living there with his girlfriend. Following advice from an architect early in 2004 that it would be cheaper to demolish the existing house and rebuild rather than renovate, the existing house was duly demolished. Further funds were advanced by the taxpayer's friend to assist with the rebuilding costs, and the taxpayer moved into his girlfriend's house during construction. The house was completed in the summer of 2005, but by this time the taxpayer found it increasingly hard to finance the works and decided to sell the new house as soon as it was finished. He moved into the partially completed house for a few months prior to its sale, although the witness statements suggested that the house was at that stage barely habitable, and the property was put on the market shortly afterwards. The property was sold in February 2006. HMRC sought to deny relief on the basis that (i) the house that was purchased in 2003 was not the same 'dwelling house' (given its ordinary meaning under TCGA 1992 s 222(1)) as the property sold in 2006 and (ii) that the taxpayer had not occupied the property as his principal or main residence prior to sale. As to the *first* contention, although the First-tier Tribunal noted (and HMRC agreed) that if an existing dwelling house was fundamentally remodelled and renovated it would still be classified as the same dwelling house, the Tribunal Judge held that the words 'dwelling house', given their ordinary meaning, referred to the building itself rather than to the land and if one house is completely demolished and a new house is built in its place, then the new house is not the same 'dwelling house'. *Second*, whilst it was accepted that the original house had been the taxpayer's main residence and that, on construction of the new house, he did not have any other property that would so qualify, the Tribunal found that the taxpayer did not occupy the property as his principal or main residence. Drawing on the previous case law, including *Goodwin v Curtis*, the Tribunal highlighted the distinction between 'occupation' and 'residence' and asked whether the nature of the taxpayers' occupation had carried 'some assumption of permanence, some degree of continuity, some expectation of continuity to turn mere occupation into residence'. To answer this question, it was necessary to look not only at the length of occupation but also, and importantly, at the quality of the occupation. That the decision to sell was made before the taxpayer moved into the property in the late summer of 2005 together with the fact that the property was still in an unfinished state when the taxpayer moved in suggested that there was never any 'assumption of permanence' or 'expectation of continuity'. The decision in this case raises a number of important issues. *First*, in respect of the Tribunal's decision that the newly constructed house did not constitute the same 'dwelling house' as the original house, the Tribunal was of the view that the term 'dwelling house' referred only to the building itself rather than to the land upon which the dwelling was built together with the building. This seems to be at odds with the decision in *Makins v Elson* (1977) (see [**23.21**]), in which case it was decided that a caravan situated on the site on which a house was in the course of construction and in which the taxpayer and his family lived whilst building works were taking place was a dwelling house, emphasis being placed on the fact that it had become part of the land through its connection to the electricity, telephone and water supplies and because its wheels were not on the ground. Moreover, in reaching their decision on this issue, the Tribunal in *Gibson* relied on the dictionary definition of dwelling house, concluding that it meant the building itself. According to the Concise Oxford Dictionary, the term 'dwelling' means 'a house or other place of residence' and 'dwelling house' is 'a house used as a residence rather than for a business'. The Tribunal clearly took a literal approach to the term dwelling house, but in doing so seemed to overlook the established case law that has held that a dwelling can refer to more than one building, thus departing from a literal interpretation of the dictionary meaning of the term. *Second*, in considering the question of whether the taxpayer occupied the newly constructed house as his principal or main residence, the Tribunal paid little or no heed to the taxpayer's intention to live in the property when it was completed, such intention being supported by the fact that the taxpayer had no other residence at the relevant time. Again, this seems at odds with previously decided cases such as *Goodwin v Curtis, Susan Bradley v R & C Comrs* and *David Morgan v R & C Comrs* that laid emphasis on the taxpayer's intention. Instead, the Tribunal concentrated on the quality of the occupation and the fact that the taxpayer had been 'camping' in the newly built house for an unspecified period in the months before its sale, at a time before the building works had been completed, and in the knowledge that the property was to be sold upon completion.

In the recent case of *Paul Munford v R & C Comrs* (2017), HMRC challenged a private residence relief claim, but because a discovery assessment was made outside the normal time limits, the burden of proof as to whether the property had been occupied as his main residence moved from the taxpayer to HMRC, and HMRC could not discharge that burden. [23.22]

3 A 'residence': the entity test

So far as the term 'a residence' is concerned, a major problem is whether, in any given situation, two or more units can constitute a single residence. Selling a house with additional accommodation available either for staff or aged relatives is not unusual and there now exists a substantial body of case law, but from which no clear or satisfactory guidelines have emerged. In *Batey v Wakefield* (1982), the first in the series of cases, a separate bungalow within the grounds of the taxpayer's house and found by the General Commissioner as fact to have been used by a caretaker to enable him to perform the duties of his employment with the taxpayer, was considered by the Court of Appeal to be exempt from CGT on its sale. The court concluded that it was necessary to identify the entity that could properly be described as constituting the residence (the 'entity' test). Fox LJ commented:

> 'in the ordinary use of English, a dwelling house, or a residence, can comprise several dwellings which are not physically joined at all'.

In his view, the fact that the bungalow was physically separate from the main dwelling house was 'irrelevant'.

This was followed by Vinelott J in *Williams v Merrylees* (1987) who echoed the words of Fox LJ when he summarised the approach to be taken:

> 'what one is looking for is an entity which can be sensibly described as being a dwelling house though split into different buildings performing different functions.' **[23.23]**

4 The curtilage test

However, in *Markey v Sanders* (1987), Walton J, ignoring the entity test, indicated that two conditions had to be satisfied: *first*, that occupation of the 'secondary' building had to increase the taxpayer's enjoyment of the main house and, *second*, that the other building had to be 'very closely adjacent' to the main building. He decided that a staff bungalow some 130 metres distant from the main residence and standing in its own grounds did not satisfy the second of the two conditions and so could not be treated as part of a single residence, with the result that, on its disposal, CGT was chargeable.

The Court of Appeal had the opportunity to review these decisions in *Lewis v Rook* (1992) which concerned the sale of a cottage some 200 yards from the main house and which had been occupied by the taxpayer's gardener. Giving the judgment of the court, Balcombe LJ concluded that no building could form part of a dwelling house that included the main house unless the building was 'appurtenant to, and within the curtilage of the main house' (the 'curtilage' test). In applying what he believed to be 'well-recognised legal concepts' in the interpretation of the term 'dwelling house' or 'residence' and rejecting the previous approach of treating the matter as a question of fact, Balcombe LJ concluded that the main residence exemption was inapplicable.

It is a cause for concern that the word 'curtilage' appears nowhere in the CGT legislation, although in other contexts it has been held to mean 'a small area about a building', and that the court appears to be preferring the restrictive approach in *Markey v Sanders* to the flexibility of *Batey v Wakefield* and *Williams v Merrylees*.

Honour v Norris (1992) largely turned on its own facts with the judge rejecting as an 'affront to common sense' the suggestion that a number of separate flats in a square could constitute a single dwelling house.

Revenue thinking in this area was set out in RI 75 August 1994 where it is stated:

> 'Where more dispersed groups of buildings have a clear relationship with each other they will fall within a single curtilage if they constitute an integral whole. In the Leasehold Reform Act case of *Methuen-Campbell v Walters*, quoted with approval in *Lewis v Rook*, the Court held that "for one corporeal hereditament to fall within the curtilage of another, the former must be so intimately associated with the latter as to lead to the conclusion that the former in truth forms part and parcel of the latter". Whether one building is part and parcel of another will depend primarily on whether there is a close geographical relationship between them. Furthermore, because the test is to identify an integral whole, a wall or fence separating two buildings will normally be sufficient to establish that they are not within the same curtilage. Similarly, a public road or stretch of tidal water will set a limit to the curtilage of the building. Buildings which are within the curtilage of a main house

will normally pass automatically on a conveyance of that house without having to be specifically mentioned. There is a distinction between the curtilage of a main house and the curtilage of an estate as a whole and the fact that the whole estate may be contained within a single boundary does not mean that the buildings on the estate should be regarded as within the curtilage of a main house.' (See also CG 64245.)
[23.24]–[23.41]

III HOW MANY RESIDENCES CAN QUALIFY FOR THE EXEMPTION?

1 Spouses and civil partners

Spouses and civil partners (see generally [51.130]) can have only one main residence whilst they are living together (TCGA 1992 s 222(6); see *Benford v R & C Comrs* (2011) where despite protestations to the contrary by the taxpayer, the Tribunal found that the taxpayer was to be treated as living with his wife for CGT purposes and could thus claim relief for only one residence). For the operation of the election (which is considered below) when a couple marry or enter into a civil partnership, see CG 64525. [23.42]

2 Where the taxpayer has more than one residence

a) *General rule*

The question of whether a particular property is a taxpayer's only or main residence is sometimes a difficult one to answer. If only one property is occupied by him as a residence the exemption *prima facie* applies to that property. Where the taxpayer has two or more residences, only the residence which is his main residence can qualify for relief. Any problems that might arise in deciding which of two residences is the main residence are obviated since the taxpayer can elect for one to be treated as his main residence (TCGA 1992 s 222(5) as amended by FA 2015 Sch 9). Such an election is conclusive as to which residence is the main residence. Where a husband and wife made an election that determined which of the two residences was their main residence, HMRC were unable to argue that the residence was not the taxpayers' main residence (*Ellis v R & C Comrs* (2013)). Of course, the election is only available in respect of 'residences' and cannot be used to convert a dwelling house which is not in use as a residence into one for the purpose of obtaining relief. In *Harrison v R & C Comrs* (2015), the taxpayer was of the view that he could make an election where he owned and occupied two properties at the same time and he did so in respect of a large number of properties, which he referred to as his 'second homes'. The First-tier Tribunal held that any election under s 222(5) must be as between two *residences*; an election does not transform a property into an only or main residence. Accordingly, the first question that had to be answered was whether any of the properties subject to an election by the taxpayer was a residence. From the wealth of case law on the issue, the Tribunal was of the view that a residence was not a house, or indeed, a home that a person simply stays in from time to time and which necessarily lacks the degree of permanence, continuity or expectation of continuity that is required of a residence. Given that this described the taxpayer's occupation of his various properties, his claim for relief was rejected (see also *Harte v R & C Comrs* (2012) and CG 64465). The election can be backdated for up to two years to the date when the second residence was acquired and can be varied at any time, the variation also being effective for the two previous years. In *Griffin v Craig-Harvey* (1993), the taxpayer's argument that an election could be made at any time during the period of ownership of a dwelling house to take effect for a period of up to two years prior to the date of the notice, was rejected. Vinelott J held that an election could only be made within two years of the acquisition of a second or subsequent residence. This decision has practical implications for taxpayers owning more than one residence who may find themselves out of time to make the necessary election.

Failure to make an election means that the self-assessment return of the taxpayer has to resolve the question on the basis of the facts and this may be decided not simply by the periods of time spent in each residence. An election can and should be made if a taxpayer occupies a property as a residence under a tenancy agreement (but not under a licence, where the occupier has only a personal, and not a proprietary, interest) whilst at the same time owning a second property. Where the property that is not owned has no more than a negligible capital value on the open market, say, a weekly rented flat, the time limit for nominating one of those residences as the main residence is extended where the taxpayer was unaware that such a nomination could be made (see ESC D21). [23.43]

EXAMPLE 23.1

Barber, having owned and lived in a house in Spitalfields for many years, acquires a luxury flat on the Essex coast in June 2013. At the same time he puts the Spitalfields house up for sale. When the house is sold he intends to rent a *pied-à-terre* in London.

(1) By June 2015 he should have elected which of Spitalfields or the flat was his main residence in respect of the period from June 2013.

(2) For sales of property where exchange of contract took place before 6 April 2014, the last three years of ownership were ignored in applying the main residence exemption (s 223(1): see [**23.83**]) and so if Spitalfields was sold at any time up to 6 April 2014, an election by Barber for the flat to be his main residence would have been beneficial: the flat would be covered by the s 222 exemption and the house would also be exempt under the same provision since the last three years of ownership would be ignored under s 223(1). However, the reduction of the final period for which relief can be given from 36 months to 18 months where exchange of contract takes place on or after 6 April 2014 would mean that Barber would be liable to CGT (on an apportionment basis) on whichever property that was not subject to the election.

(3) When he acquires the rented property in London he will again have two residences and should therefore elect within two years for the Essex flat to be his main residence.

(4) If, instead of renting a property in London, he moves into job-related accommodation under a service-occupancy agreement, an election *cannot* be made and relief will remain available for the Essex flat. This is because his rights, which derive from the contract of service, are personal only and create no proprietary rights in his favour (for residences occupied under licence, see CG 64536).

b) *Changes following the non-resident CGT charge: FA 2015 s 7 and Sch 9*

Because the new non-resident CGT charge (see **[23.2]** and **[27.43]**) is subject to private residence relief, the rules for elections where an individual has more than one residence have had to be amended. Otherwise, without any change, non-residents with both UK residential property and property outside of the UK would be able to elect for the UK property to be their PPR and thereby avoid the new CGT charge on the sale of that property. The new rules will restrict the availability of PPR relief for both non-UK residents with property in the UK and UK residents with property located in another country. **[23.44]**

From 6 April 2015, any property owned by a UK or non-UK resident individual can qualify for PPR if it is located in a territory in which the individual, their spouse or civil partner is resident or, where it is located in a different territory, the individual meets the 'day count test' in relation to the residence.

In determining the residence status of an individual, the Statutory Residence Test (SRT –see **[27.17]**–**[27.40]**) will apply in the UK. For other territories an individual will be treated as resident there in a tax year if either:
(i) they are liable to tax in that territory for more than half the tax year by virtue of their residence or domicile; or
(ii) by applying the same tests of the UK SRT but by substituting the other territory for references to the UK, they would be resident there.

If the individual is not tax resident in the territory, the day count test applies so that the individual (or his spouse or civil partner) must spend at least 90 midnights in the property in the UK tax year (between them). Time spent in another property owned in the territory can also be applied towards the 90-day count so that the total days in all properties in the territory are aggregated. Where the individual owns the property for a part only of a tax year, the 90-day threshold in the day count test will be reduced pro-rata. **[23.45]**

As with the current rules, an individual has two years from the acquisition of the second property to make an election for PPR, provided that the new conditions are met for that property.

Where a previous election has been made in respect of a property but, from 6 April 2015, that property no longer qualifies for PPR because the residence and day count tests are not met, a new election for another property must be made, prior to 5 April 2017, to avoid PPR relief from being wasted. **[23.46]**

Where a claim for PPR is made by trustees or personal representatives in respect of properties occupied by beneficiaries and legatees respectively, the residence and day count tests are applied in respect of the individual in respect of whom the relief is being claimed. **[23.47]**

Although the new rules will have virtually no impact upon UK tax residents, who will continue to obtain PPR relief for their UK homes in the same way that they did prior to the 6 April 2015, a UK tax resident with a second home abroad must now satisfy the 90-day rule (unless they are also resident in the relevant territory) even if they have already elected for the second home overseas to be their main residence for the purposes of PPR relief. Moreover, an individual who retires abroad but keeps a home in the UK will be treated as entitled to PPR relief for the years spent in the UK, but will be subject to the 90-day rule thereafter for each tax year from 2015–16 (apart from the last 18 months of ownership – see [23.83]). [23.48]–[23.60]

IV MISCELLANEOUS PROBLEMS

1 Land used with the house

Land of up to half an hectare (or permitted larger area) is exempt only if it is being used for the taxpayer's own occupation and for the enjoyment of his residence. In *Longson v Baker* (2001), the court had to determine whether 7.56 hectares (18.6 acres) of land should be included with a sizeable farmhouse and stabling for the purpose of obtaining the relief. It was held that the test for deciding whether a larger area of land was 'required' for the reasonable enjoyment of the dwelling house was an objective one based on the facts. Accordingly, it followed that the particular requirements of the owner of the house (in the present case, the grazing of horses) were irrelevant. Evans-Lombe J commented as follows:

> 'In my judgment it cannot be correct that the dwelling house at a farm *requires* an area of land amounting to more than 18 acres in order to ensure its reasonable enjoyment as a residence, having regard to its size and character.
>
> I have come to the conclusion that it may have been desirable or convenient for the taxpayer to have a total area of 7.56 hectares to enjoy with the farm, but such an area is not in my judgment required for the reasonable enjoyment of the farm as a residence having regard to its size and character.'

(For a criticism of the case, see *Taxation*, 8 February 2001, p 429. The objective nature of the permitted area test has since been applied in *Hencke v R & C Comrs* (2006).)

It should be noted that the legislation as it relates to the *land* (in contrast to the *dwelling house*) refers to the position at the date of disposal. Thus, a gain made on a disposal of land will not be exempt if the residence has already been sold. In *Varty v Lynes* (1976) the taxpayer sold his house and part of the garden. Later he sold the remaining part of the garden with the benefit of planning permission. It was held that this second disposal was chargeable and the whole gain, including that which had accrued whilst the garden land was occupied by the taxpayer along with the house, was taxed. Had the taxpayer sold the garden before or at the same time as the house, any gain would have been exempt. Brightman J suggested that his construction of s 222(1)(b) created an anomaly in that 'if the taxpayer goes out of occupation of the dwelling house a month before he sells it, the exemption will be lost in respect of the garden'. However, the current Revenue practice as explained in CG 64387 is not to apply arguments based upon that *dictum*, so that contemporaneous sales of the house and the garden (even if for development) benefit from the exemption. Where land is sold but the dwelling house is retained, the same principle applies, namely, that the land must have been used for the enjoyment of the residence at the time of the disposal.

This is an issue that tends not to arise, but HMRC was of the view that it did so in *Anne Dickinson v R & C Comrs* (2013). In that case, the taxpayer owned a house with a large garden and grounds, including a tennis court. She sold part of the tennis court to Ilex Developments Limited, a company of which she was a director, for the development of four dwelling houses, payment of the consideration being deferred and payable by instalments on completion of the sale of each house. Having signed her part of the contract and assuming erroneously that contracts had been exchanged, the taxpayer gave the company permission to start on the groundwork for the development. Contracts were formally exchanged some seven weeks later. Believing that private residence relief was available, the sale of the land was not disclosed on the taxpayer's tax return. HMRC argued that the relief was not available because the land was under development on the date that contracts were exchanged and thus could no longer be regarded as garden or grounds at that date. The First-tier Tribunal, allowing the taxpayer's appeal, held that the fact of the company entering onto the land and starting the works did not constitute a disposal of the land at that time. This decision was explained on the basis that (i) the company was allowed onto the land to start foundation work on a purely informal basis; (ii) at any stage prior to formal exchange of contracts either party was at liberty to withdraw from the transaction; and (iii) in the event that the transaction did not progress to completion, it would be difficult to conclude that the land had temporarily ceased to be 'garden or grounds', only to then revert to its original status.

Where land is purchased, upon which a dwelling-house is subsequently built, any gain attributable to the land accruing on the subsequent disposal of the dwelling and/or land (provided the land is not disposed of after the dwelling) must be apportioned to take account of the time when the land alone could not have qualified as a 'principal private residence' (*Hencke v R & C Comrs* (2006)). Of course, the situation may be different if the owner of the land lived in, say, a caravan on the land during the construction of the dwelling.

What constitutes land for the enjoyment of a principal private residence was considered in *Wakeling v Pearce* (1995). In that case, the taxpayer had cultivated a garden and maintained a washing-line in a field which was separated from her residence by another property not owned by her. The use of the field declined over the years, but it continued in a reduced form until its eventual sale as two building plots. The Special Commissioner held that the field was enjoyed with the residence and that there was no statutory requirement that the land should adjoin or be contiguous with the residence. Following its decision not to appeal against this decision because of the particular circumstances of the taxpayer, the Revenue published its interpretation of the legislation (see CG 64360 and CG 64367). Attributing to the terms 'garden' and 'grounds' their normal, everyday meaning, the Revenue regards a garden as land devoted to cultivation of flowers, fruit or vegetables but that grounds cover 'enclosed land serving chiefly for ornament or recreation surrounding or attached to the dwelling house or other building'. So, where land surrounds the residence and both are in the same ownership, the land qualifies for relief unless it is used for other purposes such as trade or agriculture. Relief will not be lost by reason only of the fact that the land is not used exclusively for recreational purposes or if there is a building on the land, provided that it is not being used for business purposes. Where land is physically separated from the residence, relief cannot be claimed merely by reason of the fact that it is used as a garden and that the two are in common ownership; by the same token, mere separation is not by itself sufficient to deny relief.

The practice of the Revenue is to allow a claim in respect of land which can be shown to be 'naturally and traditionally the garden of the residence, so that it would normally be offered to a prospective purchaser as part of the residence'. The First-tier Tribunal considered the Revenue's interpretation of the legislation in *Fountain v R & C Comrs* (2015). The taxpayers in this case had been owners of a house and had used the area behind the house, comprising a workshop and parking area, for their haulage business. Following the closure of the business, some of the land was divided into five building plots. One of the plots (Plot 4) was retained by the Fountains and they built a new home on it. After moving into it, they sold their original home and subsequently sold another of the plots (Plot 2). The taxpayers claimed that plots 4 and 2 were formed from the gardens of their original residence and argued that Plot 2, which comprised an area of land with no direct access from the main residence and which appeared to have been covered by tarmac at the time of sale, should be subject to private residence relief since it had been used as a garden. In refusing relief, the First-tier Tribunal held that there was no clear evidence to demonstrate that it was being used as garden at the time it was sold; that using an area for 'domestic use and enjoyment' or for parking a caravan or storing building materials is not enough to constitute a 'garden'. Further, and importantly, whilst there are instances where HMRC will accept separation of the garden from the main residence (for example, the garden being across the road from the house), in this case the separation of Plot 2 from the Plot 4 was not one of them, the Tribunal noting that 'Plot 2 was separated from Plot 4 by Plot 3 (which at this point had a house built on it) ...'. [23.61]

EXAMPLE 23.2

(1) Bill is the owner of a village house that he purchased along with a small garden across the road from the residence. He later bought a further area of land upon which he built a tennis court. This land is separated from his house by the neighbouring property, and is reached by means of an informal path. Bill has recently sold all of his land, whilst retaining his residence.

It is common in villages for a garden to be across the road from the residence. If it can be shown that this was such a village, then Bill is entitled to relief under TCGA 1992 s 222(1)(b) for this part of his garden, even though separated from his residence, on the ground that it is a garden that would 'normally be offered to prospective purchasers as part of the residence'. The land upon which the tennis court stands is unlikely to qualify for relief. Although Bill may regard it as part of the garden, it was bought because the existing garden was inadequate for a tennis court, and could not be viewed as being 'naturally and traditionally' the garden of the residence.

(2) Assume that Sally owns a property with 7 hectares of land. It is accepted that some 6 hectares of the land does not attract the principal private residence relief and the relief is given on the land 'which, if the remainder were separately occupied, would be the most suitable for occupation and enjoyment with the residence' (see TCGA 1992 s 222(4)). Difficult valuation

issues may arise: for instance, the non-qualifying land may well have no permitted access. Is this a factor to be taken into account in apportioning the sale consideration if the whole property is sold? (See *Oates v R & C Comrs* (2014) for a discussion of whether development value should be apportioned between the house, which qualified for PPR relief, and the land, which did not, or attributed solely to the land.)

2 Houses held in trust

Where trustees dispose of a house that is the residence of a beneficiary who is entitled to occupy it by the terms of the settlement, private residence relief applies (TCGA 1992 s 225). (It does not matter that the beneficiary pays rent to the trustees or, indeed a one-off payment: see *Wagstaff v R & C Comrs* (2013).) Relief is only available where an actual claim is made by the trustees. Where trustees hold more than one residence for the benefit of the beneficiary, they must elect which residence is the main residence for the purpose of the relief (see **[23.47]**). *Sansom v Peay* (1976) decided that the section applied both where the relevant beneficiary enjoyed an interest in possession in the property and where the trust was discretionary so that occupation was entirely a matter for the discretion of the trustees. The decision in this case has repercussions for IHT since the Revenue will argue that the beneficiary in whose favour the discretion has been exercised thereby acquires an interest in possession in the settlement (see SP 10/79). **[23.62]**

EXAMPLE 23.3

'Westwinds' is held in trust for Julian for life remainder to his children on attaining 40. In exercise of their overriding powers the trustees advance £10 on trust for the children with separate trustees and then grant those trustees a reversionary lease over Westwinds to commence in ten years time when Julian will be aged 90.

Notes:
(i)   It is not considered that this arrangement creates reservation of benefit problems for IHT purposes. Although Julian makes a transfer of value he does not make a gift.
(ii) If the house were to be sold during Julian's life, it is considered that the trustees would benefit from the full principal private residence exemption (subject to a claim for it being made) albeit that Julian's residence was by virtue of the encumbered freehold interest. This is because the settlement is treated as a single composite settlement for CGT purposes and because the wording of s 225 merely requires occupation of trust property by a beneficiary as his main residence.

3 Use of a house for a business

If part of the house is used exclusively for business purposes, a proportionate part of the gain on a disposal of the property becomes chargeable (TCGA 1992 s 224). However, as long as no part is used *exclusively* for business purposes no part of the exemption will be lost.

Where a person cares for an adult under a local authority placement scheme, their contract with the local authority may require them to set aside one or more rooms exclusively for the use of the adult in care. F(No 3)A 2010 s 16 preserves private residence relief for such individuals who dispose of the property on or after 9 December 2009. **[23.63]**

4 Letting part of the property

Where the whole or part of the property has been let as residential accommodation, this may result in a partial loss of exemption. However, the gain attributable to the letting (calculated according to how much was let and for how long) will be exempt from CGT up to the lesser of £40,000 and the gain attributable to the owner's occupation. This relief does not apply if the let portion forms a separate dwelling (TCGA 1992 s 223(4)). The Revenue has stated that the taking of lodgers will not result in a loss of any of the exemption provided that the lodger lives as part of the family and shares living accommodation. 'Shared accommodation' in this context means any part of the property other than stairs, halls, passageways or storage space. Accordingly, while a tenant in a self-contained flat would not be considered to be sharing accommodation with the landlord, even someone who has most of their own facilities but shares a toilet would. Even if the occupier only shares accommodation with a member of the landlord's family, the arrangement will still be counted as a sharing one if the landlord himself also lives in the house.

In *Owen v Elliott* (1990) the taxpayer carried on the business of a private hotel or boarding house on premises which he also occupied as his main residence and argued that he was entitled to relief since taking in hotel guests amounted to 'residential accommodation'. The Court of Appeal accepted this and rejected the argument that the occupation had to be by persons making their home in the premises let as opposed to paying guests staying overnight or on holiday. Leggatt LJ stated that:

> 'The expression "residential accommodation" does not directly or by association mean premises likely to be occupied as a home. It means living accommodation, by contrast, for example, with office accommodation. I regard as wholly artificial attempts to distinguish between a letting by the owner and a letting to the occupant; and between letting to a lodger and letting to a guest in a boarding house; and between a letting that is likely to be used by the occupant as his home and one that is not.' **[23.64]**

EXAMPLE 23.4

A sells his house which he has owned for 20 years realising a gain of £120,000. He occupied the entire house during the first ten years. For the next six years he let one-third of it and for the final four years he let the entire property.

		£	£
Total gain			120,000
Less: exemption for owner-occupation			
(i)	10 years' occupation	60,000	
(ii)	6 years' occupation of 2/3		
	(£120,000 × 2/3 × 6/20)	24,000	
(iii)	final 18 months' ownership		
	(£120,000 × 1.5/20)	9,000	93,000

	£	£
Gain attributable to letting		27,000
Gain is chargeable only to the extent that it exceeds the lesser of (i) £40,000 and (ii) the exempt gain (ie £93,000). Thus,		
Chargeable portion		NIL

5 Disposals by PRs

The benefit of the PPR exemption is extended to PRs on their disposal (on or after 10 December 2003) of a private dwelling house which, both before and after the death, was the only or main residence of one or more individuals who, on the death of the testator, are entitled to 75% of the net proceeds of sale from the house, either absolutely or for life (TCGA 1992 s 225A: see **[21.104]**). The relief is only available where a claim for it is actually made by the personal representatives. Where there is more than one residence, the PRs must elect which residence is the main residence for the purpose of the relief (see **[23.47]**). **[23.65]**

6 Disposals by legatees

A spouse or civil partner who inherits a dwelling house on the death of the other spouse/civil partner also inherits the period of ownership of the other spouse/civil partner for the purpose of calculating the relief (TCGA 1992 s 222(7)(a); and see TCGA 1992 s 62). In other cases, the beneficial period of ownership begins on the date of death and, if the beneficiary does not become resident until a later date, the period prior to becoming resident will not qualify for relief (unless falling within the final 18-month period prior to disposal). **[23.66]–[23.80]**

V EFFECT OF PERIODS OF ABSENCE

1 General rule

To qualify for the exemption, the taxpayer must occupy the property as his only or main residence throughout the period of his ownership: for these purposes only the period of ownership after 31 March 1982 counts (TCGA 1992 s 223(7)). As a general rule, therefore, the effect of periods of absence is that on the disposal of the residence a proportion of any gain will be charged. That proportion is calculated by the formula:

$$\text{Total gain} \times \frac{\text{period of absence}}{\text{period of ownership}}$$

[23.81]

2 Spouses and same-sex couples

Special rules operate for spouses and same-sex couples who have entered into a civil partnership (see **[51.130]**) since, in deciding whether a house has been occupied as a main residence throughout the period of ownership, one spouse can take advantage of a period of ownership of the other (TCGA 1992 s 222(7)(a): see [21.104] for an illustration of this rule). [23.82]

3 Permitted absences

Despite the general rule that absences render part of the gain chargeable, certain permitted absences are ignored. These include, by concession, the first 12 months of ownership in cases where occupation was delayed because the house was being built or altered, or up to a period of two years where there are good reasons for exceptional delay (ESC D49). More important, the last 18 months of ownership are likewise ignored where exchange of contracts took place on or after 6 April 2014 (TCGA 1992 s 203(1) as amended; for exchange of contracts before that date, the applicable period is 36 months) and this may prove helpful on a matrimonial breakdown. It also means that a taxpayer owning two houses can, by careful use of his election, obtain a tax advantage, subject, of course, to the necessity of making the election within two years of the second or subsequent acquisition. The reduction of the final period for which relief can be given from 36 months to 18 months limits such tax advantage. [23.83]

EXAMPLE 23.5

Janet acquires a property in Raynes Park in June 2010 that she lets until June 2012. She then occupies the property as her main residence until selling it in April 2013. Because she has occupied the property as her residence there is no CGT charge on any gain arising during her final three years of ownership. If, however, Janet acquired the property in June 2013, let it until June 2015, and then occupied ii until it was sold in June 2016, only the final 18 months are ignored, meaning that a charge will arise in respect of part of the period during which the property was let (June 2013 until December 2014).

4 Periods allowed under s 223

TCGA 1992 s 223(3) allows other periods of absence to be ignored provided that the owner had no other residence available for the exemption during these periods and that as a matter of fact he resided in the house *before and after* the absence in question. These periods are:
(1) any period or periods of absence not exceeding three years altogether;
(2) any period when the taxpayer was employed abroad; and
(3) a maximum period of four years where the owner could not occupy the property because he was employed elsewhere.
The proviso for residing in the house before and after an absence does not require that it should be immediate. Note that the legislation does not specify any minimum period of occupation; it is the quality of the occupation as a residence that is important, and thus it must be more than merely temporary accommodation.

Under the new rules (see [23.44]–[23.60], non-residents must re-occupy the property for a minimum of 90 days. [23.84]

5 Absence because of employment

The Revenue accepts that if the absence exceeds the permitted period in (1)–(3) above, then it is only the excess which does not qualify for the exemption.

The requirement that the taxpayer should reside after the period of absence will not apply in (2) and (3) if that is prevented by the terms of his employment (TCGA 1992 s 223(3) as amended by SI 2009/730 and s 223(3A)). If he is required either by the nature of his employment or as the result of his trade or profession to live in another accommodation ('job-related accommodation') he will obtain the exemption if he buys a house intending to use it in the future as a main residence. It does not matter that he never occupies it and that it is let throughout, provided that he can show that he intended to live there. He should, of course, be advised to make the main residence election since he is occupying other (job-related) property (unless this occupation derives from his contract of service). [23.85]–[23.100]

VI EXPENDITURE WITH A PROFIT-MAKING MOTIVE

The principal private residence exemption does not apply if the house was acquired wholly or partly for the purpose of realising a gain, nor to a gain attributable to any expenditure that was incurred wholly or partly for the purpose of realising a gain (TCGA 1992 s 224(3)). The acquisition of a freehold reversion by a tenant with a view to selling an absolute title to the property would appear to fall within this provision. If so, the portion of the gain attributable to the reversion would be assessable. The Revenue has, however, indicated that expenditure incurred in obtaining planning permission or obtaining the release of a restrictive covenant would be ignored for the purpose of s 224(3). The requirement of motive makes this provision difficult to apply, but the Revenue view is that only where the *primary purpose* of the acquisition was an early disposal at a profit will it be invoked. In *Jones v Wilcock* (1996) the taxpayer and his wife had lived in their home for nearly five years. In trying to establish an allowable loss, he argued that the exemption should not apply since he had acquired his home with the object of selling it at a profit. The Special Commissioner rejected this argument, saying that the word 'intention' did not always equate with 'purpose' and that the taxpayer had bought the property in order to provide himself and his wife with a home. An eventual gain was a hope, possibly an expectation, but it was not a 'purpose' within s 224(3). [23.101]–[23.120]

VII SECOND HOMES

Principal private residence relief is not available on second homes and taxpayers will commonly find that on the disposal of such properties a substantial chargeable gain is produced. It is not possible for husband and wife to have separate main residences and the Revenue will resist any suggestions that a minor child has acquired a main residence separate from his parents. Where the taxpayer has more than one home, an election should be made by him to determine which is the principal private residence for the purposes of the relief (see **[23.43]–[23.60]**). Further, by virtue of FA 2004, principal private residence relief is no longer available for disposals on or after the 10 December 2003 if the gain includes a gain that was held over on one or more previous disposals, for example, on the house being transferred into trust (TCGA 1992 s 226A). **[23.121]**

If the relief is not available, FA 2016 provides that gains realised on a disposal of UK residential property are subject to the 18% and 28% charge to CGT (despite the general reduction in the rates to 10% and 20% respectively for other gains realised on or after 6 April 2016). Moreover, it was announced in the Autumn Statement 2015 that, from 6 April 2019, the CGT due on such a disposal (and this includes overseas properties) will be payable within 30 days from completion of the disposal. This should be compared with the current position, when the payment date is between 10 and 22 months from the date of disposal. **[23.122]**

Since 6 September 2013, the affairs of those who have sold properties in the UK or abroad that are not their main residence (ie second homes), but who did not inform HMRC of this by 6 September 2013, and who appear to have paid no CGT, will be scrutinised by HMRC. **[23.123]–[23.140]**

VIII LINK UP WITH IHT SCHEMES

A number of arrangements have been entered into in recent years with a view to mitigating IHT on main residences. For instance:

(i) *'Ingram arrangements'* Under these arrangements the taxpayer reserved a lease for (say) 20 years and gifted the freehold interest to his children.

(ii) *Reversionary leases*: In practical terms a similar arrangement to (i) but conceptually quite distinct. The taxpayer grants a long lease (commonly 999 years) to his children to take effect in (say) 21 years. He continues to occupy the property as a result of his retained freehold interest.

(iii) On the death of Mr H his will provides for the IHT nil rate sum to be held on discretionary trusts with the residue passing to Mrs H (his wife). Mr H's share in the main residence (he will frequently be a tenant in common as to a 50% beneficial share) will often be held by the trustees of the nil rate trust. Because of the ability to transfer to the surviving spouse any unused part of the deceased spouse's nil rate band (see **[51.74]**), this arrangement will no longer be necessary.

In these cases, whilst IHT saving is the goal, it is important that the arrangements do not ignore any potential CGT liability. Thus, if in due course the property will be sold (typically by the children on the death of the parents), then in all these cases there is likely to be a chargeable gain given that the children will not acquire the property for market value on the death of their parents. There is, therefore, a risk that IHT savings will be offset (at least in part) by subsequent CGT liabilities. **[23.141]**

24 CGT – gifts and sales at an undervalue

Updated by Jackie Anderson, Chartered Accountant and Chartered Tax Adviser, LHA Consulting Ltd

I   Introduction [24.2]
II Gifts of business assets [24.4]
III Gifts of assets attracting an immediate IHT charge [24.22]
IV Disposals from accumulation and maintenance trusts and children's trusts [24.27]
V   Miscellaneous cases [24.28]
VI Payment of CGT [24.29]

'Mr Turner has really argued his case on broader lines than I have so far indicated, and has used language, though moderate and reasonably temperate, as to the ways of Parliament in misusing language and in effect "deeming" him into a position which on any ordinary use of the words "capital gains" was impossible to assert. He in effect says "Here is a discreditable manipulation of words. The Statute is not truthful. Words ought to mean what they say".'
(Russell LJ in *Turner v Follett* (1973) 48 TC 614 at 621.)

[24.1]

I INTRODUCTION

1 A gift as a disposal at market value

Generally speaking, the disposal of an asset 'otherwise than by way of a bargain made at arm's length' is treated for CGT purposes as made for consideration equal to the market value of the asset (Taxation of Chargeable Gains Act 1992 (TCGA 1992) s 17(1)(a)).

A disposal 'otherwise than by way of a bargain made at arm's length' is made where an asset is gifted, or is sold for consideration less than market value. A disposal between 'connected persons' (see TCGA 1992 s 286 and [19.15]) is always treated as a transaction made 'otherwise than by way of a bargain made at arm's length' (TCGA 1992 s 18(2)).

The donor (or transferor) is, therefore, deemed to receive the market value of the asset that he has given away, even where he has in fact received nothing (*Turner v Follett* (1973)), and the donee (or transferee) is similarly deemed to have paid market value, even where he has paid nothing.

EXAMPLE 24.1

Jackson sells a valuable Ming vase to his son Pollock for £10,000 which is the price that he had paid for it ten years before. The market value of the vase at the date of sale is £45,000. This disposal between connected persons is deemed to be made otherwise than by way of bargain at arm's length so that market value is substituted for the price actually paid and Jackson is deemed to have received £45,000. Pollock is treated as acquiring the vase for a cost price of £45,000.

One of the main exceptions to the market value rule is for disposals between spouses (and civil partners) living together, which are automatically deemed to take place on a 'no gain, no loss' basis (TCGA 1992 s 58 and see [51.58]). CGT relief is also given automatically for certain gifts, including gifts to charities and Community Amateur Sports Clubs (CASCs). [24.2]

2 IHT consequences

In addition to being treated as a disposal at market value for CGT purposes, a gift of assets may be chargeable (or potentially chargeable) to IHT. IHT is not normally taken into account in calculating the liability to CGT, but limited relief is available against this potential double tax charge.

First, in calculating the fall in value of the transferor's estate for IHT purposes, any CGT liability is ignored. IHT is not, therefore, charged on CGT paid by a donor (see [28.63]).

Second, if the CGT is paid not by the transferor but by the transferee, the value transferred for IHT purposes will be reduced by that amount (Inheritance Tax Act 1984 (IHTA 1984), s 165). Note that CGT is payable by the transferor but there is nothing to stop the transferee from agreeing to discharge the burden instead.

On a subsequent disposal by the transferee, any IHT paid on the gift (including, for example, IHT which subsequently became chargeable in relation to a PET) may be deducted in calculating the chargeable gain in certain circumstances, but not so as to turn a gain into a capital loss (TCGA 1992 s 165(10)).

EXAMPLE 24.2

Mr Big transfers a freehold office block to his daughter Martha Big. Assume that the value of the freehold (ignoring IHT business property relief) is £750,000 and that the CGT amounts to £250,000.
(1) If the CGT is paid by Mr Big the diminution in his estate for IHT purposes is £750,000 (ie it is *not* £750,000 + £250,000).
(2) If the CGT is paid by Martha the diminution in Mr Big's estate is reduced to £500,000 (ie £750,000 − £250,000). [24.3]

II GIFTS OF BUSINESS ASSETS (TCGA 1992 S 165)

A claim under TCGA 1992 s 165 acts to reduce both the transferor's chargeable gain arising on the gift (or transfer at undervalue), and the consideration for which the transferee is deemed to have acquired the asset. [24.4]

1 When does TCGA 1992 s 165 apply?

There must be: (i) a disposal by an individual (the transferor), (ii) of a 'business asset', (iii) 'otherwise than under a bargain at arm's length' – which includes both gifts and undervalue sales.

In general, the recipient can be any 'person' – including individuals, trustees and companies. However, relief is not available when shares or securities are transferred to a company (s 165(3)(ba)). Note that all other business assets attract the relief if gifted to a company. **[24.5]**

2 What property is included?

The section is limited to the gift (or transfer at undervalue) of 'business assets', defined as follows (s 165(2)):

'an asset is within this sub-section if –
(a) it is, or is an interest in, an asset used for the purposes of a trade, profession or vocation carried on by –
    (i)   the transferor, or
    (ii) his personal company, or
    (iii) a member of a trading group of which the holding company is his personal company,
or
(b) it consists of shares or securities of a trading company, or of the holding company of a trading group, where –
    (i)   the shares or securities are not listed on a recognised stock exchange, or
    (ii) the trading company or holding company is the transferor's personal company.'

Accordingly, under s 165(2)(b)(i), AIM shares can benefit from the relief (as they are not 'listed' for these purposes). **[24.6]**

a) Which assets qualify?

It should be noted that *any* asset is included provided only that it is used for the purposes of a trade, profession or vocation. (This can be contrasted with roll-over reinvestment relief (see **[22.72]**) which is limited to certain categories of asset). A mere disposal of an asset suffices: it is not necessary for the disposal to be of (part of) the business. The availability of s 165 hold-over relief in such circumstances could have particular significance given that relief from IHT may also be available in relation to the transfer of individual assets of a business, following the decision in *Trustees of the Nelson Dance Family Settlement v R & C Comrs* (2009) (see **[31.43]**).

Non-business assets do not attract relief. Similarly, if the assets disposed of are shares, the amount of the gain eligible for hold-over relief may be restricted if the company owns chargeable assets other than business assets. However, this restriction only applies if the company is the transferor's personal company (ie he owns at least 5% of the voting rights), or if at any time in the previous 12 months the trustees making the disposal had at least 25% of the voting rights. Where the restriction applies the proportion of the gain eligible for the relief is the proportion which the market value of the company's business assets bears to the market value of the company's total chargeable assets (TCGA 1992 Sch 7 para 7). **[24.7]**

b) *Used for the purposes of a trade*

Whether an asset is used for the purposes of a trade may be a moot point: for instance, would the relief be available on a gift of a valuable oil painting (*The Sick Corpse*) which has adorned the offices of a funeral parlour for many years?

Where the asset has been used for a trade for only part of the period of ownership or, in the case of a building, where only part of the building has been used for a trade, the gain eligible for the relief is, in each case, reduced proportionately (TCGA 1992 Sch 7 paras 5 and 6). **[24.8]**

c) *Agricultural Property Relief (APR) land*

Land qualifying (or which would qualify on a chargeable transfer being made) for APR for IHT purposes is specifically included as a business asset for CGT purposes (TCGA 1992 Sch 7 para 1) – for more on APR see **[31.62]**). Accordingly, land that is let may qualify for the relief. Unlike IHT relief for agricultural land, hold-over relief is not restricted to the agricultural value of the land.

EXAMPLE 24.3

The lease of agricultural land was owned by the trustees of the Milford Grandchildren's Trust, established in 1992. In February 2006, Debbie became entitled to an interest in possession in the entire trust fund. In December 2012, the trust ended.

For IHT purposes, the ending of the trust in December 2012 was not an occasion of charge (see IHTA 1984 s 53(2)).

For CGT purposes, the ending of the trust resulted in a deemed disposal under TCGA 1992 s 71 (see **[25.47]**), but hold-over relief under s 165 *would not have been available* because the land would not attract APR. Although the land was owned by the trustees for more than the seven years required by IHTA 1984 s 117 (where land is owned but not occupied by the transferor), in February 2006 – when Debbie became entitled to an interest in possession – a new IHT ownership period began and, of course, *she* had owned the land for less than seven years.

However, as a result of the changes to the IHT treatment of trusts introduced by FA 2006 the acquisition of an interest in possession in most trusts *after* 21 March 2006 will not now trigger a new ownership period for IHT. Accordingly, had Debbie become entitled to an interest in possession in the trust fund in, say, April 2006, s 165 relief may have been available. **[24.9]**

d) *Meaning of 'personal company' and 'trading company'*

A 'personal company' is of particular relevance in the case of the disposal of an asset rather than shares. (Most disposals of shares that qualify for the relief will do so simply by virtue of being unlisted shares). An individual's 'personal company' is defined as one in which the individual holds at least 5% of the voting rights (TCGA 1992 s 165(8)(a)). 'Trading company' has the same meaning as it used to have for taper relief (see **[20.53]**). The expression, now separately defined in TCGA 1992 s 165A, means 'a company carrying on trading activities whose activities do not include to a substantial extent activities other than trading activities'. 'Trading activities' is then defined and extends to include activities preparatory to carrying on a trade and the acquisition of an interest in a company that becomes a trading subsidiary. **[24.10]**

e) *Trustees*

These definitions and requirements are modified in the case of business assets owned by trustees. Broadly, in the case of assets, the relevant 'trade, profession or vocation' must be carried on either by the trustees or by a beneficiary with an interest in possession in the settled property immediately before the disposal. Further, the definition of a 'personal company' requires the trustees to hold at least 25% of the voting power. **[24.11]**

3 The election

Hold-over relief under s 165 will only be given on a claim being made in the prescribed form by both transferor and transferee (save where the transferee is a trustee, when only the transferor need elect) (s 165(1)). The donor is treated as disposing and the donee as acquiring the asset for its market value at the date of the gift *minus* the chargeable gain which is held-over. This postponement of tax continues until the donee disposes of the asset (although, if the donee in turn makes a gift of the asset, a further hold-over election may be available). In the event of an individual donee dying still owning the asset, the entire gain is wiped out by the death uplift in value.

Since the election is to hold-over a gain which would otherwise be chargeable, in principle it is necessary to agree the amount of that gain with HMRC so that the election should be accompanied by relevant valuations. In SP 8/92, however, the Inland Revenue published a revised statement of practice whereby computation of the gain (and hence a formal valuation of the asset) is in many cases not required. Both transferor and transferee must request this treatment in writing and provide full details of the asset transferred (the date of its acquisition and the allowable expenditure) or, alternatively, a calculation of the gain based on informally estimated valuations. Once such a request has been accepted it cannot subsequently be withdrawn. In the majority of cases, taxpayers will be only too happy to avoid the time and trouble (not to mention the expense) involved in agreeing valuations with HMRC.

EXAMPLE 24.4

(1) Sim gives his ironmonger's business to his son, Sammy. For CGT purposes any gain resulting from this gift of chargeable business assets may be held-over under s 165 on the joint election of Sim and Sammy.

(2) Jim settles his ironmonger's business on trust for his son, Jack, absolutely contingent on becoming 30 (Jack is aged 10). As in (1) above, s 165 will apply; however, in this case only Jim need elect. When the trust ends, eg on Jack becoming absolutely entitled to the business, a further hold-over election may then be made under s 165 by the trustees and Jack to postpone payment of tax which would otherwise arise under TCGA 1992 s 71.

(3) Oliver is the sole shareholder and director of an unlisted trading company (ACC Ltd) and owns the freehold site used by the company. He gives away

his shares to his four daughters equally and the freehold to his son. Section 165 relief is available to postpone tax on all five gifts. The gift of the freehold qualifies for the relief because ACC Ltd is Oliver's personal company.

When the election is made, then under s 165(4):

'(a) the amount of any chargeable gain which, apart from this section, would accrue to the transferor on the disposal, and
(b) the amount of the consideration for which, apart from this section, the transferee would be regarded for the purposes of capital gains tax as having acquired the asset or, as the case may be, the shares or securities,
shall each be reduced by an amount equal to the held-over gain on the disposal.'

EXAMPLE 24.5

Smiley gives Karl shares in his family company worth £35,000. Smiley's allowable expenditure (his acquisition cost) for CGT purposes is £10,000. They make a joint election under s 165 so that Smiley's chargeable gain (£35,000 – £10,000 = £25,000) is reduced to nil. Smiley is effectively treated as disposing of the shares for £10,000 and, as his allowable expenditure is £10,000, he has made neither a gain nor a loss. Karl is treated as acquiring the shares for the market value consideration (£35,000) less the held-over gain (£25,000) ie for £10,000.

If, within 12 months of the gift, Karl sells the shares for £41,000 – incurring deductible expenses of £2,000 - he will be assessed to CGT on a gain calculated as follows:

	£	£
Sale proceeds		41,000
Less:		
Acquisition costs	10,000	
Deductible expenses	2,000	
		12,000
Chargeable gain		£29,000

Notes:
(1) Of this gain, £4,000 is attributable to Karl's period of ownership (£29,000 – £25,000) and £25,000 represents the gain held-over on the gift from Smiley. The whole gain is chargeable on Karl.
(2) If the sale by Karl took place before 6 April 2008, Karl's deemed acquisition costs would include the value of Smiley's indexation allowance until April 1998 (if any), but any taper relief built up by Smiley would be lost. Both taper relief and the pre-1998 indexation allowance were abolished by FA 2008 for disposals on or after 6 April 2008 (see generally **Chapter 20** and [**24.13**]).

No time limit for making this election is prescribed in the section and hence the general rule laid down in TMA 1970 s 43 applies. For claims made up to 31 March 2010, the claim must be made within five years from 31 January in the tax year following that in which the disposal occurred (ie a period of some five years and ten months). For claims from 1 April 2010, under FA 2008 the claim must be made within four years from the end of the tax year in which the disposal occurred. There is a standard claim form which *must* be used in all cases (although photocopies of the form will be accepted). [**24.12**]

4 The effect of taper relief on disposals pre-6 April 2008

For disposals taking place up to 5 April 2008, taper relief reduced the amount of gain on which tax was charged; it did not affect the calculation of the gain itself. By contrast, indexation relief (which taper relief replaced) operated as a further deduction in computing the gain. This contrast was significant when calculating the gain under a pre-6 April 2008 disposal that was to be held-over under either s 165 or s 260. In contrast to the position with indexation relief, the donee under such a disposal received no credit for the accrued taper relief of the donor; his taper relief (if any) was calculated by reference only to the period for which he personally owned the asset. [24.13]

5 The interaction of entrepreneurs' relief and hold-over relief

Entrepreneurs' relief was introduced by FA 2008 primarily to reduce the effective rate of CGT from 18% to 10% on the first £1,000,000 of gains made by individuals and trustees selling a business, business assets or shares in a trading company (see **Chapter 20**). However, the relief (now available on the first £10,000,000 of gains made on disposals on or after 6 April 2011) applies to any 'qualifying business disposal' and therefore operates also to gifts (or sales at an undervalue) of such assets, as well as to ordinary arm's length sales. Indeed, it is noteworthy that the key expression 'trading company', and the associated expressions 'holding company' and 'trading group', are defined for the purposes of entrepreneurs' relief in exactly the same way as they are for hold-over relief. The definitions in TCGA 1992 s 165A apply to both reliefs.

For disposals on and after 24 June 2010, entrepreneurs' relief operates by simply applying a reduced 10% rate to gains arising from 'qualifying business disposals'. However, for disposals up to 23 June 2010 the reduced rate was instead achieved by reducing the chargeable gain which accrued to the taxpayer by 4/9 ths and then applying the usual flat CGT rate of 18%. This meant that if a hold-over election was also made the held-over gain was likewise reduced and this had an effect on the donee's acquisition cost.

EXAMPLE 24.6

In May 2010, James settled 10% of the shares in his family trading company on his adult children and the market value of the holding was agreed with HMRC at £1,500,000. The allowable expenditure (acquisition cost) was £600,000. James elected for both entrepreneurs' relief and hold-over relief. The effect of the claim for entrepreneurs' relief was as follows:

	£	
Market value of shares on disposal	1,500,000	
Less acquisition cost	(600,000)	
Gain	900,000	
Reduced by entrepreneurs' relief (4/9)	(400,000)	
James's chargeable gain	500,000	(which if taxed at 18% would have resulted in CGT of £90,000)

Because entrepreneurs' relief has been claimed £500,000 is the chargeable gain which accrues to James. The hold-over election means that this is the amount – not £900,000 – by which the market value (£1,500,000) is reduced for the purpose of ascertaining the trustees' acquisition cost, which will accordingly be £1,000,000 (£1,500,000 – £500,000), not £600,000 (£1,500,000 – £900,000). By claiming both hold-over relief and entrepreneurs' relief James has given the trustees a higher base cost than would have applied if he had elected just for hold-over relief. He has, however, used up 90% of his then £1 million lifetime allowance for entrepreneurs' relief.

Now that 'qualifying business disposals' (up to the new £10 million limit) attract their own CGT rate of 10% with effect from 24 June 2010, the hold-over position is different. If in the above *Example* the shares were settled in March 2014 James would not be able to use entrepreneurs' relief as a way of giving the trustees a higher base cost than £600,000. The effect of an election for entrepreneurs' relief now would be just that James would have a CGT liability of £90,000. The trustees' acquisition cost would be £1,500,000, and the chargeable gain £900,000, in the normal way. If, in the alternative, James were to make a hold-over election he would avoid the personal CGT liability and the trustees' base cost would be £600,000. Because entrepreneurs' relief no longer works by reducing the taxpayer's chargeable gain, the scope no longer exists for combining an election under TCGA 1992 s 169M with a hold-over election so as to give rise to a higher base cost for the trustees.
[24.14]

6 The annual exemption

The legislation does not permit the CGT annual exemption (see [19.50]) to be combined with an election under TCGA 1992 s 165 – in other words, it is not possible to set off the annual exemption against part of a chargeable gain and apply hold-over relief to the balance. Either the whole chargeable gain must be held-over or it must be subject to CGT but with the benefit of the annual exemption. Where any gain will not exceed the annual exemption, the s 165 election should not be made (so as to maximise the transferee's base cost); and even if the gain just exceeds the exemption it may be preferable to pay a small CGT charge. In appropriate cases it may be preferable to obtain the best of both worlds by making two disposals, the first of an asset where the gain is covered by the annual exemption, and the second of other business assets where hold-over relief under s 165 is claimed. [24.15]

7 Sales at undervalue

Although s 165 applies both to gifts and sales at undervalue, the excess of any actual consideration paid on a disposal over the allowable CGT deductions of the transferor is subject to charge. It is only the balance of any gain (ie the amount by which the consideration is less than the full value of the business asset) which may be held-over under s 165.

EXAMPLE 24.7

Julius sells shares in his family company worth £25,000 to his brother Jason for £16,500. Julius has allowable deductions for CGT purposes of £11,500. The CGT position is:
(1) Total gain on disposal: £25,000 – £11,500 = £13,500.
(2) Excess of actual consideration over allowable deductions:
£16,500 – £11,500 = £5,000.
(3) Gain subject to CGT ((2) above) is £5,000. After deducting Julius' annual exemption the tax payable will be nil.
(4) Balance of gain, £8,500 (ie (1) – (2)) can be held-over under s 165.

If the partial consideration is less than the allowable deductions it is ignored so that a CGT loss cannot be created.

EXAMPLE 24.8

Assume in *Example 24.7* that the sale price was £11,500 and that the allowable deductions were £16,500 instead of the other way around. The total gain of £8,500 could be held-over under s 165. The sale price of £11,500 would be ignored: Julius would not have made a loss for CGT even though he sold the shares for an amount less than his allowable deductions; and Jason's initial base cost would still be £16,500 (market value less held-over gain) and would be unaffected by the actual consideration paid by him. **[24.16]**

8 The effect of IHT on hold-over relief

Some of the interaction between CGT and IHT in the context of lifetime gifts and gratuitous undervalue transfers has already been noted at **[24.3]**.

When chargeable gains are held-over under s 165 the transferee can add to his CGT acquisition cost all or part of any IHT paid on the lifetime chargeable transfer (s 165(10)). This principle applies whether the transferor or the transferee pays the IHT.

EXAMPLE 24.9

Wendy gives shares in her family cookery company ('Cook-Inn & Co') worth £175,000 to her daughter, Kim. The chargeable gain arising of £100,000 is held-over under s 165 and Kim therefore acquires the shares at an acquisition cost for CGT of £75,000. For IHT purposes the gift by Wendy is a PET when made and therefore no tax is payable at that stage. Assume, however, that Wendy dies within seven years so that the gift then becomes chargeable and that IHT of £20,000 is paid. Kim can add that sum to her acquisition cost for CGT purposes which therefore becomes £95,000 (£75,000 + £20,000).
Notes:
(1) A similar principle applies in the case of lifetime gifts which are subject to an immediate IHT charge. The IHT payable on the lifetime chargeable transfer, including the increased amount payable if the transferor dies within the following seven years, can be added to the transferee's base cost for CGT.
(2) It may be that Kim has already disposed of the shares before the death of her mother. Nevertheless, she is entitled to have her allowable expenditure increased by the IHT resulting from Wendy's death and therefore an adjustment will be made to any CGT paid on the disposal of the shares.

There are two limits on the amount of IHT that can be added to the donee's CGT acquisition cost under s 165(10).

First, the maximum amount permissible is the IHT 'attributable to the value of the asset'. This means that if IHT had been paid by the transferor on a chargeable lifetime gift so that 'grossing-up' applied, it is only the IHT charged on the value of the gift received by the donee which can be used (grossing-up is discussed at **[28.124]**).

Second, IHT which is added to the transferee's acquisition cost cannot be used to create a CGT loss on a later disposal by the transferee. Accordingly, in *Example 24.9* above, if Kim were to sell the shares after the death of Wendy for £90,000 she would only be able to use £15,000 of the IHT payable on Wendy's death since this would be sufficient to wipe out the chargeable gain. She could not use the remaining £5,000 to create a CGT loss. **[24.17]**

9 Non-UK residents

a) *Individuals*

Section 165 hold-over relief is not available if the transferee is an individual who is not resident in the UK (TCGA 1992 s 166). This limitation is necessary since disposals by such a person are outside of the CGT net! In addition, any held-over gain will be triggered if, whilst still owning the asset in question, the transferee emigrates before six complete tax years have expired after the tax year of the disposal to him (TCGA 1992 s 168).

EXAMPLE 24.10

In May 2010, Imelda's father gave her shares in the family trading company. A gain of £80,000 was held-over so that she had an acquisition cost of £10,000. In February 2017 she took up permanent residence in Spain. The held-over gain of £80,000 becomes chargeable 'immediately before' she ceased to be UK resident at the rates in force in the tax year of emigration.

If the shares had increased in value to £130,000 by 2017, there is no question of charging that increase which is attributable to her own period of ownership; any loss would likewise be ignored.

The CGT in such cases is payable primarily by the transferee, but if tax remains unpaid 12 months after the due date it can be recovered from the transferor (TCGA 1992 s 168(7)). In such an event the transferor is given a right to recover a corresponding sum from the transferee (TCGA 1992 s 168(9)) although, if HMRC has not obtained payment from the transferee, the transferor may be unlikely to succeed!

The emigration charge will not apply if the transferee leaves the UK because of work connected with his office or employment and performs all the duties of that office or employment outside the UK, provided he resumes UK residence within three years of his departure, without having disposed of the asset (other than to his spouse or civil partner) in the meantime (TCGA 1992 s 168(5)).

It will obviously be unnecessary to invoke this emigration charge if, before becoming non-resident, the transferee had made a disposal of the asset (TCGA 1992 s 168(1)(b)). That disposal will either have triggered the held-over gain or, if it was by way of gift and a further s 165 election had been made, the asset pregnant with gain will now be owned by another UK resident, so that HMRC is not threatened with a loss of tax. If that prior disposal was merely a part disposal, so triggering only a part of the held-over gain, the balance will be chargeable on emigration (TCGA 1992 s 168(2)).

An exception to the provision that the transferee who emigrates after the disposal of the asset will not be subject to a charge is when that prior disposal is to the emigrating transferee's spouse. If that spouse had also disposed of the asset, however, resulting in a CGT charge on the gain originally held-over, that further disposal will be treated as if it had been by the transferee so that the emigration charge will not apply (TCGA 1992 s 168(3)).

Further to the introduction of non-resident CGT from 1 April 2015 (see **[19.6]**), relief under s 165 is extended to permit it to be claimed on the gift of UK residential property to a non-resident individual, partner or trustee (TCGA 1992 s 167A). A residential property might be used, for example, as a furnished holiday letting to meet the 'trade' requirement in this context.

Further, where a s 165 donee becomes non-resident, the resultant held over gain can be further held over on the deemed disposal (TCGA 1992 s 168A).
[24.18]

b) *Companies*

TCGA 1992 s 167 prevents hold-over relief from being available on gifts to foreign-controlled companies: a company is foreign-controlled for these purposes if it is controlled by a person or persons who are not resident in the UK and who are connected with the disponer. (For the meaning of 'control', see CTA 2010 s 450 and **[41.123]**).

EXAMPLE 24.11

Z, a UK resident, transfers his business to Q Ltd, a company which is owned as to 51% by Z himself and as to 49% by an offshore structure. Hold-over relief under s 165 will be available.

Note that the extended s 167A relief (see **[24.18]**) extends to a gift of UK residential property to a non-resident close company (TCGA 1992 s 167A).

In the recent First Tier Tribunal case of *William Reeves v R & C Comrs* (2017), a gift relief claim under s 165 to hold-over the gain on the transfer of a business to a company failed under s 167. Although the transferee company was incorporated and resident in the UK, and was controlled by a UK resident individual, his control was attributed to his non-resident wife and children under TA 1988 s 416(6). [24.19]

10 **Other triggering events**

A gain held-over on the transfer of assets to a settlement under which a beneficiary was entitled to an interest in possession on 22 March 2006 will become chargeable on that beneficiary's death or, if his interest is replaced by a transitional serial interest (TSI) – see **Chapter 32** - on the death of the TSI-beneficiary. The same principle applies in the less common case of assets being transferred, with a hold-over election, to a will trust under which a beneficiary has an immediate post-death interest – on that beneficiary's death the held-over gain will become chargeable.

EXAMPLE 24.12

In 2002, Herbert settled some of the shares of his successful engineering company on trust for his middle-aged son Tony for life, electing for the gain of £2.5m to be held-over. Tony had taken little interest in the company and, following FA 2006, the trustees took legal advice. After consultations within the family, they exercised a power of appointment in 2007 to terminate Tony's life interest and confer a life interest instead on his son Guy who was making his career in the company. In July 2016, Guy unexpectedly died.

Guy had a transitional serial interest and, on his death, the trustees are deemed to have made a disposal of the trust assets but TCGA 1992 s 74 limits their gain to the amount of the gain previously held-over. The trustees will thus become liable to CGT on the gain of £2.5m held-over on Herbert's settlement of the shares in 2002.

A subsequent sale of the gifted property by the transferee will of course result in the held-over gain becoming taxable. By contrast, a subsequent gift of the property by the transferee will not trigger a charge – assuming a further election is made – and on the death of the second transferee any held-over gain is wiped out.

EXAMPLE 24.13

Samuel settled his family trading company shares on trusts for his companion, Justin, for life, remainder to his mother, Iris. Under a power in the settlement the trustees subsequently advanced the shares to Justin. No CGT arose on the creation of the settlement provided that Samuel so elected (in this case an election by the settlor alone sufficed) nor on the deemed disposal under TCGA 1992, s 71(1) resulting from the termination of the settlement when the property was advanced *in specie* to Justin (provided that the trustees and Justin so elected). As in the case of outright gifts, therefore, CGT may be postponed until the assets are eventually sold.

[24.20]

11 Anti-avoidance

Anti-avoidance provisions have been in place since 10 December 2003 to deny hold-over relief (under both TCGA 1992 s 165 and s 260 – see **[24.26]**) on a transfer to a settlor-interested settlement (TCGA 1992 s 169B–169G). For this purpose, a settlor has an interest in a settlement where any property in the settlement (or any property derived from that property) may be, or is, used for the benefit of the settlor or his spouse (or civil partner) *or* any minor unmarried child of his (who is not in a civil partnership). 'Child' includes stepchild. The extension to cover minor unmarried children came into effect for disposals from 6 April 2006 (FA 2006) and applies to all settlements, whenever created. Many settlements which were not settlor-interested for CGT purposes automatically became so on 6 April 2006 as a result of this provision.

The legislation is designed partly to prevent a gain being, in effect, transferred to trustees who are in a position to realise the gain at a lower tax cost (because of available reliefs or losses) than the settlor, with the settlor then able to benefit directly or indirectly from the resulting funds. The legislation also counteracts the so-called *Melville Mark II* schemes: see **[32.93]**.

The obvious counter of transferring property to a settlement that is not a settlor-interested settlement but which subsequently becomes settlor-interested is prevented by means of a clawback of hold-over relief (and a corresponding increase in the trustees' base cost). This occurs if the settlement becomes settlor-interested within six years of the end of the tax year in which the gift was made. One effect of the FA 2006 legislation is that a settlement could become settlor-interested inadvertently, eg if a settlor makes a settlement for the benefit of his children, all whom are adult at the time the settlement is made, and he then acquires minor step-children on re-marriage. It should also be noted that for the purposes of the FA 2006 legislation (as for most other tax purposes), a 'settlor' includes anyone who has directly or indirectly provided property for the purposes of the settlement. Hence, if hold-over relief has been claimed on the initial transfer of assets to the settlement by, say, the grandparents of the beneficiaries, it could be disastrous for the beneficiaries' parents to add funds to the settlement at any time within six years of the initial transfer of assets and at a time when any of their children (the beneficiaries) were still under 18. The settlement would thereupon become 'settlor-interested' and the initial hold-over relief would be clawed back as well as denied to the parents' transfer. But a saving provision applies for pre-6 April 2006 disposals to a settlement from which the (or any) settlor's minor children could, and still can, benefit; if hold-over relief under s 165 was claimed on such a disposal there will not be a clawback of the relief as a result of the extended meaning now given to settlor-interested settlements.

Note: All the held-over gains are clawed back irrespective of the amount of the benefit taken by the settlor, spouse or minor unmarried children. The claw-back provisions also operate if a beneficiary becomes a settlor, perhaps by adding to the settlement to meet trust expenses, irrespective of the amount of bounty provided by the beneficiary-settlor. There is no de minimis or pro-rata let-out. Note also that if held-over gains were clawed back and charged to CGT by virtue of the settlement becoming settlor-interested before 6 April 2008, there was no taper relief on those gains even though taper relief would have been available if the settlor had chosen to pay the CGT and not elect for hold-over relief. **[24.21]**

III GIFTS OF ASSETS ATTRACTING AN IMMEDIATE IHT CHARGE (TCGA 1992 S 260)

The second situation where hold-over relief is available on a gift or undervalue sale, is if the relevant disposal 'is a chargeable transfer within the meaning of the Inheritance Tax Act 1984' or would be such a transfer but for the availability of the annual exemption.

A chargeable transfer of business or agricultural property qualifying for 100% relief from IHT is also eligible for relief under this provision notwithstanding that no IHT will actually be due.

However, a gain arising on the disposal of a qualifying corporate bond (QCB) cannot be held over under this section. **[24.22]**

1 When is there an immediate IHT charge on inter vivos gifts?

Lifetime transfers which are PETs do not attract an immediate IHT charge: accordingly, in such cases hold-over relief under s 260 is not available, and this applies even if the PET subsequently becomes chargeable because of the death of the transferor within seven years.

The circumstances in which s 260(2)(a) hold-over relief is available have been considerably enlarged as a consequence of the changes to the IHT treatment of trusts introduced by FA 2006, with most disposals into, and out of, settlements now being chargeable transfers for IHT. Relief under s 260(2)(a) is available in the following cases with effect from 22 March 2006:

(1) on the lifetime disposal of assets to all trusts created on or after 22 March 2006 (except disposals to disabled trusts under IHTA 1984 ss 89 or 89A which will mostly be PETs);
(2) on the lifetime disposal of assets on or after 22 March 2006 to all pre-existing trusts (whether discretionary, interest in possession or ex-accumulation and maintenance);
(3) on the disposal of assets by trustees out of all trusts created on or after 22 March 2006, except where the disposal is made on the lifetime termination of an immediate post-death interest (see [33.4]) in favour of a beneficiary absolutely entitled (such a disposal will be a PET). Note that disposals to minors from trusts under IHTA 1984 ss 71A or 71D are not chargeable transfers for IHT but nevertheless qualify for hold-over relief under new paragraphs of s 260(2), inserted by FA 2006 (see [24.27];
(4) on the disposal of assets by trustees out of:
    - pre-existing discretionary trusts
    - pre-existing interest in possession trusts, except where the disposal is made on the lifetime termination of the pre-existing interest in possession, or of a transitional serial interest (see [33.4]), in favour of a beneficiary absolutely entitled (such a disposal will be a PET)
    - pre-existing accumulation and maintenance trusts which entered the IHT relevant property regime on 6 April 2008 or on an interest in possession arising before that date. (For hold-over relief on disposals from such trusts prior to their entering the relevant property regime see [24.27]).

In addition, relief under s 260(2)(a) is available:
(5) On a gift between individuals, or on the creation of a disabled trust, in circumstances where such gifts fall outside the definition of a PET. Such cases are rare: see [28.41].

Because s 260 specifies that to come within its terms the disposal must be to and by either an individual or the trustees of a settlement, gifts to and by companies do not attract hold-over relief even though they are not PETs (unless, of course, the gift to a company is of a business asset other than shares, when relief may be available under s 165 as discussed at [24.5]).

The non-resident CGT regime introduced from 1 April 2015 (see [19.6]) has led to an extension of s 260 relief to permit it to be claimed on the gift of a UK residential property to a non-resident individual (TCGA 1992 s 261ZA).

[24.23]

2 The relief

The relief afforded by s 260 is broadly the same as that given under s 165, with s 260 relief taking precedence (TCGA 1992 s 165(3)(d)). This override may have attractions when what is contemplated is a transfer of shares in a family trading company which owns non-business assets, since there is no apportionment requirement under s 260 (see [24.7]).

An election is similarly required under TCGA 1992 s 260; the effect of holding over the gain is the same (ie the asset is disposed of and acquired at market value less held-over gain); the transferee must be UK resident and subsequent emigration may trigger the charge. Unlike s 165 there is, however, no restriction on the type of asset for which relief may be claimed. [24.24]

3 Practical uses of s 260(2)(a)

Until FA 2006, hold-over relief under s 260(2)(a) was mainly employed when a discretionary trust was either created or ended. These were the principal occasions on which an immediate IHT charge arose and on which a gain on a chargeable asset entering or leaving a trust could therefore be held-over. The following example illustrates the various permutations that are now available for s 260(2)(a) hold-over relief following the considerable extension of IHT lifetime chargeable transfers by FA 2006.

EXAMPLE 24.14

(1) In May 2016, Jake transfers his portfolio of stocks and shares (worth £500,000) into a new trust under which his adult children have interests in possession; the transfer results in an immediate IHT charge and therefore any gain on the investments can be held over if Jake (alone) elects under s 260(2)(a). Note that any IHT paid by Jake (ignoring grossing-up) can be deducted by the trustees in arriving at the CGT charge on a subsequent disposal of the shares (and this IHT sum may be increased should an extra tax charge result from the death of Jake within seven years of establishing his trust: see [24.17]).

(2) Joseph establishes a new trust by transferring a cottage worth £255,000 to the trustees. As his first chargeable transfer, IHT will not be payable since it falls within Joseph's nil rate band. Despite this, hold-over relief under s 260(2)(a) is available since the transfer by Joseph is chargeable to IHT, albeit at a nil rate. This gives the best of all worlds – no IHT but CGT hold-over. (Note that s 260(2)(a) also applies if a transfer of value which would otherwise attract an immediate IHT charge is covered by the transferor's annual exemption.)

(3) Were the trustees of Joseph's trust subsequently (say, six months later) to appoint the cottage to a beneficiary outright, there should still be no IHT charge but again CGT hold-over relief will be available.

(4) Thal and Thad, trustees of the Mallard discretionary trust, appoint chargeable assets to Billy Beneficiary. This being a trust of 'relevant property' for IHT (see [28.1]–[28.20]), an 'exit' charge will arise (see [34.23]) and therefore any chargeable gain can be held over on the joint election of Thal, Thad and Billy. Note, however, that an appointment out of a relevant property trust within three months of its creation, or within three months after a 10-yearly anniversary, does not give rise to any IHT charge (see [34.25] and [34.28]) and that appointments out of a relevant property trust established by will

made within two years of the testator's death are 'read back' into that will (see **[30.145]**). Therefore, CGT hold-over is not available in any of these cases.

(5) Trustees Tom and Ted, in exercise of powers conferred on them by the settlement, resettle the trust property (non-business assets) into a new settlement. This is a deemed disposal under s 71(1) for CGT purposes but any resulting gain may only be held over if it is also a chargeable event for IHT. With many inter-settlement transfers after 22 March 2006 this will not be the case since the property will have moved from one 'relevant property' settlement to another and no IHT 'exit' charge will arise due to the operation of IHTA 1984 s 81 (see **[34.32]**) which deems the property to remain comprised in the transferring settlement. If, by contrast, trustees exercise their powers so as to appoint new trusts of the *same* settlement (eg by terminating a pre-22 March 2006 life interest and appointing fresh discretionary trusts) then although this will give rise to a lifetime chargeable transfer for IHT there will be no deemed disposal at all for CGT purposes since the trust assets will not have left the settlement (and so hold-over relief will not need to be considered).

(6) In 1990 Seth made an accumulation and maintenance settlement in favour of his infant grandchildren, Gus and Zac, by which each would acquire a life interest in an equal half share on reaching 25. Gus acquired an interest in possession in his share under Trustee Act 1925 s 31 on reaching 25 in January 2005 and he was then treated as becoming the beneficial owner of his share for IHT under IHTA 1984 s 49(1). Zac, however, did not acquire an interest in possession in his share until reaching 25 in November 2007 and, as a result of FA 2006, IHTA 1984 s 49(1) did not apply to his share at that point, and the share entered the IHT relevant property regime instead. The trustees now consider both Gus and Zac to be financially responsible and, in order to curtail the IHT charges on Zac's share, they decide in March 2017 to exercise their powers of advancement by terminating the settlement in its entirety and transferring the assets out to Gus and Zac. Many of the assets are standing at a substantial gain.

The disposal of assets to Gus will not be a chargeable transfer for IHT since he is already deemed to be the beneficial owner of his share. Accordingly hold-over relief under s 260(2)(a) will not be available for the disposal to him. The disposal of assets to Zac, however, will result in an IHT 'exit' charge, and therefore hold-over relief under s 260(2)(a) will be available on the disposal of assets to him.

(7) In July 1995 property was settled on A&M trusts for Sid by which he was to acquire a life interest in the trust fund on attaining the age of 25. Sid will reach 25 in September 2017 and, because of the trustees' express power to accumulate the income until that time, he has not become entitled to an interest in possession under Trustee Act 1925 s 31 even though he is now over 18. To reduce future IHT charges to acceptable proportions, however, the trustees decided to alter the terms of the trust with effect from 6 April 2008 so that Sid will now become absolutely entitled to the capital on reaching 25; the trust also satisfied the other conditions of IHTA 1984 s 71D. The special charge prospectively payable under IHTA 1984 s 71E on transfers to the beneficiary between the ages of 18 and 25 was considered an acceptable price to pay in order to avoid the heavier 10-yearly anniversary charge that would otherwise be due under the relevant property regime in July 2017 shortly before Sid reaches 25. The trustees have exercised their power of advancement to transfer some of the trust assets to Sid over the period from April 2008 and the remainder will be transferred to him when

he becomes absolutely entitled on attaining age 25 in September 2017. Each such transfer to Sid will be a chargeable transfer for IHT (by virtue of IHTA 1984 s 71E) and will therefore qualify for hold-over relief under TCGA 1992 s 260(2)(a).

Note: If a transfer is made from an IHTA 1984 s 71D trust during the first three months after the beneficiary has reached 18, a 'chargeable transfer within the meaning of the IHTA 1984' takes place because a charge to tax under IHTA 1984 s 71E will arise; hence, hold-over relief under TCGA 1992 s 260(2)(a) will be available. This is so even though, under the detailed formula set out in IHTA 1984 s 71F, no IHT will actually be payable in these circumstances. The position is to be contrasted with that arising where transfers are made from a relevant property trust during the first three months after its creation or a 10-yearly anniversary: see (4) above.

[24.25]

4 Anti-avoidance

The anti-avoidance measures described at [24.21] in relation to transfers to settlor-interested settlements apply equally to hold-over relief under TCGA 1992 s 260. However, hold-over under s 260 is subject to an additional anti-avoidance provision in relation to main residence relief (see TCGA 1992 s 226A; and for main residence relief see **Chapter 23**). Where hold-over relief has been claimed under s 260, private residence relief is denied under TCGA 1992 s 222. The legislation was designed to prevent arrangements such as that in the following example.

EXAMPLE 24.15

Tarquin owns a house that is not his only or main residence. It has a market value of £500,000 and would realise a chargeable gain of £400,000 if he sold it. Tarquin would like to sell the house and give the proceeds to his adult son, Torquil.

Tarquin therefore gifts the house into a trust for Torquil, claiming relief under s 260(2)(a) (note that if the settlement were settlor-interested, the anti-avoidance provision described at [24.21] would be in point). Under the terms of the settlement, the trustees allow Torquil to occupy the house as his main residence. A few months later, Torquil leaves the house, and the trustees sell it for £510,000. Until 10 December 2003, none of the resultant gain of £410,000 would have been chargeable because of main residence relief (see [23.62]), and the trustees could have distributed the entire proceeds to Torquil.

The anti-avoidance provisions (introduced by FA 2004) now operate to deny main residence relief in these circumstances.

Because of the time allowed to make a hold-over election (see [24.12]) it may be that the trustees' disposal takes place before a hold-over claim has been made, so that the anti-avoidance rule would not be in point. If a claim is made subsequent to the trustees' disposal, main residence relief will be withdrawn and all necessary tax adjustments made.

Conversely, if a hold-over election is in place, and it is desired to make main residence relief available, the claim may be revoked. [24.26]

IV DISPOSALS FROM ACCUMULATION AND MAINTENANCE TRUSTS AND CHILDREN'S TRUSTS (TCGA 1992 S 260(2)(D), (DA) AND (DB))

Accumulation and maintenance (A&M) trusts were the creature of the original IHT legislation under which they were accorded privileged treatment and kept out of the relevant property regime with its anniversary and 'exit' charges. With effect from 22 March 2006, A&M trusts can no longer be created and the privileged IHT treatment for existing ones ended on 6 April 2008 at the latest, unless their terms were changed before that date so that the beneficiaries become absolutely entitled to the capital by the time they reached 18.

The hold-over position under s 260(2)(a) on disposals made now *to* ex-A&M trusts is dealt with in **[24.23]**.

Whilst a trust still qualified as an A&M trust prior to 6 April 2008, the disposal of assets by the trustees to beneficiaries – whether on the termination of the trust or on an advance to a beneficiary – qualified for hold-over relief even though this was not a chargeable transfer for IHT. This was by virtue of the special hold-over relief that has always applied to disposals from A&M trusts under s 260(2)(d). It should however be noted that relief under s 260(2)(d) was not available if the beneficiary had acquired an interest in possession before 22 March 2006, since the trust will have ceased to qualify as an A&M trust at that time: the position of Gus in (6) in *Example 24.14*. (A beneficiary under an A&M trust often acquired an interest in possession at age 18 or 21, even though the trust deed gave him a life or absolute interest only on reaching 25.)

Indeed, hold-over relief under TCGA 1992 s 260(2)(d) is still available on disposals from trusts which have preserved their A&M status by changing their terms before 6 April 2008 so that the beneficiaries become absolutely entitled to the capital at 18. As a result of the IHT changes introduced by FA 2006, the acquisition by a beneficiary of an interest in possession between 22 March 2006 and 5 April 2008 caused the trust to enter the IHT relevant property regime. In any event the trust will have entered the regime on 6 April 2008 at the latest unless its terms were changed before that date in the manner indicated above. If an ex-A&M trust has entered the relevant property regime in either of these ways then disposals of the trust assets will qualify for hold-over relief under s 260(2)(a) (see Zac in (6) in *Example 24.14*).

EXAMPLE 24.16

(1) Some time before 22 March 2006, property was settled on an A&M trust for Floyd on attaining 25 with the trustees having the power to accumulate the trust income until then. Floyd reached 25 in January 2017 and became absolutely entitled to the assets; the ex-A&M trust ended, and a hold-over election is possible under s 260(2)(a) (whatever the nature of the trust assets).

(2) Assume in (7) in *Example 24.14* that the trustees, instead of converting the A&M trust to a IHTA 1984 s 71D trust, calculated that less IHT would be payable if they allowed the trust to enter the relevant property regime on 6 April 2008, but transferred several of the trust assets out to Sid in March 2008, just before the trust ceased to qualify as an A&M trust and entered the

relevant property regime. Such transfers to Sid will have been free of IHT and hold-over relief under TCGA 1992 s 260(2)(d) will have been available on the disposals (whatever the nature of the trust assets).

FA 2006 established two successors to A&M trusts:
(1) Trusts for minors under IHTA 1984 s 71A (see [34.102]). These can be set up by will or intestacy or under the Criminal Injuries Compensation Scheme. The main condition is that the minor has to be entitled to the capital on attaining the age of 18 (or earlier).
(2) Trusts under IHTA 1984 s 71D (see [34.103]–[34.110]). The main condition here is that the beneficiary has to be entitled to the capital on attaining the age of 25 (or earlier). Trusts under s 71D can come into existence in one of two ways only one of which is still available. *First*, like s 71A trusts, they can be created by will or intestacy or under the Criminal Injuries Compensation Scheme. *Second*, they could be created out of a former A&M trust by the trustees altering the terms of the trust so that it satisfied the s 71D conditions immediately it ceased to qualify as an A&M trust (which would have been on 6 April 2008 at the latest).

Both s 71A and s 71D trusts are outside the IHT relevant property regime of anniversary and 'exit' charges, and the special charge imposed on transfers out of s 71D trusts applies only on transfers when the beneficiary is aged between 18 and 25. Accordingly transfers from a s 71A or s 71D trust to the beneficiary up to (or on) his/her 18th birthday are not chargeable transfers for IHT but, as with disposals from A&M trusts, a special hold-over relief is accorded to such disposals: TCGA 1992 s 260(2)(da) and (db).

EXAMPLE 24.17

In 2000 property was settled on A&M trusts for Harry, then aged 5, by which he would obtain an interest in possession in the trust fund on reaching 25. In March 2008, just before the trust was to lose its A&M status on 6 April 2008, and would otherwise enter the IHT relevant property regime, the trustees exercised their powers so that the trust satisfied the s 71D conditions with effect from 6 April 2008 – including the principal requirement that Harry would become entitled to the capital at 25. Shortly before Harry reaches 18 in 2013 the trustees decide to avoid all IHT charges and end the trust by advancing all the trust assets out to Harry on the occasion of his 18th birthday. The transfers will be free of IHT and the disposals will qualify for hold-over relief under TCGA 1992 s 260(2)(db).   **[24.27]**

V MISCELLANEOUS CASES

Hold-over relief under TCGA 1992 s 260(2) is also available in the following situations where the relevant transfer is exempt from any IHT charge:
(1) gifts to political parties under IHTA 1984 s 24;
(2) gifts to maintenance funds for historic buildings under IHTA 1984 s 27;
(3) gifts of designated property under IHTA 1984 s 30; and
(4) gifts of works of art under IHTA 1984 s 78.

Relief claims must be made jointly by the donor and donee, or just by the donor for gifts into trust (TCGA 1992 s 260(1)(c)).   **[24.28]**

VI PAYMENT OF CGT

1 General rule

CGT must generally be paid on or before 31 January following the tax year when the disposal occurs (TMA 1970 s 59B). **[24.29]**

2 Payment by instalments

TCGA 1992 s 281 provides for the payment of CGT by instalments where the CGT liability arises from gifts of certain types of property, and also from deemed disposals of settled property. However, there is no instalment option for sales at undervalue (as opposed to outright gifts).

The ability to pay by instalments will broadly be available only if the relevant chargeable gain could not have been held-over under either TCGA 1992 s 165 or s 260, or where the held-over gain is less than the otherwise chargeable gain. It should be noted, therefore, that the tax cannot be paid by instalments where a hold-over claim could have been made, but was not.

Under TCGA 1992 s 281(3), CGT may be paid by instalments in relation to any of the following assets:
(1) land;
(2) a controlling shareholding in any company; or
(3) a minority holding in an unquoted company.

Note that there is no restriction to business assets.

The person paying the CGT must give notice if he wishes to pay by instalments (TCGA 1992 s 281(2)) – tax is then paid by ten equal yearly instalments, starting on the 31 January following the tax year of the disposal. Interest is charged on the unpaid CGT and is added to each instalment (TCGA 1992 s 281(5)).

The outstanding tax can be paid off at any time, and must be paid off if the gift was to a connected person, or was a deemed disposal of settled property, and the relevant assets are subsequently sold for valuable consideration (TCGA 1992 s 281(7)).

EXAMPLE 24.18

In July 2014 Bob gave his seaside cottage to his daughter, Thelma. The resulting CGT of £50,000 may be paid by ten equal annual instalments on the appropriate notice being given by Bob (who is to pay that tax). The first instalment of £5,000 falls due on 31 January 2016 and subsequent instalments will carry interest on the unpaid balance of the CGT. **[24.30]**

3 Payment by a donee

TCGA 1992 s 282 provides that if a donor fails to pay the tax referable to the gift then HMRC may look to the donee for payment; the donee is then entitled to recover any amounts paid from the donor (TCGA 1992 s 282(2)).

[24.31]

25 CGT – settlements

Updated by Sarah Laing, CTA, Chartered Tax Advisor

I	What is a settlement? **[25.2]**
II	The creation of a settlement **[25.21]**
III	Actual and deemed disposals by trustees **[25.41]**
IV	Resettlements and separate funds **[25.81]**
V	Disposal of beneficial interests **[25.111]**
VI	Relief from, and payment of, CGT **[25.141]**
VII	Trusts with vulnerable beneficiary **[25.149]**

The legislation distinguishes between UK-resident trusts and non-resident trusts. The latter are considered in **Chapter 27A**. So far as the former are concerned, the legislation generally seeks to tax gains that arise (or are deemed to arise) on property comprised in the trust fund and not on a disposal of the interests of the beneficiaries. Actual disposals by the trustees and certain deemed disposals may trigger a charge, but disposals of beneficial interests will normally be exempt. **[25.1]**

I WHAT IS A SETTLEMENT?

1 Definition

A 'settlement' is sometimes referred to as a trust, implying that they share the same meaning. However, a settlement can include any disposition, trust, covenant, agreement, arrangement or transfer of assets (see *Wagstaff v R & C Comrs* (2014) for a reminder of the three certainties that are necessary to establish a valid trust, namely certainty of intention, subject matter and objects).

The definition of settled property was refined from 6 April 2006 as any property held in trust other than property held as nominee, bare trustee for a person absolutely entitled, an infant or disabled person (TCGA 1992 s 60). References in the legislation to a settlement are construed as references to settled property and the meaning of settlement is determined by case law. This measure effectively aligned what is treated as a settlement for the general purposes of income tax and tax on chargeable gains. The effect is that income tax will be charged on income arising to the trustees of a 'settlement' with the definition of settlement being derived from existing trust law and case law, and 'settled property' being defined in the tax legislation (TCGA 1992 s 68A).

[25.2]

2 Nominees and bare trusts

Property is not settled where 'assets are held by a person as nominee for another person, or as trustee for another person absolutely entitled as against the trustee'. The provision covers nomineeships and bare or simple trusts.
[25.3]

EXAMPLE 25.1

Tim and Tom hold 1,000 shares in DNC Ltd on trust for Bertram, aged 26, absolutely. This is a bare trust since Bertram is solely entitled to the shares and can at any time bring the trust to an end (see *Saunders v Vautier* (1841)). The shares are treated as belonging to Bertram so that a disposal of those shares by the trustees is treated as being by Bertram and any transfer from the trustees to Bertram is ignored.

3 Beneficiaries under a disability

Where the property is held on trust 'for any person who would be [absolutely] entitled but for being an infant or other person under a disability' it is not settled. [25.4]

EXAMPLE 25.2

(1) Topsy and Tim hold property for Alex absolutely, aged nine. Because of his age Alex cannot demand the property from the trustees and the trust is not simple or bare. Alex is, however, a person who would be absolutely entitled but for his infancy and he is (for CGT purposes) treated as owning the assets in the fund.

(2) Teddy and Tiger hold property on trust for Noddy, aged nine, contingent upon his attaining the age of 18. At first sight it would seem that there is no material difference between this settlement and that considered in (1) above since, in both, the beneficiary would be absolutely entitled were it not for his infancy. Noddy, however, is not entitled to claim the fund from the trustees. Unlike (1) above, Noddy's entitlement is contingent upon living to a certain age, so that, were he to ask the trustees to give him the property, they would refuse because he has not satisfied the contingency. This distinction would be more obvious if the settlement provided that the contingency to be satisfied by Noddy was the attaining of (say) 21 (see *Tomlinson v Glyns Executor and Trustee Co* (1970)). The property in this example is, therefore, settled for the purposes of CGT.

4 Concurrent interests

Where property is held for 'two or more persons who are or would be jointly [absolutely] entitled' the property is not settled. The word 'jointly' is not limited to the interests of joint tenants, applying to concurrent ownership generally. It does not, however, apply to interests that are successive, but only covers more than one beneficiary concurrently entitled 'in the same interest' (see *Kidson v MacDonald* (1974); *Booth v Ellard* (1980); and *IRC v Matthew's Executors* (1984)). [25.5]

EXAMPLE 25.3

(1) Bill and Ben purchase Blackacre as tenants in common in equal shares. The land is held on a trust of land, but for the purposes of CGT the property is not settled and is treated as belonging to Bill and Ben equally (*Kidson v MacDonald* (1974)).

(2) Mr T and his family hold 72% of the issued share capital in T Ltd (their family company). They enter into a written agreement as a result of which the shares are transferred to trustees and detailed restrictions, akin to pre-emption provisions in private company articles, are imposed. The beneficial interests of Mr T and his family are not, however, affected. Subsequently the shares are transferred out again to the various settlors. In such a 'pooling arrangement' the shares will be treated as nominee property with the result that there is no disposal for CGT purposes on the creation of the trust nor on its termination (cp *Booth v Ellard* (1980) and see *Jenkins v Brown* and *Warrington v Sterland* (1989) in which a similar result was arrived at (surprisingly?) in the case of a pooling of family farms. See further [**22.83**]).

(3) Thal and Tal hold property on trust for Simon for life, remainder to Karl absolutely. Both are adult. Although Simon and Karl are, in common parlance, jointly entitled to claim the fund from the trustees, they are not 'jointly absolutely entitled' within the meaning of s 60. The property is settled for CGT purposes.

5 Meaning of absolute entitlement

It is the concept of being 'absolutely entitled as against the trustee' which lies at the root of the three cases mentioned in TCGA 1992 s 60. Section 60(2) provides that:

'It is hereby declared that references in this Act to any property held by a person as trustee for another person absolutely entitled as against the trustee are references to a case where that other person has the exclusive right, subject only to satisfying any outstanding charge, lien or other right of the trustees to resort to the property for payment of duty, taxes, costs or other outgoings, to direct how that property shall be dealt with.'

The various rights against the property possessed by trustees and mentioned in s 60(2) refer to personal rights of indemnity; they do not cover other beneficial interests under the settlement.

EXAMPLE 25.4

Jackson is entitled to an annuity of £1,000 pa payable out of a settled fund which is held in trust for Xerxes absolutely. The property is settled for CGT purposes (*Stephenson v Barclays Bank Trust Co Ltd* (1975) and contrast *X v A* (2000) where in exercise of their lien trustees retained trust property against a beneficiary absolutely entitled – it is considered that in this case the property had ceased to be settled for CGT purposes).

A person can become absolutely entitled to assets without being 'beneficially' entitled (see [**25.81**]). [**25.6**]

6 Crowe v Appleby *and trustee appropriations*

Section 60(2) does not offer any guidance on the question of when a beneficiary has 'the exclusive right ... to direct how [the] property [the settlement] shall be dealt with'. Under general trust law beneficiaries will not be able to issue such directions unless they have the right to end the trust by demanding their share of the property (see eg *Re Brockbank* (1948)). Difficulties may arise where one of a number of beneficiaries is entitled to a portion of the fund.

EXAMPLE 25.5

A trust fund is held for the three daughters of the settlor (Jane, June and Joy) contingent upon attaining 21 and, if more than one, in equal shares absolutely. Jane, the eldest, is 21 and is, therefore, entitled to one-third of the assets. Whether she is absolutely entitled as against the trustees to that share depends upon the type of property held by the trustees and the terms of the settlement. The general principle is that she will be entitled to claim her one-third share, but not if the effect of distributing that slice of the fund would be to damage the interests of the other beneficiaries and nor if the trustees are given an express power of appropriation.
(1) If Jane is absolutely entitled to her share that portion of the fund ceases to be settled (even though Jane leaves her share in the hands of the trustees).
(2) But, if the fund consists of land, Jane will not be absolutely entitled (see *Crowe v Appleby* (1975)). Hence, the settlement will continue until all three daughters either satisfy the contingency or die before 21. Only then will the fund cease to be settled since one or more persons will, at that point, become jointly absolutely entitled. (For problems that can arise on a division of a controlling shareholding see *Lloyds Bank plc v Duker* (1987).)

What assets other than land are subject to a similar rule? HMRC (at CG 37560) comment as follows:

'In *Stephenson v Barclays Bank Trust Co Ltd* Walton J said that as regards shares in a private company in very special circumstances, and possibly mortgage debts, the person with a vested interest in a share of the property might have to wait for sale before he could call upon the trustees to account to him for his share. The principle of *Crowe v Appleby* therefore may apply to other indivisible assets. A good example would be an Old Master painting or valuable antique, or indeed a single share in a company.'

If the trustees have an express power to appropriate assets in satisfaction of the share of a beneficiary, HMRC's view is:
(1) that any gain on the deemed disposal is calculated on the assets actually appropriated and not on a proportion of the total gain on all assets in the settlement; and
(2) pending the trustees making an appropriation, tax is not charged.

[25.7]

7 Class closing

In deciding whether the class of beneficiaries has closed so that those in existence (who have satisfied any relevant contingency) have become absolutely entitled the medical impossibility of further beneficiaries being born to a living person is ignored. Hence a settlement on the children of A who attain 21 and if more than one in equal shares will remain settled property until the death of A even though he may have become incapable of having further children before that time (*Figg v Clarke* (1996)).

[25.8]–[25.20]

II THE CREATION OF A SETTLEMENT

1 General rule

A transfer into settlement, whether revocable or irrevocable, is a disposal of the entire property notwithstanding that the transferor has some interest as a beneficiary under the settlement and notwithstanding that he is a trustee, or the sole trustee, of the settlement (TCGA 1992 s 70; CG 33120). If chargeable assets are settled, a chargeable gain or allowable loss will result unless holdover relief is available (as to which see **Chapter 24**). [25.21]

2 The 'connected persons' rule

As the settlor and his trustees are connected persons (TCGA 1992 s 18(3): see [19.14]), any loss resulting from the transfer will only be deductible from a gain realised on a subsequent disposal by the settlor to those trustees. Apart from being connected with the settlor, trustees will also be connected with persons connected with the settlor who will often be beneficiaries. However, it has been confirmed by HMRC that:

> 'if the settlor dies the connection with the trustees and relatives and spouse of the settlor is broken. Therefore if, for instance, the beneficiaries of the settlement are the children of the late settlor, the trustees are not connected with those beneficiaries, even if one or more of the children are trustees' (RI 38, February 1993). [25.22]–[25.40]

EXAMPLE 25.6

(1) Roger settles his Van Gogh sketch 'Peasant with Pig' worth £200,000. His allowable expenditure totals £50,000. He also settles his main residence. The beneficiaries are his wife Rena for life with remainder to their two children, Robina and Rybina. For CGT purposes, the following rules apply:
    (a) *Main residence* This is exempt from CGT.
    (b) *The Van Gogh* This is treated as disposed of for its market value (£200,000) and, hence, Roger has made a gain of £150,000.
(2) Robin wishes to sell his share portfolio but that will realise a substantial gain. He owns real property (which he wishes to retain) that would realise a loss if sold. Robin transfers both assets to trustees on a life interest trust for himself. This triggers the gain on the investments that will be offset by the loss on the land. The trustees immediately sell the portfolio (in due course the trustees may under a power in the settlement return the assets to Robin). Robin has therefore sheltered his gain.

III ACTUAL AND DEEMED DISPOSALS BY TRUSTEES

A charge to CGT may arise as a result of either actual or deemed disposals of property by the trustees. Chargeable gains are generally computed in the usual manner. Trustees' expenses may be relieved as allowable expenses and they may set their annual exemption against any resulting gain. FA 2016 reduced the rate of CGT for trustees for 2016–17 and subsequent years from 28% to 20% (TCGA 1992 s 4(3) as amended by FA 2016). However, this reduction does not apply in two particular cases:
- 'upper rate gains' remain chargeable at 28% (TCGA 1992 s 4(3), as amended). 'Upper rate gains' are residential property gains (as defined in TCGA 1992 s 4BB).
- 'non-resident capital gains' (NRCGT gains) continue to be chargeable at 28%. Residential property gains are gains accruing on the disposal of residential property interests (defined in TCGA 1992 Sch B1 and Sch BA1) situated in the UK or overseas that are not NRCGT gains (TCGA 1992 s 4BB).

The gains of property held on bare trusts are treated as if made by the beneficiary and taxed accordingly. [25.41]

1 Transfers of property on a change of trustees

When the property is transferred from old to new trustees this is not treated as a CGT disposal since trustees are treated as a single and continuing body (TCGA 1992 s 69(1)). Note, in particular:
(1) the position when UK resident trustees are replaced by non-residents (see [27.57]);
(2) if part only of the trust property is appointed into trusts administered by non-resident trustees, given that there is a single composite settlement for CGT purposes the continuing UK trustees will be accountable for gains realised offshore (see *Roome v Edwards* (1981) and [25.82]).
[25.42]

2 Actual disposals and trust losses

When chargeable assets are sold by trustees, normal principles apply in calculating the gain (or loss) of the trustees. If the disposal generates a loss it may be set off against gains of the same year or of future years made by the trustees, subject to the restriction for the use of losses arising on transfers between connected persons. [25.43]

3 Use of trust losses by a beneficiary

a) *Assets leaving the trust*

If the deemed disposal of the asset(s) leaving the trust produces a loss, it is set first of all against other trust gains of the same year. However, to the extent that a loss remains unused in the trust, it may be 'inherited' by the beneficiary recipient of that asset. Until June 1999, that loss could be used by the beneficiary against his general gains. Now, however, it can be offset only against a gain arising on disposal of the asset advanced to him out of trust or, if the asset was land, against some other interest in land deriving its value from that land (TCGA 1992 s 71(2)–(2D)).

EXAMPLE 25.7

In May 2017, Daisy becomes absolutely entitled to one half of the assets in her grandmother's trust. At that time the trustees have unused capital losses of £25,000 and the assets to which Daisy becomes entitled are worth £30,000 less than when acquired by the trustees.
(1) None of the realised losses of £25,000 accrue to Daisy: they remain available for use by the trustees against future disposals of trust property.
(2) The loss that occurs on the s 71 deemed disposal is, however, available to Daisy but only to be set against future gains on a disposal of that trust property. (*Note*: This loss would not be available to Daisy if the trustees could use it either against gains realised earlier in the tax year 2017–18 or against gains arising on the s 71 deemed disposal.) **[25.44]**

b) *Adding property to the trust*

EXAMPLE 25.8

The Jokey Trust has unused realised capital losses. Bill purchases an interest in the trust; adds assets to the trust which are pregnant with gain (claiming holdover); those assets are sold by the trustees thereby utilising the trust losses and the cash is paid out to Bill.

TCGA 1992 s 79A provides that in the circumstances of *Example 25.8* the trustees' losses may not be set against the gain. Note that for this section to apply:
(1) a transferor must add assets to the settlement claiming holdover relief; *and*
(2) that person (or someone connected with him) must purchase an interest in the settlement.

Accordingly an original beneficiary may add property to use the trust losses. **[25.45]–[25.46]**

4 The exit charge: TCGA 1992 s 71(1)

a) *The general rule*

Section 71(1) provides for a deemed disposal of the chargeable assets in the trust fund, whenever a person becomes absolutely entitled to any portion of the settled property (an 'exit charge'). The section is a 'deeming' provision and treats the assets in the fund as being sold by the trustees (so that it is the trustee rate of CGT which is relevant) for their market value at that date and immediately reacquired for the same value, thereby ensuring that any increase in value in the chargeable assets is taxed (except in the situation discussed below). The deemed reacquisition by the trustees is treated as the act of the person who is absolutely entitled to the fund as against the trustees (see TCGA 1992 s 60(1)). **[25.47]**

EXAMPLE 25.9

Shares in Dovecot Ltd are held by trustees for Simone absolutely, contingent upon her attaining the age of 25. She has just become 25 and the shares are worth £100,000. The trustees' allowable expenditure is £25,000. She is now absolutely entitled to the fund and the trustees are deemed to sell the shares (for £100,000) and to reacquire them (for £100,000). On that deemed disposal they have realised a chargeable gain of £75,000 (£100,000 − £25,000) that may benefit from entrepreneurs' relief in the normal way (see [25.148]). The shares are now treated as Simone's property so that if she directs their sale in the future and £107,000 is raised she will have a chargeable gain of £7,000 (£107,000 − £100,000).

b) *Losses*

A loss arising on the deemed disposal which occurs under s 71 will be deducted from 'pre-entitlement gains', defined as gains accruing to the trustees in that same tax year (but before the s 71 deemed disposal) or accruing on the deemed disposal (s 71(2A)). Subject to that, the loss is passed to the beneficiary under s 71(2) as discussed in [25.45]. How is this rule affected by the existence or otherwise of connected persons? HMRC have confirmed that the beneficiaries' entitlement to the loss under s 71 is *not* affected by this rule. Indeed, it seems odd that there was ever any doubt about the matter bearing in mind that the utilisation of losses is only restricted if the relevant disposal is to a connected person. On the termination of a trust the legislation provides not for a disposal of the settled property to the relevant beneficiary but rather for a deemed disposal by the trustees (see RI 38, February 1993). [25.48]

c) *Deemed disposal triggered by the death of a beneficiary entitled to an interest in possession: TCGA 1992 s 73*

The termination of an interest in possession because of the death of the beneficiary may result in a deemed disposal by the trustees under s 71(1) if on that occasion the settlement ends (ie a person becomes absolutely entitled to the trust assets). Although there is a deemed disposal and reacquisition, no CGT (or loss relief) is charged (or allowed) on any resultant gain (loss): see [25.54] for the definition of an interest in possession. This corresponds to the normal CGT principle that on death there is an uplift in value but no charge to tax (see **Chapter 21**; and, for the IHT consequences, **Chapter 33**).

EXAMPLE 25.10

Property consisting of shares in Zac Ltd is held on trust for Irene for life, or until remarriage and thereafter to Dominic absolutely.

(1) *If Irene dies* There will be a deemed disposal and reacquisition of the shares at market value by the trustees (TCGA 1992 s 71(1)), but CGT will not be charged. The property henceforth belongs to Dominic.
(2) *If Irene remarries* The life interest will cease with the same consequences as in (1), save that CGT may be chargeable.

If the interest is in a part only of the fund, the death of the beneficiary will result in an uplift in the appropriate portion of each asset in the fund without any CGT charge thereon (TCGA 1992 s 73(2)) although assets may be appropriated by the trustees in satisfaction of that share in which case the uplift is in respect of those assets only (see **[25.7]**).

The above treatment also applies to interests in possession which are not life interests but which came to an end on death. For instance, if the income of a trust fund was settled on A until the age of 40 and thereafter the entire fund passed to B and A died aged 35 (see, for the definition of an interest in possession, **[25.54]**). **[25.49]**

d) *Reverter to settlor*

If the death causes the property to revert to the settlor, the 'reverter to disponer' exception applies (see TCGA 1992 s 73(1)(b) and **[33.21]**). The death of the beneficiary in these circumstances does not lead to a charge to IHT and, hence, the normal tax-free uplift provisions are modified to ensure that there is no double benefit. For CGT therefore the death will cause a deemed disposal and reacquisition, but for such a sum as will ensure that neither gain nor loss accrues to the trustees (a no gain/no loss disposal). Curiously, the position is different if property reverts to the settlor as life tenant. In this case a full uplift is given. **[25.50]**

EXAMPLE 25.11

In 2005, Sue settled property on trust for Samantha for life. In 2016, Samantha dies whereupon the property reverts to Sue and the acquisition value and allowable expenses of the trustees are then £15,000 (value at the death of Samantha is £25,000). There is a deemed disposal and reacquisition by the trustees for £15,000 (to ensure neither gain nor loss). Contrast, however, the position if on Samantha's death the property reverted to Sue on a life interest trust. Despite the IHT exemption still applying, for CGT purposes the usual death uplift applies (see **[25.54]**).

e) *Holdover relief and the tax-free death uplift*

Normally, a tax-free uplift occurs when the death of the interest in possession beneficiary gives rise to a s 71(1) disposal. However, if the settlor had made an election to holdover his gain when he created the settlement, that held-over gain is not wiped out on the subsequent death of the life tenant but instead is chargeable at that time (TCGA 1992 s 74: for holdover relief, see generally **Chapter 24**).

Transfers into and out of a trust that come within the IHT relevant property rules will automatically be eligible for holdover relief under TCGA 1992 s 260(2)(a). It should be noted, however, that the ability to elect for this relief to apply is generally removed where a settlement is created for the benefit of a settlor's minor children. Where assets remain in trust following the death of life tenant, there will be no CGT-free uplift on death unless a succeeding interest in possession meets the IHT rules.

EXAMPLE 25.12

Property was settled on trust for Frank for life with remainder to Brian absolutely. The settlor elected to holdover the gain of £12,000 when he created the settlement.

When Frank dies, the *total* gain on the deemed disposal made by the trustees under s 71 is £40,000. The CGT position is:
(1) There will be a tax-free uplift on the death of Frank, but only for gains arising since the creation of the settlement. Of the total gain of £40,000, £28,000 is, therefore, free of CGT.
(2) The remaining £12,000 gain (the gain held over by the settlor) is subject to tax on Frank's death (unless a further claim for holdover relief is made at that time).

The result of s 74 is a partial revival of the CGT charge on death that is explicable as an anti-avoidance measure. Assume that Bertha wished to give her daughter Brenda an asset on which there was a large unrealised capital gain and on a gift of which a holdover election was available. They could have elected for holdover relief, but that would have resulted in Brenda taking over the gain. As an alternative, therefore, Bertha could have settled the asset on an aged life tenant, who was expected to die imminently, and given the remainder interest to Brenda. No CGT would have arisen on the creation of that settlement if Bertha elected for holdover relief and, were it not for s 74, the death of the life tenant would have wiped out all gains leaving Brenda with the asset valued at its then market value. [25.51]

f) *The anti flip-flop legislation*

FA 2000 inserted provisions (TCGA 1992 s 76B and Sch 4B) aimed at 'flip-flop' arrangements which were widely employed in non-UK resident trusts. The legislation is, however, drafted sufficiently widely to catch UK trusts where the only benefit of the scheme was a 6% tax saving. Where these anti-avoidance rules apply, the trustees are deemed to dispose of and to reacquire trust assets at market value. The provisions are considered at [27A.87]. [25.52]

g) *Allowable expenditure on a deemed disposal*

By its very nature a deemed disposal will rarely lead to any expenditure. TCGA 1992 s 38(4) (which prohibits notional expenditure) seems somewhat redundant, especially in the light of *IRC v Chubb's Settlement Trustees* (1971) which permitted the deduction of *actual* expenses incurred upon the partition of a fund (see [19.22]). [25.53]

5 The termination of an interest in possession on the death of the beneficiary, the settlement continuing (TCGA 1992 s 72)

The death of a beneficiary entitled to an interest in possession, in cases where the settlement continues thereafter (ie where TCGA 1992 s 71(1) does not operate), results in a deemed disposal and reacquisition of the assets in the fund by the trustees at their then market value (TCGA 1992 s 72). CGT will not normally be imposed, and the purpose of s 72 is the familiar one of ensuring a tax-free uplift.

The termination of an interest in a part of the fund, where the settlement continues thereafter, results in a proportionate uplift in the value of all the assets.

An interest in possession for these purposes includes an annuity – the relevant provisions in s 72 are as follows:

'(3) This section shall apply on the death of the person entitled to any annuity payable out of or charged on, settled property or the income of settled property as it applies on the death of a person whose interest in possession in the whole or any part of settled property terminates on his death.

(4) Where, in the case of any entitlement to an annuity created by a settlement some of the settled property is appropriated by the trustees as a fund out of which the annuity is payable, and there is no right of recourse to, or to the income of, settled property not so appropriated, then without prejudice to subsection (5) below, the settled property so appropriated shall, while the annuity is payable, and on the occasion of the death of the person entitled to the annuity, be treated for the purposes of this section as being settled property under a separate settlement.'

EXAMPLE 25.13
Property is held on trust for Walter for life and thereafter for his son Vivian contingently on attaining 25. Walter dies when Vivian is 24. The CGT consequences are:
(1)   *Death of Walter*: There is a deemed disposal of the property under TCGA 1992 s 72; there is a tax-free uplift. The settlement continues because Vivian is not yet 25.
(2)   *Vivian becomes 25*: There is a further deemed disposal under s 71(1) and CGT may be charged on any increase in value of the assets since Walter's death.

As with deemed disposals under s 71(1) (see **[25.51]**) on the death of a life tenant the full tax-free uplift on death does not apply to a gain held over on the creation of a settlement which becomes chargeable. The uplift does, however, apply if the property becomes held on an interest in possession trust for the settlor ('reverter to settlor' no gain/no loss treatment (s 73(1)(b)), see **[25.50]**) is limited to the s 71 charge). **[25.54]**

6 Conclusions on deemed disposals under TCGA 1992 ss 71 and 72

The ending of general holdover relief in 1989 had important consequences for settlements. In particular, if it is no longer possible to postpone payment of the tax, the termination of a trust may result in a substantial tax liability. For instance, in the case of a life interest settlement rather than bringing the settlement to an end (whether by agreement between the beneficiaries or by exercise of overriding trustee powers), it may be preferable to wait for the death of the life tenant. In the case of discretionary trusts, because there will normally be a chargeable transfer for IHT on the settlement ending, it remains possible to holdover any capital gains.

Resettlements of property (considered at **[25.80]**) should normally be avoided since the act of resettlement will (in most cases) itself trigger a CGT charge. Note, however, that not every change in beneficial interests results in a deemed disposal: for instance, if a life interest terminates, for a reason other than the death of the beneficiary and the settlement continues, there is no deemed disposal for CGT purposes. This is also the case when a beneficiary merely acquires a right to the income of the trust. **[25.55]–[25.80]**

EXAMPLE 25.14

Property is settled upon trust for Belinda for life or until remarriage, and thereafter for Roger contingent upon his attaining 25. If Belinda remarries when Roger is ten, the CGT position is:
(1) *The remarriage of Belinda*: Belinda's remarriage terminates her life interest, but there is no deemed disposal as Roger is not at that time absolutely entitled to the fund. Hence, there are no CGT consequences.
(2) *When Roger attains 18*: He will become entitled to the income from the fund as a result of the Trustee Act 1925 s 31. There is no CGT consequence.
(3) *When Roger attains 25*: There is a deemed disposal under s 71(1), and (unless the property comprises business assets) holdover relief will not be available.

IV RESETTLEMENTS AND SEPARATE FUNDS

1 Basic rule

From 6 April 2006, where property is transferred from the trustees of one settlement to another, the settlor of the property disposed of by the trustees of the first settlement is treated from the time of the disposal as having made the second. Property which was provided for the purposes of the first settlement, or which is derived from it, is treated from the time of the disposal as having been provided for the purposes of the second settlement (TCGA 1992 s 68B).

When property is transferred from one settlement into another, different, settlement a CGT charge may arise under TCGA 1992 s 71(1) because the trustees of the second settlement (who may be the same persons as the trustees of the original settlement) become absolutely entitled to that property as against the original trustees (see *Hoare Trustees v Gardner* (1978)).

[25.81]

2 When does property become comprised in a separate settlement?

Exactly when a resettlement occurs as the result of the exercise by trustees of dispositive powers (eg of appointment and advancement) contained within the trust deed is still a matter of uncertainty (see especially *Roome v Edwards* (1981); *Bond v Pickford* (1983); and *Swires v Renton* (1991)). In *Roome v Edwards*, Lord Wilberforce stressed that the question should be approached 'in a practical and common sense manner' and suggested that relevant indicia included separate and defined property, separate trusts and separate trustees, although he emphasised that such factors were helpful but not decisive and that the matter ultimately depended upon the particular facts of each case. He contrasted special powers of appointment which, when exercised, will usually not result in a resettlement of property, with wider powers (eg of advancement) which permit property to be removed from the original settlement.

In *Bond v Pickford* (1983), the Court of Appeal distinguished between two types of power:
(1) a power *in the narrower form* (such as a power of appointment); and
(2) a power *in the wider form* (typically a power of advancement).

The distinction depends on whether the trustees are permitted to free settled property from the original settlement and transfer it into a new settlement. In the absence of an express provision enabling them to do this such action would be prohibited because of the principle that trustees cannot delegate.

Powers in the narrower form cannot create a new settlement: so far as powers in the wider form are concerned *their exercise will not necessarily* create a new settlement. In *Swires v Renton* (1991), Hoffmann J stressed that the classic case involving a new settlement would be where particular assets were segregated, new trustees appointed, and fresh trusts created exhausting the beneficial interest in the assets and providing full administrative powers so that further reference back to the original settlement became redundant. The absence of one or more of these features leaves open the question whether a new settlement has arisen: the question then has to be decided on the basis of intention. In the *Renton* case, for instance, despite exhaustive beneficial trusts, the administrative powers of the original settlement were retained and the appointment made other references to it thereby indicating that a new settlement had not been created. SP 7/84 generally conforms to the recent cases and indicates that the exercise of a power in the wider form will *not* create a new settlement if it is revocable, non-exhaustive, or if the trustees of the original settlement still have duties in relation to the advanced fund.

In order to provide maximum flexibility, settlements should have dispositive powers which are in the narrower and wider form so that the trustees can then decide whether it is their wish to create a new settlement or not. [25.82]

3 Separate funds within a single settlement

It is common for settlements (and especially A&M trusts) to split into separate funds that often have separate trustees managing assets which have been appropriated to that fund. Because these funds are treated as part of a single settlement (a 'composite settlement') for CGT purposes various difficulties arise as illustrated in the following example. [25.83]–[25.110]

EXAMPLE 25.15

The Bladcomb family trust was created in discretionary form in 1965 since when 90% of the assets have been irrevocably appointed on various interest in possession trusts with the remaining 10% being appointed on A&M trusts for infant beneficiaries. The various funds are administered by the original trustees of the 1965 discretionary trust. On these facts the property has remained comprised in the original settlement for CGT purposes. Accordingly:

(1) Even if separate trustees are appointed for part of the assets held on interest in possession trusts, the trustees of the original 1965 trust will remain liable for any CGT attributable to that portion of the assets.

(2) Only one annual exemption is available for gains realised in any part of the settled fund.

(3) A loss made in one fund will be used to offset a gain in another (because the settlement is a single entity). Should some form of 'compensation' be paid to the fund losing the benefit of the loss (but, if so, how is this calculated?)

V DISPOSAL OF BENEFICIAL INTERESTS

1 The basic rule

The basic rule is that there is no charge to CGT when a beneficiary disposes of his interest (TCGA 1992 s 76(1): contrast the disposal of an interest in an unadministered estate). The rationale is that gains in the trust are taxed (see above) so that to charge tax on the disposal of the interest of a beneficiary would be a form of double taxation. There is, however, a growing list of exceptions – which is added to each year as tax avoidance schemes seek to exploit the basic exemption. And, of course, if a trust is viewed as akin to a company, in which not only are corporate gains taxed but also disposals of shares are chargeable, it may be thought that the rationale behind the general rule is misconceived. [25.111]

2 Position of a purchaser

Once a beneficial interest has been purchased for money or money's worth, a future disposal of that interest will be chargeable to CGT. The consideration does not have to be 'full' or 'adequate': ie any consideration however small will turn the interest into a chargeable asset. An exchange of interests by two beneficiaries under a settlement is not, however, treated as a purchase so that a later disposal of either interest will not be chargeable.

When a life interest has been sold, the wasting asset rules (see [19.37]) may apply on a subsequent disposal of that interest by the purchaser. [25.112]

EXAMPLE 25.16

Ron is the remainderman under a settlement created by his father. He sells his interest to his friend Algy for £25,000. No CGT is charged. If Algy resells the remainder interest to Ginger for £31,000, Algy has made a chargeable gain of £6,000 (£31,000 – £25,000).

3 Purchaser becoming absolutely entitled to any part of the settled property

The termination of the settlement may result in the property passing to a purchaser of the remainder interest (of course, he may also become entitled to such property in other situations, eg if an advancement is made in his favour). As a result, that purchaser will dispose of his interest in return for receiving the property in the settlement (TCGA 1992 s 76(2)). The resultant charge that he suffers does not affect the deemed disposal by the trustees (and the possible CGT charge) under s 71(1). [25.113]

EXAMPLE 25.17

Assume, in *Example 25.16*, that Ginger becomes entitled to the settled fund which is worth £80,000. He has realised a chargeable gain of £49,000 (£80,000 – £31,000). In addition, the usual deemed disposal rules under s 71(1) operate.

4 Disposal of an interest in a non-resident settlement

TCGA 1992 s 85(1) provides that the disposal of an interest in a non-resident settlement is chargeable: the basic exemption conferred by s 76(1) is therefore excluded in such cases although it is expressly provided that no charge arises under s 76(2) if the beneficiary becomes absolutely entitled to any part of the trust fund (this charge is therefore restricted to a purchaser of the interest). When the trust was originally UK resident the appointment of non-resident trustees triggers an exit charge (see [27A.38]) and some protection against a double charge if a beneficial interest is subsequently sold is provided by s 85(3):

> '[in] calculating any chargeable gain accruing on the disposal of the interest the person disposing of it shall be treated as having:
> (a) disposed of it immediately before the relevant time, and
> (b) immediately reacquired it,
> at its market value at that time.'

Although not happily drafted, the purpose of the subsection is to fix the acquisition cost of the disponor at the date when the trustees emigrated (ie his acquisition cost will take into account the gains then realised and subject to UK tax). On first reading, the provision might be thought to impose a second charge at that time but this is not thought to be the case.

An infelicity in the drafting is that the provision is said to be relevant for the purpose of calculating the chargeable gain of the disponor: it should also be relevant in arriving at any allowable loss which he may have suffered!

EXAMPLE 25.18

The Halibut trust was set up in 1989, with Jason Halibut being entitled to the residue of the trust on the death of his sister, Rose. The trustees became non-UK resident in 2010 and Jason sold his remainder interest shortly afterwards for £150,000.
Analysis:
(1) Jason has made a chargeable disposal (TCGA 1992 s 85(1));
(2) in order to compute his chargeable gain (if any) the market value of his interest when the trust became non-resident needs to be ascertained.

FA 2000 amended s 85 to prevent what might be termed 'the in and out scheme'. Assume that a non-resident trust has stockpiled gains (for the meaning of this term, see [27.112]) and is now a cash fund. UK trustees are appointed so that the trust becomes resident and subsequently it is exported (by the appointment of further non-resident trustees). On the latter event s 85(3) would operate to increase the base costs of all the beneficial interests but, given that the assets in the trust are sterling, there will be no exit charge. Accordingly a beneficiary could sell his interest (effectively extracting stockpiled gains) tax free. From 21 March 2000 the disposal of a beneficial interest in a settlement that had stockpiled gains at 'the material time' (ie when it ceased to be UK resident) will not benefit from the uplift in value under s 85(3). [25.114]

5 Disposal of an interest in a settlement that had at any time been non-resident (TCGA 1992 s 76(1A), (1B) and (3))

This provision was introduced by FA 1998 and was something of a panic measure aimed at various schemes intended to avoid any charge on gains which had accrued in foreign trusts by repatriating the trust and a beneficiary then disposing of his interest. Various points should be noted about this provision:

(1) it catches the disposal of an interest if the settlement had at any time been non-resident or if it had received property from a non-resident settlement;
(2) like s 85(1) there is no charge if (or to the extent that) the beneficiary becomes entitled to the trust property;
(3) it would seem to overlap with s 85 and, in effect, makes that provision redundant. [25.115]

6 Sale of an interest in a 'settlor interested' trust (TCGA 1992 s 76A and Sch 4A)

a) *Basic rule*

These rules took effect from 21 March 2000 and when they apply the trustees, provided that they are UK resident, are treated as disposing and reacquiring trust assets at market value (ie there is a deemed disposal). Tax is then calculated at either the settlor rate (if the settlor still has an interest in the trust) or at the rate applicable to trusts and may be recovered by the trustees from the beneficiary who sold the interest. [25.116]

b) *When is a settlor interested in his trust?*

The normal provisions of TCGA 1992 Sch 4A apply. For a charge to apply, the trust must either have been a settlor interested trust at any time in the previous two years or must contain property derived from a trust which had been settlor interested at any time in the previous two years. Notice that the disposal can be by *any* beneficiary: the legislation is not limited to disposals by the settlor. The settlor must, however, be resident in the UK.

The definition of a settlor-interested trust now includes accumulation and maintenance trusts set up by parents. The legislation provides that a settlor has an interest in a settlement where property is or may be comprised in a settlement, or may become payable for the benefit of the settlor's dependent child, or the child derives any benefit from it whatsoever either directly or indirectly. [25.117]

c) *The mischief under attack*

The intention is to prevent exploiting the s 76(1) exemption by individuals who place assets in trusts (instead of selling the assets) and retain an interest that is subsequently sold. However, the scope of the legislation is not so limited and may catch the wholly innocent. [25.118]–[25.140]

EXAMPLE 25.19

(1) Dodgy put assets into a trust making a holdover election to avoid the payment of any CGT. He is absolutely entitled to those assets on attaining 35 (which is, say, in three months' time). He sells this interest to Tug and Thug, trustees of a settlement with realised capital losses.
    (a) under general principles the sale by Dodgy will not attract a CGT charge (TCGA 1992 s 76(1));
    (b) when Tug and Thug become absolutely entitled a further holdover election is available and when they dispose of the assets they can offset the resultant gain by their unused trust losses.

In these circumstances s 76A and Sch 4A provide that when Dodgy sells his interest the trustees make a deemed disposal of the trust property and the tax charge (at Dodgy's rates) will be borne by him.

(2) The Tinkerbell estate was resettled in 1990 and Teddy, the current life tenant, will therefore be considered to be a settlor. His son, Syd, is the remainderman but is tired of waiting for his inheritance and so sells his interest. Section 76A will apply and Syd will suffer a wholly undeserved CGT charge!

VI RELIEF FROM, AND PAYMENT OF, CGT

1 Payment

CGT attributable to both actual and deemed disposals of settled property is assessed on the trustees at a rate of either 20% or 28% (for 2016–17 onwards – see [**25.41**]): in exceptional cases the settlor's rate will apply. If the tax is not paid within six months of the due date for payment, it may be recovered from a beneficiary who has become absolutely entitled to the asset (or proceeds of sale therefrom) in respect of which the tax is chargeable. The beneficiary may be assessed in the trustees' name for a period of two years after the date when the tax became payable (TCGA 1992 s 69(4)). [**25.141**]

2 Exemptions and reliefs

Exemptions and reliefs from CGT have been discussed in **Chapter 22**, but note the following matters in the context of settled property:

Main residence exemption May be available in the case of a house settled on both discretionary and on interest in possession trusts (see *Sansom v Peay* (1976) and [**52.62**]). However, there are restrictions where holdover relief is claimed on the property entering the trust (see [**25.55**]). [**25.142**]

The annual exemption Trustees are generally allowed half of the exemption appropriate to an individual (for 2017–18, half of 11,300 = £5,650). Note that trusts for the mentally disabled are entitled to the full annual exemption (£11,300 in 2017–18). [**25.143**]

Death exemption As already discussed, the tax-free uplift will be available for most trusts. [**25.144**]

Roll-over relief Available only if the trustees are carrying on an unincorporated business. **[25.145]**

Trust rate band. A £1,000 rate band is available to all trusts paying tax at the trust rate. **[25.146]**

Deferral relief for chargeable gains Available if the beneficiaries are either individuals or charities. **[25.147]**

3 Entrepreneurs' relief and trusts

Broadly, entrepreneurs' relief means that the first £10m of gains (limit applying from 6 April 2011) arising on or in connection with disposals of the whole or part of trust business assets will be charged to capital gains tax at the rate of 10% (FA 2011 s 9) (see generally **Chapter 20**). To qualify for the relief, three conditions must be satisfied:

(1) the trustees of a settlement dispose of 'settlement business assets'. These are assets that are part of the settled property of the settlement and are:
- shares in or securities of a company, or interests in such shares or securities; or
- assets that have been used for the purposes of a business, or interests in such assets.

(2) an individual is a 'qualifying beneficiary' of the settlement. The individual must have an interest in possession (other than an interest in possession which has a fixed term) in the whole of the settled property of the settlement or in a part of the settled property that contains the settlement business assets disposed of.

(3) one of two 'relevant conditions' is satisfied. The first condition must be satisfied if the settlement business assets are shares in or securities of a company, or interests in such shares or securities. Throughout a period of one year ending within the three years up to the date of the disposal:
- the company must be the qualifying beneficiary's personal company;
- the company must be a trading company or the holding company of a trading group; and
- the qualifying beneficiary must be an officer or employee of the company or of one or more companies that are members of the group.

The second condition applies in the case where the settlement business assets are assets (or interests in assets) that have been used for the purposes of a business. Throughout a period of one year ending within the three years up to the date of the disposal, the settlement business assets must be used for the purposes of a trade carried on by the qualifying beneficiary, and the qualifying beneficiary must cease to carry on the business at some time during that three-year period. **[25.148]**

VII TRUSTS WITH VULNERABLE BENEFICIARY

1 Introduction

Trusts set up for the most vulnerable, for example, for the disabled, are taxed as if the beneficiary had received the income and gains directly. The income tax aspects of the provisions are dealt with in **Chapter 16**. The CGT aspects are summarised in the following paragraphs.

FA 2005 ss 23–45 created a new trust tax regime for certain trusts with vulnerable beneficiaries (defined by s 23 as disabled persons or relevant minors). These provisions determine which trusts and beneficiaries can elect into the regime and where a claim for special tax treatment is made for a tax year, provide for no more tax to be paid in respect of the relevant income and gains of the trust for that year than would be paid had the income and gains accrued directly to the beneficiary.

A statutory meaning of 'disabled person' was introduced by FA 2013 with effect from 17 July 2013 (FA 2005 Sch 1A).

FA 2013 also introduced a measure to allow small payments of income and capital to non-vulnerable beneficiaries without the trust losing its favoured status. The annual limit is set at the lower of £3,000 and 3% of the amount which is the maximum value of the settled property during the period in question. A claim for special tax treatment for a tax year may be made by trustees if (FA 2005 s 25(1)):

'(a) in the tax year income arises (or is treated as arising) to the trustees of a settlement from property held on qualifying trusts for the benefit of a vulnerable person ("qualifying trusts income"), and
(b) a claim for special tax treatment under this Chapter for the tax year is made by the trustees.' **[25.149]**

2 Qualifying trust gains: special capital gains tax treatment

The provisions relating to trust gains are set out in FA 2005 s 30. This section applies to a tax year if:
(a) in the tax year chargeable gains accrue to the trustees of a settlement from the disposal of settled property which is held on qualifying trusts for the benefit of a vulnerable person ('the qualifying trusts gains');
(b) the trustees would (if not for the new regime) be chargeable to capital gains tax in respect of those gains;
(c) the trustees are resident in the United Kingdom during any part of the tax year; and
(d) a claim for special tax treatment under s 30 for the tax year is made by the trustees.

It is worth noting that a claim cannot be made if the vulnerable person dies during the year in question (FA 2005 s 30(3)). **[25.150]**

3 UK-resident vulnerable persons: amount of relief

Under the 'Trusts with vulnerable beneficiary' regime, a charge to CGT on the settlor with an interest in the settlement will apply in relation to the qualifying trusts gains as if:
(a) the vulnerable person were a settlor in relation to the settlement;
(b) the settled property disposed of, and any other settled property disposed of at any time when it was relevant settled property, originated from him; and
(c) he had an interest in the settlement during the tax year.

Property is 'relevant settled property' at any time when it is property held on the qualifying trusts for the benefit of the vulnerable person, and the trustees would (if not for these rules) be chargeable to CGT in respect of any chargeable gains accruing to them on a disposal of it (FA 2005 s 31). FA 2014 includes provisions which extend the CGT uplift on death provisions so that they apply to a vulnerable beneficiary where such beneficiary dies on or after 5 December 2013. [25.151]

4 Non-UK resident vulnerable persons: amount of relief

The trustees' liability to CGT for the tax year will be reduced by an amount equal to (FA 2005 s 32):

TQTG – VQTG

Where:

TQTG is the amount of CGT to which the trustees would (if not for these new rules) be liable for the tax year in respect of the qualifying trusts gains, and

VQTG is calculated using the formula TLVA – TLVB

Where:

TLVB is the total tax liability of the vulnerable person (see below), and

TLVA is what the total tax liability of the vulnerable person would be if it included tax in respect of notional s 77 gains).

TLVB is the total amount of income tax and capital gains tax to which the vulnerable person would be liable for the tax year:
(a) if his income for the tax year were equal to the sum of his actual income for the tax year (if any) and the amount of the trustees' specially taxed income (if any) for the tax year; and
(b) if his taxable amount for the tax year (under TCGA 1992 s 3) were equal to his deemed CGT taxable amount for the tax year (if any).

TLVA is what TLVB would be if the vulnerable person's taxable amount for the tax year (under TCGA 1992 s 3) were equal to the sum of the amount mentioned in (b) above and his notional gains for the tax year. [25.152]

26 CGT – companies and shareholders

Updated by Helen McGhee, Senior Associate,
Joseph Hage Aaronson LLP

I   CGT problems involving companies [**26.1**]
II Capital distributions paid to shareholders [**26.21**]
III The disposal of shares [**26.41**]
IV Value-shifting [**26.61**]

I CGT PROBLEMS INVOLVING COMPANIES

1 CGT and corporation tax

Companies and unincorporated associations are not subject to CGT; instead chargeable gains are assessed to corporation tax. Broadly, and with the important exception of indexation relief, the principles involved in computing the chargeable gain (or allowable loss) are the same as for individuals.

Disposals from one company in a group (as defined) to another will generally be treated as taking place at a value giving rise to neither gain nor loss (TCGA 1992 s 171). Any gain is deferred until the asset is sold outside the group or if the company owning the asset leaves the group within six years of the transfer (TCGA 1992 s 179). [**26.1**]

2 Company reorganisations

The basic principle is that there is neither a disposal of the original shares nor the acquisition of a new holding: instead, the original shares and new holding are treated as a single asset acquired when the original shares were acquired. When new consideration is given on a reorganisation (for instance, on a rights issue), that is added to the base cost of the original shares and treated as having been given when they were acquired (TCGA 1992 ss 126–131). However, if there is an election under TCGA 1992, s 169Q, a claim for entrepreneurs' relief can be made as if the re-organisation involved a disposal of the original shares, and s 127 will not apply. [**26.2**]

3 Company takeovers and demergers

If the takeover is by means of an issue of shares or debentures by the purchasing company (a 'paper for paper exchange'), CGT on the gain made by the disposing shareholder may generally be postponed until the consideration shares are sold (TCGA 1992 ss 135–137). If the consideration for the acquisition is partly shares and partly cash, the cash element is treated as a part disposal of the shareholding and s 135 will apply to the balance. The purchaser must obtain more than 25% of the shares in the target company (subject to a number of conditions) for these rules to apply. Furthermore the transaction must be effected for *bona fide* commercial reasons and not form part of any scheme or arrangement of which the main purpose or one of the main purposes is to avoid a liability to CGT or corporation tax. An advance clearance may be sought (TCGA 1992 s 138) to ensure the bona fide commercial reasons test is met.

Where the assets of the target company are acquired for a cash consideration, any chargeable gain arising on this disposal of those assets will be chargeable on the target company. An exemption might apply, such as the substantial shareholdings exemption, see **[41.75]** or a deferral such as roll-over relief under TCGA 1992 ss 152–159 (see **[22.72]**). From the point of view of the target's shareholders, they may be left with the problem of what to do with a 'cash shell' company: see **Chapter 47**.

TCGA 1992 s 192 contains provisions aimed at facilitating arrangements whereby trading activities of a single company or group are split up in order to be carried on either by two or more companies or by separate groups of companies, see **Chapter 47** (demergers). [26.3]

4 Incorporation of an existing business

TCGA 1992 s 162 provides relief in cases where an unincorporated business is transferred to a company as a going concern in return for the issue of shares in the company. The relief enables the gains on the business assets transferred to the company to be rolled over into the acquisition of the shares. (For detailed examination of the rules see **[47.2]**.) [26.4]–[26.20]

II CAPITAL DISTRIBUTIONS PAID TO SHAREHOLDERS

A capital distribution (whether in cash or assets) is treated in the hands of a shareholder as a disposal or part disposal of the shares in respect of which the distribution is received (TCGA 1992 s 122(1)). 'Capital distribution' is restrictively defined to exclude any distribution that is subject to income tax in the hands of the recipient (s 122(5)(b)). As the definition of a distribution is extremely wide (see **[42.1]**) the CGT charge is confined to repayments of share capital and to distributions in the course of winding up.

EXAMPLE 26.1

(1) Prunella buys shares in Zaba Ltd for £40,000. Some years later the company repays to her £12,000 on a reduction of share capital. The value of Prunella's remaining shares immediately after that reduction is £84,000.

The company has made a capital distribution for CGT purposes and Prunella has disposed of an interest in her shares in return for that payment. The part disposal rules must, therefore, be applied as follows:

(i) consideration for part disposal: £12,000

(ii) allocation of base cost of shares:

$$£40,000 \times \frac{A}{A+B} = £40,000 \times \frac{£12,000}{£12,000 + £84,000} = £5,000$$

(iii) gain on part disposal: £12,000 − £5,000 = £7,000.

(2) Stanley buys shares in Monley Ltd for £60,000. The company is wound up and Stanley is paid £75,000 in the liquidation. Stanley has disposed of his shares in return for the payment by the liquidator and, therefore, has a chargeable gain of £15,000 (£75,000 − £60,000).

If the company had been insolvent so that the shares were worthless, Stanley should claim loss relief on the grounds that his shares had become of negligible value (see TCGA 1992 s 24(2); *Williams v Bullivant* (1983); and [**19.69**]). He has an allowable loss of £60,000. Income tax relief may be available for this loss under ITA 2007 s 131 (see [**11.121**]).

These rules are also applied when a shareholder disposes of a right to acquire further shares in the company (TCGA 1992 s 123). The consideration received on the disposal is treated as if it were a capital distribution received from the company in respect of the shares held.

Under s 122(2), if HMRC are satisfied that the amount distributed is small, the part disposal rules are not applied but the capital distribution is deducted from the allowable expenditure on the subsequent disposal of the shares, with the result of increasing the subsequent gain (in effect the provision operates as a postponement of CGT). For these purposes, a capital distribution is treated as small if it amounts to no more than 5% of the value of the shares in respect of which it is made. However, a revised approach was announced in *Tax Bulletin* 27 in February 1997 as a result of *dicta* in *O'Rourke v Binks* (1992) which noted that the purpose of the legislation was to avoid the need for an assessment in trivial cases, an approach that would have regard to the likely costs of carrying out the part disposal computation and the likely tax consequences in each case. As a result, in addition to the 5% test, HMRC now considers that s 122(2) can apply in cases where the distribution is £3,000 or less (see CG 57836).

Under s 122(4) where the allowable expenditure is *less than* the amount distributed the taxpayer may elect that the part disposal rules shall not apply and that the expenditure shall be deducted from the amount distributed. In *O'Rourke v Binks* (1992), the Court of Appeal held that the capital distribution must be small for the purpose of this subsection and that what was 'small' would be a question of fact for the Tribunal to decide.

On a liquidation there will often be a number of payments made prior to the final winding up and each is a part disposal of shares (subject to the relief for small distributions) but the shares will not necessarily need to be valued each time a distribution is made (see Statement of Practice D3).

EXAMPLE 26.2

Mark purchased 5,000 shares in Rothko Ltd for £5,000. The company makes a 1:5 rights issue at £1.25 per share. Mark is, therefore, entitled to a further 1,000 shares but, having no spare money, sells his rights to David for £250. At that time his 5,000 shares were worth £7,500. As the capital distribution (£250) is less than 5% of £7,500 the part disposal rules will not apply. Therefore, £250 will be deducted from Mark's £5,000 base cost. (NB Mark may have preferred the part disposal rules to apply since any gain resulting may be covered by his annual exemption.) **[26.21]–[26.40]**

III THE DISPOSAL OF SHARES

1 Introduction

a) *Pre-FA 1982 system*

Before FA 1982, the CGT rules were relatively straightforward and involved treating identical shares as a single asset. This 'pooling' system involved a cumulative total of shares with sales being treated as part disposals from the pool and not as a disposal of a particular parcel of shares. Special rules applied where all or part of a shareholding was acquired before 6 April 1965. **[26.41]**

b) *FA 1982 regime – operative from 6 April 1982 to 6 April 1985*

Shares of the same class acquired after 5 April 1982 and before 6 April 1985 were not pooled. Instead, each acquisition was treated as the acquisition of a separate asset. A disposal of shares was then matched with a particular acquisition in accordance with detailed identification rules that applied even where the shares were distinguishable from each other by, for instance, being individually numbered. Shares were therefore treated as a 'fungible' asset. These rules were introduced because of the indexation allowance which made it necessary to know whether the shares disposed of had been acquired within 12 months (when no allowance was available) or, in other cases, to calculate the indexation allowance by reference to the original expenditure. **[26.42]**

c) *The 1985 regime – operative from 6 April 1985 to 6 April 1998*

Major changes in the indexation allowance in 1985 enabled a form of pooling to be re-introduced. Shares of the same class acquired after 5 April 1982 and still owned by the taxpayer on 6 April 1985 were treated as one asset and further acquisitions of the shares after that date formed part of this single holding (TCGA 1992 s 104). There was an indexed pool of expenditure for each class of share and, if shares in the pool were acquired between 1982 and 1985, the initial value of this pool on 6 April 1985 comprised the acquisition costs of the relevant shares together with the indexation allowance (including an allowance for the first 12 months of ownership) that would have been given had the shares been sold on 5 April 1985.

If identical shares were acquired after 6 April 1985 they were added to the share pool with the cost of their acquisition increasing the indexed pool of expenditure (a similar result occurred if a rights issue was taken up).

When some of the shares were sold the part disposal rules were applied to both the qualifying expenditure and the indexed pool of expenditure. The indexation allowance was then found by deducting a proportion of the qualifying expenditure from a proportion of the indexed pool. The indexation allowance could only be used to reduce a gain – not to create or increase a loss. **[26.43]**

2 The regime introduced by FA 1998

a) *Basic rule*

With the introduction of taper relief in 1998, which depended upon the length of ownership of an asset, pooling was ended for individuals, PRs and trustees. As a result:
(1) acquisitions of shares on or after 6 April 1998 were not pooled (except for reorganisations being rights or bonus issues under TCGA 1992 s 127 (see **[26.2]**));
(2) pools at 5 April 1998 were preserved as a single asset (a 's 104 holding').

[26.44]

Where shares of the same class are acquired on the same day they were treated as having been acquired by a single transaction.

b) *The identification rules*

Each acquisition of shares was treated as a separate asset and new acquisition rules prescribed the order of disposals on the basis of 'last in first out' (LIFO). The order of disposals is therefore as follows (subject to what is said in the next section about bed and breakfasting):
(1) the most recently acquired unpooled shares;
(2) shares from a s 104 holding (this is treated as a single asset when the pool first came into being);
(3) 1982 pools (see **[26.43]**);
(4) shares held on 6 April 1965 (see **[26.41]**);
(5) later acquired shares. [26.45]

c) *Bed and breakfasting*

In simple terms, bed and breakfasting involved the disposal of shares on day one and their repurchase on day two: a transaction that was commonly employed to realise a loss on the shares for relief against other gains, or to realise a gain to enable the annual exemption to be utilised.

EXAMPLE 26.3

Alberich has unused CGT losses. He owns shares which have an unrealised gain and which he wishes to retain. He sells the shares at close of business one day, reduces or extinguishes the gain with his losses and repurchases the shares at the start of business the next.

TCGA 1992 s 105 was introduced to match securities bought and sold on the same day but was able to be avoided by buying back the following day. FA 1998 introduced a more widespread provision aimed at stopping bed and breakfasting by providing that disposals are to be matched with acquisitions in the following 30-day period (matching with the first securities acquired during this period): see TCGA 1992 s 106A(5). This brought an end to traditional bed and breakfasting whilst leaving some continuing opportunities: for instance, A sells his shares and his wife purchases an identical shareholding; or the disposal is triggered by the transfer to a trust for A. These simple arrangements are not caught by this provision but any transfers into trust must now take into account the inheritance tax implications following the FA 2006. It may now be necessary to consider the impact of the General Anti Abuse Rule (GAAR) in these circumstances (see **[3.79]–[3.82]**).

The '30-day rule' may produce surprising results, see the example below.

[26.46]

EXAMPLE 26.4

(1) Rover is returning to the UK after a period of non-residence. He 'bed and breakfasts' his investment portfolio with the intention that on his return to the UK his base cost will be market value. The 30-day rule will apply and needs to be taken into consideration by Rover (see *Tax Bulletin*, April 2001, p 839).

(2) With effect from 22 March 2006 the rules were amended so that they do not now apply where the person acquiring the shares is not resident in the UK. This followed the case of *Davies v Hicks* (2005) which highlighted the mismatch of the bed and breakfast rules with the exit charge arising when a trust ceases to be resident in the UK. In that case the trustees successfully argued that the exit charge under TCGA 1992 s 80 involved a deemed disposal and reacquisition of the shares by trust. However, under TCGA 1992 s 106A(5), the bed and breakfast rules applied to eliminate the gain on the deemed disposal. To correct this anomaly s 106A(5) will not apply to any acquisition on or after 22 March 2006 by a person who is not resident, or a person who is resident but is treated as non-resident by reason of a Double Taxation Agreement: s 106A(5A).

3 Simplification of pooling from 6 April 2008

From 6 April 2008, and with the abolition of taper relief, the position is considerably simplified and all shares will now be included in the s 104 pool and matched as follows:

(1) assets acquired on the date of disposal;
(2) assets acquired in the 30 days following disposal;
(3) assets in the s 104 pool.

These changes only apply to individuals and capital gains tax. The rules for corporation tax are unchanged. [26.47]

4 Shares acquired before 6 April 1965

For unquoted shares any gain is deemed to accrue evenly (the 'straight-line method') and it is only the portion of the gain since 6 April 1965 that is chargeable. The disponer may elect to have the gain computed by reference to the value of the shares on 6 April 1965. This election may only reduce a gain; it cannot increase a loss or replace a gain with a loss. Where different shares are disposed of on different dates the general rule of identification is last in, first out (LIFO) (TCGA 1992 Sch 2 paras 18–19).

For listed shares and securities the general principle is that a gain is calculated by reference to their market value on 6 April 1965 (the rules for ascertaining the market value are laid down in TCGA 1992 Sch 2 paras 1–6). If, however, a computation based upon the original cost of the shares produces a smaller gain or loss, it is the smaller gain or loss that is taken. If one calculation produces a gain, and one a loss, there is deemed to be neither. [26.48]–[26.60]

IV VALUE-SHIFTING

Complex provisions designed to prevent 'value-shifting' are found in TCGA 1992 ss 29–31. Although the sections are not limited to shares, the commonest examples of value-shifting involve shares.

Under s 29 three types of transaction are treated as disposals of an asset for CGT purposes, despite the absence of any consideration, so long as the person making the disposal could have obtained consideration. The three circumstances are outlined below. Section 29 provides that in these circumstances, the disposal is deemed not to be at arm's length and the substituted market value of the asset for the CGT computation is the consideration actually received plus the value of the 'consideration foregone'. Instances of value-shifting are to be found in the following paragraphs. [26.61]

1 **Controlling shareholdings (see CG 58853)**

Section 29(2) applies when a person having control (defined in CTA 2010 s 449) of a company exercises that control so that value passes out of shares (or out of rights over the company) in a company owned by him, or by a person connected with him, into other shares in the company or into other rights over the company. In *Floor v Davis* (1979) the House of Lords decided that the provision could apply where more than one person exercised collective control over the company, and that it covered inertia as well as positive acts. [26.62]

EXAMPLE 26.5

Ron owns 9,900 ordinary £1 shares in Wronk Ltd and his son, Ray, owns 100. Each share is worth £40. A further 10,000 shares are offered by the company to the existing shareholders at their par value (a 1:1 rights issue). Ron declines to take up his quota and all the shares are subscribed by Ray. Value has passed out of Ron's shares as he now holds a minority of the issued shares. He is treated as making a disposal of his shares by reason of s 29(2).

2 **Leases**

Section 29(4) provides as follows:

'If, after a transaction which results in the owner of land or of any other description of property becoming the lessee of the property, there is any adjustment of the rights and liabilities under the lease, whether or not involving the grant of a new lease, which is as a whole favourable to the lessor, there shall be a disposal by the lessee of an interest in the property.' (And see CG 58860.) [26.63]

EXAMPLE 26.6

Andrew conveys property to Edward by way of gift, but reserves to himself in the conveyance a long lease at a low rent. As the lease is valuable, the part disposal will give rise to a relatively small gain. Andrew later agrees to pay a rack rent so that the value of Edward's freehold is increased. When the rent is increased tax is charged on the consideration that could have been obtained for Andrew agreeing to pay that increased sum.

3 Tax-free benefits resulting from an arrangement

In contrast to s 29, s 30 applies only if there is an actual disposal of an asset. It strikes at schemes or arrangements, whether made before or after that disposal, as a result of which the value of the asset in question (or a 'relevant asset', as defined) has been reduced and 'a tax-free benefit has been or will be conferred on the person making the disposal or a person with whom he is connected; or on any other person'.

When it applies, the inspector is given power to adjust, as may be just and reasonable, the amount of gain or loss shown by the disposal (s 30(4)). This widely drafted provision will not operate if the taxpayer shows that the avoidance of tax was not the main purpose, or one of the main purposes, of the arrangement or scheme. Further, it does not catch disposals between husband and wife (within TCGA 1992 s 58); disposals between PRs and legatees; or disposals between companies that are members of a group. TCGA 1992 s 31 (as amended by FA 2011 Sch 9) extends the scope of these provisions to arrangements whereby the value of shares is materially reduced, for example where a distribution is made out of profits created by an intra group transfer to reduce the value of a shareholding prior to sale.

EXAMPLE 26.7

H Ltd has two subsidiaries, A Ltd and B Ltd. A Ltd is to be sold for a gain of £1 million. A Ltd has distributable profits of only £300,000 but it has a valuable property which it sells intra group to B Ltd for a profit of £700,000. No tax arises on this transfer by reason of TCGA 1992 s 171 but A Ltd still increases its distributable profits.

A Ltd pays a dividend of £1 million to H Ltd and A Ltd is then sold for a nominal sum. The idea is for the tax on the £1 million to be avoided.

Section 31 applies here to bring s 30 into play, allowing HMRC to make a just and reasonable adjustment to the capital gain to counteract the tax-free benefit intended to be obtained from these arrangements. **[26.64]**

27 CGT – Offshore matters for individuals

Updated by Robin Vos, Macfarlanes LLP

I Residence **[27.1]**
II Capital gains tax liability of non-residents and residents; temporary non-residents **[27.41]**
III The capital gains tax regime for foreign domiciliaries **[27.81]**
IV Non-resident companies and UK resident individuals **[27.111]**

I RESIDENCE

1 Introduction

A statutory residence test which applies to individuals for both income and capital gains tax purposes was introduced with effect from 6 April 2013. Ordinary residence has been abolished in the tax legislation and 'overseas work day relief' put on a statutory footing. These changes are discussed below (see **[27.17]–[27.40]**).

This chapter discusses the rules governing an individual's residence for capital gains tax purposes both before and after 2013. The chapter then goes on to discuss the capital gains tax regimes for non-residents including temporary non-residents and for foreign domiciliaries from April 2008. The next chapter discusses the capital gains tax regime for offshore trusts. **[27.1]**

2 The general law on residence up to 5 April 2013 – problems

Residency is the principal connecting factor in determining whether an individual is subject to income tax and capital gains tax. However, it was never previously defined in the UK's tax legislation. All that statute did (prior to the 2013 changes) was to provide three specific rules qualifying the general meaning of the term if certain conditions are met. See ITA 2007 ss 829–832 and TCGA 1992 s 9.

The difficulties caused by the lack of definition were compounded by the fact that one was dealing with not one term but two, namely 'residence' and 'ordinary residence'. Some tax liabilities were governed by residence, some by ordinary residence and some by both. For capital gains tax purposes it was enough if the taxpayer was resident or ordinarily resident in the UK.

The lack of statutory definition meant that the law on what constitutes residence or ordinary residence rested largely on decided cases. The case law presents three problems:

The first is that many of the cases are old, relating to a very different world in terms of travel and ease of communications. See for example *Levene v IRC* (1928) and *Lysaght v IRC* (1927). Hence judicial reasoning, while binding, is often inappropriate to modern conditions. Moreover many of the older cases do not clearly indicate whether days of arrival and departure have been included in the day count largely because it was often irrelevant (taxpayers could not then flit in and out of the country in the way that they can do now.)

The second problem is that because 'residence' and 'ordinary residence' are not defined for tax purposes, cases decided in other areas of the law where the term residence is used are also relevant. Thus the leading case on ordinary residence, *Shah v Barnet LBC* (1983), concerned not tax but eligibility for student grants. Similarly, cases on residence have arisen not in tax but in the context of determining whether a defendant is able to be sued in the UK under the Civil Jurisdiction and Judgments Act 1982 s 41 which in large measure turns on whether the defendant resides in the UK (*High Tech International v Deripaska* (2006); *Cherney v Deripaska* (2007) and *Yugraneft v Abramovich* (2008)).

The third problem is that the issue of whether an individual is resident or ordinarily resident is one of fact, to be determined by the tax tribunal. The higher courts will only interfere if the fact finding tribunal has erred in law or reached a conclusion so unreasonable that no reasonable body could have reached it. As a result most of the tax cases do not set out issues of principle on what constitutes residency but are decisions based on a set of facts. Very similar facts can give rise to the opposite results. The decision cannot be appealed unless it can be shown that the tribunal was not entitled to find as it did. In practice, unless the tribunal has clearly misdirected itself as a matter of law, a successful appeal is very difficult. [27.2]–[27.3]

The problems of the case-by-case approach were perceived long ago and a precise definition of residence was called for by both the Committee on Codification of Income Tax Law in 1936 and by the Royal Commission on the Taxation of Profits and Income in 1955. The 1936 Committee concluded that:

> 'the present state of affairs under which an enquirer can only be told that the question whether he is resident or not is a question of fact for the Commissioners but that by the study of the effect of a large body of case law he may be able to make an intelligent forecast of their decision is intolerable and should not be allowed to continue.'

Disputes over residence decreased after that statement because of HMRC's published guidance and practice eventually embodied in booklet IR20 (but in existence before then) which essentially imposed a day count test. The 1955 Royal Commission noted that this was 'unsatisfactory' in that it operated on the good faith of HMRC rather than on the rule of law. But IR20 was a pragmatic solution and practitioners followed it as rigorously as if it were a code of law. Eventually, however this compromise broke down and the number of residence cases and disputes greatly increased, demonstrating that the law was not satisfactory as it stood.

In particular there was dispute (no doubt caused by increased mobility) as to whether IR20 did set out 'clear bright lines' and whether if a taxpayer spent less than 91 days in the UK over a four-year period this was sufficient in itself to lose UK resident status or whether the taxpayer had to 'leave' the UK before the 91-day test became relevant at all. IR20 became subject to judicial review.

In *R (on the application of Davies and another) v IRC and R (on the application of Gaines-Cooper)* (2011) the taxpayers brought an application for judicial review in respect of whether HMRC was bound by IR20 and if they were so bound whether the taxpayers were within its scope. With Lord Mance dissenting, the Supreme Court found in favour of the Revenue on the basis that, although the guidance was in principle binding, on the particular facts the two sets of taxpayers had not satisfied the conditions set out in paragraphs 2.7–2.9 of IR20 because they had not demonstrated 'a distinct break'. Lord Wilson noted that, in his view, these paragraphs in IR20 showed two important features were required, namely (a) that the individual must take steps to create a permanent home abroad; and (b) that he must come to the UK as a visitor. The taxpayer had to leave the UK in a more profound sense than merely spending fewer days here, namely permanently or indefinitely leave or leave for full-time employment abroad and relinquish 'his usual residence' in the UK. In summary, Lord Wilson said:

> 'The reference to visits to the UK therefore underlined the need for a change in the individual's usual residence and therefore, by ready inference, for a distinct break in the pattern of his life in the UK ... it might be permissible for him to maintain in the UK not a home but property ... for his use but ... if he did so, he would fail to secure non-resident status unless his reason for doing so survived the test of consistency with his stated aim. (i.e. the UK property was used for the purpose of visits rather than as a place of settled residence.)'

The problems increased for both arrivers and leavers because HMRC ceased to give formal rulings on which the taxpayer could rely and showed an increased tendency to litigate even on quite low day counts. This uncertainty affects liability not only in one year but in subsequent years because the length of time an individual has been in the UK will be relevant for other tax purposes, for example in terms of ordinary residence, liability for the £30,000/£60,000/£90,000 remittance basis charge and inheritance tax and deemed domicile.

A person naturally wants to know where he is resident. A double tax treaty may not resolve the issue satisfactorily and will not necessarily apply for all taxes, eg deemed domicile and the remittance basis charge. Unlike the US, foreigners visiting the UK for extended periods could not safely assess their residence status simply on the basis of day-counting.

These problems and uncertainty were the driver for the introduction of a comprehensive statutory residence test (which took effect on 6 April 2013). See **[27.17]–[27.40]**.

For years prior to April 2013, taxpayers will need to determine their residence status based on the case law although clearly prior to April 2009 taxpayers can rely on IR20 as explained in the Supreme Court decision, above.

Although the statutory residence test provides a right for the taxpayer to elect that in determining residence status for 2013–14 onwards the statutory test can be applied for earlier years, this election only applies for the purpose of determining whether someone is an arriver or leaver for the purposes of the statutory residence test from 2013–14 and not for determining an individual's actual residence status in earlier tax years.

In this chapter Revenue practice is set out first, followed by the limited statutory provisions and then an analysis of the case law. The new statutory residence test which applies from 6 April 2013 is then explained briefly. For a full explanation see **Chapter 18**. [**27.4**]

a) *HMRC practice – IR20: 'Residents and non-residents: liability to tax in the United Kingdom' and HMRC 6*

As noted earlier, the fact that there was conflicting case law on residence did not really matter for much of the latter half of the 20th century, as the then Inland Revenue formulated practical rules, published in the booklet IR20 *'Residents and non-residents'*. These rules operated more or less unchanged from the 1940s and gave rise to the belief that if you did not spend more than 90 days in the UK each year you would not be treated as UK resident. IR20 was withdrawn from 6 April 2009 and replaced by HMRC 6.

IR20 was described as a concession and could not be used for tax avoidance purposes. It was prefaced by the comment that it set out only the main factors to be taken into account and that each case had to be determined on its own facts. However, IR20 seemed to be a clear statement of practice which could be relied on by taxpayers in cases which clearly fell within its terms. Even before it was withdrawn disputes had surfaced over its interpretation, no doubt reflecting the more mobile workforce; the ease of travel in and out of the UK and the fact that a day count test alone in determining residence was proving inadequate to stop significant tax leakage.

Coming to the UK

Under IR20 an individual was stated to be UK tax resident for a tax year if he met one of the following conditions:
(i) he was physically present in the UK for 183 days or more: '*the 183 day rule*'. Until 6 April 2008 it was normal practice to ignore days of arrival and departure. From 6 April 2008 midnights were included in the 183-day computation unless the person was 'in transit';
(ii) he visited the UK regularly on average 91 days or more in each tax year. The average was taken over a period of up to four years from the year of departure (so does not include days in years when he was UK resident): the '*91-day rule*';
(iii) he came to the UK with the intention of residing here permanently or for at least three years, in which case he was resident (and ordinarily resident) in the UK from the date when he arrived;
(iv) he came to the UK for a settled purpose (eg to take up employment) which meant he remained in the UK for at least two years. In this situation he was also resident in the UK from the date he arrived;
(v) he intended from the start to make regular visits of the type described in (ii), in which case he was treated as resident and ordinarily resident from 6 April of the first tax year;

(vi) he decided, before the fifth year, that he was going to make such visits, in which case he was resident and ordinarily resident from the beginning of the tax year in which he made that decision;
(vii) he was both UK resident and ordinarily resident and had left the UK only for occasional residence abroad.

Leaving the UK

An individual leaving the UK was therefore regarded as non-resident under IR20 if he satisfied the 183-and 91-day rules and fell into one of the following categories:
(i) he had emigrated permanently;
(ii) he or his spouse had left the UK to work full time abroad under a contract of employment or on a self-employed basis for a period which included at least one complete tax year;
(iii) he went abroad for some other settled purpose which lasted for at least one complete tax year.

An individual who departed without satisfying any of the above was treated as remaining UK resident. However, if, in fact, he satisfied the 183- and 91-day rules for three complete tax years his status was reviewed.

IR20 therefore suggested that residence was basically a question of counting days and given that days of arrival and departure did not normally count as days in the UK before 6 April 2008, it was possible in theory for an individual living abroad to work for four days each week in the UK for 45 weeks in the year and still be non-resident.

In *Tax Bulletin* 52 the Revenue began to move away from a pure day count when they stated that mobile workers who retained a home and settled domestic life in the UK but worked abroad in the week to such an extent that they were under the 90-day limit (eg lorry drivers) nevertheless remained UK resident.

IR20 broke down further in *Shepherd v R & C Comrs* (2005), where an airline pilot's claim to have been non-resident was examined in detail and rejected by the Special Commissioner. Although he satisfied the conditions of IR20 in terms of a strict day count, HMRC contended that this was not enough to establish non-residence. Subsequently, the High Court confirmed that the Special Commissioner had not misdirected herself in law but had accurately set out the legal test that she was required to apply. In that case, the taxpayer spent half the year outside the UK flying. He rented a flat in Cyprus and was in the UK for less than 90 days from 1999 to 2000 (excluding days of arrival and departure). However he continued to live mostly in the matrimonial home when returning to the UK (despite being separated from his wife) and was not granted an immigration permit in Cyprus until February 2000. He had to be in the UK before and after each flight. The Special Commissioner concluded that he had never left the UK: there was no distinct break in the pattern of his life and even if he was resident in Cyprus during that year this was not sufficient to lose UK residence.

Matters came to a head in *Gaines-Cooper* (2007) (SCD); domicile status affirmed (2008); judicial review application in *R (Davies) v R & C Comrs* (2010); *Gaines-Cooper* (2011) (Supreme Court decision. See **[27.4]**). This is perhaps the most celebrated case on non-residence. **[27.5]**

The Gaines-Cooper litigation

The saga began in October 2006. Gaines-Cooper was English by birth and at no time gave up his British passport. He was born in 1937 and owned a home in the UK through an offshore structure. He began a manufacturing business in the Seychelles in 1975, bought a house there and was granted a residency permit. From 1976 to 1980, he let his UK house and, in fact, ended up letting his Seychelles house between 1976 and 1979 for financial reasons. He spent 50 days or less per year in the UK during that period and appears to have been treated as non-resident for exchange control purposes. He spent between 100 and 200 days per year in the Seychelles from 1976 to 1980. He was also carrying on business and living in California from 1979 to at least 1986. However, he had international businesses operating in the Seychelles, California and the UK. In 1993, he remarried and his second wife was Seychellois. She had been living in the UK since 1977 and in 1994 she took British nationality. After her marriage, she spent most of her time in the UK home working in the UK operation. Their child, James, was born in 1998 and went to school in the UK until 2005.

Gaines-Cooper argued that he was non-resident from 1993–94 onwards on the basis of IR20. However, before proceedings began, he made a significant concession: he accepted that he was UK resident in 1992–93 because of what was then perceived to be the 'available accommodation' rule. It is arguable that this concession was unnecessary – see below. If he had not made it, he could have argued that he had never come to the UK and was therefore not a leaver. He would not then have had to show a distinct break. Hence he would not have had to satisfy the greater criteria that the Court of Appeal has held was required under IR20 for leavers.

A key part of Gaines-Cooper's case was that he had spent less than 91 days a year in the UK ignoring days of arrival in and departure from the UK. The Special Commissioners did not follow the day-counting rules in IR20 but adopted a midnight test. The result was that until at least 2000–01 he was held to have spent more than 120 midnights in the UK for all years after 1992–93. The Special Commissioners expressly did not follow IR20 but applied the case law. They took a multi-factor approach, in particular:

(i) he had a settled abode in Henley where he dwelt permanently or indefinitely;
(ii) he spent more time in the UK than he spent in the Seychelles or anywhere else;
(iii) he had both family and business ties in the UK;
(iv) his wife and son lived in the UK and his wife considered herself UK resident;
(v) he purchased and restored expensive UK business property.

The Special Commissioner decided that he was not a visitor who was in the UK for temporary purposes but an ordinarily resident individual who had left the UK merely for occasional residence abroad. He was not here for a casual purpose but rather in pursuance of 'the regular habits of life':

> 'A decision to visit the UK on a large number of days each year to be with one's wife and child is not a temporary purpose.'

Gaines-Cooper did not challenge the decision of the Special Commissioners on his residence status although he did appeal on the domicile point, losing that case as well in the High Court. However, he pursued judicial review proceedings on the residence issue on the basis that he had followed the terms of IR20, and therefore had a legitimate expectation that HMRC would apply it, *regardless of whether those terms accorded with the actual law*.

In Brief 1/2007 issued in early 2007, HMRC effectively asserted what they later argued in the judicial review proceedings, namely, that even if they were bound by IR20 as a matter of principle, Gaines Cooper had not satisfied IR20 because he had misinterpreted the 90-day rule which applied only to individuals who had left the UK or to visitors coming here. It did not apply in determining whether an individual had 'left' the UK in the first place. In deciding this latter question, Brief 1/2007 stated that HMRC considers all relevant evidence, including the pattern of presence in the UK and elsewhere. Hence the retention of family and accommodation would suggest the individual had not left. HMRC summarised the position as follows:

'In considering the issues of residence, ordinary residence and domicile in the *Gaines-Cooper* case, the Special Commissioners needed to build up a full picture of the taxpayer's life. A very important element of the picture was the pattern of his presence in the UK compared to the pattern of his presence overseas. The Special Commissioners decided that, in looking at these patterns, it would be misleading wholly to disregard days of arrival and departure. They used the taxpayer's patterns of presence in the UK as part of the evidence of his lifestyle and habits during the years in question. Based on this, and a wide range of other evidence, the Special Commissioners found that he had been continuously resident in the UK. From HMRC's perspective, therefore, the 91-day test was not relevant to the *Gaines-Cooper* case since the taxpayer did not leave the UK.'

Gaines-Cooper pursued his judicial review proceedings along with two other taxpayers, Messrs Davies and James. He said he had abided by the terms of IR20 and therefore should be treated as non-resident. He had a legitimate expectation that HMRC would follow their own guidance and had relied on it to his detriment. HMRC initially resisted this, because of words in the Preface to IR20 which said:

'... the booklet offers general guidance on how the rules apply, but whether the guidance is appropriate in a particular case will depend on all the facts of that case ...'

and because of words in para 1.1 which said:

'This booklet sets out the main factors that are taken into account, but we can only make a decision on your residence status on the facts in your particular case ...'

despite the unequivocal wording of Chapters 2 and 3. They also argued that IR20 cannot be allowed to produce a different result in any individual case from the strict law of residence because to have issued such a booklet would have been '*ultra vires*', outside HMRC's 'care and management' powers; and further, that once a person's residence status on the strict law has been decided against him by the Tax Tribunal, any 'legitimate expectation' the person had to be treated as non-resident would have become 'illegitimate'.

HMRC therefore strongly resisted Gaines-Cooper's application for permission to bring judicial review proceedings. As noted above, the Court of Appeal accepted that IR20 was subject to judicial review but did not accept that Mr Gaines Cooper had followed its terms. This decision was eventually upheld in the Supreme Court (see [27.4]). [27.6]

HMRC 6

This replaced IR20 in April 2009 and was far less prescriptive. It was amended in December 2010 and November 2011 but is heavily caveated throughout to avoid any argument that it raises a legitimate expectation. About the only useful part on which a taxpayer can rely relates to those working full-time abroad:

> '8.5 Leaving the UK to work abroad as an employee
>
> If you are leaving the UK to work abroad full-time, you will only become not resident and not ordinarily resident from the day after the day of your departure, as long as:
> - you are leaving to work abroad under a contract of employment for at least a whole tax year
> - you have actually physically left the UK to begin your employment abroad and not, for example, to have a holiday until you begin your employment
> - you will be absent from the UK for at least a whole tax year
> - your visits to the UK after you have left to begin your overseas employment will
>   - total less than 183 days in any tax year, and
>   - average less than 91 days a tax year. This average is taken over the period of absence up to a maximum of four years.
>
> 8.6 Returning to the UK after working abroad
>
> If you were not resident and not ordinarily resident when you were working abroad and you return to the UK when your employment ends, you will be not resident and not ordinarily resident in the UK until the day before you return to the UK. You will become resident and ordinarily resident on the day you return to the UK unless you can show that your return was simply a short visit to the UK between two periods of full-time employment abroad.
>
> However, if you have previously been resident in the UK and are returning to become resident here again after a period of residence abroad, you might need to consider whether your absence from the UK was a period of "temporary non-residence". If you were temporarily non-resident in the UK, this may affect your liability to UK tax when you return to become resident in the UK again.'

HMRC accept that up to ten days' work in the UK is permitted in addition to any incidental duties here. However, there is no justification for arguing that those who leave the UK for a purpose only become non-resident when the purpose commences as distinct from when they leave the UK. For example someone leaving for full-time work abroad will rarely start such work immediately. They may well settle into new accommodation first during the school holidays. On HMRC's view they do not lose UK residence until the day the work commences. Hence someone leaving for full time work in March will need to commence such work prior to 6 April. [27.7]–[27.8]

b) *Statutory provisions*

Prior to 2013 there were three statutory income tax rules, not all of which were replicated in the capital gains tax legislation.

Occasional residence abroad

ITA 2007 s 829 applied to an individual if:
- he had left the UK for the purpose of only occasional residence abroad, and
- at the time of leaving he was both resident and ordinarily resident in the UK.

Where s 829 applied, the individual was charged to income tax as if he were still residing in the UK. The section was of very limited impact, and there is no reported case where it alone resulted in liability to tax. This is because an individual is normally found to retain residence in the UK if he has left the UK for only occasional residence abroad. Thus in *Levene v IRC*, the taxpayer was found to have left the UK for only occasional residence abroad, but equally he was resident in the UK all along (see below). Conversely, in *IRC v Combe* (1932), the taxpayer went to serve an apprenticeship in New York for three years and that was found not to be for the purposes of occasional residence abroad.

The leading case on occasional residence is *Reed v Clark* (1985). Here the taxpayer was absent for only a little over a year, but there was a distinct break in the pattern of his life and throughout his absence he had made his permanent home and place of business in California. On these facts Nicholls J decided his residence in California was not occasional. Section 829 did not apply to CGT. This presumably is because ordinary residence alone rendered a person subject to CGT (TCGA 1992 s 2). Section 829 is discussed further at **Chapter 18**. However, in *Reed v Clark* the judge noted that 'the researches of very experienced Counsel have not revealed any reported decision in which a claim to tax has succeeded only by virtue of [statutory provisions]'.

In *Grace v R & C Comrs* (2008), HMRC having at one point agreed that s 829 did not apply and that Mr Grace had not left the UK for the purpose only of occasional residence abroad, then argued at the rehearing that they were not bound by this concession and that his residence in Cape Town was not occasional but for settled purposes as part of a regular order of his life adopted voluntarily. The argument was dismissed. This case was first heard by the Special Commissioner Nuala Brice who found in favour of the taxpayer (2008), whose decision was reversed on appeal by HMRC to the High Court (2008). The taxpayer appealed to the Court of Appeal successfully (2009) and the case was then remitted back to the First-tier Tax Tribunal for a rehearing where he lost (2011). The case is discussed further below at **[27.14]**.

Lord Wilson made some helpful comments on the context of s 829 in *Gaines-Cooper* (2011). He explained this section as follows:

'it is therefore clear that whether in order to become non-resident in the UK, or *whether at any rate to avoid being deemed by the statutory provision still to be* resident in the UK, the ordinary law requires the UK resident to effect a distinct break in the pattern of his life in the UK. The requirement of a distinct break mandates a multifactorial inquiry. In my view however the controversial references in the judgment of Moses LJ in the decision under appeal of the need in law for "severance of social and family ties" pitch the requirement at any rate by implication, at too high a level. The distinct break relates to the pattern of the taxpayer's life in the UK and no doubt it encompasses a substantial loosening of social and family ties; but the allowance to which I will refer, of limited visits to the UK on the part of the taxpayer who has become non-resident, clearly foreshadows *their continued existence in a loosened form.* "Severance" of such ties is too strong a word in this context.'(emphasis added)

The above comments of Lord Wilson are important in demonstrating that a taxpayer does not have to sever all ties; what he has to show is that he has not gone abroad for occasional purposes. In recent years HMRC have tended to elide this requirement with those for domicile and argued all ties must be broken with the UK. In the light of Lord Wilson's comments, the Revenue's approach is clearly wrong and should be resisted. **[27.9]**

Temporary purposes in the UK

This was relevant to both income tax and capital gains tax. ITA 2007 ss 831 and 832 applied to an individual if he was in the UK:
- for some temporary purpose only; and
- with no view to establishing his residence there.

Where these conditions were met, the relevant foreign income of the individual was not taxed (s 831) and he was treated as non-resident for the purposes of taxing employment income (s 832). But if he spent 183 days or more in the tax year in the UK, his relevant foreign income was taxable and he was treated as UK resident in taxing employment income. A similar provision was found for capital gains tax purposes in TCGA 1992 s 9 although this seemed more clearly in the nature of a relieving provision: the visitor who would otherwise be resident here was not treated as resident for capital gains tax purposes if he came here for temporary purposes and his stay was not more than 183 days. If his stay was more than 183 days then unlike ITA 2007 s 831(4) he was not automatically deemed to be UK resident. Instead he just lost the benefit of s 9(3) protection and his residence status was determined under general law although HMRC did and do not accept someone can be present for 183 days and not also *automatically* UK resident.

In determining whether the conditions of s 9 (or ss 831–832) were met, since 1993 living accommodation in the UK was ignored.

In computing how many days the individual spent in the UK a day counted only if the individual was in the UK at the end of the day. This, the so-called midnight rule, was first enacted in 2008 (FA 2008 s 24 and TCGA 1992 s 9(5)). An exception was made, and the day of arrival was disregarded, if the individual left the UK on the next day and did not while in the UK engage in activities unrelated to his passage through the UK. This was called 'the transit rule' and protected passengers who needed to stay overnight near an airport to get a connecting flight.

In *Grace v R & C Comrs* (see above), the Court of Appeal confirmed that ss 831 and 832 (and TCGA 1992 s 9) were not substantive rules as to residence. They conferred relief where the temporary visitor was UK resident or, had he exceeded the 183-day threshold, imposed income tax (but not necessarily capital gains tax) as if he were resident even if in fact he was not.

Grace also emphasises that what has to be temporary was not the individual's presence in the UK but his purpose (ibid at para 36). Was the reason for being in the UK casual or transitory? In *Grace* itself, the taxpayer was a BA pilot who had to be in the UK both before and after flights. This, the judge held, was not casual or transitory as it would continue from year to year so long as the pilot remained employed. Further guidance as to the meaning of temporary purposes was given in *Cooper v Cadwalader* (1904). Here an American had taken a lease of a shooting-lodge in Scotland, and he spent a continuous period of two months there each year during the grouse-shooting season. His principal residence and the place where he worked were in New York. The General Commissioners found that he was not resident in the UK, but this finding was reversed by the Court of Session. The question then arose of whether he was exempted by what later became s 831. All three judges who gave reasoned opinions held that it did not apply as the shooting-lodge was a residence and so meant he was in the UK with the view or intent of establishing his residence here. This point has been reversed by the 1993 change and so is now not good. But Lords Adam and McLaren then gave an additional reason for s 831 not applying, namely that coming to Scotland year after year for the shooting season was not a temporary purpose. In a significant passage Lord McLaren observed that 'temporary purposes means casual purposes as distinguished from the case of a person who is here in pursuance of his regular habits of life'. If this case is correctly decided then a person who spent less than three months in the UK and worked full-time abroad was nevertheless held to be UK resident, a result that seems directly to contradict HMRC stated practice and would catch many foreign domiciliaries with homes in London. It appears that those who came in and out of the UK for a few days each time without a settled purpose in mind may not be UK resident even if they have spent the same amount of time in the UK as those who come for a more settled purpose over a fixed length of time (see *Yugraneft v Abramovich* (2008)). **[27.10]**

Full-time work abroad

ITA 2007 s 830 applied if an individual worked full time in a foreign employment or a foreign trade. Where this condition was met, any UK living accommodation was ignored in determining whether he was UK resident for income tax purposes.

All duties other than incidental duties (narrowly defined) must have been performed outside the UK. Note that this did not say that a person was non-UK resident, only that accommodation was ignored in determining the question of residence. This is discussed further in **Chapter 18**. **[27.11]**

c) *Case law on residence*

A number of problems arise from the case law, some of which are summarised below.

(i) *Out of date case law*

Levene and *Lysaght* are the leading cases on the general meaning of the term 'residence' but they go back to the 1920s. In both cases, the taxpayers were

British subjects who had sold their homes in the UK. Mr Levene left the UK in December 1919, and for the next five years spent no more than 22 weeks per year in the UK. He had no permanent home abroad until January 1925. He stayed in hotels and visited the UK in the summer, also staying in hotels. In *Lysaght*, the taxpayer was a director of a substantial family company in England. In 1920 he gave up his home in England and moved permanently to a house he had acquired in Ireland. However, he came to England for a week every month to attend board meetings and during these visits stayed at the same hotel in Bath. His days in the UK averaged less than 90 days pa.

In both cases the Special Commissioners decided the taxpayer was resident in the UK for the years in issue. In Mr Levene's case they reached this conclusion having regard to his past and present habits of life, the regularity and length of his visits to the UK, his ties with the UK, and his freedom of attachments abroad. In Mr Lysaght's case the Commissioners gave no reasons for their decision. The Special Commissioners' decisions were upheld in the House of Lords as being ones they could properly reach, although in *Lysaght* it is clear the House would equally have upheld the opposite conclusion and Viscount Cave dissented.

It was emphasised in *Lysaght* that residence has no special meaning for tax purposes. The emphasis was on the settled place of abode. However, it was accepted that difficult cases arise where a person has no home in any country or multiple homes in a number of place, particularly a foreigner who has never resided in the UK. The latter is apparently less likely to be regarded as resident here than a British subject who leaves.

Some more modern guidance as to what constitutes residence comes from decisions under s 41 of the Civil Jurisdiction and Judgements Act 1982. In *Dubai Bank Ltd v Abbas* (1996), the Court of Appeal founded itself on the general passage quoted above from Lord Cave's speech in *Levene*.

The defendant's wife and son lived in a flat in London and he spent some two months per year in England. The Court of Appeal held he was not UK resident. The flat was owned by a company. The taxpayer had been involved in its acquisition and refurbishment but stated he stayed in hotels rather than at the flat and asserted he was effectively separated from his wife. On that basis the Court of Appeal said:

> 'A person is resident ... in a particular part of the United Kingdom if that part is for him a settled or usual place of abode ... A settled or usual place of abode connotes some degree of permanence or continuity.'

It continued:

> 'Depending on the circumstances of the particular case time may or may not play an important part in determining residence. For example, a person who comes to this country to retire and who buys a house for that purpose and moves into it, selling all his foreign possessions and cutting all his foreign ties, would to my mind be likely to be held to have become immediately resident here. In other cases it may be necessary to look at how long the person concerned has been here and to balance that factor with his connections abroad.' [27.12]

(ii) Multiplicity of factors vs settled abode

It seems unclear whether one adds up and balances a number of factors or simply looks at where the taxpayer has his settled place of residence. The case law in tax cases takes a different approach from the case law in relation to non-tax cases. However, the comments of Lord Wilson in *Gaines Cooper* (2011) do give some assistance in reconciling the case law, emphasising that the starting point in losing UK residence must be the requirement to lose one's settled abode in the UK.

In *Grace v R & C Comrs* (2008), Lewison J described a summary of the law given by the Special Commissioner in *Shepherd v R & C Comrs* (2005) as impeccable:

> 'From these authorities I derive the following principles: (i) that the concept of residence and ordinary residence are not defined in the legislation; the words therefore should be given their natural and ordinary meanings (*Levene*); (ii) that the word "residence" and "to reside" mean "to dwell permanently or for a considerable time, to have one's settled or usual abode, to live in or at a particular place" (*Levene*); (iii) that the concept of "ordinary residence" requires more than mere residence; it connotes residence in a place with some degree of continuity (*Levene*); "ordinary" means normal and part of everyday life (*Lysaght*) or a regular, habitual mode of life in a particular place which has persisted despite temporary absences and which is voluntary and has a degree of settled purpose (*Shah*); (iv) that the question whether a person is or is not resident in the United Kingdom is a question of fact for the Special Commissioners (*Zorab*); (v) that no duration is prescribed by statute and it is necessary to take account all the facts of the case; the duration of an individual's presence in the United Kingdom and the regularity and frequency of visits are facts to be taken into account; also, birth, family and business ties, the nature of visits and the connections with this country, may all be relevant (*Zorab; Brown*); (vi) that a reduced presence in the United Kingdom of a person whose absences are caused by his employment and so are temporary absences does not necessarily mean that the person is not residing in the United Kingdom (*Young*); (vii) that the availability of living accommodation in the United Kingdom is a factor to be borne in mind in deciding if a person is resident here (*Cooper*) (although that is subject to s 336); (viii) that the fact that an individual has a home elsewhere is of no consequences; a person may reside in two places but if one of those places is the United Kingdom he is chargeable to tax here (*Cooper* and *Levene*); (ix) that there is a difference between the case where a British subject has established a residence in the United Kingdom and then has absences from it (*Levene*) and the case where a person has never had a residence in the United Kingdom at all (*Zorab; Brown*); (x) that if there is evidence that a move abroad is a distinct break that could be a relevant factor in treating an individual as non-resident (*Combe*); and (xi) that a person could become non-resident even if his intention was to mitigate tax (*Reed v Clark*).'

Unlike *Dubai Bank Ltd v Abbas*, this summary of the law suggests that a multiplicity of factors must be looked at although the author believes the correct view is that the above factors do no more than help establish the question of whether the UK is indeed the taxpayer's usual or settled place of abode (see Lord Wilson's comments above at **[27.9]**). **[27.13]**

(iii) Leavers vs arrivers; the concept of distinct break

Grace was a long running case and demonstrates many of the problems with the current law: in particular the difficult question of whether a distinct break is needed for those who leave the UK and whether a higher burden is imposed on them. It is discussed in some detail below because in the Court of Appeal the factors that are important to consider in determining residence were clearly laid out. It now seems clear that the taxpayer who wants to become non-UK resident must keep to a lower day count in the UK than a foreigner coming to or visiting the UK who wishes to remain non-UK resident. A distinction between arrivers and leavers is reflected in the statutory residence test: leavers must have fewer connecting factors in the UK if they want to lose non-UK residence or spend less time here.

The *Grace* case

Mr Grace appealed against a notice of determination that he was ordinarily resident in the UK for the six years from 1997–98 to 2002–03 inclusive. The Special Commissioner decided in his favour that he was neither resident nor ordinarily resident in the UK. The Revenue successfully appealed this decision and Lewison J concluded that the Special Commissioner had made errors of law in arriving at her decision and, further, that the only possible conclusion from the primary facts was that Mr Grace was resident in the UK. On appeal the Court of Appeal unanimously concluded that the Special Commissioner had misdirected herself but that there was *not* only one possible conclusion and therefore the decision had to be remitted to the First-tier Tribunal (Tax Chamber) which had by then replaced the Special Commissioners. That re-hearing took place at the end of 2010 with the decision released in 2011. In the event Mr Grace was held to be UK resident and ordinarily resident under general law.

The facts of that case were as follows. Mr Grace was a British citizen born in South Africa in 1952 and he lived there until 1979. He qualified as an airline pilot and worked for UK airlines from 1987. He lived in the UK from 1986 and owned a house near Gatwick. In August 1997, the first year when he claimed to be non-UK resident, he set up home in South Africa and bought a house there in 1998 but continued to work for British Airways, retaining his house near Gatwick which he shared at one point with a girlfriend. He used his house before and after flights and when sick. He spent at least some of his remaining time when not flying in South Africa. He remained on the UK electoral roll and continued to use his UK bank and credit cards. It was accepted throughout that he had a well-structured social network; a doctor and dentist in South Africa; had purchased land there; joined clubs there; his most important personal effects were in South Africa. However, the UK property was fully furnished with computer and broadband access with vacant possession and he remained on the electoral roll. Post was sent to that address and he kept a car in the UK. He had had no contact with his children or wife for over 30 years and he planned to retire to South Africa when 60.

The Court of Appeal noted:
(i) the word 'reside' is a familiar English word which means 'to dwell permanently or for a considerable time, to have a settled or usual abode to live in or at a particular place'.

(ii) Physical presence in a particular place does not necessarily amount to residence in that place where, for example, a person's physical presence there is no more than a stop-gap measure. In considering a person's presence, one must consider the amount of time he spends in that place: the nature of his presence and his connection with that place.
(iii) Residence in a place connotes some degree of permanence, continuity or expectation of continuity.
(iv) Short but regular periods of physical presence may amount to residence, especially if they stem from the performance of a continuous obligation such as a business obligation, and the sequence of visits excludes the elements of chance and of occasion: see *Lysaght*.
(v) Although a person can have only one domicile at a time, he may reside in more than one place or in more than one country.
(vi) It is wrong to conduct a search for the place where a person has his permanent base or centre adopted for general purposes or to look for his real home.
(vii) Although residence must be voluntarily adopted, a residence dictated by the exigencies of business will count as voluntary residence: see *Lysaght*.
(viii) Where a person has had his sole residence in the UK, he is unlikely to be held to cease to reside in the UK unless there has been a definite break in his pattern of life: see *Re Combe*.
(ix) No duration is prescribed by statute and it is necessary to take into account all the facts of the case: the duration of an individual's presence in the UK and regularity and frequency of the visits. Also birth, family and business ties, the nature of business and the connections with the country may all be relevant: see *Zorab* (1926) and *Brown* (1926);
(x) The availability of living accommodation in the UK is a factor to be borne in mind in deciding if a person is resident here: see *Cooper v Cadwalader* (1904).
(xi) The fact that an individual has a home elsewhere is of no consequence. A person may reside in two places. However the fact that a home elsewhere is of no consequence is not to be understood as meaning that the other home is entirely irrelevant to the necessary enquiry. That would be inconsistent with the obligation to take into account all the facts of the case. But the existence of another home is not decisive because of the possibility of simultaneous residence in several places. In fact the point that Mr Grace spent relatively little time in South Africa did turn out to be relevant.
(xii) There were only two respects in which a person's state of mind is relevant in determining ordinary residence. First the residence must be voluntarily adopted; and second there must be a degree of settled purpose: see *Shah* (1983).

When the case was remitted back for rehearing to the First-tier Tribunal the judge considered whether Mr Grace needed to make a distinct break as a UK resident leaving the UK. This point had already been considered by Moses LJ in the judicial review proceedings of *Gaines Cooper* where he concluded that, construed as a whole, paragraphs 2.7 to 2.9 of IR20 required the taxpayer to show that he had left the UK permanently or indefinitely and to visit no more than the maximum number of days expressed. Moses LJ went on to say that in order to show that the taxpayer had left permanently or indefinitely, the taxpayer needed to demonstrate a distinct break and in particular that 'he had severed his ties to the extent that his previous social and family ties in the UK are no longer retained'.

It was acknowledged by the First-tier Tribunal that these comments were relevant in interpreting IR20, not necessarily in deciding residence under general law. The judge commented:

> 'My conclusion from this is that in *Gaines-Cooper* and *Levene*, the Court of Appeal considered a distinct break with the UK was essential if a person is claiming to have left the UK permanently or indefinitely for the purposes of s 334 and therefore IR20. This is not surprising: unless there has been a distinct break with the UK a person will only have left temporarily. However I find that the Court did not, as it did not need to, consider whether a distinct break is essential for someone shedding common law residence. On the contrary, all their comments on distinct break are in the context of it as a test of permanent or indefinite absence abroad.' (para 35)

However, the Tribunal noted that it was unlikely that residence would be lost unless there was a distinct break:

> 'Someone who has had UK residence needs to demonstrate that they have lost it, which is something a non UK resident does not have to do in order to demonstrate that they are not UK resident. The deciding cases on the common law meaning of residence have not held that it is essential that a distinct break is shown. However, although I agree with (Counsel for the taxpayer) that it is not essential to show a distinct break, it must be difficult to show that UK residence has been lost unless a distinct break in the taxpayer's pattern of life has occurred. I can envisage a set of circumstances where a taxpayer gradually runs down his connections with and presence in the UK to the extent that ultimately he becomes non resident without actually ever one year or another making a distinct break. However the point is not relevant in the context of this case where it is not suggested that Mr Grace gradually ran down his connections with the UK. The question is whether the change in circumstances in September 1997 were sufficient to convert his resident status to non resident: so in practice Mr Grace will have to show a sufficient break in his pattern of life.' (para 38)

Despite the original decision in *Grace* by the Special Commissioners, at the rehearing new witness statements and evidence was produced, and HMRC were allowed to introduce log books and diaries for some of the years in dispute. As a result the day count became much more adverse for Mr Grace. HMRC's argument was that the pattern of UK work was predictable with regular short stays.

The First-tier Tribunal found in HMRC's favour for the following reasons:

(i) Mr Grace in fact spent some leisure time in Horley and although his visits were short, nevertheless they were very frequent. His house was not like a hotel for him: he kept his car parked there; he paid council tax and received mail; he read his post; he caught up on paperwork and he had a girlfriend who lived with him there.

(ii) He had a social life here, at least for 2000–01, but the fact that he spent most of his social life in South Africa did not mean that he could not be resident in the UK. Like *Lysaght*, he was here for the purposes of employment. He spent a third to a half of the year neither in the UK nor in South Africa. Although there was a distinct decrease in the amount of time spent in the UK in September 1997, he was not in the UK merely for the purposes of work because the greater part of his time spent in the UK was in fact enforced rest days at intervals of about four to five days between work flights. He did have a settled abode in the UK because he was predictably staying at his house once a month. His presence in the UK was not a stop gap but indefinite and he had an expectation of continuity.

(iii) He had a real home in Cape Town and he had a different nature of life in South Africa but his social life was not greatly different before and after September 1997 in the UK.

(iv) His occupation of his own house gave a different quality to his time in the UK than if he had stayed in hotels. A very important part of his life, namely his employment, remained in the UK, and he had a home here. He did not demonstrate a sufficient break. He simply went from being a person resident in one country to being a person resident in two.

In *OJSC Oil Co Yugraneft v Abramovich* (2008), Mr Abramovich spent an average of 141 whole or part days in the UK in the calendar years 2003 to 2007, and 68 complete days. He had available accommodation and made regular visits in connection with his substantial business interest, Chelsea Football Club. Despite this, Clarke J held that for the purposes of s 41 of the Civil Jurisdiction Act he was non-resident in 2007. This may be reconciled with the *Grace* decision on the basis that he did not work here; unlike Grace he was an arriver and he did not come for a settled purpose. Equally it seems hard to see how he did not have a settled abode in the UK. Like Grace he had a home here and he used it more than just for visits.

Summary of residence position prior to April 2013

In conclusion it remains unclear if, when an individual leaves the UK and makes his home and place of business in one particular place abroad while retaining links with the UK such as family and accommodation, there needs to be a distinct break in order to establish non residence, although recent cases in the First-tier Tax Tribunal and the Upper Tribunal have very much proceeded on the basis that such a break is necessary (see *Yates v R & C Comrs* (2012), *Rumbelow v R & C Comrs* (2013 – First Tier and 2015 – Upper Tier) and *Glyn v R & C Comrs* (2013)) . Available accommodation is still regarded as a factor to consider in determining residence under general law despite the 1993 changes which only explicitly changed the limited statutory provisions.

The starting point in determining residence for any taxpayer should be to look at the comments of Lord Wilson in *Gaines Cooper*. He said that 'since 1928, if not before, it has therefore been clear that an individual who has been resident in the UK ceases in law to be so resident only if he ceases to have a settled or usual abode in the UK'. Clearly, retention of accommodation in terms of a 'settled abode' is problematic for a taxpayer who wants to lose UK residence prior to April 2013.

The next step is to examine whether the taxpayer has gone abroad permanently or for occasional purposes only. Section 829 appears to envisage that some form of distinct break is required. The taxpayer should also have regard to IR20 and after April 2009 to HMRC6 in determining whether he can fall within the scope of this guidance if his status under case law and statute remains unclear. [27.14]

(iv) Misinterpretation of the available accommodation rule.

Another problem has been confusion over the relative importance to be given the retention of accommodation in the UK. Until 1993 HMRC practice was to regard a taxpayer as UK resident if he had accommodation available to him in the UK and he set foot in the UK for even a day during the year unless he was working full-time abroad. In the 1993 Budget, the then Conservative Government announced its intention to abolish this 'available accommodation rule'. However, instead of simply enacting that accommodation should be disregarded in determining residence for all purposes, it merely amended the predecessor legislation to ITA 2007 ss 831 and 832 so that the relevance of accommodation remained unchanged for the purposes of the general law.

It is clear from the case law that there never was an available accommodation rule in the sense stated by HMRC: ie someone was not automatically UK resident under general law if he set foot in the UK for a day simply because he had a UK house. Both *Gaines Cooper* and *Grace* confirm that it is merely one factor to be taken into account under general law. Retention of accommodation does not in itself mean that a taxpayer has a settled abode here.

Levene suggests that available accommodation does mean a lower day count will result in residence. However, compare *Withers v Wynyard* (1938) where the taxpayer was held to be non-UK resident under general law despite spending three and a half months here in that year and owning a lease and using a London flat. It appears that the quality of residence is also important and having a UK home may suggest a greater intention to settle here. Someone who comes in and out of the UK at infrequent unplanned intervals is much less likely to be treated as UK resident than someone who comes to the UK for continuous periods of time staying in the same place each time, even if overall the period spent in the UK is the same.

More recently in *High Tech International v Deripaska* (2006), *Cherney v Deripaska* (2007) and *Yugraneft v Abramovich* (2008) (all non-tax cases but where the same criteria apply in determining residence) accommodation was not decisive since all of them were held to be non-UK resident for the purposes of serving proceedings despite having accommodation here. The individuals concerned had UK houses which they used and they also had houses elsewhere, but it was held that the quality of the use of their houses resembled that of a hotel. It was not a place where they 'habitually and normally resided for a settled purpose'. Hence they were held to be non-UK resident.

It is clear from these cases that the accommodation rule has been misinterpreted by HMRC in determining a person's residence status under general law, otherwise all of these people would have been UK resident. Critically, in *Gaines-Cooper* it was conceded, without further discussion, that the mere existence of available accommodation meant that the taxpayer was UK resident in 1992–93 prior to the rule change. This concession made a material difference to the taxpayer because he became a leaver rather than an arriver in 1993–94 and therefore had to show a distinct break. The conclusion is that available accommodation continues to be relevant in determining whether someone has 'left' the UK for the purposes of general law although it is not relevant in determining whether someone has come to the UK for a temporary purpose. It is also specifically ignored if someone leaves the UK for full time employment abroad. In the statutory residence test which now applies, 'available accommodation' is regarded as one connecting factor in determining residence status, confirming that it is relevant but not conclusive.

If a person has a home elsewhere, that is highly relevant in determining his residence status in the UK. The importance of this point is often underestimated. A person can be resident in more than one country but the Court of Appeal said in *Grace* that, while not decisive, the existence of a home elsewhere must be taken into account. Again this is reflected in the statutory residence test. If a person has a home in the UK and nowhere else, from April 2013 they are treated as conclusively resident in the UK.

Note that to be 'available' under current case law the accommodation does not have to be owned by the taxpayer if it is available to him: see *Lowenstein* (1926), where the house was owned by a foreign company owned by the taxpayer. The same approach is taken in the statutory test. [27.15]

Conclusions on the law prior to introduction of a statutory residence test in April 2013

It remains unclear whether the correct approach in determining residence is that set out in *Shepherd* and *Gaines-Cooper*, ie the multiple factor approach, or whether the right line is simply to look at the settled place of abode. The author considers that in the light of Lord Wilson's comments in *Gaines Cooper*, the correct approach is to determine whether a taxpayer has a settled place of abode in the UK. In order to lose a settled abode in the UK it is almost inevitable that a leaver will need to establish a settled abode abroad rather than simply be a 'wanderer'. This means that a low day count is not sufficient.

The role of available accommodation remains unclear. It is not directly relevant to the statutory provisions but continued use of the UK family home in the same way as prior to departure will clearly lead to the conclusion that the individual has retained a settled abode in the UK even if he has also established one abroad; therefore he remains UK resident under general law.

It is particularly unclear in relation to leavers just what is required for them to have 'left' the UK both for the purposes of establishing that they have not gone abroad for occasional purposes (the statutory test in s 829) and for the purposes of IR20 and HMRC 6. The question of whether the day count is definitely less for arrivers as opposed to leavers remains unresolved but clearly a leaver will need to show that he has lost his settled abode in the UK as well as establishing that he has not gone abroad for occasional purposes, and this at least raises a greater burden of proof on leavers.

HMRC 6 remains unclear in a number of areas, and comparison with decided cases suggests that it is in many respects at variance with law.

The concept of ordinary residence is equally unclear.

See in particular *Genovese v R & C Comrs* (2009) and *Tuczka v R & C Comrs* (2010). See also **Chapter 18**. This case law is not reflected in HMRC 6.

[27.16]

3 The statutory residence test

a) *Introduction*

The statutory test, which came into effect on 6 April 2013, is discussed below (taking into account HMRC's guidance which runs to over 100 pages – HMRC document RDR3).

Ordinary residence has been abolished for tax but not NI purposes.

[27.17]

b) *Outline of the legislation*

The legislation introduced in FA 2013 Sch 45 is split into four parts:
(1) Part 1 contains the rules to be applied in determining whether a person (referred to as 'P' in the legislation) is or is not UK resident for a particular tax year ('year X' in the legislation).
   There are three separate tests as follows:
   (a) The automatic UK tests whereby a person satisfying any of these tests will be UK resident.
   (b) The automatic overseas tests whereby a person satisfying any of these tests will be non-resident and importantly a person satisfying any of the automatic overseas tests cannot be UK resident under the automatic UK tests.
   (c) The sufficient ties test. This will apply to persons who are neither automatically resident under the automatic UK tests nor automatically non-resident under the automatic overseas tests. A number of ties are counted in relation to such a person in determining whether or not they are UK resident for a particular year.
(2) Part 2 is headed 'Key concepts' and contains definitions of the terms used for the three tests in Part 1. There are further definitions in Part 5 which should also be referred to where appropriate.
(3) Part 3 is headed 'Split year treatment' and defines where a tax year can be split between a resident and non-resident period (see **[27.50]**).
(4) Part 4 is headed 'Anti-avoidance'. This Part puts on a more comprehensive statutory basis the definition of temporary non-residence and the tax position of persons who are temporarily non-resident (see **[27.50]**).

[27.18]

c) *The three tests of residence*

An individual (P) is resident in the UK for a tax year ('year X') if:
(1) the automatic residence test is met for that year; or
(2) the sufficient ties test is met for that year.

If neither of these tests is met for the year or if one of the automatic overseas tests is met, P is not resident in the UK for that year.

The automatic UK tests

An individual will be UK resident if any one of the three automatic UK tests is met and none of the automatic overseas tests is met. The automatic UK tests are as follows:
(1) The first automatic residence test will be satisfied if P spends at least 183 days in the UK in year X.
(2) The second automatic residence test will be satisfied if:
   (a) P has a home in the UK during all or part of the year;
   (b) P is present in the UK home on at least 30 days (individual or consecutive days) during year X; and
   (c) while P has that UK home, there is a period of 91 consecutive days at least 30 days of which fall within year X when P:
      (i) has no overseas home; or
      (ii) has one or more overseas homes in none of which P is present on more than 29 days (not necessarily consecutive days) during year X.
   This wording means that P can be resident even if he has overseas homes, unless P has been present in one of them on at least 30 days in year X.
(3) The third automatic UK test is satisfied if:
   (a) P works full time in the UK for 365 days or more;
   (b) during that period there are no significant breaks from UK work;
   (c) all or part of that period falls within year X;
   (d) more than 75 per cent of the days in the 365 day period when P does more than three hours of work are days on which P does more than three hours of work in the UK; and
   (e) at least one day in year X is a day on which P does more than three hours of work in the UK.

For the purposes of the third automatic UK test a significant break from UK work is a period of at least 31 days none of which are days on which P does more than three hours' work in the UK or are days on which P would have done so but for being on sick leave or a reasonable amount of annual or parenting leave.

There is a fourth automatic UK test applying where P dies during year X.

The automatic overseas tests

There are three automatic overseas tests.
(1) P was resident in the UK for one or more of the three tax years preceding year X and the number of days in year X that P spends in the UK is less than 16.
(2) P was resident in the UK for none of the three tax years preceding year X and the number of days P spends in the UK in year X is less than 46.
(3) The third automatic overseas test is satisfied if:
   (a) P works full time overseas for year X;
   (b) during year X, there are no significant breaks from overseas work (with a 'significant break' having the same meaning as under the third automatic UK test);
   (c) the number of days in year X on which P does more than three hours' work in the UK is less than 31; and

(d) the number of days in year X that P spends in the UK is less than 91 (and for this purpose ignoring the deeming rule in the definition of days spent in the UK referred to below under Key Concepts).

There are two further automatic overseas texts which apply if P dies in year X.

The sufficient ties test

The number of ties that P will require in order to have 'sufficient' UK ties (defined below at [27.21]) to be treated as UK resident depends on whether P was resident in the UK in any of the previous three tax years and the number of days that P spends in the UK in year X.

The table below shows how many UK ties are sufficient in a case where P was resident in the UK in one or more of the three tax years immediately preceding year X:

Days spent by P in the UK in year X	Number of UK ties that are sufficient	UK ties
More than 15 but Fewer than 46	4	a family tie an accommodation tie
More than 45 but Fewer than 91	3	a 90-day tie a work tie
More than 90 but Fewer than 121	2	a country tie
More than 120	1	

The table below shows how many UK ties are sufficient in a case where P was resident in the UK for none of the three tax years preceding year X:

Days spent by P in the UK in year X	Number of UK ties that are sufficient	UK test
More than 45 but Fewer than 91	All 4	a family tie an accommodation tie
More than 90 but Fewer than 121	3	a 90-day tie a work tie
More than 120	2	

[27.19]

d) *UK ties*

This definition is relevant for the sufficient UK ties test of residence. The number of UK ties that will be relevant will depend on whether P was resident in the UK for one or more of the three tax years preceding year X.

If P was resident in the UK for one or more of the preceding three tax years, the following ties count as a UK tie: a family tie, an accommodation tie, a work tie, a 90 day tie and a country tie.

If P was resident in the UK for none of the prior three tax years, the country tie is disregarded.

Family tie

P has a family tie for a year if he or she has a spouse or civil partner or unmarried partner from whom P is not separated or P is a parent of a child under the age of 18 and the partner or child concerned is resident in the UK for that year. The fact that P has a minor child is disregarded if P sees the child in the UK for fewer than 61 days in the year.

A child of P who is under 18 and in full time education and only UK resident because of their education in the UK is treated (for the purposes only of the family tie test) as non-resident if the number of days the child spends in the UK outside of term-time is less than 21 (half-term breaks being treated as part of term-time for this purpose).

In applying the family tie test, the residence of the other person is determined without reference to the question of whether P is UK resident.

Accommodation tie

The accommodation tie is satisfied if P has a place to live in the UK which is available for a continuous period of at least 91 days during the year provided that P spends at least one night at that place in year X. There is no requirement for P to have an interest in or a legal right to occupy the accommodation.

If the accommodation belongs to a close relative of P, the accommodation tie will only be satisfied if P spends a total of at least 16 nights there.

If P has a property in the UK which he has let out commercially, it will not constitute an accommodation tie unless he has retained a right to use the property.

Work tie

A person has a work tie for a year if he or she works in the UK for at least 40 days (whether continuously or intermittently) in year X. For this purpose P works in the UK for a day if P does more than three hours' work in the UK on that day.

90-day tie

This tie is satisfied if P has spent more than 90 days in the UK in the tax year preceding year X, the tax year preceding that tax year, or in each of those tax years.

Country tie

P has a country tie for year X if the country in which P is present for the greatest number of days at the end of the day is the UK. If P is present at the end of the day for an equal number of days in more than one country and one of those countries is the UK the country tie will be met if that number of days is the greatest number of days spent in any country in year X. **[27.20]**

e) *Key concepts*

A number of key concepts are defined in Part 2. These include the following:

Days spent

The day count test is based on the existing test.

If P is present in the UK at the end of a day, that day counts as a day spent by P in the UK. There are now three exceptions:
(1) A day does not count if P is in transit through the UK and does not engage in activities that are to a substantial extent unrelated to P's passage through the UK.
(2) P's presence is disregarded if P would not be present in the UK at the end of the day but for exceptional circumstances beyond P's control that prevent P from leaving the UK if P intends to leave the UK as soon as circumstances permit.

Annex B to the guidance note sets out HMRC's interpretation of 'exceptional circumstances'. HMRC take a relatively narrow view, indicating that local or national emergencies or a sudden serious or life threatening illness or injury to the individual (or their partner or dependent child) may be treated as exceptional, whereas life events (such as marriage or death) or travel problems will not usually be regarded as exceptional. In any event, a maximum of 60 days in the UK can be disregarded under this rule.
(3) P is deemed to be present in the UK even if not here at the end of a day if:
   (i) P has at least three UK ties in year X;
   (ii) the number of days in year X when P is present in the UK at some point during (but not at the end of) the day is more than 30; and
   (iii) P was resident in the UK for at least one of the three tax years preceding year X.

If these conditions are satisfied, P will be deemed to have spent each such day after the first 30 such days in the UK. This deeming rule does not apply in deciding if P has a 90-day tie (see below) in ascertaining whether P has three UK ties for the purpose of this deeming rule.

Section 7 of HMRC's guidance note advises the taxpayer to keep records of travel details or tickets and boarding cards.

Home

A home can be any place (including a vehicle or vessel) which an individual uses with a sufficient degree of permanence or stability. There is no requirement that P has any legal ownership or interest in the property concerned so, for example, if P lives with his parents then their property may be his home.

As set out in Annex A to the guidance note, HMRC 'consider that a person's home is a place that a reasonable onlooker with knowledge of the material facts would regard as that person's home'. A place may be a home even if not occupied by P, for example if occupied by P's spouse and children or temporarily unavailable because of renovation.

A property will not be P's home if made available to let commercially, provided P and his family retain no right to live there. Furthermore, a property which is used as nothing more than a holiday home, temporary retreat or similar where P spends time for occasional short breaks which provide 'distinct respite from [P's] ordinary day to day life' will not be a home. However, if P's use of the holiday home is such that he in fact uses it as a home for parts of the year, it will be treated as a home for the purposes of the statutory residence test.

Section 7 of HMRC's guidance note indicates that in reviewing whether or not P has a home at a particular place, HMRC will consider (amongst other factors) the level of usage demonstrated by utility bills, membership of clubs, mobile phone usage, engagement of domestic staff, insurance documents, the address to which personal post is sent, where P's driving licence is registered, registration with local doctors, payment of local municipal taxes and bank accounts linked to the address.

This can be a trap for people leaving the UK if, on arrival in their new country of residence, they stay in temporary accommodation, for example while they are looking for a house or where they have bought a house but decide to renovate it before they start living in it. There may be a question as to whether the temporary accommodation is a 'home'. If it is not and they have retained their house in the UK, they may find that they remain resident in the UK under the second automatic UK test (having a UK home and having no overseas home).

Work

P is considered to be working if he or she does something in the performance of the duties of an employment or in the course of a trade carried on by P. Trade includes anything treated as a trade for income tax purposes which would therefore include a property rental business.

A voluntary post for which P has no contract of service does not count as work for the purpose of the statutory residence test.

Time spent working includes travelling time to the extent that P works during the journey or the cost would have been a deductible expense for tax purposes if incurred by P himself. Time spent working can also include time on-call or on stand-by.

Section 7 of HMRC's guidance note sets out the kind of records taxpayers should keep in relation to their work, including contracts of employment and a calendar indicating hours worked, nature and location of work, leave taken and breaks from work.

Location of work

Work is done where it is actually done, regardless of where the employment is held or the trade carried on by P. Work done in the course of travelling to or from the UK is assumed to be done overseas.

Full time work

P works full time in the UK or overseas if the number of hours per week averaged over the period is 35 hours or more. [27.21]

f) *Commencement*

The statutory residence test applies to the year 2013–14 and future years. Likewise, the concept of ordinary residence was abolished with effect from 6 April 2013.

An individual may elect that their residence status for tax years prior to 2013–14 be determined applying the statutory residence test for the purpose (but only for the purpose) of determining whether they are resident in the UK in the years 2013–14 to 2015–16 This election is irrevocable and must be made in writing by the first anniversary of the end of the relevant tax year. [27.22]

g) *Summary*

The effect of the statutory test is that a 'leaver' will be able to establish non-UK residence even if he retains accommodation here provided he:
(a) spends less than 91 midnights in the UK in any tax year;
(b) establishes a base abroad where he spends more time than in the UK;
(c) works fewer than 40 days in the UK (whether or not abroad) (a day of work being more than three hours a day); and
(d) has no family here.

An 'arriver' (ie someone not UK resident in the three preceding tax years) can retain non-UK residence if he never spends more than 90 midnights in the UK, even if his family are resident in the UK, he has available accommodation here and works in the UK on more than 40 days (provided he is not working full time in the UK).

In essence this broadly returns to the position under IR20 as it was understood by most taxpayers prior to the *Gaines Cooper* litigation. [27.23]

4 Members of Parliament

From 2010–11 MPs and members of the House of Lords are deemed resident, ordinarily resident and domiciled in the UK for all tax purposes. This applies even if that person is a member of Parliament for only part of the tax year and regardless of whether or not they are on a leave of absence (see Part 4 of the Constitutional Reform and Governance Act 2010). [27.24]–[27.40]

II CAPITAL GAINS TAX LIABILITY OF NON-RESIDENTS AND RESIDENTS; TEMPORARY NON-RESIDENTS

An individual who is resident in the UK during any part of the tax year is taxed on his worldwide chargeable gains made during that year. There are four qualifications to this general proposition. [27.41]

First, where the gain arises on a disposal of overseas assets and cannot be remitted to the UK because of local legal restrictions, executive action by the foreign government or the unavailability of the local currency, CGT will only be charged when those difficulties cease – TCGA 1992 s 279.

Second, an individual who is resident, but not domiciled, in the UK and who elects to be taxed on the remittance basis is liable to CGT only on such gains on overseas assets as are remitted to the UK. This is discussed in Section III below.

Third there are special rules to tax temporary non-residents on gains realised while they were abroad and these are discussed further below.

Fourth there is a clawback of the held over gain if an individual emigrates. See TCGA 1992 s 168 and [24.18]. [27.42]

By contrast, a person who is not resident in the UK is generally not liable to CGT on gains even if resulting from a disposal of assets situated in the UK (TCGA 1992 s 2). His domicile or the situs of the assets is generally irrelevant. Hence non-UK resident trusts and companies do not generally suffer CGT.

In order to prevent UK residents avoiding tax by transferring all their assets into offshore trusts or companies which then realise gains, a series of provisions have been introduced to catch gains realised by offshore trusts or companies where the settlor/beneficiary/shareholder is UK-resident. The provisions which apply to non-UK resident trusts are discussed in **Chapter 27A**.

From 6 April 2013, all companies including non-resident companies are liable to capital gains tax on disposals of UK residential property worth more than £2m. This is referred to as ATED-related CGT as it was introduced as part of a package of measures, including the annual tax on enveloped dwellings, designed to encourage individuals to own UK property directly rather than through companies. The charge does not apply to non-UK resident trusts, nor to industrial or commercial property, nor to properties which are let out commercially to third parties. Only any increase in value after 5 April 2013 will be taxed.

With effect from 6 April 2015, this capital gains tax charge applies to residential properties worth more than £1 million and from 6 April 2016 applies to residential properties worth more than £500,000. In each case, it is only any increase in value after the rules came into force on which the non-resident will be taxed.

In addition to this, from 6 April 2015 all non-residents are now taxable on gains realised on a disposal of UK residential property. It makes no difference what the property is worth and there is no exemption for properties which are let out to third parties. The legislation refers to this new charge as 'non-resident CGT'.

If a non-UK company is liable both to ATED-related CGT and non-resident CGT, there are complicated rules which apply but the basic principle is that ATED-related CGT takes precedence – principally because, in calculating non-resident CGT for companies, the company can take the benefit of indexation and only pays tax at 20% whereas, for ATED-related CGT, there is no indexation and the tax rate is 28%.

The only real exemption from non-resident CGT is principal private residence relief. As a result of the introduction of non-resident CGT, the rules for principal private residence relief have been amended. These amendments apply to all taxpayers, and not just non-residents (see **Chapter 23**).

For a non-resident to qualify for principal private residence relief he or his spouse/civil partner must spend at least 90 nights in the property in question or in another UK property in which one of them has an ownership interest. It is quite difficult (although not impossible) to do this without becoming UK resident.

A non-resident who is within the scope of non-resident CGT must submit a return and pay any tax due within 30 days of any disposal of UK residential property. The only exception to this is where the individual is already within the UK self-assessment system in which case he must still file a return within 30 days of the disposal but has until the normal time (31 January after the end of the tax year in question) to pay the tax which is due.

It is only any increase in value of the property since 6 April 2015 which is subject to non-resident CGT. When calculating the amount of chargeable non-resident gains accruing in the relevant tax year the only losses which can be deducted are losses on disposals of UK residential property interests accruing to the taxpayer in that year or unused losses from an earlier tax year.

Non-resident trusts and individuals are likely to pay non-resident CGT at the same rate as UK residents (28% – or 18% where the individual's UK income/gains are within the basic rate band). Although the main rates of CGT were reduced to 20% and 10% with effect from 6 April 2016, the 28%/18% rates continue to apply to gains on residential property. **[27.43]**

A non-UK resident individual (or trust) is also subject to CGT if it is trading in the UK through a branch or agency. In this event the branch or agency assets are subject to tax (TCGA 1992 s 10). The charge cannot be avoided by removing assets from the UK or by ceasing to trade in the UK. In both cases a deemed disposal at market value will occur (compare the deemed disposal which results from the emigration of a UK resident company). **[27.44]–[27.45]**

EXAMPLE 27.1

Peter has become non-UK resident and owns a portfolio of UK let properties in London plus UK farmland which he farms through a manager. He sells all the UK land/properties in June 2016. He will pay non-resident CGT on any gains in respect of the let properties since 6 April 2015 at 18%/28%. He is also subject to CGT in respect of gains on the UK farmland (as the farmland is used in his UK farming trade) at 10%/20%. A roll over claim could be made in respect of the gain on the farmland (see TCGA 1992 s 152; see **[22.72]**). If he had sold the farming business *prior* to becoming non-UK resident and rolled over the gain by reinvesting in the assets of a new business situate abroad there is no clawback of relief (TCGA 1992 s 152 onwards).

1 The temporary non-resident individual

As CGT is generally only charged on individuals who are resident in the UK it could be avoided by the simple expedient of becoming resident outside

the UK and then disposing of the asset. FA 1998 (as amended by F(No 2) A 2005 and FA 2013) therefore introduced the concept of temporary non-residence for CGT purposes (now contained in TCGA 1992 ss 10A and 10AA and FA 2013 Sch 45 Pt 4). An individual who is 'temporarily non-resident' (as defined) is taxed on certain gains realised whilst non-resident but only when he returns to the UK. These rules came into effect from 17 March 1998 and apply if the following conditions are satisfied:
(1) the individual was UK resident for at least some part of four of the seven tax years preceding the year of departure;
(2) the individual becomes non-UK resident for five years or less. This means that, unless split-year treatment applies (see [27.50]), an individual must be non-UK resident for six tax years in order to avoid the application of the temporary non-residence rules. A period of absence of exactly five years is not enough;
(3) during his period of absence he disposes of assets which he had owned when he left the UK or he receives capital payments from an offshore trust (TCGA 1992 s 87) or a trust of which he was the settlor realises a gain in circumstances where he would be taxed on those gains on an arising basis if he were UK resident and domiciled (TCGA 1992 s 86); or gains of an offshore company are attributed to him (TCGA 1992 s 13).

[27.46]

In these situations, the individual is taxed as if the gains accrued to him in the year of return to the UK. Because no distinction is made between one intervening year and another it follows that the CGT annual exempt amount is only available for the year of return (that being the year in which the gains are deemed to accrue) and that losses realised in later intervening years of non-residence may be offset against gains from earlier years deemed to accrue in the year of return. This is an exception to the rule that losses cannot be carried back. The rate of tax is the rate in force in the year of return, not the rate which applied in the year the disposal took place. Although the capital gains tax rate changed to 28% for disposals made on or after 23 June 2010 by those who pay the higher rate of income tax, it was provided that for those who resumed residence in 2010–11 (whether before or after 23 June) all such gains deemed to come into charge in that year were deemed to arise before 23 June and therefore were liable at 18%. [27.47]

It is noteworthy that unlike in the US, the Government chose not to impose an 'exit charge' on individuals becoming non-resident. Instead they simply extended the length of period it was necessary for the individual to stay abroad before any CGT advantages could be obtained. It is thought this was partly due to EU constraints on the imposition of an exit charge. [27.48]

A number of further points should be noted about these provisions:
(1) the charge applies to losses as well as gains;
(2) the charge does not (with certain exceptions) apply to disposals of assets which the taxpayer acquired at a time when he was non-resident (TCGA 1992 s 10AA(1)) ('the after-acquired assets rule');

(3) the normal limitation period for CGT assessments is extended to two years after 31 January next following the year of return;
(4) gains (and losses) are calculated in the normal way at the time when the asset is disposed of, as if the taxpayer were then UK resident. Tax will, however, be charged at rates current in the year of return so even though the disposal was made in a year of non-residence when the rate might have been 28%, if the taxpayer returns within five years but after 5 April 2016 the rate would only be 20% (if he is a higher rate taxpayer and assuming the gain did not relate to residential property – where the rate remains 28%);
(5) there are special rules to prevent a possible double charge under TCGA 1992 ss 86 and 87;
(6) until Budget 2005 it was thought that the charge could be neutralised by relief under a double tax treaty (see former TCGA 1992 s 10A(10)). HMRC do not accept this view was ever correct and since 16 March 2005 it is now expressly provided that treaties cannot override the s 10A charge (see former TCGA 1992 s 10A(9C) and now TCGA 1992 s 10AA(4));
(7) the concept of temporary non-residence has from 6 April 2008 been extended by FA 2008 Sch 7 (see para 53 onwards) to cover non-domiciliaries who leave the UK for fewer than five years and remit relevant foreign income or foreign chargeable gains to the UK (realised or arising prior to non-residence) during the period of absence. See TCGA 1992 s 10A(9). Hence for the foreign domiciliary who leaves the UK, the five-year rule applies:
    (a) to foreign chargeable gains realised before leaving where such gains are remitted while non-UK resident or after the individual has returned to the UK;
    (b) to foreign chargeable gains on assets acquired prior to departure and realised and remitted during the period of non-residence: these are treated as remitted in the year of return;
    (c) to foreign chargeable gains realised during the period of non-residence and remitted in a subsequent year of residence (assuming the assets were acquired prior to departure);
(8) from 6 April 2013 the temporary non-residence rule also catches certain types of income received during a period of temporary non-residence including dividends from private companies, certain employment income, pension income and gains on life insurance policies. [27.49]

EXAMPLE 27.2

Don was resident and domiciled in the UK but on 30 March 2014 he leaves the UK to take up a three-year contract of employment in Belgium starting on 6 April 2014. His broker liquidates his portfolio on 3 April 2014 and, in January 2016, Don sells his country cottage and a valuable Ming vase given to him by his wife as a leaving present. He returns to the UK in May 2018 having extended his original contract. The CGT position is as follows:
(1) Don remains resident in the UK in the tax year 2013–14 so that the disposal of shares on 3 April 2014 is chargeable (note that split year treatment does not apply as he does not start work until 6 April 2014).

(2) Because Don returns in May 2018 he has not been out of the UK for more than five complete tax years so that the gain on the disposal of the country cottage up to 5 April 2015 is brought into charge in tax year 2018–19 (his year of return). The gain from 6 April 2015 to January 2016 is taxed in the 2015–16 tax year under the non-resident CGT rules.

(3) Any gain on the sale of the Ming vase is also taxed in the year of return. Although Don only acquired the vase after he left the UK, because it was acquired from a spouse, the gain is not excluded under the after-acquired assets rule.

(4) If Don acquires an asset such as a picture in the tax year after departure, ie while non-resident (and not relying on the split year) and sells the picture in the tax year before he returns to the UK, any gain is not chargeable on him. Equally any loss would not be allowable.

(5) If Don had gone abroad on or before 16 March 1998 he would not be chargeable on gains made while not resident or ordinarily resident on any of the assets even though he may return within five years.

(6) If Don was not UK domiciled, any foreign chargeable gains realised *while he was UK resident* and subject to the remittance basis are not taxable unless and until remitted. If he remitted such gains to the UK while non-resident he is treated as remitting them in the year of return and taxed at the rates prevailing then. Gains realised while non-UK resident are taxed if realised on assets acquired before non-residence and (assuming the gains are foreign gains) such gains are remitted before or after the temporary period of non-residence.

2 Split year treatment

As already discussed, CGT is charged on individuals who are UK resident at any time during a tax year on gains made during the course of that year. Until 5 April 2013, ESC D2 enabled the year to be split so that gains arising after a person ceases to be resident are untaxed whilst gains arising before he becomes UK resident are similarly outside the tax net. Observe the following restrictions, however:

(1) the concession did not apply to trustees;
(2) like any concession it would not apply 'if any attempt is made to use it for tax avoidance' (see *R v IRC, ex p Fulford-Dobson* (1987));
(3) an individual leaving the UK on or after 17 March 1998 would only benefit from split-year treatment if he was not resident in four out of the seven years of assessment preceding that of his departure.

From 6 April 2013, following the introduction of the statutory residence test, split year treatment is only available in certain limited circumstances.

Where the taxpayer meets the criteria for split year treatment under more than one case, special rules determine which case will apply. In many cases, priority is given to the case where the overseas part of the year is the shortest.

Case 1: starting full time work overseas

This will apply if:
(a) the taxpayer was resident in the previous tax year and on a day in the relevant tax year the taxpayer starts to work full time overseas for a period which continues until the end of the relevant tax year;

(b) in the part of the tax year beginning with that day, the number of days on which the taxpayer does more than three hours' work in the UK and the number of days the taxpayer spends in the UK (but ignoring the deeming rule in the definition of days spent under Key Concepts above) must not exceed 30 days and 90 days respectively.

These numbers of days are reduced to a lower figure by reference to the number of months in the year before the taxpayer commences full time work overseas. For example if the taxpayer left the UK on 6 October (six months into the tax year) the days after the taxpayer leaves that he works in the UK for more than three hours and the days he spends in the UK should not exceed 15 and 45 respectively; and

(c) the taxpayer is not resident in the UK in the next tax year after the person left the UK under the third automatic overseas test (full time work abroad).

Case 2: accompanying spouse leaving the UK

Where a person leaves the UK to work overseas the split year treatment can also apply to an accompanying spouse, civil partner or unmarried partner.

Case 3: leaving the UK to live abroad

The split year treatment will apply where:
(a) on a day in the relevant tax year the taxpayer ceases to have any home in the UK and from then onwards the taxpayer has no home in the UK for the rest of the year;
(b) in the part of the relevant tax year beginning with the day that the taxpayer ceases to have any home in the UK, he or she must spend fewer than 16 days in the UK;
(c) the taxpayer is not resident in the UK for the next tax year; and
(d) by the end of the period of six months beginning with the day the taxpayer ceases to have a home in the UK he or she has a sufficient link with a country overseas. The taxpayer has a sufficient link with a country overseas if:
  (i) he or she is resident there under the local law;
  (ii) he or she is present in the that country at the end of each day in the six month period; or
  (iii) his or her only home or homes are in that country.

Case 4: persons coming to live in the UK

This will apply if the taxpayer:
(a) was not resident in the UK in the previous tax year;
(b) during the relevant tax year the taxpayer begins for the first time in that year to meet the only home test and continues to meet that test for the rest of the tax year. The only homes test is satisfied if the taxpayer's only home or homes are all in the UK; and
(c) did not have sufficient UK ties in the period before meeting the only homes test in the year.

Case 5: persons coming to work full time in the UK

This will apply if the taxpayer:
(a) was not resident in the UK in the previous tax year;
(b) during the relevant tax year begins a period of at least 365 days of full time work in the UK; and
(c) did not have sufficient UK ties in the part of the relevant year before beginning work.

Case 6: persons ceasing full time work overseas

This will apply if:
(a) the taxpayer was not resident in the UK in the previous tax year because the taxpayer met the third automatic overseas test for that year (working full-time abroad) but was resident in the UK for one of the four tax years before that;
(b) on a day within the relevant tax year the taxpayer ceases full time work overseas;
(c) in the part of the tax year ending on that day, the number of days in which the taxpayer does more than three hours of work in the UK and the number of days the taxpayer spends in the UK (ignoring the deeming rule) must not exceed 30 days and 90 days respectively (with those limits being apportioned according to the number of whole months of the tax year remaining after the overseas work period ends); and
(d) the taxpayer is resident in the UK for the next tax year.

Case 7: accompanying spouse arriving in the UK

Where a person arrives in the UK on ceasing to work full time overseas, the split year treatment can also apply to an accompanying spouse, civil partner or unmarried partner.

Case 8: starting to have a home in the UK

This provision, unlike Case 4, enables a person who retains a home abroad to benefit from the split year treatment. The split year treatment will apply where:
(a) the taxpayer was not resident in the UK in the previous tax year;
(b) at the start of the year the taxpayer had no home in the UK but there comes a day for the first time in that year when the taxpayer does have a home in the UK and continues to do so for the rest of that year and the whole of the next tax year;
(c) for the part of the year before the taxpayer acquires a UK home he or she does not have sufficient UK ties; and
(d) the taxpayer is resident in the UK for the whole of the next tax year.

It should be noted that, under the statutory rules, the taxpayer is not actually non-resident for the period before he comes to the UK or after he leaves the UK. Instead, the legislation amends the existing taxation rules so that most income and capital gains arising during the 'non-resident' part of the tax year are taken out of the charge to UK tax. [27.50]

3 Other matters

Two other matters should be noted. *First*, any CGT losses should be realised prior to departure; and, *second*, care should be taken to ensure that arrangements with a potential purchaser, made before going non-resident, do not amount to a disposal at that time. Accordingly, careful thought is required before a conditional contract is concluded or put and call options granted (see CG 25800 onwards for HMRC's view on this). [27.51]–[27.53]

HMRC may argue that a binding contract has been reached particularly where there is a sale of shares. Put and call options should be used with care. HMRC accept that there can be no binding agreement for the disposal of land unless the contract is in writing. [27.54]

If shares in a company have been sold in consideration of receiving shares or loan notes issued by the purchasing company, HMRC may argue that TCGA 1992 s 135 does not apply (see *Example 27.3*). Even if a clearance has been obtained under TCGA 1992 s 138 this will be invalidated if the taxpayer had definite plans to go abroad at the time of the sale and he did not disclose this in the clearance. See *Snell v R & C Comrs* (2006) (upheld in the High Court (2007)), where a company was sold for a mixture of shares and loan notes. The main shareholder subsequently became non-resident and disposed of his loan notes free of capital gains tax. HMRC successfully argued that the arrangements for the issue of loan notes in exchange for shares had a tax avoidance motive and therefore no deferral relief was available. The Special Commissioner held that the paper for paper provisions were not intended to be an exemption mechanism for somebody who wished to use them as a prelude to becoming non-resident: 'We find that he had the purpose of becoming non-resident before redeeming the loan notes and accordingly that one of his main purposes, indeed the only main purpose of effecting the arrangement, was the avoidance of capital gains tax'. See also *Coll v R & C Comrs* (2010) where the s 137 restriction applied because the taxpayer had taken loan notes as consideration with a view to avoiding capital gains tax when non-UK resident, even though he had not decided where to go. [27.55]

EXAMPLE 27.3

Luke owns all the shares in a food distribution company, S Limited. He receives an offer from a rival company, FD Limited, to buy S Limited for £20m cash. Luke and the purchaser reach an informal agreement on terms in February 2007. Luke emigrates in March 2007 and the actual agreement is signed on 6 April 2007. HMRC may ask to see the papers surrounding the sale in order to establish whether a binding oral agreement had been reached in February before Luke left the UK.

Alternatively Luke sells the company in March just before emigration in consideration of receiving guaranteed loan notes from the purchaser which he cashes in six months after the sale in October 2007 after he has left the UK intending to stay away for five complete tax years. In the light of *Snell*, HMRC may well successfully argue on the above facts that there was a chargeable disposal in March 2007 and not in October 2007 when the loan notes were encashed and that TCGA 1992 s 137(1) applies so that there is no s 135 relief. Luke should not investigate or consider any emigration plans until the sale is concluded.

In this example if Luke returned during the 2009–10 tax year even if the gains had been realised on disposals in 2007–08 the rate of tax on return would be 18%. If he returned within five years but after 5 April 2010, the rate of tax would be 28% if he was a higher rate taxpayer. Any past taper relief entitlement would be ignored.

See also *Schofield v R & C Comrs* (2012) where the Court of Appeal found in favour of HMRC in relation to a tax avoidance scheme where the taxpayer created an artificial loss prior to emigration through use of put and call options. HMRC simply argued that the scheme was tax avoidance caught by the *Ramsay* principle (see **Chapter 2**).

4 Finance (No 2) Act 2005 changes

The capital gains tax rules on non-residence were tightened up further in 2005. As noted above, the general rule in TCGA 1992 s 2 is that gains accruing on the disposal of an asset only attach to taxpayers who are resident in the UK in the tax year of disposal. As also discussed, TCGA 1992 s 10A provides for an exception: where a UK resident becomes non-resident but resumes UK residence within five tax years then any gains in the intervening years of non-residence on disposals of assets acquired before becoming non-resident become chargeable to capital gains tax as if such gains 'were gains ... accruing to the taxpayer in the year of return'. However, s 10A was stated to be 'without prejudice to any right to claim relief in accordance with any double taxation relief arrangements' (s 10A(10)). [27.56]

Hence it had been assumed that a capital gains article in a standard double tax treaty (such as between Belgium and the UK) which gave sole taxing rights on disposals of most assets to the country where the alienator was resident at the time of disposal, would apply to prevent a charge under s 10A in the year of return. This also appeared to be HMRC's stated view – see what used to be CG 26290:

> 'although section 10A requires gains accruing in the intervening years between UK departure and return to be assessed to tax there is no intention that this charging provision should override the terms of any double taxation agreement. This will mean any exemption agreement specifically given under an agreement between the UK and another taxing state should be taken into account in arriving at any UK liability.'

In fact it became HMRC practice in treaty negotiations (see for example Canada, South Africa and France) to reserve the UK's right to tax gains realised within six years of departure. [27.57]–[27.58]

HMRC now state that, while they originally accepted the view that a DTA can override a charge under s 10A, this is no longer the case. F(No 2)A 2005 s 32(6) simply omits TCGA 1992 s 10A(10) and, since 16 March 2005, it is expressly provided that treaties cannot override the s 10A charge (s 10A(9C)). The change has effect in any case in which the year of departure is 2005–06 onwards. However, the explanatory notes state 'the reason it is being removed is that it is considered unnecessary: its continuing presence in s 10A might cause doubt to be cast on the effects of other tax provisions which do not contain a corresponding statement'. HMRC suggest that the only double taxation relief is that the individual is allowed to obtain a credit for the foreign tax he has paid (if any) and that even those individuals who emigrated prior to March 2005 cannot rely on treaty relief to protect gains when they return within five years! [27.59]

F(No 2)A 2005 s 32 also deals with persons who are dual resident but are treated under the tie-breaker provisions in the relevant double tax treaty as resident in the foreign state, so are treaty non-resident. Such persons were never within the scope of TCGA 1992 s 10A at all because, although treaty non-resident, they never ceased to be resident in the UK. Hence they did not need to rely on a five-year absence provided they maintained residence in both states and under the tie-breaker provisions could be treated as resident in the foreign state. [27.60]

Whenever a person becomes treaty non-resident on or after 2005–06 they will in future be treated as non-resident for the purposes of TCGA 1992 s 10A. Hence they will need to do their full five (or six) years abroad in order to avoid a capital gains tax charge on disposals of assets. However, as with non-residents under general law, assets acquired and disposed of while treaty non-resident will not be subject to the five-year rule. [27.61]

Although a treaty non-resident taxpayer will now be treated as non-resident for the purposes of TCGA 1992 s 10A, gains attributed to him under the ss 86–87 offshore settlement regime and TCGA 1992 s 13 will not be postponed until the tax year of arrival back in the UK. In effect gains attributed under such provisions will continue to be taxed as at present, ie on the basis that the taxpayer is treated as resident in the UK throughout the time. [27.62]

If HMRC's view is correct, prior to 16 March 2005, persons who were genuinely non-resident in a jurisdiction where there was a double tax treaty protecting them from gains are worse off than persons who remained UK-resident under general law who were merely treaty non-resident! On HMRC's view, the former have had to stay out for five years throughout the period since March 1998. The latter have not had to, unless their departure is on or after 16 March 2005. (See *Example 27.4.*) [27.63]–[27.80]

EXAMPLE 27.4

Assume the facts are as in *Example 27.2* but Don left the UK in 2003 (returning in 2006) and never loses his UK residence (eg he spends at least 120 days here each year). However, he has a permanent home in Belgium and no such home in the UK. Under the tie-breaker tests in the double tax treaty he is treated as resident in Belgium and should not be chargeable on his return in May 2006 on the gain on the sale of the Ming vase.

III THE CAPITAL GAINS TAX REGIME FOR FOREIGN DOMICILIARIES

1 General points

Significant changes to the tax treatment of UK residents who remain domiciled abroad were enacted in FA 2008.

In the July 2015 Budget, further significant changes were announced. It was originally intended that these changes would take effect from 6 April 2017. However, as a result of the 2017 General Election, the provisions were removed from FA 2017. It may well be that the changes are still introduced with effect from that date, although it is possible that any changes will be deferred until 6 April 2018.

Under the proposals, individuals who have been resident in the UK for 15 out of the previous 20 years will be deemed to be domiciled in the UK for all tax purposes, including capital gains tax. Similarly, individuals who were born in the UK with a UK domicile of origin will be deemed to be domiciled in the UK for all tax purposes (including capital gains tax) at any time when they are UK resident. At the time of writing, full details of the proposed changes are not yet known but there is no doubt that they will have a significant impact on those individuals who are affected.

The general rule for some years has been that an individual who is resident, but not domiciled, in the UK is chargeable to CGT only on the remitted gains from overseas assets, ie the foreign chargeable gains – see TCGA 1992 s 12. To obtain the benefit of the remittance basis on such gains, an individual must *claim* to be taxed on a remittance basis under ITA 2007 ss 809B–809E ie be a remittance basis user unless he comes within the limited exceptions in s 809D discussed in [18.34] (including total unremitted foreign income and gains not exceeding £2,000). If he claims the remittance basis of taxation then he will lose all personal allowances and the annual capital gains tax exemption. In addition if he has been UK resident in at least seven out of the nine tax years immediately preceding the tax year in question and is over 18 he will need to pay £30,000 for the privilege of retaining the remittance basis of taxation on both foreign income and gains (s 809C and see [18.34] for further discussion). If UK resident in at least 12 out of the 14 tax years immediately preceding the tax year in question and over 18, he will need to pay £60,000 to retain the remittance basis of taxation; and if UK resident for at least 17 out of the 20 tax years immediately preceding the tax year in question and over 18, he will need to pay £90,000 (see ITA 2007 s 809C). **[27.81]**

The wider definition of what constitutes a remittance as set out in ITA 2007 s 809L (as amended by FA 2008) applies for capital gains tax purposes and is discussed further below.

The 2016 Budget papers noted that provision would be introduced for those becoming deemed domiciled on 6 April 2017 as a result of having spent 15 years in the UK as described above, enabling them to treat the base cost of non-UK assets for CGT purposes as being the market value as at 6 April 2017.

It was also announced that all non-domiciliaries who have in the past paid tax on the remittance basis would have two years from 6 April 2017 to separate out accounts which contained a mixture of income, capital and capital gains.

This would allow capital to be remitted to the UK in priority to income or capital gains which, as described below, would not otherwise be the case.

As mentioned above, all of these changes were removed from FA 2017 as a result of a General Election being called. It is, however, likely that the changes will still be implemented and may still have effect from 6 April 2017; although it is possible that the changes will only take effect from a later date (either the date of any post-election announcement or 6 April 2018).

Given the current uncertainty, these changes are not addressed in detail in this edition but will be covered in the next edition assuming that they have been implemented. [27.82]

2 When is an asset situate outside the UK for capital gains tax purposes?

TCGA 1992 s 275A provides that the situs of any intangible asset will be treated as being in the UK if any right or interest comprised in the asset is governed by, exercisable in or enforceable under or is subject to the law of the UK. The same is true of futures or options over such intangibles. The situs of such futures or options is governed by the situs of the underlying asset. [27.83]

Furthermore, all shares (including bearer shares) in and debentures of UK-incorporated companies, whether registered or not, are treated as situated in the UK. [27.84]

A debt is situated in the UK if the creditor is resident in the UK. [27.85]

3 Losses

Until April 2008 there was no relief for any overseas losses. In practice this was often not a problem because foreign domiciliaries tended to hold appreciating assets through trusts and thus avoid capital gains tax (see **Chapter 27A**). Foreign domiciliaries are now subject to capital gains tax in respect of capital payments received from foreign trusts. Partly to compensate for this, FA 2008 Sch 7 introduced limited loss relief for overseas losses from 6 April 2008 if a foreign domiciliary on the remittance basis of taxation so elects (see Sch 7 para 62 and TCGA 1992 s 16ZA as amended). [27.86]

EXAMPLE 27.5

Henri arrives in England and sells his French property for a gain of £50,000 and his French shares for a loss of £40,000 after allowing for currency gains and losses. He mixes the proceeds of both and remits £20,000 in 2007 to the UK thinking his net gain ignoring annual exemption is £10,000. In fact he is treated as remitting a gain of £20,000. Note that from 2008 if no loss election is made all the gain is treated as being remitted first, not part of the gain proportionate to the total sale proceeds or the gain net of the loss.

A number of conditions apply to overseas loss relief:
(1) An irrevocable election must be made in the first year when the remittance basis is claimed. If no election is made, foreign losses of that tax year and all future tax years will not be allowable losses even if the

individual later opts to be taxed on an arising rather than remittance basis unless he accepts he is domiciled in the UK under general law.

(2) Foreign chargeable gains remitted to the UK in a tax year later than that in which the foreign asset was disposed of cannot be reduced by losses of a later year or of any year later than that in which the gains arose (s 16ZB).

EXAMPLE 27.6

A realises foreign gains of £50,000 in 2010 and has elected to be taxed on a remittance basis. He realised foreign losses in 2011–12 and remitted the £50,000 gains in 2012–13. He cannot use the losses to reduce the taxable remittance.

(3) If the remittance basis is claimed for the tax year in which the foreign chargeable gains arise, the allowable losses are deducted first from foreign chargeable gains that both arise and are remitted in that tax year, then against foreign chargeable gains arising but not remitted in that year and then from any UK chargeable gains arising in that year.

[27.87]

EXAMPLE 27.7

B realises foreign gains of £50,000 in 2012–13 and foreign losses of £60,000 plus UK losses of £3,000. He realises gains on UK assets of £15, 000 and remits £20,000 of the foreign gains. The losses (including UK losses) are set against the remitted gains first (£20,000) and then against the remaining unremitted foreign gains arising in that year (but not against foreign gains in earlier years) and then against the UK gains – leaving £2,000 of UK gains chargeable.

The election is irrevocable. Foreign losses cannot be deducted against gains chargeable under TCGA s 87 or against gains remitted in a year later than that in which they arose. If no election is made, only UK losses remain relievable in full. Only foreign losses from 2008–09 are allowable under this provision.

4 Segregation of gains

It is not possible to separate out the gain from the original capital and remit only the capital. The position is different from a separation of income and capital. [27.88]

EXAMPLE 27.8

Pauline invested £1m in shares in a German bio-tech company, BTI Limited. These produce £20,000 dividends each year which is paid into her overseas income account. She eventually sells the BTI shares for £2m. She remits £1m to the UK. She cannot successfully argue that the £1m represents the original capital and that the gain has not been remitted even if the sale proceeds have been split up. Prior to 6 April 2008 HMRC would tax her on half the remittance on the basis that remittances are treated as taxable gain in the proportion that the gains bear to the total amount in the account. (See old CG 25401.) However, post 5 April 2008 the mixed fund rules in ITA 2007 s 809Q as inserted by FA 2008 Sch 7 apply to treat the first remittance of £1m as entirely gain.

The dividend income that has been paid into the overseas income account can continue to be segregated and is not taxable unless remitted.

If the proposed changes to the taxation of non-domiciliaries referred to above at [27.82] are implemented, Pauline would have a window of opportunity to split the original £1 million invested in the shares from the £1 million of gain. This would then allow her to remit the £1 million of original capital in priority to the £1 million of gain and so avoid any liability to tax on the £1 million remittance.

5   What constitutes a remittance?

ITA 2007 s 809L aims to set out a comprehensive code to determine what is a remittance on or after 6 April 2008. The position on what constitutes a remittance post 5 April 2008 has been discussed in **Chapter 18** and so the following is only a brief summary. [27.89]

Income or gains of an individual are treated as remitted to the UK if Conditions A and B are met; or if Condition C is met; or if Condition D is met. Condition C aims to cover gifts to non-relevant persons where a relevant person still benefits and condition D aims to counteract reciprocal arrangements. Conditions C and D are not discussed further here but see [18.34]. [27.90]

Condition A is that *money or other property is* brought to, received in or used in the UK by or for the benefit of a relevant person or a service is provided in the UK to or for the benefit of a relevant person. [27.91]

Condition B is that:
(1) the property service or consideration for the service is wholly or in part the income or chargeable gains; or
(2) derives wholly or in part and directly or indirectly from the income or chargeable gains and in the case of property or consideration is property of or consideration given by a relevant person; or
(3) the income or gains are used outside the UK directly or indirectly in respect of a relevant debt; or
(4) anything deriving from the income or chargeable gains is used in respect of the debt. [27.92]

a) *Relevant persons*

Relevant person is defined in ITA 2007 s 809M as the individual, the individual's spouse, cohabitee, civil partner, minor child or minor grandchild, any UK or overseas close company in which any of those people are participators, trusts where any of those people are beneficiaries and any body connected with such a company or trust. Note that adult descendants are not relevant persons.

The definition of relevant persons in ITA 2007 s 809M was widened with effect from 6 April 2010 by FA 2010 to clarify the position in relation to subsidiary companies. A specific definition of 51% subsidiaries of companies that would be close companies if they were resident in the UK has been inserted. FA 2009 had already amended ITA 2007 s 809M(2)(e) to include 51% subsidiaries of UK close companies. Remittance basis users will therefore no longer have the opportunity to use 51% subsidiaries of companies to make remittances that may have been outside the scope of the original legislation. [27.93]

However, in relation to gains arising prior to 6 April 2008 the definition of relevant person is restricted to the individual foreign domiciliary. [27.94]

The effects of all of this can be seen in the following examples.

EXAMPLE 27.9

(1) A sells some foreign land at a gain and gives the proceeds to his wife who invests them in the UK in shares. There is no benefit to A but A is taxed on the gain unless it arose from a disposal made prior to 6 April 2008 in which case there is only a taxable remittance if A benefits. The rate of tax is determined by the rates of tax at the date of remittance except that in relation to remittances in 2010–11 the time of remittance will determine the rate of tax, depending on whether it arises before or on or after 23 June 2010. No taper relief is available from 2008–09 even if the disposal took place before 2008–09 because the gain is treated as accruing when remitted.

(2) B gives the sale proceeds of the above land to his adult son (non-UK resident) who settles it into trust which invests in the UK. B cannot benefit but his minor grandchild can. There is a taxable remittance unless the gain arose prior to 6 April 2008 or one can argue that the trust was not in contemplation at the time of the gift to the adult son and that it is not derived from the proceeds of B's gift. B may not know that his adult son has set up a trust!

(3) C gives the proceeds of the land sale to his adult son who invests it in the UK. There is no taxable remittance by either since it is capital in the son's hands and an adult son is not a relevant person in relation to C. The son then sells the UK assets and gives the proceeds to a trust which subscribes the capital to an underlying company which invests in the UK. The trust is one from which C, spouse etc cannot benefit but could be added. This is a taxable remittance.

There are still advantages for a foreign domiciled taxpayer who is UK-resident to hold assets which are likely to show a gain through a trust. The use of a trust will avoid CGT on UK situated assets but as noted later in **Chapter 27A** can complicate the remittance rules. Instead of looking at the gain on the actual asset it will now be necessary to compute all the stockpiled gains of the trust when remitting capital to the UK. [27.95]

b) *Business investment relief*

The remittance rules discouraged investment into the UK and so a new business investment relief was introduced with effect from 6 April 2012 by FA 2012 Sch 12. Section 809VA of ITA 2007 (as inserted by Sch 12) states that foreign income or gains are not to be treated as remitted to the UK for tax purposes if the income or gains are used to make qualifying investments. These are broadly investments in a company (whether or not UK resident and whether by share capital or loan) for qualifying purposes of a 'commercial trade' (see ITA 2007 s 809VE as amended and **Chapter 18**). The company can be a trading company or one which invests in rental properties. However, the individual must claim the new relief on his tax return and there is a raft of anti-avoidance provisions.

The most difficult of these is contained in s 809VH which imposes a 'potentially chargeable event' and therefore a taxable remittance in the event that the extraction of value rule is breached or the target company does not start operating within two years of the investment. The extraction of value rule can be breached if value is received by the taxpayer or any relevant person (see above) from any 'involved company' (ie from any connected company of the taxpayer) anywhere in the world. Return of value includes any value in money or money's worth that is not subject to income tax or would not be subject to income tax or is not provided on arm's length terms. In practice this will deter many foreign domiciliaries from using the relief: any other company they own, even though completely unconnected with this one and whose activities are entirely abroad, could nevertheless be subject to HMRC scrutiny.

As part of the package of changes to the taxation of non-domiciliaries referred to at **[27.82]**, it is proposed that this trap should be removed and that any extraction of value will only lead to a clawback of relief if it is in some way connected with the investment which qualifies for business investment relief and not if value is received from an entirely unconnected company which the taxpayer happens to own. **[27.96]**

c) *Sales of exempt art*

By virtue of FA 2012 Sch 12, art that is brought to the UK on or after 6 April 2012 for the purposes of sale at arm's length to a person other than a relevant person is not a taxable remittance even if it was purchased using foreign income or gains (see ITA 2007 s 809YA as amended). The sale proceeds must be taken abroad within 45 days of receipt. The work of art must not be in the UK for more than 275 days (in total since April 2008) even if solely here for the purposes of sale unless held at an 'approved establishment', which includes Christies or Sothebys.

The taxpayer must claim relief under s 809YA on his tax return. In addition, if the sale of the art itself generates a chargeable gain in the UK then the gain (that would normally be immediately chargeable on the individual foreign domiciled owner) is deemed to be a foreign chargeable gain and taxable on the remittance basis. The proceeds must be taken out of the UK within 45 days of each instalment of the sale price being received. **[27.97]**

6 **Rate of tax**

As noted above, the rate of tax is determined by the time of remittance. The rate of tax is 18% flat rate for gains remitted between 6 April 2008 and 22 June 2010 whatever the income tax position of the taxpayer.

If funds are remitted after that date but before 6 April 2016 then the rate of tax is 28% if the taxpayer is a higher rate taxpayer. In fact even this is a simplification. The gains arising after 22 June 2010 have to be added to the taxpayer's total income for the year to determine whether they are taxed at the higher 28% rate or the lower 18%. Only to the extent that they bring the taxpayer over the higher rate limit are they taxed at 28%. One ignores gains realised prior to 23 June 2010 in determining the higher rate tax limit for the 2010–11 tax year and the annual capital gains tax exemption and personal losses can be used to reduce post 22 June gains in priority to pre 23 June gains (see **[21.61]**).

The only exception to the rate of tax is if ITA 2007 s 809J (the mixed fund rules) applies. In that event it is not the actual income or gain which is treated as remitted but those established by that section that are deemed to be remitted in a particular order. For 2010–11 these deemed gains will be treated as remitted prior to 23 June 2010 and taxed at 18%.

Gains remitted after 5 April 2016 will be taxed at 20% for a higher rate taxpayer or 28% if the gain relates to residential property or carried interest.

[27.98]

7 Disposals for less than full consideration

Prior to 2008, it was possible for a non-domiciliary to avoid capital gains tax by gifting a foreign asset pregnant with gain to a trust. [27.99]

EXAMPLE 27.10

Freda who is non-UK domiciled buys £200,000 worth of shares in the German company, Z Limited, using capital. In 2005 she settles the shares in an offshore trust from which she can benefit at a time when they are worth £1m. Under the pre April 2008 rules there is no deemed remittance and the trust acquires the shares at market value of £1m. The trustees sell the shares two years later realising a gain of £500,000. The trustees then pay capital to Freda in the UK. Under the pre April 2008 regime there was no taxable remittance by Freda of either the £800,000 pre-settlement gain or the £500,000 post settlement gain since neither TCGA 1992 ss 86 nor 87 applied and s 12 was not applicable. The gains had been 'washed out'.

Even if the trustees reinvested the proceeds in UK assets and sold at a gain and distributed the proceeds to her in the UK, there would still have been no tax chargeable on Freda.

The loophole has been closed by ITA 2007 s 809T which treats the asset in the hands of the donee as derived from the chargeable gain realised by the donor. The donor is then treated as making a taxable remittance if the donee is a relevant person and brings the asset to the UK or if the donee gives the asset or its proceeds back to the donor who then remits it to the UK.

EXAMPLE 27.11

The facts are as above except Freda settles the shares into trust in 2012. The trust acquires the shares at market value and there is no deemed remittance at that point. However, if the trust then sells the shares and pays say £500,000 to Freda or her spouse, minor child or grandchild, cohabitee or company owned by her and the £500,000 is brought to the UK, *Freda* is treated as having remitted £500,000 of pre-settlement gain and is taxed accordingly. In addition the beneficiary who receives the capital payment from the trust will now also suffer a s 87 charge based on the *trust gains of £500,000*. This s 87 charge will fall on the person who receives the capital payment to which the trust gains of £500,000 can be matched, not necessarily on Freda. If, however, the trust paid £500,000 to an adult son resident here, then Freda is not taxed on the £500,000 pre settlement gain because the son is not a relevant person. The son will be liable to tax under s 87 by reference to the trust gains of £500,000 only not the pre-settlement gains. See **Chapter 27A** for further discussion.

If Freda had settled the shares into trust in 2005 and the trust had sold the shares in June 2008 but no payment was made to her until say 2009, the question arises as to whether the pre-settlement gains of £800,000 can be subsequently taxed on her if she receives a payment in the UK or whether she is only taxed under the s 87 settlement code on trust gains of £500,000. The let out in Sch 7 para 86(4) makes it clear that if the trustees distribute to a spouse or other relevant person, Freda cannot be taxed on the £800,000 pre-settlement gains because references to a relevant person are restricted to her as the donor individual. However, the position is less clear where the payment of pre April 2008 gains is made to Freda. The better view is that such gains are not taxed on her even if the payment is made after 6 April 2008 although of course she could be taxed under s 87 on trust gains of £500,000 as a capital payment – see **Chapter 27A**. [27.100]

8 Foreign currency gains

The computation of foreign currency gains was an area of some dispute between HMRC and the professional bodies. Foreign currency is an asset for capital gains tax purposes (TCGA 1992 s 21). Any withdrawal from a foreign currency account was therefore a disposal unless the currency was acquired for personal expenditure abroad. Foreign bank accounts are foreign situs and therefore a capital gains tax computation was required whenever money was withdrawn from the bank account and remitted by the foreign domiciliary. The base cost was the aggregate value of all prior credits to the account, the sterling value of each being fixed by the exchange rates prevailing when each deposit was made.

FA 2010 s 34 introduced TCGA 1992 Sch 8A which was intended to clarify the treatment of foreign currency bank accounts held by non-domiciliaries and took effect in relation to disposals on or after 16 December 2009. (See also technical note issued by HMRC on 23 December 2009 explaining the operation of the new rules. See also HMRC's announcement in January 2010 that SP 10/84 would be extended to foreign domiciliaries so that all bank accounts in any particular foreign currency would be treated as a single account.)

Fortunately, TCGA 1992 s 252 was amended in 2012 so that all sums within an individual, estate or trust's foreign currency bank accounts are removed from the scope of capital gains tax so that neither a chargeable gain nor allowable loss can arise, with effect for disposals occurring on or after 6 April 2012. The change is not retrospective so disposals on foreign currency bank accounts prior to this date still need to be computed. [27.101]–[27.110]

IV NON-RESIDENT COMPANIES AND UK RESIDENT INDIVIDUALS

1 General rule

A non-resident company is generally excluded from liability to CGT except when it trades in the UK through a branch or an agency. Thus, a non-resident investment company is not normally liable to CGT.

As an exception to this general rule, gains realised by a non-UK company on the disposal of a UK residential property for more than £2 million (known as ATED-related gains) will potentially be subject to CGT in the UK. This is part of a package of measures introduced in 2013 aimed at discouraging the ownership of high value residential property in the UK through offshore entities. It is only any increase in value since 5 April 2013 which will be taxed.

If a property is jointly owned, split up into different interests or only part of the interest held by the company is sold, the £2 million threshold is proportionately reduced in determining whether the company is subject to CGT.

There are a number of reliefs which apply, the most important of which is that gains are not chargeable in respect of any period during which the property is let commercially to an unconnected third party.

As mentioned at [27.43], the ATED-related CGT regime was extended from 6 April 2015 to properties worth more than £1 million and further extended from 6 April 2016 to properties worth more than £500,000. In each case, it is only any increase in value from the relevant date which will be taxed.

In addition, from 6 April 2015, even if there is no ATED-related CGT charge (eg if the property is let to a third party) non-resident companies have been taxable on any disposal of an interest in UK residential property in the same way as any other non-resident. The company will, however, benefit from indexation and will only pay tax at 20% rather than the 28% rate of ATED-related CGT. [27.111]

2 Anti-avoidance

There have always been provisions designed to prevent UK-resident and domiciled individuals from using these rules to avoid the payment of CGT by the formation of non-resident companies. The legislation is contained in TCGA 1992 s 13. It applies to UK residents in the following circumstances:

(1) Chargeable gains must accrue to a company which is not resident in the UK but which would be a close company if it were so resident (note that such gains are calculated by reference to a continuing indexation allowance): for the definition of a close company, see [41.122].

(2) The gain is attributed to any UK resident participator to the extent of that person's interest in the company and there is an attribution process that involves looking through multiple layers of intermediate holdings with final attribution being on a just and reasonable basis. 'Participator' has the CTA 2010 s 454 meaning as further amplified and will catch all interests in shares as well as the interest of loan creditors. Trustees can be participators but the provisions do not 'look through' to their beneficiaries (ie the gains are attributed to the trust but further provisions may then charge the gain on the settlor (see TCGA 1992 s 86) or attribute it to the beneficiaries (see TCGA 1992 s 87)).

(3) No tax is payable if the participator's interest in the company (together with the interests of any connected persons) is less than 25% (increased from 10% in 2013 which was in turn increased from 5% by FA 2001).

(4) Gains made on the disposal of most assets of a trading company that are used in the trade are not apportioned (TCGA 1992 s 13(5)). From 6 April 2012, gains on the disposal of an asset used for the purpose of

an 'economically significant activity' carried on wholly or mainly outside the UK are also exempt. In practice, there are likely to be very few activities which qualify which do not amount to a trade. Thus, problems really arise only for participators in a non-resident investment or holding company.

(5) Also from 6 April 2012, a gain is exempt if it can be shown that neither the disposal, acquisition nor holding of the asset by the company had the avoidance of CGT or corporation tax as one of its main purposes. This is sometimes referred to as the 'motive defence'.

(6) Gains on the disposal by the company of an interest in UK residential property are excluded if those gains are taxed on the company itself under the ATED-related CGT or non-resident CGT regime (see **[27.43]** and **[27.111]**).

(7) Losses made by the non-resident company cannot be used to reduce its gains before apportionment, nor can the losses as such be apportioned except to the extent that a shareholder has had a gain apportioned to him in that tax year under s 13 and the apportioned loss would eliminate or reduce the gain. See *Example 27.12*.

(8) A shareholder can be reimbursed by the company for tax paid on apportioned gains without a further charge. Otherwise, he can deduct the tax paid from any gain made on a subsequent disposal of the shares.

(9) If, following the disposal by the company, the gain is distributed by way of dividend, distribution of capital or on a winding up of the offshore company, any tax paid on the gain is allowed as a credit against any liability arising on the distribution. The distribution must occur before the earlier of:
    (a) three years from the end of the period of account in which the gain accrued; and
    (b) four years from the date on which the gain accrued.

(10) If the non-resident company is situated in a country with which the UK has a double tax treaty, gains realised by the company may be protected by the treaty and so be outside s 13 (see *Bricom Holdings v IRC* (1997)). FA 2000 altered this position in the case of trustee shareholders by providing that 'nothing in any double taxation relief arrangements' shall prevent the attribution of gains to trustees under s 13 (see TCGA 1992 s 79B inserted by FA 2000). Individuals remain protected by treaty relief in these circumstances.

(11) Until 6 April 2008 s 13 did not apply if the UK-resident participator was not domiciled here. From 6 April 2008 s 13 does apply to UK resident foreign domiciliaries. See TCGA 1992 s 14A. The result is that if foreign companies realise foreign gains then the foreign domiciliary is taxed on the remittance basis on such gain (assuming such foreign domiciliary is electing to be taxed on the remittance basis). If a foreign close company realises a gain on a UK asset then the foreign domiciliary is taxed on an arising basis. Unlike the position for companies owned by trusts there is no automatic rebasing to 6 April 2008 so gains accruing prior to that date can still be taxed if the disposal takes places later.   **[27.112]**

EXAMPLE 27.12

Xcon Limited is a Guernsey company owned as to 70% by two non-UK residents and 30% by Eddie, a UK resident and domiciled person. Xcon Limited holds equities. Subject to the application of the motive defence, Eddie will suffer a charge under s 13 on 30% of the indexed gains realised by Xcon.

In 2015–16 Xcon realises losses of £2m and gains of £1m from the disposal of some equities. The losses can be set off against the gains made by Xcon Limited in the same tax year and can be used against gains made in the same *tax year* by other non-resident companies in which Eddie has an interest and which have been apportioned to Eddie under s 13. However, Eddie cannot use the surplus losses in Xcon Limited against his personal gains nor can those Xcon losses be carried forward to use against future gains Xcon may make in later tax years. If not used in 2015–16 they are lost forever.

EXAMPLE 27.13

Eddie, a foreign domiciliary who is a remittance basis user is UK resident and owns personally all the shares in a Jerseyco which holds a UK property. The house was acquired in 2005 and at April 2008 showed gains of £400,000.

The company sells the house in June 2008. All the gains are taxable on Eddie on an arising basis. If the company had sold the house prior to 6 April 2008 there would have been no tax. If Eddie transferred the company shares into trust and the company then sold the house there would be no immediate tax charge on Eddie (although tax charges would arise if he subsequently received benefits from the trust – see **Chapter 27A**).

If the sale took place after 5 April 2015 the company would pay tax on any increase in value since 6 April 2015 (and possibly on any increase in value since 6 April 2013 if the proceeds were more than £2 million) and Eddie would only pay tax on the balance.

EXAMPLE 27.14

The facts are as above except the company owns an Italian house which is sold at a gain after 6 April 2008. No tax charge arises on Eddie unless and until the gain is remitted to the UK. If the company reinvests the proceeds in a UK house there is a remittance at that point by Eddie of the foreign chargeable gain and, unless the motive defence applies, a tax charge will arise. If the company also realises losses in the year of disposal, such losses cannot reduce the foreign chargeable gain taxed on Eddie in the event of subsequent remittance.

Notice that the provisions whereby the profits of a 'controlled foreign company', including an investment company, may be apportioned to its UK resident corporate members do not apply to its chargeable gains (see TIOPA 2010 s 371SB(3)(b): and see [**41.161**]).

27A Offshore trusts and CGT

Updated by Robin Vos, Macfarlanes LLP

I   Background **[27A.1]**
II Exporting a UK trust; trustee residence **[27A.21]**
III Taxing the UK domiciled settlor of an offshore trust (TCGA 1992 s 86, Sch 5) **[27A.71]**
IV Taxing UK resident beneficiaries of a non-resident trust (UK domiciled and non-UK domiciled) (TCGA 1992 ss 87 ff) **[27A.111]**
V   Other offshore matters **[27A.171]**

I BACKGROUND

Trustees of a trust who are treated as non-UK resident (see **[27A.25]**–**[27A.33]**) are generally outside the scope of CGT (in common with other non-residents). Instead, various anti-avoidance provisions seek to tax trust gains either on the settlor or on the beneficiaries of the offshore trust. **[27A.1]**

Since 1991 the capital gains tax treatment of offshore trusts has been subject to continuous change. Until FA 2008 these changes did not significantly affect foreign domiciled beneficiaries. FA 2008 provided for the first time that foreign domiciliaries who are UK resident can be subject to capital gains tax under TCGA 1992 s 87. These changes are discussed in Section IV. **[27A.2]**

The history of these provisions can be summarised as follows.

a) *From 1965–81*

FA 1965 s 42 imposed a charging system for non-UK-resident trusts that led to major difficulties and was ultimately abandoned in 1981. **[27A.3]**

b) *From 1981–91*

FA 1981 s 80 charged capital gains tax on capital distributions received by UK domiciled and resident beneficiaries provided that the trust had been established by a UK domiciled settlor (now called the s 87 charge – see Section IV and TCGA 1992 s 87). One consequence was that provided no capital was distributed to beneficiaries, offshore trusts could be used to defer the payment of CGT indefinitely even if the settlor could benefit. In addition, there was no exit charge when a UK trust migrated. Nor was there any capital gains tax charge even when capital was distributed if the settlor was not UK domiciled, irrespective of whether the beneficiary receiving the capital payment was UK resident and domiciled. **[27A.4]**

UK domiciled settlors therefore found that there was no disadvantage in holding assets through offshore trusts. If the trust realised the gain no tax was payable until distributions were made to a beneficiary which might be many years hence. If by that time the beneficiary was non-UK resident or a lower rate taxpayer then the tax could be minimised. In the meantime the trustees could invest the gross gain and thereby in theory obtain a higher return. **[27A.5]**

Settlements established by foreign domiciled or non-UK resident settlors were at an even greater advantage because neither they nor any beneficiaries (wherever domiciled) of the trust were subject to capital gains tax under s 87 on capital receipts while the settlor remained non-UK domiciled or non-UK resident. The trustees were not chargeable to capital gains tax because the trust was non-UK resident. Hence potential tax charges were limited to income tax on income and on offshore income gains. **[27A.6]**

c) *From 1991–98*

Interest charge. To encourage trustees to distribute capital early an interest charge was imposed on a UK domiciled and resident beneficiary resulting in tax rates of up to 64% when capital was distributed some years after gains were realised. Contrary to the Government's expectations though this further discouraged trustees from making any distributions. *See Example 27A.13* and Section IV. **[27A.7]**

Settlor charge TCGA 1992 s 86. In addition FA 1991 provided that new offshore trusts set up by UK domiciled and resident settlors were no longer able to defer capital gains tax unless the trust was not able to benefit the settlor, spouse or children. Instead the settlor was liable for tax on trust gains under s 86. So the deferral advantages of new offshore trusts by UK settlors were limited to those set up for grandchildren or other beneficiaries not including children, spouses, settlor. However, new or old trusts set up by foreign domiciled settlors were still able to distribute capital tax free to any beneficiary. In addition pre 1991 existing untainted offshore trusts set up by UK settlors continued to operate under the old deferral regime. Such trusts were therefore able to avoid capital gains tax under s 86 provided there was no 'tainting'. See Section III below. **[27A.8]**

Exit charge. From 19 March 1991 an exit charge was levied on UK trusts which emigrated: see TCGA 1992 ss 80–84 and *Example 27A.4* and Section II. **[27A.9]**

d) *FA 1998 changes – see section III*

There were further changes for UK domiciled and resident beneficiaries/settlors as follows:
(1) the TCGA 1992 s 86 settlor charge was extended to settlements created before the 1991 changes (before 1998 the settlor charge was only

relevant to settlements created or 'tainted' on or after 19 March 1991). This meant that almost all the pre 1991 trusts which had been set up by UK domiciled and resident settlors keen to defer capital gains tax were now caught and such a settlor from 1998 paid tax on an arising basis on all future trust gains;

(2) 'grandchildren' were now included in the definition of 'defined person' for the purpose of the settlor charge if the trust was established or tainted after 16 March 1998;

(3) the capital payments charge under s 87 was extended so that UK resident and domiciled beneficiaries who received payments from offshore trusts matched to trust gains were chargeable even where the settlor was not domiciled or resident in the UK;

(4) the tax charge on disposals of beneficial interests in a settlement was extended; see Section IV below and TCGA 1992 ss 85, 76.

(5) new rules were introduced to ensure that a settlor or beneficiary could not avoid the ss 86/87 charges by becoming non-resident unless they did so for at least five years.

This process was continued by anti-avoidance measures in FA 2000, FA 2003 and F(No 2)A 2005 mainly aimed at stopping people circumventing the settlor's 's 86' charge or the beneficiary's 's 87' charge. **[27A.10]**

e) *FA 2008 changes – see Section IV*

(1) The s 86 settlor charge remains restricted to UK domiciled settlors. Non-UK domiciled settlors are not subject to the s 86 charge provided they remain foreign domiciled under general law even if they are otherwise taxed on an arising basis because they have not opted to be remittance basis users. See **Chapter 18**. Hence there are no changes to s 86.

(2) There were major changes to s 87. FA 2008 substituted a new s 87 to take effect from 6 April 2008. The basic principle remains the same. If the trustees make chargeable gains those gains are treated as accruing to the beneficiaries to the extent that beneficiaries receive capital payments from the trustees. Whether there is a charge to capital gains tax depends on the general rule in TCGA 1992 s 2. This imposes a charge to capital gains tax on UK-resident persons. So if the gain accrues to a person who is not UK resident there is no charge to capital gains tax but s 87 still applies to match the gain.

(3) However, capital payments to foreign domiciled and UK resident beneficiaries are not only matched to trust gains but (for the first time) such beneficiaries can from 6 April 2008 be chargeable to capital gains tax under TCGA 1992 s 87 and Sch 4C. This applies to all UK resident beneficiaries whether or not the settlor or such beneficiaries are domiciled here.

(4) A non-UK domiciled beneficiary who claims the remittance basis is chargeable to CGT only if the trust gain is matched to a capital payment which is remitted to, or is a benefit received in, the UK. The situs of assets on which the trust gain is realised is irrelevant to the remittance basis. What matters is whether the beneficiary has remitted the capital into the UK under the extended remittance rules in ITA 2007 s 809L (see **Chapter 27**) or received the benefit in the UK.

(5) Capital payments made to non-UK domiciliaries before 6 April 2008 are not taxed even if matched with post 5 April 2008 gains and irrespective of whether the beneficiary is a remittance basis user provided that when matched to post 5 April 2008 gains the foreign domiciliary is still domiciled outside the UK as a matter of general law.

(6) Non-UK domiciliaries are not taxed in respect of capital payments made to them after 5 April 2008 where such capital payments are matched to gains realised prior to 6 April 2008, whether or not the beneficiary is a remittance basis user.

(7) Trustees have an option to rebase assets within trusts and certain underlying companies as at 6 April 2008. (For shares this will be a 7 April 2008 valuation.)

(8) Transitional rules apply to payments made between 12 March 2008 and 5 April 2008.

(9) The FIFO (first in, first out) rule no longer applies to match gains with capital payments (see Section IV below). Instead capital payments are matched first to gains of the current year before being matched to gains of earlier years on a LIFO (last in, first out) basis. The result is that the supplemental charge has reduced in respect of many capital payments.

(10) Gains realised prior to 6 April 2008 have the benefit of any taper relief. This was to prevent the pool of stockpiled gains realised prior to 6 April 2008 from having to be recalculated.

(11) For 2010–11 only, any capital payments made prior to 23 June 2010 were only taxed at 18% even if matched to gains realised later in that tax year 2010–11. However, if the capital payment made prior to 23 June 2010 is matched to gains realised in a *future* tax year (say 2012–13) then the tax rate is 28% (or 20% after 5 April 2016). Similarly if the gain is realised in 2010–11 but matched to a capital payment made after 23 June 2010 then the rate of tax is 28% (or 20% after 5 April 2016 assuming the taxpayer is a higher rate taxpayer). In fact, if the gain is not matched in the year it is realised or in the following year, the supplemental charge could mean that the tax rate is higher than 28%/20%

(12) In calculating trust gains for the purposes of s 87, the concept of the 's 2(2) amount' is introduced. This is defined as the amount on which the trustees would be liable to capital gains tax if they had been resident in the UK during the year. As in the original s 87 this is the amount of the gains after deducting trust losses and without giving any annual exempt amount (but reducing the s 2(2) amount by the amount of any gains charged on the settlor under s 86). The matching rules are in ss 87A and 87C. [27A.11]

f) *Proposed 2017 changes*

In the July 2015 Budget, it was announced that non-domiciled individuals who had been resident in the UK for 15 out of the previous 20 years would, from 6 April 2017, be treated as domiciled in the UK for all tax purposes. However, it was also announced that special protections would apply to these individuals so that (with the exception of UK source income) they would not be taxed on income and gains arising within an offshore trust set up before becoming deemed domiciled until they receive a distribution or benefit from the trust. Implementing this will require significant changes to the anti-avoidance provisions discussed in this chapter.

It is anticipated that this legislation would take effect from 6 April 2017. However, as a result of the general election, the draft legislation was removed from Finance Act 2017. It is, however, still expected that the changes will be made and this chapter does therefore contain some references to the proposals given the importance of the changes. **[27A.12]–[27A.20]**

II EXPORTING A UK TRUST; TRUSTEE RESIDENCE

a) *What are the advantages of a non-UK resident trust?*

Moving a trust offshore has sometimes been undertaken in order to obtain all or some of the following benefits: protection from a reintroduction of exchange control; deferment or avoidance of CGT; and deferment or avoidance of income tax. More recently, establishing a non-resident trust, particularly one subject to foreign law, has sometimes been seen as a surer way of defeating creditors' claims, particularly matrimonial claims. The settlor may find it easier to resist, or at least delay, payments to a spouse if the trust is subject to say Cayman law since any order by the English courts will not necessarily be recognised or enforced in Cayman, particularly if the assets are situated outside the UK. **[27A.21]**

So long as the settlor and any spouse or civil partner are excluded from benefit, UK income tax will be avoided on income received by a non-resident discretionary trust which has no direct UK source income unless either UK resident and domiciled beneficiaries receive income distributions from the trustees or a beneficiary who is resident in the UK receives a benefit and income has been accumulated within the trust or holding company structure (ITA 2007 s 731 onwards and see **[18.111]**). However, the rate of tax will be by reference to the beneficiary's level of income and personal allowances and not necessarily levied at 45%. The remittance basis is also available in such cases.

A will trust can therefore offer income tax deferral advantages if the trust is exported soon after the settlor's death even if he was UK resident and domiciled and the capital gains tax problems raised by TCGA 1992 s 86 below do not apply once the settlor has died.

If the trust is non-interest in possession and receives UK source income directly the rate of tax will be 45%, even if the income is less than £150,000. The trustees have no personal allowances. If the trustees wish to avoid UK income tax then they have the following options (in all cases the settlor/spouse/civil partner will need to be wholly excluded or non-UK resident otherwise the trust income is taxed on the settlor):

(a) they can sell the UK income producing assets;
(b) they can transfer the UK assets to an underlying offshore company (so that no UK income is received at the trust level);

(c) the trustees can appoint revocable interests in possession (which following the FA 2006 changes will have no IHT consequences). The income will then belong to the interest in possession beneficiary and be taxed at his highest rate. [27A.22]

Non-UK resident trusts have capital gains tax advantages for foreign domiciliaries because s 86 does not apply to them irrespective of whether they are remittance basis users (ie those who claim the remittance basis of taxation and, in the case of those who have been resident here for seven out of the preceding nine tax years, pay their £30,000 (£60,000 if UK resident for 12 out of the 14 preceding tax years or £90,000 if UK resident for 17 out of the preceding 20 years)). Moreover if the trust realises gains on a UK situated asset such as UK shares, then there is no capital gains tax charge unless and until the trust provides benefits to the settlor or other beneficiary in the UK. By contrast, if the foreign domiciled settlor owned such UK shares direct or through an underlying company he would be taxed on an arising basis on any gains. So where gains are likely to be realised on UK situated assets a non-UK trust is likely to prove useful as a means of deferral for a UK resident foreign domiciled settlor. The capital can then be distributed at a time when the settlor beneficiary is non-UK resident. [27A.23]

However, offshore trusts can sometimes be more problematic for remittance basis users if they receive benefits in the UK.

EXAMPLE 27A.1
Henry is the foreign domiciled settlor of an offshore trust established some years ago which owns two houses. He lives in the UK house and the other (Italian) house is rented out. The trust eventually sells the Italian house realising a gain of £100,000 in May 2010. There are no other unmatched gains. It is estimated that the benefit to him of living rent free in the UK house is about £30,000 pa. Although there are no gains on the UK house (because it qualifies for main residence relief and in any event has not yet been sold) nevertheless he pays tax under s 87 on £90,000 (three years of benefits from 6 April 2008 matched to the gains) with £10,000 unmatched gains carried forward. In 2011–12 when he receives a further benefit of £30,000 the untaxed balance of the gains (ie £10,000) is matched to that benefit so he pays tax on that £10,000.

By contrast if he owned the UK house direct and not through the trust there would be no capital gains tax charge on disposal of the UK house due to main residence relief and the gains realised on the sale of the Italian house can be retained abroad.

Although there are ways of minimising the above tax charge on Henry in the example above (eg by the trustees distributing the whole £100,000 gain to him abroad in the same year it is realised so the gain is mostly matched to a capital payment that is not remitted – see Section IV below), nevertheless the general rule that beneficiaries pay tax by reference to the total trust gains irrespective of whether the asset or capital they actually enjoy in the UK shows a gain can be problematic for foreign domiciliaries.

Note. In the above example there should not be any income tax charge under s 720 but, if Henry was merely a beneficiary rather than the settlor, there might in certain circumstances be a charge under ITA 2007 ss 731–735.

If the settlor is UK domiciled but is dead, offshore trusts are still useful as a way of deferring capital gains tax and therefore enabling a gross sum to be invested. However, the penalty or supplemental charge referred to in Section I(c) above may make the tax advantages marginal for UK-resident and domiciled beneficiaries unless the trust is regarded as a long term investment vehicle.

There are no IHT advantages in a non-resident trust. Whether or not the trust is outside the IHT net and is excluded property depends on (a) the domicile of the settlor and (b) the situs of the assets. [27A.24]

b) *When is a trust non-resident?*

The rules on trust residence changed in FA 2006 with effect from 6 April 2007. Prior to 6 April 2007, a trust was non-UK resident for CGT purposes when a majority of the trustees were neither resident nor ordinarily resident in the UK *and* the general administration of that trust was ordinarily carried on outside the UK (TCGA 1992 s 69(1)). There was a proviso to s 69(1) for professional trustees. Where a person who was resident in the UK carried on a business consisting of or including the management of trusts and was acting as a trustee in the course of that business he was treated in relation to the trust *for capital gains tax purposes only* as non-resident if the whole of the settled property consisted of or derived from property that was provided by someone not at the time of making that provision domiciled, resident or ordinarily resident in the UK. Note, however, that this let-out did not apply for income tax purposes and therefore was of limited use unless the beneficiary was a UK resident and domiciled life tenant, in which case they would pay income tax on trust income anyway. See **Chapter 18**. [27A.25]

FA 2006 Sch 12 amended TCGA 1992 s 69 so that, from 6 April 2007, the test for residence of trustees is the same for income tax and capital gains tax purposes. The rules were aligned with the income tax rules with one important addition discussed at **[27A.29]**. From 6 April 2007, where a trust is created by a settlor who is resident or domiciled in the UK, all the trustees must be resident outside the UK if the trust is to be non-resident. If the settlor is non-resident *and* not domiciled in the UK at the time he funds the trust (including at the date of any additions or resettlements) it is only necessary that there is one non-resident trustee for the trust to be treated as non-resident for both income tax and capital gains tax purposes. If the settlor is not UK domiciled but is UK resident (or vice versa) at the date of setting up or subsequently adding to the trust, all trustees must be non-resident. Note that the place where the administration of the trust is carried out is no longer relevant for capital gains tax purposes. [27A.26]

Despite representations from the various professional bodies, the previous exemption for UK resident professional trustees was abolished on the basis that it constitutes 'state aid'. The basis for this official view remains unclear. [27A.27]

Note that, if the trust property is transferred from one trust to another, the residence of the settlor has to be tested both at the time the original trust was funded and at the time of the transfer or resettlement. See TCGA 1992 ss 68B and 69(2C).

EXAMPLE 27A.2

Mr A was not resident or domiciled here when he died leaving assets in trust. The trustees comprise two friends resident in the UK and one non-resident. The trust is non-resident for income tax purposes but prior to April 2007 was UK resident for capital gains tax purposes unless one of the UK friends was acting as a trust professional. From 6 April 2007 it became non-resident here for capital gains tax purposes unless the trustee carries on a business in the UK through a permanent establishment, branch or agency here – see below.

By contrast:

EXAMPLE 27A.3

Mr A was resident but not domiciled here when he died leaving assets in trust. The trustees comprise one UK resident and two non-UK residents and the general administration was carried on abroad. Prior to 6 April 2007, the trust was resident here for income tax purposes and non-resident for capital gains tax purposes. From 6 April 2007 it became UK resident for capital gains tax purposes and income tax purposes. **[27A.28]**

Split year treatment (see **[27.50]**) does not apply to trustees so that the UK trustees may be taxed on gains realised later in the tax year after foreign-resident trustees have been appointed. **[27A.29]**

As noted above there is an additional requirement for a trust to be non-UK resident which is a particular problem for capital gains tax purposes. This is the requirement in s 69(2D) which states that 'a trustee who is not resident in the UK shall be treated as if he were resident in the UK at any time when he acts as trustee in the course of a business which he carries on in the UK through a branch, agency or permanent establishment there'. (The comparable income tax provisions can be found in ITA 2007 ss 474–476). Acting as a trustee 'in the course of a business' means the business of providing professional trustee services for a fee. The terms 'branch, agency or permanent establishment' have been the subject of great controversy. Guidance has been agreed by HMRC (in July 2009 but expanded in 2015) and published by STEP and the CIOT.

If a trust becomes UK resident even for a day this could have disastrous capital gains tax consequences because on exporting the trust again there is a deemed disposal of all the trust assets at market value with the result that the worldwide gains of the trust become subject to UK tax. **[27A.30]**

Provided the settlor was not domiciled or resident at the date he made and funded the trust, the rule can be avoided by having one non-resident individual trustee who is unpaid. Then the trust cannot become UK resident even if one of the other trustees is deemed to be UK resident. However, for trusts where the settlor was UK resident or domiciled at any time when the trust was funded or at the date when any resettlement was made, this option will not work as a single UK resident (or deemed UK resident) trustee will cause the trustees as a body to be treated as UK resident. **[27A.31]**

HMRC accept that for trustees the 'branch' and 'agency' tests apply to non-corporate trustees and the 'permanent establishment' test to corporate trustees. Corporate non-resident trustees therefore need only be concerned about being treated as UK resident if they have a permanent establishment (as opposed to a branch or agency) in the UK (see CTA 2010 ss 1141–1153). Essentially it requires a fixed place of business in the UK through which all or part of the business of the company is carried on or an agent acting on behalf of the company who has and habitually exercises in the UK authority to do business on behalf of the company.

Agents of independent status acting in the ordinary course of business are excluded as are investment managers within the terms of the investment management exemption. Hence UK professionals such as lawyers and accountants providing services on an arms length basis to the trustees will not mean the trust has a permanent UK establishment. HMRC accept this applies even if the trustee and the service provider are members of the same group provided that the terms of engagement are commercial. Similarly an investment manager cannot be a permanent establishment of the trustee even if within the same group provided that he acts on commercial terms, carrying out normal investment transactions such as investment in stocks and shares, securities, unit trusts, options, futures etc. Options and futures relating to land are excluded. [27A.32]

The Commentary to the OECD Model Tax Convention provides further details on the meaning of 'permanent establishment'. A fixed place of business includes a place of management; a branch; office; factory or building site. So this could include the case where meeting rooms are regularly used by trustees in the UK to meet beneficiaries. (The rooms do not necessarily have to be owned or leased although the HMRC Guidance assumes this.)

The test is applied on a trust by trust basis. So while a trustee for more than one trust might be acting as a trustee in relation to one trust at a fixed place of business in the UK, it must be considered separately whether he is acting as a trustee through a fixed place of business in the UK in connection with another trust.

So far HMRC appear to have taken a fairly sensible line in interpreting the term 'permanent establishment'. Generally trustee meetings should be outside the UK and regular use of UK premises for trustee/beneficiary meetings should be avoided. The core business of the trust (which HMRC regard as including the general administration of the trust: investment strategy and decisions as to distributions) should take place outside the UK. Hence even if the trustees meet the settlor or beneficiaries in the UK, this should be more in the nature of fact-finding and discussion. The ultimate decisions should be taken (and be seen to be taken) outside the UK. There should be a formal report before the trustees when they come to make that decision and minutes should demonstrate that the matter was genuinely discussed at that meeting and not merely rubber-stamped. [27A.33]

c) *Can UK trusts be exported?*

A trust is exported from the UK if the UK trustees retire in favour of non-residents. As noted above, all the new trustees must be non-UK resident unless all persons who have funded the settlement were neither resident nor domiciled in the UK when they did so (or at the date of any resettlement).

830 *Offshore trusts and CGT*

Many trusts start off abroad but where a trust is to be moved abroad, what is the position where the trust is originally UK and all the beneficiaries are resident here? The equitable rules on the appointment of overseas trustees were set out by Pennycuick VC in *Re Whitehead's Will Trusts* (1971) as follows:

> 'The law has been quite well established for upwards of a century that there is no absolute bar to the appointment of persons resident abroad as trustees of an English trust. I say "no absolute bar" in the sense that such an appointment would be prohibited by law and would consequently be invalid. On the other hand, apart from exceptional circumstances, it is not proper to make such an appointment, that is to say, the court would not, apart from exceptional circumstances, make such an appointment; nor would it be right for the donees of such a power to make an appointment out of court. If they did, presumably the court would be likely to interfere at the instance of beneficiaries. There do, however, exist exceptional circumstances in which such an appointment can properly be made. The most obvious are those in which the beneficiaries have settled permanently in some country outside the UK and what is proposed to be done is to appoint new trustees in that country.'

This dictum would suggest that in the absence of an express power, appointing non-resident trustees is not void but may be 'improper'. (Trustee Act 1925 s 36(1) might imply that residence outside the UK for more than 12 months is unacceptable for a trustee whilst s 37(1)(c) may create difficulties for emigrations pre 1 January 1997 given that a non-UK corporate trustee cannot be a 'trust corporation': see *Adam & Co International Trustees Ltd v Theodore Goddard* (2000).) However, in *Re Whitehead's Will Trusts* the judge did approve emigration of a trust and in any event judicial attitudes have changed so that provided that the export can be shown to be for the beneficiaries' advantage (eg in saving tax) even if the beneficiaries are not living in that country the courts are not likely to interfere (see *Richard v Hon A B Mackay* (1987); see also *Lewin on Trusts* (19th edn) para 14.53 ff.)   **[27A.34]**

HMRC may not be able to object to the appointment since they do not have locus standi but any UK trustee should consider taking indemnities from the new overseas trustees in case beneficiaries at some future date allege that breaches of trust have been committed and seek to set aside the appointment. It is also sensible to include in any trust instrument an express power for the existing trustees to retire in favour of non-resident trustees. Moreover, note below the tax consequences of export – for which UK-resident retiring trustees can be made liable.   **[27A.35]**

Trustee Act 1925 s 37(1)(c) must be considered carefully when a trust migrates. It provides as follows:

> 'It shall not be obligatory, save as hereinafter provided, to appoint more than one new trustee where only one trustee was originally appointed, or to fill up the original number of trustees where more than two trustees were originally appointed, but, except where only one trustee was originally appointed, and a sole trustee when appointed will be able to give a valid receipt for all capital money, a trustee shall not be discharged from his trust unless there will be either a trust corporation or at least two persons to act as trustees to perform the trust.'   **[27A.36]**

A trust corporation is specifically defined (TA 1925 s 68) and does not include a corporate trustee in offshore jurisdictions. Hence, the appointment of new trustees may be valid, but unless the trust deed expressly provides otherwise UK-resident trustees do not get a good discharge (and hence the trust is likely to remain UK resident) unless there are at least two non-resident trustees. Until 1 January 1997 the non-resident trustees had to include at least two *individuals* but the latter requirement was changed by the Trusts of Land and Appointment of Trustees Act 1996 Sch 3 para 3(12) to two persons. The case of *Jasmine Trustees v Wells & Hind* (2007) confirmed that references to 'individuals' cannot include a corporate trustee and, therefore, prior to 1997 it was necessary to retire in favour of two individuals not merely two persons unless there was express provision to the contrary in the trust deed. [27A.37]

d) *The CGT export charge (TCGA 1992 s 80(2))*

When trustees of a UK settlement become not resident in the UK, they are deemed to have disposed of the assets in that settlement and immediately to have reacquired those same assets. This deemed disposal is closely modelled on that which applies when a person becomes absolutely entitled to settled property (see [25.47]) and on the exit charge which is levied when a non-UK incorporated company ceases to be UK-resident (TCGA 1992 s 185: see [41.154]). [27A.38]

This raises the question as to when trustees become non-UK-resident? This is when the status or identity of the trustees is changed eg by non-UK trustees being appointed in place of UK trustees or a UK trustee dying or expatriating. See s 69(1) where it is provided that:

'For the purposes of this Act the trustees of a settlement shall, unless the context otherwise requires, together be treated as if they were a single person (distinct from the persons who are trustees of the settlement of the settlement from time to time).' [27A.39]

So far as timing is concerned, the deemed disposal is said to take place 'immediately before' the relevant time (ie the moment the trustees, as a body, cease to be UK resident): accordingly the disponors are the retiring UK trustees who, given that the CGT year cannot generally be split, therefore also remain liable for gains realised by the new trustees in the tax year in which they are appointed (SP 5/92 para 2).

EXAMPLE 27A.4

Trustees of the Fisher Trust hold valuable land. The settlor is dead. The land shows a substantial gain. They decide that they wish to sell the land. If they sell the land they will realise a gain taxed at 20% (or 28% if the land is residential property). They, therefore, decide instead to retire in favour of Jersey trustees in February 2017 and in May 2017 the Jersey trustees sell the land.

The effect of s 80 is that there is a deemed disposal of the land in February 2017 and therefore that the original trustees of the Fisher Trust realise a gain at that point. They still pay tax at 20%/28% and will need to ask the Jersey trustees for funds if the UK trustees have not made a sufficient retention to pay this tax.

[27A.40]

Who is liable to pay the export charge? Because the deemed disposal is by the retiring UK trustees they are primarily responsible. It is therefore important that they retain sufficient assets to cover this liability. TCGA 1992 s 82 further provides that if tax is not paid by those trustees within six months of the due date, any former trustees of that settlement who held office during the 'relevant period' can be made accountable. The relevant period (broadly) means the 12-month period that ends with the emigration. Assume, for instance, that A and B, two professional trustees, retire on 1 January 2017 in favour of two family members. Those family trustees subsequently (on 1 July 2017) retire in favour of two non-UK resident trustees, C and D, such retirement being without the prior knowledge of A and B. On these facts, the appointment of C and D constitutes the 'relevant time' for s 80 purposes and tax on any gain arising as a result of the deemed disposal will therefore be payable on 31 January in the following tax year (ie on 31 January 2018). If not paid within six months of that date HMRC may demand that tax from all or any of A, B and the family trustees. However, a former trustee can escape liability if he shows that 'when he ceased to be a trustee of the settlement there was no proposal that the trustees might cease to be resident in the UK' (s 82(3) and SP 5/92 para 4). It is advisable to put a suitable clause in all deeds of retirement (where appropriate) to demonstrate that all trustees acknowledge that emigration was not in mind at the date the trustee stepped down. [27A.41]

The deemed disposal is of 'defined assets' which (predictably) includes all the assets that constitute the settled property at the relevant time. The term does not include UK assets used for the purpose of a trade carried on by the trustees through a UK branch or agency. This is because such assets remain within the UK tax net even after the trustees become non-resident: hence there is no need to subject them to the deemed disposal (see **Chapter 27**). If the trustees own UK residential property and any gain would be within the scope of non-resident CGT on a subsequent disposal, the trustees can elect that no gain should arise on the export, but only on a later disposal of the property.

Note that if the assets of the trust are owned through a holding company then there is no deemed disposal of those assets, only of the settled property ie the property held directly by the trustees being the shares of the holding company. [27A.42]

Section 81 deals with involuntary exports and imports. Assume that the trustees of a settlement are Adam (UK-resident) and Cedric (a Jersey-resident accountant) who does all the paperwork and performs the administrative tasks for the trustees. The settlor was UK resident at the date he funded the trust so it is UK resident. Adam dies with the result that the conditions laid down in s 69(1) are satisfied and the trust ceases to be UK resident.

On these facts, there was no intention to export the trust. Imposing an exit charge in such a case would be unjust and hence s 81 prevents the charge arising *provided that* within six months of Adam's death the trustees of the settlement become again UK resident. Not surprisingly, the exit charge remains in force for those defined assets that are disposed of during the period of non-UK residency (ie between the death and the resumption of residence). **[27A.43]**

Finally, the converse situation (a non-resident settlement becoming UK resident because of the death of a trustee) is provided for in sub-ss (5)–(7). Reverting to non-resident status within six months of the death will not generally trigger the s 80 export charge subject only to an exception where the period of UK residence has been used to add assets to the settlement claiming holdover relief on that transfer. Resuming non-resident status will result in a deemed disposal at market value of such assets. **[27A.44]–[27A.50]**

The position of beneficiaries who dispose of their interests in a trust after it has been exported is considered in Section IV: see *Example 27A.16*. **[27A.51]**

Note that gains accruing on disposals after migration but in the same tax year are fully chargeable on the UK resident trustees because split year treatment has never applied to trusts. This rule applies even if the new trustees are resident in a treaty territory whose treaty with the UK gives the territory sole taxing rights over capital gains (see TCGA 1992 s 83A). Note also that later gains of a non-resident trust can be attributed to beneficiaries who receive capital payments in the same year as the gains accrue or who have received unallocated payments in earlier years. If capital payments are made to beneficiaries when a trust was resident they can be brought into account if made in anticipation of a disposal by the trustees when non-resident.
[27A.52]

In the light of the decisions of the European Court of Justice in *de Lasteyrie du Saillant v Ministere* (2005) and *Cadbury Schweppes plc v IRC* (2006), it is arguable as to whether the s 80 exit charge is compatible with European Union law when trusts emigrate to another EU country on the basis that this may be against freedom of establishment (it is arguably not against the free movement of capital – see *Van Hilten v Inspecteur* (2008) although in fact a transfer of capital is involved when trustees retire and new ones are appointed). It may be that the charge is proportionate and justified particularly if the tax charge is delayed until the asset is sold. **[27A.53]**

Note that any trustee borrowing should be paid off before emigration if it is not within the let-outs in TCGA 1992 Sch 4B. Outstanding trust borrowing may become relevant under Sch 4B once the trust is non-UK resident (see Section V below). **[27A.54]**

Importing a non-resident trust

By contrast, the immigration of a non-resident trust to the UK by the appointment of UK-resident trustees triggers no deemed disposal and no immediate capital gains tax charge.

A non-resident trust which was within s 86 (where gains are taxed on the settlor) will from 6 April 2008 be taxed as a separate entity for capital gains tax purposes from the tax year in which it is imported. See Section III below.

Immigration of a trust can be complicated in terms of trust losses and some care is needed.

The rules can be summarised as follows:

(1) Losses realised when the trust was either UK resident or was non-UK resident but not within s 86 are not allowable against gains arising when the trust is non-UK resident and within s 86 but are allowable against gains realised when the trust is either UK resident or is non-UK resident and within s 87. See Sch 5 para 1(6).

(2) Losses realised when the trust was non-UK resident and within s 86 ('s 86 losses') are not allowable against gains realised when the trust was non-UK resident and not within s 86. Nor are they allowable against gains realised once the trust becomes UK resident whether or not it remains settlor-interested.

EXAMPLE 27A.5

Aby is a UK domiciled and resident settlor and since 1999 the life tenant of a non-resident trust which realises losses of £100,000 in 2000. These are s 86 losses. The trust is imported in 2009 but otherwise the terms are not changed. The trust then realises gains of £50,000. The losses cannot be set against the trust gains. The trust should have realised the gains in the tax year prior to immigration.

However, losses realised by non-UK resident trustees of a trust not within s 86 can be deducted against future s 87 gains realised by them and thereby reduce the amount of s 87 gains attributable to a beneficiary who receives a capital payment. This is the case even if the trust later becomes UK resident and realises gains. See s 87(4) and s 97(6) (which allows losses (including brought-forward losses) to be set against trust gains despite the fact that the trustees are non-UK resident and s 16(3) normally disallows such losses for non-residents). See also s 97(6) (which allows s 87 trust losses realised in a year of non-residence to be carried forward and used against gains in a later tax year and even if the trust is by then UK resident).

EXAMPLE 27A.6

The X Settlement is an offshore settlement primarily for the benefit of Andrew and the settlor is dead. In 2008 it realises £100,000 gains. These are not taxed on the trustees or any beneficiary but go into the s 87 pool because no previous capital payments have been made.

In 2009 the trust realises £40,000 losses. The losses cannot be carried back.

In 2010 the trust realises £30,000 gains. The 2009 losses are set against this gain thereby reducing it to zero. There are unrelieved losses of £10,000.

In 2011 the trust is imported and makes further gains of £10,000. The loss carried forward can be used to reduce this gain. (Similarly if the losses had been realised by the trust when UK resident they could be set against later gains realised by the trustees when non-UK resident. TCGA 1992 s 97(6) gives loss relief only to those losses realised when the trust is non-UK resident but this would not appear to stop such trusts claiming loss relief under s 2(2) where the losses have been realised when the trust was UK resident, even if the gains are realised when the trust was non-UK resident (provided it was not then within s 86)).

Importation of the trust should have no effect on the IHT position. If the trust has a s 87 pool then this remains and the gains are taxed on beneficiaries in the future when matched to capital payments. See Section IV below.

[27A.55]–[27A.70]

III TAXING THE UK DOMICILED SETTLOR OF AN OFFSHORE TRUST (TCGA 1992 S 86, SCH 5)

1 Introduction

Unlike TCGA 1992 s 77 which from 6 April 2008 was repealed in relation to disposals made by *any* UK resident settlor interested trusts, s 86 remains in place so that UK domiciled and resident settlors continue to be liable for capital gains tax on any gains realised by a non-resident trust where any 'defined persons' can benefit. [27A.71]

When s 86 applies, gains realised by the trustees, which would have attracted a UK CGT charge had the trustees been resident, are taxed as gains of the settlor and form the top slice of his taxable gains for that year (although such gains can be reduced by the 'personal' losses of the settlor – see point 7 below). [27A.72]

The gains are not reduced by a trustee annual exemption. Losses realised by the trustees (although available to reduce current year gains or to be set against future gains) are not treated as losses of the settlor. The settlor is given a statutory right to recover from his trustees any tax that he suffers (TCGA 1992 Sch 5 para 6) and such a right neither causes the trust income to be assessable on him under ITTOIA 2005 s 624 if he and his spouse/civil partner are excluded, nor constitutes a reservation of benefit for inheritance tax purposes, nor is a capital payment for s 87 purposes. However, the extent to which this right may be enforced in a foreign jurisdiction is uncertain, particularly if the settlor has been excluded from benefit (see *Example 27A.9*). It is not, however, thought that a right of reimbursement is the same as the enforcement of foreign revenue laws: see Lord Mackay of Clashfern in *Williams & Humbert Ltd v W & H Trade Marks (Jersey) Ltd* (1986) where he commented that 'the existence of (an) unsatisfied claim to the satisfaction of which the proceeds of the action will be applied appears to me to be an essential feature of the principle (that foreign revenue laws will not be enforced)'.

The proper law of the settlement may also be relevant here. Where the settlement is governed by English law, in practice reimbursement may be easier to enforce. See discussion in *Trusts and Estates Law and Tax Journal*, July/August 2004, p 5; see also the Jersey case of *Re the T Settlement* (2002) mentioned in *Example 27A.9* and Private Client Business 2008, where the courts effectively allowed reimbursement of the settlor on the basis that it was for the benefit of the beneficiaries to satisfy moral obligations.

The right of reimbursement is not part of the trust's governing law so foreign courts will have difficulty in recognising it where the settlor is expressly excluded unless an argument along the lines of *Re the T Settlement* can be brought. The settlor may need to bring proceedings in the English courts and seek leave to serve the trustees out of the jurisdiction, although even here it is not clear whether leave can be granted when the claim is not being brought by HMRC. See *Prestwich v RBC* (1998). [27A.73]

In determining whether a settlor is subject to s 86, two key questions need to be answered. *First*, which non-UK resident settlements are caught by s 86 and, *second*, when does a settlor retain an interest for these purposes? The answers to both questions were affected by changes made in FA 1998.

In summary a settlor will suffer a capital gains tax charge on all trust gains under s 86 if the following conditions are satisfied:

(1) the trust is non-UK resident for the entire year when the gain is realised. If the trust becomes UK resident half way through the year the trustees not the settlor are assessed on any gains;
(2) the settlor is domiciled and resident in the UK in the tax year when the gain is made (see **Chapter 27** for rules on temporary non-residence);
(3) any defined person can or could benefit in that tax year or can be added (defined persons includes settlor, spouse, civil partner, children and grandchildren and their spouses/civil partners unless the trust was set up before March 1998 and not tainted, in which case grandchildren and their spouses can benefit without the settlor suffering a s 86 charge). See para 5 and *Example 27A.11* below for explanation of defined persons.

Prior to 6 April 2008 the rate of tax on capital gains was the settlor's highest personal rate. From 6 April 2008 to 5 April 2011 all trust gains taxed on the settlor under s 86 were charged at 18% irrespective of whether he was a higher rate taxpayer. For disposals by the trustees after that date but before 6 April 2016, trust gains are taxed on the settlor at 18% or 28% depending on whether he is a higher rate taxpayer. For disposals after 5 April 2016, the tax rate is 10% or 20% unless the asset disposed of comprises residential property in which case the 18%/28% rates continue to apply. As noted earlier, trust gains can be reduced by the settlor's personal losses if there are insufficient trust losses realised in that tax year albeit trust losses cannot be set against the settlor's personal gains. [27A.74]

There are limited exceptions to the s 86 charge where a trust would otherwise be caught (eg where the trust is a protected settlement – see below). If the settlor dies in the course of the tax year, s 86 does not apply to any trust gains whether realised before or after the death. Trust gains will then be free of tax since the trust is non-UK resident and such gains will then go into the s 87 pool but can become chargeable on beneficiaries who receive (or have received) capital payments. (See Section IV below.) It may be that s 86 is an unjustified restriction under EU law given that a settlor of a UK trust is not subject to capital gains tax on trust gains and particularly given that s 86 imposes a tax charge on the settlor, even if he is excluded, if his children or grandchildren can benefit. [27A.75]

2 'Qualifying settlements'

Section 86 originally applied to 'qualifying settlements' which were defined in Sch 5 para 9 as non-UK resident settlements created 'on or after 19 March 1991' which could benefit defined persons. Pre March 1991 settlements were therefore generally outside the scope of the rules (and were known as 'golden trusts') *but* para 9(2) provided that in four situations such settlements could *become* qualifying settlements (see further SP 5/92): this is known as '*tainting*' and is discussed further in *Example 27A.7* below).

Tainting could arise if any one of four conditions was satisfied on or after 19 March 1991:

(1) property or income was added to the trust (by anyone, unless the transaction was at arm's length);
(2) the settlement was UK resident and became non-UK resident;
(3) the terms of the settlement were varied so that a defined person became for the first time a person who would *or* might benefit from the trust;
(4) a defined person (within para 9(7): see definition of defined persons below) who was not capable of benefiting from the trust before 19 March 1991 enjoyed a benefit for the first time.

EXAMPLE 27A.7

(1) The Jones Family UK Trust was set up in 1982. The settlor can benefit. In 1996 the trustees become non-UK resident. Not only did that event trigger an exit charge but, in addition, because the settlement was exported after 18 March 1991 it became a 'qualifying settlement'.

(2) The Popeye Settlement had been resident in Liechtenstein since 1989. In 1996:

(a) A court order was obtained in Vaduz whereby the beneficial class was widened to include the settlor. This had the effect of turning the trust into 'a qualifying settlement'. By contrast, in settlements where the trustees have always had the power to *add* beneficiaries and exercised that power to add a 'defined person' after March 1991 it was not thought that the terms of the trust had been varied so that it became a 'qualifying settlement'. (In SP 5/92 it is stated that 'where the terms of the trust include a power to appoint anyone within a specified range to be a beneficiary, exercise of that power after 19 March 1991 will not be regarded as a variation of the settlement'. When the trust has a general power to add *anyone* the position remains unclear but in the author's view exercising such a power of addition should not constitute tainting in the second case if it does not constitute tainting in the first.)

(b) The trustees distributed funds to the settlor's spouse who was not a beneficiary. The effect of this breach of trust was to convert the trust into 'a qualifying settlement' since she was now a person who had enjoyed a benefit (and was a 'defined person') and she was not a person who might have been expected to have enjoyed such a benefit from the settlement after 18 March 1991.

(c) On 1 March 1992 Julian Popeye added property to his father's trust. Such an addition, whether by the settlor or another, had the effect of turning the trust into a 'qualifying settlement' and the trust would now fall within s 86. This provision had to be watched carefully: it did not apply in cases where there was an accretion to settlement funds (eg where the trust received dividends or bonus shares from a company in which it had investments) nor if the settlor added property to discharge the administrative expenses of the trust (not those of the company) to the extent that such expenses could not be discharged out of trust income. (On the meaning of 'administrative expenses' and further details on tainting see the important SP 5/92 para 26.)

[27A.76]

3 The 1998 changes to 'qualifying settlements'

From 6 April 1999, *all* pre 19 March 1991 non-UK resident settlements capable of benefiting a 'defined person' (see below) were brought within the s 86 tax charge on the UK resident and domiciled settlor irrespective *of whether there has been any tainting*, ie all trust gains realised on or after that date by an untainted non-resident trust set up before or after March 1991 are taxed on the settlor if (broadly) the settlor, spouse, civil partner, his children or their spouses/civil partners or any company connected with the above can benefit in any circumstances (FA 1998 s 132 and see Sch 5). [27A.77]

If the trust was set up before March 1998 and all the above are excluded but grandchildren can still benefit the trust remains a non-qualifying settlement and gains are not taxed on the settlor unless and until the trust is tainted.

If the non-UK resident trust is set up by a UK domiciled and resident settlor on or after 17 March 1998 or is tainted from that date (see [27A.76]) and any of the above including grandchildren and their spouses/civil partners can benefit then it is qualifying and gains are taxed on the settlor under s 86.

[27A.78]

The following matters are worthy of note:
(1) From 17 March 1998 to 6 April 1999 there was a 'transitional period'. During this time the trust could, for instance, have become UK-resident, been wound up, or been converted into a 'protected settlement' (considered below). However, if the trust remained offshore and was not converted into a protected settlement, gains realised during this period were also taxed on the settlor (unless the trust did not benefit defined persons) but they were deemed to accrue in the following tax year, ie on 6 April 1999.
(2) The settlor charge could have been avoided if during the transitional period all 'defined persons' were excluded from benefit. Alternatively, the charge was avoided for pre March 1998 untainted settlements if the beneficiaries were limited to infant children of the settlor; and/ or to grandchildren; to unborn persons, to future spouses etc, albeit that these persons would be within the class of 'defined persons'. Such a trust is known as a 'protected settlement' (see TCGA 1992 Sch 5 para 9(10A)). A settlement cannot be made protected after 6 April 1999.

(3) A settlement which is currently qualifying because it benefits defined persons can be made non-qualifying *at any time* and the settlor will then escape the s 86 charge on future trust gains provided the trust is non-qualifying for the *entire* tax year when the gain is made. The rules for making a settlement non-qualifying differ depending on whether the trust was set up pre or post 17 March 1998.

EXAMPLE 27A.8

The Larg Jersey Trust was set up in 1987. The settlor, Joseph, is life tenant with remainder to his infant children. With the introduction of the 1998 changes:
(1) The trustees immediately and in exercise of powers under the settlement appointed half the fund to Joseph absolutely. This was a deemed disposal by the trustees on which Joseph was subject to CGT both on the gains realised by the trustees from the deemed disposal of the trust assets and also separately on the capital payment if this could be matched to stockpiled s 87 gains realised prior to 17 March 1998 (see Section IV below). So for example if the value of the trust assets appointed to him was £1m, the gains realised on these assets was £100,000 and the s 87 gains were £1m he would suffer tax of £40,000 under s 86 (which could be reimbursed by the trustees without being treated as a capital payment) and up to 64% on the £1m capital payment (which could not be reimbursed by the trustees without being treated as a further capital payment!)
(2) The trustees then (and before 6 April 1999) excluded Joseph from all future benefit in the trust with the result that as the only beneficiaries were his infant children the settlement became a 'protected settlement'. So long as it retains this status, future gains will not be taxed on the settlor.
(3) Protected settlement treatment is lost if the settlement is tainted (see above). In addition, privileged treatment ceases in a year where the conditions are not satisfied: notably in the tax year following a beneficiary attaining 18 (in *Example 27A.8* above, the year *after* the first child of Joseph Larg becomes 18).
(4) The 1998 changes could cause difficulties for settlors given that they are not always able to recover tax from the trust.

EXAMPLE 27A.9

On his divorce in 1990, Joseph K set up a Jersey trust for the benefit of his children under which he was prohibited from benefiting. He is estranged from his children. In 2000 the children become absolutely entitled to the trust fund leading to a gain of £2m. Joseph is taxed on this gain with little prospect of recovering tax either from the trustees or his children. (Given that the trust is governed by Jersey law it is far from certain that courts in that country will recognise Joseph's right to reimbursement even if it does not amount to the enforcement of a foreign revenue debt.) See, however, the Jersey case of *Re the T Settlement* (2002) where the settlor was expressly excluded from benefit but the Court nevertheless permitted a variation of the trust in order to allow the trustees to reimburse her the capital gains tax due under s 86. It was held that the variation would be for the benefit of unborn beneficiaries in that it included the discharge of certain moral obligations on their behalf. If the trust is made UK-resident, future gains realised will not be taxable on Joseph since it will no longer be a settlor-interested trust. **[27A.80]–[27A.81]**

4   Which settlors are caught by the offshore trust provisions in s 86?

Apart from the settlement needing to 'qualify', the legislation under which gains realised by offshore trusts are taxed on the settlor only applies in years when the settlor is *both* domiciled and resident (or, prior to 6 April 2013, ordinarily resident) in the UK. Gains realised in other years are not taxed as the settlor's and nor are gains realised in the tax year when the settlor dies. Thus s 86 does not apply to offshore trusts provided the settlor is not domiciled in the UK as a matter of general law. This is still the case even after 6 April 2008 and the settlor does not need to be a remittance basis user provided he is a foreign domiciliary.

It was announced in the Budget on 8 July 2015 that an individual who was born in the UK with a UK domicile of origin will, from 6 April 2017, be deemed to be domiciled in the UK at any time when he or she is resident in the UK. It is intended that s 86 will apply in those circumstances to any offshore trust created by the individual even if he or she is not domiciled in the UK under general law.

It was also announced that any non-domiciliary who has been UK resident for more than 15 years in any 20-year period would be treated as UK domiciled for all tax purposes. It is proposed that s 86 will apply to such long term deemed domiciliaries except where the trust has been set up before the individual becomes deemed domiciled and no property has been added to the settlement by the settlor (or by another trust of which he is the settlor or a beneficiary) at a time when he is deemed domiciled in the UK. Assuming these changes are made, it is going to be very important going forward to ensure that trusts set up by individuals who are now deemed domiciled in the UK are not tainted by additions.

Following the introduction of the concept of 'temporary non-residence' by FA 1998, difficulties may arise if a settlor – who would otherwise be subject to the s 86 charge – ceases to be UK-resident. As a result the capital payment rules in s 87 will apply (see section IV below); but if the settlor returns to the UK within five years of his departure, gains during his absence can also be attributed to him on his return (see **[27.49]**). To prevent a double charge (once on the settlor and also on a beneficiary) such gains will not include capital payments made to UK-resident beneficiaries (although note that no deduction is made for payments to non-resident beneficiaries: see TCGA 1992 s 86A).

EXAMPLE 27A.10

Red (domicile of origin New Zealand) is the settlor and life tenant of an offshore trust that realises substantial gains in 2015. He is aged 60 and until now has successfully claimed he is not UK domiciled even though he has lived in the UK for many years. He does not pay tax on any gains realised by the trustees under s 86 even if he is not a remittance basis user (ie he does not pay the £30,000/£60,000/£90,000 annual charge). However, if he receives benefits or capital payments in the UK then as a beneficiary he will be subject to tax under s 87A (see below). In 2016–17, HMRC successfully determine that he is domiciled here because he now has no intention to leave the UK. He will be taxed on an arising basis under s 86 on all gains realised by the trustees from 2016–17, whether or not they make capital payments to him. In addition any gains realised prior to 2008 which remain unmatched under the s 87 regime are now potentially taxable on him if he receives capital payments since the transitional regime applicable to foreign domiciliaries will no longer apply (see Section IV below). He will no longer obtain the benefit of rebasing.   [27A.82]

5 Meaning of a 'defined person'

Gains will be taxed on the settlor only if a 'defined person' benefits or will or may become entitled to a benefit in either the income or the capital of the settlement. When the rules were introduced in 1991 a 'defined person' was identified as follows:

'(a)   the settlor;
(b)   the settlor's spouse/civil partner;
(c)   any child of the settlor or of the settlor's spouse [no age limit];
(d)   the spouse/civil partner of any such child;
(e)   a company controlled by a person or persons falling within paragraphs (a) to (d) above;
(f)   a company associated with a company falling within paragraph (e) above.'

[27A.83]

The list was formidable and it was particularly worthy of note that children (including step-children) *of whatever age* were included. Note the trap that exists for a settlor in cases where a UK trust has been created in favour of his children which is then exported. Although the settlor is otherwise excluded from all benefit under the rules of the trust, the effect of the export is to create a qualifying settlement with the result that gains will be taxed as the settlor's since defined persons (his children – even if they are geriatric adults) will or may benefit.   [27A.84]

The only exclusion of real significance from the above list of defined persons was grandchildren and this omission was rectified by FA 1998. In respect of offshore trusts created on or after 17 March 1998 the list of defined persons is extended to catch:
(1)   any grandchild of the settlor or his spouse/civil partner;
(2)   the spouse or civil partner of any such grandchild; and
(3)   companies controlled by such persons and companies associated with such companies.   [27A.85]

Note, however, that grandchildren trusts established before 17 March 1998 are not brought within the settlor charge unless the trust is tainted (eg by the addition of further property). Therefore, if the settlor wishes to avoid a s 86 charge a trust established before 17 March 1998 can be made exclusively for the benefit of the grandchildren and their issue at any time thereafter provided it is not tainted.

EXAMPLE 27A.11

Johnny set up an offshore trust for himself and his issue and his brothers and sisters and their issue in 1990. The trust has realised no gains since 1998. It has not been added to or tainted. In 2003–04 the trustees want to realise a substantial gain from the sale of a piece of land. Provided that Johnny, his spouse/civil partner, children and their spouses/civil partners and any company controlled by them are permanently excluded from any benefit in the tax year before the disposal: ie in 2002–03, then any gains realised by the trustees in the following tax year will not be taxed on Johnny. The only beneficiaries will then be his siblings, their issue and his grandchildren and remoter issue. None of these are defined persons in respect of settlements established before 17 March 1998. Note that the settlement is not a protected settlement and therefore the change in beneficiaries does not need to be done prior to April 1999 but can be done at any point provided the trust is not tainted after 16 March 1998. However, if no change to the class of beneficiaries is made in 2002–03, any gains realised in 2003–04 by the trustees will be taxed on Johnny under s 86 unless he dies in that year. [27A.86]

6 Anti-flip-flop legislation

TCGA 1992 s 76B and Sch 4B (inserted by FA 2000) were introduced to prevent the settlor charge under s 86 being avoided by a 'flip-flop' arrangement. These provisions have been supplemented by further changes in FA 2003 to Sch 4C although these latter changes do not increase the s 86 charge but affect the s 87 pool (see Section V below).

EXAMPLE 27A.12

Year 1: Trustees of the offshore A Trust, which has no stockpiled gains and only unrealised gains, borrow against the security of the trust assets and advance the cash to the B Trust (which includes eg the settlor as a beneficiary); they then exclude 'defined persons' from the A Trust.

Year 2: A Trust disposes of assets to pay off the loan, whilst the cash is advanced out of B Trust to the settlor.

Under this arrangement the intention was that no gains were transferred from the A Trust to the B Trust (because there were no stockpiled gains which had been realised before *Year 2*) so that the distribution (in *Year 2*) from B Trust was tax free: the only disposal in the A Trust occurred at a time when the settlor charge does not apply.

Such flip-flop schemes were also used to avoid the charge under s 77 on the settlor on gains realised by UK resident settlor-interested trusts before 6 April 2008. These UK resident schemes were held not to work anyway in *West v Trennery* (2005) but this decision was based on the specific wording in s 77 and in particular the references to 'derived property'. This wording is not found in s 86 and in *Burton v R & C Comrs* (2009), the First-tier Tribunal has upheld the effectiveness of the scheme in relation to offshore trusts. [27A.87]

Amending legislation introduced by FA 2000 aimed to stop flip-flop schemes. The legislation applies if three conditions are satisfied:
(1) the trustees make a transfer of value (as defined: for instance, the transfer of moneys, to B Trust);
(2) in the year of transfer, s 86 (the settlor charge) or s 87 (the capital payments charge) or (before 6 April 2008) s 77 (UK trusts settlor charge) applies to the trust;
(3) that transfer of value is linked with trustee borrowing. [27A.88]

If these conditions are satisfied, then if a transfer of value occurs on or after 21 March 2000, the trustees are deemed to dispose of the settled property of A Trust and immediately reacquire such property at market value. (Note that the deemed disposal is not of all the assets in the structure but only of the settled property held by the trustees directly.) In a case where s 86 applies the resultant gain will be taxed on the settlor in the normal way. If s 86 does not apply, any resulting gain realised on the deemed disposal also passes into the Sch 4C pool and becomes a Sch 4C pool of gains. Such gains of pre April 2008 Sch 4C pools cannot be 'washed out' by payments to non-UK residents or foreign domiciliaries. Indeed, gains matched to capital payments made to non-residents in the year the transfer of value takes place are added back in calculating the amount of the Sch 4C pool. See also Section V below for the effect of FA 2000 and FA 2003 on beneficiaries of non-settlor interested offshore trusts and on the s 87 pool of gains. Note that there is no motive test, so innocent transactions which involve no tax avoidance can be caught if the conditions are satisfied – (i) transfer of value, and (ii) trust borrowing which is not applied for ordinary trust purposes.

From 6 April 2008 Sch 4C can apply to foreign domiciled beneficiaries but only in respect of Sch 4C pools created after that date. In some ways this is advantageous for UK domiciled beneficiaries since now Sch 4C gains arising after 6 April 2008 can be washed out by payments to UK resident foreign domiciliaries. See Section V below for further details. **[27A.89]**

7 Attributed trust gains and personal capital losses

a) *Background*

The gains of offshore settlor-interested trusts are attributed to settlors under TCGA 1992 s 86. Before April 2008 taper relief operated and the original rule was that, where there were attributed gains, taper relief would already have been taken into account in computing the figures; therefore, settlors could not deduct their personal (untapered) losses from the tapered trust gains attributed to them. Equally trust losses could not generally be deducted from personal gains. **[27A.90]**

An individual who had large personal capital losses brought forward and whose only chargeable assets were held in a settlor-interested trust could not, from 1998–99 onwards, make any further use of those losses as and when his trust realised gains. **[27A.91]**

b) *FA 2002 changes*

FA 2002 provided that the gains attributed to settlors for 2003–04 onwards were the amount of the trust gains before the deduction of taper relief. If the settlor had personal capital losses, he set them against his own chargeable gains first, but they could then be deducted from the gains attributed to him under TCGA 1992 s 86. Taper relief was then applied (on disposals prior to 6 April 2008). **[27A.92]**

The settlor was assessed to tax on the tapered gains and was then entitled to claim from the trustees of the settlement reimbursement of the tax paid in respect of the attributed gains. **[27A.93]**

Although this regime did not come into force until 6 April 2003, a settlor could *elect* for these new arrangements to apply for the tax years 2000–01, 2001–02 and 2002–03. Elections could be made for one, two or all three of these years. Elections had to be made no later than 31 January 2005.
[27A.94]

c) *Current position*

The current position remains that settlors can use their personal losses against gains which are attributed to them under TCGA 1992 s 86. TCGA 1992 s 4B allows individuals to allocate losses in the way which is most beneficial. For example, if the settlor has realised a personal capital gain on a disposal of a residential property and has gains attributed to him under TCGA 1992 s 86, he would choose to set losses first against the personal gain as residential property gains are taxed at a maximum rate of 28% whereas gains attributed to a settlor under s 86 are taxed at a maximum rate of 20% (even if the gains relate to the disposal by the trustees of residential property). [27A.95]

Note that trust losses of non-UK resident settlor-interested trusts cannot be set against personal gains of the settlor. [27A.96]

If the trust is imported past trust losses realised while the trust was in the s 86 regime remain unused. See [27A.54]. Similarly if the settlor dies then such s 86 losses will be lost forever. Hence a trust with significant past unrealised losses may wish to trigger gains before the settlor has died. (However, if the settlor dies with a qualifying interest in possession then unrealised gains on assets held directly by the trustees will be eradicated anyway. The trustees would then be better ensuring that any underlying company realised gains while the settlor was alive so that the surplus losses can be set against these gains.) [27A.97]–[27A.100]

IV TAXING UK RESIDENT BENEFICIARIES OF A NON-RESIDENT TRUST (UK DOMICILED AND NON-UK DOMICILED) (TCGA 1992 SS 87 FF)

1 **Basic rules for UK domiciled and resident beneficiaries**

Until 6 April 2008 TCGA 1992 ss 87 ff and Sch 4C applied only to tax UK resident *and* domiciled beneficiaries on capital payments or benefits received from an offshore trust or from a UK trust which had previously been offshore and which had 'stockpiled gains'. Section 87 gains could be matched to capital payments made to foreign domiciliaries but were not chargeable. Hence a way of washing out s 87 gains and avoiding any tax (but not Sch 4C gains – see Section V below) was to make capital payments to foreign domiciliaries in a year before capital payments were made to UK domiciliaries. However, from 6 April 2008, UK resident but foreign domiciled beneficiaries can also suffer a capital gains tax charge in respect of capital payments but generally only if matched to capital payments that are remitted or treated as remitted to the UK under s 809L (see **Chapters 18** and **27**). The treatment of foreign domiciliaries is discussed later in this section. [27A.101]

Prior to 17 March 1998 for s 87 to apply at all the settlor had to be domiciled *and* either resident or ordinarily resident in the UK at some time during the tax year or when the settlement was made. Hence, if the settlor was UK domiciled and resident at the date of the trust's creation the rules of s 87 *always* applied. If the settlement was originally created by a non-domiciled settlor, who subsequently became a UK domiciliary, it was caught by these rules only for those years when the settlor was UK resident and ceased to be caught on his death. Capital payments from trusts set up by non-resident but UK domiciled settlors were not caught by s 87 until the settlor became resident here. [27A.102]

As a result of disquiet caused by the 'Robinson trust' (named after a former Paymaster General, Geoffrey Robinson in relation to his own non-resident trust), any capital payments received by UK resident and domiciled beneficiaries on or after 17 March 1998 were potentially subject to capital gains tax under s 87 if the trust had stockpiled gains; the residence and domicile of the settlor became irrelevant. Section 87 ff, therefore, potentially extended to all non-resident trusts (or non-settlor interested trusts which had realised gains while non-resident) irrespective of when they were set up and whether or not the avoidance of UK tax was one of the motives of the settlor. (Contrast the provisions of ITA 2007 ss 720–735, which are subject to a 'purpose' defence in ss 736–742: see [18.113].) However, in the case of trusts set up by a non-domiciled settlor only those trust gains (and losses) realised post 16 March 1998 were generally attributable to beneficiaries.

This exemption for pre March 1998 gains and losses has continued after FA 2008 provided the settlor remains foreign domiciled or non-UK resident. However, in a curious way the exemption is now disadvantageous for foreign domiciliaries. For these beneficiaries it is desirable that the pre April 2008 pool of gains to which capital payments can be matched is as large as possible because under the transitional provisions they are not then taxed on such payments. In many cases the pool of 'tax-free' gains which can be used to frank capital payments and ensures that they are not taxable in the future when post April 2008 gains are realised is limited to 10 years from 1998. See *Example 27A.20*. [27A.103]

'Settlement' and 'settlor' are defined as for income tax (see ITOIA 2005 s 620(1)) to include an arrangement (so bounty is required) and settlor includes the testator or intestate when the settlement arises under a will or intestacy (TCGA 1992 s 87(6) as amended by FA 2008). This means that s 87 is in principle capable of applying to non-trust arrangements such as a civil law foundation or a usufruct. [27A.104]

EXAMPLE 27A.13

(1) Sergei, domiciled and resident in France, settled his holiday home in Nice on an overseas trust in 1980 for his daughter, Nina, who is domiciled and resident in England. The trust realised significant gains between 1980 and 1998. From 17 March 1998 capital payments (including the use of the property by Nina) are subject to capital gains tax under s 87 on Nina but only if the trust realises gains from that date unless Sergei becomes UK resident and domiciled here. Assuming that no chargeable gains are realised in the trust, any tax charge will be postponed until, for instance a beneficiary becomes entitled to the property or it is sold.

(Note that the property may benefit from main residence relief so no chargeable gains may arise anyway).

If Sergei becomes UK resident but not domiciled here then there is still no charge under s 87 on Nina by reference to the pre 1998 gains and no charge on Sergei under s 86 (because he is not domiciled **and** resident in the UK). However, Sergei could be subject to tax under TCGA 1992 s 87B if he receives benefits in the UK after 5 April 2008 to which gains realised after 5 April 2008 can be matched – see below.

(2) John Kaput moved to the West Indies in 1920 and settled his island paradise on trust for his Scottish descendants who become absolutely entitled to the property in 2009 when the trust period ends. On this occasion a tax charge will arise and, since the beneficiaries receive a capital payment on absolute entitlement, it will be necessary for beneficiaries to include in their tax returns a calculation showing gains realised by the trust since 17 March 1998! However, note that from 6 April 2008 the capital payment will be matched first to gains realised most recently under the LIFO rule. See below.

(3) The trustees of a non-UK settlement set up by Irek, a Russian actor now deceased, hold the trust property for Irek's four grandchildren; two of whom, A and B, are now resident and domiciled in the UK. The other two C and D are UK resident but not UK domiciled. Any capital payments made by the trustees to A and B prior to 17 March 1998 are not chargeable on them even if gains are realised post 17 March 1998. Gains and losses accruing to the trustees before 17 March 1998 and capital payments received before 17 March 1998 are wholly ignored. However, any capital payments A and B receive after 16 March 1998 can be taxed on them if matched to post 1998 gains. No payments to C and D are chargeable if made prior to 6 April 2008 whenever the gains are realised unless they are UK domiciled and resident at the time of matching. If payments are made to C and D after 5 April 2008 then they are chargeable if matched to post 5 April 2008 gains.

In summary TCGA 1992, s 87 ff apply to non resident trusts in respect of gains made from 1981–82 onwards where the trustees are not resident in the UK during the tax year or, if the settlor was resident or domiciled outside the UK, only in respect of gains made after 16 March 1998. Note, however, that if s 86 (the settlor charge) applies, no s 87 gains arise on disposals. Until 6 April 2008 TCGA 1992 s 87 ff applied only to tax UK resident *and* domiciled beneficiaries on capital payments or benefits received from an offshore trust or a UK trust which had 'stockpiled gains'. From that date, UK resident but foreign domiciled beneficiaries can also suffer a capital gains tax charge but (where the remittance basis applies) only if capital payments are remitted to the UK. [27A.105]

2 Operation of the s 87 charge for UK resident and domiciled beneficiaries

The charging system operates as follows:

a) *Trust gains ('stockpiled gains')*

The trust gains for each year are calculated on the assumption that the trustees are UK resident ('the amount on which the trustees would have been chargeable to tax ... if they had been resident in the UK in that year' – see s 87(4)). Non-resident trustees are *not* entitled to the benefit of a CGT annual exemption, but the normal uplift in value in the settled assets will occur on the death of a life tenant with a qualifying interest in possession (see **[25.49]**);

the principal private residence exemption may apply (see **Chapter 23**); and taper relief is applied to reduce any gain that has arisen *on a disposal made prior to 6 April 2008*. For trust disposals on or after 6 April 2008 no taper relief operates but even if capital payments are made after that date if they are matched to pre April 2008 gains then such gains are still calculated taking into account the taper relief available at the date of disposal (and then taxed at the rate prevailing at the time of matching with any supplemental charge if appropriate).

Note the following transitional provisions in F(No 2)A 2010 Sch 1 para 22:
(1) Any capital payment made between 6 April 2008 and 23 June 2010 that is matched to gains on trust disposals realised prior to 6 April 2011 is taxed at 18%.
(2) Any capital payment made after 22 June 2010 that is matched to trust gains realised prior to or after that date is taxed at 28% (or 20% if after 5 April 2016) if the taxpayer is a higher rate taxpayer plus any relevant supplemental charge.
(3) Any capital payment made before 23 June 2010 that is matched to gains on trust disposals realised after 5 April 2011 is taxed at 28% (or 20% if after 5 April 2016) (assuming that is the relevant rate for a higher rate taxpayer).

Although, after 5 April 2016, gains on disposals of residential property are still taxed at 18%/28%, there is nothing in the legislation which applies this to gains attributed to a beneficiary under s 87. The beneficiary will therefore only pay tax at 10%/20% (plus any supplementary charge) even if the gains attributed to him relate to gains realised by the trustees on a disposal of residential property. **[27A.106]**

In computing the amount of stockpiled gains in a trust, gains made in offshore companies may be attributed to the trustees (see TCGA 1992 s 13(10)).
[27A.107]

If trust gains are not 'matched' to benefits received by a beneficiary in that year they are carried forward and matched to future benefits. In addition if benefits have been received by beneficiaries from the trust in the past which have not yet been matched to trust gains then the gains realised in that later year are matched to the earlier benefits. To the extent that trust gains realised in a particular year cannot be matched to past or current year benefits they are carried forward and become 'stockpiled' so they are matched to future benefits. All of this is discussed in further detail below. Hence the pool of stockpiled gains goes up or down depending on the level of benefits received in any year. Remember that s 87 gains (but not Sch 4C gains – see Section V below) can be matched to benefits received by non-residents (even though there is no tax charge on such non-residents) so can be 'washed out'.

As part of the package of changes which were proposed to have effect from 6 April 2017, a new anti-avoidance provision was to be inserted which would prevent capital payments made to non-residents from being matched against the pool of gains in the trust. This would mean that, in future, the pool of s 87 gains would not be reduced by capital payments made to non-UK resident beneficiaries (but could still be reduced by distributions to beneficiaries who are resident but not domiciled in the UK even if they are taxed on the remittance basis and do not therefore pay tax on the distribution as it is kept offshore).

It is currently expected that this change will be introduced in Finance Act 2018 and will have effect from 6 April 2018. [27A.108]

b) *Capital payments*

The gains realised by the trustees will be attributed to the beneficiaries to the extent that they receive 'capital payments' that are matched to such trust gains. A payment is not a capital payment if it is otherwise taxed as income (for example) under the transfer of assets provisions (ITA 2007 ss 731–735). A 'capital payment' is widely defined (see TCGA 1992 s 97(1) and (2)) to include, *inter alia*, the situation where a beneficiary becomes absolutely entitled to the trust property as well as to 'the conferring of any other benefit'. [27A.109]

This can include, for example, rent-free occupation of houses owned by a trust, use of pictures owned by a trust as well as loans to beneficiaries which are not on commercial terms. A tax charge can arise even if the benefits are received outside the UK. [27A.110]

In *Billingham v Cooper; Edwards v Fisher* (2001) it was decided that the provision of an interest-free loan which was repayable on demand conferred a benefit on the borrower (a beneficiary of the trust) every day for which the loan was left outstanding. That benefit was a 'payment' within s 97(2) and a capital payment by virtue of s 97(1). The value of the benefit could be quantified retrospectively and the legislation would be applied year by year. Two other matters are worthy of note:

(1) It was accepted that a fixed period loan (eg for 10 years) conferred a benefit once and for all at the date of the loan and that there was no subsequent conferment of a benefit.

(2) The Court of Appeal rejected the argument that no benefit was received (or its value was nil) on the basis that if interest had been charged it would have gone to the beneficiary (who was life tenant of the settlement). The following extract from the judgment of Lloyd J at first instance was expressly approved by the appeal court:

> 'It seems to me that the legislation does not call for or permit a comparison of the position that the recipient might have been in if a different transaction had been undertaken by the trustees. There are too many different possible comparisons for that to be a tenable approach. The proper comparison is with the position of the recipient if the actual loan had not been made rather than if some other transaction had been entered into. The recipient of the actual loan, if it had not been made, would not have had the use of the money lent.
>
> It seems to me that this is particularly clear from the fact that the sections are directed to attributing gains not only to beneficiaries but also among beneficiaries in circumstances in which more than one beneficiary has received a capital payment, which of course is not true of either of these cases.
>
> I accept it is not sensible to suppose that the person entitled to income has a special status which exempts him from this treatment or requires him to be treated more favourably than other beneficiaries.'

Another controversial area is the use of rent-free accommodation by a beneficiary. If the trustees allow the beneficiary to occupy such property, HMRC maintain that the capital payment is equal to the rent that would normally be payable. If the beneficiary occupies property jointly owned by the trustees and beneficiary, eg 75% trust and 25% beneficiary, HMRC argue that the taxable benefit for the beneficiary is 75% of the full market rent. However, a contrary argument would be that the beneficiary is entitled to occupy the property by virtue of the 25% he owns (see Trusts of Land and Appointment of Trustees Act 1996). It may be argued that the true benefit is therefore only the benefit of having *exclusive* occupation and this is much lower: essentially the rent that the trustees could have obtained from a lodger sharing occupation with the beneficiary. **[27A.111]**

One of the proposals which was due to be included in FA 2017 (and which is still expected to take effect from 6 April 2017) is a new statutory regime for valuing certain capital payments. This related to loans, the use of chattels and the occupation of property. Assuming that these proposals are implemented as anticipated, the position will be as follows:

(1) *Loans* – the amount of the benefit where the trustees make a loan to a beneficiary will be the 'official rate' of interest (the rate applicable under FA 1989 s 178 for the purposes of ITEPA 2003 Chapter 7 of Part 3 – currently 2.5%) less the amount of any interest actually paid by the beneficiary to the trustees in the tax year in question. Therefore, even if the loan provides for interest to be paid at the official rate, there will still be a tax charge unless the interest is in fact paid each year.

(2) *Use of chattels* – the value of the benefit is again based on the official rate of interest. In this case, the official rate is applied to the cost of the chattel and tax is only charged for the number of days on which the property is made available to the beneficiary. The value of the benefit is reduced by any amounts paid by the beneficiary to the trustees during the tax year in question by way of 'rent' for the chattel or in respect of its repair, insurance, maintenance or storage.

EXAMPLE 27A.14

The trustees of the Ariadne Trust, a non-settlor interested offshore trust, own a painting. On 6 October 2017, they make the painting available to John, a beneficiary of the settlement. John is resident and domiciled in the UK and the painting hangs in his house in London. The painting cost £100,000. John agrees to insure the painting but does not pay anything else for the use of the painting.

The value of John's benefit for the 2017–18 tax year will be 2.5% x £100,000 = £2,500 ÷ 2 (as he has only had the use of the painting for half of the tax year) = £1,250 less the cost of insuring the painting for the relevant part of the tax year.

(3) *Occupation of land* – the benefit is linked to the market rent for the property in question. The value of the benefit is the market rent for the year less any rent actually paid by the beneficiary and any other amount paid by the beneficiary in relation to the repair, insurance or maintenance of the property. This is similar to the way in which the benefit would be calculated today. The main difference is that a deduction is only allowed for amounts actually paid during the tax year.

As with loans, there will still be a taxable benefit even if the agreement with the trustees provides for a market rent to be paid but the parties agree that the payment of the rent should be deferred. **[27A.112]**

HMRC have sometimes suggested that a settled advance by the trustees in favour of a particular beneficiary can be a capital payment within s 97. Suppose the trustees of a discretionary offshore trust with a dead UK domiciled settlor decide that they wish to defer Michael's absolute entitlement to capital at 25? He is UK domiciled and resident. He would otherwise become entitled to one-third of the trust fund and be subject to capital gains tax on the stockpiled gains. (Since he is the eldest child he will have the disadvantage of being taxed on all the stockpiled gains so far realised and effectively then 'wash out' the gains to the benefit of the others.) **[27A.113]**

The trustees of a non-resident trust may have no overriding powers of appointment. They do have a wide power of advancement. Therefore they exercise this power so as to make a settled advance for the benefit of Michael perhaps by way of resettlement of one-third of the trust fund (say £2m) so that he does not become absolutely entitled. Is this a capital payment? Even if he has no right to demand the capital can HMRC argue that he has received a capital payment up to the value of the assets advanced? Michael may only be given a revocable life interest (which post March 2006 will not be qualifying) – in these circumstances can he really be taxed on the whole capital value?
[27A.114]

Section 97(2) provides that a payment includes the conferring of any benefit and s 97(5)(b) then states that a payment is received by the beneficiary if it is paid or 'applied for his benefit'. The power of advancement can only be exercised if it is for the benefit of a beneficiary. It has been suggested that the precise terms of the settlement under which a child takes is irrelevant and the value of that interest is also immaterial because if the application is for his benefit it is squarely within s 97(5)(b).

The alternative view is that s 97(5)(b) is concerned with payments made to a third party but where the beneficiary still receives full value and s 90 (which deals with transfers between trusts) has a separate mechanism for carrying forward outstanding trust gains to a new settlement. For example, payments made to the school in settlement of fees that are a parent's liability on behalf of a child could be classed as payments applied for the benefit of a parent. In the above example, Michael has not in reality received anything like £2m since the actual value of his settled interest is far less than this. If a settled advance could be treated as a capital payment and the s 87 charge applies he would have to pay capital gains tax out of his personal funds yet he has received no capital personally. **[27A.115]**

The guidance issued by HMRC suggests that they do not take this point in practice although despite extensive examples the precise definition of capital payment is never discussed. In the case of *Burton v R & C Comrs* (2009), HMRC argued that a resettlement for the benefit of a particular taxpayer (here the settlor) was a capital payment within s 97(5) not because the advance was itself a capital payment but because the benefit was the removal of the liability to tax under s 86 by virtue of the resettlement. The decision of the tribunal was that even if a resettlement was a capital payment (about which they were divided) it had no economic value since the taxpayer was no better off afterwards than before and therefore the payment had a nil value.

In the case of *Herman v R & C Comrs* (2007) and also in the case of *Bowring v R & C Comrs* (2013), HMRC successfully argued in the First-tier Tribunal that an onward distribution from a transferee settlement could be characterised as a capital payment received indirectly from the original settlement. In both cases the resettlement and subsequent distribution from the settlement were part of a scheme implemented over a very short period. **[27A.116]**

However, on appeal the Upper Tribunal in *Bowring v R & C Comrs* (2015) overruled the First-tier Tribunal. They found that whilst it was conceivable that a separate settlement could, depending on the circumstances, constitute an intermediary, the First-tier Tribunal had erred in holding that s 97(5)(c) permitted the same capital payments to be treated as having been 'received from' the trustees of one settlement directly and the trustees of another settlement indirectly. Despite the trustees of each trust knowingly participating in the scheme, the original trust's property had been transferred to the new trust and the payments made by the trustees of the new trust were entirely at their discretion. **[27A.117]**

c) *Method of attribution*

Trust gains are attributed and therefore matched to *all* beneficiaries (unless the beneficiary is not resident here and the trust is caught by the FA 2003 changes – see Section V below) who receive capital payments. As mentioned above, there are proposals to introduce an anti-avoidance provision which would mean that trust gains are no longer matched against distributions to non-resident beneficiaries.

Gains are matched first against capital payments received in the tax year in which the gain arises. If the gains exceed the capital payments of that year, they are matched against capital payments in previous years, starting with the immediately preceding year and working backwards. When more than one capital payment is made in a single tax year, gains are attributed to the payments *pro rata* (TCGA 1992 s 87(5)). This is sometimes referred to as the 'last in, first out' method of matching. This can produce unfair results: assume, for instance, that Bill and Ben, UK domiciled and resident, become absolutely entitled to an overseas trust fund worth £200,000 in equal shares when they become 25. The trust fund has realised s 2(2) gains of £100,000 by the time Ben becomes 25 (Bill will become 25 in a following tax year). *All the gains are attributed to Ben.* See s 87A and **[27A.119]** for further details.

If a capital payment is made at a time when there are no trust gains, subsequent gains may be attributed to that beneficiary (s 87(4)).

Assume that the trustees advance capital to Ben after 2007–08 in Year 1 at a time when no trust gains have been realised. The capital payment is not taxed. They advance capital to Bill in Year 2. In Year 3 the trustees realise trust gains. Under the old pre FA 2008 rules, the gains would have been attributed to Ben first. Under the current rules, the trust gains are attributed to Bill first and taxed on him. **[27A.118]**

If there are no unmatched capital payments, trust gains are carried forward indefinitely until such a payment occurs (s 87(2)) but the last in first out rule will mean that gains carried forward are matched after gains realised in the year of capital payment. This can affect the rate of tax payable (see [**27A.136**]–[**27A.138**]). (For the position of a non-UK domiciled or resident beneficiary who receives capital payments, see below.)

EXAMPLE 27A.15

A non-resident discretionary settlement has four beneficiaries, two of whom (A and B) are UK resident and domiciled. Over three years the trust has no income and makes the following net gains and capital payments. No capital payments have been made to the non-UK resident or domiciled beneficiaries.

		A	B
Year 1	£	£	£
Capital payments		10,000	5,000
Net gains £6,000 apportioned		4,000	2,000
Capital payments c/f		6,000	3,000
		A	B
Year 2	£	£	£
Capital payments		3,000	6,000
Including payments b/f		9,000	9,000
Trust gains	20,000		
Amount apportioned	18,000	9,000	9,000
Gains c/f	£2,000		
		A	B
Year 3	£	£	£
Capital payments		15,000	5,000
Trust gains	10,000		
Gains b/f	2,000		
Amount apportioned	£12,000	9,000	3,000
Capital payments c/f		£6,000	£2,000

Note that from 6 April 2008 the trust gains realised in the year of capital payment are matched before earlier years' gains. This reduces the supplemental charge. However, when calculating the s 87 pool as it stands at 5 April 2008 the old rules (first in, first out) apply. Section 87A sets out the new rules.

EXAMPLE 27A.16

(1) The s 2(2) amounts (trust gains taxable under s 87) are:

2005–06	£50,000
2006–07	£60,000
2007–08	£60,000
2008–09	£50,000

Up to and including 2007–08, capital payments of £50,000 have been received by beneficiaries (all in 2007–08). These payments were allocated against the s 2(2) amounts using the FIFO rules in para 120 of Sch 7. Hence the 2005–06 gains are reduced to nil leaving £120,000 pre 2008–09 gains.

In 2008–09 capital payments of £70,000 are received by beneficiaries. These payments are matched under the LIFO rules in new s 87A that applies for matching in 2008–09 and later years. £50,000 is matched against the 2008–09 gains and no supplemental charge arises. £20,000 is matched against the 2007–08 gains. £100,000 total gains are carried forward available for future allocation: £40,000 from 2007–08 and £60,000 from 2006–07.

(2) In the same way that it is necessary to deal with unmatched s 2(2) amounts for a year before 2008–09 it is also necessary to deal with unmatched capital payments received before 2008–09. Paragraph 122 of Sch 7 deals with this.

2005–06	Capital payment received	£20,000
	Trust gains to which payment matched	£5,000
2007–08	Capital payment received	£10,000
	No trust gains	
	Unmatched capital payments - £15,000 for 2005–06 and £10,000 for 2007–08	
2008–09	Trust gains	£10,000

These 2008–09 gains are matched against the 2007–08 capital payment first.

If in 2007–08 trust gains had been realised of £20,000 then under the FIFO rule they would have been matched against the 2005–06 capital payment first. This leaves an unmatched capital payment of £15,000 brought forward from 2007–08 and this is matched against the trust gains realised in 2008–09 unless capital payments are made in 2008–09 in which case applying LIFO these payments are matched first.

See also **[27A.118]** for further details of the unfairness that can arise.

A charge under s 87 can be deferred so long as the trustees avoid making capital payments. The charge can be avoided altogether if such payments are made to non-UK resident beneficiaries or to a non-UK domiciled beneficiary who is a remittance basis user and does not remit the payment or if distributions are made to UK-resident and domiciled beneficiaries which do not exceed their annual capital gains tax exemptions.

Even if capital payments are made to a UK domiciled and resident beneficiary or to a remittance basis user who then remits the payments, capital gains tax can be avoided or at least deferred if there are no s 2(2) trust gains to which the capital payment can be matched and trust gains realised in subsequent years are matched to later capital payments. **[27A.119]**

EXAMPLE 27A.17

Year 1: capital payment to A	£20,000
Trust gains	Nil
Year 2: capital payment to B (non-UK resident) £30,000	
Trust gains	£20,000

Trust gains are all attributed under LIFO to the payment to B and not matched to A's capital payment. B pays no tax because he is non-UK resident. A's payment remains untaxed.

Trust gains c/f	Nil
Unmatched capital payment: £10,000 from year 2 and £20,000 from year 1	
Year 3: trust gains	£20,000
£10,000 matched to capital payment in year 2 to B	nil tax
£10,000 matched to capital payment in year 1 and charged on A	
Trust gains c/f	Nil
Unmatched capital payment: £10,000 from year 1.	

d) *Interaction with the transfer of assets abroad regime (ITA 2007 s 731)*

A capital payment made by trustees may be treated as income in the hands of the beneficiary under ITA 2007 s 731 (see **Chapter 18**). Such payments are charged to income tax up to the relevant income within the trust structure (including subsidiary companies) for that year; income from previous years is included to the extent that such income has not already been charged to a beneficiary. It is only the excess that is treated as a capital payment for s 87 purposes and subject to capital gains tax.

So in *Example 27A.16*, if the trust had accumulated income of £17,000 in 2005–06, £17,000 of the capital payment would be subject to income tax and only £3,000 would be subject to capital gains tax. The remaining £2,000 of 2005–06 gains would be carried forward and matched against the 2007–08 capital payment.

Offshore income gains realised by a non-resident trust are subject to a more complex regime discussed in **Chapter 18**. Broadly, all offshore income gains are charged to income tax rather than capital gains tax. However, in the case of foreign domiciled UK resident beneficiaries the transitional provisions discussed below are relevant and can mean that pre 2008 offshore income gains remain free of tax. **[27A.120]**

e) *Payments to a non-UK resident/domiciled beneficiary*

As discussed already, prior to 6 April 2008 a beneficiary who received a capital payment was only subject to CGT on the attributed gains if UK domiciled and resident (old TCGA 1992 s 87(7)). Even after 5 April 2008, a UK resident remittance basis user will only be taxable if the payment/benefit is received in or remitted to the UK (see **[27A.145]** ff). Accordingly, a non-UK resident or domiciled beneficiary could have trust gains attributed to him (subject to FA 2003 – see Section V below) *but not suffer any tax on those gains* even if the gains arise on UK assets held by the trust. Such gains are washed out and so distributions to non-residents or foreign domiciliaries could reduce the s 87 charge on a subsequent capital payment to a UK resident domiciliary.

FA 2013 introduced a general anti-abuse rule (GAAR) into UK tax law. HMRC published guidance as to the sorts of transactions which are likely to fall foul of the GAAR and confirmed that a decision by trustees to make a capital payment to non-resident beneficiaries in a tax year before making payments to UK resident and domiciled beneficiaries will not fall foul of the GAAR.

However, there are circumstances in which HMRC would consider that the GAAR will apply. One example that is given is a situation where an offshore trust owns a company which in turn owns a UK property. Both the property and the shares in the company are standing at a gain of £2 million. The company is liquidated and the property becomes held by the trustees. This realises a gain on the disposal of the shares and a gain on the disposal of the property. The total gains are £4 million. Beneficiary A occupies the property and would therefore be taxed on the gains that have been realised. In order to avoid this, the non-domiciled settlor adds £4 million of cash to the trust. The trustees use the cash to make a capital payment of £4 million to the settlor. In the next year, the trustees distribute the property to Beneficiary A who is UK resident.

Although, on the face of it, the trust gains have been washed out by the capital payment to the settlor, HMRC would seek to apply the GAAR so as to ignore the transfer of cash to the trust and its subsequent distribution to the settlor. The result is that Beneficiary A would pay tax on the £4 million of gains.

As previously mentioned, it may be that, in the future, gains cannot be washed out by distributions to non-resident beneficiaries. It should, however, still be possible to wash out gains by making distributions outside the UK to beneficiaries who are resident but not domiciled in the UK and who pay tax on the remittance basis. **[27A.121]–[27A.125]**

f) *Use of personal losses/rates of tax*

Unlike in the case of a settlor to whom gains are attributed under TCGA 1992 s 86, personal losses of a UK beneficiary of an offshore trust cannot be set against s 87 gains imputed to that beneficiary following the receipt of a capital payment (although curiously, by an oversight, personal losses can be set against Sch 4C gains). In *Futter v Futter* the trustees' failure to remember this meant that they appointed capital to beneficiaries in the mistaken belief that the beneficiaries could use personal losses to reduce their liability under s 87. This led to an initially successful so-called *Hastings Bass* application so that the appointments were set aside (2010). This decision was reversed in an important decision of the Court of Appeal (2011).

In two appeals heard together, *Pitt v Holt* and *Futter v Futter* (2011), the Court of Appeal declared that the law had taken 'a wrong turn'. According to Lloyd LJ, the true ratio of the *Hastings-Bass* case was set out at paras 40H–41C of Buckley LJ's judgment and is as follows:

> 'Trustees considering an advancement by way of sub-settlement must apply their minds to the question whether the sub-settlement as a whole will operate for the benefit of the person to be advanced. If one or more aspects of the provisions intended to be created cannot take effect, it does not follow that those which can take effect should not be regarded as having been brought into being by an exercise of the discretion. That fact, and the misapprehension on the part of the trustees as to the effect that it would have, is not by itself fatal to the effectiveness of the advancement ... If the provisions that can and would take effect cannot reasonably be regarded as being for the benefit of the person to be advanced, then the exercise fails as not being within the scope of the power of advancement. Otherwise it takes effect to the extent that it can.'

Lloyd LJ concluded that to challenge the exercise of a discretion successfully, there must be a breach of duty by the trustees. He identified two types of case in which the exercise of discretions can be challenged. In one the exercise is void; in the other voidable.

(i) If what is done is not within the scope of the power, it will be void. For instance:
- A procedural defect, such as the use of the wrong kind of document, the failure to obtain a necessary prior consent or the wrong people executing the document.
- A substantive defect, such as an unauthorised delegation, or an appointment to someone who is not within the class of objects (cases of a fraud on a power are similar).
- A defect under the general law, such as the rule against perpetuities, the impact and significance of which will depend on the extent of the invalidity.

(ii) If what is done is within the terms of the power, but the trustees have in some way breached their duties in respect of that exercise, then (unless it is a case of a fraud on the power) the act is not void but it may be voidable at the instance of a beneficiary who is adversely affected (subject to equitable defences and the court's discretion).

Where tax matters are relevant it is likely to be the duty of the trustees to take proper advice. But where trustees have taken advice from appropriate and reputable advisers on how to proceed in a tax efficient manner which they follow, they will not be in breach of duty if that advice turns out to be wrong. Hence, in the absence of any other basis for a challenge, the trustees will not be in breach of their fiduciary duty for a failure to have regard to relevant matters. Accordingly in such a case the trustees' act is not voidable.

Applying the principles set out above as the trustees in both *Futter* and *Pitt v Holt* had acted within their powers and taken and relied on proper advice, the exercise of their discretion was not voidable.

The Supreme Court (2013) upheld the decision of the Court of Appeal as far as *Hastings-Bass* was concerned. However, it decided that the transaction in *Pitt v Holt* should be set aside on the grounds of mistake (in that case, as to the inheritance tax consequences of creating a settlement).

The decision will be particularly pertinent to offshore trusts, where the complexity of the UK tax system has led to trustees on a number of occasions successfully setting aside earlier acts which turned out to have an adverse tax consequence. Their ability to do so in the future is now much more limited, although some offshore jurisdictions have not followed the lead of the English courts. Jersey, for example, has put in place legislation which preserves the previous understanding of the *Hastings-Bass* case (ie that no breach of duty is required). **[27A.126]**

Although a beneficiary cannot deduct his personal losses from the s 2(2) gain attributed to him under s 87 he may deduct his annual exemption and the balance would, before 6 April 2008 (if the beneficiary is UK resident and domiciled), then attract tax at 10%, 20% or 40% as appropriate (plus the surcharge, if applicable – see **[27A.136]–[27A.138]**). Gains attributed to a beneficiary in respect of capital payments made on or after 6 April 2008 but before 23 June 2010 attract capital gains tax at 18% (plus the surcharge, if applicable) provided they were matched to gains realised before 6 April 2011 so the maximum tax rate under s 87 reduced from 64% to 28.8% on capital payments before 23 June 2010. The maximum tax rate including the supplemental charge for a beneficiary receiving capital payments between 23 June 2010 and 5 April 2016 was 44.8%. After 5 April 2016, the maximum rate including the supplemental charge is 32%. **[27A.127]**

In calculating the beneficiary's CGT liability the gains attributed to him under s 87 will be treated as the *lowest part* of his total gains for the year (thereby enabling him to benefit from the beneficiary's annual exemption and, in appropriate cases, reducing any surcharge). **[27A.128]**

h) *Use of trust losses*

If non-resident trustees make losses these will be set off against future gains made by those trustees in the normal way for the purposes of calculating s 87 gains attributable to a beneficiary. Note, however, important qualifications to the general provisions dealing with losses:
(1) Such losses do not pass to a beneficiary who becomes absolutely entitled to the trust assets (see TCGA 1992 ss 16(3) and 97(6)).
(2) If losses have been realised in the trust prior to a time when it falls within the s 86 charge (eg in the case of a 'pre 1991 trust'), the existing realised losses cannot be used to reduce future gains which are taxed on the settlor. Such gains may be reduced by losses that are also realised during the period of the settlor charge. The existing losses from the period when the trust was outside the settlor charge may be used against future trust gains arising after the settlor charge has ceased to apply, eg when the settlor has died or the trust is imported.
(3) Losses which have arisen during a period of settlor charge cannot be used by the trustees against future gains that may otherwise be taxed under s 87 (eg after the settlor has died) or in respect of gains realised after the trust has immigrated to the UK. **[27A.129]–[27A.135]**

3 The supplementary (interest) charge

A 'supplementary' charge may apply to beneficiaries who receive capital payments on or after 6 April 1992 and are chargeable. From 6 April 2008 it can therefore apply to capital payments to UK resident foreign domiciliaries. **[27A.136]**

The charge operates as an interest charge on the delayed payment of CGT following a disposal of chargeable assets by non-resident trustees. It is, however, limited to a six-year period. The time covered by the charge begins on the *later* of (a) 1 December in the tax year following the year in which the disposal occurred, and (b) 1 December six years before 1 December in the year of assessment following that in which the capital payment was made. It ends in November of the year of assessment following that in which the capital payment is made.

The rate of charge is 10% pa of the tax payable on the capital payment (this percentage may be amended by statutory instrument). The minimum period is two years so the minimum charge is 20%. For a higher rate taxpayer, the effective maximum rate on which he could be charged under s 87 was 64% prior to 6 April 2008. This was reduced to 28.8% for capital payments received after that date and before 23 June 2010 even if matched to gains realised prior to 6 April 2008. If, following the capital gains tax rate changes on 23 June 2010, the gains were chargeable at 28% then the maximum supplemental charge was 16.8% giving a top tax rate of 44.8%. As a result of the reduction of the top rate of CGT to 20%, the maximum supplemental charge after 5 April 2016 is 12% giving a top rate of tax of 32%.

EXAMPLE 27A.18

The Moisie Liechtenstein Trust realises capital gains in the tax year 1998–99 and a capital payment was made to a UK domiciled and resident beneficiary on 1 July 2004.
(1) That beneficiary will be assessed to CGT on the capital payment received (at the then rate of say, 40%).
(2) The interest charge will apply for the period from 1 December 1999 to 30 November 2005 at 4% per annum (10% of 40%) so that the interest charge continues to run after the capital payment has been made. In all, six years were subject to the additional charge (being 24%) thereby giving a capital gains tax rate of 64% (40 + 24) Note that if the beneficiary does not suffer a CGT charge – for instance because he is able to set his annual exemption against the gains attributed to him – there is no interest charge.
(3) If he received the capital payment on or after 6 April 2008 but before 23 June 2010 since the gains to which such payment are matched qualify for the maximum surcharge he is taxed at 28.8%.
(4) If he received the capital payment after 22 June 2010 but before 6 April 2016, the rate of tax with supplemental charge is 44.8%.
(5) If he receives the capital payment after 5 April 2016, the rate of tax with supplemental charge is 32%. **[27A.137]**

The precise mechanics governing the supplementary charge are complex. Prior to 6 April 2008 capital payments were matched first with total trust gains at 6 April 1991 and then on a first in, first out basis. Trustees are given at least 12 months in which to distribute gains since the interest charge does *not* apply to gains realised in the same or immediately preceding year of assessment.

EXAMPLE 27A.19

In 1996–97 the Cohen Offshore Settlement realises trust gains of £100,000. Although the interest charge begins to run on 1 December 1997 no charge is levied on capital distributions made before 6 April 1998.

From 6 April 2008 capital payments to both UK and non-UK domiciled beneficiaries are matched with gains on a last in, first out basis (see FA 2008 Sch 7 para 112). This is advantageous because the supplementary charge is then reduced where trust gains have been realised in recent years. It can, however, result in rather arbitrary allocations of gains. See *Example 27A.16* and **[27A.118]**.
[27A.138]–[27A.144]

4 Operation of the s 87 charge for UK resident foreign domiciled beneficiaries from 6 April 2008

a) *General principles*

Capital payments made from 6 April 2008 to non-UK domiciled beneficiaries will generally be chargeable to tax and matched with gains on a last in, first out basis. The remittance basis will apply if the non-UK domiciled beneficiary is a 'remittance basis user' (ie where he has claimed the remittance basis under ITA 2007 s 809B or is entitled to it under s 809C) in the year when trust gains are treated as accruing to him. This will be so whether the trust gains accrue on UK or on non-UK assets. A capital distribution will be treated as remitted if the distributed property is received in or brought to the UK. Benefits-in-kind will be treated as remitted if enjoyed or used in the UK. [27A.145]

The legislation does not change the tax position of non-UK domiciled beneficiaries who received capital payments on or before 5 April 2008 and does not tax non-UK domiciled beneficiaries on future capital payments where these are matched to trust gains realised prior to 6 April 2008. This is so irrespective of whether the non-UK domiciled beneficiary is a remittance basis user provided he continues to be foreign domiciled. [27A.146]

Surplus capital payments brought forward from 2007–08 will not be taxed unless the non-UK domiciled beneficiary is both resident and domiciled in the UK when trust gains are treated as accruing to him or they can be matched to relevant income under ITA 2007 s 731. [27A.147]

Surplus capital payments to non-UK domiciled beneficiaries made prior to 12 March 2008 can be matched against post 5 April 2008 trust gains, although only to the extent that there are no capital payments made after 5 April 2008 to which the post 5 April 2008 gains can be attributed first. No charge will arise whether or not the beneficiary is a remittance basis user where the payment was received prior to 6 April 2008: FA 2008 Sch 7 para 124. [27A.148]

Capital payments made to non-UK domiciled beneficiaries between 12 March 2008 and 5 April 2008 which are not matched to pre 6 April 2008 gains will be left out of account in 2008–09 and subsequent years for the purposes of s 87 and will not be matched to any trust gains unless the beneficiary becomes UK domiciled in the future in which case such surplus capital payments can be matched to trust gains realised then (FA 2008 Sch 7 para 125).

EXAMPLE 27A.20

(1) A receives a £1m capital payment on 13 March 2008. This cannot be matched to pre April 2008 gains because the trust has insufficient gains. In 2008–09 the trust realises gains of £1m. These are not matched to that capital payment. In 2016–17 A becomes domiciled in the UK under general law. The trust realises gains which can then be matched to the 13 March 2008 payment.

(2) If A had received the £1m payment on 11 March 2008, the payment would have been fully matched to the 2008–09 gains. No tax is payable even if A is not a remittance basis user. The s 87 gains are 'washed out' and the payment

is fully matched. There would then have been no tax charge on A in 2016–17 by reference to that capital payment when A became domiciled here even if the trust subsequently realises gains.

There are special rules for offshore income gains which are outside the scope of this chapter.

If the proposed amendments which it is still expected will be introduced from 6 April 2017 are in due course enacted, long term deemed domiciliaries (those who have been UK resident for more than 15 out of the previous 20 years) will not benefit from the remittance basis and so will pay tax on the arising basis on gains attributed to them as a result of the receipt of a capital payment after they have become deemed domiciled. However, it is proposed that, as long as the deemed domiciliary has not actually become domiciled in the UK, he will continue to benefit from the 2008 transitional provisions and so would not, for example, be taxed on a pre-2008 capital payment, even if that capital payment is only matched against gains arising after the individual has become deemed domiciled in the UK. **[27A.149]**

Surplus trust gains brought forward from 2007–08 and treated under s 87(4) as accruing to non-UK domiciled beneficiaries by virtue of capital payments made on or after 6 April 2008 will not be taxed unless the non-UK domiciled beneficiary has become both resident and domiciled in the UK. Although the capital payment is received after 5 April 2008, if it is matched to trust gains realised prior to 6 April 2008 or to the pre 6 April 2008 element of any gain on a rebasing election (see **[27A.154]**), it is not necessary for the non-UK domiciled beneficiary to be a remittance basis user in order to escape tax.

Again, if the anticipated deemed domicile rules are introduced, a long term deemed domiciliary would still benefit from these transitional provisions and would not be taxed on gains arising prior to 6 April 2008 even if those gains are matched against a capital payment received after the individual had become deemed domiciled in the UK (as long as the beneficiary was not actually domiciled in the UK).

EXAMPLE 27A.21

(1) B receives a £1m capital payment in 2008–09 and remits it to the UK. No gains are realised by the trust in 2008–09 but there are surplus gains brought forward from 2007–08 of £2m. The payment is matched to those gains and no tax is charged on B, whether or not a remittance basis user. See FA 2008 Sch 7 para 124. If gains had been realised in 2008–09 of £500,000 these would have been matched first to the capital payment and the balance of £500,000 matched to the 2007–08 gains so then B would have paid tax at 18% on half the capital remitted. It is unclear what the position is if B only remits half the capital to the UK – can it be treated as comprising that capital matched to pre April 2008 trust gains and therefore not taxable? It is thought that the gains and capital payments remitted are examined over the entire year and a proportionate part is taxed.

(2) B receives a £1m capital payment in 2008–09 and does not remit it to the UK at any time while UK resident. As long as B has elected to be taxed on the remittance basis, no tax is payable even if the payment is matched to post

April 2008 gains because it has not been remitted here (see s 87B – remittance basis). In determining whether capital has been remitted consider the wider rules in ITA 2007 s 809L and **Chapter 27**. [27A.150]

Trusts which were non-UK resident on 6 April 2008 have the option to elect for rebasing to market value as at 6 April 2008 in relation to all assets held by the trust both directly and by its underlying companies. The effect is that the pre 6 April 2008 element of any trust gains treated as accruing to non-UK domiciled beneficiaries after that date will not be taxed even if the gain has not been realised prior to 6 April 2008. See FA 2008 Sch 7 para 126. The rebasing election is subject to certain time limits – see [27A.153]. In practice most trusts with foreign domiciled beneficiaries made the election in January 2010 whether or not the time limit was due to expire. The rebasing election is of no value to UK domiciled beneficiaries. [27A.151]

Any supplemental charge under TCGA 1992 s 91 for remittance basis users will be calculated based on the year in which the capital payment is made by the trustees, not the year in which it is remitted to the UK by the non-UK domiciled beneficiary. However, the rate of capital gains tax is governed by the year of remittance.

EXAMPLE 27A.22

B, a remittance basis user, receives a £1m capital payment in 2008–09 which is matched to gains realised in that tax year (and assume no rebasing election is made). He remits it to the UK in May 2010. The tax rate is 18%. If he remits it to the UK in 2011 the tax rate is 28%. If, however the trustees had only made the payment to him in 2012 the supplemental charge would have operated if the capital payment was matched to 2008–09 gains. However, as discussed previously from FA 2008 the last in first out matching rule applies to capital payments made on or after 6 April 2008. This will apply to all beneficiaries, not just non-UK domiciled beneficiaries. See *Example 27A.16* and [27A.118].

Hence when a capital payment is made on or after 6 April 2008:
- trust gains of the current year will be treated as accruing to the beneficiary before gains of previous years, and trust gains of later previous years before those of earlier previous years. This was to stop foreign domiciled beneficiaries from obtaining an advantage by capital payments being matched to pre April 2008 payments; and
- current year capital payments will be matched with trust gains before capital payments of previous years and capital payments of later previous years before those of earlier previous years;
- there is still no charge to tax on capital payments to non-UK resident beneficiaries, although capital payments made on or after 6 April 2008 will be matched to trust gains in the same order as for other beneficiaries (LIFO). This could be advantageous for a foreign domiciled UK resident beneficiary (because the payment to the non-resident washes out the most recent gains which would be taxed on him allowing capital payments made now to be matched to pre April 2008 gains). Depending on the order of payments it may be less advantageous for the UK domiciled beneficiary because the most recent gains are washed out on the payment to the non-resident leaving him subject to tax on earlier gains which carry the supplemental charge. As has previously been discussed, provisions may in any event soon be introduced

which would prevent distributions to non-resident beneficiaries from being matched against trust gains.

Note that one looks at the position over the entire year not on a payment by payment basis.

The result is that:
(1) remittance basis users will be taxable on a remittance basis on trust gains accruing to them under s 87 if and to the extent that the trust gains *and* the capital payments relate to the period after 5 April 2008. If they are not remittance basis users, they will be taxed on an arising basis;
(2) even if the capital payment was made after 5 April 2008 and is matched to trust gains made after 5 April 2008 and the payment is remitted here, there is still no tax payable if the payment is matched to a trust gain deemed to accrue before 6 April 2008 on a rebasing election – see [27A.153]. [27A.152]

No additional notification requirements have been imposed on non-UK domiciled settlors of non-UK resident trusts and there is no change to the existing reporting provisions contained in TCGA 1992 Sch 5A (see [27A.177]). [27A.153]

b) *Rebasing – FA 2008 Sch 7 para 126*

The trustees of any trust which is non-UK resident as at 6 April 2008, whatever the domicile of the settlor, have the right to elect that, for one limited purpose, the following will be deemed to have been disposed of and reacquired at market value on 6 April 2008:
(1) assets owned by the trust on 6 April 2008;
(2) assets owned by an underlying company on 6 April 2008, in so far as:
    (a) on the disposal of any such asset the gain (if any) is apportionable to the trust under s 13(10), and
    (b) it would have been so apportionable if in fact realised on 6 April 2008. [27A.154]

The election cannot be made on an asset by asset basis but, once made, will apply to all assets of the trust and any underlying companies. [27A.155]

The election is irrevocable and must be made on or before 31 January following the tax year in which the first of the following occurs:
• a capital payment is made to any beneficiary (or person treated as a beneficiary) who is UK resident; or
• a part of the trust fund which is less than the whole is transferred after 5 April 2008 to a new settlement in circumstances where s 90 applies. [27A.156]

So the earliest possible deadline for an election was 31 January 2010. The information required on the form is minimal. The trustees need to give the name of the trust and the fact that they are making an election but no details of settlor or beneficiary are requested or required under the legislation. In some cases HMRC have been known to issue a form 41G when an election has been submitted in order to obtain further information but there is no statutory requirement for the trustees to complete this form. Trustees are permitted to make the election early even if one of the triggering events above has not yet occurred. [27A.157]

The election will not in itself trigger any deemed disposal. The one limited purpose of the election is simply that, when there is a later actual disposal of the asset, the trust gains realised on that disposal will be split between the pre 6 April 2008 and post 5 April 2008 elements. Non-UK domiciled beneficiaries will not be taxed in so far as any capital payments are matched to the pre 6 April 2008 element of gain. So there will still be one trust pool with capital payments matched on a LIFO basis to trust gains but trustees will need to keep a record of pre 6 April 2008 and post 5 April 2008 gains for the purposes of being able to tell non-UK domiciled beneficiaries whether they are taxable on the gains matched to their payment. Obviously for gains realised in 2008–09 it was likely that much of the gain represented a pre April 2008 element and will therefore not be taxable. [27A.158]

The effect of Sch 7 para 126(9) can be curious in relation to a house that qualifies for main residence relief. Paragraph 126(9) requires the gain that would arise to be computed on the assumption that every asset in the trust had been sold and reacquired on 6 April 2008. If a trust owns a house that was only occupied as a beneficiary's main residence before April 2008 then the rebasing election may not prove advantageous since none of the post April 2008 gain will qualify for relief. The total chargeable gain accruing over the entire period is then likely to be lower because the trustees will be able to claim the last 18 months ownership as exempt. The trustees are permitted to take whatever results in the lower gain overall and in these circumstances will ignore the effect of the rebasing election.

By contrast if the house has first been occupied as a main residence since April 2008, rebasing may prove particularly advantageous because all or most of the post April 2008 gain will be exempt for foreign domiciled beneficiaries. [27A.159]

The election has no impact on the calculation of the supplemental charge under s 91 nor does it accelerate any charge under s 86 on a UK domiciled and resident settlor. This is because the election does not alter the fact that the entire gain continues to be treated for all purposes as having arisen only on the date of actual disposal, even if part of the gain is allocated to the pre 6 April 2008 pool for the purposes of determining whether a non-UK domiciled beneficiary is taxable under s 87. [27A.160]

Where a capital payment made after 5 April 2008 is less than the trust gains, the LIFO rule will mean that the gains of later years will be treated as accruing to the beneficiary before the gains of earlier years. However, where a rebasing election has been made by the trustees the legislation provides that the post 5 April 2008 element of the trust gains of a given year will be treated as accruing proportionately with the pre 6 April 2008 element of those gains in respect of capital payments made on or after 6 April 2008.

Generally trustees may not consider it worthwhile making a rebasing election where they are only making capital payments to UK domiciled and resident beneficiaries and/or to non-resident beneficiaries. For a UK domiciliary a rebasing election has no relevance. However, the time limits still run. Hence if in 2008–09 the trustees distribute capital to A and B,

A being UK domiciled and resident and B being foreign domiciled and non-UK resident, the rebasing election needs to be made by January 2010 even though it has no relevance for A. If B later becomes resident in the UK it may be advantageous for the trustees to have made the rebasing election so he can avoid tax on capital payments he receives while UK resident that are matched to trust gains accruing prior to April 2008.

EXAMPLE 27A.23

A receives a £100,000 capital payment in 2008–09. He is a remittance basis user. The trust realises gains of £1m in that year of which £100,000 accrued post April 2008 and £900,000 before April. It makes a rebasing election. The realised gain is matched proportionately so one-tenth represents the post April 2008 element and nine-tenths the pre April 2008 element. Hence even if the whole £100,000 is remitted, only one-tenth is taxable.

If A is foreign domiciled but not a remittance basis user then whether or not he remits the £100,000 payment, one-tenth will still be taxable but the part attributable to the pre April 2008 element will not be taxed. [27A.161]

Since any gain resulting from a rebasing election will not be brought into account on 6 April 2008 but only when the asset is disposed of, the notional pool of pre 6 April 2008 gains will fluctuate in the future because:
(1) when assets owned on 6 April 2008 are disposed of at a gain, the pool of pre 6 April 2008 gains will increase; and
(2) capital payments will reduce the pre 6 April 2008 pool to the extent that there are no post 5 April 2008 gains to which the payment can be allocated in that year.

EXAMPLE 27A.24

(1) B who is foreign domiciled but not a remittance basis user is in receipt of a surplus capital payment made in January 2008 of £1,000. The trust makes a rebasing election.
The trust realises gains in 2009–10 of £3,000 – the pre April 2008 element is £1,000 and the post April 2008 element is £2,000. No capital payments have been made since 2007–08. One-third of the pre April 2008 element gain is matched to the January 2008 capital payment. None of it is taxed because the capital payment was received before April 2008 but the matching rules will affect the chargeability of future capital payments.
(2) C (a remittance basis user) receives a £1,000 capital payment in 2009–10 and a rebasing election has been made. Gain in that year is £3,000 – pre April 2008 element is £1,500 and post is £1,500. One half of the capital payment is taxable if remitted since it is matched to the post April 2008 element. If only part of the £1,000 is remitted presumably only a proportionate part of the post April 2008 gain is taxed. If C is not a remittance basis user then one-half is still not taxed (because it relates to a pre April 2008 element) and the balance is taxed on an arising basis. [27A.162]

The timing of capital payments can be important.

EXAMPLE 27A.25

The trustees hold a UK house through a company. The house is occupied by B, a non-UK domiciliary, who therefore receives taxable UK benefits totaling, say, £500,000. The trustees sell the company in 2010–11 for a gain of £1m having made a rebasing election. All the gain realised on the disposal accrued pre 6 April 2008; the trustees should not make a cash distribution to B abroad in 2010–11. If they do, they are 'wasting' tax free gains on a capital distribution that would not be taxed on B anyway because he receives it abroad and does not intend to remit it.

If they do not make any distributions to him in that tax year £500,000 of those £1m gains (deemed to accrue pre April 2008 'pre April 2008 election gains') would then be matched to the earlier capital payments of £500,000 (ie the deemed benefit from the occupation of the house) and no tax is payable on B even though part of the capital payment was received after 5 April 2008. £500,000 gains are carried forward to be matched against future capital payments. However, since these gains are also pre April 2008 election gains they are not taxed on B in the future even if he is not a remittance basis user.

Hence it is better to match pre April 2008 election gains to capital payments received in the UK by the foreign domiciliary because no tax is paid and match post April 2008 election gains to capital payments received outside the UK.

Conclusions Where trustees have made a rebasing election, have several assets they wish to sell and have unmatched capital payments they should consider the position carefully. If asset 1 shows mainly a pre April accrued 2008 gain and asset 2 shows mainly a post April 2008 gain and capital payments have all been received in the UK, the trustees would be advised to sell asset 1 in the tax year before the sale of asset 2. However, if capital payments have been received outside the UK and are never likely to be remitted, then the trustees should sell asset 2 first so that chargeable post April 2008 gains are matched to the payments received abroad. Remember that the use of a company may double up gains and therefore tax charges!

Where a beneficiary is vulnerable to losing foreign domicile (not merely cease to claim the remittance basis), consider whether it is worth making capital payments to them prior to their losing such domicile if those capital payments can be matched to pre April 2008 realised gains or to gains that accrued prior to April 2008.

Finally care should be taken to ensure that capital payments made to a beneficiary while non-UK resident or non-UK domiciled are fully matched to trust gains, If this does not happen and the trust later makes gains after he becomes UK resident or UK domiciled, those gains could be matched to the earlier capital payment and taxed on the beneficiary then. **[27A.163]**

5 Disposal of a beneficial interest in an offshore trust

The basic rule is that disposals of beneficial interests in non-resident trusts are subject to charge on the disposing beneficiary (TCGA 1992 s 85(1) disapplying s 76(1)). In many cases the interest in question (eg a life interest) may be a wasting asset or have a nil base cost, resulting in a high tax charge on the beneficiary. The following points should be noted about this section.
[27A.164]

First, what happens if the interest of a beneficiary terminates not as a result of any voluntary action on his part but by act of the trustees: eg where a life interest is terminated by the trustees under a power reserved to them in the settlement? In this case it is thought that the termination will not amount to a disposal for CGT purposes since, whilst it is true that under the legislation certain involuntary disposals (eg a sale under a compulsory purchase order), are subject to charge (so that a voluntary act on the part of the disponor is not always required) even in these cases there is a transfer of assets as opposed to a mere forfeiture of rights. So far as a forfeiture of rights is concerned there is no disposal unless a capital sum is paid or deemed to be paid on that event (TCGA 1992 ss 22–24). If the trustees, therefore, exercise overriding powers of appointment and, say, terminate the settlor's life interest in favour of trusts for his children, there should be no tax charge on the settlor because he has made no disposal of his beneficial interest.

If the trustees can exercise their overriding powers only with the consent of the settlor, is there any disposal in these circumstances? The better view is that the giving of consent by the settlor in relation to an offshore trust is not a disposal within s 85 although HMRC's view is not entirely clear on this point. In the past HMRC have indicated that if no consideration is given for the consent there is no disposal by the beneficiary. The beneficiary in question may be able to release the requirement for his consent before any appointment by the trustees is actually contemplated. **[27A.165]**

Note that if the consent is treated as some sort of disposal of a chose in action asset for capital gains tax purposes, variations of any settlement whether UK-resident or not, where the beneficiary has to consent might be problematic!
[27A.166]

Second, the effect of s 85 may be that even if the settlor wants to be excluded from the trust (along with all defined persons) in order to avoid the s 86 charge, it may not be possible to do this easily without triggering a s 85 charge on the settlor as the disponor because the terms of the trust are such that the settlor can only be excluded if he positively surrenders his life interest. This would be regarded as a deemed disposal on which the settlor would be liable to capital gains tax (since the life interest is likely to have a low or nil base cost.) The only alternative to avoiding the s 86 charge is to wait until the death of the settlor before realising gains. Even if the trust is imported before the settlor surrenders there would be a s 76/s 85 charge – see the fifth point below). For this reason it is generally sensible to ensure that all offshore trustees have wide powers of appointment, exclusion etc in order to be able to rearrange the beneficial interests without triggering unexpected charges under s 85. **[27A.167]**

Third, the section makes it clear that although a disposal of such an interest is subject to charge this does not apply when the beneficiary becomes absolutely entitled as against the trustees in respect of any property (eg if an advance is made to him or on the deemed disposal occurring on the termination of the trust). **[27A.168]**

Fourth, if a UK-resident trust is exported thereby triggering a deemed disposal of the settled property (Section II above) a beneficiary is treated as disposing of his interest at that time for the purpose of providing him with a market value at that date which will be used in calculating his gain on a subsequent disposal of the interest (see **[25.113]**). This provision was used to avoid tax as illustrated in the following example:

EXAMPLE 27A.26

The Itchyfoot Settlement has substantial stockpiled gains and is a cash fund. The trust is imported and then exported. The beneficiaries then disposed of their interests at no gain so no charge arose under s 85 and in addition the s 87 charge was avoided.

FA 2000 amended s 85 so that from 21 March 2000 there is no uplift in the value of the interests of the beneficiaries if a settlement is exported at a time when it has stockpiled gains. [27A.169]

Fifth, disposals of beneficial interests in a trust which was *at any time* non-UK-resident (or which had received property from such a trust) are brought into charge in respect of disposals occurring on or after 6 March 1998. This matter is considered further at [25.105]. [27A.170]

V OTHER OFFSHORE MATTERS

1 Anti-flip flop legislation – TCGA 1992 Schs 4B and 4C

As noted earlier, FA 2000 attempted to stop flip flop schemes by introducing TCGA 1992 Schs 4B and 4C. Essentially where Trust A borrows and does not apply the borrowing for 'normal trust purposes' (narrowly defined) but makes a 'transfer of value' (widely defined to include capital transfers, loans on commercial terms etc) there is a deemed disposal of all or part of the trust assets remaining in Trust A (resultant gains fall into the 'Sch 4C pool'). FA 2000 prevented the use of old-style flip flop schemes which had effectively worked by delaying the realisation of gains until a later year. The pre 2000 flip flop schemes generally involved settlor interested trusts where the intention was to avoid a s 86 charge on future gains. [27A.171]–[27A.172]

The FA 2000 provisions created a number of problems: in particular there is no motive test so perfectly innocent transactions which involved no tax avoidance and no diminution in the trust assets could be caught. For example a trust that borrowed from one underlying company and lent funds to another wholly owned company to enable that company to make an investment would be caught. The safest course for offshore trusts (and for UK-resident trusts which had s 87 gains or prior to 6 April 2008 were settlor-interested, being within s 77) is to avoid trustee borrowing at all, although curiously, companies wholly owned by trustees can borrow and are not caught by the legislation (see *Tax Bulletin* 66 p 1048). [27A.173]

However FA 2000 introduced a loophole. This was contained in s 90(5)(a) which prevented s 87 gains from being carried across to the transferee settlement (trust B) to the extent that the transfer was (under Sch 4B) linked with trustee borrowing. The legislation that had aimed to stop s 86 avoidance thus opened up extensive opportunities for s 87 tax avoidance as illustrated in the following example.

EXAMPLE 27A.27

Offshore Trust A has £1m stockpiled gains and is worth £1m. It holds mostly cash or assets showing no gain. It borrows £1m and in 2002 appoints all the borrowed funds of £1m to Trust B. On a simple reading under the pre FA 2003 legislation, since there was a transfer of value linked to trustee borrowing, s 90(5)(a) provided that the stockpiled gains of £1m did not pass across into Trust B. Trust B took £1m free of the stockpiled gains. There was a deemed disposal of the assets remaining in Trust A but since these showed no gains this did not matter. There was nothing to go into the Sch 4C pool. **[27A.174]**

Such 'section 90' schemes were widely used in an attempt to get rid of the stockpiled gains which could not easily be washed out where all the beneficiaries were UK-resident. Often the penalty charge meant that if any capital payments were made to beneficiaries these would be taxed at 64% prior to 6 April 2008. Therefore the incentive to get rid of the stockpiled gains was high. **[27A.175]**

In *Herman v R & C Comrs* (2007) the scheme was found to be pre-ordained and not to work: in a somewhat unsatisfactory decision it was held that the payments to beneficiaries from the transferee settlement made shortly after resettlement could be matched to the gains in the transferor trust. In an even more unsatisfactory decision in *Bowring v R & C Comrs* (2013) the First-tier Tribunal held that any future distributions from the second settlement should be treated as indirectly received from the first settlement.

However, the movement in this direction has been somewhat slowed by the Upper Tribunal in *Bowring v R & C Comrs* (2015), where it was held that (although the transfer was part of a scheme), the trustees of the transferee trust had full discretion as to payments made out of that trust. The trustees of the offshore trust had no control over the funds and there was no settled intention to pay the funds to the beneficiaries. The assets were not therefore received indirectly from the first settlement by the beneficiaries. It was not possible for the beneficiaries to have received capital payments from both trusts (one directly and one indirectly).

In any event, the Government response to the s 90 avoidance scheme was aggressive. FA 2003 s 163 introduced further changes to Sch 4C. These changes are complex but the effects can be summarised as follows:

(1) FA 2003 changes are relevant wherever trustees of a settlement have made a transfer of value linked to trustee borrowing after 20 March 2000 even if the original settlement (Trust A in the above example) has ceased to exist. Since, as noted above, a transfer of value linked to trustee borrowing can occur in a number of unexpected instances where there is no avoidance motive, the position must be checked wherever trustees have borrowed.

(2) The FA 2003 changes do not affect beneficiaries who have received capital payments from Trust B prior to 9 April 2003. Thus in *Example 27A.27* if Trust B had distributed the entire £1m to the relevant beneficiaries by 9 April 2003, such beneficiaries were not caught by the FA 2003 legislation and such payments are tax free if the s 90 scheme works (although the scheme may fail for other reasons and see case law above.)

(3) As a result of FA 2003 the Sch 4C pool comprises not only the Sch 4B gains realised on the deemed disposal but also any outstanding s 87 gains in the transferor settlement at the end of the tax year in which the transfer was made. Thus in *Example 27A.27*, Trust B no longer takes £1m cash free of the s 87 gains. All those s 87 gains fall into the Sch 4C pool (along with any deemed Sch 4B gains) and can be allocated to any future payments made to beneficiaries of either Trusts A or B.
(4) The fact that (as in *Example 27A.27*) no gains may be realised on the deemed disposal under Sch 4B is irrelevant. If there is a transfer of value linked to trustee borrowing then the anti-avoidance legislation is triggered and a Sch 4C pool is formed comprising the Sch 4B trust gains plus the s 87 stockpiled gains.
(5) For the purposes of calculating the Sch 4C pool, the outstanding s 87 gains are calculated ignoring payments to non-resident beneficiaries which are matched in the tax year of the transfer of value (or in any later year). Since 2008, distributions to non-domiciled beneficiaries will reduce the Sch 4C pool even though the attributed gains will only be taxed if the distribution is remitted to the UK.
(6) The old s 87 stockpile in Trust A is reduced to nil. There is just one Sch 4C pool overhanging both trusts.

EXAMPLE 27A.28

In 2013–14, Trust A borrows £2m and appoints the cash to Trust B in June 2013. There is a deemed disposal of all the assets remaining in Trust A as at June 2013 (say shares in RS Limited worth £0.6m with a base cost of £0.1m) which disposal, therefore, realises a Sch 4B gain of £0.5m ignoring taper relief. The level of stockpiled s 87 gains in Trust A at the end of 2013–14 is £1m. The Sch 4C pool is therefore £1.5m and can be attributed to future capital payments made to UK resident beneficiaries out of either trust.

In 2015 Trust B makes distributions of £1.5m to Eric and John, neither of whom are resident in the UK. The following tax year Trust B distributes the balance of the fund, being £0.5m to Fiona who is resident and domiciled here. The distributions to Eric and John in 2015 do not reduce the Sch 4C pool of gains (which remains at £1.5m) although Eric and John do not suffer a CGT charge. Fiona pays tax on the entire £0.5m distributed to her. Similarly, if Trust A makes any distributions to Eric and John, such distributions will not reduce the Sch 4C pool hanging over Trust A and future capital payments to UK-resident beneficiaries will be taxed (unless the beneficiary is a non-domiciliary who is taxed on the remittance basis and the distribution is not remitted to the UK).

(7) Gains realised in subsequent years do not go into the Sch 4C pool unless there is another transfer of value linked with trust borrowing. Instead they form a separate s 2(2) amount.
(8) There are no changes as respects Sch 4C pools existing as at 5 April 2008 and such Sch 4C gains still cannot be washed out by payments to non-domiciliaries. A further Sch 4B transfer on or after 6 April 2008 will result in the creation of a separate Sch 4C pool.
(9) The deemed disposal of the assets in the original settlement means that those assets are rebased for all future purposes.

EXAMPLE 27A.29

Facts as in *Example 27A.28* except that Trust A actually sold RS shares 11 months later in May 2004 for £0.7m. The gain realised then would be £0.1m (which gain would not fall into the Sch 4C pool unless a further transfer of value is made) not £0.6m.

(10) Until 5 April 2008 taper relief was available on any deemed disposal calculated on a period of ownership from the date of acquisition up to the date of the deemed disposal.
(11) The interest charge can also apply to Sch 4C gains and again the FIFO rule has been changed to LIFO from April 2008.
(12) There are wide anti-avoidance provisions catching further transfers to other trusts. Thus if in *Example 27A.28* any of Trusts A or B later makes a further transfer of value to Trust C creating a further Sch 4C pool then gains in that pool can be attributed to any of the beneficiaries who receive capital payments from Trusts A, B or C even if say, the beneficiaries are excluded from the Trust which made the further transfer of value.
(13) It is potentially useful that post April 2008 pools of Sch 4C gains can now be washed out on payments to foreign domiciliaries.

Conclusions

When considering the tax treatment of payments to UK resident beneficiaries the rules are extremely complicated but in broad terms for non-settlor beneficiaries who receive distributions from offshore trusts, the order is as follows:

(1) First match the benefit to any relevant income under the transfer of assets provisions unless the motive test is in point. In the case of the remittance basis user, consider whether the payment or benefit has been remitted to the UK or whether the income has a UK source.
(2) Next match any excess capital payment or benefit to any offshore income gains within the structure. These are matched in priority to s 2(2) gains taxed under s 87 or Sch 4C gains and will be taxed at income tax rates, again on a remittance basis. Foreign domiciliaries will generally obtain the benefit of the transitional provisions (rebasing and exemption for pre April 2008 OIGs and capital payments) in respect of such OIGs unless such OIGs have been matched to a capital payment to a non-resident.
(3) If the payment is still unmatched, then consider whether there are any Sch 4C gains (in the case of foreign domiciliaries only post April 2008 Sch 4C gains pools are relevant). For foreign domiciliaries the remittance basis is in point, as are the transitional reliefs (rebasing, exemption for pre April 2008 capital payments).
(4) Only then can the payment be matched to s 87 gains and taxed under the provisions outlined in this chapter, again with the benefit of the remittance basis and transitional reliefs for foreign domiciliaries.

[27A.176]

2 Offshore trusts: information (TCGA 1992 s 98A, Sch 5A)

FA 1994 widened the information provisions to catch all non-resident trusts, not just those in which a defined person retains an interest. Accordingly, they apply to additions to an existing trust; to the establishment by a UK settlor of a foreign settlement and indeed to a foreign settlement created by a non-UK resident and domiciliary who subsequently becomes resident and domiciled and, finally, to the export of a UK trust. In all cases details of the date when the settlement was created; name and address of persons delivering the return and details of the trustees must be provided. Trusts that made the rebasing election were not required to give the name of the settlor or beneficiaries to HMRC. Although in some cases submission of the rebasing election led to HMRC issuing a long questionnaire to the trustees, they were under no statutory obligation to respond to such letter and were generally advised not to do so.

In some cases such trustees have also been issued with a tax return. Trustees are under a statutory obligation to submit the return if it is issued to them even if it is a nil return but in practice if they inform HMRC in advance that the trust has no UK source income and is not otherwise liable to UK tax and has realised no gains, eg it is a dry trust, HMRC accept that the tax return does not need to be completed. Formal confirmation should be obtained from HMRC on this point before the trustees ignore the return. [27A.177]

Section 4 Inheritance tax

Chapters
Introduction – from estate duty to inheritance tax
28   IHT – lifetime transfers
29   IHT – reservation of benefit
30   IHT – death
31   IHT – exemptions and reliefs
32   IHT – settlements: definition and classification
33   IHT – settlements with an interest in possession: the old and new regimes
34   IHT – relevant property: settlements without an interest in possession and those treated as settlements without an interest in possession
35   IHT – excluded property and the foreign element
36   Relief against double charges to IHT

Section 4　Inheritance tax

Introduction – from estate duty to inheritance tax

Updated by Sandra Eden, Senior Lecturer, University of Edinburgh

Many countries impose some kind of wealth tax, either an annual tax on the capital value of wealth owned by an individual, or a transfer tax, either on property inherited or on the value of a deceased's estate on death. In the UK estate duty was introduced in 1894 as a tax on a deceased's property whether passing under a will or on intestacy. Over its long life the tax was extended from its originally narrow fiscal base (property passing on death) to catch certain gifts made in the period before death and at the time of its replacement by capital transfer tax (CTT) it extended to gifts made in the seven years before death. By the 1970s estate duty was, however, widely condemned as an unsatisfactory tax. 'A voluntary tax'; 'a tax on vice: the vice of clinging to one's property until the last possible moment' – were typical descriptions.

In 1972 the Conservative Government considered replacing estate duty with an inheritance tax (Cmnd 4930). The idea was that a beneficiary would keep a cumulative account of all gifts that he received on death and pay tax accordingly. Nothing came of this proposal, largely because such a tax would have been too costly to administer and because the Conservative government fell from office.

The Labour Government, which came to power in 1974, was committed to achieving a major redistribution of wealth. As a first stage (without any prior consultation) it introduced CTT in the 1974 Budget. This tax had '... as its main purpose to make the estate duty not a voluntary tax, but a compulsory tax, as it was always intended to be' (Mr Healey, the then Chancellor of the Exchequer). CTT, as initially introduced, was a tax on all gifts throughout a person's lifetime, with the estate on death representing the final transfer, with rates of up to 75%. It was introduced as a precursor to a proposed annual wealth tax (Cmnd 5074), which in the end was never introduced. Although in concept it was a brilliantly simple tax, which removed the arbitrariness of the old estate duty, in reality CTT never achieved its espoused redistributive purpose partly because it was substantially altered during its passage through Parliament in 1974–75, and partly because a number of very wealthy individuals left the country to avoid paying it.

The advent of a series of Conservative Governments in 1979 saw a steady erosion of the principles underlying CTT. The idea of a fully comprehensive cradle to grave gifts tax was abandoned in 1981 in favour of ten-year cumulation, thresholds were raised, and a new relief introduced for agricultural landlords.

By 1986, as a percentage of GNP, CTT yielded less than one-third of the revenue formerly produced by estate duty.

To some extent, the changes made by FA 1986, which resulted in the move to the current inheritance tax, merely completed this process. Ten-year cumulation was reduced to seven years and the majority of lifetime gifts made more than seven years before death were removed from charge. As in the days of estate duty, therefore, tax is now levied on death gifts and gifts made within seven years of death. In an attempt to prevent schemes whereby taxpayers could 'have their cake and eat it' (ie give property away but continue to enjoy the benefits from it) there was a further echo from estate duty in the reintroduction of rules taxing gifts with a reservation of benefit. These changes did not amount to a replacement of CTT by estate duty but did represent a welding of certain estate duty rules onto the already battered corpse of CTT. The end result is simply a mess and to call this amalgam an inheritance tax is to confuse matters further: this term normally refers to a tax based on how much a beneficiary receives, whereas the current UK tax looks to how much the donor gives. Neither is the current UK tax a true tax on inheritances, since certain lifetime transfers are subject to charge. 'There has been no attempt at reform. The Chancellor has merely given us some reasons for making a shabby handout to the very rich. Not only has he reverted to the old estate duty, he has falsified the label' (Cedric Sandford, *Financial Times*, 26 March 1986).

Capital transfer tax was rechristened inheritance tax as from 25 July 1986 and the former legislation (the Capital Transfer Tax Act 1984) *may* be cited as the Inheritance Tax Act 1984 from that date (FA 1986 s 100). Despite the permissive nature of this provision the new title for this Act will be used in this book and inheritance tax abbreviated to IHT. All references to CTT take effect as references to IHT and, as all references to estate duty became references to CTT in 1975, they subsequently became references to IHT.

The position has now been reached whereby what was intended as a general tax on gifts has been limited (in the main) to gifts on or within seven years of death.

There have been a few significant changes to IHT since 1986. The more important include the treatment of lifetime transfers into certain trusts, the introduction in 2007 of the facility to transfer unused nil rate band to a surviving spouse or civil partner and, from 2017–18, an additional nil-rate band when a residence is passed on death to either children or grandchildren of the deceased. However, in 2017, the structure of the tax remains very similar to the regime introduced in 1986. The number of estates bearing IHT rose sharply in the early 2000s, largely as a result of rising house prices, although the introduction of the transferable nil rate band and the decline in house prices temporarily reversed this trend from 2007–08 to 2009–10. Nevertheless, IHT receipts are now rising again and, indeed, in 2015–16 (the latest year for which figures are available) IHT receipts are almost double those in 2009–10. Of course, the additional nil rate band attributable to residences coming into effect in 2017–18 is likely to slow this growth.

28 IHT – lifetime transfers

Updated by Sandra Eden, Senior Lecturer, University of Edinburgh

I Definition of a 'chargeable transfer' [**28.2**]
II What dispositions are not chargeable transfers? [**28.21**]
III When are lifetime transfers subject to IHT? The potentially exempt transfer (PET) [**28.41**]
IV On what value is IHT calculated? [**28.61**]
V 'Associated operations' (IHTA 1984 s 268) [**28.101**]
VI How is IHT calculated? [**28.121**]
VII Special rules for close companies [**28.151**]
VIII Liability, accountability and burden [**28.171**]
IX Administration and appeals [**28.201**]
X Timing of disposals [**28.231**]

For a charge to IHT to arise there must be a *chargeable transfer*. Whether tax is levied on a transfer depends upon whether it is:
(1) *chargeable immediately* at 'lifetime rates', with the possibility of an extra charge if the transferor dies within seven years, or
(2) *potentially exempt* which is a temporary status: the transfer is deemed to be exempt unless and until the donor dies within seven years of that transfer, when it becomes *chargeable* (see [**28.41**]), or
(3) *exempt*, in which case no tax will ever be charged (see **Chapter 31**).

[**28.1**]

I DEFINITION OF A 'CHARGEABLE TRANSFER'

IHTA 1984 s 1 states that 'IHT shall be charged on the value transferred by a chargeable transfer'. A chargeable transfer is then defined in IHTA 1984 s 2(1) as having three elements: a transfer of value; made by an individual; which is not exempt. [**28.2**]

1 A transfer of value

A *transfer of value* is defined in IHTA 1984 s 3(1) as any disposition which reduces the value of the transferor's estate. It includes certain deemed transfers of value ('events on the happening of which tax is chargeable *as if* a transfer of value had been made': see IHTA 1984 s 3(4)). Examples of

878   *IHT – lifetime transfers*

deemed transfers of value include death (see **Chapter 30**); the termination of certain interests in possession in settled property (see **Chapter 33**) and transfers of value made by a close company which are apportioned amongst its participators (see **[28.152]**).

'Disposition' is not defined, but the ordinary meaning is wide and includes any transfer of property whether by sale or gift; the creation of a settlement; and the release, discharge or surrender of a debt but not, it is thought, a consent (eg to an advancement of trust property). It includes a disposition effected by associated operations (see **[28.101]**). **[28.3]**

2   Omissions

By IHTA 1984 s 3(3), a disposition includes an omission to exercise a right. The right must be a legal right and the omission must satisfy three requirements:
(1) The estate of the person who fails to exercise the right must be reduced in value.
(2) Another person's estate or a trust must be increased in value.
(3) The omission must be deliberate, which is presumed to be the case in the absence of contrary evidence.

Examples of omissions include failure to sue on a debt which becomes statute-barred; failure to exercise an option either to sell or purchase property on favourable terms; and failure by a landlord to exercise his right to increase rent under a rent review clause. An omission to take up pension rights in certain circumstances, for example in the knowledge of terminal illness, was formerly an example (*Fryer (Arnold's PR) v R & C Comrs* (2010)) although this specific omission has been reversed by legislation with effect for deaths after 5 April 2011 (IHTA 1984 s 12(2ZA)).

The omission will constitute a transfer of value at the latest time when it was possible to exercise the right, unless the taxpayer can show (1) that the omission was not deliberate but was a mistake of fact (eg he forgot) or of law (eg failure to realise that the debt had become statute-barred) or (2) that it was the result of a reasonable commercial decision involving no element of bounty (eg failure to sue a debtor who was bankrupt). There may also separately be an argument that there is no transfer of value by reference to some other provision, eg IHTA 1984 s 10 (see **[28.21]**). **[28.4]**

3   Examples of transfers of value

(1) A gives his house worth £60,000 to his son B.
(2) A sells his car worth £4,000 to his daughter C for £2,000.
(3) A grants a lease of his factory to his nephew D at a peppercorn rent. The factory was worth £100,000; the freehold reversion after granting the lease is worth only £60,000. A's transfer of value is of £40,000.
(4) A is owed £1,000 by a colleague E. A releases the debt so that his estate falls in value and E's estate is increased in value. **[28.5]**

4   Transfers of value and gifts contrasted

It will be noted that IHT is based on the concept of a 'transfer of value': curiously, however, the reservation of benefit rules – introduced in

1986 – only come into play if an individual makes a 'gift' (this term is not defined). Whilst the two concepts generally overlap (the examples of transfers of value in **[28.5]** are probably also gifts) there will be exceptional cases where, for instance, there will be a deemed transfer of value which will not involve the individual making a gift (see generally **[29.41]**). **[28.6]–[28.20]**

II WHAT DISPOSITIONS ARE NOT CHARGEABLE TRANSFERS?

1 Commercial transactions (IHTA 1984 s 10(1))

A disposition is not a transfer of value and, therefore, is not chargeable if the taxpayer can show that he did not intend to confer a gratuitous benefit on another. This excludes from charge commercial transactions which turn out to be bad bargains. The transferor must not have intended to confer a gratuitous benefit on *any* person. Hence any disposition reducing the value of the transferor's estate may trigger a liability to IHT (by analogy to a crime the disposition may be seen as the *actus reus*) unless the taxpayer can show that he did not have the necessary *mens rea* for the liability to arise, ie that he had no gratuitous intent.

> **EXAMPLE 28.1**
>
> A purchases a holiday in the Bahamas in the name of C. A must show that he had no intention to confer a gratuitous benefit on C which he may succeed in doing if, for instance, C was being rewarded for being a valued employee (see *Postlethwaite's Executors v IRC* (2006)).

In order for a disposition between two *unconnected* persons not to be a transfer of value, the transferor must show that he had no gratuitous intent and that the transaction was made at arm's length. In the case of a disposition to a *connected* person, in addition to proving no gratuitous intent, the taxpayer must show that the transaction was a commercial one such as strangers might make. A 'connected person' is defined as for CGT (IHTA 1984 s 270: see TCGA 1992 s 286 and **Chapter 19**) and includes:

(1) spouses, civil partners and relatives, extended for IHT to include uncle, aunt, nephew and niece;
(2) trustees, where the terms 'settlement', 'settlor' and 'trustees' have their IHT meaning (IHTA 1984 ss 43–45, see **Chapter 32**);
(3) partners (for certain purposes only); and
(4) certain close companies.

> **EXAMPLE 28.2**
>
> (1) T sells his house valued at £270,000 to his daughter for £200,000. T will not escape a potential liability to IHT unless he can show that he never intended to confer a gratuitous benefit on his daughter and that the sale at an undervalue was the sort of transaction that he might have made with a stranger (eg that he needed money urgently and, therefore, was prepared to sell to anyone at a reduced price).

(2) Z sells his lease to his son Y subject to an obligation on Y to grant Z a leaseback for 20 years at a peppercorn rent. (This period has been arrived at on the basis of Z's life expectancy.) The price paid by Y reflects the existence of the lease and hence is substantially discounted.

Note:
(a) There will be a substantial loss in Z's estate (namely, a loss of 'marriage value') which, provided that s 10 applies, is not a PET.
(b) HMRC apparently accepts that in a case like this a lease for life can be granted to Z but this practice is open to question since, unless the lease is granted for full consideration, it will be treated for IHT as a settlement with Z enjoying an interest in possession (see **Chapter 32**). Hence it is considered safer to select a suitable term of years.
(c) In Z's hands the lease is a wasting asset and so this arrangement may be especially attractive when Z is elderly and unlikely to survive a PET by seven years.

In *IRC v Spencer-Nairn* (1991) the court had to consider the sale at an undervalue between two persons who were unknowingly connected. The taxpayer owned a farm in Scotland which was in need of significant repair. It was let to a tenant, and it was wrongly assumed that the landlord, the taxpayer, was responsible for the cost of repair, estimated at £80,000. A decision was made to sell the farm to a Jersey company for a sum in the region of £100,000. The farm was never advertised for sale and the taxpayer entered into the sale on the recommendation of his adviser: interestingly, neither the taxpayer nor the adviser were aware at the time that the company was 'connected' with the taxpayer.

For CGT purposes the Lands Tribunal for Scotland determined the market value of the farm at £199,000 on the basis that, contrary to the adviser's view, the taxpayer was not liable to pay for the improvements demanded by the tenant. In due course (not surprisingly!) HMRC raised a CTT assessment on the basis of a transfer of value of £94,000. It was generally accepted that the taxpayer did not have a gratuitous intention: but HMRC argued that the transfer was not such as the taxpayer would have made in an arm's length transaction with an unconnected person.

For s 10 to be relevant the transferor must be shown to have entered into a disposition as a result of which his estate has been diminished, and, once that is shown, the taxpayer is then forced into the position of having to prove that he did not intend to confer any benefit *and* that what he did would satisfy the test of an objective commercial arrangement. HMRC had taken a restricted view (some would say a minimalistic view!) of the section. In effect it had argued that if there was a substantial fall in the transferor's estate that was the end of the matter. In *Spencer-Nairn* the Lord President dismissed arguments of this nature in summary fashion:

'The fact that the transaction was for less than the open market value cannot be conclusive of the issues at this stage, otherwise the section would be deprived of its content. The gratuitous element in the transaction becomes therefore no more than a factor, which must be weighed in the balance with all the other facts and circumstances to see whether the onus which is on the transferor has been discharged.'

Had the burden of repairs rested on the landlord the actual sale price which he received would not have been unreasonable.

The sole question for the court was whether the sale was such as would have been made with a third party at arm's length. In applying this test, although it is basically drafted in objective terms, they found it necessary to incorporate subjective ingredients. The hypothetical vendor must be assumed to have held the belief of the landlord that the value of the property was diminished by his obligation to rebuild the piggeries. A wholly unreasonable (and in the event mistaken) belief will not presumably be relevant.

The *Spencer-Nairn* case is unusual in that the parties did not know that they were connected: in a sense therefore they were negotiating *as if* they were third parties on the open market.

> 'A good way of testing the question whether the sale was such as might be expected to be made in a transaction between persons not connected with each other is to see what persons who were unaware that they were connected with each other actually did' (Lord President Hope).

The following conclusions are suggested:
(1) whether the transferor has a gratuitous intent is entirely subjective;
(2) there can be a sale at arm's length for the purposes of the second limb of s 10 even though the price realised is not approximately the same as the 'market value';
(3) in considering what amounts to an 'arm's length' sale, features of the actual sale (such as the reasonably held beliefs of the vendor) must be taken into account – this limb is not a wholly objective test. **[28.21]**

There are special rules in the following cases:

a) *Reversionary interests*

A beneficiary under a settlement who purchases for value any reversionary interest in the same settlement may be subject to IHT on the price that he pays for the interest and s 10(1) cannot apply to the transaction (IHTA 1984 s 55(2): for the rationale of this rule see **[33.4]**). **[28.22]**

EXAMPLE 28.3

Property is settled on A for life, remainder to B absolutely. B has a reversionary interest. A buys B's interest for its commercial value of £50,000. A has made a potentially exempt transfer of £50,000.

b) *Transfer of unquoted shares and debentures*

A transferor of unquoted shares and securities must show, in addition to lack of gratuitous intent, *either* that the sale was at a price freely negotiated at that time, *or* at such a price as might have been freely negotiated at that time (IHTA 1984 s 10(2)). In practice, such shares are rarely sold on an open market. Instead the company's articles will give existing shareholders a right of preemption if any shareholder wishes to sell. Provided that the right does not fix a price at which the shares must be offered to the remaining shareholders, but leaves it open to negotiation or professional valuation at the time of sale, HMRC will usually accept that the sale is a *bona fide* commercial transaction satisfying the requirements of IHTA 1984 s 10(1). **[28.23]**

EXAMPLE 28.4

The articles of two private companies make the following provisions for share transfers:
(1) *ABC Ltd:* the shares shall be offered *pro rata* to the other shareholders who have an option to purchase at a price either freely negotiated or, in the event of any dispute, as fixed by an expert valuer.
(2) *DEF Ltd:* the shares shall be purchased at par value by the other shareholders.

Position of shareholders in ABC Ltd: they will be able to take advantage of IHTA 1984 s 10(1) since the price is open to negotiation at the time of sale.

Position of shareholders in DEF Ltd: s 10(1) will not be available with the result that if the estate of a transferor falls in value (if, for instance, a £1 share has a market value of £1.50 at the time of transfer) IHT may be charged *even in the absence of gratuitous intent.* (Note that articles like those of DEF Ltd may also cause problems for business property relief, see **[31.53]** and that valuing shares in such circumstances is subject to an artificial rule, see **[28.72]**.)

c) *Partnerships*

Partners are not connected persons for the purpose of transferring partnership assets from one to another. **[28.24]**

EXAMPLE 28.5

A and B are partners sharing profits and owning assets in the ratio 50:50. They agree to alter their asset sharing ratio to 25:75 because A intends to devote less time to the business in the future. Although A's estate falls (he has transferred half of his partnership share to B), he will escape any liability to IHT if there is a lack of gratuitous intent. Assuming that A and B are not connected otherwise than as partners, lack of gratuitous intent will be presumed, since such transactions are part of the commercial arrangements between partners.

2 **Other non-chargeable dispositions**

Excluded property (IHTA 1984 s 6) No IHT is charged on excluded property (see **Chapter 35**). The most important categories are property sited outside the UK owned by someone domiciled outside the UK and reversionary interests under a trust. **[28.25]**

Exempt transfers (IHTA 1984 Part II) Exempt transfers are not chargeable transfers and hence are not subject to charge (see **Chapter 31**). Examples are:
(1) transfers between spouses and civil partners, whether *inter vivos* or on death;
(2) transfers up to £3,000 in value each tax year;
(3) outright gifts of up to £250 pa to any number of different persons.
[28.26]

Waiver of remuneration and dividends (IHTA 1984 ss 14, 15) A waiver or repayment of salaries and other remuneration assessable as employment income by a director or employee is not a chargeable transfer; the remuneration is formally waived (by deed) or if paid, repaid to the employer who adjusts his profits or losses to take account of the waiver or repayment. It should be noted that HMRC take the view that the waiver must occur before the salary is paid to or put at the disposal of the employee – see HMRC Manual EIM 42705.

A person may, in the 12 months before the right accrued (which time is identified in accordance with usual company law rules), waive a dividend on shares without liability to IHT. A general waiver of all future dividends is only effective for dividends payable for up to 12 months after the waiver and should, therefore, be renewed each year. [28.27]

Voidable transfers (IHTA 1984 s 150) Where a transfer is voidable (eg for duress or undue influence) and is set aside, it is treated for IHT purposes as if it had never been made, provided that a claim is made by the taxpayer. As a result any IHT paid on the transfer may be reclaimed. Tax on chargeable transfers made after the voidable transfer, but before it was avoided, must be recalculated and IHT refunded, if necessary. [28.28]

Although not excluded property, business or agricultural property which qualifies for 100% relief will not attract any IHT charge (see **Chapter 31**). [28.29]–[28.40]

III WHEN ARE LIFETIME TRANSFERS SUBJECT TO IHT? THE POTENTIALLY EXEMPT TRANSFER (PET)

If the taxpayer makes an *inter vivos* transfer, IHT may be charged at once. Alternatively, the transfer may be potentially exempt (a PET). In the latter case, IHT is only levied if the taxpayer dies within seven years of the transfer: otherwise the transfer becomes exempt. During the 'limbo' period (being the period of seven years following the transfer or, if shorter, the period ending with the transferor's death) the PET is treated *as if it were exempt* (IHTA 1984 s 3A(5)) so that despite the legislation calling the transfer potentially exempt it would be more accurate to refer to it as potentially chargeable. With the exception of transfers involving trusts and transfers to companies (and by close companies), the majority of lifetime transfers are PETs. [28.41]

What is a PET?

A PET is defined in IHTA 1984 s 3A(1). It must satisfy two preliminary requirements: *first*, it must be made by an individual on or after 18 March 1986; and *second*, the transfer must, apart from this section, have been a chargeable transfer (hence exemptions – such as the annual £3,000 exemption – are deducted first). Beyond this, the range of transfers which fall within the definition of a PET was altered by FA 2006 Sch 20, with the post-FA 2006 rules being considered at **[28.43]**, and the old rules at **[28.46]**. The most important change is that the range of trusts to which a PET can be made is significantly reduced under the new rules. **[28.42]**

a) *Gifts by individuals made on or after 22 March 2006*

i) *Outright gifts to individuals*

A transfer which is a gift to another individual is a PET so long as *either* the property transferred becomes comprised in the donee's estate *or*, by virtue of that transfer, the estate of the donee is increased (s 3A(2)). **[28.43]**

EXAMPLE 28.6
(1) Adam gives Bertram a gold hunter watch worth £5,000: this is a PET.
(2) Claude pays Debussy's wine bill of £10,000. Although property is not transferred into the estate of Debussy, the result is to increase Debussy's estate by paying off his debt. Accordingly this also is a PET.
(3) Edgar who owned 51% of the shares in Frome Ltd transfers 2% of the company's shares to Grace who had previously owned no shares in the company. Edgar suffers a substantial drop in the value of his estate (since he loses control of Frome Ltd) which exceeds the benefit received by Grace. The whole transfer is a PET.

ii) *Transfers to trusts for the disabled*

These trusts are discussed in **Chapter 16**. The transfer into a trust for the disabled is treated as a PET *to the extent that the value transferred was attributable to property which by virtue of the transfer becomes settled*: IHTA 1984 s 3A(3A). The alternative condition, noted in **[28.43]** in relation to individuals, namely that the estate of the donee is increased, does not apply to trusts, so indirect transfers do not qualify (see *Example 28.7(2)*). **[28.44]**

iii) *Other transfers which are treated as PETs*

The following lifetime transfers are also treated as PETs:
(1) a transfer into a bereaved minor's trust on the coming to an end of an immediate post death interest (see **[32.51]**),
(2) certain terminations of pre-22 March 2006 interests in possession (see **[33.11]**).

As in relation to trusts for the disabled, the property must become settled as a result of the transfer. **[28.45]**

EXAMPLE 28.7
(1) A settles £100,000 on a trust for C who is disabled. This transfer is a PET.
(2) B settles an insurance policy, taken out on his own life, on a trust for D who is disabled. This transfer is a PET. He subsequently pays premiums on that policy and, although the payments are transfers of value, they are not attributable to property which becomes settled property and are not, therefore, PETs. B should, therefore, consider making a gift of that sum each year to the trustees to enable them to pay the premiums on the policy (alternatively,

the problem will be avoided if B's payments are exempt from IHT as normal expenditure out of income: see [31.4]).

b) *Gifts by individuals made before 22 March 2006*

i) *General*

The range of transfers which could be PETs prior to the changes implemented by FA 2006 included, as now, lifetime transfers to individuals and trusts for the disabled, but in addition extended to lifetime transfers into interest in possession trusts (including certain termination of such interests during the lifetime of the beneficiary) and transfers into accumulation and maintenance trusts. [28.46]

ii) *Interest in possession settlements*

Prior to the 2006 changes, the lifetime creation of an interest in possession trust was a potentially exempt transfer. The beneficiary entitled to an interest in possession was treated as owning the capital of the trust (for IHT purposes – see **Chapter 33**). This meant that any reduction or termination of the interest was taxed as if the beneficiary himself had made the transfer. So an *inter vivos* termination of his interest was treated as a PET if the capital went to another individual, an exempt transfer if it went to a charity, and a chargeable transfer if the property went into a discretionary trust (the lifetime termination of his interest cannot be a PET, since the PET definition has always excluded the creation of discretionary trusts (see [28.47])). [28.47]

EXAMPLE 28.8–28.9

In December 2005, Wilbur Wacker settles £100,000 on trust for his brother Willie for life, thereafter to his sister Wilma for life, with remainder to his godson Wilberforce. Wilbur's transfer is a PET. (Had it been made post 21 March 2006, it would be a chargeable transfer.) In February 2006, he settles a life insurance policy on the same trusts and continues to pay the premiums to the insurance company (as in *Example 28.7(2)* above). The premiums (if not already exempt as normal expenditure out of income) will also be PETs Assume also that the following events occur:
(1) Willie surrenders his life interest on 10 March 2006, his fiftieth birthday: this deemed transfer of the property in the trust is a PET made by Willie.
(2) Wilma purchases Wilberforce's remainder interest on 19 March 2006 for £60,000 (see *Example 28.3* above). The payment of £60,000 by Wilma is a PET (see *Example 28.3*). The eventual termination of the interest itself is not a transfer of value, as she is already deemed to own the underlying property.

c) *The limits of PETs*

For gifts made either before or after 22 March 2006, the following traps should be noted:
(1) Jack pays the school fees of his infant grandson Jude *or* Simon buys a holiday for his uncle Albert. In neither case does property become comprised in the estate of another by virtue of the transfer, and

neither Jude's nor Albert's estate is increased as a result of the transfer. Accordingly, both Jack and Simon have made immediately chargeable transfers of value (by contrast, a direct gift to each donee would ensure that the transfers were PETs).

(2) The reservation of benefit provisions are analysed in **Chapter 29** and it should be noted that, when they apply, property which has been given away is brought back into the donor's estate at death. The original gift will normally have been a PET (provided that, if it was made on or after 22 March 2006, it was either an outright gift to an individual or a gift into a disabled trust) and, therefore, there is a possibility of a double charge to IHT should the donor die within seven years of that gift at a time when property is still subject to a reservation. (This double charge will normally be relieved by regulations discussed in **Chapter 36**.)

(3) 'Where, under any provision of this Act other than s 52, tax is in any circumstances to be charged *as if* a transfer of value had been made, that transfer shall be taken to be a transfer which is not a PET.' (IHTA 1984 s 3A(6))

This provision ensures that deemed transfers of value cannot be PETs. For example, PETs are limited to lifetime gifts because, on death, a person is deemed to transfer his estate immediately before death. It also means that tax charges will arise when close companies are used to obtain an IHT advantage (see **[28.151]**). [28.48]

d) *CGT tie-in*

CGT hold-over relief continues to be available in cases where a gift falls outside the PET definition (ie is an immediately chargeable transfer) provided that it is made *by* an individual or trustees to an individual or trustees (TCGA 1992 s 260). Both the creation and termination of a discretionary trust will generally satisfy this wording so that the CGT that would otherwise be levied on the chargeable assets involved may be held over. By contrast, gifts to close companies do not involve gifts between individuals and trustees so that, unless the property given away is business property within the definition in TCGA 1992 s 165, hold-over relief will not be available (for the CGT position on gifts generally, see **Chapter 24** and note that hold-over relief is no longer available on gifts of shares to companies). [28.49]

e) *The taxation of PETs*

As already noted there is no charge to tax at the time when a PET is made and that transfer is treated as exempt unless the transferor dies within the following seven years. *There is, therefore, no duty to inform HMRC that a PET has been made and for cumulation purposes it is ignored.* All of this, however, changes if the donor dies within the following seven years: the former PET then becomes chargeable; must be reported; and the transfer must be entered into the taxpayer's cumulative total *at the time when it was made*. As a result, IHT on subsequent chargeable lifetime transfers may need to be recalculated (these transfers may in any event attract a supplementary charge). These consequences are illustrated in *Example 28.10* and explained further in **Chapter 30**. [28.50]–[28.60]

EXAMPLE 28.10

(1) On 1 May 2011 Ian gave £3,000 to Joyce.
(2) On 1 May 2012 he settled £500,000 on discretionary trusts in favour of his family.
(3) On 1 May 2013 he gave £60,000 to his daughter.
(4) On 1 May 2017 he died.

Ian died within seven years of all three transfers. The transfer in 2011 ((1) above) is, however, exempt since it is covered by his annual exemption (see [**31.3**]).

Transfer (2) was a chargeable lifetime transfer and attracted an IHT charge when made. Because of Ian's death within seven years a supplementary IHT charge will arise (the calculation of this additional IHT caused by death is explained in **Chapter 30**).

Transfer (3) was a PET. Because of Ian's death it is rendered chargeable and is subject to IHT. Further, Ian's cumulative total of chargeable transfers made in the seven years before death becomes (if we assume the non-availability of the £3,000 annual exemption in both 2012 and 2013) £560,000. Had Ian lived until 1 May 2020, transfer (3) would have become an exempt transfer (ie free from all IHT).

IV ON WHAT VALUE IS IHT CALCULATED?

1 What is the cost of the gift?

a) *General*

When an individual makes a chargeable disposition (including a PET rendered chargeable by death within seven years) IHT is charged on the amount by which his estate has fallen in value as a result of the transfer. A person's estate is the aggregate of all the property to which he is beneficially entitled (IHTA 1984 s 5(1)). **[28.61]**

b) *Meaning of 'property' (IHTA 1984 s 272)*

Property 'includes rights and interests of any description'. It includes property (other than settled property) over which an individual has a general power of appointment (IHTA 1984 s 5(2), because he could appoint the property to himself), but not property owned in a fiduciary or representative capacity: eg as trustee or PR. *Melville v IRC* (2001) decided that a general power exercisable over settled property amounted to a 'right or interest' and was property within the definition in s 272 (see further on this case [**32.93**]) but FA 2002 reversed this decision by adding to s 272 the words 'but does not include a settlement power' and a settlement power is then defined in IHTA 1984 s 47A as 'any power over, or exercisable (whether directly or indirectly) in relation to settled property or a settlement'. **[28.62]**

EXAMPLE 28.11

Mac transfers property worth £500,000 into a discretionary trust. He retains a power to revoke the trust after (say) three months. Although Mac can recover the entire £500,000 by exercise of this power his estate falls in value by the full £500,000. The power to revoke is a 'settlement power' and so not 'property' for IHT purposes. (Similarly a reversionary interest acquired in the circumstances set out in s 55 does not form part of the taxpayer's estate: see [**28.22**].)

888 IHT – lifetime transfers

c) *Calculating the fall in value of an estate*

In theory the transferor's estate must be valued both before and after the transfer and the difference taxed. In practice, this is normally unnecessary since the transferor's estate will only fall by the value of the gift although in unusual cases, the cost to the transferor of the gift may be more than the value of the property handed over (see *Example 28.14*). However, IHTA 1984 s 5(4) provides that, for the purpose of calculating the loss to the donor's estate, any IHT paid by the transferor must be taken into account. This does *not* extend to any other tax nor any incidental costs of transfer. Thus, in *Example 28.12*, A's estate falls only by the value of the land and by the IHT that he pays.

[28.63]

EXAMPLE 28.12

A gives £500,000 to a discretionary trust. A is going to pay any IHT on the transfer.

In order to find the loss to A's estate, one needs to find the sum which, after IHT has been paid on that sum by A, leaves £500,000. It is not correct to find the IHT by calculating tax on £500,000 because this is not the loss to his estate. This means that the £500,000 must be grossed up at the appropriate rate of IHT to discover the full cost of the gift to A (see **[28.124]** for details on how to gross up).

The £500,000 is a 'net' gift (this means that it needs to be grossed up to find the gross gift, which is the loss to the donor's estate). Assuming that A has used up his nil rate band and annual exemption for the year then that rate of tax is chargeable on the larger (gross) figure (here £625,000) which, after payment of IHT at 20%, leaves £500,000 in the trustees' hands.

Were he to give the trust land worth £500,000, A may also incur conveyancing fees and other taxes such as CGT. Such fees and other taxes are excluded from the value of the transfer.

EXAMPLE 28.13

A gives £500,000 to a discretionary trust.

First assume that the trustees are going to pay any IHT on the transfer.

The loss to A's estate is simply £500,000, so this is the sum on which tax will be calculated. The tax will come out of the gift.

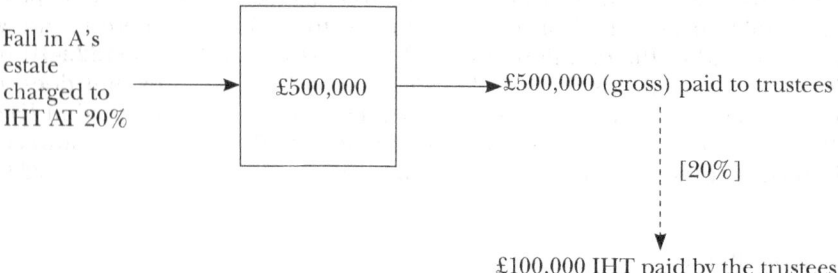

If, instead of the trustees paying the tax, it was agreed that the A would pay the IHT, the loss to the estate is no longer £500,000, it is the figure which, after tax, leaves the trustees with £500,000. The result would be:

On what value is IHT calculated? 889

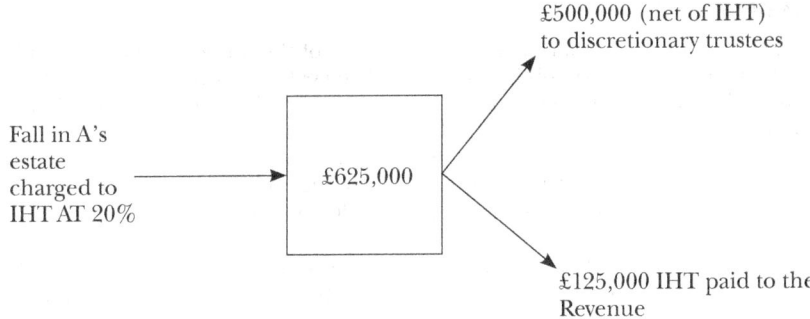

d) *Relationship between the fall in value of the donor's estate and the increase in value of the donee's estate*

IHT is generally calculated on the fall in value of the transferor's estate, not on the increase in value of the transferee's estate. This can work to the taxpayer's advantage, or disadvantage.

EXAMPLE 28.14

Compare
(1) A gives B a single Picasso plate, value £20,000; B agrees to pay any IHT that may fall due. B owns the remaining plates in the set (currently worth £150,000) and the acquisition of this final plate will give B's set a market value of £200,000. Although B's estate has increased in value by £50,000, IHT will only be charged on the fall in value in A's estate (£20,000).
(2) A owns 51% of the shares in A Ltd. This controlling interest is worth £100,000. He gives 2% of the shares to B who holds no other shares. 2% of the shares are worth (say) £2 but A, having lost control, will find that his estate has fallen by far more than £2 – say to £80,000. It will be the loss to A (£20,000) not the gain to B (£2) which is taxed.

Note that for an omission to exercise a right to be chargeable, another person's estate must be increased in value (see s 3(3) and **[28.4]**).   **[28.64]**

2 Problems in valuing an estate

Any calculation of IHT will require a valuation of the property transferred (see generally IHTA 1984 Part VI Chapter 25). As a general rule it is valued at the price that it would fetch on the open market. No reduction is made for the fact that the sale of a large quantity of a particular asset might cause the price to fall (IHTA 1984 s 160).   **[28.65]**

a) *Examples of the value transferred*

Liabilities The value of property which is burdened with a debt will normally be reduced by the value of that debt, subject to anti-avoidance rules (see **[30.14]**–**[30.20]**) (IHTA 1984 s 162(4)).   **[28.66]**

EXAMPLE 28.15

A gives his house to his son B. The market value of the house is £700,000, but it is subject to a mortgage to building society of £200,000 which B agrees to discharge. Hence, the property is valued for IHT purposes at £500,000. This position will commonly arise when a death gift of a house is made since, in the absence of a contrary intention stated in the will, the Administration of Estates Act 1925 s 35 and Succession (Scotland) Act 1964 s 14(3) provide that debts charged on property by the deceased must be borne by the legatee or donee of that property.

Co-ownership of property If land worth £100,000 is owned equally by A and B, it might be assumed that the value of both half shares is £50,000. In fact the shares will be worth less than £50,000 since it will be difficult to sell such an interest on the open market (see the Lands Tribunal cases of *Wight v IRC* (1984), *Charkham v IRC* (2000), *Barrett v IRC* (2005), *St Clair-ford v Ryder* (2006) and *HSBC Trust Co v Twiddy* (2006)). Whoever purchases will have to share the property with the other co-owner and, in practice, a discount of 10–15% is reasonable in England and Wales, although the starting point in Scotland, where land is concerned, is a flat rate reduction of £4,000, because of the right of each owner to obtain a court order to sell the property and divide the proceeds. Because of the related property rules – see **[28.70]** – there will, however, be no discount when the co-owners are husband and wife. Co-ownership of chattels poses other problems and it may be argued that, because of the difficulty of enforcing a sale, a larger discount is in order, although not in Scotland, again because of the right of division and sale.

[28.67]

Shares and securities When listed shares and securities are transferred, their value is taken (as for CGT; see **Chapter 19**) as the lesser of the 'quarter-up' and 'mid-price' calculation.

Valuation of unquoted shares and securities is a complex topic. A number of factors are taken into account, eg the company's profit record, its prospects, its assets and its liabilities. The percentage of shares which is being valued is a major factor. A majority shareholding of ordinary voting shares carries certain powers to control the affairs of the company (it will, for instance, give the owner the power to pass an ordinary resolution). A shareholding representing more than 75% confers greater powers, notably the power to pass special resolutions. Correspondingly, a shareholder who owns 50% or less of the voting power (and, even more so, a shareholding of 25% or less) has far fewer powers (he is a minority shareholder). When shares are subject to a restriction on their transfer (eg pre-emption rights) they are valued on the assumption of a sale on the open market with the purchaser being permitted to purchase the shares, but then being subject to the restrictions (*IRC v Crossman* (1937) and see **[28.72]**). [28.68]

b) *Special rules*

IHTA 1984 Part VI Chapter 1 contains special valuation rules designed to counter tax avoidance. [28.69]

Related property (IHTA 1984 s 161) IHT savings could be engineered by splitting the ownership of certain assets (typically shares, sets of chattels, and interests in land) amongst two or more taxpayers. The saving would occur when the total value of the individual assets resulting from the split was less than the value of the original (undivided) asset. A pair of Ming vases, for instance, would be worth more as a pair than the combined values of the two individual vases. When it is desired to split the ownership of such assets, however, it should be remembered that the transfer needed to achieve this result will normally be potentially chargeable and, as any tax will be charged on the fall in value of the transferor's estate, no tax saving may result. Inter-spouse transfers are, however, free of IHT and hence, were it not for the related property provisions, could be used to achieve substantial savings by asset splitting. To frustrate such schemes the related property rules provide that, in appropriate circumstances, an asset must be valued together with other related property and a proportion of that total value is then attributed to the asset (compare the CGT provisions on asset splitting: **[19.16]**). An obvious situation in which property is related is where a house is owned jointly between spouses. The First-tier Tribunal in *Price's Executor* (2010) confirmed that when valuing the share of one spouse, the starting point is to take the value of the whole house with vacant possession, then pro-rata it between the spouses according to their respective shares (rather than aggregating the value of each share, neither of which gave rise to vacant possession, as argued by the taxpayer).

EXAMPLE 28.16

X Ltd is a private company which has a share capital of £100 divided into 100 £1 shares. Assume that shares giving control (ie more than 50%) are worth £100 each and minority shareholdings £20 per share. If Alf owns 51% of the shares the value of his holding is £5,100 (£100 per share). Assume that Alf and Bess are married. Alf transfers 26% of the company's shares to Bess. Alf becomes a minority shareholder with shares worth £500 but pays no IHT because transfers between spouses are exempt. Bess also has a minority holding worth £520. If Alf and Bess then each transfer their respective holdings to their son Fred, they may be liable to pay IHT on a value of £1,020, whereas if Alf had transferred his 51% holding to Fred directly he would be potentially liable to tax on £5,100.

To prevent this IHT saving Alf and Bess's holdings are valued together as a majority holding worth £5,100. Accordingly, when Alf transfers his 25% holding to Fred this is 25/51 of the combined holding and is valued, therefore, at £2,500 (ie 25/51 of £5,100). Once Alf has disposed of his holding, Bess's 26% holding is then valued in the normal way on a subsequent transfer: ie as a minority holding worth £520 (in certain cases the associated operations rule or the GAAR might be invoked; see **[28.101]** and **Chapter 2**).

Inter-spouse/civil partner transfers are the main instance of transfers which attract the related property provisions. However, the rules also catch other exempt transfers (eg to a charity or political party) in circumstances where the transferor could otherwise obtain a similar tax advantage.

EXAMPLE 28.17

As *Example 28.16*, Alf owns 51% of the shares in X Ltd. He transfers 2% to a charity paying no IHT because the transfer is exempt. He then transfers the remaining 49% to Fred. Alf is a minority shareholder and the loss to his estate is only £980 compared with £5,100 if he had transferred the entire 51% holding directly to Fred. Some time later Fred might purchase the 2% holding from the charity for its market value of £40. Unless the two transfers (ie to the charity and to Fred) are more than five years apart, the charity's holding is related to Alf's so that his 49% holding is valued at £4,900 on the transfer to Fred.

The related property rules apply to the deemed transfer on death subject to the proviso that if the property is sold within three years after the death for a price lower than the related property valuation, it may be revalued on death ignoring the related property rules (see **Chapter 30**). [28.70]

Property subject to an option (IHTA 1984 s 163) When property is transferred as a result of the exercise of an option or other similar right created for full consideration, there is no liability to IHT.

Where an option is granted for less than full consideration, however, there will be a chargeable transfer or a PET at that time and there may be a further charge when the option is exercised. A credit will be given against the value of the property transferred, when the option is exercised, for any consideration actually received and for any value that was charged to IHT on the grant of the option. [28.71]

EXAMPLE 28.18

(1) Harold grants Daisy an option to purchase his house in three years' time for its present value of £120,000. Daisy pays £30,000 for the option which represents full consideration. When Daisy exercises the option three years later the house is worth £250,000.

Harold has not made a transfer of value and is not liable to IHT since (as the option was granted for full consideration) the house is only worth £120,000 to him.

(2) Assume instead that Daisy gives no consideration for the option which is worth £30,000. IHT may, therefore, be chargeable on that sum. On the exercise of the option IHT may be payable on £100,000 ((£250,000 – £120,000) minus the sum that was chargeable on the grant of the option (£30,000)).

Property subject to restrictions on transfer In *IRC v Crossman* (1937) the testator owned shares in a private company the articles of which imposed restrictions on alienation and transfer. By a bare majority the House of Lords held that in valuing those shares for estate duty purposes the basis to be taken was the price which they would fetch on the open market on the terms that a purchaser would be registered as the owner of the shares but would in turn be subject to the restrictions contained in the company's articles of association. The view contended for by the executors would have resulted in property which could not be sold in the open market escaping the tax net altogether. The *Crossman* case was subsequently followed by the House of Lords in *Lynall v IRC* (1972) and has been adopted in a series of cases concerning IHT. For instance, in *Alexander v IRC* (1991) a Barbican flat was purchased under the 'right to buy' provisions of the Housing Act 1980. All or part of the discount under that legislation had to be repaid in the event of the flat being sold within five years of its purchase. The taxpayer, however, died in the first year. The Court of Appeal – following *Crossman* – held that for valuation purposes an open market value must be taken and the flat was to be valued on the basis of what a purchaser would pay to stand in the deceased's shoes: ie taking over the liability to repay the discount should he sell the property within the prescribed period. It is inherent in this approach that the valuation thereby obtained may result in a higher figure than would actually be the case if the property were sold by the executors (and it appears that such a sale, even if occurring within four years of death, will not result in revaluation relief under IHTA 1984 s 190: see **Chapter 30**). [28.72]

Non-assignable agricultural tenancies The vexed question of whether a non-assignable agricultural tenancy had any value was decided in the affirmative by the Lands Tribunal for Scotland on *Crossman* principles (see generally **[31.72]**). Once it was accepted that *Crossman* applied, the issue is one of fixing the correct value. In the Scottish case, *Baird's Executors v IRC* (1991), this matter was not argued and the 'robust approach' of the District Valuer in taking 25% of the open market value was accepted. The Court of Appeal decision in *Walton v IRC* (1996), confirmed that there can be no hard and fast valuation rule in such cases. The tenancy will not automatically be valued on the basis of a percentage of the freehold value on the assumption that the landlord will always be a special purchaser: in *Walton*, for instance, the freeholder had no interest in acquiring the tenancy. Evans LJ commented that 'the sale has to take place "in the real world" and account must be taken of the actual persons as well as of the actual property involved'. [28.73]

Life assurance policies Life assurance policies normally involve the payment of annual premiums in return for an eventual lump sum payable either on retirement or on death. Special valuation rules, which do not apply on death (see **Chapter 30**), are provided by IHTA 1984 s 167 to prevent a tax saving when the benefit of such a policy is assigned. [28.74]–[28.100]

EXAMPLE 28.19

A gives the benefit of a whole life policy effected on his own life to B when its open market value is £10,000. A has paid five annual premiums of £5,000, so that the cost of providing the policy is £25,000 to date. For IHT purposes the policy is valued at the higher of its market value or the cost of providing the policy. As a result tax may be charged on £25,000.

V 'ASSOCIATED OPERATIONS' (IHTA 1984 S 268)

Before considering the anti-avoidance rules specific to IHT, it should be noted that the GAAR, introduced in 2013, also applies to IHT (FA 2013 s 203(3)(e)).

The IHT legislation, however, also contains specific provisions to prevent a taxpayer from reducing the value of a gift or the IHT chargeable by a series of associated operations.

'Associated operations' are defined in IHTA 1984 s 268 as:

'(1) ... any two or more operations of any kind, being –

    (a) operations which affect the same property, or one of which affects some property and the other or others of which affect property which represents, whether directly or indirectly, that property, or income arising from that property, or any property representing accumulations of any such income; or

    (b) any two operations of which one is effected with reference to the other, or with a view to enabling the other to be effected or facilitating its being effected, and any further operation having a like relation to any of those two, and so on; whether those operations are effected by the same person or different persons, and whether or not they are simultaneous; and "operation" includes an omission.

(2) The granting of a lease for full consideration in money or money's worth shall not be taken to be associated with any operation effected more than three years after the grant, and no operation effected on or after 27 March 1974 shall be taken to be associated with any operation effected before that date.

(3) Where a transfer of value is made by associated operations carried out at different times it shall be treated as made at the time of the last of them; but where any one or more of the earlier operations also constitute a transfer of value made by the same transferor, the value transferred by the earlier operations shall be treated as reducing the value transferred by all the operations taken together, except to the extent that the transfer constituted by the earlier operations but not that made by all the operations taken together is exempt under s 18 (spouse exemption).' **[28.101]**

In a series of cases the courts have imposed restrictions on this widely drafted section.

1 Macpherson, Reynaud and 'relevant' associated operations

In *IRC v Macpherson* (1989) trustees entered into an agreement which reduced the value of the settled property and subsequently appointed that property in favour of a beneficiary. The House of Lords held that the two transactions were associated operations, which formed part of an arrangement designed to confer a gratuitous benefit, this benefit being conferred by the appointment (see further **Chapter 31**). Lord Jauncey (in a speech with which the other Law Lords concurred) identified the boundaries of the associated operations provisions as follows:

'If an individual took steps which devalued his property on a Monday with a view to making a gift thereof on Tuesday, he would fail to satisfy the requirements of s 20(4) (now s 10(1)) because the act of devaluation and the gift would be considered together ... The definition in s 44 (now s 268) is extremely wide and is capable of covering a multitude of events affecting the same property which might have little or no apparent connection between them. It might be tempting to assume that any event which fell within this wide definition should be taken into account in determining what constituted a transaction for the purposes of s 268. However, counsel for the Crown accepted, rightly in my view, that some limitation must be imposed. Counsel for the trustees informed your Lordships that there was no authority on the meaning of the words "associated operations" in the context of capital transfer tax legislation but he referred to a decision of the Court of Appeal in Northern Ireland, *Herdman v IRC* (1967) in which the tax avoidance provisions of ss 412 and 413 of the Income Tax Act 1952 had been considered [the transfer of assets abroad legislation, now in ITA 2007 Part 13, Chapter 2: see **[18.111]**]. Lord MacDermott CJ upheld a submission by the taxpayer that the only associated operations which were relevant to the subsection were those by means of which, in conjunction with the transfer, a taxpayer could enjoy the income and did not include associated operations taking place after the transfer had conferred upon the taxpayer the power to enjoy income. If the extended meaning of "transaction" is read into the opening words of s 20(4) the wording becomes:

> "A disposition is not a transfer of value if it is shown that it was not intended, and was not made in a transaction including a series of transactions and any associated operations intended, to confer any gratuitous benefit ..."

So read it is clear that the intention to confer gratuitous benefit qualifies both transactions and associated operations. If an associated operation is not intended to confer such a benefit it is not relevant for the purpose of the subsection. That is not to say that it must necessarily *per se* confer a benefit but it must form a part of and contribute to a scheme which does confer such a benefit.'

In *Reynaud v IRC* (1999) brothers transferred shares into trusts from which they were wholly excluded: the following day the company bought back those shares from the trustees. The Special Commissioners held that, although both operations were associated, no disposition had been effected by associated operations since the value of the brothers' estates had been diminished by the gift into settlement alone:

> 'the purchase of own shares contributed nothing to the diminution which had already occurred and was not therefore a relevant associated operation.' **[28.102]**

2 The Hatton case

Hatton v IRC (1992) involved a tax avoidance scheme. Within the space of 24 hours two settlements were created. In the first, the settlor (Mrs C) reserved a short-term life interest; in the second, the reversionary interest in the first settlement was itself settled (by Mrs H) on Mrs C for a further 24-hour period with the property then being held absolutely for Mrs H. The creation of the original settlement by Mrs C involved no loss to her estate (under the relevant legislation she was treated as still owning the property by virtue of her interest in possession: see **Chapter 33**). The creation of the second settlement was likewise tax free since it involved the settlement by Mrs H of excluded property (the reversionary interest: see now IHTA 1984 s 48 and **Chapter 33**). Because the termination of Mrs C's first interest in possession was immediately succeeded by an interest in possession in the second settlement it attracted no tax charge (see now IHTA 1984 s 52(2)). Finally, the termination of that second interest in possession was also tax free since the settled property thereupon resulted to Mrs H, the settlor of that second settlement (see FA 1975 Sch 5 para 4(2): amended to prevent such schemes by FA 1981 s 104(1), now enacted as IHTA 1984 s 53(5)(b): see **Chapter 33**).

So far as the associated operations provisions were concerned, the judge concluded that the first settlement was made with a view to enabling or facilitating the making of the second (see IHTA 1984 s 268(1)(b)). Accordingly there was a disposition by associated operations which was treated as a single disposition of property from Mrs C into the second settlement of which she therefore became a settlor (see the definition of a settlement in IHTA 1984 s 43(2): **Chapter 32**).

It is not unusual for there to be two or more settlors of a single settlement. For instance, A and B could both transfer identified assets into a single trust. Under the IHT legislation, when circumstances require, that property may be treated as comprised in two separate settlements (see s 44(2)). For instance, A might settle £100 and B £50 and the resulting settlement fund could, when appropriate, be split into A's settlement (as to two-thirds) and B's settlement (as to one-third). Chadwick J concluded, however, that there could be circumstances where a division of the settlement property in this way was impractical and so, given that more than one settlor existed, the legislation must, in appropriate circumstances, treat each settlor as having created a separate settlement comprising, in each case, *the whole of the settled property*. This position can be illustrated in the *Hatton* case itself where Mrs C was, by dint of the associated operation rules (and, according to the Special Commissioners, because she was a person who had provided funds directly or indirectly), a person who had settled all the property in the second settlement. Mrs H was also a settlor; she was named as the settlor and had provided property in the shape of her reversionary interest in the first settlement. Given the nature of the property settled by these two settlors, Chadwick J was forced to conclude that each had created a separate settlement of the entirety of the property in the second settlement. Under the settlement created by Mrs C, the reverter to settlor rules did not apply.

This approach (treating each settlor as having established a separate settlement of the entirety of the settled property) would, the judge suggested, also apply to reciprocal settlements. In a simple case A would settle property on X for a limited interest in possession and as a *quid pro quo* B would settle property on Y for a similar interest. In both cases the reverter to settlor provisions would, at first sight, apply on the termination of X and Y's respective interests. Once it is accepted, however, that A is also a settlor of B's trust and *vice versa* (see s 44(1)) that analysis does not hold good. Instead, because B is a settlor of 'A's settlement' on the termination of X's limited interest an IHT charge may arise. The judge viewed the situation as one in which A and B were settlors of two separate settlements rather than accepting the view propounded by HMRC that B should be seen as 'a dominant settlor' of A's trust.

Presumably the judge's approach would not be applied in cases where a full tax charge would, in any event, arise. Take, for instance, the situation where A as part of a reciprocal arrangement settles property on B's son for life with remainder to B's daughter and B creates a similar trust in favour of A's son and daughter. Although there are reciprocal settlements, on the death of (say) B's son a full tax charge would then arise on the property in 'A's settlement' so that even though the analysis may be that B is also a settlor of the whole of the property in that trust there can surely be no question of imposing a further tax charge on the ending of B's son's interest in possession.

Finally, the analysis is not easy to apply in cases where property is settled on trusts lacking an interest in possession by two settlors, one who has made chargeable lifetime transfers and one who has not. Will HMRC be able to argue, in appropriate cases, that the former is to be treated as the settlor of the entirety so that in arriving at the IHT charge on the settlement his previous chargeable transfers will be taken into account? **[28.103]**

3 The problem of multiple settlements

In *Rysaffe Trustee Co (CI) Ltd v IRC* (2003) a taxpayer established five 'mirror' discretionary settlements: ie in each case the beneficiaries and trustees were the same; each comprised an initial sum of £10 and private company shares were subsequently added to each trust. The settlements were dated on different days. HMRC sought to impose tax on the basis that the taxpayer had made only a single settlement since the various transfers were associated and so amounted to a single disposition (see further **Chapter 34**). Park J (and a unanimous Court of Appeal) rejected HMRC's arguments as follows:

(1) 'the practical operation of the associated operations provisions is comparatively limited. It is not some sort of catch-all anti-avoidance provision which can be invoked to nullify the effectiveness of any scheme or structure which can be said to have involved more than one operation and which was intended to avoid or reduce IHT ... section 268 is not an operative provision which of itself imposes IHT liabilities. It is a definition of an expression (associated operations) which is used elsewhere. The definition only comes into effect so far as the expression "associated operations" is used elsewhere, and then only if the expression in another provision is relevant to the way in which that other provision applies to the facts of the particular case.'

(2) although a 'disposition' in s 272 can include a disposition effected by associated operations, associated operations are, however, only relevant if in substance there is a single disposition which has been divided into a number of separate 'operations'.

In addition, Park J made two further points:

(1) the transfers of the shares to the five trusts were not effected with reference to each other (s 268(1)(b)):

> 'It is true that each transfer was a part of one plan or scheme, but the transfer of parcel 1 to settlement 1 made no reference to the transfer of parcel 2 to settlement 2; and vice versa. Each transfer was effected in the knowledge that the other was being effected as well, but that does not seem to me to be the equivalent of saying that each transfer was effected "with reference to the other".'

(2) the five parcels of shares did not amount to the same property (see s 268(1)(a)).

Legislation to limit the effectiveness of so called 'pilot trusts' was included in F(No 2)A 2015 (see [34.24]). [28.104]

4 The effects of s 268 applying

It enables HMRC to tax as one transaction any number of separate transactions (including omissions) which, when looked at together, reduce the value of the taxpayer's estate. The transactions need not be carried out by the same person nor need they be simultaneous. Apparently the lifetime act of making a will can amount to an associated operation although the subsequent death will not! (*Bambridge v IRC* (1955).) Intestacy is covered by the reference to an omission.

Section 268(1)(a) is concerned with the channelling of gifts, in particular between spouses (where the transfers are exempt). In such dispositions the transferor is deemed to have made a transfer equivalent to the value of all the operations at the time when the last of them is made. If one of the operations involved a transfer of value by the same transferor, he is entitled to a credit for that value against the aggregate value of the whole operation unless the transfer was anyway exempt because it was made to a spouse (IHTA 1984 s 268(3)).

EXAMPLE 28.20

It is certain that H will die shortly whereas his wife is in good health. Any transfer H makes to his son (S), although a PET, will, therefore, be made chargeable by his death. Accordingly, he transfers £20,000 to his wife (W). W then passes the £20,000 to the son. Under IHTA 1984 s 268(1)(a) HMRC could argue that the transfers (H to W and W to S) are 'associated'. H is deemed to have made a transfer of value equivalent to the value transferred by all the associated operations, ie £40,000, £20,000 (H to W) and £20,000 (W to S). However, on his death, IHT is only chargeable on £20,000 as his transfer of £20,000 to W is exempt as an inter-spouse transfer. It is unclear whether under s 268(3) IHT could also be charged on her gift of £20,000 to S. The preferable view is no since the one charge on H should cover all the relevant transfers; but assume that H also gives £3,000 to his son which is exempt by his annual exemption (but see the *Hatton* case [28.103]). All three transfers (H to S, H to W and W to S) are associated at the time of the last of them (W to S). Under IHTA 1984 s 268(3) on H's death IHT is not charged on the aggregate value of all three transfers (ie £43,000) but on £20,000 only because he has a credit for any previous (associated) transfers of value (the £3,000 transfer to S) and the inter-spouse transfer of £20,000.

Commenting upon the associated operation provisions, Mr Joel Barnett (then Chief Secretary to the Treasury) stated that they would only be used to attack inter-spouse transfers in blatant tax avoidance cases:

'... where the transfer by a husband to a wife was made on condition that the wife should at once use the money to make gifts to others, a charge on a gift by the husband might arise under [s 268].'

(Official Report, Standing Committee A (13 February 1975) col 1596.)

Thus, spouses may channel gifts in order to utilise the poorer spouse's exemptions, eg the £3,000 annual exemption and the exemption for gifts on marriage of up to £5,000, and to obtain income tax and CGT benefits resulting from the independent taxation of spouses.

EXAMPLE 28.21

H is wealthy, his wife, W, is poor. Both wish to use up their full IHT exemptions and to provide for their son who is getting married. It would be sensible for the following arrangement to be adopted:

Stage 1 H transfers £11,000 to W which is exempt as an inter-spouse transfer. This will enable W to utilise two years' annual exemption of £3,000 (£6,000 in all) plus the £5,000 marriage exemption.

Stage 2 Both spouses then each give £11,000 to the son.

Section 268 will not be invoked provided that the gift to W is not made on condition that she pass the property to S.

Section 268(1)(b) also enables HMRC to put two separate transactions together.

EXAMPLE 28.22

(1) A owns two paintings which together are worth £60,000, but individually are worth £20,000. A sells one picture for £20,000. This is a commercial transaction (s 10(1)) and, therefore, not subject to IHT. A then sells the second picture, also for £20,000, to the same purchaser.

As a result of the two transactions, the purchaser has paid only £40,000 but received value of £60,000 and A's estate has fallen in value by £20,000. The effect of s 268(1)(b) is that HMRC can put the two transactions together and in appropriate cases tax the loss to his estate (ie £20,000) provided there is a gratuitous intent. Where the transactions are with a connected person the presumption of gratuitous intent will be hard to rebut. If both sales were to a commercial art gallery, however, it is likely that, despite s 268, no tax would be chargeable.

Contrast: assume as above that A owns two paintings but wishes to give one to his son. Accordingly, he settles that picture on trust for himself for life, remainder to his son. Provided that the settlement commenced prior to 22 March 2006, no IHT would have been charged on creation of that settlement since A would have been treated as owning the picture (see **Chapter 33**). A then surrenders his life interest and as a result tax appears to be chargeable on the value of the picture in the settlement: ie on £20,000 only (IHTA 1984 s 52(1)). Could it be argued by an application of s 268 that A has directly disposed of the picture to his son so that £40,000 is subject to IHT? (Alternatively, might the GAAR apply to produce that result?) Note that for interest in possession trusts (apart from disabled trusts) created during the settlor's lifetime on or after 22 March 2006, there is an immediate IHT charge.

(2) A owns freehold premises worth £200,000. A gives the property to his nephew (N) in two stages. He grants a tenancy of the premises to N at a full market rent thereby incurring no potential liability to IHT. Two years later, he gives the freehold to N which being subject to a lease is worth only £100,000. Hence, there is a potential liability for IHT on £100,000 only, although A has given away property worth £200,000.

(3) Under IHTA 1984 s 268(1)(b) HMRC can tax the overall loss to his estate. IHTA 1984 s 268(2), however, provides an exemption where more than three years have elapsed between the grant of the lease for full consideration and the gift or sale of the reversion.

(3) A wants to give his annual exemption of £3,000 to B each year. Although he has no spare cash, he owns a painting worth £30,000. Accordingly, A sells the painting to B for £30,000 which is left outstanding as a loan repayable on demand. Each year A releases as much of the outstanding loan as is covered by his annual exemption. After ten years the loan is written off. The painting is then worth £40,000. A loan which is repayable on demand is not chargeable to IHT (see [28.131]) and the release of part of the loan each year, although a transfer of value, is covered by A's annual exemption.

These may be associated operations under IHTA 1984 s 268(1)(b). HMRC has intimated that it *might* regard the overall transaction as a transfer of value by A of the asset at its market value (£40,000) at the date when the loan is written off. A would have a credit for his previous transfers of value, ie £30,000 (s 268(3)), and there would, therefore, be a potential charge to IHT on the capital appreciation element only, ie £10,000.

For HMRC's view in *Example 28.22(3)* to be upheld it would have to show that the donor retained ownership of the painting throughout the period of ten years. In support, it could be argued that the transferor's estate must be valued immediately after the disposition and that in the case of a disposition effected by associated operations that means at the time of the last of those operations (see IHTA 1984 ss 3(1), 268(3)). The counter-argument is that the value transferred is the difference between the value of the painting immediately before the first stage in the operation (ie £30,000) and the value of the debt after the last operation (nil) so that the loss to the transferor is £30,000, all of which is covered by the annual exemptions.

[28.105]–[28.120]

VI HOW IS IHT CALCULATED?

1 Cumulation and rates of tax

a) *Cumulation*

Each individual has a nil rate band available of, currently, £325,000. Any transfers falling within this band are chargeable at 0%. Although it has in the past been indexed for inflation, the nil rate band has been fixed at this level since April 2009 and no further increase is expected until at least 2020–21. The nil rate band is not simply a one-off lifetime allowance: it is available over a rolling seven-year period. The question to ask, each time one is considering whether there is any nil rate band on a particular transfer, is 'What chargeable transfers have taken place in the last seven years?', as these will use nil rate band. Accordingly, each individual must keep a cumulative account of all the chargeable transfers made by him. The current seven-year period (from 18 March 1986) contrasts with the original CTT legislation, which provided for unlimited cumulation, and the ten-year period from 1981 to 1986.

[28.121]

b) *Rates of tax*

From 6 April 2017 IHT rates are as follows (unchanged from 2009):

Portion of value		Rate of tax
Lower limit	Upper limit	Per cent
£	£	Nil*
0	325,000	40*
325,000	–	

* Chargeable lifetime transfers (for instance into a discretionary trust) are charged at half rates (ie at 0% or 20%). [28.122]

EXAMPLE 28.23

(Ignoring exemptions, reliefs and assuming that current IHT rates apply throughout and that the donee pays the tax.) A makes the following chargeable transfers (ie none of the transfers is a PET):
(1) *June 2010* £100,000
    The £100,000 falls within the nil rate band.
(2) *June 2016* £235,000
    The cumulative total of transfers is £335,000, and IHT is charged at rates applicable to transfers from £100,000 to £335,000: there is £25,000 of nil rate band left after the June 2010 transfer so
    ie first £225,000 is taxed at nil%
    the final £10,000 is taxed at 20% (paid by donee).
(3) *July 2017* £50,000
    The 2010 gift of £100,000 drops out of the account as it was made more than seven years before this gift. This means that £235,000 of nil rate band is used up by the June 2016 transfer, leaving £90,000 available for the July 2017 transfer. IHT is, therefore, charged at 0%.

c) *Taxing PETs*

PETs are presumed to be exempt *unless and until* the transferor dies within seven years of the transfer. If the donor does die within seven years the PET becomes a chargeable transfer (thereby necessitating the payment of IHT). In cases where the deceased taxpayer had made a mixture of chargeable transfers and PETs in the seven years before death, tax paid on the chargeable transfers may have to be recalculated, *first* because the PETs are converted into chargeable transfers from the date when they were made and, *second*, because of the death within seven years of making the chargeable transfer.

EXAMPLE 28.24

T makes the following transfers of value (ignoring annual exemptions):
Year 1 PET of £75,000
Year 2 chargeable transfer of £300,000
Year 4 T dies.
    IHT charged on the chargeable transfer in *Year 2* will have been calculated ignoring the PET made in *Year 1*. Accordingly it will have proceeded on the basis that T had made no prior chargeable transfers. As a result of his death in *Year 4*,

however, the PET of £75,000 is chargeable in *Year 1* so that IHT on the Year 2 transfer must be recalculated on the basis that when it was made T had made a prior chargeable transfer of £75,000. Hence it is recalculated using the IHT rates applicable in *Year 2*. £250,000 (the remaining nil rate band) of the year 2 transfer is chargeable at 0% and the balance, £50,000, is chargeable at 40%.

The effect of death on chargeable lifetime transfers and PETs is considered more fully in **Chapter 30**. [**28.123**]

2 Grossing-up

As already stated, IHT is charged on the fall in value in the transferor's estate. If tax was to be calculated on the basis of the gift as it stands, this would result in too little tax being payable: the loss to the donor is not just the gift, it is the gift PLUS the tax on the gift. Accordingly, any IHT payable by the transferor on the gift is treated as part of that fall in value. This means that the gift must be grossed up when the transferor is going to pay the tax. Take the example of A, who has made no previous chargeable transfers and who settles £341,000 on discretionary trusts. IHT payable by A can be calculated as follows:

Step 1 Deduct from the transfer any part of it that is exempt. A has an available annual exemption of £3,000 plus a further exemption carried forward from the previous year (see further [**31.3**]): there is, therefore, a chargeable transfer of £335,000.

Step 2 Calculate the rate(s) of IHT applicable to the chargeable transfer. The first £325,000 falls within the nil rate band and, therefore, IHT is payable only on the balance of £10,000.

Step 3 If A pays the IHT on the gift, his estate falls in value by £335,000 (after the annual exemptions) plus the IHT payable on the £10,000, ie A is charged on the cost of the gift by treating the £335,000 as a gift net of tax.

Therefore, the part of the gift on which IHT is payable (here £10,000 – the first £325,000 is covered by the nil rate band and 'taxed' at 0%) must be 'grossed up' to reflect the amount of tax payable on the gift by using the formula:

$$\frac{100}{100-R}$$

where R is the rate of IHT applicable to the sum in question. In A's case the calculation is:

£10,000 × 100/80 = £12,500 gross. Tax at lifetime rates (20%) on £12,500 is £2,500.

As a result:
(1) *Position of A:* Gift to trust (£341,000) plus IHT liability (£2,500) means a total cost of £343,500;
(2) *Position of the trust:* Receives from A £341,000.

The position is exactly the same if A gives £343,500 to the trust and requires that the trustees pay any tax due (see *Example 28.25(1)*).

Another way of doing this, once the taxpayer's cumulative total exceeds the nil rate band (currently £325,000), is to levy tax at 25% on the excess. For instance, if A gives £50,000 to his close company (a chargeable lifetime transfer) at a time when his cumulative total exceeds £325,000, tax on that transfer, if paid by A, will be 25% × £50,000 = £12,500, giving a gross transfer of £62,500. [**28.124**]

3 Effect of the tax being paid by a person other than the transferor

Grossing-up establishes the cost to a donor of making a gift where the donor is paying the IHT. On lifetime gifts, this is limited to lifetime chargeable transfers where the donor pays the IHT due: there is no grossing-up if the tax is paid by any other person, as the loss to the donor is not increased by the tax.

In relation to any *extra* tax payable on lifetime transfers (PETs or chargeable transfers) as a result of death, any IHT that is eventually charged will be due after the transferor's death and, irrespective of whether this IHT is collected from the donee or the personal representatives of the deceased (see [28.171]), the tax is not treated as increasing the original loss to the estate. It will not, therefore, be necessary to gross up in the computation of this extra tax. In such cases the extra tax is calculated on the original *fall in value* of the transferor's estate, according to the previous chargeable transfers of the donor. [28.125]

EXAMPLE 28.25

(1) A has made no previous chargeable transfers and has used up his annual exemptions. He gives £337,500 to discretionary trustees who agree to pay the IHT due on the chargeable transfer. A has made a chargeable transfer of £337,500. After deducting the nil rate band of £325,000, £12,500 is chargeable on the trustees at the rate of 20% (£2,500). A's estate falls in value by only £337,500. If A had paid the tax, the total tax would increase by £625 (he would have paid tax at a rate of 25% on £12,500 = £3,125). This does not mean that the tax is charged at a higher rate if A pays the tax, as we are not comparing like with like: the loss to A's estate is greater and the trust ends up with more property if he pays the tax. A further result of the trustees paying the tax is that A's cumulative total of gross chargeable transfers is lower for the purposes of future chargeable transfers, ie £337,500, rather than £340,625.

Compare

(2) If the trustees are to pay the IHT on A's gift to them and A wants them to retain a net sum of £337,500 after paying the tax, A must give a larger sum (£340,625) to enable them to pay the tax of £3,125. The result is that whether donor or donee pays the IHT, HMRC will receive £3,125 tax and the total cost to A will be the same.

4 Transferring non-cash assets the cheapest way

When the gift is of a non-cash asset such as land, IHT is calculated as before, but the question of who pays the tax and how much has to be paid will be of critical importance since neither party may have sufficient cash to pay the IHT without selling the asset. If the donor pays the IHT, the value of the gift must be grossed up. In addition, the tax must be paid in one lump sum. If, however, the donee (normally trustees on a chargeable lifetime transfer) pays the tax, there is no grossing-up so that the transfer attracts less IHT. Additionally, in the case of certain assets the tax can be paid by the donee in ten yearly instalments (IHTA 1984 s 227). If the asset is income producing, the donee may have income out of which to pay, or contribute towards, the instalments. Alternatively, the donor can fund the instalments paid by the

donee by gifts utilising his annual exemption. The assets on which IHT may be paid by instalments are:
(1) land, whether freehold or leasehold;
(2) a controlling shareholding of either quoted or unquoted shares;
(3) a minority shareholding of unquoted shares in certain circumstances (see **[30.54]**);
(4) a business or part of a business, eg a share in a partnership.

However, in the case of a transfer of land ((1) above), interest on the outstanding tax is charged when payment is made by instalments. **[28.126]**

EXAMPLE 28.26

A wants to settle his landed estate which is valued at £575,000 on discretionary trusts. A has made no previous chargeable transfers. If A pays the tax (ignoring exemptions and reliefs) the gift (£575,000) must be grossed up so that the total cost to A is £637,500 (£575,000 net gift less £325,000 nil rate band = £250,000 grossed up at 100/80 = £312,500, add back the part covered by the nil rate band ie £325,000 = £637,500). The IHT payable is £62,500; A must pay this in one lump sum. If the trust pays the tax, the £575,000 is a gross gift on which the IHT at A's rates is £50,000. Thus, there is a tax saving of £12,500. Further, the trust can pay the tax in instalments out of income from the estate.

5 Problem areas

a) *Transfers of value by instalments (IHTA 1984 s 262)*

Where a person buys property at a price greater than its market value, the excess paid will be a transfer of value (assuming that donative intent is present). If the price is payable by instalments, part of each is deemed to be a transfer of value. That part is the proportion that the overall gift element bears to the price paid. **[28.127]**

EXAMPLE 28.27

A transfers property worth £40,000 to B for £80,000 payable by B in eight equal yearly instalments of £10,000. Hence, after eight years there will be a transfer of value of £40,000 divided between each instalment as follows:

$$\text{Annual instalments} \times \frac{\text{value of gift}}{\text{price payable}} = £10,000 \times \frac{£40,000}{£8,000} = £5,000$$

b) *Transfers made on the same day (IHTA 1984 s 266)*

If a person makes more than one chargeable transfer on the same day and the order in which the transfers are made affects the overall amount of IHT payable, they are treated as made in the order which results in the least amount of IHT being payable (IHTA 1984 s 266(2)). This will be relevant where the transfers taken together straddle different rate bands and the donor does not pay the tax on all the transfers. Where this is the case the overall IHT will be less if the grossed-up gift is made first. In other cases an average rate of tax is calculated and applied to both transfers. When a PET made on the same day as a chargeable transfer is rendered chargeable by the donor's death within seven years these rules apply. [28.128]

c) *Transfers reported late (IHTA 1984 s 264)*

When a transfer is reported late (for the due date for reporting transfers, see **[28.172]**) after IHT has been paid on a subsequent transfer, tax must be paid on the earlier transfer and an adjustment may have to be made to the tax bill on the later transfer. The tax payable on the earlier transfer is calculated as at the date of that transfer and interest is payable on the outstanding tax as from the date that it was due. If there is more than seven years between the earlier and the later transfers, no adjustment need be made in respect of the later transfer since the seven-year limit on cumulation means that the later transfer is unaffected by the earlier transfer. When there is less than seven years between the two transfers the extra tax charged on the later transfer is levied on the earlier transfer in addition to the tax already due on that transfer. The recalculation problems that arise when PETs become chargeable are considered in **Chapter 30**. [28.129]

d) *Order of making lifetime transfers*

If the taxpayer wishes to make both a chargeable transfer (eg the creation of a discretionary trust) and a PET (eg a gift to a child) it is generally accepted that the chargeable transfer should be made *before* the PET. This means that even should the PET become chargeable, it does not form part of the tax calculations relative to the settlement (see **Chapter 34**). This also ensures the most efficient use of the annual exemption (see **[31.3]**). [28.130]

e) *Non-commercial loans*

There are no special charging provisions for loans of property and accordingly (subject only to IHTA 1984 s 29 which ensures that the usual exemptions and reliefs are available) tax will be charged, if at all, under general principles (ie has the loan resulted in a fall in value of the lender's estate?). In the case of money loans it is necessary to distinguish between interest-free loans repayable after a fixed term and loans repayable on demand. If A lends B £20,000 repayable in five years' time at no interest, A's estate is reduced in value because of the delay in repayment and (assuming gratuitous intent) A makes a PET equal to the difference between £20,000 and the value of the right to receive £20,000 in five years' time.

If, instead, A lent B £20,000 repayable on demand with no interest charged, A's estate either does not fall in value because it includes the immediate right to £20,000 or, alternatively, any fall is likely to be *de minimis*. Accordingly, A has not made a transfer of value and there is no question of any charge to IHT. Loans repayable on demand may be employed so that the use of property, and any future increase in its value, is transferred free from IHT to another.

If a commercial rate of interest is charged on a loan, the transaction is not a chargeable transfer since the estate of the lender will not have fallen in value.

Further, any interest may (normally) be waived without any charge to IHT by using the exemption for regular payments out of income (see **Chapter 31**).

[28.131]

EXAMPLE 28.28

Jasmine benefits her children without attracting a potential liability to IHT as follows:
(1) She lends her daughter £100,000 repayable on demand. The money is invested in a small terraced house in Fulham which quickly trebles in value. That increase in value belongs to the daughter who is merely obliged to repay the original sum loaned if and when Jasmine demands it.
(2) She allows her son to occupy her London flat rent free. The son enjoys the benefit of living there during the winter and lets the property to wealthy summer visitors. As there is no loss to Jasmine's estate the son's benefits are not subject to IHT (but note in such cases the possibility of an income tax charge under Settlement Provisions in Income Tax (Trading and Other Income) Act (ITTOIA 2005)): see **Chapter 16**).

f) *Relief against a double charge to IHT*

In a number of situations there is the possibility of a double charge to IHT:

EXAMPLE 28.29

Gustavus gives Adolphus his rare Swedish bible (a PET). Two years later the bible is given back to Gustavus who dies shortly afterwards. As a result of his death within seven years the original gift of the bible is chargeable and, in addition, Gustavus' estate on death, which is subject to IHT, includes the bible.

Regulations made under FA 1986 s 104 provide a measure of relief and are discussed in **Chapter 36**. [28.132]–[28.150]

VII SPECIAL RULES FOR CLOSE COMPANIES

Only transfers of value made by *individuals* are chargeable to IHT (IHTA 1984 s 2(1)). An individual could, therefore, avoid IHT by forming a close company and using that company to make a gift to the intended donee, or a controlling shareholder in a close company could alter the capital structure of the company or the rights attached to his shares, so as to reduce the value of his shareholding in favour of the intended donee.

EXAMPLE 28.30

(1) A transfers assets worth £100,000 to A Ltd in return for shares worth £100,000. A's estate does not fall in value so that there is no liability to IHT. The company then gives one of the assets (worth £50,000) to A's son B. The company and not A has made a transfer of value.

(2) A Ltd has an issued share capital of £100 all in ordinary £1 shares owned by A. The company is worth £100,000. The company resolves:
 (i) to convert A's shares into non-voting preference shares carrying only the right to a repayment of nominal value on a winding up;
 (ii) to issue to B a further 100 £1 ordinary shares at par value.
The result is that the value has passed out of A's shares without any disposition by A.

IHTA 1984 Part IV contains (*inter alia*) provisions designed to prevent an individual from using a close company to obtain a tax advantage in either of these ways. For these purposes 'close company' and 'participator' have their corporation tax meaning (see **Chapter 41**) except that a close company includes a non-UK resident company which would be close if it was resident in the UK and participator does not include a loan creditor (IHTA 1984 s 102).

[28.151]

1 Transfers of value by close companies (IHTA 1984 s 94)

When a close company makes a transfer of value, it is apportioned amongst the participators in proportion to their interests in the company, so that they are treated as having made the transfer ('lifting the veil') (IHTA 1984 s 94(1)). Thus, in *Example 28.30(1)* above, assuming A is the only shareholder in A Ltd, he is treated as having made a transfer of value of £50,000. For s 94(1) to apply the company must have made a transfer of value, ie its assets must fall in value by virtue of a non-commercial transaction (IHTA 1984 s 10(1)). The value apportioned to each participator is treated as a net amount which must be grossed up at the participator's rate of IHT. Any participator whose estate has increased in value as a result of that transfer can deduct the increase from the net amount (ignoring the effect that the transfer may have had on his rights in the company). The transfer in these circumstances is a deemed transfer of value and cannot be a PET (see **[28.48]**). IHT is therefore chargeable.

EXAMPLE 28.31

A Ltd is owned as to 75% of the shares by A and 25% by B. It transfers land worth £100,000 to A. By IHTA 1984 s 94, A and B are treated as having made net transfers of value of £75,000 and £25,000 respectively. B will be charged to IHT on £25,000 grossed up at his rate of IHT. A, however, can deduct the increase in his estate (£100,000) from the net amount of the apportionment (£75,000), so that he pays no IHT. If A's shares (and B's) have diminished in value, that decrease is ignored.

Apportionment is not always as obvious as it may seem. For instance, in calculating a participator's interest in the company, the ownership of preference shares is usually disregarded (IHTA 1984 s 96). Further, where trustees are participators and the interest in the company is held in a settlement subject to the interest in possession regime (see **Chapter 33**), the apportioned amount is taxed as a reduction in the value of the life tenant's estate (IHTA 1984 s 99(2)(a)). In trusts subject to the relevant property regime, the apportioned amount is taxed as a payment out of the settled property by the trustees (IHTA 1984 s 99(2)(b)). Finally, where a close company is itself a participator in another close company any apportionment is then sub-apportioned to its own participators (IHTA 1984 s 95).

In two cases no apportionment occurs. *First*, if the transfer is charged to income tax or corporation tax in the donee's hands, there is no IHT liability (IHTA 1984 s 94(2)(a)). *Second*, where a participator is domiciled abroad, any apportionment made to him as a result of a transfer by a close company of property situated abroad is not charged to IHT (IHTA 1984 s 94(2)(b)).

EXAMPLE 28.32

(1) A Ltd (whose shares are owned 50% by A and 50% by B) pays a dividend. The dividend is not chargeable to IHT in A or B's hands because income tax is charged on that sum under ITTOIA 2005 Part 4 Chapter 3 (tax on dividends and other distributions).

(2) A Ltd in (1) above provides A with free living accommodation and pays all the outgoings on the property. If A is a director or employee of A Ltd, these items are benefits in kind on which A pays income tax under ITEPA 2003 (earnings income) (see **Chapter 8**). If A is merely a shareholder in the company these payments are treated as a distribution by A Ltd and are charged to income tax in A's hands under ITTOIA 2005 Part 4 Chapter 3 (tax on dividends and other distributions). However, if A was not a member of A Ltd, there would be no income tax liability, so that the participator, B, would be treated for IHT purposes as having made a chargeable transfer of value under IHTA 1984 s 94(1).

(3) An English company, A Ltd, in which B and C each own 50% of the shares, gives a factory in France worth £100,000 to B, who is domiciled in the UK. C is domiciled in France and, therefore, the amount apportioned to him (£50,000) is not chargeable under IHTA 1984 s 94(1).

Participators can reduce their IHT liability on sums apportioned by the usual lifetime exemptions with the exception of the small gifts exemption and the exemption for gifts on marriage. In so far as the transfer by the company is to a charity or political party it is exempt. Participators are also entitled to 100% business relief if the close company transfers part of its business or shares in a trading subsidiary.

The company is primarily liable for the tax. If it fails to pay, secondary liability rests concurrently with the participators and beneficiaries of the transfer. A participator's liability is limited to tax on the amount apportioned to him; for a non-participator beneficiary it is limited to the increase in value of his estate. [28.152]

2 Deemed dispositions by participators (IHTA 1984 s 98)

When value is drained out of shares in a close company by an alteration (including extinguishment) of the share capital or by an alteration in the rights attached to shares, this is treated as a deemed disposition by the participators although the section does not deem a transfer of value to have been made. When such a transfer occurs, liability under IHTA 1984 s 98 rests solely on the participators and not on the company. There is no deemed transfer of value under s 98, but such transfers are expressly prevented from being PETs by IHTA 1984 s 98(3) (see *Example 28.33*(3) below). [28.153]–[28.170]

EXAMPLE 28.33

(1) Taking the facts of *Example 28.30*(2) above there is no actual transfer of value by A or A Ltd. However, under IHTA 1984 s 98 there is a deemed disposition by A equivalent to the fall in value of his shareholding. From owning all the shares and effectively all the assets he is left with a holding of 100 shares worth (probably) only their face value.

(2) A owns 60% and B 40% of the shares in A Ltd. Each share carries one vote. The articles of association of the company are altered so that A's shares continue to carry one vote, but B's shares are to carry three votes each. There is a deemed disposition by A to B equivalent to the drop in value in A's estate resulting from his loss of control of A Ltd.

(3) Zebadee, the sole shareholder in Zebadee Ltd, arranges for a bonus issue of fully paid preference shares which carry the right to a fixed dividend. He retains the shares but gives his valuable ordinary shares to his daughter. This familiar tax planning rearrangement depends in part upon the gift of the ordinary shares being a PET. Under s 98(1) the alteration in the share structure is treated as a disposition by Zebadee but as the bonus shares are at that stage issued to him, he does not then make any transfer of value. Accordingly, the subsequent gift of the ordinary shares will be a PET. It is thought that HMRC will not normally seek to argue that the bonus issue and later gift are associated operations falling within s 98(1) as an extended reorganisation (so that the gift of the shares is not prevented from being a PET by s 98(3)).

VIII LIABILITY, ACCOUNTABILITY AND BURDEN

1 Liability for IHT (IHTA 1984 Part VII)

The person primarily liable for IHT on a chargeable lifetime transfer is the transferor (IHTA 1984 s 199), although in certain cases, his spouse may be held liable as a transferor to prevent him from divesting himself of property to that spouse so that he is then unable to meet an IHT bill (IHTA 1984 s 203).

EXAMPLE 28.34

H makes a gross chargeable transfer to a discretionary trust of £1m and fails to pay IHT. He later transfers property worth £50,000 to his wife W which is exempt (inter-spouse). W can be held liable for H's IHT not exceeding £50,000.

If HMRC cannot collect the tax from the transferor (or his spouse) it can then claim it, subject to specified limits, from one of the following:

(1) The transferee, ie any person whose estate has increased in value as a result of the transfer. Liability is restricted to tax (at the transferor's rates) on the value of the gross transfer after deducting any unpaid tax.

EXAMPLE 28.35

A makes a *gross* chargeable transfer to discretionary trustees of £40,000 on which IHT at A's rate of 20% is £8,000. A emigrates without paying the tax. HMRC can only claim £6,400 in tax from the trustees, ie:

	£
Gross chargeable transfer by A	40,000
Less: unpaid tax	8,000
Revised value transferred	£32,000
Trustees are liable for IHT at 20%	£6,400

(2) Any person in whom the property has become vested after the transfer. This category includes a person to whom the transferee has in turn transferred the property; or, if the property has been settled, the trustees of the settlement and any beneficiary with an interest in possession in it; or a purchaser of the property unless he is a *bona fide* purchaser for money or money's worth and the property is not subject to an HMRC charge. The liability of these persons is limited to tax on the net transfer only and liability is further limited, in the case of trustees and beneficiaries, to the value of the settled property and, in the case of a purchaser, to the value of the property. Also included within this category is any person who meddles with property so as to constitute himself a *trustee de son tort* and any person who manages the property on behalf of a person under a disability.

(3) A beneficiary under a discretionary trust of the property to the extent that he receives income or any benefit from the trust. Liability is limited to the amount of his benefit after payment of any income tax.

The liability to pay additional IHT on a gift because of the transferor's death within seven years, and liability to tax on a PET which becomes a chargeable transfer is considered at **[30.28]**.

Quite apart from those persons from whom they can claim tax, HMRC has a charge for unpaid tax on the property transferred and on settled property where the liability arose on the making of the settlement or on a chargeable transfer of it (IHTA 1984 s 237). The charge takes effect in the same way as on death (see **Chapter 30**) except that for lifetime transfers it extends to personal property also. It will not bind a purchaser of land unless the charge is registered and in the case of personal property unless the purchaser has notice of the facts giving rise to the charge (IHTA 1984 s 238). There is no charge on heritable property in Scotland (IHTA 1984 s 237(4)).

Once an account has been submitted and IHT on a chargeable transfer has been paid and accepted by HMRC, liability for any further tax ceases four years after the later of the date when the tax was paid or the date when it became due (IHTA 1984 s 240(2)). However, if HMRC can prove that a loss of tax was caused by either the carelessness of the person liable for the tax (or his agent), or deliberately, this period is extended to six years and 20 years respectively (IHTA 1984 s 240(4) and (5)) If no account has been submitted, the period is 20 years from the date of the transfer. When HMRC is satisfied that tax has been or will be paid, it may, at the request of a person liable for the tax, issue a certificate discharging persons and/or property from further liability (IHTA 1984 s 239). **[28.171]**

2 Accountability and payment

a) *Duty to report*

An account should only be delivered in respect of a chargeable transfer which is not a PET: in the case of PETs an account is only required if the transferor dies within seven years (IHTA 1984 s 216). HMRC need not be notified of a transfer of excluded property or of a transfer that is wholly exempt (eg within the annual exemption or inter-spouse).

In addition, in certain situations chargeable transfers are 'excepted' from the duty to account (SI 2008/605):
(1) where the gift is of cash and/or quoted shares by an individual and, together with previous chargeable transfers in the last seven years, the gift does not exceed the nil rate band;
(2) where the gift is of assets other than cash or quoted shares, together with previous chargeable transfers in the last seven years it must not exceed 80% of the nil rate band.

Similar rules apply where the value is transferred on the termination of certain interests in possession in settled property (a pre 2006 interest, an IPDI, a TSI, a bereaved minor trust or an interest in a trust for the disabled – see **Chapter 32**). (There are also exempting regulations for 'excepted settlements': see SI 2008/606 and **[34.21]**.)

When the transfer is by a close company, nobody is under a duty to account, but in practice the company should do so in order to avoid a charge to interest on unpaid tax.

As a general rule, the person who is primarily liable for the IHT must deliver the account (ie the transferor in the case of a lifetime chargeable gift).

Form IHT 100 is used for all lifetime transfers including transfers of settled property on life or death with an interest in possession.

The account must be delivered within 12 months from the end of the month when the transfer was made, or within three months from the date when that person first became liable to pay IHT (if later). In practice, the account should be delivered earlier, since the tax is due before this date. Trustees of a relevant property trust must both report a chargeable event and pay the tax six months after the chargeable event.

Once death has taken place, there may be a duty on both the donees and the PRs to report lifetime payments within seven years of death and to account for tax on these. This is covered at **[30.28]**.) **[28.172]**

b) *Payment of tax*

For all lifetime chargeable transfers of unsettled property made between 6 April and 30 September, the tax is due on 30 April following and for transfers made between 1 October and 5 April it is due six months from the end of the month when the transfer was made (IHTA 1984 s 226). The optimum date to make a chargeable transfer is therefore 6 April which gives a 12-month delay before tax is due. Where trust tax is due on a chargeable event, as noted at [28.172], it is due 6 months after the chargeable event. [28.173]

Payment by instalments Generally IHT must be paid in one lump sum. IHTA 1984 s 212 provides that any person liable for the tax (except the transferor and his spouse) can sell, mortgage or charge the property even if it is not vested in him, so that if, for instance, A gives property to B who settles it on C for life, either B, the trustees, or C (if called upon to pay the tax) can sell, mortgage or charge the property in order to do so.

As an exception to the general rule, if the transferee pays the IHT he can elect in the case of certain assets to pay the tax in ten yearly instalments; the first becoming due when the tax is due (IHTA 1984 s 227). This lifetime instalment option is available for the same assets as on death (see [**30.51**]), except for the transfer of a minority holding of unquoted shares or securities within category (4) (relief when the IHT on instalment property amounts to 20% of the total bill). Trustees or beneficiaries who are liable for the tax on transfers of settled property can elect to pay in instalments provided that the property falls within one of the specified classes. Despite this election, the outstanding tax (and any interest due) may be paid at any time and if the relevant property is sold or transferred by a chargeable transfer the tax must be paid at once (IHTA 1984 s 227(4)). [28.174]

Interest Interest is charged on any tax which is not paid by the due date (IHTA 1984 s 233). Where the tax is to be paid by instalments, interest is charged on overdue instalments only, except in the case of land where interest is charged on all the outstanding tax. [28.175]

Satisfaction of tax HMRC has a discretion to accept certain property in satisfaction of tax (see IHTA 1984 s 230 and **Chapter 31**). [28.176]

Adjustments to the tax bill Subject to the limitation periods (see [28.171]) if HMRC proves that too little tax was paid in respect of a chargeable transfer, tax underpaid is payable together with interest. Conversely, if too much tax was paid, HMRC must refund the excess together with interest, which is free of income tax in the recipient's hands (IHTA 1984 s 235). [28.177]

3 Burden of tax

The question of who, as between the transferor and the transferee, should bear the tax on a lifetime transfer is a matter for the parties to decide as discussed above. The decision may affect the amount of tax payable (see [**28.125**]). The parties can agree at any time before the tax becomes due and HMRC will accept their decision so long as the tax is paid. However, the agreement does not affect the liability of the parties, so that if the tax remains unpaid, HMRC can collect it from persons liable under Part VII of the legislation (see [28.171]). [28.178]–[28.200]

IX ADMINISTRATION AND APPEALS

1 Calculation of liability

IHT is not assessed by reference to the tax year. Instead, when HMRC is informed of a chargeable transfer of value it raises an assessment called a determination (IHTA 1984 s 221). If it is not satisfied with an account or if none is delivered when it suspects that a chargeable transfer has occurred, it can raise a 'best of judgment' or estimated determination of the tax due. A determination of IHT liability is conclusive against the transferor and for all subsequent transfers, failing a written agreement with HMRC to the contrary or an appeal. [28.201]

2 Penalties

Inheritance tax has been brought within the unified penalty regime contained in FA 2008 Sch 36 (see [4.25] ff). [28.202]–[28.220]

3 Appeals

If the taxpayer disputes the determination he can appeal to the First-tier Tribunal (Tax) within 30 days (IHTA 1984 s 222), and from there to the Finance and Tax Chamber of the Upper Tribunal. Appeals substantially confined to an issue of law may go straight to the Upper Tribunal (with leave and with the consent of both parties). Appeal then lies in the usual way to the Court of Appeal or Court of Session and, with leave, to the Supreme Court (or by the 'leap frog' procedure direct to the Supreme Court). The disputed tax is not payable at the first stage of the appeal (IHTA 1984 s 242). However, if there is a further appeal, the tax becomes payable; if this appeal is then successful, the tax must be repaid with interest. [28.221]–[28.230]

X TIMING OF DISPOSALS

Obviously the timing of a disposal can be of critical importance, for example in determining whether seven years have passed before death, for the purposes of taper relief and for the purposes of allocating the annual exemption. Whilst on death, the deceased is deemed to have made a transfer of the estate immediately before his death by virtue of IHTA 1984 s 4, there is no statutory rule for lifetime transfers, so recourse must be made to general law to determine when the transfer of value takes place.

In most cases, where there is a gift of corporeal property involved, it will be the date that the gift was completed, which will normally be the date of the deed of gift or trust or delivery of the property, whichever is relevant. In relation to sums of money gifted by cheque, the date that the cheque clears is the relevant date rather than the handing over of the cheque, as the gift is revocable until clearing has taken place (*Curnock v IRC* (2003)).

In relation to immoveable or heritable property, where the property is by way of gift the relevant date in England and Wales, is the execution of the formal transfer, conveyance or assignment of the property or of a declaration of trust evidenced by writing (Law of Property Act 1925 s 53(1)(b)). In Scotland, the view of HMRC was that the relevant date was the date of registration of the disposition in favour of the donee, as this is when the ownership in the property passes. However, in *Marquess of Linlithgow v R & C Comrs* (2010) the Court of Session decided that this view was incorrect and that the relevant date is the date of delivery of the disposition. At this point, even though the transferor remains legal owner of the property until registration takes place, personal rights in the property have been transferred and this is sufficient to constitute a transfer of value. [28.231]

29 IHT – reservation of benefit

Updated by Sandra Eden, Senior Lecturer, University of Edinburgh

I   Legislative history [29.1]
II IHT consequences if property is subject to a reservation [29.21]
III When do the reservation rules apply? [29.41]
IV Exceptions – when the rules do not apply [29.71]
V   Identifying property subject to a reservation [29.101]
VI Reserving benefits after FA 1986 [29.121]
VII Pre-owned assets [29.142]
VIII Liability to account for tax on a gift with reservation [29.146]

I LEGISLATIVE HISTORY

It was possible, under the CTT regime, for taxpayers to give away property but at the same time retain the benefit and control of it. Typical arrangements included:

EXAMPLE 29.1
(1) Joe creates a discretionary trust and includes himself amongst the beneficiaries.
(2) Arty owns a fine Constable landscape. He transfers legal ownership to his daughter by deed of gift but the picture remains firmly hanging up in his house until his death.
(3) Sam gives his Norfolk farm to his son and continues to live in the farmhouse.

These arrangements were ideal for the moderately wealthy since, although the original transfer might attract tax (to the extent that it was not covered by the annual exemption and the nil rate band) future increases in value of the gifted property occurred outside the transferor's estate whilst, should the need arise (and especially if the property was settled as in *Example 29.1(1)*), the property could be recovered by the transferor. The widespread use of such arrangements made it likely that they would be attacked by legislation and the switch from CTT to IHT, which included the introduction of PETs, made this inevitable. Accordingly, provisions were introduced to deal with property subject to a reservation (see FA 1986 s 102 and Sch 20) which apply to lifetime gifts made on or after 18 March 1986.

916   *IHT – reservation of benefit*

The legislation is closely based on earlier estate duty provisions and the estate duty authorities remain relevant in construing the legislation (as was confirmed in the *Ingram* case which is considered below).   **[29.1]–[29.20]**

II   IHT CONSEQUENCES IF PROPERTY IS SUBJECT TO A RESERVATION

A gift of property subject to a reservation is treated, so far as the donor is concerned, as a partial nullity for IHT purposes. This is because he is deemed to remain beneficially entitled to the gifted property immediately before his death. It is clear from the wording of s 102(3) that the property only returns into the estate of the donor at this moment although, if the benefit reserved ceases during the lifetime of the donor, he is treated as making a PET of the property at that time (a deemed PET). No advantage therefore flows from releasing any reserved benefit just before death. Possible double charges to IHT in this area are dealt with in the regulations discussed in **Chapter 36**. It should be remembered that the reservation of benefit rules only apply to the donor for the purposes of IHT; accordingly, although the property may be taxed as part of the death estate of the donor, there is no question of such property benefiting from the CGT uplift on death. Further, the property is also comprised in the estate of the donee so that IHT charges can arise on his death.

The legislation is widely drafted to catch a benefit reserved in the gifted property itself and a 'collateral advantage' (defined in s 102(1)(b) as 'any benefit to [the donor] by contract or otherwise').

EXAMPLE 29.2

(1)   In 2012 A gives his daughter his country cottage (then worth £50,000) in return for an annuity of £500 pa payable for the next four years. The annuity ends in 2016 and A dies in 2017. By stipulating for the payment of an annuity A reserved a benefit.
  (i)   *The original transfer:* In 2012 was a PET. The value transferred was reduced because of A's annuity entitlement.
  (ii) *On the ending of the annuity in 2016:* A made a PET equal to the then value of the cottage. (Note that because this was a 'deemed' PET the value transferred is not reduced by A's annual exemption.)
  (iii) *With his death in 2017* both the earlier transfers became chargeable.
(2)   Had A died in 2013 the reservation would have been operative at his death so that, in addition to the 2012 PET being chargeable, the value of the cottage in 2012 would have formed part of his death estate.
      For relief against a double IHT charge, see **Chapter 36**.
(3)   Zac gives his house to Jim and they live in it together. Unless Zac pays Jim full market rent (see **[29.72]**) the gift is caught by the reservation of benefit rules so that:
  (a)   on Zac's death the house will be taxed as part of his estate. There will be no CGT death uplift;
  (b)   on Jim's death, because he owns the house, it will be taxed as part of his estate with the usual CGT uplift.

As a result of including the property in the deceased's estate immediately before death, it is necessary to value it at that time (and not at the time of the gift). Hence, where a transferor makes a gift with reservation there is no 'asset freezing' advantage. It also follows, of course, that as the value of the property swells the size of the estate, it may increase the estate rate of IHT (see [**30.29**] for 'estate rate') that is charged on the rest of the estate. Primary liability to pay the IHT attributable to reservation property lies with the donee (who should submit an account within 12 months of the end of the month of death) although the donor's PRs are liable if tax remains unpaid at the end of 12 months from the death. PRs who have made a final distribution of the assets in the estate may therefore be faced with a wholly unexpected claim for more IHT and this matter is considered in detail at [**30.49**]. As already noted, although the gifted property is included in the estate for IHT purposes it does *not* form part of the estate otherwise and hence does not benefit from the CGT uplift on death with the result that the donee may be faced with a substantial CGT liability on selling the property. [**29.21**]–[**29.40**]

III WHEN DO THE RESERVATION RULES APPLY?

1 There must be disposal of property by way of gift

To base liability on the making of a gift does not fit in with the general scheme of the IHT legislation which bases the tax charge upon chargeable transfers of value (see [**28.2**]). The resultant difficulties perfectly illustrate the problems of attempting to weld legislation from estate duty onto the CTT structure. Obviously, the gift must have been completed (and it should be remembered that the courts have no general power to perfect an uncompleted gift: see *Milroy v Lord* (1862)) but it may be assumed that the reservation provisions apply not just to pure gifts but also to the situation where, although partial consideration is furnished, there is still an element of bounty (see *A-G v Johnson* (1903)). A bad bargain, on the other hand, lacks any element of gift. The distinction between a gift (the basis of the reservation rules) and a transfer of value (the basis for IHT liability) is illustrated in the following example: [**29.41**]

EXAMPLE 29.3

(1) Adam owns a pair of Constable watercolours and sells one to his daughter, Jemima. He retains possession of the picture. Each picture is worth £10,000: as a pair they are worth £35,000. Jemima pays Adam £10,000 for the picture.
   (i) There is a *transfer of value* of £15,000 (drop in value of Adam's estate). This transfer is a PET (see [**28.42**]).
   (ii) Is there a *gift* of property so that the reservation rules apply? As Jemima has paid full value for the picture that she has acquired there is no element of gift, so the rules are inapplicable.
(2) Before 22 March 2006, Sam settles property on trust retaining the right to income until he is aged 50 with the remainder being settled on discretionary trusts for his family (including Sam). Assume that the trustees have the power to terminate Sam's life interest which they exercise six months after the creation of the trust.
   (i) There is no *transfer of value* when Sam creates the settlement since he was the life tenant (IHTA 1984 s 49(1)).
   (ii) Does Sam, however, make a gift at the time when he sets up the trust? Arguably, on general principles, he does: after all he has given property

to trustees reserving only a life interest. If this is correct then once that life interest ends he will be caught by the reservation rules given that he is one of the discretionary beneficiaries.

(iii) When his life interest terminates Sam makes a chargeable *transfer of value* but does not make a *gift* (contrast the position if he had voluntarily surrendered his interest). With the cessation of the life interest the fund is now held on discretionary trusts and (see (ii) above) may be property subject to a reservation (FA 1986 Sch 20 para 5(1)).

An asset, purchased with a gift of cash, from which the donor receives a benefit is not subject to the reservation of benefit rules, although this may be subject to the pre-owned asset regime (see [**29.142**]).

2 Possession and enjoyment of the property by the donee

The reservation rules apply if full possession and enjoyment of the gifted property is not enjoyed by the donee either at or before the beginning of the *relevant period*. For this purpose the relevant period is the period ending with the donor's death and beginning either seven years before that date or (if later) on the date of the gift. [**29.42**]

EXAMPLE 29.4

(1) By deed of gift A gives B the family silver but he retains it locked in a cupboard till his death; *or*

(2) A gives full possession and enjoyment of the family silver to B and dies two years later; *or*

(3) Assume in (1) above that the deed of gift was made in 2002 but that A only hands over the silver in 2008 and dies in 2017; *or*

(4) A gives the family silver to B in 2002 but borrows it back just before his death in 2017.

In (1) possession of the silver is never enjoyed by B so that there is a gift with reservation and the silver forms part of A's estate on death.

In (2) full possession and enjoyment is obtained at the beginning of the relevant period. (Hence no reservation although there is, of course, a failed PET.)

In (3) full possession and enjoyment is obtained more than seven years before death. (No reservation.)

In (4) although full possession and enjoyment was given to B, the return of the silver to A is fatal because of the next requirement.

3 Exclusion of donor from benefit

The reservation rules also apply if the donor has not been excluded from benefit *at any time* during the relevant period. In *Example 29.4(4)* the return of the silver shortly before the donor's death results in the property being subject to a reservation at A's death and, accordingly, it is subject to IHT. [**29.43**]

EXAMPLE 29.5

In 1924 the taxpayer created a settlement for the benefit of his infant daughter contingent upon her attaining 30. He was wholly excluded from benefit. In 1938 (just before she became 30) he arranged with her to borrow the income from the trust fund in order to reduce his overdraft. Until 1943 he borrowed virtually all the income: he finally died in 1946 (see *Stamp Duties Comr of New South Wales v Permanent Trustee Co* (1956)). On these facts the Privy Council held that a benefit had been reserved for estate duty purposes and the same would be true for IHT. Notice that the settlor had no enforceable right to the income: he merely made an arrangement with his daughter that she could have revoked at any time.

4 The two limbs

The requirement that the donor must be excluded from all benefit during the relevant period is comprised in two alternative limbs. Limb I requires his exclusion from the gifted property, whilst Limb II stipulates that he should not have received any benefit 'by contract or otherwise'.

So far as Limb I is concerned, in order to determine whether the donor has been entirely excluded from the gifted property, it is necessary to decide what that property comprises. There is a distinction of some subtlety between keeping back rights in the property (ie making only a partial gift) and giving the entire property but receiving a subsequent benefit therein from the donee (but note the limitations on this principle in the case of land resulting from FA 1999: see **[29.130]**). Once the gift is correctly identified, the donor must be entirely excluded both in law and in fact (see *Example 29.5*).

EXAMPLE 29.6

A father owned two properties on which an informal farming partnership was carried on with his son. Profits were split two-thirds to the father, one-third to the son. The father gave one of the properties to his son, free of all conditions, so that the son could have farmed it independently. In fact both continued to farm the property sharing the profits equally. It was held that the father had not been entirely excluded from the gifted property (*Stamp Duties Comr of New South Wales v Owens* (1953)).

Limb II, that the donor must be excluded from any benefit by contract or otherwise, is sufficiently widely drafted to catch collateral benefits that do not take effect out of the gifted property.

EXAMPLE 29.7

(1) Charlie gives land in Sussex to his son Jasper who covenants, at the same time, to pay Charlie an annuity of £500 pa for the rest of his life. The land is property subject to a reservation (cp *A-G v Worrall* (1895): '... it is not necessary that the benefit to the donor should be by way of reservation' *per* Lopes LJ).

(2) Adam sells his farm to Bertram for £100,000 when its true value is £500,000. As a sale at undervalue there is an element of gift. However, it is not easy to see how there can be a benefit reserved. The estate duty cases do not go this far and even if it is accepted that there is a reserved benefit, it presumably ceases at the moment when the £100,000 is paid to Adam with the result that there may be a deemed PET on that date. Accordingly, the somewhat absurd result is that on the same day there would be a PET of £400,000 (value of farm less consideration received) and a further PET of £500,000 (value of

property in which the reservation has ceased). It is understood that HMRC will *not* argue that on these facts there is a benefit reserved.

(3) Claude wishes to give his farm to his son Dada subject to Dada taking over the existing mortgage thereon. If the arrangement is structured in this manner, the provision for the discharge of his mortgage would appear to result in Claude reserving a benefit. However, HMRC has commented, with reference to this example, that 'the gift would be the farm subject to the mortgage and it would be an outright gift'. Were he to sell the farm for the amount of the outstanding mortgage that sale for partial consideration is not thought to involve a reservation (see (2) above); Dada could raise a mortgage on the security of the land; Claude would pay off his existing mortgage and any capital gain resulting from the consideration received (the gift element is subject to the hold-over election under TCGA 1992 s 165). Note also the stamp duty land tax implications: see FA 2003 Sch 4 para 8.

Although the benefit need not come from the gifted property itself, it must be reserved as part of a linked transaction: a purely accidental benefit in no way connected with an earlier gift is ignored. In determining whether there is such a connection, account must be taken of any associated operations (see FA 1986 Sch 20 para 6(1)(c) incorporating for these purposes IHTA 1984 s 268: see [**28.101**]).

Limb II is concerned with benefits reserved 'by contract *or otherwise*'. According to estate duty authority these words should be construed *eiusdem generis* with contract and, therefore, as requiring a legally enforceable obligation (see the unsatisfactory case of *A-G v Seccombe* (1911)). It seems most unlikely that courts today would permit obligations binding in honour only to slip through this net, however, and the statutory associated operations rule (discussed above) is couched in terms of conduct (ie what actually happened) not of legal obligation. Not surprisingly, HMRC has confirmed that 'for IHT purposes [the words 'or otherwise'] should be given a wider meaning than they had for estate duty'.

A further refinement of the second limb took place in *Buzzoni v R & C Comrs* (2013), to the effect that even where there is a benefit to the donor, the reservation rules do not bite unless that benefit impacts on the donee's enjoyment of the property. In *Buzzoni*, a long leaseholder granted a reversionary sub-lease to a trust in 1997. The subtenants undertook certain covenants in favour of the leaseholder, inter alia indemnifying the leaseholder against any service charges she was required to pay to the landlord. This was determined to be a benefit which she had reserved out of the gift – the taxpayer's argument that any benefit was separate from the gift rather than reserved out of the gift failed. However, the Court of Appeal found that the second limb, which looks to the enjoyment of the property to the exclusion of the donor, required more than consideration of the donor's position alone. In addition, it must be asked whether the donor's reservation impacts on the *donee's* enjoyment of the property. Under normal circumstances, a reservation would usually have this effect, but in *Buzzoni*, the subtenants had not only bound themselves to the covenants in the lease in the underlease, they had separately obliged themselves to observe and perform the same covenants in the Licence to Underlet, entered into with the owners of the property. This meant that the benefit the donor had reserved in the sublease made no difference to the subtenants because they were subject to exactly the same obligations by virtue of the Licence to Underlet. Any benefit to the donor was not at the expense of the donee.

Buzzoni was subsequently distinguished by the First-tier Tribunal in *Hood v R & C Comrs* (2016). In *Buzzoni* the subtenants had directly undertaken the lease obligations with the headlessor so the fact that they also relieved the donor of the obligations did not affect the subtenants' enjoyment of the property. In contrast, in *Hood* the subtenants undertook no obligations directly with the headlessor, so their undertaking to relieve the sublessor of her obligations to the headlessor did affect their enjoyment of the property, and a gift with reservation was found to exist. **[29.44]–[29.70]**

IV EXCEPTIONS – WHEN THE RULES DO NOT APPLY

1 De minimis

Certain benefits to the donor are specifically ignored. FA 1986 s 102(1) requires the entire exclusion or *virtually* the entire exclusion of the donor from the gifted property. 'Virtually the entire exclusion' had no predecessor in the estate duty legislation and is apparently designed to cover, for instance, occasional visits by the donor to a house which he had earlier given away (including short holidays! For HMRC's views on this matter see IHTM 14333). The covenant of the sub-tenant to pay £9,000 in respect of service charges to the over-landlord, thus relieving the tenant's obligation to pay, was regarded as 'far from a nominal amount' by the First-tier Tribunal in *Buzzoni v R & C Comrs* (2011) (overturned on different grounds by the Court of Appeal (see **[29.44]–[29.70]**). **[29.71]**

2 Full consideration

A second exclusion is available where the donor furnishes full consideration for the benefit enjoyed (FA 1986 Sch 20 para 6(1)(a) and ss 102A(3), 102B(3)(b)). The consideration must be 'full' throughout the donor's period of use – hence rent review clauses should be included in any letting agreement. The gifted property, however, must be an interest in land or a chattel and to come within the exclusion actual occupation, enjoyment or possession of that property must have been resumed by the donor (see *Example 29.8*). **[29.72]**

EXAMPLE 29.8

(1) Gift of land but donor is subsequently given shooting/fishing rights or rights to take timber. So long as full (not partial) consideration is furnished there is *no reservation* of benefit.

(2) Gift of Ming vase – returned to donor in return for the payment of full rent. *No reservation.*

(3) As in (1) save that donor sub-lets his rights. *Outside Sch 20 para 6(1)(a)* since actual enjoyment is not resumed and therefore there is a reservation of benefit.

(4) Gift of shares: donor continues to enjoy dividends and pays full value for that right. *Outside Sch 20 para 6(1)(a)* since the property in question is neither land nor chattels. Hence a benefit is reserved.

3 Hardship

Additionally, a benefit may be ignored on hardship grounds but this provision is restrictive and is concerned solely with the occupation of gifted land by a donor whose circumstances have changed since the original gift and who has become unable to maintain himself for reasons of old age or infirmity. Further, the donee must be related to the donor (or his spouse) and the provision of occupation must represent reasonable provision for the care and maintenance of the donor (FA 1986 Sch 20 para 6(1)(b) and see s 102C(3)).

[29.73]–[29.100]

V IDENTIFYING PROPERTY SUBJECT TO A RESERVATION

FA 1986 Sch 20 paras 1–5 contain complex tracing rules for identifying property subject to a reservation and make provision, in particular, for: what happens if the donee ceases to have possession and enjoyment of the property, whether by sale or gift; for the effect of changes in the structure of bodies corporate when the original gift was of shares or securities; for the position if the donee predeceases the donor; and, finally, for the effect of changes in the nature of the property when the original gift was settled. The rules distinguish between settled and unsettled gifts and, in the latter case, gifts of cash are not traced through to any property bought with that cash.

When property subject to the reservation qualified for agricultural or business relief at the date of the gift that relief may also be available if IHT would otherwise be charged because of the retained benefit (see [31.60]).

The case of *Sillars v IRC* (2004) concerned a deposit account held in the joint names of the deceased and her two daughters. The daughters each regarded one-third of the balance in the account as theirs. When the deceased died, the deceased's share in the account was returned as a one-third share. HMRC contended that the whole balance of the account fell within the deceased's estate because the account was property where the deceased had a general power or authority enabling her to appoint or dispose of the property as she thought fit (IHTA 1984 s 5(2)). Alternatively, that the deceased had reserved a benefit in the account because the daughters did not have possession and enjoyment of the account and because the deceased was not excluded from benefit. The Special Commissioner held that the deceased did have a general power to dispose of the balance of the account as she thought fit. The property was therefore within her estate for IHTA 1984 s 5(2) purposes. Alternatively, the deceased had reserved a benefit in the account because the deceased was not excluded from benefiting from the account and the daughters had not assumed possession or enjoyment of the account. The deceased's gift was a gift of a chose in action of the whole account and not just of two-thirds of the initial balance.

This case was followed in *Perry v IRC* (2005) and *Matthews v IRC* (2012). However, in each of these cases, the deceased had provided all the funds in the account. HMRC indicate in their notes to the form IHT205 that the full amount of the bank account should only be included where the deceased was the sole contributor. If the deceased did not contribute at all, or was only a partial contributor, either nothing, or a reduced amount, should be included on the form. This is clearly correct in the context of the reservation of benefit rules, although perhaps dubious in the context of beneficial entitlement – see [30.2]. [29.101]–[29.120]

VI RESERVING BENEFITS AFTER FA 1986

1 General matters

The avowed purpose behind the provisions of FA 1986 was to prevent the 'cake and eat it' arrangements that had flourished in the CTT era. To what extent do the new rules achieve their purpose? When it is necessary to identify the property given away, it may be that there is a defect in the rules of FA 1986 Sch 20 with regard to gifts of cash. Such gifts are expressly excluded from the rules and it is arguable that once the money is spent by the donee there is no property in which a benefit can be reserved (a similar principle applies if property originally given was turned into cash by the donee and that cash was either dissipated or used to purchase a replacement asset). A further loophole related to inter-spouse gifts (apparently closed in the wake of the *Eversden* case: see [29.140]) whilst the rules do not prevent the retention of control over the property given (see [29.134]). [29.121]

2 Drafting: reservation or partial gift ('shearing')

'[By retaining] something which he has never given, a donor does not bring himself within the mischief of [the statutory provisions] ... In the simplest analysis, if A gives to B all his estates in Wiltshire except Blackacre, he does not except Blackacre out of what he has given; he just does not give Blackacre' (Lord Simonds in *St Aubyn v A-G* (1952)).

This principle has given rise to a number of schemes which seek to exploit the range of interests which can exist in property, particularly land, for example ownership, interest in possession, lease, mortgage and covenant or servitude (in Scotland). If an individual can retain one of these interests whilst gifting others, he cannot be said to have reserved a benefit out of the gift.

EXAMPLE 29.9

(1) A owned freehold land. In 1909, a sheep farming business was carried on in partnership with his six children on it.
1913: he gave the land to his children. The partnership continued.
1929: A died.
What had he given away in 1913? Only his interest in the land subject to the rights of the partnership. Accordingly there was no property subject to a reservation of benefit (see *Munro v Stamp Duties Comr* (1934)). It is thought that the FA 1999 changes would now result in a reserved benefit (see [29.130]).

(2) In 1934 a father made an absolute gift of grazing land to his son. In 1935 that land was bought into a partnership with, *inter alia*, the father. On the death of the father in 1952 it was held that he had reserved a benefit in

the land because of his interest in the partnership. (See *Chick v Stamp Duties Comr* (1958): contrast (1) above in that interest of the father arose *after* the absolute gift.)

(3) T owns Whiteacre. He grants a lease to a nominee, assigns the freehold reversion to his daughter, and continues to occupy the property. Has T made a partial gift (of the reversion) so that the reservation of benefit rules do not apply?

It should be noted that in *Munro* (*Example 29.9(1)*, above) not only was there a substantial time gap between the grant of the lease and the gift of the freehold but, at the time when the lease was granted, the donor had no intention of making a gift of the freehold: ie it was both prior and demonstrably independent.

Doubts about shearing operations that involved the use of a nominee were caused by *Kildrummy (Jersey) Ltd v IRC* (1990), a case decided in the Scottish Court of Session and concerning a stamp duty avoidance scheme. Attempting to avoid duty, the taxpayers formed a Jersey company to which they granted a lease over property that they owned outright: the Kildrummy estate. That Jersey company executed a declaration that the lease was held 'in trust and as nominee for' the taxpayers. Just over one month later the freehold was disposed of to a second Jersey company. The Court of Session decided, unanimously, that the grant of the lease to the nominee company was null and void. Lord Sutherland commented as follows:

> 'There is no doubt that it is perfectly competent for a person to enter into a contract with his nominee but such a contract would normally be of an administrative nature to regulate the relationship between the parties and to describe the matters which the nominees are empowered to do by their principal. A contract of lease, however, is in my opinion of an entirely different nature. It involves the creation of mutual rights and obligations which can only be given any meaning if the contract is between two independent parties.'

The whole question of 'shearing operations' of this type was considered by the courts in the *Ingram* litigation. [29.122]

3 Ingram v IRC

a) *The facts*

In *Ingram v IRC* (1999), Lady Jane Ingram transferred landed property to a nominee in 1987; the following day (on her directions) he granted her a 20-year rent-free lease in the property and on the next day transferred the property (subject to the lease) to trustees who immediately executed declarations of trust whereby the property settled was held for the benefit of certain individuals, excluding Lady Jane. The arrangements, all part of a pre-planned scheme, amounted to a classic carve-out or shearing operation. Lady Jane died in 1989 and HMRC issued a determination that, because of the reservation of benefit rules, the gifted property still formed part of her estate at her death. [29.123]

b) *HMRC's claim*

HMRC argued that the grant of a lease by a nominee in favour of his principal was a nullity with the result that, although it was accepted that the trustees took the property subject to the interest of Lady Jane (as per the abortive lease), that interest took effect by way of a leaseback. Hence Lady Jane's interest could only arise contemporaneously with the gift made to the trustees, thereby resulting in a reservation of benefit. Alternatively, and even if the nominee lease was effective, the same result would probably follow as a result of applying the GAAR (see [3.77]–[3.82]). [29.124]

c) *The approach of the House of Lords*

Lord Hoffmann referred to the long history of the legislation in this area and noted that the decided cases showed that although its provisions prevent a donor from 'having his cake and eating it', there is nothing to stop him from 'carefully dividing up the cake, eating part and having the rest'. He decided the appeal on the assumption that the lease granted by the nominee was a nullity, ie on the basis that the leasehold interest came into existence only at the time when the freehold was acquired by the trustees. The consequences of such a 'contemporaneous carve-out' involved a consideration of the estate duty case of *Nichols v IRC* (1975) which had concerned a gift by Sir Philip Nichols of his country house and estate to his son, Francis, subject to Francis granting him an immediate leaseback. Goff J, giving the judgment of the Court of Appeal, concluded that such an arrangement involved a reservation of benefit by Sir Philip:

> '… we think that a grant of the fee simple, subject to and with the benefit of a lease-back, where such a grant is made by a person who owns the whole of the freehold free from any lease, is a grant of the whole fee simple with something reserved out of it, and not a gift of a partial interest leaving something in the hands of the grantor which he has not given. It is not like a reservation or remainder expectant on a prior interest. It gives an immediate right to the rent, together with a right to distrain for it, and, if there be a proviso for re-entry, a right to forfeit the lease. Of course, where, as in *Munro v Commissioner of Stamp Duties (NSW)* (1934) the lease, or, as it then may have been, a licence coupled with an interest, arises under a prior independent transaction, no question can arise because the donor then gives all that he has, but where it is a condition of the gift that a lease-back shall be created, we think that must, on a true analysis, be a reservation of benefit out of the gift and not something not given at all.'

In the event the *Nichols* case fell to be decided on the basis of the covenants given by the son in the lease in which he assumed the burden of repairs and the payment of tithe redemption duty, which covenants themselves amounted to a reservation. (See also *Buzzoni v R & C Comrs* (2013), [29.44]–29.70]) where covenants in a sublease to pay service charges to the over landlord, thus relieving the tenant of the obligation to pay these charges, were also regarded as a reservation of benefit by the tenant.) The wider statement of Goff J quoted above to the effect that a leaseback must *by itself* involve a reservation constituted the main authority relied upon by HMRC (and the comment that the *Munro* case involved a 'prior independent transaction' had subsequently been widely debated).

Lord Hoffmann unequivocally rejected this approach:

> 'It is a curious feature of the debate in this case that both sides claim that their views reflect the reality, not the mere form of the transaction, but HMRC's version of reality seems entirely dependent upon the *scintilla temporis* which must elapse between the conveyance of the freehold to the donee and the creation of the leasehold in favour of the donor. For my part I do not think that a theory based on the notion of a *scintilla temporis* can have a very powerful grasp on reality ... If one looks at the real nature of the transaction, there seems to me no doubt that Ferris J was right in saying that the trustees and beneficiaries never at any time acquired the land free of Lady Ingram's leasehold interest.' **[29.125]**

d) *The nominee lease*

Given that no reservation was involved even if the nominee lease was a nullity, it was not strictly necessary for their Lordships to express any view on the validity of such an arrangement. Lord Hoffmann, however, indicated that he was of the opinion that such a lease was valid as a matter of English law for reasons given by Millet LJ in the Court of Appeal. (Nominee leases are in fact widely used in practice.) It should, however, be appreciated that nothing in the speeches affects the proposition that a man cannot grant a lease to himself (see *Rye v Rye* (1962)) nor the position under Scots law (see *Kildrummy (Jersey) Ltd v IRC* (1990)). **[29.126]**

e) *Ramsay*

Given the conclusion that a leaseback did not involve any reservation of benefit, the question of the *Ramsay* principle being used to nullify the nominee lease did not arise, and neither Lord Hoffmann nor Lord Hutton expressed any views on this matter. **[29.127]**

f) *The meaning of 'property' in FA 1986 s 102*

Lord Hoffmann pointed out that s 102 is concerned with a gift of 'property' and that term does not necessarily refer to something that has a physical existence such as a house, but is used in a technical sense and requires a careful analysis of the nature of what has been gifted. A landowner may, for instance, gift an unencumbered freehold interest in his house in which case were he to continue to occupy that property (in the absence of a payment of full consideration and assuming that such occupation was more than on a *de minimis* level) then he would reserve a benefit. By contrast, he might retain a leasehold interest and only give away the encumbered freehold interest, in which case no benefit would be reserved in the property gifted (which would be the encumbered freehold). Of course, if the donor in the latter situation continued to occupy the house after the expiry of the retained lease, then that would (subject to what is said above about full consideration and *de minimis*) amount to a benefit retained in the freehold interest gifted. As Lord Hoffmann concluded, s 102 'requires people to define precisely the interest which they are giving away and the interest, if any, which they are retaining'. **[29.128]**

g) *The use of shearing arrangements*

The speeches demolished the argument that the creation of the lease and the gift of the encumbered freehold had to be independent transactions. The lease could be carved out contemporaneously with the gift. Accordingly a prior nominee arrangement is not necessary; the arrangement could be structured as a gift and leaseback. However, it was essential that all the relevant terms of the lease were agreed before the freehold gift was made so that it is clear that the proprietary interest retained was defined with the necessary precision. [29.129]

4 FA 1986 ss 102A–102C

Unsurprisingly the *Ingram* decision was reversed in respect of gifts of interests in land made after 8 March 1999, but the reversing legislation is narrowly targeted and, it would seem, does not otherwise change the reservation of benefit rules. If the following conditions are met the donor is treated as reserving a benefit in the gifted property with the normal consequences:
(1) There must be a gift of an interest in land (other assets are not included). Note that as with the original legislation the trigger is a gift.
(2) The donor must retain 'a significant right or interest ... in relation to the land' (in certain circumstances it will be sufficient if this is retained by his spouse) or be party to a significant arrangement in relation to the land. A right or interest is not 'significant' if the donor pays full consideration for it nor if the interest was obtained at least seven years before the gift (hence it is possible to grant a lease; wait seven years and then gift the freehold interest without falling foul of these rules).

It is not thought that these rules apply where a property is divided (eg lodge/main house) and one is gifted, one retained. [29.130]

EXAMPLE 29.10
(1) *A carves out a lease (using a nominee arrangement) and gifts the encumbered freehold interest to his daughter.* Because A has given away an interest in land and retained an interest in the same land, the gifted interest is caught by the reservation rules: hence it will form part of A's estate on his death (s 102A(2));
(2) *As above except that having carved out the lease A waits seven years before giving away the freehold.*
The reservation rules do not apply to the gifted freehold interest (s 102A(5)).
(3) *A is the life tenant of a settlement created by his grandfather and which owns his main residence. The trustees exercise overriding powers to appoint an encumbered freehold interest on continuing trusts for A's children leaving a leasehold interest in the life interest fund.*
Although A makes a transfer of value (to the extent of the freehold interest ceasing to be subject to his life interest) he does not make a gift and so the reservation rules will not apply.

5 Reversionary leases

Reversionary leases are almost the reverse of Ingram cases. Instead of reserving a lease, the owner enters into a lease which does not come into effect for a number of years, at low rent. The owner continues to reside in the property. There will be a PET when the lease is granted, but the value will be low as the lease does not come into effect immediately. The value of the property diminishes as the date of commencement of the lease approaches. The pre-owned asset rules (see **[29.142]**) introduced in 2005, have made reversionary leases much less attractive.

EXAMPLE 29.11

Tom owns the Red House. He grants a 350-year lease to his son at a peppercorn rent to begin in 21 years' time. Meanwhile he continues to occupy the property.

It appears, following *Ingram and Buzzoni*, that this arrangement is outside the original gift with reservation rules as it would constitute an effective carve out. It would appear to be affected by the 1999 legislation, except where the freehold interest was acquired at least seven years before the deferred lease is granted. This is because the 1999 legislation does not apply to the retention of rights or interests acquired more than seven years prior to the making of the gift. (FA 1986 s 102A(5)) Alternatively, the 1999 rules may not apply if the freehold was acquired for full consideration, ie where the donor bought the property (s 102A(3)).

Where the grantor of the reversionary lease is not the owner of the freehold but is a long leaseholder, there is a risk of triggering the reservation rules if the sub-tenant takes on the donor's covenants in the overlease, given that the benefit to the long-leaseholder of the covenants undertaken by the sub-tenants in the underlease would normally constitute a reservation of benefit (*Buzzoni* and *Hood*; see **[29.44]**–**[29.70]**). **[29.131]**

6 Settlements

a) *Retaining an interest*

If the settlor reserves an interest for himself under his settlement, whether he does so expressly or whether his interest arises by operation of law, there is no reservation of benefit and he is treated as making a partial gift (see *Re Cochrane* (1906) which involved a reversionary interest). **[29.132]**

b) *The object of a discretionary trust*

The position with regard to discretionary trusts is more problematic. If the settlor is one of the beneficiaries he is not entirely excluded from the property with the result that the entire fund will be included as part of his estate. In view of the limited nature of a discretionary beneficiary's rights (see *Gartside v IRC* (1968)), he cannot be treated as making a partial gift (see *IRC v Eversden* (2003)). If the donor could be added as a beneficiary under a power to add contained in the settlement it is thought that again the property is subject to a reservation. **[29.133]**

c) *The settlor as paid trustee*

A danger arises if the settlor is one of the trustees and is entitled to remuneration as trustee. According to the estate duty case of *Oakes v Stamp Duties Comr* (1954) he has reserved a benefit (although at present HMRC does not follow this case). In any event there is no problem if the settlor/trustee is not entitled to remuneration and so it is possible for a donor to retain control over the settled property without infringing the reservation of benefit rules. [29.134]

d) *The termination of an interest in possession*

Where an individual either became entitled to an interest in possession before 22 March 2006 or, if after that time, the interest was an immediate post-death interest, a transitional serial interest or a disabled person's interest (for definitions, see **Chapter 32**), and is accordingly treated as owning the property itself (see **Chapter 33**), a termination of the interest in the individual's lifetime on or after 22 March 2006, where the property continues to be settled after that termination, will be treated as a gift for the purposes of the gift with reservation rules. Thus, if such an individual retains the use of the settled property after their interest in it ends, it will remain chargeable in their hands. [29.135]

> **EXAMPLE 29.12**
>
> In November 2002, Cliff settled his country house on trust for Richie for life or until he should re-marry, thereafter to Richie's ex-wife Maddie for life, with remainder to his niece, Saphron. Richie re-married in September 2008 and, since Maddie had settled in France, the trustees permitted Richie to remain living in the house. Should Richie die in, say, December 2015, the value of the house will form part of his estate for IHT purposes in the same way as if he had formerly owned it outright.

7 Benefits that are permitted

a) *Statutory 'get outs'*

It is only necessary for the property to be enjoyed *virtually* to the entire exclusion of the donor, thereby permitting the occasional visit or holiday (see **[29.71]**). More important is the exception where the donor provides full consideration for the benefit retained. [29.136]

> **EXAMPLE 29.13**
>
> Dad gives his farm to Phil but continues to reside in the farmhouse under a lease which requires him to pay a full rent. Dad's continued use of a part of the gifted property does not bring the reservation rules into play.

b) *Co-ownership*

FA 1986 s 102B (inserted by FA 1999) was introduced to deal with gifts of a share in land and provides that there will be no reservation of benefit if:
(1) there is a gift of a share in land;
(2) both donor and donee occupy the land;
(3) the donor does not receive any benefit other than a negligible one which is provided by the donee for some reason connected with the gift.

There is no need for the interests of the occupiers of the property to be equal so the gift may be of (say) a 90% interest in the property. Note also that the donor can, if he wishes, continue to pay all the running costs of the property. [29.137]

EXAMPLE 29.14

Sally owns a five-bedroom property at the seaside and is regularly visited by her daughter and two children (who live in Tooting). She gives a 50% beneficial interest in the house to the daughter who comes and goes as she pleases and leaves possessions in the rooms of the house (eg her bedroom). Although it is not the daughter's main residence and is not her 'family home' it is nevertheless felt that s 102B(4) applies so that Sally has not reserved any benefit in the gifted share. The daughter is 'in occupation' in much the same way as owners of a country cottage would be in occupation. Take care in relation to the division of expenses: Sally must not receive any benefit from the daughter in any way connected with the gift. She should, for instance, continue to bear her own day-to-day living expenses and her proportionate share (she could pay all!) of the property expenses.

8 Reservation and spouses

The reservation of benefit rules do not apply in the case of an inter-spouse gift (see FA 1986 s 102(5)). [29.138]–[29.140]

EXAMPLE 29.15

S creates a discretionary trust. He is the unpaid trustee, his wife is one of the beneficiaries. S has not reserved any benefit although it appears that *if* his wife benefits under the trust and *if* he shares that benefit HMRC will argue that he has not been excluded from enjoyment or benefit in the gifted property.

9 Post-death variations

Instruments of variation and disclaimer provide an ideal way of transferring wealth without resulting in any IHT or CGT liability and permit the disponor to reserve a benefit in the property (see generally [**30.153**]). [**29.141**]

EXAMPLE 29.16

(1) Father dies leaving his country cottage to his daughter. She continues to use it for regular holidays and at all bank holidays but transfers it to her son by instrument of variation made within two years of father's death and read back into his will.

The crucial point is that the variation is treated as made by father for *all* IHT purposes so that his daughter has not made a gift of property capable of falling within the reservation of benefit provisions.

(2) On H's death property (including the second home) is left to his wife on a terminable life interest, remainder to the son. The trustees terminate the spouse's life interest in the country cottage but the son permits her to continue to use it on a regular basis. The reservation of benefit rules do not apply because the termination of the interest in possession, although a transfer of value (a PET) by the spouse, is not a gift (see [**29.41**]).

VII PRE-OWNED ASSETS

1) Introduction

With HMRC and the taxpayer playing something of a cat and mouse game under the reservation of benefit rules and several successful schemes being closed by subsequent legislation, a different tack was taken by the Government in FA 2004 s 84 and Sch 15. The pre-owned asset rules apply where an individual continues to enjoy a benefit from an asset which he previously owned, in which case the individual may be subjected to an income tax charge on the benefit. The rules apply from 2005–06, but only where the inheritance tax gift with reservation of benefit rules do not apply, so are largely targeted at avoidance schemes. However, because they are drafted more widely, they may catch other transactions which were outside the scope of IHT, for example where an individual receives a benefit from an asset purchased with money given by him to another person. [29.142]

2) When a charge arises

There are three forms of pre-owned assets: land, chattels and intangible property in a settlor-interested trust, and slightly different rules apply to each category.

In relation to land, a charge to income tax under these provisions will arise in respect of a 'chargeable amount' where an individual ('the chargeable person') occupies any land ('the relevant land'), whether alone or together with other persons, and either the 'disposal condition' or the 'contribution condition' is met as respects the land.

The disposal condition is met where, at any time after 17 March 1986, the chargeable person owned an interest in the relevant land (or other property the proceeds on the disposal of which were applied, directly or indirectly, by another person in acquiring the relevant land), and the chargeable person has disposed of all or part of his interest in the relevant land otherwise than by an 'excluded transaction' (see [29.145]).

The contribution condition is, broadly, satisfied where the chargeable person has funded some other person, otherwise than by an excluded transaction, to acquire an interest in the relevant property.

Very similar rules apply to chattels.

The rules which apply to intangible property are less similar. There is no disposal or consideration condition: instead, the charge applies where intangible property has been placed in a settlement which is a settlor interested trust for income tax purposes (ignoring any benefit to the settlor's spouse). [29.143]

3) How is the charge calculated?

The chargeable amount for any taxable period is, in relation to land, the appropriate rental value less the amount of any payments which, in pursuance of any legal obligation, are made by the chargeable person during period to the owner of the relevant landing respect of the occupation by the chargeable person of the relevant land.

The equivalent provision for chattels is based on a notional amount of interest arising on the value of the asset.

In relation to intangible assets, the settlor is charged on the notional amount of interest on the value of relevant property in the settlement, less any tax paid by the settlor under the various income tax provisions which apply to such settlements. **[29.144]**

4) Exclusions and exemptions

Excluded transactions, which apply only in relation to land and chattels, are set out at FA 2004 Sch 15 para 10 and include transfers to the spouse of the chargeable person, arm's length transactions, gifts by virtue of which the relevant property became settled property in which the spouse or former spouse has an interest in possession and transfers falling within the exemptions set out at IHTA 1984 ss 11, 19 and 20.

Exemptions from charge apply in relation to all three categories of assets under FA 2004 Sch 15 para 11. These include situations where the chargeable person's estate includes the relevant property (ie the person is once again the owner) and where the property is treated as owned by him under the reservation of benefit rules. It also covers most of the situations in which the gift, had it otherwise been caught by the reservation of benefit rules, would have been given relief under the reservation of benefit rules:

(i) gifts to charities, political parties, housing associations, etc.
(ii) gifts of a *pro indiviso* share of land followed by joint occupation of donor and donee.
(iii) gifts where full consideration for use is paid by the donee, (FA 1986 Sch 20 para 6(1)(a)).
(iv) 'changed circumstances' through old age and infirmity (FA 1986 Sch 20 para 6(1)(b)).

FA 2004 Sch 15 does not apply in any year where the former owner is not UK resident. If the chargeable person is UK-resident but non-domiciled, then the charge only applies in relation to UK situs property. The charge does not apply to disposals of property by persons who were non-domiciled at the time of the disposal but who have since acquired UK domicile.

There is a *de minimis* amount set of £5,000. Benefits falling below this figure will not be chargeable under FA 2004 Sch 15, although benefits of £5,001 will be chargeable in full.

Where post-death variations have been effected, the persons who owned the property which is the subject of the variation are not treated for the purposes of FA 2004 Sch 15 as having previously owned the property (FA 2004 Sch 15 para 16). **[29.145]**

VIII LIABILITY TO ACCOUNT FOR TAX ON A GIFT WITH RESERVATION

Where the reservation has ceased during the lifetime of the donor (within seven years of the donor's death), this is treated as a failed PET and the donee of the original gift is treated as primarily responsible under normal principles (see [30.28]). The normal principles on tax on lifetime gifts will also apply where there is, during the seven years before death, both an actual gift and the relinquishment of a reservation (see **Chapter 36**).

Where property is treated as forming part of the estate on death by virtue of the gift with reservation of benefit rules, again, the normal rules for liability for tax on the estate on death apply (see [**30.46**] et seq). This means that PRs are liable for the tax under IHTA 1984 s 200, concurrently with others, including the donee.

However, if the PRs do pay the tax, they would normally have a statutory right of recovery from the donee under IHTA 1984 s 211(3). This applies where:

(1) tax is due on a chargeable transfer made on death (ie this right of recovery does not apply to tax/additional tax on lifetime transfers within seven years of death which PRs may also be called upon to pay under IHTA 1984 s 199); and

(2) the tax is *not* treated as part of the general and testamentary expenses of the estate. To be so treated, the tax must be on property which vests in the PRs (IHTA 1984 s 211(1)): reservation property does not vest in the PRs.

An interesting scenario can arise if the property subject to a reservation was disposed of by transfer within seven years of death and the reservation was still operative at the date of death. In this case, there is both a real transfer (with its real tax consequences) and a deemed transfer on death. In order to avoid double taxation, regulations provide for each transfer to be ignored in turn and the tax calculated (see [**36.3**]). If treating the property only as part of the estate on death gives rise to higher tax than looking only at the lifetime transfer, a credit is given for the tax due on the lifetime transfer against the tax payable on the property as part of the death transfer – only the excess will be payable under IHTA 1984 s 200(1) by the PRs. Whilst the PRs could also separately be required under IHTA 1984 s 199 to pay the tax due on the lifetime transfer if the donee does not pay, it is only the excess payable under s 200(1) which is payable on a 'chargeable transfer made on death', the condition for recovery under s 211(3), so it would only be this excess which would be covered by the statutory indemnity. [**29.146**]

30 IHT – death

Updated by Sandra Eden, Senior Lecturer, University of Edinburgh

I General [30.1]
II How to calculate the IHT bill on death [30.21]
III Payment of IHT – incidence and burden [30.41]
IV Problems created by the partially exempt transfer [30.91]
V   Abatement [30.121]
VI Specific problems on death [30.141]

I GENERAL

IHTA 1984 s 4(1) provides that:

> 'on the death of any person tax shall be charged as if immediately before his death he had made a transfer of value and the value transferred by it had been equal to the value of his estate immediately before his death …'.

Accordingly, there is a deemed transfer of value that occurs immediately before the death and which must be cumulated with chargeable transfers made by the deceased in the preceding seven years.

In addition to causing a charge on his estate at death, death also has the effect of:
(i) turning potentially exempt transfers made in the seven years before death into chargeable transfers; and
(ii) possibly leading to a supplementary IHT charge on chargeable transfers made in that same period. [30.1]

1 **Meaning of 'estate'**

The definition of 'estate' has already been considered in connection with lifetime transfers (IHTA 1984 s 5(1); see [**28.62**]. Rights of the deceased to the estate of another, for example under an intestacy, are 'property' for IHT purposes and hence form part of a taxpayer's estate, see *Daffodil v IRC* (2002). On death, the estate does not include excluded property (see [**35.21**] for the meaning of excluded property) although it does include property, given away by the deceased, in which he had reserved a benefit at the time of his death (see **Chapter 29**). Property owned by the deceased in a fiduciary capacity, for instance as 'treasurer' for his family, does not form part of his estate (*Anand v*

IRC (1997)). As the transfer is deemed to occur immediately before the death, the estate includes the share of the deceased in jointly owned property that passes by operation of law (*jus accrescendi*) at the moment of death.

EXAMPLE 30.1

Bill and his sister Bertha own their home as beneficial joint tenants, or in Scotland, under a title with a destination in favour of the survivor, so that on the death of either that share will pass automatically to the survivor and will not be transferred by will. For IHT purposes the half share in the house will be included in their respective death estates and will be subject to charge (for the valuation of the half share, see **[28.67]**).

The estate at death also includes a gift made before death in anticipation of death and conditional upon it occurring (a *donatio mortis causa*). Hence, although dominion over the property will have been handed over, it is still taxed as part of the deceased's estate at death.

Joint bank accounts can give rise to unexpected consequences on death. *Ownership* of joint bank accounts has caused difficulties outside the tax world, but ownership is not necessarily the test for IHT. The meaning of estate for IHT includes property over which a person has a general power of appointment (IHTA 1984 s 5(2)). Irrespective of the ownership of a bank account, in the case that any signatory could withdraw the whole amount without reference to the other signatories each signatory could reasonably be described as having a power of appointment over the whole amount. Several cases, most recently *Matthews v R & C Comrs* (2012) have considered joint accounts. In *Matthews* the question was whether the full sum in a joint account, provided entirely by the deceased but operable by 'either signature' which was held in the names of the deceased and her son, should be treated as part of the estate of the deceased for IHT purposes, or just to the extent of one half. The Tribunal held that the funds in the account were entirely part of the deceased's estate on two grounds. *First,* because each party could have withdrawn the funds, the full amount was included as part of the deceased's estate under s 5(2) as each party had the power of appointment. *Alternatively,* even though the deceased could have been regarded as making a PET of at least some of the account when it was opened in joint names, recalling that the deceased provided all the funds, she had reserved a benefit over the part given away as she was not excluded from it (see **[29.101]**–**[29.120]**). In the event that each signatory only has a restricted right of access over the account, the general power of appointment would be limited to that part over which the deceased had a right of access.

Despite *Matthews,* which suggests that an unrestricted signatory has a power of appointment over the whole account, irrespective of who contributed the funds in the account, HMRC provides the following advice on valuing joint assets: 'If the person who died provided all the money in the account but had it in joint names for convenience, include all the money in your valuation. If another person provided some of the money, only include the amount provided by the person who died.' This distinguishes on the basis of who contributed the funds, which does not appear to be correct if the test is whether each joint owner can access them in full. **[30.2]**

2 Valuation

a) *A hypothetical sale*

(See also [**28.61**] ff.)

In general, assets must be valued at 'the price which the property might reasonably be expected to fetch if sold in the open market at that time'. No reduction is allowed for the fact that all the property is put on the market at the same time (IHTA 1984 s 160). This hypothetical sale occurs immediately before the death and if the value is ascertained for IHT purposes it becomes the value at death for CGT purposes and, hence, the legatee's base cost (TCGA 1992 s 274: see [**21.21**]). Reliefs that reduce the IHT value (notably business property relief) are ignored for CGT purposes. For IHT, low values ensure the least tax payable but will give the legatee a low base cost and so a higher capital gain when he disposes of the asset. **[30.3]**

b) *Lotting*

In valuing an estate at death, 'lotting' requires a valuation on the basis that 'the vendor must be supposed to have' taken the course which would get the largest price for the combined holding 'subject to the caveat ... that it does not entail undue expenditure of time and effort'. For instance, if a taxpayer dies possessed of a valuable collection of lead toy soldiers they will not be valued individually but rather as a collection (see *Duke of Buccleuch v IRC* (1967)).

In *IRC v Gray* (1994) the deceased (Lady Fox) had farmed the Croxton Park Estate in partnership with two others and the land was subject to tenancies that Lady Fox, as freeholder, had granted to the partnership. HMRC sought to aggregate (or lot) the freehold in the land with her partnership share as a single unit of property so that the value of Lady Fox's freehold reversion was an appropriate proportion of the aggregate value of that reversion and her partnership interest treated as a single item of property (in effect therefore the reversion was being valued on a vacant possession basis with an allowance for the partnership interests of the other partners). It may be noted that under the partnership deed she was entitled to 92 1/2% of profits (and bore virtually all the losses). The Court of Appeal reversed the Lands Tribunal, holding that lotting was appropriate since that was the course that a prudent hypothetical vendor would take to obtain the best price. The fact that the two interests could not be described as forming a 'natural unit of property' was irrelevant. Hoffmann LJ commented that:

> 'The principle is that the hypothetical vendor must be supposed to have "taken the course which would get the largest price" provided that this does not entail "undue expenditure of time and effort". In some cases this may involve the sale of an aggregate which could not reasonably be described as a "natural unit" ... . The share in the farming partnership with or without other property, was plainly not a "natural" item of commerce. Few people would want to buy the right to farm in partnership with strangers. Nevertheless [s 160] requires one to suppose that it was sold. The question for the Tribunal was whether, on this assumption, it would have been more advantageous to sell it with the land.'

In many ways this was not a typical case involving the fragmentation of farm land within a family and therefore it should not be assumed that this judgment will apply in all such cases. **[30.4]**

c) *Funeral expenses*

Although the general rule is that assets must be valued immediately before death, IHTA 1984 Part VI permits values to be amended in certain circumstances, eg reasonable funeral expenses can be deducted including the cost of flowers, refreshments for mourners and a headstone. HMRC have indicated the deceased's background and profession should be taken into account in determining what is reasonable (IHTM 10373). **[30.5]**

d) *Changes in value resulting from the death*

If the value of assets changes as a result of the death, it is the post-death value which is taken into account (IHTA 1984 s 171), although the termination or passing of an interest on death is excluded from this provision. **[30.6]**

EXAMPLE 30.2
(1) A took out a whole life insurance policy for £100,000 on his own life. Its value immediately before death would be equal to the surrender figure, say £80,000. As a result of A's death, £100,000 rather than £80,000 will accrue to A's estate and hence the value of the policy for IHT purposes is treated as that figure (IHTA 1984 s 167(2)).
(2) A and B were joint tenants of a freehold house worth £500,000. Immediately before A's death his joint interest would be worth in the region of £250,000. Although immediately after death its value to A's estate is nil as it has passed to B by survivorship, because the interest has passed on death the change in value is not taken into account (IHTA 1984 s 171(2)). £250,000 is included in A's estate.

e) *Post-death sales*

In three cases the pre-death valuation can be altered if the asset is sold within a short period after death for less than that valuation. Relief is not given merely because the asset falls in value after death; *only if it is sold by bargain at arm's length is the relief available*. Normally the sale proceeds will be substituted as the death valuation figure if an election is made by the person liable for the IHT on that asset (in practice this will be the PRs who should elect if IHT would thereby be reduced). Where such revaluations occur, not only must the IHT bill (and estate rate) on death be recalculated but also, for CGT purposes, the death valuation is correspondingly reduced so as to prevent any claim for loss relief by the PRs on disposal. The three cases when this relief is available are: **[30.7]**

Related property sold within three years of death (IHTA 1984 s 176) The meaning of related property has already been discussed (see **[28.70]**). So long as a 'qualifying sale' (as defined) occurs, the property on death can be revalued ignoring the related property rules (ie as an asset on its own). Although the sale proceeds need not be the same as the death value, if the sale occurs within a short time of death the proceeds received will offer some evidence of that value. **[30.8]**

EXAMPLE 30.3

Sebastian's estate on death includes one of a pair of Constable watercolours of Suffolk sunsets. He leaves it to his son; the other is owned by his widow, Jemima. As a pair, the pictures are worth £200,000. Applying the related property provisions, the watercolour is valued at £100,000 on Sebastian's death. If it were to be sold at Sotheby's some eight months after his death for £65,000, the death value could, if a claim were made, be recalculated ignoring the related property rules. It would be necessary to arrive at the value of the picture immediately before the death.

Quoted shares and securities sold within 12 months of death (IHTA 1984 ss 178 ff) If sold for less than the death valuation the sale proceeds can be substituted for that figure. It should be noted that if this relief is claimed it will affect *all* such investments sold within the 12-month period; hence, the aggregate of the consideration received on such sales is substituted for the death values. Special rules operate if investments of the same description are repurchased. The shares or securities must be listed on a recognised stock exchange or dealt with on the Unlisted Securities Market, so that the provisions do not apply to private company shares. Relief is also available in cases where the investments are either cancelled without replacement within 12 months of death or suspended within 12 months of death and remain suspended on that anniversary. In the former case, there is deemed sale for a nominal consideration of £1 at the time of cancellation; in the latter a deemed sale of the suspended investments immediately before the anniversary at their then value. [30.9]

Land sold within four years of death (IHTA 1984 ss 190 ff) The relief extends to all interests in land and is similar to that available for quoted securities although it enables a higher as well as a lower figure to be substituted. It will not normally be advantageous to have the higher figure substituted, as this will increase any inheritance tax on the estate and an election is not possible where there is no inheritance tax due (an election might in such circumstances be advantageous for capital gains tax purposes): in *Stonor v IRC* (2001), no claim could be made in relation to properties left to charities as, because there was no tax due, there was no 'appropriate person' to make the claim (see [30.11]). All sales within the four-year period are included in any election. Note, however, that in the fourth year the election is not available if the sale value would exceed the probate value (IHTA 1984 s 197A). The date of the sale is the date of the contract to sell, but an abortive exchange of contracts does not constitute a 'sale': see *Jones (Balls' Administrators) v IRC* (1997). [30.10]

EXAMPLE 30.4

MacLeod left his entire estate to his wife Tammy on his death including land valued at death at £10,000. As a result of new regional development plans, the land now has hope value and is worth in the region of £100,000. Accordingly, it is now to be sold. An election to substitute the sale proceeds for the probate value would be beneficial in CGT terms. However, because there is no appropriate person (since IHT is not payable on MacLeod's death), that election cannot be made. Neither will HMRC accept a claim where the property is not subject to tax because it is within the nil rate band rather than being left to charity.

940   IHT – death

In the case of both quoted shares and land, the election to substitute the sale proceeds must be made by the 'appropriate person', who is defined in the legislation as 'the person liable for inheritance tax attributable to (the property)'. This will normally be the PRs. [30.11]

f) *Provisional valuations*

The valuation of certain assets (notably private company shares) may take some time and the PRs may wish to obtain a grant immediately. In such cases it is possible to submit a provisional estimate for the value of the property that must then be corrected as soon as the formal valuation has been obtained (see IHTA 1984 s 216(3A) and the *Robertson* case, considered at [30.43]). [30.12]

3 Liabilities

a) *General rule*

Liabilities only reduce the value of an estate if incurred for consideration in money or money's worth, eg an outstanding mortgage and the deceased's unpaid tax liability (IHTA 1984 s 5(5)). This means that the deceased cannot simply grant an IOU in favour of a member of his family or friend without receiving consideration from that family or friend. Furthermore, in relation to deaths after 17 July 2013, debts of the deceased which are not repaid will not be deductible, unless there is a commercial reason for the debt not being repaid and it is not part of a tax avoidance scheme (IHTA 1984 s 175A). [30.13]

b) *Artificial debts*

FA 1986 s 103 introduced further restrictions on the deductibility from an estate at death of debts and incumbrances created by the deceased. These provisions supplement s 5(5) in relation to debts or incumbrances created after 17 March 1986. Broadly, their aim is to prevent the deduction of 'artificial' debts, where the deceased gives assets away and then buys them back leaving the payment outstanding. A deduction is denied to the extent that any value given for the debt was 'derived from the deceased'.

EXAMPLE 30.5

Berta gives a picture to her daughter Bobby in 2014. In 2017 Berta buys it back, leaving the purchase price outstanding until the date of her death.
(1)   The gift is a PET and escapes IHT if Berta survives seven years.
(2)   The debt owed to Bobby is incurred for full consideration (the picture) and hence satisfies the requirements of IHTA 1984 s 5(5). Deduction is, however, prevented by FA 1986 s 103 as the consideration given for the debt, the picture, derived from the deceased.

Section 103(1) provides that debts must be abated in whole or in part if any portion of the consideration for the debt was *either* derived from the deceased *or* was given by *any* person to whose resources the deceased had contributed. In the latter case contributions of the deceased are ignored, however, if it is shown (ie by the taxpayer) that the contribution was not made with reference to or to enable or facilitate the giving of that consideration.

Accordingly, unless property derived from the deceased furnished the consideration for the debt, a causal link is necessary between the property of the deceased and the subsequent debt transaction.

EXAMPLE 30.6

(1) In *Example 30.5* the consideration for the debt is property derived from the deceased and therefore the debt may not be deducted in arriving at the value of her estate. (NB: it does not matter that the gift of the deceased occurred before 17 March 1986 so long as *the debt* was incurred after that date.)

(2) In 1994 Jake gave a diamond brooch to his daughter (Liz). In 2004 she in turn gave the brooch to her sister Sam. In 2016 Sam lends £50,000 to Jake who subsequently dies leaving that debt still outstanding.

The consideration for the debt was not derived from property of the deceased and Sam would (presumably) be able to show that, although she received property from a person whose resources had been increased by the gift of deceased, the disposition of that property by the deceased was not linked to the subsequent transaction. Had Jake bought the brooch back from Liz in 2016 (leaving the price outstanding as a debt) the consideration for the debt would then be property derived from him so that the debt would not be deductible.

Debt schemes, which are likely to be less attractive following the introduction of the transferable nil rate band, were designed to preserve the nil rate band of the first spouse to die, whilst making assets available to the second spouse. They were especially useful where most of the estate was tied up in a house. There were a variety of different schemes on offer, but the general idea was that on the death of the first spouse, property was transferred to the surviving spouse, subject to a debt. This debt, which was created on the death of the first spouse in favour of a third party, for example a discretionary trust, had the effect of utilising the nil rate band of the first to die. So, although the survivor's estate on death includes any assets bequeathed by the first spouse, the estate is reduced by the debt in favour of the third party. In *Phizackerley v R& C Comrs* (2007), a debt scheme was used but failed as a result of being caught by FA 1986 s 103. On Mrs Phizackerley's death her share of the house was left to her husband, subject to him agreeing to pay a sum equal to the then current nil rate band, on demand, to a discretionary trust created on her death. On his death, the issue arose as to whether the executor's obligation to pay this sum to the trust was deductible from his estate. HMRC successfully argued that s 103 applied to prevent the deduction of the obligation because in this case, the husband had effectively contributed all the purchase price of their home, half of which he gave to her during her lifetime. This meant that the consideration which was received in return for him entering into the debt, namely the house, 'derived' from the husband. Had the deaths been in the reverse order, the debt scheme would not have been caught by s 103.

When a debt, which would otherwise not be deductible on death because of s 103(1), is repaid *inter vivos* the repayment is treated as a PET (a deemed PET). This provision is essential since otherwise such debts could be repaid immediately before death without any IHT penalty. However, the application of this rule when a taxpayer repurchases property that he had earlier given away is a matter of some uncertainty. Take, for instance, the not uncommon case where A, having made a gift of a valuable chattel, subsequently decides that he cannot live without it. Accordingly, he repurchases that chattel paying full market value to the donee. Has A made a notional PET under s 103(5) at the time when he pays over the purchase price or, if the money is paid as part and parcel of the repurchase agreement, did A never incur any debt or incumbrance falling within the section? It is thought that the latter view is correct since if the purchase price is paid at once a debt will never arise.

An element of multiple charging could arise from the artificial debt rule (in *Example 30.5*, for instance, the PET is made chargeable if Berta dies before 2022; the debt is non-deductible and the picture forms part of Berta's estate). However, the regulations discussed in **Chapter 36** prevent the multiple imposition of IHT in such cases.

Finally, although a debt may not be deducted in order to arrive at the value of the deceased's estate for IHT purposes, it must still be paid by the PRs and it is, therefore, treated as a specific gift by the deceased (see further [**30.56**]).

[**30.14**]

EXAMPLE 30.7

(1) S settled property on discretionary trusts in 1990. In 2017 the trustees lend him £6,000. This debt is non-deductible. It does not matter when the trust was created.

(2) Terry-Testator borrows £50,000 from the Midshire bank which he gives to his son. The debt that he owes to the bank is deductible on his death: in no sense is this an 'artificial debt'.

c) *Further anti-avoidance rules*

In 2013 and 2014, further anti-avoidance rules were introduced to limit the availability of deduction of debts from the estate on death. The purpose of these rules is to restrict the deduction of debts in the computation of the estate where the funds raised are used to acquire (or improve) particular assets outside the charge to UK tax.

Debts incurred to purchase or improve excluded property Excluded property is considered in more detail in **Chapter 35**, but for present purposes the most important example is property situated outside the UK, owned by a person domiciled outside the UK. Such debts are not deductible unless the excluded property has been disposed of by the date of death and the consideration is no longer excluded property, or to the extent that the debt exceeds the value of the excluded property at the date of death, subject to further anti-avoidance tests (IHTA 1984 s 162A). Debts to finance bank accounts in a currency other than sterling, (technically not excluded property although not included in the estate) are similarly not deductible (IHTA 1984 s 162AA).

EXAMPLE 30.8

Will, domiciled outside the UK, borrows £500,000 using his Wiltshire home as security. He uses it to purchase property in New Zealand. On his death he still owns the New Zealand property and the debt of £500,000 is disallowed.

If he had sold the New Zealand property and used the proceeds to buy shares in a UK listed company, the debt would be allowed. If he had simply given away the overseas property, the debt would be disallowed.

Debts incurred to purchase property eligible for APR, BPR or WR Debts which have been incurred to acquire or improve property subject to agricultural property relief, business property relief or woodland relief must be set first against the value of that property, even if they are secured against other property (eg a security on a house to purchase relievable property) (IHTA 1984 s 162B).

[**30.15**]

Timing aspects – when the anti-avoidance provisions apply

The anti-avoidance rules outlined above have differing commencement rules.

In relation to debts related to excluded property, the rules apply to deaths and other chargeable events that occur on or after 17 July 2013. In relation to debts used to finance non-sterling bank accounts, the rules apply in relation to deaths on or after 17 July 2014. In each case, it does not matter when the liability was incurred, so in a sense the changes are retrospective.

Where the debt was used to acquire, enhance or maintain assets that qualify for agricultural, business or woodlands relief, the restrictions only apply to liabilities incurred on or after 6 April 2013. Debts incurred before this date are not subject to these anti-avoidance rules. [**30.16**]–[**30.20**]

II HOW TO CALCULATE THE IHT BILL ON DEATH

Tax is calculated according to the rates set out in the following table:

Gross cumulative transfer (£)	*Rate (%) – Death*	*Rate (%) – Lifetime transfers within 7 years of death*
0–325,000*	0	0
Above 325,000	40	40

* This assumes that no nil rate band has been transferred from a predeceasing spouse – see [**30.27**], that there is no residential nil rate band available – see [**30.28**], and that the special rate of 36% a result of charitable donations does not apply – see [**30.30**].

These rates (which came into force on 6 April 2009 and have been extended to 5 April 2021) are applied to the estate at death and, in addition, when that death occurs within seven years of a chargeable lifetime transfer or PET made by the deceased the following results occur:
(1) In the case of a *chargeable transfer*, IHT must be recalculated either in accordance with the rates of tax in force at the donor's death if these are less than the rates at the time of the transfer or, alternatively, by using full rates at the time of the transfer. Subject to taper relief, extra tax may then be payable (IHTA 1984 s 7(4), Sch 2 para 2).
(2) In the case of a PET, the transfer is treated as a chargeable transfer so that *first*, IHT must be calculated (subject to taper relief) at the rates

current at the donor's death (again provided that these rates are less than those in force at the time when the transfer occurred: otherwise the latter apply: see Sch 2 para 1A), and *second*, the PET must now be included in the total transfers of the taxpayer for cumulation purposes which may necessitate a recalculation of the tax charged on other chargeable transfers made by the donor and, where a discretionary trust is involved, the recalculation of any exit charge.

These problems will be considered in order, looking first at the effect of death upon the chargeable lifetime transfers of the deceased and then at the taxation of the death estate. The consequences for discretionary trusts are considered at **[34.22]**. **[30.21]**

1 Chargeable transfers of the deceased made within seven years of his death

As already explained (see **[28.122]**) IHT will have been charged, at half the then death rate, at the time when the transfer was made. In computing that tax, chargeable transfers in the seven preceding years will have been included in the cumulative total of the transferor. As a result of his death within the following seven years, IHT must be recalculated on the original value transferred at the full rate of IHT in force at the date of death. After deducting the tax originally paid, extra tax may be payable. **[30.22]**

a) *Taper relief (IHTA 1984 s 7(4))*

If death occurs more than three years after the gift, taper relief ensures that only a percentage of the death rate is charged. The tapering percentages are as follows:

(1) where the transfer is made more than three but not more than four years before the death, 80%;
(2) where the transfer is made more than four but not more than five years before the death, 60%;
(3) where the transfer is made more than five but not more than six years before the death, 40%; and
(4) where the transfer is made more than six but not more than seven years before the death, 20%.

EXAMPLE 30.9

Danaos settles £375,000 on discretionary trusts in July 2009 (IHT is paid by the trustees). He dies:

(1) on 1 January 2011
or (2) on 1 January 2015
or (3) on 1 January 2017.

The *original transfer* in 2009 was subject to IHT at one half of rates in force for 2009–10 (see Table at **[30.21]** for the current rates).

In (1) he dies within three years of the gift: accordingly, a charge at the full tax rates for 2010–11, the year of death, must be calculated, tax paid in 2009 deducted, and any balance is then payable.

In (2) he dies more than five but less than six years after the gift: therefore only 40% of the full amount of tax on death at 2014–15 rates is calculated, the tax paid in 2009 deducted, and the balance (if any) is then payable.

In (3) death occurs more than seven years after the transfer and therefore no supplementary tax is payable.

If it is assumed that the current rates of IHT apply throughout this period, the actual tax computations are as follows (assuming that the 2009 transfer was the first chargeable transfer of Danaos and ignoring annual exemptions):

(a) *IHT on the 2009 chargeable transfer is as follows:*

first £325,000	–	Nil
Remaining £50,000 at 20%	–	£ 10,000

total IHT payable by the trustees is therefore £10,000.

(b) *If death occurs in 2011 it is within three years of the transfer and there is no taper relief:* tax on a transfer of £375,000 at the then death rates is:

first £325,000	–	Nil
remaining £50,000 at 40%	–	£ 20,000

Total IHT is therefore £20,000 which after deducting the sum paid in 2009 (£10,000), leaves a further £10,000 to be paid.

(c) *If death occurs in 2015* the calculation is as follows:
    (i)   full IHT at death rates £20,000 (as in (b) above)
    (ii) take 40% (taper relief) of tax at (i): £20,000 × 40% = £8,000
    (iii) as that sum is less than the tax actually paid in 2009 *there is no extra IHT to pay.*

It should be noted in *Example 30.9* that even though the result of taper relief may be to ensure that extra IHT is not payable because of the death, it does not lead to any refund of the original IHT paid when the chargeable transfer was made: in such cases the taper relief is inapplicable, see IHTA 1984 s 7(5). Taper relief is moreover of no benefit if the gift fell within the donor's nil rate band since, although using up all or part of that band, no tax is actually paid and taper relief operates by reducing the tax payable.   **[30.23]**

b) *Fall in value of gifted property*

If the property given falls in value by the date of death, the extra IHT is calculated on that reduced value (IHTA 1984 s 131). This relief is not available in the case of tangible movables that are wasting assets and there are special rules for leases with less than 50 years unexpired. A claim must be made within four years of death.

EXAMPLE 30.10

In Year 1 Dougal gave a Matisse figure drawing worth £375,000 to his discretionary trustees (who paid the IHT). He died in Year 3 when the Matisse was worth only £332,000.
(1)   Assuming it was Dougal's first chargeable transfer, IHT paid on the Year 1 gift was £10,000 ([£375,000 – £325,000] × 20%).
(2)   IHT on death (assume rates unchanged) is calculated on (£332,000 – £325,000) × 40% = £2,800.

Hence extra IHT payable is nil.

Had the property been sold by the trustees before Dougal's death for £332,000 (£43,000 less than its value when given away by Dougal) the extra (death) IHT would be charged on the sale proceeds with the same result as above. If, however, the property had been given away by the trustees before Dougal's death, even though its value might at that time have fallen by £43,000 since Dougal's original gift, no relief is given, with the result that the extra charge caused by Dougal's death will be levied on the full £375,000.

The value of a chargeable lifetime transfer for *cumulation* purposes is not reduced in the seven-year period since s 131 merely reduces the value that is taxed (not the value cumulated) whilst taper relief is given in terms of the rate of IHT to be charged on that transfer. Hence the full value of the life transfer remains in the cumulative total of the transferor and there is no reduction in the tax charged on his death estate. [30.24]

2 PETs made within seven years of death

The PET becomes a chargeable transfer and is subject to IHT in accordance with the taxpayer's cumulative total *at the date when it was made* (ie taking into account chargeable transfers in the preceding seven years). The value transferred is frozen at the date of transfer unless the property has fallen in value by the date of death in which case the lower value is charged (the rules concerning the fall in value of assets are the same as those considered at [30.24]). Despite these provisions, which look back to the actual date of the transfer of value, the IHT is calculated by reference to the rates in force at the date of death unless those rates have increased in which case the rates at the time of the transfer are taken (subject to taper relief, as above).
[30.25]

EXAMPLE 30.11

In October 2013 Zanda gave a valuable doll (then worth £335,000) to her granddaughter Cressida. She died in July 2017 when the value of the doll was £327,000. Assuming that Zanda had made no other transfers of value during her life, ignoring exemptions and reliefs, the IHT consequences are:
(1) The 2013 transfer was potentially exempt. However, as Zanda dies within seven years, it becomes chargeable.
(2) As the asset has fallen in value by the date of death IHT is charged on the reduced value, ie on £327,000.
(3) IHT at the rates current when Zanda died is:
first £325,000 = nil
next £2,000 at 40% = £800
Total IHT = £800.
(4) Taper relief is, however, available since Zanda died more than three years after the gift. Therefore:
£800 × 80% (taper relief on transfers between 3–4 years before death) = £640.
Note: Although IHT is calculated by reference to the reduced value of the asset, for cumulation purposes (and for CGT purposes) the original value transferred (£335,000) is retained.

3 Position where a combination of PETs and chargeable transfers have been made within seven years of death

PETs are treated as exempt transfers unless the transferor dies within the following seven-year period. Accordingly, they are not cumulated in calculating IHT on subsequent chargeable transfers. Consider the following illustration (which ignores annual exemptions):

EXAMPLE 30.12

In July 2013 Planer gives shares worth £327,000 to his son.

In April 2017 he settles land worth £335,000 on discretionary trusts and pays the IHT himself (so that grossing-up applies: see [28.124]).

He dies in February 2018. (Assume no other transfers of value were made by Planer; ignore exemptions and reliefs; current IHT rates apply throughout.)

(1) The transfer in 2013 was a PET.
(2) In calculating the IHT on the chargeable transfer in 2017, the PET is ignored. The net gift is £335,000. £325,000 of this is covered by the nil rate band, leaving £10,000 to be grossed up at 10/8 to £12,500. The chargeable transfer is £337,500 (£325,000 – the amount of the gift covered by the nil rate band – plus the grossed up element of £12,500) and the tax thereon is £2,500.
(3) As a result of his death within seven years the PET is made chargeable and the IHT calculation is as follows:
　(a) *On the 2013 transfer* IHT at the rates when Planer died is subject to 60% taper relief (gifts more than four, less than five years before death). Hence IHT at death rates is:
　　first £325,000 – nil
　　next, £2,000 (£327,000 – £325,000) at 40% = £800
　　Taper relief at 60% (between 4 and 5 years between transfer and death): £800 × 60% = £480 (tax due on 2013 transfer)
Note: Primary liability for this tax falls upon the donee (see [30.28]). Grossing-up does not apply again on the calculation when IHT is charged, or additional tax is payable, because of death.
　　(b) *On the 2017 transfer* IHT must be recalculated on this transfer since the transferor has died within seven years, and the former PET must now be included in the cumulative total of Planer at the time when this transfer was made. Hence:
　　　(i) cumulative transfers of Planer in 2017 = £327,000
　　　(ii) value transferred in 2017 = £337,500 (note this figure includes the tax Planer paid in 2017)
　　　(iii) Nil rate band in 2017 used up by previous transfers within the last seven years (the PET in 2013). Taper relief is not available on this transfer since Planer dies within three years.
so the IHT is £337,500 × 40% = £135,000
Deduct IHT paid in 2017: £135,000 – £2,500 = £132,500
Additional IHT payable on the 2017 transfer is £132,500.
Note: The cumulative total of transfers made by Planer at his death (which will affect the IHT payable on his death estate) is £327,000 + £337,500 = £664,500.

When a PET is made after an earlier chargeable transfer and the transferor dies in the following seven years, tax on that PET will be calculated by including the earlier transfer in his cumulative total. In this sense the making of the PET means that there is no reduction in his cumulative total for a further seven years and the result is that IHT could eventually turn out to be higher than if the PET had never been made ('the PET trap'!). [30.26]

EXAMPLE 30.13

Ignoring annual exemptions, Yvonne made a chargeable transfer of £325,000 on 1 May 2009 and on 1 May 2015 made a gift of £330,000 to take advantage of the PET regime. She dies on 1 May 2017 (by which date the 2009 transfer has dropped out of cumulation).

(1) IHT on the former PET in 2015 (at current rates) is £132,000 (£330,000 × 40%) since the 2009 transfer forms part of Yvonne's cumulative total at the time when the PET was made in 2015 and uses up all the nil rate band. Tax on the death estate will then be calculated by including the 2015 transfer (the former PET) in Yvonne's cumulative total, which means the estate on death is taxed at 40%.

(2) Had Yvonne not made the 2015 PET so that £330,000 continued to form part of her death estate, the 2009 transfer has dropped out of cumulation and so the tax thereon is £2,000 (£330,000 − £325,000 × 40%).

Extra IHT resulting from the making of the PET is therefore £132,000 − £2,000 = £130,000

4 The transferable nil rate band

The introduction in 2007 of the ability to transfer any unused nil rate band on death to the surviving spouse has removed the necessity for much IHT planning for middle wealth couples, much of which was concerned with how to utilise the nil rate band on the first to die, without excluding the surviving spouse from access to the assets formerly owned by the first spouse. It used to be a question of 'use it or lose it'. Now, because any unused nil rate band is available to the surviving spouse, the effects of aggregating estates on the second death is mitigated.

The change is retrospective in the sense that no matter how long ago the first spouse died, if the second spouse dies on or after 9 October 2007, any proportion of unused nil rate band of the first spouse becomes available on the death of the second. The unused proportion is available on the second death, not the unused amount, as seen in the following example.

The Court of Appeal in *Loring v Woodland Trust* (2014), was asked to consider the impact of the introduction of the transferable nil rate band on a will entered into prior to the change. Here the testator bequeathed 'assets or cash of an aggregate value equal to such sum as is at the date of my death the amount of my unused nil-rate band for Inheritance Tax' to a trust for various beneficiaries, with the balance going to charity. The charity argued, unsuccessfully, that this should be interpreted as a transfer of a single nil rate band. The Court held that the intention of the testator was clearly to make a bequest of whatever could be transferred free of tax, which meant that the charity received £325,000 less than it would have received under the pre-2007 position. [30.27]

EXAMPLE 30.14

Ken died in October 1987, when the available nil rate band was £90,000. He left £30,000 to Jill, his daughter, using up one-third of his nil rate band, with the remainder of his estate going to his surviving spouse, Fiona. Fiona died on 12 January 2017 when the nil rate band is £325,000. Assuming neither party made any lifetime transfers, there will be £541,667 of nil rate band available on Fiona's death, made up of her own nil rate band of £325,000, and two-thirds of £325,000 (£216,667) from Ken's death.

It is important to note that the nil rate band may only be used on the death of the second spouse and will not be available to cover any lifetime chargeable transfers of the second spouse at the time they are made. It will, however, cover lifetime transfers when one comes to recalculate tax on transfers within seven years of death.

EXAMPLE 30.15

Taking the facts from *Example 30.14*, above, assume that Fiona makes a lifetime chargeable transfer, after annual exemptions, of £400,000 three months before her death. Tax will be payable during her lifetime (assuming no grossing up) on £75,000 at 20% (she only has her own nil rate band of £325,000 available for the lifetime transfer).

On the recomputation of the tax on the lifetime gift after death, both her own nil rate band and the transferred nil rate band are available against the lifetime chargeable transfer, so there is no extra tax to pay (but the lifetime tax is not refundable). Of the combined nil rate bands of £541,667, £400,000 is used up on the lifetime transfer leaving only £141,667 of nil rate band available for her estate.

It is possible to acquire unused nil rate band from more than one spouse, but subject to a maximum of 100% extra nil rate band. So If Alf is predeceased by spouse Binny (who only used up 50% of her nil rate band), then remarries and is predeceased by Cathy, who only used up 25% of her nil rate band, Alf is only entitled to 100% extra nil rate band on his death, not 125%.

A claim must be made for the transfer to be made within broadly two years of the second death (IHTA 1984 s 8B).

5 The residential nil rate band

When a residence is passed on death to a lineal descendant, an additional nil rate band, the residential nil rate band (RNRB) was introduced with effect for deaths from 6 April 2017 (IHTA 1984 ss 8D–8M). The RNRB is reduced where the estate is over £2 million. There are provisions for any unused RNRB to be transferred to a surviving spouse or civil partner.

Year of death	Maximum RNRB (excluding any transferrable RNRB – see **[30.33]**)
2017–18	£100,000
2018–19	£125,000
2019–20	£150,000
2020–21	£175,000

From 2121–22 onwards, the band will increase in line with the Consumer Price Index. **[30.28]**

a) *Qualifying residential interest (IHTA 1984 s 8H)*

The deceased's estate must include an interest (usually ownership but other interests, for example an interest in possession, are included) in a 'dwelling house' which has been his 'residence'. It need not have been his main residence, and it is not necessary that he is residing in it at the date of his death. There is no statutory definition of residence or dwelling house, except that it includes:

- 'garden or ground' – no area restriction here, in contrast to CGT (see [**23.61**]; and
- a house which the deceased intended to make his residence but is living elsewhere in job related accommodation before death. Job related has the same restrictive meaning as for capital gains tax – see [**23.85**]–[**23.100**].

It excludes trees and underwood.

If there is only one such dwelling house at the date of death, that is the qualifying interest. If there is more than one, an election can be made for any to be treated as the qualifying residential interest. There is no requirement that the main residence must be chosen, so, for example, if a person lived briefly in a large house which they still own, but has been living for the last several years in a small flat, it is the large house which could be chosen.

b) *Closely inherited (IHTA 1984 ss 8J and 8K)*

The dwelling house must be transferred, generally on death, to the 'lineal descendants' (children, grandchildren etc) of the deceased. Also included as lineal descendants are step-children, adopted children and foster children and any minors (under the age of 18) if the deceased is that minor's guardian. Unusually, adopted children are treated as qualifying descendants of both their natural and adoptive parents (s 8K(4)). Any descendants of individuals in this list are included.

Also included within the definition of 'closely inherited' are spouses or civil partners of a lineal descendant. However this is limited in one respect: where the lineal descendant pre-deceased the deceased, and the surviving spouse/civil partner has in the meantime remarried/entered into a civil partnership, the surviving spouse/civil partner is no longer in the qualifying list. For example, if Andy's son Jack has predeceased him, Jack's widow Kate is on the list unless and until she remarries.

Turning to 'inherited', a person inherits the property if there is a disposition of it whether effected by will, intestacy 'or otherwise' (s 8J(1)). The property can be specifically mentioned in the will or can pass as part of the residue of the estate. It is not exactly clear to what 'or otherwise' extends. HMRC have specifically stated that property passing to a descendant under a deed of variation will be included and, presumably, the relief applies to assets transferred under a joint tenancy or survivorship clause. HMRC also say that the house itself does not need to be transferred to the descendant as long as the personal representatives sell the property and transfer the proceeds to the descendant. This suggests that if, for example, the house constituting the residue is left to a descendant but has to be sold to meet other legacies, this is treated as inherited property to the extent that cash is passed to the descendant. If the house and other assets of equal value form the residue which is left equally between a qualifying and a non-qualifying person, it also suggests that 50% of the house is treated as closely inherited irrespective of what actually happens to the house. [30.29]

There are specific provisions in relation to trusts.
There are two situations where the relief will extend to property in trust.
(1) The transfer of the house into a trust will be included within the scope of the relief if the trust is a bare trust, an immediate post-death interest (IPDI – see [33.6]), an 18–25 trust (see [33.111]) or a trust for a bereaved minor (see [33.71]–[33.72]) (of course the beneficiary in each case must be in the appropriate relationship with the deceased) (s 8J(4)).
(2) Where the deceased has an interest in possession in the property on death, the property qualifies if the descendant etc becomes beneficially entitled to it on the deceased's death (s 8J(5). Property placed in a discretionary trust on the deceased's death does not qualify. [30.30]

Where the property is treated as included in the estate on death as a result of the reservation of benefit rules, if the original transfer was a gift to one of the persons mentioned above (lineal descendants etc), the property is treated as being inherited by that person on the deceased's death (s 8J(6)). This means, for example, that if Andy gave son Jack a property many years ago, but continued to reserve a benefit over it up until his death, and bequeathed a house to daughter Jill on death, an election could be made for either house. However, if the benefit had ceased before death, triggering a PET which might become chargeable on death, there would be no election possible, and only the house to Jill could qualify. (It is worth noting here that if the value of the house to Jill is under the maximum RNRB available, and the value of the property given to Jack was higher, there should be a downsizing addition available – this is discussed further below.) [30.31]

c) *The residential enhancement*

The additional amount of nil rate band available is termed the residential enhancement (s 8D).

The residential enhancement is reduced once the estate exceeds the value of the taper threshold of £2 million. For these purposes, the term 'estate' is defined as 'the value of a person's estate immediately before the person's death' (s 8D(5)(d)) – in other words, debts are taken into account, but not property reduced by reliefs such as agricultural property relief (APR – see [31.62]–[31.78]) or business property relief (BPR – see [31.42]–[31.61]), or, importantly, transfers to the surviving spouse or civil partner (see [31.41]).

The residential enhancement is reduced by £1 for each £2 of the excess over the taper threshold.

EXAMPLE 30.16

Juno dies in 2017–18 leaving a total estate for IHT purposes of £2,150,000. Assuming all other conditions are satisfied, her RNRB is:
Table B

Maximum RNRB in 2017–18	£100,000
Less the taper reduction:	
£2,150,000	
–£2,000,000	
£150,000/2	£ 75,000
RNRB available after taper	£ 25,000

The RNRB is tapered to zero for estates of £2.2 million or more in 2017–18. Strategies to reduce estates in the taper range may include making PETS and possibly limiting aggregation of estates on the death of the first spouse/civil partner by bequeathing property to other legatees (see *Example 30.17*).

[30.32]

EXAMPLE 30.17

Alan and Betty, spouses, own a house in equal shares. On Alan's death in 2017, he leaves his share of the house (1/2 share worth £400,000) and his other estate, valued at £700,000 to Betty.

Betty dies in 2020, owning the house, then worth £1 million, which she leaves to the children, plus other estate valued at £1.7 million, ie, total estate of £2.7 million.

In the absence of the taper, Betty would have had her own RNRB and a full transferred RNRB from Alan (see **[30.33]**), in total £350,000. However, because her estate is £700,000 over the taper limit, the RNRB is reduced to zero.

Had Alan left the £700,000 'other estate' on his death to someone other than Betty, for example directly to the children, then, assuming that Betty's estate is reduced by the equivalent value, she will die owning property valued at £2 million. There will be no taper and she will be entitled to the full combined RNRB of £350,000, a saving of tax of £140,000.

d) *The transferable RNRB*

Any unused RNRB (called the 'brought forward allowance' in s 8G) on the first death of one of a married couple or civil partnership can be transferred to the surviving partner. In similar fashion to the transferable basic nil rate band, it is the unused percentage of the RNRB rather than unused amount which is transferred (see *Example 30.14*). Furthermore, it is only the second death which has to take place on or after 6 April 2017; the first death can be at any point in time.

In order to determine how much, if any, RNRB can be transferred, two issues have to be addressed. First, did the first to die claim any RNRB on his death? If not, perhaps because there was no 'qualifying residential interest' in the estate of the first to die or because it was left to someone other than a lineal descendant (the surviving spouse for example), then the survivor will inherit an extra 100% RNRB on her death. If part of the RNRB was used, the unused percentage is transferred. Where the first death took place before

6 April 2017 there is obviously no nil rate band which could have been claimed, so potentially 100% can be transferred.

The second issue is the application of the taper on the first death. In order to assess this in relation to deaths before the RNRB legislation takes effect, the allowance is assumed to be £100,000 and the taper threshold £2 million. In other cases, the actual rate in place at the date of the first death is used.

EXAMPLE 30.18

(1) Charles dies in 2017–18, leaving a share of a residence valued at £50,000 to his children. His total estate is under £2 million. He has used only 50% of the available RNRB. Barney, his surviving civil partner, dies in 2020–21. B receives a maximum of 150% of £175,000, ie £262,500.

(2) Dylan dies in 2016–17, leaving an estate of £2.15 million. The excess over the taper threshold is £150,000, so the notional allowance of £100,000 is reduced by £1 for each £2 of the excess, ie £75,000. Accordingly, the £100,000 allowance is reduced by £75,000 to £25,000. This is 25% of the untapered allowance. The proportion of RNRB which is transferred to Dylan's spouse is 25%.

In relation to those surviving serial marriages/civil partnerships, a maximum of 100% of one transferable allowance is permitted.

The RNRB is used first, before the ordinary NRB. On the whole, the order of the relief does not much matter, although it can matter on the second death of a couple where RNRB has been transferred. On the first death, it does not matter from a computational perspective in which order it is given, but on the second death it could be important to distinguish between the transferred normal NRB and the transferred RNRB because the latter is restricted to a particular type of property and is subject to taper. The priority rule has the effect of maximising the amount of (the more useful) general NRB which is transferred forward, so would appear to benefit the taxpayer. [30.33]

e) *Downsizing*

The policy objective behind the downsizing rules is clear – it is to remove the disincentive to downsize to a smaller property or sell up altogether. Implementing the policy has been rather more difficult. Essentially it permits additional NRB (called the 'downsizing addition') where the deceased formerly owned qualifying property which has been disposed of before death. The downsizing addition is only available to the extent that the deceased leaves assets to his descendants.

The downsizing rules require that:

- the deceased formerly owned property which would have qualified had it been retained until death;
- the RNRB is not fully used by another home owned at the date of death (any residential property left to someone other than a descendant also counts against available RNRB for these purposes); and
- assets (net of any secured debt) are left to direct descendants. This includes any property treated as part of the estate at death under the GWR rules, provided this was originally gifted to a direct descendant. The value of these other assets left to descendants determine the amount of RNRB (subject to the maximum available to that person).

The downsizing rules apply where the original property was disposed of on or after 8 July 2015 and to deaths after 5 April 2017. If there is more than one such property which qualifies, one must be nominated. Apart from this there are no time limits between the disposal of the property and death, and no restriction on the number of moves.

If the maximum available RNRB has not been used by a residential interest in the estate on death, and if the value of the former qualifying residential interest is greater than the qualifying residential interest in the estate on death, some downsizing addition may be available.

Further complexities arise because the downsizing addition may have to be tapered in accordance with the amount of estate left on death, and any transferred RNRB may also have to be taken into account. [30.34]

EXAMPLE 30.19

Freda sold her house for £300,000 in 2017–18 and died in 2020–21 without owning residential property. As the house sold exceeds the available RNRB at the date of death, she has effectively lost 100% of her allowance. On her death she is entitled to a maximum downsizing addition of £175,000, the maximum allowance for the year of death. This will require to be tapered should her estate be over the maximum for that year and, of course she will have to leave other assets to her descendants.

6 Accountability and liability for IHT on lifetime transfers made within seven years of death

The donee of a PET which becomes chargeable by virtue of the subsequent death of the transferor must deliver an account to HMRC within 12 months of the end of the month of death (IHTA 1984 s 216(1)(bb): PRs of the deceased must also report such transfers, see s 216(3)(b)). Tax itself is payable six months after the end of the month of death and interest on unpaid IHT runs from that date. There is no question of interest being charged from the date of the PET. Primary liability for the tax is placed upon the transferee although HMRC may also claim the IHT from any person in whom the property is vested, whether beneficially or not, excluding, however, a purchaser of that property (unless it was subject to an HMRC charge for the tax owing: see generally [28.171]).

To the extent that the above persons are not liable for the IHT *or* to the extent that any tax remains unpaid for 12 months after the death, the deceased's PRs may be held liable (IHTA 1984 s 199(2)).

An application for a clearance certificate in respect of IHT that may be payable on a PET may not be made by the executors before the expiration of two years from the death of the transferor (except where the Board exercises its discretion to receive an earlier application). If the property transferred qualified for the instalment option (see [28.174]) the tax resulting from death within seven years may be paid in instalments if the donee so elects and provided that he still owns qualifying property at the date of death (IHTA 1984 s 227(1A)).

So far as additional tax on chargeable lifetime transfers is concerned the same liability rules apply. Primary liability rests upon the donee although the deceased's PRs can be forced to pay the tax in the circumstances discussed above.

The problems posed for PRs by this contingent liability for IHT on PETs and *inter vivos* chargeable transfers are considered at **[30.49]**. **[30.35]**

7 Calculating IHT on the death estate

Having considered the treatment of PETs and the additional IHT on lifetime transfers that may result from the death of the transferor, it is now necessary to consider the taxation of the death estate (which includes property subject to a reservation and settled property in which the deceased was the life tenant). To calculate the IHT the following procedure should be adopted:

Step 1 Calculate total chargeable death estate; ignore, therefore, exempt transfers (eg to a spouse) and apply any available reliefs (eg reduce the value of relevant business property by the appropriate percentage).

Step 2 Find the nil rate band available on death by adding up all the chargeable transfers made in the seven years before death by the deceased. This cumulative total must include both transfers that were charged *ab initio* and PETs brought into charge as a result of the death. Include any transferable nil rate band and any residential nil rate band.

Step 3 Calculate death IHT bill.

Step 4 Convert the tax to an average or estate rate – ie divide IHT *(Step 3)* by total chargeable estate (arrived at in *Step 1*) and multiply by 100 to obtain a percentage rate. It is then possible to say how much IHT each asset bears. This is necessary in cases where the IHT is not a testamentary expense but is borne by the legatee or by trustees of a settlement or by the donee of property subject to a reservation (see **[30.49]**). If the deceased had exhausted his nil rate band as a result of lifetime transfers made in the seven years before death, his death estate will be subject to tax at a rate of 40% which will be the estate rate.

EXAMPLE 30.20

Dougal has just died leaving an estate valued after payment of all debts etc at £300,000. A picture worth £10,000 is left to his daughter Diana (the will states that it is to bear its own IHT) and the rest of the estate is left to his son Dalgleish. Dougal made chargeable transfers in the seven years preceding his death of £125,000. To calculate the IHT on death:

(1) Ascertain nil rate band available: £325,000 less £125,000 (lifetime chargeable transfers in the seven years before death) = £200,000
(2) Calculate IHT on an estate of £300,000:

	£
£200,000 × 0%	0
£100,000 × 40%	40,000
	£40,000

(3) Calculate the estate rate:

$$\frac{£40,000 \ (IHT)}{£30,000 \ (Estate)} \times 100 = 13.13$$

(4) Apply estate rate to picture (ie 13.33% × £10,000) = £1,333. This sum is payable by Diana.
(5) Residue (£290,000) is taxed at 13.33% = £38,666. The balance is paid to Dalgleish.

956   IHT – death

Property subject to a reservation and settled property in which the deceased had enjoyed an interest in possession at the date of death is included in the estate in order to calculate the estate rate of tax. The appropriate tax is, however, primarily the responsibility of the donee and the trustees. The IHT position on death can be represented as follows:

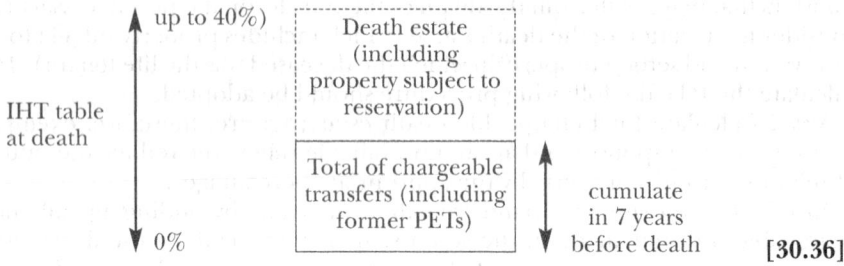

8   Charitable giving – reduced rate of inheritance tax

FA 2012 introduced a lower rate of inheritance tax in respect of deaths from 6 April 2012 where 10% or more of the estate over the nil rate band qualifies for the exemption for gifts to charity (see [31.88]) (IHTA 1984 Sch 1A). In such cases the rate of IHT charged on the chargeable element is reduced to 36%.

The charitable legacy is compared to the chargeable estate after the nil rate band. In the straightforward case, where there is no interest in possession in settled property and no property passing by survivorship or special destination, the available nil rate band on death (including any transferred nil rate band) is deducted from the chargeable estate. The chargeable estate for these purposes is the estate, less liabilities and after exemptions and reliefs, such as the surviving spouse exemption and agricultural or business property relief. The charitable gift is at this stage left in the chargeable estate and is not deducted. Provided the charitable gift is at least equal to 10% of the chargeable estate over the nil rate band, the estate is taxed at 36% rather than 40%. The effect of this provision may result in some individuals deferring donating to charity until death, rather than making lifetime gifts, in order to reach the 10% threshold.

EXAMPLE 30.21

D dies having made chargeable transfers within the last seven years of £25,000. He leaves £10,000 to charity, £390,000 to his children and the residue of his estate, £600,000, to his surviving spouse.

The chargeable estate for the purposes of the 10% calculation is £400,000, ie including the charitable gift but ignoring the exempt gift to the spouse. From this, £300,000 of the nil rate band which remains after the lifetime gifts have been taken into account can be deducted, leaving £100,000. It is this amount which is used when judging whether the 10% limit has been achieved.

In this case, the 10% condition is satisfied by the £10,000 gift to charity.

This means that the tax on the estate is:

Chargeable estate	£390,000
	(the gift to charity is deducted at this stage)
Less nil rate band	£300,000
	£ 90,000 at 36% = IHT of £32,400

Tax on the estate had the gift to charity been left to the children instead would be:
£100,000 @ 40% or £40,000.
So, whilst the charity has received £10,000, the cost to the beneficiaries (here, it will be the surviving spouse who bears the cost) is only £2,400.

The relief has a cliff edge nature – if the 10% limit is not reached, there is simply no relief. In appropriate cases, a variation of the will might be considered in order for the 10% to be achieved. [30.37]

The position is more complex where the chargeable estate contains property subject to a survivorship destination and/or an interest in possession in settled property as well as general estate. In this case, broadly, each component of the estate is treated separately and any charitable gifts are linked to the part of the estate out of which they are payable. The net value of each component of the chargeable estate is ascertained. The available nil rate band is then allocated proportionately to each component. Then the charitable gift or gifts are added back onto their respective components. Finally, the 10% test is applied, comparing the charitable gift to its respective part. If the test is satisfied in relation to one component, the 36% rate applies to that part only, although there are provisions for an election to be made for two or more components to be aggregated. This might be useful where a charitable gift forms a large percentage of one component. [30.38]–[30.40]

III   PAYMENT OF IHT – INCIDENCE AND BURDEN

If the deceased was domiciled in the UK at the time of his death, IHT is chargeable on all the property comprised in his estate whether situated in the UK or abroad. If he was domiciled elsewhere, IHT is only chargeable on his property situated in the UK. (For the extended meaning of domicile in this context, see [35.4].) [30.41]

1   Who pays the IHT on death?

a)   *Duty to account*

The deceased's PRs are under a duty to deliver to HMRC within 12 months of the end of the month of the death an account specifying all the property that formed part of the deceased's estate immediately before his death and including property:
(1) in which the deceased had a beneficial interest in possession (eg where the deceased was the life tenant under a settlement); and
(2) property over which he had a general power of appointment (this property is included since such a power enabled the deceased to appoint himself the owner so that in effect the property is indistinguishable from property owned by him absolutely).

In practice, the PRs will deliver their account as soon as possible because they cannot obtain probate and, therefore, administer the estate until an account has been delivered and the IHT paid; further, they must pay interest on any IHT payable on death and which is unpaid by the end of the sixth month after the end of the month in which the deceased died (for instance, a death in January would mean that IHT is due before 1 August and, thereafter, interest is payable). **[30.42]**

b) *Estimated values and penalties: the* Robertson *case*

The practice of sending in provisional valuations in order to obtain a grant of representation has been noted at **[30.12]**. IHTA 1984 s 216(3A) is in the following terms:

> 'If the personal representatives, after making the fullest enquiries that are reasonably practicable in the circumstances, are unable to ascertain the exact value of any particular property, their account shall in the first instance be sufficient as regards that property if it contains –
>
> (a) a statement to that effect;
> (b) a provisional estimate of the value of the property; and
> (c) an undertaking to deliver a further account of it as soon as its value is ascertained.'

In *Robertson v IRC* (2002) the executor wished to obtain an early grant of representation in order to sell the deceased's house in Scotland. In his IHT calculation he estimated a value for the deceased's personal chattels at £5,000 (subsequently valued at £24,845) and for a property in England at £50,000 (subsequently valued at £315,000). HMRC considered that the return had been prepared negligently and that a penalty of £9,000 was due (see IHTA 1984 s 247). (Since 2004, the maximum penalty has been £3,000.) Corrective valuations were submitted within six months of the deceased's death so this was not a case where there had been any loss of tax and nor was any interest payable. A Special Commissioner decided that no penalty was payable and the following matters may be noted:

(1) The executor had acted in accordance with standard practice and with common sense.
(2) The values were clearly marked as estimates and corrective accounts submitted.
(3) There was a need to obtain the grant as a matter of urgency.
(4) A penalty is only payable if an incorrect account has been negligently produced and the executor had not been negligent.
(5) In the subsequent decision, *Robertson v IRC (No 2)* (2002), the costs of the Commissioners' hearing were awarded against HMRC on the basis that it had acted 'wholly unreasonably' in connection with the hearing.

In cases where a grant is required urgently and the PRs are in difficulties in completing the IHT account, a helpline is available and HMRC may then confirm its acceptance of estimated values. **[30.43]**

c) *'Excepted estates' (SI 2004/2543)*

No formal account need be delivered in the case of an 'excepted estate', although certain information on the deceased, his family and his estate must be produced to the probate registry, a sheriff or the Probate and Matrimonial Office within one week of the grant of probate or confirmation.

There are three categories of excepted estate:
(1) the small estate, where gross value at death is covered by the nil rate band (Reg 4(2)).
(2) the exempt estate, where the gross value at death does not exceed £1m (including certain lifetime transfers) and, apart from any legacies covered by the nil rate band, the estate is left to a surviving spouse and/or charity, and the estate of a deceased who has never been UK domiciled, where the estate in the United Kingdom consists only of cash or quoted shares or securities with a gross value not exceeding £150,000 (Reg 4(3)).
(3) The deceased has never been domiciled or deemed to be domiciled in the UK and the value of the person's estate in the UK consists only of cash or quoted shares or securities, the value of which does not exceed £150,000 (Reg 4(5)).

In relation to the first two categories, the taxpayer must die domiciled in the UK; must have made no chargeable lifetime transfers other than 'specified transfers' where the value did not exceed £150,000; must not have been deemed to own property of more than £150,000 as a life tenant under a settlement; his death estate must not include property subject to a reservation, he must not have owned at death foreign property amounting to more than £100,000 and there must be no charge in relation to an alternatively secured pension fund.

HMRC reserves the right to call for an account within 35 days of the issue of a grant of probate or within 60 days of confirmation in Scotland, but if it does not do so, the PRs are then automatically discharged from further liability.
[30.44]

d) *IHT form*

In cases other than (c) above, to obtain a grant of probate or confirmation, the PRs must submit an HMRC account (IHT Form 400). [30.45]

e) *Liability for IHT (IHTA 1984 Part VII)*

Personal representatives PRs must pay the IHT on assets owned beneficially by the deceased at the time of death and on land comprised in a settlement which vests in them as PRs. Their liability is personal, but limited to assets which they received as PRs or might have received but for their own neglect or default (IHTA 1984 s 204 and see *IRC v Stannard* (1984) which establishes that overseas PRs or trustees may find that their personal UK assets are seized to meet that liability). For the liability of PRs in the event of a gift with reservation, see [29.146]. [30.46]

Other Persons If the PRs fail to pay the IHT other persons are concurrently liable, namely:
(1) Executors *de son tort*, ie persons who interfere with the deceased's property so as to constitute themselves executors or, in Scotland, vitious intromitters. Their liability is limited to the assets in their hands (see *IRC v Stype Investments (Jersey) Ltd* (1982)).
(2) Beneficiaries entitled under the will or on intestacy in whom the property becomes vested after death. Their liability is limited to the property that they receive.

(3) A purchaser of real property if an HMRC charge is registered against that property (such a charge does not apply in Scotland). His liability is limited to the value of the charge.
(4) Any beneficiary entitled to an interest in possession in the property after the death. Liability is generally limited to the value of that property.
[30.47]

Trustees Where the deceased had an interest in possession in settled property at the date of his death, it is the trustees of the settlement who are liable for any IHT on the settled property to the extent that they received or could have received assets as trustees. Should the trustees not pay the tax, the persons set out in (3) and (4) above are concurrently liable. [30.48]

Contingent liability of PRs In three cases PRs may incur liability to IHT if the persons primarily liable (the donees of the property) have reached the limits of their liability to pay or if the tax remains unpaid for 12 months after the death. These occasions are, *first*, when a lifetime chargeable transfer is subject to additional IHT because of the death; *second*, if a PET is brought into charge because of the death; and *third* if the estate includes property subject to a reservation. The following example illustrates the type of problem that may arise:

EXAMPLE 30.22

Mort dies leaving an estate (fully taxed) of £650,000. The PRs are unaware of any lifetime gifts and, therefore, pay IHT of £130,000 and distribute the remainder of the estate. Consider the following alternatives:

(1) After some years a lifetime gift by Mort of £300,000, which had been made six years before his death and was potentially exempt when made, is discovered. Although no IHT is chargeable on that gift the PRs are accountable for extra IHT on the death estate of £120,000; or
(2) A gift of £1,000,000 made one year before Mort's death is discovered. In this case not only will the PRs be accountable for extra IHT of £120,000 as above but, in addition, if the donee fails to pay IHT on the £1,000,000 gift the PRs will be liable to pay that IHT (limited to the net assets in the estate which have passed through their hands).

Contingent liabilities present major problems for PRs and the following matters should be noted:

(1) Their liability may arise long after the estate has been fully administered and distributed (eg a PET may be discovered which is not only itself taxable but also affects the charge on subsequent lifetime chargeable transfers and on the death estate). It may therefore be desirable for PRs to obtain suitable indemnities from the residuary beneficiary before distributing the estate although such personal indemnities are of course always vulnerable (eg in the event of the bankruptcy of that beneficiary).
(2) The liability of PRs is limited to the value of the estate (as discussed above). However, even if IHT has been paid on the estate and a certificate of discharge obtained they are still liable to pay the further tax that may arise in these situations.

(3) If PRs pay IHT no right of recovery is given in IHTA 1984 against donees who were primarily liable except in the case of reservation of benefit property (in this situation s 211(3) affords a right of recovery), although such a right may exist as a matter of general law (see *Private Client Business* (1998) p 58). There is, of course, nothing to stop a donor taking an indemnity from his donee to pay any future IHT as a condition of making the PET. Such an arrangement would be expressed as an indemnity in favour of his estate and does not involve any reservation of benefit in the gifted property. As noted above, personal indemnities are, of course, vulnerable in the event of the bankruptcy or emigration of the donee.

(4) It will not be satisfactory for PRs to retain estate assets to cover the danger of a future tax liability. Apart from being unpopular with beneficiaries there is no guarantee that PRs will retain an adequate sum to cover tax liability on a PET which they did not know had been made: only by retaining all the assets in the estate will they be wholly protected!

(5) Insurance would seem to be the obvious answer to these problems. PRs should give full information on matters within their knowledge and then seek cover (up to the limit of their liability) in respect of an unforeseen IHT liability arising. It would seem reasonable for testators to give expressly a power to insure against these risks. It is understood that cover can be arranged on an individual basis in such cases.

Limited comfort to PRs is afforded by a letter from the Inland Revenue to the Law Society dated 11 February 1991 (reiterated in IHTM 300044) which states:

> 'The Capital Taxes Office will not usually pursue for inheritance tax personal representatives who
>
> - after making the fullest enquiries that are reasonably practicable in the circumstances to discover lifetime transfers, and so
> - having done all in their power to make full disclosure of them to the Board of Inland Revenue
> - have obtained a certificate of discharge and distributed the estate before a chargeable lifetime transfer comes to light.
>
> This statement ... is made without prejudice to the application in an appropriate case of s 199(2) Inheritance Tax Act 1984.' **[30.49]**

Land In addition to persons who are liable for IHT on death, real property (except in Scotland), including a share in land under a trust for sale, is automatically subject to an HMRC charge from the date of death until the date when the IHT is paid (IHTA 1984 s 237(1)(a) and see *Howarth's Executors v IRC* (1997)). **[30.50]**

f) *Payment of tax: the instalment option (IHTA 1984 ss 227, 228)*

To obtain a grant of representation, PRs must pay all the IHT for which they are liable when they deliver their account to HMRC.

However, in the case of certain property the tax may, at the option of the PRs, be paid in ten-yearly instalments with the first instalment falling due six months after the end of the month of death. The object of this facility is to prevent the particular assets from having to be sold by the PRs in order to raise the necessary IHT.

The instalment option is available on the following assets:
(1) land, freehold or leasehold, wherever situate;
(2) shares or securities in a company which gave the deceased control of that company ('control' is defined as voting control on all questions affecting the company as a whole);
(3) a non-controlling holding of shares or securities in an unquoted company (ie a company which is not quoted on a recognised Stock Exchange) where HMRC is satisfied that payment of the tax in one lump sum would cause 'undue hardship';
(4) a non-controlling holding as in (3) above where the tax on the shares or securities and on other property carrying the instalment option comprises at least 20% of the tax due from that particular person (in the same capacity);
(5) other non-controlling shareholdings in unquoted companies, where the value of the shares exceeds £20,000 and either their nominal value is at least 10% of the nominal value of all the issued shares in the company, or the shares are ordinary shares whose nominal value is at least 10% of the nominal value of all ordinary shares in the company; and
(6) a business or a share in a business, eg a partnership share.

An added attraction of paying by instalments is that, generally, no interest is charged so long as each instalment is paid on the due date. In the event of late payment the interest charge is merely on the outstanding instalment. Interest is, however, charged on the total outstanding IHT liability (even if the instalments are paid on time) in the case of land that is not a business asset and shares in investment companies. If the asset subject to the instalment option is sold, the outstanding instalments of IHT become payable at once. Note that the definition of 'qualifying property' for these purposes is not subject to the same limitations as business property relief with regard to investment businesses and excepted assets: see [31.58]. [30.51]

Exercising the option: cashflow benefit If the instalment option is exercised the first instalment is, as already mentioned, payable six months after the month of death. Hence, PRs will normally exercise the option *in order to pay as little IHT as possible before obtaining the grant*. Once the grant has been obtained they may then discharge the IHT on the instalment property in one lump sum. PRs should, however, bear in mind that some IHT will usually be payable before the grant. The necessary cash may be obtained from the deceased's account at either a bank or a building society; from the sale of property for which a grant is not necessary; or by means of a personal loan from a beneficiary. If a loan has to be raised commercially, the interest thereon will qualify for income tax relief for 12 months from the making of the loan so long as it is on a loan account (not by way of overdraft) and is used to pay the tax attributable to personal property (including leaseholds and land held on trust for sale: ITA 2007 ss 403–405.

After the grant has been obtained, if the remaining tax is not paid off at once, PRs may vest the asset in the relevant beneficiary on the understanding that he will discharge the unpaid instalments of tax. Adequate security should, however, be taken in such cases because if the beneficiary defaults, the PRs remain liable for the outstanding IHT (see *Howarth's Executors v IRC* (1997)).

In the case of a specific gift which bears its own IHT and that qualifies for the instalment option, the decision whether to discharge the entire IHT bill once probate has been obtained should be left to the legatee. PRs should not make a unilateral decision (see further [30.56]). [30.52]

Certificates of discharge Once PRs have paid all the outstanding IHT they are entitled to a certificate of discharge under IHTA 1984 s 239(2). [30.53]

Instalments on chargeable lifetime transfers As already discussed, the instalment option may also be available when a chargeable *inter vivos* transfer is made (see [28.174]) and when IHT becomes payable on a PET or additional IHT on a chargeable transfer. In these situations, however, further requirements must be satisfied before the option can be claimed. The donee must have retained the original property or, if it has been sold, have used the proceeds to purchase qualifying replacement property (for a discussion of these requirements in the context of business relief see [31.59]). Further, when the property consisted of unquoted shares or securities those assets must remain unquoted from the date of transfer to the date of death (IHTA 1984 s 227(1A)). [30.54]

2 Allocating the burden of IHT

a) *The general rule*

HMRC is satisfied once the IHT due on the estate has been paid. As far as the PRs and beneficiaries under the will are concerned, the further question arises as to how the tax should be borne as between the beneficiaries: eg should the tax attributable to a specific legacy be paid out of the residue as a testamentary expense or is it charged on the property (the specific legacy)? The answer is particularly important when specific legacies are combined with exempt or partially exempt residue, since, if the IHT is to be paid out of that residue, the grossing-up calculation under IHTA 1984 s 38 (see [30.99] ff) will be necessary and will result in more IHT being payable. [30.55]

b) *Impact on will drafting*

As a general rule, a testator can, and should, stipulate expressly in his will where the IHT on a specific bequest is to fall. If the will makes no provision for the burden of tax, the general principle is that IHT on UK unsettled property which vests in the personal representatives is a testamentary expense. This means that it will come out of the residue and the residuary legatees share will be reduced by it. Under the estate duty regime land had, in such cases, borne its own duty, but the Scottish case of *Re Dougal* (1981) decided that the IHT legislation drew no distinction between realty (heritable property) and personalty (moveable property) and the matter was put beyond doubt by IHTA 1984 s 211.

So although the PRs may well account for all the tax on the estate in the first instance in order to obtain probate or confirmation, tax paid on property that is not a testamentary expense (ie on all gifts which are declared to be tax bearing in the will, joint property and foreign property), they have a right to recover that sum from the person in whom the property is vested (IHTA 1984 s 211(3)).

EXAMPLE 30.23

In Lyslie's will his landed estate is left to his son and his stocks and shares to his daughter. The residue is left to his surviving spouse. In addition he owned a country cottage jointly with his brother, Ernie.
(1) IHT on the specific gifts of the land and securities is borne by the residue in the absence of any provision to the contrary in Lyslie's will. Note that the spouse exemption therefore only applies to exempt from charge what is left after the payment of IHT on the specific gifts.
(2) IHT on the joint property will have been paid by the PRs in order to obtain probate or confirmation. However, such property passes under the title and so does not vest in the PRs, so they are given the right to recover that tax from the other joint tenant(s): IHTA 1984 s 211(3).

In drafting wills and administering estates the following matters should be borne in mind:
(1) When drafting a new will, expressly state whether bequests are tax-bearing or are free of tax.
(2) IHT on foreign property and joint property will always be borne by the beneficiary unless the will provides to the contrary. If the will provides for a legacy to be 'tax free' these words are likely to be limited to UK tax: accordingly if it is intended that the estate should also pay any foreign taxes an express statement to that effect needs to be included (see *Re Norbury* (1939)).

Assuming that the will contains a specific tax-bearing legacy, how will the IHT, in practice, be paid on it? As the PRs are primarily liable to HMRC for the IHT, they will pay that tax in order to obtain probate and either deduct it from the legacy (eg if it is a pecuniary legacy) or recover it from the legatee. For specific legacies of other property (eg land or chattels), the PRs have the power to sell, mortgage or charge the property in order to recover the tax. If they instead (usually at the legatee's request) propose to transfer the asset to him, they should ensure that they are given sufficient guarantees that the tax will be refunded to them. [30.56]

c) *IHTA 1984 s 41;* Re Benham's Will Trusts *and* Re Ratcliffe

IHTA 1984 s 41 As a qualification to the general rules stated above, a chargeable share of residue must always bear its own tax so that the burden of tax cannot be placed on an exempt slice of residue and any provision to the contrary in a will is void (IHTA 1984 s 41). [30.57]

The Benham case The implications of IHTA 1984 s 41 in the context of a will containing both chargeable and exempt gifts of residue were considered in *Re Benham's Will Trusts, Lockhart v Harker, Read and the Royal National Lifeboat Institution* (1995) in which residue was left as follows:
(1) upon trust to pay debts, funeral and testamentary expenses;
(2) subject thereto 'to pay the same to those beneficiaries as are living at my death and who are listed in List A and List B hereunder written in such proportions as will bring about the result that the aforesaid beneficiaries named in List A shall receive 3.2 times as much as the aforesaid beneficiaries named in List B and in each case for their own absolute and beneficial use and disposal'.

List A contained one charity and a number of non-charitable beneficiaries; and List B contained a number of charities and non-charitable beneficiaries.

By an originating summons, the executor asked whether, in view of IHTA 1984 s 41 and the terms of the will, the non-charitable beneficiaries should receive their shares subject to IHT, or whether their shares should be grossed up.

On this question, there were three theoretical possibilities:
(1) the non-charitable beneficiaries received their respective shares subject to IHT, which would mean that they would receive less than the charities; *or*
(2) the non-charitable beneficiaries should have their respective shares grossed up, so that they received the same net sum as the charities; *or*
(3) the IHT was paid as part of the testamentary expenses under clause 3(A), so that the balance was distributed equally between the non-charitable beneficiaries and the charities.

The court agreed that the third possibility was precluded by s 41. However, it did not agree that the charities should receive more than the non-charitable beneficiaries. The plain intention of the testatrix was that each beneficiary, whether charitable or non-charitable, should receive the same as the other beneficiaries on the relevant list. The court therefore concluded that the non-charitable beneficiaries' shares should be grossed up. [30.58]

The available options In analysing the effect of this case, consider an estate of £100,000 to be divided between wife and daughter (although remember that the problem arises whenever residue is divided between exempt and chargeable beneficiaries: for instance, between relatives on the one hand and a charity on the other).

EXAMPLE 30.24

Net residue of £100,000 to be divided equally between surviving spouse and daughter. Estate rate 40%.
(1) *Option 1*: deduct tax on £50,000 and divide balance (£80,000) equally: prohibited by s 41.
(2) *Option 2*: divide equally so that spouse gets £50,000 and daughter's £50,000 then bears tax so that she ends up with £30,000.
(3) *Option 3*: gross up daughter's share so that both end up with the same:
ie x + (100/60) × = £100,000
x = £37,500
Both receive £37,500; gross value of daughter's share is £62,500.

	Spouse (£)	*Daughter (£)*	*Tax man (£)*
Option 1	40,000	40,000	20,000
Option 2	50,000	30,000	20,000
Option 3	37,500	37,500	25,000

The difficulty posed by *Benham* lies in the court's assertion that:

'the plain intention of the testatrix is that at the end of the day each beneficiary, whether charitable or non-charitable, should receive the same as the other beneficiaries ...'.

On one view the case therefore depends upon its own facts and, in particular, on the wishes of the testatrix. However, the ready inclusion (as a matter of construction) of a grossing-up clause in all cases where:
(1)   the residue is left to exempt and non-exempt beneficiaries;
(2)   the will provides for them to take in equal shares and there is no evidence that the testator did not intend *Benham* to apply; and
(3)   the value of the estate is such that IHT is payable on the chargeable portion of residue;
would have gone against the existing practice which had been to apply s 41 (*Option 2*, in *Example 30.24* above) in such cases. [30.59]

Will drafting after Benham It is important that the whole matter is explained to the testator (with a suitable example to illustrate the fiscal and other consequences of the grossing-up route) and that the will is then drafted *either* to provide for a division of residue into shares before imposing the tax liability *or* to incorporate a grossing-up clause. The drafting should make it clear whether *Option 2* or *Option 3* is being adopted. [30.60]

The Ratcliffe case Re Ratcliffe (1999) was brought as a test case to resolve the problems which had resulted from the *Benham* decision. The testatrix left some £2.2m to be divided in accordance with the following residue clause:

> '4 I give devise and bequeath all my real and personal estate whatsoever and wheresoever not hereby otherwise disposed of unto my Trustees upon trust to sell and convert the same into money with power at their absolute discretion to postpone any such sale and conversion for so long as they shall think fit without being answerable for any loss and after payment thereout of my debts and funeral and testamentary expenses to stand possessed of the residue as to one-half part thereof for John Hugh McMullan and Edward Brownlow McMullan (the sons of my cousin Helen McMullan) in equal shares absolutely ... and as to the remainder of my estate upon trust for the following Charities in equal shares ...'

If *Option 2* in *Example 30.24* above were followed the charities would receive £1.12m; the chargeable beneficiaries £720,000 and tax payable would be £400,000; if *Option 3*, the charities and chargeable beneficiaries would each share £870,000 and the IHT would rise to £500,000.

Blackburne J indicated that the matter turned on a true construction of the will that, in this case, pointed to the intention to divide equally the residuary estate including the tax attributable to the chargeable beneficiaries' share (ie the *Option 2* approach). He accepted that a will could result in grossing-up the chargeable beneficiaries' share (ie *Option 3*) but 'much clearer wording would be needed than the common form wording actually used'. He dismissed the decision (and comments of the judge) in *Benham* as follows:

> 'If I had thought that *Re Benham's Will Trusts* laid down some principle, then, unless convinced that it was wrong, I would have felt that I should follow it. I am not able to find that it does and, accordingly, I do not feel bound to follow it.'

Although the case was set down for appeal, a compromise was agreed. [30.61]

Administering estates after Ratcliffe In cases where the will does not put the matter beyond doubt practitioners are now faced with two conflicting decisions, *Benham* and *Ratcliffe*. Of the two, the latter is to be preferred given that the judge carefully reviewed all the authorities including *Benham*: that case had involved, of course, a most obscurely drafted will and the wide *dicta* on grossing-up were not relevant to the case itself. [30.62]

3 Cases where IHT has to be recalculated

In a limited number of instances IHT paid on a deceased's estate will need to be recalculated. [30.63]

Cases where sale proceeds are substituted for the death valuation (see [30.7] ff.) [30.64]

As the result of a variation or disclaimer Such instruments, if made within two years of the death, may be read back into the original will which *may* necessitate a recalculation of the tax payable (see [30.153]). [30.65]

Discretionary will trusts If the conditions of IHTA 1984 s 144 are satisfied, tax is calculated as if the testator had provided in his will for the dispositions of the trustees (see [30.145]). [30.66]

Orders under the Inheritance (Provision for Family and Dependants) Act 1975 When the court exercises its powers under s 2 of the 1975 Act to order financial provision out of the deceased's estate for his family and dependants, the order is treated as made by the deceased and may result in there having been an under- or overpayment of IHT on death (IHTA 1984 s 146). Any application under this Act should normally be made within six months of the testator's death, so that the PRs will have some warning that adjustments to the IHT bill may have to be made. Further adjustments to the tax bill may be required if the court makes an order under s 10 of the Act reclaiming property given away by the deceased in the six years prior to his death with the intention of defeating a claim for financial provision under the Act. In this case, the deceased's cumulative total of chargeable lifetime transfers is reduced by the gift reclaimed. This, of itself, may affect the rate at which tax is charged on the deceased's estate on death. Also the value of the reclaimed property and any tax repaid on it falls into the deceased's estate thus necessitating a recalculation of the IHT payable on death.

These rules are bolstered by a somewhat obscure anti-avoidance provision in IHTA 1984 s 29A. It is relevant when there is an exempt transfer on death (eg to the surviving spouse) and that beneficiary then, in satisfaction of a claim against the estate of the deceased, disposes of property 'not derived from the death transfer'. [30.67]–[30.90]

EXAMPLE 30.25

A dies leaving everything to Mrs A. Dependant B has a claim against A's estate but is 'bought off' by Mrs A making a payment (out of her own resources) of £150,000.
(1) *In the absence of specific legislation:* the arrangement would probably be a PET by Mrs A to B and so free from IHT provided that Mrs A survived by seven

years. Alternatively it could be argued that there was no transfer of value since the compromise was a commercial arrangement under IHTA 1984 s 10. No IHT was, of course, charged on A's death.

(2) *Position under s 29A:* A's will is deemed amended to include a specific gift of £150,000 to B with the remainder (only) passing to Mrs A. Accordingly a recalculation will be necessary and an immediate IHT charge will arise.

IV PROBLEMS CREATED BY THE PARTIALLY EXEMPT TRANSFER

1 When do ss 36–42 apply?

In many cases the calculation of the IHT bill on death will be straightforward. Difficulties may, however, arise when a particular combination of dispositions is made in a will. IHTA 1984 ss 36–42 provide machinery for resolving these problems with a method of calculating the gross value of the gifts involved and, accordingly, the IHT payable. Consider, first, a number of instances where the calculation of the IHT on death poses no special difficulties: **[30.91]**

Where all the gifts are taxable A leaves all his property to be divided equally amongst his four children. In this case the whole of A's estate is charged to IHT. **[30.92]**

Where all the gifts are exempt eg A leaves all his property to a spouse and/or a charity. In this case the estate is untaxed. **[30.93]**

Where specific gifts are exempt and the residue is chargeable eg A leaves £100,000 to his spouse and the residue of £500,000 to his children. Here the gift to the spouse is exempt, but IHT is charged on the residue of £500,000 so that only the balance will be paid to the children. **[30.94]**

Where specific gifts are chargeable under the terms of the will and the residue is exempt If the gifts bear their own tax, the total chargeable part of the estate is the chargeable gift: eg A leaves a specific tax-bearing gift of £300,000 to his niece and the residue to his spouse. The spouse receives the residue after deduction of the £300,000 gift; IHT is calculated on the £300,000 and is borne by the niece. If the gifts do not bear their own tax, the chargeable estate is the gift plus the tax on the gift (IHTA 1984 s 38(3)), so the gift has to be grossed up at death rates, ie by 5/4 to the extent that it exceeds the nil rate band.

For example, A's estate on death is valued at £630,000 and he leaves £346,000 to his daughter with remainder to his surviving spouse. As previously explained, the specific gift of £346,000 will be free of tax unless the will provides to the contrary. The problem that arises is to decide how much IHT should be charged on the specific gift and this involves grossing-up that gift. With the simplified IHT rate structure, grossing-up has become relatively straightforward and, in the tax year 2016–17, the IHT payable will be two-thirds of the amount by which the chargeable legacies exceed the available nil rate band. Hence, assuming that A has an unused nil rate band of £325,000,

tax payable on the daughter's legacy will be two-thirds of £346,000 − £325,000: ie £14,000. As a result:
(1) The gross value of the legacy becomes £360,000. The daughter receives the correct net sum of £346,000 after deducting IHT at 40% on the amount by which the gross legacy exceeds the available nil rate band.
(2) The £14,000 tax is paid out of the residue leaving the surviving spouse with £270,000. [30.95]

Where there are specific gifts bearing their own tax and tax-free specific gifts, or where part of the residue is exempt, part chargeable, the calculation of the IHT is not so obvious, and it becomes necessary to apply the rules in ss 36–42, discussed at [30.99]–[30.140]. [30.96]

Business and agricultural property When business property is specifically given to a beneficiary that person will benefit from the appropriate relief but in other cases the benefit of the relief is apportioned between the exempt and chargeable parts of the estate (IHTA 1984 s 39A). [30.97]

EXAMPLE 30.26

Deceased's estate is valued at £1m and includes business property (qualifying for 50% relief) worth £600,000. He left a £600,000 legacy to his widow and the residue to his daughter.

	£
Estate	1,000,000
Less: 50% relief on business property	300,000
Value transferred	700,000

(1) Legacy of £600,000 to widow is multiplied by

$$\frac{R \text{ (value transferred)}}{U \text{ (estate before relief)}} = \frac{£700,000}{£1,000,000} = £420,000$$

(2) Accordingly the value attributed to the residue (given to the daughter) is:

$$400,000 \times \frac{R \ (£700,000)}{U \ (£1,000,000)} = £280,000$$

(3) IHT is therefore charged on £280,000.
Notes:
(1) Had relief at 100% been available the taxable sum would have been £160,000.
(2) The lowest tax bill results if the agricultural or business property is specifically given to a non-exempt beneficiary. 'Specific gift' is inadequately defined in IHTA 1984 s 42(1), and the following points may be noted:
  (i) an appropriation of business property in satisfaction of a pecuniary legacy does not count as a specific gift;
  (ii) a direction to pay a pecuniary legacy 'out of' business property is likewise not a specific gift of business property (IHTA 1984 s 39A(6));

(iii) it is possible to employ a formula to leave business property equal in value to the testator's nil rate band *after* relief at 50%;
(iv) a defectively drafted will may be cured by an instrument of variation whereby a specific gift of business property is 'read back' into the will.
(3) Difficulties can be caused if a nil rate band clause is used in a will and the estate includes business or agricultural property as illustrated in the following example.

EXAMPLE 30.27

(1) Jill leaves an estate valued at £1.3m that includes a shareholding in a private company (qualifying for 100% business property relief (BPR)) valued at £650,000.

If she leaves the shares to her son Paul by way of specific gift and residue to her husband Jack, no tax is payable.

If she leaves a cash gift of £650,000 to son Paul (this gift to bear its own tax) and residue to husband, the son's gift and the residue will each attract their appropriate portion of the relief of £650,000. The amount of relief allocated to the gift to Paul is £650,000 × £650,000/£1,300,000, ie £325,000. The gift to Paul after deduction of the relief is £325,000. After the nil rate band, the taxable value is nil.

(2) Jill instead leaves a will which provides that her son will take 'a cash sum which is the largest amount that can be given without any Inheritance Tax being payable on the transfer of value of my estate which I am deemed to make immediately before my death'. She had anticipated that her son would take £325,000 (being the amount of the nil rate band legacy) although she was aware that if she made chargeable lifetime gifts within seven years of her death, the amount her son would take under the will on her death would be reduced.

With 100% BPR, however, the amount which her son will take, assuming her nil rate band is unused on death, is £650,000, which for IHT purposes will be reduced by its share of BPR (£325,000) to £325,000, the amount of the nil rate band. The consequence will be that Jill's husband Jack will receive less than his wife had anticipated when the will was drafted. The effect would be even more dramatic if business property in the estate was worth, say, £1,000,000. In this case, the cash gift that Paul could take without payment of tax would leave Jack with nothing!

(3) This unintentional result would have been avoided if the will had stated that her son should take:

'a cash sum which is the lesser of:
(i) the largest amount that can be given without any Inheritance Tax being payable on the transfer of value of my estate which I am deemed to make immediately before my death, and
(ii) the upper limit of the nil rate band in the table of rates of tax applicable on my death in Schedule 1 to the Inheritance Tax Act 1984.'

2 Effect of previous chargeable transfers on the ss 36–42 calculation

In considering the application of ss 36–42, it has so far been assumed that the deceased had made no previous chargeable lifetime transfers in the seven years before his death. If he has, any specific gift on death must be grossed up taking account of those cumulative lifetime transfers because they may affect the rate at which tax is charged on the estate on death. [30.98]

EXAMPLE 30.28

A's estate on death is valued at £250,000 and he leaves £90,000 tax-free to his son and the residue to a charity. A had made gross lifetime transfers in the previous seven years of £325,000.

The lifetime gifts have wiped out A's nil rate band and therefore IHT on the specific legacy of £90,000 is two-thirds of £90,000 = £60,000. Accordingly, the gross legacy is £150,000 so that the charity is left with £100,000.

3 Double grossing-up

IHTA 1984 ss 36–42 also deal with the more complex problems that arise if specific tax-free gifts are combined with chargeable gifts bearing their own tax, and an exempt residue. [30.99]

a) *The problem*

Assume that B makes a specific bequest of £328,000 tax free to his son, and leaves a gift of £90,000 bearing its own tax to his daughter with residue of £400,000 (before deducting any IHT chargeable to residue) going to his spouse. To gross up the specific tax-free gift of £328,000 as if it were the only chargeable estate would produce insufficient IHT bearing in mind that there is an additional chargeable legacy of £90,000. On the other hand, if the £328,000 were grossed up at the estate rate applicable to £418,000 (ie the two gifts of £328,000 and £90,000) the resulting tax would be too high because the £90,000 gift should not be grossed up. Further, to gross up £328,000 at the estate rate applicable to the whole estate including the exempt residue would produce too much tax because this assumes, wrongly, that the residue is taxable. [30.100]

b) *The solution*

The solution provided in ss 36–42 is to gross up the specific tax-free gift at the estate rate applicable to a hypothetical chargeable estate consisting of the grossed-up specific tax-free gift and the gifts bearing their own tax. The procedure, known as double grossing-up, is as follows:

Step 1 Gross up the specific tax-free gift of £328,000 by multiplying excess over nil rate band by $\frac{5}{3}$: £3,000 × $\frac{5}{3}$ = £5,000

$$£5,000 + £328,000 = £333,000$$

Step 2 Add to this figure the tax-bearing gift of £90,000 making a hypothetical chargeable estate of £423,000.

Step 3 Calculate IHT on £423,000 assuming full nil rate band available: £423,000 − £325,000 at 40% = £39,200.

Then convert to an estate rate: namely

$$\frac{39{,}200}{423{,}000} \times 100 = 9.27\%$$

Step 4 Gross up the specific tax-free gift a second time at this rate of 9.27%:

$$£328{,}000 \times \frac{100}{100 - 9.27} = £361{,}512$$

Step 5 The chargeable part of the estate now consists of the grossed-up specific gift (£361,512) and the gift bearing its own tax (£90,000) = £451,512.
Step 6 On the figure of £451,512, IHT is recalculated:

$$£451{,}512 - £325{,}000 = £126{,}512 \text{ @ } 40\% = £50{,}605.$$

This is again expressed as a percentage of the chargeable estate.

$$\frac{50{,}605}{451{,}512} \times 100 = 11.21\%$$

Step 7 The grossed-up specific tax-free gift (£361,512) is then charged at this rate (11.21%) = tax of £40,525.

It should be noted that the IHT on specific tax-free gifts must always be paid from the residue, so this tax comes out of the spouse's share.

The estate is thus distributed as follows:

	Net Receipt	Tax	
Gross estate			£818,000
Tax-free gift to son	£328,000	£40,525	
Net of tax to daughter	£79,911	£10,089	
	£407,911 +	£50,614 =	£458,525
Residue to spouse			£359,475

[30.101]

c) *Conclusion*

Sections 36–42 are relevant whenever a tax-free specific gift is mixed with an exempt residue, and, if tax-bearing gifts are also included in the will, then a double grossing-up calculation is required. Logically, to gross up only twice is indefensible since the estate rate established at *Step 6* should then be used to gross up further the £328,000 (ie repeat *Step 4*) and so on and so on! Thankfully, the statute only requires the grossing-up calculation to be done twice with the consequence that a small saving in IHT results! [30.102]

4 Problems where part of residue is exempt, part chargeable

So far we have been concerned with a wholly exempt residue. What, however, happens if part of the residue is chargeable? For example, A, whose estate is worth £500,000, leaves a specific tax-free gift of £328,000 to his son; a tax-bearing gift of £90,000 to his daughter; and the residue equally to his widow and his nephew.

The method of calculating the IHT is basically the same as in the double grossing-up example above in that the chargeable portion of the residue (half to nephew) must be added to the hypothetical chargeable estate in *Step 2* to calculate the assumed estate rate. The difficulty is caused because, although IHT on grossed-up gifts is payable before the division of residue into chargeable and non-chargeable portions, the IHT on the nephew's portion of the residue must be deducted from his share of residue after it has been divided (IHTA 1984 s 41). To take account of this, the method for calculating the IHT payable in such cases is amended as follows:

Step 1 Gross up the specific tax-free gift of £328,000 to £333,000 (see step 1 in [**30.101**]).

Step 2 Calculate the hypothetical chargeable estate by adding to the grossed-up gift of £333,000: (1) the tax-bearing gift of £90,000 and (2) the chargeable residue:

	£	£
Estate		500,000
Less: grossed-up gift	333,000	
tax-bearing gift	90,000	423,000
		77,000

The nephew's share (the chargeable residue) is half of £77,000 = £38,500. This results in a hypothetical chargeable estate of:

$$£333,000 + £38,500 + £90,000 = £461,500$$

Step 3 Calculate the 'assumed estate rate' on £461,500:
IHT on £461,500:
£325,000 nil rate band left, so £136,500 at 40% = £54,600
Estate rate is

$$\frac{54,600}{461,500} \times 100 = 11.83\%$$

Step 4 Gross up the specific tax-free gift at this rate of 11.83%:

$$£328,000 \times \frac{100}{100 - 11.83} = £372,001$$

Step 5 The chargeable part of the estate now consists of:

	£	£
Estate		500,000
Less: grossed-up gift	372,001	
tax-bearing gift	90,000	462,001
		37,999

Nephew's share is ½ × £37,999= £19,000
Therefore, total chargeable estate is
£19,000 + £90,000 + £372,001 = £481,001
Step 6 Calculate the estate rate on the chargeable estate of £481,001:
IHT on £481,001:
£325,000 nil rate band left so £156,001 at 40% = £62,400
Estate rate is

$$\frac{62,400}{481,001} \times 100 = 12.97\%$$

Step 7 The grossed-up specific tax-free gift of £372,001 is taxed at the rate of 12.97% = £48,248.

Step 8 The tax-bearing gift of £90,000 is taxed at 12.97% = £11,673. This tax is paid by the daughter.

Step 9 The residue remaining is £500,000 − (£328,000 + £48,248 + £90,000) = £33,752. This is then divided:
Half residue to spouse = £16,876
Half residue to nephew = £16,876 less IHT calculated at a rate of 12.97% on £16,876 (ie the nephew's share of the residue at *Step 5*, above). Therefore, the tax on the nephew's share is £2,189 so that the nephew receives £14,687.

[30.103]–[30.120]

V   ABATEMENT

Although ss 36–42 are mainly concerned with calculating the chargeable estate in cases where there is an exempt residue, they also deal with certain related matters:

Allocating relief where gifts exceed an exempt limit A transfer may be partly exempt only because it includes gifts which together exceed an exempt limit, eg a transfer to a non-UK domiciled spouse which exceeds the nil rate band. To deal with such cases IHTA 1984 s 38(2) provides for the exemption to be allocated between the various gifts as follows:
(1) Specific tax-bearing gifts take precedence over other gifts.
(2) Specific tax-free gifts receive relief in the proportion that their values bear to each other.
(3) All specific gifts take precedence over gifts of residue. [30.121]

Abatement of gifts If a transferor makes gifts in his will which exceed the value of his estate, those gifts must be abated in accordance with IHTA 1984 s 37. There are two cases to consider:
(1) Where the gifts exceed the transferor's estate without regard to any tax payable, the gifts abate according to the general rules of abatement (eg in the Administration of Estates Act 1925) and tax is charged on the abated gifts.

EXAMPLE 30.29

A testator's net estate is worth £300,000. He left his house worth £100,000 to his nephew, the gift to bear its own tax, and a general tax-free legacy of £300,000 to a charity. Under IHTA 1984 s 37(1) the legacy must abate to £200,000 to be paid to the charity free of tax. The house will bear its own tax.

(2) Where the transferor's estate is only insufficient to meet the gifts as grossed up under the rules in ss 36–42, abatement is governed by IHTA 1984 s 37(2). The order in which the gifts are abated depends on the general law. **[30.122]–[30.140]**

VI SPECIFIC PROBLEMS ON DEATH

1 Commorientes

a) *The problem*

Where A and B leave their property to each other and are both killed in a common catastrophe or otherwise die in circumstances such that it is not clear in what order they died, LPA 1925 s 184 stipulates that the younger is deemed to have survived the elder. In Scotland, neither party is to be treated as having survived the other (Succession (Scotland) Act 2016 s 9). Similarly in Northern Ireland, the common law rule is that, where it is uncertain who died first, deaths are presumed to have been at the same time.

So, in England, if A was the elder, he is presumed to have died first, so that his property passes to B, and IHT will be chargeable. B's will leaving everything to A will not take effect because of the prior death of A so that his assets (including his inheritance from A) will pass on intestacy. IHT would *prima facie* be chargeable. The result is that property bequeathed by the elder would (subject to quick succession relief) be charged to IHT twice. **[30.141]**

b) *The IHT solution*

To prevent this double charge, IHTA 1984 s 4(2) provides that A and B 'shall be assumed to have died at the same instant'. This is effective at avoiding aggregation of estates, as a person must survive another in order to inherit, and so A's estate is charged only once – on his death. The question as to whether this subsection also operates to determine the *destination* of the estates for other IHT purposes is less clear, and this is important for the operation of exemptions. **[30.142]**

EXAMPLE 30.30

(1) Fred (aged 60) and his wife Wilma (aged 55), domiciled in England, are both killed in a car crash. Fred and Wilma had each left all their property to the other, whom failing, to their son Barnie. Fred's estate is valued at £500,000 and Wilma's at £400,000. According to LPA 1925 s 184, the order of deaths is Fred then Wilma, and Fred's property, therefore, passes to Wilma and thence to Barnie. The effect of IHTA 1984 s 4(2) is to ensure that Fred's estate is not aggregated with Wilma's as she is treated as not surviving him. However,

is the inter-spouse exemption under IHTA 1984 s 18 available? The view of the HMRC is that, because the property *actually* goes to Wilma first under LPA 1925 s 184, the exemption is available. In other words, the presumption in section 4(2) does not operate for all IHT purposes. So, on this view, not only is Fred's estate not aggregated with Wilma's, but it is also eligible for exemption under section 18. So there is no charge on Fred's death and on Wilma's death; only the £400,000 in her estate before Fred's death is charged.

An alternative view is that the effect of section 4(2) is to determine the IHT treatment for all purposes. In this example, Fred's estate is treated as a transfer of value to Barnie, which would exclude the operation of section 18, and Fred's and Wilma's estates are both fully chargeable (subject to any available nil rate band). (See [1995] BTR 390.)

Had the couple been domiciled in Scotland or Northern Ireland, or had they died intestate, the spouse exemption would not apply: in neither case would the property have passed through the spouse under the relevant laws of deemed survivorship on succession.

Compare:
(2) Assume that Fred and Barnie are killed in the same crash and that Fred had left his property to Barnie, whom failing to charity, and that Barnie had left his estate to charity. The statutory presumption under LPA 1925 s 184 is, again, that Barnie survives Fred and thus inherits Fred's estate. On the limited interpretation of section 4(2), although there is no aggregation of Fred's estate with Barnie's, the charity exemption would not be available on Fred's estate, as one looks to where the property goes in the first instance under the relevant laws of succession, which is to Barnie. The exemption would only be available to Barnie's original estate. In contrast, on the view that section 4(2) not only determines aggregation but destination, the charity exemption would be available on Fred's estate and, separately, on Barnie's.

2 Survivorship clauses

To inherit property on a death it is necessary only to survive the testator so that if the beneficiary dies immediately after inheriting the property, the two deaths could mean two IHT charges. Some relief is provided by quick succession relief (see **[30.144]**), but the prudent testator may provide in his will for the property to pass to the desired beneficiary only if that person survives him for a stated period. Such provisions are referred to as survivorship clauses and IHTA 1984 s 92 states that provided the clause does not exceed six months there will be (at most) only a single IHT charge.

EXAMPLE 30.31

T leaves £100,000 to A 'if he survives me by six months. If he does not, the money is to go to B'.

The effect of IHTA 1984 s 92 is to leave matters in suspense for up to six months and then to read the will in the light of what has happened. Hence, if A survives for six months it is as if the will had provided '£100,000 to A'; if he dies before the end of that period, it is as if the will had provided for £100,000 to go to B. Accordingly, two charges to IHT are avoided; there will merely be the one chargeable occasion when the testator dies.

Specific problems on death 977

In principle, it is good will drafting to include survivorship clauses. The danger of choosing a period in excess of six months is that IHTA 1984 s 92 will not apply so that the bequest will be settled property to which ordinary charging principles will apply. If a longer period is essential, insert a two-year discretionary trust into the will (see [30.145]). [30.143]

3 Quick succession relief (IHTA 1984 s 141)

Quick succession relief offers a measure of relief against two charges to IHT when two chargeable events occur within five years of each other.

For unsettled property quick succession relief is only given on a death where the value of the deceased's estate had been increased by a chargeable transfer (*inter vivos* or on death) to the deceased made within the previous five years. It is not necessary for the property then transferred to be part of the deceased's estate when he dies. The relief reduces the IHT on the second chargeable occasion. IHT is calculated in the usual way and then reduced by a sum dependent upon two factors. First, the length of time between the first chargeable transfer and the subsequent death. The percentage of relief is available as follows:

100% if previous transfer one year or less before death
80%   if previous transfer one–two years before death
60%   if previous transfer two–three years before death
40%   if previous transfer three–four years before death
20%   if previous transfer four–five years before death.

The second factor is the amount of IHT paid on the first transfer. IHTA 1984 s 141(3) states that the relief is 'a percentage determined as above of the tax charged on so much of the value transferred by the first transfer as is attributable to the increase in the estate of the second transferor'. This is not straightforward.

HMRC use the following formula:

$$A/D \times B \times C$$

where A = the increase in the estate of the person receiving the first gift, B is the tax on that transfer, C is the percentage based on the time gap between the first and second transfer and D is the value of the first chargeable transfer.

EXAMPLE 30.32

(1) *Free of tax legacy on death:* Zeb, who has made no previous chargeable transfers, dies leaving an estate of £650,000 out of which he leaves a free of tax legacy of £325,000 to Yo. Yo dies 18 months later leaving an estate of £475,000.
A = £325,000
B = £65,000 (half the tax on the whole estate, which is £325,000 at 40% = £130,000
C = 80% (between one and two years between A's death and B's)
D = £325,000 (there is no need to take account of the IHT paid in calculating D as it was not borne by Yo)

So, Yo receives QSR on his death as follows:

$$\frac{£325,000}{£325,000} \times £65,000 \times 80\% = £52,000$$

(2) *Legacy bearing own tax on death*: Having made sufficient lifetime transfers to use up his nil rate band, Eric leaves £20,000 to Ernie, the legacy to bear its own tax. All of Eric's estate is chargeable. Ernie dies three and a half years later.
A = £12,000 (after tax of £8,000 on £20,000 at 40%)
B = £ 8,000
C = 40%
D = £20,000 (the legacy)
Ernie receives QSR of

$$\frac{£12,000}{£20,000} \times £8,000 \times 40\% = £19,20$$

(3) *Lifetime gift*: Diego gives £25,000 to Madonna in October 2015 (a PET). Madonna dies in July 2016 and Diego in January 2017. As a result of Diego's death, the PET is chargeable and IHT of (say) £5,000 is paid by Madonna's estate, as a recipient of a failed PET.
A = £20,000 (the original gift less the tax which became due by Madonna's estate)
B = £5,000
C = 80% (between one and two years between A's death and B's).
D = £25,000
Madonna's estate receives QSR of

$$\frac{£20,000}{£25,000} \times £5,000 \times 80\% = £3,200$$

In the case of settled property the relief is only available (and necessary) for interest in possession trusts. It is given whenever an interest in possession terminates and hence can be deliberately activated by the life tenant assigning or surrendering his interest. The earlier transfer in the case of settled property will be the creation of the settlement.

EXAMPLE 30.33

S, who had settled property by will on B for life, C absolutely, dies in year 1. In year 2 B dies.
Year 1 IHT will be chargeable on S's estate.
Year 2 Quick succession relief is available on A's death. The chargeable transfer in the previous five years was the creation of the settlement in year 1.

[30.144]

4 Flexible will drafting (IHTA 1984 s 144)

Transfers out of certain trusts created on death (broadly, discretionary trusts) *within two years* of his death are treated as if they were made by the testator by will. Such a trust enables wills to be drafted with some flexibility and is advantageous where, for example, the testator is dying and desires his estate to be divided between his four children, but is not sure of the proportions. By inserting the two-year trust a decision about the final distribution of the estate can be postponed for a further two years. The IHT that would normally arise under the discretionary trust charging rules 'shall not be charged but the Act shall have effect as if the will had provided that on the testator's death the property should be held as it is held after the event' (s 144(2)). Section 144 cannot be disapplied by election.

In general, for s 144 to apply, the transfer out of the trust must *otherwise attract a tax charge*, see *Frankland v IRC (1997)*. However, by virtue of FA 2006 Sch 20, both pre- and post-22 March 2006 appointments of immediate post-death interests, trusts for bereaved minors or age 18-to-25 trusts (which would not otherwise be the occasion of a charge – for definitions, see **Chapter 32**), may also be made without an IHT charge and back-dated to the death.
[30.145]

a) *IHT consequences*

IHT will be charged at the estate rate on the property settled at death but if the ultimate distributions made by the trustees are 'read back' into the will that IHT may need to be recalculated. For example, if the will creates a discretionary trust (in relation to which inheritance tax is payable) and the trust is ended within two years in favour of the testator's surviving spouse, the reading back provisions result in a repayment of any IHT charged on the death estate. [30.146]

b) *Theoretical problems and practical uses of s 144*

Because at the date of death property is left on a discretionary trust or, for deaths on or after 22 March 2006, an interest in possession trust that is not an immediate post-death interest or a disabled person's interest, that property is subject to IHT and, in normal circumstances, tax will need to be paid before the PRs can obtain a grant of probate. In cases where the trust is ended (as in *Example 30.30(1)*) by appointment to a surviving spouse there will then be a refund of the tax paid, but nonetheless the estate may have been put at a cashflow disadvantage. In *Fitzwilliam v IRC* (1993) the testator's residuary estate was settled on trusts that gave the trustees power in the 23 months following the death to appoint amongst a discretionary class of beneficiaries. After the expiration of that period the trustees were to pay the income to the testator's widow for the remainder of her life. The executors indicated that they intended to appoint the property to the surviving spouse and the Winchester District Probate Registry therefore accepted that the estate was spouse exempt. This conduct was criticised by the then Inland Revenue but Vinelott J did not join in that criticism and pointed out that because the estate was largely composed of agricultural land and chattels it would have been very difficult for the executors to have paid such a bill. This matter was not raised in the higher courts. [30.147]

c) *Vesting of property issue*

It is not necessary that either the administration of the estate has been completed or an express assent of property by the PRs to the trustees has taken place before any appointment can be made. HMRC now accepts that such trusts are immediately constituted at the date of the testator's death: see further *Capital Taxes News*, July 1990, p 98. **[30.148]**

d) *CGT tie-in*

There is one remaining disadvantage: namely that if an appointment is made out of such a trust which is duly read back under s 144 there can be no question of CGT hold-over relief being available unless the property in the trust qualifies as business assets. There is no equivalent relief to s 144 permitting reading back in CGT legislation. If the estate is not fully administered at the relevant time HMRC does, however, accept that the beneficiaries take *qua* legatees at probate value (see **[21.103]**). **[30.149]**

e) *Uses*

This trust can be used as an alternative to a survivorship clause. Say, for instance, that the testator wants Eric to get the property if he survives him by 18 months failing which Ernie is to receive it. This cannot be achieved by a conventional IHT survivorship clause (which must be limited to six months; see **[30.143]**). If Eric and Ernie are made beneficiaries of a discretionary trust, however, and the trustees know the testator's wishes concerning the distribution of the fund, there is no risk of a double IHT charge in carrying out his wishes.

Such a trust is also attractive as compared with variations and disclaimers. If there is any doubt about who should be given the deceased's estate, it is better to use a trust than to rely upon an appointed legatee voluntarily renouncing a benefit under the will. All the most convincing fiscal arguments will often fail to persuade people to give up property and they cannot be compelled to vary or to disclaim!

Finally, if the estate includes business property which *may* attract IHT relief at 100%, consider leaving that property on discretionary trusts for a beneficial class including surviving spouse and issue. If it turns out that relief is *not* available the trustees can appoint the business to the spouse with reading back under s 144. Hence any IHT charge has been avoided. **[30.150]**

f) *Precatory trusts*

Instead of imposing a trust, the deceased may be content to leave property subject to a non-binding memorandum of wishes. Such 'precatory trusts' are dealt with by IHTA 1984 s 143 (which provides that if the legatee carries out the wishes within two years of the testator's death there is reading back) and should not be confused with the s 144 'two-year' trust (see *Harding (Loveday's Executors) v IRC* (1997)). **[30.151]**

5 Channelling through a surviving spouse

In cases where the testator is survived by his spouse, a flexible life interest trust in favour of that spouse might be considered. The creation of the trust was, and remains post 2006, an exempt transfer. The trustees are given power to revoke the life interest, say in favour of the children, and the revocation is a PET. Provided the surviving spouse survived for seven years, the transfer would become exempt and even if she did not survive, the position was not worsened.

The advantage this arrangement had over the two-year discretionary trust is that no tax is paid on the first death.

Accordingly, a simple alternative would be for the property to be left to the spouse absolutely and to rely upon her to then make PETs. The transferable nil rate band between spouses ([30.27]) may increase the attractiveness of this option. However, wealthy testators may be reluctant to leave matters in the control of the surviving spouse. [30.152]

6 Disclaimers and variations (post mortem tax planning)

It will often be desirable to effect changes in a will after the death of the testator, for instance, to rearrange the dispositions with a view to saving tax (and especially IHT) or to provide for someone who is omitted from the will or who is inadequately provided for. In these cases, persons named in the original will reject a portion of their inheritance; hence, they will (usually) be making a gift. Similar problems arise on an intestacy – indeed the statutory intestacy provisions will often prove even less satisfactory than a will.

So far as both IHT and CGT are concerned certain changes to a will, or to the intestacy rules, are permitted, if made within two years of death, to take effect as if they had been provided for in the original will or intestacy (for IHT, see IHTA 1984 s 142; for CGT, TCGA 1992 s 62(6)–(9): the CGT rules are considered at [21.121]). The effect of 'reading back' these changes into the will or amending the intestacy rules is to avoid the possibility of a second charge to IHT and to require a recalculation of the IHT charged on death.

EXAMPLE 30.34

T by will leaves property to his three daughters equally. He omits his son with whom he had quarrelled bitterly. The daughters agree to vary the will by providing that the four children take equally and, for the capital taxes, T's original will can be varied to make the desired provision. Provided that the rearrangement is made in writing within two years of T's death no daughter will be taxed on the gift of a part of her share to her brother. Instead tax will be charged as if T had left his estate to his four children equally (so that the IHT liability will be unchanged).

To take advantage of these provisions there must be a voluntary alteration of the testamentary provisions; in the case of enforced alterations: eg as a result of applications under the Inheritance (Provision for Family and Dependants) Act 1975, different provisions apply, although to similar effect: see [30.67].

No specific alterations were made to IHTA 1984 s 142 by FA 2006. Accordingly, where a testator died prior to 22 March 2006, and a variation to the will has been made on or after that date giving rise to an interest in possession, it will be treated as an interest in possession in existence prior to 22 March 2006 and subject to the former regime applying to interests in possession (see **Chapter 33**). Where the death occurs on or after 22 March 2006, followed by a variation which creates an interest in possession, the new interest in possession will be an immediate post-death interest. This means that it remains possible to take advantage of the spouse/civil partner exemption for interests in possession created by deed of variation within s 142 whenever the deceased died. [30.153]

a) Permitted ways of altering the will or intestacy

There are two methods of altering the dispositions of a will or intestacy; by disclaimer or by variation. A *disclaimer* operates as a refusal to accept property and, hence, to be valid, should be made before any act of acceptance has occurred (such as receiving any benefit). When a disclaimer is effected the property passes according to fixed rules of law. It is not possible to disclaim in favour of a particular person. Hence, if a specific bequest is disclaimed the property falls into the residue of the will; if it is the residue itself which is disclaimed the property will pass as on an intestacy. Property can also be disclaimed on intestacy. A disclaimer is, therefore, an all or nothing event; it is not possible to retain part and disclaim the rest of a single gift. If, however, both a specific bequest and a share of residue are left to the same person, the benefit of one could be accepted and the other disclaimed. For a consideration of when a disclaimer can be implied by conduct, see *Cook (exor of Watkins Dec'd) v IRC* (2002).

In a *variation*, the deceased's provisions are altered at the choice of the person effecting the alteration so that the gift is redirected and the fact that some benefit had already accrued before the change (and that the estate had been fully administered) is irrelevant. Any part of a gift can be redirected. Unlike a beneficiary who disclaims, the person who makes the variation has owned an interest in the property of the deceased from the death up to the variation. [30.154]

b) The IHT rules on variations and disclaimers

If the following conditions are satisfied the variation or disclaimer is not itself a transfer of value but instead takes effect as if the original will or intestacy had so provided:

(1) The variation or disclaimer must occur within two years of death. In the case of disclaimers it is likely that action will need to be taken soon after the death otherwise the benefit will have been accepted.

(2) The variation or disclaimer must be effected by an instrument in writing executed by the beneficiaries who are adversely affected by the variation. A formal deed is not necessary for tax purposes but is in practice often used for other reasons (for example enforceability in light of the lack of consideration).

(3) A variation or disclaimer cannot be for money or money's worth, except where there are reciprocal disclaimers or other beneficiaries also disclaim for the ultimate benefit of a third person. In *Lau* (2009), a child disclaimed a legacy, thus increasing the value of the exempt residue which was left to the surviving spouse. The Special Commissioner held that the disclaimer had no effect for the purposes of IHT, as the surviving spouse undertook to make a payment to the child should the disclaimer be entered into and thus the disclaimer was made for money or money's worth.

(4) All property comprised in the deceased's estate immediately before death can be redirected under these provisions *except for* property which the deceased was treated as owning by virtue of an interest in possession in a settlement (although in this case relief may be afforded

Specific problems on death 983

by a disclaimer under IHTA 1984 s 93) and property included in the estate at death because of the reservation of benefit rules.

EXAMPLE 30.35

(1) A and T were beneficial joint tenants of the house they lived in. On the death of T, A can redirect the half share of the property that he acquired by right of survivorship taking advantage of IHTA 1984 s 142.

(2) T by will created a settlement giving C a life interest. C can redirect that interest under IHTA 1984 s 142 (but see below for the position if after C's death it is desired to effect the variation).

(3) T was the life tenant of a fund – the property vests in D absolutely on T's death. D cannot take advantage of IHTA 1984 s 142 to assign his interest in the settled property, although under IHTA 1984 s 93, D could disclaim the interest without that disclaimer being subject to IHT.

(4) Mort had been life tenant of a trust fund and on his death the assets passed to his sister Mildred absolutely. He left his free estate equally to his widow and daughter. By a post-death variation the widow gave her half share to the daughter. Assuming that this variation is read back for IHT purposes the extra tax charged on Mort's death will adversely affect the trustees who are not required to consent to the election and are not protected by a deed of discharge (IHTA 1984 s 239(4)).

(5) Father leaves £100,000 shares in J Sainsbury plc to his daughter. She gives those shares to her son, within two years of his death, but continues to be paid the dividends. She elects to read the gift back into the will of her father and as her gift thereupon takes effect *for all IHT purposes* as if it had been made by the deceased the reservation of benefit rules are inapplicable (see **[29.141]**).

(6) Boris, domiciled in France, leaves his villa in Tuscany and moneys in his Swiss bank account to his son Gaspard, a UK resident. By a variation of the terms of his will made within two years of Boris' death, the property is settled on discretionary Liechtenstein trusts for the benefit of Gaspard's family. For IHT, reading back ensures that the settlement is excluded property (see **[35.20]**). For the CGT position, see *Example 22.10*.

In the case of variations, the choice to elect or not to elect is with the taxpayer. A similar election operates for CGT but it is not necessary to exercise both IHT and CGT elections; either can be exercised (see **[21.123]**).

PRs of deceased beneficiaries can enter into variations and disclaimers which can be read back into the original will, as long as the property left to that deceased beneficiary was not an interest in possession (see **[30.157]**). Further, the estate of a beneficiary alive at the testator's death can be increased by such a variation or disclaimer. **[30.155]**

EXAMPLE 30.36

(1) T leaves property to his wealthy brother. The brother wishes to redirect it to grandchildren. An election for IHT purposes is advisable since (a) it will not increase the IHT charged on T's death and (b) it will avoid a second charge at the brother's rates if the brother were to die within seven years of the gift (for which quick succession relief would not be available – see **[30.144]**).

(2) T leaves residue to his widow. She wishes to redirect a portion to her daughter. If the election is made, the IHT on T's death may be increased because an exempt bequest is being replaced with one that is chargeable. If the election is not made, on T's death the residue remains spouse exempt but the widow will make a PET. If she survives by seven years, no IHT will be payable: if she survives by three years, tapering relief will apply. Even if the PET becomes chargeable, any IHT may be reduced by the widow's annual exemption (in the year when the transfer is made) and the chargeable transfer may fall within her nil rate band. In cases like this, it will be advantageous to ensure that T's nil rate band is fully used up by a reading back election but, once that has been done, given a single rate of tax (40%), there is no advantage in reading back the variation since the rate of tax on the death of the widow will be the same and, moreover, tax will not be charged at once.

(3) In examples like (2) above a variation may be employed to redirect a posthumous increase in the value of the estate without any IHT charge. Assume for instance that the death estate of £300,000 has increased in value to £385,000. T's widow could vary the will (electing to read the charge back) to provide for a specific legacy of £300,000 to herself with the residue to her daughter. Under the provisions of IHTA 1984 ss 36–42 the death estate (£300,000) is attributed to the exempt legacy.

(4) H leaves £1m to his only daughter, D. His widow, W, dies soon afterwards leaving a small estate to D. D should consider varying H's will so that (say) she retains £325,000 (to use up H's nil rate band) and the remainder is left to W. D will then receive that sum from W's estate and gets the benefit of W's full nil rate band.

Note: In (4) above the variation may be considered artificial since it is designed solely to reduce the total IHT bill. D is left with all the property. Accordingly it may be vulnerable to attack either under the GAAR or on the basis that the dispositions of H's will have not been varied (although it is understood that HMRC does not at present take this point). Were D to redirect the benefit to her own children it would be more difficult to view the arrangement as wholly artificial.

c) *Other taxes*

So far as *stamp duty* is concerned variations in writing made within two years after the death are not subject to *ad valorem* duty provided that the appropriately worded certificate is included (normally Category L, see **Chapter 49**). No duty is payable on disclaimers which are treated as a refusal to accept, not a disposition of, property. No stamp duty land tax charge arises in respect of post-death variations made within two years of the death (FA 2003 Sch 3 para 4). A variation is not a notifiable transaction for stamp duty land tax purposes (FA 2003 s 77(3)).

There are no specific relieving income tax provisions for variations and disclaimers. Accordingly, income arising between the date of death and the date of a variation will be taxed in accordance with the terms of the will and the rules governing the treatment of estate income (as to which see **Chapter 17**). Of course, residuary income is taxed only when actually paid to the beneficiary: consequently if no income has been paid to a beneficiary who effects a variation of his residuary entitlement, income tax will be charged only on future distributions to the 'new' beneficiary. To this extent a form of reading back can apply for income tax purposes.

A variation made by a beneficiary in favour of his own infant unmarried child creates a settlement for income tax purposes within the settlement provisions in ITTOIA 2005 s 619 et seq (see **[16.95]**). Hence, income arising from the redirected property will be assessed as that of the parent (unless accumulated in a capital settlement). A disclaimer will escape these problems, if it is accepted that the property has never been owned by the disclaiming beneficiary. [30.156]

d) *Technical difficulties and traps*

A number of technical problems have arisen in connection with instruments of variation.

First, HMRC requires that the variation must indicate clearly the dispositions that are subject to it and vary their destination from that provided in the will or under the intestacy rules. The notice of election must refer to the appropriate statutory provisions, although rectification of a variation which failed to make reference to statute was permitted in *Vaughan Jones v Vaughan Jones* (2015). A formal deed is not necessary and, provided the correct information is present, a letter from the beneficiary/ies is acceptable.

Second, although it is not necessary that all variations affecting an estate or in favour of or by one beneficiary are made in one deed an election, once made, is irrevocable and s 142 will not apply to an instrument redirecting any item or part of any item that had already been redirected under an earlier instrument. The decision of *Russell v IRC* (1988) confirmed that a redirection of property already varied does not fall within s 142. Variations covering a number of items should ideally be made in one instrument 'to avoid any uncertainty', although HMRC accepts that multiple variations by a single beneficiary are not, as such, prohibited.

In *Lake v Lake* (1989) Mervyn Davis J held that a deed of variation can be rectified by the court if words mistakenly used mean that it does not give effect to the parties' joint intention. It does not matter that the rectification achieves a tax advantage nor that it is made more than two years after the death. The courts must, however, be satisfied that the deed as executed contains errors: in this case the variation was designed to give legacies to children of the deceased but, as the result of a clerical error, such gifts were expressed to be 'free of tax'. As residue passed to an exempt beneficiary (the surviving spouse), grossing-up was therefore necessary (see **[30.96]**). The order for rectification substituted 'such gifts to bear their own tax' for 'free of tax' (see also *Matthews v Martin* (1991) and *Schnieder v Mills* (1993)).

EXAMPLE 30.37

Under Eric's will £50,000 is left to his brother Wally and £100,000 to his surviving spouse Berta. The following events then occur within two years of Eric's death:
(1) Wally executes a deed of variation in favour of his own children.
(2) Berta executes a deed varying £2,500 in favour of her sister Jennie and subsequently a second variation of £47,500 to Jennie.
(3) Jennie executes a deed of variation of £25,000 in favour of her boyfriend Jonnie.
The variations in (1) and (2) satisfy the requirements of IHTA 1984 s 142 as interpreted by HMRC and so may be read back into Eric's will, whereas the variation in (3) will not be so treated and, accordingly, will be a PET by Jennie.

Third, s 142(4) contains a trap for the unwary by providing that if a variation results in property being held for a person 'for a period which ends not more than two years after the death' the interest of that person is ignored in applying the section.

EXAMPLE 30.38

Dan died on 1 January 2017 leaving all his estate to his daughter Delia. By a deed of variation dated 1 January 2018 she gave her mother, Sarah, a six-month interest in possession in that property remainder to her children and made the necessary election. As Sarah's interest ends before two years after Dan's death, it will be ignored under s 142(4) and IHT calculated as if Dan had left his estate directly to his grandchildren.

Finally, whilst the executors of a person inheriting property outright may enter into a variation on behalf of the deceased legatee, the position is different where the deceased beneficiary is given an interest in possession. The executors of the deceased beneficiary may not vary the interest in possession as they have no property to vary once the person with the life interest has died (*Soutter's Executry v IRC* (2002)) This is based on the somewhat curious idea that variations have to operate in the real world! [30.157]

7 IHT and estate duty

Up to 13 March 1975 the estate duty regime operated. The various transitional provisions for estate duty are beyond the scope of this book although mention should be made of IHTA 1984 Sch 6 para 2 that preserves for IHT purposes the estate duty surviving spouse exemption. This exemption provided that where property was left to a surviving spouse in such circumstances that the spouse was not competent to dispose of it (for instance was given a life interest therein) estate duty would be charged on the first death but not again on the death of the survivor. This exemption was continued into the CTT (and now IHT) era by IHTA 1984 Sch 6 para 2 which excludes such property from charge whether the limited interest is terminated *inter vivos* or by the death of the surviving spouse. All too often this valuable exemption may be overlooked and an over-emphasis on the attractions of making PETs may have unfortunate results. [30.158]

EXAMPLE 30.39

(1) On his death in 1973, Samson left his wife Delilah a life interest in his share portfolio. She is still alive and in robust health and the trustees have a power to advance capital to her. Estate duty was charged on Samson's death but because of IHTA 1984 Sch 6 para 2 there will be no charge to IHT when Delilah's interest comes to an end. At first sight, there appear to be advantages if the trustees advance capital to Delilah which she then transfers by means of a PET. However, this arrangement carries with it the risk of that capital being subject to an IHT charge if Delilah dies within seven years of her gift. Accordingly, an interest which is tax free is being replaced by a potentially chargeable transfer.

(2) Terminating Delilah's interest during her life may, however, have other attractions. In particular, the exemption from charge in IHTA 1984 Sch 6 para 2 is limited to the value of the property in which the limited interest subsists but that property may, by forming part of Delilah's estate, affect the value of other assets in that estate. Assume, for instance, that Delilah owns 30% of the shares in a private company (Galilee Ltd) in her own name and that a further 30% are subject to the life interest trust. When she dies she will be treated as owning 60% of the shares: a controlling holding which will be valued as such. Although one half of the value of that holding will be free from charge under para 2, the remaining portion will be taxed. Accordingly, it may be better in such cases for her life interest to be surrendered *inter vivos* even if that operation is only carried out on her deathbed.

31 IHT – exemptions and reliefs

Updated by Sandra Eden, Senior Lecturer, University of Edinburgh

I   Lifetime exemptions and reliefs [**31.3**]
II Death exemptions and reliefs [**31.21**]
III Exemptions for lifetime and death transfers [**31.41**]

1 Policy issues

Predictably, although in marked contrast to CGT, whole categories of property are not exempted from the IHT net. Hence, *excluded property*, which is ignored if transferred *inter vivos* and not taxed as part of the death estate, is restrictively defined in IHTA 1984 s 6 (see [**35.20**]).

Exemptions and reliefs apply in a number of situations: some for lifetime transfers only; some for death only; and some for all transfers, whether in lifetime or on death.

Some exemptions may be justified on cultural or social grounds, for example maintenance of the family, wedding gifts or gifts to charity. Some exemptions are based on administrative convenience, eg the small gift exemption. Others, in the case of reliefs applicable to particular property, exist because it is desirable that the property should be preserved and not sold to pay the tax bill (eg business and agricultural property where relief up to 100% of the value is available). [**31.1**]

2 The nil rate band

The nil rate band (currently £325,000) (see [**28.121**]) is not an exempt transfer since transfers within this band are chargeable transfers, albeit taxed at 0%. Accordingly, exemptions and reliefs should be exhausted first so that the taxpayer's nil rate band is retained intact as long as possible. [**31.2**]

I LIFETIME EXEMPTIONS AND RELIEFS

1 Transfers not exceeding £3,000 pa (IHTA 1984 s 19)

Up to £3,000 can be transferred free from IHT each tax year (6 April to 5 April). To the extent that this relief is unused in any one year it can be rolled forward for one tax year only. There is no general roll-forward since only where the value transferred in any year exceeds £3,000 is the shortfall from the previous year's £3,000 used.

EXAMPLE 31.1

A makes chargeable transfers of £2,500 in 2015–16; £2,800 in 2016–17; and £3,700 in 2017–18.

For 2015–16: no IHT (£3,000 exemption) and £500 is carried forward.

For 2016–17: no IHT (£3,000 exemption) and £200 only is carried forward. The £500 from 2015–16 cannot be carried forward to 2017–18.

For 2017–18: IHT on £500 (£3,200 is exempt).

The relief can operate by deducting £3,000 from a larger gift. Where several chargeable gifts are made in the same tax year, earlier gifts will be given the relief first; if several gifts are made on the same day there is a *pro rata* apportionment of the relief irrespective of the actual order of gifts. The relief applies also to settlements with interests in possession although in this case it will only be given if the life tenant so elects (see **[33.22]**).

The relationship between the annual exemption and the PET depends on the definition of a PET in IHTA 1984 s 3A:

'a transfer of value ... which, apart from this section, would be a chargeable transfer (or to the extent which, apart from this section, it would be such a transfer) ... '.

The position can therefore be stated in two propositions:
(1) a transfer of value which is wholly covered by the annual exemption is not a PET but *an exempt transfer in its own right*;
(2) a transfer of value which exceeds the annual exempt amount is *to that extent a PET*.

EXAMPLE 31.2

(1) Peta gives her father £2,500. This gift is an exempt transfer.
(2) In the same tax year Beta, who made no gifts in the previous year, gives her mother £6,500. Two annual exemptions mean that £6,000 is exempt: £500 is a PET.
(3) Cheeta intends to set up a discretionary trust for his family and to make an outright gift to his sister. He should make the discretionary trust first thereby using up his annual exemption and on a subsequent day make a PET to his sister.

Where a PET and a chargeable transfer are made in the same year, IHTA 1984 s 19(3A)(a) provides that the PET is ignored for the purpose of the annual exemption and, should the PET subsequently become a chargeable transfer (because of the death of the donor within seven years), IHTA 1984 s 19(3A)(b) provides that PETs shall be treated as having been made *after* any chargeable transfers in the same year. It is clearly intended that the annual exemption should be allocated to the chargeable transfer, even if it took place after the PET. There is a drafting difficulty with s 19(3A): it applies to PETs but, using the definition of a PET in s 3A, specifically that a PET is a transfer or part of a transfer which would otherwise be *chargeable*, the part of the transfer which is covered by the annual exemption cannot be a PET. So a strict reading of s 19(3A) with s 3A has the result that the part of the transfer covered by the annual exemption continues to take place before the chargeable transfer, and continues to use up the annual exemption! This, at least, is the view taken by HMRC – see IHTM 14143.

What should a would-be donor do who does not wish to transfer assets/money to the value of £3,000, but at the same time is reluctant to see the exemption lost? One solution is to vest an interest in property in the donee whilst retaining control of the asset (although great care must be taken to ensure that a benefit is not retained in the portion given since a transfer falling within the annual exemption is still a gift for the reservation of benefit rules: see **Chapter 29**). Selling the asset with the purchase price outstanding and releasing part of the debt each year equal to the annual exemption may fall foul of the associated operations rules (see [**28.101**]). [**31.3**]

2 Normal expenditure out of income (IHTA 1984 s 21)

Section 21 provides as follows:

> 'a transfer of value is an exempt transfer if, or to the extent that, it is shown –
>
> (a) that it was made as part of the normal expenditure of the transferor,
>
> (b) that (taking one year with another) it was made out of his income, and
>
> (c) that, after allowing for all transfers of value forming part of his normal expenditure, the transferor is left with sufficient income to maintain his usual standard of living.'

The legislation does not define (nor indeed seek to explain) 'usual standard of living' but HMRC accepts that the gifts do not have to be of cash: regular gifts of shares will, for instance, suffice. Particular difficulties are presented by requirement (a): what evidence is required to prove that payments (or any payment) constitute normal expenditure? A pattern of payments is presumably required and this is most easily shown where the taxpayer is committed to making a series of payments as, for instance, where he enters into a deed of covenant. In other cases (eg where there is no legal commitment to make a series of payments) it has usually been assumed that a number of payments would have to be made before there was sufficient evidence of regularity.

Bennett v IRC (1995) casts some light on this problem. Mrs Bennett was the life tenant of a will trust established by her late husband, the gross annual income from which was, until 1987, £300 pa. In that year, as a result of the sale of the trust assets, the income of the trust increased enormously and Mrs Bennett (a lady of settled habits) indicated to the trustees that she wished her sons to have surplus trust income above what was needed to satisfy her relatively modest needs. Accordingly in 1989 each of the three sons received a distribution of £9,300 and in the following year £60,000. Mrs Bennett then unexpectedly died. The Inland Revenue contended that the 1989 and 1990 payments were failed PETs: the executors argued that they were exempt under s 21. The court acknowledged that requirements (b) and (c) were satisfied and so the matter turned on the meaning of 'normal expenditure'. This was explained by Lightman J as follows:

> 'the term "normal expenditure" connotes expenditure which at the time it took place accorded with the settled pattern of expenditure adopted by the transferor.
>
> The existence of the settled pattern may be established in two ways. First, an examination of the expenditure by the transferor over a period of time may throw into relief a pattern, eg a payment each year of 10% of all income to charity or members of the individual's family or a payment of a fixed sum or a sum rising with inflation as a pension to a former employee. Second, the individual may be shown to have assumed a commitment, or adopted a firm resolution, regarding his future expenditure and thereafter complied with it. The commitment may be legal (eg a deed of covenant), religious (eg a vow to give all earnings beyond the sum needed for subsistence to those in need) or moral (eg to support aged parents or invalid relatives). The commitment or resolution need have none of these characteristics but nonetheless be likewise effective as establishing a pattern, eg to pay the annual premiums on a life insurance qualifying policy gifted to a third party or to give a pre-determined part of his income to his children.
>
> For expenditure to be "normal" there is no fixed minimum period during which the expenditure should have occurred. All that is necessary is that on the totality of the evidence the pattern of actual or intended regular payment shall have been established and that the item in question conforms with that pattern. If the prior commitment or resolution can be shown, a single payment implementing the commitment or resolution may be sufficient. On the other hand if no such commitment or resolution can be shown, a series of payments may be required before the existence of the necessary pattern will emerge. The pattern need not be immutable; it must, however, be established that the pattern was intended to remain in place for more than a nominal period and indeed for a sufficient period (barring unforeseen circumstances) in order for any payment fairly to be regarded as a regular feature of the transferor's annual expenditure. Thus a "deathbed" resolution to make periodic payments "for life" and a payment made in accordance with such a determination will not suffice.
>
> The amount of the expenditure need not be fixed in amount nor indeed the individual recipient be the same. As regards quantum, it is sufficient that a formula or standard has been adopted by application of which the payment (which may be of a fluctuating amount) can be quantified eg 10% of any earnings whatever they may be, or the costs of a sick or elderly dependant's residence at a nursing home.'

On the basis of this analysis he concluded that the two payments were exempted under s 21. In the later case of *Nadin v IRC* (1997) not only did the payments exceed the taxpayer's income for the year but there was no evidence of a prior commitment or resolution and the payments did not form part of any pattern of expenditure.

In *McDowall v IRC* (2004) an attorney under a power of attorney purported to make lifetime gifts in keeping with the taxpayer's established practice of making gifts to his children, their spouses and grandchildren. The power of attorney contained no express power for gifts to be made. The Special Commissioners held that the gifts were invalid because the attorney was not permitted by the power of attorney to make gifts. However, had the gifts been valid, they would have been exempt under IHTA 1984 s 21 because there was a settled pattern of making gifts and the gifts were made out of income.

EXAMPLE 31.3

A takes out a life insurance policy on his own life for £60,000 with the benefit of that policy being held on a trust for his grandchildren. A pays the premiums on the policy of £3,500 pa. He makes a transfer of value of £3,500 pa but he can make use of the normal expenditure exemption to avoid IHT so long as all the requirements for that exemption are satisfied. Alternatively, the £3,000 annual exemption would relieve most of the annual premium. (It is thought that even if the first premium was paid *before* the policy was settled, the normal expenditure exemption would apply to the value of the policy settled.)

Anti-avoidance rules provide that:
(1) The normal expenditure exemption will not cover a life insurance premium unless the transferor can show that the life cover was not facilitated by and associated with an annuity purchased on his own life (IHTA 1984 s 21(2)).
(2) Under IHTA 1984 s 263 (unless the transferor can disprove the presumption of associated transactions, as above) an IHT charge can arise when the benefit of the life policy is vested in the donee. In general, if a charge arises, the sum assured by the life policy is treated as a transfer of value.

These special rules exist to prevent tax saving by the use of back-to-back insurance policies, as in the following example:

EXAMPLE 31.4

Tony pays an insurance company £50,000 in return for an annuity of £7,000 pa for the rest of his life. At the same time he enters into a life insurance contract on his own life for £50,000 written in favour of his brother Ted. The potential advantages are that on the death of Tony the sum of £50,000 is no longer part of his estate and the annuity has no value when he dies but can be used during his life to pay the premiums on the life insurance contract. The insurance proceeds will not attract IHT because they do not form part of his estate and Tony could claim that the premiums amounted to regular payments out of his income and so were free of IHT. HMRC accepts that such arrangements are effective so long as the policies are not linked and, ideally, are taken out with different companies.

As with the annual exemption, this exemption does not prevent a gift from being caught by the reservation of benefit rules. [31.4]

3 Small gifts (IHTA 1984 s 20)

Any number of £250 gifts can be made in any tax year by a donor provided that the gifts are to different donees. It must be an outright gift (not a gift into settlement) and the sum cannot be severed from a larger gift. The section provides that the transfers of value made to any one person in any one year must not exceed £250: accordingly, it is not possible to combine this small gifts exemption with the annual £3,000 exemption. A gift of £3,250 would, therefore, be exempt as to £3,000 (assuming that exemption was available) but the excess of £250 would not fall under s 20 even if the gift had been structured by means of two separate payments. [31.5]

4 Gifts in consideration of marriage (IHTA 1984 s 22)

The gift must be made before or contemporaneously with the marriage and only after marriage if in satisfaction of a prior legal obligation. It must be conditional upon the marriage taking place so that should the marriage not occur the donor must have the right to recover the gift (if this right is not exercised, there may be an IHT charge on the failure to exercise that right under IHTA 1984 s 3(3)). A particular marriage must be in contemplation; it will not suffice, for instance, for a father to make a gift to his two-year-old daughter expressed to be conditional upon her marriage on the fatalistic assumption that she is bound to get married eventually!

The exemption can be used to settle property, but only if the beneficiaries are limited to (broadly) the couple, any issue, and spouses of such issue (see IHTA 1984 s 22(4)). Hence, a marriage cannot be used to effect a general settlement of assets within the family.

The sum exempt from IHT is:
(1) £5,000, if the donor is a parent of either party to the marriage. Thus, each of four parents can give £5,000 to the couple.
(2) £2,500, if the transferor is a remoter ancestor of either party to the marriage (eg a grandparent or great-grandparent) or if the transferor is a party to the marriage. The latter is designed to cover ante nuptial gifts since after marriage transfers between spouses are normally exempt without limit (see [**31.41**]).
(3) £1,000, in the case of any other transferors (eg a wedding guest).

When a gift of property is an exempt transfer because it was made in consideration of marriage, the reservation of benefit provisions do not apply.
[**31.6**]

EXAMPLE 31.5
(1) Father gives son a Matisse sculpture on the occasion of the son's marriage. It is worth £5,000. Possession of the piece is retained by the father but as the transfer is covered by the marriage exemption his continued possession does not fall within the reservation rules (FA 1986 s 102(5)).
(2) Mum gives daughter an interest in her house equal to £5,000 when the daughter marries. Although Mum continues to live in the house the reservation rules do not apply.

5 Dispositions for maintenance etc (IHTA 1984 s 11)

Dispositions listed in IHTA 1984 s 11 are not transfers of value and so are ignored for IHT purposes. HMRC takes the view that this exemption only applies to *inter vivos* dispositions, because 'disposition' does not cover the deemed disposition on death.
[**31.7**]

a) *Maintenance of a former spouse (IHTA 1984 s 11(1)(a))*

Even without this provision such payments would in many cases escape IHT. If made before decree absolute, the exemption for gifts between spouses (see [**31.41**]) would operate and even after divorce they might escape IHT as regular payments out of income; or fall within the annual exemption; or be non-gratuitous transfers. What s 11 does is to put the matter beyond all doubt.

Two problems may be mentioned. *First,* maintenance is not defined, so that whether it would cover the transfer of capital assets (eg the former matrimonial home) is uncertain but the Special Commissioner's decision in *McKelvey v R & C Comrs* (2008) suggests that capital transfers might be covered (see **[31.10]**). *Second,* if the payer dies but payment is to continue for the lifetime of the recipient, the position is unclear in the light of HMRC's view that this exemption is limited to *inter vivos* dispositions. **[31.8]**

b) *Maintenance of children*

Provision for the maintenance, education or training of a child of either party to a marriage (including stepchildren and adopted children) is not a transfer of value (IHTA 1984 s 11(1)(b): HMRC accepts that 'party to a marriage' includes a widow or widower). The maintenance can continue beyond the age of 18 if the child is in full-time education. Thus, school fees paid by parents escape IHT. Similar principles operate where the disposition is for the maintenance of a parent's illegitimate child (IHTA 1984 s 11(4)). Relief is also given for the maintenance of other people's children if the child is an infant and not in the care of either parent; once the child is 18, not only must he be undergoing full-time education, but also the disponer must (in effect) have been *in loco parentis* to the child during his minority (IHTA 1984 s 11(2)). Hence, payment of school and college fees by grandparents will seldom escape IHT under this provision. **[31.9]**

c) *Care or maintenance of a dependent relative*

The provision of care or maintenance whether direct or indirect must be reasonable and the relative (as defined in IHTA 1984 s 11(6)) must be incapacitated by old age or infirmity from maintaining himself (although parents and parents-in-law are always dependent relatives). The transfer of two capital assets were thought to be for the care (although not the maintenance) of a relative in *McKelvey v R & C Comrs* (2008). However, the value of the transfer went beyond that which was objectively reasonable at the date of the transfer, and an apportionment was made, with part of the value transferred falling outside the exemption. **[31.10]–[31.20]**

II DEATH EXEMPTIONS AND RELIEFS

1 **Woodlands (IHTA 1984 ss 125–130)**

This relief takes effect by deferring IHT on trees and underwood growing on land in the UK or another state within the European Economic Area (EEA) that form part of the deceased's estate. Their value is left out of account on the death, but is charged when the timber is disposed of or is transferred on a subsequent death. An election must be made for the relief by written notice given (normally) within two years after the death (s 125(3)). It is not available where the woodlands qualify for agricultural relief (see **[31.62]**) and commercial woodlands will commonly qualify for business property relief

(BPR) (see **[31.42]**): with the introduction of 100% BPR in 1992 for 'relevant business property', woodland relief has become less important).

To prevent deathbed IHT saving schemes the land must not have been purchased by the deceased in the five years before his death (note, however, that the relief is available if the woodlands were obtained by gift or inheritance within the five-year period). If the timber is transferred on a second death no tax is chargeable on later disposals by reference to the first death (s 126). The relief does not apply to the land itself, but any IHT charged as a result of death can be paid in instalments. The deferred tax on the timber may become chargeable as follows: **[31.21]**

a) *Sale of the timber with or without the land*

Once the timber is sold, IHT will be charged on the net proceeds of sale, but deductions can be made for costs of selling the timber and also for the costs of replanting. The net proceeds are taxed according to full IHT rates at the date of the disposal and the tax is calculated by treating those proceeds as forming the highest part of the deceased's estate. Business property relief (at 50%) may be available where the trees or underwood formed a business asset at the date of death and, but for the deferment election, would have qualified for that relief at that time (see s 127 and **[31.42]**). In such cases the relief is given against the net proceeds of sale (IHTA 1984 s 127). **[31.22]**

b) *A gift of the timber*

Not only is the deferred charge triggered by a gift of the timber, but also the gift itself may be subject to IHT subject to the availability of BPR. In calculating the tax payable on the lifetime gift the value transferred is reduced by the triggered IHT charged on the death and the tax can be paid by interest-free instalments (whoever pays the IHT) spread over ten years (IHTA 1984 s 229).
[31.23]

EXAMPLE 31.6

(1) Wally Wood dies in January 1991 with a death estate of £200,000. In addition, he owns at death woodlands with the growing timber valued at £40,000 and the land etc valued at £30,000. The woodlands exemption is claimed by his daughter Wilma. In 1998 she sells the timber; the net proceeds of sale are £50,000.

  (i) *Position on Wally's death:* The timber is left out of account. The value of the rest of the business (£30,000) attracts 50% business relief (the relevant level of relief in 1991: see (3) below), so that only £15,000 will be added to the £200,000 chargeable estate.

  (ii) *Position on Wilma's sale:* The IHT charge is triggered. The net proceeds are reduced by 50% business relief to £25,000 which will be taxed according to the rates of IHT in force in 1998 for transfers between £215,000 (ie Wally's total chargeable death estate) and £240,000.

(2) As in (1), above except that Wilma settles the timber on her brother Woad in 1998 when its net value is £50,000. The deferred charge will be triggered as in para (ii) of (1), above. IHT on Wilma's gift will be calculated according to IHT rates in force for 1998. She can deduct from the net value of the

timber the deferred tax ((1), above) and any IHT can be paid by instalments whether it is paid by her or by Woad.

(3) With the increase in the level of BPR to 100% in 1992, the woodlands election should not be made if the woodlands form part of a qualifying business: instead of a partial deferment of charge the business is wholly tax free.

c) *PETs and estate duty*

Estate duty was not charged on the value of timber, trees, wood or underwood growing on land comprised in an estate at death. Instead, tax was deferred until such time as the woodlands were sold and was then levied at the death estate rate on the net proceeds of sale (subject to the proviso that duty could not exceed tax on the value of the timber at the date of the death). Pending sale, duty was therefore held in suspense and this deferral period only ceased on the happening of a later death when the woodlands again became subject to duty. The introduction of a charge on lifetime gifts with the advent of CTT resulted in this deferral period terminating immediately after the first transfer of value occurring after 12 March 1975 in which the value transferred was determined by reference to the land in question (subject only to an exclusion if that transfer was to the transferor's spouse and therefore exempt from CTT: see FA 1975 s 49(4)). In such cases, the deferred estate duty charge was superseded by a charge to CTT on the transfer value.

With the introduction of the PET it was realised that a transfer of value of woodlands subject to estate duty deferral to another individual would, *prima facie*, be a PET but that the transfer would have the effect of ending the deferral period thereby cancelling any charge to duty without a compensating charge to IHT. Hence, IHTA 1984 Sch 19 para 46 provides that transfers of value which fall within FA 1975 s 49(4) and thereby bring to an end the estate duty deferral period *shall not be PETs*. Accordingly, such transfers remain immediately chargeable to IHT at the transferor's rates (with the possibility of a supplementary charge should he die within the following seven years).

[31.24]

EXAMPLE 31.7

On his death in May 1973 Claude left his landed estate to his son Charles. That estate included woodlands valued, in 1973, at £6,000. Consider the tax position in the following three situations:

(1) *If Charles sells the timber in 1999 for £16,000*: The net proceeds of sale will be subject to an estate duty charge levied at Claude's estate rate but duty will be limited by reference to the value of the timber in 1973 (ie it will be charged on £6,000).

(2) *If Charles retains the timber until his death in 1999 when it passes to his daughter*: This transfer of value will end the estate duty deferral period so that the potential charge to duty will be removed. However, the transfer to his daughter will be subject to an IHT charge unless the woodlands deferral election under IHTA 1984 s 125 ff is claimed.

(3) *If Charles makes an inter vivos gift of his estate (including the woodlands) in August 1999 to his daughter*: Such a gift will not be potentially exempt because of IHTA 1984 Sch 19 para 46. Accordingly, it will terminate the estate duty suspense period, and will result in an immediate IHT charge levied according to Charles' rates. From the wording of para 46 it is not clear whether any part of

this transfer can be potentially exempt or whether the entire value transferred is subject to an immediate charge. Undoubtedly the value of the timber will attract such a charge and likewise it would seem that the value of the land on which the timber is growing will fall outside the definition of a PET (see the wording of FA 1975 s 49(4)). What, however, if the transfer of value made by Charles includes other property, eg other parts of a landed estate which are not afforested? There was a danger that none of the value transferred would be a PET since para 46 is not limited to that part of any transfer of value comprising the woodlands. The injustice is recognised by ESC F15 which states that 'the scope of [para 46] will henceforth be restricted solely to that part of the value transferred which is attributable to the woodlands which are the subject of the deferred charge'.

2 Death on active service etc (IHTA 1984 ss 153–155A)

The estates of persons dying on active service have long been exempt from IHT. This provision has been generously interpreted to cover a death arising many years after a wound inflicted whilst on active service, so long as that wound was one of the causes of death; it need not have been the only, or even the direct cause (*Barty-King v Ministry of Defence* (1979)). Although a *donatio mortis causa* is covered by the exemption it does not apply to lifetime transfers. This exemption was extended to emergency personnel such as police and the fire service and to emergency service personnel responding to emergency circumstances for deaths on or after 19 March 2014.   **[31.25]–[31.40]**

III EXEMPTIONS FOR LIFETIME AND DEATH TRANSFERS

1 The inter-spouse/civil partners exemption (IHTA 1984 s 18)

This most valuable exemption from IHT for transfers between spouses is unlimited in amount except where a UK-domiciled donor spouse makes a gift to a donee spouse who is not domiciled in the UK, when the amount excluded from IHT was for many years £55,000 until it was increased to the value of the nil rate band in relation to transfers after 6 April 2013 (see **[51.68]** ff). There have been a couple of attempts to extend the scope of this exemption using the HRA 1998. In *Holland (Exor of Holland Deceased) v IRC* (2003) the Special Commissioners expressed the view that this did not involve discrimination against unmarried couples under the HRA 1998 and further decided that a couple who had lived together as husband and wife for 31 years did not qualify for the spouse exemption. A spouse for this purpose was a person who was legally married. In *Burden and Burden v UK* (2008), two elderly sisters living together in the family house claimed before the European Court of Human Rights that to deny them an exemption constituted discrimination and infringed their right to peaceful possession of property. The majority of the Grand Chamber of the ECtHR decided that the applicants, as cohabiting sisters, could not be compared to a married or civil partnership couple (see below) and that, accordingly, their case failed (see **[55.42]**).

The Civil Partnership Act 2004 introduced the concept of 'civil partnerships' with the aim of putting same-sex couples on a similar footing to married couples. For tax purposes, this has been achieved through

Exemptions for lifetime and death transfers 999

FA 2005, and regulations that provide for reliefs applying to married couples to apply equally to civil partners eg the inter-spousal exemption. For the sake of simplicity, references to spouses in the inheritance chapters in this book will generally be deemed to include civil partners.

The use of this exemption is considered in different parts of this book and the following points represent a summary of those sections:

(1) For tax planning purposes the received wisdom until the introduction of the inter-spousal transferable nil rate band (see [**30.27**]) was that the lowest total IHT bill was produced if both spouses use up their nil rate bands (see [**51.74**]). Particular problems resulted on the death of the first to die if the only substantial asset in his estate was the main residence, needed by his surviving spouse: for an example see *IRC v Lloyds Private Banking* (1998), [**32.28**]. The ability to transfer unused nil rate bands between spouses has reduced the necessity of schemes to preserve the nil rate band of the first to die. However, the introduction of the residential nil rate band (RNRB) may encourage some individuals to avoid leaving all their estate to the survivor. This additional nil rate band is withdrawn once an estate exceeds £2 million so, on the first death, there may in some cases be a tax advantage in leaving property to others rather than to the surviving spouse or civil partner – see [**30.32**].

(2) Each spouse should take advantage of the lifetime exemptions. HMRC will normally not invoke the associated operations provisions to challenge a transfer between spouses even if it enables a transfer by the donee spouse to occur ([**28.101**]).

(3) The rules for related property are designed to counter tax saving by splitting assets between spouses (see [**28.70**]).

(4) IHT on a chargeable transfer by one spouse to a third party may be collected from the other spouse in certain circumstances (see [**28.171**]).

[**31.41**]

2 Business property relief ('BPR': IHTA 1984 ss 103–114)

Business (and agricultural property) relief was introduced in order to ensure that businesses were not broken up by the imposition of an IHT charge. BPR takes effect by a percentage reduction in the value transferred by a transfer of value and, prior to 10 March 1992, that reduction was at either 50% or 30%. For transfers made on and after that date the levels were increased to 100% and 50% with the result that most family businesses and farms were taken outside the tax net. The relief is given automatically. [**31.42**]

a) *Meaning of 'relevant business property'*

Business property relief is given in respect of transfers of 'relevant business property' which is defined as any of the following:

(1) *A business:* For example, that of a sole trader or sole practitioner (s 105(1)(a)). A sole trader who transfers a part of his trade falls within this category and this may include a transfer of settled land (of which he is the life tenant) which is used in the business (*Fetherstonehaugh v IRC* (1984)). Until the case of *Nelson Dance Family Settlement v R & C Comrs* (2009), the view of HMRC was that the property transferred had to be

whole or part of a business. In other words the transfer of an asset (as opposed to a part of the business) would not be given relief. In *Nelson Dance*, the High Court decided that assets transferred out of a farming business were eligible for relief even though they did not themselves come under the definition of 'relevant business property' as they were not themselves 'a business' or 'an interest in a business'. The important point was that the farming business, which *was* relevant business property, was reduced in value as a result of the transfer and, given the loss to the donor principle, it was appropriate to look at the property which had lost value, rather than the property which was being transferred. This case confirms that assets of a business are eligible for relief. For a note of indicia of a business, see *McCall v R & C Comrs* (2009) and *Pawson's Executors v R & C Comrs* (2012), upheld by the Upper Tribunal in 2013 (discussed further at [**31.48**]). These include whether or not there was a serious undertaking earnestly pursued, whether it was pursued with reasonable or recognisable continuity and whether it was conducted in a regular manner.

(2) *An interest in a business:* For example, the share of a partner in either a trading or professional partnership (s 105(1)(a)).

(3) *Listed shares or securities which gave the transferor control of the company (s 105(1) (cc)):* Control itself does not have to be transferred; the requirement is simply that *at the time of transfer* the transferor should have such control (see [**31.55**]).

(4) *Unquoted securities which gave the transferor control of the company* (s 105(1) (b)): Similar comments to those in (3) apply: unquoted shares include shares dealt in on the Alternative Investment Market (AIM).

(5) *Any unquoted shares in a company* (s 105(1)(bb)).

(6) *Any land or building, plant or machinery which immediately before the transfer was used by a partnership in which the transferor was a partner or by a company of which he had control* (s 105(1)(d)).

Control for these purposes requires a majority of votes (50%+) on all questions affecting the company as a whole (see (3) and (4), above). Hence, an apparently unjust result is produced if the appropriate asset is used by a company in which the transferor owned a minority of the ordinary shares when no relief will be available, whereas had the asset been used by a partnership, then, irrespective of his profit share, relief would be available. Relief is also available if the asset is held in a trust but is used by a life tenant for his own business or by a company which he controls. The relief is given irrespective of whether a rent is charged for the use of the asset.

In *Beckman v IRC* (2000) H retired as a partner and her capital account (reflecting capital introduced into the business) was left outstanding as a debt of the business. On H's subsequent death she had ceased to own a share in the business of which she had become a creditor. No relief was therefore available. [**31.43**]

b) *Relief is on the net value of the business*

Relief is given on the net value of the business and IHTA 1984 s 110(b) states that the net value is:

> '... the value of the assets used in the business (including goodwill) reduced by the aggregate amount of any liabilities incurred for the purposes of the business.'

A number of matters are worthy of note in connection with the above definition:
(1) The definition is limiting – there will be assets and liabilities which are connected with the business but which do not satisfy the wording of s 110(b). Such assets and liabilities will, of course, still form part of the estate of the taxpayer under s 5 but will not benefit from the relief (or, in the case of liabilities, will not reduce the relief).

EXAMPLE 31.8

(a) In *Hardcastle v IRC* (2000) H was a Lloyd's Name at the time of his death. He had deposited funds at Lloyd's and had borrowed moneys to fund those deposits. At his death he owed amounts on accounts for which a result had not been announced. The Special Commissioner decided that the amounts owed on those accounts were trading losses and did not reduce the assets on which relief was available (although these liabilities did reduce the value of H's estate under s 5(4): see **[30.13]**). It was accepted that the deposited sum and borrowings taken out in connection with it fell within s 110(b) as being assets used in the business and liabilities incurred for the purposes of the business but the losses were trading losses and not liabilities incurred for the purposes of the business. Rather, they arose out of the running of the business: in the language used in a line of income tax cases, they were the fruit (income) produced by the tree (capital) (see, for instance, *Van den Berghs Ltd v Clark* (1935) at **[10.106]**). Of course, in this case the result produced enhanced BPR but the position will often be the opposite since trading receipts will not constitute assets used in the business. HMRC has indicated that it considers the case to be limited to its own facts but this does not appear to be correct.

(b) Sid acquires Roy's flower business with the aid of a loan from Finance for Flowers (FFF). That debt is not incurred for the purposes of the business (it was incurred in order to acquire the business) and so does not reduce the value of the business assets under s 110(b) although, since 6 April 2013, it will be set against the business assets under the new rules relating to debts incurred to purchase property subject to agricultural or business property relief (see (2) below and **[30.15]–[30.20]**).

(2) It was not entirely clear whether the value qualifying for BPR could be increased by charging business debts on non-business property: on the one hand liabilities are normally deducted first from the assets against which they are charged (IHTA 1984 s 162(4)); on the other, the value of business property is the net value after deduction of debts incurred for the purpose of the business. The matter will become less important over time, as debts entered into for the purposes of acquiring business property (or its maintenance or enhancement) from 6 April 2013 are deducted first from the business property, irrespective as to whether there is a charge in relation to the debts (see *Example 31.18* in the context of APR) (IHTA 1984 s 162B). The new rules apply only to debts entered into for the purposes of acquiring etc business property, and do not apply to general business related debts secured over non-business property. **[31.44]**

c) *Amount of relief*

Relief is given by percentage reduction in the value of the business property transferred. The chargeable transfer will be of that reduced sum. Business property relief is applied before other reliefs (for instance, the £3,000 *inter vivos* annual exemption). The appropriate percentage depends upon which category of business property is involved.

100% relief is available for businesses, interests in businesses, and all shareholdings in unquoted companies (ie categories (1), (2), (4) and (5), above).

50% relief is available for controlling shareholdings in listed companies (category (3), above) and for assets used by a business (category (6), above).

[31.45]

EXAMPLE 31.9

Topsy is a partner in the firm of Topsy & Tim (builders). He owns the site of the firm's offices and goods yard. He settles the following property on his daughter Teasy for life: (1) his share of the business (value £500,000) and (2) the site (value £50,000). Business property relief will be available on the business at 100% so that the value transferred is reduced to nil and on the site at 50% so that the value transferred is £25,000.

Notes:
(1) Topsy's total transfers amount to £25,000 which may be further reduced if other exemptions are available.
(2) IHT may remain payable on business property after deducting the 50% (and any other) relief(s). Whether the chargeable transfer is made during lifetime or on death, it will usually be possible to pay the tax by interest-free instalments (see [31.58] for a discussion of the position when IHT or additional IHT is charged because of death within seven years of a chargeable transfer and for the clawback rules).

d) *The two-year ownership requirement*

In general, relevant business property which has been owned for less than two years attracts no relief (IHTA 1984 s 106). However, the incorporation of a business will not affect the running of the two-year period (IHTA 1984 s 107) and if a transfer of a business is made between spouses on death, the recipient can include the ownership period of the deceased spouse. This is not, however, the case with an *inter vivos* transfer (IHTA 1984 s 108). If the spouse takes the property as the result of a written variation read back into the will under IHTA 1984 s 142 the recipient is treated as being entitled to property on the death of the other spouse. When entitlement results from an appropriation of assets by the PRs this provision would not, however, apply.

[31.46]

EXAMPLE 31.10

(1) Solomon incorporated his leather business by forming Solomon Ltd in which he holds 100% of the issued shares. For BPR the two-year ownership period begins with the commencement of Solomon's original leather business.
(2) Solomon set up his family company one year before his death and left the shares to his wife in his will. She can include his one-year ownership period towards satisfying the two-year requirement. If he made a lifetime gift to her, aggregation is not possible.

(3) If Mrs Solomon had died within two years of the gift from her husband (whether that gift had been made *inter vivos* or on death) business relief will be available on her death so long as the conditions for relief were satisfied at the time of the earlier transfer by her husband (IHTA 1984 s 109). A similar result follows if the gift from her husband had been by will and she had made a lifetime chargeable transfer of the property within two years of his death (in this case relief could be afforded under s 109 and, if Mr Solomon had not satisfied the two-year requirement, his period of ownership could be aggregated with that of Mrs Solomon under s 108).

e) *Non qualifying activities*

'Business' is a word of wide import and a landlord who lets properties with a view to profit may fall within its ambit. IHTA 1984 s 105(3) makes clear, however, that there are certain businesses for which relief is not available ('if the business ... consists *wholly or mainly* of one or more of the following, that is to say, dealing in securities, stocks or shares, land or buildings or making or holding investments'). There are thus three issues:
(1) whether a particular activity constitutes a business (see [31.43]);
(2) assuming a single mixed activity business, whether the business is *wholly or mainly* investment;
(3) where there is a combination of business activities, whether there are two businesses or a single mixed activity business.

The legislation does not define the phrase 'wholly or mainly'. This means that a taxpayer may conduct, within a single business, two activities – one of which may fall on the 'investment' side of the line, eg a trade may have income from managed investments held as a reserve, but the wholly or mainly test may result in that entire business attracting relief. The business must be carried on with a view to making a profit (*Grimwood Taylor v IRC* (1999)).

[31.47]

f) *Investment businesses*

The issue as to whether a business constitutes an investment activity has generally arisen in relation to the use of land and the increasing body of case law here demonstrates how difficult it is for the taxpayer to show that the receipt of income from land is anything other than investment activity. Any suggestion that a line can be drawn between 'active' and 'passive' management of investment property (each falling on different sides of the dividing line between investment and other business) has been clearly rejected (see *Martin (Executors of Moore) v IRC* (1995); *Burkinyoung (Executor of Burkinyoung) v IRC* (1995), *IRC v George (Stedman Dec'd)* (2003)). In *R & C Comrs v Pawson's Executors* (2013), in relation to the running of furnished holiday lettings, Henderson J in the Upper Tribunal noted that the following services were all directed at 'maintaining or enhancing the capital value of the property, and obtaining a regular income from its letting' and could not be considered as separate from investment activity: 'the taking of active steps to find occupants, making the necessary arrangements with them, collecting payment of the rent, the incurring of expenditure on repairs, redecoration and improvement of the property, maintenance of the garden and grounds in a tidy condition, and keeping the property insured'. Looking at the services provided in relation to the holiday letting business, eg cleaning, provision of electricity, hot water etc, these were insufficiently substantial to bring the activity as a whole away from being 'mainly' the holding of an investment. Similarly the taxpayer failed to show that the supporting activities went sufficiently beyond normal management activities in the context of the provision of managed office premises (*Trustees of David Zetland Settlement v R & C Comrs* (2013)) and grazings (*McCall (personal representatives of McLean) v R & C Comrs* (2009)). In the latter case it was noted 'where a landowner derives income from land he will be treated as having a business of holding an investment notwithstanding that in order to obtain the income he carries out incidental maintenance and management work, finds tenants and grants leases'.

However, where goods or services are provided as well as rent for the use of land, the activity moves away from investment towards trading. In *George (Stedman Dec'd)*, which concerned caravan parks, the Court of Appeal rejected the contention that one should identify the 'very business' and then classify all activities relating to that business in the same way as the core business. HMRC had argued in that case that because the receipt of site fees from the caravan owners was a receipt for the use of land, which is an investment business, all ancillary services should be treated in the same way. According to Carnwath LJ in this case, the legislation:

> 'does not require the opening of an "investment bag", into which are placed all the activities linked to the caravan park, including even the supply of water, electricity, and gas, simply on the basis that they are "ancillary" to that investment business.'

Instead, the relative importance of the non-investment activities to the business as a whole requires to be identified. This is a welcome decision for the taxpayer because it now means that activities will not be classified as investment just because they support or are related to an investment activity.

So one can contrast *George (Stedman Dec'd)* where the residential caravan park provided both a high level of services in relation to the caravans and club facilities for the owners with *Powell* (1997), where the site was in a run-down state and there was no evidence of any business activity beyond the receipt of income from caravan parks. In the first relief was available, in the second it was refused.

See also in relation to caravan parks *Furness v IRC* (1999), a success for the taxpayer, and *Hall (Executors of Hall) v IRC* (1997), *Weston v IRC* (2000), successes for HMRC.

Moving away from land, it was held in *Phillips v R & C Comrs* (2006) that a company whose activity was the *making* of loans to related companies was not in the business of *investing* in loans and, accordingly, could not be classed as a company whose business consisted wholly or mainly in the making or holding of investments. However, the Special Commissioner made it clear that it could never be said that the making of loans was never the making of an investment or that it always was; it 'was necessary to have regard to all the facts in the round'. [31.48]

g) *Mixed businesses: one business or two?*

It is a question of fact as to whether a mixed business is carried on as a single composite business, or two separate businesses. The issue was considered by the Upper Tribunal in the case of *Brander (Executor of Balfour)* (2010), a case with rather unusual facts. In that case, the Earl of Balfour died owning a large estate which was made up of a number of in-hand farms, woodlands, let farms, and a significant number of let cottages. On their own, the let farms and the cottages would have constituted investments.

The Earl had only owned the estate outright for eight months and prior to that it had been subject to a trust in which the Earl had an interest in possession. (This meant that the Earl satisfied the two year ownership period in relation to the property through his interest in possession: **[31.54]**.) However, the in-hand farms which, until 1999, had been farmed in a partnership of the Earl and another person, had had separate accounts from the rest of the estate and HMRC argued that there were in fact two businesses – the farming business and the letting business. The court did not regard separate accounts as meaning that there were two separate businesses. The fact that there had been a partnership at least until 1999 was one factor which had necessitated separate accounts and it was a practice continued after the Earl managed the in-hand farms on his own. There was much evidence that the Earl was personally involved in both the day-to-day and strategic management of the whole estate, including the let elements, and there was no clear demarcation between the in-house farms and the others. Staff worked for the whole estate. The view of the Upper Tribunal was that there was no basis on which to overturn the decision of the First-tier Tribunal that there was one business.

[31.49]

h) *Mixed businesses: the wholly or mainly test*

Should it be determined that there is a single composite business, the next question is whether or not the business is wholly or mainly an investment business. For both HMRC and the taxpayer, this is an all or nothing position. If the position is accepted that there are two separate businesses, one which qualifies for relief and the other which does not, then some assets which receive relief and some will not. If the mixed business is determined to be wholly or mainly an investment business, recalling that letting activities are regarded as investment businesses, relief will be lost entirely. The question whether a business consists wholly or mainly of making or holding investments is a question of fact for the Tribunal.

Determining the issue involves looking at all the activities 'in the round' in order to determine whether the main business is one of investment. Factors which are likely to be relevant at this stage (*Farmer* (1999) and *Brander (Balfour's Executor) v R & C Comrs* (2010), *Best (Buller's Executor) v R & C Comrs* (2014)) are:

(1) the level of profitability and turnover of each part of the business;
(2) the capital employed in each part;
(3) the amount of management and employee time spent on each part;
(4) in the case of a farming business, the relative acreage.

All these factors must be considered in the context of the case in hand: for example, if land is unlikely to be sold, the relative capital values are not so important. **[31.50]–[31.51]**

j) Excepted assets

Non-business assets cannot be included as a part of the business in an attempt to take advantage of the relief (IHTA 1984 s 112). Problems commonly arise when surplus cash is retained within the business: relief will only be available if that cash 'was required at the time of transfer for future use for (the purposes of the business)' (see s 112(2)(b)) and *Barclays Bank Trust Co Ltd v IRC* (1998)). HMRC may also query sums held in deposits at Lloyd's by Names. [31.52]

k) Contracts to sell the business and options

Relief is not available for transfers of the sale proceeds from a business and the relief does not extend to business property subject to a 'buy and sell' agreement. Arrangements are common in partnership agreements and amongst shareholder/directors of companies to provide that if one of the partners or shareholder/directors dies then his PRs are obliged to sell the share(s) and the survivors are obliged to purchase them. As this is a binding contract, the beneficial ownership in the business or shares has passed to the purchaser so that business relief is not available.

EXAMPLE 31.11

The shares of Zerzes Ltd are owned equally by the four directors. The articles of association provide that on the death of a shareholder his shares *shall* be sold to the remaining shareholder/directors who *must* purchase them. Business relief is not available on that death. If the other shareholders had merely possessed pre-emption rights or if the arrangement had involved the use of options, as no binding contract of sale exists, the relief would apply.

Particular problems may arise in the context of partnership agreements: professional partnerships, for instance, commonly include automatic accruer clauses whereby the share of a deceased partner passes automatically to the surviving partners with his estate being entitled to payment either on a valuation or in accordance with a formula. After some uncertainty HMRC now accepts that accruer clauses do not constitute binding contracts for sale and nor do option arrangements (*Law Society's Gazette*, 4 September 1996, p 35, IHTM 25292). It appears that the section applies only if the contract is to sell a business or part of a business: by contrast a contract to sell assets used in a business is not caught. [31.53]

l) Businesses held in settlements

For interest in possession trusts the relief is given, as one would expect, by reference to the life tenant. (It should be noted that the changes made by FA 2006 in respect of interests in possession do not appear to affect the issue of business property relief as it applies to settled property, because all that is required for the relief to be claimed is for the transferor to have a 'beneficial interest in possession'; the deemed ownership of the underlying capital is not at issue in these circumstances. Whether this was intentional or an oversight

remains to be seen). So long as the life tenant satisfies the two-year ownership test, relief will be given at the following rates:
(1) *100% relief* for all unquoted shares and for businesses belonging to the trust;
(2) *50% relief* for controlling shareholdings in listed companies held in the trust; and
(3) *50% relief* for the assets listed in (6) at **[31.43]** which are held in the trust and which are either used by the life tenant for his own business or by a company controlled by him.

Fetherstonehaugh v IRC (1984) concerned the availability of relief when land held under a strict settlement was used by the life tenant as part of his farming business (he was a sole trader absolutely entitled to the other business assets). The Court of Appeal held that 100% (then 50%) relief was available under s 105(1)(a) on the land in the settlement with the result that the subsequent introduction of 50% (then 30%) relief is apparently redundant in such cases. HMRC now accepts that in cases similar to *Fetherstonehaugh* the maximum 100% relief will be available since the land will be treated as an 'asset used in the business' and, as its value is included in the transfer of value, the land will be taxed on the basis that the deceased was the absolute owner of it.

For trusts without interests in possession, relief is given so long as the conditions are satisfied by the trustees. The relief will be given against the anniversary charge and when the business ceases to be relevant property (eg when it leaves the trust) on fulfilment of the normal conditions. **[31.54]**

m) *'Control'*

Control is defined as follows:

'a person has control of a company at any time if he then has the control of powers of voting on *all questions* affecting the company as a whole which if exercised would yield a majority of the votes capable of being exercised thereon ...' (IHTA 1984 s 269(1)).

Hence, control of more than 50% of the votes exercisable in general meeting will ensure that the transferor has 'control' for the purposes of BPR. A transfer of his shares in a listed company will attract 50% relief and a transfer of qualifying assets used by a company which the taxpayer controls 50% relief (control is also important in the context of APR: see **[31.69]**–**[31.70]**). In calculating whether he has control, a life tenant can aggregate shares held by the settlement with shares in his free estate, whilst the related property rules (see **[28.70]**) result in shares of husband and wife being treated as one holding.

In *Walker v IRC* (2001) a Special Commissioner decided that a 50% shareholder, who was the chairman of the company and who had a casting vote at meetings, was able to control a majority of votes at any meeting as required by s 269. In *Walding v IRC* (1996) Knox J decided that all votes had to be taken into account for the purpose of deciding whether the s 269 test was satisfied. The fact that shares were held by a five-year-old child did not therefore mean that those votes could be ignored for this purpose. **[31.55]**

n) Relief for minority shareholdings in unquoted companies

For transfers of value made and other events occurring on or after 6 April 1996 relief at 100% is available for all minority shareholdings in unquoted companies (including companies listed on AIM). Prior to that date relief at 100% was only available for substantial minority shareholdings (ie 25% plus) in such companies with smaller shareholdings attracting only 50% relief. As a result of the change all shares in unquoted companies may now attract 100% relief irrespective of the size of holding: the continuing distinction in the legislation between controlling shareholdings and others remains important, however, where assets are owned outside the company. [31.56]

o) Switching control

It might be assumed that because of the two-year ownership requirement, both the business property (eg the shares) and control must have been owned throughout this period. This, however, does not appear to be the case for relief under s 105(1)(b) since it is only the shares transferred which must have been owned for two years and control is only required immediately before the relevant transfer. Thus the taxpayer may – for instance as the result of a buy-back – obtain control of the company many years after acquiring his shares.

EXAMPLE 31.12

Of the 100 issued ordinary shares in Buy-Back Ltd Zack owns 40, Jed 40 and the remaining 20 are split amongst miscellaneous charities. Assume that in July 2015 Buy-Back buys Zack's holding. As those shares are cancelled the issued capital falls to 60 shares of which Jed owns 40. Were he to die in September 2015, his shareholding would fall under s 105(1)(b).

It may be possible for the partners in a quasi-partnership company to ensure that each obtains control for a short period (eg one month) to produce enhanced business relief. [31.57]

EXAMPLE 31.13

The shares in ABCD Ltd are owned as to 25% each by A, B, C and D. The shares are divided into four classes in December 2015 which will carry control in January, February, March and April 2016 respectively. In January 2016 A transfers his shares.
(1) As A has control (under s 269(1)) in January 2016 he is entitled to relief at 50% on land which he transfers and which had been used by the company.
(2) Might temporary shifts of control be nullified under the GAAR? It is arguable that, as the legislation expressly requires control at one moment only (namely immediately before the transfer), that is an end to the matter. It is, however, desirable that A should at the time of transfer actually possess control of the business: ie the other shareholders must accept that A could, if he wished, exercise his voting control over the affairs of the company.

p) Business relief and the instalment option

Any value transferred after deduction of BPR may be further reduced by the normal IHT exemptions and reliefs which are deducted *after* business relief so that a lifetime gift, for instance, may be reduced by the £3,000 annual exemption. Further, any tax payable may normally be spread over ten years and paid by annual interest-free instalments (see [**30.51**]). This instalment election is only available, in the case of lifetime gifts, if the IHT is borne by the donee: on death the election should be made by the PRs. Although there is a similarity between assets which attract business relief and assets qualifying for the instalment option, the option may be valuable where there are excepted assets or where the business is disqualified under the s 105(3) test (see [**31.47**]). This is because the definition of 'qualifying property' for the purposes of s 227 (the instalment option) and s 234 (interest-free instalments) is wider than for the purposes of BPR. There are limitations on the availability of instalment relief in the case of a transfer of unquoted shares not giving control (see [**31.55**]), as the following table indicates:

Relevant business property (IHTA 1984 Part V Chapter 1)	*Instalment assets* (IHTA 1984 Part VIII)
s 105(1)(a): a business or an interest in a business	*s 227*: a business or an interest in a business
s 105(1)(b): shares etc, giving control	*s 227(2)*: land *s 228(1)(a)*: shares etc, giving control
s 105(1)(bb): unquoted shares	*s 228(1)(b)*: on death, unquoted shares being at least 20%, of the total transfer
	s 228(1)(c): unquoted shares with hardship
	s 228(1)(d) and *228(3)*: unquoted shares within the 10% and £20,000 rule
	s 229: woodlands.

These limitations on the instalment option have been defended by HMRC on the grounds that 'it has been considered inappropriate for the instalment facility to apply in cases involving less than substantial interests in unquoted companies' (see further (1985) 6 *CTT News* 284). [**31.58**]

q) *Clawback*

When a transferor makes a lifetime chargeable transfer or a PET and dies within seven years, the IHT or extra IHT payable is calculated on the basis that business relief is not available unless the original (or substituted) property remains owned by the transferee at the death of the transferor (or at the death of the transferee if earlier) and would qualify for business relief immediately before the transferor's death (ignoring, however, the two-year ownership requirement) (IHTA 1984 s 113A). This 'clawback' of relief is anomalous: relief on death is not similarly withdrawn if the business property is sold after the death. Of course, the instalment option is similarly restricted since it is only available if the original or substituted business property is owned by the transferee at death. Relief is given for substituted property when the entire (net) proceeds of sale of the original property are reinvested within three years (or such longer period as the Board may allow) in replacement qualifying property.

Note that in the event of death within seven years of the transfer, the relief affects the value of the lifetime gifts for two separate IHT purposes – the first is in the recalculation of tax or extra tax on the transfer itself. The second relates to the value of the transfer for the purposes of calculating unused nil rate band available for future transfers. In relation to the first, it makes no difference whether the original transfer was a PET or a chargeable transfer – in both cases any additional tax is calculated on the transfer with no relief. However, for the purposes of the nil rate band, the transfer which was originally chargeable continues to be given relief, in contrast to the transfer which was originally a PET (see *Example 31.15*).

EXAMPLE 31.14

(1) Sim gave his ironmonger's business to his daughter, Sammy, in 2012 (a PET) and died in 2018. Sammy has continued to run the business. Although the PET became chargeable because of Sim's death within seven years, 100% relief is available (qualifying property retained by donee).

(2) As in (1) save that Sammy sold the business (or the business was closed down) in 2014.

No business relief is available on Sim's death. The value of the business in 2012 is taxed and forms part of Sim's cumulative total of gifts on death.

(3) As in (1) save that Sammy had incorporated the business late in 2012 and had continued to run it as the sole shareholder/director.

Business relief is available on Sim's death (substituted qualifying property).

EXAMPLE 31.15

Jock settles his business (then worth £500,000) on discretionary trusts in 2013 (a chargeable lifetime transfer). He dies in 2018 when the business has been sold by the trustees.

(1) *On the 2013 transfer*: 100% relief is available so that the value transferred is nil.

(2) *On his death in 2018*: the clawback operates. No relief is given for the purposes of calculating the extra IHT, which is calculated on a value transferred of £500,000. However, for the purposes of the nil rate band, the transfer is still treated as zero, so in the absence of other gifts, the full nil rate band will be available on death.

(3) In contrast, had the 2013 transfer been a PET, no relief is available for any purpose, and there is no nil rate band available on Jock's death. [31.59]

r) *Business property subject to a reservation*

Business property subject to a reservation is treated as comprised in the donor's estate at death (if the reservation is still then subsisting) or, if the reservation ceases *inter vivos*, as forming the subject matter of a deemed PET made at that time (see **Chapter 29**). In both cases business relief may be available to reduce the value of the property subject to charge. Whether the relief is available or not is generally decided by treating the transfer as made by the *donee* who must therefore satisfy the BPR requirements (FA 1986 Sch 20 para 8). However, for these purposes, the period of ownership of the donor can be included with that of the donee in order to satisfy the two-year requirement.

Any question of the size of the holding of shares or securities must be decided as if the shares or securities transferred continued to be owned by the *donor* and had been owned by him since the date of the gift. Accordingly, other shares of the donor (or related property of the donor) will be relevant in deciding if these requirements are satisfied. [31.60]

EXAMPLE 31.16
(1) Wainwright gives his ironmonger's business to his daughter Tina and it is agreed that he shall be paid one half of the net profits from the business each year (a gift with reservation).
  (i) At the time of the original gift (a PET) the property satisfied the requirements for business relief. If the PET becomes chargeable as the result of Wainwright's death within the following seven years, relief continues to be available if Tina has retained the original property or acquired replacement property.
  (ii) The business is also treated as forming part of Wainwright's estate on his death under FA 1986 s 102, but business relief may be available to reduce its value under FA 1986 Sch 20 para 8. Whether relief is available (and if so at what percentage) is decided by treating the transfer of value as made by the *donee*. Accordingly, Tina must satisfy the conditions for relief although she can include the period of ownership/occupation of Wainwright before the gift. (A similar provision applies if the reservation ceases during Wainwright's lifetime so that he is treated as making a PET.)
(2) Assume that Wainwright owns 100% of the shares in Widgett's Ltd and gives 20% of those shares to Tina subject to a reserved benefit. Assuming that he dies within seven years:
  (i) Relief at 100% was originally available under s 105(1)(b) when the gift was made and continues to apply to that chargeable PET if Tina has retained the shares.
  (ii) The shares are treated as forming part of Wainwright's estate because of the reserved benefit. Business relief will be available if Tina satisfies the basic requirements: ie she must have retained the original shares which must still qualify as business property in relation to her. For the purposes of deciding the size of the holding, the 20% is aggregated with the shares continued to be held by Wainwright at his death.

Note: Where property attracting 100% relief is transferred by outright gift it may be argued that this is an exempt gift under IHTA 1984 s 20 (the small gifts exemption – see [**31.5**]) with the result that the reservation of benefit rules cannot apply (see FA 1986 s 102(5)(b)).

s) *The consequences of relief at 100%*

The introduction of 100% relief has had far-reaching consequences. For instance:
(1) It is more important than ever to ensure that full relief is not lost because of a technicality. Consider, for instance, whether cash reserves will be excepted assets: are they required for use in the business? (see [**31.52**]).
(2) Consideration should be given to the structuring of business activity so that the relief is readily available: simple structures are likely to be best and fragmentation arrangements that have been common in the past may prove disadvantageous.

(3) Relief at 100% is equally available in the case of unquoted companies, sole traders and partnerships.
(4) In contrast to the relief available for heritage property, there is no clawback of the 100% relief on death if the heir immediately sells the assets: if heritage property is or can be run as a business it would be more attractive to use BPR than the heritage exemption.
(5) If lifetime gifts are made and the donor dies within seven years, relief may not be available if the donee has already sold the assets (see [31.59]). Because there is no clawback on death, taxpayers may be encouraged to delay passing on property qualifying for 100% relief.
(6) If it is feared that the new reliefs will be withdrawn in the future, a gift of property on to flexible trusts under which the donor retains control as trustee should be considered (note, however, the trap if it is envisaged that the property will be distributed within the first ten years of the trust: see [34.34]).
(7) Wills should be reviewed to ensure that, whenever this is practicable, property which is eligible for 100% BPR is left to a person other than a surviving spouse so that BPR is not lost.

EXAMPLE 31.17

Assume that X owns a farm worth £1m; farmhouse worth £400,000 and investments worth £1.5m. Mrs X will run the farm on his death and he therefore envisages a will in the following terms:
(i)   nil rate band (£325,000) to his children;
(ii)   residue to Mrs X.
No IHT will be payable on Mr X's death but the position would be much improved if the will had provided:
(i)   farm and nil rate band to/on trust for children;
(ii)   residue to Mrs X.
Again no IHT will be payable but assets passing tax free to the children now total £1,325,000.

And after X's death Mrs X purchases the farm for £1m – there is no clawback of the APR (see below)/BPR.

By her will Mrs X leaves everything to the children (including the farm) and provided that she has owned the farm for two years 100% relief is again available.
Notes:
(a) In cases where Mrs X cannot afford the purchase price, consider leaving the sum outstanding.
(b) To ensure that Mrs X will acquire the farm, consider granting her an option in the will.
(c) Stamp duty land tax will be payable on the sale.
(d) In cases where the availability of the relief is in doubt (for example, because there is a mixed business) consider leaving the business in a discretionary trust so that if relief turns out not to be available the property can be appointed out to the surviving spouse under IHTA 1984 s 144. Alternatively if relief is available the trust may continue in being or the property can be appointed out to the children.

(8) Business property relief is intended to benefit businesses as opposed to investments but this objective has not been fully achieved. Investments in limited partnerships may attract 100% relief and an AIM portfolio, qualifying for relief at 100%, may be attractive.

(9) In some cases it may be worth de-listing: ie turning the fully quoted company back into an unquoted company or one dealt in on AIM because of the higher levels of relief available. **[31.61]**

3 Agricultural property relief ('APR': IHTA 1984 ss 115–124)

IHTA 1984 ss 115–124 contains rules, introduced originally in FA 1981, giving relief for transfers of agricultural property situated in the UK or other EEA state. As with BPR, this relief is given automatically. The old (pre-1981) regime will not be considered save for a brief mention of the transitional provisions.

Relief is given for transfers of value of *agricultural property*, defined in s 115(2) as follows:

> '"Agricultural property" means agricultural land or pasture and includes woodland and any building used in connection with the intensive rearing of livestock or fish if the woodland or building is occupied with agricultural land or pasture and the occupation is ancillary to that of the agricultural land or pasture; and also includes such cottages, farm buildings and farmhouses, together with the land occupied with them, as are of a character appropriate to the property.'

There are thus three separate dimensions of the definition: (a) the land, (b) woodland and buildings occupied as ancillary to the land, and (c) farmhouses etc, each of which is now considered. **[31.62]**

a) *Agricultural land or pasture*

The land must be used for agricultural purposes. In *Dixon v IRC* (2002) the property comprised a cottage, garden and orchard totalling 0.6 acres. Although surplus fruit was sold it was decided that the property was not agricultural land or pasture: rather there was a residential cottage with land. In *Wheatley (Executors of Wheatley) v IRC* (1998), it was decided that a paddock used by a neighbour for grazing horses was not for the purposes of agriculture. Contrast, however, the position if the grazing agreement had related to cattle or sheep, when it is accepted that a farming operation (the sale of grass) is being carried on, provided that it can be shown that the taxpayer is doing something (replanting, maintaining fences, etc) other than just receiving rent.

This definition includes habitat land and land used for short rotation coppice (this being a way of producing renewal fuel for bio-mass-fed power stations – in simple terms, willow or other cuttings are planted on farmland and, after the first year, are harvested every three years or so and then made into chips which are used as fuel). *Starke v IRC* (1995) concerned a 2.5 acre site containing within it a substantial six-bedroomed farmhouse with the rest substantially covered by an assortment of outbuildings. It was used as part of a medium-sized farm, owned by the family company, carrying on mixed farming. The court concluded that the relevant property did not constitute 'agricultural land' within the above definition of 'agricultural property' as it was covered by buildings. And, although not argued, it therefore follows that the buildings did not qualify as there was no land for them to be ancillary to. The decision is hardly surprising but it does point to the dangers of a farmer giving away the bulk of his farm retaining only the farmhouse and a relatively small area of land. Such retained property will rarely qualify for relief, either on this ground, or under the 'ancillary' or 'character appropriate' tests, considered below. **[31.63]**

b) *Buildings in connection with intensive farming*

Buildings are not land (*Starke*), so if they are to qualify for relief, they must fall within either this heading or the next.

The occupation of a building must be with agricultural land and ancillary to it. In *Williams (personal representatives of Williams deceased) v IRC* (2005), 21/2 acres of a farm on which broiler houses were situated were let to a company. The first question was whether the rest of the farm could be taken into account when considering with what 'land' the building was occupied. It was decided that it could not: only the land occupied by the same person as was occupying the building, ie the company, was relevant. The second question was whether the occupation was ancillary to the 'land' as determined, and it was held that it was not: the broiler houses would qualify only if they were occupied as an 'add-on' to or as a subsidiary part of the purposes of a larger agricultural enterprise carried out on the other land with which they were occupied. So, for example, broiler houses situated on a large farm, all of which was occupied by the farmer, would qualify. Here, where they occupied almost 1/4 of all the land occupied, they did not. **[31.64]**

c) *Farmhouses*

Two tests have to be satisfied here – first, is the property in question a farmhouse; second, if so, is it of a character appropriate to the property (see generally *Private Client Business* (2013), parts 1 and 2).

In relation to the first, the issue is very much one of fact, looking at the size, content and layout relative to the land and function. In *Arnander v R & C Comrs* (2006), a substantial seven-bedroomed house with a music room, with the land farmed by contractors, was not a farmhouse at all. **[31.65]**

The question of whether a farmhouse is of a character appropriate to the property is very much a question of fact. Issues which will be considered are the relative size of the house and the farm, the layout, the history of the farming operation, and how the 'educated rural layman' would regard the house. The case law (all decided by the Special Commissioners) may be summarised as follows:

In *Lloyds TSB (PRs of Antrobus deceased) v IRC* (2002) it was agreed that Cookhill Priory (a listed six-bed country house) was a farmhouse and that the surrounding 125 acres (plus 6.54 acres of tenanted land and buildings including a chapel) were agricultural property. The Special Commissioner decided that the character appropriate test was also satisfied.

In *Higginson's Exors v IRC* (2002) Ballywood Lodge, formerly a nineteenth-century hunting lodge of six beds with 63 acres of agricultural land, three acres of formal gardens and 68 acres of woodland and wetland around Ballywood Lake, was considered not to be a farmhouse ('not the style of house in which a typical farmer would live').

In *Arnander* (see **[31.65]**), an early seventeenth-century manor house on an estate of 188 acres was not considered appropriate to the land.

Of the three, the most important decision in terms of laying down a guiding principle is the *Antrobus* case in which the Commissioner summed up the factors to be taken into account in applying the character appropriate test as follows:

> 'Thus the principles which have been established for deciding whether a farmhouse is of a character appropriate to the property may be summarised as: first, one should consider whether the house is appropriate by reference to its size, content and layout, with the farm buildings and the particular area of farmland being farmed (*Korner*); one should consider whether the house is proportionate in size and nature to the requirements of the farming activities conducted on the agricultural land or pasture in question (*Starke*); thirdly, that although one cannot describe a farmhouse which satisfies the "character appropriate" test one knows one when one sees it (*Dixon*); fourthly, one should ask whether the educated rural layman would regard the property as a house with land or a farm (*Dixon*); and, finally, one should consider the historical dimension and ask how long the house in question has been associated with the agricultural property and whether there was a history of agricultural production (*Dixon*).'

No one factor is decisive but the factors are considered in the round and the eventual decision based upon 'the broad picture'. In practice expert evidence (especially evidence of comparables) is of crucial significance.

The Upper Tribunal have recently been asked to consider the issue of 'character appropriate' in *R & C Comrs v Hanson* (2013) in a particular context. The issue here was, in determining whether the house has a character appropriate to the agricultural property, must the agricultural property all be owned by the person owning the house? In *Rosser* (2003) it was suggested that it should, but this was doubted in *Hanson v R & C Comrs* (2012).

In *Hanson*, the deceased had a life interest in a farmhouse in which his son lived at the date of the deceased's death. Because of the interest in possession, the deceased was treated as owning the farmhouse. The house was occupied (see **[31.69]**) by the son for the purposes of the farming operation which took place over 200 acres of land owned by various persons, including 128 acres owned by the son and 25 acres part-owned by the deceased. Looking at the totality of farming operations carried on from the farmhouse, it was accepted by both sides that the house was of a character appropriate to *that* property. If, however, 'property' simply referred to the 25 acres remaining in the ownership of the deceased at the date of death, it was not appropriate. In the view of the Upper Tribunal, 'property' included all the land farmed from the farmhouse, including property that was not in the ownership of the deceased, and relief was given.

Farm cottages included in the definition of 'agricultural property' must have been occupied for the purposes of agriculture (see s 117(1)); ESC F16 extends relief in such cases to include a cottage occupied by a retired farm employee or his surviving spouse provided that either the occupier is a statutorily protected tenant or the occupation is under a lease granted to the farm employee for his life and that of any surviving spouse as part of his contract of employment by the landlord for agricultural purposes.

A farmhouse will be primarily a 'residential' property – hence CGT roll-over relief is not available on it (see **[22.72]**) and nor will business property relief usually be available (save for any part used 'exclusively' for business purposes). **[31.66]**

d) *'Agricultural value' (IHTA 1984 s 115(3))*

It is the *'agricultural value'* of such property which is subject to the relief: defined as the value which the property would have if subject to a perpetual covenant prohibiting its use otherwise than as agricultural property. Enhanced value attributable to development potential is not subject to the relief. This means that in practice BPR is a more useful relief as it may apply to this excess value in the case of farmland although not in the case of the farmhouse: in practice the agricultural value is often considered to be around two-thirds of open market value, although in current market conditions a much smaller discount may be appropriate. This point was made by the Special Commissioner in the *Higginson* case when he commented:

> 'A property may command a high price in the open market because of potential for development; and subsection (3) clearly caters for that situation. But it seems to me that the notional restrictive covenant would have much less of a deprecatory effect in a case where the property has a value greater than ordinary not because of development potential but rather because of what I might call "vanity value" on account of its site, style or the like. In the light of my decision the point is academic.'

The general rule is that the value of any debt which is an encumbrance on property will first be set against the value of that property (IHTA 1984 s 162(4)). This means that a charge on agricultural property will reduce its value. For loans taken out prior to 6 April 2013, the general rule will continue to apply and a charge against non-agricultural property will optimise the impact of agricultural property relief as the debt will have the effect of reducing the value of chargeable estate rather than estate subject to relief. However, with effect from 6 April 2013, loans taken out to purchase agricultural property are to be set against the value of that property, rather than the property against which they are secured. In contrast to BPR, the starting point of valuation is the value of the property, rather than the net value of the business (see **[31.44]**) (see *Example 31.18*, below; IHTA 1984 ss 5(5)). Further, it is not necessary to transfer a farming business or part thereof in order to obtain relief which can be given on a mere transfer of assets. **[31.67]**

EXAMPLE 31.18

A farmer owns a farm qualifying for 100% agricultural relief and worth £1.5m, subject to a mortgage of £500,000. His other main assets are investments worth £800,000. The value of his estate on death for IHT purposes would be £800,000, representing the investments, and the farm is entirely covered by APR. In this situation, the debt is set off against property which qualifies for relief at 100% and is thus 'wasted'.

Suppose, however, that before his death and before 6 April 2013, the farmer arranged with the appropriate creditor to switch the mortgage from the agricultural land to the investments. The result then would be that on death the value of his estate would be only £300,000 as the debt would now be set first against the investments, reducing chargeable assets. The farm, as before, is entirely covered by APR.

e) *The level of relief (IHTA 1984 s 116)*

Section 116 provides (subject to the provisions of s 117 which are considered in [31.69]) that the level of APR is 100% and is available unless the property is subject to a tenancy beginning before 1 September 1995, in which case the 100% relief is only available where:

> 'The interest of the transferor in the property immediately before the transfer carries the right to vacant possession or the right to obtain it within the next 12 months.'

This is extended by ESC F17 to cases where the transferor's interest in the property immediately before the transfer *either:*
(1) carried the right to vacant possession within 24 months of the date of transfer; *or*
(2) is notwithstanding the terms of the tenancy valued at an amount broadly equivalent to vacant possession value.

The former situation would cover the service of notices under the terms of the Agricultural Holdings Act 1986 and so-called '*Gladstone v Bower* arrangements' while the second situation would be relevant in cases akin to that of Lady Fox (*IRC v Grey* (1994), discussed at [31.74]).

Otherwise the level of relief is at 50%. [31.68]

f) *Ownership and occupation requirements (IHTA 1984 s 117)*

However, relief is not available unless the further requirements of s 117 are satisfied:

> 's 116 does not apply to any agricultural property unless:
>
> (a) it was *occupied* by the transferor for the purposes of agriculture throughout the period of *two* years ending with the date of the transfer, or
>
> (b) it was *owned* by him throughout the period of *seven* years ending with that date and was throughout that period occupied (by him *or another*) for the purposes of agriculture.' (See *Harrold v IRC* (1996) for when a farmhouse is 'occupied'.)

Occupation by a partnership of which the transferor was a partner, or by a company controlled by the transferor, is treated as occupation by the transferor (IHTA 1984 s 119).

The Upper Tribunal in *Atkinson v R & C Comrs* (2011) had to consider the position of a farmer who had left the farmhouse to become resident in a care home for four years before his death. Although the house was not sold and his belongings remained there, there was insufficient 'occupation for the purposes of agriculture' in these four years and no relief was given. [31.69]

EXAMPLE 31.19

(1) Dan started farming in 2012 and died in April 2017. As an owner-occupier he is entitled to APR at 100%.

(2) Bill's farm was tenanted when he acquired it in 2001 but in 2016 the lease was surrendered. In August 2017 Bill died. He was the owner-occupier at death but did not satisfy the requirements of s 117(a) as he did not occupy it for two years. He has, however, owned the farm for at least seven years, so 117(b) will be satisfied and he will be entitled to 100% APR.

(3) Jack acquired his farm as an investment in 2012 and died in 2017. No APR is available as he has not owned it for seven years.

g) *Trusts and companies*

The relief (at 100% or 50% as appropriate) is available in three further cases: *first*, where agricultural property is held on discretionary trusts (100% relief, if the trustees have been farming the land themselves); *second*, where agricultural property is held on trust for a life tenant under an interest in possession trust; and *finally*, where agricultural property is held by a company in which the transferor of the shares has control. 'Control' has the same meaning as for BPR (see [31.55]). To claim the relief the appropriate two- or seven-year period of ownership must be satisfied by the company (*vis-à-vis* the agricultural property) and by the shareholder/transferor (*vis-à-vis* the shares transferred). [31.70]

EXAMPLE 31.20

Muckspreader dies owning shares in a company owning agricultural land in circumstances when APR is available in respect of the shares. He leaves the shares to his widow. She dies within two years.

On the widow's death no APR is available because she does not get the benefit of Muckspreader's period of ownership of the shares. This is anomalous (compare the position for BPR). The position would have been different if Muckspreader had owned the agricultural land itself and left it to his widow; see IHTA 1984 s 120; cf s 123(1)(b).

h) *Technical provisions*

As with BPR there are technical provisions relating to replacement property and clawback (see [31.59]), transfers between spouses, and succession from a donor (see [31.46]). Similarly, a binding contract for the sale of the property results in APR not being available (see [31.53]). [31.71]

i) *Agricultural tenancies*

The grant of a tenancy of agricultural property is not a transfer of value provided that the grant is for full consideration in money or money's worth (IHTA 1984 s 16). Hence, it is not necessary for the lessor to show (particularly in the case of transfers within the family) that he had no gratuitous intent and that the transaction was such as might be made with a stranger (see IHTA 1984 s 10(1)). For difficulties that may arise in ascertaining the market value of agricultural tenancies, see *Law Society's Gazette*, 1984, p 2749, *Law Society's Gazette*, 1985, pp 420 and 484, *Baird's Executors v IRC* (1991) and *Walton v IRC* (1996) (considered at [28.73]). [31.72]

j) *Clawback*

The availability of the relief when extra IHT is payable, or a PET becomes chargeable, because of a death within seven years is subject to the same restrictions as apply for BPR (see [**31.59**]). [**31.73**]

k) *Lotting*

In valuing an estate at death, 'lotting' requires a valuation on the basis that 'the vendor must be supposed to have' taken the course which would get the largest price for the combined holding 'subject to the caveat ... that it does not entail undue expenditure of time and effort' (see further [**30.3**]).

In *IRC v Gray* (1994) the deceased had farmed the Croxton Park Estate in partnership with two others and the land was subject to tenancies which Lady Fox, as freeholder, had granted to the partnership. HMRC sought to aggregate or lot together the freehold in the land with her partnership share as a single unit of property. It may be noted that under the partnership deed she was entitled to 92 1/2% of profits (and bore all the losses). The Court of Appeal, reversing the Lands Tribunal, held that lotting was appropriate since that was the course which a prudent hypothetical vendor would take to obtain the best price. The fact that the interests could not be described as forming a 'natural unit of property' was irrelevant. The arrangement employed in this case was commonly undertaken (before the introduction of 100% APR) in order to reduce the tax charge on agricultural property. An alternative involved leases being granted to a family farming company and HMRC seeks to apply this decision to those arrangements. As a result of ESC F17 noted in [**31.68**] transfers in *Fox*-type cases now attract 100% relief. [**31.74**]

l) *Transitional relief; double discounting*

Under the rules which prevailed up to 1981 APR was available where L let Whiteacre to a partnership consisting of himself and his children M and N. On a transfer of the freehold reversion (valued on a tenanted, not a vacant possession, basis) 50% relief was available. The ingredient of 'double discounting' consisted of first reducing the value of the property by granting the lease and then applying the full (50%) relief to that discounted value. As a *quid pro quo* HMRC argued that the grant of the lease could be a transfer of value even if for a full commercial rent.

Double discount is not available under the present system of agricultural relief and the grant of the tenancy will not be a chargeable transfer of value if for full consideration (IHTA 1984 s 16). On a transitional basis, however, where land was let, as in the above example, on 10 March 1981 so that any transfer by L immediately before that date would have qualified for relief, on the next transfer of value, that relief will still apply but at the current level of 100%. (Note that the relief was limited to £250,000 of agricultural value (before giving relief) or to £1,000 acres, at the option of the taxpayer.) The transitional relief will not apply in cases where the pre-10 March 1981 tenancy has been surrendered and regranted but similar transitional relief applies where before 10 March 1981 the land was let to a company which the transferor controlled (IHTA 1984 s 116(2)–(5)). [**31.75**]

EXAMPLE 31.21

For many years Mary has owned agricultural land which has been let to a family farming company in which she owns 100% of the shares. On her death 50% relief only will be available on the land since she is not entitled to obtain vacant possession (the company being a separate legal entity). If, however, the arrangements had been in place before 10 March 1981, Mary may be entitled to 100% relief under the 'Double Discount Rule' (for instance, if she was a director of the company immediately before 10 March 1981). Relief will only be available up to a maximum of 1,000 acres or land which at 10 March 1981 was worth up to £250,000.

m) *Milk quota*

Following *Cottle v Coldicott* (1995) HMRC now considers that milk quota comprises a separate asset distinct from the land. Accordingly it will not qualify for APR but 'with an owner occupied dairy farm, business relief at the same rate will normally be available in the alternative' (see *Inheritance Tax Manual* IHTM 24506). This treatment appears at odds with the BPR provisions (see *Taxation*, 3 June 1999, p 244). **[31.76]**

n) *Inter-relation of agricultural and business property reliefs*

Although the two reliefs are similar and overlap, the following distinctions are worthy of note:
(1) APR is given in priority to BPR (IHTA 1984 s 114(1)).
(2) Differences exist in the treatment of woodlands, crops, livestock, deadstock, plant and machinery, and farmhouses etc. When APR does not apply, consider whether BPR is available.
(3) APR is only available on property situated in the UK, Channel Islands, Isle of Man and the EEA whereas BPR is not so restricted. **[31.77]**

o) *Relief at 100%*

Many of the comments made at **[31.61]** in the context of BPR apply equally to agricultural property. In addition:
(1) there is no longer any attraction in the type of fragmentation arrangements illustrated in the *Fox* case (see **[31.74]**). Maximum relief is available for in-hand land;
(2) in-hand land need not be farmed by the owner himself. He can enter into contract farming arrangements without jeopardising 100% relief provided that these are correctly structured;
(3) the grant of new tenancies after August 1995 will not jeopardise 100% relief: thought should be given to terminating or amending (eg by adding a small area of extra land) existing tenancies so that a new tenancy resulting in 100% relief for the landlord arises;
(4) complex structures should no longer be set up but what should be done with existing structures? The costs of unscrambling may be considerable and it is worth reflecting that, assuming that the value of tenanted land is one half of the vacant possession value, the effect of 50% APR is to reduce the tax rate to 10% of vacant possession value and as that tax can be paid in ten instalments, the annual tax charge is a mere 1%. **[31.78]**

4 Relief for heritage property

(1) Heritage property can be given for national purposes or for the public benefit without any IHT or CGT charge arising (IHTA 1984 s 25). This includes transfers under the Cultural Gifts Scheme. The list of bodies to which such property may be given can be found in Sch 3. This exemption is extended to gifts of national property outside any special scheme (for example a gift to a relative) which were PETS when made, and where the property is subsequently donated for national purposes or sold by private treaty to a national body (see [31.86]) by the recipient or accepted in lieu of tax (see [31.90]). In each case, the subsequent donation, sale or offer in lieu of tax must have taken place before the original PET became a chargeable transfer as a result of the original donor's death within seven years (IHTA 1984 s 26A).

EXAMPLE 31.22

Jeremy made an inter vivos gift to Katherine of some handwritten Beatles lyrics (a potentially exempt transfer). Katherine later donated these to the British Library. Subsequently, but within seven years of the original gift, Jeremy died. The donation by Katherine is exempt under IHTA 1984 s 25 and the PET by Jeremy, which would otherwise be chargeable as a result of his death within seven years, is exempt under IHTA 1984 s 26A.

(2) In certain circumstances an application can be made to postpone the payment of IHT on transfers of value of heritage property made available to the public. Such claims now have to be made within two years of the transfer of value or relevant death or within such longer period as the Board may allow (IHTA 1984 s 30(3BA) inserted by FA 1998). As tax can be postponed on any number of such transfers, the result is that a liability to IHT can be deferred indefinitely (similar deferral provisions operate for CGT: TCGA 1992 s 258(3)). Tax postponed under these provisions may subsequently become chargeable under IHTA 1984 s 32 on the happening of a 'chargeable event'. If the transfer is potentially exempt, an application for conditional exemption can only be made (and is only necessary) if the PET is rendered chargeable by the donor's death within seven years. [31.79]

a) *Conditions to be satisfied if IHT is to be deferred*

In order to obtain this relief, *first*, the property must fall into one of the categories set out in IHTA 1984 s 31(1):

Category 1: any relevant object which appears to the Board to be pre-eminent for its national, scientific, historic or artistic interest (this category was restricted by FA 1998 by the inclusion of the requirement that the object must be pre-eminent): see IHTA 1984 s 31(1)(a).

Category 2: land of outstanding scenic, historic, or scientific interest (IHTA 1984 s 31(1)(b)).

Category 3: buildings of outstanding or architectural interest and their amenity land (s 31(1)(c), (d)) and chattels historically associated with such buildings (s 31(1)(e)).

Second, undertakings have to be given with respect to that property to take reasonable steps for its preservation; to secure reasonable access to the public (see HMRC, *Capital Taxation and the National Heritage* for more information)); and (in the case of *Category 1* property) to keep the property in the UK. In appropriate cases of *Category 1* property, it had been sufficient for details of the object and its location to be entered on an official list of such assets and concern had been expressed that proper access for the public was not always available. FA 1998 accordingly provided that the public must have extended access (ie access not confined to access when a prior appointment is made) and for greater disclosure of information about designated items (IHTA 1984 s 31(4FA), (4FB) inserted by FA 1998, see also [31.79]).

The undertaking must be given by 'such person as the Treasury think appropriate in the circumstances of the case'. In practice, this will mean a PR, trustee, legatee or donee.

A *third* requirement exists in the case of lifetime transfers of value. The transferor must have owned the asset for the six years immediately preceding the transfer if relief is to be given. Notice, however, that the six-year requirement can be satisfied by aggregating periods of ownership of a husband and wife and that it does not apply in cases where the property has been inherited on a death and the exemption has then been successfully claimed. It is surprising that the six-year requirement is limited to *inter vivos* transfers thereby permitting deathbed schemes. **[31.80]**

b) *Reopening existing undertakings*

With the aim of securing greater public access, FA 1998 provided that in the case of claims for conditional exemption made on or after 31 July 1998 open access (ie other than merely by prior appointment) must be given (s 31(4FA)). Further, the terms of any undertakings must be published. In addition, a procedure was introduced as a result of which existing undertakings (given from 1976 onwards) can be varied by agreement or, in certain circumstances, a variation in their terms might be imposed (s 35A). **[31.81]**

c) *Effect of deferring IHT*

Where relief is given the transfer is a 'conditionally exempt transfer'. So long as the undertakings are observed and the property is not further transferred IHT liability will be postponed. If there is a subsequent transfer, the existing exemption may be renewed and a further exemption claimed.

Three '*chargeable events*' cause the deferred IHT to become payable: *first*, a breach of the undertakings; *second*, a sale of the asset; and *third*, a further transfer (*inter vivos* or on death) without a new undertaking. **[31.82]**

d) *Calculation of the deferred IHT charge*

Calculation of the deferred IHT charge will depend upon what triggers the charge. If there is a breach of undertakings, the tax is charged upon the person who would be entitled to the proceeds of sale were the asset then sold. The value of the property at that date will be taxed according to the transferor's rates of IHT. When he is alive, this is by reference to his cumulative total at the time of the triggering event (any PETs that he has made are ignored for these purposes even if they subsequently become chargeable); when he is dead, the property is added to his death estate and charged at the highest rate applicable to that estate but at half the IHT table rates unless the conditionally exempt transfer was made on his death.

EXAMPLE 31.23

In 2012 Aloysius settled a Rousseau painting (valued at £500,000) on discretionary trusts. The transfer was conditionally exempt, but, in 2017 (when the picture is worth £650,000), the trustee breaks the undertakings by refusing to allow the painting to be exhibited in the Primitive Exhibition in London. If Aloysius is still alive in 2017, IHT is calculated on £650,000 at Aloysius' rates according to his cumulative total of chargeable transfers in 2017. Had Aloysius died in 2017 with a death estate of £1,000,000, £650,000 would be charged at half the rates appropriate to the highest part of an estate of £1,650,000. As can be seen from this example, considerable care should be exercised in deciding whether the election should be made. If the relevant asset is likely to increase in value, it may be better to pay off the IHT earlier assuming that sufficient funds are available.

If the deferred charge is triggered by a sale, the above principles operate, save that it is the net sale proceeds that will be subject to the deferred charge. Expenses of sale, including CGT, are deductible. If there is a disposal of *part* of a property which is conditionally exempt the designation of the *whole* is reviewed: if the disposal has not materially affected the heritage entity then the designation for the remainder stays in force and the IHT charge is limited to the part disposal. However, if the part disposal results solely from the leasehold enfranchisement under the Leasehold Reform, Housing and Urban Development Act 1993 (or Leasehold Reform Act 1967) these rules do not apply: instead there is no review of the retained property and the charge is limited to the part sold.

Calculation of the deferred charge is more complex where it is triggered by a gift since two chargeable transfers could occur; the first on the gift and the second by the triggering of the deferred charge. If the gift is a chargeable event (excluding PETs) the tax payable on that gift is credited against the triggered deferred charge. Where the gift is a chargeable transfer, but not a chargeable event, as the triggering charge does not arise the credit will be available against the next chargeable event affecting that property.

EXAMPLE 31.24

Eric makes a conditionally exempt transfer to Ernie on his death in 2012. Ernie in turn settles the asset on discretionary trusts in 2017 and (although the asset is pre-eminent) the trustees do not give any undertaking.

The creation of the settlement is a chargeable transfer by Ernie. IHT will be calculated at half rates in 2017.

The triggered charge: the value of the asset in 2017 will be subject to IHT at Eric's death rates. A tax credit for IHT paid on the 2017 gift which is attributable to the value of the asset is available.

If the trustees had given an appropriate undertaking in 2017 (since Ernie inherited the property on Eric's death, the six-year ownership requirement does not need to be satisfied by Ernie), the trust would be taxed as above. The transfer is not a chargeable event so that no triggering of the conditionally exempt transfer occurs. The tax credit is available if this charge is triggered at a later stage, eg by the trustees selling the asset.

If a conditionally exempt transfer is followed by a PET which is a chargeable event with regard to the property, IHT triggered is allowed as a credit against IHT payable if the PET becomes chargeable.

Where there has been more than one conditionally exempt transfer of the same property, and a chargeable event occurs, HMRC has the right to choose which of the earlier transferors (within 30 years before the chargeable event) shall be used for calculating the sum payable. [31.83]

EXAMPLE 31.25

Z gives a picture to Y who gives it to X who sells it. There have been two conditionally exempt transfers (by Z and Y) and HMRC can choose (subject to the 30-year time limit) whether to levy the deferred IHT charge according to Z or Y's rates.

e) *Settled property*

Where heritage property is subject to an interest in possession trust created prior to 22 March 2006, or to one of the limited exceptional interest in possession trusts (that is, not a trust for a bereaved minor or a disabled person's trust) created on or after that date (see **[33.4]**), it is treated as belonging to the life tenant and the above rules are applied. The exemption may also be available for heritage property held in a discretionary trust (IHTA 1984 ss 78, 79) and for interest in possession trusts created on or after 22 March 2006 that do not fall within one of the exceptional categories, which are treated in the same way as discretionary trusts.

Where a relevant property trust comprises heritage property which has not been the subject of conditional exemption, it is potentially subject to the IHT charge on ten-year anniversaries. To gain exemption from the charge the current position requires trustees to make a claim and obtain a heritage property designation before the ten-yearly charge arises. This departs from the general regime for conditional exemption and can cause difficulties for trustees and parties engaged in designating heritage status. Amendments made to IHTA 1984 s 79 by F(No 2)A 2015 now allow trustees to make a claim for exemption within two years of the ten-year charge arising, giving them more time and putting them on the same footing as trustees and individuals subject to other IHT charges. [31.84]

f) *Maintenance funds*

IHTA 1984 ss 27, 57(5) and Sch 4 paras 1–7 provide for no IHT to be charged when property (whether or not heritage property) is settled on trusts to secure the maintenance, repair etc of historic buildings. Such trusts also receive special income tax treatment (TA 1988 ss 690 ff) and, for CGT, the hold-over election under TCGA 1992 s 260 is available.

These funds can be set up with a small sum of money so long as there is an intention to put in further sums later. The introduction of the PET in 1986 has, however, produced a dilemma for an estate owner. He could give away property to his successor as a PET and rely upon living for seven years in order to avoid IHT. Alternatively, he could transfer that property by a conditionally exempt transfer into a maintenance fund. It is not possible to make a gift of the property and then, if the donor dies within seven years, for the donee at that point to avoid the IHT charge by transferring the property into a maintenance fund.

Settled property will be free of IHT on the death of the life tenant if within two years after his death (three years if an application to court is necessary) the terms of the settlement are altered so that the property goes into a heritage maintenance fund (IHTA 1984 s 57A). **[31.85]**

g)   *Private treaty sales*

Property subject to the conditional exemption may be given or sold by private treaty (not at an auction) to heritage bodies listed in IHTA 1984 s 25(1) and Sch 3 with the result that the conditional exemption is not withdrawn, but the original transfer becomes completely exempt (IHTA 1984 s 32(4)). (Note that FA 2016 transfers the power to add national institutions to Sch 3 from HMRC to the Treasury.) A sale by private treaty can offer substantial financial advantages for the owner – the withdrawal of conditional exemption which would otherwise result from a sale on the open market does not take place, and in addition, there is no liability to CGT. Not surprisingly, because of these fiscal benefits the vendor will have to accept a lower price than if he sold on the open market. Broadly, the market value is agreed with the public body, the tax saving is deducted to give *net* value of the asset (ie market price less prospective tax liability) and then a certain amount of the tax saving is added back on to the net value and paid to the taxpayer. The tax saving (known as 'the douceur') is thus shared between the public body and the taxpayer. 25% of the tax saving is added back on in the case of chattels and 10% for land.
[31.86]

5   Gifts to political parties (IHTA 1984 s 24)

Gifts to qualifying political parties are exempt without limit from IHT, whether made during life or on death. The definition of a qualifying party is related to Westminster MPs elected at general elections: either two MPs must have been elected or one MP and the party received at least 150,000 votes. Some parties move in and out of qualification, for example the Ulster Unionists and UKIP (both currently not qualified). The Green Party has qualified since 2010.

The Finance Bill 2017 contained proposals to update the definition to include members of devolved legislatures and candidates elected at by-elections, but these proposals were a casualty of the decision to call a General Election in 2017 and were not part of the slimmed down FA 2017.

There are detailed provisions which deny relief where the gift is delayed, conditional, made for a limited period, or could be used for other purposes (IHTA 1984 s 24(3), (4)). Any capital gain that would otherwise arise can be held over under TCGA 1992 s 260. **[31.87]**

6 Gifts to charities (IHTA 1984 s 23)

Gifts to charities and certain sports clubs are exempt without limit. As with gifts to political parties, detailed provisions deny the exemption if the vesting of the gift is postponed, conditional, made for a limited period or if it could be used for non-charitable purposes. From 1 April 2012, IHT relief is given to gifts to charities situated in the EU, Norway and Iceland provided that the charities would be charities under the law of England and Wales if they were established there, and are registered by the local equivalent of the Charity Commission in their home country, if their home country requires this.

Chapter 53 covers the definition of charities and qualifying sports clubs in detail. [31.88]

For deaths after 5 April 2012, where 10% or more of the estate over the nil rate band qualifies for the exemption for gifts to charity, the rate of IHT charged on the chargeable element is reduced to 36% (see [**30.37**]). [31.89]

7 Acceptance in lieu (IHTA 1984 s 230)

An asset can be offered to HMRC in lieu of tax (see IHTA 1984 s 230(1)). The Secretary of State has to agree to accept such assets and it should be noted that the standard of objects which can be so accepted is very much higher than that required for the conditional exemption.

Under these arrangements the offeror obtains the benefit of any rise in the value of property between the date of the offer and its acceptance by HMRC, but he has to pay interest on the unpaid IHT until his offer is accepted. As an alternative, therefore, taxpayers can elect for the value of the property to be taken at the date of the offer (thereby avoiding the payment of any interest but forgoing the benefit of any subsequent rise in the value of the property: F(No 2)A 1987 s 97 and see SP 6/87). [31.90]

32 IHT – settlements: definition and classification

Updated by Sandra Eden, Senior Lecturer, University of Edinburgh

I   Introductory [32.1]
II Definitions [32.2]
III Classification of settlements [32.21]
IV Payment of IHT [32.71]
V   Creation of settlements [32.91]
VI Reservation of benefit [32.94]

I INTRODUCTORY

In framing the original IHT rules taxing settled property, the objective was to ensure (1) that it is the capital of the settlement which is subject to tax and not just the value of the various beneficial interests, and (2) that settled property is taxed neither more nor less heavily than unsettled property. There are broadly two regimes. One is the relevant property regime, discussed in **Chapter 34**, in terms of which the trust is treated more or less as an independent entity for tax purposes (although acquiring certain characteristics of the settlor), with periodic charges and charges when property leaves the trust. The main type of trust to fall within the relevant property regime was the discretionary trust, although its scope was substantially extended by FA 2006, which now covers most trusts created on or after 22 March 2006 during the lifetime of the settlor, as well as a considerable range of trusts created on death. The other regime, discussed in **Chapter 33**, covers certain trusts in which the beneficiary has an interest in possession, which is broadly a right to receive any income of the trust. This regime treats the trust property as being owned by the person with the interest in possession, and charges inheritance tax on the trustees by reference to that beneficiary. Most interests in possession created before 22 March 2006 will be subject to this regime although, for trusts created on or after that date, this treatment applies to a rather narrower range of interests in possession, most commonly those created on the death of the settlor. [32.1]

II DEFINITIONS

1 What is a settlement?

a) *Definition*

'Settlement' is defined in IHTA 1984 s 43:

> '(2) "Settlement" means any disposition or dispositions of property, whether effected by instrument, by parole or by operation of law, or partly in one way and partly in another, whereby the property is for the time being –
> (a) held in trust for persons in succession or for any person subject to a contingency; or
> (b) held by trustees on trust to accumulate the whole or part of any income of the property or with power to make payments out of that income at the discretion of the trustees or some other person, with or without power to accumulate surplus income; or
> (c) charged or burdened (otherwise than for full consideration in money or money's worth paid for his own use or benefit to the person making the disposition), with the payment of any annuity or other periodical payment payable for a life or any other limited or terminable period; ...
> (3) A lease of property which is for life or lives, or for a period ascertainable only by reference to a death, or which is terminable on, or at a date ascertainable only by reference to, a death, shall be treated as a settlement and the property as settled property, unless the lease was granted for full consideration in money or money's worth, and where a lease not granted as a lease at a rack rent is at any time to become a lease at an increased rent it shall be treated as terminable at that time.' **[32.2]–[32.3]**

EXAMPLE 32.1

(1) Property is settled on X for life remainder to Y and Z absolutely (a fixed trust; see sub-s (2)(a) above).
(2) Property is held on trust for 'such of A, B, C, D, E and F as my trustees in their absolute discretion may select' (a discretionary trust; see sub-s (2)(b) above).
(3) Property is held on trust 'for A contingent on attaining 18' (a contingency settlement; see sub-s (2)(a) above).
(4) Property is held on trust by A and B as trustees for Z absolutely (a bare trust, although for IHT purposes there is no settlement and the property is treated as belonging to Z).
(5) A and B jointly purchase Blackacre. Under LPA 1925 ss 34 and 36 (as amended) there is a statutory trust of land with A and B holding the land on trust (as joint tenants) for themselves as either joint tenants or tenants in common in equity. For IHT purposes there is no settlement and the property belongs to A and B equally. Ownership by two or more persons in common does not create a trust in Scotland.
(6) A grants B a lease of Blackacre for his (B's) life at a peppercorn rent. This is a settlement for IHT purposes and A is the trustee of the property (IHTA 1984 s 45). Under LPA 1925 s 149 the lease is treated as being for a term of 90 years that is determinable on the death of B.

b) *Associated operations*

In *Rysaffe Trustee Co (CI) Ltd v IRC* (2003), Park J and the Court of Appeal decided that for the purposes of s 43 'dispositions' had its ordinary meaning and was not extended to include a disposition by associated operations. In simple terms therefore provided that a trust lawyer would say that five separate trusts had been established with identical property (in *Rysaffe* it was private company shares) then the IHT legislation must be applied on that basis. The use of the plural 'dispositions' in s 43(2) deals with the situation where property is added to an existing settlement whether by the settlor or by some other person. [32.4]

c) *The contrast with income tax*

A 'settlement' for IHT purposes is in one sense narrower and in another sense wider than for income tax purposes. It is narrower in that the very wide definition for anti-avoidance purposes in the income tax legislation does not apply (see [16.93]). There will normally be a trust in some recognisable form before IHT consequences follow. But the scope is wider because the income tax restriction to cases where there is an element of bounty (see [16.61]) does not apply, and hence commercial arrangements (eg landlord sinking funds) may have IHT ramifications. [32.5]

d) *Resettlements*

As discussed in [25.82] difficulties have arisen in identifying, for CGT purposes, when property has been resettled (ie when a new settlement has been created out of an existing settlement). Difficulties may also occur when it is necessary to determine whether the settlor has created one or more settlements. There are similar problems in IHT.

In *Minden Trust (Cayman) Ltd v IRC* (1984) an appointment of settled property in favour of overseas beneficiaries was held to amend the terms of the original settlement so that the terms of that appointment read with the original settlement were dispositions of property and, therefore, a settlement.
[32.6]

EXAMPLE 32.2

Each year Sam creates a discretionary trust of £3,000 (thereby utilising his annual exemption) and his wife does likewise. At the end of five years there are ten mini discretionary trusts. As a matter of trust law, and assuming that each settlement is correctly documented, there is no reason why this series should be treated as one settlement. So far as the IHT legislation is concerned the settlements are not made on the same day (see IHTA 1984 s 62); the associated operations provisions (IHTA 1984 s 268) would seem inapplicable (the facts are quite different from those in *Hatton v IRC* (1992) and in no sense is this a series of operations affecting the same property: see the *Rysaffe* case considered above. The separate trusts should be kept apart (there should be no pooling of property) and each settlement should be fully documented.

2 Settlors

In the majority of cases it is not difficult to identify the settlor, since there will usually be one settlor who will create a settlement by a 'disposition' of

property (which may include a disposition by associated operations; see IHTA 1984 s 272). A settlement may have more than one settlor:
IHTA 1984 s 44(2) states that:

'Where more than one person is a settlor in relation to a settlement and the circumstances so require, this Part of this Act (except s 48(4)–(6)) shall have effect in relation to it as if the settled property were comprised in separate settlements.'

Thomas v IRC (1981) indicates that this provision only applies where an identifiable capital fund has been provided by each settlor. The fund will be treated as two separate settlements in the case of discretionary trusts where both the incidence of the periodic charge and the amount of IHT chargeable may be affected. IHTA 1984 s 44(1) defines settlor (in terms similar to those for income tax purposes) thus:

'In this Act "settlor", in relation to a settlement, includes any person by whom the settlement was made directly or indirectly, and ... includes any person who has provided funds directly or indirectly for the purpose of or in connection with the settlements or has made with any other person a reciprocal arrangement for that other person to make the settlement.' [32.7]

3 **Additions of property**

A further problem arises where a settlor adds property to the settlement; is this for IHT purposes one settlement or two? This creates no problems in the interest in possession settlement, but is significant in relation to trusts within the relevant property regime with regard to timing and rate of the periodic and inter-periodic charges. As a matter of trust law, there will be a single settlement where funds are held and managed by one set of trustees for one set of beneficiaries, so that such additions will usually not lead to the creation of separate settlements.

Settled property is excluded if it is situated outside the UK and the settlor was non-UK domiciled at the time of the creation of the settlement (IHTA 1984 s 48(3)). If the settlor becomes UK domiciled and adds non-UK property to the trust, is the addition also excluded? If it is treated as part of the same settlement, then it is excluded because the settlor was not UK domiciled when the settlement was made. If it is treated as a separate settlement, it is not excluded. However, HMRC appear to regard material additions as separate settlements:

'The settlor must have been domiciled outside the UK at the time the settlement was made (or at the date of any additions, if the added property is material).'
(IHTM 16162) [32.8]

4 **Trustees**

The ordinary meaning is given to the term 'a trustee', although by IHTA 1984 s 45 it includes any person in whom the settled property or its management is for the time being vested. In cases where a lease for lives is treated as a settlement the lessor is the trustee. [32.9]–[32.20]

III CLASSIFICATION OF SETTLEMENTS

The Finance Act 2006 brought about a substantive change in the categorisation of trusts for IHT purposes. Because trusts in existence on 22 March 2006 (Budget day) will, on the whole, continue to be governed by the 'old' regime, both the old and the 'new' regime will be considered. Moreover, the term 'interest in possession' continues to be of importance to both regimes, and is considered at some length.

To place a particular trust into its correct category is important for two reasons. *First*, because the IHT treatment of each is totally different, both as to incidence of tax and as to the amount of tax charged; and *second*, because a change from one category to another will normally give rise to an IHT charge.

The relevant property regime is the residual category, and will apply to the settlement unless it falls within one of the other categories. The other categories are, for settlements created before 22 March 2006, the interest in possession trust, the accumulation and maintenance trust and the disabled trust. In relation to settlements created on or after 22 March 2006, they are the 'immediate post-death interest', the transitional serial interest, the bereaved minor trust and the disabled trust. [**32.21**]

1 The meaning of an 'interest in possession'

Whilst the term 'interest in possession' is not, in itself, as significant under the new regime as it was under the former regime (which continues to apply to those interests created prior to 22 March 2006), it remains important, as [**32.21**] above demonstrates. Normally, trusts can easily be slotted into their correct category. Problems were principally caused by the borderline, according to whether the settlement had an interest in possession or not. In the majority of cases, no problems arose: at one extreme stood the life interest settlement; at the other the discretionary trust. However, what of a settlement which provides for the income to be paid to Albert, unless the trustees decide to pay it to Bertram, or to accumulate it; or where the property in the trust is enjoyed *in specie* by one beneficiary as the result of the exercise of a discretion (eg a beneficiary living in a dwelling house which was part of a discretionary fund)? To resolve these difficulties, the phrase an 'interest in possession' needs definition. Except for a provision relating only to Scotland (see [**32.25**]), the legislation did not, and still does not, assist; instead, its meaning must be gleaned from a Press Notice of HMRC and *Re Pilkington (Pearson v IRC)* (1981) which largely endorses the statements in that Press Notice. [**32.22**]

> *IR Press Notice (12 February 1976)* provides as follows:
>
> 'an interest in settled property exists where the person having the interest has the *immediate entitlement* (subject to any prior claims by the trustees for expenses or other outgoings properly payable out of income) *to any income* produced by that property as the income arises; but ... a discretion or power, in whatever form, which can be exercised *after income arises* so as to withhold it from that person negatives the existence of an interest in possession. For this purpose a power to accumulate income is regarded as a power to withhold it, unless any accumulation must be held solely for the person having the interest or his personal representatives.

On the other hand the existence of a mere power of revocation or appointment, the exercise of which would determine the interest wholly or in part (but which, so long as it remains unexercised, does not affect the beneficiary's immediate entitlement to income) does not ... prevent the interest from being an interest in possession.'

The first paragraph is concerned with the existence of discretions or powers which might affect the destination of the income after it has arisen and which prevent the existence of any interest in possession (eg a provision enabling the trustees to accumulate income or to divert it for the benefit of other beneficiaries). The second paragraph concerns overriding powers which, if exercised, would terminate the entire interest of the beneficiary, but which do not prevent the existence of an interest in possession (eg the statutory power of advancement). Administrative expenses charged on the income can be ignored in deciding whether there is an interest in possession, so long as such payments are for 'outgoings properly payable out of income'. A clause in the settlement permitting expenses of a capital nature to be so charged is, therefore, not covered and HMRC has argued that the mere presence of such a clause is fatal to the existence of any interest in possession (see [**32.27**]).

[**32.23**]

Re Pilkington (Pearson v IRC) (1981) The facts of the case were simple. Both capital and income of the fund were held for the settlor's three adult daughters in equal shares subject to three overriding powers exercisable by the trustees: (1) to appoint capital and income amongst the daughters, their spouses and issue; (2) to accumulate so much of the income as they should think fit; and (3) to apply any income towards the payment or discharge of any taxes, costs or other outgoings which would otherwise be payable out of capital. The trustees had regularly exercised their powers to accumulate the income. What caused the disputed IHT assessment (for a mere £444.73) was the irrevocable appointment of some £16,000 from the fund to one of the daughters. There was no doubt that, as a result of the appointment, she obtained an interest in possession in that appointed sum; but did she already have an interest in possession in the fund? If so, no IHT would be chargeable on the appointment (see [**33.15**]); if not, there would be a charge because the appointed funds had passed from a 'no interest in possession' to an 'interest in possession' settlement.

HMRC contended that the existence of the overriding power to accumulate and the provision enabling all expenses to be charged to income deprived the settlement of any interest in possession. It was common ground that whether such powers had been exercised or not was irrelevant in deciding the case. The overriding power of appointment over capital and income did not prevent there from being an interest in possession (see the second paragraph of the Press Notice at [**32.23**] above).

For the bare majority of the House of Lords the presence of the overriding discretion to accumulate the income was fatal to the existence of any interest in possession. 'A present right to present enjoyment' was how an interest in possession was defined and the beneficiary did not have a present right. 'Their enjoyment of any income from the trust fund depended on the trustees' decision as to accumulation of income' (*per* Viscount Dilhorne). No distinction is to be drawn between a trust to pay income to a beneficiary,

but with an overriding power to accumulate, and a trust to accumulate, but with a power to pay. Hence, in the following examples there is no interest in possession:
(1) to A for life but trustees may accumulate the income; and
(2) on trust to accumulate the income but with a power to make payments to A.

For an application of the principles in *Re Pilkington (Pearson v IRC)*, see *Oakley (as Personal Representatives of Jossaume) v IRC* (2005). [32.24]

Interest in possession in Scotland

Interest in possession is defined for Scots law purposes as 'an interest under a settlement by virtue of which the person in right of that interest is entitled to the enjoyment of the property, or would be so entitled if the property were capable of enjoyment' (IHTA 1984 s 46). It was accepted in *Miller & Ors v IRC* that the *Pilkington* test applied in Scotland. [32.25]

2 Problems remaining after Pilkington

The test laid down by the majority in the House of Lords established some certainty in a difficult area of law and it is possible to say that the borderline between trusts with and without an interest in possession (under the old regime) is reasonably easy to draw; where there is uncertainty about the entitlement of a beneficiary to income, it is likely that the settlement will fall into the relevant property regime. [32.26]

The following are some of the difficulties left in the wake of *Pilkington*:

Dispositive and administrative powers For there to be an interest in possession the beneficiary must be entitled to the income as it arises. Were this test to be applied strictly, however, even a trust with a life tenant receiving the income might fail to satisfy the requirement because trustees may deduct management expenses from that income, so that few beneficiaries are entitled to all the income as it arises. This problem was considered by Viscount Dilhorne as follows:

> 'Parliament distinguished between the administration of a trust and the dispositive powers of trustees ... A life tenant has an interest in possession but his interest only extends to the net income of the property, that is to say, after deduction from the gross income of expenses etc properly incurred in the management of the trust by the trustees in the exercise of their powers. A dispositive power is a power to dispose of the net income. Sometimes the line between an administrative and a dispositive power may be difficult to draw but that does not mean that there is not a valid distinction.'

In *Pilkington* the trustees had an overriding discretion to apply income towards the payment of any taxes, costs, or other outgoings which would otherwise be payable out of capital and the Revenue took the view that the *existence* of this overriding power was a further reason for the settlement lacking an interest in possession. Was this power administrative (in which case its presence did not affect the existence of any interest in possession) or dispositive (fatal to the existence of such an interest)? Viscount Dilhorne decided that the power was administrative. Acceptable though this argument may be for management expenses, is it convincing when applied to other expenses and taxes (eg CGT and IHT) which would normally be payable out of the capital of the fund? It must be stressed that the House of Lords did not have to decide whether the Revenue's contention was correct or not, and that Viscount Dilhorne's observations were *obiter dicta*. In *Miller v IRC* (1987) the Court of Session held that a power to employ income to make good depreciation in the capital value of assets in the fund was administrative

[32.27]

Beneficiary's occupation of a dwelling house There are two issues here – *first*, do the terms of the trust itself give a right of occupation? *Second*, have the trustees exercised a power under the terms of the trust to give a beneficiary a right of occupation? The first issue continues to be important after the 2006 changes since, if the right to occupy does amount to an interest in possession, and if the right is created on the death of the settlor, the property will be subject to the interest in possession regime as an immediate post-death interest (IPDI: see [32.51]). However, the second issue has become less important after 21 March 2006 as, if the right arises as a result of the exercise of the trustees' discretion, the right will not be an IPDI or other special interest in possession, and will be subject to the relevant property regime, whether or not there is an interest in possession. The second issue is not discussed further.

Normally the trust deed is clear as to whether an interest in possession is created, but there have been some examples where, in the context of a discretionary trust, the trustees have been directed to protect the occupation of a particular individual. Usually this has arisen where the settlor has left property to a discretionary trust (in order to take advantage of the nil rate band), whilst at the same time trying to protect the continued occupation of the surviving spouse. In such cases, the existence of an interest in possession largely defeats the purpose of the exercise, which may be to avoid aggregation of the property with the estate of the surviving spouse on his or her death. In *IRC v Lloyds Private Banking Ltd* (1998), Mr and Mrs E owned their house as beneficial tenants in common. On her death, Mrs E left her half share on trust providing that:

> 'While my husband ... remains alive and desires to reside in the property and keeps the same in good repair and insured comprehensively to its full value ... and pays and indemnifies my Trustees against all rates taxes and other outgoings in respect of the property my Trustee shall not make any objection to such residence and shall not disturb or restrict it in any way and shall not take any steps to enforce the trust for sale on which the property is held or to obtain any rent or profit from the property.'

Subject to the above, the property was held on trust for her daughter absolutely. It was held that the above clause gave Mr E a life interest in the property since it elevated him to the status of a sole occupier of the entirety free from any obligation to pay compensation for excluding the daughter from occupation and free from the risk that an application would be made to court for sale. See also *Woodhall (Woodhall's Personal Representative) v IRC* (2000), *Faulkner (Adam's Trustee) v IRC* (2001), the comments by Lightman J and the Court of Appeal in *IRC v Eversden* (2002), (2003), and *Oakley (Jossaume's Personal Representative)* (2005). [32.28]

Interest-free loans to beneficiaries It has been suggested that a free loan to a beneficiary would create an interest in possession in the fund. This is thought to be wrong: as the beneficiary becomes a debtor (to the extent of the loan), one wonders in what assets his interest subsists; the moneys loaned would appear to belong absolutely to him and he would not seem to enjoy any such rights in the IOU. [32.29]

Position of the last surviving member of a discretionary class If the class of beneficiaries has closed, the sole survivor is entitled to the income as it arises so that there is an interest in possession, although since 2006 it is not treated as such for tax purposes. [32.30]–[32.50]

3 Immediate post-death interest

An immediate post-death interest ('IPDI') is a creature created by FA 2006. It is not subject to the relevant property regime, but to the rather different interest in possession regime. An IPDI is an interest in possession (see [32.22]–[32.50]) which satisfies the following conditions (IHTA 1984 s 49A):
(1) it is in a settlement effected by will or under the laws relating to intestacy;
(2) the beneficiary became entitled to the interest on the death of the testator or intestate; and
(3) that the interest is not, and never has been, in a bereaved minor trust or a disabled trust. [32.51]

EXAMPLE 32.3

Finn left property on his death to the Moomin discretionary trust. The trustees exercised their discretion to create an interest in possession in favour of Snufkin. This is not an IPDI as it is neither effected by will, nor does Snufkin become entitled on the death of the testator. Accordingly, the property remains subject to the relevant property regime.

4 The Transitional Serial Interest

The transitional serial interest (TSI) is another creature of FA 2006 and is also subject to the interest in possession rather than the relevant property regime. It is an interest in possession which immediately follows upon a 'prior interest', ie an earlier interest in possession which was created before 22 March 2006 but which terminates before 6 October 2008 or, if the prior interest terminates after 5 October 2008, it terminated on the death of the beneficiary and the beneficiary was the spouse of the person now becoming entitled (IHTA 1984 ss 49C, 49D and 49E). There are similar provisions concerning interests in possession in contracts of life insurance.

Finally, the interest is not a TSI if it is in a trust which qualifies as a bereaved minor trust or a disabled trust. [32.52]

EXAMPLE 32.4

(1) Henry was given an interest in possession upon James' death in January 2005. James' will provided that, upon Henry's marriage, Henry's interest is to cease and Jill's interest is to commence. Henry marries in June 2007. Jill's interest is a TSI. Had Henry married in June 2009, Jill's interest would not be a TSI, and the property would become subject to the relevant property regime.

(2) Janet's father created an interest in possession in favour of Janet in 1986, followed by an interest in favour of Janet's spouse, Ken, on Janet's death. Janet dies in July 2016. Ken's interest is a TSI. If the trustees had terminated Janet's interest during her lifetime in October 2007, Ken's interest is still a TSI. If the termination by the trustees had taken place in October 2009, Ken would not have a TSI.

5 The Accumulation and Maintenance Trust

Prior to FA 2006, accumulation and maintenance (A&M) trusts were useful in providing for children up to the age of 25. Lifetime transfers to an A&M trust were PETs and thereafter, the trust operated in an IHT vacuum provided various conditions were satisfied. A&M trusts qualifying for such privileged tax treatment can no longer be created (see previous editions of this book for more details). Transitional arrangements for A&M trusts in existence at 22 March 2006 were provided until 6 April 2008 (see **[33.67]**). **[32.53]–[32.57]**

6 The Bereaved Minor Trust and 18–25 trust

i) *The Bereaved Minor Trust (IHTA 1984 ss 71A–71C)*

The bereaved minor trust is far less flexible than the accumulation and maintenance trust which it replaced. It can only arise after the death of a parent. Moreover, on his or her eighteenth birthday, the beneficiary must become entitled to the property.

Broadly, a trust is a 'trust for bereaved minors' if property is held on statutory trusts for minors that arise on intestacy or on trusts established under the will of a deceased parent of the bereaved minor or on trusts established under the Criminal Injuries Compensation Scheme. Trusts of the latter two types must fulfil additional conditions. *First*, the bereaved minor must, on attaining 18 years of age (if not earlier), become absolutely entitled to the settled property, any income arising from such property and any income from such property that has been accumulated before the bereaved minor turned 18. *Second*, while the bereaved minor is under the age of 18, any income or capital payment out of the settled property must be provided for the benefit of the bereaved minor. *Third*, while the bereaved minor is under 18 years of age, either the bereaved minor is entitled to all the income arising from any settled property or no such income may be used to benefit any other person. **[32.58]**

ii) *Age 18–25 trusts (IHTA 1984 s 71D)*

18–25 trusts are trusts established under IHTA 1984 s 71D, which applies to settled property (including property settled before 22 March 2006) if the property:
- is held on trusts for the benefit of a person who is under 25 years of age;
- at least one of the person's parents has died;

- the trusts were established under the will of the deceased parent or under the Criminal Injuries Compensation Scheme; and
- the terms of the trusts satisfy the further conditions that *first*, the beneficiary must on attaining 25 years of age (if not earlier), become absolutely entitled to the settled property, any income arising from such property and any income arising from such property which has been accumulated before the beneficiary turned 25; *second*, while the beneficiary is under the age of 25, any benefit provided out of the settled property is provided to him; and *finally*, while the beneficiary is under 25 years of age, either the beneficiary is entitled to all the income arising from any settled property or no such income may be used to benefit any other person.

Despite being known as 18–25 trusts, such trusts can be for beneficiaries of any age under 25. They have an advantage over the BMT as they can delay absolute entitlement until the beneficiary's 25th birthday, albeit with a possible additional tax charge (see [33.111]). [32.59]

7 Trusts for the disabled

Trusts for the disabled continue to be given special treatment for IHT purposes, namely the creation of the trust is capable of being a PET and, even where the nature of the trust is discretionary in nature, they are treated under the interest in possession regime.

A disabled person is defined (IHTA 1984 s 89) as a person who is incapable by reason of mental disorder of administering his property or managing his affairs, or a person in receipt of attendance allowance or disability living allowance.

A trust for a disabled person may be a discretionary trust, ie a trust with no interest in possession, in which case no less than half the property in the trust must be applied for his benefit during his lifetime. There are no restrictions on the application of *income* which can therefore be used for the benefit of other members of the class of beneficiaries. This can be particularly useful where the application of income to the 'principal' disabled beneficiary could jeopardise his entitlement to state benefits. At least one half of any *capital* benefits must be paid to the 'principal' beneficiary. A trust in which the disabled person has an interest in possession continues to be subject to the interest in possession regime, in contrast to most interests in possession created after 21 March 2006 which are subject to the relevant property regime.

In addition, in 2006 a new type of disabled trust was introduced: the self-settlement by a person whom it is 'reasonable to expect' will become a disabled person within the definition of s 89. [32.60]–[32.70]

IV PAYMENT OF IHT

Primary liability for IHT arising during the course of the settlement rests upon the settlement's trustees. Their liability is limited to the property which they have received or disposed of or become liable to account for to a beneficiary and such other property which they would have received but for their own neglect or default.

If trustees fail to pay, HMRC can collect tax from any of the following (IHTA 1984 s 201(1)):
(1) Any person entitled to an interest in possession in the settled property. His liability is limited to the value of the trust property, out of which he can claim an indemnity for the tax he has paid.
(2) Any beneficiary under a discretionary trust up to the value of the property that he receives (after paying income tax on it) and with no right to an indemnity for the tax he is called upon to pay.
(3) The settlor, where the trustees are resident outside the UK, since, should the trustees not pay, HMRC cannot enforce payment abroad. If the settlor pays, he has a right to recover the tax from the trust. [32.71]–[32.90]

V CREATION OF SETTLEMENTS

1 IHT on creation

With effect from 22 March 2006, the transfer of property to a settlement will be a chargeable transfer of value by the settlor unless it is an *inter vivos* transfer to a trust in favour of a disabled person (IHTA 1984 s 3A). If the burden of paying the IHT is put upon the trustees of the settlement, HMRC accepts that the settlor of an *inter vivos* trust will not thereby retain an interest in the settlement under the income tax settlement provisions in ITTOIA 2005 s 619 et seq (SP 1/82) (see [16.91]).

The *inter vivos* creation of a settlement before 22 March 2006 was a PET in the following cases:
(1) If it created an interest in possession.
(2) If the trust had satisfied the definition of an A&M trust (see [32.53]–[32.57]) or disabled trust.

In other cases before 22 March 2006 (and notably when a discretionary trust was created), there was an immediately chargeable transfer. For settlements created before 22 March 2006, even if the settlement as created had contained an interest in possession, the termination of that interest during the lifetime of the settlor and within seven years of the setting up of the trust would have triggered the anti-avoidance rules in IHTA 1984 s 54A if a discretionary trust then arose (see [33.18]). The anti-avoidance rules continue to apply in the same fashion on the termination of a disabled person's interest. [32.91]

2 The nil rate band

In an attempt to both simplify the IHT treatment of trusts and limit the scope for reducing IHT on trusts by the creation by the same settlor of a number of trusts each with a £325,000 tax-free nil rate band, a consultation (*Inheritance tax: A fairer way of calculating trust charges*, 6 June 2014) proposed giving each individual one settlement nil rate band to be divided between the trusts created by each settlor. This proposal was not well received in the consultation exercise and was abandoned. Provisions were eventually included in F(No 2) A 2015, which do now restrict the use of multiple nil rate bands, but apply only where multiple trusts are set up and topped up on the same day; these rules do not apply where the trusts are set up and topped up on different days.
[32.92]

3 CGT and hold over relief

Whilst general CGT hold-over relief is no longer available, it remains possible to defer the payment of tax if the settlor makes a chargeable transfer (eg on the inter vivos creation of most trusts): see TCGA 1992 s 260 and [24.22].

[32.93]

EXAMPLE 32.11

(1) Sid puts assets worth £300,000 into a discretionary trust. For *IHT* purposes, the transfer, although chargeable, falls within his nil rate band so that no tax is payable. For *CGT*, hold-over relief is available as the transfer is chargeable, even though chargeable at 0%.

(2) Hopeful puts assets worth £1m, and showing a substantial gain, into a discretionary trust which he retains a power to revoke. For *IHT* purposes, a vexed question was whether he had made a transfer of value at all and, if so, of how much. If he could have revoked the trust as soon as it was created, it was argued that he had lost nothing so that he had made no transfer of value, and CGT hold-over relief was accordingly unavailable. In *Melville v IRC* (2001) a discretionary settlement included the settlor as a potential beneficiary and gave him (90 days after creation of the trust) the right to direct the trustees to exercise their discretionary powers (for instance, by appointing the property to himself). The Court of Appeal held that the right possessed by the settlor was property for IHT purposes which could be exercised to (in effect) revoke the settlement. Therefore, there was a transfer of value (given the 90-day period) but of a relatively small amount. The result of that decision was reversed by FA 2002 which inserted a new provision into IHTA 1984 s 272 restricting the definition of 'property' by excluding settlement powers. Accordingly, if Hopeful were to create his settlement today, his estate would fall in value by the £1m of assets settled, and the power reserved would be ignored. Hence, he would suffer a substantial IHT charge. The 2002 legislation was, however, restrictively drafted, and a *Melville Mark II* variant emerged, which was itself closed by IHTA 1984 s 81A with effect from 9 December 2009.

VI RESERVATION OF BENEFIT

The creation of *inter vivos* settlements can cause problems in the reservation of benefit area and the following matters are especially worthy of note:

(1) *If the settlor appoints himself a trustee of the settlement*, that appointment will not by itself amount to a reserved benefit. If the terms of the settlement provide for his remuneration, however, there may then be a reservation in the settled property (*Oakes v Stamp Duties Comr* (1954): it appears that this point is not taken by the Capital Taxes Office provided the remuneration is not excessive: see IHTM 14394). Alternatively, the settlor/trustee could be paid an annuity, since such an arrangement will not constitute a reserved benefit and the ending of that annuity will not lead to any IHT charge (IHTA 1984 s 90). Particular difficulties are caused if the settlor/trustee is a director of a company whose shares are held in the trust fund. The general rule of equity is that a trustee may not profit from his position and this means that he will generally

have to account for any director's fees that he may receive. It is standard practice, however, for the trust deed to provide that a trustee need not in such cases account for those fees. When the settlor/trustee is allowed to retain fees under the deed it is arguable that he has reserved a benefit in the trust assets within the ruling in the *Oakes* case. HMRC has, however, indicated that it will not take this point so long as the director's remuneration is on reasonable commercial terms.

(2) *If the settlor reserves an interest for himself under his settlement,* whether he does so expressly or whether his interest arises by operation of law, there is no reservation of benefit and he is treated as making a partial gift (see **Chapter 29**).

EXAMPLE 32.12

S created a settlement for his infant son, absolutely on attaining 21. No provision was made for what should happen if the son were to die before that age, and therefore there was a resulting trust to the settlor. The settlor died whilst the son was still an infant and was held to have reserved no benefit. Instead, he was treated as making a partial gift: ie a gift of the settled property less the retained remainder interest therein (*Stamp Duties Comr v Perpetual Trustee Co* (1943); and see *Re Cochrane* (1906) where the settlor expressly reserved surplus income).

The position with regard to discretionary trusts in which the settlor is included in the class of beneficiaries has been more problematic. In view of the limited nature of a discretionary beneficiary's rights (see *Gartside v IRC* (1968)) it is unlikely that he can be treated as making a partial gift. HMRC's view is that in all cases where a settlor is a discretionary beneficiary he will be treated as having reserved a benefit in the entire settled fund despite the fact that he may receive no payments or other benefits under the trust. This has now been accepted by the High Court in *IRC v Eversden* (2002) and was agreed between the parties on the appeal. The inclusion of the settlor's spouse as a discretionary beneficiary does not by itself result in a reserved benefit. Were that spouse to receive property from the settlement, however, and that property was then shared with or used for the benefit of the settlor, HMRC may then argue that there is a reserved benefit. Finally, the reservation rules do not apply to an outright exempt gift to a spouse although the FA 2003 amendments mean that reserved benefits can no longer be channelled through a spouse: see **Chapter 29**. [32.94]

33 IHT – settlements not subject to the relevant property regime

Updated by Sandra Eden, Senior Lecturer, University of Edinburgh

I   Settlements covered by the interest in possession regime [**33.2**]
II   Basic principles: the interest in possession regime [**33.4**]
III When is IHT charged? [**33.9**]
IV The taxation of reversionary interests [**33.61**]
V   Accumulation and maintenance trusts (IHTA 1984 s 71) [**33.63**]
VI Trusts for bereaved minors and 18–25 trusts [**33.71**]
VII Other special trusts [**33.112**]

Whilst most settlements are now subject to the relevant property regime, which operates on the basis of anniversary charges and exit charges, there are still important groups of settlements which have special treatment. Of particular note are those settlements subject to the interest in possession regime, under which the property in the trust is broadly treated for IHT purposes as if the person with the interest of possession owns it, taxing the termination or transfer of an interest as if the beneficiary had made a transfer of the property in which the interest subsisted. There are also other particular types of settlement which receive privileged treatment and these are considered at the end of this chapter. The relevant property regime is considered in **Chapter 34**.

[**33.1**]

I SETTLEMENTS COVERED BY THE INTEREST IN POSSESSION REGIME

a) *General*

Prior to the FA 2006 changes, virtually all trusts in which an interest in possession subsisted (see [**32.21**]) were subject to the interest in possession regime, but this Act introduced substantial changes to the tax treatment of settlements with beneficial interests in possession and now, with limited exceptions, the *inter vivos* creation of an interest in possession settlement will give rise to an immediate chargeable transfer, and the property held within the settlement will be subject to the relevant property regime. This means it will not be deemed to form part of the life tenant's estate and will instead be subject to periodic and exit charges. The result of the changes is that, in effect, two sets of rules operate for trusts with an interest in possession: one, referred to here as the interest in possession regime, for those where the interest arose prior to 22 March 2006 together with certain interests created on or after that date, and the second, the relevant property regime, covering other post-21 March 2006 interests in possession. [33.2]

b) *Settlements taxed under the interest in possession regime*

The beneficiary with an interest in possession who:
(i) became entitled to the interest prior to 22 March 2006; or
(ii) becomes entitled on or after 22 March 2006 to:
    (a) an immediate post-death interest; or
    (b) a disabled person's interest; or
    (c) a transitional serial interest;
(see **Chapter 32** for definitions). [33.3]

II BASIC PRINCIPLES: THE INTEREST IN POSSESSION REGIME

1 General

a) *Charging method*

A person who became entitled to the income of a fund prior to 22 March 2006 (usually the life tenant) and someone who becomes entitled to particular types of interests in possession on or after 22 March 2006 (see [**33.3**]) is treated '*as beneficially entitled to the property in which the interest subsists*' (IHTA 1984 s 49(1)). This rule is, of course, a fiction since a life tenant has no entitlement to capital. Although the section does not expressly provide for the deduction of trust liabilities, in practice it is the *net* value of the trust fund that is attributed to the relevant beneficiary.

As all the capital is treated as being owned by the life tenant, for IHT purposes it forms part of his estate, so that the inheritance tax consequences of any property subject to the interest ceasing to be subject to the interest is taxed as if the life tenant had made the transfer.

EXAMPLE 33.1

1   In October 2000, Colin is given an interest in possession in a settlement in which there are assets valued at £100,000. In June 2017, the trustees exercise their power to make an advancement of capital of £20,000 to Judith. This is treated as a PET by Colin. If Judith had been Colin's spouse, it would have been an exempt transfer.

2   Geoffrey has a pre-2006 interest in possession in property which, on his death, passes to his son. The value of the settled property is aggregated with Geoffrey's other estate for the purposes of calculating the inheritance tax on his death, and the tax is allocated pro-rata between his PRs and the trustees (see, further, *Example 33.2*).

The settlement itself is not a taxable entity, although primary liability for IHT falls upon the trustees. [33.4]

b) Other interests

As the life tenant of a trust with an interest in possession is treated as owning all the capital in the fund (IHTA 1984 s 49), other beneficiaries with 'reversionary interests' own nothing. IHTA 1984 s 47 defines reversionary interests widely to cover:

> 'a future interest under a settlement, whether it is vested or contingent (including an interest expectant on the termination of an interest in possession which, by virtue of section 50 ... is treated as subsisting in part of any property).'

Generally, reversionary interests are excluded property and can be transferred without a charge to IHT (see **[33.61]**). Despite the breadth of this definition, the term would not appear to catch the interests of discretionary beneficiaries since such rights as they possess (to compel due administration; to be considered; and jointly to wind up the fund) are present rights. Their interests are neither in possession nor in reversion. 'Settlement powers' (including a power to revoke the settlement) are not 'property' for IHT purposes and hence fall out of charge. **[33.5]**

2 Who is treated as owning the fund?

a) Life interests

The beneficiary with the interest is treated as being beneficially entitled to the trust property, or to an appropriate part of that property in which the interest subsists (IHTA 1984 s 49(1); if there is more than one beneficiary, it is necessary to apportion the capital in the fund (IHTA 1984 s 50(1)).

EXAMPLE 33.2

(1) Bill and Ben, beneficiaries under a family settlement created prior to 22 March 2006, jointly occupy 'Snodlands', the ancestral home, which is worth £1,500,000. This capital value must be apportioned to Bill and Ben in proportion to the annual value of their respective interests. Assuming their interests are equal, the apportionment will be as to £750,000 each.

(2) Eddie died in September 2008, leaving his entire estate to his wife, Clarrie, for life, with remainder to his son William absolutely. Clarrie's interest is an immediate post-death interest and thus qualifies as an interest in possession for the purposes of IHTA 1984 s 49. On Eddie's death, the transfer to Clarrie is exempt under the spouse exemption (IHTA 1984 s 18; see **[31.41]**); on Clarrie's death, the value of the capital in which her interest in possession subsists will be added to her free estate.

(3) In 1992, Phil left his residuary estate to his wife Jill for life, thereafter to his son David for life with remainder to his grandson Josh absolutely. Jill dies in 2007. David's interest is a transitional serial interest (it arises in immediate succession on or after 22 March 2006 but before 6 October 2008 to an interest in possession subsisting before 22 March 2006 under a trust created before then – see **[32.52]**), and thus qualifies as an interest in possession for the purposes of s 49.

(4) In 1996, Peggy settled her considerable holding of Marks & Spencer shares on her daughter Jenny for life, thereafter to Jenny's husband Brian for life with

remainder to Jenny and Brian's children. Jenny dies on 1 May 2009. Brian's interest is a transitional serial interest and thus is an interest in possession for the purposes of s 49. If, rather than dying, Jenny surrenders her interest on 1 May 2009, then Brian's interest would not be a transitional serial interest. If, instead, Jenny surrenders her interest in December 2007, Brian's interest will qualify as a transitional serial interest under (2) above. **[33.6]**

b) *A beneficiary entitled to a fixed amount of income*

Difficulties may arise where one beneficiary is entitled to a fixed amount of income each year (eg an annuity) and any balance is paid to another beneficiary. If the amounts of income paid to the two were compared in the year when a chargeable event occurred, a tax saving could be engineered. Assume, for instance, that the annuity interest terminates so that IHT is charged on its value. The proportion of capital attributable to that interest and, therefore, the IHT would be reduced if the trustees had switched investments into assets producing a high income in that year. A relatively small proportion of the total income would then be payable to the annuitant who would be treated as owning an equivalently small portion of the capital. When a chargeable event affects the interest in the residue of the income (eg through termination) the trustees could switch the assets into low income producers, thereby achieving a similar reduction in IHT.

IHTA 1984 s 50(3) is designed to counter such schemes by providing that the Treasury may prescribe higher and lower income yields which take effect as limits beyond which any fluctuations in the actual income of the fund are ignored (see SI 2000/174).

EXAMPLE 33.3

The value of the settlement is £100,000; income £4,000 per annum. A is entitled to an annuity of £2,000 pa; B to the balance of the income. If there is a chargeable transfer affecting the annuity, A is not treated as owning a half of the capital (despite receiving, as he does, one half of the income) but instead is treated as owning capital in the proportion that his income bears to total *notional* trust income, using the Treasury 'higher rate' yield. Assume that the higher rate is 5% on the relevant day; the calculation is, therefore:

Notional income = 5% of £100,000 = £5,000.

A's share of capital is, therefore, [£2,000 ÷ £5,000] × £100,000 = £40,000.

This calculation is used whenever the actual income yield exceeds the prescribed higher rate. The calculation cannot lead to a charge in excess of the total value of the fund!

When a chargeable transfer affecting the interest in the balance of the income occurs, if the actual income produced falls below the prescribed lower rate, the calculation proceeds as if the fund yielded that rate. If both interests in the settlement are chargeable on the same occasion, the prescribed rates do not apply because the entire fund is chargeable. **[33.7]**

c) *A lease treated as a settlement*

When a lease is treated as a settlement (eg a lease for life or lives: see **[32.2]**), the lessee is treated as owning the whole of the leased property save for any part treated as belonging to the lessor. To calculate the lessor's portion it is necessary to compare what he received when the lease was granted with what would have been a full consideration for the lease at that time (IHTA 1984 ss 50(6), 170).

EXAMPLE 33.4
(1) Land worth £100,000 is let to A for his life. The lessor receives no consideration so that A is treated as owning the whole of the leased property (ie £100,000). The granting of the lease is a PET by the lessor of £100,000.
(2) As above, save that full consideration is furnished. The lease is not treated as a settlement (see [**32.2**]). No IHT will be charged on its creation as the lessor's estate does not fall in value.
(3) Partial consideration (equivalent to 40% of full consideration) is furnished so that the value of the lessor's interest is 40% of £100,000 = £40,000. The value of the lessee's interest is £60,000 and the granting of the lease is a CT of £60,000.

HMRC accepts that if A, the owner of Blackacre, were to sell it for full consideration arrived at on the basis that he reserves a lease for life, then that lease has been granted for full consideration and so does not involve the creation of a settlement. This approach is questionable. [**33.8**]

III WHEN IS IHT CHARGED?

For tax on the creation of a settlement with an interest in possession, see **Chapter 32**.

This section is concerned with the tax whenever an interest subject to the interest in possession regime terminates, in whole or in part. This event may occur *inter vivos* or on the death of the life tenant: whilst there will always be a charge on death (unless the event is subject to an exemption, such as the spouse exemption (IHTA 1984 s 18)), in the former case the beneficiary will often be treated as making a PET, provided that the property in the trust fund then devolves on someone absolutely, or to a disabled trust. There are anti-avoidance rules to prevent the indirect creation of discretionary trusts via short-lived interests in possession (see [**33.18**]). [**33.9**]

1 Terminations on death

Where an interest subject to the interest in possession regime is terminated on the death of the life tenant, as the assets in the settlement are treated as part of his estate, IHT is charged on the settled fund at the estate rate appropriate to the life tenant's estate. The tax attributable to the settled property must be paid by the trustees. Although the trustees pay this tax, the inclusion of the value of the fund in the deceased's estate may increase the estate rate, thereby causing a higher percentage charge on the deceased's free estate. [**33.10**]

EXAMPLE 33.5

The settlement consists of securities worth £100,000 and is held for Albinoni for life with remainder to Busoni. Albinoni has just died and the value of his free estate is £170,000; he made chargeable lifetime transfers of £145,000. IHT will be calculated as follows:

(1) Chargeable death estate: £170,000 + £100,000 (the settlement) = £270,000.
(2) Chargeable transfers in the last seven years £145,000 (point reached by lifetime transfers) leaving £180,000 nil rate band (£145,000 + £180,000 = £325,000).
(3) Calculate IHT on death: £36,000 (£180,000 at 0%, £90,000 at 40%).
(4) Convert to estate rate:

$$\frac{tax}{estate} \times 100: ie \times \frac{36,000}{270,000} \times 100 = 13.33\%$$

(5) IHT attributable to settled property is 13.33% of £100,000 = £13,330.

2 Inter vivos terminations

The termination of an interest subject to the interest in possession regime occurring during the life of the relevant beneficiary is a transfer of value which follows the treatment which would have applied had the transfer been made by the individual. So, until the Finance Act 2006 changes, a lifetime termination was treated as a PET by the person with the life interest, provided that the property was, after that event, held for one or more beneficiaries absolutely (so that the settlement was at an end), or for a further interest in possession or on A&M or disabled trusts. IHT was only payable in such cases if the former life tenant died within seven years of the termination. Otherwise (eg where after the termination the fund was held on discretionary trusts), there was an immediate chargeable transfer by the person whose life interest was terminated in whole or in part.

Following FA 2006, the post-21 March 2006 lifetime termination of an interest subject to the interest in possession regime will qualify as a PET only if the outright transfer would have been a PET, so if, after termination, the property is held by an individual outright or on a disabled trust, this is treated as a PET by the person with the interest in possession. Otherwise, for example if the property is subject to a further interest in possession or a discretionary trust, it is a chargeable transfer. [33.11]

EXAMPLE 33.6

(1) In 2005, Sam settles property on his daughter Sally for life, remainder to charity. The creation of the trust is a PET by Sam and on Sally's death the fund will be exempt from charge (see IHTA 1984 s 23 for the charity exemption). If the property had been settled on 23 March 2006, there would have been an immediate chargeable transfer at half the death rates (unless Sally qualified as a disabled person: see **Chapter 32**) and the property would be subject to the relevant property regime (see **Chapter 34**). On Sally's death, the property ceases to be subject to the relevant property regime as the charity becomes entitled to the property. Because the property goes to charity, it is still an exempt transfer, although now by the trustees rather than by Sally (see [**34.51**]).

(2) In 2005, Sid settles property on a stranger, Jake Straw, for life or until such time as the trustees determine and thereafter the property is to be held on discretionary trusts for Sid's family and relatives. The creation of the trust is a PET; a later termination of Jake's life interest (whether before or after 22 March 2006) will be a chargeable transfer and may trigger the anti-avoidance rules. As with (1) above, had the property been settled after 21 March 2006, there would have been an immediate IHT charge.

(3) In 2005, Sam settles property on Susan, his daughter, for life, remainder to her twins contingently on attaining 21. Susan surrenders her life interest before 22 March 2006 when the twins are (i) 17, (ii) 18, (iii) 21.

The creation of the trust is a PET as is the surrender of Susan's life interest. If it is surrendered at (i), the fund is then held for A&M trusts (a PET); if surrendered at (ii), the transfer is to the twins as interest in possession beneficiaries (a PET); while, if surrendered at (iii), the twins are absolutely entitled and so it will be an outright gift which is also a PET. (Note the differing CGT results, see **Chapter 25**). If Susan surrenders her interest after 21 March 2006, both (i) and (ii) are chargeable transfers as neither come within the post-2006 definition of PETs, whilst transfer (iii) is a PET as an outright transfer. Had Susan's life interest come into effect after 22 March 2006, its surrender would have been subject to the relevant property regime, and an exit charge would be levied (see **Chapter 34**). Furthermore, the relief formerly afforded to A&M trusts is no longer available for trusts created on or after 22 March 2006 (see **Chapter 34**).

a) *Actual terminations*

Any charge will be calculated on the basis that the life tenant had made a transfer of value of the assets comprised in the trust fund when the interest terminates (IHTA 1984 s 52(1)). **[33.12]**

EXAMPLE 33.7

(1) Before 2006, £100,000 is held on trust for Albinoni for life or until remarriage and thereafter for Busoni. If Albinoni remarries (irrespective of whether this is before or after 22 March 2006), his life interest terminates and he is treated as having made a transfer of value which is a PET. Accordingly, should he die within seven years, IHT will be charged on the value of the fund at the time when his interest ended. (The trustees should bear this in mind before making any distribution to Busoni.) Note, had the interest been created post-21 March 2006, it would be subject to the relevant property regime rather than the interest in possession regime.

If Albinoni never remarried, but consented to an advancement of £50,000 to Busoni, his interest in that portion of the fund ends and he is treated as making a transfer of value which is a PET of £50,000. Assume that, three years later, Albinoni surrenders his life interest in the fund, worth at that time £120,000. This is a further transfer of value which is a PET; IHT may therefore be charged (if he dies in the seven years following the advancement) on £170,000. Notice that in all cases any tax charge is levied on a value transferred which is 'equal to the value of the property in which his interest subsisted' (see s 52(1)). The principle of calculating loss to donor's estate (see **[28.61]**) does not apply.

(2) Claude owns 49% of the shares in his family investment company, Money Box Ltd, and is the life tenant under a pre-2006 settlement which owns a further 12% of those shares. The remainder beneficiary under the trust is Claude's

daughter. No dividends are paid by the company. The tax position if Claude surrenders his interest in possession is as follows:
(a) The surrender of a beneficial interest in a settlement is generally free from CGT (TCGA 1992 s 76(1)). Assuming that the settlement ends, there will be a deemed disposal under TCGA 1992 s 71(1): see **Chapter 25**.
(b) For IHT purposes, Claude will be treated as making a transfer of value which is a PET, but the value transferred is limited to the value of the shares in the settlement (IHTA 1984 s 52(1)). Thus only the value of a 12% minority holding will be subject to tax in the event of Claude's death within seven years.

On Claude's death his estate will then comprise only a 49% minority shareholding.

The merit of this arrangement was that the substantial loss to Claude's estate resulting from his loss of control of the company did not attract a tax charge: instead, both shareholdings were valued separately. Surrender of the life interest could have occurred on Claude's deathbed but the advantages would not, of course, have been obtained if the life interest had been retained and the 49% holding given away!

b) *Deemed terminations*

IHTA 1984 s 51(1) provides that if the beneficiary disposes of his beneficial interest in possession, that disposal '*shall not be a transfer of value but shall be treated as the coming to an end of the interest*'. By providing that the disposal is not a transfer of value, s 51 has the effect of excluding the provisions which apply to transfers of value, for example, absence of gratuitous intent. As with actual terminations, the life tenant is *deemed* to have made a transfer of value.
[**33.13**]

EXAMPLE 33.8

Assume in the following examples that the life interests are either created prior to 22 March 2006, or fall within one of the special categories (eg IPDIs, TSIs) and are thus not within the relevant property regime.
(1) Albinoni (see *Example 33.7*) assigns by way of gift his life interest to Cortot. IHT will be charged as if that life interest had terminated, and Albinoni is treated as making a PET of the value of the property in which his interest subsists. Cortot becomes a tenant *pur autre vie* and, when Albinoni dies, Cortot's interest in possession terminates, so raising the possibility of a further IHT charge. Cortot is treated as having made a transfer to Busoni, which will also be a PET (for quick succession relief, see [**33.29**]).
(2) If, instead of gifting his interest, Albinoni sold it to Cortot for £20,000 (full actuarial value) and the trust fund was then worth £100,000, Albinoni's interest is deemed to have thereby terminated so that he made a transfer of value of £100,000. However, as he had received £20,000, he made a PET equal to the fall in his estate of £80,000 (£100,000 − £20,000: IHTA 1984 s 52(2)).

c) *Partition*

A division of the trust fund between a life tenant and a remainderman causes the interest in possession to terminate and IHT may be charged (in the case of a PET, if the life tenant dies within seven years) on that portion of the fund passing to the remainderman (IHTA 1984 s 53(2)). [**33.14**]

EXAMPLE 33.9

Albinoni and Busoni agreed to partition the £100,000 trust fund in the proportions 40:60. Albinoni would have been treated as making a PET of £60,000 (£100,000 − £40,000). Any IHT would have been payable out of the fund which is divided.

d) *Advancements etc to life tenant*

If all or part of the capital of the fund is paid to the life tenant, or if he becomes absolutely entitled to the capital, his interest in possession will determine *pro tanto*, but no IHT will be charged since there will be no fall in the value of his estate (IHTA 1984 s 53(2)). [33.15]

e) *Purchase of a reversionary interest by the life tenant (IHTA 1984 ss 10, 55(1))*

As the life tenant who acquired his interest before 22 March 2006 (or, if later, the interest was an immediate post-death interest, a disabled person's interest or a transitional serial interest) is treated as owning the fund, his tax bill could be reduced were he to purchase a reversionary interest in that settlement. Assume, for instance, that B has £60,000 in his bank account and is the life tenant of a fund with a capital value of £100,000. For IHT purposes he is treated as owning an estate worth £160,000. If B were to purchase the reversionary interest in the settlement for its market value of £60,000, the result would be as follows: *first*, B's estate has not fallen in value. Originally it included £60,000; after the purchase it includes a reversionary interest worth £60,000 since, although excluded property, the reversionary interest must still be valued. *Second*, B's estate now consists of the settlement fund valued at £100,000 and has been depleted by the £60,000 paid for the reversionary interest so that a possible charge to IHT on £60,000 has been avoided.

To prevent this loss of tax, IHTA 1984 s 55(1) provides that the reversionary interest is not to be valued as a part of B's estate at the time of its purchase (thereby ensuring that his estate has fallen in value) whilst IHTA 1984 s 10 (see **[28.21]**) is excluded from applying thereby ensuring that the fall in value may be subject to charge even though there is no donative intent. Hence, by paying £60,000 for the reversionary interest B has made a PET which will be taxed if he dies in the following seven years. [33.16]

f) *Transactions reducing the value of the property*

When the value of the fund is diminished by a depreciatory transaction entered into between the trustees and a beneficiary (or persons connected with him), tax is charged as if the fall in value were a partial termination of the interest in possession (IHTA 1984 s 52(3)). A commercial transaction lacking gratuitous intent is not caught by this provision.

In *Macpherson v IRC* (1988) the value of pictures held in a trust fund was diminished by an arrangement with a person connected with a beneficiary as a result of which, in return for taking over care, custody and insurance of the pictures, that person was entitled to keep the pictures for his personal enjoyment for some 14 years. Although this arrangement was a commercial transaction, lacking gratuitous intent when looked at in isolation, it was associated with a subsequent operation (the appointment of a protected life interest) which did confer a gratuitous benefit so that the exception in s 10 did not apply and the reduction in value of the fund was subject to charge. [33.17]

EXAMPLE 33.10

Trustees grant a 50-year lease of a property worth £100,000 at a peppercorn rent to the brother of a reversionary beneficiary. As a result the property left in the settlement is the freehold reversion worth only £20,000. The granting of the lease is a depreciatory transaction which causes the value of the fund to fall by £80,000 and as it is made with a person connected with a beneficiary, IHTA 1984 s 52(3) will apply and IHT may be levied as if the life interest in £80,000 had ended. (Contrast the position if the lease had been granted to the brother on fully commercial terms.)

3   Anti-avoidance (IHTA 1984 ss 54A and 54B)

Note that whilst these provisions apply in respect of all interest in possession trusts created prior to 22 March 2006, where the beneficiary became entitled to the interest in possession on or after that date, s 54A applies only where that interest is a disabled person's interest or a transitional serial interest (IHTA 1984 s 54A(1A) inserted by FA 2006 Sch 20 para 16).

a)   *When do the rules apply?*

The three prerequisites are that:
(1)   an interest in possession trust is set up by means of a PET;
(2)   it terminates either as a result of the life tenant dying or by his interest ceasing *inter vivos*; and
(3)   at that time a no interest in possession trust (other than an A&M trust) arises.

If the termination occurs within seven years of the creation of the original interest in possession trust and at a time when the settlor is still alive, the anti-avoidance rules then apply.   [33.18]

b)   *Operation of the rules*

The IHT charge on the property at the time when the interest in possession ends is taken to be the higher of two alternative calculations. First, the IHT that would arise under normal charging principles, ie by taxing the fund as if the transfer had been made by the life tenant at the time of termination. The rates of charge will be either half rates (when there is an *inter vivos* termination) or full death rates when termination occurs as a result of the death of the life tenant. The alternative calculation involves deeming the settled property to have been transferred at the time of termination by a hypothetical transferor who in the preceding seven years had made chargeable transfers equal in value to those made by the settlor in the seven years before he created the settlement. For the purpose of this second calculation half rates are used.   [33.19]

EXAMPLE 33.11

In 2005 Sam settled property worth £90,000 on trust for Pam for life or until remarriage and thereafter on discretionary trusts for Sam's relatives and friends. His cumulative total at that time was £200,000 and he had made PETs of £85,000.

Pam remarried one year later at a time when she had made chargeable transfers of £50,000, PETs of £45,000; and when the settled property was worth £110,000.
(1) The anti-avoidance provisions are relevant since the conditions for their operation are satisfied.
(2) Normally IHT would have been calculated at Pam's rates, ie on a chargeable transfer from £50,000 to £160,000. Alternatively under these provisions the tax could have been calculated by taking a hypothetical transferor who had Sam's cumulative total at the time when he created the trust; ie the £110,000 would have been taxed as a chargeable transfer from £200,000 to £310,000. In this example the second calculation would have been adopted since a greater amount of IHT results. Tax must be paid by the trustees.
(3) Assume that either Sam or Pam died after the termination of the interest in possession trust. This may result in a recalculation of the IHT liability (in this example PETs made by that person in the seven years before death would become chargeable). So far as the anti-avoidance rules are concerned, however, there is no question of disturbing the basis on which the IHT calculation was made in the first place. Hence, as was shown in (2) above, the greater tax was produced by taking the hypothetical transferor and, therefore, the subsequent death of Pam is irrelevant since it cannot be used to switch the basis of computation to Pam's cumulative total. By contrast, the death of Sam may involve additional IHT liability since his PETs of £85,000 will now become chargeable and thus included in the hypothetical transferor's total when the settlement was created.

c) *How to avoid the rules*

First, if the interest in possession continues for seven years these rules do not apply.

Second, they are not in point if the settlement was created without an immediate interest in possession (eg there was an A&M trust which subsequently became an interest in possession trust), or if the settlement was created by means of an exempt transfer (eg if a life interest was given to the settlor's spouse and that interest was subsequently terminated in favour of a discretionary trust).

Third, trustees can prevent the rules from applying if, *within six months* of the ending of the interest in possession, they terminate the discretionary trust either by an absolute appointment or by creating a further life interest.

Fourth, it is always possible to channel property into a discretionary trust by a PET, if an outright gift is made to another individual (a PET) who then settles the gifted property on the appropriate discretionary trusts (a chargeable transfer but taxed at *his* rates). Of course the transferor will have no legal right to force the donee to settle the outright gift.

Finally, the rules are only triggered by a PET. Post 2006, the creation of an interest in possession is generally not a PET but a chargeable transfer.

[33.20]

4 Exemptions and reliefs

a) *Reverter to settlor/spouse (IHTA 1984 s 53(3)–(5))*

If, on the termination of an interest in possession subject to the interest in possession regime, property reverts to the settlor, there is no charge to IHT unless that interest had been acquired for money or money's worth. This exemption also applies when the property passes to the settlor's spouse or (if the settlor is dead) to his widow or widower so long as that reverter occurs within two years of the settlor's death (for the CGT position, see **Chapter 25**).

[33.21]

EXAMPLE 33.12

(1) In 2005, Janacek created a settlement of £100,000 in favour of K for life (a PET). When K dies and the property reverts to the settlor no IHT will be charged.

Contrast the position, if the settlement provided that the fund was to pass to L on the death of K, but Janacek's wife had purchased that remainder interest from L, and given it to her husband as a Christmas present. On the death of the life tenant K, although the property will revert to Janacek and the normal charge to IHT will apply as the interest had been purchased. (For the CGT position, see **Chapter 25**.)

(2) Bert and his wife, Bertha, own their house as tenants in common. On Bert's death in 2008 he left his share to his daughter, Bettina. In 2009, she settled it on trust for her mother (Bertha) for life; remainder to herself (Bettina) for life with remainders over. This is a chargeable transfer.

On Bertha's death in February 2018, Bettina was still alive and the IHT reverter to settlor exception applied. Because Bettina only enjoys a life interest, the CGT uplift on death is available (which it would not have been if Bettina had then become absolutely entitled). The arrangement provides added security for Bertha without forfeiting any IHT benefits (contrast *IRC v Lloyds Private Banking Ltd* (1998) at **[32.28]**).

b) *Use of the life tenant's exemptions*

The spouse exemption was available on the termination of the interest in possession before 22 March 2006 if the person who then became entitled, whether absolutely or to another interest in possession, was the spouse of the former life tenant. This exemption no longer applies where the interest terminates on or after 22 March 2006 during the lifetime of the spouse with the interest and, on that occasion, an interest in possession in the other spouse arises. This is now a chargeable transfer, although the inter-spouse exemption continues to be available on the death of the spouse. Other exemptions which continue to be available are the life tenant's annual exemption (IHTA 1984 s 57), and the exemption for gifts in consideration of marriage on the *inter vivos* termination of an interest in possession if the life tenant so elects (see IHTA 1984 s 57(3), (4)). The exemptions for small gifts (£250) and normal expenditure out of income cannot be used.

EXAMPLE 33.13

Orff is the life tenant of the fund. His wife and son are entitled equally in remainder. If he surrenders the life interest, there will be no tax on the half share passing to his wife (spouse exemption). The chargeable half share passing to his son is a PET and, should it become chargeable because of his death within seven years, the annual exemption and, if surrender coincides with the marriage of the son, the £5,000 marriage gift relief will be available.

Although the making of a PET is not reported, the appropriate notice should be given to the trustees by the life tenant indicating that he wishes the transfer to be covered by his relevant exemption (the annual or marriage exemptions) so that it can then be submitted (if needed) to HMRC as required by s 57(4) (and see SI 2008/605). [33.22]

c) *The surviving spouse exemption*

The carry-over of this estate duty relief is discussed at [30.158]. The first spouse must have died before 13 November 1974 and the relief ensures that IHT is not charged on the termination of the surviving spouse's interest in the property whether that occurs *inter vivos* or on death (IHTA 1984 Sch 6 para 2). [33.23]

d) *Excluded property*

If the settlement contains excluded property, IHT is not charged on that portion of the fund (IHTA 1984 ss 5(1), 53(1)). [33.24]

e) *IHTA 1984 s 11 dispositions*

If the interest in possession is disposed of for the purpose of maintaining the disponer's child or supporting a dependent relative, IHT is not charged (see [31.7]). [33.25]

f) *Charities*

Tax is not charged if on the termination of the interest in possession the property is held on trust for charitable purposes. [33.26]

g) *Protective trusts*

The forfeiture of a protected life interest is not normally treated as the termination of an interest in possession (see [33.118]). [33.27]

h) *Variations and disclaimers*

Dispositions of the deceased may be altered after his death by means of an instrument of variation or disclaimer and treated as if they had been made by the deceased. Disclaimers are possible in the case both of settlements created by the will or intestacy of the deceased (IHTA 1984 s 142) and pre-existing settlements in which the death has resulted in a person becoming entitled to an interest in the settled property (IHTA 1984 s 93). Variations are only permitted for settlements created on the relevant death, not for settlements in which the deceased had been the beneficiary. If an interest in possession is created under a variation made on or after 22 March 2006 and is deemed to arise on the deceased's death pre-22 March 2006, it will be treated as an interest in possession in existence before that date, and so will be subject to the pre-22 March 2006 rules. Where the deceased dies on or after 22 March 2006, the new interest in possession will be an immediate post-death interest and, accordingly, it should still be possible to obtain the spouse/civil partnership exemption for interests in possession created by deed of variation within s 142 whenever the deceased might die. [33.28]

EXAMPLE 33.14

Poulenc, the life tenant of a settlement created by his father, has just died. His brother Quercus is now the life tenant in possession and if he assigns his interest within two years of Poulenc's death, the normal charging provisions will apply. (*Note:* (1) he could disclaim his interest without any IHT charge (IHTA 1984 s 93); (2) see [30.155] for problems caused to trustees when other property of the deceased is varied or disclaimed.)

i) *Quick succession relief (IHTA 1984 s 141)*

This relief is similar to that for unsettled property (see [30.144]). The first chargeable transfer may be either the creation of the settlement or any subsequent termination of an interest in possession (whether that termination occurs *inter vivos* or on death). Hence, it can be voluntarily used (by the life tenant surrendering or assigning his interest) whereas in the case of unsettled property it is only available on a death. The calculation of the relief in cases where there is more than one later transfer is dealt with in IHTA 1984 s 141(4). [33.29]

EXAMPLE 33.15

(1) A life interest settlement is created on A's death in January 2012; (2) the life interest ends in half of the fund in March 2015; (3) the life interest ends in the rest of the fund in February 2016.

Quick succession relief is available at a rate of 40% on event (2); and again at a rate of 20% on event (3). Generally, relief is given in respect of the earlier transfer first ((2) above). To the extent that the relief given represents less than the whole of the tax charged on the original net transfer ((1) above), further relief can then be given in respect of subsequent transfers ((3) above) until relief equal to the whole of the tax (in (1) above) has been given.

j) *Business reliefs*

In a settlement containing business property that relief is available to the life tenant provided that he fulfils the conditions for relief (IHTA 1984 ss 103–114). Note that the relief appears to be unaffected by the changes introduced by FA 2006.

EXAMPLE 33.16

Satie is the life tenant of the settlement. He holds 30% of the shares in the trading company Teleman Ltd, and the trust holds a further 25%. Further, the trust owns the factory premises which are leased to the company. On the death of Satie, IHT business relief is available as follows:
(1) *On the shares*: the relief (assuming that the two-year ownership condition is satisfied) is at 100% on Satie's shares and on those of the fund. The life tenant is treated as having controlled the company since he held 30% (his own) and is treated as owning a further 25% of the shares.
(2) *On the land*: the relief is at 50% since the asset is used by a company controlled by the life tenant. (But see *Fetherstonehaugh v IRC* (1984).)

Similar rules operate for agricultural relief: ie the life tenant must satisfy the conditions of two years' occupation or seven years' ownership (ownership by the trustees being attributed to the life tenant).

The requirement in relation to BPR and APR on lifetime gifts within seven years of death that the same person must own the property immediately after the gift and at the date of death (the clawback – see [31.59]) means that there is potentially a trap where settlements are concerned. If the trustees have appointed property out of the trust to a beneficiary at the date of death, the property is not owned by the same person at the date of the gift and the date of death and tax on the lifetime transfer will be calculated without relief.

[33.30]–[33.60]

IV THE TAXATION OF REVERSIONARY INTERESTS

a) **General rule: excluded property**

Reversionary interests are generally excluded property so that their assignment or transfer does not lead to an IHT charge. (The purchase of a reversionary interest by the life tenant has been considered at [33.16].) [33.61]

EXAMPLE 33.17

A fund is settled on trust for A for life (A is currently aged 88); B for life (B is 78); and C absolutely (C, A's son, is 70).

This settlement is likely to be subject to three IHT charges within a fairly short period. The position would be much improved if B and C disposed of their reversionary interests:

(1) B should surrender his interest. Taking into account his age it has little value and is merely an IHT trap.
(2) C should assign his interest to (ideally) a younger person.

The result of this reorganisation is that the fund is now threatened by only one IHT charge (on A's death) in the immediate future.

b) *Exceptions*

In four cases reversionary interests are not excluded property. This is to prevent their use as a tax avoidance device.

First, the sale of a reversionary interest to a beneficiary under the same trust, who is entitled to a prior interest (see [33.16]).

Second, the disposition of a reversionary interest which has at any time, and by any person, been acquired for a consideration in money or money's worth. (For special rules where that interest is situated outside the UK, see [35.85].)

EXAMPLE 33.18

Umberto sells his reversionary interest to Vidor (a stranger to the trust) for its market value, £20,000. If the general rules operated the position would be that:

(1) Umberto is disposing of excluded property so that no IHT is chargeable.
(2) Vidor has replaced chargeable assets (£20,000) with excluded property so that were he to die or make an *inter vivos* gift IHT would be avoided.

IHTA 1984 s 48(1)(a) and s 48(3) prevent this result. The reversion ceases to be excluded property once it has been purchased (even for a small consideration) so that a disposition by Vidor may lead to an IHT charge.

Third, a disposition of a reversionary interest is chargeable if it is one to which either the settlor or his spouse is, or has been, beneficially entitled (IHTA 1984 s 48(1)(b)).

EXAMPLE 33.19

In 2003 Viv settled property worth £100,000 on trust for his father Will for life (Will is 92). Viv retained the reversionary interest which he then gave to his daughter Ursula. If the general rules were not modified the position would be that:

(1) The creation of the settlement would have been a PET by Viv (this is prior to the 2006 changes) but the diminution in his estate would have been very small (the difference between £100,000 and the value of a reversionary interest in £100,000 subject only to the termination of the interest of a 92-year-old life tenant!).
(2) The transfer of the reversion by Viv would have escaped IHT since it is excluded property.

IHTA 1984 s 48(1)(b) ensures that the transfer of the reversion is a PET so that Viv achieved no tax saving (and, indeed, was left with the danger of a higher IHT bill than if he had never created the settlement since the death of Will is a chargeable event).

This may be used to the taxpayer's advantage in a *'Melville* type' scheme: namely, where it is desired to create a discretionary trust in order to obtain hold-over relief whilst ensuring that any IHT transfer of value is kept within the nil rate band (see [32.93]).

Fourth, the disposition of a reversionary interest is chargeable where that interest is expectant upon the termination of a lease which is treated as a settlement (typically one for life or lives; IHTA 1984 s 48(1)(c)). The lessor's reversion is treated in the same way as a reversionary interest purchased for money or money's worth so that on any disposition of it, IHT may be charged.

[33.62]

V ACCUMULATION AND MAINTENANCE TRUSTS (IHTA 1984 S 71)

Accumulation and maintenance (A&M) trusts were, before FA 2006, a useful part of the armoury in providing for the family and in particular for children up to the age of 25. Lifetime transfers to an A&M trust were PETs and thereafter, the trust operated in an IHT vacuum provided various conditions were satisfied. FA 2006 made significant changes. It effectively ended the category of A&M trusts for tax purposes created after 21 March 2006 and, for existing trusts, provided limited transitional arrangements until 6 April 2008.

[33.63]

1 A&M trusts created pre-22 March 2006

Rather than make outright gifts to minor children, it has been fairly common to settle the property in trust (often subject to the satisfaction of a contingency, eg 'attaining the age of 21') for their benefit. The creation of an accumulation trust was to mitigate the tax consequences of the making of gifts to the young, when a trust was preferable to an outright gift. In brief, accumulation trusts were treated more sympathetically for IHT purposes than other discretionary trusts – the creation during lifetime was a PET, there were no exit charges when a qualifying beneficiary became entitled to property and there were no anniversary charges.

Since 2006, no new accumulation and maintenance trusts can be created and, except for certain limited exceptions where the trust is created on the death of a parent, no special inheritance tax rules operate to protect settlements in favour of children. **[33.64]–[33.66]**

2 Transitional provisions

An A&M trust created prior to 22 March 2006 and still in existence at that date continued to enjoy the advantages outlined above (no periodic charges and no exit charges) until 6 April 2008. There is one exception to this: A&M trusts which satisfied the conditions *as to beneficiaries* of the bereaved minor trust (BMT) converted automatically to the BMT regime on 22 March 2006, with all the consequences of that regime (IHTA 1984 s 71(1B)). The conditions of the BMT which concern *the settlor* do not need to be satisfied (see **[32.58]**).

On 6 April 2008, if the trust was immediately before that date still an A&M trust and it satisfied the requirements of the 18–25 regime relating to beneficiaries, the trust simply automatically converted into an 18–25 trust. There is no charge to IHT until property starts leaving the trust, calculated on the basis of the number of years between the later of the beneficiary becoming 18 and 6 April 2008 (s 71F(5)(a); see **[33.111]**).

If, on 6 April 2008, the trust did not satisfy the requirements of the 18–25 regime, the property in the trust became subject to the relevant property regime. There was no charge on 6 April 2008, but from that date, the trust will be subject to anniversary charges and exit charges.

EXAMPLE 33.20

Assume that all the following A&M trusts are created on 1 January 2000:
(1) 'to each of X's grandchildren in equal shares, contingent on attaining the age of 18'. This satisfies the requirements of the BMT and on 22 March 2006, the trust automatically becomes a BMT. There is no anniversary charge and no exit charge when the children reach the age of 18.
(2) 'to each of X's grandchildren in equal shares, contingent on attaining the age of 21'. Grandchild A attains the age of 21 on 1 January 2008, grandchild B on 1 January 2009.
   This does not satisfy the requirements of the BMT as the beneficiaries become absolutely entitled over the age of 18. The A&M regime continues to operate until 6 April 2008, so when A becomes entitled to the property on 1 January 2008, this is not a chargeable transfer. Assuming no interest in possession arises by operation of Trustee Act 1925 s 31 in B, the trust converts into an 18–25 trust on 6 April 2008. There will be a limited exit charge on B's 21st birthday on 1 January 2009 calculated by reference to the period from 6 April 2008 to 1 January 2009.
(3) 'at the discretion of the trustees, for the education and maintenance of A, B and C, with each of A, B and C becoming entitled to an interest in possession

in their prospective share on attaining the age of 21 with absolute entitlement at the age of 26.'

A turns 21 on 1 January 2008, B on 1 January 2009 and C on 1 January 2011.

A becomes entitled to an interest in possession during the transitional period. Under the A&M regime, there is no chargeable transfer on entitlement to an interest in possession under the age of 25, and this continues to apply. On 6 April 2008, as the beneficiaries do not become *absolutely* entitled to the property before the age of 25, the conditions for the 18–25 regime are not satisfied so, on that date, the property becomes subject to the relevant property regime. There will be no charge on 6 April 2008. Neither will there be any charge when each of B and C become entitled to an interest in possession, as with limited exceptions, interests in possession which arise after 22 March 2006 are also subject to the relevant property regime, so there is no exit charge. On 1 January 2010, there will be an anniversary charge on the trust's 10-year anniversary, and further exit charges when B and C become entitled to the property outright. **[33.67]–[33.70]**

VI   TRUSTS FOR BEREAVED MINORS AND 18–25 TRUSTS

In place of A&M settlements, there are two new trust regimes – the 'trust for bereaved minors' and '18–25 Trusts'. The rules governing these trusts are contained in IHTA 1984 ss 71A–71G (introduced by FA 2006). **[33.71]**

1   Trusts for bereaved minors (IHTA 1984 ss 71A–71C)

The conditions for the bereaved minor trust (BMT) are set out at **[32.58]**.

The creation of a BMT which is normally on the death, will be a chargeable transfer. On the child becoming entitled to the property or any accumulated income from the trust at or before the age of 18, there is no exit charge, neither are there any anniversary charges. Neither is there any charge on the death of the bereaved minor under the age of 18.

To the extent that property leaves the trust other than as described, there are provisions for a tapered exit charge, depending on how long the property has been in the trust. **[33.72]–[33.110]**

2   18–25 trusts (IHTA 1984 ss 71D–71G)

The conditions for the 18–25 trust are set out at **[32.59]**.

In line with the BMT, there is no charge where the beneficiary becomes absolutely entitled to the settled property at or before the age of 18, or of payment of income arising or accumulated income at or under the age of 18, or where the beneficiary dies under the age of 18. Neither is there any charge where the trustees pay out income to the beneficiaries or trust expenses (s 71E(2)–(4)). Apart from this, a charge to tax arises when settled property ceases to be property to which s 71D applies ('the exit charge'), or where the trustees enter into depreciatory transactions (IHTA 1984 s 71E(1)).

There are two types of charge that may arise: what might be regarded as the 'normal' charge under s 71F, broadly a low exit charge, in line with the rates applicable to the relevant property regime, although running only from the date the beneficiary became 18, when property leaves the trust in certain ways; and an exceptional rather higher rate under s 71G, when the property leaves the trust in any other way.

The section 71F charge arises if, after the age of 18, the beneficiary becomes absolutely entitled to the property or the property is applied for his benefit or is by advancement, or he dies.

The tax payable is *Chargeable amount x relevant fraction x settlement rate* (s 71F(3)).

The *chargeable amount* is the drop in the value in the property in the trust, which means that a net transfer must be grossed up.

The *relevant fraction* is calculated in similar fashion to the 'appropriate fraction' in the relevant property regime (see [**34.25**]), except that the time runs from the later of the beneficiary becoming 18 and the property being subject to the 18–25 regime.

The *settlement rate* is calculated in the same fashion to the effective rate in the relevant property regime (see [**34.27**]).

The maximum rate of charge is 4.2% if absolute entitlement is on attaining the age of 25.

The section 71G charge is unlikely to be applied as, given the restrictive conditions for qualifying for an 18–25 trust, virtually all of the ways in which property will leave the trust will be covered by s 71F. One example would be where the trustees entered into a depreciatory transaction. In the event that a section 71G charge is applied, it is calculated on a tapered basis. [**33.111**]

VII OTHER SPECIAL TRUSTS

1 **Charitable trusts**

If a trust is perpetually dedicated to charitable purposes, there is no charge to IHT and the fund is not 'relevant property' (IHTA 1984 s 58). Transfers to charities are exempt, whether made by individuals or by trustees of discretionary trusts (IHTA 1984 s 76).

IHTA 1984 s 70 is concerned with temporary charitable trusts defined as 'settled property held for charitable purposes only until the end of a period (whether defined by a date or in some other way)' and ensures that, when the fund ceases to be held for such purposes, an exit charge will arise. That charge (which is calculated in the same way as for A&M trusts; see above) will never exceed a 30% rate which is reached after 50 years. [**33.112**]

2 **Trusts for the disabled (IHTA 1984 ss 89–89B)**

These trusts enjoy certain tax advantages.

The *inter vivos* creation of this trust is a PET.

A qualifying trust for a disabled person is subjected to the interest in possession regime rather than the relevant property regime, even where the trust is discretionary in nature. This means there are no exit charges or anniversary charges and, where capital is appointed to the disabled person, there is no deemed transfer of value by the disabled person.

A charge to IHT will arise on the death of the disabled person, whose deemed interest in possession will aggregate with his free estate in the normal way. Although disabled trusts can also obtain CGT advantages (eg a full annual exemption for the trustees), to qualify the disabled beneficiary must be entitled to at least one half of the income or be the sole income beneficiary (see TCGA 1992 Sch 1 para 1 and *Private Client Business* (1993) p 161). [33.113]

3 Pension funds (IHTA 1984 s 151)

A superannuation scheme or fund approved by HMRC for income tax purposes is not subject to the rules for no interest in possession trusts. This exemption from IHT extends to payments out of the fund within two years of the member's death. It is common practice for the member to settle the 'death benefit' on discretionary trusts: this trust will be subject to normal charging rules, although HMRC consider that IHTA 1984 s 81 applies to deem the property to remain comprised in the original fund, eg for the purpose of 10-year anniversary dates (see [34.21]). [33.114]

4 Employee trusts (IHTA 1984 s 86)

These trusts will not in law be charitable unless they are directed to the relief of poverty amongst employees (see *Oppenheim v Tobacco Securities Trust Co Ltd* (1951)). They may, however, enjoy IHT privileges. Their creation will not involve a transfer of value, whether made by an individual (IHTA 1984 s 28) or by a discretionary trust (IHTA 1984 s 75). Once created, the fund is largely exempted from the IHT provisions governing discretionary trusts, especially from the anniversary charge. To qualify for this treatment, the fund must be held for the benefit of persons employed in a particular trade or profession together with their dependants. These provisions are extended to cover newspaper trusts (see IHTA 1984 s 87); approved profit-sharing schemes and the FA 2000 employee share ownership plan. [33.115]

5 Compensation funds (IHTA 1984 ss 58, 63)

Trusts set up by professional bodies and trade associations for the purpose of indemnifying clients and customers against loss incurred through the default of their members are exempt from the rules for no interest in possession trusts. [33.116]

6 Maintenance funds for historic buildings (IHTA 1984 s 77, Sch 4)

IHT exemptions are available for maintenance funds where property is settled and the Treasury give a direction under IHTA 1984 Sch 4 para 1. Once the trust ceases, for any reason, to carry out its specialised function, an exit charge, calculated in the same way as for A&M trusts, occurs. [33.117]

7 Protective trusts (IHTA 1984 ss 73, 88)

A protective trust may be set up either by using the statutory model provided for by the Trustee Act 1925 (TA) s 33, or by express provisions.

These trusts have always been subject to special IHT rules and, as originally enacted, the rules offered scope for tax avoidance (see IHTA 1984 s 73 and *Thomas v IRC* (1981)). Accordingly, the rules were changed with effect from 11 April 1978 by providing that the life tenant is deemed to continue to have an interest in possession for IHT purposes despite the forfeiture of his interest (IHTA 1984 s 88). It follows that the discretionary trust regime is not applicable to the trust that arises upon such forfeiture. Should the capital be advanced to a person other than the life tenant, a charge to IHT will arise and on the death of the beneficiary the fund will be treated as part of his estate for IHT purposes (*Cholmondeley v IRC* (1986)). As a result of these rules there is the curious anomaly that, after a forfeiture of the life interest, the interest in possession rules apply to a discretionary trust although it should be borne in mind that ordinary rules apply for other taxes. Thus for income tax a 40% rate applies once the life interest is forfeited and there is no CGT uplift on the death of the principal beneficiary.

One cautionary note should be added; this system of charging only applies to protective trusts set up under the TA 1925 s 33 or to trusts 'to the like effect'. Minor variations to the statutory norm are, therefore, allowed; but not the inclusion of different beneficiaries under the discretionary trust (such as the brothers and sisters of the principal beneficiary), nor a provision that enables a forfeited life interest to revive after the lapse of a period of time. In such cases, the normal rules applicable to interest in possession and discretionary trusts apply (see *Law Society's Gazette*, 3 March 1976 and SP E7). [**33.118**]

34 IHT – the relevant property regime
Updated by Sandra Eden, Senior Lecturer, University of Edinburgh

I   Introduction and terminology [**34.1**]
II The method of charge [**34.21**]
III Exemptions and reliefs [**34.51**]
IV Discretionary trusts created before 27 March 1974 [**34.71**]

I INTRODUCTION AND TERMINOLOGY

Prior to the changes introduced by FA 2006, relevant property referred to property held in a settlement lacking an interest in possession. The method of charging settlements of this nature is totally different from that for settlements with an interest in possession (see **Chapter 33**). Instead of attributing the fund to one of the beneficiaries, the settlement itself is the taxable entity. Like an individual, a record of chargeable transfers must be kept although, unlike the individual, it will never die and so will only be taxed at half rates. Taking into account the FA 2006 changes, this chapter will discuss the rules by reference to relevant property. Until those changes, the discretionary trust was the most significant trust with relevant property, although in fact the category is wider than discretionary trusts catching, for instance, the settlement in the *Pilkington* case ([**32.24**]) and trusts where the beneficiaries' interests are contingent. These rules will now also apply to a post-21 March 2006 trust with an interest in possession that is not a transitional serial interest, an immediate post-death interest or disabled person's interest (see **Chapter 33**).

EXAMPLE 34.1
(1) A fund of £100,000 is held upon trust for such of A, B, C, D, E and F as the trustees may in their absolute discretion (which extends over both income and capital) think appropriate. The trust is one without an interest in possession.
(2) Dad settles property on trust for Sonny absolutely contingent on his attaining 30. Sonny is aged 21 at the date of the settlement and the income is to be accumulated until Sonny attains 30. There is no interest in possession because Sonny's interest is contingent.
(3) On 1 April 2015, Mum settles property on trust for her daughter Tamsin for life, with remainder to her grandson Victor absolutely. Although there

is an interest in possession, it arises post-22 March 2006 and, not being a transitional serial interest, an immediate post-death interest or disabled person's interest (and nor is it a 'special trust' considered in Sections VI and VII of **Chapter 33**), it will be subject to the relevant property regime.

IHT is charged on '*relevant property*' (IHTA 1984 s 58(1)), defined as settled property (other than excluded property) in which there is no qualifying interest in possession (with the exception of property settled on the 'special trusts' considered in **Chapter 33**). (See **[32.22]** ff for the meaning of an interest in possession.)

A 'qualifying interest in possession' is an interest to which an individual became beneficially entitled before 22 March 2006 or, where that interest arose on or after 22 March 2006, a transitional serial interest, an immediate post-death interest or disabled person's interest (IHTA 1984 s 59).

It is an interest owned beneficially by an individual or, in restricted circumstances, by a company. If within one settlement there exists an interest in possession in a part only of the settled property, these rules applied to the portion which lacks such an interest. **[34.1]**

The changes made in 2006 to the IHT taxation of trusts left a gap in the legislation concerning pre-22 March 2006 settlements where the settlor or their spouse had an interest in possession when the trust came into being and the spouse or settlor had a succeeding life interest. It was possible for the second life interest to fall outside the settlement rules altogether. This was corrected with effect from 19 November 2015, and settled property now becomes relevant property once the second spouse takes their life interest and such property will then be subject to the relevant property charges. Transitional provisions will apply to such trusts, and the new rules do not apply until any interest in possession in existence on 19 November 2015 terminates. **[34.2]–[34.20]**

II THE METHOD OF CHARGE

The central feature is the *periodic charge* imposed upon relevant property at 10-yearly intervals. The anniversary is calculated from the date on which the trust was created rather than the date, if different, when the settlement property becomes 'relevant property' (IHTA 1984 s 61(1)). In the case of settlements initially established with a nominal sum (eg £10), it is from the date when that nominal sum is received by the trustees.

EXAMPLE 34.2

(1) Silas creates a discretionary trust on 1 January 2018. The first anniversary charge falls on 1 January 2028; the next on 1 January 2038 and so on. If the trust had been created by will and he had died on 31 December 2017, that date marks the creation of the trust (IHTA 1984 s 83). A similar principle applies if the trust was established by an instrument of variation falling within IHTA 1984 s 142 (see **[30.153]**).

(2) Sebastian creates (on his death in 2017) a settlement in favour of his wife Selina for life; thereafter for such of his three daughters as the trustees may in their absolute discretion select. Selina dies in 2020. For IHT purposes, the discretionary trust is treated as having been created by Selina on her death (IHTA 1984 s 80) although the 10-year anniversary runs from 2017 (IHTA 1984 s 61(2)).

(3) On 1 April 2005 (ie before the 2006 trust regime came into effect), Eddie settles property on trust for his daughter Trudy for life, thereafter on discretionary trusts for his grandchildren. Trudy dies on 20 September 2013. Although the trust is not subject to the relevant property regime until Trudy's death, the first anniversary charge in respect of the trust will fall on 1 April 2015.

Apart from the periodic charge, IHT is also levied (the '*exit charge*') (see [**34.23**]) on the happening of certain events. In general, the IHT then charged is a proportion of the last periodic charge (see [**34.26**], [**34.29**]). Special charging provisions operate for chargeable events which occur before the first 10-year anniversary (see [**34.23**]). [**34.21**]

1 The creation of the settlement

This will, generally, be a chargeable transfer of value by the settlor for IHT purposes. The following matters should be noted: *first*, if the settlement is created *inter vivos*, grossing-up applies unless IHT is paid out of the fund (see **Chapter 28**).

Second, the cumulative total of chargeable transfers made by the settlor forms part of the cumulative total of the settlement on all future chargeable occasions (ie his chargeable transfers in the seven years prior to the creation of the settlement never drop out of the cumulative total). Therefore, in order to calculate the correct IHT charge it is essential that the trustees are told the settlor's cumulative total at the date when he created the trust.

Third, a '*related settlement*' is one created by the same settlor on the same day as the trust with relevant property (other than a charitable trust). Generally such settlements should be avoided (because related settlements can increase the amount of IHT payable: see [**34.27**]).

Fourth, additions of property by the original settlor to his settlement may create problems, particularly where property is added to more than one trust on the same day. If property is added by a person other than the original settlor, the addition will often be treated as a separate settlement (see [**32.7**]).

Problems may arise for the trustees if the settlor dies within seven years of creating the trust. PETs made *before* the settlement was created and within seven years of his death then become chargeable so that tax on creation of the settlement and the computation of any exit charge made during this period may need to be recalculated. If extra tax becomes payable this is primarily the responsibility of the settlement trustees and their liability is not limited to settlement property in their hands *at that time*. Given this danger it will be prudent for trustees who are distributing property from the trust with relevant property within the first seven years to retain sufficient funds or take suitable indemnities to cover any contingent IHT liability. [**34.22**]

EXAMPLE 34.3

Sumar makes the following transfers of value:

May 2014 £300,000 to his sister Sufi (a PET).
May 2015 £75,000 to a family discretionary trust (CT).

In May 2016 the trustees distribute the entire fund to the beneficiaries and in May 2017 Sumar dies.

As a result of his death, the 2014 PET is chargeable (the resultant IHT is primarily the responsibility of Sufi) and in addition tax on the creation of the settlement must be recalculated.

When it was set up the PET was ignored so that the transfer to the family trust fell within Sumar's nil rate band. With his death, however, IHT must be calculated, at the rates in force in May 2017. Taking into account the now chargeable PET of £300,000, there is £25,000 nil rate band left for the 2015 transfer, leaving £50,000 of the transfer to be taxed at 40%. Tax is thus 40% of £50,000, ie £20,000. In addition it is likely that no IHT will have been charged on the distribution of the fund in 2016 and therefore a re-computation is again necessary with the trustees being liable for the resulting tax.

2 Exit charges before the first 10-year anniversary

a) *When will an exit charge arise?*

A charge is imposed whenever property in the settlement ceases to be 'relevant property' to the extent of the property ceasing to be held (IHTA 1984 s 65). This will usually be as a result of an outright transfer but, before 22 March 2006, it would also include an occasion when an interest in possession arose in any of the fund, as interests in possession were all outside the relevant property regime. If an interest in possession arises over settled property on or after 22 March 2006, the property only ceases to be relevant property to the extent that it is a disabled person's interest: this becomes subject to the interest in possession regime (by definition, it cannot be one of the other interests which, post 2006, are subject to the interest in possession regime, namely an immediate post-death interest or a transitional serial interest). If the resultant IHT is paid out of the property that is left in the discretionary trust, grossing-up will apply. A charge is also imposed if the trustees make a disposition as a result of which the value of relevant property comprised in the settlement falls (a 'depreciatory transaction'; notice that in this case there is no requirement that the transaction must be made with a beneficiary or with a person connected with him).

The exit charge does not apply to a payment of costs or expenses (so long as it is 'fairly attributable' to the relevant property), nor does it catch a payment which is income of any person for the purposes of income tax (IHTA 1984 s 65(5)). **[34.23]**

b) *Calculation of the 'effective rate'*

The effective rate (IHTA 1984 s 68) is found by calculating IHT on a hypothetical transfer, on top of hypothetical previous transfers. The calculation of the rate of IHT is based upon half the full IHT rates, even if the trust was set up under the will of the settlor.

Step 1 This hypothetical transfer is made up of the sum of the following:
(1) the value of the relevant property in the settlement immediately after it commenced;
(2) the value (at the date of the addition) of any added relevant property;
(3) the value of relevant property in a related settlement (valued immediately after it commenced (IHTA 1984 s 68(5));
(4) the value of any 'same day addition' (see below), and
(5) the value of property in any other settlement which received a 'same day addition'.

No account is taken of any rise or fall in the value of the settled fund and the value comprised in the settlement and in any related settlement can include property subject to an interest in possession.

Step 2 Tax at half rates on this hypothetical transfer is calculated by taking into account chargeable transfers made by the settlor in the seven years before he created the settlement. Other chargeable transfers made on the same day as the settlement are ignored and, therefore, if the settlement was created on death, other gifts made in the will or on intestacy are ignored (IHTA 1984 s 68(4)(b)).

Step 3 The resultant tax is converted to an average rate (the equivalent of an estate rate) known as the effective rate.

EXAMPLE 34.4

Justinian settles £100,000 on discretionary trusts on 6 April 2017. His total chargeable transfers immediately before that date stood at £235,000. He pays the IHT. If an exit charge arises before the first 10-year anniversary of the fund (6 April 2027) the settlement rate would be calculated as follows:

Step 1 Calculate the hypothetical chargeable transfer. As there is no added property, no related settlement and no same day additions, it comprises only the value of the property in the settlement immediately after its creation (ie £100,000).

Step 2 Calculate the tax on £100,000 taking into account the previous chargeable transfers of Justinian at the date of creation of the trust (ie £235,000). There is thus £90,000 nil rate band remaining. Taking the IHT rates in force in April 2016, tax on the £100,000 at lifetime rates is 20% of £10,000 (the remaining £90,000 is covered by the nil rate band) = £2,000.

Step 3 The tax converted to a percentage of the transfer of £100,000 rate is 2%. This is the effective rate.

In most cases, it is only the value of the trust in question which will need to be taken into account. However, the provisions which bring into account related settlements and same day additions are both anti-avoidance provisions, aimed at fragmentation of trusts and require a little more explanation.

A settlement is related to another settlement if each was created on the same date. The provisions in relation to these are necessary because transfers made on the same day as the creation of the settlement are normally ignored and, therefore, an IHT advantage could be achieved if the settlor were to set up a series of small funds on the same day rather than one large fund.

The 'same day additions' rules are to counteract pilot trusts – small trusts set up on different days (to avoid the related property rules) to which sums are added subsequently, usually on death.

The provisions in respect of same day additions, introduced by F(No 2)A 2015, make the use of pilot trusts less attractive since, if there is an increase in value of more than one trust on the same day, not only the same day addition but also the initial value of the trust become part of the computation.

A same day addition occurs where there is a transfer of value to one relevant property settlement and, on the same day, whether by the same transfer of value or another, there is an increase in value of another relevant property settlement and both share the same settlor (s 62A).

Same day additions are ignored if (ss 62B and 62C):
- either or both the trusts are charitable trusts;
- the same day addition takes place under a will executed before 10 December 2014 and there were no additions to the settlement after that date, but only in relation to deaths before 6 April 2017;
- in relation to lifetime additions only, broadly, the increase in value to the trust in question does not exceed £5,000;
- the same day additions were regular payments of premiums on life insurance policies.

EXAMPLE 34.5

Angie, who has made previous chargeable transfers of £25,000, creates a relevant property trust in August 2010 with an initial value of £500,000. In August 2011 she creates another relevant property trust with an initial value of £200,000. In August 2016, on the same day, she adds £50,000 to each trust. In August 2017 there is a distribution from the first settlement.

Step 1 – the hypothetical chargeable transfer is the total of the sum of the value in the first trust after creation, the addition to the first trust, the same day addition to the second trust and the value of the second trust immediately after creation. This is £800,000.

Step 2 the nil rate band remaining is £300,000 as Angie has made chargeable transfers prior to the creation of the trust of £25,000. Thus £500,000 of the hypothetical chargeable transfer is hypothetically charged at 20%, or £100,000.

Step 3 the effective rate is £100,000 as a percentage of the hypothetical transfer of £800,000, or 12.5% **[34.24]**

c) *The tax charged*

The charge is on the fall in value of the fund. The rate of charge is the 'appropriate fraction' of the 'effective rate'. The appropriate fraction is 3/10ths multiplied by 1/40th for each complete successive quarter that has elapsed from the creation of the settlement to the date of the exit charge.

EXAMPLE 34.6

Assume in *Example 34.4* that on 25 March 2019 there was an exit charge on £20,000 ceasing to be relevant property. The IHT is calculated as follows:

Step 1 Take completed quarters since the settlement was created, ie seven.

Step 2 Take 7/40ths x 3/10ths (21/400ths) of the 'effective rate' of 2% to discover the rate to charge = 0.105%.

Step 3 This is applied to the fall in value of the relevant property (£20,000). The IHT will, therefore, be £21 if the tax is borne by the beneficiary; or £21.02 if borne by the remaining fund.

There is no charge on events that occur in the first three months after the settlement is created (IHTA 1984 s 65(4)) nor, in certain circumstances when the trust was set up by the settlor on his death, on events occurring within two years of that death (see [30.145]). [34.25]

3 The charge on the first 10-year anniversary

a) *What property is charged?*

The charge is levied on the value of the *relevant property* comprised in the settlement immediately before the anniversary (IHTA 1984 s 64). Income only becomes relevant property, and thus subject to charge, when it has been accumulated. Pending accumulation it is not subject to the anniversary charge and can be distributed free from any exit charge (see [34.23]). Note that the income arising in a post-22 March 2006 interest in possession trust that now falls within the definition of relevant property will, by definition, not be accumulated; it will be paid to the beneficiary with an interest in possession. Accumulation occurs once an irrevocable decision to that effect has been taken by trustees. In the absence of such a decision the position used to be that it was deemed to have been accumulated after a reasonable time for distribution has passed but with effect from 6 April 2014, for the purposes of calculating the anniversary charge, income received more than five years before the anniversary which has not been distributed by the date of the anniversary is deemed to have been accumulated. The legislation gives no guidance on what income is treated as being distributed first but HMRC have stated that they would accept first-in-first-out treatment.

The assets in the fund are valued according to general principles and, if they include business or agricultural property, the reliefs appropriate to that property will apply, subject to satisfaction of the relevant conditions. Any IHT charged on such property may be payable in instalments. [34.26]

b) *Calculation of the rate of IHT*

Half rates will be used and, as with the exit charge, the calculation depends upon a hypothetical chargeable transfer.

Step 1 Calculate the hypothetical chargeable transfer which is made up of the sum of the following:
(1) the value of relevant property comprised in the settlement immediately before the anniversary;
(2) the value, immediately after it was created, of relevant property comprised in a 'related settlement';
(3) the value of any 'same day addition'; and
(4) the commencement value of the relevant property in any other trust which received a 'same day addition'.

Again, normally the hypothetical chargeable transfer will be made up exclusively of property falling within (1) above. (2), (3) and (4), which affect the rate of IHT to be charged without themselves being taxed, are anti-avoidance measures (see [34.24]].

Step 2 Calculate tax at half rates on the hypothetical chargeable transfer, taking into account the cumulative total of:
(1) chargeable transfers of the settlor made in the *seven* years before he created the settlement; and
(2) chargeable transfers made by the settlement in the first *ten* years. Where a settlement was created after 26 March 1974 and before 9 March 1982, distribution payments (as defined by the IHT charging regime in force between those dates) must also be cumulated (IHTA 1984 s 66(6)).

Settlements with relevant property will, therefore, have their own total of chargeable transfers with transfers over a 10-year period being cumulated (contrast the seven-year period used for individuals). The unique feature of a settlement's cumulation lies in the inclusion (and it never drops out) of chargeable transfers of the settlor in the seven years before the settlement is created.

Step 3 The IHT is converted to a percentage (the 'effective rate') and 30% of that rate is then taken and charged on the relevant property in the settlement (IHTA 1984 s 66).

The highest rate of IHT is 20% (half of 40%). The highest chargeable rate (anniversary rate) is, therefore, 30% of 20%, ie 6%. Where the settlement comprises business property qualifying for 50% relief, this falls to 3% and assuming that the option to pay in instalments is exercised, the annual charge over the 10-year period becomes a mere 0.3%. If the property qualifies for 100% business or agricultural relief there is no charge. **[34.27]**

EXAMPLE 34.7

Take the facts of *Examples 34.4 and 34.6* (namely, original fund £100,000, exit charge on £20,000; previous transfers of settlor £235,000). In addition, assume Justinian had created a second settlement of £35,000 on 6 April 2017.

The original fund is worth £105,000 at the first 10-year anniversary.
(1) Relevant property to be taxed is £105,000

(2)	Calculate hypothetical chargeable transfer:	£
	Relevant property, as above	105,000
	Property in related settlement	35,000
		£140,000
(3)	Settlement's cumulative IHT total:	£
	Settlor's earlier transfers	235,000
	Chargeable transfers of trustees in preceding 10 years	20,000
		£255,000

(4) There is £70,000 nil rate band remaining for the hypothetical transfer of £140,000. Tax at half rates on the remaining £70,000 at 20% = £14,000 so that, as a percentage of the hypothetical transfer, the effective rate is 10%.
(5) The actual rate is 30% of 10% = 3%.
Tax payable is £105,000 × 3% = £3,150

4 Exit charges after the first anniversary charge and between anniversaries

The same events will trigger an exit charge after the first 10-year anniversary as before it. The IHT charge will be levied on the fall in value of the fund with grossing-up, if necessary. The rate of charge is a proportion of the rate charged at the first 10-year anniversary. That proportion is one-fortieth for each complete quarter from the date of the first anniversary charge to the date of the exit charge (IHTA 1984 s 69).

EXAMPLE 34.8

Continuing *Example 34.7*, exactly 15 months later the trustees appoint £25,000 to a beneficiary. The IHT (assuming no grossing-up) will be:
£25,000 × 3% × 5/40 (five quarters since last 10-year anniversary) = £93.75.

If the rates of IHT have been reduced (including the raising of the rate bands) between the anniversary and exit charges, the lower rates will apply to the exit charge and, therefore, the rate of charge on the first anniversary will have to be recalculated at those rates (IHTA 1984 Sch 2 para 3). So long as the IHT rate bands remain linked to rises in the retail prices index (IHTA 1984 s 8) recalculation will be the norm.

No exit charge is levied if the chargeable event occurs within the first quarter following the anniversary charge. [34.28]

5 Later periodic charges

The principles that applied on the first 10-year anniversary operate on subsequent 10-year anniversaries. So far as the hypothetical chargeable transfer is concerned the same items will be included (so that the value of property in a related settlement and of non-relevant property in the settlement is always included). The cumulative total of the fund will, as before, include the chargeable transfers of the settlor made in the seven years before he created the settlement and the transfers out of the settlement in the ten years immediately preceding the anniversary (earlier transfers by the settlement fall out of the cumulative total). The remaining stages of the calculation are unaltered. [34.29]

6 Technical problems

The basic structure of the charging provisions in IHTA 1984 ss 58–69 is relatively straightforward. The charge to IHT is built on a series of periodic charges with interim charges (where appropriate) which are levied at a fraction of the full periodic charge. [34.30]

a) *Reduction in the rate of the anniversary charge*

If property has not been in the settlement for the entire preceding ten years (as will be the case when income is accumulated during that period) there is a proportionate reduction in the charge (IHTA 1984 s 66(2)). The reduction in the periodic rate is calculated by reference to the number of completed quarters that expired before the property became relevant property in the settlement.

EXAMPLE 34.9

Assume in *Example 34.7* that £15,000 had become relevant property on 30 April 2023.

The IHT charge on the first 10-year anniversary (on 6 April 2027) would now be calculated as follows:
(1) £90,000 (the value of the property which has been in the trust for the full 10 years: £105,000 – £15,000) at 3% =£2,700.
(2) The £15,000 will be charged at a proportion of the periodic charge rate: namely 3% reduced by 24/40 since 24 complete quarters elapsed from the creation of the settlement (on 1 April 2017) to the date when the £15,000 became relevant property. As a result the IHT charged is £15,000 × 1.2% (ie 3% × 16/40) = £180.

This proportionate reduction in the effective rate of the periodic charge will not affect the calculation of IHT on events occurring after the anniversary, ie any exit charge is at the full effective rate.

The legislation does not contain provisions which enable specific property to be identified. Thus, the reduction mentioned above applies to the value of the relevant property in the fund at the 10-year anniversary 'attributable' to property which was not relevant property throughout the preceding ten years. Presumably a proportionate calculation will be necessary where the value of the fund has shown an increase.

Accumulated income caught by the anniversary charge is not given a proportionate reduction (see [34.26]). [34.31]

b) *Transfers between settlements*

IHTA 1984 s 81 prevents a tax advantage from switching property between settlements of relevant property, by providing that such property remains comprised in the first settlement. Accordingly, property cannot be moved out of a discretionary trust to avoid an anniversary charge; property cannot be switched from a fund with a high cumulative total to one with a lower total; and the transfer of property from one discretionary fund to another will not be chargeable. [34.32]

c) *Added property*

Special rules operate if, after the settlement commenced (and after 8 March 1982), the settlor made a chargeable transfer as a result of which the value of the property comprised in the settlement was increased (IHTA 1984 s 67(1)). Note that it is only additions by the settlor that trigger these provisions and that it is the value of the fund which must be increased and not necessarily the amount of property in that fund. Transfers which have the effect of increasing the value of the fund are ignored if they are not primarily intended to have that effect and do not in fact increase the value by more than 5%.

EXAMPLE 34.10

Sam, the settlor, creates in 2007 a discretionary trust of stocks and shares in Sham Ltd and the benefit of a life insurance policy on Sam's life.
(1) Each year Sam adds property to the settlement, equal to his annual IHT exemption.
(2) Sam continues to pay the premiums on the life policy each year.
(3) Sam transfers further shares in Sham Ltd.

The method of charge 1073

The special rules for added property will not apply in either case (1) or (2), since Sam is not making a chargeable transfer; the first transfer is covered by his annual exemption and the second by the exemption for normal expenditure out of income. The transfer of further shares to the fund, however, is caught by the provisions of IHTA 1984 s 67.

If the added property provisions apply, the calculation of the periodic charge which immediately follows the addition will be modified. For the purposes of the hypothetical chargeable transfer, the cumulative total of the settlor's chargeable transfers will be the higher of the totals (1) immediately before creating the settlement plus transfers made by the settlement before the addition; and (2) immediately before transferring the added property, deducting from this latter total the transfer made on creation of the settlement and a transfer to any related settlement. The settlor should normally avoid additions, since they may cause more IHT to be charged at the next anniversary and it will be preferable to create a separate settlement.

[34.33]

d) *The timing of the exit charge*

Assume, for example, that a discretionary trust has been in existence for nearly ten years and that the trustees now wish to distribute all or part of the fund to the beneficiaries. Are they better off doing so just before the 10-year anniversary or should they wait until just after that anniversary? Generally, it will be advantageous to distribute *before* an anniversary because IHT payable will be calculated at rates then in force but on historic values, ie on the value of the fund when it was settled or at the last 10-year anniversary. By contrast, if the trustees delay until after the anniversary, IHT (still at current rates) will then be assessed on the present value of the fund. To this general proposition one major exception exists which may well be the result of defective drafting in the legislation. It relates to a fund consisting of property qualifying for either business relief or agricultural relief at 50%. In this situation trustees *should not* break up the fund immediately before the first anniversary. [34.34]

EXAMPLE 34.11

A discretionary settlement was created on 1 January 2008. At all times it has consisted of agricultural property which will qualify for 50% relief. Assume no earlier transfers by settlor and that the value of the property is £500,000 throughout. Consider the effect of agricultural property relief if:

(1) *the trustees distribute the entire fund on 25 December 2017* The distribution occurs before the first 10-year anniversary. The entire value of the property in the settlement immediately after it commenced must be included in the hypothetical transfer of value since there is no agricultural property relief reduction. Therefore £500,000 must be included (IHTA 1984 s 68(5)(a)). The rate thus calculated is then applied to the fund as reduced by business relief. Hence, although the amount subject to the charge is only £250,000 (£500,000 minus 50% relief), a higher rate of IHT will apply. (Notice that if 100% relief were to be available in 2017 this trap would not arise as the property leaving the trust would be fully relieved at that point.)

(2) *the trustees distribute the entire fund on 3 January 2019*. Now the exit charge is after a ten year anniversary, and is based on the most recent anniversary charge. Section 66, which governs the calculation of the anniversary charge

is structured differently from s 68 and enables business and agricultural property relief to be incorporated in the calculation. So in this case the property subject to the anniversary charge will be reduced by 50% relief to £250,000; and for the purpose of calculating the hypothetical chargeable transfer the value of the property is similarly reduced by 50%.

7 Using discretionary trusts

Discretionary trusts are likely to remain attractive in the following situations:
(1) Small *inter vivos* discretionary settlements. Notice that two discretionary settlements can be used to create two nil rate band trusts when the transferor is transferring one and a half times his nil rate band.

EXAMPLE 34.12
A taxpayer transfers agricultural property (qualifying for 50% relief) into two discretionary trusts as follows:
Into Discretionary Trust 1 property which reduces his estate by £125,000 after 50% agricultural property relief.
Into Discretionary Trust 2 property which reduces his estate by £62,500 after 50% agricultural property relief.
In both cases, assume that the agricultural property is sold by the trustees. The result is that the first discretionary trust is worth £250,000 and, in working out any IHT charges, the settlor's cumulative total when the trust was created was nil. The second discretionary trust is worth £125,000 and was set up at a time when the cumulative total of the settlor was £125,000. Accordingly, the two trusts are nil rate band trusts, but remember that, to avoid the related settlement rules, they should be created on separate days.

(2) In will drafting, the use of the mini (£325,000) discretionary trust remains attractive for the smaller estate and, for flexibility the 'two-year' trust (see [**30.145**]). [**34.35**]–[**34.50**]

III EXEMPTIONS AND RELIEFS

Many of the exemptions from IHT do not apply to trusts with relevant property, eg the annual exemption, the marriage exemption, and the exemption for normal expenditure out of income. There is no exemption if the settled fund reverts to either the settlor or his spouse (and note that if the settlor is a beneficiary, the reservation of benefit provisions apply, see **Chapter 29**). Business and agricultural property relief may, however, be available, provided that the necessary conditions for the relief are met by the trustees. There is no question of any aggregation with similar property owned by a discretionary or other beneficiary.

Exit charges are not levied in certain cases when property leaves the settlement, eg:
(1) Property ceasing to be relevant property within three months of the creation of the trust or of an anniversary charge or within two years of creation (if the trust was set up on death and the conditions in IHTA 1984 s 144(1) are satisfied) is not subject to an exit charge ([**34.25**]).

(2) Property may pass, without attracting an exit charge, to such privileged trusts as employee trusts (IHTA 1984 s 75); maintenance funds for historic buildings (IHTA 1984 Sch 4 para 16); permanent charities (IHTA 1984 s 76(1)); and political parties in accordance with the exemption in IHTA 1984 s 24 (IHTA 1984 s 76(1)(b); and see **Chapter 31**).

If a discretionary fund contains excluded property (and property qualifying for 100% business or agricultural relief) the periodic and exit charges will not apply to that part of the fund. [34.51]–[34.70]

IV DISCRETIONARY TRUSTS CREATED BEFORE 27 MARCH 1974

Discretionary settlements created before 27 March 1974 are subject to special rules for the calculation of tax which generally result in less tax being charged (see generally IHTA 1984 ss 66–68). [34.71]

1 Chargeable events occurring before the first 10-year anniversary

The rate of IHT is set out in IHTA 1984 s 68(6). As the settlement is treated as a separate taxable entity only transfers made by the settlement are cumulated. Such chargeable transfers will either be distribution payments (if made under the regime in force from 1974 to 1982) or chargeable events under IHTA 1984 s 65. Once the cumulative total is known, the rate of tax will be calculated at half rate and the charge will be at 30% of that rate. [34.72]

2 The first anniversary charge

No anniversary charge applied before 1 April 1983. Thus, the first trust to suffer this charge was one created on 1 April 1973 (or 1963; 1953; 1943 and so on).

The amount subject to the charge is calculated in the normal way. In calculating the rate of charge, however, it is only chargeable transfers of the settlement in the preceding ten years that are cumulated (as the settlement predates CTT/IHT the settlor has no chargeable transfers to cumulate). Property in a related settlement and non-relevant property in the settlement are ignored. As before, the rate of charge is reduced if property has not been relevant property throughout the decade preceding the first anniversary. The danger of increasing an IHT bill by an addition of property by the settlor (see [**34.33**]) is even greater with these old trusts. If such an addition has been made, the settlor's chargeable transfers in the seven-year period before the addition must be cumulated in calculating the rate of tax on the anniversary charge (IHTA 1984 s 67(4)). The effective rate of charge for the anniversary charge is (as for new trusts) 30% of the rate calculated according to half the table rates. [34.73]

3 Chargeable events after the first anniversary charge

The position is the same as for new trusts. The charge is based upon the rate charged at the last anniversary. [34.74]–[34.90]

EXAMPLE 34.13

In November 1975 Maggie settled £400,000 on discretionary trusts for her family. The following events have since occurred:

In May 1981: a distribution payment of £100,000.

In May 1984: trustees distribute a further sum of £85,000 (tax borne by beneficiary).

In November 1985: the first 10-year anniversary. The value of relevant property then in the fund is £300,000.

IHT will be charged as follows:

(1) *May 1984*: The distribution is a chargeable event occurring before the first 10-year anniversary. IHT is calculated by cumulating the chargeable transfer of £85,000 with the earlier transfer made by the settlement (the distribution payment of £100,000).(Notice that there is no proportionate reduction in the effective rate for exit charges levied on old discretionary trusts before the first anniversary.)

(2) *November 1985*: The anniversary charge will be calculated on the relevant property in the settlement (£100,000). The cumulative total of transfers made by the settlement is £185,000 (£100,000 plus £85,000).

35 IHT – excluded property and the foreign element

Updated by Sandra Eden, Senior Lecturer, University of Edinburgh

I   Domicile and *situs* [35.3]
II What is excluded property? [35.20]
III Double taxation relief for non-excluded property [35.41]
IV Miscellaneous points [35.61]
V   Foreign settlements, reversionary interests and excluded property [35.81]

1 Ambit of IHT

As a general rule, IHT is chargeable on all property situated within the UK regardless of its owner's domicile and on property, wherever situated, which is beneficially owned by an individual domiciled in the UK. [35.1]

2 Excluded property

Any transfer of 'excluded property' is not chargeable to IHT (IHTA 1984 ss 3(2) and 5(1)). The main example of excluded property is 'property situated outside the UK ... if the person beneficially entitled to it is an individual domiciled outside the UK' (IHTA 1984 s 6(1)). In determining whether property is excluded property, relevant factors include not only the domicile of the transferor who is the beneficial owner of the property and the situation of the property (*situs*), but also the nature of the transferred property, since certain property is excluded regardless of its *situs* or the domicile of its owner. [35.2]

I DOMICILE AND SITUS

1 Domicile

a) *General rules*

An individual cannot, under English or Scots law, be without a domicile which connotes a legal relationship between an individual and a territory. There are three kinds of domicile: domicile of origin, domicile of choice and domicile of dependence.

A person acquires a *domicile of origin* at the moment when he is born. In England, Wales and Northern Ireland, he will usually take the domicile of his father unless he is illegitimate, or born after his father's death, or his parents are not living together and he is living with his mother, in which case he takes the domicile of his mother (Domicile and Matrimonial Proceedings Act 1973 s 4). In Scotland, from 2006, a child is normally domiciled in the same country as his parents, whether married or unmarried, where both are domiciled in the same country, failing which in the country where he has the closest connection (Family Law (Scotland) Act 2006 s 22). A domicile of origin may be superseded by a domicile of dependence or choice, but will revive if the other type of domicile lapses.

A person cannot acquire a *domicile of choice* until he is 16 or marries under that age. Whether someone has replaced his domicile of origin (or dependence) by a domicile of choice is a question of fact which involves physical presence in the country concerned and evidence of a settled intention to remain there permanently or indefinitely (*animus manendi*).

Unmarried infants under the age of 16 may find their domicile of origin changing where their father's domicile changes (in Scotland, where the child's parents' domicile changes) to a *domicile by dependence*. Women who married before 1 January 1974 acquired their husband's domicile by dependence.

[35.3]

b) *Deemed domicile*

If a person's domicile under the general law is outside the UK, he may be deemed to be domiciled in the UK, *for IHT purposes only*, in two circumstances (IHTA 1984 s 267).

First, if a person was domiciled in the UK on or after 10 December 1974 and within the three years immediately preceding the transfer in question, he will be deemed to be domiciled in the UK at the time of making the transfer (IHTA 1984 s 267(1)(a)). This provision is aimed at the taxpayer who moves his property out of the UK and then emigrates to avoid future IHT liability on transfers of that property. In such a case he will have to wait three years from the acquisition of a new domicile of choice for his property to become excluded property under IHTA 1984 s 6(1) (see *Re Clore (No 2)* (1984)).

Second, a person will be deemed domiciled in the UK if he was resident for income tax purposes in the UK on or after 10 December 1974 and in not less than 17 out of the 20 income tax years ending with the income tax year in which he made the relevant transfer (IHTA 1984 s 267(1)(b)). It is expected that this will change to 15 out of the preceding 20 years as provisions to this effect were in the original Finance Bill 2017. These rules catch the person who has lived in the UK for a long time even though he never became domiciled here under the general law. Residence is used in the income tax sense (see **Chapter 18**), and does not require residence for a period of 17 complete years. This is because the Act is concerned with a person who is resident *in a tax year* and such residence may be established with relatively limited presence.

Another tightening up of the rules in the Finance Bill 2017 which fell victim of the 2017 election was the creation of a new category – the 'formerly domiciled resident'. This specifically relates to individuals born in the UK with a UK domicile of origin but who have since acquired a domicile of choice elsewhere. Such individuals, after having been resident in the UK for a certain time, will acquire 'formerly domiciled resident' status. These individuals will be treated as UK domiciled for IHT purposes. A further impact will be in relation to trust property as currently, if the settlor is non-UK domiciled at the time the settlement is made and the property is outside the UK, the property is and remains excluded property, even if the settlor subsequently becomes UK domiciled. The proposed amendments would remove excluded property status of such property during any period during which the settlor is a formerly domiciled resident. [35.4]

EXAMPLE 35.1
(1) Jack who was domiciled in England moved to New Zealand on 1 July 2016 intending to settle there permanently. He died on 1 January 2018 when according to the general law he had acquired a domicile of choice in New Zealand. However, because Jack had a UK domicile and died within three years of losing it, he is deemed under s 267(1)(a) to have died domiciled in the UK. Accordingly, all his property wherever situated (excluding gilts; see below) is potentially chargeable to IHT. Jack would have had to survive until 1 July 2018 to avoid being caught by this provision.
(2) On 5 June 2016, Jim who is domiciled under the general law in Ruritania and who is a director of BB Ltd (the UK subsidiary of a Ruritanian company) gives a house that he owns in Ruritania to his son. By virtue of his job Jim has been resident for income tax purposes in the UK since 1 January 1986, but he intends to return to Ruritania when he retires. For IHT purposes Jim is deemed to be domiciled in the UK under s 267(1)(b); the gift will, therefore, be subject to IHT if Jim dies within seven years.

c) *Election for non-UK domiciled spouse*

A person who is not UK domiciled but who has a UK domiciled spouse may elect to be treated as UK domiciled for most IHT purposes. An election is not only permitted during the lifetime of the UK-domiciled spouse or civil partner, but also after that person's death on or after 6 April 2013. The election must be made within two years of death, but is backdated to immediately before death, thus exempting inter-spousal transfers on death. The date at which the person is to be deemed to be UK domiciled cannot be prior to 6 April 2013, but eventually, it will be possible to elect for a date up to seven years before the election is made.

The downside of the election is that the non-UK domiciled person now has all his or her assets within the scope of UK IHT.

Whilst the election cannot be revoked once made, it automatically ceases if the individual who has made the election is not resident in the UK for income tax purposes for any four successive tax years, beginning after the election (or the death, in the case of a post-death election) (IHTA 1984 s 267ZA). [35.5]

2 Situs

Subject to contrary provisions in double taxation treaties (and special rules for certain property) the *situs* of property is governed by common law rules of England, Scotland and Northern Ireland and depends on the type of property involved. For instance:

(1) An interest in land (including a leasehold estate or rent charge) is situated where the land is physically located.
(2) Chattels (other than ships and aircraft) are situated at the place where they are kept at the relevant time.
(3) Registered shares and securities are situated where they are registered or, if transferable upon more than one register, where they would normally be dealt with in the ordinary course of business.
(4) Bearer shares and securities, transferable by delivery, are situated where the certificate or other document of title is kept.
(5) A bank account (ie the debt owed by the bank) is situated at the branch that maintains the account. (Special rules apply to non-residents' foreign currency bank accounts: [35.26].)
(6) Debts are normally situated in the country in which the borrower resides.

[35.6]–[35.19]

II WHAT IS EXCLUDED PROPERTY?

1 Property situated outside the UK and owned beneficially by a non-UK domiciliary (IHTA 1984 s 6(1))

Property falling into this category is excluded regardless of its nature.

Settled property situated abroad will be excluded property only if the settlor was domiciled outside the UK at the time when he made the settlement (IHTA 1984 s 48(3): note that the position of the interest in possession beneficiary is irrelevant in this case). If the settlor retains an interest in possession either for himself or his spouse, and a discretionary trust arises on the termination of that interest, an additional test is imposed in determining whether property is excluded property. This test looks at where the settlor or the spouse (if the interest was reserved for him) was domiciled when that interest in possession ended (IHTA 1984 s 82). As this provision only applies where the property is *initially* settled with a life interest on the settlor or his spouse, it may be circumvented if the trust commences in discretionary form and is then converted into a life interest.

If a non UK domiciliary establishes a discretionary trust with excluded property under which he can benefit and subsequently acquires a UK domicile, the property remains excluded and the reservation of benefit rules are inapplicable. [35.20]

EXAMPLE 35.2

(1) Franc, domiciled in Belgium, intends to buy a house in East Anglia costing £500,000. If he buys it in his own name it will be subject to IHT on his death. If he buys it through an overseas company, however, he will then own overseas

assets (the company shares) that fall outside the IHT net. Note that if he occupies the house and is a director of the overseas company, HMRC will tax him on an emolument equal to the value of the property each year under the provisions of ITEPA 2003 s 102 (see **[8.116]**). This charge will also arise if Franc is a shadow director of the company: see *R v Allen*; *R v Dimsey* (2001). Note also that it will be subject to the annual tax on enveloped dwellings (see **[49.86]**).

The Finance Bill 2017 contained provisions to bring UK residential property owned indirectly by a non-domicile into the IHT net, so that owning property through an overseas company or partnership will no longer have the desired effect. These were dropped but are expected to re-emerge. Depending on transitional arrangements, the shares owned by Franc will no longer be excluded property under the 2017 provisions to the extent that their value is represented by UK residential property.

HMRC has confirmed that where a UK-resident individual is provided with rent-free accommodation by an overseas resident company and that company is for the purposes of the transfer pricing legislation (TIOA 2010 Part 4 – see **[41.44]**) under the control of the UK-resident individual, it will not be their practice to impute rental income to the overseas resident company (see *Tax Bulletin*, April 2000, p 742).

(2)   Erik, domiciled in Sweden, settles Swedish property on discretionary trusts for himself and his family. He subsequently acquires an English domicile of choice. Although it might appear, because of the reservation of benefit rules, that he may be treated as owning the property in the trust in the event of his death, this is not the case as a result of FA 1986 s 102(3). The settlement remains excluded property for IHT purposes as FA 1986 s 102(3) only applies to property immediately before death. However, should Erik become excluded from all benefit during his life, a deemed PET would then occur under s 102(4) (IHTM 14396). Again, legislation is expected which will mean that excluded property trusts may change status where they were set up by someone who was not at that time UK domiciled but who had a UK domicile of origin and who reacquires UK domicile status.

(3)   Boris, domiciled in France, died in February 2016 and left his villa in Tuscany and moneys in his Swiss bank account to his son Gaspard, a UK resident and domiciliary. By a variation of the terms of his will made within two years of Boris' death the property is settled on discretionary Liechtenstein trusts for the benefit of Gaspard's family. *For IHT*, reading back ensures that the settlement is of excluded property. *For CGT*, however, although the variation is not itself a disposal, Gaspard is treated as the settlor of the trust and hence the provisions in TCGA 1992 s 86 will apply (see **[27A.90]** and *Marshall v Kerr* (1994)).

2   Property that is exempt despite being situated in the UK

a)   *Government securities*

Certain Government securities (gilts) owned by a person resident outside the UK are exempt from IHT (IHTA 1984 s 6(2): see **[18.77]** – FOTRA securities). The domicile of the taxpayer is irrelevant. If these securities are settled they will be excluded property if either the person beneficially entitled to an interest in possession (eg a life tenant) is not resident in the UK, or, in the case of a discretionary trust, if none of the beneficiaries are resident in the UK (IHTA 1984 s 48(4)).

IHTA 1984 s 48(5) contains anti-avoidance provisions:
(1) If gilts are transferred from one settlement to another they will only be excluded property if the beneficiaries of *both* settlements are non-UK resident. This prevents gilts from being channelled from a discretionary trust where they were not excluded property (because some of the beneficiaries were UK ordinarily resident) to a new settlement with non-ordinarily resident beneficiaries only, where they would be excluded property (as was done in *Minden Trust (Cayman) Ltd v IRC* (1984)).
(2) When a close company is a beneficiary of a trust, any gilts owned by the trust will be excluded property only if all participators in the company are non-UK resident, irrespective of the company's residence. This aims to prevent individuals from using a company to avoid IHT. [**35.21**]

b) *Holdings in an authorised unit trust and shares in an open ended investment company*

These securities are excluded property if the person beneficially entitled is an individual domiciled outside the UK (IHTA 1984 s 6(1A) inserted by FA 2003). If held in a settlement these assets will be excluded property unless the settlor was domiciled in the UK at the time when the settlement was made (IHTA 1984 s 48(3A) inserted by FA 2003). [**35.22**]

c) *Certain property owned by persons domiciled in the Channel Islands or Isle of Man*

Certain savings (eg national savings certificates) are excluded property if they are in the beneficial ownership of a person domiciled and resident in the Channel Islands or the Isle of Man (IHTA 1984 ss 6(3), 267(4)). [**35.23**]

d) *Visiting forces*

Certain property owned in the UK by visiting forces and staff of allied headquarters is excluded property (IHTA 1984 s 155). [**35.24**]

e) *Overseas pensions*

Certain overseas pensions (usually payable by ex-colonial governments) are exempt from IHT on the pensioner's death regardless of his domicile (IHTA 1984 s 153). [**35.25**]

f) *Non-sterling bank accounts*

On the death of an individual domiciled and resident outside the UK there is no IHT charge on the balance in any 'qualifying foreign currency account' (IHTA 1984 s 157). This exemption does not apply to *inter vivos* gifts of the money in such an account.

For the inter-relationship of excluded property and settlements, see [**35.81**].
[**35.26**]–[**35.40**]

III DOUBLE TAXATION RELIEF FOR NON-EXCLUDED PROPERTY

Non-excluded property may be exposed to a double charge to tax (especially on the death of the owner); once to IHT in the UK and again to a similar tax imposed by a foreign country. Relief against such double charge may be afforded in one of two ways.

First, the UK may have a double taxation treaty with the relevant country when the position is governed by IHTA 1984 s 158. The provisions of the treaty will override all the relevant IHT legislation (eg the deemed domicile rule) and common law rules regarding the *situs* of property.

Under these treaties, the country in which the transferor is domiciled is generally entitled to tax all property of which he was the beneficial owner. The other country involved usually has the right to tax some of that property, eg land situated there. In such cases the country of domicile will give relief against the resulting double taxation. Most of these treaties also contain provisions to catch the individual who changes his domicile shortly before death to avoid tax.

Second, where no double tax treaty exists, unilateral relief is given in the form of a credit for the foreign tax liability against IHT payable in the UK (IHTA 1984 s 159). The amount of the credit depends on where the relevant property is situated; in some cases no credit is available if the overseas tax is not similar to IHT, although some relief is, effectively, given since, in calculating the reduction in the transferor's estate for calculating IHT, the amount of overseas tax paid will be disregarded (IHTA 1984 s 5(3)). This relief is less beneficial than a tax credit.   [35.41]–[35.60]

IV MISCELLANEOUS POINTS

1 Valuation of the estate – allowable deductions

Certain liabilities of a transferor are deductible when calculating the value of his estate for IHT purposes (see [30.13]), although there are limitations as to how far this is permitted and often these limitations relate to property situated outside the UK or relate to individuals outside the UK.

Any liability of a non-UK resident is deductible as far as possible from a transferor's foreign estate before his UK estate unless the liability has to be discharged in the UK (IHTA 1984 s 162(5)). This applies irrespective of the domicile of the transferor although it is more likely that a foreign domiciliary who is chargeable to IHT on his UK assets will have incurred liabilities to a non-UK lender. However, the general rule that a liability which is an encumbrance on property is taken to reduce the value of that property continues to apply to property situated outside the UK subject to the anti-avoidance rules introduced in 2013. These provisions were introduced to restrict the deductibility of debts incurred to acquire, maintain or enhance excluded property (IHTA 1984 s 162A). This will primarily affect foreign domiciliaries. A loophole was spotted in relation to liabilities incurred to place money in bank accounts in foreign currency in 2014. Such bank accounts are generally 'left out of account' in valuing the estate of a deceased who was not UK resident or domiciled but are not technically 'excluded property'. It would have been possible to circumvent the 2013 rules by borrowing money to place it in a foreign currency account but this route has been closed by IHTA 1984 s 162AA. [35.61]

EXAMPLE 35.3
Adolphus dies domiciled in Ethiopia. His estate includes sterling in a London bank account, shares in UK companies and a house in Weybridge that is mortgaged to an Ethiopian bank. He owes a UK travel company £500 for a ticket bought to enable his daughter to travel around Texas and £200,000 to a Dallas horse dealer. IHT is chargeable on his UK assets. However, the mortgage debt is deductible from the value of his house (as it is property in the UK) and £500 is deductible from the UK estate generally. There is no reduction for the debt of £200,000 assuming that he has sufficient foreign property.

2 Expenses of administering property abroad (IHTA 1984 s 173)

Administration expenses are not generally deductible from the value of the deceased's estate. However, the expense of administering or realising property situated abroad on death is deductible from the value of the relevant property up to a limit of 5% of its value. [35.62]

3 Enforcement of tax abroad

On the death of a foreign domiciliary with UK assets, the deceased's PRs cannot administer his property until they have paid any IHT and obtained a grant of probate. However, the collection of IHT on lifetime transfers by a foreign domiciliary presents a problem if both the transferor and transferee are resident outside the UK and there is no available property in the UK that can be impounded. [35.63]

4 Foreign assets

If a foreign Government imposes restrictions as a result of which UK executors cannot immediately transfer to this country sufficient of the deceased's foreign assets for the payment of IHT attributable to them, they are given the option of deferring payment until that transfer can be made. If the amount that is finally brought into the UK is less than the IHT, any balance will be waived (see ESC F6). [35.64]–[35.80]

V FOREIGN SETTLEMENTS, REVERSIONARY INTERESTS AND EXCLUDED PROPERTY

1 Foreign settlements

As a general rule, settled property which is situated abroad is excluded property if the settlor was domiciled outside the UK when the settlement was made (IHTA 1984 s 48(3)). Therefore, the domicile of the individual beneficiaries in such cases is irrelevant, so that even if the beneficiary is domiciled in the UK, there will be no charge to IHT on the termination of his interest in possession nor on any payment made to him from a discretionary trust. As noted at [**35.4**], this is likely to be changed by future legislation in the event that the settlor subsequently acquires a UK domicile. [**35.81**]

EXAMPLE 35.4

Generous, domiciled in the USA, settles shares in US companies on his nephew, Tom, for life. Tom is domiciled and resident in the UK. The property is excluded property, being property situated abroad settled by a settlor domiciled at that time outside the UK, so that there will be no charge to IHT on the ending of Tom's life interest.

If, however, those shares were exchanged for shares in UK companies, the property would no longer be excluded and there would be a charge to IHT on the termination of Tom's life interest.

If Generous had settled those same US shares on discretionary trusts for his nephews, all of whom were UK domiciled, the property would be, for the same reason, excluded property, so that the normal discretionary trust charges would not apply.

2 Reversionary interests

a) *Definition*

For IHT purposes any future interest in settled property is classified as a reversionary interest (IHTA 1984 s 47). The term, therefore, includes an interest dependent on the termination of an interest in possession, whether that interest is vested or contingent. A contingent interest where the settlement does not have an interest in possession is also a reversionary interest for IHT purposes.

EXAMPLE 35.5

Property is settled on the following trusts:
(1) A for life, remainder to B for life, remainder to C. B and C both have reversionary interests for IHT purposes.
(2) A for life, remainder to B for life, remainder to C if he survives B. C's contingent remainder is a reversionary interest for IHT purposes.
(3) To A absolutely contingent upon his attaining the age of 21. A is currently aged six and has a reversionary interest for IHT purposes.

The interest of a discretionary beneficiary is not, however, a 'reversionary interest', being in no sense a future interest. Such a beneficiary has certain present rights, particularly the right to be considered by the trustees when they exercise their discretion and the right to compel due administration of the fund. The value of such an interest is likely to be nil, however, since the beneficiary has no right to any of the income or capital of the settlement. He has merely a hope (*spes*). [**35.82**]

b) *'Situs' of a reversionary interest*

A reversionary interest under a trust for sale is a *chose in action* rather than an interest in the specific settled assets be they land or personalty (*Re Smyth, Leach v Leach* (1898)). In other cases the position is unclear; but by analogy with estate duty principles it will be a *chose in action* if the settled assets are personalty; but an interest in the settled assets themselves if they are land. Since a *chose in action* is normally situated in the country in which it is recoverable (*New York Life Insurance Co v Public Trustee* (1924)), in some cases the reversionary interest will not be situated in the same place as the settled assets. [35.83]

c) *Reversionary interests – the general rule*

A reversionary interest is excluded property for IHT (IHTA 1984 s 48(1); see [33.61]) with three exceptions designed to counter tax avoidance:
(1) Where it was purchased for money or money's worth.

EXAMPLE 35.6

There is a settlement on A for life, remainder to B. B sells his interest to X who gives it to his brother Y. X has made a transfer of value (a PET) of a reversionary interest (which can be valued by taking into account the value of the settled fund and the life expectancy of A).

(2) Where it is an interest to which the settlor or his spouse is beneficially entitled.
(3) Where a lease for life or lives is granted for no or partial consideration, there is a settlement for IHT (IHTA 1984 s 43(3)) and the lessor's interest is a reversionary interest (IHTA 1984 s 47). Such a reversionary interest is only excluded property to the extent that the lessor did not receive full consideration on the grant (see IHTA 1984 s 48(1)(c) for valuation of the lessee's interest in possession and IHTA 1984 s 170 for the valuation of the lessor's interest). [35.84]

EXAMPLE 35.7

L grants a lease of property worth £30,000 to T for £10,000 for T's life. T is treated for IHT purposes, as having an interest in possession and, therefore, as absolute owner of two-thirds of the property (£30,000 – £10,000). L is treated as the owner of one-third of the property (because he received £10,000). Therefore, one-third of his reversionary interest is not excluded property.

d) *Reversionary interests – the foreign element*

Under IHTA 1984 s 48(1) a reversionary interest (with the three exceptions above) is excluded property regardless of the domicile of the settlor or reversioner or the *situs* of the interest. Where the settled property is in the UK, but the reversionary interest is situated abroad (see [35.83]) and beneficially owned by a foreign domiciliary, the interest probably is excluded property in all cases under the general rule of IHTA 1984 s 6(1).

Foreign settlements, reversionary interests and excluded property 1087

However, the status of a reversionary interest in settled property situated outside the UK is cast into some doubt by virtue of IHTA 1984 s 48(3) to which s 6(1) is expressly made subject (IHTA 1984 s 48(3)(b)). Section 48(3) states:

'where property comprised in a settlement is situated outside the UK
(a) the property (but not a reversionary interest in the property) is excluded property unless the settlor was domiciled in the UK at the time the settlement was made; and
(b) section 6(1) above applies to a reversionary interest in the property, but does not otherwise apply in relation to the property.'

This provision appears to exclude the operation of s 48(1) by saying that a reversionary interest in settled property situated abroad is only excluded property (under the general rule in s 6(1)) if it is itself situated abroad and owned by a foreign domiciliary.

However, it is thought that s 48(3) only prevails over s 48(1) in cases of conflict and that there is no conflict here since the words 'but not a reversionary interest' in s 48(3)(a) mean that whether a reversionary interest is excluded property depends not on the *situs* of the settled property nor on the settlor's domicile, but on the general rule in s 48(1).

In summary, therefore, a reversionary interest is always excluded property regardless of *situs* or domicile with four exceptions (see **[33.62]**). Even if the interest falls within one of the exceptions, it will still be excluded property if the interest (regardless of the whereabouts of the settled property) is situated outside the UK and beneficially owned by a foreign domiciliary (IHTA 1984 s 6(1)); or if the reversionary interest is itself settled property, is situated abroad and was settled by a foreign domiciliary (IHTA 1984 s 6(1) and s 48(3)). **[35.85]**

36 Relief against double charges to IHT

Updated by Sandra Eden, Senior Lecturer, University of Edinburgh

I   Case 1 – Mutual Transfers [**36.2**]
II   Case 2 – Gifts with a reservation and subsequent death [**36.3**]
III   Case 3 – Artificial debts and death [**36.4**]
IV   Case 4 – Chargeable transfers and death [**36.5**]

The risk of a double charge to IHT arises in a number of situations and FA 1986 s 104 enabled the Board to make regulations to give relief to taxpayers in certain cases. The Regulations were made on 30 June 1987 and came into force on 22 July 1987, although the relief is given for transfers of value made, and other events occurring on or after 18 March 1986 (Inheritance Tax (Double Charges Relief) Regulations 1987, SI 1987/1130). All the examples in this chapter are based on illustrations given in the Regulations themselves. It is assumed that current IHT rates apply throughout; grossing-up does not apply to lifetime transfers; and that no exemptions or reliefs are available.   [**36.1**]

I   CASE 1 – MUTUAL TRANSFERS

The first case, in reg 4, is concerned with the area of mutual transfers, ie where property is transferred (by a PET which becomes chargeable) but at the death of the donor he has received back property from his donee (either the original property or property which represents it) which is included in the donor's death estate. The position is illustrated in the following example.

EXAMPLE 36.1

July 2013	A makes a gift of a Matthew Smith oil painting (value £100,000) to B (a PET)	
July 2014	A makes a gift into a discretionary trust of £350,000	IHT paid £5,000
Jan 2015	A makes a further gift into the same trust of £30,000	IHT paid £6,000
Jan 2016	B dies and the Smith picture returns to A	
Apr 2017	A dies. His death estate of £400,000 includes the picture returned to him in 2016 which is still worth £100,000	

If no relief were available, A in *Example 36.1* would be subject to IHT on the value of the picture twice: once when it was given away in 2013 (the chargeable PET) and a second time on its value in 2017 (as part of his death estate). In addition A's cumulative total would be increased by the 2013 PET, thereby necessitating a recalculation of the tax charged on the 2014 and 2015 transfers and resulting in a higher charge on his death estate.

Regulation 4 affords relief in this situation and provides for two alternative IHT calculations to be made and for the higher amount of tax produced by those calculations to be payable. The alternative calculations may be illustrated as follows:

EXAMPLE 36.1 CONTINUED

First calculation:
Charge the picture as part of A's death estate and ignore the 2013 PET:

July 2013	PET £100,000 ignored	Tax nil	
July 2014	Gift £350,000: tax £10,000	Tax payable =	£5,000
	Less: £5,000 already paid		
Jan 2015	Gift £30,000: tax £12,000	Tax payable =	£6,000
	Less: £6,000 already paid		
Apr 2017	Death estate £400,000	Tax payable =	£160,000
Total tax due as result of A's death			£171,000

(*Note:* because the 2013 PET is ignored A's cumulative total is unaltered and a recalculation of tax on the 2014 and 2015 transfers is unnecessary.)

Second calculation:
Charge the 2013 PET and ignore the value of the picture on A's death

		Tax
July 2013	PET £100,000:	£nil
July 2014	Gift £350,000: tax £50,000	£45,000
	Less: £5,000 already paid	
Jan 2015	Gift £30,000: tax £12,000	£6,000
	Less: £6,000 already paid	
Apr 2017	Death estate £300,000	£120,000
Total tax due as result of A's death		£171,000

Tax payable: The tax payable is equal in amount under the two calculations: see *Example 36.3* below.

It may be that reg 4 is capable of being exploited to the benefit of the taxpayer as can be seen from the following illustration. Assume that Adam gives property worth £100,000 to his daughter Berta in 2013 and buys the property back for £75,000 (which represents less than full consideration) in 2014. He then dies in 2017. Under reg 4 the value of the property (£100,000) will remain subject to IHT but Adam's estate has been reduced by the £75,000 paid for the property (see especially reg 4(3)(a)). **[36.2]**

II CASE 2 – GIFTS WITH A RESERVATION AND SUBSEQUENT DEATH

This case covers the situation where a gift with a reservation (either immediately chargeable or a chargeable PET) is followed by the death of the donor at a time when he still enjoys a reserved benefit or within seven years of that benefit ceasing (ie within seven years of the deemed PET). The situation is illustrated in *Example 36.2*.

EXAMPLE 36.2

		Tax
Jan 2011	A makes a PET of £150,000 to B	
Mar 2015	A makes a gift of a house worth £375,000 into a discretionary trust but continues to live in the property. The gift is of property subject to a reservation	£10,000
Feb 2018	A dies still living in the house. His death estate is valued at £525,000 including the house which is then worth £400,000	

Regulation 5 prevents double taxation of the house in this example by providing for two separate IHT calculations to be made as follows: [36.3]

EXAMPLE 36.2 CONTINUED

First calculation:
Charge the house as part of A's death estate and ignore the gift with reservation in 2015

		Tax
Jan 2011	PET (now exempt)	Nil
Mar 2015	Gift with reservation ignored	Nil
Feb 2018	Death estate £525,000: tax £80,000	
	Less: £10,000 already paid	£70,000
	Total tax due as a result of A's death	£70,000

(*Note:* credit for tax already paid on the gift with reservation cannot exceed the amount of death tax attributable to that property. In this example the tax so attributable is £62,500 (ie £80,000 × £400,000/£512,000) – hence credit is given for the full amount of £10,000.)

Second calculation:
The gift with reservation is charged and the value of the gifted property is ignored in taxing the death estate:

		Tax
Jan 2011	PET (now exempt)	Nil
Mar 2015	Gift of house £375,000: tax £20,000	£10,000
	Less: £10,000 already paid	
Feb 2018	Death estate £125,000 (ignoring house)	£50,000
Total tax due as result of A's death:		£60,000

Tax payable: the first calculation yields a higher amount of tax. Therefore the gift of the house in 2015 is ignored and tax on death is charged as in the first calculation giving credit for IHT already paid.

III CASE 3 – ARTIFICIAL DEBTS AND DEATH

Relief is afforded under reg 6 when a chargeable transfer (or chargeable PET) is followed by the transferor incurring a liability to his transferee which falls within FA 1986 s 103 (the artificial debt rules).

EXAMPLE 36.3

Nov 2011	X makes a PET of cash (£100,000) to Y
Dec 2011	Y makes a loan to X of £100,000
May 2012	X makes a gift into a discretionary trust of £20,000 (chargeable transfer)
Apr 2017	X dies. His death estate is worth £320,000 but the loan from Y remains outstanding

Under s 103 the deduction of £100,000 would be disallowed so that the 2011 PET and the disallowed debt would both attract an IHT charge. Relief is provided, however, under reg 6 on the basis of the following alternative calculations: [36.4]

EXAMPLE 36.3 CONTINUED

First calculation:
Ignore the 2011 gift but do not allow the debt to be deducted in the death estate:

		Tax
Nov 2011	PET ignored	Nil
May 2012	CT £20,000	Nil
Apr 2017	Death estate £320,000	£6,000
Total tax due as result of X's death		£6,000

Second calculation:
Charge the 2011 gift but allow the debt to be deducted from the estate at death.

		Tax
Nov 2011	PET £100,000	Nil
May 2012	CT £20,000	Nil
Apr 2017	Death estate (£320,000 – loan of £100,000)	£6,000
Total tax due as result of X's death		£6,000

Tax payable: The total tax chargeable is equal in amount under the two calculations and reg 8 provides that in such cases the first calculation shall be treated as producing a higher amount: accordingly the debt is disallowed against the death estate and the PET of £100,000 is not charged. Although the amount of tax paid is the same, the liability for the tax can be different, depending on whether the value is in the lifetime gift or the estate on death – see [29.146].

IV CASE 4 – CHARGEABLE TRANSFERS AND DEATH

Under FA 1986 s 104(1)(d) regulations can be made to prevent a double charge to IHT in circumstances 'similar' to those dealt with in the first three cases above.

Regulation 7, made in pursuance of this power, applies when an individual makes a chargeable transfer of value to a *person* after 17 March 1986, and dies within seven years of that transfer, at a time when he was beneficially entitled to property which either directly or indirectly represented the property which had been transferred by the original chargeable transfer.

For relief to be given under this regulation it is important to realise that the lifetime transfer must have been chargeable when made. Prior to the changes made by FA 2006, the majority of transfers to individuals would not have fallen within its ambit since they would have been PETs. Since that is no longer the case, the regulation may now be of increased significance and will be of importance in the following cases:

(1) When the chargeable transfer is to a discretionary trust which subsequently returns all or part of the property to settlor.
(2) When the chargeable transfer creates a beneficial interest in favour of the settlor.
(3) When the chargeable transfer is to a company with, again, that property being returned to the transferor.

As with the other cases, relief under reg 7 is given on the basis of two alternative calculations. The first includes the returned property in the death estate but ignores the original chargeable transfer (although there is no question of any refund of tax paid at that time). The second calculation taxes the original chargeable transfer (ie it may be subject to a supplementary charge on death and remains in the taxpayer's cumulative total) but ignores the returned property in taxing the transferor's death estate. [36.5]

Section 5 VAT

Chapters
37 VAT – the foundations
38 VAT – UK provisions
39 VAT on property
40 Practical application of VAT

37 VAT – the foundations

Hartley Foster, Partner, Fieldfisher LLP

I   Taxation of value added [37.1]
II Introduction of value added tax [37.2]
III The Single Market [37.3]
IV EU Member States [37.4]
V   The Recast Directive (Council Directive 2006/112) [37.5]
VI The future of VAT in Europe [37.9]
VII The future of VAT in the UK [37.11]

I TAXATION OF VALUE ADDED

Value added tax (VAT) is a means of collecting revenue for governments. It is, in economic terms, intended to be a tax on the value added by traders to the purchases of all raw materials, goods and services prior to resale.

The four basic elements that can be used in the calculation of 'value added' are:
(1) profit;
(2) wages and salaries;
(3) inputs (ie purchases of raw materials, goods and services); and
(4) outputs (ie sales).

Value added can be calculated by either the additive method (value added = profit + wages and salaries) or the subtractive method (value added = outputs – inputs).

In addition, tax on value added can be operated on either a direct or an indirect basis. The direct (or accounts) method uses businesses' profit and loss accounts as a basis of calculation and represents a combination of a corporation profits tax and a payroll tax borne by the trader. The indirect (or invoice) method gives rise to a tax charge on individual sales; it is a tax on consumer expenditure.

The method used in the European Union (EU) is the indirect subtractive approach. The basic principle of the common system of value added tax in the EU is to apply to goods and services a general tax on consumption that is exactly proportional to the price of those goods or services, whatever the number of transactions that take place in the production and distribution process before the stage at which tax is charged. On each transaction, VAT (output tax) (which is calculated on the price of the goods or services at the rate applicable to such goods or service) is chargeable after deduction of the amount of VAT (input tax) borne directly by the various cost components, unless specifically prohibited or restricted.

The broad effect is that businesses are not affected economically by the imposition of VAT. VAT is actually borne by the final consumer, and so it should be economically neutral. However, certain transactions are excluded, which can create distortions. [37.1]

II INTRODUCTION OF VALUE ADDED TAX

In 1960, the European Commission appointed a number of working groups to research the possibility of harmonising turnover taxes in the EEC (as it was then known). Following recommendations by the Commission, Member States were required by the First and Second Directives to introduce a tax on turnover called 'value added tax' in accordance with a common system to replace their present system of turnover taxes. The First Directive (of 11 April 1967) defined the principle of the common system of value added tax and the Second Directive (of the same date) required Member States to establish the structure of the common system of value added tax, and the procedures for applying it. These provisions gave Member States a measure of discretion in relation to specified matters and were subject to transitional provisions.

The implementation of the First and Second Directives was the first stage in the harmonisation of turnover taxes within the EEC. However, the Directives gave Member States such a wide discretion that, as at 1973, nine different and separate systems of national laws existed. The national rules regarding, for example, where and when services were deemed to be provided varied considerably. This resulted in double taxation (or no taxation), which distorted intra-Community trade.

Accordingly, further harmonisation was sought within the EU. On 17 May 1977, the European Council adopted the Sixth VAT Directive (Directive (EEC) 77/388), which set out the structure of the common system of VAT and the procedures for applying it. The Sixth VAT Directive incorporated the basic structure and procedures previously set out in the Second VAT Directive, which ceased to have effect in each Member State from the date on which the provisions of the Sixth VAT Directive were brought into application.

The uniform basis of assessment was provided by:
(1) clarifying the transactions chargeable to tax;
(2) extending the tax base for services;
(3) extending the tax to retail transactions;
(4) abolishing certain derogations previously allowed under the Second Directive;
(5) providing common exemptions; and
(6) making provision for special schemes in respect of small undertakings, farmers and used goods.

Member States were permitted to retain taxes, duties or charges that cannot be characterised as turnover taxes (see *Rousseau-Wilmot SA v Caisse de Compensation de l'Organisation Autonome Nationale de l'Industrie et du Commerce (Organic)* (Case 295/84) (1986)). Also, Member States were permitted to derogate from the directive unilaterally in accordance with a consultation procedure or by decision of the Council.

What is now Art 113 of the Consolidated Version of The Treaty on the Functioning of the European Union (which replaced Art 93 TEC) sets out the basis for the EU's approach towards harmonisation of indirect taxation. It provides:

> 'The Council shall, acting unanimously in accordance with a special legislative procedure and after consulting the European Parliament and the Economic and Social Committee, adopt provisions for the harmonisation of legislation concerning turnover taxes, excise duties and other forms of indirect taxation to the extent that such harmonisation is necessary to ensure the establishment and the functioning of the internal market and to avoid the distortion of competition.' [37.2]

III THE SINGLE MARKET

Completing the internal market became a political priority in the early 1980s. The Commission set out its views of the measures on value added tax that were necessary in order to complete the internal market in a White Paper on 14 July 1985 and a Global Communication of 5 August 1987. The Commission proposed that the origin system be introduced in relation to supplies between Member States. This would involve charging VAT in, and at the rate applicable in, the country of origin of the goods and services. Input tax would be recovered from the tax authorities of the Member States of the customers. A central EC clearing house system would reallocate VAT revenues between Member States to compensate those that would lose revenue. For this system to work effectively, rates of VAT would need to be approximated throughout the EC. For this reason (and others), the Commission's proposals were not accepted by the Member States. As can be seen since the financial crash of 2008, Member States have used rates of VAT for fiscal and economic management purposes.

The VAT system adopted was a compromise and was intended to be transitional. In so far as business-to-business supplies of goods are concerned, the VAT system remains based on a destination, rather than an origin, system of taxation. The transitional regime was intended to apply until whichever was the later of 31 December 1996 and the date that a definitive system (based on the origin system) was introduced. However, there is still no agreement as to the definitive origin system and no date for the ending of the 'transitional regime' is anticipated any time soon. Moreover, in practice, the VAT system, over recent years, has largely moved away from the origin system.

On 1 January 1993, the text of the Sixth VAT Directive was substantially amended to provide for the introduction of the Single Market. The import procedures for the movement of goods between Member States that were in force before 1 January 1993 were abolished and the provisions with respect to imports and exports were restricted to movements of goods to and from a place outside Member States.

The operation of VAT on supplies of goods between Member States is based on:
(1) zero-rating by the supplier of intra-EU supplies of goods to a registered business customer in another Member State and the self accounting

for VAT by the registered business customer on the acquisition of such goods at the rate applicable in the Member State of destination (eg a UK supplier supplies goods to a French VAT registered entity, the UK supplier will zero-rate the supply of goods from the UK to France. The French customer will then self account (under what is termed 'the reverse charge' mechanism) for French VAT on the value of the acquisition at the relevant VAT rate applicable in France); and
(2) the charging of VAT on intra-EU supplies of goods to non-VAT registered persons by the supplier in the country from which they are supplied (eg a UK supplier of goods to a French non-registered person will charge UK VAT on the value of the supply). This is subject to exceptions that prevent distortions that might otherwise arise from cross-border shopping.

Special rules apply to supplies of goods made by an entity in one Member State to non-VAT registered persons (ie individuals, charities, public bodies and fully exempt businesses) in another Member State where the value of such 'distance sales' supplies exceeds what is termed the 'distance selling threshold' applied in the consumer's Member State. This typically occurs when a consumer purchases goods via mail order or over the internet. Each Member State has the option of applying a distance selling threshold of €35,000 or €100,000 (or its own currency equivalent) per calendar year. The UK's annual threshold is £70,000. Once the distance selling threshold is exceeded, the place of supply becomes the consumer's Member State and so the supplier is required to register and account for VAT in that Member State.

Businesses are required to submit regular statistical returns, such as intra-EU sales lists and Intrastats. Since statistical information relating to intra-EU movements is no longer available from official import/export documentation (as this documentation no longer exists) larger traders must also submit regular statistical declarations.

For reasons of clarity and rationalisation, the Sixth VAT Directive was recast by Council Directive 2006/112 EC of 28 November 2006 ('the Recast Directive'). The Recast Directive repeals a number of VAT Directives and consolidates the European legislation in this area. The Recast Directive has not brought about any material changes to the existing legislation; it has rearranged the structure and contents of the Sixth VAT Directive. All references to Articles below, unless otherwise stated, are to Articles in the Recast Directive. Ultimately, the domestic UK VAT legislation must be interpreted by reference to the Recast Directive. [37.3]

IV EU MEMBER STATES

In accordance with VAT Notice 725 (January 2014), the VAT territory of the EU consists of:
- Austria
- Belgium
- Bulgaria
- Croatia
- Cyprus
- Czech Republic

- Denmark (excluding the Faroe Islands and Greenland)
- Estonia
- Finland (excluding the Aland Islands)
- France (including Monaco but excluding Martinique, French Guiana, Guadeloupe, Reunion and St Pierre and Miquelon)
- Germany (excluding Busingen and the Isle of Heligoland)
- Greece excluding Mount Athos (Agion Oros)
- Hungary
- Ireland
- Italy (excluding the communes of Livigno and Campione d'Italia and the Italian waters of Lake Lugano)
- Latvia
- Lithuania
- Luxembourg
- Malta
- The Netherlands (excluding the Netherlands Antilles)
- Poland
- Portugal (including the Azores and Madeira)
- Romania
- Slovakia
- Slovenia
- Spain (including the Balearic Islands but not Canary Islands, Ceuta or Melilla)
- Sweden
- United Kingdom (including the Isle of Man but not the Channel Islands or Gibraltar) (although see VII below).

The UK comprises England, Scotland and Wales (which together constitute Great Britain) and Northern Ireland. In the VAT legislation, references to 'the UK' include the territorial sea of the UK. The VAT legislation has effect as if the Isle of Man, but not the Channel Islands, was part of the UK. This deeming provision is subject to any contrary provisions of specified legislation. Following the enactment of the European Union Notification of Withdrawal Act 2017, the Prime Minister sent a notification of the UK's withdrawal from the EU to the European Council President on 29 March 2017. As a matter of international law, the UK remains subject to its treaty obligations and EU law until 29 March 2019. [37.4]

V THE RECAST DIRECTIVE (COUNCIL DIRECTIVE 2006/112)

As noted above, the Sixth VAT Directive (the predecessor to the Recast Directive) had the objective of making progress towards a common system of VAT and it required Member States to comply with its terms by 1 January 1978. Variation from the general rules is possible where the language of the Directive is permissive rather than mandatory or where Member States are granted a specific derogation (see arts 370–390 of the Recast Directive).

Transitional rules were introduced by Directive (EEC) 91/680 with the advent of the Single Market in 1993 and the Sixth Directive was recast by the Recast Directive of 28 November 2006. In broad outline, and subject to the transitional provisions, the structure and content of the Recast Directive is as follows:

Title I	Article 1	Introductory	
	Articles 2–4	Subject Matter and Scope of tax	The common system of VAT is to apply, broadly, to the 'supply' (see [37.6]) of all goods (refer Article 14) and services (refer Article 24) for 'consideration' (see [37.7]) throughout the Member States and for the importation of goods.
			Article 2(1)(a) of the Recast Directive effectively excludes from the scope of the tax any person who habitually provides services free of charge (*Staatssecretaris van Financiën v Hong Kong Trade Development Council*, Case 89/81).
Title II	Articles 5–8	Territorial Scope	These articles set out the territories in which the Recast Directive applies.
Title III	Articles 9–13	Taxable persons	A taxable person is defined as any person who independently carries out in any place any 'economic activity', whatever the purpose or results of that activity. Specific circumstances are also considered and various matters are left to the discretion of each Member State.
			A person undertaking acts preparatory to the carrying on of an economic activity qualifies as a 'taxable person' (*DA Rompelman & EA Rompelman-van-Deelen v Minister van Financiën*, (Case 268/83).
Title IV		Taxable transactions	
Chapter 1	Articles 14–19	Supply of Goods	A supply of goods is defined as the transfer of the right to dispose of tangible property as owner. Further elaboration as to what constitutes a supply of goods is set out in the subsequent Articles up to Article 19.
			The CJEU has held that the production of goods from materials supplied by customers only took place where the contractor produced a new article, ie one the function of which was different from that of the materials provided. Repairs, however extensive, did not amount to the supply of goods (*Van Dijk's Boekhuis BV v Staatssecretaris van Financiën*, Case 139/84).

Chapter 2	Articles 20–23	Intra-Community Acquisition of goods	An intra-Community acquisition of goods is defined as the acquisition by a person of the right to dispose as owner of movable tangible property that has been dispatched or transported to them and the goods are acquired by that person in a Member State other than that in which the dispatch or transport of the goods began.
Chapter 3	Articles 24–29	Supply of Services	A supply of services is defined as any transaction that is not a supply of goods. Transactions that Member States may treat as a supply of services are set out in Article 25 and those that Member States must treat as a supply of services are set out in Article 26.
	Article 30	Importation of Goods	An importation arises when goods which are not in free circulation within the Community enter the Community.
Title V		Place of taxable transactions	
Chapter 1	Articles 31–39	Place of supply of goods	In general terms, where goods are not dispatched or transported, the place of supply is the place where the goods are located when the supply takes place. Where goods are transported, the relevant place of supply is where the goods are located when the transport begins. Where goods come from a third country (non-EU) the place of supply is where the goods are following importation. Derogations can apply in specific scenarios.
			Where goods are supplied on board ships, aircraft or trains during the section of passenger transport operation effected within the Community, then the place of supply is deemed to be at the point of departure of the passenger transport operation.
Chapter 2	Articles 40–42	Place of an intra-Community acquisition of goods	The place of an intra-Community acquisition of goods is deemed to be the place where dispatch or transport of the goods to the person acquiring them ends. There are exceptions.

Chapter 3	Article 43	Place of supply of services (see [**37.8**])	Whether a person is a 'taxable person' determines whether certain place of supply rules apply. A taxable person who also carries out the provision of non-taxable supplies shall be treated as a taxable person in respect of all services rendered to it for these purposes. A non-taxable person who is registered for VAT shall be regarded as being a taxable person. The primary fiscal point of reference for determining the place of supply of services supplied to a taxable person is the place of establishment of the recipient of the services. If the recipient of the services is a non-taxable person, then the place of supply is where the supplier has established his business. Where a supplier has a place of establishment in one Member State and a fixed establishment in another Member State, regard should be had to the establishment from which the service is supplied. Exceptions to the above rule are as follows:
	Article 46		services rendered to a non-taxable person by an intermediary acting in the name and on behalf of another person are supplied 'where the underlying transaction is supplied'
	Article 47		services that are 'connected with immoveable property' are supplied where the property is located;
	Article 48		supplies of passenger transport are treated as made in the place where the transport takes place;
	Article 49		transport of goods services (other than the intra-Community transport of goods) to non-taxable persons are supplied where transport takes place;
	Article 50		the place of supply for intra-Community transport of goods to non-taxable persons is the place of departure of the transport;

	Article 53		certain services (defined by this Article), including cultural, sporting, entertainment or similar activities are supplied where those services are physically carried out;
	Article 55		the place of supply of restaurant and catering services (other than those on board means of passenger transport) is the place 'where the services are physically carried out';
	Article 56		supplies of short-term hiring of a means of transport are supplied 'where the means of transport is actually put at the disposal of the customer'; supplies of long-term hiring to a non-taxable person are supplied at the place where the customer is established;
	Article 57		supplies of restaurant and catering services on board means of passenger transport are treated as supplied at 'the point of departure of the passenger transport operation';
	Article 58		supplies of electronic services to non-taxable people established in a Member State by a taxable person established outside the Community shall be supplied where the non-taxable person is established;
	Article 59		Where the following supplies are made to a (non-taxable) customer outside the EU, the place of supply is where the customer is established: ● transfers and assignments of copyright, patents, licences, trademarks and similar rights; ● advertising; ● services of consultants, engineers, consultancy firms, lawyers, accountants and other similar services, data processing and provision of information; ● acceptance of any obligation to refrain from pursuing or exercising, in whole or part, a business activity or any right referred to in Article 59;

				<ul><li>banking, financial and insurance services;</li><li>provision of access to, and of transport or transmission through, natural gas, and electricity distribution systems and the provision of other directly linked services;</li><li>the supply of staff; and</li><li>hiring out moveable tangible property other than all means of transport.</li></ul>
	Article 59a			This article allows Member States to employ 'effective use and enjoyment' rules within their domestic legislation to prevent double taxation or non-taxation.
				As is evident from the above, it is necessary to identify the nature of the service that is being provided before the place of supply can be ascertained.
				In *RAL (Channel Islands) v Customs & Excise Comrs* (Case C-452/03), the CJEU held that the place of supply of gaming machines installed in amusement arcades established in the territory of a Member State was to be regarded as constituting entertainment or similar activities within the meaning of Art 9(2)(c) (now Article 53) so that the place of supply of those services was where they were physically carried out.
				In *HM Revenue & Customs v Zurich Insurance* (2007) the place of supply rules, in so far as they related to the place of establishment of the customer, were considered by the Court of Appeal.

			Zurich Insurance had its headquarters in Switzerland, and a number of branches worldwide. Zurich Insurance instructed PwCAG, a Swiss management consultancy company, to assist in the installation of a new system. In so far as the installation of the new system into the UK branch was concerned, PwCAG subcontracted this matter to PwCUK. PwCUK invoiced PwCAG, and PwCAG invoiced Zurich Insurance in Switzerland who then recovered the cost from the UK branch. HMRC assessed Zurich Insurance to VAT on the value of the services supplied by PwCAG on the basis that the place of supply of the services was the UK as the customer of the service was established in the UK. The Tribunal held that the place of supply of the service was Switzerland. This was the place where the recipient of the consultancy services was located, and taking all factors into account, the Tribunal considered that the place of contracting was the most important factor. The Court of Appeal, having considered *Berkholz*, *DFDS and RAL* upheld the decision of the High Court and said that, on the facts found by the Tribunal, the only tenable outcome of the proper application of Art 9(2)(e) was the conclusion that the place of supply was the UK. In particular, the Court of Appeal disagreed that the place of contracting was the most important factor and held that greater weight should be given to the place where the services were actually provided.

		Article 59b		Following the changes to the place of supply rules for consumer supplies of telecoms, broadcasting and electronic services (see [**37.7**]), Article 59b was repealed with effect from 1 January 2015.
Chapter 4		Articles 60–61		Imported goods are supplied in the Member State in which the goods are located when they enter the Community.
Title VI		Articles 62–71	Chargeable Event and Chargeability of VAT	Tax is chargeable on the occurrence of a 'chargeable event'. Generally, a chargeable event arises where goods are delivered, services are performed or goods are imported. For completeness, it should be noted that, under the UK VAT legislation, a chargeable event or tax point arises on the earlier of the following: (a) the time the invoice is issued in respect of the supply; or (b) the time that payment is received.
Title VII		Articles 73–79	Taxable amount	In so far as the supply of goods or the supply of services are concerned, the taxable amount includes everything which constitutes the consideration obtained or to be obtained by the supplier in return for the supply from the customer and/or from a third party. The taxable amount does not include price reductions by way of discount for early payment, price discounts or rebates granted to customers.
				In circumstances where a supplier supplied goods to a retailer for less than the normal retail price, and where the retailer undertook to arrange gatherings at which the wholesaler's goods could be sold, the CJEU held that, for the purposes of Article 11A1(a) of the then Sixth VAT Directive (now Article 73 of the Recast Directive), the taxable amount included not only the monetary consideration actually paid by the retailer for the product but also the value of the services

			provided by the retailer in obtaining and rewarding hostesses (being the difference between the normal wholesale price and the amount actually paid by the agents), so that VAT was chargeable on the whole of the normal wholesale price. *Naturally Yours Cosmetics Ltd v C & E Comrs (No 2)* (Case C-230/87).
	Article 85	Importation of goods	In so far as the importation of goods is concerned, the taxable amount is the value for customs purposes. Article 86 elaborates on the factors that should be included in determining the taxable amount of imported goods.
Title VIII	Articles 93–130	Rates	The rate applicable to taxable transactions is that in force at the time of the chargeable event. A minimum standard rate of 15% is specified, with certain optional reduced rates of not less than 5% on a restricted list of products. Derogations are also specified. (The UK now has 13 groups of supplies of goods and services that are liable to VAT at the reduced rate (VATA 1994 Sch 7A) (see **[38.6]**).)
Title IX	Article 132	Exemptions for certain activities in the public interest	This Article sets out the supplies in the public interest which are to be exempt from VAT and includes public postal services, hospital and medical care and the supply of services and of goods closely linked to welfare and social security work. These transactions are referred to in the Recast Directive as 'exempt'. However, in the UK, these transactions are referred to as 'zero-rated' supplies. The difference between an exempt transaction and a zero-rated transaction in UK 'VAT speak' is that any VAT that is directly attributable to an exempt supply is not recoverable whereas that attributable to a 'zero-rated' supply is recoverable.

	Articles 135–166	Exemptions for other activities	Article 135 lists a number of transactions that are exempt from VAT and includes insurance and reinsurance, the granting and negotiation of credit and a number of other financial transactions. There are also provisions permitting Member States to allow taxpayers the option of taxation in cases of letting and leasing of immovable property and certain other land transactions and financial transactions. There are also provisions dealing with reliefs for certain imports, exports and international transport.
Title X	Articles 167–192	Deductions	When deductible tax becomes chargeable, a corresponding right to deduct arises (*Lennartz v Finanzamt München III* (Case C–97/90) (1995)). The general rule is that a taxable person is entitled to deduct VAT where the goods or services on which the VAT was incurred relate to (a) a taxable supply (b) a supply that was 'zero-rated' (as referred to above) or (c) a supply that was a financial supply where the supply is made to a customer outside of the Community. Articles 173–175 set out the circumstances in which partial deductions ('partial recovery') can be made and the means of calculation. Article 176 sets out the restrictions that apply on the right to deduct and Articles 178–192 set out the manner in which adjustments to deductions should be made.
			Conditions for exercising the right to deduct, such as the requirement to hold an invoice relating to the deduction and rules for calculating the deductible proportion, together with adjustments for initial deductions (as in the Capital Goods Scheme, Article 187 – [38.89]–[38.94]), are outlined.

			The CJEU has held that input tax is only deductible under what was Art 17 of the Sixth Directive (now Article 167 of the Recast Directive) if the goods or services in question had a direct and immediate link with taxable transactions *BLP Group plc v C & E Comrs* (Case C-4/94).
Title XI	Articles 193–216	Obligations of Taxable Persons and Certain Non-taxable Persons and Payment Arrangements	The persons who are liable to pay tax to the authorities and matters such as registration requirements, duty to keep records and tax invoices are outlined. The detailed rules for declarations and payments in respect of imports are left to the Member States to determine.
	Articles 217–240	Invoicing	These Articles set out the requirements and formalities for issuing an invoice and the matters that lie within the discretion of Member States in this area. The Articles also set out the formalities that must be complied with where invoices are sent by electronic means.
	Articles 241–280	Accounting and Returns	These Articles set out the requirements for keeping accounts, submitting VAT returns and other formalities.
Title XII	Articles 281–369	Special schemes	These Articles permit certain simplifications to apply when the VAT system applies to small enterprises, a common flat-rate scheme for farmers, a special scheme for travel agents and special arrangements for second-hand goods, works of art, collectors' items and antiques, investment gold and electronically supplied services and for sales by public auction.
Title XIII	Article 370–396	Derogations	Member States may apply to the European Commission for permission to introduce special measures derogating from the provisions of the directive in order to achieve procedural simplifications or prevent tax avoidance.

			The CJEU ruled that Article 27(1) of the Sixth VAT Directive (now Article 395(1) of the Recast Directive) was not confined to situations where there was a deliberate intention to avoid tax, but included business arrangements undertaken for genuine commercial reasons, if the effect of such arrangements was that tax was avoided (*Direct Cosmetics Ltd v C & E Comrs (No 2); Laughtons Photographs Ltd v C & E Comrs* (Joined Cases 138/86 and 139/86)).
Title XIV	Articles 397–414	Miscellaneous	As noted above, the arrangements in place under the Recast Directive are transitional. Article 403 provides that the Council shall adopt Directives appropriate for the purpose of supplementing the common system of VAT and, in particular, for the progressive restriction or the abolition of derogations from that system. Article 404 provides that every four years, starting from the adoption of the Recast Directive, the Commission shall present a report to the European Parliament and to the Council on the operation of the common system of VAT in the Member States and, in particular, on the operation of the transitional arrangements for taxing trade between Member States. That report shall be accompanied, where appropriate, by proposals concerning the definitive arrangements.

[37.5]

1 **'Supply' of goods**

In two Netherlands cases, the CJEU held that the illegal sale of drugs such as amphetamines or hashish was not an 'economic activity' and thus not a 'supply' for VAT purposes. The principle of fiscal neutrality precludes 'a generalised differentiation between lawful and unlawful transactions', and so, in principle, unlawful transactions fall within the scope of the Recast Directive and are subject to VAT, unless the activity has special characteristics that take it completely outside the lawful economic sector. Supplies of narcotic drugs fall outside the scope of the Directive 'because of their very nature, they are subject to a total prohibition on their being put into circulation in all the Member States, with the exception of strictly controlled economic channels for use for medical and scientific purposes'. *Mol v Inspecteur der Invoerrechten en Accijnzen* (Case 269/86); *Vereniging Happy Family Rustenburgerstrat v Inspecteur der Omzetbelasting* (Case 289/86). By contrast, the operation of an unlawful game of roulette falls within the scope of VAT, since it is in competition with lawful gambling activities (see *Optigen Ltd, Fulcrum Electronics Ltd, Bond House Systems Ltd v Commissioners of Customs and Excise* (Joined Cases C-354/03, C-355/03 and C-484/03)).

KapHag Renditefonds v Finanzamt Charlottenburg (Case C-442/01) concerned a German partnership that admitted a new partner. The CJEU held that no supply was being made under Art 2(1) of the Sixth Directive, by either the individual partners or the partnership to the incoming partner in return for the capital contribution. [37.6]

2 'Consideration' for a supply

'Consideration' for a supply is an EU law concept and for VAT purposes it must have a direct link with the services supplied and must be capable of being expressed in money. *Staatssecretaris van Financiën v Cooperatieve Vereniging 'Cooperatieve Aardappelenbewaarplaats GA'* (Case 154/80). [37.7]

3 Place of supply of services

Two Directives, one on the place of supply of services (Council Directive 2008/8/EC), the other on VAT refunds (Council Directive 2008/9/EC) to taxable persons established in a Member State outside the Member State of refund, were adopted by the EU Council of Ministers on 12 February 2008. Various changes to the place of supply rules took effect as of 1 January 2010: the Recast Directive has been amended to reflect the changes and the above table incorporates these changes as well.

With regard to telecoms, broadcasting and electronic services, the introduction of the new rules on the place of business to consumer supplies was delayed until 1 January 2015. From that date, these services are taxed in the country where the consumer is established. Suppliers will be allowed to fulfil their VAT obligations in their home Member State using a 'one stop' scheme which will enable them to account for VAT on the supplies to private customers in other Member States via a single VAT return. The supplier will identify in that VAT return the value of supplies made to customers in each Member State and then account for VAT on the value of such supplies at the rate applicable in each of the identified Member States. The VAT revenue from these services will then be transferred from the country where the supplier is located to that where the customer is situated. In order to ensure a smooth transition, the Member State of establishment will retain a proportion of the VAT collected until 31 December 2018. This proportion amounts to

30% from 1 January 2015 until 31 December 2016; it will amount to 15% from 1 January 2017 until 31 December 2018 and 0% from 1 January 2019 onwards.
[37.8]

VI THE FUTURE OF VAT IN EUROPE

On 6 December 2011, the Commission published a communication on the future of VAT: 'Communication from the Commission to the European Parliament, the Council and the European Economic and Social Committee on the future of VAT – Towards a simpler, more robust and efficient VAT system tailored to the single market'.

The accompanying press release set out the four overriding objectives which emerged from the communication:
(1) a simpler, more transparent VAT system would relieve administrative burdens and make VAT more workable for businesses;
(2) VAT must be made more efficient in supporting Member States' fiscal consolidation efforts and sustainable economic growth;
(3) tackling uncollected VAT and fraud; and
(4) creating a modern EU VAT system which is based on VAT collection in the country of destination.

The Communication elicited a number of actions to be taken by the Council and the Commission. The most notable action is the Opinion of the VAT Expert Group, which was adopted on 12 June 2014. This identified that the transitional VAT system which has been in place for more than 20 years is 'causing significant administrative burdens and unacceptable risks …'. The VAT Expert Group identified four objectives which are similar to those stated by the Commission in 2011 (see above). It stressed the need for all stakeholders to work together to 'make Europe more competitive'. In the Opinion, the Group urges the Commission, the Council and the European Parliament to prioritise agreement on the definitive VAT system as soon as possible (and by 2019 at the latest). [37.9]

On 7 April 2016, the Commission presented an 'Action Plan' setting out ways to amend the current EU VAT system to make it simpler, more fraud-proof and business-friendly. According to the Commission's press release:

> 'The current VAT rules urgently need to be updated so they can better support the Single Market, facilitate cross-border trade and keep pace with today's digital and mobile economy.'

The Action Plan provides an outline of various steps the Commission intends to take, including:
(1) to modernise and simplify VAT for cross-border e-commerce (in particular for SMEs);
(2) urgent measures to tackle the 'VAT gap'; and
(3) working towards a modernised rates policy.

In the Action Plan, the Commission calls on the European Parliament and the Council to provide clear political guidance on the options put forward by the Commission and to confirm their support for the suggested reforms.

Some steps have been taken consequent on the Action Plan (such as the adoption by the Commission of a proposal for a directive that would introduce a generalised reverse charge mechanism in relation to supplies of goods and services above a certain threshold) but the intended actions by the European Parliament and the Council are taking longer to achieve than that which is set out in the plan.. [37.10]

VII THE FUTURE OF VAT IN THE UNITED KINGDOM

1 Brexit

As indicated above, the UK remains subject to EU law, unless and until an Article 50 withdrawal agreement comes into force. After the UK has left the EU, the Government will have the freedom to amend VAT law or even to abolish it. The value of VAT that is collected (£111.4 billion in 2015–16) means that it is inconceivable that there will not be some form of VAT (or sales tax) system in place in a post-Brexit UK. However, as at the date of writing, there is a fundamental lack of certainty regarding the post March 2019 system. [37.11]

2 Office of Tax Simplification VAT review

On 8 December 2016, the Office of Tax Simplification (OTS) published its terms of reference for its review of VAT (which had been announced in the 2016 Autumn Statement). The aim of the review is to develop recommendations to simplify VAT and to ease the administrative burden for businesses. On 28 February 2017, the OTS published its interim report on reform of VAT, comprising a progress report and call for evidence. Amongst the areas that it identified as requiring consideration were:

- The current VAT registration threshold. The UK's is the highest in the EU.
- The multiple VAT rates and exemption, which are complex. Simplified definitions, having only a standard rate, or discontinuing exemption are options to be considered.
- Partial exemption, the option to tax (including consideration of a central database of exercised options) and the capital goods scheme.
- Special accounting schemes, the tour operators margin scheme (which could be narrowed) and whether retail schemes, the agricultural flat rate and annual accounting schemes are needed.
- Improved HMRC guidance.
- Making Tax Digital. [37.12]

38 VAT – UK provisions
Hartley Foster, Partner, Fieldfisher LLP

I   Background [**38.1**]
II Taxable persons and transactions [**38.21**]
III Registration, accounting for tax and penalties [**38.49**]
IV The recovery of VAT, partial exemption and the Capital Goods Scheme [**38.81**]
V   International supplies of goods and services [**38.101**]

I   BACKGROUND

On becoming a member of the European Community (EC), the UK replaced two taxes (purchase tax and selective employment tax) with Value Added Tax (VAT), which was introduced by Finance Act 1972. Many of the provisions in FA 1972 (effective from 1 April 1973) and the subsequent Finance Acts and statutory instruments were consolidated in the VAT Act 1983 and then again in the Value Added Tax Act 1994 (VATA 1994). [**38.1**]

1   UK legislation and administration

UK legislation relevant to VAT is derived from two sources:
(1) EU legislation having direct applicability or direct effect in the UK; and
(2) legislation enacted by Parliament, together with subordinate legislation made thereunder.

The basic domestic legislation is VATA 1994. Many of the detailed rules are set out in orders, rules and regulations made by Statutory Instruments (VATA 1994 s 97). Notices and leaflets issued by HM Revenue & Customs (HMRC) set out their views on the operation of the legislation and do not generally have the force of law. However, certain parts of these are issued under statutory authority. This includes, for example, parts of Notice 700 (The VAT Guide), Notice 727 and associated leaflets dealing with retail schemes and Notice 703 in regard to evidence of export. Extra-statutory concessions are contained in notices and leaflets (listed and catalogued in Notice 48).

HMRC are responsible for the collection and management of VAT (VATA 1994 Sch 11 para 1). Appeals against decisions of HMRC on specified matters lie to the First-tier Tribunal, Tax Chamber (VATA 1994 s 83). Further appeals can be made, with permission, to the Upper Tribunal, the Court of Appeal and, finally, to the Supreme Court.

Under what is now Article 267 of the consolidated versions of the Treaty on European Union and the Treaty on the Functioning of the European Union (formerly Art 234 of TEC and Art 177 of the EC Treaty), the Court of Justice of the European Union ('ECJ') has jurisdiction to give preliminary rulings on matters of the interpretation of EU law referred to it by national courts (which includes the First-tier Tribunal, Tax Chamber). As noted in **Chapter 54**, the ECJ's sole function (under Article 267) is to decide what the EU law is. The ECJ will not interpret national law or apply its interpretation of EU law to the facts of the case; and the ECJ will leave it to the national courts to implement its ruling. The decision to make a reference is one for the particular national court; an individual has no direct right of access to the ECJ (see, for example, *Naturally Yours Cosmetics Ltd v C & E Comrs* (1988)). The First-tier Tribunal and the Upper Tribunal can make a reference to the ECJ (as can the courts). The general rule is that, where a question concerning EU law arises before a national court or tribunal, the matter may be referred to the ECJ if a decision on the question is necessary to enable the national court to give judgment. However, under Art 267, the matter must be referred if there is no right of appeal from a decision of the court or tribunal. Thus, courts of last resort (such as the Supreme Court in the UK) do not have a discretion as to whether to make a reference on an EU law issue which it is necessary to resolve before judgment can be given (although the court in question retains its discretion to decide whether a decision on a question of EU Law is necessary to enable it to give judgment (see *R v Henn and Darby* (Case 34/79)). If the answer to the EU law point is '*acte claire*' (in essence, so obvious that there is no scope for any reasonable doubt), then there is no obligation to refer, but the Supreme Court, as the last court of appeal in the UK, is bound to make a reference if there is any question of doubt about the interpretation of EC law. An illustration of this is the case of *C & E Comrs v Sinclair Collis Ltd* (2001). The Court of Appeal had held that the agreement under which a pub owner allowed a company operating cigarette vending machines to site a machine in the pub was an exempt supply of a licence to occupy land. Three of the members of the House of Lords disagreed with the Court of Appeal, but two agreed. Hence their Lordships decided that a reference to the ECJ was appropriate. (Ultimately, the ECJ rejected HMRC's assertions that the installation of a vending machine in a public house constituted the 'letting or leasing of immovable property' (and restored the decision that the VAT Tribunal had reached in the case six years previously)).

As indicated in **Chapter 5**, on 23 June 2016, an 'In/Out' referendum was held in the UK. The decision (by a small margin) was to leave the European Union. Following the enactment of the European Union Notification of Withdrawal Act 2017, the Prime Minister sent a notification of the UK's withdrawal from the EU to the European Council President on 29 March 2017. The UK remains subject to EU law unless and until an Article 50 withdrawal agreement comes into force; and the CJEU has confirmed that it will consider all references that have been made to it by UK courts prior to March 2019. Accordingly, the above explanation as regards references to the ECJ remains accurate (see *BAT Industries PLC v R & C Comrs* [2017] UKFTT 558 (TC)).

[38.2]

2 Mechanics of VAT

VAT is an indirect tax (ie it is levied on consumption rather than on income) that is collected at each stage of a commercial chain.

In *Example 38.1* below, a VAT rate of 20% is assumed throughout and, for the sake of illustration, it deals with a single transaction. In reality, VAT is calculated on outputs during a given period and on 'inputs' (see note (1) to the example below) during that period, not on particular transactions (see further note (3) to the example).

EXAMPLE 38.1

	Costs (£) (excluding VAT)	Sale (£) (excluding VAT)	VAT (£) on costs (input)	VAT (£) on sale (output)	Paid to HMRC (£)
Producer	–	20,000	–	4,000	4,000
Manufacturer	20,000	30,000	4,000	6,000	2,000
Wholesaler	30,000	45,000	6,000	9,000	3,000
Retailer	45,000	60,000	9,000	12,000	3,000
Customer	60,000	–	12,000	–	–
					£12,000

Notes:
(1) Each taxable person in the chain must charge VAT on supplies made to customers (outputs) (this is subject to certain exceptions). This VAT is termed 'output tax' and must be accounted for to HMRC in the taxable person's periodic VAT return. In so far as the taxable person incurs VAT on supplies which he has received, this VAT (which is referred to as 'input tax') can be recovered from HMRC, provided that it is attributable to a taxable supply made or to be made (VATA 1994 s 26) and appropriate evidence is held. If input tax exceeds output tax, the excess can be recovered in full from HMRC provided, as stated above, that it is attributable to a taxable supply (VATA 1994 s 25(3)). Output tax is only charged on supplies made in the course or furtherance of a business; input tax is generally refunded only if inputs are used or are to be used for business purposes.
(2) The final tax (£12,000 in the illustration) is wholly borne by the customer. For VAT purposes, a customer means someone who cannot recover VAT because he is not registered or he is not entitled to recover the amount under one of the relevant exceptions or he does not make any taxable outputs (ie the supplies made are entirely exempt outputs) (what is meant by 'exempt supplies' is set out below).
(3) The VAT mechanism is intended to ensure that, ultimately, the net VAT paid (ie the £12,000) is exactly 20% of the taxable value (£60,000). However, since supplies of goods or services which are exempt or outside the scope of VAT may have borne VAT which is not identified and not recoverable, this objective is not always achieved.

In order to ensure that all consumption is taxed, provision exists for the taxation of goods and services imported into the UK in certain circumstances (see [38.103]). [38.3]

3 Overview of the characterisation of supplies and applicable rate

When determining the VAT consequences of any transaction, the starting point is to ascertain whether there is a 'supply' for VAT purposes. VATA 1994 s 5 sets out what constitutes a supply of goods and what constitutes a supply of services. Once it is established that there is a supply, the characterisation of that supply is necessary for the purpose of determining: (a) the place of that supply and whether the supply is within the charge to UK VAT; and, if so (b) the rate at which VAT is chargeable on the supply. The place of supply rules are set out in detail below.

In so far as the rate of VAT is concerned, the general rule is that all supplies that are made in the United Kingdom are subject to VAT at the standard rate of 20% (from 4 January 2011). However, there are two specific reliefs from the obligation to charge VAT at this rate. *First*, a reduced rate of VAT (of 5% – VATA 1994 s 29A) applies to, for example, fuel and power, certain sanitary products, bases for child car seats, and the importation of certain antiques and collectors' items (where an effective rate of 5% is achieved by reducing the taxable value (VATA 1994 s 21(4))). *Second*, a zero rate applies to most food, books and magazines (VATA 1994 s 30). The effect of a supply being 'zero-rated' is that a taxable person is not required to charge VAT on the supply but retains the right to recover input tax incurred on costs attributable to making that supply.

Also, a supply may be exempt from VAT (VATA 1994 s 31). Here, a taxable person is not required to charge VAT on the exempt supplies and he has no right to recover input tax incurred on costs attributable to making an exempt supply. Zero-rating takes precedence where a supply is potentially both zero-rated and exempt.

Supplies of goods and services made outside the UK are outside the scope of UK VAT. [38.4]

a) *The standard rate*

This rate applies to most transactions. On 25 May 2016, the European Council adopted a directive maintaining for a further two years the minimum standard rate of 15%. The minimum standard rate is aimed at preventing an excessive divergence in VAT rates applied by Member States, and the structural imbalances or distortions of competition that could arise as a result.

As indicated above, at the time of writing, the rate in the UK is 20% (this rate is used for all examples in this chapter unless otherwise indicated). The rate rose from 17.5% as of 4 January 2011. The rates in force since the introduction of VAT have been as follows:

- 1 April 1973 to 28 July 1974: 10% (FA 1972 s 9(1))
- 29 July 1974 to 17 June 1979: 8% (VAT (Change of Rate) Order 1974)
- 18 June 1979 to 31 January 1991: 15% (F(No 2)A 1979 s 1(1)(b))
- 1 April 1991 to 30 November 2008: 17.5% (FA 1991 s 13; and VATA 1994 s 2(1))
- 1 December 2008 to 31 December 2009: 15% (Value Added Tax (Change of Rate) Order 2008)

- 1 January 2010 to 3 January 2011: 17.5% (FA 2009 s 9))
- 4 January 2011 onwards: 20% (VATA 1994 s 2(1) and F(No 2)A 2010 s 3(1))

The rate may be changed by SI upwards or downwards by up to 25% of the rate then applicable (VATA 1994 s 2(2)). [38.5]

b) *The reduced rate*

The range of reduced rate supplies is gradually being extended, albeit subject to extensive conditions, to include items such as child car seats, women's sanitary products, fuel for qualifying use, residential conversions, renovation and alteration of dwellings and installation of energy-saving materials and smoking cessation products that can be sold 'over the counter' (VATA 1994 Sch 7A).

Infraction proceedings were commenced by the European Commission in relation to the UK's reduced VAT rate on the supply and installation of energy-saving materials (on the basis that the reduced rate in the circumstances went beyond what is allowed under the Sixth VAT Directive). The ECJ published its decision on 4 June 2015 (Case C-161/14). It agreed with the Commission that the UK had implemented the relief in a way that was not in accordance with EU law; the UK had applied the reduced rate too widely, and not as part of a social policy. Consequently, FA 2016 amended VATA 1994 Sch 7A Group 2.

Following the decision of the European Council on 17–18 March 2016 regarding 'increased flexibility for Member States with respect to reduced rates of VAT', HMRC announced on 24 March 2016 that the reduced rating for women's sanitary products would be withdrawn and the same legislation would be inserted by FA 2016 s 126 as VATA 1994 Sch 8 Group 19, with the effect of making supplies of women's sanitary products subject to the zero-rate. No date has been set for the introduction of this change, although it is not expected before April 2018. [38.6]

c) *Zero-rated supplies*

A supply that is zero-rated is a taxable supply that is taxed at a 0% VAT rate. Consequently, a person who makes zero-rated supplies is able to recover any input tax incurred in making those supplies provided that that person is registered for VAT.

The zero-rate was introduced for social and political reasons and covers, for example, supplies of most food, books and newspapers and children's clothing. Formerly, the ambit of zero-rating was wider (it included, in particular, all new construction work), but the ECJ held that some aspects were in breach of the Sixth VAT Directive (which was then the relevant EC legislation for VAT purposes) and the UK law was amended accordingly.

The following heads of supply (which are subject to restrictions and exemptions) are zero-rated (see VATA 1994 Sch 8):

Group 1	Food
Group 2	Sewerage services and water
Group 3	Books, magazines and other printed matter

Group 4	Talking books for the blind and handicapped and wireless sets for the blind
Group 5	Construction of buildings etc
Group 6	Protected buildings
Group 7	International services
Group 8	Transport
Group 9	Caravans and houseboats
Group 10	Gold
Group 11	Bank notes
Group 12	Drugs, medicine, aids for the handicapped etc
Group 13	Imports, exports etc
Group 14	Tax-free shops (repealed with effect from 1 July 1999)
Group 15	Charities etc
Group 16	Clothing and footwear
Group 17	Emissions allowances (repealed with effect from 1 November 2010)
Group 18	European research infrastructure consortia (from 1 January 2013)
Group 19	Women's sanitary products

[38.7]

d) *Exempt supplies*

A number of consequences flow from making an exempt supply:
(1) no tax is charged on such a supply;
(2) its value is not taken into account in determining whether a trader is liable to be registered or has ceased to be liable to be registered;
(3) a trader who makes only exempt supplies is neither required nor entitled to be registered (except, in the case of a corporate body, as a member of a VAT group); and
(4) the amount of input tax for which a trader who makes both taxable and exempt supplies is entitled to credit is restricted to such proportion as is attributable to his taxable supplies.

By contrast to zero-rated supplies, exempt supplies are not taxable supplies. A business that makes exempt supplies does not charge output VAT on those supplies and cannot recover any input VAT incurred for the purpose of making those supplies. The following (listed in VATA 1994 Sch 9) are the heads of exempt supply:

Group 1	Land (exceptions apply)
Group 2	Insurance and reinsurance
Group 3	Postal services
Group 4	Betting, gaming and lotteries
Group 5	Finance
Group 6	Education

Group 7   Health and welfare
Group 8   Burial and cremation
Group 9   Subscriptions to trade unions and professional bodies and other public interest bodies
Group 10   Sports, sports competitions and physical education
Group 11   Works of art etc
Group 12   Fund-raising events by charities and other qualifying bodies
Group 13   Cultural services etc
Group 14   Supplies of goods where input tax cannot be recovered
Group 15   Investment gold
Group 16   Supplies of services by groups involving cost sharing

The above paragraphs apply to determine the rate of VAT applicable to a 'supply' of goods or a 'supply' of services, as appropriate.

In order to ascertain if the supply is within the charge to UK VAT, it is necessary to ascertain where the place of supply is. This is because supplies that are made outside the UK are generally outside the scope of VAT and thus not liable to UK VAT. There are complex rules for determining the place of supply. Sections 7 and 7A of VATA 1994 implement the place of supply rules. In summary, and on a general basis, these rules are as follows:

(1) Goods imported into the UK are liable to UK VAT, and it is HMRC who are responsible for the imposition of VAT in such circumstances.
(2) Where a supply of goods does not involve the removal of goods from the UK, the goods are treated as supplied in the UK.
(3) Where a supply of goods involves the installation and assembly of the goods outside the UK, the goods are supplied outside the UK.
(4) Where a supply of goods involves the removal of goods from the UK the goods are treated as supplied in the UK unless the supply is to another Member State and the distance selling rules apply (VATA 1994 s 7(5)), in which case the goods are treated as supplied outside the UK.
(5) The place of supply of a service is dependent upon whether it is a 'business to business' (B2B) supply (the recipient is a 'relevant business person' as defined in VATA 1994 s 7A(4)) or a 'business to consumer' (B2C) supply (the recipient is not a 'relevant business person'). The general rule is that the place of supply of a B2B supply is the country in which the recipient belongs and that the place of supply of a B2C supply is where the supplier belongs.
(6) Services relating to land are treated as made where the land in connection with which the supply is made is situated (VATA 1994 Sch 4A para 1).
(7) Services supplied to someone who is not a relevant business person that consist of cultural, artistic, sporting, scientific, educational or entertainments services or exhibitions, conferences, are supplied where performed VATA 1994 Sch 4A para 14A).

Supplies that are outside the scope of UK VAT but would, if made in the UK, give rise to an entitlement to recover input tax, are treated as being equivalent to zero-rated supplies, ie no VAT is charged on the supply, but input VAT incurred on expenditure in relation to the supply is recoverable. Conversely, supplies that would not give rise to an entitlement to recover input tax are treated as exempt. This is subject to an exception, namely input tax incurred on certain exempt financial services will give rise to input VAT recovery where the supplies are made to a person who 'belongs outside the Member States'. These supplies are referred to as 'out of scope with recovery supplies' (this is elaborated upon later in this chapter).

Businesses that make a mixture of taxable (including zero-rated) and exempt supplies are referred to as partially exempt. The input VAT directly attributable to taxable supplies is recoverable. That which is directly attributable to exempt supplies is irrecoverable; and that which cannot be directly attributed (eg VAT on general overheads) may be recovered in part.

Certain business expenses (such as wages and salaries and local authority rates) are wholly outside the scope of VAT. Not all input tax is recoverable even if attributable to taxable supplies: examples include VAT on the cost of entertaining customers; on expenses incurred by a company in providing domestic accommodation to directors and their families; and on expenditure other than for business purposes. There are anti-avoidance provisions preventing VAT being avoided by overcharging on insurance premiums where exempt insurance is supplied in a package with other goods or services liable to VAT. [38.8]

EXAMPLE 38.2 – MIXED SUPPLIES – CREDIT

Stefano, a computer supplier, also provides hire-purchase facilities directly to his customers. A customer buys a PC and accessories for £2,400 + VAT under an HP agreement over three years. The interest over the three years will be £200. So long as the documentation given to the customer shows the £200 as a separate charge, the total payments made will be £2,400 + £480 VAT (assuming a 20% VAT rate) for the goods and £200 exempt credit.

e) *The VAT fraction*

In *Example 38.1* above, the purchaser pays a total price of £60,000 + £12,000 (at 20%) = £72,000 for the goods. VAT as a percentage of that gross price is therefore £12,000/£72,000 = 1/6. This *'VAT fraction'* is used to calculate tax in cases where the price is 'tax inclusive'. It is particularly important at the retail level, where it is common for the price of goods to include VAT. If no mention is made of VAT and the contract does not provide otherwise, the consideration paid for the supply is VAT inclusive and the supplier must account for the tax. (See, however, VATA 1994 s 89, which provides that if, after the entering into of a contract, there is a change in the VAT rate (or a change in the VAT liability of a supply) then, unless the contract otherwise provides, the contractual price will be altered to take account of the change.) [38.9]

4 Relationship between VAT and other taxes

a) *Capital gains tax*

Statement of Practice D7 provides, in the context of CGT, that in cases where VAT paid on the purchase of an asset is recoverable, the CGT acquisition cost of the asset will exclude VAT. If no recovery is available the price will be VAT inclusive. On the disposal of an asset, VAT chargeable is ignored in computing the capital gain. Subsequent adjustments to VAT recovery, eg under the Capital Goods Scheme (see [**38.89**]), are treated as additional capital expenditure or disposal provisions in the period of adjustment. [**38.10**]

b) *Income tax*

For income tax purposes, irrecoverable VAT may be deducted as a business expense (see SP B1), except to the extent that it forms part of the cost of a capital item (where capital allowances may be available). [**38.11**]

EXAMPLE 38.3

Ben, a retailer, acquired a Steinway concert grand piano for £24,000 (including VAT at 20%). He has just sold it to a customer, Charlie, for £50,000 (excluding VAT).

(1) *VAT:* Ben must charge the customer output tax of £10,000. Input tax of £4,000 is fully recoverable.

(2) *Income tax:* The purchase price, £20,000 net of VAT, is a deductible business expense (CTA 2009 s 46). The sale consideration of £50,000 is an income receipt.

(3) *CGT:* Charlie's acquisition cost for CGT purposes is £50,000 + £10,000 (VAT) = £60,000, assuming that Charlie cannot recover the VAT.

c) *Stamp duty land tax*

Stamp Duty Land Tax ('SDLT') was introduced in December 2003. 'Chargeable consideration' for the purposes of SDLT includes the amount of VAT due on the consideration at the time of the transaction (the 'effective date' for SDLT purposes) (ie in this instance, SDLT is a tax on a tax). [**38.12**]–[**38.20**]

II TAXABLE PERSONS AND TRANSACTIONS

VAT is charged on *taxable supplies of goods* and *services* made in the UK by a *taxable person* in the course or furtherance of a *business* carried on by him (VATA 1994 s 4(1)). It is possible for a taxable person to make supplies otherwise than in the course or furtherance of his business, eg an individual who sells a private asset or a charity which makes a charitable disposal. Such supplies fall outside the scope of VAT. Goods imported into the UK from outside the EU are also chargeable (subject to a *de minimis* limit for small value items imported by post and certain other reliefs) irrespective of whether they are imported for business purposes and whether the importer is a taxable person. With regard to goods acquired from another Member State see [**38.104**]. Certain services received from abroad are also chargeable to VAT on acquisition, but this only applies if the services are received by a taxable person for the purpose of his business, and on a self-supply basis (see [**38.30**]). By contrast, exports of goods are generally zero-rated and some (although not all) exported services are zero-rated (see [**38.102**]). [**38.21**]

1 A taxable supply

The UK legislation defines 'supply' (in VATA 1994 s 5(2)) simply by stating that it 'includes all forms of supply, but not anything done otherwise than for a consideration'.

In order to be a supply that gives rise to a charge to tax, the supply must be a taxable supply. A supply must meet the following conditions to be a taxable supply:
(1) it must be made for a consideration (a number of free transactions are, however, specifically stated to be supplies, so as to be charged to tax);
(2) it must be a supply of goods or services;
(3) it must be made in the UK;
(4) it must be made in the course of furtherance of business; and
(5) it must not be exempted from tax.

Good title does not have to pass for a transfer of goods to be a 'supply' for VAT purposes. The transfer of possession of goods in circumstances where it is contemplated that title will pass in the future may be a supply of goods.
[38.22]

2 A supply of goods

VATA 1994 Sch 4 prescribes those supplies that are to be treated as supplies of goods and those that are supplies of services for VAT purposes. In some instances the definitions are not consistent with the general domestic law. For example, the sale of a freehold interest in land or the grant, assignment or surrender of a lease exceeding 21 years is treated as a supply of goods (VATA 1994 Sch 4 para 4).

Where goods forming part of the assets of a business are disposed of so as no longer to form part of those assets, whether or not for a consideration, there is generally a supply of goods (VATA 1994 Sch 4 para 5(1)).

Where a person ceases to be a taxable person, goods then forming part of the assets of the business carried on by him are deemed to be supplied by him and VAT must be accounted for. There are two relieving provisions. The first exempts specific goods (namely items in respect of which input tax was not claimed) from the deemed supply and the second exempts all goods in specified circumstances. The second relieving provision applies, inter alia, if, on the occasion on which the person ceases to be a taxable trader:
(i) the business is transferred as a going concern to another taxable trader (VATA 1994 Sch 4 para 8(1)(a) – see [38.26]);
(ii) the taxable person has died, or become bankrupt or incapacitated, and the business is carried on by some other person; or
(iii) tax on the deemed supply does not exceed £1,000.

A gift of goods is not regarded as resulting in a supply provided it is made in the course or furtherance of the business and, subject to conditions, the cost to the donor, together with the cost of any other business gifts made to the same person in the same year, does not exceed £50 or is a sample of any goods (see *Example 38.4(5)*). [38.23]

3 A supply of services

Section 5(2)(b), VATA 1994 states that 'anything which is not a supply of goods but is done for a consideration ... is a supply of services'. The issue of shares or the coming into existence of a partnership interest following the subscription of funds by the investor/partner is not 'anything ... done for a consideration' (see *KapHag Renditefonds v Finanzamt Charlottenburg* (Case C-442/01)). In *Kretztechnik AG v Finanzamt Linz* (Case C-465/03) the Advocate-General said:

> 'Although Article 6(1) of the Sixth Directive defines a supply of services as any transaction which does not constitute a supply of goods, that definition clearly cannot be taken to its literal extreme. It might be more reasonable to interpret it as intended to define a service as anything supplied which is not a good.'

[38.24]

EXAMPLE 38.4

(1) Monopoly supplies heating and lighting to X & Co. A supply of *goods* (Sch 4 para 3).

(2) X & Co assign the remaining 30-year term on their lease to Fred. A supply of *goods* (Sch 4 para 4).

(3) Big and Bob jointly own a stallion. Big sells his undivided share to Breeder & Co. A supply of *services*. Contrast the position if Big and Bob sold the horse to Breeder & Co (ie both shares were sold at the same time) when this would be a supply of *goods* (Sch 4 para 1).

(4) Concrete hires tools and machinery (a supply of *services*); it also sells goods on hire purchase (a supply of *goods*) (Sch 4 para 1(2)).

(5) A, a publisher, gives a glossy calendar to a valued customer as a goodwill gesture. As an exception to the general rule in Sch 4 para 5(1) that the transfer of goods out of a business is a supply, even if no consideration is furnished, a gift of goods made in the course or furtherance of the business is not regarded as a supply provided that the cost of the goods – the calendar – to A does not exceed £50 (VATA 1994 Sch 4 para 5(2)(a)).

(6) Sally sells power tools. One Saturday she borrows an item of trading stock for her own use. This is a supply of services and VAT will be charged on the cost (taken as being the depreciation for the period of use) of supplying the power tool (VATA 1994 Sch 4 para 5(4) and Sch 6 para 7).

4 Composite and multiple supplies

A taxable person may supply a combination of goods or services as part of what is nominally a single transaction. Where the liability of the individual supplies of goods and services would be the same as the liability of the goods or services regarded as a single package, no problems arise. However, disputes frequently arise as to whether there is a single (composite) supply or several different individual supplies, even though there is apparently a single consideration. Examination of this complex area of VAT is beyond the scope of this chapter. In essence, the test of whether or not two identifiable supplies within a single transaction should be regarded as a single supply or not depends on whether they can be regarded as economically 'dissociable' from each other

(see *EC Commission v UK* (1988) and whether certain supplies are ancillary to a single dominant supply (see *Card Protection Plan Ltd v C & E Comrs* (1999)).
[38.25]

5 Transfer of a business as a going concern (VATA 1994 s 49)

When the provisions of the VAT (Special Provisions) Order 1995 (SI 1995/1268) are satisfied, certain supplies of assets of a business as a going concern are treated as neither supplies of goods nor services and no VAT is chargeable on the consideration. This is not a matter of choice: if the conditions are satisfied and the vendor charges VAT in error, then the purchaser is not entitled to recover the amount as input tax.

The conditions are that the assets must be used by the transferee in carrying on the same line of business as the transferor with no significant break (refurbishment or redecoration is acceptable); if the transferor is registered for VAT the transferee must likewise either be registered or become registered and where the assets form part only of the business, that part must be capable of separate operation. Where land is included in the transfer, certain other conditions may have to be satisfied.

Where the rules apply the transferee will become responsible in relation to the assets transferred for any future input tax adjustments under the Capital Goods Scheme (as to which see **[38.89]** and *Example 38.20*).

When assets are acquired as a transfer of a going concern and the assets are used exclusively to make taxable supplies, the VAT incurred on the costs of acquiring those assets will be attributed to those taxable supplies and is recoverable in full. Correspondingly, input tax relating to the disposal of such assets will also be recoverable in full (see *Abbey National plc v C & E Comrs* (2001) and *Higher Education Statistics Agency Ltd*) (2000)).

The transfer of shares in a company cannot be a transfer of a business as a going concern, irrespective of the size of the shareholding, 'unless the holding is part of an independent unit which allows an independent economic activity to be carried out' (see *Staatssecretaris van Financiën v X BV* (Case C-651/11))
[38.26]

6 A taxable person

A taxable person is one who is either registered or required to be registered (VATA 1994 s 3). If the taxable supplies are, or will be, in excess of a ceiling (usually adjusted annually) the taxpayer is required to register with HMRC by submitting Form VAT 1 to, usually, his local VAT office (VATA 1994 Sch 1). The current threshold is £85,000 per annum. The de-registration threshold is £83,000 per annum.

The registration requirement is laid on the *person* rather than the business. An individual may therefore operate several businesses but will have only one VAT registration. By contrast a company is a distinct entity from its proprietors (for group registration, see **[38.50]**). For VAT purposes a partnership is treated as a separate taxable entity (VATA 1994 s 45). [38.27]

7 A business

Supplies must be made in the course or furtherance of a business (VATA 1994 s 4(1)). Section 94 states that a business 'includes any trade, profession or vocation'. 'Business', however, has a wider meaning than either trade or profession (see also the IHT provisions on 'business property relief'): and there is no requirement of profit motive. The Recast Directive (see [37.5]) uses the term 'economic activity' (Art 9), which is probably a wider term than 'business'. In *C & E Comrs v Lord Fisher* (1981), Gibson J identified the following indicia that should be considered in determining whether the activities carried on amounted to a business:

(1) whether the activity is a 'serious undertaking earnestly pursued' or 'a serious occupation not necessarily confined to a commercial or profit making undertaking';
(2) whether the activity is an occupation or function actively pursued with reasonable or recognisable continuity;
(3) whether the activity has a certain measure of substance as measured by the quarterly or annual value of taxable supplies made;
(4) whether the activity was conducted in a regular manner and on sound and recognised business principles;
(5) whether the activity is predominantly concerned with the making of taxable supplies to consumers for a consideration;
(6) whether the taxable supplies are of a kind which, subject to differences of detail, are commonly made by those who seek to profit by them.

The letting of property on a continuing or regular basis, for example, is a business activity.

In *C & E Comrs v Morrison's Academy Boarding Houses Association* (1978) the company ran boarding houses for students of Morrison's Academy. It was in all respects, carrying on an activity within the ordinary meaning of the word 'business' save that it charged rents which would produce neither profit nor loss and it reserved its accommodation for students of the Academy. It was decided that it supplied services in the course of a business. By contrast, in *Three H Aircraft Hire v C & E Comrs* (1982) the court decided that, although a single adventure could constitute a business or trade under other areas of the law, it did not amount to a business activity for VAT purposes.

The taxable supply must be made in the course '*or furtherance*' of a business. Activities that would not normally be thought of as falling in the normal course of a business may be taxable (such as the sale of assets to assist in the financing of the business). [38.28]

8 The value of a supply

VATA 1994 s 2 provides that VAT is charged on the value of the supply, determined in accordance with the Act.

Section 19(2) states that if the consideration for a supply is money 'its value shall be taken to be such amount as, with the addition of the tax chargeable, is equal to the consideration'. Accordingly, if £120 is paid for a supply taxable at the standard rate, then the value of that supply is £100. If there is a supply made for no consideration (eg a gift) or for a consideration not wholly in money (eg an exchange), then the value of the supply is 'such amount in money as, with the addition of the tax chargeable, is equivalent to the consideration' (VATA 1994 s 19(3)). (However, if services are performed for no consideration, then there is generally no supply for VAT purposes.) [38.29]

EXAMPLE 38.5
(1) A supplies goods to B for £1,800 inclusive of VAT. The value of A's supply is £1,500 being £1,800 minus the relevant VAT determined in accordance with the VAT fraction (see [**38.9**]): ie £300. A is responsible for the payment of this VAT to HMRC.
(2) A supplies goods to B who as a *quid pro quo* replaces A's existing windows. So far as A is concerned, the value in money of the work done by B (less VAT: see s 19(3)) is the consideration for his supply. For B, it is the value of A's goods.
(3) Silas, a solicitor, gives free tax advice to Mr Big, a local businessman, in the hope of obtaining Big's commercial business. No consideration is provided and there is no supply of services for VAT. Had Mr Big, for example, agreed not to pursue a claim against Silas in return for the tax advice, then this would constitute consideration.

9 The reverse charge and self-supply

A number of occasions arise where a UK taxable person is required to account for VAT as if he had made a supply of goods or services to himself. Output tax is accounted for to HMRC and the taxable person may recover such tax in the usual way if he can attribute it in whole or in part to a taxable supply. One such charge arises under VATA 1994 s 8 where a UK taxable person receives certain services from abroad (see [**38.106**]). This method of accounting for VAT is termed '*a reverse charge*'. Where the reverse charge applies, all the same consequences follow as if the recipient had himself supplied the goods or services in the UK in the course or furtherance of his business and that supply were a taxable supply.

EXAMPLE 38.6
In the course of his business, Paul receives legal advice from the lawyers Antonio and Carreras (Madrid) on the requirements of Spanish company law. He is charged £10,000. Under VATA 1994 s 8, Paul is deemed to supply himself with these services and must account for output VAT on the value of the supply. Accordingly, VAT in the sum of £2,000 is payable. That same sum is also treated as input tax for Paul and, subject to the normal rules, can be recovered by Paul.

The 'reverse charge' is also applied to goods which are acquired by a business from another EU Member State (see [**38.104**]).

Goods produced for internal use in a business, or trading stock appropriated for such use, may also lead to a VAT charge. Such cases are referred to as '*self-supplies*' and the Treasury has powers to make orders that VAT should apply as if the relevant goods or services had been both supplied to a person for the purpose of his business and supplied by him in the course or furtherance of that business (VATA 1994 s 5(5)).

In 2006, the UK made an application to the European Commission for a derogation from the provisions of the Sixth Directive to enable it to introduce a reverse charge procedure for transactions between VAT-registered businesses in certain goods that are used in Missing Trader Intra-Community (MTIC) fraud (such as, for example, mobile telephones, and computer chips). Primary legislation was enacted in FA 2006 and was brought into force by Treasury Order with effect from 1 June 2007 (Value Added Tax (Section 55A) (Specified Goods and Excepted Supplies) Order 2007). This Order was repealed and replaced with effect from 1 November 2010 by the Value Added Tax (Section 55A) (Specified Goods and Services and Excepted Supplies) Order 2010. The 2010 Order reproduces the effect of the 2007 Order in its application to supplies of mobile telephones and computer chips. It provides that supplies of 'specified goods' with a VAT exclusive value of £5,000 or more, are subject to a reverse charge when made by a UK registered business to another UK registered business and the latter is acquiring the goods for business purposes. It lists the goods to which the reverse charge regime applies and includes mobile phones, computer chips and central processing units (CPUs). The 2010 Order was introduced after evidence emerged of MTIC trading involving supplies of emissions allowances and other units which are recognised for the purposes of the European Union greenhouse gas emission allowance trading scheme ('EU-ETS'). In order to tackle this fraud on a Europe-wide basis, a new Article 199a was added to the Sixth VAT Directive with effect from 16 March 2010. When it was implemented, Article 199a allowed Member States to apply a reverse charge to supplies of emissions allowances and similar units used by businesses to comply with the EU-ETS scheme until 30 June 2015. That date has since been extended to 31 December 2018.The reverse charge operates as a way of reducing the incidence of MTIC fraud.

The UK introduced a further reverse charge on wholesale supplies, between UK counterparties, of gas through a network or system within a Member State and electricity with effect from 1 July 2014. Again, this was with the aim of countering MTIC fraud. [38.30]

EXAMPLE 38.7

Bonzo Motors acquired three cars for resale and has appropriated them for the purpose of its business. It is treated as making a supply of the cars itself and must account for output VAT.

10 Place and time of supply

a) *Place of supply*

VAT only applies to supplies made in the UK (VATA 1994 s 1).

Goods

In the case of a supply of *goods* which are located in the UK, the supply is deemed to be in the UK so that UK VAT is chargeable (VATA 1994 s 7(2)).

1132   *VAT – UK provisions*

If those goods are exported the supply is then generally (see [**38.101**]) zero-rated. Goods supplied outside the UK and which do not enter the UK fall outside the UK VAT net.   [**38.31**]

Services

Prior to 1 January 2010 the basic rule was that services were treated as being supplied in the place where the supplier belongs, which need not be the same place as where the services themselves are performed (on the concept of 'belonging', see VATA 1994 s 9). See, however, [**38.105**] for the many exceptions to this rule.

Two Directives, one on the place of supply of services, the other on VAT refunds (see **Chapter 37** for both), were adopted by the EU Council of Ministers on 12 February 2008. In so far as the place of supply of services is concerned, from 1 January 2010, the rules on the place of supply of services means that B2B supplies of services are taxed where the customer is situated, rather than where the supplier is located. The basic rule for B2C customers did not change (ie VAT generally will continue to be due in the country in which the supplier is established). FA 2009 contained provisions that amended the UK's place of supply of services rules so as to bring them in line with the new European rules. The new basic rule for B2B transactions is that VAT will be due where the business customer (as opposed to the supplier) is established.

The changes to the place of supply rules were phased in – some changes took effect on 1 January 2010, others on 1 January 2011 and others on 1 January 2013. A new regime for electronically supplied services came into effect on 1 January 2015.

There are exceptions to the basic rules set out above. Notably:
(1)   VAT is due on supplies of restaurant and catering services where such services are physically performed;
(2)   supplies of certain intangible services to non-business customers outside the EU continue to be supplied where the customer belongs;
(3)   under the new rules, from 1 January 2011, where supplied to business customers, VAT is due on most supplies of cultural, artistic, sporting, scientific, educational, and entertainment services in the country in which the customer is established. VAT will continue to be due on admission fees to such events, however, in the country where the event takes place.

With regard to telecoms, broadcasting and electronic services, new rules on the place of business to consumer supplies apply since 1 January 2015. Since that date, these services are taxed in the country where the consumer is established. Suppliers may choose either to register for VAT in that country, or to fulfil their VAT obligations in their home Member State using a 'one stop' scheme which allows them to account for VAT on the supplies to private customers in other Member States via a single quarterly VAT return. The supplier identifies in that VAT return the value of supplies made to customers in each Member State and then accounts for VAT on the value of such supplies at the rate applicable in each of the identified Member States. The VAT revenue from these services will then be transferred from the country where the supplier is located to that where the customer is situated. In order to ensure a smooth transition, the Member State of establishment will retain a proportion of the VAT collected until 31 December 2018. This proportion was 30% from 1 January 2015 until 31 December 2016; it is 15% from 1 January 2017 until 31 December 2018 and will be 0% from 1 January 2019 onwards.

[38.32]

b) *Time of supply*

The time of supply (the *tax point*) usually determines both the rate of tax and the accounting period into which the supply falls. The general rule in the case of *goods* is that this is the time when they are removed by the customer or, if not removed, when they are made available to him (VATA 1994 s 6(2)) (the general rules for time of supply may be overridden by statutory instrument (see especially VAT Regulations 1995, SI 1995/2518 Part XI). In the case of *services* it is the time when they are performed (VATA 1994 s 6(3)). If a VAT invoice is issued or payment made before goods are supplied or services are performed, then this will bring forward the time of supply (VATA 1994 s 6(4)) to the date of the invoice or the date on which payment was made. [38.33]

c) *E-commerce*

Much has been made of the potential consequences of e-commerce. As regards the supply of goods, the issues arising are the same as those encountered when using more conventional methods of trading. The place and timing of the supply of goods is unaffected by the method of procurement/delivery. As regards services, the use of new technology poses a range of problems. The basic rule that the place of supply is where the supplier belongs is overridden in the case of specified services (see [38.105]). A major issue arises as to the nature of the service being provided. By way of illustration, where music or text is downloaded is the supply one of data or a limited copyright? A further issue is the need to consider whether a server may comprise a fixed place of business. The nature of digitised goods and the need to prevent wholesale tax avoidance through the location of servers etc in a low tax jurisdiction (or even outside the EU) are issues that are being addressed by the Member States and the EU Commission.

HMRC gives guidance in *VAT: businesses supplying digital services to private consumers* on what constitutes digital services (such as broadcasting, telecommunications, and electronically supplied e-services eg e-books and music) in the context of the recent place of supply rule changes affecting such services. Since 1 January 2015, for all businesses supplying digital services to private individuals in the EU, the place of supply of such services is treated as the place where the customer is established and suppliers need to register and account for the VAT due in that Member State. In order to avoid suppliers having to register and account for VAT in each Member State in which they make supplies to private individuals, a special regime has been introduced whereby the supplier need only register in one Member State (detailed provisions are set out in Sch 3B to VATA 1994). [38.34]–[38.48]

III REGISTRATION, ACCOUNTING FOR TAX AND PENALTIES

1 Registration requirements (VATA 1994 Sch 1)

A person must be registered if:
(1) at the end of any month the value of his taxable supplies over the previous 12 months exceeds £85,000 exclusive of VAT; or
(2) at any time there are reasonable grounds for believing that the value of the taxable supplies that he will make in the next 30 days will exceed £85,000 exclusive of VAT.

HMRC must be notified within 30 days of the end of the relevant month or within 30 days after the date on which reasonable grounds first existed. Registration can be avoided if HMRC are satisfied that, although taxable turnover in the previous 12 months exceeded £85,000, it will not exceed the de-registration threshold of £83,000 in the next 12 months.

A business that is required to be registered because it exceeds the registration limits, can, at HMRC's discretion, be exempted from the requirement to be registered if it makes all or mostly zero-rated supplies and its input tax amounts would normally exceed its output tax amounts (VATA 1994 Sch 1 para 14).

A business that is not required to register under the above rules may still do so on a voluntary basis if it can satisfy HMRC that it is making taxable supplies by way of business (VATA 1994 Sch 1 para 9(a)). This may be helpful for small businesses (whose customers can recover their input tax) that wish to recover input VAT.

A person who is able to satisfy HMRC that he is carrying on activities preparatory to the making of taxable supplies (eg a feasibility study) is entitled to be registered for VAT (see *Merseyside Cablevision Ltd v C & E Comrs* (1987) (VATA 1994 Sch 1 para 9(b)).

Failure to register does not enable a person to escape his VAT obligations. Registration will be backdated when notification is made outside the prescribed time periods and the person will be required to account for output tax from the earlier date whether he has in fact charged it to his customers or not. Penalties may be payable (see **[38.68]**).

A business, which is not required to be registered under the provisions because, for example, it only makes exempt supplies, may nevertheless have to register for VAT if it receives supplies of goods from other EU Member States where their value exceeds £85,000 (VATA 1994 Sch 3 para 1). **[38.49]**

2 Group registration

Corporate bodies who are legally independent, but who are closely bound to one another by financial, economic and organisational links, may obtain a single or 'group' VAT registration. The consequence of this is that supplies of goods or services within the group are disregarded for VAT purposes (VATA 1994 s 43). This is particularly attractive when one or more companies in the group make exempt supplies and, hence, suffer restrictions on the recovery of input tax. Group registration does not affect the characterisation of supplies made by a group member to persons outside the group (see *Canary Wharf Ltd v C & E Comrs* (1996)).

Registration is in the name of a 'representative member'. The representative member becomes liable for VAT in respect of all group companies. Each individual company in a group remains jointly and severally liable for the tax payable by the representative member. Companies may join and leave a group on making an application to HMRC.

To qualify for group registration:
(a) companies must be resident or have an established place of business in the UK; and
(b) there must be 'control' between the members.

Two or more companies are eligible to be treated as members of a group if either:
- one of them controls each of the others (control depends on majority voting rights or rights to appoint or remove a majority of board directors);
- one person (whether a body corporate or individual controls all of them); or
- two or more individuals carrying on a business in partnership control all of them.

When a company ceases to fulfil the control requirements, HMRC can issue a notice to the company terminating its membership of the group from a specified date.

The Value Added Tax (Groups: Eligibility) Order 2004 was introduced as an anti-avoidance measure. This requires that 'specified bodies' must satisfy two additional conditions; the 'benefits condition' and the 'consolidated accounts condition'. What constitutes a 'specified body' is set out in Article 3 of the Order. The measures only apply to businesses that are in VAT groups or are intending to join a VAT group, where the VAT group concerned has turnover exceeding £10 million a year. Articles 5 and 6(1) set out the details of the conditions. In summary, the measure ensures that the economic benefits from the VAT group do not accrue to a third party. If the entity's accounts are not, or would not be, consolidated in the group accounts of the person controlling the VAT group, a VAT group will not be permitted. These additional rules only apply where the entity managed for the benefit of the third party makes, or intends to make, positive-rated supplies to a member of the VAT group and the VAT group would be unable to recover VAT on such supplies in full.

Under current UK legislation, it is possible for non-taxable persons (eg holding companies and dormant companies) to be included within a VAT group. This applies also in The Netherlands, Ireland, Finland, Czech Republic and Denmark. The Commission considered that the legislation in these six Member States is incompatible with the EU rules on VAT grouping and referred these six Member States to the ECJ. The ECJ confirmed on 25 April 2013 (see *Commission v UK* (C-86/11)) that the UK's VAT grouping rules do not contravene EU law by permitting non-taxable persons to be members of a VAT group. The ECJ gave similar decisions in *Commission v Netherlands* (C-65/11), *Commission v Finland* (C-74/11), *Commission v Denmark* (C-95/11), *Commission v Czech Republic* (C-109/11) and *Commission v Ireland* (C-85/11).

In 2016, HMRC met with business representatives to discuss the VAT grouping in the light of the ECJ's decisions in *Beteiligungsgesellschaft Larentia*

+ *Minerva mbH & Co. KG v Finanzamt Nordenham* (Case C-108/14), *Finanzamt Hamburg-Mitte, v Marenave Schiffahrts AG* (Case C-109/14) and *Skandia America Corp. (USA), filial Sverige v Skatteverket* (Case C-7/13). Changes that may be introduced include extending VAT grouping to non-corporate bodies and replacing the current 'control' test with new rules that adopt a test of 'close, economic, financial and organisational' links for corporate and non-corporate bodies. [38.50]

3 De-registration

HMRC may cancel a registration if satisfied that the business was not registrable at the time when it did in fact register or has since ceased to be registrable (VATA 1994 Sch 1 para 13(2) and 13(3)). A registered 'intending trader' must notify HMRC within 30 days if he will not now make taxable supplies, otherwise penalties may be imposed (VATA 1994 Sch 1 para 11).

If a business permanently ceases to make taxable supplies it *must* notify HMRC within 30 days. A business may voluntarily de-register if it is expected that its taxable turnover will fall below £83,000 in the coming year. Unless there are very unusual circumstances, deregistration cannot be effected retrospectively. [38.51]

4 Accounting for VAT

a) *General rule*

Generally, VAT on supplies of goods and services must be accounted for on a quarterly basis with quarterly accounting periods being allocated to the trader at the time of his registration. The tax operates on the basis of self-assessment. From 1 April 2012, virtually all VAT-registered businesses have been required to submit their VAT returns (Form VAT 1) online; and penalties may be imposed by HMRC for filing paper returns.

Any tax payable must be received by HMRC by the end of the month following the end of the relevant quarter period. A seven-day extension is allowed if payment is by credit transfer, but this has been withdrawn for businesses within the 'payments on account' provisions.

The taxpayer must pay the difference between output and input tax applicable to supplies during the quarter period. HMRC will repay excess input tax, normally within ten working days of receiving the return (VATA 1994 s 25(3)). If a taxpayer has, by mistake, overpaid tax in an earlier period HMRC must refund that amount (VATA 1994 s 80) unless the taxpayer would be unjustly enriched by the repayment (VATA 1994 s 80(3)). [38.52]

b) *The 'capping' provisions*

FA 1997 introduced a three-year time limit on the refunding of claims made under VATA 1994 s 80 (understated or overpaid VAT) with effect from 19 March 1997 and with retrospective effect. With effect from 1 May 1997, the three-year cap was extended further (by an amendment to reg 29 of SI 1995/2518) so as to include, amongst other things, late claims for input tax.

The legality of these provisions has been the subject of extensive litigation. In particular, the legality of the unjust enrichment provisions and the 'three-year cap' provisions were challenged by Marks & Spencer in litigation that started in the 1990s. In 1991, the VAT Tribunal held that a 'Jaffa cake' was a (zero-rated) chocolate-covered cake and not a (standard-rated) chocolate-covered biscuit. In 1994, HMRC agreed that chocolate-covered marshmallow teacakes should have been zero-rated since 1973, and that all those (including Marks & Spencer) who had been accounting for VAT at the standard rate on their sales of teacakes were, in principle, entitled to a refund. Marks & Spencer's claim for all the amounts overpaid by way of VAT since 1973 was, however, resisted on two grounds: unjust enrichment and the three-year cap.

HMRC considered that, until the law was changed in 2005, the unjust enrichment defence could be used only against a specific category of claimants, namely payment traders (ie those who had made an overpayment by way of VAT to Customs & Excise in the relevant period). It could not apply to those who had underclaimed input tax (repayment traders). Marks & Spencer (through its sales of clothing and other standard-rated goods) was in most periods a payment trader, and most other sellers of teacakes (selling mainly zero-rated food) were repayment traders. This meant that it was possible that a claim by one business could be refused whilst a similar claim from another business could not. Marks & Spencer claimed that this breached the EC law principle of equal treatment and challenged the discriminatory nature of the legislation. On the three-year cap issue, Marks & Spencer argued that its introduction with retrospective effect was contrary to the EC law principles of effectiveness (the exercise of rights must not be rendered impossible in practice) and legitimate expectation. Ultimately, the ECJ agreed with Marks & Spencer, concluding that:

(1) where the UK has misinterpreted its own zero-rating legislation so that a trader has been overcharged VAT, the general principles of EC law apply so as to give such a trader a directly enforceable EC law right to recover the overpayments;
(2) if the UK wished to enact an unjust enrichment defence in its domestic legislation, it had to do so having regard to EC law principles, in particular the principles of equal treatment and fiscal neutrality; and
(3) there could be no objective justification for discrimination between 'payment traders' and 'repayment traders'.

The ECJ said that the existence and degree of any unjust enrichment required a full economic analysis, which is a matter for the national court. The case was remitted to the House of Lords. However, 'after thirteen years of litigation, HMRC decided that they did not wish to pursue these matters'.

In June 2003, Condé Nast claimed an input tax deduction for expenditure on staff entertainment that it had mistakenly failed to deduct in past periods, going back as far as 1973. Whilst the Revenue accepted that the claim was valid, they asserted that reg 29 time-barred the claim. Condé Nast argued that because reg 29 had been introduced with effect from 1 May 1997 without adequate transitional provisions to restrict its immediate effect, it was in breach of EC law, and should be disapplied. The House of Lords agreed (in the joined cases of *Fleming and Condé Nast Publications Ltd v C & E Comrs* (2008)). They held that that the three-year cap was unlawful in so far as it purported to apply to claims for input VAT that had accrued before 1 May 1997, but had not been claimed before that date. This was because it had not been introduced with a 'reasonable transitional period', ie taxpayers did not have a reasonable opportunity to submit late accrued claims before the introduction of the new regime. The lack of adequate transitional arrangements in relation to the three-year cap that could have allowed taxpayers the opportunity to bring claims which the previous law would have allowed them to make breached the EU law principle of effectiveness. The House of Lords held that unless and until Parliament or HMRC announced to all taxpayers that a transitional period was being introduced, the three-year limitation period could not start to run.

As a result of these cases, FA 2008 introduced a transitional period (that ended on 31 March 2009) during which businesses could submit claims for:
(1) output tax overpaid in accounting periods ending before 4 December 1996, and
(2) input tax incurred in accounting periods ending before 1 May 1997 and not claimed (subject to the holding of the required evidence).

The effect of the legislation was that:
(1) the requirement, under VATA 1994 s 80(4) that a claim under that section must be brought within the appropriate time limit does not apply in respect of claims for output tax overpaid in periods ending before 4 December 1996, provided that the claim was made before 1 April 2009; and
(2) the requirement, under VATA 1994 s 25(6) (via SI 1995/2518 reg 29(1A)) that an input tax claim may not be made outside the appropriate time limit, does not apply in respect of claims where the tax was chargeable, and in respect of which the claimant held the required evidence, in a period ending before 1 May 1997, provided the claim is made before 1 April 2009.

Corresponding measures allow HMRC to raise an assessment where the payment of such a claim is subsequently found to be incorrect.

The time limit for submitting a claim for input tax was extended from three years to four years with effect from 1 April 2009.   [38.53]

c) *Tax invoice requirements*

A taxable person must keep detailed records and accounts for six years, together with full supporting documents. These are open to inspection by HMRC.

In order to recover input tax, a taxable person must be in possession of a valid tax invoice. Unless HMRC allow otherwise, a VAT invoice must show the following particulars:
(1) an identifying number;
(2) the time of the supply, ie tax point;
(3) the date of issue of the document;
(4) the name, address and registration number of the supplier;

(5) the name and address of the person to whom the goods or services are supplied;
(6) a description sufficient to identify the goods or services supplied;
(7) where services are supplied, a description of the services may be taken as sufficient to describe also the type of supply under (6) above and their extent under (8) below. For professional services, a description such as 'professional services rendered' is acceptable;
(8) for each description, the quantity of the goods or extent of the services, the rate of VAT and amount payable, excluding VAT, expressed in any currency;
(9) the unit price. This applies to 'countable' goods and services. For services, the countable element might be, for example, an hourly rate or a price paid for standard services. If the supply cannot be broken down into countable elements, the total VAT-exclusive price is the unit price. Additionally, the unit price may not need to be shown at all if it is not normally provided in a particular business sector and is not required by the customer (VAT Information Sheet 16/03, para 3.2.);
(10) the gross amount payable, excluding VAT, expressed in any currency;
(11) the rate of any cash discount offered; and
(12) the total amount of VAT chargeable expressed in sterling.

With effect from 1 January 2013, where the consideration for a supply does not exceed £250, a simplified invoice may be issued. The details shown on a simplified invoice can be limited to:
(a) the name, address and registration number of the supplier;
(b) the time of the supply;
(c) a description sufficient to identify the goods or services supplied;
(d) the total amount payable including VAT; and
(e) for each rate of VAT chargeable, the gross amount payable including VAT, and the VAT rate applicable. [38.54]

d) *Monthly returns*

Businesses likely to obtain a refund of input tax (typically an export business) may submit monthly returns (SI 1995/2518 reg 25). [38.55]

e) *Monthly payments on account*

'Very large' VAT payers (defined as those whose liability in the year ending on the last day of the last VAT quarter before the previous 1 December, or after the previous 30 November, exceeds £2.3m in a year – see VAT Notice 700/60) are required to make monthly VAT payments on account, based on the VAT liability in an annual reference period, generally at the end of each of the second and third months of every VAT quarter following the quarter in which that threshold was breached. The reference period is the year ending before the previous 30 September, 31 October or 30 November, depending on whether the first month of the quarter in which the payment on account liability begins is April, May or June. A business that is within the payments on account scheme may leave it only if its liability falls below £1.8 million.
[38.56]

f) Annual returns

Completing four VAT returns per year may present a burden to smaller businesses. As an alternative, such businesses with an annual value of taxable supplies not expected to exceed £1.35 million within 12 months may make an annual VAT return. (If a business already makes annual returns, it can continue to do so until its estimated VAT taxable turnover exceeds £1.6 million.) On the basis of the previous year's results, nine monthly payments (or three quarterly payments) must be made by direct debit; the final payment (adjusted as appropriate) together with the VAT return must then be made in the two-month period following the end of the year. [38.57]

g) Cash accounting

Businesses whose annual value of taxable supplies are not expected to exceed £1.35 million may also be assisted by electing to make VAT returns on a cash basis: ie by reference to output tax actually collected in the quarter less input tax paid in that same period. In other cases returns are on the basis of invoices issued and received rather than cash received or paid. (If a business already uses cash accounting, it can continue to do so until its estimated VAT taxable turnover exceeds £1.6 million.) [38.58]

h) Bad debt relief

In general, VAT is charged on the basis of invoices issued to customers irrespective of whether payment has been received. However, VAT relief in respect of bad debts can be granted pursuant to VATA 1994 s 36.

The requirements for relief are that the taxpayer must have:
(1) supplied goods or services;
(2) accounted for and paid VAT on that supply; and
(3) written off the whole or part of the consideration in his accounts; if an invoice is outstanding for six months, then the debtor will be obliged to repay the VAT to HMRC. In addition:
  (a) six months must have elapsed from the date on which payment became due and payable or, if later, the date of supply; and
  (b) claims must be made within four years and six months of the date on which payment became due or the date of supply, whichever is the later.

The result of a successful claim will be either a reduction in output VAT payable in the relevant quarter or, in appropriate circumstances, a refund of VAT. [38.59]

EXAMPLE 38.8 – BAD DEBT RELIEF – GENERAL

HMS submits returns for the VAT periods ending 31 January, 30 April, 31 July and 31 October and issued an invoice to a customer on 30 April for £20,000 + £4,000 VAT. Payment terms are 30 days from the tax point so settlement should have been received by 30 May. However, payment had still not been received by the end of October. Bad debt relief is available six months from 30 May. The claim would be made in the January return.

EXAMPLE 38.9 – BAD DEBT RELIEF DETAIL

Patrick is a trader who makes both standard-rated and zero-rated sales. He has made the following sales:

Date of Supply	Due Date for Payment	Rate	Price excluding VAT	VAT	Total
			£	£	£
4 April	31 May	Standard	2,100	420	2,520
10 May	30 June	Zero	1,430	–	1,430
10 June	31 July	Standard	1,200	240	1,440
15 August	30 September	Standard	1,520	304	1,824
31 August	30 September	Zero	800	–	800
			7,050	964	8,014

Patrick received the following payments on account:

	£
18 July	1,800
7 September	850

At a meeting of the creditors on 1 November the debt due to Patrick was proved and a resolution to wind up the company was passed.

Patrick submits his VAT returns quarterly for the periods ending 31 January, 30 April, 31 July and 31 October.

The bad debt relief that Patrick may claim for VAT purposes is as follows:

Bad debt relief claimable under VATA 1994 s 36

Tax point	Payment Date	Gross Debt	Payment Received (FIFO*)	Unpaid	VAT Fraction	VAT
		£	£	£	£	£
4 April	31 May	2,520	2,520	–	–	–
10 May	30 June	1,430	130	1,300	–	–
10 June	31 July	1,440	–	1,440	$\frac{1}{6}$	240
15 August	30 September	1,824	–	1,824	$\frac{1}{6}$	304
31 August	30 September	800	–	800	–	–
			2,650	5,364		504

Bad debt relief claimable:

Input Tax	Payment Due Date	Relief Claimable From	In Quarter Ended
£			
240	31 July	31 January	31 January
304	30 September	31 March	30 April
Debt to be claimed from liquidator			£5,364

[38.60]–[38.67]

5 Penalties

Introduction

FA 2007 s 97 and Sch 24 introduced a revised system of penalties in respect of inaccuracies made on documents sent by taxpayers to HMRC. The purpose of the change was to create, following the merger of the revenue departments, a single penalty framework for VAT, income tax, capital gains tax, corporation tax, PAYE, NIC and deductions made under the construction industry scheme. In relation to VAT, this regime has replaced, for the most part, the provisions in VATA relating to dishonest evasion of VAT, the misdeclaration penalty and the repeated misdeclaration penalty. The new regime came into force on 1 April 2008. However, in order to give taxpayers the opportunity to familiarise themselves with the regime, no penalties were issued before 1 April 2009.

The system has been amended since its introduction. Of particular relevance is that, since 1 April 2010, HMRC has been able to impose a penalty under FA 2008, Sch 41 for (a) failing to inform HMRC about a tax obligation at the correct time (eg that the turnover of the business has reached the VAT registration threshold) and (b) 'VAT and excise wrongdoing', which includes, for example, issuing an invoice that includes VAT the person is not entitled to charge.

The new regime provides a 'compliance spectrum', within which an 'inaccuracy' falls into one of the following categories:

(1) one which has arisen despite the fact that the taxpayer has taken 'reasonable care';
(2) one which has arisen as a result of failure to take 'reasonable care';
(3) a deliberate understatement or overclaim; and
(4) an aggravated deliberate understatement/overclaim, ie one where the taxpayer has concealed his action (but not to such a degree as to warrant criminal prosecution).

Inaccuracies that fall within category 1 do not attract a penalty. Those that fall into categories 2–4 attract penalties of increasing severity. Mitigation may be applied according to: (1) the category of inaccuracy; (2) the manner in which the inaccuracy is disclosed; and (3) the 'quality' of the disclosure. The defence of 'reasonable excuse' is, in effect, replaced by the 'reasonable care' provision in category 1. [38.68]–[38.80]

IV THE RECOVERY OF VAT, PARTIAL EXEMPTION AND THE CAPITAL GOODS SCHEME

1 The deduction principle

A taxable person is only entitled to deduct the VAT that he has incurred from the output tax for which he must account if it was incurred in the course or furtherance of a business and incurred in the making of (a) taxable supplies, (b) supplies which are outside the scope of VAT because they were made outside the UK but which would have been taxable if made in the UK, or (c) supplies of 'out of scope' services to a person that does not belong in a Member State (ie certain qualifying financial supplies that are exempt if supplied in the UK but give rise to a right to recover input tax incurred in making them when they are made outside the EU). Input tax on post cessation expenditure may continue to be regarded as deductible provided that there is a direct and immediate link between the payments made and the commercial activity and that the absence of any fraudulent or abusive intent has been established (*I/S Fini H v Skatteministeriet* (Case C-32/03)). **[38.81]**

2 The need for apportionment

In *Lennartz* (Case C-97/90), the ECJ held that where a person acquires goods partly for business and partly for non-business use, he is entitled to full input tax recovery, but output tax will be due on the supply that is deemed to take place when and to the extent that, the goods are put to a private or non-business use. UK legislation provides that where goods or services are obtained for both a business and a non-business purpose, the VAT should be apportioned, with only that proportion that relates to the business activity being treated as input tax. Thus, as a general rule, UK taxpayers have the option of recovering input tax in full and accounting for output tax on the private or non-business element under the *Lennartz* principle, or recovering only that proportion of the tax which relates to business use. Where a taxable person has made any supplies otherwise than in the course or furtherance of his business, he must carry out an apportionment in order to identify and exclude that VAT from deduction. The remaining VAT is recoverable to the extent that it can be attributed to taxable supplies and does not fall within a category of expense for which there is no right to recover (see examples below).

EU changes abolishing the *Lennartz* rule on VAT input tax recovery on the purchase of an interest in real property, boats and aircraft have been implemented with effect from 1 January 2011 to ensure that VAT recovery is restricted to the business use of such assets (Value Added Tax (Amendment) (No 4) Regulations 2010, SI 2010/3022). **[38.82]**

EXAMPLE 38.10 – BUSINESS GIFTS

(i) Sophie buys 200 bottles of whisky and gives two each to 100 customers as Christmas gifts. Each bottle costs £10. Sophie may recover input tax in full on the purchase and no output tax is due because the value to each recipient is less than £50.

(ii) Michael buys 200 bottles of whisky and gives four each to 50 customers as Christmas gifts. Each bottle costs £20. Michael may recover input tax in full on the purchase but as the value to each recipient is more than £50 (ie £80), output tax is due on the cost. Michael must pay as output tax the same amount as has been claimed as input tax.

EXAMPLE 38.11 – INPUT TAX

(1) Jack has a chain of bicycle shops and wishes to expand into Germany. He has identified suitable properties and engages the services of a local solicitor who charges €5,000. The invoice does not show VAT. Davies converts the value to sterling, say £4,000, adds £800 VAT at 20%, then on his next return pays £800 output tax and claims £800 input tax.

(2) Anne Ltd imports parts from Germany. The latest assignment was for €10,000 without VAT. The company converts this to sterling, say £8,000, adds £1,600 VAT, and includes this as payable in its next return (ie the £1,600 is added to other output tax). It then claims back the same amount as input tax.

EXAMPLE 38.12 – PRE-TRADING

Adam sets up in business as a house builder. His plan is to buy land, build houses and sell them. He cannot start the business until he has worked his notice at his current employment. Before he leaves, he incurs the following set-up costs:

- Tools   £6,000 + £1,200 VAT
- Solicitors fees   £1,000 + £200 VAT
- Accountants fees   £1,200 + £240 VAT

He may register immediately and reclaim the £1,640 input tax on his first return. He would probably complete returns monthly because all of his outputs (sales of houses) would be zero-rated and he would always be claiming a refund from HMRC.

EXAMPLE 38.13 – LATE CLAIM

Angela runs a clothing shop and is VAT registered, completing returns to the end of March, June, September and December. She bought a computer for £2,400 + £420 VAT (at 17.5%) on 30 June 2013. She also had some shop repairs carried out. The invoice was for £4,000 + £800 VAT (at 20%) and dated 30 December 2016. She failed to claim the input tax on either at the time.

When completing her September 2017 return, she realises the error. She can still reclaim the £800 on this return but the £420 cannot be claimed because the supply took place more than three years ago.

EXAMPLE 38.14 – ABORTIVE EXPENDITURE

Both Andy Ltd and Nash Ltd start research into a vaccine on 30 September 2015 and register for VAT as intending traders. On 31 December 2016, Andy Ltd launches its new successful product and starts making taxable supplies. However, Nash Ltd is unsuccessful and the research stops on 30 September 2017. Neither has made exempt supplies so all input tax reclaimed prior to making taxable supplies/ceasing research will not be disturbed and will not be clawed back by HMRC.

3 Partial exemption

A business that makes a combination of taxable and exempt supplies must attempt to attribute VAT either to its taxable business or its exempt business. Businesses such as insurance companies, banks and property developers usually make exempt supplies (see [**38.8**]) and are obviously affected, but other businesses may also be caught. Typically, rent received from property may give rise to an exempt output and so 'taint' the VAT recovery position of the business. When a business makes exempt supplies the question is how much input tax should be attributed to those exempt supplies and so be irrecoverable (this is referred to as 'exempt input tax'). For the purposes of this apportionment, supplies that are outside the scope of VAT, because they were made to a person who belongs outside the UK, are to be regarded as giving rise to a right of recovery (see *C & E Comrs v Liverpool Institute of Performing Arts* (1999)). [38.83]

4 The solution (VATA 1994 ss 25 and 26; SI 1995/2518)

The following rules apply:

First, input tax directly attributable to goods and services exclusively used or to be used in making taxable or other supplies carrying a right to recovery is fully recoverable.

Second, input tax directly attributable to goods and services exclusively used or to be used in making exempt supplies or in any other non-taxable activity is irrecoverable.

Third, the residual input tax must then relate to both taxable and exempt (or non-taxable) activities (a common example is the cost of VAT incurred on overheads). This remaining tax must be apportioned in accordance with the 'standard method' (a turnover based method) (see [38.86]) or in accordance with a reasonable method agreed with HMRC (referred to as the 'special method').

In *Schemepanel Trading Ltd v C & E Comrs* (1996), the legislation was summarised by Lord Brightman as follows:

> 'If the business activities of the taxpayer are such that all the supplies which he makes are subject to output tax (whether positive rated or zero rated) he recovers all the tax which he pays on the inputs of that business ... If all the supplies he makes are exempt supplies, he can recover none and the probability is that he will not even be registered. If the supplies which he makes are partly taxable supplies and partly exempt supplies there is to be an apportionment of the tax and that which is attributable to the exempt supplies is not recoverable.' [38.84]

5 Apportionment methods

A variety of methods are possible. However, regardless of whether the standard (ie turnover-based) method or a special method is used, if input tax is incurred partly in relation to exempt supplies and partly in relation to other supplies, then the taxpayer can recover only that amount of such input tax used in making taxable supplies (VAT Regulations 1995, SI 1995/2518 reg 101). [38.85]

a) *'Standard method'*

The standard method seeks to achieve apportionment according to the ratio of value of taxable supplies to total supplies (taxable and exempt) in a VAT period. The fraction is reduced to a percentage. The fraction must be calculated for each VAT accounting period (monthly or quarterly) using the percentage rounded down to the nearest whole number. At the end of the VAT accounting year (called a 'longer period'), the values must be aggregated and an annual adjustment performed. The percentage is rounded up for the annual adjustment. Certain supplies made by the taxpayer, such as supplies of capital goods, incidental real estate transactions, incidental financial services and self-supplies are ignored for the purpose of this calculation (VAT Regulations 1995, SI 1995/2518 reg 101(3)), ie the income derived from such transactions is not included as turnover. The standard method must be used unless and until an alternative method is approved by or imposed by HMRC.

A standard method override notice can be issued by HMRC where the results of the standard method do not reflect the use made of the purchases. Businesses must adjust the input tax deductible under the standard method at the end of their tax year if that amount is substantially different from an attribution based on the use of purchases. 'Substantially' means £50,000 or greater, or 50% or more of the value of the residual input tax but not less than £25,000. [38.86]

EXAMPLE 38.15

A taxpayer suffers the following input tax:

		£
(i)	That attributed to taxable supplies	500,000
(ii)	That attributed to exempt supplies	150,000
(iii)	Residual input tax	350,000
		£1,000,000

His taxable supplies total £10m and exempt supplies £2m.

To calculate the amount of residual input tax recoverable under the standard method:

(i) calculate (as a percentage) the ratio of taxable supplies to all supplies, ie:

$$\frac{10,000,000}{12,000,000} \times 100 = 83.33\% \ (rounded \ up \ to \ 84\%)$$

(ii) multiply residual (or 'non-attributable') input tax by this percentage to obtain input tax recoverable:
$$£350,000 \times 84\% = \underline{£294,000}$$

b) *Special methods*

By virtue of SI 1995/2518 reg 102, HMRC may approve or direct the use of any other method of apportioning residual input tax. Again, supplies of capital goods, incidental real estate transactions, incidental financial services and self-supplies must be ignored in making the calculation (SI 1995/2518 reg 102(2)). A special method is unique to a business as it deals with that business's particular circumstances. One alternative way of apportioning residual input tax is by employing the fraction (the 'input tax' based method, which was formerly the standard method):

$$\frac{input \ tax \ directly \ attributable \ to \ taxable \ outputs}{input \ tax \ directly \ attributable \ to \ taxable \ and \ exempt \ outputs}$$

A special method must be approved in writing in order to be valid. HMRC will approve a special method if it is fair and reasonable. A special method override notice allows HMRC or a business to correct the results of an unfair special method until a replacement method is implemented. [38.87]

EXAMPLE 38.16

Taking the facts of *Example 38.16* the input tax based method would produce the following:
(i) multiply residual input tax by the formula. Using the numbering in *Example 38.16* this becomes:

$$\frac{(i)}{(i)+(ii)}$$

(ii) tax recoverable is:

$$£350,000 \times \frac{500,000}{650,000} = £269,230$$

EXAMPLE 38.17 – ALTERNATIVE SPECIAL METHOD

A partly exempt business receives £4,000,000 taxable income excluding VAT and £2,000,000 exempt income. Total input VAT for the quarter is £300,000 of which £120,000 is directly attributable to taxable supplies, £100,000 is directly attributable to exempt supplies and £80,000 is non-attributable.

The non-attributable input VAT is apportioned as follows:

$$£80,000 \times \frac{4,000,000 \ (\textit{value of taxable supplies})}{4,000,000 + 2,000,000 \ (\textit{value of taxable supplies})}$$

The ratio must be expressed as a percentage rounded up to the next whole number (in this case 66.66% rounded up to 67%) so here the recoverable amount is:

$$£80,000 \times 67\% = £53,600.$$

Total VAT recoverable for the period is therefore £120,000 (direct attribution) + £53,600 (partial exemption calculation) = £173,600.

6 De minimis

EU law provides that where the amount of input tax which is not deductible by a taxable person is insignificant, Member States may allow it to be treated as nil (ie it may be recovered in full). The *de minimis* rules provide that, when the exempt input tax of a trader is not more than £625 per month on average and provided this exempt input tax is no more than 50% of all input tax in the relevant period, all input tax shall be treated as attributable to taxable supplies so that the taxpayer is fully taxable and able to recover *all* input tax (SI 1995/2518 reg 106). This test must be applied for each VAT return and again when the annual adjustment is calculated at the end of the year.

In calculating whether the *de minimis* rules apply, input tax attributable to certain exempt supplies (such as a deposit of money) may be ignored provided the taxpayer's business is not that of a bank or certain other financial institutions. Such input tax may be treated as attributable to taxable supplies and therefore ignored in applying the *de minimis* rules. This provision is intended to permit small businesses to avoid partial exemption. [38.88]

EXAMPLE 38.18 – DETAILED ILLUSTRATION OF PARTIAL EXEMPTION

For the VAT year ended 31 March 2017 Sophie had the following transactions:

	£
General sales (standard rate VAT)	240,000
General sales (zero rate VAT)	20,000
Plant sold to UK trader	10,000
Plant sold to a trader in Australia and exported to him	10,000
Exempt supplies made	200,000
Wages to employees	150,000
New motor car purchased March 2004 for use by salesman (petrol only provided for business use)	24,000
(None of the above amounts include VAT)	
Input tax:	
Attributable to taxable supplies	20,000
exempt supplies	12,000
Overheads	8,000
purchase of car	4,200

The total amount of output tax for which Sophie is required to account and her deductible input tax for the year ended 31 March 2017 is as follows:

Output tax and input tax for year ended 31 March 2014

	£	£	£
Outputs chargeable at standard rate:			
Sales	240,000		
Plant sold to UK trader	10,000	250,000	
Outputs chargeable at zero rate:			
Sales	20,000		
Plant sold to Australian trader	10,000	30,000	
Total taxable outputs		280,000	
Exempt outputs		200,000	
Total outputs		480,000	
Output tax on taxable outputs of 250,000 at 20%			50,000
Input tax attributable to taxable supplies		20,000	
Input tax attributable to overheads	8,000		
Allowable proportion:			
$\frac{260,000}{460,000} = 75\% \times £8,000$		4,560	24,560
Net payment to HMRC for year			£25,440

Note

The sales of capital items, ie the plant sold to UK and Australia, traders, are distortive and left out of the fraction.

The irrecoverable input tax of £15,440 (£12,000 + (£8,000 – £4,560) = £3,440) will be treated as an allowable expense in computing Sophie's profit for income tax purposes.

The input tax on the purchase of the car is also irrecoverable and will count as part of the cost of the car for capital allowances purposes.

7 The Capital Goods Scheme

The 'requirement to make adjustments to the deduction of input tax on capital items' scheme, more commonly known as the 'Capital Goods Scheme', was introduced with effect from 1 April 1991. It was introduced in response to concerns that certain traders were recovering input tax in circumstances where the goods on which the input tax was incurred were not, in the long term, being used in a fully taxable business (reflecting the fact that capital expenditure will normally benefit a business over a period of time (ie in contrast to income expenditure that is primarily for the benefit of the current period of account)). For example, a person who made taxable supplies only, but who was planning subsequently to make exempt supplies also, could purchase a computer system and obtain credit for the whole of the VAT incurred in a period in which he only made taxable supplies, and then subsequently use that computer system in his exempt business. Similarly, a person who buys a boat for business use but plans to later also use it for non-business purposes could obtain credit for the whole of the VAT incurred if it was a period in which he made only taxable supplies. Under the scheme, input tax deducted in respect of capital items supplied to, or acquired or imported by, traders is adjusted where the extent to which those items are used for taxable/exempt supplies or business/non-business use fluctuates.   **[38.89]**

Assets within the scheme

Expenditure on the following assets is within the scheme:
(1) a computer or item of computer equipment to a value of at least £50,000;
(2) aircraft, ships, boats and other vessels to a value of at least £50,000; and
(3) land, buildings and civil engineering works to a value of at least £250,000.
[38.90]

Initial deduction

In the year that an asset within the scheme is first acquired, a business calculates the proportion of VAT on the asset that it is entitled to deduct, in accordance with the usual rules (see **[38.81]–[38.88]**).   **[38.91]**

Subsequent adjustments

In the second and subsequent 'adjustment intervals', the business must adjust the VAT initially claimed if the extent to which the asset is used for the purposes of the business's taxable supplies is greater or less than the extent to which it was used in the initial period.   **[38.92]**

Period of adjustment

The number of 'adjustment intervals' depends on the nature of the asset. In the case of an interest in land, buildings and civil engineering works, the VAT deducted is adjusted over ten intervals. There are only five adjustment intervals for computers, aircraft, ships, boats and other vessels. The adjustment interval is the 'longer period' (see [38.85]), normally a year, ending on 31 March, 30 April or 31 May.

Where the asset is sold as part of the transfer of a going concern, an adjustment period will end on the day the asset is transferred. The transferor must then make an adjustment based on the use for that period. The transferee inherits the obligation to make any adjustments over the remaining number of intervals. An adjustment interval will also end where a company leaves or joins a VAT group. Therefore, although the adjustment interval is normally a year, it does not have to be and the adjustment period may therefore be less than ten years or five years. [38.93]

Making the adjustment

At the end of each interval following the first interval (the year of acquisition) it is necessary to compare the input tax recovery percentage of the business with the recovery percentage in the year of acquisition. If that subsequent recovery percentage is *less* than the initial percentage, input tax has been over-recovered and an amount is payable to HMRC; if the then recovery percentage is *greater* than the first year's, a repayment is due from HMRC. Special rules apply where the capital item is disposed of during the period of adjustment and F(No 2)A 1997 introduced anti-avoidance provisions to prevent the artificial manipulation of the disposal price. [38.94]–[38.100]

EXAMPLE 38.19

What to plc purchases a computer for £200,000 exclusive of VAT that is £40,000. The company is partly exempt throughout the following four years but then leases the computer to another business for the fifth year.

Year	% of use taxable	Input tax claims (£)	Adjustment %	Amount of adjustment (£)
1	51	20,400		
2	46		−5	−400
3	49		−2	−160
4	52		+1	+80
5	100		+49	+3,920

Notes:
(1) The adjustment each year is:

$$\frac{total\ input\ tax}{total\ years\ (5)} \times the\ adjustment\ percentage$$

For instance, in *year 2*:

$$\frac{40{,}000}{5} \times 5\% = £400$$

(2) The total input tax recovered (net of payments made to HMRC) is £*23,840*.
(3) Leasing the computer to another person results in 100% taxable use in *year 5*.

EXAMPLE 38.20

X Ltd purchases a new commercial property in June 2014 for £1m plus VAT. It exercises the option to tax and lets out the building for 10 years. All VAT is therefore recovered. In June 2015 it sells the building to Y Ltd for £900,000 and Y Ltd exercises the option to tax (see **[39.27]**). Because Y buys subject to the existing letting, the sale is treated as the transfer of a business as a going concern so that no VAT is charged. Y Ltd now steps into X Ltd's shoes for the purposes of the scheme. In June 2017, Y Ltd obtains vacant possession of the premises and goes into occupation for the purposes of its own partially exempt business (property investment).

The consequence is that for the last seven years of the 10-year period, the building will not be used for fully taxable purposes and Y Ltd must repay part of the input tax recovered by X Ltd.

V INTERNATIONAL SUPPLIES OF GOODS AND SERVICES

1 General principle

The VAT treatment of the import and export of goods depends on whether or not the movement is between EU countries. Movements to and from non-EU countries are taxed on a destination basis: zero-rated VAT is charged on direct exports and certain indirect exports (since October 2013, indirect exports to non-UK resident persons, overseas authorities and traders with no UK business establishment from which taxable supplies are made are also zero-rated, provided conditions are met concerning evidence of export), and VAT is chargeable on imports. The treatment of goods movements between Member States depends on whether or not the person receiving the goods is a taxable person and registered for VAT purposes.

The treatment of international services is more complex. *First*, it depends on the categorisation of the service for VAT purposes. Certain services fall outside the scope of UK VAT because they are regarded as being supplied where the customer is established or where the use and enjoyment of the service takes place. These exceptions apply notwithstanding the fact that the supplier is based within the UK. Similarly, services received from abroad may be regarded as supplied within the UK and, in principle, subject to UK VAT. *Second*, there is no absolute zero-rating of services supplied to any persons outside the UK.

It is also important to note that, in the case of both goods imported from within the EU (acquisitions – VATA 1994 s 1(3)) and certain services (VATA 1994 s 8), the liability to account for VAT is shifted to the person importing the goods and services (the customer). **[38.101]**

2 Export of goods to countries outside the EU

Under VATA 1994 s 30(6), a supply of goods is zero-rated if HMRC are satisfied that the person supplying the goods has (a) exported them to a place outside the EU, or (b) has shipped them for use as stores on a voyage or flight to an eventual destination outside the UK (other than for a private purpose) (see also VAT Regulations 1995 (SI 1995/2518)).

It is generally necessary for exports to be made directly to a customer for zero-rating to apply. However, as mentioned above, there is an exception in the case of indirect exports

In order to justify zero-rating it is essential to be able to produce evidence of export to HMRC, such as the airway bill or shipped bill of lading.

The retail export scheme under the VAT Regulations applies to 'overseas visitors' to the UK, and allows retailers to zero-rate supplies of certain goods. The taxable person is at risk if the goods are not exported and the safest course for the taxable person is to take a deposit of the VAT and return this to the customer when evidence of export has been provided. [38.102]

3 Import of goods from outside the EU

VAT is currently charged on the import of goods into the UK from outside the EU as if it were customs duty, and this is so whether or not the importer is a taxable person. The UK includes England, Scotland, Wales, Northern Ireland, territorial waters and, for this purpose, the Isle of Man.

Evidence of VAT paid on import (in the form of a certificate C79) must be obtained by a taxable person and retained as evidence for input tax recovery. VAT paid on import can be recovered as input tax in accordance with normal rules.

VATA 1994 s 21 deals with the value of imported goods.

Payment of VAT on imported goods is due at the time of importation unless the importer or his agent has been approved under a scheme for deferral of tax which enables payment to be deferred until the fifteenth day of the month following import.

Currently, a number of exemptions from the VAT charge on importation apply. Some deal with temporary imports only (under various statutory instruments such as SI 1961/1523, SI 1995/2518 and EU Regulations 2913/92 and 2454/93), and others are dealt with in SI 1984/746. Limited categories of goods are also exempted from VAT on import as personal reliefs: see SI 1992/3193.

It is also possible to defer payment of VAT on import by placing the imported goods in certain types of warehouse. Payment of VAT can by this method be deferred until the goods leave the warehouse and enter into free circulation in the EU. [38.103]

4 Transfers of goods between EU countries

Under regulations made under VATA 1994 s 30(8), where a registered taxable person in the UK despatches goods to a registered taxable person in another EU Member State, the supply will normally be zero-rated. No VAT will be paid as the goods cross the frontier. The customer will acquire the goods and will account for VAT on his own VAT return at the rate in force in the country of receipt. Where a UK registered business acquires goods from another EU country, he must now, instead of paying VAT on importation, account for VAT on the goods through his own VAT return.

Where a taxable person in one EU country despatches goods to a person who is not a VAT registered taxable person in another EU country, the supplier will generally charge VAT at the rate in force in the country of despatch. Thus, UK taxable persons who supply goods to customers in the EU who are not registered for VAT may not zero-rate those supplies. In addition, if the goods the supplier dispatches to unregistered persons exceeds certain limits, the supplier must register for, and charge, local VAT instead of UK VAT. This is known as distance selling.

From 1 January 2005, VAT on the wholesale (B2B) supply of natural gas and electricity was accounted for in the place where the customer is established. Since 1 July 2014 supplies of wholesale gas through a network or system within a Member State and electricity made between UK counterparties have been subject to the reverse charge procedure; and for other supplies, the place of supply is where the natural gas and electricity is consumed. [38.104]

5 International services

As noted above, the place of supply of a service is dependent upon whether it is a 'business to business' (B2B) supply (the recipient is a 'relevant business person' as defined in VATA 1994 s 7A(4)) or a 'business to consumer' (B2C) supply (the recipient is not a 'relevant business person'). The general rule is that the place of supply of a B2B supply is the country in which the recipient belongs and that the place of supply of a B2C supply is where the supplier belongs.

There are some exceptions to the general rules, for example, in relation to land, any supply of services which consists of the grant, assignment or surrender of an interest in land or a licence to occupy land or any lesser contractual right over land (as well as construction services and services of surveyors etc) is treated as made where the land is situate.

Since 1 January 2015, digital services (broadcasting, telecommunications and e-services) provided by a business to a consumer are taxable where the consumer is located and the supplier has responsibility for accounting for the VAT in that Member State at the relevant VAT rate. Such services provided to business customers normally fall within the general place of supply rule.

EXAMPLE 38.22

(1) Cayco, a Cayman investment company, purchases a building in the UK and grants a five-year lease, having exercised the option to tax the building (see [**39.27**]). The grant is a supply of services made in the UK and Cayco must charge UK VAT.
(2) Lex and Lax (solicitors) provide for Hiram, in the USA, estate planning advice in connection with becoming UK resident and ultimately domiciled. This service is outside the scope of UK VAT; by contrast services in connection with the acquisition of a flat for him in London are standard-rated.

(3)   Alternatively, they provide for François, a French resident who is not registered for VAT in France, advice in connection with his personal affairs. This service is standard-rated.

A further exception, 'use and enjoyment' provisions, also apply to the hiring of goods, telecommunication and broadcasting services, and the provision of electronically supplied services to a relevant business person. If the service supply would otherwise be treated as provided in the UK, but it is effectively used and enjoyed in another, non-EU, country, that country is held to be where the supply is made. Likewise, if the service would otherwise be treated as provided in a non-EU country, but is effectively used and enjoyed in the UK, the UK is held to be the place of supply. Services rendered by UK taxable persons to persons belonging outside the UK therefore, subject to the above provisions, are standard-rated unless they fall within the categories specified in VATA Sch 8 Group 7 or would be zero-rated if supplied in the UK, eg air travel, in which case zero-rating will apply. The services under this heading were substantially amended from 1 January 1993 and now comprise only:

(1)   the supply of services of work carried out on goods intended for export outside the EU; and
(2)   the supply of services comprising the making of arrangements for the export of goods or supply of services outside the EU or for a supply of services detailed in (1) above. [38.105]

6 The reverse charge

The 'reverse charge' applies, by virtue of VATA 1994 s 8, where services are supplied by a person who belongs outside the UK to a person who belongs in the UK for the purpose of a business carried on by him. The recipient of the services will be treated as if the services had been supplied by himself to himself and must account for output tax (unless the services fall within an exempt or zero-rated category) and may recover the input tax charged to himself in accordance with normal procedures if it is attributable to taxable supplies he intends to make (ie the recipient accounts for VAT in the relevant VAT return, then claims a simultaneous tax deduction).

If the services provided are within VATA 1994 Sch 4A Parts 1 and 2, then the recipient must be VAT registered to be within the reverse charge.

Anti-avoidance provisions prevent the routing of services tax free via an overseas branch of one of the companies forming a VAT group. [38.106]

39 VAT on property
Hartley Foster, Partner, Fieldfisher LLP

I   Introduction [39.1]
II Land, buildings and construction [39.19]

I   INTRODUCTION

The law of VAT on property is complex. In part, this arises because of the tension between many of the fundamental concepts of English land law (which have been evolving over many hundreds of years) and the principles of VAT (which: (a) have a more recent origin; and (b) which derive from EU law). Depending on the circumstances, land can be zero-rated, standard-rated, exempt, or outside the scope of VAT. In this chapter, an overview of the main points is provided.

The VAT treatment of supplies of land and buildings and construction services changed significantly in 1989. Prior to Finance Act 1989, most transactions in land were exempt from VAT, and only a limited number of supplies were standard-rated. There was also a significant category of zero-rated supplies – construction and sale of commercial property. In *EC Commission v UK* (Case C–416/85) (1988), the ECJ held that the UK, by allowing that zero-rating, had contravened the provisions of the Sixth Directive. As a result, the UK was obliged to impose VAT on the construction and freehold sale of new commercial buildings and civil engineering works. If such a property was let, this VAT would be irrecoverable (because it would relate to an exempt supply). In order to mitigate this consequence, the 'option to tax' system was introduced with effect from 1 August 1989. This allows businesses to convert the exempt supply into a standard-rated taxable supply, thus allowing input tax recovery on related costs and requiring the charging of VAT on the rent. FA 1989 also extended the standard rated exceptions to the basic rule (that the grant of any interest in or right over land or any licence to occupy land is exempt) and reduced the categories of zero-rated supply.

The legislation relating to the option to tax is primarily contained in VATA 1994 Sch 10. This schedule has been amended a number of times (primarily to introduce various anti-avoidance provisions). A rewritten version was introduced with effect from 1 June 2008. The amendments were not only made with the aim of simplifying the legislation, but also to introduce a provision for the revocation of the option after 20 years. Notice 742A

(April 2014) explains the effect of the option to tax. Notice 742 (May 2012) (dealing with land and property) provides helpful guidance as to HMRC's practice in relation to property transactions and when transactions involving land and buildings are exempt from VAT.

Construction services are generally taxable at the standard rate. However, certain supplies relating to the construction of new dwellings and other limited categories of residential/charitable buildings, works of alteration to some listed buildings and conversions of commercial property into residential are zero-rated (see [39.23]). Following proposals in (a) the 2001 Budget to help with urban regeneration, and (b) further changes that were introduced with effect from 1 June 2002 via FA 2002, VAT is chargeable at the reduced rate of 5% on:

(1) renovating and converting dwellings that have been empty for more than two years;
(2) converting housing into a different number of flats, or a house into flats; and
(3) converting housing into a care home or bed-sit accommodation.

Notice 708 (June 2016) contains examples of where subcontractors' work cannot be reduced or zero-rated. [39.1]

General summary of the VAT rules on property

Zero-rated supplies

(i) construction and first grant of the freehold sale or long lease (over 21 years) of dwellings and certain other buildings by the developer;
(ii) conversion of non-residential buildings into dwellings (and certain other buildings);
(iii) supply, in the course of construction or conversion of dwellings (and certain other buildings), of certain construction-related services; and
(iv) certain alterations.

Reduced rate of 5%

(i) certain conversion and renovation work, as summarised above at [39.1].

Exempt supplies

(i) sales and leases of existing property, including unbuilt on land (but NB 'option to tax').

Standard-rated

(i) sales of commercial buildings up to three years old;
(ii) construction of new buildings (except for dwellings and certain others);
(iii) work on existing buildings (unless certain conversion and renovation work (5%));
(iv) the provision of holiday accommodation; and
(v) supplies by sub-contractors:
   (a) in respect of communal residential buildings or buildings used by charities;
   (b) of disabled adaptations and mobility aids for over-60s;

(c) to a relevant housing association; and
(d) of renovation or alteration in connection with a single household dwelling vacant for the previous two years. **[39.2]–[39.18]**

II LAND, BUILDINGS AND CONSTRUCTION

1 A grant of an interest in, or right over, land (exempt supply)

The exemption for transactions relating to land is derived from Articles 135(1)(j)–(l) of the Recast Directive. These articles concern the leasing or letting of immovable property, including land that has not been built on, other than building land. The Recast Directive provides for certain exclusions from the exemption, and allows Member States to apply further exclusions. The domestic exemption for certain transactions in land is conferred by VATA 1994 Sch 9 Group 1.

The grant of any 'interest in or right over land' or any 'licence to occupy land' is exempt (subject to certain exceptions). **[39.19]**

The grant of any 'interest in or right over land'

'Land' includes buildings, civil engineering works, walls, trees, plants, and other structures and natural objects in, under, or over the land provided that they remain attached to it. '*Any interest in or right over land*' is confined to legal or equitable estates or interests in land. In *Rochdale Hornets Football Club Co Ltd v C & E Comrs* (1975), the VAT tribunal held that:

'the expression [interest in or right over land] clearly covers inter alia legal estates in fee simple, terms of years absolute and easements and also profits à prendre recognised as such by the law, that is to say rights of pasture, piscary, turbary and estovers.'

A grant of an interest in land includes a freehold sale as well as the grant, assignment or surrender of a lease. A grant of a right over land includes a grant of mineral rights or easements.

In relation to the grant of a lease, the premium or rent payable is generally consideration for an exempt supply. Thus, unless the landlord has exercised the option to tax, VAT will not be charged.

A 'grant' includes an assignment or a surrender. In *Lubbock Fine v Customs & Excise Comrs* (Case C–60/96) (1994), the ECJ held that:

'1. The term "letting of immovable property" ... covers the case where a tenant surrenders his lease and returns the immovable property to his immediate landlord.
2. [Article 135] ... which allows Member States to apply further exclusions to the scope of the exemption for the letting of immovable property, does not authorise them to tax the consideration paid by one party to the other in connection with the surrender of the lease when the rent paid under the lease was exempt from VAT.'

A 'reverse surrender' (where the landlord pays the tenant for the surrender of the tenant's interest in land) involves a supply by the landlord (namely the release of the tenant from the obligations under the lease in consideration of the reverse premium). The supply by the landlord will be exempt (unless the option to tax has been exercised). The actual surrender of the lease by the tenant to the landlord does not constitute a supply: see *AA Insurance Services Ltd v C & E Comrs* (1999).

HMRC's view that an 'inducement' to accept a lease should be distinguished from a surrender and constitutes a standard-rated supply of services by the person accepting the lease (on the basis that as the person accepting the lease has, at the time of the transaction, no interest in the property in question, he cannot make any form of grant in relation to it) was considered by the ECJ in *Cantor Fitzgerald* (Case C-108/99) and *Mirror Group plc* (Case C-409/99). The ECJ held that:

(1) a tenant who undertakes, even in return for payment from the landlord, solely to become a tenant and to pay the rent does not, so far as that action is concerned, make a supply of services to the landlord;
(2) the tenant could be regarded as making a supply of services for a consideration if the presence of that tenant was likely to attract further tenants (the supply in such a case would be one of (taxable) advertising services);
(3) where a person agrees to take on the rights and obligations of an existing lease from a third party, that is a standard rated supply of services.

In light of the decision of the ECJ, HMRC amended its previously-held view and set out its position in *VAT Notice 742* (June 2012) that: '*there is no supply for VAT purposes by a prospective tenant if* [the landlord pays] *that prospective tenant for doing no more than entering into a lease*'. However, where the tenant provides any additional benefit to the landlord, then there is a supply and the VAT treatment of such supply will depend on the nature of the particular benefit provided. **[39.20]**

Licence to occupy land

A licence is given by the occupier of land; and it permits the licensee to do some act that would otherwise be a trespass. It is a right that is personal to the licensee and no interest in the property to which it relates is created by the issue of a licence.

It is not necessary for the occupier to be granted exclusivity, ie a clearly defined area or site to the exclusion of other people, for the licence to be an exempt licence to occupy land (see *Altman Blane & Co v C & E Comrs* (1994), where the VAT Tribunal noted that although exclusivity of occupation is an essential condition of a tenancy, it is not an essential condition of a licence; and *Belgium v Temco Europe SA* (Case C-284/03)).

HMRC's views on the characteristics that must be present for a licence to occupy land to qualify for exemption are set out in *VAT Notice 742* (June 2012):

(1) the licence must be granted in return for a consideration paid by the licensee;
(2) the licence to occupy must be of a defined area of land;
(3) the licence must be for an agreed duration; and
(4) the licensee must have the right to occupy that defined area as owner and to exclude others from enjoying that right.

There have been a number of cases concerning the question of whether the installation of a vending machine amounts to the grant of a licence to occupy land. In *Sinclair Collis Ltd v C & E Comrs* (Case C-275/01), the ECJ held that the grant, by the owner of a public house, of a right to install, maintain and operate cigarette-vending machines on the premises, did not amount, in the absence of exclusive occupation of a defined area or space, to the letting of immovable property.

The cases have to be considered on their own merits; and there have been many cases concerning the grant of facilities to hairstylists at hairdressing salons. An example is *Holland (trading as The Studio Hair Company) v R & C Comrs; Vigdor Ltd v R & C Comrs* (2008) where the High Court upheld the decision of the VAT Tribunal that there was no exempt supply of a licence to occupy:

> 'the licence to occupy the area floor space ... is artificial. There is no defined area, no duration and no real exclusivity. It is virtually irrelevant to the stylist's needs ... What the stylist wants is a chair and mirrors, lighting, heating and water, use of the reception facilities and of stock in the dispensary and a laundered towel service.'

With effect from 1 October 2012, 'the grant of facilities to a person who uses the facilities wholly or mainly to supply hairdressing services' has been excluded from exemption under VATA 1994 Sch 9 Group 1 Item 1. A supply is not excluded from exemption if the grant provides for the exclusive use by the person to whom the grant is made of a whole building, a whole floor, a separate room or clearly defined area, unless the person making the grant (or a connected person) provides or makes available hairdressing services for the use of the person to whom the grant is made.

In *VAT Notice 742*, HMRC provide a list of examples of supplies that they consider are licences to occupy land and examples of supplies that they do not consider are licences to occupy land. Examples of the former include the granting of space to place a fixed kiosk on a specified site, such as a newspaper kiosk or flower stand at a railway station; and examples of the latter include the granting of an ambulatory concession, such as an ice cream van on the sea front or a burger van at a football match.

In *R & C Comrs v UK Storage Company (SW) Limited* (2012), the Upper Tribunal upheld HMRC's appeal against the First-tier Tribunal's decision that a storage company granted customers a VAT-exempt licence to occupy land. The Government had previously announced (in the 2012 Budget) the removal of the VAT exemption for self-storage facilities, with effect from 1 October 2012, to ensure that all supplies of self-storage receive the same standard-rated treatment and to counter avoidance (see FA 2012 Sch 26 and VATA 1994 Sch 9 Group 1).

EXAMPLE 39.1

(1)   On Saturday, Sid pays £35.25 to watch Arsenal FC. This is not a licence to occupy land: rather it is a licence to go on land and the supply is standard-rated.

   On Sunday, he goes fishing on the Thames, paying £15 for a day licence. This is also a standard-rated supply.

(2)   Jack sells his freehold interest in two acres of freehold land to Jill and before completion she resells to Eric. Both have disposed of (exempt) interests in land. **[39.21]**

2 Standard-rated supplies of land and buildings

VATA 1994 Sch 9 Group 1 sets out the following exceptions to the basic rule (that grants of interests in or rights over land are exempt):

(1) Freehold sales of uncompleted or new commercial buildings. The legislation does not, in fact, use the term 'commercial building' but refers to a building that is neither designed as a dwelling nor intended solely for a relevant residential or charitable purpose (see **[39.23]**).

(2) New civil engineering work. The phrase 'civil engineering work' is not defined, but envisages the construction of a work of public utility. It includes bridges, tunnels, roads, canals, drainage works, or gas and water works. A building or civil engineering work is 'new' if it was completed within the last three years. It is treated as completed when the certificate of practical completion is issued or when it is fully used, whichever happens first.

EXAMPLE 39.2

- Dan Developer completes the construction of an office block on 1 August 2014 and on the same day sells the freehold interest to X-Ray for £5m. VAT at the standard rate is charged.
- If on 31 July 2017, X-Ray sells the freehold interest to Mad Mac Burgers for £7.5m, VAT at the standard rate is charged. Had the sale been delayed until 1 August 2017 the supply would have been exempt as the sale would have taken place over 3 years after the completion of the building (unless X-Ray had exercised the option to tax: see **[39.27]**).
- A similar result would follow if X-Ray had effected an immediate sub-sale in favour of Mad Mac and the freehold had been conveyed directly from Dan Developer to Mad Mac.
- Instead of selling the freehold Dan Developer grants a long leasehold interest at a premium. The grant is an exempt supply.

(3) The grant of any interest in, right or licence consisting of a right to take game or fish except where, at the same time, the grantor also supplies the freehold to the grantee. Where land that includes the right to take game or fish is leased rather than sold freehold, standard rated VAT is chargeable on the proportion of the premium or rent attributable to the sporting rights if the value of that right exceeds 10% of the value of the whole supply.

EXAMPLE 39.3

Sid sells his freehold interest in a strip of the River Foul for £75,000. The freehold carries with it mooring and fishing rights. The sale of the freehold is an exempt supply and there is no question of apportioning the price to arrive at a value for the mooring rights or fishing rights.

(4) A supply made pursuant to a developmental tenancy, developmental lease or developmental licence.
(5) The provision of accommodation in an hotel, boarding house or similar establishment.

(6) The grant of an interest in, right over or licence to occupy holiday accommodation.
(7) The provision of seasonal pitches for caravans and the grant of facilities at caravan parks to persons for whom such pitches are provided.
(8) The provision of facilities for camping.
(9) The grant of facilities for parking a vehicle.
(10) The grant of a right to fell and remove standing timber.
(11) The grant of facilities for housing or storage of an aircraft or for mooring or storage of a ship, boat or other vessel.
(12) The grant of a right to occupy a box, seat or other accommodation at a sports ground, theatre, concert hall or other place of entertainment.
(13) The grant of facilities for playing sport or participating in physical recreation.
(14) The grant of any right (such as an option) to call for or be granted an interest or right falling within (1)–(13) above (except 4).

Certain of the grants falling within (13) are nevertheless exempt if made by certain 'not for profit' bodies.

In addition to these taxable transactions, grants of interests in or rights over land or licences to occupy land which would otherwise be exempt may be converted to taxable supplies if the landowner concerned has exercised the option to tax (see [39.27]).

In *Colaingrove Ltd v R & C Comrs* (2013), the First-tier Tribunal held that the supply of power was a (reduced-rated) supply that was separate from the provision of holiday accommodation, notwithstanding that the charge for power did not relate to the amount of power actually used. In *The Honourable Society of Middle Temple v R & C Comrs* (2013), the Upper Tribunal reversed the decision of the First-tier Tribunal that the provision of cold water to premises was a separate (zero-rated) supply from the supply of the lease of those premises. It emphasised that whether there is a single, composite supply or multiple supplies for VAT purposes must be determined on the facts of each particular case. [39.22]

3 Dwellings, qualifying residential and charitable buildings (zero-rated supplies)

The first grant or assignment of a major interest (defined to mean the freehold or a tenancy for a term certain exceeding 21 years) in certain qualifying buildings is zero-rated (VATA 1994 Sch 8 Group 5 Item 1).

To qualify, the building subject to the grant or assignment must have been:
(a) a building, constructed by the grantor as a dwelling, number of dwellings or solely for a relevant residential or charitable purpose; or
(b) a non-residential building or part thereof, which has been converted by the grantor into a dwelling, number of dwellings or solely for a relevant residential purpose (VATA 1994 Sch 8 Group 5 Notes 7 and 7A provide that buildings that have not been used for residential purposes for 10 years can be treated as non-residential buildings for this purpose).

A 'dwelling' includes a garage constructed (or converted into) at the same time as the dwelling for occupation with it (VATA 1994 Sch 8 Group 5 Note (3)). The conversion of a garage that was previously occupied with a dwelling is not zero-rated (VATA 1994 Sch 8 Group 5 Note (8)). Similarly, the conversion of a non-residential building that already contains a residential part, is not zero-rated, unless the effect of the conversion is to create an additional dwelling or dwellings or is a conversion for relevant residential use (VATA 1994 Sch 8 Group 6 Note (9)). A useful summary of the zero-rating of renovated properties is contained in the notes to form VAT 431C.

Languard New Homes Ltd v R & C Comrs and DD & DM MacPherson v R & C Comrs (2017) concerned two joined cases where the First-tier Tribunals had reached different conclusions.

MacPherson bought a village shop that comprised office space and associated storage on the ground floor, and living accommodation on the ground and first floors. It converted the village shop into two semi-detached dwellings. Each of the dwellings occupied areas that previously formed part of the living accommodation and the commercial areas. Languard bought a public house, which comprised a non-residential ground floor and two upper floors that were residential. It converted the public house into four maisonettes. The two lower maisonettes each occupied part of the ground floor and part of the first floor. The two upper maisonettes each occupied part of the second floor and part of a newly built third floor. Both MacPherson and Languard sold their interests in the maisonettes and dwellings, and sought to zero-rate their supplies. HMRC denied zero-rating.

In *MacPherson*, the First-tier Tribunal held that the sales of the dwellings were not zero-rated; in *Languard*, the First-tier Tribunal held that the sales of the maisonettes were zero-rated.

On appeal, the Upper Tribunal held that the first grants of major interests in the converted dwellings could not be zero-rated, because each dwelling comprised partly a former dwelling and partly a non-residential part. It held that a part of a building is only a non-residential part if it contains only non-residential space. It cannot be a non-residential part if it comprises some commercial space and some residential space. Accordingly, the converted dwelling must have been converted entirely from formerly non-residential space, for zero-rating to apply.

EXAMPLE 39.4

(1) Dick, the developer, builds a new house and grants a 99-year lease of it. The premium or first payment of rent is treated as consideration for a zero-rated supply. Further payments of rent are treated as consideration for an exempt supply.

(2) By contrast if he granted a lease for less than 21 years then he would make an *exempt* supply (so that input tax would be restricted).

(3) Fred Archer converts a barn into a dwelling that he then sells. The supply is zero-rated.

Use for a 'relevant residential purpose' includes use as a residential children's home or old people's home, residential accommodation for school children or students and certain other similar purposes (see **[39.38]**) (VATA 1994 Sch 8 Group 5 Note (4)).

Use for a 'relevant charitable purpose' means use either for something other than a business purpose or as a village hall or providing similar social or recreational facilities for a local community (VATA 1994 Sch 8 Group 5

Note (6)). HMRC had previously issued guidance on a concession (ESC 3.29) that allowed zero-rating for charitable buildings which had an insignificant business use (less than 10%). This concession was withdrawn with effect from 1 July 2010. HMRC now accept that the 'solely' requirement in VATA 1994 Sch 8 Group 5 Item 1 is met only if a building is intended for 95% use for a relevant charitable purpose (see HMRC Brief 32/10).

'Construction' does not include the conversion, reconstruction or alteration of an existing building and a building only ceases to be an existing building when either demolished completely to ground level or when the part remaining above ground level consists of no more than a single facade (or in the case of a corner site a double facade) the retention of which is a condition of a planning or similar permission (VATA 1994 Sch 8 Group 5 Notes (16) and (18)).

In *Central Sussex College v R & C Comrs* (2014), the First-tier Tribunal held that a phased redevelopment of a college and planned subsequent demolition of existing buildings, if funding permitted, was not a zero-rated construction of buildings.

EXAMPLE 39.5

Fred Fletcher constructs a building. The third floor is designed as a dwelling; the two lower floors as offices. He sells the property to Fred Archer. An apportionment of the consideration must be made: that portion attributable to the supply of the top floor is zero-rated whereas the remainder is standard-rated. **[39.23]**

Protected buildings

The first grant of a major interest in a 'protected building' by the person who has substantially reconstructed it is zero-rated, provided that the building is intended solely for use as a dwelling, a number of dwellings or for relevant residential or charitable use (VATA 1994 Sch 8 Group 6 Item 1).

There have been a number of cases on the meaning of substantial reconstruction. Reconstruction involves replication of what was there previously. Thus, the appearance and function of the building will be substantially the same as that which previously existed: see *C & E Comrs v Marchday Holdings Ltd* (1997). HMRC's views are set out in VAT Notice 708 (June 2016); substantial reconstruction involves major work to a building's fabric, and either complete gutting of the building or at least 60% of total reconstruction cost being eligible for zero-rating as 'approved alterations'. The term 'protected buildings' covers listed buildings and certain other scheduled monuments. **[39.24]**

Construction services

Supplies of construction services are generally standard-rated. However, where a builder provides supplies in the course of the construction of a new dwelling or qualifying residential or charitable building, those works are zero-rated (VATA 1994 Sch 8 Group 5 Item 2 and see *Example 39.6*).

Zero-rating is extended to building materials incorporated in a building (VATA 1994 Sch 8 Group 5 Item 4 and Group 6 Item 3). Input tax on materials incorporated in a building that are not building materials is not recoverable (VAT (Input Tax) Order 1992, SI 1992/3222, art 6).

DIY builders are able to obtain a refund of VAT incurred on goods used in the construction of buildings that would qualify for zero-rating (VATA 1994 s 35) (see below). [39.25]

EXAMPLE 39.6
Lucky, a developer, owns Fairacre. He engages Brad, a builder to construct a residence on the land. Brad supplies carpets and fitted bedroom furniture. Subsequently Lucky sells the completed house to Sad.
(1) Brad will zero rate the construction works (a supply in the course of the construction of the dwelling: Group 5 Item 2). Brad can also zero rate building materials. Lucky cannot reclaim the input tax attributable to the carpets and fitted furniture.
(2) Lucky makes a zero-rated supply and can reclaim VAT paid in connection with the project (eg professional fees).

Approved alterations to protected buildings

Prior to 30 September 2012, a supply of an 'approved alteration' in respect of a listed building was zero-rated (under VATA 1994 Sch 8 Group 6 Item 2). Generally, alterations that required listed building consent fell within the ambit of Item 2. Any work of repair and maintenance, and any incidental alteration that resulted from the carrying out of maintenance or repair work, was excluded. There were a number of cases in respect of the division between the two. For example, the decisions in *DH Carr v R & C Comrs* (2005) (VAT Decision 19267 (alteration)) and *GGN Builders Ltd v R & C Comrs* (2010) (TC00488 (repair and maintenance)) demonstrated that installation of damp-proofing and insulation in a building where it did not exist previously may or may not be a work of alteration; it depended on whether the work was principally to protect and preserve the existing structure, or was principally new work.

The zero-rating relief for approved alterations to protected buildings was removed with effect from 1 October 2012. The rationale for the change was set out in the 'VAT: Addressing Borderline Anomalies' consultation document (21 March 2012):

'45. Although some alterations restore or enhance the unique character of a building or prolong its active life, the majority of the work covered by the relief consists of extension work which is not necessary for heritage purposes. The current rules therefore give a perverse incentive for change as opposed to repair. Alteration work on other types of building is standard-rated so owners of listed buildings receive a tax advantage over owners of other types of building. Removing the zero rate removes the perverse incentive to change listed buildings rather than repair them and ensures that all alteration work receives the same tax treatment ...

46. The borderline between alterations and repairs and maintenance is also a major source of confusion, resulting in a high volume of taxpayer queries and error. Removing the relief will make the VAT rules simpler for businesses to understand and for HMRC to administer and will reduce the scope for error and non compliance.'

Transitional arrangements provided for the continued zero-rating of 'relevant supplies' until 30 September 2015. 'Relevant supplies' were, in broad terms, supplies of approved alterations to protected buildings pursuant to a written contract entered into before 21 March 2012. Anti-forestalling legislation came into force with effect from 21 March 2012. [39.25A]

4 Reduced rate: conversions and alterations

The scope of the reduced rate is dealt with in *VAT Notice 708* (June 2016). The table below is based on paragraph 7.2 of that document.

	Single household dwelling(s) *after* conversion	Multiple occupancy dwellings *after* conversion	Relevant residential purpose building *after* conversion
Single household dwelling(s) *before* conversion	Normally standard-rate; reduced-rate applies if the number of dwellings is altered	Reduced-rate	Reduced-rate
Multiple occupancy dwelling(s) *before* conversion	Reduced-rate	Standard-rate	Reduced-rate
Relevant residential purpose building *before* conversion	Reduced-rate	Reduced-rate	Standard-rate
Any building not listed above *before* conversion, such as a building that has never been lived in	Reduced-rate	Reduced-rate	Reduced-rate

[39.26]

5 Commercial buildings: the option to tax

An exempt supply (under VATA 1994 Sch 9 Group 1) can be converted into a taxable supply by the exercise of the option to tax by the landowner or (if the landowner is a body corporate) by another company within the same VAT group (VATA 1994 Sch 10).

The consequence of exercising the option to tax is that all supplies of the land or building made thereafter by that person (subject to any exercise by the taxpayer of the right to revoke) are taxable supplies, save to the extent that they relate to a dwelling or a building intended solely for a relevant residential purpose or relevant charitable purpose, other than an office.

Where one company in a VAT group has exercised the option over a building or land, it affects all other companies in the same group.

The main purpose of electing is to enable a landlord who has incurred input tax on the purchase or refurbishment or reconstruction of a non-residential building to recover that tax against a taxable supply (the grant of a lease or other interest in the land or sale of the freehold) that he makes. **[39.27]**

What is affected by the option?

The option may be exercised over specified land or buildings, or generally over all land and buildings in the taxpayer's ownership. An option has no effect in relation to any grant in relation to a building that is intended for use as a dwelling or solely for a relevant residential purpose.

Where the option is exercised in relation to part of a building, it will affect the whole. For this purpose, buildings linked internally or by a covered walkway and complexes consisting of a number of units grouped around a fully enclosed concourse are taken to be a single building. If a taxpayer constructs a new building on land that it has opted to tax, the building will be covered by the option to tax unless the taxpayer notifies HMRC that it wishes to exclude the building from the effect of the option. If a building is demolished or destroyed, then the option to tax will still apply to the land on which the building stood and to any future buildings that are constructed on the land.

Notification of the exclusion of a new building from the effect of an option to tax (for the purpose of para 27 of Sch 10 VATA 1994) must be made on form VAT 1614F and must contain the information requested on that form.

EXAMPLE 39.7

Lex, a property investor, owns a building which has shop premises on the ground floor, offices on the two floors above and a residential suite on the top floor. He exercises the option to tax. The consequence will be that all rents received thereafter in relation to the ground, first and second floors will be taxable, but the rent attributable to the residential suite will continue to be exempt. The rents will have to be apportioned to calculate the VAT liability. **[39.28]**

Mechanics of exercise

There are two stages in opting to tax. The first stage is making the decision to opt and the second stage is notifying HMRC of the decision. This must be done within 30 days of the decision to opt. Notification must be done by way of form VAT 1614A. The notification must state clearly what land or building the taxpayer is opting to tax and the date from which the option is to take effect. A taxpayer can make an irrevocable real estate election ('REE'), which has the effect of treating each property which is subsequently acquired by the taxpayer as individually opted (to the extent that the conditions to opt are satisfied in respect of each property) and should notify HMRC of the decision by way of form VAT 1614E. An REE may be helpful for a large business with many property interests, as the election avoids the need to complete a VAT 1614A in respect of each acquisition.

Where the taxpayer has previously made exempt supplies of the land or buildings concerned within the 10 years prior to the date it wishes the option to take effect from then, unless one or more of the conditions giving rise to automatic permission are satisfied, the taxpayer will need prior consent from HMRC to exercise the option. HMRC will consent to the exercise of the option to tax only if they are satisfied that there will be a fair and reasonable attribution of input tax. The option to tax must be exercised after the consent is received.

The automatic permission conditions are that:
(1) The previous supplies by the taxpayer related to a mixed use development and the only exempt supplies were in relation to the dwellings.
(2) The taxpayer does not wish to recover any input tax in relation to the land or buildings incurred before the option to tax has effect *and*:
   (a) the consideration for exempt supplies up to the date the option to tax is to take effect has been solely by way of rents or service charges and excludes any premiums or payments in respect of occupation after the date on which the option takes effect (payments are considered regular where the intervals between them are no more than a year and where each represents a commercial or genuine arm's length value); and
   (b) the only input tax relating to the land or building that the taxpayer expects to recover after the option to tax takes effect will be on overheads such as regular rental payments, service charges, repairs and maintenance costs (this condition is not met if the taxpayer expects to claim input tax in relation to refurbishment or redevelopment of the building).
(3) A prescriptive output-based requirement and, where applicable, an inputs-based requirement, is met (Conditions A and B, introduced from 1 May 2009 – see below for further details).
(4) The exempt supplies have been incidental to the main use of the land or building. For example, where the taxpayer has occupied a building for taxable purposes, the following would be seen as incidental to the main use and the condition would be met:
   • allowing an advertising hoarding to be displayed;
   • granting space for the erection of a radio mast;
   • receiving income from an electricity sub-station.
   The letting of space to an occupying tenant, however minor, is not incidental.

Even if an automatic condition is satisfied, the taxpayer must notify HMRC of the option to tax and specify the condition that has been satisfied.

From 1 May 2009, condition (3) was replaced by a provision that states that automatic permission may be granted where condition A and, if applicable, Condition B, are satisfied. Condition A is that:
(1) the taxpayer does not intend that any supply which will be taxable as a result of the option will be made to a connected person, unless that person will be entitled to recover at least 80% of the VAT on that supply; or
(2) the taxpayer does not intend that any supply which will be taxable as a result of the option will arise from an agreement under which an exempt supply in respect of a right to occupy the property has been or will be made, with that right beginning or continuing after the effective date of the option.

Condition B only applies where the taxpayer has been, or expects to be, entitled to credit for any part of the input tax incurred on capital expenditure on the property by virtue of the option. It is as follows:

The taxpayer does not intend or expect to use any part of the capital expenditure for the purposes in (1) or (2) below:
(1) making exempt supplies which do not confer a right to credit under VATA 1994 s 26(2)(c), unless:
   (a) all the exempt supplies:
      (i) are to an unconnected person and fall within VATA 1994 Sch 10 paras 5–11; or
      (ii) are permissible exempt supplies; or
      (iii) are incidental supplies falling within VATA 1994 Sch 9 Group 5; or
   (b) exempt supplies are made but it is intended or expected that input tax on capital expenditure on the property that is attributed to those exempt supplies will not exceed £5,000; or
   (c) the taxpayer expects to be entitled to full credit for all input tax incurred on capital expenditure on the property under VATA 1994 s 33(2).
(2) for private or non-business purposes, other than those giving right to a refund under VATA 1994 s 33, 33A, or 41(3).

The new Condition 3 is deliberately detailed in order to try to ensure that it is not used for tax avoidance purposes. HMRC published a flow diagram at Annex 2 of *VAT Notice 742A* (June 2010) to assist taxpayers with the understanding of this condition. It (and the other automatic conditions listed above) has the force of law.

Before 1 May 2009, Condition 3 was that the only input tax recovered in relation to the land or building before the option to tax took effect related solely to tax charged by the tenant or tenants upon surrender of a lease; and the building (or relevant part of the building) had been unoccupied between the date of the surrender and the date the option was to take effect; and there would be no further exempt supplies of the land or building; and the taxpayer did not intend or expect that it would occupy the land or building other than for taxable purposes. [39.29]

Revocation

Prior to 1 March 1995, the option to tax was irrevocable. Between 1 March 1995 and 1 June 2008, a taxpayer could (with the written consent of HMRC) cancel the exercise of the option within three months of the exercise provided that no VAT had in the meantime become payable or credit for input tax had been claimed as a result of its exercise and provided also that in the intervening period the land concerned had not been included in a transfer of a business as a going concern. Since 1 June 2008, the 'cooling off' period has been extended to six months and HMRC's permission is not needed where four revocation conditions and one of three additional conditions are satisfied.

The rules for revocation during the six month 'cooling off' period were relaxed from 1 April 2010 under the VAT (Buildings and Land) Order 2010. It used to be a condition of revocation that the taxpayer had not made use of the land since the option had effect.

The four revocation conditions are that:
(1) less than six months have passed since the day on which the option had effect;
(2) no tax has become chargeable on a supply of the land as a result of the option;
(3) no transfer of a going concern has occurred; and
(4) HMRC have been notified of the revocation (form VAT 1614C).

In addition to conditions (1) to (4) above, one of the following additional conditions must be satisfied in order for an option to tax to be automatically revoked:
(1) neither the person who exercised the option to tax ('the opter') nor any relevant associate of the opter has recovered extra property input tax;
(2) by virtue of the revocation, the opter and all relevant associates of the opter would be liable to account to HMRC under reg 107 or 108 of the Value Added Tax Regulations 1995 (the 'VAT Regulations') for all of the extra property input tax they have recovered; or
(3) extra property input tax has been recovered entirely on one capital item and amounts to less than 20% of the total input tax incurred on that item.

'Extra property input tax' is defined as input tax attributable to supplies which, if made at a time when the option has effect, would be taxable supplies by virtue of the option.

A 'capital item' means a capital item to which Part 15 of the VAT Regulations applies by virtue of reg 113 of the VAT Regulations.

An option may be automatically revoked where it relates to a property where no interest has been held for over six years. An option can also be revoked once at least 20 years have elapsed since the option first had effect where condition (1) below is satisfied or all of conditions (2) to (5) are satisfied:
(1) the taxpayer (or a relevant associate connected to the taxpayer) has no relevant interest in the building or land at the time when the option is revoked and if the taxpayer or a relevant associate of the taxpayer has disposed of such an interest, no such supply for the purpose of the charge to VAT in respect of the disposal is yet to take place, or would be yet to take place if one or more conditions (such as the happening of an event or the doing of an act) were to be met;
(2) the taxpayer (or a relevant associate connected to the taxpayer) held a relevant interest in the building or land which is (a) after the time from which the option has effect and (b) more than 20 years before the option is revoked;
(3) the land or buildings subject to the option at the time it was revoked does not fall for input tax adjustment as a capital item;
(4) the taxpayer (or a relevant associate connected to the taxpayer) has made no supply of a relevant interest in the building or land subject to the option in the 10 years immediately before revocation of the option that was for a consideration that was less than the open market value of that supply or arose from a relevant grant;
(5) no part of a supply of goods or services made for consideration to the taxpayer (or a relevant associate connected to the taxpayer) before the option is revoked will be attributable to a supply or other use of the land

or buildings by the taxpayer more than 12 months after the option is revoked.

Paragraph 8.3.3 of VAT Notice 724A sets out definitions of the terms 'taxpayer', 'relevant interest in the building or land', 'relevant grant' and 'relevant associate'. [39.30]

Output tax

Following exercise of the option, the landlord must account for output tax on all supplies, including rent. Even though a tenant need not have been consulted before the landlord opted, nonetheless he will be liable to pay VAT in addition to the contractually agreed rent following exercise of the option unless the lease expressly provides that the agreed rent is to be inclusive of any VAT. This is because VATA 1994 s 89(3) provides that the exercise of the option to tax is equivalent to a change in the tax charged on a supply: see [38.9]. [39.31]–[39.32]

Should the option be exercised?

Given that the main purpose is to enable input tax to be recovered, if little or no such tax has been or is to be incurred then there is probably no need to exercise the option. Moreover, even if substantial input tax is to be incurred, the impact of the exercise of the option on lettings and sales of the property must be considered. Exempt or partially exempt tenants (such as banks, insurance companies, building societies, trade unions, charities, schools, and private health care associations) may be unable to recover the whole of the VAT charged to them and may seek a lower rent if VAT is imposed. Alternatively, existing leases may be VAT inclusive so that any VAT may be effectively borne by the grantor of the lease. This will in turn deplete the capital value of the property.

EXAMPLE 39.8

Lenny purchases the fee simple in a newly constructed office block and intends to grant the Bond St Bank a 99-year lease of the premises in return for a substantial premium.
(1) Lenny will suffer input VAT on the price paid for the freehold.
(2) If Lenny registers for VAT and exercises the option to tax, the Bond St Bank will suffer input VAT on the premium paid and on rent and service charges payable under the lease. As a partly exempt business full VAT recovery will be denied (although non-recoverable VAT will be added to the expenditure for direct tax purposes – potentially getting relief at the applicable corporation tax rate). From Lenny's point of view he is able to reclaim his input tax as he is charging output tax on the taxable grant. [39.33]

The capital goods scheme

The capital goods scheme allows for adjustments to be made to the initial amount of input tax claimed by a taxable person on capital items. The requirement to make adjustments to the deduction of input tax on capital items was introduced with effect from 1 April 1990 in response to concerns that some traders were recovering input tax in circumstances where the goods on which the input tax was incurred were not, in the long term, being used in a fully taxable business. A person who was making taxable supplies and who was planning to make exempt supplies could purchase, say, computers and obtain credit for the whole of the VAT incurred in a period in which he made taxable supplies, even if he subsequently used those computers in his exempt business. The purpose of the scheme is to reflect the use of capital goods in a business over a period of time ('the adjustment period'). If there is a change in the proportion of taxable use of a capital item during an adjustment period, then an adjustment must be made to the input tax claimed in respect of that item. The scheme applies, inter alia, to capital items that are land and buildings with a value of £250,000 (net of VAT) or more.

The relevant adjustment periods for land and buildings are 10 intervals. For capital items for which the period of adjustment had not started before 1 January 2011, the first interval starts with the first use of the asset. For capital items for which the period of adjustment had started before 1 January 2011, the first interval is the period from the date of purchase of the capital item (or the date of first use if this is more relevant or the date of registration where the owner is not registered for VAT on the date that they first use the item). In each case, the first interval ends on the day before the start of the next partial exemption tax year (eg the partial exemption year starts on 1 April 2012, a capital item is purchased on 5 August 2011, the first interval is the period from 5 August 2011 to 31 March 2012). If there is no change in use between the first and second interval, and the length of the two intervals together is less than 12 months, then the two intervals are rolled together and treated as the first interval. All subsequent intervals are normally in line with the partial exemption year.

From 1 January 2011, the adjustment period is aligned with the taxpayer's interest in the asset. Where the number of intervals comprising the normal period of adjustment (ie five or ten) exceeds the number of complete years that the taxpayer has an interest in the asset by more than one, the period of adjustment is reduced to a number of intervals equal to the number of complete years plus one down to a minimum of three intervals. For example, a business acquires a seven year interest in an asset for which the normal period of adjustment is ten years. As ten exceeds seven by more than one, the period of adjustment for the asset is reduced to the number of complete years plus one, ie eight intervals.

EXAMPLE 39.9 – INPUT TAX ON CAPITAL GOODS

R & L Finance is a firm that specialises in the provision of financial advice and investment products. It is VAT registered and its VAT year ends on 30 April. It is assumed for the purposes of this example that the standard rate of VAT was and remained 20% at all relevant times.

(a) On 10 July 2015 R & L took possession of a new office block. The purchase price was £1,000,000 plus VAT of £200,000 (at 20%). The offices are used by all aspects of the business and the agreed exempt proportion as at 10 July 2011 is 60%.
(b) Subsequently, the 2016 annual partial exemption adjustment revised the exempt proportion to 65%.
(c) The 2017 annual partial exemption adjustment revised the exempt proportion to 75%.

(d) Due to expansion, on 1 January 2018 the business divided its activities into two parts. The taxation advice remained in the office block acquired in July 2015, and the sales of insurance etc became administered wholly from premises owned prior to July 2015. The 2018 annual partial exemption adjustment gave an exempt proportion of 67%.

R & L – purchase of office building

(a) 10 July 2015 – VAT input tax recoverable

	£	£
Building – input tax adjustment period – 10 intervals i.e. to 30.4.25	200,000	
Recovery percentage (100 – 60) × 40%		£80,000

This claim should be included in the quarterly VAT return to 31.7.15.

(b) 2016 annual partial exemption adjustment

	£
Revised recovery percentage (100 – 65) 35% × 200,000	70,000
Original recovery	80,000
Payable on quarterly VAT return to 31.7.16	£(10,000)

(c) 2017 annual partial exemption adjustment

First year recovery percentage (as adjusted)	35%
2017 recovery percentage (100 – 75)	25%
Adjustment percentage	– 10%
	£
Buildings $\dfrac{200{,}000}{10 \text{ years}} \times 20.3\%$	(2,000)
Payable on quarterly VAT return to 31.7.17	£(2,000)

(d) 2018 annual capital goods scheme adjustment

Building is in 33% taxable use from 1.5.2017 to 31.12.2017 = 245 days, and in 100% taxable use from 1.1.18 to 30.4.18 = 120 days. The percentage of taxable use for the year as a whole is therefore:

$$\dfrac{33\% \times 245 + (100\% \times 120)}{365} = \quad 55.03\%$$

First year recovery percentage	35%
Adjustment percentage	+ 20.03%
Buildings $\dfrac{200{,}000}{10 \text{ years}} \times 20.3\%$	4,006
Amount to be recovered on quarterly VAT return to 31.7.18	£4,006

[39.34]–[39.36]

6 Application of the transfer of a business rules (TOGC)

As the exploitation of property by the receiving of rental income amounts to a business for VAT, the sale of a let or partially let building can be treated as a transfer of part of that business as a going concern. Under the provisions of the VAT (Special Provisions) Order 1995, SI 1995/1268, it is necessary, where the sale of the building would otherwise be a taxable supply (because it is the freehold sale of a new commercial building or it is the sale of a commercial building in relation to which the vendor has exercised the option to tax), that not merely is the transferee registered for VAT (assuming that the vendor was a taxable person) but that he has, prior to the date of transfer, exercised the option to tax the building and notified HMRC of this. Due to perceived abuses of the TOGC rules to enable input tax recovery to be indirectly provided to a non-taxable business, there is requirement to tell the transferor whether or not the option they have made will be disapplied as a result of para 12 of Sch 10.

The impact of the Capital Goods Scheme when a building is purchased under the transfer of business rules needs to be considered.

Particular care needs to be taken when a property is sold via a nominee or by way of a sub-sale. As regards nominee purchases HMRC will accept the sale is a TOGC provided the nominee is acting as a disclosed agent and the nominee, beneficial purchaser and vendor sign a declaration.

In *Abbey National plc v C & E Comrs* (Case C-408/98) the ECJ held that the input tax attributable to the transfer of a business as a going concern is entirely deductible where the assets are those of a business making only taxable supplies (such as when the option to tax has been exercised).

Prior to the decision of the First-tier Tribunal in *Robinson Family Limited v R & C Comrs* (2012), it was considered that the creation of a lease out of a superior interest could not be treated as a TOGC. It was stated, for example, in *HM Revenue and Customs Notice* 700/9 that an existing asset had to be transferred for there to be a TOGC.

The First-tier Tribunal held that, despite the fact that the transferor was not in a position to transfer the headlease (and consequently granted a sublease to the transferee), a TOGC took place. HMRC has accepted this decision. In *Business Brief* 30/12, HMRC acknowledge that where the holder of a superior interest is subject to a lease and the seller grants an intermediate lease to the buyer, the acquisition of the intermediate lease subject to the lease will be treated as the transfer of a going concern 'provided the interest retained is small enough not to disturb the substance of the transaction'. HMRC go on to say that they 'will accept that a reversion retained by the transferor is sufficiently small for TOGC treatment to be capable of applying if the value of the interest retained is no more than 1% of the value of the property immediately before the transfer (disregarding any mortgage or charge)'. HMRC's change in policy was made with retrospective effect.

On 9 July 2014, HMRC issued *Revenue & Customs Brief* 27/14, which contains details of changes to, and clarifications of, HMRC's policies on the application of the TOGC rules. *Revenue & Customs Brief* 27/14 provides as follows:

Lease surrenders

A surrender of a lease can be a TOGC as long as the normal conditions for TOGC treatment are met. Accordingly, TOGC treatment may be available if, for example: (i) a tenant surrenders a lease with the benefit of subtenants; or (ii) a retailer sells its retailing business to its landlord (including a surrender of the lease of the retail premises).

This reflects the decision in *Robinson Family*.

Lease grants

The policy set out in *Revenue & Customs Brief* 30/12 that a grant of a lease can be a TOGC applies generally, and not just to property letting businesses.

Denial of TOGC where tenant introduced by buyer

In *R & C Comrs v Royal College of Paediatrics and Child Health, and Coleridge (Theobalds Road) Ltd* (2015), the Upper Tribunal ruled that TOGC treatment did not apply on a sale of land where the buyer introduced the tenant to the seller and the lease formed part of the sale arrangements.

New developments of residential and charitable buildings

For the purposes of the first grant exemption, 'person constructing' status moves to the transferee of a completed residential or charitable building on a TOGC. This means that the transferee may make a zero-rated first major interest grant if all of the following apply:
(a) a zero-rated grant of (a relevant part of) the completed building has not already been made by a previous owner (ignoring the TOGC);
(b) the TOGC transferee would suffer an unfair VAT disadvantage if its first major interest grant were treated as exempt; and
(c) the TOGC transferee would not obtain an unfair VAT advantage by being in a position to make zero-rated supplies (for example, by recovering input tax on a refurbishment of an existing building). [39.37]

7 Builders and contractors

The activities of builders and contractors may be conveniently split into:
(1) Work related to the construction of buildings for:
 (a) use as dwellings;
 (b) relevant residential use; or
 (c) relevant charitable use.
(2) Civil engineering work for the development of a permanent park for residential caravans.
(3) Services in the course of an approved alteration to a protected building.
(4) Construction of other buildings and civil engineering works (generally commercial construction).

(5) The supply of materials and fittings in connection with the work in (1)–(4) above.

The activities under (1)–(3) are zero-rated, those under (4) are standard-rated whilst the liability of items under (5) generally follows the liability of the works.

'Relevant residential purpose' is use as one of the following:
(1) a children's home;
(2) a home providing residential accommodation with personal care for persons in need of personal care by reason of old age, disablement, past or present dependence on alcohol or drugs, or past or present mental disorder;
(3) a hospice;
(4) residential accommodation for students or schoolchildren;
(5) residential accommodation for members of the armed forces;
(6) a monastery, nunnery or similar establishment; or
(7) an institution which is the sole or main residence of at least 90% of its residents.

Hospitals, prisons or similar institutions and hotels, inns or similar establishments are not regarded as being used for relevant residential purposes.

'Relevant charitable purpose' means use by a charity other than in the course or furtherance of a business, or as a village hall or similar in providing social or recreational facilities for a local community. A building to be used by a charity as, eg, a church would qualify under this relief.

Where the supply of only part of a building qualifies for zero-rating, eg a shop with a flat over it, it is necessary to apportion the value of the supply between the zero-rated and other parts. **[39.38]**

a) *Soft landscaping*

As regards new buildings for charitable or domestic use, HMRC accept that planting as well as just turfing can be eligible for zero-rating. Zero-rating can apply to both the labour element and the plants themselves. The soft landscaping must be:
(1) done at the same time or immediately after the construction;
(2) part of the planned construction;
(3) shown on the landscaping scheme approved by the local authority.
[39.39]

b) *Supply of materials and fittings*

VAT Notice 708 (June 2016) contains HMRC's policy on the VAT recovery for businesses developing or constructing a building, and describes when VAT incurred on materials used in the construction of new buildings is non-deductible. The rules for 'blocking' VAT incurred apply to goods used in showhouses in the same way as for other houses on the development.

The supply of materials and builders' hardware ordinarily installed in conjunction with zero-rated construction services is zero-rated, provided that it is supplied to the recipient of the building services. There has been a considerable amount of litigation regarding wardrobes, cupboards etc.

HMRC's guidance on these is comprehensive. HMRC accept the following as qualifying:
(a) airing cupboards, under stair storage cupboards, cloaks/vestibule cupboards, larders, closets and other similar basic storage facilities which are formed by becoming part of the fabric of the building;
(b) items which provide storage capacity as an incidental result of their primary function. Such items include shelves formed as a result of constructing simple box work over pipes, and basin supports which contain a simple cupboard beneath the basin; and simple bedroom wardrobes installed on their own with the characteristics outlined below.
(c) basic wardrobes installed on their own with **all** the following characteristics:
- The wardrobe encloses a space bordered by the walls, ceiling and floor. But units whose design includes, for example, an element to bridge over a bed or create a dressing table are furniture and are not building materials.
- The side and back use three walls of the room (such as across the end of a wall), or two walls and a stub wall. But wardrobes installed in the corner of a room where one side is a closing end panel are furniture and are not building materials.
- On opening the wardrobe you should see the walls of the building. These would normally be either bare plaster or painted plaster. Wardrobes that contain internal panelling, typically as part of a modular or carcass system, are furniture and are not building materials.
- The wardrobe should feature no more than a single shelf running the full length of the wardrobe, a rail for hanging clothes and a closing door or doors. Wardrobes with internal divisions, drawers, shoe racks or other features are furniture and are not building materials.

The following are generally recognised by HMRC as builders' hardware ordinarily installed in dwellings or other relevant buildings that qualify for zero-rating:
(1) window frames and glazing;
(2) doors;
(3) letter boxes;
(4) fireplaces and surrounds;
(5) guttering;
(6) power points (including combination shaver points/lights but not light bulbs or tubes);
(7) outside lights (provided they are standard fittings but not light bulbs or tubes);
(8) immersion heaters, boilers, hot and cold water tanks;
(9) radiators;
(10) built-in heating appliances;
(11) burglar alarms;
(12) fire alarms;
(13) smoke detectors;
(14) air conditioning equipment;
(15) equipment to provide ventilation;

(16) dust extractors;
(17) lifts and hoists;
(18) work surfaces or fitted cupboards in kitchens (including those fitted in utility rooms);
(19) kitchen sinks;
(20) baths;
(21) basins;
(22) vanity units;
(23) lavatory bowls and cisterns;
(24) bidets;
(25) shower units;
(26) fixed towel rails; toilet roller holders; soap dishes etc;
(27) 'communal' TV aerials in blocks of flats etc; and
(28) warden call systems.

The following are examples of fixtures in particular buildings used for relevant charitable purposes (but not as dwellings or for relevant residential purposes) that qualify for zero-rating:

Schools
(1) blackboards/ whiteboards fixed to or forming part of the walls;
(2) gymnasium wall bars;
(3) notice and display boards; and
(4) mirrors and barres (in ballet schools).

Churches
(1) altars;
(2) church bells;
(3) pipe organs;
(4) fonts;
(5) lecterns; and
(6) pulpits.

General
(1) external lighting systems (excluding non-fixed bulbs and tubes);
(2) blinds and shutters;
(3) mirrors;
(4) safes.

VAT Notice 708 describes the above items and also describes items of fitted furniture that are not to be treated as builders' hardware ordinarily installed as fixtures. **[39.40]**

c) *Other commercial construction and civil engineering work*

All construction work, unless expressly zero-rated or outside the scope as relating to land situated outside the UK, is standard-rated.

The supply of demolition services is normally standard-rated. Where the demolition work is carried out as an integral part of a contract for the construction of a zero-rated building and carried out prior to first occupation, the demolition services are zero-rated. Where building services are supplied in the course of construction of a building only part of which will qualify for zero-rating, eg a shop with a flat above, the supply has to be apportioned between the standard-rated and zero-rated elements. This provision applies only where an identifiable part of a building is to be used for a qualifying residential or qualifying charitable purpose.

Non-business charity buildings are often used indiscriminately by charities, sometimes for their non-business activities and sometimes not. HMRC have stated that they will ignore indiscriminate business use for non-business charity buildings (or non-qualifying use of a relevant residential building) where it is not expected to exceed 5% of the time the building is normally available for use. [39.41]

d) *Refund of VAT to 'do-it-yourself' house builders*

Normally credit for VAT suffered as input tax is only available to a registered person where it is incurred for the purpose of any business carried on by him. Exceptionally, however, VAT may be reclaimed on goods supplied (or imported) by an individual lawfully building a dwelling or dwellings otherwise than for the purpose of a business carried on by him (VATA 1994 s 35). The goods must be:
(1) incorporated in the dwelling or its site; and
(2) such that they would rank for input tax deduction as materials, builders' hardware, sanitary ware or other articles of a kind ordinarily installed by builders as fixtures.

Claims may also be made in relation to the conversion of a non-residential building and restoration to use of residential buildings not used as such in the last 10 or more years. Recovery of VAT under these provisions is subject to a number of conditions, eg:
(1) there must be documentary evidence of completion from the local authority;
(2) all tax invoices in support of the claim must be attached to the completed VAT forms (form VAT 431NB for new dwellings and form VAT 431C for conversions);
(3) claims must be made within three months of completion.

[39.42]–[39.43]

8 Estate agents

The supply of services provided by an estate agent in arranging the purchase, sale or lease of a client's property is standard rated if the property is situated in the UK or the Isle of Man. Where the property is situated outside the UK or the Isle of Man then the supply will be 'zero-rated': technically outside the scope with input tax credit. The place of supply of services relating to land, and this specifically includes 'services such as are provided by estate agents', is where the land is situated.

The supply by the agent constitutes a single supply of services and it is not possible to break the service down into its constituent parts. Any payment received for expenses incurred when a sale is not made is also a single supply of services and standard-rated. [39.44]

Property management

It is common practice for a landlord to appoint a managing agent to manage a property on his behalf, ie collect rents, deal with expenses such as insurance, repairs, porters' wages and so on. Thus tenants, suppliers, etc find themselves dealing with the managing agent rather than the landlord and rent demands and invoices may well be in the agent's name. The services rendered are by the agent and do not follow the liability of the property (*Nell Gwynn House Maintenance Fund Trustees v C & E Comrs* (1999)). However, HMRC operate a concession (ESC VAT 3.18) exempting certain services that the resident is obliged to accept because the service is supplied to the estate of buildings or blocks of flats as a whole.

This may lead to problems where the landlord has exercised the option to tax a particular property as it is vital that rent demands from the landlord meet the tests for VAT invoices. HMRC have indicated that one of the following invoicing procedures is acceptable to them:
(1) the landlord invoices the tenant direct; or
(2) the agent invoices the tenant in his own name and applies the agency procedure in accounting to the landlord. This leaves the agent with the primary liability to account for the output tax on the rent invoices, pending recovery from the landlord; or
(3) the agent invoices the tenant using the landlord's invoice with only the landlord's name, address and VAT registration number shown on the invoice. The agent's name may also appear on the invoice but only as the person through whom payment should be made.

Expenses incurred by the agent in looking after the property should be treated as disbursements incurred on behalf of the landlord. The agent's own charges for managing the property will bear tax at the standard rate. **[39.45]**

40 Practical application of VAT

Hartley Foster, Partner, Fieldfisher LLP

I   Introduction [**40.1**]
II Business activities [**40.22**]

I INTRODUCTION

The VAT legislation is drawn in general terms so that it can be applied to all types of business, person and supply. The legislation also contains special provisions that either supplement these general rules or derogate from them, so as to meet specific circumstances. Transactions vary too widely in character for a uniform set of rules to apply to them all. A mixture of social, economic, administrative and political pressures have led to many exemptions, reliefs and anti-avoidance provisions being introduced. These (often competing) pressures mean that it can be difficult to isolate which rules apply to a particular business activity and how they operate. Some of these special arrangements or Extra Statutory Concessions (ESC) are described in leaflets or notices (see Notice 48 for ESCs and Notice 700/57 (August 2014) for certain special administrative arrangements) published by HM Revenue and Customs (HMRC). [**40.1**]

Analysis of transactions

A particularly important factor to consider is whether the relevant person is accountable to VAT or not. The VAT legislation draws distinctions between different classes of person for a number of purposes, principally registration, business, exemption, zero-rating, special schemes and refunds of tax. Separation is carried out according to a number of criteria that differ from one provision to another. The following concepts are fundamental to an understanding of VAT:
(1) Legal personality: largely, but by no means exclusively, relevant to registration.
(2) Duties: these are imposed under the legislation and differ according to whether a person is or is not treated as a taxable person. A distinction is also drawn between taxable persons according to whether they make taxable supplies, they intend to make taxable supplies or they neither make nor intend to make taxable supplies. This distinction is important in determining whether a trader is liable to register or merely eligible for registration.

(3) Capacity: the legislation draws a distinction between traders who act on their own behalf (as principal) and those who act on someone else's behalf (as agent).
(4) Residence: a number of reliefs depend, in broad terms, on the country where a person is resident (more specifically, by reference to a concept of belonging).
(5) Quality: some reliefs are dependent upon some personal quality, eg as a charity, handicapped person or diplomatic mission.
(6) Activity: some reliefs are dependent upon the supplier carrying out a specific activity.
(7) Identity: some reliefs are given to named persons, eg zero-rating, refunds of tax. In other cases, supplies made by a named person may be treated in a specified manner (eg the Post Office).
(8) Supplies: the classification of supplies between goods and services can have tax consequences. **[40.2]–[40.21]**

II BUSINESS ACTIVITIES

In order to explain the application of some of the principles of VAT, specific aspects of a selection of commercial activities are considered below. The range and variation in activities are such that this approach clearly cannot be comprehensive. In this chapter: (i) food and drink; (ii) social and welfare; (iii) leisure; (iv) business services; (v) professional services; (vi) governmental bodies; and (vii) special arrangements are considered. Property transactions are dealt with in the preceding chapter. **[40.22]**

1 Food and drink

a) *Catering*

The supply of food and drink in the course of catering is standard-rated. This includes:
(1) any supply for consumption on the premises; and
(2) any supply of hot food for consumption off the premises.

Brockenhurst College (Case C-699/15) concerned courses run by the college in various subjects, including catering and hospitality. To teach catering and hospitality students practical skills, the college ran a restaurant in which all the catering functions were carried out by students. The restaurant was open to the public, who paid for their meals (as in any restaurant), but at discounted prices. The issue before the CJEU was whether the services supplied by the college were exempt (in the same way as the courses delivered by it) or standard rated, as supplies of food and drink. HMRC argued that the supplies of catering did not differ from similar supplies made by commercial bodies, and therefore were standard-rated. The College asserted that such supplies were exempt, being 'closely related' to supplies of exempt education. The CJEU agreed. It held that both the conditions in Article 134 (that the supply in question is essential to the education being provided; and that the basic purpose of the supply is not to obtain additional income for the institution in question through transactions that are in direct competition with those of commercial operators) were met. **[40.23]**

'Catering' is not a defined term. According to HMRC's VAT Notice 709/1 (October 2013), its ordinary meaning includes the supply of prepared food and drink and that it is characterised by a supply involving a significant element of service. It is intended to cover the supply of food and drink at functions such as conferences, wedding receptions and parties. It also includes ready-to-eat food or meals delivered to a customer at home (but not a supply that requires significant further preparation by the customer), at work or at a social event, and preparing and cooking food for parties.

[40.24]

Premises are the areas occupied by a retailer and/or those areas which have been specifically provided for the retailer's customer to consume food purchased. VAT Notice 709/1 indicates that this includes:
(1) a restaurant (or similar café, canteen type business) – the whole restaurant area, plus any chairs/tables on the pavement, concourse or similar areas adjacent to the main premises;
(2) a retail outlet in a shopping centre – the outlet itself and any chairs and tables in designated areas belonging to that outlet or provided for the exclusive use of that outlet;
(3) a retailer in a shopping centre with a food court – the premises are the retail outlet, plus the tables and chairs within the food court;
(4) a supermarket – any seating areas within the shop, plus any areas of chairs and table outside the shop for use of customers;
(5) a stall in a sports stadium, amusement park, exhibition, gallery or similar pay-entry venue – the premises are the stall itself, plus any facilities provided adjacent to the stall for the use of customers; and
(6) a retail outlet within an office building – the premises are the outlet, plus any area for consumption around or next to the outlet, that is, a seating or dining area.

Supplies of hot food for consumption off the premises are standard-rated for VAT purposes. It follows that the supply of food which is not hot is zero-rated. In *Sub One (t/a Subway) v R & C Comrs*, Subway argued that it was entitled to treat its supplies of toasted sandwiches and meatball marinara as zero-rated. The First-tier Tribunal (2010) dismissed the appeal, finding that the sandwiches and marinara had been heated 'for the purposes of enabling them to be consumed at a temperature above the ambient air temperature'. The Upper Tribunal (2012) and the Court of Appeal (2014) agreed that the supplies were standard rated. Subway argued that by treating its supplies as standard rated, HMRC infringed the European law principle of fiscal neutrality, as similar products had been found to be zero rated in previous decisions. The Court of Appeal agreed that, as supplies 'which are identical or similar from the point of view of the customer and meet the same needs of the consumer' (see *Rank* (C-259/10)), there was a breach of fiscal neutrality. The Court noted, however, that Subway's supplies were clearly standard rated under UK law and the varying decisions of the courts were isolated and numerically insignificant. Accordingly, it concluded that the principle of fiscal neutrality could not be relied upon by Subway to overturn HMRC's decision.

b) Licensed trade

There are three main categories of public houses: managed, free or tied. The categorisation of the public house has implications for the purposes of VAT registration and accounting. [40.27]

Managed houses

As the name implies, these are run by a manager who is an employee of the brewery that actually owns the public house.

The retail sales are those of the brewery and so for the sale of beers, wines, spirits and intoxicating liquors the managed house will be VAT registered under the name of the brewery which will account for VAT on the sales.

It is often the case that the managed house also provides a catering service that is the private business of the manager. In this situation such catering activities fall to be considered separately for VAT registration purposes and the normal liability rules will apply if the registration limits are exceeded.

A similar position applies if the owner is not a brewery but another owner which runs the public house business through a manager. That owner is then the person liable to be registered for VAT and to account for output tax on the sales. [40.28]

Free houses

These are public houses independently owned by a publican (or let by the publican from someone other than a brewery) and consequently have no restrictions on which beers, wines, spirits and soft drinks can be purchased.

The VAT position is similar to that for a tenanted house in that a licensee will likely be a self-employed person and therefore will be responsible for the corresponding VAT. [40.29]

Tenanted houses

Most pubs are owned by the breweries and now, more frequently, by pub-owning/operating companies. The companies let the pubs to the tenants. The tenant is 'tied' to mainly purchasing beers, wines and spirits for sale in the pub from the brewery. For VAT purposes, the tenant will usually be a separate legal entity and is responsible for accounting for VAT (assuming that he meets the registration requirements).

If the brewery exercises its option to tax in respect of the property, then VAT will be due by the tenant on the rent charged by the brewery. Normally, the option to tax cannot apply to domestic accommodation. However, residential accommodation within a public house can be an exception (see *AJ White* (1998) VAT Decision 15388).

A variant of tenanted house is the 'leased house'. This arrangement is very similar to tenanted houses; the difference with a leased house is that, generally, there will be no requirement to purchase stock from the brewery that owns the premises. The VAT position is the same and the lessor is required to account for output VAT (subject to meeting the registration requirements).

If a public house is also supplying other services, such as providing meals or overnight accommodation, then the precise nature of the services provided will need careful consideration in order to ensure that the VAT treatment applied is correct. **[40.30]–[40.31]**

2 Social and welfare

a) *Charities and the voluntary sector*

Any body based in England or Wales that has been recognised as a charity by the Charity Commission and entered on the register will be accepted as a charity by HMRC for tax purposes. It should be noted that some charities are not required to register with the Charity Commission. However, an unregistered charity wishing to take advantage of VAT relief must apply to HMRC for recognition of its charitable status. There is a general presumption that charities and similar non-profit making ventures intended for the benefit of the community, whether broadly or narrowly defined, should not be liable to taxation. Indeed, charitable bodies benefit from broad (though not total) exemptions from income tax, corporation tax and capital gains tax. However, this benevolence does not extend in such a broad way to VAT. There are various reliefs from VAT for charities, either by the exemption or zero-rating of certain supplies made both by and to such bodies. However, the reliefs are drawn quite specifically. It is essential that those concerned with running charities are advised as to the precise scope of the reliefs and thus their potential application to their particular operation.

A charity's work may constitute economic activity that comes within the scope of 'business', giving rise to a possible liability to VAT. However, there are a number of activities that charities may carry on that do not constitute 'business' activities and are therefore not liable to VAT. These include the following:

(1) Charges for advertisements in charity brochures, programmes, annual reports and the like, where these are clearly of a non-commercial nature and where 50% or more of the total advertisements in the publication are clearly placed by private individuals, in which case, the charity can treat all sums received as donations (which are outside the scope of VAT).

(2) The sale, hire or export of donated goods by a charity is zero rated provided that:
    (i) the goods were donated to the charity or trading subsidiary; and
    (ii) the goods must be made available to the general public, or to two or more persons who are disabled and/or receiving certain means tested benefits.

(3) Where catering is provided as part of a fund-raising event, the proceeds are exempt from VAT.

(4) Income from events (eg admission fees) clearly organised and promoted primarily to raise money for the benefit of the charity are exempt from VAT.

In order to treat a donation as outside the scope of VAT, it is generally important that nothing is supplied in return for the donation. For example, if admission to premises is conditional upon making a payment, that payment is not a donation and the charity must account for output VAT on it.

Further information in relation to the VAT obligations of charities can be found in VAT Notice 701/1 (October 2014). [40.32]

EXAMPLE 40.1 – CHARITY

A charity organises three concerts each year to raise funds. The event falls within the definition of a qualifying event for exemption from VAT. Therefore, all income generated from the events is exempt although much of it, eg admission charges and sponsorship, would normally be standard-rated.

The disadvantage is that VAT on any standard-rated costs of running the event (eg practitioners' fees, catering charges) would normally be irrecoverable under the partial exemption rules.

b) *Education*

Articles 132(1)(i), (j) and (o) of the Recast VAT Directive provide for exemption of a range of services related to education, together with the incidental supply of goods. The exemptions are specifically targeted. The provision of other services or the supply of goods by educational entities may result in an obligation to register and account for VAT. These EU provisions are reflected in VATA 1994 Sch 9 Group 6.

According to HMRC (see Notice 701/30 (February 2014)), 'education' means a course, class or lesson of instruction or study in any subject, regardless of when and where it takes place and it includes: (i) lectures, educational seminars, conferences and symposia, recreational and sporting courses; and (ii) distance teaching and associated materials. In terms of VAT treatment, in broad terms:

(1) If education is provided at no charge, there is no 'business' for VAT purposes: only sales of goods not closely related to the education provided and non-educational services are subject to VAT;
(2) If education is provided for a charge and the provider is an 'eligible body' (see below): the education provided and closely related goods or services are exempt; and the sales of other goods or services are subject to VAT; and
(3) If education is provided for a charge and the provider is not an 'eligible body' (see below): all goods and services provided are subject to VAT.
[40.33]

Eligible bodies

An 'eligible body' is defined in VATA 1994 Sch 9 Note 1 to Group 6. The term includes schools, universities and sixth form colleges. The term also includes 'a body which acts under any enactment or instrument for public purposes and not for its own profit and which performs functions similar to those of a government department or local authority' (VATA 1994 Sch 9 Note 5 to Group 7). [40.34]

Private tuition

Generally, if private tuition is provided by a sole trader or an individual in a partnership and the subject taught is one that is taught regularly in schools and/or universities, such tuition is exempt. The services of any other tutor who is not that individual are standard-rated. **[40.35]**

c) *Health*

The provision of health care services is primarily exempt from VAT (VATA 1994 Sch 9 Group 7). Whilst exemption is granted by reference to the supplier, rather than solely by reference to the service, nonetheless care must be taken to ensure that particular services fall within the scope of the exemption.
[40.36]

Supplies by qualified persons

The exemption extends primarily to the services performed by qualified medical personnel whose names appear in certain specified registers (see below) and to the supply of drugs, dressings and similar goods by such persons in connection with their supply of medical services where: (i) the services are within the profession in which they are registered to practise; and (ii) the primary purpose of the services is the protection, maintenance or restoration of the health of the person concerned. The exemption is not limited to supplies purely within the National Health Service (NHS) but extends to the private health sector.

The registers concerned are as follows:
(1) the register of medical practitioners;
(2) the register of dentists, dental hygienists, dental therapists, dental nurses, clinical dental technicians or orthodontic therapists;
(3) the register of optometrists and dispensing opticians;
(4) any register kept under the Health Professions Order 2001 (eg chiropodists, dieticians, etc);
(5) the register of osteopaths;
(6) the register of chiropractors; and
(7) the register of qualified nurses, midwives and health visitors; and
(8) the register of pharmacists.

Any supply of professional medical services by a person or by a company which is not registered or enrolled in any of the statutory registers mentioned above nevertheless qualifies for exemption when the services are performed or directly supervised by a person who is so registered or enrolled. The services concerned must clearly be within the ambit of the qualification of the person concerned in order to qualify for the exemption, eg chiropractic services provided by a state registered nurse would not be eligible for exemption.

The exemption does not extend to any other registers, including acupuncturists, hypnotherapists, herbalists or masseurs. Such services are, accordingly, always standard-rated. The CJEU has held that the exclusion of a particular profession or activity must be capable of objective justification on the grounds of professional qualifications and, thus, on the presumed quality of the services provided (*JE van den Hout – van Eijensbergen* (C–444/04)).

Further, the exemption does not now apply to goods supplied in connection with medical care. This affects mainly spectacles, contact lenses and hearing aids bought from private hearing aid dispensers, the supply of which is standard-rated. In *C & E Comrs v Leightons Ltd* (1995), it was held that the supply of spectacles by a dispensing optician is, in part, a supply of exempt dispensing services and, in part, a supply of standard-rated goods. The price paid must be apportioned accordingly. Although HMRC indicated that they considered that *Card Protection Plan Ltd v C & E Comrs* (Case C–349/96) (1999) overruled *Leightons* (with the result that the provision of spectacles or contact lenses was a single supply), the VAT Tribunal confirmed that their earlier decision in *Leightons* stands – see *Leightons Ltd and Eye-Tech Opticians v C & E Comrs* (2001) VAT Decision 17498. [40.37]

Provision of care in hospitals etc

VATA 1994 Sch 9 Group 7 Item 4 provides an exemption for the provision of care or medical or surgical treatment and, in connection with it, the supply of any goods, in any hospital or state-regulated institution.

Services provided by qualifying institutions (such as hospitals and certain hospices or nursing homes) are exempt where: (i) the services provided by the institution consist of care or medical or surgical treatment in connection with the health of the beneficiary of such services; and (ii) such treatment or care is provided under the terms of an approval, licence, registration or an exemption from registration under the relevant legislation (see VAT Notice 701/31 (August 2014)). The provision of care or medical or surgical treatment extends to cover such items as accommodation (including accommodation for parents sharing a room in a hospital with their sick children), catering, medical and nursing services and drugs, appliances, etc. HMRC interpret the term 'medical care or treatment' to include: performing medical or surgical procedures with the aim of protecting, maintaining or restoring the health of an individual; nursing sick or injured patients in a hospital, hospice or nursing home; and meals and accommodation provided to in-patients, resident or other care beneficiaries (see VAT Notice 701/31 (August 2014)). [40.38]

Pharmacists

The supply of any services by a person registered on the register of pharmaceutical chemists is exempt, but must be distinguished from the goods that might be sold through a chemist's shop. An example of an exempt supply would be a pregnancy test, carried out by the pharmacist, whereas the supply of a pregnancy testing kit would be standard-rated.

The supply by a registered pharmacist of any 'qualifying goods' dispensed to an individual for that individual's personal use on the prescription of a doctor is zero-rated (VATA 1994 Sch 8 Group 12). 'Qualifying goods' means any goods designed or adapted for use in connection with any medical or surgical treatment (except hearing aids, dentures, spectacles and contact lenses) (VATA 1994 Sch 8 Group 12 Note 2A).

This applies where the goods are dispensed on the NHS. HMRC are of the view that drugs dispensed against private prescriptions are standard rated (refer VAT Information Sheet 03/2006 *Dispensing Doctors and VAT Registration*). Any supplies that are not supplied under a prescription are not within the zero-rating provision and therefore fall to be standard-rated. [40.39]

Opticians

Registered ophthalmic or dispensing opticians can exempt the supply of their professional services to a patient and also the supply in a hospital of spectacles, contact lenses and other appliances designed to correct or relieve a defect of sight if they are supplied in connection with ophthalmic services. HMRC may seek to argue that the supply is a mixed supply, comprising an exempt supply of services and a standard-rated supply of goods, or a single supply of goods (standard-rated) rather than a single exempt supply of services. [40.40]–[40.42]

3 **Leisure**

a) *Entertainers/performers*

An individual who normally lives abroad but who performs in the UK may come within the scope of VAT in the UK as cultural, educational or entertainment services provided to a non-business customer are considered to be supplied where performed (see VATA 1994 Sch 4A para 14A). Accordingly the performer may need to register for VAT in the UK and account for VAT. The reverse charge obliges UK VAT registered customers to account for the VAT due on services supplied by an overseas supplier regarded as supplied in the UK (unless the overseas supplier is registered for VAT in the UK). Registering for VAT does not in itself bring the individual within the scope of UK income tax (or corporation tax in the case of a company) as this is determined by different criteria.

Cultural, educational or entertainment services provided to a 'relevant business person' are subject to the 'business to business' general rule (see further **Chapter 38**); accordingly, the place of supply is where the customer belongs.

It should be noted that performances outside the UK, particularly in other EU countries, may give rise to a liability to register for VAT in that country. In such circumstances, it would be necessary to account for VAT (as output tax) on all receipts whilst claiming a refund for VAT suffered on costs, subject to the normal rules of the country concerned. [40.43]

It is common practice for some entertainers to contract their services to a single theatrical agent for an agreed period and fee. In such circumstances, it is the agent who is acting as principal in making supplies to the venue. On this basis the agent must account, as output tax, for VAT on the full value of the receipt from the venue. From this amount the agent will deduct his commission and any expenses according to the terms of the contract and pass the balance to the artist. This amount represents the output of the entertainer with the consequence that VAT must be accounted for by him accordingly. In such circumstances, it is not unusual for the agent to generate the individual's invoice under a self-billing arrangement. The amount paid over to the entertainer will represent an input to the agent.

Compare this with the situation where an agent introduces an entertainer to a venue for a fee or commission. In this instance the entertainer is the principal in the transaction and will invoice the venue directly. Similarly the agent will invoice the entertainer for his commission. [40.44]–[40.48]

b) *Clubs, associations and societies*

In order to confirm the VAT treatment on services they provide, clubs and similar associations first need to consider whether such services are 'business activities' or not.

Business activities include:
(1) the provision by a club, association or organisation (for a subscription or other consideration) of the facilities or advantages available to its members;
(2) the admission for a consideration of persons to any premises; and
(3) providing catering and other facilities to non-members for a charge.

What constitutes a club, association or organisation should be a matter of fact as determined by its constitution.

Clubs may also carry on non-business activities that are outside the scope of VAT. These are mainly activities for which no payment is made to the club or, where there is a payment, no benefit is provided in return. These include:
(1) free admission to premises for non-members; and
(2) providing free literature to non-members.

Subscriptions, donations and fund raising

VAT Notice 701/5 (October 2013) provides guidance as the VAT treatment of subscription amounts received by clubs and associations from their members.

Generally, if the whole of a subscription is a voluntary payment and secures nothing or only nominal benefits in return, this is a donation and can be treated as being outside of the scope of VAT.

In other cases, the VAT liability in relation to any subscription will depend on the membership benefits which are provided by a club or association in return. It will be necessary to consider whether multiple supplies are being made and, if so, the VAT liability associated with each such supply. VAT Information Sheet 2/01 provides further information on single and multiple supplies.

Where members receive zero-rated materials, such as a journal or handbook, or exempt services (eg the making of arrangements for the provision of insurance), it should be possible to agree an apportionment of the subscription between standard-rated, zero-rated and exempt elements.

A body with objects in the public domain and of a political, religious, philanthropic, philosophical, civic or patriotic nature is not treated as carrying on a 'business' for VAT purposes. Accordingly, its subscriptions are not subject to tax (see VATA 1994 Sch 9 Group 9 para 1(e)). **[40.49]**

Guidance and Memorandum of Understanding (MoU) with CIPFA

A long-standing Memorandum of Understanding (MoU) between HMRC and the Chartered Institute of Public Finance and Accountancy (CIPFA) sets out the various scenarios relating to the provision of local authority leisure services and their VAT consequences. In the MoU, it is explained that the VAT treatment generally depends on the circumstances in which the payments are made and, in particular, who is making the relevant supplies: in some cases they are simply grants and therefore outside the scope, whilst in others they are consideration for a supply. In the joined appeals of *Edinburgh Leisure, South Lanarkshire Leisure and Renfrewshire Leisure* – EDN 03/22, 03/29 and 03/30, the appellants were non-profit-making leisure trusts established by local authorities to take over the provision of leisure. It was agreed that the local authority would pay an amount to the leisure trust to cover any shortfall between operating costs and actual income. The issue related to the determination of the VAT status of that payment. The Tribunal decided that the payment was consideration for a supply as it was the local authority's statutory obligation to ensure that there was adequate provision of leisure facilities for inhabitants of their area; but also, it was the local authority's duty to ensure adequate facilities were available for people who cannot, for social and economic reasons, make use of facilities supplied for profit which as a result are costly. HMRC did not appeal this decision. In *Business Brief 01/05*, HMRC stated that, in all cases, the terms of the payment and the direct benefit received by the funding body must be considered. **[40.50]–[40.53]**

Sports

Sporting services supplied by 'eligible bodies' are exempt under VATA 1994 Sch 9 Group 10.

The question of what is a 'sport' is currently before the CJEU (*The English Bridge Union Limited v R & C Comrs* (Case C-90/16)). The English Bridge Union (EBU) is the national body for duplicate bridge in England. It organises contract bridge tournaments and charges players an entry fee to play in those tournaments. The EBU made a claim to recover VAT that had been paid in respect of those entry fees, claiming that the fees were exempt (under Article 132(1)(m)). The Upper Tribunal referred questions to the CJEU, including:

> 'What are the essential characteristics which an activity must exhibit in order for it to be a "sport" ... In particular must an activity have a significant (or not insignificant) physical element which is material to its outcome or is it sufficient that it has a significant mental element which is material to its outcome?'

On 15 June 2017, Advocate General Szpunar released his opinion: a not insignificant physical element which is material to its outcome is not necessary; it is sufficient that the activity has a significant mental element which is material to its outcome. He opined that, on that basis (and having noted that bridge is now an Olympic sport), contract bridge is a sport.

Exemption applies to services closely linked and essential to sport or physical education where it is supplied by an 'eligible body' to an individual. An 'eligible body' in this context means:
(1) it is non-profit making;
(2) its constitution contains certain restrictions on the distribution of profits; and
(3) it is not subject to 'commercial influence'.
(See VATA 1994 Sch 9 Note 2A to Group 10.)

A club is subject to commercial influence (VATA 1994 Sch 9 Note 4 to Group 10), if, at the time of the sports supply (eg the due date for paying subscriptions or other charges to members), over the 'relevant period' (the

'relevant period' is the three years leading up to the time of the sports supply) the club has:
(1) paid a salary or bonus calculated by reference to its profits or gross income to anyone who was an officer or a shadow officer of the club (or was connected with such an officer); or
(2) purchased certain goods or services (called 'relevant supplies') from anyone who was:
  (a) an officer or a shadow officer of the club;
  (b) acting as an intermediary between the club and the officer; or
  (c) connected with any such person.

Included in the exemption are, for example:
(1) membership subscription of paying members;
(2) subscriptions to sports governing bodies for sporting services; and
(3) hiring of equipment and facilities to members.

HMRC has published a list of sports that it considers qualify for exemption. These are listed in VAT Notice 701/45 (May 2016).

HMRC have agreed that commercial clubs are able to treat the fees as a disbursement for VAT purposes provided prescribed conditions are met (see VAT Notice 701/45 (May 2016)).

Prior to 1 January 2015, supplies made by a non-profit making body operating a membership scheme to non-members were not included in the exemption. This position was revised following the CJEU's decision in *Bridport and West Dorset Golf Club Ltd* (C-495/12). The CJEU held that supplies to non-members could not be excluded from the exemption. Accordingly, HMRC (in Business Brief 25/14) conceded that 'supplies of sporting services to both members and non-members of non-profit making sports clubs qualify to be treated as exempt from VAT. This is provided that the services are closely linked and essential to sport and are made to persons taking part in sport'. This change came into effect on 1 January 2015 (see the Value Added Tax (Sport) Order 2014 (SI 2014/3185)). **[40.54]–[40.55]**

Participation and match fees

Charges for playing games and sports, such as court and green fees, payable by non-members are standard-rated. This includes match fees levied to offset overheads incurred, eg travelling expenses. The value for VAT is the gross receipts before payments of any kind (including commission to club professionals). Payments for snooker tables, squash courts, tennis courts, etc, which are illuminated by coin operated switches, or where extra charges are made for floodlighting, are also standard-rated as charges for the provision of sports facilities, and not regarded as the supply of electricity.

Payments for the right to enter a sporting competition are generally standard-rated unless:
(1) the whole of the money is returned as prizes (money, goods, trophies); or
(2) the sporting competition is organised by a non-profit making body established for the purpose of sport or physical recreation,

in which case the supply is exempt (VATA 1994 Sch 9 Group 10). However, if the fee includes elements that are standard or zero-rated supplies, apportionment may be required. This restriction does not apply if the competition is run on some other organisation's ground and it is that body which normally makes charges for admission or the use of facilities when there is no competition. Cash prizes and the award of cups and other trophies that remain the property of the club are outside the scope of VAT. As a general rule, goods given as prizes or as presentations to officials or visitors will not give rise to any output tax if the cost to the donor is not more than £50; if it is more than that amount, then there may be liability to account for output tax on that cost, unless it can be argued that the supply of the trophies is an incidental element in the overall supply –that of participating in the ceremony (*C & E Comrs v Professional Footballers Association (Enterprises) Ltd* (1993)). In either case input tax on the goods or trophies given may be reclaimed. **[40.56]–[40.62]**

c) *Museums and galleries*

Museums that do not charge for entrance are not 'in business' for VAT purposes, and cannot recover VAT on their costs. For publicly funded bodies this increases the funding requirement. Certain national museums and galleries are to be allowed to recover VAT on their costs when they provide free entry to the public (VAT (Refund of Tax to Museums and Galleries) Order 2001, see VAT Notice 998 (May 2016)). **[40.63]**

4 Business services

a) *Financial services*

A feature of the growth in financial services over recent years has been the increasing complexity of the services being provided. Arranging a loan may now, for example, involve one swap arrangement as a safeguard against interest changes and another to minimise the effect of the volatility of foreign exchange rates. Quite apart from deciding whether such transactions are exempt or zero-rated, there are often problems of identifying the supply and consideration and the partial exemption implications. Thus it is necessary to be familiar with many aspects of VAT law in order to ensure that such transactions are given the correct VAT treatment. This is particularly so in relation to the outsourcing of services. **[40.64]**

Dealings with money

Dealings with money are exempt from VAT. 'Money' in this context is defined (in VATA 1994 s 96(1)) to include currencies other than sterling. According to HMRC (see VAT Notice 701/49 (January 2013)), 'money' includes coins and bank notes denominated in sterling or in any other currency, when supplied as legal tender in financial transactions. The sorts of transactions which are regarded as falling within this category include the acceptance of money on account, money transfer services and exchange of legal tender. The CJEU has tried to identify mechanisms for containing the broad scope of the exemption. Most relevantly, in a line of cases starting with *Sparekassernes Datacenter (SDC) v Skatteministeriet* (1997), it has developed, and applied, the question: 'does the transfer effect a change in the legal and financial situation existing between the person giving the order and the recipient?' to determine whether the transaction falls within the exemption.

The value for VAT purposes of transactions of this type varies. For dealings in currency, following the decision in *First National Bank of Chicago v C & E Comrs* (1998), HMRC accept that where there is no specific consideration for the transaction plus any fees or commission charged, the value of the supply is the net result of the transactions over a period of time (ie the net profit), and not the values of the currencies exchanged (see VAT Finance Manual 2740 and *Business Brief* 16/98 (28 July 1998) and *Republic National Bank of New York v C & E Comrs* (1992)).

HMRC accept that there may be circumstances involving a foreign exchange contract that do not involve any consideration and, as such, there may not be a supply (see *Business Brief* 21/05).

Dealings in money that are not exempt include:

(1) Dealings with bank notes or coins supplied as collectors' pieces or investment articles (eg proof coins, Maundy money). Such supplies are taxable at the standard rate of VAT on their full selling price. It should be noted, however, that there is a secondhand scheme for supplies of collectors' pieces (see VAT Notice 718 (April 2011)).

(2) The first issue of notes by the Bank of England and Scottish and Northern Irish banks payable to the bearer on demand. Such supplies are zero-rated.

(3) Certain money flows which are not consideration for a VAT supply. Examples are the payment and receipt of dividends, and receipt of pension contributions and the payment of pensions out of a pension fund. This money flow does not create VAT supplies but any VAT incurred in connection with it may not be recoverable.

(4) The provision of Automatic Teller Machines (ATMs) and the software to run them. These supplies together with services provided in connection with the routine operation of an ATM, are taxable supplies.

As regards virtual currencies such as Bitcoins, HMRC has confirmed (in Brief 09/14) that, for VAT purposes:

(1) Bitcoin mining activities do not constitute 'economic activities' such that income from them will generally be outside the scope of VAT because there is an insufficient link between any services provided and any consideration received;

(2) income received by Bitcoin miners for other activities, such as for the provision of services in connection with the verification of specific transactions for which specific charges are made, will be exempt;

(3) when Bitcoins are exchanged for Sterling or other currencies, no VAT will be due on the value of the Bitcoins themselves; and

(4) charges (in whatever form) made over and above the value of the Bitcoin for arranging or carrying out any transactions in Bitcoin will also be exempt.

Supplies of goods or services in exchange for Bitcoins attract VAT in the normal way. The value of the supply of goods or services on which VAT is due will be the Sterling value of the Bitcoins at the point the transaction takes place. **[40.65]**

Securities for money

The supply of securities is exempt from VAT. 'Security for money' is not defined statutorily, but HMRC consider that it includes:

(1) bills of exchange;

(2) financial guarantees; and
(3) promissory notes (see VAT Notice 701/49 (January 2013)).

This exemption also applies to issues of certain bonds, guarantees and other forms of indemnity provided by financial institutions for money which include only a guarantee or indemnity which:
(a) is secondary to the primary contract; and
(b) is a contract of security issued by a guarantor or surety obliging him to indemnify a party to the primary contract for any loss arising from the failure or default of the other party to fulfil his obligations under the primary contract. **[40.66]–[40.67]**

Loans; deposits and granting credit

The making of loans and the granting of credit are exempt supplies. The value for VAT purposes is the gross interest and/or any other sum received by whoever makes the loan or grants the credit. The exempt supply of a loan or of granting credit is often referred to as the exemption of interest. At the risk of stating the obvious it should always be remembered that it is the interest a business receives which is the consideration for its supply of a loan or credit and not the interest it pays.

Interest received on money deposited with a bank or building society is exempt as the consideration for the supply of an advance. **[40.68]**

Instalment credit finance

Instalment credit finance covers supplies of credit by way of a hire-purchase agreement, conditional sale agreement or credit sale agreement. Each such agreement involves a supply of goods or services and a supply of credit if a separate charge is made for the credit that is disclosed to the customer. The supply of goods or services is subject to the appropriate rate of VAT, but any supply of credit is exempt. The measure of the value of the supply of credit is the amount of interest received with each payment. If the amount of the charge is not disclosed to the customer then the whole amount is subject to VAT at the rate applicable to the goods or services supplied. The full amount of VAT on the goods is accounted for at the time of supply, which is usually when the goods are delivered. **[40.69]–[40.71]**

b) *Dealings in securities*

The issue, transfer or receipt of, or any dealing with, any security or secondary security is exempt (following the CJEU decision in *Kretztechnik*, which is discussed below, the initial issue of shares is not treated as a supply for VAT purposes – see VATA 1994 Sch 9 Group 5 Item 6 and VAT Supply and Consideration Manual VATSC 97600). 'Securities' are defined as:
(1) shares, stock, bonds, notes (other than promissory notes), debentures, debenture stock or shares in an oil royalty;
(2) any document relating to money, in any currency, which has been deposited with the issuer or some other person, being a document which recognises an obligation to pay a stated amount to bearer or to order, with or without interest, and being a document by the delivery

of which, with or without endorsement, the right to receive that stated amount, with or without interest, is transferable;
(3) any bill, note or other obligation of the Treasury or of a Government in any part of the world, being a document by the delivery of which, with or without endorsement, title is transferable, and not being an obligation which is or has been legal tender in any part of the world;
(4) any letter of allotment or rights, any warrant conferring an option to acquire a security included in this item, any renounceable or scrip certificates, rights coupons, coupons representing dividends, or interest on such a security, bond mandates or other documents conferring or containing evidence of title to or rights in respect of such a security; or
(5) units or other documents conferring rights under any trust established for the purpose, or having the effect of providing, for persons having funds available for investment, facilities for the participation by them as beneficiaries under the trust, in any profits or income arising from the acquisition, holding, management or disposal of any property whatsoever.

In contrast with the value of a supply of security for money, the value for VAT purposes of a supply of any of these securities is the total consideration for any such supply together with any gross interest derived from the holding of these securities. The receipt of any dividend in respect of any of these securities is outside the scope of VAT.

In *Kretztechnik*, the CJEU ruled that the first issue of shares by a public limited company is not a supply and the VAT incurred on the costs of such an issue is deductible input tax to the extent that the company is entitled to recover VAT under its partial exemption calculation. In *Business Brief 21/05*, HMRC set out its position on share issues following this decision. HMRC accept that the issue of shares is not a supply and that the *Kretztechnik* principles are not affected by the type of company issuing the shares or other types of security, such as bonds, debentures or loan notes, when the purpose of the issue is to raise capital for the issuer's business. However, transfers and dealings in existing shares remain exempt for VAT purposes. **[40.72]**

c) *Brokerage services*

The intermediary services of mortgage brokers and money brokers in making arrangements for any advance of money or the granting of any credit are exempt.

Commission paid by building societies to agents for the introduction of investment business or mortgage transactions and commission paid by finance houses and other institutions to retailers and dealers for the introduction of hire purchase and other credit business is also usually exempt, although if the person receiving the commission does no more than make the introduction, the supply is standard-rated.

Brokerage charges in respect of securities for money are exempt, as are those in respect of other securities and secondary securities. Any charge made by a broker for advice, investment guidance or similar services is chargeable with VAT at the standard rate unless these services fall within the description of the intermediary services in relation to the making of arrangements for the issue or transfer of shares in which case they are exempt.

Brokerage charges in respect of securities, other than those for money, are out of scope with recovery if they relate to a supply of securities that is itself out of scope under the rules relating to certain types of services exported to persons belonging in countries outside the EU. The effect is that VAT is not chargeable but input tax is recoverable. **[40.73]–[40.76]**

d) *Supplies connected with financial services*

The following supplies connected with financial services are not exempt and attract VAT at the standard rate:
(1) debt collection and credit control;
(2) equipment leasing;
(3) executor and trustee services and the administration of estates;
(4) investment, finance and taxation advice;
(5) management consultancy;
(6) merger and take-over advice;
(7) nominee services (unless for acting as a nominal holder of securities);
(8) portfolio management;
(9) registrar services;
(10) safe custody services; and
(11) service companies' activities, eg, administration, payment of salaries and wages. **[40.77]**

e) *Insurance*

The basic insurance transaction involves a person guaranteeing to make a payment to or otherwise compensate some other person in certain circumstances. It is seen for VAT purposes as a supply by the insurer to the insured, the consideration for which is normally the gross premium. Where the insurer is permitted to carry on insurance business in the UK such supplies are normally exempt from VAT.

Insurance supplied by the Export Credits Guarantee Department is generally exempt (formerly, specifically under VATA 1994 Sch 9 Group 2 Item 3; now incorporated into new item 1).

The introduction of an insurance premium tax (IPT) was announced in the 1993 Autumn Budget. The tax is under the care and management of HMRC (see Notice IPT 1, May 2015). The tax is based upon the premium written and is due at a standard rate of 9.5% (up from 6%) on contracts of insurance for specified risks and a higher rate of 20% for insurance supplied with selected goods and services. The detailed operation of the tax is beyond the scope of this book. Many of the concepts and procedures appropriate to VAT have been adapted for the purposes of IPT. From 1 October 2016 the rate of IPT will increase to 10%.

Changes were announced as a result of *Card Protection Plan*, which was referred to the CJEU by the House of Lords. CPP, who were not insurers, were able to procure insurance for their customers under a block insurance policy. The CJEU ruled that businesses in such a position should qualify for the exemption. The CJEU also said that the VAT exemption could not be restricted to authorised insurers. HMRC implemented the decision of the CJEU and legislative changes were made which came into effect from 1 January 2005. In summary, the VAT exemption is extended to businesses that procure insurance cover under a block policy, under similar circumstances to CPP, or to businesses who provide insurance that have not previously been authorised to do so by the FSA, in addition to authorised insurers. **[40.78]**

Marine, aviation and transport (MAT)

If insurance falls within certain classes of risk, it is classed as MAT insurance. The VAT liability of MAT insurance is to be generally determined by the country in which the recipient belongs. The place of belonging is to be determined using a set of rules agreed between HMRC and the Association of British Insurers, Lloyd's of London, the Institute of London Underwriters and the British Insurance and Investment Association (see details in Notice 701/36 (February 2013) and 700/57 (August 2014)). Input tax recovery is still available if the insurance covers the export of goods to a non-EU country. The previous concession allowing apportionment on a 50:50 basis for risks partly in and partly out of the EU is available in a modified form. It is now necessary to identify specific exports of goods in order to be able to recover attributable input tax. **[40.79]**

Reinsurance

Reinsurance contracts are those under which an insurer takes over a specific risk from another insurer (the principal insurer), thus spreading the insurance risk of the principal insurer. Generally the VAT liability of reinsurance follows the VAT liability of insurance, and so supplies of reinsurance are exempt for the most part. Supplies of reinsurance are treated as supplies made to the principal insurer. **[40.80]**

Brokers and other intermediary services

HMRC's view (in VAT Notice 701/36 (February 2013)) is that most of the services provided by 'traditional' insurance brokers or agents by profession will fall within VATA 1994 Sch 9 Group 2 Item 4 and will therefore be exempt supplies. HMRC also consider that even if a taxable person is not an insurance broker or agent by profession, then that person may, nevertheless, qualify for exemption. Regardless of who is supplying insurance related services, such services will be exempt only where the supplier is acting in an 'intermediary capacity' between an insurer and an insured party.

VATA 1994 Sch 9 Group 2 Note 2 provides that an insurance broker or insurance agent is acting 'in an intermediary capacity' wherever he is acting as an intermediary ... between: (a) a person who provides any insurance or reinsurance, and (b) a person who is or may be seeking insurance or reinsurance or is an insured person.

In *Riskstop Consulting Ltd v R & C Comrs* (2015), the First-tier Tribunal has held that supplies made by a company that analysed risk for insurers were standard rated, because the supplier was not an agent for the purposes of VATA 1994 Sch 9 Group 2 Item 4 – it did not bring together insurers and those seeking insurance. **[40.81]**

Claims handling

Claims handling is normally exempt when supplied to an insurer belonging in the UK, outside the scope without recovery if in another EU Member State and with recovery if outside the EU. Input tax recovery is available if the customer belongs outside the EU. However, the term 'handling' is interpreted narrowly by HMRC. It covers claims checking which is necessary to enable final settlement of a claim to be made but does not extend to specialist and professional services such as those of loss adjusters, average adjusters, motor assessors, surveyors and lawyers. However, if such a specialist does act as an agent for an insurer, providing a service of investigation and claims settlement, his services would be exempt or zero-rated, following the underlying insurance.

In order to treat claims handling services as exempt, in accordance with VATA 1994 Sch 9 Note 9 to Group 2:

(1) the services must be provided under a contract of insurance or reinsurance;
(2) the person handling the claim must be authorised when doing so to act on behalf of the insurer or reinsurer;
(3) that person's authority to act must include written authority to determine whether to accept or reject any claim; and
(4) where accepting a claim in whole or in part, the service provider must have the insurer's or reinsurer's written authority to settle the amount to be paid on such claim.

By concession the VAT treatment may follow that of the underlying insurance if the claims handling service is performed by the broker who arranged the original policy.

The High Court has held that expenses incurred in respect of claims relate to the insurance supplied and the VAT on the expenses should be directly attributable and thus fully deductible or fully disallowed (*C & E Comrs v Deutsche Ruck UK Reinsurance Co Ltd* (1995)). HMRC has confirmed that following *Deutsche Ruck* (see HMRC ABI: Partial Exemption Guidance for the Insurance sector), it considers that such expenses are a cost component of the supply of services, even though they are incurred long after the premium has been paid. HMRC had previously considered that such expenses related to general overheads and that VAT on them was subject to the partial exemption method. [40.82]

Other intermediaries

Where professional advisers such as accountants, solicitors or estate agents provide insurance brokerage, their services are generally exempt or out of scope with recovery under the same conditions as apply to the services of insurance brokers. It should, however, be borne in mind that this VAT treatment only applies if these businesses provide a comparable service to insurance brokers. Where the services of these businesses amount to no more than an introduction to an insurer or broker, any charge for this service is subject to the standard rate of VAT even if the recipient of the service belongs outside the EU. [40.83]–[40.85]

5 Professional services

Barristers

The normal VAT rules for registration and accounting for VAT apply for barristers. However, there are special rules laid down in reg 92 of the Value Added Tax Regulations 1995 for determining the tax point of services provided whilst practising and consequent upon ceasing to practise, as to which see below.

A barrister should be registered as a sole trader at the chambers where he practises. Registration will need to cover any other business making taxable supplies, eg lecturing.

A barrister is regarded as making supplies of legal services to the instructing solicitor that are generally subject to VAT at the standard rate. The value for VAT on the supply of those services will be determined by reference to the consideration. The consideration will normally be the value of the fee charged by the barrister to the instructing solicitor. If a barrister is instructed by a solicitor who 'belongs' outside the UK, his fees may be zero-rated.

Special rules apply in identifying the time of supply of the services supplied by a barrister (acting in that capacity) so that these are treated as taking place at whichever is the earliest of the following:
(1) when the fee in respect of those services is received;
(2) when the barrister issues a VAT invoice in respect of them; or
(3) the day when the barrister ceases to practise.

Barristers will not normally issue a VAT invoice until receipt of payment of their fee; instead they may be expected to issue a request for payment endorsed 'This is not a VAT invoice'. This must not contain all the necessary ingredients that would constitute a VAT invoice. In particular it must avoid showing the VAT number.

On ceasing to practise the barrister must notify his local VAT office within 30 days of cessation using Form VAT 7 (either by post or online). In accordance with *VAT Notice* 700/44 (October 2015) HMRC will allow the payment of VAT on outstanding fees at the time of ceasing to practise to be deferred until such a time as the fees are actually received or a VAT invoice is issued, whichever is the earlier, provided that the barrister asks to adopt the special procedures permitted.

When a barrister dies, the deceased barrister's clerk should notify HMRC's National Advice Service of the death as soon as possible. The personal representatives should state whether they wish to pay VAT on the barrister's outstanding professional fees forthwith or to defer payment. This should be done within ten days of the grant of probate or letters of administration.

[40.86]

Solicitors

Supplies of legal services are generally chargeable to VAT at the standard rate. Where services are supplied to a person who belongs outside the EU, or to a person in business in another Member State then, subject to exceptions, the place of supply of the service is outside the UK. The supply is thus outside the scope of VAT. The Law Society has issued guidance on the steps to be taken before treating a supply as outside the scope of VAT. Input tax on related expenses is recoverable and the value of the services should still be included in the turnover figures for VAT purposes. Indeed for partial exemption purposes VAT-exclusive values should be recorded if a value based method is used. **[40.87]**

Time of supply of legal services

The rules regarding the tax point for legal services are dependent on whether the supply is a single supply, eg preparation of a will, or a continuous supply, eg trustee work.

Work done over a period to enable a single supply to be made or a series of separate jobs for the same client over a period does not amount to a continuous supply. **[40.88]**

Single supply

The basic tax point occurs when the supply of services is known to be completed and tax must normally be accounted for at this time.

This will usually be straightforward to determine and it is essentially a question of fact to be decided case by case.

This basic point can only be overridden if either:
(1) a VAT invoice is issued or payment is received before the basic tax point (if the amount invoiced or received constitutes only part of the consideration for the supply, the basic tax point is overridden only to the extent of that part); or
(2) a VAT invoice is issued within 14 days following completion of the service. In such circumstances the actual tax point becomes the date of issue of the VAT invoice or the date payment is received, whichever is the earlier.

The 14-day rule is extended to three months (under an agreement between the Law Society and HMRC – see Law Society Practice Note: VAT change (24 November 2010)) where a fee is not ascertained or ascertainable at or before the time when the services are completed, eg because the solicitor uses the services of an outside cost draftsman. Provided a VAT invoice is issued no later than three months after completion of the relevant services, the date of the invoice will be the tax point. Failure to issue a VAT invoice within the extended period will cause the actual tax point to revert to the basic tax point.
[40.89]

Continuous supply

There is no basic tax point for a continuous supply of services. A tax point occurs when a VAT invoice is issued or payment is received, whichever is the earlier. A typical case is where a regular payment is made on a retainer basis.

It should be noted that once a VAT invoice has been issued the tax shown on the invoice must be accounted for in the VAT return relevant to the VAT period in which the VAT invoice was issued. **[40.90]–[40.93]**

Credit notes

When a VAT credit note is issued in accordance with the procedure recognised by HMRC, the solicitor issuing the credit note should adjust his VAT account in the period in which the credit note is issued to reflect the reduction in tax due. The issue of VAT credit notes can, however, only take place consistently with normal commercial practice. In the context of a solicitor's practice this will include the issue of a VAT credit note following a compulsory reduction in fees and it would also include cases in which fees are reduced voluntarily by agreement with the client in lieu of the latter seeking a remuneration certificate or taxation. [40.94]

Barristers' services

The services of barristers may be rendered to the instructing solicitor, who then makes an onward supply to the client, or the client directly. A taxpayer is only entitled to recover VAT on expenditure on goods or services supplied to the taxpayer. HMRC accept the practice of redirecting invoices, addressed to the solicitor, to the client where the client pays the bill directly. The invoice addressed to the solicitor, suitably endorsed by the solicitor, is acceptable as adequate documentation to support a claim for input tax credit. [40.95]

Commission

When a taxable person receives a commission (usually for arranging insurance or for introducing an investor to a stockbroker) from a third party in connection with making a supply to a client, and the commission must be accounted for to the client, then VAT is chargeable on the net fee. A commission for providing intermediary services (ie acting as an intermediary in arranging finance or for arranging insurance) is exempt. [40.96]

Disbursements

A solicitor often makes payments on behalf of his client that are the contractual responsibility of that client, eg stamp duty; these may not be subject to VAT. The solicitor should indicate clearly on the VAT invoice that such payments are disbursements in order to avoid having to include the value of such payments in the value of the invoice on which VAT is to be added.

Expenses which a solicitor incurs in order to provide his services to his client, eg air fares, train fares, stationery, postage, etc cannot be treated as disbursements and must be included in the value of the invoice on which VAT is to be added (*Rowe & Maw v C & E Comrs* (1975)).

The Law Society has, following discussions with HMRC, issued detailed guidance on the VAT treatment of disbursements (in Practice Note: VAT on disbursements (11 March 2011)), including confirmation that the telegraphic transfer fees are not disbursements and must therefore be subject to VAT when passed on to the client. [40.97]

6 Government

The increase in privatisation and competitive tendering for services that are being contracted out increased the need for central and local Government to be aware of the VAT consequences of transactions. In the absence of any specific provision for recovery of input VAT, such recovery would be generally restricted to the extent that it relates to non-business or exempt activities. However, VATA

1994 s 33 applies to certain public bodies (including, for example, the BBC (see further [**40.100**]) and enables those bodies to recover input tax related to non-business activities. Under VATA 1994 s 33(3), the Treasury has power to add to the list of bodies which are eligible for relief under s 33.

Specific provision is made for the Crown and for local authorities and other statutory bodies: where the goods and services supplied by these bodies would lead to significant distortion of competition then such supplies will result in their being treated as taxable persons. A number of activities are specifically stated (in Annex I of the Recast VAT Directive) to give rise to a need to consider the body as a taxable person unless the scale of activities is negligible. Such activities include:
(1) telecommunications;
(2) supply of water, gas, electricity and steam;
(3) transport of goods;
(4) port and airport services;
(5) passenger transport;
(6) supply of new goods manufactured for sale;
(7) transactions of agricultural intervention agencies; and
(8) running of trade fairs and exhibitions.

The classification of activities undertaken is of importance in determining the basis for recovering VAT on expenditure, and guidance has been provided by HMRC in Notice 749 (February 2016). [**40.98**]

a) *Local authorities*

When a local authority regularly makes taxable supplies (including zero-rated supplies) in the UK in the course or furtherance of its business it is required to register for VAT (VATA 1994 s 42). The special refund scheme is available in respect of VAT on expenditure and care needs to be exercised in order to ensure that it is operated correctly. Failure to do so may lead to penalties. A 'local authority' is defined (in VATA 1994 s 96(4)) to mean the council of a county, county borough, district, London borough, parish or group of parishes (or in Wales, community or group of communities), the Common Council of the City of London, the Council of the Isles of Scilly, and any joint committee or joint board established by two or more of the foregoing and in relation to Scotland, a council constituted under the Local Government etc. (Scotland) Act 1994 s 2, any two or more such councils and any joint committee or joint board within the meaning of the Local Government (Scotland) Act 1973 s 235(1).

Local authority purchasing consortia are not considered to be acting as public bodies. [**40.99**]

b) *Statutory bodies*

Specified bodies may make a claim to obtain a refund of VAT charged on supplies to them of goods purchased, imported or acquired for non-business purposes. Where the supply is partly for business and partly for non-business, then HMRC may apportion the VAT. The apportionment will only be important where some of the business supplies are exempt and a restriction will be made under the partial exemption rules.

Among the bodies specified are:
(1) a local authority;
(2) a river purification board or a water development board;
(3) an internal drainage board;
(4) a passenger transport authority or executive;
(5) a port health authority, a port local authority or a joint port local authority;
(6) a police authority and the Receiver for the Metropolitan Police District;
(7) a development corporation, a new towns commission and the Commission for the New Towns;
(8) a general lighthouse authority;
(9) the BBC;
(10) a nominated news provider (previously ITN); and
(11) any body specified by Treasury order.

The normal rules apply to statutory bodies so that they may register voluntarily and where supplies made exceed the statutory threshold they will be required to register.

Separate registration is normally required for every 'person' and this may give rise to an obligation on a committee or other body that is separate from but has close links to the body, eg a police authority or a joint committee of two or more bodies. An application may be made for this obligation to be waived if it is wished to account for VAT through the registration of the main body.

The acquisition of goods from a supplier in another Member State may also give rise to an obligation to register. **[40.100]**

c) *Refund scheme*

The main objective of the refund scheme provided for in VATA 1994 s 33 is to avoid the movement of funds from one public pocket to another. Only where it is necessary to avoid distortion of competition in the single market is it necessary for VAT to be a commercial consideration. The scheme applies to goods and services supplied direct to the qualifying body. It is therefore necessary for the order to be placed by the body, for VAT invoices to be addressed to it and for payment to be made from its own funds.

Purchases made with trust funds where the local authority acts as sole trustee of funds and the objects of the trust relate closely to the activities of the authority, eg operating a village hall, also qualify for a refund provided that certain conditions are met. Relief may also be available for purchases made by the authority for its own purposes with funds given for specific purposes. No refund is generally available for the VAT on the acquisition of motor cars but VAT on entertainment relating to non-business activities is refundable.

Where a claim is made by a registered body, the claim will be made by including the refundable amount in the VAT return. Unregistered bodies may make claims for periods of at least one month and if the amount is less than £100 then the period must be of at least one year. **[40.101]**

d) *Government departments and other public bodies*

The Crown is not excluded from VAT and the normal provisions apply when it makes taxable supplies. Previously, the Treasury was enabled (pursuant to VATA 1994 s 41(2)) to make an order that directed that certain supplies made by a Government department that are similar to supplies made by taxable persons should be treated as supplies in the course or furtherance of a business, but this provision did not extend to other public bodies.

Section 41(2) was repealed with effect from 17 July 2012 and replaced by s 41A (supply of goods or services by public bodies). This new section was introduced to put the effective implementation of Article 13 of the Recast VAT Directive beyond doubt. Previously, there had been no express transposition of Article 13(1) into UK legislation; HMRC had given effect to the Article by interpreting existing legislation in a way that achieved the correct result for the Article's purposes. Section 41A provides that, where public bodies supply goods or services pursuant to public statute that is unique to them, they are not regarded as doing so in the course or furtherance of a business carried on by them unless:

(1) the exemption would cause distortion of competition; or
(2) the supplies arise from activities described in Annex I of the Recast VAT Directive (as listed above) which are engaged in to a degree which is more than merely negligible.

A Government department includes a National Health Service trust, a Northern Ireland health and social services body, any body of persons exercising functions on behalf of a Minister of the Crown and any part of such a department designated for this purpose by the Treasury (see VATA 1994 s 41(6), (7)). **[40.102]–[40.104]**

7 Special arrangements

a) *Retailers*

The majority of businesses which deal direct with the public are not required to issue detailed invoices for their sales nor, because they deal very largely for cash, do they need to keep their sales records in the same detail or format as manufacturing or wholesaling businesses would expect to do. They therefore do not have the same discipline of issuing VAT invoices that other businesses have and consequently would find difficulty in determining sales and output tax by conventional means. The retail schemes published by HMRC therefore offer an alternative calculation methodology for businesses that would find it difficult to issue invoices for a large number of supplies made to a large number of individuals.

HMRC have authority to allow retailers to operate special arrangements for determining the amount of output tax which they have to account for on their retail sales. It should be noted that 'exceptionally' under the relevant regulations, certain parts of VAT Notice 727 (May 2012) and the accompanying notices dealing with individual schemes have legal force.

A business making both retail and non-retail sales can use a retail scheme for the retail part of its business only. An adjustment may be required where stocks of goods are transferred between the retail part and the non-retail part.
[40.105]

Gross takings

All retail schemes require the retailer to keep a record of the value of their retail sales, called 'daily gross takings'. Retailers must include in their daily gross takings:
(1) all payments as they are received for cash sales;
(2) the full value (including VAT) of all credit or other non-cash sales; and
(3) any adjustments to the daily gross takings record. [40.106]

Choosing a retail scheme

There are a number of retail schemes that could apply. The standard schemes are:
(1) the Point of Sale scheme (see VAT Notice 727/3 (January 2013));
(2) two Apportionment schemes (see VAT Notice 727/4 (January 2013)); and
(3) two Direct Calculation schemes (see VAT Notice 727/5 (January 2013)).

If a business is eligible to operate more than one scheme, it is important to understand the implications of each scheme and to choose the correct retail scheme from the outset. The choice of scheme can affect a retailer's cashflow and they have differing record-keeping requirements – the wrong choice can prove expensive.

HMRC have the power to refuse permission to use a scheme (because, for example, they consider that it will not reflect the proper liability or because they reasonably believe that the relevant retailer can account for VAT in the normal way). The retailer has the right to appeal against such refusal (to the First-tier Tribunal, Tax Chamber).

HMRC allow a retrospective change of scheme only in exceptional circumstances. In particular, a retailer who uses a scheme for which he is eligible will not be entitled to change his scheme retrospectively on the basis that a lower overall liability would have been achieved. This is another reason why it is important that great care is taken prior to using a particular scheme.

It is open to a retailer not to use a retail scheme and to account for VAT in the normal way. However, a retailer with an annual turnover exceeding £130m who wishes to use a retail scheme must agree a bespoke scheme with HMRC. Consideration must be given to the administrative costs involved in operating a particular scheme, as well as the resulting VAT liability. VAT Notices 727/2 to 727/5 provide further information on the standard schemes and agreeing bespoke schemes. [40.107]

Second-hand goods

VATA 1994 s 50A provides for a margin scheme to operate for the sale of second-hand goods. This means that the calculation of output tax is based on the margin achieved on the goods, rather than on the total price of the goods. The scheme is voluntary, but it does provide for a reduced VAT liability. Certain conditions must be fulfilled.

Where second-hand goods meet certain conditions, in particular those with a purchase price below £500, retailers may use the global accounting scheme. This enables them to cumulate their sales of second-hand goods, rather than issuing an invoice for each transaction.

Where retailers make sales of new and second-hand goods, their records must be sufficient to allow them to analyse sales and purchases accurately.

Further details about the margin scheme and its operation can be found in VAT Notice 718 (April 2011). **[40.108]**

EXAMPLE 40.2 – MARGIN SCHEME

Cost price of relevant item – £2,000 including VAT
Selling price of relevant item – £2,800 including VAT
Profit margin = £800 including VAT
No input tax is claimed. Output tax is £800 × 1/6 = £133.33

EXAMPLE 40.3 – SECOND-HAND CARS

Tracey uses the margin scheme for second-hand car sales and meets all the required conditions for the scheme. In the quarter ended 31 June 2017 (all the amounts being stated inclusive of VAT where appropriate) the transactions are:

		Purchase Price £	Repair Costs £	Selling Price £
Second-hand car	(i)	900	112	805
Second-hand car	(ii)	4,250	140	5,895
Second-hand car	(iii)	6,900	853	7,370
Second-hand van	(iv)	2,961	1,000	3,760
Second-hand van	(v)	4,230	480	5,875
New car	(vi)	17,860	–	19,975
New car	(vii)	11,750	–	–*
			2,585	

The second-hand vans were purchased on tax invoices from registered traders. The cars were taken in part exchange from private customers.

* Used by Tracey personally – list selling price £14,995.

The VAT consequences:

Second-hand car margin scheme	Cost £	Selling Price £	Margin £		£
(i)	900	805	(Loss)		
(ii)	4,250	5,895	1,645		
(iii)	6,900	7,370	470		
		14,070	2,115	× 1/6 =	352.50

Other outputs:			£		
(iv)	Van		3,760		
(v)	Van		5,875		
(vi)	New car		19,975		
(vii)	Self-supply new car		11,750		
			41,360	× 1/6 =	6,893.33
					7,245.83

Inputs		£		
Repair costs		2,585		
Second-hand cars (i) (ii) and (iii)		–		
Vans	(iv)	2,961		
	(v)	4,230		
New	(vi)	17,860		
cars	(vii)	11,750		
		39,386	× 1/6 =	(6,564.33)
VAT payable				£681.50

Children's clothes. Children's clothes are generally zero-rated for VAT purposes. For young children's clothing and footwear (not made of fur) to qualify for relief from VAT the items of clothing must be:
(1) designed for young children (the design test); and
(2) not suitable for older persons (the suitability test).

Further details as to the requirements for zero-rating of clothes made for children can be found in VAT Notice 714 (March 2015). **[40.109]**

b) *Tour operators*

Under the normal place of supply rules, the provision of services such as passenger transport, catering and accommodation to a person travelling within the EU would create a liability for the supplier of those services to be registered for VAT in each of the Member States in which the services were provided. To avoid this, EU legislation (the tour operators' margin scheme, or 'TOMS') provides that such services may be taxed by reference to the profit margin achieved in the Member State in which the supplier is established or has a fixed establishment from which the services were provided. TOMS came into effect in the UK on 1 April 1988 and has been subject to substantial amendments on a number of occasions. Detailed guidance is provided in Notice 709/5 (February 2016).

The scheme is similar to the second-hand goods schemes. However, one fundamental difference is that, whereas the second-hand goods schemes are optional to the dealer, TOMS is compulsory for those who are defined as within its scope (except for a *de minimis* exception for incidental supplies).

The essence of the scheme is that tour operators do not charge output tax on the full value of supplies made by them and may not recover input tax on supplies bought in by them for resale. Instead they are required to account for output tax on the 'margin', ie the difference between the selling price and the bought-in cost.

However, unlike the second-hand goods schemes, the margin is calculated on the basis of the eligible supplies made during a full financial year. The trader is required to make a provisional calculation each quarter, based on the previous year's results. After the end of the year, the trader makes a final calculation for the year and accounts for any adjustment with his next VAT return. It should be noted that the calculations are made by reference to the trader's financial year; the concept of the 'tax year' that is used for partial exemption purposes does not apply here.

The term 'tour operator' (defined in VATA 1994 s 53(3)), includes a travel agent acting as principal and any other person providing for the benefit of travellers services of any kind commonly provided by tour operators or travel agents.

This definition is much wider than the term 'tour operator' is commonly understood. It includes any person who provides inclusive travel arrangements. Thus, it could apply to a coach operator or a 'freebie' newspaper that offers a package holiday to members of the public as a promotional effort.

Secret Hotels2 Ltd v R & C Comrs (2014) concerned a UK established holiday accommodation broker (known in the industry as a 'bed bank') that was owned by lastminute.com, and which operated a website that marketed holiday accommodation. HMRC issued assessments on the basis that it was liable for UK VAT under TOMS. The broker appealed, arguing that it was a disclosed agent or intermediary that earned commission from accommodation owners. The Supreme Court said that the interpretation of the broker's status must come from the written agreements with the accommodation providers and the customers. These clearly represented the economic reality that the broker was the agent of the accommodation providers. It held that there were 'no grounds to support any other conclusion' than that the broker qualified as an intermediary, outside of TOMS. [40.110]

Travellers

This term covers a person who receives a supply of a designated travel service, whatever the purpose of their journey, eg people who make their own travel arrangements but who buy accommodation or other services from a tour operator. [40.111]

Territorial scope

The scheme applies to supplies enjoyed by travellers to any part of the world, including journeys solely within the UK. Tax is only accounted for on the margin on supplies enjoyed within the EU, including the UK and the Isle of Man. [40.112]

Margin scheme

The goods and services covered by the scheme are those bought in from third parties and are referred to as 'margin scheme supplies'. These are at present split into two categories: margin standard-rated and margin zero-rated. The whole of the tour operators' margin is standard-rated, except to the extent that designated travel services are enjoyed outside the EU. These supplies must be brought into the calculations before deducting any agents' commission. In-house supplies are not included in the scheme. [40.113]

Margin standard-rated supplies

The following are *always* margin scheme supplies:
(1) hotel and other accommodation (including hire of tents and spaces on campsites);
(2) passenger transport;
(3) trips or excursions;
(4) services of tour guides;
(5) use of special lounges at airports;
(6) hire of cars, taxis, bicycles, boats.

Other supplies, such as catering, admission tickets and sports facilities will also be margin scheme supplies if they are:
(i) bought in and sold on without material alteration, for the direct benefit of a traveller; and
(ii) provided as part of a package with one or more of the suppliers listed above. [40.114]

Margin zero-rated supplies

Included under this head are margin standard-rated supplies when enjoyed in a non-EU country.

In the case of cruises, the margin will have to be calculated by separating any zero-rated transport element from the standard-rated accommodation/catering elements. [40.115]

In-house supplies

These are supplies provided by the tour operators from their own resources rather than bought in from a third party. For example, if a tour operator owns an aircraft, or charters one without a crew, he is supplying travel in-house. On the other hand if a supply of passenger transport is made to a tour operator by a third party, that is a bought-in supply even if the transport is supplied under a charter-party contract. If a hotel is taken on a long lease so that day-to-day management of the hotel passes to the operator, the supply by the operator will be treated as an in-house supply. Accommodation that has been block booked is not treated as an in-house supply when sold by a tour operator.

In-house supplies are not within the scheme and are dealt with in accordance with the normal rules. The VAT liability of such supplies is therefore different to the liabilities applicable to the margin scheme supplies. If a package is supplied which contains both in-house and bought-in supplies, then the figures for the two types of supply have to be separated so that the proper liability under the scheme can be calculated. [40.116]

Wholesale supplies

Where a tour operator makes supplies to other businesses for onward supply, ie wholesale supplies, these supplies do not fall within TOMS (and should be accounted for under the normal VAT rules). Prior to 1 January 2010, the supplier could elect to treat all of its wholesale supplies as being accounted for under TOMS. Following infraction proceedings having been taken by the EC against the UK, this concession is no longer available. [40.117]

Input tax

Tax incurred from third parties on margin scheme supplies as above cannot be treated as input tax. VAT incurred on overheads in respect of non-margin supplies may be reclaimed in the usual way. Where passenger transport is supplied 'in-house' outside the UK, the supply is regarded as outside the scope of UK VAT; it can therefore be ignored for all purposes of the margin calculation in the UK. [40.118]

Foreign currency

Where margin scheme supplies are purchased from a third party, and billed in a foreign currency, the currency must be converted into sterling at the appropriate rate of exchange detailed in VAT Notice 709/5 (February 2016).

One of the following methods must be chosen to determine the rate of exchange to apply:
(1) the rate of exchange published in the *Financial Times* using the Federation of Tour Operators' base rate current at the time of costing by the supplier;
(2) the commercial rate of exchange current at the time that the supplies in the holiday brochure were costed;
(3) the rate published in the *Financial Times* for the date that payment is made;
(4) the rate of exchange which was applicable to the purchase of the foreign currency which was used to pay for the relevant supplies; and
(5) the period rate of exchange published by HMRC for customs purposes at the time the relevant supplies were paid for. (The VAT business advice centre in the relevant area will provide details of particular period rates.)
[40.119]

Time of supply

The normal rules for determining this do not apply. Instead the tour operator has the choice of either of the following as his tax point:
(1) the date of the customer's departure or the date on which the hotel accommodation is made available, whichever happens first; or
(2) the date of the customer's departure or the date of receipt of the main payment for the 'package'. The receipt of a deposit will not establish a tax point under this option provided that it is less than 20% of the total price. **[40.120]**

Exception for incidental supplies

Some businesses whose main activity does not consist of making supplies of accommodation or travel that have been purchased from a third party may nevertheless make some purchases for resale to other margin scheme suppliers. One example is a hotelier who buys in car hire for re-supply to some of his hotel guests; another is a coach operator who buys in tickets for admission to a stately home for re-supply to his passengers. Provided that the value of the margin scheme supplies not consisting of accommodation or travel does not exceed 1% of the value of his total supplies the trader may apply to his local VAT office for approval (which should be obtained in writing) not to operate the margin scheme and so to account for VAT under the normal rules. **[40.121]–[40.122]**

Agents

Travel agents acting as true agents – arranging a supply between two other parties – are not affected by these provisions. Travel agents must, however, charge VAT on any commission they receive from a UK operator for arranging a margin scheme supply to any destination. In practice, such commission will almost certainly be self-billed to the travel agent by the operator and it is important therefore that the agent appreciates that the payment he receives contains a VAT element which he must account for to HMRC.

Prior to 1 January 2010, supplies could be treated as not being designated travel services where:
(1) supplies of goods and services were acquired by a tour operator from another taxable person; and
(2) those goods and services were on-supplied without material alteration or further processing to a taxable person who ordered the supply for use in the UK for the purpose of his business other than by way of re-supply.

Following infraction proceedings against the UK (on the ground that the term 'traveller' includes businesses that pay for employee travel, and local authorities who provide school trips), this provision was revoked with effect from 1 January 2010. In order to meet the 'sticking' VAT problem that this change gave rise to (if a business books, say, hotel accommodation through a hotel booking agent, the agent will normally act as undisclosed agent, and the supply to the business now falls within TOMS), HMRC issued *Revenue and Customs Brief* 21/10 that sets out details of an agreement with representative bodies of the business travel sector about invoicing for supplies under the arrangement known as 'hotel billback'. In the *Brief*, it is provided that HMRC do not object to the hotel booking agent being regarded as a disclosed agent (such that the principal supply is from, say, the hotel to the business customer, and consequently TOMS does not apply) provided that:

- invoices from the hotel are addressed c/o the hotel booking agent for payment (in order to show that the invoice has been issued to the hotel booking agent in its capacity as an agent);
- the booking field on the hotel invoice identifies the hotel guest, their employer and ideally carries a unique reference number;
- the hotel booking agent arranges for payment of the invoice, but does not recover the input tax thereon;
- the hotel booking agent sends the customer a payment request/ statement of the expenditure incurred by the hotel booking agent on its behalf, separately identifying the value of its supplies, VAT, etc;
- it is indicated on the payment request/statement that the VAT shown is the customer's input tax, which can be reclaimed subject to the normal rules;
- the customer uses the payment request/statement as a basis for his input tax reclaim;
- the hotel booking agent retains the original hotel invoice;
- the hotel booking agent sends a VAT invoice for its own services, plus the VAT; and
- the hotel booking agent charges its client the exact amount charged by the billback supplier, as a disbursement. **[40.123]–[40.124]**

EXAMPLE 40.4 – TOUR OPERATORS' MARGIN SCHEME REGISTRATION

Hillingdon Manor Tours (HMT) starts trading on 1 January 2017 and sells 60 package holidays between 1 January and 30 June 2017 for £1,000 each. Therefore, total turnover to 30 June is £60,000. HMT only sells this type of holiday that consists entirely of designated travel services. HMT buys in each package for £500. Therefore, the total cost to 30 June is £30,000. HMT need not register yet because the margin between the aggregate selling and buying prices is only £30,000.

By the end of November 2017, HMT has sold £180,000 worth of package holidays and its total costs are £85,000. The margin is now £90,000. This is above the registration threshold of £83,000 (that applied until 31 March 2017), so HMT must now register.

c) *Auctioneers*

An auctioneer's services to his principal are taxable in the normal way unless he offers goods for sale as an agent of the seller, and he must account for tax in the same way as any other taxable person.

The normal rules for agents also apply to auctioneers. The charge for these services must for VAT purposes be treated separately from charges to the principal for other supplies. Similar considerations apply where agricultural goods are sold on behalf of a flat rate farmer. Where certain secondhand goods, works of art or collectors' items are sold, either the general margin scheme, the special margin scheme or the normal agents' rules are applied. **[40.125]**

Auctioneers' margin scheme

An auctioneer is defined in the VAT (Special Provisions) Order as a person who sells or offers for sale goods at any public sale where persons become purchasers by competition. The scheme was developed to allow auctioneers to take advantage of the facility to account for VAT on the margin. The scheme is optional and may be applied to some transactions whilst others are excluded. The requirements for the scheme are that the seller must not be registered for VAT, or a VAT registered person selling under a margin scheme or global accounting or an insurance company selling goods it has acquired under an insurance claim or a finance house selling goods it has repossessed.

The margin scheme calculations are detailed in Notice 718/2 (revised March 2011) which sets out the charges to be included/excluded under the scheme, together with the record-keeping requirements. **[40.126]**

EXAMPLE 40.5 – AUCTIONEERS

Alison handles the following transaction:
1. Hammer price – £10,000
2. Commission charged to vendor – £1,000
3. Miscellaneous costs charged to vendor – £200
4. Net amount paid to vendor (1 – 2 – 3) = £8,800
5. Buyer's premium – £600
6. Costs recharged to buyer – £300

The scheme purchase price is 1 – 2 – 3 = £8,800
The scheme selling price is 1 + 5 + 6 = £10,900
Therefore, the margin is £10,900 – £8,800 = £2,100
Alison's output tax due on this transaction is £2,100 × 1/6 = £350

Section 6 Business enterprise

Chapters
41 Corporation tax
42 Company distributions and shareholders
43 Corporate groups
44 The taxation of partnerships
45 Limited liability partnerships
46 Choice of business medium
47 Incorporations, acquisitions and demergers
48 Capital allowances

41 Corporation tax

Updated by Stephen Whitehead, KPMG LLP (UK)

I Introduction [41.1]
II General principles – rates of tax [41.21]
III How to calculate the profits of a company [41.41]
IV Raising finance [41.91]
V Close companies [41.121]
VI The overseas dimension [41.151]
VII Corporate self-assessment [41.181]

I INTRODUCTION

Corporation tax applies to all resident bodies corporate including authorised unit trusts and unincorporated associations (see *Blackpool Marton Rotary Club v Martin* (1990)) but not to partnerships (although certain limited liability partnerships are treated as companies) or local authorities. It is levied on the profits of a company that are made up of income, charged to tax in accordance with the provisions of the Corporation Tax Acts 2009 and 2010, and chargeable gains computed generally in accordance with the principles applying for CGT.

The UK system of corporation tax was, until April 1999, generally referred to as the *imputation* system as part of the tax paid by the company was imputed to the shareholder by means of a tax credit attached to dividends paid to shareholders. Thereafter, a tax credit, at a reduced rate, continued to be attached to dividends but was no longer linked to tax paid by the company and could not be paid out to the shareholder. From 6 April 2016, the last vestiges of the imputation system were eliminated with the abolition of dividend tax credits.

The Corporation Tax Act 2009 (CTA 2009), dealing with trading, property and miscellaneous income, has effect for accounting periods ending on or after 1 April 2009. Remaining corporation tax matters are to be found in the Corporation Tax Act 2010 (CTA 2010) and in the Taxation (International and Other Provisions) Act 2010 (TIOPA 2010), the latter relating mainly to international matters affecting companies, and both of these Acts apply for corporation tax purposes to accounting periods ending on or after 1 April 2010.

Under this legislation, companies are taxed on different types of income under provisions that mirror the format of those in ITTOIA 2005, and there are specific corporation tax rules that are explained below for matters such as loan relationships and gains on 'new' intangible assets. In this chapter, reference will be made where appropriate to the previous legislation, found in the Income and Corporation Taxes Act 1988 (TA 1988) and subsequent Finance Acts. [41.1]–[41.20]

II GENERAL PRINCIPLES – RATES OF TAX

Corporation tax is charged by reference to financial years (FY) that run from 1 April to 31 March and are referred to by the calendar year in which they commence. Hence, FY 2016 means the financial year from 1 April 2016 to 31 March 2017. Where companies are wound up, the rate charged during their final financial year is generally that fixed for the preceding financial year (CTA 2010 s 628, TA 1988 s 342(2)). With effect from 1 April 2015 a single rate of corporation tax applies to all companies except in relation to ring-fence profits (for which see [41.24]). This rate is 19% for FYs 2017–2019 and, as provided in FA 2016, is to be reduced to 17% for FY 2020.

Before 1 April 2015 there were two rates of corporation tax:
(1) the small profits rate (20% for FY 2014, see [41.23]);
(2) the full rate (21% for FY 2014).

The rates applicable for FY 2007 to FY 2017 are shown in the following table:

FY	Main rate	Small profits rate
FY07	30%	20%
FY08	28%	21%
FY09	28%	21%
FY10	28%	21%
FY11	26%	20%
FY12	24%	20%
FY13	23%	20%
FY14	21%	20%
FY15–FY16	20%	not applicable
FY17	19%	not applicable

Corporation tax is charged on a current year basis on the company's profits for the financial year. Therefore, where a company's accounting period straddles two financial years the profits must be apportioned on a time basis (CTA 2009 s 8(5)). The following example illustrates the computation problem with a change in the full rate.

EXAMPLE 41.1

Grr Ltd makes up its accounts to 31 December 2017 and its trading profits are £2,000,000. The rate of corporation tax for FY 2016 is 20% and for FY 2017 is 19%. The tax will be calculated as follows:
Profits of £2,000,000 apportioned:
1 January 2017–31 March 2017:

$^{3}/_{12}$ of £2,000,000 = £500,000 taxed at 20% (FY 2016)
1 April 2017–31 December 2017:
$^{9}/_{12}$ of £2,000,000 = £1,500,000 taxed at 19% (FY 2017)

For all except large companies the tax is payable within nine months and one day after the end of the company's accounting period. Hence, in *Example 41.1* the tax would normally be due by 1 October 2018. The position of large companies is considered at [41.185]. [41.21]

1 Capital gains

Capital gains realised by a company are included in its profits and charged to corporation tax at the same rate as the company's income. The corporation tax rate on chargeable gains for FY 2017 is thus 19%. Where the accounting period straddles two financial years, chargeable gains are apportioned between them on a time basis in the same way as income (see *Example 41.1*), so that the rate does not depend on the financial year in which the gain actually accrues.

Unlike individuals, companies are not entitled to an annual exemption; the indexation allowance continues to apply to capital gains made by companies.

Disposals of shareholdings in other companies may be exempt from tax subject to the conditions of the Substantial Shareholdings Exemption (see [41.75] below).

Intangible assets created or acquired after 1 April 2002 are outside the rules for corporation tax on chargeable gains and are covered by special rules contained in CTA 2009 Part 8 (FA 2002 Sch 29). [41.22]

2 The small profits rate (CTA 2010 s 18)

The small profits rate (previously, but less accurately, called the 'small companies' rate') applied to any company (other than a close investment holding company: see [41.129]) whose profits, both income and capital, did not exceed the 'lower limit' in the accounting period.

Where a company's profits exceeded the lower limit but not the upper limit a marginal relief was available. For financial years prior to 2014 the lower limit was £300,000 and the upper limit was £1,500,000. The effect of this was (for FY 2014) to impose corporation tax at the rate of 21.25% on profits above £300,000 but below £1,500,000. For FY 2007 this marginal rate was 32.5%, for FY 2008 to FY 2010 it was 29.75%, for FY 2011 it was 27.5%, for FY 2012 25% and for FY 2013 23.75%. For this purpose profits included franked investment income (FII) (see [41.46]) unless received from a company in the same 51% group or, subject to certain conditions, from a company owned by a consortium of which the receiving company is a member (see also [42.91]). If the company had associated companies (see below), the lower and upper limits were divided by the total number of associated companies including the taxpayer company.

If a company wished to take advantage of CTA 2010 s 18 it was required to submit a claim in the company's return that the profit should be charged at the small profits rate or that marginal relief was appropriate. Any such statement also needed to indicate whether or not there were associated companies (see SP 1/91; for the treatment of companies between which there was no substantial commercial interdependence, see ESC C9 and, for accounting periods ending after 31 March 2011, FA 2011 s 55; for the position of holding companies, see SP 5/94 and for companies which were not carrying on any trade or business at any time during the accounting period, see *Jowett v O'Neill and Brennan Construction Ltd* (1998), *Land Management Ltd v Fox* (2002) and *R & C Comrs v Salaried Persons Postal Loans Ltd* (2006)). Non-resident companies could be associated companies as could companies controlled by spouses, certain relatives and business partners and also companies owned by trusts in relation to which a connected person was a settlor (see *R v CIR, ex p Newfields Developments Ltd* (2001), HL).

Changes in the small profits rate and in the lower and upper limits may be tabulated as follows:

FY	Small profits' rate (%)	Lower limit (£)	Upper limit (£)	Marginal rate (%)
1993	25	250,000	1,250,000	35
1994–95	25	300,000	1,500,000	35
1996	24	300,000	1,500,000	35.25
1997	21	300,000	1,500,000	33.5
1998	21	300,000	1,500,000	33.5
1999–01	20	300,000	1,500,000	32.5
2002–06	19	300,000	1,500,000	32.75
2007	20	300,000	1,500,000	32.5
2008–10	21	300,000	1,500,000	29.75
2011	20	300,000	1,500,000	27.5
2012	20	300,000	1,500,000	25
2013	20	300,000	1,500,000	23.75
2014	20	300,000	1,500,000	21.25

EXAMPLE 41.2

(1) Zee Ltd makes up its accounts to 31 March each year. For the year ending 31 March 2015 the company had trading profits of £80,000 and made chargeable gains of £42,000.

The profits of Zee Ltd for corporation tax purposes were:

	£
Trading (ie income) profits	80,000
Chargeable gains	42,000
Chargeable profits	£122,000

Zee Ltd, therefore, qualified for the small profits rate so that corporation tax was charged as follows:

Chargeable profits (£122,000) at 20% = £24,400

(2) Had the income profits of Zee Ltd been £280,000 then, with the addition of chargeable gains (£42,000), the small company threshold of £300,000 would

have been exceeded by £22,000 so that the small profits relief would have applied as follows:

		£
(i)	Corporation tax payable:	
	£322,000 (ie £280,000 + £42,000) × 21%	67,620
(ii)	Less: marginal relief (CTA 2010 s 19):	
	(upper relevant amount − profits) × statutory fraction	
	ie (£1,500,000 − £322,000) × $\frac{1}{400}$	2,945
(iii)	Total tax ((i) − (ii))	£64,675

Two points should be stressed in connection with the small profits rate: *first*, as noted above, provisions were made to prevent the fragmentation of a business among associated companies in an attempt to create a series of small companies (CTA 2010 s 24(3)). This restriction only applied if the associated company was carrying on a trade or business at any time in the relevant accounting period: see s 25(3) and *Jowett v O'Neill and Brennan Construction Ltd* (1999) in which retaining a large sum of money in a bank account was not considered to involve a trade or business; for further discussion, see also *Land Management Ltd v Fox* (2002) and *R & C Comrs v Salaried Persons Postal Loans Ltd* (2006).

EXAMPLE 41.3

X Ltd has three wholly owned operating subsidiaries. The companies are associated and hence the lower and upper limits for each company are divided by one plus the number of associated companies. The lower and upper limits for each company in the X Group for FY 2014 are, therefore, £75,000 and £375,000.

A company was treated as an associated company of another company if the same person controlled both companies (see *Steele v EVC International NV* (1996) and CTA 2010 s 25(5): control for these purposes was construed in accordance with CTA 2010 s 450, formerly TA 1988 s 416 on which see *R v IRC, ex p Newfields Developments Ltd* (2001)). A concession (extra-statutory concession C9) that relieved certain companies where there was no commercial interdependence was replaced by an amended s 27 of CTA 2010 with effect for accounting periods ending on or after 1 April 2011.

Second, the marginal rate applied where profits fell between the lower and upper limits, and the tax on profits in excess of the lower limit was therefore charged at an effective rate in excess of the main rate. This is because the purpose of the small profits relief was to increase gradually the average rate of corporation tax from the lower rate payable by a company with profits at or below the lower limit to the higher rate payable by a company with profits at or above the upper limit. To achieve this result the rate applicable to the slice of profits between the lower and upper limits had to *exceed* the main rate. For FY 2014 this marginal rate was 21.25% calculated as follows:

Tax on £300,000 at 20%	=	£60,000
Tax on £1,500,000 at 21%	=	£315,000
Difference (£315,000 − £60,000)	=	£255,000

Therefore, £255,000 corporation tax has to be raised on profits falling between £300,000 and £1,500,000 (ie on £1,200,000).

Hence, as a percentage, tax on £1,200,000 would have been:

$$\frac{255{,}000}{1{,}200{,}000} \times 100 = 21.25\%$$

Thus, continuing *Example 41.2(2)* above:
Corporation tax of £64,675 on profits of £322,000 could be analysed as:

		£
First £300,000 of profits at 20%	=	60,000
Final £22,000 of profits at 21.25%	=	4,675
		£64,675

In determining whether small profits relief was available, dividends received from other UK companies (franked investment income) were taken into account, but not dividends from the company's own subsidiaries (see **[42.91]** ff for further explanation of franked investment income and for an illustration of how this affected small profits relief).

The fact that a company's profits might just exceed the lower limit thereby attracting this higher marginal rate on the excess was of practical significance when considering how much money the directors of family companies should take by way of remuneration (or how much should be paid into the company's pension scheme). The marginal corporation tax rate exceeded the basic rate of income tax so that it could be advantageous to pay out such moneys in the form of salaries or by making increased contributions to the company pension scheme. Thus, in *Example 41.2(2)* above, the directors of Zee Ltd might have considered paying increased salaries or bonuses of £22,000 for the year. In this way, the company's taxable profits for that accounting period would be reduced by £22,000 which would otherwise have been taxed at 21.25%, a saving of £4,675; this would be advantageous if the tax and NICs liability on the salaries paid did not exceed this amount: see further **Chapter 46**.

If the company was a member of a group and losses were available for group relief from other group members, the marginal tax rate in each group company had to be considered when deciding how to surrender losses. Losses would be surrendered to companies with higher marginal rates (eg 21.25%) of tax before other members of the group.

With the reduction of the main corporation tax rate to 20% from FY 2015, the small profits rate no longer applies to most companies although there is still a differential rate in respect of ring fence profits (see **[41.25]**). As a result of the unification of corporation tax rates the rules for identifying associated companies are no longer needed and have been repealed. Small profits relief for ring-fence profits is instead given by reference to the number of 'related 51% group companies' – that is, active companies within a 51% group. The provisions relating to capital allowances for long-life assets, patent box small company treatment and corporation tax instalment payments, which previously depended on the definition of associated companies, were also amended accordingly. **[41.23]**

3 Corporation tax on ring fence profits

With effect from FY 2007 separate rates and fractions apply to corporation tax on ring fence profits of North Sea oil companies. The rates for FY 2007–2017 are given in the table below:

Financial year	2007–17
Main tax rate	30%
Small profits rate	19%
Lower limit	£300,000
Upper limit	£1,500,000
Marginal relief fraction	11/400
Marginal rate	32.75%

Where companies have both ring fence profits and other profits, there are special rules which have the effect of applying the appropriate rates to each part of the total profits.

As explained above (see [**41.23**]), a company's franked investment income, though not subject to tax, was taken into account in applying the profit limits for small profits relief. With effect from 6 April 2016, following the abolition of dividend tax credits, the net amount of any exempt distributions is included and this amount is identified as 'exempt ABGH distributions'.

[**41.24**]–[**41.40**]

III HOW TO CALCULATE THE PROFITS OF A COMPANY

Profits of a company are defined as including both income profits and capital gains (CTA 2009 s 2(2)). [**41.41**]

1 Income profits

a) *General principles*

CTA 2009 marked a decisive move away from the former dependence of corporation tax law on income tax rules, and also from the system of schedules and cases which was first introduced by Addington in 1803. The rules for computation of income for corporation tax purposes are now set out in full in CTA 2009 itself, in CTA 2010 and in TIOPA 2010.

Thus, a trading company having no other income will compute its profits in accordance with the rules set out in CTA 2009 Part 3. In general the rules for what expenditure is deductible by companies correspond to those applying to individuals and partnerships (discussed at [**10.130**]). Accordingly, for example, the salaries and fees paid to the company's directors and employees will be allowable expenses under CTA 2009, Part 3, Chapter 4.

However, the moves taken to align tax treatment of company profits with accounting treatment have resulted in some divergences of corporation tax rules from income tax rules. The loan relationship rules (see [**41.50**]) and the rules for taxation of intangible assets in CTA 2009 Part 8 are two examples.

So far as income from land is concerned, FA 1998 extended treatment of property rental income as a deemed business to companies and this is now dealt with in CTA 2009 Part 4 (for the income tax provisions relating to property income, see **Chapter 12**). In particular, so far as companies are concerned:

(1) rental income from non-UK property is treated as the receipts of a separate business;
(2) in the context of group relief a distinction is drawn between 'true' trading losses and losses from a property business;
(3) CTA 2010 Part 14, Chapter 3 deals with changes in ownership of a company with investment business (see **[41.67]**);
(4) in computing property business income, related interest costs, exchange gains and losses etc are dealt with under the separate loan relationship rules which apply to companies (see **[41.50]** ff).

A problem in the case of a corporate group may arise from the common assumption that it represents a single commercial entity. This is not the case for tax purposes and so an expense may be non-deductible in the hands of the paying company if that expense was incurred for 'dual purposes': eg to benefit other group members (*Commercial Union Assurance Co Ltd v Shaw* (1998); however, see also *Vodafone Cellular Ltd v Shaw* (1997) where the Revenue was unsuccessful with a similar argument and **[43.21]**). As a separate matter, a special rule introduced with effect from 19 March 2014 denies a deduction where there is an avoidance scheme involving a transfer of profits within a corporate group (CTA 2009 s 1305A).

An enhanced relief system of tax credits for small and medium-sized companies (SMEs) in respect of research and development (R&D) was introduced in 2000 and can be found in CTA 2009 Part 13. The definition of an SME is based on EU guidelines and is not the same as for UK company law. The relief was extended to all companies from 1 April 2002. The relief operated so as to enhance the deduction by 50% for an SME and 25% for other companies. For an SME, if the result is that a loss is created or enhanced then the loss may be surrendered in return for a payment equal to a specified percentage of the loss (14.5% for expenditure incurred on or after 1 April 2014). For accounting periods ending before 1 April 2012 this payment was limited to the amount of PAYE Tax and NIC accounted for by the company. Changes to these reliefs were made in FA 2008, extending the scope of the SME scheme to some larger companies and increasing the enhanced deduction to 75% for SMEs (effective from 1 August 2008 following EU approval) and 30% for large companies from April 2008. The enhanced deduction for SMEs was further increased to 100% from 1 April 2011, 125% from 1 April 2012 and 130% from 1 April 2015. FA 2008 also set a cap on the total aid that can be received for a project under the SME scheme. An alternative scheme for an 'above the line' tax credit of 10% of qualifying expenditure was introduced by FA 2013 with effect from 1 April 2013. This is intended to encourage R&D activity by large companies and to provide greater financial and cash flow support to companies with no corporation tax liability. This scheme replaced the old large company scheme from 1 April 2016. With effect from 1 April 2015 the credit was increased to 11%.

An enhanced deduction is also available for costs in relation to removing harmful substances from contaminated land. Essentially, a company may claim an enhanced deduction of 150% of costs relating to land remediation. If this deduction creates or increases a loss then a tax credit of 16% of the qualifying loss can be claimed from HMRC; this is not limited to PAYE payments as under the R&D scheme (CTA 2009 Part 14). A Government proposal to abolish this relief, as part of its commitment to simplifying the tax system, was abandoned in 2011 following consultation.

The system of capital allowances applies to companies with suitable modifications (see **Chapter 48**). The specific difficulties that may arise when an existing business is transferred to a company are dealt with in **Chapter 47**.

Agreed terms of reference for a review of the corporation tax computation by the Office of Tax Simplification were published on 12 May 2016. The report was published on 3 July 2017 and included an extensive range of proposals, some of which were characterised as 'quick wins' while other more radical reforms were proposed for the medium or long term. The Government's response to this report is awaited. [41.42]

b) *Foreign exchange gains and losses and financial instruments for managing interest rate and currency risk*

For accounting periods beginning on or after 1 October 2002 the rules for the taxation of exchange gains and losses and on interest rate and derivative contracts are included in the rules which apply to loan relationships in CTA 2009 Part 5; see CTA 2009 s for exchange gains and losses and CTA 2009 Part 7 for derivative contracts. [41.43]

c) *Transfer pricing (TIOPA 2010 Part 4)*

The transfer pricing legislation is aimed at transfer pricing arrangements entered into by multi-national corporations. Such corporations can exploit the tax rules in the various jurisdictions to obtain a tax advantage. The rules on transfer pricing aim to eliminate such activity by requiring companies to calculate their taxable profits as if the arrangements had been effected on normal commercial terms. The rules provide that where any two persons have entered into a transaction which confers on one of them a UK tax advantage, the profits and losses of the advantaged party must be computed as if the transaction had been undertaken on arm's length terms. The company has to be satisfied that its transfer pricing policy meets HMRC's requirements and that arm's length prices are adopted in order to be sure that the profits and the tax in its CTSA return are calculated correctly. If the company fails to consider whether its arrangements are in accordance with the arm's length principle, penalties apply. The other party to the transaction may obtain relief through the competent authority procedure and, in the case of UK to UK transfer pricing rules, through corresponding adjustments.

Non-UK resident companies can also be subject to the transfer pricing regime. For example, a property investment company resident in Jersey may seek to eliminate any UK tax liability on rents received from a property situated in this country by borrowing the purchase price from an associated company and claiming the interest on that loan as a deduction from the rents. If the loan is not one that would have been made between non-associated companies dealing at arm's length and a UK tax advantage has resulted, the transfer pricing rules can operate to disallow the interest deduction and therefore to increase the UK taxable property income of the Jersey company.

HMRC sought to extend this principle to third party loans which are supported or guaranteed by a connected person (eg a group member) and to disallow part or all of the interest paid on such a loan (see *Tax Bulletin* 46, April 2000). Arguably, the extension of transfer pricing to all 'provisions' made between connected persons, from 1 April 2004, now deals with this issue. HMRC may also use CTA 2009 s 443 to deny interest relief where arrangements have been entered into with the sole or main benefit being the obtaining of a deduction for the interest paid.

The transfer pricing rules apply in a wide variety of circumstances where transactions are undertaken between connected persons. A company will be connected with another if it is directly or indirectly 'controlled' by that other or both are controlled by a third company. There is a wide definition of 'control'. A person can also be connected with another by virtue of indirectly participating in the management, control or capital of the other person and this will include circumstances where the person has the right to acquire control at a future date.

The rules also cover joint venture arrangements by providing that a person can be deemed to control a company where that person has a 40% interest and another person also has 40% of the company. The scope of the rules was further extended from 4 March 2005 to apply where persons 'act together' in order to finance a company, even though none of these persons has control for the purposes of the transfer pricing legislation. These rules are mainly aimed at private equity-funded companies but may catch other arrangements.

From 1 April 2004, transfer pricing applies to UK-to-UK transactions as well as those involving counterparties who are not UK taxpayers. There is, however, an exclusion for small enterprises and a more limited relief for medium-sized enterprises and for dormant companies.

The definition of small and medium is derived from EU rules:
- Medium-sized
    - fewer than 250 employees; and
    - either turnover less than €50m (c £45m); or
    - assets less than €43m (c £38m)
- Small
    - fewer than 50 employees; and
    - turnover or assets less than €10m (c £9m).

Detailed guidance has been provided by HMRC to assist businesses to comply.

The measures abolish separate thin capitalisation requirements and subsume them within general transfer pricing requirements and allow the connected UK business to make a corresponding adjustment in the calculation of its taxable income. In recognition of the practical issues for businesses in introducing or adapting systems to enable them to comply with transfer pricing requirements, there was a temporary relaxation of penalties for failing to keep evidence to demonstrate that a result is an arm's length result. This relaxation lasted until 31 March 2006.

TIOPA 2010 Part 5 sets out the procedure to be followed by companies wishing to come to an advance agreement with HMRC on their transfer pricing policy (an 'advance pricing agreement'). This process also applies to

Advance Thin Capitalisation Agreements and Statement of Practice 1/12 sets out how the legislation will be applied in practice in such cases. [41.44]

d) *Employee trusts*

Payments into employee trusts may constitute deductible expenditure if they are of an income nature (see *Heather v P-E Consulting Group* (1978), discussed at [**10.133**]). See also *Mawsley Machinery Ltd v Robinson* (1998) where the payments were disallowed as they were for the purpose of providing a fund to purchase the company's shares and *McDonald v Dextra Accessories Ltd* (2005) where payments were not allowed as a result of the restriction imposed under CTA 2009 s 1288 where emoluments are not paid within nine months of the end of the accounting period. In this case a deduction will only be given when emoluments are actually paid to employees.

For accounting periods ending on or after 27 November 2002 a tax deduction for contributions to an employee trust (which includes a payment of money or the transfer of an asset) is only allowed to the extent that the money or the asset is used within nine months of the end of the accounting period in providing qualifying benefits. These are payments or transfers of assets that give rise to a charge to income tax and NIC (see CTA 2009 ss 1290–1297). These new rules do not apply to most retirement benefit schemes or to share-related benefits where a statutory tax deduction is allowed. [41.45]

e) *Dividends and income taxed at source*

With effect from 1 July 2009, dividends and other income distributions received are generally exempt from corporation tax whether or not the paying company is resident in the UK, provided they fall into an exempt class and are not caught by anti-avoidance provisions. Different rules apply depending on whether or not the recipient company is classed as small, but the anticipated effect is that the great majority of distributions received in each case will be exempt. Until 5 April 2016 a UK-resident company which received an exempt qualifying distribution, whether or not paid by a UK-resident company, was entitled to a tax credit equal to one-ninth of the distribution, although this credit was not payable to the company and was not taxable. The dividend together with the tax credit constituted franked investment income (FII). The rules are contained in Part 9A of CTA 2009, which was inserted by FA 2009 and formed part of the 'foreign profits package' (see further [**41.98**]).

Schedule 3 to F(No 3)A 2010 extended the exemption to certain distributions of a capital nature with retrospective effect, subject to an opt-out provision for distributions made before 22 June 2010.

Different rules applied to dividends and other distributions received before 1 July 2009. Such amounts were excluded in calculating income profits only if received by one UK company from another (CTA 2009 s 1285), see [**42.91**]. Notice, however, that FII was included in the profits of a company for the purpose of determining the availability of the small profits relief, although this income is not itself taxed (CTA 2010 s 32 and see *Example 42.12*).

The pre-2009 treatment was challenged on EU law grounds in two complex and long-running test cases, *Test Claimants in the FII Group Litigation v R & C Comrs* and *Prudential Assurance Co Ltd v R & C Comrs*. While these cases have still not been concluded, the Court of Appeal confirmed in 2016 that the UK legislation should be given a conforming interpretation under which, although foreign dividends were not exempt from corporation tax, the UK recipient company was entitled to a credit against its corporation tax liability equal to at least the nominal rate of foreign tax applying to the profits out of which the dividends were paid.

When income is received by a company net of income tax deducted at source, the gross income is included in the profits of the company and a credit is given from the corporation tax payable for the tax deducted at source.

Interest and other annual payments made after 31 March 2001 do not need to have income tax deducted at source where the recipient company is UK resident or where it is a non-resident company carrying on a trade in the UK through a permanent establishment and the payment is brought into charge in the UK.

EXAMPLE 41.4

Lexo Ltd makes up its accounts to 31 March each year. The accounts for the period ending 31 March 2018 show the following:

		£
Trading profit		260,000
Profit from lettings		40,000
Royalty received:		
Net	£60,000	
plus tax deducted	£15,000	
Gross		75,000
Total profits		£375,000
		£
Corporation tax payable:		
£375,000 at 19% (FY 2017)		71,250.00
Less: tax deducted		15,000.00
		£56,250.00

Notes:
(1) The trading profit is calculated according to the rules of CTA 2009 Part 3, and the profit from lettings according to the rules of CTA 2009, Part 4.
(2) If the tax deducted exceeded the corporation tax payable, the excess would be repaid to the company. **[41.46]**

2 Capital gains

a) *Basics*

A company's chargeable gains are computed in the same way as those of an individual. The definition of chargeable assets and the occasions when a disposal occurs are common to both individuals and companies. The annual exemption (£11,300 for 2017–18) is not available for disposals by companies and nor is entrepreneurs' relief (replacing taper relief for 2008–09 onwards)

How to calculate the profits of a company 1229

(although the company retains the indexation allowance which in the case of assets with a high base cost is an advantage). The rules for the exemption of tax on the disposals by a trading company of a substantial shareholding in another trading company under TCGA 1992 Sch 7AC are examined at **[41.75]**. **[41.47]**

b) *Intra-group disposals*

A disposal between companies in the same group is treated as giving rise to neither gain nor loss until the asset is disposed of outside the group or the recipient company leaves the group within six years (see **[43.122]**). **[41.48]**

c) *Dangers of a double charge*

A disadvantage suffered by a company and its shareholders is that on any capital gain realised by the company there may be an element of double taxation. Not only will the company suffer corporation tax on the gain, but the shareholder whose shares may have increased in value as a result of the capital profit (albeit after tax) will suffer CGT when he disposes of those shares.

EXAMPLE 41.5

S Ltd (a company wholly owned by John) makes a chargeable gain of £100,000. It will suffer corporation tax of £19,000 (19%) on that gain. John's shares will have increased in value by, say, £81,000 so that were he to sell them he would suffer CGT of up to £16,200 if the entire gain is taxed at 20% (ignoring exemptions and reliefs). Effectively, therefore, the corporate gain has been subject to tax at 35.2% (19% paid by the company and 16.2% by John).

The effect of entrepreneurs' relief, available to individuals and trustees, will have an impact. If full entrepreneurs' relief for a business asset (giving a rate of tax of 10% for smaller gains instead of 20%) is available then the total tax would be 27.1% (19% plus 10% of 81%).

Holding appreciating assets in private companies therefore can be tax-inefficient and in some circumstances it may be better for the shareholder to retain those assets and lease them to the company. However, this judgment needs to take into account other reliefs (such as entrepreneurs' relief), and the effect on other taxes such as inheritance tax and stamp duty. **[41.49]**

3 Taxation of a company's loan relationships

a) *Principles of the loan relationships regime (CTA 2009 Parts 5–7)*

The intention is to bring the profits and losses on all 'loan relationships' within the corporation tax code on income. This is achieved on the basis of the accounting treatment in the company's statutory accounts; see CTA 2009 ss 307 ff. Significant changes were made in FA 2002 and the impact of the move towards the use of International Accounting Standards was addressed in FA 2005. With effect from 1 October 2002, the taxation of derivative contracts and foreign exchange gains and losses was also brought within these rules.

A consultation on proposals for reforming the corporation tax treatment of loans and financial instruments was launched on 6 June 2013. While maintaining the basic principles underlying the current regime, these proposals were intended to make it simpler and clearer and to reduce the scope for tax avoidance. Some amendments to the rules relating to bond funds and degrouping charges were legislated in 2014, and further changes were introduced with effect from 1 January 2016. **[41.50]**

b) *Meaning of 'loan relationship' (CTA 2009 s 302)*

A loan relationship can arise in one of two ways:
(1) Where a company is either a debtor or creditor in respect of a money debt that arose from a transaction for the lending of money. A money debt is defined as a debt that falls to be satisfied by the payment of money or the transfer of rights under a debt which itself is a money debt.
(2) Where a company issues an instrument as security for a money debt.

Whether a debt arises from a transaction for the lending of money may not always be clear. In *MJP Media Services v R & C Comrs* (2012) the First-tier Tribunal considered that these words did not extend to a payment to a third party to discharge another person's debt, although this decision was upheld on other grounds on appeal. Subsequently in *Aspect Capital v R & C Comrs* (2014) the Upper Tribunal held, in a different legislative context, that a payment to a third party could constitute the making of a loan.

The regime does not apply to shares nor to any debt arising from rights conferred by shares (eg rights to a dividend or share capital) nor to gains or losses arising by reference to fluctuations in the value of securities which are convertible/exchangeable into shares and where there is (at the date of issue) more than a negligible likelihood that the conversion, etc, right will be exercised and the securities are not issued at a deep discount. Also excluded are trade debts including debts arising on the purchase of property or other goods or on the supply of services. A number of transactions in relation to debts that are not loan relationships are brought within the loan relationship rules. These are:
(1) Interest payable or receivable.
(2) Foreign exchange gains and losses.
(3) Impairment losses (and gains on reversal of impairment losses) in respect of trade or property business debts.
(4) Certain discounts.

It should be noted, however, that the rules do not deem non-loan relationship debts to be loan relationships, and the loan relationship rules only apply to such debts in relation to the matters mentioned above.

The effect of bringing impairment losses within the loan relationship rules is that the former TA 1988 s 74(1)(j), which disallowed general bad debt provisions, no longer applies. HMRC considers, however, that a general bad debt provision does not represent an impairment loss and is therefore not allowable (Corporate Finance Manual, CFM 41040). **[41.51]–[41.52]**

c) *Extent*

The regime covers all profits, gains and losses including those of a capital nature arising as a result of a company's loan relationships and related transactions. Certain charges and expenses incurred by the company for the purpose of its loan relationships are taken into account: such as those incurred in bringing a loan relationship into existence; in entering into or giving effect to a related transaction and in making any payments under a loan relationship. In addition, relief is available for abortive expenditure incurred in connection with loans.

Interest or a discount that is treated as a distribution for income tax purposes is excluded (for the definition of a 'distribution', see [42.1] ff). With effect from 5 December 2013, a special anti-avoidance rule restricts debits in respect of disguised distribution arrangements involving derivative contracts (CTA 2009 s 695A). [41.53]

d) *Trading profits, losses and expenses*

When a loan relationship is entered into for the purposes of a trade any profits and gains are taxable and interest charges, expenses etc are deductible in computing the company's trading profits (CTA 2009 s 297). This means that no adjustment is normally needed in respect of bank interest paid on a loan raised for trading purposes and commitment fees, commission and interest are all relievable on an accruals basis. While many companies are likely to have borrowed money for trading purposes, and are therefore entitled to a trading deduction for interest paid, HMRC considers that there are very few instances, other than banks and other financial institutions, where a company will be a creditor to a loan relationship for trading purposes giving rise to interest taxable as trading income. [41.54]

e) *Non-trading profits, losses and expenses*

If the loan relationship is entered into for non-trading purposes any profits, gains and interest receivable are taxed as loan relationship income and losses, interest payable, expenses and charges are tax deductible (CTA 2009 s 301). For each accounting period it is necessary to calculate the aggregate of non-trading credits less non-trading debits. If in any period the debits exceed the credits, tax relief is available as follows:

(1) As a deduction against the total profits of the company (ie which arise from any source) for the same accounting period. This relief is given before setting off trading losses for the same period or non-trading deficits carried back from a later period.
(2) By way of group relief against the current profits of other group companies in the corresponding accounting period (for group relief see [43.41]).
(3) By carry-back against profits from non-trading loan relationships of the company for the previous year.

Finally, deficits that cannot be relieved as above are carried forward against non-trading profits (including capital gains) in subsequent accounting periods. [41.55]

f) *Connected parties*

Although there are no rules specifically applying to intra-group loans there are provisions dealing with connected parties that are relevant in this situation. Because of the accruals basis it is not possible to achieve any timing benefit by having group lender and borrower companies with different accounting periods.

The loan relationship rules stipulate that gains and losses on a loan relationship must be calculated in accordance with generally accepted accounting practice. Where a loan relationship exists between two parties that have a connection, those parties must account for gains and losses in respect of that loan relationship using an amortised cost basis of accounting (as opposed to any other valid method, for example mark to market). For this purpose, parties have a connection if, at any time in the accounting period, one controls the other or both are controlled by the same person. Control in this case means the ability to secure that the affairs of the company are conducted according to one's wishes by means of the holding of shares or voting power or as a result of any powers conferred by the company's constitutional documents.

Impaired debt

If a company is party to a loan relationship then, in the first instance, all profits and losses arising from that relationship are taxable or allowable. Hence, a company that is a creditor in a relationship may recognise an impairment loss on a debt which is bad and obtain a tax deduction for that impairment. Conversely, if a debtor company has its debt released then that will result in a taxable credit arising.

This general principle is subject to a number of important exceptions. Where a debt is released, generally no taxable credit will arise if the parties to the relationship are connected. Likewise, if the parties to the relationship are connected, impairment losses cannot generally give rise to allowable debits. Similar rules apply in certain circumstances involving liquidations and capitalisation of debt.

Late interest

Where parties to a loan relationship are connected, interest is deductible on an accruals basis (based on generally accepted accounting principles). If, however, the creditor to a loan relationship is taxable on a receipts basis (eg an individual) or is not chargeable to UK tax (eg an overseas company) there could be an opportunity to accrue tax deductions with no corresponding taxable credit.

Rules were therefore included to prevent a deduction being claimed if interest was not paid in respect of a debtor loan relationship within 12 months of the end of the period in which it was accrued, if that interest would not give rise to a credit under the loan relationship rules in respect of the creditor. These rules applied where:
(1) the creditor was a company which had a connection with the debtor;
(2) the debtor was a close company and the creditor was:
    (a) a participator in the debtor company (or a person who controlled a company which was such a participator);
    (b) the associate of a person who was or who controlled a company which was such a participator or associate of a participator;

(c) a company controlled by a participator or a person who controlled a company which was such a participator; or
(d) a company in which such a participator had a major interest;
(3) the debtor had a major interest in the creditor company, or vice versa; or
(4) the creditor was a retirement benefit scheme.

For accounting periods beginning after 31 March 2009, the restrictions in relation to (1) to (3) above were disapplied where the creditor was a company unless it was resident in a 'non-qualifying territory' (broadly, a tax haven) (CTA 2009 s 374(1A)). This could present practical difficulties where companies obtained funding from multi-investor partnerships such as private equity funds, since in principle the loan relationship rules look through the partnership to individual corporate partners. HMRC has published guidance which suggests that a 'paid basis' will be accepted in instances where it is difficult to establish whether or not the partner companies are resident in non-qualifying territories (Corporate Finance Manual, CFM 35980).

Although intended to prevent manipulation of the loan relationship provisions, these rules themselves were found to give scope for manipulation. In anticipation of the planned wider changes to the loan relationship legislation (see [41.50]), they were repealed for new loan relationships with effect from 3 December 2014, although they continued to apply to existing loan relationships until 31 December 2015. [41.56]

4 Charitable donations relief

a) *Charges and qualifying charitable donations*

CTA 2010 Part 6 provides a specific relief for 'qualifying charitable donations'.
[41.57]–[41.58]

b) *Deduction against profits*

'1) Qualifying charitable donations made by a company are allowed as deductions from the company's total profits ...

2) ... after any other relief from corporation tax other than group relief.' (CTA 2010 s 189(1) and (2))

It follows that such donations may be set against all the company's profits, including chargeable gains. Any payment which is otherwise deductible from total profits, or in calculating any component of those profits (for example as a trading deduction), cannot be deducted a second time under this section (CTA 2010 s 190(2)). As s 189(4) only allows a deduction for donations made in the accounting period, it is important for a company to organise, so far as possible, its donations to be made at the end of one accounting period rather than at the beginning of the next in order to obtain the earliest possible tax relief. [41.59]

EXAMPLE 41.6

Z Ltd makes the following payments in the year ended 30 April 2017:

1234   Corporation tax

(1) £5,000 pa to the Society to Promote Antiquarian Studies (a registered charity); and
(2) £8,000 pa to the trustees of a trust fund set up by the company to educate the children of its employees and to provide evening classes in arts and crafts for its employees.

The payment of £5,000 pa: will be deductible so long as it is a qualifying donation within CTA 2010 Part 6 Chapter 2. The fact that the payment is recurring (and is for instance provided for in a deed of covenant) will not by itself enable the payment to be deducted: it must satisfy the detailed requirements.

The payment of £8,000 pa: is not a charitable payment (see *Oppenheim v Tobacco Securities Trust Co Ltd* (1951)) and will only be an allowable deduction if it can be shown to be allowable as a trading expense or otherwise.

5 Loss relief

Different relieving provisions apply depending upon the type of loss that the company has made. In all cases, however, it is only the company (or another company in the same group: see **[43.41]**) that is entitled to the relief and never the shareholders of the company. The loss is thus 'locked into' the company and this is a matter of some significance in deciding whether to commence business as a company or partnership.

Losses are deducted from the appropriate profits of the company in priority to qualifying charitable donations.

With effect from 18 March 2015, the use of certain brought-forward reliefs is restricted where the profits from which they would be deducted arise from arrangements which are intended to reduce the taxable profits of the group by creating new in-year reliefs or deductions (CTA 2010 Part 14B). A separate restriction was introduced for banking companies with effect from 1 April 2015 preventing them from covering more than 50% of their profits with losses arising before that date (CTA 2010 Part 7A). This limit was reduced to 25% with effect from 1 April 2016.

A significant reform of the loss relief rules was announced in the 2016 Budget, to take effect from 1 April 2017. Under these proposals, carried-forward losses arising from April 2017 onwards would be available to set against profits from other income streams or from other companies within a group. At the same time, however, the amount of profit within any one group of companies that can be fully offset by brought-forward losses (whenever arising) would be limited to £5m, with relief in excess of this amount restricted to 50% of profits. These rules would apply to trading losses, non-trading loan relationship deficits, management expenses, property business losses and non-trading losses on intangible fixed assets, but not to capital losses. The legislation was omitted from FA 2017 as enacted following the announcement of a general election but is to be included in a further Finance Bill later in 2017 with the original 1 April 2017 commencement date.   **[41.60]**

a)   *Relief for trading losses: 'carry-forward' (CTA 2010 s 45)*

A trading loss can be carried forward and set against trading profits (not capital gains) from the *same* trade in the future.

Relief is given automatically by reducing the trading income of the succeeding accounting period or periods. In cases where such trading income is insufficient to absorb the full loss, interest and dividends received by the company may be treated as trading income for the purpose of loss relief (CTA 2010 s 46) provided that such income would have been taxed as trading income if tax had not been assessed under other provisions. Dividends received by a company whose trade involves dealing in shares fall into this category but in *Nuclear Electric plc v Bradley* (1996) it was held that income produced by moneys set aside (although not placed in a segregated fund) for meeting future liabilities could not be treated as trading income:

> 'Whether income from investments held by a business is trading income must ultimately depend upon the nature of the business and the purpose for which the fund is held. At one end of the scale are insurance companies and banks part of whose business is the making and holding of investments to meet current liabilities. It has been suggested that tour operators might fall into this category but without a good deal more information I do not feel able to express an opinion on this matter. At the other end of the scale are businesses of which the making and holding of investments form no part. In between these two ends there will no doubt fall other types of businesses whose position is not so clear. However in this case it is absolutely clear that the business of NE was to produce and supply electricity. The making of investments was neither an integral nor any part of its business. Furthermore the investments which it did make were in no sense employed in the business of producing electricity during the year of assessment.' (Lord Jauncey)   **[41.61]**

b)   *Relief for trading losses against current and previous profits (CTA 2010 s 37)*

A company may set its trading loss against profits of the same accounting period. As the relief sets the loss against other profits it follows that *all* current profits can be used, including capital gains.

EXAMPLE 41.7

Haw Ltd's accounts for the financial year show the following: a trading loss of £6,000; rental income of £5,000; chargeable gains of £3,000; and qualifying charitable donations of £1,000. The corporation tax computation would be:

	£
Property income	5,000
Chargeable gains	3,000
	8,000
Less: trading loss	6,000
	2,000
Less: charitable donations	1,000
Profits for corporation tax	£1,000

Where a loss cannot be relieved, or cannot be fully relieved, against profits of the same accounting period a claim may be made to carry that loss back against profits of the accounting periods falling within the previous 12 months. The company must have been carrying on the same trade in the earlier period and the claim has to be made within two years of the end of the accounting period in which the loss was incurred (CTA 2010 s 37(7), subject to HMRC's discretion to extend that period). Any claim for loss relief will take effect before charitable donations are deducted but *after* any loss made in that earlier year.

EXAMPLE 41.8

How Ltd prepares its accounts for the year ended 31 May. Its accounts show the following:

	Trading profits (losses)	Property business profits	Qualifying charitable donations
	£	£	£
Year to 31 May 2016	(5,000)	4,000	Nil
Year to 31 May 2015	(7,000)	4,000	1,000
Year to 31 May 2014	2,000	4,000	1,000

In respect of the year ended 31 May 2015 a claim for s 37 relief would result in the following corporation tax computation:

31 May 2015	£		Loss memorandum £
Property business	4,000	Trading loss	7,000
Less trading loss	(4,000)	Used in year	(4,000)
Taxable profits	Nil	Losses remaining	3,000

31 May 2014	£		£
Property business	4,000		
Trading profits	2,000		
Total	6,000		
Loss carried back	(3,000)	Carried back	(3,000)
	3,000		
Less charitable donations	(1,000)		
Taxable profit	2,000		Nil

As a result of the claim any tax paid on the 2014 profit will be recovered to the extent that losses cover profits of that year.

In respect of the year ended 31 May 2016, a claim under s 37 would result in all of the company's £4,000 property business profit being covered by losses arising in the year with £1,000 remaining unused. This excess £1,000 cannot be carried back as there are no available profits in the year ended 31 May 2015. The losses must be carried forward under s 45.

A number of technical points should be made in connection with the relief under CTA 2010 s 37.

First, in the case of a terminal loss the carry-back period is three years (see CTA 2010 s 39(2)). A scheme to take advantage of this extended relief, by transferring the trade to a person outside the charge to corporation tax, was blocked by CTA 2010 s 41 (formerly TA 1988 s 393A(2E), introduced by FA 2009 with effect from 21 May 2009).

Second, a limited and temporary extension of the carry-back period to three years was announced in the 2008 Pre-Budget Report and is contained in FA 2009 Sch 6 para 3. For accounting periods ending in each of the 12-month periods ending on 23 November 2009 and 23 November 2010, losses of up to £50,000 could be carried back for up to three years instead of only for one. The limit of £50,000 was reduced proportionately for accounting periods of less than a year.

Third, on a claim being made a terminal loss will be set against profits of earlier accounting periods falling in the previous three years. It is not possible to claim to set the loss against a particular year in that three-year period: rather it must be offset against *later* periods first. A 2016 loss, for instance, will be offset against 2015; then 2014, and, finally, against the 2013 accounting period.

Fourth, capital allowances may increase the loss to be relieved under s 37 although it should be noted that capital allowances carried forward from an earlier period cannot be included as part of the loss. **[41.62]**

c)   *General restrictions on the availability of trading loss relief*

There are restrictions on the availability of trading loss relief under CTA 2010 s 37 and s 45. **[41.63]**

A commercial purpose The trade must be carried on commercially with a view to the realisation of a gain if s 37 relief is to be available. Carry-forward (s 45) relief will, however, always apply. **[41.64]**

Acquiring a tax loss company CTA 2010 s 674 can operate to prevent the use of trading losses where, after the loss has been incurred, there has been a change in the ownership of the company's shares. The purpose of these provisions is to stop the practice of purchasing companies in order to utilise their accumulated trading losses or their past profits (and note that these provisions are extended to cover the sale of investment companies with surplus management expenses and companies which have property business losses: see **[41.67]** and **[41.70]**).

There are two relevant factors to be considered in deciding whether loss relief is available:
(1)   whether there has been a change of ownership; and
(2)   what has happened to the business of the company.

CTA 2010 s 719 contains detailed rules setting out what constitutes a change in ownership; basically it amounts to a change in the beneficial ownership of more than 50% of the ordinary share capital. A change is disregarded where the company continues to be a 75% subsidiary of the same parent company (s 724) and also, from 1 April 2014, where a new holding company is inserted on top of an existing group (s 724A).

So far as the business of the company is concerned the rules in s 674 apply if either:
(1)   there is a change in ownership accompanied by a major change in the nature or conduct of the trade and both changes occur within a

three-year period (for the interpretation of 'major' see *Willis v Peeters Picture Frames Ltd* (1982); *Purchase v Tesco Stores Ltd* (1984) and SP 10/91); or
(2) a change in ownership follows a period when the trade carried on by the company has become small or negligible and only after that change of ownership has there been a revival, not necessarily within a three-year period.

HMRC accepts that a major change does not occur if changes are introduced to increase efficiency; to keep pace with developing technology; or to rationalise the business by withdrawing unprofitable items. SP 10/91 provides the following illustrations of what does and does not amount to a 'major' change:

'*Examples where a change would not of itself be regarded as a major change*
- (a) A company manufacturing kitchen fitments in three obsolescent factories moves production to one new factory (increasing efficiency).
- (b) A company manufacturing kitchen utensils replaces enamel by plastic, or a company manufacturing time pieces replaces mechanical by electronic components (keeping pace with developing technology).
- (c) A company operating a dealership in one make of car switches to operating a dealership in another make of car satisfying the same market (not a major change in the type of property dealt in).
- (d) A company manufacturing both filament and fluorescent lamps (of which filament lamps form the greater part of the output) concentrates solely on filament lamps (a rationalisation of product range without a major change in the type of property dealt in).
- (e) A company whose business consists of making and holding investments in UK quoted shares and securities makes changes to its portfolio of quoted shares and securities (not a change in the nature of investments held).

Examples where a major change would be regarded as occurring
- (f) A company operating a dealership in saloon cars switches to operating a dealership in tractors (a major change in the type of property dealt in).
- (g) A company owning a public house switches to operating a discotheque in the same, but converted, premises (a major change in the services or facilities provided).
- (h) A company fattening pigs for their owners switches to buying pigs for fattening and resale (a major change in the nature of the trade, being a change from providing a service to being a primary producer).
- (i) A company switches from investing in quoted shares to investing in real property for rent (a change in the nature of investments held).'

A further set of anti-avoidance rules, designed to counter targeted loss-buying, was inserted as CTA 2010 ss 730A–730D with effect from 20 March 2013. These sections restrict the ability to offset trading losses against other profits following a 'qualifying change', where the loss arises from the deduction of a trading expense and arrangements have been made of which a main purpose is to enable such amounts to be deducted and offset. They also restrict the ability to deduct trading and other expenses and non-trading debits where arrangements have been made to transfer profits so as to enable relief to be obtained for such deductions. The definition of 'qualifying change' is found in CAA 2001 s 212C and is significantly different from that of 'change in the ownership of a company' in CTA 2010 s 719.

[41.65]

Corporate reconstructions If a company ceases to carry on a trade (eg when the trade is sold), the trade is treated as discontinued even though it may subsequently be carried on by another company (CTA 2009 s 41(2)). This means that losses cannot be carried forward although carry-back relief may be available.

Where a reconstruction has occurred as a result of which the trade passes from one company to another and both companies are under similar control, CTA 2010 ss 944 and 948 (formerly TA 1988 s 343) permit losses and capital allowances to be carried forward from the predecessor to the successor company.

There are restrictions on the amount of loss that can be carried forward, typically relevant when the transferor company is insolvent at the time of the transfer. Broadly, if the successor company fails to take over all the liabilities of the transferor (as when part only of the trade – the successful part – is being hived-down into a new 'clean' company) and the transferor has insufficient assets to cover them, the losses which can be transferred are reduced by the amount by which the predecessor's liabilities not transferred exceed the aggregate of the purchase consideration and the assets not transferred.

For s 944 to apply the same person or persons must, at some time within the period of two years after the change, directly or indirectly own the trade (or not less than a three-quarter share in it) and must have owned that trade or the same interest therein within the period of one year before the change. Ownership is normally determined by reference to ordinary share capital, which is given by CTA 2010 s 1119 a wider definition than its normal meaning and includes all issued share capital except shares which carry a fixed rate dividend and no other interest in the profits of the company.

A normal hiving-down operation satisfies these requirements although restrictions on the amount of loss that can be carried forward have removed some of its attractions: when only a part of the transferor's trade is transferred (as in the typical hive-down) apportionments must be made to determine what fraction of the loss can be carried forward.

The successor company can amalgamate the predecessor's trade with another enterprise already carried on, although, in this situation, HMRC's view is that the carried-forward loss relief will only be available against future profits arising from the old trade (see *Falmer Jeans v Rodin* (1990)). In *Leekes Ltd v R & C Comrs* (2016), the Upper Tribunal held that this restriction applied under the former TA 1988 s 343 where the original trade was carried on as part of a larger trading operation by the successor as well as where the successor only took over the activities of the former trade and not the trade itself. [41.66]

EXAMPLE 41.9

The ordinary share capital of Zee Ltd and Pee Ltd is owned as follows:

	Zee Ltd	Pee Ltd
Alan	10	8
Ben	6	12
Claud	30	40
Dennis	29	20
Others	25	20

A transfer of a trade from Zee Ltd to Pee Ltd would fall within s 944 since the 75% common ownership test is satisfied albeit that the relevant shares in Pee Ltd are owned by the same persons in different proportions.

d) *Relief for income losses other than trading losses*

Losses of a UK property business are calculated in the same way as losses of a trade; however, they are relieved differently. UK property business losses arising in any year must first be used to reduce total profits of that year. Any unrelieved loss cannot be carried back to the preceding period but must be carried forward to the next period (CTA 2010 s 62). Property business losses brought forward to an accounting period are treated as losses arising in that period and so must be relieved against total profits of that period.

If a company with UK property business losses ceases to carry on its UK property business, but continues to carry on an investment business, the property business losses become excess management expenses. If the company does not have any investment business following the cessation of the UK property business, the losses will be extinguished.

Losses from miscellaneous transactions may be set against miscellaneous income for either the current or first available future accounting period (CTA 2010 s 91).

On a change of ownership of a company carrying on a property business, CTA 2010 s 683 restricts the carry-forward of property business losses in a similar way to the rules for trading losses in s 674 (see **[41.65]**). With effect from 20 March 2013, CTA 2010 ss 705C–705E impose similar restrictions on non-trading debits and losses on intangible fixed assets on a change of ownership of a 'shell company' (a company which is not a company with investment business and does not carry on a trade or a property business). New anti-avoidance rules restricting the use of non-trading debits following a 'qualifying change' took effect from the same date (see **[41.65]**). **[41.67]**

e) *Relief for capital losses*

Losses which accrue on disposals of assets are computed in the same way as chargeable gains (see **[41.22]**) and can be set against the first available chargeable gains made by the company. Such losses cannot be offset against income profits although losses on shares held under the Corporate Venturing Scheme may be set against other profits (see **[41.73]**). **[41.68]**

6 Management expenses

a) *The basic rule*

Companies with investment business may deduct sums paid out in management expenses (such as salaries and general office expenditure – for a consideration of the meaning of 'management expenses', see *Camas plc v Atkinson* (2004)) from their total profits to the extent that the expenses are in respect of so much of the company's investment business as consists in the making of investments provided the investments concerned are not held by the company for an unallowable purpose (ie not chargeable to UK tax) during the accounting period. Management expenditure that is capital in nature is not deductible and relief that is available is given only when any management expenses are charged to the profit and loss account (CTA 2009 Part 16). Hence capitalised expenditure will only be relieved if amortised.

HMRC has issued guidance on its view as regards the dividing line between revenue and capital expenditure and on the 'unallowable purpose' test.

If such expenditure is unrelieved, it can be carried forward and offset in future years, but cannot be carried back to a previous accounting period. Unrelieved qualifying charitable donations can likewise be carried forward and treated as management expenses in future years so long as they were 'made for the purposes of the company's investment business' (CTA 2009 s 1223(1)–(2)).

A company with investment business means any company whose business consists wholly or partly in the making of investments; there must be a 'business' with a financial return (see further *Cook v Medway Housing Society Ltd* (1996)). This extends to non-resident companies undertaking an investment activity through a permanent establishment.

Anti-avoidance measures include provisions that disallow expenses of management to the extent that they are connected with any arrangements that had, as their main purpose, obtaining a tax advantage (CTA 2009 s 1248).

For companies whose business consists of managing land, expenses involved in administering that land will be deductible in computing the property business income, whereas the general running costs of the company will be management expenses. Difficulties may arise in obtaining a deduction for expenses such as brokerage and stamp duty relating to the sale of investments which may be classified as part of costs of purchasing and selling (ie as being of a capital nature). [41.69]

b) *Sales of surplus management expenses companies*

CTA 2010 s 682 applies to sales of companies with surplus management expenses. As with the rules dealing with trading losses there has to be a change in the ownership of the company and the management expenses cannot be carried forward to periods beginning after that change in a number of situations. In addition to those that apply for trading losses there is a further provision designed to prevent the purchaser pumping cash into the acquired company which would be invested to produce income to absorb the management expenses. [41.70]

1242 Corporation tax

c) *Special treatment of trading companies*

Whether or not a company is a trading company may be important in that:
(1) reliefs from capital taxes (CGT and IHT) may be available only to shareholders in trading companies: see, for instance, business property relief for IHT;
(2) favourable tax treatment for certain corporate transactions, for example repurchase of shares or demergers, is only available to trading companies.

A *trading company* exists 'wholly or mainly' for the purpose of carrying on a trade. In practice HMRC considers, in doubtful cases, that this phrase means more than 50% and will look at turnover, net profits, net assets and management time to see if this requirement is met. When a holding/subsidiary structure is used the holding company will often not itself be a trading company albeit that its main function is to hold shares in trading subsidiaries.

There is, however, nothing to prevent a trading company from claiming relief for management expenses. Any company with investment business may deduct expenses of management to the extent that the expenses are in respect of so much of the company's business as consists in the making of investments, provided the investments concerned are not held by the company for an unallowable purpose (ie for the purpose of activities which are not commercial or not chargeable to UK tax) during the accounting period. [41.71]

7 Corporate Venturing Scheme (FA 2000 s 63, Sch 15)

This is a tax incentive scheme (closely mirrored on the EIS and VCT provisions that apply to individuals) designed to encourage companies to invest in small trading companies. [41.72]

a) *The reliefs*

The investor company obtains tax relief at 20% on sums invested in new ordinary shares that are held for at least three years. For instance, if Xerxes Ltd makes a qualifying investment of £100,000, its corporation tax liability will be reduced by £20,000. When the shares are sold, tax that would otherwise arise may be deferred if the gain is reinvested (up to a year before and three years after the time when the gain is realised) in another qualifying shareholding. If the shares produce a loss on disposal the investor obtains relief for that loss (net of investment relief) against income if the losses are not deducted against gains. [41.73]

b) *The requirements*

These largely follow the EIS/VCT requirements but the following may be noted:
(1) the corporate investor cannot obtain relief if it controls the small company in which it invests (control, subject to two modifications, is defined in CTA 2010 ss 450, 451: see FA 2000, Sch 15 para 8);

(2) the corporate venturer's stake in the company must not exceed 30% taking into account ordinary share capital and share and loan capital which can be converted into ordinary share capital; and
(3) the issuing company must not be quoted (although it may subsequently become quoted without relief being forfeited) and at least 20% of its ordinary shares must be owned by one or more independent individuals (FA 2000, Sch 15 para 18).

The gross assets test is the same as for EIS relief as is the trading activities requirement. [41.74]

8 Relief for disposals of substantial shareholdings (TCGA 1992 s 192A, Sch 7AC)

A new relief that had been the subject of extensive consultation was introduced on 1 April 2002 to provide an exemption from tax in respect of gains on the disposal by a company of a substantial shareholding in another company.

The relief applies to capital gains realised by a trading company (or member of a trading group) on the disposal of shares in a trading company (or a member of a trading group). Such gains will be exempt from tax providing the shareholding was 'substantial', that is to say 10% or more of the ordinary share capital, and has been held for a continuous period of 12 months during the two years before the disposal. Some key points are as follows:

(1) The relief applies only to companies.
(2) It applies to disposals of shares in overseas companies as well as UK companies.
(3) The company making the disposal must have been a trading company or member of a trading group not only before the disposal but immediately afterwards. This may have the effect of denying the relief to a holding company with a single trading subsidiary.
(4) A company qualifies as a trading company if its activities do not include to a substantial extent non-trading activities.
(5) A company qualifies as a member of a trading group if, broadly, the activities of the members of the group taken together do not include to a substantial extent non-trading activities. The meaning of substantial in this context is more than 20% of the activities based on earnings, assets and employee time/expenses (see CG 53116).
(6) Where different companies in a group hold shares in a subsidiary, these may be aggregated for the purposes of establishing whether a 10% shareholding exists.
(7) Provided at least 10% of the ordinary shares have been held for the requisite period, the relief applies to disposals of all types of shares and also of 'assets related to shares', a category that includes options over shares and securities convertible into shares.
(8) In addition to holding at least 10% of the ordinary shares the company making the disposal must have been beneficially entitled to at least 10% of its distributable profits and at least 10% of its assets on a winding up.
(9) A capital loss made on the disposal of a shareholding that would qualify for the exemption will not be eligible for relief.

Clearance is available to taxpayers where there is uncertainty over the application of this exemption to a proposed disposal as part of HMRC's non-statutory clearance service.

A consultation on possible reforms to the substantial shareholdings exemption was launched in May 2016 with the intention of increasing its simplicity, coherence and international competitiveness. Legislation removing or relaxing some of the requirements for exemption was omitted from FA 2017 following the announcement of a general election but is to be included in a further Finance Bill later in 2017 with effect for disposals on or after 1 April 2017. [41.75]–[41.90]

IV RAISING FINANCE

1 The sources of company finance

There are two major sources of corporate finance. Money can be raised by an allotment of *shares* so that the contributors become members of the company and will generally expect to receive dividends on those shares. Alternatively, money can be borrowed with the company creating *debentures* and paying interest to the debenture holders.

Interest may attract tax relief but dividends are not deductible in arriving at the company's profits. As a result of the limited imputation system (until 5 April 2016) and the partial exemption of dividend income (thereafter) a full double charge to tax is avoided but not all the corporation tax paid by the company is offset by reliefs available to the shareholders and so there remains a discrimination in favour of debentures and against raising funds by a share issue. [41.91]

2 Qualifying corporate bonds

a) *Basic rules for companies*

Certain loans to traders that prove to be irrecoverable qualify for capital gains loss relief (TCGA 1992 s 253). The majority of company loans, however, do not fall within this provision since they are 'debts on security' which are excluded from that section. Until 14 March 1989 this did not matter since relief was separately available for losses incurred by such investors under TCGA 1992 s 251 (relief for debts on security). From that date the law in this area has undergone a series of changes. It is important to appreciate at the outset that the rules for companies and the rules for individuals and trusts are different. For companies, profits and losses on loans are generally included in the company's income computation in accordance with the loan relationship rules so that the CGT rules do not apply. The following discussion is therefore concerned with the position of individuals and trusts. [41.92]

b) *Definition of a QCB (TCGA 1992 s 117)*

Qualifying corporate bonds (QCBs) are wholly exempt from CGT. Gains are therefore tax-free and no relief is available for losses. The original definition of a QCB involved a sterling denominated bond, debenture or loan stock whether secured or unsecured but restricted to securities which were *either* themselves quoted on the UK Stock Exchange *or* issued by a body with other securities so quoted.

FA 1989 widened the definition of a QCB to embrace such securities *whether or not issued by a quoted body*. The consequence was to extend the definition to include virtually all company securities. As a result, the disposal of such securities was wholly exempt from CGT with the result that losses incurred on that disposal were not tax allowable. Not surprisingly, attention was focused on the definition of a QCB in order to draw up an agreement which fell *outside* that definition but which still amounted to a debt on a security thereby enabling loss relief to be available under TCGA 1992 s 251. **[41.93]**

c)   *Preserving loss relief for debts on security*

Two devices were commonly employed. *First*, a QCB must be 'expressed in sterling and in respect of which no provision is made for conversion into or redemption in a currency other than sterling' (TCGA 1992 s 117(1)(b)). Accordingly, provisions for redemption in another currency or by reference to another currency could be included to take the bond outside the QCB definition. In *R & C Comrs v Trigg* (2016) the Upper Tribunal held that a clause providing for a bond to be redenominated in another currency following a change in the currency of the United Kingdom was such a provision.

An *alternative* lay in the requirement that to be a QCB the debt in question must represent and have at all times represented a normal commercial loan (TCGA 1992 s 117(1)(a) and, for the definition of a normal commercial loan, TA 1988 Sch 18 para 1). Providing a right of conversion into shares would ensure that the test was *not* met so that the security was not a QCB.
[41.94]–[41.95]

d)   *'Rolling into' a QCB*

Special rules exist to deal with the situation where a gain is 'rolled into' a QCB. Assume, for instance, that Toby sells his company to Vulture Ltd in consideration for an issue of securities in Vulture that fall within the definition of a QCB. Toby's gains on the disposal of his shares can be rolled into the replacement securities by virtue of TCGA 1992 ss 135–137. If the replacement securities are QCBs, special rules in TCGA 1992 s 116 apply and the gain is not 'rolled over' but merely postponed, to be triggered on a subsequent disposal of the QCB. In effect the gain is held in suspense and will arise *even if* the QCB is sold at a loss or is written off. Toby may therefore realise nothing on his QCB and yet be left with a tax liability. To add insult to injury, relief under TCGA 1992 s 254 will not be available even if the security has become of negligible value because the loan in question will not have been used wholly for trading purposes; it was created to enable Vulture Ltd to acquire Toby's company. If Toby dies still owning the QCB the suspended gain will pass to his personal representatives and fall into charge when they dispose of the bond. HMRC has, however, confirmed that the deferred charge can be avoided if a disposal is made to a charity within TCGA 1992 s 257. There will be no charge on the gift by the donor nor on the subsequent disposal of the bonds by the charity. **[41.96]**

1246 *Corporation tax*

e) *Paper for paper exchanges*

With the introduction of taper relief, it could sometimes be more attractive to sell a company's shares in exchange for loan notes which were not QCBs so as to preserve entitlement to taper relief. Taper relief was, however, discontinued for 2008–09 onwards and replaced by entrepreneurs' relief: **Chapter 20**. For the transitional relief which applies where shares were exchanged for QCBs before 6 April 2008 see **[20.36]** and for the treatment of subsequent re-organisations involving QCBs see **[20.37]** and **[20.38]**. [**41.97**]

3 **Financing a UK subsidiary ('thin capitalisation')**

From 1 April 2004 the UK thin capitalisation rules were subsumed into the transfer pricing rules. Hence, arm's length rates and gearing levels must be applied to loans made between companies where one controls the other, or the same person can control both. As explained in **[41.44]** above, the definition of control used here is very wide.

Whether particular financing arrangements will meet the arm's length standard depends very much on the business sector of the company concerned, the assets which might provide security, cash flow and the general state of the economy. *Tax Bulletin* 17 (June 1995) indicated that the Revenue would normally accept arrangements which gave a debt–equity ratio of something less than 1:1 and income cover of at least 3:1, provided they otherwise met the arm's length test. Current guidance, however, stresses that the UK does not operate a 'safe harbour' and that OECD principles and guidance must be applied to the facts and circumstances of each case (see in particular INTM 516050 and INTM 517040).

Before 1 April 2004, thin capitalisation was effectively covered by the former TA 1988 s 209(2)(da). This provision applied to treat the excessive amount of the interest as a distribution where:

(1) either the borrower is a 75% subsidiary of the lender or both are 75% subsidiaries of a third company; and
(2) the whole or any part of the interest paid is greater in amount than would have been paid between unconnected companies.

In practice, the position was usually governed by double tax treaties, but this was not satisfactory since some treaties did not contain any override; in other cases the override did not apply where a 'special relationship' existed between borrower and lender. The interpretation of the 'special relationship' provisions is clarified by TIOPA 2010 s 131, which specifies that all factors must be taken into account, including whether the loan would have been made at all, and the amount in which the loan would have been made, in the absence of the special relationship, unless these factors are expressly excluded by the wording in the particular treaty.

In addition, the ECJ decision in the *Thin Capitalisation Group Litigation test case* (C-524/04) has stated that, even where the debt is not arm's length, so long as the arrangements between companies are put in place for genuine commercial reasons, there should be no need for an adjustment under the thin capitalisation rules. Furthermore, adjustments under the thin capitalisation rules should not be made between the UK and the EU unless a corresponding adjustment in the EU country can also be made.

Following consultation, HMRC introduced a new set of measures as part of a package of measures on the taxation of foreign profits, which apply to accounting periods beginning after 31 December 2009 (TIOPA 2010 Part 7). This limits the overall tax deduction that can be obtained for finance expense by UK companies in a group by reference to the group's consolidated gross finance expense.

In the light of recommendations published by the OECD as part of its Base Erosion and Profit Shifting (BEPS) project, the Government has announced the introduction of new rules to limit corporate interest deductions with effect from 1 April 2017. These will incorporate a fixed ratio rule limiting corporation tax deductions for net interest expense to 30% of a group's UK earnings before interest, tax, depreciation and amortisation (EBITDA). There will also be a group ratio rule based on the net interest to EBITDA ratio for the worldwide group. There will be a group *de minimis* threshold of £2m net UK interest expense per annum. The existing debt cap legislation will be repealed but rules with a similar effect, limiting a group's UK net interest deductions to the amount of its worldwide net third party interest expense, will be incorporated in the new scheme. A consultation document on the detail of the proposals was issued in May 2016 and legislation was introduced in the 2017 Finance Bill, but omitted from FA 2017 following the announcement of a general election. It is to be included in a further Finance Bill later in 2017 with the original 1 April 2017 commencement date.
[41.98]–[41.120]

V CLOSE COMPANIES

Companies controlled by one person or by a small group of individuals could be operated so as to secure tax advantages unavailable to the individual taxpayer or to the larger corporate taxpayer. As a result there have been special rules since 1922 aimed at preventing such arrangements.
[41.121]

1 What is a close company?

A close company is a company in relation to which one of two conditions is met. Condition A is that it is:

'under the control —
(a) of 5 or fewer participators, or
(b) of participators who are directors'

(CTA 2010 s 439(2))

Hence, it may be either director-controlled (irrespective of the number of directors involved) or controlled by five or fewer participators. Condition B is an alternative test based on the participators' entitlement to assets in a winding up (CTA 2010 s 439(3)). [41.122]

1248   Corporation tax

a)   *The meaning of 'control'*

A person (or two or more persons taken together) is deemed to have control of a company if:
(1) he can exercise control over the company's affairs, in particular by possessing or acquiring the greater part of the share capital or voting power; or
(2) he possesses or is entitled to acquire:
   (a) such part of the issued share capital as would give him a right to the greater part of the income of the company if it were all to be distributed; or
   (b) the right to the greater part of the assets available for distribution among the participators on a winding up or in any other circumstances.

In deciding whether a person has control there may be attributed to him any rights vested in his nominees, his associates and companies controlled by him or his associates. A 'nominee' is a person holding assets for another.
[41.123]

b)   *The meaning of 'participator', 'associate' and 'director'*

'*Participator*' is defined as a person having a share or interest in the capital or income of the company and includes a person who is entitled to acquire share capital or voting rights and loan creditors, but not a bank lending in the ordinary course of its business (CTA 2010 s 454, 453(4)).

'*Associate*' of a participator includes: (1) any person related to him as spouse, parent, remoter forebear, sibling, child or remoter issue, or as partner; (2) the trustees of any settlement set up by him or by any person related to him (see, for instance, *R v IRC, ex p Newfields Developments Ltd* (2001)); and (3) fellow beneficiaries under a trust of the company's shares or entitled to shares in the company under the will of a deceased shareholder (CTA 2010 s 448).

'*Director*' is defined as a person who occupies that post; any person in accordance with whose instructions the directors act; and a manager of the company who, with his associates, owns or controls 20% of the company's ordinary share capital (CTA 2010 s 452). [41.124]

c)   *Companies that are not close*

The following companies that would otherwise fall within the above definition are treated as not being close companies:
(1) any non-resident company;
(2) companies which are registered industrial and provident societies;
(3) companies controlled by or on behalf of the Crown;
(4) companies which are controlled by one or more companies which are not close companies and cannot be treated as close except by taking a non-close company as one of the five or fewer participators (therefore, the subsidiary of a non-close company is normally not a close company): note, however, CTA 2010 s 444(4), which has the effect that the UK subsidiary of a foreign parent will be close if the parent would be close were it UK resident;

(5) companies whose shares have been listed and dealt in on a recognised stock exchange during the preceding 12 months, provided that shares carrying at least 35% of the voting power are beneficially held by the public. Shares are not held by the public if (*inter alia*) they are held by a director of the company or his associates, and the exception does not apply when the principal members (ie the five members who hold the greatest voting power in the company, but excluding any who hold less than 5% of the voting power) possess more than 85% of the total voting power. [41.125]

d) *Illustrations of the definition*

Most small private companies will be close. Where there are fewer than ten shareholders the company must be close since five or fewer shareholders must control it. [41.126]

EXAMPLE 41.10

Aviary Ltd has an authorised and issued share capital of 60,000 ordinary shares of £1 each. Each share carries one vote. The shares are held as follows:

	Ordinary shares
Mr A Robin, Chairman	5,000
Mr B Raven, Managing Director	2,800
Mr C Crow, Director	2,400
Mr D Hawk, Director	4,400
Mr E Thrush, Director	2,200
Mr F Robin, son of A Robin	1,800
Mr G Magpie, Sales Manager	3,600
Mr H Magpie, father of G Magpie	3,000
Mrs J Eagle, sister of G Magpie	3,000
Mrs K Wren, sister of G Magpie	2,400
Sundry small shareholders	29,400
	60,000

Is Aviary Ltd a close company? It will be necessary to consider voting control and to discover whether it is either a company controlled by five or fewer participators or a company controlled by directors who are participators.

Participator/holding		Five largest shareholdings	Shareholdings of all 'directors'
G Magpie – Sales Manager	3,600		
Add: associate holdings:			
H Magpie – father		3,000	
Mrs J Eagle – sister		3,000	
Mrs K Wren – sister		2,400	
	12,000	12,000	12,000
A Robin – Chairman	5,000		

Add: associate holding:

F Robin – son	1,800		
	6,800	6,800	6,800
D Hawk – Director		4,400	4,400
B Raven – Managing Director		2,800	2,800
C Crow – Director		2,400	2,400
E Thrush – Director		–	2,200
Total shares		28,400	30,600

Although not controlled by five or fewer participators, Aviary Ltd is a close company because it is controlled by its directors. Notice that for this purpose, Mr G Magpie, the sales manager, is treated as a director because with his associates he holds 20% of the company's shares (CTA 2010 s 452).

2 Special rules that apply to close companies

a) *Extended meaning of 'distribution' (CTA 2010 s 1064)*

Close companies are treated as making distributions when they incur expenses in providing living accommodation or other benefits in kind for a participator or his associates. This rule does not apply in cases where the benefit is subject to taxation under the provisions of ITEPA 2003 Part 3, and is designed to catch benefits conferred upon shareholders and debenture holders who are neither directors nor higher-paid employees of that company. The normal rules that govern the taxation of distributions apply (see **Chapter 42**). [41.127]

EXAMPLE 41.11

DB Ltd, a close company, provides free holidays costing £1,500 each for Barry, a director, Barney, a shareholder and Betty, a debenture holder.

(1) *Barry's holiday* The cost will be a deductible business expense of DB Ltd. Barry will be assessed under the ITEPA 2003 rules on the benefit of £1,500 which he has received.

(2) *Barney's and Betty's holiday* In neither case will the expense be charged under ITEPA 2003 but, as both are participators, the expense will be treated as a distribution.

b) *Loans to participators and their associates (CTA 2010 s 455)*

A close company which makes a loan to a participator or his associate is obliged to pay to HMRC an amount equal to 32.5% of the loan (25% for loans made before 6 April 2016). The loan itself is not a distribution and the borrower is not entitled to any tax credit. The payment to HMRC may best be described as a 'forced' loan so that when the participator repays the loan, HMRC will repay the amount paid. The amount will also be repaid if the loan is either released or written off but in those cases the participator will be assessed to income tax at the appropriate dividend rate (subject to the annual tax-free dividend allowance from 6 April 2016) on the amount of the loan in the year of release (for the meaning of a release in this context see *Collins v Addies; Greenfield v Bains* (1992)). For releases taking place before 6 April 2016, income tax is charged at the dividend upper or additional rate, if applicable, on the amount of the loan grossed up at the dividend ordinary rate for the year of release and the participator will be treated as having paid tax (which, however, cannot be reclaimed) at the dividend ordinary rate. The company must notify HMRC of the making of such a loan (for a consideration of when a debt was incurred, see *Gold v Inspector of Taxes; HCB Ltd v Inspector of Taxes* (1998)). The tax is due along with the corporation tax for the accounting period (nine months after the end of the accounting period). No payment is necessary if the loan has been repaid at the time the amount becomes payable. New rules introduced from 20 March 2013 withdraw relief in certain cases where a further payment is made within 30 days of a repayment or where there are arrangements for a further payment to be made.

Where the loan is released or written off after 23 March 2010, CTA 2009 s 321A prevents the company from obtaining a deduction under the loan relationships legislation (see [41.50] ff) in respect of the amount released or written off.

These provisions also catch debts owed to the company, save for the situation where goods or services have been supplied in the ordinary course of the business of the company and the period of credit is normal or does not exceed six months. Debts assigned to the company are likewise treated as loans but the misappropriation of a company's funds does not create a debt since the necessary consensus is lacking (*Stephens v Pittas* (1983)). With effect from 20 March 2013, arrangements conferring a benefit on a participator or associate may also be caught.

The rules do not apply to loans made in the ordinary course of a company's business of money lending nor to loans not exceeding £15,000 to someone who works full-time for the company and who does not have a material interest in it (a material interest is normally 5% of the ordinary shares).

Two other points must be mentioned. *First*, if the loan is to a director or higher-paid employee, income tax may also be charged under ITEPA 2003, on the beneficial loan based on the interest foregone; and, *second*, loans to directors must, in general, be approved by a resolution of the company's members under CA 2006 s 197.

A consultation document outlining various options for the reform of these rules was published by HMRC on 9 July 2013. In the light of responses received, the Government decided not to undertake fundamental reform of the regime but some specific anti-avoidance provisions were introduced by FA 2013 (see CTA 2010 ss 464A–464D). [41.128]

c) *Close investment-holding companies*

Special rules applied before 1 April 2015 to close companies which were not trading companies or members of a trading group. For these purposes a company was trading if it existed wholly or mainly for the purposes of trading so that it did not necessarily have to trade in every accounting period in order to satisfy the test. Companies that dealt in land, shares or securities were trading companies for these purposes and a company carrying on property investment on a commercial basis was likewise treated as a trading company and therefore was not a CIC.

The consequence of being a CIC was that the small profits rate of corporation tax was not available: instead, the company suffered corporation tax at the main rate whatever its level of profits. **[41.129]–[41.150]**

VI THE OVERSEAS DIMENSION

1 Liability to tax

A company that is resident in the UK is liable to corporation tax on all its profits wherever arising (CTA 2009 s 5(1)) except where specific exemptions apply (as to which see, in particular, the foreign branch exemption discussed in **[41.155]**). In the past a non-resident company has been liable to corporation tax only if it was trading in the UK through a permanent establishment and liability was restricted to the chargeable profits from that permanent establishment (CTA 2009 s 5(2)–(3)). New provisions introduced by FA 2016 have extended the scope of the charge to profits, wherever arising, from a trade of dealing in or developing UK land, whether or not the trade is carried on through a UK permanent establishment. Further provisions, contained in Part 8ZB of CTA 2010, define the circumstances in which a profit or gain of a company from a disposal of land in the UK is to be treated as arising from such a trade – broadly, this applies where land has been acquired or developed with the purpose of realising a profit on disposal or is held as trading stock. These provisions apply in relation to disposals on or after 5 July 2016. Where they apply, they displace any charge to income tax which would otherwise arise on the company (see below). Legislation to extend this charge to all profits recognised in accounts on or after 8 March 2017, regardless of when the contract was entered into, was included in the 2017 Finance Bill but omitted from FA 2017 following the announcement of a general election.

Except as mentioned above, a non-resident company having income arising in the UK but not trading through a permanent establishment cannot be assessed to corporation tax but may be subject to UK income tax. This will frequently be the position where a non-resident company owns investment property in the UK giving rise to rental income. In such cases, as the company will probably not have any UK presence, the UK Revenue may have problems of tax collection. In the case of rental income the problem is resolved by the obligation on the tenant to deduct tax from the rents. A charge to corporation tax under the CGT rules will only arise on the trade assets of non-resident companies trading through a permanent establishment in the UK (TCGA 1992 s 10B). See, however, **[27.111]** for the CGT charge applying to non-resident companies from 6 April 2013 on disposals of UK residential property. This charge was further extended from 6 April 2015 but, with effect from 5 July 2016, ceased to apply where the disposal is within the scope of the new corporation tax charge. **[41.151]**

2 Computation of profits

The basic rule is that companies must compute and express their profits and losses and their corporation tax liability in sterling. However, companies that satisfy the relevant conditions must compute the profit or losses of a trade in either the company's accounting currency or its functional currency. That basic profit or loss is then translated into sterling at an appropriate exchange rate. CTA 2010 Part 2 Chapter 4 sets out the conditions that have to be met if a currency other than sterling is to be used: in simple terms the question depends on the currency the accounts are drawn up in and its functional currency. Functional currency is defined in CTA 2010 s 17(4) as the '... currency of the primary economic environment in which the company operates'.

In the past a company's capital gains have had to be computed in sterling, whether or not this was its functional or accounting currency. Provisions in FA 2013 allow companies with a non-sterling functional currency to compute capital gains and losses on certain assets (ships, aircraft, shares or interests in shares) in their functional currency. A corresponding change has been made to the treatment of any loan or derivative used to hedge the foreign exchange risk on the asset. This legislation took effect from 1 September 2013. [41.152]

3 The meaning of 'residence'

Formerly, companies were treated as UK resident and taxed accordingly if their central management and control was situated in the UK. The law developed in a series of cases and where precisely management and control is exercised is a factual question of some difficulty. Generally, of course, such powers will be vested in the board of directors, so that the problem becomes one of identifying where the board exercises its powers (see, for instance, *Untelrab Ltd v McGregor; Unigate Guernsey Ltd v McGregor* (1995)). Two general points should be stressed. *First*, that the overseas country where the company was incorporated is usually of small significance when it is a question of establishing UK residence. *Second*, it is possible under English law for a company to be 'dual resident', ie resident in more than one country.

This residence test is supplemented by an additional test based upon the place of company incorporation. UK incorporated companies will *always* be taxed as UK resident irrespective of where central management and control is exercised. This is subject to the qualification that 'dual resident' companies that would not be regarded as UK resident under the 'tie-breaker' provisions of a double tax treaty are not treated as UK resident. Subject to this qualification, there is now a dual test in operation as a result of which a company will be UK resident if *either* it was incorporated here *or*, in the case of companies incorporated abroad, its central management and control is located here (SP 1/90 sets out HMRC's views on these rules). There are exceptions and transitional provisions for certain companies which were carrying on business before the incorporation test came into effect.

The case of *Wood v Holden* (2006) emphasised that, if an overseas company holds its board meetings outside the UK, *prima facie* the central management and control of the company is outside the UK unless it can be shown that a UK resident 'outsider' had dictated or usurped the powers of the board.

A board acting on the proposals and advice of another (rather than that other dictating the decisions to be taken) is still effectively managing and controlling the company. However, in the later case of *Laerstate BV v R & C Comrs* (2009), the facts were found to show that while the board meetings took place outside the UK, the high-level decisions were not made by the board but were made, predominantly in the UK, by one of the directors. The company's central management and control was therefore in the UK.

The Special Commissioners in *News Datacom Ltd v R & C Comrs* (2006) clarified that, if a company is claiming not to be UK resident, it is not necessary to identify a non-UK territory in which the company is resident. [41.153]

EXAMPLE 41.12

(1) Styx Ltd, a UK incorporated company, was trading on 15 March 1988 (when the supplementary test based on UK incorporation was introduced) and, because its management was located in Liechtenstein, was then treated as non-UK resident. As the transitional period has expired it is now treated as UK resident unless it qualifies for one of the exceptions to the incorporation rule.

(2) Aster Ltd was incorporated in the UK on 31 March 1995 and is managed and controlled from Liechtenstein. It is resident in the UK.

(3) Rambo Ltd is incorporated in Panama and controlled by directors resident and exercising central management and control in the UK. It is resident in the UK.

4 Tax consequences of ceasing to be UK-resident

Subject to the 'tie-breaker' provisions, a UK incorporated company cannot lose its UK residence. In the case of overseas companies, however, if central management and control becomes located elsewhere, UK residence will cease and in that event a tax charge will arise on the unrealised gains of the company immediately prior to its change of residence. TCGA 1992 s 185 deems the company to have disposed of all its assets at market value immediately before it becomes non-resident and to have immediately reacquired them (note that if the tax is not paid within six months from becoming payable it may be collected from other persons: TCGA 1992 s 190). If at any later time the company carries on a trade in the UK through a permanent establishment the deemed disposal does not apply to any assets that are situated in the UK and are used in or for the trade, or are used or held for the permanent establishment.

EXAMPLE 41.13

On 1 August 2017 Rambo Ltd (see *Example 41.12*, above) ceases to be UK resident. At the relevant time it owns chargeable assets worth £200,000 on which its allowable expenditure is £50,000. Immediately before its change in residence it is deemed to sell the assets for £200,000, immediately reacquiring them, and thereby realising a chargeable gain of £150,000 (subject to the indexation allowance) in FY 2017.

The company must inform HMRC in advance of its intention to cease UK residence (TMA 1970 s 109B; see SP 2/90 for the procedure to be followed) and this should be done by notice in writing specifying the time when this change will occur and should include a statement of UK tax payable together with particulars of how that tax is to be paid. The tax in question will include any PAYE for which the company is liable. If such tax remains unpaid for more than six months, it may then be recovered from, *inter alia*, a controlling director or another company in the same group. Failure by the company to comply with the notification procedures before ceasing to be UK resident may lead to a penalty on both the company and certain other persons: the maximum amount payable being equal to the tax unpaid at the time when the company ceased to be resident.

With effect from 11 December 2012, companies which cease to be resident in the UK as a result of a transfer of their place of management to another EU or EEA Member State can opt for deferred payment arrangements in respect of exit charges. [41.154]

5 Taxing resident companies

All profits wherever made by a UK resident company will be charged to corporation tax subject to any available double taxation reliefs and to certain exceptions as mentioned below.

When a trade is to be carried out by a UK company in a foreign country there are three possible methods of operation available.

First, the trade may be with that country so that there is no trading presence within the country and foreign tax is avoided (typically a representative office is established in the foreign country).

Second, a branch may be opened overseas which, from a UK tax point of view, has historically resulted in any profits being subject to corporation tax. It also meant that loss relief would be available. A move to a more territorial basis for taxing the profits of foreign branches was introduced with effect from 19 July 2011 (see CTA 2009 ss 18A–18S), with consequential amendments to other legislation. The effect is to allow a UK resident company to elect for profits and losses of foreign permanent establishments, including gains or losses on the disposal of relevant assets, to be left out of account for UK corporation tax. There is a rule to prevent diversion of profits to low-tax territories. There are also rules to recapture losses which have been offset against other profits before the exemption took effect.

If a foreign branch is incorporated by the formation of a subsidiary company in the foreign jurisdiction it is possible to postpone the payment of UK tax on capital gains that would otherwise result: see TCGA 1992 s 140.

Third, a subsidiary non-resident company may be formed with the result that corporation tax is generally avoided on profits until they are distributed to the UK by way of dividend. The attractions are obviously considerable when the tax rates in the overseas country are low in comparison with those in the UK and there are provisions to prevent tax avoidance by the use of controlled foreign companies (see [41.161]).

Until recently, the UK group relief rules did not permit losses arising in overseas companies to be surrendered to cover profits in UK resident companies. Following the decision in *Marks & Spencer plc v Halsey* at the European Court of Justice, group relief has been extended to allow losses arising in subsidiaries based in the European Economic Area (EEA) to be surrendered against profits of that company's UK parent and the parent's UK subsidiaries in certain circumstances. In particular, it is required that the loss has not been and cannot be relieved in any period in the EEA territory. This change has a very limited scope and does not address a number of other situations (for example group relief between an EEA company and a UK company that have a common parent company which is not resident in the UK). In *Commission v UK* (2015) a challenge to certain aspects of the legislation (the fact that it was not retrospective and the time at which the test relating to relief of losses elsewhere must be satisfied) was unsuccessful. Further changes seem likely following the UK's referendum vote to leave the EU (see also [43.44]). [41.155]

6 Double tax relief

(a) *General principles*

Double tax relief permits the set-off of foreign tax against UK corporation tax on the profits of the branch or distributions from a subsidiary company either by virtue of a double tax treaty with the relevant country (TIOPA 2010 s 6) or by unilateral relief (TIOPA 2010 s 9). It may be noted that double tax relief for companies has become less significant as many distributions and overseas branches are now exempt from UK tax (see [41.46]). [41.156]

EXAMPLE 41.14

	£
UK profits	2,000,000
Overseas branch profit (income and gains)	80,000
(overseas tax paid £25,000)	
	£2,080,000
Corporation tax (19%)	395,200
less relief (restricted)	15,200
UK tax payable	£380,000

Notes:
(1) At its simplest double tax relief cannot exceed the amount of corporation tax attributable to the foreign income or gains; hence the maximum relief in this example is 19% of £80,000 = £15,200.
(2) Double tax relief became substantially more complex following changes made in FA 2000 and FA 2001 to deal with perceived abuse of mixer companies (see [41.159]).

(b) *Double tax agreements*

A large number of bilateral agreements are currently in place. Under these arrangements, certain classes of income derived from the participating countries are given complete exemption from income and capital gains taxes in the country from which they arise. In other cases relief from UK taxation is generally given in the form of a credit, calculated by reference to the foreign tax suffered. The credit is set against the UK tax chargeable on the doubly taxed income or gain.

Where double tax relief applies no deduction for foreign tax is generally allowed in assessing the foreign income or gain. If, however, a taxpayer does not take the credit allowable by an agreement, any foreign tax paid on that income, in the place where it arises, is deductible from the income for purposes of the UK tax assessment. Double tax agreements normally contain a 'mutual agreement procedure' that enables a taxpayer to present his case to the competent authority in his state of residence if he considers that the action of a tax authority has resulted, or will result, in taxation not in accordance with the agreement. The UK competent authority is HMRC. **[41.157]**

(c) *Unilateral relief*

Where tax on overseas income is not relieved, or is only partly relieved, under an agreement, unilateral relief will normally apply.

The mechanics and limits are substantially the same as those under which the bilateral agreements operate. **[41.158]**

(d) *Double tax relief and mixer companies*

Example 41.15 illustrates the use of the credit method of giving double tax relief. Much of the foreign tax relieved in the UK is underlying tax, ie tax paid on the profits out of which a foreign company pays a dividend. The purpose of a mixer company was to mix (or average out) foreign taxes paid in different countries to set against the UK tax charged on the single dividend that was paid out of the mixer company.

EXAMPLE 41.15

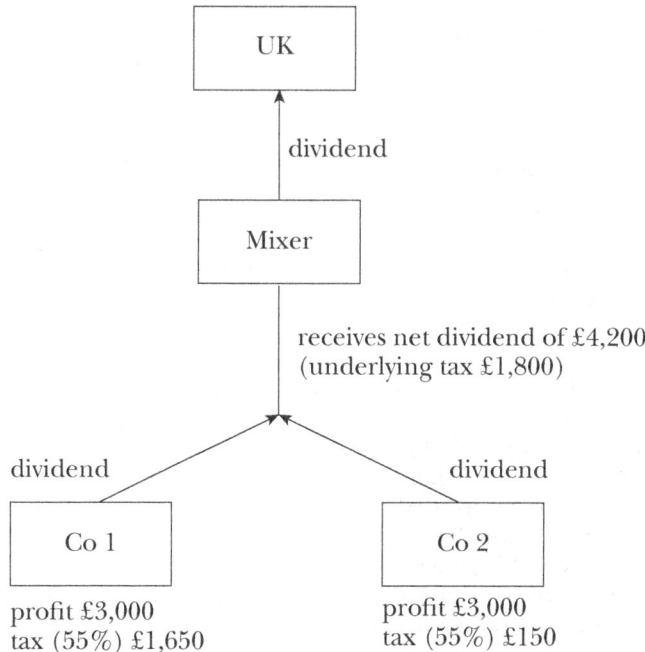

Corporation tax

Notes:

		£
(1)	Dividend paid to UK parent	4,200
	Underlying tax	1,800
		6,000
	UK corporation tax (say 30%)	1,800
	Credit for foreign tax (restricted to maximum UK corporation tax payable)	1,800
	Tax payable	Nil

(2) If Co 1 had been directly owned by the UK company only 900 of the foreign tax suffered would have been relieved (*viz* 30% × £3,000).

In FA 2000 the Government restricted the use of mixer companies by introducing provisions to eliminate the tax advantage of routing overseas dividends through mixer companies in favourable foreign jurisdictions (such as the Netherlands). This applies to claims for credit relief made on or after 31 March 2001. The restriction applies to the relievable underlying tax in respect of any dividend paid up through an overseas subsidiary. Relief for underlying tax is generally restricted to the full corporation tax rate in force when the dividend is paid. However, a partial relief from this capping restriction is provided by the concurrent introduction of a system of 'onshore pooling' of certain foreign dividends. In such cases, relief is available up to a maximum of 45% in total. Relief may similarly be obtained up to the same overall 45% limit for unrelieved withholding and underlying tax on dividends received directly from overseas subsidiaries. The two main exclusions from the onshore pool are dividends paid by controlled foreign companies to satisfy the acceptable distribution policy test (see **[41.161]**), or dividends representing such dividends, and dividends for which relief is itself restricted.

[41.159]–[41.160]

7 Controlled foreign companies (CFCs): TIOPA 2010 Part 9A

This legislation enables HMRC to tax UK companies on profits made by certain overseas corporations. Chargeable profits of the overseas entity are apportioned to those with an interest in the CFC and a UK resident company holding, with connected persons and associates, at least a 25% interest in the CFC will be assessed on its apportioned share of the profits. The provisions only apply if the CFC is under UK control and is resident in a 'low tax' area, defined as one where the tax is less than three-quarters of what would have been charged in the UK. 'Under UK control' for these purposes includes cases where a company is controlled jointly by a UK resident person and a foreign resident person and each of them has at least 40%, but not more than 55%, of their joint controlling interest (the test is aimed at joint ventures). There is a low profits exemption which applies if accounting profits or assumed taxable profits do not exceed £50,000 or if either of these does not exceed £500,000 and the amount representing non-trading income does not exceed £50,000 (these thresholds are reduced if the period is less than a full year). The provisions do not cover chargeable gains which may, however, be apportioned amongst UK shareholders under TCGA 1992 s 13 when the overseas company is one which would be close under UK rules.

In their original form these provisions applied to controlled foreign companies generally, but subject to various exemptions which were designed to ensure that the charge would only arise where a CFC was used with the object of avoiding tax and to exclude CFCs that were pursuing an 'acceptable distribution policy', or that carried on 'exempt activities'. So far as the former is concerned, companies had to distribute 90% of their taxable profits less capital gains and foreign tax in order for the company to be pursuing an acceptable distribution policy. So far as the exempt activities test is concerned, the rules restricted the use of intra-group service companies and limited the cases where an overseas holding company qualified for exemption.

The decision of the ECJ in *Cadbury Schweppes* (Case C-196/04) indicated that the UK CFC rules were, to an extent, incompatible with EU law. Essentially, an EU subsidiary of a UK company should not be subject to the UK CFC rules even if the establishment of that company was done explicitly to benefit from more favourable tax rates. This basic position, however, could be overridden if the overseas company had no real substance in the overseas territory, ie it had no proper establishment there, its services were not actually performed there or the services performed by the company had no real value such that the profits arising in that company did not reflect the commercial reality. New legislation was introduced with effect from 6 December 2006 that applied to subsidiaries of UK companies which were subject to an apportionment under the CFC rules and had a business establishment in an EEA territory. The rules excluded from any CFC apportionment profits representing the net economic value of work carried out by individuals working for the CFC in business establishments in other EEA territories.

In June 2007 the Government published a discussion document on the taxation of foreign profits of companies, which included proposals for a radical reform of the CFC rules. Following further consultation, substantial changes to the CFC rules were introduced in FA 2009 Sch 16 as part of the 'foreign profits package' (see **[41.98]**). The effect of these was to remove the exemption for companies pursuing an acceptable distribution policy and to remove the exempt activities exemption from companies other than local holding companies. The post-election Budget in June 2010 announced that new CFC rules were to be legislated in spring 2012. As a first step, consultation took place in the summer of 2010 on interim improvements which were included in FA 2011 and applied to accounting periods beginning on or after 1 January 2011. These included exemptions for companies with a limited UK connection and an alternative *de minimis* exemption threshold based on accounting profits rather than a UK tax calculation.

A completely revised scheme of legislation in respect of controlled foreign companies was introduced by FA 2012 and applies for accounting periods commencing on or after 1 January 2013. The legislation is contained in new Part 9A of TIOPA 2010. It introduces the concept of a 'CFC charge gateway' through which profits of a CFC must pass in order to be chargeable profits. Depending on whether certain initial criteria are satisfied, profits are considered for the purposes of the gateway if they are attributable to UK activities, if they are finance profits (trading or non-trading), if they derive from captive insurance business or in a case involving solo consolidation (an arrangement whereby an unregulated subsidiary is treated for regulatory purposes as if it were a division of a regulated company). There are exemptions for companies which are newly under UK control, for companies carrying on business in excluded territories, and for companies with low profits or low profit margins. There is also an exemption for finance profits arising from intra-group loan relationships, which may cover 75% of the profits or may exempt the whole amount to the extent that the loan is funded out of resources derived from the ultimate debtor's territory of residence. With effect from 5 December 2013, this exemption does not apply where there are arrangements whose main purpose is to divert non-trading finance profits from a UK-resident company to a CFC.

Under corporate self-assessment, companies need to have in place systems which will allow them to collect all information necessary to decide whether the CFC legislation will apply because if so, the company must account for any tax due. [41.161]

8 Taxing non-UK resident companies

Companies not resident in the UK are subject to corporation tax on income arising from a trade carried on in the UK through a permanent establishment. The crucial factor in establishing a liability to UK tax is, therefore, whether a trade is carried on within the UK or not (see further **Chapter 18**). Other income arising from a UK source may be charged to income tax in the non-resident company's hands (CTA 2009 s 3, but see also [**41.151**]). Hence, a property investment company with no permanent establishment in the UK, but owning land in the UK, would be subject to income tax on the profits arising from that land (but not on profits arising from a disposal where this is within the charge to corporation tax as explained in [**41.151**]).

Capital gains are chargeable only if they arise from property associated with the trade carried on by the permanent establishment (CTA 2009 s 19(3); TCGA 1992 s 10B). In the case, therefore, of a non-resident property company owning land in the UK, no chargeable gain will arise on a disposal of its capital assets (for exceptions to this see [**27.111**]). A UK resident subsidiary of an overseas company is a separate legal entity from the overseas company and will be subject to UK tax on its worldwide income. If a UK permanent establishment is transferred to a UK resident company in the same worldwide group as the transferor company the transfer falls within the capital gains group rules (TCGA 1992 s 171).

In his Autumn Statement in November 2016, the Chancellor announced that the government was considering bringing all companies receiving taxable income from the UK into the corporation tax regime. A consultation document, issued in March 2017, set out a more limited proposal which would apply only to property and trading income and indicated that the government would respond to the consultation in the Autumn. [41.162]

9 Taxing non-resident shareholders of resident companies

The tax credit and FII provisions for periods before 6 April 2016 only applied to a resident shareholder. Therefore, a non-resident was not (subject to the provisions of a double tax treaty) entitled to any tax credit. The non-resident is not liable to income tax on the dividend (ITA 2007 ss 811–814). **[41.163]**

10 Diverted Profits Tax

An entirely new tax called Diverted Profits Tax was introduced with effect from 1 April 2015. This is charged at a rate of 25% (55% for ring fence profits) and applies in two separate sets of circumstances: where non-UK resident companies have diverted profits from the UK by avoiding a taxable presence, and where UK-resident companies have diverted profits from the UK by the use of entities or transactions lacking economic substance. Credit may be given for UK or foreign tax paid on the same profits. Companies are required to notify HMRC within three months of the end of the accounting period if they are potentially liable and HMRC may then issue a preliminary notice which allows the company the opportunity to make representations. HMRC may then issue a charging notice and any liability must be paid within 30 days. Unusually, there is no immediate right of appeal against the notice. Instead, the legislation provides for a 12-month review period during which HMRC may reduce the amount charged or issue a supplementary charging notice. Following the review period, the company has 30 days in which it can appeal against the original and any supplementary charging notice. The tax charged remains payable notwithstanding the appeal.

The rules are extremely complex and their practical impact (and interaction with other tax liabilities and with double taxation agreements) is not yet clear. The rate of tax is higher than the corporation tax rate and is clearly intended to have a deterrent effect. **[41.164]–[41.180]**

VII CORPORATE SELF-ASSESSMENT

1 Introduction

Self-assessment for companies was introduced for accounting periods ending on or after 1 July 1999 (see FA 1998 s 117 and Schs 18 and 19). **[41.181]**

2 The operation of corporate self-assessment

a) *Payment of tax and filing returns*

Since the introduction of Corporation Tax Self Assessment in 1999, HMRC no longer issues assessments of the company's tax liability. The tax return itself must include a self-assessment of the tax payable for that accounting period based upon the information contained in the return and taking into account any claims for relief or allowances. The self-assessment must include any sums due under eg CTA 2010 s 455, the transfer pricing and the CFC legislation. In addition, it is necessary for the return to contain details of any tax 'schemes' that need to be disclosed under the Tax Avoidance Schemes (Information) Regulations introduced in FA 2004.

In general, the company's taxable profits will automatically be determined on the basis of the self-assessment. HMRC may, by notice to the company, correct a return or make an amendment to a return for obvious errors or omissions within certain time periods. HMRC is also entitled to 'enquire' into the return and if it does so the taxable profits will be determined at the end of the enquiry.

The filing deadline for the corporation tax return is normally 12 months after the end of the period to which the return relates. When filing the return the company must deliver computations showing how the figures in the return were calculated and a copy of its audited accounts for the period. Company tax returns for periods ending after 31 March 2010 must be submitted online in Inline XBRL format.

Claims for group relief, capital allowances and certain tax credits must be made through the completed tax return. Under corporate self-assessment, the rules provide that claims and consents to the surrender of group relief can no longer be amended but must formally be withdrawn and replaced, if appropriate, by a new claim.

The requirement to make a return is not automatic. A company is only required to make a return if a notice to that effect is sent to it. However, a company that is liable to pay corporation tax in respect of an accounting period must notify HMRC of this fact within 12 months of the end of that accounting period. Furthermore, the company must pay its estimated corporation tax liability by the normal due date.

FA 2004 s 55 introduced a requirement for companies to notify HMRC (within three months) of the beginning of its first accounting period, and of the beginning of any subsequent accounting period that does not immediately follow the end of a previous accounting period. Although this requirement remains in effect, the penalty for non-compliance was abolished with effect from 1 April 2010.

In December 2015, the government published a 'roadmap' for 'Making Tax Digital', outlining proposals which would transform the tax compliance of most businesses and companies. This was followed by a series of more detailed consultation documents from HMRC in August 2016. Under these proposals, businesses would be required to provide HMRC with quarterly updates and to submit an 'End of Period statement' following the year or period end, effectively replacing the existing tax return. Although the proposed timetable would mean that corporation tax would be brought within the scope of this reform by 2020, the consultation to date has focused mainly on income tax, and detailed proposals for companies are still awaited. **[41.182]**

b) *Interest*

Although tax returns need not be filed until 12 months after the end of the relevant accounting period, the normal due date for payment of corporation tax remains. For most companies this will be nine months after the end of the accounting period. Large companies (as defined by SI 1998/3175) may have obligations under the quarterly payments system (see **[41.185]**). Interest will run as from the date for payment if the tax has not been paid. Interest on any overpayment or underpayment will also be calculated from the due date. Not surprisingly, the interest on overpayments will not be as high as the interest on underpayments, and the rates of interest are closely linked to market rates.

[41.183]

c) *Late and incorrect returns (FA 1998 Sch18 paras 17–20)*

If a completed return is not delivered to HMRC within the 12-month period, the following rapidly escalating penalties are automatically imposed:

Return filed within 12 months	:	no penalty
Return filed within 15 months	:	£100
Return filed within 18 months	:	£200
Return filed within 24 months	:	£200 + 10% of unpaid tax
Return filed outside 24 months	:	£200 + 20% of unpaid tax

Companies which are guilty of persistent failure to make returns are subject to more severe penalties since, if a penalty has been levied in respect of both of the two previous accounting periods, and the return for the third period is also late, the flat rate penalties become £500 (instead of £100) and £1,000 (instead of £200). FA 2007 introduced a new system of penalties for incorrect returns in which the amount of penalty is explicitly linked to the behaviour leading to the error and to the quality of disclosure by the company. This applies to returns which are due after 31 March 2009 in respect of periods commencing after 31 March 2008. FA 2008 provides for a similar system of penalties for failure to give notice of chargeability to corporation tax. A new system of penalties for late returns and late payment of tax, covering multiple taxes, is contained in FA 2009 Sch 55 and 56 and was to take effect for corporation tax from a date to be announced. It is now unclear whether this will ever happen, since options for a revised penalty system arising from the 'Making Tax Digital' proposals were outlined in a consultation document issued in March 2017. **[41.184]**

EXAMPLE 41.17

A Ltd makes up its accounts to 31 October each year. Its corporation tax return for the year ended 31 October 2013 is submitted on:
(1)   15 November 2014; or
(2)   15 March 2015; or
(3)   15 January 2016: no tax was unpaid on 1 May 2015; or
(4)   15 January 2016: £1,000 tax was unpaid on 1 May 2015, but was paid by 10 June 2015.

The penalties levied under each of these alternatives are:
(1)   £100 (£500 if the returns for the previous two accounting periods were also late);
(2)   £200 (£1,000 if the returns for the previous two accounting periods were also late);
(3)   £200 (or £1,000 – no tax-related penalty is due);
(4)   £400 (or £1,200 – a tax-related penalty (20% × £1,000) is added to the flat rate penalty).

For the purposes of calculating penalties, 'unpaid tax' means the amount owing after 18 months, account being taken of credit for income tax withheld.

d) *Quarterly payments*

For accounting periods ending on or after 1 July 1999 large companies have to pay their corporation tax in instalments calculated according to their anticipated final tax bill for the current period. A large company is a company whose taxable profits in any accounting period exceed £1,500,000. The regulations provide, however, that a company is not a large company for the purposes of the quarterly payment regulations if its total tax liability for the accounting period does not exceed £10,000. There is a further exclusion in circumstances where the profits for the period do not exceed £10m and the company was not a large company in the 12 months preceding the accounting period. The idea is that companies within the new payment system are those which have sophisticated accounting and administrative systems in place already that can handle the quarterly payment charge quite easily. In determining whether a company is large or not any related 51% group companies (associated companies for periods beginning before 1 April 2015) must be taken into account. The £1,500,000 limit and the £10m profit limit are reduced by dividing them by the number of companies in the group. The *de minimis* exclusion where the total liability does not exceed £10,000 continues to apply. All the above limits are reduced proportionately for periods of less than one year.

In the case of a large company with a 12-month accounting period the payment dates for corporation tax are as follows:
(1) six months and 14 days from the start of the accounting period;
(2) nine months and 14 days from the start of the accounting period;
(3) 14 days after the end of the accounting period;
(4) three months and 14 days from the end of the accounting period.

There are provisions for HMRC to repay tax to a company which believes that it has over-estimated the instalments which become due. Interest is payable on late paid instalments and HMRC will pay interest on overpaid tax.

For accounting periods commencing on or after 1 April 2019, these payments are to be brought forward by four months in the case of companies with profits in excess of £20 million (divided by the number of group companies where appropriate), so that all instalments are payable before the end of the year to which they relate. [41.185]

e) *Duties of senior accounting officers*

FA 2009 Sch 46 introduced a new obligation for senior accounting officers of 'qualifying' companies, applying to financial periods of such companies commencing on or after 21 July 2009. The definition of 'qualifying company' broadly extends to companies incorporated under the UK Companies Acts where the aggregate turnover of all such companies within the same group exceeds £200m or their aggregate balance sheet total exceeds £2bn. The senior accounting officer is required to take reasonable steps to ensure that the company establishes and maintains appropriate tax accounting arrangements, ie arrangements that enable the company's 'relevant liabilities' (ie liabilities to specified UK taxes and duties) to be calculated accurately in all material respects. For each financial year of the company, the senior accounting officer must provide HMRC with a certificate stating whether such arrangements were in place throughout the year and explaining any shortcomings. A penalty of £5,000 can be imposed on the senior accounting officer for failing to take such steps, for failing to give the required certificate or for giving a certificate that includes a careless or deliberate inaccuracy. In addition, the company is liable to a penalty of £5,000 if it fails to ensure that HMRC is notified of the name of the senior accounting officer. There are provisions to prevent multiple penalties from arising where the same individual is the senior accounting officer for more than one company in a group. [41.186]

3 **Anti-avoidance: company purchase schemes**

When the ownership of a company changes hands and that company fails to pay corporation tax for any period before the date of the change, the tax may be assessed on any person who had control of the company before the change (or any company which that person controlled: see CTA 2010 Part 14 Chapter 6, TA 1988 s 767A and s 767B). The relevant circumstances are similar to those which apply in relation to carry forward losses under CTA 2010 s 674 (see **[41.65]**) and typically involve the vendor first stripping out trading assets to another group company then selling the company to a purchaser who leaves the company unable to pay its tax liabilities. Accordingly, great care needs to be exercised in structuring sales of companies and in drafting suitable tax indemnities. [41.187]

42 Company distributions and shareholders

Updated by Stephen Whitehead, KPMG LLP (UK)

I   Meaning of a distribution (CTA 2010 Part 23 Chapters 2 and 3) **[42.1]**
II Distributions and company buy-backs **[42.21]**
III Taxation of 'qualifying distributions' **[42.41]**
IV Taxation of individuals (and charities) who receive distributions **[42.76]**
V   Taxation of other persons who receive distributions **[42.91]**
VI Taxation of 'non-qualifying' distributions **[42.121]**
VII Exempt distributions and scrip dividends **[42.141]**

I MEANING OF A DISTRIBUTION (CTA 2010 PART 23 CHAPTERS 2 AND 3)

The term 'distribution' is widely defined to cover not only the payment of dividends but any method of transferring the company's profits to its members.

For the company, a distribution is not deductible in arriving at its profits for corporation tax: distributions are made out of profits after tax.

For individual shareholders the amount of the distribution (including the associated tax credit up to 5 April 2016) is treated as income falling under Schedule F until 5 April 2005 and as savings and investment income under ITTOIA 2005 Part 4 thereafter.

Distributions received by corporate shareholders, together with the accompanying tax credit, were referred to in the legislation for periods up to 5 April 2016 as 'franked investment income' (FII). Thereafter, where distributions need to be taken into account for some corporation tax purpose (for example, in calculating small company relief for ring fence profits (see **[41.24]**)), they are known by the slightly less elegant term 'exempt ABGH distributions'. **[42.1]**

The intention is to catch not merely the payment of profits to shareholders in the form of a dividend, but all payments and transfers by a company to its members other than repayment of capital subscribed, including the purchase by the company of its own shares (see **[42.21]**); other examples are discussed below. **[42.2]**

1 **Any distribution out of the assets of the company which is made in respect of shares except in so far as it is a repayment of capital or equal to any new consideration received (CTA 2010 s 1000(1)B)**

When sums are returned to shareholders on a reduction of capital, they will not be treated as distributions provided that they do not exceed the original amount subscribed (including any premium paid on the allotment of the shares). Payments to members on a winding up are expressly excluded from the definition of a distribution (such sums will usually be liable to CGT in the hands of the shareholders). The issue of bonus shares is not itself a distribution, but a repayment of share capital in the following ten years will be a distribution up to the amount paid up on the bonus issue: see CTA 2010 s 1026; see also [42.4]). [42.3]

EXAMPLE 42.1

U Ltd has a share capital of 100 ordinary £1 shares. It makes a 1:1 bonus issue by capitalising £100 of reserves. Later it repays the shareholders 50p per share on a reduction of capital. Each shareholder is treated as receiving a distribution on the reduction in capital.

Position of a shareholder: Originally, he owned one £1 share. After the bonus issue, he owns two £1 shares. After the reduction in capital, he owns two 50p shares and has £1 in cash. The shareholder is in the same position as if he had received a £1 dividend and is taxed as such.

2 **A reduction of share capital followed by a bonus issue (CTA 2010 s 1022)**

Essentially, this is the same operation as described at [42.3] but in a different order and it has similar taxation consequences. These consequences will not follow if the gap between repayment and the bonus issue exceeds ten years providing the bonus issue is not of redeemable shares and the company is not a relevant company within CTA 2010 s 729. In addition, the bonus issue cannot be regarded as a distribution if the repaid share capital consisted of fully paid preference shares. [42.4]

EXAMPLE 42.2

U Ltd has a share capital of 100 £1 shares. It makes a reduction of share capital by repaying 50p per share. It then issues 100 50p bonus shares (ie a 1:1 issue).

Position of a shareholder: originally, he held one £1 share. After the repayment of capital, he owns one 50p share and has 50p in cash. After the bonus issue, he owns two 50p shares and has received 50p in cash. Hence, he has shares of identical aggregate par value to the one share held at the start and has received a 50p payment from the company which will be treated as a distribution.

3 **The issue of bonus redeemable shares and securities (CTA 2010 s 1000(1)C–D)**

A bonus issue of redeemable shares (ie shares which the company has express authority or an obligation to redeem in the future) and of securities is a distribution. Unlike the other types of distribution, this was, until 5 April 2016, a '*non-qualifying*' distribution. With effect from 6 April 2016, this terminology has been abandoned and this type of distribution is referred to as a '*CD distribution*'. The taxation consequences of such distributions are considered at [**42.121**]. It should be noted that the company is not, at the time of the distribution, paying out money to shareholders, but is entering into a commitment to do so in the future. The value of the distribution will, in the case of shares, be the nominal value together with any premium payable on redemption. In the case of other securities, it will be the amount secured together with any premium payable on redemption. When redeemable shares and securities are redeemed, the redemption would normally be a qualifying distribution, until 5 April 2016, and thereafter a '*non-CD distribution*'. [**42.5**]

4   **A transfer by a company to its members of assets or liabilities which are worth more than any new consideration furnished by the member (CTA 2010 s 1020)**

The excess of the value of any assets or liabilities transferred by a company to its members over any new consideration furnished by the members is a distribution. [**42.6**]

EXAMPLE 42.3

John is a member of J Ltd. He sells his house to J Ltd for £200,000 when the market value of the house is only £150,000. The excess £50,000 value will be taxed as a distribution in his hands.

5   **Certain interest payments (see generally CTM 15500 et seq)**

Interest payments geared to the profits of the company (irrespective of the reasonableness of the rate) or excessive interest (that which exceeds a reasonable commercial return) may be treated as distributions by CTA 2010 s 1000(1)E–F. Interest payments on bonus securities and on securities that are convertible whether directly or indirectly into shares in the company (unless listed on a recognised stock exchange) are distributions. These rules do not apply if the payment is to another company within the charge to corporation tax, except to the extent that the interest exceeds a reasonable commercial return (and subject to certain other exceptions).

For the position of interest paid by one company to an associated or connected party (UK or overseas) see the transfer pricing rules in TIOPA 2010 Part 4 discussed at [**41.44**]. [**42.7**]

EXAMPLE 42.4

Zee Ltd borrows £50,000 from Con at a rate of interest of 10% pa. A reasonable commercial rate would be 6%. The company pays £5,000 pa to Con of which £3,000 is deductible from profits for corporation tax purposes. The excess (£2,000 pa) is a distribution on which Con will be taxed as savings and investment income under ITTOIA 2005 Part 4.

The intention of this provision is to prevent equity investment being artificially characterised as a loan in order to obtain corporation tax relief on the payment of the interest. It does not catch 'ratchet loans': *viz* commercial loans with interest rates linked to profit so that the rate of interest reduces as business profits improve (or conversely the rate increases as business results deteriorate): see CTA 2010 s 1017(1).

6 'Equity notes'

Equity notes are perpetual debt instruments issued by UK resident companies. The term itself is defined in CTA 2010 s 1016. A typical illustration is a security with no fixed date for redemption. The UK formerly taxed payments under the instrument as 'interest' but the above provisions now reclassify such payments as distributions. Holding companies chargeable to UK corporation tax are generally unaffected (CTA 2010 s 1032). [42.8]

7 The stock dividend option (see CTM 17005)

ITTOIA 2005 s 410(2) provides that where shares are offered to shareholders instead of a cash dividend, those shares will be treated as income in the shareholders' hands (see further [42.150] for a consideration of the enhanced stock dividend). [42.9]

8 Special rules for close companies

Where a close company provides a benefit for a participator the cost of providing the benefit is treated as a distribution: see CTA 2010 s 1064 and [41.127]. [42.10]–[42.20]

II DISTRIBUTIONS AND COMPANY BUY-BACKS

The Companies Act 2006 Part 18 (before 1 October 2009, Companies Act 1985 ss 159–181) allows companies to purchase their own shares. Generally, such purchases must be paid for out of distributable profits, but private companies may use the proceeds of a fresh issue of capital. Any payment to a shareholder in excess of the sum originally subscribed on the allotment of the shares is treated as a distribution, unless the repayment occurs on a winding up of the company. CTA 2010 s 1033 provides that, where certain conditions are satisfied, a purchase by a company of its own shares will *not* be treated as a distribution so that any profit made will be within the scope of capital gains tax. If the conditions of s 1033 are not satisfied the buy-back will be treated as a distribution. The conditions are as follows. [42.21]

1 The company

The company must be unquoted: that is to say, its shares must not be listed on the official list of a stock exchange but its shares may be dealt in on AIM. It must be either a trading company or the holding company of a trading group. A trading group is a group, the business of whose members taken together consists wholly or mainly of the carrying on of one or more trades. [42.22]

2 The vendor of the shares

a) *Qualifying vendors*

The vendor may be an individual, a trustee, the PR of a deceased shareholder, or a company. He must be resident and, if an individual, ordinarily resident in the UK throughout the tax year. Normally, the shares must have been owned for the whole of the five years ending with the transfer and it is not possible to aggregate different ownership periods. Accordingly, where assets are transferred to a trust or distributed by trustees to a beneficiary, the transferor must satisfy the five-year period. In the exceptional cases of husband/wife and of the deceased/his PRs and legatees, aggregation is permissible and in the latter case the aggregated ownership period need only be three years.

[42.23]

b) *The 'substantial reduction' test*

The vendor must 'substantially reduce' his shareholding which means that his interest in the company must go down by at least 25%. In determining whether a substantial reduction has been achieved it should be remembered that shares bought back by the company are normally treated as cancelled (see Companies Act 2006 ss 688, 706; Companies Act 1985 s 160(4))). [42.24]

EXAMPLE 42.5

A Ltd has 100 shares in issue held by:

A	40
B	30
C	20
D	10
	100

A Ltd buys back 10 of A's shares. A will then have 30 shares compared with the 40 shares he previously owned, which looks like a 25% reduction in his shareholding. However, when his 10 shares are purchased by A Ltd they are cancelled and the issued share capital is reduced to 90; A's shares therefore represent a 33.33% holding which is more than 75% of his previous holding. This will not satisfy the substantial reduction test.

For A to satisfy the substantial reduction test he would need to sell at least 15 shares so that his holding is reduced to 25 shares out of a total of 85: a 29.4% holding which is less than 75% of his previous holding of 40%.

c) *The 'connected' test*

After the purchase the vendor must not be 'connected' with the acquiring company (CTA 2010 s 1042(1)). For this purpose 'connected' means holding more than 30% of the company's:
(1) issued ordinary share capital;
(2) share and loan capital (loan capital is widely defined in CTA 2010 s 1063(1) to include, eg, a director's loan account); or
(3) voting power. [42.25]

d) *Other matters*

In calculating these fractions, spouses and associates are treated as one person. As any transactions in the same shares within 12 months of the sale will form part of the same transaction, it follows that replacement shares must not be acquired within a period of one year. [42.26]

3 **The reason for the sale**

There are two permissible reasons. First, the purchase by the company must benefit its trade (or that of a 75% subsidiary) and not be part of a scheme designed to enable the shareholders to participate in the company's profits without receiving a dividend or otherwise to avoid tax. The requirement that the purchase must be a 'benefit to the trade' is not an easy test to satisfy. For instance, the buying out of dissident shareholders is certainly for the benefit of the company but that is not necessarily the same as being for the benefit of the trade – unless it can be shown that the continued dissension was harming the management and therefore the trade of the company (contrast the position if money was needed urgently by the vendor, eg to fund a divorce settlement). In practice, HMRC has stated (see SP 2/82) that it will expect the requirement to be satisfied in such cases and where the vendor shareholder is genuinely giving up his entire interest in the company.

EXAMPLE 42.6
(1) It is proposed that WW Ltd (an unquoted trading company) purchases the shares of Mr Wam, one of the original founders of the company. He is willing to sell a 60% holding but wishes to keep a small (5%) holding for sentimental reasons. Mr Wam is retiring in favour of a new management team. On HMRC practice the transaction would be regarded as for the benefit of the trade of WW Ltd and, the other conditions being satisfied, the payment for the shares will not be a distribution.
(2) Sal is the sole shareholder in Sal Ltd, an unquoted trading company. Profits amount to £100,000 for the present accounting period and Sal Ltd plans to use them to purchase 50% of Sal's shares. This proposal will not be within the provisions of CTA 2010 s 1033 because:
    (i) it would appear to be a scheme designed to pass the profits to Sal without declaring a dividend;
    (ii) Sal is not substantially reducing her holding since she will still own all the shares in Sal Ltd;
    (iii) the purchase is not for the benefit of Sal Ltd's trade.

The second permitted reason for the sale of the shares is where the whole, or substantially the whole, of the proceeds of sale are to be used by the recipient in discharging his IHT liability charged on a death. The money must be so used within two years of death and it has to be shown that the IHT cannot be paid without undue hardship unless the shares are sold back to the company. In this case the above requirements as to the vendor of the shares do not apply. The IHT need not be due in respect of the shares. [42.27]

EXAMPLE 42.7

(1) Sam inherits the family residence on his father's death. Under the terms of the will it is to bear its own IHT which can be raised by the sale of Sam's shareholding in Sham Ltd (a trading company which is not listed). The only alternative would involve the sale of the family house. If the shares are sold to Sham Ltd, the purchase money will not be treated as a distribution.

(2) Sue inherits 30% of the share capital of Carruthers Ltd. She does not want the shares and arranges for the company to buy them back. Although this arrangement falls outside the relief for hardship on a death, there will be no distribution since such a payment will be for the benefit of the trade (see SP 2/82).

4 Position if the vendor is a UK company

If the vendor of the shares is a UK company and the payment is not treated as a distribution, it will be taxed as a chargeable gain in the ordinary way.

If the payment does not satisfy the s 1033 requirements it will be treated as a distribution in the hands of the vendor company. In the past, distributions were generally not liable to corporation tax by reason of CTA 2009 s 1285 and its predecessor, TA 1988 s 208 which read:

> 'Except as otherwise provided by the Corporation Tax Acts, corporation tax shall not be chargeable on dividends and other distributions of a company resident in the UK nor shall any such dividends or distributions be taken into account in computing income for corporation tax.'

Accordingly it might have seemed to be attractive for a company to arrange for a disposal of shares by means of a buy-back falling outside what is now CTA 2010 s 1033 (formerly TA 1988 s 219) so that the proceeds would escape all taxation.

HMRC took the view (see SP 4/89) that the proceeds could still be brought into charge to tax on chargeable gains. It said that TA 1988 s 208 had nothing to do with capital gains and merely excluded the distribution from a charge to tax as income. It did not exempt the distribution from tax as a chargeable gain. Although TCGA 1992 s 37 excludes from the computation of a capital gain amounts actually taxed as income, the receipt was not taxed as income and there was nothing to prevent it being charged as a capital gain.

This Statement of Practice attracted immediate criticism (see *Taxation*, 21 September 1989) and remained controversial until the decision of the Court of Appeal in *Strand Options and Futures Ltd v Vojak* (2003) which upheld HMRC's position. For good measure, the point was dealt with explicitly in CTA 2009 s 1285(3). With effect from 1 July 2009 s 1285 is replaced by Part 9A of CTA 2009 (see **[42.91]**), under which the exemption, where it applies, relates only to the charge to corporation tax on income. Further legislation to clarify the situation under both the old and the new system of dividend taxation was included in F(No 3)A 2010 Sch 3. The effect of this is to preserve capital gains treatment for distributions arising on transactions such as share buy-backs, while ensuring that the exemption applies to other distributions which are capital in nature including distributions out of reserves arising from a reduction in share capital.   **[42.28]**

EXAMPLE 42.8

KP Ltd owns 500 shares in SJ Ltd for which it subscribed £1 each in March 1988. SJ Ltd buys the shares back for £10 each in June 2017.

(1) If the purchase is within CTA 1988 s 1033 KP Ltd's tax position would be as follows:

	£
Sale proceeds for CGT purposes	5,000
Less: price paid by SJ Ltd	500
Capital gain (ignoring indexation)	£4,500

(2) If the purchase is outside s 219, and treated as a distribution, the distribution would not be taxed as income but it would be brought into charge to capital gains tax in the same way.

5 Advantages if the distribution rules apply

When the distribution rules apply, it is only the excess of the purchase proceeds over the amount originally subscribed for the shares that is treated as a distribution. As the sum treated as a distribution must then be ignored in calculating the individual vendor's CGT position (see TCGA 1992 s 37(1)), it is possible for him to make a CGT loss whilst selling the shares at a profit.

EXAMPLE 42.9

Risker subscribed for 50 shares in BB Ltd at par value of £1 per share. He sold the shares two years ago to Tusker for £500 and BB Ltd has now bought back the shares for £950. Assuming that the sale is taxed as a distribution Tusker's tax position is as follows:

a) Income tax	£
Total consideration received	950
Net distribution subject to income tax (950 – 50)	900
b) CGT	£
Sale proceeds	950
Less: charged to income tax	900
	50
Less: price paid by Tusker	500
CGT loss	(£450)

Note:
There is a distribution to the extent that the sale proceeds exceed the sum originally subscribed for the shares (ie the sum paid by Risker).

Entrepreneurs' relief should also be taken into account where available as it can make a substantial difference to the tax payable. **[42.29]**

(2) there is shadow ACT of £10,000 (25% of £40,000) on account of its dividend payments;
(3) the effect is to restrict the set-off of past surplus advance corporation tax to £14,000 (£24,000 less £10,000); and
(4) its corporation tax liability is therefore reduced by £14,000, as is the figure for past surplus ACT carried forward to the next accounting period.

A group cannot use surplus ACT in any company in the group until a home has been found within the group for the notional offset of all shadow ACT generated by that group. **[42.48]**

Notes:

(1) Companies used to suffer corporation tax to the extent that dividends had been paid. With the abolition of ACT there is no minimum tax bill.
(2) A company paying no corporation tax could still pass tax credits to its shareholders if it paid a dividend before 6 April 2016.
(3) A company with no taxable income can fund itself as efficiently by shares (probably preference shares) as by debt. **[42.49]–[42.75]**

IV TAXATION OF INDIVIDUALS (AND CHARITIES) WHO RECEIVE DISTRIBUTIONS

Dividends and other distributions received by UK shareholders are assessed to income tax under ITTOIA 2005 s 385. Until 5 April 2016 this assessment was on the gross sum: ie on the dividend actually paid together with the appropriate tax credit (ITTOIA 2005 ss 397(1), 398(1)).
(1) The tax credit was 10% (and the 'tax credit fraction' was one-ninth).
(2) Individuals and charities were not entitled to a repayment of any tax credit. Charities were entitled to compensation from the government as a percentage payment of their dividend income over a transitional period until 2003–04.
(3) Although these provisions concerning repayment of tax credits did not apply to non-resident shareholders, the size of the tax credit coupled with the imposition of a withholding tax would normally have produced little or no refund of the credit.
(4) Individuals subject to tax at either lower (abolished from April 2008) or basic rate had no further liability since the 'dividend ordinary rate' applicable in such cases was 10% (ITA 2007 s 8). Higher rate taxpayers were liable to the 'dividend upper rate' of 32.5% or the 'dividend additional rate' which was introduced from 6 April 2010 at 42.5% but reduced to 37.5% from 6 April 2013. Trusts were charged at the 'dividend trust rate' which was the same as the dividend additional rate. There is a special relief for trusts to exclude the first £1,000 of income which would otherwise be chargeable (in the case of dividend income) at the 'dividend trust rate', subject to anti-splintering rules (see **[42.96]**).
(5) With effect from 2016–17 the dividend tax credit is abolished. In its place, a dividend tax allowance of £5,000 per annum has been introduced for individuals. Dividend income in excess of the allowance is taxed at 7.5% for basic rate taxpayers, 32.5% for higher rate taxpayers and 38.1% for

additional rate taxpayers. There is no dividend nil rate allowance for trusts: dividend income included in the first £1,000, treating the dividend income as the highest slice of income, is taxed at the dividend ordinary rate of 7.5%, and any excess at the dividend trust rate of 38.1% (from 2016–17). A proposal to reduce the dividend tax allowance to £2,000 with effect from 2018–19 was included in the 2017 Finance Bill but omitted from FA 2017 following the announcement of a general election. **[42.76]–[42.90]**

V TAXATION OF OTHER PERSONS WHO RECEIVE DISTRIBUTIONS

1 UK companies

a) *No tax liability on distributions*

In the past, dividends and other distributions received by one UK company from another were not generally subject to corporation tax in the recipient's hands (CTA 2009 s 1285). With effect from 1 July 2009, however, this simple exemption was replaced by Part 9A of CTA 2009 which exempts all dividends, whether or not paid by UK companies, provided that they satisfy certain conditions (see further **[41.46]**). In practice, most dividends paid by UK companies continue to be exempt under the new rules. Until 5 April 2016 the sum paid, together with the tax credit thereon, was known as 'franked investment income' (FII). **[42.91]**

b) *Refund of tax credit*

Companies and pension funds were not entitled to any refund of tax credits. **[42.92]–[42.93]**

c) *Small profits relief*

As noted at **[41.23]**, in determining whether the small profits relief is available to a company, for periods before 1 April 2015 or for ring fence profits, its exempt distribution income is taken into account. In relation to periods up to 5 April 2016, the relief is not available on the profits of a company in so far as those profits include FII, other than FII received from a member of the same 51% group of companies or from certain consortium-owned companies. For ring fence profits for periods from 6 April 2016, the references to FII are replaced by references to 'exempt ABGH distributions', ie distributions which are treated as such only because they fall within paragraph A, B, G or H in s 1000(1) of CTA 2010 and which are exempt under Part 9A of CTA 2009. The following example shows how the small profits relief calculation is affected by FII for periods before 6 April 2016: **[42.94]**

EXAMPLE 42.12

HN Ltd makes up accounts to 31 March each year. For the year ended 31 March 2015 the company had trading profits of £300,000 and received FII of £200,000 from another (non-group) UK company (ie £180,000 + £20,000 tax credit).
The corporation tax calculation was as follows:

(i)   Tax at 21% on £300,000   £63,000

(the dividend income was ignored at this stage)
(ii) Less: small profits relief calculated as follows:
(upper relevant amount − profits) × statutory fraction × basic profits/profits
'basic profits' means profits subject to corporation tax;
'profits' means basic profits plus FII, ie:

$$(1{,}500{,}000 - 500{,}000) \times \frac{1}{400} \times \frac{300{,}000}{500{,}000} = £1{,}500$$

(iii) Total tax ((i)−(ii)) = £61,500

2 Trusts and estates

a) *Interest in possession trusts*

The beneficiary receives the tax credit on dividend income and the income is taxed in his hands in the same way as with an individual directly entitled. Accordingly, any additional liability depends upon the level of that beneficiary's taxable income. **[42.95]**

b) *Distributions received by discretionary trusts*

A special tax rate, the dividend trust rate, applies to distributions received by discretionary trusts. This rate was 25% up to 5 April 2004, 32.5% from 6 April 2004 to 5 April 2010, 42.5% from 6 April 2010 and was reduced to 37.5% with effect from 6 April 2013 in line with the reduction in the additional rate of income tax. These rates were applied to the gross dividend including the 10% tax credit. From 6 April 2016, following the abolition of the tax credit, the rate was increased to 38.1%.

An example of the calculation, involving a tax credit, for the tax year ended 5 April 2016 is given below.

EXAMPLE 42.13

		£		£
Net dividend				80.00
Tax credit @ $\frac{1}{9}$ of net	(10%)			8.89
Gross dividend				88.89
Tax at Trust rate	37.5%	37.78		
				33.33
				£55.56

The first £1,000 (for 2017–18) of income arising to a trust chargeable at the rate applicable to trusts or the dividend trust rate is, instead, chargeable at the basic, lower or dividend ordinary rate depending on the type of income: ITA 2007 s 491 (see **[16.21]**).

There are also measures to group trusts made by the same settlor for the purposes of sharing one basic rate band between them.

The position of beneficiaries who receive distributions from the trust and the tax charge under ITA 2007 s 493 are considered at [16.66]. [42.96]–[42.120]

VI TAXATION OF 'NON-QUALIFYING' DISTRIBUTIONS

Until 5 April 2016, an issue of bonus redeemable shares or securities was a non-qualifying distribution (CTA 2010 ss 1000(1)C–D and 1136). It was taxed in two stages: *first*, on the issue of the securities the recipient could be assessed at the dividend upper or dividend additional rate less the tax credit. *Second*, when the shares were redeemed, the redemption was a qualifying distribution with the normal taxation consequences, save that, if the shareholder was then liable for income tax at the dividend upper or dividend additional rate, a deduction was made for any tax which he originally paid on the non-qualifying distribution: ITTOIA 2005 ss 400–401.

These rules have been recast following the abolition of dividend tax credit from 6 April 2016. There is now no special treatment for a CD distribution (as non-qualifying distributions are now termed), but on the subsequent receipt of a linked non-CD distribution which consists of the repayment of the shares or security issued in the earlier distribution, the tax liability is reduced by the lesser of the tax on the CD distribution and the tax that would otherwise be charged on the non-CD distribution. Both the CD distribution and the non-CD distribution are assumed to be the lowest slice of the person's dividend income in the year in which they are made, except that if they both take place in the same year the CD distribution is assumed to be a lower slice than the non-CD distribution. This could constitute a (presumably unintended) disincentive to issuing and repaying bonus shares or securities in the same year. [42.121]–[42.140]

VII EXEMPT DISTRIBUTIONS AND SCRIP DIVIDENDS

1 Demergers and the ICI test case

The general topic of demergers is considered in **Chapter 47** where a distinction is drawn between 'direct' and 'indirect' demergers. From a tax point of view, provided that the requirements of CTA 2010 ss 1075–1085 are satisfied (see **[47.51]**), the transfer of shares in the demerged company to the shareholders is not treated as a distribution and, for CGT purposes, the distributed shares are treated as a company reorganisation (TCGA 1992 ss 127, 192(2)). If the shareholder sells the shares in either the original or the demerged company, the original cost of the shares is apportioned between the shares in the distributing company and the demerged company. For individuals, therefore, demergers can be effected without the necessity for a liquidation and without attracting fiscal penalties. Unfortunately this has not been the case in certain situations where the shares are owned by trustees (see generally CG 33921 et seq). To understand why problems arose it is first necessary to consider the background trust and company law. [42.141]

a) *Company and trust law*

Hill v Permanent Trustee Co of New South Wales Ltd (1930), a Privy Council case, confirmed that a company can only part with its assets to its shareholders by way of a distribution of profits unless it is in liquidation or making an authorised reduction in share capital.

> 'A limited company not in liquidation can make no payment by way of return of capital to its shareholders except as a step in an authorised reduction of capital. Any other payment made by it by means of which it parts with moneys to its shareholders must and can only be made by way of dividing profits. Whether the payment is called "dividend" or "bonus" or any other name, it still must remain a payment on division of profits ... Moneys so paid to a shareholder will (if he be a trustee) *prima facie* belong to the person beneficially entitled to the income of the trust estate. If such moneys or any part thereof are to be treated as part of the corpus of the trust estate there must be some provision in the trust deed which brings about that result. No statement by the company or its officers that moneys which are being paid away to shareholders out of profits are capital, or are to be treated as capital, can have any effect upon the rights of the beneficiaries under a trust instrument which comprises shares in the company.' (Lord Russell)

In the simple *direct* demerger, a company first declares a dividend out of distributable profits and then satisfies that dividend by an allocation of shares which it owns (accordingly the demerger will typically be of a subsidiary). By contrast in an *indirect* demerger the company will transfer part of its business into a newly formed company which will issue shares directly to the shareholders. Following on from the above statement the demerged shares will be income in the hands of the recipient. If they were owned by trustees of an interest in possession trust, the consequence was that those shares belonged to the life tenant. The consequences for the trust fund could be startling: for instance when Thomas Tilling Ltd made a distribution (which was considered by the courts in the case of *Re Sechiari* (1950)) the effect was to reduce the price of the company's shares by 77%. A windfall for income beneficiaries and a glaring injustice for those interested in the capital of the fund! **[42.142]**

b) *The position of trustees on the assumption that the demerged shares were income*

On commonsense grounds and in the interests of fairness between the beneficiaries, trustees might wish to ensure that the trust capital is not depleted as the result of a proposed demerger.

The trustees could dispose of their shareholdings *before* the dividend was declared and demerger occurred and the trustees could subsequently buy back shares in either or both of the demerged companies. The acquired shares would then form part of the capital of the settlement. However, the sale of original shares might be commercially undesirable as it would represent a disposal (and possibly trigger a charge to capital gains tax).

The decision to sell might itself raise difficulties for the trustees: the deprived life tenant might argue that the decision was motivated solely to prevent him receiving income from the trust.

Alternatively, the life tenant might agree that the shares should be added to the capital of the settlement. Were he to do so, not only might he suffer a CGT charge (disposing of shares which have become his property) but he would add property to the settlement and to that extent become a settlor himself.
[42.143]

c) *Tax position if the shares were trust income*

An individual who receives demerged shares, provided that the necessary conditions are met, will obtain an exempt distribution so that there will be no question of any income tax liability. Any CGT charge will be postponed until a disposal occurs. [42.144]

Trustees of life interest trusts. The income of a life interest trust (including the demerged shares if treated as income) belongs to the life tenant (subject only to the trustees' lien for costs) and, assuming that the relevant conditions are satisfied, that would be an exempt distribution for income tax purposes. For CGT purposes the position is not so straightforward and two approaches are possible. The shares could be treated as part of the trust fund to which the life tenant then became absolutely entitled. This raises the prospect of a charge under TCGA 1992 s 71. Alternatively, because the life tenant is treated as owning income as it arises, it could be argued that the distributed shares never became trust property so that s 71 is not in point. After initial doubts HMRC accepted that the income belongs to the life tenant as a result of the *Archer-Shee* decision so that TCGA 1992 s 71 is not in point (see CG 33931).

One effect of the above is that the base costs of the trust cannot be apportioned to the life tenant and must be attributed only to the original shares (despite the diminution in their value flowing from the demerger). Accordingly, the trustees may realise a loss when those shares are sold (the oddness of this result in the case of direct demergers is well illustrated in *Private Client Business*, 1995, p 128). Turning to the life tenant, what is the base cost of the shares that he has received? HMRC has concluded that in the case of a *direct demerger* the allowable cost to the life tenant is the market value of the demerged shares as a result of TCGA 1992 s 17(1): see [19.14]. The disposal by the company would be the corresponding disposal for the purpose of s 17(2) (see CG 33931). In the case of an *indirect demerger*, however, there is no corresponding disposal (because the company did not dispose of the shares); accordingly the life tenant has no allowable cost.

As compared with individual shareholders, therefore, the life tenant could be placed at a CGT disadvantage in the case of indirect demergers (following the ICI test case (see [42.148]) it is, however, likely that such shares would have been capital and so not belonging to the life tenant).

If the terms of a settlement provide for the payment of an annuity and for the balance of the income to be paid elsewhere the above analysis does not hold good. The reasoning in *Archer-Shee* cannot apply: the shares have become part of the trust funds and a CGT charge under s 71 may arise when they are paid out to a beneficiary. [42.145]

Discretionary and accumulation trusts where the demerged shares are accumulated. The trustees have received the shares as an exempt distribution so that there is no liability to income tax under ITTOIA 2005 s 383. Although the shares are 'income' in the trustees' hands, provided that they exercise their powers to accumulate there are no further fiscal consequences. [42.146]

Discretionary and accumulation trusts where the shares are paid out to a beneficiary. Because the shares have been received as income by the trustees, if those shares (or their cash equivalent) are paid to a beneficiary the rules of ITA 2007 Part 9 Chapter 7 will be in point. Given that the trustees received an exempt distribution, no Part 9 Chapter 3 credit will be available, so that (subject to any unused credit in the tax pool) the payment is likely to attract an income tax charge. If the shares (rather than any cash equivalent) are paid out to a beneficiary, for CGT purposes a charge under TCGA 1992 s 71 may arise in addition to any income tax liability. A hold-over election is, however, generally available when property ceases to be held on discretionary trusts (see [24.22]). [42.147]

d) *The ICI test case: are demerged shares income after all?*

The ICI demerger was 'indirect': the bio-chemical part of ICI's business was transferred to a new company (Zeneca plc) and the shares in that company were transferred directly to the ICI shareholders. *Sinclair v Lee* (1993) considered the position of trustees of an interest in possession will trust in receipt of Zeneca shares. The Vice-Chancellor concluded that the Zeneca shares formed part of the capital of the fund and that the *Hill* line of cases could be distinguished.

The judgment was deeply disappointing. Whilst it is true that ICI, for its own tax reasons, chose to effect its demerger by the 'indirect' method, to concentrate on that as a way of escaping from the manacles of precedent was hardly satisfactory. There should be no difference between the case where a shareholder receives as a distribution shares which had been owned by his company (the so-called direct demerger) and that where the company instead procures the issue of shares by a third party (as occurred in the *ICI* case). Having said that, there are *dicta* towards the end of the judgment that could, if the need arises, be used as ammunition against a mechanical application of the *Hill* decision:

> 'In the last analysis, the rationale underlying the general principles enunciated in *Hill's* case is an endeavour by the law to give effect to the assumed intention of the testator or settlor in respect of a particular distribution to shareholders. When the inflexible application of these principles would produce a result manifestly inconsistent with the presumed intention of the testator or settlor, the court should not be required to apply them slavishly. In origin they were guidelines. They should not be applied in circumstances, or in a manner, which would defeat the very purpose they are designed to achieve.' [42.148]

e) *Confusion resolved?*

In 1991, Racal Electronics plc distributed its shareholding in Racal Telecom plc to its shareholders (a direct demerger) whereas in the following year it demerged the Chubb Group by the indirect route. It is interesting to consider the position of an interest in possession trust owning Racal shares. In the first case the Racal Telecom shares should have been handed over to the life tenant whereas in the second we now know that the shares formed part of the trust capital. How many trustees got it right? How many simply assumed – without even addressing the problem – that the shares must be added to the trust capital? And how many have retained the shares waiting for the matter to be cleared up? The best that could be said of *Sinclair v Lee* was that it solved half the problem.

Finally, the generally favourable tax treatment for interest in possession trusts in the case of direct demergers does not necessarily apply where the settlement is governed by foreign law. This will only be the case where the relevant law treats a life tenant as deriving his income directly from the trust investments in accordance with *Baker v Archer-Shee* principles.

Meanwhile, for settlements under English law, legislation to clarify the situation was proposed in a report by the Law Commission in May 2009 (*Capital and Income in Trusts: Classification and Apportionment*). A consultation document incorporating a draft Bill was issued by the Ministry of Justice in March 2010 and, following consultation and minor modifications, the Trusts (Capital and Income) Act 2013 received Royal Assent on 31 January 2013. Under s 2, with effect from 1 October 2013, corporate receipts from tax-exempt demergers are classified as capital rather than income, with a corresponding power for trustees to make payments to income beneficiaries. **[42.149]**

2 Scrip dividends

a) *The enhanced scrip (or stock) dividend*

The stock dividend option has been considered at **[42.9]**. In the absence of any element of 'enhancement', the shares are income in the hands of trustees. However, where the alternative to the cash dividend is shares which are worth significantly more, there is a degree of value enhancement which is particularly acute where the shareholders are offered the possibility of converting the scrip into cash by an immediate sale. An example of a scrip offer illustrates all these points: the net cash dividend of 16.75p per existing share was well exceeded by the scrip offer of 25.125p per share and, if the shareholder wished to sell this scrip, the company had arranged a sale price of 23.87p per share. **[42.150]**

b) *Tax treatment*

For the shareholder there is no liability to income tax at the basic or dividend ordinary rate; the higher or additional rate taxpayer, however, is subject to a tax charge at the dividend upper or additional rate on the cash equivalent of the stock dividend, grossed up at the dividend ordinary rate for stock dividends received before 6 April 2016, but treated as having paid tax at the dividend ordinary rate on the same amount (ITTOIA 2005 ss 409–414). The cash equivalent is normally the amount of the cash alternative, but if the market value of the scrip exceeds the cash dividend by 15% or more of the market value, the cash equivalent is the market value.

These rules apply to:
(1) individual shareholders;
(2) trustees of discretionary or A&M trusts; and

(3) life tenants who are entitled to receive the scrip dividend (see further on the position of interest in possession trusts [**42.152**]). [**42.151**]

EXAMPLE 42.14

Jenni, a higher rate taxpayer, and an ordinary shareholder in Wizzo Ltd, opts to take an enhanced scrip dividend. Instead of receiving a cash dividend for £50 she accepts paid up shares having a value of £90. Her 2015–16 tax position is:

(1) *Income tax*: The market value of the scrip exceeds the cash alternative by more than £13.50 (15% of £90), so that the cash equivalent is the market value (£90). This must be grossed up at 10% (to £100) and Jenni will then be subject to an income tax charge at the dividend upper rate on this amount (ie to a tax charge of 32.5% less the tax credit, resulting in a liability of £22.50). If she were liable at the dividend additional rate of 37.5%, the tax liability would be £27.50. See ITTOIA 2005 ss 409–414.

(2) *CGT*: The shares are treated as a newly acquired asset and the cash equivalent of the share capital (£90) is her base cost: see TCGA 1992 s 142.

Notes:

(i) The same rules will apply if the shares had been received by trustees of an A&M trust and for the purpose of the income tax charge the dividend trust rate (37.5%) would give an income tax liability of £27.50.

(ii) Similarly, if the shares had been treated under an interest in possession trust as belonging to the life tenant, the above rules apply and, for CGT purposes under TCGA 1992 s 142, the shares are treated as acquired for a base cost equal to the cash equivalent of the share capital. Where, under the terms of an interest in possession trust, the shares are either treated as capital or, alternatively, the value is split between the life tenant and capital, the position is set out in the following paragraph.

(iii) If the scrip dividend had been received after 5 April 2016 Jenni's tax charge, assuming she had used her dividend nil rate allowance elsewhere, would be on the cash equivalent (£90) at the dividend upper rate of 32.5%, giving tax of £29.25. Tax at the dividend ordinary rate of 7.5% (£6.75) is treated as paid although this tax is not repayable. Her resulting tax liability is therefore £22.50 as before.

c) *Interest in possession trusts (and see SP 4/94)*

As with demergers it is interest in possession trusts which pose problems for scrip dividends. Traditionally, trustees have opted for cash rather than scrip: however, if there is a substantial element of enhancement, trustees should at least consider whether to take the scrip. If they do so, a familiar problem arises: are the shares income (and so the property of the life tenant) or must they be added to the capital of the trust? The normal non-enhanced scrip dividend will be treated in the same way as a cash dividend and so belong to the life tenant. In cases of enhanced value, however, there is some authority that the value of the scrip must be apportioned with the life tenant being entitled to the value of the cash dividend. Hence, although the shares themselves are added to the trust capital, the trustees must raise this sum and pay it to the life tenant (and so they may find it necessary to sell the shares). This was the result in *Re Malam, Malam v Hitchens* (1894). (Contrast, however, *Bouch v Sproule* (1887) in which the shares were allocated to capital, and the *Hill* line of cases where they were treated as income.) Presumably the theory underlying apportionment is that the element of enhancement must be attributed to the value of the existing shares (and so treated as a form of capital reorganisation: see further *Law Society Gazette*, July 1993, p 17).

The tax treatment depends on how the shares are treated as a matter of trust law (this is expressly recognised by HMRC in SP 4/94 and a similar rule applies in the case of non-UK trusts). There are therefore three possibilities:

(1) *Shares treated as trust capital:* No income tax liability arises and, for CGT purposes, the trustees acquire a new asset but apparently at a nil base cost (since ITTOIA 2005 ss 409–414 do not apply to fixed interest trustees, proceeding on the assumption that the shares belong to the life tenant).

(2) *Shares treated as income:* The beneficiary with the interest in possession is treated as entitled to the income and taxed in the same way as an individual shareholder: see **[42.151]**.

(3) *A Malam apportionment:* The income tax position of the life tenant in a *Malam* type case is (according to SP 4/94) that he will be taxed on the income when it is paid out to him by the trustees under TA 1988 s 687 (see now ITA 2007 Part 9 Chapter 7) and, as the trustees are not treated as having paid income tax on the scrip dividend, basic rate income tax must be accounted for by those trustees and the usual credit passed to the life tenant. The life tenant will be treated as receiving income equivalent to the cash dividend plus tax (at the basic rate) and this will be income taxable as savings and investment income. The treatment applies whether the payment is made out of the proceeds of sale of the shares, out of other capital of the trust or by a distribution of some of the shares comprised in the scrip issue.

So far as the trustees' tax position on receipt of the shares is concerned, there is no question of any further income tax liability arising, since ITTOIA 2005 ss 409–414 have no application to interest in possession trusts. For CGT purposes, the scrip falls outside the provisions that enable the base cost of the shares to be equal to the 'cash equivalent of the share capital'. Accordingly, shares retained by the trustees will be treated as a new asset with a nil acquisition cost. These startling results arise because the relevant legislation proceeds on the assumption that the shares must belong to the life tenant in such cases who would be liable for higher rate income tax but would also be credited with an uplifted CGT base. If some of the shares are transferred to the life tenant there is a part disposal for CGT purposes.

An argument that TA 1988 s 249(6) (the predecessor to ITTOIA 2005 s 410(3)) had the effect of requiring a scrip dividend to be treated as income for trust law purposes was accepted by the High Court in *Pierce v Wood* (2009), but this decision was not followed by the Upper Tribunal in *Gilchrist v R & C Comrs* (2014). In the inheritance tax case of *Seddon v R & C Comrs* (2015), the First-tier Tribunal considered itself bound by the decision in *Gilchrist*.

EXAMPLE 42.15

In 2016–17 the trustees of the Dari Will Trust accept an enhanced scrip dividend from ABC plc under which, instead of receiving a cash dividend worth £80, they receive shares to a value of £120. The trustees decide under the terms of the trust that they are obliged to distribute the value of the cash dividend to the life tenant.

(1) The life tenant will receive £80 together with a credit for the basic rate income tax deducted at source (ie £100 in all). The trustees must, according to SP 4/94, pay income tax to HMRC under ITA 2007 s 901 of £20.

(2) So far as the scrip dividend is concerned the trustees will not suffer any income tax liability thereon but the shares will be acquired at a nil base cost. Were the shares to be sold by the trustees a gain of £120 would result and accordingly they would face a CGT liability of £24. On these particular facts therefore the trustees would be out of pocket as a result of accepting the scrip dividend since their costs total £80 + £20 + £24 = £124, whereas the value received was only £120.

In the *Malam* case, Stirling J decided that 'the proceeds of the realisation of the shares should be applied in payment first of the dividend (to which the tenant for life is entitled ...) and the balance ought to be applied as capital'. Pending sale of the shares, the life tenant would have a charge upon those shares equal to the value of the dividend. The view of HMRC – that the life tenant is to be treated as receiving an annual payment falling under ITTOIA 2005 Part 5 – is not free from doubt. It is arguable that any 'compensation' payment by the trustees does not constitute income and so escapes the income tax net altogether. [42.152]

43 Corporate groups
Updated by Stephen Whitehead, KPMG LLP (UK)

I   Operating structures [43.1]
II What is a group? [43.21]
III Group and consortium relief (CTA 2010 Part 5) [43.41]
IV Group arrangements for payments of instalments of corporation tax [43.101]
V   Capital gains [43.120]
VI Depreciatory transactions and value shifting (TCGA 1992 s 176 and s 31) [43.151]
VII VAT [43.191]
VIII Stamp duty land tax [43.211]

I OPERATING STRUCTURES

Assume that R and E plan to set up in business together: R is a chef of renown and E has run (with some success) a hamburger chain. A corporate structure, rather than a partnership, is considered appropriate. A single company with two divisions – the catering/food production portion and the restaurant outlet – is one possibility. From a tax and risk perspective the company will be a single accountable entity (the fact that it is run as two separate divisions is purely for internal management purposes). Forming two separate companies – R Ltd and E Ltd – with different shareholdings may not meet their wishes and a group structure may be advantageous. A holding company – with shares owned 50:50 by R and E – may own two subsidiaries, R Ltd and E Ltd. From a risk and tax perspective there are then three separate legal entities: accordingly the insolvency of the restaurant business of E Ltd would not necessarily bring down R Ltd nor the holding company.

Commercially, groups of companies have obvious attractions: different enterprises can be segregated into different corporate units each with its limited liability and separate identity. Each trade will, to a greater or lesser extent, have a separate management and, in the event of a decision to sell any part of the enterprise, the appropriate company can be sold to the purchaser. From a taxation point of view, however, and despite the various reliefs considered below, forming a group has historically been disadvantageous because the various grouping provisions have not caused all the companies to be treated as one for tax purposes and, accordingly, certain reliefs have been restricted. Up to 1 April 2015, one significant problem with using groups was the application of the small profits rate of tax to the members of the group. Where the companies were 'associated', the upper and lower limits for each associated company for calculating whether the small profits rate of corporation tax was available were divided by the number of associated companies. This led to the loss of relief and hence a failure by the group as a whole to take full advantage of the small profits rate.

If the associated companies formed a group, it could be possible to arrange for profits within the group to be configured in a way which minimised the tax payable. If the group overall had profits below the lower limit for small profits relief, it was usually best that they were distributed evenly around the group in order to avoid them falling within the marginal relief band. The requirement that transactions between companies satisfying the 'participation condition' (TIOPA 2010 s 148) be treated for tax purposes as if taking place at arm's length could make this more difficult to achieve, although this requirement does not, in general, apply to small and medium-sized enterprises. From 1 April 2015, this issue has been eliminated as there is from this date a single rate of corporation tax, 19% for FY 2017.

Another example (which continues to be relevant post 1 April 2015) is the quarterly payments system where a large group could result in a number of relatively small companies becoming subject to instalment payments. For periods up to 31 March 2015, the profit limits for instalment payments, like those applying to the small profits rate, were divided by the number of associated companies, but for periods ending after that date the calculation is instead based on the number of related 51% group companies.

[43.1]–[43.20]

EXAMPLE 43.1

F Ltd has one wholly owned subsidiary, B Ltd. Both companies make up their accounts to 31 March and for the year ending 31 March 2015 both have taxable profits of £150,000. The lower limit for each company is £150,000 (£300,000 ÷ 2) and therefore both are taxed at 20%, making £60,000 tax payable in total.

If F Ltd had profits of £250,000 and B Ltd profits of £50,000, the position would be different. F Ltd has profits falling within the marginal band and therefore pays tax of £51,250 (£250,000 × 21% – (£750,000 – £250,000) × 1/400) and B Ltd pays £10,000 – making a total of £61,250, an increase of £1,250.

EXAMPLE 43.2

W Ltd makes profits of £400,000 and has three subsidiaries whose results are as below for the year ended 31 March 2015:

Rock Ltd	profit	£25,000
Stone Ltd	loss	£10,000
Granite Ltd	loss	£5,000

There are four associated companies, so not only does W Ltd pay tax at the full rate of 21% (because the upper limit of £1.5 million is divided by 4, so that the company pays the full rate when profits exceed £375,000), but the quarterly payments system also applies to W.

II WHAT IS A GROUP?

A group of companies will comprise at least a parent company (a holding company) which controls another company known as a subsidiary. Groups may consist of any number of interlocking companies and 'company' is defined as a body corporate which includes an industrial and provident society and a UK building society. Commercially, a group may be regarded as a single entity; however, as far as the law is concerned the companies are generally treated as separate legal entities. The tax legislation confers a number of useful reliefs upon companies in a group. These reliefs depend upon the structure of the group: some are available to '51% groups'; some to '75% groups'; and some to 'consortia'. For 'consortium' structures, provision is made for cases where: (i) a company (so-called 'link company') is both a member of a ('linked') group and one of the joint owners of a consortium company (CTA 2010 s 133); and (ii) a company is both a member of a group and owned by a consortium (CTA 2010 s 153(3), and see also ss 148–149).

A '51% group' exists where more than 50% of the ordinary share capital of one company is beneficially owned, directly or indirectly, by another company; and a '75% group' where at least 75% of the ordinary share capital of one company is so owned (CTA 2010 s 1154). Certain privileges may be available even if the 75% or 51% group requirement is not satisfied, in cases where a company is owned by a consortium of corporate members. A company is owned by a consortium if 75% or more of the ordinary share capital is beneficially owned by companies of which none owns less than a 5% share and none owns 75% or more (CTA 2010 s 153).

How does the existence of a group affect the tax position of an individual shareholder? For entrepreneurs' relief purposes, a disposal of shares in the holding company of a trading group may qualify for the lower rate of capital gains tax provided that certain conditions are satisfied. Relief may also be available under the IHT business property relief provisions provided that the conditions in IHTA 1984 s 105(4)(b) and s 111 are met.   **[43.21]–[43.40]**

III GROUP AND CONSORTIUM RELIEF (CTA 2010 PART 5)

1 When is relief available?

Group relief applies to 75% groups and to consortia. In addition to the requirements as to the ownership of share capital, certain economic ownership tests must also be met. CTA 2010 s 151(4) provides that for group relief to be available the parent company must also be entitled to not less than 75% of the profits available for distribution and not less than 75% of the assets available for distribution on a winding up. For consortium relief a consortium member's interest in the consortium company is taken as the lowest of the percentage share capital, entitlement to profits available for distribution and entitlement to assets on a winding up. In addition, consortium relief is restricted by direct voting power held by a consortium member in a consortium company (CTA 2010 ss 143–144).   **[43.41]**

2 The international dimension

Until 1 April 2000, the group relief legislation required the relationship between the surrendering company and the claimant company in a group relief claim to be established having regard solely to companies which were UK residents. This restriction in the UK legislation was tested in the courts in an EU context on the basis that EU companies should benefit from arts 52 and 58 of the EC Treaty (now arts 49 and 54 of the Treaty on the Functioning of the European Union (TFEU)) providing for freedom of establishment. The argument was that the UK group relief legislation restricted freedom of establishment by providing that tax benefits were not available to non-UK companies. So far as consortium relief was concerned, the case of *ICI v Colmer* (1996) was particularly significant and involved two UK-resident companies each owning shares in a holding company with a number of wholly owned trading subsidiaries, the majority of which were non-UK resident (although a minority were resident in the EU). The Revenue contended that the holding company did not fall within the definition in TA 1988 s 413(3)(b) because the subsidiary trading companies had to be UK resident. The matter was referred to the European Court of Justice (ECJ) which decided that the UK restriction was not contrary to EC law but that it should be possible to establish a group or consortium relationship through companies resident in the EU. After the matter had been referred back to the House of Lords by the ECJ, ICI contended that since the effect of the decision of the ECJ was that, if a majority of the subsidiaries concerned had been resident in countries within the EU, consortium relief could not have been denied, it was no longer permissible for the UK to limit the relief to companies resident in the UK. The House of Lords said that although it might seem anomalous, if a majority of a company's subsidiaries were non-UK and non-EU companies, the business of that company was not a 'holding company' within the terms of the group relief legislation and so no relief was available. Had the company had a majority of EU subsidiaries things would have been different.

This matter was resolved by FA 2000 which amended the group relief rules to permit groups and consortia to be established through companies resident anywhere in the world. This means that fellow UK resident subsidiaries of a non-UK company can surrender losses etc between themselves (see the discussion concerning the *Marks & Spencer* case below for whether a foreign parent can surrender down losses for use by a UK subsidiary).

Group relief has also been extended to UK permanent establishments (PEs) of non-resident companies so that, for example, the UK PE of a US company could surrender the losses of the UK trade to a UK subsidiary of the same US company. Such losses would need to be attributable to activities of the UK PE within the charge to UK corporation tax, which would not be exempt from such tax by virtue of any double taxation arrangement and which are not relievable against non-UK profits of any person for the purposes of any foreign tax (CTA 2010 s 107). This last condition was the subject of a referral to the Court of Justice of the European Union (CJEU) in *Philips Electronics UK Ltd* (2012) (C-18/11). The CJEU found in favour of the taxpayer and FA 2013 s 30 has introduced amendments to the UK group relief provisions to allow companies resident in the European Economic Area to surrender losses arising in UK branches to other UK companies via group relief from 1 April 2013. Importantly, new CTA 2010 s 107(6A) and (6B) contain restrictions to this basic rule where the losses surrendered are also used against non-UK profits.

The position is therefore as follows:

EXAMPLE 43.3

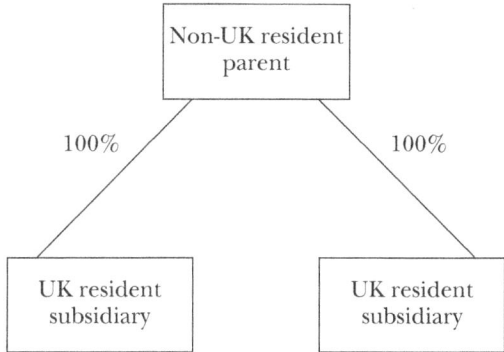

In *Example 43.3* the two UK subsidiaries are now members of the same group, whatever the country of residence of the parent. The two UK subsidiaries will therefore be able to claim and surrender group relief between each other.

In addition, if the non-UK resident parent trades in the UK through a PE, the PE will be able to claim group relief from the UK resident subsidiaries. It will also be able to surrender losses and other amounts to the UK resident subsidiaries providing those amounts are not relievable against non-UK profits in the overseas country.

EXAMPLE 43.4

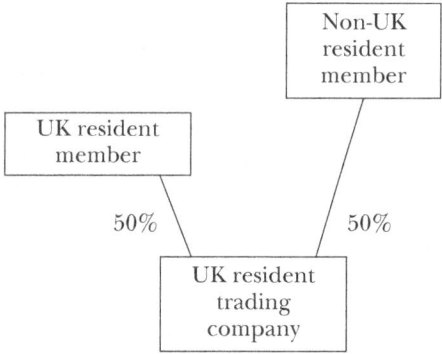

In *Example 43.4* the two holding companies form a consortium, whatever the country of residence of the non-UK resident member. The UK resident member of the consortium and the UK resident trading company are able to claim and surrender group relief between themselves.

In *Felixstowe Dock and Railway Company Ltd v R & C Comrs* (2014), the CJEU found that consortium relief should be available in groups where there is an EEA link company. UK law was previously changed (F(No 3)A 2010) in this regard but only with effect from accounting periods commencing on or after 12 July 2010. Further, the CJEU rejected other restrictions previously found in CTA 2010 ss 133(5)–(8). Legislation in F(No 2)A 2015 has now removed all location requirements for consortium relief with effect for accounting periods beginning on or after 10 December 2014. [43.42]

3 Operation of the relief

EXAMPLE 43.5

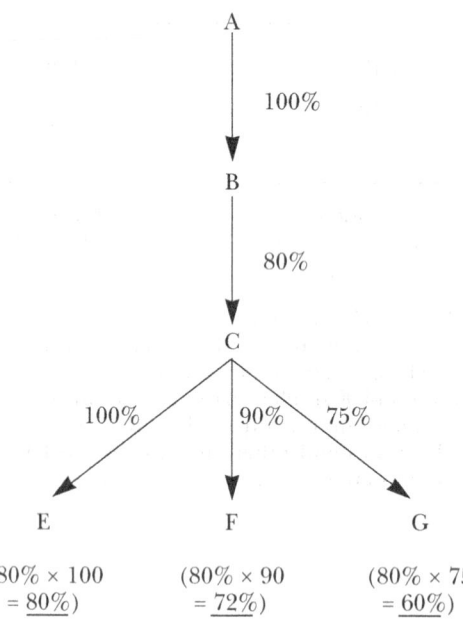

A, B, C and E form a 75% group. A only owns 72% of F and 60% of G. The latter two companies cannot, therefore, form part of a 75% group with A. However, C, E, F and G form a further group.

The relief enables trading losses or non-trading deficits on loan relationships, or management expenses and certain other items (see CTA 2010 s 99), to be surrendered to another company in the group or consortium, except that such items may not be surrendered by a dual resident investing company to another member of a UK group (CTA 2010 s 109). Generally, however, these amounts can be used to reduce the taxable profits of the 'claimant' company on being given up by the 'surrendering' company. It is not necessary to make a payment for group relief but if one is made it is ignored in computing profits and losses of both companies for tax purposes provided the payment does not exceed the amount of loss surrendered.

The amount of available loss or expense which it is possible to surrender is the amount generated in the part of the accounting period of the surrendering company which overlaps with the accounting period of the claimant company. The maximum loss which may actually be surrendered is restricted to the profit of the claimant company attributable to the overlapping period. There are certain further restrictions where the surrendering company has profits against which the loss etc can be offset (CTA 2010 s 105). The relief is more restrictive in the case of consortia since losses may be surrendered to the consortium members only in proportion to their percentage interest in the consortium company. Similarly, losses may be surrendered by the consortium members only up to the amount of the consortium company's profits corresponding to their percentage interest in the consortium company.

EXAMPLE 43.6

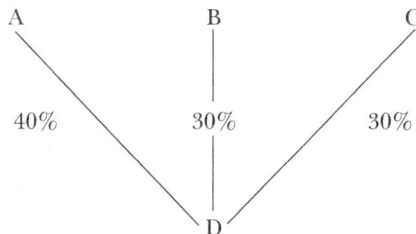

D makes a loss of £60,000. It can be surrendered to A, B and C as follows:
A = £24,000 (40% of £60,000)
B = £18,000 (30% of £60,000)
C = £18,000 (30% of £60,000).
If D had made profits of £100,000 and A and B had made losses of £50,000 and £40,000 respectively then they could have surrendered losses to D as follows:
From A = £40,000 (40% of £100,000)
From B = £30,000 (30% of £100,000).

The claimant company must use the relief in the year of surrender; it cannot be carried back or forward and is deducted from total profits after any charges on the income of the claimant company. It need not be surrendered in full (contrast loss relief under CTA 2010 s 37 where the full loss must be relieved if there are sufficient profits).

EXAMPLE 43.7

Little Ltd is the wholly owned subsidiary of Big Ltd. Both companies make up accounts to 31 March and for the year ended 31 March 2017, Little Ltd has trading losses of £20,000 and Big Ltd profits of £400,000. All the loss could be surrendered to Big Ltd resulting in the profits being reduced to £380,000. If Big Ltd were to pay up to £20,000 for the surrender, that sum would be ignored for tax purposes. Alternatively, Little Ltd might carry back all or a part of the loss under CTA 2010 s 37 and merely surrender the balance. [43.43]

4 The Marks & Spencer Case

The effect of European law on group relief has been further accentuated by the case of *Marks & Spencer plc v Halsey* (2005) C-446/03. Marks & Spencer established subsidiaries in Belgium, France and Germany but the retail operations were not a success and substantial losses were incurred. Group relief was claimed but the claim was denied by HMRC. One of the conditions for group relief in the UK at the time was that the surrendering companies needed to be resident in the UK or at least carrying on business in the UK through a branch or agency, so under domestic legislation Marks & Spencer were clearly not entitled to the relief.

However, they claimed that the domestic group relief provisions were discriminatory and contrary to what is now Art 49 TFEU (freedom of establishment).

Broadly, the ECJ concluded that the freedom of establishment provisions did not preclude provisions of a member state which generally prevented a resident parent company from deducting from its taxable profits losses incurred by a subsidiary resident in another member state. However, it was contrary to the freedom of establishment provisions to prevent a resident parent company from doing so where the non-resident subsidiary had exhausted the possibilities in its state of residence of having the losses taken into account for the current or any previous accounting period and where there were no possibilities for those losses to be taken into account in its state of residence for future periods either by the subsidiary itself or a third party. The court did not deal explicitly with the situation where a UK-resident company claims relief for losses incurred by its non-resident parent company or by a non-resident subsidiary of such a parent.

In the FA 2006 the Government changed the law to accommodate the decision in the *Marks & Spencer* case. The principal features of these changes, which have effect from 1 April 2006, are as follows:

- The surrendering (ie loss-making) company must be within the charge to tax under the law of any EEA territory either because it is resident there or because it trades through a PE in that EEA territory.
- The surrendering company must be a subsidiary of a claimant company which is resident in the UK or the surrendering company and the claimant company must be 75% subsidiaries of a third party which is resident in the UK (note consortium group relief is not available under these provisions).
- The surrendering company must have sustained an overseas loss equivalent to the items which can be surrendered as group relief. The overseas loss must be determined under the law of the relevant EEA territory.
- The overseas loss must not have been relieved in any territory outside the UK or be capable of being relieved in the relevant EEA territory or other specified territories for any period, including future periods.
- The actual loss surrendered by the company is limited to the amount determined applying UK tax rules.

As mentioned, these provisions came into effect on 1 April 2006. Before that date taxpayers had to rely on the judgment in *Marks & Spencer* to obtain relief for overseas losses. The Court of Appeal gave its judgment in *Marks & Spencer* (2007) as to how the ECJ decision should be applied in practice. A further decision on the actual claims made by Marks & Spencer plc was given by the First-tier Tribunal on 2 April 2009, and was substantially upheld by the Upper Tribunal, subject to some differences regarding time limits, in June 2010. Both the company and HMRC applied for permission to appeal to the Court of Appeal, the Government taking a narrower view of the ECJ's judgment in *Marks & Spencer* than that adopted by the Court of Appeal in 2007. In this appeal (2011) the Court of Appeal upheld Marks and Spencer's contention that the time at which the conditions relating to the use of the loss (the so-called 'no possibilities test') must be satisfied is the time when the claim is made, rather than the end of the period in which the loss arises. It also confirmed that the overseas loss can be split into parts for the purpose of applying the no possibilities test, so that relief can be claimed in the UK for part of the loss even though the remaining part has been or can be relieved elsewhere. Where timing differences between the overseas and UK tax calculations mean that losses arise in different years, relief can be claimed on the basis of the UK calculation.

HMRC appealed to the Supreme Court, which unanimously dismissed HMRC's appeal on the 'no possibilities' test without the need for further reference to the CJEU (2013). The remaining issues were held over to a subsequent hearing and the judgment was handed down on 19 February 2014. It was decided, in part, that: (i) Marks & Spencer is entitled to make sequential/consequential claims in respect of the same accounting period, ie amend and/or replace an original claim; (ii) Marks & Spencer is not allowed to make fresh claims for periods covered by the old 'pay and file' regime rather than Corporation Tax Self-Assessment; and (iii) Marks & Spencer's method of loss calculations was preferable to HMRC's and should result in a company claiming no more or less than it would if UK tax resident.

In February 2015, the CJEU found against the European Commission in its contention that it was virtually impossible to satisfy the 'no possibilities test' within CTA 2010 and that this meant the UK had failed to fulfil its obligations under the Treaty on the Functioning of the European Union. This decision has been treated by HMRC, controversially, as calling into question the approach taken by the Supreme Court in *Marks and Spencer* (2013) in relation to the time at which the 'no possibilities' test is to be applied, not only for periods after 31 March 2006 to which the new EEA group relief provisions apply, but also for earlier periods. There remains no clear resolution for taxpayers on this subject, while the UK's vote to leave the EU raises the prospect of further legislative change. [43.44]

5 The European Vinyls Case

In *Steele v EVC International* (1996) ('the *European Vinyls* case') the court held that a shareholders' agreement providing for the constitution and control of a jointly owned company caused the shareholders to be connected to each other for the purposes of TA 1988 s 839(7) (now CTA 2010 s 1122(4)).

It was feared that this case, although not directly concerned with consortium relief, could have had a serious impact on its availability in the case of consortia where the owners had agreed to implement a policy for the company and especially in joint ventures. This is because if all the owners of the company are deemed to be connected, they are each deemed to control not less than 75% of the votes so there will be no consortium relief by virtue of TA 1988 s 410(2) (now CTA 2010 s 155(3) Effect 3). HMRC confirmed in *Tax Bulletin* 26, December 1996 that where members of a consortium had entered into an ongoing agreement to operate the consortium company in accordance with their collective will the case would be applied to consortia and could deny relief. As a result FA 1997 s 68 (arguably retrospectively) was enacted to disapply the connected persons test of s 839(7) (now CTA 2010 s 1122(4)) in the context of claims for group or consortium relief (see explanatory definitions in CTA 2010 s 155(3) Effect 3). [43.45]

6 Claims

A claim for relief must be made by the first anniversary of the filing date, which normally means within a two-year period from the end of the accounting period. However, if there is an enquiry into the tax return the time limit is extended to 30 days after the enquiry is concluded, the return amended by HMRC or any appeal determined.

A claim for group relief must be made in the claimant company's tax return for the accounting period for which the claim is made. The claim can be made in the original or amended return. The claim must specify the amount of relief claimed and the name of the surrendering company. A claim for group relief requires the written consent of the surrendering company and, in the case of a consortium, all the members of the consortium must consent in writing. It is possible for a group to enter into arrangements with HMRC under which claims and consents can be made in a single document (often referred to as a joint amended return). [43.46]

7 Tax avoidance

CTA 2010 s 154 is designed to prevent artificial manipulation of the group relief provisions: in particular, the forming of groups on a temporary basis and in order to obtain the relief. Under the terms of this section a company will not be regarded as a member of a group if '*arrangements*' are in existence for the transfer of that company to another group or for any person to take control of the company but not the other companies within the group. For the meaning of 'arrangements', see SP 3/93 and on the general interpretation of this section *Pilkington Bros Ltd v IRC* (1982). CTA 2010 ss 155A and 155B make provision for certain joint venture and mortgage arrangements not to constitute 'arrangements' for these purposes. These provisions effectively enact ESC C10 into legislation. Relief is not available during any period when such arrangements are in force. In *Shepherd v Law Land plc* (1990), for instance, arrangements (an option to purchase the shares of the subsidiary company) came into existence on 6 January 1983 and ceased five weeks later on 11 February 1983 (the option was never taken up). In the accounting period ending 31 March 1983 group relief was therefore not available for that five-week period.

In *J Sainsbury plc v O'Connor* (1991) a joint venture company (Homebase) was formed by Sainsbury's and a Belgian company in which Sainsbury's held 75% of the issued share capital and the Belgian company the remaining 25%. There was, in addition, a cross-option agreement whereby 5% of that share capital could be acquired by the Belgian company. The options were not exercisable for a five-year period and, in the event, were never exercised. Did their existence prevent Sainsbury's being entitled to group relief? The Court of Appeal decided that they were so entitled: *first*, because mere existence of the options did not deprive Sainsbury's of their beneficial ownership in the relevant shares: accordingly they satisfied the 75% test. *Second,* because the existence of the options did not amount to arrangements which affected the rights of the relevant shares within the test for such arrangements laid down in TA 1988 Sch 18 (now CTA 2010 Part 5 Chapter 6). Legislation was introduced (now found within CTA 2010 ss 169 ff) whereby 'arrangements' was extended to include such changes in the ownership of shares that could arise under options to buy and sell. [43.47]

8 **Future changes**

A radical restructuring of the corporate loss relief provisions is to be introduced from 1 April 2017, once the Finance (No 2) Bill 2017 has been passed (see **[41.60]**). In relation to losses arising on or after the commencement date, this will move away from the principle that losses can be offset against profits of other group companies only in the period in which they arose. Instead, such losses will be available for offset against group profits of subsequent periods as well as against other income streams within the same company. Each group will have an allowance of £5m profit per annum which can be relieved in full and this can be allocated among group companies at the group's discretion. Relief for profits in excess of this allowance will be limited to 50% of the excess. [43.48]–[43.100]

IV GROUP ARRANGEMENTS FOR PAYMENTS OF INSTALMENTS OF CORPORATION TAX

Groups of companies can arrange to account for corporation tax on a group basis. The idea is that the group, via a nominated member company, can enter into a binding arrangement with HMRC under which the nominated company undertakes to pay the corporation tax liability of all the companies in the specified group. To be eligible to enter into the group payment arrangements, the participating members of a group constitute parent companies and their subsidiaries and also their subsidiaries, all the way down a chain of holding. Although an indirect holding by the ultimate parent in a company at a lower tier might be considerably less than 50%, the whole tier can benefit from these arrangements as long as each company in the tier owns more than 50% of the equity capital in the company at the tier below it. Not all group companies eligible to participate in such an arrangement need to do so. It is also possible to have several group payment arrangements in place for a wider group each comprised of different specified members. Group members still need to file individual self-assessment returns separately and each needs to compute its own corporation tax liability for the accounting period. However, each company's liability is met out of an allocation of the group payments made under these arrangements. Interest on underpaid tax will remain the liability of the individual group company as will any late fine or penalty that may be incurred.

If companies in a group do not participate in the group payment arrangements, amounts of instalments overpaid by one group member (and presumably amounts overpaid under the group payment arrangement) can be surrendered between companies.   **[43.101]–[43.119]**

V CAPITAL GAINS

Note that for companies special rules apply to intangible assets acquired on or after 1 April 2002 and loan relationships. Subject to certain exceptions, these assets are not chargeable assets for corporation tax purposes and the capital gains rules do not apply.   **[43.120]**

1 What is a group for these purposes?

For chargeable gains purposes, a group consists of a principal company and all its 75% subsidiaries. If any of those subsidiaries also have 75% subsidiaries they are included within the group provided they are effective 51% subsidiaries of the principal company (TCGA 1992 s 170).   **[43.121]**

EXAMPLE 43.8

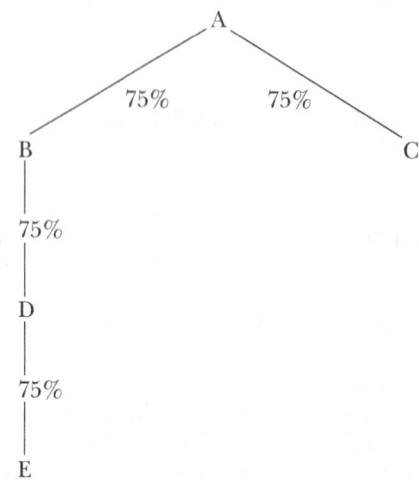

A, B, C and D form a s 170 group. E is not in the group as it is not a 51% subsidiary of A, the principal company.

2 Intra-group transfers

The transfer of an asset within a group is treated as being for a consideration that gives rise to neither gain nor loss (TCGA 1992 s 171: for the IHT position if the disposal involves a transfer of value, see IHTA 1984 s 97). The result is to defer any gain until the asset is disposed of outside the group or until the company owning the asset leaves the group, if this happens within six years (TCGA 1992 s 179). A potential purchaser of a company should, therefore, check whether the company will be subject to such 'exit' charges in the event of its leaving its existing group, or whether any company in a group they acquire has any member company with such a potential 'exit' charge. FA 2011 recast these provisions so that, broadly speaking, the s 179 gain (or loss) on the asset transferred is, in certain circumstances, added to (or subtracted from) the gain or loss on disposal of the shares in the transferee company. If this gain or loss is exempt under the substantial shareholdings exemption then the exit charge will not apply. This amendment has effect where the transferee company is sold on or after 19 July 2011 but it was possible to elect on a group basis for these provisions to apply on or after 1 April 2011.

FA 2011 also introduced a new procedure for claiming a reduction in an exit charge where one does arise in a target company (TCGA 1992 s 179ZA). The procedure allows a company to make a claim to HMRC that a gain giving rise to an exit charge be reduced by a just and reasonable amount, eg in case of double charging.

FA 2000 updated the rules for chargeable gains and companies. The changes were intended to allow the tax-neutral transfer of assets between companies in a wider variety of circumstances. In particular it changed the definition of a 'group' for these purposes and enabled transfers of assets within a group even if the relevant members of the group were not resident in the UK. The rules allow any company, whatever its country of residence, to be a member of a group but transfers within the group will only be on a tax neutral basis if the asset remains within the UK tax net.

Prior to FA 2000, if company B (in the structure set out in *Example 43.9* below) transferred an asset to company C, company B was treated as making a disposal of the asset at its market value, and charged to corporation tax on any gain arising.

EXAMPLE 43.9

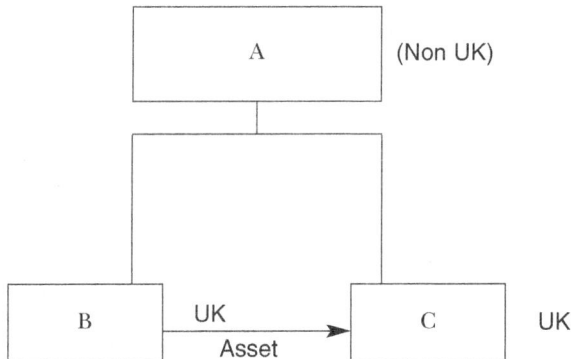

The FA 2000 changes mean that even though company A is not resident in the UK, company B and company C can transfer assets between themselves on a no gain/no loss basis, as if company A were UK resident.

The changes to the rules also mean that a UK subsidiary can transfer assets to a non-UK subsidiary of the same parent provided that the asset will be used by that non-UK subsidiary for its trade in the UK. Since the assets will remain within the corporation tax charge after the transfer, the no gain/no loss treatment applies. The de-grouping rule was amended so that TCGA 1992 s 179 focuses on a company leaving the worldwide group. [43.122]

3 Sub-groups

Where two or more companies which between themselves would form a group leave the group at the same time no exit charge arises on assets which they acquired from each other; such companies are known as associated companies (as defined in TCGA 1992 ss 179(2ZA) and 179(2ZB) and see further *Dunlop International AG v Pardoe* (1999)). TCGA 1992 s 179(2A) may apply to create an exit charge in situations where, after the sub-group has left the original group, the recipient company of the earlier intra-group transfer leaves the subsequent group (note that FA 1998 strengthened this provision by widening the 'common control' test in s 179(2B)). The detailed requirements of this legislation have been further examined in the case of *Johnston Publishing (North) Ltd v R & C Comrs* (2008). It had been thought prior to this case that the transferor and transferee companies need only be associated when they leave the group. In this case it was decided that the transferee and transferor must be associated (ie capable of forming a group on their own) both at the time of the intra-group transfer *and* when they leave the group. FA 2011 Sch 10 made it clear that for this exemption to apply, the companies must be part of the same sub-group at all times from the time of the intra-group transfer of the asset until immediately after they leave the original group. This amendment has effect where the transferee company leaves the group on or after 19 July 2011. [43.123]

4 Triggering a loss

Before 5 December 2005 it was possible to use TCGA 1992 s 179 to crystallise a capital loss as the following example illustrates. [43.124]

EXAMPLE 43.10

Alpha Ltd transfers a chargeable asset showing a capital loss to subsidiary company Beta Ltd which has realised capital profits. TCGA 1992 s 171 ensures that the transfer is at no gain/no loss. Beta Ltd then issues shares to a non-group company (Omega Ltd) so that there is a deemed disposal of the asset under TCGA 1992 s 179 and the loss is thereby realised and can be used to offset Beta's capital gains. (The loss is not reallocated under the FA 2011 provisions described above as there is no disposal of shares in Beta.) Omega then sells the shares to Alpha Ltd. Notice that the transaction has resulted in a permanent change in the capital structure of Beta Ltd.

Provisions introduced by FA 2006 and incorporated within TCGA 1992 (see ss 184A to 184F) have effect for disposals on or after 5 December 2005 and are likely to deny the offset of any loss crystallised in this way. The provisions are far-reaching and apply to any arrangements of which the main purpose or one of the main purposes is to secure a tax advantage. HMRC has issued guidance notes to explain when they consider these provisions apply. Broadly, they state that a loss is likely to be caught if there is no commercial loss or no commercial disposal.

5 Trading stock

If the asset transferred had not formed part of the trading stock of the transferor but is appropriated to the trading stock of the transferee, the transfer itself is covered by the no gain/no loss rule of s 171; but the transferee is then given an election when the asset is appropriated to his stock (see TCGA 1992 s 173). *Either* that appropriation is taxed as a disposal at market value thereby triggering any capital gain (or loss) *or*, alternatively, the transferee may elect to convert that gain into a trading profit (or loss) by postponing any tax until the asset is sold.

In *Coates v Arndale Properties Ltd* (1984) an attempt to take advantage of the election to obtain group relief for a loss on a capital asset was unsuccessful. The House of Lords concluded that the transferee never acquired the asset as trading stock because it was immediately resold to another member of the same group. Hence, the transaction was not covered by the election. This 'constructional' approach to a tax relieving provision may be contrasted with the House of Lords decision in *Furniss v Dawson* (1984). In *Reed v Nova Securities Ltd* (1985) the House of Lords were again concerned with the question of when assets are acquired as trading stock and concluded that not only must those assets be of a kind which were sold in the ordinary course of the company's trade, but they must also have been acquired with a view to resale at a profit. [43.125]

6 Capital losses

The group relief provisions do not provide for the surrender of capital losses. In the past it was common for chargeable assets to be transferred within the group (taking advantage of TCGA 1992 s 171 which prevents any chargeable gain arising: see above) to enable losses to be utilised.

EXAMPLE 43.11

Subsidiary company Alpha intends to sell land to P, but will realise a capital gain of £80,000 on that sale. Assume that another subsidiary company (Beta) has unused capital losses of £100,000. The land could be sold to Beta for full value and then resold by Beta to P.
(1) *On the sale to Beta:* the disposal is on a no gain/no loss basis irrespective of the actual consideration paid (TCGA 1992 s 171: above). No gain is, therefore, realised by Alpha.
(2) *On the sale to P:* the gain of £80,000 is realised by Beta, which can use its losses to avoid any corporation tax charge.

FA 2000 changed the position by enabling two companies within a group to elect that an asset can be treated as though it had been transferred between themselves immediately before being sold to a person outside the group. The idea was to enable groups to bring together (in effect) chargeable gains and allowable losses in a single company without the need to make an actual transfer of ownership of the asset within the group. The election had to be made within two years of the end of the accounting period of the company that made the actual disposal (TCGA 1992 s 171A). Where such an election was made the incidental costs of disposal incurred by the actual disponor were treated as made by the notional disponor. Note that this election could only be made where an asset was disposed of outside the group; the election could not be made in respect of other events which can give rise to capital gains disposals. FA 2009 made further amendments to these provisions. It is now possible to elect for a chargeable gain or allowable loss that arises on any actual or deemed disposal (or any part thereof) to be transferred between companies in a capital gains group. [43.126]

7 Anti-avoidance

In *News International v Shepherd* (1989) Vinelott J held that the acquisition of a loss-making company to which the parent then transferred shares for sale on the Stock Market did not involve a composite transaction so that the *Ramsay* principle was inapplicable. Crucially, in that case the terms of the actual sale had not been arranged before the intra-group transfer. It did not matter that the subsidiary was acquired for the express purpose of utilising its unrelieved losses. The *News International* case reawakened interest in the acquisition of a company by a group in order to take advantage of its capital losses. FA 1993 inserted s 177A into TCGA 1992 and a new Sch 7A providing for capital losses brought into a group to be 'ring fenced'.

Broadly, these rules mirror the legislation that deals with income losses in similar cases. The rules were widely drafted to catch unrealised as well as realised losses and apply to a loss-making company joining a group if gains are realised that would otherwise be set against those losses. These anti-avoidance issues were complex and still allowed some capital losses to be transferred to a third party; furthermore it was possible for companies with potential gains to be sold to groups with actual or potential losses which could be used to shelter these gains.

FA 2006 contained further anti-avoidance provisions, which were enacted as TCGA 1992 ss 184A–184F, designed to reinforce the ring-fencing of capital losses and ensure they can only be offset against gains which are realised on assets owned by the same group which has sustained the loss. FA 2007 strengthened these anti-avoidance measures by providing that allowable capital losses do not include any losses which arise in consequence of arrangements designed to secure a tax advantage. FA 2011 made further amendments to simplify some of the rules in Sch 7A. [43.127]

8 Roll-over relief

For roll-over relief, trades carried on by companies in a 75% group are treated as a single trade (TCGA 1992 s 175). HMRC considers that this section means that a chargeable gain made by one group member on a disposal of an asset outside the group can be rolled over into an asset acquired from outside the group by another group member (SP D19).

EXAMPLE 43.12

R Ltd, S Ltd and Q Ltd are members of a 75% group. The following transactions occur:
(1) R Ltd disposes of an office block with a base cost of £100,000 to Q Ltd when its value is £150,000;
(2) Q Ltd sells that asset to T Ltd for £150,000; and
(3) S Ltd acquires a new office block for use in its business for £200,000.

The taxation consequences of these transactions (ignoring indexation allowances) are:
(1) *The intra-group transfer from R Ltd to Q Ltd* This is treated as being for no gain/no loss so that tax on the gain (£50,000) is postponed. Q's base cost is, therefore, £100,000.
(2) *The sale by Q Ltd to T Ltd* The asset leaves the group so that a chargeable gain of £50,000 arises to Q Ltd.
(3) *The replacement asset purchased by S Ltd* On a claim being made by both companies (Q Ltd and S Ltd) the gain of Q Ltd can be rolled over into the purchase by S Ltd. Hence, S Ltd's base cost of the new asset will be £150,000 (£200,000 − £50,000) and Q Ltd will not be assessed on a gain as a result of the disposal to T Ltd.

In *Campbell Connelly & Co Ltd v Barnett* (1992) doubt was cast on this view:

'It was submitted to me that the inference should be drawn in relation to [s 175(1)] that not only should the trades carried on by members of a single group of companies be treated as a single trade and thereby the same trade but that members of a group of companies should be treated as a single person and thereby the same person. That does not seem possible to me as a matter of construction, given the very startling difference Parliament provided in the clearest possible way in [s 175(3)].'

(Knox J whose judgment was affirmed by the Court of Appeal (1993).)

The result was to leave the interpretation of s 175(1) in a state of confusion and the Financial Secretary indicated that irrespective of the *Campbell Connelly* case:

'The Revenue's practice seems to me to be sensible and to reflect how commercial transactions are commonly organised. We will ensure that it continues to apply. What needs to be done will depend on the outcome of the appeal.'

As from 29 November 1994 this view was given statutory effect (in what is now s 175(2A)): relief is available provided that the disposing and acquiring companies are members of the group at the time of *their own* transaction. They do not have to be members of the group at the time of both events.

[43.128]

9 'Roll around' relief

FA 1995 contained provisions preventing roll-over relief from being available where a company which had realised a gain on disposal of an asset acquired a replacement asset from another group member (this commonly being referred to as 'roll around' relief). The replacement asset was acquired on a no gain/no loss basis so that the amount deemed to be invested was linked to the original cost to the group of the asset (together with any indexation allowance). Nonetheless this device could be used to shelter a gain and had the merit of avoiding the payment of cash outside the group. (See TCGA 1992 s 175(2C).) [43.129]

10 Group property companies

Roll-over relief is limited to trading companies and so, as a matter of strict law, was not applied to non-trading companies within a group which held assets for use by the trading companies. In fact, relief was extended by means of ESC D30: this concession was given statutory force by FA 1995 and that company is now treated as if it were carrying on the 'group trade' in relation to disposals or acquisitions used wholly for the purposes of the group trade (TCGA 1992 s 175(2B)). It is thought that the non-trading company may hold assets used by non-group members and that this will not jeopardise the above relief although such assets will not themselves be eligible for roll-over relief.
[43.130]

11 Compulsory acquisition of land

TCGA 1992 s 247 applies when land is compulsorily acquired to enable the vendor to roll over his gains into the acquisition of other land. FA 1995 extended this relief to the situation where the replacement land is acquired by a company in the same capital gains group as the company which made the compulsory disposal. [43.131]

12 Linked transactions

The CGT rules in TCGA 1992 ss 19–20 (dealing with assets disposed of in a series of linked transactions) do not apply to transactions between companies in the same (75%) group which, under TCGA 1992 s 171, give rise to neither gain nor loss. Thus such transactions do not count as part of any linked series (contrast the situation where there is a transfer between spouses). Special provision is, however, made for the following case. [43.132]

> **EXAMPLE 43.13**
> Asset 1 is transferred by a series of intra-group transfers from Slim Ltd to Short Ltd; then to Tall Ltd and finally from Tall Ltd to a connected outsider Wilbur. Asset 2 is transferred directly by Slim Ltd to Wilbur. So long as Wilbur is connected with both Tall Ltd and Slim Ltd the disposal of Asset 1 is treated as having been made by Slim Ltd to him and hence can be linked to the disposal of Asset 2. Any increase in the tax chargeable on the disposal of Asset 1 remains the liability of Tall Ltd (TCGA 1992 s 19(6)).

13 Roll-over claims

Roll-over claims under s 175(2A) must be made jointly by the two companies involved. [43.133]–[43.150]

VI DEPRECIATORY TRANSACTIONS AND VALUE SHIFTING
(TCGA 1992 S 176 AND S 31)

Anti-avoidance provisions within the legislation may apply to prevent the exploitation of the rules for transfer of assets around groups to secure a tax advantage. TCGA 1992 s 176 operates to restrict allowable capital losses made on a disposal of shares by a group member following an earlier depreciatory transaction which resulted in the value of the share being reduced. FA 2011 restricted the timing of this provision to a disposal of shares within six years of the depreciatory transaction.

TCGA 1992 s 31 deals with value shifting and operates to restrict allowable losses and increase capital gains in certain circumstances. The value shifting provisions were substantially simplified in FA 2011 with the repeal of certain of the existing mechanistic provisions and the replacement of these with more general 'purposive' provisions. These new provisions, which have effect from 19 July 2011, are aimed at countering all transactions which do not solely consist in the making of an exempt dividend payment and which seek to reduce the value of shares in a company, thereby obtaining a tax advantage.

[43.151]–[43.170]

EXAMPLE 43.14

Bigco Ltd intends to sell its subsidiary Smallco Ltd for £5,000. The base cost of the Smallco shares is £1,000 which would give Bigco a gain of £4,000 (ignoring indexation). Before the sale Smallco transfers one of its assets which has a market value of £2,000 to Bigco for £500. Smallco originally paid £1,000 for the asset. As a result of the transfer Smallco is only worth £3,500 and on the sale Bigco makes a gain of £2,500. At the same time Bigco sells the asset for £2,000 making a gain of £1,000 (as Bigco took over Smallco's base cost). The total gain made by Bigco has been reduced from £4,000 to £3,500, so the value shifting rules would be applied to increase the gain.

(If it could be shown that the asset was transferred for *bona fide* commercial reasons and not as part of a scheme to avoid tax, the value shifting provisions would not apply.)

[43.171]–[43.190]

VII VAT

Two or more associated corporate bodies may register as a VAT group allowing the companies to account for VAT as a single taxable person. Subject to anti-avoidance rules being triggered, this typically results in supplies of goods or services within the group being disregarded for VAT purposes (VATA 1994 s 43) meaning no VAT is accounted for, nor any VAT invoices issued. This may be particularly attractive when one or more companies in the group make taxable supplies to another group company that is unable to recover its VAT in full, as it may reduce the overall VAT burden of irrecoverable VAT. As long as the group makes taxable supplies outside the group, it should still be able to recover the input tax attributable to those outside taxable supplies.

The decision of the High Court in *C & E Comrs v Kingfisher plc* (1994) determined that the effect of the grouping provisions went further than merely allowing a number of VAT entities to account for VAT under a single registration (as HMRC had contended) and created a single taxable entity. The CJEU decision in *European Commission v United Kingdom of Great Britain and Northern Ireland* (2013) (C-86/11) confirmed the current position of the UK that a 'non-taxable person', such as certain types of holding company, is eligible to join a VAT group.

Registration is made in the name of a chosen 'representative member' who becomes liable to report VAT in respect of all business carried out by group companies. Each individual company, however, remains jointly and severally liable for the VAT position of the group. To qualify, the two or more companies must be established, or have a fixed establishment in the UK and satisfy the control test. Whether a company has control of another is defined by reference to the Companies Act 2006 (s 1159) meaning of a 'holding company'.

In general, supplies between the UK establishment and non-UK establishments of a company included in a UK VAT group are also disregarded, subject to anti-avoidance. However, following the CJEU decision in *Skandia America Corporation* (2014), HMRC confirmed that the overseas establishment will be regarded as a separate taxable person where it is included in a VAT group in any of certain EU Member States that operate alternative VAT grouping regimes.

HMRC may refuse an application to form a group or an application by any company to join or leave a group if they perceive a VAT avoidance motive. VATA 1994 Sch 9A contains further provisions giving HMRC extensive powers to counter VAT avoidance using the group registration rules. Section 4 of VAT Notice 700/2 sets out HMRC's policy in applying these provisions.

In *Larentia + Minerva v Finanzamt* (2015) the CJEU held that national legislation could not restrict membership of a VAT group to entities having legal personality and linked to the controlling company of the group in a 'relationship of subordination', except where those requirements were appropriate and necessary to prevent abusive practices or combat evasion or avoidance. Following that decision HMRC issued a consultation document on changes to the grouping rules, seeking views on the impact of extending grouping to non-corporate bodies and on alternatives to the current control test. The Government's response to the consultation is awaited.

Applications for group treatment take effect from the dates they are received by HMRC or such other time as HMRC may allow. HMRC have 90 days from the receipt of an application to make enquiries and, if necessary, refuse group treatment. HMRC have powers to remove companies from groups on ineligibility or Revenue protection grounds.   **[43.191]–[43.210]**

VIII STAMP DUTY LAND TAX

Stamp duty land tax (SDLT) applies to acquisitions of interests in land in England, Wales and Northern Ireland. (From 1 April 2015, SDLT in Scotland has been replaced by Land and Buildings Transaction Tax.) SDLT group relief may apply to acquisitions of land interests including grants of leases between companies within a 75% group, as defined for the purposes of group relief for corporation tax, and with the same tests of direct or indirect economic entitlement to not less than 75% of the profits available for distribution and not less than 75% of the assets on a winding up. An unrestricted relief of this nature would make it easy for corporate vendors of UK real estate to transfer land into a single purpose company within the group and then to sell the company thereby avoiding the SDLT charge (though some stamp duty might be payable). So there are numerous restrictions for SDLT group relief to apply and, in some cases, provisions to claw back the value of the relief subsequently.

The detailed requirements to be met before SDLT group relief can apply so that SDLT is not charged on land transactions are in FA 2003 Sch 7. For group relief to be available one of the companies must beneficially own, directly or indirectly, at least 75% (by nominal value) of the ordinary share capital of the other, or a third company must beneficially own, directly or indirectly at least 75% of the ordinary share capital of each.

Amongst other conditions, SDLT group relief does not apply if there is an arrangement to de-group the transferee company at the time of the land transfer or if the consideration for the transfer is provided, directly or indirectly, by a person outside the group. Group relief will also be unavailable if there are arrangements for a change of control of the transferee. In addition a motive test must be met before group relief is available, there must be a bona fide commercial purpose for the transfer and it must not form part of arrangements of which a main purpose is to avoid tax – including direct taxes (but not VAT). Relief must be claimed in a land transaction return or an amendment of such a return. Even when group relief is validly claimed there is a three-year period during which a charge equal to the tax saving may apply if the transferee de-groups from the vendor. A claw-back may also apply if the vendor is de-grouped first and there is subsequently a change in ultimate control of the transferee. **[43.211]**

44 The taxation of partnerships

Updated by Anna Jarrold, Head of Professional Services Tax, BDO LLP

I   Income tax [**44.2**]
II Capital gains tax [**44.31**]
III Inheritance tax [**44.51**]
IV Value added tax [**44.71**]

In the UK there are three common forms of 'partnership'; a partnership formed under the Partnership Act 1890 (often called a general partnership), a limited partnership formed under the Limited Partnership Act 1907 and a limited liability partnership (LLP) formed under the Limited Liability Partnerships Act 2000. The latter is more akin to a company in its commercial obligations, but has taxation characteristics similar to a partnership. This chapter concentrates on the first two forms of partnership. **Chapter 45** deals with limited liability partnerships.

Partnerships and LLPs have been the subject of review by HMRC since the beginning of 2013 and a number of aspects are subject to new rules. Prior to these changes the taxation of partnerships and partners was largely governed by general principles, actual practice and HMRC guidance and concessions. Now, however, there is a substantial body of legislation that needs to be considered.

These new rules include major changes in the treatment of the loans to participators rules, the tax status of members of LLPs, allocations of profit and entrepreneurs' relief and were included in Finance Acts 2013, 2014 and 2015. Whereas the pace of change has slowed in F(No 2)A 2015 and FA 2016, they did contain measures which materially affect partners and LLP members. F(No 2)A 2015 also contained changes to the taxation of carried interest and further provisions with regard to the treatment of disguised investment management fees, which are prevalent in private equity structures. FA 2016 saw changes to the way in which dividends are taxed and the introduction of new 'nil' rate bands for both dividend and investment income from 2016–17.

HMRC published the outcome of a consultation entitled 'Partnership Taxation: Proposals to Clarify Tax Treatment' in March 2017 covering a variety of aspects, including the use of nominee arrangements and the reporting requirements for multi-tier partnership structures. Legislation is expected to be included in the second Finance Bill 2017.

Partnerships may have partners who are either individuals or corporate bodies. This chapter deals with the taxation of individuals. Although the statutory references may differ, the principles outlined in this chapter frequently apply to corporate partners.

Unlike companies and unincorporated associations, a partnership, whether trading or professional, is not subject to special rules of taxation. A partnership is fiscally transparent, and the normal principles of income tax and CGT apply to each partner individually. For IHT the partners are taxed individually on their interest in the partnership, but the assets of the partnership are not treated as the assets of the individual partners. The position is different for VAT, where a partnership is treated as a separate taxable entity (VATA 1994 s 45). [44.1]

I INCOME TAX

The income from a trading or professional partnership is charged to tax under ITTOIA 2005 Part 9. Individual partners are required to include their share of partnership profits in their own tax return. However a partnership return is required to enable the calculation of the partnership profits to be dealt with centrally (TMA 1970 s 12AA). The online and paper filing dates for the partnership return are respectively 31 January and 31 October following the end of the tax year. This assumes a partnership comprised solely of individuals. Where there is at least one corporate partner, the return must be filed by the later of 31 January following the tax year or 12 months from the end of the relevant period where it is filed online. Where a paper return is filed, it is the later of 31 October following the tax year or 9 months from the end of the relevant period. The relevant period is the period to which the partnership makes up accounts and will end on the accounting date of the partnership ending in the tax year. For example, if the return is filed online, for a partnership with a corporate partner and a year end of 31 March 2016, the filing deadline is 31 March 2017 (ie later than 31 January 2017). [44.2]

1 How to calculate the profits of the partnership

a) *Contrast the sole trader/practitioner*

The rules for calculating the profits of a partnership are the same as for the sole trader or practitioner (see **Chapter 10**). The extent that a sum paid to a partner is a tax deductible amount or a profit share needs consideration when preparing the partnership tax computation.

In *MacKinlay v Arthur Young McClelland Moores & Co* (1989) the Court of Appeal (although later reversed by the House of Lords, see below) allowed a partnership to deduct removal costs paid to encourage two partners to move house: in one case from London to Southampton, in the other from Newcastle to Bristol. In both cases the move was desirable from the point of view of the firm's business and neither partner would have agreed to move had his relocation expenses not been borne by the firm. Slade LJ explained the

Court of Appeal decision and distinguished the *Mallalieu* case (see [**10.137**]) as follows:

> 'The analogy between the case of expenses incurred by a sole trader of which he is the beneficiary and the case of expenses incurred by a partnership, of which one partner is the beneficiary, is a misleading one. Section 74(a) ... directs attention to the object of the *spender*, not the recipient. In the first of those two cases it is impossible to differentiate between the objects of the taxpayer *qua* spender and *qua* beneficiary; ... in the second case, where the payer and the beneficiary are not the same, it is clearly possible to evaluate the objects of the payer in incurring the expenditure separately and distinctly from those of the beneficiary ... The Revenue [must] ascertain the purpose of the expenditure at least primarily by what was referred to in argument as the "collective purpose" of the partnership in incurring it.'

The House of Lords reversed the Court of Appeal decision and, in so doing, restated the principles underlying the rules governing the deduction of business expenditure. Their Lordships held, *first*, that there was no difference for these purposes between a partnership – even a large professional body run by a management committee on corporate lines – and a sole practitioner. In both cases, to be deductible, expenditure must be 'wholly and exclusively laid out or expended for the purposes of the trade, profession or vocation'. Only in very limited situations is an English partnership a separate entity for tax purposes and the speeches of the Law Lords emphasised again that tax rules applicable to individuals must apply to unincorporated bodies. In some cases, this is easier said than done: for instance, the application of CGT principles to partnerships is far from straightforward, as will be discussed later.

A *second* principle to emerge from the speeches was that (in the words of Lord Oliver) 'a partner working in the business or undertaking of the partnership is in a very different position from an employee'. Crucially, he is also a proprietor and accordingly any money which he withdraws from the business whether in the form of a share of profits, 'salary', or interest on partnership capital, must be treated as a share of profits. However, it is an over-simplification to assume that *no sums* paid out by the firm to a partner can amount to a deductible business expense for the firm (see [**44.6**] and [**45.22**]).

The context of an allowable deduction was further explored in *R & C Comrs v Peter Vaines* (2016). This case considered whether the taxpayer was entitled to a deduction, under the 'wholly and exclusively' principles, from his share of partnership profits for an out of court settlement of a bank claim relating to a previous firm. The taxpayer argued that if the claim was not settled he could have been made bankrupt thus preventing him from continuing in his current trade. The First-tier Tribunal held that the payment to the bank was wholly and exclusively for the purposes of the taxpayer's trade. The Tribunal also found that as the payment was to preserve and protect the taxpayer's professional career or trade, it followed that the expense was a revenue and not capital payment. However, the decision was overturned on appeal to the Upper Tribunal, where, it was accepted that such a payment could qualify as wholly and exclusively expended for the purposes of the trade. However, the deduction of the payment had to be justifiable in the context of his current firm's trade carried on collectively. The payment inevitably resolved what was essentially a personal matter rather than one related to the conduct of the trade of his new firm. The payment was therefore not incurred wholly and exclusively for the purpose of his trade. [**44.3**]

b) *The basis of assessment*

The taxable profits of a partnership are based on the accounting profits, usually calculated using Generally Accepted Accounting Principles (UK GAAP), although some firms may choose to adopt International Accounting Standards, including work-in-progress for the accounting year ended in the tax year (see **Chapter 10**). Historically partnerships were able to account for profit (and calculate tax liabilities) on a cash basis (ITTOIA 2005 s 160) but work-in-progress has been required to be accounted for from 1999–2000 onwards. There was a further change to accounting requirements with the issue of UITF 40 in March 2005. Both of these changes resulted in accounting adjustments. There were two types of transitional relief available for professional practices in general and barristers/advocates in particular. These reliefs took the form of spreading the adjustment arising on the change of accounting basis in 1999–2000 (and in particular the inclusion of professional work-in-progress) over a period of up to 10 years (ITTOIA 2005 Part 2 Chapter 17 and ITTOIA 2005 s 860) and spreading the adjustment in respect of UITF 40 over three to six years. UK GAAP changed with the introduction of FRS 102, which applies to accounting periods commencing on or after 1 January 2015 and impacts partnerships. From 6 April 2013, small businesses with a turnover of under £ 83,000 (the VAT threshold) can elect to use a form of the cash basis in certain circumstances and this can include partnerships and barristers (or advocates in Scotland) but not LLPs. [**44.4**]

c) *Arriving at a firm's taxable profit*

ITTOIA 2005 s 24 and s 25 require generally accepted accounting principles to be used in arriving at the taxable profit. The accounting results are then subject to any adjustment required by law in calculating taxable profits. The following specific matters merit comment: [**44.5**]

Limited company partners If the partnership has both individual and corporate partners, there will be a requirement for two different tax calculations to be prepared, one using the principles applicable to income tax and the other reflecting the corporation tax rules. It should be noted that there are some significant differences that affect these calculations, such as the loan relationship rules and intangible fixed asset regime, which only apply to corporation tax. If the partnership is made up entirely of limited company partners the tax computation only needs to reflect the corporation tax rules. (See [**44.10**] concerning the FA 2014 rules on the allocation of profits after 6 April 2014 to corporate members of partnerships with both individual and corporate members.)

Salary paid to partners How a partner's salary is taxed depends on whether he is a partner or merely an employee of the firm. The terms used by the parties themselves are not decisive of the matter; it is the substance of the relationship between them that, as determined from the partnership agreement, needs to be considered. In view of the high level of national insurance contributions (NIC) payable by an employer in respect of higher-paid employees, the firm should consider carefully how it wishes new 'partners' to be taxed and draft the partnership agreement accordingly. (See [**45.22**] for comments regarding changes introduced in FA 2014 and effective from 6 April 2014 relating to UK LLPs.)

If the individual is an employee, the salary paid is a deductible partnership expense on which he should be assessed as earnings from an employment, with tax deducted at source under PAYE. If the individual is a partner, the salary is not an allowable expense of the firm but an appropriation of profits. The firm's accounts must show the profits as including salaries paid to non-employee partners that are then taken into account when apportioning those profits amongst the partners. [**44.6**]

EXAMPLE 44.1

Balthazar, Mountolive and Justine are in partnership sharing profits in the ratio 3:2:1 after deducting salaries agreed at £5,000, £10,000 and £15,000 respectively. In the year ended 31 December 2016 the business profits (after deducting 'salaries') were £60,000.

This profit will be divided between the partners in accordance with their profit sharing arrangements in the year ended 31 December 2016.

For 2016–17, the current year basis applies and the assessment will be on £90,000 (the salaries being treated as part of the profit shares) attributed to the partners as follows:

Balthazar:	£5,000	(salary) plus	£30,000	(3/6 × £60,000)	=	£35,000
Mountolive	£10,000	(salary) plus	£20,000	(2/6 × £60,000)	=	£30,000
Justine:	£15,000	(salary) plus	£10,000	(1/6 × £60,000)	=	£25,000
	£30,000	(salaries) +	£60,000	(balance of profits)	=	£90,000

Interest paid to partners Partners may be paid interest on capital contributed to the firm. As with partners' 'salaries', the interest is not a tax deductible expense, but is treated as an appropriation of profit. The profits must be adjusted by adding back the interest and the share of each of the partners in the profits then calculated. [**44.7**]

Rent paid to a partner Where premises are owned by one partner and leased to the firm, any rent paid will be an allowable deduction from the firm's profits, unless the amount exceeds the market rate. The partner concerned will be taxed on that rent as property income. It may be more attractive for the premises to be let to the partnership at a nominal rent and for the partner to receive an increased share of the profits. This will not be tax deductible by the firm, but the partner concerned will be taxed on the income as trading profits (rather than as property income) and, thus could give greater scope in the event of loss relief. However, the additional Class 4 NIC liability and restrictions on the availability of tax relief for pension contributions can tip the balance of advantage back to property income treatment.

When the partner has taken out a loan for the purchase or improvement of the premises which are used by the firm, he needs to ensure that the interest paid on the loan qualifies for income tax relief. If he receives rent from the firm or if the firm discharges the interest payments (which will be treated as 'deemed rent') income tax relief will be obtained by setting the interest due against the rent (or the deemed rent arising from the interest paid by the firm). If the premises belong to all the partners they cannot let those premises to the firm since a person cannot let property to himself (see *Rye v Rye* (1962)).

Should a partner lease property to a partnership, the position concerning entrepreneurs' relief (ER) should be considered. If the property is used in a qualifying business and is disposed of together with the business, or a share of the business, the property disposal may also qualify for ER on the basis that it is an 'associated disposal' (TCGA 1992 s 169K). However, where rent has been charged by the partner, after 6 April 2008, the relief available will be restricted. These provisions were tightened in FA 2015 so that there must be a disposal of at least 5% of the business to qualify. **[44.8]**

Losses Tax Losses incurred by the partnership are apportioned between the partners in the same way as any profits (ITTOIA 2005 s 850), each partner dealing with his share of the loss under the normal relieving provisions (see **Chapter 11**). There are restrictions on the ability to allocate a loss to one partner and a profit to another partner such that only the net firm position is reflected by the allocation, whether a loss or profit (ITTOIA 2005 s 850A). Legislation has been enacted to counteract arrangements devised to allocate losses to partners in excess of their financial contribution or where initial losses of the partnership are allocated to partners, who then leave the partnership before profits are generated. The provisions apply to trades (but not to professions) and restrict the extent to which partners can offset losses against other sources of income (ie restrict the availability of sideways loss relief). It does not restrict the extent losses can be carried back or carried forward against income of the same trade. In any instance where a trade is undertaken by a partnership, the losses that are eligible for sideways loss relief cannot exceed the capital contributed by the individual to the partnership (as defined in ITA 2007 s 105). For these purposes loans from partners to partnerships do not count as capital contributions. (See **[45.12]** for comments regarding changes introduced in FA 2014 and effective from 6 April 2014 relating to UK LLPs.)

For losses sustained on or after 2 March 2007, there is a second sideways loss relief restriction which is considered after the test based on partners' capital contributions. For non-active and limited partners there is a ceiling of £25,000 of losses which are available for sideways loss relief. A non-active partner is defined in ITA 2007 s103B as a partner who does not spend, on average, 10 hours a week in the performance of his duties as a partner.

These restrictions apply to all forms of partnership undertaking a trade, including limited liability partnerships.

In addition, there is a specific anti-avoidance rule regarding sideways relief for losses arising from exploiting films. For non-active and limited partners, relief is blocked for losses arising on or after 22 July 2004, in the first four years of a trade.

FA 2008 included provision to extend the loss carry-back provisions for companies and unincorporated businesses, including LLPs. Originally, the losses to which the new provisions applied were those arising in accounting periods ending in the period 24 November 2008 to 23 November 2009 (for companies) and 2008–09 (for unincorporated businesses). Further legislation was introduced in FA 2009 so that losses arising in accounting periods from 24 November 2009 to 23 November 2010 (for companies) and 2009–10 (for unincorporated businesses) are also eligible for the extended loss carry-back provisions. In this context, a partner in an LLP is treated individually, so that the amount referred to relates to the individual partner's share of the loss.

For these years, the amount of trading losses that can be carried back to the preceding year remains unlimited. After carry back to the preceding year, a maximum of £50,000 of unused losses were available for carry-back to the earlier two years. The £50,000 limit applies separately to the unused losses of each 12-month period or tax year. For example, for a member of an LLP, a separate cap applied to the extended carry-back of losses made in each of the tax years 2008–09 and 2009–10.

The majority of previously unlimited income tax reliefs that may be deducted from income under ITA 2007 s 24 are, from 5 April 2013, capped at the greater of £50,000 or 25% of the individual's total income liable to income tax. Note that sideways loss relief for trading losses, opening year trade losses and post-cessation trade relief are caught by these provisions. There is no cap on the amount of losses that can be carried forward for offset against future profits from the same trade or carried back in a terminal loss relief claim (ITA 2007 s 89). There is also no cap in respect of overlap relief crystallised on the retirement of a partner or on the change of accounting reference date.

Under self assessment, it is the partner's responsibility to calculate any restrictions on losses and any exit charges. [44.9]

d) *Allocating profits/losses to members – mixed member partnerships*

HMRC had previously accepted the principle that the partners are free to allocate the profits/losses amongst themselves in accordance with their own partnership agreement or otherwise by agreement amongst themselves.

FA 2014 introduced restrictions on the allocation of profits and losses where a partnership or LLP is a 'mixed member' partnership. A 'mixed member' partnership is a partnership or LLP that has, as partners or members, both individuals and persons who are not individuals. Examples of non-individuals include companies and trustees. These rules have effect from 6 April 2014 and are subject to anti-forestalling rules from 5 December 2013. Where the rules apply, profits or losses allocated to a non-individual partner may be taxed upon the individual partners of the business. This can also extend to an individual who is not a partner in the LLP in certain circumstances. On 27 March 2014, HMRC issued guidance to assist with the application and interpretation of these new rules (Partnerships: A review of two aspects of the tax rules – Mixed Membership Partnerships – Alternative Investment Fund Managers – Transfers of Assets & Income Streams Through Partnerships).

Outline of the rules

The rules target profit allocations that are viewed as diverting an individual partner's profit to a non-individual member (usually a corporate member that is not liable to income tax) of a partnership or LLP. Where an excess amount of the partnership profits are allocated to the non-individual member (ie more than its 'appropriate notional profit'), HMRC has the power to reallocate the profit to the individual member for tax purposes – even in cases where individuals try to circumvent the rules, eg by ceasing to be personal members.

Similar rules now allow HMRC to restrict the claimable amount of a loss where there is an excess allocation of losses from a partnership member who is not chargeable to UK income tax to members that are.

Detailed conditions

Before HMRC can invoke its power to reallocate profits from non-individual to individual partners, two conditions must be met.

First, it must be 'reasonable to suppose' that the profits of the non-individual member (usually a company or a trust) represent deferred profits of the individual members (ie profits that would have otherwise been taxable on the individual members but for the artificial allocation to the non-individual member). The individual partner or partners must also save or defer tax as a result of the arrangement.

Second, there is a commerciality test. This involves testing whether the profit allocated to the non-individual member is an 'appropriate' return on the capital or assets it has contributed to the partnership (see below). It must also be 'reasonable to suppose' that any excess profit over the appropriate return that is allocated to the non-individual member arose because an individual member had the 'power to enjoy' those profits at a later date and he or she saved tax in the meantime.

Who has a 'power to enjoy' the diverted profits?

An individual member will be regarded as having a power to enjoy profits allocated to a non-individual member if he or she is connected to the non-individual member. The fact that the individual and the non-individual are both members of the partnership will not alone make them connected for these purposes. However, where:
- an individual member controls the non-individual member (alone or with someone connected to him or her); and
- the individual member or a person connected to him or her (a very wide class of relatives, business partners and entities) can benefit in any way, at any time, from the profits received by the non-individual member,

then the individual member is deemed to have a 'power to enjoy' profits allocated to the non-individual member.

EXAMPLE 44.2

Mrs Hill is a member of an LLP in which Hill Ltd is also a partner. Hill Ltd is owned by Mrs Hill's children and she is a director of the company. Hill Ltd has never paid any dividends to shareholders nor a salary to Mrs Hill but it receives a profit share from the LLP.

Mrs Hill has a power to enjoy the profits allocated to Hill Ltd under the rules. Therefore, any excess profit that is allocated to Hill Ltd may end up being reallocated to Mrs Hill.

In other commercial situations, perhaps where an outside investor has injected cash into a partnership through a corporate member, the individual members may derive some benefit from the presence of the corporate member. However, if the individual members do not control the corporate member there is no 'power to enjoy' so no profit reallocation will be made.

What is the appropriate notional profit?

To calculate whether there is any excess profit that must be taxed on individual members, HMRC must first establish what level of profit it is 'appropriate' for the non-individual member to receive from the partnership. In general terms, what is appropriate is determined by considering the usual arm's length return that would apply between unconnected parties, ie a commercial rate of return for the capital it supplies or the services it provides to the partnership.

When assessing how much capital the non-individual member has contributed, the rules set out that it is only the money or property that the non-individual member has contributed to the 'permanent endowment' of the partnership that can be counted. This means that balances on current, tax or drawings accounts (including undrawn profit share) within the partnership are ignored and only long term capital is counted.

Where services are provided by the non-individual member to the partnership, a commercial rate for those services must be assessed. However, any services provided directly by the individual member of the partnership through his or her company are ignored – even if there is a chain of intermediaries such that the service company is not a non-individual member of the partnership.

In practice, it should be relatively straightforward to agree an appropriate notional rate of return on capital for a non-individual partner but agreeing appropriate rates for services it provides to a partnership through its employees (who are not also members of the partnership) may be more time consuming – particularly if the entity does not provide services to unconnected third parties.

EXAMPLE 44.3

Jupiter LLP has four partners, one a company, Saturn Ltd, and three individuals. Saturn Ltd is owned by two of the other partners and has provided the capital to the business of £1 million; it provides no other services, assets or facilities to the LLP. Under the terms of the partnership agreement, Saturn Ltd is entitled to 30% of the profits of the business. For the year ended 30 April 2016, Jupiter LLP will have taxable profits of £2 million. For accounting purposes, Saturn Ltd is entitled to £600,000 of the taxable profit.

However, the new mixed member partnership rules apply and under these rules it is clear that two of the individual partners of Jupiter LLP have the 'power to enjoy' the profits of Saturn Ltd. Let us assume that the commercial rate of interest applicable for a loan from a third party on terms similar to the Saturn Ltd capital account is 10%. The taxable profits will need to be reallocated for tax purposes such that Saturn Ltd's share of the taxable profit will be reduced to £100,000, being 10% of £1 million. The balance of the profit share allocated to Saturn Ltd, £500,000, will then need to be reallocated for tax purposes, on a just and reasonable basis, to the two individual partners who have the power to enjoy the profits of Saturn Ltd.

When profit is reallocated by HMRC

Where the rules are applied, HMRC will seek to tax the individual members on their share of any profit deferred (ie via payments to the non-individual member they control that are in excess of a normal commercial rate of return to which it would be entitled). In almost all cases, this will require the partnership's advisers to agree a just and reasonable split of disputed profits with HMRC.

Double taxation is prevented by treating payments made to the individual member from the corporate member (that stem from excess partnership profit that it has received over appropriate notional profit) as non taxable income for the individual. For example, for a dividend paid by the company to its owner (or any other individual) where both are members of the partnership, only that part of the dividend that is derived from the company's appropriate notional profit is taxable on the individual as savings income; the balance is taxed on the individual but as his or her own partnership profit share when it arose and was allocated to the corporate member.

Equally, where the rules apply, the non-individual member's taxable profit must be reduced to reflect the increase in the individual member's share.

However, there will be situations where simple numerical adjustments are not appropriate because of computation differences between income and corporation tax. In such circumstances, a just and reasonable adjustment will need to be negotiated with HMRC. For partnerships treated as alternative investment fund managers (AIFM), special rules will apply where deferred profit is treated as allocated to the firm itself and taxed on the firm at personal tax rates.

Following such adjustments, partners involved in a mixed membership partnership are likely to be no worse off than they would have been had there been no attempt to defer tax. However, the administrative burden that this process creates will be significant and most partnerships will wish to amend their arrangements so that they are not necessary.

International businesses

There are no special rules to exempt members of international partnerships. However, it is important to remember that, in most cases, where partnership structures have been set up for commercial reasons while there may well be a mixed membership partnership in the UK, there may be no effective reduction in the individual member's taxable profit from the UK partnership. In such cases, the rules will not apply.

Where a structure does result in deferral of UK tax and HMRC applies the rules to reallocate profits to individual partners in the UK, this could easily result in double taxation and individuals may not be able to set overseas tax paid on the same profits against their UK tax liability under double taxation agreements.

Losses

The rules targeting artificial allocation of excess losses are aimed at partnerships used as investment vehicles rather than professional partnerships. However, they can apply in all situations where there is a mixed membership partnership that has been used (mainly or in part) to avoid tax through the artificial use of trade or property business losses.

For example, where individual members of a partnership subscribe capital and are allocated the losses in the initial year/s of a business (including excess capital allowances), the loss relief at income tax rates is effectively the return on their investment. In later years when capital has effectively been returned, individual members may have only a small profit share with the corporate member taking most of the profits which are then taxed at lower corporation tax rates. Under the new rules, no loss relief will be given to individual members in such cases.

Asset transfers

Alongside the FA 2014 rules for partnership profits and losses, the Government introduced anti-avoidance rules to target the transfer of assets (including income streams) using partnerships. Such arrangements take advantage of the fact that the transferee and transferor are subject to differing tax rates (eg a company and an individual, residents and non-residents, traders and investors etc) to avoid tax. The new rules apply to all partnerships, not just mixed membership partnerships (although not where the parties concerned are close relatives).

An example of such a technique might be where a company contributes capital to a partnership in return for a share of the profits from a trade (an income stream) transferred into the partnership by an individual. HMRC regards the individual as having effectively sold his or her income stream, receiving the capital in exchange. Where the legislation applies, an amount is charged to tax as if it were income of the transferor, being the higher of the amount of consideration given for the asset and its market value.

Accounting periods straddling 6 April 2014

All partnership profits arising after 6 April 2014 may be subject to the FA 2014 rules, even where the accounting period started much earlier and straddles 6 April 2014.

The rules include anti-forestalling clauses to target action that partners took between 5 December 2013 and the end of their partnership's accounting period (where this straddles 6 April 2014) to divert profits to a non-individual member of the partnership. For example, where a partnership has an annual accounting date of 30 June, any action taken between 5 December 2013 and 30 June 2014 to reallocate excess profits to a non-individual member will trigger HMRC's reallocation powers. The rules enable a recast of the profit shares for all the partners for the accounting year to 30 June 2014, on a 'just and reasonable' basis. The profits would be time-apportioned between two deemed periods: 1 July 2013 to 5 April 2014 and 6 April 2014 to 30 June 2014. For the latter period, the individual partners would become taxable on any reallocated profit.

As promised in the initial consultation on these proposals, there will be no reallocation by HMRC for profits treated as arising prior to 6 April 2014. Therefore, mixed member partnerships will not be subject to the new rules for accounting periods ending on or before 5 April 2014. **[44.10]**

2 Interest relief on loans to acquire a share in a partnership

Tax relief is available for interest on money which is borrowed to acquire a share in a partnership that undertakes a trade or profession, or is lent to the firm for its business, or to acquire machinery or plant to be used by the firm. It is important to be able to demonstrate the purpose of the borrowing. In *Lancaster v IRC* (2000), the taxpayer failed to convince the Special Commissioner that the purpose of borrowing money was to use it within the business rather than funding a transfer of value to his spouse. This case highlights the need to carefully arrange matters when considering the funding of a partnership interest.

The relief operates by enabling the borrower to deduct the interest from his income (ITA 2007 s 383/s 398; see **[7.48]**). In contrast, where the firm borrows money, any interest paid is normally a deductible business expense (ITTOIA 2005 s 29; see **[10.130]**).

It should be noted that, in order for the borrower to obtain relief, there must exist significant uncertainty as to whether the level of return will secure a post-tax surplus for the investor. An individual who uses a scheme that exploits s 383 by means of an arrangement that eliminates any investment risk will be denied tax relief for the interest paid (ITA 2007 s 384A: see **[14.31]**).

The restrictions referred to in **[44.9]** also apply to qualifying loan interest from 5 April 2013. These cap the allowable income tax deduction for interest and other appropriate reliefs to the greater of £50,000 or 25% of the individual's total income liable to income tax. **[44.11]**

3 Changes in the partnership

Partnership changes are considered in detail in **Chapter 10**. **[44.12]**

4 Leaving the partnership

a) *Consultancies*

An outgoing partner may be retained as a consultant whereupon he will often be paid a fee in return for some continuing duties. For income tax purposes, the consultant is not a partner so that any sum paid to him by the firm will be a deductible business expense assuming that it can be justified under the 'wholly and exclusively' test (**[10.130]** and **[10.137]**). If the expenditure has more than one purpose, ITTOIA 2005 s 34(2) permits a deduction for the portion incurred wholly and exclusively for the business. This is statutory confirmation of the decisions in *Copeman v Flood* (1941); and *Earlspring Properties Ltd v Guest* (1995)).

The consultant may be an employee so that PAYE must be operated and he may benefit from joining the firm's pension scheme for a few years. Even if a PAYE obligation does not arise directly, the individual may be within the personal service company rules in ITEPA 2003 Part 2 Chapter 8. He may be able to establish that he is exercising a profession or vocation and should be assessed under ITTOIA 2005 s 847. This treatment is more likely to apply where the individual holds consultancies with several different bodies. In view of the increased NIC payable in respect of employees, the firm should consider whether it will be preferable to retain the individual as a partner with a reduced profit share rather than as a consultant; however, the parties should also consider the potential impact of a reduced profit share on the availability of overlap relief on an eventual exit (see [10.201]).

If the outgoing partner retains an interest in a corporate member of the partnership, it is likely that HMRC will consider the use of its profit reallocation powers (see [44.10]). [44.13]

b) *Payment of annuities by continuing partners*

Payment of annuities to retiring partners may be an efficient way of dealing fairly with a retiring partner where partners are not formally paid for goodwill. These are becoming less common within partnerships and are typically excluded from LLP structures due to the fact that such annuities must be accounted for as a liability on the firm's balance sheet.

Annuities are paid net of basic rate tax (see **Chapter 14**). The paying partners do not get relief for the payment in the partnership return (as the annuity is paid net of tax) and must claim tax relief for higher rates of tax through their own self assessment return. They are not subject to PAYE.

Annuities are taxable as income in the hands of the recipient (see [44.16]).

Professional partnership agreements may make provision for the payment of annuities to retiring partners in consideration for the outgoing partner surrendering his share of the firm's goodwill and of its capital assets (see [44.34]). It is largely a matter of commercial expediency whether such annuities are payable and if so for how long and for what amount. The recipient may prefer an annuity linked to the profits of the business (eg 10% of the net profits) rather than a fixed sum, as this should offer 'inflation proofing', but may not be beneficial where profits are falling. [44.14]

Position of paying partners It is usual for the cost of an annuity to be borne by the partners in the same proportion as they share the profits. The annuity will be tax-effective provided that it is payable under a partnership agreement to a former member of that partnership, or his widow or other dependants (where the partner is dead the annuity must not be payable for more than ten years) and is an arms length transaction (ITTOIA 2005 s 627(2)). The annuity will also be an effective annual payment if it is paid in connection with the acquisition of a share in the business of the outgoing partner.

The partnership agreement will often provide for any incoming partner to take over the cost of an appropriate share of the annuity and that, should the firm cease to exist, the outstanding years of the annuity are to be valued and treated as a debt owed by the partners in the partnership at the date of its cessation. For partnerships which have converted to LLP structures, the annuity arrangements may have been left as a liability of the former partners of the predecessor partnership. Typically, a prior share of profit will be allocated to the annuity paying partners of the LLP in order to facilitate the payment of the annuity liability. [44.15]

Position of the recipient The recipient will be liable to income tax on the annuity with a credit for basic rate tax deducted at source. Prior to 6 April 2006 the annuity was taxed in the recipient's hands as earned income to the extent that the amount payable did not exceed one half of the average of that individual's best three years' profits out of the last seven; any excess was unearned income (TA 1988 s 628). The differential between earned and unearned income was repealed by FA 2004 with effect from 6 April 2006. This was a consequence of simplification of pension legislation generally (see **Chapter 50**). However, these payments are not relevant for lifetime allowance/annual allowance purposes.

If the annuity is payable after the recipient's death to a widow(er) or dependants, they may have problems enforcing the payments should the continuing partners default (see *Beswick v Beswick* (1967)). [44.16]

EXAMPLE 44.4

The partnership agreement of Falstaff & Co provides for retiring partners to be paid an annuity for ten years after retirement amounting to 10% of the annual net profits of the firm earned in the preceding accounting year.

Hal retires as a partner on 5 April 2016. In the tax year 2016–17, Falstaff & Co's net profits amount to £90,000. The continuing partners will pay Hal £7,200, ie 10% × £90,000 = £9,000 less basic rate income tax deducted at source. Hal must enter the gross amount of the payment (£9,000) in his income tax calculation for 2016–17 with a tax credit for £1,800 (basic rate tax of 20%).

c) *Retirement annuities and personal pension schemes*

In addition to or instead of (b) above, partners as self-employed individuals could provide for their retirement by making pension contributions personally. Prior to 1 July 1988, such insurance had to take the form of a retirement annuity contract approved under TA 1988 s 619. However, in order to bring retirement provision for the self-employed into line with that available to employees, TA 1988 ss 630–655 required both employees who contract out of occupational pension schemes and partners who provide for their retirement to enter personal pension scheme arrangements. These requirements commenced from 1 July 1988. On 6 April 2006, the UK pension regime was further simplified with an annual contributions limit subject to an overriding fund value cap. FA 2009 and subsequent Finance Acts have significantly complicated the tax relief position by restricting relief for individuals. Major changes to the pension regime were introduced in FA 2014 and implemented from 6 April 2015 which allow individuals in most circumstances to access their pension benefits directly and without limitation. These changes are considered further in **Chapter 50**.

II CAPITAL GAINS TAX

1 General

The application of CGT principles to partnerships causes difficulties which are mainly due to the failure of the legislation to make express provision for the treatment of partnerships. It is, therefore, necessary to apply rules designed for individuals to firms and rely on SP D12, SP 1/79 and SP 1/89 as a substitute for proper legislation in this field. SP D12 was revised in September 2015 following the report of the Office of Tax Simplification. The latest update includes a new section 5 covering the situation where a partner contributes an asset to a partnership by means of a capital contribution, which follows the approach outlined by HMRC in the Revenue & Customs Brief 03/08. It also contains a new s 14 detailing the CGT loss reliefs that may be applicable. Apart from these, there is some revision of language but the basic principles have not changed in the new version. The Office of Tax Simplification commented that SP D12 had stood the test of time and was well understood. Fundamental change or actual legislation is therefore not anticipated.

Where the partnership is carrying on a trade, any dealings with the assets of the partnership are treated as dealings by the partners individually (TCGA 1992 s 59). In the absence of any specific agreement, the treatment of capital gains and losses follows the profit sharing arrangements although often partners agree that the asset surplus entitlement will be different from the profit sharing ratio to reflect the partners' contributions to the capital of the business. At times it may be uncertain whether a particular asset is partnership property or owned by one of the partners and merely used, often without any formal arrangement being entered into, by the firm (see, in relation to milk quota, *Faulks v Faulks* (1992)). [44.31]

EXAMPLE 44.5

(1) Flip & Co, a partnership trading in goods from the East, has three partners, Flip, Flap and Flop, who share asset surpluses in the ratio 3:2:1. In 1998 the firm acquired a painting which was put on display in the firm's reception area at a cost of £60,000; they sell it subsequently for £180,000. The total gain (ignoring any incidental costs of disposal) is £120,000. CGT must be calculated separately for each partner:

Flip owns 3/6 of the asset and, therefore, has a base cost of £30,000 and is entitled to 3/6 of the sale proceeds (£90,000); his gain is £60,000 (ie he is entitled to 3/6 of the partnership gain).

Flap's base cost is 2/6 of £60,000 (£20,000) and his share of the proceeds is 2/6 of £180,000 (£60,000) so that his gain is £40,000.

Flop's base cost is 1/6 of £60,000 (£10,000) and his share of the proceeds is 1/6 of £180,000 (£30,000) so that his gain is £20,000.

(2) Assume that the painting is given to Flip in recognition of his 25 years' service with the firm. It is worth £180,000 at the date of the gift. The position of Flap and Flop is basically unchanged and they have made gains of £40,000 and £20,000 respectively. Tax may be postponed by an election under TCGA 1992 s 165 if the donors and Flip agree. In that event Flap will dispose of his 2/6 share for £20,000 and Flop his 1/6 share for £10,000.

The position of Flip is that since he is given the asset he is not treated as making a disposal of his original 3/6 share in the asset (see SP D12, para 3).

Hence, the only difficulty is to discover Flip's base cost. Under general principles it will be:

	£	
	30,000	(cost of original 3/6 share)
Plus	60,000	(market value of Flap's 2/6 share at date of gift)
Plus	30,000	(market value of Flop's 1/6 share at date of gift)
	£120,000	

The result is that Flip's own gain (£60,000) is held over until such time as he disposes of the painting.

If claims are made under TCGA 1992 s 165 Flip's base cost becomes:

	£	
	30,000	(as above)
Plus	20,000	(balance after deducting held-over gain on Flap's share)
Plus	10,000	(balance after deducting held-over gain on Flop's share)
	£60,000	

2 Changing the asset surplus sharing ratio

CGT may be triggered when the asset surplus sharing ratio is altered.

Old partners	*New partners*	*Old asset surplus sharing ratio*	*New asset surplus sharing ratio*
(1) AB	ABC	1:1	1:1:1
(2) AB	AB	1:1	2:1
(3) ABC	ABD	1:1:1	2:2:1

In all the above cases, there has been a change in the entitlement to asset surpluses (and, therefore, to the beneficial ownership of the capital assets). No asset has been disposed of outside the firm, but there has been a disposal of a share of the assets between the partners.

In (1), above, A and B formerly owned the assets equally; C now joins the firm and is entitled to 1/3 of the asset surpluses. A and B have each made a disposal of 1/3 of their original share in the assets (or 1/6 of the total). A, for instance, is now entitled to 1/3 instead of 1/2 or, to put the matter another way, they have together made a disposal of 1/3 of the total assets to C. In (2), although the partners remain the same, the sharing ratio is altered so that B is making a disposal to A of 1/2 of his share of the assets. In (3), C is disposing of a 1/3 share in the assets amongst the continuing partners, A, B and D (A and B each acquire an extra 1/15 of the assets and D 3/15).

Such changes in the asset sharing ratio are likely to occur principally in three cases: (i) on the retirement of a partner; (ii) on the introduction of a new partner; and (iii) on the amendment of the partnership agreement. It should be noted that the mere revaluation of an asset in the accounts of the firm has no CGT consequences since the revaluation is neither a disposal of an asset nor of a share in assets. However, a charge will arise if an adjustment to the profit sharing ratio is made as a result of, or after, the revaluation.

Where the revaluation is credited to the partners' accounts and there is a change in profit sharing ratio, a capital gain arises, despite the fact that no actual disposal of the asset takes place. SP D12 paragraph 4 only applies where no revaluation of the asset concerned has occurred.

EXAMPLE 44.6

(1) Fleur and Camilla have been in partnership sharing profits and asset surpluses equally. The only substantial chargeable asset of the business is the freehold shop that cost £40,000 in 1998. Fleur now sells her share to Charlotte for £75,000.

Fleur has made a disposal of her half share in the asset and her gain is calculated as follows (ignoring any incidental costs of disposal):

	£
Consideration received	75,000
Less: base cost (50% of £40,000)	20,000
Gain	£55,000

(2) Slick and Slack are in partnership owning asset surpluses in the ratio 2:1. The main capital asset is the firm's premises which cost £30,000 in 1998 and have recently been revalued in the firm's accounts at £75,000. The two partners have the following interests in this capital asset:

	Slick £	*Slack* £
Original expenditure	20,000	10,000
Share of increased value	30,000	15,000
	£50,000	£25,000

Sloth joins the firm and Slick disposes of ½ of his share to Sloth with the result that the sharing ratio becomes 1:1:1. The capital account of Slick will be credited with the value of the share transferred and ultimately he will be paid that sum of money. Slick has thus disposed of ⅓ of the asset (or ½ of his share) which has a value of £25,000. That sum will be credited to his capital account with the result that he will have made a chargeable gain of £25,000 (consideration for the share disposed of) less £10,000 (base cost of the share disposed of) = £15,000.

Slick will be assessed to CGT on this gain despite the fact that he may not be entitled to receive the £25,000 until the firm is dissolved or until he leaves it. So far as the incoming partner Sloth is concerned, he will acquire a ⅓ share of the capital asset, of a value of £25,000, and that figure will be his base cost (it will often be the capital sum that he will pay into the firm on becoming a partner).

(3) If in (2) above Slick and Slack had never revalued the premises (which appear in the accounts at their original cost price of £30,000), on the change in profit sharing ratio Slick will be treated as transferring half of his share for its book value (£10,000) with the result that he will have made no gain. Correspondingly, Sloth's base cost will be £10,000.

A failure to revalue an asset, with a subsequent transfer of it at cost, might be viewed as a gift to the incoming partner so that market value should be substituted for the share transferred. In *Example 44.6* this would produce a gain for Slick of £15,000 (£25,000 − £10,000). However, although partners are generally connected persons, they are not so treated in respect of transfers of partnership assets (TCGA 1992 s 286(4)). Hence, the market value rule will not apply unless the partners are connected in some other capacity, eg parent and child, and even in those circumstances HMRC states that 'market value will not be substituted ... if nothing would have been paid had the parties been at arm's length' (SP D12, para 7). In all cases, therefore, there will be no question of market value being substituted *so long as the transaction can be shown to be one entered into at arm's length*. Normally, the commercial nature of the arrangement will be assumed. However, where the parties to the transaction are connected persons, otherwise than by solely being partners in the business, the onus is on the taxpayer to show that identical transactions would have been made with a stranger. This onus will usually be discharged by showing that the incoming partner was assuming a large share of responsibility for the running of the business and, thus, furnishing consideration for his share of the assets.

If the bounty element is so great that the transfer must be treated as a gift, HMRC has stated that 'the deemed disposal proceeds will fall to be treated in the same way as a payment outside the accounts'. In such a case any CGT can be postponed by the parties electing to hold over the gain under TCGA 1992 s 165. [44.32]

EXAMPLE 44.7

Jake and Jules are brothers and are in business together sharing profits equally. The chargeable assets of the firm cost a total of £20,000 and are now worth £200,000 although they have not been revalued in the firm's books. Jake now transfers his 50% share to his two sons, Jason and Jasper without any requirement for them to work in the business. This would clearly not be a bargain at arm's length and a disposal for CGT at market value would arise giving rise to a charge to CGT. However, Jake, Jason and Jasper could potentially make a claim under TCGA 1992 s 165 to hold over Jake's gain.

3 Goodwill

Goodwill is a chargeable asset for CGT purposes. Thus, the disposal of the whole or part of a firm's goodwill may be an occasion of charge to CGT. As accounting results must be prepared using UK GAAP or FRSs, goodwill is most commonly recognised on a balance sheet subsequent to an acquisition of trade and assets. Problems have arisen in recent years (especially with regard to professional partnerships) when the existing partners decided not to charge future incoming partners for any share of existing goodwill and, therefore, to write off the goodwill in the partnership's balance sheet. On the question as to whether those partners who originally paid for a share of that goodwill (usually on becoming partners in the firm) can then claim immediate CGT loss relief, the following principles may be suggested.

First, on an actual disposal of the goodwill, whether on retirement or to an incoming partner, provided that its value has been written off in the partnership's balance sheet, an allowable loss for CGT purposes may be claimed by the disposing partner.

EXAMPLE 44.8

Alfie is a partner in Cockney Films & Co. When he joined the firm in 1995 he paid £10,000 for a share in the goodwill. The firm has decided to write off goodwill since incoming partners will no longer be expected to pay for a share of it. When he retires and a new partner, Slicker, joins there will be no payment for Alfie's share of goodwill and Alfie will have made a loss for CGT purposes of £10,000 (being the difference between what he originally paid for the asset and the consideration received on its disposal).

Second, at the time when the goodwill is written off in the balance sheet, the partners may wish to claim immediate loss relief under TCGA 1992 s 24(2) which allows a claim for loss relief when 'the Inspector is satisfied that the value of an asset has become negligible'. HMRC does not agree that the mere writing off of goodwill has this result but takes the view that goodwill retains its value even though no longer paid for by incoming partners or shown in the firm's balance sheet, on the grounds that if the business were sold, the consideration would include a sum for goodwill (see CGT Manual, CG 68080). [**44.33**]

4 Payment of annuities

When a partner leaves the firm any annuity payments that he receives from the continuing partners will be subject to income tax ([**44.13**]). In addition to charging the annuity to income tax, its capitalised value may be treated as consideration for the disposal of a share of the partnership assets (TCGA 1992 s 37(3)) and CGT levied on any resultant gain. The capitalised value will not be subject to CGT if it is paid on retirement by reason of age or ill health and the annuity is a reasonable recognition of past services. For these purposes SP D12 para 8 considers 'reasonable recognition' to be a best three of seven years test. It reads:

> 'The capitalised value of the annuity will only be treated as consideration for the disposal of his share in the partnership assets, if it is more than can be regarded as a reasonable recognition of the past contribution of work and effort by the partner to the partnership. Provided that the former partner had been in the partnership for at least ten years an annuity will be regarded as reasonable for this purpose if it is no more than two-thirds of his average share of the profits in the best three of the last seven years in which he was required to devote substantially the whole of his time to acting as a partner.'

For lesser periods the following fractions will be used instead of the two-thirds:

Complete years in partnership	Fraction
1–5	$1/60$ for each year
6	$8/60$
7	$16/60$
8	$24/60$
9	$32/60$

1330 The taxation of partnerships

In addition to an annuity, a retiring partner may receive a lump sum. This will always be charged to CGT. Where the partner receives both an annuity and a lump sum, the lump sum may also cause the capitalised value of the annuity to be charged to CGT unless the following requirement is met:

'If the outgoing partner is paid a lump sum and an annuity, the Revenue will not charge CGT on the capitalised value of the annuity provided that the annuity and one-ninth of the lump sum together do not exceed the relevant fraction of the retired partner's average share of the profits.' (SP 1/79) **[44.34]**

EXAMPLE 44.9

(1) Charles and Claude agree to pay their partner, Clarence, who retires on 5 April 2017 after 18 years as a partner, an annuity of £20,000 pa for the next ten years. His share of the profits in the last seven years of the partnership was as follows:

Tax year	Profits £	Tax year	Profits £
2015–16	30,000	2012–13	20,000
2014–15	34,000	2011–12	40,000
2013–14	34,000	2010–11	15,000
		2009–10	12,000

The annuity does not exceed ⅔ of Clarence's average share of profits in the best three years of the last seven years before retirement, ie ⅔ × £108,000 divided by 3 = £24,000. Therefore, no CGT is paid on the capitalised value.

Contrast the position if Clarence had been paid an annuity of £25,000 pa. As the permitted £24,000 figure is exceeded the entire capitalised value of that annuity would be subject to CGT.

(2) Assume that, in addition to the annuity, of £20,000 for 10 years it is agreed that Clarence is to receive a lump sum of £54,000. His position is as follows:
  (i) the annuity will be subject to income tax;
  (ii) the lump sum (£54,000) will be subject to CGT in so far as it represents consideration for a disposal of chargeable assets; and
  (iii) the capitalised value of the annuity will also be included for CGT purposes since the annuity (£20,000) plus ⅑ of the lump sum (£6,000) exceeds the ⅔ limit of £24,000.

To the extent that the recipient is subject to CGT, the remaining partners have generated a base cost for future transactions.

In summary, an annuity is always charged to income tax on the recipient, and a lump sum is always charged to CGT. The capitalised value of an annuity may also be charged to CGT.

5 CGT Reliefs

CGT reliefs of particular relevance to partnerships are: **[44.35]**

Hold-over relief Under TCGA 1992 s 165 for gifts of business assets (see **[24.4]–[24.21]**). **[44.36]**

Roll-over (business asset replacement) relief (TCGA 1992 s 152) The extension of the relief in two circumstances should be noted. *First*, it applies to assets which are owned by an individual partner and used by the firm, so long as the entire proceeds of disposal are reinvested in another business asset used by the firm or used in a new trade carried on by the partner. *Second*, where land (or another qualifying asset) is partitioned between the partners, it is treated as a new asset for the purpose of this relief provided that the firm is dissolved immediately afterwards (see ESC D23). (See generally **[22.72]**–**[22.81]**.)

[44.37]

Roll-over (incorporation) relief (TCGA 1992 s 162) This relief is available on the incorporation of a partnership (see **[22.100]**–**[22.103]**). Care is needed over the impact of this on entrepreneurs' relief as it is possible that the conditions for this relief may not be met after incorporation and, therefore, on a subsequent share sale. If such a scenario is likely to apply it may be beneficial to disapply incorporation relief such that the gain is crystallised at a time when entrepreneurs' relief is available and of value. [44.38]

Disincorporation Relief (FA 2013, ss 58–60) may be due when a company transfers its business as a going concern to some or all of its shareholders who have held shares for more than 12 months and the transfer date falls within the period of five years from 1 April 2013 to 31 March 2018. It applies where all the assets of a business (except cash) are transferred and have a total value of less that £100,000. As the transfer must be to 'individuals' this relief applies to general partnerships only and not LLPs. Broadly, the effect of disincorporation relief is to defer a capital gain until the shareholder disposes of the asset. This is set out in new TCGA 1992 ss 162B and 162C and CTA 2009 s 849A.

6   Entrepreneurs' relief (TCGA 1992 s 169H–169S)

- Entrepreneurs' relief (ER) can be claimed in respect of certain qualifying disposals, enabling gains up to a lifetime allowance of £10 million to be taxed at a rate of 10% (TCGA 1992 s 169N(4A)). Qualifying disposals include an interest in a business. For disposals up to 22 June 2010, the relief worked by only bringing ⁵⁄₉ of the qualifying gain into charge and applying the then rate of CGT, 18%, giving an effective tax rate of 10%. After 22 June 2010, the tax rate applicable to the gain is 10%. The relief only applies to qualifying disposals which include disposals of an interest in a trading partnership or LLP.
- Changes introduced in FA 2015 restricted the availability of entrepreneurs' relief on disposals of goodwill, associated disposals and companies whose trading status derived from their ownership of a trading LLP (FA 2015 ss 41–43). However, following widespread criticism of these measures, which were seen to penalise taxpayers who were not the intended targets of the legislation, FA 2016 introduced provisions that, in some cases, restore the pre-FA 2015 position. The amendments are backdated to the date on which the relevant FA 2015 measure came into effect (18 March 2015 or 3 December 2014).

- In particular, the definition of trading company/group has been revised for ER purposes where the shares are held in a company which invests in a joint venture company or partnership. ER will now be available where the person has at least a 5% indirect interest in the shares, and effectively controls 5% voting rights of the joint venture company or where the person is entitled to at least 5% of the assets and profits of the partnership and also controls 5% of the voting rights of the corporate partner. There remains, however, some ambiguity as to the operation of these definitions and dialogue with HMRC regarding the definition of trading company/group for these purposes continues.
- There is also an extension of the availability of ER for associated disposals to include, in some cases, a disposal of a privately-held asset when there is an accompanying disposal of business assets to a family member. The relief can now also be claimed where the disposal does not meet the current 5% partnership share requirement, provided the individual making the disposal has held a 5% interest in the partnership's assets for at least three of the eight years ending with the date of the disposal.
- ER can now be claimed in respect of transfers of goodwill to a close company where the transferor holds less than 5% of the shares and voting rights in that company. Relief will also be due where the individual holds more than 5% of the shares or voting power if the transfer of the business is part of arrangements for the company to be sold to a new independent owner [44.39]–[44.50]

III INHERITANCE TAX

For IHT purposes a partnership is not a separate legal entity but a collection of individuals, and inheritance tax applies to each partner as an individual in respect of his interest in the partnership. For these purposes, the partnership is not transparent and the partnership assets are not treated as the assets of the partners.

Normally, the share of a retiring partner in the firm will pass to the continuing partners. There will be no IHT charge where full consideration is paid, or if the transfer is a commercial transaction within IHTA 1984 s 10(1).

EXAMPLE 44.10

Big & Co has 20 partners all equally entitled to profits. The following changes occur:
(1) Partner Zack is retiring and is to receive an annuity. His share of goodwill is to pass automatically under the partnership deed to the continuing partners.
(2) Partner Uriah is to devote less time to the business and will receive a reduced share of the profits (including capital profits). At the same time, partner Victor is to be paid an increased profit share to reflect his central position within the firm.
(3) Partner Yvonne is retiring and her place is to be taken by her daughter Brenda. No payment is to be made by Brenda.

The IHT consequences of these transactions are as follows:
(1) *Zack* There is no risk of an IHT charge since consideration is given for his assets (there may not even be a fall in value in his estate). Regarding the

automatic accrual of goodwill, it is generally thought that the estate duty case of *A-G v Boden* (1912) is still good law for IHT. Mutual covenants by the partners that goodwill shall pass to the surviving partners on death or retirement without any cash payment will make the transfer of goodwill non-gratuitous within IHTA 1984 s 10(1). This principle should apply even where the other parties are, or include, connected persons since it should be possible to show that identical arrangements would have been made with partners who were not so connected.

(2) *Uriah* The loss to Uriah's estate is the result of a commercial bargain since he is being allowed to devote less time to the business; no transfer of value arises. Likewise, increasing the profit sharing ratio of Victor is merely a commercial judgement by the other partners of his importance to the firm.

(3) *Yvonne* The new partner is a connected person and Brenda's acquisition of an interest in the partnership will be treated as a transfer of value by Yvonne unless the same arrangement would have been made with a new partner who was not connected to Yvonne.

The major IHT reliefs applicable to trading and professional partnerships will be business property relief, agricultural relief, and the instalment option. There are three points of particular relevance to partnerships:

First, on a transfer of assets held outside the firm and consisting of land, buildings and machinery or plant, business property relief at 50% may be available. If the asset is owned by the partnership, the full 100% relief may apply on the partners' interest in the partnership.

Second, the IHT business reliefs are not available where a partner's share is subject to a binding contract of sale at the time of transfer (see IHTA 1984 s 113). If it is desired to ensure that on the death or retirement of a partner his share shall pass to the survivors whilst at the same time preserving IHT business property relief, the partnership deed should avoid either imposing an obligation on the remaining partners to purchase his share or even providing for his share to accrue automatically to them. Instead the deed should give the surviving partners *an option* to purchase that share (see *Law Society Gazette*, 4 September 1996, at p 35).

Finally, in *Gray v IRC* (1994), HMRC succeeded before the Court of Appeal in combining the deceased's freehold interest in a landed estate with her share in a farming partnership which owned a lease over the land thereby causing a much higher value to be attributed to the property. The case represents a considerable extension of the old authorities, especially with regard to the rejection of any requirement that for valuation purposes property must form a 'natural unit'. It may turn out, however, that the actual decision turned on particular facts since the other partners were not members of the family and had no wish to continue in the business, being only too willing to sell their partnership shares to the hypothetical purchaser of the entire estate: (*Private Client Business* (1994) Issue 4). [44.51]–[44.70]

IV VALUE ADDED TAX

A partnership is regarded as a separate person for VAT registration purposes. The registration of persons carrying on business in partnership may be in the name of the firm. A notification of liability to register by a partnership is to be accompanied by Form VAT 2, which shows the name, address and signature of each partner.

The admission of a new partner or retirement of an existing partner creates a new partnership. However for VAT, in determining whether goods or services are supplied to or by persons carrying on a business in partnership, no account is taken of any change in the partnership. This does not apply to a change if there is an outright sale of the business by one group of individuals to another and the value of taxable supplies exceeds the registration threshold.

Where the same individuals carry on two separate and distinct businesses in partnership, there need not be separate registrations in respect of each partnership (*C & E Comrs v Glassborow* (1974)). This decision was distinguished where two limited partnerships existed, see *Saunders v C & E Comrs* (1980).

Changes in the composition of a continuing partnership must be notified to the Commissioners in the same way as other changes affecting the registered particulars of a taxable person. Until such time as a retirement is notified, a former partner is regarded as a continuing partner for the purposes of VAT and, therefore, remains liable for any ongoing VAT liability. [44.71]

45 Limited liability partnerships

Updated by Anna Jarrold, Head of Professional Services Tax, BDO LLP

I   Background [45.1]
II Non-tax aspects of an LLP [45.4]
III Taxing profits and gains [45.9]
IV Tax on cessation of activities [45.17]
V   Transfer of an unincorporated business to an LLP [45.20]
VI Anti-avoidance: investment and property investment LLPs [45.22]
VII Other taxes [45.23]

I BACKGROUND

1 The options

The main choice of business vehicle for many new businesses has historically been between a sole trader, a partnership or a company. With the exception of the rules for personal service companies, the tax advantages of operating a company are, primarily, the lower rates of tax on retained profits and the absence of national insurance contributions (NIC) on profits extracted by way of dividends. In some circumstances, where profits are not retained in the business, a partnership can be almost as tax-efficient as a limited company. A significant benefit of a partnership is that it may be able to flex the income and capital sharing ratios, which is not easily achieved with a company's share capital.

If profits are to be generated and extracted then use of a company leads to two layers of tax. Tax first arises within the company, and is then levied on the shareholders as the company pays them salary or dividends. Use of a partnership overcomes this double charge as profits are taxed as they arise, whether they are extracted or not and thus there is no second layer of taxation on extraction. However, with the continuing reduction of the corporation tax rate and the increase in personal tax/self employed NIC, the effective tax rates of extracting via a dividend from a company compared to a partnership profit share became much closer than in previous years and, by 2015, marginally favoured the company dividend option. The position of salary versus profit share favoured the partnership/LLP structure but this needed to be balanced to take account of the tax on disallowable expenditure. However, the change in treatment of tax on dividends, involving the scrapping of the tax credit system and the creation of a dividend nil rate band, together with an investment income nil rate band introduced by FA 2016 have shifted the fulcrum again. These measures seen against the backdrop of falling corporation tax rates, the FA 2014 provisions with regard to mixed member partnerships, the salaried partners rules and the FA 2015 and FA 2016 changes to the availability of entrepreneurs' relief mean this is an increasingly complex area to which careful consideration must be given (see further **Chapter 46**).

Traditionally the main commercial advantage of a company was the ability to limit liability. A further, not inconsiderable, advantage was the increased credibility of the corporate business due to its public reporting requirements. This included, for example, the enhanced ability to raise funds with floating charges and the ability to enter into asset finance leases. [45.1]

2 Limited partnerships

The Partnership Act 1890 was followed by the Limited Partnerships Act 1907, which permitted limited liability. Probably the most significant requirement of these provisions is that a partner with limited liability may not take any part in the management of the firm. Since active partners will often exercise management and control, they will be disqualified from the limited liability protection otherwise available. Accordingly, as a general business vehicle, the limited partnership has not enjoyed the popularity of the limited liability company. It has, however, gained acceptance as a vehicle for investment funds as, typically, the limited partners are the investors in the fund. A limited partnership requires one partner to have unlimited liability and frequently, this 'General Partner' will be a limited company. As the investors do not undertake management of the fund they are the limited partners, and thus have limited liability. The fund has tax transparency and so the investors are taxed directly on their share of fund income and gains.

Limited partnerships are often used in conjunction with LLP's (see also [**45.14**]) and companies in hybrid structures within the financial services and private equity investment arenas and the operation of these can be quite complex. A detailed consideration is beyond the scope of this chapter, but FA 2015, F(No 2)A 2015 and FA 2016 contain some provisions which may materially affect partners in such structures. Briefly, they are:

- The retention of the 28% CGT rate for gains attributable to carried interest.
- FA 2015 s 21 treats certain sums as profits of a trade rather than capital gains if they are derived from investment management services, ie in other words, they are deemed to be received as part of the investment managers' remuneration rather than through a genuine carried interest or co-investment arrangement. The definition of investment management services is drafted very widely.
- F(No)2 A 2015 denied the operation of 'base cost shift', the reallocation of CGT base cost between partners without tax consequences under SPD 12, to carried interest partners. There were also some fundamental changes to the taxation of carried interest for non-domiciled partners.
- FA 2016 has introduced a minimum 'holding period' for investments in funds (40 months) for carry payments to qualify for CGT treatment.

Carry payments related to shorter holding periods will be treated as income payments.

3 LLP's – general

Since 6 April 2001, the limited liability partnership (LLP) has been a business vehicle available in the UK. It provides a mechanism whereby the partners (including those that are active) enjoy a measure of limited liability whilst continuing to benefit from the tax transparent nature of a partnership. In legal terms, an LLP is a 'body corporate' and it has the same reporting requirements as those of a limited company. This means that it has its own separate legal personality and can contract in its own name (as opposed to being an agent for its partners). Also, its management acts on behalf of the LLP and not on behalf of the partners (who are called members). The biggest attraction of an LLP is that an LLP which is undertaking a trade, profession, or other business with a view to profit is tax transparent whilst the members are provided with limited liability. Individual members of the LLP are protected from debts or liabilities arising from negligence, wrongful acts or misconduct of *another* member, employee or agent of the LLP. They may have unlimited liability for their own misdeeds. The LLP Act 2000 refers to members rather than partners of a UK LLP. In this chapter, we refer to both partner and member as it is commonly accepted that both titles mean the same in the context of a UK LLP. [45.3]

II NON-TAX ASPECTS OF AN LLP

1 LLPs and companies

At a practical level, it is essential to remember that an LLP is a body corporate, and not an unincorporated entity. The price of limited liability is that an LLP must follow the Companies Act requirements for public disclosure of information such as reporting of members details and of filing annual accounts. These requirements are almost identical to those that apply to limited companies. The major difference between the company and LLP financial regimes is that no maintenance of capital principle applies to LLPs (although LLPs within the financial industry will have their own capital maintenance requirements).

The key non-tax features of an LLP are:
- the LLP has full legal capacity;
- it needs to register with the Registrar of Companies;
- it needs to comply with disclosure requirements eg to file annual accounts (audited if necessary) on a UK Generally Accepted Accounting Principles (UK GAAP) basis or using International Accounting Standards;
- the members of the LLP are in a similar position to company directors regarding wrongful trading etc;
- the Insolvency Act 1986 applies with necessary amendments.

The reason that the LLP has similar commercial obligations to those of a company arises from the fact that the Limited Liability Partnerships

Act 2000 (LLPA 2000) is a framework Act. It provides a basic framework and anticipates secondary legislation to provide much of the practical detail. The Limited Liability Partnerships Regulations 2001 (LLPR 2001) is an example of such detail and operates in two ways. It either states the legislation applicable to LLPs or imports considerable amounts of existing legislation (eg the Companies Act 1985 as amended by the Companies Act 2006 and the Insolvency Act 1986), and then directs amendments to the imported legislation. Where legislation has been imported, this has been to different extents – for example, only certain parts of the Companies Act 1985 have been imported by LLPR 2001, whereas virtually the whole of the Insolvency Act 1986 (as applicable to companies) applies to LLPs. A consequence of this legislative approach is that an LLP is closer to a modified form of private limited company than to a partnership. This is borne out by LLPA 2000's 1(5), which states that the law relating to partnerships does not apply to a limited liability partnership unless otherwise provided.

The impact of Companies Act 2006 on LLPs has been the subject of some debate. However it has been confirmed that LLPs have the same accounts filing deadline and audit requirements as companies and these apply to LLPs for accounting periods beginning 1 October 2008.

Similarly, any changes to the Companies Act 2006 concerning companies acting as directors of other companies are expected to be extended to corporate members of LLPs in some form when the Department of Business Innovation and Skills' proposals in its consultation on Transparency and Trust are enacted. [45.4]

2 Limited liability

The liability of a member of an LLP is limited to:
- the capital contributed, or agreed to be contributed; and
- the amount that the member agrees to contribute in the event of the LLP being wound up.

There are some exceptions. In particular, there will not be a limitation where a member has accepted a personal duty of care to a third party or a personal contractual commitment. In this case, it is possible for the member to have unlimited liability. In practice, limitation of liability is only likely to be an issue in an Armageddon situation, that is, where the LLPs assets are extinguished to settle a claim. This is an area where the LLP is more akin to a general partnership than a company.

There may also be additional liabilities in the event of an LLP becoming insolvent. For example, the 'claw back' rules apply to an LLP. The 'claw back' rules relate to any amounts withdrawn by members in the two years leading up to a winding up where the member knew, or ought to have known, that after the withdrawal there was no reasonable prospect that the LLP would pay its debts or avoid insolvent liquidation. The 'claw back' rules are a direct consequence of the application of parts of the Insolvency Act 1986 (by virtue of the Limited Liability Partnership Regulations 2001).

Members must ensure that they make it clear that the firm is an LLP (eg notepaper, trading name, promotional material, etc) otherwise it may be argued that there was, in fact, an ordinary partnership with unlimited liability. A member will also have unlimited liability if that person is the sole member for a period in excess of six months – for example, on the death of the only other member. The sole member will be liable for the LLP's debts after the six month period has passed. [45.5]

3 Members' Agreement

Every member is deemed to be an agent of the LLP. The extent of the agency can be limited by the constitutional documents. With the exception of a basic default structure, members must create the necessary legal relations between themselves and between members and the LLP. The general law of partnerships or companies will not determine those relationships.

It is, therefore, advisable for a comprehensive agreement to be drawn up to govern these relations (and indeed the law expects one to be created (LLPA 2000 s 5)). This is often known as the Members' Agreement and will deal with profit sharing and ownership issues. The Members' Agreement is akin to the Articles of Association of a company and protects the interests of the members. However, it is not filed at Companies House and remains a private document.

If a Members' Agreement does not exist, then the LLPR 2001 contains direction as to the default position in respect of eleven fundamental matters, such as the sharing of capital and income profits and the extent that members may take part in the management of the LLP. As the default terms in LLPR 2001 may not be appropriate for all businesses, and nor may they be practical to operate, it is always recommended that a Members' Agreement is created. Most agreements are based on the model of traditional partnership agreements.

A Members' Agreement should include:
- the management of the LLP;
- the decision-making process;
- the capital contributions required of the members, both while a going concern and (if any) on liquidation;
- the division of profits and losses (both income and capital);
- procedures for changes to the membership;
- procedures for dispute resolution;
- the designated members of the LLP;
- termination of the LLP;
- provision for amendment of the LLP agreement;
- property ownership by the LLP and members;
- the extent that certain terms of the agreement are governed by a law other than English law;
- indemnity for a member by the LLP;
- restrictions on competing business undertaken by partners;
- the authority of partners and limits of that authority;
- restrictive covenants applying to partners. [45.6]

4 Accounts

As noted, the accounting and audit provisions of the Companies Act 2006 apply to an LLP. All relevant FRSs, SSAPs and SORPs and their international relatives IFRSs or IASs also apply to an LLP.

Accounting practice is important in determining both the quantum of profit and the timing aspect of recognising income and expenditure. In view of the specific issues arising as regards LLPs, a SORP has been produced on LLP accounting and was most recently updated in January 2017. The consequences of the SORP should be understood by the partners before adopting LLP status. This is because the publicly disclosed accounts of an LLP will differ from those of a company whose commercial results are identical.

LLPs are subject to the changes in UK GAAP arising on the introduction of FRS 102 which applies to accounting periods commencing on or after 1 January 2015 (See [**44.4**]). [**45.7**]

5 International

The extent to which an overseas jurisdiction treats the LLP as tax transparent or opaque (ie similar to a company) can only be ascertained on a jurisdiction-by-jurisdiction basis.

It is not uncommon for overseas jurisdictions to request a residency certificate from the UK tax authorities before granting the benefits of a double tax treaty to the UK taxpayer. For companies this is relatively easy to obtain. In its international tax manual, HMRC has indicated that it is not possible to obtain a residency certificate for an LLP, but instead that such certificate should be obtained in respect of each of its members (INTM 162033). This has led to additional administrative requirements when certificates are sought.

Where a UK LLP only has non-resident members, there will be no liability to tax in the UK if there is no business carried out in the UK. If there is a business carried on in the UK, the non-resident members are only subject to UK tax on the UK profits. Where there are both UK resident and non-resident members, two tax computations are required, one showing just UK profits and one showing total profits.

The position of overseas entities for UK taxation purposes, and whether they are treated as opaque or transparent, is complex as there is no set rule as to whether an LLP incorporated outside of UK law will be treated as look through for direct tax purposes. Each individual entity should be considered based on its specific governance and the legislation under which it has been incorporated. The case of *Anson v R & C Comrs* (2013) has demonstrated, in the context of a Delaware LLC, that the precise nature of an entity incorporated overseas should not be taken at face value but considered in the context of its structure and the rules under which it is governed. The Supreme Court (2015) overturned the Court of Appeal's decision, finding that double tax relief was due in respect of the US tax paid in respect of US profits remitted to the UK.

This chapter focuses on the UK LLP structure and not that of an LLP formed under the law of another territory. In particular, the new partner status rules introduced in the FA 2014 have been targeted at the UK LLP and do not apply to an LLP formed using the law of another territory irrespective of whether the business of the LLP is carried on within the UK. Not all international LLP structures operating in the UK will be taxed as a partnership and the UK tax status should be checked against the list published by HMRC (INTM 180030).

[**45.8**]

III TAXING PROFITS AND GAINS

1 General

As noted, LLPs are treated as tax transparent partnerships for UK tax purposes in most circumstances. The main exceptions to this general rule relate to LLPs in liquidation, property investment LLPs, and LLPs that are not carrying out a business with a view to profit. [45.9]

2 LLPs undertaking a business with a view to profit

Where an LLP carries on a trade, profession or business with a view to profit, the members will be treated for the purposes of income tax, corporation tax and capital gains tax as if they were partners carrying on that business in partnership. Hence, an LLP undertaking a trade, profession or business will be treated as tax transparent for both income and capital gains and the detailed provisions discussed in **Chapter 44** will be relevant as regards each member (ITTOIA 2005 s 863 and TCGA 1992 s 59A). These rules apply equally to corporate members (CTA 2009 s 1259 and TCGA 1992 s 59A). Concern that this vehicle could be 'abused' resulted in special rules being introduced that apply to 'investment' and 'property investment' LLPs (see [45.13]).

In *R & C Comrs v Peter Vaines* (2016) (see [44.3]), the First-tier Tribunal held that whilst Mr Vaines was carrying on a trade at a law firm, each partner in the LLP was personally carrying on a trade, albeit collectively with other partners. Although HMRC were successful in their appeal to the Upper Tribunal, the above principle was explicitly acknowledged in the written judgment. This demonstrates and supports the tax transparent nature of the LLP structure and the fact that the activities of the partners in an LLP are treated for tax purposes as being carried on by the partners themselves. [45.10]

3 Partner status/salaried member rules

a) *The position up to 5 April 2014*

The taxation and NIC position of members of an LLP has been complex and involved some uncertainty. Where a partner satisfies all of the normal badges of self-employment, they will be treated as self-employed. However, until 5 April 2014, all salaried members, who were registered at Companies House as members of the LLP, were treated by HMRC as self-employed for these purposes following the provisions set out in ITTOIA 2005 s 863. However, LLPA 2000 s 4(4) clearly allowed for employee members, which would imply that such salaried members could be treated as employees of the LLP. It was the view of the author of this chapter that if it was intended that 'salaried members' were to be taxed as self-employed their arrangements should be capable of meeting the normal criteria of self-employment. Typically this would include the requirement for the members in question to provide capital to the LLP and participate in the variable profits of the business (and possibly losses to some degree) (see the discussion at [12.13]).

Where members of an LLP are treated as partners, not employees, the self-employed (Class 2 and Class 4) rates of NIC will apply and there will be no liability to employers NIC.

FA 2014 introduces new rules that take away this uncertainty. **[45.11]**

b) *The position from 6 April 2014*

FA 2014 introduced rules to determine the tax status of members of a LLP. These rules apply from 6 April 2014. Where a member of a LLP is deemed under the rules to become an employee for income tax purposes, their self-employment is deemed to have come to an end on 5 April 2014, ie in the tax year 2013–14. The rules apply for tax matters only and do not affect the member's status in other respects, such as employment law, liability on a winding up etc. These rules apply to UK LLPs (LLPA 2000) only and do not apply to partners in a general partnership, a limited partnership or an LLP formed under the law of another territory.

The salaried member rules ensure that a member is taxed as an 'employee' if three conditions are *all* met:

Condition A: Disguised salary. The condition is met if there are arrangements in place under which:
- the member is to provide services for the LLP; and
- it is reasonable to expect that the amounts payable by the LLP in respect of the member's performance of those services will be wholly, or substantially wholly, 'disguised salary'. The legislation explains that the rules will apply where it is reasonable to expect that at least 80% of the amount payable by the LLP for the member's services will be 'disguised salary'. This is a forward-looking test on the basis of what is anticipated and the fact that the profits of the firm do not produce the anticipated result does not preclude this test being failed.

Condition B: Significant influence. The condition is met if the mutual rights and duties of a member and the LLP do not give the member significant influence over the affairs of the LLP.

Condition C: Capital contribution. This condition is met if the member's contribution to the LLP is less than 25% of the disguised salary (see Condition A above).

HMRC has produced guidance relating to how they see the new rules applying (Partnerships: A review of two aspects of the tax rules – Salaried Members Rules: Revised Technical Note and Guidance).

Condition A – Disguised salary

The disguised salary test relates to an amount that meets any of the following requirements:
- it is fixed; or
- it is variable, but varied without reference to the overall amount of profits or losses of the LLP; or
- it is not, in practice, affected by the overall profits or losses of the LLP.

For the third of these tests, HMRC see the test as operating based upon the practical position rather than a hypothetical situation that is unlikely to arise.

EXAMPLE 45.1

Priestfield LLP is a firm with 100 partners whose profits have exceeded £10 million for each of the last three years. For the year ended 31 March 2017 the firm achieved a total profit before fixed shares of £12.5 million.

The 10 junior partners have agreed profit shares ranging from £50,000 to £75,000. Their agreement with the firm is that these profit shares are payable as a first tranche of the firm's profit but, if there is insufficient profit, then these fixed shares are abated. As it is reasonable to presume that profits of Priestfield LLP will exceed the profits allocated to the junior partners the junior partners will meet Condition A.

Hessenthaller is a recent lateral hire from a competitor firm. His package includes a fixed sum of £75,000 plus a commission of 25% of the billings on any new clients that he introduces to Priestfield LLP. For the last year, Hessenthaller had a good year and was allocated additional profit based on his commission arrangement of £150,000. Hessenthaller has two elements to his profit share. Both the fixed sum and the commission are 'disguised salary' as they are not dependent upon the overall profitability of the firm. However, this is the historic position; the test is forward looking and it will be necessary to understand the expectation for the firm's profits in the future as well as what the expectations are for the ongoing commission arrangements. If they are to continue, Hessenthaller will meet Condition A based upon his historic position.

Barrett, the senior partner, is nearing retirement and has agreed to reduce his hours for an increased fixed profit share. Last year his package was based upon a fixed first tranche of £75,000 plus a 3% profit share of profits over the total fixed shares of £7,500,000. The profit for the year was £12.5 million resulting in a total profit share for Barrett of £225,000. Had these arrangements remained in place, Barrett would have failed Condition A and would continue to be taxed as self-employed. Going forward, Barrett will be working a three-day week and his new profit share will be a fixed first tranche of £110,000 plus 0.5% of profits over £7.5 million. The historic position does not impact upon the new tests for partner status. If the firm's profits are expected to be £13 million or less then Barrett's variable profit share will be less than 20% of his total and Condition A will be met with Barrett being taxed as an employee.

Taylor, the managing partner, receives a first tranche profit of £50,000 together with 5% of the profits over the fixed shares of £7,500,000. Taylor fails Condition A.

Condition B – Significant influence

The target of this part of the legislation is to deny self-employed status to those members of a UK LLP that do not have any significant influence over the day-to-day affairs of the business and are merely working within the business. Those who are in senior management roles will typically fail Condition B and be self-employed for tax purposes. It will be appreciated that in large UK LLPs, where there are many partners, most partners will meet Condition B and will only be able to maintain/establish self-employment through the other two tests.

EXAMPLE 45.2

Continuing from *Example 45.1*:

Taylor, being the managing partner, will have a significant influence and will fail Condition B. However, Barrett has clearly held an influential position being the senior partner and may still maintain significant influence over the affairs of the LLP. Subject to Barrett's continuing role, he may be able to satisfy the significant influence test and fail Condition B but further detail would be required to support this view.

Priestfield LLP has a management committee of eight partners that undertakes to deal with the day-to-day running of the business. The management committee will therefore have a significant influence on the business and the partners on the committee will fail Condition B.

Condition C – Capital contribution.

This test recognises that typical partners will have invested their own funds in their self-employed business which is at risk in the day-to-day dealings of the business. The condition is met if the partner's contribution is less than 25% of the disguised salary (see Condition A). As a transitional measure for individuals who were members of a UK LLP on 5 April 2014, putting a firm commitment in place by 6 April 2014 and making the contribution to take them over the 25% threshold by 5 July 2014, means that it is the new level of capital that HMRC will take into account in determining whether Condition C is met.

For new members after 5 April 2014, a two-month period is allowed to provide the contribution, again subject to there being a firm commitment to make the contribution from the day of becoming a member.

The legislation and guidance is slightly confusing about 'contribution', 'capital' and 'capital contribution'. In correspondence, HMRC has confirmed that it is less concerned about what the funding is called but rather their focus is to ensure the funding being provided to the business is for the permanent endowment of the firm and not something that can be readily removed or varied without the agreement of the members of the firm as a whole. The rules specifically exclude the following from being counted:

- sums that the individual may be called upon to pay at some future date (but note the position above re new partners);
- undrawn profits, unless by agreement they have been converted into capital;
- sums that are held by the LLP for the member, for example, sums held in a taxation reserve account;
- amounts of capital that are part of arrangements to enable the individual to 'avoid' being treated as employed where there is no intention that they have permanent effect or otherwise give rise to no economic risk to the member.

EXAMPLE 45.3

Stones LLP are a 30 partner firm of insolvency practitioners. Each partner has an obligation under the LLP Members Agreement to provide capital to the firm of £5,000 plus a loan based upon 50% of the partners expected profit share based upon the annual budget. This funding requirement can only be adjusted via a 75% majority vote of the partners. In this case, Condition C is failed by all of the members of Stones LLP and the partners are all taxed as self-employed.

Members of an LLP, who are individuals, will be entitled to claim interest relief on the loans they take out for the purposes of the business of the LLP, provided that the relevant conditions of the relief are met (ITA 2007 s 398 and 399; see [7.45]). Relief will not, however, be available for funds provided to an investment or property investment LLP (ITA 2007 s 399(2)(b): see [45.14]). In these circumstances, consideration should be given to raising any required finance via the LLP itself. This is subject to changes set out at [44.11].

[45.12]

4 Losses

For loss relief purposes, active members of trading (but not professional) LLPs are subject to the restrictions as outlined at [44.9]. Consequently, for active partners of an LLP the ability to set losses, etc against income or profits from other activities will be limited by reference to the amount of the capital contribution made plus the amount of agreed liability on a winding up. For non active partners, there is a further restriction to £25,000 of losses which are available for sideways relief for losses sustained on or after 2 March 2007 (ITA 2007 s 103C/s 107).

In this case, the member's contribution to the LLP is measured at the end of the loss making period and is made up of two parts:
- *Part 1* – any amounts contributed to the LLP less any repayments (this includes repayments in the five years following the use of the loss).
- *Part 2* – The amount of the member's liability on a winding up of the LLP where that is not part of the capital in Part 1 above.

The restriction in relief is calculated on a cumulative basis thereby restricting the relief from being offset sideways to the total contribution, during the period of partnership. There is nothing to prevent losses from being carried forward and offset against profits of the same trade.

Undrawn profits of a member of an LLP cannot normally be added to their subscribed capital in order to calculate the limit of relief for any trading losses.

The loss relief restrictions do not apply to professional partnerships. This means that the whole loss is available to the partners of a professional LLP irrespective of whether the partners are required to make good the loss by making a contribution to the assets of the LLP. In cases where a professional LLP has become insolvent, the partners are able to offset their share of the total loss against their income liable to taxation depending on the general loss relief provisions, including terminal loss relief (see [11.102]). There is no statutory definition of a professional partnership but case law has been the historic indicator of the extent that an activity is a trade or a profession. Case law will therefore need to be reviewed to differentiate between a trade or profession.

[45.13]

5 Investment LLPs and property investment LLPs

a) *An 'investment LLP' (ITA 2007 s 399)*

As a specific anti-avoidance measure, the Taxes Acts have introduced the concept of an investment LLP and a property investment LLP. The definition of an investment LLP closely follows the definition of an investment company so that the case law and guidance relating to the definition of an investment company may be applied to LLPs (ITA 2007 s 399(6)). A representative period will be taken to form a view as to whether the principal part of the LLP's income is derived from the business so that an LLP is an investment or property investment LLP, but that view will then be taken to apply for the whole period of account.

b)   A 'property investment LLP' (ITA 2007 s 1004)

The definition of a property investment LLP builds on that of an investment LLP. Two particular rules should be noted:
(1) As regards property activities, individuals will not be able to obtain interest relief on loans to buy into a property investment LLP (ITA 2007 s 399(2)). On one level this is not surprising, since interest relief is currently restricted for limited partners in a limited partnership registered under the Limited Partnership Act 1907 (ITA 2007 s 399(2)(a)). The restriction for LLPs matches this restriction.
(2) Exemptions for income and gains will not apply for pension funds, the pension business of life insurance companies and the tax-exempt business of friendly societies where the income and gains are received in their capacity as a member of a property investment LLP (TA 1988 s 659E). [45.14]

6   Capital gains

A member's interest in a trading or professional LLP will not be regarded as a separate chargeable asset, and the members will be taxable on their share of chargeable gains arising on the disposal of the LLP's assets (TCGA 1992 s 59A). The exception to this position is where a liquidator or receiver is appointed to the LLP, as this event results in the LLP ceasing to be transparent for tax purposes (see [45.19]). The favourable capital gains tax treatment afforded by SP D12 applies (see [44.31]) to members of an LLP. [45.15]

7   Corporate members and mixed member LLPs

Not being a company, an LLP cannot be a member of a capital gains tax group. Nor can it be a member of a group for corporation tax group relief purposes. This has reduced the attractiveness of utilising LLPs in corporate structures. Where assets are transferred from a corporate member to the LLP, this will be treated as a disposal for CGT purposes and can also be treated as a distribution from the company to the members of the LLP. This disposal takes place at market value. As an alternative, the corporate member could consider contributing the asset as its capital, which may not be treated as a disposal for CGT purposes (although consideration should be given to the impact of the change in ownership of capital assets between members).

A further consequence of admitting a corporate member into an LLP is that the LLP will be classified as a mixed partnership and, as such, not qualify for an annual investment allowance (AIA) for capital allowance purposes. A partnership or LLP will only qualify for an AIA if all members are individuals

(CAA 2001 s 38A(3)(b)). However, this will not prevent the corporate member from claiming allowances in its own right.

FA 2015 s 43 provided that for the purposes of entrepreneurs' relief, the status of a corporate member is no longer determined by the status of the LLP of which it is a member. However, FA 2016 modifies these provisions and a summary of the new provisions is set out at [44.39] ff. As mentioned, the interpretation of the FA 2016 revision is not necessarily clear and is the subject of ongoing discussion. However, it represents a welcome relaxation compared with the blanket denial of relief resulting from the FA 2015 position.

Where an LLP is classified as a mixed partnership, the allocation of profits and losses between members falls within the new rules introduced by FA 2014. These new rules came into effect from 6 April 2014 and are subject to anti-forestalling rules from 5 December 2013. Where the new rules apply, profits or losses allocated to a non-individual partner may be taxed upon the individual partners of the business. This can also extend to an individual who is not a partner in the LLP in certain circumstances (see [44.10]).

From 20 March 2013, HMRC have extended the provisions under CTA 2010 s 455 to include partnerships and LLPs where the partners consist of at least one individual and one company and an individual partner is also a participator in the company. In this scenario, a penalty tax charge may arise if the company makes a loan or transfers value to the partnership or LLP, and this funds withdrawals by the partners or value passes to the partners, eg where the company leaves undrawn profits on the partnership's capital account. [45.16]

IV TAX ON CESSATION OF ACTIVITIES

1 General

The LLP is treated as being transparent for tax purposes until it ceases to carry on a trade or business either at the end of a winding-up process or by going into liquidation. In these circumstances, the LLP reverts to corporate status. This will also be the case should the LLP cease to meet the criteria of operating a business with a view to a profit.

In order to prevent avoidance of tax when an LLP ceases to be transparent, there is a charge to tax based on an amount equal to any chargeable gains previously postponed or gains which have not come back into charge as a result of a gift of business assets (TCGA 1992 s 169A).

Any gains previously postponed as a result of a replacement of business assets will also fall into charge (TCGA 1992 s 156A). The temporary cessation of trading will not, however, change the normal tax treatment. [45.17]

2 Winding up and liquidation

a) *Winding up*

Where the members of an LLP proceed to wind up the LLP's affairs without the formal appointment of a liquidator, the transparency of the LLP will

be preserved during the period in which the assets are being disposed of provided that:
(1) the LLP is not being wound up for reasons connected in whole or in part with the avoidance of tax; and
(2) the period of winding up is not unreasonably protracted (*Tax Bulletin* 50 (December 2000)).

If these conditions are not met, then the tax transparency of the LLP may be regarded as coming to an end before the informal winding-up process has been completed. [45.18]

b) *Liquidation*

The appointment of a liquidator means that the LLP is no longer carrying on a trade or profession with a view to profit, and tax transparency will be lost (*Tax Bulletin* 50, December 2000). In the liquidation period, the LLP's capital gains will be treated in exactly the same way as for any other body corporate (ie, they will fall within the corporate tax legislation). Chargeable gains will be computed by reference to the date on which assets were first acquired by the LLP and their cost at that date (TCGA 1992 s 8(6)). Indexation will, therefore, be available on the disposal of the LLP's assets. As with shareholders, LLP members will be taxed on any gain (or granted relief for losses) that arises on the disposal of their capital interests in the LLP. The allowable acquisition cost of each partner's interest is determined according to the historical capital contributions made as if the LLP had never been transparent. This treatment does not extend to any pre-liquidation asset disposals: their tax treatment remains undisturbed. It should be noted that the tax base cost of a partner's capital interest is not equal to the market value of that interest at the time when transparency is lost – there is no rebasing. Accordingly, the impact of going into liquidation should be carefully considered. [45.19]

V TRANSFER OF AN UNINCORPORATED BUSINESS TO AN LLP

The limitation of liability, whilst retaining tax transparency, has made the LLP an attractive vehicle for professional practices. This has led to many partnerships converting to LLP status. The effect of a transfer of a partnership to an LLP has been set out in *Tax Bulletin* 50, December 2000. The key points to note are:
- *Capital allowances* – No balancing charges or allowances will arise.
- *Interest relief* – Members continue to enjoy tax relief for interest on qualifying borrowings. ITA 2007 s 409 reflects this.
- *Cessation* – Incorporation as an LLP will not, of itself, involve the cessation of the trade or profession.
- *Overlap relief* – no overlap relief will be utilised or created unless there is a change of accounting date.
- *Tax returns* – If a conventional partnership incorporates as an LLP *during* an accounting period, then if the partners so wish, a single partnership return may be made for the accounting/tax year in question.

- *PAYE returns* – a single return may be made for the tax year in which a conventional partnership incorporates as an LLP.
- *Annuities* – assuming that the rights remain substantially the same:
  - the transfer of a partner's annuity rights and/or
  - the transfer of annuity obligations to former members will not be regarded as a chargeable disposal
  - the same treatment is accorded where an annuitant agrees to the substitution of the LLP for the predecessor partnership as the payer of the annuity.
- *Inheritance* tax – there will not be a break in the period of ownership of a business interest for IHT purposes. [45.20]

It will be a matter of fact as to whether an LLP has succeeded to the business of a partnership. The basic test is whether or not the business carried on by the LLP is recognisably 'the business' previously carried on by the old partnership. The issues to be considered in determining whether or not a succession has occurred are set out in SP 9/86. Where only part of an existing trade or profession is transferred, the cessation of business provisions may apply to the old partnership. In this case, the previous overlap relief will be crystallised and commencement provisions will apply to all members of the LLP giving rise to fresh overlap profits. [45.21]

VI ANTI-AVOIDANCE: INVESTMENT AND PROPERTY INVESTMENT LLPS

Provisions introduced by FA 2001 Sch 25 (as rewritten by ITA 2007 and FA 2007) are intended to discourage the use of LLPs for purposes other than trading and professional activities. The property investment LLP is particularly identified to prevent pension funds investing in property through LLPs.

Ordinary investment LLPs (those 'whose business consists wholly or mainly in the making of investments and the principal part of whose income is derived there from') are penalised by prohibiting interest relief under ITA 2007 s 399(2) on borrowings to subscribe capital, lending to the LLP, etc for individual members.

Interest relief will, however, be available if an individual investor can satisfy the conditions of other interest relieving provisions, eg property income. [45.22]

VII OTHER TAXES

1 **Stamp Duty Land Tax (SDLT)**

The Limited Liability Partnership Act 2000 s 12 provides for relief from stamp duty on the transfer of assets from a partnership to an LLP. This relief is replicated for SDLT in FA 2003 s 65. The relief is available for transfers on conversion or within 12 months of the date of incorporation of the

LLP. Technically, the legislation does not fit in with the proper analysis of a member's interest in an LLP. However, HMRC (in *Tax Bulletin* 50 December 2000) says that it will not take the point. The key practical considerations are:
- the partners' proportional interests in the assets transferred to the LLP must correspond to those held by them through the LLP immediately after incorporation; or
- if there are any changes, the proportions have not been changed for tax avoidance reasons; and
- the people making the transfers (ie the partners in the old firm) must be exactly the same as the members of the LLP immediately after incorporation.

SDLT applies to partnerships and LLPs with effect from 23 July 2004. However, the Finance Act 2006 has brought in changes to remove most transactions between partners from the charge to SDLT. A charge may arise on the contribution of a property to a partnership or LLP. The detailed rules are beyond the scope of this chapter – see **Chapter 40** for further detail.
[45.23]

2 National insurance and salaried members

Where a member of a UK LLP fails one of the conditions referred to at [45.12], the member will be liable to self-employed NIC being typically contributions for Class 2 and 4 NIC. However, where a member satisfies all of those conditions he or she will be taxed as an employee and will be liable for employee NIC and the LLP will be liable for employer NIC. Since 6 April 2015 both Class 2 and Class 4 NIC have been collected via the self-assessment process by way of the annual tax return. HMRC announced that from 6 April 2013 sleeping and inactive partners would also be regarded as self-employed workers and be subject to the Class 2 and Class 4 NIC charge. It was announced in the 2016 Budget that Class 2 NIC will be abolished from 6 April 2018. [45.24]

3 VAT

Business Brief 3/2001 sets out the VAT position of LLPs. The basic rules of VAT apply to any form of business. As regards the incorporation of a partnership, broadly, the LLP will need to apply for a separate registration unless the partnership ceases to trade at the same time. Where the partnership ceases at the same time the existing registration can be transferred to the LLP. This will, generally, not give rise to a VAT charge as it will be a transfer of a going concern (TOGC) subject to the normal rules, so no VAT will be payable. Although an LLP cannot be a member of a direct tax group, it can be a member of a VAT group. This facility may make the LLP attractive when compared to an ordinary partnership or limited partnership when it is desired to limit the VAT leakage on management fees (eg where the recipient of the fee cannot recover input VAT in full) whilst retaining favourable NIC treatment. [45.25]

46 Choice of business medium

Updated by Helen McGhee, Senior Associate, Joseph Hage Aaronson LLP

I   Introduction – the available options [46.1]
II Non-tax factors [46.21]
III The taxation factors [46.41]
IV General conclusions [46.81]

I INTRODUCTION – THE AVAILABLE OPTIONS

When commencing a business the participators will normally have an unrestricted choice between operating through the medium of a company or partnership. Professions which operate through the medium of a partnership may set up a company to service the running of their premises and to provide staff, furniture and equipment. The limited liability partnership has been introduced as a hybrid between the limited liability company and the unlimited liability of the traditional partnership.

The typical company will be the private limited company and the typical partnership will consist of a number of partners with unlimited personal liability. [46.1]

There are, however, other possibilities such as:

The public company: Its attraction is the ability to raise funds from the public (contrast the restriction on private companies: (Companies Act 2006 s 755(1)). In practice, of course, it is unlikely that a new business would commence as a public company since the costs involved are considerable and only in very limited cases would a Stock Exchange listing or permission to deal in the company's shares on the Alternative Investment Market be granted for a completely new enterprise. [46.2]

The unlimited company: This suffers from the disadvantage that the liability of the shareholders is unlimited – hence, they are in the same position as partners (albeit with the convenience of corporate personality). However, the unlimited company need not file the statutory company accounts, enabling it to preserve a greater degree of confidentiality. Many of the restrictions which apply to limited companies for the protection of creditors do not apply. [46.3]

The old style limited partnership under the Limited Partnerships Act 1907: The creation of an old style limited partnership is regulated by formalities similar to those which have to be satisfied if a company is to be formed and although there can be partners whose liability for the debts of the firm is limited, there must also be at least one general (or unlimited) partner. Furthermore, if a limited partner takes any part in the management of the firm, he loses the protection of his limited liability and becomes a general partner. Thus, a limited partner who has put capital into the firm might be obliged to allow his money to be lost by inept management since any attempt to interfere would put at risk the whole of his personal fortune. In recent years the investment and tax planning opportunities afforded to limited partnerships have proved attractive both for income tax and IHT as the partnership interest may qualify for business property relief at 100%. [46.4]

The limited liability partnership (LLP): This form of legal entity was introduced by the Limited Liability Partnership Act 2000 (see **Chapter 45**). An LLP is a body corporate which exists as a legal person separate from its members. The introduction of this legislation stemmed from the concerns felt by professional partnerships over the unlimited liability of the partners and the unsatisfactory operation of the Limited Partnerships Act. An increasing number of professional partnerships are converting to LLPs although some will be deterred by the company law disclosure requirements that apply. The existing tax rules for partnerships and partners generally apply to LLPs and members of LLPs which are carrying on businesses as if they were partnerships and partners respectively. Accordingly whether to operate through a general partnership or an LLP is tax neutral and converting an existing partnership into an LLP will not normally lead to any tax charge. [46.5]

Partnerships with companies: This hybrid arrangement involves an individual joining in partnership with a limited company. If the individual is also a director of the company concerned, making him a limited partner offers attractions since he can participate in the management of the business in his capacity as director of the company. The particular advantages afforded by the arrangement lie in the regulation of profit sharing ratios to take account of different income and corporation tax rates and to maximise the use of business losses. FA 2014 significantly cut across the advantages of this arrangement as it inserted s 850C, 850D and 850E into ITTOIA 2015, which allows HMRC in certain circumstances to redistribute profit allocation from the non-individual partner to the individual partner. [46.6]

It is worth noting the IHT and business property relief (BPR) considerations in using these hybrids. Where, as above, a partnership is carrying on a trade but there is a corporate member, then the corporate share would qualify for BPR. However, in the reverse, if an LLP holds an interest in an underlying company, HMRC assert that the LLP is not transparent for IHT purposes and BPR will only be available if the LLP is 'trading', notwithstanding the underlying trade of the company (see IHTM 25094 on the interpretation of IHTA 1984 s 267A), although see *R & C Comrs v Neton Dance* (2009) for a counter argument.

IR 35 and managed service companies (see **[8.32]**–**[8.40]**): It will not be attractive for a taxpayer to form a company in circumstances where these rules apply, although there might be strong commercial pressures to do so despite the tax disadvantages. **[46.7]–[46.20]**

II NON-TAX FACTORS

1 Limited liability

A limited company is a separate legal entity and is solely liable for its debts and obligations. The shareholders' liability is restricted to the sum invested by way of share capital and this liability cannot be increased without their consent (Companies Act 2006 s 25). The limited company offers the ideal vehicle for the individual who wishes to set up in business, but who is not prepared to risk his entire personal fortune in the venture.

EXAMPLE 46.1

Brian is the sole shareholder in Wretched Ltd. The company is in liquidation with total debts of £50,000 and assets of only £20,000. Brian has a personal wealth of £100,000, but because of the limited liability of the company, the creditors of Wretched Ltd cannot generally look to Brian for payment of the shortfall.

There are exceptions to the principle of limited liability and in certain circumstances the 'veil of incorporation' has been lifted to make shareholders liable for the company's debts. Although these instances are rare, the director of a private company should be aware that there are circumstances in which he might be liable for the debts of the company. For example, a director of a company which has entered insolvent liquidation who is found guilty of wrongful trading under the Insolvency Act 1986 s 214 can be ordered by a court to contribute to the assets of that company. The Supreme Court has recently considered the circumstances in which the corporate veil may be pierced in *Prest v Petrodel Resources Ltd* (2013), a case concerning financial provision for a wife following divorce.

On a practical level, in order to obtain finance for his company a shareholder/director will often be required to give security for the liabilities of the company by way of a personal guarantee. To the extent that personal guarantees are given, limited liability will be illusory. However, it is only major lenders, lease finance companies and landlords who are likely to require guarantees – not trade creditors and certainly not customers. **[46.21]**

2 Corporate personality

Obviously a company can never die: it can only be liquidated or dissolved. The death of a shareholder does not affect the company; the only result will be a transmission of some of the shares of the company. Sole traders enjoy no such advantages, because the assets of the business will be vested in them so that death will bring the business to an end. Further, from the point of view of simple estate planning, the company's shares are easy to transfer and easy to divide into separate parcels. A large shareholding can be fragmented between different members of the shareholder's family whereas the ownership of an unincorporated business is not so easily divisible. The popularity of the Family Investment Company has grown over recent years.

The existence of a separate legal entity (the company) means that the shareholder/proprietor can enter into legally binding contracts with it (see *Lee v Lee's Air Farming Ltd* (1961)). The shareholder in the small private company will be concerned in the management of the business as a director and may enter into a lucrative long-term service contract with the company. Amongst a number of advantages that such contracts offer will be the protection in the event of the employment being prematurely terminated and preferential treatment for arrears of wages in the event of the company's insolvency.

Incorporation will have an effect on the valuation of the interest in the business. A 10% partner, for instance, is treated as owning 10% of the firm's assets but a 10% minority shareholding would be valued at a substantial discount (because of the very limited rights possessed by a 10% shareholder). This can give rise to an advantage for tax purposes and incorporating a business may be a useful first step as a prelude to a gift of part of the business.

[46.22]

3 Obtaining finance

Companies have advantages when it comes to raising finance. Apart from issuing risk capital in the form of shares, money can also be raised by loans secured by fixed and floating charges. The fixed charge is common to both incorporated and unincorporated businesses (eg the land mortgage), but a floating charge is only applicable to companies. It operates as a charge over (usually) the entire undertaking and has the advantage of leaving the company free to deal with the assets of the business as it sees fit save to the extent that the terms of the charge provide otherwise. The floating charge will only crystallise on liquidation or when a default, as specified in the deed of charge, occurs.

How advantageous is the floating charge? This question can only be answered by considering whether creditors will be satisfied with the protection afforded by it and in many cases they will not be. Quite apart from the inherent defects of a non-crystallised charge, the existence of preferential creditors on an insolvency has weakened the attractions of such charges. Accordingly, the characteristic feature of company charging in recent years has been the practice of creditors to demand fixed security (see, eg *Siebe Gorman & Co Ltd v Barclays Bank Ltd* (1979) and the growth of *Romalpa* clauses). [46.23]

4 Formality, rigidity and costs

By comparison with the unincorporated business, a company suffers from formality and rigidity and has greater operating costs. A partnership or sole trader can establish a business with negligible documentation and formality. A company can be bought 'off the shelf' quite cheaply but the costs of a tailor-made company are usually higher. The obligation to file forms is a regular feature of a company's life, especially the annual return and it is necessary to submit annual accounts to the Registrar of Companies. Such requirements, however, are probably a small price for the benefits of limited liability and, in practice, the costs of a well-drafted partnership deed may be equal to the expense involved in company formation.

Previously, as an artificial entity, a company had to be formed for specific purposes set out in the objects clause of its memorandum of association. However, for companies formed under the Companies Act 2006, the company's objects will be unrestricted (ie it may carry on any trade or business whatsoever) unless the articles specifically restrict the objects of the company. Actions outside the scope of restricted or prescribed objects are *ultra vires* and are void. **[46.24]–[46.40]**

III THE TAXATION FACTORS

The formation of a company generally means that the company will be taxed as an entity distinct from its members and distributions from the company will be taxed in the hands of the shareholders, resulting in double taxation. Specific provisions dilute this problem, but it remains a major argument against incorporation. Any comparison, however, cannot be just between the taxation of individuals and the taxation of companies, since there is also the need to consider the individual as a director or employee of the company. The topic must, therefore, include some discussion of the pros and cons of being employed as opposed to self-employed. **[46.41]**

1 Taxation of income profits

a) *Rates of tax*

Profits of a partnership or sole trader will be charged to income tax at 40% when the individual's taxable income for 2017–18 exceeds £33,500 and at 45% for those with income in excess of £150,000. Corporation tax is charged on the profits of the company at a flat rate of 19% for 2017–18. What was the 'marginal rate' of tax for companies with profits between £300,000 and £1,500,000 is no longer applicable (see **[41.21]**).

Dividends are taxed in a special way and three different rates apply depending upon the level of the individual's income. On 6 April 2016, the dividend tax system was overhauled. The tax credit system of taxing dividends, considered to be overly complex, was abolished.

From April 2016, all individuals are entitled to a £5,000 dividend tax free allowance (the government has proposed that this be reduced to £2,000 from 6 April 2018, although the relevant measures were removed from FA 2017). For someone who is liable to tax only at the basic rate, any excess dividend over the £5,000 is taxed at 7.5%. For an individual whose taxable income exceeds £33,500 but is less than £150,000, the rate is 32.5% and for those whose income exceeds £150,000 the rate of tax on dividends is 38.1%. The £5,000 allowance is really a zero tax rate band, as it still forms part of an individual's income when considering in which band they are assessed.
[46.42]

b) *National Insurance contributions*

The rates for 2016–17 are set out as **Appendix A** at the end of this chapter. National insurance contributions (NIC) costs must be borne in mind when extra salary/bonuses are paid out to directors and employees. **[46.43]**

1356 Choice of business medium

c) *The effect of paying all the profits out as remuneration*

Employees' remuneration is deductible as a business expense of the company and will be subject to income tax as earnings in the hands of the employee. The amount paid to a full-time working director is unlikely to be challenged as excessive so that, if all the profits are paid out as remuneration, the company will pay no corporation tax (contrast *Copeman v William J Flood & Sons Ltd* (1941) and *Earlspring Properties Ltd v Guest* (1993) which illustrate that excessive payments to a director's family may be challenged). The only differences between a shareholder/director who extracts all the profits as salary and the self-employed sole trader are as follows:

(1) Dates for paying the tax: this is discussed in more detail at **[46.45]** below.
(2) Pension entitlements: the pensions available for employees and for the self-employed are discussed in **Chapter 50**. It should be remembered that, although the pension choices are now similar in both cases, one advantage for employees is that tax deductible contributions to their pension schemes can also be made by their employer (ie by the company), thus boosting their eventual entitlement. However for those earning over £150,000 for years after 2009–10 tax relief for pension contributions has been reduced. For 2017–18 the annual allowance of £40,000 is tapered down and reduced by £1 for every £2 income over £150,000 to a minimum of £10,000.
(3) Social security aspects: the salary paid to employees, including directors, attracts Class 1 NIC payable by both employer (the company) and the employee. **[46.44]**

d) *Dates for paying tax*

Companies have a maximum delay of nine months from the end of the accounting period to the payment of corporation tax. The system of quarterly payments for corporation tax means that large companies have to pay tax during the accounting period. Where company profits are all paid out in directors' fees, the tax and NIC will be deducted and paid under the PAYE system.

For individuals the self-assessment regime involves profits charged for a tax year being those shown in the accounting period ending in the year of assessment (this tax is paid in two instalments, on 31 January in the year of assessment and on the following 31 July). A final, balancing, payment is then made the following 31 January. Drawing up accounts to end early in the tax year (eg on 6 April) therefore produces the longest delay before the tax liability is finally settled. **[46.45]**

e) *Trading losses*

The relief for trading losses is generally more advantageous with an unincorporated business. Company losses are 'locked in' so that they cannot be used by the owners to set against their other income, and instead relief will only be given when the company makes profits (see **[41.60]**). Formerly, the ability to set a trading loss against capital gains in the year in which the loss was incurred was the one real advantage that the company had over the unincorporated trader. However, an unincorporated trader can now set trading losses against capital gains for the year of the loss and the following year (see [11.61]). The unincorporated trader is also able to set his trading losses against his other income under the provisions of ITA 2007 s 64 and, so far as early losses are concerned, against previous income as a result of ITA 2007 s 72. It is often argued that, when a new business is likely to show early losses, it is best to start the business as an unincorporated trade and to incorporate the business when it becomes profitable. However, if early losses exceed the wildest expectations of the trader, the advantage of income tax loss relief will not compensate for the disaster of bankruptcy. Had the loss been realised by a company, the limited liability may have protected the proprietors from bankruptcy. [46.46]

EXAMPLE 46.2
Having worked in the Civil Service for many years, Samantha has resigned to open a boutique. She anticipates trading losses in the early years. She has a substantial private income.
(1) If she forms a company to run the business, trading losses can be relieved only against future corporate profits.
(2) If she operates as a sole trader the losses can be set against her private income (and capital gains) for the year of the loss (ITA 2007 s 64) or against her income, including that from the Civil Service, in previous years (ITA 2007 s 72) or against both (*Butt v Haxby* (1983)).

f) *Interest relief*

Income tax relief is generally available on the interest paid on loans to acquire a share in either a partnership or a close company. To qualify, there is no longer a requirement for the taxpayer to work for the greater part of his time in the business (see generally **Chapter 7**). Relief is also available on loans raised for the benefit of the close company or partnership. Interest paid on loans to finance the business will usually be a deductible business expense; companies are subject to special rules whereby all profits and losses (whether as borrowers or lenders) are treated as income with interest payments taxed or relieved as they accrue rather than as they are paid. [46.47]

g) *Corporate investment reliefs*

Various reliefs have been introduced in an attempt to stimulate investment in qualifying trading companies. [46.48]

Loss relief (ITA 2007 s 131) Section 131 is intended to encourage the subscription of shares in certain unquoted trading companies by allowing a loss on disposal of the shares (including failure of the venture) to be relieved against income (see further [11.121]). It is not available for money lost in an unincorporated enterprise, but the partner who lends money to the partnership may be able to claim a capital loss under TCGA 1992 s 24 if the partnership defaults and the debt is a debt on a security, or otherwise under TCGA 1992 s 253 (debt relief for loans to traders). [46.49]

Enterprise Investment Scheme (ITA 2007 Part 5) Subject to detailed provisions being satisfied, limited income tax relief at 30% on the sum invested in a qualifying company is available and the investment may also enable unlimited capital gains to be sheltered (see **Chapter 15**). There is a maximum qualifying investment of £1m per year. **[46.50]**

Seed Enterprise Investment Scheme (SEIS) The Enterprise Investment Scheme was extended in respect of shares issued after 6 April 2012 to create an improved relief for newer, smaller companies – the provisions to be satisfied broadly mirror those of EIS but relief is limited to £100,000 for income tax relief at 50%. Capital gains on disposals are exempt up to £50,000 by relying on SEIS investment.

Investors' Relief (IR) Budget 2016 announced an extension in entrepreneurs' relief for external investors in unlisted trading companies. The IR applies a 10% rate of CGT up to a maximum investment of £10m on the disposal of ordinary shares in an unlimited trading company where, perhaps, the EIS requirements were not met. **[46.51]**

h) *Illustration*

EXAMPLE 46.3

Business profits are estimated to be £40,000 in the year ended 31 March 2018 and the proprietor will take £15,000, leaving the remainder in the business to finance expansion.

(1) If an unincorporated business:

		£	£
Taxable income (ignoring reliefs)			£40,000.00
Income tax on £40,000:			
33,500 at 20%		6,700.00	
6,500 at 40%		2,600.00	
		£9,300.00	
NIC			
Class 2		148.20	
Class 4		2,865.24	
		£3,013.44	

			£
Profit:			40,000.00
Less	Income tax	9,300.00	
	NIC	3,013.44	12,313.44
			£27,686.56

(2) If the company paid out £15,000 as emoluments and the balance retained:

Employee:	£	£
Taxable income (ignoring reliefs)		15,000
Tax on £15,000 @ 20%	3,000	
NIC on £6,836 @ 12%	820.32	3,820.32
Total amount received after tax and NIC		£11,179.68

Company:		£
Total profits		40,000
Less: remuneration	15,000	
NIC on remuneration @ 13.8%	943.37	15,943.37
Taxable profits		24,056.63
Corporation tax at 19%		4,570.76
Retained profit		£19,485.87

(3) In summary, the amount of tax and NIC payable as a sole trader amounts to £12,313.44 whereas the total amount of tax paid with the company paying out a salary of £15,000 and retaining the remainder amounts to £8,391.08, a saving of £3,922.36; the saving will vary depending upon the amount of profit retained or paid out by the company.

If the business is generating profits in excess of the needs of the proprietor(s), the ability to use the lower corporation tax rates to retain profits represents one of the attractions of incorporation. Hence, the retention of profits is a factor of importance in most businesses. **[46.52]**

2 Extracting cash from the business

One of the drawbacks of a company is exposed when the individual wishes to extract surplus profits for his own benefit. The company is a separate taxable entity and the funds extracted will be charged to tax on the individual. As the company's profits have already been charged, there is a risk of double taxation. The major methods of 'extracting' profits are: **[46.53]**

Paying dividends: Dividends are taxed as income in the hands of the shareholder and attract a £5,000 tax free allowance (which the government has proposed be reduced to £2,000 from 6 April 2018); thereafter they are then taxed at 7.5% if the individual shareholder is liable to tax only at the basic rate. For those liable to tax at the higher rate, the tax payable on the dividend is 32.5% and for those liable to tax at the additional rate, which applies to incomes over £150,000 the rate of tax is 38.1%.

A shareholder may waive his entitlement to a dividend before it is declared and it will not then be treated as paid to him since he never becomes entitled to it. Accordingly, it does not form part of the income of the shareholder for income tax purposes. Further by IHTA 1984 s 15, a dividend waiver will not be a transfer of value for inheritance tax purposes if it is made within one year before the dividend is declared. Two common uses of the waiver may be noted: *first*, to enable the company to pay a larger dividend on the other shares; *second*, to enable profits to be extracted by shareholders who are not directors by the latter waiving their dividend and taking additional remuneration. However it is necessary to consider the NIC implications and the settlement provisions in ITTOIA 2005 Part 5 Chapter 5 in respect of any proposed dividend waiver.

A dividend waiver is certainly capable of being a settlement where there exists an element of bounty. Accordingly a dividend enabling another shareholder to receive an increased dividend would be a settlement within the meaning of ITTOIA 2005 s 624. The person waiving the dividend would be the settlor and would remain taxable on the whole of the amount waived. (See *Buck v R & C*

Comrs (2008) SpC 716. See also Ministerial Statement 26 July 2007 and TSEM 4000 following *Jones v Garnett* (2007) for further examples of settlements.) The case of *Donovan and McLaren v R & C Comrs* (2014) demonstrated that great care is needed where such waivers operate between husband and wife. In this case there were four shareholders: two husbands owning 40% each and two wives holding 10% each. The husbands waived their rights to their dividends in order for the wives to receive them, taxable at their basic rate. HMRC won their argument that such regular waivers were arrangements that amounted to settlements within ITTOIA 2005 s 620 and, as the transactions were not arm's length and there was therefore an element of bounty, the husbands were liable to income tax on the dividend income (see **[16.93]**).

The case also highlighted that consideration of the validity of the waiver is necessary, along with the distinct rules that apply to interim or final dividend waivers. Specifically, a final dividend cannot be waived once it has been declared at a general meeting; it can only be waived before this entitlement arises since otherwise, as in this case, there must be an element of bounty. An interim dividend can be waived at any time before it is actually paid as this is when the entitlement arises.

A dividend waiver is now necessary on settlement. A dividend waiver is the temporary abandonment of a contingent right to future income. It does not necessarily increase the amount payable to any other shareholder unless the dividend is declared for a fixed monetary amount. **[46.54]**

EXAMPLE 46.4

Magna is a higher rate taxpayer with 7,500 shares representing a 75% shareholding in Magna Ltd. His daughter Minima has 2,500 shares, a 25% shareholding.

(a) Magna waives his rights to dividend and the company declares a dividend of £50,000. The whole of the dividend is therefore paid to Minima. She would have received only £12,500 if Magna had not waived his dividend and the extra £37,500 is therefore a settlement and will be taxed on Magna.

(b) If the company had instead declared a dividend of £20 per share Minima would receive £50,000 but Magna would receive nothing. His waiver would not have affected her dividend; it would merely have eliminated his dividend. The waiver would not be a settlement – subject to (c) below.

(c) If the company had insufficient distributable profits to pay a dividend on all the shares, there would be a settlement. If the company only had £160,000 distributable profits, Minima would only have been entitled to a maximum of £40,000 and it is only because of the waiver by Magna that she was able to receive more. This excess £10,000 will be taxed on Magna as a settlement (see *Buck v R & C Comrs* (2008)).

(d) Although the dividend waiver might not itself be a settlement, the payment of the dividend or the generation of profits could be a settlement. Magna might take a very low salary from the company with the intention of boosting the profits that are paid out by dividend to Minima. This could be a settlement because the provision of services would be bounteous, enabling income to be transferred to Minima (see *Jones v Garnett* (2005)).

Interest payments: Excessive interest payments, and any attempt to link the interest to the profits of the company, may result in the interest being treated as a distribution and not tax deductible from the company's profits (see **[42.7]**). Interest payments have to be in respect of *bona fide* loans. **[46.55]**

Lending the profits: Apart from restrictions on the making of loans to directors in the Companies Act 2006, the company will usually be a close company so that the provisions of CTA 2010 s 455 will apply (see [**41.128**]). This means that any loan to a shareholder will give rise to a payment of notional tax by the company of 32.5% (from April 2016) of the loan. This notional tax is repayable to the company only when the loan is repaid. In addition, the recipient may be liable to income tax on a benefit in kind from the receipt of a beneficial loan. FA 2013 extended the scope of s 455 to additionally cover loans and advances to:

> '(b) the trustees of a settlement one or more of the trustees or actual or potential beneficiaries of which is a participator in the company or an associate of such a participator, or
> (c) a limited liability partnership or other partnership one or more of the partners in which is an individual who is:
> (i) a participator in the company, or
> (ii) an associate of an individual who is such a participator.' [**46.56**]

EXAMPLE 46.5

An individual (Mr X) owns 100% of the shares in C Ltd. X and C set up an LLP with themselves as the partners. C makes a loan to the LLP.

Prior to the changes introduced in FA 2013, this arrangement would not have given rise to a s 455 charge. However, it is now within s 455(1)(c) as Mr X owns 100% of the shares in C Ltd.

Extracting the profits by selling the shares: Profits made by the company will be reflected in the value of the shares. Hence, a sale of the shares will ensure that the profit is obtained by the shareholder as a capital gain. This will inevitably give rise to double taxation since not only will the company's profit be subject to corporation tax, but also the proceeds of sale of the shares will be taxable on the shareholder.

Where a shareholder wishes to extract value from the company by ultimately liquidating the company, from 6 April 2016 he will need to be mindful of a new targeted anti-avoidance rule (TAAR) in conjunction with the anti-avoidance regime known as the transactions in securities (TIS) rules (see [**3.30**]–[**3.50**]). The TIS rules give HMRC the power to deem a transaction that is taxable as capital to instead be taxable as income where there is a tax avoidance motive as part of a transaction being undertaken between a close company and its owner. This new TIS TAAR needs to be considered in the context of any liquidation of a company going forward. The new TAAR was designed to counter practices known as 'phoenixing' or 'moneyboxing' but is considered to be more far reaching than this. [**46.57**]

EXAMPLE 46.6

Hoco Ltd makes profits of £100. Corporation tax at 19% is £19 so that £81 is retained by Hoco Ltd. If all the shares are owned by Mr Hoco they would be worth £81 more. Therefore, were Mr Hoco to sell his shares for the asset value, he would make a gain of £81 subject to CGT at 20% = £16.20 (ignoring capital gains tax allowances). The total tax attributable to the company's £100 profit is therefore

£35.20 (£19 paid by Hoco Ltd and £16.20 paid by Mr Hoco.) The tax would be less if the shares qualified for entrepreneurs' relief or, if Mr Hoco was a basic rate tax payer as this could reduce the capital gains tax on the shares to a rate of only 10%.

Buy-backs: This topic is considered at **[42.21]**: reference should be made to CTA 2010 s 1033 and SP 2/82. **[46.57]**

Extraction in the form of remuneration: As already discussed, this method avoids any double charge to tax since the sum paid will be deductible for corporation tax and subject only to income tax and NIC in the hands of the individual. In the typical private company, where the shareholders are also full-time working directors, profits may easily be extracted in this fashion. (See *Ebrahimi v Westbourne Galleries Ltd* (1973) for a practical illustration of such a private company and for a salutary lesson in what can happen if things go wrong!) The amount of NIC borne by the company (discussed above) should also be borne in mind when fixing levels of remuneration. However, it is likely that extraction of profits by dividends will give rise to a lower tax burden (see **[46.52]**). **[46.59]**

Tax-efficient benefits: Modest savings can be obtained by the provision of certain benefits in kind (see generally *Taxation*, 28 September 2000, p 664): for instance:
(1) holiday accommodation or a second home subject to a possible benefit in kind charge;
(2) assets which directors can use for a limited time so as to keep the benefit at a low level (for instance, use of a yacht/aircraft etc otherwise used for the purposes of the business);
(3) are there still attractions in the company car and company fuel? It is necessary to compare the cost savings to the individual by having the car purchased and paid for by the company, with the tax and NIC payable on the benefits in kind. The use made of the car will be crucial in this calculation and the alternative of a mileage allowance (tax-free under the Approved Mileage Allowance Payments Scheme). In extreme cases the provision of a van as a second car may be attractive since this will result in no taxable benefit if the employee is prohibited from any private use other than ordinary commuting. However, the benefit in kind is £3,230 if the restricted private use condition is not satisfied, subject to reductions where the van is pooled, the van cannot be used for 30 days in a row or the employee pays to privately use the van;
(4) as far as NIC mitigation is concerned the loopholes in this area have been steadily reduced over the years and NIC now also applies to most benefits in kind. **[46.60]**

Dividends or remuneration? The main choice facing proprietors of a private company is between dividends and salary. The payment of salary has obvious attractions being fully deductible by the company and, for example, potentially being qualifying expenditure for companies undertaking R&D and claiming R&D relief. The increasing level of NIC has improved the position of the dividend, and reverses the advantages of paying salaries: see **[46.51]**. In cases where husbands and wives are both engaged in the business of a private company it is necessary to give detailed consideration to the possible application of ITTOIA 2005 s 624. In *Jones v Garnett* (2007) (more popularly known as *Arctic Systems Limited* – see [**16.102**]) the company provided computer consultancy services that were supplied by Mr Jones. Mrs Jones dealt with all the financial administrative requirements. Mrs Jones took a small salary and the profits were mainly extracted by way of dividend. HMRC argued that the arrangements represented a settlement for the purposes of s 624 so that the dividend paid to Mrs Jones could be treated as the income of Mr Jones. There were two important issues – *first*, whether these arrangements represented a settlement by Mr Jones and *second*, whether such a settlement could be excluded from these provisions by the exemption provided by s 626 for outright gifts from one spouse to another of property which is not wholly or substantially a right to income.

These issues have been hotly debated, and the passage of the case through the courts has merely added to the uncertainty. However, the House of Lords concluded the various questions as follows:

(a) The arrangements did represent a settlement by Mr Jones. In the leading speech, Lord Hoffmann said that this was not a normal commercial transaction between two adults; it only made sense on the basis that they were married to each other.

(b) The arrangements represented an outright gift by Mr Jones to Mrs Jones. This was a more complex matter because Mrs Jones had originally subscribed for her share in the company rather than it being given to her by Mr Jones. However, Lord Hoffmann explained that the arrangement involving the acquisition by Mr Jones of her share was a gift by Mr Jones.

(c) The property (ie the share) was not wholly or substantially a right to income.

The share was an ordinary share, conferring all the conventional rights of ordinary shares and much more than just a right to income. Accordingly, the exemption provided by s 626 applied, and the dividends were taxable on Mrs Jones and not on Mr Jones. See also the failed dividend waiver case *Donovan and McLaren v R & C Comrs* (2014) (see [**46.54**]). (Note also the case of *PA Holdings v R & C Comrs* (2011) where HMRC succeeded in treating dividends as earnings for income tax and NIC purposes.) [**46.61**]

3 **Capital taxes**

a) *General*

Recent changes in the capital taxation of companies have placed the small company in an improved position compared with the unincorporated business.

Sole traders and partners are subject to CGT at a rate of 20% with an annual exemption (for 2017–18) of £11,300. For partnerships, the rules for calculating the CGT liability of the individual partners are applied in accordance with SP D/12 (see **Chapter 44**). So far as companies are concerned, capital gains are taxed at the normal corporation tax rate, ie 19%.

In many cases individuals and companies will be able to defer a charge by claiming roll-over relief under TCGA 1992 s 152 (see [**22.72**]) or by EIS deferral relief. Capital profits can be taken out of the company by means of a dividend. In this way, a shareholder who is liable to tax only at the basic rate and who wishes to realise the capital profit on his shares can avoid the double charge to tax that would otherwise result when he sells those shares (see *Example 46.7*). [46.62]

EXAMPLE 46.7

In its accounting period ending 31 March 2018, Kafka Ltd, a small company, makes a capital gain of £30,000. K, a higher rate taxpayer, is the sole shareholder/director and wishes to obtain the benefit of this profit.

(1) *Sale of shares:* Kafka Ltd incurs a corporation tax charge of £5,700 on the capital gain and the net amount of £24,300 is retained in the company. If K were to sell his shares for a price reflecting this retained profit he would be subject to CGT of £4,860 being 20% on the retained profit. Hence, assuming K has already utilised his CGT annual exemption, the total tax attributable to the company's capital profit will be 35.2%). (£5,700 corporation tax + £4,860 CGT).

(2) *Payment of dividend:* If, instead of selling his shares, K arranges for Kafka Ltd to distribute the profit by way of dividend the tax position is as follows:

	£
Dividend	24,000
Dividend allowance	5,000
	£19,000
Taxed on K at 32.5%	6,175

Note, however, that no account has been taken of the availability of entrepreneurs' relief on a sale of the shares by K which would reduce K's CGT to £2,430.

b) *Retention of assets outside the business*

It is a common practice to keep appreciating capital assets out of a company. In part, this is to avoid any risk of a double charge to CGT: but undoubtedly the most compelling reason is very often the desire of the owner of the asset to retain all of any future profits made from the sale of that asset! In such a case, therefore, the relevant shareholder will allow the asset to be used by the company, but will retain its ownership.

On its disposal, any gain will be subject to CGT only in the hands of the shareholder. The difficulty is that although a double charge may be avoided, other problems can be created, for instance:

(1) *IHT business property relief:* Relief may be available on such an asset, but only at 50% and, in the case of an asset used by an unquoted company, only if the owner is a controlling shareholder (which limits the relief to those cases where the individual has more than 50% of the company's voting shares). For a partner the relief at 50% is available whatever the size of his share in the partnership (see [31.43]). The possibility of 100% relief is a crucial factor which may encourage assets to be held within partnerships and companies.

(2) *Payment for use of the asset:* Apart from such payments being subject to income tax as property income they will restrict the availability of IHT business property relief. Hence, it may be better for the taxpayer to take

an increased share of the profits instead or, in the case of a company, a greater salary. If rent is paid the company should obtain a corporation tax deduction (provided that it is not excessive): rent in excess of a market rent paid to a shareholder is treated as a distribution. Interest paid on a loan to acquire property can only be set against rental income whereas interest on a loan to purchase shares in, or make a loan to, the company can be deducted from the taxpayer's total income.

(3) *Section 162 relief.* The relief for CGT on the incorporation of a business will not be available if assets (except cash) are retained outside the company.

(4) *Paying IHT by instalments* is generally not available in the case of assets held outside a company except for land (when interest will be charged on the unpaid IHT). **[46.63]**

c) *VAT aspects*

If a new commercial building is acquired, the purchaser may have to pay VAT on the purchase price. If this VAT is to be recovered, the purchaser will need to register for VAT and to charge VAT on the rent which he receives. **[46.64]**

4 Stamp duty land tax

Sales of a business involving land will give rise to a charge to stamp duty land tax. On a share transfer stamp duty or stamp duty reserve tax is charged at an *ad valorem* rate of only 1/2%. If the business to be sold consists of valuable dutiable assets, the purchaser may (obviously depending on other commercial considerations) prefer to reduce his stamp duty cost by acquiring the shares.
[46.65]–[46.80]

IV GENERAL CONCLUSIONS

Although non-taxation factors tend to favour incorporation (notably the benefit of limited liability), tax considerations will favour the unincorporated trader at lower levels of profit and incorporation when higher profits are made. Note, however, in particular:

(1) The rate of corporation tax (19%) is less than the higher rates of income tax (40% and 45%) and applies to both income and capital profits, which encourages retention of profits in a company.

(2) Dividends are still taxed at lower rates and carry a small tax free allowance to offset (at least in part) tax suffered by the company.

(3) The danger of an investor being 'locked-into' the private company has been reduced by the 'buy-back' provisions (see **[42.21]**).

(4) Taxpayers are given incentives to invest in corporate trades through the Enterprise Investment Scheme, Seed Enterprise Investment Scheme and CGT deferral relief.

Two final points may be mentioned. *First*, questions of commercial 'prestige' favour incorporation: the label 'company director' is more impressive than 'sole trader'. *Second*, and by way of a cautionary note, considerable tax reliefs are given to encourage firms to incorporate and new corporate businesses to commence, but the same is not true on disincorporation. A company is easier to get into than out of, and this is a factor to be remembered when the decision to incorporate is taken. **[46.81]**

APPENDIX A: TABLE OF RATES OF NATIONAL INSURANCE CONTRIBUTIONS FOR 2017–18

The table below shows the rates of national insurance contributions for the year 2017–18.

CLASS 1 (EMPLOYMENT) – NOT CONTRACTED OUT		
	Employer % of all earnings	*Employee*
Weekly earnings bands		
£0–£157	0%	0%
£158–£866	13.8%	12%
Over £866	13.8%	2%
Men 65 and over and women 60 and over	13.8%	Nil
Class 1A – on benefits	13.8%	Nil
Class 1B – on PAYE settlement agreements	13.8%	Nil
Class 2 Self-employed		£2.85 per week
Limit of net earnings for exception		£6,025 pa
Class 3 Voluntary		£14.25 per week
Class 4 Self-employed on profits		
£8,164–£45,000		9%
over £45,000		2%

At Budget 2016 the Government announced that Class 2 NIC will be abolished from April 2018.

47 Incorporations, acquisitions and demergers

Updated by Helen McGhee, Senior Associate, Joseph Hage Aaronson LLP

I   Transfer of an unincorporated business to a company [47.2]
II Company acquisitions [47.31]
III Demergers and reconstructions [47.51]
IV Management buy-outs [47.71]

Some aspects of business takeovers will be considered in this chapter, although in view of the complexities and technicality of the subject all that is attempted is a general introduction to the problems involved. [47.1]

I TRANSFER OF AN UNINCORPORATED BUSINESS TO A COMPANY

This section is concerned with the issues that arise when an existing unincorporated business is transferred to a company. There are a variety of ways in which this might happen, for instance:
(1) The business could be transferred to an existing company or to a company formed or purchased 'off the shelf' by the proprietor to take over the business.
(2) The business might be acquired by the company in return for shares in the company, loan notes, cash, deferred or contingent consideration or a combination of all four. [47.2]

1 Income tax

Until 6 April 2005 unincorporated businesses were subject to income tax under Schedule D Case I but now the code is contained in ITTOIA 2005 Chapter 2. The principles on which income tax is charged are unchanged and where the business is transferred to a company the closing year rules will apply. Where assets only are sold and the proprietor continues the same trade, there will not be a cessation of the business and he will continue to be taxed according to the current year rules.

Termination of a business may lead to a claim for terminal loss relief (ITA 2007 s 89). As an alternative, where the business is transferred to a company wholly or mainly for shares, the taxpayer can elect for any year throughout which he retains beneficial ownership of the shares to set off unrelieved trading losses against income that he receives from the company. The set-off must first be used against salary if the proprietor is employed by the company but any balance can be relieved against dividends paid by the company (ITA 2007 s 86). The loss cannot be transferred to the company.

A discontinuance of the trade may result in a clawback of capital allowances by a balancing charge. Where the transfer is to a company controlled by the transferor, an election can be made by both parties, in the case of machinery and plant, that the company takes over the assets at written down value for capital allowances. That election must be made within two years of the date of succession (CAA 2001 s 266). [47.3]

2 Capital gains tax

a) *The available reliefs*

The incorporation of the business will involve the transfer of chargeable assets to the company with a consequent risk of a CGT charge. A number of reliefs may be available: [47.4]

Where the transfer is in exchange for shares: relief is provided by TCGA 1992 s 162 which operates to roll any gain on the business assets into the shares acquired in exchange (see **[22.100]**–**[22.103]**). The capital gain will, therefore, be postponed until the shares are sold. (Note, however, that the company acquires the business assets at market value, ie there is a tax-free step up which will reduce the capital gain on a disposal of the assets by the company.) For the relief to apply, all the business assets (except cash) must be transferred to the company in exchange for shares. It follows that retention of appreciating business assets prevents s 162 from applying. Any attempt to remove those assets from the business prior to incorporation (eg by transferring them to a spouse) may result in HMRC denying the relief on the grounds that not all the assets of the business had been transferred. If the consideration is partly shares and partly cash an appropriate portion of the gain will be subject to charge and only the balance will be rolled into the shares (see ESC D32 where liabilities of the business are taken over). Special rules operate if part of the consideration is a qualifying corporate bond.

In finding for the taxpayer (who had undertaken various activities ancillary to the letting of five investment flats) in *Elizabeth Moyne Ramsay v R & C Comrs* (2013), the Upper Tribunal defined a business to be one where the 'activities were a serious undertaking earnestly pursued or a serious occupation; or the activity was an occupation or function actively pursued with reasonable or recognisable continuity' and where 'the activity had a certain amount of substance in terms of turnover ... was conducted in a regular manner and on sound and recognised business principles, and ... were of a kind which, subject to differences of detail, are commonly made by those who seek to profit by them.' A simple transfer of an income stream, a particular contract or anything short of all assets of the business (excluding cash) will not be enough to satisfy s 162 – see *Paul Roelich v R & C Comrs* (2014).

Where the incorporation of the trade is into a corporate member (possibly incorporated as a result of the change in law in relation to attribution of profits within mixed member partnerships under FA 2014), HMRC confirmed to the Chartered Institute of Taxation that they consider, with effect from

30 April 2016, that s 162 relief is not available on such incorporations because the assets of the partnership deemed to be held by the corporate member before incorporation are not regarded as having been transferred to that member. Where s 162 relief is not available, then s 165 gift relief may be useful to defer any gains to the extent it is a trading company. **[47.5]**

A transfer for cash: Roll-over relief under TCGA 1992 s 152 (see **[22.72]–[22.81]**) may be available if the transferor reinvests the proceeds of sale in one of the relevant classes of assets specified in s 155, in the same or a new trade within the prescribed period. This is unlikely to arise if the trade has been transferred. **[47.6]**

A gift to the company: Where business assets are transferred to the company for no consideration or at an undervalue the disposal will be treated as taking place at market value as the business owner and the company are deemed to be connected persons for the purposes of TCGA 1992 s 18. The gain arising can be held over under TCGA 1992 s 165 (see **[24.4]**). The use of this hold-over election under s 165 should, however, be carefully considered since the effect is to transfer any capital gain in the assets to the company (as opposed to rebasing them with a section 162 transfer). Accordingly it can lead to a double charge when that gain is ultimately realised by the company (see further **Chapter 46** and *Example 47.1*, below). A charge to Stamp Duty Land Tax will apply on a transfer of land to the company. **[47.7]**

The retention of appreciating assets outside the company: The double charge which may arise when capital gains are realised by a company means that where a business is incorporated there may be attractions in retaining outside the company those assets which are likely to appreciate substantially in value and to allow the company to use or lease those assets. TCGA 1992 s 162 will not apply to the incorporation in these circumstances so that, unless hold-over relief is available, gains on the incorporation will be subject to charge. A gift of the retained asset should attract hold-over relief under TCGA 1992 s 165 and ultimately business property relief for IHT at a rate of 50% for the transferring owner so long as he 'controls' (within the IHTA 1984 s 269 definition) the company (but note that 100% business property relief will *not* be available). There would be no immediate IHT charge under IHTA 1984 s 3 on incorporation as the assets are not leaving the estate of the transferring owner; he is simply converting them into shares. **[47.8]**

The tax efficient practice of a trading business selling its trade and/or assets to a close company at market value (liable to CGT at the 10% entrepreneurs' relief rate) and leaving the proceeds outstanding on the new director's loan account to be extracted tax free, has been curtailed since 3 December 2014 by the introduction of new TCGA 1992 s 167LA and CTA 2009 ss 849B–849D.
[47.8A]

EXAMPLE 47.1

Slick intends to incorporate his existing business. Accordingly, Slick Ltd is formed with £100 share capital. Slick then sells to Slick Ltd goodwill for a nominal sum and other assets at their CGT base cost. The consideration may either be paid in cash or left outstanding as a loan to Slick Ltd. An election under TCGA 1992 s 165 is then made. The following matters should be noted:

(1) Slick is free to retain the ownership of whichever assets he desires (hence avoiding the restrictions of s 162).

(2) Under s 165 the gain is rolled over to reduce Slick Ltd's base cost of the assets whereas under s 162 it is the base cost of the shares held by the shareholder that is reduced, the company acquiring the assets at market value. Note, however, that Slick Ltd will obtain the benefit of the CGT indexation allowance only on the uplifted base value of the assets transferred (not on the original base value). A major problem which may arise if s 165 is used is that the postponed gain may be taxed twice – once on disposal by the company of chargeable assets and the second time when the shares showing an increased value are sold.

b) *Valuation*

In *Tax Bulletin* 76 (April 2005) HMRC explained their practice on the treatment of goodwill when a sole trader transfers their business to a company in which they have a controlling interest. The transfer of the goodwill represents a transaction between connected parties and market value needs to be substituted for the actual consideration: TCGA 1992 s 17. Where the goodwill is over valued HMRC will treat the excess not as a capital gain but as earnings or as a benefit in kind, chargeable to income tax and class 1 NIC. Where there is no evidence that any excess value constitutes earnings (for example, it may have been received in his capacity as a shareholder rather than employee) they consider the excess would be regarded as a distribution, providing there are sufficient distributable profits for such a distribution to be lawful.

Where the excess value arises inadvertently (because neither side intended to transfer the goodwill as an excess value) HMRC will allow the transaction to be unwound by the company repaying the excess value to the sole trader or rewriting the loan account to remove the excess amount.

It should be noted that HMRC assert that the goodwill attributable to the personal skill of a proprietor of a business cannot be transferred to a company.

The valuation of goodwill is a difficult topic and HMRC set up a specialist team to consider the position in late 2013. The result was a 12 page Guidance Note from the Valuation Office setting out their views on the approach to be taken on goodwill as well as other assets. The note is not a full exposition of the view of HMRC as it is quite short and covers many assets but it is a useful source of information and contains references to pertinent cases. [47.9]–[47.10]

3 **Stamp duty and SDLT**

The transfer of a business to a company may involve a charge to stamp duty land tax (SDLT). SDLT will only be charged on the land, as a charge to stamp duty on intellectual property was abolished by FA 2000 and on goodwill in 2002. SDLT will also be charged on any mortgage over the land taken over by a purchaser.

The transfer of trade debtors or the benefit of contracts may be subject to stamp duty. It may be necessary to apportion the consideration between dutiable and non-dutiable items on a just and reasonable basis, incorporating a certificate of value if appropriate. [47.11]

4 Problems for a purchasing company

Where the business is not being incorporated but is being sold to an existing company, other difficulties for that purchaser should be noted. For instance, if the business is acquired as a going concern it must be treated separately for corporation tax purposes from any existing trade already carried on by the company. The price paid for items such as land, plant, machinery and goodwill will constitute the purchaser's base cost for the purpose of computing any future capital gains. So far as capital allowances are concerned, a conflict of interest is likely with the vendor wishing to attribute as small a sum as possible to such assets in order to avoid a balancing charge whilst for the purchaser a high figure will give him a greater capital allowance. The agreed apportionment will normally be accepted by HMRC, but will probably only be reached after hard bargaining between the parties. **[47.12]**

From 1 April 2014 for the purchaser to claim capital allowances the vendor must have included the relevant plant and machinery in his tax computations, even if he was not claiming allowances. This may require an extra step in the pre-sale negotiations. **[47.13]**

5 Other matters

A number of ancillary matters should also be considered on incorporation or sale of a business. The following summarises the more important aspects:

(1) If an existing trade is incorporated, contracts of employment automatically transfer with the business. Where assets alone are sold, however, claims for redundancy will occur if staff are reduced. (See especially the Employment Rights Act 1996 and the Transfer of Undertakings (Protection of Employment) Regulations 2006.)

(2) If the vendor of the business is a director of the purchasing company (this will normally be the case when a business is being incorporated), a general meeting of the company will usually have to approve the agreement under Companies Act 2006 s 190. If new shares are to be issued it will be necessary to ensure that the company has available authorised share capital although most companies incorporated after 2006 do not have authorised share capital (if necessary, the authorised share capital should be increased: see CA 2006 s 617); that the directors have the power to allot such shares (see CA 2006 s 549); and that any pre-emption provisions in the articles of association have either been satisfied or do not apply to shares issued in return for a non-cash consideration.

(3) Providing the company is registered for VAT before the transfer of the business as a going concern, there will be no charge on the transfer of items which would otherwise be subject to VAT on the sale of the business (VATA 1994 s 49). VAT may be charged on a mere transfer of assets.

(4) Ensure that all necessary consents are obtained and/or documents amended, eg a landlord's consent to the assignment of a lease.

(5) A property letting business can qualify as a business for the purposes of s 162 where the business is transferred to the company in exchange for shares (*Elizabeth Moyne Ramsay v R & C Comrs* (2013)).

(6) If the business is sold for cash, the vendor should remember that for IHT purposes, business property relief and the instalment option will be lost because an asset which qualifies for relief for IHT is being exchanged for cash that enjoys no such relief. **[47.14]–[47.30]**

II COMPANY ACQUISITIONS

A sale of a company may take different forms. The assets of the target company may be purchased; or the shares of that company may be acquired. In the former, the shareholders of the target will be left with a company whose sole asset is cash; in the latter, the shareholders themselves will be left with cash. Alternatively, the takeover may be by a share exchange in which case the vendors will be left with shares in the purchaser. On a share acquisition, the purchaser will have acquired the entire enterprise as a going concern and, if a corporate purchaser, will have acquired a subsidiary company. In an assets takeover, the purchaser may simply amalgamate those assets with his existing business so that instead of acquiring a new enterprise he may simply be expanding his existing business. **[47.31]**

1 Considerations on an assets sale

a) *The vendor*

If the vendor company intends to continue in business, an assets sale has the advantage that the vendor company may be able to roll over any gains (under TCGA 1992 s 152) into the purchase of new assets within the permitted time. It is possible to reinvest in a completely different trade (see SP 8/81). A disposal of trading stock results in a corporation tax charge and a disposal of machinery and plant may lead to balancing charges.

If the company plans to discontinue trading permanently, the consequences are far from satisfactory. The company will be liable to tax on any capital profits made on the sale. The normal carry-back of losses to the previous year will be available, but carry-forward relief will be lost. Problems will arise if the shareholders wish to extract the cash from the company. The result will be either an income tax charge on a distribution, or a charge to CGT on a liquidation in addition to the tax charge already borne by the company. Generally, if the vendors plan to discontinue the business, and to obtain all the sale proceeds personally, the company should not sell its assets; it is better for the shareholders to sell the shares. However, where the shareholders have no real need for the money other than to invest, they may prefer to arrange for the company to sell its assets and for the proceeds to be invested by the company. In this way the tax on the disposal might be lower and the return on the investment of the proceeds will be taxed at a lower rate inside the company than if they invest the money themselves. **[47.32]**

b) *The purchaser*

The *first* and most obvious attraction is that the purchaser can select which assets he wants to acquire since he will not be acquiring the entire entity.

Second, save in respect of employees (which the purchaser will take over if there is a transfer of a business as a going concern), the purchaser will not run the risk of acquiring liabilities which he does not want and/or of which he is not aware. *Third*, the purchaser may be entitled to capital allowances (eg on the purchase of plant and machinery) and to roll over relief on the purchase of qualifying assets. [47.33]

2 Considerations on a share sale

a) *The vendor*

The sale of shares will be a disposal for CGT purposes. Because the company is sold, there is no change of owner of the business so that continuity of employment is automatically preserved and all debts and liabilities effectively pass to the purchaser. The vendors will normally be required to give certain undertakings and warranties to the purchaser so that there will be some continuing personal liability.

If the purchase money is to be paid in instalments, CGT will still be charged on the total sum at the outset unless HMRC allows the tax to be paid by instalments (see TCGA 1992 s 280). Where the consideration is partly deferred, the deferred consideration may need to be brought into charge immediately if it is able to be quantified, or at its present value at the date of the contract if it is unable to be ascertained or quantified at that date (*Marren v Ingles* (1980), see **[19.8]**).

If the vendors intend to stay in business, a share sale may not be ideal since, for CGT, gains on the sale of the shares can only be rolled over into the purchase of replacement shares in a qualifying EIS or SEIS company. It is therefore likely that they will have a gain immediately chargeable to tax at a rate of either 10% or 20% (depending on whether they are higher rate taxpayers). However, it may be that the vendors can qualify for entrepreneurs' relief, meaning that even if the individuals are higher rate taxpayers tax will be chargeable on the gain at 10% on the first £10m of the gain (this is a lifetime limit) for disposals after 5 April 2011 and they might regard that as an acceptable result. The position of the vendor if consideration for the sale is in the form of shares or loan notes is considered below. [47.34]

b) *The purchaser*

The acquisition of the company's shares will usually ensure continuity of the business. However, there will be no tax relief for the purchase of the shares themselves. It is possible to carry forward trading losses suffered by the company prior to the sale of the shares but by CTA 2010 s 99 these losses may only be set against profits *in the same trade*. If the trade has ceased, carry-forward is not possible even if an identical trade is later started. Further, CTA 2010 s 673 prevents relief in the event of a 'major change in the nature or conduct of the trade' within a period of three years of the sale (see *Willis v Peeters Picture Frames Ltd* (1983) and SP 10/91; see **[41.65]**). The prudent purchaser should tread warily for three years before attempting any major revitalisation of the target company if he wants to preserve any losses which may be available in the company.

It is essential for the purchaser to ascertain what skeletons are hidden in the target company's cupboards. To protect himself, warranties and indemnities will normally be sought. In a typical share acquisition agreement the vendor will be asked to warrant at the time of sale that the company has no undisclosed tax liabilities. Since the function of tax warranties is not only to protect the purchaser against future liabilities but also to extract for the purchaser information about the company, tax warranties normally involve detailed points. For example, the vendor will be asked to warrant that the company has duly and punctually paid all taxes, has operated the PAYE system correctly and has not been involved in any anti-avoidance scheme. It is usual to back up these warranties with a deed of tax indemnity whereby the vendor indemnifies the purchaser against any tax liability of the company which comes to light after the sale but by reference to a pre-completion event and which was not disclosed to the purchaser. As a result of *Zim Properties Ltd v Proctor* (1985) (see **[19.66]**) payments made under such indemnities were thought to be taxable in the hands of the recipient as the proceeds of the disposal of a *chose in action* (ie the right to sue was considered a separate asset). This led to the practice of inserting a 'grossing-up' clause in the deed of indemnity to ensure that the amount payable in the event of a claim would equal the liability under the deed plus the tax payable by the purchaser thereon. However, ESC D33 makes it clear that, *provided that payments under indemnities are made to the purchaser*, they will be regarded as a reduction in the purchase price and therefore not subject to tax (contrast the position if payments are made to the company). Notwithstanding this, grossing-up clauses are often still found in deeds of tax indemnity.

When purchasing a company out of a group, special considerations arise. In particular, there may be a clawback charge under TCGA 1992 s 179 in respect of assets transferred to the subsidiary by another group company on a no loss/no gain basis under s 171. FA 2011 changed the way the de-grouping charge is allocated on a transfer of shares: the charge was previously allocated to the transferee company but now the value of the charge is added to the consideration received by the transferor. The effect of these changes brought in by FA 2011 mean that any de-grouping charge exposure is just as pertinent for the vendor as it is for the purchaser. **[47.35]**

c) *Pre-sale dividend strip*

The use of a pre-sale dividend to extract value from a subsidiary before its sale was once a well-used tax saving device subject to the availability of distributable profits and the value shifting rules (see **[26.61]**). At one time, the pre-sale dividend strip was popular with individual vendors of private companies as a means of reducing the CGT liability on sale. However, with the reduction in the top rate of CGT to 20% (ignoring the higher rate for gains on residential property and carried interest) for most taxpayers (and the possibility of entrepreneurs' relief on the first £10m from 6 April 2011, which reduces the rate of CGT to 10%) a straightforward sale is likely to give rise to a much lower tax liability than that arising from a pre-sale dividend. (See also **[26.61]** for the interaction with the value shifting provisions). **[47.36]**

EXAMPLE 47.2

SJ Ltd has substantial undistributed profits. The owner, Mr Wise has been offered £2m for his shares which do not qualify for entrepreneurs' relief, producing a capital gain of £1.2m which, taxed at 20%, would lead to a CGT liability of £240,000.

If, shortly before the sale, a dividend of £1m is paid to Mr Wise and the sale price is reduced accordingly, he will suffer a CGT liability of £40,000 on his reduced gain of £200,000 plus income tax of approximately £360,000 on his dividend. Thus, Mr Wise would pay tax totalling over £400,000 so he would be better off not taking a pre sale dividend now that the rate of CGT has been reduced even further.

d) *Pre-sale stock dividends*

Instead of a pre-sale cash dividend the vendors may receive a stock dividend from the company prior to sale (the tax treatment of stock dividends is considered at **[42.9]**). Such arrangements have been commonly used where the company has insufficient reserves to pay a pre-sale cash dividend. Typically, the company declares a stock dividend alternative that should be as early as possible in the company sale process. Each shareholder is offered a choice between a cash dividend and an issue of new shares at par. Shortly before the sale, the shareholders take up their stock dividend entitlements. This reduces the risk of the sale falling through after the dividend has been taken up, which could leave the shareholders with an income tax charge but no cash with which to pay it. For company law purposes, the amount charged to reserves is the *nominal* value of the new shares not their market value. There is no longer any tax saving likely to arise from a pre-sale stock dividend because the dividend rate of 32.5% if the shareholder is paying tax at the higher rate (less the £5,000 tax free allowance) is much higher than the CGT rate of 20%.

[47.37]

3 Acquisition by means of a share issue

Shares or assets in the target may be acquired in exchange for an issue of shares in the acquiring company. In such an event:

(1) On a share exchange CGT will not usually be payable by the vendors since a roll-over deferral is available provided that the arrangement is *bona fide* commercial and, generally, that more than 25% of the target's shares are owned or acquired by the purchaser (TCGA 1992 s 135 and s 137). Deferral is also available if the exchange is as a result of a general offer made to the shareholders of the target that is conditional upon the purchaser acquiring control of the target and is for *bona fide* commercial purposes. A clearance can be obtained from HMRC under s 138 that this requirement is satisfied. It is also possible to exclude s 135 so that a gain is crystallised (in whole or in part) when the vendor wishes to take advantage of EIS deferral relief or entrepreneurs' relief under s 169Q.

(2) *Marren v Ingles* (see **[19.8]**) can present problems in share-for-share transactions where shares in the vendor are transferred to a purchaser in return for an immediate issue of shares in the purchaser together with a future right to further consideration, possibly in the form of shares (an arrangement sometimes referred to as an 'earn-out' since

the further consideration is often made dependent on a future profit target being met). These future shares (ie the deferred consideration) do not fall within TCGA 1992 s 135 and accordingly cannot benefit from the deferral. A number of arrangements were employed to avoid this difficulty usually involving an issue of loan stock by the purchaser that was ultimately converted into shares (ie the deferred shares) in the purchaser. The immediate exchange of shares for convertible loan stock fell within TCGA 1992 s 135 whilst the subsequent conversion of the loan stock was free from CGT under TCGA 1992 s 132.

The problems of earn-outs were eased by ESC D27, which provided that:

'where an agreement for the sale of shares or debentures in a company creates a right to an unascertainable element (whether or not subject to a maximum) against the purchaser which is acquired by the vendor at the time of disposal and that right falls to be satisfied wholly by the issue of shares or debentures, then, notwithstanding a concurrent right to consideration other than in the form of shares or debentures, the Board are prepared to treat the right to shares or debentures in the hands of the vendor as a security within the meaning of [TCGA 1992 s 132].'

Relief under s 135 was therefore available if the other conditions are satisfied. The concession was not happily worded but HMRC applied it to the extent that the future consideration could only be satisfied by an issue of shares or debentures and therefore ignored the existence of a concurrent or separate right to a cash payment. The concession was revised by the insertion of a final paragraph in two situations that extended its ambit. *First*, if the original purchaser was itself subsequently purchased on a share-for-share basis by another company (not in the same group) and the initial vendor's earn-out rights were exchanged for similar rights in the new purchaser and, *second*, if there was a subsequent variation in the terms of the original sale agreement (eg by extension of the earn-out period or to record an agreed settlement). In both cases the original s 135 roll-over was not prejudiced.

TCGA 1992 s 138A put the extra-statutory concession onto a legislative basis: the legislation is, however, more detailed; for instance, it defines 'unascertainable' and it is clear that although the relief is only available if the earn-out is satisfied by paper, there can be two separate earn-outs, one for cash and one for paper.

EXAMPLE 47.3

Jon owns shares in J Ltd that is taken over by P Ltd. For his shares Jon receives an initial cash sum together with a right to further (deferred) consideration depending on the profits of J Ltd and to be satisfied by an issue of shares in P Ltd (at the time of the takeover the value of the deferred consideration is unascertainable). Jon's CGT position is as follows:
(i) under general principles the consideration for the disposal of his shares will include the value of the earn-out right (which is a separate asset: see *Marren v Ingles* (1980));
(ii) under s 138A any gain that would have resulted from the value attributed to this right is deferred;

(iii) when the right is satisfied by an issue of shares this can be treated as a conversion of securities so that the charge is further deferred until such time as Jon sells the P Ltd shares;
(iv) if the earn-out is satisfied by an issue of securities in the form of qualifying corporate bonds the legislation makes it clear that the postponed tax will be charged on the disposal of the qualifying corporate bond.

(3) If assets of the target are transferred in return for shares by way of a *bona fide* commercial arrangement with the target going into liquidation, there will be no corporation tax on the transfer of assets by the target. Instead, the assets will be transferred at no gain/no loss, so that tax will be deferred until the purchaser sells (TCGA 1992 s 140). The shares in the purchaser company received by the vendor's shareholders are not subject to CGT until sold (TCGA 1992 s 136): but see the case of *Snell v R & C Comrs* (2008). Clearance is available under both these provisions.
[47.38]

4 **Acquisition by means of loan notes**

The vendor should ensure that the loan arrangements are structured as a debt on security (see [22.44]). The paper-for-paper exchange will fall under the roll-over provisions of TCGA 1992 s 135 and the vendor may be able to spread his gain by encashing the notes in different tax years. Sometimes an individual vendor will prefer to arrange that the security is not a qualifying corporate bond so that he would be entitled to loss relief in the event that the purchasing company defaults (see [41.94]). [47.39]–[47.50]

III DEMERGERS AND RECONSTRUCTIONS

Splitting up groups of companies or splitting a company into separate parts under separate ownership is the subject of relieving provisions. CTA 2010 s 1074 takes distributions which are made to achieve a demerger outside the normal income tax treatment of distributions (under CTA 2010 s 999) whilst TCGA 1992 s 192(2) prevents the shareholders from suffering a CGT charge by treating the demerged shares as if they had been received on a reorganisation of share capital. It should, however, be noted that the demerger code under the CTA 2010 does not deal either with the company's CGT position or with stamp duty land tax.

The conditions to be satisfied are technical and cannot be used to separate trades from investments (see generally SP 13/80). In general, three types of transaction constitute a demerger and qualify for advantageous tax treatment:
(1) A transfer to ordinary shareholders of shares in another company of which the transferor owns at least 75% of the ordinary share capital. This is the so-called '*direct demerger*' in the sense that the shares pass directly to the shareholders of the demerged company and the distributing company may suffer a CGT charge on the distribution.
(2) Pursuant to an agreement between the transferor company, its shareholders and the transferee company, the transferor declares a

dividend *in specie* of part of its undertaking which it transfers to the transferee in return for an issue of shares to the shareholders of the transferor. This and (3) below are '*indirect demergers*' since the trades or subsidiaries pass first to a company which then issues shares to the original shareholders in the demerged company (this was the type of demerger carried out by ICI and considered by the court in *Sinclair v Lee* (1993)). In both cases a CGT charge on the company is prevented by TCGA 1992 s 140.

(3) An amalgamation of (1) and (2): namely, shares in company 1's 75% subsidiary are transferred to company 2 in return for an issue of shares in that company.

Even where a transaction would appear to fall within one of these categories, further conditions have to be satisfied if relief is to be available. Only trading companies and groups are covered, and each entity resulting from any split must be a trading entity. Further, the reason for the split must be to benefit some or all of the trading activities that before the distribution were carried on by a single company and after the distribution by two or more companies. The purpose of the demerger must not be to save tax nor must it be intended as a means of transferring control of the company to a third party. A clearance procedure is available and the form of application is set out in SP 13/80.

The transfer of an 'undertaking' is exempt from stamp duty land tax under FA 1986 s 75 and a direct demerger, because it involves no sale, is not potentially subject to duty.

The demerger procedure may be employed to effect a partition as illustrated in the following example: [47.51]

EXAMPLE 47.4

Audivis Ltd carries on two separate trades as a result of a merger of two existing businesses (Audi and Vis). Its shareholders are family A and family V who are concerned in the running of the different trades. The merger has failed and so two classes of share are created (A and V shares); a dividend is declared in respect of the A shares which is satisfied by the transfer of the 'Audi' trade to a transferee company which issues shares to the A shareholders.

There are two other types of demerger, notably an Insolvency Act 1986 s 110 demerger or a Companies Act 2006 Part 26 demerger, both of which are widely used. [47.52]–[47.70]

IV MANAGEMENT BUY-OUTS

The distinction between an MBO and an employee buy-out is that in the latter the business is purchased by all or a part of the workforce not just by the managers. There are three typical situations when a buy-out may occur; *first*, when a subsidiary (or division) is purchased from a group of companies; *second*, when the owners sell the family company or its business; and *third*, when a receiver or liquidator sells all or a part of the failed undertaking often by means of a hive-down. As with any takeover the management may purchase either shares of the target company or the assets of the business and similar considerations to those discussed at [47.32] apply in deciding which is the most advantageous method for vendor and purchaser.

When the company is purchased (ie a share purchase) the normal indemnities and warranties should be sought by the management team although the vendors will often take the view that if there are 'skeletons in the cupboard', this is a matter of which the managers will have knowledge.

The major difficulties involved in buy-outs relate to the financing of the purchase since the management team will lack sufficient funds to purchase the business out of their own resources. Accordingly the bulk of the finance must be supplied by institutional investors and the target company or business is generally purchased by a newly formed company ('Newco') in which the managers have voting control but in which the majority of the finance has been provided by the institutions (this will normally be in the form of unsecured loan stock and convertible preference shares).

It may be possible to use the assets of the target company to assist in the purchase of its own shares (see CA 2006 Chapter 4). Dividends or loans may be paid to Newco to enable it to discharge interest payments to the institutions (care should be taken to ensure that when Newco is a holding company it has sufficient profits against which to obtain tax relief for the interest payments). Finally, the target could be liquidated after its purchase and its assets transferred up to Newco. This would have the attraction of ending the holding company/trading subsidiary structure but care should be taken to ensure that the transfer of assets does not trigger a CGT charge (see TCGA 1992 s 122). Accordingly, it might be more satisfactory to transfer the business of the target as a going concern at book value and to leave the consideration outstanding on an inter-company loan account. The target would then be left as a 'shell' company.

So far as the managers are concerned, apart from using their own personal wealth to purchase shares in Newco, it will often be necessary for them to raise additional funds by way of loans. Income tax relief may be available on the interest paid on such loans (see generally *Lord v Tustain* (1993) and **Chapter 7**). ITA 2007 s 383 relief is given if the taxpayer works for the greater part of his time in the actual management or conduct of the company. When the buy-out is arranged through Newco, it is essential to ensure that it satisfies the test for a close trading company if ITA 2007 s 383 relief is to be available (see *Lord v Tustain* (1993): a company formed to acquire a business existed for the purpose of carrying on that business). In practice, this means ensuring that 75% or more of its income is derived from trading subsidiaries and HMRC accepts that, so long as it is in receipt of the appropriate amount of dividends or income from the target during its first accounting period, this requirement will be treated as satisfied at the time when the managers make their investment. Thus, if at some later date Newco ceases to satisfy the conditions of ITA 2007 s 383, relief will not be withdrawn. Relief may alternatively be available under ITA 2007 s 401. Newco must be employee-controlled (ie full-time employees should control more than 50% of the ordinary share capital and votes) and it must be an unquoted trading company or the holding company of a trading group. For the purpose of this requirement, Newco may qualify even though it has only the one trading subsidiary. If the company ceases to be employee-controlled, however, tax relief is withdrawn. Reference has already been made to the potential income tax liability of managers under ITEPA 2003 Part 7 Chapter 2 resulting from an acquisition of shares in their capacity as employees (see further **Chapter 9**). Further, if shares are offered at below market price, an income tax liability under the general provisions taxing benefits in kind could arise. [47.71]

48 Capital allowances

Updated by Martin Wilson, Chairman, The Capital Allowances Partnership Limited

---

I   The general scheme of capital allowances [48.1]
II Plant and machinery [48.11]
III Industrial buildings [48.91]
IV Other categories of expenditure eligible for capital allowances [48.121]

I THE GENERAL SCHEME OF CAPITAL ALLOWANCES

In general, taxpayers cannot deduct capital expenditure in arriving at their taxable income or profits (an exception was the Private Landlord's Energy Saving Allowance – see [48.126]). Nor is depreciation in commercial accounts allowed as a deduction for tax purposes. Capital allowances, broadly speaking, take the place of depreciation charged in commercial accounts and allow the cost of certain capital assets to be written off over a period against a business's taxable profits. Some capital allowances have a secondary purpose, that of providing an incentive for certain types of expenditure for wider political reasons, such as the 100% FYAs for expenditure on environmentally beneficial plant or machinery (see [48.35]).

1 The legislation

The governing legislation for capital allowances is the Capital Allowances Act 2001 (CAA 2001).

References to sections, without more, are references to sections of CAA 2001. [48.1]

2 The different forms of allowances

Capital allowances give taxpayers relief for certain kinds of capital expenditure. CAA 2001 deals with who gets relief for what expenditure, when and how. Part 1 of CAA 2001 sets out the basic rules on how allowances affect the calculation of tax, defines some of the key terms used throughout the Act and

stops double relief. Each of the next 11 Parts deals with a specific allowance, providing allowances for expenditure on:
(1) *plant and machinery* (Part 2);
(2) *industrial buildings* – abolished from April 2011 but still of relevance where property is acquired (Part 3);
(3) *business premises renovation* (Part 3A) (abolished from April 2017);
(4) *agricultural buildings* – abolished from April 2011 but still of relevance where property is acquired (Part 4);
(5) the renovation and conversion of vacant space above shops and commercial properties to provide flats for rent ('*flat conversion allowances*' – abolished from April 2013) (Part 4A);
(6) *mineral extraction* (Part 5);
(7) *research and development* (Part 6);
(8) the acquisition of certain industrial information or techniques ('*know-how*') (Part 7);
(9) the purchase of *patent rights* (Part 8);
(10) *dredging* (Part 9).
(11) the construction of *dwelling houses let on assured or certain other tenancies* (Part 10) (abolished from April 1992).

Part 11 deals with contributions one person makes to another's expenditure, and Part 12 deals with miscellaneous issues such as capital allowances for life assurance businesses, the interaction between capital allowances and the VAT capital items legislation, partnerships, and the succession and transfer of businesses.

Where an allowance is made, under one of the above codes the taxpayer cannot obtain an allowance under another in respect of the same expenditure.

[48.2]

3 **Capital expenditure**

a) *Problems in identifying expenditure of a capital nature*

Capital allowances are generally due only in respect of *capital* expenditure provided that it is also qualifying expenditure for the particular form of allowance being claimed. Usually taxpayers will prefer the expenditure to be classed as *revenue* expenditure so as to obtain a deduction for it in arriving at their profits and thus receive 100% tax relief immediately: ie for the chargeable period related to the accounting period in which the expenditure was incurred. By contrast, much capital expenditure is not deductible at all; and even capital expenditure which qualifies for capital allowances does not usually entitle the taxpayer to a 100% deduction in the first year, although, temporarily, such a deduction is available for a limited amount of capital expenditure using the annual investment allowance (see [**48.28**]). (There are further exceptions of limited application: see the 100% allowances for energy-saving and water-conserving plant and machinery expenditure ([**48.29**]–[**48.35**]), the recently abolished 100% allowances for flat conversions ([**48.122**]), for R&D expenditure ([**48.123**]), the renovation of business premises (([**48.124**]) and the landlord's energy saving allowance ([**48.126**]).) Accordingly, the distinction between capital and revenue expenditure is very significant.

What is capital expenditure and what is a capital sum? The legislation is unhelpful, only stating what capital expenditure is *not*, ie it cannot include:
(1) in relation to the payer, expenditure which is deductible in computing the taxable profits or gains of a trade, profession, office, employment or vocation, or
(2) in relation to the recipient, a sum which in his hands counts as a receipt in computing his trading profits, or
(3) annual payments within ITA 2007 Part 15 Ch 6, eg rent and royalties which are made after deduction of tax at source: s 4.

Viscount Cave's test in *Atherton v British Insulated and Helsby Cables Ltd* (1925) has stood the test of time:

'... when an expenditure is made, not only once and for all, but with a view to bringing into existence an asset or an advantage for the enduring benefit of a trade ... there is very good reason (in the absence of special circumstances leading to an opposite conclusion) for treating such an expenditure as properly attributable not to revenue but to capital'.

The distinction between capital and revenue expenditure is often difficult to draw when considering expenditure on an existing asset, namely, whether the expenditure is a repair (revenue) or an improvement (capital). Is the expenditure for the purpose of maintaining the asset in its present condition or at its present value (revenue), or is the effect to alter the very nature of the asset so as virtually to bring into existence a new asset (capital)? Also, where *part* of an asset is replaced there can be circumstances in which the replacement is regarded as a separate asset in itself so that the expenditure will be capital expenditure: see, for instance, *O'Grady v Bullcroft Main Collieries Ltd* (1932).

Certain expenditure that would otherwise be classed as capital may be treated as revenue expenditure by virtue of specific provisions in the tax legislation. The most common example is a premium paid by a trader on a short lease, part of which can be deducted from his trading income over the duration of the lease: ITTOIA 2005 ss 60–65 (see [12.85]).

Conversely, where expenditure on an integral feature (for example, repairs) is more than 50% of the (notional or hypothetical) cost of replacing that integral feature, it must be treated as capital expenditure by virtue of s 33B even though it would otherwise be classed as revenue (see [48.61]).

CAA 2001 sometimes makes specific provision for the demolition costs of an asset to be treated as qualifying expenditure for capital allowances purposes, eg s 26, in respect of the demolition costs of plant and machinery. [48.3]

b) *Contributions*

Part 11 of CAA 2001 (ss 532–543) contains special provisions relating to subsidies and other contributions paid by one person to another person's capital expenditure. Broadly, ss 532 and 535 provide that a recipient cannot obtain capital allowances on expenditure to the extent that it is funded by a contribution (not counting insurance moneys), but ss 537 ff enable the contributor to do so if the contribution is made for the purposes of a trade or 'relevant activity' carried on by him and the recipient is an unconnected person whose expenditure would (but for s 532) have entitled the recipient to claim allowances.

'Relevant activity' is defined by s 536(5) to include not only a profession or vocation but also a property business, including that of furnished holiday lettings and an overseas property business, and also the management of an investment company.

It should be noted in particular that expenditure is not treated as incurred by a person if it has been met, directly or indirectly, by a central or local Government grant (there are exceptions to this, for instance, Northern Ireland regional development grants): ss 532 and 534.

All expenditure qualifying for a contributions allowance has to be allocated to a single asset pool: s 538(3) and see [48.54]. [48.4]

c) *The VAT element*

The treatment of the VAT element of capital expenditure qualifying for allowances will depend on a person's VAT status. The treatment is as follows:

(1) For a person who is not a taxable person for VAT the cost of an asset for capital allowance purposes will include the VAT. His input VAT forms part of his expenditure for tax purposes generally.

(2) A person whose output is wholly taxable for VAT (whether at the standard rate or zero rate) will be able to reclaim input VAT suffered. Therefore, for him the cost of an asset for capital allowance purposes is exclusive of VAT (with the exception of motor cars where reclaiming VAT is expressly prohibited).

(3) For a taxable person whose supplies are partly exempt, the VAT inputs which cannot be reclaimed must be attributed, however approximately, to the individual items of expenditure to which they relate. If such an item is an asset qualifying for capital allowances, its cost for that purpose will be its net cost plus the proportion of the VAT suffered thereon which cannot be reclaimed.

Where the capital expenditure is incurred on a 'capital item' within the VAT Capital Goods Scheme (see [38.89]) detailed provision is made in the various allowances for account to be taken of any VAT adjustments caused by the operation of the Scheme. Broadly speaking, any additional VAT which a person becomes liable to pay during the VAT adjustment period (because the proportion of exempt use has risen) is to be treated as capital expenditure incurred by that person; and any additional VAT which a person becomes entitled to deduct during the VAT adjustment period (because the proportion of exempt use has fallen) is regarded as a (or as an additional) 'disposal value' reducing his qualifying expenditure for future writing-down allowances. See, for example, CAA 2001 Part 2 Chapter 18 in respect of plant and machinery allowances. [48.5]

4 Claiming capital allowances

For both individuals and companies the granting of capital allowances is not automatic: allowances have to be claimed (s 3(1)). Similarly, it is not compulsory to claim the maximum amount of writing-down allowances (WDAs): a taxpayer claiming WDAs for any chargeable period may claim a reduced allowance of whatever amount he chooses: see s 56(5). Occasionally a taxpayer may have good reason not to claim allowances, or to claim only a reduced WDA, for a particular chargeable period, for example, to maximise the amount of taxable income or profits available in the period for other tax reliefs (including personal allowances that would otherwise be wasted) or for the offsetting of trading losses brought forward. With WDAs calculated on a reducing balance basis (eg for plant and machinery: see [48.37]) the effect of not claiming the allowance, or of making a reduced claim, for a particular period is to increase the balance of qualifying expenditure carried forward to the succeeding period. Thus the allowances for the succeeding period will be greater (and any balancing charge will be less) than would otherwise have been the case. The taxpayer does not lose the benefit of allowances not claimed, it is merely deferred.

It is important to remember that capital allowances are given for a period of account (or 'chargeable period'). This will not (except by coincidence) be the same as a tax year, except for qualifying activities other than trades (see [48.12]) which are subject to income tax rather than corporation tax. [48.6]

5 When is capital expenditure incurred?

It is often important to determine the time when capital expenditure is incurred, because an allowance will be available for a chargeable period only if the expenditure has been incurred in that (or a previous) period. If the expenditure is incurred in a chargeable period, the allowance generally becomes available even if the asset has not been brought into use in the business in that period (Industrial Buildings Allowances, now abolished, were an exception).

Subject to certain exceptions, an amount of capital expenditure is treated as incurred as soon as there is an unconditional obligation to pay it (when title will normally pass) even though the agreement may provide a credit period for payment: s 5(1) and (2).

One of the exceptions to the above is where there is a credit period exceeding four months from the date when the obligation to pay becomes unconditional. In this event the expenditure is treated as incurred on the date by or on which, under the credit agreement, it is required to be paid: s 5(5).

Furthermore, as an anti-avoidance measure, if the obligation to pay arises earlier than normal commercial usage for that trade would dictate, and the only or main benefit that results is the bringing forward of capital allowances to an earlier chargeable period, the expenditure will be deemed to be incurred on the later date by or on which payment must actually be made: s 5(6).

A 'chargeable period' means, broadly, for a company, partnership or self-employed individual, an accounting period; and for an employee the tax year: s 6. [48.7]

6 How is a capital allowance given?

For both income tax and corporation tax, first year allowances, writing-down allowances and balancing charges are generally treated as expenses and receipts of the trade for the accounting period in which they arise (see, eg ss 247–252 in relation to plant and machinery allowances). FA 2010 introduced restrictions on the use that may be made of a loss deriving from capital allowances in cases where a *main purpose* of a transaction was to secure a tax advantage by obtaining an annual investment allowance (see [**48.28**]) to create a loss which may be offset against other income (ITA 2007 s 127A), or where a loss-making company is acquired essentially for the inherent value of its unclaimed capital allowances (ss 212A–212S). [**48.8**]

a) *Trading losses*

For individuals and partnerships, a trading loss can be carried forward and set against future profits of the same trade (under ITA 2007 s 83). Alternatively, the taxpayer may elect to set the loss against his general income of the year when the loss arises, or of the preceding year (ITA 2007 ss 64, 71). Once this has been done, the taxpayer may offset against capital gains in those same years or, if appropriate (ie, the loss occurs in any of the first four years of trading), he can elect to carry it back under ITA 2007 s 72 (see **Chapter 11** for a consideration of loss relief). If the individual's involvement in a trade is a non-active one (ie less than ten hours per week), relief against other income under s 64, 71 or 72 is restricted to £25,000 (ITA 2007 s 74A).

Relief under ITA 2007, s 64, 71 or 72 is not permitted where the loss arises directly or indirectly in consequence of, or otherwise in connection with, 'relevant tax avoidance arrangements', which are essentially arrangements aimed at obtaining relief under these sections (ITA 2007 s 74ZA).

For companies carrying on trades the provisions of CTA 2010 s 45 and s 37 have a broadly similar effect in that trading losses can be carried forward indefinitely against that trade or (by election) carried back for a period of one year, in each case to be offset against total profits. Profits are defined as income and chargeable gains (CTA 2009 s 2(2)). [**48.9**]

b) *Property losses*

Capital allowances and balancing charges are treated similarly as regards the property business of an individual, partnership or company (including a business of furnished holiday lettings), ie as expenses or receipts of that business: see, for example, ss 248 and 249. If capital allowances result in a property business loss, then contrary to the general principle that applies to property business losses generally, that loss may be relieved against other income (but not gains) of the taxpayer in question for the year of the loss or the following year, in either order (but only to the extent that the loss is attributable to capital allowances – ITA 2007 s 120). However, there is no offset against other income if the loss is incurred in a business of furnished holiday lettings (FHL). Furthermore, UK-based FHL properties are treated as one business and EEA-based FHL properties are treated as an entirely separate business; losses on one cannot be set against the other.

Offsetting the loss against general income is not permitted if the loss relates to the annual investment allowance (see [**48.28**]), and that Annual Investment Allowance (AIA) arose in connection with a transaction, a main purpose of which was to obtain an AIA in order to create a loss for use against general income (ITA 2007 s 127A).

Property losses suffered by a company may be offset against total income (including gains) of the year in which the loss is incurred, or the following year, or carried forward against future profits of the same property business (CTA 2010 s 62).

Capital allowances are also given for plant and machinery used in the management of an investment company: s 253. **[48.10]**

II PLANT AND MACHINERY

1 **The conditions**

Section 11 is the general provision by which plant and machinery allowances are granted. The effect of this section is that allowances are granted under CAA 2001 Part 2:
(1) to a person carrying on a *qualifying activity*
(2) who *incurs*
(3) *capital expenditure*
(4) on the provision of *plant* or *machinery*
(5) *wholly or partly* for the purposes of that qualifying activity
(6) provided the plant or machinery is then *owned* by that person as a result of incurring the expenditure.

Each of these constituent elements will be examined in turn. If elements (3)–(6) are met the capital expenditure is called *qualifying expenditure*.
[48.11]

a) *'A person carrying on a qualifying activity'*

Under CAA 2001 s 15, entitlement to plant and machinery allowances is by virtue of carrying on a 'qualifying activity' (in effect, a business activity). This includes both a trade and certain non-trading activities, such as:
(1) a UK property business;
(2) a furnished holiday lettings business;
(3) an overseas property business;
(4) a profession or vocation;
(5) the management of an investment company;
(6) an employment or office.

In each case, the activity only qualifies to the extent that the profits or gains are chargeable to tax (or would be if there were any) (s 15(1)).

Items (1), (2) and (3) in the list above highlight the availability of capital allowances for fixtures in investment properties, held either by UK investors or by non-resident investors (non-resident investors benefit from capital allowances because they are liable to UK income tax on the net profits of their UK property business).

Note, however:
(a) Plant and machinery for use in a *dwelling-house* does not qualify for capital allowances if the expenditure is incurred by a landlord carrying on a property business (UK or overseas): s 35. An exception is where the landlord is carrying on a business of FHL (as defined by statute, which imposes certain letting period criteria). For non-holiday furnished lettings the taxpayer historically could take advantage of ESC B47 and deduct 10% of the rent (net of council tax and water rates) as an allowance for the cost of renewing furniture, furnishings and chattels

(see [**12.45**]). However, the 10% wear and tear allowance was abolished from 6 April 2016. In its place landlords are able to deduct the actual costs of replacing furnishings in a property (FA 2016 ss 73–74, ITTOIA 2005 ss 250A, 311A).

(b) Plant and machinery such as heating, lighting alarms, entry systems and lifts in the common parts of blocks of flats will be allowable as they are not being used in a dwelling house.

In 2010, HMRC revised its view of what constitutes a dwelling-house (Revenue & Customs Brief 45/10), defining a dwelling-house as a property (or part of a property) that provides the facilities required for day-to-day private existence.

Finally, although a person may be carrying on a qualifying activity, a particular allowance may be restricted by the legislation to a specified category of taxpayer: for example, the annual investment allowance available to individuals or corporations, but not to mixed partnerships (see [**48.28**]).

Furnished holiday accommodation is defined by reference to its use and not its nature. It should be noted that in order to qualify for allowances the property must meet certain conditions:

(a) it is available for letting to the public generally as holiday accommodation on a commercial basis for at least 210 days (not necessarily consecutive); and
(b) it is actually so let for at least 105 days; and
(c) for a period of at least seven months (which need not be continuous but must include those months which contain the 70 qualifying days) it is not normally in the same occupation for a continuous period exceeding 31 days (ITTOIA 2005 ss 323, 325 in relation to income tax and CTA 2009 ss 265(3) and 267(1)–(6) in relation to corporation tax).

Where accommodation is actually let for less than 105 days in the year of assessment, or the period of 12 months, it may nevertheless still qualify on the making of an 'averaging' claim. A person who lets two or more sets of accommodation may elect, within two years after the end of the year of assessment or period, to average the number of days let for each accommodation. If the average number of days let amounts to at least 105, all of the accommodation included in the claim is deemed to have been let for at least 105 days. Accommodation may not be included in more than one such claim for any year of assessment or period. It is important to note that the election does not have to include all holiday lettings. The lettings may be specified in the election on a selective basis so the lettings likely to reduce the average days below 105 may be excluded (ITTOIA 2005 ss 324–326 in relation to income tax and CTA 2009 s 268(1)–(5) in relation to corporation tax).

A so-called 'period of grace election' is permitted by ITTIOA 2005 s 326A and CTA 2009 s 268A, which allows a non-qualifying FHL year to be treated as a qualifying year if the FHL qualified in the previous year.

If the property still fails the occupancy threshold in the next year the election can be made for a further year (provided the election was made for the first non-qualifying year) and it is even possible to make the claim if the property only qualifies in the first year as a result of an averaging election. If the property fails to meet the occupancy condition in the fourth year (after two years being treated as qualifying) then it will no longer qualify as a FHL.

It is important to note that there must be a genuine intention to meet the occupancy threshold for all years covered by the claim.

Where a FHL property fails to meet the conditions, the FHL business may be treated as ceasing and capital allowances will no longer be available. A balancing charge, based on the market value of the assets, will crystallise, but no sale proceeds will be received with which to pay the tax. However, this interpretation relies on the failure to meet the conditions being regarded as tantamount to a permanent cessation of the FHL business. If the FHL business is continuing, with the intention that a qualifying level of letting may be achieved in future years, it is understood that HMRC accepts that there has been no permanent discontinuance. **[48.12]**

b) *'Who incurs'*

This has already been considered in relation to capital allowances generally; see **[48.4]** and **[48.7]**. **[48.13]**

c) *'Capital expenditure'*

This has also been considered in relation to capital allowances generally, see **[48.3]**.

It should be noted that expenditure on plant or machinery held as *stock in trade* will be revenue not capital expenditure and will not qualify for allowances (instead, a trading deduction will be given as part of cost of sales). Therefore, in the case of a property company it is important to ascertain whether the property is held in a trading or investment portfolio because capital allowances will not be available on plant and machinery in properties held in a trading portfolio. Such items, like the properties themselves, will be stock in trade: for instance, plant in properties held by a property dealer or in properties being constructed by a development company for sale, as opposed to letting.

There are special rules relating to the ascertainment of the capital expenditure incurred on plant and machinery in the common situation where a building, with plant and machinery already installed as fixtures, is purchased for a single price. These are considered in detail at **[48.64]** ff.

If a taxpayer is given an asset which he then uses for a qualifying activity, he will be entitled to writing-down allowances as if he had incurred capital expenditure equal to the open market value of the asset at the time it was brought into use: s 14. If however, the donor and the taxpayer are 'connected' the taxpayer's expenditure will generally be taken to be the cost of the asset to the donor if this is less than its open market value when brought into use: ss 213(3) and 218. Similar rules apply where an asset is inherited.

First year allowances are not generally available where an asset is received as a gift. **[48.14]**

d) *'On the provision of plant or machinery'*

Definition

Prior to the implementation of the 'integral features' legislation in April 2008 (see **[48.61]**), the terms 'plant' and 'machinery' were never defined in legislation. However, ss 21 and 22 provide that buildings, structures, land and alterations to land *cannot* qualify as plant and, furthermore, set out categories of assets (now List A in s 21(3) and List B in s 22(1)) which are deemed to be included in the expressions 'building' and 'structure' and so fall outside the definition of plant and machinery (such as walls, ceilings, mains services, lift shafts, stairs). But these provisions only seek to identify what is *not* plant and machinery.

These rules, whilst setting out categories of assets included in the expressions 'building' and 'structure', must be read in conjunction with s 23, which sets out a list of assets which, although comprised within buildings and structures, are *not* automatically excluded from plant and machinery. This is now List C in s 23(4). These assets can still be considered on their own merits and on the basis of the relevant case law (see [48.17] and [48.17]). Examples include gas and sewerage systems provided mainly to meet the particular requirements of the qualifying activity, sprinkler systems, burglar alarm systems, moveable partitions, swimming pools, dry docks and grain silos. Interestingly, this list also includes 'decorative assets provided for the enjoyment of the public in the hotel, restaurant or similar trades', reflecting increasing recognition by the courts that in such trades the ambience or setting is part of what the trader is selling. For all such items, as well as the innumerable capital assets which do not form part of a building or structure, it is case law alone which determines whether they qualify as plant or machinery.

Case law is still therefore extremely important.

The intention of section 23

The Revenue's published view is that assets in s 23 are not automatically regarded as plant, but rather that they must in addition meet the usual tests set out by case law. However, it was the clear intention of the legislators that the assets listed in s 23 should be treated as plant and machinery (provided, of course, that they are used in a relevant business activity). When the relevant legislation was first introduced, the Inland Revenue wrote to the Institute of Taxation:

> 'The intention behind the legislation is therefore to strengthen the current boundary (between plant and buildings or structures) and to ensure that no further erosion takes place. ... The broad aim is to provide exclusions for assets currently regarded as plant as a result of court decisions, so as to leave the present position unchanged. The specific amendments which ministers have introduced ... are intended to ensure that this is so.'

The 'specific amendments' included the items towards the end of what is now List C in s 23.

In conclusion, the application of case law principles to a type of asset in List C will generally determine that that asset is plant, as it was those same case law principles that determined the composition of List C when first enacted.

[48.15]

Case law: Machinery 'Machinery' is easier to identify than 'plant'. Assets with moving parts, with or without power supplies, are invariably accepted as machinery. [48.16]

Case law: Plant 'Plant', on the other hand, is more difficult to identify. The meaning has been the subject of litigation for over 100 years. From the early case of *Yarmouth v France* (1887) the broad distinction developed between (a) assets which are used in the course of a trade (plant) and (b) assets which form part of the premises in which the trade is carried on (non-plant). Over the years the usefulness of this broad distinction was seen to have its limitations. The case law often appeared contradictory. Hence the same type of item (light fittings) was allowed as plant for a fast food chain company, on the ground that the volume of light was important for that trade rather than just being for general illumination (*Wimpy International Ltd v Warland* (1988)), but not for a department store, where the indoor lighting was regarded as merely a part of the setting in which the trade was carried on (*Cole Bros Ltd v Phillips* (1982) but contrast the specialist window lighting of the store which was accepted as plant because it was designed to attract custom). Note that with effect from April 2008, a lighting system will be treated as an 'integral feature' qualifying for plant allowances (see **[48.61]**).

It was against this unsatisfactory case law background that FA 1994 introduced the schedules of assets included in the expressions 'building' and 'structure' referred to above, and now in ss 21 and 22. The Revenue explained to the Chartered Institute of Taxation at the time:

> 'Court cases have, over the years, increasingly reclassified expenditure on buildings and structures as being expenditure on plant. This erosion has affected Exchequer receipts and has itself created continuing uncertainty. The intention behind the legislation is therefore to strengthen the current boundary [between plant and premises] and to ensure that no further erosion takes place.'

This legislative intent with regard to post-29 November 1993 expenditure on buildings and structures has been supplemented, in relation to expenditure on buildings and structures incurred on or before that date, by a change in the judicial approach to the boundary between premises and plant, illustrated by three cases in which exalted status has been given to the premises test. The Court of Appeal (upholding the decision of the High Court) in *Gray v Seymours Garden Centre* (1995) in relation to a structure in a garden centre designed to maintain plants in a favourable condition; the Court of Appeal (again upholding the decision of the High Court) in *Attwood v Anduff Car Wash Ltd* (1997) in relation to a car wash hall; and the High Court in *Bradley v London Electricity* (1996) in relation to an underground substation, all overruled decisions of the General or Special Commissioners in favour of the taxpayer and applied the 'premises' test *in addition to* the 'business use' test. The fact that the structure in question performed some business purpose did not save it from disqualification since its *function* (or primary function) was not as apparatus with which the business was carried on but rather as the premises upon which the business was carried on. To paraphrase Hoffmann J in *Wimpy*, it was 'more appropriate' to regard it as part of the premises, rather than as having retained a separate identity. In the words of Fox LJ in *Wimpy* (quoted with approval by the Court of Appeal in both *Seymours Garden Centre* and *Anduff*): 'The fact that the building in which a business is carried on is, by its construction, particularly well-suited to the business, or indeed was specially built for that business, does not make it plant ... it remains the place in which the business is carried on and is not something with which the business is carried on'.

The interaction of s 23 with the 'premises test'

Section 23 lists assets unaffected by ss 21 and 22 (which deny plant allowances on assets held to be 'buildings' or 'structures'). If an exempted asset is a building, a structure or an alteration of land, then s 23 acts to disapply ss 21 and 22; if it is not a building, a structure or an alteration of land (and is not land), it is difficult to see how it can be regarded as part of the premises.

It would seem illogical to have specifically exempted assets from the operation of the new rule (which was, after all, stated by the Revenue to be a tightening of the existing tests) if those assets were not plant anyway. Consequently, most of the items listed in s 23 are quite clearly plant.

This is only to be expected – s 23 was stated, both by the Inland Revenue and by the Financial Secretary to the Treasury, to reflect and maintain existing case law and practice. At the time this legislation was first brought forward, case law principles (including the 'premises test') were well established. So, assets which were exempted by s 23 were in fact assets which had previously qualified as plant in line with case law principles.

It should therefore be no surprise to discover that, when the case law principles are applied to any item in s 23, those principles direct that the item be regarded as plant. In a sense, it is superfluous to say that s 23 assets must additionally pass the case law tests, because they are the very assets that established the case law tests in the first place. **[48.17]**

Building alterations Where a person carrying on a qualifying activity incurs capital expenditure on alterations to an existing building *incidental* to the installation of plant or machinery for the purposes of his qualifying activity then that expenditure will be treated as if it were incurred on the provision of the plant and machinery and therefore as eligible for capital allowances, see s 25. Note that 'incidental' has a wider meaning than 'necessary': see *IRC v Barclay Curle & Co Ltd* (1969).

This provision can enable an item to qualify for capital allowances which would not otherwise do so. For example, expenditure on a lift shaft does not normally qualify since it counts as part of the 'building' in List A in s 21(3)). However, the installation of a new lift in an existing building may require the construction of a new lift shaft and this could count as building alterations connected with the installation of the lift and thus fall within s 25.

The question of incidental expenditure was considered by the Special Commissioners/First-tier Tribunal and Upper Tribunal in *JD Wetherspoon plc v R & C Comrs* (2007/2009 and 2012). In a somewhat confusing decision, strengthened upper floors were held to be incidental to commercial cooking equipment, panelled cubicles were incidental to toilet fittings and splash-backs were incidental to sinks, but wipe-clean surfaces were not incidental to kitchen equipment and nor were blockwork cubicles incidental to toilet fittings. **[48.18]**

Demolition costs Where any plant or machinery is demolished and replaced the demolition costs (net of any moneys received for the remains of the items) are treated as part of the expenditure incurred on the replacement items: s 26(2).

If the demolished items are not replaced the net demolition costs are added to the taxpayer's pool of 'qualifying expenditure' for the purpose of future WDAs (see [48.54]: s 26(3)). [48.19]

Other expenditure treated as being on plant and machinery Certain expenditure which would not normally be described as being on the provision of plant or machinery is nevertheless treated as such by statute for the purposes of capital allowances. The theme of such expenditure is one of safety, for instance:
(1) Expenditure on thermal insulation of an existing building, for the purposes of a qualifying activity (qualifying at 10% pa [48.38], [48.62]): s 28.
(2) Expenditure in taking steps specified in a safety certificate issued for a regulated stand at a sports ground (s 31) or for a ground designated under the Safety of Sports Grounds Act 1975 (s 30). This provision is abolished for expenditure incurred after April 2013.
(3) Expenditure by individuals and partnerships (not companies) on security assets used to meet a special threat to an individual's personal physical security arising from his trade, profession or vocation: s 33.
[48.20]

e) *'Wholly or partly for the purposes of the qualifying activity'*

This expression cannot be taken at face value because CAA 2001 Chapter 15 (ss 205–208) restricts allowances (and balancing charges) for plant and machinery which is used only partly for the purposes of a qualifying activity: see [48.63].

If a taxpayer purchases an asset for private use, or for some other purpose which does not qualify for capital allowances, and subsequently uses that asset for a qualifying activity, he is treated as if he had incurred capital expenditure on the provision of the asset for the purposes of the qualifying activity; but the qualifying expenditure is the open market value of the asset at the time it is brought into use for the qualifying activity or, if lower, the original cost to the taxpayer: s 13.

Where an asset is transferred from trading stock, there is a deemed sale at market value (ITTOIA 2005 s 172B (income tax), CTA 2009 s 157 (corporation tax)). However, for capital allowances purposes, the qualifying expenditure is the original cost (CA 11530). Section 13 (use for qualifying activity of plant or machinery provided for other purposes) would not apply because the 'actual expenditure' was not capital expenditure.

This is confirmed by HMRC guidance, which states:

'If expenditure on the provision or construction of an asset was revenue expenditure and the asset is later permanently appropriated to fixed assets WDAs may be given. The expenditure that qualifies for WDAs is the original expenditure incurred and not the market value of the asset at the time of the appropriation. You should not accept that an asset has been permanently appropriated to fixed assets unless you are satisfied that any profit on sale would be capital rather than revenue.' (CA 11530) [48.21]

1394 Capital allowances

f) *'Provided that person owns the plant or machinery as a result of incurring the expenditure'*

The general rule is that to qualify for capital allowances the plant and machinery must be 'owned' by the person incurring the capital expenditure: s 11. An exception is where plant is leased under a long funding lease (generally one of more than five years), in which case, provided various conditions are met, allowances are available to the lessee, rather than to the lessor, who is the actual owner of the plant (FA 2006 Sch 9). This provision does not apply to fixtures and plant leased with a building.

Special rules are needed to deal with fixtures, since land law usually treats them as belonging to the owner of the freehold. In many cases this will mean that the person incurring expenditure on them for use in a qualifying activity (eg the tenant) will not become the legal owner of the fixture. In the absence of special rules, many taxpayers incurring capital expenditure on fixtures would thus fail to qualify for allowances. **[48.22]**

Installation of fixtures by tenant The general position is now contained in s 176(1). This provides that if a person who has an 'interest in land' incurs capital expenditure in providing a fixture (eg on the construction or refurbishment of a building) for the purpose of a qualifying activity carried on by him, he will be treated as the owner of the fixture. An 'interest in land' for this purpose is broadly defined to include a freehold or leasehold estate, an agreement to acquire the same, an easement and a licence to occupy: ss 175(1) and 174(4). Thus a tenant can be entitled to capital allowances for fixtures he installs even though as a matter of property law he may not own the fixtures in question. **[48.23]**

Acquisition of property with fixtures already installed The provisions of s 176(1) are supplemented by those of s 181 the effect of which is that where, after an item has become a fixture, a person acquires an existing interest in the land (freehold or leasehold) and the consideration given by him includes an element for the fixture, the fixture is generally treated as belonging to him, whatever the position under property law.

Grant of a new interest The provisions of s 176(1) are further supplemented by those of ss 183 and 184 which apply where a lease (ie a new interest) is granted to a tenant for a premium which includes an element for fixtures already installed. If the landlord is (or would be) entitled to allowances in respect of the fixtures, the landlord and tenant may jointly elect within two years after the grant of the lease for the tenant to be treated as the owner of the fixtures for capital allowances purposes: ie for the allowances to be transferred to the tenant: s 183. If no joint election is entered into, then the allowances vest (or continue to vest) in the landlord. For this reason if a prospective vendor suggests that, instead of selling the freehold, he grants a long leasehold interest to the prospective purchaser for a premium, the purchaser may wish to seek an undertaking from the vendor-landlord that he will enter into a joint election under s 183.

Where the landlord is not entitled to claim allowances (as where he is a non-taxpayer or property dealer) the tenant is automatically treated as the owner of the fixtures: s 184. **[48.24]**

Joint expenditure on fixtures The 'deeming' provision of s 176(1) could result in two or more persons with different interests in the land 'owning' the same fixture at one and the same time: for instance, if a landlord and tenant share the cost of installing a fixture. In these circumstances s 176(2) and (3) lays down an order for priority of entitlement whereby only one person can own the fixture at a time generally the person with the most subordinate interest.
[48.25]

EXAMPLE 48.1

Two property investment companies, L and T, plan to purchase and redevelop a property jointly for letting, sharing the eventual occupational rents. To make their eventual interests more marketable L and T adopt a vertical structure whereby L buys the property and grants a 150-year lease to T on a rent formula which effectively secures 50% of the eventual occupational rents for L. L and T enter into a separate development agreement providing for equal sharing of the redevelopment costs including the substantial expenditure on plant and machinery which are to become fixtures in the building.

T's expenditure on the plant and machinery will qualify for capital allowances under normal principles. However, allowances would be available to L under the 'contributions' rules (Part 11 – see [48.4]).

Disposal of property with fixtures The 'deemed ownership' provisions of ss 176, 181, 183 and 184 are mirrored by s 188 which provides that where a person who is treated as the owner of a fixture by any of those sections ceases to hold the 'qualifying interest' (eg the lease) he is generally treated as ceasing to be the owner of the fixture at the same time, with the consequence that a disposal value then has to be brought into account (see [48.53]).

Exceptions to the above apply:
(1) where a lease merges into a superior interest acquired by the tenant;
(2) where a lease terminates and a new lease of the same property is granted to the same tenant;
(3) where a lease terminates but the tenant remains in possession with the consent of the landlord: s 189. [48.26]

Equipment lessors Equipment lessors are also the beneficiaries of 'deemed ownership' provisions resulting in connection with fixtures. Basically an 'equipment lessor' is a person who installs a fixture on another's property and lets out that item (a 'fixtures lease') to the occupier: s 174. Under the general rule in s 176(1), the equipment lessor would be denied capital allowances because he would have no interest in the land itself, one of the conditions under that section for him to be treated as the owner of the fixture. Section 177(1) deals with this by making provision for the equipment lessor and the equipment lessee to elect that the equipment lessor shall be treated as the owner of the fixtures.

Note, however, that this election cannot generally be made if the fixture is not provided for the purpose of a qualifying activity carried on (or to be carried on) by the equipment lessee or if the equipment lessee is a non-taxpayer, such as a pension fund, local authority or charity: ss 178(a) and (b). The latter measure was introduced by FA 1997 and was aimed at arrangements whereby non-taxpayers could indirectly benefit from capital allowances to which they were not entitled, for instance, by the equipment lessor passing back the value of the capital allowances via reduced leasing charges. (There are exceptions, even where the fixture is not provided for the purpose of a qualifying activity of the equipment lessee or where the equipment lessee is a non-taxpayer, in the case of leases of fixtures attached to land rather than to buildings, eg street furniture such as bus shelters (s 179); and also in the case of leases of domestic heating equipment installed as part of the Affordable Warmth Programme (s 180). Both s 179 and s 180 contain additional conditions to be met in those cases.)

The effect of an election under s 177 is that the equipment lessor is treated as the owner of the fixture (and thus entitled to capital allowances) from the time he incurred the expenditure or, if later, from the time the equipment lessee begins to carry on the qualifying activity. [48.27]

2 Annual Investment Allowance (AIA) and first-year allowances (FYAs)

a) *Annual investment allowance*

A 100% Annual Investment Allowance (AIA) is available in respect of expenditure on plant or machinery (which the person incurring the expenditure then owns – s 51A), up to a maximum of £200,000 (formerly at rates between £25,000 and £500,000) per annum.

It is available to individuals, companies and partnerships of which all the members are individuals. Mixed partnerships and trusts are not within the definition. This was confirmed in *Drilling Global Consultant LLP v R & C Comrs* (2014).

It was first available with effect from 6 April 2008 (income tax) or 1 April 2008 (corporation tax) at the rate of £50,000 per annum. The limit was increased to £100,000 with effect from 6 April 2010 (income tax) or 1 April 2010 (corporation tax), and was reduced to £25,000 with effect from 6 April 2012 (income tax) or 1 April 2012 (corporation tax). However, in a reversal of policy, the allowance was then increased to £250,000 from 1 January 2013, initially for a stated period of two years. However, that two-year period was subsequently extended to 31 December 2015, and the limit was doubled to £500,000 with effect from 6 April 2014 (income tax) or 1 April 2014 (corporation tax). After 31 December 2015, it was planned to reduce the limit to £25,000, but in the Budget of July 2015 it was announced that the amount would instead be £200,000. In each case where the limit changes, transitional rules apply for accounting periods overlapping the relevant dates, time-apportioning the maximum AIA. [48.28]

b) *FYAs for all businesses (2009–10)*

FYAs were available for all businesses, regardless of size at the rate of 40%, for expenditure incurred in the 12-month period beginning 1 April 2009 (corporation tax) and 6 April 2009 (income tax). [48.29]

c) *FYAs for small or medium-sized enterprises: ss 44 and 46–52*

FYAs for plant and machinery expenditure by small and medium-sized enterprises were available from 1 July 1997 to 31 March 2008, before being abolished by FA 2008 s 72. [48.30]

d) *100% FYAs for expenditure on designated energy-saving plant and machinery: ss 45A–45C and 46*

Sections 45A–45C were introduced by FA 2001 as part of a package of measures to encourage investment in a new generation of environmental technologies. To qualify for these 100% FYAs the expenditure must be incurred on or after 1 April 2001 on new plant or machinery of a description, and meeting energy-saving criteria, specified by the government.

For this purpose, the Department of Business, Energy and Industrial Strategy has published Energy Technology Criteria and Product Lists – see https://etl.beis.gov.uk/engetl/fox/live/ETL_PUBLIC_PRODUCT_SEARCH.

The disqualifying provisions of s 46 (see **[48.29]**) apply to 100% FYAs for energy-saving plant and machinery in the same way as they do to 40% (or 50%) FYAs. With effect from 1 April 2006, the allowance for such assets which are leased is restricted to those cases where the assets concerned are 'background plant or machinery' (generally fixtures in a property).

Section 45AA prevents FYAs in Great Britain from being available for expenditure on plant (for example, solar panels or combined heat and power (CHP) systems) where that plant generates electricity or heat that attracts tariff payments under either the Feed-in Tariffs or the Renewable Heat Incentive schemes as set out in the Energy Act 2008 or (for Northern Ireland) the Energy Act 2011. **[48.31]**

e) *100% FYAs for expenditure on new low-emission cars: ss 45D and 46*

In FA 2002 the Government continued its policy of encouraging the development of environmentally friendly technologies by introducing 100% FYAs for expenditure (by any business, large or small) on new cars which either emit no more than 75 grams of CO_2 per kilometre driven (95 g/km between 1 April 2013 and 1 April 2015, 110 g/km between 1 April 2008 and 1 April 2013, 120 g/km prior to 1 April 2008) or are electrically propelled. These FYAs initially applied to expenditure incurred from 17 April 2002 to 31 March 2008. FA 2008 extended these allowances until 31 March 2013, FA 2013 extended them for a further two years, then they were further extended by the Capital Allowances Act 2001 (Extension of First-year Allowances) (Amendment) Order (SI 2015/60) re expenditure on or after 1 April 2015 until 31 March 2021. The disqualifying provisions of s 46 (see **[48.29]**) apply.

For the capital allowances treatments of cars generally, and the changes to the system from April 2009, see **[48.74]–[48.76]**). **[48.32]**

f) *100% FYAs for expenditure on new natural gas, hydrogen and biogas refuelling equipment: ss 45E and 46*

FA 2002 also introduced 100% FYAs for expenditure on plant and machinery installed at gas refuelling stations for use solely in connection with refuelling vehicles with natural gas or hydrogen fuel. Again, the expenditure initially had to be incurred between 17 April 2002 and 31 March 2008, but the latter date was changed to 31 March 2013 by FA 2008 s 75. The same legislation extended the relief to biogas refuelling equipment from 1 April 2008. Further extensions were made initially to 31 March 2015 and then to 31 March 2018 (SI 2015/60).

Expenditure incurred on natural gas and hydrogen refuelling equipment for leasing also initially qualified for the new 100% FYA. With effect from 1 April 2006, the allowance for such assets which are leased is withdrawn (FA 2006 Sch 9 para 11). The other disqualifying provisions of s 46 (see **[48.29]**) apply. **[48.33]**

g) *100% FYAs for expenditure on plant and machinery used wholly for a 'ring-fence' trade: ss 45F–45G and 46*

A 'ring-fence' trade is a trade for the extraction of oil or gas in the UK or on the UK Continental Shelf, and a company carrying on such a trade is subject to a supplementary charge to corporation tax on its profits from that trade (TA 1988 s 501A). FYAs at a rate of 100% are given on expenditure incurred by a company on equipment used wholly for the purposes of a ring-fence trade.

Section 45G contains provisions for the withdrawal of the FYA if the equipment is not used, or not used exclusively, for a ring-fence trade throughout the first five years after the expenditure was incurred or, if shorter, throughout the company's ownership of the equipment. **[48.34]**

h) *100% FYAs for expenditure on environmentally beneficial plant or machinery: ss 45H–45J and 46*

FA 2003 s 167 introduced 100% FYAs for expenditure incurred from 1 April 2003 on new environmentally beneficial plant or machinery of a description, or meeting environmental criteria, specified by Treasury Order. The idea is to promote the use of technologies and products designed to prevent or remedy damage to the physical environment or natural resources. These are currently water-saving or quality improving.

For this purpose, the Department for Environment, Food and Rural Affairs has published Water Technology Criteria and Product Lists – see http://www.watertechnologylist.co.uk/.

Assets which are 'long-life' assets (see **[48.62]**) do not qualify and the disqualification provisions of s 46 (see **[48.29]**) also apply. With effect from 1 April 2006, the allowance for such assets which are leased is restricted to those cases where the assets concerned are 'background plant or machinery' (generally fixtures in a property).

Section 45J provides for the apportionment of expenditure where some, but not all, of the components of the plant or machinery meet the description specified by Treasury Order. **[48.35]**

First year tax credits

With effect from 1 April 2008, it is possible for such allowances to be converted into a repayable tax credit, to the extent that they give rise to a loss. Certain restrictions apply. The rules are contained in CAA 2001 Sch A1, introduced by FA 2008 Sch 25.

Broadly, a company (and only a company) which has a 'surrenderable loss' may claim a first year tax credit, equal to 19% of that loss (Sch A1 para 2), subject to an upper limit. This percentage applies, regardless of size of company, so there may be instances where it is better not to claim the tax credit, but to carry the loss forward to be set against subsequent years' profit, when tax may be payable at a higher rate. Any loss used as the basis for a tax credit cannot be carried forward in the normal way. A claim for a first year tax credit can be restricted to only part of the total amount claimable.

The amount of the loss which is 'surrenderable' is the lower of (i) the amount of the first year allowance and (ii) the actual loss. So if a first year allowance of £100,000 is deducted in computing a loss of £60,000, the tax credit payable will be 19% of £60,000, ie £11,400. If a first year allowance of £100,000 is deducted in computing a loss of £150,000, the tax credit payable will be 19% of £100,000, ie £19,000.

Repayments are limited to the lower of:
(a) the total amount of the company's PAYE and NIC liabilities for payment periods ending in the chargeable period; and
(b) £250,000.

The tax credit will normally be paid to the company; however, it may be used to discharge any outstanding liability to corporation tax. HMRC do not have to make a repayment where the company has outstanding PAYE or NIC liabilities.

A payment in respect of a first year tax credit does not count as income of the company for any purpose.

Where a first year tax credit is claimed in respect of an asset, and that asset is then sold before the end of the 'clawback period', the tax credit is paid back to HMRC and the relevant loss reinstated. The clawback period is defined as ending four years after the end of the chargeable period for which the first year tax credit was paid.

A credit will not be allowed where arrangements have been entered into which have the claiming of a tax credit as a main purpose. **[48.36]**

i) *100% FYAs for expenditure on plant and machinery for use in designated assisted areas: s 45K–45N*

100 per cent FYAs are available for expenditure on plant and machinery for use in designated assisted areas within specific Enterprise Zones. It should be noted that FYAs are available only for expenditure within designated assisted areas, which are not identical to the Enterprise Zones themselves. Maps of the areas can be found at https://www.gov.uk/government/publications/enterprise-zones.

The expenditure must be incurred in the period after the area is designated as an assisted area. Initially, expenditure had to be incurred before 1 April 2017, but this was extended to 1 April 2020 by FA 2014 s 64(5)(a) with effect from 17 July 2014.

However, the existence of a specific end-date (ie 2017 or 2020) meant that the relief was less beneficial in areas which were designated later rather than earlier. Consequently, FA 2016 s 69 amends the rules so that first-year allowances are available for expenditure incurred in a period of eight years beginning with the date on which the area is (or is treated as) designated.

The relief is restricted to UK resident companies liable to corporation tax in respect of a trade or a mining, transport or similar undertaking, and the expenditure must be on new and unused plant. There are sundry exceptions to eligible companies based on European Union rules on state aid. Thus, for example, agricultural firms do not qualify, and nor do vehicles or transport equipment acquired by transport undertakings.

The plant must be acquired for use primarily in a designated assisted area, and anti-avoidance rules exist to ensure this requirement is not abused. Inter alia, there is scope for a claw-back of allowances if the plant begins to be used primarily *outside* of the designated assisted area within five years. Furthermore, the expenditure must be incurred for the purposes of expanding a business or starting a new type of business not previously carried on by the company.
[48.37]

j) *100% FYAs for expenditure on zero-emission goods vehicles: s 45DA*

Expenditure on new *zero-emission goods vehicles* in the period 1 April 2010 to 31 March 2018 (for corporation tax) and 6 April 2010 to 5 April 2018 (for income tax) qualifies for a 100% first-year allowance. This relief is subject to certain conditions imposed by Brussels State aid rules (ss 45DA, DB as inserted by F(No 3)A 2010 Sch 7). [48.38]

3 **Writing-down allowances (WDAs)**

a) *WDAs: the basic idea*

The various FYAs for plant and machinery have been considered at **[48.29]**–**[48.38]**. The main form of plant and machinery allowance however is not a FYA but the annual writing-down allowance (WDA).

Taking the case of a single asset of plant or machinery, a WDA is available at (generally) the rate of 18% per annum of the unrelieved 'qualifying expenditure' attributable to the asset, on a reducing balance basis. The unrelieved qualifying expenditure means the original 'qualifying expenditure' (see **[48.11]**) less any FYAs or WDAs already given. Prior to April 2012, the rate was 20%, and before April 2008, the rate was 25%. The rate was reduced to 18% per annum for accounting periods ending on or after 6 April 2012 (income tax) or 1 April 2012 (corporation tax) (s 56, amended by FA 2011 s 10).

For certain types of expenditure (so-called 'special rate expenditure, including long-life assets, thermal insulation, solar panels and integral features (see **[48.61]**, **[48.62]**), the rate of WDA is 8% with effect from 1 April 2008 (corporation tax) and 6 April 2008 (income tax) (s 56, amended by FA 2011 s 10). From 2008 to 2012, the corresponding rate was 10%. **[48.39]**–**[48.52]**

EXAMPLE 48.2

Wildhern Property Company Ltd, a new property investment company, made its first acquisition in March 2017) and incurred, as an apportionment of the purchase price of the property, capital expenditure of £800,000 on plant (it is assumed that all of the plant is special rate plant and that the AIA is used elsewhere). Wildhern will be entitled to claim WDAs during each year that the plant remains in its ownership as follows:

Year 1	£
Capital expenditure on plant	800,000
Less: 8% WDA	64,000
Unrelieved qualifying expenditure carried forward	736,000
Year 2	£
Less: 8% WDA	58,880
Unrelieved qualifying expenditure carried forward	677,120

Thus in each of the first two years WDAs of £64,000 and £58,880 could be offset against Wildhern's taxable profits from its property business. This would continue until the property was sold, when a disposal value would be brought into account (see [48.53]).

If a chargeable period is more or less than a year the rate of WDA for that period is proportionately increased or reduced (in contrast to FYAs). It is similarly reduced proportionately if the qualifying activity has been carried on for only part of the chargeable period.

A WDA is not however available in the chargeable period in which the qualifying activity ceases: s 55(4). Instead, there is either a balancing allowance or a balancing charge: see [48.53].

b) *Disposals and balancing allowances/charges: the basic idea*

When an item of plant or machinery is disposed of, the 'disposal value' of that item must be brought into account to ensure that the allowances which have been given correspond to the actual depreciation cost of the item to the business: s 61(1). A disposal (or 'disposal event', to use the CAA 2001 expression) occurs for these purposes whenever:

(1) the taxpayer ceases to own the asset, for instance by selling it;
(2) the asset ceases to be in his possession, for instance by theft;
(3) the asset ceases to exist, for instance by destruction or dismantling;
(4) the asset ceases to be used wholly for the purposes of the qualifying activity;
(5) the qualifying activity is permanently discontinued, for instance, on a sale or incorporation of the business.

The 'disposal value' will usually be the net sale proceeds or insurance moneys or in other cases the open market value of the item: see the table set out in s 61(2). Where different assets are sold together (for example a building and fixtures), the disposal value of the assets must by default be established by a just apportionment under s 562 (see [48.65]). Accounts net book value and tax written-down value are irrelevant.

Where an asset is sold out of the special rate pool, the anti-avoidance provisions of s 215 potentially apply. If the asset is disposed of for less than its tax written-down value, as part of a scheme or arrangement having the obtaining of a tax advantage as a main purpose, then notional tax written-down value is substituted for the actual disposal value.

From 25 November 2015, the rules were amended further by FA 2016 s 70 in order to counter tax avoidance schemes which sought to reduce disposal values of plant or machinery for capital allowances purposes below the actual full value attributable to the disposal of those assets, the difference in value being received, directly or indirectly, in such a way as to not form part of the disposal value for capital allowances purposes.

The changes take effect for transactions involving an 'avoidance purpose' on or after 25 November 2015. On or after that date, s 215 is amended so that that the term 'avoidance purpose' includes not only the obtaining of a more favourable allowance, but also the avoidance of a liability for the whole or part of a balancing charge to which a person would otherwise be liable.

Furthermore, where on or after 25 November 2015, all or part of a receipt for the disposal of plant would not otherwise be taken into account in determining the disposal value of that plant, and hence gives rise to a tax advantage, the disposal value of the plant or machinery is adjusted in a just and reasonable manner so as to cancel out the tax advantage.

EXAMPLE 48.3

(continuing from *Example 48.2*)
Year 3
Wildhern Property Company switches out of property investment and sells the building. £400,000 of the net sale proceeds is attributed to the plant. This is the disposal value and, since it is less than the unrelieved qualifying expenditure of £677,120, Wildhern will have a *balancing allowance* of £277,120, which is deductible in calculating the profits of its property business for the chargeable period in which the sale took place.

If the proportion of the net sale proceeds attributable to the plant (the disposal value) had been £700,000 there would be a *balancing charge* of £22,880, taxed as a receipt of the property business in the chargeable period of sale.

Notwithstanding s 61(2), however, the disposal value of any plant or machinery cannot exceed the qualifying expenditure incurred by the taxpayer when he acquired it: s 62. In the event of an item of plant or machinery being sold at a gain, the excess of the net sale proceeds over the acquisition cost may be chargeable to CGT: see **[19.66]**.

Moreover, despite the table of disposal values in s 61(2), the disposal value is nil if the taxpayer gives the item of plant or machinery to a charity or disposes of it in circumstances where a tax charge arises under ITEPA: s 63 (eg a gift to an employee).

A disposal value also has to be brought into account where a person who has been treated as the owner of a fixture subsequently ceases to hold the qualifying interest (usually the lease) and is thereby treated by s 188 as ceasing to own the fixture (see **[48.26]**). Section 196 contains the detailed rules. A tenant is not, however, treated as ceasing to hold the qualifying interest, and hence no disposal value has to be brought into account, where any of the exceptions referred to in **[48.26]** apply. Moreover, s 196(1) provides that where a tenant ceases to own a fixture by virtue of the expiry of his lease, his disposal value will be nil unless he receives compensation for the fixture.

It should be emphasised at this point that a balancing allowance (ie an allowance equal to the amount by which the disposal value is less than the unrelieved qualifying expenditure) is available only if there is a permanent discontinuance of the qualifying activity, as in *Example 48.2*: ss 55(4) and 65. If Wildhern had remained in property investment the disposal value would simply have been deducted from the WDA of £677,120 before calculating the 8% WDA for Year 3: see 'Pooling' below. [48.53]

4 Pooling

a) *General*

For ease of explanation, *Example 48.2* has shown the operation of WDAs and balancing allowances/charges by reference to a taxpayer, Wildhern, which acquired a single building, containing a single item of plant. In practice, however, it is more usual for property investment companies to acquire a number of properties (and for them and traders to acquire a number of items of plant and machinery) over a period of time. In such circumstances the qualifying expenditure has to be 'pooled' to calculate WDAs and balancing allowances or charges: s 53. 'Pooling' effectively means including expenditure in a calculation of potential allowances, whether or not those allowances are actually claimed. It is generally assumed that the pooling must be reflected on a tax return. However, whilst the corporation tax return (CT600) includes a box for showing expenditure incurred, there is no equivalent on income tax returns. Where it is important to demonstrate that expenditure has been pooled (for example where the mandatory pooling requirements of s 187A apply – see **[48.73]**) the return should contain a statement that expenditure has been incurred, even where no allowances are claimed. HMRC have said 'There is no specific required form for pooling. If it is clear on the face of the return or attachments thereto sent to HMRC that assets have been pooled then the pooling requirement will be satisfied.'

There are in fact three different kinds of pools:

(1) A *'single asset pool'* The principal single asset pools are those for expenditure on expensive cars (see **[48.74]**); short-life assets (see **[48.59]**); assets used only partly for a qualifying activity (see **[48.63]**); and assets to which the taxpayer has made a capital contribution (see **[48.4]**): s 54(3). Each single asset pool may not contain expenditure in respect of more than that one asset: s 55(2). WDAs will be available until the first chargeable period in which a disposal event occurs (see **[48.53]**). This is the 'final chargeable period' for a single asset pool and will trigger a balancing allowance or a balancing charge.

(2) *'Class pools'* There is now just one class pool for 'special rate expenditure'. Long-life assets were previously dealt with in a separate class pool (see **[48.62]**), but from 2008–09 are dealt with in the special rate pool (see **[48.60]**).

(3) The *'main pool'* Qualifying expenditure falls into the main pool if it does not have to be allocated to a single asset pool or a class pool: s 54(6).

For both a class pool and the main pool the 'final chargeable period' means the chargeable period in which there is a permanent discontinuance of the qualifying activity. Only in this period can a balancing allowance arise in these pools. Note there is no balancing allowance in a pool simply because all the assets in that pool have been disposed of, unless that coincides with the permanent discontinuance of the qualifying activity.

If a person carries on more than one qualifying activity, expenditure relating to the different activities must not be allocated to the same pool: s 53(2). Thus a property company which engages in both property investment (an ordinary property business) and property development (a trade) will need to maintain two main pools; and if it incurs expenditure on long-life assets or integral features in each of its activities it will similarly need to maintain two class pools for its long-life assets, one for each qualifying activity.

WDAs and balancing allowances and charges for each chargeable period are determined separately for each pool. The key concepts are:

(a) AQE, which means the *available qualifying expenditure* in the pool for that period. This will consist of:
  (i) any qualifying expenditure allocated to the pool for that period *together with*
  (ii) any unrelieved qualifying expenditure carried forward from the previous chargeable period: s 57(1).

  A person is generally free to allocate or not allocate qualifying expenditure to the appropriate pool in any chargeable period, ie he may add qualifying expenditure to the appropriate pool in a chargeable period after the one in which the expenditure was incurred.

(b) TDR, which means the *total of disposal receipts* to be brought into account in that chargeable period. 'Disposal receipts' means the actual disposal values which have to be brought into account as the result of any disposals, taking account of the effect of sections such as s 62 and s 63 which, if applicable, will limit the disposal values specified in the table set out in s 61(2) (see [48.53]). [48.54]

b) *Pooling: WDAs*

Except in relation to the special rate pool, the amount of WDAs for a chargeable period is 18% of the excess of AQE over TDR, adjusted up or down if the chargeable period is more or less than a year or if the qualifying activity is carried on for less than the whole chargeable period: s 56(1), (3) and (4).

For the special rate pool the amount of WDAs is 8% of the excess of AQE over TDR: s 102. [48.55]

c) *Pooling: balancing allowances and charges*

As stated, the 'pooling' provisions mean that, except in relation to single asset pools, so long as the business continues no balancing allowances will arise and it is unlikely that any balancing charges will become due. Whether the disposal value of any plant or machinery is more or less than the unrelieved qualifying expenditure (the written-down value) of that item considered in isolation, the disposal value will simply be used to reduce the AQE of all the remaining items in the pool on which future WDAs will be calculated. Therefore any negative tax effect on disposal will be spread over many years rather than hitting the taxpayer immediately.

EXAMPLE 48.4

Wildhern Property Company buys three investment properties in successive years incurring, as an apportionment of the respective purchase prices, the following capital expenditure on the plant and machinery within those properties (it is assumed that all of the plant is special rate plant and that the AIA is used elsewhere):

Year 1	Property A plant and machinery expenditure of £600,000
Year 2	Property B plant and machinery expenditure of £800,000
Year 3	Property C plant and machinery expenditure of £1,000,000

	£
Year 1 Capital expenditure AQE (Property A)	600,000
Less: 8% WDA for year	48,000
Unrelieved qualifying expenditure carried forward	652,000
Year 2 Add capital expenditure (Property B) to pool	800,000
AQE in pool	1,452,000
Less: 8% WDA for year	116,160
Unrelieved qualifying expenditure in pool carried forward	1,335,840
Year 3 Add capital expenditure (Property C) to pool	1,000,000
AQE in pool	2,335,840
Less: 8% WDA for year	186,867
Unrelieved qualifying expenditure in pool carried forward	2,148,973

Suppose that in *Year 4* Wildhern sells property A with the disposal value of the plant and machinery being £453,125:

Year 4	
AQE in pool	2,148,973
Less: disposal value	453,125
	1,695,848
Less: 8% WDA for year	135,668
Unrelieved qualifying expenditure in pool carried forward	1,560,180

A balancing charge will, however, arise in any chargeable period in which TDR exceeds AQE: s 56(6). In a class pool or the main pool this could occur before the permanent discontinuance of the qualifying activity, if sale proceeds exceed the written-down value of the pool.

A balancing allowance will arise in a class pool or in the main pool only in the chargeable period in which the qualifying activity is permanently discontinued (the final chargeable period) and then only if the AQE for that period exceeds TDR: s 56(7). **[48.56]**

Small pools

With effect from 6 April 2008 (income tax) or 1 April 2008 (corporation tax), where the written-down value of a pool is no more than £1,000, businesses may claim a writing-down allowance equal to the value of the pool.

This simplification measure is aimed at removing the need to carry forward small pools of expenditure and calculate ever-diminishing writing-down allowances (s 56A).

This applies to the general pool and to the 'special rate' (8%) pool, but not to single asset pools. **[48.57]**

d) *Sale of business*

As stated, in the chargeable period in which a business terminates there is no WDA. Instead, there will either be a balancing allowance (if the TDR of the plant and machinery is less than the AQE) or a balancing charge (if it is greater): s 56.

Where the termination of the business is by reason of its sale the amount of the purchase price attributed to the plant and machinery is calculated on the basis of a just apportionment under s 562.

Balancing allowances and charges can be avoided on the occasion of a sale or transfer of a business between connected persons. The connected persons can jointly elect within two years after the sale or transfer that the disposal value shall be an amount which gives rise to neither a balancing allowance nor a balancing charge, ie the transferee takes over the allowances position of the transferor: ss 266 and 267. This election will normally be used when a business is incorporated. **[48.58]**

e) *Single asset pools for short-life assets, by election: ss 83–89 (Part 2 Chapter 9)*

The taxpayer may irrevocably elect within two years after the end of the chargeable period in which the expenditure on the asset was incurred for that asset to be a short-life asset. The qualifying expenditure in respect of the asset will then be allocated to a single asset pool (a 'short-life asset pool') on which the WDAs will be calculated separately from the WDAs on the main pool of qualifying expenditure. If the short-life asset is then disposed of within eight years after the end of the chargeable period in which the expenditure was incurred ('the eight-year cut-off'), the disposal proceeds will trigger an immediate balancing allowance (or, less likely, balancing charge) for the taxpayer, instead of effecting only a reduction in the qualifying expenditure in the main pool. The eight-year period was formerly four years. The change takes effect for expenditure incurred on or after 1 April 2011 (corporation tax) or 6 April 2011 (income tax).

A short-life election is not available for integral features, ships, cars, and certain leased items. It is intended for, although not specifically limited to, assets with an anticipated working life of less than eight years, typically computers. Note, however, that the important factor is the length of ownership by the person making the election, not the whole life of the asset. The election is not available for assets which are acquired only partly for the purpose of a qualifying activity and partly for some other purpose (see **[48.63]**).

Thus the cost of a short-life asset can effectively be written off for tax over the same period that it is likely to depreciate. The only occasion on which a short-life election might have an adverse effect is where the asset is sold before the end of the eight-year period for more than its unrelieved qualifying expenditure (or 'written-down value').

If the asset is not disposed of within eight years, then at that time the AQE (the written-down value) must be transferred to the main pool.

To prevent the short-life election from being abused by a sale to a connected person before the eight-year cut-off, s 89(4) and (5) provide that the purchaser in such a case will be deemed to have made a short-life election and the existing eight-year cut-off will be preserved, ie the purchaser must transfer the asset into his main pool on the same date as the vendor would otherwise have done. The connected vendor and purchaser may, however, jointly elect within two years after the end of the chargeable period of the sale for the asset to have been transferred between them at its AQE rather than its market value, with the result that the vendor at least avoids a balancing charge (or allowance) on that occasion: s 89(2) and (6). **[48.59]**

f) *Special rate pool*

The special rate pool was introduced by FA 2008, for certain expenditure incurred on or after 6 April 2008 (income tax) and 1 April 2008 (corporation tax). The definition of 'special rate expenditure' (CAA 2001 s 104A includes:
(a) new expenditure on thermal insulation under CAA 2001 s 28;
(b) new expenditure on integral features under CAA 2001 s 33A;
(c) new expenditure on long-life assets under CAA 2001 Chapter 10;
(d) 'old' expenditure on long-life assets not previously allocated to a pool;
(e) some cars (see **[48.75]**); and
(f) solar panels, where the expenditure was incurred from April 2012.

[48.60]

Integral features

After a year-long consultation process, FA 2008 legislated for a new category of plant and machinery, to be known as 'integral features' (CAA 2001 s 33A). That section defines integral features as:
(a) electrical and lighting systems;
(b) cold water systems;
(c) space or water heating systems, powered systems of ventilation, air cooling or air purification (including floors or ceilings comprised in such a system);
(d) lift, escalators and moving walkways;
(e) external solar shading.

However, permanent floors, walls and ceilings are excluded. Active facades (typically, external cladding with two glazing layers separated by a ventilated cavity) are regarded as falling within item (c).

Changes to the list may be made by Treasury Order only to include expenditure which would not otherwise qualify for plant allowances, or to exclude expenditure if it would otherwise qualify for a higher rate of plant allowances.

These assets qualify for writing-down allowances at the 'special rate' of 8% pa (s 104A(1)). So far as integral features are concerned, there are no 'grandfathering' provisions, which is to say that each purchaser must consider afresh whether an asset is an integral feature – the treatment in the hands of the vendor is irrelevant. On a positive note, an asset which pre-dated the introduction of the integral features rules and which would not then have qualified for allowances, may fall within the definition of an integral feature qualifying for allowances when acquired by a subsequent purchaser.

1408   Capital allowances

There are, inevitably, anti-avoidance provisions to ensure connected persons cannot transfer assets simply to trigger the integral features rules to their advantage.

The rules apply where expenditure is on the *provision or replacement* of an integral feature. The term 'replacement' is extended by s 33B. Broadly, if expenditure on an integral feature (for example, repairs) is more than 50% of the cost of replacing that integral feature, that expenditure will be treated as being in respect of a replacement. In essence, the usual process for determining whether expenditure is capital or revenue is reduced to a mathematical comparison. Theoretically, repairs costing 50% of the cost of replacing a heating system could be allowed as repairs, but if that figure were 50.1% they would automatically be treated as capital. It is not possible to circumvent the 50% rule by fragmenting repair expenditure, as the calculation must be based on the cumulative total of expenditure incurred over a rolling 12-month period (s 33B). [**48.61**]

g)   *The class pool for long-life assets (pre- April 2008): ss 90–104*

Expenditure on long-life assets incurred from April 2008 is included in the special rate pool (see [**48.59**]).

A 'long-life asset' is plant or machinery which it is reasonable to expect will have a useful economic life of at least 25 years (or where such was the reasonable expectation when it was new). However, these rules do not apply to expenditure incurred on fixtures in a dwelling house, retail shop, showroom, hotel or office. Once an asset has been treated as a 'long-life asset' it cannot be reclassified as non-long-life in the hands of a subsequent purchaser: s 103. This differs from the treatment of integral features (see [**48.61**]), where each subsequent purchaser must consider whether an asset is an integral feature, regardless of the historical treatment in the hands of the vendor.

There is also a *de minimis* limit below which these 'long-life asset' provisions do not operate, currently £100,000 for a chargeable period of 12 months (adjusted up or down if the chargeable period is more or less than a year). If the limit is exceeded, all the relevant expenditure is long-life asset expenditure. [**48.62**]

h)   *Single asset pools for assets used only partly for a qualifying activity: ss 205–208 (Part 2 Chapter 15)*

Section 11 grants plant and machinery allowances where the expenditure is incurred 'wholly or partly' for the purposes of a qualifying activity. CAA 2001 Part 2 Chapter 15 explains how the allowances are computed if the qualifying use is only 'partly for the purposes of a qualifying activity'. The idea is that the allowances are reduced proportionately for the non-qualifying use, eg for private use in the case of a sole trader. It would be impossible to achieve the correct adjustment if the expenditure was pooled with expenditure on other plant or machinery, so where expenditure is incurred on an item only partly for the purposes of a qualifying activity this expenditure is kept outside the main pool and allocated to a single asset pool.

Further, if an asset in the main pool ceases to be used wholly for the qualifying activity and becomes only partly so used, this is treated as a disposal of the asset (see [**48.53**]). The disposal value of the asset reduces the qualifying expenditure in the main pool but an amount equal to the disposal value is transferred to a single asset pool in the same chargeable period. The disposal value will be the market value, derived from the table in s 61(2).

In both the above cases, WDAs on the single asset pool for any chargeable period are reduced to such an extent as is just and reasonable having regard in particular to the extent to which the asset is used for the purposes of the qualifying activity in that period. It is however the full amount of the WDA, before the reduction, that is deducted in determining the amount of unrelieved qualifying expenditure carried forward to the following chargeable period.

If the asset is disposed of (which includes ceasing to use it for the purposes of the qualifying activity at all) the disposal value of the asset will give rise to a balancing allowance or charge. That allowance or charge will be reduced in the same proportion that the total amount of allowances previously given bears to the amount which would have been available had there been no non-qualifying activity use.

Furthermore, if in any chargeable period there is a reduction in the amount of qualifying use of an asset, and at the end of that period the open market value of the asset is greater than the AQE by more than £1m, a disposal value has to be brought into account for that chargeable period (s 208). By the table set out in s 61(2) the disposal value will be the open market value, with the result that a balancing charge will arise. The taxpayer is then treated in the following chargeable period as incurring qualifying expenditure, equal to the disposal value, on the fresh provision of the asset. This measure, introduced by FA 2000, is aimed mainly at non-residents and other persons, the degree of whose taxable trading (or property business) activities in the UK is liable to vary. Where the rule applies its effect is to adjust the allowances given so that they are brought into line with the depreciation actually suffered. [48.63]

5 Allowances: ascertaining the 'qualifying expenditure' on fixtures in purchased buildings

a) *Basic principles*

In order to claim capital allowances it is first necessary to identify the qualifying expenditure. In the case of a purchase of a 'stand-alone' asset the qualifying capital expenditure is simply established by reference to the actual cost incurred in its acquisition by the taxpayer. Similarly, capital expenditure incurred on plant and machinery fixtures installed in the construction of a new building, or in the alteration or refurbishment of an existing building, may be readily established in most cases by separating out the assets in question and abstracting the cost of providing and installing them directly from invoices or priced documentation.

In the case of the purchase of an existing building containing fixtures, however, the only known cost will usually be the price paid by the purchaser for the entire building. Within that purchase price would be an element for the lifts, heating, sanitary ware etc which qualify for capital allowances. The question arises as to how the price for those fixtures is to be determined. [48.64]

b) *The 'just apportionment' under s 562*

The position in such circumstances is governed by s 562. This provides for 'a just and reasonable apportionment' of the sale price of a single bargain in order to arrive at the proportion properly attributable to the plant and machinery.

This applies even if a separate price is, or purports to be, agreed for the plant and machinery and even if the plant and machinery is sold, or purportedly sold, under a separate contract. Since the largest of capital allowances claims are made on plant and machinery fixtures within the acquisition cost of existing buildings, the operation of s 562 is particularly important.

For the purposes of a s 562 valuation, a property purchaser is regarded as acquiring three main assets: the land, the building and the plant and machinery within the building. Under the valuation method approved by the Revenue, it is necessary, in broad terms, to ascertain three figures, ie the value of the land as a cleared site (with planning permission for a contemporary equivalent of the building *in situ*), the reinstatement cost of the building excluding plant, and the reinstatement cost of the plant and machinery itself. The actual purchase price must then be apportioned between these three elements. The proportion of the total purchase price attributable to the plant and machinery is the same proportion as the plant and machinery reinstatement cost bears to the total of the three elements described.

The preferred method of the Valuation Office Agency (VOA) for achieving an apportionment is known as the *multiplier formula* and this is by far the most commonly used method in practice:

$$Q = P \times \frac{A}{(B + C)}$$

where Q = qualifying expenditure
A = replacement cost of the qualifying assets
B = replacement cost of the building (including plant content)
C = land value (ie bare site value)
P = purchase consideration.

This methodology was challenged by a taxpayer in *Bowerswood House Retirement Home Ltd v R & C Comrs* (2015), but the challenge was rejected by the First-tier Tribunal – 'taking into account our finding that the formula used by [VOA] has been used over many years in this context we accept that it does give a just and reasonable apportionment on the facts of this case'.

EXAMPLE 48.5

In 1990 a pension fund redeveloped a building for investment, incurring expenditure of £200,000 on the plant and machinery installations. (Being a non-taxpayer, the pension fund would not have claimed capital allowances on that plant and machinery.)

In 2017 Wildhern Property Company purchased the building for £2.2m. Under the approved valuation method the three constituent elements are valued as follows:

	£
Land as cleared site	200,000
Reinstatement cost of plant and machinery	300,000
Reinstatement cost of building	1,900,000
	2,400,000

A s 562 apportionment of the £2.2m sale price would produce a proportion for the plant and machinery of:

$$\frac{300,000}{2,400,000} \times 2,200,000 = £275,000$$

Wildhern's opening qualifying expenditure for the plant and machinery is more than the sum spent on the initial plant and machinery installation, and obviously far more than the written-down value (unrelieved qualifying expenditure) of the plant and machinery at the time of the 2017 sale. The effect of a s 562 apportionment of the sale price is that the valuation of the plant and machinery actually reflects any increase in property prices generally.

The fundamental points to bear in mind with regard to a s 562 apportionment are:
(1) The exercise is aimed at arriving at the proportion of the total *purchase price* which is properly attributable to the plant and machinery. The written-down value, market value, and original cost of the machinery and plant are in the first instance irrelevant to the s 562 computation (but see restrictions discussed below).
(2) It is not only the purchaser to whom s 562 applies. The vendor is also required to apportion the total sale price in order to ascertain the disposal value of his plant and machinery: see item 1 of the table in s 196(1).
(3) However, the ascertainment of the sale/purchase price of the fixtures by a s 562 apportionment does not necessarily determine the vendor's disposal value that he has to bring into account for the fixtures sold; or the purchaser's qualifying expenditure that he can add to his pool.

As far as the vendor is concerned, his disposal value cannot exceed the expenditure he incurred in acquiring the items (see s 62(1) and [48.53]). Thus, if in *Example 48.5* a taxpaying property investor, instead of a pension fund, had redeveloped the property and subsequently claimed capital allowances on the £200,000 incurred on plant and machinery, the disposal value for the plant and machinery on the sale in 2017 would have been £200,000, not £275,000.

As far as the purchaser is concerned, there are now a number of statutory provisions which limit, or determine, the amount of expenditure which qualifies for capital allowances in his hands. These provisions are now considered. **[48.65]**

c) *Transactions between connected persons, sale and leasebacks and transactions with a main purpose of obtaining a tax advantage: ss 214–218*

Where:
(1) the vendor and purchaser of plant and machinery (whether fixtures or not) are connected, *or*
(2) the plant and machinery continues to be used for the purposes of a qualifying activity carried on by the vendor, for instance on (but not limited to) a sale and leaseback of a building, *or*
(3) the relevant transaction is a transaction to obtain allowances

then no FYA is available (where one would otherwise be due) and the amount of qualifying expenditure which the purchaser can allocate to the relevant pool for his WDAs cannot exceed the disposal value brought into account by the vendor.

If no disposal value is brought into account by the vendor (as where the vendor is a non-taxpayer or the sale was on trading account) the amount of the purchaser's qualifying expenditure cannot exceed the lower of:
(a) the open market value of the plant and machinery;
(b) the capital expenditure (if any) incurred by the vendor, or any connected person, on the plant and machinery. It should be noted that this particular limitation will not apply where the vendor is a property trader since his expenditure on the plant and machinery will not have been *capital* expenditure (see s 4(2)).

By ss 227, 228 the limitation in (a) above to open market value will not apply if an election is made to that effect by the vendor and the purchaser (usually a finance company), and
(1) the vendor incurred capital expenditure on the provision of the asset, thus ruling out property traders and other vendors who acquired equipment as trading stock;
(2) the asset was new when acquired by the vendor and the sale occurs within four months after it was brought into use;
(3) the vendor did not himself acquire the asset through a sale and leaseback transaction or from a connected person; and
(4) the vendor has made no claim for allowances in respect of the expenditure incurred on the asset.

By removing the restriction to open market value for the purchaser's (finance company's) qualifying expenditure, this rule facilitates businesses financing the purchase of new equipment through leasing.

Where a transaction, scheme or arrangement has an avoidance purpose then the purchaser's allowances are restricted so as to cancel the tax advantage. To this end, the restriction may be:
- to reduce the rate at which the allowances are calculated (if the tax advantage the purchaser would otherwise obtain is allowances at a rate that is too high); or
- to reverse any timing advantage sought by the purchaser so that he is, in both cases, in the position that he would have been in without the tax advantage; or
- (in other situations) to restrict the purchaser's qualifying expenditure to an amount that has the effect of negating the tax advantage.

If appropriate, more than one restriction may be made to the purchaser's allowances. If a transaction with an avoidance purpose is also a connected person transaction or a sale and leaseback, the existing rules in s 218 or s 228 must also be considered and the largest applicable restriction made. **[48.66]**

d) *The first general restriction applying to fixtures: FA 1985*

The first general restriction aimed at limiting a purchaser's qualifying expenditure on fixtures was introduced by FA 1985. This provided that a purchaser's qualifying expenditure in respect of any fixtures could not exceed the disposal value brought into account by the vendor on those items. However, this restriction applied only if the immediate vendor had made a claim for plant and machinery allowances in respect of the fixtures (for expenditure incurred after 11 July 1984). Thus if the vendor was a non-taxpayer or not entitled to claim capital allowances (or omitted to do so) then the purchaser would still have been entitled to an unrestricted claim for allowances based upon what is now a s 562 'just apportionment' of his total purchase price (the majority of cases in practice). There was no requirement to look back at the treatment adopted by earlier owners.

If this provision had not been amended, most buildings would have become unrestricted at some point in time and so qualifying expenditure on the plant and machinery would then have been 'regenerated' reflecting the increase in property values. Partly as a consequence of this, the FA 1985 provision was replaced by more far-reaching provisions introduced by FA 1997 (now CAA 2001 s 185). [48.67]

e) *Fixtures acquired after 23 July 1996 and on which any former owner had claimed an allowance: s 185 and Sch 3 para 38*

Where fixtures are acquired on the purchase, etc of property the amount of the purchaser's qualifying expenditure can be no greater than the disposal value brought into account (for the purposes of capital allowances) by the vendor *or by any other previous owner on a disposal after 23 July 1996*. The effect is that the purchaser is restricted to the most recent post-23 July 1996 disposal value brought into account, whether by the vendor or any previous owner; and the purchaser will be restricted to the disposal value of *all* the fixtures on which the vendor (or previous owner) claimed allowances, including any on which the expenditure was incurred pre-July 1984.

It follows from this that a purchaser needs to establish whether any previous owner had made a claim because this also could restrict his entitlement. As time passes, this becomes increasingly unworkable, and a pragmatic approach has generally been adopted, not least by HMRC, in most cases. In practical terms, if the immediate vendor was required to bring in a disposal value, the purchaser's qualifying expenditure will be restricted to that disposal value, which will be limited to the vendor's original qualifying expenditure, and that in turn will have been restricted to the disposal value brought into account by the previous vendor. Therefore HMRC's main concern has been to ensure that any claim is limited to the current seller's disposal value. The provisions of s 185 requiring consideration of previous owners has historically only had a significant impact where a taxpayer sells to a non-taxpayer (eg a pension fund), who later sells again to a taxpayer. However, this effectively changes under rules introduced by FA 2012 with effect for transactions taking place on or after 6 April 2012 for income tax or 1 April 2012 for corporation tax (s 187A). See [**48.73**].

It should, however, be noted that notwithstanding s 185 there will still be no restrictions on a s 562 apportionment for a purchaser in respect of fixtures on which the vendor has not claimed capital allowances (as where the vendor is a non-taxpayer such as a charity or pension fund, or a property developer holding the building on trading account) as long as there has not been any post-23 July 1996 sale by an owner who *did* claim allowances on those fixtures. In respect of any such fixtures, the purchaser will be entitled to capital allowances based on a s 562 'just apportionment' of his purchase price of the property, unrestricted by past disposal values brought into account by any owners before the vendor. Until April 2014, the same principles applied where the seller could have claimed allowances, but omitted to do so (typically because they were loss-making). However, from April 2014, in order for the purchaser to claim allowances on fixtures, they will first need to persuade the seller to make a claim, before passing on the benefit (see [48.73]). Once the seller has made a claim (albeit only at the purchaser's request) s 185 will now apply to restrict allowances.

As illustrated in *Example 48.5*, if a taxpaying property investor, instead of a pension fund, had redeveloped the property, and claimed capital allowances, his disposal value for the plant and machinery on the sale in 2017 would have been limited by s 62(1) to the original cost, £200,000. The effect of s 185 is that, because this sale took place after 23 July 1996, no subsequent purchaser of the property can have qualifying expenditure for these plant and machinery items of more than £200,000 (their original cost). Where there has been a post-23 July 1996 sale, s 185 ensures that no s 562 apportionment on a subsequent sale can have the effect, for instance in a rising property market, of 'regenerating' the qualifying expenditure for these items to a level higher than their original cost.

It is, of course, in the interest of a vendor to enter as low a disposal value as he can justify. It is not unknown for a vendor who is selling at a substantial profit to try to avoid doing a s 562 apportionment at all, to include a disposal value in his tax return well below original cost (or no disposal value at all) and to succeed in getting this accepted incorrectly by his inspector without enquiry. If this should happen, a purchaser might find that his inspector insists on applying s 185 in these circumstances, even though the low disposal value has been accepted incorrectly by the vendor's inspector. As a last resort, the purchaser could go to the Tax Tribunal under s 563, with (if the vendor's approach has clearly been unreasonable) a high chance of success. It is made explicit under s 187A that the seller is required to account for a disposal value, even if the purchaser fails to meet the requirements of that section, such that the purchaser's claim is nil. [48.68]

f) *Conclusions for a purchaser*

It follows from the above that a purchaser who is concerned about his capital allowances position should seek to establish, before contracts are exchanged, the following:

(1) What plant and machinery items have been the subject of capital allowance claims by the vendor?
(2) What was the vendor's original expenditure on those items?
(3) Are there any other plant and machinery items in the building? Will the seller agree to a claim on those assets?
(4) If so, has any previous owner claimed allowances on these and brought a disposal value into account (eg on a sale of the property) *after* 23 July 1996?

In regard to (3), it should be noted that many property investors, mainly small or medium-sized companies, on purchasing a building with fixtures for refurbishment, claim allowances for the plant and machinery they install as part of the refurbishment, but omit to claim allowances for the items that were in the building at the time they purchased and which were incorporated within the refurbishment. Unless the company purchased the property post-23 July 1996 from an owner who had himself claimed allowances on these items, when the company sells the property its purchaser will be able to claim allowances on those items based on a s 562 apportionment unrestricted by s 185 (however from April 2014 this is subject to the pooling requirement – see [48.73]).

Solicitors acting for a purchaser should, however, note that if the vendor has not made a claim for allowances he will nevertheless be entitled (subject to satisfying certain conditions) to make a retrospective claim after his disposal of the property. If this should happen the purchaser could unwittingly find his s 562 claim limited by s 185. It will therefore be advisable for the purchaser's solicitor to insert into the sale contract clauses to establish what claims are to be made, and who is to have the benefit of any allowances arising.

Even a purchaser who is not entitled to claim allowances (eg a gross fund or a property dealer) would be well advised to ascertain the full capital allowances history so that he can give this information to a subsequent purchaser. This is normally dealt with using the 'CPSE.1' Commercial Property Standard Enquiries form. Use of form CPSE.1 is not mandatory, and other in-house enquirers exist. A short-form version called CPSE.7 is available for low value transactions, but is of no practical use for capital allowances purposes and should be avoided. [48.69]

g)   *Election between vendor and purchaser: s 198*

From 19 March 1997 a vendor of property who has claimed capital allowances on fixtures has been able to enter into a s 198 (or s 199 for leases) joint election with the purchaser to determine the amount of the total sale price that is to be apportioned to the fixtures. This determines both the disposal value to the vendor and the amount of qualifying expenditure for the purchaser. It also binds HMRC, unlike an apportionment specified in a contract for sale.

An election once made is irrevocable.

Note that a s 198 election can be made only in respect of fixtures on which the vendor has claimed allowances.

The amount specified in the election may not exceed either the cost of the fixtures to the vendor or the total purchase price paid by the purchaser (so in *Example 48.5* an election could not have been made at a figure above £200,000). In most cases the 'cap' for the election will be the vendor's cost.

If the parties contemplate making an election at a figure less than the 'notional written-down value' there may be a risk of the anti-avoidance provisions of s 197 applying, by which the notional written-down value will be substituted. These provisions apply only if there is a tax avoidance objective to the whole transaction, not merely to the making of a s 198 election. 'Notional written-down value' is defined to mean, broadly, the value which the items would currently have for capital allowances if allowances had been claimed on them individually and separately from any pool, ie the value which, as a disposal value, would give rise to neither a balancing allowance nor a balancing charge.

Subject to these anti-avoidance provisions there can be particular advantages in having a s 198 election where one party to the transaction has a significantly higher overall tax rate than the other, ie an election favouring the former, with a suitable adjustment of other terms of the transaction.

There are also cases in which a purchaser is not greatly concerned about the capital allowance position: for instance, if the purchaser is a non-taxpayer or a property dealer and is not entitled to claim allowances, or if he has present and pending losses which are likely to mean that any allowances he has are unlikely to benefit him for a few years and his main concern is simply to purchase the investment property. In these cases the vendor is in a good position to get a low disposal value agreed by a joint election under s 198. The purchaser should, however, be aware that a low disposal value agreed by him may have an adverse impact on the price he can get when he sells the property since this disposal value will determine the maximum amount a purchaser from him can claim by way of qualifying expenditure.

A purchaser should note at the pre-contract stage whether the vendor is proposing a s 198 election and, if so, the proposed sale price for the fixtures. He can then take specialist advice as to whether this is a reasonable figure for the fixtures in question or whether (as would generally be the case) he is likely to fare better with a s 562 apportionment subject to any restriction under s 185.

Elections must be made within two years after the date of the purchaser's acquisition of his interest. For other rules about the content of elections and procedure, see ss 200 and 201. It is important from the purchaser's point of view that the election is very specific as to the particular plant it relates to, so that he clearly retains the right to a s 562 apportionment (subject to any s 185 'cap' applicable) in relation to plant not intended to be covered by the election.

Strictly, since the fixtures rules in CAA 2001 work on an asset-by-asset basis a s 198 election would need to be made in relation to each individual fixture. In practice, HMRC normally accept a single s 198 election covering a group of fixtures in a single building but not one covering fixtures in different properties eg where a portfolio of properties is being sold. It has been noted that many s 198 elections are arguably invalid for a variety of reasons, including:

(1) a failure to adequately identify the assets purportedly subject to the election;
(2) purportedly including non-fixtures within the election;
(3) making an election for assets on which the vendor has not claimed allowances;
(4) including within the election assets that do not in any case qualify for allowances;
(5) including within the election assets that do not actually exist (eg lifts in a single-storey building).

Historically, HMRC has been reluctant to challenge or reject elections. However, with effect from April 2012, such rejections have become more common. A taxpayer (purchaser or vendor) who is relying on an election which is rejected may find he is already out of time to amend the election or apply to the tribunal (see [48.72]). [48.70]

h) *Agreed sale price of fixtures without election*

Sale contracts sometimes specify the proportion of the sale price which the parties agreed should be attributed to fixtures. This is rarely done with capital allowances in mind. An allocation such as this would not be binding on the Revenue or, if it conflicts with the requirements of s 562 for a just apportionment, on the parties to the contract: s 562(2), *Fitton v Gilders & Heaton* (1955) and *Tapsell (Mr & Mrs) & Lester (Mr) (trading as Partnership 'The Granleys') v R & C Comrs* (2011). [48.71]

i) *Additional procedural requirements from April 2012: s 187A*

For property acquisitions from April 2012, where the seller (or in some cases, a previous owner) has claimed allowances on fixtures, the purchaser may only claim where he can satisfy a new 'fixed value requirement'.

The fixed value requirement is met when one of two outcomes occurs. That is, either:
- 'a relevant apportionment of the apportionable sum has been made' (see below);
- or the current owner has obtained certain statements where the property is acquired from someone other than 'the past owner' (a rare exception not discussed further).

A 'relevant apportionment' is made if:
- a Tribunal has determined the part of the sale price that constitutes the disposal value of the fixtures, on an application made by one of the affected parties within two years of the purchaser's acquisition; or
- there has been a joint election, under either s 198 or s 199, as appropriate, between the past owner and the purchaser within two years of the acquisition.

The overwhelming majority of commercial property transactions involving second-hand fixtures should involve a relevant apportionment, so that there will be the requirement for a reference to the tribunal, or for a joint election to be made, within two years of a sale. If this requirement applies, but is not met, the purchaser is deemed to have claimed on £nil. This not only rules out a claim by the purchaser, but also by any future purchaser of those same fixtures (their claim will be restricted under s 185 to the first purchaser's disposal value, which under s 62 cannot exceed that purchaser's deemed claim of £nil).

It should be remembered that the underlying legislation has not changed, and therefore in the absence of an election, the default position is that the seller should suffer a claw-back of allowances, with the purchaser being able to claim (generally) on no less than the seller's original cost. A negotiated election is almost certain, therefore, to be detrimental to the purchaser.

These additional requirements have effect:
- for income tax purposes, in relation to new expenditure incurred on or after 6 April 2012; and
- for corporation tax purposes, in relation to new expenditure incurred on or after 1 April 2012.

A key point to note is that until April 2014, the new 'fixed value requirement' rules only applied where the seller had claimed allowances on the fixtures. If the seller had not so claimed, the previous rules were unaffected. [48.72]

1418 Capital allowances

j) Further change from April 2014

From April 2014, the 'fixed value requirement' applies not only where the seller has claimed allowances, but also where the seller was entitled to claim but did not do so. This is achieved by imposing a second new requirement, that the seller's expenditure on qualifying fixtures must be pooled before the subsequent transfer to a purchaser (the 'pooling requirement'). In effect, after April 2014, where a purchaser wants to claim allowances on fixtures, then if the seller has not claimed allowances, the purchaser must require the seller to make a claim before passing on the value to the purchaser. This will, of course, only apply where the seller is entitled to make a claim, so will not affect purchases from non-taxable entities, or assets on which the seller *could not* have claimed allowances. Nor will it apply to any assets on which the seller could not have claimed, because the items were not plant in his hands. The most common example of this will be where the seller incurred expenditure on cold water systems, general electrical or lighting systems, and external solar shading before April 2008. These items are now accepted as integral features qualifying for plant allowances (see **[48.61]**), but before April 2008 they were not accepted as plant so, by definition, the seller could not claim allowances.

For the purpose of determining whether expenditure was incurred on or after 1 or 6 April 2012 or 2014, the effect of s 12 is ignored. Section 12 relates to expenditure incurred before commencement of the qualifying activity (commonly called pre-trading expenditure) and deems that expenditure to have been incurred on the first day that the qualifying activity is carried on. For example, if a property was acquired in 2011 but was first let in 2013, s 12 would deem any qualifying expenditure to have been incurred in 2013, but it would not be subject to the fixed value requirement. **[48.73]**

6 Allowances on cars and other vehicles

a) Introduction

The treatment of cars will depend on whether they were acquired before or after 6 April 2009 (for income tax) or 1 April 2009 (for corporation tax). Before those dates, the key point was whether they cost in excess of £12,000. After that date, the emphasis changes, and allowances instead depend on carbon dioxide emission levels. Expenditure incurred before April 2009 continued to be subject to the old rules for a further five years, that is, until April 2014 (FA 2009 Sch 11 para 29). Any balance of expenditure not yet written-off at that point was transferred to the main pool at the start of the first chargeable period to commence on or after 1 or 6 April 2014 (FA 2009 Sch 11 para 31).

This section discusses the emission-based system now in place, although some matters, including definitions, are common to both old and new systems.

A 'car' is defined as 'any mechanically propelled road vehicle' but there are a number of exclusions, the first being vehicles which are of a construction primarily suited for conveyance of goods: s 268A. Lorries and vans are therefore generally excluded from the special treatment accorded to cars. Some vehicles can be designed either for goods or for passengers, and their tax treatment will depend on the precise construction of the relevant vehicle. The Revenue has confirmed that Land Rovers are capable of falling within this exclusion; Range Rovers and estate cars are not.

If a vehicle is not a 'car' it is dealt with in the same manner as most other items of plant, ie as part of the main pool. However, expenditure on new *zero-emission goods vehicles* in the period 1 April 2010 to 31 March 2018 (for corporation tax) and 6 April 2010 to 5 April 2018 (for income tax) qualifies for a 100% first-year allowance. This relief is subject to certain conditions imposed by State aid rules (ss 45DA, DB as inserted by F(No 3)A 2010 Sch 7).

Cars are excluded from the operation of the provisions relating to short-life assets (s 84) and long-life assets (s 96). **[48.74]**

b) *Expenditure on or after 1 or 6 April 2009*

With general effect from 6 April 2009 (for income tax) and 1 April 2009 (for corporation tax), capital allowances for new expenditure cars are based on carbon dioxide emissions (FA 2009 Sch 11 para 26). Electrically-propelled cars, and those with very low carbon dioxide emissions (defined as equal to or less than 75g per kilometre) continue to qualify for a 100% first year allowance (CAA 2001 s 45D).

Cars with carbon dioxide emissions of between 75g and 130g per kilometre will continue to qualify at the 'main rate' of writing down allowance, currently 18% per annum. This rate will also apply to all cars first registered before 1 March 2001 (FA 2009 Sch 11 para 8).

Expenditure on other cars, that is, those with carbon dioxide emissions in excess of 130g per kilometre, will be allocated to the special rate pool (alongside, for example, long-life assets and integral features), qualifying at a rate of 8% per annum (FA 2009 Sch 11 para 7).

Lower emission limits applied prior to 1 April 2015. **[48.75]**

Cars and accelerated allowances

Sundry provisions prevent cars from qualifying for accelerated allowances. These are:
- CAA 2001 s 46 which prevents cars (other than those with very low carbon dioxide emissions) qualifying for the first year allowances;
- CAA 2001 s 81, which prevents cars qualifying for the annual investment allowance;
- CAA 2001 s 84, which prevents cars from being treated as short-life assets. **[48.76]**

Anti-avoidance

CAA 2001 s 104F prevents the artificial creation of balancing allowances in groups where one company carries on the business of providing cars for other companies in the group. This applies only to 'special rate cars'. **[48.77]**

The 100% first year allowances (FYAs) introduced by FA 2002 for new low-emission cars are explained in **[48.32]**. **[48.78]**

c) *Expenditure before 1 or 6 April 2009*

(i) *'Inexpensive cars'*

The term 'inexpensive car' is not an expression defined in the legislation but is used here to indicate a car (other than a low-emission car in respect of which a 100% FYA is available under the new s 45D) with a cost to the present taxpayer of £12,000 or less and which is used wholly in the taxpayer's qualifying activity.

Under the old system, an 'inexpensive car' is treated for capital allowances in the same way as most other items of plant, ie as part of the main pool.

It should, however, be noted that a car costing £12,000 or less which is used partly for private purposes will still need to be kept outside the main pool and allocated to a single asset pool under CAA 2001 Part 2 Chapter 15 (see **[48.63]**). Separate records will thus still continue to be required for such cars.

[48.79]

(ii)   'Expensive cars': ss 74–82 (Part 2 Chapter 8)

Under the old system, the term 'expensive car' means a car (other than a low-emission car in respect of which a 100% FYA is available under the new s 45D) with a cost to the present taxpayer of more than £12,000. These are dealt with in CAA 2001 Part 2 Chapter 8.

Expenditure incurred before April 2009 will continue to be subject to the old rules for a further five years, ie, until April 2014 (FA 2009 Sch 11 para 29).

Any balance of expenditure not yet written off at that point will be transferred to the main pool at the start of the first chargeable period to commence on or after 1 or 6 April 2014 (FA 2009 Sch 11 para 31).

In the case of a new car 'cost' is accepted as including factory-fitted extras but not additions made after the car has been brought into use unless these were contracted for at the time of the acquisition of the car. Subsequent additions are added to the main pool.

There are two special features of the capital allowances treatment of 'expensive' cars:

(1)   The expenditure on such a car has to be allocated to a single asset pool: s 74. It follows from this that, unlike disposals from the main pool (or the old car pools), a balancing adjustment will arise whenever an individual 'expensive' car is disposed of.

(2)   The annual WDA for 'expensive' cars is restricted to £3,000, proportionately adjusted where the chargeable period is more or less than a full year: s 75.

In general terms it will often be advantageous for a taxpayer with a fleet of cars to buy an 'expensive' car rather than add another 'inexpensive' car to his main pool, especially where it is anticipated that the car will be sold after a relatively short time for a low value. With the expenditure being kept in its own single asset pool, the disposal proceeds will trigger an immediate balancing allowance for the taxpayer, instead of effecting only a reduction in the overall qualifying expenditure in the main pool.

The WDA for an 'expensive' car is proportionately reduced in the following circumstances:

(a)   Where the taxpayer receives a contribution, eg from an employee, towards the purchase price: s 76. The person making the contribution can also claim allowances, although his WDAs will be restricted to such proportion of £3,000 as his contribution bears to the total expenditure: s 76(4).

(b) If the car is used partly for purposes other than the purposes of the actual qualifying activity: s 77(2). In these circumstances the WDAs will be reduced according to what is 'just and reasonable' in the same way as under CAA 2001 Part 2 Chapter 15. This often ends up being negotiated between the taxpayer and the inspector after an enquiry into the taxpayer's own assessment of the appropriate reduction. The reduction is commonly based on the proportion which private mileage bears to total mileage. It is understood that in practice cars used by employees and directors are normally regarded by inspectors as used wholly for the business purposes of the employing company for capital allowances purposes, notwithstanding that they might be used privately by the employee or director. A tax charge would normally arise on the benefit in kind under the benefits code of ITEPA 2003 Part 3.

HMRC may also seek to restrict allowances where there is a 'blatant incongruity' between the type of car and the size and nature of the business (Revenue Manual CA 2422).

If an expensive car bought wholly for a qualifying activity later begins to be used partly for other (eg private) purposes there is no disposal event (and hence no balancing adjustment) as there would normally be under s 61(1): s 77(1). The single asset pool under Chapter 8 takes the place of the single asset pool that would normally be required under Chapter 15 in this event and the 'just and reasonable' reduction rules in Chapter 8 take effect in the same way as the corresponding rules in Chapter 15.

To prevent traders circumventing the allowance restriction for 'expensive cars' by leasing rather than buying and then claiming the deduction of the whole rental as a business expense, the deduction permitted in calculating profits under CTA 2009 s 46 (previously the deduction under TA 1988 s 74) is limited to the proportion that £12,000 plus one half of the excess above £12,000 bears to the total cost of the car when new: CTA 2009 s 56 (TA 1988 s 578A), ITTOIA 2005 s 48. **[48.80]**

EXAMPLE 48.6

Footsore hires a car, which cost £16,000, for business use at a rent of £1,020 for one year. The hire charge that he can treat as a business expense is limited to:

$$\frac{£12,000 + \frac{1}{2}\,(£16,000 - £12,000)}{£16,000} \times £1,020 = £3,892.50$$

7 Hire purchase: ss 67–69 (Part 2 Chapter 6)

In the absence of specific legislation, a person acquiring plant (eg a car) under a hire-purchase agreement would not be able to fulfil the 'ownership' requirement (see **[48.22]**) because title would not generally pass until all instalments have been paid. Special rules apply however where a taxpayer incurs capital expenditure on plant or machinery under a contract which provides that he 'shall or may become the owner of the machinery or plant on the performance of the contract': s 67(1). Thus these special rules apply to leases which contain an option under which it is possible for the hirer to acquire the asset at the end of the period of hire; and to contracts where title to the asset passes automatically to the purchaser on payment of the final instalment of the purchase price. HMRC's view is that expenditure is incurred 'under a contract' only if the contract is legally binding and commits the taxpayer to incur that expenditure.

In such cases s 67 has two effects:
(1) the 'ownership' requirement is treated as satisfied at any time when the taxpayer is entitled to the benefit of the contract, and
(2) all capital expenditure to be incurred under the contract after the time when the plant or machinery is brought into use for the purposes of the qualifying activity is treated as having been incurred at that time.

It is of course only the capital element of the hire-purchase instalments that is treated in the way described in (2) above. The interest element is generally a fully deductible business expense in the year it is paid.

There are two exceptions to the operation of s 67 on hire-purchase contracts:
(a) Section 67 does not apply to hire-purchase contracts for fixtures. Fixtures have their own 'deemed ownership' provisions (see **[48.23]**) and these apply even if the fixture is acquired under a hire-purchase contract.
(b) For chargeable periods ending on or after 2 July 1997, the effect of (2) above does not apply where the plant or machinery is let under a finance lease: s 229(3). Where this is the case, capital expenditure on the asset will qualify for allowances only as and when it is incurred and not when the asset is first brought into use.

Where s 67 does apply, and the taxpayer subsequently ceases to be entitled to the benefit of the contract, he is treated as ceasing to own the asset at that time and has to bring a disposal value into account. The disposal value is the total of any sums he receives by way of compensation or insurance money plus the residue of the expenditure still to be paid under the contract.
[48.81]–[48.90]

III INDUSTRIAL BUILDINGS

Capital allowances in the form of Industrial Buildings Allowances (IBAs) were available under CAA 2001 Part 3 if expenditure was incurred in the construction of an industrial building or certain other buildings. However, they have been phased out so that, with effect from 6 April 2011 for income tax (1 April 2011 for corporation tax), IBAs are no longer available.

Nonetheless, the purchaser of an industrial property will still need to know whether, and to what extent, industrial buildings allowances have been claimed by previous owners. A purchaser may wish to claim plant and machinery allowances on fixtures in the property, and these may in the past have qualified for industrial buildings allowances, in which case the purchaser's claim will be restricted under s 186. For this ongoing reason, the definition of an industrial building is summarised below. A more complete description of industrial buildings allowances was included in the 30th and earlier editions of *Revenue Law: Principles and Practice.* **[48.91]**

Unlike plant and machinery, an industrial building was defined in detail in CAA 2001 (in Part 3, Chapter 2). The main type of 'industrial building' was a building or structure which was *in use* for the purposes of a 'qualifying trade'. Thus the trade carried on by the tenant or other occupier was all important. **[48.92]**

Table A in s 274 set out seven trades which are qualifying trades; and Table B in the same section set out ten undertakings which were qualifying trades if they were carried on by way of trade. The Table A trades included all manufacturing and processing trades, certain storage trades, agriculture contracting, and fishing. The Table B undertakings included undertakings for the generation or distribution of electricity, the supply of water and hydraulic power, and transport, highway, tunnel, bridge and dock undertakings. **[48.93]**

Other buildings which qualified as 'industrial buildings' for capital allowances were:
(1) certain hotels, ie hotels in which there are at least ten letting bedrooms, which offer breakfast and an evening meal, and are open for at least four months between April and October: s 279;
(2) sports pavilions provided for the workers of a trade: s 280;
(3) commercial buildings, eg offices, in relation to 'qualifying enterprise zone expenditure': s 281. **[48.94]**

Buildings used as dwelling-houses, retail shops, showrooms, hotels (other than those referred to above) and offices outside enterprise zones were not generally industrial buildings: s 277. **[48.95]–[48.120]**

IV OTHER CATEGORIES OF EXPENDITURE ELIGIBLE FOR CAPITAL ALLOWANCES

1 Agricultural buildings (CAA 2001 Part 4)

Agricultural Buildings Allowances (ABAs) have been phased out, so that, with effect from 6 April 2011 for income tax (1 April 2011 for corporation tax), they are no longer available. Nonetheless, the purchaser of an agricultural property will still need to know whether, and to what extent, agricultural buildings allowances have been claimed by previous owners. A purchaser may wish to claim plant and machinery allowances on fixtures in the property, and these may in the past have qualified for agricultural buildings allowances, in which case no claim for fixtures allowances is possible by virtue of s 9(1). For this ongoing reason, the rules relating to which buildings may have qualified for ABAs are summarised below.

ABAs were previously given for capital expenditure on the construction of farmhouses, farm buildings, cottages, fences and other works for the purposes of husbandry on land in the UK. The meaning of 'husbandry' has been examined by the courts on several occasions over the years and its meaning is expressly widened by the legislation to include commercial fishing: s 362. The following points should be noted:

(1) The building, etc need not be standing on the relevant agricultural land. What was required is that it was used for the purposes of husbandry carried out on that land.
(2) A landlord could claim ABAs in relation to buildings, etc let to a tenant carrying on husbandry on the related agricultural land. [48.121]

2 Flat conversions (CAA 2001 Part 4A)

This legislation gave 100% capital allowances (and in some cases WDAs) for qualifying expenditure incurred in connection with the conversion or renovation of part of a 'qualifying building' into a 'qualifying flat'. This relief was withdrawn for expenditure incurred on or after 1 April 2013 for businesses within the charge to corporation tax, and on or after 6 April 2013 for businesses within the charge to income tax. The entitlement to claim writing down allowance on any outstanding residue of qualifying expenditure also ceased with effect from the same dates. [48.122]

3 Research and development (CAA 2001 Part 6)

There is a 100% allowance for qualifying expenditure on research and development. The provisions are found in CAA 2001 Part 6 (ss 437–451).

To qualify as R&D the activity must fall within guidelines issued by the Secretary of State for Trade and Industry on 5 March 2004 (replacing previous guidelines issued on 28 July 2000). These guidelines are now the responsibility of the Department of Business, Energy and Industrial Strategy (formerly the Department for Business, Innovation and Skills (BIS), and before that the Department of Trade and Industry) (DTI).

The key theme is that the activities must be creative or innovative work in the fields of science or technology, and undertaken with a view to the extension of knowledge (that is, seeking an 'advance'). R&D is characterised by work that contains an appreciable element of innovation and aims to resolve scientific or technological uncertainties. Such works can range from research in areas that are purely theoretical to applied research and experimental development directed towards a practical aim or product. But commercial development undertaken without such scientific or technological investigation, or undertaken only after the resolution of such uncertainty, is not R&D.

For capital allowances purposes R&D expressly includes oil and gas exploration and appraisal.

Qualifying expenditure means capital expenditure incurred by a person on R&D:
(a) undertaken either by him or on his behalf; and
(b) that relates to a trade he is carrying on or has commenced since incurring the expenditure: s 439.

Expenditure on land does not qualify for R&D allowances, but expenditure on acquiring an existing building or structure, or plant and machinery in such a building or structure, is capable of qualifying. For this purpose a 'just and reasonable' apportionment will need to be made to identify the non-qualifying proportion attributable to the land: s 440.

An R&D allowance is generally given in the chargeable period in which expenditure is incurred, at the rate of 100%. If the trade is yet to commence, however, the allowance is given in the chargeable period of commencement: s 441. A claim for a reduced allowance may be made although, as there is no provision for the remainder to be claimed in later years through WDAs, such a claim is unlikely in practice.

Strict rules apply for the recovery of an R&D allowance where an asset representing allowable expenditure is transferred or sold by the person who incurred the expenditure. In this event, or if the asset is demolished or destroyed, a balancing event occurs and if the proceeds exceed the amount of any unclaimed allowance a balancing charge will arise equal to the excess. The 'proceeds' means, in the event of an arm's length sale, the net sale proceeds; in the event of any other sale or transfer, the market value; and in the event of the demolition or destruction of the asset any amount received for the remains plus any insurance moneys or other compensation. If the balancing event occurs after the permanent cessation of the relevant trade, the balancing charge is made in the chargeable period of the cessation: ss 441–444.

Finally, R&D allowances are not to be confused with the tax relief/credit scheme for *non*-capital expenditure on R&D that was introduced by FA 2000 for small and medium-sized companies, and then extended to all companies and also enhanced in value (particularly in relation to R&D on vaccine research) by FA 2002, and improved further by subsequent Finance Acts. The definition of R&D is subtly wider for capital expenditure than non-capital expenditure because 'qualifying indirect activities' (ie activities that are related to the R&D but do not directly contribute to it such as information services, maintenance and security etc) are R&D under the BERR definition so qualify for R&D capital allowances. However, they do not qualify for the R&D tax relief/credit because this is only available for staff and other costs *directly/actively* engaged in the R&D.

It is possible in some cases to seek advance assurance from HMRC that an activity does qualify as R&D. The main benefit of advance assurance is to provide the company with a guarantee that HMRC will not raise further questions about the initial R&D claim, and for R&D claims submitted for the next two accounting periods.

The advance assurance procedure can only be used by companies which have not claimed R&D tax relief before, and which meet these criteria:
- fewer than 50 employees; and
- annual turnover of no more than £2 million.

New companies which have yet to start trading can also apply for advanced assurance. However, where the company is part of a group, advance assurance will not be given if another member of the group has claimed R&D tax relief in the past.

This HMRC practice is published at https://www.gov.uk/guidance/research-and-development-tax-relief-advance-assurance. [48.123]

4 Renovation of business premises allowance (CAA 2001 Part 3A)

Between April 2007 and April 2017, there existed a 100% allowance for expenditure on the renovation of business premises, whether owned or let, with the intention that those premises are brought back into business use.

The allowance was available from 11 April 2007 (SI 2007/945), initially for a period of five years (s 360B). The scheme was later extended until 31 March (corporation tax) or 5 April 2017 (income tax) (SI 2012/868). **[48.124]**

The premises must have been vacant for a year or more and be situated in a designated disadvantaged area. They must last have been used for the purposes of a trade or as an office. In *Senex Investments Ltd v Commissioners for HM Revenue and Customs* (2011), a church run on commercial principles was held to be a trade for this purpose.

As a result of the requirement for 12 months' vacancy, the legislation potentially encouraged a taxpayer whose premises had been vacant for a few months, and who was considering work of this kind, to postpone the works until such time as the property had been vacant for a full year, so as to ensure the 100% allowance could be claimed.

Uptake of the allowances was limited. According to the Chief Financial Secretary to the Treasury, in 2014–15, only around 1,350 taxpayers made a claim. **[48.125]**

5 Landlord's energy saving allowance (ITTOIA 2005 s 312, CA 2009 s 251)

Prior to 6 April 2015 (income tax) and 1 April 2015 (corporation tax), relief was available for landlords who incurred capital expenditure installing energy-saving insulation to residential property. This was available for non-corporate landlords from 6 April 2004 (Income Tax (Trading and Other Income) Act 2005 (ITTOIA 2005) s 312) and for corporates from 8 July 2008 (CTA 2009 s 251 and SI 2008/1520). **[48.126]**

This Landlord's Energy Saving Allowance provided a tax deduction in computing rental income of up to a maximum of £1,500 for the installation of:
- cavity wall insulation and loft insulation
- solid wall insulation
- hot water system insulation and draught proofing
- floor insulation. **[48.127]**

Section 7 Stamp taxes

Chapters
49   Stamp taxes

49 Stamp taxes

Jonathan Legg CTA, Partner, Mishcon de Reya LLP

I   Introduction [49.1]
II Stamp duty land tax (SDLT) (including annual tax on enveloped dwellings) [49.22]
III Stamp duty reserve tax (SDRT) [49.92]
IV Stamp duty on stock and marketable securities [49.107]

I INTRODUCTION

The first stamp duties were introduced in 1694 during the reign of William and Mary as a temporary measure to fund the war against the French. Whilst relations with our Gallic neighbours are now much more civilised, stamp duties have since remained a feature of the fiscal landscape (although substantial changes to the regime have been made, notably in 1986 and 2003). The cardinal feature of stamp duty, and one that distinguished it from the other direct taxes, had been that it was strictly a charge on *instruments* and not on either transactions or on persons. Indeed, historically, the bulk of the revenues from stamp duty had become focused on two main areas: conveyances of UK land and transfers of shares in UK companies. Stamp duty was cheap for the Stamp Office to collect – since taxpayers and their advisers did most of the work. But the arrival of the electronic age, and the ingenuity of those who sought to carry out transactions without creating stampable documents, resulted in the introduction of numerous anti-avoidance provisions and, ultimately, two brand new *self-assessed* transaction taxes – viz Stamp Duty Reserve Tax ('SDRT') in 1986 and Stamp Duty Land Tax ('SDLT') in 2003.

More recently, high-value residential property has been targeted by both the Coalition and Conservative Governments in various ways. First, came the abolition of the old 'slab' system of SDLT for *residential* property with effect from 4 December 2014, replacing it with a new 'slice' system whereby different rates of tax are now paid to the extent that the price of a property falls within different bands. More controversial is the introduction of new 'higher rates' of SDLT for certain residential transactions with effect from 1 April 2016 (the new higher rates add an additional 3% to the applicable rate of SDLT in each band where it applies). This means that the rate of SDLT on the top slice of a residential property transaction where the additional rates apply is now 15%. All of this is in addition to the anti-avoidance rules, introduced in 2012, which levy a *flat rate* of 15% SDLT on certain purchases of homes by *companies* and which introduced a restricted form of mansion tax, the Annual Tax on Enveloped Dwellings.

The Government also abolished the old 'slab' system of SDLT for *non-residential and mixed use* property (from 17 March 2016). Under the new 'slice' system, the top rate of SDLT is 5%. It will be apparent that the distinction between what is 'residential' versus 'non-residential and mixed use' property has now gained increasing importance given the differential in the rates of SDLT. [49.1]–[49.20]

1 Current structure of Stamp Taxes

The current 'Stamp Taxes' regime can be broken down into three distinct parts:

(a) Stamp duty land tax (SDLT) applies to transactions in UK land, including acquisitions of existing land interests, the creation of new interests and variations and surrenders. It also applies to transfers of partnership interests in certain property investment partnerships. The tax is mandatory with modern enforcement powers and the taxpayer has to self-assess, and send in a return and the associated payment within 30 days of a transaction.

(b) Stamp duty reserve tax (SDRT) applies, with full enforcement powers, to agreements to transfer chargeable securities (essentially UK equities). However, except for electronic transfers related to deals on a trading platform, the charge is generally by-passed by submitting a stock transfer form for stamping.

(c) Stamp duty applies to documents relating to transactions involving shares (including bearer shares) and 'marketable securities' (a security which is capable of being sold in any stock market in the UK) and is not in general mandatory – though absence of stamping impedes the use of documents for registration and as court evidence. Significantly, this means that a company registrar is not entitled to register the transferee under a stock transfer form as a member of the company unless a properly stamped form (or form which has been properly certified as not chargeable to stamp duty) is presented.

The words 'stamp' and 'duty' are confusingly included in the names of SDRT and SDLT, notwithstanding that neither directly involve stamps and they are taxes rather than duties. But the naming of taxes is a political matter and these names were no doubt chosen to emphasise continuity with the long-standing predecessor rather than their novelty as new taxes. [49.21]

II STAMP DUTY LAND TAX (SDLT)

The legislative provisions are in FA 2003 Part 4, as extensively amended by subsequent Finance Acts and statutory instruments. References in this section are to FA 2003 unless otherwise specified.

SDLT replaced stamp duty on land from 1 December 2003. There is no interaction with stamp duty legislation – except in so far as the transitional provisions determine which tax applies to transactions that started while stamp duty applied and finish when SDLT applies. A knowledge of stamp duty is not required in order to understand SDLT – even though many features were carried forward in some form to the new tax. But the Government's anti-avoidance motive for introducing the tax led to key SDLT provisions being designed around the structure of specific stamp duty mitigation schemes. This starting point led to the extraordinary complexity of the charging provisions for ordinary conveyances and lease grants. Some references to the stamp duty schemes will therefore be made to help the reader to understand why the SDLT provisions are structured in the way that they are. [49.22]–[49.24]

1 Scope of the tax

The scope of SDLT is limited to land in the UK (s 48(1)(a)) but it does not matter how or where the transaction was effected or whether any party to the transaction is present or resident in the UK (s 42(2)).

The charge applies to 'land transactions' (s 43) which are acquisitions of 'chargeable interests' (s 48) that are widely defined and include freeholds, leaseholds and options relating to land. But licences to occupy land and security interests over land such as mortgages are excluded as exempt interests and do not trigger a charge to SDLT.

Transfers of interests in 'property investment partnerships' are brought within the scope of SDLT and there are special rules when partners transfer land into partnerships and vice-versa. [49.25]

2 Basics

The basic elements of SDLT are as follows:
(a) There must be a *land transaction* (s 43) which is defined as the *acquisition* of a *chargeable interest* (s 48). But 'acquisition' is given an extended meaning to include the creation, surrender, release or variation of a chargeable interest.
(b) The *purchaser* (s 43) is potentially liable to the tax and is responsible for self-assessment, payment of any tax, and delivery of *land transaction return* (s 76) if the transaction is *notifiable* (ss 77 and 77A).
(c) There is no tax consequence until the *effective date* of the transaction (s 119) – notification and any payment are required within 30 days of that date.
(d) The amount of tax payable is based on the *chargeable consideration* (Sch 4) and is charged at rates as set out below. [49.26]

3 The new slice system

In the Autumn Statement in December 2014, the Government announced a fundamental change in the way SDLT was calculated on residential property, moving to the so-called 'slice system' of SDLT with effect from 4 December 2014 (although with transitional rules for contracts entered into before this date but completing after). Similarly, with effect from 17 March 2016 (again with transitional rules), the same 'slice' principle was extended to non-residential and mixed use property.

Previously, the SDLT on both 'residential' and 'non-residential and mixed use' properties was calculated pursuant to the so-called 'slab' system. Under the slab system, SDLT was paid as a fixed percentage of the *entire* price, depending on the band in which the price fell. This system for SDLT had long been criticised for its unfairness and distortion of the market – for example, a person paying £250,000 for a home paid 1% SDLT on the entire purchase price (£2,500) whereas a person paying £251,000 paid 3% SDLT (£7,530). For both residential and non-residential and mixed use property, this system has now been ripped up and replaced by a more progressive system – the so-called 'slice' system. Rather than paying a single rate of SDLT on the full purchase price of the property, a buyer now pays different rates of SDLT to the extent the price of the property falls within different bands, as set out in the 'Table of SDLT rates' below.

In making the change to the calculation of SDLT on *residential* property, the Government highlighted the fact that 98% of homeowners would pay less SDLT. When compared to the SDLT due under the old rules, the 'break even' price is £937,500 – so at prices below this, it is correct that buyers will pay less SDLT under the new rules. However, at prices above this, buyers will pay more; and at the top end very considerably more. Even at £2 million, the typical price of a terraced house in many non-prime inner London suburbs, SDLT will increase by over 50% from £100,000 to £153,750.

Note that, as an anti-avoidance rule to discourage individuals buying homes in companies, there is a flat rate of 15% (payable on the entire price, as per the slab system) where a company or other 'non-natural person' buys a home for over £500,000 (although note that certain reliefs for genuine business activity, including letting to third parties and property developers, are available; this is considered further in the Anti-Avoidance section). **[49.27]**

4 The higher rates of SDLT on purchases of additional residential property

FA 2016 introduced new higher rates of SDLT, which have applied to purchases of 'additional residential properties' since 1 April 2016 and are intended to catch the purchase of second homes and buy-to let properties by adding an additional 3% to each 'slice' of the price.

The higher rates are relevant on the purchase of a 'major interest' in one or more 'dwellings'. For these purposes, 'major interest' means a freehold interest or lease which was originally granted for seven years or more. 'Dwelling' means a building:
- used as a dwelling;
- suitable for use as a dwelling; or
- in the process of being constructed or adapted for such use.

Note that certain types of use are excluded from the definition of dwelling including, it appears, residential student accommodation (although HMRC considers only purpose-built student accommodation to be outside the scope of the additional rate). The new rules may also catch certain off-plan purchases, but will *not* apply to non-residential or mixed use property, where the consideration is less than £40,000 or to caravans, houseboats and mobile homes.

The higher rates will apply to the purchase of a major interest in a single dwelling by an individual, if at the end of the day of purchase, Conditions A to D are met (that is, if any of the conditions are *not* met, then the higher rates cannot apply). **[49.28]**

Conditions A–D

- Condition A – the chargeable consideration is £40,000 or more;
- Condition B – the dwelling is not subject to a lease which has more than 21 years to run at the date of purchase;
- Condition C – the purchaser owns an interest in another dwelling, which has a market value of £40,000 or more and is not subject to a lease which has more than 21 years to run at the date of purchase of the new dwelling; and
- Condition D – the dwelling being purchased is not replacing the purchaser's only or main residence.

(See the 2016 Guidance Note: https://www.gov.uk/government/uploads/system/uploads/attachment_data/file/570876/SDLT_Higher_rates_for_additional_properties.pdf)

The rules relating to Condition C in particular need to be considered carefully. In deciding whether a buyer owns another dwelling, any properties in which that person has an interest (however small) and wherever in the world the other dwelling is have to be considered. Any interest held by a spouse or joint buyer must also be taken into account (unless the spouses are separated or not living together in circumstances which are likely to become permanent). Similarly, the interest of a beneficiary under a trust where they have a right to income from a dwelling or right to occupy a dwelling for life must also be taken into account (since there must be a *right* to receive income or occupy the dwelling, this cannot apply where the trust is discretionary). Finally, if a child is absolutely entitled to a dwelling under the terms of a trust, the parents of the child (and their spouse) are deemed to have an interest in a dwelling.

Condition D will effectively exclude many acquisitions from the ambit of the higher rates. There are essentially two parts to a replacement of a purchaser's main residence relief:

- there must be a disposal of the buyer's or their spouse/civil partner's previous main residence; and
- the dwelling acquired must be intended to be occupied as the individual's only or main residence.

There are two situations where the relief will apply. *First*, where the disposal of the 'old' dwelling occurred up to three years before, or on the day of, the purchase of the 'new' dwelling (although note that the three years can be extended in certain circumstances where the new acquisition occurs on or before 26 November 2018). In this case, the higher rates will not apply to the purchase of the new dwelling. *Second*, where the purchase of the 'new' dwelling happens first and then the disposal of the 'old' dwelling happens in the three years afterwards. In this case, the higher rates must be paid on the acquisition of the 'new' dwelling, but the excess SDLT can be claimed back if the 'old' dwelling is sold within three years.

Whether a property is somebody's main residence is a question of fact, and HMRC states that you cannot simply look at where they split their time. In their guidance, HMRC state that the following may be useful in establishing which residence is an individual's main residence if they own more than one:

- If the individual is married or in a civil partnership, where does the family spend its time?
- If the individual has children, where do they go to school?
- At which residence is the individual registered to vote?
- Where is the individual's place of work?
- How is each residence furnished?
- Which address is used for correspondence?
- Where is the individual registered with a doctor/dentist?
- At which address is the individual's car registered and insured?
- Which address is the main residence for council tax?

Note that purchases or *two or more* dwellings will usually be caught by the higher rates (provided that Conditions A and B above are met). Further, any purchase or a single dwelling by a company or a discretionary trust will always be caught by the higher rates if Conditions A and B above are met.

One significant omission from the final legislation was any relief from the higher rate for the purchase of '15 or more' dwellings, which had been suggested in the original consultation. This was clearly bad news for investors into Private Rented Sector (although there is a relief for buildings let as student accommodation). [49.29]

Table of SDLT rates

Table A: Residential

Relevant consideration	Percentage	Percentage with higher rates
Up to £125,000	0%	3%
The next £125,000 (the portion from £125,001 to £250,000)	2%	5%
The next £675,000 (the portion from £250,001 to £925,000)	5%	8%
The next £575,000 (the portion from £925,001 to £1.5 million)	10%	13%
The remaining amount (the portion above £1.5 million)	12%	15%
More than £500,000 (for acquisitions by companies and other 'non-natural persons')	15%	

Table B: Non-residential or mixed

Relevant consideration	Percentage
Up to £150,000	0%
The next £100,000 (the portion from £150,001 to £250,000)	2%
The remaining amount (the portion above £250,000)	5%

Distinction between residential versus non-residential and mixed use property

Given the new top rates of tax for dwellings of 12%/15% under the new 'progressive' rates and higher rates and the flat rate of 15% for residential property acquired by non-natural persons, it is increasingly important to be able to distinguish between what is residential property, and what is non-residential or mixed property.

The legislation provides that residential property is a building or part of a building that, at the date of the relevant transaction is:
- used as a dwelling;
- suitable for use as a dwelling; or
- in the process of being constructed or adapted for such use.

This includes land which forms part of the garden or grounds of such a building.

Whilst the distinction may seem obvious, it is not always so. For example, would an office in a house mean that it becomes 'mixed' and therefore not subject to the top rate of tax? HMRC's answer (which must be correct) is that mere use of a room or area in a home as an office will not cause it to be mixed use, as the room would still be suitable for use as a dwelling. Similarly, a pool, gym or similar would be residential as it contributes to the enjoyment of the residential premises.

The legislation specifies that certain uses are always residential, such as residential accommodation for school pupils and accommodation for students (other than halls of residence). Further, the sale of six or more dwellings as part of a single transaction will generally be considered to be 'non-residential'.

There is also a charge on the rental element of new leases (and sometimes on the rental element of an existing lease which is assigned) – see below for details. **[49.30]**

5 Land transactions

A land transaction is defined by s 43(1) as an 'acquisition' of a 'chargeable interest' in land. So we need to consider s 48 to see the scope of these interests.
[49.31]

a) *Chargeable interests*

Only land in the UK is to be considered. The definition of the UK is not extended to include territorial waters and therefore stops at the low water mark. Section 121 tells us that land includes buildings and structures, and land covered by water.

Then things become more difficult since s 48 has a very wide definition of 'chargeable interest' from which certain categories of interest are exempted.

The wide definition comprises:
(1) an estate, interest, right or power in or over land in the UK; and
(2) the benefit of an obligation, restriction or condition affecting the value of any such estate, interest, right or power.

The first part of the definition includes freehold and leasehold interests. And it includes equitable as well as legal interests. The inclusion of rights over land brings in the granting of easements. Powers over land include powers of appointment by trustees where a beneficiary might pay consideration in order to vary a land interest. The second part brings payments to vary restrictive covenants into the charge, for example.

Section 48 excludes, as exempt interests:
(1) security interests;
(2) licences to use or occupy land;
(3) tenancies at will; and
(4) advowsons, franchises, or manors.

Security interests are defined as 'an interest or right (other than a rentcharge) held for the purpose of securing the payment of money or the performance of any other obligation'. This means that lenders or creditors taking a charge over property will not be acquiring a chargeable interest in land. In particular, normal mortgages or re-mortgages will not trigger payments of SDLT.

Licences are exempt interests and are not specially defined for SDLT purposes. The *Street v Mountford* (1985) authorities on the distinction between leases and licences will therefore be of use in determining whether a particular contract is within the scope of SDLT.

Leases are defined for the purposes of SDLT in Sch 17A para 1 as:
(1) an interest or right in or over land for a term of years (whether fixed or periodic); or
(2) a tenancy at will or other interest or right in or over land terminable by notice at any time.

There will, of course, be situations where it is difficult to distinguish between a contractual licence (a personal right) and a lease (a proprietary right). The important point to note is that the substance of the relevant transaction must be considered – simply calling an agreement a 'licence' does not necessarily mean it is a licence. **[49.32]**

b) *Acquisitions*

Where an existing land interest is transferred it is clear that the transferee acquires the interest. But the scope of chargeable land transactions is wider than transfers. To achieve this, the definition of 'acquisition' is extended (s 43), with corresponding extensions of the concepts of 'vendor' and 'purchaser'. These extensions are as follows, and in each case the person or persons deemed to 'acquire' the interest are specified:

Event	*Deemed acquisition and purchaser*
the creation of an interest	an acquisition by the person becoming entitled to the new interest
the surrender or release of an interest	an acquisition by the person whose interest is benefited or enlarged by the transaction
the variation of an interest (other than a lease)	an acquisition by the person benefiting from the variation

the variation of a lease	an acquisition by the person benefiting from the variation, but only if it takes effect or is treated (for the purposes of SDLT) as a new lease;
	the amount of rent or the term of the lease is reduced; or
	other variations where the lessee provides consideration in money or money's worth (other than an increase in rent) for the variation.

[49.33]

c) *The purchaser*

The purchaser is the person who is responsible for any SDLT and the administrative responsibilities. So, once there is a chargeable land transaction, we must identify the purchaser or purchasers. Based on the extended definition of 'acquisition', the purchaser is the person who acquires the chargeable interest. Four cases identify the purchaser as follows:

Transaction	*Purchaser*	*Example*
Transfer	The transferee	Purchaser of an existing freehold or leasehold interest
Creation	The person becoming entitled to the new interest	The tenant to whom a lease is granted
Surrender	The person whose interest is benefited or enlarged	The landlord when a lease is surrendered
Variation	The person who benefits from the variation	The tenant who pays the landlord to agree to a rent reduction
		The landlord who pays the tenant to reduce the term

But s 43(5) restricts the definition by specifying that a person is only treated as a purchaser if he is a party to the transaction or has given consideration for it. This prevents the owners of land interests related to the subject matter of a land transaction from inadvertently becoming subject to an SDLT charge by virtue of an indirect benefit to their own land interest. But it does not widen the scope of the charge to include everyone who is a party to a land transaction or who provides consideration. A 'purchaser' must 'acquire' a chargeable interest *and* also be a party to the transaction or provide consideration.

[49.34]

d) *The effective date*

For a land transaction the 'effective date' is the trigger to notify and pay tax within 30 days, so it is crucial to identify it. The general rule in s 119 is that the effective date is the date that the transaction is completed. However, different rules apply where a contract is entered into which is to be completed by a conveyance (s 44); this will cover most common transactions involving freehold and leasehold interests where an agreement is normally followed by a later transfer. **[49.35]–[49.36]**

6 Contract and conveyance

a) *The simple case*

Section 44 gives the basic rule where a contract for a land transaction is entered into and is to be completed by a conveyance. The term 'contract' includes any agreement (including an agreement for lease) and 'conveyance' is defined to include any instrument (including a lease). So the rules here cover standard purchases of freehold and leasehold interests and grants of new leases unless they come within the special rules in Sch 17A (considered further below).

Where completion follows a contract for sale, the basic position is as follows:
(i) Completion occurs without an earlier *substantial performance* of the contract
   In this case the contract and conveyance are treated as a single land transaction with the date of completion as the effective date.
(ii) *Substantial performance* occurs before completion.
   Section 44(4) deems there to be a land transaction as if all of the transaction envisaged in the contract had occurred on the date of substantial performance. The effective date is therefore the date of substantial performance.
   The subsequent completion is a separate land transaction and is notifiable in its own right. But it is chargeable only to the extent (if any) that the amount of tax chargeable on it is greater than the amount of tax chargeable on the contract. It will therefore be rare for an additional charge to apply at completion.
   If, after substantial performance, a contract is rescinded or annulled (wholly or partly) then the tax paid can be (proportionately) reclaimed (s 44(9)).
   Agreements for lease are subjected to special treatment in Schedule 17A instead of s 44 and are considered further below.

The statutory definition of substantial performance is contained in s 44(5)–(7). Any of the following are sufficient to trigger substantial performance:
(1) payment of 90% or more of the part of the consideration which is not rent (the statute merely says 'a substantial amount' but HMRC practice is to use 90% or more as their interpretation;
(2) the purchaser (or a connected person) taking possession of the whole, or substantially the whole, of the property, even if this is under a licence;
(3) (in the case of a lease) paying rent;
(4) receiving or becoming entitled to profits or rents derived from the land interest.

So the effective date, and therefore the timing of any tax payment, depends on whether or not substantial performance occurs before completion.

[49.37]

The following example illustrates a simple case of a house sale.

EXAMPLE 49.1

Cook agrees to buy Strauss' house for £300,000. The contract is entered into on 1 January 2018. Collingwood pays a 5% deposit, but does not get the keys to the door until completion that occurs on 1 February 2018.

Because this transaction is completed without previously being substantially performed:

(a) Entering into the contract is not regarded as being a land transaction.
(b) Contract and completion are regarded as a single transaction with the effective date of the transaction being 1 February 2018 (s 44(3)).
(c) Cook must deliver a 'land transaction return' before the end of the period of 30 days after 1 February 2018 (s 76(1)) and must at the same time pay the tax (s 86(1)).
(d) The sale will not be registered at the Land Registry unless a certificate of compliance with the SDLT provisions is produced. A Revenue Certificate will be issued following acceptable filing of the land transaction return.

b) *Pre-completion transactions ('Sub-sales')*

A may contract to sell a property to B, and before completion B contracts to sell to C or assigns his rights under the original contract to C. Both contracts may then be completed by A conveying to C (at B's direction).

The SDLT legislation has historically provided a form of relief for B in this situation under the so-called sub-sale rules. However, due to on-going 'abuse' of this form of relief, FA 2013 substantially re-wrote the rules. Since 17 July 2013 (Royal Assent of FA 2013), the new rules for 'pre-completion transactions' have applied to the types of situation noted above.

For the pre-completion transaction rules to be relevant, there must be a contract for a land transaction within the meaning of FA 2003, s 44. Prior to the 'original contract' being substantially performed or completed, the purchaser under that contract may enter into a further agreement as a result of which another person is entitled to call for the conveyance of all or part of the subject-matter of the original contract. It is this further agreement which is known as a pre-completion transaction.

A pre-completion transaction can be an 'assignment of rights' or a 'free-standing transfer'. The transferee (ie the ultimate purchaser) is not regarded as entering into a land transaction by reason of the pre-completion transaction but the following rules apply:

Assignment of rights

The legislation provides that the transferor (ie the purchaser under the original transaction) enters into a 'notional land transaction' where there is an assignment of rights. The consideration under the notional land transaction is any consideration given under the original contract by either the transferee or the transferor.

Free-standing transfers

Where there is a sub-sale, the legislation adds any consideration given for the pre-completion transaction to the consideration otherwise given by the transferee.

It is not necessary for the legislation to deem the transferor to have entered into a notional land transaction because, if the free-standing transfer is a sub-sale, the original contract will be completed (or substantially performed) so the transferor will be the purchaser under a land transaction as normal.

Relief for the purchaser under the original contract?

Where the transferor (ie the purchaser under the original contract) enters into an assignment of rights or a sub-sale, the new rules make it necessary for the transferor to claim relief from SDLT in a land transaction return. In relation to a sub-sale, the original contract must be substantially performed or completed at the same time as, and in connection with, the substantial performance or completion of the sub-sale contract. The requirement to claim relief in a land transaction return is a key part of the new provisions – this was not previously the case under the old rules, and meant that many aggressive SDLT planning arrangements could not be adequately policed by HMRC.

There are various belt and braces anti-avoidance rules which are intended to stop future misuse of this relief. These include denying relief where it is reasonable to conclude that the transferor had a main purpose of securing an SDLT advantage for any person. Where the parties are connected, there are also rules which require the ultimate purchaser to be liable for SDLT based on a certain minimum consideration.

An example of sub-sale relief is as follows: [49.38]

EXAMPLE 49.2

Lloyd enters into a contract to sell land to Botham for £1m paying a deposit of £100,000. Botham goes into occupation of the land to build a house. Botham then sells his rights under the contract to Atherton for £200,000, and requires Lloyd to convey the land directly to Atherton, who pays the balance of £900,000 to Lloyd. SDLT is triggered by each agreement as follows:

Lloyd and Botham: as a result of Botham's substantial performance of the contract, SDLT is payable by Botham on the consideration of £1m.

Botham and Atherton: Atherton will be liable to SDLT based on (a) the sum paid to Botham for the assignment (£200,000) plus (b) the sum paid to Lloyd to complete the Lloyd/Botham contract (£900,000). SDLT is therefore payable by Atherton on £1.1m.

It should be noted that, if Botham had not gone into occupation of the land (and had not otherwise substantially performed the contract), he could have avoided an SDLT charge on completion of the sub-sale. Under the new rules, this relief would need to be claimed in a land transaction return.

c) *Development agreements providing for sub-sale*

Sections 44A and 45A were introduced by FA 2004 to clarify the SDLT position on certain development contracts. For example, a developer may contract with a landowner such that he will build houses on the land, arrange their sale, and then direct the landowner to convey the relevant parcel of land to the end purchaser. Section 44A ensures that, where there is a contract between A and B under which B may subsequently direct A to convey to C, who is not a party to the initial contract, then B has entered into a land transaction if he substantially performs the contract. If the development proceeds, B obviously will substantially perform since he will take possession of the site to build the houses. Section 45A covers the position when B assigns rights under such a contract to D. This provision is essentially an anti-avoidance provision (introduced by FA 2004) designed to stop developers avoiding an SDLT charge where the parties stop short of entering into a contract of sale to the developer.

What is in some doubt is whether these provisions are restricted to development situations. Section 44A states that a contract merely has to provide for B to have the right to direct A to convey to C, and this is allowed for in many standard contracts. So there is some doubt as to whether ss 44A and 45A apply in only the limited range of circumstances envisaged. However, it seems to be the view of HMRC that in situations where s 44 and s 44A are both capable of applying then s 44 will take precedence. This will leave s 44A and s 45A to apply when B did not have a contract for a land transaction within the scope of s 44 – or at least where it is unclear whether s 44 applies.
[49.39]

7 Options

Options and rights of pre-emption appear to be provided for in s 46. In fact most options to purchase land are covered in the general definition of land transaction and s 46(4) expressly excludes the application of s 46 to options covered elsewhere. The purpose of the section is to bring 'put' options relating to land interests within the scope of SDLT and to remove doubt about options under Scots Law.

The acquisition of an option is a separate land transaction from the subsequent exercise of the option, and has an effective date when it is acquired (rather than when it becomes exercisable).

The acquisition of an option and its exercise (if it is exercised) may well be 'linked' transactions (see below). [49.40]

8 What is chargeable consideration?

a) *The general rule*

The chargeable consideration for a land transaction is defined in Schedule 4. The general rule is that it includes any consideration in money or money's worth given for the subject-matter of the transaction, directly or indirectly, by the purchaser or a person connected with him. Then there are rules about debt, apportionment, exchanges, and extensions to the definition in relation to building services and other services. The special rules are summarised below. [49.41]

b) Special rules

i) Value added tax

Chargeable consideration includes value added tax chargeable in respect of the transaction, so SDLT is a tax that is charged on a tax. VAT is not included in the chargeable consideration if the vendor has not elected to waive the exemption from VAT (under VATA 1994 Sch 10 para 2) prior to the effective date. [49.42]

ii) Postponed consideration

There is no discount where the payment of consideration is postponed. (However, see below for the rules on uncertain consideration.) [49.43]

iii) Just and reasonable apportionment

Where an overall bargain contains more than one land transaction or relates to other matters as well as land transactions, the consideration is to be apportioned on a just and reasonable basis in order to determine the amount of chargeable consideration for the land transaction or land transactions within the bargain. For example, a purchaser may purchase land for a price, and also pay a sum for chattels (which are not part of the land and hence outside the scope of SDLT). However, the sums paid for chattels must not exceed a 'just and reasonable' sum, otherwise SDLT may be due on some or all of these sums (as the sums are, in effect, disguised consideration for the sale of the land). [49.44]

iv) Exchanges

Exchanges of land interests are treated as two land transactions. The general rule is that each party to the exchange is deemed to have paid consideration which is the higher of the actual consideration or the market value of the land interest that it acquires, so long as a major interest in land (a freehold or leasehold) is involved in the exchange. Detailed rules are in Sch 4 para 5. It should be noted that this treatment is less advantageous than that which existed under the old stamp duty regime, where an exchange could be treated as the sale of the more valuable property (hence, only one stamp duty charge arose). [49.45]

v) Partition or division

For land transactions giving effect to a partition or division of a chargeable interest to which persons are jointly entitled, the share of the interest held by a purchaser immediately before the partition or division is disregarded in calculating the chargeable consideration. [49.46]

vi) Non-monetary consideration

Chargeable consideration that is not in the form of cash or debt is generally included at its market value at the effective date of the transaction. [49.47]

vii) Debt as consideration

The rules are in Sch 4 para 8.
  Where chargeable consideration includes:
(1) the satisfaction or release of debt due to the purchaser or owed by the vendor; or
(2) the assumption of existing debt by the purchaser;
     then the amounts of debt satisfied, released or assumed are included in the chargeable consideration for the transaction.
  But, if the effect of this is that the amount of the chargeable consideration for the transaction exceeds the market value of the subject matter of the land transaction, the amount of the chargeable consideration is treated as limited to that value.
  Reference should also be made to the SDLT Manual (SDLTM 04040) which is intended to put 'beyond doubt that there is an assumption of debt by the transferee when the rights or liabilities of any party to the transaction are changed in relation to the debt'. **[49.48]**

viii) Foreign currency

Amounts in foreign currency are converted to sterling by reference to the London closing exchange rate on the effective date of the transaction (unless the parties have used a different rate for the purposes of the transaction).
[49.49]

ix) Carrying out of building works

Generally, the value of works is taken into account as chargeable consideration, calculated on the basis of their open market value. However, there are special rules in Sch 4 para 10 where the whole or part of the consideration for a land transaction consists of the carrying out of works of construction, improvement or repair of a building or other works to enhance the value of land.
  That is, works are not chargeable consideration if:
(1) the works are carried out *after* the effective date of the transaction;
(2) the works are carried out on land acquired or to be acquired by the purchaser, or on any other land held by the purchaser or a connected person; and
(3) it is not a condition of the transaction that the vendor carries them out on the purchaser's behalf.
Where there are two effective dates because the contract was substantially performed before completion, it is sufficient for the works to be carried out after the earlier effective date (para 10(2A)).
  HMRC have given the following example in SDLTM 4060a:

EXAMPLE 49.3

  P Ltd, a construction company, enters into a contract to acquire a plot of land from V Ltd.
  Under the terms of the contract, P Ltd is to pay £1m and to build a new workshop for V Ltd on a plot of land owned by V Ltd in a nearby town.

The cost of constructing the workshop is £750,000.
The chargeable consideration for Stamp Duty Land Tax is £1,750,000.
The relief in Sch 4 para 10 does not apply here because the works are not being carried out on land owned by P Ltd or a person connected with P Ltd. **[49.50]**

x) Provision of services

Where the provision of services (other than building works) is consideration for a land transaction, the value of that consideration is the amount that would have to be paid in the open market to obtain those services. **[49.51]**

xi) Employer-provided accommodation

Schedule 4 para 12 applies where a land transaction is entered into by reason of the purchaser's employment, or that of a person connected with him, if the transaction gives rise to a charge to tax under the ITEPA 2003 Part 3 Chapter 5 (taxable benefits: living accommodation). The cash equivalent chargeable to income tax is added to the consideration for the transaction.
[49.52]

xii) Obligations under a lease

On the grant of a lease, the usual undertakings and obligations of a tenant do *not* comprise chargeable consideration, under the provisions of Sch 17A para 10. Nor does an assignee's taking on of rent or other tenant obligations comprise chargeable consideration (para 17). See the lease section below for more on leases. **[49.53]**

xiii) Reverse premium

A reverse premium (ie value given by the vendor, rather than the purchaser) does not count as chargeable consideration. **[49.54]**

xiv) Indemnity given by purchaser

Where the purchaser agrees to indemnify the vendor in respect of liability to a third party arising from breach of an obligation owed by the vendor in relation to the land that is the subject of the transaction, neither the agreement nor any payment made in pursuance of it counts as chargeable consideration.
[49.55]

c) *Contingent, uncertain or unascertained consideration*

All or part of the consideration for a transaction may be unclear at the effective date. Section 51 provides for this. **[49.56]**

i) *Contingent consideration*

'Contingent' here means that an amount is to be paid or is not to be paid if some uncertain future event occurs. An example is where a plot of land is acquired for a consideration of £1 million, and an additional contingent payment of £1.5 million should planning permission be obtained for an intended development.

In the first place, tax is chargeable on the basis that the contingent amount is paid (or does not cease to be paid). In other words, SDLT is charged on the maximum amount for any contingency or set of contingencies. But see below for the rules on deferment. [49.57]

ii) Uncertain or unascertained consideration

Consideration is defined as 'uncertain' where the amount depends on uncertain future events occurring after the effective date. An example is where a developer buys a plot of land and agrees that he will pay to the vendor an overage payment of a percentage of profits or turnover when the buildings are completed and sold on to third parties. By definition, it is impossible to quantify this amount on the effective date of the transaction, hence it is 'uncertain'.

An 'unascertained' amount is an amount that can in principle be determined at the effective date – it does not depend on future events – but in practice is unknown. For example, the consideration may be based on a set of business accounts to be made up to the day before signing the agreement. Until the accounts have been settled, the amount of consideration is not determined.

In both cases, SDLT is chargeable on the basis of a reasonable estimate of the total consideration that will be paid, subject to the provisions relating to deferment considered below. [49.58]–[49.59]

iii) Adjustments

Section 80 provides for an adjustment where a contingency crystallises, or uncertain or unascertained consideration becomes ascertained. If the effect is to increase liability for SDLT or to make a transaction notifiable (ie if the reasonable estimate was too low), the adjustment or notification must be made as if the effective date was the date of the event that removed the uncertainty. If the adjustment is downwards (ie if the reasonable estimate was too high), the taxpayer is entitled to claim repayment of the overpaid tax. [49.60]

iv) Deferred payment of SDLT

Section 90 provides for a purchaser to apply to HMRC to defer payment of SDLT in respect of contingent or uncertain consideration. An application can only be made in respect of consideration that falls to be paid or provided on one or more future dates of which at least one falls, or may fall, more than six months after the effective date of the transaction.

The rules that HMRC will apply when deciding whether to allow deferments are in the Stamp Duty Land Tax (Administration) Regulations, SI 2003/2837, Part 4 (regs 10–28). See SDLTM 50910. [49.61]

v) Contingent, uncertain or unascertained consideration in the form of rent

The adjustment and deferral provisions do not apply to consideration in the form of rent. See the lease section below for the special rules. **[49.62]**

d) Transfers of land to a connected company

SDLT generally applies to the actual consideration given for a land transaction. For example, gifts do not usually even require a land transaction return to be filed.

However, where the purchaser is a company 'connected' to the vendor, s 53 deems the consideration for a land transaction to be no less than the market value of the land transferred. This is an anti-avoidance provision to prevent a person gifting land into a wholly owned company and then selling the shares in the company to a third party (this would have allowed a vendor to 'package' land into a company, meaning that the purchaser was only liable to stamp duty at 0.5% (or possibly 0% if an offshore company was used) rather than SDLT at up to 4%).

It should be noted that a transfer to a connected company might be subject to a relief (for example, the relief for transfers within corporate groups), in which case the amount of consideration would be irrelevant. **[49.63]**

e) Linked transactions

Linked transactions are defined in s 108 as those which form part of a single scheme, arrangement or series of transactions between the same vendor and purchaser or, in either case, persons connected with them. The purpose of this anti-avoidance rule is to prevent the fragmentation of land deals so as to gain the advantage of lower rates. However, note that since 19 July 2011 it has been possible to claim relief on the acquisition of multiple dwellings. Where the relief applies, the rate of tax which applies is that which would have applied had the dwelling been acquired independently (ie the fact that it is 'linked' to the purchase of other dwellings would not affect the rate of SDLT which applied; see **[49.125]** ff).

EXAMPLE 49.4

A vendor advertises a house with a garden for sale at an asking price of £650,000. Mr and Mrs X are interested in the property and, after negotiations, the purchase is structured so that Mr X buys the house for £500,000 and Mrs X buys the gardens for £100,000.

HMRC will regard these purchases as linked transactions. The rate of tax is determined by reference to the sum of the chargeable considerations (£600,000) and a rate of 4% applies to each land transaction, giving a total tax charge of £24,000. Had it not been for this rule, Mr X would have paid 3% of £500,000 (£15,000) and Mrs X would have paid nothing on her transaction below the £125,000 threshold for residential property.

A circumstance where transactions are linked is where a property portfolio is acquired under a single negotiated deal. This can be contrasted with the position where a number of properties are acquired as separate lots at a public auction. Stamp duty case law established that separately struck deals made in this manner are not regarded as a 'series' of transactions to be aggregated as one transaction. **[49.64]**

9 **Leases**

a) *The charge on a new lease*

What distinguishes the lease regime is that there is an additional charge in relation to the rent that is payable under the lease. SDLT, like the other stamp taxes, makes a single charge when a transaction is carried out (subject to subsequent corrections if some or all of the consideration is uncertain). So, rather than charge the rent paid each year, SDLT charges in relation to the 'net present value' (NPV) of the rent calculated over the whole lease term when the lease is granted (but see below about agreements for lease).

Schedule 5 (as amended) contains the rules for calculating the amount of tax chargeable. Schedule 17A contains further provisions relating to leases.

[49.65]

b) *Tax chargeable on a premium*

When a new lease is granted, SDLT is charged on a premium in accordance with the 'slice' system examined above. For example, if a tenant of a non-residential property gives a premium of over £250,000, then SDLT will be due. There are also anti avoidance provisions where the annual rent for the lease exceeds £1,000: in such cases, there is no zero band for the premium (ie the minimum charge is 1%).

Readers will also note that reverse premiums paid by the landlord to the tenant are not charged (Sch 17A para 18). [49.66]

c) *Tax chargeable on rent*

SDLT also introduced a controversial additional charge on the grant of a lease, chargeable by reference to the 'net present value' (NPV) of the lease. SDLT is due to the extent that the NPV exceeds the relevant threshold (a 'slice' system). The rates and thresholds are as follows (Sch 5 para 2). The detail of the NPV calculation is set out below for completeness; although note that in practice HMRC has provided a calculator on its website which will do the calculation for you.

Table a: residential

Rate bands	*Percentage*
£0 to £125,000	0%
Over £125,000	1%

Table b: non-residential or mixed

Rate bands	*Percentage*
£0 to £150,000	0%
The portion from £150,001 to £5,000,000	1%
The portion above £5,000,000	2%

[49.67]

i) NPV of the rent

How does a taxpayer calculate the NPV of a lease? The NPV is based on totalling the rent over the whole lease term, but with a discount factor that counts a decreasing percentage of the rent for future years. Here is the formal definition from Sch 5 para 3:

Definition of net present value of rent payable over the term of the lease

The net present value of the rent payable over the term of a lease is calculated by applying the formula

$$\text{NPV} = \sum_{i=1}^{n} \frac{r_i}{(1+T)^i}$$

where:

NPV is the net present value.

ri is the rent payable in year i. (However, this is modified by Sch 17A para 7 to substitute for years 6 onwards the maximum rent payable in any 12-month period in the first five years of the lease.)

i is the first, second, third, etc year of the term.

n is the term of the lease.

T is the temporal discount rate, initially set at 3.5% (it seems unlikely that this rate will change, even though Sch 5 para 8 provides a power to do so by regulation).

Thus, the net present value is the total of the net present values of the rents each year.

Whilst the calculation is complex, an SDLT calculator is available on the Stamp Office website (www.hmrc.gov.uk/so) to assist in the calculation of the net present value of rents. Provided that the term and the rents are entered into the calculator, it carries out the complex calculations (see example below) for you.

EXAMPLE 49.5 – A SIMPLE COMMERCIAL LEASE

A lease is granted for a term of four years at a rent of £100,000 a year. VAT is not chargeable. The calculation of NPV is as follows:

Year	Rent	Rent discounted
1	£100,000	£96,618
2	£100,000	£93,351
3	£100,000	£90,194
4	£100,000	£87,144
Total	£400,000	£367,308

Note the following:

The rent for the first year of the lease is discounted. The formula specifies that the rent for year 1 be divided by 1.035, giving the result £96,618.

For year 2, the rent is divided by 1.035 twice. That is to say: £93,351 = £100,000/(1.035 × 1.035).

The NPV for rent in years 3 and 4 is calculated in a similar manner and the four figures totalled to obtain the NPV for the entire lease term as £367,308 (compared with the total undiscounted rent of £400,000).

Since the lease is non-residential, the threshold is £150,000, and only £217,308 of the NPV is chargeable to tax at 1%. This gives a tax charge of £2,173.

EXAMPLE 49.6 – NPV CALCULATION WHERE THE RENT VARIES

A lease has a fixed term of five years, and the rent payable in each year is as follows:

Year 1	£4,000
Year 2	£5,000
Year 3	£6,000
Year 4	£7,000
Year 5	£8,000
Total	£30,000

The net present value of the rental over this period is calculated as follows:

Year 1 4,000/(1+0.035)	£3,864.73
Year 2 5,000/[(1+0.035) × (1+0.035)]	£4,667.55
Year 3 6,000/[(1+0.035) × (1+0.035) × (1+0.035)]	£5,411.65
Year 4 7,000/[(1+0.035) × (1+0.035) × (1+0.035) × (1+0.035)]	£6,100.09
Year 5 8,000/[(1+0.035) × (1+0.035) × (1+0.035) × (1+0.035) × (1+0.035)]	£6,735.78
Total	£26,779.82

The net present value is £26,779, which is below the threshold.   **[49.68]**

ii) Variable or uncertain rents

As already noted, the calculation of NPV on the grant of a lease is based on the pattern of rents over the first five years (rents for the later years in the formula being taken as the maximum rent for any 12-month period within the first five years). Schedule 17A para 7 provides special rules where any rent within the first five years of the lease is uncertain. Except for adjustments in line with the retail prices index, which are ignored, the taxpayer must make a 'reasonable estimate' of any future changes when filing the land transaction return on grant. A second land transaction return is then required, either at the five-year point or earlier if all the uncertainties crystallise earlier.

For example, if a lease has an open market rent review at the end of year three, then the taxpayer must make a reasonable estimate of the rents arising in years 4 and 5 in order to calculate the NPV on the grant of the lease. When the rent review is settled (say at the beginning of year 4), the taxpayer must submit a further land transaction return. Further SDLT may be due, or a refund given, depending on the accuracy of the reasonable estimate.

[49.69]

iii) Increase in rent in first five years

The charge on the NPV of rents was controversial since it greatly exceeded the corresponding stamp duty charge for commercial occupational leases – often by more than a factor of five. The Government therefore became particularly sensitive about avoidance of this aspect of the charge.

The legislation in Sch 17A para 13 provides that where a lease is varied so as to increase the amount of rent as from a date before the end of the fifth year of the term of the lease, the variation is treated as if it were the grant of a lease in consideration of the additional rent made payable by it. However, any increase of rent before the end of the fifth year pursuant to a provision contained in the lease (eg a rent review clause) does not fall within this rule. The term of the deemed lease will be equal to the unexpired residue of the term of the actual lease. If this is seven years or more, then a land transaction return will be required if the rent increase is £1,000 or more (annually). If the term of the deemed lease is less than seven years, then it will only be notifiable if SDLT is actually payable (ie if the net present value of the deemed lease is over the nil rate threshold). **[49.70]–[49.71]**

iv) Assignment of lease treated as grant of lease

The charge on the NPV of rent usually applies only to the grant of a lease. Mindful that a lease for rent might be eligible for a relief or exemption and that it might then be assigned for a small premium (leases at market rent have little capital value), Sch 17A para 11 was introduced to trigger the NPV charge in such a case on the first assignment of a lease which was not covered by a list of specified exemptions. The exemptions in the list include group relief and charities relief (see below).

For example, if A grants a lease at a market rent to a wholly owned subsidiary B and group relief is claimed, and B subsequently assigns the lease to a third party (C) for £1, then C is liable to SDLT as if the lease were granted to him or her – hence, SDLT is due by reference to both the premium and the NPV. **[49.72]**

d) *Surrenders and re-grants*

When an existing lease is surrendered in return for a new lease, Sch 17A para 16 removes the Sch 4 para 5 rules for exchanges and states that the grant is not treated as consideration for the surrender or vice versa.

Paragraph 9 provides that the NPV charge on the new lease is based only on rent in so far as it is additional to rent already taken into account for SDLT purposes on the surrendered lease. This effectively gives a credit for SDLT already paid and is considered below in the context of agreements for lease. It will be apparent that no credit is given if the original lease was subject to the old stamp duty regime – SDLT by reference to a full NPV will be due on the grant of the new lease. **[49.73]–[49.74]**

10 Partnership transactions

a) *Introduction*

Transfers of partnership interests, where the partnership owns 'chargeable interests', are subject to SDLT under a special regime in Part 3 of Sch 15. The new rules stem from HMRC's desire to halt what they considered to be unacceptable SDLT planning involving partnerships.

The detail of the special regime is complex, but broadly applies to three types of transaction:
(1) transfers of a chargeable interest from a partner to a partnership (para 10);
(2) transfers of an interest in a property investment partnership (paras 14, 17, 31, 32);
(3) transfers of a chargeable interest from a partnership to a partner (para 18).

'Partnership' is defined for the purposes of SDLT as including general partnerships within the Partnership Act 1890, limited partnerships within the Limited Partnerships Act 1907, and limited liability partnerships under the Limited Liability Partnerships Act 2000. Entities of a similar character formed under a foreign jurisdiction are also included (para 1).

Further general provisions disregard the legal personality of a partnership (if it has one) and treat its holding of chargeable interests and entering into land transactions as being done by or on behalf of the partners. And partnerships are deemed not to be unit trusts or open-ended investment companies (paras 2–4).

Normal rules apply to land transactions to which the partnership is a party and which do not fall within the three special categories. So an acquisition by a partnership from a vendor who is independent of the partnership is subject to a charge under the normal rules.

The three elements of the special regime apply broadly as follows:
(1) When a partner transfers a chargeable interest to a partnership (or a person transfers a chargeable interest to a partnership in exchange for a partnership share), the SDLT charge is based on a proportion of the market value of the interest. The proportion, expressed as a percentage, is 100 less that partner's percentage share of the partnership after the transaction. In determining the transferor's share after the transaction, the interests of individuals 'connected' with the transferor can be included (the interests of certain corporate trustees 'connected' with the transferor can also be included). So, where the partner owns 100% of a property and transfers it to a partnership in which he or she has a 15% share, he or she is taken to have disposed of 85% of the property to the other partners of the partnership, and 85% of the market value is charged to SDLT.
(2) When a partner transfers an interest in a property investment partnership (viz a partnership whose sole or main activity is investing or dealing in chargeable interests (whether or not that activity involves the carrying out of construction operations on the land in question)) to someone else, the transferee is charged to SDLT on a proportion of the market value of any chargeable interests held by the partnership – that proportion being the acquired proportionate interest in the partnership that has been acquired. Leases for a market rent (with reviews to market rent) and other specified land interests are excluded from the valuation of the land in the partnership for these purposes. (It should be noted that Finance Act 2007 significantly widened the definition of when there is the transfer of a partnership interest – but this appears to have been remedied by the FA 2008 (see below)). The charge on the transfer of an interest in a property investment partnership only applies to transfers of interests in partnerships whose sole or main activity is investing in, dealing in, or developing property (so professional partnerships are excluded).
(3) When a partnership transfers a chargeable interest to a partner or former partner, the SDLT charge is based on a proportion of the market value of the interest. In general terms, the proportion, expressed as a percentage, is 100% less that partner's percentage share of the partnership before the transaction. In determining the partner's share before the transaction, the interests of individuals 'connected' with the partner can be included (the interests of certain corporate trustees 'connected' with the partner can also be included). So, where the

partner has a 15% share in the partnership before the land transfer he is taken to have acquired 85% of the property (since he already effectively held 15%), and 85% of the market value is charged to SDLT.

It is important to note that the legislation (Sch 15 para 34(2)) defines a partnership share as 'the proportion in which he is entitled at that time to share in the income profits of the partnership'. Hence, a partner's entitlement to *capital* profits is irrelevant for the purposes of these rules.

There are various exceptions to the rules considered above. For example, Sch 15 paras 27 and 27A provide that, where a partner (or transferor who receives a partnership interest) transfers a chargeable interest to a partnership within the meaning of (1) above, the SDLT charge may be reduced by reference to interests held by other corporate partners in the same group as the transferor. This is subject to clawback provisions should the parties cease to be associated within three years.

EXAMPLE 49.7

A and B establish a partnership, each making a capital contribution of £1 million. So each has a 50% interest. A owns a property with a market value of £0.5 million and this is to be transferred to the partnership in one of two possible ways.

(i) A transfers the land to the partnership and receives cash consideration of £0.5 million.

In this case A would not have a larger share of the partnership after the transaction since the cash he has received matches the capital item he has transferred.

SDLT is charged in respect of a total of £250,000, which is 50% of the market value on the basis that A in effect retains 50% of the property by virtue of his 50% partnership interest.

(ii) A transfers the land to the partnership and receives no cash consideration, but his partnership share is adjusted to allow for the fact that he has contributed a total of £1.5 million to the partnership whereas B contributed £1 million. After the transaction, therefore, A has a 60% interest.

SDLT is charged on 40% of the £0.5 million market value (£200,000) on the basis that after the transaction, A in effect retains 60% of the property.

After the position reached by (ii), C buys A's partnership interest for £1.5 million.

This is deemed to be a land transaction. The chargeable consideration is taken to be 60% (the partnership interest acquired) of the market value of the land held by the partnership (£0.5 million), that is to say £300,000.

Exemptions and reliefs generally apply to partnership transactions – in some cases with amended wording to explain the detailed application of a relief (para 25).

There is also an anti-avoidance provision that provides that a withdrawal of money other than income profit by a partner within three years of his transferring land into a partnership is subject to a charge as a deemed land transaction (para 17A).

Finally, a stamp duty charge is not removed from documents transferring partnership interests (Sch 15 paras 31–33). It seems that the aim is to protect the 0.5% stamp duty charge where the property of the partnership consists largely of UK equities. The stamp duty charge does not exceed the charge to stamp duty that a transfer of the underlying stock and marketable securities would incur.

b) *Finance Acts 2007 and 2008*

It should be noted that FA 2007 significantly widened the potential for SDLT charges with regard to transfers of interests in property investment partnerships. This was a result of the extension of the definition of what constitutes the transfer of an interest in a property investment partnership. After FA 2007, any change in the income-sharing ratios of a partnership amounts to the transfer of an interest in that partnership – a very wide definition. It is of course very common for income-sharing ratios for change as new investors arrive and old investors retire, when profit 'hurdles' are reached and certain partners receive an increased income share etc. Due to extensive lobbying by the industry, the Government accepted that changes needed to be made.

How did FA 2008 seek to remedy these problems? The first point to note is that the definition of 'transfer of an interest in a property investment partnership' remains in its wide state – ie it will continue to include changes in income-sharing ratios. The main change was to the definition of what is 'relevant partnership property'. Prior to FA 2008, 'relevant partnership property' meant, broadly, all land held by the partnership 'immediately after the transfer' of the partnership interest. So, if A and B were equal partners in a partnership which owned land with a value of £1m, and A transferred its 50% partnership interest to C, then SDLT was due by reference to 50% of the 'relevant partnership property' – ie the value of the land held immediately after the transfer to C (50% of £1m in this example). FA 2008 now creates a distinction between 'Type A' transfers and 'Type B' transfers. Where the transfer is a 'Type A' transfer, the existing rules continue to apply. However, if the transfer is a 'Type B' transfer, then a more generous regime applies. In general terms, the transfer of a partnership interest will be a 'Type A' transfer where an existing partner's interest is acquired for *consideration in money or money's worth* by another person, or where a new partner joins, an existing partner leaves and the exiting partner *withdraws money or money's worth* from the partnership. Every other transfer is a Type B transfer.

Crucially, any transfer for *no consideration* will be a Type B transfer. This means that a gift of a partnership interest will be a Type B transfer. Similarly, an incoming partner who becomes entitled to a proportion of the partnership's income (in exchange for subscribing for an appropriate amount of partnership capital only) should also result in a Type B transfer – this is on the assumption that no other 'consideration' is being paid to any outgoing partner or a partner whose share reduces. Clearly, whether 'consideration' is being provided is a critical question, and it is hoped that HMRC will produce guidance to clarify its view of this area in due course.

The benefit of having a Type B transfer is that a Type B SDLT computation ignores land which is acquired in certain circumstances, so that no SDLT is due in respect of that land. This includes:

- land whose transfer to the partnership did not fall within para 10(1)(a), (b) or (c) of Sch 15 to FA 2003;
- land in respect of whose transfer to the partnership an election has been made under para 12A of Sch 15 to FA 2003 (see below);
- land that was transferred to the partnership on or before 22 July 2004;
- land that is not attributable economically to the interest in the partnership that is transferred.

So, if a partnership acquires land and pays full SDLT on its acquisition, the land can be ignored where there is a Type B transfer. This would appear to solve some of the problems faced by property investment partnerships.

It will be noted that if land has been put into the partnership and relief claimed under 'paragraphs 10(1)(a), (b) or (c)', then the benefits of Type B cannot be claimed. This will broadly be the case where a *partner* transfers land to a partnership or where a person transfers land into a partnership in exchange for a partnership interest. As noted above, the para 10 calculation, whilst on the face of it exceedingly complicated, normally subjects the partnership to SDLT by reference to the proportion of property 'given away' by the partner/incoming partner who contributes the land. This means that a partner/incoming partner who retains a 99% interest in a partnership will not usually crystallise a material SDLT charge when the land is contributed. The logic here is clear: if a person has not paid SDLT on the full market value of land which they have put into a partnership, then the benefits of Type B transfer of partnership interests are not available.

It follows that, if full market value SDLT is paid where land is contributed by a partner/incoming partner, then the benefits of Type B apply. This can be achieved under the new para 12A – this simply allows the partner/incoming partner to elect that SDLT will be paid on the full market value of the land contributed.

HMRC guidance is still awaited in relation to when the land is not 'attributable economically' to the interest in the partnership transferred.

Finally, it should be noted that HMRC has introduced a further anti-avoidance rule. Where the targeted anti-avoidance rule in FA 2003 s 75A applies (see below), then the rules providing for relief from SDLT on a contribution into a partnership do not apply. The rule is rather unsatisfactory, in that where it applies, the precise SDLT analysis on a contribution to a partnership is unclear. Taxpayers would be best advised to seek a non-statutory clearance from HMRC where there is doubt about the correct tax treatment. [49.75]

11 Exemptions and reliefs

Under stamp duty, many of the reliefs were subject to 'adjudication' that required the taxpayer to submit the relevant documents and claim the relief. Adjudication of a relief gave certainty, usually fairly quickly. In contrast, under SDLT the taxpayer has to self assess and enter a code in the relevant box in the land transaction return if he considers that he is entitled to a relief. Provided that the land transaction return is ostensibly in order, HMRC will issue an SDLT certificate to the taxpayer (it operates a 'process now, check later' system). HMRC has a period of nine months during which it can open an enquiry and challenge the availability of the relief.

[49.76]–[49.77]

a) *Group relief*

This corresponds to the relief available under the old stamp duty rules under FA 1930 s 42 and provides for exemption from SDLT for transfers of properties between companies within a group. Companies are members of the same group if one is the 75% subsidiary of the other, or both are 75% subsidiaries

of a third company. A company (company A) is the 75% subsidiary of another company (company B) if company B:
(i) is beneficial owner of not less than 75% of the ordinary share capital of company A;
(ii) is beneficially entitled to not less than 75% of any assets available for distribution to equity holders of company A; and
(iii) would be beneficially entitled to not less than 75% of any assets of company A available for distribution to its equity holders on a winding up.

Group relief is not available if at the time of the land transaction there are 'arrangements' in existence by virtue of which any person could obtain control of the purchaser but not the vendor. Further, relief will not be available if the transaction is part of 'arrangements' under which (a) the consideration for the transaction is to be provided (directly or indirectly) by a person other than a group company (although financing from a third party bank is usually acceptable); or (b) the vendor and purchaser are to cease to be members of the same group by reason of the purchaser ceasing to be a 75% subsidiary of the vendor or a third company.

FA 2005 introduced a further test for group relief to apply. This is that there must be a *bona fide* commercial motive and that avoidance of tax (including stamp duty, income tax, corporation tax and capital gains tax) is not a main motive.

The relief is subject to a clawback if certain corporate events occur within three years of the effective date of the transaction or under arrangements entered into before the end of the three-year period. These include the transferee company leaving the group while it or a relevant associated company holds the chargeable interest and certain cases when control of the transferee changes following successive transactions eligible for group relief.

FA 2008 did contain a material amendment to these claw-back rules. It has always been the case that, if A transfers land to B and group relief is validly claimed, when A (ie the transferor) leaves the group, this does not give rise to any SDLT clawback. This is consistent with the policy objective noted above, as the land remains in the same economic group and hence it would be inequitable to levy an SDLT charge in these circumstances. However, HMRC became aware of certain 'schemes' which were designed to avoid the claw-back rules by utilising this 'carve-out'. It was argued that, where the transferor left the group first (or was liquidated), a subsequent de-grouping of the transferee did not give rise to an SDLT charge. The argument was therefore that A could sell land to a newly incorporated sister company B, A could be liquidated and B could then be sold to a third party without SDLT claw-back. FA 2008 sought to fill any perceived gap in the legislation by providing that, if there is a change in control of the purchaser after the vendor leaves the group, then the claw-back rules continue to apply. The legislation provides that there is a change of control of the purchaser where a person who controls the purchaser (alone or with others) ceases to do so, a person obtains control of the purchaser (alone or with others) or the purchaser is wound up.

Unfortunately, the legislation has much wider ramifications than may at first appear to be the case. What if a group transfers land from one company to another as part of an internal reorganisation and then liquidates the transferor? This is an entirely common scenario, as the group may not wish to leave a redundant company in its group; however, this would lead to a clawback of the relief if the acquiring entity was ever sold to a third party. Representations were made to the Government during the passage of Finance Bill 2008, but the only concession is that the clawback will not apply where there is a change in control of the purchaser because a loan creditor obtains control of, or ceases to control the purchaser, and the other persons who controlled the purchaser before that change continue to do so.

HMRC have published administrative and technical guidance including a description of how they will interpret the group relief rules and in particular the 'arrangements' test in *Tax Bulletin* 70 which is available on the HMRC website (largely derived from SP 3/98 which provides equivalent guidance in relation to stamp duty). [49.78]

b) *Reconstruction and acquisition reliefs*

These reliefs (s 62, Sch 7 Part 2) match those available for stamp duty under FA 1986 s 75 or 76 as follows:
(1) Reconstruction relief provides a full exemption from SDLT where a land transaction is in connection with a scheme of reconstruction of the 'target' company in exchange for non-redeemable shares and, possibly, the assumption or discharge of liabilities of the target company by the 'acquiring' company.
(2) Acquisition relief reduces the rate of SDLT to 0.5% where the land transaction is entered into in connection with the acquisition of an undertaking of the target company in exchange for non-redeemable shares or for such shares and cash up to 10% of the nominal value of the shares and also, possibly, the assumption or discharge of liabilities of the target company by the 'acquiring' company.

Both reliefs are subject to the motive test as for group relief and may be withdrawn in the following circumstances:
(1) The transferee company leaves the group within three years of the effective date of the transaction (or under arrangements entered into before the end of the three-year period) while still holding an interest in property (or an interest derived from it) which it held at the date of the transaction.
(2) There is a change of control of the transferee company within three years of the effective date of the transaction (or under arrangements entered into before the end of the three-year period) while still holding an interest in property (or an interest derived from it) which it held at the date of the transaction. [49.79]–[49.80]

c) *Multiple dwellings acquisitions*

Where interests in more than one dwelling are acquired, relief may apply to reduce the rate of tax which applies to the transaction. Where it applies, the rate of SDLT which applies is calculated by reference to the consideration divided by the number of dwellings (ie the mean consideration), subject to a minimum rate of 1%. The policy intention of this was to encourage investment in the residential sector, primarily the private rented sector. However, note that the new additional 3% rate can apply when calculating the rate of relief available (unless the property is not considered to comprise 'dwellings', like purpose-built student accommodation). This has made the relief much less valuable on the purchase of residential property portfolios, and means that on the purchase of six or more dwellings it will often be more valuable to simply account for SDLT at the non-residential/mixed use rate of SDLT (see Section 4 above).

The relief can be claimed where there is a 'relevant transaction'. This is either a transaction, the main subject matter of which includes interests in more than one dwelling or a transaction which is one of a number of linked transactions (where the transaction and the linked transactions are dwellings). Significantly, a superior interest (eg a freehold or headlease) over a property which includes dwellings is treated as if it were an interest in the dwellings. However, the superior interest does not qualify for the relief if it is subject to a lease in excess of 21 years (again, reflecting the policy objective that the relief is aimed at investment in the private rented sector, where leases are shorter).

For example, if the freehold of a purpose built student accommodation block is purchased for £2.5m (where none of the leases are subject to long leases) the SDLT would be as follows:
- this is a relevant transaction as there is more than one dwelling in the property;
- the freehold is treated as if it were an interest in each of the dwellings;
- the consideration divided by the number of flats is £125,000. This is below the 2% residential threshold of £125,000, although the minimum rate of tax under this relief is 1%. So the SDLT due is 1% of £2.5m = £25,000.

There are clawback provisions in the event that the number of dwellings changes in the three years after the effective date of the transaction. **[49.81]**

d) *Exemptions under Schedule 3*

Whereas the reliefs considered in (a)–(c) and (e) have to be claimed in a land transaction return (which is submitted to HMRC), the exemptions under Sch 3 do not give rise to an SDLT charge and do not need to be notified to HMRC. The exemptions include:

Exempt land transactions (under Schedule 3)	*Statutory reference*
Gifts (transactions where there is no chargeable consideration)	s 50, Sch 3, para 1
Certain grants of leases by registered social landlord	Sch 3, para 2
Transactions in contemplation of or in connection with divorce or separation	Sch 3, para 3
Variation of testamentary dispositions, etc	Sch 3, para 4

Care should be taken in relation to gifts of land to companies which are 'connected' to the transferor, since a market value consideration will be imputed in this case (s 53). The exemption would not therefore apply in such situations unless the market value of the land was nil. **[49.82]**

e) *Other reliefs*

A land transaction return is needed for these other reliefs (if the transaction would have been notifiable, absent the relief).

Reliefs	Statutory reference
Leaseback element of sale and leaseback	s 57A
Certain acquisitions of residential property	s 58A, Sch 6A
Part-exchange (house building company)	s 58A, Sch 6A
Acquisition by property trader	s 58A, Sch 6A
Re-location of employment	s 58A, Sch 6A
Transfers involving multiple dwellings	s 58D, Sch 6B
Compulsory purchase facilitating development	s 60
Compliance with planning obligations	s 61
Group relief	s 62, 126, Sch 7, Part 1
Reconstruction relief	s 62, Sch 7, Part 2, paras 7, 9–13
Acquisition relief (tax limited to 0.5%)	s 62, 127, Sch 7, Part 2, paras 8–13
Demutualisation of insurance company	s 63
Demutualisation of building society	s 64
Incorporation of limited liability partnership	s 65, Sch 15
Transfers involving public bodies	s 66
Transfer in consequence of reorganisation of parliamentary constituencies	s 67
Charities	s 68, Sch 8
Acquisition by bodies established for national purposes	s 69
Right to buy transactions	s 70, Sch 9
Registered social landlords	s 71
Alternative property finance	ss 72, 73
Collective enfranchisement by leaseholders (does not apply in Scotland) – this relief is widened by FA 2009	s 74
Crofting community right to buy (applies in Scotland only)	s 75
Private Finance Initiative (PFI) transactions	Sch 4, para 17

[49.83]

g) *Clawbacks*

Four reliefs are subject to clawbacks if 'disqualifying events' occur within three years. For group relief, clawback is potentially triggered by corporate-level events that de-group the purchaser (see the earlier discussion of the scope of this clawback in 'Partnership transactions' at **[49.75]** above). For acquisition and reconstruction reliefs, change of control of the purchaser can cause a clawback. And for charities relief the clawback may result from loss of charitable status or a disqualifying change of use of the land by the purchaser. If a disqualifying event occurs a land transaction return is required within 30 days. **[49.84]**

12 Anti-avoidance

a) *Section 75A*

Section 75A introduced, with effect from 6 December 2006, wide anti-avoidance rules for SDLT purposes. The new rules apply where:
(i) a vendor (V) disposes of a chargeable interest, and another person (P) acquires either it or an interest in land deriving from it;
(ii) a number of transactions (including the disposal and acquisition) are involved in connection with the disposal and acquisition ('the scheme transactions'); and
(iii) the sum of the amounts of SDLT payable in respect of the scheme transactions is less than the amount that would be payable on a 'notional land transaction' effecting the acquisition of V's chargeable interest by P on its disposal by V.

If the section applies, the scheme transactions are disregarded, and SDLT is payable on the notional transaction by reference to 'the largest amount (or aggregate amount) given or received by or on behalf of any one person in respect of the scheme transactions'.

For example, the rules are designed to counter:
(i) 'lease break' arrangements. This may involve V granting a long lease to an unconnected nominee (the lease containing a landlord's break clause). V sells the freehold reversion to P for a nominal amount. P then pays V a large sum to break the lease;
(ii) variations to the 'lease-break' arrangements described above. For example, V grants a long lease to an unconnected nominee and V sells the freehold reversion to P for a nominal amount. P pays V a large sum to vary the lease to insert a break clause; P then pays V a nominal sum to break the lease;
(iii) arrangements involving SDLT 'sub-sale' relief. For example, V contracts to sell property to a Subco of P. Subco declares a dividend in specie of the property to P. The contracts are completed and the property transferred to P.

It is not overstating the case to say that this is a fairly ground-breaking piece of legislation, certainly in the SDLT context. Whereas, previously, HMRC had been content to introduce specific anti-avoidance legislation at either Pre-Budget Report or Budget time to counteract 'schemes' it became aware of, s 75A is an attempt to stop any future 'schemes' in their tracks.

Section 75A has caused a significant amount of concern, given the wide-ranging nature of the provisions. After representations from the industry, HMRC did enact ss 75B and 75C, which are intended to remove many common transactions from the ambit of the anti-avoidance rule. For example, a business sale will often include the transfer of various assets including goodwill, premises, stock, employees etc, and a buyer will be liable to SDLT in relation to the part of the consideration attributable to the premises. The original s 75A appeared to change this position so that SDLT was due by reference to the entire consideration paid by the buyer, even the consideration which was not attributable to the land; this is not now the case. **[49.85]**

b) *High Value Residential Property: 15% SDLT, the Annual Tax on Enveloped Dwellings ('ATED') and CGT changes*

In the Government's consultative document on *Modernising Stamp Duty* published in 2002, the proposal was made that transfers of interests in 'land-rich' entities should be subject to an SDLT charge on the proportion of the underlying land that was effectively transferred. The issue, highlighted by the press in the context of the sale and purchase of companies owning homes in expensive areas of London, was simply that the sale of shares in a non-UK incorporated company will not usually give rise to a stamp duty or SDLT charge (unlike the sale of the underlying property directly). However, the proposal was not implemented.

However, the issue gained new momentum in the Emergency Budget in June 2010, which stated that the Coalition Government would:

'examine whether further changes to the rules on stamp duty land tax on high value property transactions are needed to prevent avoidance in this area.'

The following measures have now been introduced:
(1) a new rate of 15% SDLT for acquisitions of dwellings with a value in excess of £500,000 by companies and certain other 'non-natural' persons. There are various reliefs for genuine businesses (as the rules are intended to catch owner occupiers only who hold their properties in companies). The legislation includes reliefs for genuine property developers, landlords and traders;
(2) an 'annual charge' for companies and certain other 'non-natural' persons' holding dwellings with a value in excess of £1m. This is known as the 'Annual Tax on Enveloped Dwellings' ('ATED') and applies from 1 April–31 March each year. For the year from April 2017–31 March 2018, the rates are:

Property Value	£500,000 to £1m	£1m to £2m	£2m to £5m	£5m to £10m	£10m to £20m	Greater than £20m
Annual Charge	£3,500	£7,050	£23,550	£54,950	£110,100	£220,350

Again, there are various reliefs for genuine businesses (as the rules are intended to catch owner occupiers only who hold their properties in companies). A self-assessment return must be completed each year (including if a relief is to be claimed).

It should be noted that the relevant value of the property at present is the value at April 2012. This value then fixes the ATED from April 2013 until April 2018 (so a property worth £4.95m in April 2012 would be in the £23,550 ATED bracket for 2017–18, even if its value has increased to more than £5m in the meantime). For the five years from April 2018, the ATED will be based on the value of the property at April 2017;
(3) the loss of the capital gains tax exemption for non-resident companies and certain other non-natural persons where a dwelling with a value over £2m is disposed of. This change came into force for disposals by non-resident companies after April 2013, although it only applies to gains arising from April 2013 (so there is effectively a 're-basing' to April 2013 for the purposes of the new charge). Again, there are various reliefs for genuine businesses (as the rules are intended to catch owner occupiers only who

hold their properties in companies). Although outside the scope of this chapter, the Government also introduced a new CGT charge for *all* non-resident investors in UK residential property with effect from April 2015.

The policy aim of the Government is clear: it wishes to stop individuals holding high-value homes in companies and other 'non-natural' entities (so-called 'enveloping') as this may allow the property to be disposed of SDLT free in some cases (by virtue of selling the shares in the company/entity rather than the property). **[49.86]**

c) *Disclosure of Tax Avoidance Scheme ('DOTAS') rules*

SDLT was originally excluded from the original DOTAS rules; however, SDLT has been brought within the ambit of the rules with effect from 1 August 2005. In general terms, the rules oblige 'promoters' of arrangements designed to avoid to notify HMRC. HMRC will then provide the 'promoter' with a scheme reference number which the taxpayer will then need to use to notify HMRC. The intention of the legislation is for HMRC to get an 'early warning' about arrangements that it may consider objectionable.

A 'scheme' must be disclosed if:
- its use might be expected to give rise to a 'tax advantage';
- that tax advantage is the main benefit, or one of the main benefits, that might be expected to arise from using the scheme; and
- the arrangements are prescribed in regulations.

SDLT is prescribed in regulations where the land includes commercial property, where the aggregate value of the commercial property element is at least £5m and none of the exceptions apply (see below). Since 1 April 2010, the disclosure rules have also caught residential property with a value over £1m.

HMRC has made it clear that the rules are not limited to new and innovative tax-planning schemes. They catch any arrangement where SDLT is mitigated.

Since the ambit of the new legislation is so wide, the regulations include a 'white list' of matters that do not need to be disclosed. This white list contains six steps (A–F). You do not therefore need to disclose arrangements comprising one or more of:
- Step A: the transfer of land to a company created for the purpose ('a special purpose vehicle');
- Step B: claims to relief: sale and leaseback relief, group relief and most other reliefs (but oddly not including sub-sale relief);
- Step C: the sale of shares in a special purpose vehicle which holds land to an unconnected purchaser;
- Step D: not exercising the election to waive exemption from VAT;
- Step E: arranging the transfer of a business in such a way that it is a transfer of a going concern for VAT purposes;
- Step F: the creation of a partnership to which land is transferred.

Although arrangements are excluded from the disclosure rules if they comprise one or more of Steps A to F, this is subject to two provisos.

First, the arrangements must not include any step not in the white list that is necessary for the purpose of securing a tax advantage. Significantly, sub-sale relief is not included in the white list, so any of the steps in the list coupled with a sub-sale transaction would give rise to a requirement to disclose.

Second, certain combinations of steps are not excluded from the disclosure rules. That is, arrangements that include all or at least two of Steps A, C and D or involve more than one instance of A, C or D. This means, for example, that while the transfer of property to a company and a sale of shares in a property company considered independently do not give rise to a disclosure requirement because both are listed, the use of both in the same sequence of transactions must be disclosed. [49.87]

Who must make the disclosure?

It is usually the 'promoter' who must disclose the scheme to HMRC. If the 'promoter' of the scheme cannot disclose the matter to HMRC due to legal professional privilege (as will usually be the case for a firm of solicitors) then it is the client who must notify HMRC, unless the client waives the right to privilege. There is a strict time limit in relation to notification, which is usually five days from the date on which the 'promoter' makes a proposal available for implementation, or the date on which the 'promoter' first becomes aware of any transaction forming part of the arrangements. [49.88]

Recent developments

As noted above, with effect from 1 April 2010, the ambit of the disclosure rules were extended to include arrangements where the subject matter is residential property (with a market value of at least £1m) or mixed use property where the subject matter of the arrangements contains non-residential property with a market value of at least £5m and/or residential property with a market value of at least £1m. The rules have also been amended so that certain schemes involving 'sub-sale' relief, which previously did not have to be disclosed under the so-called 'grandfathering' rules, now have to be disclosed.

FA 2014 also contained additional powers for HMRC to tackle what the Government considers to be unacceptable tax schemes. For example, HMRC will be able to issue so-called 'Follower' Notices on taxpayers who have taken part in arrangements which are similar to those of another taxpayer who has 'lost' in the courts. The rules are intended to remove the timing benefit for those who have taken part in such schemes, as the Notices will force them to account upfront for the tax in dispute. Similarly, taxpayers who have made DOTAS disclosures may be forced to account for tax upfront. These rules are controversial as they give significant discretion to HMRC to assess SDLT upfront unilaterally without having to take a taxpayer to the Tax Tribunal. Together with the new general anti-avoidance rule (GAAR, which has effect from 17 July 2013 (Royal Assent of FA 2013)) HMRC now has very extensive and sophisticated weaponry to tackle artificial SDLT avoidance schemes. [49.89]

13 Administration

If a land transaction is notifiable (s 77), it is necessary to file a land transaction return and pay any tax due (s 76). The land transaction return comprises form SDLT1 together with SDLT2, SDLT3 and SDLT4 as appropriate (copies can be obtained from HMRC or submitted online). This requirement to render land transaction returns is also linked to the process of land registration since, for a notifiable transaction, a Revenue Certificate is needed for the purposes of registration of the land interest.

Even when HMRC has issued a certificate, it has a period of nine months after the filing date to open an enquiry into the land transaction return – longer in the case of non-disclosure, negligence, etc (s 78, Sch 10).

The legislation, as amended by Finance Act 2008 now provides that the following are notifiable:
(1) an acquisition of a 'major interest' (ie a leasehold or freehold interest) which does not fall within one of the exceptions in s 77A of the Finance Act 2003;
(2) an acquisition of a chargeable interest other than a major interest where the chargeable consideration results in SDLT being due (or being due but for a relief).

The exceptions set out in s 77A (inserted by FA 2008) include the following:
(1) any of the exemptions in Sch 3 to the Finance Act 2003 (see above);
(2) a transaction (other than the grant, assignment or surrender of a lease) involving residential or non-residential land where the chargeable consideration for the transaction (including 'linked transactions') is less than £40,000;
(3) the grant of a lease for a term of seven years or more where:
    – the chargeable consideration other than rent is less than £40,000; and
    – the annual rent is less than £1,000;
(4) the assignment or surrender of a lease where:
    – the lease was originally granted for a term of seven years or more;
    – the chargeable consideration for the assignment or surrender other than rent is less than £40,000; and
    – the rent is less than £1,000;
(5) the grant, assignment or surrender of a lease for a term of less than seven years where the chargeable consideration does not exceed the zero rate threshold.

Schedule 10 Part 2 establishes a duty for purchasers to keep and preserve records relating to a land transaction return for at least six years. There is a corresponding requirement in Sch 11 Part 2 in relation to self-certificates.

[49.90]

14 Transitional provisions

Land transactions may or may not be 'SDLT transactions' to which SDLT rather than stamp duty applies under the transitional provisions set out in Sch 19. HMRC Stamp Taxes produced the following flowchart to indicate whether a transaction attracts SDLT. Royal Assent of FA 2003 was on 10 July 2003 and implementation of SDLT was on 1 December 2003.

The main categories of document which are executed on or after 1 December 2003 but which are still subject to stamp duty rather than SDLT are:
(1) Conveyance executed to complete a contract for sale executed before 11 July 2003, without any variation of the contract or intervening assignment of rights or subsale or exercise of an option, etc.
(2) Leases granted in conformity with agreements for lease executed before 11 July 2003 without any variation, etc.

These circumstances are by now unusual. However, there are still a reasonable number of agreements for lease in relation to new developments where the lease will only be granted on completion of the building works. Even for these, if material variations in the agreement are made the subsequent grant of the lease will fall within SDLT. The other circumstance where stamp duty applies in practice is where granting of the lease has been overlooked – landlord and tenant having had no legal difficulties in relying on the agreement for lease – and a formal grant becomes desirable.

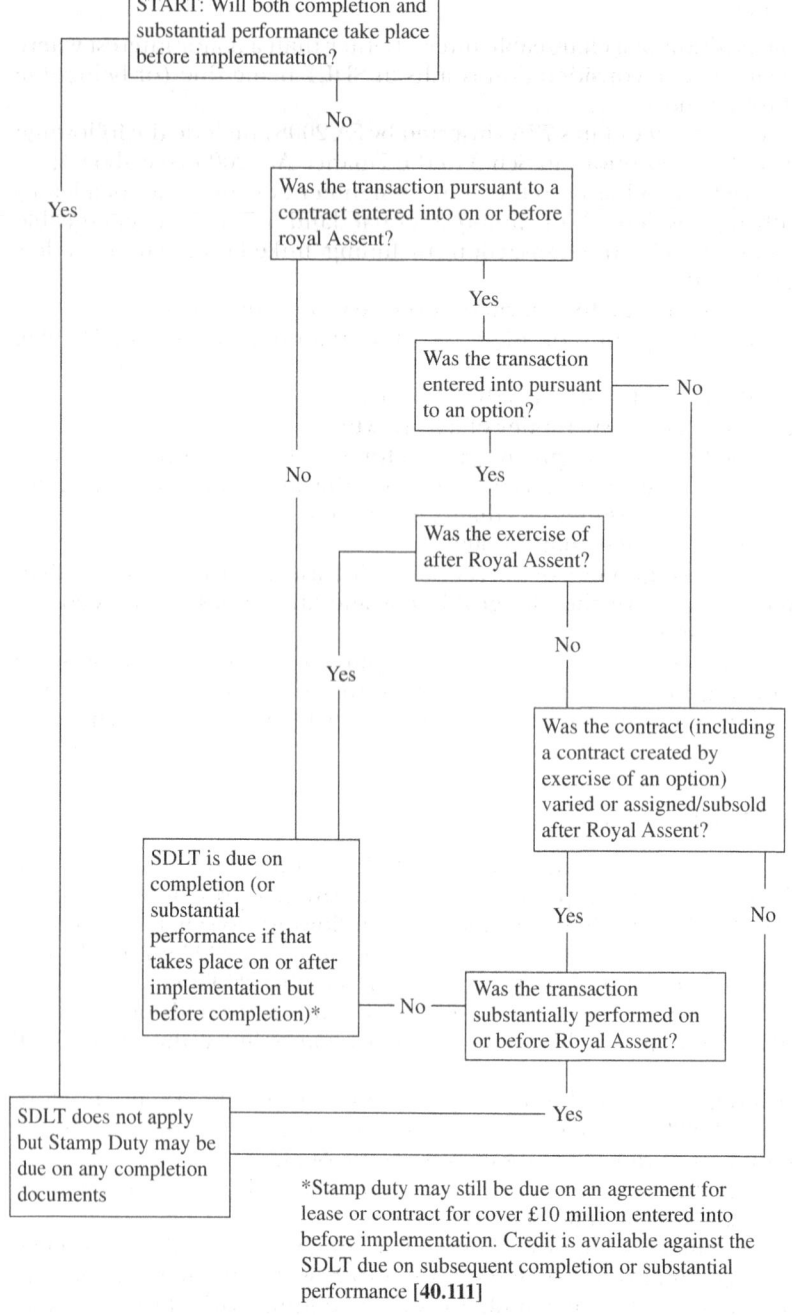

[49.91]

III STAMP DUTY RESERVE TAX (SDRT)

FA 1986 introduced SDRT to protect the revenue as the trading of shares entered the electronic age. SDRT is a mandatory tax with modern enforcement provisions charged on the transferee whenever there is an *agreement* to transfer shares within the scope of the tax. It is aimed at transactions rather than instruments. But stamp duty on *instruments* transferring shares remained (and remains) in place. A double charge to both taxes is prevented since the liability to SDRT is removed if an instrument transferring the relevant shares is duly stamped within six years of a transaction. This also provides continued access to certain reliefs against stamp duty that have not been replicated in the SDRT provisions. Other than for deals carried out on Stock Exchanges and settled electronically, it is generally necessary to submit stock transfer documents for stamping to enable the registration of changes in legal ownership of shares in private companies or in the subsidiaries of public companies.

A reform envisaged in FA 1990 would have removed both stamp duty and SDRT from all transactions in shares to coincide with the introduction of paperless dealing under the Stock Exchange's planned share transfer system ('Taurus'). In the event the collapse of Taurus meant that the charge on shares was left in place. By the time the replacement system, Crest, went live in 1996, the political desire to abolish this source of revenue had waned and the Crest system automatically collects SDRT on share transactions that it settles electronically.

The statutory provisions for SDRT (mostly in FA 1986 Part 4) ensure that the substantial revenues from stamp taxes on UK shares continue to be paid. SDRT imposes a charge on the transferee whenever there is an agreement to transfer chargeable securities (FA 1986 s 87) with modern administrative, compliance, and enforcement procedures (SI 1986/1711). There is a separate SDRT regime for surrenders of units in UK unit trusts and shares in open-ended investment companies (OEICS) (FA 1999 Sch 19).

But, with the important exception of those who play a direct role in the financial markets, most taxpayers need take little notice of SDRT. This is because stamp duty applies to documents that transfer shares and the vast bulk of off-market share transactions require a stamped stock transfer form to enable registration of the change in legal ownership. And a number of important reliefs can only be obtained by claiming stamp duty relief on a transfer document. A stamped transfer document removes the SDRT charge on the associated agreement (FA 1986 s 92) or allows the reclaim of SDRT already paid.

This Part describes SDRT as it applies to market transactions where no physical document is required and to the relevant minority of non-market transactions. The next Part describes stamp duty which, in its shrunken form, now only applies to documents relating to stock and marketable securities.

[49.92]–[49.100]

1 **The basics**

a) *Territorial scope*

SDRT applies wherever agreements are made or effected, ie whether or not the transaction is effected in the UK and any party is resident or situated in the UK (FA 1986 s 86(4)). [49.101]

b) The principal charge

SDRT is a charge on agreements to transfer stocks and shares issued by UK incorporated companies. Securities issued by a Societas Europaea (SE) (a new European company created by Council Regulation (EC) 2157/2001, 8 October 2001) are within the scope of the charge if the SE has its registered office in the UK, irrespective of where the SE was incorporated.

The principal charge (FA 1986 s 87) applies when A agrees with B to transfer 'chargeable securities' (defined in detail in FA 1986 s 99(3) onwards), whether or not to B, for a consideration in money or money's worth and is charged at 0.5% of consideration. The principal charge is cancelled if an instrument of transfer covering those securities is executed in pursuance to the agreement and duly stamped within a period of six years (FA 1986 s 92). B is liable to the tax though others, such as the broker who arranges the deal, may also be accountable under administrative regulations.

The definition of chargeable securities includes interests in or rights arising out of stocks, shares or loan capital. So transfers of derivative financial instruments are within the scope of the tax, though the issue of a derivative will not trigger the principal charge; nor will there be a charge if a derivative contract is settled by a cash payment.

The SDRT charge does not apply to securities that are exempt from all stamp duties (FA 1986 s 99(5)) this includes gilt-edged securities and other loan capital exempt under FA 1986 s 79, see [**49.124**]); nor to stock or securities subject to charge under the bearer head of stamp duty (FA 1999 Sch 15).

Since 1996 the electronic system CREST has settled deals made on the London Stock Exchange without the use of physical stock transfer forms. The tax is levied on the consideration paid except where an exemption can be claimed by the use of flags in CREST transactions, and share registers are automatically updated, CREST (and any other approved paperless system) has a statutory obligation to collect and account for SDRT on transactions carried out within its system or reported through it for regulatory purposes.

[**49.102**]

c) The higher charge

SDRT applies at a higher rate to shares converted into depositary receipts (FA 1986 s 93) and to shares put into a clearance system (FA 1986 s 96). It supplements the charge to duty on depositary receipts (see [**49.121**]) and is charged at a rate of 1.5% subject to an option, in FA 1986 s 97A, enabling as an alternative clearance services to opt for the normal SDRT charges to apply to transactions within the service. The higher charge acts as a 'season ticket' up-front charge since subsequent effective changes in ownership of the underlying UK shares are not subject to any charge. For this reason, issues of new shares are subject to the higher charge as well as transfers of existing shares – unlike the principal charge that does not apply to new issues.

There are reliefs for transfers of shares between systems, where the higher charge applied on the original entry to such a system (FA 1986 ss 97AA and 97B). However, other transfers of shares out of such a system bring them back into the scope of the principal charge.

Notwithstanding the above, the European Court of Justice in the case of *HSBC Holdings Ltd and Vidacos Nominees v R & C Comrs* (Case C-569/07) effectively ruled that the UK rule levying a 1.5% charge on the issue of shares into an EC clearance system is unlawful. HMRC has accepted this in respect of shares in UK companies which have been issued into EC based systems and has conceded that taxpayers may wish to make claims reclaims for amounts paid to date. Further, in *HSBC Holdings plc and Mellon v R & C Comrs* (2012), the First-tier Tribunal held that the charge to SDRT on a transaction where shares in a UK incorporated company were transferred into a non-EU incorporated depositary receipt system 'as in integral part of the raising of capital' was also incompatible with the Capital Duty Directive. HMRC has accepted that the *Mellon* decision also applies to a debt security which falls within the scope of the relevant Capital Duty Directive (eg loan notes and corporate bonds) (*Stamp Taxes Bulletin* 2/2012), and has stated that other forms of security will be dealt with on a case-by-case basis. [49.103]

2 Exemptions for certain financial market transactions

When shares are bought on the financial markets there are likely to be a series of transactions carried out by brokers, market makers, etc to effect the one trade. Some of these intermediate dealers may act as agents for others. But others act in a principal capacity and would be charged to SDRT. The intention of the SDRT provisions is just to charge the end purchaser. So there are reliefs from stamp duty and SDRT for market intermediaries (FA 1986 ss 80A and 88A) and for additional transactions in relation to public issues (FA 1986 s 89A) as well as for within-market stock lending (FA 1986 s 89AA). It should be noted that the scope of the reliefs continues to be extended. For example, FA 2010 s 65 introduced amendments to existing legislation to make it clear the members of clearing houses may obtain relief under both stamp duty and SDRT when clearing chargeable share trades. [49.104]

3 Off-market transactions subject to SDRT

The existence of SDRT protects the stamp duty charge on changes in ownership of UK shares. In particular, avoidance schemes which depend on restricting the need for stock transfer documents are ineffective, since any agreement to transfer shares which does not require the execution of a stampable document triggers a free-standing SDRT charge.

Some examples where SDRT, but not stamp duty, applies are as follows:

EXAMPLE 49.8
(1) Adam receives a renounceable letter of allotment of shares in Zeta Ltd.
    (i) If he applies to be registered there will be no charge to duty since there has been no transfer of the rights comprised in the letter.
    (ii) If he renounces the rights and transfers the letter of allotment to Bertha who in turn transfers to Charles, SDRT may apply to those transfers.
(2) Bertram buys and sells securities within the same Stock Exchange account or there is a purchase of shares that are registered in the name of a nominee acting for both seller and purchaser. Given that in both cases there is an agreement to transfer chargeable securities for consideration, Bertram is subject to SDRT. [49.105]

4 The charge on units in unit trusts

Unlike the principal charge to SDRT, the special regime for units in UK unit trusts operates as a free-standing tax regime without any overlap or interaction with stamp duty. The provisions are in FA 1999 Sch 19 which removes stamp duty from instruments relating to units under a unit trust scheme (para 1) except that units are treated as stock where they are consideration in relation to an otherwise stampable document (para 19) or where they fall within the bearer instrument regime.

Subject to the proposed changes noted below, the SDRT charge applies to surrenders of units and is in the first place charged at 0.5% on the market value of the units. The taxpayers are the trustees of the unit trust who will undoubtedly ensure that the trust deed provides for any tax to be financed out of the fund or from charges to unit holders. FA 1986 s 99(5A) exempts from the charge unit trusts with no register in the UK and no UK-resident trustees.

The full 0.5% charge is proportionately reduced by two formulae. *First*, the tax amount is multiplied by I/S if I, the number of units issued in the week of the surrender and the week after, is smaller than S, the total number of surrenders in the same two-week period. This may seem odd. The tax policy rationale is that if all redeemed units are re-issued then the full charge should apply since, in effect, the ownership of the underlying property (eg shares) has changed hands and there would have been a charge to stamp duty or SDRT if that property had changed ownership directly. If, in contrast, there are no new issues within a reasonable time of the surrender then the unit trust is likely to have to sell the underlying assets corresponding to the surrendered units. In this case the stamp duty or SDRT charge on the sale of the assets (albeit charged on the purchaser) means that the charge on the surrender can be removed without net effect on total revenues. The formula reduces the SDRT charge to the extent that issues match surrenders.

The *second* proportionate reduction is also based on looking through the units to the underlying property. This reduction is to multiply by the formula $N/(N+E)$ where N is the value of non-exempt investments and E is the value of exempt investments in the fund. Exempt investments are defined in FA 1986 s 99(5A)(b) and are in broad terms securities outside the scope of stamp duty (eg non-UK shares) and units in unit trusts that only invest in bonds.

The unit trust regime is applied to OEICS, with appropriate changes in terminology, by regulations in SI 1997/1156. Regulation 4A specifically relates to the FA 1999 Sch 19 regime.

It should be noted that the Coalition Government did announce in its Emergency Budget in 2010 that it would review the Sch 19 system, the abolition of which the relevant trade associations have lobbied for for some time.

It should be noted that there is an exemption where the unit trust or OEIC invests in non-chargeable securities such as bonds, gilts etc. FA 2011 has now widened the circumstances in which interests in underlying schemes are classed as exempt for the purposes of Sch 19.

FA 2014 abolishes the SDRT charge on unit trusts and open-ended investment companies in Sch 19 Part 2. Following consultation, the legislation has been revised to retain an SDRT charge on non pro-rata in specie redemptions. These changes have effect from 30 March 2014 and are intended to make UK domiciled unit trusts and OEICs more competitive. [49.106]

IV STAMP DUTY ON STOCK AND MARKETABLE SECURITIES

1 General structure of stamp duty

Stamp duty depends primarily upon the Stamp Act 1891 and the Stamp Duties Management Act 1891 as amended by subsequent Finance Acts. From 1 December 2003, when SDLT commenced, FA 2003 s 125 restricts stamp duty to instruments relating to stock and marketable securities. (NB some documents relating to land stayed within stamp duty under the transitional provisions for SDLT.)

Since 13 March 2008, transfers where the consideration is £1,000 or less will no longer attract stamp duty. This is a major simplification. A new certificate has been added to the reverse of a stock transfer form, to be completed when a share transfer is 'otherwise' exempt from stamp duty or no chargeable consideration is given for the transfer. Old versions of a stock transfer form continued to be accepted until 5 September 2012 (with the certificate being added manually to the reverse of the form).

Once the transfer has been properly certified, it can be sent directly to the company registrar. Similarly, the stamp duty on share buybacks has, since 13 March 2008, only applied where the consideration for the repurchase is more than £1,000. Again, Forms 169 and 169(1)B now include a form of certification. The only exceptions are for duplicate or counterpart documents or substitute bearer instruments. These must still be presented to HMRC to be stamped to indicate that the original document was stamped with the correct amount of stamp duty. [49.107]

a) *Written instruments*

Stamp duty applies to any 'instrument' (the term includes 'every written document') which falls within the description of what were termed 'Heads of Charge' in the Stamp Act 1891 and were restated in FA 1999 Schs 13 and 15, and is not covered by an exemption. If a transaction transferring chargeable securities is effected without a written instrument then SDRT is likely to apply. [49.108]

b) *Rates, interest and penalties*

The amount of stamp duty to be paid will usually be *ad valorem* duty calculated by reference to the amount or value of the consideration recorded in the instrument (rounded up, if necessary, to a multiple of £5). SA 1891 s 15 (amended by FA 1999) provides that an instrument may be stamped after execution 'on payment of the unpaid duty and any interest or penalty payable'. Note the following:
(1) *Interest (s 15A)*: after 30 days interest is payable at a rate fixed by regulations but not if the interest is less than £25. This charge applies to all documents that are chargeable, including those executed overseas. In all cases the 30-day period runs from the date of execution.
(2) *Penalties (s 15B)*: after the 30-day period a penalty arises. If the document is presented for stamping within one year of the end of the 30-day period the maximum penalty is £300 or, if less, the amount of duty. After one year, the maximum penalty is the amount of the duty or, if more,

£300. Where an instrument is executed and retained offshore, the 30-day period for the penalty is delayed to the point where it is brought into the UK. However, this is of little practical importance where SDRT potentially applies.

(3) There is a power for the Commissioners to mitigate any penalty (s 15B(4)) and 'no penalty is payable if there is a reasonable excuse for the delay in presenting the instrument for stamping' (s 15B(5)). An appeal against late stamping penalties may be made to the Special Commissioners and then to the High Court (FA 1999 Sch 12).

(4) The '30-day rule' may create problems in cases where the amount of duty is uncertain (for instance when the sale price depends upon a set of accounts yet to be prepared) or where a statutory exemption from duty is claimed. **[49.109]**

c) *Who is accountable for duty?*

The legislation does not generally state who is accountable for the duty. Apart from the fact that SDRT is enforceable on the transferee in relation to transfers of chargeable securities, the main sanction for non-payment is that, unless properly stamped, no document executed in the UK or relating to any property that is situated in the UK, will be admissible in evidence in any civil proceedings (SA 1891 s 14(4)) and company registrars are not permitted to register changes without having a stamped document (SA 1891 s 17). There is, however, a penalty for failure to submit bearer instruments for stamping in accordance with FA 1999 Sch 15 para 1. **[49.110]**

d) *Administration*

The administration of stamp duty is under the Commissioners of Revenue & Customs. In the event of a dispute there will normally be an adjudication followed by the stating of a case by the commissioners with a hearing in the Chancery Division of the High Court. There is a right of appeal to the Court of Appeal and, ultimately, to the House of Lords. Unlike other taxes the taxpayer (or, rather, the person who wishes the document to be duly stamped) has to pay the assessed duty before the appeal is heard. **[49.111]**

e) *Adjudication*

If required to do so the commissioners must state whether, in their opinion, any executed instrument is subject to a stamp duty charge and if so must state the amount of duty chargeable (the *adjudication* process: SA 1891 s 12). Adjudication may be voluntary, in which case the individual will be asking the commissioners to confirm that no duty is payable on the instrument, or, alternatively it may be necessary to ascertain the correct duty to be paid. In certain cases, however, legislation makes adjudication compulsory to ensure that the correct amount of duty is paid or to ensure that an instrument is covered by an exemption from duty (eg where there is a transfer between associated companies or a company reconstruction and exemption from duty is sought: see **[49.125]** and **[49.126]**). Such instruments are deemed not to have been properly stamped unless adjudicated bearing a stamp to that effect.

Stamp duty on stock and marketable securities 1471

The process of adjudication is an essential step in the appeals procedure and it also provides a definitive means by which a third party can be satisfied as to the correctness of the stamp duty paid – since the Stamp Office cannot change its mind about the stamp duty payable on a document after formal adjudication. This ability to require HMRC to take a binding view as to the tax position is in contrast to the provisions for modern taxes. The norm in recent legislation is for the taxpayer to be required to self-assess and take the risk if, on enquiry, he turns out to have underpaid. Statutory clearance procedures are relatively rare (and new ones have not been included in recent years) and administrative procedures for rulings tend to be restricted to areas where the meaning of the law is in doubt in a particular circumstance. **[49.112]**

2 Instruments subject to stamp duty on sale

a) *Conveyance or transfer on sale (FA 1999 Sch 13(1))*

Stamp duty is chargeable on a document which transfers stock or marketable securities on sale and the duty charged is *ad valorem* at a rate of 0.5% of consideration (rounded up to a multiple of £5 if necessary). Generally these documents will be stock transfer forms though they may, for example, be declarations of trust or letters of direction to a nominee where these effect a transfer.

'Sale' is not defined but there must be a vendor, a purchaser, and consideration (although there is no requirement that the consideration must be adequate). Duty is charged on the amount or value of the consideration and where it is in sterling, there will be no problem. If the consideration is in foreign currency, duty is charged on the sterling equivalent at the rate of exchange applying on the date of execution of the instrument (FA 1985 s 88).
[49.113]

i) *Meaning of 'consideration'*

Although the consideration for a sale will often be money, for stamp duty purposes stock or marketable securities and debts and other liabilities are also treated as chargeable sale consideration (SA 1891 ss 55, 57). A right to receive shares or securities in the future is dutiable consideration: for the purpose of valuing, that consideration and the possibility that it may not be issued is ignored (s 55(1A)). Reorganisations of corporate groups often involve share for share exchanges. If shares are transferred and the consideration is an issue or transfer of other shares, then the consideration shares must be valued to calculate the amount of stamp duty payable. **[49.114]**

ii) *Unascertainable consideration and the contingency principle*

Consideration may be uncertain at the time of the sale due to elements that depend on future events. For example, the shares in a company which runs a business might be sold for an amount which depends on the amount of profits over, say, the three years following the sale. If there is a specified *maximum* consideration provided for under contingencies which are provided for, then *ad valorem* duty is charged on that amount even though there may be little practical likelihood of it being paid. If there is no maximum sum stated but a minimum figure, *ad valorem* duty is charged on the minimum figure. If, however, there was no maximum nor minimum figure the consideration is wholly unascertainable with nothing to stamp (see *Coventry City Council v IRC* (1978); *LM Tenancies 1 plc v IRC* (1996), CA; affd (1998), HL. **[49.115]**

b) *Partnership dissolutions*

Documents relating to partnerships may be within the scope of stamp duty if the partnership owns stock or marketable securities (FA 2003 Sch 15 para 33). On the dissolution of a partnership, the division (or partition) of the assets between the partners will not be treated as a sale (*MacLeod v IRC* (1885)) but, if an outgoing partner is 'bought out', the instrument effecting that arrangement will be a sale (*Garnett v IRC* (1899)). A partition document is subject to a fixed duty. The mere withdrawal of partnership capital does not attract any charge and neither does the introduction of cash by an incoming partner. However, when an incoming partner pays for an interest in the business, the relevant document may operate as a conveyance on sale. Given these permutations, considerable care should be exercised in structuring both the admission of new partners and the retirement of old partners. To the extent that partnership property consists of interests in land, SDLT special rules apply and require even more care (see **[49.73]**).

EXAMPLE 49.9

Dave joins the partnership of Bob, Mick and Tom that has no land assets. He contributes capital of £100,000. This by itself will not amount to a sale. If, however, he pays the money to the other partners or they make a simultaneous withdrawal of capital, the deed or instrument of partnership effecting the transaction will be charged as a conveyance or transfer on sale of partnership property to Dave. However, the amount of stamp duty to be charged will depend on the extent to which partnership property consists of chargeable securities.

[49.116]

c) *Exchanges of shares*

An exchange of shares is a sale not an exchange (*Chesterfield Brewery Co v IRC* (1899)). FA 2000 s 122 ensures that both transfers are stampable *ad valorem* (unless exempt). This overrides a former practice under which a sale of shares for shares as consideration resulted in only one charge to *ad valorem* duty – the other transfer being stamped at £5. **[49.117]–[49.122]**

3 **The higher charge for depositary receipt systems and clearance services (FA 1986 ss 67–72A)**

A 1.5% charge is generally imposed when UK shares are converted into depositary receipts or transferred to a clearance service that enables UK shares to be bought and sold without payment of stamp duty or SDRT. The charge is levied on the consideration paid if the transfer is on sale: otherwise it is levied on the value of the shares at that time. This provision complements the higher charge of SDRT (see further **[49.102]** and see FA 1986 s 97A).

As noted above, it should be noted that the European Court of Justice (*HSBC Holdings plc, Vidacos Nominees Ltd v Comrs of HMRC* (Case C-569/07)) has stated that the UK rules breach EC law. HMRC now accepts that shares issued by a UK company into an EC clearance system should not be subject to the 1.5% entry charge, and accepts that taxpayers may be able to make reclaims in respect of previous transactions (subject to the usual time limits).

[49.123]–[49.124]

4 Exemptions and reliefs from stamp duty

The stamp duty reliefs include the following:

a) *Transfers between associated companies 'group relief' (FA 1930 s 42)*

Conveyance or transfer duty is not charged on an instrument by which one company transfers shares to an associated company. The detailed requirements are in FA 1930 s 42 which requires that one of the companies in question must beneficially own, directly or indirectly, at least 75% of the ordinary share capital of the other, or a third company beneficially owns, directly or indirectly at least 75% of the ordinary share capital of each. There is no residence restriction: foreign companies may benefit from the relief and their inclusion in a group will not prevent the group qualifying for the relief (*Canada Safeway v IRC* (1973)). The 'grouping' test was tightened up by FA 2000: to have regard to the tests in TA 1988 Sch 18. The test of association is also not satisfied if a person or persons together has or have or could obtain control of one (but not both) of the otherwise associated companies (see new s 42(2C) and for the interpretation of such clauses *Pilkington Bros Ltd v IRC* (1982)).

FA 1967 s 27(3) contains provisions to prevent abuse of the s 42 relief. In particular the consideration for the transfer must not be provided from outside the group. The relief will not be allowed if it forms part of an arrangement whereby the transferor's interest in the transferee's share capital will be reduced below 75%.

It is necessary to apply for adjudication of the instrument effecting the transfer in order to obtain the relief (currently letters should be sent to the Birmingham Stamp Office). Claims for group relief require a formal (but not statutory) declaration by a director or company secretary of the company establishing the group (see SP 3/98) and *Stamp Taxes Manual* 6.163 onwards). In contrast to the corresponding group relief in SDLT, there is no motive test or clawback rule for group relief on shares. [49.125]

b) *Reconstructions where there is no real change of ownership (FA 1986 ss 75–77)*

Exemption from *ad valorem* duty is given when, pursuant to a scheme of reconstruction of the target company, the whole or part of its undertaking (s 75), or the whole of its issued share capital (s 77), is acquired by the acquiring company for an issue of non-redeemable shares and perhaps the assumption or discharge of liabilities. Section 76 formerly provided a partial relief for transfers of land but has no utility for share transfers since it merely restricts the duty to 0.5%. For the meaning of a scheme of reconstruction, see SP 5/85 and see also *Fallon v Fellows* (2001) and the provisions in FA 2002 putting the practice on a statutory basis.

From the day after Royal Assent to FA 2006, the statutory provision no longer requires the registered office of the acquirer to be within the UK for these reliefs. On 22 July 2005, HMRC announced that: 'Following legal advice, the Government now accepts that this requirement is defective in law. HMRC will, therefore, from the date of this announcement, and provided that all other conditions for the relief are satisfied, accept claims to relief where the registered office of the acquiring company is in any EEA State.' The condition will not be applied in future and reclaims will be made for transfers within the two years preceding the announcement, provided that other conditions were satisfied. It is assumed that EU law is the law that makes this provision defective, but neither HMRC nor the Government chose to reveal their analysis.

Section 77 enables the interposition of a holding company and s 75 provides for demergers. Other conditions for these reliefs are that, apart from the assumption of liabilities consideration must be in the form only of shares which must be issued to all shareholders of the target company only (and not to that company itself). The acquisitions must be for *bona fide* commercial reasons and not have any tax avoidance as a main purpose. After the acquisition each shareholder in the target company must hold shares in the acquirer and *vice versa* and the proportion of the shares of one company held by any shareholder must be the same as the proportion of the shares in the other company held by that same shareholder. From FA 2006 the conditions in ss 75 and 77 reliefs that the proportions must be 'the same proportion' has been softened to read 'the same proportion, or as nearly as may be the same proportion' to allow for circumstances where precise matching cannot be achieved for practical reasons. Section 77 also requires that share classes of the target match the classes of the consideration shares in the acquiring company.

Any instrument employed to convey or transfer property under any of the reconstructions requires adjudication. These arrangements normally take place pursuant to TCGA 1992 s 139 in respect of which a clearance procedure is available under s 138 (this will usually be accepted by the Stamp Office). Given these requirements, which ensure that the undertaking is held by the same shareholders before and after the acquisition, this exemption is extremely limited. A reconstruction under the Insolvency Act 1986 ss 110–111 may fall within this relief as illustrated in *Illustration 1* below:

Illustration 1

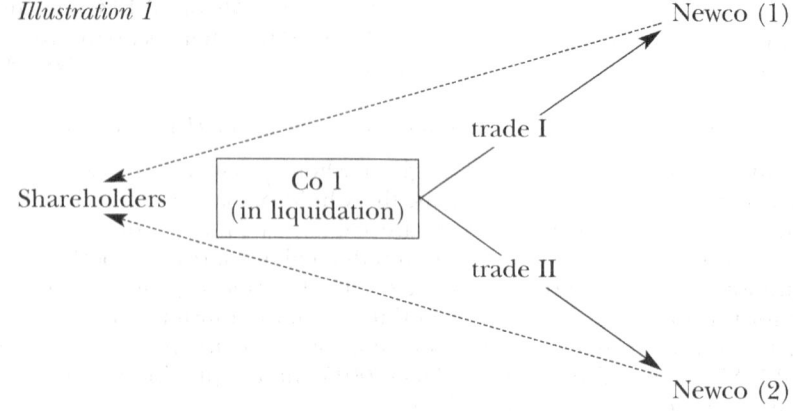

Company 1 is liquidated and its two component trades are split with the ownership being transferred to Newco (1) and Newco (2). Those companies then issue shares to the shareholders of Company 1. This reconstruction qualifies for relief: contrast, however, the following illustration (a demerger) that does not:

Illustration 2

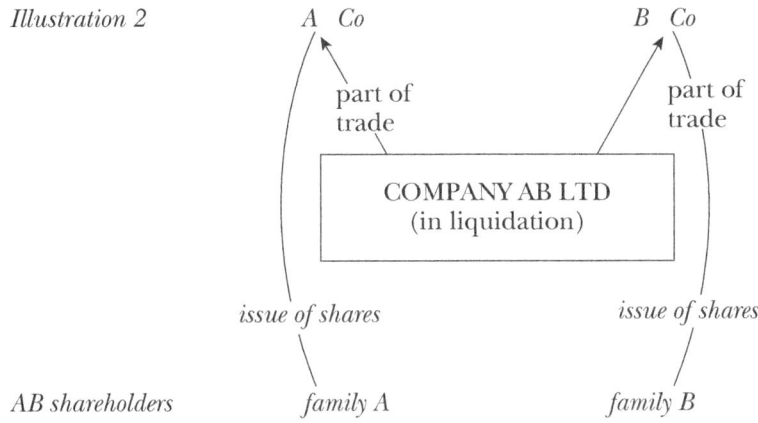

In *Illustration 2* there is a similar partition but, instead of the shares in the two new companies being divided amongst all the original shareholders, the shares in A Co now pass only to the original shareholders who comprised the A family and the B Co shares to the B family.

There are equivalents to FA 1986 ss 75 and 76 reliefs in SDLT (in FA 2003 Sch 7) relating to the transfer of land assets. There are some detailed differences, including clawback rules. **[49.126]**

5 Recent developments

Provisions in FA 2014 have abolished the stamp duty charge on transfers of shares traded on the Alternative Investment Market ('AIM') of the London Stock Exchange and certain other listed growth markets (which includes SDRT). The changes have had effect since 28 April 2014. **[49.127]**

Section 8 Pensions

Chapter
50   Pensions

50 Pensions

Written by Rosalind Connor, Partner, ARC Pensions Law LLP

I   An introduction to pension schemes [**50.1**]
II Tax treatment prior to A-day [**50.5**]
III Present day tax treatment of pensions [**50.9**]
IV Unregistered pension schemes [**50.51**]

I AN INTRODUCTION TO PENSION SCHEMES

Pension arrangements generally provide benefits (usually by way of an income stream) in old age, once an individual has retired from paid work, but often also provide an income on ill-health (where this prevents the individual from working) or for dependants on death. Pensions are also provided at a modest rate by the state, but this chapter does not focus on what might be termed 'social security pensions' but instead the tax treatment of private pensions, provided by the employer, by an individual for themselves, or, most often, by a combination of the two.

The pensions area has always been heavily regulated and the regulation is under continual revision. A combination of a wish to protect elderly people, a number of high-profile scandals and a requirement not to cripple businesses with unpayable costs has led to several pensions statutes in recent years which continue in force. The industry maintains a Pensions Regulator, a Pensions Ombudsman, a Pension Protection Fund for schemes of which the employer is insolvent, an excellent free advice service (the Pensions Advisory Service), as well as being subject in parts to the Financial Conduct Authority.

The vast amount of regulation has made pension schemes increasingly complex to operate and has given rise to a lot of pension specific terminology. As much as possible, this chapter avoids jargon, but it is important to note that pension schemes may be occupational (established by an employer) or personal (arranged by the individual). They may be defined benefit (where a level of benefit is promised by the scheme) or defined contribution (where the only promise is as to the level of contribution). The scheme itself may also be referred to as a plan or a fund, particularly in the USA, where the term 'scheme' is pejorative, but the terms are interchangeable. Individuals within a scheme are referred to as members.

A scheme may be structured a number of different ways. According to FA 2004 s 150, a pension scheme is any arrangement 'comprised in one or more instruments or agreements' which provides benefits on retirement, death, reaching a certain age or serious ill-health. However, in practice, pension schemes and in particular those subject to the favourable tax treatment under FA 2004 are set up either by an arrangement under trust or by way of an insurance contract with a long-term insurer. [50.1]

1 Trust based schemes

An occupational scheme set up by an employer for its employees is generally set up under trust. The trust will be declared in a trust deed which will establish the employer and, to the extent they make contributions, the employees as settlors and appoint individuals or a company to act as trustee. It is technically possible for the trustee to be the employing company itself, although this is highly unusual because the regulatory requirements as to the identity and election of directors of a trustee company would impinge on the business operations of the employer. The beneficiaries of the trust are the members, their dependants or nominees (who may receive death benefits) and in some circumstances the employer which may receive a surplus if the pension becomes overfunded.

Pension trust documents consist of a declaration of trust, often referred to as the 'definitive deed' and contain the administrative provisions and an appended set of rules which set out the benefits provided under the scheme. Given the complexity of the operation of pension schemes, these documents often run to over 100 pages of details.

The operation of trusts in these circumstances allows the import of a significant body of trust case law to ensure that the trust operates for the purpose for which it was established, which is often slightly less accurately characterised as 'acting in the interests of members'. It also ensures that the assets remain separate from those of the employer and are not accessible either to the employer or before receipt of pension to beneficiaries who, as a result of the Pensions Act 1995 s 91, are generally unable to assign, charge or waive their rights to benefits under the pension scheme. Trust law can also have unintended consequences to pension schemes. For example, in *Air Jamaica v Charlton* (1999) it was held by the Privy Council that the occupational pension scheme for employees of Air Jamaica was void for perpetuity, meaning that the pensions already paid were available for return to the creditors of the insolvent employer.

Trust based schemes are also often used outside the private occupational pension environment, where the pension is provided by a third party provider such as an insurance company. The trust structure can be seen as a convenient one for pension provision and also has the advantage of giving a degree of comfort to customers as to the care taken of their benefits. The growth of demand for smaller defined contribution pensions has given rise to a number of 'master trusts' where a financial services provider provides a trust structure to which employer customers can adhere. The provider then provides a board of trustees who will manage the investments for employees of each of the many and unconnected employers that are its customers. Master trusts are now becoming subject to their own regulation and authorisation process as a result of the Pension Schemes Act 2017. [50.2]

2 Contract based schemes

For a scheme to obtain the benefits of tax registration under FA 2004 it must either be set up as an occupational scheme or alternatively by a person authorised to do so under the Financial Services and Markets Act 2000 (see FA 2004 s 154). A scheme established by authorised persons will on the whole (with the exception of the use of master trusts referred to above) be set up under a simple insurance contract. From a legal point of view this is a contract directly between the provider (the long term insurance company which is the authorised person) and the employee.

The employer has no legal obligation here except in relation to any direct contractual arrangement it has with the employee that it will make payments into its pension arrangement. In practice, however, employers often offer their pension contributions to employees through a single provider for ease of administration. These are usually badged as group personal pension schemes but in legal terms they are a series of individual contracts between employees and a single provider, and any agreement between the provider and the employer is simply for the employer to distribute access to the provider's product to its employees.

Personal pension schemes have historically included the concept of stakeholder pensions. Stakeholder pensions were introduced under the Welfare Reform and Pensions Act 1999 and were a form of low fee, easy access personal pension scheme to attract lower paid workers. Employers were obliged to provide access to these pension schemes but not provide contributions to them, and as a result the take up of these schemes was small. The requirement to provide them fell away when the provisions of the Pensions Act 2008 came into effect requiring employers instead to automatically enrol employees into a pension scheme and make contributions in relation to them.　　　　[50.3]

3 Self-invested schemes

Most pension schemes operate so that the investments available are either chosen directly by the trustees of the scheme on behalf of members or are chosen by members from a list of funds available. Generally personal pension schemes will have a very wide range of funds available and a smaller list will apply for an occupational scheme. In each case most of the funds are investment funds in which the member may purchase units. In addition, pension schemes will operate a default fund, being the fund into which members who have not made a choice are entered. Most members of most schemes do not make any investment choice and find themselves invested in the default fund.

However, some individuals wish to use the tax advantageous environment of their pension arrangement to make individual investment decisions, and self-invested schemes are available on the market to provide this. Self-invested personal pensions (or 'SIPPs') are personal pension schemes where, rather than choosing from a range of funds, the individual can nominate investment directly into assets. Most providers place a number of restrictions on the investments that can be made and inevitably the charges relating to these types of products are such as to make them only attractive for the large funds of sophisticated investors.

It is also possible to operate a self-invested occupational pension scheme known as a small self-administered scheme (or 'SSAS') which operates where there are fewer than 12 members, all of whom are trustees. SSASs tend to be used in family businesses where the only members are owner directors who therefore exercise significant control over the employer as well as being the trustees of the SSAS.

SIPPs and SSASs usually operate as investment-regulated pension schemes, as defined at FA 2004 Sch 29A para 1. Certain restrictions on investments discussed at [**50.13**] ff hold for these schemes. [**50.4**]

II TAX TREATMENT PRIOR TO A-DAY

The tax treatment of pension schemes underwent a revolution on 6 April 2006 when the provisions of Part 4 of FA 2004 came into force. This date was referred to both by HMRC and the pensions industry as 'A-day' and the term is still referenced in documentation about pension tax treatment. Set out below is a short summary of the pre-A-day provisions and how changes were transitioned as these are relevant to older and legacy schemes. [**50.5**]

1 Approval and IR12

Prior to A-day, pension schemes operated under the provisions of the Income and Corporation Taxes Act 1988 (TA 1988) and previous Acts which granted favourable tax treatment so long as a pension scheme was approved by the then Inland Revenue ('the Revenue', now HMRC). Occupational schemes would be established by an interim trust deed which included very limited details of benefits but contained the most important administrative provisions, including a requirement to put in place a full, definitive trust deed and rules within two years. Approval for the interim deed would be received relatively swiftly from the Revenue and the main rules would then be drafted.

The drafting of rules was required to be in accordance with the Revenue's manual IR12 which set out the maximum benefits for which it would permit approval. In order to ensure that benefits remained within the limits of IR12, most schemes would include an appendix setting out the IR12 limits and a rule stating that to the extent the benefits were in excess of those limits they would not be paid. The more detailed rules would then be submitted to the Revenue where they would be reviewed to ensure that they did indeed fall within the IR12 provisions before approval was granted of the definitive deed.

A large number of other changes, such as other amendments to rules and adherence of further employers to the scheme required the approval of the Revenue before they could be brought into force, and many pension scheme rules still refer to approval by the Revenue as part of the process of amendments for coming into operation, although that term is now obsolete. Any treatment of pension schemes or payment of benefits outside the provisions in IR12 could result in significant tax charges and, in extremis, the withdrawal of approval, meaning that all previous tax advantages would be lost. The threat of this was sufficient to ensure that pension schemes kept conservatively within those rules.

A similar process existed for personal pension schemes. The Revenue manual in this case was IR76. [50.6]

2 The Revenue limits and grandfathering of benefits

The limits set out in IR12 were relatively generous and separately covered a number of different benefits. For instance, they provided a salary cap above which no salary should be taken into account for defined benefit purposes, a cap on the level of a lump sum to be provided at the commencement of the pensions in an occupational pension arrangement, the limit on accrual in a defined benefit arrangement and the level of contributions under a defined contribution scheme. Several of these limits and even the methodologies differed between IR12 and IR76 resulting in different limits for members in terms of both contributions and benefits, depending on whether their scheme was occupational or personal.

In addition to this complexity, a number of reductions to the IR12 limits to make them less generous were 'grandfathered', which means that the benefits provided to those who were already members of the pension scheme were subject to old limits and new limits applied only to new joiners. The end result of this was a very complex process where limits were difficult to understand and calculate, as well as being very time-consuming for the Revenue itself.
[50.7]

3 A-day and the Modification Regulations

When FA 2004 came into force at A-day the changes were very significant. In particular, the different benefits provided for different groups and the distinction between occupational and personal schemes as well as most of the differences between defined benefit and defined contribution schemes were swept away in an attempt to simplify the process. This meant that existing schemes needed to be modified to cope with an entirely new regime and amendments needed to be made to all existing approved pension schemes to deal with the new provisions.

There was a particular concern that the new provisions would mean that schemes which were drafted on the understanding of the IR12 limits pre-A-day would suddenly find that they were providing much more generous benefits once those limits ceased to apply, as the limits referred to in their rules fell away. As a result, the Registered Pension Schemes (Modification of the Rules of Existing Schemes) Regulations 2006 (SI 2006/364) were brought into force. By virtue of these regulations, any pension scheme that had not amended its provisions to deal with the A-day changes in advance of A-day was subject to provisions to ensure that it did not make unauthorised payments under the new rules and that certain of the old limits, such as the limit that the salary cap imposed for the purposes of calculating defined benefit pensions and for contribution rates, were kept in place. The provisions had a transitional effect and continued in force until the scheme made its own amendments with a longstop date of 6 April 2011, when they fell away again.
[50.8]

III PRESENT DAY TAX TREATMENT OF PENSIONS

1 General concept

The tax treatment made available to pension schemes is particularly generous and one of the more generous treatments of pensions globally. In general, contributions are not taxed as income of the individual member and an employer's contribution is generally deductible against corporation tax. In addition, there is generally no taxation on capital growth or income received by the pension fund itself. Benefits are instead taxed on receipt in the hands of the recipient at their marginal tax rate, but even this is limited as members can obtain a lump sum of up to 25% of the size of the fund free of tax. Some commentators argue that tax is merely deferred as the growth of the fund tax free increases the size of the fund available for taxation on receipt, but the treatment of pensions savings from a tax point of view is generally considered generous and is designed to attract people to save for their old age so as to reduce the social security cost to the Treasury of those who have retired.

In July 2015, HM Treasury announced a consultation to consider whether this tax structure, known as the EET structure ('*e*xempt on the contribution, *e*xempt on growth, *t*axed on receipt') should be radically changed. In particular, the consultation proposed a consideration of a TEE structure, similar to ISA savings vehicles, by which contributions are made out of taxed income and growth and receipt are tax exempt. No changes were made and commentators suggested that the change of Chancellor means that this is now unlikely. However, the possibility of such a change remains tempting for government as it accelerates tax receipts. [50.9]

2 Registration process

To take advantage of the favourable tax treatment, a pension scheme must be registered with HMRC under Part 4 of FA 2004. In contrast to the approval process discussed in [50.5] ff, registration is generally a swift and straightforward process. In order to be registered, a pension scheme must either be an occupational scheme or alternatively a personal pension or stakeholder scheme established by a person with the relevant permissions.

An occupational pension scheme is defined under FA 2004 s 150(5) as one that is established by an employer and being 'capable of having effect' so as to provide benefits for employees of that or another employer. This broad drafting was considered in *Pi Consulting (Trustee Services) Ltd v The Pensions Regulator and ors* (2013). In this case, the court held that a scheme can simply be established with the ability to permit one or more directors or employees of an employer to join even if all other members of the scheme are entirely unrelated. Indeed, in this case the court held that a company that merely had a director (whether or not paid) could be the employer for these purposes so long as the scheme clearly permitted directors as well as employees to become members of the scheme. In general, however, occupational pension schemes are established by an employer for its employees and those of group companies, but there are a number of industry-wide schemes which take advantage of this provision to provide benefits for employees of a large number of unconnected employers and also a growing number of 'master trusts' which similarly are established by a provider and then offered to a range of different customers for the benefit of their employees.

A personal pension scheme may be registered if it is established by someone with permission under the Financial Services and Markets Act 2000 (FSMA 2000) to establish a personal pension scheme or stakeholder pension scheme. For these purposes, the establishment and management of a personal pension scheme or a stakeholder pension scheme is a regulated activity in accordance with the FSMA 2000 s 22 and therefore only those with authorisation from the FCA for these purposes may establish a personal pension scheme which is then registered.

The registration process requires the scheme to have an administrator. The scheme administrator is responsible for the day-to-day administration of the scheme, including meeting any compliance requirements. In the absence of a nomination, the administrator will be the trustees or, for a personal pension, the authorised person. Most schemes use this default position.

The registration process under the legislation was designed to require HMRC to register pension schemes except in certain circumstances, so as to make the process much more certain and much speedier. The application must be made by the scheme administrator who must be a resident of the UK or an EU or EEA state and is appointed to hold that role (FA 2004 s 270). The scheme administrator must make a number of declarations in order to register a pension scheme, in particular:

- that the scheme documents do not entitle any person to unauthorised payments (although unauthorised payments may be made by a registered scheme);
- the information in the application is correct and complete;
- the administrator will discharge the functions properly and understands the penalties for not doing so;
- the scheme administrator is a suitable and proper person;
- the scheme will be maintained for the purposes of providing the benefits that fall within FA 2004 s 164(1).

The concern about some of the pension schemes that have been put in place (in particular liberation schemes discussed in [50.21] below) has led to an increase to the list of bases on which HMRC can decide not to register a scheme (from an initial list that the information is incorrect or the declaration is false). It now includes the administrator failing to provide information or obstructing an inspection or it appearing that the scheme has not been established or maintained for the purposes of providing benefits under s 164(1). It also allows HMRC not to register a scheme if the administrator is not a fit and proper person for the role. In addition, there are now a number of powers pursuant to which HMRC may require information and impose penalties for failure to provide information or providing inaccurate information.

It is possible to appeal against decisions not to register for a 30-day period following notification of the decision. If the First-tier Tribunal upholds the appeal, the scheme is then treated as registered from the date chosen by the Tribunal.

HMRC also has the power to deregister a scheme withdrawing the registration with effect from a stated date, giving rise to a de-registration charge against the administrator of 40% of the fund. The causes of the de-registration include the scheme not being maintained wholly or mainly for the purpose of making payments under s 164(1), the administrator not being a fit and proper person, chargeable payments being above HMRC's threshold, failure to pay substantial tax, failure to provide information or documents or providing inaccurate information, obstruction of an inspection or there being no scheme administrator. De-registration is, of course, an extreme response and in general HMRC tends to use it either only as a last resort or when it believes that the registration itself had been in error. [50.10]

3 Taxation of contributions

a) *The taxing of contributions in detail*

Contributions to a registered pension scheme are generally made from gross income. For contributions made on an employee's behalf from their salary, the employer may deduct this from gross salary before the deduction of PAYE. The contributions made by the individual are subject to a tax credit by which the administrator may claim back income tax at the basic 20% rate, which is then added to the contributions. Higher or additional rate taxpayers can claim tax relief on the additional 20% or 25% income tax via their returns.

Salary sacrifice arrangements are common for pension schemes. In these circumstances, an employee agrees that, rather than make a pension contribution, he or she will receive a salary reduced by the amount of the contribution and the employer will make that contribution instead. In effect, the employee has the same level of pension contribution and the same level of post-pension salary, but the lower actual salary reduces the national insurance contributions. HMRC generally accepts salary sacrifice arrangements, so long as the amendment to salary is properly agreed between employer and employee in advance. There has been some recent criticism of the arrangements, but changes to these rules announced in the March 2017 budget specifically excluded salary sacrifice arrangements in place for pension schemes and certain other benefits.

Contributions made by an employer as an employee benefit to the pension scheme are not taxed under ITEPA 2003 s 201 but, instead, give rise to no income tax. In addition, such contributions are in general deductible against corporation tax for the employer.

Employer contributions that benefit from corporation tax relief under FA 2004 s 196 are subject to some limitations, in particular in relation to asset backed contributions in certain circumstances. In addition, employers making contributions of more than £500,000 (which exceed 210% of the contributions in the previous charging period) must then spread relief over a period of between one and three future years. Contributions only receive relief in circumstances where the contribution is 'wholly and exclusively' for the purpose of the business of that employer. Difficulties in claiming such relief can arise where contributions are made in relation to employees on secondment, particularly overseas and where there is no commercial benefit for the actual employer in making such a contribution. [50.11]

b) *The annual allowance and carry forward*

Contributions to a pension scheme for, by or on behalf of an individual (including contributions by the employer) are subject to a charge if they are above the annual allowance amount.

The annual allowance charge is made on all contributions above the annual allowance amount. The charge is made at the marginal rate of tax for the individual in order to effectively remove the tax free advantage of these contributions.

When FA 2004 first came into force, the annual allowance amount was £215,000. It rose to £255,000 in 2011–12 but then fell sharply to £50,000 and was further reduced to £40,000 from 2014–15 onwards and may be amended by Treasury Order.

From 2016–17, the annual allowance has been reduced for higher earners. The annual allowance falls by £1 for every £2 that the individual's gross income is above £150,000 for the year, falling to a minimum of £10,000 for those with incomes of over £210,000. There are further provisions to prevent avoidance using salary sacrifice.

The annual allowance is personal to the individual and may relate to contributions to several different pension schemes. The total input to be calculated against the annual allowance is easy to calculate in relation to a defined contribution arrangement as it is equal to contributions made. However, if the arrangement includes any form of defined benefit arrangement the annual allowance relates to the increase in a member's rights under the scheme, which are calculated in accordance with the provisions of FA 2004 ss 229–237 and effectively assess the value of those benefits at the end of the year and deduct from them the value at the beginning of the year to give an increase in value.

It is possible to carry forward any unused annual allowance for up to three years. In short, the unused annual allowance can be credited and added to the annual allowance for the next year (or two subsequent years) in order to use up the allowance amount.

The annual allowance is reduced to £10,000 for a member who has commenced flexi-access drawdown, received an uncrystallised funds pension lump sum or a flexible annuity. This provision was introduced with the changes that came into effect from 6 April 2015 as described at **[50.18]** in order to ensure that employers did not avoid national insurance contributions by making contributions in lieu of salary to older employees, which were immediately drawn down by the individual. A further reduction of the annual allowance in these circumstances to £4,000 was announced in the 2017 Budget with effect from 6 April 2017. However, it was removed from the Finance Bill following the call of the 2017 General Election. It is expected that, if re-elected, the Conservative government will bring this into force in a later Finance Act. **[50.12]**

4 **Taxation of a pension fund**

a) *Growth of the fund*

The general tax position is that there is no capital gains or income tax on any returns to, or growth of, the pension fund itself. The fund retains a tax free environment whilst the monies remain within the registered pension scheme. This operates by way of a series of exemptions to the taxation of various investment income amounts (such as income from investments and deposits, from futures and options contracts, certificates of deposit and underwriting commissions) and capital gains on exemptions. This treatment does not therefore apply to trading income, that is, income from carrying on a business, which will fall outside this series of investments. Although carrying on a business does not run any risk of de-registration, it will not be exempt from tax in the same way that investment income and capital gains are, and so it is highly unusual for pension schemes to carry out trading activities.

[50.13]

b) VAT

Pension schemes are not generally VAT registered because they cannot be carrying on a business. Historically, this has meant that schemes have paid very significant irrecoverable VAT amounts on service charges incurred by pension schemes, such as on fees paid to legal advisors, fund managers, accountants and actuaries, whose fees will include a VAT charge.

Historically, HMRC has taken the view that VAT must be charged to pension schemes. However, where a VAT registered employer paid expenses on behalf of the pension scheme, HMRC allowed the employer (if VAT registered) to recover some of the VAT. In this regard HMRC distinguished between investment costs and other charges and held that the employer could not recover (or set off against output VAT) the VAT in respect of scheme investment costs that it paid. Invoices that covered investments and other administrative costs were subject to a split by which only 30% of the VAT on the relevant invoice was capable of being recovered by the employer. This position was significantly altered in late 2014 following a number of European cases in relation to the VAT treatment of pension schemes and the treatment of the payment of scheme expenses by employers.

The first case in relation to this is *Wheels Common Investment Fund Trustees Limited v R & C Comrs* (2013), where the question was whether the Wheels common investment fund, which was an investment fund used purely by the pension schemes operated by a group of companies, should have the benefit of an exemption for VAT under article 135(1)(g) of Council Directive 2006/112/EC for special investment funds. The CJEU held that the defined benefit pension scheme and the common investment fund did not satisfy the criteria of a special investment fund for the purposes of such exemption. The Court particularly focused on the fact that the fund was not open to the public and on the lack of a link between the fund's performance and the benefits received by the individuals (as the fund was defined benefit and therefore the benefit received by individuals depended on the defined benefit promise rather than the performance of investments from time to time).

Fiscale Eenheid PPG Holdings BV CS Te Hoogezand v Inspecteur Van De Belastingdienst/Noord/Kant Oor Groningen (2013) then took a slightly different approach in relation to a Dutch pension scheme. In this case, the scheme was not VAT registered but its costs were paid by a VAT registered employer (including payments for investment related services). The CJEU held that the payments made by the VAT registered employer were business expenses of the employer and therefore the VAT was recoverable. It was held that since the pension scheme was run for the incentivisation of employees, it was an expense of the business in its business activities, and therefore VAT could be recovered.

The case of *ATP Pension Service A/S v Skatteministeriet* (2014) further improved the position of pension schemes in relation to VAT, with the CJEU deciding that a pension scheme could in fact be a special investment fund (even though the *Wheels* scheme had not been) if it is:

- funded by members;
- invested using a risk-spreading principle; and
- one where the members bear the investment risk.

This focused on the feature of the member bearing risk referred to in the *Wheels* case and implied that a defined contribution arrangement in the UK may well be VAT exempt as a special investment fund.

The first effect of these cases was an interim provision by HMRC. An initial HMRC Brief in February 2014 (Brief 2014/6) responded to the *PPG* case by allowing VAT to be recovered by the employer in respect of invoices that covered both investment and other matters, but still denied VAT recovery in relation to investment only invoices. In November 2014, a replacement brief (Brief 2014/43) stated that the investment and non-investment distinction would no longer be used and VAT would be recoverable by employers where services were provided to the employer rather than to the scheme. HMRC proposed that contemporaneous evidence that the services were provided to the employer would be required. In a further update (Brief 2015/8 published on 26 March 2015) HMRC acknowledged that the services are in fact provided to the scheme rather than to the employer but that it would expect the employer to be a party to these agreements. Difficulties may of course arise for a scheme which has included the employer as a party particularly where the trustees seek independent advice. It may well be that HMRC's position, which does not appear consistent with the CJEU's view in the *PPG* case, oversteps the requirements so that in fact the contemporaneous evidence of the employer being a party is not required. HMRC, in acknowledgement of the practical difficulties, has confirmed it is still consulting on the issue with the industry, and in the meantime has extended the transitional period when schemes and employers can opt to use the pre-2014 approach, initially until the end of 2016, under Brief 2015/17 and now to 31 December 2017 by Brief 2016/14. The resolution of this matter is further complicated by Brexit, and it may well be that HMRC takes no further action on this issue until the Great Repeal Bill is developed. In any event, a number of schemes are looking to reclaim VAT paid over a number of years and the repayments could be significant.

HMRC also issued a further brief in relation to defined contribution pension schemes in November 2014 (Brief 2014/44), in which HMRC accepted that a pension scheme will be VAT exempt if:

- it is solely funded by people to whom the benefit is paid (including indirect payments by way of employer contributions);
- the customer bears the pensions risk (as is the case for defined contribution arrangements);
- the fund is pooled and spread over several different investments.

Again, there is a process for reclaiming overpaid VAT by such schemes which is expected to be widely if not universally used by defined contribution schemes. [50.14]

c) *Tax penalties and specific investments*

Historically, pension schemes have excluded a large number of investments which were deemed not suitable for a pension environment, particularly those of short term or depreciating value or those with limited liquidity as well as assets which may suggest an attempt to use the pension scheme to avoid inheritance tax. These limits have reduced over time but still apply for certain assets of investment regulated schemes.

Under the provisions of FA 2004 Sch 29A, the taxable property provisions relate to the holding of residential property and to chattels or tangible movable property and effectively require that any holding of those by investment regulated pension schemes gives rise to a tax charge.

Investment regulated pension schemes (which comprise most self-invested schemes as described at [50.4]) are subject to further restrictions. Personal pension schemes fall within this definition where the member or someone related to them is able to direct, influence and advise on the matter of investment of the funds in the pension scheme (related persons being 'connected persons' under ITA 2007 s 993). An occupational pension scheme is investment regulated if there are 50 or fewer members and one or more of those members is able to direct, influence or advise in the manner of investment, and the same provisions hold for a separate self-controlled section of a larger pension scheme.

The holding of such property gives rise to a charge based on 10% of the value of the property, or the profits received if higher. The charge is the scheme sanction charge of 40% of this amount.

Borrowing by all registered pensions schemes is subject to limits. Schemes are authorised to borrow an aggregate amount of total current borrowings of up to 50% of the net value of the fund immediately before the borrowing has taken place. Borrowing above this amount gives rise to a scheme sanction charge of 40% of the excess. [50.15]

5 Tax treatment of payments by pension scheme

a) *Benefit crystallisation events and the lifetime allowance*

As well as the limit on contributions contained in the annual allowance, registered pension schemes are subject to a charge on the value of the fund above the lifetime allowance. At the time of retirement, the fund is assessed against the lifetime allowance and, to the extent that it is in excess of that amount, is subject to the lifetime allowance charge defined under FA 2004 s 214. The charge is made at 25% of the fund, rising to 55% in relation to any amount given to the member as a lump sum (FA 2004 s 215).

The lifetime allowance was originally £1.5 million at the time that FA 2004 came into effect in 2006, rising to £1.8 million in 2010–11 and then falling to £1.5 million in 2012–13, £1.25 million in 2014–15 and finally to £1 million for the tax year 2016–17. It remains £1 million for the tax year 2017–18.

The lifetime allowance is assessed at the time of any benefit crystallisation event. The benefit crystallisation events are set out in FA 2004 s 216 and effectively cover any situation in which the member obtains a pension or funds from the pension arrangement, or pensions or lump sums are paid on their death. In addition, reaching the age of 75 is a benefit crystallisation event for funds not already crystallised.

In relation to a benefit crystallisation event, the amount crystallised is also set out in s 216 and is effectively the value of the fund that is crystallised at that time. As such, if the crystallisation event relates only to half the pension fund it is only that half which is assessed at that time against the lifetime allowance. If the benefit taken is a defined benefit pension, the relevant revaluation factors set out in FA 2004 s 276 will be used to convert the annual pension to a nominal amount crystallised. Currently, the factors used multiply the annual pension by 20 to produce the nominal amount.

Following a benefit crystallisation event, a lifetime allowance for an individual is then reduced by the amount crystallised so that any later benefit crystallisation events will be assessed against the reduced lifetime allowance. If the lifetime allowance has changed between the first and the second benefit crystallisation events, the fund from the earlier benefit crystallisation event amount is prorated down (if the lifetime allowance is reduced) or up (if the lifetime allowance is increased) to be assessed against the present lifetime allowance.

Further provisions relate to benefit crystallisation events relating to non-residence and overseas pension schemes to ensure that the assessment is carried out on proportionate grounds. [50.16]

b) *Methods of taking pension benefits*

Historically, pension schemes would allow members to take benefits in one of two structures: a lump sum and a pension. Lump sums are discussed at [50.19] but the pension amount (which is subject to income tax, at the individual's marginal rate) could be taken either as a pension paid out by the scheme itself or by the purchase of an annuity policy. The annuity policy is an insurance policy by which the insurer, in return for a capital sum, pays an income for the remainder of the individual's life (and therefore the risk insured is the life expectancy of the individual). Either an annuity can be bought by the pension scheme and held within its own funds or, as is more common in a defined contribution arrangement, it is provided in the name of the individual who then has no further claims under the scheme itself.

Annuities have given rise to significant complaints over some years on the perceived grounds of being poor value for money. Certainly the industry is relatively small, but it should be borne in mind that many in the actuarial profession (which assesses the risks and likely cost of pension liabilities) continue to assert that this criticism is overstated and is at least in part due to an under-estimate of life expectancy by individuals. In short, people often expect to receive their annuity pension for a shorter period than that for which they do in fact receive it. Certainly life expectancy has been increasing significantly and the criticism of annuities as poor value for money has persisted despite the fact that annuities bought many years ago (and criticised as poor value for money at that time), are now acknowledged to be a very significant advantage for the individual and costly for the insurer because of increased longevity.

The growing criticism of annuities has given rise to a number of other methods which have been available for those with a defined contribution pension to take it on a tax efficient basis. These methods, collectively known as drawdown, have generally allowed funds to be removed from the pension pot at and following retirement so long as sufficient funds are retained to ensure a pension can be provided. The processes for the different forms of drawdown have been relatively complex and historically have required significant administration to ensure that the drawdown was within the appropriate limits.

The changes to FA 2004 introduced under the Taxation of Pensions Act 2014 (TPA 2014) have replaced some methods of drawdown with a simple flexi-access drawdown arrangement. These changes came into effect from 6 April 2015 and allow members of a defined contribution scheme to allocate some or all of their fund for flexi-access drawdown. The allocated fund can be removed from the pension arrangement without limit and subject to no restrictions except for those imposed by the pension provider. The principle is that pension savings can be used as any other savings account once retirement is reached. This allows members to take a large sum when this is required and retain money within the scheme when less is required. It does not guarantee that there are sufficient sums for retirement or old age but the political principle behind this has been that individuals can be trusted to make these decisions for themselves.

In addition, capped drawdown remains, allowing members to drawdown up to a fund limit of 150% of the annuity the fund would provide. Those in capped drawdown may elect to be treated as in flexi-access drawdown and will be automatically treated as having done so if drawdown exceeds the capped amount. In addition, flexible drawdown pensions automatically changed to flexi-access drawdown from 6 April 2015.

In any form of drawdown, the benefit crystallisation event is the allocation of the fund or part of the fund for drawdown and the allocated amount is then the crystallised amount. This allows a member to allocate their fund for drawdown within the lifetime allowance and pay no lifetime allowance charge on the growth of the fund thereafter.

The development of drawdown has drawn a significant distinction between defined benefit and defined contribution schemes. None of the drawdown options relate to a defined benefit scheme where the pension, of a defined amount, is paid either by an annuity or direct from the funds of the scheme at the option of trustees. It is also worth noting that the drawdown options are not universally available for those in defined contribution schemes. Most occupational schemes are not presently offering most of these options and some FCA regulated providers have put limits on when they will do so. Up to retirement, members can transfer their funds from one scheme to another, allowing them to move their funds to a scheme that allows drawdown, and it may well be that this method is used more regularly to allow members to access benefits by way of drawdown.

It is worth noting that the TPA 2014 also relaxed a number of restrictions on the terms of an annuity bought with a defined contribution pension, in particular under FA 2004 Sch 28 para 3(1)(d), which required annuities not to decrease in payment over time. The broadening of annuities under para 3(1A) of that Schedule has arguably increased the attractiveness of annuities to members of defined contribution schemes. [50.17]

c) *Timing of payments*

In general, pension schemes have a normal retirement date at which pensions are generally drawn. However, whereas that date is of significant importance to a defined benefit scheme (with a pension usually reduced if it is taken early or increased if it is taken late) it is of less significance for a defined contribution scheme when a pension taken relates merely to the fund that is available.

Of more significance from a taxation viewpoint is normal minimum pension age, as defined in FA 2004 s 279. This is the earliest age at which a pension may be drawn within the HMRC rules.

In general, a pension may not be taken before normal minimum pension age except if the member suffers from ill-health, which is defined in FA 2004 Sch 28 para 1 as the 'ill-health condition'. This is effectively that the scheme administrator (the manager or trustees) has received evidence from a doctor that the member is and will continue to be incapable of carrying out their occupation because of a physical or mental impairment, and that the member has ceased to do so. Most pension schemes are established to allow members to take the pension early in circumstances of ill-health but the effect of this requirement is that a tax charge will arise in respect of such an unauthorised payment if the relevant medical evidence has not been received or the member is still carrying out their occupation whatever the terms of the scheme rules. It should be noted that the ill-health condition does not require the employee to be incapable of carrying out *any* occupation and it is not uncommon for someone to receive an ill-health pension and then take another role elsewhere.

The normal minimum pension age is 55 but was 50 up to 5 April 2010. In addition, if a pension scheme gave members a right (not subject to discretion) to an early retirement from age 50, which was in place on 5 April 2006 and in relation to which the member had a right to that benefit on or before 10 December 2003 or joined the scheme after that date (but before 6 April 2006) with their right subject to those pre-10 December 2003 provisions, the limit of 50 still applies. This complexity means that there are a number of schemes which have some members with a normal minimum pension age of 55 and some with a normal minimum pension age of 50. This can make a transfer from one pension scheme to another substantially less attractive for those who retain this right, as the right may be lost in the transfer. [50.18]

d) *Lump sums and tax treatment*

Generally, pension funds are used to provide an income stream but lump sum payments can be made in certain circumstances without adverse tax consequences and, for some, with beneficial tax consequences.

The following lump sums may be paid with the following tax consequences:

(i) *Pension commencement lump sum*

A pension commencement lump sum (PCLS) is paid free of any tax charge. This is a lump sum paid whilst a member has some lifetime allowance available and it is paid in connection with a pension or drawdown becoming available at any time between the six months before and the year after the member first becomes entitled to it. Because a pension is payable, the member must either satisfy the ill-health condition or have reached a normal minimum pension age. Exclusions apply in relation to a lump sum which is provided alongside a pension for which the sole or main purpose of the pension is to give rise to the lump sum.

The lump sum is subject to a maximum amount, which is one-third of the value of the pension provided and therefore 25% of the total pension fund (one part being used for the lump sum for every three to be used for the pension). The lump sum must also be no more than 25% of the lifetime allowance (reduced by any benefit crystallisation events that have already occurred). A member who had a right to a lump sum in excess of 25% of their benefits already accrued on A-Day may obtain a larger pension commencement lump sum under the provisions of FA 2004 Sch 36 para 31.

Pension commencement lump sums that were paid in relation to the purchase of an annuity which was since cancelled following the announcement of the introduction of flexi-access drawdown in March 2014 continue to be treated as pension commencement lump sums even if the time limits are breached because of a delay occasioned by the pension moving into drawdown.

(ii)   Serious ill-health lump sum

If the administrator has received evidence from a doctor that the member is expected to live for less than one year, a serious ill-health lump sum is payable at any time, including before normal minimum pension age. The lump sum includes the full value of the member's benefit and is only available if there is some lifetime allowance available, there has been no benefit crystallisation event, and the member has not reached the age of 75.

(iii)   Uncrystallised funds pension lump sum

Another change introduced under the TPA 2014 alongside flexi-access drawdown allows a member of a defined contribution scheme who has reached normal minimum pension age or in respect of whom the ill-health condition is met to take some or all of his or her funds as a lump sum. Taking the fund is in itself a benefit crystallisation event and requires sufficient lifetime allowance to be available. An uncrystallised funds pension lump sum is generally not available for those with enhanced or primary protections (see **[50.22]**), pension credits from divorce settlements or non-residents or overseas pension arrangements. Taxation of this lump sum is at the marginal rate in the hands of the individual but only charged on 75%, to give credit as if a pension commencement lump sum had been taken for 25% of the sum.

(iv)   Short service refund lump sum

A short service refund lump sum is a sum payable from an occupational pension scheme where a member has left the scheme at a time where he does not have a right to benefits being retained within the scheme under the Pension Schemes Act 1993 s 71 (so-called 'short service benefit'). This relates in general to a member who has less than three months service in a scheme or between three months and two years where he or she has not elected to take a transfer elsewhere. For a member who joined a defined contribution scheme on or after 1 October 2015, the maximum period of service is 30 days. The sum must be equal to the member's contributions and the returns on it and excludes the employer's contributions for these provisions to apply. The charge on this fund is 20% for the first £20,000 and 50% thereafter.

(v) Refund of excess contributions lump sum

Where a member has made or had made in respect of him or herself a contribution in excess of the annual allowance, a refund of that excess is payable, upon which income tax is not payable.

(vi) Trivial commutation lump sum

On the surrender of a member's rights under a pension scheme (between the ages of 60 and 75) because the rights are too small to provide an economic pension, a trivial commutation lump sum is paid. It is now only available in respect of defined benefit schemes (for which uncrystallised funds pension lump sums do not apply) and requires that the member's rights under all pension schemes do not exceed £30,000 and there has been no previous payment in the last 12 months of a trivial commutation amount. The taxation of this amount is at the marginal rate in the hands of the individual. Alternatively, the total pension rights under one scheme (ignoring all others) can be surrendered if it is £10,000 or lower as a de minimis payment. This is taxed in the same way.

(vii) Winding up lump sum

A winding up lump sum is a payment to the member because their occupational pension scheme was wound up and the value of the member's fund does not exceed £18,000. It is only payable when there is lifetime allowance available and the employer is not making, and has not in the previous five years made, contributions to another pension arrangement for that individual and will not do so for the following year. Taxation of a winding up lump sum is in the hands of the recipient at their marginal rate.

(viii) Lifetime allowance excess lump sum

A lifetime allowance excess lump sum is an authorised payment that a member of a registered pension scheme can receive if his or her benefits exceed the lifetime allowance. Payment can only be made if the member is under the age of 75 or meets the ill-health condition and is taxed by way of the lifetime allowance charge of 25% to 55% as described at **[50.16]**.

(ix) Transitional 2013–14 lump sum

A transitional 2013–14 lump sum is a new authorised payment that permits a lump sum to be paid which has become a trivial commutation lump sum

because of the increase in the trivial commutation limit between 2014 and 2015 where an initial lump sum on pension commencement had been paid before that announcement. No income tax is payable on this lump sum.
[50.19]

e) *Payments to employers*

A number of payments may also be made to the employer of an occupational pension scheme where the rules of the scheme allow. Authorised employer payments can be made in the following circumstances:
(i) a payment of surplus where the scheme rules allow this and where this is paid in accordance with the Registered Pension Schemes (Authorised Surplus Payments) Regulations (SI 2006/574), either on the winding up of the pension scheme or otherwise where there is a surplus in the scheme. The surplus charge is 35% and is not charged if the sponsoring employer is a charity or otherwise exempt from income tax or corporation tax in respect of payments at the relevant time;
(ii) a compensation payment which is a payment permitted under the pension scheme and the provisions in the Pensions Act 1995 s 91 in relation to a compensation for loss caused by the criminal or negligent act or omission of the member whose benefits are then forfeited to make such a payment. There is no taxation on such payments, other than any treated as income in the hands of the employer;
(iii) authorised employer loans which are loans made to the employer of no more than 50% of the value of the pension fund and subject to HMRC conditions as to interest, repayment and security to ensure that the loan is at market rate; and
(iv) scheme administration employer payments which are payments by the pension scheme to the employer for costs that the employer has incurred in the administration of the pension scheme, most commonly by employing pension managers and others whose work relates to the pension scheme. These are not unauthorised payments and therefore are not subject to unauthorised payment charges and surcharges.
[50.20]

f) *Unauthorised payments*

Any payment not falling into the categories set out above or within the rules on payments on death set out at [50.31] ff below is an unauthorised payment by the pension scheme. As described at [50.10], registered pension schemes may not entitle anyone to an unauthorised payment but unauthorised payments can still be made by a pension scheme. As well as an actual payment, FA 2004 Pt 4 Ch 3 sets out a range of other acts which will constitute an unauthorised payment, including the assignment or surrender of benefits, the provision of a benefit other than by way of a payment, the acquiring of an interest in taxable property for an investment regulated pension scheme or the shifting of value by the creation or amendment of rights in relation to assets held by the pensions scheme.

Any unauthorised payment is subject to an unauthorised payment charge of 40% of the unauthorised payment in the hands of its recipient. In addition, if the payment is worth 25% or more of the fund held by the pension scheme for that individual (or 25% of the total fund size in relation to a payment to an employer), it is subject to an unauthorised payment surcharge of 15%. In addition to this, the scheme administrator is liable for a scheme sanction charge of 40% of the unauthorised payment or 15% if the unauthorised payment charge and surcharge has been paid.

In recent years HMRC and authorities in general have become concerned about the growing trend for pension schemes to be established to encourage members of legitimate pension schemes to take a transfer into the scheme for the purposes of releasing the cash directly and paying any necessary tax charges. So-called 'pensions liberation' gives rise in many circumstances to individuals obtaining access to their pension fund at below normal minimum pension age, often unaware and even misled about the charges that will be made. In addition, very significant charges are levied by the providers and a number of cases now brought before the Pensions Ombudsman suggest that the receiving pension scheme may have fraudulently forwarded the funds in their entirety to the scheme manager.

In an attempt to combat pensions liberation, FA 2014 added provisions allowing HMRC more grounds to refuse registration or to de-register pension schemes, in particular relating to the scheme not having been established or maintained for making authorised payments under FA 2004 s 164(1)(a) or (b), and providing greater powers for HMRC to demand documentation. In addition, provisions have been introduced to allow independent trustees, who have been appointed by the Pensions Regulator under its powers under the Pensions Act 1995, to replace trustees of a liberation scheme in order that the scheme may be properly governed in the future, and to accept the appointment without becoming liable for the scheme sanction charge because of unauthorised payments made before. However, the issue of pensions liberation persists and continues to give rise to the concern that individuals are being encouraged to transfer their pension funds to a scheme which will provide unauthorised payments without fully understanding the costs involved. A consultation by HM Treasury in December 2016 proposed more radical measures to deal with this issue, including penalties for cold calling pensioners, and increased powers for trustees to refuse to make transfers (whereas they are presently required to do so if instructed by the member).

[50.21]

g) *Protection of accrued benefits*

The introduction of the lifetime allowance and the changes to it have, over time, given rise to individuals whose pensions have been accrued on the basis of earlier rules for whom it seemed unfair to impose taxation merely because the rules had changed. As a result, the original simplifying concept of the FA 2004 has been diluted by attempts to provide grandfathered protection to those who have already operated under the old system.

(i) *Changes in April 2006: enhanced and primary protection*

FA 2004 originally permitted two forms of protection that could be applied for by those who had already accrued benefits under their pension arrangement. Those applying for enhanced or primary protection were required to do so before 6 April 2009, although limited opportunities for later application are available for those who had a 'reasonable excuse' for missing the deadline (under reg 12 of the Registered Pension Schemes (Enhanced Lifetime Allowance) Regulations (SI 2006/131)).

Primary protection gives a lifetime allowance enhancement factor to be added to the lifetime allowance at the time of retirement, which is based on the percentage amount by which the fund at 6 April 2006 was in excess of the lifetime allowance. In addition, following the fall of the lifetime allowance in 2012, if a member's first benefit crystallisation event occurs after 6 April 2012, the enhancement amount is the higher of the enhancement factor to the current lifetime allowance and that enhancement factor to the £1.8 million lifetime allowance in April 2012. A member with primary protection can continue to contribute to the pension scheme but contributions and increases in value of the fund cannot take it over the new enhanced lifetime allowance without incurring the lifetime allowance charge.

Enhanced protection is available for those who do not wish to accrue further under their pension arrangement. Enhanced protection allows the member's fund to be free of the lifetime allowance charge whatever the growth in the fund so long as the member does not make any contributions or accrue any benefits or have any contributions made for it to any pension fund.

(ii) Changes in April 2012: fixed protection

On 6 April 2012 the lifetime allowance fell from £1.8 million to £1.5 million. Under FA 2011 Sch 18, fixed protection allowed members of pension schemes to apply prior to 6 April 2012 to retain a lifetime allowance of £1.8 million or such higher amount as the standard lifetime allowance rises to in the future. As with enhanced protection, it is not possible to make any future accrual of pension or accept any contributions into any arrangement without losing fixed protection.

(iii) Changes in April 2014: fixed and individual protection

In 2014, the lifetime allowance was reduced from £1.5 million to £1.25 million and protection was again offered. For fixed protection, application would need to have been made before 6 April 2014 and as with fixed protection in 2012, no further accrual of pension can be made. A person applying for fixed protection in 2014 retained a lifetime allowance of £1.5 million, which falls away if the lifetime allowance rises above this in the future.

In addition, individual protection is available for those who expect their pension savings at retirement to be more than £1.25 million. Individual protection can be applied for up to 5 April 2017. Individual protection freezes lifetime allowance at the value of pension savings as at 5 April 2014 but it does allow future contributions to be made. Individual protection is used by those who wish to make further pension contributions and wish to limit, if not remove, the lifetime allowance charge to the value of the fund as at April 2014. Applications for individual protection can be made by people who already have fixed protection or enhanced protection and the individual protection will remain dormant and only come into effect if the other protections fail (presumably from making further pension accruals).

(iv) Changes in April 2016: fixed and individual protection

Both fixed and individual protection are provided for the fall to £1 million in order to protect those who expect their retirement fund to be over £1 million. These work similarly to the 2014 protections except that, as the relevant legislation was not put in place in advance of 6 August 2016, applications may be made retrospectively. However, Fixed Protection 2016 is not available if the individual accrued any benefits after 5 April 2016.

(v) Auto enrolment and the protections

Under the Pensions Act 2008, all employers are required to automatically enrol employees into a pension scheme, with the employee able to opt out retrospectively only once they have been enrolled. This has caused significant concerns for those with protections that require no further pension accrual because the quite severe penalties for non-compliance with auto enrolment on the part of employers means that many have auto enrolled individuals who then risk losing their protection as a result. HMRC has generally taken the view that an immediate opt out is sufficient, but with effect from 1 April 2015, an employer can opt not to auto enrol any individual with any of the above-mentioned protections, although this may not prevent it occurring, particularly if the individual has not notified his employer of his protected position. [50.22]

(h) *Divorce settlements and the lifetime allowance*

The effect of divorce under the provisions of the Welfare Reform and Pensions Act 1999 is that it is possible for the court to issue a pension sharing order as part of a divorce settlement. This transfers part of the pension from one party to the divorce to the other (referred to in the legislation as the 'ex-spouse'). The effect of a pension sharing order is that the pension still counts towards the lifetime allowance of the original member rather than the recipient ex-spouse, whose lifetime allowance is unaffected by the receipt of the shared pension. [50.23]–[50.30]

6 Pensions benefits on death

a) *Pensions and lump sums*

Most pension arrangements offer some type of benefit on death. The rules as to death benefits under the pre A-day changes were complex and have been greatly simplified under FA 2004. Effectively, a pension may be paid to a dependant, which includes:
- a spouse or civil partner (including someone who held that position at the time that the member's pension came into payment);
- a child (generally including stepchildren) under the age of 23 or otherwise dependent due to physical or mental impairment; and
- any other person who is either financially dependent on the member at the time of their death or had a relationship of financial interdependency or alternatively was dependent because of physical or mental impairment.

The rules of the scheme may limit this list further but payments of pensions to such persons fall to be authorised member payments.

A lump sum payment can also be made in relation to the rights and benefits of the member under the scheme. In general, trust based schemes will retain a discretion as to the recipient within the scheme so that the payment is a discretionary trust payment and therefore falls outside the deceased's estate for inheritance tax purposes. A lump sum payment is often insured and calculated as several times salary and can easily place a member above inheritance tax thresholds. As such, it is common for occupational schemes to retain this discretion, and personal pension schemes often exclude a death benefit, which is instead provided under a separate trust in order to retain this inheritance tax benefit. Other lump sum death benefits may be authorised payments, in particular a payment to a charity on death or a payment of the full value of an individual's pension which is less than £30,000 as a trivial commutation lump sum death benefit.

Payments on death are crystallisation events, and so will be reviewed against the lifetime allowance as discussed in [50.16]. As a result, there has been a growth in recent times in the popularity of excepted life policies under Income Tax (Trading and Other Income) Act 2005 s 480, which may give rise to inheritance tax charges, but will not count against the lifetime allowance.

[50.31]

b) *Pension benefits and inheritance tax planning*

With the advent of drawdown pensions under FA 2004, there was distinct concern that a pension fund would be used for inheritance tax planning rather than for retirement planning. In effect, there were concerns that those with more resources would use their pension scheme to hold assets which could then be provided to the next generation outside the inheritance tax regime as a fund held on trust. As a result, there were a number of punitive measures introduced in relation to lump sums paid from a pension scheme on death, giving rise to a charge if the member died over the age of 75, except for lump sums paid to a charity, trivial commutation and winding up lump sums. In addition, the same charge arose for annuity protection lump sums and drawdown lump sums on death at any age. The charge, initially at 35% and only for certain of these benefits, rose to 55% in 2011, and this was viewed as an attempt to ensure that funds were drawn from the pension on retirement, and not simply left to the next generation as an IHT-efficient vehicle. Benefits could be drawn down by dependants and taxed as a pension in the normal way, and often this was much more tax efficient than a lump sum payment.

The changes brought in under the TPA 2014 reduced the charge to 45%. However, it also broadened the drawdown of funds to include nominees and successors as well as those who were actually dependants of the deceased, which continue to be taxed at the marginal rate in the hands of the recipient. The nominee may be nominated either by the member or by the administrator of the scheme and so gives a very wide range of individuals who could receive the funds and be taxed themselves at marginal rates, and the nomination can follow more than one generation. However, there will be no tax at all on the fund if the member is under the age of 75 at the time of death. These provisions certainly allow more scope for use of a pension as an inheritance tax planning vehicle, although there is an ongoing debate as to whether nominees enjoy benefits free from inheritance tax. **[50.32]**

7 Obligations to pay

Generally, pensions paid under a scheme are paid net of tax with the scheme administrators operating a PAYE system. Trustees of occupational schemes and personal pension schemes are therefore registered for PAYE and operate in the same way as a normal employment payroll. These obligations relate not only to members' pensions but to pensions payable to dependants.

Unauthorised payment charges are taxed in the hands of the recipient. The same is true of both the lifetime allowance and annual allowance charge. If an annual allowance charge exceeds £2,000, the member has a right under FA 2004 s 237B to render the scheme jointly liable for the charge, although the scheme administrator may apply to HMRC for a discharge of its liabilities on the grounds that the payment would be a substantial detriment to the interests of members of the scheme and it would not be just and reasonable to apply the charge. **[50.33]–[50.50]**

IV UNREGISTERED PENSION SCHEMES

Historically, there have been a number of arrangements in place to provide pensions for people whose benefits exceed the limits of tax efficient pension benefits. Such schemes have become less popular as the tax treatment has become less favourable over time but there are a number of historical arrangements still in place.

It was once quite common to find funded unapproved retirement benefit schemes ('FURBS') and unfunded unapproved retirement benefit schemes ('UURBS'). These operated for senior executives as a top up to the pension provided under the approved or later registered pension scheme. FURBS were generally set up under trust and often in an off-shore tax favourable location such as the Channel Islands. An UURBS could easily be a simple promise added to an employment contract and it is not uncommon to find UURBS that are created in error by promises set out in letters to senior executives from businesses that have not taken prior advice as to their effect.

In recent years, FURBS have been referred to as employer–financed retirement benefit schemes ('EFRBS'). EFRBS are referred to and described in ITEPA 2003 Pt 6 Ch 2. EFRBS are simply unregistered schemes that operate to provide pension benefits on retirement and none of the tax reliefs relating to pensions under FA 2004 apply to EFRBS. Tax charges lie with the individual once a benefit is received, including by way of a loan to the individual.

Depending on the wording of the EFRBS, if it is established as a trust under which benefits are 'earmarked' to an individual, or involves any loan or other payment by a third party to an employee, it is likely to give rise to a charge under the so-called disguised remuneration regime set out in ITEPA 2003 Pt 7A. This gives rise to a charge to PAYE and national insurance once the contribution is made (and therefore, generally, long before the benefit is received). The disguised remuneration regime excludes pre-6 April 2006 EFRBS and lump sums accrued prior to 6 April 2011 under an EFRBS, but the risk of the disguised remuneration regime applying for arrangements that are not specifically exempted has resulted in a significant fall in popularity for these arrangements. [50.51]

Section 9 The family

Chapters
51 Taxation of the family unit
52 Matrimonial breakdown

51 Taxation of the family unit

Updated by Jackie Anderson, Chartered Accountant and Chartered Tax Adviser, LHA Consulting Ltd

I   Introduction **[51.2]**
II Income tax **[51.11]**
III Capital gains tax **[51.56]**
IV Inheritance tax **[51.68]**
V   Stamp duty and stamp duty land tax **[51.91]**
VI Administration **[51.111]**
VII Civil partnerships **[51.130]**
VIII Comparisons in the treatment of spouses and cohabitees **[51.131]**

'If you're from an ordinary working class family, life is much harder than many people in Westminster realise. You have a job but you don't always have job security. You have your own home, but you worry about paying a mortgage. You can just about manage but you worry about the cost of living and getting your kids into a good school.

If you're one of those families, if you're just managing, I want to address you directly.

When it comes to taxes, we'll prioritise not the wealthy, but you.'

Theresa May's first statement as Prime Minister in Downing Street (13 July 2016)

[51.1]

I INTRODUCTION

Historically, the impact of taxation on the family unit concerned, in the main, tax allowances, particularly those for married couples, and mortgage interest relief (MIRAS). The election of the New Labour government in 1997 brought an end to this, with the abolition of the married couples' allowance (apart from the age-related married couple's allowance (see **[51.20]**–**[51.23]**) and what remained of MIRAS. Instead, we had to learn the new language of tax credits, introduced to reduce poverty in families, particularly amongst children, and to provide an incentive to work by making work pay.

Following the election of the Coalition Government in May 2010, and then the Conservative Government in 2015, the policy changed, with an emphasis once again on personal allowances in order to remove more people from the tax net. As well as increasing personal allowances, FA 2014 provided that, since

2015–16, a spouse or civil partner has been able to elect to transfer part of their personal allowance to their spouse or civil partner (see **[51.12]–[51.18]**).

At the same time, significant changes to the tax credit system are taking place. Universal Credit is to replace virtually the whole of the benefit system, including tax credits (see *Universal Credit: welfare that works* (Cm 7957, DWP, November 2010; Welfare Reform Act 2012). It is being implemented in stages, with completion expected in 2022.

Importantly for the purposes of this book, the new system of Universal Credit will be administered by just one department – the Department for Work and Pensions (DWP) – meaning that HMRC will relinquish the task of looking after a system with which it was never really comfortable.

Of critical importance is the parity of treatment (from 5 December 2005) between married couples and civil partners (see **[51.130]**) and, in each case, those treated as such. Whilst this chapter continues, in the main, to refer to 'spouses', the equal treatment of civil partners should be borne in mind. Further, following the Marriage (Same Sex Couples) Act 2013, a reference to marriage is to be read as including a reference to marriage of a same sex couple, a reference to a married couple is to be read as including a reference to a married same sex couple and a reference to a person who is married is to be read as including a reference to a person who is married to a person of the same sex. **[51.2]–[51.10]**

II INCOME TAX

1 Independent taxation of husband and wife

From 6 April 1990, every taxpayer resident in the UK has been entitled to a personal allowance that can be set against all types of income, both earned and unearned. For 2017–18, the allowance is £11,500 irrespective of age, reducing where the income is above £100,000 by £1 for every £2 of income above the £100,000 limit. This means that for 2017–18, those with income over £123,000 will have their personal allowance removed completely. That every taxpayer is entitled to a personal allowance is in stark contrast to the position that existed prior to 6 April 1990 when a married woman's income chargeable to income tax was deemed to be that of her husband for income tax purposes.

It should be noted that CTC and WTC are determined on the basis of the income of the family, marking a return to the assessment of joint income, albeit only for the purposes of tax credits (see **[51.27]**). **[51.11]**

2 Transferable tax allowance for married couples and civil partners (ITA 2007, ss 55A–55E)

From 6 April 2015, taxpayers who are married or in a civil partnership have been able to elect to transfer a fixed part of their personal allowance to their spouse or civil partner provided that the following conditions are met: (i) the transferring spouse must have income of £11,500 or less for 2017–18 (plus up to £5,000 of tax free savings interest); (ii) the recipient spouse must be liable to pay tax at the basic rate (in other words they must have income of between £11,500 and £45,000 in 2017–18); (iii) neither party can claim the tax reduction for married couples and civil partners born before 6 April 1935 (see **[51.20]**); and (iv) they must be UK resident.

The transferable sum for 2017–18 is £1,150 (10% of the personal allowance), and the recipient is eligible to a tax reduction of 20% of this amount, ie, £230 for 2017–18. Claims can be backdated to include any tax year since 5 April 2015. **[51.12]–[51.19]**

EXAMPLE 51.1

In 2017–18 Alan, who was born on 5 October 1965 has income of £8,000. His spouse, Becky, who was born on 17 April 1957, has income of £30,000.

(a) Alan is entitled to a personal allowance of £11,500 but as his taxable income is only £8,000 he will waste £3,500 of the allowance unless he elects to reduce his allowance by £1,150 and transfers it to Becky. His personal allowance then becomes £10,350.

(b) Becky is also entitled to a personal allowance of £11,500. As she is a basic rate taxpayer she can claim a tax reduction of 20% of the transferable tax allowance of £1,150, saving her tax of £230.

3 The age-related married couple's allowance

Where at least one of the parties to the marriage was born before 6 April 1935, the married couple's allowance is retained (for 2017–18, the maximum allowance is £8,445). Whilst new claims can no longer be made when one of the spouses reaches the age of 65, where a person born on or before 6 April 1935 newly marries, they or their spouse will be eligible to claim the relief. The claimant's entitlement is by way of a *reduction in respect of the income tax liability* arising on his total income, in other words, a tax credit. This tax credit is an amount equal to a percentage of the allowance, 10% for 2017–18 or, if less, an amount that would reduce the claimant's tax liability to nil. **[51.20]**

a) *Basic requirements*

A man who is married and whose wife is living with him for any part of the tax year is entitled to a married couple's allowance for that year in addition to the personal allowance. ITA 2007 s 1011 defines the phrase 'living together' as follows:

'Individuals who are married to, or are civil partners of, each other are treated for the purposes of the Income Tax Act as living together unless –

(a) they are separated under an order of a court of competent jurisdiction,

(b) they are separated by deed of separation, or

(c) they are in fact separated in circumstances in which the separation is likely to be permanent.'

For income tax purposes, therefore, a marriage ends at the time of actual separation. Continuing to live in the same house will not normally amount to separation, although if the building is divided into two flats that are self-contained, it is likely that the couple will be living apart for income tax purposes. In *Holmes v Mitchell* (1991) the husband and wife had ceased to be one household in 1972 and become two households even though they continued to live under the same roof and there was no physical division of the dwelling space. With the husband's subsequent declaration of intent to seek a divorce some 10 years later, the circumstances of the separation were then such that it was likely to be permanent.

The allowance can still be claimed if the couple are unable to live together because of illness or old age, working away from home, an armed forces posting, being in prison or training and education. **[51.21]**

b) *Restriction of relief*

The allowance of £8,445 is reduced if, for 2017–18, the taxpayer's income exceeds the income limit of £28,000, although it cannot fall below £3,260. The restriction applies by reducing the allowance by £1 for every £2 of income above £28,000.

EXAMPLE 51.2

Porgy, who celebrated his 65th birthday in March 2000, and Bess are married and living together throughout the tax year 2017–18. Porgy's gross income (all earned) is £50,000; Bess has no income.

Porgy's income tax liability for 2017–18 is computed as follows:

		£
Income		50,000
Deduct: personal allowance		11,500
		£38,500
Income tax liability:		
£32,000 at 20% = £6,400		
£6,500 at 40% = £2,600		9,000
Deduct: relief for age-related MCA (restricted due to income limit):		
£3,260 × 10%		326
Net income tax liability		£8,674

If, instead, Porgy's gross income for 2017–18 was only £13,000, his tax liability would be computed in the following way:

		£
Income		13,000
Deduct: personal allowance		11,500
		1,500
Income tax liability:		
£1,500 at 20%		300
Deduct:	relief for age-related MCA: £8,445 × 10% = £844.50	
	restricted to £300	300
Net income tax liability		Nil

A claimant's tax liability is determined *after* giving effect to any deductions in respect of any qualifying maintenance payments (see **[52.3]**) (ITA 2007 ss 24, 26, 27). Further, any double taxation relief to which the claimant may be entitled either unilaterally or by virtue of a double taxation agreement is ignored. **[51.22]**

c) *Use of the allowance*

The allowance went automatically to the husband for marriages before 5 December 2005, but there are now provisions that allow a married couple to decide how to allocate part of the allowance between them. Before the beginning of the appropriate tax year *either* the couple may elect jointly that the wife should be allocated the whole of the specified amount, *or* the wife can elect to receive one half of the specified amount. In either case, the wife will become entitled to a reduction from her income tax liability of an amount equal to 10% (for 2017–18) of the specified amount or of her allocated portion of the specified amount. The allowance is claimed either by completing the Married Couple's Allowance section of the self-assessment tax return or, where no tax return is completed each year, by contacting HMRC. Where the relief afforded in respect of the married couple's allowance cannot be fully utilised, whether by the husband or the wife, because his or her tax liability is insufficient to absorb the allowable percentage reduction, that spouse may give notice that the other spouse should be entitled to an income tax reduction calculated by reference to the unused part of the allowance.

EXAMPLE 51.3

Susan who was born after 5 April 1948 and Nicholas, who was born before 6 April 1935, are a married couple living together throughout the tax year 2017–18. Nicholas has a part-time job bringing in £12,000 pa. Susan earns £22,000 pa and has elected to receive one half of the specified amount of the age-related married couple's allowance. Relief in respect of this allowance will be split between them in the following way:

Nicholas

		£
Income		12,000
Deduct: personal allowance		11,500
		£500
Income tax liability: £500 at 20%		100
Deduct:	relief for age-related MCA (full amount less Susan's portion): £8,445 × 1/2 × 10% = £422.25	
	restricted to £100	100
Net income tax liability		Nil

As Nicholas has used only £100 of the possible £422.25 in reducing his tax liability to nil, the remaining £322.25 should be transferred to Susan to further reduce her income tax liability.

Susan

		£
Income		22,000
Deduct: personal allowance		11,500
		10,500
Income tax liability:	£10,500 at 20%	2,100
Deduct:	her portion of relief for age-related MCA: £8,445 × 1/2 × 10% = £422.25 plus unused part transferred from Nicholas of £ 322.25	744.50
Net income tax liability		£1,355.50

If the married couple's allowance has been reduced in the year of marriage (see [51.24]), it is that reduced allowance that forms the maximum amount which can be transferred to the other spouse.

It is important to note that a husband and wife eligible for the age-related married couple's allowance cannot also avail themselves of the provisions allowing for the transfer of part of the personal allowance to the other spouse or civil partner, which apply only to spouses or civil partners born after 5 April 1935. [51.23]

4 Tax in year of marriage

The personal allowance is available to both husband and wife in the year of marriage in the normal way. However, the age-related married couple's allowance for the year of marriage is reduced by one-twelfth for each complete tax month before the date of marriage (ITA 2007 s 54). For example, in the case of a couple marrying on 4 August where there has been no election as to the allocation of the allowance, the man would lose three-twelfths of the married couple's allowance since there are three complete tax months in that tax year during which the couple are not married.

Where a man who is already entitled to the age-related married couple's allowance (because of a previous marriage in the same tax year) marries, only one allowance is available.

If a married couple separate in one tax year but are reconciled in a later year, and were not divorced in the meantime, the husband will get the full age-related married couple's allowance in the year of reconciliation. There is no *pro rata* reduction, as there is for the year of marriage. [51.24]

5 Death of either spouse

If the wife dies, the husband will get the full age-related married couple's allowance for that tax year, in addition to his personal allowance. For subsequent years he will receive only the personal allowance (assuming that he does not remarry). If the husband dies, in addition to her personal allowance the wife will receive any unused relief in respect of the age-related married couple's allowance. The widow's bereavement allowance was abolished with effect from April 2000. [51.25]

6 Blind person's allowance

A taxpayer who is a registered blind person for the whole or part of the year of assessment receives an additional relief (for 2017–18) of £2,320. If a husband and wife or civil partners, are both registered blind they can each claim the blind person's allowance. A blind person who is married or in a civil partnership may transfer any surplus allowance to their spouse or civil partner; it is irrelevant that the transferee spouse or civil partner may not be blind. [51.26]

7 The child tax credit and the working tax credit

a) *Introduction*

In an attempt to improve work incentives, simplify the benefits system and tackle administrative complexity, the Welfare Reform Act 2012 provides for the introduction of a 'Universal Credit', a new single monthly payment for people in or out of work, to replace a range of existing means-tested benefits and tax credits for people of working age. The provisions of the Act have been effective since 2013 and initially applied to new claims in certain areas of the country. It will be phased in for existing tax credit recipients but, until that time, the basic structure of the child tax credit (CTC) and the working tax credit (WTC) remains the same. It should also be noted that WTC is to be frozen for four years from 2016–17 and CTC will be largely limited to two children for children born after 5 April 2017.

The original aim of CTC and WTC was to separate the support for working adults in a household from support for children to ensure both that children may be properly provided for within out of work households as well as in working households, and that those who are low-paid receive more financial help whether or not they have children. Accordingly, CTC may be claimed irrespective of whether an adult in the household is in work, and WTC may be claimed even though there may be no children in the household.

Tax credits must actually be claimed by use of the appropriate form (TC600). A claimant who makes a tax credit claim can have this backdated by up to one month if they meet all the entitlement conditions. An individual or family's award is based on two factors: *first*, their current circumstances (for example, for CTC, how many children they have, and for WTC, how many hours they work and the amount of eligible childcare costs), and *second*, their gross income (or the joint gross income of a couple). A 'couple' is defined as a man and a woman who are married (which definition will now include two persons of the same sex who are married – see Marriage (Same Sex Couples) Act 2013 Sch 3, para 1(1)(b)), or two people of the same sex who are civil partners of each other (see [51.130]), and not separated (Tax Credits Act 2002 s 3(5) as amended), or a man and a woman, or two people of the same sex, living together as if they were married or civil partners, a matter of fact that is likely to be determined by reference to the social security approach.

CTC and WTC run from 6 April in any year for a period of 12 months and, generally, awards will be made on the basis of the claimant's current circumstances and previous year's gross income, with changes in circumstances (for example, the birth of a new child) or in income during that period being reflected in the amount paid to the claimant (see **[51.37]–[51.38]**). This 'responsiveness' is achieved through a three-stage process. On a claim for a tax credit being made, HMRC make an initial decision as to whether an award should be made, and the rate at which to award it. Following notification of a change of circumstances during the year, HMRC may revise their initial decision and amend the award from the date of the change. At the end of the period of award, that is, at the end of the tax year in which the award was made, the person to whom a tax credit was awarded is required to confirm that the circumstances/income affecting their entitlement to tax credits were the same for the current year as for the previous year or, if they were not, to declare how they differ. HMRC will then make a final decision as to entitlement and any underpayment is refunded only after the award has been finalised at the end of the tax year. Overpayments are recovered either by a notice to repay a specified sum within 30 days of service of the notice or, since October 2014, HMRC may automatically claw back outstanding overpayments in respect of old claims from new ongoing tax credit awards by cross-claim recovery. By this process, households with live tax credit awards and with outstanding overpayments from claims that have ended and which included the same claimant(s) will be able to have the old debts recovered by a reduction of 25% in tax credit payments from the ongoing award, limited to a 10% reduction where the claimant(s) receives maximum tax credit award. This will not apply where the debt arose on an old joint claim and the new joint claim is made with a new partner. Further, where the old debt is already being repaid directly to HMRC, it will not be included for cross-claim recovery from ongoing payments. **[51.27]**

b) *Child Tax Credit*

(i) *Elements of the credit*

There are two basic elements:
(1) 'the family element' up to a maximum of £545 (for 2017–18) per year;
(2) 'the child element' for *each* child within the family up to a maximum of £2,780 (for 2017–18) per year.

An extra credit for each child with a disability and a further severely disabled child element is available (£3,175 and £1,290 respectively for 2017–18).

Unlike WTC (see **[51.31]**), there is no additional second adult element that distinguishes between couples and lone parents; CTC is independent of the status of the adults in the family or the number of parents in or out of work, and the calculation of the credit is based on the *children* in the household. Further, in contrast to the abolished Child Tax Credit, a claim for CTC will be based on the *joint* income of a couple.

The actual award of CTC is based on the aggregate of these separate elements, which is then adjusted according to the claimant's income. For 2017–18, CTC is paid at the maximum rate until the income of the family reaches £16,105 pa (the first threshold for those entitled to CTC only). Thereafter, the award is gradually reduced at the rate of 41p for every pound of gross income over the threshold; the family element also tapers away at the rate of 41p for every pound of gross income. **[51.28]**

(ii) Conditions of entitlement

A claim may be made in respect of a child or children of a family irrespective of whether one or both of the adults are working. The support continues until 1 September following the child's 16th birthday or, for those who continue in full-time secondary education, until the young person's 19th birthday. It is also now available in respect of 16–19 year olds on unwaged work-based training programmes. [51.29]

(iii) Payment of the credit

CTC (along with the childcare element of WTC (see [51.35])) is paid directly to the main carer, who is frequently the mother. The persons or families with whom the child normally lives may decide which of them is mainly responsible but, if they do not decide, HMRC will decide on the basis of the available information; it cannot be split between the main and minority carer. In *Humphreys v R & C Comrs* (2012), the Supreme Court held that the 'no-splitting' rule was a reasonable rule for the state to adopt and the indirect sex discrimination was justified and not a breach of Art 14 of the European Convention on Human Rights. Giving the judgment of the court, Lady Hale referred to the rationale behind the introduction of CTC, namely, the reduction in/alleviation of child poverty and said:

> 'If funds are targeted at one household, it is likely that a child living in that household will be better off than he or she would be if the funds are split between two households with modest means. The state is, in my view, entitled to conclude that it will deliver support for children in the most effective manner, that is, to the one household where the child principally lives. This will mean that that household is better equipped to meet the child's needs. It also happens to be a great deal simpler and less expensive to administer, thus maximising the amount available for distribution to families in this way.'

(See [55.44].) [51.30]

c) *Working Tax Credit*

(i) Elements of the credit

There are broadly four elements:
(1) a basic element in respect of all persons entitled to the credit, up to a maximum of £1,960 per year (for 2017–18);
(2) an element in respect of persons being a couple (whether married or not) or a lone parent, up to a maximum of £2,010 per year (for 2017–18);
(3) a 30 hour element giving extra credit to a person who, or persons who between them, works for more than 30 hours per week, up to a maximum of £810 per year (for 2017–18); and
(4) a childcare element of 70% of eligible childcare costs, up to maximum costs of £175 per week for one child, and £300 per week for two or more children (for 2017–18).

There is an additional element for disabled and severely disabled workers (£3,000 and £1,290 respectively for 2017–18).

As with CTC, a WTC award is the aggregate of these separate elements, adjusted according to the claimant's income. For 2017–18, individuals and couples with income below £6,420 per year receive the maximum amount of credit; for those whose income exceeds that threshold, the award is gradually reduced at the rate of 41p for every pound of gross income above the threshold. Claimants eligible for both WTC and CTC have their maximum awards reduced in the following order:
- WTC apart from the childcare element;
- the childcare element of WTC;
- CTC apart from the family element; and
- the family element of CTC. [51.31]

(ii) Conditions of entitlement

1 Couples with children and workers with a disability
Couples with children and workers with a disability are eligible for WTC provided they are over the age of 16 and, for 2017–18, work at least 24 hours per week unless either (i) one partner is over the age of 60 and works 16 hours; or (ii) one partner qualifies for the disability element and works 16 hours; or (iii) one partner works 16 hours and the other is ill, an inpatient in a hospital or in prison; or (iv) one partner works 16 hours a week or more, and the other is entitled to Carer's Allowance. Couples with children are eligible for an extra credit element if jointly they work at least 30 hours per week, provided that one of them works at least 16 hours. Where the claim for the credit is made jointly, the couple are entitled to a further second adult element. [51.32]

2 Lone parents
Single persons are eligible provided they are over the age of 16 and work at least 16 hours per week. They are further entitled to additional elements in respect of working at least 30 hours per week and for claiming as a single parent. [51.33]

3 Workers with no children and no disability
This category was not available under the former WFTC, eligibility for which was dependent upon a claimant having responsibility for children, whether as a lone parent or as a couple. The claimant must be aged 25 or over, and working for at least 30 hours per week. In the case of a joint claim, the couple will be entitled to the second adult element, provided that one of them works at least 30 hours per week. There has been criticism that those below the age of 25 and without children are not eligible for tax credits, since research has revealed in-work poverty in the 18–25 age-group. [51.34]

(iii) Childcare element

Families will be eligible for the childcare element of WTC where a lone parent or both partners in a couple work for at least 16 hours per week and incur relevant childcare charges. For these purposes, a person is a child until the last day of the week in which falls 1 September following the child's 15th birthday (or 16th if the child is disabled). The childcare element is available for approved childcare schemes, and in England these would include registered minders, foster-carers, nurseries, play schemes, nannies and out of school hours clubs. For 2017–18, the childcare element will provide help with 70% of eligible costs. [51.35]

(iv) Payment of the credit

WTC (apart from the childcare element) is paid directly by HMRC to both the employed and the self-employed. For couples, it is paid to the partner who is engaged in remunerative work, and if both work at least 16 hours per week, they can decide between them which of them is to receive the payments. In the event that they do not reach a decision, HMRC will decide to which partner the credit will be paid. [51.36]

d) *Changes in circumstances*

Although a change in circumstances will generally only affect the rate of entitlement, an award will come to an end prior to the end of the tax year if eligibility for the credit ceases, for example, because there is no longer a 'child' or 'young person' in the family. Further, an award will only last until either a couple who have made a joint claim separate, or a single person who has made a claim becomes part of a couple (at which time, a new claim would have to be made). In these circumstances, there is a formal requirement to notify HMRC of such a change within one month of its occurrence. In the case of a new claim being made thereafter, the award will be backdated for up to 31 days only. Notification is also required where there are changes in work status and the number of children for whom the family can claim support. There is a further requirement to notify HMRC when the claimant or partner leaves the UK permanently or for more than eight weeks, or where the claimant goes abroad due to an illness, family illness or bereavement for more than 12 weeks. Where a change merely affects the rate of the award, formal notification of the change, again within one month, is only required where there is either a cessation of, or a significant reduction in, childcare costs. With respect to any other changes, there is no formal requirement to notify where the change might have the effect of reducing the rate of entitlement (the overpayment of a tax credit, with the need to pay it back at the end of the year, is a deterrent to not notifying. With the reduction of the income rise disregard to £2,500 for 2016–17 and subsequent years – see [51.38] – it is even more crucial that claimants inform HMRC of changes to income as they occur), but where it would have the effect of increasing the rate of entitlement, for example the birth of a new child, or an increase in the number of hours worked (giving rise to eligibility for the 30-hour element), then provided HMRC is notified, the tax credit award will be backdated for up to one month. Any other changes not notified to HMRC in the course of the year and not requiring notification, will come to light at the end of year (see [51.27]). [51.37]

e) *Changes in income*

In the case of the initial decision on an award of a tax credit, a determination is made on the basis of the income of the previous tax year. However, entitlement is only finally determined at the end of the tax year for which the claim is made, and consideration must then be given to both the previous tax year and the year in which the claim is made, the current tax year. Where there is an increase in the family income during the current year, it is the current year income that will form the basis of the final award, subject to a £2,500 disregard (for 2016–17; the previous income rise disregard of £5,000 will continue to be used to finalise 2015–16 claims in the summer of 2016);this disregard means that if the current year income is no more than £2,500 higher than that of the previous year, it is the income of the previous year that is taken (TCA 2002 s 7(3)(a) and the Tax Credits (Income Thresholds and Determination of Rates) Regulations 2002 as amended). If there is a fall in income, a fall of up to £2,500 will be disregarded (for 2016–17). A fall greater than £2,500 will cause the award to be adjusted, but the first £2,500 will be ignored. [51.38]

EXAMPLE 51.4

Edwina is a lone parent who has been awarded CTC and WTC for 2017–18. Her gross income for 2016–17 (the 'previous' year income) was £20,000. Her final award, determined at the end of 2017–18, will depend upon her gross income for the current year, 2017–18.

(1) If Edwina's income for 2017–18 is £22,000, the final award will continue to be based on the income of the previous year (TCA 2002 s 7(3)(a)). This is because the current year income exceeds the previous year income by no more than £2,500.

(2) If Edwina's income for 2017–18 is £25,000, the final award will be based on the income of the current year reduced by £2,500, ie £22,500 (TCA 2002 s 7(3)(b)). This is because the current year income exceeds that of the previous year by more than £2,500.

(3) If Edwina's income for 2017–18 is £18,000, the final award will continue to be based on the income of the previous year. This is because the fall in income is less than £2,500.

(4) If Edwina's income for 2017–18 is £15,000, the final award will be based on the current year income, ignoring the first £2,500 of the reduction (ie the income to be taken into account for tax credit purposes for 2017–18 is £17,500).

f) *Appeals*

(i) *The appeals process*

Although it was the clear intention of Parliament at the time of the enactment of the TCA 2002 that tax credits appeals should be heard by the then Commissioners of Income Tax (TCA 2002 s 39), possibly because of the impending changes to the tax tribunals, all appeals go to the Social Entitlement Chamber of the First-tier Tribunal (TCA 2002 s 63 as amended by the Transfer of Tribunal Functions and Revenue and Customs Appeals Order 2009) until the Treasury directs otherwise. Although it had been announced that the transfer of all tax credit appeals to the Tax Chamber would take place once the new tribunal structures had 'bedded down', in light of the introduction of the new Universal Credit, the administration of which will rest with the DWP, it is unlikely that this will now happen. The appeals procedure, which is a compromise between the Social Security Act 1998 and the Social

Security Decisions and Appeals Regulations on the one hand, and TCA 2002 and TMA 1970 on the other, has changed considerably for decisions made on or after 6 April 2014. Claimants who disagree with the initial decision, a decision to terminate an award, any other revision or refusal to revise, a decision as to entitlement after the final notice at the end of the period of award (which could include a challenge to an overpayment if the claimant believes that the underlying calculation that led to the overpayment is wrong) and any later revision, *but not* a decision by HMRC to *collect* an overpayment, must first request a review of the decision (mandatory reconsideration) by HMRC's appeals team in the Tax Credit Office within 30 days of the date of the decision notice (a late application for reconsideration may be lodged in certain circumstances) and be issued with a mandatory reconsideration notice showing the outcome of the reconsideration. If the claimant remains dissatisfied, there is then an appeal to the First-tier Tribunal; if the case is a 'difficult' one, then membership of the tribunal must include a financially qualified person. Further appeals lie, in the first place, to the Administrative Appeals Chamber of the Upper Tribunal on a matter of law and with permission (on matters of fact, the decision of the First-tier Tribunal is usually final) and thereafter to the Court of Appeal, again with permission and on a point of law. For decisions made prior to 6 April 2014, an appeal was to the First-tier Tribunal with no prior mandatory reconsideration. [51.39]

(ii) Disputes

There is no appeal against a decision for the repayment of an overpayment. However, where a claimant has actually received more than their entitlement in a year but does not think that it should be paid back because they believe that they have met their responsibilities under COP26 and that HMRC have made a mistake, the dispute process, which is governed by COP26 and is subject to a three month time limit, will apply. Disputes are decided within HMRC by the Customer Service and Support Group in the Tax Credit Office and any further challenge is limited to the Adjudicator and Parliamentary Ombudsman. [51.40]

g) *A Case Study*

EXAMPLE 51.5

Alan and his wife Charlene have three children, Alice aged nine, Ben aged six, and Claire who was born on 6 April 2017. Their joint gross income for 2016–17 was £17,000 and £66,000 for 2017–18. They have always worked in excess of 40 hours each week.

Since both Alan and Charlene are away from home during the day, they incur childcare costs. Prior to the birth of Claire, these amounted to £120 per week, but thereafter rose to £320 per week.

1. **Calculating the initial award**
(a) *Entitlement to claim*
The family will be entitled to claim tax credits in respect of the tax year 2017–18 by completing form TC600. The initial claim will be based upon the income for 2016–17, the preceding tax year.
(b) *Calculating initial entitlement to CTC*
The basic entitlement to CTC comprises:

	£
Family element	545.00
Child element (£2,780) for 2 children	5,560.00
Maximum basic CTC entitlement	£6,105.00

However, the detailed rules of calculation convert each element to a daily sum, rounding certain (but not all) figures up or down, and then converting the result back into an annual sum. This exercise is done to allow for the extra day occurring in a leap year. The result of this is that the basic entitlement on the initial claim becomes:

	£
Family element	547.50
Child element for two children	5,562.60
Maximum basic CTC entitlement	£6,110.10

(c) *Calculating entitlement to WTC*

The basic entitlement to WTC comprises:

	£
Basic element	1,960.00
Second adult element	2,010.00
30-hour element	810.00
Maximum basic WTC entitlement	£4,780.00

Applying the conversion rules discussed above, the basic entitlement on the initial claim becomes:

	£
Basic element	1,960.05
Second adult element	2,011.15
30-hour element	810.30
Maximum basic WTC entitlement	£4,781.50

There is entitlement to the childcare element, which is limited to 70% of the childcare costs up to a maximum of £175 per week for one child and, with more than one child, to a maximum of £300 per week. In this case, the amount paid at the time of the initial application was less than £300, and the entitlement is:

	£
Childcare cost of £120.00 per week	6,240.00
Childcare element: 70% of £6,240	£4,368.00

(d) *Calculating maximum initial tax credits award*

The initial award is the aggregate of CTC, WTC and the childcare element of WTC:

	£
CTC	6,110.10

	£
WTC	4,781.50
Childcare element of WTC	4,368.00
Maximum initial award	£15,259.60

(e) *Calculating the reduction in the initial award*
(i) WTC is reduced by 41% of the amount by which the claimant's income, calculated as above, exceeds the threshold (£6,420 for 2017–18). The reduction in the award is thus:

	£
Income	17,000.00
Less threshold	6,420.00
	10,580.00
Reduction in award: 41% × £10,580	4,337.80

(ii) CTC is reduced by 41% of the amount by which the claimant's income exceeds the threshold (£16,105 for 2017–18). The reduction in the award is thus:

	£
Income	17,000.00
Less threshold	16,105.00
	895.00
Reduction in award: 41% × £895.00	366.95

(iii) Reductions are made in the following order:
 WTC
 Childcare element of WTC
 Child element of CTC
 Family element of CTC

(f) *Calculating the actual award*

	£	£
WTC		4,781.50
Less: reduction in award		4,337.80
Actual WTC award		443.70
Childcare element of WTC	4,368.00	
Less: reduction in award	366.95	
Actual childcare element award		4001.05
CTC		6,110.10
Total tax credits payable		10,554.85

2. Calculating the effect of the change in circumstances following the birth of Claire

Provided that HMRC were notified of this change in circumstances (which will have the effect of increasing the tax credits award) within one month of the date of the change, the revised award takes effect from the date of change. Otherwise, the award will only be effective as from the date of notification.

The birth of Claire and the increase in childcare costs will both cause the tax credits award to be revised:

	£	£
CTC (applying the conversion rules):		
Family element	547.50	
Child element for 3 children	8,343.90	
Revised CTC award		8,891.40
Childcare element of WTC (limited to £300 per week and taking into account the reduction)		10,920.07
WTC remains the same		443.70
Total tax credits payable after the birth of Claire		£20,255.17

3. Calculating entitlement after the final notice at the end of the tax year 2016–17

The award is reassessed at the end of the year, and a comparison is made between the income of the previous year (2016–17 on the facts of this case study) and that of the current year (2017–18).

	£
Gross joint income for 2016–17	17,000.00
Gross joint income for 2017–18	66,000.00

At this level of income, the whole of the award would be withdrawn including the family element of CTC that is restricted by 41% of the amount by which the income for the relevant period exceeds £16,105 (£66,000–£16,105 × 41% = £20,456.95).

	£	£
WTC		0
Childcare element of WTC		0
CTC (apart from family element)		0
Family element of CTC	547.50	
Less: restriction	(20,456.95)	0
Initial revised award		20,255.17
Final award		0
Overpayment		£20,255.17

If Alan and Charlene have no current entitlement to tax credits (which seems likely), they will be asked to repay £20,255.17 within 30 days of notice being given to them by HMRC. Wherever possible, a previous year's overpayment will be collected by reducing the claimant's payments for the current tax year (see *Tax Credits Manual* and **[51.27]**). Whilst there is a statutory right of appeal against the decision giving rise to an overpayment, a decision by HMRC to collect the overpayment is not subject to appeal. **[51.41]**

8 Childcare support

There are several forms of tax-free childcare support:
(1) Employers may provide childcare facilities for children under 18 without an employee benefit charge arising on the employed parent (ITEPA 2003 s 318).
(2) Employers could provide childcare vouchers to their employees to pay for qualifying childcare for up to £55 per week. Tax relief was restricted to basic rate from April 2011.
(3) From September 2017, 3- and 4-year-olds may be entitled to an additional 15 hours free childcare per week (in addition to the 15 hours per week to which they are already entitled).
(4) Tax-Free Childcare is the new scheme introduced from April 2017 – this is considered further below.

Following consultation and changes to the original proposals, the scheme will be available to all eligible families, and is not dependent upon employers offering the scheme. This means that self-employed parents will also be able to get support with childcare costs.

Eligibility

To qualify:

- There must be children under the age of 12 within the first year of the operation of the scheme, or children with disabilities up to the age of 17.
- Parents must either be (i) in work, earning at least £120 per week and not more than £100,000 per year. To support newly self-employed parents, the government is introducing a 'start-up' period, during which self-employed parents: (i) will not have to earn the minimum income level of £50 a week; or (ii) could be on paid sick leave or paid and unpaid statutory maternity, paternity and adoption leave.

Parents may not use Tax-Free Childcare at the same time as they receive childcare vouchers, Universal Credit or tax credits.

The relief

Parents will be able to open an online account, through the government website (https://childcare-support.tax.service.gov.uk/par/app/applynow), which they (and other persons such as grandparents, other family members and employers) can pay into as and when they like to cover the cost of childcare with a registered provider. For every 80p paid into the account, the government will top it up with an extra 20p, *equivalent to* income tax at the basic rate, with a cap of £10,000 of childcare costs for any one child (ie there is a limit of £2,000 HMRC top-up per child per year). [51.42]

9 Child Trust Fund

The child trust fund, provided for by the Child Trust Funds Act 2004, was intended as a new long-term savings and investment account for children. Its aim was to ensure that all children had a financial asset behind them when they reached the age of 18, and to encourage a savings culture for both families and children. However, soon after it was elected in May 2010, the Coalition Government made clear its intention to end all contributions in due course. Accordingly, the child trust fund was withdrawn for children born after 2 January 2011. Accounts will continue for eligible children born between 1 September 2002 and 2 January 2011 but, from August 2010, government contributions to child trust funds at birth were reduced from £250 to £50 and children reaching the age of seven on or after 1 August 2010 no longer receive the universal government contribution of £250 formerly made to all eligible seven year olds (Child Trust Funds (Amendment No 3) Regulations 2010, SI 1894/2010). [51.43]

In light of the changes made to child trust funds and the Government's intention to end all government payment into accounts eventually, any provider of child trust funds is now permitted to stop accepting vouchers but may continue to act as a provider for the Child Trust Fund accounts it already holds (Child Trust Funds (Amendment No 4) Regulations 2010, SI 2599/2010).

Children, parents, family and friends, together with institutions or organisations such as businesses, community groups, charities and local authorities, are able to contribute up to £4,128 (for 2017–18) to each account. There exists no provision for income tax relief on such a subscription and any payment by an individual is taken into account in determining the annual exempt amount for inheritance tax purposes (see [31.3]), unless it is made on a regular basis and qualifies for exemption as normal expenditure out of income (see [31.4]). Until the child reaches the age of 16, the account is managed by the person with parental responsibility. On reaching 16, a child may manage his own child trust fund account, but there is no access to the money until he reaches the age of 18, at which time he may use it as he chooses.

Junior Individual Savings Accounts (see [15.26]) were launched in November 2011 as the long term replacement for Child Trust Funds. These tax-free savings accounts for those under the age of 18 allow for savings or investment of up to £4,080 per year (for 2016–17). The account remains tax-free until the child's 18th birthday, when it gets converted into an adult ISA. Most children born before 1 September 2002 or after 2 January 2011 are eligible to start a Junior ISA, but a child cannot have both a CTF and a Junior ISA. However, since April 2015, parents and guardians may transfer existing CTFs into Junior ISAs, allowing for better rates of interest. [51.44]

Neither the child nor the account provider is liable for any income tax on the income from CTF savings and investments, including dividends, interest (which may be made gross to the account provider) and bonuses, on any annual profits or gains treated by ITA 2007 Part 12 Chapter 2 (the accrued income scheme: see [42.100]) as having been received by them in respect of account investments, or on an offshore income gain arising from a disposal of an account investment that would otherwise be treated as a profit or gain by virtue of ITA 2007, s 535 (see [13.6]). Importantly, income arising from account investments is not deemed to be that of the parent subscriber under ITTOIA 2005 s 629 (see [16.95]). Further, the child pays no capital gains tax arising on the disposal of account investments. However, the child trust fund investments are effectively ring-fenced from any other investments held by the child concerned, since any capital losses arising on the disposal of child trust fund investments are not deductible from any capital gains made outside the child trust fund. [51.45]

10 High income Child Benefit charge

As part of the Coalition Government's cost-cutting measures and policy of targeting reliefs at those who need them most, FA 2012 provides for an income tax charge with effect from 7 January 2013 on taxpayers whose income is more than £50,000 and who receive Child Benefit or whose partner receives Child Benefit. Where both partners have income of more than £50,000, the charge applies to the partner with the highest income. The amount of the charge is collected through either self-assessment or PAYE. HMRC notify all of those whose income is over £50,000 of the liability to the charge.

Child Benefit is unaffected by this charge (subject to the election: see [51.49]) and will continue to be paid in full even if the claimant or their partner is liable to the charge. [51.46]

a) *The charge*

(i) For taxpayers whose income is between £50,000 and £60,000, the charge is 1% of the amount of Child Benefit for every £100 of income that exceeds £50,000.
(ii) For taxpayers whose income exceeds £60,000, the charge is equal to the full amount of Child Benefit.

EXAMPLE 51.6

Claude and Claudia have two children and Claudia is eligible to receive Child Benefit of £1,788.80 (£20.70 per week for the first child and £13.70 per week for the second child for 2017–18). Claude's income is £57,000. Claudia has no income. Claude will be charged £1,252.16 (1% of the amount of Child Benefit for every £100 of income above £50,000, ie, 70%). If Claude's income had been, say, £63,000, he would be charged £1,788.80, the whole amount of the Child Benefit. The amount of the charge is collected through either self-assessment or PAYE. [51.47]

b) *The measure of income*

The measure of income that is used is the individual's adjusted net income, which is calculated in a series of steps:
(i) find the net income, ie the total of the individual's income subject to income tax less specified deductions such as trading losses and payments made gross to pension schemes;
(ii) the net income is reduced by the grossed-up amount of the individual's gift contributions and the grossed-up amount of pension contributions which have received tax relief at source;
(iii) add back any relief payments to trade unions or police organisations deducted in arriving at the individual's net income. The result is the individual's adjusted net income. [51.48]

c) *The election*

If a claimant or their partner does not wish to pay the new charge, they can elect not to receive the Child Benefit to which they are entitled, and may later withdraw that election if they or their partner cease to be liable to pay the charge (ie because the claimant's income or that of their partner falls below £50,000). **[51.49]**

11 Reliefs and exemptions

b) *Enterprise Investment Scheme and Seed Enterprise Investment Scheme*

(i) The Enterprise Investment Scheme (EIS), which applies to new eligible shares issued in qualifying companies and provides income tax relief at 30%, 'aims to incentivise investment in smaller, higher risk companies' and 'plays a significant role in the provision of venture capital for small businesses' (*The Enterprise Investment Scheme: A Consultation Document* (HM Treasury, March 2008) (see **[15.51]–[15.81]**). Husband and wife each have their own maximum limit for EIS relief on qualifying share subscriptions (£1 million since 6 April 2012) meaning that a husband and wife can claim relief on subscriptions totalling £2m. Where shares are issued to joint owners, such as husband and wife or civil partners, each is treated as having subscribed the same amount for an identical number of shares irrespective of the fact that one of them might have paid the whole amount. For example, if W pays £3,000 for 3,000 shares but in the joint names of W and H, each will be treated as having subscribed £1,500 for 3,000 shares. Inter-spouse transfers do not result in withdrawal of the relief: the transferee spouse is instead treated as the original subscriber for the shares.

(ii) The Seed Enterprise Investment Scheme (SEIS – see generally **[15.128]–[15.134]**), which applies to shares issued on or after 6 April 2012, was introduced as one of a number of measures aimed at stimulating the economy. Specifically, it is designed to help small, early-stage companies to raise finance by offering income tax and capital gains tax reliefs to individual investors who purchase new shares in those companies. Complementing EIS, SEIS is intended to recognise the particular difficulties which very early stage companies face in attracting investment by offering tax relief at a higher rate than that offered by EIS. When the SEIS legislation was introduced in FA 2012, it was originally envisaged that the scheme would run for a five-year fixed period only. However, because of its success, it has now been made permanent. The rules for SEIS mirror those for EIS, so that a husband and wife each have their own maximum annual investment limit (£100,000 for 2017–18) meaning that a husband and wife can claim relief at 50% of the cost of the shares totalling £200,000. TCGA 1992 s 150G and Sch 5BB provides for CGT relief for reinvestment in SEIS shares, gains not being chargeable to CGT to the extent that they were matched by qualifying SEIS investment (see **[15.92]**). This relief was limited to gains accruing to the SEIS investor in 2012–13; FA 2013 extended relief, but for only half the qualifying re-investment amount. This 50% reinvestment relief continues to apply for 2017–18. **[51.50]**

c) *Close company loans*

Close companies are exempt from a tax charge on loans to full-time employees without a material interest in their company if the sum of outstanding loans to the employee does not exceed £15,000 (CTA 2010 s 456). Under independent taxation there are separate £15,000 limits for husband and wife if both are employees of the company. [51.51]

d) *Capital allowances and charges*

Capital allowances due by way of discharge or repayment are given against income of a specified class or, on election, against other income for the year or the following year. Such allowances can be set only against the income of the person who incurred the expenditure. So far as charges on income are concerned, for example the payment of an annuity, if a married couple are jointly liable to make a payment, the amount each person *actually pays* is the amount of his or her charge for tax purposes. If it is unclear how much each person pays, HMRC will adopt a 50:50 split. [51.52]

12 Trading losses

The trading loss of one spouse cannot be offset against the income of the other spouse. Instead, any unused loss may be carried forward to set against the income in the following year of the spouse who incurred the loss. [51.53]

13 Jointly held property

In order to give a clear and simple basis of taxation without the need for enquiries where assets, such as rental property, are jointly owned by both spouses, special rules exist whereby income from assets held in the names of a husband and wife who are living together is treated as income to which husband and wife are entitled equally (ITA 2007 s 836). Thus, if husband and wife have a joint building society account, even if they have contributed to it in unequal proportions, for income tax purposes each is treated as owning one-half of the interest arising, and taxed accordingly. Indeed, some spouses actively rely on the 50:50 rule when, in fact, the asset is owned between them in different proportions. Say, for example, the husband owns an income-producing asset worth £1,000. He might transfer it into the joint names of himself and his wife but only give his wife a 1% beneficial interest in the asset. Despite this, under the 50:50 rule the wife will be taxed on 50% of the income. Nevertheless, the husband will remain the owner of 99% of the asset. However, since April 2004, the general 50:50 rule has not applied in a variety of circumstances, and in particular where the property in question is shares in a close company, and one spouse is beneficially entitled to all of the shares and income, or the spouses are entitled to the shares and income in equal or unequal proportions (ITA 2007 s 836(3)). Close company shares are given the same meaning as in CTA 2010 ss 1072(4), 1113(6), 1114(3)(6), 1115(1) and 1117(1). This provision is aimed at preventing the general measure from being used as a device to circumvent the anti-avoidance settlements legislation.

EXAMPLE 51.7

Jimbo Ltd provides the services of Jim as a consultant to a number of clients working in the telecommunications industry. Jim is the sole director of the company. His wife, Tanya, takes no active part in the company and has no other income. The company's share capital is £100 consisting of 100 £1 shares, for which Jim and Tanya subscribed jointly. By virtue of a declaration of trust, Jim is entitled to 99% of the beneficial ownership of the shares, with Tanya being beneficially entitled to the remaining 1%. During the tax year 2003–04, on a turnover of £100,000, the company incurred expenses of £5,000, Jim received a salary of £10,000 and a dividend of £70,000 was declared. Although Jim controls the company, when the dividend was paid out TA 1988 s 282A deemed the income from the shares to arise 50:50, so that for tax purposes £35,000 was treated as Jim's and £35,000 as Tanya's. It had been thought that the settlements legislation in ITTOIA 2005 Part 5 Chapter 5, which was designed to prevent individuals from securing a tax advantage by transferring their own income to another individual who is taxed at a lower rate, would not have applied since Jim had not given anything away – apart from 1% of the shares and income, to which the settlements legislation could apply – thus saving Jim and Tanya significant amounts of tax. However, this assumption was questioned in the case of *Jones v Garnett* (2007) (see **[51.55]**), although the House of Lords found in favour of the taxpayer on the particular facts of the case. In any event and in contrast, if the same facts occurred during the tax year 2017–18, ITA 2007 s 836(3) would require that Jim and Tanya be taxable on the actual income to which they are entitled. Accordingly, Jim would be taxed on 99% of the income, and Tanya would be taxed on 1%.

More generally, the 50:50 rule does not apply to income to which neither spouse is beneficially entitled; to partnership income from a trade or profession; to the income of a married couple who are separated; to the situation where property is held in the name of one party only; or where some other legislation (eg that governing settlements) directs that the income should be taxed in a different way.

However, by virtue of ITA 2007 s 837, it is possible for the general 50:50 rule to be displaced (eg in respect of income to which one spouse only is beneficially entitled or in respect of income to which they are beneficially entitled in unequal shares). For the rule to be displaced, an appropriate declaration must be made specifying the shares in which the income is, in fact, beneficially enjoyed by one or both spouses. Any declaration must relate to both the income arising from the property and the property itself, and the income cannot be shared in different proportions from the capital. It has effect in relation to income arising on or after the date of the declaration.

Notice of any declaration must be given to the appropriate tax inspector within the period of 60 days beginning with the date of the declaration and must be made on the prescribed Form 17. If no such notice is given, despite the contrary intentions of the spouses, the 50:50 rule will apply (*Koshal v R & C Comrs* (2013)).

EXAMPLE 51.8

John and Susan jointly own £1,000 10% loan stock in XYZ plc producing annual interest of £100. Each will be taxed on one half of the income. They may enter into a declaration of trust giving John a 1% beneficial interest in the stock and Susan a 99% beneficial interest. If, following that trust, the appropriate declaration is made on Form 17 and submitted to the Revenue within 60 days, as from the date of that declaration Susan will be taxed on 99% of the income and John on 1%. **[51.54]**

14 Planning opportunities

The rules offer planning opportunities to many couples. In particular, if one spouse or civil partner is a higher or additional rate taxpayer and the other is subject to the basic rate only, it will be advantageous for income tax purposes for the former to transfer income-producing assets to the other spouse to ensure that the personal allowance and basic rate band is fully utilised. There may be other advantages (see **[51.59]**). However, care must be taken to ensure that any transfer is an outright gift of assets with 'no strings'. Certain gifts will *not* be treated as outright gifts, namely:

(1) a gift not carrying the right to the whole of the income from the property given; or
(2) a gift which is wholly or substantially a right to income (without being a gift of the underlying capital); or
(3) a gift subject to conditions; or
(4) a gift where the property given or any income or property derived from it is or might be paid to or for the benefit of the donor.

In such circumstances, the gift will be treated as a settlement and any income arising treated as the donor's for income tax purposes (ITTOIA 2005 s 624(1), formerly TA 1988 s 660A). To be certain that the inter-spouse gift is effective for income tax purposes it is vital to ensure that the gift is outright, incapable of being revoked, unconditional and of matching proportions of income and capital. For a gift that was considered to be wholly or substantially a right to income, see *Young v Pearce, Young v Scrutton* (1996) (see **[16.102]**). In fact, that case was one of the first cases to reveal just how widely HMRC is prepared to use the settlement legislation to combat what it views as a transfer of income between co-shareholders or partners where the effective reward by way of dividend or partnership share is not commensurate to the way in which the money is earned (see *Tax Bulletin*, April 2003, p 1011 and February 2004, p 1085).

This important issue was revisited by the House of Lords in the case of *Jones v Garnett* (2007), otherwise known as the *Arctic Systems* case (see **[16.93]** and **[16.102]**). In that case, the only business of a company, which was owned equally by husband and wife, each paying £1 for the purchase of the shares, was the supply of consultancy services provided by the husband alone. The husband was the sole director and the wife provided some administrative services. Both received small salaries from the company; although substantial dividends were paid equally to husband and wife in certain years. Bearing in mind the modest services being provided by the wife, the Revenue was of the view that the dividends were being paid in lieu of a salary in order for the income to be taxed at the lower rate applicable to the wife rather than to the higher rate of the husband. Accordingly, the question to be decided was whether the dividend income paid to the wife during those years was income arising under a settlement made by the husband and thus to be treated as the income of the husband as settlor under s 660A(1) (now ITTOIA 2005 s 624(1)). There were two main questions to be decided: *first*, was there a settlement, which term includes an arrangement, within the meaning of the relevant statutory provisions; and *second*, did the outright gift exclusion in TA 1988 s 660A(6) (now ITTOIA 2005 s 626: see **[16.102]**) apply so as to prevent the anti-avoidance rules from having effect? As Lord Neuberger pointed out, these two issues were difficult enough to spawn quite a considerable difference in judicial opinion. Thus, the senior Special Commissioner found for the Revenue on both issues, whilst the junior Commissioner found against the Revenue on both issues. Park J found for the Revenue on both issues, but his main reason on the second one was different from that of the senior Special Commissioner.

The Court of Appeal found against the Revenue on the first issue and, although they did not have to make a decision because of their conclusion with respect to the first issue, would have been for the Revenue on the second issue, although disagreeing with the reasoning of the senior Commissioner! For its part, the House of Lords held (i) that there was an arrangement amounting to a settlement; but that (ii) the taxpayers fell within the exception created by ICTA 1988 s 660A(6) (now ITTOIA 2005 s 626). As far as the first issue was concerned, the House of Lords, following the decision in *IRC v Plummer* (1980), confirmed the opinion of the lower courts that, for a transfer of property to amount to a settlement for the purposes of the legislation in question, there needed to be an 'element of bounty' in the transaction (although Baroness Hale refused to use such demeaning language). However, unlike the Court of Appeal, but following Park J, the House of Lords took the view that the taxpayers' dealings were driven not for commercial reasons, but by tax considerations. This was not 'a normal commercial transaction between two adults'; it was not an arrangement into which Mr Jones would have entered with someone with whom he was dealing at arms' length. It was 'natural love and affection' that provided the consideration for the benefit he intended to confer upon his wife, and that was sufficient to provide the necessary 'element of bounty'. As for the second issue concerning the exception to applying ICTA 1988 s 660A (now ITTOIA 2005 s 624) by means of an 'outright gift' to the donor's spouse, the House of Lords concluded that, despite the fact that Mrs Jones had paid for her one share in the company, given that it was Mr Jones' consent to the transfer of the share with the expectation of dividends to Mrs Jones that gave the transfer the 'element of bounty' for the purposes of the first issue, by the same token it made the transfer a 'gift' for the purposes of the exclusion. Moreover, contrary to the view of Park J and the *obiter* opinion of the Court of Appeal, the House of Lords held that the transfer of the share was the essence of the arrangement; the expectation of other future events gave that transfer the necessary element of bounty, but the events themselves did not form part of the arrangement. Accordingly, the transfer itself of the one share to Mrs Jones did amount to an 'outright gift'. Finally, taking a different view from Park J, but in accordance with that of the Court of Appeal, the House of Lords was of the opinion that the share was not 'wholly or substantially a right to income'. It was an ordinary share conferring other rights additional to the right to receive income. Lord Hope said:

> '... so long as the shares from which the income arises are ordinary shares, and not shares carrying contractual rights which are restricted wholly or substantially to a right to income, the settlement will fall within the exception created by section 660A(6).'

It was the fact that the share was an ordinary share that distinguished this case from *Young v Pearce* (1996). The message given by Lord Hope is a very clear one: future transactions of this kind will escape the rigours of ITTOIA 2005 s 624 provided that the shares gifted by one spouse to the other are ordinary shares and not of a class which, in effect, restricts the holder's right to little more than income.

This view has been confirmed by subsequent cases: see *Bird v R & C Comrs* (2008); *Buck v R & C Comrs* (2008); *Donovan & McLaren v R & C Comrs* (2014). In deciding whether there had been an 'arrangement' within s 660A (now ITTOIA 2005 s 624), the Special Commissioners and the First-tier Tribunal followed Lord Hoffmann's lead by taking a 'realistic' view of the matter. In the first case, the issue of shares to their minor daughters by Mr and Mrs Bird enabling the daughters to take a 60% share in a business that had previously been owned by Mr and Mrs Bird, amounted to an arrangement within the scope of the settlement provisions. In the second and third, waivers, and subsequent payment of, dividends by husbands in favour of their wives were held in each case to have been part of a plan to use a company's shares to divert income, and fell within the meaning of an arrangement within the legislation. In neither *Buck* or *Donovan & McLaren* was the outright gift between spouses exemption applicable; there was no evidence that the share allotments in favour of the wives were gifts. Even if the shares allotted to the wives could be characterised as gifts, *Jones v Garnett* could be distinguished on the facts because the essential arrangement was not the transfer of the shares from the husbands to their wives but the waiver of dividends.

Patmore v R & C Comrs (2010), a First-tier Tribunal decision, was decided on a very different, and possibly questionable, basis. In this case, on the retirement of its controlling shareholder, the taxpayer and his wife purchased a small company of which the taxpayer was a director. The purchase was funded partly by a mortgage on their home, which they owned jointly. Following the purchase, although the wife was equally liable for the loans raised to purchase the company, she received a much smaller percentage of the shares in the company than the taxpayer. The company's shares were reorganised into two classes, with the wife owning 2% of the A shares and 10% of the non-voting B shares. Dividends were paid in respect of the B shares in the tax years 1999 to 2003, and were paid immediately into the taxpayer's loan account to set against the outstanding payments in relation to the purchase of the company. HMRC argued that the taxpayer was liable to tax on the dividend paid in respect of the B shares as the settlor under a settlement within TA 1988 s 660A (now ITTOIA 2005 s 625) on the basis that the taxpayer owned the company and used his control of it to declare significant dividends in favour of his wife so that they would attract a lower rate of income tax. However, his wife never received the dividends because they were effectively retained by the taxpayer to repay the purchase debt. The Tribunal had to decide whether there was a settlement of (i) the B shares and (ii) the dividends from those shares for the purpose of what is now ITTOIA 2005 s 625. In respect of the first issue, the judge, having decided that there was an arrangement between the taxpayer and his wife that would never have been the subject of a commercial, arm's length deal, held that it amounted to a settlement. However, and crucially, in distinction to the cases of *Buck* and *Bird*, the judge could find no element of bounty. This was because she held that there was a constructive trust in the wife's favour: she contributed half of the capital to buy the shares by being jointly liable with her husband on the purchase loan and on the mortgage of the jointly owned house. The purchase of the company was a joint enterprise by the taxpayer and his wife to secure their financial future. The wife did not intend to give her half-share to her husband. The couple took the advice of their accountant, which was to allot to her B shares rather than transfer to her half of the 85 A shares they had jointly purchased. The B shares were not a fair recognition of her investment as they were almost valueless, carrying no voting rights and no rights to any dividend; any dividend paid was entirely at the taxpayer's discretion. As a result, there arose a constructive trust over half of the A shares in the wife's favour when they were purchased; she was entitled to half of the A shares but she received only two and a promise of almost valueless B shares. Accordingly, when the 10 B shares were allotted to the wife, although the arrangement was not commercial, it was not gratuitous either: it was a recognition of her rights to shares in the company. If the taxpayer had transferred to her 42.5 of his A shares it would not have been gratuitous as she was entitled to them (under the constructive trust); the judge said that it followed that the allotment instead of the almost valueless B shares (presumably in lieu) could not therefore be gratuitous.

As to the second issue of whether the *dividends* from the B shares were settled on the wife, following the approach of Lord Hoffmann in taking 'a broad and realistic view of the arrangements', the judge found that, consistently with the decision in *Buck*, choosing to pay a dividend on only one kind of share (the B shares) could amount to a settlement of that dividend. However, as with the allotment of the shares themselves, s 660A could only apply where there was present in the arrangement some element of bounty or gratuity. Because the taxpayer held the A shares in trust for his wife, the dividends he caused to have paid to her, albeit on the B shares, were dividends to which she was entitled, at least in part. Thus, to the extent that she was entitled to the dividends, there was no gratuity and therefore no settlement within s 625.

To the extent that the dividends paid to the wife exceeded her entitlement as the beneficial owner of half of the A shares, there was a settlement within s 625 and, because the property given, the dividends, were 'wholly or substantially a right to income', the judge concluded that the exception in s 626 for outright gifts could not apply.

This decision is questionable because (i) it seems to ignore the House of Lords decision in *Stack v Dowden* (2007) on the imposition of constructive trusts and (ii) because, if there does exist an implied trust here, it looks more like a resulting than a constructive trust. It might be harder to argue that the interest in particular property arising by virtue of the resulting trust can, in effect, be transferred to different property.

In a ministerial statement given in July, 2007, the Exchequer Secretary to the Treasury expressed the Government's view that 'individuals involved in these arrangements should pay tax on what is, in substance, their own income and that the legislation should clearly provide for this' and announced that proposals for changes to legislation to ensure this was the case would be brought forward. Expected changes in FA 2009 following wide consultation on draft provisions did not appear and have not appeared since, but we may yet expect legislation in the future that may change the structure of small company taxation following the review by the Office for Tax Simplification of small business taxation (March 2016). The rules above do not catch a gift where the donee, of his or her own accord, chooses to apply the income or capital in some way that might benefit the donor. The previous Inland Revenue practice whereby property which might return to the donor following the death of the donee under the donee's will or under the intestacy rules would not, for that reason, fail to be treated as an outright gift is now expressly enacted in ITTOIA 2005 s 625(4)(c), formerly TA 1988 s 660A(3)(c).

As noted above, one way of making an outright gift of unequal amounts of income and capital is to arrange for the capital to be owned jointly, albeit in unequal shares, and then to rely upon the presumption of equality to ensure that half of the income is taxed as that of the spouse with the small capital entitlement. Such presumption will not apply where the assets concerned are shares in a close company. [51.55]

III CAPITAL GAINS TAX

1 Separate taxation of gains

The gains of each spouse are calculated separately and each is entitled to an annual exemption (£11,300 for 2017–18). [51.56]

2 Losses

The losses of a spouse can only be offset against his or her own chargeable gains and not set against the gains of the other spouse. [51.57]

3 Inter-spouse transfers (TCGA 1992 s 58)

The disposal of an asset by one spouse to another, or from one civil partner to the other, is treated as being for such consideration as gives rise to neither gain nor loss. This rule operates whether or not any consideration is furnished for the transfer and in spite of the couple being connected persons. Effectively, therefore, gains are held over and the asset will be acquired at the base cost of the disponer spouse together with any incidental costs involved in the disposal. For disposals before 6 April 2008, the indexation allowance (available only for periods up to April 1998) will be included in the deemed consideration. In respect of disposals on or after 6 April 2008, the indexation allowance has been abolished in its entirety.

EXAMPLE 51.9

Jim gives his wife Judy two birthday presents on 1 June 2007, a Ming vase which he acquired from Christie's on 1 April 1988 and a painting by William Roberts acquired on 10 April 1986.

The disposal by Jim will be at no gain/no loss and Judy's base costs will include an indexation allowance on the vase from April 1988 to April 1998 and on the picture from April 1986 to April 1998. (The indexation allowance was abolished for the months after April 1998 in the case of individuals.)

Had the gift been made instead on 1 June 2017, Judy's base cost would not include the benefit of an indexation allowance for either the vase or the painting because, for disposals on or after 6 April 2008, the indexation allowance is abolished in its entirety.

The rule in s 58 applies only so long as the spouses or civil partners are 'living together', and a couple will remain living together for these purposes, and therefore taxed as a married couple, where one is, but the other is not, resident in the UK during a year of assessment. [51.58]

4 Taper relief

Taper relief only applied in respect of disposals made before 6 April 2008. When an asset was transferred between spouses before 6 April 2008, taper relief on the eventual disposal of that asset was based on the combined period of ownership of both spouses. [51.59]

5 Entrepreneurs' relief

Entrepreneurs' relief was introduced by the FA 2008 (see generally **Chapter 20**), and is available in three circumstances. First, in respect of gains made on the disposal of all or part of a business; secondly in respect of gains made on the disposal of assets following the cessation of a business; and finally in respect of gains made by an individual on the disposal of shares in a trading company where that individual was an officer or employee of the company and held at least 5% of its shares and voting rights. For disposals made on or after 6 April 2011, qualifying gains up to a lifetime limit of £10m are charged to CGT at a rate of 10% (for lifetime limits on respect of chargeable gains made before that date, see **[20.1]**). An important drawback is that, unlike taper relief, periods of ownership of an asset by the two spouses cannot be aggregated. Accordingly, if one spouse owns 3% of the ordinary voting rights of a company, and the other owns 4%, the two cannot be added together and, consequently, neither spouse will qualify for entrepreneurs' relief as neither will own the necessary 5% holding in the company. [51.60]

6 Cohabitees and children

General CGT principles operate for disposals between cohabitees and between parents and their children. In the case of disposals to children the connected persons rules operate with the result that any disposal will be deemed to be made at market value (TCGA 1992 ss 17, 18). In distinction, cohabitees are not connected for the purposes of CGT. [51.61]

7 Principal private residence

Only one principal private residence exemption is available where a married couple live together (TCGA 1992 s 222(6) and see **[23.42]**). [51.62]

8 Jointly held assets

Where assets are disposed of which were held in joint names of husband and wife, each spouse will be regarded as owning a half share of the asset and charged to CGT accordingly. This is subject to the couple having made a declaration that the asset is held in different shares: in such a case the gain is charged *pro rata* according to their respective shares in the property.

Any declaration that has been made for income tax purposes regarding jointly held property will have a corresponding effect for CGT purposes.

[51.63]

9 Planning opportunities

If one spouse's annual CGT exemption will not be utilised whilst the other spouse's is fully utilised, it may be worth the couple transferring assets (at no gain/no loss under s 58 – see [51.58]) to the 'poorer' spouse so that both exemptions are used. There are two rates of CGT in force and, for disposals on or after 6 April 2016, these are the standard rate of 10% for basic rate income taxpayers, and the higher rate of 20% for those paying higher rates of income tax. Accordingly there are obvious CGT benefits in spouses transferring assets from one to the other where one is a basic rate income taxpayer and the other a higher rate taxpayer. [51.64]–[51.67]

IV INHERITANCE TAX

1 General principles

There is no aggregation of spouses' chargeable transfers for IHT purposes. They are treated as separate taxable entities, each entitled to the full exemptions and reliefs. It is immaterial whether they are living together and, unlike the position with respect to income tax and CGT, a couple remain married for IHT purposes until the decree absolute that terminates the marriage. If care is taken with the associated operations and related property rules, transfers between spouses offer an opportunity to mitigate IHT since they are exempt without limit (except where the donee spouse is domiciled abroad – see [51.71]). [51.68]

a) *Both spouses domiciled in the UK*

The inter-spouse exemption means that full use may be made of both spouses' exemptions and reliefs and benefits may be obtained by ensuring that the nil rate band (currently £325,000, and frozen at that level until the end of 2020–21) of each spouse is fully used. Where any spouse or civil partner to die first has not fully utilised their nil rate band, any unused part may be transferred to the estate of their surviving spouse or civil partner who dies on or after 9 October 2007 (see [30.27]). This ensures that a married couple or civil partners are entitled between them to a nil rate band of £650,000 (until the end of 2020–21). For transfers on or after 6 April 2017, an additional (main residence) nil rate band (£100,000 for 2017–18; £125,000 for 2018–19;

£150,000 for 2019–20; and £175,000 for 2020–21) will be available when a residence is passed on death to a direct descendant (see [**30.28**]). The main residence nil-rate band will be transferable where the second spouse or civil partner of a couple dies on or after 6 April 2017 irrespective of when the first of the couple died. This means that for 2017–18, the combined entitlement of a married couple or civil partners to a nil rate band is increased to £850,000.

[**51.69**]

b) Donee spouse domiciled abroad

(i) Spouse exemption

Where the donee spouse is domiciled abroad, the position since 1982 has been that only £55,000 may be transferred free of IHT. However, for transfers of value made after 6 April 2013, FA 2013 provided for an increase in the cap for gifts to non-domiciled spouses or civil partners to the same figure as that for the prevailing nil rate band, ie £325,000 until 2020–21. [**51.70**]

(ii) Domicile election

FA 2013 also provides that, subject to satisfying one of two conditions, an election after 17 July 2013 may be made in writing to HMRC for the non-domiciled spouse to be UK domiciled (for IHT purposes only; the election does not affect the spouse's income tax or CGT position). This will enable the spouses to benefit from an unrestricted spouse exemption on gifts from the domiciled spouse, but it will also mean that, from the time of the election, the donee spouse's worldwide estate will be liable to IHT.

The two conditions are:
(a) if the election is made during the lifetime of the donor spouse, the donee must not be UK domiciled and the donee's spouse must be UK domiciled at the time of the election;
(b) if the election is made on the death of the donor spouse, the donor spouse died UK domiciled on or after 6 April 2013 and the donee was not UK domiciled at that time. The lifetime and death elections have effect on a 'date specified'. In the absence of such a date, the lifetime election will take effect from the date the election is made. The death election is treated as taking effect immediately before any transfer treated as made by IHTA 1984 s 4 immediately before the death of the spouse.

(See [**31.41**]) and also Private Client Business 2013, Issue 2.)

EXAMPLE 51.10

In September 2017 Rob, who is domiciled in the UK, considers buying a gastropub costing £1.5m in the name of his wife, Carole, who is domiciled in Italy.
(i) If no election is made, the first £325,000 of the transfer of value will be exempt, the remainder being a PET, which Rob will have to survive for seven years to avoid an IHT charge.
(ii) If Carole makes an election, the transfer will be fully exempt.

Where the donor UK domiciled spouse has died, the non-UK domiciled surviving spouse, ie the donee, (or the donor's personal representatives) may make the election within two years of the death (or such period as the Revenue may allow), allowing for dispositions taking effect on death to benefit from the uncapped IHT exemption.

EXAMPLE 51.11

Bob, who is domiciled in the UK, died on 10 September 2017, leaving the bulk of his estate situated in the UK to his spouse, Pam, who is domiciled in Spain.
(i) If no election is made, only the first £325,000 of the disposition will be exempt from IHT.
(ii) Pam or Bob's personal representatives may make an election for Pam to be UK domiciled for IHT purposes at any time before 10 September 2019. If this is done, the disposition will benefit from the uncapped spouse exemption. The Revenue may permit an election to be made after 10 September 2019 on the facts of the particular case.
(iii) In the event that Bob had made a lifetime transfer of value in favour of Pam on 10 September 2010, resulting on his death in a failed PET, but Pam had made no election at the time of the transfer, any election she or Bob's personal representatives might make following Bob's death will be ineffective for the uncapped spouse exemption and only the first £325,000 of the disposition will be exempt.

A lifetime election will be effective from the date specified in the notice, which must be on or after 6 April 2013, and within the seven-year period immediately preceding:
- the date on which the election is made (if a lifetime election); or
- the date of the deceased's death (if a death election).

EXAMPLE 51.12

In September 2013 Rob, who is domiciled in the UK, buys a gastropub costing £1.5m in the name of his wife, Carole, who is domiciled in Italy. Realising that she could have made an election for the spouse exemption to apply, Carole makes the election, choosing a date specified of October 2013.

The gift is spouse exempt so that no charge would arise if Rob should die within seven years of making the gift.

EXAMPLE 51.13

In August 2013, Jane who is domiciled in the UK, makes a substantial gift to her husband, Edmund, who is domiciled in Norway. She dies in August 2019.

Edmund can make a death election specifying a date of August 2013 and, rather than the gift being a failed PET, it would be spouse exempt.

Once made, the election cannot be revoked but, if the person making it is not resident for income tax purposes for four successive tax years beginning at any time after the election is made, the election ceases to have effect at the end of that period.

EXAMPLE 51.14

In *Example 51.13*, Carole is not UK domiciled and not resident.
(i) She makes an election in September 2013. The four year period begins with the year of the election, 2013–14 and consequently will remain in force until the tax year 2017–18 if she remains non-resident throughout 2014–15, 2015–16 and 2016–17.
(ii) If Carole becomes UK resident in 2015–16, the election remains in force. Had she become resident in 2017–18, the election would have ceased to have effect. [51.71]

2 PETs and the nil rate band

Generally, there are only two rates of tax (0% and 40%), although for deaths on or after 6 April 2012, a lower rate of 36% will be charged where 10% or more of the deceased person's net estate is left to charity. The *ideal* IHT planning for spouses should ensure that full use is made of PETs, the nil rate band and, of course, charitable giving if this can be afforded. [51.72]

a) *Making full use of PETs*

Whenever practicable, PETs should be employed to transfer wealth *inter vivos* to future generations. The spouse with the greater life expectancy should make the bulk of such transfers in order to minimise the risk of the PET failing. Since the making of any kind of *inter vivos* trust, apart from a trust for a disabled person, on or after 22 March 2006, will now be subject to the same inheritance tax regime that formerly only applied to discretionary trusts, it is suggested that outright gifts should be made to avoid any charge that might arise in respect of property of a value in excess of the nil rate band (see **[28.41]**–**[28.42]**). If necessary, property can be transferred from the wealthy to the poorer spouse to enable the transfer to be made without the risk of the associated operations provisions applying. [51.73]

b) *Making full use of the nil rate band*

The ability to transfer to the surviving spouse any unused part of the nil rate band of the first spouse to die and, from 2017–18, any unused part of the main residence nil-rate band where the second spouse dies on or after 6 April 2017, (see **[30.27]** and **[51.69]**), has removed the necessity for much IHT planning for middle wealth couples, which was mainly concerned with how to utilise the nil rate band on the first to die, without excluding the surviving spouse from access to the assets formerly owned by the first spouse. One device by which this was achieved was through a 'mini discretionary trust', details of which can be found in earlier editions of this book. Because any unused nil rate band is now available to the surviving spouse, such devices are no longer needed.

EXAMPLE 51.15

Husband (H) had an estate of £500,000; wife (W) an estate of £150,000. If H died first and left all to W:

IHT on H's death   Nil (spouse exemption)
IHT on W's death   Nil (on £650,000) (allowing for the transfer to W of H's full nil rate band)

This measure has saved the family IHT of £130,000 (ie 40% × £325,000).

It remains desirable, if possible, to leave property attracting 100% business or agricultural property relief to someone other than the surviving spouse.

EXAMPLE 51.16

Bill owns a farm (qualifying for 100% agricultural property relief (APR)) worth £1m. On his death it will be run by his wife, Daisy. If he leaves it to her in his will, APR will be lost since the gift will be spouse exempt. Bill should therefore consider leaving the farm to his daughter, Tulip. Because of APR at 100% IHT will not be charged on that gift. Tulip could then sell the farm to her mother, Daisy, for its market value of (say) £1m with the result that:
(i) on Daisy's death APR may again be available at 100% provided that she occupies the farm for two years (the relief has been 'recycled');
(ii) if Daisy's mother cannot afford £1m, consider leaving the price outstanding on an interest-free loan. [51.74]

3 How to leave property to a spouse: outright and limited gifts

A separate problem is whether a spouse gift should be absolute or for a limited (for example, life) interest. So far as IHT is concerned, both types of gift fall within the spouse exemption so that the tax is neutral. Accordingly, the decision can be made on non-fiscal grounds.

The *outright gift* has the attraction of flexibility. The surviving spouse is free to use the property for any purpose and may therefore employ it to the best advantage of the family in the future. As a corollary, however, because the assets are given free from all conditions, an imprudent spouse may fritter away the inheritance and leave nothing for the children.

A *life interest* avoids the dangers inherent in the absolute gift by ensuring that the capital assets will eventually pass to persons entitled in remainder (usually children or grandchildren). Giving an interest in income may, however, be inadequate for the needs of the surviving spouse. A sudden emergency requiring a substantial capital outlay, for instance, may arise and if the absolute gift suffers from being too flexible the limited interest may well prove too inflexible! It had been the Government's intention to treat for inheritance tax purposes such an immediate post-death interest in possession trust in the same way as a discretionary trust from 22 March 2006, but it subsequently changed its mind in the face of extreme criticism from a number of professional bodies.

An alternative to the two major types of gifts considered above is for a limited interest to be conferred on the spouse, but for the trustees of the will to be given a power to advance capital sums to the spouse. Such a power can then be exercised should the need arise, bearing in mind that capital sums advanced to the interest in possession beneficiary are free from IHT (IHTA 1984 s 52(2)). Giving only a life interest to a surviving spouse may give rise to a further disadvantage in restricting the ability of that person to pass on the property by means of potentially exempt lifetime transfers. It is true that by including a power to advance capital as set out above, the problem can be partly solved: however, the end result is somewhat cumbrous with the trustee advancing assets to the life tenant in order for that person to make PETs of the same property.

A life interest may, however, be employed *to ensure that the surviving spouse makes a PET*. Assume, for instance, that a husband wishes the bulk of his estate to pass on his death to his grandchildren on trust. His wife is much younger but he is concerned that, should he leave the property to her absolutely, it will never find its way to the grandchildren. On these facts the husband should be advised to settle property in his will with his spouse being given an immediate interest in possession. The trustees should then be given the power to terminate the interest (say six months after his death) whereupon the will should provide for the property to be held on the desired trusts for the grandchildren. There is no IHT charged on the husband's death because of the spouse exemption and the subsequent termination of the interest in possession will be a PET by the surviving spouse. However for deaths occurring on or after 22 March 2006, while the spouse exemption would still apply, the subsequent termination of the interest in possession is the occasion of a chargeable transfer (see **Chapter 30** for a discussion). [51.75]

4 Cohabitees and children

The general principles of IHT apply to transfers between cohabitees (so that *inter vivos* transfers will be PETs: death transfers chargeable) and between parents and children. In the latter case the connected person rules apply. [51.76]

5 Post mortem adjustments

The rules governing *post mortem* rearrangements (see **Chapter 30**) are bolstered up by an anti-avoidance provision in IHTA 1984 s 29A which is relevant when there is an exempt transfer on death (for example, to the surviving spouse) and the recipient then, in satisfaction of a claim against the estate of the deceased, disposes of property 'not derived from the death transfer' (see **Chapter 30**). [51.77]–[51.90]

V STAMP DUTY AND STAMP DUTY LAND TAX

A gift between spouses is (like other voluntary dispositions) exempt from *ad valorem* duty; a sale between spouses is subject to *ad valorem* duty only if it is made otherwise than in connection with the breakdown of the marriage (see FA 1985 s 83, and **Chapter 49**) and where the consideration is less than £1,000 (see FA 2008 s 98). [51.91]–[51.110]

VI ADMINISTRATION

From 1990–91 each spouse's tax affairs have been dealt with separately, not necessarily by the same tax office. It is each spouse's own responsibility to furnish, if required, a tax return in respect of his or her income and gains for the tax year in question.

HMRC are not permitted to disclose information regarding one spouse's tax affairs to the other without the spouse in question's written permission.

From 5 December 2005, these principles have applied with equal force to same-sex civil partners (see [51.130]). [51.111]–[51.129]

VII CIVIL PARTNERSHIPS

CPA 2004, which came into force on 5 December 2005, created a new legal status of civil partner, giving same-sex couples in the UK the opportunity of acquiring a legal status for their relationship, and gaining rights and responsibilities that mirror those available to a married couple. Although taxation measures were not provided for in the Act itself, the Tax and Civil Partnership Regulations 2005 provide for similar treatment for civil partners and civil partnerships as is given to married persons and marriage. The effect of this means that, since 5 December 2005, tax charges and reliefs, together with the various anti-avoidance rules, have applied to married couples and civil partners alike. The most significant change is the exemption from inheritance tax of transfers between civil partners during their lifetime or on death.

Same sex couples (like cohabitees: see [51.131]) had argued for some considerable time that the exemption in favour of married couples, but not in favour of those who were not legally married, was discriminatory and, taken together with Article 1 of Protocol No 1, was a breach of the European Convention on Human Rights (see [55.21], [55.42]–[55.60]). Whilst this argument was discounted in respect of heterosexual cohabitees, who had the choice of whether or not to marry (see [55.42]–[55.60]), it was believed that same sex couples might have been successful had such argument been brought before the domestic courts under the HRA 1998.

Another area affected includes the capital gains tax legislation where: (i) only one property owned by a couple who are civil partners may be treated as the principal private residence of either of them at any time for the purpose of the principal private residence exemption; (ii) transfers of assets between persons who are civil partners who are living together are on a no gain no loss basis; (iii) civil partners are treated as 'connected persons' and are also connected with other persons such as close relatives of their civil partner in the same manner as husbands and wives; and (iv) a settlement of assets by one civil partner under which the other partner can benefit may result in the settlor being liable to capital gains tax on capital gains realised by the trustees, provided other conditions are met (see [19.49]).

As far as income tax is concerned: (i) where one of the partners was born before 6 April 1935, the partners are entitled to an allowance equivalent to the married couple's allowance (see **[51.20]**); and (ii) the income tax anti-avoidance provisions dealing with transfers of assets abroad where, as a result of the transfer, income becomes payable to a person resident or domiciled outside the UK, also apply to civil partners. Pension tax legislation amendments provide that references to husband, wife, ex-husband, ex-wife, spouse, ex-spouse, surviving spouse, widow and widower now include civil partner, former civil partner and surviving civil partner. Pension tax simplification legislation, which came into force on 6 April 2006, also reflects the terms of the CPA 2004. Finally, there is an exemption from stamp duty and stamp duty land tax for transactions effected in connection with the dissolution of a civil partnership so that transfers of shares or the transfer of an interest in the partners' home into the sole ownership of one of the ex-partners is exempt (see **[52.65]**).

Note that where a same sex couple choose to marry (as opposed to forming a civil partnership), following the Marriage (Same Sex Couples) Act 2013, a reference to marriage is to be read as including a reference to marriage of a same sex couple, a reference to a married couple is to be read as including a reference to a married same sex couple and a reference to a person who is married is to be read as including a reference to a person who is married to a person of the same sex. **[51.130]**

VIII COMPARISONS IN THE TREATMENT OF SPOUSES AND COHABITEES

The withdrawal of the married couple's allowance from 2000–01, together with the uniform personal allowance for all individuals irrespective of marital status, has meant that married and cohabiting couples are now on a par with each other for income tax purposes (although this has changed, once again, from 2015–16 with the introduction for eligible married couples and civil partners of an election to transfer part of the personal allowance of one spouse/civil partner to the other (see **[51.2]**–**[51.10]**). In a similar fashion, for CGT purposes, the annual exempt amount (up to £11,300 for 2017–18) is available to *all* taxpayers (and hence as much to the advantage of both husband and wife as to each of a cohabiting couple), whilst for IHT, the general exemptions (£3,000 pa, gifts in consideration of marriage and normal expenditure out of income) are available to all.

No distinction is made between married and cohabiting couples for the purposes of working tax credit and child tax credit: both credits are available irrespective of whether a couple are married or living together as husband and wife. They are also available to lone parents. These credits (which are gradually being replaced by Universal Credit), particularly CTC, are concerned mainly with children; it is the children who make up the family, and it is the children who should be supported irrespective of whether their parents or carers are married or not. It was believed by some that to treat cohabitation on a par with marriage for taxation purposes would be impractical in cases where that relationship was likely to be transitory; in other cases (notably situations falling within the old idea of 'common law marriage') a different argument could be thought persuasive, albeit that deciding when a temporary arrangement had become permanent could be far from easy. These concerns are no longer critical when it is the *child* of the relationship that is being supported rather than the relationship itself.

That having been said, the distinction in tax law between a married couple and those living together as husband and wife (and those living together as civil partners) persists in other important areas. Crucially, special reliefs are available to a married couple that enable assets to be transferred *inter se* without the risk of any tax charge. For IHT purposes this relief is unlimited in amount save for the situation where the donee spouse is a non-UK domiciliary (and therefore potentially outside the UK tax net).

For CGT purposes, disposals between spouses are treated on a no gain/no loss basis (see TCGA 1992 s 58). As some (limited!) compensation, it may be noted that various anti-avoidance rules based upon a 'connected persons' test will not normally apply to cohabitees. In such cases transactions between the cohabiting couple will be taxed in the same way as transactions between strangers. Take, for instance, IHTA 1984 s 10, which is intended to ensure that IHT does not catch a transfer that is a bad bargain. In the case of a transfer between cohabitees, in order to avoid any question of an IHT charge, it is only necessary to show an absence of gratuitous intent on the part of the transferor. It is not necessary to go further, as is the case when the transferee is a connected person, and to show the transfer in question is one that would have been entered into with a third party. Admittedly this is small beer in the majority of cases where the crucial point in any case where property is transferred between a couple (whether married or otherwise) will be the exemption from charge for inter-spouse transfers.

Consider, however, as a second illustration the CGT rules which tax the settlor on the gains realised by his trustees in cases where he has retained an interest in his trust. For UK trusts, TCGA 1992 ss 77, 78 limit the charge to situations where the settlor or his spouse (no mention of other members of the family, nor of cohabitees) can benefit directly or indirectly from property in the settlement (see **Chapter 19**). The legislation on offshore trusts goes further: a settlor has an interest if a benefit may be enjoyed by a category of 'defined persons' which includes children (plus their spouses), stepchildren, grandchildren and companies controlled by such persons (including any company controlled by that company). Still no mention of the cohabitee!

Those small advantages aside, it is the absence of any capital tax relief for transfers *inter se* which is the greatest disadvantage facing cohabitees. Elementary tax planning schemes are, as a result, fraught with difficulties. For income tax purposes, for instance, ensuring that a couple take full advantage of their individual allowances and of the basic rate tax band will frequently involve an outright transfer of an income-producing asset. In the case of cohabitees, care must be taken to ensure that if that transfer is of a chargeable asset it falls within the transferor's annual CGT exemption whilst, for IHT purposes, if that transfer exceeds the £3,000 annual exemption it will constitute a potentially chargeable transfer. Will drafting for the cohabitor is likewise a problematic exercise: if everything is left to his cohabitee, the estate will be subject to a 40% tax levy once the £325,000 nil rate band has been exhausted. There is no exempt transfer to shelter behind in such cases: no simple channelling operation which can be performed to make any tax liability disappear as in the case of married couples.

A common trap which may arise is as follows. Assume that Terry and June cohabit in No 44 Railway Cuttings, a house which they own as joint tenants. Terry dies without having made a will (a negligent death) with the result that his free estate (ie his property other than his share of Railway Cuttings) passes to his parents. June is not entitled to any property on his intestacy although she could bring an action for reasonable financial provision under the Inheritance (Provision for Family and Dependants) Act 1975 provided she can show that she was financially dependent on Terry. In cases where both cohabitees have had full-time jobs this is unlikely to be the case. To return to the example, assume that the total value of Terry's estate exceeds the IHT nil rate threshold: say, for instance, that Terry's half share in the house is worth £200,000 and that his free estate is likewise worth £200,000. (It may in passing be noticed that in valuing Terry's half share in the house a discount on the basis of the joint occupation should be allowed. Such a discount is not, of course, available in the case of a half share owned by husband and wife because of the related property rules in IHTA 1984 s 161: see **Chapter 28**.) The IHT bill (£30,000 assuming that Terry had an intact nil rate band) will result in an estate rate of 7.5% and June will be accountable for the £15,000 attributable to Terry's share in the house since the burden of IHT charged on joint property falls on that property. She has received nothing under Terry's intestacy and given that his parents may be unwilling to make any contribution towards the IHT charge on Railway Cuttings, the end result is that unless she can afford to raise a mortgage or alternatively to pay the tax in instalments (with interest) she will end up being forced to sell the house.

Successive governments have made it very clear that they will not entertain the idea of equating cohabitation of couples with marriage, although an exception has been made in part of the statutory residence test (the family tie – see **[27.20]**). Moreover, a Special Commissioner has explained (in an *obiter dictum*: see *Holland v IRC* (2002)) that the treatment of cohabitees is not in breach of the European Convention on Human Rights and that it is permissible for Parliament to legislate for different tax provisions to apply to married persons, since this reflected the mutual rights and obligations brought about by marriage (see **[55.42]**–**[55.60]**) The later decisions of the ECtHR in *Burden v UK* (2006), a case concerning two elderly sisters who had lived together for all of their lives, and *Courten v UK* (2008) (concerning a co-habiting same-sex couple) confirm this view. (The outcome of the later appeal in *Burden* to the Grand Chamber of the ECtHR was the same, but the court reached its conclusion on a different ground that would not be relevant to cohabitees (see **[55.43]**)). **[51.131]**

52 Matrimonial breakdown

Updated by George Duncan, Partner, Charles Russell Speechlys LLP

I   Income tax [**52.2**]
II   Capital gains tax [**52.21**]
III Inheritance tax [**52.41**]
IV Stamp duty [**52.60**]
V   The matrimonial home [**52.61**]

Matrimonial breakdown necessarily has financial and tax repercussions. The financial implications of divorce have been the subject of three high-profile decisions, two of the House of Lords and one, *Charman v Charman* (2007), of the Court of Appeal. In *Miller v Miller* (2006), the question that needed to be determined was how capital assets should be divided following only a brief marriage. In contrast, the issue in *McFarlane v McFarlane* (2006) concerned the role of periodical payments in circumstances where, following a marriage lasting 16 years, the available capital, although substantial, was not sufficient to enable an immediate clean break, but the husband was a very high-earner and would continue to be so in the coming years. Different again, the issue in *Charman v Charman*, where the marriage had lasted for some 28 years and the capital assets were vast, was the extent to which the husband's 'special contribution' to the marriage in amassing a huge fortune due to his own talent and endeavour should enable the court to depart from the principle of equality expounded in the earlier case of *White v White* (2001).

What is important to note is that, although matters of taxation may have led the parties to take certain decisions during the marriage (see particularly the High Court decision in *McFarlane v McFarlane* (2003) and the Court of Appeal in *Charman v Charman*), they are no longer an issue on matrimonial breakdown. Where once it used to be an occasion that afforded scope for tax planning, such opportunities have, in the main, been removed altogether since, from 5 April 2000, income tax relief on maintenance payments has no longer been available at all unless one or both of the parties to the marriage was over the age of 65 on or before 5 April 2000.

It should also be noted that, since 5 December 2005, references to 'marriage' and associated terms include 'civil partnerships', and the term 'spouses' includes 'civil partners' (see [**51.130**]). Cohabitees, however, are treated as single people with a lack of legal remedies on separation and on death (for the conceptual difficulties that arise in this context with respect to the beneficial ownership of the home, see the discussion by the Court of Appeal and the Supreme Court in *Jones v Kernott* (2010 and 2011 respectively) about the House of Lords decision in *Stack v Dowden* (2007). Although the Law Commission published a consultation paper (No 179 (2006)), which put forward proposals that would enable eligible cohabiting couples who had provided the necessary contributions or sacrifices to the relationship to obtain financial relief on a breakdown of the relationship, nothing has yet come of this and it seems likely that it is to be left to a pioneering Supreme Court to continue the advances already made in *Stack v Dowden* and *Jones v Kernott* in respect of the beneficial interests in the family home.

A point to be noted is the Marriage (Same Sex Couples) Act 2013, which provides that a reference to marriage is to be read as including a reference to marriage of a same sex couple, a reference to a married couple is to be read as including a reference to a married same sex couple and a reference to a person who is married is to be read as including a reference to a person who is married to a person of the same sex. [52.1]

I INCOME TAX

1 General principles

On the breakdown of a marriage the parties revert to single status. For income tax purposes marriage ends when the parties separate 'in such circumstances that the separation is likely to be permanent'. Because of independent taxation, both parties will, in any event, have been taxed separately whilst married, so that each will have been entitled to the personal allowance (£11,500 for 2017–18, but which reduces by £1 for every £2 of income above £100,000).

Where one or both of the separating spouses was born on or before 5 April 1935, relief in respect of the age-related married couple's allowance (see [51.21]) will continue to be given for the tax year of separation. Until replaced by Universal Credit, Child Tax Credit may continue to be claimed in respect of children under the age of 16, or of those young persons under the age either of 19 where they remain in full-time secondary education or of 18 where they have left school within the previous 20 weeks and have registered with the Careers Service. The tax credit is paid to the 'main carer' (see [51.27]). [52.2]

2 The treatment of maintenance payments

Tax treatment of qualifying maintenance payments (ITA 2007 Part 8 Chapter 5)

Limited tax relief is available for maintenance payments for the benefit of a spouse or civil partner where one or both of the parties to the marriage was born on or before 5 April 1935. Relief is also available for payments to a spouse or civil partner for the maintenance of a child, where either the payer or the recipient was born before 6 April 1935. Payments of maintenance, whether to spouses or for children have three key tax consequences.

First, the payer is not entitled to deduct the sum paid as a charge on his income and is therefore forced to make the payment out of taxed income.

Second, the sum is paid over gross to the recipient: there is no question of deducting income tax at source.

Finally, the sum is received free from income tax: ie it does not fall under ITTOIA 2005 s 683 as an annual payment. The position is the same in respect of payments arising outside the UK (see ITTOIA 2005 s 730).

Only limited compensation for the payer is offered, whereby the payer's tax liability on his total income is reduced by a percentage (10% for 2017–18) of a specified amount (£3,260) or, if lower, the actual amount of the maintenance paid. If the payer's income tax liability is insufficient to offset the whole of the reduction, relief is given by reducing the liability to nil; he cannot claim any repayment of tax (ITA 2007 Part 2 Chapter 3). In determining what a payer's income tax liability is for this purpose, tax at the basic rate that the claimant is entitled to deduct or retain out of charges on income is excluded. Further, any income tax reduction to which he may be entitled by reason of the age-related married couple's allowance is ignored.

It should be noted that this relief is only available in the case of payments to a former or separated spouse, either for the maintenance of that spouse or for the maintenance of a relevant child of theirs (following the decision of the ECtHR in *PM v UK* (2005) (**[55.43]**), relief has been extended to cover payments for children between parents who were never married): it is not available in the case of maintenance payments made directly to children. Nor is it sufficient merely that such payments are made directly to the former or separated spouse; the court order or agreement under which such payments are made must specify that the payments are to be made to the other parent for the maintenance of the child and not to the child itself (*Billingham v John* (1998)).

Remarriage by the former recipient spouse precludes the payer from obtaining relief, and it is immaterial that the second marriage may also have ended in divorce (*Norris v Edgson* (2000)). The payments must be made under a UK court order or agreement or under court orders of countries that are members of the EU or assessed by the Child Support Agency (see *Otter v Andrews* (1999): voluntary payments of mortgage interest were not qualifying maintenance payments). **[52.3]**

EXAMPLE 52.1

Under a court order made on 1 July 2010 Eric, who celebrated his 65th birthday on 14 December 1999, is obliged to make annual payments of £3,500 to his former wife Erica. Eric's income for the year 2017–18 is £47,000.

	£
Income	47,000
Deduct: personal allowance	11,500
	£35,500
Income tax liability: £33,500 at 20% = £6,700	
£2,000 at 40% = £800	7,500
Deduct: relief in respect of maintenance payment, subject to a maximum amount of £3,260 = £3,260 × 10%	326
Net income tax liability	£7,174

3 Pensions and divorce

Apart from the matrimonial home, the asset of greatest value to a married couple, typically, is the accumulated pension provision of the money earner. For the older divorcing couple, the financial arrangements made for their retirement will need adjusting since they will no longer be living in one household.

How to treat pensions on divorce has, in the past, proved to be a major problem, stemming from the fact that, on divorce, the accrued pension rights of the parties are not usually equal: the spouse who has remained at home to care for the family is less likely to have built up pension entitlement than the working spouse. High profile was given to this problem by *Brooks v Brooks* (1995), in which case the House of Lords held that a pension fund set up by the husband's company during the course of the marriage, and which specifically provided for a pension for his spouse, was a post-nuptial settlement which could be varied by the court in order to provide the wife with an immediate annuity and a pension on the termination of the marriage. In a previous case, *Griffiths v Dawson & Co* (1993), the court had held a solicitor, acting on behalf of a wife who was being divorced, negligent for failure to hold up the proceedings in order to investigate any possible rights she may have had in the pension fund linked to her husband's employment. (It is also arguable that a pension established prior to the marriage may be varied as an ante-nuptial settlement.)

Provided both that the rules of the pension fund allow for the other spouse (frequently the wife) to claim such benefits and that the wife is of an age to take advantage of those benefits, and that third party rights are not prejudiced, these cases seem to provide an alternative means of providing income for a divorced spouse through contributions paid by the employed spouse which had not suffered tax. (It would seem that a variation of settlement order may be available in relation to any type of pension scheme apart from an unfunded statutory scheme. A retirement annuity contract or personal pension can only be varied insofar as the benefits will be approved by HMRC.)

It should be noted that this solution is only available as a consent incorporated in the preamble of the consent order by way of undertaking (WRPA 1999 Sch 3 para 3).

A method frequently employed to ensure that a divorcing spouse benefited from the other spouse's pension, and one that may still be utilised, is offsetting. This, in effect, trades one spouse's pension against other assets from the marriage (see **[52.11]**). **[52.4]–[52.10]**

a) *Offsetting*

At a time when the courts were unable to compel a pension holder to set aside any of his pension benefit for the ex-spouse, the courts took account of the value of the pension by offsetting this against other assets, and such a method of allowing a divorcing spouse to enjoy the benefits of the ex-spouse's pension continues today. Effectively, the ex-spouse gets another asset, or share of another asset (up to the appropriate value of the share of the pension) instead of the share of the pension. Frequently, this would involve the ex-spouse getting a larger share of the matrimonial home to compensate for the pension share.

As far as the valuation of the pension is concerned during divorce negotiations, a starting point is typically a 25% reduction. This figure reflects, in part, a deduction for valuing a gross pension fund knowing that it would suffer income tax in the hands of the receiver. It also takes into account the willingness of the parties to trade off the pension fund's uncertain future income stream for the certainty of cash in their pockets today.

EXAMPLE 52.2
Harry and his spouse Harriet are divorcing. Harry has a personal pension fund valued at £300,000 and the family home is worth £450,000 with no mortgage. There are no other assets or liabilities.

Harry and Harriet's total assets are worth £750,000 If the court was to award each of the divorcing spouses a settlement of 50%, this would result in a value of £375,000 for each party so that:
(a) Harriet would get £375,000 of the equity in the home; and
(b) Harry would keep his pension (valued at £300,000) and get £75,000 of the equity in the home, to bring his share up to the £375,000. If he is under age 55, he will not be able to access his share of the assets until he is eligible to take pension benefits.

However, this example is unrealistic since there are likely to be other factors to consider: it may be the case that the property would need to be sold to allow each party to purchase a property of their own, or the pension may be the biggest single asset and there are insufficient assets to trade against it. For this reason, it may be that one of the other ways in which a divorcing spouse may enjoy the benefits of the ex-spouse's pension is to be preferred. [52.11]

b) *Pension attachment*

The courts have a duty to consider the loss of pension rights in a divorce settlement (or on judicial separation) and can require the trustees of an occupational scheme to make a payment to the other party to the marriage when payment under the scheme becomes due to the party with the pension rights (see Matrimonial Causes Act 1973 ss 25B–25D).

Periodical payments under a pension attachment order are regarded as deferred maintenance for income tax purposes. Such payments are therefore not taxable in the hands of the payee, but are regarded as the income of the scheme member. [52.12]

c) *Pension sharing*

Although the basic state pension is not shareable, it is possible for the State Second Pension (formerly the State Earnings related Pension Scheme – SERPS) and additional pension to be shared.

Pension sharing enables the court to split a pension into any percentage at the time of divorce so that, for example, the wife may either become a member of the husband's scheme in her own right or, as an alternative, may take a transfer of an amount into her own pension scheme. It has been stated that provision for, say, a wife from a husband's pension did not introduce an 'entitlement-driven' system of pension-loss compensation (*T v T (Financial Relief: Pensions)* (1998); *Burrow v Burrow* (1999)); rather, their application should be based upon the needs of the claimant. However, in light of the decisions in *White v White* (2001) and *Miller v Miller* (2006), *McFarlane v McFarlane* (2006) and *Charman v Charman* (2007), it is suggested that the court, in operating the principles of fairness, equality and non-discrimination, should consider not just the needs of the claimant, but also the requirement of compensation for any economic disadvantage generated by the relationship and the sharing of the fruits of the matrimonial partnership. (For the question of how pensions are valued for these purposes, see *Martin-Dye v Martin-Dye* (2006).)

In contrast to periodical payments under a pension attachment order, periodic pension payments under a pension sharing order are taxable at the payee's marginal rate of tax. It will therefore be appreciated that 'sharing' carries a considerable tax advantage, with each spouse having allowances/ basic rate of tax to set against the income resulting from the split.   **[52.13]**

d) *Pension flexibility*

Pension flexibility, introduced in April 2015 by the Taxation of Pensions Act 2014 whereby individuals with money purchase savings are able to access their entire pension fund flexibly, may provide greater flexibility for those going through the divorce process who are already 55 or over, or those close to 55. In the majority of cases, each spouse will want to ensure that they can afford a home of their own following a settlement. The 2015 changes, which allow individuals the option to release funds from their personal pension early, could help to relieve the financial burden of finding a deposit for a new property.

The new flexibility raises further issues around how pensions are considered on divorce, which affect all three of the options discussed above:

(i)   *Offsetting* A pension fund need no longer be regarded as an income product but more like a readily realisable liquid asset, with the result that there should be less of a reduction in valuing the fund.

(ii) *Pension attachment* Flexibility may potentially leave scope to circumvent the requirements set out in the attachment order. For example, the pension-owning spouse may be able to avoid the payment of the income as set out in the attachment order by choosing to take all benefits as an uncrystallised funds pension lump sum (UFPLS). If the attachment order does not specify exactly when and how benefits must be taken, and/or does not specify 'tax-free lump sum' (called the pension commencement lump sum (PCLS)), by taking the UFPLS (which does not pay a PCLS), there are no pension funds left to crystallise and no income left to be covered by an income earmarking order.

(iii) *Pension sharing* The non-pension owning spouse may prefer to have cash rather than a share of a pension fund. Where the member is over 55 this is possible, even if the spouse is much younger, as the right to access the pension fund is linked to the age of the pension policyholder.   **[52.14]**

4   Life insurance policies and divorce

Where a court makes an order for ancillary relief under MCA 1973 which results in *either* a transfer of rights under a life insurance policy, capital redemption policy or a purchased life annuity from one spouse to the other *or* a formal ratification of an agreement reached by the divorcing parties that deals with the transfer of assets including a life insurance policy etc, the Revenue view is that the transfer of ownership of the policy is not for money or money's worth. As a consequence, no gain arises upon which income tax could be chargeable. This revised interpretation represents a change of view on the part of the Revenue in response to the decision in *G v G* (2002) (see *Tax Bulletin*, December 2003). [52.15]

5 **Tax credits**

Where a joint claim for an award of tax credits is made either by a husband and wife or civil partners, or by a couple living together as husband and wife or as civil partners, the award will come to an end when the couple separates or when they cease to live together as husband or wife or as civil partners. There is a formal requirement to notify HMRC within one month of such a change in circumstances if it occurs during the year for which an award has been made (Tax Credits Act 2002 s 6(3); Tax Credit (Claims and Notification) Regulations 2002 (SI 2002/2014) reg 21 as amended by the Tax Credit (Claims and Notification) (Amendment) Regulations 2006 (SI 2006/2689)). The penalty for not making the required notification is a fine not exceeding £300.

Once the couple stop living together, a new claim must then be made, if appropriate, by each party, and any new award of the child tax credit and the childcare element of the working tax credit will only be made to the person who is the main carer of the child. In the case of a new claim being made, the award will be backdated for up to 31 days. [52.16]–[52.20]

II CAPITAL GAINS TAX

1 **The parameters of s 58**

Disposals between spouses (which term includes married same sex persons and civil partners) are not subject to CGT and are treated as made for a consideration that will produce neither gain nor loss (see TCGA 1992 s 58, **Chapter 19** and [51.58]).

Once the spouses separate this provision ceases to apply and the ordinary rules of CGT operate (but note *Gubay v Kington* (1984)). Hence, a transfer of chargeable assets between spouses after their separation may be subject to CGT (see, for instance, *Aspden v Hildesley* (1982)). It may therefore be crucial that the reorganisation of capital assets on the breakdown of a marriage should be arranged, so far as possible, to come within s 58. That section only applies in cases where the disposal is between spouses who 'in that year of assessment' were living together. Accordingly, if assets are not transferred in the year of separation, the no gain/no loss rule will be inapplicable.

Although the exemption for inter-spouse transfers is lost in the tax year following separation, the couple remain connected persons until decree absolute so that disposals between separation and divorce are deemed not to be bargains at arm's length, but are treated as for a consideration equal to the market value of the property (TCGA 1992 s 18). However, following the decision of *G v G* (2002), where there is a transfer of business assets pursuant to a court order, HMRC will now permit hold over relief (see [**24.5**]), thereby deferring any CGT liability to the recipient on a future disposal. This policy will not apply to the transfer of business assets between spouses without recourse to the courts, unless the parties are able to demonstrate that there was a substantial gratuitous element in the transfer and that no consideration passed in the form of a surrender of rights.

With the current rate of 20% for those who pay higher rate tax this policy may be of increased importance for future disposals. [**52.21**]

2 The annual exemption

For the year 2017–18, husband and wife are each entitled to their own annual CGT exemption (£11,300), and this entitlement will remain unaffected by separation. [**52.22**]

3 Orders for the payment of a lump sum under MCA 1973 s 31(7B)

Under MCA 1973 s 31, the court has the power to vary, discharge or suspend an order for financial provision for a party to a marriage or former marriage. It may, for instance, under s 31(7A) discharge an order for periodical payments and then under s 31(7B) make a supplemental provision, for example for the payment of a lump sum. The Revenue accepts that in awarding the lump sum the court is exercising its discretion afresh and hence that sum is not derived from an asset (namely the now discharged right to periodical payments). Hence, TCGA 1992 s 22(1) (see [**19.64**]) does not apply and the lump sum is free of CGT (see *Tax Bulletin*, April 2001, p 840). [**52.23**]–[**52.40**]

III INHERITANCE TAX

For IHT purposes marriage continues until the decree absolute so that outright transfers between spouses after separation and before divorce continue to be exempt. After decree absolute, the general rules operate, unless the dispositions are exempt under IHTA 1984 s 11 (see **Chapter 31**). Maintenance payments fall within s 11 and are, therefore, exempt from IHT. However, s 11 is probably not wide enough to cover maintenance paid by way of a transfer of a capital sum or of a capital asset which may, therefore, be chargeable unless it does not reduce the transferor's estate (for example because it is in satisfaction of outstanding financial claims by the former spouse), or lacks gratuitous intent. In most cases the absence of gratuitous intent ensures no tax charge for transfers between former spouses that result from the breakdown of the marriage (see the statement of the Senior Registrar of the Family Division made with the agreement of the Revenue (1975) 119 SJ 396) and IHTM 04165). [**52.41**]–[**52.59**]

IV STAMP DUTY

A wide exemption from stamp duty for transfers in connection with divorce is contained in FA 1985 s 83. [**52.60**]

V THE MATRIMONIAL HOME

1 The difficulties

The matrimonial home will often be the only valuable asset owned by a couple and, given the steep rise in the value of property in recent years, it may be very valuable indeed, so that its destination on divorce poses a number of tax problems.

Before considering these, however, it is important to discover who owns the home. One spouse may be the sole owner at law but the other spouse may have acquired an equitable interest in the property either expressly (eg by agreement between the parties in writing) or under a resulting trust arising from that spouse's monetary contribution to the purchase of the property (see, for example, *Gissing v Gissing* (1971)), or under a constructive trust. A constructive trust may arise in one of two ways. *First*, there may be evidence of an express agreement or an express representation that the property is to be shared beneficially and that the other spouse has acted to his or her detriment in relying on that agreement or representation. *Alternatively* there may be evidence based on the conduct of the parties from which can be inferred a common intention to share the property beneficially, such conduct normally being a direct financial contribution by the spouse who is not the legal owner (*Lloyds Bank plc v Rosset* (1991)).

On the question of the beneficial shares enjoyed by each of the parties where the property is in joint names, see *Stack v Dowden* (2007) and *Jones v Kernott* (2011), both cases concerning cohabitees, where the House of Lords and the Supreme Court respectively exhaustively reviewed the authorities, and noted that resulting trusts may not be appropriate for deciding the beneficial ownership of the family home. It is suggested that although these cases did not concern consideration of whether one of the parties had acquired an interest in the home, the reasoning by their Lordships/Justices may have an impact on any future cases to be decided on this issue, and a less restrictive stance than that taken in *Rosset* may well emerge.

If the house is to be sold on divorce, or its ownership transferred in whole or in part from one (former) spouse to the other, problems of income tax, CGT and (exceptionally) IHT may arise. [52.61]

2 CGT

Before separation any disposal of the matrimonial property will be exempt from CGT if it is the spouses' main residence although the exemption may be restricted for example by a period of non-residence. Once the parties separate, however, an absent spouse who has an interest in the property may incur a CGT liability on a disposal of it. Difficulties principally arise in two cases: assume in each case that the husband owns the house which he has left, and that the wife remains in occupation throughout. [52.62]

Case 1 The house is to be transferred to the wife. This disposal by the husband will not fall within the no gain/no loss rules of TCGA 1992 s 58 since the parties have been separated throughout the relevant tax year. Further, the husband has been absent from the house since the date of separation. So long as the disposal occurs within 18 months of that date (for disposals after 6 April 2014;

for disposals before that date, the period is three years), no charge will arise on any part of the gain (TCGA 1992 s 223(1) as amended), but once that 18-month period expires, the proportion of the total gain that is deemed to have accrued from the end of that period may be chargeable (the appropriate calculation is described at [**23.83**]).

Any charge is, however, avoided if TCGA 1992 s 225B applies. This section applies where a married couple or civil partners cease to live together and the marriage or civil partnership is later dissolved or annulled, and one partner ceases to occupy the main residence. It provides that where that partner subsequently disposes of the home, or an interest in it, to the other partner, as part of a financial settlement, the home may be regarded for the purpose of TCGA 1992 s 222–224 as continuing to be a residence of the transferring partner from the date his or her occupation ceases until the date of transfer, provided that it has been the other partner's only or main residence throughout that period.

Thus, where a husband leaves the matrimonial home while still owning it, the usual capital gains tax exemption or relief for a taxpayer's only or main residence would be given on the subsequent transfer to the wife, provided she has continued to live in the house and the husband has not elected that some other house should be treated for capital gains tax purposes as his main residence for this period. This could occur many years after the separation.
[**52.63**]

Case 2 The house is to be sold. If the sale occurs more than 18 months after the separation (three years if the sale took place before the 6 April 2014), TCGA 1992 s 225B is not available (because the disposal is not to the wife), so that there will be a charge on a proportion of the total gain. [**52.64**]

3   IHT and stamp duty land tax

Transactions involving the matrimonial home will not usually involve IHT. Either the inter-spouse exemption still applies or, after divorce, there is no gratuitous intent (see **Chapter 28**). Moreover, provided that a transfer of assets on divorce to a former spouse is pursuant to a court order, transferors should escape any possible liability under the pre-owned asset regime (see [**29.140**]). The transfer of property between spouses and former spouses as a result of the breakdown of marriage are not subject to stamp duty land tax whether the transfer is made pursuant to a court order or by the agreement of the parties alone (see FA 2003 Sch 3 para 3). [**52.65**]

4   The taxation consequences of typical court orders

In order to consider the taxation implications of four typical court orders dealing with the matrimonial home on divorce, assume throughout that the spouse who has left (H) owns the matrimonial home. [**52.66**]

a)   *The order for outright transfer (the 'clean-break')*

H is ordered to transfer the entire ownership of the house to W (see *Hanlon v Hanlon* (1978)). H may also be ordered to make maintenance payments covering, *inter alia*, any mortgage payments to be made by W. [**52.67**]

CGT The disposal to W attracts no charge if it occurs within 18 months of separation (or three years if the transfer took place before 6 April 2014); if it occurs later, there is no charge if TCGA 1992 s 225B applies. **[52.68]**

IHT No charge arises as a transfer pursuant to a court order lacks gratuitous intent. **[52.69]**

b)   *H and W become joint owners of the house with sale postponed*

H is ordered to transfer an interest in the house to W. The couple will be beneficial tenants in common. W will be entitled to live in the house to the exclusion of H and the sale will be postponed until (for instance) the children reach 18 (see *Mesher v Mesher* (1980)). **[52.70]**

CGT When the half interest in the house is transferred to W the result is as in a) above. On the eventual sale of the house, a proportion of the gain on H's share will be chargeable (corresponding to his period of absence), unless it can be argued that the effect of the order is to create a settlement. Normally, jointly owned land is not settled (TCGA 1992 s 60; *Kidson v MacDonald* (1974) and **Chapter 25**). It may, however, be argued that because W has an exclusive right to occupy under the terms of the order the parties are not 'jointly absolutely entitled' since they do not have identical interests in the property.

Accordingly, if the property is settled, no CGT will be charged upon its disposal so long as a claim is made, because it will have been occupied by W 'under the terms of the settlement' (see TCGA 1992 s 225). This is understood to be the Revenue view (see CG 65365). **[52.71]**

IHT The position is unclear and will depend to some extent upon the drafting of the court order. However, if the property is settled for CGT it is likely that it will also be settled for IHT. See **[52.74]**. **[52.72]**

c)   *Settling the house*

W is given the right to live in the house for her life, or until remarriage, or until voluntary departure, whichever happens first. Thereafter, the house is to be sold and the proceeds divided equally between H and W (see *Martin v Martin* (1977)). **[52.73]**

CGT The creation of the settlement will not be chargeable (as in a) above) and on the termination of the life interest although a deemed disposal under TCGA 1992 s 71(1) will occur (see **[25.47]**), no charge to CGT will arise because of the main residence exemption (TCGA 1992 s 225) so long as a claim is made. **[52.74]**

IHT There will be no charge on the creation of the settlement (see **[52.69]**). However, pursuant to FA 2006, the property within the settlement will become relevant property and, when W's interest comes to an end, will be subject to the exit charge (**[34.23]**). Since H and W are settlors their reversionary interests are not excluded property and are therefore part of their estates and exposed to IHT (IHTA 1984 s 48(1); (see **[33.62]**). **[52.75]**

d)   *Outright transfer subject to a charge over the property in favour of the transferor*

H transfers the house to W, but is granted a charge over the property either for a specific sum (as in *Hector v Hector* (1973)), or for a proportion of the sale proceeds (as in *Browne v Pritchard* (1975)). Sale and payment may be postponed until the children attain 18 or until W dies or wishes to leave the house. [52.76]

IHT Depending upon the details of the arrangement, the property is not settled, but belongs to W – no charge. [52.77]

CGT The transfer to W should not be chargeable on the principles in a) above. On the eventual sale, the position is not entirely clear. If H's charge is for a specific sum, this must be a debt due to H. Therefore, when the house is finally sold and the debt repaid there will be no charge to CGT on the repayment (TCGA 1992 s 251; see **[22.42]**).

If the charge is for a proportionate share of the proceeds of sale, however, H's right is not a debt, but a *chose in action*, ie the right to a future uncertain sum; see *Marren v Ingles* (1980) and **Chapter 19**. As a result, when the house is eventually sold and a sum of money paid to H, there will be a chargeable disposal of that *chose in action*. However the tax treatment of any profit realised by H is obscure and will depend to some extent upon the details of the arrangements. [52.78]

e)   *Conclusions*

It must be stressed that taxation factors are not the most important considerations to be borne in mind when considering financial adjustments upon a matrimonial breakdown. The outright transfer may currently be the ideal for tax purposes, but it leaves the husband with no interest in the former matrimonial home and so deprives him of any capital appreciation. Further, the court has no power to adjust property orders once made, so they must be correct at the start. Finally, a transfer of the house or an interest therein is quite different from a declaration (normally under the Married Women's Property Act 1882) that a woman owns, and has always owned, a share in the asset. No transfer is involved in such cases and the taxation consequences of transfers discussed above are irrelevant. [52.79]

Section 10 Charities

Chapters
53   Tax treatment of charities

53 Tax treatment of charities
Updated by Alison Paines, Anna Sumner and Graham Elliott, Withers LLP

I   Qualifying charities [**53.21**]
II   Tax relief on charitable income and gains [**53.41**]
III Expenditure by a charitable body [**53.61**]
IV   Effective charitable giving [**53.79**]
V   Value added tax [**53.121**]
VI   Stamp duty land tax [**53.130**]
VII Community Infrastructure Levy [**53.131**]
VIII Annual tax on enveloped dwellings [**15.132**]
IX   Employment allowance [**15.133**]

Charity law has undergone a fundamental reassessment in recent years. For centuries the law had been governed with reference to the Preamble to the Statute of Elizabeth of 1601, as interpreted by the dicta of Lord Macnaghten in *IRC v Pemsel* (1891). However, the first years of the 21st century saw a major review of the law, which culminated in the Charities Act 2006. Since that time, the key charity legislation (including the 2006 Act) was consolidated (but not amended) in the Charities Act 2011. Further reform is possible following the Law Commission's second consultation on 'Technical Issues in Charity Law' which supplements the consultation it held in 2015 and which raised additional questions, concerning issues such as changing a charity's purpose and trust corporations. The supplemental consultation closed in October 2016 and, at the time of writing, the Law Commission was preparing its final recommendations and a draft Bill for publication in September 2017.

Although the changes introduced in the 2006 Act did not specifically amend the taxation of charities, they constituted the widest-ranging reform of charity law for four centuries. They will therefore inevitably impact heavily on the content of this chapter, and the adviser will need to refer to the latest editions of the standard works on the subject, which take into account the enactment of the 2006 Act.

There have, in addition, been many changes to the tax treatment of charities since the turn of this century, in particular the revision of Gift Aid in FA 2000, the extension of income tax relief to gifts of quoted shares and land in FA 2001 and 2002, the introduction by FA 2006 of the 'substantial donors' rules and its subsequent repeal in 2011 and replacement by the 'tainted donations' rules, and the new definition of 'charity' for tax purposes contained in FA 2010. [**53.1**]–[**53.20**]

I QUALIFYING CHARITIES

1 General

Tax reliefs are generally only available to bodies which are, in English law, charities. Most charities in England and Wales are now obliged to register with the Charity Commission (and registration is widely seen as a 'badge' of charitable status). Provisions under FA 2010 (see below) require new charities also to register with HMRC after registering with the Charity Commission if they wish to be recognised as charities for tax purposes.

Some charities, however, do not need to register with the Commission (Charities Act 2011 s 30(2)); these include exempt charities under Charities Act 2011 Sch 3, any charity which is excepted by either an order of the Charity Commission or regulations and whose gross income does not exceed £100,000 and any charity whose income does not amount to more than £5,000 a year (unless the charity is a charitable incorporated organisation; CIOs must be registered with the Charity Commission irrespective of their income). **[53.21]**

2 Charity law and tax law definitions of 'charity'

The Charities Act 2006 substantially revised the legal definition of charity in English law. The relevant provisions (see below) came into force on 1 April 2008, and are now contained in the Charities Act 2011.

However, the previous definition which applied until 1 April 2008 still retains some relevance, as it continues to impact on the new statutory definition, and it is therefore worth briefly reviewing the previous position.

The principal themes were drawn together by Lord Macnaghten (in *Income Tax Special Purposes Commissioners v Pemsel* (1891)), who classified charitable purposes under the following four headings, which formed the legal definition of 'charitable' in English law up until 1 April 2008:

(i) the relief of poverty
(ii) the advancement of education
(iii) the advancement of religion
(iv) other purposes beneficial to the community.

In addition, there was a general requirement that charities must be for the benefit of the public at large, or a sufficient section of the public – the 'public benefit test'. Under the old law, there was a (rebuttable) presumption that a charity promoting any of the first three heads would be for the public benefit, whereas charities seeking to qualify under the fourth head had actively to show that they would benefit the public.

The fourth category was of course a very broad sweep-up head, which allowed the law to evolve to include numerous additional purposes, for example, the relief of unemployment, the protection of the environment and the promotion of amateur sport, provided of course that they were deemed to satisfy the public benefit test mentioned above.

The Charities Act 2006 definition

Charities Act 2006 introduced a definition of a charity (now contained at Charities Act 2011 s 1) as an institution which is established for charitable purposes only, and which falls subject to the jurisdiction of the High Court.

The definition of 'charitable purposes' comprises a two-stage test.

First, to qualify as charitable, a purpose has to come under one of the following 13 heads:
- (a) the prevention or relief of poverty;
- (b) the advancement of education;
- (c) the advancement of religion;
- (d) the advancement of health or the saving of lives;
- (e) the advancement of citizenship or community development;
- (f) the advancement of the arts, culture, heritage or science;
- (g) the advancement of amateur sport;
- (h) the advancement of human rights, conflict resolution or reconciliation or the promotion of religious or racial harmony or equality and diversity;
- (i) the advancement of environmental protection or improvement;
- (j) the relief of those in need, by reason of youth, age, ill-health, disability, financial hardship or other disadvantage;
- (k) the advancement of animal welfare;
- (l) the promotion of the efficiency of the armed forces of the Crown, or of the efficiency of the police, fire and rescue services or ambulance services; and
- (m) a sweep-up category including:
  - (1) any purposes not within (a)–(l) but recognised as charitable purposes under existing charity law or by virtue of s 5 of the Charities Act 2011 (relating to recreation and similar trusts);
  - (2) any purposes that may reasonably be regarded as analogous to any purposes within paragraphs (a)–(l) or (1) above; and
  - (3) any purposes that may reasonably be regarded as analogous to, or within the spirit of, any purposes which have been recognised under charity law as falling within paragraph (2) above or this paragraph.

Second, all charities also need to satisfy the public benefit test, thereby effectively removing the presumption of public benefit which previously applied to the first three heads of charity as mentioned above.

However, it should be noted that what satisfies the public benefit requirement can vary between different types of charitable purposes, and the 2006 Act did not (subject to what follows) alter this position. In November 2011, the Charities Tribunal determined a reference by the Attorney-General in relation to the charitable status of benevolent funds, which seek to relieve poverty amongst a restricted group of people (sometimes defined by reference to an individual or single organisation). The Tribunal confirmed that with respect to such charities, while they must still show public benefit in the sense that their purpose must be such as to be a benefit to the community, it is not necessary that a 'sufficient section' of the public can benefit. The judgment states:

> 'The 2006 Act has not, in our judgment, changed [the legal position]…The "public benefit" as that term was understood for the purposes of the law of charity required, in the context of a trust for the relief of poverty, only that public benefit in the first sense should be shown.'

More recently, however, the Charity Commission has placed a question mark over whether pre-2006 case law can be relied on as being good law in respect of public benefit. In 2014 the Charity Commission initially refused to register the Preston Down Trust, a meeting house of the Plymouth Brethren Christian church, on the grounds that it did not meet the public benefit requirement.

Prior to 2006, the advancement of religion was prima facie charitable and a High Court case, *Holmes v AG* (1981) had confirmed a trust of the Exclusive Brethren was charitable. Despite this, the Charity Commission's view was that the 2006 Act required public benefit to be shown in all cases and indicated that religious groups must demonstrate that benefit is provided to the wider community, notwithstanding pre-2006 case law. In the end, the Preston Down Trust was registered as a charity.

Many of the 13 purposes are of course very similar to the previously recognised purposes (and paragraphs (d) to (l) largely codify purposes which had been recognised under the old fourth head). That said, paragraph (h), concerning the advancement of human rights, is an example of how the Act has assisted the development of the law in certain respects. In the case of *The Human Dignity Trust v Charity Commission* (2013), the First-tier Tribunal noted that 'the advancement of human rights' does not yet have a specific meaning in charity law and, as such, it is an 'evolving concept'. It held that the organisation in question, established to support those who challenge same-sex discrimination in the law worldwide, was charitable.

An important category to highlight is the 13th head, which retains a sweep-up provision, and which importantly will include any other existing recognised purposes and also purposes 'analogous to, or within the spirit of', any previous purpose. This should allow the Courts and the Charity Commission flexibility to continue to develop the law. In 2011, for example, a new organisation established to promote and support public access to open-source online content was registered as a charity on the grounds that it provided a public resource akin to a reading room or library, which case law from the 19th century had found to be charitable.

The Charity Commission has a statutory duty (by virtue of Charities Act 2011 s 17) to issue guidance on public benefit in order to promote understanding of this public benefit requirement, and charity trustees have a statutory duty to have regard to this guidance when exercising their powers and duties. The Commission published its first general guidance in January 2008, followed by supplementary guidance on public benefit in relation to specific types of charity (such as fee-charging charities). However, in 2011 the Independent Schools Council challenged the legal basis of the Charity Commission's guidance in relation to fee-charging in the case *Independent Schools Council v Charity Commission* (2011) and was partially successful. As a result, the Charity Commission withdrew its public benefit guidance in so far as it was affected by the judgment and has since published revised guidance in September 2013, which was updated in February 2014.

Charity trustees must report in their charity's annual report how they provide public benefit, and certify that they have had regard to the Commission's guidance on public benefit: Charities (Accounts and Reports) Regulations 2008 and the relevant provisions of the Charities Act 2016. **[53.22]**

The Finance Act 2010 definition and foreign charities

Paragraph 1 of Sch 6 to FA 2010 introduced a new definition of 'charity' for tax purposes, following recent developments in European law. Until FA 2010, the UK, along with many other jurisdictions, only granted favourable tax treatment to domestic charities, and gifts made to them. Two key judgments of the European Court of Justice, *Stauffer v Finanzamt München* (2006) and

Persche v Finanzamt Lüdenscheid (2009), however, stated that it is a breach of EC Treaty Arts 56 and 58(3), concerning the free movement of capital, to discriminate against charities established in other EU Member States simply because they are foreign.

FA 2010 Sch 6 has therefore extended favourable tax treatment to certain foreign charitable organisations in the EU, Norway, Iceland and Liechtenstein. To be eligible, these organisations (along with UK charities) must fall within FA 2010's meaning of a charity, defined as a body of persons or trust that:
(a)   is established for charitable purposes only;
(b)   meets the jurisdiction condition;
(c)   meets the registration condition; and
(d)   meets the management condition.

The first two conditions are aligned to the Charities Act 2011 definition: 'charitable purposes' is cross referred to Charities Act 2011 s 2 (see above); and the jurisdiction condition is met if the organisation is subject to the control of a relevant UK court or any other court in the exercise of a corresponding jurisdiction under the law of a 'relevant territory' – being another EU member state, or Norway, Iceland or Liechtenstein.

The registration condition requires that the organisation has either complied with any requirement to be registered with the Charity Commission, or with equivalent requirements to be registered.

Finally, an organisation meets the management condition if its 'managers are fit and proper persons to be managers'. 'Managers' are defined as 'persons having the general control and management of the administration of the body or trust', which repeats word-for-word the definition of a trustee under Charities Act 2011 s 177.

HMRC has published detailed guidance on this final condition, which raised concerns amongst the sector. In particular, HMRC intends to apply the term 'managers' more widely than to a charity's trustees alone (the guidance refers to a charity's 'Chairperson, Treasurer, Secretary' or its Executive Board), and it is unclear when precisely a manager would fail to qualify as fit and proper, as this remains at HMRC's discretion (although the guidance does contain a non-exhaustive list of examples where a manager could fail this condition). In March 2017, HMRC updated its guidance on the 'fit and proper person' test, which now includes a detailed description, with reference to the Disclosure of Tax Avoidance Schemes (DOTAS) rules and the general anti-abuse rule, of the circumstances in which a charity manager who has used or been involved in the design or promotion of tax avoidance schemes may be deemed not to be a fit and proper person. HMRC also notes in its guidance that an individual will not be considered to be actively involved in designing or promoting tax avoidance schemes simply because they work for, or in, the same organisation or partnership as an individual who has been actively designing or promoting schemes. HMRC stated that, in all cases, it will consider all of the relevant circumstances, such as the nature and size of the scheme, the extent of the manager's involvement and the likelihood of their future participation in such schemes. New charities must now register with HMRC, even if they have already registered with one of the UK charity regulators.

The new definition of 'charity' was initially in force in respect of Gift Aid only, but, since 1 April 2012, has applied to all charitable reliefs, and so any charity in the UK or the rest of the EU or Norway or Iceland, must meet this test in order to benefit from any of the UK reliefs available to charities.

In practice, very few non-UK charitable organisations have been recognised as charities by HMRC, and it remains common for a non-UK charitable organisation seeking to raise UK funds to establish a UK supporter or 'friends of' charity.

It is not yet known how Brexit will affect the definition of 'charity' for tax purposes, if at all. It might be caught up in a general repeal or addressed more directly, depending on how other EU Member States treat UK charities, for example. In 2014, the government consulted on options for changing the definition of charity for tax purposes in order to tackle tax avoidance. The proposal was subsequently abandoned, it being considered not sufficiently targeted and having the potential for unintended negative consequences for legitimate charities. [53.23]

3 Charitable work outside the UK

The charitable purposes do not have to be carried out exclusively in the UK: the same public benefit guidance applies to charities working abroad as it does to charities operating in England and Wales.

The Charities Act 2011 and the Charity Commission are limited in their application and operations to England and Wales. In Scotland, the Charities and Trustee Investment (Scotland) Act 2005 established an independent regulator, the Office of the Scottish Charity Regulator, whose responsibilities include the maintenance of a register of Scottish charities. It is worth noting that the 2005 Scottish Act introduced a separate statutory definition of charitable purposes applying in Scotland. This is very similar, but not identical, to the definition in the Charities Act 2011. Similarly, the Charities Act (Northern Ireland) 2008, which received Royal Assent in September 2008, has created the Charity Commission for Northern Ireland, which began registering charities in December 2013.

Further, the Charity Commission's jurisdiction is restricted to charities which fall within the definition in the Charities Act 2011 s 1, being 'an institution which is established for charitable purposes only, and falls to be subject to the control of the High Court in the exercise of its jurisdiction with respect to charities'. Overseas charities will, in practice, only come within this definition if a majority of the trustees or the bulk of the funds are subject to the control of the High Court and therefore to supervision by the Attorney-General. [53.24]

4 Non-charitable purpose trusts

English law has generally refused to accept that non-charitable purpose trusts are valid. Amongst the reasons given for this attitude are that, in a number of cases, the purposes have been so imprecisely drafted that it would be difficult to control the trustees in the exercise of their functions; in other cases the purposes would continue forever and therefore breach the rule against perpetual duration; whilst certain purposes have been stigmatised as useless or capricious (see, for instance, *McCaig v University of Glasgow* (1907) in which the court set aside a will trust that would have involved building statues of the deceased and other 'artistic towers' at prominent points on his estate).
[53.25]

5 The policy of conferring tax reliefs on all charities

There has been debate in the past as to whether all charities should automatically receive the uniform tax benefits available and there have been suggestions that only some charities should qualify, for example, those whose operation is for the public benefit to a sufficient degree (see Lord Cross of Chelsea in *Dingle v Turner* (1972)).

This debate has been brought into sharper focus by the provision in the Charities Act 2011 (introduced by the Charities Act 2006) that all charities must be for the public benefit (referred to above). This has generated an amount of public debate, focusing in particular on fee-charging charities such as private schools and hospitals. For some time, a specific statutory definition of public benefit had been suggested, but in the end, the Act simply provided a statutory duty on the Charity Commission to issue guidance on the meaning of 'public benefit' (see [**53.22**]), and the position has not changed since. To date, therefore, no fundamental distinctions between different types of charity are made so far as tax relief is concerned (although in VAT some types of supply are treated differently, eg medical supplies). Community amateur sports clubs, however (which are not of themselves charitable), have a slightly different tax treatment from fully qualifying charities – see [**53.101**].

[**53.26**]–[**53.40**]

II TAX RELIEF ON CHARITABLE INCOME AND GAINS

1 Relief from direct taxes

CTA 2010 ss 468–493 (for corporation tax purposes), ITA 2007 ss 520–532 and TCGA 1992 s 256 confer relief from income tax, CGT and corporation tax in respect of:

(1) rent from land and property (for charitable trusts, ITA 2007 s 531; for charitable companies, CTA 2010 s 485);
(2) interest and dividends (for charitable trusts, ITA 2007 ss 532 and 533; for charitable companies, CTA 2010 ss 486 and 487);
(3) single gifts by companies and individuals (Gift Aid) (for charitable trusts, ITA 2007 ss 520–522; for charitable companies, CTA 2010 ss 471–473 and 475);
(4) grants from other charities (for charitable trusts, ITA 2007 s 523; for charitable companies, CTA 2010 s 474); and
(5) chargeable gains (TCGA 1992 s 256).

In cases where tax has been deducted at source, the recipient charity is normally entitled to a refund by application to HMRC Charities division; (the special position of charities which receive distributions (including dividends) from companies is discussed in **Chapter 42**). The relevant income must form part of the income of a charity or be applicable, and applied, for charitable purposes only (CTA 2010 s 493 and see *IRC v The Helen Slater Charitable Trust Ltd* (1982)).

FA 2006 introduced some changes to the mechanism for providing relief to charities (see [**53.61**]) and added some further rules which denied relief to charities involved in 'transactions with substantial donors'. These rules have since been repealed but still apply to donations received between 22 March 2006 and 31 March 2011 – see [**53.116**] for more detail. [**53.41**]

2 Trading

Trading income is exempt from tax in the following circumstances:
(1) Where the trade carries out a primary purpose of the charity or is ancillary to the primary purpose (eg an educational charity running a school or sale of food and drink to visitors by a museum) – CTA 2010 s 478 and ITA 2007 s 524.
(2) Where the work is done mainly by beneficiaries of the charity (eg a charity set up to provide work for the disabled) – CTA 2010 s 478 and ITA 2007 s 524.
(3) Where profits are from a fund-raising event, such as a ball or concert, which has exemption from VAT under VATA 1994 Sch 9 Group 12 (see [**53.127**]). The event must be organised primarily to raise money for the charity and the exemption only applies if not more than 15 events of the same type are held in the same location in a financial year. Events where weekly gross takings do not exceed £1,000 do not count towards the 15 events allowed for the purposes of this exemption – CTA 2010 s 483 and ITA 2007 s 529. (See ESC C4.)
(4) Where the total annual turnover of trades which are not otherwise exempt does not exceed £5,000 (or 25% of all the charity's incoming resources if greater – maximum £50,000). The exemption also applies if at the beginning of the period the charity had a reasonable expectation that the annual turnover would not be exceeded – CTA 2010 s 480 and ITA 2007 s 526.
(5) Where the profits derive from certain types of lottery, including lotteries which are exempt under the Gambling Act 2005 (CTA 2010 s 484 and ITA 2007 s 530).

Where charities carry out mixed trades (ie where some of the trade qualifies for relief and some does not), they previously had to rely on an HMRC concession to the effect that relief would be allowed pro rata, so that the non-qualifying element of the trade did not taint the qualifying element. CTA 2010 s 479 and ITA 2007 s 525 have regularised the position by ensuring that the practice is given a statutory footing, by treating the qualifying element as a separate trade from the non-qualifying element.

In those cases where the proposed trade does not satisfy the tests mentioned above, the device that has been commonly adopted by charities is to incorporate a company to carry out the work and for the profits thereby produced to be paid as tax-deductible charitable donations to the charity under Part 6 CTA 2010, or the 'corporate Gift Aid' scheme. The result of so doing is that the taxable profits of the company are kept at zero and the sums received by the charity do not themselves attract tax. It is important that the right amount is paid by the company, for if the Gift Aid payment turns out to be *less than* the profit, the company is left with a corporation tax liability. To avoid this problem it is now provided that, if a Gift Aid payment is made within nine months after the end of an accounting period and the paying company is wholly owned by a charity, the company can claim to treat the Gift Aid payment as made in that accounting period (CTA 2010 s 199). This means that a company, which is wholly owned by a charity, can calculate its profits for an accounting period and then make a Gift Aid payment to the charity within nine months of the end of the period, and thereby reduce its taxable profits to nil. An alternative method, for the profits to be paid to the charity by means of a dividend, is not recommended, since not all the tax suffered by the company is recovered (see generally *Charities – Trading and Business Activities*, HMRC website).

The use of trading subsidiaries came under scrutiny in the case of *Noved Investment Co v R & C Comrs* (2006). However, FA 2006 s 57 clarified that the treatment mentioned above will continue to apply, and indeed offered a concession, effectively extending the relief by allowing the Gift Aid mechanism described above to apply where a trading subsidiary company is jointly owned by a number of charities.

On the other hand, the abolition of the corporation tax nil rate band in FA 2006 had a knock-on effect for charities and their trading subsidiary companies, which had previously been able to make use of this to build up working capital to the nil rate band limit.

The Diverted Profits Tax (FA 2015 Part 3 ss 77–116), effective in respect of profits arising from 1 April 2015, does not apply to payments to charity, thereby exempting charity trading subsidiaries from the tax. **[53.42]**

3 Land transactions

It is worth noting that, although charities are exempt from the usual charge to income tax on receipts representing rents and profits from land, they are not automatically exempt from the charge to income tax on gains of a capital nature realised from transactions in land which fall within CTA 2010 Part 18 or ITA 2007 ss 755 and 756 (see **[12.101]–[12.113]**). **[53.43]–[53.60]**

III EXPENDITURE BY A CHARITABLE BODY

To qualify for the tax benefits set out in this chapter, the charity must spend its money *only for charitable purposes*. Such expenditure will, of course, include the cost of its own charitable activities; buying assets to be used to further its work; administrative and fund-raising costs; and the payment of money to bodies established to carry out the work of the charity. It is crucial to bear in mind, however, that spending money on non-charitable purposes, or investing or lending money in ways which are not for the benefit of the charitable objects or within the charity's constitutional or other powers, will not only result in a withdrawal of tax relief so far as both the charity and (in certain cases) its donors are concerned, but may also constitute a breach of trust/fiduciary duty by the trustees. A charity can be treated as incurring non-charitable expenditure to the extent that it makes any investment which is not an approved charitable investment (as defined in CTA 2010 s 512 or ITA 2007 s 558), or makes a loan which is not an approved charitable loan (as defined in CTA 2010 s 514 or ITA 2007 s 561). The Charities (Protection and Social Investment) Act 2016 introduced an express power of social investment for charities.

When making payments to a non-UK body, charities have to take 'such steps as the Commissioners for Her Majesty's Revenue and Customs consider are reasonable' to ensure the funds will be applied for purposes recognised as charitable under English law (CTA 2010 s 500 and ITA 2007 s 547).In September 2011 HMRC issued guidance (contained in its Annex II guidance on non-charitable expenditure) on the steps it might consider 'reasonable in the circumstances', last revised in July 2017. The guidance states that HMRC will have regard to: the charity's knowledge of the overseas body; previous relations with the overseas body; the previous history of the overseas body; the amounts given in both absolute and relative terms; and the charity's observance of its own internal financial, management and decision making procedures, and whether or not these were adequate. Essentially, a charity should tailor its approach to payments on a risk and proportionality basis. HMRC advises that 'the trustees must be able to describe the steps they take, explain how those steps ensure charitable application of funds, demonstrate that those steps were reasonable and produce evidence that the steps were, in fact, taken'. Funds not applied for charitable purposes as English law understands the term will fall within a charity's non-charitable expenditure.

The precise mechanism for denying tax relief for non-charitable expenditure makes a direct link between non-charitable expenditure incurred by a charity and loss of tax relief, so that income and gains eligible for tax relief will be restricted by £1 for every £1 of non-charitable expenditure. The provisions allow for excess non-charitable expenditure to be carried back to be set off against previous income and gains of the charity for up to the six previous tax years if necessary (CTA 2010 ss 493–517 and ITA 2007 ss 540–564).

The effect of incurring non-charitable expenditure was illustrated in *IRC v Educational Grants Association Ltd* (1967). In that case, the Educational Grants Association had been established for the advancement of education and had a close relationship with the Metal Box Company Ltd in that the bulk of its income came from a deed of covenant executed in its favour by that company. On a repayment claim for income tax deducted at source being made, it transpired that between 76% and 85% of the income of the charity was applied for the education of children of persons connected with the Metal Box Company Ltd. Accordingly the claim for repayment failed since the court was not convinced that the income of the charity was being applied for 'charitable purposes only'. In deciding that the organisation had expended money for non-charitable purposes, the judge accepted that this involved concluding that the managers had acted *ultra vires* in spending the Association's income: he therefore concluded: 'it is of course open to a comparable body to frame its objects so as to make clear that its income may be applied for private as well as public purposes, but in that case it may not obtain tax relief. It does not seem to me that such a body can have it both ways'. **[53.61]–[53.78]**

IV EFFECTIVE CHARITABLE GIVING

Prior to the enactment of FA 2010, tax relief for charitable giving had last been radically overhauled in FA 2000. Before that date:
(1) Gift Aid was available for one-off donations of £250 or more; and
(2) deeds of covenant could be made which involved a legally enforceable obligation to make payments to a charity over a period which had to be capable of exceeding three years. There were no maximum or minimum financial limits.

As a measure of simplification the Gift Aid scheme was extended by FA 2000 and donations under deed of covenant brought within the scheme.

The Budget of 2012 made provision for a cap on tax reliefs applicable to charitable gifts to come into effect from April 2013; however, the Government withdrew the proposal following significant pressure from the charity sector, which cited the damage it would cause to UK philanthropy. **[53.79]**

1 Gift Aid (ITA 2007 ss 413–430)

a) *Gift Aid after FA 2000*

The changes made by FA 2000 achieved a large measure of simplification as well as extending the scope of the relief. As from 6 April 2000 the £250 minimum payment was abolished and *any* gift to charity is entitled to income tax relief provided:

(1) it is a gift of money;
(2) the donor makes a Gift Aid declaration;
(3) any benefits to the donor are within the limits discussed at **[53.84]** below;
(4) it is not associated with the purchase of property from the donor (so the donor cannot make a Gift Aid gift to a charity to enable the charity to purchase property from him); and
(5) the donor is charged income tax and/or capital gains tax for the year of donation at least equal to the tax treated as deducted from all their Gift Aid donations.

If the gift qualifies for Gift Aid relief the donor is treated as having deducted income tax at the basic rate from his gift. Thus if he makes a gift of £80 to a charity he is treated as having made a gift of £100 from which tax of £20 has been deducted. The 20% tax deemed to have been deducted by the donor can be recovered by the charity from HMRC.

The donor's basic rate tax limit (ie his higher rate threshold) is increased by the gross amount of the gift. Thus, if the donor makes a gift of £80 (gross value £100), the higher rate threshold will be increased from the usual figure (£45,000 in 2017–18) by £100 to £45,100. This means that if the donor is a higher rate taxpayer, he will pay income tax at 20% instead of 40% on taxable income between £45,000 and £45,100 (see diagram below). This will save him 20% of £100 (£20) on his tax bill.

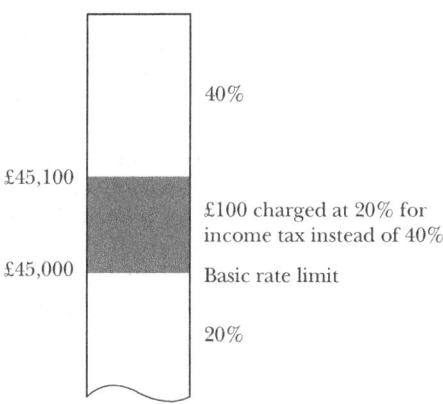

If the taxpayer pays less income tax and CGT than the amount recovered by the charity, he will be assessed for tax equal to the difference. Thus if the donor has given £80 to the charity (£100 gross), but has only paid £10 income tax and CGT, he will be required to refund to HMRC the difference between the £20 tax recovered by the charity and the £10 tax he has paid, ie a further £10 will be added to his tax bill.

Taxpayers subject to the higher or additional rate tax band (40 or 45% for 2017–18) are able to reclaim the higher or additional tax paid on donations to charity, which will arguably mean a greater incentive for additional rate taxpayers to donate at higher values.

Similarly, taxpayers earning more than £123,000 who are subject to a withdrawal of their personal allowance will attract tax relief at their highest rate of tax on charitable donations.

Charities may apply to HMRC to reclaim Gift Aid tax for donations made up to four years beforehand. [53.80]

The Small Donations Scheme

In line with a Government pledge to continue to explore ways of improving Gift Aid, the Small Donations Scheme took effect from 6 April 2013, giving charities and community amateur sports clubs (CASCs) the ability to apply for a Gift Aid *style* repayment on small donations – a 'top-up payment' of 25p for each £1 of eligible donation – without the need to obtain Gift Aid declarations for those donations. The aim is to simplify procedures for charities collecting donations in circumstances such as bucket collections at fund raising events where it might be difficult to obtain all the donor information necessary under the Gift Aid Scheme.

A 'small donation' has been set at £20 or less, and the total amount of small donations on which the repayment can be claimed is capped as of 6 April 2017 at £8,000 per year, per charity (unless a charity is 'connected' with another, in which case the £8,000 limit is shared between the connected charities. Broadly speaking, a charity is connected to another in a tax year if they have the same or substantially similar purposes and are controlled by the same or connected persons). The £8,000 cap may be increased if a charity operates from 'community buildings', such as town halls, to reflect that a single charity may operate distinct community activities. The community buildings rule does not apply to CASCs.

The Small Charitable Donations Act 2017 ushered in several key changes to the Small Donations Scheme with effect from 6 April 2017. The Act amends the Scheme by:

(1) removing the 'start-up period' and 'recent Gift Aid claims' requirements completely (under which charities were only eligible if they had existed for at least two tax years before the tax year of the claim and had made successful Gift Aid claims in at least two of the previous four tax years with no greater than a two-year period between claims) in order to allow more small and new charities to benefit more quickly;

(2) permitting contactless payments to be eligible in an effort to ensure that the Scheme continues to take account of modern fundraising needs;

(3) allowing for charities, or groups of charities, to claim under the main allowance or under the community buildings allowance, but not both. Significantly, for connected charities this means that it will no longer be permissible for one of the charities to claim under the main allowance while another one claims under the community buildings allowance; and

(4) updating the community buildings rules to permit donations received outside of the community building but within the same local authority area to qualify. The aim of this final measure is to enable more charities to benefit from the crucial work that they provide to their local communities.

Penalties: a charity will not be able to make a claim under the Small Donations Scheme if it incurs a penalty relating to Gift Aid or the Small Donations Scheme in that tax year or the previous tax year. The Small Donations Scheme differs from the usual Gift Aid scheme in a number of ways. As well as the £8,000 limit and the absence of a Gift Aid declaration, donations must be received as bank notes or coins (or via contactless payment for donations made after 6 April 2017); donations made by cheque, credit card or bank transfer do not count. Eligible organisations will have to claim under the Scheme within two years of the end of the tax year in which donations are collected (as opposed to four years for usual Gift Aided donations), and donors must not receive any benefits in return for their donations other than a 'small token of negligible value', such as a 'lapel sticker'. Claims will be based on the tax year from 6 April, regardless of the claiming charity's accounting year. Donations made with Gift Aid declarations cannot be included under the Scheme.   [53.81]

b)   *Gift Aid declarations (see a model form declaration below)*

The donor must make an oral, handwritten or electronic declaration (it can be made over the internet). The rules covering such declarations are set out in the Donations to Charity by Individuals (Appropriate Declarations) Regulations 2000 (SI 2000/2074), as amended, and more detailed procedures are provided for in HMRC guidance with the aim of ensuring that the law behind Gift Aid is more fully explained to donors making declarations.

There is no prescribed form for Gift Aid declarations, although many charities choose to use the HMRC model declaration. However, as a minimum, all Gift Aid declarations must contain:
- the name of the charity or CASC;
- the donor's name;
- the donor's home address;
- whether the declaration covers only the present donation, or past and/or future donations as well;
- a statement or verbal confirmation that Gift Aid is to apply.
- confirmation that the donor has been given an explanation that he or she must pay at least as much UK income and/or capital gains tax for the year of the donation as the amount that will be claimed by the charities or CASCs to which he or she donates in that period.

(1)   Oral declarations

Oral declarations may be made in person or by telephone, and the recipient charity may keep an audible recording of such declarations.

If an audible recording is not made, the charity must send the donor a written confirmation of their declaration including certain information, set out in HMRC guidance. Oral declarations are not effective until such written confirmation is sent.

(2)   Written declarations

Written declarations may be made on paper forms or electronically.

Neither paper nor electronic declarations can be made by default; there must be a positive decision, such as a tick box option, to indicate that a donor agrees that the Gift Aid scheme should apply to their donation.

A single declaration may cover any number of donations already made or intended to be made in the future (hence it replaces the deed of covenant although, unlike a deed of covenant, the declaration is not legally binding).

HMRC provides three different model declarations: in respect of a one-off donation; a specific donation and qualifying past and/or future donations (example below); and a sponsorship form. These differ from the single model declaration which was made available until February 2012, and provide greater explanation to the donor about the Gift Aid scheme. In particular, they were updated in October 2015 to refer to the donor's liability to HMRC in circumstances where they have paid insufficient tax to cover the Gift Aid claim made by the charity.

Gift Aid declaration – for past, present and future donations

Charity Gift Aid Declaration – multiple donation

Boost your donation by 25p of Gift Aid for every £1 you donate

Gift Aid is reclaimed by the charity from the tax you pay for the current tax year. Your address is needed to identify you as a current UK taxpayer.

In order to Gift Aid your donation you must tick the box below:

I want to Gift Aid my donation of £_____ and any donations I make in the future or have made in the past 4 years to:

Name of Charity _____

I am a UK taxpayer and understand that if I pay less Income Tax and/or Capital Gains Tax than the amount of Gift Aid claimed on all my donations in that tax year it is my responsibility to pay any difference.

My Details

Title _____ First name or initial(s) _____

Surname _____

Full Home address _____

_____

_____

Postcode _____ Date _____

Please notify the charity if you:
- want to cancel this declaration
- change your name or home address
- no longer pay sufficient tax on your income and/or capital gains

If you pay Income Tax at the higher or additional rate and want to receive the additional tax relief due to you, you must include all your Gift Aid donations on your Self-Assessment tax return or ask HM Revenue and Customs to adjust your tax code.

[53.82]

(3) Gift Aid declarations provided through an intermediary

FA 2015 amends ITA 2007 with a view to reducing the administrative burden on intermediaries receiving donations on behalf of a charity. Regulations can be introduced relieving intermediaries, such as independent fundraisers, of the need to receive a Gift Aid declaration from donors giving to multiple charities, for example. [53.83]

c) *Receipt of benefits*

There are limits on benefits which a donor may receive in return for each donation he makes. These rules have always applied to individual donors and to close companies, but FA 2006 extended them to apply to all corporate donors (see **[53.86]**). FA 2011 increased the level of benefits which a donor can receive. The rules are surprisingly complicated. If the donation is to qualify for Gift Aid any benefits must satisfy both the 'relevant value' test and the 'aggregate value' test.

The 'relevant value test' means that benefits to donors must not exceed the amounts below:

Gifts up to £100	25% of the donation
Gifts of £101 to £1,000	£25
Gifts of £1,001+	
• Made between 6 April 2007 and 5 April 2011	5% of the donation (up to a maximum of £500)
• Made on or after 6 April 2011	5% of the donation (up to a maximum of £2,500)

These limits are applied separately to each unconnected gift. Thus if the donor makes four unconnected gifts to a charity in a year, and only one gift exceeds the above limit, the remainder of the gifts can qualify for Gift Aid. However, connected gifts to the same charity in the same year must be considered together, and adjustments are made if the gifts are made for a period of less than a year. Thus if a £5 monthly subscription is paid to a charity for six months, this will be adjusted since it is only payable for half a year.

EXAMPLE 53.1

Subscription of £5 a month paid to charity under an open-ended standing order. This will be 'annualised' and treated as a gift of £60 (12/1 × £5). A one-off benefit up to £15 would be within the relevant value test.

Where the benefits are received for a period of less than 12 months, both the benefits and the gifts are adjusted.

EXAMPLE 53.2

Donor gives a gift of £240 to charity. He is given a six-month subscription to a computer magazine worth £15 (not just a magazine publicising the work of the charity which would not count as a benefit). The benefit is annualised £15 × 12/6 = £30.

The gift is also annualised £240 × 12/6 = £480. The maximum benefit allowed is £25 so the relevant value test is not satisfied.

In addition to the relevant value test, the gifts must also satisfy the 'aggregate value' test. This means that if the aggregate value of benefits given by a charity to any one donor in consequence of his Gift Aid donations in the same tax year exceeds £2,500 (or £500 for donations made between 6 April 2007 and 5 April 2011), his donation will not qualify for Gift Aid.

The benefit rules may be avoided if a donor specifies that part of his payment to a charity is for benefits and part is a donation. This must be specified at or before the time the donation is made. It is too late to specify this after the gift. This can only be done where the item received by the donor has an easily ascertainable value and the excess paid by the donor has a clear donative purpose. The charity and the donors should keep evidence of how the payment was made. Alternatively, separate payments could be made. Such rules are particularly relevant for charity auctions.

The restrictions discussed above do not apply to the benefit of any right of admission to view property, the preservation of which is the sole or main purpose of the charity; or to observe wildlife, the conservation of which is its sole or main purpose, provided that the opportunity to make such gifts is available to members of the public (ITA 2007 ss 420 and 421). Thus if a member of a zoological society is given the right of free entry to the zoo, this does not count as a benefit.

However, in the 2005 Budget, the Government stated its intention to stop charities reclassifying admission fees as donations in order to benefit from Gift Aid, on the basis that this is outside the spirit and purpose of the Gift Aid rules, which were introduced with the intention of encouraging additional donations to charity. Provisions were enacted in F(No 2)A 2005 s 11 (now reflected in ITA 2007 ss 420 and 421) which have the effect that, from 6 April 2006, if a visitor makes a donation to a charity in order to view property falling within the exemption *instead* of paying the admission charge, Gift Aid will only apply in the following two alternative situations:

- where a right of admission given in return for the gift is valid for a period of at least one year at all times that the general public can gain admission; or
- if the right of admission is for less than one year, the gift must be at least 10% more than the amount that any member of the public would have to pay to gain the same right of admission.

However, the scope of the exemption has been broadened to apply to any charity which charges the public to view property *preserved, maintained, kept or created* by the charity in relation to its charitable work. 'Property' for these purposes includes plants, animals and works of art (but not performances).

Although the amendment has resulted in a reduction in the income of some charities, this has to some extent been offset by the benefits being extended to a broader range of charities. [53.84]

d) *Avoiding a 'Double-Dip'*

It had been thought that Gift Aid could be employed to achieve a 'have your cake and eat it' result. For IHT purposes there are certain situations where 'reading back fictions' are available. For instance, a deed of variation falling within IHTA 1984 s 142 may be read back into the will of the testator (and therefore taxed as if that testator had made the relevant disposition of property) and, similarly, a precatory gift, falling within IHTA 1984 s 143, attracts IHT reading back. The fiction in both these cases holds good for IHT but not for income tax where the analysis remains that the original gift became the property of the named beneficiary who then in turn transferred that property to another person.

Assume, therefore, that Berta, who has just died, has left the residue of her estate (worth £400,000) to her daughter Janice. Janice now wishes to make a substantial donation to charitable causes. She enters into an instrument of variation whereby Berta's will is amended to provide for a gift of £10,000 to the charity (IHT free; if the tax has been paid, a refund is in order) with the remaining £390,000 being paid to Janice. She may seek full income tax relief for the £10,000 under Gift Aid by combining Gift Aid with an instrument of variation. Unfortunately the Revenue successfully challenged the availability of Gift Aid relief on the basis that to qualify 'neither the donor or any person connected with him [must] receive a benefit in consequence of making [the gift]'. In an unsatisfactory judgment a Special Commissioner decided that the saving in IHT amounted to such a benefit thereby preventing relief (*St Dunstan's Educational Foundation v Major* (1997)). A more recent case, *Harris v R & C Comrs* (2010), with a similar set of facts, came to the same conclusion.

However, it would seem that the variation of a non-residuary legacy would not give a benefit to the donor (since any tax saving would swell the residue), and would be eligible for Gift Aid provided that no one connected with the donor benefits from the IHT saving. In addition, the provisions for gifts of qualifying investments and land (see **[53.99]** and **[53.100]**) have different benefit rules: in simple terms the amount on which relief is given is reduced by the value of any benefit received. Hence if 40% IHT relief is obtained which benefits the donor, 60% of the value of the gifted property is still capable of attracting relief for gifts of qualifying investments or interests in land. **[53.85]**

e) *Corporate Gift Aid*

Companies (and unincorporated associations which are assessable to corporation tax) can claim tax relief for qualifying charitable donations. Such donations can be set against the company's profits for corporation tax purposes, to the extent that the company may have no chargeable profits at all. The payment must be a sum of money (distributions of profit related to a shareholding do not qualify). As payments are made gross, the charity cannot make a Gift Aid claim on any such donations.

The same restrictions on benefits received by individuals also apply to companies (see **[53.84]**).

It is common for charities to engage in trading activities as a means of fundraising. However, income produced by such activities will normally attract income tax (see **[53.42]** for the exceptions). The problems arising are usually solved by carrying on the trade through a separate company which is wholly owned by the charity. Corporate profits may then be donated to the charity under the Corporate Gift Aid scheme (see **[53.42]**). **[53.86]**

2 Deeds of covenant

Prior to the introduction of the Gift Aid scheme by FA 2000, sums paid to charity under deed of covenant were tax effective (ie they reduced the income of the payer) provided that the covenant was capable of lasting for more than three years. This requirement could be satisfied if either a fixed period in excess of three years was chosen (hence the popularity of the four-year covenant) or, alternatively, if a period of uncertain duration was chosen which might exceed three years.

FA 2000 removed the separate tax relief for payments made under deed of covenant (see [14.13]). Tax relief for such payments is now given under the Gift Aid scheme. As a transitional measure payments made under deeds in existence on 6 April 2000 do not require a Gift Aid declaration: the deed of covenant in effect performs this function. To obtain tax relief for payments made under covenants executed after 5 April 2000, or to cover gifts larger than the amount covenanted, a Gift Aid declaration is required.   [53.87]

3 Payroll giving (ITEPA 2003 ss 713–715)

The 'payroll deduction scheme' is discussed in **Chapter 8**. In broad terms, it involves employers who wish to set up a scheme for their employees entering into a contract with an agency approved by HMRC. Employees who wish to join the scheme authorise their employer to deduct the relevant amount from their pay before calculating PAYE tax due and to pay over the relevant amount to the agency. The function of the agency is to act as a clearing house, distributing the appropriate sums to the individual charities which have been nominated by the employees. There is no upper limit to the amount which may be given.

The Government announced in the 2011 Budget that it would explore how to increase the take-up of payroll giving, and a consultation took place at the beginning of 2013. The consultation document revealed that only 2% of employers offer Payroll Giving schemes, with just 3% of employees donating. The Government's proposals included a reduction in the processing time of donations from 60 to 35 days, a service level agreement between charities and payroll giving agencies and the creation of an improved web presence for payroll giving. In March 2015, it signed an agreement with charity representatives and payroll giving agencies to raise payroll giving's performance and profile.

[53.88]

4 Relief from capital taxes

a) *CGT*

TCGA 1992 s 257 provides that for CGT purposes gifts to charity are at no gain/no loss (compare the similar rule for inter-spouse gifts under TCGA 1992 s 58). In appropriate cases it may be better, however, to sell the asset (perhaps to realise a capital loss) and then gift the cash to charity taking advantage of the Gift Aid rules. HMRC accepts that the CGT exemption in TCGA 1992 s 256 applies to capital payments received from trusts which have stockpiled gains (on 'stockpiled gains' see further [27A.121]).   [53.89]

b) *IHT*

For IHT purposes, charitable gifts are exempt transfers of value under IHTA 1984 s 23. Relief under this section is given in the following terms:

> 'transfers of value are exempt to the extent that the values transferred by them are attributable to property which is given to charities or registered clubs.'

However, HMRC accepts that relief will be given in a case where the fall in value of the donor's estate exceeds the benefit received by the charity:

> 'Where the value transferred (i.e. the loss to transferor's estate as a result of the disposition) exceeds the value of the gift in the hands of a charity, etc, the Commissioners for Her Majesty's Revenue and Customs take the view that the exemption extends to the whole value transferred.' (See SP E13.)

Three points may be made in connection with gifts to charity by will.
[53.90]

i) Gift to a non-exempt foreign charity (note the effect of FA 2010 Sch 6 having come fully into force for EU, Norwegian, Icelandic and Liechtenstein charities)

Assume that a will provides:

> 'I leave the residue of my estate to the X Foundation (a New York charity).'

No IHT relief is available: consider solving the problem by a deed of variation redirecting the gift to an English sub-charity. [53.91]

ii) Drafting the will/making a lifetime gift

Assume that the client wishes to make the following gift:

> 'I wish to give £50,000 to the University of Pennsylvania.'

Consider making the gift to a UK charity (eg the Charities Aid Foundation) whose objects allow it to carry on charitable activities abroad. It may, in due course, transfer the property to a foreign charity without loss of IHT relief (in the case of a gift by will beware IHTA 1984 s 143: 'precatory trusts').
[53.92]

iii) Residuary gifts to charity and chargeable persons

When the residue of an estate is to be split between one or more charities on the one hand and chargeable persons (eg relatives of the deceased) on the other, problems have arisen in calculating the IHT payable on the chargeable portion (this is often referred to as a '*Benham*' problem). This matter is considered in detail in **Chapter 30** and it is felt that *Re Ratcliffe* (1999) now affords general guidance which will apply in all save exceptional cases.
[53.93]

IHT relief on charitable legacies of 10% or more of a testator's net estate

With effect from 6 April 2012, a reduced IHT rate of 36%, as opposed to 40%, applies where a testator leaves 10% or more of their net estate to a 'qualifying' charity – ie one which has been recognised as a charity for tax purposes by HMRC.

The value of a testator's net estate is the sum of all assets after deducting any debts, liabilities, reliefs, exemptions and available nil-rate band; and will depend on how the testator's assets are held – whether jointly; in trust; or outright by the testator, or as tenants in common.

Beneficiaries under wills of individuals who died after 5 April 2012 may wish to consider whether entering into a deed of variation directing that 10% of the net estate be given to charity will result in a more appealing distribution of assets.

Budget 2015 (March) announced a review of deeds of variation used for tax purposes. Further to a consultation, the Government responded in December 2015 by stating that it would not introduce new restrictions on how deeds of variation can be used for tax purposes, but that it would continue to monitor their use. **[53.94]**

5 Gifts in kind

Businesses can obtain tax relief for the cost of gifts of trading stock and equipment which they sell or use in the course of their business (typical examples are computers, photocopiers, minibuses and furniture). The relief is, however, restricted as explained below. **[53.95]**

a) *Gifts of trading stock*

CTA 2009 ss 105 and 106 provide relief for gifts of trading stock for the purposes of a charity, CASC or educational establishment.

The relief applies to gifts by companies of items of equipment either manufactured or sold in the course of their trade. The corresponding rule for unincorporated businesses is found at ITTOIA 2005 s 108. The relief operates by overriding the rule that disposals of stock other than in the course of trade should be treated as a trade receipt at its market value. Further, items of equipment used in the course of the donor's trade, and on which capital allowances have been given, are treated as having been disposed of at nil value, so that the balance of allowances due on the asset will be given to the business in the normal way. **[53.96]**

b) *Gifts of medical supplies and equipment*

Similar relief is available under CTA 2009 s 107 where a company makes a gift from trading stock of medical supplies or equipment for humanitarian purposes, and the supplies or equipment are for human use. **[53.97]**

c) *Other gifts of assets*

Donations of other types of assets are not eligible for tax relief (excluding the relief for gifts of qualifying investments and land discussed at **[53.99]** and **[53.100]**, and gifts of pre-eminent property discussed at **[53.111]**).

However, HMRC's guidance notes have clarified that Gift Aid can apply where a donor appoints a charity as his agent to sell an asset on his behalf and then voluntarily makes a gift of the sale proceeds to the charity. This allows goods offered to a charity shop to be brought within the Gift Aid scheme, which applies only to donations of money. A Gift Aid declaration will need to be completed. Since 6 April 2016, the procedure has been simplified so that donors can authorise a gift of up to £100 of sales proceeds (if the charity is operating the shop directly) or £1,000 (if the goods are sold by a charity trading subsidiary) without the shop having to seek the donor's subsequent confirmation that these sale proceeds should be treated as donations under Gift Aid, as was the previous requirement. HMRC provides template letters which may be used by shops when these limits are exceeded. [53.98]

6 Gifts of qualifying investments

Qualifying investments comprise quoted stocks and shares on recognised stock exchanges (which include many exchanges around the world); units in an authorised unit trust; shares in an open-ended investment company; an interest in an offshore fund; and shares quoted on the AIM and PLUS markets. A qualifying investment can also include an interest in land, which is discussed in the subsequent section. The relief applies to gifts on or after 6 April 2000 in the case of individuals (see ITA 2007 s 431) and on or after 1 April 2000 in the case of companies (CTA 2010 s 203). The donor obtains an income tax (or corporation tax) deduction for the full market value of the qualifying investment at the date of the gift (plus incidental costs of transfer). If the charity pays any money for the shares, or gives any other benefits, this is deducted from the tax relief.

The assets on which this relief is available benefit from an easily discoverable value, thereby minimising the costs of obtaining a valuation and reducing the possibilities of abuse.

In addition to this income tax relief, the usual CGT exemption (see [53.89]) also applies. This means that it can be very tax efficient to give shares to charity.

The legislation prevents donors from obtaining income tax relief in excess of the benefit received by a charity from the donation of a qualifying investment by providing that where a person places an obligation on the charity that results in the value of the gift in the hands of the charity being less than the gift in the hands of the donor, the income tax relief that can be claimed by the donor is restricted to the lower amount.

In addition, further to amendments effected by the FA 2010, where a donor has acquired a qualifying investment at below market value as part of a scheme or arrangement, or the market value of the qualifying investment is artificially inflated at the date of the gift to charity, the rules operate by adjusting the amount of relief to the donor to the cost of acquiring the investment, where:
(1) the qualifying investment gifted to the charity was acquired within four years of the date of disposal; and
(2) the main purpose, or one of the main purposes, of acquiring the qualifying investment was to dispose of it to a charity and claim tax relief.
(CTA 2010 ss 209–212 and ITA 2007 ss 437–440). [53.99]

EXAMPLE 53.3

Arthur purchased shares in A plc for £4,000. He sells them to a charity for £4,000 when they are worth £10,000. Arthur pays no CGT and can deduct £6,000 gift element from his income. If Arthur is a higher rate taxpayer who has used his CGT annual exemption this will save him £6,000 × 28% = £1,680 CGT *and* £6,000 × 40% = £2,400 income tax. It follows that it has only cost Arthur £1,920 (£6,000–£4,080) to give a £6,000 benefit to the charity.

7 Gifts of qualifying interests in land

Donors may also obtain tax relief on gifts of leasehold or freehold interests in land (CTA 2010 ss 205–206 and ITA 2007 ss 433–434). Although the donor must usually dispose of the whole of his interest in the land, it is specifically provided that the grant of a lease for a term of years absolute in the whole or part of the land qualifies for the relief. Where land is owned jointly all owners must dispose of their interests if the gift is to qualify.

In order to claim the relief the donor must receive a certificate from the charity describing the interest in land, giving the date of the disposal and stating that the charity has acquired the interest. There are provisions for cancelling the tax relief if the donor becomes entitled to an interest in the land, or enjoys rights over it, before the 31 January which falls more than five years after the gift (in the case of a company before the sixth anniversary of the end of the accounting period in which the gift was made). Thus if an individual gives land to a charity on 1 June 2014, the tax relief will be cancelled if he enjoys any rights over the land before 31 January 2020. The cancellation provisions do not apply if the donor gives full consideration in money or money's worth for the interest or right he enjoys.

The anti-avoidance rules set out in [53.99] in respect of qualifying investments (of which a qualifying interest in land is one kind) also apply.

[53.100]

8 Community amateur sports clubs (CTA 2010 Part 13 Chapter 9; Community Amateur Sports Clubs Regulations 2015)

Amateur sports clubs, which are open to the whole community, charging membership within prescribed limits, and which provide facilities for and promote participation in one or more eligible sports (for a list of eligible sports please visit https://www.gov.uk/government/publications/community-amateur-sports-clubs-detailed-guidance-notes) may register with HMRC for the following corporation tax exemptions:

(1) Exemption for trading income which does not exceed £50,000 a year (£30,000 a year before 1 April 2015).
(2) Exemption for interest.
(3) Exemption for property income which does not exceed £30,000 a year (£20,000 a year before 1 April 2015).
(4) Exemption for chargeable gains. Where the club incurs expenditure for non-qualifying purposes the amount of income or gains exempted is reduced. If a club is deregistered by HMRC, or ceases to hold property for qualifying purposes, there is a deemed disposal and the capital gain may be chargeable to corporation tax.

Gifts of money to the club qualify as Gift Aid donations, so the club will be able to reclaim basic rate tax on the gross amount of the gift and the donors will be able to claim higher rate tax relief as if the sports club were a charity. However, membership fees do not count as gifts, so no tax relief is available to members or the club on membership fees. Gifts to sports clubs also qualify for exemption from inheritance tax. Gifts by a business of trading stock and used machinery and plant are given the same relief as applies to similar gifts to a charity (see **[53.96]** above).

Once registered as a CASC, a club cannot apply to be recognised as a charity. To convert a registered CASC to a charity involves winding up the CASC and transferring over the assets and activities to a new charity.

An amateur sports club may register with the Charity Commission, rather than applying to HMRC as a CASC. The advancement of amateur sport was recognised as a 'fourth head' charitable purpose by the Charity Commission and was expressly included in the Charities Act 2006 as one of the new 13 charitable purposes. Registering as a charity may be more favourable to the club from a tax point of view as the payroll deduction scheme and gifts of qualifying investments and land discussed above do not apply to sports clubs registered with HMRC. However, registration with the Charity Commission is still likely to be more onerous for the club with the need to submit to Charity Commission regulation and to submit accounts and reports to it. **[53.101]**

9 Gifts treated as made in previous tax year

Where a gift is made on or after 6 April 2003, the taxpayer may elect to treat the gift as made in the previous tax year for the purposes of claiming higher rate tax relief (ITA 2007 s 426). The election can be made up to the date the taxpayer submits his income tax return for the previous year (but not after 31 January). The election will not affect claims made by the charity.

This provision means that a taxpayer can make a gift to charity before he submits his tax return and then get immediate higher rate tax relief against the income in the return. However, it may encourage delay in submitting tax returns as once the return is submitted it will not be possible to backdate gifts to the previous year. **[53.102]**

10 Gifts of tax repayments to charity

SA donate was a scheme introduced on 6 April 2004 enabling taxpayers to nominate a charity on their self-assessment tax returns to receive all or part of a tax repayment. The scheme was not used often and was withdrawn with effect from 6 April 2012, as it apparently would have needed an extensive update to safeguard it from fraud. **[53.103]–[53.110]**

11 Cultural Gifts Scheme – gifts of pre-eminent objects and works of art to the nation

As a part of the Government's commitment to 'encouraging charitable giving and building a more socially conscious society', it launched a consultation in June 2011 on proposals to encourage lifetime gifts of pre-eminent works of art and historical objects to the nation by the introduction of a new relief. Until that point, the only tax relief applicable for gifts of a pre-eminent object to the nation was that under the 'Acceptance in Lieu' scheme, through which donors can offer such items in full or part to HMRC to settle part or all of an inheritance tax liability.

Provisions were included in FA 2012 Sch 14 following the 2011 consultation, which now afford relief to individuals or companies in respect of 'pre-emininent property' to be held for the benefit of the public or the nation.

'Pre-eminent property' includes pictures, books, manuscripts, works of art, scientific objects or other things which the relevant Minister is satisfied is/are pre-eminent for its/their national, scientific, historic or artistic interest.

The scheme operates by enabling UK taxpayers to offer an object they consider to be a pre-eminent object as a gift to the nation, stating their self-assessed value of the object. An expert panel will consider whether the object is pre-eminent. If it agrees that it is, it will make a recommendation to the relevant Minister, and if that Minister agrees with the recommendation, the panel informs the prospective donor. The potential value of the tax relief will be based on a set percentage (30% for individuals and 20% for companies) of the agreed value of the object that is being donated. The panel will inform HMRC of the agreed terms of the donation.

If accepted as a gift to the nation, the donor will also be exempt from CGT or IHT on the gift.

The scheme operates alongside the Acceptance in Lieu scheme, with both schemes sharing a joint £40 million annual limit (with effect from the year 2014–15) and being administered by the Arts Council. (See *Private Client Business* (2013) at 239.) [53.111]–[53.115]

12 Anti avoidance provisions – tainted donation rules

The tainted donation rules are the successor rules to the controversial substantial donor rules, which were introduced in FA 2006 but repealed with effect from 1 April 2011 following significant pressure from the charity sector. The substantial donor rules operated to remove some of a charity's tax relief if that charity entered into certain transactions with any of its 'substantial donors' (a donor of at least £25,000 in any 12-month period; or of at least £150,000 over any period of six years – with donors meeting these tests continuing to qualify as a substantial donor for the following five tax years). Those transactions included the exchange of property between a charity and substantial donor; the provisions of services by a charity to a substantial donor, or vice versa; the provision of financial assistance by a charity to a substantial donor, or vice versa; and the investment by a charity in the business of a substantial donor (if not listed on a recognised stock exchange). Subject to certain exemptions, the most important applying where the transaction was on an arm's length basis, any payment by the charity to the substantial donor would be non-charitable expenditure.

The substantial donor rules were introduced without consultation, and a close examination of them revealed a number of possible anomalies, some of which arose from the inclusion in the rules of a provision deeming references to a 'substantial donor' to include references to a connected person of the donor. In addition, the onus on policing was effectively on charities themselves, which have the duty under self-assessment to report all transactions that might be relevant. The position was made more difficult by the fact that there was no advance clearance procedure. Formal consultation on the substantial donor rules was commenced in 2008, culminating in the Pre-Budget Report of 2009 announcing that these rules would be replaced with new ones based on a purpose test. Informal consultation on a proposed new test took place in Autumn 2010, following which the tainted donation rules were introduced in FA 2011. The relevant statutory provisions were inserted as ITA 2007 ss 809ZH to 809ZR; CTA 2010 ss 939A to 939I; and TCGA 1992 s 257A, which had effect in respect of gifts made on or after 1 April 2011. The two most noteworthy changes are that there are no longer thresholds on the level of donation above which the rules apply, so that the concept of a 'substantial donor' has disappeared, and that the primary burden on a breach of the rules lies with the donor, rather than the charity (although charities can suffer penalties if they were a party to the arrangements).

The rules will apply to tax relievable gifts which satisfy the following conditions:

(1) The donor or a 'connected' person enters into arrangements with a charity and it is reasonable to assume that the donations and arrangements would not have been entered into independently of one another ('Condition A');
(2) The main purpose or one of the main purposes of the arrangements is to obtain a financial advantage directly or indirectly from the charity or a connected charity ('Condition B'); and
(3) The donor is not a 'qualifying charity-owned company' (such as a trading subsidiary) ('Condition C').

If all three conditions are satisfied, the donation is a 'tainted donation'. The effect of making a tainted donation is the removal of income tax, corporation tax or capital gains tax relief, as relevant, from the gift.

An 'arrangement' may include the sale or letting of property; the provision of services; the exchange of property; the provision of a loan or other financial assistance; and the investment in a business. Permissible Gift Aid benefits; financial advantages applied solely for charitable purposes by the recipient; and financial advantages attributable to gifts of qualifying investments, interests in land or trading stock to charity are expressly excluded from the remit of the rules.

The new rules did not reduce the complexity of the anti-avoidance provisions, and some commentators still argue that they deal with instances which would already be denied tax relief under other existing legislation, such as that surrounding permissible Gift Aid benefits or non-charitable expenditure. [53.116]–[53.119]

13 Social Investment

Budget 2013 announced the introduction of a new tax relief to encourage private investment in social enterprises and to help social enterprises access new sources of finance. Following a consultation exercise, the Chancellor announced during Budget 2014 that the rate of relief would be set at 30%. FA 2014 introduced new sections to ITA 2007 and TCGA 1992 and made consequential changes to other legislation. Draft provisions were published intended for FA 2017 which would enlarge the scheme, but these were put on hold when the 2017 general election was called. It is assumed that they will be brought into effect in due couse, to apply to investments with effect from 6 April 2017.

Under Part 5B to ITA 2007, individual investors (who must be UK taxpayers with a direct interest in the investment or an interest via a nominee fund) making an eligible investment at any time from 6 April 2014 will be able to deduct 30% of the cost of their investment from their income tax liability either for the tax year in which the investment is made or the previous tax year (if 2014–15 or later). Individuals will also be able to defer their CGT liability if they invest their gain in a qualifying social investment and will pay no CGT on any gain on the investment itself.

The investment must be in newly issued shares or newly qualifying debt investments and must be held for a minimum of three years. Each eligible organisation can receive up to a maximum of approximately £290,000 over three years (due to EU state aid rules) and individual investors can invest up to £1,000,000 in more than one social enterprise. Relief is not available on any investment in respect of which the investor has obtained relief under the Enterprise Investment Scheme, the Seed Enterprise Investment Scheme or the Community Investment Tax Relief scheme.

To be eligible a social enterprise must:
- be either a registered charity (a company or a trust), a community benefit society, or a community interest company;
- carry out a qualifying trade; and
- have fewer than 500 employees and less than £15 million in assets.

The monies used from the investment must be used for a qualifying trade or the investor will lose their tax relief. Excluded trades include dealing in land, banking and property development. Social enterprises will need to apply to HMRC to confirm that they meet the requirements of the scheme and investors will be able to claim tax relief once this confirmation has been given.

The changes that had been expected in FA 2017 before the general election was called included an increase in the cap on which a social enterprise can raise from £290,000 to £1,500,000. [53.120]

V VALUE ADDED TAX

Unlike other taxes, there are only a few special VAT exemptions which apply to charities and most of the VAT rules which apply to commercial organisations will continue to be relevant (see generally **Chapters 37–40**). Further useful guidance on this topic can be found in HMRC Notice 701/1. [53.121]

1 Inputs – supplies made to the charity

Supplies made to the charity are usually taxable if they would be taxable when made to a non-charity. Taxable supplies are either charged to VAT at standard rate, currently 20%, reduced (5%) or zero. Where the supply is zero-rated, the charity is not charged VAT and the supplier is able to recover any VAT he has paid on his costs. Some supplies are exempt from VAT. This is less favourable as although the charity will not be charged VAT, the supplier will not be able to recover the VAT he has had to pay on costs. It may thus result in a higher price paid by the charity. [53.122]

a) *Zero-rated supplies to charities*

The following supplies are zero-rated if supplied to a charity (VATA 1994 Sch 8). The list is not exhaustive. In many cases the charity must make an eligibility declaration to the supplier that the goods are being purchased or imported by a charity, or being used for particular purposes (for examples of declarations see HMRC Notice 701/6 (Supplement) (April 1997)).

(1) Advertising services supplied to charities whatever the purpose of the advertising (VATA 1994 Sch 8 Group 15 items 8–8C). The zero-rating extends to advertisement design and production services but excludes advertising where members of the public are 'selected' (ie by direct mailing, or telephone sales), website creation and design, and internal overheads related to advertising. By concession the relief will also apply to goods used by charities for the purposes of collecting monetary donations, ie collection boxes, lapel badges, and giving envelopes which are pre-printed with a fund raising message.

(2) Equipment supplied to charities for producing talking newspapers and books for the blind, and radios and recorders supplied to charities for free loan to the blind (VATA 1994 Sch 8 Group 4).

(3) The supply, repair and maintenance of lifeboats and the supply of fuel for use in a lifeboat (VATA 1994 Sch 8 Group 8 item 3).

(4) The donation of goods by a VAT registered person to a charity (or a company which has agreed in writing to pay all its profits to charity) for the purpose of sale, hire or export by the charity (or company) (VATA 1994 Sch 8 Group 15 item 2). The effect is to avoid an unfair deemed VAT liability payable by the donor.

(5) The construction of a new building, or purchase of a freehold or lease exceeding 21 years of a new building if the building is used 'solely' for relevant charitable purposes (ie for non-business purposes or as a village hall) (VATA 1994 Sch 8 Group 5). HMRC interprets 'sole' use as use of at least 95% for the qualifying use. It allows any reasonable method of calculation to establish this ratio.

(6) Medical and scientific equipment and ambulances, if purchased with charitable or voluntary funds for donation to health authorities or charities providing rescue services or care for the sick and disabled (VATA 1994 Sch 8 Group 15 items 4 and 5).

(7) Medicines supplied to a charity caring for patients or animals (VATA 1994 Sch 8 Group 15 item 9).

(8) Goods and services designed specifically for the disabled and certain building alterations for the disabled (eg bathroom adaptations) (see VATA 1994 Sch 8 Group 12 items 2, 2A, 4–7, 9, 11–13 and 17–19).

[53.123]

b) *Supplies of fuel and power*

The supply of fuel and power for a qualifying use, such as in a residential care home or for use in charitable non-business activities (relevant charitable purposes), benefits from the reduced rather than standard rate. The reduced rate is currently 5%. If the supply does not exceed the *de minimis* limits (eg 1,000 kilowatt hours a month of electricity or 2,300 litres of gas oil per delivery), it is automatically treated as being for a qualifying use. Where the use is part qualifying and part not, provided at least 60% is for qualifying use, VAT is also charged at the reduced rate instead of at the standard rate. Where these limits are exceeded an apportionment must be made between qualifying and non-qualifying use, and an apportioned part is chargeable at the reduced rate. The fuel supplier requires the charity to issue a certificate specifying the level of reduced rate supplies for which it qualifies. [53.124]

EXAMPLE 53.4

A charity uses 50% of its building solely for non-business activities but 50% for business purposes. The supply of fuel exceeds the *de minimis* limits. One half of its purchase of fuel would be charged at the reduced rate, the remainder at the standard rate.

2 Outputs—supplies made by the charity

A charity, like anyone else, is generally liable to VAT on supplies made by it if the charity is a taxable person, and the supply is in the course of business and not exempt. A charity is a taxable person if its taxable supplies exceed the registration threshold (£83,000 a year from 1 April 2016). It must then register for VAT. It is able to register voluntarily at lower levels of taxable turnover. Certain imported services and goods count towards the limits even though they are not supplied by the charity. [53.125]

a) *Supplies must be in the course of business*

Some supplies by a charity are not in the course of business and are therefore outside the scope of VAT. In addition, donations and grants freely given to the charity are not consideration for any supply and thus are outside the scope of VAT. By concession, charges for advertisements in charity brochures are regarded as outside the scope of VAT provided at least 50% of the advertisements are private rather than trade. Further, welfare services supplied at least 15% below cost for the relief of distress, such as soup supplied to the distressed poor (eg in a soup queue), are regarded as non-business supplies. Voluntary services supplied free of charge, such as first aid, rescue at sea and rights of worship, are also regarded as outside the scope of VAT. In this case, if the beneficiary chooses to make a donation, it must clearly be a matter of choice whether or not to do so, and not made to secure the benefit.

On the other hand, the receipt of subscriptions by a charity for which the charity provides goods or services is usually regarded as a supply in the course of business. This does not apply if the only benefits received are a right to vote at meetings and to receive reports, or are nominal benefits such as a lapel badge. Thus if a charity receives more than the registration threshold in the form of subscriptions and other taxable supplies, it will usually have to register for VAT and account for VAT on the subscriptions it receives.

That said, a limited exemption applies to subscriptions to certain philanthropic or civic membership bodies (VATA 1994 Sch 9 Group 9 wwitem 1(e)). The definition of 'philanthropic' is not clear and caution in applying this exemption needs to be exercised (at the time of writing a tribunal decision appeared to confer a broad ambit for this exemption).

The sale or letting of goods by a charity is in the course of business. However, the sale or hire by a charity of donated goods is zero-rated either where the sales are to the general public as a whole or to certain narrowly defined categories of people (VATA 1994 Sch 8 Group 15 items 1 and 1A). However, sales of bought-in goods do not qualify for zero-rating and are taxed at the standard rate of VAT (unless of course they are zero-rated by law such as children's clothes). Sales from a hospital trolley to patients in hospital are VAT exempt, but sales to members of the staff are standard-rated.

Certain welfare services provided by a charity are exempt from VAT. This includes services for the elderly, sick, distressed, and disabled, and services for 'protecting' children and young people. Goods and services supplied incidental to the provision of spiritual welfare by a religious community are in the course of business, but are exempt if supplied otherwise than for profit (VATA 1994 Sch 9 Group 7 item 10).

Examples of other supplies made by a charity in the course of business include admission fees (generally standard rated, unless falling within the exemption for cultural supplies), the hiring of charity buildings (usually exempt but sometimes taxed under the 'option to tax') and sponsorship payments for which the business receives advertisement or promotion (standard rated). Part of the initial payment made to a charity (or usually its subsidiary) under an affinity credit card scheme (at least 20%) must be treated as standard rated and the remainder outside the scope of VAT by long-standing concession. **[53.126]**

b) *Exemption for fund-raising events*

Fund-raising events organised by a charity or its wholly owned subsidiary, or more than one charity, are, subject to certain conditions, exempt from VAT if the primary purpose is the raising of money and the events are promoted for that purpose (though there is doubt as to whether it needs to be a 'primary purpose'). The exemption extends to events organised by a company which is wholly owned by the charity and has agreed in writing to transfer all its profits to the charity. The exemption does not apply if more than 15 events of the same kind are held by the charity in the same location in one financial year, although events do not count towards this limit if gross takings from all similar events at the location do not exceed £1,000 a week, eg coffee mornings. However, if such coffee mornings are regular activities carried out more than once or twice a week they may not be 'events' and therefore may not qualify for exemption. Events where more than two nights' accommodation are provided are excluded, as are all events which are likely to distort competition with VAT registered traders (VATA 1994 Sch 9 Group 12).

Fund-raising events over the internet qualify as exempt if the same conditions are met. For these purposes the whole of a charity's website is regarded as a single location.

If a fund-raising event does not qualify for exemption it is worth considering selling tickets for a lower price, and inviting voluntary donations. So long as the price of the tickets is not less than the usual price charged for a commercial event (in the case of events such as theatre performances), or is sufficient to cover the organiser's total costs (in the case of events such as dances) and, provided the position is reflected in the publicity material and on the tickets,

VAT will not be charged on the voluntary donation. That donation must, however, be entirely voluntary and not a condition of participation.

Certain 'charity challenge events', whereby participants raise sponsorship through physical/mental endurance activities, may be subject to VAT, however. Where the events include: a package of both travel and accommodation; or bought-in accommodation; or more than two-nights accommodation from a charity's own resources, the events will not qualify for the fund-raising VAT exemption. The key risk here is that any sum ultimately payable by the participant to allow him to take part is consideration for a taxable supply even if covered by donations from supporters. [53.127]

VAT cost-sharing exemption

With effect from July 2012, a new class of exempt supply applies under VATA 1994 Sch 9 Group 16 (generally known as the 'cost-sharing exemption'). This is of particular relevance to charities making VAT exempt supplies or performing non business activities which may wish to share costs with one another but which, under normal rules, are subject to VAT charges on their supplies of services to one another. There are five key provisions which must be met in order to benefit from the exemption:

(1) the group must be independent, and should therefore be free of third party ownership;
(2) members of the group must make exempt and/or non-taxable supplies;
(3) supplies by the group to its members must be at cost measured over a normal business cycle (ie the group cannot make a profit);
(4) the services must be 'directly necessary' to the members' exempt and/or non-taxable supplies (as defined somewhat obscurely in HMRC 'guidance' but not in the legislation); and
(5) cost-sharing, using the exemption, must not cause a distortion of competition. [53.128]

3 **Payment of VAT**

Like any other business, a charity which makes taxable supplies pays VAT each quarter which is calculated by taking its output tax (the tax on its outputs, ie on supplies made *by* the charity) and deducting its input tax (the tax on its inputs, ie on supplies made *to* the charity). If its input tax exceeds its output tax it may claim a repayment of VAT. If the charity makes supplies which are exempt or outside the scope of VAT it can only deduct part of its input tax (see **Chapter 38**).

It may be possible for a small charity to join a flat rate scheme whereby VAT is calculated as a fixed percentage of its turnover (including VAT). With effect from 1 April 2017 the usual range of percentages applicable under this scheme has been superseded by a high rate of 16.5% for any 'low cost' trader. The definition of this is specific and involves situations where the user buys a relatively low value of goods. This could easily affect charities which may find themselves pushed to this high rate. In that case the administrative benefits of the flat rate scheme remain, but the potential for saving tax no longer applies. Such a scheme may save some administrative work, but the VAT calculation is not so exact as under the normal scheme and could result in the charity paying more VAT. On the other hand, the VAT might work out to be less than under the usual scheme. This would need careful consideration by the charity. See HMRC Notice 733 (August 2011) and SI 2002/1142 (and amending SIs) for details of the flat rate scheme. The main 'catch' in the scheme is that the flat rate applies to exempt as well as taxable turnover.

Subject to certain conditions, it may be possible for a charity and its trading subsidiaries to register as a VAT group (see HMRC Notice 700/2 (September 2011)). [53.129]

VI STAMP DUTY LAND TAX

Charities will be exempt from stamp duty land tax provided the conditions in FA 2003 Sch 8 para 1 are met. *First*, the charity must intend to use the purchased land for qualifying charitable purposes (ie in furtherance of its charitable purposes or as an investment the profits of which are applied towards its charitable purposes). *Second*, the transaction must not have been entered into in order to avoid tax. This relief does not apply to purchases made by charity subsidiary companies.

The first requirement creates some uncertainty. For example, while premises purchased for running as a care home or for the administration of the charity would clearly qualify as being used in furtherance of a charity's objects, what if a charity were to purchase a shop from which to sell goods, thereby using the premises in furtherance of the charity's business purposes (for example, where the charity is carrying on *de minimis* trade directly not using a trading company) rather than direct charitable purposes? Although it is currently understood that the Stamp Taxes Office will extend the exemption to property used for business or other activities the profits of which are applied for the charity's charitable purposes, there has been no formal clarification of this.

The exemption will be withdrawn if a 'disqualifying event' occurs within three years of the transaction (FA 2003 Sch 8 para 2). A disqualifying event would occur if the charity still had an interest in the land and either the charity ceased to be established for charitable purposes or the land ceased to be used for a qualifying charitable purpose. [53.130]

VII COMMUNITY INFRASTRUCTURE LEVY

Part 11 of the Planning Act 2008 introduced the Community Infrastructure Levy, a fee which local authorities may charge developers on developments of over 100 square metres so that the local authority can fund any work required to improve or change the local infrastructure as a result of the development.

The levy applies only to developments of buildings into which people normally go (as opposed to developments of structures such as wind turbines, or buildings into which people go only intermittently in order to inspect or maintain plant and machinery). The charge is dependent on the release by the relevant local authority of charging schedules. For example, in March 2012, the Mayor of London released the CIL charging schedule applicable to London boroughs, with the charge ranging from £20–£50 per square metre depending on the borough, and which applies to development consented to on or after 1 April 2012. Local authorities were generally expected to adopt charging over the course of 2014.

Section 210 of the Planning Act 2008 states that local authorities must exempt charities from the levy if the development property is to be used wholly or mainly for a charitable purpose of the charity – 'mandatory relief'. In addition, regulation 44 of the Community Infrastructure Levy Regulations (SI 2010/948) allows local authorities to provide discretionary relief where charities are to hold the developed land for investment purposes. Whether this is offered at all will depend on the local authority in question. The exemptions cannot apply where the charity owns the land jointly with a non-charity, or to charity trading subsidiaries. There is clawback on the exemption if the charity no longer qualifies for the relief within the subsequent seven years. [53.131]

VIII ANNUAL TAX ON ENVELOPED DWELLINGS

Charitable companies are exempt from the tax payable with effect from 1 April 2013 by companies that own residential property valued at greater than £500,000 where the property is held to further the charitable purposes of the charity or of another charity, or as an investment from which the profits are (or are to be) applied to the charitable purposes of the charity. [53.132]

IX EMPLOYMENT ALLOWANCE

From April 2014, all business and charity employers are able to offset an annual allowance of up to £3,000 against their Class 1 National Insurance contributions (NICs) liability. [53.133]

Section 11 Europe and human rights

Chapters
54   The impact of EU law
55   Human rights and taxation

54 The impact of EU law
Hartley Foster Partner, Fieldfisher LLP

I   Introduction [54.1]
II   Leaving the EU [54.2]
III   The institutions of the EU [54.4]
IV   Sources of EU law [54.11]
V   Underlying principles [54.21]
VI   The fundamental freedoms: introduction [54.31]
VII   The fundamental freedoms: scope [54.41]
VIII The fundamental freedoms: breach and justification [54.51]
IX   The fundamental freedoms: abuse of right [54.71]
X   Prohibition of State aid [54.81]
XI   Directives [54.91]
XII   Common Consolidated Corporate Tax Base [54.97]
XIII European companies [54.99]

I INTRODUCTION

The United Kingdom became a member of the European Economic Community (EEC) and a party to the treaties establishing the Community with effect from 1 January 1973. It took some time for the full legal effect of this (and the UK's implementing legislation) to become clear. However, it is now beyond doubt that the UK Parliament no longer has complete power to determine the laws in force in the UK. UK legislation, even if validly passed by Parliament, is ineffective to the extent that it conflicts with EU law.

This has wide-reaching implications for UK revenue law, just as it does for all other areas of UK law. EU law acts as an important restraint on the UK's fiscal sovereignty. VAT (which is dealt with in **Chapter 37**) and customs duties (which are outside the scope of this work) are directly governed by detailed EU legislation passed under the provisions of the treaties. But, even where there is no detailed legislation (such as in the case of direct tax), EU law has a very significant role to play. Although the Court of Justice of the European Union (CJEU) has reiterated consistently that direct taxation 'is a matter that falls within the competence of Member States' (see, for example, *Gschwind* (1999)), it has also made clear that Member States must exercise that competence 'in accordance with EU law'. The effect of this is that, where there is a conflict between EU law and domestic direct tax law, EU law will prevail and the relevant domestic rule will have no effect.

The rules of EU law that most particularly affect the UK direct tax code are the 'fundamental freedoms' set out in the EU Treaty. These rules require Member States to enable goods, services, persons and capital to move freely within the Community, in order to ensure the creation of an internal market. Ever since the treaties first came into force, the fundamental freedoms have been interpreted purposively, so as to strike down domestic legal rules incompatible with an internal market or with the 'ever closer union' that is envisaged in the Treaty of Rome. The freedoms have been applied specifically by the CJEU in the context of direct tax.

The chapter comprises 13 sections. After this introductory section, the next section addresses briefly, the likely consequences (as at the date of writing) of the June 2016 referendum in the UK, how a Member State may leave the EU. The next two sections comprise a brief overview of the EU institutions, and the sources of EU law respectively. The next five sections deal primarily with the impact of the EU case law on the UK direct tax code, considering both cases that have arisen in a tax context and (to the extent necessary) general law cases. Sections X, XI and XII deal with three other areas of EU law: State aid, the tax directives and the Common Consolidated Corporate Tax Base; and the final section deals briefly with a structure that could lead, ultimately, to the introduction of a common set of rules for calculating EU-wide tax profits: the European Company or Societas Europaea (SE).

Before proceeding, it is necessary to make one short explanatory point. The treaty that established the EEC in 1957 was called the Treaty of Rome. The Treaty of Rome was renamed the European Community Treaty in 1992 by the Treaty on European Union signed at Maastricht on 7 February 1992 (TEU, sometimes called the 'Maastricht Treaty'). The European Community Treaty was renamed the Treaty on the Functioning of the European Union (TFEU) by the Treaty of Lisbon (which came into force on 1 December 2009). The Treaty of Lisbon amended and renumbered the TEU in the process of turning it into the TFEU.

The TFEU is referred to as the 'EU Treaty' in this chapter. All references to Article numbers in this chapter are to the TFEU (post-Treaty of Lisbon) numbers save where specifically stated otherwise.

The Treaty of Lisbon also introduced a number of other changes of nomenclature, including the following:
- the 'European Community' or EC ceased to exist and instead the terms European Union or EU are used in all circumstances where 'EC' would have been used previously;
- the term 'common market' was replaced for all purposes by 'internal market';
- the 'Court of First Instance' was renamed the 'General Court'; and
- the court system was renamed 'The Court of Justice of the European Union' (CJEU).

For ease, both pre and post 2009 decisions of the court are referred to as decisions of the CJEU. [54.1]

II LEAVING THE EU

Article 50

Article 50 of the TEU allows a Member State to notify the EU of its withdrawal:

'(1) Any Member State may decide to withdraw from the Union in accordance with its own constitutional requirements.

(2) A Member State which decides to withdraw shall notify the European Council of its intention. In the light of the guidelines provided by the European Council, the Union shall negotiate and conclude an agreement with that State, setting out the arrangements for its withdrawal, taking account of the framework for its future relationship with the Union. That agreement shall be negotiated in accordance with Article 218(3) of the Treaty on the Functioning of the European Union. It shall be concluded on behalf of the Union by the Council, acting by a qualified majority, after obtaining the consent of the European Parliament.

(3) The Treaties shall cease to apply to the State in question from the date of entry into force of the withdrawal agreement or, failing that, two years after the notification referred to in paragraph 2, unless the European Council, in agreement with the Member State concerned, unanimously decides to extend this period.'

On 23 June 2016, an 'In/Out' referendum was held in the UK. The decision (by a small margin – 37.4% of the registered electorate voted 'Leave') was to leave the European Union. There was considerable debate subsequently regarding two matters. First, whether the Prime Minister could invoke Article 50 by use of the royal prerogative and, secondly, whether the UK could leave the EU by repealing the European Communities Act 1972 (rather than notifying the EU under Article 50). In *R (on the application of Miller and another) v Secretary of State for Exiting the European Union* (2017), the Supreme Court held that an Act of Parliament was required before Article 50 could be invoked. Following the enactment of the European Union Notification of Withdrawal Act 2017, the Prime Minister sent a notification of the UK's withdrawal from the EU to the European Council President on 29 March 2017.

As a matter of international law, the UK remains subject to its treaty obligations and EU law until 29 March 2019. Technically, the UK is able to participate in EU business as normal, save as regards discussions pertaining to its withdrawal, but, practically, the UK's involvement has diminished.

Article 218(3) of the EU Treaty and guidelines issued by the European Council provide the framework for the negotiations between the UK and the European Commission, as EU negotiator. The start of the negotiations was delayed by, *first*, the UK general election, and, *second*, the fact that no party achieved an overall majority. The negotiations began on 19 June 2017.

As at the time of writing, the two issues that have been discussed are the issue of payments by the UK to the EU and the rights of UK citizens in Europe and European citizens in the UK. As regards the first, the UK Government quickly capitulated on its previous position that there would be simultaneous discussions regarding exit and future relationships. The UK Government has accepted that exit (which includes the financial consequences of exit) needs to be addressed first. It seems also to be accepted by the UK Government that the UK is likely to make payments to the EU in order to secure a preferential working relationship with the EU; there remains much speculation and conjecture as to the quantum of such payments, and the period over which they would be paid. The second issue concerns matters such as rights of movement, citizenship, abode, education, medical treatment and pensions. As at the time of writing, the UK and the EU remain in disagreement in relation to a number of these matters.

The two-year negotiating period can be extended only by agreement of all EU Member States. If no extension is agreed, the UK will cease automatically to be a member of the EU on 29 March 2019. The concept of there being a transitional period, during which the UK retains some aspects of EU membership, after 29 March 2019 has been suggested by a number of members of the UK Government; whether this approach would be acceptable to the EU is not yet known. [54.2]–[54.3]

II THE INSTITUTIONS OF THE EU

The main institutions of the EU that were set up by the EU Treaty to carry out the Community's tasks are:
(i) the Parliament;
(ii) the Council;
(iii) the European Commission; and
(iv) the CJEU.

There are different powers ascribed to each of the institutions; and the way that they interact is designed to ensure that checks and balances prevent any one institution from becoming too powerful. The powers of the respective institutions have evolved over time and each revision of the treaties has seen an increase in the power of the Parliament in comparison to the other institutions.

A number of other institutions – such as the European Central Bank – have been established that have specific roles in the EU; these are outside the focus of this chapter. [54.4]

a) *The European Parliament*

The European Parliament is directly elected, with the number of Members of the European Parliament (MEPs) per country being based on the population of each Member State. Elections take place every five years, on the basis of universal adult suffrage. There is no uniform voting system; each Member State is free to choose its own system, subject to certain restrictions, which include that the system must be a form of proportional representation. The MEPs represent c.500 million citizens. Following the European Parliamentary elections in May 2014, there are 751 MEPs.

The European Parliament shares legislative power equally with the Council of the European Union. With regard to the adoption of new legislation, there is a distinction between the ordinary legislative procedure ('the co-decision procedure'), where the Parliament is on an equal footing with the Council, and the special legislative procedures that apply in specific cases where Parliament has only a consultative role ('the consultation procedure'). The co-decision procedure was introduced by the TEU and extended by the

Amsterdam Treaty (1999). Approximately two-thirds of European laws are adopted through the co-decision procedure. However, taxation matters are dealt with under the consultation procedure; here the European Parliament will give only an advisory opinion. [54.5]

b) *The European Council*

The Council's task is to ensure that the objectives set out in the EU Treaty are attained. It has the final power of decision in relation to most secondary legislation. However, in most cases, it may act only on the basis of a proposal from the Commission.

The Council consists of one representative from each Member State. The representative must be 'at ministerial level, authorised to commit the government of that Member State'. The Council presidency is a rotating one: it is held by each Member State in turn for a six-month period. In the case of tax legislation, the Council of Ministers will comprise ministers from national governments with fiscal responsibility. This composition of the Council is known as 'ECOFIN'. The number of areas where qualified majority voting is used has been increased significantly. However, fiscal measures still require unanimous approval. [54.6]

c) *European Commission*

The European Commission was created to represent the European interest that is common to all Member States. It has a number of roles.

First, the European Commission acts as the guardian of the treaties. Under Art 4 of the Lisbon Treaty, Member States are obliged to 'take any appropriate measure ... to ensure fulfilment of the obligations arising out of the Treaties or resulting from the acts of the institutions of the Union' and they shall 'refrain from any measure which could jeopardise the attainment of the Union's objectives'. It is the role of the Commission to ensure that these objectives are met by the Member States and it has a discretionary power to end any infringements of EU law by Member States, if necessary by taking proceedings under Art 258 of the EU Treaty to the CJEU (see *Lütticke GmbH v Commission* (1966)). In support of this, it has extensive investigatory powers that it can use to require Member States to provide information.

Second, the European Commission is the initiator of Community action. The Commission is responsible for implementing common policies (such as the common agricultural policy); it administers the budget; and it sets the legislative timetable for the year. However, although the Commission has the right to take any step that it considers is appropriate in order to attain the objectives of the treaties, in practice, most proposals that it puts forward will be in response to a specific request for action from another institution, a Member State or from interested parties.

The European Commission is the only body authorised to put forward proposals for legislation. The fundamental EU principles of subsidiarity and proportionality must be respected: the Commission should only propose legislation if it is more effective to do so on the EU level than at the domestic level and it should ensure that the legislation goes no further than is necessary to achieve the desired objectives. The Commission is divided administratively into Directorates General; the one concerned with tax is known as the

Directorate General for Taxation and Customs Union (DG TAXUD). In preparing early drafts the various Directorates General consult with national governments and civil servants, representatives of trade and professional bodies and other interested parties. This process is known as 'comitology'. When the text of a draft is settled, it will be formally adopted by the full Commission and will be published in all EU languages in the *Official Journal* (OJ) as a formal proposal. At that stage, the Economic and Social Committee and the European Parliament will consider the proposal and, in doing so, will listen to the views of third parties. [54.7]

d) *The CJEU*

The jurisdiction of the CJEU is defined in the EU treaty. It has jurisdiction on the following matters:
(1) failure by a Member State to fulfil an obligation under the EU Treaty;
(2) legality of acts of the Council and Commission;
(3) failure to act by the Council or Commission; and
(4) preliminary rulings.

Under Art 267, the CJEU has jurisdiction to give preliminary rulings concerning:
(a) the interpretation of the EU Treaty; and
(b) the validity and interpretation of acts of the institutions, bodies, officers or agencies of the Union.
(c) the interpretation of the statutes of bodies established by an act of the Council.

The CJEU comprises 28 judges (one per Member State). Given the continuing high number of references to the CJEU it has been proposed recently that the number of judges be doubled to two per Member State; that has yet to be implemented. There are 11 Advocates-General. The CJEU may sit as a full court, in a Grand Chamber of 13 judges or in Chambers of three or five judges. More than 80% of cases are heard by three judges and it is rare for the CJEU to sit as a full court. It may do so where a case of exceptional importance is concerned; and there are particular cases prescribed by the Statute of the Court (such as proceedings to dismiss the European Ombudsman or a Member of the European Commission who has failed to fulfil his or her obligations) where it must. It sits in a Grand Chamber when a Member State or an institution which is a party to the proceedings so requests, and in particularly complex or important cases (including some tax cases). A representative of the Court (the 'Juge Rapporteur') gives the single judgment in each case, the text of which will have been agreed following discussions between the judges who sat on the case. This process is called 'delibere'. Decisions of the CJEU are generally, but not always, preceded by a detailed report ('opinion') from an Advocate-General (A-G)) that also has considerable weight, and is often cited later in implementing legislation. But, it is not binding on the CJEU. When deciding a case, the CJEU will often (but not invariably) follow the A-G's opinion. All cases before the CJEU are allocated a number, the last two digits of which refer to the year in which the action was started in the Court of Justice.

In matters of EU law, domestic courts and tribunals should refer points of dispute relating to EU law to the CJEU if they consider that a decision of the CJEU is necessary to enable them to give judgment. This process is known as a 'preliminary reference' under Article 267. It is by far the most common method by which tax cases end up before the CJEU. Decisions of the CJEU on preliminary references bind domestic courts (of all Member States) on the interpretation of EU law.

The general rule is that, where a question concerning EU law arises before a national court or tribunal, the matter may be referred to the CJEU if a decision on the question is necessary to enable the national court to give judgment. However, under Art 267, the matter *must* be referred if there is no right of appeal from a decision of the court or tribunal. Thus, courts of last resort (such as the Supreme Court in the UK) do not have a discretion as to whether to make a reference on an EU law issue which it is necessary to resolve before judgment can be given (although the court in question retains its discretion to decide whether a decision on a question of EU law is necessary to enable it to give judgment (see *R v Henn and Darby* (1979)). If the answer to the EU law point is 'acte claire' (in essence, so obvious that there is no scope for any reasonable doubt), then there is no obligation to refer.

The decision to make a reference is a matter for the national court or tribunal, not for the parties to the case. The court is not even bound to accept a joint submission by the parties that an issue of EC law that is not acte claire arises (see *Rheinmuhlen-Dusseldorf v Einfuhr-und Vorratsstelle fur Getreide und Futtermittel* (1974)). Similarly, a reference may be made by a court against the wishes of all the parties (see, for example, *Direct Cosmetics v Customs & Excise Commissioners* (1984)). Thus, if one of the parties disagrees with the decision, that party must appeal under national law – there is no direct right of access to the CJEU (see for example, *Marks and Spencer v Halsey* (2003). The Special Commissioners declined to refer; their decision was appealed to the High Court, where Park J referred questions to the CJEU).

In *R v International Stock Exchange, ex p Else* (1993) Sir Thomas Bingham (as he then was) set out guidelines that courts should be mindful of when deciding whether or not to refer issues of EU law to the CJEU. *First*, if the issues are almost certain to be conclusive of the outcome of these appeals, and, *second*, if it cannot be said that the court can resolve the issue itself 'with complete confidence', the issues should be referred. If the delay and costs of an appeal can be avoided by the making of a reference at an early stage, then that is a relevant consideration for a court to consider (see Bingham J in *C and E Comrs v Samex ApS and Hanil Synthetic Fiber Industrial Co Ltd* (1983)).

Until an Article 50 withdrawal agreement is concluded, that remains the position in the UK. It is understood that the CJEU will consider all references that have been made to it by UK courts prior to March 2019. In *BAT Industries Plc v R & C Comrs* (2017), the appellants urged the Tribunal to refer questions to the CJEU, given 'the current state of affairs in relation to Brexit'. The Tribunal refused to make a reference and said that the test remains as enunciated in *ex p Else*.

It is the responsibility of the UK court, rather than the parties, to settle the terms of the reference, although, in practice, the parties are normally involved in the drafting process. Practice Direction 68 of the Civil Procedure Rules 1998 states that the 'reference should identify as clearly and succinctly as possible the question on which the court seeks the ruling of the European Court. In choosing the wording of the reference, it should be remembered that it will need to be translated into many other languages'.

If a reference is made and not withdrawn the CJEU will give a decision. It will not concern itself with the question of whether or not a reference was necessary. However, where it considers that the subject matter of the reference has been adequately dealt with in its previous jurisprudence, it may give its view by way of a 'reasoned order' that refers to that previous jurisprudence. This will usually take place without there having been a hearing or an opinion delivered from an A-G.

The CJEU's sole function under Art 267 is to decide what the EU law is. This has two important consequences. *First*, the CJEU will not interpret national law or apply its interpretation of EU law to the facts of the case. *Second*, the CJEU will leave it to the national courts to implement its ruling (see eg *Cadbury Schweppes v IRC* (2006) where the CJEU held that the CFC legislation in the UK was contrary to EU law, but then referred back to the domestic court the issue as to whether that legislation could be justified; it was for the UK government to show that its CFC legislation could be interpreted as giving rise to a charge to UK tax only where 'wholly artificial arrangements' that do not reflect economic reality and which are aimed at circumventing the application of the legislation have been created). [54.8]–[54.10]

III SOURCES OF EU LAW

EU law comprises:
(1) the various treaties;
(2) regulations, directives and decisions made by EU institutions; and
(3) decisions of the CJEU.

EU law, in effect, imposes obligations on Member States to amend national law and, in certain instances, creates rights and obligations having direct effect in the legal systems of Member States without separate enactment by national legislatures. The following general conclusions can be drawn:
(1) EU law affects both Member States and their nationals. Provisions having direct effect in Member States create rights and impose obligations on individuals, which may be enforced in national courts. Other provisions affect the relations of Member States, inter se, or impose obligations upon them to enact national legislation giving effect to common policies.
(2) EU law has a uniform application in all Member States. The CJEU is the only body competent to give an authoritative ruling on the interpretation and application of the treaties, although national courts are required to give effect to the treaties purposively (whatever the national rules of legal interpretation) and, in the UK are increasingly doing so without having made a reference to the CJEU (see, for example, *The Trustees of the BT Pension Scheme v R & C Comrs* (2013)). Member States cannot restrict the operation of EU law by failing to implement or repeal national legislation, or by passing legislation, which is inconsistent with it.

(3) EU law takes precedence over national law (and bilateral treaties). Inconsistent national legislation is overridden by EU law, and directly enforceable rights are to be given effect as part of national law whether or not national legislation has been implemented. However, a Member State cannot rely on such directly enforceable rights as against an individual national. [54.11]

a) *The treaties*

The original Treaty of Rome that established the EEC in 1957 was primarily an economic treaty that was concerned with creating a single market in Europe. However, as well as traditional free-trading aims, it expressly included a number of purely social goals. The Single European Act (SEA) (which entered into force on 1 July 1987) further extended the scope of Community competence. One of the key objectives of the SEA was to ensure that the EC's internal market would be completed by the end of 1992. It included a formal framework for co-operation by Member States which led ultimately to Maastricht. On 1 November 1993, the TEU, which had been signed at Maastricht on 7 February 1992, brought into being a new legal and political entity – the European Union.

The Treaty of Amsterdam (TA) was signed in October 1997 and entered into force on 1 May 1999. Its aim was to change the composition and functioning of the institutions, which was considered politically necessary in order to enable enlargement of the EU, particularly with regard to applicants from central and eastern Europe. TA adopted the principle of 'closer co-operation', which provides that a limited number of Member States may establish rules that, in relation to a certain matter, apply only to themselves and not to any non-participating Member States, but nonetheless are within the institutional framework of the EU.

Articles 2 to 6 of the EU Treaty set out the main objectives of the EU and identify the means by which those objectives are to be met. They do not impose any particular legal obligations on Member States. They have interpretative value and may be used to clarify the parameters of the more specific treaty provisions that do impose legal obligations on Member States. [54.12]

b) *Secondary legislation*

There are two forms of secondary legislation that may be adopted at Community level by the Council of Ministers or the Commission acting under a specific provision of the EU Treaty or by the Commission acting under powers delegated to it by the Council of Ministers:
(1) regulations: this form of legislation has automatic effect in all Member States, without the need for any endorsement at national level. Regulations override inconsistent national legislation, whether adopted before or after the regulation; and
(2) directives: these are addressed to Member States and are binding as to the result, but leave to the individual Member States responsibility for taking decisions about the manner and form of their implementation.

Directives specify the regime to apply and require Member States to adjust their national laws and administrative practices accordingly. A directive shall 'leave to the national authorities the choice of form and methods' as to the result to be achieved. Each directive specifies the period within which national laws must be amended. Legal action may be taken by the Commission against the Member State in question under Art 258 or by another Member State under Art 259 for failure to implement a Directive.

Article 258 provides that:

'If the Commission considers that a Member State has failed to fulfil an obligation under the Treaties, it shall deliver a reasoned opinion on the matter after giving the State concerned the opportunity to submit its observations.'

If the State concerned does not comply with the opinion within the period laid down by the Commission, the latter may bring the matter before the CJEU (OJ C83, 30 March 2010, p 160). Article 259 further provides that:

'A Member State which considers that another Member State has failed to fulfil an obligation under the Treaties may bring the matter before the Court of Justice of the European Union.

Before a Member State brings an action against another Member State for an alleged infringement of an obligation under the Treaties, it shall bring the matter before the Commission.

The Commission shall deliver a reasoned opinion after each of the States concerned has been given the opportunity to submit its own case and its observations on the other party's case both orally and in writing.

If the Commission has not delivered an opinion within three months of the date on which the matter was brought before it, the absence of such opinion shall not prevent the matter from being brought before the Court.'

A Member State which is found by the CJEU to be in breach of its obligations must, under Art 260 take measures to comply with the judgment. If a Member State does not comply with a judgment of the CJEU, the Commission may ask the CJEU to fine it for non-compliance. The first stage involves the Commission issuing a letter of formal notice. This is a request to the government of the Member State to notify it of what measure has been taken to comply with the judgment of the CJEU. Failure to comply can result in very large daily penalties being imposed.

Directives have 'vertical' direct effect, ie they may be invoked by private individuals against Member States (and emanations of Member States, such as HMRC) where the Member State has failed properly to implement the provision within the period prescribed for that purpose. Directives cannot be invoked against private individuals (ie they do not have 'horizontal' direct effect). [54.13]–[54.20]

IV UNDERLYING PRINCIPLES

1 Precedence of EU law over UK law, and comparison with bilateral treaties

EU law matters in the UK for the simple reason that the UK Parliament has passed an Act requiring it to be taken into account. As a matter of UK law, international treaties do not give rise to enforceable rights as between the UK State and private individuals. Treaties (and other rules of international law) do not take effect in that way unless and until specifically incorporated into domestic law by a domestic statute. In other words, from a theoretical Public International Law perspective the UK has a 'dualist' system.

Standard bilateral tax treaties are governed by international law, rather than by domestic laws, and usually under the auspices of the Vienna Convention on the Law of Treaties. The general rule is that the provisions contained within treaties override those of domestic tax law.

Article 18 of the Vienna Convention reads:

'A State is obliged to refrain from acts which would defeat the object and purpose of a treaty when:

(a) it has signed the treaty or has exchanged instruments constituting the treaty subject to ratification, acceptance or approval, until it shall have made its intention clear not to become a party to the treaty; or

(b) it has expressed its consent to be bound by the treaty, pending the entry into force of the treaty and provided that such entry into force is not unduly delayed.'

The central tenet of the Vienna Convention is that treaties are concluded 'in good faith' and there is a presumption that a State will not want to override its treaties. A UK illustration of this is *R & C Comrs v FCE Bank Plc* (2012). FCE Bank Plc ('FCE') and Ford Motor Company Limited ('FMCL') were UK-resident subsidiaries of Ford Motor Company ('FMC'), which was resident in the USA. Under the UK tax rules in force in 1994 (which had been put in place in 1988 in their then current form), FCE was not entitled to relief for losses incurred by FMCL because the two companies had no common parent resident in the UK (the 'link rules'). FCE claimed that this represented discrimination against the two UK companies, because of their ownership by a US resident. Such discrimination is prohibited by the double taxation agreement between the UK and US (which entered into force in 1980). FCE was therefore entitled to relief for the losses surrendered by FMCL. HMRC's argument was that the non-discrimination article did not apply in circumstances where, in theory, the company could have restructured its affairs in order to escape the link rules. There was no argument about what would happen if it was found that the treatment was discriminatory: if the UK tax rule was discriminatory, it fell foul of the non-discrimination article and was to be disapplied. The UK courts held that the UK rule was discriminatory. Accordingly FCE was entitled to relief for the losses of FMCL.

The situation is more complicated if the treaty has been overridden intentionally. Can a taxpayer still rely on the treaty? How easily treaty provisions can be intentionally overridden by domestic law is a function of the way that a state's constitution incorporates treaties into its laws. Generally speaking, it depends on whether the State perpetrating the treaty override is a common law State (such as the UK) or a civil law State, such as Germany or France.

In a common law jurisdiction, treaty law has the same status as domestic law and therefore, using the general principle that a later law overrides an earlier law, the treaty override is usually effective. So if, as in the UK, a parliamentary statute is required to give effect to a treaty, subsequent domestic law may override the treaty. This is the case despite the fact that TIOPA 2010 s 6 (formerly TA 1988 s 788(3)) provides that a double tax treaty is to be given effect 'notwithstanding anything in any other enactment'.

The general UK constitutional principle is that Parliament cannot bind its successors. The above statement in law does not mean that a new provision in domestic law expressly designed to override a treaty provision is not possible.

The UK courts have found that if the statutory wording is clear, there may well be 'no scope for application of any presumption against ... breach of International Law' (*Padmore v IRC (No.2)* (2001) per Lightman J). In the case of *Padmore*, a UK-resident individual was a partner in a partnership, resident in Jersey, which dealt with patents and which partnership was considered opaque. This Jersey partnership acquired a share in a UK partnership which operated out of London, was considered resident in the UK and which paid UK income tax. Mr Padmore claimed that the part of the profits of the London partnership which were attributed to him ought to have been exempt from UK tax under the terms of the then UK/Jersey double tax agreement. In the first case which Mr Padmore brought, he won. However, following that decision, F(No 2)A 1987 s 62 was enacted, which overturned the court's decision for future income. Mr Padmore returned to court once more, arguing that a treaty could not be overridden by subsequent domestic legislation. By the time the case reached court, s 62 had been consolidated into TA 1988. Some rationalisation of the wording of the legislation had been undertaken as part of the consolidation process. Mr Padmore therefore argued, additionally, that the consolidated version of s 62 did not unequivocally state that it was intended to override the UK/Jersey tax treaty, and therefore had to be interpreted as being subsidiary to the terms of the UK/Jersey treaty. The court noted that the provisions in F(No 2)A 1987 were supplemented by provisions preventing the new rules from applying prior to certain dates. These were the dates of Mr Padmore's first court case. By the time his first case had reached the High Court, s 62 had already been enacted and these additional conditions were needed so as not to prejudice his case. In the second *Padmore* case, the courts held that the intention of the legislators was clear and the intention was to override the terms of the UK/Jersey treaty from the date of the enactment of that legislation (as well as any other treaties where the same point concerning foreign controlled partnerships applied). Therefore, Mr Padmore could not continue to rely on the UK–Jersey treaty. In short, bilateral treaty override in the UK is possible where it is the clear intention of the legislator to achieve it.

However, with the coming into effect of the EC Treaty and the establishment of the European Community, a 'new legal order' came into being, under which Member States of the Community limited their sovereign competences within the framework of the structure and objectives of the European Community. From the outset, the rules of the EC Treaty had a significant interaction with the direct tax systems of the Member States.

Three early cases help illustrate the immediate impact that this 'new legal order' had on the domestic legal systems of the Member States: *Humblet* (1960), *Van Gend en Loos* (1963) and *Costa v ENEL* (1964). **[54.21]**

a) *Transfer of competency to the Community*

In *Humblet* (1960) the right of the Member States to tax Community officials came under scrutiny as competence in relation to the taxation of salaries of

Community officials had been transferred to the Community (and remains there to this day).

Mr Humblet was a Community official of Belgian nationality. By taking Mr Humblet's salary into account when determining the progressive tax rate to be applied to his wife, Belgium attempted to indirectly tax Mr Humblet's salary by using an exemption with progression method under its domestic rules. Mr Humblet argued this was contrary to Art 16 of the protocol on privileges and immunities to the Treaty on the European Coal and Steel Community.

The CJEU noted that even though a number of double tax conventions had been entered into by the Member States containing a clause allowing for the application of the 'exemption with progression' method, no such reservation had been included in the Community's Treaties.

Accordingly it found that remuneration paid to Community officials was withdrawn from 'the Member States' sovereignty in tax matters'. It drew a distinction between income subject to the control of the national tax authorities of the Member States and the salaries of Community officials as the latter were subject to Community law alone as regards 'liability to tax while the other income of officials remains subject to taxation by the Member States'.

The Court determined that any taxation of Mr Humblet's salary, direct or indirect, was not within the jurisdiction of the Member States and so his salary could not be taken into account when determining the progressive tax rate on other income earned by his spouse. In other words, the Belgian domestic tax rules at issue were found to be incompatible with Community law and had to be amended. [54.22]

b) *Direct effect of Community rules*

Van Gend en Loos (1963) is key to understanding that community law is not susceptible to later national or bilateral agreements. In September 1960 the complainant had imported a quantity of ureaformaldehyde into the Netherlands from Germany. Under a protocol to the tariff of import duties then in force, the rate of duty on this substance had been raised from 3% to 8% as of March 1960.

Van Gend en Loos appealed on the basis that Art 12 of the EEC Treaty prohibited Member States from introducing new customs duties or from increasing those which already applied, and that that Article had direct effect without any further measures of implementation.

The Netherlands Government argued that an alleged infringement of the treaty was only justiciable by the court on the initiative of another Member State or the Commission; alternatively that the EEC Treaty did not differ from a standard international treaty and the intentions of parties in entering into the treaty were relevant.

The Court found that the EEC Treaty was decidedly more than an agreement which merely creates mutual obligations between Member States. The conclusion it drew from this was a far-reaching one: 'that the community constitutes a new legal order of international law for the benefit of which the states have limited their sovereign rights, albeit within limited fields, and the subjects of which comprise not only Member States but also their nationals. Independently of the legislation of Member States, Community law therefore not only imposes obligations on individuals but is also intended to confer upon them rights'. These rights of nationals of the Member States could be invoked before national courts and tribunals. Consequently, certain Community law rules had direct effect in the domestic legal systems of the Member States – including on their direct taxation systems. [54.23]

c) *Supremacy of EU law*

In *Costa v ENEL* (1964) an Italian citizen who owned shares in an electricity company, and was opposed to the nationalisation of the electricity sector in Italy, refused to pay his electricity bill (which amounted to about a pound), in protest. He was sued for non payment by the newly created State electricity company, ENEL. In his defence, he argued that the nationalisation of the electricity industry violated the Treaty of Rome. The Milan court referred the case to the Italian Constitutional Court and to the CJEU. The Italian Constitution Court ruled that, whilst the Italian Constitution allowed for the limitation of sovereignty for international organisations such as the EEC, it did not upset the normal rule of statutory interpretation that where two statutes conflict the later one prevails. As a result, the Treaty of Rome, which had been incorporated into Italian law in 1958, could not prevail over the electricity nationalisation law which was enacted in 1962. In light of the decision of the constitutional court, the Italian government submitted to the CJEU that the Italian court's request for a preliminary ruling from the CJEU was inadmissible on the grounds that as the Italian court was not empowered to set aside the national law in question, a preliminary ruling would not serve any valid purpose. The CJEU determined that EU law was supreme over the national laws of the Member States. The Court derived this entitlement from a variety of factors: from the spirit of the EU's Treaties; from the fact that a new legal system had been established, which had created new rights for individuals in Member States' legal systems; from the creation of the EU's framework and institutions; and from the limitations imposed on the sovereignty of the Member States together with the transfer of powers to the EU. The Court also noted that Community Regulations were binding and directly applicable in all Member States and that EU law had to apply uniformly in the Member States. But, the CJEU went on to comment that:

> 'the obligations undertaken under the Treaty establishing the Community would not be unconditional, but merely contingent, if they could be called into question by subsequent legislative acts of the signatories. Wherever the Treaty grants states the right to act unilaterally, it does this by clear and precise provisions.'

Accordingly,

> 'The transfer by the States from their domestic legal system to the Community legal system of the rights and obligations arising under the Treaty carries with it a permanent limitation of their sovereign rights, against which a subsequent unilateral act incompatible with the concept of the Community cannot prevail.'

In the UK, Parliament has passed an Act requiring EU law to be given precedence: the European Communities Act 1972 (ECA 1972).

The two key provisions of ECA 1972 are s 2(1) and s 2(4). ECA 1972 s 2(1) provides for all 'rights, powers, obligations and restrictions' under the relevant treaties to take effect as a matter of UK domestic law. ECA 1972 s 2(4) provides that all UK legislation, whether passed before or after the introduction of ECA 1972, shall have effect subject to s 2(1) and to the other provisions of s 2. Some (though not all) parts of EU law are expressed so as to give rise to enforceable rights (they are 'directly effective'). Therefore, ECA 1972 s 2 has the effect of requiring that directly effective provisions of EU law have the force of law in the UK, and prevail over any inconsistent UK legislation.

Despite some initial doubts as to the acceptability of this interpretation under traditional constitutional law theory, the English courts, from 1990 onwards, have adopted it. In *Factortame Ltd v Secretary of State for Transport* (1990) Lord Bridge said that ECA 1972 s 2(4) has 'precisely the same effect as if a section were incorporated in [the relevant legislation] which in terms enacted that the provisions [set out there] were to be without prejudice to the directly enforceable Community rights of nationals of any Member State of the EEC'. A number of questions were referred to the CJEU and in a subsequent related case (*R v Secretary of State for Transport, ex p Factortame Ltd* (1991)) the House of Lords swept away any final constitutional doubts by saying that it was the implied intention of Parliament, by enacting ECA 1972, to limit its sovereignty by accepting the supremacy of EU law. Since that time, there has been no doubt that unless and until the UK Parliament renounces the EU Treaty (and repeals ECA 1972), the UK courts will accord supremacy to directly effective EU law by applying it directly in priority to inconsistent UK law.

The UK Government has indicated that it intends to repeal ECA 1972 and transpose all directly applicable EU law into UK law as part of the UK's exit from the EU. The European Union (Withdrawal) Bill has that aim. Its first reading was on 13 July 2017. It is intended that the European Union (Withdrawal) Act will not come into force until the date that the UK leaves the EU. [54.24]

2 **The impact of EU law on UK law**

The substantive provisions relating to the fundamental freedoms are discussed below. However, first, a few key underlying propositions stated by the CJEU are set out. It should be understood that this is nothing more than the briefest summary of the key rules with regard to the impact of EU law. For a fuller understanding, reference should be made to a specialist legal text.

(1) In order for the aims of the EU to be achieved, it is necessary for there to be uniformity of application of EU law throughout the EU, and that requires EU law always to be supreme (see *Costa v ENEL* (1964) and *Internationale Handelsgesellschaft mbH* (1970)).

(2) A domestic national court that is required to apply provisions of EU law is under a duty to give full effect to those provisions by refusing to apply any conflicting national legislation; the domestic court should not wait for such conflicting national legislation to be set aside by legislative or other means (*Simmenthal SpA* (1978)).

(3) A finding that a national provision is inapplicable because of incompatibility with EU law does not mean that that domestic provision is ultra vires and thus is to be disregarded in its entirety. The CJEU has

made it clear that national courts are to disapply national measures in order to safeguard enforceable Community law rights only to the extent that those measures are incompatible with Community law (See *IN CO GE '90 Srl* (1998) and *ICI v Colmer* (1996)). Otherwise, the offending national provisions remain in force.

(4) The obligation to give full effect to EU law applies not only to national courts, but also to domestic administrative agencies such as, for example, HMRC (see *Gervais Larsy v INASTI* (2001)). [54.25]–[54.30]

V THE FUNDAMENTAL FREEDOMS: INTRODUCTION

Prior to the amendments introduced by the Treaty of Lisbon, the four 'fundamental freedoms' (or, simply, 'freedoms') first appeared in Art 3 of the Treaty of Rome. That Article provided that the broad aim of the EU Treaty was to ensure the creation of 'an internal market characterised by the abolition, as between Member States, of obstacles to the freedom of movement of goods, persons, services and capital'. In other words, the freedoms were central to the treaty and its aims. The freedoms now appear in the following terms at Art 26:

'1. The Union shall adopt measures with the aim of establishing or ensuring the functioning of the internal market, in accordance with the relevant provisions of the Treaties.
2. The internal market shall comprise an area without internal frontiers in which the free movement of goods, persons, services and capital is ensured in accordance with the provisions of the Treaties.'

Detailed rules for each of them are set out in Arts 28 to 66, and they are each described more fully in [54.42]–[54.50]. The freedoms primarily play an economic role, namely to assist in the abolition of barriers to the internal market. Although the four freedoms are addressed to Member States, the relevant Articles have been held by the CJEU to be directly effective. Accordingly, individuals and companies have the right to invoke any one or more of those freedoms to challenge the validity of domestic law provisions (including tax law) that represent an obstacle to their utilisation of such freedom(s).

However, in any such challenge, it is necessary to identify the particular freedom that it is asserted that a provision breaches. This is partly because the freedoms are different in scope. It is also because, as described below, there are certain grounds on which an obstacle to a freedom may be justified, so as to be protected from challenge; and those grounds are not identical for each of the four freedoms.

In certain circumstances, it is very clear which freedom is in play. The dividing line between, for example, 'goods' and 'persons' is very easy to identify. However, other boundaries, particularly the ones between 'goods' and 'capital' and between 'goods' and 'services' are less distinct. The CJEU cases suggest that in such cases there are no hard and fast rules: rather, it is a matter of degree. For example, the CJEU has held that, although collectors' coins are 'goods', legal tender in circulation falls within the provisions relating to 'capital' (*Bordessa* (1995)).

In other circumstances, although the freedoms are mutually exclusive in scope, it will be clear that a single domestic rule may represent an obstacle to two or more freedoms. In such circumstances, it is necessary to determine whether the rule should be tested against each of those freedoms, or only one of them. The position seems to be that any freedom that is only affected in an indirect or ancillary way is to be ignored in these circumstances (this has much in common with the test in the VAT case of *Card Protection Plan Ltd v C & E Comrs* (1999) see **[38.25]**). This rule emerges from *C & E Comrs v Schindler* (1994), a case where both 'goods' and 'services' were potentially relevant. In that case, the CJEU said that if goods are supplied in a form that is not an end in itself, but is ancillary to the supply of a service (such as advertising materials) then the activity should be treated as the movement of services, but not the movement of goods. A similar approach was recommended by A-G Tesauro in *Safir* (1998) in relation to the boundary between 'capital' and 'services'. He opined that, where possible, the domestic rule should be considered only in relation to the freedom that it restricts 'directly', and not as an obstacle to any other freedoms that it affects indirectly. This passage was cited and relied upon by A-G Alber in *Baars* (2000) and by A-G Geelhoed in *Reisch* (2004).

Although the CJEU has not always been so punctilious (in *Svensson & Gustavvson* (1995), the CJEU held that certain aspects of Luxembourg law breached both the free movement of capital and services provisions, but it did so without providing an analysis of how each provision applied to the relevant law), in more recent cases (see eg *Fidium Finanz AG* (2006) and the *Test Claimants in the Thin Cap Group Litigation* (2007)), it has adopted a similar approach to that suggested by A-G Alber in *Baars* (2000). The approach taken by the CJEU in these cases is analysed further at **[54.49]**.   **[54.31]–[54.40]**

VI   THE FUNDAMENTAL FREEDOMS: SCOPE

As noted above, the EU Treaty provides four fundamental freedoms on which individuals and companies can rely, in accordance with the framework described above. However, although the framework is constant, each of those four freedoms applies in slightly different ways. This section addresses the specific circumstances in which specific tax rules have fallen (or will fall) within the scope of one of the freedoms, so as to be disapplied in order to give effect to the Member State's duties and the taxpayers' rights under that freedom.

It should be noted that at this stage that, in certain circumstances, rules that appear to restrict a fundamental freedom may nonetheless be considered to be justified, in which case they will not be disapplied (similarly, rules which are wholly non-discriminatory, both in theory and practice, will generally be permitted). Any justification will either be by reference to one of a list of overriding objectives set out in the Treaty itself, or by reference to one of a (separate, and open-ended) class of objectives which do not appear in the EU Treaty but which have been inferred by the CJEU. The justifications set out in the EU Treaty are dealt with in this section. The rather more important issues associated with the class of justifications clarified by the CJEU are discussed (together with the question of wholly non-discriminatory rules) in Section VII below. [54.41]

1   **Free movement of goods (Arts 28 to 32)**

As the EEC originated as a free trade area, the free movement of goods is often regarded by Community lawyers as the most important of the fundamental freedoms.

However, although many of the principles of the application of the fundamental freedoms were developed in the context of the free movement of goods, from a substantive point of view it is of little relevance to direct tax (being rather more concerned with indirect taxes such as customs and excise duties, which are beyond the scope of this work, and with VAT, which is discussed in the self-contained section in **Chapters 37–40**). Accordingly, specific instances of its application are not discussed here. [54.42]

2   **Free movement of persons (Arts 45 to 55)**

Uniquely amongst the four fundamental freedoms, free movement of persons comprises two quite distinct limbs: (i) the freedom of workers to travel to other Member States and to be able to accept employment there (Art 45); and (ii) the right of establishment for citizens of Member States (Art 49) and companies and firms incorporated in the EU or with their central administration here (the benefit of Art 49 is extended to such companies by Art 54).

Of the four freedoms, free movement of persons (particularly the 'establishment' arm) has had, perhaps, the most significant impact on direct tax. This is because most European tax systems were set up, prior to the advent of the EEC, in a way whose underlying philosophy is in direct conflict with the requirements of Art 49. In accordance with conventional international tax theory, the UK and most (if not all) of the Member States have proceeded on the basis that resident taxpayers are to be treated differently from non-resident taxpayers. They have also assumed that, from a 'parent company' perspective, branches and subsidiaries within the State can be treated differently from those that are abroad (and that branches owned locally can be treated differently from those parented in another jurisdiction). Finally, their laws tend to provide for cross-border transactions or activities to be taxed differently to purely domestic ones, principally to avoid the loss of tax to the particular State's fiscal authority. However, the clear result of the obligation on Member States to ensure free movement of persons within the EU is that there are very significant restrictions on a State's ability to do any of these things. [54.43]

a)   *Free movement of workers: Art 45*

As noted above, this Article guarantees the freedom of workers to travel to other Member States and to be able to accept employment there. There is no definition of 'worker' in the Treaty; and the CJEU has interpreted the term in a wide sense. In *Levin* (1982), it said that if what is proposed involves: 'the pursuit of effective and genuine activities to the exclusion of activities on such a small scale as to be regarded as purely marginal and ancillary', then the person is a 'worker'; to define the term more restrictively would be contrary to the overarching principles of the EU Treaty. In *Wallentin v Riksskatteverket* (2004), the CJEU held that Mr Wallentin could rely on Art 45 to claim a refund of Swedish withholding tax that had been imposed on his wages when he undertook a three-week holiday job with the Church of Sweden.

The main set of issues that have arisen in this context relate to personal tax advantages, such as personal allowances (see **[7.103]**) that are expressed to be dependent upon residence. Broadly, subject to questions of discrimination and justification (see below), the CJEU has held that Member States are required to treat migrant workers as if they were residents. The leading case in relation to personal tax advantages for migrant workers remains *Schumacker* (1995). Mr Schumacker was a Belgian resident employed in Germany. Over 90% of his income was earned in Germany and he was exempted from Belgian tax on this foreign-source income. As there was no Belgian tax due in respect of which he could credit his Belgian personal allowances and deductions, he instead sought similar allowances from the German State. Under German law, he would only have been entitled to such allowances if he were a German resident. The CJEU agreed that he should be entitled to such allowances. Other cases are discussed below in relation to the question of discrimination.

It should be noted that there is no automatically corresponding right for companies to move their central management to another Member State under Art 45 (see *ex p Daily Mail and General Trust plc* (1988)). Whether this right is protected by the right to freedom of establishment is addressed in the Exit Taxes section below. **[54.44]**

b) *Freedom of establishment: Arts 49 and 54*

The right enshrined in Arts 49 and 54 is a right to establish a business in a Member State (whether by way of branch or subsidiary of an existing business, or otherwise) and to do so on terms that that business undertaking will not be discriminated against on the ground of the owner's nationality (or in the case of a company, its seat). Where the 'establisher' has only a part-interest in the establishment, this freedom will be engaged only if that interest allows him to participate in the management or control of entity or business and allows him to exercise definite influence (*Baars* (2000)). This is generally considered to be a non-numerical test, though the better view is that large minority holdings would qualify, provided that the 'establisher' does actually involve himself in the management or control of the establishment. This article has been considered to suggest the need to disapply domestic tax rules in each of the following situations.

(1) More stringent taxation on an individual resident abroad with a local business than a local resident:

Wielockx (1995) – a rule confining to residents the right to deduct payments to a pension scheme when computing business profits.

(2) More stringent taxation on a branch than a locally incorporated subsidiary:

Commission v France (1986) (the 'avoir fiscal' case) – the inability of a French branch of a German company to claim a tax credit that would have been available to a French company in corresponding circumstances;

Compagnie de Saint-Gobain (1999) – the unavailability of treaty relief on dividend income received by a German branch of a French company, in circumstances that a German company would have been entitled to such relief; and

Royal Bank of Scotland plc v Greek State (1999) – the application of a flat rate of corporation tax to branches of overseas companies, when a lower rate was available in certain circumstances to Greek companies.

(3) More stringent taxation on a foreign-owned company than one that is domestically owned:

Metallgesellschaft/Hoechst (2001) – the inability of the UK subsidiary of a non-resident company to make a group income election, which would have enabled it to pay a dividend to its parent companies without having to account for advance corporation tax (very broadly speaking, a collection mechanism for corporation tax triggered by the payment of a dividend); and

Lankhorst-Hohorst (2002) – the application of German thin capitalisation rules to a loan received by the German subsidiary of a Dutch parent company, which rules would not have applied had the loan been granted by a German-resident parent company.

Thin Cap (2007) – the application of UK thin capitalisation rules to recharacterise interest payments as dividends.

Group Steria SCA (2015) – the French taxation of EU-source dividends that involved including 5% of dividends received from EU subsidiaries in French taxable income but fully exempting dividends received from French tax-consolidated subsidiaries.

(4) More stringent taxation on a person or entity with foreign establishments than one with local establishments:

Imperial Chemicals Industries plc v Colmer (1996) – the application of a UK rule that consortium relief for losses was conditional on the holding company being a company whose business consisted wholly or mainly of the holding of shares of companies that are its 90% subsidiaries and that in determining this only UK resident companies could be considered;

Baars (2000) – the denial of the Netherlands wealth tax exemption to holdings in foreign companies, when it applied to holdings in domestic companies;

Bosal Holding BV (2001) – the denial of relief for interest expenses in relation to monies borrowed to acquire shares in a non-Netherlands company;

X&Y (2002) – the denial of a CGT deferral on transfer of an asset to an associated but non-resident company, when that deferral would have been available on the transfer to an associated resident company; and

de Baeck (2004) – imposition of a CGT charge on transfer of an asset to an associated but non-resident company (this case is much the same as *X&Y* (2002) except that the domestic rule allowed for the transfer to be wholly tax-free).

(5) A tax charge applying directly on transfer of residence of the person or business abroad (but, see the section entitled Exit taxes below (at [**54.46**]) for a more detailed analysis):

De Lasteyrie (2003) – a deemed disposal for French CGT purposes of assets when the individual moved his residence from France; and

N v Inspecteur van de Belastingdienst Oost (2006) – A-G Kokott opined that, although the exit charge regime in The Netherlands restricted the exercise of freedom of establishment, it could be justified as it pursued the legitimate objective of maintaining a proportional tax system based on the principles of territoriality and coherence; the CJEU decided the case in the same way as it had decided *De Lasteyrie*.

(6) More stringent loss surrender and offset rules for a resident entity with an (EU) non-UK corporate parent when compared to a resident entity with a UK corporate parent:

Marks & Spencer v Halsey (2005) – denial of offset of terminal French losses against UK profits;

Philips Electronics (2012) – denial of ability to offset losses of a UK branch against UK subsidiary profits where there was a non-UK intermediate parent; and

Felixstowe Dock (2014) – denial of consortium relief within structures with an EEA link company where it would have been allowed had the link company been subject to UK corporation tax.

(7) Rules re-characterising foreign subsidiary profits as domestic parent profits in circumstances where that would not happen with a domestic subsidiary:

Cadbury Schweppes (2006) – UK rules under which the profits of a controlled foreign company were attributed to the resident company and taxed in its hands.

It will be noted that Art 43 will disapply any establishment-related rule of more stringent taxation, whether that taxation applies to the establisher or the establishment itself. It will also be noted that in some of these cases, the right of establishment has disapplied not only rules which affect the establishment itself, but also rules which affect subsequent dealings between the establisher and the establishment (see, in particular, *X&Y* (2002) and *Lankhorst-Hohorst* (2003)). This is now a relatively uncontroversial proposition. [**54.45**]

Exit taxes

The purpose of exit taxes is to secure taxation in respect of unrealised gains in assets (whether they be shares in a company, intellectual property or real estate) that might otherwise escape taxation in the 'home' jurisdiction as a result of the taxpayer leaving that jurisdiction. They usually operate by deeming the exiting company to have disposed of and immediately reacquired its assets for market value. Whilst it is evident that there is a justification for them (balanced allocation of taxing power), they do act as a serious hindrance to the exercise of free movement of rights: any gain is both accelerated and notional; it could be many years before the relevant asset is sold and any eventual sale price could be less than the value on exit.

The jurisprudence of the CJEU shows a distinction between companies and the emigration of individuals. Companies derive their existence from a national legal system, which may take away that existence when they transfer their real seat abroad, whereas individuals exist, irrespective of any particular national law.

In *R v HM Treasury and IRC, ex p Daily Mail and General Trust* (1988), Daily Mail sought to remain incorporated in the UK, but transfer its central management to the Netherlands before disposing of part of its assets. At the time, consent of the Treasury was required. The Treasury refused to consent unless Daily Mail triggered the gain in part before it migrated. The CJEU upheld the UK's provisions, stating that a UK company that retained its status as a UK incorporated company could be restricted from transferring its place of central management and control to another Member State.

In a number of subsequent cases, the CJEU has upheld the reasoning in *Daily Mail*, but two more recent cases (*Cartesio* (2008) and *National Grid Indus* (2011)) demonstrate that the lawfulness of exit charge provisions in respect of companies depends on whether or not they are proportionate.

Cartesio Oktató és Szolgáltató bt v Hungary (2008) concerned a Hungarian limited partnership that sought to transfer its seat to Italy. Under Hungarian law this triggered a dissolution of the Hungarian entity and a corporate exit tax. Advocate General Maduro concluded that the Hungarian rules that provide that a company incorporated in Hungary cannot transfer its operational headquarters to another Member State without the company having been previously dissolved (thereby creating a tax charge on disposal of its assets) are incompatible with Arts 49 and 54. Whilst it may be acceptable to have rules that set conditions on the transfer, in order to guard against abuse (ie where wholly artificial arrangements exist), that was not the situation in relation to Hungarian provisions. Thus, in Advocate General Maduro's opinion, the provisions should be disapplied. However, the CJEU disagreed, holding that, in the absence of a uniform community law definition of the companies which may benefit from Art 49 on the basis of a single connecting factor (as opposed to multiple factors, such as registered office, central administration or principal place of business), the question as to whether Art 49 applies to a company is a preliminary matter that can be resolved by the applicable national law only. In this regard, there is a distinction between 'incorporation doctrine' states and 'real seat' States. Incorporation doctrine states confer legal recognition by reference to the place of incorporation and maintenance of a registered office, ie regardless of where a company's operations are carried on. Real seat States require a substantial connection between where a company's central or controlling operations are carried on and its place of incorporation; without that connection, recognition of the legal status of the company may be denied. The implication of the CJEU's decision is that real seat doctrine countries that prohibit the transfer of the central administration of locally registered companies may continue to do so, but where incorporation doctrine states permit the transfer of the corporate seat (and in consequence a national company becomes subject to the company law of another Member State), Art 49 is engaged and any restriction in either the originating or receiving State is impermissible unless justifiable.

In *National Grid Indus BV* (2011), a Dutch incorporated company was set up to participate in a joint venture in Pakistan. The joint venture did not materialise and it lent the money that was to be invested into the joint venture back to the UK group. Four years later, the decision was taken to move the residence of the company to the UK; it would, however, remain a Dutch incorporated company. One consequence of this was that an inherent foreign exchange profit on the loan would not be subject to tax in the future. The Dutch tax authorities sought to tax this gain by means of an exit charge, imposed when the residence was moved.

The Advocate General asked whether the charge was in the public interest as a balanced allocation of the right to tax and, if so, was the charge proportionate or did it go beyond what was necessary to achieve this aim? She opined that, in principle, Member States could seek to tax latent monetary gains, but, to be proportionate, there was a further question that had to be answered: was it appropriate to tax the gain at the time of departure or should it be deferred? If it is practical to tax the gain at the time of realisation and not at exit, that is the preferred option. Whether it is practical depends on the nature of the asset; if it can be 'traced' so that the later gain can be taxed, taxing on exit would be disproportionate. If it cannot be traced, so that there is a risk that the gain would escape tax, an exit tax could be proportionate and therefore justifiable.

The CJEU adopted a similar approach and held that an exit tax which does not give the right to defer payment until the gain becomes realised is not proportionate. The CJEU suggested that exit tax legislation should include two options: (i) the immediate payment of tax on unrealised gains; (ii) a deferment until the disposal of the asset (potentially with interest).

In *Verder* (2015) a limited partnership under German law, which dealt solely with the administration of patent, trademark and model rights, had transferred those rights to its permanent establishment in the Netherlands. The German tax authority sought to impose a charge to tax on the limited partnership in Germany based on the unrealised capital gains inherent in the assets at the time of the transfer of the assets. The unrealised capital gains were charged to tax on a straight line basis over ten years. The Court found that there was a restriction on the freedom of establishment within the meaning of Article 49 TFEU, but that the restriction was appropriate and proportionate for ensuring the preservation of the allocation of taxing rights, by reason of the need to take account of the risk of non-recovery of the tax, which increases with passage of time. [54.46]

Derogations under Arts 51 and 52

Article 51 exempts activities which are connected 'with the exercise of official authority'. This derogation has been given a very narrow interpretation and a similar set of exceptions in relation to the free movement of goods has been narrowly construed. Article 52 provides a list of exceptions to the free movement of workers and the freedom of establishment. They are of limited application in the context of direct tax: the right of persons to move freely does not override domestic rules providing for special treatment of foreign nationals based on public policy, public security or public health. It is expected that these exceptions would be construed narrowly. [54.47]

3 Freedom to provide services (Art 56)

Article 56 sets out the third freedom. It provides that nationals of Member States are guaranteed the right freely to provide services cross-border. As with freedom of establishment, the right is accorded to EU nationals and to companies that have either their registered office, central administration or place of business in a Member State. The freedom to provide services is a subsidiary freedom to the three other fundamental freedoms: the services in question are those 'normally provided for remuneration, insofar as they are not governed by the provisions relating to freedom of movement for goods, capital and persons' (Art 50(1)). Again, where domestic law provides that a cross-border provider of services is subject to more stringent taxation than a domestic provider, the relevant domestic rule will be disapplied. A recent example of this is *Brisal-Auto Estradas do Litoral SA v Fazenda Pública* (2016). The issue here was whether the system that provided for (i) withholding tax on gross interest paid to a non-resident lender and (ii) tax that was collected later from resident lenders, at a higher rate but on their net profit, was permissible. The CJEU, unsurprisingly, held that non-resident lenders and resident lenders should be in a similar position with regards to the deduction of business expenses, both directly connected with the activity being taxed and also as a proportion of overheads.

It is frequently said that the right to provide services includes the right to receive services (see *Eurowings Luftverkehrs AG* (1999)). In that case, German companies leasing assets could claim a certain tax deduction only if they leased the assets from a domestic lessor. The CJEU held that this amounted to a restriction on the freedom to receive services from other Member States, and that the taxpayer should be entitled to such a deduction, even if it leased the assets from a foreign lessor. However, this is simply a manifestation of the fact that the more stringent tax treatment tends to apply in the hands of the recipient of the services rather than the provider. Therefore, in *Laboratoires Fournier* (2005) the limitation of an increased deduction for R&D expenditure to expenditure incurred in France was held to affect the right of non-French subcontractors to supply their services, even though the limitation applied to the tax position of the French company that had (or could have) sub-contracted the services in the first place. Further, this freedom can even affect an unfavourable tax treatment in the hands of a third party: in *Commission v Spain* (2004) the CJEU held that a rule which granted more favourable tax treatment to dealings in shares listed on the Spanish stock market restricted the right of other stock markets to provide their services to Spanish undertakings, thereby benefiting neither the stock market nor the undertaking, but an owner of shares in the undertaking.

As with free movement of persons and free movement of goods, the freedom to provide services is subject to derogation on the grounds of 'public policy, public security or public health' (under Art 62). Again, it is expected that these derogations would be construed narrowly, and (in particular) so as to exclude economic aims. [54.48]

4 Free movement of capital (Arts 63 to 66)

The final freedom is set out in Art 63. Article 63(1) provides that: 'within the framework of the provision set out in this Chapter, all restrictions on the movement of capital between Member States and between Member States and third countries shall be prohibited'. These current provisions have been in force only since 1 January 1994; before that date, the provisions on free movement of capital were restricted to the EU & EEA. The current provisions on movement of capital, like the provisions in respect of the free movement of goods, are expressed by reference to the object of protection, namely 'capital', rather than by reference to the rights of a given entity. Article 63(2) is in identical terms to Article 63(1), but applies to 'payments' rather than to 'movements of capital'.

These provisions apply to all measures that impose a more stringent tax regime on or in respect of cross-border movements of capital. In *Lenz* (2004) and *Manninen* (2004), the CJEU held that a tax system that taxed dividends from local shares (Austrian and Finnish, respectively) more favourably than dividends from shares in non-resident companies was within Art 63, the cross-border capital movement being the original investment in the shares. In *Weidert & Paulus* (2004), a rule which allowed the acquisition costs of shares in domestic companies to be deducted from taxable income (but not the acquisition costs of shares in non-resident companies) also fell within Art 63 (it will be noted that this is a very similar case to *Bosal* (2001), but applying in circumstances where the level of investment was insufficient to create an establishment). As with freedom of establishment, Art 63 can disapply rules in either State: in *Fokus Bank* (2004), a case very similar to *Lenz* (2004) and *Manninen* (2004), the EFTA court (the corresponding court to the ECJ for the European Free Trade Area) found that the free movement of capital was impeded even though the tax regime in question applied in the State of the dividend payer, rather than in the shareholder's State.

Article 65(1)(b) provides for similar derogations to those in play for free movement of goods, services and persons. Again, it is to be expected that they will be construed narrowly.

However, although, so far, free movement of capital seems to apply in very much the same way as the other three freedoms, there are four significant points of difference.

First, Art 65 contains specific additional grounds on which measures that affect the free movement of capital can be justified. These must be considered in each case, notwithstanding that the CJEU currently restricts their scope. Article 65(1)(a) allows Member States to apply tax provisions which restrict free movement of capital within the EU insofar as they discriminate between 'tax-payers who are not in the same situation with regard to their place of residence or with regard to the place where their capital is invested'. However, although this ground appears to be quite wide-ranging in its scope, the Court has made clear that as Art 65(1)(a) is a derogation from a fundamental freedom, it is interpreted strictly (in an analogous way to Art 36). Thus, Art 65(1)(a) absolutely does not mean that any tax legislation that distinguishes between taxpayers by reference to the place where they invest their capital is automatically compatible with the Treaty. Further, by virtue of Art 65(3), in order to justify differential tax treatment under this provision, there must be an underlying difference that justifies the differing treatment. The decisions of the CJEU in *Manninen* (2004) and, particularly, *Weidert & Paulus* (2004) have put it almost beyond doubt that the effect of this is that Art 65(1)(a) adds nothing to the case law on justifications, discussed below.

Article 65(1)(b) indicates that measures which affect the free movement of capital can be justified to the extent necessary 'to prevent infringements of national law and regulations, in particular in the field of taxation and the prudential supervision of financial institutions, or to lay down procedures for the declaration of capital movements for purposes of administrative or statistical information'. However, again, Art 65(3), applies and as appears from *Verkooijen* (2001), this restricts the impact of Art 65(1)(b) in much the same way as it restricts Art 65(1)(a).

The second distinction is the limited nature of Art 63. It is obvious that, in certain cases, there is a real overlap between free movement of capital and the other freedoms (particularly freedom of establishment); it is now clear that Art 63 is to be treated as a subsidiary freedom, not to be considered where any impact on the free movement of capital arises indirectly from a limitation on another freedom (as in, for instance, *X&Y* (2002)). Although it was considered previously that potentially Art 63 always could be raised in the alternative in the event that, for whatever reason, it was found that there was no breach of freedom of establishment (see A-G Alber in *Safir* (1998)), a limitation on that approach was introduced by the CJEU in *Fidium Finanz AG* (2006) and the *Test Claimants in the Thin Cap Group Litigation* (2006)). The correct test to apply when a national measure potentially contravenes Art 63 and Art 49 is as follows. The measure must be considered, to determine which is the most appropriate freedom against which it is to be measured. If it can be shown that the two freedoms are directly affected by the offending provision, then, as it is necessary for the domestic rules to comply with both freedoms (as A-G Alber said in *Baars* (2000), relying on *Konle* (1999)), the CJEU is bound to analyse the provision in the context of both Art 49 and Art 63. However, if the measure primarily affects freedom of establishment, then the CJEU will only examine the provision in the context of that measure. Any restrictive effect caused by the legislation on the free movement of capital will be viewed as an unavoidable consequence of any restriction on freedom of establishment that will not justify an independent examination of the legislation in the light of Art 63 (see also *Omega* (2004)). There is doubt that the decision that the Amsterdam Tax Court of Appeal reached in a case in March 2005, where it held that Art 63 could apply even in circumstances where the transaction is one to which (in a purely EU context) the rules on freedom of establishment would be given effective priority, is correct following *Test Claimants in the Thin Cap Group Litigation* (2006). The priority as between capital and services (both of which consider themselves to be subsidiary freedoms) is not considered to be a significant issue in practice.

Finally, uniquely amongst the four freedoms, Art 63 applies even in respect of transactions with non-EU countries (as in *Ospelt* (2003)). The scope of this rule is currently somewhat uncertain, and recent cases in a tax context suggest that extending EC non-discrimination arguments to entities outside the EU can be difficult.

The key substantive limitation to the above is that found in Art 64(1), which permits the retention of any national or Community law measures that existed on 31 December 1993 that affect movements of capital to or from third countries 'involving direct investment (including investment in real estate), establishment, the provision of financial services or the admission of securities to capital markets'. The derogation in Art 64 applies to 'movements of capital', whilst Art 63 applies to 'payments' (under Art 63(2)) and 'movements of capital' (under Art 63(1)). Thus, it had been argued that the derogation in Art 64 applied only to movements of capital. In *NEC Semi-Conductors Ltd v IRC* (2003), Park J in the High Court held that Art 64 applies both to 'movements of capital' and 'payments', and the Court of Appeal disagreed (2006). However, the House of Lords (*Boake Allen Ltd v R & C Comrs* (2007)) considered that the decision of the CJEU in *Test Claimants in the FII Group Litigation* (2006) answered this question definitively by confirming that the derogation in Art 64 applies to Art 63 as a whole. In *X v Staatssecretaris van Financiën* (2015), the CJEU held that the exception to the free movement of capital contained in Art 64(1) was not limited to restrictions on the movement of capital that relate solely to the categories referred to in Art 64(1). As such, it could apply to general measures, such as the extended time period for the recovery of tax on foreign income that was in issue, provided that the particular case involved one of the prescribed types of capital movement.

It is necessary to determine when a measure is to be regarded as having existed prior to December 1993. In *Sanz de Lera* (1995) the CJEU held that this derogation is to be construed strictly: no new restrictions on the movement of capital to or from third countries can be created by Member States and the only permissible exceptions are in respect of the types of movements specified in the Article (although they also found that rules of equal application to EU and non-EU transactions will be protected by this standstill provision for non-EU transactions). However, in *Holböck* (2007) and *Test Claimants in the FII Group Litigation* (2006) the CJEU interpreted the derogation more widely. The CJEU held that any national measure adopted after 1993 is not, by that fact alone, automatically excluded from the derogation laid down in the Community measure in question. If the provision is, in substance, identical to the previous legislation or is limited to reducing or eliminating an obstacle to the exercise of Community rights and freedoms in the earlier legislation, it will be covered by the derogation. In *Holböck* (2007), the CJEU held that the Austrian legislation which was amended in 1996 should be regarded as having existed on 31 December 1993 and was therefore protected under Art 64.

A-G Geelhoed suggested in *FII Group Litigation* (2006) that 'different considerations' apply to justification where non-EU countries are concerned. Freedom of movement of capital is a constituent element in economic and monetary union; once that union is complete, there will be complete unity in terms of movement of capital and payments. However, that is not the context in relation to capital moving to non-EU countries.

There was a useful discussion of what these 'different considerations' might be in *Skatteverket v A* (2007). Under the 1999 Swedish Law on Income Tax, dividends paid to a Swedish-resident individual are normally subject to income tax in that State. However, under para 16 of Chapter 42 of that law there was an exemption for dividends received from Swedish companies. In 2001 this exemption was extended to companies corresponding to a Swedish limited company established in States within the EEA and any other State with which Sweden had concluded a DTC that contained a provision on exchange of information. The 1965 DTC between Sweden and Switzerland, which deals with the taxation of dividends and interest in Arts 10 and 11, does not contain an express provision on exchange of information. However, a 1993 arrangement (which did not have the status of a protocol to the treaty) set out the procedure to be followed by an individual to obtain tax relief under those articles. A owned shares in X, which had its registered office in Switzerland. X was considering distributing the shares that it held in one of its subsidiaries. A applied to the Revenue Commission for a preliminary decision on whether such a distribution was exempt from income tax. A stated that X corresponded to a Swedish limited liability company and that the conditions for tax exemption imposed by the law, other than those relating to the location of the registered office of the company, were satisfied. The Revenue Commission concluded that the distribution of shares contemplated by X should be exempt from income tax under the provisions of the EC Treaty on free movement of capital since although the Mutual Assistance Directive did not apply, the 'Arrangement appeared to make it possible for the Swedish tax authorities to obtain the information required for the application of domestic tax legislation'. The tax authority appealed on the basis that the provisions on free movement of capital were unclear with regard to the movement of capital between Member States and third countries, and in particular in the case of those third countries which oppose exchanging information for purposes of fiscal supervision. They argued that in relations with third countries, compliance with the prohibition laid down in Art 63(1) would lead to unilateral liberalisation on the part of the European Community without the Community securing a guarantee of equivalent liberalisation on the part of the third countries concerned. A maintained that the provisions in the arrangement could be treated as if they were a provision on the exchange of information in the DTC, and, in any event, para 16a of Chapter 42 was a restriction on the free movement of capital that could not be justified. The question, in essence, was whether the provisions of the Treaty on free movement of capital were to be interpreted as precluding legislation of a Member State which provided that exemption from income tax in respect of dividends distributed in the form of shares in a subsidiary might be granted only if the distributing company is established in a State within the EEA or in a State with which a taxation convention providing for the exchange of information had been concluded by the Member State imposing the tax.

The Court noted that Art 63(1) lays down a clear and unconditional prohibition for which no implementing measure was needed. Even if the liberalisation of the movement of capital with third countries might pursue objectives other than that of establishing the internal market it was clear that, when the principle of free movement of capital was extended, pursuant to Art 63(1), to movement of capital between third countries and the Member States, the Member States chose to enshrine that principle in that article and in the same terms for movements of capital taking place within the Community and those relating to relations with third countries.

The Court accepted that, because of the degree of legal integration that exists between Member States, and, in particular by reason of the presence of Community legislation that seeks to ensure cooperation between national tax authorities, such as Directive 77/799, the taxation by a Member State of economic activities having cross-border aspects which take place within the Community is not always comparable to that of economic activities involving relations between Member States and third countries. The Court further accepted that it might also be that a Member State will be able to demonstrate that a restriction on the movement of capital to or from third countries is justified for a particular reason in circumstances where that reason would not constitute a valid justification for a restriction on capital movements between Member States. But, even so, the Court rejected the pleas of Member States that one-sided liberalisation was a serious danger. It found that legislation such as the Swedish legislation entailed a restriction of the movement of capital between Member States and third countries which, in principle, is prohibited by Art 63(1). It then proceeded to limit its own decision:

(1) The rules might be covered by the grandfathering clause, as they had existed in a substantially identical form before 31 December 1993 and thus might fall under the exception provided for in Art 64(1).

(2) Under Art 65(1)(b), Art 63 was without prejudice to the right of a Member State to take all requisite measures to prevent infringements of national law and regulations, in particular in the field of taxation. The Court thus recognised that the need to guarantee the effectiveness of fiscal supervision constitutes an overriding requirement of general interest capable of justifying a restriction on the exercise of a fundamental freedom.

(3) The Court held that that case law that relates to restrictions on the exercise of freedom of movement within the Community, could not be transposed in its entirety to movements of capital between Member States and third countries, since such movements take place in a different legal context from that of the cases which gave rise to that jurisprudence.

Accordingly, the Court held that where the legislation of a Member State makes the grant of a tax advantage dependent on satisfying requirements, compliance with which can be verified only by obtaining information from the competent authorities of a third country, it is, in principle, legitimate for that Member State to refuse to grant that advantage if, in particular, because that third country is not under any contractual obligation to provide information, it proves impossible to obtain such information from that country. **[54.49]–[54.50]**

VII THE FUNDAMENTAL FREEDOMS: BREACH AND JUSTIFICATION

1 Introduction

The previous section discussed the content of the fundamental freedoms, and specific carve-outs to them as set out in the EU Treaty. Generally speaking, a domestic rule that affects the exercise of one of the freedoms and is not protected by a carve-out will be disapplied. However, as noted above, it is not necessarily the case that all such rules will be disapplied in this way. Certain rules will be permitted because they apply in a wholly non-discriminatory way as between comparable parties. Even those that are not permitted for that reason may nonetheless be permitted on the basis that they are justified as a means of achieving one of the 'overriding objectives', which do not appear in the treaty, but which have been approved by the CJEU. **[54.51]**

a) *Barriers to market*

Measures which are wholly non-discriminatory and apply (in practice, as well as in theory) equally to cross-border taxpayers and transactions as they do to domestic ones will be disapplied to the extent that they act as a genuine barrier preventing access to the market of one or more Member States.

This was resolved first in the context of the free movement of goods: the CJEU held in *Keck and Mithouard* (1994) that non-discriminatory measures would be struck down if they 'prevented' (or, according to A-G Jacobs in *Leclerc-Siplec* (1995) 'substantially impeded') access to market. Similar questions subsequently arose in respect of the other fundamental freedoms; and in the 1990s the CJEU started gradually to apply this principle across the board. In the context of free movement of workers under Art 39, *Bosman* (1995) and *Graf* (2000) establish that non-discriminatory restrictions will be prohibited only if they have an effect akin to actual exclusion from a particular market. In the context of freedom to supply services, in *Alpine Investments* (1995) the CJEU referred only to provisions which 'directly affect' access to the market.

These cases establish that for non-discriminatory barriers to the market to be prohibited a relatively severe test must be satisfied. Therefore, although the existence of corporation tax in the UK is a disincentive to doing business here, it is not a barrier to the UK market that the CJEU would disapply. Accordingly, it is not considered likely that a tax rule would be disapplied under this heading. [54.52]

b) *Comparability, discrimination and restriction*

The position is different for discriminatory rules (ie those which apply differently to comparable domestic and cross-border situations). Rules that impose any sort of discriminatory disincentive will be disapplied even if their actual impact is slight. There is not even any need for evidence that, on the facts of the case, the rule in question actually affected the decision making process of the relevant persons. In *Gebhard* (1995) the CJEU said that the rule need only be 'liable to hinder or make less attractive the exercise of the fundamental freedoms'. In *de Lasteyrie* (2004) the CJEU considered it to be uncontroversial that a rule would be disapplied even if it was of limited scope or minor importance (albeit, that in this case, the CJEU did say that, on the facts, there was a substantial effect). Indeed, even a difference in treatment that is purely procedural in nature can lead to the disapplication of a rule. In *Vestergaard* (2000) the CJEU held that a rule which introduced a rebuttable presumption that travel to conferences abroad was partly holiday (so that the reimbursement of expenses by the employer should be seen as a taxable benefit) fell foul of the provisions on free movement of services.

It was rules that discriminated directly on the grounds of nationality (or, in practice in every case other than *Gilly* (1998), residence) that it was first appreciated could be struck down for breach of EU law even where the rules did not act as a substantial barrier to market access. However, the case law of the CJEU has developed such that there are also two other types of discriminatory disincentive to the exercise of the fundamental freedoms that may be prohibited: 'indirect discrimination' and (if different) 'restriction'. The distinction here is important.

The fundamental freedoms: breach and justification 1621

If a measure is 'directly discriminatory', then it will be prohibited, unless it is permitted by one of the specific carve-outs provided in the EU Treaty, described above.

However, if it is only 'indirectly discrimination' or a 'restriction', then it will be capable of being saved by a general justification, in the way and subject to the rules described at [**54.61**] ff (including particularly the principle of proportionality, which is dealt with separately at [**54.66**] ff). [**54.53**]

c) *Methodology*

The CJEU follows a standard analytical process to decide whether a national rule conflicts with EU law.

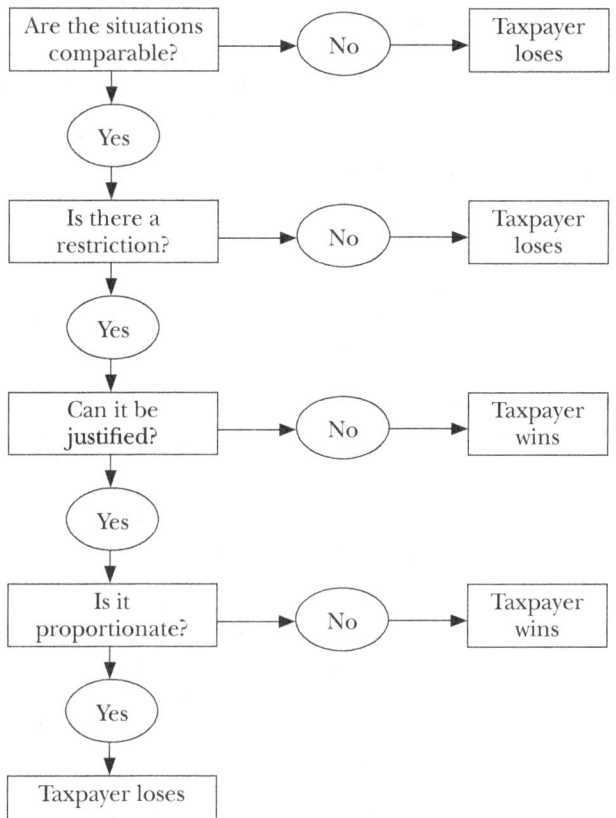

This figure shows the decision making process where a taxpayer has alleged a breach of EU law and a preliminary reference has been made. *First*, the CJEU asks whether the situation of the complainant is comparable to that of the comparator who receives the advantageous treatment the complainant seeks. *Second*, the CJEU asks whether there is a restriction of a directly effective right under EU law (usually manifested by some form of differential treatment). If the CJEU finds that there is then it asks whether that restriction is permissible (or justifiable). Such a restriction is permissible only if it pursues a legitimate objective compatible with the Treaty and is justified by imperative reasons in the public interest. It is further necessary that the restriction be proportionate, that is, its application is appropriate to ensuring the attainment of the objective thus pursued and does not go beyond what is necessary to attain it. [54.54]

2 Comparability

a) *Comparability in general*

The first question to be answered, in determining whether a rule, which is not a substantial barrier to market but nonetheless acts as an obstacle to a fundamental freedom, will be disapplied, is whether the rule is discriminatory. In general terms, discrimination can arise in one of two ways. The first is where persons in a comparable situation are treated in a dissimilar way. The second is where two persons, not in a comparable position, are treated in a similar way. Discrimination in the context of direct tax is generally not within the 'traditional' framework of sex, nationality, colour or race: rather, it proceeds by reference to nationality, residence, or place of doing business.

The key issue here is to determine whether two people are in a comparable situation. However, this exercise is not always straightforward in an international tax context. Many of the rules which fall within the scope of a fundamental freedom apply differently to residents and non-residents, because conventional international tax theory recognises that there is a distinction between residents and non-residents with regard to tax burden.

The fundamental function of international tax law is to distinguish, in each country's case, between the tax jurisdiction of that country and the tax jurisdiction of all other countries. In relation to the taxation of non-residents and of foreign-source income, the national laws of most countries, and the tax treaties that they conclude with other countries, aim at territorial partition of the tax base, normally on the basis of, *first*, the principle of 'source taxation' (ie if a person earns income in a country other than the country of his residence, then that country also is entitled to tax that person, because it provides the local infrastructure for him to earn that income, but only in respect of that locally earned income: see, for a general discussion, *Whitney v IRC* (1926)) and, *second*, by preventing double taxation where the claims overlap. This is reflected in the OECD Model Tax Convention on Income and Capital (the 'OECD Model'), which recognises a distinction between residence taxation (residents of a country are taxable in that State in respect of all income, no matter where it arises, because a resident benefits from the public expenditure of his home State and enjoys the benefits of its laws for the protection of his person and his property ('worldwide taxation')) and source taxation. Moreover, the OECD Model does not treat residents and non-residents as comparable for tax purposes; it prohibits only direct discrimination based on nationality (see Art 24). In contrast, EU law regards the following as indirect discrimination (and thus, in principle, prohibited: (i) non-residents receiving a different treatment to residents; (ii) domestic source income receiving a different treatment to income from another Member State.

The way in which the CJEU has tried to balance the competing demands of the internal market and settled international tax law is by accepting that residents and non-residents are, in principle, not comparable for taxation purposes; and that Member States may apply simultaneously the source principle (for non-residents) and the worldwide principle (for residents); but that Member States may only do so provided that the differences in tax treatment that follow from the application of those principles of international tax law can be 'justified' either by reference to a relevant difference of fact or by one of the justifications, such as the need to combat abuse. [54.55]

b) *Comparability and territoriality*

The CJEU will, in certain cases, allow distinctions between resident and non-resident taxpayers to be made if this can be justified by objective differences between them. In *Futura* (1997) Luxembourg law dictated that for Luxembourg purposes a loss-making Belgian-resident company with a Luxembourg branch could carry forward only the Luxembourg element of its losses for set-off against Luxembourg profits. It also required the company to prepare Luxembourg-specific accounts to demonstrate those losses. The CJEU upheld the rule in question. As an entity that was objectively only properly taxable in Luxembourg according to its local income Futura was held to be in an objectively different position to a Luxembourg-resident company, and so Luxembourg was entitled to insist that only its Luxembourg losses be brought into account, even though those rules did not apply to Luxembourg residents. To put it another way, because the Luxembourg fiscal authority did not seek to tax the non-branch income, it did not have to give relief for the non-branch losses.

Another example is *ACT IV GLO* (2006). This case concerned the UK's tax rules on dividends paid by a UK resident company to its shareholders resident in other Member States or non-member countries. The UK did not impose a withholding tax on dividends but in certain circumstances granted a tax credit (if the ultimate shareholders were resident in the UK or in a Member State that had concluded a double tax convention with the UK containing a provision extending the tax credit on a full or partial basis) and then taxed the tax credit. However, no tax credit was granted if the relevant double tax convention did not contain such a provision. The Court found that where the UK granted a tax credit as a result of a DTC, but then sought to tax that tax credit, it had to treat the recipient in the same way as a UK company. The extension of the tax charge (on the tax credit) to non-resident companies meant that those companies risked incurring a series of charges to tax on any distributed profits received from a UK company. Consequently, this was a restriction on the freedom of establishment of non-resident companies that had established subsidiaries in the UK. However, where no tax credit was payable, there was no extra-territorial exercise of taxing jurisdiction, and so there was no requirement to provide equal treatment.

This doctrine does not permit Member States to apply different rules to cross-border transactions across the board, even if those transactions only apply differently to residents and non-residents. This point has been argued (and rejected) repeatedly, see eg *Laboratoires Fournier* (2005). A-G Jacobs noted that it was an essential part of the rationale of *Futura* (1997) that non-resident companies were treated no less favourably than resident ones.

In addition, this rule seems restricted to situations where the taxpayer is genuinely subject to taxation on only part of his income in the State in question. Therefore, in *Schumacker* (1995), the Court relied (in striking down the domestic rule denying personal allowances to migrant workers) on the proposition that, as he earned almost his entire income in Germany, Mr Schumacker was in a substantially comparable position to a German resident with regard to personal allowances and deductions. In the subsequent cases of *Gschwind* (1999), *Asscher* (2002) and *de Groot* (2002), the Court seemed to have moved to a more sensitive test, under which such a migrant worker will be in a comparable position to a local resident for these purposes only if by deriving the main part of his taxable income locally he was missing out on a corresponding benefit from his home State. In *D v Inspecteur van be Belastingdienst* (2005), the CJEU held in the context of Art 63, that an individual, who had only 10% of his wealth in a State in which he was not resident, was not in a comparable situation to the residents of that State.

[54.56]

c) *Comparability by reference to other issues*

There are also indications in the case law of other circumstances in which taxpayers will or will not be treated as in comparable positions. This typically depends on the nature of a given enterprise (or facts applying to it: see *Schumacker* (1995) above) and the qualitative nature of the rules which apply to it in the particular context. Therefore, although (as noted above under freedom of establishment, see eg *'Avoir Fiscal'* (1986)) branches and subsidiaries are typically considered to be in comparable positions (and so to be treated the same), this is probably not the case when dealing with the ability of a given enterprise to use or surrender losses: the fact that a company with a branch in State X is taxable in that country on its local income, whereas a company incorporated there is taxable on its worldwide income, may well mean that the two are not in a comparable position for these purposes (see, for instance, the Opinion of A-G Maduro in *Marks and Spencer* (2005)). The relevant rules can be rules of local law (as in *Marks and Spencer* (2005)) or the law of another State: see the statements in *Manninen* (2004) that the comparability of a local and cross-border situation might depend on the effectiveness of the law of the other State to mitigate double taxation. However, differences in applicable tax rates will generally not lead to non-comparability (see A-G Tizzano in *Lenz* (2004)) because the taxpayers are in principle in the same situation: full taxpayers in their local Member State.

[54.57]

3 Discrimination and restriction

a) *Direct discrimination*

Article 12 of the EC Treaty provides a fundamental guarantee for EU nationals which prohibits direct discrimination on the grounds of nationality. It is now also clear that each of the fundamental freedoms also carries with it a specific right for discriminatory domestic rules not to be enforced in the area of that freedom. This prohibition on overt discrimination on grounds of nationality ('direct discrimination') is a cornerstone of the EU. In a tax context, direct discrimination occurs where the domestic tax provision expressly confers or denies a different tax treatment on the grounds of nationality (or, in practice, residence) in circumstances where there are no material differences for those purposes between a resident and a non-resident (as in *Schumacker* (1995)). Any such direct discrimination will be prohibited.

For completeness, it should be noted that there has been considerable discussion over the years about whether a regime in a Member State which discriminates between different cross-border situations, treating dealings with nationals of one Member State less well than dealings with those of another Member State, will also be prohibited, and the tax authority will be required to extend the more favourable treatment in both situations. This question (the so-called most-favoured nation (MFN) issue) was dealt with decisively in *D* (2005), The CJEU rejected an argument based on MFN. It held that it is inherent in a bilateral tax treaty that the reciprocal rights and obligations under the treaty apply only to persons resident in either of the two contracting Member States. Thus, a national of a Member State that is not party to the treaty is not in a comparable situation to a national of a contracting Member State. [54.58]

b) *Indirect discrimination*

It is now clear that a measure will be prohibited if, even though not expressly discriminatory by reference to nationality (or residence), it does have that effect in practice ('indirect discrimination'). An indirectly discriminatory provision is one that does not expressly include nationality (or residence) as a criterion for its application, but has the consequence that non-nationals (or residents) are treated less favourably than nationals.

The prospect of such measures being prohibited first arose in the context of the free movement of goods (under Art 28) in the '*Cassis de Dijon*' case (*Rewe* (1979)). In this case, the CJEU had to consider a measure that was discriminatory on the grounds of nationality in practice only. German law specified a minimum alcohol content of 15–20% for certain spirits, including cassis. German cassis complied with this stipulation, but French cassis did not. The German rules were not directly discriminatory: they applied without distinction to domestic and imported goods. However, the result of the rules was effectively to ban French cassis from the German market. The issue was whether Germany could prevent the importation of goods lawfully marketed in France on the grounds that they did not comply with German product regulations. The CJEU concluded that the disparity between the French and German product regulations was, in principle, an obstacle to free movement of goods, within the scope of Art 28. Therefore, even though not directly discriminatory, it was capable of being disapplied. [54.59]

c) *Restriction*

The CJEU no longer frames its judgments in terms of 'discrimination' but rather in terms of 'differences in treatment' or 'restrictions'. Analysis of when a difference in treatment would be treated as discriminatory was originally considered important; generally, the key issue there was identification of the relevant domestic comparator. A gradual shift since the opinion of A-G Jacobs in *Danner* (2001) means that the burden of proof in respect of restrictions has effectively switched from the taxpayer to the fiscal authorities. All that the taxpayer needs to do is establish a difference in treatment between a cross-border situation and a purely domestic situation. It then falls to the fiscal authorities to seek to demonstrate that the difference is justified by some objective difference between the domestic and cross-border situation (see *Laboratoires Fournier* (2005)) or, failing that, one of the true justifications dealt with in the next section.

It is understood that this approach grew up as a matter of administrative convenience, since it almost always transpired that there was no objective justification for the difference in treatment (and so discrimination was established). In this way, the CJEU could avoid the difficult questions of whether a measure is directly or indirectly discriminatory: it dealt with this question only when it absolutely has to (such as in *Haahr Petroleum Ltd* (1997)). However, the position here is now clear. The taxpayer need only point to a difference in treatment. Unless the Member State can demonstrate that it involves no discrimination, or is justified, then the relevant rule will be disapplied. [54.60]

4 The 'Rule of Reason' and Justifications

If it can be established that a restriction has arisen, the next question is whether it is capable of being justified. As noted above, the list of justifications is no longer confined to those set out in the EU Treaty. Over the past 20 years, a doctrine has emerged from the CJEU that, in some circumstances, such measures may be justified on general principles, rather than as a matter of a specific provision in the EU Treaty. This particularly has been by the adoption from US competition law (and application to the fundamental freedoms) of the concept of 'rule of reason': that certain measures, even though in principle prohibited, will be permitted if they are justified by pressing matters of public importance.

The application of the concept of the 'rule of reason' can be taken, for present purposes, to stem from *Cassis de Dijon* (1979), as noted above. In this case, as outlined above, the indirectly discriminatory measures were found to breach Art 34, and not be protected by Art 36. However, the CJEU recognised that this could be harsh in its effects on Member States. The CJEU held that certain measures, even if prohibited in principle, will, in appropriate circumstances, be upheld if 'recognised as being necessary in order to satisfy mandatory requirements relating in particular to the effectiveness of fiscal supervision, the protection of public health, the fairness of commercial transactions and the defence of the consumer'. In *Cassis de Dijon*, the CJEU made clear that the 'rule of reason' would not apply to directly discriminatory measures. This was later applied to services in *Säger* (1991). Then, in *Gebhard* (1995) (a case that involved the freedom of establishment) the CJEU indicated that a uniform approach should be followed in respect of all the freedoms. Since that case, it is clear that a measure will be treated as justified under the rule of reason only if:
(1) it is applied in a non-discriminatory (ie not directly discriminatory) manner;
(2) it is justified by imperative reasons in the public interest;
(3) it is suitable for securing the attainment of the objective pursued; and

(4) it does not go beyond what is necessary to attain that objective (the so-called 'proportionality test').

The first of these criteria was discussed in the last section. The second is discussed here. The third and fourth (suitability and proportionality) are discussed in the next section.

Outside the context of direct tax, the 'rule of reason' has been invoked to save measures from prohibition on a number of occasions. However, in the direct tax field, such arguments have succeeded rarely (notably in *Bachmann* (1992)). In particular, the following ideas have been rejected as not amounting to 'imperative reasons in the public interest': lack of reciprocity on the part of other Member States by not granting corresponding tax treatment to non-residents (*Eurowings* (1999) and *Commission v France* (1986)); economic aims such as the need to encourage investment in domestic companies (*Verkooijen* (2000) and, particularly, prevention of loss of tax revenue for that Member State (see *St Gobain* (1999) and *Weidert & Paulus* (2004)). In the tax sphere, the only overriding requirements in the public interest capable of justifying restrictions on the exercise of fundamental freedoms that the CJEU has recognised even as potentially applicable are: (1) fiscal cohesion; (2) prevention of tax avoidance; and (3) fiscal supervision. These are discussed in turn below.

It should be noted that the class of justifications is not closed. In *Laboratoires Fournier* (2005), both A-G Jacobs and the CJEU considered the prospect that the promotion of research and development might be an overriding requirement of general interest. However, no decision had to be taken on the facts of the case. In any event, A-G Jacobs noted that any such objective would have to be pursued on a Community-wide basis to be capable of justifying an obstacle to a fundamental freedom. It is likely that that analysis will apply also to any further justifications that may be mooted in the future. [54.61]

a) *Fiscal cohesion*

The first time that the doctrine of fiscal cohesion was applied by the CJEU was in *Bachmann* (1992). Mr Bachmann was a German national, resident and employed in Belgium. Prior to his move to Belgium, he had taken out sickness, invalidity and life insurance policies with German insurance companies. Belgian tax law provided, *first*, that the contributions paid on such policies were deductible only if they were paid 'within Belgium' (ie to a Belgian resident undertaking); and, *second*, that sums subsequently payable by insurance companies (whether resident in Belgium or abroad) under such policies were liable to tax in the hands of the recipients, unless there had been no deduction of contributions.

The CJEU ruled that such provisions amounted to indirect discrimination on the ground of nationality and so were capable of contravening the rules on the free movement of workers (Article 45) and freedom to provide services (Article 56). However, it also accepted the justification offered by Belgium, namely the need to maintain the coherence of its national tax system. In the Belgian system, there was a direct link between the deductibility of contributions and the taxation of benefits. The loss of revenue resulting from the deduction of insurance contributions was offset by the taxation of the sums payable by the insurers. Belgium could not tax the benefits paid to non-residents under policies with foreign insurers; and so if the Belgian system of tax allowed deductions for contributions in respect of such policies, then fiscal coherence would be disrupted.

Since *Bachmann*, the fiscal coherence justification has been widely criticised and until recently it had not been applied in any subsequent CJEU case. Broadly speaking, the CJEU has imposed two key restrictions on the principle. *First*, if there is a double taxation convention (see para **[13.17]**) in force between the two relevant States, the defence of fiscal cohesion cannot be invoked, since the State is taken to have addressed any such concerns in that convention (see *Wielockx* (1995), where the failure in *Bachmann* to consider the relevance of double taxation conventions was criticised, and *Danner* (2001), where a case on almost identical facts to *Bachmann* was decided in favour of the taxpayer, at least in part on the grounds of the existence of a double taxation convention). *Second*, the requirement for a direct link (a 'symmetry') between the fiscal advantage and the corresponding fiscal disadvantage has been rigidly applied: the advantage and disadvantage must relate to the same tax and the same taxpayer (*Verkooijen* (2000) and *Lankhorst-Hohorst* (2003)). In both *Manninen* (2004) and *Weidert & Paulus* (2004) there was a strong indication that coherence must be judged on an EU-wide (or, possibly, even world-wide) basis; any argument that a disadvantage is linked to a corresponding advantage, but that corresponding advantage is simply that the Member State has relinquished taxing power in a related situation in favour of another Member State, will be treated as an argument not as to fiscal cohesion, but as to reduction in tax revenue.

It is now settled case law that that the need to preserve the cohesion of a tax system may justify a restriction on the exercise of the freedoms of movement guaranteed by the Treaty (see *Krankenheim* (2008) and *Commission v Belgium* (2011). However, it is equally settled that the existence of a direct link must be established between the tax advantage concerned and the offsetting of that advantage by a particular tax levy (*Commission v Belgium* (2011)), the direct nature of that link falling to be examined in the light of the objective pursued by the rules in question (see *Fininvest* (2009)). **[54.62]**

b) *Fiscal supervision*

It is now clear from settled case law that the need to ensure the effectiveness of fiscal supervision constitutes an overriding reason relating to the general interest capable of justifying a restriction on the exercise of the fundamental freedoms guaranteed by the Treaty and that a Member State is authorised to apply measures which enable the amount of costs deductible in that Member State, which were incurred in another Member State, to be ascertained clearly and precisely.

This possible justification was mentioned specifically in *Cassis de Dijon*. In the direct tax field, its role as a possible justification has been repeatedly confirmed (see also *Laboratoires Fournier* (2005)), but the leading case is still *Futura* (1997) in relation to direct taxes. The facts of this case are set out above (see **[54.56]**).

In *Laboratoires Fournier* the CJEU recognised that adequate fiscal supervision could be an imperative reason in the public interest to justify the requirement for Luxembourg accounts to be kept and Luxembourg losses to be computed on local principles, so justifying the restriction of a fundamental freedom.

However, the CJEU did not uphold the domestic rule on this ground. This was because the rule failed to meet one of the other *Gebhard* criteria: proportionality. The CJEU concluded that, in this case, the stringency and retroactive nature of the evidence requirements were not proportionate and, therefore, that the defence could not apply. Where fiscal supervision fails as a defence it is usually on the grounds of proportionality.

In *de Lasteyrie* (2004) the CJEU said that the only substantive tax rules that may be justified are those that have the specific object of excluding any tax advantage from purely artificial schemes having the purpose of circumventing the law. Measures intended to allow the data underlying a return or claim to be ascertained clearly and precisely can also be justified under this ground (see *Laboratoires Fournier* (2005), confirming *Baxter* (1999); and see also A-G Kokott in *Manninen* (2004)).

However, for a restrictive measure to be justified, it must observe the principle of proportionality, in that it must be appropriate for securing the attainment of the objective it pursues and must not go beyond what is necessary to attain it (see eg *Persche* (2009)).

It should be noted that the jurisprudence concerning fiscal supervision within the EU cannot be transposed in its entirety to the freedoms guaranteed by the EEA Agreement with third countries, since the exercise of the latter take place in a different legal context (see eg *Finnish Tax Authorities v A* (2012)). In general terms, the bar for a successful fiscal supervision defence is lower for counterparties outside the EU. [54.63]

c) *Prevention of tax avoidance*

This was first asserted as a defence in *Commission v France* (1986), where it was rejected by the CJEU without consideration. In later cases, the CJEU has recognised that the need to prevent tax avoidance could be a justification for restrictions. The first case in which the CJEU analysed the defence (and referred to the concept of a 'wholly artificial arrangement') was *Imperial Chemicals Industries plc v Colmer* (1998). In that case, the CJEU said at para 26:

> 'As regards the justification based on the risk of tax avoidance, suffice it to note that the legislation at issue in the main proceedings does not have the specific purpose of preventing wholly artificial arrangements, set up to circumvent United Kingdom tax legislation, from attracting tax benefits, but applies generally to all situations in which the majority of a group's subsidiaries are established, for whatever reason, outside the United Kingdom. However, the establishment of a company outside the United Kingdom does not, of itself, necessarily entail tax avoidance, since that company will in any event be subject to the tax legislation of the state of establishment.'

The approach of the CJEU in *ICI* was that only legislation introduced for the specific purpose of precluding tax avoidance by preventing the setting up of wholly artificial arrangements that were designed to avoid domestic legislation for tax reasons could be justified by reference to the defence of 'prevention of tax avoidance'. Its existence as a valid defence was confirmed in *de Lasteyrie* (2004), citing *Hoechst/Metallgesellschaft* (2001), and *X&Y* (2000).

In *de Lasteyrie*, the CJEU clarified that tax avoidance, for these purposes, means obtaining a tax advantage from a purely artificial scheme that has the purpose of circumventing the law. The CJEU said at para 50:

> 'As regards justification based on the aim of preventing tax avoidance, referred to by the national court in its question, it should be noted that Article 167a of the CGI is not specifically designed to exclude from a tax advantage purely artificial arrangements aimed at circumventing French tax law, but is aimed generally at any situation in which a taxpayer with substantial holdings in a company subject to corporation tax transfers his tax residence outside France for any reason whatever (see, to that effect, *ICI*, paragraph 26, and *X and Y*, paragraph 61).'

The CJEU made it clear that the principle can extend to tax evasion or fraud. The rule in question was found not to be justified on the basis of anti-avoidance, by virtue of failing the *Gebhard* (1995) appropriateness and proportionality tests.

The reasoning of the CJEU in cases such as *Eurowings* (1999) and *de Lasteyrie* (2004) suggests that, provided an item of profit remains capable of being taxed in one of the Member States, a rule which seeks to tax that profit in a given Member State will not be capable of justification on this ground. At this stage, the defence lapses into the unsustainable 'protection of tax revenue' argument.

However, it is clearly the case that the CJEU has become troubled by taxpayers 'enjoining the Court to explore the boundaries of the application of the Treaty' (to adopt the wording of A-G Geelhoed in *Test Claimants in Class IV of the ACT Group Litigation* (2006) at para 1). In essence, there are now two different types of case. The first of these concerns cross-border money flows. In these cases, dividends or interest is paid from one person to another and the recipient is treated differently depending on whether the source of the income is located in the same or another Member State. Here, no restriction is allowed. The cases are clear. See, for example, *Manninen* (2004); *Lenz* (2004); *Meilicke* (2007); *Fokus Bank* (2005) (an EFTA decision); *Denkavit* (2007); *Commission v UK* (2014). In such cases, the basis of this jurisprudence is that the 'wholly artificial' doctrine is limited – that is, it is only where legislation has the specific purpose of ensuring that artificial arrangements aimed at circumventing the domestic law for a tax advantage that, potentially, that legislation may be capable of being defended; and then it must be analysed whether that legislation meets the *Gebhard test* of proportionality.

The second category is 'other cases'. Here, the result is less predictable. There have been a number of decisions of the CJEU released post *Marks & Spencer* (2005) which do not concern cross-border money flows where the court has expressed concern as to the balance between taxpayers and Member States. In these cases, references to 'fiscal sovereignty' and 'balanced allocation of taxing powers' (which had all but disappeared) have started to creep in. In *Cadbury Schweppes* (2006) (which concerned the UK's CFC regime), A-G Léger noted that the language used in the description of the anti-avoidance justification reproduced the wording of the abuse of rights doctrine. Whether the justification of anti-avoidance will be developed by the CJEU into a special ground that may justify a restriction, ie either a stand-alone doctrine of 'abuse' or a sub-set of the doctrine of 'abuse of rights', is currently an open question.

The question that was referred to the CJEU in *Cadbury Schweppes* was whether the company, in establishing and capitalising companies in another Member State solely because of a more favourable tax regime available in that Member State, was exercising the fundamental freedoms, or whether it is an abuse of such freedoms. The mere fact that a company transfers its place of management to another Member State cannot set up a general presumption of tax avoidance and justify a measure that compromises the exercise of a fundamental freedom guaranteed by the Treaty (see *Commission v France* (2004) and, for a re-statement, the Opinion of A-G Kokott in *Philips Electronics* (2012)). **[54.64]**

d) *Conclusion*

The list of possible justifications is certainly not closed. However, it is becoming increasingly clear, in practice, that, subject to the development of the anti-avoidance principle into a general abuse doctrine, any taxing rule that is, in principle, an impediment to the internal market, is likely to be struck down. In particular, the only justification for which the CJEU has shown any sustained sympathy is that described in the opinion of A-G Fennelly in *Hoechst/Metallgesellschaft* (2001), namely the prospect of tax evasion in both relevant countries ('it would seem that the true scope for fiscal cohesion as a justification for the differentiated treatment of non-residents would concern only situations in which there is a real and substantial risk that extending equal treatment in respect of a particular benefit would potentially facilitate tax evasion in both the host Member State and the Member State of residence of the claimant non-resident taxpayer'). In *Marks and Spencer* (2005), the CJEU considered the three justifications together in terms of preserving a balanced allocation of the power to impose taxes (ie tax sovereignty), guarding against the danger of double usage of losses (or 'double-dipping'), and guarding against the risk of tax avoidance through relieving losses in high-tax jurisdictions; but more recent case law suggests these justifications retain an independent existence. **[54.65]**

5 Justifications (2): Suitability and Proportionality

As noted above, even if a rule is justifiable in principle, it will nonetheless be struck down (as it was in *Futura Participations*) if it is not suitable for the objective that it seeks to meet, and is not proportionate to that objective: that is to say, if it goes beyond what is absolutely necessary in order to pursue the aim in question. As will be seen, the two criteria are somewhat similar in nature. **[54.66]**

a) *Suitability*

This criterion has been considered particularly in the context of the prospective justification of 'tax avoidance'. The CJEU has repeatedly indicated that measures intended to prevent tax evasion or avoidance (the CJEU on occasion uses the terms as synonyms) will be considered disproportionate if they are not directly aimed at avoidance transactions (see *Futura Participations* (1997) and also *Lankhorst-Hohorst* (2003)). Therefore, in *de Lasteyrie* (2004), a purported anti-avoidance rule that sought to approximate tax avoidance intention by reference to the period for which certain assets were held was struck down. However, the criterion applies equally across all prospective justifications. [54.67]

b) *Proportionality*

Proportionality is a fundamental principle of EU law, developed as long ago as in *Internationale Handelsgesellschaft mbH* (1970). No matter how important the end, if the means used to achieve it is not proportionate to that end, then the relevant measure will be prohibited. In determining this, the CJEU will consider whether the particular measure is necessary by analysing whether the end could have been achieved by other, less restrictive, measures (see A-G Tizzano in *Lenz* (2004)). Thus, for example, in *Cassis de Dijon* (1979), the aims pursued by the German Government potentially could have been achieved merely by labelling the bottles with their alcohol content. As the regulations were not proportionate, they could not be justified.

In the direct tax context, in *Laboratoires Fournier* (2005) the CJEU held that a measure that imposed a blanket disallowance of foreign expenditure could not be justified on the grounds of fiscal supervision (the argument being that it was difficult for the local tax authority to prove to its satisfaction that foreign expenditure had been validly incurred). Similarly the CJEU in *Lenz* (2004) suggested that withholding tax arrangements are unlikely to be considered proportionate. In *de Lasteyrie* (2004) the CJEU said that *Hoechst/Metallgesellschaft* (2001) is authority for the proposition that fiscal cohesion can never justify the collection of taxes in advance in respect of non-residents; and in the context of a defence which can only be invoked in the event of tax evasion or fraud, A-G Mischo said that it is disproportionate to have a presumption of tax evasion in a cross-border context, although the tax authorities should be free to seek to demonstrate it on a case-by-case basis.

Both the CJEU in *Laboratoires Fournier* (2005) and A-G Maduro in *Marks and Spencer* (2005) indicated that a measure that made the desired tax treatment conditional upon the provision of information might well be proportionate. This will, of course, mean that obtaining the desired tax treatment in a cross-border situation will involve some additional procedural steps, but it appears that that is acceptable, provided that the steps imposed are the minimum necessary in view of the difference in situation (see A-G Kokott in *Manninen* (2004), where she said there that the principal limitation was to ensure that those proof requirements did not prevent the cross-border taxpayer from having an 'effective' and 'equivalent' remedy (as required by *Cassis de Dijon* (1979) and *Grundig Italia* (2002)). There are practical difficulties here, associated with enforcing the collection of data or tax liabilities assessed on non-residents. The CJEU has shown itself unsympathetic to such pleas in relation to the EU because of the availability of the Mutual Assistance Directives (even when the former was either not in force or ineffective), but, as noted above (see eg *Finnish Tax Authorities v A* (2012)) more sympathetic to the tax authorities regarding their dealings with EEA States and with third countries.

Finally, it should be said that the concept of proportionality in EU law is similar to the concept in European human rights law, where the European Court of Human Rights (ECHR) has held that the interpretation of the Articles of the Convention must aim to strike a balance between: 'the demands of the general interests of the community, and the requirements of the protection of the individual's fundamental rights' (*Soering v UK* (1989)) (see **Chapter 55**). The balancing test essentially involves weighing up the impact of the restriction imposed, and evaluating whether this is justified by the importance of the end to be achieved. Central to this doctrine of proportionality is the idea that there must be a 'fair balance' between the societal interest and the individual's rights, which is analogous to the balancing in Community law between the matter of general interest and the fundamental freedom. Accordingly, it may be that, in the future, it will be possible to take guidance from the case law under European human rights law. [54.68]–[54.70]

VIII THE FUNDAMENTAL FREEDOMS: ABUSE OF RIGHT

1 Introduction

Given the extensive rights granted by EU law for individuals and companies to engage in cross-border activities without fear of disadvantageous tax treatment, it is clear that an opportunity exists for companies and individuals to rely on EU law as part of their tax planning. Profits are taxed in different ways in the different Member States, and it may well be advantageous to arrange for particular profits to be taxed in one State rather than another; an obvious example is the low rates of corporation tax in (say) the Republic of Ireland, which makes it clearly desirable to arrange for business profits to be taxed there rather than in (say) France. Further (as is clear from cases such as *Lankhorst-Hohorst* (2002)) domestic anti-avoidance provisions designed to prevent this kind of behaviour may well themselves fall foul of EC law and so be ineffective.

However, in cases of abuse, there is a limitation on the rights granted by EU law under the doctrine of 'abuse of right'. Under this doctrine, in at least some circumstances, a taxpayer who purports to exercise his rights, but does so solely for tax avoidance reasons, will be unable to rely on those rights, because he is not in fact exercising those rights at all. Abuse of right is a well-developed concept in many European civil law systems that has come to be applied by the CJEU to rules of EU law. It is a protective doctrine that qualifies rights that are defined in broad terms. The basis of the doctrine is that rights granted by the law can be relied upon only to the extent that they are used for the purposes they were designed for (the classic formulation is by the French writer Plainiol in his *Traité e élémentaire de droit civil* (Vol 2, p 871) 'la droit cesse là où l'abus commence': 'the right ceases where abuse begins').

It seems that the application of the principle by the CJEU has been intended to ensure the operation of the single market. If transactions have no genuine economic substance, and are carried out purely to obtain a beneficial treatment that should not be available in such circumstances, then they do not assist the operation of the single market, and so are not entitled to the protection of the rules regulating the market. Thus, the purpose of the doctrine is to prevent a distortion of competition. However, whether the doctrine is simply an aspect of a purposive interpretation of the fundamental freedoms (ie the fundamental freedoms apply only to the extent that they are

exercised for a genuine economic purpose or exists as a stand-alone general principle of EU law, such as proportionality, remains an open question.
[54.71]

2 The relevant case law

a) *The basic rule:* Emsland-Stärke

In the customs duty case of *Emsland-Stärke GmbH* (2000), the taxpayer exported goods from Germany to Switzerland and received export refunds from Germany (on the basis of EC Regulation 2730/79). Immediately after the goods had been released for home use in Switzerland, they were transported back into the EU where they entered free circulation after payment of import customs duties, which were about half of the amount of the export refunds paid by Germany. The CJEU held that the German tax authority was entitled to revoke its decision granting the export refund. It said that rights under EU law could not be relied upon where (1) although the conditions for the application of those rights had been met in form, they had not been met in substance, and (2) the taxpayer had an intention to obtain an advantage from the Community rules by creating artificially the conditions to formally come within the scope of a right. [54.72]

b) Centros *and its possible limitations*

The formulation of abuse by the CJEU in *Emsland-Stärke* stated by the CJEU in *Centros* (1999) in the following way: if a person is seeking to exercise an EU right 'unreasonably to derive, to the detriment of others, an improper advantage, manifestly contrary to the objective pursued by the legislator in conferring that particular right on the individual' then that person will be denied the benefit of the relevant EU law (see also *Holleran v Daniel Thwaites plc* (1989)). At this time, the most directly relevant cases to taxation arose in the context of company law, where a person resident in Member State A has wished to avoid certain rules of local company law (such as minimum capital requirements (*Centros* (1999)) or reporting requirements (*Inspire Art* (2003)) and so has set up a company in Member State B with a view to conducting business in Member State A through that company. In both *Centros* (1999) and *Inspire Art* (2003), the CJEU held that efforts by Member State A to make such steps ineffective were contrary to Art 49, and so impermissible. In particular, the CJEU found that there had been no 'abuse of right' sufficient to prevent the Member State B company from relying on Art 49, even though the structure as a whole had no purpose other than to circumvent the company law rules in question. However, the doctrine may not be quite as weak as would appear from this. In both cases, the CJEU relied on the fact that the rules of Member State A sought to inhibit the activities of the company incorporated in Member State B, and that the company itself genuinely wished to exercise its right of establishment for its own economic aims. Therefore, the conditions for the application of Art 49 had been met in both form and substance. Neither case addressed the legitimacy of a rule affecting the ability of the resident of Member State A to set up the shell company in Member State B in the first place. It is considered that a rule restricting that right could well apply, despite the impact of any fundamental freedom, to prevent abusive activities.
[54.73]

c) *The VAT experience*

In the UK, HMRC has used the abuse of right principle as a means to challenge VAT avoidance arrangements. The underlying basis of HMRC's approach to these cases is that VAT avoidance is not an economic activity under EU law. Thus, as VAT law is directed only to activities carried on with a business purpose, any 'abusive' steps are to be ignored. This approach was first raised in *BUPA Hospitals Ltd and Goldsborough Developments Ltd* (2002); and is analysed more fully in the later VAT Tribunal case of *Blackqueen Ltd* (2002). A number of questions on the point have been referred to the CJEU in various cases. However, the CJEU declined to deal with the point in *RAL (Channel Islands) Ltd* (2005), and the decisions of the CJEU in *Bond House Systems* (2005) and *Halifax/BUPA/University of Huddersfield* (2005) indicate that, although the *Emsland-Stärke* (2000) formulation remains good law, there are features of the VAT system (in particular that the taxpayer's 'right' arises under a provision of EU law (namely under the Recast Directive)), which require the doctrine to be applied there rather differently than in the context of direct tax.

In *Halifax*, the CJEU confirmed that the abuse of rights doctrine can apply to VAT. The CJEU held that it may apply if the transactions 'result in the accrual of a tax advantage the grant of which would be contrary to the purpose of [the legal provisions]' and it is apparent 'from a number of objective factors that the essential aim of the transactions concerned is to obtain a tax advantage'. However, the prohibition of abuse is not relevant 'where the economic activity carried out may have some explanation other than the mere attainment of tax advantages'. If abuse is present, then the transactions involved must be 'redefined so as to re-establish the situation that would have prevailed in the absence of the transactions constituting abusive practice'. That may give rise to practical difficulties.

Two post-Halifax cases are *Weald Leasing Limited* (2010) and *RBS Deutschland Holdings GmbH* (2010). *Weald Leasing* concerned arrangements that had been put in place to avoid tax. Those elements of the structure that staggered the input tax charge were held to be within the contemplation of the Directive and did not run counter to its purpose; the introduction of non-commercial terms had a potential artificiality, such that it was held that they were contrary to its purpose. The CJEU did not wholly redefine the transaction, but limited the reconstruction to the artificial element of the leasing arrangements. In *RBS*, the CJEU held that the transactions were genuine and commercial; it was just that, by using the group's German subsidiaries, the group could exploit a difference between the UK and German rules. That arose because one of those Member States had failed to implement the Directive properly, and the Directive could not be interpreted as containing provisions that remedied its inadequate implementation. [54.74]

d) Cadbury-Schweppes v IRC

In the UK, three references to the CJEU were made with regard to the impact of EC law on the controlled foreign companies rules: *Cadbury Schweppes* (2006); *CFC GLO* (reasoned order 2008) and *Vodafone* (later withdrawn). In each of the references, a question regarding abuse was included.

In the first of these references (*Cadbury Schweppes*), A-G Léger answered the question whether the establishment by a parent company of a subsidiary in another Member State for the purpose of enjoying the more favourable tax regime of that other State constitutes, in itself, an abuse of freedom of establishment negatively. Such a decision could not, by itself, be an abuse of EU law. As the CJEU held in *Inspire Art* (2003), the reason why a company chooses to incorporate in a Member State is irrelevant with regard to the application of the freedom of establishment. *A contrario*, in assessing whether there is abuse, the starting point is whether the objective pursued by the EU law provision relied upon is fulfilled. Establishment within the meaning of Art 49 involves the actual pursuit of an economic activity in the host State. Thus, if the subsidiary carries on a genuine economic activity, the purpose of Art 49 is met – it cannot be abusive. In terms of deciding whether there is 'genuine and actual pursuit of an activity' by the subsidiary in the Member State in which it was established, A-G Léger set out certain objective criteria that are to be applied on a case-by-case basis. These are:

- the degree of physical presence of the subsidiary in the foreign country;
- the genuine nature of the activity provided by the subsidiary; and
- the economic value of that activity with regard to the parent company/group.

However, the Opinion of A-G Léger was only followed in part by the CJEU. The focus of the CJEU was very much on the first limb of the tests: were genuine activities being carried on in the host Member State? ie the contrast is to an entity that is just a 'brass plate' company. The CJEU referred to *Eurofood* (2006). In *Eurofood*, the issue was whether the Irish authorities could carry out insolvency proceedings or whether it should be carried out by the Italian authorities. Eurofood was registered in Ireland in 1997 as a 'company limited by shares' with its registered office in the International Financial Services Centre in Dublin; it was a wholly owned subsidiary of Parmalat SpA, a company incorporated in Italy, whose principal objective was the provision of financing facilities for companies in the Parmalat group. The answer to which Member State could carry out the proceedings depended on where the 'main interests of the debtor' were sited. The CJEU said that:

> 'in determining the centre of the main interests of a debtor company, the simple presumption laid down by the Community legislature in favour of the registered office of that company can be rebutted only if factors which are both objective and ascertainable by third parties enable it to be established that an actual situation exists which is different from that which locating it at that registered office is deemed to reflect. That could be so in particular in the case of a "letterbox" company not carrying out any business in the territory of the Member State in which its registered office is situated.' (para 35)

The reference to 'letterbox' and 'not carrying on any business' reinforces the view that 'genuine' in the context of genuine economic activity means having the consequences that they should have. Thus, it is similar to the approach taken by the domestic courts in relation to the issue of residence in *Wood v Holden* (2006): one looks at the whole package and determines whether or not it is a sham.

The decision of the CJEU was that the UK's CFC legislation is incompatible with the Treaty if it can apply to situations other than wholly artificial arrangements, but it is for the domestic court to analyse the legislation as a whole: does it only apply to wholly artificial arrangements or can it apply in other situations? The CJEU indicated that it was of the view that there should be a division of responsibilities between the courts being observed. However, it does raise the question: if the legislation is incompatible with Treaty provisions, why refer it back to the domestic court? The CJEU had the facts and the CFC legislation before it. The author is of the view that the CJEU could have determined whether the motive test, as defined by the legislation on CFCs, lends itself to an interpretation which enables the taxation provided for by that legislation to be restricted to wholly artificial arrangements.

In the *CFC GLO case* (2008), the CJEU indicated that the decisions in *Cadbury Schweppes*, and in three GLO cases, namely, *ACT Class IV* (2006), *FII* (2006) and *Thin Cap* (2007) resolved the questions in this reference. This reinforces that the test of abuse is as described above. **[54.75]**

e) *Post* Cadbury-Schweppes *cases*

All the above cases suggest that the CJEU requires the analysis of the question as to whether or not abuse is present to be undertaken on an individual 'case by case' basis (often by the domestic court). The same test is to be applied in direct and indirect tax cases (and in non-tax cases), namely whether 'wholly artificial arrangements' exist, that is, is there, *first*, an intent to obtain, through artifice, benefits not intended to be received by that entity, and, *second*, the situation that the granting of those benefits would be contrary to the purpose of the provisions of EU law relied on by the entity. However, in a number of cases decided after *Cadbury-Schweppes*, the CJEU has accepted a general presumption of abuse in entire categories of cross-border cases. These cases move the focus of the doctrine away from the perspective of the taxpayer and towards the perspective of the Member States.

In *Van Hilten-Van der Heijden* (2006), the CJEU endorsed a Netherlands inheritance tax provision that treated emigrating nationals who died within ten years of emigration as if they had remained resident in the Netherlands by reason of being 'justified by the concern to prevent a form of tax evasion'. No intent to avoid tax was shown (nor needed to have been shown) by the Member State. In *Thin Cap GLO* (2007), the CJEU accepted the 'arm's length test' as a generalised method for determining whether (and to what extent) the deduction of interest paid abroad on a group loan constitutes a 'wholly artificial arrangement' and in the *FII Group Litigation* (2006), the CJEU allowed a tax measure that excluded cross-border dividends from the base exemption granted in respect of domestic dividends on the generalised basis that such measures could be justified as preventing profits from being shifted abroad. **[54.76]–[54.80]**

IX PROHIBITION OF STATE AID

There is one further provision of the EU Treaty that must be borne in mind in appropriate cases: Art 107, which deals with State aid. The State funding a particular undertaking, in principle, can give rise to a distortion of the free market and thus hinder its efficiency. However, it is recognised by the EU that the freedom for an individual Member State to aid particular sectors or undertakings must be maintained. State aid is an important economic and social tool that may be particularly necessary in areas of high employment or sectors that face localised economic difficulties, both in terms of economic growth and social cohesion. Moreover, it has been argued that even if certain State aid measures distort the competitive balance between Member States these measures may, nonetheless, be beneficial for the competitiveness of the EU as a whole in the global market-place. Thus, for example, the introduction of measures that aim to develop the economies of the States that acceded to the EU in May 2004 potentially may be sought to be justified on the ground that strengthening the economic development of these States will increase the economic power of the EU.

The regulation of State aid is sensitive and the provisions in the EU Treaty aim to balance the competing interests of individual member States and the internal free market. This balancing act is achieved in two ways.

First, the granting of State aid that, 'distorts or threatens to distort competition by favouring certain undertakings or the production of certain goods', is broadly prohibited (under Art 107(1)), but this is subject to express and extensive derogations in Art 107(2) and (3), which allow aid that serves the purpose of protecting legitimate economic and social goals. Article 107(2) specifies the categories of aid that are compatible with the internal market (such as, for example, 'aid having a social character, granted to individual consumers, provided that such aid is granted without discrimination related to the origin of the products concerned'); and Art 107(3) lists those aids that may be compatible (such as, for example, 'aid to facilitate the development of certain economic activities or of certain economic areas, where aid does not adversely affect trading conditions to an extent contrary to the common market').

The *second* limb of the balancing act is regulation of all State aid by the Commission. The Commission is required to keep 'under constant review all systems of aid'; and must 'be informed, in sufficient time to enable it to submit its comments, of any plans to grant or alter aid' (under Art 108(3)). Thus if a State wishes to introduce a tax measure that constitutes a State aid prohibited under Art 107, then it must notify the Commission prior to its implementation. Failure to notify the Commission timeously renders the aid illegal.

The term 'State aid' is not defined in the EU Treaty. The understanding of its scope, in practice, comes primarily from reports by the Commission and judgments of the CJEU. Each has construed it broadly. The Commission has indicated that four cumulative elements must be shown for a measure to constitute fiscal State aid: There must be: (1) favourable tax treatment (such as a reduction in the tax base); (2) granted by a Member State or through State resources (which includes the State foregoing revenue that it would otherwise have collected); (3) that actually or potentially affects trade between Member States; (4) by favouring certain undertakings or the production of certain goods.

For a measure to be classified as State aid, it must be specific in terms of its application. Any measure intended to exempt firms in a particular sector will be caught, no matter how broadly that identifiable sector is defined; whereas a mere propensity for a measure to favour one sector rather than another cannot amount to selectivity. Thus, States remain free to take such measures as, for example, abolishing capital gains tax, even though the impact of this measure would be greater in certain sectors of the economy.

The boundary between a measure that is aimed at benefiting only certain sectors and a measure that may have that consequence is, however, often hard to discern. In order to determine whether a fiscal measure is specific, the common tax system must be determined. Then, it must be examined whether the measure is justified 'by the nature or general scheme' of the tax system, ie whether it 'derive[s] generally from the basic or guiding principles of the tax system in the Member State concerned. If this is not the case, then State Aid is involved' (Commission Notice on State aid, OJ C384, 10 December 1998, p 3). If the measure is a general one, but the State retains a discretionary power in respect of the administration of that rule, then that measure will be treated as if it is specific (*Ecotrade Srl v Altiformi e Ferriere di Servola SpA* (1998). For example, on 19 January 2005, the European Commission started an investigation into the UK's system of business rates that applies to the telecommunications industry. One of the bases of complaint was that there existed a number of different methods of valuation of hereditaments within the UK rating system and that there was discretion given to the Valuation Officer to choose the methodology to use. Aid that falls within Art 107(1) is not limited to direct subsidies; it may be in 'any form whatsoever'. Thus any preferential tax treatment, consisting of a tax concession or a relief, gives rise to aid (*De Gezamenlijke Steenkolenmijnen in Limburg* (1961). In *Portuguese Republic v EC Commission* (2006), the reduced rates of income tax and corporation tax introduced by the Azores Regional Assembly were held to be State aid, and not justified in so far as they applied to financial services and intra-group services; the CJEU held that 'the activities do not contribute sufficiently to regional development to be declared compatible' with the Treaty.

On 7 October 2014, the European Commission started an investigation into whether the tax ruling on transfer pricing given by Luxembourg's tax authorities to Amazon in Luxembourg complied with the EU rules on State aid. Tax rulings are comfort letters by tax authorities giving a specific company clarity on how its corporate tax will be calculated. In particular, they are used to confirm transfer pricing arrangements. This influences the allocation of the group's taxable profit between its subsidiaries located in different countries. Tax rulings as such are not problematic. However, tax rulings on transfer pricing arrangements may involve State aid within the meaning of EU rules if they are used to provide selective advantages to a specific company or group of companies. The tax ruling in relation to Amazon dates back to 2003 and is still in force. It applies to Amazon's subsidiary Amazon EU Sàrl, which is based in Luxembourg and records most of Amazon's European profits. Under the ruling, Amazon EU Sàrl pays a tax deductible royalty to a limited liability partnership established in Luxembourg but which is not subject to corporate taxation in Luxembourg. As a result, most European profits of Amazon are recorded in Luxembourg but are not taxed in Luxembourg. The concern of the Commission is that this may constitute State aid.

All Member States have been asked to provide copies of previous rulings to the Commission for review.

In October 2015, the European Commission decided that the tax rulings provided to Fiat by Luxembourg and to Starbucks by the Netherlands constituted unlawful State aid.

In August 2016, the European Commission concluded that tax rulings issued by the Irish tax authorities in favour of two Apple subsidiaries, which operated in Ireland until 2015, constituted illegal State aid that allowed Apple to allocate profits in a way that reduced the taxes payable in Ireland by up to €13bn. The decision required Ireland to recover this amount, plus interest, from Apple. Both the Irish Government and Apple have appealed the decision to the Court of Justice.

The imposition of a detriment in the form of a tax on one party can amount to aid elsewhere (this is often referred to as 'negative State aid'), if its imposition gives rise to a corresponding advantage to identifiable business competitors of those who have to bear the detriment (see *R (on the application of Professional Contractors Group Ltd) v IRC* (2002)). Thus, for example, a windfall tax on privatised industries could constitute State aid. Similarly, in *Weidert & Paulus* (2004), the CJEU noted that the Luxembourg provision giving beneficial tax treatment for investments in Luxembourg companies, which was unlawful for not being extended to non-resident companies, could alternatively have been prohibited as a State aid (subject to Commission approval under Art 108(3)).

The consequence of a measure being unlawful State aid is that the measure must be stopped. A business that has been the recipient of unlawful State Aid will be required to repay the aid even if this has consequence that the business must be wound up (*Commission v Belgium* (1986)). Therefore, in the *Weidert & Paulus* (2004) situation, State aid proceedings would have involved the aid being clawed back, instead of (in the case of proceedings for breach of a fundamental freedom) the benefit being extended to other taxpayers. The Commission publishes an annual survey of its proceedings relating to State aid in the *Official Journal* and publishes details in its annual report on competition policy. Due to this openness, a recipient of unlawful State aid will not, save in exceptional circumstances, be able to challenge repayment on the ground that it had a legitimate expectation that the aid had been granted in accordance with Art 108. [54.81]–[54.90]

X DIRECTIVES

In addition to the impact of the fundamental freedoms and State aid, there is one other key article of the EU Treaty relevant to direct tax: Art 115. This allows for the adoption of harmonising measures in the field of direct tax. Prior to the recent publication of the OECD's work on Base Erosion and Profit Shifting ('BEPS'), there had been only three substantive direct tax directives adopted under Art 115: the Merger Directive (Directive 90/434/EEC) and the Parent-Subsidiary Directive (Directive 90/435/EEC), both of which were adopted on 23 July 1990; and the Interest and Royalties Directive (Directive 2003/49/EC) of 3 June 2003. There are also two directives that primarily concern the exchange of information between Member States: the Mutual Assistance Directive (Directive 2011/16/EU) and the Savings Directive (Directive 2003/48/EC). All have been subject to sporadic revision, updating, and consolidation since their inception.

The BEPS project has resulted in the introduction of the Anti-Tax Avoidance Directive. As its *fons et origo* was the Common Consolidated

Corporate Tax Base project, it is considered separately below in that section
(see [54.97] ff). [54.91]

1 **The Cross-border Merger Directive**

In 1990 the Council adopted Directive 90/434/EEC on a common system of taxation applicable to mergers, divisions, transfers of assets and exchanges of shares concerning companies in different Member States, It sought to remove fiscal obstacles to cross-border reorganisations.

Nearly every Member State's tax system contains rules that allow capital gains to be deferred on a takeover of or merger with another company. However, cross-border mergers would not benefit from this treatment. The aim of the Merger Directive was to ensure that there is no difference in tax treatment between domestic and cross-border mergers, as any difference could hinder the cross-border expansion of groups of companies. It provided for a common system for deferral of capital gains tax on four types of operation: (i) legal merger (where one company transfers all its assets and liabilities to another company, which company becomes legal successor to it, and then 'dissolves'); (ii) legal division (where one company transfers all its assets and liabilities to two or more companies, which companies become legal successors to it, and then dissolves); (iii) transfer of assets (a company transfers one or more branches to another company in return for shares in that company, but remains in existence); and (iv) exchange of shares (a company acquires a majority of shares in another company in return for its shares, but remains in existence).

The Directive contains a general anti-abuse provision, which provides that Member States may deny the beneficial capital gains treatment if one of the principal aims of the operation is tax avoidance. Such an aim may be presumed if the operation is 'not carried out for valid commercial reasons'. The scope of the anti-abuse clause was considered by the CJEU in *Leur-Bloem* (1997). The CJEU said that, although the domestic legislation may stipulate that if the operation is not carried out for valid commercial reasons, a presumption of tax avoidance arises, national authorities must still examine each particular transaction and cannot simply apply predetermined general criteria. Thus, a general rule that automatically excluded certain categories of operations from the tax advantage is not allowed; it would not be proportionate. The CJEU also said that in order for an operation to be carried out for a valid commercial reason, it cannot be entered into only for the attainment of a purely fiscal advantage.

The Mergers Directive was amended by Directive 2005/19/EC (which came into force in 2006), so as to expand the list of companies to which the Mergers Directive applies to include SEs and to introduce measures that deal with transfers of registered office by an SE where the assets remain connected with a permanent establishment in the relevant Member State.

In 2009 the Council of Ministers adopted Directive 2009/133/EC which codified in a single text all Directives relating to Mergers. This included the initial Directive, the amendments introduced by Directive 2005/19/EC and Directive 2006/98/EC adding the required references following the accession of Bulgaria and Romania to the EU. This codification was prior to the accession of Croatia to the European Union which led to a further Directive, Directive 2013/13/EU.

One particular area of difficulty in the UK is that UK company law does not allow for 'legal merger' or 'division' as those terms are defined in the Directive (as a matter of UK company law, a company that has transferred its assets and liabilities to another company still exists unless and until it is subsequently dissolved). [54.92]

2 The Parent/Subsidiary Directive

If a subsidiary company remits its profits to its parent company in another Member State, then there are two potential tax charges that may arise. The first is a withholding tax on the payment of the dividends by the subsidiary; and the second is a tax on the parent company on the receipt of the dividends (which have been subject to underlying tax in the state of the subsidiary). The Parent-Subsidiary Directives have sought to abolish these potential hindrances to the free movement of capital and the freedom of establishment.

The first relevant Directive affecting this area is Council Directive 88/361/EEC on the free movement of capital, but the one bearing the name 'Parent/Subsidiary Directive' is Council Directive 90/435/EEC. The current version is as amended by Council Directive 2003/123/EC which was adopted to broaden the scope and improve the operation of 90/435/EEC.

The main features of the Directive are, *first*, that it, generally requires a full exemption from withholding tax on dividends paid by a subsidiary in one Member State to its parent company in another Member State; and *second*, it requires that Member States either should exempt parent companies from corporate tax on such dividends (exemption method), or give parent companies a credit against their tax liability for the corporate tax paid by the subsidiary (indirect credit method). The Directive applies to qualifying EU parent companies holding an interest of (currently) at least 10% in qualifying EU subsidiary companies.

The Directive is designed not to affect imputation systems that seek to prevent economic double taxation of the same profit (ie in the hands of the company that generated the profit and again in the hands of a parent company receiving a distribution representing that profit). Article 7(1) of the Directive provides that the requirement for advance payment of corporation tax in a subsidiary's State of residence is not a withholding tax; and Art 7(2) provides that the Directive will not affect agreements among Member States that are designed to mitigate economic double taxation of dividends (including the payment of tax credits to recipients of dividends). In *Océ van der Grinten NV* (2003) the CJEU held Art 7 of the Directive is to be construed in a broad-brush way, so that provisions that form part of a body of rules protected by Article 7 will themselves be protected, even if, when considered alone, they would fall outside that protection.

As with the Merger Directive, the Parent Subsidiary Directive contains anti-abuse provisions. In line with the general move to defend corporate tax bases, in November 2013 the Commission proposed amendments to the Directive with the twofold objective of tackling hybrid loan mismatches and introducing a general anti-abuse rule.

In May 2014, the Council decided to split the proposal and to address these two issues separately. In July 2014, it adopted as a first step provisions to prevent corporate groups from using hybrid loan arrangements to benefit from double-non taxation under the directive. Meanwhile work continued on the anti-abuse clause, and agreement on that was reached in December 2014. The Anti-Tax Avoidance Directive is addressed below. [54.93]

3 The Interest and Royalties Directive

The Interest and Royalty Directive is designed to eliminate withholding tax obstacles in the area of cross border interest and royalty payments between groups of companies. It was adopted in June 2003 and Member States have been required to apply it (with various temporary derogations, all of which have now expired) since 1 January 2004.

In the UK, FA 2004 ss 97–105 implemented the directive with retrospective effect from 1 January 2004. These sections provided that certain interest or royalty payments were exempt from income tax, provided that: (i) the person making the payment is either a UK company, or a UK permanent establishment of an EU-resident company; (ii) the beneficial owner of the income is either an EU company, or its permanent establishment (other than one in the UK or outside the EU); (iii) both companies are 25% associates (both companies are 25% associates if one directly holds at least 25% capital or voting rights in the other, or alternatively if a third company directly holds at least 25% capital or voting rights in each of them); (iv) and HMRC has issued an exemption notice. This legislation is now to be found in ITTOIA 2005 ss 757–767.

In 2011 the Commission proposed a revised directive that would reduce the 25% associates figure to 10% and extend the list of companies to which it is applied. This proposal was not accepted by the European Parliament. [54.94]

4 The Mutual Assistance Directive

Mutual assistance between Member States in the field of taxation has been established for a long time but for direct tax was formalised in the 1997 Mutual Assistance Directive (Council Directive 77/799/EEC). This applied in relation to direct taxes, certain excise duties and insurance premium tax. It required Member States to exchange information in order to enable each State to 'effect a correct assessment of taxes'. Information could be 'spontaneously' provided by a tax authority of one Member State to that of another Member State if the first Member State suspected a loss of tax in the other Member State. Restrictions as to whom the information could be passed applied under the Mutual Assistance Directive as applied under individual double taxation conventions (in particular that similarly strict standards of confidentiality would be observed by the tax authority in the other Member State).

There was a growing consensus that the Mutual Assistance Directive was not fit for purpose in the modern globalised era. It effectively lapsed, before being replaced by Council Directive 2011/16/EU which provided for much more comprehensive, and timely, exchanges of information. In the same way that many double taxation conventions have in recent years been amended to allow for automatic exchange of financial account information between contracting states, this Directive was amended by Council Directive 2014/107/ EU which extended the cooperation between tax authorities to automatic exchange of financial account information (see further below with regard to the Savings Directive).

The Directive was amended again, on 25 May 2016, as part of the first element of the January 2016 package of Commission proposals to strengthen rules against corporate tax avoidance. Directive 2016/0010 builds on the 2015 OECD recommendations to address BEPS. It implements OECD anti-BEPS action 13, on country-by-country reporting by multinationals, into a legally binding EU instrument. It covers groups of companies with a total consolidated group revenue of at least €750 million.

There are limits on the powers of fiscal authorities to obtain information. In *Berlioz* (2015), a French subsidiary paid dividends to its Luxembourg parent without deducting tax (on the basis that the dividends were exempt). The French tax authorities requested information from the Luxembourg tax authorities, which sought the relevant information from the parent company. It refused to provide some information on the ground that the information requested was not 'foreseeably relevant'. The CJEU held that protection against arbitrary involvement by public authorities in the private activities of any natural or legal person is a basic principle of EU law. It said that an information request is lawful only if the information requested is 'foreseeably relevant' for the purposes of the tax investigation in the Member State seeking it; Member States cannot engage in 'fishing expeditions'. Accordingly, the information request was unlawful. [54.95]

5 The Savings Directive

The powers imposed by the Mutual Assistance Directive are enhanced by the Savings Directive, the purpose of which is to counter cross-border tax evasion by collecting and exchanging information about foreign resident individuals receiving savings income outside their resident State. The Directive requires banks and other financial institutions to disclose details of the recipients of interest paid by such institutions in circumstances where the recipient of the interest is resident outside the Member State where the bank is situated.

The Directive has applied since 2005 to all EU Member States. The same measures were applied as from the same date (from 1 January 2007 for Bulgaria and Romania, and from 1 July 2013 for Croatia) in ten dependent or associated territories of EU Member States through the implementation of bilateral agreements signed by each of the 28 EU Member States with those jurisdictions. Equivalent measures were applied, from the same dates, in five European third countries, including Switzerland.

The Directive allows for the levying of a withholding tax (now 35%) as an alternative to exchanges of information. However, this was only available to the three Member States (Belgium, Austria and Luxembourg) who opted out of the disclosure requirements for a transitional period (Belgium stopped exercising its withholding option and switched to exchange of information on 1 January 2010, Luxembourg from 1 January 2015). Although these States were exempted from the requirement to disclose, they could still receive disclosures from other Member States or their dependencies during the opt-out period. The UK dependencies (in particular, the Channel Islands, and the Isle of Man) all indicated originally that they would opt for the withholding tax but all have now moved to automatic exchange of information.

On 24 March 2014 the EU Council of Ministers adopted a revised version of the Savings Taxation Directive, Council Directive 2014/107/EU on administrative co-operation in the field of direct taxation. This was with the aim of closing existing 'loopholes' (in particular, by interposing trusts or foundations to enable non-disclosure) and better preventing tax evasion.

[54.96]

XI THE COMMON CONSOLIDATED CORPORATE TAX BASE

Proposals by the European Commission for a less wildly variable basis for taxation within the EU (which, it is suggested, would reduce compliance costs, especially for international groups) date back as far as 1962. However, it was not until 2011 (after ten years of focussed work) that the Commission released its proposal for a Council Directive on a Common Consolidated Corporate Tax Base (CCCTB) in the European Union.

The aims of the CCCTB were:
(i) to eliminate tax impediments that arise from 28 different corporate tax systems and hinder intra-EU cross-border activities for multinationals (MNEs) and economic growth in the Single Market;
(ii) to make the EU more attractive for cross-border investment by significantly reducing the cost and administrative burden of tax and transfer pricing compliance (in particular, because the Commission increasingly doubted that 'arms' length' pricing always, or even in the majority of cases, leads to the right answer); and
(iii) to encourage fair and transparent tax competition based on national corporate tax rates.

The key features of the proposed CCCTB were as follows:
(i) it was to be voluntary, with an opt-in system for groups of companies;
(ii) there would have been a single set of rules for calculating taxable EU source profits and losses of opted-in entities. Each member of a group would have been be subject to tax on the net profit allocated to it at the national corporate tax rate in its country of residence or, for permanent establishments, the permanent establishment's country of location;
(iii) groups would have filed one consolidated tax return, submitted by the principal taxpayer to the tax authority of the Member State of its residence;
(iv) the principal tax authority would have dealt with all aspects of the tax return (including assessments, and administrative and judicial appeals);
(v) artificial transactions carried out for the sole purpose of avoiding tax would have been ignored; and
(vi) a CFC rule which treated the tax base of the EU group as including certain non-distributed income of certain non-EU resident entities would have been included. The CFC rule would not have applied unless the general corporate tax rate of the country where the relevant entity was resident was less than 40% of the average statutory corporate tax rate applicable in all Member States.

The Commission estimated that the CCCTB could save European businesses a total of c €3 billion, €700 million of which would be saved as a result of no longer having to deal with 27 different tax administration systems. However, Ireland commissioned a study which indicated that compliance costs would *increase* by 13%. The proposal did not meet with a positive response from Member States.

However, the changed political environment and the OECD's widely-publicised work on BEPS led to the Commission presenting a strategy to re-launch the CCCTB in June 2015, in the Action Plan for Fair and Efficient Corporate Taxation. The aim of the re-launch was to kick-start negotiations on the CCCTB in Council. The Commission said that it would come forward with a new proposal in 2016 to revive the CCCTB, based on two key changes:

(i) a mandatory CCCTB, to prevent profit shifting: an optional system would not be used by companies that aggressively plan to avoid taxes; and
(ii) introduction through a step-by-step approach to make it more manageable for Member States to agree. The primary focus is intended to be on securing the common tax base, starting with international elements related to BEPS. The Commission will propose postponing consolidation until after the common base has been implemented.

The Commission also called on Member States to continue work on some international aspects of the common base, linked to the OECD BEPS project, while the revised CCCTB proposal was being prepared. The Anti-Tax Avoidance Directive takes account of the outcome of Member States' discussions on these issues in Council. [54.97]

1 **The Anti-Tax Avoidance Directive**

The Anti-Tax Avoidance Directive ('ATAD') aims to achieve a balance between the need for a certain degree of uniformity in implementing the BEPS outputs across the EU and Member States' needs to accommodate the special features of their tax systems within these new rules. It lays down principle-based rules and leaves the details of their implementation to Member States, on the understanding that they are better placed to shape the precise elements of the rules in a way that best fits their corporate tax systems. The directive covers five areas, three of which implement OECD recommendations, namely, the interest limitation rules, the CFC rules and the rules on hybrid mismatches. The two others, ie the general anti-abuse rule and the exit taxation rules, deal with anti-tax-avoidance aspects of the 2011 proposal for an EU CCCTB.

On 20 June 2016, the Economic and Financial Affairs Council of the European Union approved the ATAD for corporate taxpayers in the EU. Member States will have until 31 December 2018 to transpose most of the provisions of the directive into their national laws. As at the date of writing, whilst it is reasonably likely that the UK will still be in the EU at that date, it is unclear, nonetheless, whether the UK will seek to implement the ATAD. The five main elements of the ATAD are as follows:

a) *General interest limitation rule*

The ATAD fixes a ratio for deductibility. Deduction of net interest expenses is restricted to 30% of the taxpayer's earnings before net interest, tax, depreciation and amortisation (EBITDA) or up to €3m, whichever is higher. A grandfathering provision means that loans concluded before 17 June 2016 will not be subject to this restriction, provided no amendments are made to the loan.

b) *Exit taxation*

This measure seeks to tax any unrealised gains on assets, business of a permanent establishment or residence of a company transferred out of their Member State of origin.

c) *A general anti-abuse rule*

This measure seeks to ensure that there are no abuse gaps by reason of Member States' domestic GAARs being inadequate or non-existent. Under the ATAD, the EU GAAR will apply to artificial arrangements or a series of arrangements that have been designed to obtain a tax advantage that defeats the main, or one of the main, objects or purposes of the relevant tax provision. Where the EU GAAR applies, the arrangement or arrangements must be ignored and reconstructed by reference to economic substance and in line with the Member State's domestic law.

d) *Controlled foreign company rules*

This measure seeks to prevent companies in one Member State from artificially diverting profits to a subsidiary or exempted permanent establishment resident in a low tax jurisdiction without proportionate economic substance in the subsidiary or the permanent establishment.

The UK includes within its CFC regime a partial exemption from the CFC charge for foreign group finance or treasury companies. It is unlikely that this would be permissible under the ATAD, should the UK become subject to it.

e) *Hybrid mismatch framework*

This measure, broadly, is in line with the BEPS recommendations. It is intended to counter taxpayers exploiting differences between domestic tax systems in order to achieve a double deduction for related party expenses or a deduction for the expense but no inclusion of the income in taxable income (ie 'double non-taxation'). [54.98]

XII EUROPEAN COMPANIES

On 8 October 2004 a new legal entity, which had a gestation period of over 30 years, was finally born: the *société européenne* ('SE'). An SE is a European public limited company that is available in all Member States (and the EEA). The intention is that an SE allows companies incorporated in different Member States to merge or form a holding company or joint subsidiary, whilst avoiding (in theory) the legal and practical constraints that arise from the existence of numerous different legal systems. Use of an SE allows companies operating in several Member States to operate (in theory) with a unified management and reporting structure, and under one set of rules. Although an SE is not intended to be a tax saving vehicle (there are no specific tax rules provided in the SE regulation or directive) it is clear that it has at least the potential to assist with the Commission's proposal to work towards a common set of rules for calculating EU-wide tax profits.

As at 14 August 2017, 2,827 registrations for SEs had been made. Less than a fifth of the SEs that have been established are 'normal' SEs in the sense of having business activities and multiple employees. The remainder were either special purpose subsidiaries or shelf companies.

F(No 2)A 2005 ss 51–65 introduced provisions relating to the SE in UK law. Broadly, these sections provide that if an SE is resident in the UK, then it will be subject to UK tax and they seek to ensure that an SE can be formed without giving rise to a significant tax cost. The relevant provisions are now to be found in CTA 2009. The intention is that a UK company's decision to merge with a company in another Member State to form an SE is not disadvantaged (or driven) by tax considerations. However, the provisions, unsurprisingly, do not address the underlying incompatibility of some parts of the UK tax system with EU law. To date, the SE is very far from providing a solution to this issue.

[54.99]

55 Human rights and taxation
Updated by Robin Williamson MBE CTA (Fellow)

I   Introduction [55.1]
II The right to property: Art 1 of Protocol No 1 [55.21]
III Enjoyment of Convention rights without discrimination: Art 14 [55.41]
IV Respect for privacy: Art 8 [55.61]
V   The right to a fair hearing: Art 6 [55.81]
VI Human rights and EC law [55.101]

I INTRODUCTION

1 Background to the Human Rights Act 1998

The European Convention for the Protection of Human Rights and Fundamental Freedoms (the European Convention) is a treaty of the Council of Europe. The Council, established at the end of the Second World War, was established before the European Union and, although many nations are members of both, the two bodies are quite separate. Over the years, the European Convention has become one of the foremost agreements defining standards of behaviour across Europe and indeed the acceptance of the Convention by most European countries meant incorporation into their own domestic law. Until the late 1990s, it was believed by the UK that the rights and freedoms guaranteed by the Convention could be delivered under the common law. That this was no longer sufficient was recognised both by the increasing need of applicants to take their case to the European Court of Human Rights (ECtHR) and by the passing of the Human Rights Act 1998 (HRA 1998). The effect of this Act was to incorporate into UK law, from October 2000, a major part of the European Convention. The aim was to guarantee a wide range of rights and freedoms for everyone, whether individuals or corporate entities, guaranteed in writing and enforceable in domestic courts. [55.1]

2 The Human Rights Act 1998 and incorporation

It can be said that there has been incorporation of Convention rights by HRA 1998 only in so far as it is consistent with parliamentary sovereignty. Thus, whereas the Constitution of the USA enables the US Supreme Court to strike down Federal statutes that are inconsistent with human rights principles, HRA 1998 does not give the courts a power to strike down primary legislation that is inconsistent with the Convention and Parliament may, if it chooses, maintain in force such legislation. Moreover, the Act can be repealed in the normal way. That said, there are some who feel that the effect of judgments (in areas other than tax law) handed down by both our own judges as well as those in the ECtHR have the effect of overruling the will of Parliament and that HRA 1998 should be repealed. Taking account of these views, the Conservative party announced in their 2015 manifesto that a future Conservative Government would replace the HRA 1998 with a British Bill of Rights. This would have the effect of making the UK Supreme Court the ultimate arbiter of human rights cases in the UK. The 2017 Conservative Manifesto was more equivocal:

> 'We will not bring the European Union's Charter of Fundamental Rights into UK law. We will not repeal or replace the Human Rights Act while the process of Brexit is underway but we will consider our human rights legal framework when the process of leaving the EU concludes. We will remain signatories to the European Convention on Human Rights for the duration of the next parliament.' **[55.2]**

3 Main principles of the Human Rights Act 1998

The Act operates on three main principles. *First*, courts and tribunals are required to construe both primary and secondary legislation in a way that is compatible with the Convention rights in so far as that is possible (s 3). This is in contrast to the pre-Act position when the domestic court was only obliged to construe *ambiguous* legislation in accordance with the Convention; now the possibility exists for a claimant to challenge *any* legislation on the basis that it is not compatible with Convention rights. This process was summarised by Lord Hoffmann in *R v IRC, ex p Wilkinson* (2005):

> 'The important change in the process of interpretation which was made by section 3 was to deem the Convention to form a significant part of the background against which all statutes, whether passed before or after the 1998 Act came into force, had to be interpreted. Just as the "principle of legality" meant that statutes were construed against the background of human rights subsisting at common law ... so now, section 3 requires them to be construed against the background of Convention rights. There is a strong presumption, arising from the fundamental nature of Convention rights, that Parliament did not intend a statute to mean something which would be incompatible with those rights. This, of course, goes far beyond the old-fashioned notion of using background to "resolve ambiguities" in a text which had notionally been read without raising one's eyes to look beyond it. The Convention, like the rest of the admissible background, forms part of the primary materials for the process of interpretation. But, with the addition of the Convention as background, the question is still one of *interpretation*, i.e. the ascertainment of what, taking into account the presumption created by section 3, Parliament would reasonably be understood to have meant by using the actual language of the statute.'

Thus it was that in *Ghaidan v Godin-Mendoza* (2004), the House of Lords held that in applying to the facts of the case the provisions of the Rent Act 1977, the words 'person who was living with the original tenant as his or her husband or wife' extended not only to heterosexual couples but also to the survivor of a long-term stable same-sex relationship. Whether such interpretation would be applied in the context of taxation remains to be seen (in *Courten v UK* (2008), (see **[55.43]**), the ECtHR did not need to decide the point, the issue having been argued on the basis of an alleged violation of Art 14 – discrimination).

Second, the Act requires all public authorities to act in accordance with the Convention (s 6), and courts will be at liberty to strike down any exercise of power that infringes the Convention. This is subject to the doctrine of the 'margin of appreciation' which requires the court to consider not only whether the relevant authority acted 'reasonably, carefully and in good faith', but in addition whether the authority's action was 'proportionate to the aim pursued' and supported by 'relevant and sufficient' reasons, including 'an acceptable assessment of the relevant facts'. *Third*, although no court is able to strike down or disregard primary legislation that conflicts with the Convention, the higher courts may make a 'declaration of incompatibility', which is a first step towards correcting the primary legislation (s 4, and see **[55.44]** and **[55.86]**). **[55.3]**

4 The courts and human rights

It should be remembered that findings of the ECtHR have to be applied in about 47 states, all having very different cultures and politics. Accordingly, when dealing with human rights issues, domestic courts and tribunals will take into consideration the jurisprudence of the ECtHR; indeed they are obliged to do so by HRA 1998 s 2(1) but, like the ECtHR itself, they are not bound by any of its previous decisions. This was spelt out by Potter LJ in *Han (t/a Murdishaw Supper Bar) v C & E Comrs* (2001):

> 'Since s 2(1) of the HRA requires the court or tribunal to take into account the Strasbourg case law of the European Court of Human Rights (the Strasbourg Court) when determining a question which has arisen in connection with a Convention right, that case law provides the starting point for the domestic court or tribunal's deliberations and the court or tribunal has a duty to consider such case law for the purpose of making its adjudication. It is not bound to follow such case law (which itself has no doctrine of precedent) but, if study reveals some clear principle, test or autonomous meaning consistently applied by the Strasbourg Court and applicable to a Convention question arising before the English courts, then the court should not depart from it without strong reason.' **[55.4]**

5 Human rights and tax

How, then, have tax matters been affected by the HRA 1998? At a time when HMRC have been given the widest possible information-gathering powers (by FA 2008, Sch 36 which, it has been commented, are the tax equivalent of stop and search powers), it is essential that taxpayers should have adequate safeguards. Whether the HRA 1998 provides these is a moot point. Given that EU law has applied in the UK for over four decades, but that it is only relatively recently that its implications for income tax and corporation tax have begun to be understood (see, for example, *ICI plc v Colmer* (2000) and *Marks & Spencer plc v Halsey* (2005)), it may yet be too early to make any accurate predictions.

When it was first enacted, commentators believed that the HRA 1998 would have a substantial impact, particularly in relation to indirect taxation and, to a certain extent, that view has already been borne out (see *Han v C & E Comrs* (2001) (at **[55.82]**)). However, one particular judgment of the ECtHR shows a distinct lack of enthusiasm on the part of the majority sitting in the case for restricting state power in taxation matters (*Ferrazzini v Italy* (2001) (see **[55.83]**)). Whilst that view is tempered by the fact that there was a strong and reasoned opinion by the dissenting judges, suggesting that the precise circumstances in which Convention rights might be invoked in respect of fiscal matters remains a matter of speculation, subsequent cases have followed the majority decision (see, for example, the cases of *Significant Ltd v Farrel* (2005), *Ketko v Ukraine* (2008), *R (on the application of ToTel Limited) v The First Tier Tribunal (Tax Chamber) and HM Treasury* (2011), *R (on the application of APVCO 19 Limited) v HM Treasury and R & C Comrs* (2015) and *Walapu v R & C Comrs* (2016): see **[55.83]**).

That cases will be brought is recognised by the fact that public funding (formerly legal aid) is now available for cases before the Tax Tribunals where the proceedings concern penalties which the courts have declared to be criminal in the terms specified by the European Convention or where an applicant seeks to argue that issue, *and* it is in the interests of justice for an applicant to be legally represented. Funding is available for both legal advice prior to any hearing and for legal representation at the tribunal. This is subject to the applicant being financially eligible, with applicants on income support, income-related employment and support allowance, income-based jobseekers allowance, guarantee pension credit and universal credit being automatically eligible.

That cases *are* being brought has been confirmed by a report from Thomson Reuters showing that the number of tax cases raising human rights issues doubled from 12 in 2011–12 to 25 in 2012–13. Some, however, will not bear even a consideration. Thus, the ECtHR refused to hear an application by a group known as the 'Peace tax Seven' against the refusal of HM Treasury to create a separate fund to receive a proportion of the tax monies paid by the applicants to be used exclusively for non-military purposes. The group had argued that to force them to pay taxes, part of which would be used for military purposes, was an unjustified interference with the exercise of freedom of thought, conscience and religion (Art 9 of the Convention) and thus constituted a failure to secure the right in question. They also argued that the Government's failure to accede to their request constituted unlawful discrimination against them. The Court was of the view that the application 'did not disclose any appearance of a violation of the rights and freedoms set out in the [European] Convention' (2009). **[55.5]–[55.20]**

II THE RIGHT TO PROPERTY: ART 1 OF PROTOCOL NO 1

1 Ambit of the provision

Article 1 of Protocol No 1 to the European Convention guarantees, in substance, the right to property and, in effect, comprises three elements. The first contains the general principle of peaceful enjoyment of the possession of property; the second deals with deprivation of property and subjects that to certain conditions; the third recognises that contracting states are entitled to control the use of property, expressly reserving the right of contracting states to pass laws that they deem necessary to secure the payment of taxes. This was explained by the ECtHR in *National and Provincial Building Society v UK* (1997) in the following terms:

> 'According to the Court's well established case law, an interference, including one resulting from a measure to secure the payment of taxes, must strike a fair balance between the demands of the general interest of the Community and the requirements of the protection of the individual's fundamental rights. The concern to achieve this balance is reflected in the structure of Art 1 as a whole, including the second paragraph: there must therefore be a reasonable relationship of proportionality between the means employed and the aims pursued. Furthermore in determining whether this requirement has been met, it is recognised that a Contracting State, not least when framing and implementing policies in the area of taxation, enjoys a wide margin of appreciation and the Court will respect the Legislature's assessment in respect of such matters unless it is devoid of reasonable foundation.'

(On the question of the wide margin of appreciation see also *Georgiou v UK* (2001) and *Totel Ltd v R & C Comrs* (2014), in which case the Upper Tribunal reiterated the words of the ECtHR in *Bulves v Bulgaria* (2009) that a contracting state, not least when framing and implementing policies in the area of taxation, enjoys a wide margin of appreciation, and the ECtHR will respect the legislature's assessment in such matters unless it is devoid of reasonable foundation. The taxpayer's subsequent appeal to the Court of Appeal based on the principle of equivalence in European Union law was dismissed (2016).)

More recently, the ECtHR has said that the first and most important requirement of Art 1 of Protocol No1 is that any interference with the peaceful enjoyment of possessions should be lawful and that, accordingly, the issue of a 'fair balance' only becomes relevant once it has been established that the interference in question was not arbitrary and satisfies the requirement of lawfulness. In this context, the term 'lawful' refers to the quality of the law in question, requiring it to be accessible to the persons concerned and precise and foreseeable in its application (see *Shchokin v Ukraine* (2011), *Yukos v Russia* (2011) and *NKM v Hungary* (2013)). Whether the 'fair balance' issue should subsume the question of legality is likely to be decided on a case-by-case basis (see, for example, *R (on the application of APVCO 19 Limited) v HM Treasury and R & C Comrs* (2015) (below) where Vos LJ felt it was convenient to treat the questions separately in the context of that particular case).

The all-important term 'possessions' has been considered in a number of cases. In *Burden v UK* (2006, 2008) (see **[55.43]**), two elderly sisters who had lived together all their lives and, for the last 30 years, in a house owned by them jointly and built upon land inherited from their parents, complained to the ECtHR under Art 1 of Protocol No 1 in conjunction with Art 14 (see **[55.41]**), arguing that they should be regarded as being in a similar situation to a married or civil partnership couple, entitling them to the spouse/civil partner exemption on the first death for IHT purposes (see **[31.41]**). The ECtHR dismissed the government's argument that Art 1 of Protocol No 1 could not apply (and thus, neither could Art 14 (see [**55.41**])) because the *presumptive heir* had no property rights and, accordingly, her hope of inheriting in the event of death could not amount to a 'possession' of property. The court's view was that the applicants did not complain that they would be prevented from acquiring property, but that the survivor would be liable to pay IHT on the jointly owned property; since the duty to pay tax on existing property fell within the scope of Art 1 of Protocol No 1, that article, along with Art 14, was engaged.

The term 'possessions' was again scrutinised by the ECtHR in *NKM v Hungary* (2013). In that case, the applicant, a Hungarian civil servant, was made redundant and became entitled to statutory severance pay. A part of the amount to which she was entitled was taxed at a special rate of 98% and deducted at source. This charge resulted in an effective rate of 52% on the total severance package compared with a general personal income tax rate of 16% in the relevant period. The applicant complained, inter alia, that the imposition of such a high rate of tax constituted an unjustified deprivation of property and was thus incompatible with Art 1 of Protocol No 1. Although the applicant never in fact received the entirety of her severance pay because the special tax was withheld directly by the authorities, giving rise to the question of whether there were 'possessions' within the meaning of Art 1 of Protocol No 1, the Court took the view that a 'legitimate expectation' of obtaining an asset could also enjoy the protection of the Article, saying:

'... where a proprietary interest is in the nature of a claim, the person in whom it is vested may be regarded as having a "legitimate expectation" if there is a sufficient basis for the interest in national law, for example where there is settled case-law of the domestic courts confirming its existence. However, no "legitimate expectation" can be said to arise where there is a dispute as to the correct interpretation and application of domestic law and the applicant's submissions are subsequently rejected by the national courts ...'

In this case, the Court found that a statutory scheme that provides for severance encompasses a statutory entitlement in exchange for the service rendered. Accordingly, irrespective of whether the applicant received part of the severance pay with the obligation to declare it and pay the tax in due course or whether, as here, the tax was automatically deducted from the payment, the severance had already been earned or was definitely payable, thus turning it into a possession for the purposes of Art 1 of Protocol No 1. (The applicant was successful in her challenge under this provision: see [**55.25**].)

In contrast, in *R (on the application of APVCO 19 Limited) v HM Treasury and R & C Comrs* (2015), the taxpayers took part in a tax avoidance scheme designed to allow them to escape stamp duty land tax (SDLT) on their purchases of high value residential property. They applied for judicial review of FA 2013 s 194, which retrospectively amended FA 2003 s 45. They contended that these changes amounted to an infringement of Article1 of Protocol No1 and of Art 6 (for the arguments based on Art 6, see [**55.83**]). By way of background, FA 2003 s 45 provides that where there is a contract for sale of property and a sub-sale, as a result of which a person other than the original purchaser becomes entitled to call for a conveyance of the property, the substantial performance or completion of the original contract at the same time as, and in connection with, the substantial performance or completion of the secondary contract is disregarded with the result that the completion of the original contract in such circumstances is taken out of the charge to stamp duty land tax (SDLT). Unsurprisingly, these provisions became a target for tax avoidance schemes in relation, mainly, to residential property transactions, with HMRC seeking to combat them by a variety of measures. In March 2011, a Protocol, *Tackling Tax Avoidance* was published, providing criteria that ministers would observe 'when deciding whether to announce a change to tax law that has immediate effect', and to allow decisive action when risks to the Exchequer were identified. It was announced in the 2012 Budget that action would be taken to close down future SDLT avoidance schemes where appropriate with effect from the date of the budget, and legislation was promised to make clear that particular avoidance schemes relating to sales and sub-sales would not be effective. Such legislation was introduced by FA 2012 and, subsequently, it was announced that further retrospective legislation would be enacted with a view to closing down future SDLT schemes, with the Exchequer Secretary to the Treasury explaining that, in light of the abuse in this area and the tax at risk over the next five years (estimated to be around £160 million), the Treasury viewed the legislative changes as wholly exceptional and consistent with the Protocol. These changes duly came into force with retrospective effect. The appellants in this case contended that the changes infringed Article 1 of Protocol No 1 and Art 6 and sought a declaration of incompatibility under the HRA 1998 s 4. In agreeing with the judge at first instance, the Court of Appeal held that Article 1 of Protocol No 1 was not engaged in this case since the legislative change did not impose on the appellants a liability to pay SDLT but, rather, removed an alleged genuine, but not established, right to tax relief. According to Strasbourg jurisprudence, such a claim to tax relief is not a 'possession' within Article 1 of Protocol No 1 because possessions must exist or be claims in respect of which an individual has a legitimate expectation that they will be realised. A legitimate expectation has to be based on a legal provision or a judicial decision and cannot be based on an arguable claim or genuine dispute. In light of the clear warnings by the Chancellor that SDLT schemes would be blocked, the appellants had no legitimate expectation that they would be able to pay only a fraction of the ordinary SDLT that was due. Vos LJ explained this simply by saying that the appellants had not been deprived of the cash they would have used to pay the tax but, rather, of an argument that they were not liable to pay the tax, and the authorities show that this is insufficient to amount to an interference with a possession under Article 1 of Protocol No 1 (see also *R (on the application of Huitson) v R & C Comrs* (2011) and *Rowe, Worrall and Others v R & C Comrs* (2015), in which case taxpayers challenged HMRC's issue of partner payment notices (PPNs – see **[5.27]**)) requiring up-front payments of tax pending the resolution of enquiries into the tax arrangements, arguing that this amounted to an interference with their enjoyment of property rights as guaranteed by Article 1 of Protocol No 1). For his part, Floyd LJ said the appellants would only have been deprived of their money if the scheme had been effective to avoid SDLT. However, this had not been established and the fact that it was arguable that the scheme was effective to avoid SDLT was not enough to engage Article 1 of Protocol No 1. The Court of Appeal further agreed with the judge in holding that, even had Article 1 of Protocol No 1 been engaged, the legislative changes were not incompatible with it. Vos LJ said that the legislative change was lawful: it was not relevant that other SDLT schemes had not been blocked, and the Government's action could not be seen as a breach of their protocol on retrospective legislation. He said further that the Government's action was proportionate and 'in this case, the balance between the general interests of the community and the protection of the individual's fundamental rights falls heavily on the side of the public interest'.

Where previous legislation giving preferential treatment to companies with foreign investments (including 10 years' immunity from changes in the law governing foreign investments) was repealed, the ECtHR declared inadmissible a claim by a majority shareholder in a company with foreign investment that the subsequent legislation that sought to abrogate the immunity as regards tax and customs was contrary to his property rights guaranteed by Art 1 of Protocol No 1 (*Ketko v Ukraine* (2008)). In upholding the respondent's contention that the claimant shareholder (as opposed to the company) was not a victim of the alleged violation within the meaning of Art 34 since he was not directly affected by the measure in question, the court observed that, as a general rule, shareholders of a company (even majority ones) cannot claim to be victims of an alleged violation of a company's rights under the Convention. Moreover, the court held that there were no exceptional circumstances in the present case to justify departing from the court's normal rule of not piercing the corporate veil or disregarding a company's legal personality.   [55.21]

2   IR35 and the Professional Contractors Group

Article 1 of Protocol No 1 was one of the arguments invoked in the high profile judicial review case brought against the Inland Revenue by *inter alia* the Professional Contractors Group in respect of the imposition of the notorious IR35 legislation relating to personal service companies (*R (on the application of Professional Contractors Group Ltd) v IRC* (2001)). The later appeal by the taxpayers did not concern the issue of human rights (see **[8.31]**)). Companies subject to the IR35 legislation are primarily one-man companies, which charge out the services of the owner, ('the service contractor'), to a client for fees paid by the client to the service company in circumstances where the service contractor would be an employee of the client if he had provided his services directly to it. Out of this remuneration, the service contractor is paid a small salary, from which income tax and employees' national insurance contributions (NICs) are deducted, and the service company pays employers' NICs. From the balance will be deducted allowable expenses, and a substantial dividend out of the profit may eventually be paid to the service contractor which will not attract NICs, and in respect of which income tax will only be payable as and when the dividend is declared. Any retained profit will be assessable to corporation tax. The aim of IR35 is to treat the fees as income from employment with income tax and NICs being deductible.

The claimants' case was that a right to enjoy the benefit of a shareholding in a service company is a right of property and, by virtue of the IR35 legislation, enjoyment of that right was interfered with contrary to Art 1 of Protocol No 1 for two reasons. *First*, the imposition of income tax and NICs on the notional remuneration together with the way in which expenses are treated, meant that the 'right' was rendered more expensive. *Second*, the uncertainty as to whether a particular service contractor would be classified as an employee if he had rendered his services directly to the client would result either in a loss of enjoyment of the shareholding or it put the very existence of service companies in jeopardy. In holding that the impact of IR35 was insufficient to amount to a breach of Art 1 of Protocol No 1, Burton J considered the Strasbourg jurisprudence in relation to the claimant's first argument, and said:

> 'A financial liability arising out of the raising of taxes or contributions may adversely affect the guarantee of ownership if it places an excessive burden on the person concerned or fundamentally interferes with his financial position. However, it is in the first place for the national authorities to decide what kind of taxes or contributions are to be collected. Furthermore the decisions in this area will commonly involve the appreciation of political, economic and social questions which the Convention leaves within the competence of the Contracting States. The power of appreciation of the Contracting States is therefore a wide one.'

Accordingly, he concluded that even if the full amount of a service company's earnings (without any allowance for expenses) in a given year were treated as the remuneration of the service contractor, this would not amount to a confiscation of property, nor to a fundamental interference with the claimants' financial position, and nor would it amount to an abuse of the UK's rights to levy taxes. As to the second argument in respect of uncertainty, Burton J was of the opinion that the effect of IR35 was to submit service contractors to the same common law test of employment with respect to each engagement to which they would have been subject but for the interposition of the service company. With that in mind, he concluded that it could not offend against the concept of certainty for the common law of employment to apply to a service contractor. [55.22]

3 Use of Art 1 of Protocol No 1

Article 1 of Protocol No 1 may also be invoked in the following cases:
(1) *Recovery of overpaid tax* A taxpayer who has overpaid income or corporation tax has, from 1 April 2010, a statutory right to make a claim for repayment by way of overpayment relief (TMA 1970 ss 33, 33A as amended, and Sch 1AB inserted, by FA 2009 s 100 and Sch 52). Relief is restricted by the fact that (a) HMRC is only entitled to give such relief if the taxpayer has not had a reasonable chance to correct their tax liability any other way (by making or amending a self-assessment return or appealing against an HMRC assessment or amendment of their return); (b) where a return is made in accordance with the 'prevailing practice' at the time, recovery is prevented; and (c) any claim is subject to time limits (claims must be made within four years of the end of the tax year or accounting period to which the claim relates, unless it relates to a mistake in an individual's 2004–05 and 2005–06 self-assessment return if they were not given a notice to make the return within 12 months of the end of the tax year. The time limits for claims in these cases are 31 January 2011 and 31 January 2012 respectively). The statutory right to the recovery of overpaid VAT is restricted if the

claimant would thereby be unjustly enriched (VATA 1994 s 80). Each of the restrictions on recovery is capable of challenge under Art 1 of Protocol No 1. The claimant would have to show that the restrictions to reclaiming the overpaid tax (a possession of the taxpayer) could not be justified in the general interest and that they were disproportionate to the state's aim in providing for them. That such a claim would be successful is more doubtful since the amending legislation contained in FA 2009 came into effect.

In *R (on the application of Higgs) v R & C Comrs* (2015) the claimant, Mr Higgs, claimed a repayment of overpaid tax for the year 2006–07 under TMA 1970 s 59B(1) on the basis of his self-assessment which was filed on 11 November 2011. HMRC refused the claim on the grounds that the self-assessment was out of time under TMA 1970 s 34(1). The Upper Tribunal held that s 34(1) only applied to assessments made by HMRC, not self-assessments, and granted the claimant's appeal. It was therefore unnecessary to consider his alternative ground, that HMRC would have been obliged to use its discretion to extend the deadline imposed by s 34(1) otherwise the claimant would 'suffer disproportionate damage resulting in an infringement of his rights under Article 1 of Protocol 1'. But the judge said that if the Upper Tribunal decision on s 34(1) was reversed on appeal and it became necessary to consider the human rights point, the matter should then be remitted to HMRC for it to give 'full and proper consideration' to whether to extend the deadline to allow the claimant's self-assessment and repayment claim to be processed, having regard to (among other things) whether the decision amounts to a disproportionate interference with the claimant's rights under Art 1 of Protocol No 1. **[55.23]**

(2) *Seizure of property* Whilst the seizure of goods and documents would appear to infringe Art 1 of Protocol No 1, this may be justified depending upon the facts of each particular case. (Search and seizure may also infringe Art 8 (see **[55.61]**)). In deciding whether such provisions are necessary and proportionate, the claimant's case will largely depend upon whether the exercise of such powers is subject to effective judicial supervision and a right of appeal (see *AGOSI v United Kingdom* (1986), and also *Lindsay v C & E Comrs* (2002), and *R (on the application of Hoverspeed) v C & E Comrs* (2002), both cases concerning the seizure of vehicles following allegations of illegal importation of goods). **[55.24]**

(3) *Imposition of a one-off tax or of an excessively high rate of tax*

In the matter of imposing taxes, States are given considerable freedom to decide what taxes to levy and the rate at which they should be charged. As Judge Lorenzen said in his separate but concurring judgment in *NKM v Hungary* (2013) (see **[55.21]**):

'It has been the Court's constant case-law that the imposition of taxes as a general rule is for the States to decide and that only if the system or the way it has been applied in a particular case is arbitrary or devoid of reasonable foundation can the imposition of taxes be challenged under Article 1 of Protocol No 1.'

That having been said, it is possible that the levying of a tax such as the windfall tax on a particular taxpayer, or one type of taxpayer, may be in violation of Art 1 of Protocol No 1. To succeed, a claimant would have to show that the imposition of the tax interfered with that taxpayer's rights of ownership of its assets or its financial situation to such an extent that the tax could be considered disproportionate or an abuse of the state's right under Art 1 of Protocol No 1 to levy taxes (see *Wasa Liv Omsesidigt v Sweden* (1988) where the argument failed on the facts of the case). The imposition could also possibly be challenged under Arts 14 and 6(1) (see **[55.41]** and **[55.81]**).

As far as high rates of tax are concerned, the applicant in *NKM v Hungary* (2013) complained that the imposition of a 98% rate of tax on the upper bracket of her severance pay constituted an unjustified deprivation of property, or else taxation at an excessively disproportionate rate, in violation of Art 1 of Protocol No 1. Having reiterated the oft used phrase that States enjoy a wide margin of appreciation in matters of tax policy, in assessing whether the measure complained of was in the public interest, the Court found that, whilst it was intended to protect the public purse against excessive severance payments, this goal was not primarily served by taxation; as an alternative, the severance rules could have been changed so as to reduce the amount paid. Moreover, although the Court was of the view that the applicable tax rate is not in itself decisive, in considering the proportionality principle, it found that the tax rate imposed exceeded 'considerably' the rate applicable to other revenues, including severance paid in the private sector and that little consideration had been given to the confiscatory nature of the tax burden. Taking these factors into account, the Court concluded that the measure, as applied to the applicant, could not be justified by the legitimate public interest relied on by the Government even though it was intended to serve social justice. The applicant had acted in good faith and had a legitimate expectation that she would receive a statutorily guaranteed right; instead, she was deprived of the large part of her severance pay. In those circumstances, the measure could not be held reasonably proportionate to the aim sought to be realised. In his separate but concurring judgment, Judge Lorenzen made it clear that the judgment in this case should not be seen to interfere with the principle that it is for States to decide what taxes should be imposed.

In *Joost Lobler v R & C Comrs* (2015) one issue was whether the charge to tax on the partial surrender of a life assurance policy, which was described by the First-tier Tribunal judges as 'an outrageously unfair result', was incompatible with Article 1 of Protocol No 1. The legislation (ITTOIA 2005 s 539) taxed the entirety of the taxpayer's partial surrenders (themselves amounting to 97.5% of his life policy in total) less a mere 5% of the policy premium for each year in which the policy had been held. This resulted in tax at an effective rate of 779% of the income generated by the policy. This was a sum which the Upper Tribunal judge said 'exhausts [the taxpayer's] life savings and may bankrupt him, although he made no substantial profit or gain'. It was held that Mr Lobler made a mistake in the way in which he withdrew the policies, and he was granted rectification (following the Supreme Court in *Pitt v Holt* (2011). But a subsidiary argument, that Mr Lobler's human rights (specifically under Article 1 of Protocol No 1) were breached by the charge to tax and the statute imposing it should be read, so far as possible, in a manner that was compatible with the ECHR, was rejected. Following *NMK v Hungary*, the judge said:

'The means employed to achieve the public interest in this case amount to depriving Mr Lobler and his family of all their personal finances and leaving him in a state of possible bankruptcy. Each case must be considered individually on its own merits. Is it possible to conclude that the legislation in question is generally "devoid of reasonable foundation"? In my view the scales tip, only just, in favour of reasonable foundation because the law is not irrational or arbitrary. While it would be fairer if the gain on partial surrenders was calculated using a different and more proportionate method, the fact that it is not does not make the current method of calculating tax on partial surrenders devoid of reasonable foundation. Again, while it would be fairer if the law was simpler, the fact that it is not does not mean that there is a breach of human rights.'

Nevertheless, the Finance Bill published in April 2017 included a clause which would have enabled HMRC to substitute a 'just and reasonable' solution to cases, like that of Mr Lobler, where policyholders make wrong choices regarding partial surrender and assignment of policies and face a tax bill that is 'wholly disproportionate'. The clause was not passed in FA 2017, but it is expected to be re-introduced in a subsequent Finance Bill. If passed, it is likely that the possibility of a just and reasonable solution will counteract any future challenge under Article 1 of Protocol No 1 – see for instance *Morgan Lloyd Trustees Ltd (as administrator of the Wren Press Pension Scheme) v R & C Comrs* (2017), in which the First-tier Tribunal held that the surcharge and scheme sanction charges under FA 2004 ss 209 and 239 did not infringe Art 1 of Protocol No 1 because they were subject to s 268 under which the person charged could apply to HMRC for the liability to be discharged on 'just and reasonable' grounds. **[55.25]**

(4) *Imposition of retrospective legislation* Retrospective legislation is used most often in the area of taxation as an anti-avoidance measure by plugging a loophole. Would such legislation infringe the European Convention on the basis that it undermines the rule of law and legal certainty? In *MA and 34 Others v Finland* (2003), the ECtHR stated that retrospective tax legislation was not as such prohibited by Art 1 of Protocol No 1 and that the key question was whether the backdating struck a fair balance between those affected by the change, both positively and negatively (see also the separate but concurring judgment of Judge Lorenzen in *NKM v Hungary* (2013)). This view was confirmed in *Belmonte v Italy* (2010), where again the ECtHR held that Art 1 of Protocol No 1 does not prohibit retrospective tax legislation but that, depending upon the facts of each particular case, retrospective legislation may impose an excessive burden on an individual and thus breach that individual's rights. In that case, land was acquired by the local Italian municipality and, following an action by the original applicant (who had died by the time of the ECtHR judgment), compensation was awarded in February 1990 and became finally binding on 8 May 1991. Many delays by the local municipality meant that an initial payment of compensation was not made until 27 May 1992, with the final payment being made as late

as 4 January 1995. Following new legislation that came into force on 30 December 1991, this final payment was subject to a 20% withholding tax. The applicant complained that there had been a breach of Art 1 of Protocol No 1 on the ground that the legislation operated retrospectively to an award of compensation that had become final before the imposition of the withholding tax. Although the Strasbourg Court refused to accept that retrospectivity on its own could amount to a breach of Art 1 of Protocol No 1, it went on to hold that the application of the withholding tax in this particular case failed to meet the fair balance between the general interests of the public and the need to safeguard the fundamental rights of the individual. This was so because, had the municipality been punctual in its payment of the compensation, payment would have preceded the introduction of the withholding tax. This is a stark example of the subjective approach taken by the ECtHR towards the test of proportionality (for a discussion of this issue, see [2005] BTR 1).

This question was considered at some length by the Court of Appeal in *Huitson v R & C Comrs* (2011) (see also *Shiner v R & C Comrs* (2011) and *Rowe, Worrall and others v R & C Comrs* (2015)). The case concerned an independent contractor, resident and carrying out his trade in the UK, who sought to avoid tax through an arrangement centred on the Isle of Man that aimed to take advantage of the Double Tax Arrangement (DTA) between the UK and the Isle of Man. The combined effect of the UK legislation before it was changed and the DTA in question, which sought to give relief by charging tax in one country only, was that the taxpayer paid tax on certain income in neither country. As Kenneth Parker J aptly commented in the first instance decision (2010), 'this would appear to be a rather paradoxical result of a DTA exclusively aimed at avoiding *double* taxation'. By exploiting the arrangement over seven years, the claimant avoided income tax of £84,980 and reduced his effective rate of tax to an average of 3.5 per cent. So effective was the scheme that some 2,500 taxpayers exploited similar arrangements, with a possible loss to the Exchequer of £100m and distortion of competition between those independent contractors who availed themselves of the scheme and those who did not. Unsurprisingly, the Government enacted legislation amending the DTA with retrospective effect, thereby preventing the avoidance intended by the claimant and others. By way of judicial review, Mr Huitson claimed that provisions in FA 2008 that changed legislation regarding the DTA were incompatible with Art 1 of Protocol No 1 because of their retrospective effect, which failed to achieve a fair balance between the interests of the general body of taxpayers and the rights of the claimant as an individual, and because they were disproportionate.

In the High Court, Kenneth Parker J, with whom the Court of Appeal agreed, accepted the following, *inter alia*, to be incontrovertible:
(a) the fundamental purpose of a DTA is to avoid double taxation. It is not a purpose of DTAs to facilitate the complete avoidance of income tax in any jurisdiction;
(b) it is a legitimate and important aim of UK public policy in fiscal affairs that a DTA should do no more than relieve from double

taxation, and that a DTA should not be permitted to become an instrument by which persons residing in the UK avoid, or substantially reduce, the incidence of income tax that they would ordinarily pay on their income, including income earned from the exercise of a trade or profession. That is particularly the case where the means chosen to exploit the DTA in that way comprises artificial arrangements;

(c) such is the importance of the public policy in (b) above that the UK legislature is entitled, and can reasonably be expected, to enact legislation to ensure that any relevant DTA does not become an instrument of tax avoidance in the sense identified in (b) above; and

(d) in principle, the policy in (b) above is of such importance that retrospective legislation may be justified.

The Court of Appeal, like the High Court, duly concluded that there was no basis for the claim that the Parliamentary response in this case had been disproportionate. Parliament was entitled to pursue the rigorous policy in (b) above and to legislate to put the effect of the DTA beyond doubt and to prevent taxpayers resident in the UK from exploiting the relevant DTA in a way that would enable them to substantially reduce income tax that would otherwise be properly paid on income arising from the exercise of a trade or profession. Moreover, Parliament was entitled to legislate with retrospective effect, particularly in order to ensure a 'fair balance' between the interests of the great body of resident taxpayers who paid income tax on their income from a trade or profession in the normal way, and the taxpayers, like the claimant, who had sought to exploit, by artificial arrangements, the DTA in plain contravention of the important public policy set out above.

In March 2011, a Protocol was issued by HMRC dealing with the circumstances in which the Government would use retrospective legislation, in some cases to reduce liabilities, but mostly to prevent a loss to the Exchequer in cases of tax avoidance. Until then, the approach had been to make an announcement, the date of which was the date from which subsequent legislation would take effect. Notwithstanding its commitment to consult with regard to tax changes, the Government wanted to retain the ability to use retrospective legislation as outlined above, most likely to take effect outside of a scheduled fiscal event like the Budget and by Written Ministerial Statement. The document made it clear that pre-announcement changes would be regarded as wholly exceptional 'because such changes impose a set of legal consequences on a person in respect of actions they carried out without being able to foresee those consequences ... There is a balance to be struck between the need for a stable tax system and certainty for taxpayers and the responsibility to protect the Exchequer against risk'. Accordingly, the Protocol makes it clear that such changes will *normally* only be announced other than in the Budget where there would otherwise be a significant risk to the Exchequer, that significant new information has emerged to identify the risk or indicate its scale and changing the law immediately would be expected to prevent significant losses to the Exchequer.

Whether the government had acted in accordance with this Protocol was one of the issues arising in *R (on the application of APVCO 19 Limited) v HM Treasury and R & C Comrs* (2015) (see **[55.21]**). In holding that there had been no breach of the Protocol, Vos LJ held *first* that the promise made by the government in the Protocol only applies 'normally' and the need to make sure that further abusive schemes to avoid the existing legislation were not devised was an exceptional situation; *second*, there were significant risks to the Exchequer in that taxpayers were likely to continue to devise minor variations on tax avoidance schemes once the process of anti-avoidance legislation left a window for them to do so; *third*, and most importantly, whilst the losses envisaged (about £7 million) were not very large compared to the overall tax take, they were significant to the Exchequer because they represented a number of taxpayers deliberately doing what the government had said it intended to stop. The term used is 'significant' and not 'substantial'; and *finally*, the situation occasioning the legislative changes was indeed wholly exceptional: the fact that the appellants were avoiding only a relatively small amount of tax was not to the point. The respondents wanted, exceptionally, to demonstrate that the Chancellor had made it clear that he intended to close all loopholes so that purchasers of properties in the UK would pay their fair share of SDLT and that he would act retrospectively if they persisted in trying to find ways to defeat the clear intention of Parliament. [55.26]

(5) *Imposition of disproportionate tax penalties* It could be argued that where tax penalties are so heavy as to be disproportionate to the public benefit, there is a breach of Art 1 of Protocol No 1. In *Mondero & Others v France* (2010), a heavy penalty was imposed on the applicants who had operated an unauthorised gambling activity for profit, and who had tried, amongst other things, to interfere with witnesses. Despite the fact that total payment of duties evaded together with penalties amounted to more than three times the total assets of the applicants, the Strasbourg Court concluded that the imposition of the sanctions was not disproportionate. It was of the view that penalties came within the wide margin of appreciation enjoyed by the State in tax matters, particularly given the public interest in combating money laundering. It is suggested that this is yet another example of the Court's subjective approach to the test of proportionality. [55.27]–[55.40]

III ENJOYMENT OF CONVENTION RIGHTS WITHOUT DISCRIMINATION: ART 14

1 Article 14 is not a substantive provision

There is no general prohibition on discrimination in the European Convention. Article 14 requires that the enjoyment of the rights set out in the Convention are to be secured without discrimination. What this means is that in every case, Art 14 must be accompanied by a substantive provision. Although the application of Art 14 does not presuppose a breach of those substantive provisions, in order for it to be applied, the facts of the case must come within the ambit of one or more of them. It is likely that in the area of taxation, the substantive right that will most often be alleged to have been violated is Art 1 of Protocol No 1 (see, for example, *R (on the application of Wilkinson) v IRC* (2005) at **[55.42]** and *Burden v UK* (2006, 2008) at **[55.21]** and **[55.43]**), although it should be noted that the connection between a substantive right and Art 14 may be somewhat tenuous! **[55.41]**

2 Scope of Art 14

A challenge under Art 14 may be made, although it may not necessarily be successful, in the following cases:

(1) *Discrimination between similarly situated taxpayers* The imposition, for example, of a windfall tax on one, or only some, of a number of companies in the same sector may be challenged on the basis that it draws an arbitrary distinction between a similar group of taxpayers, but it is suggested that the chances of success are small. The application for judicial review of a refusal by HMRC to make a widower's bereavement payment to an applicant was unsuccessful (see (3) below)). One of the applicant's claims was that it was irrational or an abuse of power to treat him differently from certain other taxpayers who, unlike him, had previously petitioned the court in Strasbourg and had come to a friendly settlement with HMRC. The House of Lords dismissed this claim on the basis that, having decided that there was no justification whatever for extending the widows' bereavement allowance to men, the applicant would not be entitled to damages in either a domestic court, or at Strasbourg; that HMRC did not take this point with the other taxpayers did not mean that they were not entitled to take the point against the applicant (*R v IRC ex parte Wilkinson* (2005)). However, in *PM v UK* (2005) (see (2) below), the ECtHR was of the opinion that the Government had breached Convention rights by drawing a distinction between married and unmarried fathers for the purpose of qualifying maintenance payments. **[55.42]**

(2) *Discrimination on the grounds of marriage/civil partnership* UK legislation that provided for allowances discriminating between single and married people (and married people now include civil partners: see **[51.130]**) has been held not to be an infringement of the Convention on the grounds that it was within the discretion allowed to contracting states and that the distinction was objectively justifiable (*Lindsay v UK* (1986)). It was this case that the Government relied upon in response to the challenge in *PM v UK* (2005). Following the separation of an unmarried couple that had previously lived and had a daughter together, it was agreed under the terms of a deed of separation that the applicant, the father, would pay weekly maintenance for his daughter. He was granted tax relief for the maintenance payments made during the tax year in which they began, but it was later claimed by the UK Government that this was an error on the part of the Revenue. The applicant was refused relief for later years on the basis that he had never been married to his daughter's mother, and that, accordingly, his payments could not be qualifying maintenance payments within TA 1988 s 347(B) (the relief claimed by the applicant is no longer available unless one of the parties to the marriage or former

marriage was aged 65 or over on the 5 April 2000; see [**52.3**]). Before the ECtHR, the applicant argued that there had been a violation of Art 14 in conjunction with Art1 of Protocol No 1 on the basis that he was being treated differently from a married (or previously married) father, and that there was no objective or reasonable justification for the difference in treatment. Bearing in mind Governmental policy (manifested through the powers vested in the Child Support Agency) that parents, and fathers in particular, should be responsible for the maintenance of their children irrespective of their marital status, he was in an analogous position with a married father, since their legal obligations with respect to their children were identical. For its part, the Government submitted that, for the purpose of s 347B, paternity was not relevant in determining whether a payment was a qualifying maintenance payment; rather, it 'was the relationship of marriage that was at the core of the legislation', and that *Lindsay* precluded any argument denying the right of a government to distinguish between married and unmarried persons. The Government's alternative argument was that, in any event, there was an objective and reasonable justification for the difference in treatment, based on a policy of promoting the institution of marriage, even after the breakdown of the marriage. Holding that there had been a violation of Convention rights, the ECtHR was of the opinion that the applicant was not seeking to compare himself to a couple in a subsisting marriage, but to a married *father*; in terms of a child's welfare, a married and an unmarried father were in a relatively similar position. This case should, therefore, be more correctly placed in (1) above. The Court was of the further view that there was no justification for the difference in treatment. It said:

> 'Given that he has financial obligations towards his daughter, which he has duly fulfilled, the Court perceives no reason for treating him differently from a married father, now divorced and separated from the mother, as regards the tax deductibility of those payments. The purpose of the tax deductions was purportedly to render it easier for married fathers to support a new family; it is not readily apparent why unmarried fathers, who undertook similar new relationships, would not have similar financial commitments equally requiring relief.'

The UK tax system generally distinguishes between those who are married or civil partners of one another and those who live together as though married or civil partners, with the exception of the High Income Child Benefit Charge. Working tax credit and child tax credit, being welfare payments administered by HMRC, follow most social security benefits by making no such distinction. The view of the Strasbourg court is that the ability to legislate on the basis of a distinction between married and unmarried persons remains within a government's competence. Whether the distinction will remain justifiable with the changing attitudes of society to marriage remains to be seen, and challenges will doubtless continue. For example, in *R (on the application of Siobhan McLaughlin) v Department for Social Development* (2016), the Court of Appeal in Northern Ireland allowed an appeal by the Department against a decision by the trial judge that its refusal to grant Widowed Parent's Allowance to the applicant, who had not been married to her deceased partner, involved discrimination on grounds of marital status, contrary to Article 8 read with Article 14 of the Convention (the widowed parent's allowance is one of the very few benefits which do make a distinction between marriage/civil partnership and cohabitation). Siobhan McLaughlin has been given leave to appeal to the Supreme Court.

The issue has been tested several times in the context of inheritance tax, which allows for an exemption for gifts between spouses. In *Holland v IRC* (2002), the Special Commissioners dismissed the appellant's argument that, although she and the deceased were not legally married, they had lived together as husband and wife for 31 years before his death and so she should be treated as his spouse for IHT purposes. The Revenue having accepted that marriage was a question of status within Art 14, and that the facts of the appeal fell within both Art 1 of Protocol No 1 and Art 8, the commissioners held (albeit *obiter*, the human rights issue having been determined on the basis that the Act had not come into force at the time of the death) that it was permissible for Parliament to legislate for different tax provisions to apply to married persons, since this reflected the fact that marriage is accompanied by mutual rights and obligations between the spouses relating to maintenance both during their lives and after their deaths. Although a challenge has come from the survivor of a same-sex couple (where the death of his partner occurred prior to 5 December 2005: *Courten v UK* (2008): see below), traditionally treated in the same way as cohabitees for tax purposes, the prospect of future challenges is unlikely. From 5 December 2005, same-sex couples who have registered their partnership under the Civil Partnership Act 2004 enjoy the same rights, and are subject to the same restrictions, as married couples under both tax and the tax credit legislation (see [51.130]). Given that heterosexual couples do not fall within the ambit of the Act, despite efforts on their behalf during the passage of the Civil Partnership Bill through Parliament, it was thought that this issue remained a live one, and that challenges would be brought before the higher courts. When the challenge did eventually come, it was before the ECtHR, and from two sisters, who had lived together all their lives, and for the last 30 years in a jointly owned house which they had had built on land inherited from their parents (*Burden v UK* (2006, 2008); see [55.21]). They argued that they could properly be regarded as being in a similar situation to a married couple or civil partners, and the fact that the IHT spouse exemption was not available to them amounted to discrimination and a breach of Art 1 of Protocol No 1 along with Art 14. Although the government claimed that the applicants' position was brought about by accident of birth rather than through a voluntary commitment to one another, the sisters maintained that they had chosen to live together in a loving, committed and stable relationship, and that their actions in doing so were just as much an expression of their respective self-determination and personal development as would have been the case had they been joined by marriage or a civil partnership. In following *Lindsay v UK* (1986), the majority of the Chamber of the ECtHR (2006) decided that a state is at liberty to pursue policies to promote marriage through its tax system, and to make available the same fiscal privileges attendant on marriage to same-sex couples who had demonstrated their commitment though entering a civil partnership. However, even assuming that a comparison could be made between the sisters and married couples or civil partners, the difference in their treatment was not inconsistent with Art 14. In reaching this conclusion, the court had to assess whether the means used by the government (the IHT spouse exemption available only to spouses and civil partners) were proportionate to the aim pursued (encouraging marriage and committed single-sex unions), and whether it was objectively and reasonably justifiable to deny co-habiting siblings the IHT exemption. It said:

> '[A]ny system of taxation, to be workable, has to use broad categorisations to distinguish between different groups of taxpayers ... The implementation of any such scheme must, inevitably, create marginal situations and individual cases of apparent hardship or injustice, and it is primarily for the state to decide how best to strike the balance between raising revenue and pursuing social objectives.'

Accordingly, the policy enacted in the Inheritance Tax Act 1984 did not exceed the government's very wide margin of appreciation, and the sisters' claim was unsuccessful. Note should be taken of two dissenting judgments, one of which argued that it was not good enough for the court to recognise that there existed 'marginal situations' without at the same time justifying how such injustice could be justified and that, as far as the sisters' relationship was concerned, 'unless some compelling reasons can be shown, the legislation cannot simply ignore that such unions also exist'.

The applicants' case was more recently heard by the Grand Chamber of the ECtHR (2008) which, by a large majority, reached the same conclusion as the Chamber, but by a different and shorter route. Their analysis was simply that, for the purposes of Art 14, the applicants, as cohabiting sisters, could not be compared to a married or civil partnership couple:

> 'As with marriage, the Grand Chamber considers that the legal consequences of civil partnership under the 2004 Act, which couples expressly and deliberately decide to incur, set these types of relationship apart from other forms of cohabitation. Rather then the length or the supportive nature of the relationship, what is determinative is the existence of a public undertaking, carrying with it a body of rights and obligations of a contractual nature. Just as there can be no analogy between married and Civil Partnership Act couples, on the one hand, and heterosexual or homosexual couples who choose to live together but not to become husband and wife or civil partners, on the other hand ... the absence of such a legally binding agreement between the applicants renders their relationship of cohabitation, despite its long duration, fundamentally different to that of a married or civil partnership couple.'

Accordingly, there had been no discrimination and thus no violation of Art 14 taken in conjunction with Art 1 of Protocol No 1. Of the

17 judges who made up the Grand Chamber, two agreed with the final conclusion of the majority but preferred the earlier reasoning of the Chamber of the ECtHR, and two dissented. One of the dissenters, Judge Borrego Borrego, believed that the majority of the Grand Chamber had failed to follow protocol by not ruling on the question of 'whether or not granting inheritance tax exemption to same-sex couples in a civil partnership but not to the applicant sisters, who are also a same-sex couple, is a measure proportionate to the legitimate aim pursued'. The other dissenter, Judge Zupančič (who, interestingly, suggested that the taxation of inheritance was inherently questionable), was of the view that, in effect, marriage was the cut-off criterion for differentiation between different classes; once the Government had extended the IHT exemption to another mode of association, namely civil partners, this opened the door for a reconsideration of whether denial of the tax advantage to others was rationally related to a legitimate government interest.

The one difficulty with the majority view is that no account was taken of the fact that, unlike cohabiting heterosexual or same-sex couples, siblings are not in a position to marry (or enter into a civil partnership), and are thus excluded from the advantage of the tax exemption. It was for this reason that such a relationship was given express consideration during the passage through Parliament of the Civil Partnership Act, albeit that it was left until some later date to deal with the issue. That same issue, but this time in relation to a same-sex cohabiting couple, arose more recently in *Courten v UK* (2008). The applicant, whose same-sex partner died prior to the enactment of the Civil Partnership Act 2005, sought to distinguish *Burden* (upon which the UK Government relied) on the ground that while relationships based on consanguinity could be distinguished from married couples and civil partners, this ground of distinction could not apply to cohabiting same sex couples. Having established that he was in an analogous position to married heterosexual couples, he claimed that, at the relevant time (before 5 December 2005), he had no choice about cohabiting without a legally binding agreement and that the difference in treatment amounted to discrimination contrary to Art 14. In dismissing his claim, the court noted that legislation had subsequently been introduced to provide same-sex couples with a formal mechanism for giving legal effect to their union, including exemption from inheritance tax under the Inheritance Tax Act 1984, s 18, and confirmed the margin of appreciation afforded to Governments in relation to the timing of that legislation. The UK Government was thus exonerated from any criticism in not introducing the legislation at an earlier date, which would have enabled the applicant to benefit from the exemption. [55.43]

(3) *Discrimination on the grounds of gender* Such discrimination would appear to be hard to justify. A provision (now abolished) which allowed for a widow's bereavement allowance but not a widower's, has now been the subject of three challenges, two before the ECtHR and the other before the domestic courts. In the first case before the ECtHR, in order to avoid a hearing before the court, the UK Government conceded the point and reached a settlement of the case. This involved paying out

the same amount to the widower as would have been given to a widow (*Crossland v IRC* (1999)). However, in the wake of the Revenue's refusal to provide the same treatment for other widowers in the same position, an unsuccessful application to the High Court for judicial review of this refusal was made (*R (on the application of Wilkinson) v IRC* (2002)). Further appeals to the Court of Appeal (2003) and to the House of Lords (2005) were also unsuccessful. (It is interesting to note that, although each court reached the same ultimate conclusion, the reasoning and conclusions on particular claims differed.) In the higher courts, it was common ground that the offending provision was discriminatory, with no objective justification for the discrimination resulting from the widow's bereavement allowance, and thus incompatible with Art 14. *Prima facie*, the refusal of the allowance amounted to an unlawful act on the part of HMRC (HRA 1998 s 6(1)). The issues remaining to be decided were *first*, whether the Revenue had power to afford to the taxpayer an extra-statutory concession by way of income tax deduction equivalent to the allowance in question: if there was no such power, the Revenue could not have acted differently than it had done (HRA 1998 s 6(2)(a)), and this would provide an exclusion from s 6(1); *second*, if it did have such power, whether it was *obliged* to grant such a reduction to the taxpayer on the basis that the action was necessary to give effect to provisions which were not compatible with Convention rights (HRA 1998 s 6(2)(b)); and *third*, whether the Revenue was obliged at common law, as a matter of fairness, to give the allowance to widowers in the light of the settlement of Mr Crossland's case before the ECtHR. In respect of the first issue, the House of Lords were in total agreement with the Court of Appeal which, having reviewed the authorities dealing with both the Revenue's powers to care for, manage and collect the various taxes under TMA 1970 s 1, and their ability to make extra-statutory concessions, held that they were not authorised to grant the taxpayer an extra-statutory allowance in the form of a tax reduction.

Lord Hoffmann said:

> 'This discretion enables the commissioners to formulate policy in the interstices of the tax legislation, dealing pragmatically with minor or transitory anomalies, cases of hardship at the margins or cases in which a statutory rule is difficult to formulate or its enactment would take up a disproportionate amount of Parliamentary time. The commissioners publish extra-statutory concessions for the guidance of the public and Miss Rose drew attention to some which she said went beyond mere management of the efficient collection of the revenue. I express no view on whether she is right about this, but if she is, it means that the commissioners may have exceeded their powers under section 1 of TMA. It does not justify construing the power so widely as to enable the commissioners to concede, by extra-statutory concession, an allowance which Parliament could have granted but did not grant, and on grounds not of pragmatism in the collection of tax but of general equity between men and women.' (*R v IRC ex parte Wilkinson* (2005)).

Although the conclusion reached in respect of the first issue made argument in respect of the second untenable, the House of Lords nevertheless dealt with it briefly, taking the view that, had the Revenue the power to grant an extra-statutory allowance to widowers to match the widow's bereavement allowance, they would not have been obliged to exercise that power in order to avoid a breach of Convention rights. Lord Hoffmann said:

> 'The reason why the commissioners are protected by section 6(2)(b) is not because they were "giving effect" to section 1 of TMA by insisting that it was a discretion and not a duty. They are protected because they were giving effect to section 262 by giving the allowance only to widows. If section 6(1) "does not apply" to what they did under section 262, there is no basis for saying that a failure to make an allowance to widowers was (as a matter of domestic law) in breach of Convention rights.'

This was also the decision reached in *R (on the application of Hooper) v Secretary of State for Work and Pensions* (2005) where, despite a statutory provision in respect of certain widows' benefits, there also existed a common law power that enabled the Secretary of State to make benefits payments to widowers).

As far as the third issue was concerned, the House of Lords was unable to accept the taxpayer's argument that, in the light of the friendly settlement of *Crossland*, the HMRC's refusal to make a settlement in similar terms in the present case had caused the claimant to suffer a pecuniary loss that should be compensated by payment of damages. An award of damages is permissible under the HRA 1998, but only if it is necessary to afford the claimant 'just satisfaction'. Lord Hoffmann said that there was no justification whatever for extending the widow's allowance to men. If Parliament had paid proper regard to Art 14, it would have abolished the allowance for widows. In that event, Mr Wilkinson would not have received an allowance and no damages were therefore necessary to put him in the position in which he would have been if there had been compliance with his Convention rights. This reasoning was accepted by the ECtHR at the second hearing of the case, when *Wilkinson* re-emerged as *Hobbs v UK* (2006), with the issue of just satisfaction being the single issue to be decided. In declining to make an award in respect of pecuniary damage, the court noted that the original purpose of the allowance was to rectify an inequality that existed between widows and widowers. Prior to the tax year 2000–01, on the death of his wife, a widower was able to claim the married man's allowance in the year following her death; by contrast a widow could claim only her own single person's allowance. The widow's bereavement allowance was introduced to make up the shortfall. However, on the introduction in 1990 of independent taxation and the ability from 1993–94 onwards for married couples to choose how to share the married couple's allowance, the allowance became obsolete and, along with the married couple's allowance, it was abolished in 2000 (see [51.25]). Accordingly, between 1993–94 and 2000–01, the distinction made between widows and widowers was not reasonably and objectively justified and amounted to a violation of Convention rights. Despite this, the court was unwilling to make an award in respect of pecuniary damage on the basis that, since the underlying purpose of the allowance had ceased to exist, those widows who had received a benefit had done so as the result of an anomaly of the then current tax system. To give to widowers the equivalent of this benefit would be to perpetuate the anomaly. It should be noted that, as in the *Wilkinson/Hobbs* case, the ECtHR in *Willis v UK* (2002) held that the difference in treatment between men and women regarding entitlement to a Widow's Payment and a Widowed Mother's allowance (both social security payments) was not based on any objective and reasonable justification, and was, therefore, in violation of Art 14 of the Convention taken in conjunction with Art 1 of Protocol No 1. However, unlike the *Wilkinson/Hobbs* case, the principle of 'just satisfaction' was not in issue since the UK did not deny its obligation to pay pecuniary compensation. A further provision (now amended, see [**7.104**]) allowing for an increased allowance to a *man* married to and living with a totally incapacitated wife with a dependent child but not to a woman was similarly challenged before European Commission of Human Rights (now abolished) (*MacGregor v UK* (1997)). The Commission found that the friendly settlement of the case had been secured on the basis of respect for human rights as defined in the Convention.

Discrimination on the ground of gender was raised in *Humphreys v R & C Comrs* (2012) in relation to the receipt of child tax credit (CTC). CTC in respect of each child is payable to only one person, even where the care of the child is shared between two or more persons. Entitlement to CTC depends on who is deemed responsible for the child, and rules for determining this are set out in the Child Tax Credit Regulations 2002 (SI 2002/2007), reg 3(1). Rule 1 provides that where the child lives with one person, that person is treated as responsible. Rule 2 provides that where a child lives with two or more persons in different households, the person having 'main responsibility' for the child is treated as being responsible. In the present case, the appellant's children lived with their mother, but retained substantial contact with the appellant, spending most weekends and half of all school holidays with him. HMRC determined that the mother was the main carer, denying the appellant's claim to CTC. On appeal, he argued that the legislative scheme breached Art 14 read with Art 1 of Protocol No 1 in that it indirectly discriminated against men because, on the whole, fathers are more likely than mothers to have secondary, but nonetheless significant, responsibility for the care of their children. HMRC accepted the appellant's argument that the legislation was indirectly discriminatory, leaving the Supreme Court to answer the key question of whether that discrimination was objectively justified. In holding that it was, Lady Hale, giving the judgment of the court, said that '... the normally strict test for justification of sex discrimination ... gives way to the "manifestly without reasonable foundation" test' developed in *Stec v United Kingdom* (2006) which, she said, could apply equally to direct and indirect discrimination. In that case, which concerned state benefits, the Grand Chamber of the ECtHR confirmed that a 'difference in treatment is discriminatory if it has no objective and reasonable justification; in other words, if it does not pursue a legitimate aim or if there is not a reasonable relationship of proportionality between the means employed and the aim sought to be realized', but that when the issue concerns general measures of economic and social strategy, a wide margin of appreciation is allowed to member states. 'The Court will generally respect the legislature's policy choice unless it is 'manifestly without reasonable foundation'. However, Lady Hale said that the application of the *Stec* test did not mean that the justification put forward would escape careful scrutiny by the courts. The main factor that persuaded the Supreme Court that the rule which disallowed splitting CTC was not manifestly without reasonable justification was the very rationale for the introduction of CTC. The credit was meant to relieve child poverty and the government's view was that by paying it to the main carer in the expectation that that person would incur most of the expenditure in looking after the child was likely to be of greater benefit to the child than splitting the CTC between two carers of modest means, which could result in neither of them being able to provide adequately for the child's needs. Also of importance was the problem of how to calculate the benefit if it was to be split.

The wide margin of appreciation allowed to member states in this area was also recognised by the Supreme Court in *R (on the application of SG and others (previously JS and others)) v Secretary of State for Work and Pensions* (2015), In this case, subordinate legislation imposing a cap on the amount of welfare benefits which can be received by claimants in non-working households was challenged under the HRA 1998 primarily on the basis that it disproportionately affects single parents and domestic violence victims, who tend to be women and thus discriminates unjustifiably between men and women, contrary to Art 14 of the ECHR read with Art 1 of Protocol No 1. Amongst other grounds, the appellants argued that Parliament had not complied with its obligations to consider the best interests of the child under the United Nations Convention on the Rights of the Child (UNCRC) Art 3(1). Dismissing the appeal, Lord Reed, giving the leading judgment of the Supreme Court, said that the question was whether the established indirect discrimination was a proportionate means of meeting legitimate aims. He was of the view that the question of proportionality involved controversial issues of social and economic policy, with major implications for public spending. It was therefore necessary for the Court to give due weight to the considered assessment of a democratically-elected institution and it should be respected unless manifestly without reasonable foundation. He also stated that many of the issues in the appeal were considered by Parliament before the regulations were approved. Lord Carnwath added that the UNCRC Art 3(1) had no role in justifying discrimination against women: the treatment of the child does not depend on the sex of their parent. He stated that though the Secretary of State had failed to show how the Regulations complied with Art 3(1), the consequences were a matter of politics rather than legal. [55.44]

(4) *Discrimination between employees and self-employed persons* Different tax provisions apply to the employed (ITEPA 2003) and to the self-employed (ITTOIA 2005). One such provision permits employers to obtain a deduction for childcare expenses for employees as the provision of a benefit to its employees. Subject to certain conditions, an employee is not

taxed on that benefit. In contrast, self-employed persons can make no such deduction in respect of expenses incurred in respect of childcare. The taxpayer, a self-employed person, argued in *Carney v Nathan* (2002) that the disallowance of such expenditure constituted discrimination within Art 14 in relation to Art 1 of Protocol No 1. Her argument was dismissed by the Special Commissioner, whose brief view was that the taxpayer, as a self-employed person paying childcare expenses for herself, was not in a similar situation to an employer paying for the employee. Given that the rules allowing for deduction of expenditure are generally more generous to the self-employed than to the employed, this must be seen as a pragmatic decision. **[55.45]**

(5) *Discrimination in the exercise of a discretion in relation to a published statement of practice or extra-statutory concession* Domestic law already provides for redress on the part of a taxpayer when the Revenue refuses either to apply a published practice to a particular taxpayer, or to abide by an undertaking given after full disclosure. In light of the comments in respect of extra-statutory concessions made by both the Court of Appeal and the House of Lords in the *Wilkinson* case, it is debatable whether Art 1 of Protocol No 1 and Art 14 would provide an additional ground for redress. In any event, because of the comments made by their Lordships in the *Wilkinson* case, there has been a full review of the published extra-statutory concessions, the result of which has been that certain concessions have now been enacted and others have been withdrawn. The conclusion that must be drawn from this is that there is a belief that those concessions that remain are unlikely to prove problematic. Where extra-statutory concessions are not published, it is highly unlikely that there could be a challenge under Art 14. However, in a case where HMRC introduced a concession but deliberately did not publicise it, only offering it to certain litigants in an attempt to settle an action and to some who rang a helpline and appeared to HMRC to qualify for it, the judge remarked:

> 'What I am clear is that as a matter of *Wednesbury* unreasonable, it is unlawful to act as HMRC have done and give a concession but fail to publish it. It is a fundamental principle that HMRC should treat taxpayers equally. They cannot do this if the concession is unpublished and in effect only communicated to those who happened to be the lead appellants in the litigation or those who phoned a helpline. In this HMRC have acted as no reasonable taxing authority could have acted.'

(*L H Bishop Electrical Co Ltd & Ors v C & R Comrs* (2013) at [510]. See also **[55.49]**.) **[55.46]**

(6) *Discrimination as to prosecution* The Revenue's policy of selecting who to prosecute in cases of tax fraud has been held legitimate on the ground that the primary objective of the Board is to collect tax (*R v IRC, ex p Mead and Cook* (1992)). A taxpayer, aggrieved at being prosecuted when another guilty of a similar offence was not, may challenge the policy under Art 14. Presumably, however, the Revenue would seek to demonstrate that the policy was proportionate to the objective of collecting tax and that it was objectively justifiable. **[55.47]**

(7) *Discrimination in the use of Legal Advice Privilege (LAP)* Recently in the Supreme Court, Lord Neuberger was of the view that various decisions of the Strasbourg Court undermined the suggestion that it would be contrary to Art 14 to hold that LAP applies to communications with professional lawyers and not with other professional people such as accountants giving tax advice (*R (on the application of Prudential plc) v Special Commissioner of Income Tax* (2013); see **[55.62]**). **[55.48]**

(8) *Compulsory online filing where taxpayer disabled, elderly, etc.* In *L H Bishop Electrical Co Ltd v R & C Comrs* (2013), three of the appellants were unable to comply with regulations which required them to file their VAT returns online because of their disability, their age, or because there was little or no broadband connection in the place where they carried on their business. The First-tier Tribunal found that because of their 'disproportionate application to persons who are computer illiterate due to their age, or who have a disability which makes using a computer accurately very difficult or painful, or who live too remotely for a reliable internet connection, the regulations were an interference with Convention rights under Art 1 of Protocol No 1 and Art 8 (privacy – see IV below) combined with Art 14 which was not justified'.

HMRC did not appeal against the decision of the First-tier Tribunal. Instead, following a public consultation, they amended the regulations (VAT General Regulations 1995 (SI 1995/2518) reg 25A(6)) so that they were human rights compliant (they already contained an exemption for practising members of a religious society or order whose beliefs were incompatible with the use of electronic communications). The lessons of *Bishop* appear to have been learned at least to the extent that in the Finance Bill introduced in April 2017, the clauses intended to introduce mandatory electronic record-keeping and online quarterly reporting of business results to HMRC for income tax, corporation tax and VAT contained an exemption for those for whom it was not reasonably practicable to keep electronic records or file online by reason of disability, age, remoteness of location, or for any other reason. Those clauses were not enacted in the Finance Act 2017 but they are expected to be re-introduced in a subsequent Finance Bill. **[55.49]–[55.60]**

IV RESPECT FOR PRIVACY: ART 8

1 Scope of Article 8

Article 8 is concerned with issues of compliance. The primary protection in Art 8 is that everyone is entitled 'to respect for his private and family life, his home and his correspondence'. This does not provide a comprehensive privacy provision, and the right that is granted is subject to the limitations that any interference must be: (a) in accordance with the law; and (b) necessary in a democratic society in the interests of national security, public safety, the economic well-being of the country, the prevention of crime, the protection of health and morals and the protection of the rights and freedoms of others. In the context of taxation, a challenge to HMRC may be brought under Art 8 in respect of oppressive demands for information (*X v Belgium* (1982), *Tamosius v UK* (2002) and *Gould (t/a Garry's Private Hire) v R & C Comrs* (2007)

SpC) and searches without warrant (*Funke v France* (1993)). In *X v Belgium*, whilst the European Commission of Human Rights held that the taxpayer had suffered an interference with his privacy in having to divulge all items of his expenditure and of his receipts, it had been in the interest of the economic well-being of the country, and thus outside Art 8. A similar conclusion was reached in *Gould (t/a Garry's Private Hire) v R & C Comrs*. In dismissing a claim that an enquiry into the taxpayers' partnership accounts had been lengthy and unnecessary and a breach of Art 8, the Special Commissioner said that:

> 'while an investigation into *[the taxpayers']* private expenditure is an interference into their private life, it is in accordance with the law and is necessary in a democratic society in the economic well-being of the country that such investigation should be permitted for the purpose of establishing the true taxable profit.'

In *R (on the application of Cooke) v R & C Comrs* (2007), the court had to consider whether certain safeguards (including prior judicial sanction), which had to be satisfied where a notice is issued by a tax inspector under TMA 1970 s 20(3) (see [**4.35**]) requiring any person to produce documents relating to a taxpayer's affairs for the purpose of enquiring into his tax liability, had also to be satisfied when such notice is given instead by the Board to a barrister, advocate or solicitor in accordance with s 20B(3), albeit not specified in that provision. The central issue was whether the interference of rights protected by Art 8 was 'in accordance with the law'. This was said to mean that 'there must be a measure of protection in domestic law against arbitrary interferences by public authorities with the rights safeguarded by, *inter alia*, para 1 of Art 8' (*Olsson v Sweden* (1988)). The court was of the view that a distinction had to be made between, for example, a search made under TMA 1970 s 20C (see [**4.156**]) and a notice given under s 20(3); the former is both more intrusive than the latter, and less amenable to a pre-emptive judicial remedy by the taxpayer. Any need for judicial scrutiny where a s 20(3) notice is given by the Board in accordance with s 20B(3) is adequately met by the availability of judicial review. Accordingly, no prior judicial sanction is required in such a case. (The relevant provisions have since been replaced by powers to obtain the tax files of an agent who has either had a dishonest conduct determination made against him and either not appealed against or confirmed on appeal, which themselves are subject to prior judicial approval – FA 2012 Sch 38.) In contrast, in *Funke v France* (1992), searches were made by customs officers at a time when no judicial sanctions were in place. The taxpayer agreed to give up certain documents, but subsequently retracted. As a consequence of the searches, fines were imposed upon the taxpayer. The ECtHR held that the searches were a direct interference in privacy and that, accordingly, this was an infringement of Art 8. In looking at whether the searches were necessary and proportionate, the court took into consideration the need for adequate judicial supervision in addition to the requirement in the Article itself. [55.61]

2 Legal professional privilege

Described by the Supreme Court of the US as 'the oldest of the privileges for confidential communications known to the common law' (*Upjohn Company v United States* 449 US 383, 389 (1981), cited by Lord Sumption in *R (on the* application of *Prudential plc v Special Commissioner of Income Tax* (2013)), legal professional privilege (LPP) is a single integral privilege, whose sub-heads are legal advice privilege (LAP) and litigation privilege (*Three Rivers District Council v Governor and Company of the Bank of England (No 6)* (2005) per Lord Carswell). Where LPP attaches to a communication between a legal adviser and a client, the client is entitled to object to any third party seeing the communication for any purpose unless (i) the client agrees to or waives its right; (ii) a statute provides expressly that the privilege can be overridden; (iii) the document concerned was prepared for, or in connection with, nefarious purposes; or (iv) one of a few miscellaneous exceptions apply (*Prudential plc* (2013) per Lord Neuberger). Unsurprisingly, questions have arisen as to whether taxpayers are protected by LPP when required by the Revenue to produce documents. Although breach of a convention right is not necessarily pleaded in such cases, the domestic courts have relied upon decisions of the ECtHR in finding for the taxpayer. Thus, in *R (on the application of Morgan Grenfell & Co Ltd) v Special Commissioner of Income Tax* (2002), the issue was whether the taxpayer was protected against a notice under TMA 1970 s 20(1)) requiring production of documents covered by legal professional privilege. (This was one of the cases where breach of a Convention right had not been pleaded – the issue centred on the specific words of s 20(1)). In holding that it was, the House of Lords, citing the ECtHR case of *Foxley v UK* (2000), confirmed that privilege is a fundamental human right which can be derogated from only in exceptional circumstances. Lord Hoffmann doubted that these exceptional circumstances would include the public interest in the collection of financial information by the Revenue and suggested that if new information-gathering legislation were to be passed, then any interference with privilege would have to be shown to have a legitimate aim necessary in a democratic society. Such legitimate aim was tested in *Tamosius v UK* (2002), in which case the ECtHR rejected the complaint that the issue and execution of search warrants in connection with a Revenue investigation into an alleged tax fraud was in breach of Art 8, particularly in regard to documents covered by legal professional privilege. Whilst there was no dispute that the search constituted an interference with the applicant's rights under Art 8, because it had been carried out in accordance with the law and in pursuit of the prevention of crime and disorder, such interference was to be regarded as 'necessary in a democratic society' within the terms of Art 8(2). Scrutiny by the judge issuing the warrant, along with the prohibition on removing documents protected by legal professional privilege, provided sufficient safeguards against possible abuse.

Whilst there is little doubt that human rights command, and the courts continue to uphold, that access to legal advice on a private and confidential basis is a fundamental principle that should not lightly be interfered with (see, for example, *Bowman v Fels* (2005)), what has recently been in contention is the issue of whether LAP should extend to communications between client and accountant. In *R (on the application of Prudential plc) v Special Commissioner of Income Tax* (2010), the appellants argued that they should not be required to disclose documents relating to legal advice in connection with tax matters given to them by the accountants PwC. In the lower courts, leading counsel for Prudential submitted that previous decisions on the issue should not be regarded as binding since they were decided prior to the HRA 1998, and argued that a determining factor in the application of LAP is not the status of the advisor but, rather, the nature of the advice and thus the function of the advisor. As far as the giving of tax advice is concerned, lawyers and accountants tend to serve virtually the same function; thus, it was argued, why should both not enjoy the benefit of LPP? The Court of Appeal rejected this argument, Lloyd LJ, delivering the decision of the court, concluding that, despite arguments based on human rights, they were bound by a previous Court of Appeal decision (*Wilden Pump Engineering Co v Fusfeld* (1985)) and confirmed that LPP does not apply at common law to any professional other than a qualified lawyer, that is, a solicitor, barrister or an appropriately qualified foreign lawyer. Moreover, Lloyd LJ held further that even if they had not been bound by precedent, they would have concluded that it was not open to the court to hold that LPP applies outside the legal profession. He said:

> 'It is the essence of the rule that it should be clear and certain in its application, since it is not the subject of any ad hoc balancing exercise but is, to all intents and purposes, absolute. As applied to members of the legal profession, acting as such, it is sufficiently clear and certain. If it were to apply to members of other professions who give advice on points of law in the course of their professional activity, serious questions would arise as to its scope and application. To which accountants should it apply, given that "accountant" does not by itself denote membership of any particular professional body, or the obligation to comply with any, or any particular, professional obligations? To which other professional advisers would it apply? To what areas of the law would it apply as regards the advice of any adviser who is not a lawyer as such? These questions are serious and important, and would require a clear answer in order that the scope and application of the extended LPP should be known and understood.'

In an unsuccessful appeal to the Supreme Court, Lord Neuberger, building upon Lloyd LJ's judgment, said that to extend privilege to professional advisers other than those in the legal professions was, for three reasons, a matter for Parliament. *First*, the consequences of extending privilege were hard to assess and would lead to a clear principle becoming unclear; *second*, the whole question raises issues of policy, which should be left to Parliament to decide; and finally, Parliament had enacted legislation relating to LAP, which at the very least suggests that it would be inappropriate for the court to extend the law on LAP. It should be noted that Lord Sumption and Lord Clarke dissented and were of the view that because LPP and its constituent elements developed to protect *the client*, there was no reason to deny such privilege to the communications in question if the material requisitioned by the respondent would have been privileged if a solicitor or barrister had performed the functions that the accountant in the case had performed.

This same issue has arisen in respect of a piece of legislation (FA 2004 ss 306–319: see **Chapter 5**), which requires the 'promoter' of certain tax avoidance schemes to notify HMRC of any proposal or arrangements falling within the disclosure rules set out in attendant regulations. Following discussions with the Law Society of England and Wales on the scope of LPP, the Government decided to amend the Regulations to remove any uncertainty that tax schemes marketed and designed by lawyers had to be disclosed. The effect of the revised regulations is that (i) a lawyer who is unable to comply fully with the disclosure rules on the grounds of LPP will not be a promoter in respect of those arrangements; but (ii) the client who uses the arrangements has to disclose them instead unless there is another promoter (for example, an accountant) who is liable to comply with the disclosure requirement. Accountants who are promoters of arrangements are required to disclose them in all the circumstances specified in the regulations.   [55.62]–[55.80]

V   THE RIGHT TO A FAIR HEARING: ART 6

One of the cornerstones of the Convention, Art 6(1) entitles everyone to a 'fair and public hearing within a reasonable time by an independent and impartial tribunal established by law' in the determination of their civil rights and obligations or in respect of criminal charges against them. In the context of taxation, several issues arise. These include:
(1) the extent to which tax-related obligations are within Art 6(1), which requires either that a claimant is the subject of a criminal charge or that his 'civil rights and obligations' must have been affected;
(2) the question of the burden of proof in respect of a criminal charge;
(3) the problems concerning the privilege against self-incrimination; and
(4) whether judicial review will be found to provide a fair enough hearing to satisfy the requirements of Art 6(1). [55.81]

1   Tax-related obligations and Art 6(1)

a)   *What amounts to a criminal charge?*

The importance of establishing that a charge is a criminal one lies in the fact that the more generous protections given in Art 6 to criminal proceeding will apply (see [55.91]). Whilst it is clear that, for example, a charge under FA 2000 s 144 (fraudulent evasion of income tax) is a criminal charge, certain other provisions imposing penalties leave room for doubt. A number of decisions have been concerned with the question of whether certain tax, and ostensibly civil, penalties give rise to criminal charges within the meaning of Art 6(1). That such a penalty could be criminal in nature was confirmed by the ECtHR in *Georgiou v UK* (2001), and was applied in the High Court by Jacob J in *King v Walden* (2001), who held that the system for imposing penalties for fraudulent or negligent delivery of incorrect tax returns was criminal for the purposes of Art 6(1) because the system was punitive. When that case reached the ECtHR (*King v UK* (2004)), the court, noting that the domestic courts themselves appeared to have no doubt that the penalties should be regarded as criminal for the purposes of an examination under Art 6(1) of the Convention, affirmed that the severity of the penalties had the effect of engaging Art 6(1), and did not consider it decisive that a sentence of imprisonment was not at stake in the proceedings. In *Han v C & E Comrs* (2001), the Court of Appeal had to decide whether or not civil penalties imposed against Han and others for alleged dishonest evasion of tax provided for in the VATA 1994 s 60 gave rise to criminal charges. In upholding the decision of the Chairman of the VAT and Duties Tribunal that the penalties were 'criminal charges' for the purposes of Art 6 by a majority of two to one, the Court of Appeal's starting point was to consider the Strasbourg case law on the issue. According to the Strasbourg jurisprudence, the concept of criminal charge within the meaning of Art 6 is an autonomous one and, effectively, three criteria are applied to determine whether a criminal charge has been imposed (see *Engel v The Netherlands* (1976); *AP, MP and TP v Switzerland* (1998) and affirmed by the Grand Chamber of the ECtHR in *Ezeh and Connors v UK* (2003), a case concerning prison disciplinary offences). These are (a) the classification of the proceedings in domestic law; (b) the nature of the offence; and (c) the nature and degree of severity of the penalty that the person concerned risked incurring. In applying these criteria, Potter LJ noted that:

'... the Strasbourg Court does not in practice treat these three requirements as analytically distinct or as a three stage test, but as factors together to be weighed in seeking to decide whether, taken cumulatively, the relevant measure should be treated as criminal. When coming to such decision ... factors (b) and (c) carry substantially greater weight than factor (a).'

This means that the categorisation of the charge in domestic law is not decisive of the nature of the charge and provides only a starting point for the classification. Rather, Art 6 impels the court to look behind the appearances and examine the realities of the procedure in question. This is done by considering the second and third criteria in the cumulative rather than in the alternative. Applying the three criteria to the facts before them, the Court of Appeal was of the opinion that:

(1) the national classification of the penalties as 'civil' was merely a starting point and, moreover, that classification (which came about through the implementation of the proposals contained in the *Report of the Committee on Enforcement of Powers of Revenue Departments*, 'the Keith Report' (1983)), did not represent a decision on the part of the legislature to de-criminalise dishonest evasion of VAT;

(2) the relevant provisions applied in principle to all citizens as taxpayers and not merely to a restricted group, and sought to deter and punish rather than compensate Customs and Excise (now HMRC); and

(3) it was sufficient that the penalty was substantial and its purpose was punitive and deterrent, and there was no requirement that it should involve imprisonment.

Accordingly, looking at the substance rather than merely the form of the penalty, it was evident that it amounted to a criminal charge to which Art 6 applied. This approach was followed in *Sharkey v R & C Comrs* (2006), in which case a fixed penalty of £50 for the non-production of documents was held not to amount to a criminal charge. Although there was an element of punishment in the penalty, the High Court said that its primary function was to secure documents for the Revenue. Moreover, it was held that the possibility of further daily penalties in the future for a continued failure to produce the documents in question could not affect the classification of the fixed penalty. For its part, the ECtHR has also taken the view that 20% or 40% civil penalties were criminal for the purposes of Art 6, irrespective of the fact that no criminal intent had to be established before the penalties could be imposed (*Vastberga Taxi Association & Vulic v Sweden* (2002), and *Janosevic v Sweden* (2002) (note that the penalty in *King v UK* (2004) was of the magnitude of 80% of the lost tax). It is interesting to note that in both of these cases, the ECtHR took the view, contrary to the domestic courts, that the three criteria should be viewed as alternatives and not cumulative unless, after an analysis of each, it was impossible to reach a conclusion as to the existence of a criminal charge). The Grand Chamber of the ECtHR in *Jussila v Finland* (2006) confirmed that the second and third of the *Engel* criteria are alternatives and, although expressly agreeing with the approach in *Janosevic*, it stressed that the relative lack of severity of the penalty cannot divest an offence of its inherently criminal character. It argued that, although reference was made in *Janosevic v Sweden* to the severity of the penalty, this was a separate and additional ground for the criminal characterisation of an offence that had already been established on examination of the nature of the offence. Despite cases such as *Ali & Begum v C & E Comrs* (2002), in which the VAT Tribunal decided that serious misdeclaration penalties, default surcharges and late registration penalties were *not* criminal for the purposes of Art 6, *Jacques v R & C Comrs* (2007) where the Special Commissioners held that a penalty of £50 for non-production of documents was not a criminal charge and *Bancroft v Crutchfield* (2002) (see [55.83]), where the surcharge of 5% of unpaid tax under TMA 1970 s 59C was too small to be considered a criminal penalty, all of which seem to be at odds with the approach taken by the ECtHR (and, since *Jussila v Finland*, difficult to justify on the sole ground that the penalties imposed were far less severe than those in the two Swedish cases), the recent cases of *Bluu v R & C Comrs* (2015), *Linda Jarvis v R & C Comrs* (2015) and *Jack Dyson v R & C Comrs* (2015) have all followed the Strasbourg jurisprudence by holding that the minor nature of a penalty does not prevent it from being 'criminal' under the Convention, and that the classification under national law is not decisive. A penalty intended to punish and to deter, and which applies to taxpayers generally, is criminal in nature. Guidance originally issued to its staff by the then Inland Revenue (*Guidance to Inland Revenue Staff on Human Rights and Penalties*, Inland Revenue, 11 September 2002, see [55.85]) so as to avoid the possibility of infringing the taxpayer's right of non-incrimination and right to silence has since been incorporated into individual manuals (see, eg, IHTM 36401, dealing with human rights and penalties in connection with inheritance tax, and EM 1360, dealing with the obligations of employers).

The case of *Personal representatives of Mr Michael Wood (Deceased) v R & C Comrs* (2015) raised a slightly different issue, unconcerned with penalties (which had been dropped by HMRC in the event of the taxpayer's death and on the grounds that there could be no fair trial in the circumstances). Assessments on the personal representatives (PRs) of the deceased taxpayer were raised by HMRC under the extended time limits set out in TMA 1970 s 36(1A)(a) for the 14 tax years commencing 1992–93 in the belief that they could show that the taxpayer had acted 'deliberately' to bring about a loss of income tax or CGT. The PRs contended that the assessments should not be allowed to stand. They argued that the allegation of deliberately bringing about a tax loss constituted the taxpayer being 'charged with a criminal offence'. Since it was impossible for the PRs (without the taxpayer) to fairly contest at a hearing HMRC's allegation of deliberate behaviour by the taxpayer, especially over a period of 14 years commencing 22 years ago, forcing them to do so would be unfair and contrary to Art 6. Applying the *Engel* criteria, the judge concluded that the effect of s 36(1A)(a) is simply to enable HMRC, upon proof of the deliberate bringing about of a loss of tax, to recover from the taxpayer that which he or she could and should have paid; that recourse to the extended assessment time limit is not penal in nature – it is not to condemn or punish but simply to enable HMRC, upon proof of the deliberate bringing about of a loss of tax, to recover from the taxpayer that which he or she could and should have paid. [55.82]

b) *Civil rights and obligations*

As far as 'civil' rights are concerned, Strasbourg jurisprudence indicates that a taxpayer's obligations are outside the scope of Art 6(1) because they are 'public in nature'. It would appear that public law rights and obligations are not civil rights and obligations, whereas private law rights and obligations are. Thus, the obligations to make social security payments and to pay taxes are 'public' obligations since they derive from the citizen's 'normal civic duties in a democratic society' (see *Schouten and Meldrum v Netherlands* (1994); note also that a determination which bears directly on a person's entitlement to tax credits amounts to a determination of his civil rights: *ZM and AB v R & C Comrs* (2013)). Accordingly, in cases where the issue is one of assessment to tax, there would appear to be no guarantee of a fair hearing under Art 6(1). In *Ferrazzini v Italy* (2001), the view of the majority of the ECtHR (sitting as the Grand Chamber of 17 judges, giving an indication of the importance of the issue) was that:

> 'tax matters still form part of the hard core of public-authority prerogatives, with the public nature of the relationship between the taxpayer and the tax authority remaining predominant.'

Nonetheless, there was a strong dissenting opinion from six members of the Grand Chamber, and an indication that this might not always be the view of the court. The view was put that:

> 'as long as a dividing line between "civil" and "non-civil" rights and obligations is maintained in respect of proceedings between individuals and governments, it is important to ensure that the relevant criteria for determining what is "civil" are applied in a logical and reasonable manner – and that may make it necessary from time to time to adjust the case law in order to make it consistent in the light of recent developments.'

However, the majority decision has been affirmed by the ECtHR in *Vastberga Taxi Association Vulic v Sweden* (2002), and *Janosevic v Sweden* (2002), and was followed in *Bancroft v Crutchfield* (2002), in which case the Special Commissioner held that an appeal against a surcharge under TMA 1970, s 59C did not relate to civil rights, and in *Taylor v IRC* (2003), where the same Special Commissioner dismissed a claim by a personal representative that an appeal against a notice of determination to inheritance tax was not within a reasonable time of the death of the testator. A similar decision was reached by the High Court in *Significant v Farrell* (2005), where the applicant had claimed that the strict enforcement of a statutory provision in the domestic legislation prevented a fair hearing by the court. The same issue has been considered more recently in a number of other cases, including one in the context of

VAT, a second concerning SDLT and a third concerned with the legitimacy of the accelerated payment notice scheme (APN) and associated partner payment notice scheme, introduced by FA 2014 Chapter 3 (see [5.27]). In *R (on the application of ToTel Limited) v The First-tier Tribunal (Tax Chamber) and HM Treasury* (2011), the claimant, who was paid a refund of input tax, wished to make an appeal against HMRC's subsequent efforts to recoup that refund but was required to pay or deposit the sums assessed as payable to VAT before the hearing of appeals challenging the assessments. The First-tier Tribunal had dismissed the claimant's application that it should be relieved of making such payment on the grounds of hardship. The claimant sought to appeal that decision. Contrary to indications given by the Tribunal during the course of the hearing, there is no right of appeal on a point of law by reason of VATA 1994 s 84(3C), which provides that the decision of the tribunal as to the issue of hardship is final. One of the arguments put forward by the claimant was that the conduct of HMRC infringed its rights under Art 1 of Protocol No 1 and Art 6. Having rejected the claimant's argument under Art 1 of Protocol No 1 on grounds of the wide margin of appreciation afforded to Contracting States in the area of taxation, the High Court addressed the issue of Art 6. It concluded that that the case of *Ferrazzini* provided 'the clear and common jurisprudence of the European Court of Human Rights', which should be followed in the absence of special circumstances (per Lord Slynn, *R v Alconbury Developments Ltd* (2002)). The view of both the framers of the European Convention on Human Rights and the European Court of Human Rights is that tax disputes are excluded from the civil aspect of Article 6.1. Irrespective of the merits of the case, this part of the decision is unfortunate. There was little deep analysis by the judge of the issue and no reference to published work that argued, by analogy with social security and state employment cases, that the approach of the court towards tax cases was now outdated (ToTel's appeal to the Court of Appeal (2012) was successful on the alternative ground that the provision was *ultra vires*. Accordingly, the appeal on the substantive issue was heard by the Upper Tribunal and dismissed (2014) – see [55.21]). In *R (on the application of APVCO 19 Limited) v HM Treasury and R & C Comrs* (2015) (see [55.21]), a case concerning retrospective legislation to prevent avoidance of SDLT, in which it had been argued on behalf of the appellant that the legislative changes deprived them of a fair and public hearing before the First-tier Tribunal and the courts, the Court of Appeal firmly endorsed *Ferrazzini* and rejected the argument that an analogy should be drawn between the approach to the determination of whether there is 'any criminal charge against him' and of 'his civil rights and obligations'. Vos LJ explained that whereas in the former case, the starting point is to determine whether the offence charged is, according to national law, criminal or disciplinary or both and the autonomous definition adopted by the ECtHR then requires other factors to be addressed, there is no equivalent approach to the question of whether a right or obligation is 'civil'. He said that it 'is simply established autonomously that tax disputes are not "civil" for the purposes of article 6'. The same view was taken by Green J in *Walapu v R & C Comrs* (2016), in which case the taxpayer, who had used a marketed tax avoidance scheme for the express purpose, included in his tax return for the tax year 2007–08 a claim for a rebate of over £100,000 based on the losses arising from the scheme. HMRC paid the rebate just before its computer flagged his self-assessment record with a caution to stop repayments arising from the scheme, which had been notified under DOTAS. HMRC was unable to correct its mistake until the APN regime was introduced six years later, at which time it was able to issue notices demanding immediate payment of any disputed tax without the matter being decided by a court or tribunal. Accordingly, HMRC issued the taxpayer with an APN demanding the return of the rebate, and the taxpayer challenged the notice on various grounds including violation of his human rights. His application for judicial review claimed that the APN system gave HMRC powers that it was using unfairly and unjustly, and which gave him no right of appeal. In dismissing the claim, Green J said that the 'right' at stake should be 'civil' within the autonomous meaning of that notion under Article 6 (*A K v Liechtenstein* (2015)); applying that principle to the facts of the present case, the dispute concerned a claim for relief against income tax *already* paid (by way of PAYE) and, as such, was a 'paradigm example of a tax dispute as to the sum that is owed by the taxpayer to the state'. Accordingly, on the basis of case law, this pre-assessment tax dispute was not a 'civil' dispute but a 'public' dispute between citizen and state (see also *L H Bishop Electrical Co Ltd A F Sheldon t/a Aztec Distributors v R & C Comrs* (2013), the *obiter* comment of the First-tier Tribunal judge in *Personal representatives of Mr Michael Wood (Deceased) v R & C Comrs* (2015) – see [**55.82**] and *Rowe, Worrall & Others v R & C Comrs* (2015) – see [**55.21**]). Even more unfortunate is part of a judgment in *Ross James Anderson v R & C Comrs* (2012), a case not concerned with Art 6. In rejecting the appellant's claim under Art 1 of Protocol No 1, the First-tier Tribunal saw fit to note that in *Ferrazzini* the ECtHR said that it 'considers that tax disputes fall outside the scope of civil rights and obligations [for purposes of Article 6 of the Convention]. Despite the pecuniary effects which they necessarily produce for the taxpayer'. There was no discussion of the relevance this had to the case being decided, and with respect to the learned tribunal judges, they showed a lack of understanding of Art 1 of Protocol No 1, which has been used extensively by taxpayers and with some success.

Where the issue goes beyond that of liability to tax and quantum of tax assessed, Art 6 may be invoked where a taxpayer is given no right of appeal against a particular decision, or the right of appeal is so restricted that it is impossible to exercise, or where a taxpayer is subject to an unacceptably onerous burden of proof (see *Hodgson v C & E Comrs* (1997)). [**55.83**]

(c) *Ability to scrutinise information notices*

In *Berlioz Investment Fund SA v Director of the Direct Tax Administration, Luxembourg* (2015), the French tax administration sent a notice to the Luxembourg tax administration requesting information about Berlioz pursuant to Directive 2011/16/EU on administrative co-operation in the field of taxation. The purpose of the notice was to establish whether Berlioz had lawfully received dividends from its French subsidiary free of withholding tax. The Luxembourg administration duly issued an information order to Berlioz with which Berlioz complied only in part, arguing that the information it did not provide was not foreseeably relevant to the checks being carried out in the French administration. The Luxembourg tribunal did not determine the question of the lawfulness of the information request, whereupon Berlioz appealed to the Administrative Court of Luxembourg on the grounds that the tribunal's refusal to determine the question constituted a breach of its right to an effective judicial remedy as guaranteed by Art 6(1) of the Convention. The Administrative Court referred the matter to the European Court of Justice which held (applying the Charter of Fundamental Rights of the European Union) that Berlioz must be able to argue against the legality of the information notice and whether it was 'foreseeably relevant' for the purposes of the tax administration of the Member State seeking it. It cited the OECD Council Commentary, that:

> 'Contracting states are not at liberty to engage in fishing expeditions, nor to request information that is unlikely to be relevant to the tax affairs of a given taxpayer. On the contrary, there must be a reasonable possibility that the requested information will be relevant.' [55.84]–[55.90]

2 Rights guaranteed by Art 6: the burden of proof

The importance of the question at issue in cases such as *Han* lies in the protection afforded to taxpayers by the various minimum rights provided for by Art 6(1), (2) and (3). Article 6(1) states that everyone is entitled to a fair hearing within a reasonable time by an impartial tribunal in the determination of any criminal charge against him (see, for example, *Eloranta v Finland* (2008), concerning the excessive length of the proceedings and *Walapu v R & C Comrs* (2015) (see [55.83]) where Green J, having decided that Art 6 was not engaged, went on to decide what would have been the outcome had he decided that the dispute was civil. He noted that *first*, judicial review will provide whatever level of judicial protection is needed to ensure that an individual's Article 6 rights are protected (see [55.93]; and, *secondly*, the established APN procedures allowed recipients either to complain to HMRC or to use TMA 1970 s 28A(4) to compel HMRC to issue a closure notice within a specified period, triggering the normal rights of appeal, although neither course of action would cause cancellation of the APN. However, he added that the taxpayer had produced nothing in the facts of his own case to suggest he would be denied the right to put his arguments to the appellate tribunal). That everyone charged with a criminal offence shall be presumed innocent until proved guilty is confirmed by Art 6(2). Article 6(3) guarantees certain minimum rights to everyone charged with a criminal offence. These ensure that defendants are able to defend themselves either personally or with legal assistance, that there is adequate time to prepare a defence, the right to secure the attendance of witnesses, and that they understand the charges brought against them and have the assistance of an interpreter if necessary. This last 'right' is particularly pertinent where penalties have been raised against non-English or inadequate English speakers, as in *Han* itself. Of great importance in this context is the question of the burden of proof. It might be assumed that where it has been concluded that a penalty amounts to a criminal charge, the Revenue would have to prove its case beyond all reasonable doubt, rather than on the balance of probabilities. That this is not the case was spelt out by Mance LJ in *Han*:

> 'The classification of a case as criminal for the purpose of Art 6(3) of the Convention on Human Rights … is a classification for the purposes of the Convention only.

It entitles the defendant to the safeguards provided expressly or by implication by that Article. It does not make the case criminal for all domestic purposes. In particular, it does not, necessarily, engage protections such as those provided by the Police and Criminal Evidence Act 1984.'

However, in *Ajay Chandubhai Kumar Patel v C & E Comrs* (2001) (17248), the VAT tribunal, citing the House of Lords decision in *Khawaja v Secretary of State for Home Department* (1984), considered that:

'The standard is the civil standard of the balance of probabilities; however, under Art 6(2) the appellant is innocent until proved guilty. In any event, clear evidence is needed for a finding of dishonesty; the more serious the allegation, the more cogent the evidence must be.' [55.91]

3 The privilege against self-incrimination and the right to silence

Formerly, it was believed that issues concerning a breach of Art 6 might arise where the Revenue obtained information from the taxpayer either under threat of penalty for non-compliance, or where the *Hansard* procedure had been adopted, and that information was subsequently used in criminal proceedings against the taxpayer. (The *Hansard* procedure was adopted by the Revenue in cases of tax fraud, and permitted the Board to accept a money settlement in lieu of instituting criminal proceedings in respect of the alleged fraud. Prior to changes made to the procedure (see below) no undertaking was given that such a settlement would be accepted, even if the taxpayer had made a full confession, and the Revenue's decision to exercise its discretion in favour of the taxpayer would have been influenced by the amount of co-operation given by him.) In these circumstances, the taxpayer could well have argued that his right to a fair trial had been breached because, by providing sensitive information under threat of a penalty, he had been forced to incriminate himself. This issue was considered by the House of Lords, albeit *obiter*, in *R v Allen* (2001). In that case the taxpayer, who was being investigated for tax fraud, had failed to comply with a notice (under TMA 1970 s 20(1)) requiring him to furnish the Revenue with certain information. The *Hansard* procedure having been adopted, the taxpayer answered the Revenue's questions and furnished it with, albeit false, information. He was subsequently charged with the criminal offence of cheating the public revenue and, in the House of Lords, he argued that the demands made upon him both by s 20(1) and the *Hansard* procedure had caused the information to be given involuntarily, and was a breach of his right not to incriminate himself, thus violating his right to a fair trial under Art 6 of the Convention. In fact, the trial and conviction took place before the relevant sections of the HRA 1998 had come into force on 2 October 2000. The House of Lords held that, despite the fact that the appeal was being heard after that date, the Act did not operate retrospectively to make unsafe by reason of a breach of Art 6 a conviction which was safe under English law at the time the conviction took place. Despite this, Lord Hutton gave his opinion on the issue, and he distinguished *Allen* from *Saunders v United Kingdom* (1996), a case not concerning taxation, in which the ECtHR stated that the right to silence and the right not to incriminate oneself are 'generally recognised international standards which lie at the heart of a notion of a fair procedure under Art 6'. In Lord Hutton's opinion, just as the state would be perfectly at liberty to prosecute a taxpayer for cheating the Revenue by furnishing a standard tax return containing false information:

> '... viewed against the background that the state, for the purpose of collecting tax, is entitled to require a citizen to inform it of his income and to enforce penalties for failure to do so, the s 20(1) notice requiring information cannot constitute a violation of the right against self-incrimination.'

Moreover, to the extent that there was an inducement to provide information contained in the *Hansard* procedure, it was to give true and accurate information to the Revenue. In *Allen*, the defendant failed to respond to the inducement and gave false information. Accordingly, his argument that he was induced to provide certain information in the hope of non-institution of criminal proceedings held out by the Revenue, and that its provision was therefore involuntary and in breach of Art 6(1), was invalid. However, Lord Hutton did conclude that:

> 'If, in response to the *Hansard* Statement, the appellant had given true and accurate information which disclosed that he had earlier cheated the Revenue and had then been prosecuted for that earlier dishonesty, he would have had a strong argument that the criminal proceedings were unfair and an even stronger argument that the Crown should not rely on evidence of his admission ...'

In the light of Lord Hutton's concluding words, and as a direct result of the HRA, important changes were made to the *Hansard* procedure. Much of this procedure, together with the changes, are now to be found in the Code of Practice 9 (COP 9), a combined code that covers both direct and indirect taxes. As a consequence of the changes, a taxpayer making a full confession under COP 9 is assured that HMRC will not pursue a criminal prosecution; the discretion previously enjoyed by the Revenue as to the course of action it would take following such a confession has effectively been removed. However, in addition to giving both a full and complete confession, the taxpayer must also offer full co-operation during the investigation, including the giving of full facilities for investigation into his affairs and for examination of such books, papers, documents or information as the Board may consider necessary. Without such co-operation, the taxpayer remains at risk of prosecution. However, unlike the old *Hansard* procedure, and in accordance with the view of Potter and Mance LLJ in *Han* that these are civil matters and should not be dealt with as a criminal investigation, COP 9 does not includes the PACE requirements. This means that a taxpayer will not be cautioned as to his rights, nor will meetings be tape-recorded.

In addition to the changes made to the *Hansard* procedure and now, in effect, reproduced in COP 9, the Revenue, whilst not conceding that their penalties are criminal in nature, have also issued guidance to their staff so as to avoid the possibility of infringing the taxpayer's right of non-incrimination (and also the right to silence). Revenue staff must make the taxpayer fully aware of (i) the need to provide information; (ii) the penalties that may attach if this is not done; (iii) the formal powers that can be used to obtain the necessary information should the taxpayer be unwilling to answer questions directed to him; (iv) the fact that the extent to which the taxpayer has freely and fully offered information may be taken into account in calculating the penalty; and (v) the fact that, in the event that the Revenue are unable to agree with the taxpayer, information or documents provided during the enquiry may be used in any appeal proceedings. In practice, HMRC follow the procedure outlined in Code of Practice 9 in investigating fraud, under which a taxpayer can be investigated under a civil rather than criminal process if they have entered into a contractual arrangement to make a full disclosure (the Contractual Disclosure Facility), and made a full outline disclosure under that arrangement (Fraud Civil Investigation Manual, FCIM 201010 ff). [55.92]

4 Judicial review and Art 6(1)

The First-tier Tax Chamber and the Upper Tribunal (Finance and Tax) face an overriding difficulty. Even in cases where the taxpayer is given no rights of appeal, unless the tribunal is able to construe the domestic legislation in such a way so as to comply with Art 6(1), it will be powerless under the HRA 1998. Whilst the Act enables a 'court' to make a declaration that domestic legislation is incompatible with the European Convention (which, ultimately, paves the way for remedial action), a tribunal is not a 'court' for these purposes, even though judicial review of cases by the Upper Tribunal (Finance and Tax) has the same effect as if the review had been carried out by the High Court (England and Wales) (ARTG 12020).

However, it appears that judicial review provides a fair enough hearing to satisfy the requirements of Art 6(1). In *Walapu v R & C Comrs* (2015), Green J held that the claimant was not denied rights of access to a court either at all or within a reasonable period of time because the remedy of judicial review was available. He said:

> 'The issuance of an APN involves the taking of an administrative decision by HMRC. This decision is taken following a staged process of evidence collection and evaluation. There is therefore undoubtedly a "decision" in the administrative law sense which in principle is capable of being subjected to judicial review, just as it has been in the present case. Judicial review is, it is now trite to observe, context specific and it will also take account of the existence of other remedies. This might mean that judicial review will be refused until a person has exhausted other remedies, such as an appeal procedure; or it might limit the scope and intensity of review taking into account the existence of other remedies. The important point is that judicial review will provide whatever level of judicial protection is needed to ensure that an individual's Article 6 rights are protected.' [55.93]–[55.100]

VI HUMAN RIGHTS AND EU LAW

If the area of law in question is governed by EU law, all the principles of the European Convention, which underpin EU law, will apply in any event and every court and tribunal has power to take the provisions of the European Convention into account. This principle has been restated in *Marks & Spencer v C & E Comrs* (2002) (although, on the facts of the case, it was unnecessary to consider the arguments based on this principle). Provided that it applies, EU law is not subject to the limitations imposed by the HRA 1998 on tribunals (see **[55.93]**). This means that arguments about incompatibility of domestic law with the European Convention can be made before the Tax Tribunals (see also *Ali v Begum* (2002) where the former VAT Tribunal recognised that there might be circumstances where the Union protection of human rights confers greater procedural protection than Art 6 of the Convention). **[55.101]**

Index

[all references are to paragraph number, which appear after the text paragraph]

A

Abatement
  inheritance tax on death, and 30.121–30.122
Absolute interests in residue
  estates in administration, and 17.52–17.54
Accelerated payments
  tax avoidance, and 5.28
Acceptance in lieu
  heritage property relief, and 31.90
Accounting costs
  trading income, and 10.147
Accounting dates
  trading income, and 10.196–10.200
Accounting policies
  trading income, and 10.66
Accounting practice
  change of accounting basis 10.72
  financial reporting standards 10.64
  introduction 10.63
  materiality 10.65
  policies 10.66
  provisions 10.67
Accounting to HMRC
  employment income, and 8.199
Accounts
  limited liability partnerships, and 45.7
  trading income, and 10.61
Accrued income scheme
  And see **Tax avoidance**
  generally 3.12
  overview 3.4
Accumulation and maintenance trusts
  capital gains tax, and 24.27
  inheritance tax, and 32.53
  settlements not subject to relevant property regime, and
    created pre-22 March 2006 33.64
    introduction 33.63
    transitional provisions 33.67

Accumulation and maintenance trusts – *contd*
  settlements subject to relevant property regime, and 34.91–34.98
Acquisition of company
  considerations on assets sale
    purchaser 47.33
    vendor 47.32
  considerations on share sale
    pre-sale dividend strip 47.36
    pre-sale stock dividends 47.37
    purchaser 47.35
    vendor 47.34
  introduction 47.31
  loan notes, by 47.39
  share issue, by 47.38
Acquisition of interests
  loan interest, and
    close companies 7.45
    co-operatives 7.47
    partnerships 7.46
  stamp duty land tax, and 49.33
Acquisition relief
  stamp duty land tax, and 49.79
A-Day
  And see **Pension schemes**
  generally 50.8
Adjudication
  stamp duty, and 49.112
Adjusted total income
  net income, and 7.42
Administrative expenses
  family taxation, and 51.111
  trusts, and 16.5
Administrative machinery
  appeals
    And see **Appeals**
    First-tier Tribunal 4.201–4.209
    introduction 4.173
    legislative basis 4.173
    preliminary stages 4.178–4.185

Administrative machinery – *contd*
  appeals – *contd*
    summary of new system 4.176
    Upper Tribunal 4.210–4.213
  assessment of tax
    Code of Practice 9 4.52
    Contractual Disclosure Facility 4.53
    disclosure opportunities 4.54
    discovery assessments 4.41–4.43
    enquiries 4.33
    failure to make returns or payment on time 4.27
    fraud investigations 4.50–4.54
    Hansard procedure 4.50–4.51
    interest 4.32
    payment 4.23
    penalties 4.25–4.26
    returns 4.22
    self assessment 4.21
  Code of Practice 9 4.52
  collection of tax 4.24
  Contractual Disclosure Facility 4.53
  disclosure rules
    And see **Disclosure rules**
    accelerated payments 5.28
    annual tax on enveloped dwellings 5.15–5.16
    conclusions 5.31
    direct taxes 5.4–5.17
    DOTAS 5.4–5.17
    follower notices 5.29
    indirect taxes 5.21–5.26
    inheritance tax 5.12–5.14
    introduction 5.3
    POTAS rules 5.30
    scope 5.3
    stamp duty land tax 5.11
    VADR 5.21–5.26
    widening scope 5.12
  discovery assessments 4.41–4.43
  enquiries 4.33
  failure to make returns or payment on time 4.27
  fraud investigations
    Code of Practice 9 4.52
    Contractual Disclosure Facility 4.53
    disclosure opportunities 4.54
    Hansard procedure 4.50–4.51
  Hansard procedure 4.50–4.51
  HM Revenue and Customs
    creation 4.2
    information powers 4.54–4.168
  information powers
    And see **Information powers**

Administrative machinery – *contd*
  information powers – *contd*
    civil investigatory powers 4.161–4.168
    criminal investigatory powers 4.56–4.160
    introduction 4.54
    PACE, under 4.59–4.158
    SOCPA, under 4.160
  interest 4.32
  introduction 4.1
  payment 4.23
  penalties 4.25–4.26
  reform proposals 5.1
  returns 4.22
  self assessment 4.21
  stamp duty, and 49.111
  stamp duty land tax, and 49.90
  value added tax, and 38.2
Advance corporation tax
  And see **Distributions**
  introduction 42.41–42.42
  utilisation of surplus 42.46–42.48
Advowsons
  stamp duty land tax, and 49.32
Age allowance
  income tax, and 7.103
Age 18–25 trust
  inheritance tax, and 32.58
  settlements not subject to relevant property regime, and 33.111
Age-related married couple's allowance
  basic requirements 51.21
  introduction 51.20
  restriction of relief 51.22
  use 51.23
Agency workers
  employment income, and
    introduction 8.31
    managed services company legislation 8.34
    operation of rules 8.32
    services provided to public sector authorities 8.33
Agricultural buildings
  capital allowances, and 48.121
Agricultural expenses
  income from land, and 12.46
Agricultural property relief
  'agricultural property' 31.62
  agricultural land or pasture 31.63
  agricultural tenancies 31.72
  'agricultural value' 31.67
  amount 31.68

Agricultural property relief – *contd*
  business property relief, and 31.77
  'character appropriate' test 31.65–31.66
  clawback 31.72
  companies, and 31.70
  double discounting 31.75
  farmhouses 31.65–31.66
  intensive farming buildings 31.64
  interest in possession trusts, and 33.30
  introduction 31.62
  lotting 31.74
  milk quota 31.76
  occupation requirement 31.69
  ownership requirement 31.69
  reservations, and 31.78
  settlements not subject to relevant property regime, and 33.30
  technical provisions 31.71
  transitional relief 31.75
  trusts, and 31.70
Alimony
  foreign income, and 18.41
Alternative charges
  miscellaneous income, and 13.14
Amalgamations, reconstructions and takeovers
  capital gains tax, and
  business relief 22.104
Amateur sports clubs
  And see **Charities**
  generally 53.101
Annual allowance
  pensions, and
    divorce settlements 50.23
    generally 50.12
Annual exemption
  capital gains tax, and
    family taxation, and 51.56
    generally 19.50–19.57
    trusts 25.143
  capital gains tax on death, and 21.64
  marital breakdown, and 52.22
Annual investment allowance
  generally 48.28
  trading income, and 10.135
Annual parties and functions
  employment income, and 8.168
Annual payments
  ambit of charge 14.2
  annuities 14.15
  anti-avoidance, and 14.12
  basis of assessment 14.4
  capital gains tax, and 22.3

Annual payments – *contd*
  charge to tax
    bona fide commercial reasons 14.16
    introduction 14.14
    payment by individual 14.15
  charging provisions 14.1
  charitable covenants 14.12
  collection of tax 14.45–14.46
  companies 14.5
  deduction of tax at source
    collection of deductions 14.45–14.46
    effect of failure to make 14.26
    generally 14.22
    introduction 14.21
    operation of s 448 ITA 2007 14.23–14.24
    payments outside the tax net 14.28
    position of recipient 14.25
    use of formulae 14.27
  discretionary trusts, and 14.15
  Gift Aid, and 14.13
  income arising 14.3
  interest, and 14.17
  introduction 14.1
  maintenance payments, and 14.13
  not otherwise charged
    generally 13.6–13.8
    introduction 14.8
  partnership annuities, and 14.16
  patent royalties, and 14.44
  payments outside the tax net 14.28
  purpose 14.11
  Schedule D, and 14.1
  taxation 14.11–14.13
  terminology 14.6–14.8
Annual returns
  value added tax, and 38.57
Annual tax on enveloped dwellings (ATED)
  charitable companies 53.132
  description of arrangements 5.16
  generally 5.15
  introduction 5.7, 49.1
  overview 49.86
Annuitants
  estates in administration, and 17.44–17.47
  trusts, and 16.64
Annuities
  And see **Annual payments**
  capital gains tax
    generally 22.3
    partnerships 44.34
  deceased's estate 17.6

Annuities – *contd*
foreign employment income 18.50
income tax
  generally 14.15
  introduction 14.1
  partnerships 44.14–44.16
payment by continuing partners 14.16
  capital gains tax 44.34
  income tax 44.14–44.16
retirement annuities 44.17
Anti-avoidance
And see **Tax avoidance**
annual payments, and 14.12
annual tax on enveloped
  dwellings 49.86
charitable gifts, and 53.116
consortium relief, and 43.47
deferral relief, and 15.98
Enterprise Investment Scheme,
  and 15.57
general anti-abuse rule (GAAR)
  Aaronson Report 3.75–3.81
  experience of other
    jurisdictions 3.82
  introduction 3.74
  key principles 3.80
  proposals 5.1
groups of companies, and
  capital gains 43.127
  consortium relief 43.47
interest in possession trusts, and
  application of rules 33.18
  how to avoid the rules 33.20
  operation of rules 33.19
land, and
  application of provision 12.104
  avoiding provision 12.111
  conditions 12.104–12.107
  connected persons 12.107
  disposal of land 12.105
  effect of provision 12.103
  generally 12.101
  introduction 3.6
  opportunities to make gain 12.109
  other matters 12.112
  shares in landholding
    companies 12.108
  trading stock 12.106
  trading transactions 12.102
limited liability partnerships,
  and 45.22
loss relief, and 11.122
losses, and 19.48
non-resident companies, and 27.112
premiums, and 12.83

Anti-avoidance – *contd*
Seed Enterprise Investment Scheme,
  and 15.134
settlements not subject to relevant
  property regime, and
  33.18–33.20
stamp duty land tax, and
  annual tax on enveloped
    dwellings 49.86
  disclosure of tax avoidance scheme
    rules 49.87–49.89
  generally 49.85
  high value residential
    property 49.86
targeted anti-avoidance rules
  (TAAR) 3.1
targeted loss buying 41.65
transactions in UK land
  application of provision 12.104
  avoiding provision 12.111
  conditions 12.104–12.107
  connected persons 12.107
  disposal of land 12.105
  effect of provision 12.103
  generally 12.101
  introduction 3.6
  opportunities to make gain
    12.109
  other matters 12.112
  shares in landholding
    companies 12.108
  trading stock 12.106
  trading transactions 12.102
transfer of assets abroad, and
  chargeable income 18.118
  general 18.111
  'individuals ordinarily resident in
    the UK' 18.112
  introduction 18.110
  legislative reforms 18.127–18.128
  liability of non-transferors
    18.120–18.125
  liability of transferor 18.114–18.119
  powers to obtain
    information 18.126
  purpose 18.113
  remittance basis for non-
    domiciliaries 18.119
trusts, and
  background 16.91
  benefits received by unmarried
    infant children from parental
    settlements 16.95–16.97
  charge to tax 16.94
  conclusions 16.107

Anti-avoidance – *contd*
  trusts, and – *contd*
    effect of rules 16.92
    introduction 16.91–16.94
    receipt of capital benefits 16.106
    'settlement' 16.93
    settlor retains interest in
      settlement 16.98–16.105
  value shifting, and
    controlling shareholdings 26.62
    introduction 26.61
    leases 26.63
    overview 19.75
    tax-free benefits resulting 26.64
Anti-avoidance (trusts)
  background 16.91
  bare trusts for infants 16.97
  benefit to spouse or civil
    partner 16.102
  benefits received by unmarried
    infant children from parental
    settlements
    bare trusts for infants 16.97
    basic rule 16.95
    other points 16.96
    vulnerable beneficiaries 16.96
  charge to tax 16.94
  conclusions 16.107
  effect of rules 16.92
  introduction 16.91–16.94
  non-domiciled settlors 16.105
  receipt of capital benefits 16.106
  retention of benefit 16.101
  'settlement' 16.93
  settlor retains interest in
    settlement
    basic rule 16.98
    benefit to spouse or civil
      partner 16.102
    exceptions for certain types of
      income 16.103
    inter-relationship with former
      rules 16.100
    non-domiciled settlors 16.105
    other taxes 16.99
    retention of benefit 16.101
    settlor not to be regarded as
      retaining an interest 16.104
  vulnerable beneficiaries 16.96
Anti flip flop legislation
  generally 27A.171–27A.176
  taxing UK domiciled settlor of
    offshore trust 27A.87–27A.89
Anti-Tax Avoidance Directive
  EU law, and 54.98

Antiques
  capital gains tax, and 22.22
Appeals
  capital gains tax deferral relief,
    and 15.96
  closure notice applications 4.180
  Court of Appeal 4.213
  First-tier Tribunal
    appeals from 4.209
    basic cases 4.203
    complex cases 4.205
    costs of proceedings 4.208
    decision notices 4.207
    default paper cases 4.202
    introduction 4.201
    paper cases 4.202
    procedure 4.206
    standard cases 4.204
  inheritance tax, and 28.221
  introduction 4.173
  legislative basis 4.173
  litigation and settlement strategy of
    HMRC 4.183
  postponement of tax 4.182
  preliminary stages
    closure notice applications 4.180
    litigation and settlement strategy of
      HMRC 4.183
    postponement of tax 4.182
    referral of questions during
      enquiry 4.181
    review procedure 4.185
    right to appeal 4.178
    self-assessment closure
      procedure 4.179
    settlement agreements 4.184
  referral of questions during
    enquiry 4.181
  review procedure 4.185
  right to appeal 4.178
  self-assessment closure
    procedure 4.179
  settlement agreements 4.184
  summary of new system 4.176
  Upper Tribunal
    appeals from 4.213
    costs of proceedings 4.212
    introduction 4.210
    publication of decisions 4.211
  working tax credit, and 51.39
Appointment
  estates in the course of administration,
    and
    tax consequences 17.58
    treatment of income 17.59

Apportionment
  estates in administration, and 17.26
  miscellaneous income, and 13.17
  value added tax, and
    de minimis rule 38.88
    generally 38.82
    methods 38.85–38.87
    partial exemption, and 38.83–38.84
    special methods 38.87
    standard method 38.86
Appropriations
  stock in trade, and 19.71
Approved alterations
  value added tax, and 39.25A
Approved share schemes
  And see **Tax-advantaged share schemes**
  company share option plans 9.76
  enterprise management
    incentives 9.83–9.87
  general treatment 9.71–9.72
  NICs 9.90
  PAYE 9.88–9.89
  requirements 9.73–9.74
  savings-related share option
    schemes 9.75
  share incentive plans 9.77–9.82
Armed services personnel
  inheritance tax on death, and 31.25
Art sales
  remittances, and 27.97
Artificial debts
  double charges 36.4
  generally 30.14
Artificial transactions in land
  application of provision 12.104
  avoiding provision 12.111
  conditions
    application of provision 12.104
    connected persons 12.107
    disposal of land 12.105
    trading stock 12.106
  connected persons 12.107
  disposal of land 12.105
  effect of provision 12.103
  generally 12.101
  introduction 3.6
  opportunities to make gain 12.109
  other matters 12.112
  shares in landholding
    companies 12.108
  trading stock 12.106
  trading transactions 12.102
Assessment of tax
  Code of Practice 9 4.52
  Contractual Disclosure Facility 4.53

Assessment of tax – *contd*
  discovery assessments 4.41–4.43
  employment income, and 8.12
  enquiries 4.33
  fraud investigations
    Code of Practice 9 4.52
    Contractual Disclosure Facility 4.53
    disclosure opportunities 4.54
    Hansard procedure 4.50–4.51
  Hansard procedure 4.50–4.51
  interest 4.32
  payment 4.23
  penalties
    failure to make returns or payment
      on time 4.27
    generally 4.25–4.26
  returns 4.22
  self assessment 4.21
  savings and investment income,
    and 14.4
  trading income, and
    accounting dates 10.196–10.200
    background 10.192
    current year basis 10.193–10.194
    overlap relief 10.201
    partners 10.202–10.204
    partners joining 10.202
    partners leaving 10.203
    partnership changes 10.204
  trusts, and 16.6
Assisted areas
  first year allowances for plant and
    machinery 48.37
Associated operations
  lifetime transfers, and 28.101–28.105
Associations
  value added tax, and
    donations 40.49
    fund-raising 40.49
    introduction 40.49
    match fees 40.56
    MoU with CIPFA 40.50
    participation fees 40.56
    sporting services 40.54
    subscriptions 40.49
Auctioneers
  value added tax, and
    generally 40.125
    margin schemes 40.126
Authorised unit trusts
  capital gains tax, and 22.3
  corporation tax, and 41.2
  inheritance tax, and 35.22
Aviation insurance
  value added tax, and 40.79

B

Bad debts
  trading income, and 10.144
  value added tax, and 38.59–38.60
'Badges of trade'
  circumstances responsible for
    realisation 10.27
  frequency of similar
    transactions 10.25
  introduction 10.22
  length of ownership 10.24
  motive 10.28
  subject matter of transaction
    10.23
  work done on property 10.26
Balancing allowances and charges
  plant and machinery, and
    generally 48.56
    pooling 48.56
Bank accounts
  meaning of 'estate', and 30.2
Bank interest
  income tax, and 7.24
Bare trusts
  capital gains tax, and 25.3
  income tax, and 16.97
Barristers
  value added tax, and 40.86
'Base costs'
  capital gains tax, and 19.13
Basis of assessment
  And see **Assessment to tax**
  annual payments, and 14.4
  employment income, and 8.12
  savings and investment income,
    and 14.4
  trading income, and
    accounting dates 10.196–10.200
    background 10.192
    current year basis 10.193–10.194
    overlap relief 10.201
    partners 10.202–10.204
    partners joining 10.202
    partners leaving 10.203
    partnership changes 10.204
Bed and breakfasting
  And see **Tax avoidance**
  disposal of shares, and 26.46
  generally 3.13
Beneficial loan arrangements
  employment income, and 8.124
Beneficiaries under a disability
  capital gains tax, and 25.4
Benefit crystallisation events
  pension schemes, and 50.16

Benefits code
  beneficial loan arrangements 8.124
  by reason of employment 8.105
  cars
    fuel and other benefits 8.122
    introduction 8.117
    non-pooled 8.119–8.122
    pooled 8.118
    reducing the tax charge 8.120
    use of own car 8.121
  cash equivalent cost 8.126
  cash payments 8.127
  conclusion 8.135
  credit tokens 8.109
  employment-related benefits
    8.125
  excluded employees 8.104
  expenses payments 8.108
  fuel for vehicles 8.122
  interaction with charge on
    earnings, 8.103
  introduction 8.101
  living accommodation 8.110–8.116
  lower-paid employees 8.104
  making good 8.107
  optional remuneration
    arrangements 8.106
  prospective employees 8.128
  purpose of rules 8.102
  residual liability 8.125–8.131
  scholarships 8.130
  trivial benefits 8.131
  use of asset 8.129
  vans
    fuel and other benefits 8.122
    introduction 8.117
    non-pooled 8.123
    pooled 8.118
  vehicles
    fuel and other benefits 8.122
    introduction 8.117
    non-pooled cars 8.119–8.122
    non-pooled vans 8.123
    pooled cars and vans 8.118
    reducing the tax charge 8.120
    use of own car 8.121
  vouchers 8.109
Bereaved minor trusts
  inheritance tax, and 32.59
  settlements subject to relevant
    property regime, and 34.117
Betting winnings
  capital gains tax, and 22.3
Bicycles
  employment income, and 8.166

Biogas refuelling equipment
   first year allowances, and 48.33
Bitcoins
   value added tax, and 40.65
Blackmail payments
   trading income, and 10.148
Blind person's allowance
   income tax, and 7.105, 51.26
'Bona fide commercial'
   annual payments, and 14.16
   transactions in securities, and 3.64
Bond washing
   And see **Tax avoidance**
   accrued income scheme 3.12
   generally 3.11
   overview 3.4
   transactions in securities, and 3.29
Bonus shares
   And see **Distributions**
   following reduction of capital 42.4
   generally 42.3
   redeemable shares 42.5
'Brexit'
   Article 50 TEU 54.2
   VAT, and 37.11
Bribes
   trading income, and 10.148
Brokerage services
   value added tax, and 40.73
Builders activities
   value added tax, and 39.38
Building alterations
   capital allowances, and 48.18
Building works
   stamp duty land tax, and 49.50
Business activities
   And see **Value added tax**
   auctioneers
      generally 40.125
      margin schemes 40.126
   business services
      brokerage services 40.73
      dealings in securities 40.72
      financial services 40.64–40.69
      insurance 40.78–40.83
      supplies connected with financial services 40.77
   financial services
      Bitcoins 40.65
      connected supplies 40.77
      dealings in money 40.65
      deposits 40.68
      generally 40.64
      instalment credit finance 40.69

Business activities – *contd*
   financial services – *contd*
      loans 40.68
      securities for money 40.66
   food and drink
      catering 40.23–40.25
      free houses 40.29
      licensed trade 40.27–40.30
      managed houses 40.28
      public houses 40.27–40.30
      tenanted houses 40.30
      tied houses 40.30
   government 40.98–40.102
   health
      hospital care 40.38
      introduction 40.36
      opticians 40.40
      pharmacists 40.39
      supplies by qualified persons 40.37
   introduction 40.21
   leisure
      associations 40.49–40.56
      clubs and societies 40.49–40.56
      donations 40.49
      entertainers 40.43–40.44
      fund raising 40.49
      galleries 40.63
      match fees 40.56
      museums 40.63
      'nett' acts 40.44
      participation fees 40.56
      performers 40.43–40.44
      sporting services 40.54
      subscriptions 40.49
   professional services
      barristers 40.86
      barristers' services 40.95
      commission 40.96
      credit notes 40.94
      disbursements 40.97
      legal aid payments 40.90
      solicitors 40.87–40.90
   retailers
      choice of scheme 40.107
      gross takings 40.106
      introduction 40.105
      secondhand goods 40.108–40.109
   social and welfare 40.32–40.40
      charities 40.32
      correspondence courses 40.35
      education 40.33–40.35
      health 40.36–40.40
      hospital care 40.38
      opticians 40.40

Business activities – *contd*
  social and welfare – *contd*
    pharmacists 40.39
    voluntary sector 40.32
  tour operators
    agents 40.123
    foreign currency 40.119
    incidental supplies 40.121
    in-house supplies 40.116
    input tax 40.118
    introduction 40.110
    margin scheme 40.113–40.114
    territorial scope 40.112
    time of supply 40.120
    travel agents 40.123
    travellers 40.111
    wholesale supplies 40.117
Business investment relief
  remittances, and 27.96
Business medium, choice of
  buy-backs 46.58
  capital taxes 46.62–46.63
  conclusions 46.81
  dividends 46.54–46.55
  Enterprise Investment Scheme
    generally 46.50
    smaller companies 46.51
  income profits
    dates for payment 46.45
    Enterprise Investment
      Scheme 46.50–46.51
    illustrations 46.52
    interest relief 46.47
    loss relief 46.49
    national insurance
      contributions 46.43
    profits paid out as
      remuneration 46.44
    rates 46.42
    reliefs 46.48–46.50
    trading losses 46.46
  income tax
    benefits 46.60
    buy-backs 46.58
    dates for payment 46.45
    dividends 46.54–46.55, 46.60
    Enterprise Investment
      Scheme 46.50–46.51
    extracting cash from
      business 46.53–46.61
    illustrations 46.52
    income profits 46.42–46.52
    interest relief 46.47
    loans 46.56
    loss relief 46.49

Business medium, choice of – *contd*
  income tax – *contd*
    national insurance
      contributions 46.43
    profits paid out as
      remuneration 46.44
    rates 46.42
    reliefs 46.48–46.50
    remuneration 46.59
    share sales 46.57
    trading losses 46.46
  interest relief 46.47
  introduction 46.1–46.7
  limited liability partnership 46.5
  limited partnerships 46.4
  loans 46.56
  loss relief 46.49
  national insurance contributions
    generally 46.43
    table 46.Appendix
  non-tax factors
    corporate personality 46.22
    formality, rigidity and costs 46.24
    limited liability 46.21
    obtaining finance 46.23
  partnerships 46.1
  partnerships with companies 46.6
  personal service companies 46.7
  private limited company 46.1
  public company 46.2
  reliefs 46.48–46.50
  remuneration 46.59
  Seed Enterprise Investment
    Scheme 46.51
  share sales 46.57
  stamp duty land tax 46.65
  tax factors
    capital taxes 46.62–46.63
    extracting cash from
      business 46.53–46.61
    income profits 46.42–46.52
    introduction 46.41
    stamp duty land tax 46.65
    value added tax 46.64
  trading losses 46.46
  types 46.2–46.7
  unlimited company 46.3
  value added tax 46.64
Business premises
  renovations
    capital allowances, and
      48.124–48.125
Business services
  brokerage services 40.73
  dealings in securities 40.72

1698 Index

Business services – *contd*
  financial services 40.64–40.69
  insurance 40.78–40.83
  supplies connected with financial
    services 40.77
Business property relief (IHT)
  agricultural property relief, and 31.77
  amount 31.45
  clawback 31.59
  consequences 31.61
  contracts to sell the business 31.53
  'control' 31.55
  excepted assets 31.52
  instalment payments, and 31.58
  interest in possession trusts, and 33.30
  introduction 31.42
  investment businesses 31.48
  minority shareholdings in unquoted
    companies 31.56
  mixed businesses
    one business or two 31.49
    'wholly or mainly' test 31.50
  net value of business, on 31.44
  non-business assets 31.52
  non qualifying activities 31.47
  ownership requirement 31.46
  'relevant business property' 31.43
  reservations, and 31.60
  settlements, and 31.54
  settlements not subject to relevant
    property regime, and 33.30
  switching control 31.57
  'wholly or mainly' test 31.50
Business reliefs (CGT)
  amalgamations 22.104
  compulsory acquisition of land
    22.82–22.83
  entrepreneurs' relief
    family taxation 51.60
    generally 22.85
    trusts 25.148
  hold-over relief
    assets attracting immediate IHT
      charge, of 24.22–24.26
    business assets, of 24.4–24.21
    disposal at market value 24.2
    general 22.99
    IHT consequences 24.3
    introduction 24.1–24.3
  incorporation of business
    conditions 22.101
    deferral of tax on sale
      of unincorporated
      business 22.102
    election to disapply 22.103

Business reliefs (CGT) – *contd*
  incorporation of business – *contd*
    generally 22.100
    overview 26.4
    introduction 22.71
  reconstructions 22.104
  replacement of business assets
    basic conditions 22.72
    companies 22.77
    foreign assets 22.76
    intention to reinvest, and 22.80
    non-residents 22.76
    occupation for business
      purposes 22.75
    partnerships 22.77
    prior acquisition of replacement
      assets 22.73
    problem areas 22.79
    provisional relief 22.80
    qualifying assets 22.74
    restrictions 22.78
    wasting assets 22.78
  roll-over relief
    compulsory acquisition of
      land 22.82–22.83
    incorporation of business
      22.100–22.103
    replacement of business
      assets 22.72–22.80
  retirement relief 22.84
  takeovers 22.104
  undervalue disposals 22.99
Buy-back of company shares
  advantages if distribution rules
    apply 42.29
  choice of business medium, and 46.58
  clearance 42.31
  'connected' test 42.25
  fraction calculations 42.26
  introduction 42.21
  qualifying vendors 42.23
  reason for sale 42.27
  relevant companies 42.22
  stamp duty 42.31
  'substantial reduction' test 42.24
  trustees, from 42.30
  UK company as vendor 42.28
  vendor of shares 42.23–42.26

C

Calculation of tax
  capital gains tax, and
    annual exemption 19.50–19.57
    assets acquired before 6 April
      1965 19.29

Calculation of tax – *contd*
  capital gains tax, and – *contd*
    assets owned on 31 March
      1982 19.30–19.34
    deductible expenditure
      19.19–19.23
    disposal consideration 19.14–19.18
    introduction 19.13
    leases of land 19.39–19.43
    part disposals 19.35–19.36
    rates 19.49
    rebasing 19.30–19.34
    set-off of capital losses 19.58
    taper relief 19.28
    use of trading losses 19.59
    wasting assets 19.37–19.38
  corporation tax, and
    capital gains 41.47–41.49
    charitable donations relief
      41.57–41.59
    corporate venturing scheme
      41.72–41.74
    disposals of substantial
      shareholdings 41.75
    income profits 41.42–41.46
    introduction 41.41
    loan relationships 41.50–41.56
    loss relief 41.60–41.68
    management expenses 41.69–41.71
  income tax, and
    charging taxable income
      7.120–7.132
    introduction 7.1
    net income 7.40–7.91
    personal reliefs 7.101–7.113
    stages 7.4
    tax rates 7.2–7.3
    total income 7.21–7.27
  inheritance tax (death), and
    accountability 30.35
    chargeable transfers 30.22–30.23
    fall in value of property 30.24
    generally 30.36
    introduction 30.21
    liability for tax 30.35
    potentially exempt transfers
      30.25–30.26
    residential nil rate band
      30.28–30.34
    taper relief 30.23
    transferable nil rate band 30.27
  inheritance tax (lifetime transfers),
    and
    cumulation 28.121
    generally 28.123

Calculation of tax – *contd*
  inheritance tax (lifetime transfers),
    and – *contd*
    grossing-up 28.124
    late reported transfers 28.129
    non-cash assets 28.126
    non-commercial loans 28.131
    order of making transfers 28.130
    payment of tax other than by
      transferor 28.125
    problem areas 28.127–28.132
    rates of tax 28.122
    relief against double charge 28.132
    transfers of value by
      instalments 28.127
    transfers on same day 28.128
'Cancellation of tax advantage'
  transactions in securities, and 3.53
Capital allowances
  agricultural buildings 48.121
  annual investment allowance 48.28
  building alterations 48.18
  capital expenditure
    contributions by another
      person 48.4
    generally 48.3
    VAT 48.4
  capital gains tax, and 19.47
  cars (on or after 1 or 6 April 2009)
    anti-avoidance 48.77
    cars 48.76
    generally 48.75
    introduction 48.74
    low-emission vehicles 48.78
  cars (prior to 1 or 6 April 2009)
    expensive cars 48.80
    inexpensive cars 48.79
    introduction 48.74
  claims 48.6
  dredging 48.2
  equipment lessors 48.27
  family taxation, and 51.51
  fixtures 48.22–48.25
  flat conversions 48.122
  general scheme 48.1–48.10
  income from land, and
    generally 12.47
    introduction 12.46
  industrial buildings
    'industrial building' 48.92–48.95
    introduction 48.91
    qualifying trade 48.93
  know-how 48.2
  landlord's energy saving
    allowance 48.126–48.127

Capital allowances – *contd*
  legislative framework 48.1
  method of giving
    introduction 48.8
    property losses 48.10
    trading losses 48.9
  mineral extraction 48.2
  patent rights 48.2
  plant and machinery
    annual investment allowance 48.28
    balancing allowances/charges 48.56
    building alterations 48.18
    'capital expenditure' 48.14
    cars 48.74–48.80
    conditions 48.11–48.27
    equipment lessors 48.27
    first year allowances 48.29–48.38
    first year tax credits 48.36
    fixtures 48.22–48.25
    hire purchase 48.81
    'machinery' 48.16
    'on the provision of plant and machinery' 48.15–48.20
    'owned by that person as a result of incurring the expenditure' 48.21–48.27
    'person carrying on a qualifying activity' 48.12
    'plant' 48.17
    pooling 48.54–48.63
    qualifying expenditure 48.64–48.73
    tenants fixtures 48.23
    'who incurs' 48.13
    'wholly or partly for the purposes' 48.21
    writing down allowances 48.39–48.53
  property losses 48.10
  renovation of business premises 48.124–48.125
  research and development 48.123
  time when incurred 48.7
  trading income, and 10.135
  trading losses 48.9
  types 48.2
Capital distributions
  capital gains tax, and 26.21
Capital gains by companies
  See also **Capital gains tax**
  double taxation 41.49
  generally 41.47
  groups of companies
    anti-avoidance 43.127
    capital losses 43.126

Capital gains by companies – *contd*
  groups of companies – *contd*
    compulsory acquisition of land 43.131
    group property companies 43.130
    intra-group transfers 43.122
    introduction 43.121
    linked transactions 43.132
    roll-around relief 43.129
    roll-over claims 43.133
    roll-over relief 43.128
    sub-groups 43.123
    trading stock 43.125
    triggering a loss 43.124
  intra-group disposals 41.48
  introduction 41.22
Capital gains tax
  accumulation and maintenance trusts 24.27
  amalgamations, reconstructions and takeovers 22.104
  annual exemption
    death, and 21.64
    family taxation, and 51.56
    generally 19.50–19.57
    marital breakdown, and 52.22
  antiques 22.22
  appropriations to and from stock in trade 19.71
  background 19.2
  'base costs' 19.13
  basic principles
    chargeable assets 19.8
    chargeable disposals 19.7
    chargeable persons 19.6
    introduction 19.5
  business reliefs
    amalgamations, reconstructions and takeovers 22.104
    compulsory acquisition of land relief 22.82–22.83
    entrepreneurs' relief 22.85
    hold-over relief 22.99
    incorporation of business relief 22.100–22.103
    introduction 22.71
    postpone of CGT on gifts 22.99
    replacement of business assets relief 22.72–22.80
    retirement relief 22.84
    undervalue disposals 22.99
  calculation of the gain
    assets acquired before 6 April 1965 19.29

Capital gains tax – *contd*
  calculation of the gain – *contd*
    assets owned on 31 March
      1982 19.30–19.34
    deductible expenditure
      19.19–19.23
    disposal consideration 19.14–19.18
    introduction 19.13
    leases of land 19.39–19.43
    part disposals 19.35–19.36
    rebasing 19.30–19.34
    taper relief 19.28
    wasting assets 19.37–19.38
  calculation of tax payable
    annual exemption 19.50–19.57
    rates 19.49
    set-off of capital losses 19.58
    use of trading losses 19.59
  capital allowances, and 19.47
  capital distributions to
    shareholders 26.21
  capital sums derived from assets 19.64
  chargeable assets 19.8
  chargeable disposals 19.7
  chargeable persons 19.6
  charges 19.73
  charitable transactions 22.4
  charities, and
    generally 53.89
    introduction 53.41
  chattels
    comprising a set 22.23
    non-wasting chattels 22.22
    wasting chattels 22.21
  children 51.61
  children's trusts 24.27
  choice of business medium,
    and 46.62–46.63
  cohabitees 51.61
  companies, and
    capital distributions to
      shareholders 26.21
    disposal of shares 26.41–26.48
    generally 26.1
    incorporation of existing
      business 26.4
    mergers 26.4
    reorganisations 26.2
    takeovers 26.3
    value shifting 26.61–26.64
  compensation, and
    case law 19.66–19.67
    ESC D33 19.68
  compulsory acquisition of land
    22.82–22.83

Capital gains tax – *contd*
  conditional contracts, and 19.79
  connected persons 19.15
  consequences of realising gain 19.81
  consideration for disposal
    connected persons 19.15
    deferred consideration 19.17
    general 19.14
    market value of assets 19.16
    Marren v Ingles 19.18
  copyrights
    calculation of gain on
      disposal 19.38
    definition 19.37
  corporate bonds 22.45
  cultural gifts scheme 22.6
  damages, and
    case law 19.66–19.67
    ESC D33 19.68
  death, and
    annual exemption 21.64
    deductions and allowances
      21.62–21.64
    disclaimers 21.121–21.126
    domicile of PRs 21.3
    entrepreneurs' relief 21.63
    exempt legatees 21.105
    incidental expenses 21.62
    indexation 21.63
    inheritance provision 21.127
    introduction 21.1–21.2
    losses of deceased 21.41
    losses of PRs 21.81
    post-death variations 21.121–21.126
    principal private residence 21.65
    rate of tax 21.61
    'reading back' 21.122–21.123
    residence of PRs 21.3
    revaluations 21.23
    sale of assets by PRs 21.61–21.65
    spouse exemption 21.104
    taper relief 21.63
    transfers to legatees 21.101–21.105
    valuation of chargeable assets
      21.21–21.24
    will trusts, and 21.103
  debts
    general principle 22.42
    loans to traders 22.43
    meaning 22.41
    qualifying corporate bonds 22.45
    security, on 22.44
  deductible expenditure
    acquisition of asset 19.20
    death, and 21.62–21.64

Capital gains tax – *contd*
  deductible expenditure – *contd*
    disallowed expenditure 19.23
    disposal of asset 19.22
    enhancing value of asset 19.21
    indexation 19.24–19.27
    introduction 19.19
  deferral
    sale of unincorporated
      business 22.102
  deferral relief
    anti-avoidance 15.98
    appeals 15.96
    claims 15.100
    clawback of gain 15.97
    disposal 15.91
    EIS investments 15.93–15.94
    entrepreneurs' relief 15.94
    introduction 15.89
    qualifying investment 15.92
    relief 15.90
    taper relief 15.93
    trustees 15.99
    withdrawal 15.95
  deferred consideration 19.17
  destruction of asset 19.65
  disallowed expenditure 19.23
  'disposal'
    appropriations to and from stock in
      trade 19.71
    capital sums derived from
      assets 19.64
    charges 19.73
    compensation in damages,
      and 19.66–19.68
    destruction of asset 19.65
    exchanges of joint interests in
      land 19.77
    general 19.63
    hire-purchase agreements 19.72
    introduction 19.7
    lease extensions 19.76
    mortgages 19.73
    negligible value of asset 19.69
    options 19.70
    settled property 19.74
    timing 19.78–19.79
    total loss of asset 19.65
    value shifting 19.75
  disposal consideration
    connected persons 19.15
    deferred consideration 19.17
    general 19.14
    market value of assets 19.16
    Marren v Ingles 19.18

Capital gains tax – *contd*
  disposal of shares
    acquisition before 6 April
      1965 26.48
    basic rule 26.44
    bed and breakfasting 26.46
    current regime 26.44–26.46
    identification rules 26.45
    introduction 26.41–26.43
    pooling from 6 April 2008 26.47
  distributions to shareholders 26.21
  enhancing value of asset 19.21
  entrepreneurs' relief
    See also **Entrepreneurs' relief**
    death 21.63
    generally 51.60
  estates in administration, and 17.1
  exchanges of joint interests in
    land 19.77
  exempt assets 22.2
  exempt gains 22.3
  exempt persons 19.12
  exemptions and reliefs
    charitable transactions 22.4
    chattels 22.21–22.23
    cultural gifts scheme 22.6
    debts 22.41–22.45
    exempt assets 22.2
    exempt gains 22.3
    heritage property 22.5
    introduction 22.1
    main residence 23.1–23.141
    overview 19.9–19.10
    woodland 22.5
  expenses
    acquisition of asset 19.20
    disallowed expenditure 19.23
    disposal of asset 19.22
    enhancing value of asset 19.21
    indexation 19.24–19.27
    introduction 19.19
  extensions of lease 19.76
  family taxation, and
    annual exemption 51.56
    children 51.61
    cohabitees 51.61
    entrepreneurs' relief 51.60
    inter-spouse transfers 51.58
    jointly held assets 51.63
    losses 51.57
    planning opportunities 51.64
    principal private residence
      51.62
    separate calculation 51.56
    taper relief 51.59

Capital gains tax – *contd*
fine wine 22.22
gifts
  accumulation and maintenance
    trusts, from 24.27
  assets attracting immediate IHT
    charge, of 24.22–24.26
  business assets, of 24.4–24.21
  children's trusts, from 24.27
  designated property, of 24.28
  disposal at market value 24.2
  general 22.99
  IHT consequences 24.3
  introduction 24.1–24.3
  maintenance of historic buildings,
    for 24.28
  political parties, to 24.28
  works of art, of 24.28
gifts of assets attracting immediate
    IHT charge
  anti-avoidance 24.26
  chargeable transfers 24.23
  extent of relief 24.24
  introduction 24.22
  use of relief 24.25
gifts of business assets
  agricultural property 24.9
  annual exemption 24.15
  anti-avoidance 24.21
  application of provision 24.5
  creation of settlement 24.20
  effect of IHT 24.17
  election 24.12
  emigration of transferee 24.20
  entrepreneurs' relief, and 24.14
  hold-over relief, and 24.14
  introduction 24.4
  non-resident companies. to 24.19
  non-resident individuals, to 24.18
  'personal company' 24.10
  qualifying assets 24.7
  relevant property 24.6–24.11
  taper relief, and 24.13
  'trading company' 24.10
  triggering events 24.18–24.20
  trustees 24.11
  use for the purposes of trade 24.8
heritage property 22.5
hire-purchase agreements 19.72
historical development 19.4
hold-over relief
  assets attracting immediate IHT
    charge, of 24.22–24.26
  business assets, of 24.4–24.21
  disposal at market value 24.2

Capital gains tax – *contd*
hold-over relief – *contd*
  general 22.99
  IHT consequences 24.3
  introduction 24.1–24.3
income profits, and 19.82
income tax overlap
  generally 19.3
  leases of land 19.42
incorporation of business relief
  conditions 22.101
  deferral of tax on sale
    of unincorporated
    business 22.102
  election to disapply 22.103
  generally 22.100
  overview 26.4
indexation
  basic rules 19.26
  capital losses, and 19.27
  death, and 21.63
  rationale 19.24
  statutory changes 19.25
instalment payments
  gifts, and 24.30
  generally 19.61
inter-spouse transfers 51.58
introduction 19.1
jewellery 22.22
jointly held assets 51.63
lease extensions 19.76
leases of land
  basic rules 19.39
  income tax overlap 19.42
  premiums 19.40
  regrants 19.43
  surrenders 19.43
  wasting asset rules 19.41
limited liability partnerships, and
  corporate members 45.16
  gains 45.15
  introduction 45.9
  losses 45.13
  mixed member LLPs 45.16
  partner status 45.11–45.12
  salaried members 45.11–45.12
  trading LLPs 45.10
loans to traders 22.43
loss relief, and 11.61
losses
  anti-avoidance 19.48
  capital allowances 19.47
  circumstances in which arise 19.44
  death, and 21.41, 21.81
  family taxation, and 51.57

Capital gains tax – *contd*
  losses – *contd*
    restrictions 19.47–19.48
    set-off 19.58
    taper relief, and 19.46
    targeted anti-avoidance rule 19.48
    use 19.45
  main residence
    And see **Main residence exemption**
    availability 23.1–23.2
    definitions 23.21–23.24
    expenditure with profit-making
      motive 23.101
    family taxation, and 51.62
    IHT schemes, and 23.141
    introduction 23.1
    non-residents, and 23.2
    periods of absence 23.81–23.85
    problem areas 23.61–23.66
    qualifying residences 23.42–23.48
    second homes 23.121–23.123
  market value of assets 19.16
  marital breakdown, and
    annual exemption 52.22
    generally 52.21
    lump sum payments 52.23
    matrimonial home 52.62–52.63
  mortgages 19.73
  negligible value of asset 19.69
  no gain/no loss transactions 19.11
  non-chargeable assets 22.2
  non tax-advantaged share schemes
    acquisition of shares other than
      pursuant to pre-existing
      right 9.46–9.47
    acquisition of shares pursuant to
      employment-related securities
      option 9.50–9.56
    chargeable gain calculation 9.57
    grant of right to acquire shares to
      employee 9.49
    introduction 9.45
  offshore matters for individuals
    liability of non-residents
      27.41–27.63
    new regime for foreign
      domiciliaries 27.81–27.101
    non-resident companies
      27.111–27.112
    residence 27.1–27.30
  options
    calculation of gain on
      disposal 19.38
    definition 19.37
    disposal, and 19.70

Capital gains tax – *contd*
  part disposals
    formula not used, where 19.36
    general rule 19.35
    leases of land, and 19.39
  partnerships, and
    annuity payments by partners 44.34
    changes to asset surplus sharing
      ratio 44.32
    entrepreneurs' relief 44.39
    general 44.31
    goodwill 44.33
    hold-over relief 44.36
    incorporation relief 44.38
    reliefs 44.35–44.39
    replacement of business assets
      relief 44.37
    roll-over relief 44.37–44.38
  patent rights
    calculation of gain on
      disposal 19.38
    definition 19.37
  payment
    donee, by 24.31
    gifts, and 24.29–24.31
    instalments, by 19.61
    timing 19.60
  payment by instalments
    gifts, and 24.30
    generally 19.61
  postponement of CGT on gifts 22.99
  premiums for leases 19.40
  principal private residence
    And see **Main residence exemption**
    availability 23.1–23.2
    definitions 23.21–23.24
    expenditure with profit-making
      motive 23.101
    family taxation, and 51.62
    IHT schemes, and 23.141
    introduction 23.1
    non-residents, and 23.2
    periods of absence 23.81–23.85
    problem areas 23.61–23.66
    qualifying residences 23.42–23.48
    second homes 23.121–23.123
  purchased life interests in settled
    property
    calculation of gain on
      disposal 19.38
    definition 19.37
  qualifying corporate bonds 22.45
  rates
    companies 19.49
    entrepreneurs' relief 19.49

Capital gains tax – *contd*
  rates – *contd*
    history 19.49
    individuals 19.49
  rebasing
    basic rule 19.31
    election 19.33
    introduction 19.30
    qualifications 19.32
    technical issues 19.34
  reconstructions, amalgamations and takeovers 22.104
  reinvestment relief
    clawback of gain 15.88
    generally 15.82
  reliefs
    charitable transactions 22.4
    chattels 22.21–22.23
    cultural gifts scheme 22.6
    debts 22.41–22.45
    exempt assets 22.2
    exempt gains 22.3
    heritage property 22.5
    introduction 22.1
    main residence 23.1–23.141
    overview 19.9–19.10
    woodland 22.5
  replacement of business assets relief
    basic conditions 22.72
    companies 22.77
    foreign assets 22.76
    intention to reinvest, and 22.80
    non-residents 22.76
    occupation for business purposes 22.75
    partnerships 22.77
    prior acquisition of replacement assets 22.73
    problem areas 22.79
    provisional relief 22.80
    qualifying assets 22.74
    restrictions 22.78
    wasting assets 22.78
  reporting requirements 19.62
  retirement relief 22.84
  roll-over relief
    compulsory acquisition of land 22.82–22.83
    incorporation of business 22.100–22.103
    replacement of business assets 22.72–22.80
  Seed Enterprise Investment Scheme
    anti-avoidance 15.134
    capital gains tax exemption 15.131

Capital gains tax – *contd*
  Seed Enterprise Investment Scheme – *contd*
    capital gains tax re-investment relief 15.132
    company directors 15.133
    income tax relief 15.130
    introduction 15.128
    qualifying companies 15.129
    qualifying investors 15.133
    tax reliefs 15.130–15.132
  set-off of capital losses 19.58
  settled property 19.74
  settlements
    absolute entitlement 25.6
    actual or deemed disposals 25.41–25.55
    bare trusts, and 25.3
    beneficiaries under a disability, and 25.4
    class closing 25.8
    concurrent interests, and 25.5
    'connected persons' rule 25.22
    creation 25.21–25.22
    death of beneficiary with interest in possession trusts 25.54
    definition 25.2
    disposal of beneficial interests 25.111–25.118
    entrepreneurs' relief 25.148
    exemptions and reliefs 25.142–25.148
    exit charge 25.47–25.53
    gifts of business assets, and 24.20
    introduction 25.1
    losses 25.43–25.45
    meaning 25.2–25.8
    nomineeships, and 25.3
    payment of tax 25.141
    resettlements 25.81–25.83
    taper relief 25.148
    transfers on change of trustees 25.42
    trustee appropriations, and 25.7
    vulnerable beneficiaries 25.149–25.152
  surrenders of leases 19.43
  tangible movable property
    calculation of gain on disposal 19.38
    definition 19.37
  taper relief
    And see **Taper relief**
    death, and 21.63
    family taxation, and 51.59

Capital gains tax – *contd*
taper relief – *contd*
generally 19.28
losses, and 19.46
timing of disposal
conditional contracts 19.79
general rule 19.78
total loss of asset 19.65
transfer of unincorporated business to company, and
available reliefs 47.4–47.8
valuation 47.9
trusts
absolute entitlement 25.6
actual or deemed disposals 25.41–25.55
bare trusts, and 25.3
beneficiaries under a disability, and 25.4
class closing 25.8
concurrent interests, and 25.5
'connected persons' rule 25.22
creation 25.21–25.22
death of beneficiary with interest in possession trusts 25.54
definition 25.2
disposal of beneficial interests 25.111–25.118
entrepreneurs' relief 25.148
exemptions and reliefs 25.142–25.148
exit charge 25.47–25.53
gifts of business assets, and 24.20
introduction 25.1
losses 25.43–25.45
meaning 25.2–25.8
nomineeships, and 25.3
payment of tax 25.141
resettlements 25.81–25.83
taper relief 25.148
transfers on change of trustees 25.42
trustee appropriations, and 25.7
vulnerable beneficiaries 25.149–25.152
undervalue disposals
generally 24.16
introduction 22.99
use of trading losses 19.59
value shifting
controlling shareholdings 26.62
introduction 26.61
leases 26.63
overview 19.75
tax-free benefits resulting 26.64

Capital gains tax – *contd*
venture capital trusts
deferred relief on reinvestment 15.127
disposals by investors 15.126
introduction 15.123
trust 15.125
wasting assets
calculation of gain on disposal 19.38
chattels 22.21
definition 19.37
leases of land 19.41
replacement of business assets 22.78
wine 22.22
woodland 22.5
Capital Goods Scheme
initial deduction 38.91
introduction 38.89
method of adjustment 38.94
option to tax commercial buildings, and 39.34
period of adjustment 38.93
relevant assets 38.90
subsequent adjustments 38.92
Capital sums derived from assets
capital gains tax, and 19.64
Care of dependent relative
inheritance tax on death, and 31.10
Carry-across relief
losses, and 11.41
Carry-forward relief
corporation tax, and 41.61
income tax, and 11.21
Cars
capital allowances ((on or after 1 or 6 April 2009)
anti-avoidance 48.77
cars 48.76
generally 48.75
introduction 48.74
low-emission vehicles 48.78
capital allowances (prior to 1 or 6 April 2009)
expensive cars 48.80
inexpensive cars 48.79
introduction 48.74
fuel and other benefits 8.122
introduction 8.117
non-pooled cars 8.119–8.122
pooled cars 8.118
reducing the tax charge 8.120
use of own car 8.121

Cash accounting
  value added tax, and 38.58
Cash-backs
  miscellaneous income, and 13.28
Cash basis
  consultation 12.44
  trading income, and
    calculation of profits 10.74
    election 10.73
    moving to 10.75
Cash equivalent cost
  employment income, and 8.126
Cash handling services
  disclosure rules, and 5.22
Cash ISA
  generally 15.27
Cash payments
  employment income, and 8.127
Cash termination payments
  contemporaneous share sales 8.157
  current regime 8.150
  damages, and 8.156
  death benefits 8.152
  disability benefits 8.152
  exceptions 8.151–8.154
  first £30,000 8.154
  generally 8.148
  injury benefits 8.152
  internationally mobile
    employees 8.158
  introduction 8.101
  old regime 8.149
  PAYE 8.155
  pension benefits 8.152
  reform recommendations 8.159
  reporting requirements 8.155
Catering
  value added tax, and 40.23–40.25
Certificates of discharge
  reservation of benefit, and 30.53
Change of accounting basis
  trading income, and 10.72
Change of ownership
  transactions in securities, and 3.36
Character appropriate test
  agricultural property relief,
    and 31.65–31.66
Chargeable assets
  capital gains tax, and 19.8
Chargeable consideration
  And see **Stamp duty land tax**
  adjustments 49.60
  carrying out building works 49.50
  contingent consideration 49.56–49.57
  debt 49.48

Chargeable consideration – *contd*
  division 49.46
  employer-provided
    accommodation 49.52
  exchanges 49.45
  foreign currency 49.49
  general rule 49.41
  indemnity by purchaser 49.55
  just and reasonable
    apportionment 49.44
  lease obligations 49.53
  linked transactions 49.64
  non-monetary consideration 49.47
  partition 49.46
  postponed consideration 49.43
  provision of services 49.51
  rent 49.62
  reverse premium 49.54
  transfer of land to connected
    company 49.63
  unascertained consideration 49.58
  uncertain consideration 49.58
  value added tax 49.42
Chargeable disposals
  capital gains tax, and 19.8
Chargeable instruments
  And see **Stamp duty**
  conveyance on sale 49.113–49.114
  dissolution of partnerships 49.116
  exchange of shares 49.117
  transfer on sale 49.113–49.114
Chargeable interests
  stamp duty land tax, and 49.32
Chargeable transfers
  contrast with gifts 28.6
  death, and 30.22–30.23
  'disposition' 28.3
  double charges 36.5
  examples 28.5
  introduction 28.2
  omissions 28.4
  transfer of value 28.3
Charges
  capital gains tax, and 19.73
Charges on income
  see **Net income**
Charging provisions
  annual payments, and 14.1
  employment income, and
    'from' an employment 8.41
    generally 8.11
    termination payments 8.142–8.145
  foreign income, and 18.31
  trading income, and
    corporation tax 10.3

Charging provisions – *contd*
  trading income, and – *contd*
    income tax 10.2
    introduction 10.1
Charging taxable income
  additional tax liabilities 7.125
  dates for payment of tax 7.122
  excluded tax liabilities 7.126
  exemptions from tax
    exempt income 7.129–7.131
    exempt organisations 7.128
    introduction 7.127
    ISAs 7.132
    life assurance policies 7.132
  other tax reductions 7.124
  rates of tax 7.120–7.121
  specimen calculation 7.123
Charitable activities
  value added tax, and 40.32
Charitable buildings
  value added tax, and 39.23
Charitable donations relief
  deduction against profits 41.59
  qualifying donations 41.57–41.58
Charitable gifts
  income tax, and
    annual payments 14.12
    employment income 8.173
  inheritance tax on death, and
    death 30.37–30.38
    exemptions and reliefs 31.88–31.89
Charitable transactions
  capital gains tax, and 22.4
Charitable trusts
  settlements not subject to relevant
    property regime, and 33.112
  settlements subject to relevant
    property regime, and 34.111
Charities
  amateur sports clubs 53.101
  annual tax on enveloped
    dwellings 53.132
  anti-avoidance provisions 53.116
  capital gains tax
    generally 53.89
    introduction 53.41
  chargeable gains 53.41
  charitable work outside UK 53.24
  community amateur sports
    clubs 53.101
  community infrastructure levy 53.131
  corporate gifts 53.86
  corporation tax 53.41
  Cultural Gifts Scheme 53.111
  deeds of covenant 53.87

Charities – *contd*
  definition of 'charity'
    Charities Act 2006 53.22
    Finance Act 2010 53.23
  distributions, and 42.76
  diverted profits tax, and 53.42
  dividends 53.41
  'double-dip' 53.85
  employment allowance 53.133
  expenditure 53.61
  foreign charities 53.23
  fuel and power 53.124
  fund-raising events 53.127
  Gift Aid
    corporate gifts 53.86
    declarations 53.82–53.83
    'double-dip' 53.85
    generally 53.79
    introduction 53.41
    receipt of benefits 53.84
    scope of relief 53.80
    small donations scheme 53.81
  gifts in kind
    generally 53.95
    gift of assets 53.98
    medical supplies and
      equipment 53.97
    trading stock 53.96
  gifts of assets 53.98
  gifts to foreign charity 53.91
  gifts treated as made in previous tax
    year 53.102
  income tax 53.41
  inheritance tax
    generally 53.90
    gift in kind 53.95–53.98
    gift of assets 53.98
    gift to foreign charity 53.91
    legacies of 10% or more of testator's
      net estate 53.94
    lifetime gifts 53.92
    medical supplies and
      equipment 53.97
    residuary gifts 53.93
    trading stock 53.96
    wording of will 53.92
  interest 53.41
  introduction 53.1
  land transactions 53.43
  legacies of 10% or more of testator's
    net estate 53.94
  lifetime gifts 53.92
  medical supplies and
    equipment 53.97
  non-charitable purpose trusts 53.25

Charities – *contd*
  payroll giving 53.88
  pre-eminent objects and works of
      art 53.111
  qualifying charities
      'charities' 53.22
      foreign charities 53.24
      generally 53.21
      non-charitable purpose trusts 53.25
      work outside UK 53.24
  qualifying investments 53.99
  receipt of benefits 53.84
  residuary gifts 53.93
  social investment 53.120
  sports clubs 53.101
  stamp duty land tax 53.130
  tainted donations 53.116
  tax relief
      direct taxes, against 53.41
      policy 53.25
  tax repayments 53.103
  trading income 53.42
  trading stock 53.96
  value added tax
      cost-sharing exemption 53.128
      fuel and power 53.124
      fund-raising events 53.127
      inputs 53.122–53.124
      introduction 53.121
      outputs 53.125–53.126
      payment 53.129
      zero-rated supplies 53.123
  wording of will 53.92
  work outside UK 53.24
  works of art 53.111
  zero-rated supplies 53.123
Chattels
  capital gains tax, and
      comprising a set 22.23
      non-wasting chattels 22.22
  wasting chattels 22.21
Child benefit
  high income charge
      election 51.48
      extent 51.46
      generally 51.45
      measure of income 51.47
Child tax credit
  appeals 51.39
  case study 51.40A
  changes in circumstance 51.37
  changes in income 51.38
  conditions of entitlement 51.29
  disputes 51.40
  elements 51.28

Child tax credit – *contd*
  introduction 51.27
  payment 51.30
Child trust fund
  introduction 51.42
  operation 51.43
  reliefs 51.44
Childcare
  employment income, and 8.167
  tax-free support 51.41
Children
  capital gains tax, and
      bare trusts 25.3
      generally 51.61
  income tax, and 16.97
  inheritance tax, and 51.76
Children's trusts
  capital gains tax, and 24.27
Civil engineering work
  value added tax, and 39.41
Civil partners
  age-related allowance
      basic requirements 51.21
      generally 7.111–7.113
      introduction 51.20
      restriction of relief 51.22
      use 51.23
  income tax
      age-related 7.111–7.113,
          51.20–51.23
      transferable tax allowance
          7.115–7.117, 51.12
  main residence exemption, and
      periods of absence 23.82
      qualifying residences 23.42
  transferable tax allowance
      7.115–7.117, 51.12
Clawback
  agricultural property relief, and 31.72
  business property relief, and 31.59
  deferral relief, and 15.97
  reinvestment relief, and 15.88
  stamp duty land tax, and 49.84
Clean-break transfer
  marital breakdown, and 52.67–52.69
Clearance services
  stamp duty, and 49.123
Clearances
  distribution to beneficiaries,
      and 17.60
Close companies
  applicable rules 41.127–41.129
  'associate' 41.124
  'control' 41.123
  'director' 41.124

Close companies – *contd*
  distributions
    generally 41.127
    introduction 42.10
  examples 41.126
  excluded companies 41.125
  family taxation, and 51.50
  introduction 41.121
  investment-holding companies 41.129
  lifetime transfers, and
    deemed dispositions by participators 28.153
    introduction 28.151
    transfers of value 28.152
  loans to participators 41.128
  meaning 41.122–41.126
  'participator' 41.124
  transactions in securities, and 3.37
Clubs and societies
  value added tax, and
    donations 40.49
    fund-raising 40.49
    introduction 40.49
    match fees 40.56
    MoU with CIPFA 40.50
    participation fees 40.56
    sporting services 40.54
    subscriptions 40.49
Code of Practice 9
  fraud investigations, and 4.52
Cohabitees
  capital gains tax, and 51.61
  inheritance tax, and 51.76
Collection of tax
  annual payments, and 14.45–14.46
  employment income, and
    accounting to HMRC 8.199
    benefits in kind 8.192
    gross payments to employee 8.201
    introduction 8.191
    K codes 8.196
    non-deduction of PAYE 8.200
    part only of payment taxed 8.193
    PAYE coding 8.195
    PAYE settlement agreements 8.198
    'payment' 8.194
    problem cases 8.192–8.193
    real-time information 8.203
    recovery of tax from employee by employer 8.202
    reform proposals 8.203
    returns 8.197
    scope of provisions 8.191
    settlement agreements 8.198

Collection of tax – *contd*
  foreign employment income, and 18.51
  generally 4.24
'Combined effect of'
  transactions in securities, and 3.54
Commercial buildings
  option to tax, and
    capital goods scheme, and 39.34
    introduction 39.27
    mechanics of exercise 39.29
    output tax 39.31
    property affected 39.28
    purpose of exercise 39.33
    revocation 39.30
Commercial transactions
  lifetime transfers, and 28.21
Commission
  miscellaneous income, and 13.28
  value added tax, and 40.96
Commissioners of HMRC
  generally 4.2
Common Consolidated Corporate Tax Base
  EU law, and 54.97
Commorientes
  inheritance tax on death, and 30.141–30.142
Community amateur sports clubs
  And see **Charities**
  generally 53.101
Community infrastructure levy
  charities, and 53.131
Companies
  acquisition of
    considerations on assets sale 47.32–47.33
    considerations on share sale 47.34–47.37
    introduction 47.31
    loan notes, by 47.39
    share issue, by 47.38
  agricultural property relief, and 31.70
  annual payments, and 14.5
  business reliefs, and
    amalgamations, reconstructions and takeovers 22.104
    compulsory acquisition of land relief 22.82–22.83
    hold-over relief 22.99
    incorporation of business relief 22.100–22.103
    introduction 22.71
    postpone of CGT on gifts 22.99

Companies – *contd*
business reliefs, and – *contd*
  replacement of business assets
      relief 22.72–22.80
  retirement relief 22.84
  undervalue disposals 22.99
capital allowances
  And see **Capital allowances**
  agricultural buildings 48.121
  capital expenditure 48.3–48.5
  claims 48.6
  flat conversions 48.122
  general scheme 48.1–48.10
  industrial buildings 48.91–48.95
  landlord's energy saving
      allowance 48.126–48.127
  method of giving 48.8–48.10
  plant and machinery 48.11–48.81
  renovation of business
      premises 48.124–48.125
  research and development 48.123
  time when incurred 48.7
  types 48.2
capital gains tax, and
  capital distributions to
      shareholders 26.21
  disposal of shares 26.41–26.48
  generally 26.1
  incorporation of existing
      business 26.4
  mergers 26.4
  reliefs 22.71–22.104
  reorganisations 26.2
  takeovers 26.3
corporation tax
  And see **Corporation tax**
  generally 41.1–41.187
disposal of shares
  acquisition before 6 April
      1965 26.48
  basic rule 26.44
  bed and breakfasting 26.46
  current regime 26.44–26.46
  identification rules 26.45
  introduction 26.41–26.43
  pooling from 6 April 2008 26.47
distributions
  And see **Distributions**
  company buy-backs, and
      42.21–42.31
  exempt distributions 42.141–42.149
  meaning 42.1–42.10
  scrip dividends 42.150–42.152
  taxation of non-qualifying
      distributions 42.121

Companies – *contd*
distributions – *contd*
  taxation of qualifying
      distributions 42.41–42.49
  taxation of recipients 42.76–42.96
groups
  capital gains 43.121–43.133
  consortium relief 43.41–43.48
  depreciatory transactions 43.151
  instalment payments of corporation
      tax 43.101
  introduction 43.1
  meaning 43.21
  stamp duty land tax 43.211
  value shifting 43.151
  VAT 43.191
income tax, and
  losses 11.2
  savings and investment income 14.5
limited liability partnerships, and 45.4
rates of tax 19.49
residence, and 18.16
savings and investment income,
    and 14.5
scrip dividends, and
  generally 42.150
  interest in possession trusts 42.152
  tax treatment 42.151
transfer of unincorporated business to
  capital gains tax 47.4–47.9
  income tax 47.3
  introduction 47.2
  other issues 47.14
  problems for purchasing
      company 47.12–47.13
  stamp duty land tax 47.11
value shifting
  controlling shareholdings 26.62
  introduction 26.61
  leases 26.63
  overview 19.75
  tax-free benefits resulting 26.64
Company buy-backs
advantages if distribution rules
    apply 42.29
clearance 42.31
'connected' test 42.25
fraction calculations 42.26
introduction 42.21
qualifying vendors 42.23
reason for sale 42.27
relevant companies 42.22
stamp duty 42.31
'substantial reduction' test 42.24
trustees, from 42.30

Company buy-backs – *contd*
  UK company as vendor 42.28
  vendor of shares 42.23–42.26
Company share option plans
  tax-advantaged share schemes, and 9.76
Compensation
  capital gains tax, and
    case law 19.66–19.67
    ESC D33 19.68
  employment income, and 8.64
Compensation funds
  settlements not subject to relevant property regime, and 33.116
  settlements subject to relevant property regime, and 34.115
Composite supplies
  value added tax, and 38.25
Compulsory acquisition of land
  capital gains tax, and 22.82–22.83
  groups of companies, and 43.131
Computer equipment
  employment income, and 8.166
Conditional contracts
  capital gains tax, and 19.79
Confidentiality conditions
  disclosure rules, and 5.22
Connected persons
  capital gains tax, and 19.15
Consideration
  transactions in securities, and 3.34
Consideration for disposal
  connected persons 19.15
  deferred consideration 19.17
  general 19.14
  market value of assets 19.16
  Marren v Ingles 19.18
Consideration of marriage, gifts in
  inheritance tax on death, and 31.6
Consortium relief
  anti-avoidance 43.47
  availability 43.41
  claims 43.46
  European Vinyls case 43.45
  future changes 43.48
  international dimension 43.42
  Marks & Spencer case 43.44
  operation 43.43
Construction industry workers
  employment income, and 8.31
Construction services
  value added tax, and 39.25
Consultancies
  partnerships, and 44.13

Contingency principle
  stamp duty, and 49.115
Contingent consideration
  stamp duty land tax, and 49.56–49.57
Contingent fee arrangement
  disclosure rules, and 5.22
Contingent liabilities
  reservation of benefit, and 30.49
Contractual Disclosure Facility
  fraud investigations, and 4.53
Control
  business property relief, and 31.55
Controlled foreign companies
  corporation tax, and 41.161
Conversions
  value added tax, and 39.26
Convertible shares
  non tax-advantaged share schemes 9.25
Conveyances
  stamp duty, and 49.113–49.114
  stamp duty land tax, and 49.36–49.39
Co-ownership
  lifetime transfers, and 28.67
  reservation of benefit, and 29.137
Copyright royalties
  generally 14.40
Copyrights
  capital gains tax, and
    calculation of gain on disposal 19.38
    definition 19.37
Corporate bonds
  capital gains tax, and 22.45
  definition 41.93
  general rule 41.92
  paper-for-paper exchanges 41.97
  preserving loss relief for debts on security 41.94
  'rolling into' 41.96
Corporate venturing scheme
  introduction 41.72
  requirements 41,74
  tax relief 41.73
Corporation tax
  application 41.2
  authorised unit trusts, and 41.2
  calculation of profits
    capital gains 41.47–41.49
    charitable donations relief 41.57–41.59
    corporate venturing scheme 41.72–41.74
    disposals of substantial shareholdings 41.75
    income profits 41.42–41.46

Corporation tax – *contd*
  calculation of profits – *contd*
    introduction 41.41
    loan relationships 41.50–41.56
    loss relief 41.60–41.68
    management expenses 41.69–41.71
  capital allowances
    And see **Capital allowances**
    agricultural buildings 48.121
    capital expenditure 48.3–48.5
    claims 48.6
    flat conversions 48.122
    general scheme 48.1–48.10
    industrial buildings 48.91–48.95
    landlord's energy saving
      allowance 48.126–48.127
    method of giving 48.8–48.10
    plant and machinery 48.11–48.81
    renovation of business
      premises 48.124–48.125
    research and development 48.123
    time when incurred 48.7
    types 48.2
  capital gains
    double taxation 41.49
    generally 41.47
    groups, and 43.121–43.133
    intra-group disposals 41.48
    introduction 41.22
  charitable donations relief
    deduction against profits 41.59
    qualifying donations 41.57–41.58
  charities, and 53.41
  close companies
    applicable rules 41.127–41.129
    'associate' 41.124
    'control' 41.123
    'director' 41.124
    distributions 41.127
    examples 41.126
    excluded companies 41.125
    introduction 41.121
    investment-holding
      companies 41.129
    loans to participators 41.128
    meaning 41.122–41.126
    'participator' 41.124
  companies, and 41.2
  consortium relief
    anti-avoidance 43.47
    availability 43.41
    claims 43.46
    European Vinyls case 43.45
    future changes 43.48
    international dimension 43.42

Corporation tax – *contd*
  consortium relief – *contd*
    Marks & Spencer case 43.44
    operation 43.43
  controlled foreign companies 41.161
  corporate groups
    capital gains 43.121–43.133
    consortium relief 43.41–43.48
    depreciatory transactions 43.151
    instalment payments of corporation
      tax 43.101
    introduction 43.1
    meaning 43.21
    stamp duty land tax 43.211
    value shifting 43.151
    VAT 43.191
  corporate venturing scheme
    introduction 41.72
    requirements 41.74
    tax relief 41.73
  currency risk 41.43
  deduction at source income 41.46
  derivative contracts 41.43
  disposals of substantial
    shareholdings 41.75
  distributions, and 42.1
  dividends 41.46
  double taxation
    capital gains, and 41.49
    general principles 41.156
    mixer companies 41.159
    tax agreements 41.157
    unilateral relief 41.158
  duties of senior accounting
    officers 41.186
  employee participation, and
    amount of relief 9.128
    arbitrage receipts rules 9.129
    availability of relief 9.125–9.127
    deductibility 9.122
    introduction 9.121
    restriction of tax relief 9.123
    share type 9.127
    statutory tax relief 9.124–9.129
    tax position of employee 9.126
    timing of relief 9.129
  employee trusts 41.45
  financial years 41.21
  foreign companies
    calculation of profits 41.152
    controlled foreign
      companies 41.161
    liability to tax 41.151
    non-resident companies 41.162
    'residence' 41.153

Corporation tax – *contd*
  foreign exchange gains and
    losses 41.43
  groups of companies
    capital gains 43.121–43.133
    consortium relief 43.41–43.48
    depreciatory transactions 43.151
    instalment payments of corporation tax 43.101
    introduction 43.1
    meaning 43.21
    stamp duty land tax 43.211
    value shifting 43.151
    VAT 43.191
  income profits
    deduction at source 41.46
    derivative contracts 41.43
    dividends 41.46
    employee trusts 41.45
    foreign exchange gains and
      losses 41.43
    general principles 41.42
    income taxed at source 41.46
    interest rate contracts 41.43
    transfer pricing 41.44
  income taxed at source 41.46
  incorrect returns 41.184
  interest 41.183
  interest rate contracts 41.43
  intra-group disposals 41.48
  introduction 41.1–41.2
  late returns 41.184
  limited liability partnerships, and 41.2
  loan relationships
    connected parties 41.56
    extent of regime 41.53
    general principles 41.50
    impaired debt 41.56
    late interest 41.56
    meaning 41.51
    non-trading profits, losses and expenses 41.54
    trading profits, losses and expenses 41.53
  loss relief
    acquisition of tax loss company 41.65
    capital losses, for 41.68
    carry-forward 41.61
    'commercial purpose' 41.64
    current profits, against 41.61
    introduction 41.60
    non-trading income losses, for 41.67
    previous profits, against 41.61

Corporation tax – *contd*
  loss relief – *contd*
    reconstructions 41.66
    restrictions on availability 41.63–41.66
    targeted loss buying 41.65
    trading losses, for 41.61–41.62
  management expenses
    acquisition of surplus expenses company 41.70
    distinction between investment and trading companies 41.71
    general rule 41.69
  miscellaneous income, and 13.5
  overseas dimension
    calculation of profits 41.152
    controlled foreign companies 41.161
    double tax relief 41.156–41.159
    effect of ceasing to be UK resident 41.154
    liability to tax 41.151
    non-resident companies 41.162
    non-resident shareholders of resident companies 41.162
    'residence' 41.153
    UK resident companies abroad 41.155
  paper-for-paper exchanges 41.97
  partnerships, and 41.2
  pay and file 41.182
  payment date 41.21
  qualifying corporate bonds
    definition 41.93
    general rule 41.92
    paper-for-paper exchanges 41.97
    preserving loss relief for debts on security 41.94
    'rolling into' 41.96
  quarterly payments 41.185
  raising finance
    qualifying corporate bonds 41.92–41.97
    sources of finance 41.91
    thin capitalisation 41.98
  rates
    capital gains 41.22
    introduction 41.21
    ring fence profits of North Sea oil companies 41.24
    small profits rate 41.23
  ring fence profits of North Sea oil companies 41.24
  self-assessment
    anti-avoidance 41.187

Index 1715

Corporation tax – *contd*
 self-assessment – *contd*
  duties of senior accounting
   officers 41.186
  incorrect returns 41.184
  interest 41.183
  introduction 41.181
  late returns 41.184
  operation of pay and file 41.182
  quarterly payments 41.185
 small profits rate 41.23
 targeted loss buying 41.65
 thin capitalisation 41.98
 trading income, and 10.3
 transfer pricing 41.44
 unincorporated associations, and 41.2
Correspondence courses
 value added tax, and 40.35
Counteraction
 transactions in securities, and 3.38
Couples
 income tax, and 7.22
Court of Appeal
 See also **Appeals**
 generally 4.213
Creative artists
 trading income, and 10.172–10.173
Credit card services
 disclosure rules, and 5.22
Credit notes
 value added tax, and 40.94
Credit tokens
 employment income, and 8.109
Cultural gifts scheme (CGS)
 generally 53.111
 introduction 22.6
Cumulation
 lifetime transfers, and 28.121
Currency risk
 corporation tax, and 41.43
Current year basis
 closing years of business 10.195
 continuing business 10.193
 opening years of new business 10.194

D

D&O insurance premiums
 employment income, and 8.173
Damages payments
 capital gains tax, and
  case law 19.66–19.67
  ESC D33 19.68
  introduction 22.3
 employment income, and 8.156
 trading income, and 10.145

Dates for payment
 income tax, and 7.122
De minimis
 reservation of benefit, and 29.71
 value added tax, and 38.88
Dealings in securities
 value added tax, and 40.72
Death
 abatement 30.121–30.122
 accountability 30.35
 active service, on 31.25
 agricultural property relief
  And see **Agricultural property relief**
  generally 31.62–31.78
 anti-avoidance rules
  generally 30.15
  timing aspects 30.16
 burden of tax 30.55–30.62
 business property relief
  And see **Business property relief**
  generally 31.42–31.61
 calculation of tax
  accountability 30.35
  chargeable transfers 30.22–30.23
  fall in value of property 30.24
  generally 30.36
  introduction 30.21
  liability for tax 30.35
  potentially exempt transfers
   30.25–30.26
  residential nil rate band
   30.28–30.34
  taper relief 30.23
  transferable nil rate band 30.27
 capital gains tax, and
  annual exemption 21.64
  deductions and allowances
   21.62–21.64
  disclaimers 21.121–21.126
  domicile of PRs 21.3
  effect 21.1
  entrepreneurs' relief 21.63
  generally 51.60
  exempt legatees 21.105
  generally 30.149
  incidental expenses 21.62
  indexation 21.63
  inheritance provision 21.127
  introduction 21.1
  losses of deceased 21.41
  losses of PRs 21.81
  post-death variations 21.121–21.126
  principal private residence 21.65
  rate of tax 21.61
  'reading back' 21.122–21.123

1716 Index

Death – *contd*
  capital gains tax, and – *contd*
    residence of PRs 21.3
    revaluations 21.23
    sale of assets by PRs 21.61–21.65
    spouse exemption 21.104
    taper relief 21.63
    transfers to legatees 21.101–21.105
    valuation of chargeable
      assets 21.21–21.24
    will trusts, and 21.103
  certificates of discharge 30.53
  chargeable transfers 30.22–30.23
  charitable gifts
    death 30.37–30.38
    exemptions and reliefs 31.88–31.89
  commorientes 30.141–30.142
  contingent liabilities 30.49
  death on active service 31.25
  disclaimers 30.152–30.157
  entrepreneurs' relief 21.63
  'estate' 30.2
  excepted estates 30.44
  exemptions and reliefs
    agricultural property relief
      31.62–31.78
    business property relief 31.42–31.61
    charitable gifts 31.88–31.89
    death on active service 31.25
    heritage property 31.78–31.85
    inter-spouse transfer 31.41
    political parties, gifts to 31.87
    woodlands 31.21–31.24
  flexible will drafting 30.145–30.151
  heritage property
    And see **Heritage property relief**
    generally 31.78–31.85
  hold-over relief, and 30.148
  income tax 51.25
  inheritance provision 21.127
  instalments 30.51–30.53
  interest in possession trusts, and 33.10
  inter-spouse transfer 31.41
  introduction 30.1
  land 30.50
  liabilities
    anti-avoidance rules 30.15–30.16
    artificial debts 30.14
    general 30.13
  liability for tax 30.35
  main residence exemption, and
    disposal by legatees 23.66
    disposal by personal
      representatives 23.65
  nil rate band 31.2

Death – *contd*
  partially exempt transfers
    application of provisions
      30.91–30.97
    double grossing-up
      30.99–30.101
    effect of previous chargeable
      transfers 30.98
    residue part exempt and part
      chargeable 30.103
  payment of tax
    burden of tax 30.55–30.62
    certificates of discharge 30.53
    contingent liabilities 30.49
    duty to account 30.42
    estimated values 30.43
    excepted estates 30.44
    IHT form 30.45
    instalments, by 30.51–30.53
    introduction 30.41
    land 30.50
    person liable 30.42–30.54
    personal representatives 30.46
    recalculation 30.63–30.67
    trustees 30.48
  person liable 30.42–30.54
  personal representatives 30.46
  political parties, gifts to 31.87
  post-death variations 30.152–30.157
  potentially exempt transfers
    30.25–30.26
  precatory trusts 30.151
  quick succession relief 30.144
  recalculation 30.63–30.67
  residential nil rate band
    brought forward allowance 30.33
    closely inherited 30.30–30.31
    downsizing 30.34
    inherited 30.30
    introduction 30.28
    lineal descendants 30.30
    qualifying residential
      interest 30.29
    residential enhancement 30.32
    transferable 30.33
  settlements not subject to relevant
    property regime, and 33.10
  specific issues 30.141–30.158
  stamp duty, and 30.156
  surviving spouse 30.152
  survivorship clauses 30.143
  transferable nil rate band
    generally 30.27
    residential property 30.33
  trustees 30.48

Death – *contd*
  valuation of chargeable assets on
    death, and
    basic rule 21.21
    general conclusion 21.24
    IHT purposes, for 21.22
    IHT revaluations 21.23
  value of gift (death)
    changes in value 30.6
    funeral expenses 30.5
    introduction 30.3–30.4
    post-death sales 30.7–30.10
    provisional valuations 30.12
  vesting of property 30.148
  woodlands 31.21–31.24
Death benefits
  employment income, and 8.152
  pension schemes, and
    inheritance tax planning, and 50.32
    lump sums 50.31
Debts
  capital gains tax, and
    general principle 22.42
    loans to traders 22.43
    meaning 22.41
    qualifying corporate bonds 22.45
    security, on 22.44
  stamp duty land tax, and 49.48
Deceased's estates
  absolute interests in residue
    17.52–17.54
  administration period
    apportionments 17.26
    duration 17.20
    interest relief 17.23
    letting 17.25
    liability of personal
      representatives 17.21
    relevant tax office 17.22
    trading 17.24
  annuitants 17.44–17.47
  appointments
    tax consequences 17.58
    treatment of income 17.59
  apportionments 17.26
  capital gains tax, and 17.1
  clearances 17.60
  deceased's income
    administrative issues 17.7
    annuity contracts 17.6
    dividends 17.3
    interest on income due 17.7
    introduction 17.2
    life insurance policy 17.6
    partners 17.5

Deceased's estates – *contd*
  deceased's income – *contd*
    sole traders 17.5
    trust income 17.4
  disclaimers
    tax consequences 17.58
    treatment of income 17.59
  distributions to beneficiaries
    absolute interests in residue
      17.52–17.54
    annuitants 17.44–17.47
    basic principles 17.41
    clearances 17.60
    conclusions 17.55–17.57
    general legatees 17.42
    limited interests in residue 17.49
    residuary beneficiaries 17.48–17.54
    specific legatees 17.43
    successive interests in residue 17.57
  duration of administration 17.20
  general legatees 17.42
  interest relief 17.23
  introduction 17.1
  letting 17.25
  limited interests in residue 17.49
  personal representatives
    liability 17.21
    role 17.1
  relevant tax office 17.22
  residuary beneficiaries 17.48–17.54
  specific legatees 17.43
  successive interests in residue 17.57
  trading 17.24
  Trusts Registration Service 17.22
  variations
    tax consequences 17.58
    treatment of income 17.59
Decorations for valour
  capital gains tax, and 22.3
Deductible charges
  deduction against profits 41.59
  relevant charges 41.57
Deductible expenses
  capital gains tax, and
    acquisition of asset 19.20
    death, and 21.62–21.64
    disallowed expenditure 19.23
    disposal of asset 19.22
    enhancing value of asset 19.21
    indexation 19.24–19.27
    introduction 19.19
  charitable donations relief
    deduction against profits 41.59
    qualifying donations 41.57–41.58
  employee, by and for 8.172

Deductible expenses – *contd*
fixed rate, at
  introduction 10.161
  use of business premises as a home 10.164–10.165
  use of home for business purposes 10.163
  vehicle expenditure 10.162
foreign employment income, and 18.49
introduction 8.171
non-travel expenses 8.172–8.173
other expenses 8.175
trading income, and
  accounting costs 10.147
  annual investment allowance 10.135
  bad debts 10.144
  basic principles 10.130
  capital allowances 10.135
  damages, fines and losses 10.145
  depreciation 10.136
  designs 10.155
  doubtful debts 10.144
  employee costs 10.152
  employee payments 10.132
  employee trusts 10.133
  examples 10.139–10.157
  fines 10.145
  fixed rate, at 10.161–10.165
  impairment losses 10.144
  intellectual property 10.155
  interest 10.156
  legal costs 10.146
  losses 10.145
  outplacement counselling 10.148
  patents 10.155
  payment relating to crime 10.148
  payments to organisations 10.153
  penalties 10.156
  pre-trading expenditure 10.143
  rent for business premises 10.140
  repairs and improvements 10.142
  research and development 10.154
  restrictive covenants 10.134
  sale and leaseback arrangements 10.141
  sponsorship 10.157
  surcharges 10.156
  sum prohibited by statute 10.138
  sum to be income not capital 10.131–10.136
  tax 10.147
  trade marks 10.155
  training 10.148
  travelling expenses 10.150–10.151

Deductible expenses – *contd*
trading income, and – *contd*
  use of business premises as a home 10.164–10.165
  use of home for business purposes 10.163
  vehicle expenditure 10.162
  'wholly and exclusively' for business purposes 10.137
travel expenses 8.174
trusts, and 16.5
Deduction of tax at source
annual payments, and
  collection of deductions 14.45–14.46
  effect of failure to make 14.26
  generally 14.22
  introduction 14.21
  operation of s 448 ITA 2007 14.23–14.24
  payments outside the tax net 14.28
  position of recipient 14.25
  use of formulae 14.27
corporation tax, and 41.46
trusts, and
  dividends 16.6
Deduction principle
value added tax, and 38.81
Deductions from earnings
And see **Deductible expenses**
generally 8.171
Deeds of covenant
charities, and 53.87
Deemed disposition by participators
lifetime transfers, and 28.153
Deeply discounted securities
savings and investment income, and 14.42
Deferral of payment
sale of unincorporated business, and 22.102
stamp duty land tax, and 49.61
Deferral relief
anti-avoidance 15.98
appeals 15.96
claims 15.100
clawback of gain 15.97
disposal 15.91
EIS investments 15.93–15.94
entrepreneurs' relief, and 15.94
introduction 15.89
qualifying investment 15.92
relief 15.90
taper relief 15.93

Deferral relief – *contd*
  trustees 15.99
  withdrawal 15.95
Deferred consideration
  capital gains tax, and 19.17
Deferred gains
  entrepreneurs' relief, and
    EIS 20.40
    introduction 20.34
    qualifying corporate bonds
      20.36–20.38
    share exchanges 20.39
    social investment tax relief 20.40
    VCT 20.40
Defined benefit schemes
  See **Pension schemes**
Defined contribution schemes
  See **Pension schemes**
Demergers
  distributions, and 42.141–42.149
  generally 47.51
Depositary receipt systems
  stamp duty, and 49.123
Depreciation
  trading income, and 10.136
Depreciatory transactions
  groups of companies, and 43.151
De-registration
  value added tax, and 38.51
Derivative contracts
  corporation tax, and 41.43
Designated assisted areas
  first year allowances for plant and
    machinery 48.37
Designs
  trading income, and 10.155
Destruction of asset
  capital gains tax, and 19.65
Development agreements
  stamp duty land tax, and 49.39
Directives
  And see **EU law**
  Anti-Tax Avoidance 54.98
  Common Consolidated Corporate Tax
    Base 54.97
  Interest and Royalties Directive
    54.94
  introduction 54.91
  Merger Directive 54.92
  Mutual Assistance Directive 54.95
  Parent/Subsidiary Directive 54.93
  Savings Directive 54.96
Directors
  Seed Enterprise Investment Scheme,
    and 15.133

Disability benefits
  employment income, and 8.152
Disabled, trusts for the
  inheritance tax, and 32.59
  settlements not subject to relevant
    property regime, and 33.113
Disbursements
  value added tax, and 40.97
Disclaimers
  capital gains tax on death,
    and 21.121–21.126
  estates in the course of administration,
    and
    tax consequences 17.58
    treatment of income 17.59
  inheritance tax on death, and
    30.152–30.157
  interest in possession trusts, and 33.28
  settlements not subject to relevant
    property regime, and 33.28
**Disclosure of tax avoidance scheme
  (DOTAS) rules**
  And see **Disclosure rules**
  annual tax on enveloped dwellings
    description of arrangements 5.16
    generally 5.15
  description of arrangements 5.13
  disclosable information 5.8
  form of disclosure 5.9
  generally 5.3
  information powers 5.17
  inheritance tax 5.12–5.14
  introduction 5.4
  promoters of tax avoidance schemes
    (POTAS)
    generally 5.30
    introduction 5.5–5.6
  schemes and arrangements 5.7
  stamp duty land tax, and
    generally 49.87
    introduction 5.11
    persons required to disclose 49.88
    recent developments 49.89
  time of disclosure 5.10
  widening scope 5.12
Disclosure rules
  accelerated payments 5.28
  annual tax on enveloped dwellings
    description of arrangements 5.16
    generally 5.15
  conclusions 5.31
  direct taxes (DOTAS)
    annual tax on enveloped
      dwellings 5.15–5.16
    disclosable information 5.8

Disclosure rules – *contd*
  direct taxes (DOTAS) – *contd*
    form of disclosure 5.9
    information powers 5.17
    inheritance tax 5.12–5.14
    introduction 5.4
    promoters 5.5–5.6
    schemes and arrangements 5.7
    stamp duty land tax 5.11
    time of disclosure 5.10
    widening scope 5.12
  follower notices 5.29
  hallmarked schemes 5.23
  indirect taxes (VADR)
    designated transactions 5.22
    generally notifiable
      transactions 5.23
    hallmarked schemes 5.23
    introduction 5.21
    listed schemes 5.22
    notification 5.25
    reforms 5.26
    tax advantage 5.24
  information powers 5.17
  inheritance tax
    description of arrangements 5.13
    introduction 5.12
    required information 5.14
  introduction 5.3
  listed schemes 5.22
  promoters of tax avoidance schemes
      (POTAS) rules
    generally 5.30
    introduction 5.5–5.6
  scope 5.3
  stamp duty land tax 5.11
Discounted gift schemes
  generally 15.25
Discovery assessments
  assessment of tax, and 4.41–4.43
Discretionary trusts
  annual payments, and 14.15
Discretionary trusts
  distributions, and 42.96
  dividends 16.66
  general rules 16.65
  reservation of benefit, and 29.133
Discrimination
  human rights, and
    employees and self-employed
      persons, between 55.45
    exercise of discretion, in 55.46
    gender grounds, on 55.44
    legal advice privilege, and 55.48
    marriage grounds, on 55.43

Discrimination – *contd*
  human rights, and – *contd*
    nature 55.41
    prosecution, as to 55.47
    scope 55.42–55.48
    similarly situated taxpayers,
      between 55.42
Disguised remuneration
  tax avoidance, and 5.7
Disposal
  appropriations to and from stock in
    trade 19.71
  capital sums derived from assets
    19.64
  charges 19.73
  compensation in damages, and
    case law 19.66–19.67
    ESC D33 19.68
  consideration
    connected persons 19.15
    deferred consideration 19.17
    general 19.14
    market value of assets 19.16
    Marren v Ingles 19.18
  destruction of asset 19.65
  exchanges of joint interests in
    land 19.77
  general 19.63
  hire-purchase agreements 19.72
  introduction 19.8
  land, of 12.105
  lease extensions 19.76
  mortgages 19.73
  negligible value of asset 19.69
  options 19.70
  settled property 19.74
  shares, of
    acquisition before 6 April
      1965 26.48
    basic rule 26.44
    bed and breakfasting 26.46
    current regime 26.44–26.46
    identification rules 26.45
    introduction 26.41–26.43
    pooling from 6 April 2008 26.47
  substantial shareholdings, and 41.75
  timing
    conditional contracts 19.79
    general rule 19.78
  total loss of asset 19.65
  value shifting 19.75
Disposal of land
  transactions in UK land 12.105
Disposals of substantial shareholdings
  corporation tax, and 41.75

Disposition
 lifetime transfers, and 28.3
Dispositions for maintenance
 inheritance tax, and 31.7–31.10
Dissolution of partnerships
 stamp duty, and 49.116
Distributions by companies
 See also **Dividends**
 advance corporation tax
  introduction 42.41–42.42
  utilisation of surplus 42.46–42.48
 assets of company made in respect of shares 42.3
 bonus shares issue
  following reduction of capital 42.4
  generally 42.3
  redeemable shares 42.5
 capital gains tax, and 26.21
 close companies, and 42.10
 company buy-backs, and
  advantages if distribution rules apply 42.29
  clearance 42.31
  'connected' test 42.25
  fraction calculations 42.26
  introduction 42.21
  qualifying vendors 42.23
  reason for sale 42.27
  relevant companies 42.22
  stamp duty 42.31
  'substantial reduction' test 42.24
  trustees, from 42.30
  UK company as vendor 42.28
  vendor of shares 42.23–42.42.26
 demergers, and 42.141–42.149
 'equity notes' 42.8
 exempt distributions 42.141–42.149
 foreign income, and 18.36
 franked investment income
  generally 42.91–42.94
  introduction 42.1
 interest in possession trusts 42.152
 interest payments 42.7
 meaning 42.1–42.2
 payment on winding up 42.3
 redeemable shares 42.5
 reduction of capital
  followed by bonus issue 42.4
  generally 42.3
 Schedule F, and 42.1
 scrip dividends
  generally 42.150
  interest in possession trusts 42.152
  tax treatment 42.151
 shadow ACT 42.46–42.48

Distributions by companies – *contd*
 stock dividend option 42.9
 surplus ACT 42.46–42.48
 taxation of non-qualifying distributions 42.121
 taxation of qualifying distributions
  introduction 42.41–42.42
  utilisation of surplus ACT 42.46–42.48
 taxation of recipients
  charities 42.76
  discretionary trusts 42.96
  estates of deceased persons 42.95–42.96
  individuals 42.76
  trusts 42.95–42.96
  UK companies 42.91–42.94
 transfer to members of assets or liabilities worth more than new consideration 42.6
Distributions to beneficiaries
 absolute interests in residue 17.52–17.54
 annuitants 17.44–17.47
 basic principles 17.41
 clearances 17.60
 conclusions 17.55–17.57
 general legatees 17.42
 limited interests in residue 17.49
 residuary beneficiaries 17.48–17.54
 specific legatees 17.43
 successive interests in residue 17.57
Distributions to shareholders
 capital gains tax, and 26.21
Diverted profits tax
 charities, and 53.42
Dividend stripping
 And see **Tax avoidance**
 generally 3.10
 overview 3.4
 transactions in securities, and 3.58–3.60
Dividends
 charities, and 53.41
 choice of business medium, and 46.54–46.55
 dividends 17.3
 foreign taxpayers, and 18.78
 income tax, and 7.27
 trusts, and
  deduction of tax at source 16.6
  s 479 ITA 2007 charge, and 16.29–16.30
  s 496 ITA 2007 charge, and 16.33

Dividends – *contd*
  trusts, and – *contd*
    tax on discretionary
      beneficiaries 16.66
Division
  stamp duty land tax, and 49.46
Divorce
  annual exemption 52.22
  capital gains tax
    annual exemption 52.22
    generally 52.21
    lump sum payments 52.23
    matrimonial home 52.62–52.63
  clean-break transfer 52.67–52.69
  income tax
    general principles 52.2
    life insurance policies 52.15
    maintenance payments 52.3
    pensions 52.4–52.12
  inheritance tax
    generally 52.41
    matrimonial home 52.64
  introduction 52.1
  life insurance policies 52.15
  lump sum payments 52.23
  maintenance payments 52.3
  matrimonial home
    capital gains tax 52.62–52.63
    clean-break transfer
      52.67–52.69
    conclusions 52.79
    inheritance tax 52.64
    introduction 52.61
    joint ownership with sale
      postponed 52.70–52.72
    outright transfer with charge
      back 52.76–52.78
    settlement of house 52.73–52.75
    stamp duty land tax 52.65
  pensions
    Brooks v Brooks decision 52.4
    earmarking orders 52.12
    flexibility 52.14
    introduction 52.4
    offsetting 52.11
    pension attachment 52.12
    pension sharing 52.13
  stamp duty 52.60
  stamp duty land tax 52.65
  tax credits 52.16
DIY house builders
  value added tax, and 39.42
Domicile
  choice, of 18.25–18.26
  deemed 18.28

Domicile – *contd*
  inheritance tax, and
    deemed domicile 35.4
    election for non-UK domiciled
      spouse 35.5
    general 35.3
  introduction 18.23
  married women 18.29
  origin, of 18.24
  personal representatives 21.3
  proposed 2017 changes 18.30
  special situations 18.27
Donations
  value added tax, and 40.49
DOTAS rules
  And see **Disclosure rules**
  annual tax on enveloped dwellings
    description of arrangements 5.16
    generally 5.15
  description of arrangements 5.13
  disclosable information 5.8
  form of disclosure 5.9
  generally 5.3
  information powers 5.17
  inheritance tax 5.12–5.14
  introduction 5.4
  promoters of tax avoidance schemes
    (POTAS)
    generally 5.30
    introduction 5.5–5.6
  schemes and arrangements 5.7
  stamp duty land tax, and
    generally 49.87
    introduction 5.11
    persons required to disclose 49.88
    recent developments 49.89
  time of disclosure 5.10
  widening scope 5.12
Double charges
  inheritance tax, and
    artificial debts and death 36.4
    chargeable transfers and death 36.5
    gifts with reservation and
      subsequent death 36.3
    introduction 36.1
    mutual transfers 36.2
'Double-dip'
  Gift Aid, and 53.85
Double discounting
  agricultural property relief, and 31.75
Double taxation
  corporation tax, and
    capital gains, and 41.49
    general principles 41.156
    mixer companies 41.159

Double taxation – *contd*
  corporation tax, and – *contd*
    tax agreements 41.157
    unilateral relief 41.158
  income tax, and 18.91
  inheritance tax on death, and 35.41
Double tax treaties
  residence, and 18.22
Doubtful debts
  trading income, and 10.144
Dredging
  capital allowances, and 48.2
Dwellings
  value added tax, and 39.23

E

Earmarking orders
  pensions, and 52.12
Earned income
  income tax, and 7.23
'Earnings'
  And see **Employment income**
  expenses 8.94–8.95
  general principles 8.92–8.93
  introduction 8.91
  money or money's worth 8.92
  valuing the benefit 8.93
Earnings basis
  miscellaneous income, and 13.16
Earn-outs
  non tax-advantaged share
    schemes 9.12
E-commerce
  value added tax, and 38.34
EC law
  See **EU law**
Education
  disclosure rules, and 5.22
  value added tax, and
    eligible bodies 40.34
    generally 40.33
    private tuition 40.35
EIS
  See **Enterprise Investment Scheme**
Elections
  main residence exemption and 23.43
  value added tax on commercial
    property, and 39.27
Emoluments
  employment income, and 8.41
Employee-controlled companies
  loan interest on investments,
    and 7.48
Employee costs
  trading income, and 10.152

Employee ownership trusts
  bonus payments 9.117
  introduction 9.115
  transfer of ownership interest 9.116
Employee participation
  approved share schemes
    And see **Tax-advantaged share
      schemes**
    generally 9.2
  choice of scheme
    non-tax aspects 9.151–9.160
    other shareholders 9.164
    tax aspects 9.161–9.163
  convertible shares 9.25
  corporation tax
    amount of relief 9.128
    arbitrage receipts rules 9.129
    availability of relief 9.125–9.127
    deductibility 9.122
    introduction 9.121
    restriction of tax relief 9.123
    share type 9.127
    statutory tax relief 9.124–9.129
    tax position of employee 9.126
    timing of relief 9.129
  employee ownership trusts
    bonus payments 9.117
    introduction 9.115
    transfer of ownership interest 9.116
  employee share ownership
    plans 9.113
  employee shareholders
    CGT relief on disposal 9.34
    generally 9.32
    introduction 9.1
    tax reliefs (abolition) 9.33
  employee trusts
    introduction 9.111
    taxation 9.112
  encouraging employee share
    ownership 9.1
  equity ratchets, and 9.12
  'from' employment, and 9.2
  introduction 9.1–9.3
  loans to acquire shares 9.1
  non tax-advantaged share schemes
    And see **Non tax-advantaged share
      schemes**
    background 9.11
    capital gains tax 9.45–9.57
    conclusions 9.58
    introduction 9.11–9.13
    NICs 9.44
    PAYE 9.42–9.43
    rights to acquire shares 9.41

Employee participation – *contd*
  non tax-advantaged share
    schemes – *contd*
    share incentives 9.21–9.34
    share options 9.41
  non-tax aspects of choice
    accounting treatment 9.160
    bonus schemes 9.152
    employee retention 9.155
    'friendly' shareholdings 9.156
    introduction 9.151
    market in non-quoted shares
      9.157
    performance-related
      incentives 9.153
    retention of employees 9.155
    reward for growth in share
      value 9.154
    sense of identity between employees
      and company 9.158
    selective employee
      participation 9.159
  other shareholders, and 9.164
  priority share allocations 9.30
  reporting obligations 9.3
  research institution spin-out
    companies 9.31
  share incentives
    artificial depression of market
      value 9.26
    convertible shares 9.25
    employee shareholders 9.32–9.34
    introduction 9.1
    enhancement of market value 9.26
    meaning 9.2
    post-acquisition benefits 9.29
    priority share allocations 9.30
    research institution spin-out
      companies 9.31
    restricted shares 9.21–9.23
    shares acquired for less than market
      value 9.27
    shares disposed of for more than
      market value 9.28
  spin-out companies 9.31
  tax-advantaged share schemes
    And see **Tax-advantaged share**
      schemes
    company share option plans 9.76
    enterprise management
      incentives 9.83–9.87
    general treatment 9.71–9.72
    NICs 9.90
    PAYE 9.88–9.89
    requirements 9.73–9.74

Employee participation – *contd*
  tax-advantaged share schemes – *contd*
    savings-related share option
      schemes 9.75
    share incentive plans 9.77–9.82
  tax aspects of choice 9.161–9.163
  Treasury shares 9.114
  unapproved employee trusts
    introduction 9.111
    taxation 9.112
  unapproved share schemes
    And see **Non tax-advantaged share**
      schemes
    generally 9.2
Employee payments
  trading income, and 10.132
Employee share ownership plans
  generally 9.113
Employee shareholders
  CGT relief on disposal 9.34
  generally 9.32
  introduction 9.1
  tax reliefs (abolition) 9.33
Employee trusts
  corporation tax, and 41.45
  introduction 9.111
  settlements not subject to relevant
    property regime, and 33.115
  settlements subject to relevant
    property regime, and 34.114
  taxation 9.112
  trading income, and 10.133
Employer-provided accommodation
  stamp duty land tax, and 49.52
Employment allowance
  charities, and 53.133
Employment income
  See also **Income tax**
  accounting to HMRC 8.199
  agency workers
    introduction 8.31
    managed services company
      legislation 8.34
    operation of rules 8.32
    services provided to public sector
      authorities 8.33
  amounts counted as employment
    income
    contemporaneous share sales 8.157
    current regime 8.150
    damages, and 8.156
    death benefits 8.152
    disability benefits 8.152
    exceptions 8.151–8.154
    first £30,000 8.154

Employment income – *contd*
amounts counted as employment income – *contd*
generally 8.148
injury benefits 8.152
internationally mobile employees 8.158
introduction 8.101
old regime 8.149
PAYE 8.155
pension benefits 8.152
reform recommendations 8.159
reporting requirements 8.155
amounts treated as earnings
benefits code 8.103–8.131
introduction 8.101
payments 8.132–8.135
purpose of rules 8.102
annual parties and functions 8.168
basis of assessment 8.12
beneficial loan arrangements 8.124
benefits code
beneficial loan arrangements 8.124
by reason of employment 8.105
cash equivalent cost 8.126
cash payments 8.127
conclusion 8.135
credit tokens 8.109
employment-related benefits 8.125
excluded employees 8.104
expenses payments 8.108
fuel for vehicles 8.122
interaction with charge on earnings, 8.103
introduction 8.101
living accommodation 8.110–8.116
lower-paid employees 8.104
making good 8.107
optional remuneration arrangements 8.106
prospective employees 8.128
purpose of rules 8.102
residual liability 8.125–8.131
scholarships 8.130
trivial benefits 8.131
use of asset 8.129
vehicles 8.117–8.123
vouchers 8.109
bicycles 8.166
by reason of employment 8.105
cars
fuel and other benefits 8.122
introduction 8.117
non-pooled 8.119–8.122
pooled 8.118

Employment income – *contd*
cars – *contd*
reducing the tax charge 8.120
use of own car 8.121
cash equivalent cost 8.126
cash payments 8.127
cash termination payments
contemporaneous share sales 8.157
current regime 8.150
damages, and 8.156
death benefits 8.152
disability benefits 8.152
exceptions 8.151–8.154
first £30,000 8.154
generally 8.148
injury benefits 8.152
internationally mobile employees 8.158
introduction 8.101
old regime 8.149
PAYE 8.155
pension benefits 8.152
reform recommendations 8.159
reporting requirements 8.155
charging provisions
'from' an employment 8.41
generally 8.11
termination payments 8.142–8.145
charitable giving, and 8.173
childcare 8.167
collection of tax
accounting to HMRC 8.199
benefits in kind 8.192
gross payments to employee 8.201
introduction 8.191
K codes 8.196
non-deduction of PAYE 8.200
part only of payment taxed 8.193
PAYE coding 8.195
PAYE settlement agreements 8.198
'payment' 8.194
problem cases 8.192–8.193
real-time information 8.203
recovery of tax from employee by employer 8.202
reform proposals 8.203
returns 8.197
scope of provisions 8.191
settlement agreements 8.198
compensation for losses 8.64
computer equipment 8.166
construction industry workers, and 8.31
credit tokens 8.109
damages 8.156

Employment income – *contd*
  deductible expenses
    employee, by and for 8.172
    introduction 8.171
    non-travel expenses 8.172–8.173
    other expenses 8.175
    travel expenses 8.174
  D&O insurance premiums, and 8.173
  'earnings'
    expenses 8.94–8.95
    general principles 8.92–8.93
    introduction 8.91
    money or money's worth 8.92
    valuing the benefit 8.93
  emoluments, and 8.41
  employment-related benefits 8.125
  entertainers, and 8.31
  exemptions
    annual parties and functions 8.168
    bicycles 8.166
    childcare 8.167
    computer equipment 8.166
    gifts from third parties 8.168
    homeworker's additional
      expenses 8.165
    introduction 8.161
    long service awards 8.168
    minor benefits 8.169
    mobile phones 8.166
    outplacement counselling 8.163
    relocation costs 8.162
    subsidised meals 8.168
    third party gifts 8.168
    training 8.164
    use of assets 8.166
  expenses as earnings
    exemptions 8.95
    generally 8.94
  expenses payments 8.108
  foreign income
    annuities 18.50
    collection of tax 18.51
    deductible expenses 18.49
    emoluments for duties performed
      in UK 18.46
    introduction 18.43
    pensions 18.50
    place of work 18.48
    remittance basis 18.47
  foreign taxpayers, and 18.73
  'from' an employment
    general principles 8.42
    introduction 8.41
    past services 8.44
    third party payments 8.43
  fuel for vehicles 8.122

Employment income – *contd*
  'general earnings' 8.11
  gifts
    generally 8.62
    third parties, from 8.168
  'golden handshakes'
    contemporaneous share sales 8.157
    current regime 8.150
    damages, and 8.156
    death benefits 8.152
    disability benefits 8.152
    exceptions 8.151–8.154
    first £30,000 8.154
    generally 8.148
    injury benefits 8.152
    internationally mobile
      employees 8.158
    introduction 8.101
    old regime 8.149
    PAYE 8.155
    pension benefits 8.152
    reform recommendations 8.159
    reporting requirements 8.155
  gross payments to employee 8.201
  homeworker's additional
    expenses 8.165
  inducement payments 8.63
  introduction 8.1
  IR 35 workers
    introduction 8.31
    managed services company
      legislation 8.34
    operation of rules 8.32
    services provided to public sector
      authorities 8.33
  K codes 8.196
  liability insurance premiums,
    and 8.173
  living accommodation
    additional charge 8.112
    basic charge 8.111
    decreasing the charge 8.113
    exemptions 8.114
    increasing the charge 8.113
    introduction 8.110
    non-domiciliaries 8.116
  long service awards 8.168
  lower-paid employees 8.104
  lump sum termination payments
    contemporaneous share sales 8.157
    current regime 8.150
    damages, and 8.156
    death benefits 8.152
    disability benefits 8.152
    exceptions 8.151–8.154
    first £30,000 8.154

Employment income – *contd*
  lump sum termination payments – *contd*
    generally 8.148
    injury benefits 8.152
    internationally mobile employees 8.158
    introduction 8.101
    old regime 8.149
    PAYE 8.155
    pension benefits 8.152
    reform recommendations 8.159
    reporting requirements 8.155
  managed service companies
    introduction 8.31
    legislation 8.34
    operation of rules 8.32
    services provided to public sector authorities 8.33
  membership fees, and 8.172
  minor benefits 8.169
  mobile phones 8.166
  national insurance contributions 8.1
  non-deduction of PAYE 8.200
  office or employment
    employment status 8.22
    introduction 8.20
    'office' 8.21
    partners 8.23
    reclassification of status 8.24
  optional remuneration arrangements 8.106
  outplacement counselling 8.163
  own car use 8.22
  part only of payment taxed 8.193
  past services 8.44
  PAYE
    coding 8.195
    introduction 8.1
    settlement agreements 8.198
  payroll deduction scheme, and 8.173
  permanent health insurance 8.133
  personal service companies
    introduction 8.31
    managed services company legislation 8.34
    operation of rules 8.32
    services provided to public sector authorities 8.33
  pooled cars and vans 8.118
  post-cessation receipts, and 8.12
  problem areas
    compensation for losses 8.64
    gifts 8.62
    inducement payments 8.63
    introduction 8.61

Employment income – *contd*
  problem areas – *contd*
    unearned income 8.66
    variation of terms of employment payments 8.65
  prospective employees 8.128
  real-time information 8.203
  recovery of tax from employee by employer 8.202
  relocation costs 8.162
  residual liability 8.125–8.131
  restrictive undertakings 8.134
  returns 8.197
  Schedule E, and 8.11
  scholarships 8.130
  services provided to public sector authorities 8.33
  settlement agreements 8.198
  sick pay 8.133
  source doctrine 8.13
  subsidised meals 8.168
  tax structures 8.11–8.13
  tax year 8.12
  taxable earnings 8.11
  termination payments
    charging provision 8.142–8.144
    introduction 8.141
    payments treated as earnings 8.147
    residual charging provision 8.145
  third party gifts 8.168
  third party payments 8.43
  training 8.164
  travel expenses 8.174
  trivial benefits 8.131
  unearned income 8.66
  use of assets
    exemptions, and 8.166
    generally 8.129
  vans
    fuel and other benefits 8.122
    introduction 8.117
    non-pooled 8.123
    pooled 8.118
  variation of terms of employment payments 8.65
  vehicles
    fuel and other benefits 8.122
    introduction 8.117
    non-pooled cars 8.119–8.122
    non-pooled vans 8.123
    pooled cars and vans 8.118
    reducing the tax charge 8.120
    use of own car 8.121
  vouchers 8.109
Employment loss relief
  net income, and 7.42

Energy saving allowance
 capital allowances, and
  48.126–48.127
Energy-saving and water-conserving plant and machinery
 first year allowances, and 48.31
Enhanced protection
 pension schemes, and 50.22
Enquiries
 assessment of tax, and 4.33
Enterprise Investment Scheme (EIS)
 anti-avoidance 15.57
 capital gains tax, and 22.3
 choice of business medium, and
  generally 46.50
  smaller companies 46.51
 eligible shares 15.55
 entrepreneurs' relief, and 20.41
 family taxation, and 51.49
 introduction 15.51
 pre-arranged exits 15.57
 qualifying activities 15.56
 qualifying company 15.54
 qualifying individuals 15.53
 relief 15.52
 smaller companies, for 46.51
Enterprise management incentives
 eligible employees 9.85
 introduction 9.83
 maximum value of options 9.86
 qualifying companies 9.84
 taxation of employees 9.87
Entertainers
 employment income, and 8.31
 foreign taxpayers, and 18.74
 value added tax, and
  generally 40.43
  'nett' acts 40.44
Entrepreneurs' relief
 aggregation of gains and losses 20.5
 associated disposals
  disposal of shares 20.29–20.34
  introduction 20.29
 calculation 20.4
 claims 20.7
 death, and 21.63
 deferral relief, and 15.94
 deferred gains
  EIS 20.40
  introduction 20.34
  qualifying corporate bonds
   20.36–20.38
  share exchanges 20.39
  social investment tax relief 20.40
  VCT 20.40

Entrepreneurs' relief – *contd*
 disposal of business
  sole traders 20.20
 disposal of part of business
  sole traders 20.21
 EIS, and
  deferral relief 20.41
  deferred gains 20.40
 employment requirement 20.10
 family taxation, and 51.60
 generally 22.85
 gifts of business assets, and 24.14
 interaction with other reliefs 20.41
 introduction 20.1
 losses, and 20.6
 operation
  aggregation of gains and losses 20.5
  calculation 20.4
  interaction with losses 20.6
  qualifying disposals 20.3
 order of use of schemes 20.41
 outline 20.2
 overview 19.4
 partners
  generally 20.22
  special rules 20.23
 partnerships, and 44.39
 post cessation disposals 20.24–20.28
 qualifying corporate bonds
  election by taxpayer 20.38
  generally 20.36
  post 6 April 2008 20.37
 qualifying disposals 20.3
 rates of tax, and 19.49
 shareholders
  generally 20.8
  personal company 20.9
 social investment tax relief 20.40
 sole traders
  disposal of business 20.20
  disposal of part of business 20.21
  generally 20.19
 trading company
  HMRC ruling 20.18
  holding company 20.16
  introduction 20.11
  significant interest 20.13
  subsidiaries 20.16
  substantial extent 20.15
  trade 20.14
  trading activities 20.12
  trading group 20.17
 trusts, and 25.148
 VCT 20.40

Environmentally beneficial plant or machinery
first year allowances, and 48.35
Equipment lessors
capital allowances, and 48.27
'Equity notes'
distributions, and 42.8
Equity ratchets
non tax-advantaged share schemes 9.12
Estate
inheritance tax on death, and 30.2
Estate agents
value added tax, and
generally 39.44
property management 39.45
Estate duty
inheritance tax, and 30.158
Estates in administration
absolute interests in residue 17.52–17.54
administration period
apportionments 17.26
duration 17.20
interest relief 17.23
letting 17.25
liability of personal representatives 17.21
relevant tax office 17.22
trading 17.24
annuitants 17.44–17.47
annuity contracts 17.6
apportionments 17.26
capital gains tax, and 17.1
clearances 17.60
deceased's income
administrative issues 17.6
annuity contracts 17.6
dividends 17.3
interest on income due 17.7
introduction 17.2
life insurance policy 17.6
partners 17.5
sole traders 17.5
trust income 17.4
disclaimers
tax consequences 17.58
treatment of income 17.59
distributions to beneficiaries
absolute interests in residue 17.52–17.54
annuitants 17.44–17.47
basic principles 17.41
clearances 17.60
conclusions 17.55–17.57

Estates in administration – *contd*
distributions to beneficiaries – *contd*
general legatees 17.42
limited interests in residue 17.49
residuary beneficiaries 17.48–17.54
specific legatees 17.43
successive interests in residue 17.57
dividends 17.3
duration of administration 17.20
general legatees 17.42
interest on income due 17.7
interest relief 17.23
introduction 17.1
letting 17.25
life insurance policy 17.6
limited interests in residue 17.49
personal representatives
liability 17.21
role 17.1
relevant tax office 17.22
residuary beneficiaries 17.48–17.54
specific legatees 17.43
successive interests in residue 17.57
trading 17.24
Trusts Registration Service 17.22
variations
tax consequences 17.58
treatment of income 17.59
EU law
abuse of right 54.71–54.76
Anti-Tax Avoidance Directive 54.98
barriers to market 54.52
bilateral treaties 54.21
'Brexit'
Article 50 TEU 54.2
Common Consolidated Corporate Tax Base Directive 54.97
comparability
generally 54.55
introduction 54.53
methodology 54.54
reference to other issues, by 54.57
territoriality, and 54.56
direct effect 54.23
Directives
Anti-Tax Avoidance 54.98
Common Consolidated Corporate Tax Base 54.97
Interest and Royalties Directive 54.94
introduction 54.91
Merger Directive 54.92
Mutual Assistance Directive 54.95
Parent/Subsidiary Directive 54.93
Savings Directive 54.96

EU law – *contd*
  discrimination
    comparators, and 54.59
    direct discrimination 54.58
    indirect discrimination 54.59
    restrictions 54.60
  establishment
    exit taxes 54.46
    generally 54.45
  European companies 54.99
  fundamental freedoms
    abuse of right 54.71–54.76
    breach 54.51–54.68
    derogations 54.47
    discrimination 54.55–54.60
    establishment 54.45–54.46
    introduction 54.31
    justifications 54.61–54.68
    movement of capital 54.49
    movement of goods 54.42
    movement of persons 54.43
    movement of workers 54.44
    provision of services 54.48
    'rule of reason' 54.61
    scope 54.41
  human rights, and 55.101
  impact on domestic law 54.22
  institutions of the EU
    Council of European Union 54.6
    Court of Justice of the European Communities 54.8
    European Commission 54.7
    European Parliament 54.5
    introduction 54.4
  introduction 54.1
  justification
    anti-avoidance 54.64
    conclusions 54.65
    fiscal cohesion 54.62
    fiscal supervision 54.63
    proportionality 54.68
    'rule of reason', and 54.61
    suitability 54.66–54.67
  leaving the EU
    Article 50 TEU 54.2
  methodology 54.54
  movement of capital 54.49
  movement of goods 54.42
  movement of persons 54.43
  movement of workers 54.44
  precedence over UK law
    direct effect 54.23
    generally 54.21
    supremacy 54.24
    transfer of competency 54.22

EU law – *contd*
  proportionality 54.68
  provision of services 54.48
  'rule of reason' 54.61
  sources
    introduction 54.11
    secondary legislation 54.13
    treaties 54.12
  state aid 54.81
  supremacy 54.24
  territoriality 54.56
  transfer of competency to Community 54.22
  underlying principles 54.21–54.22
Exchange of land
  capital gains tax, and 19.77
  stamp duty land tax, and 49.45
Exchange of shares
  stamp duty, and 49.117
Excluded property
  inheritance tax, and
    domicile, and 35.3–35.5
    generally 28.25
    government securities 35.21
    introduction 35.1–35.2
    non-sterling bank accounts 35.26
    OEIC shares 35.22
    overseas pensions 35.25
    policy issues 31.1
    property owned by persons domiciled in Channels Islands or Isle of Man 35.23
    property situated outside UK and owned by non-UK domiciliary 35.20
    situs of property, and 35.6
    unit trust holdings 35.22
    visiting forces 35.24
  interest in possession trusts, and 33.24
  settlements not subject to relevant property regime, and 33.24
Exempt art sales
  remittances, and 27.97
Exempt dispositions
  commercial transactions 28.21
  excluded property 28.25
  exempt transfers 28.26
  partnerships 28.24
  reversionary interests 28.22
  transfer of unquoted shares and debentures 28.23
  voidable transfers 28.28
  waiver of remuneration and dividends 28.27

Exempt interests
  stamp duty land tax, and 49.32
Exempt supplies
  See also **Value added tax**
  generally 38.8
  property 39.19
Exempt transfers
  See also **Partially exempt transfers**
  See also **Potentially exempt transfers**
  inheritance tax, and 28.26
Exemptions and reliefs
  agricultural property relief
    'agricultural property' 31.62
    agricultural land or pasture 31.63
    agricultural tenancies 31.72
    'agricultural value' 31.67
    amount 31.68
    business property relief, and 31.77
    'character appropriate' test 31.65–31.66
    clawback 31.72
    companies, and 31.70
    double discounting 31.75
    farmhouses 31.65–31.66
    intensive farming buildings 31.64
    interest in possession trusts, and 33.30
    introduction 31.62
    lotting 31.74
    milk quota 31.76
    occupation requirement 31.69
    ownership requirement 31.69
    reservations, and 31.78
    settlements not subject to relevant property regime, and 33.30
    technical provisions 31.71
    transitional relief 31.75
    trusts, and 31.70
  business property relief
    amount 31.45
    clawback 31.59
    consequences 31.61
    contracts to sell the business 31.53
    'control' 31.55
    excepted assets 31.52
    instalment payments, and 31.58
    introduction 31.42
    investment businesses 31.48
    minority shareholdings in unquoted companies 31.56
    mixed businesses 31.49–31.50
    net value of business, on 31.44
    non-business assets 31.52
    non qualifying activities 31.47
    ownership requirement 31.46

Exemptions and reliefs – *contd*
  business property relief – *contd*
    'relevant business property' 31.43
    reservations, and 31.60
    settlements, and 31.54
    switching control 31.57
    'wholly or mainly' test 31.50
  capital gains tax, and
    charitable transactions 22.4
    chattels 22.21–22.23
    cultural gifts scheme 22.6
    debts 22.41–22.45
    exempt assets 22.2
    exempt gains 22.3
    heritage property 22.5
    introduction 22.1
    main residence 23.1–23.141
    overview 19.9–19.10
    woodland 22.5
  employment income, and
    annual parties and functions 8.168
    bicycles 8.166
    childcare 8.167
    computer equipment 8.166
    gifts from third parties 8.168
    homeworker's additional expenses 8.165
    introduction 8.161
    long service awards 8.168
    minor benefits 8.169
    mobile phones 8.166
    outplacement counselling 8.163
    relocation costs 8.162
    subsidised meals 8.168
    third party gifts 8.168
    training 8.164
    use of assets 8.166
  family taxation, and
    capital allowances 51.51
    close company loans 51.50
    Enterprise Investment Scheme 51.49
  heritage property relief
    acceptance in lieu 31.90
    calculation of deferred charge 31.83
    effect of deferred charge 31.82
    introduction 31.79
    maintenance funds 31.85
    preconditions 31.80
    private treaty sales 31.86
    reopening existing undertakings 31.81
    settled property 31.84

Exemptions and reliefs – *contd*
  hold-over relief
    assets attracting immediate IHT
      charge, of 24.22–24.26
    business assets, of 24.4–24.21
    disposal at market value 24.2
    general 22.99
    IHT consequences 24.3
    introduction 24.1–24.3
  income tax, and
    exempt income 7.129–7.131
    exempt organisations 7.128
    introduction 7.127
    ISAs 7.132
    life assurance policies 7.132
  incorporation of business relief
    conditions 22.101
    deferral of tax on sale
      of unincorporated
      business 22.102
    election to disapply 22.103
    generally 22.100
    overview 26.4
  inheritance tax, and
    acceptance in lieu 31.90
    agricultural property relief
      31.62–31.78
    armed services personnel,
      and 31.25
    business property relief 31.42–31.61
    care of dependent relative 31.10
    charitable gifts 31.88–31.89
    consideration of marriage 31.6
    death, and 31.1–31.25
    death on active service 31.25
    dispositions for maintenance
      31.7–31.10
    heritage property 31.79–31.86
    inter-spouse transfers 31.41
    introduction 31.1
    lifetime transfers, and 31.3–31.10
    lifetime and death transfers,
      and 31.41–31.89
    maintenance of children 31.9
    maintenance of dependent
      relative 31.10
    maintenance of former spouse 31.8
    marriage gifts 31.6
    nil rate band 31.2
    normal expenditure out of
      income 31.4
    political parties, gifts to 31.87
    small gifts 31.5
    spouse exemption 31.41
    timber 31.21–31.24

Exemptions and reliefs – *contd*
  inheritance tax, and – *contd*
    transfers not exceeding £3,000
      pa 31.3
    woodlands 31.21–31.24
  interest in possession trusts
    33.21–33.30
  main residence, and
    And see **Main residence exemption**
    availability 23.1–23.2
    definitions 23.21–23.24
    expenditure with profit-making
      motive 23.101
    family taxation, and 51.62
    IHT schemes, and 23.141
    introduction 23.1
    non-residents, and 23.2
    periods of absence 23.81–23.85
    problem areas 23.61–23.66
    qualifying residences
      23.42–23.48
    second homes 23.121–23.123
  partnerships, and
    entrepreneurs' relief 44.39
    general 44.35
    hold-over relief 44.36
    incorporation relief 44.38
    replacement of business assets
      relief 44.37
    roll-over relief 44.37–44.38
  reconstruction relief 22.104
  replacement of business assets relief
    basic conditions 22.72
    companies 22.77
    foreign assets 22.76
    intention to reinvest, and 22.80
    non-residents 22.76
    occupation for business
      purposes 22.75
    partnerships 22.77
    prior acquisition of replacement
      assets 22.73
    problem areas 22.79
    provisional relief 22.80
    qualifying assets 22.74
    restrictions 22.78
    wasting assets 22.78
  roll-over relief
    compulsory acquisition of
      land 22.82–22.83
    incorporation of business
      22.100–22.103
    replacement of business
      assets 22.72–22.80
  retirement relief 22.84

Exemptions and reliefs – *contd*
  settlements not subject to relevant
      property regime 33.21–33.30
  stamp duty, and
      companies, for 49.125–49.126
      group relief 49.125
      reconstructions 49.126
  stamp duty land tax, and
      acquisition relief 49.79
      clawback 49.84
      group relief 49.78
      introduction 49.76
      multiple dwellings
          acquisitions 49.81
      other 49.83
      reconstruction relief 49.79
      Schedule 3, under 49.82
  takeover relief 22.104
  transfer of unincorporated business to
      company, and 47.4–47.8
Exit taxes
  freedom of establishment, and 54.46
Expenses
  And see **Deductible expenditure**
  charities, and 53.61
  earnings, as
      exemptions 8.95
      generally 8.94
  employment income, and 8.108
  miscellaneous income, and 13.18
  trading income, and
      capital expenditure 10.77
      date at which allowable 10.78
      deductibility 10.76
      post-cessation expenses 10.81
Exporting a UK trust
  advantages of non-resident
      trust 27A.21–27A.24
  export charge to CGT 27A.38–27A.55
  procedure 8.1088.108 27A.34–27A.37
  provision of information
      requirements 27A.177
  rules on trust residence
      27A.25–27A.33
Extended approval period
  disclosure rules, and 5.22
Extensions of lease
  capital gains tax, and 19.76
Extra-statutory concessions (ESCs)
  generally 1.25

F

Fair hearing
  human rights, and
      burden of proof 55.91

Fair hearing – *contd*
  human rights, and – *contd*
      civil rights and obligations 55.83
      criminal charges 55.82
      introduction 55.81
      judicial review 55.93
      privilege against self
          incrimination 55.92
      right to silence 55.92
      scrutiny of information
          notices 55.84
      tax-related obligations 55.82–55.83
Family unit taxation
  administration 51.111
  age-related married couple's
      allowance
      basic requirements 51.21
      introduction 51.20
      restriction of relief 51.22
      use 51.23
  blind person's allowance 51.26
  capital gains tax
      annual exemption 51.56
      children 51.61
      cohabitees 51.61
      inter-spouse transfers 51.58
      jointly held assets 51.63
      losses 51.57
      planning opportunities 51.64
      principal private residence 51.62
      separate calculation 51.56
      taper relief 51.59
  child benefit high income charge
      election 51.48
      extent 51.46
      generally 51.45
      measure of income 51.47
  child tax credit
      appeals 51.39
      case study 51.40A
      changes in circumstance 51.37
      changes in income 51.38
      conditions of entitlement 51.29
      disputes 51.40
      elements 51.28
      introduction 51.27
      payment 51.30
  child trust fund
      introduction 51.42
      operation 51.43
      reliefs 51.44
  childcare support 51.41
  civil partnerships
      generally 51.130
      transferable tax allowance 51.12

Family unit taxation – *contd*
  cohabitee/spouse distinction 51.131
  death of spouse 51.25
  high income child benefit
    charge 51.45–51.48
  income tax
    age-related married couple's
      allowance 51.20–51.23
    blind person's allowance 51.26
    child tax credit 51.27–51.30
    child trust fund 51.42–51.44
    childcare 51.41
    civil partner's transferable tax
      allowance 51.12
    death of spouse 51.25
    exemptions and reliefs 51.49–51.51
    high income child benefit
      charge 51.45–51.48
    independent taxation 51.11
    jointly held property 51.54
    married couple's transferable tax
      allowance 51.12
    planning opportunities 51.55
    tax credits 51.27–51.40A
    trading losses 51.53
    transferable tax allowance 51.12
    working tax credit 51.31–51.40A
    year of marriage 51.24
  independent taxation 51.11
  inheritance tax
    both spouses domiciled in the
      UK 51.69
    children 51.76
    cohabitees 51.76
    donee spouse domiciled
      abroad 51.70–51.71
    general principles 51.68
    limited gifts 51.75
    nil rate band 51.72–51.74
    outright gifts 51.75
    post mortem adjustments 51.77
    potentially exempt transfers
      51.72–51.74
  introduction 51.1–51.2
  jointly held property 51.54
  marriage breakdown
    And see **Marital breakdown**
    annual exemption 52.22
    capital gains tax 52.21–52.23
    income tax 52.2–52.15
    inheritance tax 52.41
    introduction 52.1
    life insurance policies 52.15
    lump sum payments 52.23
    maintenance payments 52.3

Family unit taxation – *contd*
  marriage breakdown – *contd*
    matrimonial home 52.61–52.79
    pensions 52.4–52.12
    stamp duty 52.60
    tax credits 52.16
  married couple's allowance
    transferable tax allowance 51.12
  nil rate band 51.72–51.74
  planning opportunities 51.55
  post-death variations 51.77
  post mortem adjustments 51.77
  potentially exempt transfers
    51.72–51.74
  stamp duty 51.91
  stamp duty land tax 51.91
  trading losses 51.53
  transferable tax allowance
    civil partnerships 51.12
    generally 7.115–7.117
    introduction 51.1
  working tax credit
    appeals 51.39
    case study 51.40A
    changes in circumstance 51.37
    changes in income 51.38
    childcare element 51.35
    conditions of entitlement
      51.32–51.34
    disputes 51.40
    elements 51.31
    introduction 51.27
    payment 51.36
  year of marriage 51.24
Farmers
  trading income, and 10.172–10.173
Fees
  miscellaneous income, and 13.28
Films and filming
  loss relief, and 11.122
  miscellaneous income, and 13.26
Final salary schemes
  See **Pension schemes**
Financial reporting standards (FRSs)
  trading profits, and 10.64
Financial services
  value added tax, and
    Bitcoins 40.65
    connected supplies 40.77
    dealings in money 40.65
    deposits 40.68
    generally 40.64
    instalment credit finance 40.69
    loans 40.68
    securities for money 40.66

Financial years
  corporation tax, and 41.21
Fine wine
  capital gains tax, and 22.22
Fines
  trading income, and 10.145
First-tier Tribunal
  See also **Appeals**
  appeals from 4.209
  basic cases 4.203
  complex cases 4.205
  costs of proceedings 4.208
  decision notices 4.207
  default paper cases 4.202
  introduction 4.201
  paper cases 4.202
  procedure 4.206
  standard cases 4.204
Fixed income beneficiaries
  interest in possession trusts 33.7
  settlements not subject to relevant property regime, and 33.7
Fixed protection
  pension schemes, and 50.22
Fixtures
  capital allowances, and 48.22–48.25
Flat conversions
  capital allowances, and 48.122
'Flowering shares'
  non tax-advantaged share schemes 9.12
Fluctuating profits relief
  creative artists 10.172–10.173
  farmers 10.172–10.173
  introduction 10.171
  inventors 10.174
  market gardeners 10.172–10.173
Follower notices
  tax avoidance, and 5.29
Food and drink activities
  value added tax, and
    catering 40.23–40.25
    free houses 40.29
    licensed trade 40.27–40.30
    managed houses 40.28
    public houses 40.27–40.30
    tenanted houses 40.30
    tied houses 40.30
Foreign companies
  corporation tax, and
    calculation of profits 41.152
    controlled foreign companies 41.161
    liability to tax 41.151

Foreign companies – *contd*
  corporation tax, and – *contd*
    non-resident companies 41.162
    'residence' 41.153
Foreign currency sales
  capital gains tax, and 22.3
  stamp duty land tax, and 49.49
Foreign domiciliaries
  asset situate outside the UK 27.83–27.85
  disposals for less than full consideration 27.99–27.100
  foreign currency gains 27.101
  general points 27.81–27.82
  losses 27.86–27.87
  rate of tax 27.98
  remittances
    business investment relief 27.96
    introduction 27.89–27.92
    relevant persons 27.93–27.95
    sales of exempt art 27.97
  segregation of claims 27.88
Foreign element
  capital gains tax on individuals
  And see below
    liability of non-residents 27.41–27.63
    new regime for foreign domiciliaries 27.81–27.101
    non-resident companies 27.111–27.112
    residence 27.1–27.30
  corporation tax
    calculation of profits 41.152
    controlled foreign companies 41.161
    double tax relief 41.156–41.159
    effect of ceasing to be UK resident 41.154
    liability to tax 41.151
    non-resident companies 41.162
    non-resident shareholders of resident companies 41.162
    'residence' 41.153
    UK resident companies abroad 41.155
  income tax
  And see below
    anti-avoidance 18.110–18.128
    domicile 18.23–18.30
    double taxation relief 18.91
    foreign income 18.31–18.51
    foreign taxpayers 18.71–18.80
    introduction 18.1
    residence 18.2–18.22

Foreign element – *contd*
  income tax – *contd*
    transfer of assets abroad
      18.110–18.128
    proposed 2017 changes 18.30
Foreign element (capital gains tax)
  liability of non-residents
    Finance (No 2) Act 2005
      changes 27.56–27.63
    introduction 27.41–27.44
    other matters 27.51–27.55
    split year treatment 27.50
    temporary non-resident
      individuals 27.46–27.49
  new regime for foreign domiciliaries
    asset situate outside the UK
      27.83–27.85
    disposals for less than full
      consideration 27.99–27.100
    foreign currency gains 27.101
    general points 27.81–27.82
    losses 27.86–27.88
    rate of tax 27.98
    remittances 27.89–27.97
    segregation of claims 27.88
  non-resident companies
    anti-avoidance 27.112
    general rule 27.111
  proposed 2017 changes 18.30
  residence
    case law 27.12–27.16
    full-time work abroad 27.11
    Gaines v Cooper decision 27.6
    Grace decision 27.14
    general law 27.2–27.4
    HMRC practice 27.5–27.8
    introduction 27.1
    multiplicity of factors 27.13
    occasional residence abroad 27.9
    statutory provisions 27.9–27.11
    statutory residence test 27.17–27.24
    temporary purposes in the
      UK 27.10
  temporary non-resident
    individuals 27.46–27.49
Foreign element (income tax)
  anti-avoidance
    chargeable income 18.118
    general 18.111
    'individuals ordinarily resident in
      the UK' 18.112
    introduction 18.110
    legislative reforms 18.127–18.128
    liability of non-transferors
      18.120–18.125

Foreign element (income tax) – *contd*
  anti-avoidance – *contd*
    liability of transferor 18.114–18.119
    powers to obtain
      information 18.126
    purpose 18.113
    remittance basis for non-
      domiciliaries 18.119
  domicile
    choice, of 18.25–18.26
    deemed 18.28
    introduction 18.23
    married women 18.29
    origin, of 18.24
    proposed 2017 changes 18.30
    special situations 18.27
  double taxation relief 18.91
  double tax treaties 18.22
  foreign employment income
    annuities 18.50
    collection of tax 18.51
    deductible expenses 18.49
    emoluments for duties performed
      in UK 18.46
    introduction 18.43
    pensions 18.50
    place of work 18.48
    remittance basis 18.47
  foreign income
    alimony orders 18.41
    becoming resident in UK 18.42
    calculation of liability 18.32–18.33
    charge 18.34
    charging provisions 18.31
    distributions from companies 18.36
    employment income 18.43–18.51
    foreign partnerships, from 18.39
    foreign trusts, from 18.38
    off-shore 'roll-up' funds 18.40
    partnerships, from 18.39
    pensions 18.41
    professions 18.35
    property income 18.37
    remittance basis 18.34
    savings and investment
      income 18.36
    Schedule D, and 18.31
    trade profits 18.35
    trusts, from 18.38
    vocations 18.35
  foreign taxpayers
    dividends paid by UK
      companies 18.78
    employment income 18.73
    entertainers 18.74

Foreign element (income tax) – *contd*
  foreign taxpayers – *contd*
    interest from UK banks and
      building societies 18.76
    introduction 18.71
    land in the UK 18.75
    non-resident discretionary
      trusts 18.79
    professions 18.72
    sportsmen and women 18.74
    trade profits 18.72
    UK government securities 18.77
    vocations 18.72
    withholding tax on royalties 18.80
  introduction 18.1
  non-resident partnerships 18.17
  ordinary residence 18.14–18.15
  partnerships
    fiscal transparency 18.18
    non-resident partnerships 18.17
  proposed 2017 changes 18.30
  residence
    acquisition of resident status 18.7
    available accommodation 18.5
    corporations 18.16
    double tax treaties 18.22
    from 6 April 2013 18.8–18.13
    introduction 18.2
    loss of resident status 18.7
    meaning 18.2
    non-resident partnerships 18.17
    occasional residence abroad 18.6
    ordinary residence 18.14–18.15
    partnerships 18.17–18.18
    personal representatives 18.21
    prior to 6 April 2013 18.3–18.7
    statutory residence test 18.8–18.13
    the '91-day' rule 18.4
    the '183-day' rule 18.3
    'tie-breaker' clauses 18.22
    trustees 18.19
    trusts 18.20
  statutory residence test
    automatic non-residence test 18.9
    automatic residence test 18.10
    introduction 18.8
    split year treatment 18.12
    temporary non residence 18.13
    UK ties 18.11
  transfer of assets abroad
    18.110–18.128
  UK resident
    available accommodation 18.5
    introduction 18.3
    occasional residence abroad 18.6

Foreign element (income tax) – *contd*
  UK resident – *contd*
    the '91-day' rule 18.4
    the '183-day' rule 18.3
    withholding tax on royalties 18.80
Foreign exchange gains and losses
  corporation tax, and 41.43
Foreign income
  alimony orders 18.41
  becoming resident in UK 18.42
  calculation of liability 18.32–18.33
  basis charge 18.34
  charging provisions 18.31
  distributions from companies 18.36
  employment income
    annuities 18.50
    collection of tax 18.51
    deductible expenses 18.49
    emoluments for duties performed
      in UK 18.46
    introduction 18.43
    pensions 18.50
    place of work 18.48
    remittance basis 18.47
  foreign partnerships, from 18.39
  foreign trusts, from 18.38
  off-shore 'roll-up' funds 18.40
  partnerships, from 18.39
  pensions 18.41
  professions 18.35
  property income 18.37
  remittance basis 18.34
  savings and investment income 18.36
  Schedule D, and 18.31
  trade profits 18.35
  trusts, from
    generally 18.38
    introduction 16.9
  vocations 18.35
Foreign settlements
  inheritance tax, and 35.81
Foreign taxpayers
  dividends paid by UK
    companies 18.78
  employment income 18.73
  entertainers 18.74
  interest from UK banks and building
    societies 18.76
  introduction 18.71
  land in the UK 18.75
  non-resident discretionary trusts 18.79
  professions 18.72
  sportsmen and women 18.74
  trade profits 18.72
  UK government securities 18.77

1738   Index

Foreign taxpayers – *contd*
  vocations 18.72
  withholding tax on royalties 18.80
Franchises
  stamp duty land tax, and 49.32
Franked investment income
  And see **Distributions**
  generally 42.91–42.94
  introduction 42.1
'From' an employment
  employee participation, and 9.2
  general principles 8.42
  introduction 8.41
  past services 8.44
  third party payments 8.43
FRSs
  trading profits, and 10.64
Fuel for vehicles
  employment income, and 8.122
Fund raising
  value added tax, and 40.49
Furnished holiday lettings
  introduction 12.61
  other measures 12.63
  qualifying holiday lettings 12.62
  tax treatment 12.64
Furniss v Dawson
  And see **Tax avoidance**
  decision 2.23
  facts 2.22
  overview 2.4

G

Galleries
  value added tax, and 40.63
Gambling winnings
  capital gains tax, and 22.3
General anti-abuse rule (GAAR)
  And see **Tax avoidance**
  Aaronson Report
    background 3.75
    conclusions 3.76
    general overview 3.77
    operating procedures 3.79
    other matters 3.80
    scope 3.78
    thoughts on legislation 3.81
  background 3.75
  employment income, and 8.1
  experience of other jurisdictions 3.82
  general overview 3.77
  international obligations 3.80
  introduction 3.74
  operating procedures 3.79
  pre-17 July 2013 transactions 3.80

General anti-abuse rule (GAAR) – *contd*
  proposals 5.1
  scope 3.78
  use of Hansard, and 1.23
'General earnings'
  employment income, and 8.11
General legatees
  estates in administration, and 17.42
Generally accepted accounting practice (GAAP)
  trading income, and 10.62
Genuine commercial reasons
  transactions in securities, and 3.64
Gift Aid
  annual payments, and 14.13
  corporate gifts 53.86
  declarations
    generally 53.82
    oral 53.82
    provided through intermediary 53.83
    written 53.82
  'double-dip' 53.85
  generally 53.79
  introduction 53.41
  receipt of benefits 53.84
  scope of relief 53.80
  small donations scheme 53.81
Gift and loan scheme
  generally 15.23
Gifts
  accumulation and maintenance trusts, from 24.27
  assets attracting immediate IHT charge, of
    anti-avoidance 24.26
    chargeable transfers 24.23
    extent of relief 24.24
    introduction 24.22
    use of relief 24.25
  business assets, of
    agricultural property 24.9
    annual exemption 24.15
    anti-avoidance 24.21
    application of provision 24.5
    creation of settlement 24.20
    effect of IHT 24.17
    election 24.12
    emigration of transferee 24.20
    entrepreneurs' relief, and 24.14
    hold-over relief, and 24.14
    introduction 24.4
    non-resident companies. to 24.19
    non-resident individuals, to 24.18
    'personal company' 24.10

Gifts – *contd*
  business assets, of – *contd*
    qualifying assets 24.7
    relevant property 24.6–24.11
    taper relief, and 24.13
    'trading company' 24.10
    triggering events 24.18–24.20
    trustees 24.11
    use for the purposes of
      trade 24.8
  children's trusts, from 24.27
  designated property, of 24.28
  disposal at market value 24.2
  general 22.99
  IHT consequences 24.3
  income tax, and
    generally 8.62
    third parties 8.168
  introduction 24.1–24.3
  maintenance of historic buildings,
    for 24.28
  political parties, to 24.28
  third parties, from 8.168
  works of art, of 24.28
Gifts with reservation
  double charges 36.3
  liability to account for tax 29.146
Gilt edged securities
  capital gains tax, and 22.3
  inheritance tax, and 35.21
'Golden handshakes'
  contemporaneous share sales 8.157
  current regime 8.150
  damages, and 8.156
  death benefits 8.152
  disability benefits 8.152
  exceptions 8.151–8.154
  first £30,000 8.154
  generally 8.148
  injury benefits 8.152
  internationally mobile
    employees 8.158
  introduction 8.101
  old regime 8.149
  PAYE 8.155
  pension benefits 8.152
  reform recommendations 8.159
  reporting requirements 8.155
Goodwill
  partnerships, and 44.33
Government activities
  value added tax, and
    government departments 40.102
    introduction 40.98
    local authorities 40.99

Government activities – *contd*
  refund scheme 40.101
  statutory bodies 40.99
Government securities
  capital gains tax, and 22.3
  inheritance tax, and 35.21
Grant of interest in or right over land
  value added tax, and
    generally 39.19
    'interest in or right over land' 39.20
    licence to occupy land 39.21
Grant of lease
  value added tax, and 39.37
Grossing-up
  lifetime transfers, and 28.124
Gross payments to employee
  employment income, and 8.201
Group life policies
  generally 15.10
Group relief
  stamp duty, and 49.125
  stamp duty land tax, and 49.78
Groups of companies
  capital gains
    anti-avoidance 43.127
    capital losses 43.126
    compulsory acquisition of
      land 43.131
    group property companies 43.130
    intra-group transfers 43.122
    introduction 43.121
    linked transactions 43.132
    roll-around relief 43.129
    roll-over claims 43.133
    roll-over relief 43.128
    sub-groups 43.123
    trading stock 43.125
    triggering a loss 43.124
  compulsory acquisition of land 43.131
  consortium relief
    anti-avoidance 43.47
    availability 43.41
    claims 43.46
    European Vinyls case 43.45
    future changes 43.48
    international dimension 43.42
    Marks & Spencer case 43.44
    operation 43.43
  depreciatory transactions 43.151
  disclosure rules, and 5.22
  instalment payments of corporation
    tax 43.101
  intra-group transfers 43.122
  introduction 43.1
  meaning 43.21

Groups of companies – *contd*
  roll-around relief 43.129
  roll-over relief 43.128
  stamp duty land tax 43.211
  sub-groups 43.123
  trading stock 43.125
  value added tax, and
    generally 43.191
    registration 38.50
  value shifting 43.151

H

Hallmarked schemes
  disclosure rules, and 5.21
'Hallmarks'
  tax avoidance, and 5.7
Hansard procedure
  interpretation of legislation, and 1.23
  serious investigation cases, and 4.50–4.51
Hardship
  reservation of benefit, and 29.73
Health
  value added tax, and
    hospital care 40.38
    introduction 40.36
    opticians 40.40
    pharmacists 40.39
    supplies by qualified persons 40.37
Hearings
  human rights, and
    burden of proof 55.91
    civil rights and obligations 55.83
    criminal charges 55.82
    introduction 55.81
    judicial review 55.93
    privilege against self incrimination 55.92
    right to silence 55.92
    scrutiny of information notices 55.84
    tax-related obligations 55.82–55.83
'Help-to-buy' ISAs
  generally 15.29
Her Majesty's Revenue and Customs (HMRC)
  creation 4.2
  information powers
    civil investigatory powers 4.161–4.168
    criminal investigatory powers 4.56–4.160
    introduction 4.54
    PACE, under 4.59–4.158
    SOCPA, under 4.160

Heritage property relief
  acceptance in lieu 31.90
  calculation of deferred charge 31.83
  capital gains tax, and 22.5
  effect of deferred charge 31.82
  introduction 31.79
  maintenance funds 31.85
  preconditions 31.80
  private treaty sales 31.86
  reopening existing undertakings 31.81
  settled property 31.84
High value residential property
  stamp duty land tax, and 49.86
Hire of equipment
  miscellaneous income, and 13.27
Hire-purchase
  capital gains tax, and 19.72
  plant and machinery allowances, and 48.81
Historic buildings funds
  settlements not subject to relevant property regime, and 33.117
HM Revenue and Customs
  creation 4.2
  information powers
    civil investigatory powers 4.161–4.168
    criminal investigatory powers 4.56–4.160
    introduction 4.54
    PACE, under 4.59–4.158
    SOCPA, under 4.160
Holiday lettings
  introduction 12.61
  other measures 12.63
  qualifying holiday lettings 12.62
  tax treatment 12.64
Hold-over relief
  assets attracting immediate IHT charge, of
    anti-avoidance 24.26
    chargeable transfers 24.23
    extent of relief 24.24
    introduction 24.22
    use of relief 24.25
  business assets, of
    agricultural property 24.9
    annual exemption 24.15
    anti-avoidance 24.21
    application of provision 24.5
    creation of settlement 24.20
    effect of IHT 24.17
    election 24.12
    emigration of transferee 24.20

Hold-over relief – *contd*
  business assets, of – *contd*
    entrepreneurs' relief, and 24.14
    hold-over relief, and 24.14
    introduction 24.4
    non-resident companies. to 24.19
    non-resident individuals, to 24.18
    'personal company' 24.10
    qualifying assets 24.7
    relevant property 24.6–24.11
    taper relief, and 24.13
    'trading company' 24.10
    triggering events 24.18–24.20
    trustees 24.11
    use for the purposes of trade 24.8
  disposal at market value 24.2
  general 22.99
  gifts of business assets, and 24.14
  IHT consequences 24.3
  partnerships, and 44.36
Homeworker's additional expenses
  employment income, and 8.165
Hospital care
  value added tax, and 40.38
Hot food
  value added tax, and 40.23–40.25
Human rights
  courts, and 55.4
  EU law, and 55.101
  legislative framework
    background 55.1
    incorporation of rights 55.2
    main principles 55.3
  prohibition of discrimination
    employees and self-employed persons, between 55.45
    exercise of discretion, in 55.46
    gender grounds, on 55.44
    legal advice privilege, and 55.48
    marriage grounds, on 55.43
    nature 55.41
    prosecution, as to 55.47
    scope 55.42–55.48
    similarly situated taxpayers, between 55.42
  right to fair hearing
    burden of proof 55.91
    civil rights and obligations 55.83
    criminal charges 55.82
    introduction 55.81
    judicial review 55.93
    privilege against self incrimination 55.92
    right to silence 55.92

Human rights – *contd*
  right to fair hearing – *contd*
    scrutiny of information notices 55.84
    tax-related obligations 55.82–55.83
  right to protection of property
    ambit 55.21
    IR35 55.22
    use 55.23–55.27
  right to respect for private and family life
    generally 55.61
    legal professional privilege 55.62
  tax, and 55.5
Hydrogen refuelling equipment
  first year allowances, and 48.33

I

Identification rules
  disposal of shares, and 26.45
Immediate post-death interest
  inheritance tax, and 32.51
Impairment losses
  trading income, and 10.144
Importing non-resident trusts
  generally 27A.55
'In consequence of'
  transactions in securities, and 3.54
Income not otherwise charged
  miscellaneous income, and 13.9–13.11
Income profits
  capital allowances
    And see **Capital allowances**
    agricultural buildings 48.121
    capital expenditure 48.3–48.5
    claims 48.6
    flat conversions 48.122
    general scheme 48.1–48.10
    industrial buildings 48.91–48.95
    landlord's energy saving allowance 48.126–48.127
    method of giving 48.8–48.10
    plant and machinery 48.11–48.81
    renovation of business premises 48.124–48.125
    research and development 48.123
    time when incurred 48.7
    types 48.2
  capital gains tax, and 19.82
  choice of business medium, and
    dates for payment 46.45
    Enterprise Investment Scheme 46.50–46.51
    illustrations 46.52

Income profits – *contd*
  choice of business medium, and – *contd*
    interest relief 46.47
    loss relief 46.49
    national insurance contributions 46.43
    profits paid out as remuneration 46.44
    rates 46.42
    reliefs 46.48–46.50
    trading losses 46.46
  deduction at source income 41.46
  derivative contracts 41.43
  dividends 41.46
  employee trusts 41.45
  foreign exchange gains and losses 41.43
  general principles 41.42
  income taxed at source 41.46
  interest rate contracts 41.43
  transfer pricing 41.44

Income tax
  age allowance 7.103
  age-related married couple's allowance
    basic requirements 51.21
    introduction 51.20
    restriction of relief 51.22
    use 51.23
  annual payments
    And see **Annual payments**
    ambit of charge 14.2
    basis of assessment 14.4
    charge to tax 14.14–14.17
    collection of tax 14.21–14.28
    companies 14.5
    income arising 14.3
    introduction 14.1
    taxation 14.11–14.13
    terminology 14.6–14.8
  approved share schemes
    And see **Tax-advantaged share schemes**
    generally 9.2
  background 6.2
  bank interest 7.24
  blind person's allowance 7.105
  calculation
    charging taxable income 7.120–7.132
    introduction 7.1
    net income 7.40–7.91
    personal reliefs 7.101–7.113
    stages 7.4

Income tax – *contd*
  calculation – *contd*
    tax rates 7.2–7.3
    total income 7.21–7.27
  capital allowances
    And see **Capital allowances**
    agricultural buildings 48.121
    capital expenditure 48.3–48.5
    claims 48.6
    family taxation, and 51.51
    flat conversions 48.122
    general scheme 48.1–48.10
    industrial buildings 48.91–48.95
    landlord's energy saving allowance 48.126–48.127
    method of giving 48.8–48.10
    plant and machinery 48.11–48.81
    renovation of business premises 48.124–48.125
    research and development 48.123
    time when incurred 48.7
    types 48.2
  capital gains tax, and
    generally 19.3
    leases of land 19.42
  case law 6.21
  categories of income 6.41
  charging taxable income 7.120–7.132
  charities, and 53.41
  child benefit high income charge
    election 51.48
    extent 51.46
    generally 51.45
    measure of income 51.47
  child tax credit
    appeals 51.39
    case study 51.40A
    changes in circumstance 51.37
    changes in income 51.38
    conditions of entitlement 51.29
    disputes 51.40
    elements 51.28
    introduction 51.27
    payment 51.30
  child trust fund
    introduction 51.42
    operation 51.43
    reliefs 51.44
  childcare support 51.41
  choice of business medium, and
    benefits 46.60
    buy-backs 46.58
    dates for payment 46.45
    dividends 46.54–46.55, 46.60

Income tax – *contd*
  choice of business medium, and – *contd*
    Enterprise Investment Scheme 46.50–46.51
    extracting cash from business 46.53–46.61
    illustrations 46.52
    income profits 46.42–46.52
    interest relief 46.47
    loans 46.56
    loss relief 46.49
    national insurance contributions 46.43
    profits paid out as remuneration 46.44
    rates 46.42
    reliefs 46.48–46.50
    remuneration 46.59
    share sales 46.57
    trading losses 46.46
  civil partner's age-related allowance
    basic requirements 51.21
    generally 7.111–7.113
    introduction 51.20
    restriction of relief 51.22
    use 51.23
  close company loans 51.50
  copyright royalties 14.40
  couples, and 7.22
  dates for payment 7.122
  dividends 7.27
  domicile
    choice, of 18.25–18.26
    deemed 18.28
    introduction 18.23
    married women 18.29
    origin, of 18.24
    proposed 2017 changes 18.30
    special situations 18.27
  double taxation relief 18.91
  double tax treaties 18.22
  earned income 7.23
  employee ownership trusts
    bonus payments 9.117
    introduction 9.115
    transfer of ownership interest 9.116
  employee participation
    And see **Employee participation**
    choice of scheme 9.151–9.164
    corporation tax 9.121–9.129
    employee ownership trusts 9.115–9.117
    employee share ownership plans 9.113

Income tax – *contd*
  employee participation – *contd*
    employee trusts 9.111–9.112
    introduction 9.1–9.3
    non tax-advantaged share schemes 9.11–9.58
    tax-advantaged share schemes 9.71–9.90
    Treasury shares 9.114
  employee share ownership plans 9.113
  employee trusts
    introduction 9.111
    taxation 9.112
  employment income, on
    And see **Employment income**
    agency
    amounts treated as earnings 8.101–8.135
    collection of tax 8.191–8.203
    deductible expenses 8.171–8.175
    'earnings' 8.91–8.95
    earnings from an employment 8.41–8.44
    exemptions 8.161–8.169
    introduction 8.1
    managed service companies 8.31–8.34
    office or employment 8.20–8.24
    personal service companies 8.31–8.34
    problem areas 8.61–8.66
    tax structures 8.11–8.13
    termination payments 8.141–8.159
  Enterprise Investment Scheme 51.49
  estates in course of administration
    And see **Estates in administration**
    administration period 17.20–17.26
    deceased's income 17.2–17.7
    distributions to beneficiaries 17.41–17.57
    introduction 17.1
  exemptions
    capital allowances 51.51
    close company loans 51.50
    Enterprise Investment Scheme 51.49
    exempt income 7.129–7.131
    exempt organisations 7.128
    introduction 7.127
    ISAs 7.132
    life assurance policies 7.132
  family taxation, and
    age-related married couple's allowance 51.20–51.23

Income tax – *contd*
  family taxation, and – *contd*
    blind person's allowance 51.26
    child tax credit 51.27–51.30
    child trust fund 51.42–51.44
    childcare 51.41
    civil partner's transferable tax allowance 51.12
    death of spouse 51.25
    exemptions and reliefs 51.49–51.51
    high income child benefit charge 51.45–51.48
    independent taxation 51.11
    jointly held property 51.54
    married couple's transferable tax allowance 51.12
    planning opportunities 51.55
    tax credits 51.27–51.40A
    trading losses 51.53
    transferable tax allowance 51.12
    working tax credit 51.31–51.40A
    year of marriage 51.24
  foreign employment income
    annuities 18.50
    collection of tax 18.51
    deductible expenses 18.49
    emoluments for duties performed in UK 18.46
    introduction 18.43
    pensions 18.50
    place of work 18.48
    remittance basis 18.47
  foreign income
    alimony orders 18.41
    becoming resident in UK 18.42
    calculation of liability 18.32–18.33
    charge 18.34
    charging provisions 18.31
    distributions from companies 18.36
    employment income 18.43–18.51
    foreign partnerships, from 18.39
    foreign trusts, from 18.38
    off-shore 'roll-up' funds 18.40
    partnerships, from 18.39
    pensions 18.41
    professions 18.35
    property income 18.37
    remittance basis 18.34
    savings and investment income 18.36
    Schedule D, and 18.31
    trade profits 18.35
    trusts, from 18.38
    vocations 18.35

Income tax – *contd*
  foreign taxpayers
    dividends paid by UK companies 18.78
    employment income 18.73
    entertainers 18.74
    interest from UK banks and building societies 18.76
    introduction 18.71
    land in the UK 18.75
    non-resident discretionary trusts 18.79
    professions 18.72
    sportsmen and women 18.74
    trade profits 18.72
    UK government securities 18.77
    vocations 18.72
    withholding tax on royalties 18.80
  furnished holiday lettings
    introduction 12.61
    other measures 12.63
    qualifying holiday lettings 12.62
    tax treatment 12.64
  general principles 6.1
  'income' 6.43
  independent taxation 51.11
  intellectual property royalties 14.40
  interest paid by banks and building societies 7.24
  investment income 7.23
  irrecoverable peer-to-peer loans 7.92
  ISAs 7.132
  joint income 7.22
  jointly held property 51.54
  land, and
    anti-avoidance 12.101–12.112
    chargeable persons 12.41
    computation of profits 12.42–12.49
    furnished holiday lettings 12.61–12.64
    lease premiums 12.81–12.87
    rent factoring 12.88
    trading principles 12.1–12.24
  lease premiums
    anti-avoidance 12.83
    charge 12.82
    instalments, in 12.84
    introduction 12.81
    relief on trading premises 12.85
    reverse premiums 12.87
    trusts 12.86
  life assurance policies
    generally 7.132
    marital breakdown, and 52.15

Income tax – *contd*
  limited liability partnerships, and
    introduction 45.9
    losses 45.13
    trading LLPs 45.10
  loan interest
    acquisition of interest in close
      company 7.45
    acquisition of interest in
      co-operative 7.47
    acquisition of interest in
      partnership 7.46
    introduction 7.44
    investment in employee-controlled
      company 7.48
    payment of inheritance tax 7.50
    purchase of life annuity 7.51
    purchase of plant or
      machinery 7.49
  loss relief
    property losses 7.81
    trading losses deducted from
      general income 7.82–7.91
  losses
    anti-avoidance 11.122
    capital gains relief 11.61
    carry-across relief 11.41
    carry-forward relief 11.21
    final years loss relief 11.101–11.02
    initial loss relief 11.81–11.82
    introduction 11.1–11.5
    terminal loss relief 11.102
    transfer of business to
      company 11.101
    unquoted corporate trades 11.121
  maintenance payments 52.3
  marital breakdown, and
    general principles 52.2
    life insurance policies 52.15
    maintenance payments 52.3
    pensions 52.4–52.12
  married person's age-related
    allowance
    basic requirements 51.21
    generally 7.111–7.113
    introduction 51.20
    restriction of relief 51.22
    use 51.23
  miscellaneous income
    alternative charges 13.14
    annual payments not otherwise
      charged 13.6–13.8
    apportionment 13.17
    cash-backs 13.28
    charging options 13.2

Income tax – *contd*
  miscellaneous income
    commissions 13.28
    corporation tax 13.5
    earnings basis 13.16
    expenses 13.18
    fees 13.28
    filming 13.26
    full amount of income 13.19
    general charge 13.2–13.6
    hire of equipment 13.27
    income not otherwise
      charged 13.9–13.11
    income rather than capital 13.12
    income tax 13.4
    legal proceedings 13.22
    losses 13.20–13.21
    overview 13.30
    photography 13.26
    procedure 13.16–13.22
    scope 13.1
    specific cases 13.23–13.30
    specific charging provisions
      13.3–13.5
    taxable source 13.13
    taxing priority 13.14–13.15
    theatrical 'angels' 13.24
    toll charges 13.27
    trading 13.15
    volunteer drivers 13.29
    writing and publishing 13.25
  mutually exclusive rule 6.42
  net income
    calculation 7.43
    deductible reliefs 7.41–7.42
    general 7.40
    interest payments 7.44–7.51
    irrecoverable peer-to-peer
      loans 7.92
    loss relief 7.81–7.91
  non tax-advantaged share schemes
    And see **Non tax-advantaged share**
      schemes
    background 9.11
    capital gains tax 9.45–9.57
    conclusions 9.58
    introduction 9.11–9.13
    NICs 9.44
    PAYE 9.42–9.43
    rights to acquire shares 9.41
    share incentives 9.21–9.34
    share options 9.41
  ordinary residence 18.14–18.15
  overseas dimension
    anti-avoidance 18.110–18.128

Income tax – *contd*
  overseas dimension – *contd*
    domicile 18.23–18.30
    double taxation relief 18.91
    foreign income 18.31–18.51
    foreign taxpayers 18.71–18.80
    introduction 18.1
    residence 18.2–18.22
    transfer of assets abroad 18.110–18.128
  partnerships, and
    annuity payments by partners 44.14–44.16
    basis of assessment 44.4
    calculation of profits 44.3–44.10
    changes in partnership 44.12
    consultancies 44.13
    introduction 44.2
    leaving partners 44.13–44.17
    loan interest relief 44.11
    personal pension schemes 44.17
    retirement annuities 44.17
    taxable profit 44.5–44.10
  patent royalties 14.40
  payment dates 7.122
  pensions
    Brooks v Brooks decision 52.4
    earmarking orders 52.12
    flexibility 52.14
    introduction 52.4
    offsetting 52.11
    pension attachment 52.12
    pension sharing 52.13
  personal allowances 7.103
  personal reliefs
    blind person's allowance 7.105
    civil partner's allowances 7.111–7.117, 51.20–51.23
    general 7.101–7.102
    married person's allowance 7.111–7.117, 51.20–51.23
    personal allowances 7.103
  personal savings allowance 7.25
  property losses 7.81
  rates
    generally 7.120–7.121
    introduction 7.2–7.3
  rent factoring 12.88
  residence
    acquisition of resident status 18.7
    available accommodation 18.5
    corporations 18.16
    double tax treaties 18.22
    from 6 April 2013 18.8–18.13

Income tax – *contd*
  residence – *contd*
    introduction 18.2
    loss of resident status 18.7
    meaning 18.2
    non-resident partnerships 18.17
    occasional residence abroad 18.6
    ordinary residence 18.14–18.15
    partnerships 18.17–18.18
    personal representatives 18.21
    prior to 6 April 2013 18.3–18.7
    statutory residence test 18.8–18.13
    the '91-day' rule 18.4
    the '183-day' rule 18.3
    'tie-breaker' clauses 18.22
    trustees 18.19
    trusts 18.20
  savings income
    And see **Savings income**
    ambit of charge 14.2
    basis of assessment 14.4
    companies 14.5
    copyright royalties 14.40
    deeply discounted securities 14.42
    generally 7.24–7.26
    interest 14.31–14.37
    introduction 14.1
    patent royalties 14.40
    purchased life annuities 14.41
    terminology 14.6–14.8
    unauthorised unit trusts 14.44
  savings nil rate 7.25
  source doctrine 6.41
  specimen calculation 7.123
  starting rate for savings 7.26
  statutory basis 6.21–6.22
  stock dividends 7.27
  tax-advantaged share schemes
    And see **Tax-advantaged share schemes**
    company share option plans 9.76
    enterprise management incentives 9.83–9.87
    general treatment 9.71–9.72
    NICs 9.90
    PAYE 9.88–9.89
    requirements 9.73–9.74
    savings-related share option schemes 9.75
    share incentive plans 9.77–9.82
  tax-free childcare 51.41
  tax year 6.22
  territorial scope 18.1

Income tax – *contd*
  total income
    combining income from all
      sources 7.21
    couples 7.22
    dividends 7.27
    earned income 7.23
    general 7.21
    interest paid by banks and building
      societies 7.24
    investment income 7.23
    personal savings allowance 7.25
    savings income 7.24–7.26
    savings nil rate 7.25
    starting rate for savings 7.26
  trading income, on
    And see **Trading income**
    basis of assessment 10.192–10.204
    computation of profits 10.61–10.81
    deductible expenses 10.130–10.157
    introduction 10.1–10.4
    relief for fluctuating profits
      10.171–10.174
    'trade' 10.18–10.41
    trading receipts 10.101–10.119
  trading losses
    deducted from general
      income 7.82–7.91
    generally 51.53
  transactions in securities, and
    generally 3.56
    tax advantage 3.55
  transfer of assets abroad
    chargeable income 18.118
    general 18.111
    'individuals ordinarily resident in
      the UK' 18.112
    introduction 18.110
    legislative reforms 18.127–18.128
    liability of non-transferors
      18.120–18.125
    liability of transferor 18.114–18.119
    powers to obtain
      information 18.126
    purpose 18.113
    remittance basis for non-
      domiciliaries 18.119
  transfer of unincorporated business to
    company, and 47.3
  Treasury shares 9.114
  trusts and settlements
    And see **Trusts**
    anti-avoidance 16.91–16.107
    beneficiaries entitled to trust
      income 16.61–16.73

Income tax – *contd*
  trusts and settlements
    charge on discretionary
      payments 16.31–16.33
    definitions 16.2–16.4
    dividends 16.29–16.30
    general principles 16.5–16.9
    income taxed at special rates
      16.21–16.26
    introduction 16.1
    reform proposals 16.108
    vulnerable beneficiaries
      16.74–16.77
  unapproved employee trusts
    introduction 9.111
    taxation 9.112
  unapproved share schemes
    And see **Non tax-advantaged share
      schemes**
    generally 9.2
  venture capital trusts 15.122
  withholding tax on royalties 18.80
  working tax credit
    appeals 51.39
    case study 51.40A
    changes in circumstance 51.37
    changes in income 51.38
    childcare element 51.35
    conditions of entitlement
      51.32–51.34
    disputes 51.40
    elements 51.31
    introduction 51.27
    payment 51.36
  year of marriage 51.24
Income tax advantage
  transactions in securities, and 3.55
Incorporation relief
  conditions 22.101
  deferral of tax on sale of
    unincorporated business 22.102
  election to disapply 22.103
  generally 22.100
  overview 26.4
  partnerships, and 44.38
**Incorporation of unincorporated
  business**
  limited liability partnerships,
    and 45.20–45.21
Incorrect returns
  corporation tax, and 41.184
Indemnity by purchaser
  stamp duty land tax, and 49.55
Independent taxation
  generally 51.11

Indexation
  abolition 19.4
  basic rules 19.26
  capital gains tax on death, and 21.63
  capital losses, and 19.27
  rationale 19.24
  statutory changes 19.25
Individual savings accounts (ISAs)
  apportionment of investment 15.26
  capital gains tax, and 22.2
  cash ISA 15.27
  eligibility 15.26
  generally 15.26
  'help-to-buy' ISA 15.29
  income tax, and 7.132
  innovative finance ISA 15.31
  lifetime ISA 15.30
  Junior ISA 15.32
  stocks and shares ISA 15.28
  types 15.26
Inducement payments
  employment income, and 8.63
Industrial buildings allowances
  'industrial building' 48.92–48.95
  introduction 48.91
  qualifying trade 48.93
Information notices
  right to fair hearing, and 55.84
Information powers
  civil investigatory powers
    inspect businesses 4.166–4.168
    introduction 4.161
    obtain information and
      documents 4.162–4.165
  criminal investigatory powers
    introduction 4.56–4.58
    PACE, under 4.59–4.158
  excluded material 4.157
  'identity unknown notice' 4.165
  inspection of businesses
    introduction 4.166
    Sch 36 para 10, under 4.167
    Sch 36 para 11, under 4.168
  introduction 4.54
  obtaining information and documents
    differences between systems 4.163
    'identity unknown notice' 4.165
    'Taxpayer Notice' 4.162
    'third-party notice' 4.164
  PACE, under
    introduction 4.59
    production orders 4.157
    safeguards 4.158–4.159
    search powers 4.140–4.155
  production orders 4.157

Information powers – *contd*
  search powers
    introduction 4.59
    PACE, under 4.140–4.155
  SOCPA, under 4.160
  special procedure material 4.157
  'Taxpayer Notice' 4.162
  'third-party notice' 4.164
  TMA s 20BA power 4.159
Inheritance provision
  capital gains tax, and 21.127
Inheritance tax
  18–25 trusts 34.118
  abatement 30.121–30.122
  accountability
    death 30.35
    lifetime transfers 28.172
  accumulation and maintenance
    trusts 34.91–34.98
  administration
    appeals 28.221
    calculation of liability 28.201
    penalties 28.202
  agricultural property relief
    'agricultural property' 31.62
    agricultural land or pasture 31.63
    agricultural tenancies 31.72
    'agricultural value' 31.67
    amount 31.68
    business property relief, and 31.77
    'character appropriate' test
      31.65–31.66
    clawback 31.72
    companies, and 31.70
    double discounting 31.75
    farmhouses 31.65–31.66
    intensive farming buildings 31.64
    interest in possession trusts,
      and 33.30
    introduction 31.62
    lotting 31.74
    milk quota 31.76
    occupation requirement 31.69
    ownership requirement 31.69
    reservations, and 31.78
    settlements not subject to relevant
      property regime, and 33.30
    technical provisions 31.71
    transitional relief 31.75
    trusts, and 31.70
  appeals 28.221
  armed services personnel, and 31.25
  artificial debts
    double charges 36.4
    generally 30.14

Inheritance tax – *contd*
  associated operations 28.101–28.105
  bereaved minors, trusts for 34.117
  burden of tax
    death 30.55–30.62
    lifetime transfers 28.178
  business property relief
    amount 31.45
    clawback 31.59
    consequences 31.61
    contracts to sell the business 31.53
    'control' 31.55
    excepted assets 31.52
    instalment payments, and 31.58
    introduction 31.42
    investment businesses 31.48
    minority shareholdings in unquoted companies 31.56
    mixed businesses 31.49–31.50
    net value of business, on 31.44
    non-business assets 31.52
    non qualifying activities 31.47
    ownership requirement 31.46
    'relevant business property' 31.43
    reservations, and 31.60
    settlements, and 31.54
    switching control 31.57
    'wholly or mainly' test 31.50
  calculation of liability 28.201
  calculation of tax (death)
    accountability 30.35
    chargeable transfers 30.22–30.23
    fall in value of property 30.24
    generally 30.36
    introduction 30.21
    liability for tax 30.35
    potentially exempt transfers 30.25–30.26
    residential nil rate band 30.28–30.34
    taper relief 30.23
    transferable nil rate band 30.27
  calculation of tax (lifetime transfers)
    cumulation 28.121
    generally 28.123
    grossing-up 28.124
    late reported transfers 28.129
    non-cash assets 28.126
    non-commercial loans 28.131
    order of making transfers 28.130
    payment of tax other than by transferor 28.125
    problem areas 28.127–28.132
    rates of tax 28.122
    relief against double charge 28.132

Inheritance tax – *contd*
  calculation of tax (lifetime transfers) – *contd*
    transfers of value by instalments 28.127
    transfers on same day 28.128
  care of dependent relative 31.10
  certificates of discharge 30.53
  chargeable transfers
    contrast with gifts 28.6
    death, and 30.22–30.23
    'disposition' 28.3
    double charges 36.5
    examples 28.5
    introduction 28.2
    omissions 28.4
    transfer of value 28.3
  charitable gifts
    death 30.37–30.38
    exemptions and reliefs 31.88–31.89
  charities, and
    generally 53.90
    gift in kind 53.95–53.98
    gift of assets 53.98
    gift to foreign charity 53.91
    legacies of 10% or more of testator's net estate 53.94
    lifetime gifts 53.92
    medical supplies and equipment 53.97
    residuary gifts 53.93
    trading stock 53.96
    wording of will 53.92
  charitable trusts 34.111
  close companies, and
    deemed dispositions by participators 28.153
    introduction 28.151
    transfers of value 28.152
  commercial transactions 28.21
  commorientes 30.141–30.142
  compensation funds 34.115
  consideration of marriage 31.6
  contingent liabilities 30.49
  co-ownership of property 28.67
  cost of gift 28.61–28.64
  cumulation 28.121
  death
    abatement 30.121–30.122
    anti-avoidance rules 30.15–30.16
    accountability 30.35
    artificial debts 30.14
    burden of tax 30.55–30.62
    calculation of tax 30.21–30.36
    certificates of discharge 30.53

Inheritance tax – *contd*
  death – *contd*
    CGT, and 30.149
    chargeable transfers 30.22–30.23
    charitable giving 30.37–30.38
    commorientes 30.141–30.142
    contingent liabilities 30.49
    disclaimers 30.152–30.157
    duty to account 30.42
    'estate' 30.2
    estimated values 30.43
    excepted estates 30.44
    exemptions and reliefs 31.1–31.89
    flexible will drafting 30.145–30.151
    hold-over relief, and 30.148
    IHT form 30.45
    instalments 30.51–30.53
    introduction 30.1
    land 30.50
    liabilities 30.13–30.16
    liability for tax 30.35
    nil rate band 31.2
    partially exempt transfers 30.91–30.103
    payment of tax 30.41–30.67
    person liable 30.42–30.54
    personal representatives 30.46
    post-death variations 30.152–30.157
    potentially exempt transfers 30.25–30.26
    precatory trusts 30.151
    quick succession relief 30.144
    recalculation 30.63–30.67
    residential nil rate band 30.28–30.34
    specific issues 30.141–30.158
    stamp duty, and 30.156
    surviving spouse 30.152
    survivorship clauses 30.143
    transferable nil rate band 30.27
    trustees 30.48
    valuation 30.3–30.12
    vesting of property 30.148
  death on active service 31.25
  deemed dispositions by participators 28.153
  deemed domicile 35.4
  disclaimers 30.152–30.157
  disclosure rules, and
    description of arrangements 5.13
    introduction 5.12
    required information 5.14
  'disposition' 28.3
  dispositions for maintenance 31.7–31.10

Inheritance tax – *contd*
  domicile, and
    deemed domicile 35.4
    election for non-UK domiciled spouse 35.5
    general 35.3
  double charges
    artificial debts and death 36.4
    chargeable transfers and death 36.5
    gifts with reservation and subsequent death 36.3
    introduction 36.1
    mutual transfers 36.2
  double taxation relief 35.41
  duty to account 30.42
  election for non-UK domiciled spouse 35.5
  employee trusts 34.114
  'estate' 30.2
  estate duty, and 30.158
  excluded property
    domicile, and 35.3–35.5
    generally 28.25
    government securities 35.21
    introduction 35.1–35.2
    non-sterling bank accounts 35.26
    OEIC shares 35.22
    overseas pensions 35.25
    policy issues 31.1
    property owned by persons domiciled in Channels Islands or Isle of Man 35.23
    property situated outside UK and owned by non-UK domiciliary 35.20
    situs of property, and 35.6
    unit trust holdings 35.22
    visiting forces 35.24
  exempt dispositions
    commercial transactions 28.21
    excluded property 28.25
    exempt transfers 28.26
    partnerships 28.24
    reversionary interests 28.22
    transfer of unquoted shares and debentures 28.23
    voidable transfers 28.28
    waiver of remuneration and dividends 28.27
  exempt transfers 28.26
  exemptions and reliefs
    acceptance in lieu 31.90
    agricultural property relief 31.62–31.78

Inheritance tax – *contd*
exemptions and reliefs – *contd*
  armed services personnel,
    and 31.25
  business property relief 31.42–31.61
  care of dependent relative 31.10
  charitable gifts 31.88–31.89
  consideration of marriage 31.6
  death, and 31.1–31.25
  death on active service 31.25
  dispositions for maintenance
    31.7–31.10
  heritage property 31.79–31.86
  inter-spouse transfers 31.41
  introduction 31.1
  lifetime transfers, and 31.3–31.10
  lifetime and death transfers,
    and 31.41–31.89
  maintenance of children 31.9
  maintenance of dependent
    relative 31.10
  maintenance of former spouse 31.8
  marriage gifts 31.6
  nil rate band 31.2
  normal expenditure out of
    income 31.4
  political parties, gifts to 31.87
  small gifts 31.5
  spouse exemption 31.41
  timber 31.21–31.24
  transfers not exceeding £3,000
    pa 31.3
  woodlands 31.21–31.24
fall in value of an estate 28.63–28.64
family taxation, and
  both spouses domiciled in the
    UK 51.69
  children 51.76
  cohabitees 51.76
  donee spouse domiciled
    abroad 51.70–51.71
  general principles 51.68
  limited gifts 51.75
  nil rate band 51.72–51.74
  outright gifts 51.75
  post mortem adjustments 51.77
  potentially exempt transfers
    51.72–51.74
flexible will drafting 30.145–30.151
foreign settlements 35.81
gift with reservation
  double charges 36.3
  liability to account for tax 29.146
gifts, and 24.3
government securities 35.21

Inheritance tax – *contd*
grossing-up 28.124
heritage property relief
  acceptance in lieu 31.90
  calculation of deferred
    charge 31.83
  effect of deferred charge 31.82
  introduction 31.79
  maintenance funds 31.85
  preconditions 31.80
  private treaty sales 31.86
  reopening existing
    undertakings 31.81
  settled property 31.84
inter-spouse transfers 31.41
interest 28.175
interest in possession trusts
  18–25 trusts 33.111
  accumulation and maintenance
    trusts 33.63–33.67
  actual terminations 33.12
  advancements to life tenant 33.15
  agricultural property relief 33.30
  anti-avoidance 33.18–33.20
  application of rules 33.18
  basic principles 33.4–33.5
  bereaved minor trusts 33.71–33.72
  business property relief 33.30
  charging method 33.4
  charitable purposes 33.26
  charitable trusts 33.112
  compensation funds 33.116
  death, and 33.10
  deemed terminations 33.13
  disabled person's interests 33.6
  disabled persons trusts 33.113
  disclaimers 33.28
  employee trusts 33.115
  excluded property 33.24
  exemptions and reliefs 33.21–33.30
  fixed income beneficiaries 33.7
  historic buildings maintenance
    funds 33.117
  immediate post-death interests 33.6
  inter vivos terminations 33.11–33.17
  introduction 33.1–33.3
  leases 33.8
  life interests 33.6
  life tenant's exemptions, and 33.22
  maintenance of child 33.25
  maintenance of dependent
    relative 33.25
  maintenance of historic
    buildings 33.117
  operation of rules 33.19

Inheritance tax – *contd*
  interest in possession trusts – *contd*
    ownership of fund 33.6–33.8
    partition 33.14
    pension funds 33.114
    post-death variations 33.28
    protective trusts 33.27, 33.118
    purchase of reversionary interest by life tenant 33.16
    quick succession relief 33.29
    reduction of value of property 33.17
    reversion to settlor 33.21
    reversionary interests, and 33.61–33.62
    surviving spouse exemption 33.23
    time of charge 33.9–33.30
    transitional serial interests 33.6
    trusts for the disabled 33.113
    variations 33.28
  late reported transfers 28.129
  liabilities
    death 30.13–30.16
    lifetime transfers 28.66
  liabilities on death
    anti-avoidance rules 30.15–30.16
    artificial debts 30.14
    general 30.13
  liability for tax
    death 30.35
    lifetime transfers 28.171
  life assurance policies 28.74
  lifetime transfers
    accountability 28.172
    administration 28.201–28.221
    associated operations 28.101–28.105
    burden of tax 28.178
    calculation of tax 28.121–28.132
    chargeable transfers 28.2–28.6
    close companies, and 28.151–28.153
    exempt transfers 28.21–28.28
    exemptions and reliefs, and 31.3–31.10, 31.41–31.89
    introduction 28.1
    liability for tax 28.171
    nil rate band 31.2
    payment of tax 28.173–28.176
    potentially exempt transfers 28.41–28.50
    timing of disposals 28.231
    value of gift 28.61–28.74
  limited liability partnerships, and 45.24
  loan interest on payment, and 7.50

Inheritance tax – *contd*
  lotting
    agricultural property relief, and 31.74
    generally 30.4
  main residences, and 23.141
  maintenance
    children 31.9
    dependent relative 31.10
    former spouse 31.8
    historic buildings 34.116
    introduction 31.7
  marital breakdown, and
    generally 52.41
    matrimonial home 52.64
  marriage gifts 31.6
  mentally disabled persons, trusts for 34.112
  multiple settlements 28.104
  nil rate band 31.2
  non-assignable agricultural tenancies 28.73
  non-cash assets 28.126
  non-commercial loans 28.131
  non-sterling bank accounts 35.26
  normal expenditure out of income 31.4
  OEIC shares 35.22
  options on property 28.70
  overseas pensions 35.25
  partially exempt transfers
    application of provisions 30.91–30.97
    double grossing-up 30.99–30.101
    effect of previous chargeable transfers 30.98
    residue part exempt and part chargeable 30.103
  partnerships
    generally 44.51
    introduction 28.24
  payment of tax (death)
    burden of tax 30.55–30.62
    certificates of discharge 30.53
    contingent liabilities 30.49
    duty to account 30.42
    estimated values 30.43
    excepted estates 30.44
    IHT form 30.45
    instalments, by 30.51–30.53
    introduction 30.41
    land 30.50
    person liable 30.42–30.54
    personal representatives 30.46
    recalculation 30.63–30.67
    trustees 30.48

Inheritance tax – *contd*
  payment of tax (lifetime transfers)
    adjustments to bill 28.177
    generally 28.173
    instalments, by 28.174
    interest 28.175
    other than by transferor 28.125
    satisfaction of tax 28.176
  penalties
    death 30.42
    lifetime transfers 28.202
  pension funds 34.113
  pension schemes, and 50.32
  personal representatives 30.46
  political parties, gifts to 31.87
  post-death variations
    death 30.152–30.157
    lifetime transfers 29.141
  potentially exempt transfers
    CGT tie-in 28.49
    death, and 30.25–30.26
    double charges 36.2–36.3
    gifts after 21 March 2006 28.42–28.45
    gifts before 22 March 2006 28.46–28.47
    interest in possession trusts settlements 28.47
    introduction 28.41
    limits 28.48
    meaning 28.42
    outright gifts to individuals 28.43
    preconditions 28.42
    relevant transfers 28.42–28.47
    taxation 28.50
    trusts for the disabled 28.44
  precatory trusts 30.151
  pre-owned assets
    calculation of charge 29.144
    exclusions and exemptions 29.145
    forms 29.143
    introduction 29.142
    'property'
      reservation of benefit 29.128
    value of gift 28.62
  property owned by persons domiciled in Channels Islands or Isle of Man 35.23
  property situated outside UK and owned by non-UK domiciliary 35.20
  protective trusts 34.117
  quick succession relief
    gifts on death 30.144
    interest in possession trusts 33.29

Inheritance tax – *contd*
  quick succession relief – *contd*
    settlements not subject to relevant property regime, and 33.29
  rates of tax 28.122
  recalculation 30.63–30.67
  related property 28.70
  relief against double charge 28.132
  reservation of benefit
    application of rules 29.41–29.44
    chargeable transfers, and 28.6
    consequences 29.21
    co-ownership 29.137
    de minimis 29.71
    discretionary trusts 29.133
    disposal of property by way of gift 29.41
    double charges 36.3
    drafting 29.122
    enjoyment of property by donee 29.42
    exclusion of donor from benefit 29.43–29.44
    excepted circumstances 29.71–29.73
    full consideration 29.72
    hardship 29.73
    Ingram v IRC 29.123–29.126
    legislative history 29.1
    permitted benefits 29.136–29.137
    possession of property by donee 29.42
    post-death variations 29.141
    post-FA 1986 position 29.121–29.145
    pre-owned assets 29.142–29.145
    'property' 29.128
    property subject to reservation 29.101
    Ramsay 29.127
    reversionary leases 29.131
    settlements 29.132–29.135
    shearing 29.122
    spouses, and 29.138
    statutory get-outs 29.136
    use of shearing arrangements 29.129
  residential nil rate band (death)
    brought forward allowance 30.33
    closely inherited 30.30–30.31
    downsizing 30.34
    inherited 30.30
    introduction 30.28
    lineal descendants 30.30
    qualifying residential interest 30.29

Inheritance tax – *contd*
  residential nil rate band (death) – *contd*
    residential enhancement 30.32
    transferable 30.33
  restrictions on transfer of property 28.72
  reversionary interests
    definition 35.82
    foreign element 35.85
    general rule 35.84
    introduction 28.22
    situs 35.83
  satisfaction of tax 28.176
  settlements
    And see **Settlements**
    18–25 trust 32.58
    accumulation and maintenance trust 32.53
    additions of property 32.8
    associated operations 32.4
    associated operations 32.4
    bereaved minor trust 32.59
    classification 32.21–32.59
    creation 32.91–32.93
    definition 32.2–32.6
    immediate post-death interest 32.51
    'interest in possession trusts' 32.22–32.30
    interest in possession trusts, with 33.1–33.62
    interest in possession trusts, without 34.1–34.74
    introduction 32.1
    meaning 32.2–32.9
    payment of tax 32.71
    reservation of benefit 32.94
    settlers 32.7
    special trusts 34.111–34.118
    transitional serial interest 32.52
    trustees 32.9
    trusts for the disabled 32.59
    with interest in possession trusts 33.1–33.62
    without interest in possession trusts 34.1–34.74
  settlements not subject to relevant property regime
    18–25 trusts 33.111
    accumulation and maintenance trusts 33.63–33.67
    actual terminations 33.12
    advancements to life tenant 33.15
    agricultural property relief 33.30
    anti-avoidance 33.18–33.20

Inheritance tax – *contd*
  settlements not subject to relevant property regime – *contd*
    application of rules 33.18
    basic principles 33.4–33.5
    bereaved minor trusts 33.71–33.72
    business property relief 33.30
    charging method 33.4
    charitable purposes 33.26
    charitable trusts 33.112
    compensation funds 33.116
    death, and 33.10
    deemed terminations 33.13
    disabled person's interests 33.6
    disabled persons trusts 33.113
    disclaimers 33.28
    employee trusts 33.115
    excluded property 33.24
    exemptions and reliefs 33.21–33.30
    fixed income beneficiaries 33.7
    historic buildings maintenance funds 33.117
    immediate post-death interests 33.6
    inter vivos terminations 33.11–33.17
    introduction 33.1–33.3
    leases 33.8
    life interests 33.6
    life tenant's exemptions, and 33.22
    maintenance of child 33.25
    maintenance of dependent relative 33.25
    maintenance of historic buildings 33.117
    operation of rules 33.19
    ownership of fund 33.6–33.8
    partition 33.14
    pension funds 33.114
    post-death variations 33.28
    protective trusts 33.27, 33.118
    purchase of reversionary interest by life tenant 33.16
    quick succession relief 33.29
    reduction of value of property 33.17
    reversion to settlor 33.21
    reversionary interests, and 33.61–33.62
    surviving spouse exemption 33.23
    time of charge 33.9–33.30
    transitional serial interests 33.6
    trusts for the disabled 33.113
    variations 33.28
  settlements subject to relevant property regime
    accumulation and maintenance trusts 34.91–34.98

Inheritance tax – *contd*
  settlements subject to relevant property regime – *contd*
    added property 34.33
    amount of tax 34.25
    charge after ten-year anniversary charge 34.28
    charge prior to ten-year anniversary charge 34.23–34.25
    creation 34.22
    discretionary trusts, and 34.35
    exemptions and reliefs 34.51
    exit charges 34.23–34.33
    introduction 34.1–34.2
    later periodic charges 34.29
    method of charge 34.21
    pre-27 March 1974 trusts 34.71–34.74
    rate of tax 34.24, 34.37
    reduction in rate of anniversary charge 34.31
    technical problems 34.30–34.34
    ten-year anniversary charge 34.26–34.27
    timing of exit charges 34.34
    transfers between settlements 34.32
  shares and securities 28.68
  situs of property, and
    generally 35.6
    reversionary interests 35.83
  small gifts 31.5
  spouse exemption 31.41
  stamp duty, and 30.156
  surviving spouse 30.152
  survivorship clauses 30.143
  taper relief 30.23
  timber 31.21–31.24
  timing of disposals 28.231
  transfer not exceeding £3,000 pa 31.3
  transfer of unquoted shares and debentures 28.23
  transfer of value
    close companies, and 28.152
    contrast with gifts 28.6
    examples 28.5
    generally 28.3
    instalments, by 28.127
    omissions 28.4
  transfer on same day 28.128
  trustees 30.48
  unit trust holdings 35.22
  valuation of estate
    allowable deductions 35.61
    enforcement of tax abroad 35.63

Inheritance tax – *contd*
  valuation of estate – *contd*
    expenses of administering property abroad 35.62
    foreign assets 35.64
  value of gift (death)
    changes in value 30.6
    funeral expenses 30.5
    introduction 30.3–30.4
    post-death sales 30.7–30.10
    provisional valuations 30.12
  value of gift (lifetime transfers)
    co-ownership of property 28.67
    cost of gift 28.61–28.64
    fall in value of an estate 28.63–28.64
    liabilities 28.66
    life assurance policies 28.74
    non-assignable agricultural tenancies 28.73
    options on property 28.70
    problem areas 28.65–28.74
    'property' 28.62
    related property 28.70
    restrictions on transfer of property 28.72
    shares and securities 28.68
    special rules 28.69–28.74
  vesting of property 30.148
  visiting forces 35.24
  voidable transfers 28.28
  waiver of remuneration and dividends 28.27
  woodlands 31.21–31.24
Initial loss relief
  losses, and 11.81–11.82
Injury benefits
  employment income, and 8.152
Innovative finance ISAs
  generally 15.31
Inspection of businesses
  introduction 4.166
  Sch 36 para 10, under 4.167
  Sch 36 para 11, under 4.168
Instalment payments
  business property relief, and 31.58
  capital gains tax, and
    gifts, and 24.30
    generally 19.61
  groups of companies, and 43.101
Insurance
  life assurance policies
    non-qualifying policies 15.2–15.10
    qualifying policies 15.1
    taxation of insurance companies 15.3

1756 *Index*

Insurance – *contd*
  value added tax, and
    brokers 40.81
    generally 40.78
    intermediary services 40.81–40.82
    marine, aviation and
      transport 40.79
    reinsurance 40.80
Insurance companies
  corporation tax 15.3
Intellectual property
  royalties, and 14.40
  trading income, and 10.155
Interest
  annual payments, and 14.17
  banks and building societies, from
    generally 7.24
    foreign taxpayers, and 18.76
  charities, and 53.41
  corporation tax, and 41.183
  deduction of tax at source 14.32
  disguised interest 14.36
  distributions, and 42.7
  estates in administration, and 17.23
  funding bonds 14.35
  future issues 14.37
  generally 4.32
  kind, in 14.35
  legacies, on 14.34
  lifetime transfers, and 28.175
  net income, and
    introduction 7.44
    loan to buy an employee-controlled
      company 7.46
    loan to buy an interest in close
      company 7.45
    loan to invest in a co-operative 7.47
    loan to invest in a partnership 7.48
    loan to pay inheritance tax 7.50
    loan to purchase life annuity 7.51
    loan to purchase plant and
      machinery 7.49
  savings and investment income, and
    deduction of tax at source 14.32
    disguised 14.36
    funding bonds 14.35
    future issues 14.37
    kind, in 14.35
    legacies, on 14.34
    source of interest 14.33
    tax relief for payment 14.31
  source of interest 14.33
  stamp duty, and 49.109
  tax relief for payment 14.31
  trading income, and 10.156

Interest in possession trusts
And see **Settlements not subject to
  relevant property regime trusts**
  18–25 trusts 33.111
  accumulation and maintenance trusts
    created pre-22 March 2006 33.64
    introduction 33.63
    transitional provisions 33.67
  actual terminations 33.12
  advancements to life tenant 33.15
  agricultural property relief 33.30
  anti-avoidance
    application of rules 33.18
    how to avoid the rules 33.20
    operation of rules 33.19
  basic principles
    charging method 33.4
    other interests 33.5
  bereaved minor trusts 33.71–33.72
  business property relief 33.30
  charging method 33.4
  charitable purposes 33.26
  charitable trusts 33.112
  compensation funds 33.116
  death, and 33.10
  deemed terminations 33.13
  disabled person's interests 33.6
  disabled persons trusts 33.113
  disclaimers 33.28
  employee trusts 33.115
  excluded property 33.24
  exemptions and reliefs
    agricultural property relief 33.30
    business property relief 33.30
    charitable purposes 33.26
    disclaimers 33.28
    excluded property 33.24
    life tenant's exemptions, and 33.22
    maintenance of child 33.25
    maintenance of dependent
      relative 33.25
    post-death variations 33.28
    protective trusts 33.27
    quick succession relief 33.29
    reversion to settlor 33.21
    surviving spouse exemption 33.23
    variations 33.28
  fixed income beneficiaries 33.7
  historic buildings maintenance
    funds 33.117
  immediate post-death interests 33.6
  inter vivos terminations
    actual terminations 33.12
    advancements to life tenant 33.15
    deemed terminations 33.13

Interest in possession trusts – *contd*
  inter vivos terminations – *contd*
    introduction 33.11
    partition 33.14
    purchase of reversionary interest by life tenant 33.16
    transactions reducing value of property 33.17
  introduction 33.1–33.3
  leases 33.8
  life interests 33.6
  life tenant's exemptions, and 33.22
  maintenance of child 33.25
  maintenance of dependent relative 33.25
  maintenance of historic buildings 33.117
  operation of rules 33.19
  ownership of fund
    fixed income beneficiaries 33.7
    leases 33.8
    life interests 33.6
  partition 33.14
  pension funds 33.114
  post-death variations 33.28
  protective trusts
    generally 33.118
    introduction 33.27
  purchase of reversionary interest by life tenant 33.16
  quick succession relief 33.29
  reduction of value of property 33.17
  reversion to settlor 33.21
  reversionary interests, and
    generally 33.61–33.62
    inter vivos terminations 33.16
  scrip dividends, and 42.152
  surviving spouse exemption 33.23
  time of charge
    actual terminations 33.12
    advancements to life tenant 33.15
    agricultural property relief 33.30
    anti-avoidance 33.18–33.20
    application of rules 33.18
    business property relief 33.30
    death, and 33.10
    deemed terminations 33.13
    disclaimers 33.28
    excluded property 33.24
    exemptions and reliefs 33.21–33.30
    inter vivos terminations 33.11–33.17
    life tenant's exemptions, and 33.22
    maintenance of child 33.25
    maintenance of dependent relative 33.25

Interest in possession trusts – *contd*
  time of charge – *contd*
    operation of rules 33.19
    partition 33.14
    post-death variations 33.28
    protective trusts 33.27
    purchase of reversionary interest by life tenant 33.16
    quick succession relief 33.29
    reduction of value of property 33.17
    reversion to settlor 33.21
    surviving spouse exemption 33.23
    transitional serial interests 33.6
    variations 33.28
  transitional serial interests 33.6
  trusts for the disabled 33.113
  variations 33.28
Interest payments
  distributions, and 42.7
  introduction 7.44
  loan to buy an employee-controlled company 7.46
  loan to buy an interest in close company 7.45
  loan to invest in a co-operative 7.47
  loan to invest in a partnership 7.48
  loan to pay inheritance tax 7.50
  loan to purchase life annuity 7.51
  loan to purchase plant and machinery 7.49
Interest rate contracts
  corporation tax, and 41.43
Interest relief
  choice of business medium, and 46.47
  estates in administration, and 17.23
Intermediary services
  value added tax, and 40.81–40.82
Internationally mobile employees
  termination payments, and 8.158
Interpretation
  legislation 1.21
Inter-spouse transfers
  capital gains tax, and 51.58
  inheritance tax, and 31.41
Inter-vivos terminations
  actual terminations 33.12
  advancements to life tenant 33.15
  deemed terminations 33.13
  introduction 33.11
  partition 33.14
  purchase of reversionary interest by life tenant 33.16
  transactions reducing value of property 33.17

Intra-group transfers
  capital gains, and 43.122
  corporation tax, and 41.48
  stamp duty, and 49.125
Inventors
  trading income, and 10.174
Investigatory powers
  civil powers
    inspect businesses 4.166–4.168
    introduction 4.161
    obtain information and
      documents 4.162–4.165
  criminal powers
    introduction 4.56–4.58
    PACE, under 4.59–4.158
  inspection of businesses
    introduction 4.166
    Sch 36 para 10, under 4.167
    Sch 36 para 11, under 4.168
  obtaining information and documents
    differences between systems 4.163
    'identity unknown notice' 4.165
    'Taxpayer Notice' 4.162
    'third-party notice' 4.164
  PACE, under
    introduction 4.59
    production orders 4.157
    safeguards 4.158–4.159
    search powers 4.140–4.155
  production orders 4.157
  search powers
    introduction 4.59
    PACE, under 4.140–4.155
  SOCPA, under 4.160
  TMA s 20BA power 4.159
Investment businesses
  business property relief, and 31.48
Investment limited liability partnerships
  anti-avoidance 45.22
  generally 45.14
Investment income
  ambit of charge 14.2
  basis of assessment 14.4
  companies 14.5
  copyright royalties 14.40
  deeply discounted securities 14.42
  generally 7.23
  interest
    deduction of tax at source 14.32
    disguised 14.36
    funding bonds 14.35
    future issues 14.37
    kind, in 14.35
    legacies, on 14.34

Investment income – *contd*
  interest – *contd*
    source of interest 14.33
    tax relief for payment 14.31
  introduction 14.1
  patent royalties 14.40
  purchased life annuities 14.41
  terminology 14.6–14.8
  unauthorised unit trusts 14.44
Investment products
  discounted gift schemes 15.25
  generally 15.21
  gift and loan scheme 15.23
  spousal interest trusts 15.22
  trust carve out 15.24
Investment trusts
  capital gains tax, and 22.3
IR 35 workers
  introduction 8.31
  managed services company
    legislation 8.34
  operation of rules 8.32
  services provided to public sector
    authorities 8.33
ISAs
  apportionment of investment 15.26
  capital gains tax, and 22.2
  cash ISA 15.27
  eligibility 15.26
  generally 15.26
  'help-to-buy' ISA 15.29
  income tax, and 7.132
  innovative finance ISA 15.31
  lifetime ISA 15.30
  Junior ISA 15.32
  stocks and shares ISA 15.28
  types 15.26

J

Jewellery
  capital gains tax, and 22.22
Joint bank accounts
  meaning of 'estate', and 30.2
Joint income
  income tax, and 7.22
Jointly held property
  family taxation, and 51.54
Jointly held trusts
  capital gains tax, and 51.63
Junior ISAs
  generally 15.32
Just apportionment
  plant and machinery allowances,
    AND 48.65
  stamp duty land tax, and 49.44

K

K codes
  employment income, and 8.196
Know-how
  capital allowances, and 48.2

L

Land
  See also **Stamp duty land tax**
  agricultural expenses 12.46
  allowance (proposed) 12.43
  ambit of rules 12.1
  artificial transactions
    application of provision 12.104
    avoiding provision 12.111
    conditions 12.104–12.107
    connected persons 12.107
    disposal of land 12.105
    effect of provision 12.103
    generally 12.101
    introduction 3.6
    opportunities to make gain 12.109
    other matters 12.112
    shares in landholding companies 12.108
    trading stock 12.106
    trading transactions 12.102
  capital allowances
    generally 12.47
    introduction 12.46
  cash basis
    consultation 12.44
  chargeable persons 12.41
  charities, and 53.100
  computation of profits
    accountancy practice 12.42
    capital allowances 12.47
    cash basis (consultation) 12.44
    interest payments 12.45
    losses 12.46
    property income allowance (proposed) 12.43
    replacement domestic items relief 12.48
  excluded income 12.24
  foreign taxpayers, and 18.75
  furnished holiday lettings
    introduction 12.61
    other measures 12.63
    qualifying holiday lettings 12.62
    tax treatment 12.64
  income tax, and
    anti-avoidance 12.101–12.112
    chargeable persons 12.41

Land – *contd*
  income tax, and – *contd*
    computation of profits 12.42–12.49
    furnished holiday lettings 12.61–12.64
    lease premiums 12.81–12.87
    rent factoring 12.88
    trading principles 12.1–12.24
  lease premiums
    anti-avoidance 12.83
    charge 12.82
    instalments, in 12.84
    introduction 12.81
    relief on trading premises 12.85
    reverse premiums 12.87
    trusts 12.86
  lettings outside trading provisions 12.23
  property income allowance (proposed) 12.43
  property income business 12.1
  rent-a-room relief 12.49
  rent factoring 12.88
  replacement domestic items relief 12.48
  reverse premiums 12.87
  Schedule A, and 12.1
  shares in landholding companies 12.108
  trading principles 12.1–12.24
  transactions in UK land
    application of provision 12.104
    avoiding provision 12.111
    conditions 12.104–12.107
    connected persons 12.107
    disposal of land 12.105
    effect of provision 12.103
    generally 12.101
    introduction 3.6
    opportunities to make gain 12.109
    other matters 12.112
    shares in landholding companies 12.108
    trading stock 12.106
    trading transactions 12.102
  unearned income, and 12.22
Landlord's energy saving allowance
  capital allowances, and 48.126–48.127
Late filing of returns
  corporation tax, and 41.184
Late reported transfers
  lifetime transfers, and 28.129
Lease extensions
  capital gains tax, and 19.76

Lease premiums
  anti-avoidance 12.83
  capital gains tax, and 19.40
  charge 12.82
  instalments, in 12.84
  introduction 12.81
  relief on trading premises 12.85
  reverse premiums 12.87
  trusts 12.86
Leaseback agreements
  disclosure rules, and 5.22
Leases of land
  capital gains tax, and
    basic rules 19.39
    income tax overlap 19.42
    premiums 19.40
    regrants 19.43
    surrenders 19.43
    wasting asset rules 19.41
  interest in possession trusts, and 33.8
  settlements not subject to relevant
      property regime, and 33.8
  stamp duty land tax, and
    increase of rent in first five
        years 49.70
    introduction 49.32
    net present value of rent 49.68
    new leases 49.65
    obligations 49.53
    premiums 49.66
    re-grants 49.73
    rent 49.67
    surrenders 49.73
    uncertain rents 49.69
    variable rents 49.69
  value added tax, and 39.37
Legal advice privilege
  prohibition of discrimination,
      and 55.48
Legal costs
  trading income, and 10.146
Legal proceedings
  miscellaneous income, and 13.22
Legal professional privilege
  right to respect for private and family
      life, and 55.62
Legatees
  main residence exemption, and 23.66
Legislation
  Hansard, and 1.23
  interpretation 1.21
  simplification process 1.22
Letting
  estates in administration, and 17.25
  main residence exemption,
      and 23.64

Liabilities
  inheritance tax on death, and
  lifetime transfers, and 28.66
Liability for tax
  inheritance tax on death, and 30.35
  lifetime transfers, and 28.171
Liability insurance premiums
  employment income, and 8.173
Licences to use or occupy
  stamp duty land tax, and 49.32
Life annuities
  loan interest on purchase, and 7.51
Life assurance policies
  capital gains tax, and 22.3
  deceased's estate 17.6
  group life policies 15.10
  income tax, and 7.132
  lifetime transfers, and 28.74
  marital breakdown, and 52.15
  non-qualifying policies
    FA 1998 changes 15.4
    FA 2003 changes 15.8
    FA 2004 changes 15.9
    general treatment 15.5
    introduction 15.2
    offshore policies 15.6
    personal portfolio bonds 15.4
    taxation of insurance
        companies 15.3
    trusts 15.7
  qualifying policies 15.1
Life interests
  interest in possession trusts, and 33.6
  settlements not subject to relevant
      property regime, and 33.6
Lifetime allowance
  generally 50.16
  protection of accrued benefits 50.22
Lifetime ISAs
  generally 15.30
Lifetime transfers
  accountability 28.172
  administration 28.201
  agricultural property relief
    And see **Agricultural property relief**
    generally 31.62–31.78
  associated operations 28.101–28.105
  burden of tax 28.178
  business property relief
    And see **Business property relief**
    generally 31.42–31.61
  calculation of tax
    cumulation 28.121
    generally 28.123
    grossing-up 28.124
    late reported transfers 28.129

Lifetime transfers – *contd*
  calculation of tax – *contd*
    non-cash assets 28.126
    non-commercial loans 28.131
    order of making transfers 28.130
    payment of tax other than by
      transferor 28.125
    problem areas 28.127–28.132
    rates of tax 28.122
    relief against double charge 28.132
    transfers of value by
      instalments 28.127
    transfers on same day 28.128
  chargeable transfers 28.2–28.6
  close companies, and 28.151–28.153
  exempt dispositions
    commercial transactions 28.21
    excluded property 28.25
    exempt transfers 28.26
    partnerships 28.24
    reversionary interests 28.22
    transfer of unquoted shares and
      debentures 28.23
    voidable transfers 28.28
    waiver of remuneration and
      dividends 28.27
  exempt transfers 28.26
  exemptions and reliefs, and 31.3–31.10
    agricultural property relief
      31.62–31.78
    business property relief 31.42–31.61
    charitable gifts 31.88–31.89
    consideration of marriage 31.6
    heritage property 31.78–31.85
    inter-spouse transfer 31.41
    maintenance 31.7–31.10
    normal expenditure out of
      income 31.4
    political parties, gifts to 31.87
    small gifts 31.5
    transfers not exceeding £3,000
      pa 31.3
  heritage property
    And see **Heritage property relief**
    generally 31.78–31.85
  introduction 28.1
  liability for tax 28.171
  mutual transfers 36.2
  nil rate band 31.2
  payment of tax
    adjustments to bill 28.177
    generally 28.173
    instalments, by 28.174
    interest 28.175
    other than by transferor 28.125
    satisfaction of tax 28.176

Lifetime transfers – *contd*
  potentially exempt transfers
    CGT tie-in 28.49
    death, and 30.25–30.26
    double charges 36.2–36.3
    gifts after 21 March 2006
      28.42–28.45
    gifts before 22 March 2006
      28.46–28.47
    interest in possession trusts
      settlements 28.45
    introduction 28.41
    limits 28.48
    meaning 28.42
    outright gifts to individuals 28.43
    preconditions 28.42
    relevant transfers 28.42–28.47
    taxation of 28.50
    trusts for the disabled 28.44
  value of gift
    co-ownership of property 28.67
    cost of gift 28.61–28.64
    fall in value of an estate 28.63–28.64
    liabilities 28.66
    life assurance policies 28.74
    non-assignable agricultural
      tenancies 28.73
    options on property 28.70
    problem areas 28.65–28.74
    'property' 28.62
    related property 28.70
    restrictions on transfer of
      property 28.72
    shares and securities 28.68
    special rules 28.69–28.74
Limited interests in residue
  estates in administration, and 17.49
Limited liability partnerships
  accounts 45.7
  anti-avoidance 45.22
  background 45.2
  capital gains tax
    corporate members 45.16
    gains 45.15
    introduction 45.9
    losses 45.13
    mixed member LLPs 45.16
    partner status 45.11–45.12
    salaried members 45.11–45.12
    trading LLPs 45.10
  cessation of activities
    general 45.17
    liquidation 45.19
    winding up 45.18
  choice of business medium,
    and 46.5

Limited liability partnerships – *contd*
  companies, and 45.4
  corporate members 45.16
  corporation tax, and 41.2
  general 45.3
  income tax
    introduction 45.9
    losses 45.13
    trading LLPs 45.10
  incorporation of unincorporated business 45.20–45.21
  inheritance tax 45.24
  international aspects 45.7
  introduction 45.1
  investment LLP
    anti-avoidance 45.22
    generally 45.14
  limited liability 45.5
  liquidation 45.19
  loss relief 45.13
  Members' Agreement 45.6
  mixed member LLP 45.16
  national insurance contributions 45.24
  partner status 45.11–45.12
  property LLP
    anti-avoidance 45.22
    generally 45.14
  salaried members
    generally 45.11–45.12
    NICs 45.24
  stamp duty land tax 45.23
  trading LLP 45.10
  transfer of unincorporated business 45.20–45.21
  undertaking business with view to profit 45.10
  value added tax 45.25
  winding up 45.18

Limited partnerships
  choice of business medium, and 46.4
  generally 45.2

Linked transactions
  stamp duty land tax, and 49.64

Liquidation
  limited liability partnerships, and 45.19

Listed schemes
  disclosure rules, and 5.21

Living accommodation
  additional charge 8.112
  basic charge 8.111
  decreasing the charge 8.113
  exemptions 8.114
  increasing the charge 8.113

Living accommodation – *contd*
  introduction 8.110
  non-domiciliaries 8.116

Loan interest
  acquisition of interest in close company 7.45
  acquisition of interest in co-operative 7.47
  acquisition of interest in partnership 7.46
  introduction 7.44
  investment in employee-controlled company 7.48
  net income, and 7.42
  partnerships, and 44.11
  payment of inheritance tax 7.50
  purchase of life annuity 7.51
  purchase of plant or machinery 7.49

Loan notes
  acquisition of company, and 47.39

Loan relationships
  connected parties 41.56
  extent of regime 41.53
  general principles 41.50
  impaired debt 41.56
  late interest 41.56
  meaning 41.51
  non-trading profits, losses and expenses 41.54
  trading profits, losses and expenses 41.53

Loans
  acquire interest in close company, to
    generally 7.45
    introduction 9.1
  capital gains tax, and 22.43
  corporation tax, and 41.128
  net income, and
    buy an employee-controlled company 7.46
    buy an interest in close company 7.45
    introduction 7.44
    invest in a co-operative 7.47
    invest in a partnership 7.48
    pay inheritance tax 7.50
    purchase life annuity 7.51
    purchase plant and machinery 7.49
  participators, to
    corporation tax 41.128
  traders, to 22.43

Long service awards
  employment income, and 8.168

Loss relief
And see **Losses**
anti-avoidance 11.122
capital gains, against 11.61
carry-across relief 11.41
carry-forward relief 11.21
choice of business medium, and 46.49
corporation tax, and
  acquisition of tax loss
    company 41.65
  capital losses, for 41.68
  carry-forward 41.61
  'commercial purpose' 41.64
  current profits, against 41.61
  introduction 41.60
  non-trading income losses,
    for 41.67
  previous profits, against 41.61
  reconstructions 41.66
  restrictions on availability
    41.63–41.66
  targeted loss buying 41.65
  trading losses, for 41.61–41.62
early years, in 11.81–11.82
films, and 11.122
final years, in
  terminal loss relief 11.102
  transfer of business to
    company 11.101
income from property 11.3
initial loss relief 11.81–11.82
introduction
  companies 11.2
  general 11.1
  income from property 11.3
limited liability partnerships, and 45.13
partnerships, and 11.122
profession, and 11.4
property losses 7.81
restriction from 2013/14
  onwards 11.5
targeted loss buying 41.65
terminal loss relief 11.102
total income, and
  property losses 7.81
  trading losses deducted from
    general income 7.82–7.91
trade 11.4
trading losses
  deducted from general
    income 7.82–7.91
  generally 51.53
  transfer of business to
    company 11.101
unquoted corporate trades 11.121

Losses
capital allowances, and
  introduction 48.8
  property losses 48.10
  trading losses 48.9
capital gains tax, and
  anti-avoidance 19.48
  capital allowances 19.47
  circumstances in which arise 19.44
  family taxation, and 51.57
  restrictions 19.47–19.48
  set-off of capital losses 19.58
  taper relief, and 19.46
  targeted anti-avoidance rule 19.48
  use 19.45
  use of trading losses 19.59
capital gains tax on death, and
  losses of deceased 21.41
  losses of PRs 21.81
companies, and 11.2
family taxation, and 51.57
general 11.1
income from property 11.3
limited liability partnerships,
  and 45.13
miscellaneous income, and
  13.20–13.21
profession, and 11.4
restriction from 2013/14
  onwards 11.5
trade, and 11.4
trading income, and 10.145
vocation, and 11.4
Lotting
agricultural property relief, and 31.74
generally 30.4
Low-emission cars
first year allowances, and 48.32
Lower-paid employees
employment income, and 8.104
Lump sum payments
marital breakdown, and 52.23
pension schemes, and 50.19
Lump sum termination payments
contemporaneous share sales 8.157
current regime 8.150
damages, and 8.156
death benefits 8.152
disability benefits 8.152
exceptions 8.151–8.154
first £30,000 8.154
generally 8.148
injury benefits 8.152
internationally mobile
  employees 8.158

Lump sum termination payments – *contd*
  introduction 8.101
  old regime 8.149
  PAYE 8.155
  pension benefits 8.152
  reform recommendations 8.159
  reporting requirements 8.155

M

Main residence exemption
  availability 23.1–23.2
  business use 23.63
  capital gains tax on death, and 21.65
  curtilage test 23.24
  death, and
    disposal by legatees 23.66
    disposal by personal
      representatives 23.65
  definitions
    'dwelling house' 23.21
    'residence' 23.22–23.24
  degree of permanence 23.22
  disposal by legatees 23.66
  disposal by personal
    representatives 23.65
  election between residences
    generally 23.43
    non-residents, and 23.44–23.48
  entity test 23.23
  expenditure with profit-making
    motive 23.101
  family taxation, and 51.62
  IHT schemes, and 23.141
  introduction 23.1
  land used with the house 23.61
  legatees, and 23.66
  letting part of property 23.64
  non-residents, and
    generally 23.44–23.48
    introduction 23.2
  periods of absence
    civil partners 23.82
    employment-related periods 23.85
    general rule 23.81
    married couples 23.82
    other situations 23.84
    permitted absences 23.83
    same-sex couples 23.82
  personal representatives, and 23.65
  problem areas 23.61–23.66
  qualifying residences
    civil partners 23.42
    married partners 23.42
    more than one residence
      23.43–23.48

Main residence exemption – *contd*
  residence
    curtilage test 23.24
    degree of permanence 23.22
    entity test 23.23
  second homes 23.121–23.123
  trust-held houses 23.62
  use of house for business 23.63
Maintenance
  inheritance tax, and
    children 31.9
    dependent relative 31.10
    former spouse 31.8
    historic buildings 34.116
    introduction 31.7
  interest in possession trusts, and
    child 33.25
    dependent relative 33.25
  marital breakdown, and 52.3
  settlements not subject to relevant
      property regime, and
    child 33.25
    dependent relative 33.25
  settlements subject to relevant
    property regime, and 34.116
Maintenance funds
  heritage property relief, and 31.85
  settlements not subject to relevant
    property regime, and 33.117
Maintenance payments
  annual payments, and 14.13
Maintenance powers
  divesting effect 16.71
  introduction 16.70
  tax treatment 16.73
  vesting effect 16.72
Managed service companies
  introduction 8.31
  legislation 8.34
  operation of rules 8.32
Management buy-outs
  generally 47.71
Management expenses
  corporation tax, and
    acquisition of surplus expenses
      company 41.70
    distinction between investment and
      trading companies 41.71
    general rule 41.69
  trusts, and 16.23
Manors
  stamp duty land tax, and 49.32
Margin schemes
  auctioneers 40.126
  secondhand goods 40.108–40.109

Margin schemes – *contd*
  tour operators
    agents 40.123
    foreign currency 40.119
    incidental supplies 40.121
    in-house supplies 40.116
    input tax 40.118
    introduction 40.110
    margin scheme 40.113–40.114
    territorial scope 40.112
    time of supply 40.120
    travel agents 40.123
    travellers 40.111
    wholesale supplies 40.117
Marine insurance
  value added tax, and 40.79
Marital breakdown
  annual exemption 52.22
  capital gains tax
    annual exemption 52.22
    generally 52.21
    lump sum payments 52.23
    matrimonial home 52.62–52.63
  clean-break transfer 52.67–52.69
  income tax
    general principles 52.2
    life insurance policies 52.15
    maintenance payments 52.3
    pensions 52.4–52.12
  inheritance tax
    generally 52.41
    matrimonial home 52.64
  introduction 52.1
  life insurance policies 52.15
  lump sum payments 52.23
  maintenance payments 52.3
  matrimonial home
    capital gains tax 52.62–52.63
    clean-break transfer
      52.67–52.69
    conclusions 52.79
    inheritance tax 52.64
    introduction 52.61
    joint ownership with sale
      postponed 52.70–52.72
    outright transfer with charge
      back 52.76–52.78
    settlement of house 52.73–52.75
    stamp duty land tax 52.65
  pensions
    Brooks v Brooks decision 52.4
    earmarking orders 52.12
    flexibility 52.14
    introduction 52.4
    offsetting 52.11

Marital breakdown – *contd*
  pensions – *contd*
    pension attachment 52.12
    pension sharing 52.13
    stamp duty 52.60
    stamp duty land tax 52.65
    tax credits 52.16
Market gardeners
  trading income, and 10.172–10.173
Market value
  capital gains tax, and
    consideration for disposal 19.16
  income tax, and
    trading receipts 10.117–10.118
Marriage gifts
  inheritance tax, and 31.6
Married couple's allowance
  age-related
    basic requirements 51.21
    generally 7.111–7.113
    introduction 51.20
    restriction of relief 51.22
    use 51.23
  transferable tax allowance
    7.115–7.117, 51.12
Match fees
  value added tax, and 40.56
Materiality
  trading income, and 10.65
Matrimonial home
  capital gains tax 52.62–52.63
  clean-break transfer 52.67–52.69
  conclusions 52.79
  inheritance tax 52.64
  introduction 52.61
  joint ownership with sale
    postponed 52.70–52.72
  outright transfer with charge
    back 52.76–52.78
  settlement of house 52.73–52.75
  stamp duty land tax 52.65
McGuckian v IRC
  And see **Tax avoidance**
  generally 2.32–2.33
  purposive interpretation 2.36
Medals for valour
  capital gains tax, and 22.3
Members of Parliament
  residence, and 27.24
Membership fees
  employment income, and 8.172
**Mentally disabled persons,
   trusts for**
  settlements subject to relevant
    property regime, and 34.112

Milk quota
  agricultural property relief,
    and 31.76
Mineral extraction
  capital allowances, and 48.2
Minor benefits
  employment income, and 8.169
Minority shareholdings in unquoted companies
  business property relief,
    and 31.56
Miscellaneous income
  alternative charges 13.14
  annual payments
    And see **Annual payments**
    ambit of charge 14.2
    basis of assessment 14.4
    charge to tax 14.14–14.17
    collection of tax 14.21–14.28
    companies 14.5
    income arising 14.3
    introduction 14.1
    taxation 14.11–14.13
    terminology 14.6–14.8
  annual payments not otherwise charged
    corporation tax 13.8
    income tax 13.7
    introduction 13.6
  apportionment 13.17
  cash-backs 13.28
  charging options 13.2
  commissions 13.28
  corporation tax charge 13.5
  earnings basis 13.16
  expenses 13.18
  fees 13.28
  filming 13.26
  full amount of income 13.19
  general charge 13.2–13.6
  hire of equipment 13.27
  income not otherwise charged
    corporation tax 13.11
    income tax 13.10
    introduction 13.9
  income rather than capital 13.12
  income tax charge 13.4
  legal proceedings 13.22
  losses 13.20–13.21
  overview 13.30
  photography 13.26
  procedure
    apportionment 13.17
    earnings basis 13.16

Miscellaneous income – *contd*
  procedure – *contd*
    expenses 13.18
    full amount of income 13.19
    legal proceedings 13.22
    losses 13.20–13.21
  publishing 13.25
  scope 13.1
  specific cases 13.23–13.30
  specific charging provisions
    corporation tax 13.5
    income tax 13.4
    introduction 13.3
  'sweeping up' provisions
    corporation tax 13.11
    generally 13.30
    introduction 13.1
  taxable source 13.13
  taxing priority
    alternative charges 13.14
    trading 13.15
  theatrical 'angels' 13.24
  toll charges 13.27
  trading 13.15
  volunteer drivers 13.29
  writing and publishing 13.25
Misdeclaration penalties
  value added tax, and 38.68
Mixed businesses
  business property relief, and
    one business or two 31.49
    'wholly or mainly' test 31.50
Mobile phones
  employment income, and
    8.166
Modification powers
  pension schemes, and 50.8
Money purchase schemes
  See **Pension schemes**
Monthly returns
  value added tax, and 38.55
Mortgages
  capital gains tax, and 19.73
Motor vehicles
  capital gains tax, and 22.2
Multiple dwellings acquisitions
  stamp duty land tax, and 49.81
Multiple settlements
  lifetime transfers, and 28.104
Multiple supplies
  value added tax, and 38.25
Museums
  value added tax, and 40.63
Mutually exclusive rule
  income tax, and 6.42

N

National insurance contributions
choice of business medium, and
   generally 46.43
   table 46.Appendix
employment income, and 8.1
limited liability partnerships,
   and 45.24
non tax-advantaged share
   schemes 9.44
tax-advantaged share schemes,
   and 9.90

National Savings Certificates
capital gains tax, and 22.2

Natural gas refuelling equipment
first year allowances, and 48.33

Negligible value
capital gains tax, and 19.69

Net income
adjusted total income 7.42
calculation 7.43
deductible reliefs
   generally 7.41
   restriction 7.42
general 7.40
interest payments
   introduction 7.44
   loan to buy an employee-controlled
      company 7.46
   loan to buy an interest in close
      company 7.45
   loan to invest in a co-operative 7.47
   loan to invest in a partnership 7.48
   loan to pay inheritance tax 7.50
   loan to purchase life annuity 7.51
   loan to purchase plant and
      machinery 7.49
irrecoverable peer-to-peer loans 7.92
loss relief
   property losses 7.81
   trading losses deducted from
      general income 7.82–7.91

'Nett' acts
value added tax, and 40.44

Nil rate band
calculation of tax on death, and
   generally 30.27
   residential property 30.33
family taxation, and 51.72–51.74
generally 31.2
residential nil rate band
   brought forward allowance 30.33
   closely inherited 30.30–30.31
   downsizing 30.34
   inherited 30.30

Nil rate band – *contd*
residential nil rate band – *contd*
   introduction 30.28
   lineal descendants 30.30
   qualifying residential interest
      30.29
   residential enhancement 30.32
   transferable 30.33
settlements, and 32.92

'91-day' rule
residence, and 18.4

No gain/no loss transactions
capital gains tax, and 19.11

'No main object of obtaining a tax advantage'
transactions in securities, and 3.66

Non-assignable agricultural tenancies
lifetime transfers, and 28.73

Non-cash assets
lifetime transfers, and 28.126

Non-commercial loans
lifetime transfers, and 28.131

Non-corporate distribution rate
corporation tax, and 41.24

Non-deduction of PAYE
employment income, and 8.200

Non-monetary consideration
stamp duty land tax, and 49.47

Non-qualifying life policies
FA 1998 changes 15.4
FA 2003 changes 15.8
FA 2004 changes 15.9
general treatment 15.5
introduction 15.2
offshore policies 15.6
personal portfolio bonds 15.4
taxation of insurance
   companies 15.3
trusts 15.7

Non-resident companies
anti-avoidance 27.112
general rule 27.111

Non-resident discretionary trusts
foreign taxpayers, and 18.79

Non-resident individuals
See **Non-residents**

Non-resident partnerships
residence, and 18.17

Non-resident trustees
trusts, and 16.9

Non-resident trusts
anti flip flop legislation
   generally 27A.171–27A.176
   taxing UK domiciled settlor of
      offshore trust 27A.87–27A.89

Non-resident trusts – *contd*
  background
    generally 27A.1
    historical changes to
      scheme 27A.2–27A.11
    proposed 2017 changes 27A.12
  exporting a UK trust
    advantages of non-resident
      trust 27A.21–27A.24
    export charge to CGT
      27A.38–27A.55
    procedure 27A.34–27A.37
    rules on trust residence
      27A.25–27A.33
  proposed 2017 changes 27A.12
  provision of information
    requirements 27A.177
  residence of trustee 27A.21–27A.55
  taxing UK domiciled settlor of
    offshore trust
    anti flip flop legislation
      27A.87–27A.89
    attributed trust gains
      27A.89–27A.97
    'defined person' benefits
      27A.83–27A.86
    introduction 27A.71–27A.75
    personal capital losses
      27A.89–27A.97
    qualifying settlements
      27A.76–27A.81
    qualifying settlors 27A.82
  taxing UK resident beneficiaries of
    non-resident trust
    [*n.b. UK domiciled and resident
      beneficiaries*]
    attribution method
      27A.118–27A.119
    basic rules 27A.101–27A.105
    capital payments 27A.109–27A.117
    disposal of beneficial interest in
      offshore trust
      27A.164–27A.169
    interest charge 27A.136–27A.138
    offshore losses 27A.129
    operation of s 87 charge
      27A.106–27A.129
    payments prior to 6 April
      2008 27A.121
    personal losses or rates of
      tax 27A.126–27A.128
    s 731 ITA 2007 tie-in 27A.120
    'stockpiled gains' 27A.106–27A.108
    supplementary charge
      27A.136–27A.138

Non-resident trusts – *contd*
  taxing UK resident beneficiaries of
    non-resident trust – *contd*
    trust gains 27A.106
    use of personal losses or rates of
      tax 27A.126–27A.128
  taxing UK resident beneficiaries of
    non-resident trust
    [*n.b. UK resident foreign domiciled
      beneficiaries*]
    general principles 27A.145–27A.153
    rebasing 27A.154–27A.163
Non-residents
  See also **Non-resident trusts**
  See also **Overseas dimension**
  liability
    ESC D2 27.50
    Finance (No 2) Act 2005
      changes 27.56–27.63
    introduction 27.41–27.44
    other matters 27.51–27.55
    temporary non-resident
      individuals 27.46–27.49
  main residence exemption, and
    generally 23.44–23.48
    introduction 23.2
  new regime for foreign domiciliaries
    asset situate outside the UK
      27.83–27.85
    disposals for less than full
      consideration 27.99–27.100
    foreign currency gains 27.101
    general points 27.81–27.82
    losses 27.86–27.88
    rate of tax 27.98
    remittances 27.89–27.97
    segregation of claims 27.88
  non-resident companies
    anti-avoidance 27.112
    general rule 27.111
  remittances
    business investment relief 27.96
    introduction 27.89–27.92
    relevant persons 27.93–27.95
    sales of exempt art 27.97
  residence
    case law 27.12–27.16
    full-time work abroad 27.11
    Gaines v Cooper decision 27.6
    Grace decision 27.14
    general law 27.2–27.4
    HMRC practice 27.5–27.8
    introduction 27.1
    multiplicity of factors 27.13
    occasional residence abroad 27.9

Non-residents – *contd*
  residence – *contd*
    statutory provisions 27.9–27.11
    statutory residence test 27.17–27.24
    temporary purposes in the UK 27.10
  temporary non-resident individuals 27.46–27.49
Non-sterling bank accounts
  inheritance tax, and 35.26
Non tax-advantaged share schemes
  background 9.11
  'by reason of employment' 9.12
  capital gains tax
    acquisition of shares other than pursuant to pre-existing right 9.46–9.47
    acquisition of shares pursuant to employment-related securities option 9.50–9.56
    chargeable gain calculation 9.57
    grant of right to acquire shares to employee 9.49
    introduction 9.45
  choice of scheme
    non-tax aspects 9.151–9.160
    other shareholders 9.164
    tax aspects 9.161–9.163
  conclusions 9.58
  general points 9.12
  income tax
    acquisition of shares other than pursuant to pre-existing right 9.48
    acquisition of shares pursuant to employment-related securities option 9.56
    grant of right to acquire shares to employee 9.49
    introduction 9.11–9.13
  NICs 9.44
  non-tax aspects of choice
    accounting treatment 9.160
    bonus schemes 9.152
    employee retention 9.155
    'friendly' shareholdings 9.156
    introduction 9.151
    market in non-quoted shares 9.157
    performance-related incentives 9.153
    retention of employees 9.155
    reward for growth in share value 9.154
    sense of identity between employees and company 9.158

Non tax-advantaged share schemes – *contd*
  non-tax aspects of choice – *contd*
    selective employee participation 9.159
  PAYE 9.42–9.43
  residency conditions, and 9.13
  rights to acquire shares 9.41
  share incentives
    artificial depression of market value 9.26
    convertible shares 9.25
    employee shareholders 9.32–9.34
    enhancement of market value 9.26
    meaning 9.2
    post-acquisition benefits 9.29
    priority share allocations 9.30
    research institution spin-out companies 9.31
    restricted shares 9.21–9.23
    shares acquired for less than market value 9.27
    shares disposed of for more than market value 9.28
  share options 9.41
  tax aspects of choice 9.161–9.163
Normal expenditure out of income
  inheritance tax, and 31.4
North Sea oil companies
  ring fence profits 41.24
Notices to pay
  tax avoidance, and 5.28

O

Occupational pension schemes
  See **Pension schemes**
OEIC shares
  inheritance tax, and 35.22
Office of Tax Simplification
  employee benefits and expenses 8.101
Office or employment
  And see **Employment income**
  employment status 8.22
  introduction 8.20
  'office' 8.21
  partners 8.23
  reclassification of status 8.24
Office-holders
  IR 35, and 8.32
Offsetting
  pensions, and 52.11
Off-shore loop
  disclosure rules, and 5.22
Off-shore 'roll-up' funds
  foreign income, and 18.40

Offshore trusts
anti flip flop legislation
  generally 27A.171–27A.176
  taxing UK domiciled settlor of offshore trust 27A.87–27A.89
background
  generally 27A.1
  historical changes to scheme 27A.2–27A.11
  proposed 2017 changes 27A.12
exporting a UK trust
  advantages of non-resident trust 27A.21–27A.24
  export charge to CGT 27A.38–27A.55
  procedure 27A.34–27A.37
  rules on trust residence 27A.25–27A.33
proposed 2017 changes 27A.12
provision of information requirements 27A.177
residence of trustee 27A.21–27A.55
taxing UK domiciled settlor of offshore trust
  anti flip flop legislation 27A.87–27A.89
  attributed trust gains 27A.89–27A.97
  'defined person' benefits 27A.83–27A.86
  introduction 27A.71–27A.75
  personal capital losses 27A.89–27A.97
  qualifying settlements 27A.76–27A.81
  qualifying settlors 27A.82
taxing UK resident beneficiaries of non-resident trust
[*n.b. UK domiciled and resident beneficiaries*]
  attribution method 27A.118–27A.119
  basic rules 27A.101–27A.105
  capital payments 27A.109–27A.117
  disposal of beneficial interest in offshore trust 27A.164–27A.169
  interest charge 27A.136–27A.138
  offshore losses 27A.129
  operation of s 87 charge 27A.106–27A.129
  payments prior to 6 April 2008 27A.121
  personal losses or rates of tax 27A.126–27A.128

Offshore trusts – *contd*
taxing UK resident beneficiaries of non-resident trust – *contd*
  s 731 ITA 2007 tie-in 27A.120
  'stockpiled gains' 27A.106–27A.108
  supplementary charge 27A.136–27A.138
  trust gains 27A.106
  use of personal losses or rates of tax 27A.126–27A.128
taxing UK resident beneficiaries of non-resident trust
[*n.b. UK resident foreign domiciled beneficiaries*]
  general principles 27A.145–27A.153
  rebasing 27A.154–27A.163
'183-day' rule
residence, and 18.3
"One-man" companies
introduction 8.31
managed services company legislation 8.34
operation of rules 8.32
services provided to public sector authorities 8.33
Opticians
value added tax, and 40.40
Option to tax
value added tax on commercial buildings, and
  capital goods scheme, and 39.34
  introduction 39.27
  mechanics of exercise 39.29
  output tax 39.31
  property affected 39.28
  purpose of exercise 39.33
  revocation 39.30
Optional remuneration arrangements
generally 8.106
Options
capital gains tax, and
  calculation of gain on disposal 19.38
  definition 19.37
  disposal, and 19.70
  lifetime transfers, and 28.70
  stamp duty land tax, and 49.40
'Ordinary course of making and managing investments'
transactions in securities, and 3.65
Ordinary residence
And see **Residence**
generally 18.14–18.15

Outplacement counselling
  employment income, and 8.163
  trading income, and 10.148
Overseas dimension
  capital gains tax for individuals
    And see below
    liability of non-residents
      27.41–27.63
    new regime for foreign
      domiciliaries 27.81–27.99
    non-resident companies
      27.111–27.112
    residence 27.1–27.30
  offshore trusts
    And see **Offshore trusts**
    anti flip flop legislation
      27A.171–27A.176
    background 27A.1–27A.11
    exporting a UK trust
      27A.21–27A.55
    information 27A.177
    proposed 2017 changes 27A.12
    residence of trustee
      27A.21–27A.55
    taxing UK domiciled settlor of
      offshore trust
      27A.71–27A.97
    taxing UK resident beneficiaries of
      non-resident trust
      27A.101–27A.163
  corporation tax
    calculation of profits 41.152
    controlled foreign
      companies 41.161
    double tax relief 41.156–41.159
    effect of ceasing to be UK
      resident 41.154
    liability to tax 41.151
    non-resident companies 41.162
    non-resident shareholders of
      resident companies 41.162
    'residence' 41.153
    UK resident companies
      abroad 41.155
  income tax
    And see below
    anti-avoidance 18.110–18.128
    domicile 18.23–18.30
    double taxation relief 18.91
    foreign income 18.31–18.51
    foreign taxpayers 18.71–18.79
    introduction 18.1
    residence 18.2–18.22
    transfer of assets abroad
      18.110–18.128

Overseas dimension (capital gains tax)
  liability of non-residents
    ESC D2 27.50
    Finance (No 2) Act 2005
      changes 27.56–27.63
    introduction 27.41–27.44
    other matters 27.51–27.55
    temporary non-resident
      individuals 27.46–27.49
  new regime for foreign domiciliaries
    asset situate outside the UK
      27.83–27.85
    disposals for less than full
      consideration 27.99–27.100
    foreign currency gains 27.101
    general points 27.81–27.82
    losses 27.86–27.88
    rate of tax 27.98
    remittances 27.89–27.97
  non-resident companies
    anti-avoidance 27.112
    general rule 27.111
  remittances
    business investment relief 27.96
    introduction 27.89–27.92
    relevant persons 27.93–27.95
    sales of exempt art 27.97
  residence
    case law 27.12–27.16
    full-time work abroad 27.11
    Gaines v Cooper decision 27.6
    Grace decision 27.14
    general law 27.2–27.4
    HMRC practice 27.5–27.8
    introduction 27.1
    multiplicity of factors 27.13
    occasional residence abroad 27.9
    statutory provisions 27.9–27.11
    statutory residence test 27.17–27.24
    temporary purposes in the
      UK 27.10
  temporary non-resident
    individuals 27.46–27.49
Overseas dimension (income tax)
  anti-avoidance
    chargeable income 18.118
    general 18.111
    'individuals ordinarily resident in
      the UK' 18.112
    introduction 18.110
    legislative reforms 18.127–18.128
    liability of non-transferors
      18.120–18.125
    liability of transferor
      18.114–18.119

Overseas dimension (income tax) – *contd*
  anti-avoidance – *contd*
    powers to obtain
      information 18.126
    purpose 18.113
    remittance basis for
      non-domiciliaries 18.119
  domicile
    choice, of 18.25–18.26
    deemed 18.28
    introduction 18.23
    married women 18.29
    origin, of 18.24
    proposed 2017 changes 18.30
    special situations 18.27
  double taxation relief 18.91
  double tax treaties 18.22
  foreign employment income
    annuities 18.50
    collection of tax 18.51
    deductible expenses 18.49
    emoluments for duties performed
      in UK 18.46
    introduction 18.43
    pensions 18.50
    place of work 18.48
    remittance basis 18.47
  foreign income
    alimony orders 18.41
    becoming resident in UK 18.42
    calculation of liability
      18.32–18.33
    charge 18.34
    charging provisions 18.31
    distributions from companies 18.36
    employment income 18.43–18.51
    foreign partnerships, from 18.39
    foreign trusts, from 18.38
    off-shore 'roll-up' funds 18.40
    partnerships, from 18.39
    pensions 18.41
    professions 18.35
    property income 18.37
    remittance basis 18.34
    savings and investment
      income 18.36
    Schedule D, and 18.31
    trade profits 18.35
    trusts, from 18.38
    vocations 18.35
  foreign taxpayers
    dividends paid by UK
      companies 18.78
    employment income 18.73
    entertainers 18.74

Overseas dimension (income tax) – *contd*
  foreign taxpayers
    interest from UK banks and
      building societies 18.76
    introduction 18.71
    land in the UK 18.75
    non-resident discretionary
      trusts 18.79
    professions 18.72
    sportsmen and women 18.74
    trade profits 18.72
    UK government securities 18.77
    vocations 18.72
  introduction 18.1
  non-resident partnerships 18.17
  ordinary residence 18.14–18.15
  partnerships
    fiscal transparency 18.18
    non-resident partnerships 18.17
  proposed 2017 changes 18.30
  residence
    acquisition of resident status 18.7
    available accommodation 18.5
    corporations 18.16
    double tax treaties 18.22
    from 6 April 2013 18.8–18.13
    introduction 18.2
    loss of resident status 18.7
    meaning 18.2
    non-resident partnerships 18.17
    occasional residence abroad 18.6
    ordinary residence 18.14–18.15
    partnerships 18.17–18.18
    personal representatives 18.21
    prior to 6 April 2013 18.3–18.7
    statutory residence test 18.8–18.13
    the '91-day' rule 18.4
    the '183-day' rule 18.3
    'tie-breaker' clauses 18.22
    trustees 18.19
    trusts 18.20
  statutory residence test
    automatic non-residence
      test 18.9
    automatic residence test 18.10
    introduction 18.8
    split year treatment 18.12
    temporary non residence 18.13
    UK ties 18.11
  transfer of assets abroad
    18.110–18.128
  UK resident
    available accommodation 18.5
    introduction 18.3
    occasional residence abroad 18.6

Overseas dimension (income tax) – *contd*
UK resident – *contd*
the '91-day' rule 18.4
the '183-day' rule 18.3
Overseas pensions
inheritance tax, and 35.25
Own car use
employment income, and 8.22
Ownership
agricultural property relief,
and 31.69
business property relief, and 31.46
interest in possession trusts, and
33.6–33.8
settlements not subject to relevant
property regime, and 33.6–33.8

P

PACE powers
introduction 4.59
production orders 4.157
safeguards 4.158–4.159
search warrants
introduction 4.59
PACE, under 4.140–4.155
special procedure material 4.157
TMA s 20BA, under 4.159
Paper-for-paper exchange
corporation tax, and 41.97
Part disposals
formula not used, where 19.36
general rule 19.35
leases of land, and 19.39
Partial exemption
value added tax, and 38.83–38.84
Partially exempt transfers
application of provisions 30.91–30.97
double grossing-up 30.99–30.101
effect of previous chargeable
transfers 30.98
residue part exempt and part
chargeable 30.103
Participation fees
value added tax, and 40.56
Partition
interest in possession trusts,
and 33.14
settlements not subject to relevant
property regime, and 33.14
stamp duty land tax, and 49.46
Partnerships
see also **Limited liability partnerships**
allocation of profits/losses to
members 44.10
annual payments, and 14.16

Partnerships – *contd*
annuity payments by partners
capital gains tax 44.34
income tax 44.14–44.16
anti-avoidance
loss relief, and 11.122
calculation of profits 44.3–44.10
capital gains tax
annuity payments by partners 44.34
changes to asset surplus sharing
ratio 44.32
entrepreneurs relief 44.39
general 44.31
goodwill 44.33
hold-over relief 44.36
incorporation relief 44.38
reliefs 44.35–44.39
replacement of business assets
relief 44.37
roll-over relief 44.37–44.38
changes in partnership 44.12
choice of business medium,
and 46.1
consultancies 44.13
corporation tax, and 41.2
employment income, and 8.23
entrepreneurs' relief 44.39
foreign income, and 18.39
goodwill 44.33
hold-over relief 44.36
income tax
annuity payments by
partners 44.14–44.16
basis of assessment 44.4
calculation of profits 44.3–44.10
changes in partnership 44.12
consultancies 44.13
introduction 44.2
leaving partners 44.13–44.17
loan interest relief 44.11
personal pension schemes 44.17
retirement annuities 44.17
taxable profit 44.5–44.10
incorporation relief 44.38
inheritance tax
generally 44.51
lifetime transfers 28.24
interest paid to partners 44.7
introduction 44.1
leaving partners 44.13–44.17
lifetime transfers, and 28.24
limited company partners, and 44.6
loan interest relief 44.11
loss allocation 44.10
loss relief, and 11.122

Partnerships – *contd*
  losses
    allocation to members 44.10
    generally 44.9
  mixed member partnerships 44.10
  personal pension schemes 44.17
  profit allocation 44.10
  reform proposals 8.23
  reliefs
    entrepreneurs' relief 44.39
    general 44.35
    hold-over relief 44.36
    incorporation relief 44.38
    replacement of business assets relief 44.37
    roll-over relief 44.37–44.38
  rent paid to partner 44.8
  replacement of business assets relief
    generally 44.37
    introduction 22.77
  residence, and
    fiscal transparency 18.18
    non-resident partnerships 18.17
  retirement annuities 44.17
  roll-over relief
    incorporation 44.38
    replacement of business assets 44.37
  'salaried members' 8.23
  salary paid to partners 44.6
  stamp duty land tax, and 49.75
  taper relief 44.39
  taxable profit
    allocation of profits/losses to members 44.10
    interest paid to partners 44.7
    introduction 44.5
    limited company partners 44.6
    losses 44.9
    rent paid to partner 44.8
    salary paid to partners 44.6
  value added tax 44.71

Past services
  employment income, and 8.44

Patent rights
  capital allowances, and 48.2
  capital gains tax, and
    calculation of gain on disposal 19.38
    definition 19.37

Patent royalties
  generally 14.40
  trading income, and 10.155

Pay and file
  corporation tax, and 41.182

PAYE
  employment income, and
    coding 8.195
    introduction 8.1
    settlement agreements 8.198
    termination payments 8.155
  non tax-advantaged share schemes 9.42–9.43
  tax-advantaged share schemes, and 9.88–9.89

Payment of tax
  capital gains tax, and
    donee, by 24.31
    gifts, and 24.29–24.31
    instalments, by 19.61
    timing 19.60
  corporation tax, and 41.21
  employment income, and 8.199
  generally 4.23
  income tax, and 7.122
  inheritance tax on death, and
    burden of tax 30.55–30.62
    certificates of discharge 30.53
    contingent liabilities 30.49
    duty to account 30.42
    estimated values 30.43
    excepted estates 30.44
    IHT form 30.45
    instalments, by 30.51–30.53
    introduction 30.41
    land 30.50
    person liable 30.42–30.54
    personal representatives 30.46
    recalculation 30.63–30.67
    trustees 30.48
  instalments, by
    gifts, and 24.30
    generally 19.61
  lifetime transfers, and
    adjustments to bill 28.177
    generally 28.173
    instalments, by 28.174
    interest 28.175
    other than by transferor 28.125
    satisfaction of tax 28.176

Payments on account
  value added tax, and 38.56

Payments to organisations
  trading income, and 10.153

Payroll deduction scheme
  charities, and 53.88
  employment income, and 8.173

Peer-to-peer loans
  irrecoverability 7.92

Penalties
income tax, and
 failure to make returns or payment on time 4.27
 generally 4.25–4.26
inheritance tax, and
 death 30.42
 lifetime transfers 28.202
stamp duty, and 49.109
trading income, and 10.156
value added tax, and
 introduction 38.68
 mitigation 38.68
 reasonable care 38.68

Pension schemes
A-Day regime 50.8
annual allowance
 divorce settlements 50.23
 generally 50.12
attachment 52.12
auto enrolment 50.22
benefit crystallisation events 50.16
benefits on death
 inheritance tax planning, and 50.32
 lump sums 50.31
capital gains tax, and 22.3
carry forward 50.12
contract based schemes 50.3
divorce settlements 50.23
earmarking orders 52.12
EET structure 50.9
employment income, and 8.152
enhanced protection 50.22
fixed protection 50.22
foreign employment income, and 18.50
foreign income, and 18.41
generally 50.9
grandfathering benefits 50.7
growth of fund 50.13
individual protection 50.22
inheritance tax planning 50.32
introduction 50.1
IR12 50.6
lifetime allowance 50.16
lump sums 50.19
marital breakdown, and
 Brooks v Brooks decision 52.4
 earmarking orders 52.12
 flexibility 52.14
 introduction 52.4
 offsetting 52.11
 pension attachment 52.12
 pension sharing 52.13
methods of taking benefits 50.17

Pension schemes – *contd*
obligations to pay 50.33
partnerships, and 44.17
payments to employers 50.20
pension attachment 52.12
pension sharing 52.13
pre-A Day tax treatment
 approval 50.6
 grandfathering benefits 50.7
 introduction 50.5
 IR12 50.6
 Modification Regulations 50.8
 Revenue limits 50.7
primary protection 50.22
protection of accrued benefits 50.22
registration process 50.10
salary sacrifice, and 50.11
self-invested schemes 50.4
settlements not subject to relevant property regime, and 33.114
settlements subject to relevant property regime, and 34.113
sharing 52.13
structures 50.1
tax penalties 50.15
taxation of contributions 50.11–50.12
 annual allowance 50.12
 carry forward 50.12
 generally 50.12
taxation of fund
 growth of fund 50.13
 tax penalties 50.15
 VAT 50.14
taxation of payments by scheme
 auto enrolment 50.22
 benefit crystallisation events 50.16
 divorce settlements 50.23
 enhanced protection 50.22
 fixed protection 50.22
 individual protection 50.22
 lifetime allowance 50.16
 lump sums 50.19
 methods of taking benefits 50.17
 payments to employers 50.20
 primary protection 50.22
 protection of accrued benefits 50.22
 timing of payments 50.18
 unauthorised payments 50.21
timing of payments 50.18
trust based schemes 50.2
unauthorised payments 50.21
unregistered schemes 50.51
VAT 50.14

1776 Index

PEPs
  capital gains tax, and 22.2
  generally 15.33
Performers
  value added tax, and
    generally 40.43
    'nett' acts 40.44
Permanent health insurance
  employment income, and 8.133
Personal allowances
  generally 7.103
Personal Equity Plans
  capital gains tax, and 22.2
  generally 15.33
Personal injuries damages
  capital gains tax, and 22.3
Personal pensions
  And see **Pension schemes**
  partnerships, and 44.17
Personal reliefs
  And see **Exemptions and reliefs**
  age allowance 7.103
  capital gains tax, and 19.50–19.57
  civil partner's allowance
    age-related 7.111–7.113, 51.20–51.23
    transferable tax allowance 7.115–7.117, 51.12
  income tax, and
    blind person's allowance 7.105
    civil partner's allowance 7.111–7.117, 51.20–51.23
    general 7.101–7.102
    married person's allowance 7.111–7.117, 51.20–51.23
    personal allowances 7.103
  married person's allowance
    age-related 7.111–7.113, 51.20–51.23
    transferable tax allowance 7.115–7.117, 51.12
  personal allowances 7.103
Personal representatives
  And see **Estates in administration**
  domicile 21.3
  income tax, and
    liability 17.21
    residence 18.21
    role 17.1
  inheritance tax on death, and 30.46
  main residence exemption, and 23.65
  residence 21.3
Personal savings allowance
  generally 7.25

Personal service companies
  choice of business medium, and 46.7
  introduction 8.31
  managed services company legislation 8.34
  operation of rules 8.32
  services provided to public sector authorities 8.33
Pharmacists
  value added tax, and 40.39
Photography
  miscellaneous income, and 13.26
Place of supply
  e-commerce 38.34
  generally 38.31
  services 37.8, 38.32
Plant and machinery
  loan interest on purchase, and 7.49
  meaning 48.16–48.17
Plant and machinery allowances
  balancing allowances and charges
    generally 48.56
    pooling 48.56
  biogas refuelling equipment 48.33
  building alterations 48.18
  'capital expenditure' 48.14
  cars (on or after 1 or 6 April 2009)
    anti-avoidance 48.77
    cars 48.76
    generally 48.75
    introduction 48.74
    low-emission vehicles 48.78
  cars (prior to 1 or 6 April 2009)
    expensive cars 48.80
    inexpensive cars 48.79
    introduction 48.74
  conditions 48.11–48.27
  designated assisted areas, and 48.37
  energy-saving and water-conserving plant and machinery 48.31
  environmentally beneficial plant or machinery 48.35
  equipment lessors 48.27
  first year allowances
    biogas refuelling equipment 48.33
    energy-saving and water-conserving plant and machinery 48.31
    environmentally beneficial plant or machinery 48.35–48.36
    hydrogen refuelling equipment 48.33
    introduction 48.29
    low-emission cars 48.32
    natural gas refuelling equipment 48.33

Plant and machinery allowances – *contd*
  first year allowances – *contd*
    plant and machinery for use in
      designated assisted areas 48.37
    plant and machinery used wholly
      for a 'ring-fence' trade 48.34
    small or medium-sized
      enterprises 48.30
    zero-emission goods vehicles 48.38
  fixtures 48.22–48.25
  hire purchase 48.81
  hydrogen refuelling equipment 48.33
  goods vehicles
    zero-emission 48.38
  just apportionment 48.65
  low-emission cars 48.32
  'machinery' 48.16
  natural gas refuelling
    equipment 48.33
  'on the provision of plant and
    machinery' 48.15–48.20
  'owned by that person as a
    result of incurring the
    expenditure' 48.21–48.27
  'person carrying on a qualifying
    activity' 48.12
  'plant' 48.17
  plant and machinery for use in
    designated assisted areas 48.37
  plant and machinery used wholly for a
    'ring-fence' trade 48.34
  pooling
    assets used only partly for qualifying
      activity 48.63
    balancing allowances and
      charges 48.56
    generally 48.54
    integral features 48.61
    long-life assets 48.59
    sale of business 48.58
    short-life assets 48.59
    small pools 48.57
    special rate pool 48.60
    writing down allowances 48.55
  qualifying expenditure
    additional procedural
      requirements 48.72
    agreed sale price of fixtures without
      election 48.71
    basic principles 48.64
    election between vendor and
      purchaser 48.70
    fixtures 48.67–48.69
    further changes 48.73
    'just apportionment' 48.65

Plant and machinery allowances – *contd*
  qualifying expenditure – *contd*
    sale and leasebacks 48.66
    transactions between connected
      persons 48.66
    transactions with main purpose of
      obtaining tax advantage 48.66
  'ring-fence' trade 48.34
  small or medium-sized
    enterprises 48.30
  tenants fixtures 48.23
  use in designated assisted areas,
    for 48.37
  used wholly for a 'ring-fence'
    trade 48.34
  'who incurs' 48.13
  wholly for a 'ring-fence' trade,
    used 48.34
  'wholly or partly for the
    purposes' 48.21
  writing down allowances
    generally 48.39–48.53
    pooling 48.55
    zero-emission goods vehicles 48.38
Political parties, gifts to
  inheritance tax, and 31.87
Pooled cars and vans
  employment income, and 8.118
Pooling
  And see **Plant and machinery
    allowances**
  assets used only partly for qualifying
    activity 48.63
  balancing allowances and
    charges 48.56
  generally 48.54
  long-life assets 48.59
  sale of business 48.58
  short-life assets 48.59
  small pools 48.57
  writing down allowances 48.55
Post cessation expenses
  trading income, and 10.81
Post-cessation receipts
  employment income, and 8.12
  net income, and 7.42
  trading income, and 10.80
Post-death variations
  capital gains tax on death,
    and 21.121–21.126
  family taxation, and 51.77
  inheritance tax on death, and
    30.152–30.157
  interest in possession trusts,
    and 33.28

Post-death variations – *contd*
  reservation of benefit, and 29.141
  settlements not subject to relevant
    property regime, and 33.28
Post mortem adjustments
  capital gains tax on death,
    and 21.121–21.126
  family taxation, and 51.77
  inheritance tax on death, and
    30.152–30.157
  interest in possession trusts,
    and 33.28
  reservation of benefit, and 29.141
  settlements not subject to relevant
    property regime, and 33.28
Postponed consideration
  stamp duty land tax, and 49.43
Postponement
  capital gains tax, and 22.99
POTAS rules
  generally 5.30
  introduction 5.5–5.6
Potentially exempt transfers
  CGT tie-in 28.49
  death, and 30.25–30.26
  double charges 36.2–36.3
  family taxation, and 51.72–51.74
  gifts after 21 March 2006
    other transfers 28.45
    outright gifts to individuals 28.43
    transfers to trusts for the
      disabled 28.44
  gifts before 22 March 2006
    generally 28.46
    interest in possession trusts
      settlements 28.47
  introduction 28.41
  limits 28.48
  meaning 28.42
  outright gifts to individuals 28.43
  preconditions 28.42
  relevant transfers
    gifts after 21 March 2006
      28.42–28.45
    gifts before 22 March 2006
      28.46–28.47
    introduction 28.42
  taxation 28.50
  trusts for the disabled 28.44
Precatory trusts
  inheritance tax on death, and 30.151
Pre-eminent objects and works of art
  charities, and 53.111
Premium Bonds
  capital gains tax, and 22.2

Premiums (leases)
  anti-avoidance 12.83
  capital gains tax, and 19.40
  charge 12.82
  instalments, in 12.84
  introduction 12.81
  relief on trading premises 12.85
  reverse premiums 12.87
  trusts 12.86
Pre-owned assets
  calculation of charge 29.144
  exclusions and exemptions 29.145
  forms 29.143
  introduction 29.142
Prepayment between connected parties
  disclosure rules, and 5.22
Pre-trading expenditure
  trading income, and 10.143
Primary protection
  pension schemes, and 50.22
Principal private residence exemption
  availability 23.1–23.2
  business use 23.63
  capital gains tax on death, and 21.65
  curtilage test 23.24
  death, and
    disposal by legatees 23.66
    disposal by personal
      representatives 23.65
  definitions
    'dwelling house' 23.21
    'residence' 23.22–23.24
  degree of permanence 23.22
  disposal by legatees 23.66
  disposal by personal
    representatives 23.65
  election between residences 23.43
  entity test 23.23
  expenditure with profit-making
    motive 23.101
  family taxation, and 51.62
  IHT schemes, and 23.141
  introduction 23.1
  land used with the house 23.61
  legatees, and 23.66
  letting part of property 23.64
  non-residents, and
    generally 23.44–23.48
    introduction 23.2
  periods of absence
    civil partners 23.82
    employment-related periods 23.85
    general rule 23.81
    married couples 23.82
    other situations 23.84

Principal private residence exemption – *contd*
periods of absence – *contd*
permitted absences 23.83
same-sex couples 23.82
personal representatives, and 23.65
problem areas 23.61–23.66
qualifying residences
civil partners 23.42
married partners 23.42
more than one residence 23.43–23.48
residence
curtilage test 23.24
degree of permanence 23.22
entity test 23.23
second homes 23.121–23.123
trust-held houses 23.62
use of house for business 23.63
Principles-based legislation
transactions in securities, and 3.73
Priority share allocations
non tax-advantaged share schemes 9.30
Private life
human rights, and
generally 55.61
legal professional privilege 55.62
Private motor vehicles
capital gains tax, and 22.2
Private treaty sales
heritage property relief, and 31.86
Professional services
value added tax, and
barristers 40.86
barristers' services 40.95
commission 40.96
credit notes 40.94
disbursements 40.97
legal aid payments 40.90
solicitors 40.87–40.90
Professions
foreign income, and 18.35
foreign taxpayers, and 18.72
losses, and 11.4
trading income, and 10.41
Promoters of tax avoidance schemes (POTAS)
generally 5.30
introduction 5.5–5.6
Property
human rights, and
ambit 55.21
IR35 55.22
use 55.23–55.27

Property income
agricultural expenses 12.46
allowance 12.43
ambit of rules 12.1
artificial transactions
application of provision 12.104
avoiding provision 12.111
conditions 12.104–12.107
connected persons 12.107
disposal of land 12.105
effect of provision 12.103
generally 12.101
introduction 3.6
opportunities to make gain 12.109
other matters 12.112
shares in landholding companies 12.108
trading stock 12.106
trading transactions 12.102
capital allowances
generally 12.47
introduction 12.46
cash basis
consultation 12.44
chargeable persons 12.41
computation of profits
accountancy practice 12.42
capital allowances 12.47
cash basis (consultation) 12.44
interest payments 12.45
losses 12.46
property income allowance (proposed) 12.43
replacement domestic items relief 12.48
excluded income 12.24
foreign income, and 18.37
furnished holiday lettings
introduction 12.61
other measures 12.63
qualifying holiday lettings 12.62
tax treatment 12.64
income tax, and
anti-avoidance 12.101–12.112
chargeable persons 12.41
computation of profits 12.42–12.49
furnished holiday lettings 12.61–12.64
premiums 12.81–12.87
rent factoring 12.88
trading principles 12.1–12.24
lettings outside trading provisions 12.23
losses, and 11.3

Property income – *contd*
  premiums
    anti-avoidance 12.83
    charge 12.82
    instalments, in 12.84
    introduction 12.81
    relief on trading premises 12.85
    reverse premiums 12.87
    trusts 12.86
  property income allowance (proposed) 12.43
  property income business 12.1
  rent-a-room relief 12.49
  rent factoring 12.88
  replacement domestic items relief 12.48
  reverse premiums 12.87
  Schedule A, and 12.1
  shares in landholding companies 12.108
  trading principles 12.1–12.24
  transactions in UK land
    application of provision 12.104
    avoiding provision 12.111
    conditions 12.104–12.107
    connected persons 12.107
    disposal of land 12.105
    effect of provision 12.103
    generally 12.101
    introduction 3.6
    opportunities to make gain 12.109
    other matters 12.112
    shares in landholding companies 12.108
    trading stock 12.106
    trading transactions 12.102
  unearned income, and 12.22
Property income business
  income from land, and 12.1
Property limited liability partnerships
  anti-avoidance 45.22
  generally 45.14
Property losses
  capital allowances, and 48.10
  loss relief, and 7.81
  net income, and 7.42
Property management
  value added tax, and 39.45
Proportionality
  EU law, and 54.68
Prospective employees
  employment income, and 8.128
Protection of property
  human rights, and
    ambit 55.21

Protection of property – *contd*
  human rights, and – *contd*
    IR35 55.22
    use 55.23–55.27
Protective trusts
  interest in possession trusts, and 33.27
  settlements not subject to relevant property regime, and
    generally 33.118
    introduction 33.27
  settlements subject to relevant property regime, and 34.117
Provision of services
  stamp duty land tax, and 49.51
Provisions
  trading income, and 10.67
Public houses
  value added tax, and
    free houses 40.29
    generally 40.27
    managed houses 40.28
    tenanted houses 40.30
    tied houses 40.30
Publishing
  miscellaneous income, and 13.25
Purchased life annuities
  savings and investment income, and 14.41
Purchased life interests in settled property
  calculation of gain on disposal 19.38
  definition 19.37

Q

Qualifying buildings
  value added tax, and 39.23
Qualifying corporate bonds
  capital gains tax, and 22.45
  entrepreneurs' relief, and
    election by taxpayer 20.38
    generally 20.36
    post 6 April 2008 20.37
  definition 41.93
  general rule 41.92
  paper-for-paper exchanges 41.97
  preserving loss relief for debts on security 41.94
  'rolling into' 41.96
Qualifying life policies
  generally 15.1
Qualifying loan interest
  acquisition of interest in close company 7.45
  acquisition of interest in co-operative 7.47

Qualifying loan interest – *contd*
  acquisition of interest in
    partnership 7.46
  introduction 7.44
  investment in employee-controlled
    company 7.48
  net income, and 7.42
  partnerships, and 44.11
  payment of inheritance tax 7.50
  purchase of life annuity 7.51
  purchase of plant or machinery 7.49
Quarterly payments
  corporation tax, and 41.185
Quick succession relief
  inheritance tax on death, and 30.144
  interest in possession trusts,
    and 33.29
  settlements not subject to relevant
    property regime, and 33.29

R

'Ramsay' principle
  And see **Tax avoidance**
  applicability 2.34–2.45
  conclusions 2.46–2.48
  generally 2.21
  limits 2.24–2.29
  meaning 2.34–2.45
  overview 2.4
  reaffirmation 2.32–2.33
  role of courts, and 1.24
  scope 2.34–2.45
  stamp duties, and 2.43
  tax mitigation distinction 2.45
  value added tax, and 2.44
Rates of tax
  capital gains tax, and
    companies 19.49
    death, on 21.61
    entrepreneurs' relief 19.49
    history 19.49
    individuals 19.49
  corporation tax, and
    capital gains 41.22
    introduction 41.21
    non-corporate distribution
      rate 41.24
    small profits rate 41.23
  entrepreneurs' relief, and 19.49
  income tax, and 7.120–7.121
  lifetime transfers, and 28.122
  stamp duty, and 49.109
  value added tax, and
    introduction 38.4
    reduced rate 38.6

Rates of tax – *contd*
  value added tax, and – *contd*
    standard rate 38.5
    zero-rated supplies 38.7
'Reading back'
  capital gains tax on death,
    and 21.122–21.123
Real-time information (RTI)
  generally 8.203
Reasonable care
  value added tax, and 38.68
Rebasing
  basic rule 19.31
  election 19.33
  introduction 19.30
  qualifications 19.32
  technical issues 19.34
Recalculation
  inheritance tax on death, and
    30.63–30.67
Reconstruction relief
  stamp duty land tax, and 49.79
Reconstructions, amalgamations and
  takeovers
  capital gains tax, and 22.104
  generally 47.51
  stamp duty, and 49.126
Recovery of tax
  employer from employee, by 8.202
Redeemable shares
  distributions, and 42.5
Reduced rate of VAT
  generally 38.6
  property 39.26
Reduction of capital
  And see **Distributions**
  followed by bonus issue 42.4
  generally 42.3
Registration for VAT
  de-registration 38.51
  generally 38.49
  group 38.50
Reinsurance
  value added tax, and 40.80
Relevant property regime
  accumulation and maintenance
    trusts 34.91–34.98
  added property 34.33
  amount of tax 34.25
  charge after ten-year anniversary
    charge 34.28
  charge prior to ten-year anniversary
    charge 34.23–34.25
  creation 34.22
  discretionary trusts, and 34.35

Relevant property regime – *contd*
  exemptions and reliefs 34.51
  exit charges 34.23–34.33
  introduction 34.1–34.2
  later periodic charges 34.29
  method of charge 34.21
  pre-27 March 1974 trusts 34.71–34.74
  rate of tax 34.24
  reduction in rate of anniversary
    charge 34.31
  technical problems 34.30–34.34
  ten-year anniversary charge
    34.26–34.27
  timing of exit charges 34.34
  transfers between settlements 34.32
  shares and securities 28.68
  situs of property, and
    generally 35.6
    reversionary interests 35.83
  small gifts 31.5
  spouse exemption 31.41
  stamp duty, and 30.156
  surviving spouse 30.152
  survivorship clauses 30.143
  taper relief 30.23
  timber 31.21–31.24
  transfer not exceeding £3,000 pa 31.3
  transfer of unquoted shares and
    debentures 28.23
  transfer of value
    close companies, and 28.152
    contrast with gifts 28.6
    examples 28.5
    generally 28.3
    instalments, by 28.127
    omissions 28.4
  transfer on same day 28.128
  trustees 30.48
  unit trust holdings 35.22
  valuation of estate
    allowable deductions 35.61
    enforcement of tax abroad 35.63
    expenses of administering property
      abroad 35.62
    foreign assets 35.64
  value of gift (death)
    changes in value 30.6
    funeral expenses 30.5
    introduction 30.3–30.4
    post-death sales 30.7–30.10
    provisional valuations 30.12
  value of gift (lifetime transfers)
    co-ownership of property 28.67
    cost of gift 28.61–28.64
    fall in value of an estate 28.63–28.64

Relevant property regime – *contd*
  value of gift (lifetime transfers) – *contd*
    liabilities 28.66
    life assurance policies 28.74
    non-assignable agricultural
      tenancies 28.73
    options on property 28.70
    problem areas 28.65–28.74
    'property' 28.62
    related property 28.70
    restrictions on transfer of
      property 28.72
    shares and securities 28.68
    special rules 28.69–28.74
  vesting of property 30.148
  visiting forces 35.24
  voidable transfers 28.28
  waiver of remuneration and
    dividends 28.27
  woodlands 31.21–31.24
Relief against double charge
  lifetime transfers, and 28.132
Reliefs and exemptions
  agricultural property relief
    'agricultural property' 31.62
    agricultural land or pasture 31.63
    agricultural tenancies 31.72
    'agricultural value' 31.67
    amount 31.68
    business property relief, and 31.77
    'character appropriate' test
      31.65–31.66
    clawback 31.72
    companies, and 31.70
    double discounting 31.75
    farmhouses 31.65–31.66
    intensive farming buildings 31.64
    interest in possession trusts,
      and 33.30
    introduction 31.62
    lotting 31.74
    milk quota 31.76
    occupation requirement 31.69
    ownership requirement 31.69
    reservations, and 31.78
    settlements not subject to relevant
      property regime, and 33.30
    technical provisions 31.71
    transitional relief 31.75
    trusts, and 31.70
  business property relief
    amount 31.45
    clawback 31.59
    consequences 31.61
    contracts to sell the business 31.53

Reliefs and exemptions – *contd*
  business property relief – *contd*
    'control' 31.55
    excepted assets 31.52
    instalment payments, and 31.58
    introduction 31.42
    investment businesses 31.48
    minority shareholdings in unquoted companies 31.56
    mixed businesses 31.49–31.50
    net value of business, on 31.44
    non-business assets 31.52
    non qualifying activities 31.47
    ownership requirement 31.46
    'relevant business property' 31.43
    reservations, and 31.60
    settlements, and 31.54
    switching control 31.57
    'wholly or mainly' test 31.50
  capital gains tax, and
    charitable transactions 22.4
    chattels 22.21–22.23
    cultural gifts scheme 22.6
    debts 22.41–22.45
    exempt assets 22.2
    exempt gains 22.3
    heritage property 22.5
    introduction 22.1
    main residence 23.1–23.141
    overview 19.9–19.10
    woodland 22.5
  employment income, and
    annual parties and functions 8.168
    bicycles 8.166
    childcare 8.167
    computer equipment 8.166
    gifts from third parties 8.168
    homeworker's additional expenses 8.165
    introduction 8.161
    long service awards 8.168
    minor benefits 8.169
    mobile phones 8.166
    outplacement counselling 8.163
    relocation costs 8.162
    subsidised meals 8.168
    third party gifts 8.168
    training 8.164
    use of assets 8.166
  family taxation, and
    capital allowances 51.51
    close company loans 51.50
    Enterprise Investment Scheme 51.49

Reliefs and exemptions – *contd*
  heritage property relief
    acceptance in lieu 31.90
    calculation of deferred charge 31.83
    effect of deferred charge 31.82
    introduction 31.79
    maintenance funds 31.85
    preconditions 31.80
    private treaty sales 31.86
    reopening existing undertakings 31.81
    settled property 31.84
  hold-over relief
    assets attracting immediate IHT charge, of 24.22–24.26
    business assets, of 24.4–24.21
    disposal at market value 24.2
    general 22.99
    IHT consequences 24.3
    introduction 24.1–24.3
  income tax, and
    exempt income 7.129–7.131
    exempt organisations 7.128
    introduction 7.127
    ISAs 7.132
    life assurance policies 7.132
  incorporation of business relief
    conditions 22.101
    deferral of tax on sale of unincorporated business 22.102
    election to disapply 22.103
    generally 22.100
    overview 26.4
  inheritance tax, and
    acceptance in lieu 31.90
    agricultural property relief 31.62–31.78
    armed services personnel, and 31.25
    business property relief 31.42–31.61
    care of dependent relative 31.10
    charitable gifts 31.88–31.89
    consideration of marriage 31.6
    death, and 31.1–31.25
    death on active service 31.25
    dispositions for maintenance 31.7–31.10
    heritage property 31.79–31.86
    inter-spouse transfers 31.41
    introduction 31.1
    lifetime transfers, and 31.3–31.10
    lifetime and death transfers, and 31.41–31.89

Reliefs and exemptions – *contd*
  inheritance tax, and – *contd*
    maintenance of children 31.9
    maintenance of dependent
      relative 31.10
    maintenance of former spouse 31.8
    marriage gifts 31.6
    nil rate band 31.2
    normal expenditure out of
      income 31.4
    political parties, gifts to 31.87
    small gifts 31.5
    spouse exemption 31.41
    timber 31.21–31.24
    transfers not exceeding £3,000
      pa 31.3
    woodlands 31.21–31.24
  interest in possession trusts
    33.21–33.30
  main residence, and
    And see **Main residence exemption**
    availability 23.1–23.2
    definitions 23.21–23.24
    expenditure with profit-making
      motive 23.101
    family taxation, and 51.62
    IHT schemes, and 23.141
    introduction 23.1
    non-residents, and 23.2
    periods of absence 23.81–23.85
    problem areas 23.61–23.66
    qualifying residences 23.42–23.48
    second homes 23.121–23.123
  partnerships, and
    entrepreneurs' relief 44.39
    general 44.35
    hold-over relief 44.36
    incorporation relief 44.38
    replacement of business assets
      relief 44.37
    roll-over relief 44.37–44.38
  reconstruction relief 22.104
  replacement of business assets relief
    basic conditions 22.72
    companies 22.77
    foreign assets 22.76
    intention to reinvest, and 22.80
    non-residents 22.76
    occupation for business
      purposes 22.75
    partnerships 22.77
    prior acquisition of replacement
      assets 22.73
    problem areas 22.79
    provisional relief 22.80

Reliefs and exemptions – *contd*
  replacement of business assets
    relief – *contd*
    qualifying assets 22.74
    restrictions 22.78
    wasting assets 22.78
  roll-over relief
    compulsory acquisition of
      land 22.82–22.83
    incorporation of business
      22.100–22.103
    replacement of business
      assets 22.72–22.80
  retirement relief 22.84
  settlements not subject to relevant
    property regime 33.21–33.30
  stamp duty, and
    companies, for 49.125–49.126
    group relief 49.125
    reconstructions 49.126
  stamp duty land tax, and
    acquisition relief 49.79
    clawback 49.84
    group relief 49.78
    introduction 49.76
    multiple dwellings
      acquisitions 49.81
    other 49.83
    reconstruction relief 49.79
    Schedule 3, under 49.82
  takeover relief 22.104
  transfer of unincorporated business to
    company, and 47.4–47.8
Relocation costs
  employment income, and 8.162
Remittance basis
  foreign employment income,
    and 18.47
  foreign income, and 18.34
Remittances
  business investment relief 27.96
  introduction 27.89–27.92
  relevant persons 27.93–27.95
  sales of exempt art 27.97
Remuneration
  choice of business medium, and 46.59
Renovation of business premises
  capital allowances, and 48.124–48.125
Rent
  stamp duty land tax, and
    increase in first five years 49.70
    introduction 49.67
    net present value 49.68
    uncertain 49.69
    variable 49.69

Rent-a-room relief
  income from land, and 12.49
Rent factoring
  income from land, and 12.88
Rent for business premises
  stamp duty land tax, and 49.62
  trading income, and 10.140
Repairs and improvements
  trading income, and 10.142
Repayment of tax
  charities, and 53.103
Replacement domestic items relief
  property income, and 12.48
Replacement of business assets relief
  basic conditions 22.72
  companies 22.77
  foreign assets 22.76
  intention to reinvest, and 22.80
  non-residents 22.76
  occupation for business
    purposes 22.75
  partnerships
    generally 44.37
    introduction 22.77
  prior acquisition of replacement
    assets 22.73
  problem areas 22.79
  provisional relief 22.80
  qualifying assets 22.74
  restrictions 22.78
  wasting assets 22.78
Reporting requirements
  capital gains tax, and 19.62
  employment income, and 8.155
  employee participation, and 9.3
Research and development
  capital allowances, and 48.123
  trading income, and 10.154
Research institution spin-out companies
  non tax-advantaged share
    schemes 9.31
Reservation of benefit
  agricultural property relief,
    and 31.78
  application of rules 29.41–29.44
  business property relief, and 31.60
  chargeable transfers, and 28.6
  consequences 29.21
  co-ownership 29.137
  de minimis 29.71
  discretionary trusts 29.133
  disposal of property by way of
    gift 29.41
  drafting 29.122
  enjoyment of property by donee 29.42

Reservation of benefit – *contd*
  exclusion of donor from
    benefit 29.43–29.44
  excepted circumstances 29.71–29.73
  full consideration 29.72
  hardship 29.73
  Ingram v IRC 29.123–29.126
  inheritance tax, and
    generally 29.132–29.135
    introduction 32.94
    object of discretionary trust 29.133
    retention of interest 29.132
    settlor as paid trustee 29.134
    termination of IIP 29.135
  legislative history 29.1
  permitted benefits
    co-ownership 29.137
    statutory get-outs 29.136
  possession of property by donee 29.42
  post-death variations 29.141
  post-FA 1986 position 29.121–29.145
  pre-owned assets 29.142–29.145
  'property' 29.128
  property subject to reservation 29.101
  Ramsay 29.127
  reversionary leases 29.131
  settlements
    generally 29.132–29.135
    introduction 32.94
    object of discretionary trust 29.133
    retention of interest 29.132
    settlor as paid trustee 29.134
    termination of IIP 29.135
  shearing
    generally 29.122
    use of arrangements 29.129
  spouses, and 29.138
Residence
  acquisition of resident status
    18.8–18.9
  available accommodation
    non-resident individuals 27.15
    UK residents 18.5
  case law
    available accommodation
      rule 27.15
    conclusions 27.16
    distinct break concept 27.14
    Grace decision 27.14
    leavers vs arrivers 27.14
    multiplicity of factors vs settled
      abode 27.13
    old law 27.12
  corporations 18.16
  distinct break concept 27.14

Residence – *contd*
  double tax treaties 18.22
  from 6 April 2013
    accommodation tie 27.20
    automatic non-residence
      test 18.9
    automatic overseas tests 27.19
    automatic residence test 18.10
    automatic UK tests 27.19
    commencement 27.21
    country tie 27.20
    days spent 27.21
    family tie 27.20
    full time work 27.21
    generally 27.17
    home 27.21
    introduction 18.8
    key concepts 27.21
    location of work 27.21
    90-day tie 27.20
    outline of legislation 27.18
    summary 27.23
    split year treatment 18.12
    sufficient ties tests 27.19
    temporary non residence 18.13
    tests of residence 27.19
    UK ties 18.11, 27.20
    work 27.21
    work tie 27.20
  full-time work abroad 27.11
  Gaines-Cooper decision 27.6
  general law 27.2–27.4
  Grace decision 27.14
  HMRC practice
    coming to the UK 27.5
    Gaines-Cooper decision 27.6
    HMRC 6 27.7
    introduction 27.5
    leaving the UK 27.5
  introduction 18.2
  IR20 27.5
  leavers vs arrivers 27.14
  loss of resident status 18.8–18.9
  meaning 18.2
  members of House of Lords 27.24
  MPs 27.24
  multiplicity of factors vs settled
    abode 27.13
  non-resident individuals, and
    case law 27.12–27.16
    full-time work abroad 27.11
    Gaines v Cooper decision 27.14
    general law 27.2–27.4
    HMRC practice 27.5–27.8
    introduction 27.1

Residence – *contd*
  non-resident individuals, and – *contd*
    multiplicity of factors vs settled
      abode 27.13
    occasional residence abroad 27.9
    statutory provisions 27.9–27.11
    temporary purposes in the
      UK 27.10
  non-resident partnerships 18.17
  occasional residence abroad
    non-resident individuals 27.9
    UK residents 18.6
  ordinary residence
    generally 18.14–18.15
    proposed abolition 27.1
  partnerships
    fiscal transparency 18.18
    non-resident partnerships 18.17
  personal representatives 18.21, 21.2
  prior to 6 April 2013
    available accommodation 18.5
    introduction 18.3
    occasional residence abroad 18.6
    the '91-day' rule 18.4
    the '183-day' rule 18.3
  settled abode 27.13
  statutory provisions
    full-time work abroad 27.11
    occasional residence abroad 27.9
    temporary purposes in the
      UK 27.10
  statutory residence test
    accommodation tie 27.20
    automatic non-residence test 18.9
    automatic overseas tests 27.19
    automatic residence test 18.10
    automatic UK tests 27.19
    commencement 27.21
    country tie 27.20
    days spent 27.21
    family tie 27.20
    full time work 27.21
    generally 27.17
    home 27.21
    introduction 18.8
    key concepts 27.21
    location of work 27.21
    90-day tie 27.20
    outline of legislation 27.18
    summary 27.23
    split year treatment 18.12
    sufficient ties tests 27.19
    temporary non residence 18.13
    tests of residence 27.19
    UK ties 18.11, 27.20

Residence – *contd*
  statutory residence test – *contd*
    work 27.21
    work tie 27.20
  temporary purposes in the
    UK 27.10
  the '91-day' rule 18.4
  the '183-day' rule 18.3
  'tie-breaker' clauses 18.22
  trustees 18.19
  trusts 18.20
  UK resident
    available accommodation 18.5
    introduction 18.3
    occasional residence abroad 18.6
    the '91-day' rule 18.4
    the '183-day' rule 18.3
  'work day' relief 27.1
Residence in property
  And see **Main residence
    exemption** 23.66
  curtilage test 23.24
  degree of permanence 23.22
  entity test 23.23
Residential nil rate band
  death, on
    brought forward allowance 30.33
    closely inherited 30.30–30.31
    downsizing 30.34
    inherited 30.30
    introduction 30.28
    lineal descendants 30.30
    qualifying residential interest 30.29
    residential enhancement 30.32
    transferable 30.33
Residual liability
  employment income, and
    8.125–8.131
Residuary beneficiaries
  estates in administration, and
    17.48–17.54
Restrictive covenants
  trading income, and 10.134
Restrictive undertakings
  employment income, and 8.134
Retailers
  value added tax, and
    choice of scheme 40.107
    gross takings 40.106
    introduction 40.105
    secondhand goods 40.108–40.109
Retirement annuities
  partnerships, and 44.17
Retirement relief
  generally 22.84

Returns
  assessment of tax, and 4.22
  employment income, and 8.197
  trusts, and
    exceptional cases 16.7
    generally 16.6
  value added tax, and 38.55
Reverse charge
  value added tax, and
    generally 38.30
    international supplies of goods
      and services 38.106
Reverse premiums
  stamp duty land tax, and 49.54
Reverse premiums
  income from land, and 12.87
Reversion to settlor
  interest in possession trusts,
    and 33.21
  settlements not subject to relevant
    property regime, and 33.21
Reversionary interests
  definition 35.82
  foreign element 35.85
  general rule 35.84
  interest in possession trusts,
    and 33.61–33.62
  lifetime transfers, and 28.22
  settlements not subject to relevant
    property regime, and
    33.61–33.62
  situs 35.83
Reversionary leases
  reservation of benefit, and 29.131
Right to fair hearing
  burden of proof 55.91
  civil rights and obligations 55.83
  criminal charges 55.82
  introduction 55.81
  judicial review 55.93
  privilege against self
    incrimination 55.92
  right to silence 55.92
  scrutiny of information notices
    55.84
  tax-related obligations 55.82–55.83
Right to protection of property
  ambit 55.21
  IR35 55.22
  use 55.23–55.27
**Right to respect for private and
    family life**
  generally 55.61
  legal professional privilege 55.62
  tax, and 55.5

Rights to acquire shares
non tax-advantaged share schemes 9.41
Ring fence profits of North Sea oil companies
corporation tax, and 41.24
'Ring-fence' trade
first year allowances, and 48.34
Roll-around relief
groups of companies, and 43.129
Roll-over relief
compulsory acquisition of land 22.82–22.83
groups of companies, and 43.128
incorporation of business
  conditions 22.101
  deferral of tax on sale of unincorporated business 22.102
  election to disapply 22.103
  generally 22.100
  overview 26.4
  partnerships, and 44.38
partnerships, and
  incorporation 44.38
  replacement of business assets 44.37
replacement of business assets
  basic conditions 22.72
  companies 22.77
  foreign assets 22.76
  intention to reinvest, and 22.80
  non-residents 22.76
  occupation for business purposes 22.75
  partnerships 22.77
  prior acquisition of replacement assets 22.73
  problem areas 22.79
  provisional relief 22.80
  qualifying assets 22.74
  restrictions 22.78
  wasting assets 22.78

S

s 479 ITA 2007 charge
And see **Trusts**
affected trusts 16.22
beneficiary with complete right to income 16.24
'dividend trust rate' 16.21
dividends 16.29–16.30
generally 16.21–16.26
management expenses 16.23
relevant income 16.26

s 479 ITA 2007 charge – *contd*
'trust rate' 16.21
will trusts 16.25
s 496 ITA 2007 charge
And see **Trusts**
dividends 16.33
generally 16.31
'tax pool' 16.32
Salaried members
generally 45.24
introduction 8.23
Salary sacrifice
pension contributions, and 50.11
Sale and leaseback arrangements
trading income, and 10.141
Sales of exempt art
remittances, and 27.97
Save As You Earn deposits
capital gains tax, and 22.2
generally 15.33
Savings income
ambit of charge 14.2
basis of assessment 14.4
companies 14.5
copyright royalties 14.40
deeply discounted securities 14.42
distributions, and 42.1
generally 7.23
interest
  deduction of tax at source 14.32
  disguised 14.36
  funding bonds 14.35
  future issues 14.37
  generally 7.24
  kind, in 14.35
  legacies, on 14.34
  source of interest 14.33
  tax relief for payment 14.31
introduction 14.1
patent royalties 14.40
personal savings allowance 7.25
purchased life annuities 14.41
savings nil rate 7.25
starting rate for savings 7.26
terminology 14.6–14.8
unauthorised unit trusts 14.44
Savings nil rate
generally 7.25
Savings-related share option schemes
tax-advantaged share schemes, and 9.75
Schedule A
corporation tax, and 41.42
property income, and 12.1

Schedule D
annual payments, and 14.1
corporation tax, and 41.42
foreign income, and 18.31
property income, and 12.1
trading income, and 10.1–10.3
Schedule E
employment income, and 8.11
Schedule F
distributions, and 42.1
Schemes of reconstruction
generally 47.51
Scholarships
employment income, and 8.130
Scrip dividends
And see **Distributions**
generally 42.150
interest in possession trusts 42.152
tax treatment 42.151
Secondhand goods
value added tax, and 40.108–40.109
Second homes
capital gains tax, and 23.121–23.123
stamp duty land tax, and
conditions 49.29
generally 49.28
Section 479 ITA 2007 charge
And see **Trusts**
affected trusts 16.22
beneficiary with complete right to income 16.24
'dividend trust rate' 16.21
dividends 16.29–16.30
generally 16.21–16.26
management expenses 16.23
relevant income 16.26
'trust rate' 16.21
will trusts 16.25
Section 496 ITA 2007 charge
And see **Trusts**
dividends 16.33
generally 16.31
'tax pool' 16.32
'Securities'
transactions in securities, and 3.33
Security interests
stamp duty land tax, and 49.33
Seed Enterprise Investment Scheme (SEIS)
anti-avoidance 15.134
capital gains tax exemption 15.131
capital gains tax re-investment relief 15.132
company directors 15.133
generally 46.51

Seed Enterprise Investment Scheme (SEIS) – *contd*
income tax relief 15.130
introduction 15.128
qualifying companies 15.129
qualifying investors 15.133
tax reliefs 15.130–15.132
Segregation of claims
foreign domiciliaries, and 27.88
Self assessment
assessment of tax, and 4.21
corporation tax, and
anti-avoidance 41.187
duties of senior accounting officers 41.186
incorrect returns 41.184
interest 41.183
introduction 41.181
late returns 41.184
operation of pay and file 41.182
quarterly payments 41.185
trusts, and 16.5
Self-supply
value added tax, and 38.30
Serious investigation cases
Code of Practice 9 4.52
disclosure opportunities 4.54
Hansard procedure 4.50–4.51
Settled property
And see **Trusts**
capital gains tax, and 19.74
heritage property relief, and 31.84
Settlement agreements
employment income, and 8.198
Settlements
And see **Trusts**
accumulation and maintenance trust 32.53
additions of property 32.8
associated operations 32.4
associated operations 32.4
bereaved minor trust 32.59
business property relief, and 31.54
capital gains tax, and 25.1–25.152
CGT holdover relief, and 32.93
classification
18–25 trust 32.58
accumulation and maintenance trust 32.53
bereaved minor trust 32.59
introduction 32.21
immediate post-death interest 32.51
'interest in possession trusts' 32.22–32.30

Settlements – *contd*
  classification – *contd*
    transitional serial interest 32.52
    trusts for the disabled 32.59
  creation 32.91–32.93
  definition 32.2–32.6
  immediate post-death interest 32.51
  inheritance tax, and
    classification 32.21–32.59
    creation 32.91–32.93
    interest in possession trusts,
      with 33.1–33.62
    interest in possession trusts,
      without 34.1–34.74
    introduction 32.1
    meaning 32.2–32.9
    payment of tax 32.71
    reservation of benefit 32.94
    special trusts 34.111–34.118
  'interest in possession trusts'
    32.22–32.30
  interest in possession trusts, with
    And see **Settlements not subject to
      relevant property regime**
    generally 33.1–33.62
  interest in possession trusts, without
    And see **Settlements subject to
      relevant property regime**
    generally 34.1–34.74
  introduction 32.1
  meaning
    generally 32.2–32.9
    introduction 16.2
  nil rate band, and 32.92
  payment of tax 32.71
  reservation of benefit, and
    generally 29.132–29.135
    introduction 32.94
    object of discretionary trust 29.133
    retention of interest 29.132
    settlor as paid trustee 29.134
    termination of IIP 29.135
  settlors 32.7
  special trusts 34.111–34.118
  transitional serial interest 32.52
  trustees 32.9
  trusts for the disabled 32.59
**Settlements not subject to relevant
  property regime**
  18–25 trusts 33.111
  accumulation and maintenance trusts
    created pre-22 March 2006 33.64
    introduction 33.63
    transitional provisions 33.67
  actual terminations 33.12

**Settlements not subject to relevant
  property regime** – *contd*
  advancements to life tenant 33.15
  agricultural property relief 33.30
  anti-avoidance
    application of rules 33.18
    how to avoid the rules 33.20
    operation of rules 33.19
  basic principles
    charging method 33.4
    other interests 33.5
  bereaved minor trusts 33.71–33.72
  business property relief 33.30
  charging method 33.4
  charitable purposes 33.26
  charitable trusts 33.112
  compensation funds 33.116
  death, and 33.10
  deemed terminations 33.13
  disabled person's interests 33.6
  disabled persons trusts 33.113
  disclaimers 33.28
  employee trusts 33.115
  excluded property 33.24
  exemptions and reliefs
    agricultural property relief 33.30
    business property relief 33.30
    charitable purposes 33.26
    disclaimers 33.28
    excluded property 33.24
    life tenant's exemptions, and 33.22
    maintenance of child 33.25
    maintenance of dependent
      relative 33.25
    post-death variations 33.28
    protective trusts 33.27
    quick succession relief 33.29
    reversion to settlor 33.21
    surviving spouse exemption 33.23
    variations 33.28
  fixed income beneficiaries 33.7
  historic buildings maintenance
    funds 33.117
  immediate post-death interests 33.6
  inter vivos terminations
    actual terminations 33.12
    advancements to life tenant 33.15
    deemed terminations 33.13
    introduction 33.11
    partition 33.14
    purchase of reversionary interest by
      life tenant 33.16
    transactions reducing value of
      property 33.17
  introduction 33.1–33.3

Settlements not subject to relevant property regime – *contd*
leases 33.8
life interests 33.6
life tenant's exemptions, and 33.22
maintenance of child 33.25
maintenance of dependent relative 33.25
maintenance of historic buildings 33.117
operation of rules 33.19
ownership of fund
  fixed income beneficiaries 33.7
  leases 33.8
  life interests 33.6
partition 33.14
pension funds 33.114
post-death variations 33.28
protective trusts
  generally 33.118
  introduction 33.27
purchase of reversionary interest by life tenant 33.16
quick succession relief 33.29
reduction of value of property 33.17
reversion to settlor 33.21
reversionary interests, and
  generally 33.61–33.62
  inter vivos terminations 33.16
scrip dividends, and 42.152
surviving spouse exemption 33.23
time of charge
  actual terminations 33.12
  advancements to life tenant 33.15
  agricultural property relief 33.30
  anti-avoidance 33.18–33.20
  application of rules 33.18
  business property relief 33.30
  death, and 33.10
  deemed terminations 33.13
  disclaimers 33.28
  excluded property 33.24
  exemptions and reliefs 33.21–33.30
  inter vivos terminations 33.11–33.17
  life tenant's exemptions, and 33.22
  maintenance of child 33.25
  maintenance of dependent relative 33.25
  operation of rules 33.19
  partition 33.14
  post-death variations 33.28
  protective trusts 33.27
  purchase of reversionary interest by life tenant 33.16
  quick succession relief 33.29

Settlements not subject to relevant property regime – *contd*
time of charge – *contd*
  reduction of value of property 33.17
  reversion to settlor 33.21
  surviving spouse exemption 33.23
  transitional serial interests 33.6
  variations 33.28
transitional serial interests 33.6
trusts for the disabled 33.113
variations 33.28
Settlements subject to relevant property regime
accumulation and maintenance trusts 34.91–34.98
added property 34.33
amount of tax 34.25
charge after ten-year anniversary charge 34.28
charge prior to ten-year anniversary charge 34.23–34.25
creation 34.22
discretionary trusts, and 34.35
exemptions and reliefs 34.51
exit charges 34.23–34.33
introduction 34.1–34.2
later periodic charges 34.29
method of charge 34.21
pre-27 March 1974 trusts 34.71–34.74
rate of tax 34.24
reduction in rate of anniversary charge 34.31
technical problems 34.30–34.34
ten-year anniversary charge 34.26–34.27
timing of exit charges 34.34
transfers between settlements 34.32
shares and securities 28.68
situs of property, and
  generally 35.6
  reversionary interests 35.83
small gifts 31.5
spouse exemption 31.41
stamp duty, and 30.156
surviving spouse 30.152
survivorship clauses 30.143
taper relief 30.23
timber 31.21–31.24
transfer not exceeding £3,000 pa 31.3
transfer of unquoted shares and debentures 28.23
transfer of value
  close companies, and 28.152
  contrast with gifts 28.6
  examples 28.5

Settlements subject to relevant property regime – *contd*
  transfer of value – *contd*
    generally 28.3
    instalments, by 28.127
    omissions 28.4
  transfer on same day 28.128
  trustees 30.48
  unit trust holdings 35.22
  valuation of estate
    allowable deductions 35.61
    enforcement of tax abroad 35.63
    expenses of administering property abroad 35.62
    foreign assets 35.64
  value of gift (death)
    changes in value 30.6
    funeral expenses 30.5
    introduction 30.3–30.4
    post-death sales 30.7–30.10
    provisional valuations 30.12
  value of gift (lifetime transfers)
    co-ownership of property 28.67
    cost of gift 28.61–28.64
    fall in value of an estate 28.63–28.64
    liabilities 28.66
    life assurance policies 28.74
    non-assignable agricultural tenancies 28.73
    options on property 28.70
    problem areas 28.65–28.74
    'property' 28.62
    related property 28.70
    restrictions on transfer of property 28.72
    shares and securities 28.68
    special rules 28.69–28.74
  vesting of property 30.148
  visiting forces 35.24
  voidable transfers 28.28
  waiver of remuneration and dividends 28.27
  woodlands 31.21–31.24
Settlor
  And see **Trusts**
  meaning 16.3
Shadow ACT
  distributions, and 42.46–42.48
Share incentive plans
  benefits to be provided 9.78
  forfeiture 9.80
  funding the trust 9.82
  holding period 9.79
  introduction 9.77
  restrictions 9.79

Share incentive plans – *contd*
  taxation of employees 9.81
  transfer 9.80
Share incentives
  artificial depression of market value 9.26
  convertible shares 9.25
  employee shareholders
    CGT relief on disposal 9.34
    generally 9.32
    tax reliefs (abolition) 9.33
  enhancement of market value 9.26
  meaning 9.2
  post-acquisition benefits 9.29
  priority share allocations 9.30
  research institution spin-out companies 9.31
  restricted shares 9.21–9.23
  shares acquired for less than market value 9.27
  shares disposed of for more than market value 9.28
Share options
  non tax-advantaged share schemes 9.41
Share sales
  choice of business medium, and 46.57
Shares and securities
  charities, and 53.99
  lifetime transfers, and 28.68
  stamp duty reserve tax, and
    exemptions 49.104
    generally 49.92
    higher charge 49.103
    introduction 49.1
    off-market transactions 49.105
    overview 49.21
    principal charge 49.102
    territorial scope 49.101
    unit trusts 49.106
Situs of property
  generally 35.6
  reversionary interests 35.83
Shearing
  reservation of benefit, and
    generally 29.122
    use of arrangements 29.129
Sick pay
  employment income, and 8.133
Small companies
  corporation tax, and 41.23
  first year allowances, and 48.30
Small donations scheme
  Gift Aid, and 53.81

Small gifts
  inheritance tax, and 31.5
Small or medium-sized enterprises (SMEs)
  corporation tax rate, and 41.23
  first year allowances, and 48.30
Small profits rate
  corporation tax, and 41.23
Social and welfare activities
  charities 40.32
  correspondence courses 40.35
  education
    eligible bodies 40.34
    generally 40.33
    private tuition 40.35
  health
    hospital care 40.38
    introduction 40.36
    opticians 40.40
    pharmacists 40.39
    supplies by qualified persons 40.37
  hospital care 40.38
  opticians 40.40
  pharmacists 40.39
  voluntary sector 40.32
Social investment
  charitable gifts, and 53.120
Social investment tax relief (SITR)
  entrepreneurs' relief, and 20.40
Soft landscaping
  value added tax, and 39.39
Sole traders
  entrepreneurs' relief, and
    disposal of business 20.20
    disposal of part of business 20.21
    generally 20.19
Solicitors
  value added tax, and 40.87–40.90
Source doctrine
  employment income, and 8.13
Specific legatees
  estates in administration, and 17.43
Speculative developers
  value added tax, and 39.43
Sponsorship
  trading income, and 10.157
Sporting services
  value added tax, and 40.54
Sports clubs
  And see **Charities**
  generally 53.101
Sportsmen and women
  foreign taxpayers, and 18.74
Spousal interest trusts
  generally 15.22

Spouses
  capital gains tax on death, and 21.104
  inheritance tax, and 31.41
  reservation of benefit, and 29.138
Stamp duty
  See also **Stamp duty land tax**
  accountable persons 49.110
  adjudication 49.112
  administration 49.111
  chargeable instruments
    conveyance on sale 49.113–49.114
    dissolution of partnerships 49.116
    exchange of shares 49.117
    transfer on sale 49.113–49.114
  clearance services 49.123
  contingency principle 49.115
  conveyance on sale 49.113–49.114
  depositary receipt systems 49.123
  dissolution of partnerships 49.116
  exchange of shares 49.117
  exemptions and reliefs
    companies, for 49.125–49.126
    group relief 49.125
    reconstructions 49.126
  family taxation, and 51.91
  group relief 49.125
  higher charge 49.123
  interest 49.109
  intra-group transfers 49.125
  introduction 49.1
  mixed use properties, and 49.27
  penalties 49.109
  rates 49.109
  recent developments 49.127
  reconstructions 49.126
  reservation of benefit, and 30.156
  'slab' system, and 49.1
  'slice' system, and
    generally 49.27
    introduction 49.1
  structure 49.107
  transfer on sale 49.113–49.114
  unascertainable consideration 49.115
  value added tax, and 38.12
  written instruments 49.108
Stamp duty land tax
  acquisition relief 49.79
  acquisitions 49.33
  additional residential property
    conditions 49.29
    generally 49.28
  administration 49.90
  advowsons, and 49.32
  annual tax on enveloped dwellings (ATED) 49.86

1794 Index

Stamp duty land tax – *contd*
  anti-avoidance
    annual tax on enveloped
      dwellings 49.86
    disclosure of tax avoidance scheme
      rules 49.87–49.89
    generally 49.85
    high value residential
      property 49.86
  background 49.4
  basic principles 49.26
  carrying out building works 49.50
  chargeable consideration
    adjustments 49.60
    carrying out building works 49.50
    contingent consideration
      49.56–49.57
    debt 49.48
    division 49.46
    employer-provided
      accommodation 49.52
    exchanges 49.45
    foreign currency 49.49
    general rule 49.41
    indemnity by purchaser 49.55
    just and reasonable
      apportionment 49.44
    lease obligations 49.53
    linked transactions 49.64
    non-monetary consideration 49.47
    partition 49.46
    postponed consideration 49.43
    provision of services 49.51
    rent 49.62
    reverse premium 49.54
    transfer of land to connected
      company 49.63
    unascertained consideration 49.58
    uncertain consideration 49.58
    value added tax 49.42
  chargeable interests 49.32
  charities, and 53.130
  choice of business medium, and 46.65
  clawback of relief 49.84
  contingent consideration 49.56–49.57
  conveyances 49.36–49.39
  debt 49.48
  deferred payment 49.61
  development agreements 49.39
  disclosure of tax avoidance scheme
    (DOTAS) rules
    generally 49.87
    persons required to disclose 49.88
    recent developments 49.89
  disclosure rules, and 5.11

Stamp duty land tax – *contd*
  division 49.46
  effective date 49.34
  employer-provided
    accommodation 49.52
  exchanges 49.45
  exempt interests 49.32
  exemptions and reliefs
    acquisition relief 49.79
    clawback 49.84
    group relief 49.78
    introduction 49.76
    multiple dwellings
      acquisitions 49.81
    other 49.83
    reconstruction relief 49.79
    Schedule 3, under 49.82
  family taxation, and 51.91
  foreign currency 49.49
  franchises, and 49.32
  generally 49.22
  group relief 49.78
  groups of companies, and 43.211
  high value residential property
    49.86
  higher rates 49.28
  indemnity by purchaser 49.55
  introduction 49.1–49.2
  just and reasonable
    apportionment 49.44
  land transactions
    acquisitions 49.33
    chargeable interests 49.32
    effective date 49.34
    exempt interests 49.32
    introduction 49.31
    purchaser 49.34
  leases
    increase of rent in first five
      years 49.70
    introduction 49.32
    net present value of rent 49.68
    new leases 49.65
    obligations 49.53
    premiums 49.66
    re-grants 49.73
    rent 49.67
    surrenders 49.73
    uncertain rents 49.69
    variable rents 49.69
  licences to use or occupy 49.32
  limited liability partnerships,
    and 45.23
  linked transactions 49.64
  manors, and 49.32

Stamp duty land tax – *contd*
  marital breakdown, and 52.65
  multiple dwellings acquisitions
      49.81
  new leases 49.65
  non-monetary consideration 49.47
  options 49.40
  overview 49.21
  partition 49.46
  partnership transactions 49.75
  postponed consideration 49.43
  premiums 49.66
  provision of services 49.51
  Ramsay v IRC principle, and 2.43
  rates 49.30
  reconstruction relief 49.79
  reliefs
    acquisition relief 49.79
    clawback 49.84
    group relief 49.78
    introduction 49.76
    multiple dwellings
        acquisitions 49.81
    other 49.83
    reconstruction relief 49.79
    Schedule 3, under 49.82
  rent
    increase in first five years 49.70
    introduction 49.67
    net present value 49.68
    uncertain 49.69
    variable 49.69
  reverse premium 49.54
  scope 49.25
  'second dwellings'
    conditions 49.29
    generally 49.28
  security interests, and 49.33
  sub-sales
    development agreements 49.39
    generally 49.38
  tenancies at will, and 49.32
  transfer of land to connected
      company 49.63
  transfer of unincorporated business to
      company, and 47.11
  transitional provisions 49.91
  unascertained consideration
      49.58
  uncertain consideration 49.58
  uncertain rents 49.69
  value added tax
    generally 49.42
    introduction 38.12
  variable rents 49.69

Stamp duty reserve tax
  exemptions 49.104
  generally 49.92
  higher charge 49.103
  introduction 49.1
  off-market transactions 49.105
  overview 49.21
  principal charge 49.102
  territorial scope 49.101
  unit trusts 49.106
Stamp taxes
  See also **Stamp duty**
  See also **Stamp duty land tax**
  See also **Stamp duty reserve tax**
  current structure 49.21
  introduction 49.1
Standard-rated supply
  value added tax, and 39.22
Starting rate
  savings income, and 7.26
State pension provision
  See **Pension schemes**
Statements of Practice
  generally 1.25
Statutory income
  see **Total income**
Statutory residence test (SRT)
  And see **Residence**
  accommodation tie 27.20
  automatic non-residence
      test 18.9
  automatic overseas tests 27.19
  automatic residence test 18.10
  automatic UK tests 27.19
  commencement 27.21
  country tie 27.20
  days spent 27.21
  family tie 27.20
  full time work 27.21
  generally 27.17
  home 27.21
  introduction 18.8
  key concepts 27.21
  location of work 27.21
  90-day tie 27.20
  outline of legislation 27.18
  summary 27.23
  split year treatment 18.12
  sufficient ties tests 27.19
  temporary non residence
      18.13
  tests of residence 27.19
  UK ties 18.11, 27.20
  work 27.21
  work tie 27.20

Stock
  depreciation 10.136
  valuation
    discontinuance, on 10.114
    introduction 10.110
    method 10.112
    purpose 10.111
    work in progress 10.113
Stock dividends
  distributions, and 42.9
  income tax, and 7.27
Stock stripping
  And see **Tax avoidance**
  generally 3.29
Stocks and shares ISA
  generally 15.28
Sub-groups
  capital gains, and 43.123
Sub-sales
  stamp duty land tax, and
    development agreements 49.39
    generally 49.38
Subscriptions
  value added tax, and 40.49
Subsidised meals
  employment income, and 8.168
Substantial shareholdings
  corporation tax, and 41.75
Successive interests in residue
  estates in administration, and 17.57
Supplies
  exempt supplies 38.8
  introduction 38.4
  reduced rate 38.6
  standard rate 38.5
  zero-rated supplies 38.7
Supply of goods
  value added tax, and
    consideration 37.7
    generally 38.23
    introduction 37.6
Supply of services
  value added tax, and 38.24
Surcharges
  trading income, and 10.156
Surplus ACT
  distributions, and 42.46–42.48
Surrenders of leases
  capital gains tax, and 19.43
  value added tax, and 39.37
Surviving spouse
  interest in possession trusts, and 33.23
  reservation of benefit, and 30.152
  settlements not subject to relevant
    property regime, and 33.23

Survivorship clauses
  reservation of benefit, and 30.143
'Sweeping-up' provision
  corporation tax 13.11
  generally 13.30
  introduction 13.1

T

Tainted donations
  charitable gifts, and 53.116
Tangible movable property
  capital gains tax, and
    calculation of gain on
      disposal 19.38
    definition 19.37
Taper relief
  background 19.4
  changes of FA 1998, and 19.17
  death, and 21.63
  deferral relief, and 15.93
  family taxation, and 51.59
  generally 19.20
  gifts of business assets, and 24.13
  losses, and 19.38
  reservation of benefit, and 30.23
Targeted anti-avoidance rules
  and see **Tax avoidance**
  generally 3.1
  salaried members 45.24
Targeted loss buying
  anti-avoidance rules, and 41.65
Tax
  meaning 1.3
  trading income, and 10.147
Tax advantage
  tax avoidance, and 5.7
  transactions in securities, and 3.55
Tax-advantaged share schemes
  choice of scheme
    non-tax aspects 9.151–9.160
    other shareholders 9.164
    tax aspects 9.161–9.163
  company share option plans 9.76
  enterprise management incentives
    eligible employees 9.85
    introduction 9.83
    maximum value of options 9.86
    qualifying companies 9.84
    taxation of employees 9.87
  general treatment 9.71–9.72
  NICs 9.90
  non-tax aspects of choice
    accounting treatment 9.160
    bonus schemes 9.152
    employee retention 9.155

Tax-advantaged share schemes – *contd*
  non-tax aspects of choice – *contd*
    'friendly' shareholdings 9.156
    introduction 9.151
    market in non-quoted shares 9.157
    performance-related
      incentives 9.153
    retention of employees 9.155
    reward for growth in share
      value 9.154
    sense of identity between employees
      and company 9.158
    selective employee
      participation 9.159
  PAYE 9.88–9.89
  recent deregulation 9.71
  requirements
    enquiries 9.73
    exclusion of persons with material
      interest 9.74
    notification 9.73
    other 9.74
    penalties 9.73
    restrictions attached to shares 9.74
    self-certification 9.73
    share type 9.74
  savings-related share option
    schemes 9.75
  share incentive plans
    benefits to be provided 9.78
    forfeiture 9.80
    funding the trust 9.82
    holding period 9.79
    introduction 9.77
    restrictions 9.79
    taxation of employees 9.81
  tax aspects of choice 9.161–9.163
  tax regime 9.72
  transfer 9.80
Tax avoidance
  accelerated payments 5.28
  accrued income scheme
    generally 3.12
    overview 3.4
  annual tax on enveloped dwellings
    description of arrangements 5.16
    generally 5.15
  anti-avoidance, and
    And see **Anti-avoidance**
    annual payments 14.12
    consortium relief 43.47
    deferral relief 15.98
    Enterprise Investment
      Scheme 15.57
    groups of companies 43.127

Tax avoidance – *contd*
  anti-avoidance, and – *contd*
    interest in possession trusts
      33.18–33.20
    land 12.101–12.112
    limited liability partnerships 45.22
    loss relief 11.122
    losses 19.48
    non-resident companies 27.112
    premiums 12.83
    settlements not subject to relevant
      property regime 33.18–33.20
    stamp duty land tax 49.85–49.89
    targeted anti-avoidance rules 3.1
    transfer of assets abroad
      18.110–18.128
    trusts 16.91–16.107
    value shifting, and 26.61–26.64
  artificial transactions in land 3.6
  Astall v R&C Comrs 2.40
  background 2.3
  Barclays Mercantile v Mawson 2.38
  Baylis v Gregory 2.25
  bed and breakfasting 3.13
  bond washing
    generally 3.11
    overview 3.4
    transactions in securities, and 3.29
  Bowater Property Developments v IRC 2.25
  Burmah Oil v IRC
    generally 2.21
    overview 2.4
  Craven v White 2.25
  direct taxes
    annual tax on enveloped
      dwellings 5.15–5.16
    description of arrangements 5.13
    disclosable information 5.8
    form of disclosure 5.9
    information powers 5.17
    inheritance tax 5.12–5.14
    introduction 5.4
    promoters 5.5–5.6
    schemes and arrangements 5.7
    stamp duty land tax 5.11
    time of disclosure 5.10
    widening scope 5.12
  disclosure rules
    And see **Disclosure rules**
    accelerated payments 5.28
    annual tax on enveloped
      dwellings 5.15–5.16
    conclusions 5.31
    direct taxes 5.4–5.17
    follower notices 5.29

Tax avoidance – *contd*
  disclosure rules – *contd*
    indirect taxes 5.21–5.26
    inheritance tax 5.12–5.14
    introduction 5.3
    scope 5.3
    stamp duty land tax 5.11
    widening scope 5.12
  disguised remuneration 5.7
  dividend stripping
    generally 3.10
    overview 3.4
    transactions in securities, and 3.29
  DOTAS
    And see **DOTAS**
    generally 5.3–5.17
    stamp duty land tax 49.87–49.89
  Fitzwilliam v IRC 2.29
  follower notices 5.29
  Furniss v Dawson
    decision 2.23
    facts 2.22
    overview 2.4
  general anti avoidance rule (GAAR)
    Aaronson Report 3.75–3.81
    experience of other
        jurisdictions 3.82
    introduction 3.74
    key principles 3.80
    proposals 5.1
  'hallmarks', and
    direct taxes 5.7
    indirect taxes 5.23
  indirect taxes
    designated transactions 5.22
    generally notifiable
        transactions 5.23
    hallmarked schemes 5.23
    introduction 5.21
    listed schemes 5.22
    notification 5.25
    reforms 5.26
    tax advantage 5.24
  inheritance tax
    description of arrangements 5.13
    introduction 5.12
    required information 5.14
  introduction 2.1–2.2
  IRC v Scottish Provident 2.39
  legislative framework
    accrued income scheme 3.12
    bed and breakfasting 3.13
    bond washing 3.11
    dividend stripping 3.10
    generally 3.2–3.8

Tax avoidance – *contd*
  legislative framework – *contd*
    introduction 3.1
    transactions in securities 3.28–3.72
    typical schemes 3.9–3.11
  loss relief, and 11.122
  MacNiven v Westmoreland 2.37
  Mayes v R&C Comrs 2.41
  McGuckian v IRC
    generally 2.32–2.33
    purposive interpretation 2.36
  'new approach' 2.4
  promoters of tax avoidance schemes
    (POTAS)
    generally 5.30
    introduction 5.5–5.6
  R&C Comrs v Mayes 2.41
  Ramsay v IRC principle
    applicability 2.34–2.45
    conclusions 2.46–2.48
    generally 2.21
    limits 2.24–2.29
    meaning 2.34–2.45
    overview 2.4
    reaffirmation 2.32–2.33
    scope 2.34–2.45
  sale of income derived from personal
    activities 3.6
  Scottish Provident v IRC 2.39
  stamp duty land tax, and
    disclosure rules 5.11
    generally 49.87
    introduction 2.43
    persons required to disclose 49.88
    recent developments 49.89
  stock stripping 3.29
  targeted anti-avoidance rules
    (TAAR) 3.1
  'tax advantage' 5.7
  tax losses 3.8
  tax mitigation distinction 2.45
  transactions in securities
    application of provisions 3.68–3.72
    background 3.29
    'bona fide commercial' 3.64
    'cancellation of tax advantage' 3.53
    case decisions 3.71–3.72
    change of ownership 3.36
    circumstance E 3.62
    close company 3.37
    'combined effect of' 3.54
    consideration 3.34
    counteraction 3.38
    current application 3.68–3.72
    definitions 3.51–3.67

Tax avoidance – *contd*
  transactions in securities – *contd*
    dividend stripping 3.58–3.60
    'escape clause' 3.63
    genuine commercial reasons 3.64
    'in consequence or' 3.54
    'income tax' 3.56
    'income tax advantage' 3.55
    introduction 3.28–3.31
    legislative changes 3.30–3.32
    meaning 3.33
    'no main object of obtaining a tax advantage' 3.66
    'ordinary course of making and managing investments' 3.65
    overview 3.3
    principles-based legislation 3.73
    purpose of transaction 3.35
    'securities' 3.33
    'tax' 3.56
    'tax advantage' 3.55
    'transactions' 3.33
  transfer of assets overseas 3.5
  transfer pricing 3.8
  value added tax (VADR), and
    And see **VADR**
    generally 5.21–5.25
    introduction 2.44

Tax credits
  appeals 51.39
  case study 51.40A
  changes in circumstance 51.37
  changes in income 51.38
  child tax credit
    conditions of entitlement 51.29
    elements 51.28
    introduction 51.27
    payment 51.30
  disputes 51.40
  marital breakdown, and 52.16
  working tax credit
    childcare element 51.35
    disputes 51.40
    elements 51.31
    introduction 51.27
    payment 51.36

Tax exempt special savings accounts (TESSAs)
  generally 15.33

Tax-free childcare
  generally 51.41

Tax Law Rewrite project
  legislation, and 1.22

Tax losses
  tax avoidance, and 3.8

Tax mitigation
  Ramsay v IRC principle, and 2.45

Tax reliefs
  see **Exemptions and reliefs**

Tax repayments
  charities, and 53.103

Tax shelters
  capital gains tax
    deferral relief 15.89–15.100
    reinvestment relief 15.82–15.88
  deferral relief
    anti-avoidance 15.98
    appeals 15.96
    claims 15.100
    clawback of gain 15.97
    disposal 15.91
    EIS investments 15.93–15.94
    entrepreneurs' relief 15.94
    introduction 15.89
    qualifying investment 15.92
    relief 15.90
    taper relief 15.93
    trustees 15.99
    withdrawal 15.95
  Enterprise Investment Scheme
    anti-avoidance 15.57
    eligible shares 15.55
    introduction 15.51
    pre-arranged exits 15.57
    qualifying activities 15.56
    qualifying company 15.54
    qualifying individuals 15.53
    relief 15.52
  individual savings accounts
    apportionment of investment 15.26
    capital gains tax, and 22.2
    cash ISA 15.27
    eligibility 15.26
    generally 15.26
    'help-to-buy' ISA 15.29
    income tax, and 7.132
    innovative finance ISA 15.31
    lifetime ISA 15.30
    Junior ISA 15.32
    stocks and shares ISA 15.28
    types 15.26
  investment products
    discounted gift schemes 15.25
    generally 15.21
    gift and loan scheme 15.23
    spousal interest trusts 15.22
    trust carve out 15.24
  life assurance policies
    non-qualifying policies 15.2–15.10
    qualifying policies 15.1

Tax shelters – *contd*
  life assurance policies – *contd*
    taxation of insurance
      companies 15.3
  personal equity plans 15.33
  reinvestment relief
    clawback of gain 15.88
    generally 15.82
  save as you earn 15.33
  tax exempt special savings
    accounts 15.33
  venture capital trusts
    background 15.121
    capital gains tax 15.125–15.127
    generally 15.124
    income tax 15.122
    outline 15.122–15.123
Tax simplification
  generally 1.26
Tax unit
  generally 1.6
Tax year
  employment income, and 8.12
  income tax, and 6.22
Taxable earnings
  employment income, and 8.11
Taxable supply
  value added tax, and 38.22
Tenancies at will
  stamp duty land tax, and 49.32
Terminal loss relief
  losses, and 11.102
Terminal markets
  value added tax, and 40.7
Termination payments
  charging provision 8.142–8.144
  introduction 8.141
  payments treated as earnings 8.147
  residual charging provision 8.145
TESSAs
  generally 15.33
Theatrical 'angels'
  miscellaneous income, and 13.24
Thin capitalisation
  corporation tax, and 41.98
Third party gifts
  employment income, and 8.168
Third party payments
  employment income, and 8.43
Third party suppliers
  disclosure rules, and 5.22
Timber
  inheritance tax, and 31.21–31.24
Toll charges
  miscellaneous income, and 13.27

Total income
  combining income from all
    sources 7.21
  couples 7.22
  dividends 7.27
  earned income 7.23
  general 7.21
  interest paid by banks and building
    societies 7.24
  investment income 7.23
  personal savings allowance 7.25
  savings income 7.24–7.26
  savings nil rate 7.25
  starting rate for savings 7.26
Total loss of asset
  capital gains tax, and 19.65
Tour operators
  agents 40.123
  foreign currency 40.119
  incidental supplies 40.121
  in-house supplies 40.116
  input tax 40.118
  introduction 40.110
  margin scheme
    standard-rated supplies 40.113
    zero-rated supplies 40.114
  territorial scope 40.112
  time of supply 40.120
  travel agents 40.123
  travellers 40.111
  wholesale supplies 40.117
Trade
  'badges of trade'
    circumstances responsible for
      realisation 10.27
    frequency of similar
      transactions 10.25
    introduction 10.22
    length of ownership 10.24
    motive 10.28
    subject matter of transaction
      10.23
    work done on property 10.26
  commercial approach 10.20
  common sense approach 10.20
  definition 10.18
  gambling, and 10.21
  introduction 10.18
  losses, and 11.4
  mutual trading 10.29
  realisation of assets after
    discontinuance 10.30
  single activity 10.19
Trade marks
  trading income, and 10.155

Trading
  estates in administration, and 17.24
Trading company
  entrepreneurs' relief, and
    HMRC ruling 20.18
    holding company 20.16
    introduction 20.11
    significant interest 20.13
    subsidiaries 20.16
    substantial extent 20.15
    trade 20.14
    trading activities 20.12
    trading group 20.17
Trading income
  And see **Income tax**
  accounting costs 10.147
  accounting dates 10.196–10.200
  accounting policies 10.66
  accounting practice
    change of accounting basis 10.72
    financial reporting standards 10.64
    introduction 10.63
    materiality 10.65
    policies 10.66
    provisions 10.67
  accounts 10.61
  annual investment allowance 10.135
  bad debts 10.14
  'badges of trade'
    circumstances responsible for
      realisation 10.27
    frequency of similar
      transactions 10.25
    introduction 10.22
    length of ownership 10.24
    motive 10.28
    subject matter of transaction 10.23
    work done on property 10.26
  basis of assessment
    accounting dates 10.196–10.200
    background 10.192
    current year basis 10.193–10.194
    overlap relief 10.201
    partners 10.202–10.204
    partners joining 10.202
    partners leaving 10.203
    partnership changes 10.204
  capital allowances 10.135
  cash basis
    calculation of profits 10.74
    election 10.73
    moving to 10.75
  change of accounting basis 10.72
  charging provisions
    corporation tax 10.3

Trading income – *contd*
  charging provisions – *contd*
    income tax 10.2
    introduction 10.1
  charities, and 53.42
  computation of profits
    accounting practice 10.63–10.72
    accounts 10.61
    cash basis 10.73–10.75
    expenditure 10.76–10.78
    generally accepted accounting
      practice 10.62
    post-cessation receipts and
      expenses 10.80–10.81
  corporation tax 10.3
  creative artists 10.172–10.173
  crime-related expenditure 10.149
  current year basis
    closing years of business 10.195
    continuing business 10.193
    opening years of new
      business 10.194
  damages payments 10.145
  deductible expenses
    accounting costs 10.147
    annual investment allowance 10.135
    bad debts 10.144
    basic principles 10.130
    capital allowances 10.135
    crime-related expenditure 10.149
    damages, fines and losses 10.145
    designs 10.155
    depreciation 10.136
    doubtful debts 10.144
    employee costs 10.152
    employee payments 10.132
    employee trusts 10.133
    examples 10.139–10.157
    fines 10.145
    fixed rate, at 10.161–10.165
    impairment losses 10.144
    intellectual property 10.155
    interest 10.156
    legal costs 10.146
    losses 10.145
    outplacement counselling 10.148
    patents 10.155
    payment relating to crime 10.148
    payments to organisations 10.153
    penalties 10.156
    pre-trading expenditure 10.143
    rent for business premises 10.140
    repairs and improvements 10.142
    research and development 10.154
    restrictive covenants 10.134

Trading income – *contd*
  deductible expenses – *contd*
    sale and leaseback
      arrangements 10.141
    security-related expenditure 10.149
    sponsorship 10.157
    sum prohibited by statute 10.138
    sum to be income not
      capital 10.131–10.136
    surcharges 10.156
    tax 10.147
    trade marks 10.155
    training 10.148
    travelling expenses 10.150–10.151
    'wholly and exclusively' for business
      purposes 10.137
  depreciation 10.136
  designs 10.155
  employee costs 10.152
  employee payments 10.132
  employee trusts 10.133
  expenditure
    capital expenditure 10.77
    date at which allowable 10.78
    deductibility 10.76
    post-cessation expenses 10.81
  farmers 10.172–10.173
  financial reporting standards 10.64
  fixed rate expenses
    introduction 10.161
    use of business premises as a
      home 10.164–10.165
    use of home for business
      purposes 10.163
    vehicle expenditure 10.162
  foreign income, and 18.35
  foreign taxpayers, and 18.72
  generally accepted accounting
    practice 10.62
  intellectual property 10.155
  interest 10.156
  introduction 10.1–10.4
  inventors 10.174
  legal costs 10.146
  legislative framework
    corporation tax 10.3
    income tax 10.2
    introduction 10.1
  market gardeners 10.172–10.173
  materiality 10.65
  miscellaneous income, and 13.15
  non-deductible expenditure 10.138
  outplacement counselling 10.148
  patents 10.155
  payment relating to crime 10.148

Trading income – *contd*
  payments to organisations 10.153
  penalties 10.156
  policies 10.66
  post-cessation expenses 10.81
  post-cessation receipts 10.80
  pre-trading expenditure 10.143
  'profession' 10.41
  provisions 10.67
  realisation of assets after
    discontinuance 10.30
  relief for fluctuating profits
    creative artists 10.172–10.173
    farmers 10.172–10.173
    introduction 10.171
    inventors 10.174
    market gardeners 10.172–10.173
  rent for business premises 10.140
  repairs and improvements 10.142
  research and development 10.154
  restrictive covenants 10.134
  sale and leaseback
    arrangements 10.141
  Schedule D, and 10.2–10.3
  security-related expenditure
    10.149
  sponsorship 10.157
  standards 10.64
  surcharges 10.156
  tax 10.147
  'trade'
    'badges of trade' 10.22–10.28
    commercial approach 10.20
    common sense approach 10.20
    definition 10.18
    gambling, and 10.21
    introduction 10.18
    mutual trading 10.29
    realisation of assets after
      discontinuance 10.30
    single activity 10.19
  trade marks 10.155
  trading receipts
    dispositions for less than market
      value 10.115–10.119
    gifts 10.115–10.119
    introduction 10.101
    sum to be income not
      capital 10.103–10.109
    sum to be derived from
      trade 10.102
    valuation of trading stock
      10.110–10.114
  training 10.148
  travelling expenses 10.150–10.151

Trading income – *contd*
  use of business premises as a
    home 10.164–10.165
  use of home for business
    purposes 10.163
  vehicle expenditure 10.162
  'vocation' 10.41
  'wholly and exclusively' for business
    purposes 10.137
Trading losses
  capital allowances, and 48.9
  choice of business medium, and 46.46
  family taxation, and 51.53
  net income, and 7.42
Trading receipts
  appropriation of unclaimed deposits
    and advances 10.107
  cancellation of business
    contract 10.106
  dispositions for less than market value
    introduction 10.115
    market value rule 10.117–10.118
    transfer pricing 10.116
  gifts 10.115–10.119
  introduction 10.101
  release of debts 10.109
  restrictions on activity 10.104
  sale of 'know-how' 10.108
  sterilisation of an asset 10.105
  sum to be income not capital
    appropriation of unclaimed deposits
      and advances 10.107
    cancellation of business
      contract 10.106
    introduction 10.103
    release of debts 10.109
    restrictions on activity 10.104
    sale of 'know-how' 10.108
    sterilisation of an asset 10.105
  sum to be derived from trade 10.102
  trading stock
    discontinuance, on 10.114
    introduction 10.110
    method 10.112
    purpose 10.111
    work in progress 10.113
  transfer pricing 10.116
  valuation of trading stock
    discontinuance, on 10.114
    introduction 10.110
    method 10.112
    purpose 10.111
    work in progress 10.113
Trading stock
  capital gains, and 43.125

Training
  employment income, and 8.164
  trading income, and 10.148
Transactions in land
  application of provision 12.104
  avoiding provision 12.111
  conditions
    application of provision 12.104
    connected persons 12.107
    disposal of land 12.105
    trading stock 12.106
  connected persons 12.107
  disposal of land 12.105
  effect of provision 12.103
  generally 12.101
  introduction 3.6
  opportunities to make gain 12.109
  other matters 12.112
  shares in landholding
    companies 12.108
  trading stock 12.106
  trading transactions 12.102
Transactions in securities
  application of provisions 3.68–3.72
  background 3.29
  'bona fide commercial' 3.64
  'cancellation of tax advantage' 3.53
  case decisions 3.71–3.72
  change of ownership 3.36
  circumstance E 3.62
  close company 3.37
  'combined effect of' 3.54
  consideration 3.34
  counteraction 3.38
  current application 3.68–3.72
  dividend stripping 3.58–3.60
  'escape clause' 3.62
  genuine commercial reasons 3.64
  'in consequence or' 3.54
  'income tax' 3.56
  'income tax advantage' 3.55
  introduction 3.28–3.31
  legislative changes 3.30–3.32
  meaning 3.33
  'no main object of obtaining a tax
    advantage' 3.65
  'ordinary course of making and
    managing investments' 3.65
  overview 3.3
  principles-based legislation 3.73
  purpose of transaction 3.35
  'securities' 3.33
  'tax' 3.56
  'tax advantage' 3.55
  'transactions' 3.33

Transactions in UK land
  application of provision 12.104
  avoiding provision 12.111
  conditions
    application of provision 12.104
    connected persons 12.107
    disposal of land 12.105
    trading stock 12.106
  connected persons 12.107
  disposal of land 12.105
  effect of provision 12.103
  generally 12.101
  introduction 3.6
  opportunities to make gain 12.109
  other matters 12.112
  shares in landholding
      companies 12.108
  trading stock 12.106
  trading transactions 12.102
Transfer of assets overseas
  chargeable income 18.118
  general 18.111
  'individuals ordinarily resident
      in the UK' 18.112
  introduction 18.110
  legislative reforms 18.127–18.128
  liability of non-transferors
      18.120–18.125
  liability of transferor 18.114–18.119
  overview 3.5
  powers to obtain information 18.126
  purpose 18.113
  remittance basis for non-
      domiciliaries 18.119
Transfer of business as going concern
  value added tax, and
    generally 38.26
    property 39.37
Transfer of business to company
  loss relief, and 11.101
Transfer of land to connected company
  stamp duty land tax, and 49.63
Transfer of unincorporated business
  company, to
    capital gains tax 47.4–47.9
    income tax 47.3
    introduction 47.2
    other issues 47.14
    problems for purchasing
        company 47.12–47.13
    stamp duty land tax 47.11
  limited liability partnerships,
      to 45.20–45.21
Transfer of value
  close companies, and 28.152

Transfer of value – *contd*
  contrast with gifts 28.6
  examples 28.5
  generally 28.3
  instalments, by 28.127
  omissions 28.4
Transfer on sale
  stamp duty, and 49.113–49.114
Transfer pricing
  corporation tax, and 41.44
  tax avoidance, and 3.8
  trading receipts, and 10.116
Transferable nil rate band
  artificial debts, and 30.14
  calculation of tax on death, and
    generally 30.27
    residential property 30.33
Transitional serial interest
  inheritance tax, and 32.52
Transferable tax allowance
  civil partnerships 51.12
  generally 7.115–7.117
  introduction 51.1
  married couples 51.12
Transport insurance
  value added tax, and 40.79
Travel agents
  value added tax, and 40.123
Travel expenses
  employment income, and 8.174
  trading income, and 10.150–10.151
Treasury shares
  generally 9.114
Trivial benefits
  employment income, and 8.131
Trust carve out
  generally 15.24
Trustees
  And see **Trusts**
  deferral relief, and 15.99
  'dividend trust rate' 16.21
  inheritance tax on death, and 30.48
  liability at rate applicable to trusts
      (RAT)
    introduction 16.1
    s 479 ITA 2007 charge
        16.21–16.30
    s 496 ITA 2007 charge 16.31–16.33
  meaning 16.4
  powers of maintenance
    divesting effect 16.71
    introduction 16.70
    tax treatment 16.73
    vesting effect 16.72
  remuneration 16.8

Trustees – *contd*
  residence, and 18.19
  'trust rate' 16.21
Trusts
  And see **Settlements**
  agricultural property relief,
    and 31.70
  business property relief, and 31.54
  capital gains tax
    And see **Trusts (capital gains tax)**
    generally 25.1–25.152
  distributions, and 42.95–42.96
  'dividend trust rate' 16.21
  entrepreneurs' relief, and 25.148
  income tax
    And see **Trusts (income tax)**
    generally 16.1–16.108
  offshore
    And see **Offshore trusts**
    anti flip flop legislation
      27A.171–27A.176
    background 27A.1–27A.11
    exporting a UK trust
      27A.21–27A.55
    information 27A.177
    proposed 2017 changes 27A.12
    residence of trustee 27A.21–27A.55
    taxing UK domiciled settlor of
      offshore trust 27A.71–27A.97
    taxing UK resident beneficiaries of
      non-resident trust
      27A.101–27A.163
  'trust rate' 16.21
  Trusts Registration Service 17.22
Trusts for the disabled
  inheritance tax, and 32.59
  settlements not subject to relevant
    property regime, and 33.113
Trusts (capital gains tax)
  absolute entitlement 25.6
  actual disposals
    assets leaving trust 25.44
    change of trustees 25.42
    conclusions 25.55
    exit charge 25.47–25.52
    introduction 25.41
    termination of interest in
      possession trusts on death of
      beneficiary 25.54
    trust losses 25.43
    use of trust losses 25.44–25.45
  addition of property 25.45
  annual exemption 25.143
  assets leaving trust 25.44
  bare trusts, and 25.3

Trusts (capital gains tax) – *contd*
  beneficiaries under a disability,
    and 25.4
  change of trustees 25.42
  class closing 25.8
  concurrent interests, and 25.5
  'connected persons' rule 25.22
  creation 25.21–25.22
  deferral relief 25.147
  death of beneficiary with interest in
    possession trusts 25.54
  deemed disposals
    assets leaving trust 25.44
    change of trustees 25.42
    conclusions 25.55
    exit charge 25.47–25.52
    introduction 25.41
    termination of interest in
      possession trusts on death of
      beneficiary 25.54
    trust losses 25.43
    use of trust losses 25.44–25.45
  deferral relief 25.147
  definition 25.2
  disposal of beneficial interests
    absolute entitlement of purchaser to
      part of settled property 25.113
    basic rule 25.111
    non-resident settlement, in
      25.114–25.115
    position of purchaser 25.112
    settlor interested trust, in
      25.116–25.118
  entrepreneurs' relief 25.148
  exemptions and reliefs
    annual exemption 25.143
    death exemption 25.144
    deferral relief 25.147
    entrepreneurs' relief 25.148
    introduction 25.142
    main residence 25.142
    roll-over relief 24.145
    taper relief 25.148
    trust rate band 25.146
  exit charge
    allowable expenditure 25.53
    anti flip-flop legislation 25.52
    deemed disposal 25.48
    general rule 25.47
    hold-over relief 25.51
    losses 25.48
    revertor to settlor 25.50
    tax-free death uplift 25.51
  gifts of business assets, and 24.20
  introduction 25.1

1806 Index

Trusts (capital gains tax) – *contd*
  losses
    assets leaving trust 25.44
    exit charge 25.48
    generally 25.43
    use 25.44–25.45
  main residence 25.142
  meaning 25.2–25.8
  nomineeships, and 25.3
  payment of tax 25.141
  resettlements 25.81–25.83
  roll-over relief 24.145
  separate funds 25.81–25.83
  taper relief 25.148
  transfers on change of trustees 25.42
  trust rate band 25.146
  trustee appropriations, and 25.7
  vulnerable beneficiaries
    introduction 25.149
    qualifying trust gains 25.150
    UK resident vulnerable persons 25.150

Trusts (income tax)
  administrative expenses 16.5
  annuitants 16.64
  anti-avoidance
    background 16.91
    benefits received by unmarried infant children from parental settlements 16.95–16.97
    charge to tax 16.94
    conclusions 16.107
    effect of rules 16.92
    introduction 16.91–16.94
    receipt of capital benefits 16.106
    'settlement' 16.93
    settlor retains interest in settlement 16.98–16.105
  assessment to tax 16.6
  bare trusts for infants 16.97
  beneficiaries entitled to trust income
    calculating tax 16.62
    general rule 16.61
    relevant income 16.63
  charge on discretionary payments
    dividends 16.33
    generally 16.31
    'tax pool' 16.32
  deductible expenses 16.5
  deduction of tax at source 16.6
  definitions
    'settlement' 16.2
    'settlor' 16.3
    'trustees' 16.4

Trusts (income tax) – *contd*
  discretionary beneficiaries
    dividends 16.66
    general rules 16.65
  dividends
    deduction of tax at source 16.6
    s 479 ITA 2007 charge, and 16.29–16.30
    s 496 ITA 2007 charge, and 16.33
    tax on discretionary beneficiaries 16.66
  foreign source income
    generally 16.9
    introduction 18.38
  general principles
    liability of trustee at basic rate 16.5
    other 16.9
    remuneration of trustees 16.8
    returns 16.6–16.7
  introduction 16.1
  main residence exemption, and 23.62
  management expenses 16.23
  modernisation of law 16.1
  non-resident trustees 16.9
  powers of maintenance
    divesting effect 16.71
    introduction 16.70
    tax treatment 16.73
    vesting effect 16.72
  reform proposals 16.108
  remuneration of trustees 16.8
  residence, and 18.20
  returns
    exceptional cases 16.7
    generally 16.6
  s 479 ITA 2007 charge
    affected trusts 16.22
    beneficiary with complete right to income 16.24
    dividends 16.29–16.30
    generally 16.21–16.26
    management expenses 16.23
    rate applicable to trusts 16.21
    relevant income 16.26
    will trusts 16.25
  s 496 ITA 2007 charge
    dividends 16.33
    generally 16.31
    'tax pool' 16.32
  self assessment 16.5
  'settlement' 16.2
  'settlor' 16.3
  supplementing income out of capital 16.67–16.69

Trusts (income tax) – *contd*
trustees
meaning 16.4
powers of maintenance 16.70–16.73
remuneration 16.8
trustees liable at rate applicable to trusts (RAT)
introduction 16.1
s 479 ITA 2007 charge 16.21–16.30
s 496 ITA 2007 charge 16.31–16.33
vulnerable beneficiaries
background 16.74
meaning 16.75
qualifying trusts 16.76
treatment of income 16.77
will trusts 16.25
Trusts Registration Service
generally 17.22

U

UK domiciled settlor of offshore trust
anti flip flop legislation 27A.87–27A.89
attributed trust gains 27A.89–27A.97
'defined person' benefits 27A.83–27A.86
introduction 27A.71–27A.75
personal capital losses 27A.89–27A.97
qualifying settlements 27A.76–27A.81
qualifying settlors 27A.82
UK resident beneficiaries of non-resident trusts
UK domiciled and resident beneficiaries
attribution method 27A.118–27A.119
basic rules 27A.101–27A.105
capital payments 27A.109–27A.117
disposal of beneficial interest in offshore trust 27A.164–27A.169
interest charge 27A.136–27A.138
offshore losses 27A.129
operation of s 87 charge 27A.106–27A.129
payments prior to 6 April 2008 27A.121
personal losses or rates of tax 27A.126–27A.128
s 731 ITA 2007 tie-in 27A.120
'stockpiled gains' 27A.106–27A.108
supplementary charge 27A.136–27A.138
trust gains 27A.106

UK resident beneficiaries of non-resident trusts – *contd*
UK domiciled and resident beneficiaries – *contd*
use of personal losses or rates of tax 27A.126–27A.128
UK resident foreign domiciled beneficiaries
general principles 27A.145–27A.153
rebasing 27A.154–27A.163
UK taxation
classification of taxes 1.2
conclusions 1.41–1.42
features of the system
courts' role 1.24
legislation 1.21–1.23
practice 1.25
introduction 1.1
legislation
Hansard, and 1.23
interpretation 1.21
simplification process 1.22
meaning of 'tax' 1.3
purpose 1.4
statistics 1.5
tax simplification 1.26
tax unit 1.6
Unapproved share schemes
And see **Non tax-advantaged share schemes**
background 9.11
capital gains tax 9.45–9.57
conclusions 9.58
introduction 9.11–9.13
NICs 9.44
PAYE 9.42–9.43
rights to acquire shares 9.41
share incentives 9.21–9.31
share options 9.41
Unascertainable consideration
stamp duty, and 49.115
Unascertained consideration
stamp duty land tax, and 49.58
Unauthorised payments
pension schemes, and 50.21
Unauthorised unit trusts
savings and investment income, and 14.44
Uncertain consideration
stamp duty land tax, and 49.58
Undervalue disposals
generally 24.16
introduction 22.99

Unearned income
employment income, and 8.66
income from land, and 12.22
Unincorporated associations
corporation tax, and 41.2
Unincorporated business, transfer of
company, to
capital gains tax 47.4–47.9
income tax 47.3
introduction 47.2
other issues 47.14
problems for purchasing
company 47.12–47.13
stamp duty land tax 47.11
limited liability partnerships,
to 45.20–45.21
Unit trusts
capital gains tax, and 22.3
corporation tax, and 41.2
inheritance tax, and 35.22
stamp duty reserve tax, and 49.106
Unlimited companies
choice of business medium,
and 46.3
Unquoted company trades
loss relief, and 11.121
Upper Tribunal
See also **Appeals**
appeals from 4.213
costs of proceedings 4.212
introduction 4.210
publication of decisions 4.211
Use of assets
exemptions, and 8.166
generally 8.129
Use of business premises as a home
trading income, and 10.164–10.165
Use of home for business purposes
trading income, and 10.163

V

VADR regime
designated transactions 5.22
generally notifiable transactions 5.23
hallmarked schemes 5.23
introduction 5.21
listed schemes 5.22
notification 5.25
reforms 5.26
tax advantage 5.24
Valuation
See also **Value of gift**
capital gains tax on death, and
basic rule 21.21
general conclusion 21.24

Valuation – *contd*
See also **Value of gift** – *contd*
IHT purposes, for 21.22
IHT revaluations 21.23
estates, and
allowable deductions 35.61
capital gains tax on death,
and 21.21–21.24
enforcement of tax abroad 35.63
expenses of administering property
abroad 35.62
foreign assets 35.64
transfer of unincorporated business to
company, and 47.9
Value added tax
accountability 40.2
accounting
annual returns 38.57
bad debt relief 38.59–38.60
'capping' provisions 38.53–38.54
cash accounting 38.58
general rule 38.52
monthly returns 38.55
payments on account 38.56
administration 38.2
alterations to property 39.26
annual returns 38.57
apportionment
de minimis rule 38.88
generally 38.82
methods 38.85–38.87
partial exemption, and 38.83–38.84
special methods 38.87
standard method 38.86
approved alterations 39.25A
associations
donations 40.49
fund-raising 40.49
introduction 40.49
match fees 40.56
MoU with CIPFA 40.50
participation fees 40.56
sporting services 40.54
subscriptions 40.49
auctioneers
generally 40.125
margin schemes 40.126
aviation insurance 40.79
background 38.1
bad debt relief 38.59–38.60
barristers
generally 40.86
services 40.95
Bitcoins 40.65
brokerage services 40.73

Value added tax – *contd*
  builders activities 39.38
  business 38.28
  business activities
    auctioneers 40.125–40.126
    business services 40.64–40.83
    food and drink 40.23–40.30
    government 40.98–40.102
    introduction 40.21
    leisure 40.43–40.63
    professional services 40.86–40.97
    retailers 40.105–40.109
    social and welfare 40.32–40.40
    tour operators 40.110–40.123
  business services
    brokerage services 40.73
    dealings in securities 40.72
    financial services 40.64–40.69
    insurance 40.78–40.83
    supplies connected with financial services 40.77
  capital allowances, and 48.4
  capital gains tax, and 38.10
  Capital Goods Scheme
    initial deduction 38.91
    introduction 38.89
    method of adjustment 38.94
    option to tax commercial buildings, and 39.34
    period of adjustment 38.93
    relevant assets 38.90
    subsequent adjustments 38.92
  'capping' provisions
    extension to four years 38.54
    generally 38.53
  cash accounting 38.58
  catering 40.23–40.25
  charitable buildings 39.23
  charities
    cost-sharing exemption 53.128
    fuel and power 53.124
    fund-raising events 53.127
    generally 40.32
    inputs 53.122–53.124
    introduction 53.121
    outputs 53.125–53.126
    payment 53.129
  choice of business medium, and 46.64
  civil engineering work 39.41
  clubs and societies
    donations 40.49
    fund-raising 40.49
    introduction 40.49
    match fees 40.56
    MoU with CIPFA 40.50

Value added tax – *contd*
  clubs and societies – *contd*
    participation fees 40.56
    sporting services 40.54
    subscriptions 40.49
  commercial buildings (option to tax)
    capital goods scheme, and 39.34
    introduction 39.27
    mechanics of exercise 39.29
    output tax 39.31
    property affected 39.28
    purpose of exercise 39.33
    revocation 39.30
  commission 40.96
  composite supplies 38.25
  construction services 39.25
  contractors activities 39.38
  conversions 39.26
  correspondence courses 40.35
  cost-sharing exemption 53.128
  credit notes 40.94
  de minimis rule 38.88
  dealings in securities 40.72
  deduction principle 38.81
  de-registration 38.51
  disbursements 40.97
  disclosure rules, and
    designated transactions 5.22
    generally 5.3
    generally notifiable transactions 5.23
    hallmarked schemes 5.23
    introduction 5.21
    listed schemes 5.22
    notification 5.25
    reforms 5.26
    tax advantage 5.24
  DIY house builders 39.42
  donations 40.49
  dwellings 39.23
  e-commerce 38.34
  education
    eligible bodies 40.34
    generally 40.33
    private tuition 40.35
  entertainers
    generally 40.43
    'nett' acts 40.44
  estate agents
    generally 39.44
    property management 39.45
  EU harmonisation
    implementation 37.2
    Member States 37.4
    Recast Directive (2006/112) 37.5

Value added tax – *contd*
　EU harmonisation – *contd*
　　single market 37.3
　　'supply' of goods 37.6–32.8
　exempt supplies
　　generally 38.8
　　property 39.19
　financial services
　　Bitcoins 40.65
　　connected supplies 40.77
　　dealings in money 40.65
　　deposits 40.68
　　generally 40.64
　　instalment credit finance 40.69
　　loans 40.68
　　securities for money 40.66
　food and drink activities
　　catering 40.23–40.25
　　free houses 40.29
　　licensed trade 40.27–40.30
　　managed houses 40.28
　　public houses 40.27–40.30
　　tenanted houses 40.30
　　tied houses 40.30
　fund raising 40.49
　future developments
　　Action Plan 37.10
　　generally 37.9
　　UK, in 37.11–37.12
　galleries 40.63
　government activities
　　government departments 40.102
　　introduction 40.98
　　local authorities 40.99
　　refund scheme 40.101
　　statutory bodies 40.99
　grant of interest in or right over land
　　generally 39.19
　　'interest in or right over land' 39.20
　　licence to occupy land 39.21
　groups of companies, and
　　generally 43.191
　　registration 38.50
　health
　　hospital care 40.38
　　introduction 40.36
　　opticians 40.40
　　pharmacists 40.39
　　supplies by qualified persons 40.37
　hospital care 40.38
　implementation 37.2
　income tax, and 38.11
　insurance
　　brokers 40.81
　　generally 40.78

Value added tax – *contd*
　insurance – *contd*
　　intermediary services 40.81–40.82
　　marine, aviation and
　　　transport 40.79
　　reinsurance 40.80
　intermediary services 40.81–40.82
　international supplies of goods
　　export outside EU 38.102
　　general principle 38.101
　　import from outside EU 38.103
　　reverse charge 38.106
　　transfer between EU
　　　countries 38.104
　international supplies of
　　services 38.105
　introduction 37.1–37.2
　legal aid payments 40.90
　legislative framework 38.2
　leisure activities
　　associations 40.49–40.56
　　clubs and societies 40.49–40.56
　　donations 40.49
　　entertainers 40.43–40.44
　　fund raising 40.49
　　galleries 40.63
　　match fees 40.56
　　museums 40.63
　　'nett' acts 40.44
　　participation fees 40.56
　　performers 40.43–40.44
　　sporting services 40.54
　　subscriptions 40.49
　licence to occupy land 39.21
　licensed trade
　　free houses 40.29
　　generally 40.27
　　managed houses 40.28
　　tenanted houses 40.30
　　tied houses 40.30
　limited liability partnerships,
　　and 45.25
　marine insurance 40.79
　match fees 40.56
　mechanics of regime 38.2
　misdeclaration penalties 38.68
　monthly returns 38.55
　multiple supplies 38.25
　museums 40.63
　'nett' acts 40.44
　opticians 40.40
　option to tax commercial buildings
　　capital goods scheme, and 39.34
　　introduction 39.27
　　mechanics of exercise 39.29

Value added tax – *contd*
  option to tax commercial buildings – *contd*
    output tax 39.31
    property affected 39.28
    purpose of exercise 39.33
    revocation 39.30
  partial exemption 38.83–38.84
  participation fees 40.56
  partnerships, and 44.71
  payments on account 38.56
  penalties
    introduction 38.68
    mitigation 38.68
    reasonable care 38.68
  performers
    generally 40.43
    'nett' acts 40.44
  persons accountable 40.2
  pharmacists 40.39
  place of supply
    e-commerce 38.34
    generally 38.31
    services 37.8, 38.32
  practical application
    business activities 40.21–40.126
    classification of persons 40.2
    introduction 40.1–40.2
  private tuition 40.35
  professional services
    barristers 40.86
    barristers' services 40.95
    commission 40.96
    credit notes 40.94
    disbursements 40.97
    legal aid payments 40.90
    solicitors 40.87–40.90
  property, on
    alterations 39.26
    approved alterations 39.25A
    builders activities 39.38
    charitable buildings 39.23
    civil engineering work 39.41
    commercial buildings 39.27–39.34
    construction services 39.25
    contractors activities 39.38
    conversions 39.26
    DIY house builders 39.42
    dwellings 39.23
    estate agents 39.44–39.45
    exempt supply 39.19
    grant of interest in or right over land 39.19–39.21
    introduction 39.1
    materials and fittings 39.40

Value added tax – *contd*
  property, on – *contd*
    option to tax commercial buildings 39.27–39.34
    property management 39.45
    qualifying buildings 39.23
    reduced rate 39.26
    soft landscaping 39.39
    speculative developers 39.43
    standard-rated supply 39.22
    summary of rules 39.2
    transfer of business as going concern 39.37
    zero-rated supply 39.23–39.25A
  property management 39.45
  public houses
    free houses 40.29
    generally 40.27
    managed houses 40.28
    tenanted houses 40.30
    tied houses 40.30
  Ramsay v IRC principle, and 2.44
  rates
    introduction 38.4
    reduced rate 38.6
    standard rate 38.5
    zero-rated supplies 38.7
  'reasonable care' defence 38.68
  recovery
    apportionment 38.82
    de minimis rule 38.88
    deduction principle 38.81
    methods of apportionment 38.85–38.87
    partial exemption 38.83–38.84
    special methods 38.87
    standard method 38.86
  reduced rate 38.6
  registration
    de-registration 38.51
    generally 38.49
    group 38.50
  reinsurance 40.80
  retailers
    choice of scheme 40.107
    gross takings 40.106
    introduction 40.105
    secondhand goods 40.108–40.109
  returns 38.55
  reverse charge
    generally 38.30
    international supplies of goods and services 38.106
  secondhand goods 40.108–40.109
  self-supply 38.30

Value added tax – *contd*
  social and welfare activities
    charities 40.32
    correspondence courses 40.35
    education 40.33–40.35
    health 40.36–40.40
    hospital care 40.38
    opticians 40.40
    pharmacists 40.39
    voluntary sector 40.32
  soft landscaping 39.39
  solicitors 40.87–40.90
  speculative developers 39.43
  sporting services 40.54
  stamp duty, and 38.12
  stamp duty land tax
    generally 49.42
    introduction 38.12
  standard method 38.86
  standard rate 38.5
  standard-rated supplies 39.22
  subscriptions 40.49
  supplies
    exempt supplies 38.8
    introduction 38.4
    reduced rate 38.6
    standard rate 38.5
    zero-rated supplies 38.7
  supply of goods
    consideration 37.7
    generally 38.23
    introduction 37.6
  supply of services 38.24
  taxable persons
    generally 38.27
    introduction 38.21
  taxable supply 38.22
  tenanted houses 40.30
  terminal markets 40.7
  tied houses 40.30
  time of supply 38.33
  tour operators
    agents 40.123
    foreign currency 40.119
    incidental supplies 40.121
    in-house supplies 40.116
    input tax 40.118
    introduction 40.110
    margin scheme 40.113–40.114
    territorial scope 40.112
    time of supply 40.120
    travel agents 40.123
    travellers 40.111
    wholesale supplies 40.117

Value added tax – *contd*
  transfer of business as going concern
    generally 38.26
    property 39.37
  transport insurance 40.79
  travel agents 40.123
  UK provisions
    future developments 37.11–37.12
    generally 38.1–38.106
  VADR
    designated transactions 5.22
    general 5.3
    generally notifiable transactions 5.23
    hallmarked schemes 5.23
    introduction 5.21
    listed schemes 5.22
    notification 5.25
    reforms 5.26
    tax advantage 5.24
  value of a supply 38.29
  VAT fraction 38.9
  voluntary sector 40.32
  zero-rated supplies
    generally 38.7
    property 39.23–39.25
Value of gift
  inheritance tax on death, and
    changes in value 30.6
    funeral expenses 30.5
    introduction 30.3–30.4
    post-death sales 30.7–30.10
    provisional valuations 30.12
  lifetime transfers, and
    co-ownership of property 28.67
    cost of gift 28.61–28.64
    fall in value of an estate 28.63–28.64
    liabilities 28.66
    life assurance policies 28.74
    non-assignable agricultural tenancies 28.73
    options on property 28.70
    problem areas 28.65–28.74
    'property' 28.62
    related property 28.70
    restrictions on transfer of property 28.72
    shares and securities 28.68
    special rules 28.69–28.74
Value shifting
  controlling shareholdings 26.62
  disclosure rules, and
    designated transactions 5.22
    general 5.3

Value shifting – *contd*
 disclosure rules, and – *contd*
  generally notifiable
   transactions 5.23
  hallmarked schemes 5.23
  introduction 5.21
  listed schemes 5.22
  notification 5.25
  reforms 5.26
  tax advantage 5.24
 groups of companies, and 43.151
 introduction 26.61
 leases 26.63
 overview 19.75
 tax-free benefits resulting 26.64
Vans
 fuel and other benefits 8.122
 introduction 8.117
 non-pooled vans 8.123
 pooled vans 8.118
Variation of terms of employment payments
 employment income, and 8.65
Variations
 And see **Post-death variations**
 estates in the course of administration, and
  tax consequences 17.58
  treatment of income 17.59
 interest in possession trusts, and 33.28
 settlements not subject to relevant property regime, and 33.28
VAT Disclosure Regime (VADR)
 designated transactions 5.22
 general 5.3
 generally notifiable
  transactions 5.23
 hallmarked schemes 5.23
 introduction 5.21
 listed schemes 5.22
 notification 5.25
 reforms 5.26
 tax advantage 5.24
Vehicles
 employment income, and
  fuel and other benefits 8.122
  introduction 8.117
  non-pooled cars 8.119–8.122
  non-pooled vans 8.123
  pooled cars and vans 8.118
  reducing the tax charge 8.120
  use of own car 8.121
 trading income, and 10.162

Venture capital trusts (VCTs)
 background 15.121
 capital gains tax
  deferred relief on reinvestment 15.127
  disposals by investors 15.126
  generally 22.3
  introduction 15.123
  trust 15.125
 entrepreneurs' relief, and 20.40
 generally 15.124
 income tax 15.122
 outline 15.122–15.123
Vesting of property
 inheritance tax on death, and 30.148
Visiting forces
 inheritance tax, and 35.24
Vocations
 foreign income, and 18.35
 foreign taxpayers, and 18.72
 losses, and 11.4
 trading income, and 10.41
Vocational training
 disclosure rules, and
  designated transactions 5.22
  general 5.3
  generally notifiable
   transactions 5.23
  hallmarked schemes 5.23
  introduction 5.21
  listed schemes 5.22
  notification 5.25
  reforms 5.26
  tax advantage 5.24
Voidable transfers
 lifetime transfers, and 28.28
Voluntary sector
 value added tax, and 40.32
Volunteer drivers
 miscellaneous income, and 13.29
Vouchers
 employment income, and 8.109
Vulnerable beneficiaries
 And see **Trusts**
 background 16.74
 meaning 16.75
 qualifying trusts 16.76
 treatment of income 16.77

W

Waiver of remuneration and dividends
 lifetime transfers, and 28.27
Wasting assets
 calculation of gain on disposal 19.38
 chattels 22.21

Wasting assets – *contd*
  definition 19.37
  leases of land 19.41
  replacement of business assets 22.78
Water-conserving plant and machinery
  first year allowances, and 48.31
'Wholly and exclusively' for business purposes
  trading income, and 10.137
'Wholly or mainly' test
  business property relief, and 31.50
Will trusts
  And see **Trusts**
  capital gains tax on death, and 21.103
  s 479 ITA 2007 charge, and 16.25
Winding up
  distributions, and 42.3
  limited liability partnerships, and 45.18
Wine
  capital gains tax, and 22.22
Withholding tax
  royalties 18.80
Woodlands
  capital gains tax, and 22.5
  inheritance tax on death, and 31.21–31.24
Work-in-progress
  depreciation 10.136
  valuation 10.113
Working tax credit
  appeals 51.39
  case study 51.40A
  changes in circumstance 51.37
  changes in income 51.38

Working tax credit – *contd*
  childcare element 51.35
  conditions of entitlement
    couples with children 51.32
    lone parents 51.33
    workers with disability 51.32
    workers with no children 51.34
    workers with no disability 51.34
  disputes 51.40
  elements 51.31
  introduction 51.27
  payment 51.36
Works of art
  charities, and 53.111
Writing down allowances
  plant and machinery, and
    generally 48.39–48.53
    pooling 48.55
Writing and publishing
  miscellaneous income, and 13.25
Written instruments
  stamp duty, and 49.108

Y

Year of marriage
  income tax, and 51.24

Z

Zero-emission goods vehicles
  first year allowances for plant and machinery 48.38
Zero-rated supplies
  charities, and 53.123
  generally 38.7
  property, and 39.23–39.25A